Some Useful Physical Constants

heat of fusion of water at 0°C = 79.71 cal/g

heat of vaporization of water at 100°C = 539.55 cal/g

standard acceleration of gravity, g = 980.66 cm/sec

velocity of light in vacuum, c = 2.9979×10^{10} cm/sec

perfect gas constant, R = 8.3143 joule (g mole)$^{-1}$ (deg K)$^{-1}$

Avogadro's number, $N_A = 6.0226 \times 10^{23}$ molecules/g mole

Stefan-Boltzmann constant, $\sigma = 5.6697 \times 10^{-8}$ W m^{-2} °K^{-4}

Planck's constant, h = 6.6255×10^{-34} joule-sec

Boltzmann constant, k = 1.3805×10^{-23} joule/°K

Dimensions of the Physical World

DISTANCES (km): equatorial radius = 6378, polar radius = 6357, equatorial circumference = 40,074, mean elevation of continents = 0.8, mean depth of oceans = 3.8, mean distance to sun = 149.5×10^6

AREAS (km^2): total surface = 510.1×10^6, oceans = 361.3×10^6, continents and islands = 148.8×10^6, ice-free land = 133×10^6

MASSES (metric tons): Earth = 6.0×10^{21}, oceans = 1.4×10^{18}, ice caps and glaciers = 2.9×10^{16}, atmosphere = 5.2×10^{15}, lakes and streams = 1.3×10^{14}, living organisms (wet weight) = 5×10^{12}

ENERGY FLOWS (kW): solar energy striking top of atmosphere = 1.72×10^{14}, solar energy reaching surface = 8.60×10^{13}, evaporation of water = 4.13×10^{13}, gross photosynthesis = 2×10^{11}

SEA-LEVEL ATMOSPHERE: mass density = 1.225 kg/m^3, pressure = 1.013 bars, number density = 2.547×10^{19} molecules/cm^3, standard temperature = 15.0°C, molecular weight of air = 28.96, speed of sound = 331.4 m/sec

ECOSCIENCE:
POPULATION, RESOURCES, ENVIRONMENT

ECOSCIENCE: POPULATION, RESOURCES, ENVIRONMENT

PAUL R. EHRLICH
STANFORD UNIVERSITY

ANNE H. EHRLICH
STANFORD UNIVERSITY

JOHN P. HOLDREN
UNIVERSITY OF CALIFORNIA, BERKELEY

W. H. FREEMAN AND COMPANY
San Francisco

Library of Congress Cataloging in Publication Data

Ehrlich, Paul R.
Ecoscience.

First-2d ed. published under title: Population, resources, environment.
Bibliography: p.
Includes indexes.
1. Population. 2. Pollution. 3. Human ecology.
I. Ehrlich, Anne H., joint author. II. Holdren, John P., joint author. III. Title.
HB871.E35 1977 301.32 77–6824
ISBN 0–7167–0567–2
ISBN 0–7167–0029–8 pbk.

Printed in the United States of America

9 8 7 6 5 4 3 2 1

To LuEsther with deep appreciation

Contents

Preface xiii

Chapter 1 Population, Resources, Environment: Dimensions of the Human Predicament 1

The Essence of the Predicament 2
Interactions: Resources, Economics, and Politics 2
Interactions: Technology, Environment, and Well-Being 4
The Prospects: Two Views 5

SECTION I NATURAL PROCESSES AND HUMAN WELL-BEING 7

Chapter 2 The Physical World 11

Earth's Solid Surface and Below 14

The Hydrosphere 21
Atmosphere and Climate 32

Chapter 3 Nutrient Cycles 67
Dynamics of Nutrient Cycling 68
Chemistry of Nutrient Cycles 70
Cycles of the Principal Nutrients 73
Other Nutrients and Geographical Variations 92

Chapter 4 Populations and Ecosystems 97
Population Dynamics 98
Natural Selection and Evolution 122
Community Ecology 128
Biomes 145
Freshwater Habitats 160
Marine Habitats 161
Ecological Models 170

SECTION II POPULATION AND RENEWABLE RESOURCES 177

Chapter 5 The History and Future of the Human Population 181
Population Growth 181
Demographic Projections and Population Structure 202
Population Distribution and Movement 227

Chapter 6 Land, Water, and Forests 247
Land 247
Water 257
Forests 272
The Taken-for-Granted Resources 278

Chapter 7 A Hungry World 283
The Production of Food 284
The Dimensions of World Hunger 290
The Distribution of Food 297
Expanding the Harvest 328
Food from the Sea 352
New and Unconventional Food Sources 370
Should We Be Pessimistic? 376

SECTION III ENERGY AND MATERIALS 387

Chapter 8 Energy 391
Size and Sources of Contemporary Energy Use 393
Growth and Change in Energy Flows 396
Energy Resources: Supplies, Depletion, Limits 400
Energy Technology 411
Energy Use and Conservation 489
Perspectives on the Energy Problem 498

Chapter 9 Materials 515
Materials Use: Flows and Stocks 516
Prospects for New Mineral Supplies 522
Augmenting Resources: Recycling, Substitution, Low-Grade Ores 525
Conclusions 530

SECTION IV UNDERSTANDING ENVIRONMENTAL DISRUPTION 535

Chapter 10 Direct Assaults on Well-Being 541
Air Pollution 542
Water Pollution 556
Pesticides and Related Compounds 561
Trace Metals 567
Fluorides 575
Chemical Mutagens 575
Ionizing Radiation 579
The Environment and Cancer 586
Noise Pollution 596
The Work Environment 597
Geological Hazards 600
The Human Environment 601
The Epidemiological Environment 606

Chapter 11 Disruption of Ecological Systems 621
Modifying Ecosystems 623
Pollutants in Ecosystems 629
Atmosphere and Climate 672
Thermonuclear Warfare 690
Ecological Accounting 691

SECTION V THE HUMAN PREDICAMENT: FINDING A WAY OUT 711

Chapter 12 Humanity at the Crossroads 715
The Optimum Population 716
Understanding the Web of Responsibility: The First Step to Solutions 719
The Prospects 730

Chapter 13 Population Policies 737
Family Planning 738
Population Policies in Developed Countries 745
Population Policies in Less Developed Nations 761
Motivation 776
Population Control: Direct Measures 783
Population Control and Development 789

Chapter 14 Changing American Institutions 805
Religion 806
Science and Technology 813
Medicine 823
Education 824
The Legal System 829
Business, Labor, and Advertising 840
Economic and Political Change 843
Some Targets for Early Change 858
A Question of Goals 873

Chapter 15 Rich Nations, Poor Nations, and International Conflict 885
Rich World, Poor World 887
Population, Resources, and War 908
Helping the Poor: A Problem in Ethics 920
Inventing a Better Future 924
International Controls: The Global Commons 939

Chapter 16 Summary 953
Cornucopians Versus Neo-Malthusians 953
Defects in the Cornucopian Vision 954
Alternative Approaches to Technology and Well-Being 955
Epilogue 957

Appendix 1 World Demography 959

Appendix 2 Food and Nutrition 967

Appendix 3 Pesticides 979

Appendix 4 Reproduction and Birth Control 988

Acknowledgments 1001

Index of Subjects 1005

Index of Names 1029

Preface

Since the first edition of *Population, Resources, Environment* was published seven years ago, the population of the world has grown by almost one-half billion people—roughly the number that lived in the entire world when the Pilgrims landed on Plymouth Rock. In the same period, famine has stalked the nomads of the sub-Saharan region of Africa and the struggling peasants of the Indian subcontinent, an energy crisis has transformed perceptions of the world resource situation, and nuclear weapons have become increasingly accessible to the nations of the world. Since 1972, the world economy has been rocked by both monetary inflation and production recession. The significance of environmental deterioration has become inescapable, and its complex relation to economics has been brought to the attention of millions who had never previously paid attention to either. The realization has dawned that seemingly disparate events in the economic, environmental, and political spheres are interconnected. That civilization has entered a period of grave crisis is now doubted only by those afflicted with incurable Micawberism; everyone who is alertable is alerted.

But being alert to the existence of a crisis is not enough if a rational response to it is to be generated. One must also thoroughly understand the elements of the crisis and how they interact. The present book, based on *Population, Resources, Environment,* is an attempt to provide a more thorough, up-to-date understanding of the population-resource-environment predicament and to discuss strategies for dealing with it. In format and emphasis it is quite different from the earlier book.

There is a brief introductory chapter designed to give the reader a capsule overview of the predicament of humanity, a framework into which the more detailed discussions that follow can be fitted. The first major section, consisting of three chapters, gives a detailed review of the physical and biological systems of Earth. This provides background material for students who have not previously been exposed to basic geology and ecology. In this section, as in the rest of the book, a great deal of numerical data and some equations will be found. To grasp the problems humanity now faces, one must understand both their magnitudes and the rates at which they are changing. The vast majority of this material, however, calls for no mathematical sophistication beyond arithmetic and the ability to read graphs. In some cases, high school algebra is required, and, in a few, results from calculus are introduced. But the significance of the results is discussed in each case, so knowledge of calculus is not required for understanding.

The second section covers population and renewable resources—land, soil, water, forests, and food. The coverage of all these topics has been updated and considerably enlarged from that in the second edition of *Population, Resources, Environment.* The third section covers energy and materials far more comprehensively than did our previous books, with special attention paid to nuclear energy and other possible sources for the long term, as well as to the potential of energy conservation.

The material on environmental disruption in the fourth section has been updated and includes more comprehensive coverage of carcinogens, mutagens, climate modification, and many other topics. The last section on social, economic, and political change, including the issue of population control, has likewise been considerably expanded.

Extensive footnotes with references to the technical literature document key points throughout the book. In addition, at the end of each chapter there is a brief list of references, Recommended for Further Reading, containing our selection of the most generally useful works for further exploration of the topics in the chapter. This precedes the annotated chapter bibliographies that will be familiar to readers of our other books. In both footnotes and bibliographies, we have concentrated on recent additions to the literature, sometimes at the expense of important, even seminal works. We believe that the more recent contributions contain the latest thinking on a given topic, and their bibliographies often provide a full entrée to the previous literature of that subject.

We have tried throughout the book to state clearly where we stand on various matters of controversy. Our apprehension about the course of humanity expressed in *Population, Resources, Environment* and *Human Ecology* has deepened; if there is another edition of *Ecoscience,* we hope that events will then permit a more optimistic evaluation.

Paul R. Ehrlich
Anne H. Ehrlich
John P. Holdren

A Note on Documentation

To save space, most of the footnotes contain only authors' names and the titles of publications (or, after the first citation of a work within a chapter, a partial title). The complete citations are given in alphabetical order by authors' names in either the Recommended for Further Reading list or the Additional References list at the end of each chapter.

ECOSCIENCE: POPULATION, RESOURCES, ENVIRONMENT

It is clear that the future course of history will be determined by the rates at which people breed and die, by the rapidity with which nonrenewable resources are consumed, by the extent and speed with which agricultural production can be improved, by the rate at which the underdeveloped areas can industrialize, by the rapidity with which we are able to develop new resources, as well as by the extent to which we succeed in avoiding future wars. All of these factors are interlocked.

—Harrison Brown, 1954

CHAPTER 1

Population, Resources, Environment: Dimensions of the Human Predicament

Providing people with the ingredients of material well-being requires physical resources—land, water, energy, and minerals—and the supporting contributions of environmental processes. Technology and social organization are the tools with which society transforms physical resources and human labor into distributed goods and services. These cultural tools are embedded in the fabric of the biological and geophysical environment; they are not independent of it.

As the number of people grows and the amounts of goods and services provided per person increase, the associated demands on resources, technology, social organization, and environmental processes become more intense and more complicated, and the interactions among these factors become increasingly consequential. It is the interactions—technology with employment, energy with environment, environment and energy with agriculture, food and energy with international relations, and so on—that generate many of the most vexing aspects of civilization's predicament in the last quarter of the twentieth century.

This book is about that predicament: about its physical underpinnings in the structure of the environment and the character of natural resources; about its human dimensions in the size, distribution, and economic condition of the world's population; about the impact of that population on the ecological systems of Earth and the impact of environmental changes on humanity; about the technology, economics, politics, and individual behavior that have contributed to the predicament; and about the changes that might alleviate it.

THE ESSENCE OF THE PREDICAMENT

In a world inhabited in the mid-1970s by a rapidly growing population of more than 4 billion people, a massive and widening gap in well-being separates a rich minority from the poor majority. The one-third of the world's population that lives in the most heavily industrialized nations (commonly termed developed countries—DCs) accounts for 85 percent of the global personal income and a like fraction of the annual use of global resources. The people living in the less industrialized nations (often called less developed countries—LDCs) must apportion the remaining 15 percent of global income and resource use among two-thirds of the world's population. The result is an unstable prosperity for the majority of people in the DCs and frustrating, crushing poverty for the majority in the LDCs. Millions of the poorest—especially infants and children—have starved to death every year for decades; hundreds of millions have lived constantly, often consciously, almost always helplessly on the brink of famine and epidemic disease, awaiting only some modest quirk of an environment already stretched taut—an earthquake, a flood, a drought—to push them over that edge. The 1970s brought an apparent increase in such quirks—1972 and 1974 were years of flood, drought, and poor harvests. World food reserves plummeted, and millions more human beings were threatened by famine. Meanwhile, the entire population continued growing at a rate that would *double* the number of people in the world within 40 years.

The prosperity of the DCs—awesome by comparison with the poverty of the LDCs—has been built on exploitation of the richest soils, the most accessible fossil fuels, and the most concentrated mineral deposits of the entire globe—a one-time windfall. As they now struggle to maintain and even expand their massive consumption from a resource base of declining quality, the DCs by themselves appear to be taxing technology, social organization, and the physical environment beyond what they can long sustain. And the LDCs, as they try to follow the same path to economic development, find the bridges burned ahead of them. There will be no counterpart to the windfall of cheap resources that propelled the DCs into prosperity. A DC-style industrialization of the LDCs, based on the expensive resources that remain, is therefore probably foredoomed by enormous if not insurmountable economic and environmental obstacles.

The problems arising from this situation would be formidable even if the world were characterized by political stability, no population growth, widespread recognition of civilization's dependence on environmental processes, and a universally shared commitment to the task of closing the prosperity gap. In the real world, characterized by deep ideological divisions and territorial disputes, rapid growth of population and faltering food production, the popular illusion that technology has freed society from dependence on the environment, and the determined adherence of DC governments to a pattern of economic growth that enlarges existing disparities rather than narrowing them, the difficulties are enormously multiplied.

INTERACTIONS: RESOURCES, ECONOMICS, AND POLITICS

It takes water and steel to produce fuel, fuel and water to produce steel, fuel and water and steel to produce food and fiber, and so on. The higher the level of industrialization in a society, the more intimate and demanding are the interconnections among resources. Agriculture in the United States, Europe, and Japan, for example, uses far more fuel, steel, and mineral fertilizers per unit of food produced than does agriculture in India or Indonesia. The interconnections among resources also become more intense as the quality of the resource base diminishes; the amount of fuel and metal that must be invested in securing *more* fuel and metal increases as exhaustion of rich deposits forces operations deeper, farther afield, and into leaner ores.

These tightening physical links among resources have their counterparts in economic and organizational effects. Scarcity or rising prices of one commodity generate scarcity and rising prices of others, thus contributing both directly and indirectly to inflation and often to unemployment. Massive diversion of investment capital and technical resources to meet the crisis of the moment—attempting to compensate for lack of foresight with brute force applied too late—weakens a system elsewhere and thus promotes crises in other sectors later. Apparent solutions seized in haste and ignorance cut off options that may be sorely missed when future predicaments arise.

International aspects add to the complexity—and the dangers—of these interactions. Money pours across international boundaries, collecting in those parts of the world where rich deposits of essential resources still remain. In resource-importing DCs, the pressure to redress the balance-of-payments imbalance becomes the dominant determinant of what is exported, subverting other goals. Resources of indeterminate ownership, such as fish stocks in oceans and seabed minerals, become the focus of international disputes and unregulated exploitation. And foreign policies bend and even reverse themselves to accommodate the perceived physical needs.

The interactions of resources, economics, and politics were displayed with compelling clarity in the worldwide petroleum squeeze of the mid-1970s. The consequences of a slowdown in the growth of petroleum production in the principal producing countries, accompanied by almost a quadrupling of the world market price, reverberated through all sectors of economic activity in DCs and LDCs alike. The prices of gasoline, jet fuel, heating oil, and electricity soared, contributing directly to inflation. Increased demand for petroleum substitutes such as coal drove the prices of those commodities up, thereby contributing indirectly to inflation, as well. Shortages of materials and services that are particularly dependent on petroleum for their production or delivery quickly materialized, feeding inflation and unemployment still further.

The impact of the energy crisis was especially severe on the already precarious world food situation. Indeed, rising food prices, following the poor harvests of 1972, were a major factor in the decision by the Organization of Petroleum Exporting Countries (OPEC) to raise oil prices. The strong and growing dependence of agriculture on energy—especially petroleum—soon made itself felt worldwide as an important contributor to further increases in food prices. This was especially so in developed countries (where agriculture is most highly mechanized), a few of which are the main sources of the exportable food supplies that determine world market prices. The largest exporter, the United States, has gratefully responded to increased foreign demand for its food exports, which has helped to pay for the nation's increasingly expensive oil imports (but which has also contributed to raising domestic food prices). This phenomenon—the need to sell food abroad to pay for oil—may have assured continued high-quality diets for nations like Japan that can still afford to buy, but it also reduced the amount of uncommitted food reserves in the DCs that would be available to alleviate famines in LDCs too poor to buy the food they needed on the world market.

The most obvious consequence of the 1973 petroleum embargo and price rise on international political affairs was one intended by the oil-producing Arab states—a sudden diminution of DC support for the Israeli position in Middle East territorial disputes. Some less obvious effects, however, may in the long run be more significant. The United States and several other DCs export military hardware as a major source of the foreign exchange they need to pay for imported raw materials; and the intensity with which the arms exporters hustle their wares in the international market is increasing as the oil-related balance-of-payments problem worsens. The result has been to support a spiraling arms race in LDCs, which is both a pathetic diversion of funds needed there to raise the standards of living and a profoundly destabilizing force operating against world peace. The export of nuclear reactors, likewise encouraged by the DCs' need to pay for imported raw materials, may also have disastrous effects. Although intended for production of electricity, these reactors also provide their LDC recipients with the materials needed to manufacture nuclear bombs. India's nuclear explosion in 1974 demonstrated for any remaining doubters that the spread of reactors can mean the spread of nuclear weapons. And it must be assumed that the distribution of such weapons into more and more hands—and into some of the most politically troubled regions of the world—greatly increases the chances that they will be used.

INTERACTIONS: TECHNOLOGY, ENVIRONMENT, AND WELL-BEING

The relationship connecting technology, environment, and well-being would constitute a deep dilemma for civilization, even in the absence of the economic and political complexities just described. Simply stated, the dilemma is this: while the intelligent application of technology fosters human well-being directly, a reducible but not removable burden of environmental disruption by that technology undermines well-being. This negative burden includes the direct effects of technology's accidents and effluents on human life and health; the direct impact of accidents, effluents, preemption of resources, and transformation of landscapes on economic goods and services; and technology's indirect adverse impact on well-being via disruption of the vital services supplied to humanity by natural ecological systems. These free services—including, among others, the assimilation and recycling of wastes—are essential to human health and economic productivity. It is clearly possible to reach a point where the gain in well-being associated with (for example) producing more material goods does not compensate for the loss in well-being caused by the environmental damage generated by the technology that produced the goods. Beyond that point, pursuing increased prosperity merely by intensifying technological activity is counterproductive. Many people would argue that the United States has already passed that pivotal point.

The turning point where environmental costs begin to exceed economic benefits can be pushed back somewhat by using technologies that cause the least possible environmental damage. It cannot be pushed back indefinitely, however, because *no technology can be completely free of environmental impact.* This flat statement—implying that continued expansion of any technology will eventually lead to environmental costs exceeding its benefits—is true on fundamental physical grounds. It means that environmental constraints will ultimately limit economic production—the product of the number of people and the amount of economic goods and services that each person commands—if nothing else limits it first.

Despite increased scientific attention to environmental problems in recent years, most of the potentially serious threats are only sketchily understood. For many such problems, it cannot be stated with assurance whether serious damage is imminent, many decades away, or indeed already occurring—with the full consequences yet to manifest themselves. Much remains to be learned, for example, about the causation of cancer and genetic damage by low concentrations of nearly ubiquitous environmental contaminants, either alone or in combination: pesticide residues, combustion products, heavy metals, plasticizers, food additives, prescription and nonprescription drugs, and innumerable others.

The most serious and imminent peril of all may well prove to be civilization's interference with the "public service" functions of environmental processes. Agricultural production in a world already on the brink of famine depends intimately on the absence of major fluctuations in climate, on the chemical balances in soil and surface water that are governed by biological and geochemical nutrient cycles, on naturally occurring organisms for pollination of crops, and on the control of potential crop pests and diseases by natural enemies and environmental conditions. Agents of human disease and the vectors that transport those agents are also regulated in large part by climate, by environmental chemistry, and by natural enemies. Ocean fish stocks—an important source of food protein—depend critically on the biological integrity of the estuaries and onshore waters that serve as spawning grounds and nurseries. The environmental processes that regulate climate, build and preserve soils, cycle nutrients, control pests and parasites, help to propagate crops, and maintain the quality of the ocean habitat, are therefore absolutely essential to human well-being. Unfortunately, the side effects of technology are systematically diminishing the capacity of the environment to perform these essential services at the same time that the growth of population and the desire for greater affluence per capita are creating greater demand for them.

Nor can the public-service functions of the environment be safely replaced by technology if technology destroys them. Often the foresight, scientific knowledge, and technological skill that would be required to perform this substitution just do not exist. Where they do exist, the economic cost of an operation on the needed scale is almost invariably too high; and where the economic cost at first seems acceptable, the attempt to replace environmental services with technological ones initiates a vicious circle: the side effects of the additional technology disrupt more environmental services, which must be replaced with still more technology, and so on.

THE PROSPECTS: TWO VIEWS

The foregoing brief survey of the dimensions of the human predicament suggests a discouraging outlook for the coming decades. A continuing set of interlocking shortages is likely—food, energy, raw materials—generating not only direct increases in human suffering and deprivation, but also increased political tension and (perversely) increased availability of the military wherewithal for LDCs to relieve their frustrations aggressively. Resort to military action is possible, not only in the case of LDCs unwilling to suffer quietly, but, with equal or greater likelihood, in the case of industrial powers whose high standard of living is threatened by denial of external resources. The probability that conflicts of *any* origin will escalate into an exchange of nuclear weapons, moreover, can hardly fail to be greater in 1985's world of perhaps fifteen or twenty nuclear-armed nations than it has been in the recent world of five.

The growth of population—very rapid in the LDCs, but not negligible in most DCs, either—will continue to compound the predicament by increasing pressure on resources, on the environment, and on human institutions. Rapid expansion of old technologies and the hasty deployment of new ones, stimulated by the pressure of more people wanting more goods and services per person, will surely lead to some major mistakes—actions whose environmental or social impacts erode well-being far more than their economic results enhance it.

This gloomy prognosis, to which a growing number of scholars and other observers reluctantly subscribes, has motivated a host of proposals for organized evasive action: population control, limitation of material consumption, redistribution of wealth, transitions to technologies that are environmentally and socially less disruptive than today's, and movement toward some kind of world government, among others. Implementation of such action would itself have some significant economic and social costs, and it would require an unprecedented international consensus and exercise of public will to succeed. That no such consensus is even in sight has been illustrated clearly by the diplomatic squabbling and nonperformance that have characterized major international conferences on the environment, population, and resources, such as the Stockholm conference on the environment in 1972, the Bucharest Conference on World Population in 1974, the Rome Food Conference in 1974, and the Conferences on the Law of the Sea in the early 1970s.

One reason for the lack of consensus is the existence and continuing wide appeal of a quite different view of civilization's prospects. This view holds that humanity sits on the edge of a technological golden age; that cheap energy and the vast stores of minerals available at low concentration in seawater and common rock will permit technology to produce more of everything and to do it cheaply enough that the poor can become prosperous; and that all this can be accomplished even in the face of continued population growth. In this view—one might call it the cornucopian vision—the benefits of expanded technology almost always greatly outweigh the environmental and social costs, which are perceived as having been greatly exaggerated, anyway. The vision holds that industrial civilization is very much on the right track, and that more of the same—continued economic growth—with perhaps a little luck in avoiding a major war are all that is needed to usher in an era of permanent, worldwide prosperity.[1]

[1]Outstanding proponents of this view include British economist Wilfred Beckerman (*Two cheers for the affluent society*, St. Martin's Press, London, 1974): British physicist John Maddox (*The doomsday syndrome*, McGraw-Hill, New York, 1972); and American futurologist Herman Kahn (*The next 200 years*, with William Brown and Leon Martel, William Morrow, New York, 1976).

Which view of civilization's prospects is more accurate is a question that deserves everyone's scrutiny. It cannot be decided merely by counting the "experts" who speak out on either side and then weighing their credentials. Rather, the arguments must be considered in detail—examined, dissected, subjected to the test of comparison with the evidence around us. This is an ambitious task, for the issues encompass elements of physics, chemistry, biology, demography, economics, politics, agriculture, and a good many other fields as well. One must grapple with the arithmetic of growth, the machinery of important environmental processes, the geology of mineral resources, the potential and limitations of technology, and the sociology of change. It is necessary to ponder the benefits and shortcomings of proposed alternatives as well as those of the status quo; and it is important to ask where burdens of proof should lie.

Does civilization risk more if the cornucopians prevail and they are wrong? or if the pessimists prevail and *they* are wrong? Could an intermediate position be correct, or are perhaps even the pessimists too optimistic? What is the most prudent course in the face of uncertainty? Making such evaluations is, of course, a continuing process, subject to revision as new arguments, proposals, and evidence come to light. What is provided in the following chapters is a starting point: a presentation of essential principles, relevant data, and (we think) plausible analyses that bear on the predicament of humanity.

Recommended for Further Reading

Brown, Harrison. 1954. *The challenge of man's future.* Viking, New York. A landmark in the literature of the human predicament, perceptively elucidating the interactions of population, technology, and resources. Brown alerted a generation of scholars and policy-makers to the seriousness of impending problems and has worked tirelessly in national and international scientific circles to mobilize the talent to help solve them.

Ehrlich, Paul R.; Anne H. Ehrlich; and John P. Holdren. 1973. *Human ecology.* W. H. Freeman and Company, San Francisco. A predecessor of this book, providing capsule introductions to many of the topics expanded upon here.

National Academy of Sciences-National Research Council. 1969. *Resources and man.* Report of the Committee on Resources and Man of the National Academy of Sciences. W. H. Freeman and Company, San Francisco. A sober look at population, food, energy, minerals, and environment, together with forthright policy recommendations, by a group of experts both eminent and eloquent.

Osborn, Fairfield. 1948. *Our plundered planet.* Little, Brown, Boston. A prescient early plea for an integrated approach to the interlocking problems of population, resources, and environment.

That civilizations have transformed many aspects of the physical environment is beyond dispute. Indeed, the prevalence of "man-made" environments (such as cities) and intensively managed ones (such as wheat fields) makes it all too easy to suppose that such technological environments are now the only ones that matter. This supposition, which one could call the humanity-is-now-the-master-of-nature hypothesis, is partly responsible for the widespread underestimation of the seriousness of environmental problems. Regardless of such beliefs, civilizations and their technological environments continue to be embedded, as they always have been, in a larger nontechnological environment. This larger environment provides the raw materials with which technology must work, and its characteristics *together* with those of technology define the limits of what is possible at any given time.

Technology and natural environmental processes together—not technology alone—have permitted the human population and its material consumption to reach their present levels. Today human beings continue to depend on the nontechnological environment for a variety of services that technology not only cannot replace, but without which many technological processes themselves would be nonfunctional or unaffordable. Many of these services are mentioned in Chapter 1—the regulation of climate, the management of soil and surface water, the environmental chemistry of nutrient cycling and control of contaminants, and the regulation of pests and disease, among others. To understand the nature and extent of humanity's dependence on these services, and the degree of their vulnerability to disruption by mismanagement and overload, one must investigate in detail the character of the physical and biological processes that provide them. We do so in the next three chapters: "The Physical World," discussing basic geological processes, the hydrologic cycle, and climate; "Nutrient Cycles," describing the major pathways by which carbon, nitrogen, phosphorus, and other essential nutrients move from the living to the nonliving environment and back again; and "Populations and Ecosystems," an introduction to the principles of population biology and ecology essential to an understanding of the structure and functions of biological communities. The details of the actual threats to these processes posed by the activities of contemporary human beings are taken up in Chapter 11.

SECTION

I

Natural Processes and Human Well-Being

There is one ocean, with coves having many names;
a single sea of atmosphere, with no coves at all;
a thin miracle of soil, alive and giving life;
a last planet; and there is no spare.

—David R. Brower

Prehistoric human beings earned a living from their surroundings in much the same way as many other animals did (and do): they sought out and preyed upon other organisms—edible plants and killable animals—that shared the environment, they drank water where they found it, and they took shelter in trees and caves. The geographical distribution, size, and well-being of the human population under these circumstances were influenced very strongly by the characteristics of the natural environment—patterns of hot and cold, wet and dry, steep and flat, lush and sparse. These patterns of climate, topography, flora, and fauna were in turn the products of millions of centuries of interaction among natural geophysical and biological processes—continental drift, mountain-building, erosion, sedimentation, the advance and retreat of glaciers, the rise and fall of the oceans, and the evolution and extinction of various kinds of organisms.

Before the advent of agriculture, most of the natural processes and systems that so strongly influenced the human condition were themselves not much influenced by what humans did; the interaction was largely a one-way street. Fire and stone implements apparently were used even by the forerunners of *Homo sapiens* well over a million years ago, and the wielders of those early tools certainly used them to affect their local environments, both intentionally and inadvertently. But it was agriculture, which began about 10,000 years ago, that marked the sharpest transition in the capacity of *Homo sapiens* to influence the physical environment on a large scale. From that beginning, which permitted specialization and a scale of social organization not possible among hunter-gatherers, arose a long series of technological and social developments that produced the agricultural and industrial civilizations that today virtually cover the globe.

All the rivers run into the sea; yet the sea is not full.

—Ecclesiastes

CHAPTER 2

The Physical World

The *biosphere* is that part of Earth where life exists. In vertical dimension it extends from the deepest trenches in the ocean floor, more than 11,000 meters (36,000 feet)[1] below sea level, to at least 10,000 meters (m) above sea level, where spores (reproductive cells) of bacteria and fungi can be found floating free in the atmosphere. By far most living things—most of which depend directly or indirectly on the capture of solar energy by photosynthesis in plants and certain bacteria—exist in the narrower region extending from the limit of penetration of sunlight in the clearest oceans, less than 200 meters from the surface, to the highest value of the permanent snow line in tropical and subtropical mountain ranges—about 6000 meters, or 20,000 feet. (Everest, the highest mountain, rises almost 8900 meters above sea level.) By any definition, the biosphere is as a mere film in thickness compared to the size of the ball of rock on which it sits—about like the skin of an apple, in fact. The radius of Earth is about 6370 kilometers (km), or 4000 miles (mi).

Of course, conditions within the thin envelope of the biosphere are influenced by physical processes taking place far outside it: by the energy emitted by the sun, 150

[1]Throughout this book physical dimensions are given in metric units, sometimes accompanied by the English equivalent to ease the transition for readers not completely accustomed to the metric system. For more precise conversion factors, see the tables inside the covers of the book.

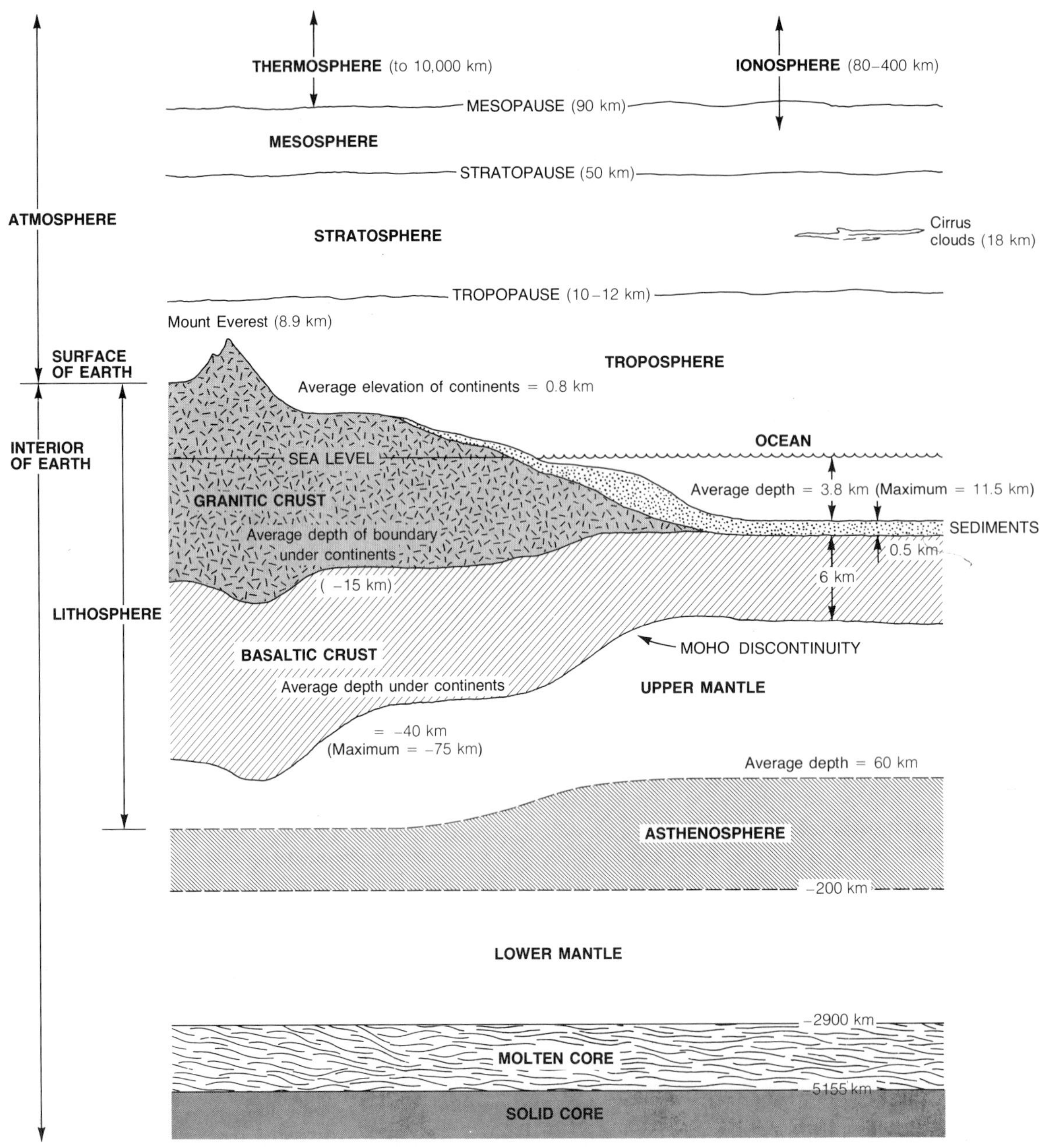

FIGURE 2-1

Vertical structure of the physical world. (Scales are greatly distorted.)

million kilometers away; by the tides originating in the relative motion and positions of Earth, sun, and moon (the distance from Earth to the moon averages about 380,000 km); by the presence of gases 20 to 400 km high in the atmosphere that screen out harmful components of incoming solar energy; by the constitution and structure of Earth's crust (to 40 km deep), which govern the availability of mineral nutrients at the surface and of metallic ores accessible to industrial civilization; by the behavior of the solid but plastically flowing[2] mantle (to 2900 km deep) on which the crustal plates "float" and move laterally; and by the motion of Earth's molten core (2900 to 5200 km deep), which produces the magnetic field that protects the planet's surface from bombardment by energetic, electrically charged particles from space. The vertical structure of Earth's atmosphere, surface, and interior is illustrated in Figure 2-1. The terminology used there for the various vertical divisions is explained in the following text, where the character of the atmosphere and Earth's interior are taken up in more detail.

In horizontal extent the biosphere covers the globe, although in the hottest deserts and coldest polar regions—as at the highest elevations—usually only dormant spores can be found. Earth's total surface area amounts to 510 million square kilometers (about 197 million mi^2), of which 71 percent is ocean and 29 percent land (see Table 2-1). The mass of all living organisms on Earth amounts to about 5 trillion metric tons,[3] three-fourths of which consists of water. Under the reasonable assumption that living matter has about the same density as water [1 gram per cubic centimeter (1g/cm^3)], this would mean that the living part of the biosphere was equivalent to a layer of material only 1 centimeter thick, covering the globe. (The range concealed in this average is from 0.0002 g of living material for each square centimeter of surface in the open ocean to 15 g or more for each square centimeter of surface in a tropical forest.)

[2] *Plastic flow* in a solid refers to continuous deformation in any direction without rupture.

[3] A metric ton (MT) equals 1000 kilograms (kg), or 2205 pounds. One trillion (in scientific notation, 10^{12}) equals 1000 billion, or 1,000,000 million.

TABLE 2-1
Surface Areas of the Globe

	Percentage of category	*Area (million km^2)*
TOTAL EARTH SURFACE		510
OCEANS		361
Pacific Ocean*	46	
Atlantic Ocean*	23	
Indian Ocean*	18	
Arctic Ocean*	4	
Mean extent of sea ice (Arctic, South Atlantic, Pacific, and Indian)	7	
LAND		149
Eurasia	36	
Africa	20	
North and Central America	16	
South America	12	
Antarctica	10	
Oceania	6	
Ice-covered land	10	
Terrain more than 3000 meters high	5	
Lakes and rivers	1	

*Mean extent of sea ice has been subtracted.
Source: Strahler and Strahler, *Environmental geoscience.*

TABLE 2-2
Masses of Constituents of the Physical World

Constituent	*Mass (trillion MT)*
Living organisms (including water content)	8
Liquid fresh water, on surface	126
Atmosphere	5,140
Ice	30,000
Salts dissolved in oceans	49,000
Oceans	1,420,000
Earth's crust (average depth, 17 km)	24,000,000
Earth (total)	6,000,000,000

The relative masses of various constituents of the physical world are shown in Table 2-2.

To study the processes that operate in any subdivision of the physical world—atmosphere, biosphere, Earth's crust—one must know something about energy: what it is, how it behaves, how it is measured. For whenever and wherever anything is happening, energy in some form is involved; it is in many respects the basic currency of the physical world. An introduction to energy and the related concepts of work and power, along with the units in which these quantities can be measured, is provided in Box 2-1. Some feeling for how much energy is stored in and flows between various parts of the physical world is conveyed in Table 2-3.

EARTH'S SOLID SURFACE AND BELOW

The outermost layer of Earth's solid surface is called the *crust.* It ranges in thickness from about 6 kilometers beneath the ocean floor to as much as 75 kilometers below the largest mountain ranges. In essence, the crust floats on the denser *mantle* beneath it. (As is elaborated below, the crust and mantle are differentiated by the different compositions and densities of the rock they comprise.) As with icebergs on the sea, the more crust extends above the surface (as in a mountain range), the more bulk is hidden below.[4] This situation is made possible by the existence of a soft, yielding layer called the *asthenosphere* in the middle of the underlying mantle. This layer's strength is low because the rock is near its melting point. The combination of the crust and the hard upper layer of the mantle is called the *lithosphere,* a term sometimes also employed in a more general sense to mean the entire solid part of Earth. Below the mantle, between the depths of 2900 and 5200 kilometers, lies Earth's *molten outer core.* This core consists largely of liquid iron (with some nickel) at a temperature of perhaps 2500° C; its properties and motion produce Earth's magnetic field.

[4]For more detailed treatment of this point and others in this section, see F. Press and R. Siever, *Earth;* and A. N. Strahler and A. H. Strahler, *Environmental geoscience.*

TABLE 2-3
Energy Flow and Storage in the Physical World

	Energy or power
STORAGE	*Trillion MJ*
Energy released in a large volcanic eruption	100
Chemical energy stored in all living organisms	30,000
Energy released in a large earthquake	100,000
Chemical energy stored in dead organic matter	100,000
Heat stored in atmosphere	1,300,000
Kinetic energy of Earth's rotation on its axis	250,000,000,000
FLOWS	*Million Mw*
Tides	3
Heat flow from Earth's interior	32
Conversion of sunlight to chemical energy in photosynthesis	100
Conversion of sunlight to energy of motion of atmosphere	1,000
Sunlight striking top of atmosphere	172,000

BOX 2-1 Work, Energy, and Power: Definitions, Disguises, and Units

Work is the application of a force through a distance. *Energy* is stored work. *Power* is the rate of flow of energy, or the rate at which work is done. All these concepts are more easily understood with the help of examples and some elaboration.

Work—force multiplied by distance—is done when a weight is lifted against the force of gravity (as with water carried upward in the atmosphere in the course of the hydrologic cycle), when mass is accelerated against the resistance of inertia (as with waves whipped up on the ocean by the wind) or when a body is pushed or pulled through a resisting medium (as with an aircraft moving through the atmosphere or a plow cutting through a field). The presence of distance in the concept of work means that work is done only if there is motion—if you push on a stalled car and it doesn't budge, there is a force, but there is no work because there is no motion.

The foregoing are examples of *mechanical work*—work involving the bulk (or *macroscopic*) motion of agglomerations of molecules. There are also various forms of *microscopic* work, such as *chemical work* and *electrical work*, which involve forces and motions on the scale of individual molecules, atoms, and electrons. To heat a substance is to do a form of microscopic work in which the individual molecules of the substance are made to move more rapidly about in all directions, without any bulk motion taking place. The demonstration that all these different manifestations of work are fundamentally the same can be found in treatises on physics and chemistry.*

If work has many guises, so must energy, which is only *stored* work. Work stored as the motion of a macroscopic object (for example, a speeding automobile or the Earth spinning on its axis) is called *mechanical energy* or *kinetic energy*. The latter term may be applied as well to the energy of motion of microscopic objects (such as, molecules, electrons). Work stored as the *disordered* motion of molecules—that is, rotation, vibration, and random linear motion not associated with bulk motion of the substance—is called *thermal energy* or *sensible heat* or (more commonly) just *heat*. Note that temperature and heat are not the same. Temperature is a measure of the intensity of the disordered motion of a typical molecule in a substance; the heat in a substance is the sum of the energies stored in the disordered motion of all its molecules. (The relation between temperature and energy is developed further in Box 2-3.)

Kinetic energy means something is happening; that is, the work is stored as motion. *Potential* or *latent* energy means something is "waiting" to happen. That is, the work is stored in the position or structure of objects that are subject to a force and a restraint; the force provides the potential for converting position or structure into kinetic energy, and the restraint is what keeps this from happening (at least temporarily). Each kind of potential energy is associated with a specific kind of force. Gravitational potential energy (an avalanche waiting to fall) and electrical potential energy (oppositely charged clouds waiting for a lightning stroke to surge between them) are associated with forces that can act between objects at large distances. Chemical potential energy (gasoline waiting to be burned, carbohydrate waiting to be metabolized) is associated with the forces that hold atoms together in molecules—that is, with chemical bonds. Nuclear potential energy is due to the forces that hold protons and neutrons together in the nucleus—the so-called strong force. Latent heat of vaporization (water vapor waiting to condense into liquid, whereupon the latent heat will be converted to sensible heat) and latent heat of fusion (liquid waiting to freeze into a solid, with the same result) are associated with the electrical forces between molecules in liquids and solids. The idea that potential energy is something "waiting" to happen needs only to be tempered by recognition that sometimes it can be a long wait—the chemical potential energy in a piece of coal buried in Earth's crust, for example, may already have waited a hundred million years.

Electromagnetic radiation is a form of energy that does not fall neatly into any of the categories we have mentioned so far. It is characterized not

(*Continued*)

*See, for example, R. Feynmann, R. Leighton, and M. Sands, *The Feynmann lectures on physics*, Addison-Wesley, Reading, Mass., 1965.

BOX 2-1 (*Continued*)

in terms of the motion or position or structure of objects but in terms of the motion of electric and magnetic forces.** Light (visible electromagnetic radiation), radio waves, thermal (infrared) radiation, and X-rays are all closely related varieties of this particular form of energy. (See also Box 2-4.)

Albert Einstein theorized, and many experiments have subsequently verified, that any change in the energy associated with an object (regardless of the form of the energy) is accompanied by a corresponding change in mass. In this sense, mass and energy are equivalent and interchangeable, the formal expression of equivalence being Einstein's famous formula $E = mc^2$. (Here E denotes energy, m mass, and c the speed of light.) Because a small amount of mass is equivalent to a very large quantity of energy, a change in mass is only detectable when the change in energy is very large—as, for example, in nuclear explosions.

Different professions use a bewildering array of units for counting work and energy. The metric system is prevailing, but so gradually that the literature of energy and environmental sciences will be littered for years to come by a needless profusion of archaic units. Since work has the dimensions of force times distance, and all energy can be thought of as stored work, it should be apparent that a single unit will suffice for all forms of energy and work. The most logical one is the *joule* (J), which is exactly the amount of work done in exerting the basic metric unit of force, 1 *newton* (N), over the basic metric unit of distance, 1 meter.† We shall use the joule and its multiples, the kilojoule (1000 J, or kJ) and the megajoule (1,000,000 J, or MJ), throughout this book.

Our only exception to the use of the joule is a concession to the enormous inertia of custom in the field of nutrition, where we reluctantly employ the *kilocalorie* (kcal). A kilocalorie is approximately the amount of thermal energy needed to raise the temperature of 1 kg of water by 1 degree Celsius (1° C);†† this unit is often confusingly written as "calorie" in discussions of nutrition. Running the bodily machinery of an average adult human being uses about 2500 kcal—about 10,000 kJ—per day.)

Besides the erg (1 ten-millionth of a joule) and the calorie (1 thousandth of a kcal), the unit of energy most likely to be encountered by the reader elsewhere is the British thermal unit (Btu), which is approximately the amount of thermal energy needed to raise 1 pound of water by 1 degree Fahrenheit (1° F). A Btu is roughly a kilojoule.

In many applications one must consider not only *amounts* of energy but the *rate* at which energy flows or is used. The rate of energy flow or use is *power. Useful power* is the rate at which the flow of energy actually accomplishes work. The units for power are units of energy divided by units of time—for example, British thermal units per hour, kilocalories per minute, and joules per second. One joule per second is a *watt* (w). A kilowatt (kw) is 1000 watts, and a megawatt (Mw) is 1,000,000 watts; these are the units we use for power in this book. These units are perfectly applicable to flows of nonelectric as well as electric energy, although you may be accustomed to them only in the context of electricity. Similarly, the kilowatt hour (kwh), denoting the amount of energy that flows in an hour if the rate (power) is 1 kilowatt, makes sense as a unit of energy outside the electrical context. A kilowatt hour is 3600 kilojoules. For example, we can speak of an automobile using energy (in this case, chemical energy stored in gasoline) at a rate of 100 kilowatts (100 kilojoules of chemical energy per second). In an hour of steady driving at this rate of fuel consumption, the automobile uses 100 kJ/sec multiplied by 3600 sec (the number of seconds in an hour) or 360,000 kJ. The same quantity of energy used in a jumbo jetliner would produce a much larger power—say, 180,000 kw—for a much shorter time (2 sec).

A complete set of conversion factors for units of energy and power appears just inside the covers of this book.

**A physicist might object at this point that it isn't always useful, or even possible, to discriminate between objects and fields of electric and magnetic force. This level of technicality will not be needed in this book.

†The units of force are units of mass multiplied by units of acceleration. One newton is a mass of 1 kg times an acceleration of 1 m per second (sec) per second ($1\ N = 1\ kg \cdot m/sec^2$). One joule equals 1 newton-meter ($1\ J = 1\ N\text{-}m = 1\ kg \cdot m^2/sec^2$).

††Zero and 100 on the Celsius, or centigrade, scale of temperature correspond to the freezing point and the boiling point of pure water. The conversion between Celsius (C) and Fahrenheit (F) is: degrees F = 1.8 × degrees C + 32.

Within the molten outer core is a *solid inner core,* also composed of iron and nickel, under enormous pressure.

Many of the characteristics of Earth's solid surface are the result of the operation of *tectonic processes*—the motion of great solid segments of the lithosphere, called *plates,* which slide about over the plastically flowing asthenosphere at a rate of a few centimeters per year. Operating over hundreds of millions of years, such motions have apparently produced displacements of thousands of kilometers. The now widely accepted theory of continental drift holds that the present arrangement of the continents arose in this way, beginning with the breakup of the single supercontinent Pangaea about 200 million years ago.[5]

Some of the main tectonic processes, as they continue to work today, are illustrated in Figure 2-2. At *divergent plate boundaries* on the ocean floor, such as the East Pacific and Mid-Atlantic Ridges, adjacent plates move apart and new crust is created in the gap by *magma* (molten rock), which rises from below and then solidifies. This phenomenon is called seafloor spreading. At *convergent plate boundaries,* as along the western edge of South America, one plate may be driven beneath the other into the asthenosphere. Heat generated by the friction in these *subduction zones* melts some of the crustal rock to produce magma, which rises to feed volcanic activity at the surface. Deep-sea trenches, steep mountain ranges, and powerful earthquakes are other characteristics of these zones of violent collision between plates. At a third type of interface between plates, the plates slide past each other, moving parallel to the boundary. These *parallel-plate boundaries* are characterized by earthquakes with large surface displacements; the San Andreas Fault, which produced the great San Francisco earthquake of 1906, marks such a boundary. The principal plate boundaries are indicated on the map in Figure 2-3.

Many other geophysical processes operate simultaneously with the tectonic motions described above to govern the shape and composition of Earth's crust. These processes include mountain-building by uplifting of the crust, the wearing-away of exposed rock surfaces by the actions of wind, rain, ice, and chemical processes (together these effects are called *weathering*), the transport

[5]See J. Tuzo Wilson, ed., *Continents adrift.*

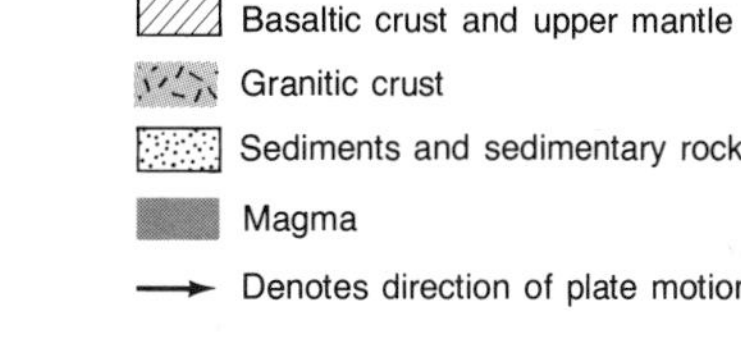

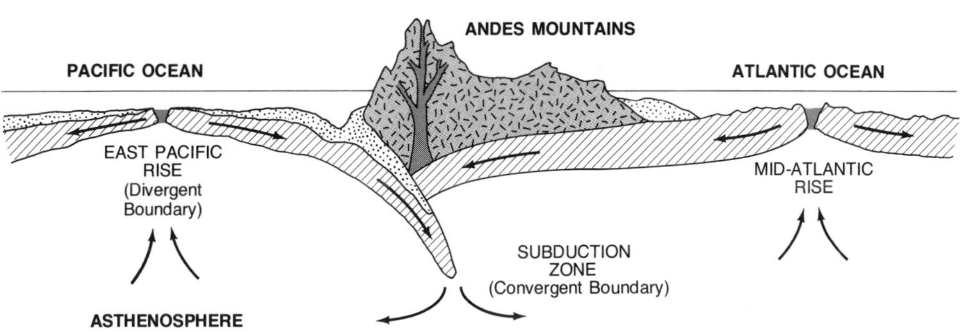

FIGURE 2-2

Tectonic processes and the Earth's surface. (From Rona, 1973.)

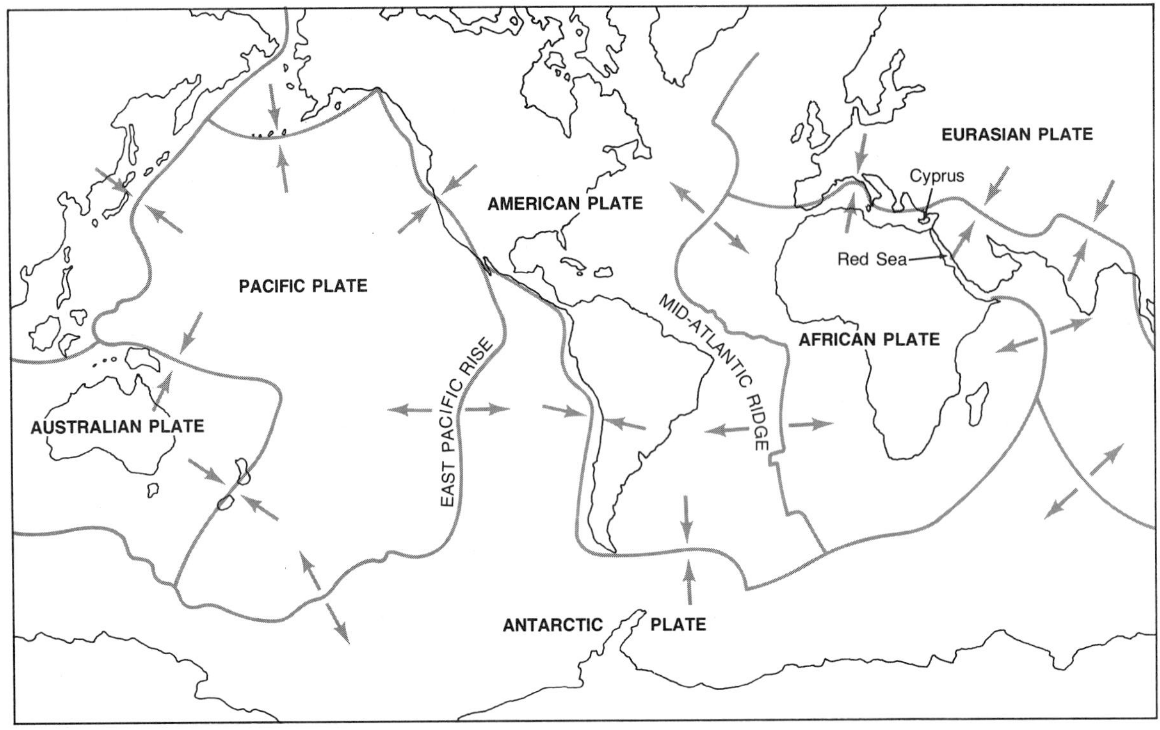

FIGURE 2-3

Six principal tectonic plates of the lithosphere.

of particles of rock and soil by water and wind *(erosion),* and the formation and transformation of new rocks from sedimentary material. The way in which these processes are linked together to produce the principal geological cycles is represented schematically in Figure 2-4.

Rock that is exposed at the surface of the crust is gradually weathered away by physical and chemical processes. The resulting particles are some of the raw materials for new soil (the formation of which also requires the action of living organisms), and some of the chemicals liberated from the rock become available to the biosphere as nutrients (see Chapter 3). Although the rock particles may sometimes be carried uphill by wind and ice, the predominant motion is downhill with the flow of water. Thus it happens over geologic spans of time (hundreds of thousands to millions of years) that large amounts of material are removed from the exposed rocky crust at high elevations and deposited on the lowlands and on the ocean floors. The accumulating weight of these sediments, consisting ultimately not only of rock fragments but also of dead plant and animal matter and chemicals precipitated out of seawater, contributes to sinking of the underlying crust and upper mantle. (Tectonic subsidence, the result of large-scale crustal motions, is more important in this sinking phenomenon than is the local accumulation of sediment weight, however.[6]) Simultaneously, crustal rise, or uplifting, under the lightened regions restores some of the loss of elevation produced by weathering and erosion. This process of sinking and uplifting is made possible by the capacity of the dense but soft (almost molten) asthenosphere to be deformed and, indeed, to flow. The folding

[6]Press and Siever, *Earth,* p. 479.

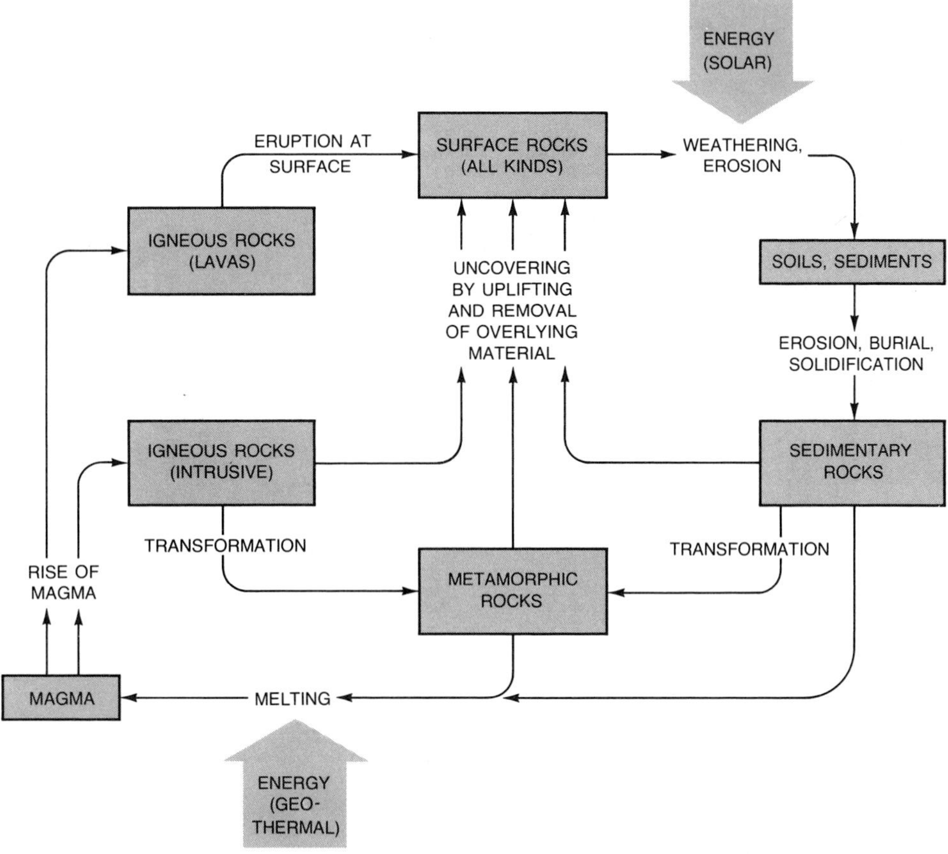

FIGURE 2-4

Geologic cycles. Intrusive igneous rocks are those that solidify from magma before reaching the surface, in contrast to extrusive igneous rocks (lava). Most sedimentation (deposition of sediments) takes place on the ocean floor. The time for material to complete a cycle is typically tens of millions to hundreds of millions of years.

and buckling of Earth's crust, which has produced much of the varied topography we see, is the combined result of the sinking-uplifting phenomenon just described and the continuous collision of the great lithospheric plates.

As layers of sediment become more deeply buried, they are subjected to temperatures and pressures high enough to initiate chemical and physical changes that transform the sediments into rock (called *sedimentary rocks*). Among the rocks formed in this way are shale, sandstone, limestone, and dolomite. Under some conditions, such as the particularly energetic geological environment where tectonic plates collide, further transformations under the action of heat and pressure produce *metamorphic rocks,* among which are slate and marble. The most abundant rocks in Earth's crust, however, are *igneous rocks*—those formed by the cooling and solidification of magma. Repeated local melting, migration, and resolidification of the rock in Earth's crust and upper mantle have led over the eons to a general stratification, with the densest material on the bottom and less dense material above. Thus, the upper layer of the continental crust consists largely of *granitic* igneous rocks—rocks rich in the relatively light elements silicon and aluminum. The oceanic crust and the lower layer of the continental crust (Figure 2-1) consist mainly of *basaltic* igneous rocks—somewhat denser material, containing substantial amounts of iron in addition to the lighter elements. The mantle below is *olivine* igneous rock, richer yet in iron and therefore denser than the overlying crust.

The average elemental composition of Earth's crust is given in Table 2-4. The predominance of the light elements is apparent: of the ten most abundant elements—accounting for 99 percent of the mass of the crust—only iron has an atomic number above 25. The crust comprises only about 0.4 percent of the mass of Earth, however. Essentially all the rest resides in the denser and vastly thicker mantle and core (Table 2-2). The composition of the entire planet (Table 2-5), reflects the predominance of iron in those inner layers. Of interest is that carbon, the basic building block of living material, is not among the most abundant elements (it ranks fourteenth in crustal abundance, at 0.032 percent).

TABLE 2-4
Average Composition of Earth's Crust

Element	*Atomic number*	*Percentage by weight*
Oxygen	8	45.2
Silicon	14	27.2
Aluminum	13	8.0
Iron	26	5.8
Calcium	20	5.1
Magnesium	12	2.8
Sodium	11	2.3
Potassium	19	1.7
Titanium	22	0.9
Hydrogen	1	0.14

Source: Brian J. Skinner, *Earth resources.*

TABLE 2-5
Average Composition of Earth (Overall)

Element	*Atomic number*	*Percentage by weight*
Iron	26	34.6
Oxygen	8	29.5
Silicon	14	15.2
Magnesium	12	12.7
Nickel	28	2.4
Sulfur	16	1.9
Calcium	20	1.1
Aluminum	13	1.1
Sodium	11	0.57
Chromium	24	0.26

Source: Brian Mason, *Principles of geochemistry.*

The energy that drives the great geological cycles has two distinct origins. Those parts of the cycles that take place on the surface—weathering, the formation of soil, erosion, the production of plant and animal matter that contributes to sediments—are powered by solar energy and its derivatives, wind and falling water. (The character of these energies is examined more closely later in this chapter.) The remaining geophysical processes (for example, the production and migration of magma and the inexorable motions of the tectonic plates) are driven by geothermal energy—heat that is produced beneath Earth's surface. It is thought that most of this heat results from the decay of radioactive isotopes that were already present when Earth was formed.[7] (The reader completely unfamiliar with the terminology and physics of radioactivity may wish to look ahead to Box 8-3.) The most important isotopes in this respect are uranium-238 (half-life 4.5 billion yr), thorium-232 (half-life 14 billion yr), and potassium-40 (half-life 1.3 billion yr). Notwithstanding the rather low concentration of these isotopes in Earth's crust, the energy released by their continuing radioactive decay is enough to account approximately for the observed rate of heat flow to the surface. The very long half-lives of these isotopes guarantee, moreover, that this source of energy for geological change will have been diminished only slightly a billion years hence.

The processes of melting and resolidification, sinking and uplifting, the motion of tectonic plates of continental scale, the gouging and pushing of massive glaciers, and the different rates of weathering and erosion associated with different climates and different combinations of exposed rocks have combined to produce a tremendous variety of geological features.[8] The importance of these features to human beings is severalfold. The landforms—plains, mountains, valleys, and so on—are one major determinant of the extent to which different parts of the planet's surface are habitable. The soils that have resulted from geological and biological processes over

[7]It is possible that there is some additional contribution by frictional heat generation resulting from tidal forces on the molten and plastic parts of Earth's interior.

[8]The reader interested in pursuing this complex but fascinating subject should consult one of the several good geology books listed at the end of this chapter.

the millennia are another (and more limiting) determinant of how many people can be supported and where. The zones of earthquakes and volcanism present serious environmental hazards to humans. And the distribution of fossil fuels and metals in scattered deposits far richer than the average crustal abundance is a geological phenomenon of enormous practical importance.

Although the processes that produced these features often act imperceptibly slowly in human terms, the temptation to consider the geological forces to be beyond human influence—or to take for granted their contributions to human well-being—must be resisted. Soil that has taken a thousand years to accumulate can be washed or blown away in a day through human carelessness; and there is evidence that the activities of human societies worldwide—cultivation, overgrazing, deforestation, construction—have doubled the prehistoric rate of sediment transport to the sea (Chapter 6 and Chapter 11). Earthquakes are widely feared and are called natural disasters, but the lack of foresight in planning and construction that has characterized the development of human settlements in active earthquake zones suggests that the consequences are due as much to human ignorance and irresponsibility as to nature's harshness. There are circumstances, moreover, in which human activities actually *cause* earthquakes (injection of liquid wastes into rock formations, for example), and conceivably there may someday be technological means by which the frequency of strong earthquakes can be diminished. Without concentrated deposits of mineral ores, industrial civilization as we know it could not have arisen; they represent a coincidental natural subsidy for society, provided by the work of natural energy flows over eons. The notion that technological civilization is now clever enough to do without this subsidy, once it is used up, by extracting needed materials from common rock is a dubious one. (We will examine this idea more closely in Chapter 9.)

THE HYDROSPHERE

Most forms of life on Earth require the simultaneous availability of mineral nutrients, certain gases, and water in liquid form. The boundaries of the biosphere—which are fuzzy, rather than sharp—can be defined as the places where the concentration of one or more of these essentials drops too low to sustain life. The principal reservoirs of available mineral nutrients are soil and sediment, the main reservoir of the needed gases is the atmosphere, and the primary supply of water is, of course, in the oceans. Where they meet, these reservoirs intermingle to produce the most fertile parts of the biosphere: the upper layers of soil, where gases and moisture readily penetrate, and the shallower parts of the oceans, where nutrients from the land and the bottom mingle with dissolved gases and light that penetrates downward from the surface.

The oceans include not only some of the planet's most hospitable environments for life (and, almost surely, the environment where life began) but also make up by far the largest single habitat on Earth's surface. They cover almost 71 percent of the planet and their volume is an almost incomprehensible 1.37 billion cubic kilometers (330 million mi^3). The term *hydrosphere* refers not only to the oceans themselves, however, but also to the "extensions" of the oceans in other realms—the water vapor and water droplets in the atmosphere, the lakes and the rivers; the water in soil and in pockets deep in layers of rock; the water locked up in ice caps and glaciers. The sections that follow here examine, first, some of the important characteristics of the oceans, then the behavior of ice on Earth's surface, and, finally, the hydrologic cycle, which makes water so widely available even far from the seas.

The Oceans

More than 97 percent of the water on or near the surface of Earth is in the oceans (Table 2-6). This enormous reservoir is a brine (salts dissolved in water) of almost uniform composition. The concentration of the dissolved salts ranges from 3.45 percent (by weight) to about 3.65 percent, varying with depth and latitude. The density of seawater varies between 1.026 and 1.030 grams per cubic centimeter, depending on depth and salinity, compared to 1.000 grams per cubic centimeter for fresh water at the reference temperature of 4° C (39° F). An average cubic meter[9] of seawater weighs 1027 kilograms

[9]One cubic meter (m^3) = 35.3 cubic feet = 264 gallons.

TABLE 2-6
Water Storage in the Hydrosphere

Storage	*Volume (1000 km³)**
Average in stream channels	1
Vapor and clouds in atmosphere	13
Soil water (above water table)	67
Saline lakes and inland seas	104
Freshwater lakes	125**
Groundwater (half less than 800 m below Earth's surface)	8,300
Ice caps and glaciers	29,200
Oceans	1,370,000

*1 km³ = 264 billion gallons.
**Twenty percent of this total is in Lake Baikal in the Soviet Union.
Source: Brian J. Skinner, *Earth resources.*

TABLE 2-7
*Composition of Seawater (excluding dissolved gases) (MT/km³)**

Elements at more than 1000 MT/km³		*Selected elements at less than 1000 MT/km³*	
H_2O	991,000,000	Lithium	175.0
Chlorine	19,600,000	Phospohorus	70.0
Sodium	10,900,000	Iodine	60.0
Magnesium	1,400,000	Molybdenum	10.0
Sulfur	920,000	Copper	3.0
Calcium	420,000	Uranium	3.0
Potassium	390,000	Nickel	2.0
Bromine	67,000	Cesium	0.4
Carbon	29,000	Silver	0.2
Strontium	8,300	Thorium	0.04
Boron	5,000	Lead	0.02
Silicon	3,100	Mercury	0.02
Fluorine	1,300	Gold	0.004

*1 MT = 1000 kg.
Source: Edward Wenk, Jr., The physical resources of the ocean, p. 167.

(1.027 MT, or 1.13 short tons), of which about 36 kilograms is dissolved salts. Although most of this material is the familiar sodium chloride, more than half of all the known elements are present in seawater at trace concentrations or more.

The concentrations of several elements in seawater are given in Table 2-7. It is thought that this composition has remained essentially unchanged during most of geologic time. This would mean that the inflow of minerals reaching the oceans from rivers, from the atmosphere, and from undersea volcanoes has been roughly balanced by the outflow—namely, the incorporation of inorganic precipitates and dead organic matter into sediments on the ocean floor.[10] In a situation of *equilibrium* of this kind (with inflow balancing outflow), it is easy to calculate the average time an atom of a given element spends in the ocean between entering it and leaving it. This is called the *residence time;* it is an important concept in the study of nutrient cycles and of pollution. The concepts of equilibrium and residence time, along with some related ideas that find widespread application in environmental sciences, are reviewed in Box 2-2. The residence times of

[10]A superb and detailed treatment of the processes maintaining the composition of the oceans appears in Ferren MacIntyre, Why the sea is salt. This and other *Scientific American* articles on the oceans referred to in this section are collected in J. Robert Moore, ed., *Oceanography.*

BOX 2-2 Flows, Stocks, and Equilibrium

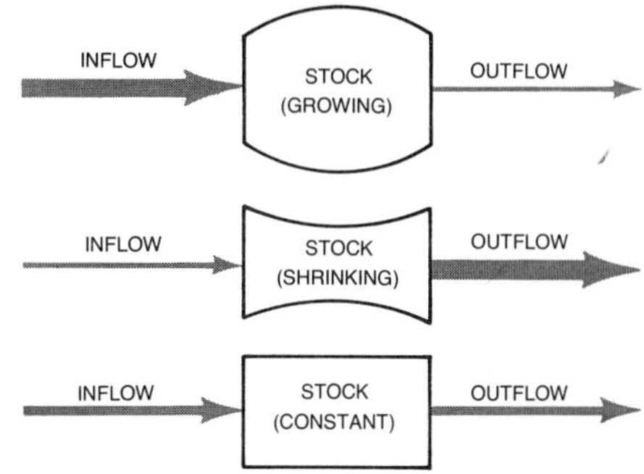

The terms *mass balance, energy balance, input/output analysis,* and *balancing the books* all refer to fundamentally the same kind of calculation—one that finds extensive application in physics, chemistry, biology, and economics and in the many disciplines where these sciences are put to use. The basic idea is very simple: everything has to go somewhere, and it is possible and useful to keep track of where and how fast it goes.

The concepts and terminology are illustrated in the diagram here. A stock is a supply of something in a particular place—money in a savings account, water in a lake, a particular element in the ocean. The stocks can be measured in terms of value (dollars), volume (liters), mass (grams), energy (joules), number of molecules, or other units, but not time. Time appears, instead, in the complementary concept of *flows,* the inflow (or input) being the amount of commodity added to the stock per unit of time and the outflow (or output) being the amount of commodity removed from the stock per unit of time. Thus, flows are measured in units like dollars per year, liters per minute, grams per day, or joules per second (watts). In the diagram, the sizes of the flows are indicated by the widths of the arrows. In a savings account, the inflow is deposits plus interest, the outflow is withdrawals, and the stock is the balance at any given time.

Clearly, if the inflow is greater than the outflow, the stock becomes larger as time passes; if outflow exceeds inflow, the stock shrinks. The change in the size of the stock in a given period is the difference between inflow and outflow, multiplied by the length of the period. (If the inflow and outflow vary during the period, one must use their averages.) In the event that the inflow and the outflow have exactly the same magnitude, the size of the stock remains constant. This last situation, where inflow and outflow balance is called equilibrium, or, more specifically, *dynamic equilibrium* (something is flowing, but nothing is changing). The more restrictive case where nothing at all is happening—that is, no inflow, no outflow—is called *static equilibrium.*

In a state of equilibrium, there is not necessarily any relation between the size of the flows (*throughput*) and the size of the stock.* For example, a small lake in equilibrium may be fed by a large river and drained by an equally large one (small stock, large throughput), or a large lake in equilibrium may be fed by a small river and drained by an equally small one (large stock, small throughput). If one divides the size of a stock in equilibrium by the size of the throughput, one obtains a very useful quantity—the *average residence time* (τ). In the example of the lakes, this is the average length of time a water molecule spends in the lake between entering and leaving. For a lake of 100 million cubic meters, fed and drained by two rivers with flows of 100 cubic meters per second each, the average residence time would be given by:

$$\tau = \frac{100{,}000{,}000 \text{ m}^3}{100 \text{ m}^3/\text{sec}} = 1{,}000{,}000 \text{ sec},$$

which is about twelve days. A smaller volume and/or a larger throughput would produce a shorter residence time.

The concept of residence time is useful not only for describing geophysical processes but also for analyzing economic and biological ones. Economic "residence times" include replacement periods for capital and labor. And, to cite an example from biology, if the stock is the world's human population, then the inflow is the rate at which people are born, the outflow is the rate at which people die, and the average residence time is the life expectancy. Clearly, a given population size could be maintained at equilibrium by conditions of high throughput (high birth rate, high death rate, short life expectancy) or by conditions of low throughput (low birth rate, low death rate, long life expectancy). This subject is taken up in more detail in later chapters.

*Throughput means just what you would think—"what flows through"—and in general has the magnitude of the smaller of the inflow and outflow in a given situation. In equilibrium, inflow and outflow and throughput are all the same number.

TABLE 2-8
Residence Times of Some Constituents of Seawater

Element	Residence time (million years)
Sodium	260
Magnesium	45
Calcium	8
Potassium	11
Silicon	0.01

Source: Strahler and Strahler, *Environmental geoscience*, p. 197.

some important constituents of seawater are listed in Table 2-8.

The absolute quantities of materials dissolved in a cubic kilometer of seawater are quite large—175 metric tons of lithium, 3 metric tons of copper, 200 kilograms of silver, and 4 kilograms of gold, to mention some elements commonly regarded as scarce. Multiplying such numbers by the total volume of the oceans gives very large numbers, indeed, and these staggering quantities, combined with the ready accessibility of the oceans, have stimulated much discussion of mining seawater for its riches. In mining, it is the *concentration* of the material that counts, however (a subject to which we return in Chapter 9). To get the three tons of copper in a cubic kilometer of seawater, for instance, this desired material must somehow be separated from the billion metric tons of other elements mixed up with it, and this is not easy.

Probably a more important reason for looking into the details of the composition of the oceans is to evaluate the seriousness of various kinds of ocean pollution. If pollutants such as lead and mercury, for example, are added to the oceans in sufficient quantities to alter substantially the natural concentrations of those elements over large areas, one might suspect that significant biochemical consequences could result. If, on the other hand, the discharge of an element into the ocean produces concentration changes small compared to natural variations in space and time of the concentration of this substance, little or no harm would be expected.

One cannot assume, of course, that substances added to the oceans are quickly diluted by this vast volume of water. How far? How deep? How fast? are the questions, and the answers are found in the rather complicated patterns of horizontal circulation and vertical mixing in the oceans, as well as in the functioning of biological systems that may concentrate them (Chapter 4). Vertical mixing is rapid only near the surface. The turbulence (violent mixing motions) produced by wave action at the surface penetrates only to a depth of from 100 to 200 meters, and this defines the thickness of the layer within which most of the absorbed solar energy is distributed.

Below this warm, well-stirred surface layer is a transitional region called the *thermocline,* where the temperature drops rapidly. In this region there is usually less vertical motion than in the surface layer. Here heat penetrates partly by conduction (molecules passing on energy by jostling their neighbors) but mostly by convection (transport of energy by bulk motion of a warm medium) in large, slow eddies. There are two reasons for the relative lack of vertical motion in the thermocline: (1) motions originating at the surface have been damped out by friction before penetrating so deep and (2) the colder water near the bottom of the thermocline tends to be denser than the warmer water near the top of this layer, stifling thermal circulation.[11] In some circumstances, however, variations in salinity can influence density enough to produce a vertical circulation, despite the countervailing influence of the temperature profile. The bottom of the thermocline lies between 1000 and 1500 meters below the surface; from this level down, the temperature is nearly uniform and lies in the range from 0° to 5° C. (Seawater freezes at −2° C, or about 28.4° F.) Like the thermocline, this deepest ocean layer is thermally stratified, with the coldest water lying at the bottom. In the deep layer, moreover, salinity increases with depth; the saltier water is, the denser it is, so the salinity profile and the temperature profile both place the densest water at the bottom, inhibiting vertical mixing.

This simplified view of the vertical layering of the oceans is illustrated schematically in Figure 2-5. Note that the stratification breaks down near the poles, where

[11]Thermal circulation, or thermal convection, occurs when warm fluid (liquid or gas), finding itself below colder, denser fluids, rises, while the colder material sinks. This is what happens when a fluid, such as water in a pan, is heated from below. The ocean is heated mainly at the top.

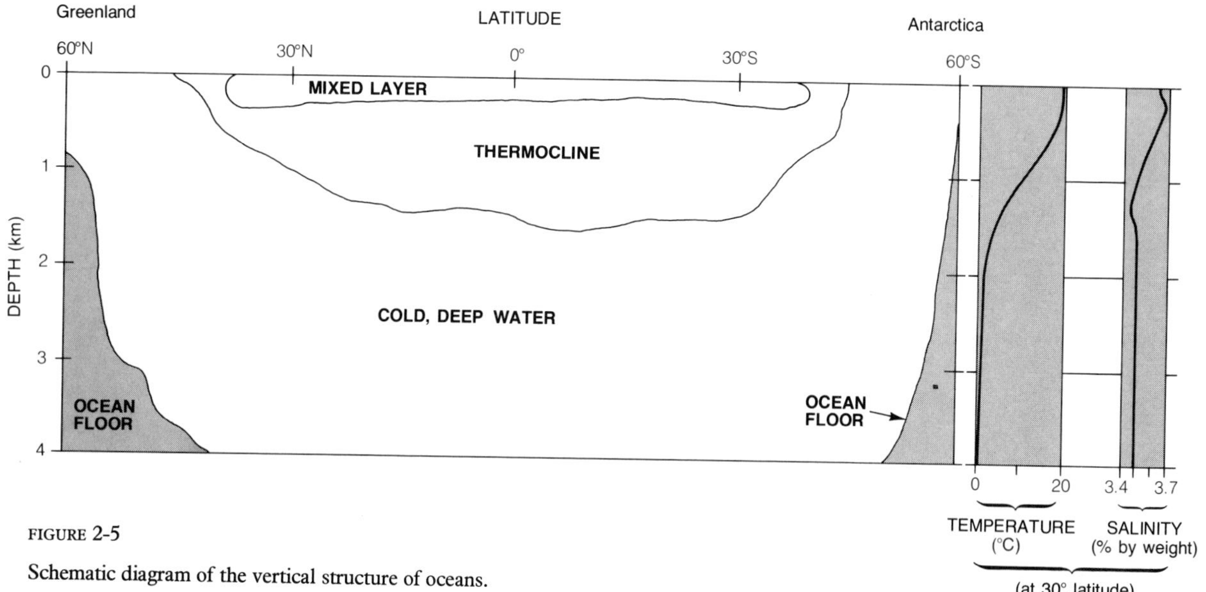

FIGURE 2-5

Schematic diagram of the vertical structure of oceans.

the cold layer extends all the way to the surface. That the surface waters in the Arctic and Antarctic oceans should be considered outcroppings of the deep layer that extends throughout the world ocean is suggested not only by patterns of temperature and salinity but also by the distribution of certain creatures. The huge Greenland shark, for example, once thought to inhabit only Arctic waters, has been photographed three or four kilometers deep in waters off Baja California and in the Indian Ocean.[12]

The stable stratification of the oceans also breaks down at scattered places and times far from the poles, as in upwellings in which winds push the surface water away from a steep continental slope and cold water rises from below to replace it (off the coast of Peru, for example) or when rapid cooling of surface water under unusual circumstances causes it to sink. The mean residence times for water in the various ocean layers illustrate the relative rarity in space and time of large vertical movements: a typical water molecule in the mixed layer may spend 10 years there, whereas one in the thermocline spends 500 years before reaching the deep layer, and a water molecule in the deep layer typically spends 2000 or 3000 years before reaching one of the upper layers. Clearly, it must be assumed that most substances added to the oceans near the surface and dissolved there will remain near the surface for years, being diluted only by the small fraction of the ocean water that makes up the well mixed top layer (between 3 and 5 percent).

Horizontal circulation in the oceans is considerably faster than vertical mixing. Water in the main currents, which generally involve only the mixed layers, typically moves at speeds of 1 kilometer per hour (km/hr), and occasionally up to 5 kilometers per hour. Thus, an object or a substance being carried in the current might easily move 1000 kilometers in a month and cross an ocean in six months to a year. (The main oceanic surface currents appear on the map in Figure 2-6.) The principal features are the circular movements, called *gyres,* centered in the subtropical latitudes (25° to 30° north and south of the equator), an equatorial countercurrent (most prominent in the Pacific) that provides a return pathway for water that would otherwise be piling up against Asia and Australia, and the Antarctic circumpolar current, flowing uninterrupted from west to east around the far southern part of the globe. These currents are produced

[12]John D. Isaacs, The nature of oceanic life.

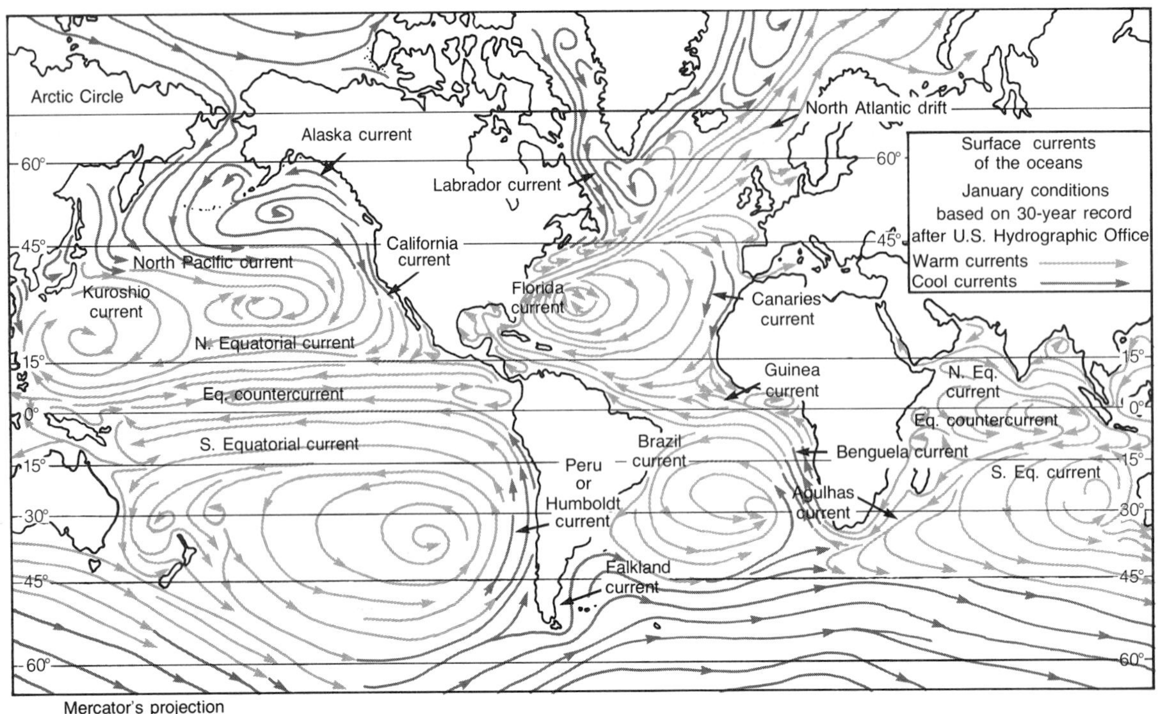

FIGURE 2-6

Main oceanic surface currents.

by a complex interaction of the effects of the winds, Earth's rotation, and the placement of continents and islands.[13] By moving enormous quantities of water—sometimes warm, sometimes cold—from one region to another, the ocean currents exert a major influence on climate, a subject taken up in more detail later. The two mightiest currents on Earth, the Antarctic circumpolar current and the main branch of the Gulf Stream, each carries some fifty times the combined flow of all the world's rivers.[14]

The horizontal circulation in the deep layer of the ocean is much less thoroughly mapped than that of the surface layer and has been widely supposed to be much less vigorous. Typical speeds in these deep currents have been thought to be on the order of 0.1 kilometer per hour or less. An increasing number of direct measurements of deep ocean currents now suggest a much more vigorous deep-ocean circulation, however, involving powerful eddies 100 kilometers or more in horizontal extent, containing currents of 0.5 to 1 kilometer per hour.[15] One would expect the general flow to be from the poles toward the equator, inasmuch as some cold water enters the deep layer from above at the poles and some rises in upwellings closer to the equator. But the actual situation is made quite complicated by Earth's rotation, by the irregular distribution of landmasses, and by the complex topography of the ocean floor.

It has been true historically and is still true today that the usefulness of the oceans to civilization and, in turn, civilization's impact on the oceans have been greatest in the shallower waters at the edges of the continents. This

[13]See, for example, R. W. Stewart, The atmosphere and the ocean.
[14]P. H. Kuenen, *Realms of water,* p. 47.

[15]F. Bretherton, Recent developments in dynamical oceanography.

is so partly for simple reasons of accessibility, and partly because of the particular fertility of the near-shore waters and the richness of the underlying sediment in minerals of economic interest. The term *continental shelf* refers to that part of the near-shore underwater topography that is actually an extension of flatlands on a continent itself. Although the outer edge of a continental shelf is often defined as the line along which the depth of the water reaches 200 meters, a less arbitrary boundary is the point where there is a marked increase in the downward slope of the bottom. The steeply sloping region just beyond this boundary is called the *continental slope.* The "foothills" leading from the ocean floor to the seaward edge of the continental slope are called the *continental rise.*

Using the definition of continental shelf just given, it has been estimated that continental shelves underlie 7.5 percent of the area of the oceans (an area equal, however, to 18 percent of Earth's land area).[16] These shelves vary in width from essentially nothing to 1500 kilometers, and their seaward edges vary in depth from 20 to 550 meters (the average depth at the edge is 133 meters). The circulation patterns in shallow, continental-shelf waters are complex, and the residence times of dissolved substances over the shelf can be surprisingly long—as much as several years to migrate from the coastline to the outer edge of a wide shelf like that off the east coast of the United States.

Glaciers and Sea Ice

Fifteen thousand years ago, much of what is now continental shelf was dry land. Sea level was 130 meters lower than it is today. Where was the 45 million cubic kilometers of water (about 12 billion billion gallons!) this difference in sea level represents? It was locked up in the great glaciers of the ice age. In the warmer period in which we find ourselves today, the water that remains frozen as ice still far exceeds all other reservoirs of fresh water on Earth (Table 2-6). Were this ice to melt, sea level would rise another 80 meters.

It is important in this connection to distinguish between *glaciers* and *sea ice.* A glacier is a sheet of ice formed *on land* when accumulated snow is compressed and hardened into ice by the weight of overlying layers. Sea ice is ice formed from seawater; it floats on the ocean's surface, although it may be attached to land at its edges.

The glaciers that usually come to mind when one hears this term are the scattered "mountain and valley glaciers" that occur throughout the world's high mountain ranges—the Himàlayas, Andes, Rockies, and Alps, for example. The larger glaciers of this variety are some tens of kilometers long, a kilometer or more across, and a few hundred meters thick. These glaciers are constantly in motion, being fed by snowfall at their surfaces in the higher elevations and moving downhill as the deep layers, under great pressure, flow as a plastic solid. (Perhaps the easiest way to visualize what is going on in such flow, which as we noted earlier also occurs in rock in Earth's mantle, is to consider the plastic solid to be an extremely viscous fluid.) The speed of advance varies along the length of the glacier, but is typically 100 meters per year or more in the main body of the larger mountain glaciers. The advance of such glaciers is terminated by melting of the tongue of the glacier at the lower end.

By far the greatest part of the world's inventory of ice—more than 99 percent—is tied up in a second kind of glacier, the land ice or ice sheets, that cover the bulk of the Greenland and Antarctic landmasses. The formation of such a sheet requires an arctic climate, sufficient precipitation, and fairly flat land. The ice layer that results covers essentially the entire landscape in a gently sloping dome, interrupted only by a few projecting mountain peaks. The Greenland ice sheet covers an area of 1.74 million square kilometers (about 80 percent of the total area of Greenland) and has an average thickness of about 1600 meters (5250 ft). The Antarctic ice sheet covers 13 million square kilometers with ice up to 4000 meters thick (13,000 ft) and averaging perhaps 2300 meters.[17] About 91 percent of the world's ice thus is in the Antarctic sheet and about 9 percent in the Greenland sheet. These ice sheets, like mountain and valley glaciers,

[16]K. O. Emery, The continental shelves.

[17]Press and Siever, *Earth,* p. 371; Strahler and Strahler, *Environmental geoscience,* pp. 434–436.

are in motion, carrying to the sea the ice formed from precipitation in the central regions. Typical speeds are some tens of meters per year on the ice sheet proper, but they can be much higher—hundreds, and even thousands, of meters per year—where certain glacial tongues meet the sea.

Where the ice sheets meet the sea in broad expanses, they may extend into the ocean as more-or-less floating ice shelves, from tens to hundreds of meters thick. In the Antarctic, these shelves reach widths of hundreds of kilometers. The largest, the Ross Ice Shelf, covers more than 500,000 square kilometers. Icebergs originate when great masses of ice break off from the tips of glacial tongues or the edges of ice shelves and are carried away (often into shipping lanes) by currents (see Figure 2-7).

Sea ice, as distinguished from floating extensions or pieces of glaciers, is formed by the freezing of seawater on the ocean surface. The North Pole ice pack, with a mean extent of about 10 million square kilometers, is a collection of slabs of sea ice floating on the Arctic Ocean. In winter, these slabs are frozen together and attached to land at various points around the ocean's periphery. In summer, some of the slabs break apart and are separated by narrow strips of open water, and the southern limit of the ice retreats northward. The sea ice, which begins to form at $-2°$ C, is porous, and the enclosed cavities often contain water saltier than seawater. Glacial ice, by contrast, consists of fresh water, being simply compacted and recrystallized snow.

The maximum thickness of sea ice is only between 3 and 5 meters. Once it reaches this thickness, the layer of ice insulates the underlying water so well that no more can freeze—heat is supplied from the deeper water faster than the surface layer can lose it through the ice. (Ice is a poor conductor of heat and snow an even poorer one, which is why snow igloos stay so warm inside.) If the average thickness of the North Pole ice pack is 2 meters, it contains less than one-hundredth as much ice as the Greenland ice sheet.[18] Of course, melting of the sea ice would have no direct effect on sea level, even if the volume of this ice were much greater; the ice is floating, thus displacing an amount of water equal to its weight, so

[18]Ten million km^2 of area multiplied by 0.002 km average thickness is 20,000 km^3 of ice in the polar pack, compared to 1.7 million km^2 multiplied by 2.2 km average thickness, or 2,700,000 km^3 of ice, in the Greenland sheet.

FIGURE 2-7

A glacier feeding ice into the sea in Paradise Bay, Antarctica. No large icebergs are visible in this picture. (Photo by P. R. Ehrlich.)

it is already contributing exactly as much to the level of the oceans as it would if it melted. Aside from the sea-level issue, however, which relates solely to glacial ice sheets, the sea ice has great importance for climate.

The Hydrologic Cycle

Although oceans and ice caps contain some 99.3 percent of all the water on Earth (Table 2-6), the fraction of 1 percent residing at any given time in the atmosphere, in lakes and streams, and in soil and subsurface layers plays unique and important roles. The flow of water on the surface is a major determinant of the configuration of the physical environment. Soil moisture is essential to most terrestrial plant life. The stocks and flows of ground and surface water are major links in the transport and cycling of chemical nutrients and important determinants of what kinds and intensities of human activity can be supported in what locations. And water in the atmosphere has several functions that are central to shaping climates.

The set of processes that maintain the flow of water through the terrestrial and atmospheric branches of the hydrosphere is called the *hydrologic cycle.* The cycle includes all three physical states of water—liquid, solid (ice and snow), and gas (water vapor). It also includes all of the possible transformations among these states—*vaporization,* or evaporation (liquid to gas); *condensation* (gas to liquid), *freezing* (liquid to solid); melting, or *fusion* (solid to liquid); and *sublimation* (gas to solid, or the reverse).

The principal flows in the hydrologic cycle are: (1) *evaporation* of water from the surface of the oceans and other bodies of water, and from the soil; (2) *transpiration* of water by plants, the result of which is the same as that of evaporation—namely, the addition of water vapor to the atmosphere; (3) horizontal *transport* of atmospheric water from one place to another, either as vapor or as the liquid water droplets and ice crystals in clouds; (4) *precipitation,* in which atmospheric water vapor condenses (and perhaps freezes) or sublimates and falls on the oceans and the continents as rain, sleet, hail, or snow; and (5) *runoff,* in which water that has fallen on the continents as precipitation finds its way, flowing on and under the surface, back to the oceans. Because it is difficult and not particularly useful to distinguish between the contributions of evaporation and transpiration on the continents, these two terms are often lumped together as *evapotranspiration.*

The magnitudes of these flows, averaged over all the continents and oceans and expressed in thousands of cubic kilometers of water per year, are shown in Figure 2-8.[19] These magnitudes are based on the assumption that the various components of the hydrosphere are in equilibrium, which is at least a good first approximation. That is, on a year-round average, inflows and outflows for the atmosphere, the oceans, and the continents all balance. (For example, in thousands of cubic kilometers, the atmosphere receives $62 + 456 = 518$ as evaporation from the surface and gives up $108 + 410 = 518$ as precipitation.)

The magnitude of the flows in the hydrologic cycle is more readily grasped if one thinks of the flows in terms of the equivalent depth of water, averaged over the surface area involved. In these terms, the world's oceans annually lose to evaporation a layer of water 1.26 meters deep (about 4 feet) over their entire surfaces, gaining back 1.14 meters from precipitation and 0.12 meters from the discharge of rivers and groundwater. The continents receive precipitation each year equivalent to a layer of water 0.73 meters (29 in) deep over their entire surface areas, of which 0.42 meters is lost to evaporation and 0.31 meters makes up the runoff.

Combining the foregoing information on equilibrium flows with the information on stocks in the hydrosphere summarized in Table 2-6 permits us to estimate the average residence time of water in the different parts of the cycle (see Box 2-2). These residence times, which are of great importance in analyzing the transport of pollutants, as well as nutrients, by the hydrologic cycle, are listed in Table 2-9. There is an enormous range, from the average nine days a water molecule spends in the atmosphere between being evaporated from the surface and falling again as precipitation, to the 10,000 years a

[19]The values presented here are at the high end of a range of published estimates, in which the differences of professional opinion amount to as much as 25 percent.

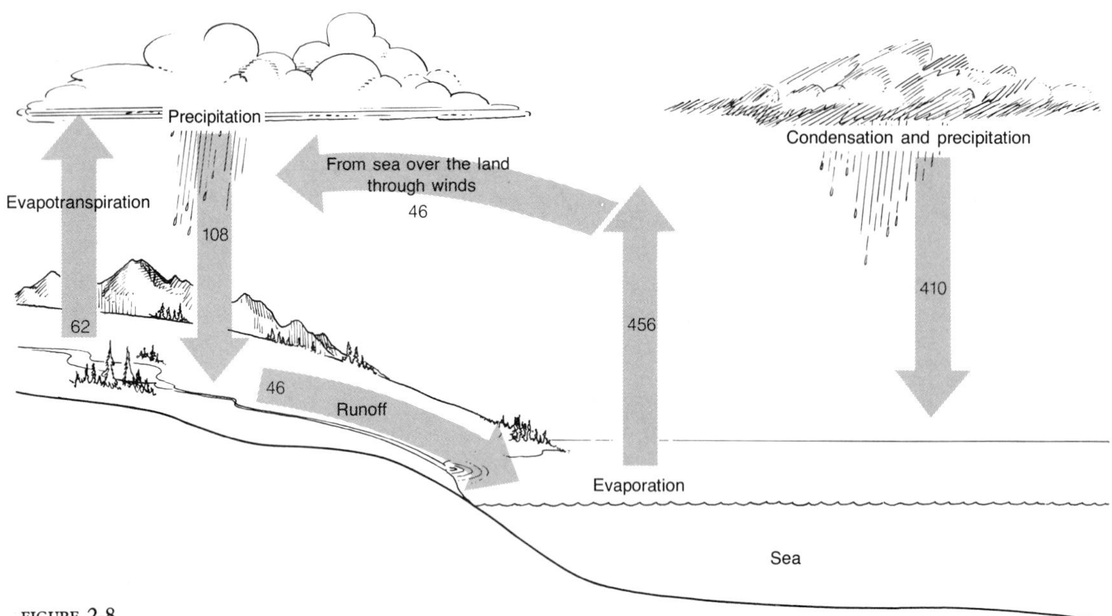

FIGURE 2-8

The hydrologic cycle (1000 km³/yr). (Data from M. I. Budyko, 1974.)

TABLE 2-9
Residence Times of Water Molecules in the Hydrologic Cycle

Location	*Residence time*
Atmosphere	9 days
Rivers (typical speed, 1 m/sec)	2 weeks
Soil moisture	2 weeks to 1 year
Largest lakes	10 years
Shallow groundwater (speed, 1–10 m/day)	10s to 100s of years
Mixed layer of oceans (1st 150 m)	120 years
World ocean	3000 years
Deep groundwater	up to 10,000 years
Antarctic ice cap	10,000 years

Sources: Computed from Table 2-6 and Figure 2-8 or adapted from SMIC, *Inadvertent climate modification,* and Strahler and Strahler, *Environmental geoscience.*

molecule of water typically spends as ice between falling in a snowflake on the Antarctic ice sheet and rejoining the ocean with the melting of an iceberg. It is also important to remember that there are large deviations from the average in any given category—a water molecule may fall in a raindrop not nine days but an hour after being evaporated from Earth's surface; another may wander not two weeks but two years in the delta of the Amazon River before reaching the sea. Nevertheless, the average residence times can provide useful insights into a variety of important problems, and the approach can be refined whenever information more pertinent than global averages is available.

The balance between precipitation and evapotranspiration varies widely from continent to continent, as shown in Table 2-10. The size of the runoff (the difference between precipitation and evapotranspiration) is a measure of how much water is potentially available for domestic and industrial uses by society (including dilution and removal of wastes) and for the other functions that flowing water performs. Note in Table

TABLE 2-10
Average Water Balance of the Continents

	Precipitation (cm/yr)	Evaporation (cm/yr)	Runoff (cm/yr)	Runoff (km³/yr)
Africa	69	43	26	7,700
Asia*	60	31	29	13,000
Australia	47	42	5	380
Europe	64	39	25	2,200
North America	66	32	34	8,100
South America	163	70	93	16,600

*Includes entire USSR.
Source: Budyko, M. I., p. 227.

2-10 the remarkable fact that South America has a runoff per unit of surface area almost three times that of North America, the continent with the next greatest runoff. It is perhaps not so surprising, then, that the discharge of the Amazon River, which drains the wettest third of South America, amounts to about a seventh of the runoff of the entire world.

Much of the runoff on the continents takes place not on the surface but beneath it. Although the quantities can only be estimated, it is clear that most rivers receive at least as much of their flow from seepage through the ground as from flow over the ground; and a certain amount of water reaches the oceans via flowing aquifers and seepage at the edges of the continents without ever joining a surface river at all.[20] Water beneath the land's surface is called *soil moisture,* or soil water, when it is distributed in the first meter or so of soil (a zone defined by the depth of penetration of the roots of most plants.) Below the zone of soil moisture is an intermediate zone where the water percolates downward through open pores in the soil and rock; and below this is the *water table,* marking the surface of the body of *groundwater* that saturates the soil or rock in which it finds itself, filling all pores and spaces in the soil or rock completely. The groundwater extends downward until it is limited by an impermeable layer of rock. In some circumstances, there are successive layers of groundwater (*aquifers*) separated by impermeable layers of rock. The absolute lowest limit of groundwater is probably about 16 kilometers from the surface, where the pressure is so great that all pores are closed and any rock becomes impermeable.

Most groundwater is flowing, albeit very slowly [10 meters per day (m/d) in coarse gravel near the surface, more commonly 1 m/d, and much more slowly at greater depths.] At 1 meter per day, of course, it takes almost three years to move 1 kilometer. Figure 2-9 is a schematic diagram of the zones and flows of subsurface water, showing the intersection of the water table and a surface river.

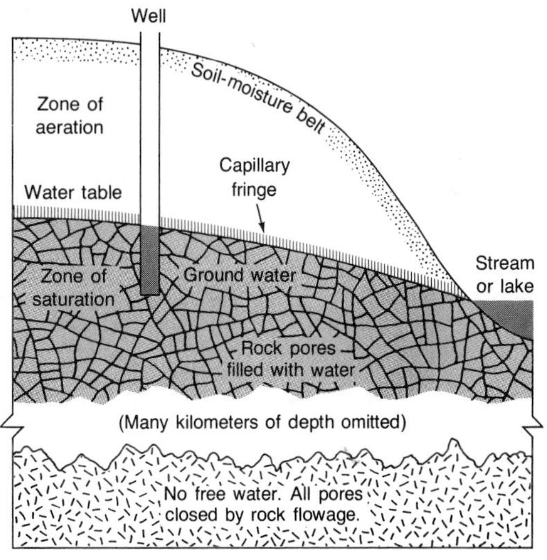

FIGURE 2-9

Zones of subsurface water. (After Ackerman, Colman, and Ogrosky, in A. N. Strahler and A. H. Strahler, *Environmental geoscience.*)

[20]See, for example, Strahler and Strahler, *Environmental geoscience,* Chapter 12, and Kuenen, *Realms of Water,* Chapter 5.

The energy that drives the hydrologic cycle is energy from the sun—indeed, this function is the largest single user of the solar energy reaching Earth's surface. The reason so much energy is required is that it takes a great deal of energy to evaporate water—2250 joules per gram at the boiling point of 100° C and 2440 joules per gram at Earth's average surface temperature of 15° C. (This is the highest heat of vaporization of any known substance.) It takes fifty times as much energy to evaporate a gram of water as it does to lift it to an altitude of 5 kilometers. The energy used to evaporate the water is stored as latent heat of vaporization (see Box 2-1), which is released to the environment as heat whenever and wherever the water vapor condenses into liquid. Thus, energy delivered by the sun at one point on Earth's surface may be released high in the atmosphere over a point 1000 kilometers away. This mechanism of redistributing energy by the transport and condensation of water vapor is a major determinant of Earth's climate.

As noted above, the energy the sun supplies at the time of evaporation reappears as heat at the time of condensation. Similarly, the smaller amount of solar energy that does the work of lifting the water vapor against the force of gravity appears as frictional heat when falling droplets of condensed vapor collide with molecules of air and when rushing mountain streams rub against their rocky beds. That all the energy the sun supplies to terrestrial processes comes back again in one form or another is not coincidence or quirk, but an illustration of the first law of thermodynamics—the law of conservation of energy. Further excursions into the machinery of the physical world—and of human technology—will require some familiarity with this law and with its companion, the second law of thermodynamics, so an introduction to both is provided in Box 2-3.

ATMOSPHERE AND CLIMATE

The blanket of gases that makes up Earth's atmosphere has many functions. Of the four elements required in greatest quantity by living organisms [carbon (C), oxygen (O), hydrogen (H), nitrogen (N)] the atmosphere provides the main reservoir of one (N), the most accessible reservoir of two others (C, O), and an essential link in the continuous recycling of the fourth (H, in the form of H_2O). The atmosphere is substantial enough to protect the organisms on Earth's surface from a variety of harmful particles and radiations that reach the planet from the sun and from space, but it is transparent enough to permit an adequate amount of life-giving sunlight to penetrate to that surface. Acting as a thermal insulator, the atmosphere keeps Earth's surface much warmer, on the average, than it would be if there were no atmosphere. And the stirrings of the atmosphere, transporting energy and moisture from one place to another, are a major part of the patterns of climate so important to the character and distribution of life.

For simplicity, we begin our investigation of the atmosphere by ignoring its internal vertical and horizontal motions and considering its properties as a static body of gas.

Air

The term *air* refers to the particular mixture of gaseous compounds making up the atmosphere. The average composition of this mixture, not including water, is shown in Table 2-11. An important property of gases is that a given number of molecules at a given temperature and pressure will occupy almost exactly the same volume, regardless of the mass or size of the molecules. This property has led to the use of the somewhat confusing terms *percent by volume* or *fraction by volume* to describe the relative abundance of the various constituents of gaseous mixtures. That is, if three-quarters of the molecules in a container of fixed volume are gas *A* and one-quarter are gas *B*, one can think of gas *A* as "occupying" three-fourths of the volume and gas *B* as "occupying" one-fourth. (What is happening in reality, of course, is that both gases, mixed together, occupy the whole volume, with gas *A* accounting for three-fourths of the pressure in the volume and gas *B* accounting for one-fourth of the pressure.) We will use the term *molecular fraction* (number of molecules of a constituent divided by the total number of molecules in the mixture), because it is unambiguous and works for solids and liquids as well as gases. The reader should simply be aware that this term is interchangeable with the term

TABLE 2-11
Average Composition of Clean Dry Air

Constituent	*Symbol*	*Molecular weight*	*Molecular fraction of air*	*Mass fraction of air*
Nitrogen	N_2	28	0.7809	0.755
Oxygen	O_2	32	0.2095	0.232
Argon	Ar	40	0.0093	0.013
Carbon Dioxide	CO_2	44	320 ppm	486 ppm
Neon	Ne	20	18 ppm	12 ppm
Helium	He	4	5.2 ppm	0.7 ppm
Methane	CH_4	16	2.9 ppm	1.6 ppm
Krypton	Kr	84	1.1 ppm	3.2 ppm
Nitrous Oxide	N_2O	44	0.5 ppm	0.8 ppm
Hydrogen	H_2	2	0.5 ppm	0.03 ppm
Ozone	O_3	48	0.01 ppm	0.02 ppm

Source: Garrels, Mackenzie, and Hunt, *Chemical cycles.*

BOX 2-3 Availability, Entropy, and the Laws of Thermodynamics

Many processes in nature and in technology involve the transformation of energy from one form into others. For example, light from the sun is transformed, upon striking a meadow, into thermal energy in the warmed soil, rocks, and plants; into latent heat of vaporization as water evaporates from the soil and through the surface of the plants; and into chemical energy captured in the plants by photosynthesis. Some of the thermal energy, in turn, is transformed into infrared electromagnetic radiation heading skyward. The imposing science of thermodynamics is just the set of principles governing the bookkeeping by which one keeps track of energy as it moves through such transformations. A grasp of these principles of bookkeeping is essential to an understanding of many problems in environmental sciences and energy technology.

The essence of the accounting is embodied in two concepts known as the first and second laws of thermodynamics. No exception to either one has ever been observed. The first law, also known as the law of conservation of energy, says that energy can neither be created nor destroyed. If energy in one form or one place disappears, the same amount must show up in another form or another place. In other words, although transformations can alter the *distribution* of amounts of energy among its different forms, the *total* amount of energy, when all forms are taken into account, remains the same. The term *energy consumption,* therefore, is a misnomer; energy is used, but it is not really consumed. One can speak of fuel consumption, because fuel, as such, does get used up. But when we burn gasoline, the amounts of energy that appear as mechanical energy, thermal energy, electromagnetic radiation, and other forms are exactly equal all together to the amount of chemical potential energy that disappears. The accounts must always balance; apparent exceptions have invariably turned out to stem from measurement errors or from overlooking categories. The immediate relevance of the first law for human affairs is often stated succinctly as, "You can't get something for nothing."

Yet, if energy is stored work, it might seem that the first law is also saying, "You can't lose!" (by saying that the total amount of stored work in all forms never changes). If the amount of stored work never diminishes, how can we become worse off? One obvious answer is that we can become worse off if energy flows to places where we can no longer get at it—for example, infrared radiation escaping from Earth into space. Then the stored work is no longer accessible to us, although it still exists. A far more fundamental point, however, is that *different kinds of stored work are not equally convertible into useful, applied work.* We can therefore become worse off if energy is transformed from a more convertible form to a less convertible one, even though no energy is destroyed and even if the energy has not moved to an inaccessible place. The degree of convertibility of energy—stored work—into applied work is often called *availability.*

Energy in forms having high availability (that is, in which a relatively large fraction of the

(*Continued*)

BOX 2-3 (*Continued*)

stored work can be converted into applied work) is often called high-grade energy. Correspondingly, energy of which only a small fraction can be converted to applied work is called low-grade energy, and energy that moves from the former category to the latter is said to have been degraded. Electricity and the chemical energy stored in gasoline are examples of high-grade energy; the infrared radiation from a light bulb and the thermal energy in an automobile exhaust are corresponding examples of lower-grade energy. The quantitative measure of the availability of thermal energy is temperature. More specifically, the larger the *temperature difference* between a substance and its environment, the more convertible into applied work is the thermal energy the substance contains; in other words, the greater the temperature difference, the greater the availability. A small pan of water boiling at 100° C in surroundings that are at 20° C represents considerable available energy because of the temperature difference; the water in a swimming pool at the same 20° C temperature as the surroundings contains far more total thermal energy than the water in the pan, but the availability of the thermal energy in the swimming pool is zero, because there is no temperature difference between it and its surroundings.

With this background, one can state succinctly the subtle and overwhelmingly important message of the second law of thermodynamics: *all physical processes, natural and technological, proceed in such a way that the availability of the energy involved decreases.* (Idealized processes can be constructed theoretically in which the availability of the energy involved stays constant, rather than decreasing, but in all real processes there is *some* decrease. The second law says that an *increase* is not possible, even in an ideal process.) As with the first law, apparent violations of the second law often stem from leaving something out of the accounting. In many processes, for example, the availability of energy in some *part* of the affected system increases, but the decrease of availability elsewhere in the system is always large enough to result in a net decrease in availability of energy overall. What is consumed when we use energy, then, is not energy itself but its availability for doing useful work.

The statement of the second law given above is deceptively simple; whole books have been written about equivalent formulations of the law and about its implications. Among the most important of these formulations and implications are the following:

1. In any transformation of energy, some of the energy is degraded.
2. No process is possible whose sole result is the conversion of a given quantity of heat (thermal energy) into an equal amount of useful work.
3. No process is possible whose sole result is the flow of heat from a colder body to a hotter one.
4. The availability of a given quantity of energy can only be used once; that is, the property of convertibility into useful work cannot be "recycled."
5. In spontaneous processes, concentrations (of anything) tend to disperse, structure tends to disappear, order becomes disorder.

That Statements 1 through 4 are equivalent to or follow from our original formulation is readily verified. To see that statement 5 is related to the other statements, however, requires establishing a formal connection between order and availability of energy. This connection has been established in thermodynamics through the concept of *entropy,* a well defined measure of disorder that can be shown to be a measure of unavailability of energy, as well. A statement of the second law that contains or is equivalent to all the others is: *all physical processes proceed in such a way that the entropy of the universe increases.* (Not only can't we win—we can't break even, and we can't get out of the game!)

Consider some everyday examples of various aspects of the second law. If a partitioned container is filled with hot water on one side and cold water on the other and is left to itself, the hot water cools and the cold water warms—heat flows from hotter to colder. Note that the opposite process (the hot water getting hotter and the cold getting colder) does not violate the first law, conservation of energy. That it does not occur illustrates the second law. Indeed, many processes can be imagined that satisfy the first law but violate the second and therefore are not expected to occur. As another example, consider adding a drop of dye to a glass of water. Intuition and the second law dictate that the dye will spread, eventually coloring all the water—concentrations disperse, order (the dye/no dye ar-

BOX 2-3 (*Continued*)

rangement) disappears. The opposite process, the spontaneous concentration of dispersed dye, is consistent with conservation of energy but not with the second law.

A more complicated situation is that of the refrigerator, a device that certainly causes heat to flow from cold objects (the contents of the refrigerator—say, beer—which are made colder) to a hot one (the room, which the refrigerator makes warmer). But this heat flow is not the *sole* result of the operation of the refrigerator: energy must be supplied to the refrigeration cycle from an external source, and this energy is converted to heat and discharged to the room, along with the heat removed from the interior of the refrigerator. Overall, availability of energy has decreased, and entropy has increased.

One illustration of the power of the laws of thermodynamics is that in many situations they can be used to predict the maximum efficiency that could be achieved by a perfect machine, without specifying any details of the machine! (Efficiency may be defined, in this situation, as the ratio of useful work to total energy flow.) Thus, one can specify, for example, what *minimum* amount of energy is necessary to separate salt from seawater, to separate metals from their ores, and to separate pollutants from auto exhaust without knowing any details about future inventions that might be devised for these purposes. Similarly, if one is told the temperature of a source of thermal energy—say, the hot rock deep in Earth's crust—one can calculate rather easily the maximum efficiency with which this thermal energy can be converted to applied work, regardless of the cleverness of future inventors. In other words, *there are some fixed limits to technological innovation, placed there by fundamental laws of nature.* (The question of how far from the maximum attainable efficiencies industrial societies operate today is taken up in Chapter 8.)

More generally, the laws of thermodynamics explain why we need a continual input of energy to maintain ourselves, why we must eat much more than a pound of food in order to gain a pound of weight, and why the total energy flow through plants will always be much greater than that through plant-eaters, which in turn will always be much greater than that through flesh-eaters. They also make it clear that *all* the energy used on the face of the Earth, whether of solar or nuclear origin, will ultimately be degraded to heat. Here the laws catch us both coming and going, for they put limits on the efficiency with which we can manipulate this heat. Hence, they pose the danger (discussed further in Chapter 11) that human society may make this planet uncomfortably warm with degraded energy long before it runs out of high-grade energy to consume.

Occasionally it is suggested erroneously that the process of biological evolution represents a violation of the second law of thermodynamics. After all, the development of complicated living organisms from primordial chemical precursors, and the growing structure and complexity of the biosphere over the eons, do appear to be the sort of spontaneous increases in order excluded by the second law. The catch is that Earth is not an isolated system; the process of evolution has been powered by the sun, and the decrease in entropy on Earth represented by the growing structure of the biosphere is more than counterbalanced by the increase in the entropy of the sun. (The process of evolution is discussed in more detail in Chapter 4.)

It is often asked whether a revolutionary development in physics, such as Einstein's theory of relativity, might not open the way to circumvention of the laws of thermodynamics. Perhaps it would be imprudent to declare that in no distant corner of the universe or hitherto-unexplored compartment of subatomic matter will any exception ever turn up, even though our intrepid astrophysicists and particle physicists have not yet found a single one. But to wait for the laws of thermodynamics to be overturned as descriptions of everyday experiences on this planet is, literally, to wait for the day when beer refrigerates itself in hot weather and squashed cats on the freeway spontaneously reassemble themselves and trot away.

fraction by volume, often used elsewhere for gases. In many applications it is also useful to work with the *mass fraction* (grams of constituent/gram of mixture). This is a more precise statement of what is meant by the common term *fraction by weight* or *percent by weight.*[21]

A *mole* of any substance is 6.02×10^{23} molecules, and the mass of a mole is equal to the molecular weight of the substance in grams. For example, the mass of a mole of nitrogen gas (N_2) is 28 grams. It is often convenient to speak of air as if it were a single substance; the term *a mole of air* means 6.02×10^{23} molecules, of which 78.09 percent are nitrogen molecules, 20.95 percent are oxygen molecules, and so on. Such a collection of molecules has a mass of about 29 grams, which is called the *molecular weight of air.* (These definitions will be of importance later in interpreting what is meant by pollution standards expressed in different ways.)

Although nitrogen and oxygen comprise 99 percent of dry air, the trace constituents carbon dioxide (CO_2) and ozone (O_3) play exceedingly important roles because of the special properties of these molecules, as described below. Methane, nitrous oxide, and hydrogen also have roles in atmospheric chemistry and physics, albeit smaller ones. Argon, helium, krypton, and neon, by contrast, are chemically inert, monatomic gases, whose presence in the atmosphere is of interest only as resources for certain applications in technology.[22]

Water Vapor

The water content of the atmosphere varies greatly from place to place and time to time. Three commonly used measures of water content are *absolute humidity, specific humidity,* and *relative humidity.* Absolute humidity is the mass of water vapor per unit volume of air, and it varies from almost zero over the driest deserts to around 25 grams per cubic meter over jungles and tropical seas. Specific humidity is the mass of water vapor per unit mass of air. (A closely related term, the *mixing ratio,* is the mass of water vapor mixed with each unit mass of *dry* air.) Relative humidity, usually expressed as a percentage, is the ratio of the actual molecular fraction of water vapor in air to the molecular fraction corresponding to saturation at the prevailing temperature. (*Saturation* refers to the condition that ensues if air is left for a long time in a sealed container partly filled with pure water; the number of molecules of water vapor per unit volume of air under these circumstances depends only on the temperature.)[23] Relative humidity usually is between 0 and 100 percent, but under special circumstances (supersaturation) it can significantly exceed 100 percent.

Under ordinary circumstances, water vapor in the atmosphere begins to condense into droplets of liquid, forming clouds, as soon as the relative humidity exceeds 100 percent by even a small amount. The process of condensation is greatly facilitated by the virtually universal presence in the atmosphere of small particles that provide surfaces where the condensation can commence. Called *condensation nuclei* when they perform this function, these particles include salt crystals formed by the evaporation of sea spray, dust raised by the wind, ash from volcanoes and forest fires, decomposed organic matter, and, of course, particles produced by various technological activities. Even in "unpolluted" air, particles that might serve as condensation nuclei are seemingly abundant in absolute terms (more than 100 particles per cubic centimeter), but the extent of condensation and precipitation apparently are related to specific physical characteristics of the condensation nuclei as well as to their number.

The molecular fraction of water vapor corresponding to saturation increases as temperature increases—warm air can "hold" more water vapor than cool air. Accordingly, there are two ways in which relative humidity can be raised from less than 100 percent to more, initiating

[21]Weight means the force exerted upon a mass by gravity. Weight and mass are more or less interchangeable (using the relation, weight equals mass multiplied by acceleration of gravity) only if one stays on Earth's surface, where gravity is nearly constant. An astronaut has the same mass on the surface of the moon as on Earth, but a very different weight, because the acceleration of gravity on the moon is much less than on Earth.

[22]For discussions of how the atmosphere came to have the composition it does, the reader should consult Preston Cloud and Aharon Gibor, The oxygen cycle; and Preston Cloud, ed., *Adventures in earth history.*

[23]The often encountered definition of saturation as "the maximum amount of water vapor air can hold at a given temperature" is not quite correct. A good discussion of this and the following points is given by Morris Neiburger, James G. Edinger, William D. Bonner, *Understanding our atmospheric environment,* Chapter 8.

condensation and perhaps precipitation: (1) more water vapor can be added to the air by evaporation from an exposed water surface; (2) the air can be cooled so that the vapor content corresponding to saturation falls. At a given vapor content (a fixed specific humidity), the temperature at which the relative humidity reaches 100 percent is called the *dew point.* Addition of water vapor to the air by evaporation is a slow process, but cooling of the air can be very rapid. Rapid cooling to below the dew point is the mechanism immediately responsible for most condensation phenomena—the appearance of dew and fog at night as air is cooled by radiation of heat to the night sky; formation of clouds and rain in updrafts as the air is cooled by expansion; and formation of beads of water on the outside of a pitcher of ice water on a hot day, as air adjacent to the pitcher is cooled by contact with the cold surface.

Pressure, Temperature, and Vertical Structure

The pressure exerted by the atmosphere on objects at Earth's surface is essentially equal to the weight of the overlying air, which at sea level amounts on the average to 10.3 metric tons per square meter (14.7 lb/in^2). This amount of pressure, defined as 1 atmosphere, is the same as would be exerted at sea level by a column of water about 10 meters high (33 ft) or a column of mercury 760 millimeters (mm) high (29.92 in). This means that the mass of the atmosphere is only equivalent to that of a 10-meter layer of water covering Earth (you can check this in Table 2-2) and that pressure under water increases by the equivalent of 1 atmosphere for every 10 meters of depth. The usual metric unit for the measurement of atmospheric pressure is the millibar; 1 millibar is 100 newtons (N) per square meter (see Box 2-1 for the definition of the newton), and 1 atmosphere is 1013.25 millibars.

Atmospheric pressure is not ordinarily perceived as a force because it acts equally in all directions (up, down, sideways); organisms are not crushed by it because the gases and liquids in tissue are also at atmospheric pressure, so the inward and outward forces balance. Pressure becomes perceptible as a (painful) pressure *difference* if the pressure outside an organism changes more rapidly than the interior pressure can accommodate (an example would be the pain in one's ears associated with a rapid change in altitude).

Unlike water, whose density at the bottom of the deepest ocean trenches at pressures of hundreds of atmospheres is only a few percentage points higher than its density at the surface, the air in the atmosphere is highly compressible—that is, density increases markedly as pressure increases. Indeed, air behaves very much like a "perfect gas," for which pressure (p), density (ρ), and temperature (T) are related by the equation

$$p = \rho R T$$

For this equation to be valid, the temperature T must be measured with respect to *absolute zero,* the temperature at which there is no molecular motion. Temperature measured from this zero point, which is the same for all substances, is called *absolute temperature,* and the corresponding unit of measurement in the metric system is the degree kelvin.[24] The R in the equation is the gas constant, which for dry air equals 287 joules per kilogram per degree kelvin. According to the perfect gas equation, the density of dry air varies in direct proportion to pressure, if temperature is held constant.

Because the atmosphere is compressible, its mass is concentrated in the lower layers. Forty percent of the air in the atmosphere lies below the altitude of the summit of Mount Whitney in California's Sierra Nevada range (4.4 km) and two-thirds lies below the altitude of the summit of Mount Everest (8.9 km). The density of air at an altitude of 12 kilometers, where most subsonic jet airliners fly, is about one-fifth the density at sea level. The average variation of pressure and temperature with altitude above sea level is shown in Figure 2-10.

The atmosphere is subdivided into horizontal layers according to the pattern of temperature variation. The lowest layer, called the *troposphere,* is characterized by a rather uniform average rate of temperature decline with altitude of 6.4° C per kilometer. Almost all the atmo-

[24]Absolute zero, or 0 degrees kelvin (K) equals −273.15° C. An attempt was made recently to standardize the unit of absolute temperature as simply the kelvin, rather than the degree kelvin, but the change has not been generally adopted.

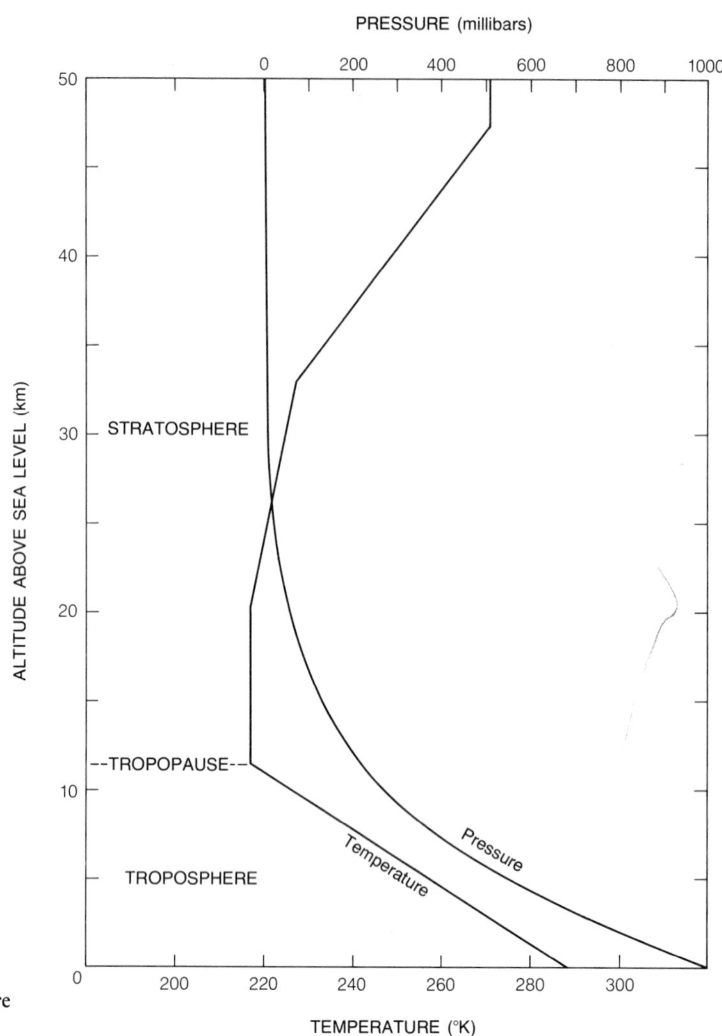

FIGURE 2-10

Variation of atmospheric temperature and pressure with altitude.

spheric phenomena that govern climate take place in the troposphere. The top of the troposphere is called the *tropopause,* where the temperature decline stops and a layer of uniform temperature at about −55° C commences. The tropopause is typically found at an altitude of from 10 to 12 kilometers, but it ranges from a low of 5 or 6 kilometers at the poles to around 18 kilometers at the equator.

The *stratosphere* extends from the tropopause up to the stratopause (about 50 km) and is characterized over much of this interval by temperatures increasing with altitude (reaching almost 0° C at the stratopause). The gaseous composition of the stratosphere is essentially the same as that at sea level, with two significant exceptions. First, there is very little water vapor in the stratosphere; the mixing ratio is typically two or three parts per million (ppm), or 1000 to 10,000 times less than is common near sea level. Second, there is a great deal more ozone in the stratosphere than in the troposphere; the maximum molecular fraction of ozone is 10 ppm near 25 km altitude, or 1000 times more than the average for the whole atmosphere.[25] The air pressure and density at the top of the stratopause are on the order of a thousandth of the values at sea level.

Above the stratosphere lies the *mesosphere* (to about 90 km), wherein the temperature again decreases with altitude. The composition of the mesosphere remains much like that of the lower layers, except for certain trace constituents such as water vapor and ozone. The troposphere, stratosphere, and mesosphere together are called the *homosphere,* referring to their relatively uniform composition. Above the mesosphere is the *thermosphere* (temperature again rising with altitude), which contains the *heterosphere* (so named because the molecular constituents are there separated into distinct layers of differing composition) and the *ionosphere* (referring to the presence of free electrons and the positively charged ions from which the electrons have been stripped). The thermosphere has no well defined upper limit; its density at 100 kilometers is around one-millionth of atmospheric density at sea level, and by 10,000 kilometers it has faded off to the density prevailing in interplanetary space.

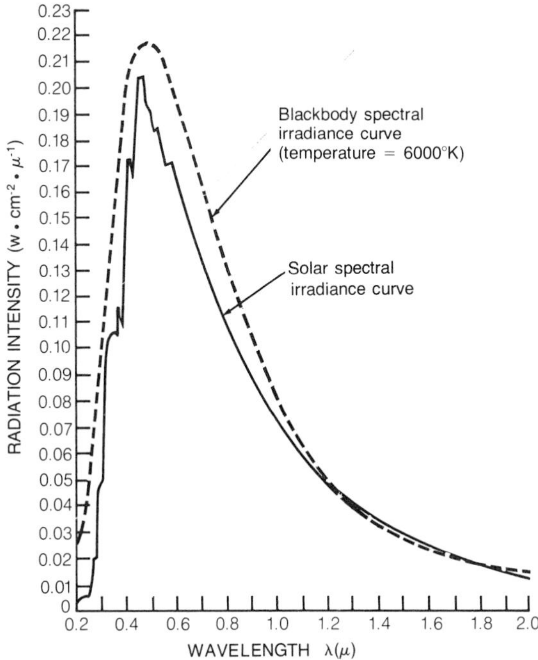

FIGURE 2-11

Solar irradiance spectrum and 6000°K blackbody radiation reduced to mean solar distance. (From Neiburger, Edinger, and Bonner, 1973.)

Radiant Energy Flow in the Atmosphere

What accounts for the complicated way in which temperature changes with altitude in the atmosphere? The answer involves the way in which different atmospheric constituents interact with radiant energy arriving from the sun and with radiant energy trying to escape Earth into space. The same processes, of course, determine how much and what kinds of energy reach Earth's surface, so they are crucial in determining the conditions that govern life. To understand these processes requires at least a modest acquaintance with the character of radiant energy (or electromagnetic radiation), and this is supplied in Box 2-4.

The energy in the electromagnetic radiation reaching the top of Earth's atmosphere from the sun is distributed over a range of wavelengths, as shown in Figure 2-11. One can determine from such a graph that about 9 percent of the total incoming energy is in the ultraviolet part of the electromagnetic spectrum, 41 percent is in the visible part of the spectrum, and 50 percent is in the infrared part. A significant part of this energy is prevented from reaching Earth's surface by gaseous constituents of the atmosphere that are opaque to certain wavelengths. This opacity is due not to reflection but to absorption (the energy in the radiation is absorbed by the gas molecules, warming the atmospheric layers where these processes take place).

The depletion of incoming radiation by absorption in atmospheric gases is summarized in Table 2-12. The main results are that ultraviolet solar radiation with wavelengths less than 0.3 microns (μ) is almost completely absorbed high in the atmosphere, and infrared solar radiation is substantially depleted through absorp-

[25]Study of Critical Environmental Problems (SCEP), *Man's impact on the global environment,* p. 41.

BOX 2-4 Electromagnetic Radiation

Light, X-rays, radio waves, infrared radiation, and radar waves are all variations of the same thing—phenomena with the interchangeable names *electromagnetic radiation, electromagnetic waves,* and *radiant energy.*

Energy in this form travels at the speed of light (c, or 299,792 km/sec in vacuum), and—as the words *in vacuum* imply—requires no material medium to support the energy flow. This property contrasts with the other, much slower forms of energy transport (conduction and convection) which do require a medium. Convection involves the bulk motion of matter; conduction involves molecular motion. What moves in the case of electromagnetic radiation is a combination of electric and magnetic fields of force.

For many purposes, it is useful to visualize this pattern as a traveling wave, as shown in the diagram here. There the curve denotes the spatial pattern of the strength of the electric or magnetic field, and the pattern is moving to the right with speed c. (Actually, there should be separate curves for the electric and magnetic fields, but this detail need not trouble us here.) The *wavelength* (λ) is the distance between successive crests or troughs.* At any fixed point along the path of the wave, the field is seen to oscillate with *frequency* (υ) related to wavelength and the speed of light by the relation $\upsilon = c/\lambda$.

*Unfortunately, there are more concepts in science than there are Greek letters. Thus, for example, lambda (λ) represents wavelength in physics and finite rate of increase in population biology (Chapter 4).

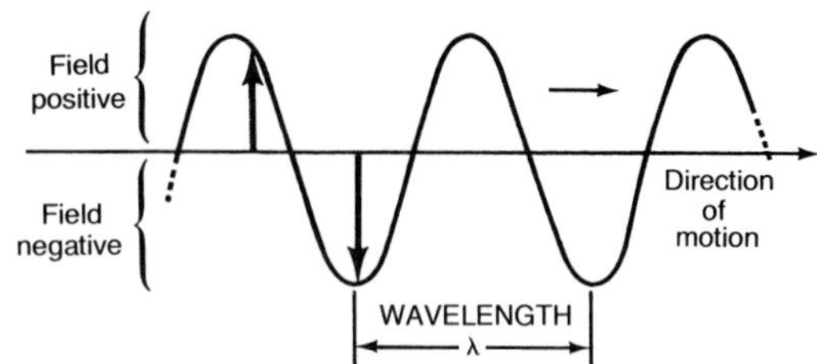

The different forms of electromagnetic energy are distinguished by their different wavelengths (or, equivalently, their frequencies, since one can be computed from the other using the relation $\lambda\upsilon = c$). Visible electromagnetic radiation has wavelengths between 0.40 microns (violet light) and 0.71 microns (red light). A micron (μ) is one-millionth of a meter. The entire range of wavelengths that have been observed, from tiny fractions of a micron to tens of kilometers, is called the *electromagnetic spectrum.* Some types of electromagnetic radiation occupying different parts of the spectrum are indicated in the table below.

Type of radiation	Wavelength range
radio	1–10 m
radar (microwaves)	1–30 cm
infrared	0.71–100 μ
visible	0.40–0.71 μ
ultraviolet	0.10–0.40 μ
X-rays	10^{-5}–10^{-2} μ

The way electromagnetic radiation interacts with matter depends in a complicated manner on the wavelength of the radiation, on its intensity (energy flow per unit of area, measured—say—in watts per square meter), and on the properties of the matter. Radiant energy that encounters matter may be transmitted, reflected, or absorbed. To the extent that radiation of a given wavelength is transmitted, the material is said to be transparent to that wavelength; to the extent that the radiation is reflected or absorbed, the material is said to be opaque to that wavelength. Most materials are transparent to some wavelengths and opaque to others. Many gases, for example, are rather opaque to most ultraviolet wavelengths but transparent to radio waves, visible light, and X-rays. Human flesh is opaque to visible light but transparent to X-rays.

Often, transmission, reflection, and absorption all take place at once. Consider a glass window in the morning sunlight: the glint off the window indicates that reflection is taking place; the room behind the window is illuminated and warmed, so there is certainly transmission; and the window itself gets warm, so absorption is happening, too.

Both transmission and reflection can be *direct* or *diffuse*. Direct means that a beam of electromagnetic radiation arriving from a single specific direction is sent on or sent back in a single specific direction. Diffuse means that the incoming beam is split up and sent on or sent back in many different directions. The phenomenon that produces diffuse transmission and reflection is called *scattering*. All light reaching the ground on a completely overcast day is diffuse light that has been scattered by the water droplets in the cloud layer.

All matter that is warmer than absolute zero can *emit* radiation. (The "machinery" by which emission occurs has to do with the behavior of the electrons in matter. We will not dwell on this machinery here, summarizing instead only the main results of its operation.) Some substances emit only radiation of certain wavelengths, and all substances can absorb only the wavelengths they can emit. A body that absorbs all the radiation that hits it in all wavelengths is called a *blackbody*, a useful idealization that is approached in the real world but never quite reached. A blackbody is not only a perfect absorber, but also a perfect emitter; the amount of electromagnetic energy emitted at any given wavelength by a blackbody of a specified temperature is the theoretical maximum that any real body of that temperature can emit at that wavelength. The total amount of radiation emitted by a blackbody is proportional to the fourth power of the body's absolute temperature. The wavelength at which a blackbody emits most intensely decreases in inverse proportion to the absolute temperature—that is, the higher the temperature, the shorter the wavelength.

The characteristics of the sun as a source of electromagnetic radiation are very closely approximated by those of a blackbody with a temperature of 5800° K. The wavelength at which its emission is most intense is 0.5 microns, corresponding to blue-green light (see Figure 2-11).

TABLE 2-12
Absorption of Solar Radiation by Atmospheric Gases

Wavelength range (μ)	*Fate of radiation*
UNTRAVIOLET	
Less than 0.12	All absorbed by O_2 and N_2 above 100 km
0.12–0.18	All absorbed by O_2 above 50 km
0.18–0.30	All absorbed by O_3 between 25 and 50 km
0.30–0.34	Part absorbed by O_3
0.34–0.40	Transmitted to Earth almost undiminished
VISIBLE	
0.40–0.71	Transmitted to Earth almost undiminished
INFRARED	
0.71–3	Absorbed by CO_2 and H_2O, mostly below 10 km

Source: Neiburger, Edinger, and Bonner, *Understanding our atmospheric environment.*

tion by carbon dioxide and (especially) by water vapor at lower altitudes. The atmosphere's gases are almost completely transparent to the visible wavelengths, where the intensity of solar radiation reaches its peak (Figure 2-11), and to the "near-ultraviolet" radiation, with wavelengths just shorter than the visible. (This near-ultraviolet radiation is an important contributor to sunburn.) Significantly, the only atmospheric gas that is opaque to ultraviolet radiation between 0.18 and 0.30 microns in wavelength is ozone. Without the trace of ozone that exists in the stratosphere, this radiation would reach Earth's surface—where it could be extremely disruptive to the life forms that evolved in the absence of these wavelengths (Chapter 11). The absorption of ultraviolet radiation by ozone in the stratosphere has a second important effect—it produces the stratospheric heating that causes temperature to increase with altitude in this layer of the atmosphere, with consequences discussed in the next section.

Some of the incoming radiation that is not absorbed by atmospheric gases is scattered by them (Box 2-4). Some of the scattered radiation returns to space (diffuse reflection), and some reaches the ground as diffuse solar radiation. The physics of scattering by the molecules in air is such that blue light is scattered much more than is red light. The sky appears blue because what reaches the eye is mostly scattered light and hence—owing to the preferential scattering of blue wavelengths by air molecules—mostly blue. That the sun appears red at sunset is precisely the same phenomenon at work; then one is looking at direct-beam radiation—the unscattered part—from which the blue has been removed (by scattering) and in which mainly the red remains.

Absorption and scattering of solar radiation are done by *aerosols* as well as by gases. An aerosol is a suspension of solid or liquid particles in a gas. Fog, clouds, smoke, dust, volcanic ash, and suspended sea salts are all aerosols. Whether a given aerosol acts mainly as an absorber or mainly as a scatterer depends on the size and composition of the particles, on their altitude, and on the relative humidity of the air they are in. Certainly, the aerosols that interact most strongly with solar radiation are clouds, which at any given time cover about half Earth's surface with a highly reflective layer.

The reflectivity of a surface or a substance is called its *albedo* (formally, albedo equals reflected energy divided by incoming energy). This property depends not only on the characteristics of the surface, but also on the angle at which the incoming radiation strikes the surface (the angle of incidence). The albedo is much higher at shallow angles of incidence than at steep (nearly perpendicular) angles. The albedo of clouds ranges from 0.25 (thin clouds, perpendicular incidence) to more than 0.90.

Averaged around the year and around the globe, the amount of energy that penetrates to Earth's surface is about half of what strikes the top of the atmosphere. Of that which penetrates, somewhat more than half is diffuse and somewhat less than half is direct. Upon

TABLE 2-13
Albedo of Various Surfaces

Surface	*Albedo*
Snow	0.50–0.90
Water	0.03–0.80
Sand	0.20–0.30
Grass	0.20–0.25
Soil	0.15–0.25
Forest	0.05–0.25

Sources: SMIC, *Inadvertent climate modification;* Neiburger, Edinger, and Bonner, *Understanding our atmospheric environment.*

reaching the surface, this energy meets several fates. Some is reflected, with the albedo varying from land to water and from one type of vegetation to another—and, of course, depending on the angle of incidence (Table 2-13). Some is absorbed by the melting or sublimation of ice or snow, or the vaporization of water. Some is absorbed to warm the surface and objects on or under it. And a tiny fraction is captured and transformed into chemical energy by the process of photosynthesis in plants.

The fate of solar energy striking the top of Earth's atmosphere is summarized in Figure 2-12. Note that the average albedo of the Earth-atmosphere system is about 0.28, of which two-thirds is accounted for by clouds.

Now from the first law of thermodynamics (Box 2-3), which says energy can neither be created nor destroyed, and from elementary considerations of stocks and flows (Box 2-2), one can draw some important conclusions about energy flow in the Earth-atmosphere system. First, the rate at which Earth's atmosphere and surface are absorbing solar energy must be matched by the rate at which the system loses energy, or else the amount of energy stored on the surface and in the atmosphere would be steadily changing. In other words, if the system is to be in equilibrium, outflow must equal inflow. Lack of equilibrium, if it occurred, would mean a changing stock of energy in the Earth-atmosphere system. This could manifest itself as an upward or downward trend in mean temperature (a changing stock of thermal energy), or in mean absolute humidity or mean volume of ice and snow

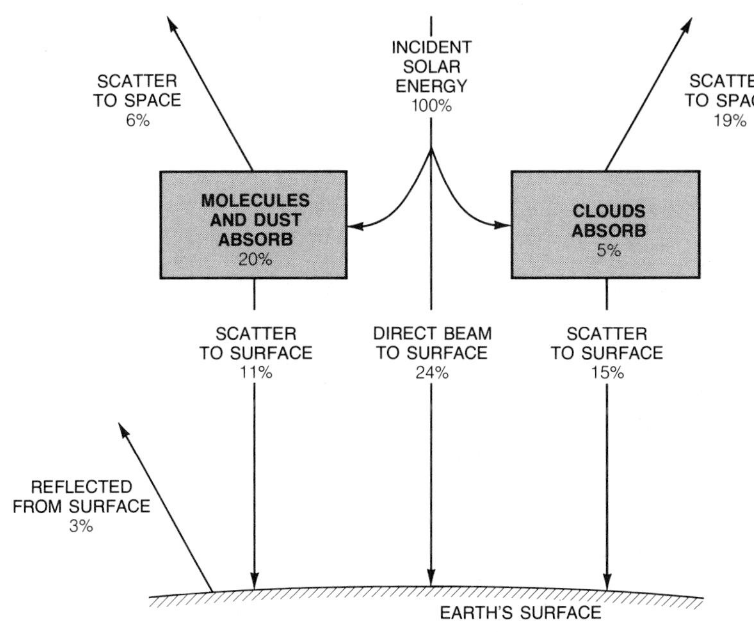

FIGURE 2-12

The fate of incoming solar radiation. Figures represent global annual averages.

(a changing stock of latent energy of vaporization and fusion), or in mean quantity of organic matter (a changing stock of chemical energy). Of course, different parts of Earth's surface and atmosphere at different times of year *are* out of equilibrium—temperature, humidity, snow cover, and quantity of vegetation generally change dramatically with seasons. Inflow and outflow of energy at a given time and place in general do not balance. But they *must* balance on a year-round average for the whole globe or else there will be year-to-year changes in the *mean* values of these indices of stored energy. Such changes have occurred in the past as cooling periods leading into ice ages and warming periods leading out of them. These changes and the potential for further ones, with or without human influence, are discussed below. As a first approximation, however, it is reasonable to assume that inflows and outflows of energy are in balance on the global, annual average.

The second conclusion is that the same considerations of inflow, outflow, and equilibrium that apply to the Earth-atmosphere system as a whole must apply separately to its components. If the atmosphere is to be in equilibrium in a global, time-averaged sense, it must be losing energy at the same rate it is receiving it. The same must hold for Earth's surface.

Clearly, then, the energy flow shown in Figure 2-12 is not the complete picture. The figure shows a net accumulation of energy in the atmosphere (gas molecules, clouds, dust) equal to 22 percent of the solar energy that strikes the top of the atmosphere and a net accumulation of energy at the surface equal to 47 percent of total incoming solar energy.

What is the fate of this absorbed energy, amounting in all to 69 percent of the solar input? The answer is this: after running the machinery of winds, waves, ocean currents, the hydrologic cycle, and photosynthesis, the energy is sent back to space as *terrestrial radiation.*

Terrestrial radiation refers to the electromagnetic radiation emitted by Earth's surface and atmosphere in accordance with the principles summarized in Box 2-4: the amount of energy radiated per unit of area is proportional to the fourth power of the absolute temperature of the radiating substance, and the wavelength of most intense radiation is inversely proportional to the absolute temperature. If the Earth-atmosphere system were a blackbody at temperature, T, the exact relation for the rate of emission of radiation, S, would be:

$$S = \sigma T^4.$$

If S is measured in watts per square meter and T is measured in degrees kelvin, then the proportionality constant σ (the Stefan-Boltzmann constant) has the numerical value 5.67×10^{-8}. On the assumption that the energy returned to space as terrestrial radiation should exactly balance the 69 percent of incoming solar energy that is absorbed, one can compute the effective blackbody temperature of the Earth-atmosphere system to be about 255° K (− 18° C or about 0° F). This is the temperature a perfect radiator would have to have in order to radiate away into space the same amount of energy per unit of area as the Earth-atmosphere system actually does radiate away, on the average.

Actually, the Earth-atmosphere system closely resembles a blackbody radiator, so the above temperature is not unrealistic. Why, then, is that temperature so much lower than the observed mean surface temperature of 288° K (15° C, or 59° F)? The reason is that most of the terrestrial radiation actually escaping from the Earth-atmosphere system is emitted by the atmosphere, not the surface. (You can see from Figure 2-10 that the temperature 255° K corresponds to an altitude of about 5 kilometers, or halfway between sea level and the tropopause.) Most of the terrestrial radiation emitted by the warmer surface does not escape directly to space because the atmosphere is largely opaque to radiation of these wavelengths. The wavelength of radiated energy, you should recall, increases as the temperature of the radiator decreases: Earth, being much cooler than the sun, emits its radiation at longer wavelengths. The peak intensity of terrestrial radiation occurs at a wavelength of around 10 microns, which is in the infrared part of the spectrum, in contrast to solar radiation's peak intensity at a wavelength of about 0.5 microns in the visible part of the spectrum.[26]

[26]There is almost no overlap in the wavelength ranges of solar and terrestrial radiation; at 3 microns, the intensity of solar radiation has fallen to 5 percent of its value at the 0.5-micron peak, while that of terrestrial radiation has only attained about 10 percent of its value at the 10-micron peak. Meteorologists often refer to solar radiation as shortwave radiation and terrestrial radiation as long-wave radiation.

The opaqueness of the atmosphere to outgoing infrared radiation from the surface is due mainly to three atmospheric constituents: carbon dioxide, water vapor, and clouds. (A more modest contribution is made by ozone.) Carbon dioxide absorbs infrared radiation in a narrow band of wavelengths around 3 microns, in another narrow band near 4 microns, and in the wavelengths between 12 and 18 microns. Water vapor absorbs infrared radiation in narrow bands around 1, 1.5, and 2 microns, and in broader ones from 2.5 to 3.5 microns, from 5 to 8 microns, and from 15 microns through the remainder of the infrared. Clouds are very much like blackbodies in the entire infrared part of the electromagnetic spectrum—they absorb most of the infrared radiation that reaches them. The infrared radiation absorbed by carbon dioxide, water vapor, and clouds is subsequently *reradiated* by these substances—much of it being sent back in the direction of Earth's surface and some escaping into space. The atmosphere, therefore, through the properties of clouds, water vapor, and carbon dioxide, acts as a thermal blanket that keeps Earth's surface about 33° C warmer than it would be without these constituents.

Because of this effect of clouds, all else being equal, clear nights are colder than cloudy nights; in the absence of clouds, more infrared radiation leaving the surface escapes directly to space without being intercepted. The additional thermal-blanket effect of water vapor and carbon dioxide is sometimes called the *greenhouse effect.* This is because glass, like carbon dioxide and water vapor, is relatively transparent to visible radiation but more opaque to infrared radiation. Light enters a greenhouse more readily than heat can escape, a situation resembling that in the atmosphere. The *main* reason a greenhouse is warmer inside than outside, however, is that the glass prevents convection from carrying away sensible heat and latent heat of vaporization.[27] Thus, the term *greenhouse effect* is not entirely appropriate for the role of carbon dioxide and water vapor in the atmosphere.

The flows of terrestrial radiation are summarized in Figure 2-13, expressed as a percentage of solar energy striking the top of the atmosphere and computed as a global annual average. Note that the rate at which infrared radiation is emitted from Earth's surface actually exceeds the rate of solar input at the top of the atmosphere and is far larger than the rate at which solar energy is directly received at the surface. This large radiation output and the high temperature responsible

[27]This fact has been demonstrated by building a greenhouse of rock salt (which is as transparent to infrared radiation as to visible radiation) next to a greenhouse of glass. The rock-salt greenhouse, simply by preventing convection, stayed almost as warm inside. (See, for example, Neiburger, et al., *Understanding.*)

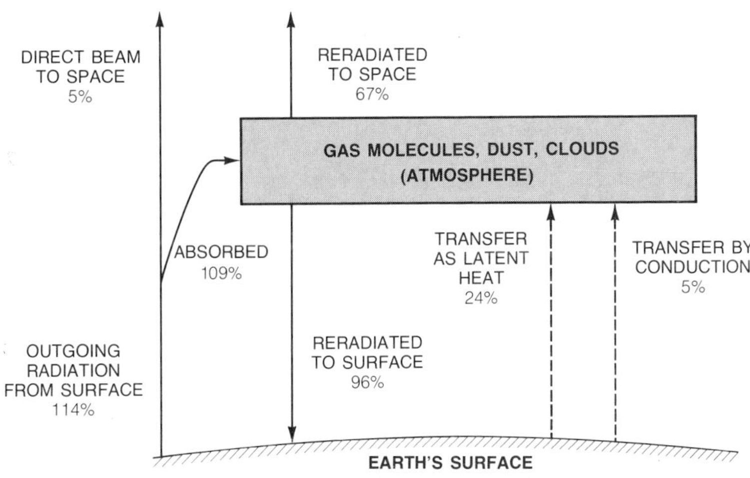

FIGURE 2-13

Flows of terrestrial radiation. Percentage of solar energy incident at the top of the atmosphere (global annual averages).

for it are made possible by the large flow of infrared radiation reradiated to the surface by the atmosphere, as discussed earlier. Any alteration of the composition of the atmosphere by pollution can have an important influence on this downward reradiated energy flow (see Chapter 11).

Two important energy flows other than radiation are represented in Figure 2-13 by broken lines. The larger of these flows is the transfer of energy from the surface to the atmosphere as latent heat of vaporization. That is, energy that has been used to evaporate water at the surface moves into the atmosphere in the form of the latent heat of vaporization that is associated with the water vapor (see Box 2-1). This energy is eventually surrendered to the atmosphere as sensible heat when the water vapor condenses. The magnitude of this surface-to-atmosphere energy flow is equal to almost a quarter of the solar energy flow reaching the top of the atmosphere. The second major nonradiative flow (perhaps a fifth as large as that of latent heat) is the transfer of sensible heat from the surface to the atmosphere by conduction—that is, the warming of the air by contact with the surface. Sensible heat transported across the interface of surface and air in this way then moves upward in the atmosphere by convection. (Of course, in some places and at some times the atmosphere is warmer than the surface, with the result that sensible heat flows from the atmosphere to the surface rather than the reverse. Remember, we have been discussing the global, annual-average situation here.)

Atmospheric Energy Balance and Vertical Motions

With the information in the preceding section, one can construct average energy balances for Earth's surface, for the atmosphere, and for the Earth-atmosphere system as a whole. Such a set of balances is given in Table 2-14, both in terms of the percentage of solar energy flow at the top of the atmosphere and in watts per square meter of Earth's surface area. Energy flow per unit of area is called *flux*. The solar flux through a surface perpendicular to the sun's rays at the top of the atmosphere is called the *solar constant* and is equal to about 1360 watts per square meter [1.95 calories (cal)/cm^2/minute (min), or 1.95 langleys/min, in units often used by meteorologists].[28] As a sphere (to a very good approximation), Earth's total surface area is 4 times the area of the cross section it presents to the sun's rays. Hence, the average amount of solar energy reaching the top of the atmosphere per square meter of Earth's surface is just one-fourth of the solar constant, or 340 watts per square meter, as indicated in Table 2-14. The average solar flux reaching Earth's surface is 173 watts per square meter of horizontal surface. Solar flux measured this way at the surface is often termed *insolation.*

The difference between the amount of energy incident on Earth's surface as radiation (solar and terrestrial) and the amount leaving as radiation is called by meteorologists the *net radiation balance,* or sometimes just net radiation. This amount of energy flow, which as shown in Table 2-14 averages 105 watts per square meter flowing into the surface for the whole globe, is of special meteorological significance because it is the amount of energy available for the climatically crucial processes of evaporation of water and surface-to-air transfer of sensible heat. Many discussions of human impact on climate use the net radiation balance, rather than the incident solar energy, as the yardstick against which civilization's disturbances are measured (Chapter 11).

The pattern of Earth-atmosphere energy flows that has been described here provides the explanation for the observed temperature distribution in the lower atmosphere. Basically, the atmosphere is heated from the bottom—by direct contact with warm land or water surfaces, by the release of latent heat of vaporization when water vapor condenses (virtually entirely in the troposphere and mostly in its lowest third), and by the absorption of terrestrial infrared radiation in water vapor, clouds, and carbon dioxide. Water vapor and clouds are most abundant in the lower troposphere, so that is where a large part of the absorption takes place. These effects, differentially heating the atmosphere near the bottom, produce the general trend of decreasing temperature with altitude in the troposphere. Only above

[28]It is actually not known exactly how constant the solar constant really is (see, for example, S. Schneider and C. Mass, Volcanic dust, sunspots, and temperature trends).

TABLE 2-14
Energy Balances for Earth's Surface, Atmosphere, and Surface-Atmosphere System (global annual averages, accurate to perhaps ± 10%)

	Percentage of solar energy flow at top of atmosphere	*Average energy flow (w/m^2)*
SURFACE-ATMOSPHERE SYSTEM		
Solar radiation reaching top of atmosphere	100	340
Total inflow	100	340
Solar radiation scattered from atmosphere	25	85
Solar radiation scattered from surface	3	10
Terrestrial direct radiation, surface to space	5	17
Terrestrial radiation, atmosphere to space	67	228
Total outflow	100	340
SURFACE		
Solar direct radiation	24	82
Solar diffuse radiation, via clouds	15	51
Solar diffuse radiation, via air, dust	11	37
Terrestrial reradiation from clouds, vapor, CO_2	96	326
Total inflow	146*	496
Reflected solar radiation	3	10
Outgoing terrestrial radiation	114	387
Latent heat to atmosphere	24	82
Sensible heat to atmosphere	5	17
Total outflow	146*	496
ATMOSPHERE		
Solar radiation interacting with clouds, air, dust	76	258
Terrestrial radiation from surface, absorbed	109	371
Latent heat from surface	24	82
Sensible heat from surface	5	17
Total inflow	214*	728
Solar radiation scattered to space	25	85
Solar radiation scattered to surface	26	88
Absorbed radiation reradiated to space	67	228
Absorbed radiation reradiated to surface	96	327
Total outflow	214*	728

*These flows exceed 100 percent of incoming solar radiation because, in addition to the solar throughput, an internal stock of energy is being shifted back and forth between surface and atmosphere.

Source: After Schneider and Dennett, Climatic barriers.

the tropopause does atmospheric heating by absorption of ultraviolet solar radiation (particularly by ozone) reverse the trend and produce temperatures that increase with altitude (refer to Figure 2-10). Ozone also absorbs outgoing terrestrial infrared radiation in a narrow wavelength band at 9.6 microns, to which other atmospheric gases are largely transparent.

The structure of the troposphere, with the warmest air on the bottom, promotes vertical instability (hot air rises, and cold air sinks). Sensible heat and latent heat of vaporization are thus transported upward by convection, and the troposphere tends to be vertically well mixed. The mixing time in the lower half of the troposphere—that is, the time it takes for a molecule at 5 kilometers

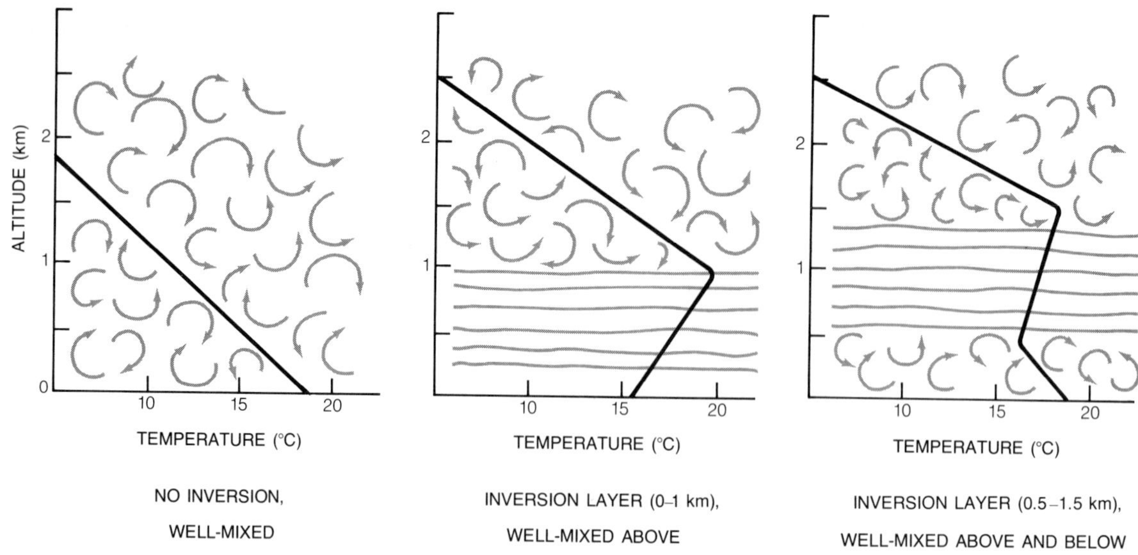

FIGURE 2-14

Inversions in the troposphere. Temperature versus altitude in different circumstances.

altitude to change places with one at the surface—is usually on the order of a few days. (In convective storms it can be hours.) The stratosphere, by contrast, is vertically stratified; like the ocean, its warmest layer is on top, with progressively colder layers below, which tends to suppress vertical motion. The vertical mixing time in the stratosphere is on the order of a year or two.

Under some circumstances, the usual temperature profile of the troposphere near the ground is altered so that temperature increases with altitude. In this situation (called an *inversion*), vertical mixing is suppressed over the altitude range where the temperature is increasing. (Vertical mixing is also suppressed in circumstances where temperature decreases with altitude but not rapidly enough to overcome the stratifying effect of the density variation.) Some of the main possibilities are indicated in Figure 2-14. Inversions are of special importance in environmental science because they inhibit the dilution of pollutants, as is discussed further in Chapter 10.

Variation of Incoming Solar Flux with Place and Season

If the vertical energy flows discussed in the preceding sections were all there were to climate, it would not be so difficult to analyze. So far, however, we have only been working with energy flows averaged over the whole globe and the whole year; the real complexity lies in the tangled patterns of energy flow that arise from differences between day and night, summer and winter, land surfaces and water surfaces, and so on.

Let us first consider the geometrical factors that produce variations from season to season and from latitude to latitude in the amount of solar radiation that strikes the top of the atmosphere. They are:

1. Earth is essentially spherical.
2. Earth travels around the sun in an orbit that is not quite circular.
3. Earth spins on an axis that is tilted 23.5° from perpendicular to the plane of its orbit.

Because Earth is a sphere, the maximum solar flux at any moment is received at the subsolar point (that is, the point that is directly "under" the sun, or equivalently, the point at which the sun appears to be directly overhead) and declining values of flux are received as one moves away from this point on the surface of the sphere. This is so because a flat surface of given area intercepts a maximum of the solar beam when the surface is perpendicular to the beam, and progressively less at angles away from the perpendicular. This situation is illustrated in Figure 2-15.

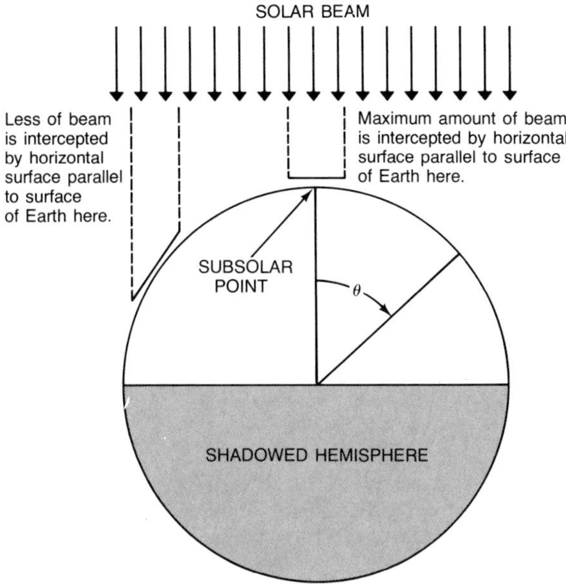

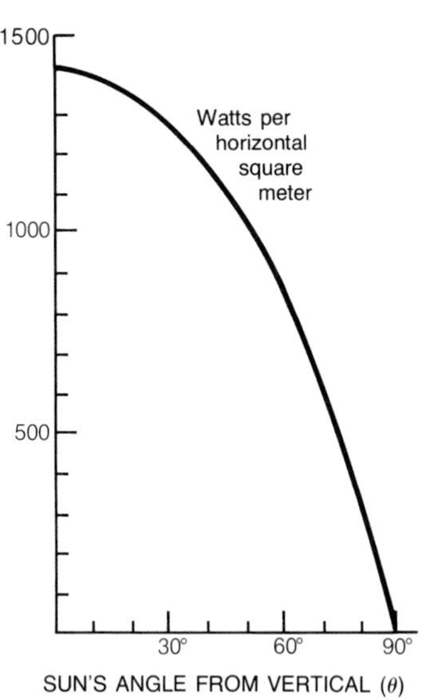

FIGURE 2-15

Insolation at the top of the atmosphere.

Earth's elliptical orbit around the sun deviates from a circle just enough to make the distance between Earth and sun vary by ± 1.7 percent from the mean value of 149.6 million kilometers. This variation in distance produces a difference of ± 3.4 percent in solar flux (that is, the solar energy flow incident on a surface perpendicular to the sun's rays above the atmosphere varies from a maximum of 1406 w/m^2 to a minimum of 1314 w/m^2, the average of 1360 w/m^2 being the "solar constant" given earlier). The minimum distance occurs in the first few days of January, when the Northern Hemisphere is having its winter and the Southern Hemisphere its summer, and the maximum occurs in the first few days of July.

Clearly, the seasons are not produced by the slight ellipticity in Earth's orbit, but rather by the tilt of Earth's axis of rotation. The orientation of this tilt remains fixed as Earth circles the sun, as shown schematically in Figure 2-16. This means that the Northern Hemisphere is tilted directly toward the sun at the June 21 solstice, corresponding to the first day of summer in the Northern Hemisphere and the first day of winter in the Southern Hemisphere, and the Southern Hemisphere is tilted directly toward the sun at the December 21 solstice. On June 21 the subsolar point is on the Tropic of Cancer (23.5° north latitude)[29] and the entire area north of the Arctic Circle (66.5° north latitude) is illuminated by the sun during all twenty-four hours of the day. On December 21 the subsolar point is on the Tropic of Capricorn (23.5° south latitude), and the entire area within the Antarctic Circle is illuminated for all twenty-four hours of the day. At the equinoxes (March 21 and September 23) the subsolar point is on the equator, and day and night are each twelve hours long everywhere on Earth (except in the vicinity of the poles, which experience continuous twilight).

The net effect of these geometrical aspects of the Earth-sun relationship is to produce strong north-south differences, or *gradients,* in the incoming solar flux perpendicular to Earth's surface at the top of the atmosphere. The size and shape of the gradients vary

[29]The subsolar point becomes a subsolar line as Earth performs its twenty-four hour rotation.

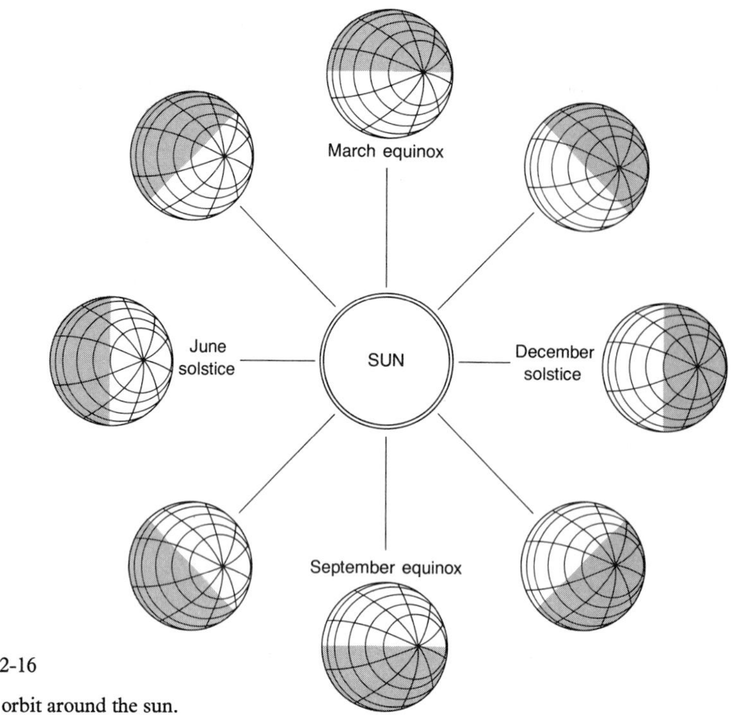

FIGURE 2-16

Earth's orbit around the sun.

with the seasons. Figure 2-17 shows the solar flux at the top of the atmosphere, in calories per square centimeter per day, as it varies throughout the year at three different latitudes in the Northern Hemisphere. Note the strong equator-to-pole contrast in the winter, which is reduced as summer approaches and actually reverses in midsummer. (The summer pole receives more energy per unit of surface area in midsummer than does the equator, because the sun is shining twenty-four hours a day at the summer pole.)

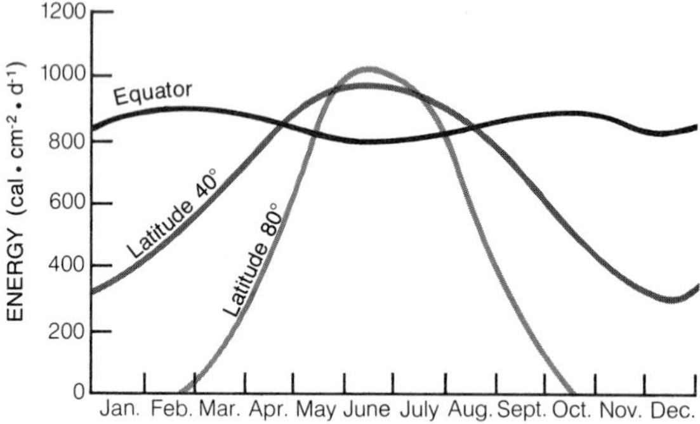

FIGURE 2-17

Seasonal variation of solar flux on a horizontal surface outside the atmosphere. (From Gates, 1971.)

The amount of solar radiation reflected back into space also varies with latitude (more is reflected at the extreme northerly and southerly latitudes, where the radiation strikes the surface at angles far from perpendicular) and with season (ice and snow reflect more than do vegetation and water). Finally, the amount of terrestrial radiation leaving the top of the atmosphere varies with latitude and season, because the emission of such radiation depends on temperature and other characteristics of the atmosphere and the surface below. An accounting of the radiation flows across an imaginary surface at the top of the atmosphere, then, must include incoming sunlight, outgoing reflected sunlight, and outgoing terrestrial radiation. Where the inflow exceeds the outflows across such a surface, it is said that the underlying column of atmosphere has a *heating excess.* Where the outflows exceed the inflow, there is said to be a *heating deficit.*

The Machinery of Horizontal Energy Flows

If there were no mechanisms to transfer energy horizontally over Earth's surface from regions of heating excess to regions of heating deficit, the result would be much greater extremes in conditions than actually exist. Energy would accumulate in the areas of heating excess until the additional outgoing infrared radiation produced by higher temperatures restored a balance; similarly, energy would be lost to space from areas of heating deficit until the drop in outgoing radiation associated with lower temperatures restored the incoming-outgoing balance in those areas. To say that the extremes of temperature on Earth's surface would be greater under these circumstances is an understatement. It is plain from Figure 2-17, for example, that the region north of 80° north latitude receives no incoming radiation at all from mid-October to late February (although, of course, the emission of outgoing terrestrial radiation continues). In the absence of energy inflows from warmer latitudes, then, the radiative energy loss in winter at the latitudes having darkness twenty-four hours a day would cool the surface rapidly and continuously toward absolute zero.

But there *are* horizontal energy flows—principally, the transport of sensible heat and latent heat of vaporization by the motions of the atmosphere and the transport of sensible heat by ocean currents. (These *convective* energy transfers are much bigger and faster than conduction. See Box 2-3, to review the difference.) These flows are driven largely by the north-south temperature differences arising from the radiation imbalances just described, and they are largely responsible for the general features of global climate. The overall pattern of the north-south energy flows on an annual average basis is indicated in Table 2-15.

The atmospheric motions that carry energy toward the poles as sensible heat and latent heat must, of course, be balanced by return flows of air toward the equator. Otherwise, air would be piling up at the poles! Two kinds

TABLE 2-15
Average Annual North-South Energy Flows (w/m^2)

Latitude zone	*Net radiation at top of atmosphere (incoming minus outgoing)*	*Net latent heat (precipitation minus evaporation)*	*Net sensible heat transport by atmosphere*	*Net sensible heat transport by ocean*
60–70°N	−65	11	43	11
50–60°N	−40	20	5	15
40–50°N	−16	12	−5	9
30–40°N	5	−17	0	12
20–30°N	19	−41	21	1
10–20°N	31	−15	−3	−13
0–10°N	39	44	−51	−32
0–10°S	41	19	−32	−28
10–20°S	37	−21	−12	−4
20–30°S	27	−43	11	5
30–40°S	12	−25	5	8
40–50°S	−11	11	−8	8
50–60°S	−39	36	−12	15

Note: Sum of entries in any given zone is zero, denoting balance of inflows and outflows averaged for year. (Positive numbers represent net inflow; negative numbers represent net outflow.)

Source: Modified from Budyko, in SMIC, *Inadvertent climate modification,* p. 91.

of circulation that move heat poleward but keep the air distributed are particularly important. The first of these is the thermal circulation illustrated in Figure 2-18A; the poleward flow is high in the troposphere; the equatorward flow, near the surface. The second is the cyclonic circulation shown in Figure 2-18B, which can be thought of as taking place in a horizontal plane. Actually, Earth's major atmospheric circulations are generally combinations of vertical and horizontal components. The term

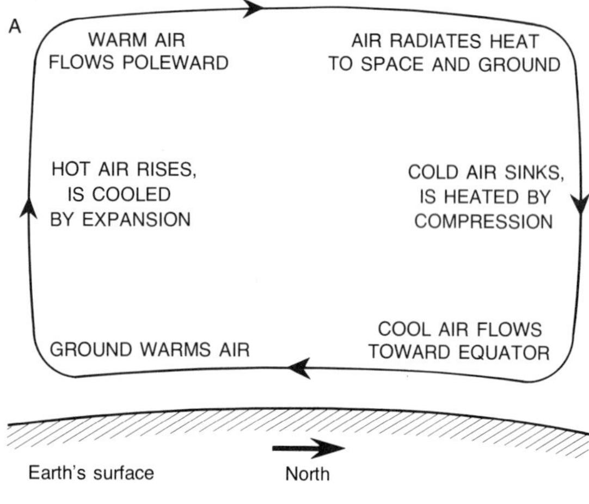

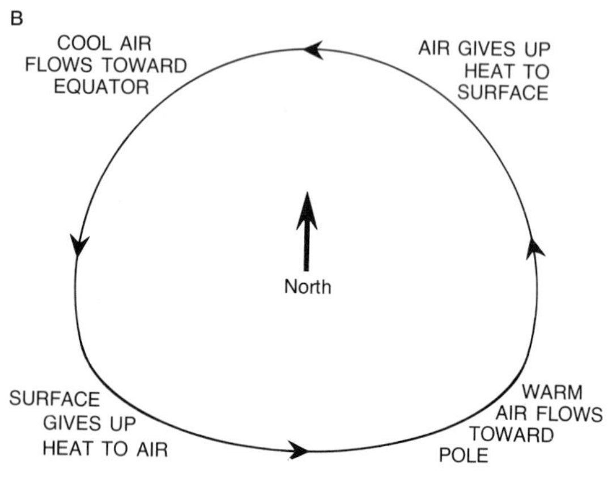

FIGURE 2-18

North-south air flows with poleward transport of heat. A. Thermal circulation, cross-section looking west, parallel to Earth's surface in the Northern Hemisphere. B. Cyclonic circulation, looking down on Earth's surface in the Northern Hemisphere.

wind is usually reserved for the horizontal motion, and the terms *updraft* and *downdraft* describe the vertical. The horizontal motion is almost always much faster than the vertical: typical wind speeds range from 1 to 20 meters per second; typical vertical speeds in large-scale atmospheric circulations are 100 times less, although local updrafts associated with clouds and mountain ranges may be 10 meters per second or more. Typically, then, a "parcel" of air (an arbitrarily defined collection of molecules whose behavior one chooses to trace) might move 100 kilometers horizontally while rising 1 kilometer.

Like solids, gases such as air move in response to the forces exerted upon them in ways described by Newton's laws of motion. One important kind of force in the atmosphere is associated with *pressure gradients.* The pressure-gradient force is a push from regions of high pressure, associated with high temperature and/or density, toward regions of low pressure. Another important force in the atmosphere is gravity, which exerts a downward pull on every molecule of air. (Vertical motions in the atmosphere generally are slow because the vertical pressure-gradient force usually balances the force of gravity almost exactly.) The distribution of regions of high pressure and low pressure in the atmosphere is complex, owing not only to the variations in insolation, reflection, and absorption with latitude and altitude, but also to local differences associated with topography and the distribution of vegetation, land, and water. But the atmospheric circulation patterns are *not* what would be expected from consideration only of the pressure gradients associated with these features, together with the force of gravity, because two other important factors come into play. These are the *Coriolis deflection* (usually inappropriately called the Coriolis force) and *friction.*

The Coriolis deflection is a complication that arises from the rotation of the planet. Specifically, Earth tends to rotate out from under objects that are in motion over its surface (for example, fired artillery shells and moving parcels of atmosphere). That is, such objects do not go quite where they seem to be heading, because the place they were heading is rotating at a different velocity than the point of origin (rotational speed is highest at the equator, where a point must move some 40,000 km/day, and lowest near the poles). Thus, in the Northern

Hemisphere a parcel of air moving north will appear to a terrestrial observer to be deflected to the right (east), the direction of the Earth's rotation, because it will carry the higher velocity of its place of origin. The Coriolis "force" is the *apparent* extra force (besides pressure gradients, gravity, and any other "real" forces that may be acting) needed to explain to an observer on Earth's rotating surface the observed paths of moving objects. We say "apparent" because no work is done to produce the deflection—it is a function of the position of the observer. A person in space observing the trajectory of an artillery shell relative to the solar system (assume, for example, that the shell were visible but the rest of Earth were invisible) would not see any Coriolis deflection. The magnitude of the Coriolis deflection is greatest at the poles and zero on the equator; the magnitude also varies in direct proportion to the speed of an object—a stationary object is not subject to Coriolis deflection.[30] The direction of the Coriolis deflection is always perpendicular to the direction of an object's motion. It changes the *direction* of motion but not the speed. Motions in the Northern Hemisphere are deflected to the right; motions in the Southern Hemisphere, to the left.

Consider the effect of the Coriolis deflection in the Northern Hemisphere on the flow of air into a region of low atmospheric pressure from surrounding regions of higher pressure. The pressure-gradient force tries to drive the flow straight in, but the Coriolis deflection bends it to the right (Figure 2-19). The resulting spiral patterns are actually visible in most satellite photographs of Earth, because the winds carry clouds along with them (Figure 2-20). The spirals associated with low-pressure centers (clockwise in the Southern Hemisphere, counterclockwise in the northern) are called *cyclones,* and the outward spirals associated with high-pressure centers (clockwise in the Northern Hemisphere, counterclockwise in the southern) are called *anticyclones.*

The force of friction adds two features to the wind patterns described thus far. It slows down the wind near Earth's surface—most dramatically in the first few tens of

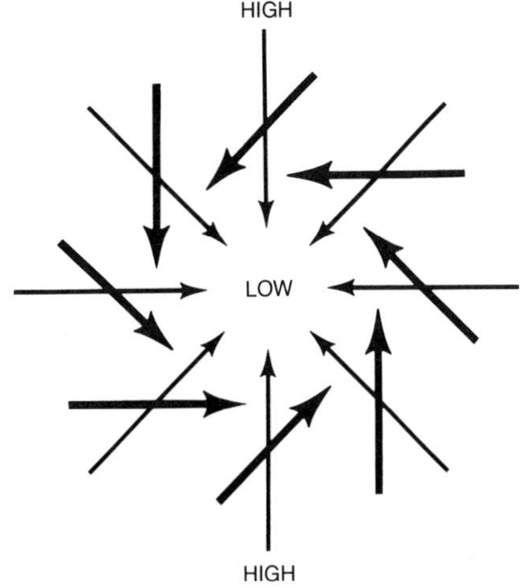

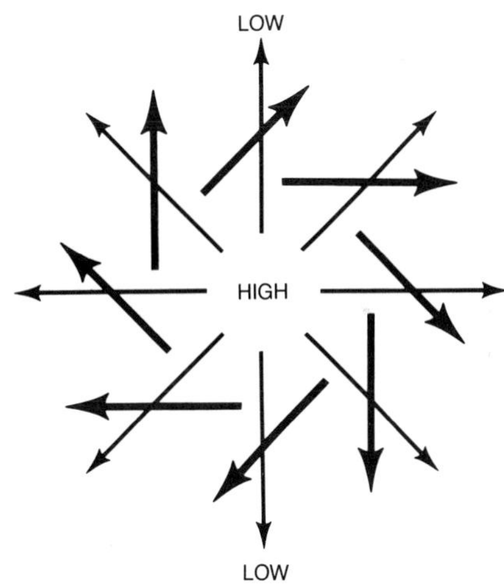

FIGURE 2-19

Coriolis deflection of the wind. Light arrows denote the direction of pressure-gradient force, which would also be wind direction on a nonrotating Earth. Heavy arrows show the Coriolis deflection of the wind directly to the right (Northern Hemisphere).

[30]The magnitude of the Coriolis deflection associated with horizontal motion at velocity v m/sec at latitude ϕ is $2\Omega v \sin\phi$/kg mass, where $\Omega = 7.29 \times 10^{-5}$ radians/sec is the angular velocity of Earth's rotation. (There are 2π radians, or 360 degrees, in one revolution.) See, for example, Neiburger, et al., *Understanding,* pp. 99–104.

FIGURE 2-20

Atmospheric circulation patterns as revealed by cloud distributions. (NASA).

meters, but still significantly at altitudes up to a few hundred meters. And, because of the way the friction force interacts with the pressure-gradient force and the Coriolis deflection, it causes the *direction* of the wind to change with altitude for the first several hundred meters. The horizontal pressure gradients themselves may be quite different at one altitude than at another, which also gives rise to significant changes in the wind patterns as one moves away from Earth's surface.[31]

[31]More detailed explanations of the operation of the friction force and the variation of pressure gradients with altitude are given in Neiburger et al., *Understanding*, pp. 109–114.

The General Circulation

The overall pattern of atmospheric motions resulting from the phenomena just described is called the *general circulation.* Its main features are illustrated in Figure 2-21. The associated variation of average sea level pressure is indicated in Figure 2-22.

The surface circulation in the tropical regions north and south of the equator is dominated by the trade winds, blowing, respectively, from the northeast and the southeast. These very steady winds are associated with the pressure drop between the subtropical highs and the

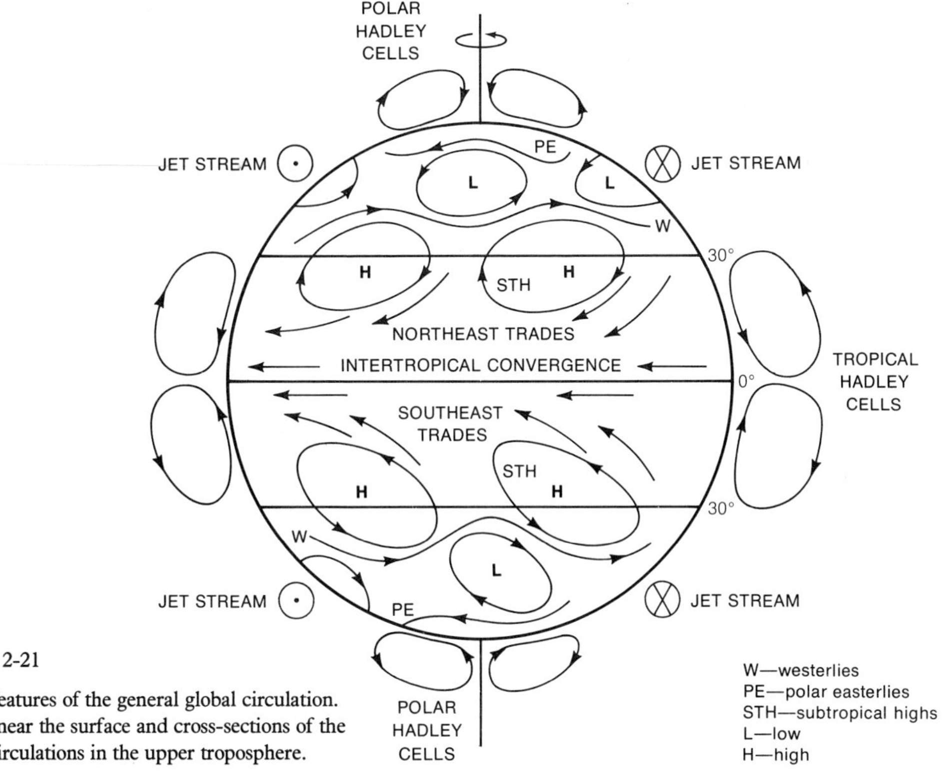

FIGURE 2-21

Main features of the general global circulation. Flows near the surface and cross-sections of the main circulations in the upper troposphere.

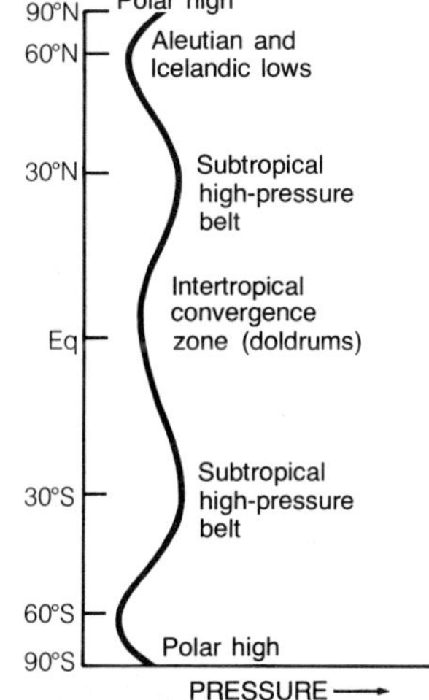

FIGURE 2-22

Variation of average sea-level pressure with latitude. (From Neiburger, Edinger, and Bonner, 1973).

low-pressure *doldrums* on the equator. The trade winds are deflected from the direction of the pressure drop by the Coriolis force—to the right in the Northern Hemisphere, to the left in the southern—as explained above. The region where the trade winds meet to form a belt of easterly winds encircling the globe near the equator is called the *intertropical convergence zone.*

The vertical part of the circulation in the tropics consists of thermal circulations of the form shown in Figure 2-18A, one immediately north of the equator and one immediately south. These are called *Hadley cells,* after the British meteorologist who first postulated their existence. In the Hadley cells, the air rising over the equator is moist as well as warm. As it rises, the air cools, whereupon some of the contained moisture condenses into droplets and falls as rain. The latent heat of vaporization released in this process helps drive the air farther upward, producing more condensation, more release of latent heat, and more rain. Thus, the air rising near the equator in the Hadley cells is largely "wrung out," producing in the process the very rainy climates for which the tropics are known. Having lost its moisture and some of its sensible heat in ascending, the air flowing poleward in the upper part of the Hadley cells continues to lose heat by radiating energy to space more rapidly than it absorbs radiant energy from the warmer atmospheric layers and the surface below. At around 30° north and south latitude, the relatively cold, dry air commences to sink. In sinking into higher pressure it is warmed by compression. This descending flow of warm, dry air in the 30° latitude belts is a major reason these belts are characterized by deserts all around the world. (The Sahara of northern Africa, the Kalahari of southern Africa, the Atacama of Chile, and the Sonoran desert of Mexico and the United States are examples.) Finally, as the dry air moves equatorward on the surface to complete its circuit, it picks up both heat and moisture from the increasingly warm surfaces of the land and water of the tropics.

Thermal circulation patterns similar to the Hadley cells of the tropics are also found in the vicinity of the poles, but they are smaller and weaker than those on either side of the equator. The temperature and pressure differences driving the polar flow are less than those nearer the equator, and the transfers of moisture and latent heat are also much smaller.

Although it was postulated at one time that there must be an indirect cell linking the equatorial and polar cells in each hemisphere—that is, a cell in which air sinks on the side toward the equator, flows poleward on the surface, and rises on the polar side—measurements indicate that this pattern is either extremely weak or entirely missing. Rather than being borne by such circulations, the poleward energy flow in the middle latitudes is accomplished instead by the great, swirling, horizontal flows associated with the subtropical highs (see Figure 2-18B, as well as Figure 2-21) and with the wavy boundary between those highs and the subpolar lows. Along that boundary in both hemispheres, the winds are predominantly westerly (that is, flowing from west to east) both at the surface and high in the troposphere.

Embedded in the westerlies at the upper edge of the troposphere and on the boundary between the subpolar lows and the subtropical highs are the *circumpolar jet streams,* encircling the globe in a meandering path covering latitudes from 40° to 60°. The core of a jet stream is typically 100 kilometers wide and 1 kilometer deep, and is characterized by wind speeds of 50 to 80 meters per second [110 to 180 miles per hour (mph)]. These high speeds are the result of a large pressure change over a relatively short horizontal distance on the boundary between low-pressure and high-pressure circulation systems. In addition to the circumpolar jet streams, there are westerly subtropical jet streams at about 30° north and south latitudes, associated with the poleward edges of the Hadley cells, and some seasonal jet streams of lesser importance.[32]

On the boundary between the subpolar lows and the polar highs, there are weak easterly winds at the surface, giving way to westerlies at higher altitudes. The high-altitude flow, then, is entirely westerly. The part of this flow lying poleward of the subtropical highs is cold air—essentially a great west-to-east spinning cap of it, draped over each pole—and is called the *circumpolar vortex.* The circumpolar vortex in the winter hemisphere is larger and wavier at the edge than the one in the summer hemisphere, because the equator-to-pole temperature difference that is the basic driving force behind these features is much greater in winter. The waviness at the edge of the circumpolar vortex is caused by cold, low-pressure circulation systems being pushed equatorward into the temperate zones, producing the cold fronts and accompanying storms common in winter.

In the summer hemisphere, the characteristics of the general circulation associated with the equator-to-pole temperature difference are much less strongly developed. The intertropical convergence crosses the equator into the summer hemisphere, the summer-hemisphere Hadley cell weakens and nearly vanishes, and the circumpolar vortex subsides. This weakening and relative disorganization of the general circulation in the summer hemisphere permits the pattern to be dominated by asymmetries connected with the distribution of land and bodies of water. Among the most important of these are

[32]Strahler and Strahler, *Environmental geoscience,* pp. 96–98.

the *summer monsoons* of Asia and sub-Saharan Africa, in which moist, cool air sweeps inland over warm landmasses, rises, and drops the moisture as rain. This climatic feature is essential to the food supply of a substantial part of the world's population.

Weather, Climate, and Climate Change

Weather and climate are not the same thing, and the difference between the two terms involves the time span in which one is interested. *Weather* refers to the conditions of temperature, cloudiness, windiness, humidity, and precipitation that prevail at a given moment, or the average of such conditions over time periods ranging from hours to a few days. The weather can change from hour to hour, from day to day, and from week to week.

Climate, on the other hand, means the *average pattern* in which weather varies in time, and the average is determined over longer periods (from a month to decades). Thus, one might speak of the climate of a given region as being characterized by hot, dry summers and severe winters. Within this region, one would still expect some periods (days or weeks) of cool weather in summer and mild weather in winter. If the weather for an entire summer were cooler than usual, one would still speak of an exceptional summer's weather or a short-term climatic fluctuation but not of climate change. But if the weather averaged over ten or twenty consecutive summers were significantly cooler than the average for the previous thirty, then one could begin to call the phenomenon a change in climate.

Local weather and climate are determined by the complicated interaction of regional and global circulation patterns with local topography, vegetation, configuration of lakes, rivers, and bays, and so on.[33] Successful weather prediction requires combining knowledge of these general patterns and known local features with the most detailed available information about the weather conditions of the moment and the past few days—not just at the location whose weather is being predicted, but at other locations, as well. That is, to predict tomorrow's weather, one must know as much as possible about today's. What happens in Los Angeles on Saturday may be largely foreseeable from what was happening in San Francisco on Friday, which could have been a storm that was in Portland on Wednesday, which originated as a disturbance in the Gulf of Alaska on Monday.

As everyone knows, forecasting the weather even one day ahead is not an exact science. This inexactitude is not because there are undiscovered physical processes at work; all the basic physical laws involved are actually known. The imperfections in prediction have two origins: first, the actual system involved—atmosphere, ocean, other water bodies, land—is far too complicated for the known physical laws to be applied exactly, even with the largest computers; second, the initial conditions—the state of the system at the time the analysis begins—can be specified only approximately, owing to fundamental monitoring limitations. The farther in advance one wishes to make a local weather forecast, the more difficult the task becomes, because the larger is the area of the globe whose present conditions can influence subsequent conditions at the place one is interested in. Also, temperature and pressure anomalies small enough to slip through the global network of weather stations today may have grown large enough in a week's time to determine the weather over large regions. Weather satellites have made the meteorologist's task somewhat easier, especially because they provide information about meteorological conditions over the oceans, where surface monitoring stations are relatively scarce; but reliable weather forecasting a week in advance is still not a reality. Because the meteorological system is so complex, reliable forecasting two weeks ahead may never be attainable.

Understanding and predicting the changes in climate that have occurred and will continue to occur over time spans of decades, centuries, and millennia is in some respects even more difficult than forecasting the weather from day to day. The weather forecaster has the disadvantage of having to deal with tremendous detail in terms of variations over short times and short distances, but the advantage of access to a tremendous body of observa-

[33]In this chapter we have emphasized the large-scale processes that govern the patterns of weather and climate over large regions, continents, and hemispheres. Investigating in detail the *microclimates* that influence intimately the human and biological communities in specific small regions would take us deeper into the demanding and technical subject of meteorology than space and the nature of this book permit. The interested reader should consult Neiburger et al., *Understanding our atmospheric environment,* or another basic meteorology text for an introduction to the micrometeorology missing here.

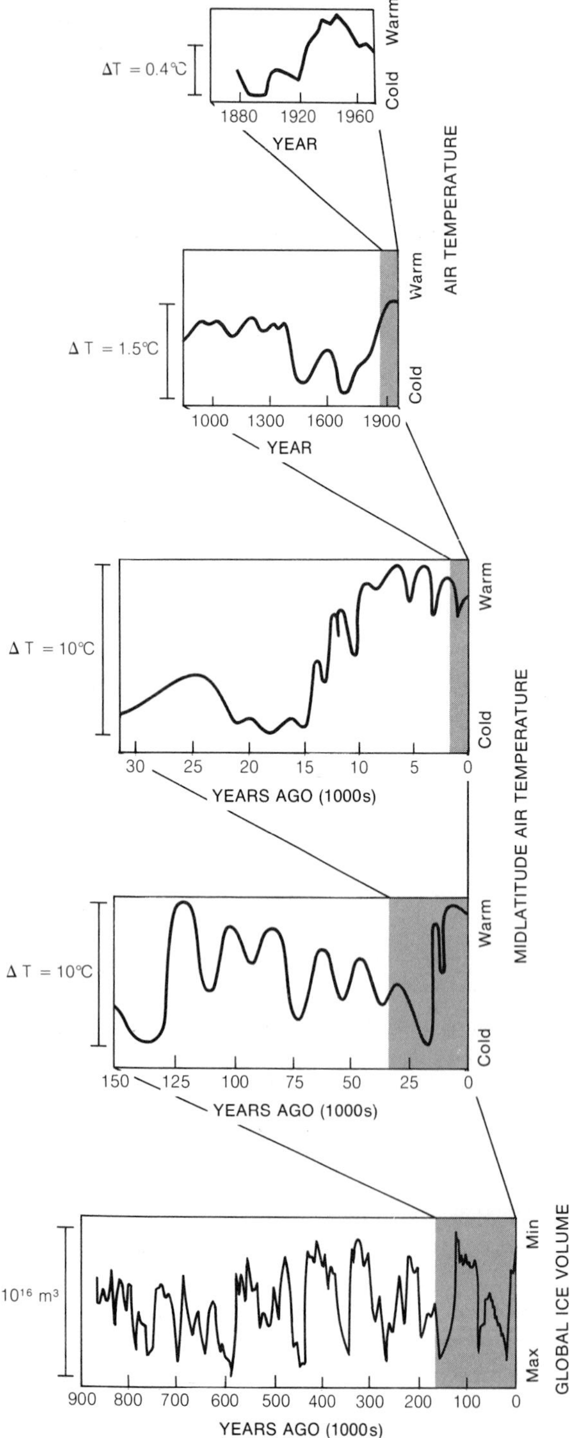

FIGURE 2-23

The Earth's climate—the past million years. (After Bolin, 1974.)

tional data—the weather happens every day, and many skilled observers with good instruments are watching and recording. The climatologist has reasonably good, direct, observational data only for the past few decades, spotty records for the past century or so, and only indirect evidence before that (scattered historical writings dating back several centuries, some archeological evidence going back a few thousand years, and only the fossil record and geological evidence before that). The plight of the climatologist is something like trying to learn all about weather on the basis of good data for the past two days, spotty data for the past two weeks, and only some fuzzy clues as to what might have happened before then.

On the basis of the limited evidence available to them, climatologists have done a remarkable job of reconstructing in a plausible way Earth's climatic history for about the past million years and, more roughly, for the past 60 million years.[34] Some of the main features of the more recent history are illustrated in Figure 2-23. It shows a series of fluctuations in average midlatitude air temperature, with different amplitudes associated with different time scales. (The amplitude of a fluctuation is the difference between the maximum and minimum values associated with it.) The amplitude of the indicated variation in the past hundred years is about 0.5° C (roughly, 1° F); the amplitude of the fluctuations with a time scale of a few hundred to a thousand or so years is from about 1.5° to 2.5° C; and the amplitude of the fluctuations with a time scale of tens of thousands of years is in the range of between 5° and 10° C.

Several points with respect to this climatic history deserve emphasis:

1. Variability has been the hallmark of climate over the millennia. The one statement about future climate that can be made with complete assurance is that it will be variable—a conclusion not without significance for food production (see Chapter 7).

2. Rather small changes in average midlatitude temperatures are likely to be associated with larger changes in the seasonal *extremes* of temperature at those latitudes,

---

[34]Study of Man's Impact on Climate (SMIC), *Inadvertent climate modification,* pp. 28–45; Bert Bolin, Modelling the climate and its variations.

and with even larger changes in the extremes nearer the poles. These extremes in temperature are likely to have a more crucial influence on flora and fauna than are the averages.

3. Modest changes in average temperature and the accompanying larger changes in temperature extremes are often associated with significant changes in the circulation patterns, humidities, amounts of rainfall, and other features that make up regional climates. These changes, too, can drastically influence the character of the plant and animal communities that exist in different regions.

4. The drop in average midlatitude temperature associated with major ice ages is as little as 4° or 5° C. It is possible that an even smaller drop could *trigger* such an ice age.[35]

5. The onset of significant climatic change in the past has sometimes been quite rapid. There is evidence to suggest, for example, that the advance of the continental ice sheets in a cooling period that commenced about 10,800 years ago destroyed living forests wholesale within the space of a single century or less.[36]

6. The world finds itself in the last part of the twentieth century A.D. in one of the warmest periods in recent climatic history. What people alive today assume is normal—namely, the climate of the past thirty to sixty years—is in reality near one of the extremes of the persistent historical fluctuations. Even without the possibility of inadvertent human influence on climate, it could not be predicted on the basis of present knowledge how much longer this present extreme climate might last. Past evidence suggests, however, that when it ends, it will end (barring human intervention) with a cooling trend.

Several questions present themselves. What has caused the climatic fluctuations of the past? If climate change is a historical fact of life, is there any reason to worry about future changes? Is civilization capable of inadvertently influencing climate—for example, by accelerating natural change or initiating a different trend? Is there any prospect of deliberate intervention to stop a threatening trend in climate? We consider the first two questions in the next few paragraphs; the last two will be touched on only briefly here and then taken up in detail in Chapter 11.

The causes of past changes in climate are not well understood. One possibility is variation in the rate at which the sun emitted energy, but there is no convincing evidence to show that this has occurred, and no convincing theory that predicts it has been proposed.[37] A second set of possibilities involves changes in atmospheric composition, influencing the transmission of incoming solar radiation and/or outgoing terrestrial radiation. For example, periods of intense volcanic activity might have added enough ash to the atmosphere to affect climate significantly, or biological and geophysical processes might have caused the atmospheric stock of carbon dioxide to deviate appreciably from its present value. Evidence to connect these possibilities with the actual onset of ice ages is lacking, however. Still another possibility is variations in Earth's orbit, which would have affected the amount and timing of incident solar energy. Such variations are known to have occurred and to be occurring, but they appear to have been too small *by themselves* to have produced the onset or retreat of ice ages.

A likely contributing factor is that the circulation patterns and other phenomena that produce the gross features of climate are not very stable. If they were stable, the systems governing climate would tend to return after any disturbance to the conditions that prevailed before the disturbance. Many examples are known in physical science of systems that are stable if the disturbances imposed on them are not too large, but unstable—that is, they fall into altogether different patterns of behavior than the initial ones—if a disturbance exceeds some threshold. The idea of stability and the related concept of *feedback mechanisms* are explored by means of some simple examples in Box 2-5.

The number of feedback mechanisms influencing the stability of the global climate, both positively and negatively, is very large.[38] Some of the more important ones are indicated in Figure 2-24. It is not unlikely, under these circumstances, that the ocean-atmosphere

[35]SMIC.

[36]H. H. Lamb, *The changing climate,* p. 236

[37]For intriguing speculations, see Schneider and Mass, Volcanic dust.

[38]W. W. Kellogg and S. H. Schneider, Climate stabilization: for better or for worse?

BOX 2-5 Stability and Feedback

In general, a system is said to be *stable* if it tends to return to its initial state after any perturbation, and *unstable* if a perturbation would cause the system to depart permanently from its initial state. Often the character of the perturbation determines whether a system is stable or unstable.

As a simple example, consider a system consisting of a marble in a round bowl, as shown in cross-section in the diagram here. The "state" of this system is the position of the marble, and in the initial state the marble is at rest at the bottom of the bowl (A). The system is stable against small sideways displacements of the marble—that is, if one pushes it to the side, the marble will roll back toward the center and eventually come to rest again in the initial state. The system is *not* stable against displacements so large that the marble is pushed out of the bowl (or against entirely different kinds of perturbations, such as turning the bowl over!). A similar system (B), in which the bowl is inverted and the marble rests on top, is unstable even against small perturbations. Any displacement causes the marble to roll away.

It seems likely that the stability properties of Earth's meteorological system are analogous to those of the third arrangement (C). In this case, there are several states of equilibrium—that is, states in which the system can remain unchanged for an extended period. Each equilibrium state is stable against small perturbations, but a large perturbation can cause the system to shift to a different equilibrium, which in turn is stable until a large enough perturbation happens along to cause another shift. Such systems are often called *metastable.*

When the forces or flows that affect the system are in balance, at least temporarily, then the system will be in equilibrium. A perturbation generally alters the forces or flows, and the *way* it alters them determines whether the system is stable or unstable. In a stable system, a perturbation sets in motion changes in forces or flows that tend to restore the initial state. Processes that work this way are called *negative feedback* (a change in the state of a system induces an effect that reduces the change). *Positive feedback* occurs when a change induces an effect that enlarges the change.

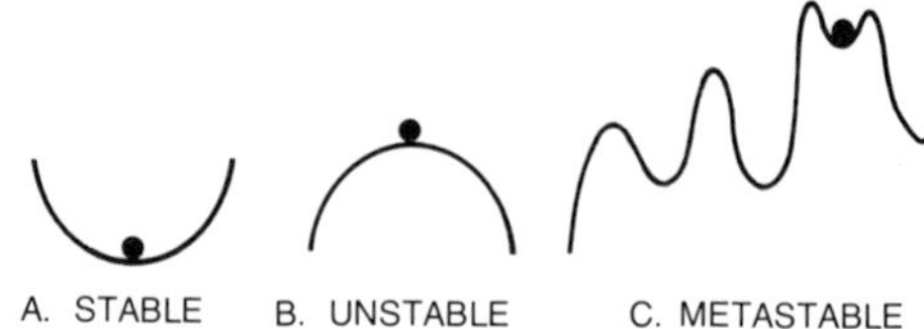

Consider the marble inside the bowl again. A displacement leads to a force that pulls the marble back toward its initial position, reducing the displacement; this is negative feedback. If the marble is on top of an inverted bowl, the force that results from any displacement acts to increase the displacement; this is positive feedback. Cause and effect relations of this kind—cause producing effect that reacts back on cause—are sometimes called *feedback mechanisms* or *feedback loops,* terms that originated in the narrower context of control systems for machinery, aircraft, and so on.

We have already considered some simple feedback mechanisms in this chapter without calling them that. An important one for climate is the negative feedback mechanism connecting surface temperature and outgoing terrestrial radiation. If a perturbation should increase the surface temperature, this would cause the rate of energy outflow in terrestrial radiation to increase; all else being equal, this would cause the surface temperature to fall, reducing the initial perturbation. If a perturbation should reduce the surface temperature, the rate of energy loss via terrestrial radiation would fall, which would tend to raise the temperature again.

Often, one must trace feedback mechanisms through two or more physical processes. Consider, for example, another mechanism involving Earth's surface temperature: an increase in surface temperature causes an increase in evaporation rate, causing increased concentration of water vapor in the atmosphere, causing an enhanced greenhouse effect, causing a further increase in surface temperature. In complicated systems such as those influencing climate, many different feedback mechanisms—some positive, some negative—are operating at the same time, and predicting the net effect of a given perturbation can therefore be very difficult.

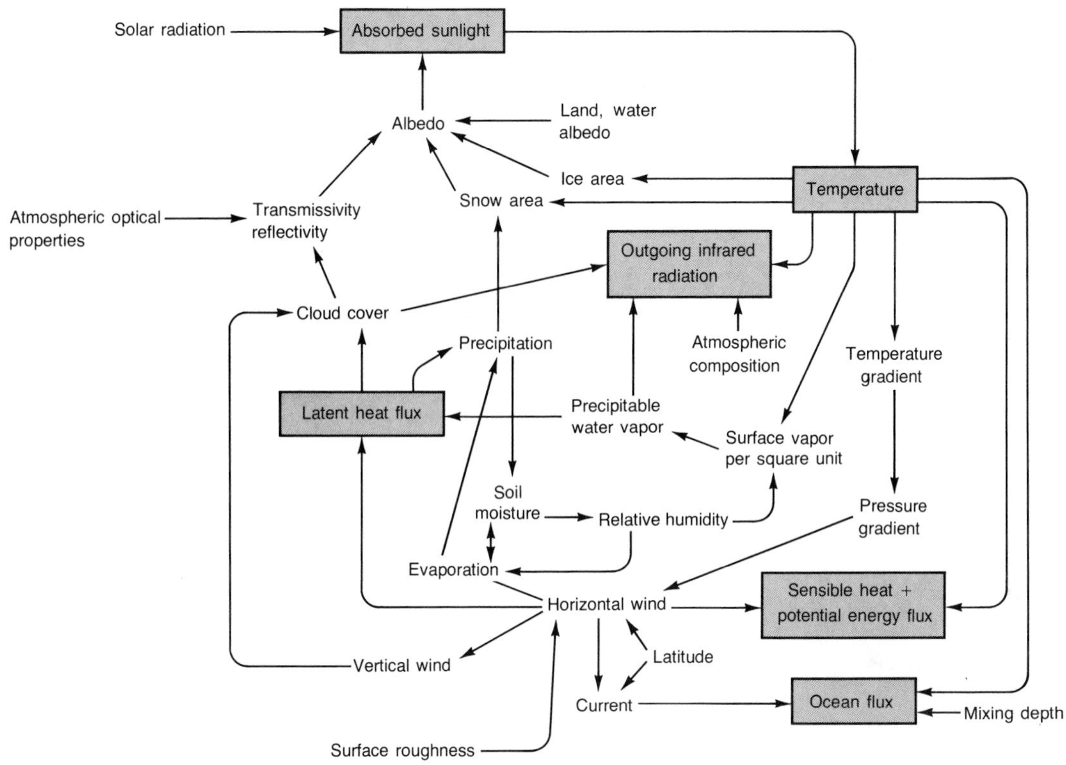

FIGURE 2-24

Some feedback loops governing global climate. (After Kellogg and Schneider, 1974.)

system governing climate belongs to the class of physical systems that are stable against small disturbances but change quite drastically and semipermanently if a larger disturbance happens along. In the case of Earth's climate, a disturbance (such as a change in solar output or in the amount of solar energy reaching Earth) need not involve an energy flow larger than the flows in the main climatic processes in order to start an instability. It would be enough that the energy associated with the disturbance be sufficient to tip the balance between two competing feedbacks, each of which might involve a much larger energy flow than that of the disturbance. Such phenomena—sometimes called *trigger effects*—are encountered frequently in environmental sciences.

There is increasing evidence suggesting that certain large variations in regional weather patterns are caused by a feedback effect in which anomalies in ocean surface temperatures play a major role.[39] The heat capacity of the oceans (that is, the amount of energy stored for each degree the temperature rises) is far greater than those of the atmosphere or the land. As a result, small changes in the temperature of large masses of ocean water absorb or release enormous quantities of heat, and this permits the oceans to serve as thermal buffers, moderating what would otherwise be more extreme changes in seasonal temperatures in the overlying atmosphere and on the adjacent landmasses. That weather and climate are largely the result of the behavior of the *ocean-atmosphere system*, and not the behavior of the atmosphere alone, has been known for a long time. More specifically, however,

[39]Jerome Namias, Experiments in objectively predicting some atmospheric and oceanic variables for the winter of 1971–72. S. A. Farmer, A note on the long-term effects on the atmosphere of sea surface temperature anomalies in the north Pacific Ocean.

recent studies indicate that weather cycles of hot and cold or wet and dry, which are observed on a time scale of ten to fifteen years in many regions, are connected with changes in ocean surface temperatures that persist over large areas for similar periods. Apparently, such changes can produce a longitudinal (east-west) shift in the wavy pattern of alternating high- and low-pressure zones at the edge of the circumpolar vortex. What causes the changes in ocean temperatures themselves is not completely understood.

A hypothesis believed by many climatologists to explain longer-term climatic change is that the historical changes in Earth's orbit have been large enough to trigger a positive feedback involving the albedo in polar regions: reduced solar input leads to more areas being covered with ice and snow, leading to increased albedo (more reflectivity), leading to less solar energy absorbed at the surface, leading to further expansion of the ice and snow.[40] Eventually, other (negative) feedbacks would come into play to limit the expansion of the ice and snow cover, but the new distribution of surface cover and associated circulation patterns—an ice age—might persist for thousands of years.

Although the causes of ice ages (also called *glaciations*) are not well understood, there is good evidence concerning the actual conditions that prevailed in the Wisconsin glaciation, which was the most recent of several Pleistocene glaciations and ended only about 10,000 years ago. Compared to today's values, mean global temperatures were lowered 5° or 6° C (9° to 11° F), and mean temperatures were lowered by 12° C or more in the vicinity of the ice sheets themselves.[41] Sea level dropped at its lowest to 125 meters below today's level, the water being tied up in the continental ice sheets that covered what is now Canada, the north central United States, Scandinavia, and much of northern Europe (see Figure 2-25).[42] The drop in sea level exposed much of what is now continental shelf, which became a richly vegetated landscape. The snow line in most mountain areas dropped 1000 to 1400 meters, and 700 to 900 meters in

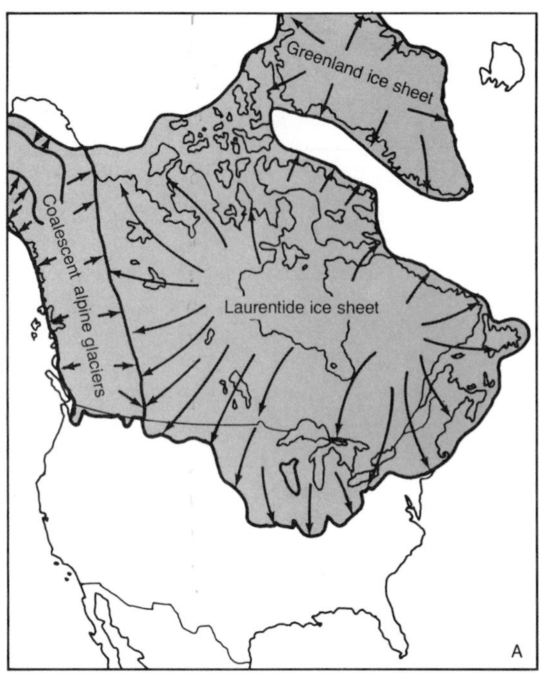

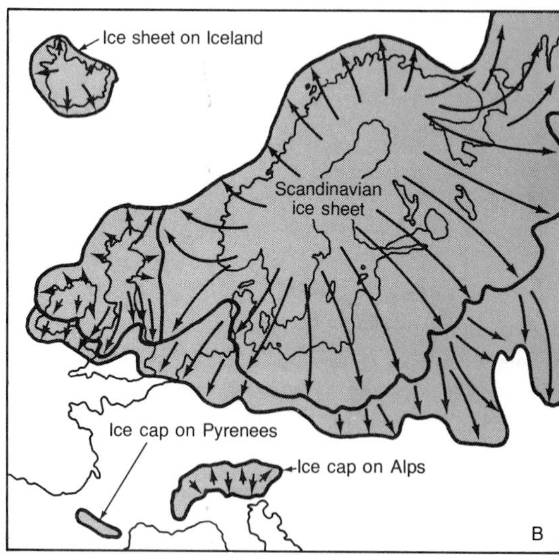

FIGURE 2-25

Maximum extent of Pleistocene glaciation in the Northern Hemisphere. A. North America. B. Europe.

[40]SMIC, pp. 125–130; Kellogg and Schneider, Climate stabilization, p. 1166.

[41]SMIC, pp. 33–34.

[42]Strahler and Strahler, *Environmental geoscience*, p. 454.

the tropics, compressing the life zones that exist between the snow line and sea level (see Chapter 4).

It is worth mentioning again that the changes producing these conditions generally may have been—and in some regions certainly were—quite rapid. Although one tends to think of glaciation as a slow process involving the plastic flow of glacial ice (as described earlier), there is a much faster mechanism available for the advance of glaciers during the onset of ice ages: snow falls over a large region, fails to melt, and is compressed under the weight of new snow the following winter. Thus, the area under a semipermanent cover of ice and snow can increase enormously in a single season. This process of rapid glaciation has aptly been termed the *snow blitz*.[43]

The evidence suggests that the departure of the Wisconsin glaciers was even more sudden than the onset. At the peak of the warming period that followed this most recent retreat of the ice sheets, average global temperatures rose to 2° or 3° C warmer than today's, sea level rose to today's level but apparently not above it, and the prevailing circulation patterns produced considerably more rainfall in the Sahara and the eastern Mediterranean lands than occurs today.[44] These conditions, called the postglacial optimum by climatologists, occurred between 5000 and 6000 years ago.

The fact that Earth has a long history of climate change offers small consolation, unfortunately, to today's human population, faced as it is with the prospect of further change in the future. Significant climate change in *any* direction—hotter, colder, drier, wetter—in the world's major food-producing regions would be likely to disrupt food production for years, and even decades, because the animals and crops now relied upon are relatively well adapted to existing climate conditions. The recent historical record and the nearness of present conditions to a temperature maximum, moreover, suggest that the most *likely* major trend to occur next is cooling. This almost certainly would disrupt food production for as long as the lowered temperatures persisted, by reducing the area and growing season available for some of the most important food crops. The dependence of agriculture on climate is explored further in Chapter 7 and Chapter 11. Other ecological effects of climate change could also have serious human consequences, which are treated in Chapter 11.

How and when human activities could themselves cause, accelerate, or prevent climate change is a complicated and imperfectly understood subject, which is also postponed until Chapter 11. What is most relevant to that discussion from the foregoing treatment of the machinery of climate and natural climate change are the complexity and probable instability of the patterns of energy flow in the ocean-atmosphere system, and the speed with which changes, once triggered, may spread and intensify.

[43]Nigel Calder, In the grip of a new ice age?
[44]SMIC, p. 37.

Recommended for Further Reading

Cloud, Preston, ed. 1970. *Adventures in earth history.* W. H. Freeman and Company, San Francisco. Many classic papers in the earth sciences.

Kuenen, P. H. 1963. *Realms of water.* Wiley, New York. Remarkably entertaining and informative treatment of water in the oceans, on land, and in the atmosphere. Splended sections on glaciers and sea ice.

Menard, H. W. 1974. *Geology, resources, and society.* W. H. Freeman and Company, San Francisco. Very readable text, especially good on recent climatic history.

National Academy of Sciences (NAS). 1975. *Understanding climatic change.* NAS, Washington, D.C. Excellent coverage of how climatologists reconstruct climatic history from fragmentary evidence, as well as of many other topics in climate.

Neiburger, Morris; J. G. Edinger; and W. D. Bonner. 1973. *Understanding our atmospheric environment.* W. H. Freeman and Company, San Francisco. Good introductory text, with emphasis on weather.

Press, Frank, and Raymond Siever. 1974. *Earth.* W. H. Freeman and Company, San Francisco. Thorough, magnificently illustrated text on the earth sciences. Emphasis on interaction of experiments and observations with theory.

Strahler, A. N., and A. H. Strahler. 1973. *Environmental geoscience.* Hamilton, Santa Barbara, Calif. Copious illustrations and clear explanations of an extraordinary range of topics in environmental earth science.

Additional References

Bolin, Bert. 1970. The carbon cycle. *Scientific American,* September, pp. 124–132. Includes discussion of carbonates in the sedimentary cycle.

———. 1974. Modelling the climate and its variations. *Ambio,* vol. 3, no. 5, pp. 180–188. Historical record of climate variation, and use of measurements and models to investigate ongoing changes.

Bretherton, F. 1975. Recent developments in dynamical oceanography. *Quarterly Journal of the Royal Meteorological Society,* vol. 101, pp. 705–722. Technical account of the emerging picture of surprisingly vigorous deep-ocean circulation, consisting of large eddies.

Budyko, M. I. 1974. *Climate and life.* Academic Press, New York. Comprehensive technical monograph by one of the world's preeminent climatologists.

Calder, Nigel. 1975. In the grip of a new ice age? *International Wildlife,* July/August, pp. 33–35. Popular treatment of the snow-blitz theory.

Cloud, Preston, and Aharon Gibor. 1970. The oxygen cycle. *Scientific American,* September, pp. 110–123. Quite technical treatment of the evolution of Earth's atmosphere and the role of the sedimentary cycle in that process.

Emery, K. O. 1969. The continental shelves. *Scientific American,* September, pp. 106–122.

Farmer, S. A. 1973. A note on the long-term effects on the atmosphere of sea-surface temperature anomalies in the north Pacific Ocean. *Weather,* vol. 28, no. 3, pp. 102–105.

Frieden, Earl. 1972. The chemical elements of life. *Scientific American,* July, pp. 52–60. Connections between sedimentary cycle and biosphere.

Garrels, R. M.; F. T. Mackenzie; and Cynthia Hunt. 1975. *Chemical cycles and the global environment.* Kaufmann, Los Altos, Calif. Concise and data-rich treatment of sedimentary cycle and chemistry of ocean and atmosphere.

Gates, David. 1971. The flow of energy in the biosphere. *Scientific American,* September, pp. 88–100. Interaction of climate and ecosystems.

Isaacs, J. D. 1969. The nature of oceanic life. *Scientific American,* September, pp. 146–162. Fascinating revelations about the fauna of the deep layers of the ocean, among other topics.

Kellogg, W. W., and S. H. Schneider. 1974. Climate stabilization: For better or for worse? *Science,* vol. 186, pp. 1163–1172 (December 27). Noted here for the useful discussion of feedback mechanisms.

Kukla, G. J., and H. J. Kukla. 1974. Increased surface albedo in the Northern Hemisphere. *Science,* vol. 183, pp. 709–714 (February 22). Changes in snow and ice cover in the Northern Hemisphere were great enough in the early 1970s to cause significant changes in the hemispheric heat balance. Satellite measurements are reported.

Lamb, H. H. 1966. *The changing climate.* Methuen, London. Methods and conclusions of historical climatology.

———. 1972. *Climate: Past, present, and future.* Methuen, London. Excellent introduction to climatology.

Leopold, Luna B. 1974. *Water.* W. H. Freeman and Company, San Francisco. Readable introduction to the hydrologic cycle.

Lorenz, E. N. 1970. Climate change as a mathematical problem. *Journal of Applied Meteorology,* vol. 9, pp. 325–329. The author argues that climate change could be caused by "internal" fluctuations that are characteristic of complicated physical systems.

McDonald, James E. 1952. The coriolis effect. *Scientific American,* May. Reprinted in J. R. Moore, ed., *Oceanography,* pp. 60–63. Readable elaboration and examples.

MacIntyre, Ferren. 1970. Why the sea is salt. *Scientific American,* November, pp. 104–115. Excellent introduction to geochemistry.

Mason, Brian. 1966. *Principles of geochemistry.* 3d ed. Wiley, New York. Good introductory text.

Miller, Albert. 1966. *Meteorology.* Merrill, Columbus, Ohio. Concise and readable paperback.

Moore, J. R., ed. 1971. *Oceanography: Readings from* Scientific American. W. H. Freeman and Company, San Francisco. Collection of articles.

Munk, Walter. 1955. The circulation of the oceans. *Scientific American,* September. Reprinted in J. R. Moore, ed., *Oceanography,* pp. 64–69.

Namias, Jerome. 1969. Seasonal interactions between the north Pacific Ocean and the atmosphere during the 1960s. *Monthly Weather Review,* vol. 97, no. 3, pp. 173–192. Early analysis of a possible controlling role for the ocean in climate fluctuations.

———. 1972. Experiments in objectively predicting some atmospheric and oceanic variables for the winter of 1971–2. *Journal of Applied Meteorology,* vol. 11, no. 8, pp. 1164–74.

Oort, Abraham H. 1970. The energy cycle of the earth. *Scientific American,* September, pp. 54–63. Sizes and functions of major natural energy flows.

Rona, P. A. 1973. Plate tectonics and mineral resources. *Scientific American,* July.

SCEP. *See* Study of Critical Environmental Problems.

Schneider, S. H.; and Roger D. Dennett. 1975. Climatic barriers to long-term energy growth. *Ambio,* vol. 4, no. 2, pp. 65–74. Contains good synopsis of knowledge about the operation of global climatic machinery.

Schneider, S. H., and C. Mass. 1975. Volcanic dust, sunspots, and temperature trends. *Science,* vol. 190, pp. 741–746 (November 21). Interesting speculations and analysis centered around the influence on climate of possible variations in the sun's output.

Sellers, William D. 1965. *Physical climatology.* University of Chicago Press. Excellent text.

Siever, Raymond. 1974. The steady state of the earth's crust, atmosphere, and oceans. *Scientific American,* June, pp. 72–79. An illuminating review of the main ideas in geochemistry.

Skinner, Brian J. 1969. *Earth resources.* Prentice-Hall, Englewood Cliffs, N.J. Capsule introduction to the hydrologic cycle, among other topics.

SMIC. *See* Study of Man's Impact on Climate.

Stewart, R. W. 1969. The atmosphere and the ocean. *Scientific American,* September, pp. 76–86. Useful summary of some ocean-atmosphere interactions, although dated somewhat by recent developments (see Jerome Namias, Seasonal interactions between the north Pacific Ocean and the atmosphere during the 1960s; Namias, Experiments in objectively predicting; and F. Bretherton, Recent developments in dynamical oceanography).

Study of Critical Environmental Problems (SCEP). 1970. *Man's impact on the global environment.* M.I.T. Press, Cambridge, Mass. Contains short summaries of main global climatic processes.

Study of Man's Impact on Climate (SMIC). 1971. *Inadvertent climate modification.* M.I.T. Press, Cambridge, Mass. A wealth of information and references on the study of climate and climate change. Moderately technical.

Wenk, Edward, Jr. 1969. The physical resources of the ocean. *Scientific American,* pp. 166–176.

Wilson, J. Tuzo, ed. 1972. *Continents adrift: Readings from* Scientific American. W. H. Freeman and Company, San Francisco. Articles on plate tectonics and continental drift.

Woodwell, George M. 1970. The energy cycle of the biosphere. *Scientific American,* September, pp. 64–74.

Wyllie, Peter J. 1975. The earth's mantle. *Scientific American,* March, pp. 50–63. Plate tectonics, earthquakes, and the composition of the planet.

All things from eternity are of like form
and come round in a circle.

—Marcus Aurelius

CHAPTER 3

Nutrient Cycles

The main flow of energy that helps shape conditions on Earth's surface comes from space; and when the energy's work here is done, to space it returns. With respect to energy, then, Earth is an open system. With respect to its chemical endowment, however, Earth is a closed system. That is, the amounts of carbon, hydrogen, oxygen, iron, gold, and other elements in the planet-atmosphere system do not change with time; the chemical arrangement and physical distribution of these elements can and do vary, but essentially nothing enters and nothing leaves the system.[1]

The elements in this closed system that are essential to life are called *nutrients.* They can be divided into three categories: the 4 main chemical building blocks of living matter (carbon, oxygen, hydrogen, nitrogen); 7 *macronutrients,* of which smaller but still significant quantities are required for life; and 13 *micronutrients,* or trace elements, of which tiny quantities perform essential functions (see Table 3-1).[2] The suitability of any terrestrial or aquatic environment for the support of life depends on the availability of nutrients in appropriate forms and quantities. The processes that govern this availability (or lack of it) are known collectively as *nutrient cycles,* because of the way the individual basic stocks of physical material move cyclically through the living and nonliving parts of the physical world.

These cycles function in support of life not merely by making nutrients continuously available—in other

[1]The main exceptions are some hydrogen escaping into space from the top of the atmosphere, some hydrogen arriving in the "solar wind" from the sun, and some iron and other elements arriving in the form of meteorites. The quantities involved in these flows are negligible for the purposes of this discussion.

[2]Frieden, The chemical elements of life.

words, by maintaining the fertility of the environment—but also by limiting the accumulation of material in quantities, forms, and places in which it would damage organisms. It is important to recognize in this connection that the same elements and compounds that serve as nutrients for some organisms in some concentrations are often toxic for other organisms, or even for the same organisms at higher concentrations. For example, molecular oxygen (O_2) is toxic to anaerobic organisms and, at high enough concentrations, even to mammals. Ammonia (NH_3) is an important source of nutrient nitrogen for many plants but is toxic to people. Hydrogen sulfide (H_2S) is a nutrient for certain types of bacteria but is extremely toxic to mammals.

TABLE 3-1
The Chemical Elements of Life

Symbol	*Name*	*Atomic number*	*Atomic weight*
BASIC BUILDING BLOCKS			
H	Hydrogen	1	1
C	Carbon	6	12
N	Nitrogen	7	14
O	Oxygen	8	16
MACRONUTRIENTS			
Na	Sodium	11	23
Mg	Magnesium	12	24
P	Phosphorus	15	31
S	Sulfur	16	32
Cl	Chlorine	17	35
K	Potassium	19	39
Ca	Calcium	20	40
TRACE ELEMENTS			
F	Fluorine	9	19
Si	Silicon	14	28
V	Vanadium	23	51
Cr	Chromium	24	52
Mn	Manganese	25	55
Fe	Iron	26	56
Co	Cobalt	27	59
Cu	Copper	29	64
Zn	Zinc	30	65
Se	Selenium	34	79
Mo	Molybdenum	42	96
Sn	Tin	50	119
I	Iodine	53	127

Source: E. Frieden, The chemical elements of life.

DYNAMICS OF NUTRIENT CYCLING

The steps that make up all nutrient cycles involve two basic processes: physical transport and chemical transformation.

The principal agents of physical transport are discussed in Chapter 2. They are: (1) the hydrologic cycle, including evaporation and precipitation as well as the flow of streams, groundwater, and ice; (2) winds; (3) ocean currents; and (4) geologic movement, especially the upward and downward motions at the boundaries of tectonic plates and geologic uplifting on continents. A fifth agent of physical transport that is important in a few circumstances is the movement of organisms. For example, fish-eating birds that deposit their excrement on land provide a significant pathway by which nitrogen and phosphorus are transferred from the sea to the land. Fish such as salmon, that feed mostly in the ocean but migrate up freshwater rivers to spawn and die, perform a similar function, as do the ocean-caught fish consumed by continent-dwelling human beings.

How the various mechanisms of transport link the principal "compartments" of the physical world is represented schematically in Figure 3-1. Obviously, the ease (and, hence, the rate) with which a given substance can move through these pathways depends on its physical state (solid, liquid, gas), on other physical properties (solubility, volatility), and on the possibility of chemical transformations that can change those properties. Such chemical transformations take place in living organisms and in the nonliving environment. They are considered in more detail below. The magnitudes of the flows in some of the principal pathways shown in Figure 3-1 are listed in Table 3-2.

Each of the compartments indicated in Figure 3-1 often is divided into subcompartments for the purpose of tracing nutrient flows. Thus, for example, it is customary to consider three subcompartments of material in both the soil and the oceans: living organic matter, dead organic matter, and the inorganic medium itself. These subcompartments can be further subdivided—for example, organic matter, into plants, animals, and microorganisms; and seawater, into the well-mixed surface layer and the stratified deeper layers. Finally, within each subdivision of each subcompartment, the magnitudes of

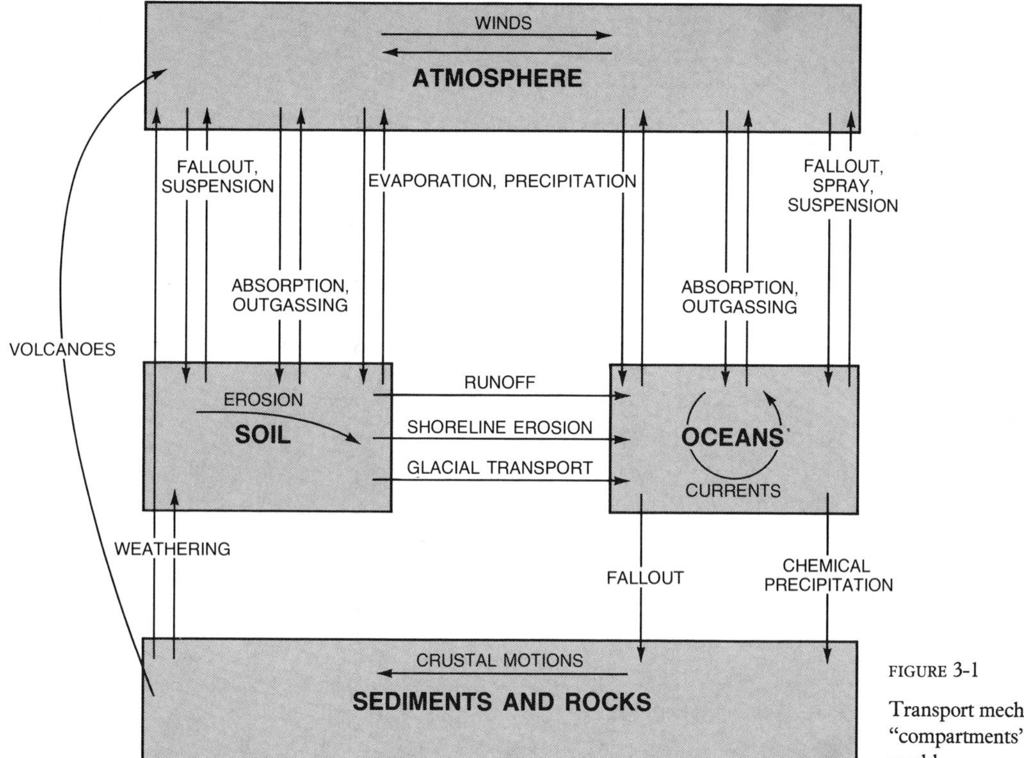

FIGURE 3-1

Transport mechanisms among the "compartments" of the physical world.

the stocks, or pools, of the important elements and compounds are of interest, as are the magnitudes of the flows into and out of the pools (where flows can mean physical movement or chemical transformation or a combination of the two).

For any pool that is in steady state—that is, for which inflows balance outflows so the size of the pool does not change with time—an average residence time for a compound can be calculated as the ratio of the size of the pool to the sum of the inflows or outflows (see Box 2-3). For example,

$$\text{residence time (yr)} = \frac{\text{pool (kg)}}{\text{sum of outflows (kg/yr)}}$$

Examination of the residence times for important pools provides quick insight into the dynamics of nutrient cycling, and, indirectly, into the probable vulnerability of specific components of nutrient cycles to disruption by human intervention. For example, a long residence time means the annual flows are small compared to the pool, which means in turn that unless human disruptions cause

TABLE 3-2
Some Global Materials Flows

Pathway	*Magnitude of flow (billion MT/yr)*
TO OCEANS	
River discharge (H_2O)	32,000
Groundwater flow (H_2O)	4,000
River-borne suspended solids (today)	18
River-borne suspended solids (prehuman)	5(?)
River-borne dissolved solids	4
Ice-sheet transport of solids	2
Shoreline erosion	0.3
TO AND FROM ATMOSPHERE	
Evaporation (H_2O)	526,000
CO_2 exchange in photosynthesis	220
CO_2 from burning fossil fuels	16
Dust and smoke from land	1(?)
Volcanic gases and debris	0.1

Note: Uncertainty in most estimates is roughly ±20 percent.
Sources: R. M. Garrels, F. T. Mackenzie, and C. Hunt, *Chemical cycles and the global environment;* Study of Man's Impact on Climate, *Inadvertent climate modification.*

TABLE 3-3
Residence Times in Some Important Nutrient Pools

Nutrient pool	*Residence time (yr)*
Nitrogen in atmosphere	64,000,000
Oxygen in atmosphere	7,500
Inorganic nitrogen in soil	100(?)
Carbon in dead terrestrial organic matter	27
Carbon in living terrestrial organic matter	17
Carbon dioxide in atmosphere	5
Carbon in living oceanic organic matter	0.10
Sulfur compounds in atmosphere	0.02

Note: Uncertainties are at least ±20 percent.

a very large alteration in inflow or outflow they will affect the size of the pool only very slowly. A short residence time, by contrast, means that significant changes in inflow or outflow can affect the size of the pool very quickly. Approximate residence times for some of the important nutrient pools appear in Table 3-3.

CHEMISTRY OF NUTRIENT CYCLES

Two kinds of chemistry play crucial roles in the principal global nutrient cycles: the chemistry of the sedimentary cycle, associated with the very slow transformation of very large pools of material, and the chemistry of life, associated with the more rapid transformation of much smaller pools. Both kinds of chemistry depend very heavily on the very special roles of water as a source of hydrogen (H^+) and hydroxyl (OH^-) ions for many chemical reactions, as a medium for holding other chemical compounds in solution where they can react, and as a vehicle for physical transport of compounds from place to place.

Sedimentary Cycle

Nutrients are mobilized in the sedimentary cycle when water comes in contact with rock. Rainwater is slightly acidic, having absorbed some atmospheric carbon dioxide to form weak carbonic acid:[3]

$$H_2O + CO_2 \longrightarrow H_2CO_3$$
$$H_2CO_3 \longrightarrow H^+ + HCO_3^-$$

[3] A good discussion of this point is given by F. Press and R. Siever in *Earth,* Chapter 6.

The pH of rainfall in areas free of industrial pollution is around 5.7. (Recall from basic chemistry that pH is the negative of the log to base 10 of the concentration of hydrogen ions in moles per liter. The pH of distilled water is 7.0, corresponding to 10^{-7} moles of hydrogen ion per liter.) This slight acidity is enough to facilitate greatly the dissolution of many minerals present in exposed rock—a process called *weathering.*

Among the most important weathering reactions is that of the common mineral feldspar (a constituent of granite):

$$\underset{\text{feldspar}}{2KAlSi_3O_8} + \underset{\text{carbonic acid}}{2(H^+ + HCO_3^-)} + \underset{\text{water}}{H_2O} \longrightarrow$$
$$\underset{\text{kaolinite}}{Al_2Si_2O_5(OH)_4} + \underset{\text{dissolved silica}}{4SiO_2} + \underset{\text{dissolved potassium and bicarbonate ion}}{2K^+ + 2HCO_3^-}$$

Kaolinite is a clay; it is left behind in this process as a contribution to the formation of soil, whereas the dissolved silica, potassium ion, and bicarbonate ion are carried away in the runoff. The mobilization and removal of positive ions such as (in this case) potassium is called *leaching.* Note that the reaction consumes some water and that it reduces the acidity of the solution (that is, it removes hydrogen ions) as it proceeds. These properties are characteristic of weathering reactions. Essentially the same reaction also occurs in the weathering of the aluminosilicates of sodium and calcium ($NaAlSi_3O_8$, $CaAl_2Si_2O_8$). Other silicate minerals also weather in the same general manner to produce kaolinite or other clays.

The weathering of certain other minerals leads to their complete dissolution; no solid trace is left behind to be incorporated into soil. The most important of these minerals are the limestones, or carbonate rocks, which undergo the following reactions:

$$CaCO_3 + H^+ + HCO_3^- \longrightarrow Ca^{++} + 2HCO_3^-$$
$$CaMg(CO_3)_2 + 2(H^+ + HCO_3^-) \longrightarrow Mg^{++} + Ca^{++} + 4HCO_3^-$$

Still other weathering reactions consume atmospheric oxygen in the oxidation of iron minerals:

$$4FeSiO_3 + O_2 + 2H_2O \longrightarrow 4FeO(OH) + 4SiO_2$$
$$4Fe_3O_4 + O_2 \longrightarrow 6Fe_2O_3$$
$$4FeS_2 + 15O_2 + 8H_2O \longrightarrow 2Fe_2O_3 + 8H_2SO_4$$

Most of the products of the weathering reactions mentioned here eventually reach the sea, either as dissolved ions or as suspended solids. Between the time they are freed from rock and the time they reach the sea, of course, some of these elements have made one or more passages through the living part of the biosphere as nutrients. In the sea, too, the nutrient substances are captured from the water by living organisms, eventually to be returned to the water or to the sediments on the ocean floor. The reverse of many of the weathering reactions also can occur in seawater in the absence of intervention by living organisms, forming solid precipitates that join the organic debris on the ocean bottom. Apparently these outputs of the major nutrient elements from the oceans roughly balance the inputs, because considerable physical evidence indicates that the salinity of seawater has been approximately constant for at least the past 200 million years.[4]

The sedimentary cycle is finally closed by the geologic processes described in Chapter 2: that is, by the processes of transformation and transportation that turn seafloor sediments into continental rocks, and by volcanic action.

Living Matter

Ecologist Edward S. Deevey, Jr., has pointed out that living matter can be regarded as a chemical compound with the empirical formula[5]

$$H_{2960}O_{1480}C_{1480}N_{16}P_{1.8}S.$$

This enormous (and completely intentional) oversimplification serves both to call attention to the chemical side of life—the side with which this chapter is concerned—and, more specifically, to illustrate the relative proportions in which the six most abundant elemental constituents of living material exist.

Actually, there is substantial variation in the ratios of the chemical elements of life in different kinds of organisms, the above formula being a weighted average in which woody plants predominate. The numbers are, in any case, not known with great accuracy. Another source gives the molar ratio H/O/C/N/S/P as 1600/800/800/9/5/1 for land plants (different from Deevey mainly in the abundances of sulfur and phosphorus) and 212/106/106/16/2/1 for living marine plants, soil humus, and organic materials in sedimentary rocks.[6] (Readers who have not studied basic chemistry or who have forgotten it should see Box 3-1 for a review of mole and mass measures.)

The basic reactions that link the water cycle, the carbon dioxide cycle, and the oxygen cycle through living matter are photosynthesis:

$$6\ CO_2 + 12\ H_2O + \text{solar energy} \longrightarrow C_6H_{12}O_6 + 6\ H_2O$$

and its opposite, respiration, or oxidative metabolism:

$$6\ O_2 + C_6H_{12}O_6 \longrightarrow 6\ CO_2 + 6\ H_2O + \text{heat.}$$

The compound $C_6H_{12}O_6$, or $(CH_2O)_6$, is glucose, the simplest carbohydrate produced by photosynthesis. The photosynthesis reaction is written with what appear to be six extra H_2O molecules on each side because twelve molecules of H_2O are actually broken up for each molecule of $C_6H_{12}O_6$ synthesized; radioactive-tracer experiments show that all twelve oxygen atoms from the 12 H_2O end up in the $6O_2$, and the oxygen in the six *new* water molecules comes from the CO_2.[7] The amount of energy transformed from light into stored chemical energy by the photosynthesis reaction is 112 kilocalories (469 kilojoules) per mole of carbon fixed. The net result of the respiration reaction is to transform the same 112 kilocalories per mole of carbon from chemical energy into heat.

Photosynthesis is carried out not only by higher green plants (such as oak trees, grasses, and ferns) but also by various kinds of algae (green, brown, red, blue-green) and by certain bacteria. In the bacteria, substances other than water serve as the sources of hydrogen for the reduction of carbon.[8] For example, the green sulfur

[4]Ferren MacIntyre, Why the sea is salt.

[5]Edward S. Deevey, Jr., Mineral cycles.

[6]R. M. Garrels, F. T. Mackenzie, C. Hunt, *Chemical cycles and the global environment.*

[7]See, for example, A. L. Lehninger, *Biochemistry,* p. 457.

[8]*Reduction* is the term for gaining electrons in chemical reactions, to be contrasted with *oxidation,* which means losing electrons. In most cases, gaining a hydrogen atom is equivalent to gaining an electron, because hydrogen effectively gives up its single electron to most elements with which it forms compounds. See, for example, L. Pauling, *General chemistry,* or any other basic chemistry text.

BOX 3-1 Moles, Molecules, and Mass Ratios

A mole of an element is 6.02×10^{23} atoms; a mole of a compound is 6.02×10^{23} molecules. This number—known as Avogadro's number—is the number of *atomic mass units* in a gram. (The atomic mass unit is defined as one-twelfth of the mass of the most abundant isotope of carbon, which is carbon-12. One atomic mass unit is approximately the mass of a proton.) It follows from these definitions that a mole of any element or compound—6.02×10^{23} atoms or molecules of it—has a mass in grams equal to the atomic or molecular weight of the substance in atomic mass units. For example, a mole of carbon (atomic weight, 12 atomic mass units) has a mass of 12 g; a mole of carbon dioxide, or CO_2 (atomic weight, 44 atomic mass units), has a mass of 44 g.

The mass ratios of elements in living matter and in other compounds differ from the molar ratios because different elements have different atomic weights. Consider the carbohydrate molecule $(CH_2O)_n$, where n is an integer telling how many times the basic CH_2O building block appears in the molecule. The ratio of moles of hydrogen to moles of carbon to moles of oxygen in this material is 2 to 1 to 1—in shorthand, $H/C/O = 2/1/1$. The ratio of the masses is obtained by multiplying the numbers in the molar ratios by the appropriate atomic weights. The mass ratio H/C/O in $(CH_2O)_n$ is $(2 \times 1)/(1 \times 12)/(1 \times 16) = 2/12/16 = 1/6/8$.

bacteria use hydrogen sulfide instead of water, according to the equation

$$12\ H_2S + 6\ CO_2 + \text{light} \longrightarrow C_6H_{12}O_6 + 6\ H_2O + 12\ S,$$

producing elemental sulfur rather than oxygen. (In fact, these bacteria are obligate anaerobes—they would be poisoned by oxygen.) The reverse reaction (respiration) consumes sulfur and carbohydrate and liberates heat, carbon dioxide, and hydrogen sulfide. Still other photosynthesis reactions use hydrogen, obtained from H_2O or H_2S or other hydrogen donors, to reduce substances other than carbon dioxide. For example, most higher plants can reduce nitrate, instead of CO_2, in photosynthesis:

$$9\ H_2O + 2\ NO_3^- + \text{light} \longrightarrow 2\ NH_3 + 6\ H_2O + 4\tfrac{1}{2}\ O_2;$$

and nitrogen-fixing photosynthetic organisms can reduce atmospheric nitrogen:[9]

$$3\ H_2O + N_2 + \text{light} \longrightarrow 2\ NH_3 + 1\tfrac{1}{2}\ O_2.$$

These variations notwithstanding, the great bulk of photosynthesis on Earth consists of the reduction of carbon dioxide, with water as the hydrogen source.

The photosynthesis and respiration reactions, as we have written them here, actually represent only the end points of vastly more complicated sequences of chemical events. For example, although burning glucose in air is described essentially completely by the respiration reaction given above,

$$6\ O_2 + C_6H_{12}O_6 \longrightarrow 6\ CO_2 + 6\ H_2O + \text{heat},$$

to achieve the same result in a living cell (at a temperature far below that of combustion) requires many intermediate steps. The intermediate steps in both respiration and photosynthesis rely heavily on three kinds of organic compounds: the energy carrier ATP (adenosine triphosphate); the electron carrier NADP (nicotinamide adenine dinucleotide phosphate); and various catalysts called enzymes. (Catalysts speed up chemical reactions without themselves being consumed.)[10]

A closer look at these compounds provides some clues to the importance of the elements nitrogen, phosphorus, and sulfur in the chemistry of life. All biochemical reactions of importance (not just photosynthesis and respiration) require enzyme catalysts if they are to proceed at significant rates. All enzymes are ***proteins.*** Proteins other than enzymes also serve as hormones; as vehicles to transport oxygen; as important structural

[9] Lehninger, *Biochemistry;* and R. Y. Stanier, M. Douderoff, and E. A. Adelberg, *The Microbial world,* Prentice-Hall, Englewood Cliffs, N.J., 1970.

[10] For detailed descriptions of the biochemistry of photosynthesis and respiration see R. P. Levine, The mechanism of photosynthesis; P. Cloud and A. Gibor, The oxygen cycle; Lehninger, *Biochemistry.*

components of skin, tendons, muscle, cartilage, and bone; and in numerous other roles. All proteins are made up of building blocks called *amino acids,* and all amino acids contain the amino group $-NH_2$. A single protein contains from fifty to some tens of thousands of amino acids, and hence at least that many nitrogen atoms. (Some amino acids contain more than one nitrogen.) The shape and stiffness of many proteins—properties essential to their functions—are governed and maintained by bonds in which sulfur plays a crucial role, so it, too, is essential to the chemistry of life.

ATP and NADP are examples of *nucleotides,* compounds consisting of a five-carbon sugar to which one or more phosphate groups ($-PO_4$) and a *nitrogen base* are attached. A nitrogen base is a ring compound containing both nitrogen and carbon in the ring structure. Nucleotides not only perform critical energy-transfer and electron-transfer functions in the chemistry of living cells, but they are also the building blocks of *nucleic acids.* Each nucleic acid molecule contains hundreds to thousands of nucleotides, the arrangement of which is a chemical means of storing information. Nucleic acids control the synthesis of proteins and a variety of other processes in living cells. The nucleic acid DNA (deoxyribonucleic acid) is the *genetic material*—the bearer of the coded information that is passed from parent cells and organisms to their offspring to "tell" them what to become. The nucleic acid RNA (ribonucleic acid) plays essential roles in carrying out the instructions coded in DNA molecules.[11]

In addition to its role as a constituent of DNA and RNA, phosphorus, in the form of phosphate, is one of the principal anions (ions with a negative charge) that maintains electric neutrality in the fluids of living organisms. Along with calcium, it is also an important component in shells and bony structures. Sulfur, besides playing its role in proteins, in the form of sulfate ($-SO_4$) is another principal anion in body fluids and cells. The third principal anion is the chloride ion ($-Cl$). The principal cations (positively charged ions) are sodium, potassium, calcium, and magnesium. Magnesium is an essential constituent of many enzymes and of the green pigment chlorophyll. Iron is a key component of many enzymes and of the oxygen-transporting protein hemoglobin.[12]

Oversimplifying considerably, one can say that the quantity of living matter in a given environment is *limited by the stock of that requisite of life that is in shortest supply.* This rather obvious proposition carries the name *Liebig's law of the minimum.*[13] Of course, the limiting factor varies from one type of organism to another and from one environment to another. Generalizations are difficult, but it is fair to say that under many circumstances the quantity of plant material in a given environment is in fact controlled by a *limiting nutrient* (although the density of a given kind of plant is often controlled by a herbivore).[14] In desert regions the limiting nutrient is generally water. Under many conditions where water is not limiting, as in freshwater lakes, the limiting nutrient turns out to be phosphorus; in the open ocean it may be iron. In some richly productive environments, nitrogen and phosphorus are jointly limiting—producing any more plant material would require supplying more of both nutrients. Obviously, the limiting nutrient in a given biological system represents a leverage point where the effects of natural or human-induced perturbations manifest themselves rapidly.

CYCLES OF THE PRINCIPAL NUTRIENTS

The cycles of many nutrients are tightly linked chemically and biologically. This is so much the case for the cycles of carbon, oxygen, and hydrogen that we consider them together. The cycles of nitrogen, phosphorus, and sulfur, on the other hand, can usefully be examined separately, as they are here.

[11]For an introductory discussion, see Paul R. Ehrlich, R. Holm, M. Soule, *Introductory biology.* More detail is available in J. D. Watson, *The molecular biology of the gene.*

[12]Material in this paragraph is treated more fully in Frieden, Chemical elements.

[13]For a more thorough discussion see E. P. Odum, *Fundamentals of ecology.*

[14]For example, Paul R. Ehrlich and L. C. Birch, The "balance of nature" and population control.

TABLE 3-4
Phytomass and Net Primary Production on Land and in the Oceans

	Phytomass (10^9 MT, dry weight)	Estimated net primary production (10^9 MT dry organic matter/yr)	(10^{15} moles carbon/yr)	(10^{18} kcal/yr)	(10^{12} watts)
On Land	1840.0	107	4.0	0.48	63
In Oceans	3.9	55	2.1	0.25	33
totals	1843.9	162	6.1	0.73	96

Note: MT = metric tons, conversions from mass to energy at 0.45 gram carbon per gram dry organic matter, 10 kcal per gram carbon. For ranges of uncertainty, see text.
Sources: After R. H. Whittaker and G. E. Likens, Carbon in the biota, in *Carbon and the biosphere,* G. H. Woodwell and E. V. Pecan, eds.

Carbon-Oxygen-Hydrogen

It is appropriate to begin our closer examination of the carbon-oxygen-hydrogen cycles with their intersection in the green plant, the basis of almost all life on Earth.

Carbon and energy in living plants. Most living plants not only fix (store) energy by means of photosynthesis but they also use some of that stored energy to drive their own life-sustaining internal processes by means of respiration. The total rate at which a plant or a plant community stores solar energy by means of photosynthesis is called *gross photosynthesis* or *gross primary production* (GPP). The figure obtained by subtracting from gross photosynthesis the amount of energy used by the plants in respiration (R) is called *net photosynthesis* or *net primary production* (NPP). In abbreviated form, then, the relation is GPP − R = NPP. Several interchangeable units are used in the biological literature for the measurement of these quantities: calories or kilocalories per unit of time, watts or kilowatts (different units for measuring the same thing—energy flow), grams of carbon fixed into organic compounds per unit of time, moles of carbon fixed per unit of time, or grams of dry organic matter produced per unit of time. The relations among these units are discussed in Box 3-2.

A wide range of estimates of global net primary production and the associated standing crop of living plants *(phytomass)* have been published.[15] One recent review indicates that the estimates of net primary production are converging on a value around 160 billion (1.60×10^{11}) metric tons per year for the globe.[16] Global phytomass was estimated in the same review as about ten times larger—1840 billion metric tons, dry weight—and gross photosynthesis was estimated to be about twice as large as net production (that is, half of gross photosynthesis is consumed in plant respiration and half remains as net production). The estimates for phytomass and net primary production, separated into terrestrial and oceanic components, are presented in Table 3-4.

The roughness of these estimates deserves emphasis. The range of recent (1970 or later) estimates of land phytomass, for example, is from about half the value given in Table 3-4 to 30 percent larger; the range of published values of ocean phytomass is from twenty times smaller than the value in Table 3-4 to three times larger.[17] The factor-of-60 range of informed opinion with respect to oceanic phytomass is especially remarkable. The range in recent published estimates of oceanic net primary production is only ±10 percent from the value in Table 3-4, and the range in terrestrial net production is from 15 percent less to 60 percent more than the value in the table.[18] The fraction of gross primary production consumed in plant respiration is known to vary between 20 percent and 75 percent, depending on type of plant and region, but the global average is unlikely to differ much from 50 percent.[19]

[15]See especially, G. M. Woodwell and E. V. Pecan, eds., *Carbon and the biosphere;* United States National Committee for the International Biological Program, *Productivity of world ecosystems.*

[16]R. H. Whittaker and G. E. Likens, Carbon in the biota, *Carbon and the biosphere,* Woodwell and Pecan, pp. 281–300.

[17]The high value of terrestrial phytomass and the low value of oceanic phytomass are from L. Rodin, N. Bazilevich, and N. Rozov, Productivity of the world's main ecosystems. The opposite extremes are found in B. Bolin, The carbon cycle.

[18]Whittaker and Likens, Carbon, p. 291.

[19]R. H. Whittaker, *Communities and ecosystems.*

BOX 3-2 Units for Energy and Material Flow in the Carbon Cycle

For the purpose of reconciling estimates of annual production presented in grams of carbon, grams of dry organic matter, and kilocalories, one widely used convention assumes that 10 kilocalories of energy are stored per gram of fixed carbon and that dry organic matter contains 45 percent fixed carbon by weight.* (The actual range of values for different kinds of dry organic matter extends roughly ± 15 percent from these nominal figures.) Thus, measurements in grams or metric tons (1 MT $= 10^6$ g) of carbon can be converted to grams or metric tons of dry organic matter by multiplying by 2.2, and 1 gram of dry organic matter can be taken to represent 4.5 kilocalories of stored energy. Useful conversions following directly from this convention are that 1 gram of dry organic matter per day corresponds to an average energy flow of about 0.2 watts; 1 gram of carbon per day, to about 0.5 watts; and one metric ton of dry organic matter per year, to about 600 watts. Also, 1 metric ton of dry organic matter contains 37,500 moles of carbon.

Although we shall use the convention just described, the reader may encounter others elsewhere. If the dry organic matter were pure carbohydrate—$(CH_2O)_n$—which stores 112 kilocalories per mole of carbon, then the appropriate conversions would be: 3.7 kilocalories per gram of dry organic matter, 9.3 kilocalories per gram of carbon, 0.4 gram carbon per gram of dry organic matter. [Actually, CH_2O *is* a good approximation of the average composition of all living matter (see Deevey's formula presented earlier) because so much of the world's biomass is cellulose tied up in woody plants, and cellulose has nearly this formula. However, most of the plant material *produced* each year is not cellulose—remember, a big pool does not necessarily mean a big flow. The annual production of organic matter contains a higher proportion of fixed carbon and higher energy content per gram than does the cellulose-dominated, slow-to-turn-over standing crop.] The rounded-off value of 4 kilocalories per gram of dry organic matter is in fairly widespread use in conjunction with the figure of 10 kilocalories per gram of fixed carbon, itself a rough average among several kinds of plant matter.

These differences in conversion values are troublesome for those seeking consistency in the ecological literature, but the differences they produce in the published figures for net production are much smaller than the uncertainties of measurement and estimation.

*See, for example, R. H. Whittaker and G. E. Likens, Carbon in the biota, in *Carbon and the biosphere*, G. H. Woodwell and E. V. Pecan, eds., pp. 281–300.

Taking the range of estimates into account, one can state several conclusions with reasonable assurance: (1) the annual NPP of the oceans is only one-third to one-half that of the continents, even though the oceans cover more than 70 percent of Earth's surface; (2) the pool, or standing crop, of living plant material on land is at least several hundred times that in the oceans; (3) the average turnover time (life expectancy) of oceanic plants must be in the range of days to weeks, in order for so small a phytomass to be associated with so large an annual production; (4) the average turnover time of terrestrial living plants, by contrast, is in the range of a decade or two;[20] (5) oceanic and terrestrial phytomasses are both so poorly known that man-induced or natural changes large enough to be very important in the long term could easily escape notice for some time. In the latter regard, although there are good reasons to suppose that the activities of civilization have diminished the terrestrial phytomass significantly, some experts consider this assertion to be debatable.[21]

Notwithstanding the uncertainties in the data, it is instructive to examine the large regional variations in plant productivity that are concealed in the global totals. Some of these figures (on which the totals in Table 3-4 are based) are summarized in Table 3-5. Of particular interest are the facts that tropical forests account for more than 40 percent of terrestrial NPP (although they cover only about 16 percent of the land area) and that up-

[20]Obviously, this longevity is strongly influenced by the high proportion of the terrestrial biomass in long-lived trees and shrubs. Most crop plants, of course, "turn over" in less than a year.

[21]See the comments in Whittaker and Likens, Carbon, pp. 295–297, and the group discussion stimulated by them (pp. 300–302).

TABLE 3-5
Variation and Distribution of Net Primary Production

	Range of NPP (g organic matter/m^2/yr)[a, b, c]	Total NPP (billion MT/yr)[a]
Tropical Forest	1300–6000	45.3
Shrubland, Grassland, Savanna	500–3200	19.8
Temperate Forest	1200–2000	14.9
Northern Forest	600–1000	9.6
Cultivated Land	350–9400	9.1
Swamps, Lakes, Marshes	1000–1500	6.2
Desert, Tundra, Alpine Meadow	3–250	2.4
Terrestrial total		107.3
Open Ocean	50–370	42.0
Continental Shelf	370–750+	9.6
Reefs, Estuaries	1800–4900	3.6
Upwelling Regions	370–750	0.2
Oceanic total		55.4

[a]R. H. Whittaker and G. E. Likens, Carbon in the biota, in *Carbon and the biosphere,* G. H. Woodwell and E. V. Pecan, eds., p. 283.
[b]L. Rodin, N. Bazilevich, and N. Rozov, Productivity of the world's main ecosystems, pp. 15–17, 22.
[c]G. H. Woodwell, The energy cycle of the biosphere, *Scientific American,* September 1970, pp. 64–74.

welling regions, continental shelves, reefs, and estuaries yield almost 25 percent of oceanic NPP while accounting for less than 9 percent of the ocean's area.

According to Table 3-4, the rate at which energy is being stored in net primary production is about 100 million megawatts, roughly two-thirds on land and one-third in the ocean. The rate of gross primary production can be assumed to be about 200 million megawatts. The net primary production is roughly twelve times the rate at which civilization used commercial energy in 1975, where commercial energy refers to energy that is sold (for example, fossil fuels, hydropower, and nuclear power, but excluding food) as opposed to energy that is gathered by the user (for example, most wood, dung).

Very little of the solar energy that reaches Earth's surface is captured by photosynthesis. The net primary production is about 0.1 percent of the incident solar energy at the surface—0.25 percent of what strikes the land and 0.05 percent of what strikes the ocean. Some of the reasons these percentages are so small are obvious. Plants do not by any means cover all of Earth's surface; in many areas of the world the growing season lasts only part of the year; and in some circumstances, as already noted, plant growth is limited by lack of one or more critical nutrients. Under favorable conditions, on the other hand—as in a well watered and fertilized cornfield or a fertile swamp—NPP may reach 2 percent or so of incident solar energy averaged over the growing season and as much as 6 percent or 7 percent of incident solar energy on the most favorable days.[22]

These numbers still seem low. One additional reason for this is that only about one-fourth the solar energy reaching the ground is in the part of the wavelength range that stimulates photosynthesis (blue and red light).[23] The other big reason is the large amount of water that must be evaporated through the leaves of plants to maintain the nutrient-bearing flow of water through them. Evaporating this water typically takes 40 percent or more of the energy that falls on a plant, and a much higher percentage of what is actually absorbed by the plant.[24] (For production of every ton of wet weight of many crops—of which about one-fourth is dry organic matter—around 100 tons of water are evaporated. This means 400 grams of water are evaporated, requiring

[22]Odum, *Fundamentals,* Chapter 3.
[23]D. Gates, The flow of energy in the biosphere.
[24]Ibid.; H. Penman, The water cycle.

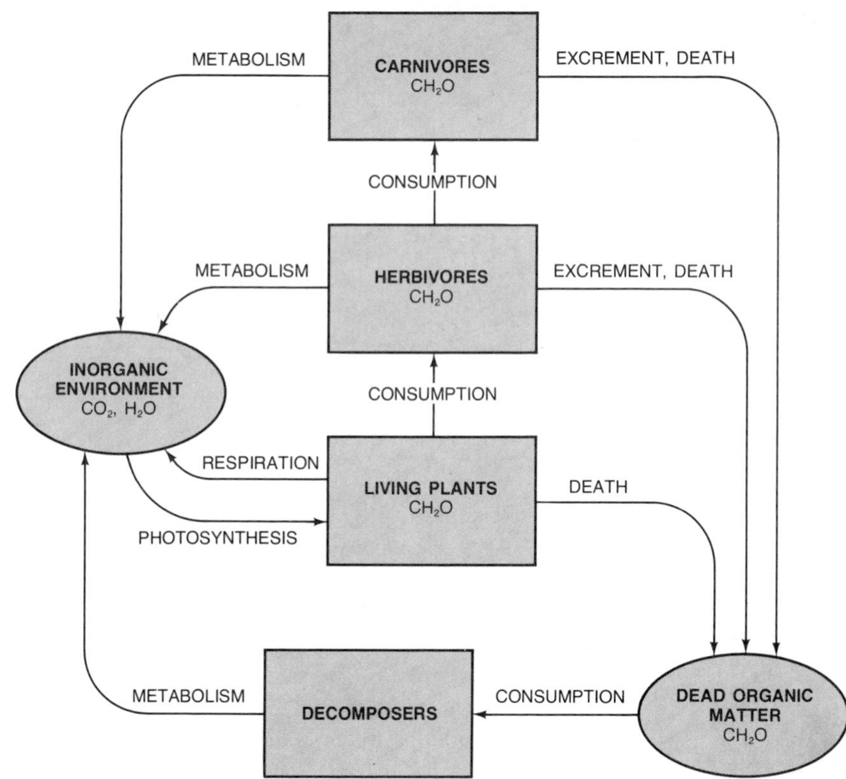

FIGURE 3-2

The cycling of carbon through organisms (simplified).

about 0.6 kilocalories per gram evaporated, for every gram or 4.5 kilocalories of dry organic matter produced. The ratio in such a case is about 50 kilocalories for evaporation per kilocalorie of net primary production.)

Oxygen balance: metabolism by animals and microbes. The overall effects of the net production of plants on the cycles of carbon, oxygen, and hydrogen are as follows: (1) more oxygen, O_2, is added to the environment than is removed from it; (2) less carbon dioxide, CO_2, and water, H_2O, are added to the environment than are removed from it; (3) the CO_2 and H_2O subtracted from the environmental pools show up as additions to the pool of stored organic matter, CH_2O, and to the atmospheric oxygen pool. Quantitatively, for every metric ton of dry organic matter produced, there is a net loss from the environment of 0.6 metric tons of water and about 1.5 metric tons of CO_2, and a net gain of about 1.1 metric tons of oxygen.

Why, then, is oxygen not building up continuously in the atmosphere, while water and carbon dioxide are depleted? Because plant matter is not accumulating, but rather is approximately in steady state. It is being broken down into carbon dioxide and water again by the metabolism of animals and microbes, using up molecular oxygen just as rapidly as new plant material and oxygen are being produced.

Consider the possible fates of plant carbohydrate produced as part of net primary production (Figure 3-2). Plants either are consumed by herbivores, or they die and add their carbohydrate to the pool of dead organic matter. Of the part consumed by herbivores, some is metabolized and thereby returned to the environmental pool of CO_2 and H_2O, some is added as excrement to the pool of dead organic matter, and some is incorporated into herbivore tissue, either to be eaten by carnivores or to be added at the herbivore's death (by causes other than being devoured) directly to the pool of dead organic matter. The same fates await the carbohydrate that reaches the carnivores. The cycle is closed by the action of decomposers—both animals and microbes (bacteria)—which by metabolizing the fixed carbon in dead organic matter return CO_2 and H_2O to the environmental pools.

There are some important side pathways in the carbon cycle not shown in Figure 3-2, in which the initial products of decomposition include methane and carbon monoxide (CH_4 and CO) in addition to carbon dioxide. The main reactions are:

$$2\,CH_2O \longrightarrow CH_4 + CO_2$$

$$2\,CH_2O + O_2 \longrightarrow 2\,CO + 2\,H_2O.$$

The CH_4 and CO may then be oxidized in the soil or in the atmosphere according to the following reactions:

$$2\,CH_4 + 3\,O_2 \longrightarrow 2\,CO + 4\,H_2O \quad \text{and}$$

$$2\,CO + O_2 \longrightarrow 2\,CO_2.$$

The details concealed by these simple formulas can be quite complex.

In steady state, the metabolism of carbohydrate by herbivores, carnivores, and decomposers returns to the environment exactly as much CO_2 and H_2O as the production of the carbohydrate by photosynthesis originally removed. And it consumes exactly as much oxygen as the photosynthesis produced. There is therefore no long-run buildup (or depletion) of oxygen in the environment as a result of this cycle, unless net photosynthesis and metabolism get out of balance.

The sequestering of fixed carbon. How did oxygen accumulate in the atmosphere in the first place? The biogeochemical evidence suggests that molecular oxygen in the atmosphere is of biological origin, there having been essentially none before the evolution of photosynthetic organisms, perhaps 2 billion years ago.[25] For oxygen produced by photosynthesis to have accumulated over the long term, part of the carbon fixed by this process must have been withdrawn from the cycle illustrated in Figure 3-2, escaping the oxidation step back to carbon dioxide. Indeed, it is precisely such a break in the carbon cycle that produced the fossil fuels. They originated as plant material that escaped breakdown by decomposers, in many cases by being buried in swamps and bogs under conditions from which both oxygen and anaerobic decomposer organisms were absent. Hundreds of millions of years of burial under considerable pressure and heat converted these plant materials into the hydrocarbon fossil fuels—coal, petroleum, and natural gas. The oxygen released when the carbon in these fuels was first fixed by photosynthesis remained in the atmosphere.[26]

The different ranks of coal—lignite, subbituminous, bituminous, anthracite—represent different ages (listed here from youngest to oldest) in terms of the origin of the plant material they derived from, and somewhat different chemical compositions.[27] Peat is the partially decomposed organic matter that is the precursor of coal. Petroleum, natural gas, oil shale, and tar sands are the results of different histories of biogeochemical transformation, but all originated, like coal, with dead organic matter.

Not all of the fixed carbon that has been sequestered out of reach of natural oxidative processes is in deposits as concentrated as the fossil fuels. A much larger amount, in fact, is dispersed in sediments whose hydrocarbon content is on the order of 1 part per 1000 (1 g of hydrocarbon material per kg of sediment) or less.[28]

Since the oxygen reservoir in the atmosphere has been built up by the sequestration of fixed carbon in various forms, could it be jeopardized by any forseeable activities of civilization that would cause the oxidation of these fixed-carbon pools? Deforestation, for example, could lead to the oxidation of part of the standing crop of fixed carbon in living organic matter, and combustion of fossil fuels oxidizes those pools. Yet, examination of the best estimates of the sizes of the fixed-carbon pools shows little cause for concern in the short term (see Table 3-6). Removal and oxidation of the entire terrestrial biomass would deplete atmospheric oxygen by at most 0.2 percent. Combustion of *all* the conventional fossil fuels (coal, petroleum, natural gas—of which about 90 percent is coal) thought to be recoverable *ever* by human effort would deplete atmospheric oxygen by 1.8 percent. This

[25]Cloud and Gibor, The oxygen cycle.

[26]Contrary to a rather widely held misconception, fossil fuels did not come mainly from dinosaurs or other animals. Because of the inefficiency of energy transfer up food chains and other factors (which are treated in Chapter 4), the rate at which fixed carbon was incorporated in animal tissues was much smaller than the rate at which it was incorporated into plant tissues.

[27]See P. Averitt, Coal; and Chapter 8 of this book.

[28]See, for example, T. H. McCulloh, Oil and gas.

TABLE 3-6
Sizes of Pools of Fixed Carbon (10^{15} moles reduced carbon)

Oceanic Biomass[a, b]	0.1–0.6
Terrestrial Biomass[a, b]	40–70
Dead Organic Matter, terrestrial[a, b]	60–750
Dead Organic Matter, dissolved and suspended in oceans[a, b]	60–250
Recoverable Coal, Petroleum, Natural Gas[c]	500
Oil Shale[c]	24,000
Reduced Carbon, dispersed in sediments[a]	1,000,000
Molecular Oxygen, in atmosphere[a, d]	38,000

[a]R. M. Garrels, F. T. Mackenzie, C. Hunt, *Chemical cycles and the global environment.*
[b]G. M. Woodwell and E. V. Pecan, *Carbon and the biosphere.*
[c]M. K. Hubbert, Energy resources.
[d]For comparison.

would reduce the oxygen content of the atmosphere at sea level to what it now is at an elevation of 150 meters. The 1975 global rate of fossil-fuel combustion would amount to a depletion of atmospheric oxygen by about 0.001 percent per year—far below the threshold of detectability with existing measurement techniques. On the other hand, the amount of reduced carbon thought to be present in oil shales is sufficient, if it were ever totally recovered and oxidized, to consume *more than half* the atmospheric oxygen pool. Some observers believe that most of the oil shales are too dispersed an energy resource ever to be economically attractive (see Chapter 8). But, in the event this view is not correct and civilization commences to use oil shale at a very high rate—say, ten times the rate at which all forms of energy were consumed worldwide in 1975—it would still take many centuries for the resulting depletion of atmospheric oxygen to become serious.

The oxygen situation is made more complicated than indicated in the foregoing paragraphs by the existence of important pools of oxygen elsewhere than in the atmosphere. It is apparent from the information in Table 3-6 that other oxygen pools must exist, because the number of moles of oxygen in the atmosphere is much smaller than the number of moles of reduced carbon in the sediments and elsewhere. The oxygen produced when all that carbon was fixed and sequestered was tied up with the oxidation of ferrous oxide (FeO) to ferric oxide (Fe_2O_3) and sulfur to sulfate (-SO_4) in sedimentary rocks. It may also have been tied up in the oxidation of carbon of inorganic origin (such as carbon monoxide from volcanoes) to carbon dioxide and carbonate (-CO_3). Although all these reactions are slow, they can account for the necessary enormous amounts of oxygen if they are assumed to have operated over geologic time spans.[29] Similarly, alterations in conditions governing the reaction rates could lead to significant changes in atmospheric composition over very long periods. On shorter time scales, however, organic carbon pools and associated reactions are almost certainly more important, and they are unlikely to produce significant changes in atmospheric oxygen in less than centuries.

Carbon dioxide. Although atmospheric oxygen depletion evidently is not a short-term threat, buildup of atmospheric carbon dioxide is. Every mole of oxygen removed from the atmosphere means a mole of carbon dioxide added. Since the number of moles of CO_2 in the atmosphere is 700 times smaller than the number of moles of O_2, a change of a specified number of moles has 700 times the effect on the CO_2 concentration as on the O_2 concentration. The combustion of fossil fuel that depletes oxygen by 0.001 percent per year augments the atmospheric CO_2 by 0.7 percent per year—not an insignificant increment.

Not all of the added CO_2 remains in the atmosphere, however. Some is absorbed by the oceans, and it is conceivable that some is being taken up in an increase in biomass. (Recall from the earlier discussion that the size of the biomass is not known with sufficient accuracy to

[29]See, for example, Cloud and Gibor, The oxygen cycle.

detect even rather substantial changes.) An increase in the concentration of CO_2 in the atmosphere should increase the rate of net photosynthesis (where other nutrients are not limiting), and this would produce a growing biomass if the rate of oxidative metabolism by consumers and decomposers did not increase correspondingly.

Accurate measurements of atmospheric CO_2 have been made since about 1957. They have been coupled with indirect evidence to produce a model of the rise of atmospheric CO_2 from about 280 molecular parts per million in preindustrial times to around 325 parts per million in 1975.[30] The possible climatic effects of this increase and its continuation are discussed in Chapter 11.

An additional kind of evidence that can shed some light on the sources and fate of the CO_2 added to the atmosphere is the abundance of radioactive carbon-14 relative to the amount of nonradioactive carbon-12 in various pools. Carbon-14 is produced naturally by bombardment of nitrogen by cosmic rays in the stratosphere and also by civilization when nuclear bombs are detonated in the atmosphere; it then mixes throughout the atmosphere and is incorporated, along with other carbon, into plant matter. Since the half-life of carbon-14 is only 5770 years, the carbon-14 buried for millions of years in fossil fuels has decayed away entirely.[31] Thus, the CO_2 added to the atmosphere by the combustion of fossil fuels contains no carbon-14, whereas CO_2 added from pools with faster turnover does contain carbon-14. The reduction in the $^{14}C/C$ ratio in the atmosphere because of the combustion of fossil fuels is called the *Suess effect*. The use of data on the Suess effect, combined with other information needed to help interpret it (such as the way the rate of natural and artificial ^{14}C production has varied over time), has allowed development of the estimate that about half of the CO_2 ever added to the atmosphere by combustion of fossil fuels has stayed there.[32] The same work indicates that the land biomass should have increased between 1 percent and 3 percent since preindustrial times, having absorbed some of the industrial CO_2, while the oceans absorbed the rest. This change in land biomass is much too small to measure, and the exact amount is a matter of controversy.

Global carbon cycle. Figure 3-3 presents an internally consistent picture of the pools and flows of the global carbon cycle. We caution the reader once more that substantial uncertainties exist about many of the numbers, as noted in detail earlier, and that further research might therefore alter the picture considerably. In this diagram, the pools of living and dead organic matter on land and in the oceans are assumed to be in equilibrium. Half the CO_2 added to the atmosphere by combustion of fossil fuels is assumed to dissolve in the surface layer of the oceans. The fossil-fuel pool shown here is somewhat larger than the figure in Table 3-6 suggests, because the latter indicated only the part of the fossil fuels estimated to be recoverable eventually. (Some will remain forever in the ground, as discussed in Chapter 8.)

Of the carbon added to the atmosphere by the respiration of animals and microbes, only a few percent is in the form of methane (CH_4) and carbon monoxide (CO), while the rest is carbon dioxide.[33] Still, the natural sources of carbon monoxide—incomplete decomposition of organic matter and partial oxidation of methane in the atmosphere—exceed man-made carbon monoxide from fossil-fuel combustion severalfold. Methane is apparently not toxic at any concentrations that occur in natural environments, and carbon monoxide is toxic only at concentrations on the order of 100 times the global atmospheric average or more.[34]

Nitrogen

The nitrogen cycle is chemically the most intricate of the major nutrient cycles, and it is probably the least well understood scientifically. The several chemical forms of nitrogen to be encountered in this discussion are identified in Table 3-7. The crucial role of nitrogen in all proteins makes this element essential to life, but most

[30]Lester Machta, Prediction of CO_2 in the atmosphere.

[31]Those unfamiliar with the basic terminology of radioactivity should look ahead to Box 8-3.

[32]R. Bacastow and C. D. Keeling, Atmospheric carbon dioxide and radiocarbon in the natural carbon cycle, pt. 2. Their actual figure for the fraction of industrial carbon dioxide remaining in the atmosphere between 1959 and 1969 was 49 ± 12 percent.

[33]Garrels, Mackenzie, and Hunt, *Chemical cycles*, p. 74.

[34]Ibid., pp. 73–75.

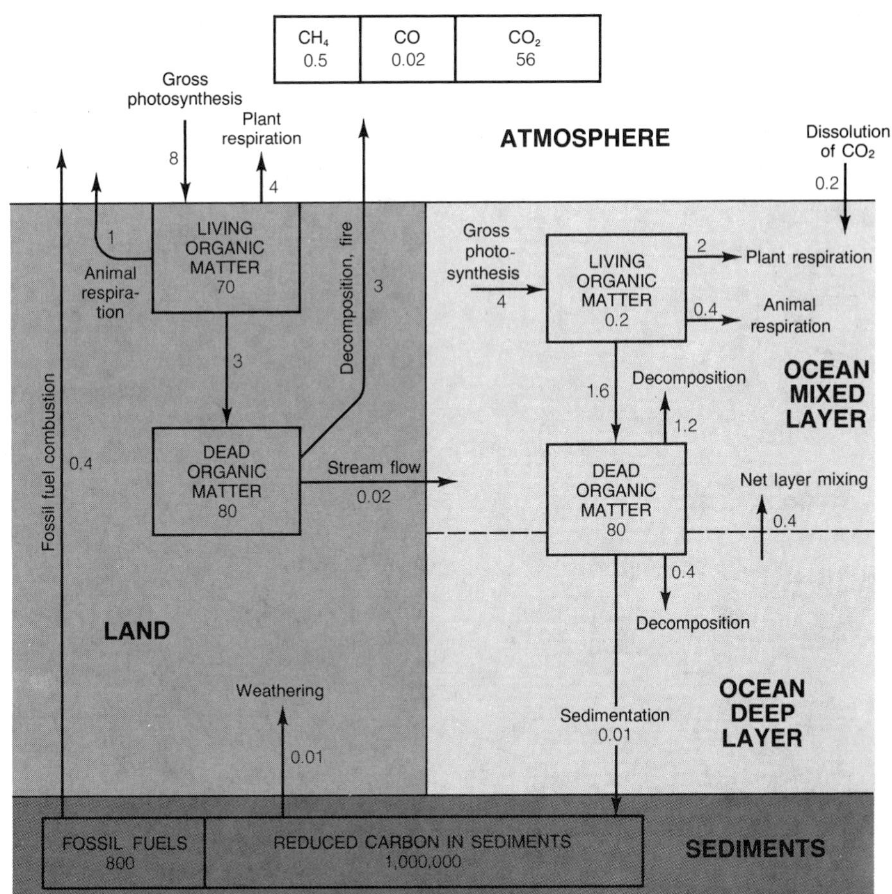

FIGURE 3-3

Pools and flows in the global carbon cycle. Arrows denote flows in 10^{15} moles per year; boxes denote pools in 10^{15} moles.

TABLE 3-7
Chemical Forms of Nitrogen

Formula	*Name*	*Oxidation number**	*Comments*
NH_3	Ammonia	−3	Major nutrient form
NH_4^+	Ammonium ion	−3	From NH_3 dissolved in water
NH_2^+	Amino group	−1	Constituent of protein
N_2	Nitrogen gas	0	Bulk of atmosphere
N_2O	Nitrous oxide	+1	Laughing gas, controls natural ozone cycle
NO	Nitric oxide	+2	Combustion product
NO_2^-	Nitrite ion	+3	Link in N cycle
NO_2	Nitrogen dioxide	+4	From NO oxidized in atmosphere
NO_3^-	Nitrate ion	+5	Principal nutrient form

*Negative oxidation numbers denote more-reduced forms, and positive oxidation numbers, more-oxidized forms.

organisms can assimilate and use nitrogen only in specific chemical forms. Only a relatively few species of bacteria and algae can convert gaseous molecular nitrogen (N_2) into the more complex compounds that can be used by plants and animals. The principal usable forms are ammonia (NH_3) and nitrates ($-NO_3$), of which the latter is needed in greater quantity by most plants. The conversion of N_2 to ammonia and nitrate is called *nitrogen fixation,* and the species that can accomplish this conversion are called nitrogen-fixing organisms. Thus, although the atmosphere represents an enormous reservoir of molecular nitrogen, the continuation of life on Earth depends absolutely on the activities of these tiny, inconspicuous organisms.

Organisms and nitrogen. The best known of the nitrogen-fixing organisms are the bacteria (genus *Rhizobium*) associated with the special nodules on roots of legumes, which are plants of the pea family. In a symbiotic relationship, the bacteria obtain from the plants the energy they need to carry out the nitrogen-fixing reaction

$$2N_2 + 6H_2O \longrightarrow 4NH_3 + 3O_2,$$

and some of the ammonia, in turn, is made available to the plants for the synthesis of amino acids, for example,

$$2NH_3 + 2H_2O + 4CO_2 \longrightarrow 2CH_2NH_2COOH + 3O_2.$$

(In this example the amino acid is glycine.) The capacity of such legumes as alfalfa, beans, peas, and clover to fix nitrogen in large quantities has led to their widespread use in crop-rotation schemes to replenish in the soil the nitrogen depleted by other crops.

Although nitrogen fixation by the legume-bacteria symbiosis is thought to be responsible for most natural nitrogen fixation, the fixation step is also carried out by some bacteria that have looser associations with plants, including the free-living *Azotobacter* (aerobic) and *Clostridium* (anaerobic), and by various species of blue-green algae.[35] Blue-green algae are apparently responsible for maintaining the fertility of rice paddies in much of Asia, which are subjected to intensive cropping without the use of nitrogen fertilizers.

The amino acids used by all organisms as the building blocks of protein are synthesized not only from ammonia but also from nitrate produced from ammonia by processes collectively called *nitrification.* The nitrification reactions yield energy, which supports the life processes of the nitrifying bacteria *(Nitrosomonas, Nitrobacter).* The actual synthesis of amino acids is carried out by bacteria (which differ widely in how many amino acids they can synthesize), by plants (which can synthesize all the amino acids needed for making proteins), and by animals (which, again, differ in the variety of amino acids they can produce).[36]

Vertebrates—including human beings—cannot synthesize all the amino acids they need and must obtain intact in the food they eat the ones they cannot synthesize. The amino acids an animal must get from its diet are called *essential amino acids;* those it can synthesize are called *nonessential.* (This terminology is unfortunate, because both essential and nonessential amino acids are needed—the distinction concerns only whether the organism can synthesize them itself.)

Fixed nitrogen that has been incorporated into organisms returns to the soil in animal wastes and in dead organisms (microbes, plants, animals) or parts of organisms (for example, leaves). Animal wastes are rich in urea—$(NH_2)_2CO$—which is the principal product of the metabolism of proteins in many organisms. The proteins of dead organisms are broken down into amino acids and other residues by bacteria and fungi of decay. The latter compounds—urea, amino acids, and other breakdown products of protein—are then converted into ammonia by yet another group of bacteria. This step is called *ammonification.* (The chemical reaction for the ammonification of an amino acid is just the opposite of amino-acid synthesis.)

So far we have described how nitrogen is fixed by living organisms and how the fixed nitrogen is further processed by them. A logical question at this point is: How is nitrogen *un*fixed? For without a mechanism for

[35]See, for example, Odum, *Fundamentals,* pp. 87–91; C. C. Delwiche, The nitrogen cycle; and Stanier, Douderoff, and Adelberg, *The microbial world.* An important recent technical monograph is R. C. Burns and R. W. F. Hardy, *Nitrogen fixation in bacteria and higher plants.*

[36]Lehninger, *Biochemistry,* Chapter 24, the biosynthesis of amino acids, and pp. 539–565, nitrogen fixation.

TABLE 3-8
Some Chemistry of Nitrogen in Organisms

Step	*Reaction*	*Energy*	*Organism*
Fixation	$2N_2 + 6H_2O \longrightarrow 4NH_3 + 3O_2$	In	*Rhizobium, Azotobacter, Gloeocapsa, Plectonema*
Amino-Acid Synthesis (ammonification is the reverse)	$2NH_3 + 2H_2O + 4CO_2 \longrightarrow 2CH_2NH_2COOH + 3O_2$	In	Many, bacteria and others
Nitrification	$2NH_4^+ + 3O_2 \longrightarrow 2NO_2^- + 4H^+ + 2H_2O$	Out	*Nitrosomonas*
Nitrification	$2NO_2^- + O_2 \longrightarrow 2NO_3^-$	Out	*Nitrobacter*
Denitrification	$4NO_3^- + 2H_2O \longrightarrow 2N_2 + 5O_2 + 4OH^-$	Out	*Pseudomonas*
Denitrification	$5S + 6KNO_3 + 2CaCO_3 \longrightarrow 3K_2SO_4 + 2CO_2 + 3N_2$	Out	*Thiobacillus denitrificans*
Denitrification	$C_6H_{12}O_6 + 6\,NO_3^- \longrightarrow 6CO_2 + 3H_2O + 6OH^- + 3N_2O$	Out	Many

Sources: Edward S. Deevey, Jr., Mineral cycles; R. M. Garrels, F. T. Mackenzie, and C. Hunt, *Chemical cycles and the global environment;* R. C. Burns and R. W. F. Hardy, *Nitrogen fixation.*

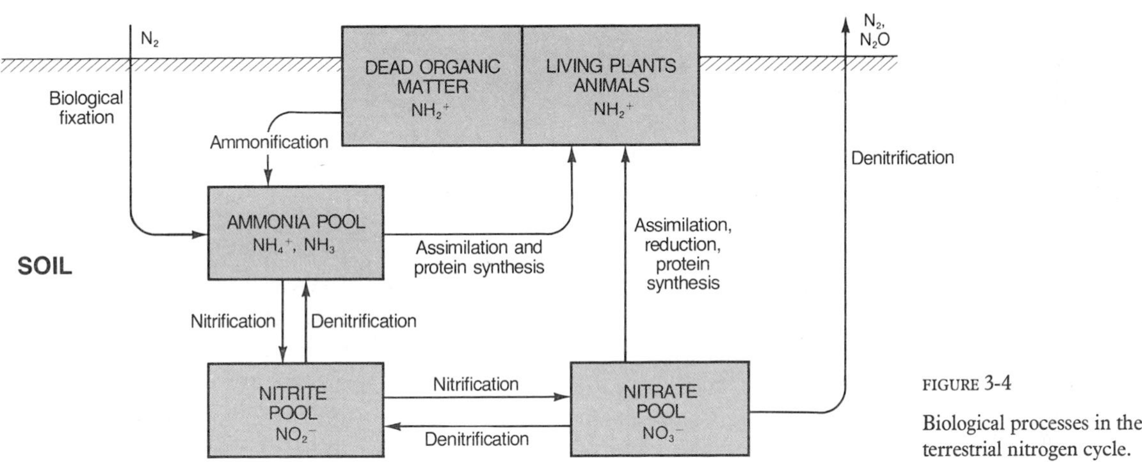

FIGURE 3-4

Biological processes in the terrestrial nitrogen cycle.

returning nitrogen to its molecular form (N_2), even the vast reservoir of this compound that exists in the atmosphere would have been depleted long ago; much of the nitrogen would be tied up as nitrates in soil, in the oceans, and in sediments.[37] The mechanism that has prevented this outcome by closing the atmospheric loop of the nitrogen cycle is the action of a relatively few groups of *denitrifying bacteria* that make their living converting nitrate to nitrous oxide (N_2O) and N_2. (These transformations release energy.) The nitrous oxide is reduced to N_2 by further bacterial action, or in the atmosphere by photochemical reactions. Another set of denitrifying reactions, also carried out by bacteria, transforms nitrate to nitrite and nitrite to ammonia.

The chemistry of the main steps in the nitrogen cycle that are mediated by bacteria is summarized (in an illustrative, not exhaustive way) in Table 3-8. For each reaction, the "energy" column indicates whether energy must be supplied to accomplish it ("in") or whether the reaction makes energy available ("out"). The part of the terrestrial nitrogen cycle directly associated with organisms is represented schematically in Figure 3-4. The oceanic cycle is substantially similar, relying both on bacteria and algae.[38]

[37]See the discussion in Deevey, Mineral cycles, p. 141.

[38]See especially Burns and Hardy, *Nitrogen fixation.*

Inorganic processes. Some important flows and transformations in the nitrogen cycle take place without the active participation of organisms. For example, some of the ammonia produced by the decomposition of organic materials enters the atmosphere by outgassing from Earth's surface. Highly soluble in water, the ammonia dissolves in atmospheric water vapor to form ammonium ion, which combines with sulfate and nitrate ions and rains out as ammonium sulfate and ammonium nitrate. Possibly, the ammonium ion is also partly removed from the atmosphere by oxidation to N_2.[39]

Nitrous oxide, produced by denitrifying bacteria, is the second most abundant form of nitrogen in the atmosphere, after N_2. No sinks for this gas are known in the troposphere—that is, no process has been identified in the troposphere that converts N_2O to other compounds—but one may yet be discovered. The presently known sink for N_2O is in the stratosphere, where it is both photochemically reduced by ultraviolet light to produce N_2 and O, and oxidized by contact with atomic oxygen to produce nitric oxide (NO).[40] The net result chemically is

$$2N_2O \longrightarrow N_2 + 2NO.$$

Nitric oxide (NO) is a very effective catalyst for the destruction of ozone (O_3) in the stratosphere. The reactions are

$$NO + O_3 \longrightarrow NO_2 + O_2,$$

$$O_3 \xrightarrow[\text{light}]{\text{ultraviolet}} O_2 + O,$$

$$NO_2 + O \longrightarrow NO + O_2,$$

from which the net effect is

$$2O_3 \xrightarrow[\text{light}]{\text{ultraviolet}} 3O_2.$$

Thus, there is a connection between the rate of biological nitrous oxide (N_2O) production in the soil and the rate of ozone destruction high in the stratosphere. This link is examined more closely in Chapter 11.

Nitric oxide is also produced in or added to the troposphere by several processes. One is the so-called juvenile addition of nitric oxide by volcanoes. Another is fixation from atmospheric nitrogen gas by lightning, where the lightning discharge supplies the high energy needed to drive the reaction:

$$N_2 + O_2 \longrightarrow 2NO.$$

The same reaction takes place as the result of combustion of fossil fuels by industrial society in automobiles, aircraft, electric power plants, and other processes. Nitric oxide, from whatever source, is oxidized in the troposphere to give nitrogen dioxide (NO_2), which in turn reacts with atmospheric water, giving nitric acid and reproducing the NO:

$$3NO_2 + 3H_2O \longrightarrow 2HNO_3 + NO.$$

The nitric acid falls in rain as HNO_3 or reacts with other atmospheric constituents (such as NH_4^+) to produce other nitrate compounds. The end result in either case is to supply fixed nitrogen to the surface.

In addition to the inadvertent production of fixed nitrogen through the combustion of fossil fuels, industrial society fixes atmospheric nitrogen intentionally for use as fertilizer. The basis of this industrial fixation process is a method invented by Haber and Bosch in 1914, in which nitrogen and hydrogen react under high pressure and in the presence of a catalyst to form ammonia. The source of the hydrogen for this process is usually methane in natural gas. Some of the ammonia produced is reacted with carbon dioxide to produce urea, and some is reacted with oxygen to form nitric acid. The nitric acid is reacted with more ammonia to make ammonium nitrate—along with urea, a widely used fertilizer.[41] These materials are often referred to as *inorganic fertilizers,* to distinguish them from the ammonia, urea, and nitrates of organic origin that are often used as fertilizer in the form of manure or plant material. (There is no chemical distinction between, say, nitrate ion of organic origin and nitrate ion produced in a fertilizer plant, but important differences in soil quality may result from the different ways in which the nitrate is actually made available to the soil in organic and inorganic fertilization. See Chapter 11 for further discussion.)

[39]Garrels, Mackenzie, and Hunt, *Chemical cycles,* p. 95.

[40]P. J. Crutzen, Estimates of possible variations in total ozone due to natural causes and human activities.

[41]Delwiche, The nitrogen cycle, p. 143.

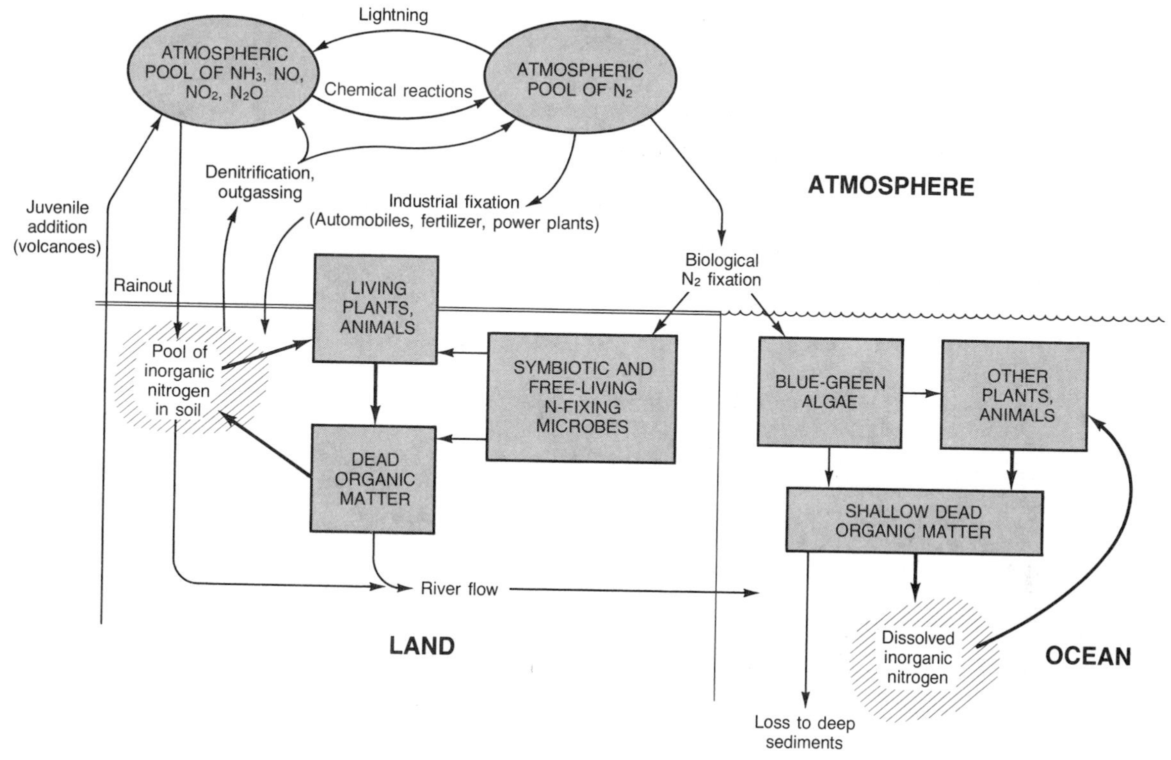

FIGURE 3-5

The global nitrogen cycle. The largest flows are denoted by the heavier arrows.

Nitrate compounds, whether put in the soil by biological processes or by rainout from the atmosphere or by application of inorganic fertilizers, are usually quite soluble; thus, those that escape uptake by plants or bacterial denitrification may be transported far and wide by the flow of surface water, or they may accumulate in the much more slowly moving reservoirs of groundwater.

Global nitrogen cycle. The biologic and inorganic steps in the global nitrogen cycle are depicted together in Figure 3-5. Estimates of the sizes of some of the major flows are summarized in Table 3-9, with an indication of the approximate uncertainties in those figures.[42]

Note that industrial nitrogen fixation may have been equal to half of natural fixation already in 1975, a very significant perturbation in a global process. It is unlikely that natural denitrification processes are keeping pace with the increased load of fixed nitrogen (although the data are far from adequate to prove this). If this is the case, fixed nitrogen must be accumulating in one or more of the pools: biomass, dead organic matter, inorganic pools in soil and oceans, or groundwater. How much increase in global river flow of nitrates has increased because of industrial fixation is quite uncertain—and controversial (see Chapter 11). Also very unclear is the partitioning between N_2O and N_2 of gas flow to the

[42]The ranges of uncertainty are from the workshop summarized by the Institute of Ecology (TIE) in *Man in the living environment,* and from comparisons of some of the principal published reviews of nitrogen cycle data and estimates, namely Garrels, Mackenzie, and Hunt, *Chemical cycles;* chapter 8; Delwiche, The nitrogen cycle; Deevey, Mineral cycles; Burns and Hardy, *Nitrogen fixation.* A set of estimates giving natural fluxes around 10 times greater than the central values presented here for some fixed-nitrogen forms appears in E. Robinson and R. C. Robbins, Gaseous atmospheric pollutants from urban and natural sources, in *Global effects of environmental pollution,* S. F. Singer, ed. Those estimates apparently were not considered credible by those attending the TIE workshop.

TABLE 3-9
Magnitudes of Flows in the Global Nitrogen Cycle

	Magnitude (10^{12} moles N/yr)	*Approximate uncertainty*
NATURAL FIXATION (TOTAL)	9	÷×2[a]
Legumes	2	±50%
Other Terrestrial Biological	4	÷×2
Oceanic Biological	2	÷×3
Atmospheric by Lightning	0.6	÷×2
Fixed Juvenile Addition	0.01	÷×3
INDUSTRIAL FIXATION IN 1975 (TOTAL)	4.9	±20%
Fertilizer Production	2.6	±10%
Combustion	2	±25%
Other Processes	0.3	±50%
ASSIMILATION AND INCORPORATION IN PROTEIN (TOTAL)[b]	520	÷×2
Terrestrial Plants	100	±50%
Terrestrial Fungi and Bacteria	100	÷×3
Oceanic Plants	300	÷×2
Oceanic Fungi and Bacteria	20	÷×5
N_2O AND N_2 TO ATMOSPHERE FROM DENITRIFICATION	6	÷×2
From Land	7	÷×2
From Ocean	3	÷×2
NH_3 TO ATMOSPHERE FROM AMMONIFICATION	8	÷×2
From Land	5	÷×2
From Ocean	3	÷×3
RAINOUT OF NH_4^+, NO_3^- TO SURFACE (TOTAL)	7	÷×2
To Land	5	÷×2
To Ocean	2	÷×2
RIVER FLOW OF FIXED NITROGEN (TOTAL)	2	÷×2

[a]The symbol ÷×2 means the value could be from 0.5 to 2 times the magnitude given.
[b]The figures for assimilation of fixed nitrogen by terrestrial and oceanic plants are derived from the net primary production (carbon) estimates of Table 3-4, using the molecular carbon/nitrogen ratios of 41/1 for terrestrial plant production and 5.7/1 for oceanic plant production (TIE, *Man*, p. 71). The figure for terrestrial plants differs from the molecular carbon/nitrogen ratio in the terrestrial pool of plants (about 90/1, according to Deevey, Mineral cycles) because the pool is mostly wood, whereas the annual production contains a much higher proportion of leaves.
Sources: C. C. Delwiche, The nitrogen cycle; R. M. Garrels, F. T. Mackenzie, and C. Hunt, *Chemical cycles and the global environment*, chapter 8. The Institute of Ecology (TIE), *Man in the living environment*, chapter 3. R. C. Burns and R. W. F. Hardy, *Nitrogen fixation in bacteria and higher plants.*

atmosphere from denitrification, and what factors control the partitioning.[43]

Perhaps the most striking feature of the data in Table 3-9 is the margin by which the rate of uptake of fixed nitrogen for incorporation into protein by plants, fungi, and bacteria exceeds the rate of new fixation by both natural and industrial processes (roughly a factor of 35). The internal loops of the nitrogen cycle, which can be summarized as uptake/synthesis → excretion/death → decomposition → uptake/synthesis (with the nitrogen remaining in the fixed state at all times), thus embody a great deal more of the cycle's total activity than do the external loops, wherein nitrogen enters and leaves the atmospheric pool of N_2 (see Figure 3-5). Among other things, this suggests that disturbances directly affecting the strong internal loops would lead much more quickly to large-scale consequences than would disturbances affecting fixation of atmospheric nitrogen.

Estimates of the sizes of some of the pools of nitrogen in the global cycle appear in Table 3-10. A significant contrast with other biogeochemical cycles considered here is the large fraction of the total reservoir of nitrogen that is tied up in the atmospheric pool; for all other

[43]For a synopsis of such insights as are available, see Burns and Hardy, *Nitrogen fixation.*

nutrients, the pools in sediments and sedimentary rocks are largest.

From the information on pools in Table 3-10 and that on flows in Table 3-9, some important characteristic times can be deduced, albeit with substantial uncertainties. For example, the assimilation of fixed nitrogen by terrestrial plants "turns over" the nitrogen in the combined dead organic matter and inorganic soil nitrogen pools roughly every 100 to 600 years; assimilation of fixed nitrogen by ocean plants turns over the corresponding ocean pools every 40 to 350 years. The stock of nitrogen in the main terrestrial and oceanic loops (biomass, dead organic matter, fixed nitogen in soil and water) is replenished by natural fixation every 1200 to 35,000 years—turnover times that apparently would be cut by 50 percent by the addition of the 1975 rate of industrial fixation. The atmospheric pool of N_2 is turned over only once every 15 million to 60 million years by natural fixation. By contrast, N_2O has an atmospheric residence time of perhaps ten to thirty years (unless its production and destruction rates have been badly misjudged), and NH_3/NH_4 and NO/NO_2 have residence times of a month or two. The shortest residence time among atmospheric nitrogen forms is that of NO_2^- and NO_3^-—perhaps a day.

Clearly, human interventions in the nitrogen cycle cannot possibly influence the atmospheric concentration of N_2 on any time scale of practical interest. On the other hand, the concentrations of other atmospheric forms of nitrogen could be influenced on time scales of a few months to a few years, and the sizes of the major pools of fixed nitrogen in the soil and surface water could be influenced in a matter of a few to a few tens of human generations. Significant local disruptions in soil and surface water can of course occur more quickly, and they have (see Chapter 11).

TABLE 3-10
Sizes of Pools in the Global Nitrogen Cycle

Pool	*Size* (10^{12} *moles N*)
LAND	
Biomass (99% in plants)[a]	400–1,000
Dead Organic Matter[a]	5,000–60,000
Inorganic Fixed Nitrogen in Soil[b, c]	5,000–15,000
OCEANS	
Biomass (80% in plants?)[a, c]	10–300
Dead Organic Matter[a, d]	9,000–60,000
Dissolved Inorganic Nitrogen in Oceans[b, c]	4,000–50,000
Dissolved N_2 in Oceans[d, e]	1,500,000 ± 10%
SEDIMENTS[c, d]	29,000,000–70,000,000
ATMOSPHERE[c, d, f]	
N_2	282,000,000
N_2O	90 ± 50%
NH_3, NH_4^+	2 ± 50%
NO, NO_2	0.4 ± 50%

[a]Based on the range of values for carbon pools in Table 3-6, with carbon/nitrogen ratios as follows: land biomass, 90/1 (Deevey, Mineral cycles; Garrels, Mackenzie, and Hunt, *Chemical cycles*); land, dead organic matter, 12/1 (Woodwell and Pecan, eds., *Carbon*, p. 369); ocean biomass and dead organic matter, 6.6/1 (Garrels, Mackenzie, and Hunt, *Chemical cycles*).
[b]The Institute of Ecology, *Man in the living environment.*
[c]Burns and Hardy, *Nitrogen fixation.*
[d]Garrels, Mackenzie, and Hunt, *Chemical cycles,* chapter 8.
[e]Delwiche, The nitrogen cycle.
[f]E. Almqvist, An analysis of global air pollution.

Phosphorus

Phosphorus, while absolutely essential to life, is required in quantities only about one-tenth as great as nitrogen.[44] Nevertheless, phosphorus probably is the limiting nutrient in more circumstances than any other element because of its scarcity in accessible form in the biosphere.

Two chemical properties of phosphorus are responsible for this natural scarcity, which is much more acute than one might expect from the size of the total phosphorus pool in sedimentary rocks. One is that phosphorus does not form any important gaseous compounds under conditions encountered in the environment.[45] The second is the insolubility of the salts formed by the phosphate anion $PO_4^{\equiv}$ and the common cations Ca^{++}, Fe^{++}, and Al^{+++}. The lack of gaseous compounds deprives the phosphorus cycle of an atmospheric pathway linking land and sea and thus slows the closing of the cycle to the almost inconceivably sluggish pace of

[44]N/P atom ratio is 9/1 in land plants, according to Deevey, Mineral cycles, and 16/1 in marine plants, according to Garrels, Mackenzie, and Hunt, p. 67.

[45]Phosphene gas produced in swamps is negligible in quantity. See, for example, Institute of Ecology, p. 50.

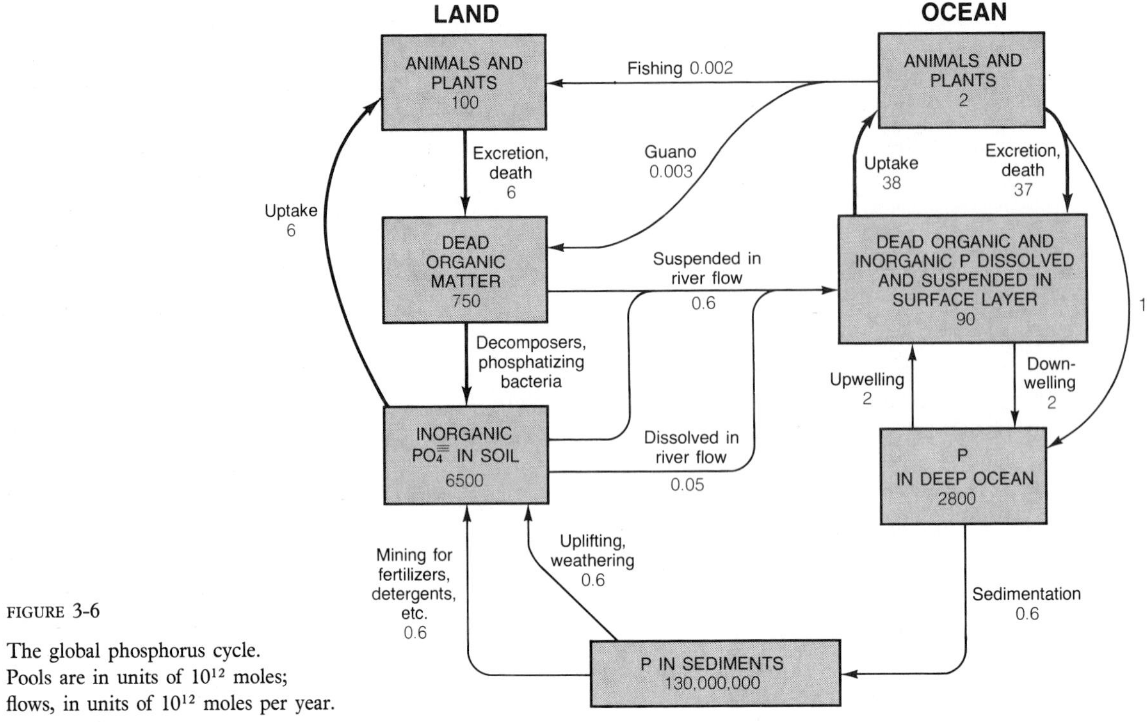

FIGURE 3-6

The global phosphorus cycle. Pools are in units of 10^{12} moles; flows, in units of 10^{12} moles per year.

sedimentation, uplift, and weathering. That phosphate forms insoluble compounds with constituents of most soils retards its uptake by plants and slows its removal and transport by surface water and groundwater.

The main characteristics of the global phosphorus cycle are indicated in Figure 3-6. The numbers given there for the organic pools and flows are based on the carbon-cycle estimates summarized in Figure 3-3, combined with the carbon/phosphorus ratios for different kinds of organic matter, as discussed above. These phosphorus numbers, therefore, should not be considered any more precise than the carbon numbers (roughly $\pm$ 50 percent in the flows, and multiplicative factors of 2 or 3 larger or smaller in the pools). In fact, they may be less precise than this, because of inaccuracy in the estimates of carbon/phosphorus ratios on a global basis.

As in the nitrogen cycle, the inner loops between living material and the soil (or ocean) pool of decomposition products appear to contain most of the flow in the phosphorus cycle. Also in analogy to the nitrogen cycle, a group of bacteria (phosphatizing bacteria) makes a living converting the phosphorus compounds characteristic of living tissue into inorganic phosphate.

The links between the terrestrial and oceanic parts of the phosphorus cycle are very weak. Little dissolved phosphorus is carried by rivers, because of the low solubility of phosphorus salts (the amount carried in suspended soil particles by erosion is about ten times as large). Aside from the slow link provided by the sedimentary cycle, the only sea-to-land transport is in fish and shellfish harvested from the sea and consumed on land, and in the excrement that fish-eating seabirds deposit on land. These flows together amount to about one-hundredth of the erosion loss. The idea that the sedimentation rate roughly balances the river flow and is balanced in turn by the rate of uplifting and weathering is an assumption, not an experimentally determined fact. The assumption amounts to supposing that the various pools have reached a natural equilibrium over geologic time and that the extra phosphorus now being mobilized by civilization's mining of phosphate rock is not yet reaching the rivers in appreciable quantities.[46] Quite possibly, the acquisition of more data shedding light on historical and contemporary phosphorus loads in rivers will change this picture.

Worldwide mining of phosphate rock amounted to 94 million metric tons in 1972, which corresponds to the 0.6 trillion moles of phosphorus represented under "mining" in Figure 3-6.[47] Seventy to 80 percent of this amount is added to the land as fertilizer—mostly in the forms of ammonium phosphate $[(NH_4)_3PO_4]$, triple phosphate $[Ca(H_2PO_4)_2]$, and superphosphate, which is a mixture of triple phosphate and gypsum $[CaSO_4 \cdot 2H_2O]$.[48] Phosphorus is also used in detergents (three-quarters of the nonfertilizer use), animal-feed supplements, pesticides, medicines, and a host of industrial applications.[49] It seems reasonable to assume that most of these uses eventually lead to the deposition of the phosphorus in the environment.

Over the long term, civilization's mobilization of phosphorus by mining phosphate rock must certainly be considered a significant perturbation in the cycle. The time in which mining at the level of the mid-1970s would double the pool of phosphate in the soil (assuming the additions all remained there, which is unlikely) would be around 10,000 years. There are some reasons to think that this very long-term problem should not be our primary worry about the phosphorus cycle, however. One is that the local perturbation of adding phosphorus to agricultural land is far greater than these global-average numbers indicate and can be important much sooner (see Chapter 11). A second is that known and suspected *minable* phosphorus resources—as distinguished from those too dispersed to recover—could not support a drain of 0.6 trillion moles of phosphorus per year for 10,000 years (see Chapter 9); this situation suggests, especially in the face of a demand for phosphorus that is not constant but, rather, is doubling about every fifteen years, that exhaustion of the concentrated supplies of phosphorus is more imminent than overloading the cycle globally. These aspects of civilization's effect on the phosphorus cycle are, of course, closely related. It is largely because society breaks the main internal loop of the phosphorus cycle on agricultural land (by "exporting" from the land the phosphorus-containing crops and crop residues and not returning the sewage that in time receives this phosphorus) that the heavy supplement of mined phosphorus is required.

[46]See, for example, A. Lerman, F. T. Mackenzie, and R. M. Garrels, Modeling of geochemical cycles.

[47]U.S. Department of Commerce, *Statistical abstract of the United States,* 1974 p. 675. *Phosphate rock* is calcium phosphate, $Ca_3 (PO_4)_2$, which is 20 percent phosphorus by weight.

[48]Raymond Ewell, Fertilizer use throughout the world; J. B. Cathcart and R. A. Gulbrandsen, Phosphate deposits.

[49]Study of Critical Environmental Problems, *Man's impact on the global environment.*

Sulfur

The sulfur cycle is important, chemically complicated, and not yet well understood quantitatively. Its importance has several dimensions: the essential role of sulfur in the structure of proteins; the circumstance that the main gaseous compounds of sulfur are toxic to mammals; the fact that sulfur compounds are important determinants of the acidity of rainfall, surface water, and soil; and the possibility that sulfur compounds may play a role in influencing the amount of molecular oxygen in the atmosphere in the very long term.[50] The complexity of the sulfur cycle, like that of nitrogen, arises mainly from the large number of oxidation states the element can assume. Some of the principal compounds and groups in which sulfur participates are listed in Table 3-11.

Many transformations among the different oxidation states of sulfur are carried out by bacteria. Which of the several kinds of sulfur bacteria (and, hence, which reactions) prevail in a given situation depends on the presence or absence of oxygen and light and the acidity or alkalinity of the environment.[51] The principal biologic sulfur transformations are summarized in Table 3-12. Essentially all of the bacterial activity probably takes place in wet media—moist soil, swamps, the muds of lakeshores and estuaries, and (to an uncertain degree) the

[50]A thorough and up-to-date review of the sulfur cycle is Missouri Botanical Garden, *Sulfur in the environment.*

[51]See, for example, H. D. Peck, Jr., The microbial sulfur cycle.

TABLE 3-11
Chemical Forms of Sulfur

Formula	*Name*	*Oxidation number*	*Comments*
H_2S	Hydrogen sulfide	−2	"Rotten egg" gas, extremely toxic
HS^-	Hydrosulfide ion	−2	Constituent of amino acids
$S^=$	Sulfide ion	−2	Forms insoluble compounds with metals
$S_2^=$	Disulfide ion	−1	Plays crucial role in stiffening protein
S_2,S_6,S_8	Elemental sulfur	0	Crystalline solid
SO_2	Sulfur dioxide	+4	Colorless, toxic gas
H_2SO_3	Sulfurous acid	+4	Weak acid from SO_2 plus water
SO_3	Sulfur trioxide	+6	Gas from oxidizing SO_2 in air
H_2SO_4	Sulfuric acid	+6	Strong acid from SO_3 plus water
$SO_4^=$	Sulfate ion	+6	Forms many compounds in atmosphere and soil

TABLE 3-12
Sulfur Chemistry of Biologic Assimilation and Decomposition

Transformation	*Mechanism*
SO_2, $SO_4^= \longrightarrow$ organic S	Assimilation and synthesis by plants
Organic S $\longrightarrow H_2S$	Many anaerobic and aerobic bacteria
Organic S $\longrightarrow SO_4^=$	Most plants and animals, many bacteria
$SO_4^= \longrightarrow H_2S$	Anaerobic bacteria (*Desulforvibrio, Desulfotomaculum*)
$H_2S \longrightarrow S \longrightarrow SO_4^=$	Aerobic bacteria (*Thiobacillus*), photosynthetic bacteria (*Chromatium, Chlorobium*)

open water of lakes and oceans.[52] The presence of dissolved oxygen favors decomposition of organic sulfur to form sulfates; the absence of oxygen favors decomposition to form sulfides.

Reactions involving the oxidation of sulfur also take place without the intervention of bacteria. Hydrogen sulfide that has been produced by bacterial decomposition is readily oxidized chemically by dissolved oxygen in water, producing sulfite and sulfate. (The mean lifetime of H_2S in water containing appreciable dissolved oxygen appears to be on the order of tens of minutes.)[53] Hydrogen sulfide emitted to the atmosphere is oxidized to sulfur dioxide (SO_2) by atomic oxygen (O), molecular oxygen (O_2), and ozone (O_3). These reactions are too slow in clean, dry air to account for the observed atmospheric residence time of H_2S of only a few hours; possibly most of the action takes place when the reacting gases are dissolved in atmospheric water droplets or absorbed on the surfaces of suspended particles.[54] Sulfur dioxide is further oxidized in the atmosphere to form sulfur trioxide and various sulfates, including sulfuric acid. Photochemical oxidation of SO_2 exists but is too slow (0.1 percent per hour) to account for the observed lifetime of SO_2 in the atmosphere (minutes to days). Much more important, apparently, is the dissolving of SO_2 in atmospheric cloud and water droplets to form sulfurous acid (H_2SO_3), followed by the oxidation of this sulfurous acid to sulfuric acid (H_2SO_4). The oxidation is sped up by various metal salts dissolved in the droplets, which serve as catalysts.[55]

The global sulfur cycle is represented in schematic and simplified form in Figure 3-7. The estimates given there

[52]F. B. Hill, Atmospheric sulfur and its links to the biota; A. R. Brigham and A. U. Brigham, Sulfur in the aquatic ecosystem.

[53]H. G. Ostlund and G. Alexander, Oxidation rate of sulfide in seawater: A preliminary study, *Journal of Geophysical Research, vol. 68* (1963), pp. 3995–3997.

[54]See R. D. Cadle, The sulfur cycle, in *Sulfur,* Missouri Botanical Garden; W. Kellogg, R. Cadle, E. Allen, A. Lazrus, E. Martell, The sulfur cycle.

[55]P. P. Gaspar, Sulfur in the atmosphere, *Sulfur,* Missouri Botanical Garden, pp. 14–38.

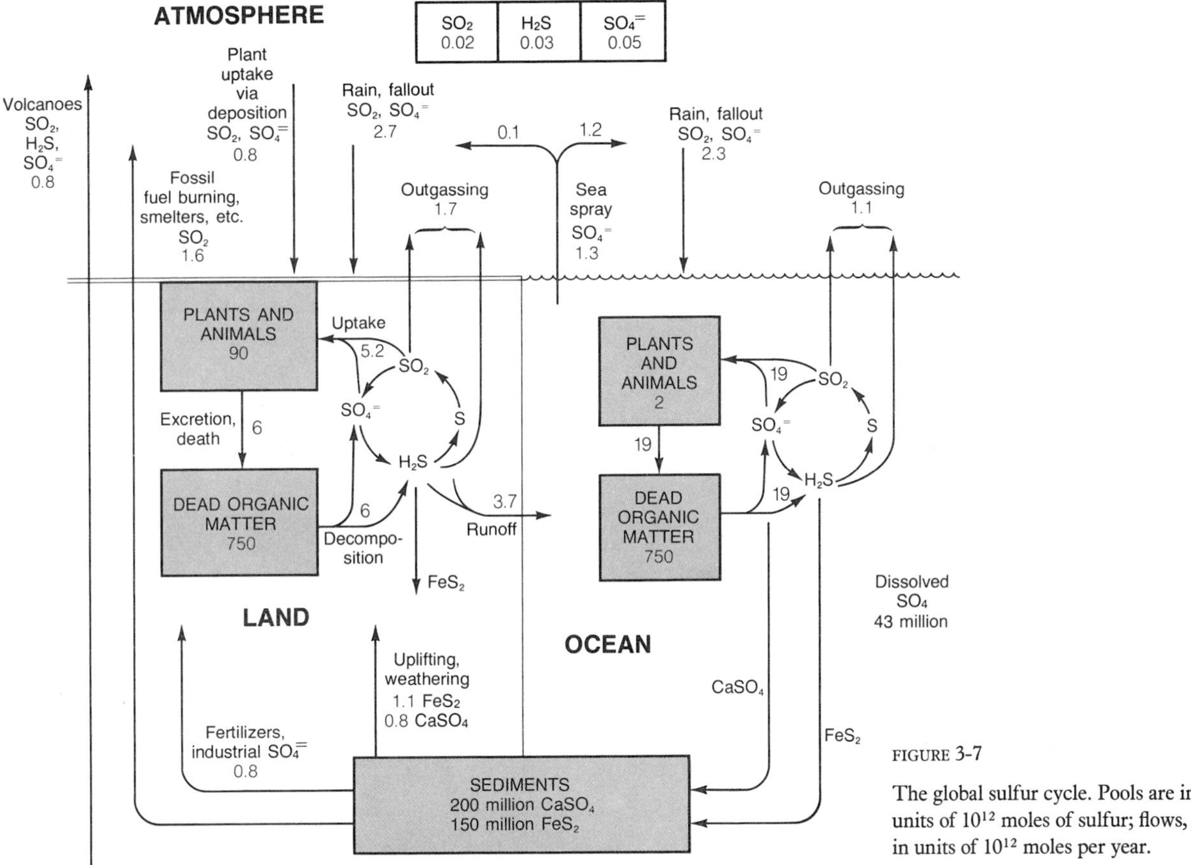

FIGURE 3-7

The global sulfur cycle. Pools are in units of 10^{12} moles of sulfur; flows, in units of 10^{12} moles per year.

for the magnitudes of pools and flows contain all the uncertainties encountered in the carbon, nitrogen, and phosphorus cycles, and more. The pools in organic matter were computed from the carbon estimates given in Figure 3-3, together with carbon/sulfur atom ratios of 800/1 in living terrestrial plants and 106/1 in marine plants and dead organic matter.[56] Uptakes were computed from the phosphorus figures in Figure 3-6 (in turn, based on carbon) with phosphorus/sulfur atom ratios of 1/1 for land plants and 2/1 for ocean plants.[57] The global average sulfur content of organic matter is not considered as well established as the carbon, nitrogen, and phosphorus contents, however.

The values for the flows to the atmosphere of SO_2 and H_2S originating in bacterial decomposition were *chosen* in Figure 3-7 to produce a balance between inputs and outputs of sulfur to the atmosphere; there are at this writing no adequate data with which to support or reject those values for the SO_2 and H_2S flows, nor are measurements of the atmospheric pools of H_2S, SO_2, and $SO_4^=$ accurate enough to determine whether they are really constant at present or not. The apparent mean lifetime of sulfur in all forms in the atmosphere (about 10^{11} moles of sulfur altogether) is about one week. The main pathways by which sulfur leaves the atmosphere are dry fallout and rainout of SO_2 and sulfates [the latter largely as H_2SO_4 and neutral ammonium sulfate, $(NH_4)_2SO_4$] and uptake of SO_2 and sulfates directly from the atmosphere by plants.[58]

[56] Ratios are from Garrels, Mackenzie, and Hunt, *Chemical cycles,* p. 67.

[57] The land-plant ratio is based on data for uptake by crops in M. B. Jones, Sulfur in agricultural lands, in *Sulfur,* Missouri Botanical Garden, pp. 141–168; the ratio for ocean plants, from Garrels, Mackenzie, and Hunt, *Chemical cycles,* p. 67, assuming high turnover tends to make P/S ratio the same in uptake as in the pool.

[58] See, for example, J. G. Severson, Jr., Sulfur and higher plants, in *Sulfur,* Missouri Botanical Garden, pp. 92–111.

Sulfates and sulfuric acid that fall on the land can usefully restore nutrient sulfur that has been removed by cropping, or they can acidify soil and surface water with possible adverse effects on ecosystems, depending on the circumstances. The human input of sulfur to the atmosphere had reached a magnitude of about half of the natural inputs by the early 1970s (if the estimates of the natural flows in Figure 3-7 are roughly correct) and had apparently caused an increase in the acidity of rainfall over large regions (see Chapter 11). The human perturbation in the sulfur cycle appears all the more significant when the additions to land and surface water of sulfur fertilizer and industrial sulfuric acid are reckoned in, since they amount to about half as much as the human sulfur inputs to the atmosphere. Figure 3-7 indicates an annual excess of 0.8×10^{12} moles of sulfur accumulating in the soil or terrestrial vegetation and leaves open the possibility that the other 1.6×10^{12} moles of the annual human sulfur input are accumulating in the oceans. Again, these are little more than educated guesses; knowledge of the magnitude of the relevant pools and flows is inadequate to determine what really is happening in this much detail. We simply know the extra sulfur must go somewhere.

Potentially capable of altering the atmospheric oxygen pool over the very long term—tens to hundreds of millions of years—is the balance or imbalance between weathering and sedimentation of highly insoluble iron sulfide (FeS_2). Weathering of FeS_2 produces sulfate, which under some circumstances can be precipitated into sediments as gypsum ($CaSO_4 \cdot H_2O$) before being reduced back to sulfide. The precipitation of gypsum, of course, takes the oxygen in the sulfate (which was extracted from the atmosphere during the weathering of the FeS_2) with it. If more sulfur is added to sediments as gypsum than is removed from sedimentary rocks as gypsum—that is, if there is an increase of sedimentary $CaSO_4 \cdot H_2O$ at the expense of FeS_2—then a steady drain on atmospheric oxygen could result. There is evidence that this phenomenon was actually occurring during the Permian period about 250 million years ago, but how much oxygen depletion occurred is unclear and controversial.[59]

[59]Garrels, Mackenzie, and Hunt, *Chemical cycles*, pp. 87–89.

One rather powerful analytic technique offers hope of resolving some of the important uncertainties about the sulfur cycle, in both its short-term and long-term aspects. The technique exploits the existence of two stable isotopes of sulfur—^{32}S and ^{34}S—the relative proportions of which differ in sulfur compounds of different origins. The average abundance ratio of ^{32}S atoms to ^{34}S atoms in nature is thought to be about 22.2/1, but sulfur in seawater has 2 percent more ^{34}S than this, biologically produced hydrogen sulfide has between 2.3 percent less and 0.6 percent more, and so on.[60] Since instruments are now available that can measure this ratio with great precision, in a sample it is possible to determine, for instance, the fraction of a given flow of sulfur that comes from different pools (if they have different ratios). This technique has been used successfully to determine the origins of pollutant sulfur in several places around the world, and to investigate the fate of sulfur in the sedimentary cycle in earlier geologic eras. Discrimination on the basis of isotope ratios also has great potential for untangling some of the complexities of the carbon, nitrogen, phosphorous, and other cycles.

OTHER NUTRIENTS AND GEOGRAPHICAL VARIATIONS

The nutrients just considered in detail are, of course, not the only important ones, nor are the quantitative relationships shown for global averages uniformly valid in different kinds of biological communities (or even in the same general kinds of communities in different places). We chose carbon-oxygen-hydrogen, nitrogen, phosphorus, and sulfur either because of their quantitative importance globally (C-O-H and N) or because of special characteristics of their biochemical roles and environmental behavior (P and S), and because a larger literature exists on these nutrients than on the others.

Other nutrients mobilized and used in large quantities include calcium, magnesium, and potassium. All of these are present in seawater in large amounts (see Table 2-7) and in rainwater and surface water in much smaller

[60]For a thorough discussion, see B. D. Holt, Determination of stable sulfur isotope ratios in the environment, *Progress in nuclear energy, analytical chemistry,* vol. 12, no. 1 (1975), pp. 11–26.

amounts, and are added to the soil by rock weathering as described above in the discussion of the sedimentary cycle. In some circumstances, dust raised by the wind and deposited as dry fallout elsewhere forms an important additional link in the cycling of these nutrients, and in other circumstances the mobilization rate from rocks is increased by the rock-splitting action of deep tree roots in the weathering process.[61]

The cycling of the macronutrients nitrogen, phosphorus, sulfur, calcium (Ca), magnesium (Mg) and potassium (K), in various kinds of biological communities—hardwood forests, jungles, deserts—has been extensively studied since the 1960s, and a large body of data is accumulating.[62] The enormous variety in the nutrient budgets of different communities in different places is indicated graphically in Figure 3-8, which summarizes some of these studies. The differences among communities of the same type (for example, the temperate hardwood forests) result from differences in soil, quantity of rainfall, local rainwater chemistry, dry fallout characteristics, and detailed species composition. (All these factors, of course, interact.)

One respect in which the presentation of global nutrient flows may be particularly misleading is in failing to reveal what part of the soil pool of nutrients is actually accessible to plants. This factor varies widely from one region to another, but it is known that in many important biological communities, such as tropical jungles, the actual availability of soil nutrients is very low. Such a cycle, in which nutrients spend a long time in a large pool of living and dead organic matter and a short time in a small pool of accessible inorganic nutrient forms, is called a tight cycle. The opposite situation, with a large pool of accesssible inorganic nutrient forms compared to the organic pool, is called a loose cycle.[63]

Another important distinction left out of the global estimates is between agricultural and nonagricultural systems. Although the human inputs of nitrogen, phosphorus, and sulfur fertilizers are already noticeable perturbations in these cycles on a global basis, their effects in the agricultural systems where they are applied are much larger than the global figures indicate. Much more extensive local studies are needed to resolve the questions that these magnified local perturbations raise (see Chapter 11).

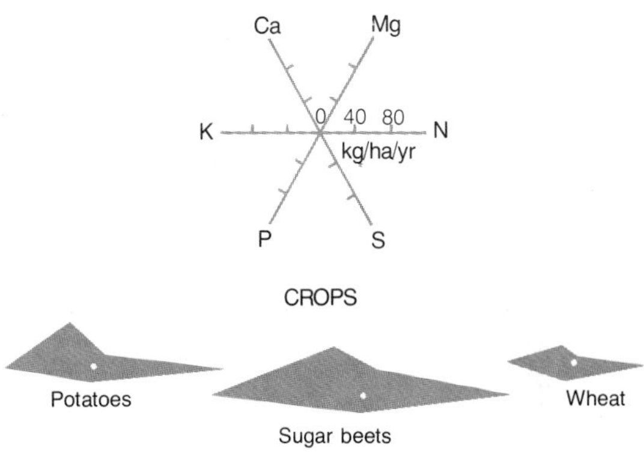

TEMPERATE DECIDUOUS FORESTS

CONIFEROUS FORESTS

STEPPES

FIGURE 3-8

Graphic representation of different nutrient budgets. The shaded polygons are formed by plotting on the axes shown the annual absorption of potassium, calcium, magnesium, nitrogen, phosphorus, and sulfur and then connecting the resulting points with straight lines. (Condensed from Duvigneaud and Denaeyer-deSmet, 1975, p. 141.)

---

[61]See, for example, Whittaker, *Communities,* chapter 5.

[62]A classic paper is F. H. Bormann and G. E. Likens, Nutrient cycling. For recent reviews, see D. E. Reichle, Advances in ecosystem analysis; P. Duvigneaud and S. Denaeyer-de Smet, Mineral cycling in terrestrial ecosystems.

[63]See Whittaker, *Communities.*

Recommended for Further Reading

Deevey, Edward S., Jr. 1970. Mineral cycles. *Scientific American,* September, pp. 148–158. A basic reference on nutrient cycles by a senior researcher in the field.

Ehrlich, Paul; R. Holm; and M. Soule. 1973. *Introductory biology.* McGraw-Hill, New York. Readable introduction to the roles of elements in living systems, among many other topics.

Garrels, R. M.; F. T. Mackenzie; C. Hunt. 1975. *Chemical cycles and the global environment.* Kaufmann, Los Altos, Calif. A good introduction to the use of simple quantitative models in the study of global chemical cycles. Indispensable for the serious student of these matters.

Stryer, Lubert. 1975. *Biochemistry.* W. H. Freeman and Company, San Francisco. Excellent text.

U.S. National Committee for the International Biological Program. 1975. *Productivity of world ecosystems.* National Academy of Sciences, Washington, D.C. Indispensible reference on the carbon cycle.

Woodwell, G. M., and E. V. Pecan, eds. 1973. *Carbon and the biosphere.* National Technical Information Service, Springfield, Va. August, CONF-720510. Proceedings of a major conference with papers by most of the prominent United States researchers on the carbon cycle, global primary productivity, and related topics.

Additional References

Almqvist, E. 1974. An analysis of global air pollution. *Ambio,* vol. 3, no. 5, pp. 161–167. A systematic survey of the magnitude of human contributions and the techniques for measuring them.

Averitt, P. 1973. Coal. In D. A. Brobst and W. P. Pratt, eds. *United States mineral resources,* Government Printing Office, Washington, D. C., pp. 133–142. A technical discussion of the geology and physical properties of coal, as well as the magnitude of resources.

Bacastow, R., and C. D. Keeling. 1973. Atmospheric carbon dioxide and radiocarbon in the natural carbon cycle. Pt. 2. In *Carbon and the biosphere,* G. M. Woodwell and E. V. Pecan, eds., pp. 86–136. Excellent technical review of a complex and often less cogently presented topic—where the carbon dioxide comes from and where it goes.

Bolin, B. 1970. The carbon cycle. *Scientific American,* September, pp. 124–132. Readable introduction by an eminent researcher.

Bormann, F. H., and G. E. Likens. 1967. Nutrient cycling. *Science,* vol. 155, pp. 424–429. A good discussion by two eminent investigators of nutrient flows in terrestrial ecosystems.

Bowen, H. J. M. 1966. *Trace elements in biochemistry.* Academic Press, New York. A classic text.

Brigham, A. R., and A. U. Brigham. 1975. Sulfur in the aquatic ecosystem. In *Sulfur in the environment,* Missouri Botanical Garden, pp. 159–175. Good quantitative survey of the pathways and chemistry of sulfur in aquatic environments.

Burns, R. C., and R. W. F. Hardy. 1975. *Nitrogen fixation in bacteria and higher plants.* Springer-Verlag, New York. Highly technical, up-to-date monograph, with an extensive bibliography. Contains substantially higher estimate of global nitrogen fixation than previous work.

Cathcart, J. B., and R. A. Gulbrandsen. 1973. Phosphate deposits. In *United States mineral resources,* D. A. Brobst and W. P. Pratt, eds. Government Printing Office, Washington, D.C., pp. 515–525. Basic reference on the geology of the phosphate resource.

Cloud, P., and A. Gibor. 1970. The oxygen cycle. *Scientific American,* September, pp. 111–123. Excellent introduction to the origins and fate of atmospheric oxygen on geologic time scales.

Crutzen, P. J. 1974. Estimates of possible variations in total ozone due to natural causes and human activities. *Ambio,* vol. 3, no. 6, pp. 201–210. A good survey of the threats to ozone, heavy on atmospheric chemistry.

Delwiche, C. C. 1970. The nitrogen cycle. *Scientific American,* September, pp. 137–146. Good starting point for anyone wishing to review the recent literature of the nitrogen cycle.

Duvigneaud, P., and S. Denaeyer-de Smet. 1975. Mineral cycling in terrestrial ecosystems. In U. S. National Committee for the International Biological Program, *Productivity of world ecosystems,* pp. 133–154. Strongly quantitative approach with emphasis on differences in nutrient flows and inventories in various ecosystems.

Ehrlich, Paul R., and L. C. Birch. 1967. The "balance of nature" and population growth. *American Naturalist,* vol. 101, pp. 97-107. Discusses the role of herbivores in limiting plant populations.

Ewell, Raymond. 1972. Fertilizer use throughout the world. *Chemtech,* September, pp. 570–575. Good compilation of historical data on fertilizer use.

Frieden, E. 1972. The chemical elements of life. *Scientific American,* July, pp. 52–60. One of the best article-length introductions to the role of chemical elements in organisms.

Gates, D. 1971. The flow of energy in the biosphere. *Scientific American,* September, pp. 89–100. An eminent physicist-turned-biologist surveys his specialty.

Hill, F. B. 1973. Atmospheric sulfur and its links to the biota. In *Carbon and the biosphere,* G. M. Woodwell and E. V. Pecan, eds., pp. 159–180. Good treatment, for the serious student of the sulfur cycle.

Hubbert, M. K. 1969. Energy resources. In *Resources and man,* National Academy of Sciences–National Research Council, W. H. Freeman and Company, San Francisco. A classic survey and introduction to quantitative estimation of resource depletion by the most well-known practitioner of this field.

Ingestad, T. 1974. Nutrient requirements and fertilization of plants. *Ambio,* vol. 3, no. 2, pp. 49–54. Discusses inefficient use of nutrients under present fertilization practices and suggests improvements.

Institute of Ecology, The (TIE). 1972. *Man in the living environment.* University of Wisconsin Press, Madison, chapter 3. Collects and summarizes the work of many authors on nutrient cycling.

Kellogg, W.; R. Cadle; E. Allen; A. Lazrus; and E. Martell. 1972. The sulfur cycle. *Science,* vol. 175, pp. 1587–1596 (February 11). Good, quantitative review article.

Lehninger, A. L. 1965. *Bioenergetics.* Benjamin, New York. Lucid treatment of energy in organisms.

———. 1970. *Biochemistry.* Worth, New York. A thorough introduction to the chemistry of life. Sometimes heavy going for the uninitiated.

Lerman, A; F. T. Mackenzie; and R. M. Garrels. 1975. Modeling of geochemical cycles. *Geological Society of America Memoir,* vol. 142, pp. 205–218. Concise presentation of some of the methods in the Garrels, Mackenzie, and Hunt book listed earlier.

Levine, R. P. 1969. The mechanism of photosynthesis. *Scientific American,* December, pp. 58–60.

McCulloh, T. H. 1973. Oil and gas. *United States mineral resources,* D. A. Brobst and W. P. Pratt, eds., pp. 477–496. Concise, fairly technical treatment of origins and occurrence of liquid and gaseous hydrocarbons.

Machta, Lester. 1973. Prediction of CO_2 in the atmosphere. In *Carbon in the biosphere,* G. M. Woodwell and E. V. Pecan, pp. 21–30. Use of computer models for predicting the accumulation and consequences of carbon dioxide in the atmosphere.

MacIntyre, Ferren. 1970. Why the sea is salt. *Scientific American,* November, pp. 104–115. A splendid introduction to geochemistry, much broader than the title implies.

Margulis, L., and J. Lovelock. 1976. Is Mars a spaceship, too? *Natural History,* vol. 85, no. 6, pp. 86–90. An informative discussion of ways in which biological processes maintain conditions of temperature, humidity, pH, and chemical composition on and near Earth's surface.

Mason, Brian. 1966. *Principles of geochemistry.* 3d ed. Wiley, New York. Good introductory text.

Missouri Botanical Garden. 1975. *Sulfur in the environment.* Saint Louis. Best available volume on the chemistry and biology of sulfur compounds in the environment. Brings together much material that is hard to find elsewhere.

Odum, E. P. 1971. *Fundamentals of ecology.* 3d ed. Saunders, Philadelphia, chapter 5. A well-known text, rich in field data and examples.

Pauling, L. 1970. *General chemistry.* 3d ed. W. H. Freeman and Company, San Francisco. Excellent basic reference.

Peck, H. D., Jr. 1975. The microbial sulfur cycle. In *Sulfur in the environment,* Missouri Botanical Garden, pp. 62–78. The often underemphasized bacterial side of this crucial nutrient cycle.

Penman, H. 1970. The water cycle. *Scientific American,* September, pp. 99-108. Readable introduction to the hydrologic cycle.

Press, F., and R. Siever. 1974. *Earth.* W. H. Freeman and Company, San Francisco. Magnificently illustrated, authoritative, and well written. The best geology book available, we think.

Reichle, D. E. 1975. Advances in ecosystem analysis. *BioScience,* vol. 25, no. 4 (April), pp. 257–264. Good survey of the nutrient-flow measurements and measurement techniques employed in the International Biological Program (IBP).

Rodin, L., N. Bazilevich, and N. Rozov. 1975. Productivity of the world's main ecosystems. In United States National Committee for IBP, *Productivity of world ecosystems,* pp. 13–26. One of the basic papers on global primary production. Indispensable for serious students of the carbon cycle.

SCEP. *See* Study of Critical Environmental Problems.

Singer, S. F., ed. 1970. *Global effects of environmental pollution.* Springer-Verlag, New York. A useful, although uneven, collection of papers on climate, nutrients, and persistent pollutants.

Study of Critical Environmental Problems (SCEP). 1970. *Man's impact on the global environment.* The M.I.T. Press, Cambridge. Remains a must as a survey of the human impact on climate and ecosystems, emphasizing effects of industrial society. Relevant to this chapter are treatments of carbon dioxide, phosphorus, and nitrogen.

Study of Man's Impact on Climate (SMIC). 1971. *Inadvertent climate modification.* The M.I.T. Press, Cambridge. Contains detailed discussion of carbon dioxide and its influence on climate, among many other topics.

TIE. *See* Institute of Ecology, The.

United States Department of Commerce. Annual. *Statistical abstract of the United States.* Government Printing Office, Washington, D.C.

Watson, J. D. 1976. *The molecular biology of the gene.* 3d ed. Benjamin, New York. The definitive treatise.

Whittaker, R. H. 1970. *Communities and ecosystems.* Macmillan, New York. Brief, well-written introduction to ecology, with good treatment of global productivity.

One of the penalties of an ecological education is that one lives alone in a world of wounds. Much of the damage inflicted on land is quite invisible to laymen. An ecologist must either harden his shell and make believe that the consequences of science are none of his business, or he must be the doctor who sees the marks of death in a community that believes itself well and does not want to be told otherwise.

—Aldo Leopold,
Round River

CHAPTER 4

Populations and Ecosystems

Humanity shares the physical vehicle of Earth with an enormous diversity of other living things—plants, animals, and microorganisms. There may be as many as 10 million different kinds—*species*—of organisms alive today. In turn, each species consists of one or more *populations,* a population being a group of individuals more or less isolated from other populations of the same species.[1] This diverse array is not static. Populations of organisms change continually in size and genetic composition in response to changes in their physical environments and in response to changes in other populations. The populations of plants, animals, and microorganisms of Earth, or of any area of Earth, make up a *biological community,* a community bound together by an intricate web of relationships. Of course, this living web is embedded in the physical environment, interacts with it, and modifies it.

The interdependence that characterizes the physical and biological elements of the environment has led ecologists to coin the term *ecosystem* (short for ecological system) for the functional unit that includes both *biotic* (living) and *abiotic* (nonliving) elements. In order to understand humanity's role in ecosystems, it is necessary

[1]The reader interested in some of the complexities of the definitions of *population* and *species* should refer to Paul R. Ehrlich, R. W. Holm, and D. R. Parnell, *The process of evolution,* chapters 5 and 13.

to have some grasp of the functioning of both biotic and abiotic elements in these systems and of their properties in combination. You have already been introduced to the major abiotic features of the environment. In this chapter the biotic elements are discussed, starting with the properties of populations and then moving on to the integration of populations into ecosystems.

POPULATION DYNAMICS

The study of changes in population size—*population dynamics*—is of enormous practical importance to humankind. People are continually in the position of wishing to predict or influence the sizes of populations of other organisms or of some group of *Homo sapiens* or of humanity as a whole. Will there be a spruce budworm outbreak next year? Are peregrines threatened with extinction? Can the present harvest of sei whales or Peruvian anchovetas be sustained? How many people will be living in the United States in the year 2000? Answering any of these questions would require some knowledge of population dynamics.

Although the details of population dynamics can be endlessly complex, the essence of analyzing changes of numbers is relatively straightforward. A number of points should be kept clearly in mind throughout the discussion.

1. The analysis basically amounts to keeping track of inputs and outputs in a population (Box 2-2).
2. The inputs are natality and immigration. (*Natality* is used instead of births because individuals that hatch from eggs or grow from seeds are not normally said to have been "born.")
3. The outputs are mortality (deaths) and emigration.
4. In most discussions in this chapter, migration is ignored, and the analyses focus on natality and mortality.
5. In populations with overlapping generations (such as human populations), the *age composition*—that is, the proportion of individuals in various age classes—has a substantial effect on the future course of population growth. In populations where adults of one generation invariably die before their offspring mature (like many insects), the generations do not overlap, and the analyses are greatly simplified.

Although the mathematics of human population dynamics is identical to that of other animal populations with overlapping generations,[2] a subtle difference in approach has developed between ecologists, who are mainly interested in nonhuman populations, and the social scientists known as demographers, who study the dynamics of human populations alone.

Demographers concern themselves primarily with factors that influence natality—that is, the birth rate. They assume that death rates in *Homo sapiens* will reach a low point and remain there as diseases and other threats are conquered, and they therefore concentrate on the interesting and important questions of how and when birth rates may change in response to social or environmental pressures.

In contrast, ecologists—especially those who work with invertebrates—tend to focus on mortality. The reproductive rates of most nonhuman organisms can change dramatically only over evolutionary time (hundreds or thousands of generations). Ecologists have considered populations to have a rather fixed *reproductive potential* (a term no longer in vogue) and have viewed varying mortality rates as the prime determinants of population size. To oversimplify, demographers have viewed the populations they study as having varying inputs and fixed outputs, whereas ecologists have viewed theirs as having fixed inputs and varying outputs. The differences of approach in the two scientific disciplines are quite interesting and can be seen by comparing this discussion with that in Chapter 5, which deals with demography.

In the remainder of this section of text, the discussion centers primarily on the dynamics of nonhuman populations, although most of the points apply to human beings as well. The treatment varies considerably in depth and complexity. The most basic concepts of population dynamics—for example, instantaneous birth and death rates, exponential growth, growth with restraint, age composition, population structure—are introduced at a

[2]For a more thorough introduction to the mathematics of population dynamics, see: C. J. Krebs, *Ecology: The experimental analysis of distribution and abundance;* R. W. Poole, *An introduction to quantitative ecology;* R. E. Ricklefs, *Ecology;* J. Roughgarden, *Theory of population genetics and evolutionary ecology, an introduction;* and E. O. Wilson and W. H. Bossert, *A primer of population biology,* Sinauer, Stamford, Conn., 1971. Only a brief outline is given here.

BOX 4-1 Symbols Used in Population Dynamics

Symbol	Meaning
N	population size
$N(t)$	population size at time t. Some texts use N_t.
$N(0)$	population size at time zero (starting population size)—sometimes written N_0.
t	time in any units
T	length of a generation
$\frac{dN}{dt}$	instantaneous rate of change of population size
IRI	instantaneous rate of increase in population size
b	birth rate
d	death rate
r	intrinsic rate of increase (instantaneous rate of increase per individual)
r_m	maximum intrinsic rate of increase
λ	lambda, the finite rate of increase, N_1/N_0
e	the base of natural logarithms (approximately 2.718)
ln	natural logarithm (*l*og *n*atural)
K	carrying capacity (the maximum number of individuals that can be supported in a given environment)
c	a constant
α	alpha, a competition coefficient
β	beta, a competition coefficient
x	age as a variable
l_x	the proportion or number of survivors of a birth cohort at age x.
m_x	the average number of female offspring produced by a female of age x
$\sum$	sum of . . .
$\sum_0^\infty$	sum from zero to infinity of . . .
R_0	net reproductive rate, $\sum_0^\infty l_x m_x$
NRR	net reproductive rate
${}_nq_x$	in life tables, the proportion of persons alive at the beginning of an age interval who die during that interval
${}_nd_x$	in life tables, the number of persons from a given birth cohort dying during an age interval
${}_nL_x$	in life tables, the number of persons in an age interval in a hypothetical stationary population supported by 100,000 annual births and subject to the actual l_x schedule of the population
T_x	in life tables, the total number of persons in the stationary population in an age interval and all subsequent age intervals. Equals $\sum_x^\infty {}_nL_x$

level that assumes no prior familiarity with the field. For the more ambitious reader, however, there are also some excursions into subtleties and details at a somewhat more mathematical level. This material (much of it displayed in boxes) can be skipped without loss of continuity but will repay the scrutiny of those who wish a clearer picture of what the study of population dynamics really entails. The notation used in this discussion is summarized in Box 4-1.

Instantaneous Rate of Increase

A logical beginning is to consider the problem of measuring the rate of change in a population—that is, the rate of increase or decrease—*at a given moment.* An average rate is easy to calculate. Suppose at the beginning of a year a population of mice contains 100 individuals and at the end of the year it contains 220. The population has grown at an average rate of 10 individuals per month, or 120 per year. This is analogous to, say, calculating the average rate of speed of an automobile trip by dividing the distance between start and finish by the time it consumes. Thus, if the car progresses 200 miles in 10 hours, the average rate of speed is 20 miles per hour (note that rates are always expressed in terms of a unit of time).

Of course, the growth of the mouse population might have been the result of 30 female mice all having litters in a single month, together with some deaths scattered evenly over the rest of the year, just as the average speed of 20 miles per hour might have been achieved by driving 80 miles an hour for a 3-hour spurt and backing up slowly for the other 7 hours. In other words, the instantaneous rate of change in both cases may have been high and positive for a brief period and negative for the rest of the time.

What we will calculate now is the *instantaneous rate of increase* (IRI) for a population—a quantity analogous to the readout on a speedometer, which tells how fast the car is going at a given instant. The IRI will be positive when the population is growing and negative when it is shrinking—a negative IRI being analogous to a speedometer reading when the car is backing up.

It is reasonable to expect that the rate of change in the size of a population (let the size be N) in the course of time (t) will itself depend on the population size. (A mathematician would say the rate of change of N is a *function* of N.) Whatever the average individual's contribution to population growth, it must be multiplied by the population size in order to determine the amount of change in the population as a whole. These simple relations, expressed in the notation of calculus, yield the most basic equation of population dynamics:[3]

instantaneous rate of increase	=	average individual contribution to population growth	multiplied by	population size	
$\frac{dN}{dt}$	=	r	$\times$	N	$= rN$

Here dN/dt is the conventional notation for instantaneous rate of change of N with t. The average individual contribution (r) is the *instantaneous rate of increase (per individual)*, usually called the *intrinsic rate of increase* by biologists.[4] Thus, at a given moment, if a population contains a million individuals (N) and is growing at that moment at the rate of 100,000 individuals per year (dN/dt), then r would be 0.10. In other words, the growth rate amounts to one-tenth of an individual per individual per year. In recent years the human population has been growing with an r of about 0.02; that is, roughly one-fiftieth of a person has been added per person per year to the total population.

The factor r is more easily understood if it is split into its input and output components. If input is b (the instantaneous birth rate) and output is d (the instantaneous death rate), then r is seen to be simply b minus d. (We are ignoring migration.) If more individuals are being born at a given instant than are dying, the population is growing, and r is positive. If more are dying than are being born, the population is shrinking, and r is negative.

[3]Some familiarity at least with the notation and fundamental approach of calculus is helpful for what follows. For an introduction or review, see E. Batschelet, *Introduction to mathematics for life scientists,* 2d ed. (Springer-Verlag, New York, 1975), or a basic calculus text.

[4]This quantity is also sometimes called *the innate capacity for increase.*

Exponential Growth

The equation $dN/dt = rN$ relates the IRI to population size itself. It does not, however, show explicitly how the size of a population (growing according to this relationship) at one time is related to the size at another time. Consider, for instance, a population whose size at an initial time ($t = 0$) is known and is denoted $N(0)$. How can one calculate the size t units of time later [$N(t)$]?[5] The answer can be derived from the equation for IRI by elementary calculus. For the case when r itself does not vary with time, one obtains:

{Size after t time units}	=	{initial size}	multiplied by	{e raised to the power of the IRI per capita multiplied by t time units}
$N(t)$	=	$N(0)$	$\times$	e^{rt}

Here e is the base of the natural logarithm; it is approximately equal to 2.7183. When the quantity e is raised to a power that is a variable—for example, the product rt—the result is called the *exponential function.* It is sometimes also written, "exp(rt)." This function has unique mathematical properties that cause it to arise naturally in the mathematical representation of many physical and biological processes. Its presence in the growth equation just presented is the basis for calling this particular process *exponential growth.*

Consider the application of the exponential growth equation to human population growth in India. The population of India in 1975 was about 620 million persons. How large would it be in 2025—fifty years later—if it continued to grow at the 1975 rate (an r of roughly 0.026 per person per year)? Using the above formula:[6]

$$
\begin{aligned}
N(0) &= 620 \text{ million} \\
t &= 50 \text{ yr};\ r = 0.026;\ rt = 1.30 \\
e^{rt} &= 2.7183^{1.30} \doteq 3.67 \\
N(t) &= N(50) = N(0)e^{rt} = 3.67 \times 620 \text{ million} \\
&= 2275 \text{ million}
\end{aligned}
$$

[5]The alternate notations N_0 and N_t are used in many biology texts.

[6]The symbol $\doteq$ means, "approximately equal to."

BOX 4-2 Interest and Growth Rates

If $N(0)$ dollars is placed in a bank at a 2-percent rate of interest, compounded semiannually, the principal plus the interest at the end of t years will be

$$N(t) = N(0)(1.01)^{2t}.$$

More generally, if the interest rate is expressed as a decimal r (where $100r =$ interest rate as a percent) and interest is compounded x times a year, then

$$N(t) = N(0)\left(1 + \frac{r}{x}\right)^{xt}. \qquad (1)$$

If interest is compounded continuously, then $x \rightarrow \infty$. Expression (1) may be rewritten, substituting $y = r/x$

$$\begin{aligned} N(t) &= N(0)(1 + y)^{rt/y} \\ &= N(0)[(1 + y)^{1/y}]^{rt}. \qquad (2) \end{aligned}$$

Those who have had calculus will understand that as $x \rightarrow \infty, y \rightarrow 0$, and in the limit

$$\lim_{y \rightarrow 0} (1 + y)^{1/y} = e.$$

The base of natural logarithms (e) is approximately equal to 2.718. Therefore, when interest is compounded continuously, (2) becomes the familiar equation of exponential population growth

$$N(t) = N(0)e^{rt}.$$

Given the growth rate, the doubling time may be computed by setting $N(t)/N(0) = 2$. Then

$$2 = e^{rt}.$$

Taking the natural logarithm (ln) of each side (and remembering that $\ln e = 1$) gives

$$\ln 2 = rt \quad \text{or} \quad \frac{\ln 2}{r} = t \quad \text{or} \quad \frac{0.6931}{r} = t.$$

For example, if the annual growth rate is 2 percent, then $1.02 = e^r$ and $r = 0.0198$, and

$$t = \frac{0.6931}{0.0198} = 35 \text{ yr}.$$

The doubling time can be closely approximated by dividing seventy years by the annual growth rate in percent. (The approximation becomes less accurate as annual growth rate gets larger, however; above a rate of 10 percent it can be significantly in error.)

Thus, in the year 2025 India's population would have grown to 2275 million (or 2.275 *billion*) persons—well over half the 1975 population of the entire Earth!

A quantity growing exponentially increases in any given period of time by a fixed percentage of its size at the beginning of the period. A savings account at a bank where interest is compounded grows exponentially. The interest becomes part of the balance and, in turn, earns more interest. As time goes on, the balance gets bigger and the additions in the form of interest get bigger, in proportion. When growth is exponential, as it approximately is now in the human population, each addition becomes a contributor of new additions. The relationship between compound interest and population growth rates is made explicit in Box 4-2, as is a derivation of *e*.

If the *percentage* of exponential growth of a population in two successive periods is the same, the *absolute* growth in the second period is larger. Between 1960 and 1970, growing at about 2 percent per year, world population increased by some 650 million persons; if the 2 percent annual rate of growth persisted through the 1970s, the population increase for that decade would be about 800 million.

Exponential growth at a constant annual percentage increase can be characterized by the time it takes for any given quantity to double. The doubling time for a population growing at 2 percent per year is about 35 years. Consumption of energy—a useful index both of resource consumption and of a population's impact on the environment—is growing worldwide at roughly 5 percent per year, corresponding to a doubling time of only 14 years. (The general relation is: doubling time is approximately equal to 70 years divided by the annual percentage increase. See Box 4-2.)

Use of the concept of doubling time emphasizes what for our purposes is the most important property of exponential growth—the rapidity with which such growth can exceed a given limit after seeming safely small for a long time. To understand this phenomenon, imagine a large aquarium with filter and aeration systems adequate to the needs of 1000 guppies. Suppose we start with 2 guppies in the tank and that the number grows exponentially with a doubling time of 1 month. It takes 8 doublings, or 8 months, for the guppy population to reach half the carrying capacity of the tank (2 → 4 → 8 → 16 → 32 → 64 → 128 → 256 → 512). For this entire period, the population seems safely small; no crisis seems imminent. Symptoms of impending disaster are unlikely to appear until the population is well over half the tank's capacity. The critical phase of the growth, when the population zooms from 512 to more than 1000, occurs within the ninth month, when the last 100 guppies are added in less than 5 days. After 265 days of apparent prosperity, exponential growth carries the population from 90 percent of capacity to a disastrous excess in less than a week.

If the subject is human beings instead of fish in an aquarium, the limits are not so obvious, but the treacherous properties of exponential population growth are just as relevant. *A long history of exponential growth does not imply a long future of exponential growth.*

Increase Without Restraint

Restraints on the growth of a population include predators, disease, and shortages of resources such as food and water. When all such restraints are removed—when there are no predators or disease and there are superabundant resources—r reaches a theoretical maximum, symbolized as r_m (*m* for "Malthusian"). Actually, r_m for a given species is not a single number but has a range of values, depending on temperature, humidity, and other conditions. For a specified set of such conditions, then, the maximum possible exponential rate of growth is the corresponding maximum intrinsic rate of increase multiplied by the population size:

$$\left(\frac{dN}{dt}\right)_{\max} = r_m N.$$

Suppose, for instance, that a grain beetle has established a population of 100 individuals in a bin of wheat in which the temperature is 29°C and the moisture content of the wheat is 14 percent. Assuming growth without significant restraint and an $r_m = 0.75$ per individual per week, how many beetles would you expect to find after 3 weeks? The calculation is of the same form as that done for population growth in India, above—although the r for the Indian population was not the theoretical maximum (r_m) for the temperature and humidity of India!

In the grain beetle case: $N(0) = 100$; $r_m = 0.75$; and $t = 3$. And $N(t)$ [$= N(3)$] is to be calculated.

$$\text{After } t \text{ weeks, } N(t) = N(0)e^{r_m t}.$$

$$\text{After 3 weeks, } N(3) = 100e^{(0.75)(3)} = 100e^{2.25} = 949.$$

Thus, one would expect to find 949 beetles after 3 weeks of unrestrained growth. After 10 weeks there would be 180,804 beetles; and in 20 weeks, 326,901,737 beetles. Essentially unrestrained growth obviously cannot continue for 20 weeks unless the wheat bin is large, since at that point more than 300 million beetles would be competing for the remaining grain. Indeed, unrestrained growth for a year would lead to:

$$N(52) = 100e^{(0.75)(52)} = 100e^{39}$$

$$N(52) = 8{,}659{,}340{,}042{,}000{,}000{,}000 \doteq 8.7 \times 10^{18}.$$

If each beetle weighed 10 milligrams on the average, the entire mass of beetles would weigh 8.7×10^{11} metric tons. After 82 weeks there would be 6.1×10^{28} beetles, and their weight of 6.1×10^{21} metric tons would be equal to that of Earth! A general rule about long-continued exponential increase is that it leads to preposterous numbers with surprising speed.[7]

Remember, in the more general case of exponential growth, where predators and disease are not eliminated (or in human populations, where some limitation of births is almost always practiced), r is substituted for r_m. Hence, growth may be exponential at a rate below the theoretical maximum. For instance, the human population is now growing roughly exponentially with $r \doteq 0.02$ per person per year, whereas r_m for human beings in most environments would probably be in the vicinity of 0.04 to 0.05. Exponential growth produces characteristic curves when numbers are plotted against time (Figure 4-1). These curves transform into a straight line if the population size is plotted on a logarithmic scale (Figure 4-2), which is why it is often called logarithmic growth.

[7]The r_m conditions in this example approximate those calculated for the grain beetle *Calandra oryzae* by L. C. Birch in Experimental background to the study of the distribution and abundance of insects, pt. 1, *Ecology,* vol. 34, pp. 698–711.

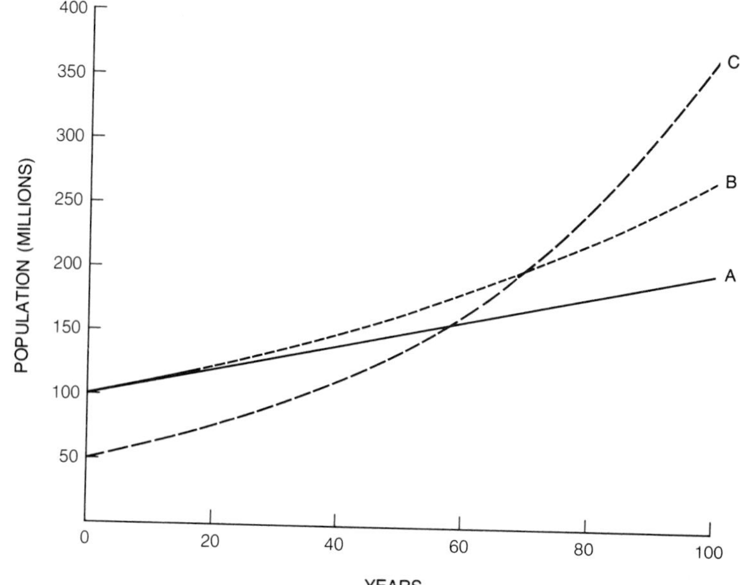

FIGURE 4-1

Exponential growth and arithmetic growth. A. Initial population of 100 million growing arithmetically at 1 million per year. B. Initial population of 100 million growing exponentially at 1 percent per year. C. Initial population of 50 million growing exponentially at 2 percent per year. Compare A and B: The difference is negligible at first, then grows dramatically. This is the effect of compound interest. Compare B and C: A higher exponential growth rate soon compensates for a smaller initial population.

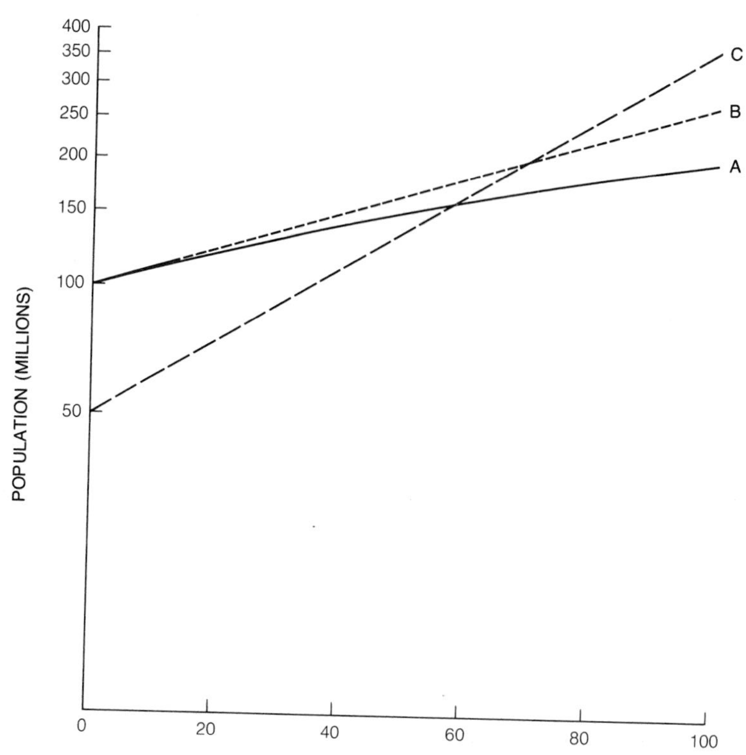

FIGURE 4-2

Curves from Figure 4-1, replotted using a logarithmic scale on the ordinate. Note that only the previously straight arithmetic growth line, A, is now curved.

It is important to keep in mind both the properties of exponential growth curves and the assumptions underlying them. Remember especially that the intrinsic rate of increase (r) is assumed to be constant and that the rate of change of population size (derivative of size with respect to time, dN/dt) is this constant, r, multiplied by the size at a particular time. Thus, when the beetle population was just 1000 individuals, the instantaneous growth rate was:

$$\frac{dN}{dt} = rN = 0.75(1000) = 750 \text{ individuals per week.}$$

The human population in 1975 was some 4 billion persons and was growing approximately exponentially at about 2 percent per year. Hence, the midyear instantaneous growth rate was roughly 0.02×4 billion $= 80$ million per year. The relation between true instantaneous rates of change and the *finite rates* that can be computed from data generally available is explored in Box 4-3.

Growth with Restraint

Suppose that, instead of being constant, an individual's reproductive contribution varies with the size of the population. Now the basic equation becomes:

$$\begin{Bmatrix}\text{Instantaneous}\\ \text{rate of}\\ \text{increase}\end{Bmatrix} = \begin{Bmatrix}\text{function}\\ \text{of}\\ \text{population size}\end{Bmatrix} \times \text{population size}$$

$$\frac{dN}{dt} = f(N) \times N$$

$$= r \times N,$$

where $f(N)$ stands for a function of N—that is, for r, which now varies with N.

The simplest mathematical model we can make of this situation is one in which r decreases linearly as N increases. That is, in this model r is not a constant but rather is given by the expression:

$$r = r_m\left(\frac{K - N}{K}\right).$$

Here K is the *carrying capacity* (the maximum number of individuals that can be supported in a given environment). According to this relation, at the beginning of the growth process (when $N = 0$), r is equal to r_m, the Malthusian rate of increase. Later, as N approaches the carrying capacity (K), r approaches zero.

The differential equation for this simple model of growth is:

$$\frac{dN}{dt} = r_m\left(\frac{K - N}{K}\right)N.$$

This can be rewritten in the form:

$$\frac{dN}{dt} = r_m N\left(\frac{K - N}{K}\right) = N\left(r_m - \frac{r_m}{K}N\right)$$
$$= N(a - bN),$$

where $a = r_m$ and $b = r_m/K$. By integrating this differential equation (expressing population size as a function of time), we obtain the following solution:

$$N(t) = \frac{K}{1 + ce^{-r_m t}},$$

where $c = [K - N(0)]/N(0)$.

This equation is that of the logistic curve (Figure 4-3)—the archetypal presentation of density dependence in ecology. Note in this figure that the growth rate of the population at each point in time depends on its density (size). Growth starts off slowly and then accelerates

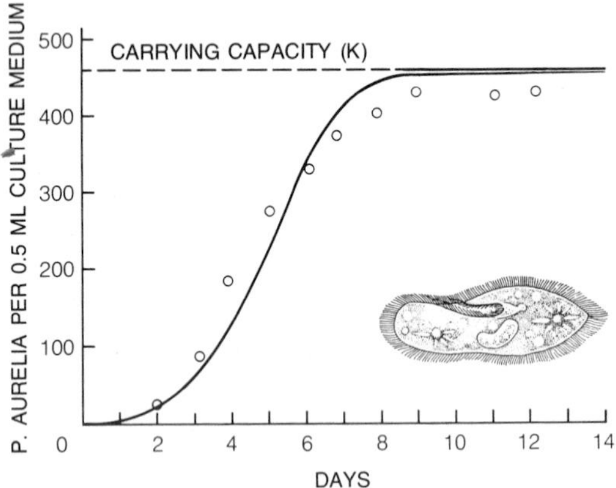

FIGURE 4-3

The logistic growth of a population of the protozoan *Paramecium aurelia* in culture. Data show observed values that are quite close to the calculated logistic curve. (Adapted from Andrewartha and Birch, 1954.)

BOX 4-3 Finite and Instantaneous Rates

Finite birth and death rates are computed by dividing the number of births (or deaths) in a period by the average population size in that period (the sum of the initial and final sizes divided by 2) or by the size of the population at the midpoint of the period. These finite rates are estimates of the instantaneous rates, and the difference between the finite birth and death rates is an estimate of r, the instantaneous rate of increase per individual.

Consider a population of rodents. Suppose there were 11,250 births and three-fourths as many (8,438) deaths in the population during a period in which the average population size was 11,250. The finite birth rate would be 1 per individual per period, and the finite death rate would be 0.75 per individual per period. The instantaneous rate of increase per individual during that period in that case can be estimated to be 0.25 individuals per individual during the period—from which one could estimate that the final population would be 1.25 times the starting size (the original number of individuals plus one-quarter of an additional individual for each of the original individuals).

The factor by which the size of a population is multiplied *during a given period* is the finite rate of increase per individual, or, simply, the *finite rate of increase* (conventionally symbolized by the Greek letter lambda, λ) for that period. Thus, if N_1 is the population size at the end of the period and N_0 is the size at the beginning,

$$N_1 = \lambda N_0 \quad \text{and} \quad \frac{N_1}{N_0} = \lambda.$$

What would λ be in our example? To find out, we must establish the initial population size (N_0) and the final size (N_1). There were 11,250 births and 8,438 deaths, so 11,250 minus 8,438, or 2,812, rodents were added to the population. We know the average population size during the period was 11,250, so the starting size (N_0) must have been 11,250 minus half the growth, or 9,844, and the final size (N_1) must have been 11,250 plus half the growth, or 12,656. Thus:

$$\lambda = \frac{N_1}{N_0} = \frac{12{,}656}{9{,}844} = 1.29.$$

What accounts for the discrepancy between 1.29 and 1.25? The basic answer is that when a population is growing, the rate per individual gives a continuously varying total rate of increase because *the number of individuals is steadily growing.* Thus, an IRI per individual of 0.25 will multiply our hypothetical population by more than a factor of 1.25 in a given finite period because the IRI per individual is applied not just to the original population of 9,844, but to a continuously growing population.

The ratio λ is known if the population sizes N_0 and N_1 are known, or it can be estimated by adding 1 to the difference between the finite birth and death rates for an interval, if those are known or can be estimated. In most theoretical work, such as mathematical models of population dynamics, one works not with λ but with r, so it is necessary to know the relation between those two quantities. This relation can be obtained easily from the solution of the exponential growth equation. If the length of the time in question is one unit, we obtain:

$$\frac{N_1}{N_0} = \lambda = e^r.$$

In the example given here, $\lambda = 1.29$, so

$$r = \ln\lambda = \ln(1.29) = 0.255.$$

Note that the estimate of $r = 0.25$, made by subtracting the finite birth rate from the finite death rate, differs from the exact value by only 0.005. When dealing in periods of time that are short in comparison with the doubling time of the population (that is, when finite rates of increase are very small), the instantaneous rate can be approximated by subtracting 1 from the finite rate. For example, rounded to two places:

	Estimate of r, $\lambda - 1$	True r
	$1.01 - 1 = 0.01$	0.01
	$1.02 - 1 = 0.02$	0.02
	$1.03 - 1 = 0.03$	0.03
	$1.05 - 1 = 0.05$	0.05
but		
	$1.20 - 1 = 0.20$	0.18
	$1.40 - 1 = 0.40$	0.34
	$2.00 - 1 = 1.00$	0.69
	$3.00 - 1 = 2.00$	1.10
	$10.00 - 1 = 9.00$	2.30

Therefore, when considering annual rates for humanity (where the finite rate is always below 1.05), the difference between finite birth and death rates is a good estimator of the average r for the year.

rapidly. The first part of the curve is sometimes called the *log phase* because, when plotted with N on a logarithmic scale (Figure 4-2), it approximates the straight line of exponential growth. Then the curve rapidly flattens out, approaching K asymptotically (that is, the difference between N and K becomes infinitesimally small as t gets very large).

There are many simplifying assumptions in the logistic equation. One is that all individuals are presumed to be alike ecologically (there is, for instance, assumed to be no change with age in the likelihood of giving birth or being eaten). There is assumed to be no time lag between a change in the environment and the reactions of the organisms—a very unrealistic assumption. Very low densities are presumed not to hinder mate-finding. And, most important, there are the assumptions that the carrying capacity (K) is constant and that r is directly proportional to $K - N$.

Despite these simplifications, the logistic curve has proven to be remarkably close to observed patterns of population growth in laboratory cultures of organisms such as yeasts, protozoa, and fruit flies. Indeed, the recent history of human population growth might represent the log phase of a logistic pattern. It is not, however, known exactly what the carrying capacity is for the global human population, although it certainly is *not* a constant. As we discuss later, any determination of the carrying capacity for *Homo sapiens* must include the question of how long that carrying capacity is expected to persist.

The question of changes in carrying capacity must be considered for any organism, although in laboratory experiments this may often be ignored. In nature, for instance, fruit flies may well show a logistic pattern of growth. A fertile female fly finds a suitable habitat—say, a pile of rotten fruit—and lays her eggs. The population then grows in a roughly logistic manner, but when the food is exhausted the population "crashes"—it is reduced to a very low level or goes extinct. This type of outbreak-crash population cycle is common in organisms that exploit temporary habitats. The species persists because dispersing individuals can find other suitable habitats. But *Homo sapiens,* as a whole, cannot follow this pattern, for there is only one known suitable habitat!

The logistic model has also proven to be a valuable building block for the construction of multispecies models, which are a means of studying interactions among different organisms. For example, a simple model can be constructed for the growth of a pair of competing species, a and b, with two differential equations:

$$\frac{dN_a}{dt} = r_{ma}N_a\left(\frac{K_a - N_a - \alpha N_b}{K_a}\right).$$

$$\frac{dN_b}{dt} = r_{mb}N_b\left(\frac{K_b - N_b - \beta N_a}{K_b}\right).$$

The subscripts a and b indicate the intrinsic rates of increase, carrying capacities, and populations of species a and b. The Greek letter alpha (α) represents the degree to which the resources of species a are reduced by each individual of species b. The letter beta (β) is the degree to which the resources of b are reduced by each individual of a. In this model, α and β are constants and are called *competition coefficients.* Depending on the relationship of K_a, K_b, α, and β, logistic competition can result in one species or the other wiping out its competitor or in the two species coexisting, depending on the initial proportions of the two populations. A considerable body of competition theory deals with such questions as the definition of ecological *niche* (the role an organism plays in an ecosystem), the degree of similarity possible between organisms in competition, and the circumstances under which they coexist or exclude one another.[8]

Age Composition and Population Growth

The assumption that all individuals are ecologically identical—equally likely, for instance, to give birth or die—is not even approximated in most animal populations and clearly is not the case in human populations. Understanding the effects of the age compositions of these populations (and changes in those compositions) on birth and death rates is critical to understanding their dynamics, especially when populations have overlapping generations.

Consider the input side of the equation first. Given the requisite information, one can construct a schedule of age-specific birth rates for a population. In bisexual

[8]These matters are beyond the scope of this book but are dealt with in fine texts by Pianka and Roughgarden. (E. Pianka, *Evolutionary ecology;* J. Roughgarden, *Theory of population genetics.*)

organisms, this schedule is the maternity function, m_x (*m* for maternity, *x* for age). It is normally presented in terms of the number of female offspring per female. Such a function is plotted in Figure 4-4 for women in the United States. The shape of the curve is rather typical for human females—a rapid rise from the midteens to the late twenties, and then a sharp tapering-off around forty-five. In populations in less developed countries, the entire curve extends farther to the left (reproduction starts earlier), and the peak usually is considerably higher because the average woman has more babies (Figure 4-5).

To make statements about population growth, however, we need to know more than what the number of female offspring per female will be in each age class. We also need to know how many females there are in each age class. For this, it is necessary to know the probability that an individual will survive to any given age (l_x, in which *l* denotes living) which can be obtained from the age-specific death rates. Again, the pattern is similar for females of most human populations. As can be seen from the plot of age-specific death rates in Figure 4-6, there is a burst of infant mortality, followed by low death rates through childhood and young adulthood, with a gradual increase starting in the late twenties. The basic U-shape of the curve holds for all human populations, but in less developed countries infant and child (ages 1–5) mortalities are considerably higher, and the high death rates of old age begin earlier.

Conventionally, however, death-rate data are presented in terms of l_x, defined either as the number of individuals surviving or the proportion of individuals surviving. Most animal populations show survivorship curves (l_x) of one of three types (Figure 4-7). Human populations in developed countries come close to having a Type I curve, in which low early mortality is followed by a period of rapidly increasing death rates in middle age. The Type II curve, in which a constant proportion of the population dies in each age interval, is approximated by adults of some butterflies, adult fishes, some adult birds, and adults in primitive human groups (all of these organisms have high juvenile mortalities). Type III curves are probably the most common in natural animal populations: extremely heavy early mortality followed by a gradual die-off of the survivors. Most marine invertebrates, fishes, and insects show this general pattern.

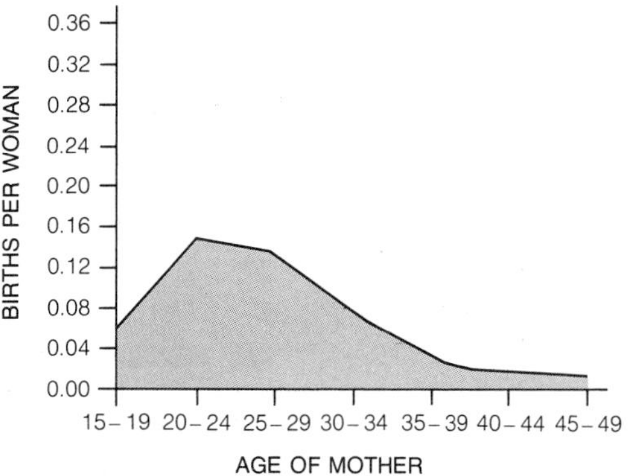

FIGURE 4-4

The maternity function for American women, 1971. The ordinate indicates the number of offspring produced by an average woman in each period. Thus an average American woman reproducing at the 1971 rate would have 0.15 children between the ages of 20 and 24. (Data from U.S. Agency for International Development.)

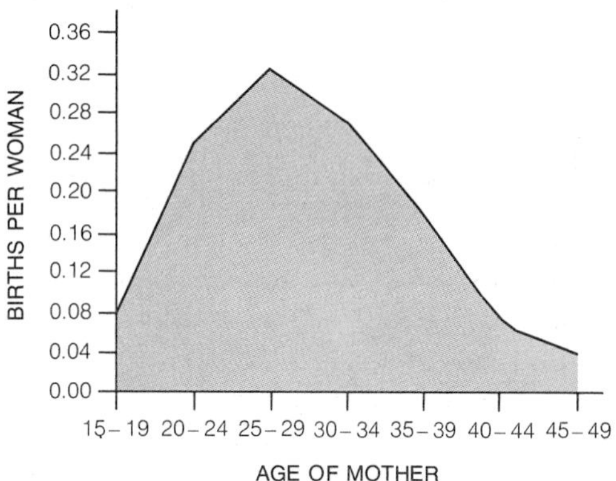

FIGURE 4-5

The maternity function for Peruvian women, 1969. If data were available, this curve would extend farther to the left than the one in Figure 4-4. (Data from U.S. Agency for International Development.)

FIGURE 4-6

Age-specific death rates of American women, 1973. Only the prereproductive and reproductive years, critical to calculation of population reproductive rates, are shown in detail.

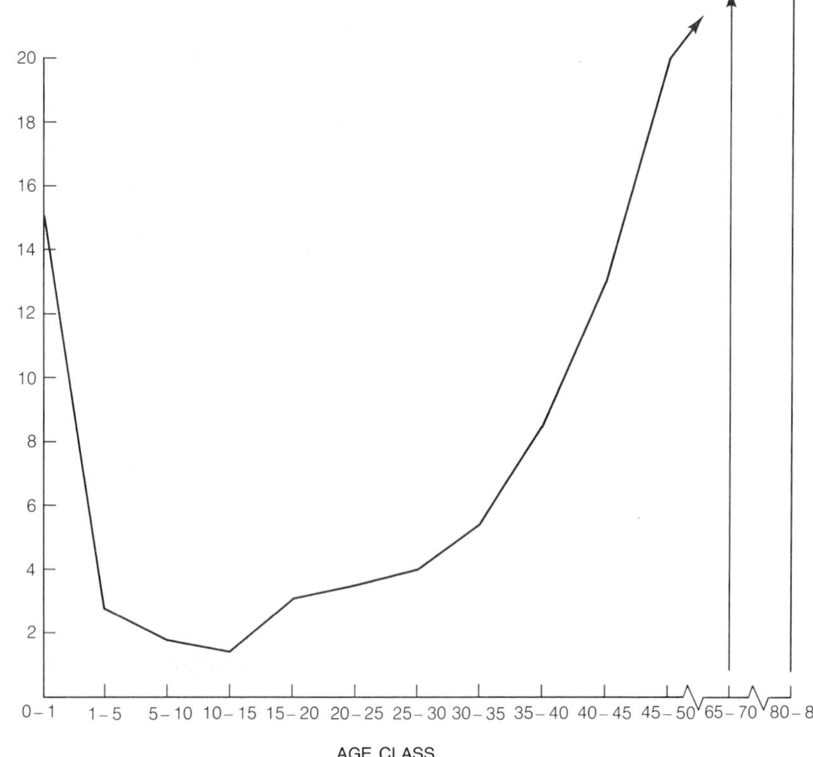

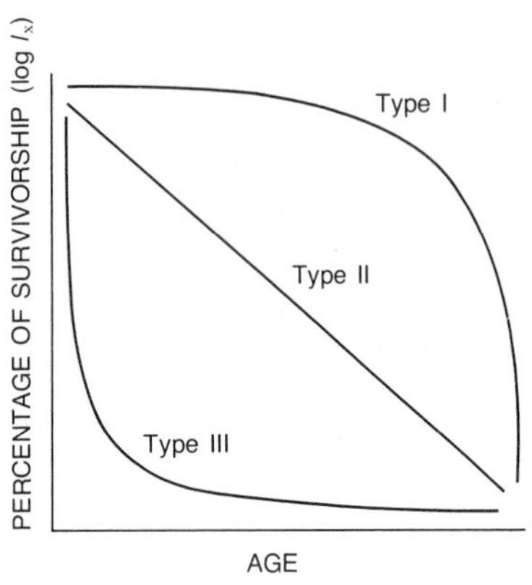

FIGURE 4-7

Three types of survivorship curve. Only the general shape of the curve is important here, not the scale.

TABLE 4-1
A Simple Life Table

x (*Age class*)	l_x (*Proportion of survivors*)	m_x (*Average number of offspring*)	$l_x m_x$
0	1.00	0.0	0.00
1	0.80	1.0	0.80
2	0.30	0.5	0.15
3	0.16	0.25	0.04
4	0.05	0.20	0.01
5	0.00	0.00	0.00
			1.00

If age-specific death- and birth-rate (l_x and m_x) data are available, it is possible to combine them in order to make some statements about population dynamics. Let us look at a single newborn female cohort (a group of females born at the same time) of a hypothetical animal. A version of a *life table* called an $l_x m_x$ table can be constructed for the cohort by observing the pattern in which it reproduces and dies. In Table 4-1, x is the designator of the age class $(x - \frac{1}{2})$ to $(x + \frac{1}{2})$—that is, if x is 5 years, all individuals $4\frac{1}{2}$ to $5\frac{1}{2}$ years old are in Class 5. In the same table, l_x is the proportion of the cohort surviving to age x, and m_x is the age-specific female birth rate. The key column is the right-hand one, the product of l_x and m_x. The sum of that column, $\Sigma_0^\infty l_x m_x$, tells the average number of female offspring produced per female of the original cohort. This sum is designated R_0 and is known as the *net reproductive rate* (NRR).

If $R_0 = 1$, as it does in this example, it means that the original female cohort has exactly replaced itself; for 1000 females in generation n, there are 1000 females in generation $n + 1$. If $R_0 = 2$, then in generation $n + 1$ there are 2000 females. If $R_0 = 0.5$, there are 500 in generation $n + 1$. If generations do not overlap—that is, if all the parents die before any of their offspring mature (as in an insect with one generation per year)—then R_0 indicates whether the population is growing, shrinking, or *stationary* (not changing in size). If R_0 is greater than 1, the population is growing; if R_0 is less than 1, the population is shrinking; if R_0 is exactly 1, the population is stationary.

If generations overlap, however, no statement about population growth at a given moment can be made on the basis of a calculation of R_0 alone. It is necessary also to know the *age composition* of the population. The way R_0 is calculated in a population with overlapping generations is analogous to that of the preceding hypothetical example. Age-specific female birth- and death-rate schedules are determined for a given period of time; and those schedules are applied mathematically to a hypothetical cohort in order to calculate R_0. The age composition of the actual population at the time of determination of the birth-rate and death-rate schedules is not taken into consideration.

Suppose that R_0 in a human population is found to be 1. Suppose further that almost half the women in the population are below reproductive age. Even if R_0 remained 1 and each *generation* were just reproducing itself, the population would continue to grow for some time because the proportion of females in their childbearing years would be increasing (raising the overall birth rate, b) more rapidly than the ranks of the elderly were increasing (raising the overall death rate, d). Remember that, ignoring migration, it is the relationship of these overall rates (not the age-specific rates) that determines whether the population is growing, shrinking, or stationary.

The relationship between R_0 and r is discussed further in Box 4-4. Confusion of the net reproductive rate (R_0) with the instantaneous rate of increase has, for example, led to many erroneous statements about population growth in the United States. When in the early 1970s the NRR was very close to 1, many commentators declared that the United States had reached ZPG (zero population growth, a stationary population). Unfortunately, this was not so (see Chapter 5).

What $R_0 = 1$ for a growing human population does mean is that if the age-specific vital (birth and death) rates that result in $R_0 = 1$ are maintained, the population will eventually reach ZPG (in about a lifetime). That is, if the NRR in the United States remained equal to 1 for some seventy-five years, and if there were no migration, the population would stop growing at the end of that time (ZPG, $r = 0$), and the size of the United States population at ZPG would be about 280 million persons.

The reason for the continued growth with NRR equal to 1 is that the age composition of the U.S. population in the early 1970s was not in a steady state. If the schedule of age-specific birth and death rates (and thus the NRR) subsequently remain constant, the *age composition* (or *age distribution,* as it is often called) will change gradually into what is known as a *stable age composition* or a *stable age distribution.*[9] When a stable age composition is reached, recruitment into each age class (births for the youngest, aging for the rest) is compensated by departures (mortality plus aging into the next older class) so the proportion of the population in each age class remains constant and each age class has exactly the same r as the entire population. This stability of age composition would be achieved in any population with constant vital rates; accordingly, a population with a stable age composition may be growing, shrinking, or stationary.

Sometimes a population with such an age composition is referred to as a *stable* population. This should not be confused with a *stationary* population. A stationary population does not necessarily have a stable age composition (although, without a stable age composition, vital rates must keep changing in complex ways if the population is to *remain* stationary). Again, stable populations are not necessarily stationary, and stationary populations are not necessarily stable.

It takes about the average life expectancy (symbolized $\mathring{e}_0$) for the age composition of a population to stabilize. The life expectancy can be calculated from a life table. Table 4-5 in Box 4-5 shows this calculation for the female population of the United States in 1973. Since $\mathring{e}_0 = 75.3$, obviously it would take about seventy-five years for the population of the United States to reach a

[9]A. J. Lotka, The stability of the normal age distribution, *Proceedings of the National Academy of Sciences,* vol. 8 (1922), pp. 339–345.

BOX 4-4 Generation Time and Calculation of r

Given a $l_x m_x$ table, and *assuming a stable age distribution,* r can be estimated easily. If T is the average length of a generation (that is, the average time between the birth of mothers and the birth of their female offspring), then the size of the female population after a generation of growth can be calculated:

$N_t = N(0)e^{rt}$, becomes $N_T = N(0)e^{rT}$

$$\frac{N_T}{N_0} = e^{rT} = \text{(by definition) the ratio of female births in two successive generations}$$

$$= R_0 = \text{NRR}.$$

Therefore, $R_0 = e^{rT}$, $\ln R_0 = rT$, and $r = \ln R_0/T$.

Thus, all that is required to estimate r is R_0 and an estimate of T, the generation time.

How is the generation time estimated? It may be approximated from the information in the $l_x m_x$ table by the formula:

$$T = \frac{\Sigma x l_x m_x}{\Sigma l_x m_x} = \frac{\Sigma x l_x m_x}{R_0}.$$

In this expression, $x l_x m_x$ is the age of the female times the average reproductive contribution for that age class. The total of the product divided by the total reproduction of that generation (R_0) gives the average age of females reproducing, weighted by the amount of reproduction of each age class. The value of T can now be used in the expression $r = \ln R_0/T$ to calculate r.

It is possible to get a more accurate estimate of the r associated with any $l_x m_x$ schedule by substituting trial values of r until a solution is found to Euler's formula:

$$\Sigma_{x=0}^{\infty} l_x m_x e^{-rx} = 1.$$

This involves calculating an e^{-rx} value for each age class (x), multiplying by the $l_x m_x$ value, and summing the products. The procedure for getting an estimate of T and then r, and then using the latter as a starting point for trials for getting a more accurate r is shown in Table 4-2. The data are for a hypothetical organism with overlapping generations, an R_0 of 1.85 and a generation time of about one and a half months. Only the first trial calculation is shown in the table (Columns 5 and 6). The calculated value for r (0.408) will, of course, only be realized when the age composition of the population is stable.

Note that the more precise estimate of r obtained with Euler's formula now permits a more accurate estimate of the generation time (T):

$$r = \frac{\ln R_0}{T} =$$

$$0.408 = \frac{0.615}{T}$$

$T = 1.51$ (0.10 months shorter than the original estimate, 1.61).

The relationships of R_0, r, and T permit us to say something about the effects of age of reproduction on population growth. If reproduction occurs earlier, T becomes shorter; if reproduction is delayed, T naturally becomes longer. But how much effect this has on r depends on the magnitude of $\ln R_0$. When R_0 is larger, a shift in generation time from, say, 20 years to 30 years greatly reduces r (slows population growth). As R_0 approaches 1, however, $\ln R_0$ approaches 0, and the influence of an increase of T from 20 to 30 years is minimal. This can be seen in Table 4-3, which shows the difference between r for 20- and 30-year generation times and different values of R_0.

From this result it can be seen that delaying the onset of reproduction (increasing T) may be a useful strategy for slowing the growth of a rapidly growing population; but the closer a population is to ZPG, the less effective this strategy will be.

TABLE 4-2

x	1 l_x	2 m_x	3(=1 × 2) $l_x m_x$	4(=1 × 3) $x l_x m_x$	5 $e^{-0.383x}$	6(=5 × 3) $e^{-0.383x} l_x m_x$
0	1.00	0.00	0.00	0.00	1.00	0.000
1	0.80	1.25	1.00	1.00	0.68	0.680
2	0.60	1.00	0.60	1.20	0.46	0.276
3	0.30	0.75	0.23	0.69	0.32	0.074
4	0.10	0.20	0.02	0.08	0.22	0.004
5	0.00	0.00	0.00	0.00	0.15	0.000
			1.85	2.97		1.034

$\Sigma l_x m_x = R_0 = 1.85$
$\Sigma x l_x m_x = 2.97$

$$T \doteq \frac{2.97}{1.85} = 1.61$$

$$r \doteq \frac{0.615}{1.61} = 0.383.$$

When $r = 0.383$, $\Sigma_{x=0}^{\infty} l_x m_x e^{-rx} = 1.034$.
When $r = 0.400$, $\Sigma_{x=0}^{\infty} l_x m_x e^{-rx} = 1.013$.
When $r = 0.410$, $\Sigma_{x=0}^{\infty} l_x m_x e^{-rx} = 0.995$.
When $r = 0.408$, $\Sigma_{x=0}^{\infty} l_x m_x e^{-rx} = 1.001$.

TABLE 4-3
Effects of Generation Time (T) on r

R_0	$\ln R_0$	$r_1(T = 20)$	$r_2(T = 30)$	$r_1 - r_2$
2.00	0.693	0.0347	0.0231	0.0116
1.50	0.405	0.0203	0.0135	0.0068
1.10	0.095	0.0048	0.0032	0.0016
1.05	0.049	0.0024	0.0016	0.0008
1.00	0.000	0.0000	0.0000	0.0000

BOX 4-5 Life Tables

Age-specific death rates in a population—especially a human population—are often presented in the form of life tables. Such tables are of great interest to the actuaries employed by insurance companies and to government planners. Also, as described in the text, if the l_x data in a life table are combined with the m_x data of a fertility table, the net reproductive rate R_0 is easy to calculate.

The 1973 life tables for males and females in the United States are given in Table 4-4 and Table 4-5. The source of the data is the United States National Center for Health Statistics. The explanation of the columns that follows is from the same source, slightly modified. Note, in particular, how the key variable, the life expectancy $\mathring{e}_x$, is calculated.

Column 1, "Age Interval" $(x–x + n)$. Column 1 gives the interval between the two exact ages indicated. For instance, "20–25" means the five-year interval between the twentieth birthday and the twenty-fifth.

Column 2, "Proportion Dying" $({}_nq_x)$. This column shows the proportion of a cohort who are alive at the beginning of an indicated age interval who will die before reaching the end of that age interval. For example, for males in the age interval 20–25, the proportion dying is 0.0111. Of every 1000 males alive and exactly 20 years old at the beginning of the period, 11.1 will die before reaching their twenty-fifth birthdays. The ${}_nq_x$ values represent *probabilities* that persons who are alive at the beginning of a specific age interval will die before reaching the beginning of the next age interval. They are the age-specific death rates. The "Proportion Dying" column forms the basis of the life table; the life table is so constructed that all other columns are derived from it.

Column 3, "Number Surviving" (l_x). This column shows the number of persons, starting with a cohort of 100,000 live births, who survive to the exact age marking the beginning of each age interval. The l_x values are computed from the ${}_nq_x$ values, which are successively applied to the remainder of the original 100,000 persons still alive at the beginning of each age interval. Thus, of 100,000 male babies born alive, 98,022 complete the first year of life and enter the second; 97,674 begin the sixth year; 96,405 reach age 20; and 13,662 live to age 85. In life tables the l_x schedule is often given as the probability of reaching an age interval (the proportion of individuals reaching that interval), as in Table 4-1.

Column 4, "Number Dying" $({}_nd_x)$ shows the number dying in each successive age interval out of 100,000 live births. Of 100,000 males born alive, 1978 die in the first year of life, 348 in the succeeding four years, 1068 in the five-year period between exact ages 20 and 25, and 13,662 die after reaching age 85. Each figure in Column 4 is the difference between two successive figures in Column 3.

Columns 5 and 6, "Stationary Population" $({}_nL_x$ and $T_x)$. Suppose that a group of 100,000 individuals is born every year and that the proportion that dies in each such group in each age interval throughout the lives of the members is exactly that shown in Column 2. If there were no migration and if the births were evenly distributed over the calendar year, the survivors of those births would make up a population that is both stationary and stable. It is stationary because in such a population the total number of persons is constant, and stable because the number of persons living in any given age group is constant. When an individual leaves the group, either by death or by growing older and entering the next higher age group, that person's place would immediately be taken by someone entering from the next lower age group. Thus, a census taken at any time in a stationary and stable community would always show the same total population and the same numerical distribution of that population among the various age groups. In such a stationary population, supported by 100,000 annual births, Column 3 shows the number of persons who, each year, reach the birthday that marks the beginning of the age interval indicated in Column 1, and Column 4 shows the number of persons who die each year in the indicated age interval. The sum of Column 4 must of course be 100,000, or the population would not be stationary.

Column 5 shows the number of persons in the stationary population in the indicated age interval. For example, the figure given for males in the age interval 20–25 is 479,389. This means that in a stationary population of males supported by 100,000 annual births and with the proportion dying in each age group always in accordance with Column 2, a census taken on any date would show 479,389 persons between exact ages 20 and 25.

Column 6 shows the total number of persons in the stationary population (Column 5) in the indicated age interval and all subsequent age intervals. For example, in the stationary population of males referred to in the discussion of Column 5 preceding, Column 6 shows that there would be at any given moment a total of 4,808,611 per-

TABLE 4-4

Life Table of Males in the United States, 1973

Age interval (years)	*Proportion of persons alive at the beginning of the age interval who die during that interval*	*Of 100,000 born alive*		*Stationary population*		*Average number of years of life remaining at the beginning of the age interval*
		INDIVIDUALS LIVING AT BEGINNING OF THE AGE INTERVAL	INDIVIDUALS DYING DURING AGE INTERVAL	INDIVIDUALS IN THE AGE INTERVAL	INDIVIDUALS IN THIS AND ALL SUBSEQUENT AGE INTERVALS	
1	**2**	**3**	**4**	**5**	**6**	**7**
x–$x+n$	${}_nq_x$	l_x	${}_nd_x$	${}_nL_x$	T_x	$\mathring{e}_x$
0–1	0.0198	100,000	1,978	98,241	6,756,651	67.6
1–5	0.0035	98,022	348	391,259	6,658,410	67.9
5–10	0.0024	97,674	236	487,740	6,267,151	64.2
10–15	0.0026	97,438	251	486,640	5,779,411	59.3
15–20	0.0080	97,187	782	484,160	5,292,771	54.5
20–25	0.0111	96,405	1,068	479,389	4,808,611	49.9
25–30	0.0103	95,337	983	474,222	4,329,222	45.4
30–35	0.0111	94,354	1,047	469,259	3,855,000	40.9
35–40	0.0151	93,307	1,411	463,244	3,385,741	36.3
40–45	0.0225	91,896	2,066	454,698	2,922,497	31.8
45–50	0.0360	89,830	3,238	441,672	2,467,799	27.5
50–55	0.0538	86,592	4,656	422,019	2,026,127	23.4
55–60	0.0854	81,936	6,996	393,097	1,604,108	19.6
60–65	0.1266	74,940	9,490	351,961	1,211,011	16.2
65–70	0.1795	65,450	11,750	298,605	859,050	13.1
70–75	0.2564	53,700	13,771	234,454	560,455	10.4
75–80	0.3610	39,929	14,416	163,517	325,991	8.2
80–85	0.4645	25,513	11,851	96,792	162,474	6.4
85+	1.0000	13,662	13,662	65,682	65,682	4.8

sons who had passed their twentieth birthdays. The population at all ages 0 and older (in other words, the total population of the stationary community) would be 6,756,651.

Column 7, "Average Remaining Lifetime" ($\mathring{e}_x$). The average remaining lifetime (also called expectation of life) at any given age is the average number of years remaining to be lived by those surviving to that age, calculated on the basis of a given set of age-specific rates of dying. In order to arrive at this value, it is first necessary to observe that the figures in Column 5 of the life table can also be interpreted in terms of a single life-table cohort without introducing the concept of the stationary population. From this point of view, each figure in Column 5 represents the total time (in years) lived between two indicated birthdays by all those reaching the earlier birthday among the survivors of a cohort of 100,000 live births. Thus, the figure 479,389 for males in the age interval 20–25 is the total number of years lived between the twentieth and twenty-fifth birthdays by the 96,405 (Column 3) males (of the 100,000 born alive) who reached the twentieth birthday. The corresponding figure in Column 6 (4,808,611) is the total number of years lived after attaining age 20 by the 96,405 reaching that age. This number of years divided by the number of persons surviving (4,808,611 divided by 96,405) gives 49.9 years as the average remaining lifetime of males at age 20.

(*Continued*)

BOX 4-5 (*Continued*)

TABLE 4-5
Life Table of Females in the United States, 1973

Age interval (years)	*Proportion of persons alive at the beginning of the age interval who die during that interval*	*Of 100,000 born alive*		*Stationary population*		*Average number of years of life remaining at the beginning of the age interval*
		INDIVIDUALS LIVING AT BEGINNING OF THE AGE INTERVAL	INDIVIDUALS DYING DURING AGE INTERVAL	INDIVIDUALS IN THE AGE INTERVAL	INDIVIDUALS IN THIS AND ALL SUBSEQUENT AGE INTERVALS	
1	**2**	**3**	**4**	**5**	**6**	**7**
x–$x+n$	${}_nq_x$	l_x	${}_nd_x$	${}_nL_x$	T_x	$\mathring{e}_x$
0–1	0.0154	100,000	1,536	98,641	7,527,880	75.3
1–5	0.0028	98,464	275	393,190	7,429,239	75.5
5–10	0.0017	98,189	169	490,482	7,036,049	71.7
10–15	0.0015	98,020	143	489,761	6,545,567	66.8
15–20	0.0031	97,877	299	488,685	6,055,806	61.9
20–25	0.0036	97,578	352	487,040	5,567,121	57.1
25–30	0.0040	97,226	393	485,191	5,080,081	52.3
30–35	0.0055	96,833	532	482,909	4,594,890	47.5
35–40	0.0084	96,301	812	479,607	4,111,981	42.7
40–45	0.0036	95,489	1,238	474,555	3,632,374	38.0
45–50	0.0200	94,251	1,888	466,843	3,157,819	33.5
50–55	0.0287	92,363	2,652	455,552	2,690,976	29.1
55–60	0.0436	89,711	3,911	439,370	2,235,424	24.9
60–65	0.0625	85,800	5,361	416,373	1,796,054	20.9
65–70	0.0910	80,439	7,321	384,903	1,379,681	17.2
70–75	0.1468	73,118	10,735	340,102	994,778	13.6
75–80	0.2366	62,383	14,762	276,405	654,676	10.5
80–85	0.3450	47,621	16,429	196,873	378,271	7.9
85+	1.0000	31,192	31,192	181,398	181,398	5.8

stable age composition once the vital rates became constant. And, *with NRR = 1, population growth would not cease until the age composition stabilized.*

Furthermore, only when there is a stable age composition is a population growing truly exponentially, that is, according to the equation

$$N(t) = N(0)e^{rt}.$$

In many human populations, growth is close enough to exponential that if you know r—that is, $b - d$—you can calculate a doubling time (Box 4-2) without significant error. Where the age composition is far from stable, however, the calculated r and doubling time would be very misleading. For instance, in the United States in the early 1970s, there was a sudden change in net reproductive rate, and the age composition was very different from the stable composition that ordinarily would be associated with the new NRR. Thus, while the difference between birth rate and death rate in 1974 (about 0.6 percent) indicated a doubling time of approximately 120 years, in fact, if the NRR remained constant, population growth would have stopped in about seventy-five years with less than a 50 percent increase in population.

If you read Box 4-3, you saw that the finite rate of increase (λ) can in theory vary from zero (when the population goes extinct) to plus infinity (the population size is increasing infinitely rapidly). Between zero and one the population size is shrinking; at one it is stationary (neither growing or shrinking); and above one it is growing. By contrast, the instantaneous rate of increase r is between zero and plus infinity if the population is increasing, zero and minus infinity if it is decreasing, and zero if it is stationary (if it has reached ZPG).

Population Structure

Very frequently ecologists wish to know what factors are influencing population size. They may need the information to design a system for exploiting a valued resource such as a stock of food fishes. Or they may wish to manipulate the population sizes of other economically important organisms—for instance, to suppress a dangerous crop pest or a vector of disease, or to increase the population size of a pollinator or a predator on pests. Whenever the dynamics of an organism is to be investigated for any reason, some of the most important data are those giving information on *population structure.* In the most general sense, population structure is simply all the factors that influence the way in which matings occur in a population. It includes such elements as age composition, mating preferences, and the patterns of distribution and movement. The latter patterns are considered in this section.

Suppose the populations of two species, the white rhinoceros of Africa and the Sumatran rhinoceros of Southeast Asia, were reduced to seventy-five individuals each. Which would have the best chance of survival? Everything else being equal, you would have to bet on the white rhino because of its population structure. It lives in herds, so mates would have little problem in finding one another (often a difficulty when a population size drops below a critical point). By contrast, the Sumatran rhino lives alone in territories, and mating apparently occurs by chance encounter during an annual period of wandering over huge areas.[10] Thus, reduction in population size is bound to have more serious consequences for this rhino than for the white rhino. Indeed, this species is severely threatened today—its numbers have been reduced to perhaps between 100 and 170 individuals, scattered over much of Southeast Asia, where expansion of human populations has led to a rapid destruction of suitable habitat. Furthermore, like other Asian rhinoceroses, the Sumatran rhino is still hunted because of the use of its horn, hide, most organs, and even urine, by Chinese pharmacists. (Many Chinese, who make up a substantial portion of the Southeast Asian population, hold a traditional belief in rhinoceros horn as a potent aphrodisiac.)[11]

It is not uncommon to find many different population structures in the same group of organisms. In California one kind of checkerspot butterfly, *Euphydryas editha,* tends to divide into many rather small populations that rarely exchange individuals. A nearly indistinguishable species occurring in the same area, *Euphydryas chalcedona,* moves around more, and its populations occupy larger areas.[12] Both of these species have small, restricted populations, however, in contrast to a nearly ubiquitous subalpine butterfly of the Rocky Mountains, *Erebia epipsodea.* Populations of *E. epipsodea* cover such enormous areas that individuals separated by more than 10 kilometers may be members of the same interbreeding unit, whereas individuals of *E. editha* separated by only 0.5 kilometers may belong to different units.[13]

A totally different pattern has been found in the long-lived tropical butterfly *Heliconius ethilla.* The temperate-zone butterflies mentioned above apparently wander more or less at random over areas where nectar sources for the adults and food plants for the larvae are widely distributed. The *Heliconius,* by contrast, have relatively ritualized daily movements. Much of their time is spent moving among widely scattered plants from which the adults collect pollen. The pollen provides amino acids which allow the butterflies to live for several months as adults. Individual *Heliconius* set up "trap lines" and move in patterns determined by whatever plants are blooming at a given time. Population units seem to consist of clus-

[10]G. E. Hutchinson and S. D. Ripley, Gene dispersal and the ethology of the Rhinocerotidae, *Evolution,* vol. 8 (1954), pp. 178–179.

[11]J. Fisher, N. Simon, and J. Vincent, *Wildlife in danger,* Viking, New York, 1969.

[12]Paul R. Ehrlich, R. White, M. Singer, S. McKechnie, and L. Gilbert, Checkerspot butterflies: A historical perspective, *Science* vol. 188 (1975), pp. 221–228 (April 18).

[13]P. F. Brussard, and Paul R. Ehrlich, Contrasting population biology of two species of butterfly, *Nature,* vol. 227 (1970) pp. 119–129.

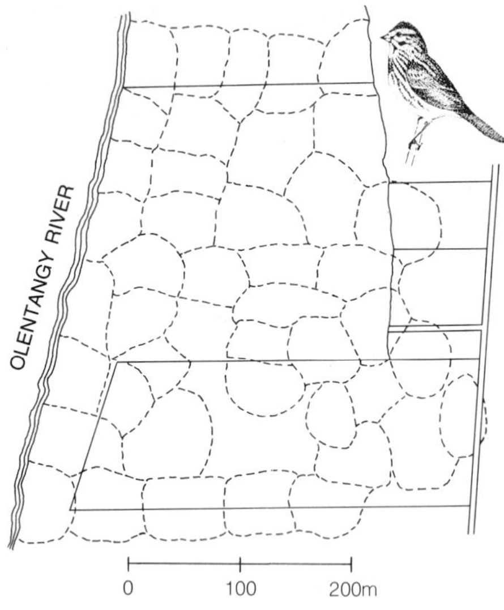

FIGURE 4-8

Territoriality in the song sparrow. The map shows dimensions and positions of territories on a tree-dotted floodplain at Columbus, Ohio (April 6, 1932). Broken lines enclose territories of forty-four males. (Adapted from Nice, 1937.)

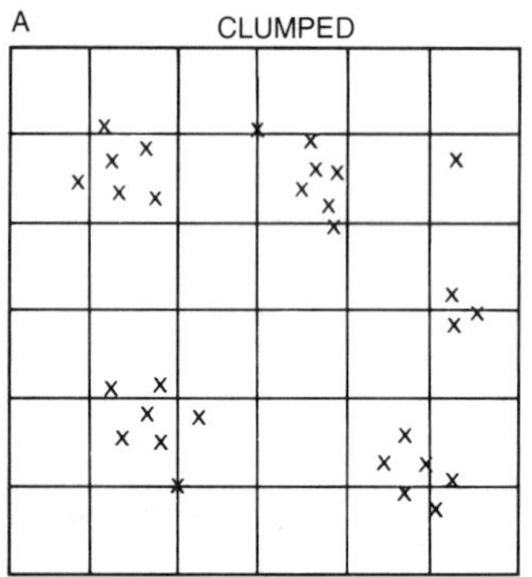

FIGURE 4-9

Kinds of distribution, Each × indicates the position of one hypothetical individual. Note that the number of empty squares increases as one goes from overdispersed to random to clumped distribution (each example includes thirty individuals).

ters of more or less circular trap lines, and movements of more than 400 meters are apparently rare.[14]

The patterned movements of *Heliconius* butterflies are also characteristic of some tropical bees with widely scattered pollen resources. But such movements are much more common among vertebrates, where an individual concentrates its activities within a single area, the *home range.* Frequently the home range, or a portion of it, is defended against other members of the same species or, more rarely, members of other species. The defended portion of the home range is called a *territory.* Territoriality may be a year-round phenomenon, as it is with many small pomacentrid fishes of coral reefs, individuals of which defend a small area of the reef against all comers (including human beings 25 or more times their length!) the year round. Other organisms may defend their territories for only a brief, specific period, usually the breeding season. For instance, many male birds maintain territories during the breeding season (their songs are announcements of intent to defend and readiness to breed), but they flock together peacefully when not breeding. *Homo sapiens*—popular literature to the contrary—does not show individual territoriality in the same sense that these other animals do.[15]

The reasons that territoriality evolved seem varied and as yet are not entirely understood. But at least one result of territoriality is clear—it tends to space individuals more or less evenly over an area (Figure 4-8). Since most territories can only be compressed so far, this also tends to limit the maximum size of a population, often keeping it well below the limits of food resources. Much may be inferred about the behavior of particular animal populations merely by plotting their distributions (Figure 4-9). If individuals are clumped (Figure 4-9A), they are probably social; if they are overdispersed (Figure 4-9C), territoriality is likely; and if they are randomly distributed (Figure 4-9B), they probably have a minimum of interaction. There are statistical tests that can distinguish these three states, tests that are applied to counts of individuals in grid squares. If there are some squares with many individuals and many with none, it indicates social groupings;

[14]Paul R. Ehrlich and L. E. Gilbert, Population structure and dynamics of the tropical butterfly *Heliconius ethilla, Biotropica,* vol. 5 (1973), pp. 69–87.

[15]For a discussion of territoriality in human beings and its relationship to territoriality in general, see E. O. Wilson, *Sociobiology.*

if most squares have one or a few individuals, that indicates territoriality. But the scale of the grid must be selected with care. On the scale of a single woodland, a population of tree-nesting birds might seem overdispersed; but on the scale of a state they might appear to be clumped, because woodlands are clumped.

Dispersion is the term for the three patterns of individual distribution just discussed; *dispersal* is the movement of individuals into and out of population units. Knowledge of dispersion can have practical application in interpreting the dynamics of populations that are important to humanity. Information on dispersal is important because, as we discuss later, invasions of communities by alien organisms may have a dramatic effect upon those communities, often to the detriment of humanity. The ability of organisms or of their propagules (eggs, seeds, and such) to move is their *vagility.* The chances for successful dispersal of an organism from one area to another depends on the vagility of the organism, the presence of barriers (for example, water for a terrestrial organism, lowlands for a mountain organism, dry land for a fish), and the availability of suitable habitat in the new area.

Mankind, of course, has played a major role in the dispersal of organisms, especially in the past century. Many plants have seeds that stick in the coats of passing mammals and are thus dispersed. Such seeds also tend to be dispersed readily on the clothes people wear. Other plants have moved around the world as seeds mixed in with the ballast of ships or with fodder carried for domestic animals on ships and trains. And, of course, many plants have been purposely transplanted, often carrying with them unwanted insects or other animals. People have also purposely dispersed animals, frequently with unhappy results (see "Extinction, Endangered Species, and Invasions," below).

Data on the Dynamics of Natural Populations

Unfortunately, relatively few sets of data on natural populations are useful in testing the theory of population dynamics. There are several reasons for this. First, censusing animals is usually difficult. Rarely is straightforward counting possible, so various procedures for estimating numbers must be employed. One technique used frequently is mark-release-recapture analysis. Individuals are marked in some way (with butterflies, coded numbers are put on the wings with felt-tipped pens), released, and allowed to mix back in with the population. Later a second sample group is taken. Suppose 100 individuals were captured and marked the first time, and, of a later sample of 100 captured, 10 had been marked previously. Then, assuming the equivalence of the ratios

$$\frac{\text{population size } (N)}{\text{sample marked } (S_1)} = \frac{\text{second sample taken } (S_2)}{\text{number of marked recaptures } (R)},$$

we can estimate N as

$$N = \frac{S_1 \times S_2}{R}.$$

Or, in our example:

$$N = \frac{100 \times 100}{10} = 1000.$$

This simple estimate is based on the assumption that if 100 marked individuals (marks) made up 10 percent of a population, the population must have 1000 individuals. Of course, in real life things are not so simple —statistical errors enter with the sampling, the marks may not mix randomly with the remainder of the population or they may be more or less readily captured than unmarked individuals, and there may be recruitment or loss to the population between the first and second samplings. Various procedures have been developed to help compensate for these problems, and despite the difficulties, mark-release-recapture analysis is widely used.

In addition to estimates of population size, this technique also provides information on population structure —for instance, the statements about butterfly population structures made earlier were based on experiments in which many thousands of individuals were marked and released. Data obtained from these experiments can also be used to estimate survivorship and longevity. For example, while temperate-zone butterflies live as adults for an average of perhaps two weeks, the tropical *Heliconius ethilla* are much longer lived—averaging about two months, with some surviving five months or more.

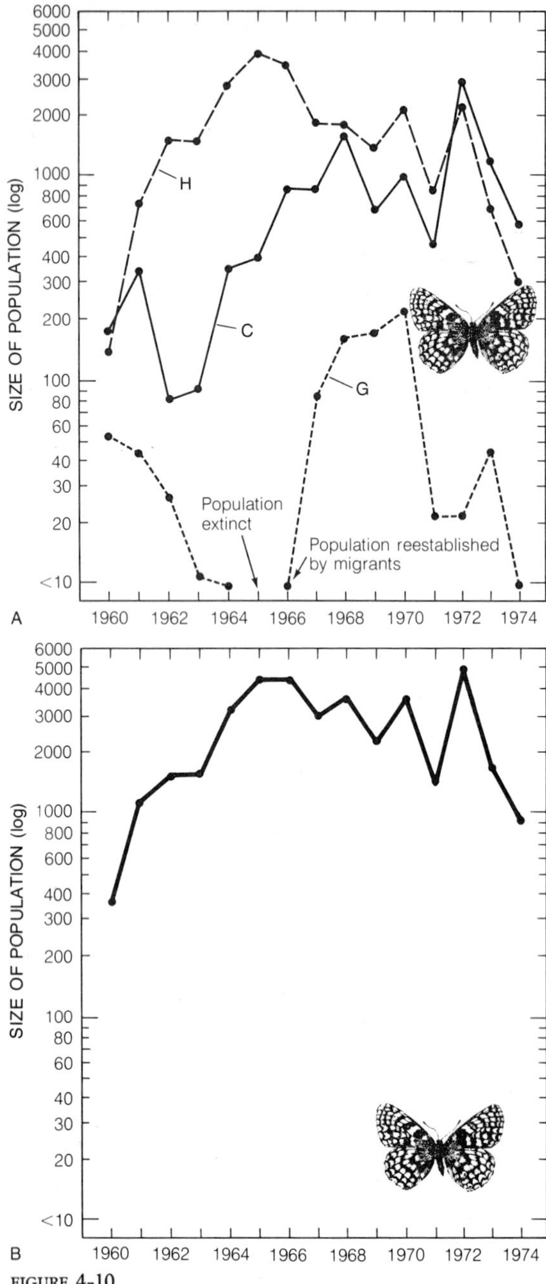

FIGURE 4-10

Changes in the size of the Jasper Ridge colony of checkerspot butterflies, *Euphydryas editha.* A. Three populations (areas C, G, and H) are plotted separately. There are discrete generations, one per year. Parents and offspring never fly together. Note two extinctions and one reestablishment of G population. B. The total size of the Jasper Ridge colony (populations C, G, and H summed). The extinctions are not detectable, so important information on the dynamics of the three units is lost.

The temperate-zone species described have only one generation per year, so their generations do not overlap. The *Heliconius* do have overlapping generations; grandparents fly with their adult grandchildren.

The importance of understanding population structure when interpreting data on population dynamics can be seen by examining changes in the size of the *Euphydryas editha* populations diagramed in Figure 4-10. When studies of the dynamics of *E. editha* were begun in 1960, it was thought that there was only a single population in the Jasper Ridge biological experimental area on Stanford University's campus. A capture-recapture analysis that year revealed that what had been thought to be a single population were three quite isolated populations. These populations occupied different parts of an island of grassland surrounded by chaparral (see the discussion under "Biomes," below) and were not separated by any obvious barriers.[16] What would have happened had this structure been overlooked and the entire three-population colony been treated as a dynamic unit? For one thing, the extinction and reestablishment of Population G would not have been detected, and for another the constancy of the overall population size would have been exaggerated (note that the line in Figure 4-10 showing changes in the total size of the colony is much smoother than that of any of the individual populations).

Why is this so important? Most of the effort in population ecology goes into attempting to understand why populations change in size as they do. Ecologists wish to understand how various environmental factors influence population size so they can predict future sizes and—where it is economically important—manipulate factors to influence future population sizes. They wish to reduce populations of pests and increase populations of beneficial organisms. One of the main ways of finding out what affects population size is to correlate observed changes in size with observed changes in an environment. But, as with the *E. editha,* if two or more populations are lumped together, an erroneous picture of changes in population size may be drawn. This is especially critical because it is thought that the influence of environmental factors on populations size *is in part a function of popula-*

[16]Paul R. Ehrlich, The population biology of the butterfly, *Euphydryas editha:* pt. 2, The structure of the Jasper Ridge colony, *Evolution,* vol. 14 (1965), pp. 327–336.

tion size; that is, the populations respond to the environment *in a density-dependent manner.*[17] For instance, the larger an animal population is, the less likely a given individual is to have an abundant food supply or a satisfactory place to shelter from the weather. Thus the availability for each individual of both food and shelter —as well as other resources—may be density-dependent.

The more that environmental factors have density-dependent effects, the less variation you would expect in the size of a population. As a population increased, the life of the average individual would become increasingly precarious, reproduction would diminish, and the population size would begin to fall. When it decreased far enough, resources per individual would become abundant again, life would be more secure, and the population would tend to increase again. The more sensitive the operation of the factors to density, the less variation may occur in population size. Thus, erroneously lumping populations C, G, and H of Jasper Ridge *E. editha* would produce data much more indicative of a density-dependent "regulation" of population size than would be warranted by the actual behavior of the individual populations.

There is no more enduring controversy in population ecology than that over whether the sizes of populations are generally regulated in a density-dependent manner.[18] Ecologists who work with insects tend to believe that the feedback effect from density on population size is minimal. Those who study territorial organisms like birds are often impressed by the way availability of space for territories regulates the sizes at least of breeding populations in a density-dependent fashion. An additional complication is that populations differ genetically and may change in their genetic compositions from generation to generation. (This concept is discussed further under "Natural Selection and Evolution.") Some workers claim that there is *genetic feedback,* because the genetic makeup of a population affects its density. Changes in population density affect the environment, which in turn (through natural selection) changes the genetic makeup of the population.

Detailed studies of *E. editha* populations indicate that, within the same species, density may have very little influence on population size in some cases, whereas in other populations it may be very important. Furthermore, there is evidence that the importance of density may change from generation to generation.[19] It seems likely that few great generalities about modes of population regulation are possible. It is obvious that at some point the growth of *any* population will be halted by factors operating in a density-dependent manner, because no resource is infinite. It is also obvious that the carrying capacity will always vary through time. But, below that point, the degree to which density at generation n will influence density at generation $n + 1$ appears to vary greatly among organisms, among populations of the same organism, and even, in some cases, between generations of the same population. Beyond that, population ecology may have to concentrate on developing procedures for investigating dynamics.[20] The reasons that populations of both Australian magpies (Figure 4-11) and *Heliconius ethilla* (Figure 4-12) are relatively constant in size may be quite different, but the approach to discovering what the critical factors are and making predictions about population sizes in the future can be very similar in both cases.

The definition of population units, for instance, is important in both cases. (This, we must repeat, is basic. For example, failure to determine whether the Peruvian anchoveta fishery is exploiting one population or two has made rational planning of that exploitation difficult.) A search for limiting factors can then be made. (It looks as if space for territories, operating in a density-dependent fashion, is the critical factor for the magpies. The situation of the *Heliconius* butterflies is more complex, but adult pollen resources appear to limit the population, also in a density-dependent fashion.)

[17]Population density is technically the number of individuals per unit area, but, since most populations have limited space, an increase in population size automatically means an increase in density. Thus *density-dependent* and *population-size–dependent* are usually synonymous, and the former is the accepted expression.

[18]An excellent, brief historical summary of the controversy can be found in Krebs, *Ecology,* p. 270–286.

[19]Ehrlich, et al., Checkerspot butterflies.

[20]The landmark publication in this area is H. G. Andrewartha and L. C. Birch, *The distribution and abundance of animals.* This book is a must for all serious students of ecology. Among other things, the authors' classification of environmental factors into four components (1) weather, (2) food, (3) other animals and pathogens, and (4) a place to live was a conceptual breakthrough. A broader classification that can be used for plant populations as well appears in Ehrlich, et al., *The process of evolution,* p. 84.

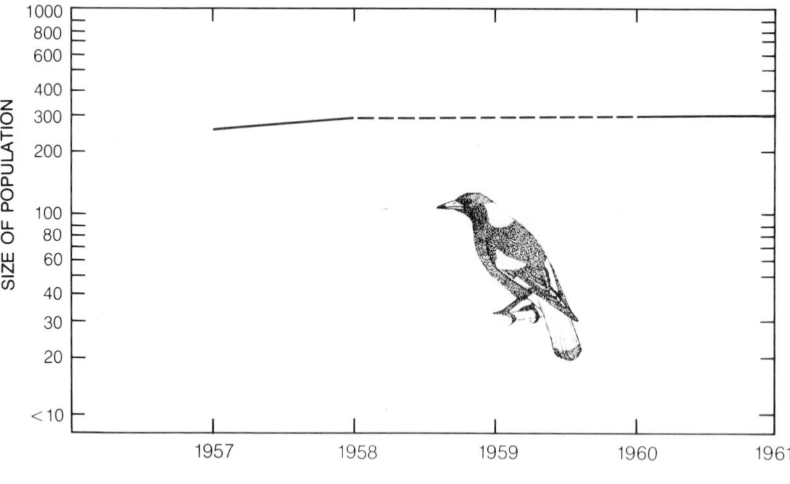

FIGURE 4-11

Changes in the size of a population of magpies, *Gymnorhina tibicen,* near Canberra, Australia. Individual birds may live for many years. The broken line indicates a significant gap in sampling. (Data from Carrick, *Proceedings of the Thirteenth International Ornithological Congress,* 1963, p. 750.)

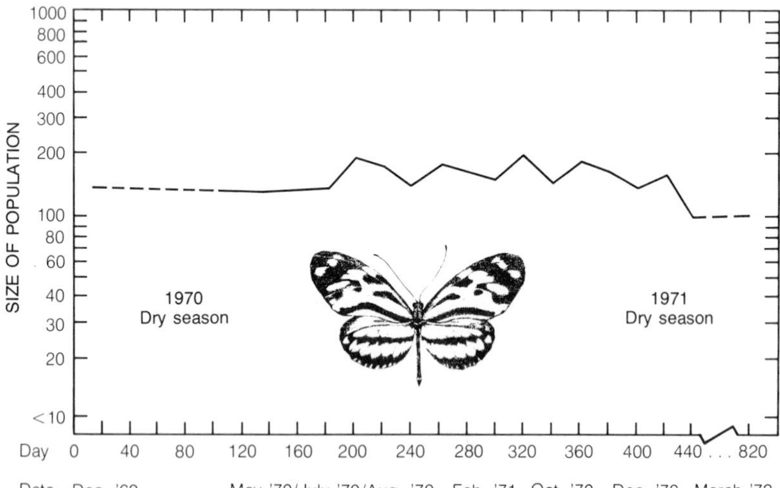

FIGURE 4-12

Changes in the size of a population of *Heliconius* butterflies, *H. ethilla,* in the mountains of northern Trinidad. Adults are long-lived (up to six months), and generations overlap; grandparents may fly alongside their grandchildren.

Multi-Species Systems

Very often population ecologists are concerned with the simultaneous behavior of two interacting populations. A great deal of attention has been paid, for example, to predator-prey systems. In part this is a response to such fascinating phenomena as the partially linked cyclic changes in the abundance of prey and specialist predators—Canadian snowshoe rabbits and lynxes, for example. In part it results from the need to understand such systems when attempting to introduce predators as biological controls of pests. Of most direct interest in human ecology are the interacting dynamics of human populations with parasites such as the plague bacterium and the influenza virus.[21]

Sometimes the dynamics of two or more populations are intertwined in a competitive situation. Competition occurs whenever two or more organisms utilize a common resource that is in short supply. Both predation and competition have been studied extensively in the laboratory, since both appear to be very important in determining the structures of natural communities. For example, competition between two species of flour beetles, *Tribolium castaneum* and *Tribolium confusum,* was stud-

[21]See K. E. F. Watt, *Ecology and resource management,* chapter 5.

ied in a series of experiments. The basic technique was to start mixed colonies in containers of flour and then see which species won the competition by eliminating its competitor under various conditions of initial density, volume of flour, temperature, humidity, the presence or absence of a parasite, and so forth. (A win invariably occurred—the two species will not coexist.)

In experiments in which temperature and humidity were varied, it was found that under some conditions *T. castaneum* always won; under other conditions *T. confusum* always won; and in intermediate conditions the outcome was "indeterminant"—sometimes *T. castaneum* won and sometimes *T. confusum.*[22] The indeterminant results proved to be caused by genetic differences in competitive ability within the species of beetles. Beetles can be selected for ability to compete; strains exist of *T. castaneum,* for instance, that invariably win in the temperature-humidity range previously thought to be indeterminant.[23] The outcome under intermediate conditions was actually determined by the genetic characteristics of the individuals used to start each culture.

One of the shortcomings of ecology in its earlier days was a tendency to ignore the genetic properties of populations under study (it was geneticists, not ecologists, who first pointed out indeterminacy as a probable cause in the flour beetle experiments). In order to understand certain key aspects of ecology, it is important to have at least a passing acquaintance with the genetic properties of populations and how they change through time—that is, an acquaintance with natural selection and evolution.

The Dynamics of Exploited Populations

Often the ecologist interested in population dynamics is asked to recommend a pattern of exploitation of some economically valuable animal population such as a fishery. Although an extensive and complex literature exists on this topic, we can only mention a few points about it here.[24] First of all, just what form the exploitation will take must be decided. In many, if not most cases, the problem from a biological point of view seems to be to design an exploitative program so that a *maximum sustainable yield* (MSY) is obtained. A maximum sustainable yield is the greatest amount of a population being exploited (fish, whale, deer, or whatever) that can be harvested without reducing future yields. MSY can be defined in terms of total numbers removed, total biomass removed, numbers of a particular age class removed, or biomass of some age class. Obtaining each of these would ordinarily require quite different harvesting strategies. In addition, the exploiter must choose either to maximize the productivity of the population or to minimize the loss to other causes of mortality. In the first case, harvesting might be concentrated on reproducers, minimizing competition for those remaining and inducing high productivity. In the second, harvesting might be concentrated on juvenile individuals because they are most subject to natural mortality.

Consider a simple model for the harvesting of a population following a logistic growth curve (Figure 4-13). A glance at the curve shows that dN/dt is maximal around the middle, where the increasing upward push of r_mN is balanced by the increasing downward push of $(K-N)/K$. ($K =$ carrying capacity.) Under this model, the MSY (numbers) could be harvested merely by removing enough individuals to keep the population size stationary at that point. A sustainable yield (SY, numbers) could be obtained by keeping the population larger or smaller, but in both cases the SY would be smaller than the MSY. Regardless of the strategy of exploitation, the MSY is always obtained by keeping populations below their maximum potential sizes, because production is higher when the population is smaller.

The model presented for MSY makes a number of biological assumptions—such as that the stock being

[22]T. Park, Experimental studies of interspecies competition: pt. 2, Temperature, humidity and competition in two species of *Tribolium, Physiological Zoology,* vol. 27 (1954), pp. 177–238.

[23]I. M. Lerner and F. K. Ho, Genotype and competitive ability of *Tribolium* species, *American Naturalist,* vol. 95 (1961); pp. 329–343; J. Park, P. H. Leslie, and D. E. Mertz, Genetic strains and competition in populations of *Tribolium. Physiological Zoology,* vol. 37 (1964), pp. 97–162. For a fine general treatment of both competition and predation, see the Krebs text, *Ecology,* chapters 12 and 13.

[24]For example, see R. J. N. Beverton and S. J. Holt, *On the dynamics of exploited fish populations,* H.M. Stationery Office, London, 1957; or E. D. LeCren and M. W. Holdgate, eds., *The exploitation of natural animal populations,* Blackwell, Oxford, 1962. A student interested in the dynamics of exploited populations should also refer to Krebs, *Ecology,* and Watt, *Ecology.*

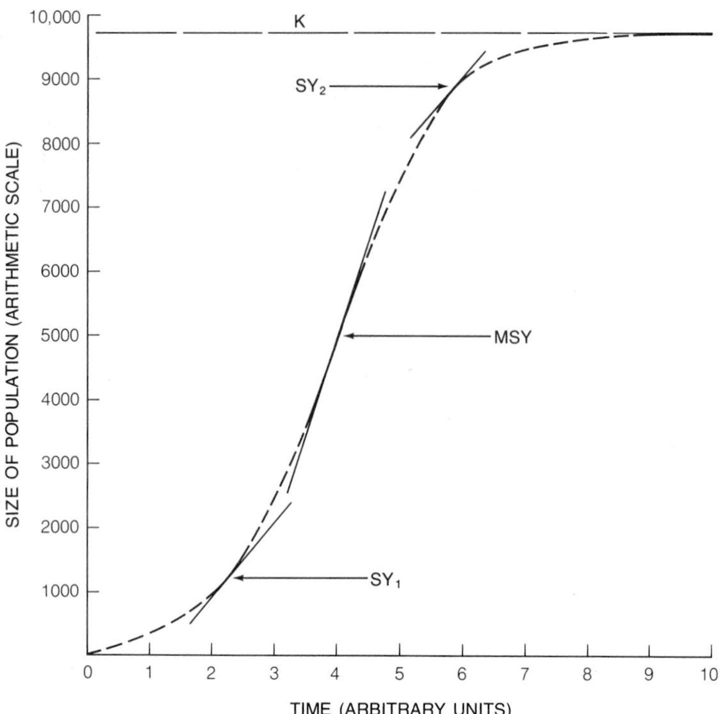

FIGURE 4-13

Sustainable yields in a hypothetical population growing according to the logistic model. The IRI (dN/dt) is indicated by tangents to the curve at three points SY_1, MSY, and SY_2. Note that the maximum sustainable yield (MSY) is obtained at the point where dN/dt is maximum, that is, when the population consists of about 5000 individuals. Sustainable yields at lower (SY_1) and higher (SY_2) population sizes would be smaller.

exploited is relatively self-contained, that K is more or less constant, and that patterns of density-dependence of reproduction do not cause large fluctuations in the amount of stock. It does not consider the social organization of the exploited population or the possible effects of exploitation on the age structure of the population. When such factors are ignored, a pattern of harvesting can lead to a population crash from which no recovery occurs.

More serious, however, is the total absence from the model of economic considerations such as the costs of harvesting, the elasticity of demand for the product, and whether the population exploited is common property (as in an oceanic fishery) or controlled by an owner (a commercial fish pond). When economic factors are included, harvesting is often pushed beyond the biological MSY, since by doing so an economic variable such as receipts can be maximized.[25]

[25]See, for example, J. A. Crutchfield and G. Pontecorvo, *The Pacific salmon fisheries: A study of irrational conservation*, pp. 28–36.

NATURAL SELECTION AND EVOLUTION

Natural selection is the creative process in evolution. It is essentially the differential reproduction of genetic types. In most animal and plant populations and in all human populations, individuals differ because each individual has a different hereditary endowment. For instance, people differ in such traits as eye color, height, and blood type, all of which are at least partially hereditary. If people with one hereditary trait (that is, one kind of genetic information) tend to have more children than those with another, then natural selection is occurring with respect to that trait. Natural selection can cause one kind of genetic information—for example, that producing people with a certain type of hemoglobin—to become more and more common in the pool of genetic information (the gene pool) of a population. This might occur as a response to an environmental change in which mosquitoes carrying malaria become more common, since individuals with one kind of hemoglobin are more resistant to malaria than those with another. Changes in the gene pool of a population constitute the basic process of *evolution.*

It is evident that in the evolutionary history of humanity, for instance, there was a selective trend toward increased brain size. This is a convenient shorthand for a more complete description that might go like this:

> In early human populations there was variation in brain size. This variation was largely caused by differences among individuals in their genetic endowment. Individuals with slightly larger brains were presumably better able to utilize the cultural information of the society. This permitted them readier access to mates, a better chance of surviving, or perhaps a better chance of successfully rearing their offspring; and they reproduced more than did individuals with smaller brains. The result was a gradual increase in the genetic information producing larger brains in the gene pools of human populations. In turn, this increased the capacity for storing cultural information and thus produced a selective advantage for further increase in brain size. This reciprocal evolutionary trend continued until other factors, such as the difficulty of getting the enlarged braincase of a baby through the female's pelvis (which was not commensurately enlarged) at birth, removed the selective premium on further increase in brain size.

Understanding natural selection will help to illuminate a number of points in this book. Chapter 11, for example, discusses the development of resistance to pesticides in insect populations, a process that occurs through natural selection. Individual insects often vary in their natural resistance to a pesticide, and this variation has a genetic basis. Insects that are naturally more resistant have a better chance of surviving, and thus of reproducing, than their less fortunate fellows. In this way an entire population may become more and more resistant when sprayed repeatedly with a pesticide, as in each generation the most resistant individuals do most of the breeding.

A key concept to bear in mind is that natural selection is the differential *reproduction* of genetic types (*genotypes,* in the shorthand of geneticists). Natural selection often involves differential survival, but differentials in reproduction may occur even when the life expectancies of all genotypes remain identical. All may live the same length of time, but some may be relatively sterile while others are highly fertile. Another key point to remember is that natural selection cannot operate unless there is genetic variability in a population. If there is no variation, all individuals are genetically identical and there can be no differential reproduction of genotypes. Such a population would be unlikely to survive for long, since it would lack the ability to make evolutionary adjustments to changed conditions.

The environmental factors that lead to natural selection are called *selective agents.* Changing weather can be a selective agent, leading to an accumulation of genotypes that thrive under new climatic conditions. DDT can be a selective agent, leading to insect populations made up of genotypes resistant to DDT. (In that case, humanity was the ultimate selective agent, but the resultant evolution was undesired.)

Artificial selection occurs when human beings purposely arrange for the differential reproduction of genotypes. Artificial selection is practiced by all plant and animal breeders as they control the differential reproduction of genotypes. The idea is to develop strains in which the characteristics most valuable to society are maximized—weight in swine, milk production in cows, egg production in chickens, shape and durability in tomatoes, height above ground for ears of corn (for ease in harvesting), beauty in flowers, and so on. These strains have undergone evolutionary processes that adapt them for a man-made environment.

Without human assistance, these strains would disappear through extinction or reversion under the countervailing pressure of natural selection. That pressure must always be reckoned with by the plant or animal breeder. Frequently, attempts to enhance a single characteristic too much upset development and diminish fertility; thus, natural selection opposes further progress under the pressure of artificial selection.

Like natural selection, artificial selection can occur only if the requisite genetic variation is present. Biologists and agronomists regard genetic variation in animals and plants as an invaluable resource that must be preserved so that new strains can be selected to meet new needs. As we discuss later, however, some of the richest sources of that variation in important crop plants are being lost at an alarming rate (see Chapter 7).

Evolutionary forces other than natural selection also can change the gene pools of populations. *Mutation* can change one form of a gene into another and thus change the constitution of the gene pool. Immigrants bringing genes into the pool of a population or emigrants taking them out may have genetic constitutions different from the population as a whole, and thus *migration* can change the pool. Both mutation and migration may increase the genetic variability of a population.

Furthermore, chance occurrences, which are inevitably involved in the passage of genetic information from one generation to the next, can also lead to changes in the gene pool. Without going into detail, one can think of the adults of generation $n + 1$ as possessing a sample of the genetic information present in those of generation n. Just as a sample of 100 flips of an honest coin usually will not produce exactly 50 heads because of *sampling error,* so the gene pool of generation $n + 1$ will not be exactly the same as that of generation n, because of sampling error. Because sampling error causes random changes in the frequency of genes in a pool, it is referred to as *genetic drift.*

The magnitude of genetic drift in a population is itself a function of the population's size. The smaller the population, the more important drift is (just as the fewer the flips of the honest coin, the larger the deviation from 50-50 is likely to be). In any sampling, some of the genes present in generation n may not be present in generation $n + 1$—that is, some of the genetic variability may be lost. Such *decay of variability* is especially severe in small populations—making it difficult, say, to maintain the variability of crops by storing small samples of seed.[26]

If a population is greatly reduced by natural catastrophe or hunting, it is likely to suffer a decay of genetic variability. If, for instance, a given gene is represented on the average in 1 of 10,000 individuals, it is highly likely that gene will be lost if the population is reduced to 100 individuals. This loss of genetic variability may greatly reduce the chances that the population can evolve appropriately in response to environmental changes and thus enhances the probability of extinction.

Even if a population increases again in size after undergoing such a genetic bottleneck, the gene pool may remain impoverished for a considerable period. For instance, the northern elephant seal, which lives on the coast of California and Baja California, went through such a bottleneck in the nineteenth century. Its population—now more than 30,000 individuals—may have been reduced to as few as 20 individuals in the 1890s. Investigations of the genes controlling a variety of enzymes indicate that the genetic variability of the population is much less today than that of its subantarctic relative, the southern elephant seal, and that of other vertebrates, and it may therefore be highly vulnerable to environmental change.[27]

Although mutation, migration, and genetic drift are all evolutionary forces, it is important to remember that natural selection is the creative force in evolution. It is selection that shapes populations and species in response to changing environments. And, as will become apparent in the next section of this text, selective interactions are major forces in the evolution of communities.[28]

Coevolution

Predator-prey systems illustrate a situation in which one can expect each population to affect the evolution of the other. When two populations are ecologically intimate, each exerts selective pressure on the other. (See Box 4-6 for descriptions of some other forms of ecological intimacy.) Hence, differential reproduction induced by a predator should bring about improvement in the escape mechanisms of the prey, and, reciprocally, selection in the prey should sharpen a predator's attack.

To put it more precisely, in each generation those genetic variants among the predators that are most

[26]Selection can also reduce variability. Any program of maintaining living samples of organisms to preserve variability inevitably selects for individuals that culture well. This, in turn, tends to reduce variability further.

[27]M. L. Bonnell and R. K. Selander, Elephant seals: Genetic variation and near extinction, *Science,* vol. 184 (1974), pp. 908–909 (May 24).

[28]This discussion of evolution is necessarily greatly simplified and abbreviated. Those interested in more detail may wish to consult Ehrlich et al., *The process of evolution,* especially chapters 6 and 7, which deal with population genetics.

BOX 4-6 Ecological Intimacies

A rather complex terminology has developed around various kinds of relationships between species. Some of the terms most commonly used in the literature are defined below.

PREDATOR. Usually this is applied to an animal that kills and devours other animals (the *prey*). The term is increasingly being used also in place of *herbivore* (plant-eater), especially when the result is the demise of an individual plant (as in *seed-predator*).

HERBIVORE. An animal that eats living plants, whether or not it kills them.

PARASITE. An organism that feeds on another organism *(host)* but normally does not kill it (or kills it only very slowly). Parasites are usually much smaller than their hosts, and predators are often larger than their prey, but the dividing line between predator or herbivore and parasite is sometimes blurred. For instance, parasites usually live out their lives in or on a single host individual, but some insects are confined to a single plant and are generally called herbivores.

PARASITOID. Usually this term is applied to insects that lay eggs on, in, or near other insects or spiders, which are their hosts. The young parasitoids live inside the host, inevitably killing it about the time the parasitoids form their pupae (a resting stage of many insects between larval and adult stages). Like parasites, parasitoids are smaller than their hosts, often more than one lives on a single host, and they do not kill their host quickly. Like predators, they always kill their hosts. Some parasitoids are important agents in biological pest-control programs (see Chapter 11).

MODEL. A distasteful or dangerous organism that another species mimics in order to escape from predation. Models usually have aposematic (warning) coloration that makes them obvious and "advertises" their obnoxious character. In *Batesian mimicry* the mimic is tasty or harmless. In *Mullerian mimicry* models mimic each other, presumably so that predators see the same advertisement associated with obnoxiousness more frequently. Predators then need to sample fewer prey in order to learn the meaning of the advertisement than they would if each model had a different aposematic pattern.

MUTUALISM. Any mutually beneficial association, such as that between two Mullerian mimics or that between a rhinoceros and a tick-bird (the bird gets food by cleaning ticks off the rhinoceros, and the rhinoceros gets rid of its parasites).

COMMENSALISM. An association of two species in which one benefits and the other is not harmed. Tiny mites living in the facial hair follicles of most people with healthy skin are good examples of commensals. Most persons are utterly unaware of the presence of these harmless residents.

SYMBIOSIS. A blanket term for parasitism, commensalism, and mutualism; in older literature it is sometimes used as a synonym for mutualism.

COMPETITION. The utilization of a resource in short supply by two or more individuals or populations. Competition may be *interspecific* (among individuals of differing species) or *intraspecific* (among individuals of a single species).

successful in attacking the prey are likely to be most successful in reproducing, and thus the efficiency of the predator can be expected to increase generation by generation. This does not mean, however, that soon the predator will be so effective that the prey population will be wiped out, for the prey evolves too. In each generation, the prey individuals that escape predation are the ones to reproduce and contribute their genes to posterity.

This kind of point-counterpoint selective process was originally described in detail for butterflies whose caterpillars (herbivores) eat plants (prey). The kinds of reciprocal evolutionary changes found in that system and in similar systems (such as predator-prey, host-parasite, model-mimic, and competitor-competitor systems) were christened *coevolution.*[29] It was pointed out that in such systems the populations were often involved in a coevolutionary race in which extinction of one or the other element was a possibility. The predator, for instance, could become so efficient as to wipe out the prey—or the prey so elusive as to starve the predator.

[29]Paul R. Ehrlich and P. H. Raven, Butterflies and plants: A study of coevolution, *Evolution,* vol. 18 (1964), pp. 586–608.

FIGURE 4-14

Stone plants *(Lithops julii* var. *reticulata)* growing in the desert at Karasburg, Southwest Africa. Various succulent plants of the family Aizoaceae have evolved extraordinarily effective camouflage that makes them closely resemble small stones. (Photo courtesy of Chester Dugdale.)

Understanding the coevolutionary aspects of ecological systems is extremely important to anyone interested in human welfare. The importance can be seen clearly in the relationship between plants and the organisms that attack them. Plants cannot escape their predators by running away, so they have evolved a variety of other defenses. Some, like the stone plants of African deserts (Figure 4-14), have evolved camouflage patterns that make them very difficult to see. More familiar are mechanical defenses against herbivores, especially the sharp spines of such plants as cacti and acacia trees. But the most nearly ubiquitous and seemingly most effective defenses of plants are biochemical.

Plants have evolved a vast array of compounds, such as alkaloids, terpenes, essential oils, tannins, and flavonoids, raphides (needlelike calcium oxalate crystals), and other crystals, all of whose roles appear to be to poison or otherwise discourage the animals, fungi, and bacteria that prey on the plants. These compounds are used by humanity in many ways. They are the active ingredients in spices (many essential oils), medicines (quinine, belladonna, digitalis, morphine), stimulants (caffeine), and other drugs (nicotine, marijuana, opium, peyote). Plant compounds are even used for their primeval purpose—as pesticides (nicotine, pyrethrin).

Insects and other predators on plants have been engaged in a long coevolutionary race with the plants, evolving strategies to avoid being poisoned. Undoubtedly, some have become extinct, but many others have persisted, some running the race so well that they are able not only to eat the poisonous plants, but in some cases even adopt the poisons as part of their own defenses against predators. For example, the monarch butterfly *(Danaus plexippus)* contains vertebrate heart poisons which it obtains from its milkweed food plants.[30] The poisons cause the blue jay predators of the monarch to vomit. Considering their evolutionary experience with poisons, it is not surprising that many wild populations of insects have become resistant to DDT and other pesticides as a result of the indiscriminate use of those poisons.

Plants have been shown to suffer heavy losses to insect predators, and yet there clearly are physiological limits to how much poison the plants can sequester without poisoning themselves or without allocating to poison-production too much of the energy they need for growth, maintenance, and reproduction. At least some plants have shown an interesting evolutionary response to this problem. In the Rocky Mountains of Colorado, populations of lupines and other leguminous plants suffer heavy attacks from the larvae (caterpillars) of small blue (lycaenid) butterflies. These butterflies, with a name longer than their wingspread *(Glaucopsyche lygdamus)*, lay their eggs on the flower buds (Figure 4-15), and their larvae devour the flowers. Of some inflorescences (groups of flowers on a common stalk), 85 percent or more of the flowers are destroyed, with a corresponding loss in seedset.[31] Therefore, considerable selective advantage should accrue to any plant genotypes that are resistant to the insect's attack. (Remember, reproductive success is the result that counts in evolution.) By counting the eggs

[30]T. Reichstein, J. V. Euw, J. A. Parsons, and M. Rothschild, Heart poisons in the monarch *(Danaus plexippus)*, *Science*, vol. 161 (1968), pp. 861–866; and L. P. Brower and S. C. Glazier, Localization of heart poisons in the monarch butterfly, *Science*, vol. 188 (1975), pp. 19–25.

[31]D. E. Breedlove and Paul R. Ehrlich, Coevolution: Patterns of legume predation by a lycaenid butterfly, *Oecologia*, vol. 10 (1972), pp. 99–104.

laid on inflorescences in several lupine populations, it was determined that the level of *Glaucopsyche* attack was much higher in some than in others. A careful analysis of the alkaloid content of plants from the various populations gave a clue to one major reason for this variability. Populations that for other reasons were unavailable to the butterflies contained small amounts of a single alkaloid. Those exposed to attack accumulated much higher amounts of alkaloids in their inflorescences. Of this exposed group, the populations that suffered heavily from predation contained a mixture of nine alkaloids that varied very little from plant to plant. The populations that were exposed but remained relatively free of attack by *Glaucopsyche,* in constrast, showed great variation from plant to plant in the mixtures of three or four alkaloids they contained and in the total quantities of alkaloid in their inflorescences.[32]

From these and related data, it was hypothesized that the variability in their alkaloid content was itself a defense mechanism against small specialized herbivores like *Glaucopsyche.* By presenting the butterfly population with a varied defense, the plants were able to retard the development of resistance to that defense. Butterflies that as larvae developed on one alkaloid type were certain to lay many of their eggs on other types. Most of the offspring of a larval generation selected by one poison regime would themselves face a different regime.

How did the plants invent such an ingenious strategy? It obviously is a result of the coevolutionary process. The more common an alkaloid type is, the more insects feed on it for several consecutive generations and thus become relatively resistant to that particular type. That type therefore suffers the heaviest seed loss and thus becomes less common in the lupine population. Thus, a *frequency-dependent* selection situation presumably is set up, in which variability is maintained because the heaviest predation is directed at the most common type.

The direct importance to agriculture of understanding this sort of coevolutionary system is obvious. It is entirely possible, for instance, that by deliberately introducing and maintaining variable biochemical defenses in crops, the need to use dangerous synthetic pesticides might be dramatically reduced. The potential for erecting such chemical defenses is especially high in crops like cotton, which people do not eat (cotton is *the* major crop in terms of insecticide use).[33] But with sufficient cleverness such defenses might be adapted for some food crops.

FIGURE 4-15

A lycaenid butterfly, *Glaucopsyche lygdamus,* laying an egg on a lupine bud, Gunnison County, Colorado. (The body, behind the wing, curves down at left to deposit the egg.) The larvae of this tiny butterfly (wingspread about 25 mm) are major predators on lupine plants. (Photo by P. R. Ehrlich.)

Similarly, it is important to keep in mind the defensive functions of many, if not all, "secondary" compounds of plants—that is, those with no obvious role in normal life processes of the plant. There is, for instance, an active research program underway to breed a strain of cotton whose seeds do not contain the poisonous compound gossypol. This would be a financial bonanza for cotton growers, since without gossypol, edible cottonseed protein could be prepared cheaply enough that the crop could probably earn a profit as a food crop, with the lint

[32]P. M. Dolinger, Paul R. Ehrlich, W. L. Fitch, and D. E. Breedlove, Alkaloid and predation patterns in Colorado lupine populations, *Oecologia,* vol. 13 (1973), pp. 191–204.

[33]About 50 percent of the pesticides used in the United States are applied to cotton and tobacco (D. Pimentel, Extent of pesticide use, food supplies, and pollution).

(fiber) serving as a bonus. But gossypol probably evolved as cotton's main chemical defense against insects and other pests. Without it, the already difficult pest problems of cotton might become insuperable.

Plants do not necessarily fight the coevolutionary battle with insects and other pests by manufacturing poisons. Nitrogen needed by seedlings is stored in grain seeds in the form of amino acids, the building blocks of proteins. These amino acids are essential nutrients for all animals, which must use them to make their own proteins. But the balance of amino acids in grains is not ideal for utilization by human beings and many other animals—in grains, for example, the essential amino acid lysine tends to be in especially short supply. This makes the seeds less nutritious both for people and for other predators, and may well be the reason low-lysine seeds evolved. Work is progressing among agronomists to select new high-lysine strains of grain as a partial answer to world protein shortages. Unfortunately, these efforts may only be short-circuiting a major defense of the grains against herbivores, thus creating pest problems that might overbalance the advantages of the new strains.[34] The attempts to find new strains of both cotton and grain may be worthwhile, but in the process careful attention should be paid to possible coevolutionary constraints on their success.

COMMUNITY ECOLOGY

The plants, animals, and microorganisms that make up a biological community in an area are interconnected by an intricate web of relationships, a web that also includes the physical environment in which the organisms exist. You will recall that the interdependent biological and physical components make up what biologists call an ecosystem. The ecosystem concept emphasizes the functional relationships among organisms and between organisms and their physical environments. These functional relationships are exemplified by the food chains through which energy flows in an ecosystem, as well as by the pathways along which the chemical elements essential to life move through that ecosystem. These pathways are generally circular—the elements pass through the system in cycles. The cycling of some elements is so slow, however, that in the time-span of interest to society, movement appears to be one-way. An understanding of the flow of energy and the cycling of materials in ecosystems is essential for perceiving what may be the most subtle and dangerous threat to human existence. This threat is the potential destruction, by humanity's own activities, of those ecological systems upon which the very existence of the human species depends.

In Chapter 3 we discussed the physical aspects of nutrient cycling in detail, but we dealt with the biological components of the ecosystems as black boxes. Now the time has come to pry the lids off those boxes and examine the living parts of those systems. A logical place to start is with the feeding sequences ecologists call food chains.

Food Chains

All flesh is grass. This simple statement summarizes a basic principle of biology that is essential to an understanding of both ecological systems and the world food problem. The basic source of food for all animal populations is green plants—"grass." Human beings and all other animals with which we share this planet obtain the energy and nutrients for growth, development, and sustenance by eating plants directly, by eating other animals that have eaten plants, or by eating animals that have eaten animals that have eaten plants, and so forth.

One may think of the plants and animals in an area, together with their physical surroundings, as comprising a system through which energy passes and within which materials move in cycles. Energy enters the system in the form of radiation from the sun. Through the process of photosynthesis, green plants are able to capture some of the incoming solar energy and use it to bond small molecules into the large (organic) molecules that are characteristic of living organisms. That process is often called *fixing* the solar energy. Basically, the energy from light is used in a complex process in which water and carbon dioxide (CO_2) are raw materials, and glucose (a

[34]Such problems have already been reported (see L. R. Brown, *By bread alone,* Praeger, New York, 1974, p. 165).

sugar) and oxygen are the ultimate end products. The chemical bonds of the products contain more energy than those of the raw materials; that added energy is derived from the sun.[35]

The plants themselves and the animals that eat plants break down the large organic glucose molecules and put to use the energy that once bound those molecules together. The process by which they mobilize the energy is called *respiration* (or, more precisely, *cellular respiration*) (see Figure 4-16). In outline, respiration is the opposite of photosynthesis—glucose is combined with oxygen (oxidized) to produce water and carbon dioxide, and the energy thus released is trapped in chemical bonds of special molecules that transport it to other points of use.[36] The animal or plant expends some of that energy in its daily activities and uses some of it to build large molecules of animal or plant substance (for growth or repair of tissue). Animals that eat other animals, once again break down the large molecules and put the energy obtained—energy that originally arrived in the form of solar energy—to their own uses.

According to the first law of thermodynamics (see Box 2-3), energy can be neither created nor destroyed, although it may be changed from one form to another (as in the change from light energy to the energy of chemical bonds in photosynthesis). The second law of thermodynamics says, in essence, that in any transfer of energy there is a loss of available energy; that is, a certain amount of the energy is degraded from an available, concentrated form to an unavailable, dispersed form. The practical expression of this law as it applies to food production is that no transfer of energy in a biological system is 100 percent efficient; some energy always becomes unavailable at each transfer. In the photosynthetic system, usually 1 percent or less of the sunlight falling on green plants is actually converted to the kind of chemical bond energy that is available to animals eating the plants. Usually something less than 10 percent of the energy in

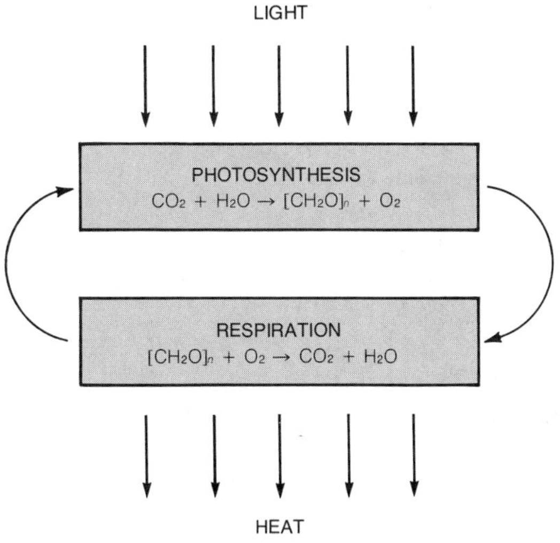

LIGHT

PHOTOSYNTHESIS
$CO_2 + H_2O \rightarrow [CH_2O]_n + O_2$

RESPIRATION
$[CH_2O]_n + O_2 \rightarrow CO_2 + H_2O$

HEAT

FIGURE 4-16

Photosynthesis and respiration are the basic metabolic processes of most living plants, which obtain their energy from sunlight. In photosynthesis, energy from light is used to remove carbon dioxide and water from the environment; for each molecule of CO_2 and H_2O removed, part of a molecule of carbohydrate (CH_2O) is produced and one molecule of oxygen (O_2) is returned to the environment. In respiration by a plant or an animal, combustion of carbohydrates and oxygen yields energy, CO_2, and H_2O. (Adapted from Gates, 1971.)

the plants is converted into chemical bonds in animals that eat the plants. Roughly 10 percent of that energy may in turn be incorporated into the chemical bonds of other animals that eat the animals that ate the plants.

Thus, one may picture the flow of energy through this system as a step-by-step progression along what is known as a food chain. A food chain starts with the green plants, which are known as the *producers* or *autotrophs* (self-feeders). They are the first *trophic* (feeding) *level.* At all other trophic levels are the *heterotrophs* (other-feeders). At the second trophic level are the *herbivores* (plant-eating animals), the *primary consumers.* At the third trophic level are the *secondary consumers,* the *carnivores* (meat-eaters), which eat herbivores. *Tertiary consumers* are the carnivores that eat other carnivores, and so forth. Human beings play many roles in the food chains, but

[35]For a fine elementary discussion of the photosynthetic process, see P. H. Raven and H. Curtis, *The biology of plants,* 2d ed., Worth, New York, 1976. For an excellent, more detailed treatment see P. M. Ray, *The living plant,* 2d ed., Holt, Rinehart and Winston, New York, 1972.

[36]For details, see Paul R. Ehrlich, R. W. Holm, and M. E. Soulé, *Introductory biology,* McGraw-Hill, New York, 1973, or any other modern biology text.

FIGURE 4-17

A food chain including a man. A mosquito feeding on the man would be a quaternary consumer.

their most common role is as a herbivore, since grains and other plant materials make up a very great proportion of the diets of most people. People can also be secondary consumers, as when they eat beefsteak (or the meat of any other herbivorous animal). When they consume fishes, they often occupy positions even farther along the food chain, because many fishes are tertiary or even quaternary consumers themselves. A food chain including human beings is pictured in Figure 4-17.

At each transfer of energy in a food chain, perhaps 90 percent of the chemical energy stored in the organisms of the lower level becomes unavailable to those of the higher level (in certain situations the percentage lost may be much greater or less than this). Since the total amount of energy entering the food chain is fixed by the photosynthetic activity of the plants, obviously more energy is available to organisms occupying lower positions in the food chain than is available to those in higher positions. For instance, as an oversimplification, it might take roughly 10,000 pounds of grain to produce 1000 pounds of cattle, which in turn could be used to produce 100 pounds of human beings. By moving people one step down the food chain, ten times as much energy would be made directly available to them—that is, the 10,000 pounds of grain used to produce 1000 pounds of cattle could be used instead to produce 1000 pounds of human beings.

It follows from this application of the second law of thermodynamics that in most biological systems the biomass (living weight) of producers is greater than that of primary consumers; the biomass of primary consumers in turn is greater than that of secondary consumers; and so forth. The weight of organisms possible at any trophic level is dependent upon the energy supplied by the organisms at the next lower trophic level; and some energy becomes unavailable at each transfer (Figure 4-18).

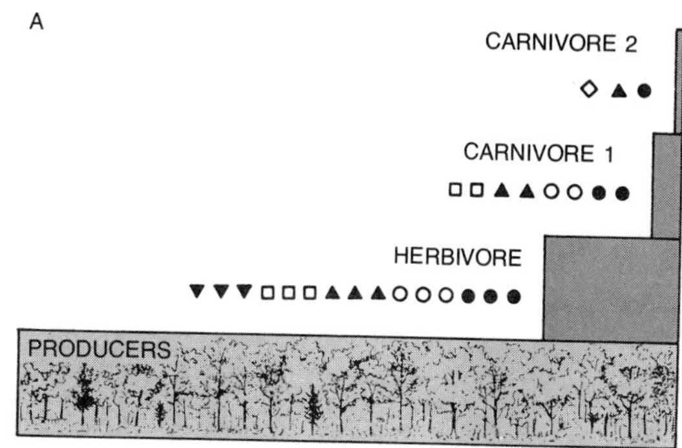

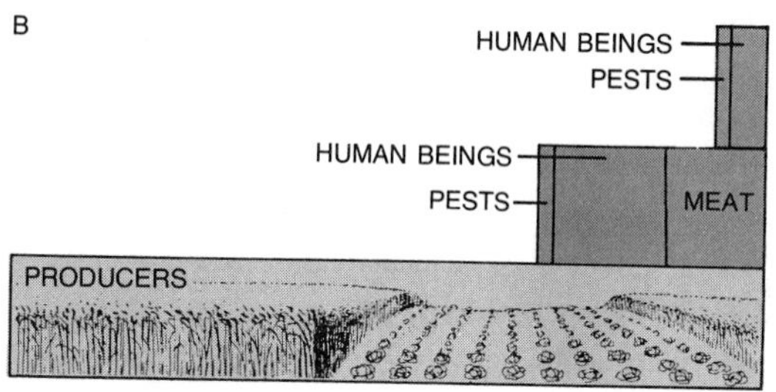

FIGURE 4-18

A. An intact natural ecosystem exemplified by a mature oak and hickory forest that supports several levels of consumers in the grazing food chain, with 10–20 percent of the energy in each trophic level being passed along to the next level. The symbols represent different herbivore and carnivore species. Complexity of structure regulates population sizes, maintaining the same pattern of energy distribution in the system from year to year. B. An agricultural ecosystem is a special case, yielding a larger than normal harvest of net production for herbivores, including human beings and the animals that provide meat for them. Stability is maintained through inputs of energy in cultivation, pesticides, and fertilizer. (Adapted from Woodwell, 1970.)

Productivity

Let us review for a moment two key concepts in the energetics of communities that were first discussed in connection with the carbon cycle (Chapter 3). Gross primary production (GPP) is a measure of the total energy fixed by a community through the process of photosynthesis. Net primary production (NPP), on the other hand, is the GPP minus the energy used by the plants themselves for respiration. The GPP for the entire Earth is on the order of 10^{18} kilocalories.[37] The global

[37]E. P. Odum, *Fundamentals of ecology*. In a concession to tradition, in this section of text we are using kilocalories (kcal) instead of kilojoules (KJ) as the units of energy. The coversion is 4.18 KJ = 1 kcal.

TABLE 4-6
*Primary Production and Biomass Estimates for the Biosphere**

1	2	3	4	5	6	7	8
Ecosystem type	*Area, 10^6 km² = 10^{12} m²*	*Mean net primary productivity, g C/m²/yr***	*Total net primary production, C/yr (columns 2 × 3)*	*Combustion value, kcal/g C*	*Net energy fixed, 10^{15} kcal/yr (columns 4 × 5)*	*Mean plant biomass, kg C/m²*	*Total plant mass, 10^9 metric tons C (columns 2 × 7)*
Tropical rain forest	17.0	900	15.3	9.1	139	20	340
Tropical seasonal forest	7.5	675	5.1	9.2	47	16	120
Temperate evergreen forest	5.0	585	2.9	10.6	31	16	80
Temperate deciduous forest	7.0	540	3.8	10.2	39	13.5	95
Boreal forest	12.0	360	4.3	10.6	46	9.0	108
Woodland and shrubland	8.0	270	2.2	10.4	23	2.7	22
Savanna	15.0	315	4.7	8.8	42	1.8	27
Temperate grassland	9.0	225	2.0	8.8	18	0.7	6.3
Tundra and alpine meadow	8.0	65	0.5	10.0	5	0.3	2.4
Desert scrub	18.0	32	0.6	10.0	6	0.3	5.4
Rock, ice, and sand	24.0	1.5	0.04	10.0	0.3	0.01	0.2
Cultivated land	14.0	290	4.1	9.0	37	0.5	7.0
Swamp and marsh	2.0	1125	2.2	9.2	20	6.8	13.6
Lake and stream	2.5	225	0.6	10.0	6	0.01	0.02
Total continental	149	324	48.3	9.5	459	5.55	827
Open ocean	332.0	57	18.9	10.8	204	0.0014	0.46
Upwelling zones	0.4	225	0.1	10.8	1	0.01	0.004
Continental shelf	26.6	162	4.3	10.0	43	0.005	0.13
Algal bed and reef	0.6	900	0.5	10.0	5	0.9	0.54
Estuaries	1.4	810	1.1	9.7	11	0.45	0.63
Total marine	361	69	24.9	10.6	264	0.0049	1.76
Full total	510	144	73.2	9.9	723	1.63	829

*All values in columns 3 to 8 are expressed as carbon on the assumption that carbon content approximates dry matter × 0.45.
**Grams of carbon per meter per year.
Source: Whittaker and Likens in *Carbon and the biosphere,* G. M. Woodwell and E. V. Pecan, eds.

NPP—the energy available to all food chains—has recently been estimated to be about 7.2×10^{17} kilocalories, or roughly 720 million billion kilocalories.[38] As Table 4-6 shows, however, the NPP varies greatly from ecosystem to ecosystem.

Some additional terminology is commonly used in discussions of community energetics. *Net community production* (NCP) is calculated by subtracting from the NPP the part of that productivity used by the heterotrophs in the community. In crop ecosystems, a farmer normally tries to maximize all three kinds of productivity as well as the ratios of NPP/GPP and NCP/GPP.[39] In other words, a crop is usually selected that will fix as much solar energy as possible and use as little energy as possible in respiration. Heterotrophs other than human beings are excluded from the system insofar as is possible. Table 4-7 shows a comparison of a crop ecosystem (an alfalfa field) and a natural ecosystem (a tropical rain forest).

In grazing agricultural ecosystems, on the other hand, human beings often try to maximize the secondary productivity of some heterotrophs such as cattle. In such a case, the NPP/GPP ratio may be high, but the NCP/GPP ratio will be low. Suppose two grazing food

[38]R. H. Whittaker and G. E. Likens, Carbon in the biota. See also H. Lieth, Primary productivity in ecosystems: Comparative analysis of global patterns, for an estimate about 6 percent higher. For an estimate some 50 percent higher, see L. E. Rodin, N. I. Bazilevich, and N. N. Rozov, Productivity of the world's main ecosystems. Both of these papers and the volumes they are in will be very useful for those interested in the problems of evaluating productivity.

[39]The measurements, of course, are done before people, as the ultimate heterotrophs in the food chain, take their share.

chains were observed: Grass 1 → cattle → people; and Grass 2 → cattle → people. One might well be interested in the ecological efficiency with which the two chains operated. This could be calculated by determining how many kilocalories of grass were eaten by the cattle and dividing that by how many kilocalories of beef were consumed by the people. Presuming that the people in both groups ate the same portions of the cattle (and that everything else was equal), this calculation would tell which of the two grasses was best to plant. Efficiency of energy transfer between trophic levels is called a *Lindeman's efficiency* and has the general form:

$$\frac{\text{energy intake at } n\text{th trophic level}}{\text{energy intake at } (n-1)\text{th trophic level}}.$$

Ecological efficiencies may also be calculated within trophic levels in the form:

$$\frac{\text{net secondary productivity at } n\text{th level}}{\text{energy intake at } n\text{th level}}.$$

A rule-of-thumb figure of 10 percent has already been given as the Lindeman's efficiency. Measurements vary, however, from community to community and between trophic levels. If anything, they are likelier to be slightly more than the 10 percent, although they are rarely more than 25 percent. Yet efficiencies as great as 70 percent have been reported for some marine food chains.[40]

Efficiencies within trophic levels vary a great deal, but tissue-growth efficiences tend to decrease as one goes up the food chain. [Tissue-growth efficiency is the ratio of net productivity at level *n* to assimilation (energy fixed in photosynthesis or food absorbed from the alimentary canal) at the same level.] For entire communities these efficiencies seem to average around 60 percent for plants, about 40 percent for herbivores and carnivores, and perhaps 30 percent for secondary carnivores.[41] Efficiencies for a particular species may be very much lower,

TABLE 4-7
Production and Respiration in Two Ecosystems (kcal/m²/yr)

	*Field of alfalfa**	*Rain forest***
Gross primary production (GPP)	24,400	45,000
Autotrophic respiration	9,200	32,000
Net primary production (NPP)	15,200	13,000
Heterotrophic respiration	800	13,000
Net community production (NCP)	14,400	essentially zero
NPP/GPP (%)	62.3	28.9
NCP/GPP (%)	59.0	0

*In the United States. Data from M. O. Thomas and G. R. Hill, Photosynthesis under field conditions. In *Photosynthesis in plants,* J. Franck and W. E. Loomis, eds., Iowa State College Press, Ames, 1949, pp. 19–52.
**Data from H. T. Odum and R. F. Pigeon, eds., *A tropical rainforest: A study of irradiation and ecology at El Verde, Puerto Rico,* National Technical Information Service, Springfield, Va., 1970.
Source: Adapted from E. P. Odum, *Fundamentals of ecology.*

however. (Of course, care must be taken in calculating efficiencies in order to avoid, say, computing the ratio of dry dog food consumed to wet weight of dog produced!)

It is important to keep in mind that basically these efficiencies are a consequence of the second law of thermodynamics— that in the respiratory process some of the high-grade energy of the chemical bonds is degraded to heat at a temperature so close to ambient that organisms have not been able to evolve a way to make it do work—in other words, it has become inaccessible to the ecosystem. It is this inexorable action of the second law that produces the pyramidal form of the diagrams in Figure 4-18. The relationships between trophic levels are conventionally illustrated by pyramid diagrams based on numbers of individuals, energy, or biomass.

Figure 4-19 shows pyramids of numbers for a grassland and for a temperate forest in summer. Note that the forest pyramid is partly inverted because of the large sizes of the individual trees. Figure 4-20 shows pyramids of biomass for a tropical forest community in Panama and the marine community of the waters of the English Channel. The numbers pyramids show the numbers of organisms that exist at an instant of time; the biomass pyramids show the dry weight of the crop of organisms at a given instant.

Note that the English Channel pyramid is also inverted—the biomass of phytoplankton is smaller than that of zooplankton. Does this mean that plankton have

[40]T. S. Petipa, E. V. Pavlova, and G. N. Mirov, The food web structure: Utilization and transport of energy by trophic levels in the planktonic community, In *Marine food chains,* J. H. Steele, ed., University of California Press, Berkeley, 1970, pp. 142–167.

[41]D. G. Kozlowsky. A critical evaluation of the trophic level concept: pt. 1, Ecological efficiencies, *Ecology,* vol. 49 (1968), pp. 48–60.

FIGURE 4-19

Pyramids of numbers for a grassland and a temperate forest community in summer. The numbers represent individuals per 1000 square meters; P = producers; H = herbivores; C = carnivores; TC = top carnivores. Microorganisms and soil animals are excluded. (Adapted from Odum, 1971.)

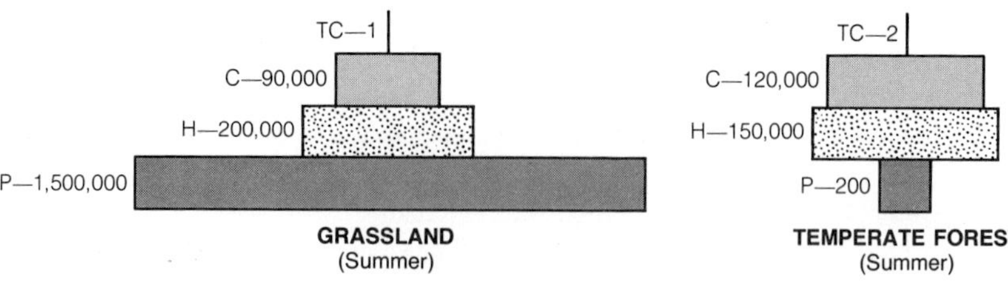

FIGURE 4-20

Pyramids of biomass for the English Channel marine and the Panamanian tropical forest communities. The numbers represent grams of dry weight per square meter; P = producers; H = herbivores; C = carnivores; D = decomposers. (Adapted from Odum, 1971.)

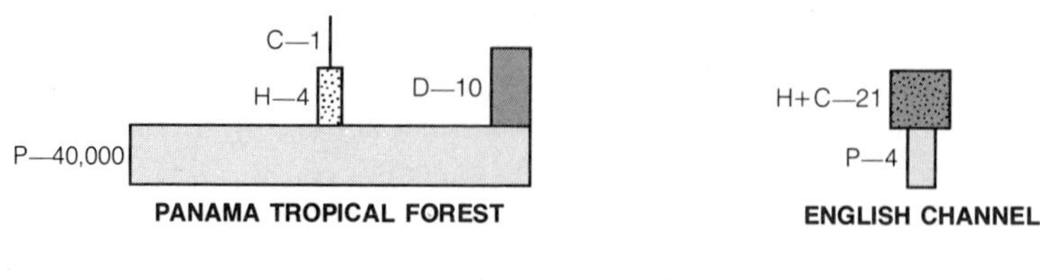

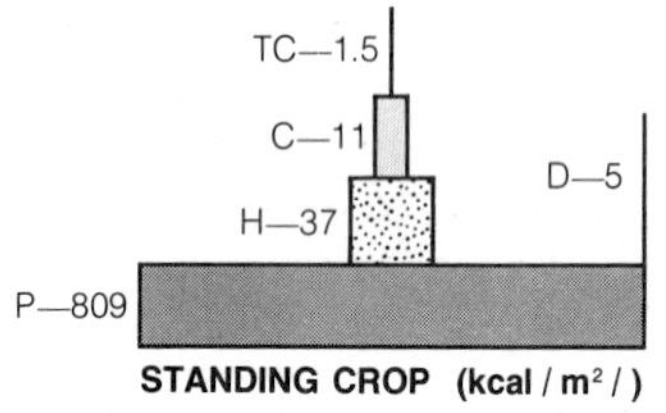

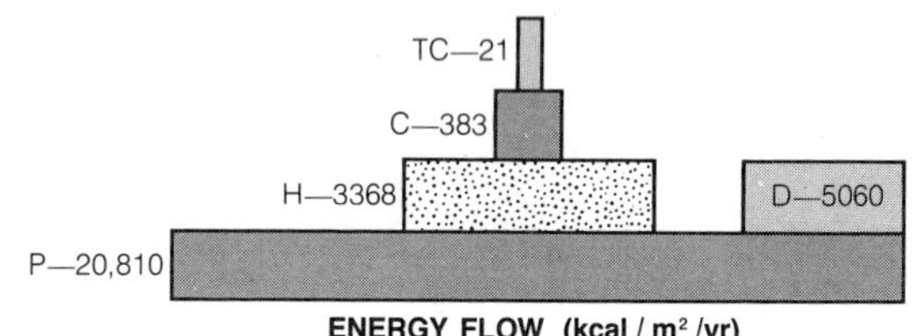

FIGURE 4-21

Standing crop and energy flow pyramids for an aquatic community at Silver Springs, Florida. P = producers; H = herbivores; C = carnivores; TC = top carnivores; D = decomposers. (Adapted from Odum, 1971.)

found a way around the second law? Hardly—the pyramid of productivity for the English Channel community is right side up. The key point is that in that community the phytoplankton have a much more rapid turnover than the zooplankton. As an analogy, suppose you had on your kitchen shelf only one day's food at a time and the shelf was restocked every night. Since a biomass pyramid represents the situation at a given point in time (rather than productivity over time) a biomass pyramid of the shelf-person system would also be inverted.

In general, small organisms use energy at higher rates (the *metabolic rate*) and reproduce more rapidly than large ones. Thus, for a given amount of energy flowing into a trophic level, the standing crop or biomass will vary directly with the size of the organisms. The biomass of elephants that could exist on a given chunk of Africa would be much greater than the biomass of a hypothetical insect population that ate precisely the same plants.

The relationships among size, standing crop (biomass), and energy flow can be seen in Figure 4-21. Note that the standing crop of decomposers (bacteria and fungi) is proportionally tiny—only 0.58 percent of the biomass of the community. In contrast, they account for 17 percent of the energy flow in the community. In a sense, the energy-flow pyramids give the most accurate assessment of the roles of organisms at various trophic levels. Numbers pyramids tend to exaggerate the importance of small organisms; biomass pyramids, to underrate them. And, as long as the second law holds, energy-flow pyramids will show no inversions!

It is, of course, extremely important to keep the difference between biomass and productivity in mind when considering the exploitation of a population. As one might expect, productivity is the critical variable. Knowledge of the total biomass of blue whales in existence is much less important in determining a rational harvesting scheme than knowledge of the weight of blue whales produced annually (there are many other important variables, as well—see Chapter 7).

Succession

Biological communities are not static. They change over relatively long periods of time—hundreds, thousands, and millions of years—as the climate of Earth changes and as their component species evolve and coevolve. They also change on a time scale of years, decades, and centuries, in a process known as *succession.* Suppose a piece of land is newly exposed by the retreat of a glacier, the lowering of a lake, or the emergence of land from the ocean by volcanic action. Gradually the exposed rock is fragmented under the action of the wind, running water, and alternate heating and cooling, and soil starts to form. Plants such as lichens invade and speed the soil formation through chemical interactions with the substrate. Grasses and herbs then move in, adding the action of their roots (and their decaying remains) to the process. Herbivores arrive, followed by carnivores that feed upon them; then the process of primary succession is well underway.

Primary succession is the development of a biological community where none existed previously. The terrestrial process begins with bare substrate and, if undisturbed, continues until a relatively stable community characteristic of the climate regime and the soil type develops. Such a community is called a *climax.* The entire sequence of communities from bare ground to the climax is called a *sere,* and intermediate communities are called *seral stages.* Primary succession, beginning with a lake and progressing to a forest, is diagramed in Figure 4-22.

The earliest studies of succession were done around the turn of the century on a sere from bare sand substrate to a beech-maple climax forest on dunes around the shore of Lake Michigan. Pioneering ecologists H. H. C. Cowles and V. E. Shelford studied the plants and animals of this successional series, and the same system was reinvestigated by J. S. Olson a half-century later.[42] In the later study it was determined through carbon dating that the entire successional process took about 1000 years—a relatively long time. This historic sere was threatened by industrial development when one of us first visited it in 1958, and efforts were being made by conservationists to preserve the dunes as a recreational area and outdoor teaching facility. At this writing the issue remains unresolved, because although Congress set aside 3360 hectares of Indiana dunes as a national park, a nuclear power plant and adjacent industrial development are threatening it.

Secondary succession occurs when a climax community is destroyed—say, by a fire or by human activities. It differs from primary succession largely in the early stages—the time-consuming process of soil-building is partially or wholly unnecessary. Human beings are often responsible for secondary succession, as when a clearing in a tropical forest is abandoned by a milpa farmer or when a dirt road or railway right-of-way is no longer used.

A great deal has been written and many names have been coined by ecologists attempting to define and classify climaxes. The problem is fundamentally one of time—how long must a community last in a changing world in order to be considered a climax? No precise answer can be given. In periods of relatively little climatic change, a penultimate seral stage (the subclimax) may last a long time before an even more persistent climax stage replaces it. In parts of northern California, a grassland disclimax (a climax maintained by disturbance) is created by overgrazing in areas that otherwise would be live-oak woodland (cattle eat the young oak saplings, leaving the grassland that appears in Figure 4-23).

There generally are significant changes in the ratio of gross production, P (or GPP), to total community respiration, R (autotrophic and heterotrophic), as succession proceeds.[43] At the early stages of normal succession, the P/R ratio is greater than 1. Material is being added to the system, and net community production is high. As the climax P/R approaches 1, the system is more or less in equilibrium, and NCP is low or 0 (Figure 4-24).

There are other differences, too. At the early stages of

[42] J. S. Olson, Rates of succession and soil changes on southern Lake Michigan sand dunes, *Botanical Gazette,* vol. 119 (1958), pp. 125–170.

[43] A fine summary of the differences between early and late seral stages was given by E. P. Odum in The strategy of ecosystem development, *Science,* vol. 164 (1969), pp. 262–270.

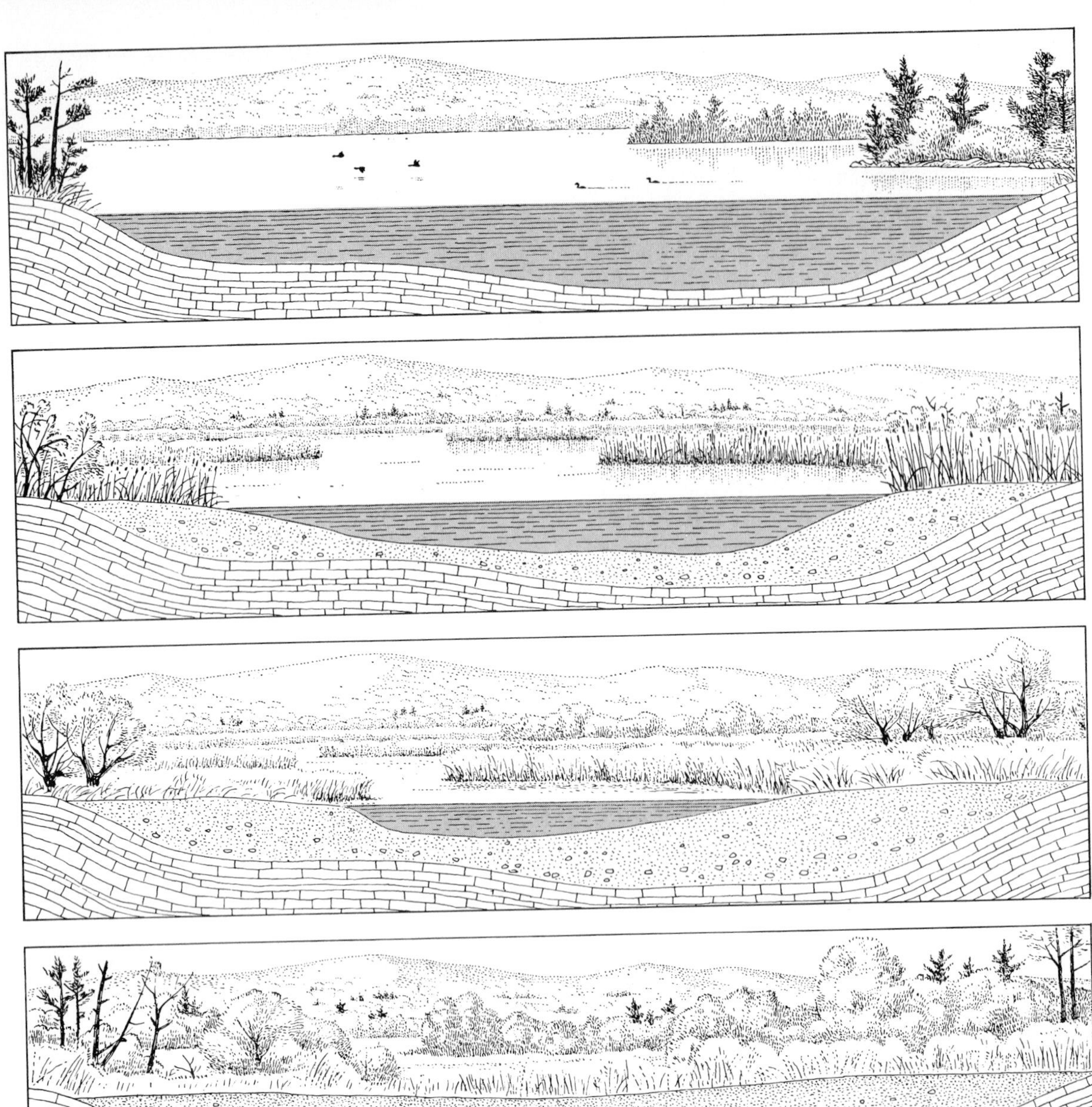

FIGURE 4-22

Primary succession leading to the obliteration of a lake. The process starts at the edge of the water *(top);* where a few bog-adapted conifers rise in a forest of hardwoods. Next the debris of shallow-water plants turns the lake margin into marsh, which is gradually invaded by mosses and bog plants, bog-adapted bushes and trees such as blueberry and willow, and additional conifers. Eventually the lake, however deep, is entirely filled with silt from its tributaries and with plant debris. In the final stage *(bottom)* the last central bog grows up into forest. (Adapted from Powers and Robertson, 1966.)

FIGURE 4-23

A grassland disclimax maintained by cattle grazing in the foothills of the Santa Cruz Mountains, central California. Notice the absence of oak seedlings. If the cattle were removed, this area would revert to oak woodland. (Photo by P. R. Ehrlich.)

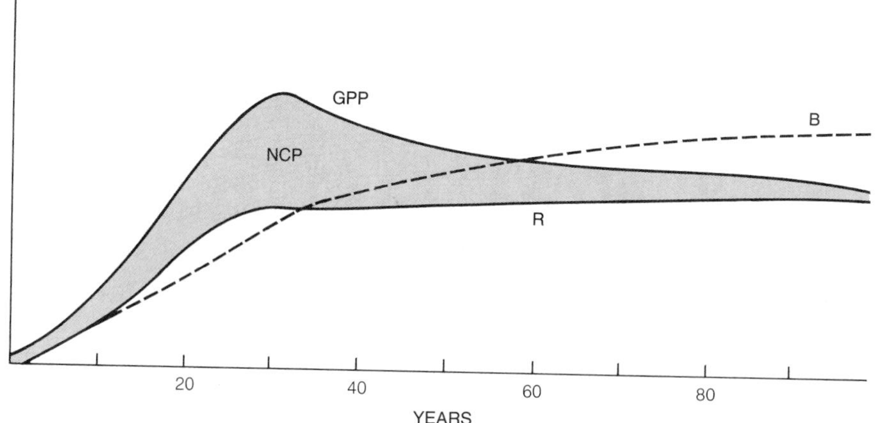

FIGURE 4-24

Succession in a forest.
GPP = grass primary production;
NCP = net community production;
R = total community respiration;
B = total biomass.
(Adapted from Odum, 1971.)

succession, food chains tend to be rather linear, and the bulk of the energy flows through the herbivores (through the so-called grazing food chain). In the climax the food chains tend to be woven into complex food webs (as discussed below), and as much as 90 percent of the NPP bypasses herbivores and goes directly into the *detritus food chain*—that is, to the decomposers.

It is useful to think of modern people as grazers—animals tied to the eating of grass—since the vast majority of human food is either grain or animals fed on grains or other grasses. It is not surprising, therefore, that a major human activity is keeping succession from proceeding beyond the early seral stages: in other words, in farming. Farms are man-made simplified ecosystems in which farmers attempt to maximize the P/R ratio. In this endeavor, considerable energy must be expended (weeding and eliminating competing herbivores) to prevent the natural processes of succession and to counteract other forces that tend to destroy what is an inherently unstable ecosystem.

Complexity and Stability

What tends to make early seral stages in general, and farms in particular, less permanent features in the landscape than, say, the oak-hickory forest climax? One explanation frequently cited is that farms are less complex. The climax contains more species of plants, animals, and microorganisms, and their food chains are more intricately interwoven.

That there is a causal connection between complexity (or diversity) and stability (which in one sense is thought of as resistance to change in species composition and numbers of individuals) in biological communities is part of the folk wisdom of ecology. Six lines of evidence for this notion were presented by the famed British ecologist Charles Elton in his classic book, *The ecology of invasions by animals and plants.*

1. Mathematical models of simple ecological systems indicate little stability; ordinarily there are great fluctuations in numbers of the population of each species.
2. In simple laboratory systems, such as those containing a single predator species and a single prey species, extinction is the normal outcome for the predator or for both species.
3. Natural communities on small islands are much more vulnerable to invasion by organisms that did not evolve with the community than are continental communities. This is especially true of oceanic islands with depauperate biotas (relatively few species present).
4. Cultivated land (communities greatly simplified by human beings) is especially subject to invasions and to population explosions of pest species.
5. Species-rich tropical rain forests are not as subject to insect outbreaks as are less-complex, temperate-zone forests.
6. Pesticide treatment of orchards has resulted in pest outbreaks by upsetting the relationships between pests and their predators and parasites.

These observations appear to be confirmed by many others. Recall that *Heliconius ethilla* in tropical forests is extremely stable in numbers, whereas populations of *Euphydryas editha* in temperate areas fluctuate greatly. In addition, the floristically rather uniform northern coniferous forest seems especially vulnerable to outbreaks of insect pests; and heavy use of pesticides has frequently created pest problems—for example, the famous Cañete Valley disaster in Peru (described in Chapter 11).

To understand one possible mechanism for the diversity-stability relationship, consider a complex food web (the intertwined food chains of a community). The food web of a Long Island estuary was thoroughly investigated by biologists George M. Woodwell, Charles F. Wurster, and Peter A. Isaacson.[44] Some of the relationships they discovered are represented in Figure 4-25. Their study illustrates several important characteristics of most food webs, one being complexity. Although the figure shows only a sample of the kinds of plants and animals in this ecosystem, it is evident that most of the consumers feed on several different organisms and that most prey organisms are attacked by more than one predator. To put it another way, the food chains are interlinked. This interlinking may be one of the reasons that complexity is associated with stability in ecosystems. Presumably, the more food chains there are in an ecosystem and the more cross-connecting links there are among them, the more chances the ecosystem has to compensate for changes imposed upon it.

For example, suppose the marsh-plant–cricket–red-wing-blackbird section of Figure 4-25 represented an isolated entire ecosystem. If that were the case, removing the blackbirds—say, by shooting—would lead to a plague of crickets. This in turn might lead to the defoliation of the plants, and then to the starvation of the crickets. In short, a change in one link of such a simple chain would have disastrous consequences for the entire ecosystem. Suppose, however, that the cormorants were removed from the larger system. Populations of flukes and eels would probably increase, which in turn might reduce the population of green algae *(Cladophora).* But there would be more food for mergansers and ospreys, so those populations would probably enlarge, leading to a reduction in the numbers of eels and flukes. In turn, the algae population would recover.

Needless to say, things do not normally happen that

[44]George M. Woodwell, Toxic substances and ecological cycles, *Scientific American,* March 1967.

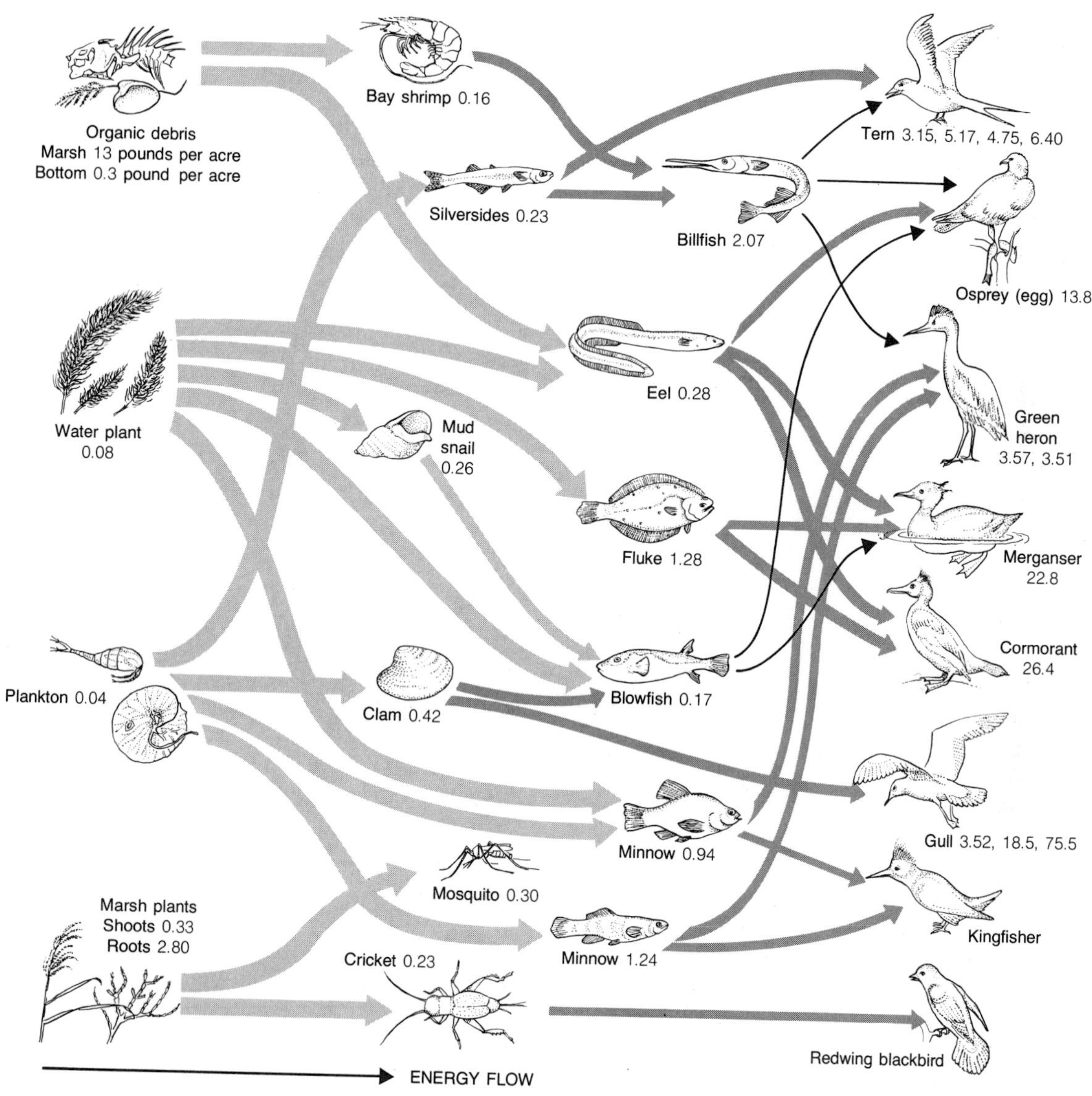

FIGURE 4-25

Portion of a food web in a Long Island estuary. The arrows indicate the flow of energy; the numbers tell how many parts per million of DDT are found in each kind of organism. (Adapted from Woodwell, 1967.)

simply and neatly in nature. But there appear to be, then, both observational and theoretical reasons to believe that a general principle holds: *stability is related to complexity.* Complex communities such as the deciduous forests that cover much of the eastern United States persist year after year if people do not interfere with them. An oak-hickory forest is quite stable in comparison with an ultrasimplified community such as a cornfield, which is a man-made stand of a single kind of grass. A cornfield has little natural stability and is subject to almost instant ruin if it is not constantly managed by the farmer. Similarly, arctic and subarctic ecosystems, which are also characterized by simplicity, tend to be less stable than complex tropical forest ecosystems. In arctic regions the instability is manifested in frequent, violent fluctuations in the sizes of populations of such northern animals as lemmings, hares, and foxes. In contrast, outbreaks of one species seldom occur in complex tropical forests. The late Robert MacArthur, who played a key role in stimulating the surge of interest in theoretical ecology in the last two decades, suggested in 1955 that the stability of an ecosystem is a function of the number of links in the web of its food chains. He developed a measure of that stability using information theory.[45]

More recent work, however, indicates that the relationship is more complicated and difficult to explain. For example, in some experimental work, an increase in diversity at one trophic level decreased stability at the next higher level; in other work it did not.[46] It turns out that both of the terms *complexity* (diversity) and *stability* have many meanings. Complexity, for instance, may refer merely to the species diversity—how many kinds of organisms are present and the equitability of their abundance. (A community consisting of 100 individuals of each of three species is more diverse than one having 10 individuals of each of two species and 280 individuals of a third.) Or the term may be used to refer to the spatial diversity or patchiness of the environment (a number of vertical layers in the vegetation; uniform fields or fields interspersed with hedgerows). It also may include the genetic diversity within populations.

Stability, as the term is most generally used, refers to the propensity of an ecosystem (or any system, for that matter) to return to equilibrium following perturbation. Since equilibria are difficult to define and measure in entire ecosystems, however, very often definitions of stability are based on the amplitude of fluctuations in the sizes of sample populations in an ecosystem.

Recently the mathematics of complexity-stability theory has been synthesized by R. M. May,[47] who has shown convincingly that stability does not increase as a simple mathematical consequence of an increase in species diversity. But the mathematical models of ecosystems considered by May involve so many simplifying assumptions—especially the absence of coevolution—that they really do not address the key question of whether diversity causes stability.

Two other reviews of the diversity-stability question, by ecologists Daniel Goodman[48] and William W. Murdoch,[49] both conclude that in natural ecosystems there is no reason to believe that diversity produces stability. Both cite numerous examples casting doubt on the classic Eltonian formulation of the relationship and the evidence that has been rallied to support that formulation. Murdoch focuses on the coevolutionary nature of species interactions in natural systems. He suggests, "The marked instability of agroecosystems (and other artificial communities), in contrast with the stability of natural communities, results from the frequent disruption of crops by humans and from the lack in crop systems of co-evolutionary links between the interacting species. This second feature of crops is caused by the haphazardness of the collection of species on any given crop field, the changing selective regime imposed by humans, and the fact that crops [crop ecosystems] have lost many species that were present in the previously existing natural communities."[50]

Subsequently, however, Jonathan Roughgarden in a theoretical study of the role of coevolution in communities has shown that it may be either a stabilizing or a

[45]Fluctuations of animal populations and a measure of community stability. *Ecology,* vol 36, pp. 533–536.

[46]L. E. Hurd, M. V. Mellinger, L. L. Wolf, S. J. McNaughton, Stability and diversity at three trophic levels in terrestrial successional ecosystems, *Science,* vol. 173 (1971), pp. 1134–1136; and C. A. Bulan and G. W. Barrett, The effects of two acute stresses on the arthropod component of an experimental grassland system, *Ecology,* vol. 52 (1971), pp. 597–605.

[47]*Stability and complexity in model ecosystems.*

[48]The theory of diversity-stability relationships in ecology, *Quarterly Review of Biology,* vol. 50 (1975), pp. 237–266.

[49]Diversity, complexity, stability and pest control.

[50]Ibid., p. 806.

destabilizing force.[51] In some circumstances coevolution can greatly enchance community stability, leading to a structure that will not collapse if a single species is removed. More frequently it leads to a configuration less stable than the original—to situations where, for example, the loss of a single species population may lead to the decay of the entire system.

The last word on the relationship between diversity and stability is clearly not in. Perhaps the best hypothesis available today is that where one finds an association between diversity and stability it is probably the result of parallel evolutionary trends rather than a direct causal relationship.[52] To put it another way, an increase in the complexity of ecological systems does not necessarily lead to an increase in their stability and, in fact, may destabilize them. But in the course of evolution the most stable complex systems are by definition those that have persisted for long periods. Unstable complex systems, on the other hand, have disappeared.

Some tentative conclusions can be drawn from this. First of all, merely adding more species to agricultural ecosystems will not necessarily stabilize them. Indeed, it may have exactly the opposite effect. Van Emden and Williams[53] cite numerous examples of this before giving a weak endorsement to the desirability of maintaining hedgerows between fields. They may take a somewhat too gloomy view of the benefits of such maintenance of spatial diversity, however, since they do not consider the positive effects of the hedgerows as pollinator refuges. But it is clear that careful evaluations of all the properties of the coevolved complexes of an ecosystem are necessary before attempting to tinker with increasing diversity in order to stabilize such systems.

On the other side of the coin, one can say that removing elements from relatively stable natural ecosystems may well destabilize them, with unfortunate consequences for *Homo sapiens,* which depends on those systems for a variety of indispensable services. For instance, in Africa a reduction in the diversity of the antelope fauna by brush clearing has destabilized the grazing ecosystem, and the game herds are diminishing. The productivity of herbivores in the new system, in which cattle are replacing the antelopes, is much less, as is the potential of that system for supporting human life.[54]

Loss of herbivore productivity is not the only possible consequence of reducing complexity. Ecologist George Woodwell has emphasized the tightness of normally complex, mature ecosystems. Several studies show that disturbance (for example, cutting down the trees of a forest) leads to a leakage of nutrients from a system. Such leakage, according to Woodwell, "may be large enough under certain circumstances to reduce the potential of the site for repair through succession and to degrade other systems by overloading them with nutrients."[55] The phenomenon of nutrient leakage is worldwide, but it seems especially critical in that most threatened of all ecosystems, the tropical rain forest.

Unhappily, there is no way to predict exactly what the consequences will be of removing even one species from an ecosystem or even of reducing the genetic variability of a species. In some cases a removal may make no discernable difference; in others it may be catastrophic. In one instance, removal of a single species from a fifteen-species intertidal community of marine invertebrates caused it to collapse to an eight-species system in less than two years.[56] Similarly, it is clear from the work in lupines and lycaenid butterflies discussed earlier that genetic diversity may be very important in the trophic relationships of plant populations.

Diversity, stability, and ecological politics. Ecologists have commonly argued for the preservation of diversity because they have believed that the stability of ecological systems may depend upon it. Now, as we have seen, considerable doubt has been thrown on the notion

[51]Coevolution in ecological systems, part 2: Results from "loop analysis" for purely density-dependent coevolution, in *Symposium on measuring natural selection in natural populations,* F. Christiansen and T. Fenchel, eds., Springer-Verlag, Aarhus, in press.

[52]R. Margalef, Diversity and stability: A practical proposal and a model of interdependence, in *Diversity and stability in ecological systems,* USAEC, Washington, D.C., Brookhaven Symposia in Biology, November 22, 1969.

[53]Insect stability and diversity in agroecosystems, *Annual Review of Entomology,* vol. 19 (1974), pp. 455–475.

[54]W. H. Pearsall, The conservation of African plains game as a form of land use, in *The exploitation of natural animal populations,* E. D. LeCren and M. W. Holdgate, eds., *Symposia of the British Ecological Society,* Blackwell, Oxford, 1962, pp. 343–383.

[55]Success, succession, and Adam Smith, *BioScience,* vol. 24, pp. 81–87.

[56]R. T. Paine, Food web complexity and species diversity, *American Naturalist,* vol. 100 (1966), pp. 65–75.

that diversity causes stability, and even on the idea that the two are associated. It therefore is important that general statements about diversity, complexity, and stability now be eliminated from the political rhetoric of the environmental movement, for that movement must give as accurate an interpretation of the current state of ecological science as possible.

It is important to note that the diversity-causes-stability argument is not necessary in order to demonstrate that extermination of populations or species, destruction of genetic variability, and other actions that simplify ecological systems are threatening not just to those systems but to humanity as well. Lessening the diversity of *both* simple and complex natural ecosystems may lead to their destabilization, with results that are extremely undesirable from a human viewpoint. As Goodman succinctly put it, "From a practical standpoint, the diversity-stability hypothesis is not really necessary; even if the hypothesis is completely false it remains logically possible—and, on the best available evidence, very likely—that disruption of the patterns of evolved interaction in natural communities will have untoward, and occasionally catastrophic, consequences."[57]

Extinction, Endangered Species, and Invasions

It should be apparent from the preceding that humanity forces populations and species to extinction at its peril. Of course, extinction is a natural phenomenon—organisms have been going extinct for billions of years. There have been episodes of "rapid" extinction in geological history, such as the disappearance of the dinosaurs about 70 million years ago. Those rapid episodes, however, were actually quite slow compared to the extinction "explosion" now occurring. Records of the disappearance of species of birds and mammals have been reasonably accurate since 1600. Since then some 130 species have become extinct—roughly 1 percent of the 12,910 species of birds and mammals alive 375 years ago.[58]

Although past rates of extinction are very difficult to estimate, if the average "life span" of a species of higher vertebrate is assumed to be between 200,000 and 2 million years, then extinction of 1 percent of the species could be expected every 2000 to 20,000 years. If so, in the period from 1600 to 1975 the rate of extinction was five to fifty times as high as in the past. Furthermore, some 300 additional species of birds and mammals are now threatened with extinction. Should one-fifth of those actually become extinct before the year 2000, the rate would be from 40 to 400 times normal. Such rates of extinction are much too rapid for the normal evolutionary processes that generate organic diversity to be able to replace them.

Human beings first became a significant force for extinction when they became hunters. There is little question that the extinction of many large mammal species during the late Pleistocene 10,000 to 12,000 years ago was accelerated by the human search for food.[59] In more recent times, however, this has declined in importance as a cause, and the destruction of the habitats of birds and mammals has become a more important element in extinction.[60] For other animals and plants, habitat destruction is the primary cause of extinction. When those much more numerous organisms are added to the bird-mammal picture, the rate of extinction then seems to be about 10,000 species per century (from a total of perhaps 10 million). If the Brazilians and others succeed in destroying the flora and fauna of the Amazon basin (as discussed in Chapter 11), perhaps *1 million* kinds of plants and animals could disappear from that region alone.[61]

Furthermore, in many (if not most) situations, saving small patches of habitat is not enough to prevent a decay of species diversity. A preserved area must be large enough to support all of the populations belonging there—and some mammalian carnivores and raptorial birds require territories of many square kilometers. Even populations of insects may require sizable areas for their maintenance. It seems likely, for example, that because of its trap-lining behavior a population of the butterfly

[57]The theory of diversity-stability, p. 261. See also Gordon H. Orians, Diversity, stability and maturity in natural ecosystems.

[58]Fisher, Simon, and Vincent, *Wildlife in danger.*

[59]P. S. Martin and H. E. Wright (eds.), *Pleistocene extinctions,* Yale University Press, New Haven, 1967.

[60]G. Vetz and D. L. Johnson, Breaking the web, *Environment,* vol. 16, no. 10 (December 1974).

[61]Scientists talk of need for conservation and an ethic of biotic diversity to slow species extinction, *Science,* vol. 184 (May 10, 1974), pp. 646–647.

Heliconius ethilla requires at least one square kilometer. Many euglossine bees also require large areas of forest, and many bee populations and species are being wiped out as the forests of Central America are decimated.[62] Their loss, in turn, is having dire consequences for the orchids and other plants that depend on them for pollination. The future well-being of the ecological systems that support our civilization may be threatened by the extinction of these species. Some of the species now endangered may be key species in systems important to people, but there is no way to tell whether they are, without the most exhaustive investigations of the ecosystems involved. Who, for instance, would have guessed that E. J. Kuenzler would discover in his study of a Georgian salt marsh[63] that a seemingly insignificant mussel was largely responsible for making phosphorus (a limiting resource) available to the community?

Thus, conservationists have a powerful argument for the protection of endangered species beyond the compassionate-esthetic-recreational arguments usually raised, although those are compelling in themselves. As far as anyone knows at this writing, the other species of organisms on Earth are our only living companions in the universe. Each one that is forced to extinction is one that our descendants will not have the opportunity to see (or exploit), just as we have no possibility of seeing alive dodos, passenger pigeons, or the Xerces butterfly. And, of course, each extinction carries with it the threat of the loss of other values as a pool of genetic information is destroyed forever. These losses range from potential sources of antibiotics and laboratory animals for medical research to genetic material useful for domestication, or, through crossing, for improving plants and animals already domesticated.

Nor is it possible to insure adequately against such loss by maintaining samples of organic diversity in zoos, experiment stations, and botanical gardens. The problems of maintaining many species in captivity are extremely complex—and, as the numbers that need to be saved grow, the task could become immense.[64] But, even if culture techniques were perfected for most species, the serious problem of the decay of genetic variability would remain.

Finally, it is important to remember that human beings decrease organic diversity, not only by directly assaulting species and by destroying habitats, but also by moving organisms around. Species transplanted are often species removed from the presence of natural enemies that keep their numbers in check, and inserted into the presence of others that have never evolved defenses against the invaders or the capacity to compete with them. In 1975 on the island of Maui in Hawaii, we were surprised to find a dense population of swallowtail butterflies. The only large butterflies on the Hawaiian islands previously had been monarchs. The new butterfly was *Papilio xuthus*, a common Asian species in a group that feeds on plants of the *Citrus* family Rutaceae. A phone call to the Hawaii Department of Agriculture revealed that *P. xuthus* had been in the Hawaiian islands for more than a year and on Maui for "about three months." In that time a population much denser than most *Papilio* populations had built up, apparently in the log phase of growth, and considerable damage was visible on the citrus trees, grown largely as ornamental plants.

What impact this import will have on native Hawaiian Rutaceae remains to be seen. The Hawaiian Islands, however, have lost a great deal of their native forests to clearing for agriculture and for urban and resort development. The unique fauna of Hawaiian honeycreepers (finchlike birds of the family Drepanididae) has already suffered severe losses. Eight of twenty-two species discovered before 1900 are now extinct or presumed extinct, and several others have lost distinct races from various islands. Forest clearing, the introduction of mongooses for rat control, and the introduction of foreign birds that both competed with the honeycreepers and carried disease, all played parts in this disaster. (The mongoose, by the way, is one of the most destructive exotic animals. Wherever it has been introduced to control rats or snakes, it has made haste to devour part of the local bird fauna as well.)

Enormous areas may be dramatically changed by introduction of a single species freed of its natural controls. The flora of much of the Mediterranean area

[62]D. H. Janzen, The deflowering of Central America, *Natural History*, April 1974.

[63]Structure and energy flow of a mussel population in a Georgian salt marsh, *Limnology and Oceanography*, vol. 6 (1961), pp. 191–204.

[64]David R. Zimmerman, Captive breeding: Boon or boondoggle, *Natural History*, December 1974, pp. 6–19.

FIGURE 4-26

A. Distribution of the major biomes of the world. (Adapted from Odum, 1971.) B. The relationship of biomes to precipitation and temperature. The broken line encloses the range of values within which either grasses or woody plants may dominate, depending on local conditions. The figure is simplified, and the positions of the divisions are approximate. (Adapted from Whittaker, 1970.)

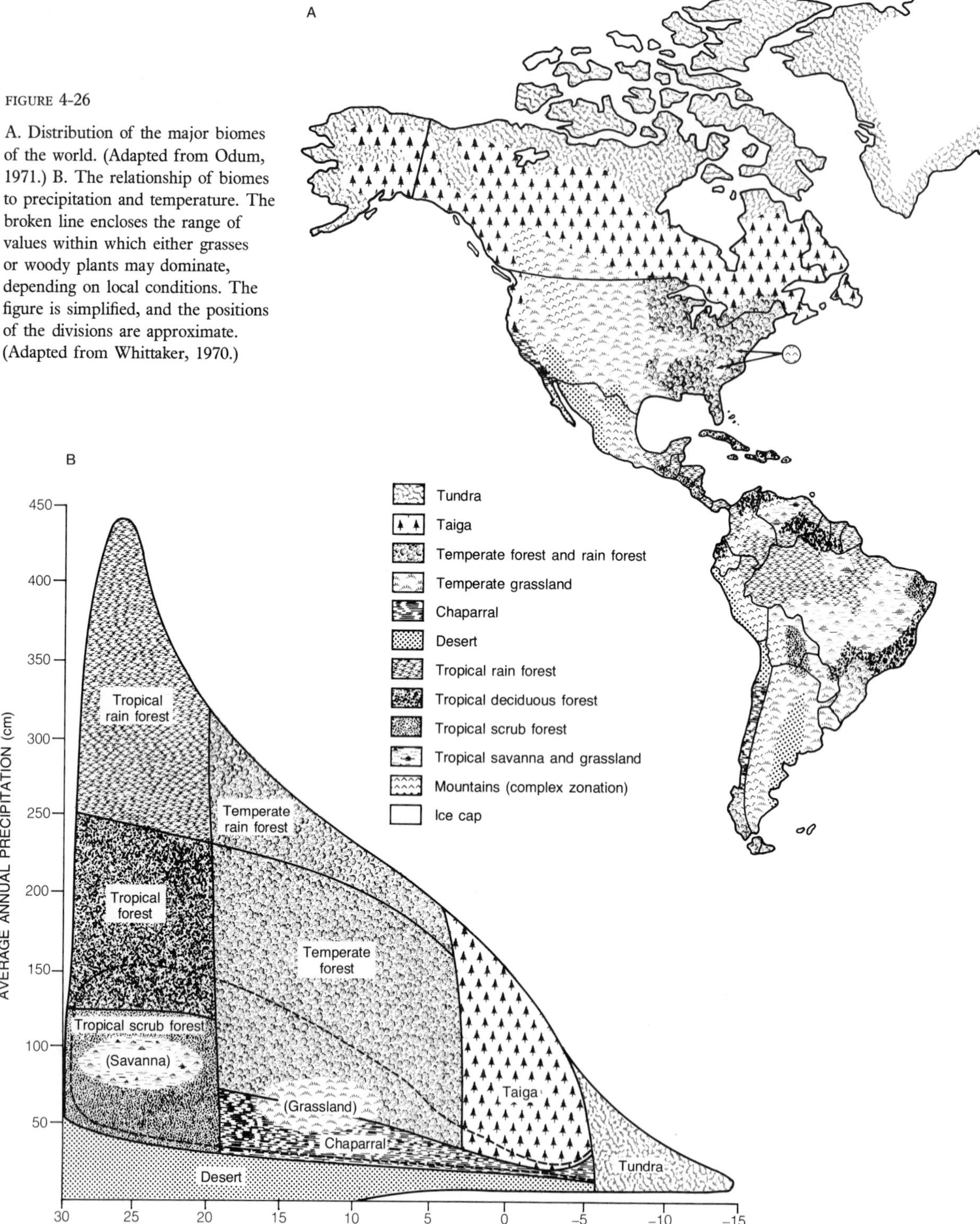

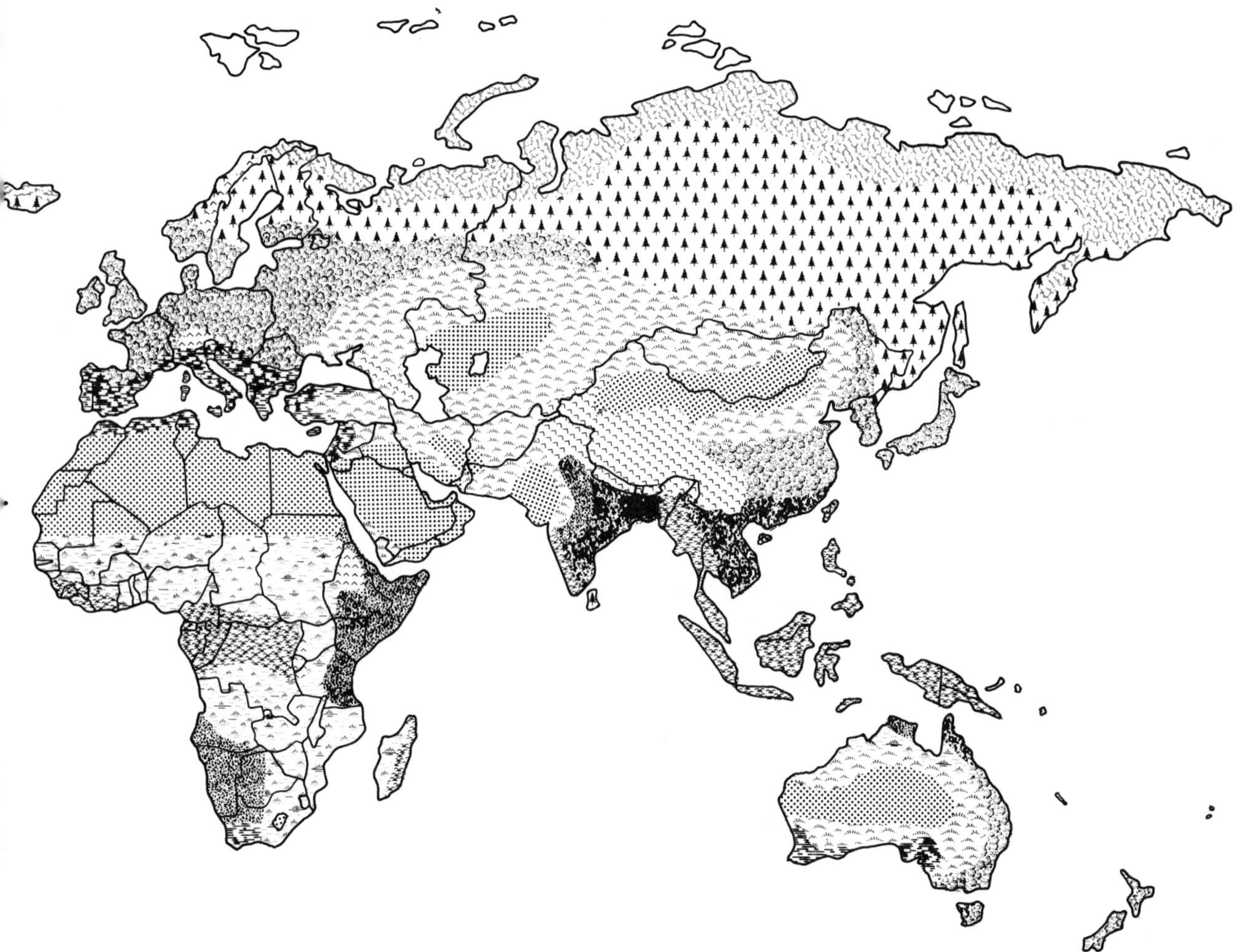

today is impoverished because of the activities of that ultraefficient grazer and browser, the goat. *Opuntia* cactus imported into Australia covered vast areas until its populations were brought under control by a moth, *Cactoblastis cactorum,* taken there for the purpose from the native haunts of the cactus in South America.

The history of human transfers of organisms, purposeful or accidental, is replete with disasters—the cabbage butterfly, the Hessian fly, the gypsy moth, the starling, and the walking catfish have made trouble in North America; rabbits overran Australia; and the grape pest *Phylloxera* nearly destroyed France's wine industry in the nineteenth century. The great ecologist and conservationist Aldo Leopold once said, "The first rule of intelligent tinkering is to save all the parts." Perhaps we should now add to that, "and don't put them in the wrong place."

BIOMES

Terrestrial communities differ dramatically from place to place. The assemblage of plants and animals observed by a resident of California or Chile, for example, is strikingly different from that familiar to a resident of New Jersey or Great Britain. The major kinds of terrestrial communities are called *biomes* by ecologists. Since the impact of human activities varies greatly from biome to biome, you should be familiar with the distribution and at least some of the characteristics of these broadest groupings of communities (Figure 4-26A).[65]

Climatic factors exert the primary control over the nature of the biota (a collective term for the organisms) of

[65]Further details on the fauna and flora of biomes can be found in the books by Kendeigh; Odum; Raven, Evert, and Curtis; and Allee et al., listed at the end of the chapter.

TABLE 4-8
Biological Productivity in Differing Biomes

Biomass	*Arctic tundra (USSR)*	*Northern taiga (USSR)*	*Beech forest (central Europe)*	*Subtropical deciduous forest (average)*	*Tropical rain forest (average)*	*Dry savanna (India)*	*Desert (USSR)*
Photosynthetic parts (%) (mostly leaves) }	30	8	1	3	8	11	13
Perennial parts (%) (stems, etc.) }		70	73	77	74	47	25
Roots (%)	70	22	26	20	18	42	62
Total	100	100	100	100	100	100	100
Litter fall (% of plant biomass)	20	4	3	5	8	27	38

Source: Modified from L. E. Rodin and N. I. Bazilevich, *Production and mineral cycling in terrestrial vegetation.*

broad geographic areas—they are responsible for the characteristic life forms that permit ecologists to distinguish biomes. The relationship of average annual precipitation, average annual temperature, and biome type is shown in Figure 4-26B. Some of the characteristics of ecosystem productivity in the various biomes are listed in Table 4-6. Table 4-8 presents a picture of the distribution of biomass among roots and above-ground parts of plants and indicates what percentage of the biomass the litter fall is, in seven biomes. There are characteristics of the ecosystem in various biomes that transcend the collection of species functioning in the ecosystems. Thus, two tropical rain forests may have entirely different floras, but they will be much more similar to each other in their productivity and in the apportionment of biomass between roots and above-ground parts than either would be to a temperate forest or a desert ecosystem.

Temperate Forest

In regions where the minimum temperature is below freezing each winter but usually does not drop below −12° C (10° F) and the annual rainfall is between about 75 and 200 centimeters (30–80 inches), the dominant plants and animals belong to the *temperate forest biome.* This is the biome familiar to most readers of this book, because it is the biome in which Western (and Chinese) civilization developed. It is typified by the deciduous forest of the eastern United States but is also found in Western Europe and Northeastern China. Where soil conditions permit, mixtures of broad-leafed deciduous trees, such as maples, hickories, and many oaks, grow in dense stands. In the American forests, characteristic mammals such as white-tailed deer, squirrels, shrews, bears, and raccoons forage; so do birds such as warblers, woodpeckers, a wide variety of thrushes and flycatchers, wild turkeys, and owls and hawks.

The deciduous nature of the dominant trees plays a critical role in determining the nature of the temperate forest biome (Figure 4-27). It permits a rich secondary flora to coexist under the trees, flowering in the early spring before the leafing of the trees shades the flora out. In turn, the members of this secondary flora are producers of major components of the temperate forest food web. Many forest insects, for example, feed on these plants of the understory. Furthermore, the deciduous habit itself can be considered an evolutionary response of basically tropical flowering plants that permits them to survive periods when low temperatures would interfere with their photosynthetic mechanisms and water balances.

Because of the annual leaf drop, temperate forests generate soils rich in nutrients, which in turn support an extravagant microbiota in the soil itself. A gram of forest soil has been found to contain 650,000 algae, and counts of microarthropods may number in the hundreds of thousands and nematodes (roundworms) in the millions per square meter.[66] Hence, soil is not just small particles

[66]L. Steubing, Soil flora: Studies in the number and activity of microorganisms in woodland soils, in *Analysis of temperate ecosystems,* David E. Reichle, ed.

worn from the rock of Earth's crust, but a complex integral part of the ecosystem, containing both plants and animals. Especially important to the fertility of the soil is its content of decomposed organic matter or *humus* (see Chapters 7 and 11).

When a temperate forest is cleared, the stored energy and nutrients in the trees are removed, as is the protection from wind and torrential rain that a forest canopy provides. Furthermore, an important source of new nutrients is lost, for the forest trees serve as nutrient pumps. Their deep roots bring vital substances up from the lower regions of the soil, and the trees deposit them at the surface when they shed their leaves.

FIGURE 4-27

A deciduous forest. (Photo by George Taylor, courtesy Friends of the Earth.)

When temperate forests are cleared, the richness of the soils can be preserved if great care is taken to see that their supplies of nutrients and decaying organic material are maintained. It is critical to remember that raising crops or grazing animals on land is, in a sense, mining the soil unless nutrients are carefully returned to it. The nutrients depart along with the crops, meat, wool, or whatever is removed. These may be returned in a variety of ways so the crucial nutrient cycles are continued (see Chapter 3). But, all too often, short-term careless exploiters have permitted soils to deteriorate or have ignored opportunities to improve them. Numerous abandoned farms in Virginia and the Carolinas show the cost to humanity of ignoring the fundamentals of soil ecology; the rich farms of, say, Bavaria show the rewards of paying careful attention to them.

Unfortunately, economic considerations often lead individuals who are exploiting an ecological system to use short-term strategies that are disastrous for humanity in the long run. Thus, it might have been uneconomical for nineteenth-century farmers in some parts of the eastern United States to maintain the nutrient supplies in the soil of their farms carefully. Perhaps they could only survive by living on the capital of nutrients in the land they cleared. In more densely crowded Europe, without competition from other farmers continually exploiting an expanding frontier, a Bavarian farmer of the same period could afford the appropriate soil husbandry—a husbandry that was part and parcel of ancient local tradition.

Deserts

In areas where rainfall is less than 25 centimeters (10 inches) a year are found the world's deserts. They are concentrated in the vicinity of the latitudes 30° north and 30° south, where the global weather system tends to produce descending masses of dry air (although special local conditions may create deserts far from these latitudes). Lack of moisture is the essential factor shaping the *desert biome.* Most deserts are quite hot in the daytime and, because of the sparse vegetation and resultant rapid reradiation of heat, quite cold at night (Figure 4-28). Some, like the fog desert of the Peruvian coast, which

FIGURE 4-28

A desert plant community, central Baja California, Mexico. Notice the variety of spiny, succulent plants and their wide spacing. (Photo courtesy of Robert Ricklefs.)

FIGURE 4-29

A fog desert on the Peruvian coast south of Lima (the shore is in the background). Note the lack of vegetation in this habitat. (Photo by P. R. Ehrlich.)

FIGURE 4-30

An Arctic rock desert, Cornwallis Island, Northwest Territories, Canada. Like the fog desert, this habitat is often nearly devoid of plants, which in this area are most abundant on the relatively nutrient-rich sites of the middens of ancient Eskimo camps. (Photo by P. R. Ehrlich.)

gets little sun over much of the year (Figure 4-29) and the arctic rock desert (Figure 4-30) are relatively cool even at midday. Both of these desert habitats can be nearly devoid of plants.

Desert plants and animals have evolved many specializations for conserving water. In plants these include unusually thick, waterproof outer layers or cuticle, modifications of breathing pores (stomata), reductions in leaf area, and specialized hairs or outgrowths that reflect light. Many desert plants also are heavily armed with spines to repel the attacks of moisture-seeking animals. They frequently are aromatic, indicating the presence of biochemical defenses against herbivores.

Plants may appear to be widely spaced in deserts, but if their roots were visible, the ground between the plants would be seen to be laced with shallow root systems that allow maximum absorption of the rain that does fall. In certain soil conditions, desert plants may have extremely long taproots to reach deep underground water supplies.

Germination of the seeds of desert plants is often inhibited by water-soluble chemicals that must be leached out by a threshold amount of rain before sprouting can occur. Other plants that grow in gravelly arroyos have seeds that require abrasion as the first rains wash them along before they will germinate. Thus, deserts appear to turn miraculously green almost overnight following significant rains, and fast-growing annual plants often create spectacular floral displays.

Proportionately more annual plants are found in the desert biome than in any other. If rainfall is relatively abundant, each individual plant may produce numerous flowers. If rainfall is sparse, many individuals produce only a single blossom each. Since the period of bloom is brief and only follows sporadic rainfall, many people who have traveled in desert areas have not seen them in bloom and remain unaware of the wonderful aesthetic resource they represent.

Desert animals also solve the problem of water shortage in diverse ways. Most are active primarily at night, remaining under cover in the heat of the day. Excretory systems are designed to conserve water, and many desert animals are able to use the water they produce in their cellular metabolism. Many desert insects are "annuals," like the plants they feed on—synchronizing their periods of activity with the evanescent desert bloom.

Desert soils contain little organic matter and must ordinarily be supplied with both water and nitrogen if they are to be cultivated. Much of the uncultivated flat land remaining in the world today is desert, and it seems inevitable that large-scale attempts will be made to expand agriculture into this biome. As we discuss in Chapter 11, irrigation is an expensive and often temporary process—very often a system cannot be maintained and once-cultivated arid lands revert to desert.

Human activities already have produced a great increase in the amount of desert and wasteland. In 1882 land classified as either desert or wasteland amounted to 9.4 percent of the total land on Earth. In 1952 that proportion had risen to 23.3 percent. (Part of this increase doubtless is the result of better information or changes in the definition of wasteland.) During the same period, land classified as carrying inaccessible forest decreased from 43.9 percent to 21.1 percent.[67] The vast Sahara itself is in part man-made, the result of overgrazing, faulty irrigation, and deforestation, combined with natural climatic changes. Today the Sahara seems to be advancing southward into the drought-stricken Sahel, its advance aided by overpopulation of people and domestic animals. The great Thar desert of western India is also partly the result of human influence. Some 2000 years ago, what is now the center of that desert was a jungle. The spread of the desert has been aggravated by poor cultivation practices, lumbering, and overgrazing. Human activities could lead to repetition of the Sahara and Thar stories in many parts of the globe.[68]

Grasslands

Where broad climatic conditions are intermediate between those favoring temperate forest and those producing desert, microclimatic factors (controlled by slope, exposure, and the like) determine whether forests grow.

---

[67]R. R. Doane, *World balance sheet,* Harper, New York, 1957.

[68]The Sahara and Thar situations are described in M. Kassas, Desertification versus potential for recovery in circum-saharan territories, in *Arid lands in transition,* Harold E. Dregne, ed., American Association for the Advancement of Science, Washington, D.C., 1970; and B. R. Seshachar, Problems of environment in India, in *Proceedings of joint colloquium on international environmental science.* U.S. Government Printing Office, Washington, D.C., 1971, Report 63-562.

Thus, tongues of forest may intrude into areas of desert climate along river valleys. The trees themselves change the microclimate in their vicinity, and if they are removed from an area otherwise suitable for their growth, a *grassland* may develop (Figure 4-23). Many ecologists feel that the great grasslands of the American prairie and Great Plains, the steppes of Russia, the vast savannas of Africa, and so forth are all zones between forest and desert where fire and/or browsing animals have prevented the spread of trees, even though rainfall is more plentiful than that which produces typical desert. Various specializations of grasses lead to their dominance in such situations.

Large animals typical of grasslands include the bison ("buffalo") and pronghorn antelope in North America; wild horses in Eurasia; large kangaroos in Australia; and zebras, giraffes, white rhinoceros, and a vast diversity of antelopes in the African savannas. The latter support the richest fauna of large grazers, and the grazers seem to have coevolved in ways that maximize the utilization of the local plant resources.[69]

Other important grassland animals include lions, cheetahs, hyenas, coyotes, and other predators; a variety of birds, ranging in size from ostriches and vultures to small sparrows; rabbits and other burrowing rodents (including the prairie dog); and grasshoppers (locusts). Some grasshoppers exist in a solitary form when their population density is low but transform under crowded conditions over a generation or so into a gregarious form that differs strikingly in both appearance and behavior. The crowded forms migrate in huge masses, laying waste to the countryside—a plague of locusts. For a long time the origins of the locust plagues were not understood because the solitary and gregarious forms were so dissimilar they were identified as different species.[70]

The grassland biome has a higher concentration of organic matter in its soil than any other biome. The amount of humus in grassland soil is about a dozen times that in forest soils. The extraordinary richness of grassland soil has led to the establishment of extremely successful agricultural ecosystems in grassland areas—in the American prairies, for example. These agricultural systems can deteriorate rapidly, however, if careful soil husbandry is not practiced.

The interlaced roots and creeping underground stems of grasses form a turf that prevents the erosion of soil by wind and water. When the turf is broken with a plow, however, the soil is exposed to those erosive influences. In addition, certain kinds of plowing can lead to the formation of a hardpan (a soil horizon nearly impervious to water and roots) below the surface. These two factors have led to rapid deterioration of agroecosystems established in some grasslands—a deterioration dramatized by the dust bowl of the American Great Plains in the 1930s, described so graphically by John Steinbeck in his classic *The Grapes of Wrath.* Indeed, lack of proper soil conservation has already led to a loss of an estimated one-third of the topsoil of the United States (see Figure 4-31).[71]

The situation elsewhere is even more serious. It is estimated that half the farmland in India is not adequately protected from erosion, and on fully one-third of the farmland, erosion threatens to remove the topsoil completely. As agronomist Georg Borgstrom has pointed out, soil conservation procedures are especially difficult to institute in areas where a population is poorly fed. He cites a study that recommended a one-fifth reduction in the amount of cultivated land and a one-third reduction in the size of livestock herds in Turkey.[72] It was hoped that these reductions would help to diminish the danger of catastrophic erosion caused by overgrazing. Unfortunately, the program was not initiated, presumably because the local people depended upon the land and the herds for food and other necessities. As so often happens, a short-run need took precedence over long-run wisdom.

Agriculture in grassland biomes can only be successful over the long term in areas where considerable effort is put into the maintenance of soil structure and nutrients. As we discuss in Chapters 6 and 11, there is considerable reason on this account for anxiety about the prospects for continued high productivity in the American Midwest.

[69]See, for example, S. J. McNaughton, Serengeti migratory wildebeest: Facilitation of energy flow by grazing, *Science,* vol. 191 (January 9, 1976), pp. 92–94.

[70]See V. B. Wigglesworth, *The life of insects,* New American Library, New York, 1968, or any standard entomology text.

[71]Kendeigh, *Ecology.*

[72]*Too many,* Georg Borgstrom, Macmillan, New York, 1969.

A

B

FIGURE 4-31

A. A dust storm approaching Springfield, Colorado, May 21, 1937. The storm caused a half hour of total darkness in the late afternoon. B. A farm abandoned in Bacca County, Colorado, after wind had blasted topsoil from fields and moved it over the farmhouse and other structures. The plow in the foreground was left at the end of a row in the field. (Photos courtesy of the U.S. Department of Agriculture, Soil Conservation Service.)

Taiga

North of the temperate forests in the Northern Hemisphere lies a broad zone of coniferous forest, generally called by its Russian name, *taiga* (Figure 4-32A). Most of the trees do not shed all their leaves in winter. Their leaves are specialized to reduce water loss, especially in the cold season when the area is, in physiological effect, a desert. The leaves in many cases are needlelike and generally last three to five years. Although one thinks of spruce, fir, and other conifers as typical of the taiga, in local regions—including disturbed areas—such deciduous trees as aspens, alders, and larches may be prominent elements of the flora (Figure 4-32B). In general, the trees are much less diverse than those in temperate forests, and the soils have a different kind of humus and are more acid.

Bears, moose, lynxes, rabbits, squirrels, and a variety of birds live in the taiga, but the diversity and abundance of warm-blooded vertebrates are generally less than those of the temperate forests. An exception to this rule are the mustelids (weasels, martins, sables, fishers, and wolverines), which are relatively richly represented. The diversity of cold-blooded vertebrates is even more dramatically restricted—snakes are uncommon, and few amphibia are to be found. Insect diversity is correspondingly low, but the existence of huge stands of one or two species of conifer provides an opportunity for periodic

A

B

C

D

FIGURE 4-32

A. Taiga along the Hay River, Northwest Territories, Canada. A growth of aspens and willows occupies the area subject to flooding along the riverbank. (Photo by P. R. Ehrlich.) B. Taiga in winter northeast of Fort Yukon, Alaska (north of the Arctic Circle). This picture shows characteristic soil polygons, formed through expansion and contraction during freezing and thawing. (Photo courtesy of the U.S. Department of Agriculture, Soil Conservation Service.) C. Taiga in summer near Great Slave Lake, Northwest Territories, Canada (south of the Arctic Circle), showing large areas of muskeg (marsh) and numerous small lakes characteristic of much of the Canadian subarctic. (Photo by P. R. Ehrlich). D. Mosquito protection is required on the Great Slave Lake, Hay River, Northwest Territories, Canada. Note the mosquitoes on the pith helmet. (Photo by P. R. Ehrlich.)

FIGURE 4-33

Nothofagus, the southern beech, on the shores of Lake Fagnano, Tierra del Fuego, Argentina. The slopes of the far shore are covered with *Nothofagus* forest. (Photo by P. R. Ehrlich.)

outbreaks of herbivores like the spruce budworm (the larva of a moth, *Choristoneura fumiferana*), which can defoliate huge areas of forest. In the early 1950s in New Brunswick, Canada, more than 6 million acres were defoliated by the spruce budworm.[73] Mosquitoes and other biting flies reach abundances in the taiga unknown elsewhere in the world and can make human life very difficult in summer (Figure 4-32D). The uniformity of the taiga ecosystem in comparison with the temperate forest and its comparative sensitivity to insect plagues has been one of the underpinnings of the notion that diversity in ecological systems tends to be associated with their stability.

First animal pelts for the fur trade and then wood were the major commodities people extracted from the taiga. Decimation of the fur-bearing animals, changes in clothing styles, and a growing demand for pulp for manufacturing paper have led to an almost total shift to logging in the exploitation of this system. Huge areas have been denuded of forest, often with little or no attempt to protect the soil, so in many places the existence of the climax coniferous forests of the taiga is threatened by erosion. Furthermore, broadcast use of insecticides against insects has been widespread, adding persistent poisons to the already heavily taxed ecosystems of the planet and normally failing to fulfill the goals of the spray program.[74]

In the Southern Hemisphere, little of the land area extends to high enough latitudes to support an extensive taiga like that of the Northern Hemisphere. A somewhat comparable ecosystem is found in the cool areas of South America and Australia, dominated by evergreen trees of the beech family in the genus *Nothofagus* (Figure 4-33). A characteristic of *Nothofagus* forests, like those of the taiga, is an extensive litter of tree trunks and branches on the forest floor, since in cold climates the action of decomposer organisms is quite slow.

Tundra

North of the taiga lie the treeless plains of the *tundra.* In those areas, where the average annual temperature is below −5° C (23° F), the ground normally thaws in summer only to a depth of less than a meter. Below that it remains permanently frozen (permafrost). Precipitation is usually less than 25 centimeters (10 inches) per year. The permafrost effectively prevents the establishment of

[73]R. F. Morris, (ed.), The dynamics of epidemic spruce budworm populations, *Memoirs of the Entomological Society of Canada,* vol. 31 (1963) pp. 1–332.

[74]Ibid. Also, see Chapter 11 for a fuller discussion of the use of insecticide.

FIGURE 4-34

Tundra biome. A. Grassy tundra at Duke of York Bay, Southampton Island, Northwest Territories, Canada. The bones in the foreground are the vertebrae of a right whale at the site of an old Eskimo encampment. The right whale is now extinct in this area. B. An Eskimo child holding a piece of white whale (beluga) skin on Coral Harbour, Southampton Island, 1953. The skin of this small whale is considered such a delicacy that the Eskimo word for it, *muktuk*, forms the root of the Eskimo word for "delicious," *a nah muktuk*. The tundra biome in most areas is relatively devoid of large food animals, the exception being migratory caribou. Therefore, primitive Eskimo groups were heavily dependent upon sea mammals and fishes for food and other resources. C. Eskimo men butchering walruses on Walrus Island in northern Hudson Bay, Canada. Walrus provide food for sled dogs, skin for making harness, and ivory for carving. D. Low tundra with extensive willow stands around lakes on Southampton Island. (Photos by P. R. Ehrlich.) E. Tundra below Mount McKinley, Alaska, showing caribou trails. (Photo by Charlie Ott, courtesy National Audubon Society.)

trees. Not surprisingly, the soil fauna is poorly developed—nearly as depauperate as that of deserts.[75] Lichens, sedges, grasses, willows (which normally reach a height of less than a meter), and members of the cranberry family are among the dominant plants (Figure 4-34A). In some areas of the central Canadian Arctic, however, rainfall is so low that a rock desert nearly devoid of vegetation occurs (Figure 4-30).

Caribou, wolves, musk-oxen, arctic foxes, rabbits, and (occasionally in summer) polar bears are among the mammals found in the tundra. In the brief arctic summer, an astounding diversity of birds (especially waterfowl), migrate to the tundra to breed, feeding on an ephemeral bloom of insects and freshwater invertebrates. Mosquitoes can make one's life nearly as miserable in the tundra as in the taiga. Reptiles and amphibians are absent. As in the taiga, animal populations in the tundra may be subject to dramatic oscillations in size. Best known are the lemming cycles, which induce cycles in the owls, jaegers (predatory gulls), and other predators that feed on them.

Because of the slow rates at which plants grow and decompose, with the low temperatures and the characteristics of permafrost, the thick, spongy matting of lichens, grasses, and sedges that characterizes the "low tundra" (that found in depressions and on plains rather than ridges and slopes) is especially slow to recover from disturbance.[76] Tracks of vehicles or animals can remain visible for decades (Figure 4-34E). Great care must be taken in building on tundra because heat from structures will melt the permafrost and cause uneven settling, which often badly distorts the structures. The tundra has been one of the least exploited biomes, but that era is also ending.

Tropical Rain Forests

Near the equator, in areas where annual rainfall is greater than about 240 centimeters (95 inches) and the mean annual temperature is more than 17° C (64° F), are found the *tropical rain forests*—the jungles of popular fiction. Tropical rain forests grow in climatic zones where neither temperature nor water is a limiting factor. They once covered much of Central America and South America, central and western Africa, Madagascar, and Southeast Asia. Tropical rain forests are characterized by a great diversity of plant and animal species and by their spacial structure.

The trees of these forests are taller than those of many temperate forests, the tallest reaching 60 meters (200 feet) or so. The tops of most trees are intertwined, to form a dense canopy 30 meters (100+ feet) or more above the ground (Figure 4-35A). The tallest trees stand out above the canopy. Beneath it little light penetrates to the ground. There are in many places more than fifty species of trees per hectare—many more species than one could find in a day's walk through a temperate forest, where the vast majority of trees represent only a few species. Characteristic of tropical forests, also, are a wide variety of epiphytes (plants that grow high on the trees in the sunlit zone whose roots do not reach down to the soil). Except where a fallen tree has created a hole in the canopy to admit light, the understory in a rain forest is sparse, unlike that of a temperate forest. Since the trees normally do not branch below the canopy, one can often walk almost unobstructed through the dimly lit depths of a mature forest (the forest's edge, in contrast, is usually a tangle of riotous growth). Most trees have shallow roots, and many develop huge buttresses for support (Figure 4-35C).

Animal species in tropical rain forests are also very diverse, with insects, amphibia, reptiles, and birds especially well represented. For example, roughly as many butterfly species can be found in a single rain forest locality as are found in the entire United States (five or six hundred), including whole groups unknown or scarcely represented in the temperate zones. Coevolutionary relationships appear to be more highly developed in this biome than in any other.

To a layman the luxuriant growth of a tropical jungle implies a rich soil. Nothing, however, could be further from the truth. Tropical forest soils are in general exceedingly thin and nutrient-poor. They cannot maintain large reserves of minerals needed for plant growth, such as phosphorus, potassium, and calcium, primarily

[75]M. S. Chilarov, Abundance, biomass and vertical distribution of soil animals in different zones, in *Secondary productivity of terrestrial ecosystems*, K. Petruzewicz, Warsaw, 1967, p. 611–629.

[76]T. A. Babb and L. C. Bliss, Effects of physical disturbance on Arctic vegetation in the Queen Elizabeth Islands, *Journal of applied ecology*, vol. 11 (1974), pp. 549–562.

A

FIGURE 4-35

A tropical rain forest. A. The canopy of a rain forest covering hills in central Costa Rica. B. In the dense understory, light penetrates into a rainforest along a stream in Sarapiqui, on the Atlantic coastal plain of Costa Rica. C. Buttresses of a rain forest tree in Sarapiqui, Costa Rica. (Photos by P. R. Ehrlich.)

B

C

because heavy rainfall and a high rate of water flow through the ground to the water table leach them from the soil. The leaching process leaves behind large residues of insoluble iron and aluminum oxides in the upper levels of tropical forest soils.

What nutrients there are in the tropical forest ecosystem are tied up in the lush vegetation itself. Those nutrients that are released by the decay of dropped leaves and fallen trees are quickly taken up by the shallow network of roots that laces the forest floor and are returned to the living vegetation. Since most tropical forest trees are evergreen, the process is continuous. A rich layer of humus does not accumulate as it does in a temperate forest, where, after a general leaf-fall, the trees are dormant each winter.

Tropical rain forests are being destroyed more rapidly than any other biome. In Central America, the forests are "vaporizing," to borrow the term of Daniel Janzen, one of the most distinguished tropical ecologists.[77] In Brazil they are being destroyed as a consequence of direct governmental action, in an effort to develop the Amazon basin. Throughout the tropics, forests are being cut down to make room for farms. The pressure of human population and ignorance are quickly robbing the world of its richest reservoir of terrestrial organic diversity.

Altitudinal Gradients

In areas where there are substantial variations in altitude, the terrestrial communities differ at different elevations. This is primarily because the temperature of the air decreases about 6° C for every 1000-meter increase in altitude, and because, especially in desert areas, rainfall increases with altitude.[78] Thus, in the mountains of Colorado above about 3500 meters, temperature conditions are similar to those of the tundra biome at sea level, and a treeless *alpine tundra* exists. As one travels northward in the Rocky Mountains, the treeline (the altitude above which tundra occurs) gradually lowers until in northern Alaska and Canada it reaches sea level.

Tundra is virtually continuous in the northern Rocky Mountains; in Colorado "islands" of mountain tundra occur as dense archipelagos. Because of this, the faunas and floras of the arctic and North American alpine tundras have many similar organisms. For instance, among the butterflies of Colorado mountaintops are numerous genera, and even a few species, also found in the sea-level tundras 3800 kilometers to the north. By contrast, the treeless zones of tropical South American and African mountains, where the treeline is around 4000 meters, superficially resemble arctic tundra (Figure 4-36)[79] but show few faunal affinities with the north. For example, satyrine butterflies of the genus *Erebia* found in the high mountains of Colorado are representatives of a circumpolar genus characteristic of cool climates. Satyrine butterflies of the high Andes that are virtually indistinguishable on the wing from *Erebia*, however, are members of the genus *Punapedaloides*, which has strictly tropical affinities.

Thus, in the mountains it is possible to find compressed into 2000 vertical meters a series of communities that would occupy a sea-level latitudinal gradient 1000 kilometers or more in length (Figure 4-37). Alpine habitats contribute greatly to the floral and faunal diversity of Earth because, although in temperature they closely resemble sea-level habitats closer to the poles, they differ in other factors, such as daylength regime and atmospheric pressure. Anyone who has been active at an altitude of more than 3500 meters knows that the stresses encountered there are quite different from those at sea level anywhere!

Other Biomes

In this brief survey, we have not touched on some less extensive but nonetheless interesting biomes. *Chaparral*, found in places with mild marine climates and winter rainfall such as the Mediterranean basin and the southwest coasts of North America, South America and

[77]Janzen, The deflowering.

[78]For example, see J. Terborgh, Distribution on environmental gradients: Theory and preliminary interpretation of distributional patterns in the avifauna of the Cordillera Vilcamba, Peru, *Ecology*, vol. 52 (1971), pp. 23–40; and R. H. Whittaker and W. A. Niering, Vegetation of the Santa Catalina mountains, Arizona, pt.5: Biomass, production and diversity along the elevation gradient, *Ecology* vol. 56 (1975), pp. 771–790.

[79]S. R. Eyre, *Vegetation and soils: A world picture.*

FIGURE 4-36

Above the tree line near La Oroya, Peru, about 4000 meters. (Photo by P. R. Ehrlich.)

Australia, and the Cape region of South Africa, is characterized by dry, aromatic, evergreen shrubs and shrubby trees (Figure 4-38). Chaparral is subject to periodic fires that maintain the dominance of the shrub vegetation; the underground parts of the perennial plants found there are fire-resistant, and some of the annuals must undergo fire before germination. In areas such as Southern California, people have built homes extensively in chaparral and suffer the consequences of the inevitable fires.

Tropical savannas are grasslands with scattered clumps of trees, which tend to be thorny. This biome covers a large portion of Africa and is familiar to all who have seen movies or television shows on the magnificent herds of hoofed mammals (and the carnivores that prey on them) that still roam in places like the Serengeti Plain. In many regions the savanna is threatened by overgrazing by cattle, but some efforts are now being made to develop systems of sustained-yield harvesting of native antelopes, which are better adapted to feeding on the savanna plants and more resistant to disease than cattle.

Tropical scrub and *tropical deciduous* (or *seasonal*) *forest* biomes are found where rainfall is intermediate between that suitable for savanna and that required for tropical rain forest. The scrub (sometimes called thorn forest) is found where the precipitation is between 50 and 125 centimeters (20 to 50 inches) per year; the deciduous forest, where it is between 125 and 250 centimeters (50 to 100 inches). The former consists of small hardwood trees, frequently thorny, as the name implies. The latter, especially where rainfall is toward the top of the range, is a full-scale forest (the monsoon forests of India and Vietnam). In both of these biomes—in contrast to tropical rainforests—there are well-defined wet and dry seasons to which both plants and animals are adapted. (The reproductive activities of many insects, for example, are timed to coincide with the wet season, with its abundance of fresh plant food.)

A key point to understand here is that an extremely wide variety of situations is covered by the term *tropical*—indeed, even by the term *tropical forest.* The tropics are far more diverse than the temperate zones. Consequently, no single system can possibly be devised to solve the problems of "tropical agriculture" because those problems vary so enormously from place to place.

One further biome, the *temperate rain forest,* deserves mention. These forests are characteristic of the northwestern coast of North America and the southwestern coast of New Zealand, areas that receive 200 to 380 centimeters (80 to 150 inches) of precipitation annually. They are characterized in North America by very tall coniferous trees such as western hemlock, Douglas fir, and redwoods, and have well-developed understories with abundant mosses (there often are epiphytic mosses—those that grow on trees and other large plants—as well). This biome is extensively exploited for timber, the redwoods being especially valued for their decay-resistant wood.

FIGURE 4-37

Altitudinal changes in vegetation in Cement Creek, Gunnison County, Colorado. The sagebrush area in the foreground is at about 3000 meters. The second growth of aspens on the slope to the left and the coniferous forest on the other slopes are at 3000–3800 meters. Treeless tundra occupies the highest areas, at about 4000 meters. (Photo by P. R. Ehrlich.)

FIGURE 4-38

Chaparral near El Cajon, east of San Diego, California. Chamise, toyon, *Ceanothus,* and other characteristic chaparral shrubs occupy the hillside; small chaparral oak species dominate the denser vegetation along the stream bottom in the foreground. (Photo courtesy of Robert Ricklefs.)

FRESHWATER HABITATS

Biological communities in fresh water are classically divided into two groups—those found in the running water of rivers and streams and those of the standing water of ponds and lakes. What ties these communities into a logical unit, however, are the physical properties of the medium in which they exist. Water, as you will recall from Chapter 2, has extraordinary properties that in many ways govern the climate of Earth and the way in which organisms have evolved here. Indeed, life as we know it is inconceivable without water. Our discussion of freshwater habitats focuses on four properties of water—its change of density at 4° C, its content of dissolved oxygen, its transparency, and its content of dissolved chemicals other than oxygen.

It is fair to say that there would be no freshwater life outside the tropics if H_2O did not reach its highest density above its freezing point. If it did not, ice would sink, and temperate and polar bodies of water would freeze solid each winter. In large lakes in the temperate zone, a decrease in water density with increasing temperature (above 4° C) creates a layering of water during the summer. An upper layer of less dense, warm water, the *epilimnion,* is formed. Deeper waters remain cool and thus more dense, to form the *hypolimnion.* Separating these two stable layers is a zone of rapid temperature change, the *thermocline.* (For a more detailed discussion, see Chapter 11.) This layering and the transparency of the water are intimately related to one of its most critical properties, its oxygen content.

The amount of light that penetrates the water decreases rapidly with depth, the longer (red) wavelengths dropping out first. By measuring oxygen production and consumption by plankton in water samples, it is possible to determine the point in the gradient of light at which photosynthesis is balanced by respiration.[80] This *compensation level* by convention is considered the dividing line between an upper *euphotic* (autotrophic) zone and a lower *profundal* (heterotrophic) zone. In summer the compensation level is usually above the thermocline; because the algae that contribute oxygen as a product of photosynthesis cannot live below that point, the amount of dissolved oxygen in the hypolimnion may drop almost to zero.

The degree of oxygen depletion (summer stagnation) in the hypolimnion is partially a function of the productivity of the lake. Lakes with low nutrient content (because of the characteristics of their drainage basins, or their ages) tend to have a low density of phytoplankton and few plants in their *littoral* zones (shallow regions where sunlight penetrates to the bottom). In such *oligotrophic* (few foods) lakes, the "rain" of dead organisms and other organic debris into the hypolimnion is relatively sparse. Since the degradation of those wastes by decomposers requires oxygen, oxygen supplies are less likely to be depleted there than where there is a heavy input of wastes. Furthermore, in some young lakes the water is so transparent that the compensation level is below the thermocline, and excess oxygen is produced in the hypolimnion by photosynthesis. Oligotrophic lakes can thus support populations of such fish as lake trout, which require both cool water and considerable oxygen.

Most oligotrophic lakes are geologically young. As they grow older, a successional process may occur as nutrients and sediments wash in and the lakes grow shallower and support more littoral vegetation. Productivity increases, and the lakes may have massive blooms of phytoplankton. The rain of organic debris into the hypolimnion is heavy, and oxygen depletion there becomes severe—especially after the die-off of a plankton bloom. Such *eutrophic* (well fed) lakes will not support some commercially valuable fishes like trout, but will support food fishes like bass and bluegills, as well as carp and other "trash fish," all of which are at home in warmer waters and tolerant of lower oxygen concentrations.

Eutrophication is a natural successional process in some lakes, but injections of nutrients in the form of pollutants can hasten the process, greatly reducing the value of a lake for recreation and fishing (see Chapter 11). Hence, one index of the degree of pollution in a body of fresh water is the *dissolved oxygen concentration* (DO); another is the difference between the production and consumption of oxygen—*biological* (or *biochemical*) *oxygen demand* (BOD). The latter may be thought of as the amount of oxygen required for the oxidative decomposition of materials in the water. The BOD is normally

[80]The technique is described by E. P. Odum in *Fundamentals of ecology,* pp. 14–16.

measured in the laboratory as the number of milligrams of O_2 consumed per liter of water over a period of five days at 20° C (see Chapter 10 for further discussion of BOD).

What happens to the stratification of a temperate lake in winter? As the upper layer cools in the autumn, it begins to sink, carrying fresh oxygen with it to the depths. The thermocline disappears, and nutrient-rich waters from the hypolimnion circulate throughout the lake. At one point the lake is *isothermal* (4° C from top to bottom). Then, when the lake freezes, the temperature (and density) gradient is established from the surface ice at 0° C to the rest of the lake at 4° C. In spring after the ice melts, the water at the surface warms to 4° C and sinks through the lighter 2° to 3° C water below, producing a spring overturn and a redistribution of oxygen and nutrients.

Tropical lakes, in which the water has high surface temperatures, have weak temperature gradients and often rather stable layering, created by the resultant slight density differences. Therefore, the ecology of those lakes is substantially different from that of temperate lakes.

The fauna of any body of fresh water, temperate or tropical, will vary somewhat with the chemical characteristics of the water. For instance, the pH of the water must be within a certain range if certain species of fish are to thrive—as every serious fancier of tropical fish has discovered. Some species, such as neon tetras, come from acid waters and do best in an aquarium if the pH is kept low. Others, such as mollies, do best in more alkaline water (high pH). Aquatic plants are similarly sensitive to pH. The concentration of calcium ions has been shown to be important in restricting the distribution of freshwater sponges and to be related to the distribution of triclad flatworms (planarians), but much still remains to be learned about the relationship between the chemistry of water and its biota.[81] This is becoming especially important as human beings increasingly change the chemistry of fresh waters with pollutants.

Streams and rivers differ from ponds and lakes primarily in their relative lack of stratification in either temperature or oxygen concentration, in their having currents, and in their proportionally greater interface with the land (the length of banks relative to the volume of water). These differences strongly influence the biota. Usually in streams producers are inadequate to supply the consumers, the difference being made up by organic materials washed from the banks. Because of the currents, most of the plants and animals of streams and rivers have evolved ways to keep from being washed downstream—using holdfasts, burrowing into the substrate, or having superb swimming ability (like brook trout). Plankton is comparatively rare in running water, but in the slower-moving parts of streams and rivers it may be an important part of a community.

The normally high oxygen content of streams and rivers has meant that animals adapted to running water generally have little tolerance for low oxygen concentration. Any addition of oxygen-reducing (high BOD) pollutants to streams or rivers is therefore likely to have a drastic effect on the fauna.

MARINE HABITATS

The oceans cover about 71 percent of Earth's surface, thus making them the most extensive habitat. As we described in Chapter 2, the oceans play major roles in the hydrologic cycle and in the global weather machine; therefore, their influence on life extends to all organisms. Considering their size, the oceans are an extraordinarily uniform environment—especially the 98 percent or so of their volume that is below the depth to which enough light penetrates for photosynthesis to occur.

Because the oceans are rather thoroughly stirred by currents, there is sufficient oxygen for heterotrophs in most areas, as well as abundant CO_2 for autotrophs. But nutrients are often in short supply, especially nitrogen and phosphorus. Productivity is highest in the oceans in areas of upwelling, as along the western coast of South America, where nutrients are brought to the surface in abundance. In those areas phytoplankton reproduce without the nutrient shortage that restricts much of the open ocean to low productivity.

Many bizarre and wonderful creatures have evolved in the sunless depths of the oceans, feeding on the organic matter that drifts down from above and often signaling one another with luminescent organs. Most of the

[81]Krebs, *Ecology*, pp. 98–101.

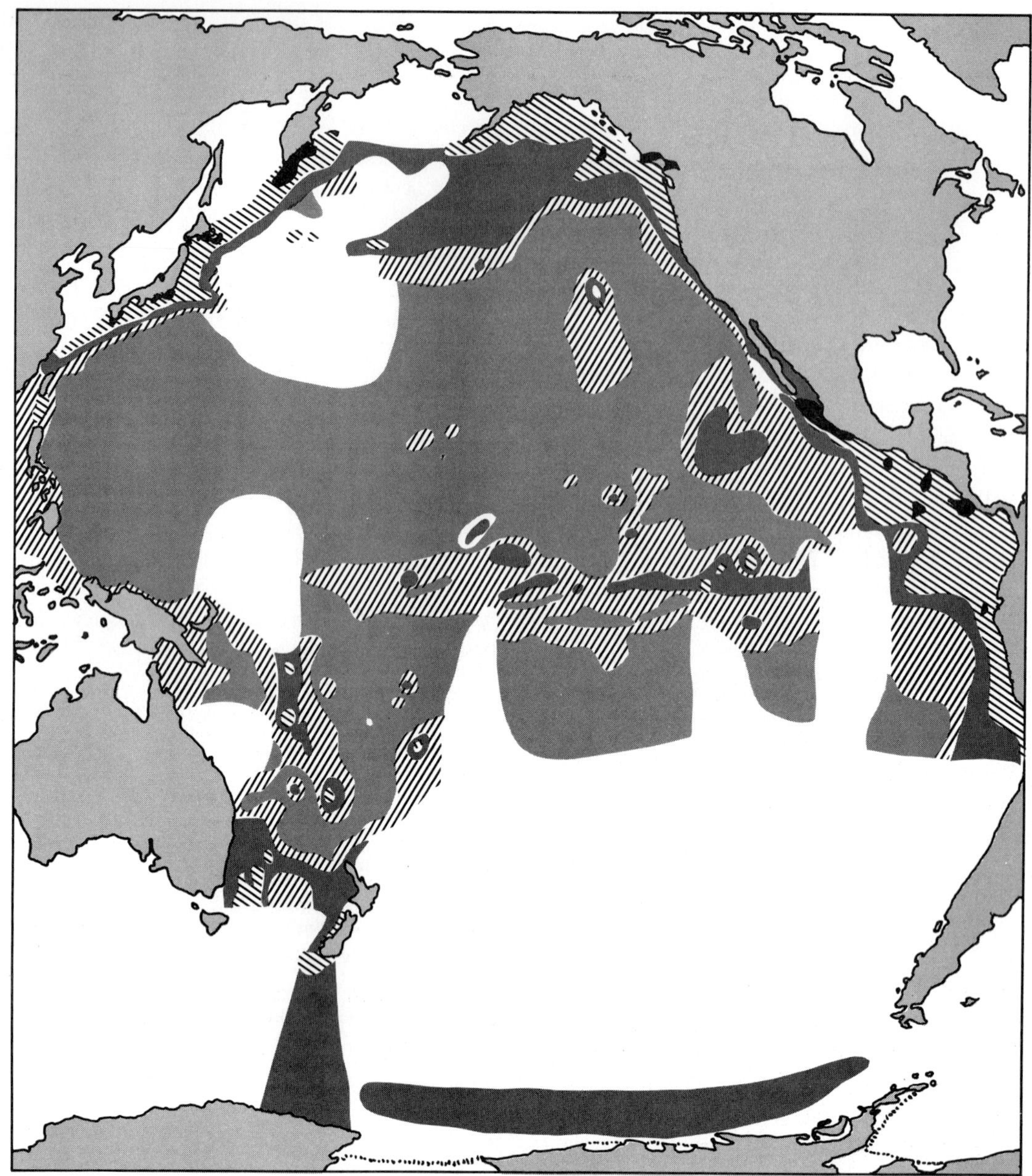

IN THE TOTAL WATER COLUMN

MILLIGRAMS OF CARBON FIXED PER DAY PER SQUARE METER		GRAMS OF CARBON FIXED PER YEAR PER SQUARE METER
100		36
100–150		36–55
150–250		55–91
250–650		91–237
650+		237+
		No data available

FIGURE 4-39

Gross primary production per unit area in the Pacific Ocean. Net primary production would be about 60 percent of the figures shown. (Data from NAS/NRC, *Resources and man.*)

biological activity of interest to humanity in the oceans, however, occurs near the surface in the *euphotic zone* (where photosynthesis exceeds plant respiration) and especially near the continents, where the availability of nutrients maximizes productivity. That is where the great fisheries are, and that is also where human inputs to the oceans are greatest (Figure 4-39).

Near the shore the marine environment becomes more complex, and intricate zonations have developed under the influence of light gradients, wave action, and tides (Figure 4-40). The most complex, and perhaps the most interesting, marine habitats are the coral reefs that fringe the shores of tropical landmasses. The reefs are made of the skeletons of coral animals that live in a mutualistic relationship with algae. In some ways the complexity of the reef habitat rivals that of a tropical rain forest, with vertical stratification and great diversity of species.[82] Roughly one-third of all fish species (both freshwater and saltwater) live on coral reefs (Figure 4-41).

BARNACLES	MYTILUS PERNA (Mussels)
CAULERPA LIGULATA (Green algae)	PATELLA COCHLEAR (Limpets)
CORALLINES (Algae)	PATELLA GRANULARIS (Limpets)
GELIDIUM PRISTOIDES (Red algae)	PLOCAMIUM CORALLORHIZA (Red algae)
HYPNEA SPICIFERA (Green algae)	POMATOLEIOS CROSSLANDI (Tube worms)
LITTORINA KNYSNAËNSIS (Snails resistant to dessication)	PYURA STOLONIFERA (Ascidian sea squirt)
Short algal turf	

FIGURE 4-40

Intertidal zonation on the south coast of Africa. A. The upper edge of the *Littorina* snail zone. B. The upper edge of the barnacle zone. C. The upper edge of the zone defined by the limpet *Patella cochlear.* D. The upper edge of the subtidal zone. The shore is shown at an exceptionally low spring tide on an unusually calm day. The zones are represented in a very diagrammatic fashion, somewhat telescoped; the *Littorina* zone is especially reduced. (Adapted from T. A. Stephenson and A. Stephenson, *Life between tidemarks on rocky shores,* W. H. Freeman and Company. Copyright © 1972.)

[82]Paul R. Ehrlich, Population biology of coral reef fishes, *Annual Review of Ecology and Systematics,* September 1975, pp. 211–247.

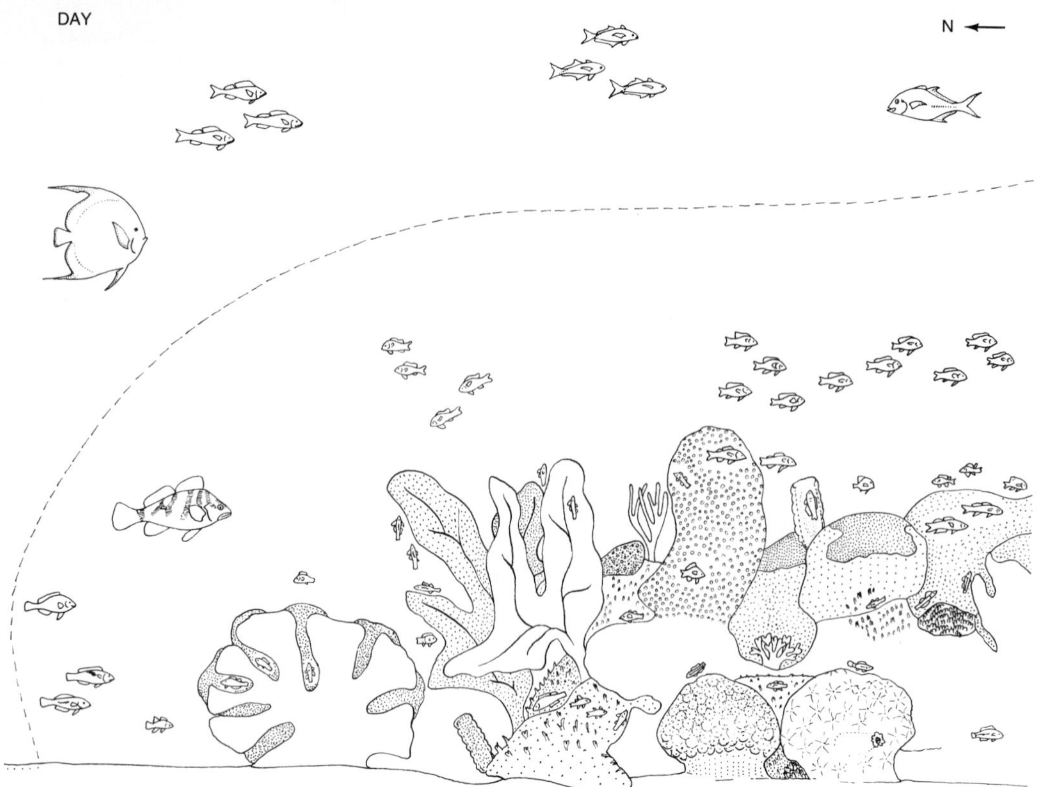

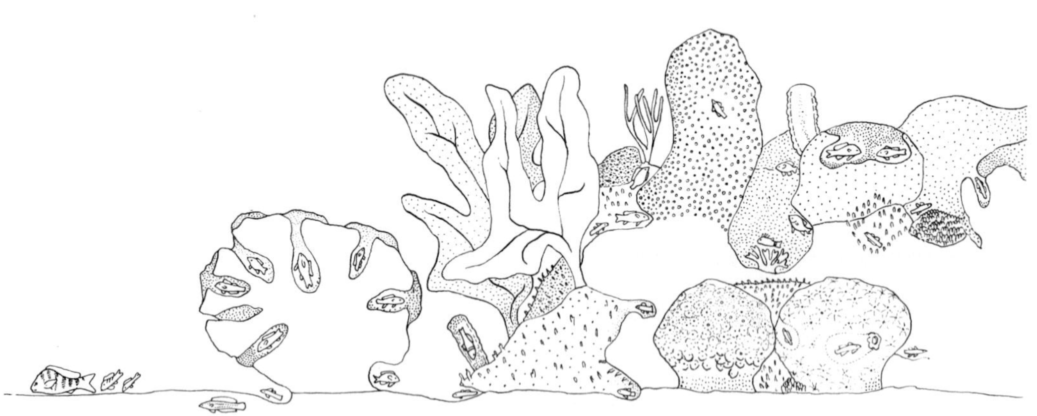

FIGURE 4-41

Complexity and diversity of a coral reef habitat is indicated by this diagrammatic cross-section of reefs off St. John, U.S. Virgin Islands, showing general distribution of 73 fish species, day and night. Reefs in the northern part of the Australian Great Barrier Reef can support up to 1000 fish species. On coral

reefs, of course, there are a great many kinds of invertebrates and algae not indicated here. (Adapted from *Results of the tektite program: ecology of coral reef fishes,* Natural History Museum, Los Angeles County, *Science bulletin,* 14, 1972.)

But even the diverse coral reef fauna shows great similarities in such far-apart places as the Society Islands of the central Pacific and the reefs fringing the East African coast—and genera of fishes found in both of those places also occur in the Caribbean. In contrast to both terrestrial and freshwater habitats, which are often isolated from each other, the oceans have a great unity.

Estuaries

Where rivers and streams flow into the oceans, and fresh and salt water intermingle in tidal ponds, rivers, and embayments are found the habitats known as estuaries. Organisms that live in estuaries must be tolerant of a wide range of salinities and usually of a wide range of temperatures also. The daily rhythm of the tides gives them an ever-changing environment.

Many organisms have evolved to live in these conditions, and the productivity of estuaries (which tend to be nutrient traps) is very high (Table 4-6). Some of this productivity is harvested at the estuary by human beings—most of the oysters and crabs people eat, for example, are estuarine. More important to *Homo sapiens,* however, is the role estuaries play as "nurseries" for commercially important marine species. Many of the shrimps and fishes that are harvested at sea have estuarine young. Indeed, it has been estimated that about two-thirds of the rich commercial fishing on the continental shelf of the eastern United States consists of species that spend part of their life cycles in estuaries.[83]

Another estimate[84] credits each hectare of estuary with contributing more than 550 kilograms of fishes per year to coastal fisheries. Using a conservative estimate of 1.4×10^6 km^2 (1.4×10^8 hectares) of estuaries worldwide, their total annual contribution to fisheries would be $550 \times 1.4 \times 10^8 = 77 \times 10^9$ kg = 77 million MT. That is somewhat more than the present global fisheries harvest and about one-third of the total estimated potential production of fishes in the sea (see Chapter 7). That estuaries are among the most threatened of all habitats today is therefore cause for considerable concern.

[83] J. L. McHugh, Management of estuarine fisheries, in *A symposium on estuarine fisheries,* American Fisheries Society, Washington, D.C., 1966, special publication 3; G. M. Woodwell, P. H. Rich, and G. A. S. Hall, Carbon in estuaries, in *Carbon and the biosphere,* Woodwell and Pecan, eds., p. 234.

[84] R. H. Stroud, in *Symposium on the biological significance of estuaries,* P. A. Douglas and R. H. Stroud, eds., Sport Fishing Institute, Washington, D.C., 1971, p. 4.

Antarctica

One further habitat deserves attention—one that contains only a small amount of land that isn't perpetually ice-covered and that supports a "terrestrial" community almost entirely dependent on marine producers. That habitat is Antarctica. There are two flowering plants (a grass and a plant of the carnation family) and a variety of mosses and lichens scattered around the fringes of the Antarctic continent. These producers support small communities of invertebrate consumers and decomposers, but all of the vertebrates found on land in the Antarctic feed on food chains based on massive summer blooms of marine phytoplankton, supported by extremely nutrient-rich upwellings in the sea. The phytoplankton support large populations of shrimplike krill, which in turn form the feeding base for animals as diverse as baleen whales and penguins (Figure 4-42).

Penguins and other seabirds breed on land in the summer[85] in enormous colonies that in their turn support populations of skuas (predatory relatives of seagulls), which feed on penguin eggs and young penguins. One antarctic seal, the leopard seal, feeds on penguins. Another, the Weddell seal, feeds on fishes and squid, and a third, the crabeater seal, belies its name by feeding mostly on krill. In turn, those seals are preyed upon by killer whales (Figure 4-43).

Of all the major habitats on Earth, Antarctica, in a physical sense, is the least disturbed by human activities. Antarctica is protected by a barrier of sea ice, so only a handful of people had ever set foot on the continent before the middle of the twentieth century. And, except for the small huts of explorers like Scott and Shackleton, the bits of land not permanently ice-covered showed no signs of human disturbance before that time.

[85] The exception to this is the emperor penguin, which breeds in winter on the ice.

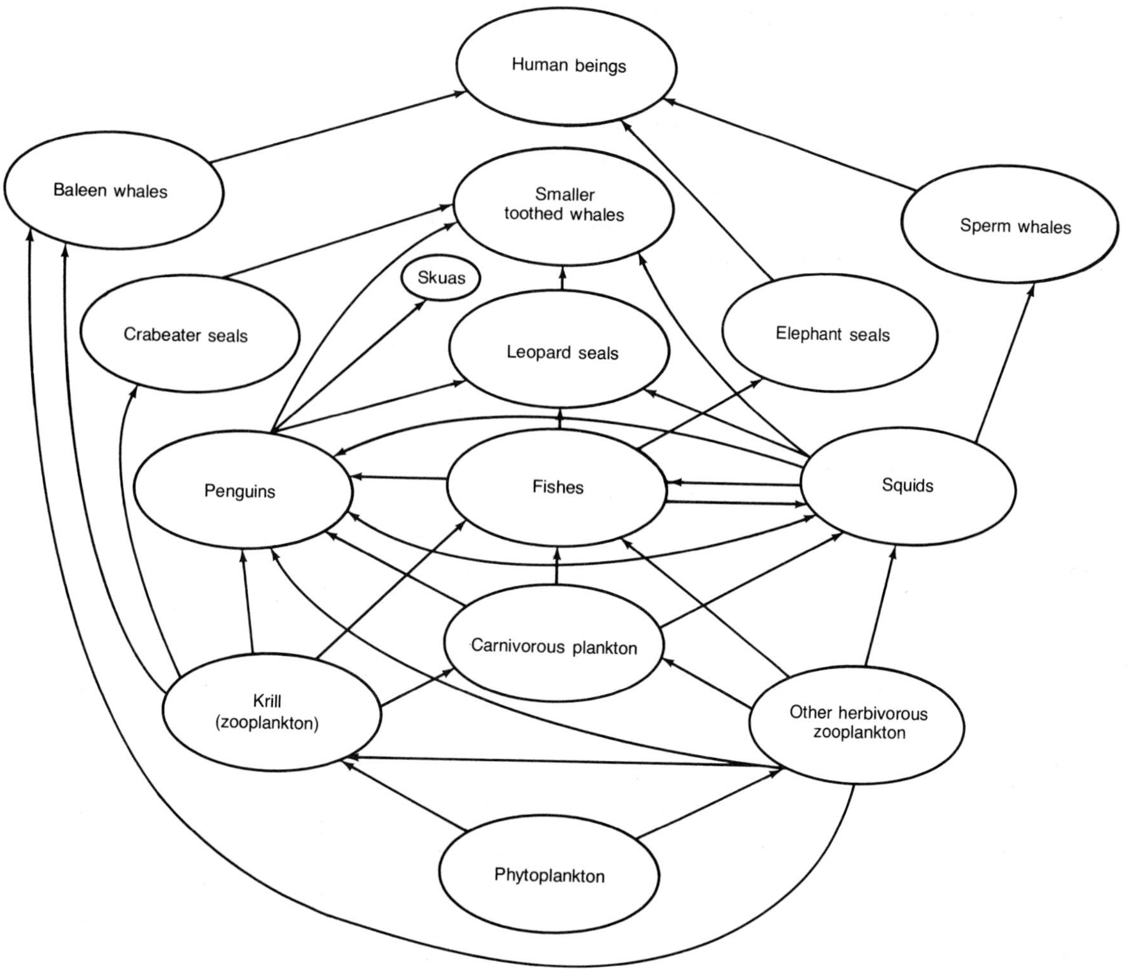

FIGURE 4-42

Antarctic food chains. Notice that even the "terrestrial" vertebrates are dependent upon marine productivity.

But long before World War II, humanity was exploiting the antarctic oceanic ecosystem that is the feeding base of all large animal life on that continent. Early in the twentieth century, whaling in antarctic waters was so intense that by 1920 the right whale, so-called because it was easy to catch and floated after harpooning (the "right" whale from a whaler's point of view!) was virtually extinct, and concern was expressed in the international community about the future of all exploited whales. After World War II, overexploitation continued (see Chapter 7 for more detail); today whales are scarce in antarctic waters. In a two-week voyage in antarctic waters in 1974/1975, the authors saw *no* whales of the species that have constituted the backbone of the whaling industry. In the very same waters in 1912, Robert Cushman Murphy reported seeing "whales in all directions," even though the slaughter of those great mammals was far enough advanced by then that the shoreline near the whaling station at South Georgia Island was "lined for miles with the bones of whales."[86]

What effect the removal of the baleen whales from the Antarctic Ocean will have on the structure of the

[86]*Logbook for grace,* Time-Life Books, New York, 1965, p. 188.

A

B
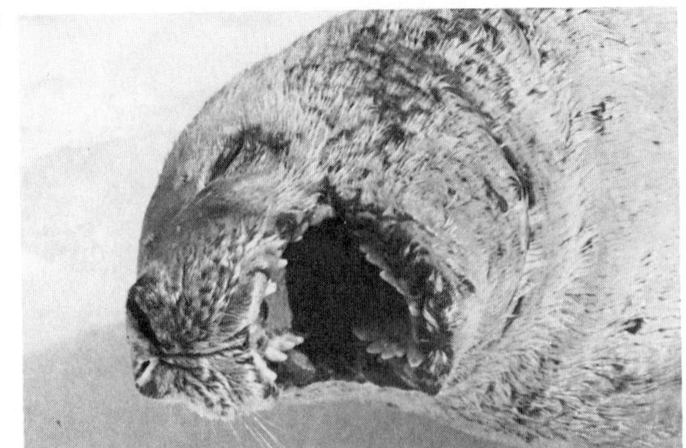

C

FIGURE 4-43

Antarctic food chains. A. Crabeater seals on an ice floe in Paradise Bay, Antarctica. In the absence of large terrestrial predators, these seals, unlike those of the Arctic (which are eaten by polar bears and hunted by Eskimos), have not evolved a fear of being approached. B. Trilobed teeth of a crabeater are used in capturing krill. C. A Weddell seal under attack by a pod of killer whales in Lemaire Channel, Antarctica. The seal can be seen on the ice just behind the head of the leading whale, which has risen from the water to look at it. Repeated coordinated rushes of the whales, which sent streams of water over the ice floe, eventually washed the seal into the sea, where it was devoured. (Photos by P. R. Ehrlich.)

FIGURE 4-44

A garbage dump at U.S. Palmer Station in Antarctica. (Photo by P. R. Ehrlich.)

ecosystem there remains to be investigated, but it must be considerable. At one time an estimated 100,000 individuals of the now virtually extinct blue whale roamed antarctic waters for four months of every year. Each individual consumed four tons of plankton, mostly krill *(Euphausia superba)*, per day; hence, the blue whale alone processed some 50 million tons of plankton annually. The dramatic reduction in the number of whales has in theory made an enormous surplus of plankton available to the seals, penguins, and fishes that also feed on it, but no studies have been made of possible changes in their population sizes. Hence, humanity, through whaling alone, has clearly had a dramatic impact on the biology of Antarctica.

In the years following World War II, land stations have been established on the antarctic continent by various nations. Some were attempts to claim sovereignty; many in the mid-1950s were cooperating in scientific research projects of the United Nations International Geophysical Year. These stations have produced local versions of the kind of environmental deterioration so commonplace in the rest of the world. The United States has produced an ugly town at McMurdo Sound, symbolically complete with a nuclear power plant, and at the Palmer Station on the Antarctic Peninsula, a typical American garbage dump (Figure 4-44), the largest on the continent. More serious than such local blights is the exploration for minerals that someday may open the Antarctic to the kind of destruction now being visited on the Arctic. Recent U.S. Navy reports of 45 billion barrels of oil in Antarctica hardly is a hopeful sign.[87]

Another hazard to the antarctic environment is the possible escape of dogs from stations. Antarctica is devoid of large terrestrial predators, and penguins in particular could easily be decimated. We have seen dogs killing them at the Argentine station at Hope Bay. The penguins nest in vast rookeries on the ground (Figure 4-45); they would be sadly vulnerable to even one or two feral dogs, which could do enormous damage before perishing in the antarctic winter.

Finally, of course, antarctic ecosystems have been polluted with chlorinated hydrocarbons, lead, and other

[87]"Today" Show, NBC, February 25, 1975.

A

B

FIGURE 4-45

A. A small portion of an Adelie penguin colony in Hope Bay, Antarctica. Like many human societies (such as the Netherlands), breeding penguin colonies are utterly dependent upon imported resources for their survival.
B. An Adelie parent, having returned from the sea, regurgitates krill for its chick. Notice the spined tongue, which helps the bird to grasp the krill, and compare with Figure 4-43B. (Photos by P. R. Ehrlich.)

products of civilization. Thus, although to the untrained eye the continent still seems remote and untouched, its biology has already been profoundly modified by human action, and further destructive change is threatened.

ECOLOGICAL MODELS

Because ecology often deals with exceedingly complex systems, it is a standard technique in the science to attempt to gain understanding by creating models of them. A model can be thought of as a simplified representation of reality. Ideally, it should be an aid to thinking about reality and should lead to an ability to make predictions about future states of reality and suggest experiments or measurements that could help define reality more precisely. For example, the logistic curve is a model of the growth processes of real populations in certain circumstances. You will recall that in our earlier discussion it was simplified in several ways—for instance, it assumed that all individuals were ecologically identical, which is never true. Models can be verbal or graphic (or hydraulic or electric), but many of the most useful are mathematical.

Mathematical models fall into two general classes—they either include the random changes that seem to characterize nature or they ignore them. The former are statistical or *stochastic* models; the latter, *deterministic.* The logistic curve is a deterministic model.

In constructing a model, one can strive to build into it one or more of the following properties: precision, realism, generality, and manageability. *Precision* is the ability of a model to predict future states of the system accurately. *Realism* is the extent to which the mathematical formulation of the model reflects the underlying biological processes of the system modeled. *Generality* is the degree to which the model applies to diverse systems. *Manageability* is the ease with which the model can be manipulated—for example, are the differential equations easy to solve, or are their solutions easy to approximate? The logistic curve model is high in manageability and generality, medium in realism, and low in precision.

Two general schools of model-building have developed in ecology: one dealing with complex computer models (systems ecology) and one dealing with simple analytic models. Systems ecology has concentrated on constructing computer models of ecosystems. The system is broken down into a series of compartments, such as herbivores, top carnivores, cities, and farms; and numbers (system variables) are used to describe the state of each compartment at a given time (say, the biomass present). Functions (transfer functions) are then produced to describe the interactions of the compartments, such as the flows of energy among them. Inputs from outside of the system that are not influenced by the system, such as arriving solar energy or fossil fuels, are described by other functions (forcing functions).

The model is then manipulated in attempts to make it simulate the past behavior of known systems satisfactorily and to see what elements of the system are especially sensitive or insensitive to changes elsewhere in the system. One simple systems model of the general type is shown in Figure 4-46, in which the system is analogized to an electric circuit. The most famous model of this class was the world model developed by Donella and Dennis Meadows and their colleagues at Massachusetts Institute of Technology and published in *The Limits to Growth.*[88] That study is discussed in greater detail in Chapter 12.

The computer models of the systems ecologists tend to be high in precision and low in generality and to lose reality as they become more general. Whereas they usually do not supply rewarding holistic insights, they can often provide clues as to how and where an ecological system might most profitably be manipulated and the converse, where a system is so robust that manipulation is likely to have little effect. One of the major drawbacks of systems ecology is the relative paucity of data available with which to develop and test models.

The modeler of the analytic school has a different approach. He or she would start with a question such as, "What would be the form of a population growth curve if the rate of increase were a linear function of size itself?" Or the question might be, "Under what circumstance of resource availability would an organism that can use two

[88]Donella H. Meadows; D. L. Meadows; J. Randers; W. W. Behrens, III, *The limits to growth,* Universe Books, Washington, D.C., 1972.

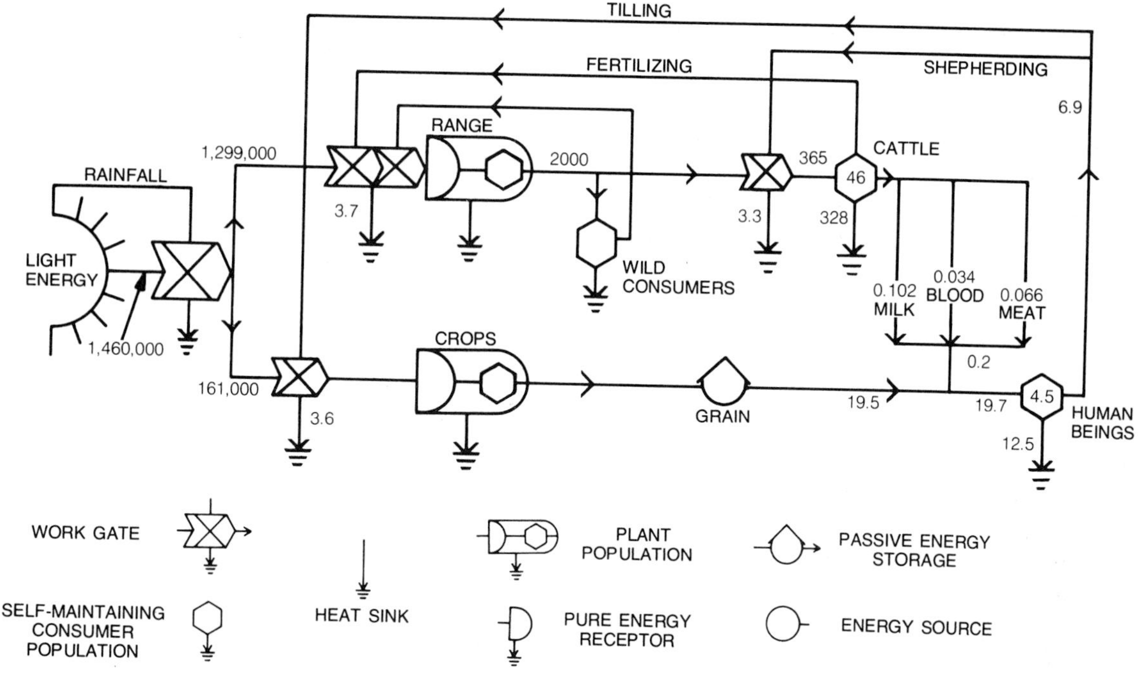

FIGURE 4-46

A simple agricultural system in Uganda. Food is derived from grains, meat, blood, and milk. Animals serve as storage units. The numbers represent kilocalories per square meter per year. Dry weights were converted to kilocalories, using 4.5 kcal per gram. There are 70 people per square mile at 150 pounds per person, 25 percent of which is dry matter, which is equivalent to 1 gram per square meter.

The basic net production of plant material for dry regions is a function of rainfall. Using 21 inches of rainfall, one is able to determine that 500 grams of dry plant material are produced per square meter of land each year. Since 1 acre is cultivated per person and there are 70 persons per square mile, 11 percent of the natural yield area is preempted by crops. At 4.5 cattle per person and 560 pounds per cow, 33 percent of which is dry weight, excluding ash and water, 10.2 grams of animal weight is produced per square meter.

By considering the monthly consumption of milk, blood, and meat, one obtains an annual caloric yield per person from the cattle of 3800 kcal of milk, 2450 kcal of meat, and 1265 kcal of blood, which provides the per-area data in the figure. The caloric requirement per person is given as 2000 kcal per person per day, or 19.7 kcal per square meter per year. The milk, meat, and blood supply only 0.2 of this requirement, so crops must provide the remaining 19.5, a net yield much less than the net yield of vegetation of the natural range. Total insolation in this area just above the equator is about 4000 kcal per square meter per day.

The work of men in tending the crops and cattle can be taken as a percentage of their time spent in this activity (primarily during the daylight hours). As the culture is intimately involved with the cattle, it is assumed that one-sixth of the daily metabolism of each man is devoted to management of the cattle and an equal amount is used for production of crops. The rationale is that the maintenance requirements of a man during his work are necessary to that work, in addition to calories directly expended.

The metabolic activites of a 650-pound steer requires 8000 kcal per day, or 365 kcal per square meter per year. Some fraction of the steer's time and metabolism goes into refertilizing the range on which it grazes, thus reinforcing and maintaining its nutrient loop. Part of a steer's day is spent on the move, and parts of its organ systems are involved in the nutrient regeneration system. One-tenth of its metabolism was taken as its work contribution to vegetation stimulation.

This system does not involve money, and an economic transactor symbol does not appear. (Slightly modified from President's Science Advisory Committee Report on the World Food Problem, 1967.)

classes of resources win out in competition with one that can use three?" Mathematical models of the situation (like the logistic curve in the first instance) are constructed, and then the model and its assumptions are tested against actual systems in nature or in the laboratory.

The models of this school tend to be high in generality and low in precision, although in some simple cases the reverse can be true. Realism, which is generally lower than in systems ecology, also tends to decline with increasing generality.

Although both schools in a sense are in their infancies, it is fair to say that systems ecology is likely to be most productive in providing tools for the solution of practical problems, whereas simple analytic models probably will be most valuable in helping ecologists understand the more general properties of ecological systems. Both schools have provided a welcome infusion of theory into academic ecology. What is badly needed now is a greater concern for applied problems among academic ecologists and a greater appreciation of the potential value of theory among agriculturalists, wildlife managers, city planners, politicians, and others directly concerned with ecological problems.

Recommended for Further Reading

Collier, B. D.; G. W. Cox; A. W. Johnson; P. C. Miller. 1973. *Dynamic ecology.* Prentice-Hall, Englewood Cliffs, N.J. A fine modern text with a systems approach and better-than-average integration of plant ecology with the other material.

Ehrlich, Paul R.; R. W. Holm; and D. R. Parnell. 1974. *The process of evolution.* 2d ed. McGraw-Hill, New York. A basic textbook of evolutionary theory.

Emlen, J. M. 1973. *Ecology: An evolutionary approach.* Addison-Wesley, Reading, Mass. A modern text especially suitable for those with a mathematical bent. (See especially the section on Leslie matrix analysis of population dynamics.)

Krebs, C. J. 1972. *Ecology: The experimental analysis of distribution and abundance.* Harper, New York. A text in the tradition of Andrewartha and Birch (see Additional References). Well written and especially good on population dynamics.

Odum, E. P. 1971. *Fundamentals of ecology.* 3d ed. W. B. Saunders, Philadelphia. The most recent edition of a classic ecology text. Comprehensive, with an excellent bibliography.

Pianka, E. R. 1974. *Evolutionary ecology.* Harper, New York. A relatively brief, well-integrated text, taking the analytical-theoretical approach.

Pielou, E. C. 1974. *Population and community ecology: Principles and methods.* Gordon and Breach, New York. Excellent with a detailed mathematical approach.

Ricklefs, R. E. 1973. *Ecology.* Chicago Press, Newton, Mass. A comprehensive text outstanding for its integration of population genetics with ecology.

Roughgarden, J. In press. *Theory of population genetics and evolutionary ecology, an introduction.* Macmillan, New York. The best brief text on the mathematical theory of evolution and ecology. Highly recommended.

Tait, R. V., and R. S. De Santo. 1972. *Elements of marine ecology.* Springer-Verlag, New York. A sound introduction.

Watt, K. E. F. 1968. *Ecology and resource management.* McGraw-Hill, New York. This is a good source for basic material on the analysis of exploited populations and the systems approach to theory.

Whittaker, R. H. 1975. *Communities and ecosystems.* 2d ed. Macmillan, New York. An excellent brief text with well-balanced, good coverage of ecological problems.

Additional References

We list here some of the works written since World War II which provide access to the vast literature of ecology and evolutionary biology. In addition to these there are many journals in which articles pertinent to subjects covered in this chapter appear. Key journals include: *American naturalist* (U.S.), *Biotropica* (U.S.), *Ecology* (U.S.), *Ecological monographs* (U.S.), *Ekologiya* (USSR, available in translation as *Soviet journal of ecology*), *Environmental entomology* (U.S.), *Evolution* (U.S.), *Genetica* (Netherlands), *Genetics* (U.S.), *Heredity* (UK), *Journal of Ecology* (UK), *Journal of experimental marine biology and ecology* (Netherlands), *Journal of theoretical population biology* (U.S.), *Marine biology* (West German Federal Republic), *Nature* (UK), *Oecologia* (West German Federal Republic), *Oikos* (Denmark), *Researches on population ecology* (Japan), and *Science* (U.S.).

Allee, W. C.; A. E. Emerson; O. Park; T. Park; and K. P. Schmidt. 1949. *Principles of animal ecology.* Saunders, Philadelphia. This massive work, known to generations of students as the Great Aepps, is far out of date but has a fine bibliography of the older literature.

Andrewartha, H. G., and L. C. Birch. 1954. *The distribution and abundance of animals.* University of Chicago Press, Chicago. The modern era of animal population ecology begins with this classic. A "must" for all those professionally interested in the environment.

Annual Reviews, Inc., *Annual review of ecology and systematics.* Published yearly since 1970. Annual Reviews, Inc. Palo Alto, Calif. All volumes contain articles of great interest to ecologists and evolutionists.

Baker, H. G., and G. L. Stebbins, eds. 1965. *Genetics of colonizing species.* Academic Press, New York. A basic source with many first-rate contributions.

Bartlett, M. S., and R. W. Hiorns, eds. 1973. *The mathematical theory of the dynamics of biological populations.* Academic Press, London. Only for the mathematically sophisticated.

Boer, P. J. den; and G. R. Gradwell, eds. 1971. *Dynamics of populations.* Center for Agricultural Publishing and Documentation, Wageningen, the Netherlands. A fine sample of recent work on diverse topics.

Cavalli-Sforza, L. L., and W. F. Bodmer. 1971. *The genetics of human populations.* W. H. Freeman and Company, San Francisco. A fine, comprehensive source on human and population genetics.

Chambers, K. L., ed. 1970. *Biochemical coevolution.* Oregon State University Press, Corvallis. Papers on important aspects of coevolution.

Cloudsley-Thompson, J. L. 1975. *Terrestrial environments.* Wiley, New York. Up-to-date descriptions of biomes, zoogeography, and so forth, including the freshwater biome.

Creed, R., ed., 1971. *Ecological genetics and evolution.* Blackwell, Oxford. A fine volume focusing on the ecological causes of genetic polymorphism.

Crutchfield, J. A., and G. Pontecorvo. 1969. *The Pacific salmon fisheries: A study of irrational conservation.* Johns Hopkins, Baltimore. Deals with interactions of biological and economic yields in exploited populations.

Dobben, W. H. van, and R. H. Lowe-McConnell, eds. 1975. *Unifying concepts in ecology.* Dr. W. Junk, The Hague. Papers from the First International Congress of Ecology on energy flow, productivity, diversity and stability, and ecosystem management.

Dobzhansky, T. 1970. *Genetics of the evolutionary process.* Columbia University Press, New York. An important source for both theoretical and experimental approaches to population genetics—a successor to Dobzhansky's classic, *Genetics and the origin of species* (New York; Columbia University Press, 3d edition, 1951). A must for anyone interested in evolution.

Elton, C. S. 1958. *The ecology of invasions by animals and plants.* Methuen, London. *The* source on this subject—a classic.

———. 1966. *The pattern of animal communities.* Methuen, London. Natural history, with much fascinating material by one of the greatest of all ecologists.

Emden, H. F. van, ed. 1973. *Insect-plant relationships.* Blackwell, Oxford. The bibliographies of many of these interesting papers are extensive and useful.

Etherington, J. R. 1975. *The environment and plant ecology.* Wiley, New York. A good basic text in physiological ecology of plants.

Eyre, S. R. 1963. *Vegetation and soils: a world picture.* Aldine, Chicago. This comprehensive work includes a section on the impact of human beings.

Ford, E. B. 1964. *Ecological genetics.* Methuen, London. *The* classic of the British school working with natural populations.

Gilbert, L. E., and P. H. Raven, eds. 1975. *Coevolution of animals and plants.* University of Texas, Austin. An excellent collection dealing with a key field in population biology.

Heywood, V. H., ed. 1973. *Taxonomy and ecology.* Academic Press, London. A wide-ranging symposium with several important papers on coevolution.

Hutchinson, G. E. 1958. Concluding remarks. *Cold Spring Harbor symposium on quantitative biology* vol. 22, pp. 415–427. The Biological Laboratory, Cold Spring Harbor, New York. A key paper which forms the basis of much recent work on niche theory.

———. 1969. Eutrophication, past and present. In *Eutrophication: Causes, consequences, correctives,* National Academy of Sciences, Washington, D.C. A fine article by one of the world's most distinguished ecologists and limnologists.

Kendeigh, S. C. 1974. *Ecology.* Prentice-Hall, Englewood Cliffs, N. J. See for material on biomes.

Kershaw, K. A. 1973. *Quantitative and dynamic plant ecology.* 2d ed. American Elsevier, New York. Excellent on statistical aspects, but like many other treatments of plant ecology totally ignores the critical role of animals in plant ecology.

Kozlowski, T. T., and C. E. Allgren. 1974. *Fire and ecosystems.* Academic Press, New York. Covers the ecological roles of fire, both harmful and beneficial.

Kummel, B. 1970. *History of the earth.* 2d ed. W. H. Freeman and Company, San Francisco. A comprehensive introduction to historical geology—a good source for those interested in the course (rather than the process) of evolution.

Lewontin, R. C., ed. 1968. *Population biology and evolution.* Syracuse University Press, New York. A good collection.

———. 1974. *The genetic basis of evolutionary change.* Columbia University Press, New York. Exciting summary and synthesis of recent work on enzyme polymorphisms and their significance in evolutionary theory.

Lieth, H. 1975. Primary productivity in ecosystems: Comparative analysis of global patterns. In *Unifying concepts in ecology,* W. H. van Dobben and R. H. Lowe-McConnell, eds., pp. 67–88. Estimates about 122×19^9 metric tons of terrestrial primary productivity (55×10^9 tons of carbon).

MacArthur, R. H. 1972. *Geographical ecology: Patterns in the distribution of species.* Harper, New York. A pioneer synthesis dealing with the factors controlling the distribution of organisms—the last work of a great pioneer in the "new ecology," published shortly before his untimely death.

McNaughton, S. J., and L. L. Wolf. 1973. *General ecology.* Holt, Rinehart and Winston, New York. An excellent text interweaving theory and examples from a very wide range of organisms.

Margalef, R. 1968. *Perspectives in ecological theory.* University of Chicago Press, Chicago. Offbeat and interesting.

May, R. M. 1973. *Stability and complexity in model ecosystems.* Princeton University Press, N.J. A theoretical consideration of the crucial problem of the resistance of ecosystems to perturbation.

Mayr, E. 1963. *Animal species and evolution.* Harvard University Press, Cambridge, Mass. This scholarly and exhaustive treatise supercedes the author's earlier classic, *Systematics and the origin of species* (Columbia University Press, 1942). *Animal species and evolution,* has been abridged as *Populations, species and evolution* (Harvard University Press, 1970). Highly recommended.

Murdoch, William W. 1975. Diversity, complexity, stability and pest control. *Journal of applied ecology,* vol. 12, pp. 795–807. A key article disputing the classic view that diversity promotes stability.

National Academy of Sciences (NAS). 1969. *Eutrophication: Causes, consequences, correctives.* NAS, Washington, D. C. A gold mine of information—see especially G. E. Hutchinson's introductory article.

Oosting, H. J. 1956. *The study of plant communities.* 2d ed. W. H. Freeman and Company, San Francisco. A classic, much of it now out of date.

Orians, Gordon H. 1975. Diversity, stability and maturity in natural ecosystems. In *Unifying concepts in ecology,* W. H. van Dobben and R. H. Lowe-McConnell, eds. A good, brief discussion suggesting that "attempts to find general relationships between diversity and 'stability' are likely to be fruitless."

Patten, B. C., ed. 1971. *Systems analysis and simulation in ecology.* Academic Press, New York. A two-volume collection.

Pielou, E. C. 1969. *An introduction to mathematical ecology,* Wiley, New York. A fine treatment for those quantitatively inclined.

Pimentel, D. 1973. Extent of pesticide use, food supplies, and pollution. *Journal of the New York Entomological Society,* vol. 81, pp. 13–33. Reports increases in crop losses despite increased pesticide use, due in part to the "practice of substituting insecticides for sound bioenvironmental pest control" (for example, crop rotation and sanitation) and also to higher consumer standards.

Pomeroy, L. R., ed. 1974. *Cycles of essential elements.* Dowden, Hutchinson and Rose, Stroudsburg, Pa. Reprints of key papers.

Poole, R. W. 1974. *An introduction to quantitative ecology.* A good introduction to mathematical analyses in ecology.

Raven, P. H.; R. F. Evert; and H. Curtis. 1976. *Biology of plants.* Worth, New York. By far the best modern botany text.

Reichle, D. E., ed. 1970. *Analysis of temperate forest ecosystems.* Springer-Verlag, New York. A fine recent summary, well integrated for a collection of separate papers.

———. J. F. Franklin, and D. W. Goodall, eds. 1975. *Productivity of world ecosystems.* National Academy of Sciences, Washington, D.C. Report of a symposium with many important papers.

Richards, P. W. 1952. *The tropical rain forest.* Cambridge University Press. A standard work, still very useful.

———. 1973. The tropical rain forest. *Scientific American,* December. A good overview of the ecosystem and its exploitation.

Rodin, L. E., and N. I. Brazilevich. 1967. *Production and mineral cycling in terrestrial vegetation.* Oliver and Boyd, London. This comprehensive review was first published in the USSR in 1965.

——— and N. N. Rozov. 1975. Productivity of the world's main ecosystems. In *Productivity of world ecosystems,* D. Reichle, J. Franklin, and D. Goodall. National Academy of Sciences, Washington, D.C., pp. 13–26. Higher estimates than R. H. Whittaker and G. E. Likens.

Simberloff, D. S., and L. G. Abele. 1975. Island biogeography theory and conservation practice. *Science,* vol. 191, pp. 285–286 (January 23). In some cases a cluster of small refuges may support more species than one large one.

Simpson, G. G. 1953. *The major features of evolution.* The most thorough and general explanation of evolutionary trends in animals, but now somewhat out of date.

Slobodkin, L. B. 1961. *Growth and regulation of animal populations.* Holt, Rinehart and Winston, New York. Partly out of date, but a landmark in its day.

Sondheimer, E., and J. B. Simeone, eds. 1970. *Chemical ecology.* Academic Press, New York. One of the first volumes in a rapidly expanding field.

Southwood, T. R. E. 1966. *Ecological methods.* Methuen, London. The source on techniques for work on populations of small animals.

Spurr, S. H., and B. V. Barnes. 1973. *Forest ecology.* 2d ed. Ronald, New York. A first-rate text.

Stebbins, G. L. 1950. *Variation and evolution in plants.* Columbia University Press, New York. Old but still essential; some more recent material may be found in his *Chromosomal evolution in higher plants,* Addison-Wesley, Reading, Mass., 1971.

———. 1974. *Flowering plants: Evolution above the species level.* Harvard University Press, Cambridge, Mass. A recent tour de force on the relationships of groups of plants. Essential for those interested in plant-animal coevolution, a topic of great importance to humanity.

Usher, M. B., and M. H. Williamson, eds. 1974. *Ecological stability.* Halstead Press, New York. A collection illustrating the diversity of views ecologists hold on this topic.

Van Dyne, G. M. 1969. *The ecosystem concept in natural resource management.* Academic Press, New York. A useful compendium with numerous examples of the analysis and modeling of ecosystems.

Watson, A., ed. 1970. *Animal populations in relation to their food resources.* Blackwell, Oxford. A symposium on the feedback from food resources to the regulation of numbers.

Weller, J. M. 1969. *The course of evolution.* McGraw-Hill, New York. A survey of the evolutionary history of major plant and animal groups.

Whittaker, R. H., and G. E. Likens. 1973. Carbon in the biota. In *Carbon and the biosphere,* G. Woodwell and E. Pecan, eds. Technical Information Center, USAEC, Washington, D.C., pp. 281–300. Discussion of productivity, previous estimates, and impact of man. (See also Rodin, Bazilevich, and Rozov, *Productivity of the world's main ecosystems.*)

Wilson, E. O. 1975. *Sociobiology.* Harvard University Press, Cambridge, Mass. This landmark volume has much to say about the ecology and evolution of social animals, from social insects to human beings. Extremely controversial, with a superb bibliography.

Woodwell, G. M., and H. H. Smith, eds. 1969. *Diversity and stability in ecological systems.* USAEC, Washington, D.C., Brookhaven Symposia in Biology, 22. A collection of papers that bears witness to the complexity of the problem and the diversity of approaches to it.

Woodwell, G. M. and E. V. Pecan, eds. 1973. *Carbon and the biosphere.* USAEC, Oak Ridge, Tenn. Numerous up-to-date articles pertinent to this chapter and chapters 2 and 3.

SECTION

II

Population and Renewable Resources

The tide of the earth's population is rising,
the reservoir of the earth's living resources is falling.

—Fairfield Osborn, 1948

Having considered the basic principles of operation of the environment in which human society is embedded, we turn now to the human population itself and certain of the demands it makes on that environment.

Chapter 5 gives a rather detailed introduction to demography—the study of the size, structure, and distribution of the human population and the ways and reasons these characteristics change. Some knowledge of the history of human population change is essential to an understanding of the present situation, and this is provided. We attempt, as well, to furnish some basis for estimating what future patterns of population change may be, while recognizing that all forecasts should be heavily qualified and surrounded by disclaimers. (Demographers in the past have been notably more successful at describing what *has* happened than at predicting what *will* happen.) Of course, there are some kinds of changes that, barring catastrophe, are extraordinarily unlikely—for example, a leveling-off of the global population size in less than several decades and at a size much smaller than about twice today's. We explore in detail the reasons for this unfortunate human "commitment" to further growth.

The primary reasons for concern with population are the pressures that population characteristics and population change impose on physical resources, environmental services, economic prosperity, social systems, and human values. The natures of many of those pressures are examined in subsequent chapters, but it is worth setting down some general observations on population pressure here to help place the demographic detail of Chapter 5 in perspective.

It is important to understand, first, that population pressure may arise from large absolute population size or from unsuitable geographical distribution of population or from high rates of change in size or distribution or from a combination of these factors. Population pressures in Europe, Japan, and the United States, for example, are associated more with the large sizes those populations have already attained than with their rates of population growth, which are relatively low. Of course, even a low rate of growth in such a country is made more significant precisely because the absolute impact of population size and the impact per person are already so high there; but saying the pressures are primarily related to size is to recognize that those regions would be experiencing essentially similar difficulties even if their rates of population growth were zero at this time.

In certain of the less developed countries, by contrast, population pressures are associated more with an inability of social and economic services to keep up with rapid population growth than with the absolute sizes of the populations. This is the situation in many countries in Latin America and Africa. The pressures are often exacerbated by high rates of change in population distribution—namely, floods of migrants into the cities from the countrysides.

Many Asian countries illustrate a third situation, in which awesome pressures arise both from the great size the populations have already reached and from continuing high rates of growth. India, Pakistan, Bangladesh, and the People's Republic of China are examples of this general situation, although they differ from each other in important respects.

A theme that emerges from these considerations and runs through Chapter 5 is that few generalizations about population and population pressure can be expected to hold worldwide. The variety of conditions and pressures in different countries is enormous. Understanding the overall demographic situation is possible only when these differences are examined in detail, and this we have undertaken to do.

Chapter 6 and Chapter 7 deal with some of the resources necessary for the support of the human population—more specifically, those resources it has become customary to call renewable. They are land, soil, water, forests, and food. Whether *renewable* is really a useful generic label for these commodities is questionable. The planet's stores of land and water are essentially fixed, and they can be used over and over again; but the same can be said of metals, usually thought of as nonrenewable. The difference is only that, when metals are dispersed in use, society must write them off or pay a heavy price in energy to reconcentrate them, whereas when water is dispersed in use, solar energy reconcentrates it "free" through the hydrologic cycle. At the same time, it is easy to think of circumstances in which soil is a highly nonrenewable resource—for example, when it is eroded by wind or water much faster than natural processes can replenish it. If soil is lost, the capacity to grow food and forests in that region is lost, too, so those become, at least locally, nonrenewable.

The resources of land, soil, water, and forests are so intimately related that we have put them together in Chapter 6. We devote more space in that chapter to the complex chemical and physical characteristics of soil than is customary in environmental science texts because we believe that soil's central role in support of human society has been widely underestimated. The complexity and subtlety of the functions performed by soil are a major reason that food production cannot be greatly expanded merely by planting crops on any reasonably flat space not otherwise occupied. That the soil is an ecosystem in itself, moreover, should serve as a warning that it may be vulnerable not only to the traditional threats of erosion, waterlogging, and salination but also to systematic disruption by the chemical assaults of industrial society. (These threats are considered in Chapter 11.)

Food, the subject of Chapter 7, is simultaneously a biological, technological, economic, social, and political problem. Eventual limits to food production by conventional methods will be imposed by limitations on the resources of soil and water, discussed in Chapter 6, and of course by the availability of sunlight. Short of these resource limits, however, society may already be pushing up against limits of another kind—limits in its ability to make available the expensive technology of high-yield agriculture, to supply and pay for the industrial energy this technology requires on a continuing basis, and to absorb the environmental burdens that expanding agriculture by any means produces. The difficulties of growing enough food are compounded by the problems of distributing the food to those who are hungry. (We are regularly discouraged to hear discussions of food "surpluses"—meaning a supply that exceeds *economic* demand—when so much of the problem is that the people who are hungry are also broke.) Like so many of the problems treated in this book, the nature of the food problem varies enormously from region to region, which makes generalizations difficult. Nevertheless, we believe that at least one generalization emerges clearly from the detailed analysis in Chapter 7: concerning the future of food supply, none dare be complacent.

Prudent men should judge of future events
by what has taken place in the past,
and what is taking place in the present.

—Miguel de Cervantes (1547–1616),
Persiles and Sigismunda

We shall see finally appear the miracle of an
animal society, a complete and definitive ant-heap.

—Paul Valéry (1871–1945)

CHAPTER 5

The History and Future of the Human Population

The first small population of human beings probably appeared on Earth more than 2 million years ago on the continent of Africa. Since then, the human population has spread out to occupy virtually the entire land surface of the planet. And in the past century or two it has exploded in numbers. Today roughly between 4 and 5 percent of all the people who have ever lived inhabit Earth—some 4 billion.[1]

[1]N. Keyfitz, How many people have ever lived on Earth? *Demography,* vol. 3 (1966), pp. 581–582. Unless otherwise noted, current population statistics are based on the United Nations *Concise report on the world population situation in 1970–1975 and its long-range implications,* 1974; The Environmental Fund, Inc., 1975 *World population estimates;* Population Reference Bureau, *1975 Population data sheet;* various annual volumes of the *United Nations Demographic yearbook* (United Nations, New York) and *Statistical abstract of the United States* (United States Department of Commerce; Washington, D.C.); and United States National Center for Health Statistics (USNCHS), *Monthly vital statistics report of the United States.*

This chapter recounts the history of population growth and explores its projected course in the future, especially the next century or so. Principles of human population dynamics (demography) are also presented here, with a view to explaining the present predicament of humanity and how the current demographic situation shapes the future and limits social options. Population size and growth have profound, if seldom noticed, effects on the course of events, and this is likely to be even more true in the future than it has been in the past.

POPULATION GROWTH

Since there are no substantial historical data on which to base estimates of population size and changes before 1650, estimates must be based on circumstantial evi-

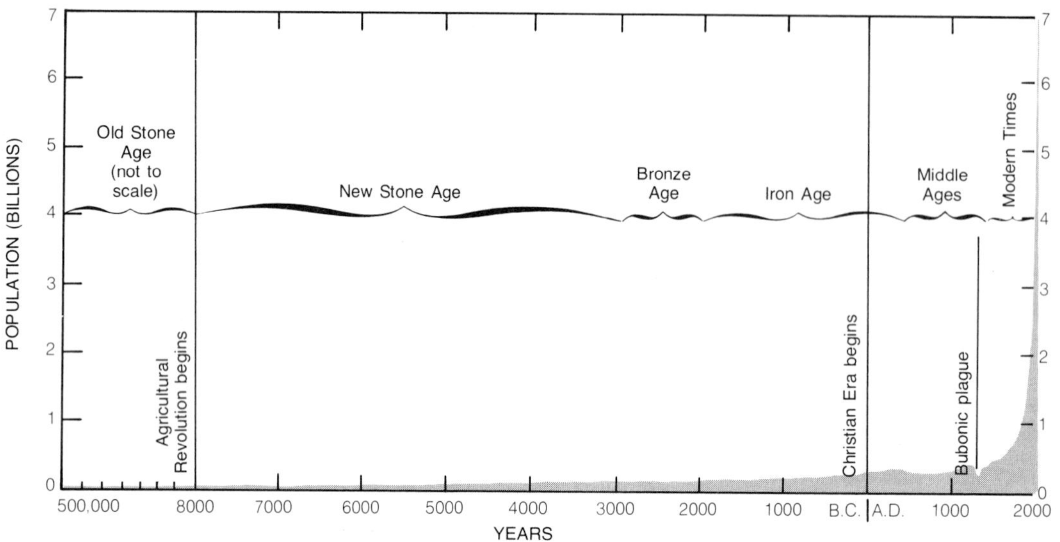

FIGURE 5-1

The growth of human numbers for the past half-million years. If the Old Stone Age were in scale, its baseline would extend about 18 feet to the left. (Adapted from *Population bulletin,* vol. 18, no. 1. Courtesy of the Population Reference Bureau, Inc., Washington, D.C.)

dence. For instance, agriculture was unknown before about 8000 B.C.; prior to that all human groups made their living by hunting and gathering. No more than 52 million square kilometers (20 million square miles) of Earth's total land area of some 150 million square kilometers (58 million square miles) could have been successfully utilized in this way by our early ancestors. From this and the population densities of hunting and gathering tribes of today, it has been estimated that the total human population of 8000 B.C. was about 5 million people.

The sizes of population at various times from the onset of the Agricultural Revolution until the first scanty census data were recorded in the seventeenth century have also been estimated. This was done by extrapolation from census figures that exist for present-day agricultural societies and by examination of archaeological remains. Such data as the numbers of rooms in excavated ancient villages have proven especially useful for calculating village populations. It is thought that the total human population at the time of Christ was around 200 million to 300 million people, and that it had increased to about 500 million (half a billion) by 1650. It then doubled to 1000 million (1 billion) around 1850, and doubled again to 2 billion by 1930. The course of human population growth is traced in Figure 5-1. Note that the size of the population has (with a few setbacks) increased continuously and that the *rate* of increase has also risen.

Perhaps the simplest way to describe the growth rate is in terms of doubling time—the time required for a population to double in size. In growing from 5 million in 8000 B.C. to 500 million in 1650, the population increased a hundredfold. This required between six and seven doublings within 9000 or 10,000 years:

$$\begin{array}{lcccccccc} \text{Population (millions):} & 5 & \rightarrow 10 & \rightarrow 20 & \rightarrow 40 & \rightarrow 80 & \rightarrow 160 & \rightarrow 320 & \rightarrow 640 \\ \text{Doublings:} & & 1 & 2 & 3 & 4 & 5 & 6 & 7 \end{array}$$

Thus, on the average, the population doubled about once every 1500 years during that period. The next doubling, from 500 million to 1 billion, took 200 years; and the

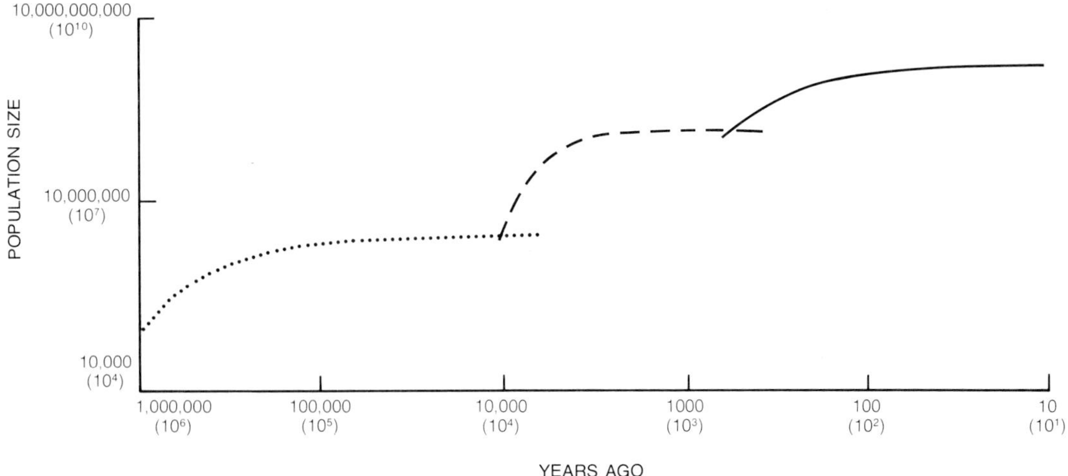

FIGURE 5-2

Human population growth plotted on a log-log scale. Plotted in this way, population growth is seen as occurring in three surges, associated with the cultural, agricultural, and industrial-medical revolutions (discussed later in this chapter). (Adapted from Deevey, 1960.)

doubling from 1 billion to 2 billion took only 80 years. The population reached 4 billion around 1975, having doubled again in only 45 years. The rate of growth in the early 1970s would, if continued, double the population in about 36 years. Table 5-1 summarizes human population history in these terms.

To take a slightly different perspective, it took 1 million or 2 million years to achieve a population size of 1 billion around 1850. The next billion was added in 80 years (1850–1930). The third billion came along in only 30 years (1931–1960), and the fourth took only about 15 years (1961–1975). If this rate of growth continued, the fifth billion would be added in just slightly more than a decade (by 1987).

The sort of graph shown in Figure 5-1 does not reveal details of trends in the long, slow growth of the human population before the current millennium. But if population size and time are plotted against one another on logarithmic scales (a log-log graph, as in Figure 5-2), a greater range of time can be shown, and more detail in the lower range of population sizes is revealed. Notice that the log-log graph shows three surges of population growth, one about 600,000 years ago, one about 8000 years ago, and one about 200 years ago.

The reasons for the patterns that appear on both graphs are reasonably well understood, but before examining them, we must consider some aspects of human population dynamics.

TABLE 5-1
Doubling Times of the Human Population

Date	*Estimated world population*	*Time in which population doubles (years)*
8000 B.C.	5 million	
		1500
1650 A.D.	500 million	
		200
1850 A.D.	1000 million (1 billion)	
		80
1930 A.D.	2000 million (2 billion)	
		45
1975 A.D.	4000 million (4 billion)	
	Computed doubling time around 1975	36

Birth and Death Rates

A human birth rate *(b)* is usually expressed as the number of births per 1000 persons per year, rather than per individual as in Chapter 4. The total number of births during the year is divided by the estimated population at the midpoint of the period. For example, in the United States there were 3,159,000 live births during the twelve months ending November 30, 1975. The population on May 30, 1975 (the midpoint of that period), was estimated to be 213,000,000. The birth rate

TABLE 5-2
Doubling Times at Various Rates of Increase

Annual increase (%)	*Doubling time (years)*
0.5	139
0.8	87
1.0	70
2.0	35
3.0	23
4.0	18

(b) for that period was therefore 3,159,000/213,000,000 = 0.0148. There were 0.0148 births per person, or 0.0148 × 1000 = 14.8 births per 1000 people. Similarly, there were 1,912,000 deaths during the period, giving a death rate *(d)* of 1,912,000/213,000,000 = 0.0090 × 1000 = 9.0 deaths per 1000 people in the year from December 1, 1974 to November 30, 1975.[2]

Growth Rate

Ignoring migration, the growth rate *(r)* is calculated by subtracting the death rate from the birth rate $(b - d)$. During the year ending November 30, 1975, the United States growth rate was 14.8 − 9.0, or 5.8 per 1000. That is, in the period from December 1, 1974, to November 30, 1975, 5.8 persons were added to each 1000 in the United States population. Technically, this is the *rate of natural increase,* since migration is ignored. To add to the confusion, demographers express this growth rate as a *percent annual increase*—that is, not as a rate per 1000 or per person, but as a rate per 100. In the example cited above, the annual increase would be 0.58 percent, a typical rate for an industrialized nation today.

Population growth for the entire world presents a different picture. In the early 1970s the estimated world birth rate was around 32 per 1000 per year and the death rate about 13 per 1000. The growth rate was thus 32 − 13 = 19 per 1000, or approximately 1.9 percent.[3] This gives a finite rate of increase (λ) of about 1.02 per year and a reasonably accurate estimate of $r = 0.019$ (doubling time, 36 yr) as discussed in Chapter 4. The age composition of the entire human population is not stable, and the growth of that population therefore is only roughly exponential. If the vital rates of the early 1970s persisted, however, the population would grow to 8 billion people around the year 2010. Table 5-2 shows the doubling times that would be associated with various annual percentage increases.

[2]USWCHS, *Vital statistics,* vol. 24, no. 11 (February 2, 1976).

[3]The Population Reference Bureau estimate for that period was b = 31.5 per 1000, d = 12.8 per 1000, r = 18.7 per 1000, or an increase of slightly less than 1.9 percent. Other sources (Lester R. Brown, World population trends: Signs of hope, signs of stress) have postulated lower rates for 1975: $b = 28.3$, $d = 11.9$, $r = 16.4$ per 1000, or 1.64 percent per year—a substantial decline since 1970.

History of Population Growth

The populations of our ancestors a few million years ago (*Australopithecus* and relatives) were confined to Africa and numbered perhaps 125,000 individuals. By that time, these ancestors of ours had already "invented" culture, the body of nongenetic information passed from generation to generation. The volume of culture is, of course, vastly greater today than in the days of *Australopithecus.* In those days human culture was transmitted orally and by demonstration from the older to the younger members of the group. It doubtless consisted of information about methods of hunting, gathering, and preparing food; rules of social conduct; identification of dangerous enemies; and the like. Today, of course, human culture includes information transmitted and stored in such diverse places as books, phonograph records, photographs, videotapes, and computer tapes.

The possession of a substantial body of culture is what differentiates human beings from the other animals. During human evolutionary history the possession of culture has been responsible for a great increase in human brain size (the australopithecines had small brains, with an average volume of only about 500 cubic centimeters). Early human beings added to the store of cultural information, developing and learning techniques of social organization and group and individual survival. This gave a selective advantage to individuals with the large brain capacity necessary to take full advantage of the culture. Larger brains in turn increased the potential store of cultural information, and a self-reinforcing coupling of the growth of culture and brain size resulted. This trend continued until perhaps 200,000 years ago, when growth of brain size leveled off at an average of some 1350 cubic centimeters, and human beings considered to belong to the same species as modern humanity, *Homo sapiens*, appeared.

The evolution of culture had some important side effects. Although the prehistoric human birth rate probably remained around 40 or 50 per 1000, cultural advances probably caused a slight decline in the average death rate. But the average death rate could not have been more than 0.004 per 1000 below the birth rate (the corresponding growth rate being 0.0004 percent or less), and there unquestionably were sizable fluctuations in birth rates and, especially, in death rates, particularly during the difficult times associated with glacial advance. Long before the Agricultural Revolution, humanity had spread out from Africa to occupy virtually the entire planet. It is known that human beings reached the Western Hemisphere some time before 45,000 B.C. As they became ubiquitous, increased hunting and gathering efficiency may have led, among other things, to the extinction of many large mammals, such as the great ground sloths, saber-toothed tigers, and woolly mammoths.[4]

The Agricultural Revolution. The consequences of cultural evolution for human population size and for the environment were minor compared with those that were to follow the Agricultural Revolution. It is not certain when the first group of *Homo sapiens* started to supplement its hunting and food-gathering with primitive farming. Archeological studies have produced firm evidence that village-farming communities functioned in the Middle East between 7000 and 5500 B.C.[5] Around that time certain groups of people in the hills flanking the Fertile Crescent, in what is now the border area of Iraq and Iran, gradually began to take up a new mode of life, cultivating a variety of crops and domesticating edible animals. Those people had previously practiced intensive food collection, as do Eskimos today, and presumably they were intimately familiar with the local flora and fauna. It would have been a natural step from gathering food to producing it.

With the beginnings of agriculture, growth of the human population started to accelerate. Two general explanations have been offered. The conventional explanation of this agriculture-related increase until recently was that the sizes of earlier populations had been kept in check by high natural mortality and that the development of agriculture tended to reduce the death rate. Agriculture not only allowed production of food to replace the constant search for it, it also permitted people to settle in one place. This in turn generated possibilities for storing vegetable foods in granaries and bins, and meat on the hoof. Farmers were able to feed more than their own families, and as a result some members of early agricultural communities were able to turn entirely to other activities. All of these changes helped to raise the general standard of life. Wheeled vehicles appeared; copper, tin, and then iron were utilized; and dramatic sociopolitical changes occurred, along with urbanization. Human existence thus began to lose some of its hazards, and the average life expectancy began to creep upward from its primitive level of perhaps twenty to twenty-five years.[6]

Recently, a rather different view of population growth just after the Agricultural Revolution has developed. It does not dispute the historical trends already described, but it does dispute that their primary cause was a lowered death rate.[7] Instead, the observed changes are attributed primarily to changes in the birth rate.

Using evidence from living populations of hunters and gatherers such as the !Kung[8] bushmen of southern Africa, from the demography of extinct human populations inferred from fossil samples, and from the behavior of nonhuman primates, supporters of this view have concluded that our ancestral hunters and gatherers consciously tried to space the births of their children. If this is true, one of the most "human" of all behavioral traits—the conscious control of reproduction—at least with respect to spacing, if not of total family size—may

[4]P. S. Martin and H. E. Wright, eds., *Pleistocene extinctions;* P. S. Martin, Pleistocene niches for alien animals; C. A. Reed, Extinction of mammalian megafauna in the Old World late quaternary. See also Chapter 4.

[5]R. J. Braidwood, The Agricultural Revolution; Wilhelm G. Solheim, II, An earlier Agricultural Revolution, *Scientific American,* April 1972, pp. 34–41.

[6]For example, J. D. Durand, A long-range view of world population growth.

[7]See D. E. Dumond, The limitation of human population: a natural history, for a summary.

[8]The exclamation point denotes a click made with the tongue against the roof of the mouth, a sound with no counterpart in English.

be many thousands of years older than was previously thought. Child-spacing (with gaps of at least three to five years) among nomadic hunters and gatherers was presumably necessitated partly by the inability of the mother to carry more than one child. Another likely reason would have been the need to nurse each child for at least three years because the environment lacked the soft food required for earlier weaning.[9] Moreover, it appears likely that prolonged breast-feeding itself may help in suppressing fertility. Infanticide may also have been practiced widely among hunter-gatherers, when children were born too soon and in times of scarcity.[10]

Anthropological research on various contemporary and recent hunter-gatherer groups (such as the !Kung bushmen) and on migratory agriculturalists such as the Polynesians indicates that those people have been quite conscious of population pressures and aware of the reasons behind many of their customs relating to marriage and child-bearing. The Polynesians are renowned for their long-distance migrations, an obvious response to population pressure. But they also practiced infanticide, polyandry, nonmarriage of landless younger sons, abstention from sexual activity for a period of time after birth of a child, coitus interruptus, and abortion.[11] Their awareness of the need to limit their numbers probably was sharpened by their confinement to small islands. Whether most hunter-gatherers have been conscious of a need to limit their final family sizes is problematical; but attention appears mainly to have focused on child-spacing.

The imperatives for child-spacing experienced by hunter-gatherers apparently disappeared when agriculture began. Although some changes at that juncture worked toward slowing population growth (for example, unlike hunters and gatherers, a significant proportion of the people in many agrarian societies remains unmarried), it is generally agreed that agriculture and high natality go hand in hand. The prime reason for this, many demographers believe, is the perceived economic value of children to farming families. (This pronatalist attitude may still be a major factor in keeping birth rates high in peasant communities today.) The increased natality in agrarian societies, not a decline in death rates, is considered in this school of thought to have been the main reason for the acceleration of population growth following the Agricultural Revolution. They claim that mortality from disease probably increased with the greater population densities of agrarian societies, especially in preindustrial cities, and that there is no persuasive evidence that death rates declined with the start of farming.

Because of the uncertainty of early demographic records and especially the problems of reconstructing prehistoric vital rates, it is difficult to evaluate the two explanations of the population explosion that followed the Agricultural Revolution. It seems clear, however, that the earlier "lowered-death-rate" explanation was at best oversimplified.

Population growth after the Agricultural Revolution. The growth of human populations was not continuous after the Agricultural Revolution. Civilizations rose, flourished, and disintegrated; periods of good and bad weather occurred; and those apocalyptic horsemen—pestilence, famine, and war—took their toll. Of course, there has been no accurate record of human population sizes until quite recently, and even today demographic statistics for many areas are unreliable. A general picture that is quite adequate for the purposes of our discussion can be reconstructed, however. Although the global trend (indicated in Figure 5-1) has been one of accelerating increase, a great many local population explosions and crashes are concealed in that trend. For example, bubonic plague (black death) killed an estimated 25 percent of the inhabitants of Europe between 1348 and 1350. From 1348 to 1379 England's total population was reduced almost by half, from an estimated 3.8 million to 2.1 million. Many cities lost half or more of their inhabitants in the second half of the fourteenth century.[12] The demographic effect of repeated visitations of plague on the European population

[9]J. B. Birdsell, Some predictions for the Pleistocene based on equilibrium systems among recent hunter-gatherers; R. B. Lee, Population growth and the beginnings of sedentary life among the !Kung bushmen; G. B. Kolata, !Kung hunter-gatherers: Feminism, diet, and birth control.

[10]Mildred Dickeman, Demographic consequences of infanticide in man.

[11]James T. Tanner, Population limitation today and in ancient Polynesia, *BioScience*, vol. 25, no. 8 (August 1975), pp. 513–516.

[12]W. L. Langer, The black death.

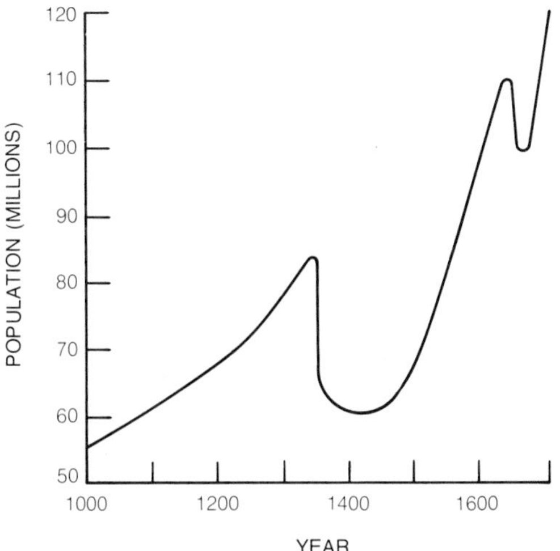

FIGURE 5-3

The effects of the bubonic plague on the size of the European population in the fourteenth and seventeenth centuries. The curve is an estimate based on historical accounts; actual data are scarce. (Adapted from Langer, 1964.)

is represented in Figure 5-3. The plague also triggered great social unrest, a typical concomitant of both dramatic increases and reductions in population size. The social and psychological effects lingered for centuries.[13] These plagues were only the most dramatic and well-known epidemic in history. Numerous other plagues have taken their tolls over the centuries. For example, the influenza epidemic of 1917/1918, a much milder disease, killed some 20 million people in one year.

Famine has also been an important recurring contributor to high death rates. Floods, drought, insect plagues, warfare, and other disasters often have pushed populations over the thin line between subsistence and famine. One study by Cornelius Walford[14] lists more than 200 famines in Great Britain between 10 A.D. and 1846 A.D. (Box 5-1). Many, of course, were local affairs, which nevertheless could be very serious in the absence of efficient transport systems for transferring surplus food from other areas. Another study counts 1828 Chinese famines in the 2019 years preceding 1911, a rate of almost one per year. Some of those famines and some in India have been known to result in millions of deaths. Even in this century famine has killed many millions. For example, perhaps from 5 million to 10 million deaths have been attributed to starvation in Russia in the first third of the century (1918–1922, 1932–1934). Perhaps as many as 4 million deaths were caused by famine in China (1920/1921) before the revolution in 1949, and unknown millions in the first decade afterward. And between 2 and 4 million deaths were caused by famine in West Bengal, India, in 1943.

Warfare has often created conditions in which both pestilence and famine thrived, but it is difficult to estimate the direct consequences of war for population size. In many areas of the world, wars must have made a major contribution to the death rate, even when the conflict was between preagricultural groups. The effect of warfare on the sizes and distribution of populations in New Guinea, for example, was rather dramatic until quite recently. For security, villages in many areas were situated exclusively on hilltops, some of them thousands of feet above the nearest available water. A likely fate for a New Guinean man, woman, or child was death at the hands of a hostile group.

Throughout the history of Western civilization, war has been essentially continuous. This doubtless helped to maintain high death rates, particularly by creating food shortages and the preconditions of plagues. Barbarian invasions of the Roman Empire (375–568 A.D.), the Hundred Years' War (1337–1453), and especially the Thirty Years' War (1618–1648) caused substantial increases in the death rate in Europe. To give a single instance from the last of those conflicts, the storming and pillaging of Magdeburg by Catholic forces in 1631 caused an estimated 20,000 deaths. Indeed, some historians feel that as many as a third of the inhabitants of Germany and Bohemia died as a direct result of the Thirty Years' War.

The Peace of Westphalia ended the Thirty Years' War in 1648, introducing a period of relative tranquility and stability. At that time the Commercial Revolution was in full swing. Power was concentrated in monarchies, after having been decentralized in a loose feudal structure, and mercantilism was the economic order of the day. Perhaps

[13] W. L. Langer, The next assignment.

[14] The famines of the world: Past and present.

BOX 5-1 Famines

A small sampling of quotes from Cornelius Walford's 1878 chronology of 350 famines will give some feel for the ubiquity in time and space of this kind of catastrophe. (Quotation marks indicate where Walford was quoting directly from his sources.) Those who have seen films of recent famines in India and Africa are unlikely to consider scenes like those described below as things of the past.

B.C. 436 *Rome.* Famine. Thousands threw themselves into the Tiber.

A.D. 160 *England.* Multitudes starved.

192 *Ireland.* General scarcity; bad harvest; mortality and emigration, "so the lands and houses, territories and tribes, were emptied."

331 *Antioch.* This city was afflicted by so terrible a famine that a bushel of wheat was sold for 400 pieces of silver. During this grievous disaster Constantine sent to the Bishop 30,000 bushels of corn, besides an immense quantity of all kinds of provisions, to be distributed among the ecclesiastics, widows, orphans, etc.

695–700 *England and Ireland.* Famine and pestilence during three years "so that men ate each other."

1193–1196 *England, France.* "Famine occasioned by incessant rains. The common people perished everywhere for lack of food."

1299 *Russia.* Ravaged by famine and pestilence.

1412–1413 *India.* Great drought, followed by famine, occurred in the Ganges-Jumna delta.

1600 *Russia.* Famine and plague of which 500,000 died.

1769–1770 *India.* (Hindustan) First great Indian famine of which we have a record. It was estimated that 3,000,000 people perished. The air was so infected by the noxious effluvia of dead bodies that it was scarcely possible to stir abroad without perceiving it; and without hearing also the frantic cries of victims of famine who were seen at every stage of suffering and death.

1770 *Bohemia.* Famine and pestilence said to carry off 168,000 persons.

1789 *France.* Grievous famine; province of Rouen.

1790 *India.* Famine in district of Barda . . . so great was the distress that many people fled to other districts in search of food; while others destroyed themselves, and some killed their children and lived on their flesh.

1877–1878 *North China.* "Appalling famine raging throughout four provinces (of) North China. Nine million people reported destitute, children daily sold in markets for (raising means to procure) food. . . . Total population of districts affected, 70 millions. . . ." The people's faces are black with hunger; they are dying by thousands upon thousands. Women and girls and boys are openly offered for sale to any chance wayfarer. When I left the country, a respectable married woman could be easily bought for six dollars, and a little girl for two. In cases, however, where it was found impossible to dispose of their children, parents have been known to kill them sooner than witness their prolonged suffering, in many instances throwing themselves afterwards down wells, or committing suicide by arsenic.

1878 *Morocco.* ". . . If you could see the terrible scenes of misery—poor starving mothers breaking and pounding up bones they find in the streets, and giving them to their famished children—it would make your heart ache."

the most basic new idea of mercantilism was that of government intervention to increase the power of the state and (more important, from our point of view) the prosperity of the nation. Planning by government was extended to provide economic necessities for the population.

The preindustrial rise of population, 1650–1850. In the middle of the seventeenth century, a period of relative peace started in a postfeudal economic environment. Simultaneously, a revolution in European agriculture—a revolution that was largely a result of the Commercial Revolution—began to gather momentum. It accelerated rapidly in the eighteenth century. Rising prices and increasing demand from the growing cities added to the commercial attractiveness of farming. The breakdown of the feudal system gradually destroyed the manorial estates. On those estates each male serf had assigned to him several scattered strips of land, which were farmed communally. The serfs grew increasingly unhappy with the communal farming, so the strips were rearranged into single compacted holdings leased by individual peasants from the landholder.

As landowners wished to put more land to the plow, they began to enclose old communal woodland and grazing lands with hedges and walls, barring the peasants from resources essential to their subsistence. This movement was especially pronounced in Great Britain, where it was promoted by a series of special acts of Parliament. Furthermore, much of the peasantry was dispossessed or forced out of agriculture by competition from the more efficient large farming operations. Agriculture was transformed into big business.

Accompanying these changes were fundamental improvements in crops and farming techniques. For instance, the role of clover in renewing soil (by replacing lost nitrogen) was discovered in England by Lord Charles Townshend. This made the practice of letting fields lie fallow every third year unnecessary. Other improvements were made in methods of cultivation and in animal breeding. Agricultural output increased and so, consequently, did the margin over famine. It seems plausible that a combination of commercial and agricultural revolutions, a period of relative peace, and the disappearance of the black death all combined to reduce the death rate and produce the European population surge that started in the mid-seventeenth century.[15] Between 1650 and 1750 it is estimated that the populations of Europe and Russia increased from 103 million to 144 million.

An additional factor that may have contributed to this acceleration in growth was the opening of the Western Hemisphere to European exploitation. In 1500 the ratio of people to available land in Europe was about 10 per square kilometer. The addition of the vast, virtually unpopulated frontiers of the New World reduced the ratio for Europe plus the Western Hemisphere to less than 2 per square kilometer. As historian Walter Prescott Webb wrote, this frontier was, in essence "a vast body of wealth without proprietors."[16] Thus, not only was land shortage in Europe in part alleviated, but several major European nations were enriched. Both factors encouraged population growth.

Furthermore, the introduction of two new foods from the New World, maize (corn) and the potato, either of which could provide sustenance for a large family from a very small plot of land, may have fueled a population increase by expanding the feeding base.[17] Maize was widespread in southern Europe by the eighteenth century, during which the populations of both Spain and Italy nearly doubled.

Although we can speculate with ease about the causes of Europe's population boom between 1650 and 1750, it is somewhat more difficult to explain a similar boom in Asia. The population there increased by some 50 to 75 percent in that period. In China, after the collapse of the Ming dynasty in 1644, political stability and the agricultural policies of the Manchu emperors doubtless led to a depression of death rates. The introduction of maize and peanuts to China in the eighteenth century may also have stimulated growth there, as the potato and maize seem to have done in Europe.

[15]The disappearance of black death was possibly due to the displacement of the black rat, which lived in houses, by the sewer-loving brown rat. This lessened contact between people and rats, and thus reduced the chances of plague-carrying fleas reaching human beings. In London the great fire of 1666 destroyed much of the city, which consisted largely of rundown wooden buildings that provided excellent shelter for the rats. By orders of the king, the city was rebuilt with brick and stone, thus making it much more secure from plague.

[16]*The great frontier.*

[17]W. L. Langer, American foods and Europe's population growth, 1750–1850.

Much of the Asian population growth during that period probably took place in China, since India was in a period of economic and political instability caused by the disintegration of the Mogul Empire. When the last of the Mogul emperors, Aurangzeb, died in 1707, India was racked by war and famine. British soldier and statesman Robert Clive and the East India Company established British hegemony in India during the period between 1751 and 1761. At a time when China may have had the world's most advanced agricultural system under the efficient Manchu government, India was a battleground for the British and French. And the rapid increase in power of the British East India Company following the Peace of Paris in 1763 did not bring rapid relief. Indeed, in a famous famine in 1770, about one-third of the population of Bengal is reputed to have perished—a circumstance that did not prevent industrious agents from maintaining the East India Company's revenue from Bengal during that year!

World population seems to have grown at a rate of about 0.3 percent per year between 1650 and 1750. The rate increased to approximately 0.5 percent between 1750 and 1850, during which time the population of Europe doubled. Because what demographic records exist are scanty, fragmentary, and often anecdotal, the causes of this acceleration are not known and have become a subject of some debate. The prevailing view has been that, in Europe at least, the surge occurred in response to a number of favorable changes that acted chiefly to reduce mortality.[18]

The most important cause of lowered death rates in preindustrial Europe seems to have been a decline in mortality from infectious diseases, especially tuberculosis (at least in England) and smallpox (resulting from the introduction of smallpox inoculation). Demographic historians T. McKeown, R. G. Brown, and R. G. Record attribute this change to "environmental improvements"—primarily, increased food production resulting from continued advances in agricultural techniques.[19] P. E. Razzell has suggested that the adoption of habits of personal hygiene following the popular introduction of soap and cheap utensils and cotton clothing had more to do with the reduction of infectious diseases than did nutritional improvement.[20] He also cites drainage and reclamation of land as possibly helping to reduce the incidence of malaria and various respiratory diseases.

Another group of historians puts an emphasis on rising birth rates as an explanation of the burst of growth in Europe's population that began in the seventeenth century. Even though agricultural socioeconomic systems (such as that of eighteenth-century Europe) generally promote high birth rates, there is evidence that through most of history, farming populations have kept their natality below the maximum. Not the least of this evidence is the relatively low growth rate during the first 10,000 years of agriculture (less than 0.1 percent.)[21] This suggests that there was a "reserve" of natality that could permit an increase when needed. Some historians think such a reserve may have helped fuel Europe's seventeenth-century growth spurt.[22] The claim is that rising birth rates played an important role in accelerating this population growth and that the decline in death rates may not have been significant or consistent until around 1900.[23] The latter suggestion is not supported, however, by evidence from several northwestern European countries for which data exist (see Figure 5-4).

Historian William Langer believes an overriding factor was the widespread acceptance of the potato as a staple food in northern Europe during the eighteenth century, particularly among peasants trying to subsist on very small pieces of land.[24] His view is that, by providing relatively abundant, nutritious food for the poor, potato cultivation encouraged couples to marry younger and raise larger families. Hence, it stimulated higher birth rates as well as contributing to the improved nutrition that led to lower death rates from disease. The potato's role in generating the population explosion in Ireland during this period (the Irish increased from 3 million to 8 million), followed by a crash when potato blight destroyed the crop in 1846 and 1847 (1 million died, and 2

[18]A. J. Coale, The history of the human population.

[19]T. McKeown, R. G. Brown, R. G. Record, An interpretation of the modern rise of population in Europe.

[20]P. E. Razzell, "An interpretation of the modern rise of population in Europe"—a critique.

[21]E. A. Wrigley, *Population and history;* Dumond, The limitation, pp. 718–719.

[22]R. Freedman, The sociology of human fertility: A trend report and bibliography; Wrigley, *Population,* p. 161 ff.

[23]Dumond, The limitation, p. 719.

[24]Langer, American foods.

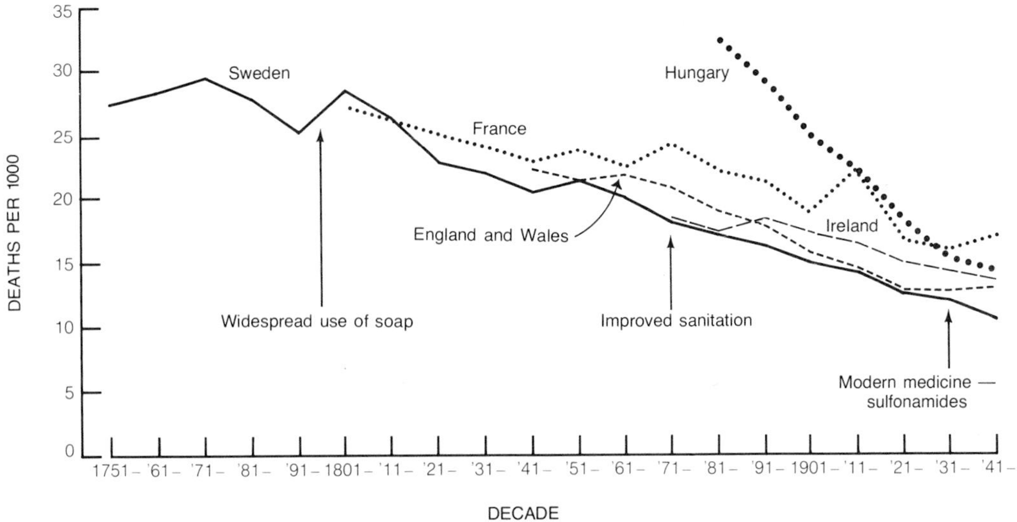

FIGURE 5-4

Mean annual death rates in England and Wales, Sweden, France, Ireland, and Hungary from the time of their initial registration. The times when some factors thought to play important roles in reducing mortality were introduced are indicated, too. Note that modern medicine–as distinct from personal and public hygiene–became an important influence only quite recently. (Adapted from McKeown, Brown, and Record, 1972.)

million emigrated), is common knowledge. Many other areas in Europe were also threatened by the blight, but because the people were less completely dependent on a potato monoculture, more survived.

Quite probably all these factors—prosperity, increased food supplies, diminished mortality from disease, improved sanitation—contributed in some measure to the acceleration in Europe's population growth between 1750 and 1850. There is little evidence to support the hypothesis that birth rates rose significantly. Indeed, in some countries they were declining well before 1800. The argument that the acceleration of growth that accompanied the beginning of agriculture was primarily caused by increased natality seems to us persuasive; the claim that a significant trend in declining death rates did not develop until the end of the nineteenth century is less so, especially since considerable evidence exists to the contrary.

Regardless of whether the growth in Europe's population between 1750 and 1850 was caused mainly by declining death rates, rising birth rates, or some combination of the two, twice as many people were living there at the end of the century as had been at the beginning. Moreover, this increase occurred despite several factors operating against it, notably a high rate of celibacy (nonmarriage) and the apparently widespread practice of infanticide.[25] Reports of infanticide in Europe extend back into the Middle Ages,[26] but by 1800 in England, France, and Germany it seems to have reached almost epidemic proportions. The vast majority of the unwanted children were born to the poor—often to unmarried domestic servants and others unable to care for them. In this connection, there seems to have been considerable social and economic pressure against marriage for the landless poor, and even for younger sons of the wealthier classes. In London and Paris—and perhaps other cities, as well—foundling hospitals were established to care for the growing numbers of abandoned babies. But the level of care provided was so poor that the main result was the disappearance of infant bodies from streets, roadsides, and streams (evidently they were a very common sight before 1800).[27] The horrors of widespread infanticide—largely suppressed and forgotten today—apparently per-

[25]W. L. Langer, Checks on population growth: 1750–1850.

[26]Dickeman, Demographic consequences; Richard Trexler, Infanticide in Florence: New sources and first results, and The foundlings of Florence, 1395–1455, *History of childhood quarterly*, vol. 1 (1973), no. 1 (spring), pp. 98–116, and no. 2 (fall), pp. 259–284.

[27]Langer, Checks.

sisted as late as 1870—perhaps not coincidentally, about the time the birth-control movement was beginning (see Chapter 13). One might speculate that both the birth-control movement and Victorian prudery (especially the powerful disapproval of extramarital sexual activity and illegitimacy) were both reactions to infanticide. It is ironic, if so, that the same prudery for decades hindered the spread of birth control!

The doubling of Europe's population between 1750 and 1850 also was achieved in the face of substantial emigration to the New World, where the population jumped from 12 million to about 60 million in the same period. The United States grew from about 4 million in 1790, when the first census was taken, to 23 million in 1850. Much of the increase was due to immigration, mainly from England, but birth rates were also high (an estimated 55 per 1000 in 1800, declining to 43.3 per 1000 in 1850).[28] Mortality data are lacking, but it is probable that the death rate in the United States was declining as it was in Europe, and for similar reasons. As just one example, mass inoculation against smallpox was first introduced and shown to be effective during the Revolutionary War.

Growth in Asia between 1750 and 1850 was slower than in Europe, amounting to an increase of about 50 percent. Most of the developments that favored a rapid increase in Europe's population were to appear in Asia only much later, if at all. Little is known about the sizes of past populations in Africa, a continent that remained virtually unknown to the outside world until well past the middle of the nineteenth century. It is generally accepted that the population there remained more or less constant at around 100 million, plus or minus 5 or 10 million, between 1650 and 1850. After that, death rates appear to have declined somewhat, perhaps because of improved food supplies and distribution and the introduction of European sanitation and medicine.

The demographic transition, 1850–1930. Death rates in Europe and North America continued to decline during the period between 1850 and 1900, probably as a result of improvements in living conditions that accompanied the Industrial Revolution. Although the horrible conditions that prevailed in mines and factories during the early stages of the rise of industry are well known to all who have read the literature of the period, the overall situation in areas undergoing industrialization actually improved. Life in the rat-infested cities and rural slums of preindustrial Europe had been grim almost beyond description. Advances in agriculture, industry, and transportation by 1850 had substantially bettered the lot of the average person in Europe and North America. Improved agriculture had reduced the chances of crop failures and famine. Mechanized land and sea transport had made local famines less disastrous by providing access to distant resources. Great improvements in sanitation—notably, the installation of sewage systems and the purification of water supplies—in the last third of the nineteenth century helped to reduce death rates further. So did discovery of the role of bacteria in infection and the introduction of inoculation against disease. (The medical advances, however, appear to have had less impact on mortality than has traditionally been attributed to them.)[29]

European death rates, which in 1850 had been in the vicinity of 22 to 24 per 1000, decreased to around 18 to 20 per 1000 by 1900 and went as low as 16 per 1000 in some countries. Combined rates for Denmark, Norway, and Sweden dropped from about 20 per 1000 in 1850 to 16 per 1000 in 1900.[30] In western and northern Europe in the latter half of the nineteenth century, low death rates (and the resultant high rate of population increase) helped stimulate massive emigration.[31]

By the end of the century, another significant trend appeared: birth rates in several Western countries, including the United States, were also declining. In Denmark, Norway, and Sweden, the combined birth rate was around 32 per 1000 in 1850; by 1900 it had decreased to 28. Similar declines occurred elsewhere. This was the start of the so-called demographic transition—a falling of birth rates that followed declining death rates in Europe

[28] *Historical statistics of the United States: Colonial times to 1957,* U.S. Bureau of the Census, Washington, D. C.

[29] McKeown, Brown, and Record (An interpretation) are of the opinion that sanitation was far more important than medicine in reducing death rates before 1935. They point out that no significant drugs effective against infectious disease existed until sulfa drugs were developed in the 1930s and modern antibiotics in the 1940s.

[30] A. J. Coale, The decline of fertility in Europe from the French Revolution to World War II, in *Fertility and family planning: A world view,* S. J. Behrman; L. Corsa, Jr.; and R. Freedman, eds.

[31] K. Davis, The migrations of human populations.

and North America, which has generally been associated with industrialization.[32] Figure 5-5 shows the progress of the demographic transition in several European countries.

What caused the decline in birth rates in the industrializing Western countries? No one knows for certain, but some rather good guesses have been made. In general, it has been assumed that the changed conditions of life caused by industrialization led to changed attitudes toward family size. In nineteenth-century western Europe, customs of late marriage (which reduces birth rates by reducing the number of years each woman is reproductively active) and a high proportion of nonmarriage were already established. Hence, declining birth rates presumably were due mainly to conscious and increasing limitation of the number of children born within marriage.

It has been observed that in agrarian societies children are commonly viewed as economic bonuses. They serve as extra hands on the farm and take care of parents in their old age. This pronatalist point of view was beautifully expressed by Thomas Cooper in 1794.[33] He wrote: "In America, particularly out of the large towns, no man of moderate desires feels anxious about a family. In the country, where dwells the mass of the people, every man feels the increase of his family to be the increase of his riches: and no farmer doubts about the facility of providing for his children as comfortably as they have lived. . . ."

As a society industrializes, the theory goes, these things change. Children are no longer potential producers; they become consumers, requiring expensive feeding and education. This is especially so once child labor is abolished and education becomes compulsory. Large families, which become more likely with lowered death rates, tend to reduce mobility and to make the accumulation of capital more difficult. Other factors affecting family size that have been mentioned are the education and employment of women, increased secularization of society, and the decline of traditional religious influence.[34]

The demographic transition in Europe, however, was not limited to urban areas, although it may have begun there. Rapid population increase created a squeeze in rural areas as well, a squeeze that was compounded by the modernization of farms. A finite amount of land had to supply a livelihood for more people. As time went on, increased mechanization, which made larger farms more efficient and reduced the need for farm labor, made it more and more difficult for a young couple to establish themselves on a farm of their own. This may effectively have outweighed any traditional advantages of large farm families. As a result, rural birth rates also dropped, and many people moved to the cities seeking jobs in commerce and industry.

Yet this traditional explanation of the demographic transition, in which industrialization is considered the prime influence, does not account for numerous exceptions. France, for example, industrialized late compared to some of its neighbors, yet it was the first country to experience declining birth rates, beginning in 1800 or earlier (Figure 5-5). The United States also had a dropping birth rate well before industrialization had progressed very far; nor was land scarcity ever a significant factor here.[35] In England, the birthplace of the Industrial Revolution, on the other hand, the birth rate *rose* slightly between the 1840s and the 1870s, after which it declined steadily.

Hungary, like most of eastern Europe, industrialized much later. Its demographic transition also began later (and proceeded faster), but the birth rate was dropping precipitously well before industrialization had taken place to any significant degree.[36] Thus it appears that, whereas industrialization (and accompanying urbanization and extension of compulsory education) may have been a factor in Europe's demographic transition, it clearly is not the whole explanation, and possibly is not even the main one.

The twentieth century. The demographic transition in Western nations continued into the twentieth century. Yet, despite declining birth rates and a high rate of emigration from Europe, many of those countries were

[32]Coale, The history.
[33]*Some information respecting America,* p. 55.
[34]Coale, The Decline.

[35]*Historical statistics of the United States.*
[36]McKeown, Brown, and Record, An interpretation; M. S. Teitelbaum, Relevance of demographic transition theory for developing countries; Coale, Decline.

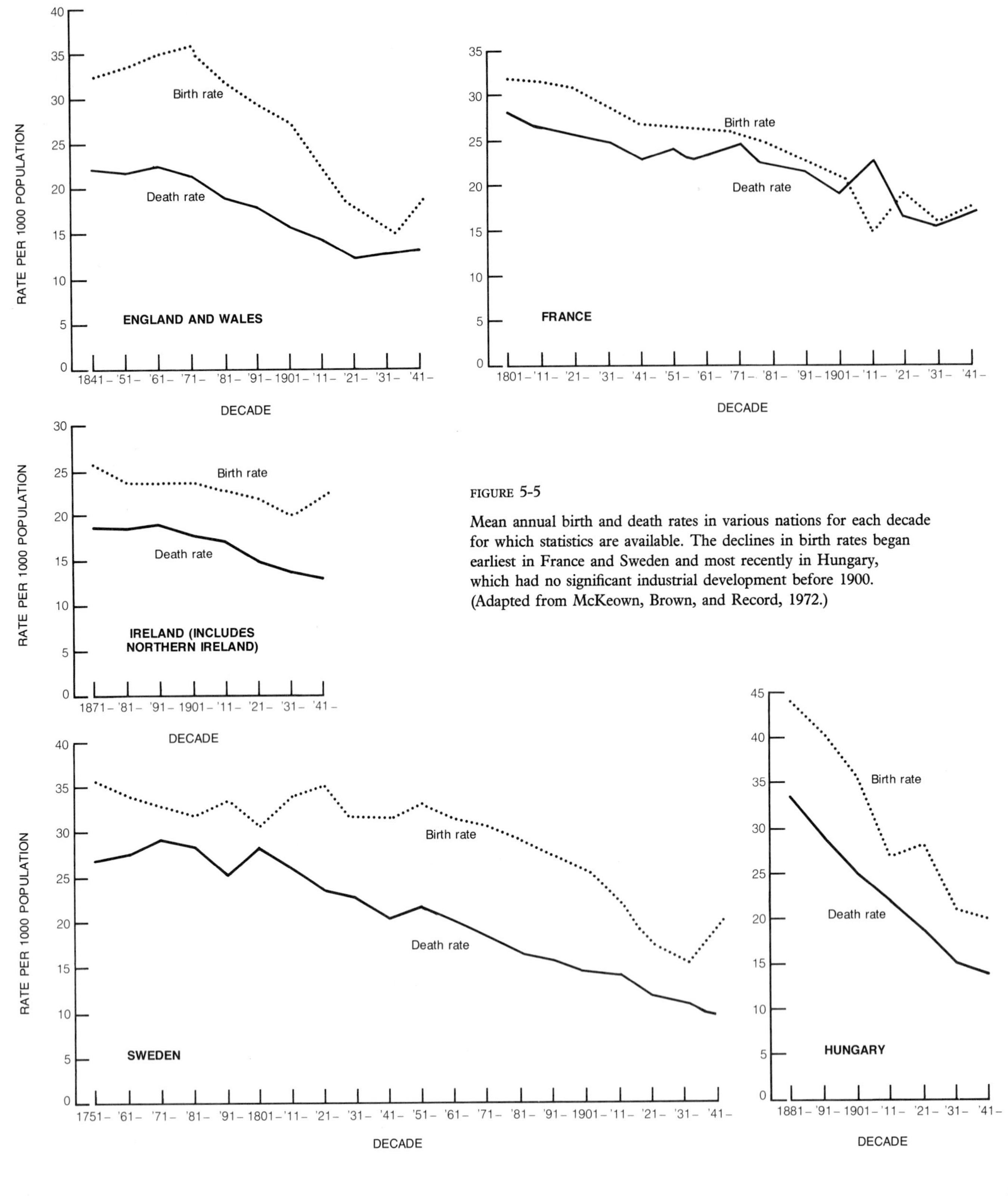

FIGURE 5-5

Mean annual birth and death rates in various nations for each decade for which statistics are available. The declines in birth rates began earliest in France and Sweden and most recently in Hungary, which had no significant industrial development before 1900. (Adapted from McKeown, Brown, and Record, 1972.)

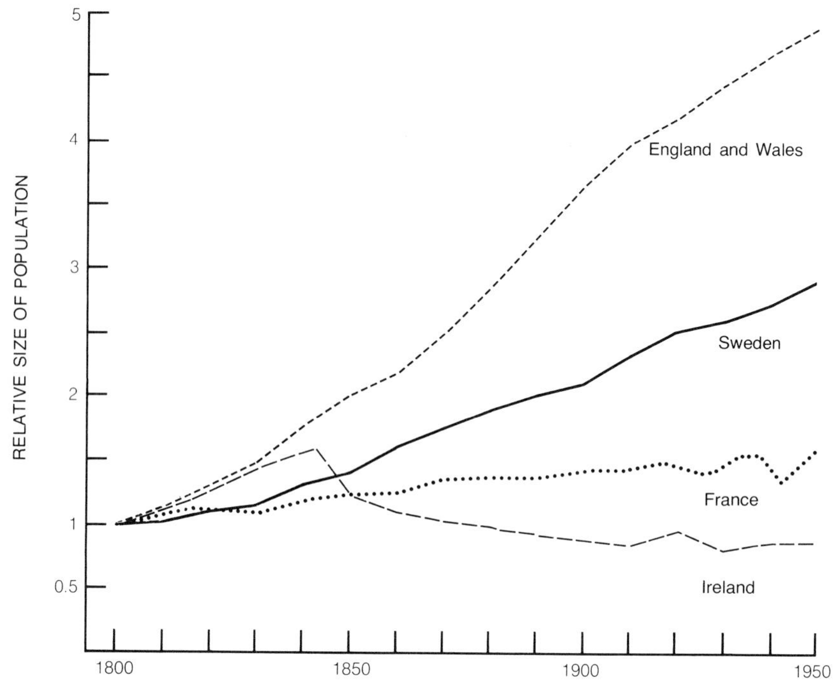

FIGURE 5-6

The growth of populations relative to their sizes in 1800. (Adapted from McKeown, Brown, and Record, 1972.)

TABLE 5-3
Populations, 1850 and 1950 (estimated, in millions)

	World	*Africa*	*North America*	*Latin America*	*Asia (except USSR)*	*Europe and Asian USSR*	*Oceania*
1850	1131	97	26	33	700	274	2
1950	2495	200	167	163	1376	576	13

Source: United Nations (1963) and estimates (somewhat modified) by Willcox, *Studies in American Demography,* and Carr-Saunders, *World Population.*

growing as rapidly as ever (Figure 5-6). Of the four nations represented in Figure 5-6, only Ireland lost population, and that was a direct result of the Irish potato famine in the 1840s. Birth rates there remained moderately high but were counterbalanced by heavy emigration. France maintained a very low rate of natural increase; Sweden and England both had relatively high ones, but Sweden's growth was much more depressed by emigration. The United States, by comparison, tripled its population between 1850 and 1900, spurred by massive immigration, even though its birth rate continued to decline steadily.

The average growth rate of the world population between 1850 and 1950 was about 0.8 percent per year. Population increased in that time from slightly more than 1 billion to almost 2.5 billion. The estimated populations shown in Table 5-3 indicate that between 1850 and 1950 the population of Asia did not quite double, whereas it more than doubled in Europe and Africa, multiplied about fivefold in Latin America, and more than sixfold in North America.

Toward the middle of the twentieth century, this pattern of relative growth rates began to change. By the 1930s declines in the birth rates in some European countries had outpaced declines in the death rates, and population growth had begun to slacken. By then the combined death rate of Denmark, Norway, and Sweden had declined to 12 per 1000, and the birth rate had dropped precipitously to about 16 (Figure 5-4). North America followed a similar path, both in lower birth rates

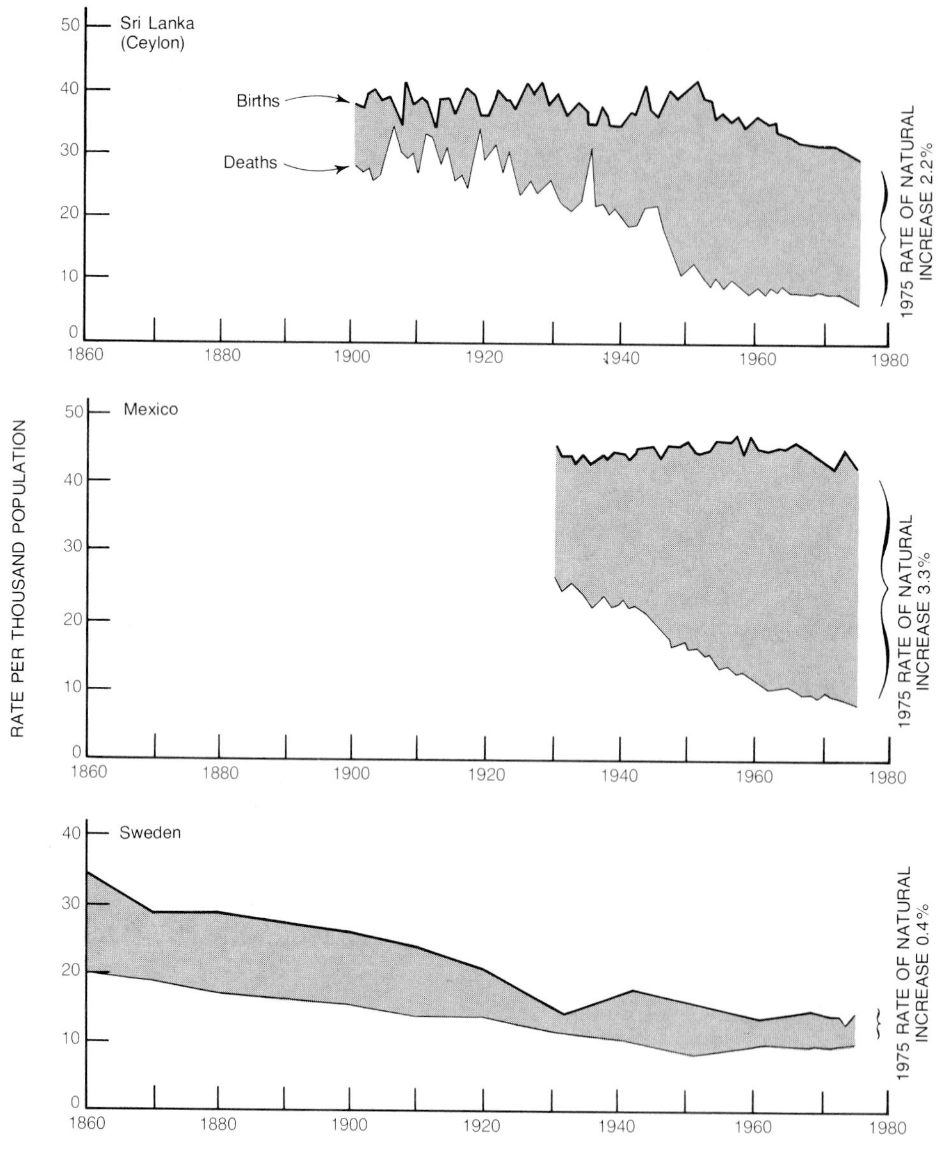

FIGURE 5-7

Different patterns of change in birth and death rates and the rate of natural increase. Death rates dropped gradually in Western industrial countries such as Sweden and precipitously in LDCs such as Sri Lanka (Ceylon) and Mexico. (Courtesy of the Population Reference Bureau, Inc., Washington, D.C.)

and in dramatically reduced immigration after the 1920s.

Stimulated by improving economic conditions and World War II, however, birth rates rose again during the 1940s and remained above replacement level in most developed countries until the late 1960s. Consequently, European growth rates generally averaged between 0.5 and 1.0 percent from 1945 to 1970. Since then, the decline in fertility has resumed, and a few countries had reached zero population growth (ZPG) by the mid-1970s.

As population growth in industrialized nations slowed in response to low birth rates around the time of World War II, a dramatic decline in previously quite high death rates occurred in the nonindustrial nations. In some countries, such as Mexico, the decline started before the war. In others, such as Ceylon (now Sri Lanka), it did not start until the end of the war. Compare, for instance, the trend in Sweden since 1860 with that in Mexico since 1930 (Figure 5-7). This decline in the death rate was caused primarily by the rapid export of modern drugs and public-health measures from the developed countries to the less developed countries. The consequent "death control" produced the most rapid, widespread change known in the history of human population dynamics: the postwar population explosion.[37]

The power of exported death control can be seen by examining the classic case of Ceylon's assault on malaria after World War II. Between 1933 and 1942 the death rate due directly to malaria in Ceylon was reported as about 2 per 1000. That rate, however, represented only a fraction of the malaria deaths, as many were reported as being caused by "pyrexia," a fancy name for fever. Actually, in 1934/1935 a malaria epidemic may have been directly responsible for fully half the deaths on the island. The death rate for those years rose to 34 per 1000. In addition, malaria, which infected a large portion of the population, made many people susceptible to other diseases and thus contributed to the death rate indirectly, as well as directly.

The death rate in Ceylon in 1945 was 22 per 1000. The introduction of the insecticide DDT in 1946 brought rapid control over the mosquitoes that carry malaria. Subsequently, the death rate on the island dropped 34 percent between 1946 and 1947, declined by about 50 percent of the 1945 level by 1955, and has continued to decline since then. In 1975 it stood at 8 per 1000. Although part of the drop was certainly due to other public health measures and the control of other diseases, much of it can be accounted for by the control of malaria.

TABLE 5-4
Change in Age-Specific Death Rates of Males in Two LDCs

	1950–1952 rate as a percentage of 1920–1922 rate	
Age class	*Jamaica*	*Ceylon*
0–1	45.1	39.8
1–5	38.3	34.7
5–10	34.6	21.7
10–15	28.7	15.6
15–20	25.9	16.1
20–40	31.7	21.4
40–60	59.2	32.4
60–70	73.1	48.2

Source: K. Davis, The population impact on children in the world's agrarian countries.

Victory over malaria, yellow fever, smallpox, cholera, tuberculosis, and other infectious diseases has been responsible for similar abrupt drops in death rates throughout the nonindustrial world. The decline has been most pronounced among children and young adults. They are the people most vulnerable to infectious diseases—the diseases most efficiently controlled by modern medical and public-health procedures. (Congenital problems in infants and degenerative diseases of old people reduce the proportionate effects of infectious disease in those age brackets.) The differential reduction of mortality can be seen clearly in data from Jamaica and Ceylon (Table 5-4).

In the decade between 1940 and 1950, death rates declined 46 percent in Puerto Rico, 43 percent in Taiwan, and 23 percent in Jamaica. In a sample of eighteen less developed areas, the average decline in death rate between 1945 and 1950 was 24 percent.[38] Figure 5-8 shows the dramatic change in death rates from the 1945 to 1949 average to the 1960/1961 average in selected Asian nations.

[37]K. Davis, The amazing decline of mortality in underdeveloped areas.

[38]Ibid.

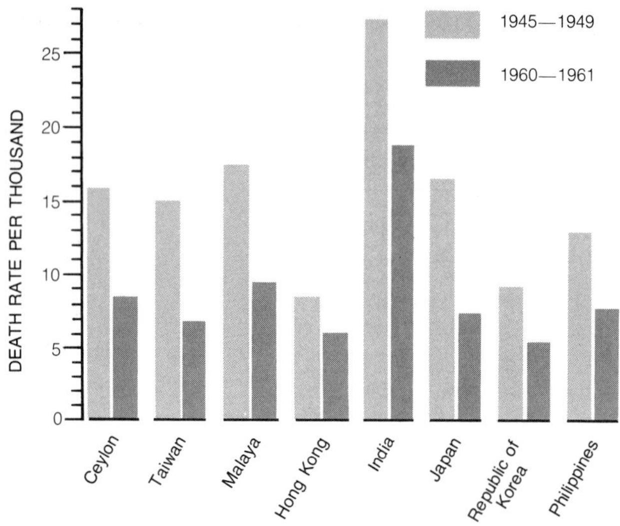

FIGURE 5-8

Changes in death rates in selected Asian nations. The average rates between 1945 and 1949 are compared with those of 1960 and 1961. (Adapted from *Population bulletin,* vol. 20, no. 2. Courtesy Population Reference Bureau, Inc., Washington, D.C.)

A critical point to remember is that this precipitous decline in death rate is different in kind from the long-term slow decline that occurred throughout most of the world following the Agricultural Revolution. It is also different in kind from the comparatively faster decline in death rates in the Western world since 1650, even though both were achieved primarily through reduction in deaths from infectious diseases. The difference is that the plummeting death rates of less developed countries are a response to a spectacular environmental change in the LDCs, not to a fundamental change in their institutions or general ways of life. Furthermore, that change did not originate within those countries but was introduced from the outside.

The factors that have been associated with a demographic transition (to lowered birth rates) in the developed countries therefore were not and still are not present in most non-Western countries, and birth rates there accordingly have remained high. For instance, the Indian birth rate in 1891 was estimated to be 49 per 1000 per year; in 1931 it was 46 per 1000, and in 1972 it was still around 40 per 1000, despite efforts to reduce it during the 1960s and 1970s (see Chapter 13). And much of that small decline can be attributed to changes in the nation's age composition (see Box 5-4).

In the decade 1930 to 1940, the populations grew in North America and Europe at 0.7 percent per year, whereas those of Asia grew at 1.1 percent, Africa at 1.5 percent, and Latin America at 2.0 percent, even though death rates were still considerably higher in the last three areas mentioned. The annual world growth rate for the decade was 1.1 percent.

Since then, the majority of the human population has moved rapidly from a situation of high birth and death rates to one of high birth rates and low death rates. The average annual world growth rate for the decade 1940 to 1950, presumably depressed by World War II, was 0.9 percent (doubling time, 77 years). It then zoomed to 1.8 percent (doubling time, 38 years) from 1950 to 1960 following the introduction of death control to the less developed regions. During the 1960s the world growth rate fluctuated between 1.8 and 2.0 percent per year. The entire population grew from about 2.3 billion in 1940 to 2.5 billion in 1950, to 3.0 billion in 1960, and 3.6 billion in 1970.[39]

According to the Population Reference Bureau, whose figures are based mainly on United Nations estimates, the world's population size in mid-1976 was 4,019 million, the annual growth rate was 1.8 percent, and the doubling time 38 years.[40] These numbers, however, conceal very large differences in rates of growth among nations and regions, which are described in Box 5-2 and summarized in Table 5-5. (Appendix 1 presents detailed population estimates for 1976, prepared by the Population Reference Bureau.)

Most LDC population figures, it should be noted, are only approximations because census data from many of them are inadequate or nonexistent. There is considerable controversy, for example, about the actual size and rate of growth of the Chinese population. China itself claimed a population of 800 million in late 1974. The United Nations put the population at 838 million in mid-1975 and the growth rate at 1.7 percent. Demogra-

[39]United Nations *Statistical yearbook, 1973,* and various other sources.
[40]*1976 World Population Data sheet.*

pher Robert Cook of the Environmental Fund is skeptical of both estimates, and he places the 1975 total at more than 900 million and the growth rate close to 2 percent.[41] (According to his figures, the world population in 1975 was growing at a rate of 2.2 percent per year and doubling in 32 years.) Another demographer, John S. Aird, of the United States Department of Commerce, has claimed that China's population exceeded 930 million in 1972 and was growing at 2.4 percent.

At the other extreme, R. D. Ravenholt, director of the population program for the U.S. Agency for International Development (AID), claims that world population growth reached a peak between 1965 and 1970 and has now begun to decline.[42] He places China's 1975 population at 876 million and its growth rate at 0.8 percent. Ravenholt also offers lower estimates than Cook's of birth rates for many LDCs with family-planning programs. Obviously, large discrepancies in estimates for China alone can induce considerable variation in estimates for the world as a whole. Table 5-6 shows the differences between three of these estimates of world population size and growth.

The most recent U.N. and U.S. government figures indicate that Ravenholt may be correct that the rate of population growth worldwide has begun to slacken since 1970.[42a] Lester Brown of Worldwatch Institute attributes the slowdown to (1) unexpectedly successful results of China's population policies and a correspondingly lower death rate and, especially, birth rate there; (2) a significant decline in birth rates in nearly all developed countries; (3) some success in lowering birth rates in some LDCs; and (4) a *rise* in death rates in several LDCs, especially in South Asia, caused primarily by food shortages in the early 1970s (see Chapter 7). To the extent that lowered birth rates may be slowing population growth, this is encouraging news. To the extent that reduced growth is caused by a rise in death rates, it is a tragic confirmation of the often-ignored warnings of ecologists and others.

TABLE 5-5
Populations, 1960, 1970, and 1975, and Rates of Growth in Major Areas and Regions of the World

Region	Population (millions)			Annual growth rate (%)	
	1960	1970	1975	1960–1970	1970–1975
WORLD TOTAL	2995	3621	3988	1.90	1.93
More developed regions*	976	1084	1133	1.05	0.88
Less developed regions	2019	2537	2855	2.28	2.36
EUROPE*	425	459	474	0.77	0.64
Eastern Europe*	97	103	106	0.62	0.64
Northern Europe*	76	80	82	0.57	0.41
Southern Europe*	118	128	132	0.78	0.74
Western Europe*	135	148	153	0.96	0.67
USSR*	214	243	255	1.25	0.99
U.S. AND CANADA*	199	226	237	1.31	0.90
OCEANIA	16	19	21	2.12	1.98
Australia and New Zealand*	13	15	17	1.92	1.83
Melanesia	2	3	3	2.44	2.56
Micronesia and Polynesia	1	1	1	3.42	2.64
SOUTH ASIA	865	1111	1268	2.50	2.64
Eastern South Asia	219	285	326	2.65	2.69
Middle South Asia	588	749	853	2.41	2.59
Western South Asia	58	77	90	2.79	2.96
EAST ASIA	787	926	1005	1.62	1.63
China	654	772	838	1.70	1.64
Japan*	94	104	111	1.03	1.26
Other East Asia	39	50	56	2.39	2.15
AFRICA	272	352	402	2.58	2.66
Eastern Africa	77	100	114	2.60	2.71
Middle Africa	32	40	45	2.41	2.35
Northern Africa	65	86	99	2.77	2.81
Southern Africa	18	24	28	2.87	2.70
Western Africa	80	101	116	2.36	2.59
LATIN AMERICA	216	284	326	2.74	2.73
Caribbean	21	26	28	2.12	2.14
Middle America	49	67	79	3.19	3.21
Temperate South America*	31	36	39	1.64	1.44
Tropical South America	116	155	180	2.93	2.91

*The regions marked with asterisks are considered as "more developed," from a demographic point of view.

Source: United Nations, *Concise Report.*

[41] *World population estimates, 1975.*

[42] Gaining ground on the population front.

[42a] Summarized in Lester R. Brown, World population trends. See also J. W. Brackett and R. T. Ravenholt, World fertility, 1976: An analysis of data sources and trends.

BOX 5-2 Population Growth: 1975 to 2000

By 1975 a striking disparity in population growth rates had arisen between the developed areas and the less developed areas of the world. Most DCs were growing very slowly, at less than 1 percent per year; many LDCs were growing at 3 percent per year or more. At 3.5 percent a population would multiply *more than thirtyfold within a century.* The world population in 1975 was about 4 billion, and the growth rate in the early 1970s was 1.9 percent per year (doubling in 36 years), according to the United Nations.* The following paragraphs outline the situation continent by continent.

North America

Canada and the United States together had a 1975 population of 237 million. A growth rate of 0.9 percent per year gave a doubling time for the area of 77 years. Depending on future birth rates and migration patterns, North America could have as many as 350 million people in the year 2000, or it could have as few as 265 million.

Latin America

This area (the Western Hemisphere south of the United States) had a 1975 population of 326 million and a growth rate of 2.7 percent, the highest rate for any major region. As a whole the population of the area was doubling every 26 years. Some Latin American countries have had extremely high growth rates and rapid doubling times in recent years. Honduras, for example, had a 1975 growth rate of 3.5 percent and a doubling time of 20 years. Doubling times for other representative countries were: Dominican Republic, 21 years; Mexico, 22 years; Peru, 24 years; Brazil, 25 years; Surinam, 27 years; Bolivia, 28 years; and Cuba, 35 years. A few countries in temperate Latin America were growing more slowly—Chile, Argentina, and Uruguay (doubling in 38, 53, and 69 years, respectively). According to various projections, the population of Latin America in the year 2000 will be between 550 and 760 million (see Figure 5-9).

Concise report on the world population situation, 1970–1975, and its long-range implications. Doubling times that follow for regions and nations are from *1975 Population Data Sheet,* Population Reference Bureau, Inc.

Europe

Europe is the demographic antithesis of Latin America. The 1975 European population (excluding European USSR and Turkey) was 474 million. The growth rate for the continent was 0.6 percent, which gives a doubling time of 116 years. The more rapidly growing countries, such as Ireland, Spain, and Yugoslavia, had doubling times of between 60 and 80 years. But most European countries were doubling much more slowly than that: Czechoslovakia, every 116 years; Italy, every 139 years; Hungary, every 173 years; and Austria, every 347 years. Both East Germany and West Germany have reached zero population growth. In the year 2000 Europe's population is projected to be about 540 million.

The Soviet Union had a 1975 population of 255 million, a growth rate of 1.0 percent, and a doubling time of 70 years. For several years its growth rate has been similar to that of the United States, but it is now higher. The population is projected to reach 315 million by the year 2000.

Africa

The 1975 population of Africa was 402 million people. Its current rate of growth is 2.6 percent, and its doubling time, 27 years. The pattern of growth is approaching that of Latin America, except that generally higher death rates in Africa result in a slightly lower growth rate. Sample doubling times were: Kenya, 21 years; Zambia, 22 years; Morocco, 24 years; Malagasy Republic, 24 years; Nigeria, 26 years; South Africa, 26 years; Egypt, 29 years; the People's Republic of Congo, 29 years; and Central African Republic, 33 years. Projections for the year 2000, based on the assumption that the death rate will continue to decline, give Africa a population of between 730 and 900 million, second only to the total projected for Asia. Some specialists on Africa cite evidence that the relatively high death rates there will drop rapidly in coming years and the birth rates will remain high. If this occurs, growth rates of 3.5 percent or even 4 percent per year could become commonplace in Africa, in which case the population estimates given here would be too low.

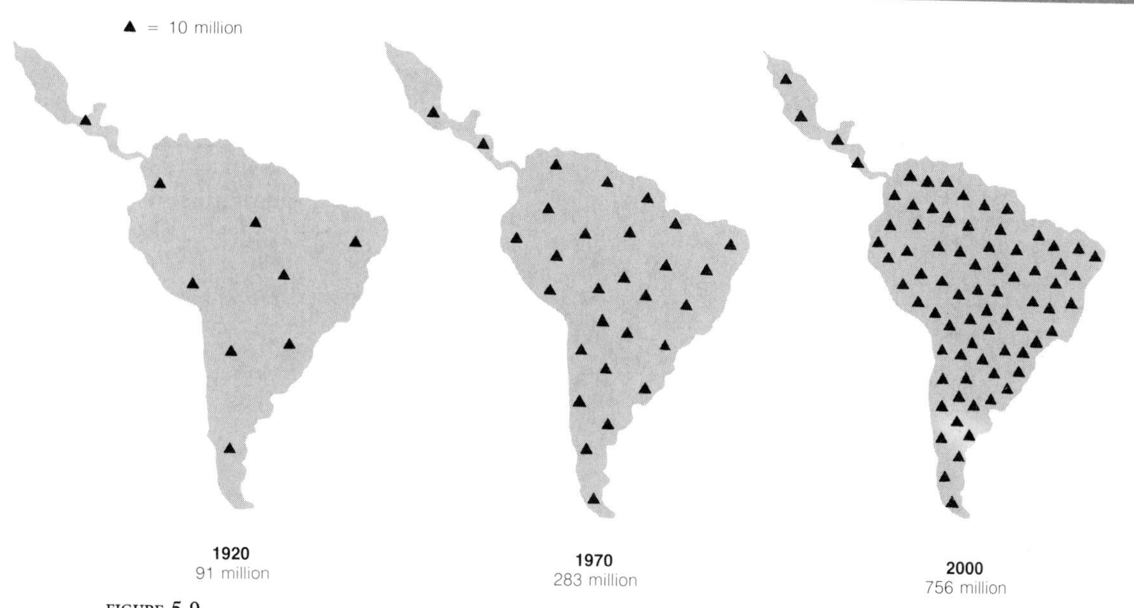

FIGURE 5-9

Population growth in Latin America, 1920–2000. If fertility rates do not drop, the population of the area will undergo more than an eightfold increase in eighty years. (Adapted from *Population bulletin,* vol. 23, no. 3. Courtesy of the Population Reference Bureau, Inc., Washington, D.C.)

Asia

Today's population giant, Asia, is inhabited by at least 2,273 million—over 2 billion—people. That figure—more than half the world's population—does not include the population of Asian USSR. It may be an understatement, moreover, if India's 1971 census results were incomplete and if some population estimates for China have been too low. Asia's 1975 growth rate was 2.1 percent, and its doubling time was 33 years. Among the Asian nations only Japan shows a growth pattern similar to those of Europe and North America, although Hong Kong, Taiwan, Singapore, and South Korea are moving in that direction. Japan's growth rate in 1975 was 1.3 percent, and its doubling time, 53 years. The doubling time for South Korea was 35 years; for Taiwan, 36 years; Singapore, 43 years; and Hong Kong, 50 years. The People's Republic of China presents a special problem. The size of its population and its growth rate are uncertain. Estimates of size range from 800 to 950 million people, the 1975 United Nations figure being 838 million. The United Nations estimated the growth rate as 1.7 percent (a 55-year doubling time), but this is basically an informed guess.

For the rest of Asia, doubling times tell the familiar story of the LDCs: Philippines, 21 years; Pakistan, 22 years; Malaysia, 24 years; Indonesia, 27 years; Afghanistan, 28 years; and India, 29 years. Among the most rapidly growing countries today are the Middle-Eastern, mainly Moslem, countries of southwestern Asia. The influx of wealth from oil in those lands in the 1970s may be effectively suppressing death rates, which until recently were relatively high. Typical 1975 doubling times were: Kuwait, 10 years; Iran, 23 years; and Saudi Arabia, 24 years. Projections for the year 2000 put Asia's population between 3000 and 4500 million and uniformly predict that that continent will continue to be the home of more than half of all *Homo sapiens.*

TABLE 5-6
World Population—Three Estimates

	United Nations	*Environmental Fund*	*U.S. Agency for International Development*
Population (mid-1975, in millions)	3988	4147	3943
Average birth rate (per 1000)	31.8 (1970–1975)	35.0 (1975)	28.2 (1974)
Average death rate (per 1000)	12.8 (1970–1975)	13.0 (1975)	11.8 (1974)
Rate of natural increase (%)	1.9 (1970–1975)	2.2 (1975)	1.63 (1974)
Annual increment in population (mid-1970s, in millions)	75	86	63

Sources: United Nations estimates appeared in United Nations, *Concise report;* those of the Environmental Fund, Inc., in *World population estimates, 1975;* and AID estimates in R. T. Ravenholt, Gaining ground.

Even the inadequate and controversial data available are nevertheless more than sufficient for our discussion. Whether there actually were only 3.8 billion people or as many as 4.3 billion in the world in mid-1976, or whether the average worldwide growth rate was 1.5 or 2.2 percent, does not significantly affect our conclusions about what that implies for the future of the planet and its inhabitants.

DEMOGRAPHIC PROJECTIONS AND POPULATION STRUCTURE

Once there was a young man who proposed a novel pay scheme to a prospective employer. For one month's work he was to receive 1 cent on the first day, 2 cents on the second, 4 on the third, and so on. Each day his pay was to double until the end of the month. The employer, a rather dull-witted merchant, agreed. The merchant was chagrined, to say the least, when he found that the young man's pay for the fifteenth day was more than $160. The merchant went bankrupt long before he had to pay the young man $167,733 for the twenty-fifth day. Had he remained in business, he would have had to pay his new employee wages of more than $10 million for the month.

This is just one of many stories illustrating the astronomical figures that are quickly reached by repeated doubling, even from a minute base. Another is about a reward that consists of a single grain of rice on the first square of a chessboard, 2 on the second, 4 on the third, and so forth, until the board is filled. It turns out that completing the reward would take several thousand times the world's annual rice crop.

Equally horrendous figures may be generated by projecting the growth of the human population into the future. Doubling time for that population fluctuated around 35–37 years between 1960 and 1974. If growth continued at that rate, the world population would exceed a billion billion people about 1000 years from now. That would be some 2000 persons *per square meter* of Earth's surface, land and sea! Even more preposterous figures can be generated. In a few thousand more years everything in the visible universe would be converted into people, and the diameter of the ball of people would be expanding with the speed of light! Such projections should convince all but the most obtuse that growth of the human population must stop eventually.

Age Composition

The discussion of the human population so far has dealt mainly with population sizes and growth rates, but of course there is more to demography than that. Populations also have structure: *age composition* and *sex ratio,* as well as *distribution* and *dispersion* (the geographic positions and relative spacing of individuals), discussed later in this chapter. These structural factors can strongly influence rates of growth and do have profound effects on the social and economic conditions under which a population lives.

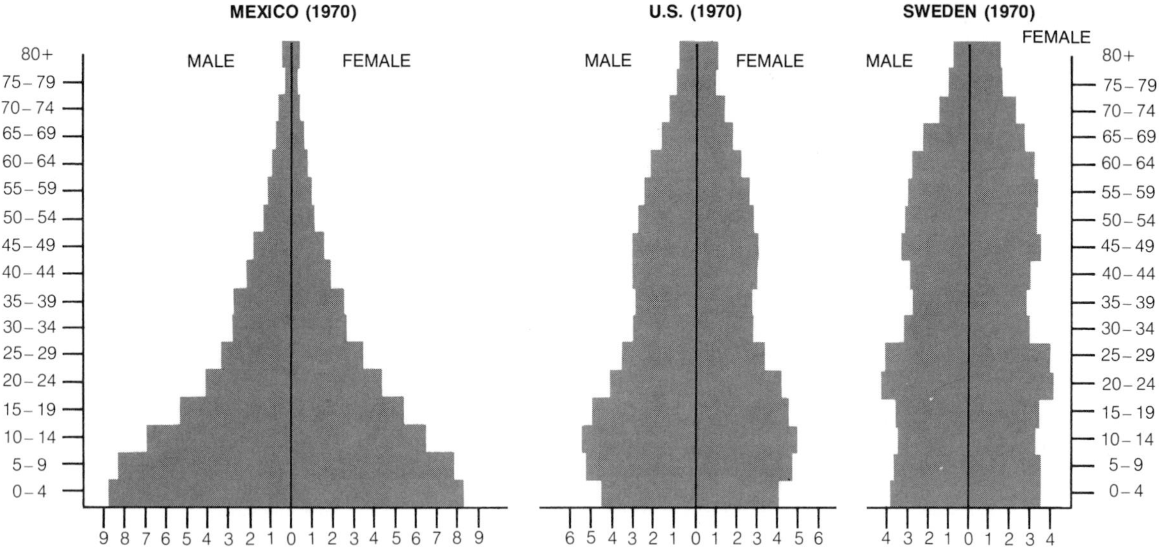

FIGURE 5-10

The age structure of a population is profoundly affected by changing fertility. In a country like Mexico, with a recent history of high fertility, the age structure is pyramidal. In a country like Sweden, with a recent history of low fertility, the structure is quite rectangular up to age 60. The U.S. age structure lies between the two extremes. (Adapted from Freedman and Berelson, 1974.)

Population profiles are a graphic means of showing the age composition of a population—that is, the relative numbers of people in different *age classes.* Look, for instance, at the age compositions of the populations of Mexico, the United States, and Sweden in 1970, as shown in Figure 5-10. Because the profiles are based on proportions, they all have the same area, despite great differences in the absolute sizes of those populations. This allows you to focus easily on their shapes, which of course reflect the different age compositions. Mexico's profile exemplifies rapidly growing countries with high birth rates and declining death rates. Most of its people are young (48 percent are under age 15). Sweden, however, has had low birth and death rates for many decades. It has a much slenderer population profile than Mexico. Only 21 percent of the people of Sweden are under age 15. The irregular profile exhibited by the United States reflects relatively large fluctuations in the birth rate over the past fifty years, particularly the baby boom of the late 1940s and the 1950s. The recent decline in American fertility is apparent in the constriction at the pyramid's base—the smaller numbers in the 1–4 and 5–9 age classes. The percentage of persons under age 15 was 27 in the mid-1970s, a somewhat higher percentage than in Sweden.

In Mexico—and most LDCs—high birth rates and increasing control over mortality (especially infants and children) have greatly inflated the younger age groups in the population since World War II. There has not yet been time for individuals born in the period of death control to reach the older age classes, whose death rates are higher than those of the younger age classes. In most LDCs the greatest declines in death rates among infants and children occurred in the late 1940s, and the large numbers of children born in that period began to reach their peak reproductive years in the late 1960s. *Their* children in turn are further inflating the lower tiers of the population pyramid.

Eventually, of course, either population control will reduce birth rates in those countries, or famine or other natural checks on population will once again increase mortality in the youngest age classes—or, possibly, in all

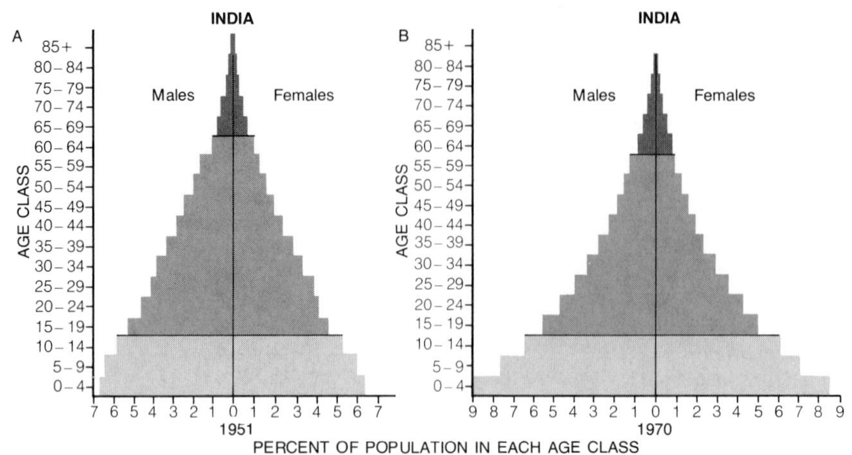

FIGURE 5-11

A. Age composition of the population of India in 1951. Declining death rates had not yet produced the pinched profile characteristic of rapidly growing LDCs like Mexico. (Adapted from Thompson and Lewis, 1965.)
B. Age composition of the population of India in 1970; the profile then resembled a typical LDC. (After *Population bulletin,* vol. 26, no. 5, Nov. 1970. Courtesy of the Population Reference Bureau, Inc., Washington, D.C.)

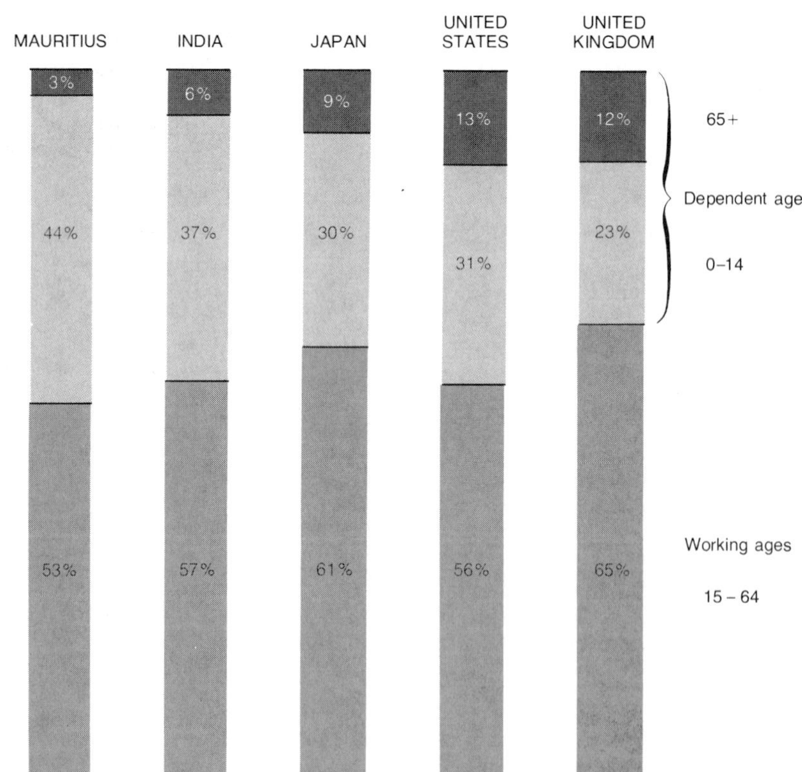

FIGURE 5-12

Dependency loads in Mauritius (1959), India (1951), Japan (1960), the United States (1960), and the United Kingdom (1959). Note the contrast in proportions of economically active people in a typical LDC, Mauritius, and a typical DC, the United Kingdom. (Adapted from *Population bulletin,* vol. 18, no. 5, courtesy Population Reference Bureau, Washington, D.C.; and Thompson and Lewis, *Population problems,* 1965.)

age classes. If birth rates are lowered, eventually there will also be rises in the death rate as the populations age and the older age classes with higher age-specific death rates become proportionately larger.

In the absence of both birth control and natural checks, however, death rates in the extraordinarily young populations of the LDCs may temporarily fall below those of the DCs. For instance, in the early 1970s the death rate in the United Kingdom was 11.7 per 1000; in Sweden, 10.5; in Belgium, 11.2; and in the United States, 9.4. In contrast, the death rate in Costa Rica was 5.9; in Mexico, 8.6; in Trinidad, 5.9; in Sri Lanka, 6.4; in Singapore, 5.2; and in Hong Kong, 5.5.[43] The low death rates are a product of the age composition of the populations in those places. They do not, for instance, necessarily reflect a better level of medical care or longer life expectancy.

One additional profile shape is common: the triangle characteristic of countries that have both high birth rates and high death rates. Such profiles must have typified most human populations until fairly recently. They lack the extremely broad base of profiles like that of Mexico (Figure 5-10) and most other LDCs today. India's profile was essentially triangular in 1951 (Figure 5-11). Since then, India's death rate has dropped by about 10 per 1000, and the base of the profile has broadened to produce the "pinched triangle" shape of other LDCs.

One of the most significant features of the age composition of a population is the proportion of people who are economically productive to those who are dependent on them. For convenience, the segment of the population in the age class 15–64 is chosen as an index of the productive portion of a population (Figure 5-12). Figures 5-10, 5-11, and 5-12 provide a comparison of the proportion of dependents in the populations we have been considering. The proportion of dependents in LDCs is generally much higher than in the DCs, primarily because such a large fraction of the population is under 15 years of age. Thus, the ratio of dependents to the total population is higher in the poor countries and lower in the rich countries, although the ratio is somewhat misleading because of the greater utilization of child labor in LDCs. This unfortunate dependency ratio is an additional heavy burden to the LDCs as they struggle for economic development (see Box 5-3).

The high percentage of people under 15 years of age in LDCs is also indicative of the explosive potential for growth of their populations. In most LDCs this percentage is 40 to 45; in a few, as high as 50. By contrast, the percentage of persons under age 15 in DCs is usually between 20 and 30. Thus, LDCs have a much greater proportion of people in their prereproductive years. As those young people enter their reproductive years, the childbearing fractions in those populations will increase greatly. In turn, their children will further inflate the youngest age groups. These masses of young people in the LDCs are the gunpowder of the population explosion.

Birth, death, and fertility rates. The birth and death rates used thus far, which are expressed in births and deaths per 1000 in a population per year, are called by demographers *crude birth rates* and *crude death rates.* They are called crude because they do not contain information about differences in the age composition of populations. They are simply estimates of b and d (Chapter 4); and the difference between them ($b - d = r$) is the annual growth rate. Crude birth rates and death rates are the most readily available *demographic statistics* (and thus most widely quoted), but although they are often quite useful, comparison of crude rates can be misleading.

An outstanding example of this was the highly publicized decline in the birth rate of the United States during the 1960s, which was widely misinterpreted as heralding the end of the United States population explosion. The birth rate in 1968 was 17.4 per 1000, a record low for the country—below the previous low of the Depression year 1936. (The trend in birth rates between 1910 and 1973 is shown in Figure 5-13.) Between 1959 and 1968 the crude birth rate declined about 25 percent. Closer examination of the data, however, shows that the decrease was caused only in part by a drop in the number of children born to the average couple. Some of the decrease was because a smaller percentage of the population was in the childbearing years. The relevant demographic statistic here is the *general fertility rate.*

[43]Population Reference Bureau, Inc., *1975 Population data sheet.*

BOX 5-3 Mauritius, Children, and the Dependency Load

Mauritius, one of the Mascarene Islands in the Indian Ocean, has one particular claim to fame—it was once the home of the now-extinct dodo, a flightless bird larger than a turkey. But Mauritius also presents another case history in population biology—this one concerning *Homo sapiens.* By 1969 more than 800,000 people were jammed onto the island—more than 440 per square kilometer—and the population had a growth rate of 2 percent a year. The story of Mauritius' population growth after World War II is similar to that of other less developed countries, and the result by around 1960 was a dependency load of 47 percent. That is, 47 percent of the population was either younger than 15 (44 percent) or older than 65 (3 percent). Although the proportion under 15 had by 1975 been reduced to about 40 percent (the growth rate had dropped to 1.7 percent), the society is still faced with a tremendous burden in the form of vast numbers of children who are nonproductive, or relatively unproductive.*

The huge proportion of young people in the population has put a tremendous strain on the Mauritius school system. Many primary schools had to go on double shifts during the 1960s, and an extreme shortage of teachers developed. In order to staff the schools, teachers had to be put in charge of classes before they completed their training. Most of the country's educational effort went into primary schools; in 1962 only 1 out of 7 elementary-school students went on to high school.

The education problem in Mauritius is a good example of what demographer Kingsley Davis meant when he said that children "are the principal victims of improvident reproduction." Many LDCs cannot afford to educate their children adequately—in part, because of a more urgent need for using their limited funds for public health and welfare. After the first five years of life, children in the LDCs enter the age class that has the lowest mortality rates. Those children desperately need education—for their own good and for the future of their societies—but the sorry fact is that in the absence of population control, solving health problems in LDCs like Mauritius makes solving the education problem extremely difficult.

High fertility and low income also tend to force children out of school and into the labor pool as early as possible. Even the chances for education in the home are reduced when families are large and mothers overburdened. Child labor is used at a very high level in less developed countries, although the productivity of that labor may be quite low. United Nations statistics, which may understate the case, show that 31 percent of males between 10 and 14 years of age are economically active in LDCs, in contrast to only 5 percent in DCs.

It is a brutal irony that children thus must bear the brunt of the population explosion. Commenting on the complacency with which many of the rich formerly regarded the plight of the poor, Davis wrote, "the old philosophy that [the children's] coming is a just and divine punishment for their parents' sexual indulgence, and therefore not to be mitigated by deliberate control is one of the cruelest doctrines ever devised by a species noted for its cruel and crazy notions."

*Most of the information here is from Kingsley Davis, The population impact on children in the world's agrarian countries.

The general fertility rate (the number of births per 1000 women 15 to 44 years old) is a more refined indicator of birth trends because it compensates for differences in sex ratio (which may be the result of wars or migration of workers) and for gross differences in age composition. Differences in age composition would be revealed if two populations had identical crude birth rates but widely differing fertility rates. This could mean, for instance, that one had a relatively small proportion of people 15 to 44 years old and a high fertility rate, whereas the other had a relatively high proportion in the 15 to 44 age group and a lower fertility rate.

As is shown in Figure 5-14, the fertility rate in the United States was declining along with the birth rate during the period between 1959 and 1968. Thus, not only were fewer babies being born in proportion to the entire population than during the 1950s, but fewer babies were being born in relation to the population of females in

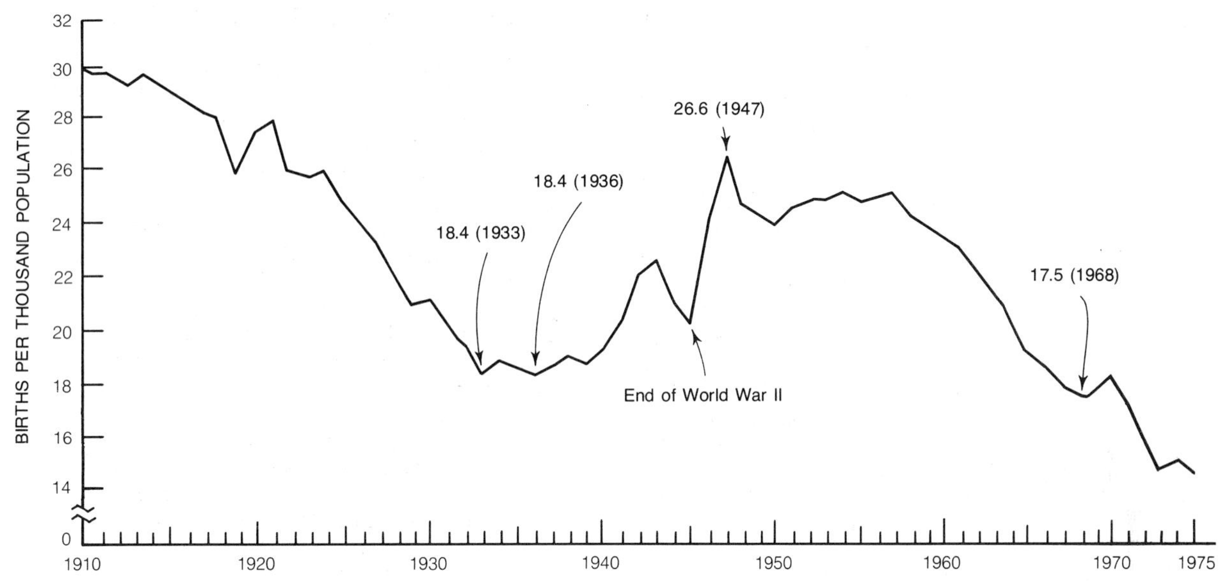

FIGURE 5-13

Birth rates in the United States, 1910–1974. (Adapted from *Population profile,* Population Reference Bureau, March 1967. Courtesy of the Population Reference Bureau, Inc., Washington, D.C. Recent data from U.S. Bureau of the Census.

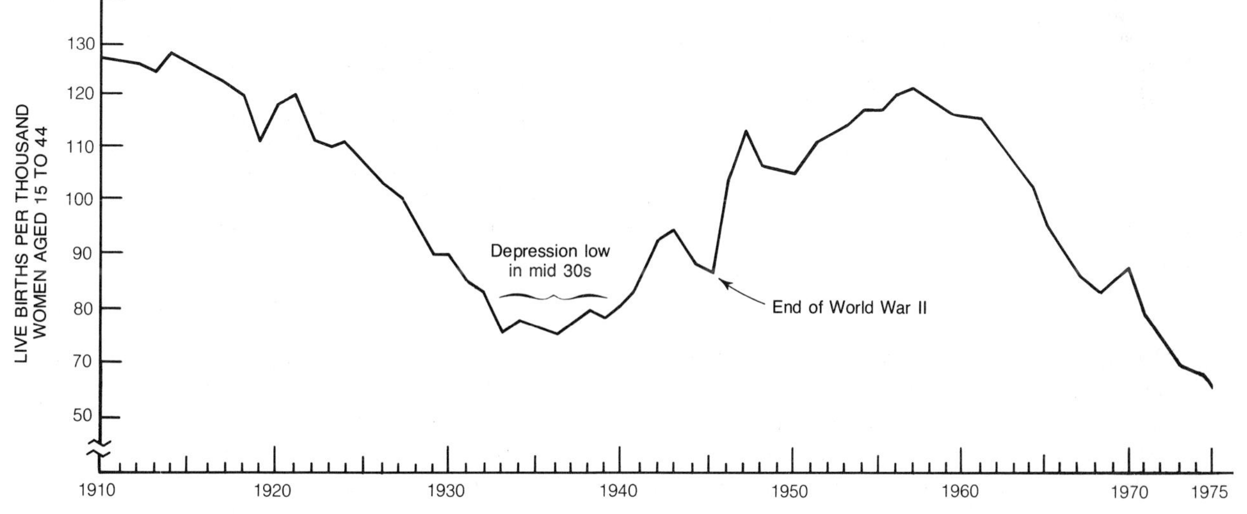

FIGURE 5-14

Fertility rates in the United States, 1910–1974. (Adapted from *Population profile,* Population Reference Bureau, March 1967. Courtesy of Population Reference Bureau, Inc., Washington, D.C. Recent data from U.S. Bureau of the Census.)

BOX 5-4 Stable Population Models

A stable population is one in which vital rates (fertility and mortality) and age composition remain constant. The population itself may be growing or shrinking, either slowly or rapidly, or its size may be stationary. The models shown in Table 5-7 represent two stationary and five growing populations resembling actual populations that exist today or that may have existed in the past. The resemblance, of course, is only general; the models are hypothetical projections of demographic factors and trends. But they are helpful for seeing how those factors and trends are related.

Model 1, for instance, is thought to be similar to early, preagricultural populations. Recent research suggests that both fertility and mortality may have been slightly lower than shown here, but in other respects the model probably fits reasonably well.* Early human populations are believed to have been close to stationary, as Model 1 is. They grew only very slowly over many thousands of years—no doubt, with many short-term fluctuations above and below the no-growth level.

Model 2 represents an agricultural population with high birth rates and mortality somewhat lower than primitive levels. If western Europe during the Industrial Revolution had maintained constant vital rates at these levels for a lifetime, the population structure would have resembled this model. Earlier favorable periods in history, such as the heyday of the Roman Empire and Japan before the Meiji Restoration, may have seen life expectancies and vital rates approaching those of Model 2. Less developed countries in the twentieth century also had similar vital rates as modern death control was introduced, but for them this stage was even more transient than it was for industrializing Europe. Demographic stability was clearly never achieved by those LDC populations.

By the 1970s mortality in most LDCs was much lower, and life expectancies and mortality rates resembling those in both Model 3 and Model 4 could be found among them. Life expectancy in India, Bangladesh, and several African countries, for example, was around 50 (Model 3). In some LDCs, on the other hand, life expectancy was approaching 70, a level typical of developed countries. Among those are Singapore, Hong Kong, Taiwan, and several Latin American countries. Many of these countries still have high birth rates and are growing very rapidly, as in Model 4.

The last three models are intended to represent developed countries that have experienced a demographic transition and have high life expectancies and low mortalities and fertilities. A few European countries have had low fertility long enough that their populations resemble Model 5 fairly closely. A life expectancy of 74.8 years, shown in Model 6 and Model 7, is postulated as the highest attainable under optimum conditions with present or foreseeable medical technology. Given this life expectancy, replacement fertility is 2.08 children per woman, and both the crude birth rate and the crude death rate would be 13.4 once stability was achieved. This is the situation in Model 7, a stable, stationary population with low fertility and mortality.

*D. E. Dumond, The limitation of human populations; and G. B. Kolata, !Kung hunter-gatherers.

their childbearing years. Yet, the 1968 fertility rate of about 85, unlike the crude birth rate, was still higher than the lows reached during the Depression (when the figure was well below 80) and the population was still growing at about 1 percent per year.

In 1970 the fertility rate began to rise, reflecting a rising proportion of women in their twenties (the prime reproductive years). The rise was brief, however; by the end of 1974 the fertility rate in the United States had dropped precipitously to 68.4. Moreover, this did not reflect a change in age composition but, rather, a significant change in reproductive behavior. For the first time in history, fertility in the United States had dropped *below replacement level*—below a net reproductive rate of 1. (The NRR at the end of 1974 was 0.9.)

Momentum of Population Growth

Let us review for a moment some of the basic population dynamics discussed in Chapter 4. If age-

TABLE 5-7
Models of Stable Populations

Feature	High-fertility models				Low-fertility models		
	Model 1	Model 2	Model 3	Model 4	Model 5	Model 6	Model 7
LEVELS OF FERTILITY AND MORTALITY, INDEPENDENT OF AGE COMPOSITION							
Children born per woman (total fertility)	6.0[a]	6.0	6.0	6.0	2.5	2.5	2.08[a]
Life expectancy (years)[b]	21.3[c]	30.0	50.0	70.0	70.0	74.8	74.8[c]
CRUDE VITAL RATES, AS AFFECTED BY ACTUAL AGE COMPOSITION							
Births per 1000 population	47.1	46.2	43.1	41.4	17.3	16.8	13.4
Deaths per 1000 population	47.1	34.1	15.5	4.9	12.1	10.7	13.4
Rate of natural increase per 1000	0.0	12.1	27.6	36.5	5.2	6.1	0.0
Infant mortality per 1000 births	361.2	264.9	121.1	28.8	28.8	13.4	13.4
Doubling time (years)	never	57.0	25.0	19.0	133.0	114.0	never
AGE COMPOSITION (% TOTAL POPULATION)							
All ages	100.0	100.0	100.0	100.0	100.0	100.0	100.0
Ages 0–14	35.2	39.3	43.7	46.1	24.0	23.7	19.7
Ages 15–64	61.8	57.9	53.5	51.1	63.8	62.8	63.4
Ages 65 years and older	3.0	2.8	2.8	3.0	12.2	13.5	16.9
Dependency ratio[d]	62.0	75.0	87.0	97.0	57.0	59.0	58.0
Median age (years)[e]	23.2	20.3	18.0	16.9	33.0	34.7	38.2

[a]That level of fertility that, at the given mortality, ensures exact replacement (NRR = 1).
[b]For both sexes combined.
[c]That level of mortality that, at the given fertility, ensures exact replacement.
[d]Numbers aged 0–14 and 65 and over per 100 aged 15–64.
[e]Age so determined that half the population is below and half is above that age.
Source: United Nations, *Concise report.*

Certain interesting relationships emerge from a comparison of the models. For instance, the birth rate drops steadily between Models 1 and 4, although the fertility per woman remains the same. The reason is changing age compositions. Lower mortality results in higher survival rates among infants and children and thus increases the proportion of people younger than the child-bearing ages. In a population with high fertility, indeed, the crude death rate can fall to a much lower level than in a low-fertility population because the proportion of old people with high age-specific death rates (even with the best medical care) is very small.

specific vital rates (birth and death) remain constant, the age composition of a population eventually becomes *stable,* a situation in which the proportion of people in each age class does not change through time. A population with a stable age composition can be growing, shrinking, or constant in size. Box 5-4 shows a series of stable population models in which the reciprocal influences of vital rates and age compositions can be seen. Five of the models represent growing populations; two represent populations that are constant in size.

When a population is constant in size (the crude birth rate equals the crude death rate), demographers refer to it as *stationary.* Colloquially, one says that zero population growth (ZPG) has been achieved. Replacement reproduction means that each married couple, on the average, is having just the number of children that will lead to the parents' replacement in the next generation: NRR = 1. (For a full explanation of NRR, refer to Chapter 4.) Where death rates are at typical DC levels, this is about 2.11 children per woman. The extra 0.11 child per woman compensates for prereproductive mortality, nonmarriage, and infertility in that generation.

The NRR (R_0) of a human population is the ratio of the number of women in one generation to that in the next. It is calculated by applying the age-specific birth and death rates of the population at a given time to a hypothetical group of 1000 newborn female babies, determining how many live female babies those females would themselves produce, and dividing that number by 1000.

If the average completed family size of a population with typical DC death rates is three children, the NRR will be about 1.3. An NRR of 1.3 means that, barring changes in birth and death rates and assuming a stable age composition, the population will grow 30 percent *per generation* (a generation is usually about 25 to 30 years). As long as the NRR is more than 1, such a population will continue to grow. An NRR of 1 (fertility at replacement level) indicates either a stationary population or one that will become stationary after time has allowed the age composition to stabilize. If the NRR drops *below* 1 and stays there, the population will shrink sooner or later (how soon depends on the initial age composition).

Note that the NRR describes what the relative sizes of *consecutive generations* will be if the age-specific vital rates (death and fertility) remain constant at the values they had when the NRR was calculated. Even if those rates (and thus the NRR) do not change, the age composition of the population must be known in order for population projections to be made, since *Homo sapiens* has overlapping generations.

Population momentum in the United States. The drop in American fertility to below replacement level between 1972 and 1975 was popularly interpreted to mean that zero population growth (ZPG) had been achieved in the United States. But growth certainly had not stopped (natural increase in 1975 was 5.8 per 1000; immigration brought the growth rate to about 8 per 1000). Nor will it stop until the crude birth rate is balanced by the crude death rate (and immigration is balanced by emigration). Because of the age composition of the population, if replacement reproduction (NRR = 1) were exactly maintained for about seventy years (one lifetime), *then* natural increase would cease. Population growth has *momentum*—growth does not stop instantaneously when each couple, on the average, just replaces itself.

If low fertility were maintained long enough, the age composition would change in response, and the median age of the United States population would gradually rise from about 28 (in 1975) to 37. The rising proportion of older people in the population would result in higher death rates; and because there would be proportionally fewer young people reproducing, the crude birth rate would decline slowly. Eventually the birth rate and the death rate (in 1975 about 14.8 and 9.0, respectively)[43a] would converge at about 13 per 1000. Past and projected changes in the age composition of the United States population from 1900, when the population was growing rapidly, to an ultimate stationary population (assuming continued replacement fertility) are presented graphically in Figure 5-15.

If the United States population maintained the below-replacement-level fertility of 1973 to 1976 (NRR = 0.9), growth would end by the year 2025 with a peak population of about 252 million (even if present legal immigration rates continued).[44] After that the population would gradually decline in size.

It is impossible to say at this point, however, whether the low fertility figures for the early 1970s signal the beginning of a sustained trend or whether they are merely examples of the short-term ups and downs that for the past few decades have confounded the demographers and economists who have tried to explain these things. Many factors can influence birth rates in addition to the number of women in their childbearing years. Severe economic conditions, epidemics, and wars may cause declines in birth rates. For instance, the shipment of young men overseas during World War I and the great influenza epidemic of 1918 together led to a drop in the United States birth rate from 28.2 in 1918 to 26.1 in

[43a]U.S. Bureau of the Census, Annual summary for the United States, 1975, *Monthly vital statistics report*, vol. 24, no. 13, June 30, 1976.

[44]United States Bureau of the Census, *Current population reports, population estimates and projections,* Washington, D.C., series P-25, no. 541, February. 1975.

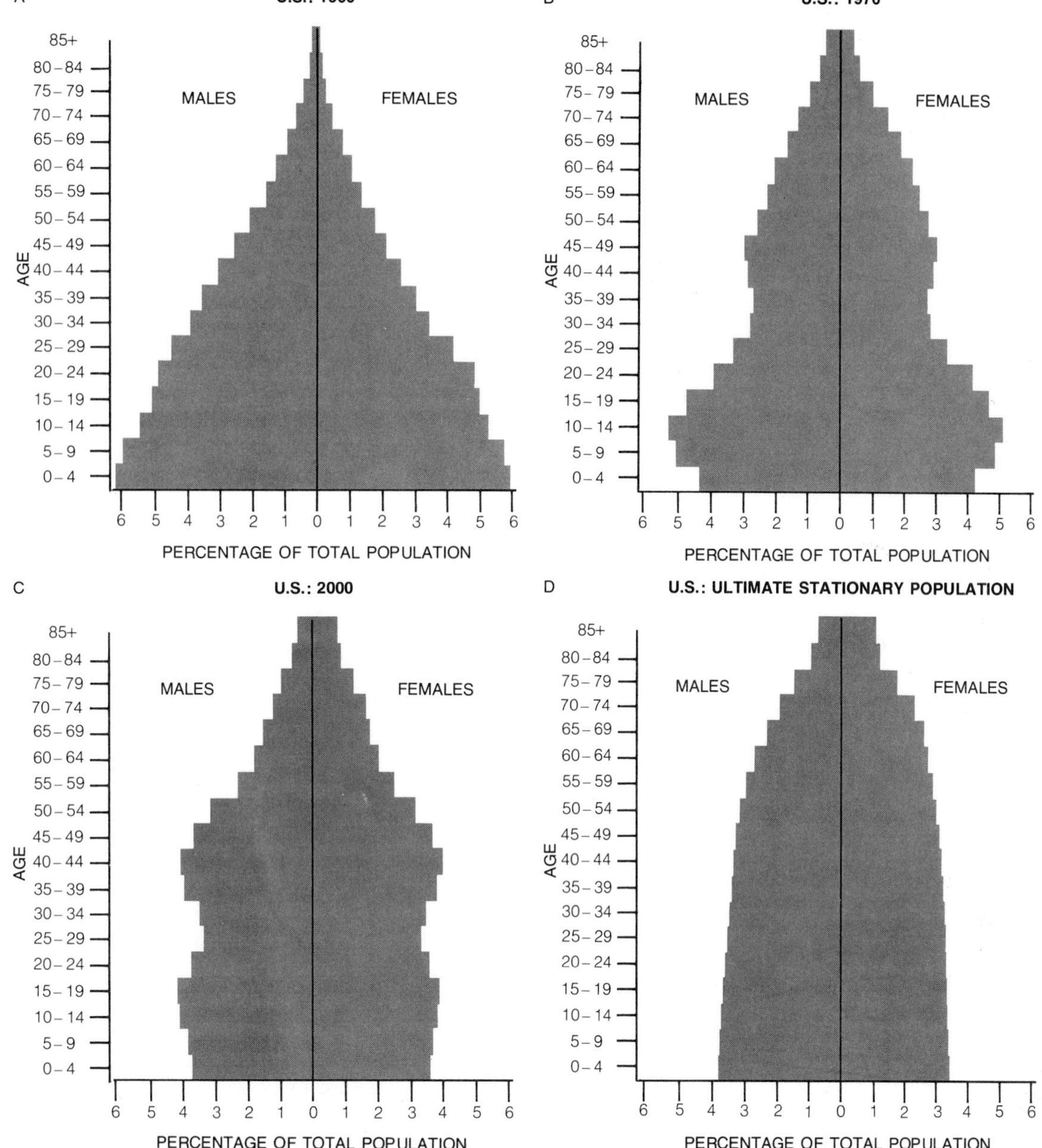

FIGURE 5-15

A. The U.S. population in 1900 had the age composition represented by this pyramid. Its triangular shape, strikingly similar to that of India in 1951 (Figure 5-11), is characteristic of a fast-growing population with high birth and death rates, where the average life expectancy is less than 60 years. A third of Americans were then under 15 years of age. B. The U.S. population of 1970 gave rise to a pyramid whose sides were pinched in because of the low birth rates that prevailed during the years of the Great Depression. The bulge centered on the 10-to-14-year-old age group is a consequence of the postwar baby boom. C. The U.S. population of the year 2000 will form this age pyramid if fertility stabilizes at replacement levels from now until the end of the century. Five-to-19-year-olds of 1970, who will then be 30 years older, will have produced a second bulge of 5-to-19-year-olds. D. An ultimate stationary population, if it is achieved in the United States during the next century, will have the age composition shown here. A third of the population will be less than 25 years of age, a third will be between 25 and 50, and another third will be over 50. (Adapted from Westoff, 1974.)

1919. Similarly, low birth rates in the United States and Europe in the 1930s have been attributed—perhaps somewhat erroneously—to the economic hardships of the Depression.[45] And improvements in economic conditions and the return of servicemen after World War II led the birth rate in the United States to jump from 20.4 in 1945 to 26.6 in 1947.

The present low fertility rate in the United States may result from a combination of social forces now at work in our society: rising public awareness of the consequences of overpopulation, the growth of the women's liberation movement, the extension of family-planning services to low-income groups, and the legalization of abortion. (See Chapter 13 for more discussion of these social influences.) If these are the most important influences on reproduction in the United States, consistently low fertility may continue into the future. If, on the other hand, fertility is determined by economic factors such as the unemployment rate among prospective fathers, then, as economic conditions improve, fertility may rise again and continue to fluctuate over the long term thereafter.

From statistics on births over the past four decades, it is known that the number of women in the 15 to 44 age class in the United States has been increasing and will continue to increase throughout the 1970s (by 12 percent between 1974 and 1980). Moreover, the age 20 to 29 subgroup, whose members bear most of the children, is increasing even faster. It will grow by about 14 percent between 1974 and 1980 and will not reach a peak until after 1980.[46] Therefore, unless fertility in the age 20 to 29 cohort falls considerably below its 1974 level, both the crude birth rate and the general fertility rate in the United States *can be expected to rise during the late 1970s and early 1980s.*

Some evidence is emerging that the extremely low fertility recorded in the early 1970s was in part a result of later marriage and postponed childbearing among young women, combined with a reduction of fertility among women over 30, most of whom had married and started their families at relatively younger ages. Although the marriage rate has been dropping and rates of divorce and separation have risen steadily, by 1975 there was a large pool of young married women—one-third of all ever-married women younger than 30—who had not borne children (in 1960 the proportion was about 20 percent). Demographers J. Sklar and B. Berkov speculated that that age group was likely to start its postponed childbearing in the late 1970s, causing a significant rise in the national birth rate by 1977.[47]

The U.S. National Fertility Survey conducted by the Bureau of the Census in 1974 indicated that 84 percent of all currently childless wives under 30 years old anticipated having one or more children, but among those over 25 the percentage dropped to 73.[48] Since other surveys have shown an aversion among Americans to having one-child families,[49] the further assumption is made that most of those women eventually will bear at least two children.

Sklar and Berkov may be right. A burst of postponed births among married women around the age of 30 could cause a rise in the birth rate and in the general fertility rate between 1975 and 1985. But by late 1976 there was no evidence of such a rise (fertility, indeed, declined further in early 1976). And what really counts in the long run is *completed family size* (the average number of children per woman, sometimes called *total fertility*). The 1974 Fertility Survey indicated a strong trend toward the two-child family, especially among younger women (Table 5-8). Wives aged 25 to 29 in 1974 expected an average total of about 2.3 children, and those 18 to 24 expected only 2.17 (approximately replacement level). If their expectations are realized and if the trend continues with younger cohorts, the population is on its way to ZPG, regardless of temporary fluctuations in the birth rate caused by differences in age composition and the timing of births.

Demographer Thomas Frejka, using 1965 as a base year, showed what could happen to the United States

[45]See, for instance, Richard A. Easterlin, *Population, labor force, and long swings in economic growth;* A. Sweezy, The economic explanation of fertility changes in the U.S. Easterlin supports the conventional view, whereas Sweezy argues that the low birth rates of the Depression years were mainly a continuation of a long-established trend.

[46]USNCHS, *Vital statistics,* vol. 23, no. 12 (February 28, 1975).

[47]J. Sklar and B. Berkov, The American birth rate: Evidences of a coming rise.

[48]United States Bureau of the Census, Prospects for American fertility: June 1974, *Population characteristics, current population reports,* Washington, D.C., series P-20, no. 269 (September 1974).

[49]Judith Blake, Can we believe recent data on birth expectations in the United States?, *Demography,* vol. 11 (1974), no. 25, pp. 25–44.

TABLE 5-8
Births to Date and Lifetime Births Expected by Married Women 18–39 Years Old, Surveyed 1967–1974

	Total 18–39	Age class at date of survey (years) 18–24	25–29	30–34	35–39
LIFETIME BIRTHS EXPECTED PER 1000 WOMEN					
1974	2550	2165	2335	2724	3091
1971	2779	2375	2619	2989	3257
1967	3118	2852	3037	3288	3300
BIRTHS TO DATE PER 1000 WOMEN					
1974	1973	848	1691	2539	3063
1971	2146	952	1949	2802	3210
1967	2427	1173	2312	3050	3214

Source: United States Bureau of the Census, Prospects for American fertility: June 1974, *Current population reports, population characteristics,* series P-20, no. 269 (September 1974).

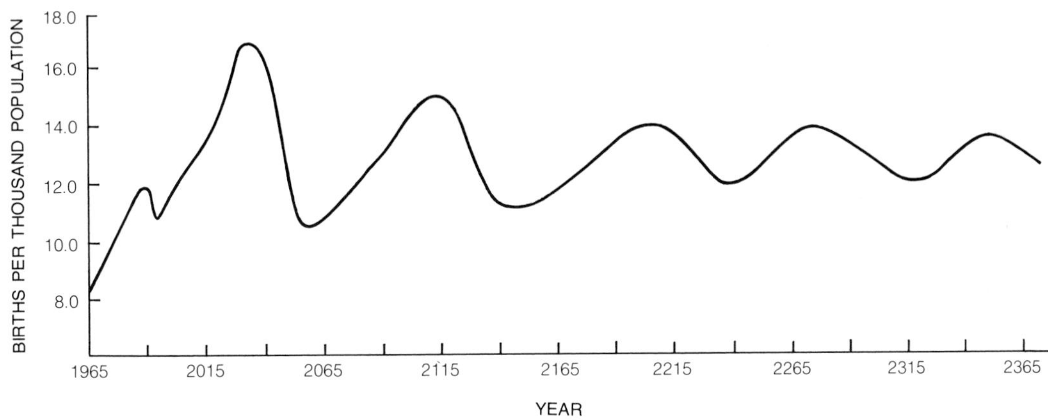

FIGURE 5-16

Projection of changes in the crude birth rate that would be necessary if the total population of the United States were to remain constant during the period from 1965 to 2365. (Adapted from Frejka, 1968.)

population under a variety of assumptions.[50] For instance, instant ZPG (a stationary population) could be achieved only by reducing the NRR to slightly below 0.6, with an average of about 1.2 children per family, between 1965 and 1985. Thus, to bring the crude birth and death rates immediately into balance (so the growth rate was 0), the average completed family size would have to drop far below the replacement level that would *eventually* lead to such a balance. After that, in order to hold the population size constant, the crude birth rate and NRR would have to oscillate wildly above and below the eventual equilibrium values for several centuries (see Figure 5-16). The age composition would correspondingly change violently, undoubtedly having a variety of serious social consequences.

The problems caused by great fluctuations in the birth rate and irregularities in the age composition could be avoided by maintaining the 1975 level of fertility (slightly below replacement). This would produce further growth, but at a slackening rate. Disregarding immigration, growth would end in about fifty years with a peak population of about 252 million, and then there would be a slow decline. Accepting some further growth followed by a period of negative population growth

[50]Reflections on the demographic conditions needed to establish a U.S. stationary population growth.

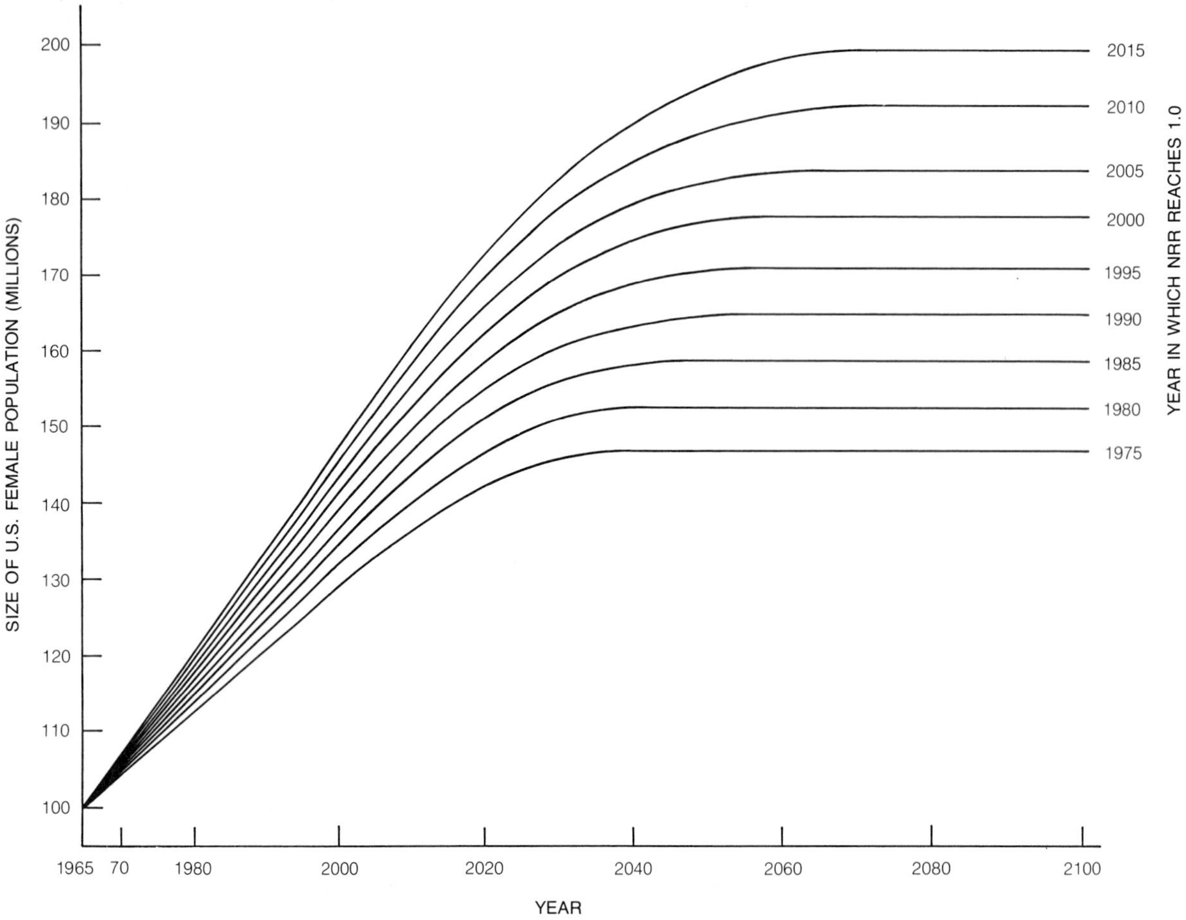

FIGURE 5-17

Projections of the course of population growth in the United States if the NRR reached 1 in various years. The total population size would be slightly less than twice the size of the female population, since there are slightly fewer men than women. (Adapted from Frejka, 1968.)

(NPG, *r* negative), rather than attempting to hold the population precisely at ZPG, would seem to be much less disruptive. And, as we discuss throughout this book, there are powerful arguments for reducing the size of the United States population well below its *present* level (to say nothing of any projected future peak).

Frejka also described what would happen if the NRR declined from the 1965 level of about 1.3 to 1 in a series of years starting with 1975 (assuming there was no immigration). The projections in Figure 5-17 clearly indicate that substantial population growth would occur after a pattern of replacement reproduction was established, no matter when that might be. For instance, if an NRR of 1 had been reached in 1985 and maintained exactly, the population would not have stopped growing until 2055, and the ultimate population would have been around 300 million (slightly less than twice the female population size shown in the figure). If the NRR of 1 reached by 1973 were more-or-less precisely maintained, the population would still grow to at least 280 million, not stopping before the year 2035. Of course, the ultimate number of people would be much higher if the NRR rose again above 1 for any significant length of time, and it would be lower if it remained below 1.

Reflecting the dropping fertility rate since the late 1950s and a rising public consciousness of population

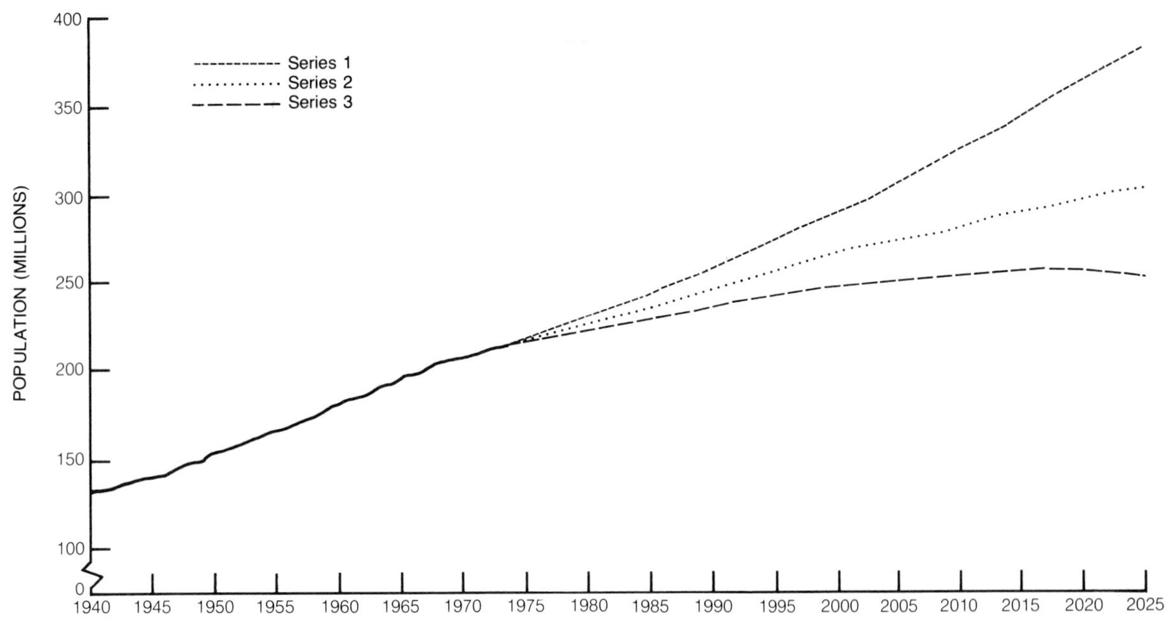

FIGURE 5-18

Estimates and projections of the population of the United States, 1940–2025. (U.S. Bureau of the Census.)

growth, the Bureau of the Census has periodically issued revised projections of U.S. population growth, each a little lower than the last. Since 1970, the bureau has given at least one alternative projection each time that was based on the attainment of replacement fertility in the 1970s, with slight fluctuations around that point between 1970 and 2000 to compensate for age composition differences. Projections issued in 1975[51] ranged between 245 million and 287 million for the year 2000 (Figure 5-18). All three projections in 1975 assumed continued net immigration (legal) at present levels (400,000 per year) and slight reductions in mortality. Fertility assumptions, however, differed: Series I assumed a completed fertility of 2.7 children per woman (as in the early 1960s), Series II assumed a completed fertility of 2.1 (approximately replacement), Series III assumed a completed fertility of 1.7. Series II (if immigration were ended) would ultimately result in a stationary population around the middle of the twenty-first century. Series III would result in a peak population of about 252 million around the year 2020, followed by negative population growth—a gradual decline.

A fertility picture resembling that of the United States prevails in other developed countries. Figure 5-19 shows fertility trends in many DCs since World War II. Many demographers now believe that what is happening is a consummation of the demographic transition, which will ultimately end in ZPG for those countries.[52] The postwar baby boom, viewed in this perspective, seems to be a temporary reversal of a long-term trend. Indeed, as the figure shows, it was either a relatively minor zig or else was virtually nonexistent in all DCs except Great Britain's former colonies—the United States, Canada, Australia, and New Zealand.

[51]Projections of the population of the United States: 1975 to 2050, *Population estimates and projections, current population reports,* series P-25, no. 601 (October 1975). For a discussion of the recent series of census bureau projections, see Leon F. Bouvier, U.S. population in 2000: Zero growth or not?

[52]C. F. Westoff, The populations of the developed countries.

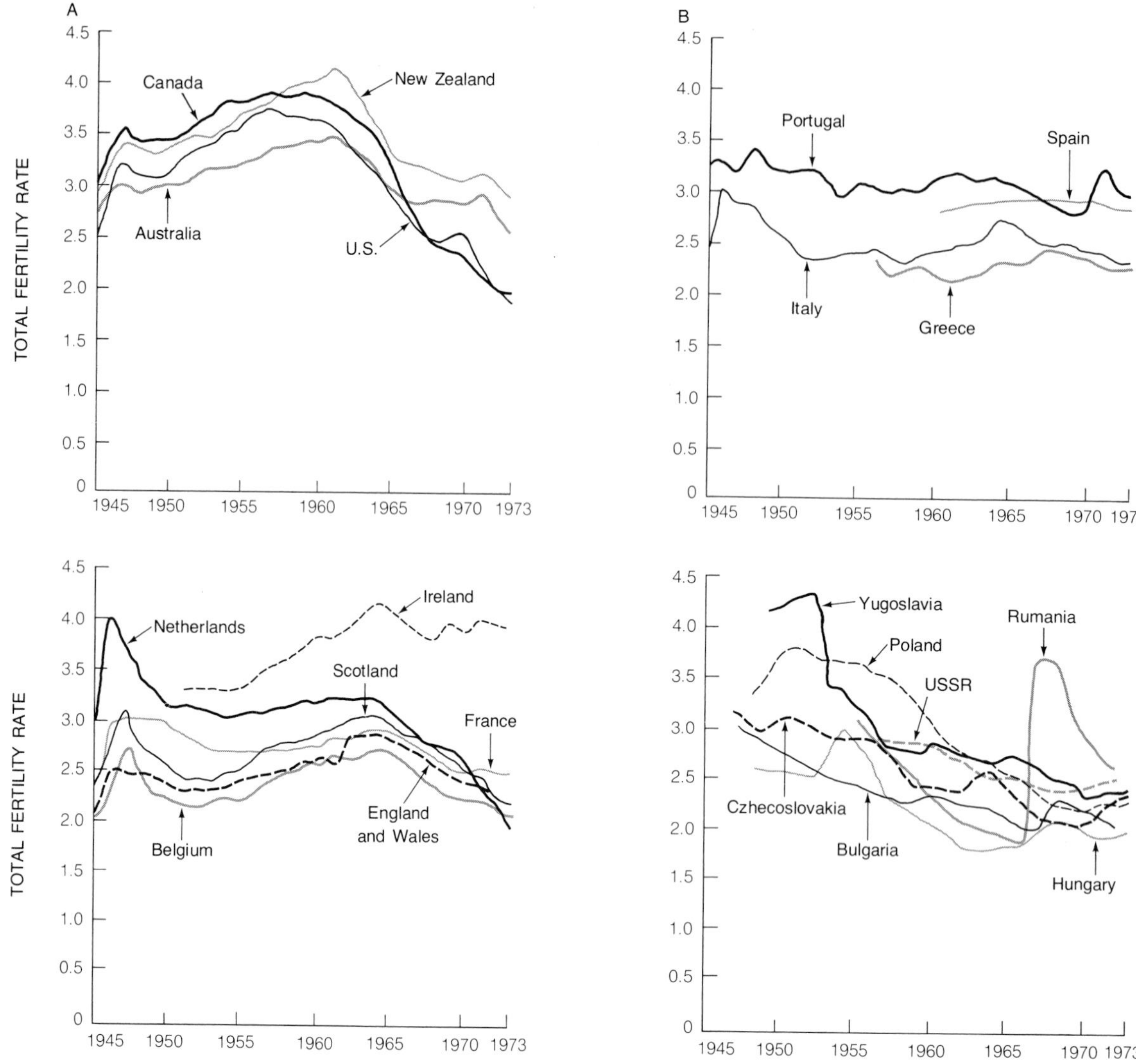

FIGURE 5-19

Fertility since 1945. Total fertility refers to average completed family size. A. Since 1945 the United States has averaged 1.9–3.8 children per family. The postwar baby boom was most pronounced among overseas English-speaking populations *(top)*. Sharp declines began in the 1960s. The postwar surge in fertility in Western Europe *(bottom)* was brief. Fertility fell sharply, climbed again slowly, and since the early 1960s has been declining. Fertility in Ireland is quite different, reflecting its unusual demographic past. B. Slow declines in fertility seem to be taking place in Portugal and Italy *(top)*. There is no clear trend in Spain or Greece, but data are limited. In the Communist countries of Eastern Europe *(bottom)*, fertility has generally been falling, except for a brief, sharp rise in Rumania

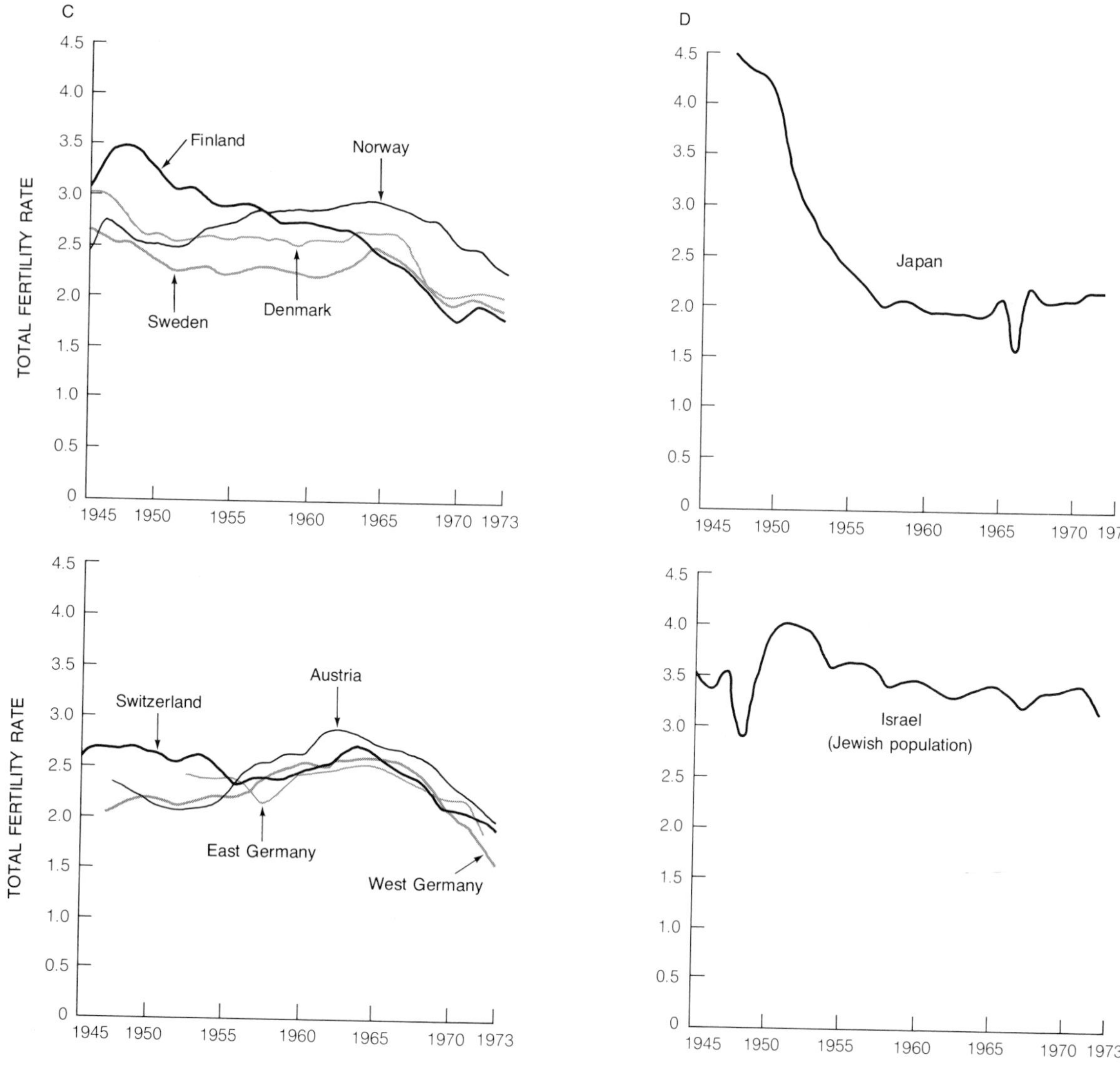

when the abortion law was tightened in 1967. C. Scandinavian countries, except for Sweden, showed only a brief postwar surge in fertility. The decline since then has been sharpest in Finland. Countries of Central Europe have followed a fertility pattern similar to that of Western Europe. West German fertility is now the lowest among all developed countries, and the country has reached zero population growth. D. Two newly developed countries, Japan and Israel, show markedly different fertility patterns. The decrease in Japanese fertility followed the adoption of a liberal abortion law. The curve for Israel applies only to the Jewish population. Fertility of the Arabs in Israel is currently more than twice as high. (Adapted from Westoff, 1974.)

The *total fertility rate* is the average number of children each woman would bear during her lifetime if age-specific fertility remained constant, and a total fertility rate of 2.1 is roughly equal to an NRR of 1 where typical DC death rates prevail. As the figure shows, many European countries have reached replacement fertility, and some have dropped even lower. A few countries with extremely low fertility or relatively high rates of emigration had achieved negative population growth (NPG) by 1975. Among those were East Germany, West Germany, Luxembourg, and the United Kingdom.[53]

In the most highly industrialized countries of Europe, fertility has been at least moderately low for nearly two generations. Relatively little momentum is therefore built into their age compositions. Eastern and southern European countries, the USSR, and especially Japan, on the other hand, have comparatively short histories of low fertility. As in the United States, considerable potential for population growth still exists in those countries.

Population momentum in LDCs. The situation in rapidly-growing less developed countries is radically different, however. The reason for the enormous growth potential inherent in the age composition of most LDCs can be seen by considering their schedules of age-specific vital rates. In those countries, roughly 40 to 50 percent of the populations are less than 15 years old. Those populations of young people will soon be moving into age classes with high age-specific fertility rates, *but it will be some fifty years more before they are subject to the high death rates associated with old age.* Fifty years is about two generations, which means that those youngsters will have children and grandchildren before they swell the upper part of the age pyramid and begin to make heavy contributions to the crude death rate. Therefore, even if the age-specific fertility rates in a population dropped precipitously to a net reproductive rate (NRR; R_0) of 1, ZPG could not be reached for more than fifty years thereafter. You will recall from Chapter 4 that it takes roughly one life expectancy after NRR (R_0) reaches 1 before a stable age distribution is reached and growth ends (r equals 0). Hence, *assuming there is no rise in the age-specific death rates,* there must be a long braking time before even very successful birth-control programs can halt growth in those nations. The momentum inherent in their age compositions means that population sizes will expand far beyond the level at which the "brakes" are successfully applied.

Demographer Nathan Keyfitz has calculated the magnitude of that momentum.[54] He demonstrated what would happen if a birth-control miracle were to occur and the average number of children born to each woman in a typical LDC (currently, the average is about six) dropped immediately to the replacement level (perhaps 2.5 children per woman, with present-day LDC death rates).[55] If such replacement reproduction were achieved overnight, a typical LDC would nonetheless continue to grow until it was about 1.6 times its present size.

Should the fertility rate of an LDC drop to replacement level gradually over the next thirty years, however, the final population would be some 2.5 times the present size. These Keyfitz numbers show why it is difficult for many scientists to see how population growth can be brought to a halt by birth-control measures before stresses on social systems or ecosystems bring growth to a halt by raising death rates. Moreover, a drop to replacement level even in thirty years is extremely unlikely to occur in most LDCs. The most optimistic U.N. demographic projections do not foresee such a pattern of fertility decline; but even such a relatively happy outcome would commit India, for instance, to an ultimate population of some *1.6 billion* people if the Indian NRR reached 1 around the year 2005.

Tomas Frejka has calculated projected paths toward ZPG in detail for the major regions and many individual countries of the world, assuming attainment of replacement fertility at different times and some decline in death rates from improvements in public health.[56] Figure 5-20 contrasts the amount of momentum built into the populations of developed countries with those of less developed countries.

[53]United Nations *Concise report.* The report on the United Kingdom is from *International journal of environmental studies,* vol. 6 (1974), p. 230.

[54]On the momentum of population growth.

[55]United Nations, *Concise report.*

[56]*The future of population growth: Alternative paths to equilibrium.* For less detailed summaries, see Population Reference Bureau, Inc., *Population bulletin,* vol. 29, no. 5 (1974); or T. Frejka, The prospects for a stationary world population.

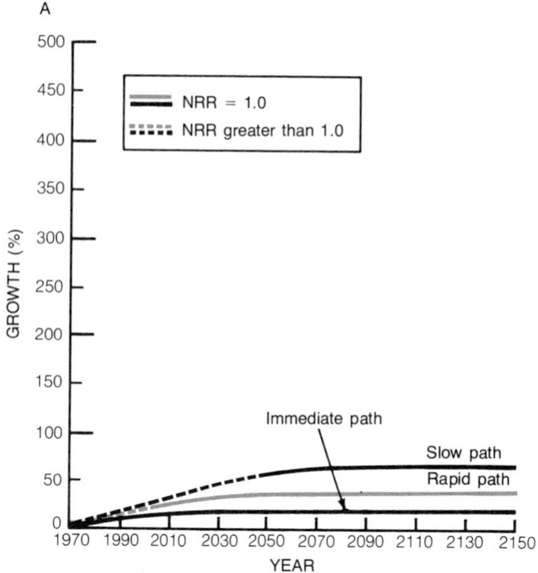

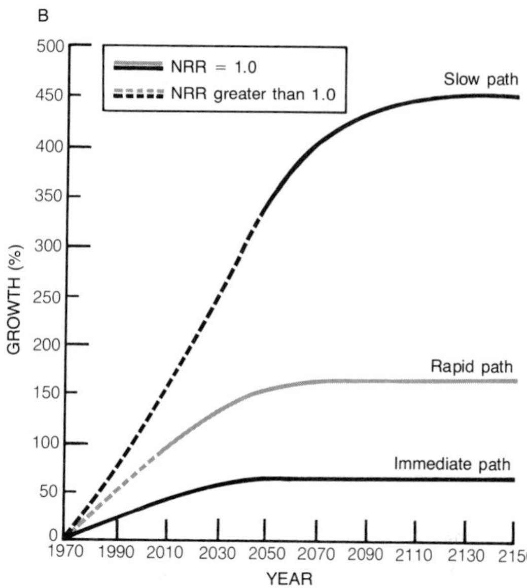

A. Potential population growth in the developed regions by selected paths, 1970–2150.
B. Potential population growth of the less developed regions by selected paths, 1970–2150.
(Adapted from Frejka, 1973.)

TABLE 5-9
Three Paths to ZPG

	Year	*Total population (billions)*	*Crude birth rate*	*Average annual growth rate*	*Average annual increment of population (millions)*	*Period*	*Net reproductive rate*	*Total fertility rate*
Base population	1970	3.6	33	2.0	68	1965–1970	1.9	4.7
	If in year		*The following characteristics are to be achieved*			*Then in period*	*The following rates are necessary*	
Immediate path	2000	4.7	18	0.8	37	1970–1975	1.0	2.5
	2050	5.6	14	0.2	9	1980–1985	1.0	2.4
	2100	5.7	13	0.0	0	1990–1995	1.0	2.3
						2000–2005	1.0	2.2
Rapid path	2000	5.9	21	1.2	70	1970–1975	1.8	4.4
	2050	8.2	14	0.3	21	1980–1985	1.6	3.7
	2100	8.4	13	0.0	0	1990–1995	1.3	2.9
						2000–2005	1.0	2.2
Slow path	2000	6.7	28	2.0	124	1970–1975	1.9	4.6
	2050	13.0	16	0.8	97	1980–1985	1.8	4.2
	2100	15.1	13	0.0	5	1990–1995	1.7	3.9
						2000–2005	1.6	3.5

Note: Changes required in demographic features in order to achieve the population levels projected in Figure 5-22 are set forth. Achievement of even the upper levels would require a significant decline in the 1970 total fertility rate.
Source: T. Frejka, The prospects for a stationary world population.

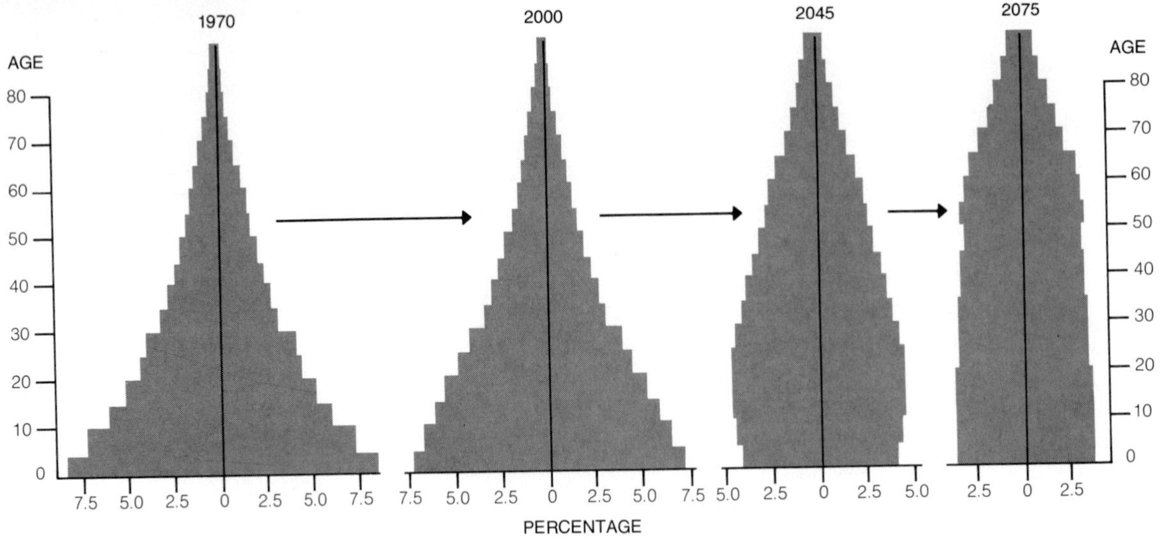

FIGURE 5-21

Age pyramids for India on the slow path to ZPG, 1970–2075. As a population moves toward the nongrowing state, a characteristic age structure emerges. Since the numbers of births and deaths change very little from year to year, all age groups are approximately the same size, although the older groups tend to be smaller because of their higher mortality. (Adapted from Frejka, 1974.)

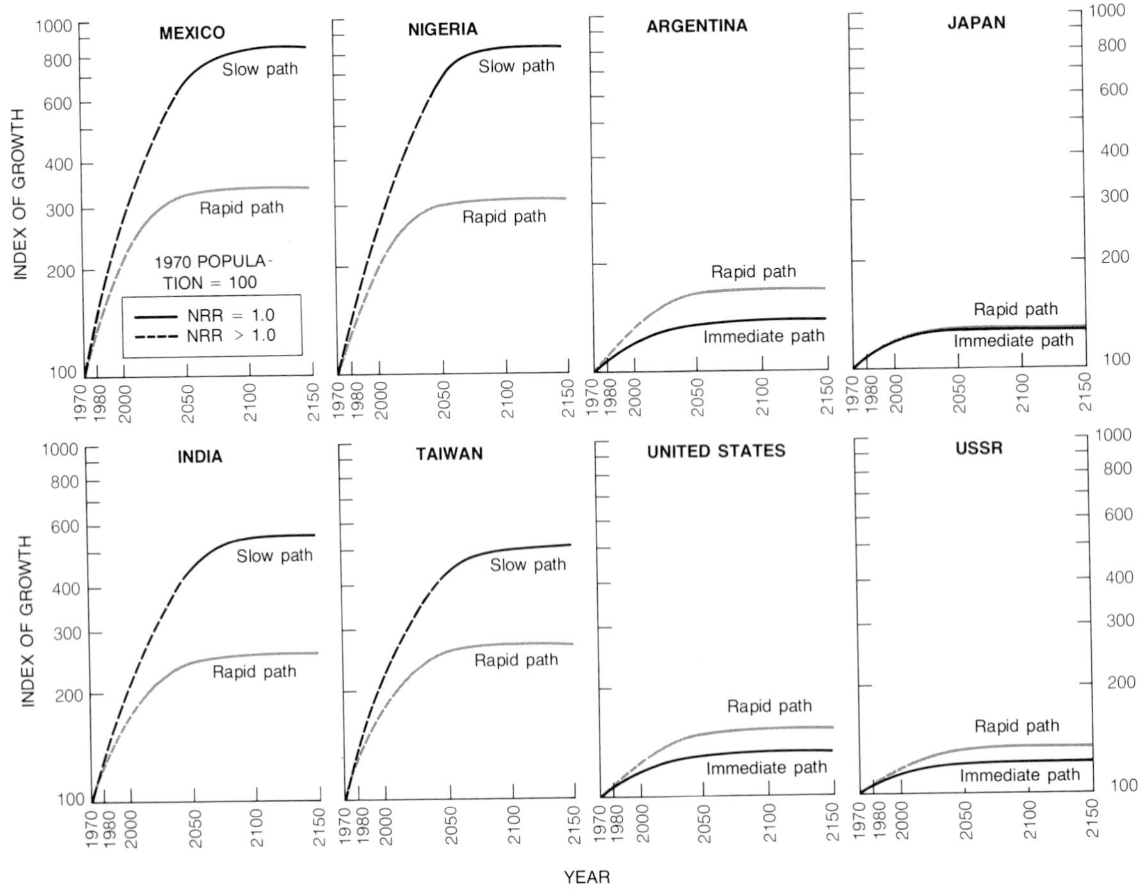

Frejka's immediate path to ZPG assumes an NRR equal to 1 starting in the early 1970s. Such a course apparently is now being followed more or less closely in many DCs, including the United States, but is impossible for LDCs, most of which would have to cut their birth rates by more than half overnight to reach it. His rapid path assumes attainment of NRR = 1 by the year 2005. This is not impossible for most LDCs, though it is highly unlikely for many. Under this scenario, the world's population would be nearly 6 billion in the year 2000 and would continue to grow during most of the twenty-first century to at least 8 billion. Frejka's slow path assumes NRR = 1 being reached by about 2045. The slow path would result in a world population of nearly 7 billion by 2000, and an ultimate population of 15 billion, reached sometime in the twenty-second century. Table 5-9 indicates the magnitude of demographic change each path would entail.

A change in fertility obviously would substantially alter the age compositions of now rapidly growing LDCs. The consequences of the slow path for India's population profile are shown in Figure 5-21. Even more radical change would occur—and more quickly—if the rapid path were followed.

How the more plausible paths would affect population growth in various individual nations is shown in Figure 5-22. (The actual projected population figures for those and other countries appear in Appendix 1.) Even by the immediate path, the United States population is projected to reach about 280 million, a 36 percent increase after 1970. Contrasting this with the United States Census Bureau projection from the subreplacement fertility rate that prevailed from 1973 to 1976 of a 252-million peak in 2024,[57] it becomes clear what a large difference a very small difference in the fertility rate can make over time. Countries with very high birth rates in 1970, such as India, Mexico, Nigeria, and even Taiwan (whose birth rate declined significantly during the 1960s), can look forward to multiplying their populations *five- to tenfold* if they follow the slow path.

Figure 5-23 shows the results of Frejka's projections

[57]United States Bureau of the Census, *Current population reports*, series P-25, no. 541 (February 1975).

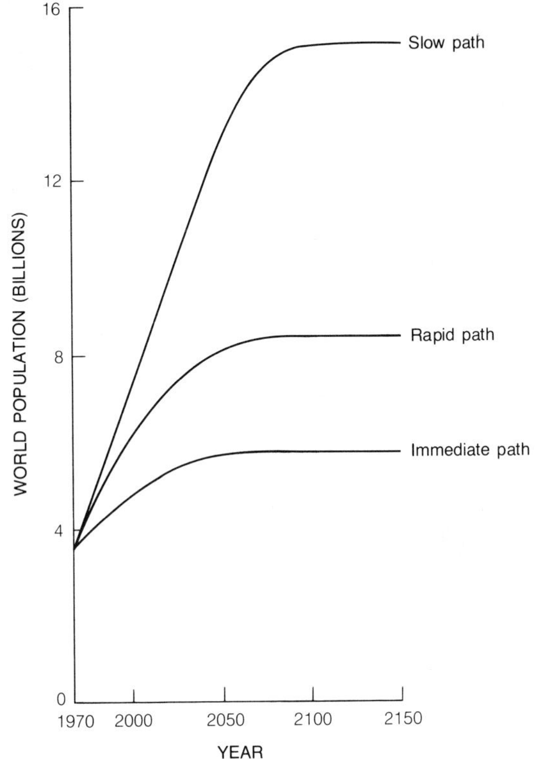

FIGURE 5-23

Population projections are based on three assumptions about when a net reproduction rate of 1 might be achieved and maintained. Reading from the bottom, the dates are 1970–1975, 2000–2005, and 2040–2045. With an index of 100 for the 1970 population, the indexes under the three projections would rise by the year 2050 to 153, 224, 357, and by the year 2150 to 156, 230, and 426, respectively. (Adapted from Frejka, 1973.)

FIGURE 5-22 (*left*)

Potential population growth of selected countries by various paths, 1970–2150. The index of growth is the percentage of the 1970 population size. (Adapted from Frejka, 1974.)

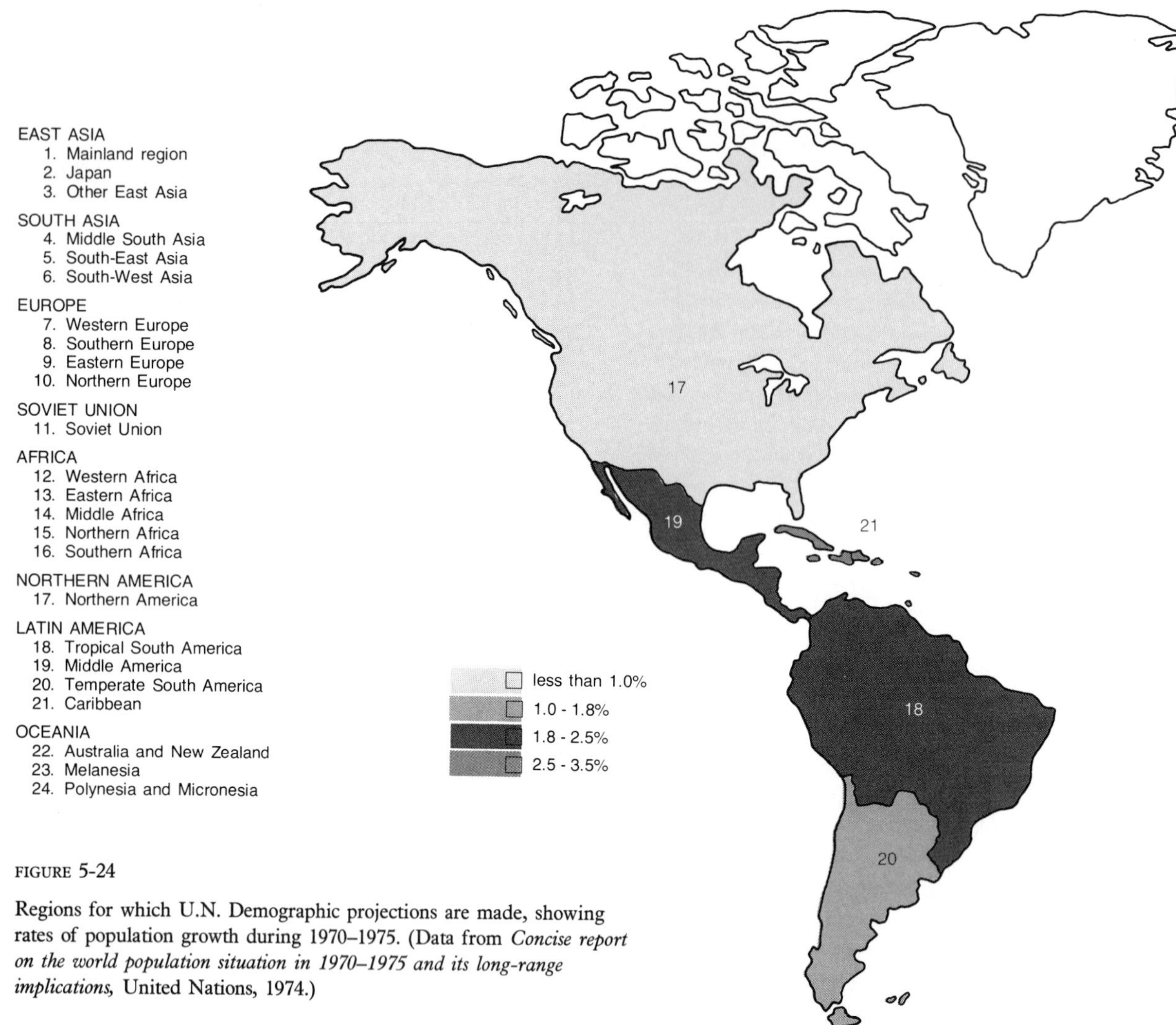

FIGURE 5-24

Regions for which U.N. Demographic projections are made, showing rates of population growth during 1970–1975. (Data from *Concise report on the world population situation in 1970–1975 and its long-range implications*, United Nations, 1974.)

on the total world population. It must be emphasized that all of these projections assume an end to population growth through birth control; they do not consider unpredictable discontinuities such as wars and mass famines. Continued growth at high rates like those of the past few decades would lead to preposterously huge populations in a surprisingly short time. Even the essentially impossible immediate path to ZPG (which would require almost halving the birth rate worldwide instantly) commits Earth to a population of nearly 6 billion human beings by 2050. On the more reasonable (but by no means easy) rapid path, the population would soar past 8 billion. The built-in momentum of population growth thus virtually guarantees that the human population *cannot be stabilized by means of birth limitation at less than 8 billion people.*

United Nations demographic projections. We have examined what is demographically possible in the way of ending population growth by means of birth control, given existing age compositions and mortalities. Now let us consider some likelier future paths of population change. Of primary interest and significance to us are predictions of population sizes during the next century. Such projections have been made by many governmental and private organizations.[58] R. T. Raven-

[58]United States Bureau of the Census, The two-child family and population growth: An international view.

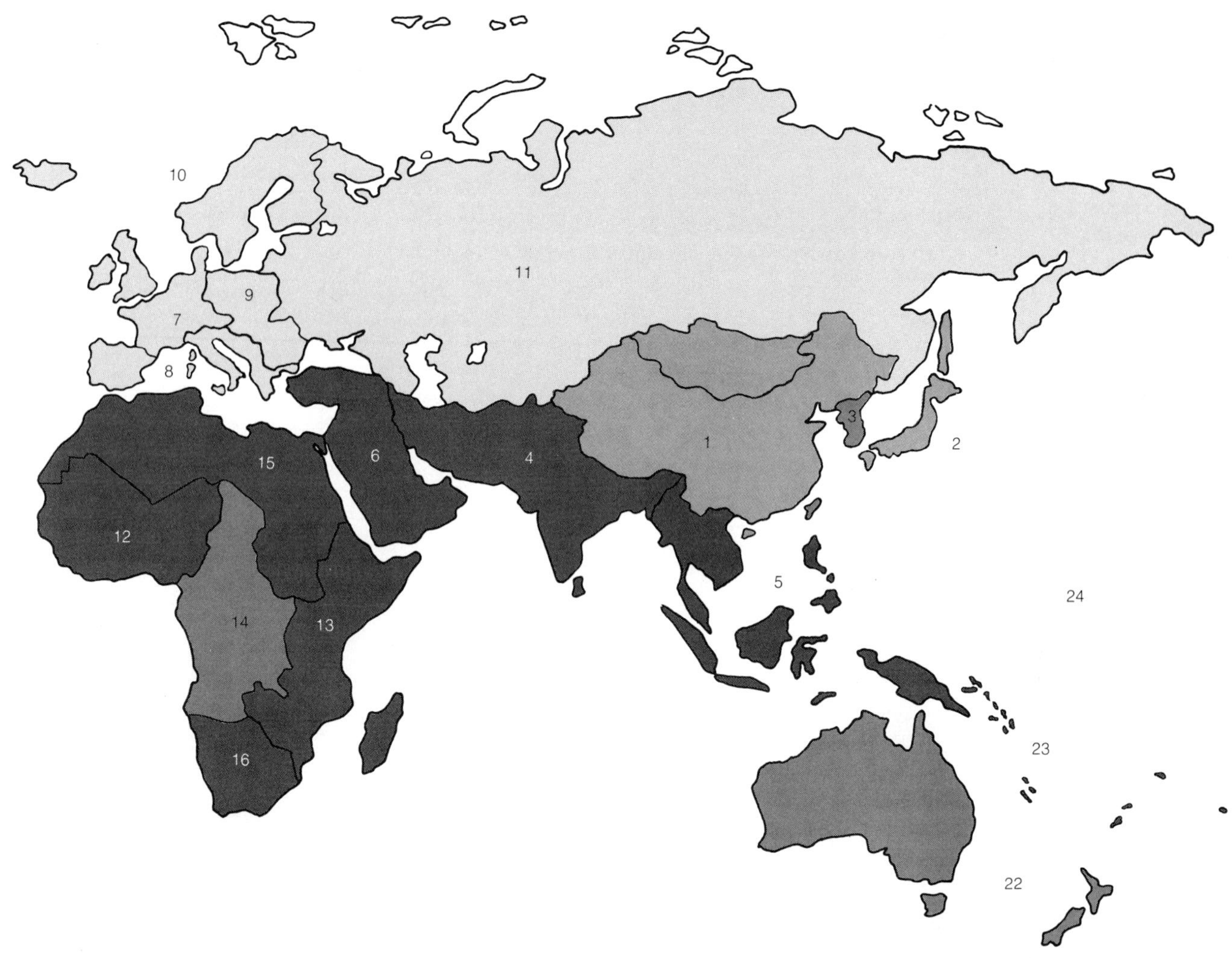

holt of the Agency for International Development (AID) has made perhaps the most optimistic forecasts (not really detailed projections) we have seen.[59] He claims that family-planning programs can reduce the average world birth rate below 20 per 1000 and the growth rate to less than 1 percent by 1985. He postulates a world population of only 5.5 billion by 2000.

Perhaps the most useful available population projections are those made periodically by the United Nations, most recently in 1974 (Figure 5-24).[60] They are not simple extrapolations of past trends or of present rates. Instead, the U.N. projections are computed on the basis of individual components; that is, individual forecasts are made of trends in age-specific fertility, death rates, migration, and so forth. The forecasts are based on the best available demographic data for nations or regions of the world, and the scope of future variation in those rates is estimated on the basis of past trends in developed and less developed areas. Possible major disasters, such as thermonuclear war or massive famines, are not considered, since they cannot be predicted.

All of the data are integrated to produce *medium, low,* and *high* projections, the latter two of which the demographers hope will bracket the actual figures. The accuracy of the projections depends, of course, on how much the realized rates differ from the predicted rates.

[59]Gaining ground on the population front.
[60]United Nations, *Concise Report.*

TABLE 5-10
Population of the World and Major Areas in 1975 and in 2075, According to High, Medium, and Low U.N. Projection Variants (in millions)

Area	1975	2075, according to: High variant	Medium variant	Low variant	Range between high and low variants
WORLD TOTAL	4,029	15,831	12,210	9,462	6,369
NORTHERN GROUP (MOSTLY DCs)	1,989	3,606	3,107	2,718	888
U.S. and Canada	243	488	340	295	193
Europe	479	669	592	533	136
USSR	256	435	400	359	76
East Asia	1,011	2,014	1,775	1,531	481
SOUTHERN GROUP (MOSTLY LDCs)	2,040	12,225	9,103	6,744	5,481
Latin America	327	1,796	1,297	1,003	793
Africa	395	3,465	2,522	1,599	1,866
South Asia	1,296	6,898	5,232	4,102	2,796
Oceania	22	66	52	40	26

Source: United Nations, *Concise report.*

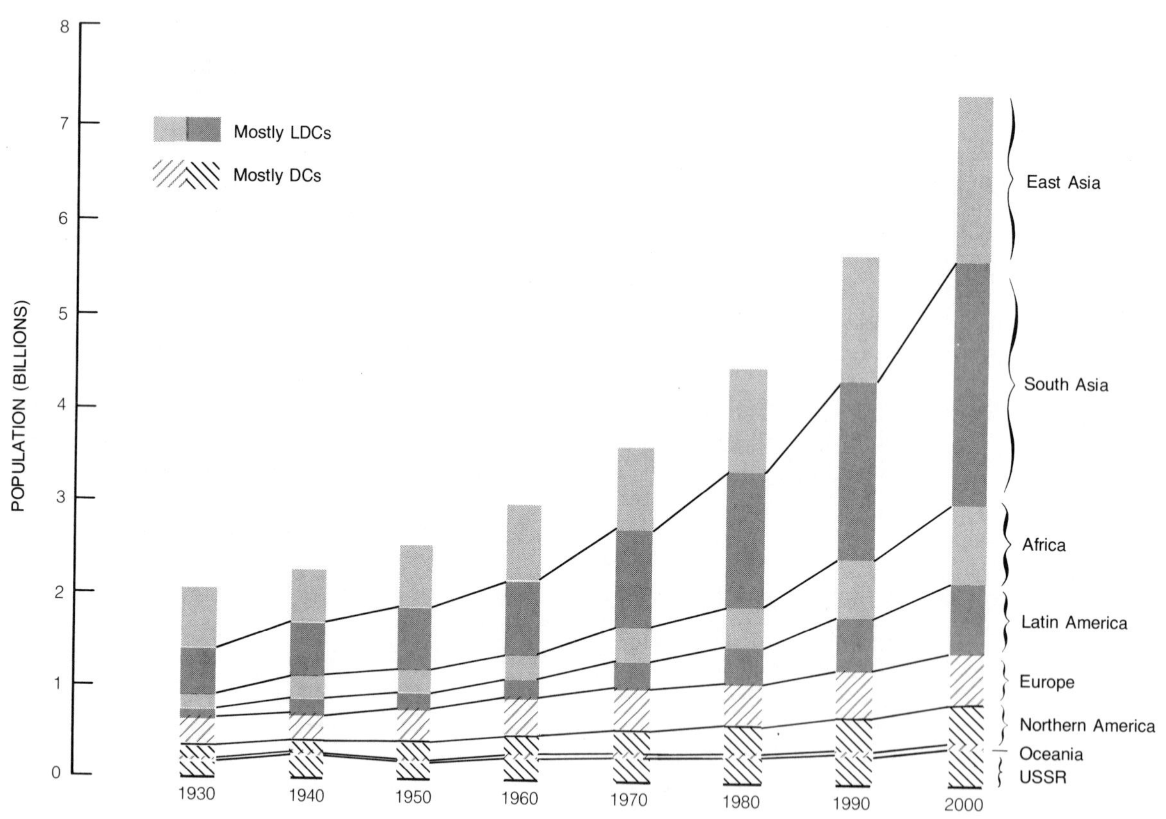

FIGURE 5-25

Projected growth of the world population, based on U.N. 1963 constant fertility projection. (Adapted from *Population bulletin,* vol. 21, no. 4. Courtesy of the Population Reference Bureau, Inc., Washington, D.C.)

Table 5-10 compares the projected low, medium, and high populations for 2075 for the world and for major regions.

The United Nations formerly made another projection, called the *constant fertility, no migration projection,* which was based on the simpler assumptions that current fertility and the recent downward trend in mortality would continue and that there would be no migration between geographical areas (Figure 5-25). Detailed presentation of this projection seems to have been abandoned, however, as forecasts beyond the year 2000 produced clearly unsustainable numbers—total world populations of 7.2 billion in 2000, more than 14 billion in 2025, 33 billion in 2050, and 80 billion in 2075![61]

In the past, population projections and forecasts have erred fairly consistently on the low side. For instance, in 1948 *Time* magazine cited the opinions of unnamed experts that a prediction (by the Food and Agriculture Organization of the United Nations) of a world population of 2.25 billion in 1960 was probably too high.[62] (The actual population in 1960 was about 3 billion.)

In 1949 economist Colin Clark predicted a world population in 1990 of 3.5 billion, and in 1950 demographer Frank Notestein predicted that by the year 2000 there would be 3.3 billion people alive. Both numbers were exceeded well before 1970. In 1957 United Nations demographers offered the following population projections for 1970: low, 3.35 billion; medium, 3.48 billion; and high, 3.5 billion, The actual population passed the high projection for 1970 sometime near the end of 1968.

In the Depression years of the 1930s it was common for demographers in Europe and the United States to show great concern over the possibility of population declines. Their apprehensions were based on projections of trends in both birth rate and death rate. But declines in birth rates during the Depression were more than compensated for by the baby boom of the 1940s and 1950s. Moreover, no one foresaw the unprecedented effect of death control exported from DCs to LDCs. How widely projected estimates can vary is illustrated in Table 5-11, which shows United Nations estimates made in different years for the world population in 1980. Not surprisingly, the latest estimates will probably be closest to the actual figure.

TABLE 5-11
Projections of World Population in 1980 (in millions) as Made by the United Nations at Several Points of Time, from 1951 to 1968

Made in	*Low variant*	*Medium variant*	*High variant*
1951	2976	–	3636
1954	3295	–	3990
1957	3850	4220	4280
1963	4147	4339	4550
1968	–	4457	–

Source: Courtesy of Nathan Keyfitz.

In 1974, reversing past experience, the United Nations revised downward its estimates of current population sizes and its projections for the future for most areas. The changes were based on new census results; on the birth-rate declines in Europe, North America, and Oceania; on lower-than-expected census results from India; and improved (though still inadequate) data on China. Population estimates for Latin America, Africa, and the Soviet Union were revised upward. The projections for the medium variant to 2075 appear in Figure 5-26 and in Table 5-12. Also, for the first time the United Nations took its projections to ZPG, on the assumption that a "complete" demographic transition in that direction will ultimately occur in all developing countries as well as in developed ones.

Whether the lowered estimates of the 1970 populations are correct is a matter of some controversy, at least with regard to the less developed areas. China appears to have made substantial progress in lowering fertility (see Chapter 13), but actual data are scanty. The lower census figures from India may have been due to undercounting, to a higher-than-expected death rate, to reduced fertility, or to a combination of all three. The United Nations postulates a trend in India to later marriage, which would have reduced fertility. If the census was incomplete, of course, then India's size and rate of growth assume even

[61]Ibid.

[62]November 8, 1948.

more alarming proportions.[63] The indicated decline in fertility, should it prove to be real, is heartening. But, as both Frejka and the United Nations demographers have clearly demonstrated, the momentum of population growth assures that the present population will at least double or triple before growth can be ended by reducing fertility. This assumes that the resource base and the economic and social fabric that support the human population can somehow be sustained under such a strain. On this, even the sober, usually optimistic United Nations appears to have doubts:

> It remains justifiable to contemplate also the possibility of severe reversals in the event of major breakdowns in international or national organization. There

[63] A. Adlakha and D. Kirk, Vital rates in India 1961–1971 estimated from 1971 census data. This study accepts the total count and estimates that mortality was higher than anticipated and that there was a small reduction in fertility. There is evidence of a trend to later marriage, but it may be compensated by there being fewer widows in the reproductive ages.

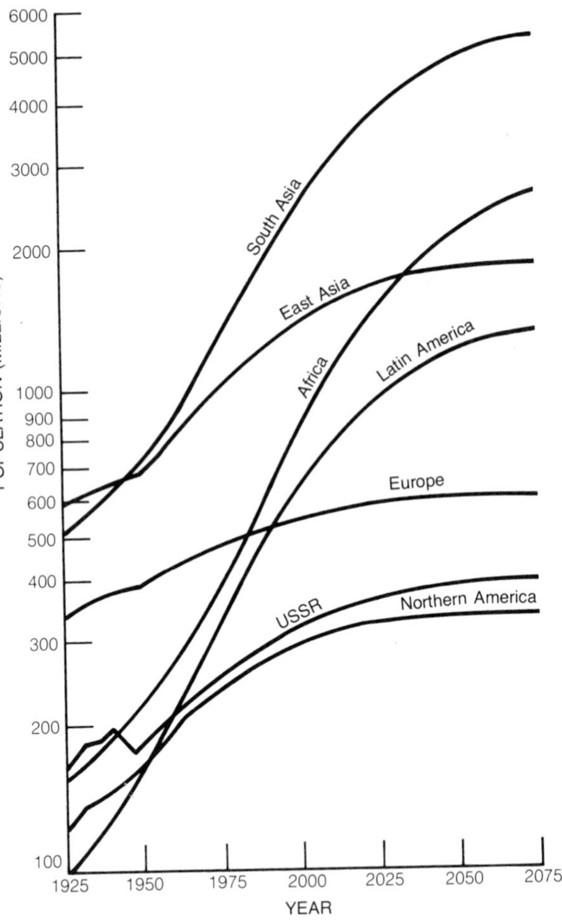

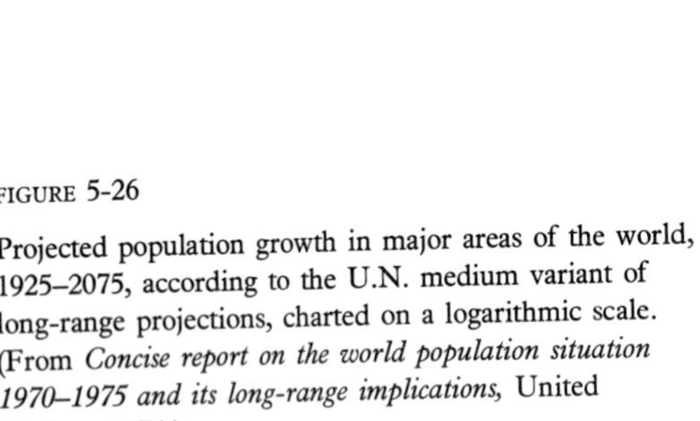

FIGURE 5-26

Projected population growth in major areas of the world, 1925–2075, according to the U.N. medium variant of long-range projections, charted on a logarithmic scale. (From *Concise report on the world population situation 1970–1975 and its long-range implications,* United Nations, 1974.)

TABLE 5-12

Population of the World and Major Areas, at 25-Year Intervals, 1925–2075 (medium variant, in millions)

Area	*1925*	*1950*	*1975*	*2000*	*2025*	*2050*	*2075*
WORLD TOTAL	1,960	2,505	3,988	6,406	9,065	11,163	12,210
NORTHERN GROUP (MOSTLY DCs)	1,203	1,411	1,971	2,530	2,930	3,084	3,107
U.S. and Canada	125	166	237	296	332	339	340
Europe	339	392	474	540	580	592	592
USSR	168	180	255	321	368	393	400
East Asia	571	673	1,005	1,373	1,650	1,760	1,775
SOUTHERN GROUP (MOSTLY LDCs)	757	1,094	2,017	3,876	6,135	8,079	9,103
Latin America	98	164	326	625	961	1,202	1,297
Africa	153	219	402	834	1,479	2,112	2,522
South Asia	497	698	1,268	2,384	3,651	4,715	5,232
Oceania	9	13	21	33	44	50	52

Source: United Nations, *Concise report.*

is no denying that catastrophic events can happen despite all safeguards to avert them . . . . Certainly, international efforts will continue to be directed at the preservation of peace, the assertion of human rights, the stimulation of economic and social improvements, the protection of the environment and relief action in disaster-stricken areas. Failure in these undertakings would have to be immense if the consequences were to have a sizable impact on the high rates of population growth which have to be foreseen. It remains imperative to create the conditions permitting a healthy life for between 10,000 and 15,000 million human beings which will probably inhabit this earth in the coming century.[64]

To be complacent about population growth, therefore, one must not only be unworried by the condition of today's 4 billion people; one must also be confident that Earth can support the population of no less than 8 billion human beings to which humanity is already inescapably committed—and (more likely) the 10 to 15 billion the United Nations expects!

Since prediction is a favorite pastime of almost everyone concerned with population, we will offer our own. We believe that United Nations projections for the year 2000 (with the possible exception of the low forecast) are *too high.* This is not, however, because we share their optimism about the future impact of family-planning programs on birth rates. Instead, for reasons we explain later, we expect that increases in death rates will either slow or terminate the population explosion, unless efforts to avoid such a tragic eventuality are mounted immediately.

POPULATION DISTRIBUTION AND MOVEMENT

Human beings are not uniformly distributed over the face of Earth. Moreover, their distribution has continuously changed throughout history, with migration and varying rates of population growth. Figure 5-27 shows the pattern of population density that prevailed in 1972. (Population density is the number of individuals per unit area.) For human populations, this figure is normally expressed as number of people per square kilometer or per square mile.

Table 5-13 shows the population density of the world's major areas in 1960 and 1975. Note that, although most people think of the developed world as being more densely populated, it is not (even though Europe is the most densely populated continent). The average density of less developed countries is more than twice as great as the average in developed countries. And both east and south Asia seem likely to overtake Europe in density within a decade or so. Of course, we must be cautious in picturing densities in terms of people per square kilometer because of the human tendency to gather in clusters. Although the United States in 1975 had about 23 people per square kilometer *on the average* (about 27 per square kilometer in the coterminous forty-eight states), there were many square kilometers that were uninhabited. Furthermore, people ordinarily are not uniformly distributed within any given square kilometer. Some samples of population densities in 1972, both moderate and extreme, were:[65]

	People per square mile	*People per square kilometer*
Earth (land area)	72	28.0
United States	59	23.0
Australia	4	1.5
Japan	744	287.0
Tokyo	20,000	7,722.0
New York City	26,000	10,039.0
Manhattan Island	68,000	26,255.0

The densities and distributions of populations, especially in relation to resources, have played critical roles in many important events in human history. Densities that are perceived as high by the members of populations themselves generate what is commonly called population pressure. Overpopulation is usually perceived in relation not to the absolute size of a population but to its density and to the resource base on which it depends. On many thousands of occasions in prehistory, one tribe or another must have decided that it had nearly exhausted the

[64]United Nations, *Concise report.*

[65]United Nations, *Statistical yearbook,* New York, 1973; U.S. Department of Commerce, *Statistical abstract of the United States,* Washington, D.C., 1974.

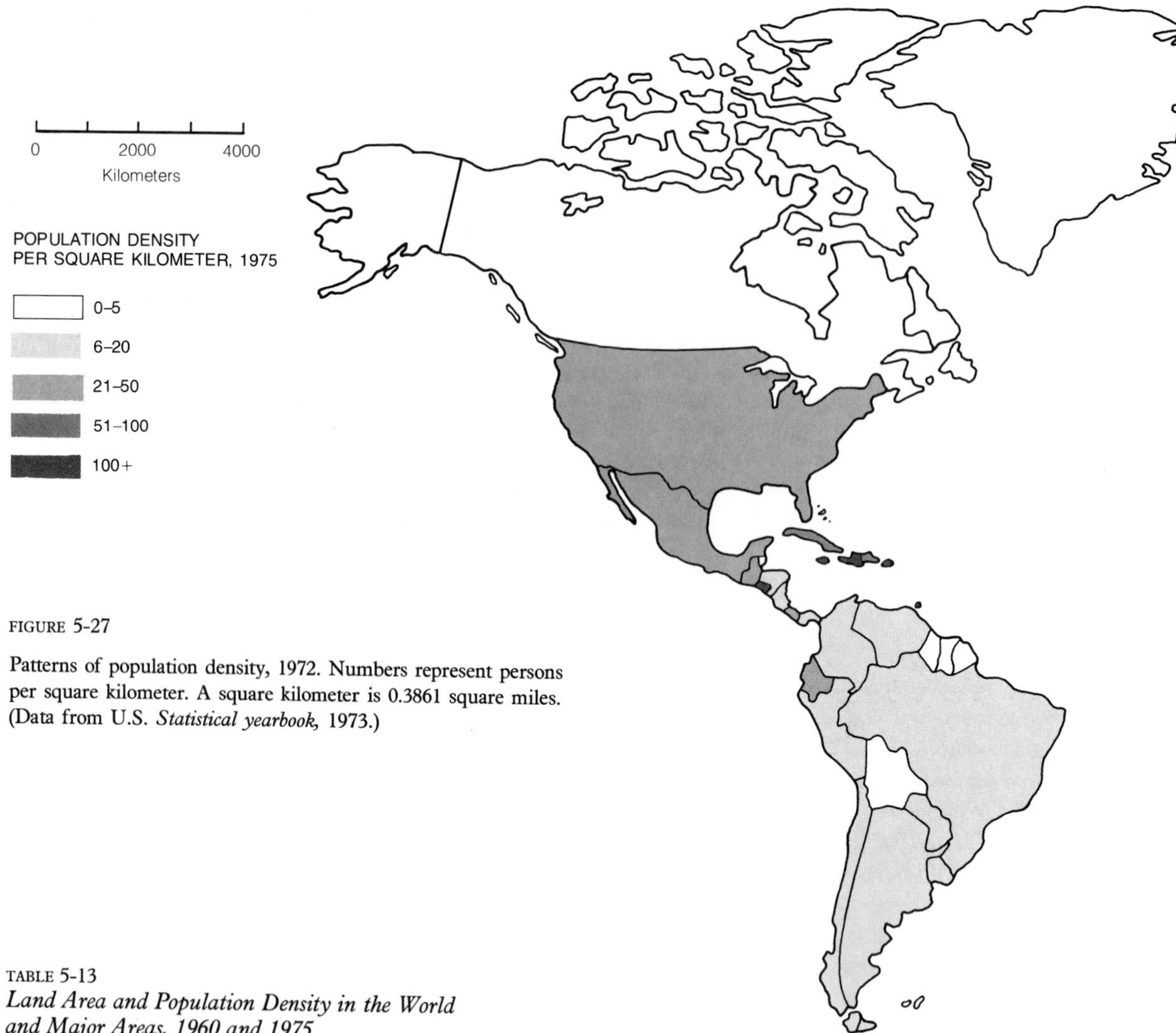

FIGURE 5-27

Patterns of population density, 1972. Numbers represent persons per square kilometer. A square kilometer is 0.3861 square miles. (Data from U.S. *Statistical yearbook,* 1973.)

TABLE 5-13
Land Area and Population Density in the World and Major Areas, 1960 and 1975

Area	Land area (1000 km²)	Inhabitants per km²	
		1960	1975
World total	135,779[a]	22.1	29.4
More developed regions	60,907	16.0	18.6
Less developed regions	74,872	27.0	39.5
Europe	4,936	86.1	96.0
USSR	22,402	9.6	11.4
U.S. and Canada	21,515	9.2	11.0
Oceania	8,509	1.9	2.5
South Asia	15,775	54.9	80.4
East Asia	11,756	67.0	85.5
Africa	30,320	9.0	13.2
Latin America	20,568	10.5	15.8

[a]Not including the Antarctic continent.
Source: United Nations, *Concise report.*

berries and game in its home territory and therefore moved in on its neighbors. Many famous migrations in history, such as the barbarian invasions of Europe in the early Christian era, may have been partly due to population pressures. In 1095 when Pope Urban II preached the First Crusade, he referred to the advantages of gaining new lands. The Crusaders were mainly second sons who had been dispossessed because of a growing trend toward primogeniture in Europe (inheritance by the firstborn son only). Considerable evidence, such as indications of attempts at land reclamation, suggests that population pressures were building up in Europe well before the fifteenth century.

Before the arrival of Europeans in what is today the continental United States, the population density was

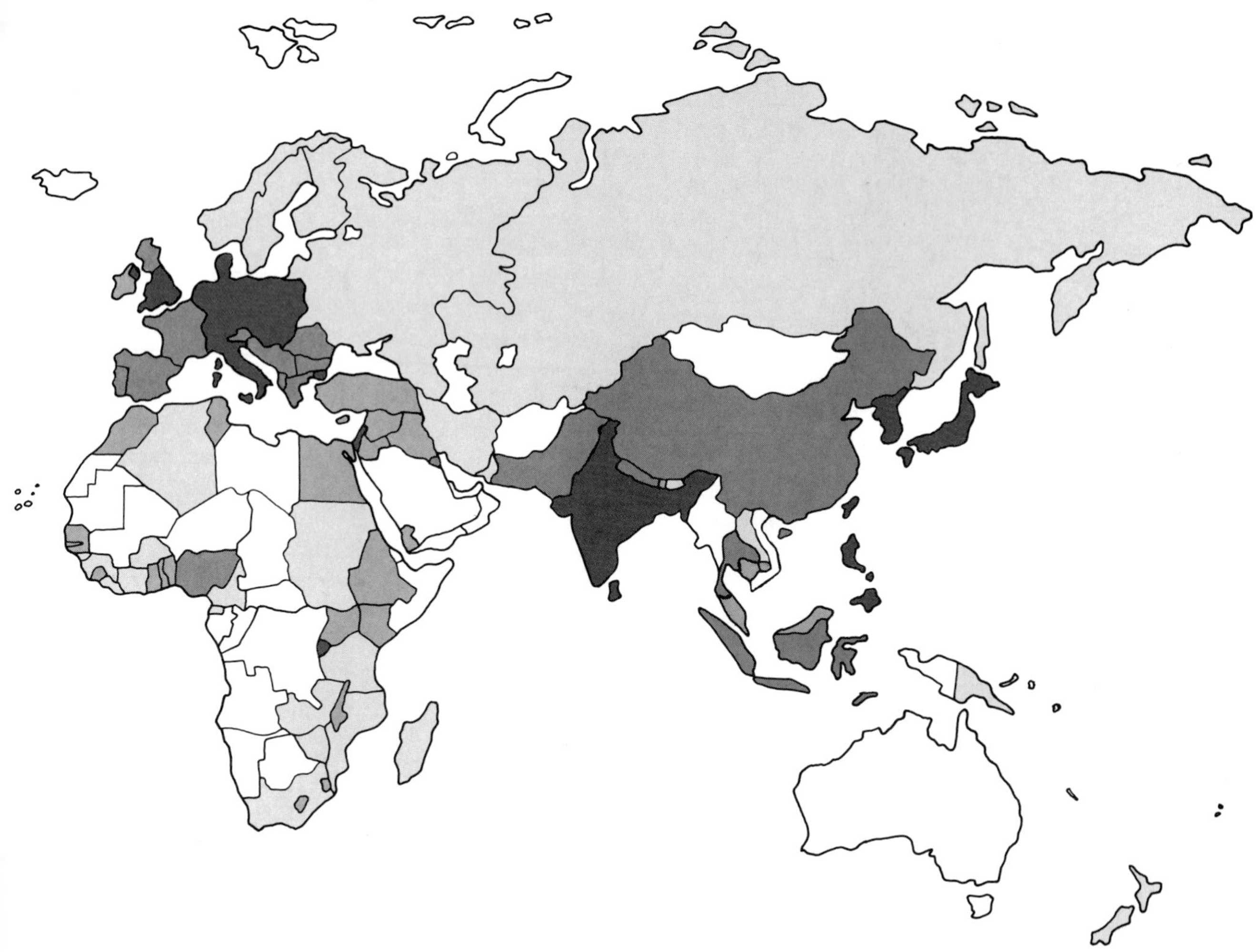

about 0.13 people per square kilometer. The addition to Europe of the sparsely populated New World at the end of the fifteenth century in effect reduced the overall population density of Europe from about 10 people per square kilometer to fewer than two people per square kilometer in the total area, and at the same time enormously expanded Europe's resource base.

European exploitation of the spatial, mineral, and other material wealth of the New World led to the creation of a basic set of institutions attuned to frontier attitudes. The ensuing economic boom lasted for 400 years.[66] At least as far as land is concerned, the boom is now plainly over. The population density of the European metropolis (western Europe and the Western Hemisphere) increased until it again exceeded 10 people per square kilometer (26 people per square mile) before 1930. Since all the materials on which the boom depended came ultimately from the land, the entire boom is clearly limited. Many of humanity's present difficulties are related to the rate at which the limits are being approached. And many of the lingering institutions and attitudes that evolved in a frontier setting now constitute major threats to the survival of the human population.

Population pressure has also been observed to lead to conflict. Many wars were fought by European nations as they scrambled to occupy the Western Hemisphere. They warred among themselves and against the technologically less advanced native populations in the New

[66]W. P. Webb, *The great frontier.*

World. More recently, in the 1930s and 1940s, population pressure contributed to Nazi Germany's famous drive to *lebensraum* (literally, *room for living*), especially in the East, where it reached its climax in Operation Barbarossa—the ill-fated invasion of the Soviet Union. Historian D. L. Bilderback has commented that in the early years of Hitler's power, "large numbers of intelligent and humane persons believed that the Eastern adventure was a matter of necessity for their own survival." Whether Germany in 1941 was overpopulated in some absolute sense is not the point. The nation perceived itself as overpopulated.

Germany is probably more pressed for space today than it was then. The Bonn government, however, in contrast to Hitler, is not calling attention to overpopulation as a problem. Indeed, only recently has it begun to realize that by many standards Germany today *is* overpopulated. During the 1950s and 1960s, West Germany was importing workers in large numbers from southern Europe and North Africa. Today that immigration has been reduced to a trickle, and fertility has declined to below replacement level in both East Germany and West Germany.

Japan's expansionist moves in the 1930s and early 1940s can be traced in part to the high population density on its small islands. The population growth of Japan in the last third of the nineteenth century and the first third of the twentieth century was unprecedented among industrialized nations. It doubled in size (from 35 million to 70 million), and therefore in density, during the sixty-three years between 1874 and 1937. When the attempt to conquer additional territory failed and population growth continued to accelerate, Japan legalized abortion and drastically reduced its population growth. But, with 111 million people in 1975 and still growing by 1.3 percent per year,[67] Japan is again feeling the pinch and is looking more and more toward the continent of Asia for at least economic *lebensraum.*

Population pressures are certainly contributing to international tensions today. The USSR, India, and other neighbors of overpopulated China have been guarding their frontiers nervously since before 1960. Population growth in China has left her few long-range choices but to expand, to starve, or to implement stiff population-control policies. Since the 1960s, China has followed the last course, but whether it will succeed remains an open question.

[67]Population Reference Bureau, Inc., *1975 Population data sheet.*

Australians are clearly apprehensive about the Asian multitudes. This attitude for a long time was reflected in their nation's "whites only" immigration laws and Western-oriented foreign policy. The racial bias of Australian immigration policies was eliminated in the 1960s, but soon afterward there was a movement to stop encouraging immigration altogether. Australians have reason to be fearful of too much immigration. Because there is a generally unfavorable and unreliable climate over much of Australia and because of the nation's history of disastrous agricultural practices, the continent, although large, lacks the resources for absorbing even a *single year's increment* to the Asian population.[68] Such an addition would more than *quintuple* Australia's population, from 13.8 million to 74 million. The number of people added annually to India's population alone (13 to 15 million) is more than the entire population of Australia today.

Population density has increased in all areas of the world and can be expected to continue increasing as the human population grows. But the varying rates of growth from region to region mean that some regions may not even double their population density in the next century (assuming growth follows projected paths), while others will increase their density from three- to fivefold. Table 5-14 shows projected density from 1925 to 2075 for various regions according to the United Nations medium-variant projection. South Asia, for instance, is projected to reach a density nearly three times as high as Europe's today, which is the highest ever known previously in a major region. And Europe today is by no means self-sufficient for resources, or even for food.

Migration

Migration is almost as characteristic of *Homo sapiens* as toolmaking. Perhaps only a few domestic animals are as widely distributed on Earth's land areas as people are.

[68]A. J. Marshall, ed., *The great extermination,* Heinemann, London, 1966. This book documents past abuse of the fragile Australian environment.

TABLE 5-14
Land Area and Inhabitants per Square Kilometer, in the World and Major Areas, 1925–2075 (United Nations medium variant)

Major area	*Land area (1000 km²)*	*Inhabitants/km²* 1925	*1950*	*1975*	*2000*	*2025*	*2050*	*2075*
WORLD TOTAL	139,450	14	18	29	46	65	80	88
NORTHERN GROUP (MOSTLY DCs)	60,574	20	23	33	42	48	51	51
U.S. and Canada	21,515	6	8	11	14	15	16	16
Europe	4,931	69	79	96	110	118	120	120
USSR	22,402	7	8	11	14	16	18	18
East Asia	11,726	49	57	86	117	141	150	151
SOUTHERN GROUP (MOSTLY LDCs)	78,786	10	14	26	49	78	103	116
Latin America	20,535	5	8	16	30	47	59	63
Africa	30,227	5	7	13	28	49	70	83
South Asia	19,557	25	36	65	122	187	241	268
Oceania	8,557	1	2	3	4	5	6	6

Source: United Nations, *Concise report.*

From their probable origins in Africa, human groups had spread out to occupy all the major land areas of the planet but Antarctica by 20,000 years ago, long before the beginnings of agriculture or written history. There is little question that the human habit of wandering has been a major factor in cultural evolution, as new ideas, and especially technical innovations, have been carried from one area to another. Agriculture, as one very important example, was transmitted largely through migrations and often by displacement of resident non-agricultural peoples. Today the only remaining groups of people who do not practice agriculture are a few isolated tribes in remote areas where a harsh climate is generally unsuitable for raising crops, such as arctic Eskimos, Bushmen of the Kalahari, aboriginal tribes in Australia's interior deserts, and the Indians of Tierra del Fuego. And all these groups are under severe pressure from modern civilization to abandon their hunter-gatherer cultures.

The impetus for the movement of people in large groups may have several sources, including overpopulation and resource pressure, as discussed earlier. Demographer Kingsley Davis argues that differences between groups in levels of technology and economic opportunity are also major causes of migration.[69] Differential technology can work both ways: people with more sophisticated technology may invade and conquer new areas, or less advanced groups may be attracted to the greater opportunities provided by a more developed society. Ancient Romans, for example, conquered vast areas in Europe, North Africa, and western Asia, seeking mineral wealth and an expanded food base. But, unlike the earlier Greeks and Phoenicians, the Romans did not colonize those regions in any great numbers. Rather, people from the outlying areas migrated to Rome, attracted by the greater economic opportunities there. Perhaps even greater numbers went to Rome involuntarily as slaves.

Waves of Asian invaders swept across Europe during the Roman Empire, as they had for centuries before. Perhaps they were partly impelled by population pressure in Asia, but probably they were also attracted by the wealth of the Mediterranean basin. Migrant barbarians were gradually assimilated into the Roman population, and, as that civilization gradually declined, the technological differences between the barbarians outside and the Romans inside probably faded. Certainly the fall of Rome in the fifth century suggests that, in warfare at least, the barbarians were equal to the Romans.

In the Middle Ages, the known major migrations were those of Islamic peoples—Arabs and Turks, some of whom in turn were responding to pressure from Genghis Khan's Mongols. But the discovery of the New World by Europeans led to a burst of exploration and exploitation followed by waves of migration from the seventeenth through the twentieth centuries. And, even as Europeans began to settle the sparsely inhabited new lands, they

[69] The migrations.

were also claiming, colonizing, and exploiting more-populated territories in Asia and Africa. Slavery and indentured labor accounted for much of the migration between 1450 and 1870, including movement of as many as 20 million people.[70]

Migration of Europeans to the New World, Australia, New Zealand, and South Africa remained at fairly low levels until the nineteenth century. Davis attributes the great acceleration of movement in that century to the Industrial Revolution (which widened the technological gap between Europe and the other continents and stimulated the search for raw materials) and to growing economic uncertainty in Europe. The early nineteenth century in northwestern Europe also was a period of declining death rates and rapid population growth. England, Ireland, and (later) Germany and Scandinavia, sent millions of migrants to North America, Australia, New Zealand, temperate South America, and South Africa. Between 1840 and 1930, at least 52 million people left their home continent, most of them for North America. Large as this emigration was, it had little effect in retarding population growth in most of Europe, although it fueled population explosions in the receiving countries. In most European countries, emigration appears to have allowed a delay in the beginning of the birth-control movement. The Irish potato famine provided a special stimulus to emigration in the 1840s and 1850s, as 2 million Irish left the country in four years. Emigration continued at a high level, and Ireland is the only European country whose population growth was reversed by it. Had the same fertility prevailed without that safety valve, the Irish population would be more than 12 million today, rather than 3 million.

It is fashionable to suppose that the era of large-scale migration ended before World War II, but that is not the case. Despite the establishment of immigration restrictions and quota systems in the 1920s and 1930s in many receiving countries (including the United States), migration has continued briskly, although there are some important differences in who migrates where. One significant change is the twentieth-century phenomenon of political refugees, who have attended each war, major or minor. One can list numerous examples: Turkish Armenians and White Russians early in the century; European Jews after World War II (not to mention millions of "displaced persons" of various national origins who settled elsewhere after that war), Palestinian Arabs, Chinese, Hungarian "freedom fighters," Cubans, and, in 1975, 150,000 Vietnamese.

Another form of involuntary migration is the expulsion or exchange of minorities by nations. Examples include the Sudeten Germans repatriated from Czechoslovakia after World War II, and the Moslems and Hindus exchanged when India and Pakistan were partitioned. Davis has estimated that altogether more than 70 million people were displaced between 1913 and 1968.

Migration by choice is also proceeding, but there have been changes. Northern and central European countries, which formerly sent emigrants to new lands, since World War II or even earlier have been receiving more migrants than they have sent out. At first the immigrants, imported to meet labor shortages, came mainly from southern European countries—Portugal, Spain, Italy, Greece, and Yugoslavia. More recently immigration from central and North Africa, India, and Pakistan has increased. Here again, as Davis points out, because the technological gap has widened betweed DCs and LDCs since World War II, migrants from less highly developed societies are moving to more developed ones in search of better jobs. Other possible factors are a reversal of relative population growth rates (earlier in the century, Western countries were growing more rapidly than non-Western countries) and the recent independence of former colonies. A part of this picture, too, is the brain drain, in which professionally trained citizens of LDCs, unable to find satisfactory employment at home, move to DCs.

A similar change in migration patterns has taken place in the United States. Before 1890, immigrants to the United States came predominantly from northern and western Europe. After the turn of the century, most came from southern Europe. The 1965 Immigration Act abolished the national quota system, and since then immigrants from LDCs, particularly Latin America, have far outnumbered Europeans.[71] Figure 5-28 shows

[70] *Ibid.*

[71] Charles B. Keely, Immigration composition and population policy.

the national origins of immigrants to the United States in 1972. While national quotas no longer apply, there are quotas for people based on other criteria: relatives of citizens or residents, skilled or unskilled workers in desired occupations, and refugees (except in unusual situations like the Cuban revolution and the Vietnamese evacuation). Hence, age and sex compositions of immigrants as a group have changed, as have their countries of origin. There has been an increase in the proportions of professionals, of married people with families, and of males rather than females since 1965.

The total number of immigrants admitted annually to the United States has been about 400,000 in recent years. Unfortunately, no useful information exists on how many have left the country permanently, so the actual contribution of *net* migration to the population growth of the United States is unknown. Usually, emigration is ignored in discussions of United States population dynamics or immigration policies.

During the nineteenth and the early twentieth centuries immigration was an important element of United States population growth. Between 1900 and 1910, it accounted for more than half the nation's growth. It reached a low of less than 6 percent in the 1930s and 1940s, but by 1973 it again comprised more than a quarter of United States population growth (see Table 5-15).

The above discussion is based only on legal immigration. But the United States also receives large numbers of illegal immigrants, mainly from Mexico (estimates range from 60 to 85 percent of illegal immigrants) but also from several other Latin American and Caribbean countries, the Philippines, China, Korea, Nigeria, Ethiopia, Italy, Greece, Iran, and some other Middle Eastern states.[72]

Although there is no way to know exactly how many illegal immigrants are now residing in the United States or how many enter each year, some estimates have been made. It is believed that by 1974 some 8 million illegal aliens were living in the United States,[73] despite the

[72]A. C. McLellan and M. D. Boggs, Illegal aliens: A story of human misery; The alien wave, *Newsweek*, February 9, 1976.

[73]The alien wave, *Newsweek*, February 9, 1976. This was confirmed by a study made by the Census Bureau in 1975, reported by CBS radio, November 7, 1975.

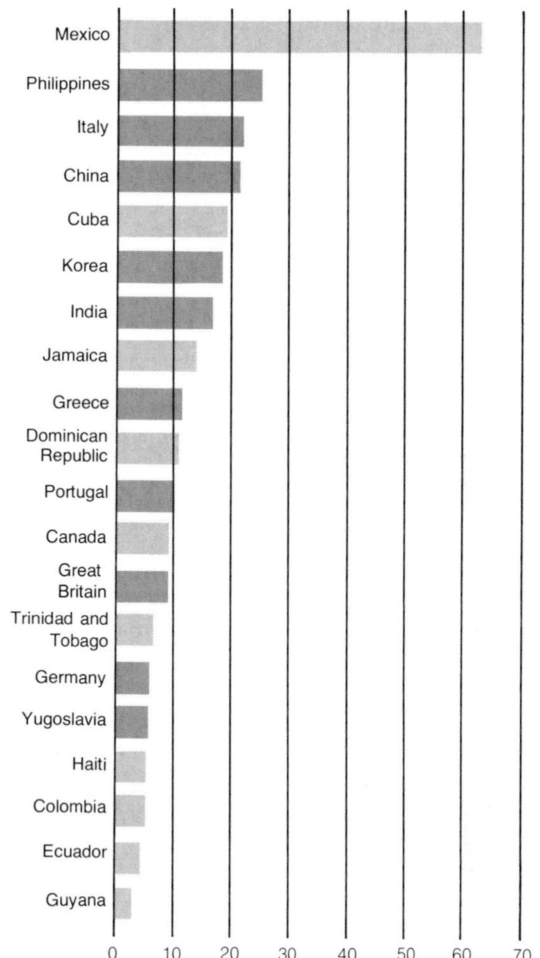

FIGURE 5-28

Sources of recent immigration to the United States are ranked here in descending order, with the top 10 countries of origin in the Western Hemisphere distinguished by shade from the top 10 in the Eastern Hemisphere. The figures for each country in the Western Hemisphere (except Cuba) represent the number of visas issued in fiscal year 1972; the figure for Cuba includes 16,380 "adjustments of status" granted by the Immigration and Naturalization Service to aliens subject to numerical limitations. The figures for the Eastern Hemisphere represent the number of visas issued in fiscal year 1972 (excluding recaptured visas) together with the number of adjustments of status and conditional entries granted to aliens subject to numerical limitation. (Data from U.S. State Department, 1973; from Davis, 1974.)

TABLE 5-15
Ratio of Immigration to Population Growth in the United States, 1820–1973

Decade ending	*Population increase (1000s)*	*Immigration (1000s)*	*Immigration as % of growth*
1830	3,227	152	5%
1840	4,203	599	14
1850	6,122	1,713	28
1860	8,251	2,598	32
1870	8,375	2,315	28
1880	10,337	2,812	27
1890	12,791	5,247	41
1900	13,046	3,688	28
1910	15,977	8,796	55
1920	13,738	5,735	42
1930	17,064	4,107	24
1940	8,894	528	6
1950	19,028	1,035	5
1960	27,766	2,515	9
1970	23,888	3,322	14
1971	2,008	370	18
1972	1,678	385	23
1973	1,499	400	27

Source: John Tanton, ZPG and Immigration: A discussion paper (Zero Population Growth, Inc., Washington, D.C., 1974 (from data of the U.S. Bureau of the Census and U.S. Immigration and Naturalization Service).

deportation of hundreds of thousands each year (more than 600,000 in 1973 and 800,000 in 1974). Estimates of annual clandestine arrivals range from 400,000 to 3 million. Illegal immigrants have often been encouraged to enter the country by prospective employers, covertly or overtly, to take very low-paying, menial jobs that are nevertheless more attractive than what is available in their home countries. Many jobs now held by illegal aliens are in urban areas, and some require highly skilled workers. The influx of foreign workers causes problems as they compete for jobs with welfare recipients and other low-income citizens, thus depressing the United States wage scale and sending funds out of the country. All of these problems were exacerbated by the recession of 1974/1975.

The demographic impact of illegal immigrants is bound to be large if they continue to arrive at the current rate. Even at the lowest estimated level of entry, their numbers equal those of legal immigrants. Demographic projections made by the organization Zero Population Growth have indicated that, if immigration proceeded at the rate of 1.2 million per year (400,000 legal and 800,000 illegal immigrants), and fertility remained at the 1975 level of 1.9 children per woman, the United States population would soar to 346 million in 2050.[74]

Like the unknown numbers of emigrants who leave the United States, illegal immigrants are left out of most estimates of United States population size and growth (with the major exception of the *World Population Estimates* of Robert C. Cook for the Environmental Fund). Efforts to pass legislation in Congress to strengthen regulations against illegal immigrants and to penalize employers for hiring them have failed so far.[75] Illegal immigrants do not enter the United States only; several countries in Europe and South America also attract them, mainly for the same reasons.

Migration, of course, can have no effect on the growth of population worldwide; there is no migration to or from Earth. But it can have significant effects on the rates of growth of individual countries, on their age compositions, and on population densities.[75a] Migration obviously increases the growth of receiving countries and reduces that of sending countries. In the case of the United Kingdom, mentioned above, net emigration produced negative population growth by 1975, even though the age composition and fertility rates should have produced a slow positive growth and immigrants from less developed former colonies were still being admitted.[76] But the number of immigrants had been reduced by tightened regulations, and the number of emigrants (mostly native-born) sharply rose in response to deteriorating economic conditions. Most emigrants went to Australia, Canada, and New Zealand.

Emigration from rapidly growing LDCs also has the effect of dampening population growth in the country of origin, perhaps providing enough of a safety valve to delay establishment of needed population programs.

[74]Melanie Wirken, Illegals threaten U.S. population stabilization, *Intercom* (Population Reference Bureau, Inc.), vol. 6, no. 4, June 1976, p. 4.

[75]The enterprising border jumpers, *Time,* May 19, 1975; The alien wave.

[75a]For a discussion of these effects and related consequences, see John Tanton, International migration.

[76]*International Journal of Environmental Studies,* p. 300, n.52.

This appears to have been the case for Mexico, which only established a family-planning program in 1974, although the nation's birth rate has been around 46 per 1000 for some time. Similarly, several Caribbean islands (Puerto Rico, Barbados, and Trinidad, for example) have for decades exported substantial fractions of their natural increase, mainly to the United States or Canada. Birth rates have fallen in several Caribbean nations since 1965, but the possibility remains that they might have fallen considerably sooner and faster without the safety valve of emigration.

Urbanization

One of the oldest of all demographic trends is the one towards urbanization. Preagricultural people by necessity were dispersed in small groups over the landscape. Hunting and gathering required perhaps a minimum of 5 square kilometers of territory to produce the food for one person. Under such conditions and without even the most primitive transportation systems, it was impossible for people to exist in large concentrations. But the Agricultural Revolution changed all that. Because more food could be produced in less area, agricultural people began to form primitive communities. The ability of farmers to feed more than their own families was obviously a prerequisite of urbanization. A fraction of the population first had to be freed from cultivation of the land before cities could develop.

But the division of labor and specialization in a nonfarming population does not seem in itself to have led immediately to urbanization. For example, some scholars believe that Egyptian agriculture and society were such that considerable numbers of people were freed from the land by the time their culture reached the stage usually considered civilized (about 3000 B.C.). But it was another 2000 years before they developed the kind of complex, interrelated society recognizable as a city. Similarly, it is doubted whether the Mayan civilization produced cities. It is thought that, in ancient Mesopotamia, at least, and perhaps in Cambodia, the development of large and complex irrigation systems helped lead to the formation of cities. Then, as today, shortages of water formed the bases of political disputes, so people may have gathered in large groups for defensive purposes. Mesopotamian cities also would have served as storage and redistribution centers for food. As anthropologist Robert M. Adams has written, "the complexity of subsistence pursuits on the flood plains may have indirectly aided the movement toward cities. Institutions were needed to mediate between herdsman and cultivator; between fisherman and sailor; between plowmaker and plowman."[77] It has also been suggested that mobilizing, working, and using metals may have stimulated concentrated settlement patterns. Whatever the actual impetus for urbanization, the first cities arose along the Tigris and Euphrates rivers between 4000 and 3000 B.C.

The trend toward urbanization continues today, as it has ever since those first cities were formed. Because of differing fertility patterns and generally much poorer health conditions, cities traditionally have been unable to maintain their populations through natural increase, let alone to grow. Hence, growth of cities before the late nineteenth century was almost entirely due to migration from rural areas. The move to the cities has at times been stimulated by agricultural advances that made possible the establishment of larger, more efficient farms. It seems also to have been stimulated by population growth in rural areas, which necessitated either the subdivision of farms among several sons or the migration of "surplus" offspring to the cities. In the past, advances in agriculture generally have been accompanied by advances in other kinds of technology, which provided new opportunities for nonagricultural employment. Beyond providing places for those displaced from the land, cities have always been attractive in themselves to people who hoped to improve their economic conditions.[78]

The movement into large urban concentrations has been especially rapid in the past century. For instance, in the United States about 6 percent of the population lived in urban areas in 1800, 15 percent in 1850, and 40 percent in 1900. Today, nearly 75 percent of the population lives in cities or their suburbs (Figure 5-29). Recent Census Bureau evidence indicates, however, that the trend to

[77]R. M. Adams, The origin of cities.

[78]For a fascinating study of the history of cities, read Lewis Mumford, *The city in history: Its origins, its transformations, and its prospects.*

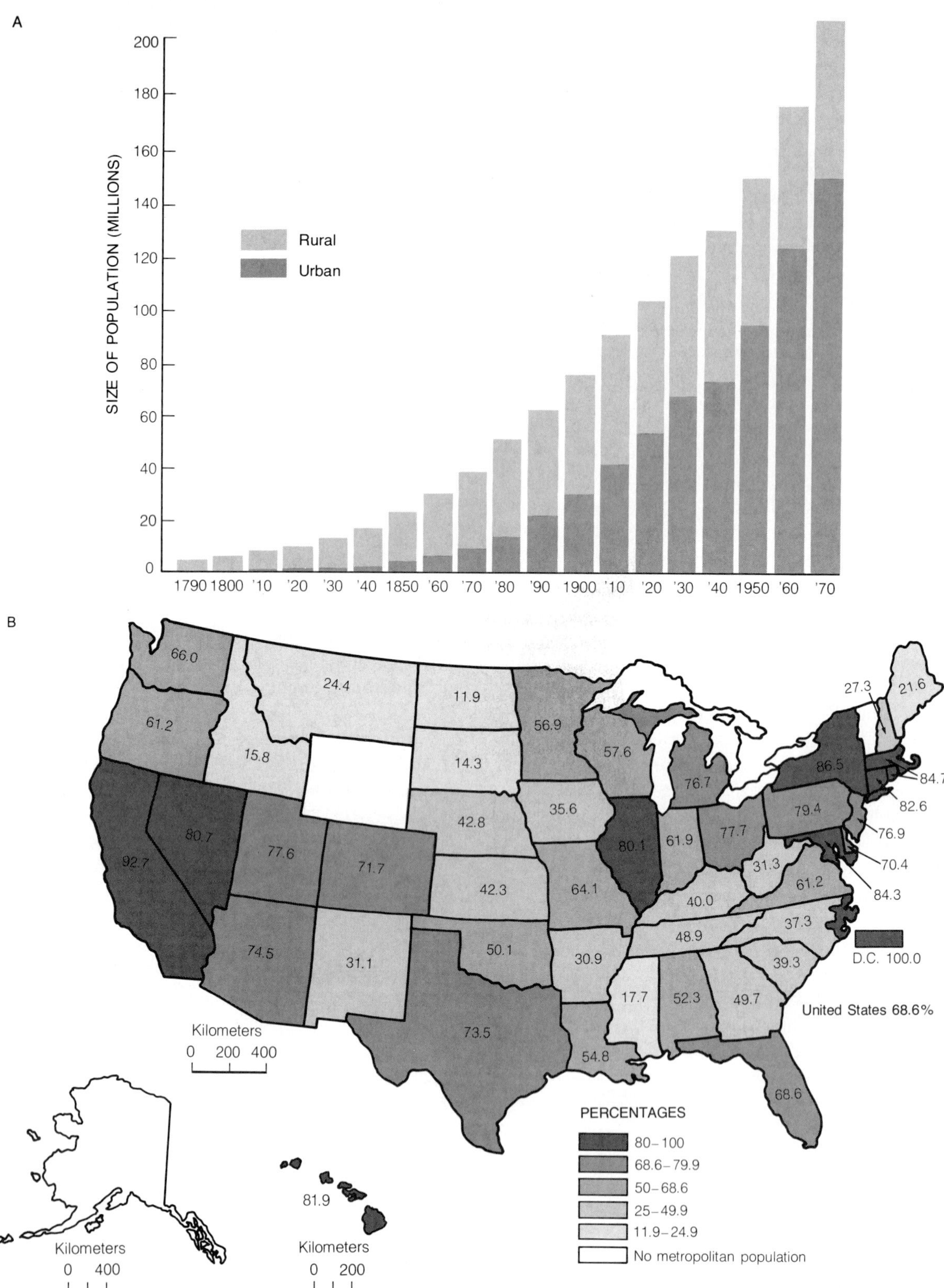

POPULATION IN STANDARD METROPOLITAN STATISTICAL AREAS 1970

urbanization in the United States may have ended—and may even have begun a reversal.[79]

Other industrialized nations are also more or less heavily urbanized, ranging from 56 percent in eastern Europe to 86 percent in Australia and New Zealand. Most LDCs are much less urbanized, but the variation among them is even greater. Tropical South America reaches European levels—59 percent—whereas East Africa is only 12 percent urbanized. The trend to urbanization is accelerating rapidly in those countries, however, attended by a variety of severe social problems. Altogether, almost 40 percent of the world's population was urban in 1970.[80] Table 5-16 traces the urbanization of major regions since 1925 and projected to 2075.

TABLE 5-16
Percentage of Total Population Living in Urban Areas in the World and Major Areas, 1925–2025

Area	1925	1950	1975	2000	2025
World	21	28	39	50	63
U.S. and Canada	54	64	77	86	93
Europe	48	55	67	79	88
USSR	18	39	61	76	87
East Asia	10	15	30	46	63
Latin America	25	41	60	74	85
Africa	8	13	24	37	54
South Asia	9	15	23	35	51
Oceania	54	65	71	77	87

Source: United Nations, *Concise Report.*

An additional change is in the proportion of the world's people who live in very large cities (those with 1 million or more inhabitants). A generation ago most such cities were in developed countries. By the 1970s more of the million-cities were in LDCs, and their aggregate population exceeded that in DCs. Table 5-17 shows the growth of million-cities between 1960 and 1975.

One problem that is inevitably encountered when discussing urbanization is the definition of an urban area. This varies from country to country, and from time to time. Furthermore, urban areas in different countries or different areas of the same country often are quite dissimilar. Los Angeles, New York, and Chicago have certain features (good and bad) in common—good art museums, major universities, slums, disadvantaged minorities, numerous TV stations, clogged streets and freeways, dangerously congested airports, diverse specialty shops, high crime rates, and air pollution, to name a few. But their differences are as apparent as their similarities. The air-pollution problems of Los Angeles and New York differ fundamentally because the smogs over the two cities have different compositions and the cities are in different physical settings. Water-supply problems are unique in each of the three cities. Los Angeles has a seemingly hopeless surface transportation problem and smoggy "sunshine slums." Mexican-Americans are one of its largest minority groups. Chicago has substantial problems with migrants from the Ozarks. New York has had great difficulty in satisfactorily absorbing masses of immigrants from Puerto Rico and the rural South, many of whom have ended up as welfare recipients. The problems of government in the three cities have their own peculiar twists, but all have more or less serious financial problems.

Urbanization seems to have one almost universal effect, the breaking-down of the traditional cultures of those who migrate to the cities—a loss of roots, or alienation. In rural or tribal societies each individual has a well-defined role in the organization of the society, a role that he or she has matured into and that is recognized by all other members of the society. In contrast, anonymity is a major feature of the city. City-dwellers typically are on close terms with no more people than are village-dwellers, and they tend to go to great lengths to

[79]Roy Reed, Rural areas' population gains now outpacing urban regions, *The New York Times,* May 18, 1975. For a more detailed description of this new phenomenon, see Peter A. Morrison, with Judith A. Wheeler, Rural renaissance in America? The revival of population growth in remote areas.

[80]United Nations, *Concise Report.*

FIGURE 5-29 (*left*)

Urbanization of the United States. In 1970, some 73.5 percent of Americans were living in towns or cities, and 68.6 percent were living in large cities and their surroundings (metropolitan areas). Since 1970 the percentage of urban Americans has passed 75. (A. Adapted from *Population bulletin,* vol. 19, no. 2. Courtesy of the Population Reference Bureau, Inc., Washington, D.C. B. U.S. Bureau of the Census, 1970.)

TABLE 5-17
Million-Cities, 1960 and 1975

Area	Number of million-cities		Population of million-cities (millions)		Percentage of total population in million-cities	
	1960	1975	1960	1975	1960	1975
World	109	191	272	516	9.1	12.8
More developed regions	64	90	173	251	17.7	21.9
Less developed regions	45	101	99	265	4.9	9.2
Europe	31	37	73	93	17.3	19.3
USSR	5	12	13	25	6.1	9.7
U.S. and Canada	18	30	52	80	26.2	32.9
Oceania	2	2	4	6	24.7	26.9
South Asia	16	34	32	88	3.7	6.8
East Asia	23	45	60	131	7.7	12.9
Africa	3	10	6	22	2.4	5.5
Latin America	11	21	31	71	14.5	21.9

Note: The 1975 estimates correspond to earlier population estimates and projections of the United Nations.
Source: United Nations, *Concise report.*

avoid "getting involved" with the vast majority of the human beings with whom they come into daily contact.

Urbanization in the United States in some ways differs dramatically from urbanization in other countries. For instance, the difference between city-dwellers and country-dwellers in the United States has become increasingly blurred, especially in recent years, with urban culture becoming dominant. Rapid transportation and mass media have exposed the country folk to the ways of the city. Furthermore, in the United States especially, the phenomenon of suburbanization has developed. Suburbanites, who take advantage of high-speed automobiles, plentiful and cheap fuel, freeways, and affluence, have attempted to enjoy the advantages of city and countryside simultaneously, by working in the former and living close to the latter.

Suburbanization has been extremely rapid since World War II and has led to some severe problems in the United States. While affluent and middle-class taxpayers have left the cities, poor and unskilled people squeezed out of rural areas largely by increasingly mechanized agriculture, have flooded to the cities seeking jobs in industry. As tax returns to city governments have dwindled, it has become more and more difficult for cities to maintain even basic services. In an effort to restore their tax losses, many cities have concentrated their urban renewal funds on building high-rise office buildings used mostly by commuting suburbanites, while the slum areas housing the poor have become even more crowded, neglected, and crime-ridden. Thus, the contemporary United States city consists largely of office buildings and slums, surrounded by affluent suburbs, freeways, and industrial areas. The central city is strangled during the day by traffic as suburbanites commute to the city and factory workers commute out of it. Nevertheless, American cities have access to the resources to solve their urban problems, difficult though they are. Their problems are largely the result of poor planning or no planning at all.

European cities, too, have been suburbanized, but not to the same degree as those of North America. Because it has greater population density, and consequently less land to spare, Europe has avoided the greatest excesses of urban sprawl. Different urban government arrangements and zoning regulations have also played a part in keeping cities relatively compact. Moreover, urbanization has proceeded more slowly in Europe than elsewhere. This is not to say there are no urban problems in Europe. Even though public transport systems are generally far superior to those in the United States, traffic congestion (largely from automobiles) is almost unmanageable in the centers of many of the largest cities. Housing shortages have plagued European cities at times; public or publicly subsidized housing has made up a substantial portion of housing built since World War II in some countries. In London, there is a serious shortage of housing as well as a growing number of abandoned buildings, some slated for demolition. Homeless families by the thousands have asserted squatter's rights by occupying the derelict structures—in some cases, even with government assistance.

While rapid urbanization has caused problems in industrialized countries, it is virtually a disaster in many LDCs.[81] There, urban problems are largely the result of cities' being overwhelmed by massive, unanticipated immigration from the countryside. Between 1950 and 1960, the populations of cities in the DCs increased 25 percent, while those of cities in the LDCs increased 55 percent. In most LDCs, especially since the end of World War II, there has been an increasing flood of impoverished peasants into urban areas. Yet employment opportunities there have not materialized. The result has been the development of huge shantytowns around the fringes of cities.

In Latin America the shantytowns are given different names in each country: *favelas* in Brazil, *tugurios* in Colombia, *ranchos* in Venezuela, and *barriadas* in Peru. In Peru, at least a million squatters live in such settlements—a substantial fraction of Peru's population of about 15 million (Figure 5-30). They are virtually a universal phenomenon around large cities in Central America and tropical South America. Most of these urban migrants become permanent residents, and among them, women outnumber men. The majority of arrivals are between 15 and 30 years old.

The trend in Africa has been similar, with hundreds of thousands migrating to the cities annually in search of better lives. Nairobi, the capital of Kenya, had a 1968 population of 460,000 and was growing at a rate of 7 percent per year. (That is more than twice the growth rate of Los Angeles in the decade 1950 to 1960.) During the 1960s, Accra, the capital of Ghana, was growing at almost 8 percent per year; Abidjan, capital of the Ivory Coast, at almost 10 percent; Lusaka, capital of Zambia, and Lagos, capital of Nigeria, both at 14 percent.[82] Unlike Latin American urban migrants, African migrants are usually young men who stay in the city only temporarily and then return to their families in the countryside. Lack of employment and housing for families are probably the reasons for the turnover.

[81]Atlas report, Cities in trouble, *Atlas,* December 1975. See also George J. Beier, Can third world cities cope? for a concise analysis of the situation.

[82]Bulging African cities where dreams die, *San Francisco Chronicle,* November 20, 1968.

FIGURE 5-30

A shantytown in the Rimac district of Lima, Peru. Many squatter houses, originally straw shacks, are being rebuilt in brick and masonry whenever the earnings of the owners permit. (Photo courtesy of William Mangin.)

The rate of urbanization in Asia has also been rapid in this century, but in most Asian countries the increases have been from a rather low base. For instance, at the turn of the century about 11 percent of India's population was urban. Today more than 20 percent of India's people live in cities. This deceptively low rate of urbanization conceals what for India is a problem of immense proportions (Figure 5-31). As in Africa, many of India's (and other Asian) urban migrants remain in the cities only temporarily.

Some of the world's fastest-growing cities are in southeast Asia, especially in Indonesia. Hong Kong and, to a lesser degree, Singapore have had rapid urbanization compounded by high rates of immigration—often illegal—from China. Although both cities have prospered as manufacturing and trading centers, they have succeeded in providing housing and services for their burgeoning populations only through strenuous efforts. Table 5-18 shows the projected growth of the world's largest and fastest-growing cities between 1970 and 1985—only fifteen years. In that time, many will double their populations and one (Bandung, Indonesia) will more than triple its population.

In most rapidly growing LDCs, the trend to the cities seems to be caused in large part by the same hope for a better life that has drawn people from rural areas of the southern United States and Puerto Rico to a slum life in New York, Chicago, and other northern metropolises, or from rural southern Europe to industrial northern Europe. But in the cities of less developed countries, where there is little industry, economic opportunities are much more limited than in the cities of the United States or Europe.

In the LDCs, communications and transportation are much less efficient than in DCs, and the peasant cultures are less influenced by the urban. The overwhelming majority of urban-dwellers in LDCs are migrants from the countryside who have brought their peasant cultures with them.[83] Unlike the majority of DC urbanites, whose specialized education, training, and skills assure them of places in the city's complex social web, the LDC immigrant has no such skills to offer. In the United States, unskilled rural immigrants are in the minority. Although they may have employment problems, most are at least literate and can be absorbed into the industrial society.

Cities in developed countries are a source of wealth and power, generated through technology and manufacturing. The goods they produce are exchanged for raw materials and food from the countryside. In contrast, many LDC cities subsist in times of shortage primarily on food imported from other countries. Attracted by the opportunity to obtain a share of the imported food, inhabitants of the countryside move into the cities when the countryside can no longer support them. Inevitably, they find that their limited skills render them incapable of contributing to the economy. As a consequence, they are not much better off than they were where they came from. In some LDC cities, squatters now make up a majority of the population. According to the United Nations, they constitute at least one-third of the urban populations of all less developed areas and are increasing by about 15 percent per year—doubling every five or six years.[84] Miserable as their condition seems to be, at least those who have settled with their families evidently prefer to remain in their squatter settlements rather than return to what they left. Many, of course, may have burned their bridges behind them and have no way of successfully returning to their former homes. Many migrants to LDC cities do, however, maintain contact with their home villages and contribute financially to their rural relatives.

Evidence is accumulating that many squatter settlements are far more successful as a way of life than would appear to Western eyes. Among the permanent migrants, modified village societies are often established within squatter settlements, thus transferring village culture to the city (a factor that may explain why their attitudes and reproductive patterns generally resemble those of rural people). Such established settlements are very different from rural slums in the United States or other DCs, which are often characterized by an absence of community coherence and efforts toward neighborhood improvements.

Squatter settlements often start out with the most

[83]N. Keyfitz, Population density and the style of social life.

[84]United Nations, *Report on the world social situation,* Center for Housing, Building and Planning, Department of Economic and Social Affairs, New York, 1974.

TABLE 5-18
Growth of the World's Cities, 1970–1985

	1970 population (millions)	1985 population (millions)	Projected growth (%)
BIGGEST CITIES			
1 New York	16.3	18.8	15
2 Tokyo	14.9	25.2	69
3 London	10.5	11.1	6
4 Shanghai	10.0	14.3	43
5 Paris	8.4	10.9	30
6 Los Angeles	8.4	13.7	63
7 Buenos Aires	8.4	11.7	39
8 Mexico City	8.4	17.9	113
9 Sao Paolo	7.8	16.8	115
10 Osaka	7.6	11.8	55
11 Moscow	7.1	8.0	13
12 Peking	7.0	12.0	71
13 Calcutta	6.9	12.1	75
14 Rio de Janeiro	6.8	11.4	68
FASTEST GROWING CITIES			
1 Bandung	1.2	4.1	242
2 Lagos	1.4	4.0	186
3 Karachi	3.5	9.2	163
4 Bogota	2.6	6.4	146
5 Baghdad	2.0	4.9	145
6 Bangkok	3.0	7.1	137
7 Teheran	3.4	7.9	132
8 Seoul	4.6	10.3	124
9 Lima	2.8	6.2	121
10 Sao Paulo	7.8	16.8	115
11 Mexico City	8.4	17.9	113
12 Bombay	5.8	12.1	109
OTHERS			
Jakarta	4.0	7.7	93
Detroit	4.0	4.9	23

Source: Adapted from *People,* vol. 1, no. 4, p. 10.

rudimentary of dwellings but progress to more permanent structures as their owners can afford to build them. The shantytowns are built by their inhabitants, who organize a community social structure in order to bring in needed services from outside, such as water, food, public transportation, schools, and health care.[85]

This pattern is especially common in Latin America. In some of the more successful cities, governments have cooperated with the settlements in providing these services and assisting the people in their community projects. Around Lima, for instance, settlements are being steadily improved through the joint efforts of the squatters and the Peruvian government.[86] Such cooperation among governments and squatters is relatively rare, unfortunately. More commonly, governments try to ignore the shantytowns, or—more ambitiously—try to clear the slums and thereby "remove" the problem (without success). Where slum clearance has been attempted, the result has often been social disaster—or at least an extremely expensive program of building urban housing for the poor.[87]

[85]W. Mangin, Squatter settlements.

[86]Sally E. Kellock, a UNICEF (United Nations Children's Fund) program officer in Peru, personal communication.

[76]United Nations *1974 Report on the world social situation.*

FIGURE 5-31

A street in Calcutta. These people live in makeshift shacks built on the sidewalk. Some of the shacks also function as shops where the "owners" sell food and handmade articles. (Wide World Photos.)

One of the major obstacles to improving conditions for urban squatters is the apparent inability of governments to find solutions in any but traditional Western approaches. Just one outstanding example is the sanitation facilities—or lack of them—in most LDC cities. Sewer systems serve only 28 percent of the LDC urban populations; 30 percent of those populations have no facilities at all.[88] Calcutta, for instance, relies on a crumbling sewer system built at the turn of the century for 600,000 people—less than one-tenth of the present population.[89] Calcutta first tried slum clearance, but has since turned to making modest improvements in the *bustees* (as the shantytowns are called), providing latrines and minimal water service.[90] Most LDCs, however, seem unable to conceive of sanitation except in terms of unsanitary latrines or western-style sewer systems, which are well beyond their means, technologically and financially, and which use too much water. So nothing is done. A program is urgently needed to develop intermediate technologies to solve this problem—perhaps along the line of the *clivus multrum* dry toilet (see Chapter 11).

Urban projections. Even more alarming than the present urban situation are projections of trends in urbanization. For instance, one projection has led to an estimate for Calcutta in the year 2000 of 66 million inhabitants, more than *8 times* today's population. Needless to say, that total will not be reached—but there is a realistic expectation that the population of this teeming city (Figure 5-31), in which several hundred thousand people live in the streets today, will increase from 7.5 million to 12 million by 1990. Calcutta is already a

[88]Richard Feacham, Appropriate sanitation.

[89]Peter Wilsher, Everyone, everywhere, is moving to the cities, *The New York Times,* June 22, 1975.

[90]Atlas report. Cities in trouble.

disaster area, and the consequences of further growth at such a rate are heartrending to contemplate.

The population of relatively prosperous Tokyo is projected to reach 40 million in the year 2000 (compared to 15 million in 1970). In a desperate attempt to create land for expansion, Tokyo has been using 7000 tons of garbage a day to fill Tokyo Bay. Flat, empty land is at a premium in mountainous, overpopulated Japan. Middle-class apartments are already so scarce that people have to wait two years to obtain them. Tokyo's dense crowding seems destined only to get worse.

Demographer Kingsley Davis has made some extrapolations of urbanization trends and has produced some startling statistics. If the urban growth rate that has prevailed since 1950 continues, half of the people in the world will be living in the cities by 1984. If the trend should continue to 2023 (it cannot!), everyone in the world would live in an urban area. Most striking of all, in 2020 most people would not just be in urban areas; half of the world's human beings would be in cities of more than 1 million population, and in 2044 *everyone* would exist in "cities" of that size. At that time the largest "city" would have a projected population of 1.4 billion people, out of a projected world population of 15 billion.[91] (The word *city* here appears in quotation marks because, should such a stage be reached, world living conditions would make the term meaningless in its historical sense.)

[91]The urbanization of the human population.

Such projections, of course, are merely extensions of recent trends. They are helpful in showing the direction in which *Homo sapiens* is headed. But, if anything, they make it clear that those trends cannot long continue. The movement to urbanization in the developed world may indeed be ending now. In much of Europe it has markedly slowed in the past decade, and in the United States it appears to have reversed slightly in the 1970s.

How long the cities of less developed countries can go on absorbing masses of unemployable peasants in makeshift slums without major social breakdown is an open question. Much probably could be done to alleviate their explosive urban growth by concentrating development effort in rural areas and smaller towns in order to provide useful employment there. But the key to solving the problem in the long run is clearly to reduce the rate of population growth as quickly as feasible. From at least one point of view, burgeoning LDC cities are both symptomatic and symbolic of humanity's predicament. There one finds juxtaposed many of the contradictions of today: wealth and poverty; modern technology and industry and illiteracy; abundance and hunger.

The future of the human population depends on much more than population dynamics. Those dynamics are limited by the physical, biological, and social environments in which the population finds itself. Furthermore, human actions can change both kinds of environments for better or worse. These interactions are explored in some detail in the following chapters.

Recommended for Further Reading

Bogue, D. J. 1969. *Principles of demography.* Wiley, New York. A good basic text.

Coale, A. J. 1974. The history of the human population, *Scientific American,* September, pp. 41–51. A concise account of demographic history.

Davis, K. 1965. The urbanization of the human population. *Scientific American,* September, pp. 41–53. (*Scientific American* offprint 659, W. H. Freeman and Company, San Francisco.) Useful article on development of early cities and modern trend toward urbanization.

———. 1974. The migrations of human populations. *Scientific American,* September, pp. 93–105. Informative and interesting discussion of causes and consequences of migration.

Dumond, D. E. 1975. The limitation of human population: A natural history. *Science,* vol. 187, pp. 714–721 (February 28). Interesting article on ways in which various societies have controlled their population growth.

Freedman, R., and B. Berelson. 1974. The human population. *Scientific American,* September, pp. 30–39. General overview of the present population situation.

Mumford, L. 1961. *The city in history: Its origins, its transformation and its prospects.* Harcourt, New York. Fascinating compendium on cities.

Population Reference Bureau (PRB). *Population Bulletin.* PRB, Washington, D.C. This is a useful source of information for the educated layperson on virtually all aspects of demography.

———. Annual. *Population data sheet.* A concise summary of population numbers and related data listed by country.

Teitelbaum, M. S. 1975. Relevance of demographic transition theory for developing countries. *Science,* vol. 188, pp. 420–425 (May 2). Suggests that demographic transition theory for Europe may not be applicable to LDCs.

Thompson, W. S., and D. J. Lewis. 1965. *Population problems.* 5th ed. McGraw-Hill, New York. A basic text.

United Nations. 1974. *Concise report on the world population situation, 1970–1975, and its long-range implications.* New York. Excellent account of present world population situation; much useful data.

Westoff, C. F. 1974. The populations of the developed countries. *Scientific American,* September, pp. 108–120. On the population situation in DCs, especially recent fertility declines toward replacement levels.

Additional References

Adams, R. M. 1960. The origin of cities. *Scientific American,* September. (*Scientific American* offprint 606, W. H. Freeman and Company, San Francisco.) An interesting paper on how and why the first cities appeared in the Middle East.

Adlakha, A. and D. Kirk. 1975. Vital rates in India 1961–71 estimated from 1971 census data. *Population studies,* vol. 28, no. 3. An analysis of the data from India's 1971 census.

Atlas report. Cities in trouble. *Atlas,* December 1975. Contains four articles on urban problems in both DCs and LDCs and some ideas for solving them.

Behrman, S. J.; L. Corsa, Jr.; and R. Freedman, eds. 1969. *Fertility and family planning: A world view.* University of Michigan Press, Ann Arbor. Useful source for recent demographic history.

Beier, George F., 1976. Can third world cities cope? *Population bulletin,* vol. 31, no. 4 (Population Reference Bureau, Inc., Washington, D.C.). Concise analysis of LDC urbanization problems.

Birdsell, J. B. 1968. Some predictions for the Pleistocene based on equilibrium systems among recent hunter-gatherers. *In Man the hunter,* R. B. Lee and J. DeVore, eds., Aldine, Chicago, pp. 229–240.

Bouvier, Leon F., 1975. U.S. population in 2000: Zero growth or not? *Population Bulletin,* vol. 30, no. 5. An analysis of census bureau projections of United States population growth.

Brackett, J. W., and R. T. Ravenholt, 1976. World fertility, 1976: An analysis of data sources and trends. *Population reports,* series J, no. 12. (November). Recent demographic trends.

Braidwood, R. J. 1960. The Agricultural Revolution. *Scientific American,* September. (Reprinted in Paul R. Ehrlich et al., *Man and the ecosphere.*)

Brown, Harrison; John P. Holdren; Alan Sweezy; and Barbara West, eds. 1974. *Population: Perspective 1973.* Freeman, Cooper, San Francisco. Articles reviewing recent developments in population around the world. See especially the articles on mainland China.

Brown, Lester R., 1976. World population trends: Signs of hope, signs of stress. *Worldwatch Paper 8.* Worldwatch Institute, Washington, D.C. (October).

Carr-Saunders, A. M. 1936. *World population.* Oxford University Press, Fairlawn, N.J. A classic source.

Cavalli-Sforza, L. L., and W. F. Bodmer. 1971. *The genetics of human populations.* W. H. Freeman and Company, San Francisco. Contains a good discussion of genetics, demography, population projection matrices, and such.

Curwen, E. C., and G. Hatt. 1953. *Plough and pasture.* Henry Schuman, New York. Early history of farming.

Dalrymple, D. G. 1964. The Soviet famine of 1932–34. *Soviet Studies,* vol. 14, pp. 250–284. An excellent and detailed account.

Davis, K. 1956. The amazing decline of mortality in underdeveloped areas. *American Economic Review,* vol. 46, pp. 305–318. An early paper on the success of death-control technology.

———. 1965. The population impact on children in the world's agrarian countries. *Population Review,* vol. 9, pp. 17–31. Contains details of the argument that children get a disproportionately bad deal in the LDCs.

Deevey, Edward S. 1960. The human population. *Scientific American,* September. (*Scientific American* offprint 608, W. H. Freeman and Company, San Francisco.) Concise history of population growth.

Demko, G. J.; H. M. Rose; and G. A. Schnell, eds. 1970. *Population geography: A reader.* McGraw-Hill, New York. Background information on population structure and distribution, urbanization, and so forth.

Dickeman, Mildred. 1975. Demographic consequences of infanticide in man. *Annual review of systematics and ecology,* vol. 6, Annual Reviews, Inc., Palo Alto, Calif. Fascinating article on motivation of family limitation—goes far beyond the phenomenon of infanticide.

Durand, J. D. 1967. A long-range view of world population growth. *Annals of the American Academy of Political Science,* vol. 369, pp. 1–8.

Easterlin, R. A. 1968. *Population, labor force, and long swings in economic growth.* Columbia Press, New York. An analysis of economic influences on fertility.

Ehrlich, Paul R., John P. Holdren, and Richard W. Holm, eds. 1971. *Man and the ecosphere,* W. H. Freeman and Company, San Francisco. Important papers from *Scientific American* with critical commentaries.

Enke, S. 1970. Zero population growth, when, how and why. *Tempo,* General Electric Co., Santa Barbara, Calif., January. A relatively nontechnical discussion of population momentum.

Environmental Fund, Inc. (Annual.) *World population estimates.* Washington, D.C. A useful data sheet on population.

Feacham, Richard. 1976. Appropriate sanitation. *New Scientist,* January 8. On the sanitation facilities in LDC cities.

Freedman, Deborah, ed. 1976. Fertility, aspirations, and resources: A symposium on the Easterlin hypothesis. *Population and Development Review,* vol. 2, nos. 3 and 4. Discussion of economic influences on fertility.

Freedman, R. 1960. The sociology of human fertility: A trend report and bibliography. *Current Sociology,* vol. 9, no. 1, pp. 35–119.

Frejka, T. 1968. Reflections on the demographic conditions needed to establish a U.S. stationary population growth. *Population Studies,* vol. 22 (November), pp. 379–397.

———. 1973. *The future of population growth: Alternative paths to equilibrium.* Wiley, New York. A detailed examination of population momentum.

———. 1973. The prospects for a stationary world population. *Scientific American,* March, pp. 15–23. Less detailed than Frejka's book, and somewhat optimistic in tone.

———. 1974. World population projections: Alternative paths to zero. *Population Bulletin,* vol. 29, no. 5. A good summary of the material in Frejka's book.

Hance, W. A. 1970. *Population, migration and urbanization in Africa.* Columbia University Press, New York.

Keely, Charles B. 1974. Immigration composition and population policy. *Science,* vol. 185, pp. 587–593 (August 16). An informative discussion of recent changes in United States immigration policies and their consequences.

Keyfitz, N. 1966. How many people have ever lived on Earth? *Demography,* vol. 3, pp. 581–582. An estimate that 4 to 5 percent of all human beings ever born are alive today.

———. 1966. Population density and the style of social life. *BioScience,* vol. 16, no. 12 (December), pp. 868–873. Information on the origin of cities and differences between DC and LDC cities.

———. 1971. On the momentum of population growth. *Demography,* vol. 8, no. 1 (February), pp. 71–80. Source of the "Keyfitz numbers."

——— and W. Flieger. 1971. *Population: Facts and methods of demography.* W. H. Freeman and Company, San Francisco. Gives life tables and other calculations for most countries where birth and death statistics exist, and explains methods used in those calculations. Age distributions, sex ratios, and population increase are among its themes. Highly recommended.

Kolata, G. B. 1974. !Kung hunter-gatherers: Feminism, diet and birth control, *Science,* vol. 185 September, pp. 932–934. Provocative discussion of birth control among hunter-gatherers.

Langer, W. L. 1958. The next assignment. *American historical review,* vol. 63, pp. 283–305. Includes an excellent discussion of the long-term effects of the black death on European society.

———. 1964. The black death. *Scientific American,* February. (*Scientific American* offprint 619, W. H. Freeman and Company, San Francisco. Reprinted in Paul R. Ehrlich et al., *Man and the ecosphere.*) Interesting historical study of the plagues in medieval Europe.

———. 1972. Checks on population growth: 1750–1850. *Scientific American,* February, pp. 92–99. Fascinating account of the prevalence of infanticide in nineteenth-century Europe.

———. 1975. American foods and Europe's population growth, 1750–1850. *Journal of Social History,* winter, pp. 51–66.

Lee, R. B. 1972. Population growth and the beginnings of sedentary life among the !Kung bushmen. *In population growth: Anthropological implications,* B. Spooner, ed. The M.I.T. Press, Cambridge, Mass. On how hunter-gatherers change their reproductive behavior when they take up agriculture.

McKeown, T.; R. G. Brown; and R. G. Record. 1972. An interpretation of the modern rise of population in Europe. *Population Studies,* vol. 26, no. 3 (November). Interesting exploration of possible causes of accelerating population growth in Europe in the eighteenth and nineteenth centuries.

McLellan, A. C., and M. D. Boggs. 1974. Illegal aliens: A story of human misery. *ZPG National Reporter,* December (Reprinted from *AFL-CIO American federationist,* August 1974.)

Mangin, W. 1967. Squatter settlements. *Scientific American,* October. (*Scientific American* offprint 635, W. H. Freeman and Company, San Francisco.) Provides some insight into lives of recent migrants into LDC cities.

Martin, P. S. 1970. Pleistocene niches for alien animals. *BioScience,* vol. 20, no. 4, (February 15) pp. 218–221. Discusses the ecological impact of Pleistocene extinctions.

——— and H. E. Wright, eds. 1967. *Pleistocene extinctions.* Yale University Press, New Haven. On the effects of early human hunting on populations of large mammals.

Morrison, P. A., and J. P. Wheeler, 1976. Rural renaissance in America? The revival of population growth in remote areas. *Population bulletin,* vol. 31, no. 3. Describes the recent shift of the U.S. population toward rural areas.

Ravenholt, R. T. 1976. Gaining ground on the population front. *War on hunger,* February, pp. 1–3, 13. An optimistic view of current population growth rates and projected trends.

Razzell, P. E. 1974. "An interpretation of the modern rise of population in Europe"—a critique. *Population Studies,* vol. 28, no. 1, pp. 5–17. Critical comment on McKeown, Brown, and Record (above) postulating the adoption of soap and sanitation as a major cause of declining death rates in eighteenth- and nineteenth-century Europe.

Reed, C. A. 1970. Extinction of mammalian megafauna in the Old World late Quaternary. *BioScience,* vol. 20, no. 5 (March 1), pp. 284–288. More on extinctions of populations of large mammals due to human activities.

Sklar, J., and B. Berkov. 1975. The American birth rate: Evidences of a coming rise. *Science,* vol. 189, pp. 693–700 (August 29). Suggests that United States birth rate will rise in late 1970s as women begin bearing postponed children.

Sweezy, A. 1971. The economic explanation of fertility changes in the United States. *Population Studies,* vol. 25, no. 2 (July), pp. 255–267. Casts doubt on economic explanations of low birth rates during Depression of 1930s.

Tanton, John H. 1976. International migration as an obstacle to achieving world stability. *The ecologist,* vol. 6, no. 6 (July). On the demographic and social effects of migration today.

United Nations Statistical Office. Annual. *Demographic yearbook.* New York. This annual compilation is *the* source for world data on population.

U.S. Bureau of the Census. 1971. The two-child family and population growth: An international view. Washington, D.C., September. Population projections for selected countries.

U.S. National Center for Health Statistics (USNCHS). Monthly. *Vital statistics report.* Washington, D.C. This report is essential for up-to-date information on vital rates and demographic trends in the United States. Other useful publications on the American population are also issued from the center.

Walford, C. 1878. The famines of the world: Past and present. *Royal Statistical Society Journal,* vol. 41, pp. 433–526. An interesting historical account.

Waterbolk, H. T. 1968. Food production in prehistoric Europe. *Science,* vol. 162, pp. 1093–1102. On beginning of agriculture in Europe.

Webb, W. P. 1964. *The great frontier.* Rev. ed. University of Texas Press, Austin. Diverting, perhaps prophetic discussion of how the frontier has shaped Western attitudes and institutions and how its disappearance may lead to ultimate disaster.

Wrigley, E. A. 1969. *Population and history.* McGraw-Hill, New York. Brief and interesting.

Young, J. Z. 1971. *An introduction to the study of man.* Clarendon Press, Oxford. Chapter 33 deals with the history of the genus *Homo.* The book as a whole is a gold mine of information on humanity as seen by one of the world's most distinguished zoologists.

We abuse land because we regard it as a commodity belonging to us. When we see land as a community to which we belong we may begin to use it with love and respect.

—Aldo Leopold, 1948

CHAPTER 6

Land, Water, and Forests

Among physical resources, land is central in importance. By land we mean not only physical space but also the characteristics that govern the uses to which land can be put. Those characteristics include the topography (the shape of the terrain—for example, flat, hilly, or mountainous), the quantity and quality of soil, the availability of water, and the nature of local climates. Of course, those features are interrelated, and together they influence and are influenced by the vegetation that grows on the land: soil is a product of the underlying rock, the climate, the topography, and the creatures living on it and in it; the availability of water depends on how much falls as rain and snow, on how much evaporates, and on how much is retained, where, and for how long; the latter properties depend on local soil and vegetation as much as they influence them.

Many of the basic physical principles underlying these relations are described in Chapter 2, Chapter 3, and Chapter 4. In this chapter we discuss the characteristics of Earth's land and its supplies of fresh water as resources—that is, in terms of their availability and suitability for the support of the human population. The closely related topics of forests and the production of timber are also treated here; production of food is the subject of Chapter 7.

LAND

Earth has a land area of 149 million square kilometers (58 million square miles), which in 1975 was occupied at an average density of about 27 people per square kilometer

(70 per square mile). This does not seem to be such a high density—it amounts to almost 4 hectares (or 10 acres) per person.

But land is a resource only insofar as its specific characteristics enable it to serve some human need. A very rough classification of global land area suggests that only about 30 percent of the land surface is potentially arable (farmable); 20 percent is uncultivable mountainous terrain; 20 percent is desert or steppe; 20 percent is characterized by glaciers, permafrost, and tundra; and 10 percent consists of other types of land with soils unsuitable for cultivation.[1]

Much of the land that is uncultivable is also so inhospitable as to be nearly uninhabitable—the Arctic and Antarctic, steep slopes, swamps, certain desert regions, and so on. For good reason, then, the human population is spread very unevenly over Earth's land surface. People have concentrated—and continue to concentrate today—in the areas that are most hospitable.

Some of the most serious land problems arise from competing, mutually exclusive uses for the same advantageously located pieces of land. Many of our cities, for example, arose in the centers of the best farmland, so some of that valuable resource has been lost beneath highways, suburbs, and airports as the cities have spread. Coastlines are in demand as desirable places to live, as a recreational resource for those who do not live there, as economical sites for electric power plants, as outlets for commerce, and as bases for the utilization of marine resources (Figure 6-1). Unfortunately, the coasts are also the location of relatively fragile communities of plants and animals, such as those in salt marshes and estuaries, upon which much of the productivity of the sea depends (see Chapter 4). Leaving essential ecological systems such as these intact may prove to be one of the most important uses of land; it may also prove to be one of the uses that is least compatible with other human activities. To assume that human beings should dare to exploit every bit of land that appears potentially capable of being exploited would be dangerous (although not unprecedented) arrogance.

In summary, there appears to be a good deal of land available if one does not inquire too carefully about what kind it is. But the most useful sorts of land are already in short supply in most parts of the world.

We note also that United States consumers (and those in many other nations that rely heavily on imports of food or raw materials) must be considered to be "occupying" a good deal of land outside their national boundaries. In this sense, DCs "occupy" coffee plantations in Brazil and rubber plantations in Laos, land used for bauxite mines in Jamaica and copper mines in Zambia, rangeland for cattle and sheep in Argentina, lumber-producing forests in Ivory Coast and Indonesia, and land used for growing soybeans in Colombia and peanuts in Nigeria.

Classification of Land by Climate, Vegetation, and Use

Closer examination of Earth's land resource can take several directions: we can classify it according to climate and vegetation, according to present use, and according to characteristics of soils. In this section of text we consider climate, vegetation, and land use, and we treat soils in the next section.

Vegetation and cultivation. Table 6-1 shows a classification of the land area of the globe into *bioclimatic* regions, carried out by Soviet scientists who have long been active in the field of biogeography. The term *bioclimatic* is merely an explicit recognition that regional climates and vegetation patterns are intimately interconnected. An alternative classification strictly by vegetation patterns, corresponding very closely in its categories to the biomes described in Chapter 4, is given in Table 6-2. In these classifications, *land* refers to the area of continents and islands, including the lakes and streams they contain. In Table 6-1 the lakes and streams constitute a separate category; in Table 6-2 they are apportioned among the biomes in which they occur. When land covered by lakes, streams, and glaciers is subtracted from the category of land area, the global land surface amounts to 133 million square kilometers. As Table 6-2 indicates, about 10 percent of that land surface is under cultivation.

In 1967 the report of the President's Science Advisory Committee panel on the world food supply estimated the

[1]Georg Borgstrom, *Too many*, p. 291.

FIGURE 6-1

An example of development on an estuary near San Rafael, California, on San Francisco Bay. Houses and boat docks are built right on the shore; a freeway interchange has been built over the water. Dikes are shown at the lower left, and even the channels are man-made. (Photo by Aero Photographers.)

TABLE 6-1
Bioclimatic Regions of the World

Bioclimate	*Total land area (million km²)*	*Percentage of total land*
Polar humid and semihumid	8.05	5.4
Boreal humid and semihumid	23.20	15.5
Subboreal humid	7.39	4.9
Subboreal semiarid	8.10	5.4
Subboreal arid	7.04	4.7
Subtropical humid	6.24	4.2
Subtropical semiarid	8.29	5.0
Subtropical arid	9.73	6.5
Tropical humid	26.50	17.7
Tropical semiarid	16.01	10.8
Tropical arid	12.84	8.6
Glaciers	13.9	9.3
Streams and lakes	2.0	1.4

Note: 100 percent = 149.3 million km^2.
Source: L. Rodin, N. Bazilevich, N. Rozov, Productivity of the world's main ecosystems, in National Academy of Sciences, *Productivity of world ecosystems,* Washington, D.C., 1975, pp. 13–26.

TABLE 6-2
Land Classification by Vegetation

Type of vegetation	*Total land area occupied (millions km²)*	*Percentage of total land*
Tropical forest	20.3	13.6
Coniferous forest	14.6	9.8
Deciduous forest	5.7	3.8
Taiga	3.9	2.6
Semiarid grasslands	22.0	14.7
Humid grasslands	14.9	10.0
Wetlands	3.3	2.2
Cultivated (grain)	7.0	4.7
Cultivated (other)	6.8	4.6
Tundra	8.5	5.7
Desert	22.4	15.0
Glacier and perpetual frost	19.7	13.2

Source: After Edward Deevey, The human population.

TABLE 6-3
Arable and Cultivated Land and Population, Worldwide

Region	Population in 1975 (millions)	Land area (million km^2)			Cultivated area per person (hectares)	Cultivated land as % of potentially arable land
		Total	Potentially arable	Cultivated		
Africa	401	30.2	7.33	1.58	0.39	22
Asia	2255	27.3	6.28	5.18	0.23	82
Australia and New Zealand	17	8.2	1.54	0.16	0.94	10
Europe	473	4.8	1.74	1.54	0.33	89
North and Central America	316	21.1	4.66	2.39	0.76	51
South America	245	17.5	6.80	0.77	0.31	11
USSR	255	22.3	3.56	2.27	0.89	64
Total	3967	131.5	31.9	13.89	0.35	43

Note: Cultivated area is called by FAO "arable land and land under permanent crops." It includes land under crops, land temporarily fallow, temporary meadows for mowing or pasture, market and kitchen gardens, fruit trees, vines, shrubs, and rubber plantations. Within this definition there are said to be wide variations among reporting countries. The land actually harvested during any particular year is about one-half to two-thirds of the total cultivated land. Populations of some islands omitted.

Source: For population: *1975 Population Data Sheet,* Population Reference Bureau, Inc., Washington, D.C. For land: President's Science Advisory Committee, *The world food problem;* Economic Research Service, United States Department of Agriculture, Foreign agricultural economic report 298, Government Printing Office, Washington, D.C., 1974.

amount of potentially arable land on Earth to be 3.19 billion hectares.[2] This amounts to only 24 percent of the total ice-free land area but is perhaps three times the area actually planted and harvested in any given year. About 1.67 billion hectares—more than half of the estimated total—lies in the tropical areas. Warm-temperate and subtropical areas account for another 0.56 billion hectares, and cool-temperate areas account for most of the rest (0.91 billion hectares). The distribution of cultivated and potentially arable land in relation to population and area of continents is shown in Table 6-3. Most of the land classified as potentially arable but not now under cultivation is in Africa and South America.

It is easy to be misled by the foregoing estimate of potentially arable land into an overoptimistic prognosis of how much more land can be brought under cultivation. Several factors make optimism unwarranted. First, rather obviously, the best agricultural land is already being cultivated. Neither subsistence nor commercial farmers are stupid; they farm first where food can be produced with the smallest investments of labor and money (this is the definition of the best land). Most land classified as potentially arable but not now under cultivation suffers from one or more important specific defects: it may be remote, subject to erosion, steep or uneven, rocky, of short growing season, deficient in water, endowed with soils deficient in nutrients, or intractable in other respects. (In Africa, for example, tsetse flies make substantial areas uninhabitable; they carry sleeping sickness and are very difficult to eradicate.) Land with such deficiencies is called *marginal,* and the difficulty of bringing marginal land into profitable cultivation is the major reason the amount of cultivated land has in fact been expanding so slowly (only about 0.15 percent per year worldwide between 1950 and 1970).[3]

Some of the shortcomings of marginal land can of course be overcome by technology. Irrigation can supply missing water, fertilizer can supply missing nutrients, terracing can level slopes and reduce erosion—but such measures are expensive. The costs of opening new land in seven sample projects in LDCs in the early 1960s ranged from \$87 to \$2400 per hectare, and the median was \$540.[4] If the very optimistic assumption is made that in

[2]President's Science Advisory Committee, *The world food problem.*

[3]University of California Food Task Force, *A hungry world: the challenge to agriculture.*

[4]President's Science Advisory Committee, *The world food problem,* vol. 2, pp. 435–439. In 1974 the United Nations estimated that the total cost of a 20-percent expansion of land under cultivation, renovation of existing irrigated areas, and development of new irrigation schemes would cost \$90 billion. For potential gains to be exploited rapidly enough, an annual investment of between \$8 billion and \$8.5 billion would be required. (*Assessment of the world food situation, present and future,* item 8, provisional agenda, U.N. World Food Conference 1974). Since the United Nations total corresponds to a cost of only \$300 per hectare of newly cultivated land, it would appear to be a substantial underestimate.

1975 land suitable to feed four persons per hectare could be brought under cultivation for $1000/hectare, then an investment of $20 billion annually would be required to keep up with present world population growth of about 75 million per year. Of course, the greater the amount of marginal land brought under cultivation, the lower will be the quality of the remaining unused pool and the higher will be the economic costs of further increments to cultivated land.

Another basis for skepticism about the potential for expanding cultivated land is that much of the land classified as potentially arable is already in use as pasture or economically productive forest. Grazing land makes up perhaps two-thirds of the presently uncultivated but potentially arable land worldwide, and accessible forest about one-third.[5] Putting grazing land under the plow delivers a smaller net yield than opening virgin land, since the former is already producing some food. Clearing forest for cultivation increases food production at the expense of actual or potential production of timber, a versatile raw material also subject to increasing demands. (The ecological consequences of changes in land-use patterns are discussed in Chapter 11.)

Land use in the United States. With a land area of 9.16 million square kilometers (about 3.5 million square miles) and a population in 1975 of around 215 million people, the United States has an average population density slightly less than that of the world as a whole—with about 24 people per square kilometer, or 62 per square mile.[6] As noted in Chapter 5, most of these people are concentrated in urban regions on the coasts and around the Great Lakes, leaving large segments of the central United States sparsely populated (by the superficial measure of land area per person). The land area of the forty-eight contiguous states (which for some purposes is more relevant than the area including Alaska and Hawaii) is 7.69 million square kilometers, and the corresponding population density is 28 people per square kilometer—about the same as the global average.

Ownership of land in the United States is categorized in Table 6-4. The holdings of the federal government amount to more than a third of the total. Most of the federal land is grazing land and forest, controlled by the Bureau of Land Management in the Department of the Interior and by the United States Forest Service in the Department of Agriculture. Land in private ownership is about 60 percent of the total, while the original occupants of the territory now comprising the United States—tribes of American Indians—control about 2 percent. If Alaska is excluded, the fraction of territory held by the federal government falls to about 20 percent, Indian land is 3 percent, and the fraction in private hands rises to about 70 percent.[7]

TABLE 6-4
Ownership of Land in the United States (including Alaska and Hawaii)

Owner	*Area (million hectares)*	*Percentage of total*
Federal government		
Department of Interior	219	
Department of Agriculture	75	
Department of Defense	12	
Other	3	
Total federal	309	33.7
State governments	46	5.0
County and municipal governments	8	0.9
Indian tribes	20	2.2
Individuals and corporations	533	58.2
Total	916	100.0

Source: United States Department of Commerce, *Statistical abstract of the United States,* 1974, p. 199.

The uses of land in the United States around 1970 are summarized in Table 6-5. The category labeled "cropland" represents the sum of cropland actually in use as well as that which is deliberately held idle for economic or political reasons. Some 12 to 14 percent of the cropland total was idle in the early 1970s, but essentially all of it had been pressed into service by 1975.[8] Urban and transportation uses of United States territory appear

[5]Borgstrom, *Too many,* p. 299.

[6]The area given is without lakes and rivers; with them, the figure is 9.37 million square kilometers. (United States Department of Commerce, *Statistical abstract,* 1975), p. 5.

[7]C. B. Hunt, *Physiography of the United States* (W. H. Freeman and Company, San Francisco, 1967), p. 121.

[8]Lester R. Brown, The world food prospect; see also Chapter 7.

TABLE 6-5
Uses of Land in the United States

Use	*Land area (million hectares)*	*Percentage of total*
Pasture and rangeland	360	39.3
Ungrazed forest	192	20.9
Cropland	155	16.9
Desert, swamp, barren, tundra (limited use)	110	12.0
Urban and transportation	27	2.9
Military	12	1.3
National wildlife refuges	12	1.3
National parks	12	1.3
Farm buildings and farm roads	11	1.2
Withdrawn from other uses by surface mining	2	0.2
Transmission line rights of way	1	0.1
Other	24	2.6

Note: The table, which includes Alaska and Hawaii, does not include lakes and reservoirs.

Sources: United States Department of Commerce, *Statistical abstract of the United States,* 1974, p. 600; National Commission on Materials Policy, *Material needs and the environment today and tomorrow,* chapter 7.

rather minor, as they involve less than 3 percent of the total land area, but it should be noted that some expanding urban centers are located in the midst of or adjacent to the best agricultural lands. The nation can ill afford to lose those prime croplands. California, where the problem of such encroachment has been particularly severe, had lost about 700,000 hectares of prime agricultural land to cities, suburbs, and highways by 1975. And of California's 8.2 million hectares of remaining prime and "potentially prime" agricultural land, another 400,000 hectares were zoned for urban development by 1985.[9] The loss of arable land to urbanization nationwide has been estimated at 5.1 million hectares between 1958 and 1974.[10]

Soil

The nature and quantity of vegetation that can be grown on a given piece of land depend strongly on the characteristics of the soil. Study of the properties and distribution of soil types is therefore essential both for an understanding of existing patterns of vegetation and for determining strategies and prospects for success in increasing the yield of plant materials used by human society.

Soil functions as a source and as a storage reservoir of water and mineral nutrients for plants, as a medium in which chemical transformations influencing the availability of those nutrients takes place, and as an anchor for the support of terrestrial as well as many aquatic plants. In composition, it is a mixture of inorganic minerals, organic matter, soil animals and microorganisms, gases, and, of course, moisture.[11]

Soil origins and structure. As described in Chapter 2, the main source of the inorganic particles in soil is the weathering of the various types of rock—igneous, sedimentary, metamorphic—by exposure near Earth's surface to temperature changes; the physical action of ice, water, and roots; and chemical attack by rainwater, surface water, and atmospheric gases. Uplifting of unconsolidated sediments from the seafloor is another, rarer source of soil materials. These sources of the mineral components of soil are called *parent materials;* the parent materials can be either *residual* (meaning the soil is formed where the weathering takes place) or *transported* (meaning the materials have been moved to the place of soil formation by the action of wind, water, ice, gravity, or a combination of these). *Alluvial* is the term given to soils deposited by river flow. *Colluvial* refers to soils whose parent materials were deposited by landslides.

Most soils are not uniform in vertical profile but rather are characterized by zones called *horizons.* The uppermost layer or zone is called the *A horizon.* It is the home of most of the soil organisms and the location of the greatest abundance of roots. It has usually been somewhat depleted of soluble substances by leaching. The next zone proceeding downward is the *B horizon.* It receives downward-moving minerals leached from above and, often, upward-migrating substances from weathered parent materials below; therefore it is called the zone of accumulation. The *C horizon* consists of the weathered rock material. The bedrock below, usually but not always the true parent material, is the *D horizon.*

[9]California Land Use Task Force, *The California land,* Chapter 3.
[10]University of California Food Task Force, *A hungry world,* p. 78.

[11]The best introductory consideration of soil we have found (on which much of this section is based) is J. Janick, R. Schery, F. Woods, and V. Ruttan, *Plant science,* chapters 12 and 16.

In soil studies more detailed than our treatment here, the horizons are often subdivided by the addition of subscripts running 1 to 3, top to bottom, (that is, A_1, A_2, A_3). In that notation, the fresh dead organic matter (called *litter*) is the A_{00} horizon; and the partially decomposed organic matter (called *duff*), just above the A_1 horizon, is the A_0 horizon.

Soils in which the layered structure is well developed and distinct are called *zoned* or *normal;* those without this well-developed vertical profile are called *azonal.* Alluvial and colluvial soils are often azonal.

Another important characteristic of soil is *texture* (meaning the size of the individual mineral particles). An international classification system defines particles with diameter less than 0.002 millimeters as *clay,* those with diameters between 0.002 and 0.02 millimeters as *silt,* and particles between 0.02 and 2 millimeters in diameter as *sand.*[12] The term *loam* is used to describe mixtures of the different size classes of soil particles. A standard classification scheme based on the proportions of clay, silt, and sand in soil is illustrated in Figure 6-2.

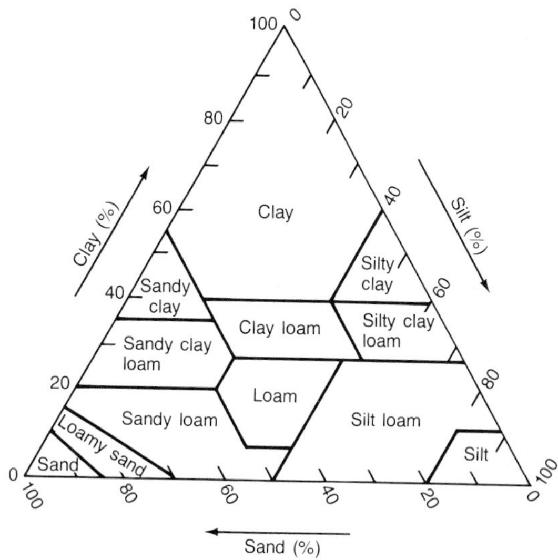

FIGURE 6-2

Soil classification by texture. (From Janick et al. Data from U.S. Department of Agriculture.)

Soil texture influences the rate at which water percolates through soil and the amount of water a soil can contain. Coarse soils are characterized by rapid infiltration, and hence low surface runoff, but they cannot retain much water. The fine-textured clays are penetrated by water only slowly but have a high storage capacity. The *pore space* in soil, which is filled in varying proportions by water and air, is typically around 50 percent in many kinds of soils; what is more important than the total volume of the pore space is the characteristic size of individual pore spaces. Few large pores make a much less satisfactory soil than many small ones. Soil organisms and organic matter are crucial in maintaining the better situation by preventing excessive coagulation of soil particles into large clods.

Soil organic matter. Dead organic matter in soil not only influences pore size, but itself serves as a sponge that soaks up and retains moisture. Through its decomposition by bacteria, it acts also as a source of carbon dioxide, water, and mineral elements. Certain constituents of dead organic matter, such as waxes, fats, lignins, and some proteinaceous materials, resist decomposition and are converted instead into the dark colloidal substance called *humus.* (A colloidal substance consists of particles larger than molecules but small enough to remain suspended in solution.) The physical and chemical properties of humus affect the character of soil out of proportion to its fraction by weight, in part because of the large surface-to-volume ratio associated with particles of such small size. The fraction by weight of dead organic matter in soil is typically in the range of 0.4 to 1.1 percent.[13]

Living soil organisms (other than the roots of plants) make up an even smaller fraction of the mass of soil (typically 0.1 percent or less).[14] (In absolute terms this is not a small quantity, however, as it amounts to several tons of living organisms per hectare.) These include: bacteria and algae, whose critical roles in nutrient cycles are described in Chapter 3; fungi, which perform some of the same functions as bacteria in nutrient cycles, as well

[12] See Janick et al., *Plant science,* p. 219, for a more complete classification, ranging up to "boulder" (diameter greater than 256 millimeters).

[13] P. Sanchez and S. Buol, Soils of the tropics and the world food crisis.

[14] Janick et al., *Plant science,* p. 224.

as being the principal producers of humus; and larger organisms such as mites, millipedes, insects, and worms, which physically cultivate the soil and help break down organic litter (see also Chapter 11).

Soil chemistry. The chemistry of a soil is governed in large measure by the properties of its clay particles and the similarly tiny particles of humus. Clay particles are platelike, with a layered internal structure that leaves negative electric charges arrayed on the surfaces of the plates. Humus particles are also negatively charged on their exteriors. These electrical properties account for the characteristic of soil exchange capacity (the ability to retain and exchange cations such as H^+, Ca^{++}, Mg^{++}, K^+, and Na^+).

This function is crucial in governing soil fertility. Without the negative charges on particles of clay and humus, the positively charged nutrient cations released to the soil by the decay of organic matter or added to the soil in fertilizer would quickly be leached away, out of reach of plant roots. Bound to the negative charges on clay and humus, however, those ions are made available to plants gradually when they are replaced at the negatively charged sites by hydrogen ions from the soil. There is actually a replacement heirarchy—hydrogen, calcium, magnesium, potassium, sodium—in which each ion listed tends to displace any that appears to its right in the list, if the two are present in equal amount; hydrogen tends to replace all of the metallic ions. If a particular cation is present in very large quantities, however, it can even replace ions to its left in the heirarchy by sheer force of numbers (that is, by mass action, to use chemical terminology).

The magnitude of exchange capacity is merely a matter of how many negatively charged sites are available in a soil. The unit of measure is milliequivalents per 100 grams, which means the number of milligrams of hydrogen ion (H^+) that will combine with 100 grams of dry soil. Different types of clay have widely varying exchange capacities (in the range of from 10 to 100 milliequivalents/100 g), whereas humus has the greatest of all (from 150 to 300 milliequivalents/100 g).[15] This chemical role of humus is perhaps even more crucial than the roles humus plays in maintaining soil texture and retaining water. The importance of all three functions provides ample reason for viewing with alarm the depletion of soil humus by certain agricultural practices (see Chapter 11).

A major source of hydrogen ions in the soil is the production of carbonic acid from the solution of carbon dioxide in water. Another source is nitric and sulfuric acid added by polluted rainfall or formed from nitrogen and sulfur compounds produced by decomposition of organic matter or added in fertilizer. Yet another is organic acids exuded by plant roots or produced by decomposition. Excessive concentrations of hydrogen ions (indicated by low pH—that is, strongly acidic soil) replace nutrient cations on clay and humus colloids faster than those nutrients can be taken up by plants; the result is that the nutrients are leached away. Acidic soils are common in humid climates. A shortage of hydrogen ions (high pH—strongly alkaline soil), on the other hand, can leave some nutrient ions too tightly bound to clay and humus to be absorbed by plants. Other nutrients, such as iron and manganese, become trapped in compounds that are extremely insoluble in basic solutions.

Crops differ rather widely in the pH ranges they tolerate. Most of the grains flourish best in slightly acidic soil, potatoes and berries in quite acidic soil, alfalfa and asparagus in neutral soil.[16] When soil is too acidic for the crops desired, it is common practice to neutralize the soil by adding lime.

Classification of soils. Differences in soils around the world arise from the mineral compositions of the parent materials and from differing climatic conditions, which together influence the organic and inorganic processes of soil development. Several major types of soil-forming regimes have been identified: the main ones are podzolization, laterization, calcification, gleization, and salinization.

Podzolization is the set of processes associated in its extreme form with cool climates, abundant precipitation, and acid upper soil layers strongly leached of mineral nutrients and the oxides of iron and aluminum. The nutrients, oxides, and humus accumulate in the deeper

[15] Janick et al., *Plant science*, p. 222; see also A. N. Strahler and A. H. Strahler, *Environmental geoscience*, Chapter 11.

[16] Janick et al., *Plant science*, p. 309.

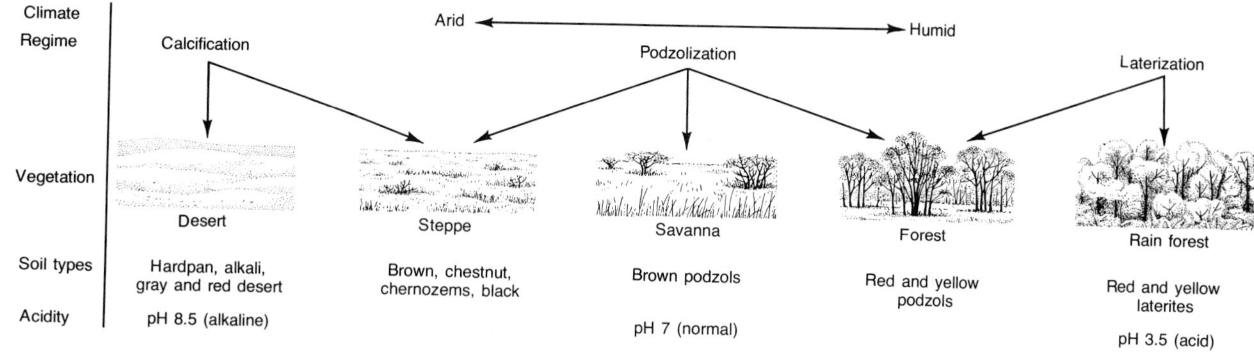

FIGURE 6-3

Relation of soil-forming regimes, vegetation, and soil types. (Adapted from Janick et al., 1974.)

layers. Fungi are the main soil-forming organisms. Those soils are characteristic of northern forests, although they exist in some circumstances well into temperate and subtropical regions.

Laterization is a set of processes associated with the humid tropics and subtropics. High mean temperatures in these regions permit sustained and rapid bacterial action, which minimizes the accumulation of plant litter and humus. In the absence of the organic acids associated with humus, the soil is neutral, rendering the oxides of iron and aluminum relatively insoluble; those oxides accumulate in the upper soil horizons as hard clays and rocklike material called *laterite* (from the Latin for brick), a mixture of $Fe_2O_3 \cdot nH_2O$ and $Al_2O_3 \cdot H_2O$.

Calcification occurs in climates where evapotranspiration exceeds precipitation. There is little leaching of the metallic cations, and microbial activity is slow, so the soils tend to be alkaline and rich in humus. Calcium carbonate in solution is carried upward from the water table by capillary action in the season of little surface moisture and is left in the upper soil horizons in solid form when the water evaporates.

Gleization is the set of processes characteristic of poorly drained environments in cool or cold climates. The low temperatures permit heavy accumulation of organic matter, and the excessive wetting produces a sticky clay underneath.

Salinization is the regime characterized by accumulation of highly soluble salts in the soil. This situation arises naturally from poor drainage in regions of low precipitation and high temperatures (deserts), and it can be brought about by faulty agricultural practices—irrigating too parsimoniously in dry climates, or using salt-laden irrigation water. Soils in the salinization regime are weakly to strongly alkaline.[17]

The geographical boundaries separating the spheres of influence of the different soil-forming regimes are often not distinct. An enormous variety of soils results from variations within regimes and from overlaps between regimes, and a quite complicated classification scheme and taxonomy for soils (the United States comprehensive system of soil classification) has been devised to help soil scientists cope with this diversity.[18] Figure 6-3 is a schematic illustration of how a few of the principal *soil types* emerge from the soil-forming regimes. Characteristics of a somewhat broader selection of soil types encountered in the literature of soil science and biogeography are summarized in Box 6-1.[19]

A somewhat more utilitarian soil classification scheme, widely used in the United States, is based on the capability of a soil to sustain various uses—the categories run from Class I (the best soils for agriculture) to Class VIII (suitable only for recreation and wildlife).[20]

Exhaustion, erosion, and regeneration. The limitations in the extent and quality of the soils with which civilization began would be serious enough,

[17]For more extensive treatments of these regimes, see Strahler and Strahler, *Environmental*, chapter 12; Janick et al., *Plant science*, chapter 12; C. B. Hunt, *Physiography*, chapter 6.

[18]See Janick et al., *Plant science*, pp. 232–235, for a summary, or United States Soil Conservation Service, *Soil classification: A comprehensive system* (Government Printing Office, Washington, D.C., 1964) for the full taxonomy.

[19]See also H. W. Menard, *Geology, resources, and society*, chapter 13.

[20]Janick et al., *Plant science*, pp. 234–236.

BOX 6-1 Characteristics of Common Soils

	Pedalfers (soils of humid regions)
Tundra soil	Dark-brown, peaty layer over gray horizons mottled with rust; substrate permanently frozen. *Climate:* frigid, humid. *Vegetation:* lichens, mosses, herbs, shrubs. *Process:* gleization (development of organic-rich, sticky, compact, clayey layer due to excessive wetting).
Alpine meadow	Dark-brown, organic-rich layer grading down at 30 to 60 centimeters to gray and rusty soil, streaked and mottled. *Climate:* cool temperate to frigid. *Vegetation:* grasses, sedges, herbs. *Process:* gleization, some calcification (deposition of calcium carbonate).
Bog and half-bog	Brown, dark-brown, or black peaty material over soils of mineral matter mottled gray and rust. *Climate:* cool to tropical; generally humid. *Vegetation:* swamp, forest, sedges, or grasses. *Process:* gleization.
Podzol, brown podzol, gray-brown podzol	Leaf litter over a humus-rich layer over a whitish-gray to grayish-brown leached layer; B horizon clayey and brown. Acid. *Climate:* cool, temperate, humid. *Vegetation:* northern forests, coniferous and/or deciduous. *Process:* podzolization (bases—Al and Fe—leached more than silica from A horizon and accumulated in B horizon).
Red and yellow podzol	Thin, dark organic layer at surface over yellow-gray or gray-brown leached layer 15 to 90 centimeters thick, over clayey B horizon over parent material mottled red, yellow, and gray. *Climate:* warm temperate to tropical humid. *Vegetation:* coniferous forest or mixed deciduous and coniferous. *Process:* podzolization superimposed on lateritization (silica leached more than the bases).
Prairie and reddish prairie	Brown in the north; reddish-brown toward the south. Grades down to lighter-colored parent material with no horizon of carbonate accumulation. *Climate:* cool temperate to warm temperate, humid. *Vegetation:* tall grass. *Process:* weak podzolization.
	Pedocals (soils of arid regions)
Chernozem	Black to gray-brown, crumbly soil to a depth of 90 to 120 centimeters, grading through lighter color to a layer of carbonate accumulation. *Climate:* subhumid, temperate to cool. *Vegetation:* tall grass. *Process:* calcification (accumulation of carbonates in lower horizons).
Chestnut, brown, reddish chestnut, and reddish brown	Brown to black surface layer in north; reddish in south; lighter color at depth and grading down to layer of carbonate accumulation. Chestnut thinner than chernozem, and brown thinner than chestnut. *Climate:* semiarid; cool to hot. *Vegetation:* mostly short grasses in north; grasses and shrub in south. *Process:* calcification.
Desert, sierozem, red desert	Light gray or brown in north; reddish in south; low in organic matter; carbonate layer generally within 30 centimeters of the surface. *Climate:* arid, cool to hot. *Vegetation:* mostly desert shrubs. *Process:* calcification.
	Other soils
Rendzina	Dark-gray or black, organic-rich, surface layers over soft light gray or white calcareous material derived from chalk, soft limestone, or marl. *Climate:* variable. *Vegetation:* mostly grassland. *Process:* the lime in these soils is derived from the parent materials.
Laterite	Thin organic layer over reddish, strongly leached soil, generally clayey and enriched in hydrous alumina or iron oxide or both; low in silica; generally many feet thick. *Climate:* tropical wet. *Vegetation:* mostly forest. *Process:* lateritization (see Red and Yellow Podzol).
Saline and alkaline	Soils in which salts including alkali have accumulated, generally in poorly drained areas. *Climate:* variable, but commonly arid or semiarid. *Vegetation:* salt-tolerant species or lacking. *Process:* salinization or alkalization (salts deposited in soil as a result of evaporation).

Source: Hunt, *Physiography of the United States.*

considering the demands that a growing population is placing on this resource. Those limitations are aggravated, however, by the loss of needed soil by urbanization, by erosion, and by the depletion or exhaustion of the fertility of some soils.

Depletion of soil nutrients and humus need not follow from intensive cropping, as demonstrated by the continued fertility of rice paddies in Asia that have been cultivated continuously for thousands of years. That success has been due to several factors: the high clay content of the soil, the annual augmentation of the alluvial topsoil in the paddies by silt eroded from hilltops, the nitrogen fixation by blue-green algae in the flooded paddies, and the practice of returning human and animal waste to the soils from which the nutrients therein came.[21] Intensive cultivation without either natural or artificial augmentation of nutrients can only exhaust soil fertility, however, and even the use of inorganic fertilizers alone does not prevent the depletion of the humus (see also Chapter 11).[22] The practical application of the detailed study of soils is to discover both the potential and the limitations of different soil types for the production of vegetation, and the procedures appropriate to using each type as a permanent or renewable resource rather than as a "mine" to be exhausted and abandoned.

Perhaps even more serious than urbanization and loss of fertility as a global threat to soils is erosion (the removal of the body of the soil itself by the action of wind and, especially, water). Cultivation of soil increases the natural rate of erosion, even when it is conducted properly on good land. Data from the United States Department of Agriculture indicate that erosion rates on cultivated land may be 100 times those on forested land receiving the same rainfall.[23] One of the most careful analyses of erosion in the United States and worldwide suggests that the transport of sediment from the land to the sea has increased more than threefold in the United States over the prehuman rate and by a factor of about 2.5 worldwide.[24] (The study estimated the sediment loads in the 1960s as 180 metric tons per year per average square kilometer of ice-free land globally and 250 metric tons per square kilometer per year in the United States.) The map in Figure 6-4 indicates the cumulative toll erosion has taken in the forty-eight contiguous states.

Loss of soil by erosion is a significant problem for the United States and other industrial nations, but it is worse by far in the poor countries. There even the modest degree of control exerted in the United States by the Soil Conservation Service is often missing, and the pressure of rapid population growth makes itself felt in overgrazing, deforestation for firewood, and the clearing of steep slopes for cultivation. The result has been an appalling increase in rates of erosion both by wind (primarily in desert lands) and by water, precisely in those parts of the world that can least afford the loss.[25] We return to the intertwined problems of cultivation practices, climate, and the loss of soil or soil fertility in Chapter 11.

The rate at which lost soil can be regenerated by natural processes varies enormously, depending on climate, other factors influencing biological activity, and availability of inorganic raw materials. Under very favorable circumstances, in which abundant new material is provided in the form of windborne or waterborne sediment or volcanic ash, a foot of soil may form in as little as from 50 to 100 years.[26] In the more common situation, in which new soil must be formed from parent rocks, the time scale is more likely to be in the range of from 200 to 1000 years per centimeter of soil—perhaps 10,000 years or more for a foot of soil.[27] In most circumstances, then, the loss of soil is irreversible on a time scale of practical human interest.

WATER

"Water is the best of all things," said the Greek poet Pindar. It is also, in the broad sense, a renewable resource, continually reprocessed and delivered to the land by the hydrologic cycle described in Chapter 2.

The central role of water in sustaining the life processes of the biosphere has been discussed in Chapter

[21] Menard, *Geology*, pp. 361–362

[22] W. A. Albrecht, Physical, chemical, and biochemical changes in the soil community.

[23] Menard, *Geology*, pp. 359.

[24] S. Judson, Erosion of the land.

[25] Erik P. Eckholm has documented this much-underrated aspect of the global predicament in a brilliant book, *Losing ground*.

[26] Menard, *Geology*, pp. 364–365.

[27] Strahler and Strahler, *Environmental*, p. 275.

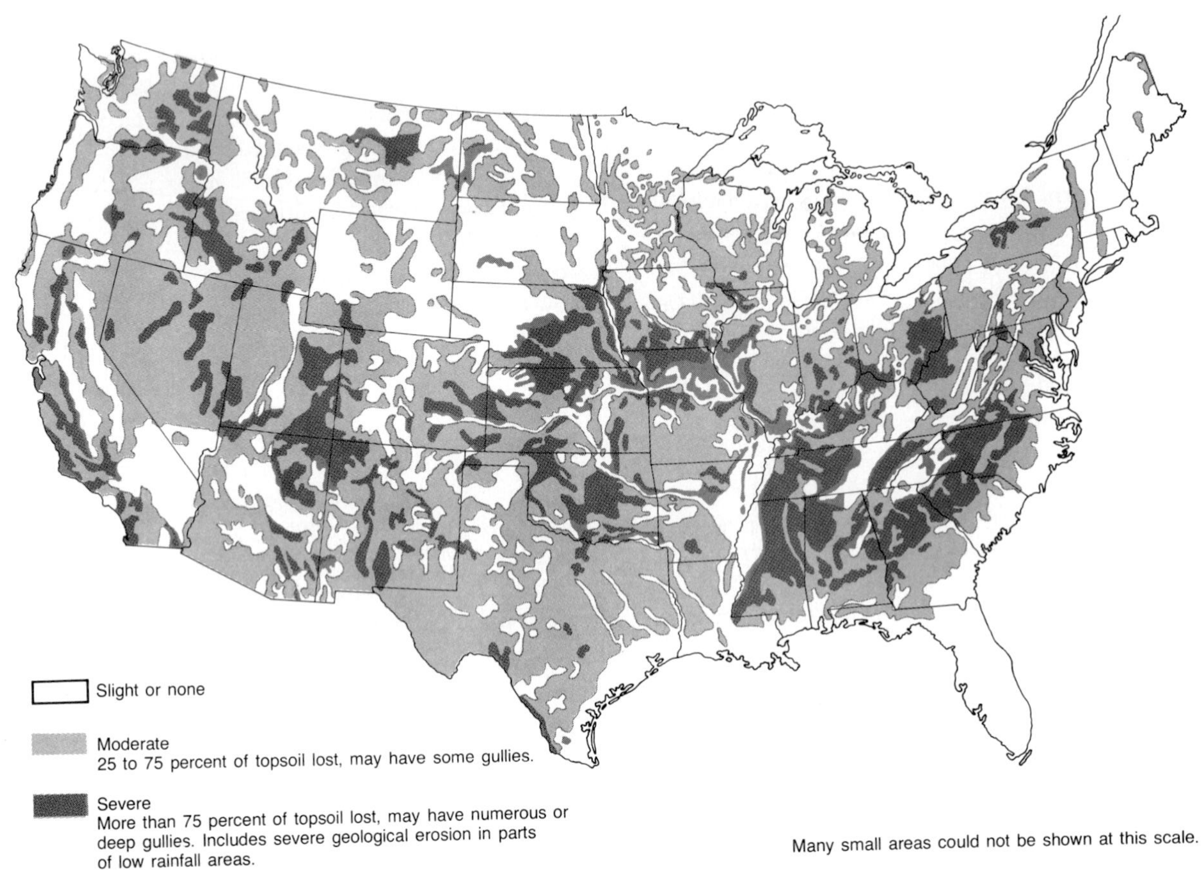

FIGURE 6-4

Cumulative effects of erosion in the United States. (Adapted from Hunt, 1974.)

3, and, from a different point of view, in the foregoing section of text on soil. Here we take up the availability and functions of water as it is used directly as a resource by civilization: for changing the natural pattern of biological productivity through irrigation; for drinking, cooking, washing, and bathing; as an industrial raw material and coolant; as a flow resource for diluting and removing waste materials, turning hydroelectric generators, and providing transportation and recreation.

We survey here the availability of water for these purposes, present and projected patterns of water use and supply, and the nature and costs of large-scale water-supply technology. Pollution of water supplies by the activities of civilization is taken up in Chapter 10.

Availability

As we discussed in Chapter 2, the amount of water available for runoff on the surface and underground (including not only what reaches the oceans but also net recharge, if any, of surface reservoirs and underground aquifers) is simply the difference between what falls as precipitation and what returns to the atmosphere as evapotranspiration. The annual runoff from major regions of the world is summarized in Table 6-6. (There is a range of about ±25 percent in the figures published by various scholars; the estimates in Table 6-6 fall at the high end of the range.) The runoff of the forty-eight contiguous states is about 1700 cubic kilometers per year,

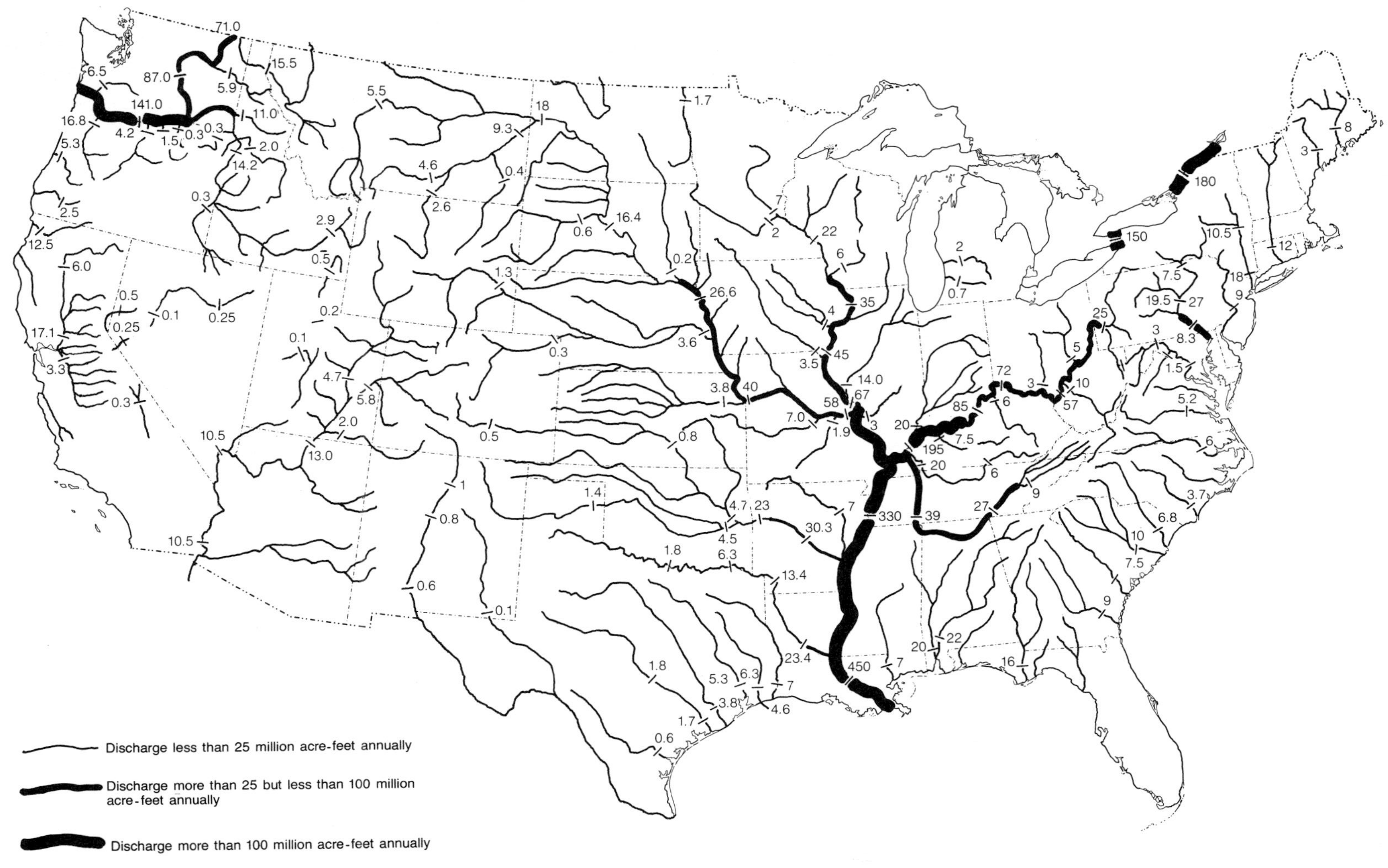

FIGURE 6-5

Flow of rivers in the United States. (millions of acre-feet per year). (Adapted from Hunt, 1974.)

TABLE 6-6
Freshwater Runoff in Major Regions of the World

Region	Annual runoff (km³)	Annual runoff (acre feet, millions)
Africa	7,900	6,400
Asia*	8,000	6,500
Australia	390	320
Europe*	1,200	970
North and Central America	8,200	6,600
South America	16,000	13,000
USSR	4,200	3,600

*Excluding USSR.
Source: Calculated from Study of Man's Impact on Climate, *Inadvertent climate modification,* p. 97; and I. P. Gerasimov, D. L. Armand, and K. M. Yefron, eds., *Natural resources of the Soviet Union,* p. 15.

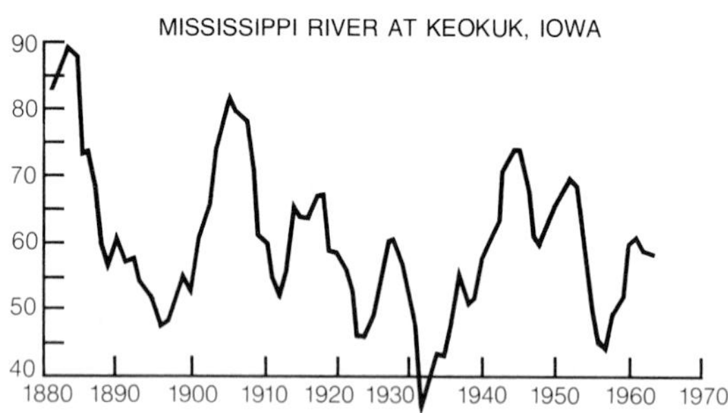

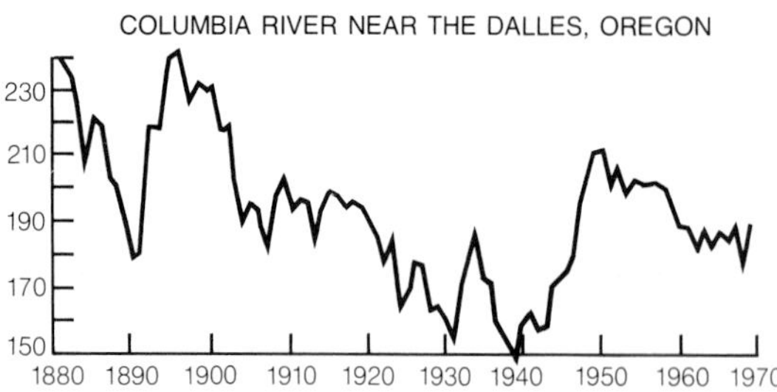

FIGURE 6-6

Historical variation in mean discharge of two American rivers. Data are five-year running averages, plotted at one-year intervals, of mean discharge rate in thousands of cubic feet per second (cfs). One thousand cfs = 2.45 million cubic meters per day = 723,000 acre-feet per year. (Adapted from Leopold, 1974.)

only a modest fraction of the total for North America and Central America together. Including Alaska and Hawaii, the United States runoff is about 2000 cubic kilometers per year.[28]

Dividing the runoff figures by the human population gives what appears at first glance to be a reassuring picture. For example, the runoff for the forty-eight contiguous states works out to about 4700 billion liters per day, or roughly 22,000 liters per inhabitant per day. The global figure is around 31,000 liters per person per day, based on a population of 4 billion.

Geographical and temporal distribution. These often-cited figures are highly misleading, however, because the water is very unevenly distributed, both geographically and in time. Worldwide, much of the runoff is in sparsely populated regions, as exemplified by the vast drainages of northern Canada (the Mackenzie and other rivers), Siberia (the Ob, Yenisey, and Lena), and the jungle of the Amazon. In the United States, the western half of the land area gets only about a third of the runoff.[29] (Flows of major United States rivers appear in Figure 6-5.)

Even more troublesome than the inconvenient geographical distribution of runoff is its uneven distribution in time. Floods and droughts, after all, are age-old problems with water supply. Difficulties are caused both by the generally predictable annual cycle of runoff, wherein much of the total flow is concentrated in a few months of wet season or spring melt, and by unpredictable year-to-year variations in the exact timing of this pattern and in the total annual flow. The fraction of the total runoff concentrated in a flood period lasting two or three months is from 40 to 70 percent over much of the United States.[30] The problem of variation in total annual flow from year to year in two of America's major rivers is illustrated in Figure 6-6.

A large variation in runoff from month to month and from day to day means that the minimum daily flow that

[28]For various runoff estimates, see Menard, *Geology,* chapter 17; Strahler and Strahler, *Environmental,* chapter 13; Hunt, *Physiography,* chapters 5 and 9; T. Van Hylckama, Water resources. One cubic kilometer (a billion cubic meters) is 264 billion gallons or 810,000 acre-feet.

[29]C. Murray and E. Reeves, *Estimated use of water in the United States in 1970.*

[30]Hunt, *Physiography,* p. 75.

BOX 6-2 Availability and Dependability: How Much Water Can One Count On?

Several indicators are in widespread use that represent how much water is *usually* available or how much can be made available in theory. (Considerable confusion has been engendered by the inconsistent use of terminology and definitions for these measures in the literature on water.) For example, the United States Geological Survey presents data for the *annual flow exceeded 9 years out of 10.* This figure amounts to about 1000 cubic kilometers for the forty-eight contiguous states as a whole (about 60 percent of the *average* annual flow), but in some drainage basins within the forty-eight states (those of great variability) the figure is less than a third of the average flow.* (It may be useful to ponder the difference between average flow and flow exceeded 9 years out of 10 for the individual rivers in Figure 6-6.)

A different indicator is *dependable flow,* which according to the water experts at Resources for the Future (a respected private think tank in Washington, D.C., which deals with resource questions) means the flow that is equaled or exceeded every day of every year.** Because of seasonal and year-to-year variations, this would be a very small fraction of annual flow indeed, without society's intervention in the form of dams to store water and regulate flows. As it is, figures for dependable flow by this definition are rarely encountered. One finds, instead, figures for the flow available 50 percent of the time or 90 percent of the time or 95 percent of the time (that is, flow rates equaled or exceeded 50 out of 100 days, and so forth). For example, the flow available 50 percent of the time for the 48 contiguous states, with the storage facilities of the mid-1950s, was 2.2 billion cubic meters per day—less than half of the daily *average* obtained by dividing the average annual flow by 365.† The flow available 95 percent of the time, according to the same analysis, was only 0.35 billion cubic meters per day, or about 7 percent of the average runoff. (The reservoir storage associated with these availabilities was 220 cubic kilometers, or 280 million acre-feet.) As noted in the text, the storage system and available flows had been much improved by 1970.

Finally, Resources for the Future defines *maximum dependable flow* as the average daily flow (the annual flow divided by 365) minus the evaporation losses that would occur in a system of reservoirs large enough to spread the flow out completely evenly over a year. If dependable supply is defined as above, this is literally the largest value it could have. Recent estimates of the maximum dependable flow for the forty-eight states are around 3.6 million cubic meters per day, or 80 percent of the average daily flow. In other words, evaporation losses from a system of reservoirs extensive enough to parcel out United States runoff uniformly over the year would amount to 20 percent of the runoff.

*C. Murray and E. Reeves, *Estimated use of water in the United States.*

**H. Landsberg, L. Fischman, and J. Fisher, *Resources in America's future,* p. 379.

†Landsberg, Fischman, and Fisher, *Resources,* p. 380.

can be counted on year-round—or even most of the time—is much smaller than the average daily flow calculated by dividing the yearly figure by 365 (see Box 6-2). To even out the flow by catching floodwaters and releasing them during dry spells, civilization has strung dams along most of the world's major rivers. As the network of dams grows more extensive and the associated reservoirs grow larger, the dependable flow becomes a bigger fraction of the average flow. The flow available 98 percent of the time (98 days out of 100) in the forty-eight contiguous states in 1970 was about 1.5 billion cubic meters per day (about a third of the average flow).[31]

It is important to recognize that increases in available flow achieved by means of reservoirs are bought at the expense of increased loss by evaporation, because of the larger surface area of the reservoirs. In other words, regularity increases; total flow decreases. This problem of evaporation is especially severe in the southwestern United States and other arid regions. The evaporative loss at Lake Mead on the Colorado River, alone, was found to be 1 cubic kilometer per year (about 4500 liters for every person in the United States),[32] and losses behind Egypt's Aswân High Dam have far exceeded initial estimates.

[31]R. G. Ridker, Future water needs and supplies.

[32]J. Hirschleifer, J. DeHaven, and J. Milliman, *Water supply,* p. 16.

BOX 6-3 Sources and Effects of Dissolved Constituents and Physical Properties of Natural Water

Constituent or physical property	*Source or cause*	*Significance*
Silica (SiO_2)	Dissolved from practically all rocks and soils, usually 1 to 30 ppm	Forms hard scale in pipes and boilers and on blades of steam turbines.
Iron (Fe)	Dissolved from most rocks and soils; also derived from iron pipes. More than 1 or 2 ppm of soluble iron in surface water usually indicates acid wastes from mine drainage or other sources.	On exposure to air, iron in groundwater oxidizes to reddish-brown sediment. More than about 0.3 ppm stains laundry and utensils. Objectionable for food processing. Federal drinking water standards state that iron and manganese together should not exceed 0.3 ppm. Larger quantities cause unpleasant taste and favor growth of iron bacteria.
Calcium (Ca) and magnesium (Mg)	Dissolved from most soils and rocks, but especially from limestone, dolomite, and gypsum.	Cause most of the hardness and scale-forming properties of water. Waters low in calcium and magnesium are desired in electroplating, tanning, dyeing, and textile manufacturing.
Sodium (Na) and potassium (K)	Dissolved from most rocks and soils.	Large amounts, in combination with chloride, give a salty taste. Sodium salts may cause foaming in steam boilers, and a high sodium ratio may limit the use of water for irrigation.
Bicarbonate (HCO_3) and carbonate (CO_3)	Action of carbon dioxide in water on carbonate rocks.	Produce alkalinity. Bicarbonates of calcium and magnesium decompose in steam boilers and hot-water facilities to form scale and release corrosive carbon dioxide gas. In combination with calcium and magnesium cause carbonate hardness.
Sulfate (SO_4)	Dissolved from many rocks and soils.	Sulfate in water containing calcium forms hard scale in steam boilers. Federal drinking water standards recommend that the sulfate content not exceed 250 ppm.

Building a system of water storage and regulation that can deal with year-to-year variations in total runoff is vastly more difficult than evening out the peaks and valleys within a single year, because a much larger amount of water would have to be stored. Even determining the average annual flow can be a difficult and precarious business, as the famous case of the Colorado River Compact illustrates. The compact, signed in 1922, divided up the rights to Colorado River water among seven contending states (Mexico was added later), based on the supposition that the average annual flow at Lees Ferry would be 22.8 billion cubic meters. (The treaty allocated absolute amounts of water, not percentages.) The estimate of the available flow was based on the record before 1922. Unfortunately for the effectiveness of the compact, a long dry spell was then entered; the average flow at Lees Ferry was 16 billion cubic meters per year in the period between 1930 and 1964, and it may well not return in this century to the value assumed by the compact in 1922.[33]

Groundwater. Much cheaper than building reservoirs to even out the variations of surface runoff is the time-honored technique of falling back on natural underground water storage—groundwater—in times of low surface flows. Reservoirs of groundwater (aquifers) are recharged naturally by seepage from the surface and underground flows at rates that depend on the permeability of surrounding rock and soil. Generally the residence time of groundwater is thousands of years, so

[33]See, for example, Menard, *Geology*, p. 494.

Constituent or physical property	*Source or cause*	*Significance*
Chloride (Cl)	Dissolved from rocks and soils; present in sewage and found in large amounts in ancient brines, seawater, and industrial brines.	In large amounts in combination with sodium gives salty taste. In large quantities increases the corrosiveness of water. Federal drinking water standards recommend that the chloride content not exceed 250 ppm.
Dissolved solids	Chiefly mineral constituents dissolved from rocks and soils, but includes organic matter.	Federal drinking water standards recommend that the dissolved solids not exceed 500 ppm. Waters containing more than 1000 ppm dissolved solids are unsuitable for many purposes.
Hardness as $CaCO_3$ (calcium carbonate)	In most water, nearly all the hardness is due to calcium and magnesium.	Consumes soap before a lather will form. Deposits soap curd on bathtubs. Hard water forms scale in boilers, water heaters, and pipes. Hardness equivalent to the bicarbonate and carbonate is called carbonate hardness. Any hardness in excess of that is called noncarbonate hardness.
Acidity or alkalinity (hydrogen ion concentration, pH)	Acids, acid-generating salts, and free carbon dioxide lower pH. Carbonates, bicarbonates, hydroxides and phosphates, silicates, and borates raise pH.	A pH of 7.0 indicates neutrality in a solution. Values greater than 7.0 denote increasing alkalinity; values less than 7.0 indicate increasing acidity. Corrosiveness of water generally increases with decreasing pH.
Dissolved oxygen (O_2)	Dissolved in water from air and from oxygen given off in photosynthesis by aquatic plants.	Dissolved oxygen increases the palatability of water. Under average stream conditions, 4 ppm is usually necessary to maintain a varied fish fauna in good condition. For industrial uses, zero dissolved oxygen is desirable to inhibit corrosion.

Source: Hunt, *Physiography of the United States.*

recharge of seriously depleted aquifers is very slow.[34]

When the rate of withdrawal of groundwater from an aquifer exceeds the rate of recharge over a period of time, the water table falls. The cost of drilling wells and of pumping out the water increases rapidly with the depth of the well, so if a water table falls too far below the surface, extracting the water becomes altogether uneconomical. In practical terms, the water in such cases is a nonrenewable resource that has been mined out. This has happened in parts of Arizona and is underway on the high plains of Texas, where extensive use of groundwater has dropped the water table as much as 30 meters.[35] Smaller but still serious declines in water tables have occurred in other parts of the United States and the world. Such declines not only represent the long-term loss of the accessible groundwater resource, but they also can lead to the reduction of surface streamflow, the drying-up of ecologically important ponds and bogs, the intrusion of salt water into freshwater aquifers in coastal regions, and subsidence.[36]

Water quality. An integral part of the issue of availability of water is its quality. Quite independent of the pollutants that have been added to water by civilization (which are discussed in Chapter 10), the quality of water varies widely because of natural factors. Aspects

[34]Menard, *Geology,* p. 483; Strahler and Strahler, *Environmental,* pp. 305–316.

[35]Van Hylckama, Water, p. 153; Menard, *Geology,* p. 491.

[36]Strahler and Strahler, *Environmental,* pp. 312–313; J. F. Poland, Land subsidence in the western U.S., in *Focus on environmental geology,* R. W. Tank, ed., Oxford University Press, London 1973.

of quality that determine the usefulness, or even the usability, of water in various industrial, domestic, and agricultural applications include color, odor, taste, temperature, oxygen content, dissolved salts, and burden of suspended organic and inorganic material. Many of these aspects are interrelated, of course.

The most widespread cause of natural water-quality problems is dissolved salts. Although rainwater itself is almost pure, its passage over and through soil and rock formations causes the water to accumulate a burden of dissolved mineral material whose chemical composition depends in detail on the specific types of soil and rock contacted. Groundwater generally carries a higher burden of dissolved material than surface water. Among the most common materials dissolved in natural waters are silica, limestone, magnesia, gypsum, and iron. They can cause hardness, discoloration, strong tastes, and the formation of troublesome solids in pipes and industrial equipment. The properties and consequences of dissolved materials are considered in more detail in Box 6-3.

Federal standards for drinking water specify that the concentration of all dissolved solids in combination should be less than 500 parts per million by weight.[37] Water containing as much as 2500 ppm can be tolerated by livestock. Some industrial uses require water with a considerably smaller proportion of dissolved solids than the drinking water standard. Water for irrigation is considered excellent to good if dissolved solids are in the range from 0 to 700 ppm, harmful to some plants under some conditions in the range from 700 to 2100 ppm, and unsuitable under most conditions at more than 2100 ppm.[38] By comparison, seawater contains about 35,000 ppm dissolved solids and the Great Salt Lake, nearly ten times that much.

A high content of dissolved solids in natural waters is a much greater problem in the Southwest and the northern plains than elsewhere in the United States (Figure 6-7). This condition results from the high leachability of the native rocks and soils in those areas, a slow rate of runoff (maximizing the contact of a given quantity of water with soil and rock), and a high evaporation rate (concentrating the salts in the diminished water volume left behind). The naturally high salinity in the Southwest has been increased further by certain activities of civilization: the construction of reservoirs has increased the evaporation rate, and the use and reuse of water for irrigation has increased both the evaporation and leaching rates. The climbing salt content in the lower Colorado River has caused political friction between states and between the United States and Mexico.[39] The inability of present water-users in this drainage to tolerate further increases in dissolved salts may limit the exploitation of western coal and oil-shale, because the water-intensive processes involved in extracting, processing, and transporting these resources would increase both evaporation and leaching of salts (see Chapter 8).

Patterns of Use and Supplies

Human and animal needs for drinking water are dwarfed by the quantities of water used for washing and flushing, and they in turn are dwarfed by the amount of water used in manufacturing and agriculture. The amounts of water needed for several functions and tasks are listed in Table 6-7. Most of the enormous water requirement for crop production is, of course, water the crop plants evaporate in conducting their life processes, *not* free water contained in the harvested plant or water fixed in the plant's carbohydrate. The even larger amount of water used for milk and beef production is almost entirely needed to grow the feed for the cows and steers. Of special importance in determining the water needs of an expanding world agriculture is that crops grown in arid or nutrient-deficient regions require *more* water per unit of edible produce than those grown in the more favorable conditions characterizing most agriculture today.[40]

To examine patterns of water use in detail, it is necessary to distinguish among three phenomena: (1) *withdrawal* of water from surface or underground flows and reservoirs, wherein part of the water may be returned after use to the same flows and reservoirs and can be used again; (2) *consumptive use* of some of the water that has been withdrawn—usually by evaporation but sometimes by embodying the water in a product or polluting it

[37]Hunt, *Physiography,* p. 80.
[38]Hirshleifer et al., *Water supply,* p. 23.
[39]Menard, *Geology,* p. 494; Hirshleifer et al., *Water supply,* p. 23.
[40]Borgstrom, *Too many,* p. 138.

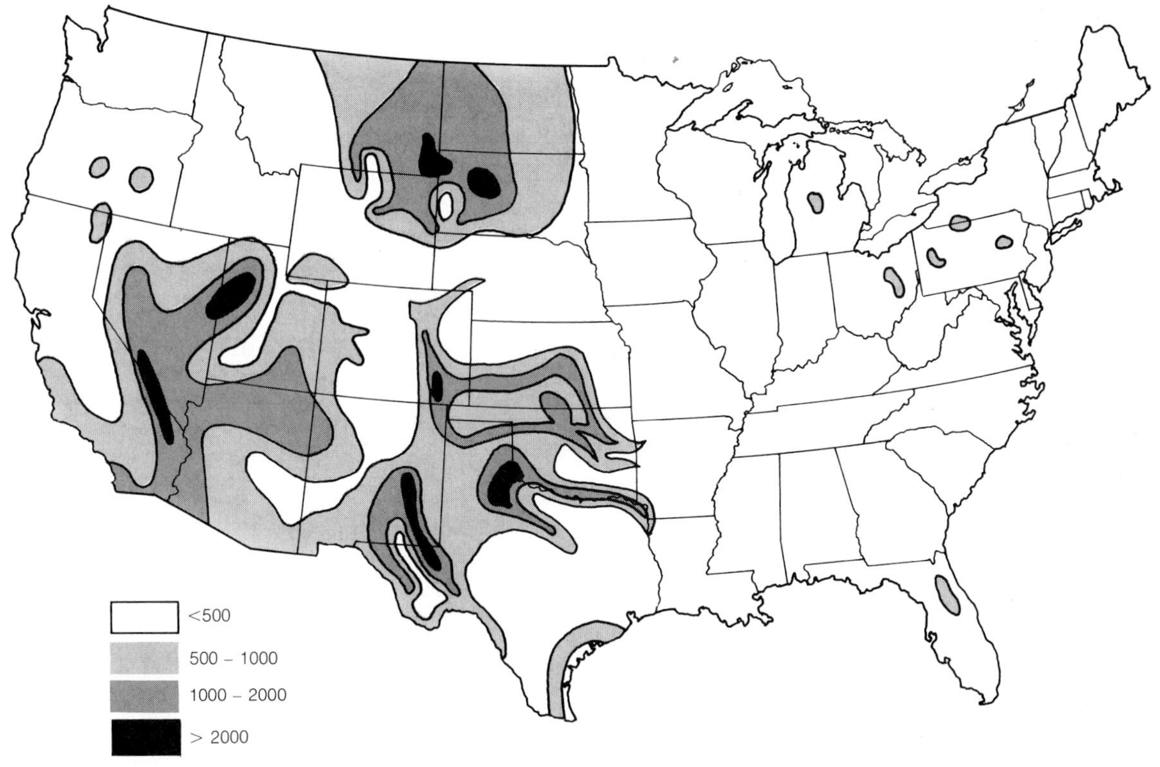

FIGURE 6-7

Burden of dissolved solids in U.S. rivers. Numbers indicate parts per million. (Adapted from Hunt, 1967.)

beyond possibility of reuse; (3) *flow requirement,* wherein the water is used *in place* for dilution of wastes, generation of hydropower, navigation, maintenance of habitat and wildlife, and recreation.

Withdrawal and consumption. The fraction of a withdrawal that is actually consumed varies widely among the different sectors of water use. For electric utilities, which use water mainly for carrying away the waste heat inevitably produced at power plants (see Chapter 8), the consumption was only 0.6 percent of withdrawals in the United States in 1970.[41] The figure is so low because most of the cooling was by the once-through technique, in which cool water from a river, lake or ocean is warmed 8° to 10° C and then returned to its source. Although the water is not consumed in the

[41]This and other 1970 United States figures in the next few paragraphs are from C. Murray and E. Reeves, *Estimated use of water in the United States in 1970.*

TABLE 6-7
Some Water Requirements

Use	*Amount of water used (m^3)*
Drinking water (adult, daily)	0.001
Toilet (1 flush)	0.02
Clothes washer (1 load)	0.17
Refine a ton of petroleum	2–50
Produce a ton of finished steel	6–270
Grow a ton of wheat	300–500
Grow a ton of rice	1,500–2,000
Produce a ton of milk	10,000
Produce a ton of beef	20,000–50,000

Note: 1 m^3 = 1000 liters = 264 gal. Tons are metric tons (= 1000 kg).

Source: Georg Borgstrom, *Too many,* p. 139; J. Hirschleifer, J. DeHaven, and J. Milliman, *Water supply,* p. 27.

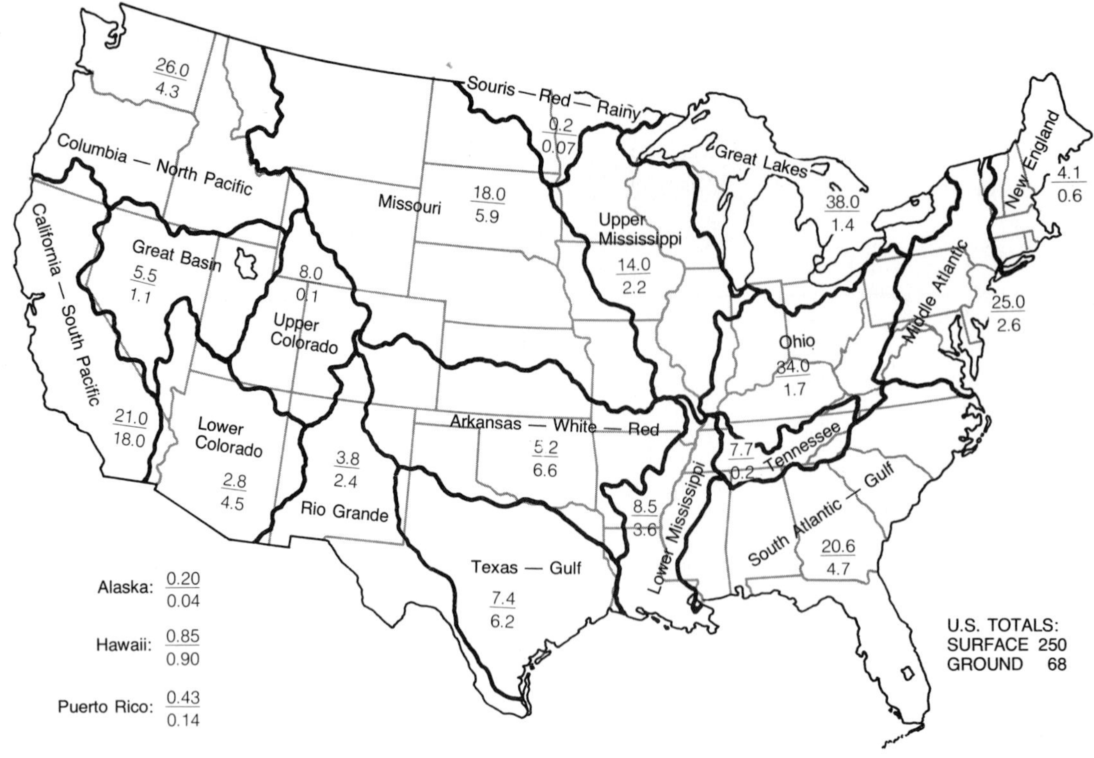

FIGURE 6-8

Freshwater withdrawals in the United States, 1970. The upper numbers represent surface water; the lower numbers, groundwater. All numbers represent million cubic meters per day (the annual amounts divided by 365). (Data from Murray and Reeves, U.S. Geological Survey, circular 676.)

process, its cooling capacity is effectively gone until it has managed, perhaps some distance away, to give up the added heat to the atmosphere. The consumed fraction of electric utility water withdrawals will increase sharply in the future, however, because regulations restricting thermal discharges to rivers, lakes, and the ocean are forcing power plants to rely more heavily on evaporative cooling systems.

Industry consumes about 11 percent of the water it withdraws, a fraction that is expected to decrease in the future as economic and regulatory incentives encourage repeated reuse of water (recirculation), once withdrawn.[42] Domestic and commercial consumption of water from municipal systems is about 22 percent of withdrawals. Irrigation, by far the largest actual consumer of water in the United States, consumes about 75 percent of the water it withdraws. As noted above, moreover, much of the water returned after irrigation carries a bigger burden of dissolved salts than the water withdrawn.

Withdrawals of fresh water for all purposes in 1970 in the United States are shown in Figure 6-8, broken down into drainage basins and into withdrawals from surface and groundwater. Notice that most withdrawals in the Northwest and Northeast are from surface water, whereas withdrawals from groundwater are roughly equal to those from surface water in the Southwest.

Table 6-8 presents, for the same geographical divisions of the country, data for total withdrawals and consumptive use compared with mean annual runoff and annual runoff exceeded 9 years out of 10. All these data are annual flows divided by 365, to give mean daily flows in millions of cubic meters. Naturally, the runoff figures for each region represent water that originates there and do not include inflow from upstream regions (for example, flow into the lower Colorado basin from the upper

[42]National Commission on Materials Policy, *Material needs and the environment today and tomorrow,* pp. 8-5–8-6.

TABLE 6-8
Freshwater Runoff, Withdrawals and Consumption in North American Hydrologic Regions

	Quantities (million m^3/day)			
Regin	*Mean runoff*	*Runoff exceeded 9 years out of 10*	*Total withdrawals*	*Consumption*
Columbia-North Pacific	796	561	116	41.7
California-South Pacific	235	114	148	83.3
Great Basin	28	11	25	12.1
Upper Colorado	49	30	30	15.5
Lower Colorado	12	4	28	19.0
Rio Grande	19	8	23	12.5
Missouri	204	110	90	45.5
Arkansas-White-Red	277	136	45	25.7
Texas (Gulf)	121	42	51	34.9
Souris-Red-Rainy	23	8	1	0.4
Upper Mississippi	246	136	61	3.0
Lower Mississippi	299	144	46	13.6
Great Lakes	284	204	149	4.5
Ohio	474	284	135	3.4
Tennessee	155	106	30	0.8
New England	254	186	18	1.5
Middle Atlantic	318	258	105	5.3
South Atlantic (Gulf)	747	849	96	12.5
Totals	4541	2831	1199	335.2

Note: All flows are mean daily figures (annual flows ÷ 365).
Source: C. Murray and E. Reeves, *Estimated use of water in the United States.*

TABLE 6-9
Water Users in the United States

	Quantities (million m^3/day)			
User	*Withdrawal*	*Surface contribution*	*Ground contribution*	*Amount consumed*
Public municipal	104	68	36	22
Rural domestic	17	3	14	13
Electric utilities	461	456	5	3
Self-supplied industry	148	118	30	16
Irrigation	479	308	171	361

Note: All figures are mean daily flows (annual ÷ 365).
Source: C. Murray and E. Reeves, *Estimated use of water in the United States in 1970.*

Colorado River). Of eighteen regions, there is 1 (the lower Colorado) in which consumptive use exceeds mean annual runoff, 3 in which consumptive use exceeds the flow available 9 years out of 10, and 6 in which total withdrawals exceed flow available in 9 years out of 10. These are the main potential trouble spots for water supply in the United States.

Not represented in Figure 6-10 or in Table 6-8 are withdrawals of salt water amounting to about 200 million cubic meters per day nationwide, mostly for cooling electric power plants.

Table 6-9 shows the breakdown of freshwater withdrawals and consumptive use in the United States in 1970 according to the category of use: municipal (in-

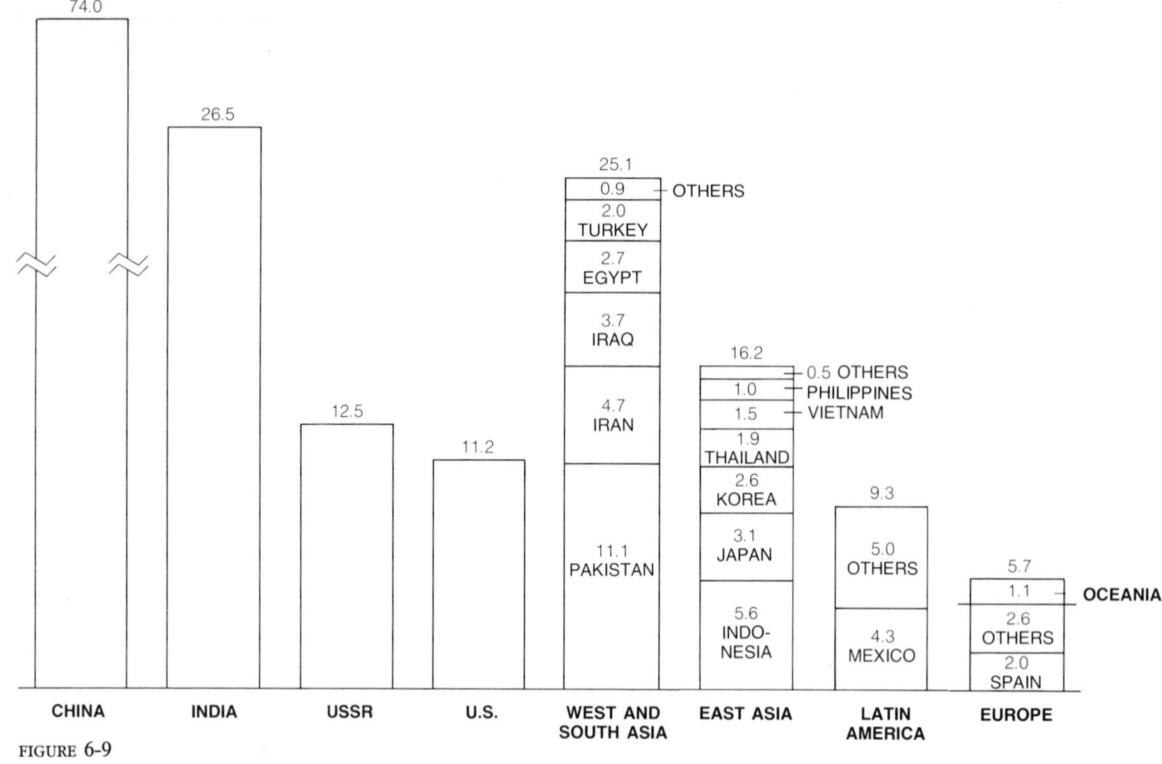

FIGURE 6-9

Irrigated land area of the globe (million hectares), 1963–1965. (Data from Borgstrom, 1969.)

cluding domestic, commercial, and some industrial uses), rural domestic, electric utilities, other self-supplied industrial, and irrigation. Irrigation accounts for about 40 percent of withdrawals but 87 percent of the consumptive use.

Projections made for the year 2000 by the United States Geological Survey show a doubling of withdrawals over the 1970 figures but an increase of about 50 percent in consumptive use of water, implying a greater degree of reuse.[43] Almost half the projected increase in withdrawals is expected to be used for cooling electric power plants; a slower rate of growth in electricity generation, which now seems likely (see Chapter 8), would significantly reduce those projected withdrawal requirements.

Even the higher forecasts of water use might be met by the national water supply, but they would certainly aggravate existing regional difficulties in the drier parts of the country. That shortages of water already exist in the arid regions bodes ill for schemes to develop their massive fossil-fuel resources and to expand irrigated land for food production. Nevertheless, on a national basis problems of water quality will probably remain more important than problems of absolute supply.

[43]National Commission on Materials Policy, *Material needs,* p. 8-5.

Irrigation. As the biggest consumer of water and a cornerstone of agricultural production in many parts of the world, irrigation deserves special attention. The practice of irrigation appears to be as old as agriculture itself.[44] The most rapid expansion of the area under irrigation has probably been in the past two centuries, however. In the nineteenth century, the amount of land under irrigation worldwide increased from about 8 million to 45 million hectares. By the mid-1960s the irrigated area was about 180 million hectares, distributed as indicated in Figure 6-9. This amounted to about 5 percent of all cultivated land.

In the United States, only about 10 percent of the harvested acreage is irrigated, but that land produces more than 25 percent of the cash value of crops grown.[45]

[44]Borgstrom, *Too many,* pp. 184–185, is the source of most of the information in this paragraph. See also Eric Eckholm, *Losing ground,* chapter 7.

[45]Edward Groth, III, Increasing the harvest.

The importance of irrigated land worldwide is probably similarly disproportionate to its fraction of the total cultivated area.

The amount of irrigated land worldwide in the mid-1970s was about 200 million hectares, out of perhaps 340 million hectares that are considered potentially irrigable.[46] The extension of irrigation to the remainder is expected to cost at least $1200 per hectare on the average, the price naturally rising as the more difficult areas are developed.[47] The quality of existing irrigation systems varies widely, moreover, and some land already counted as irrigated needs more water than the existing systems deliver if it is to be fully productive.

Waterlogging and salt accumulation on irrigated land in many parts of the world make it questionable to some observers whether optimistic projections of the continued expansion of the land area under irrigation will be realized.[48] Iraq, Pakistan, and India have each suffered severe damage by waterlogging and salination to millions of hectares of irrigated land, and a noted Soviet soil scientist goes so far as to assert that 60 to 80 percent of all irrigated lands worldwide are becoming gradually more saline, hence less fertile.[49] Sophisticated drainage technology could alleviate this problem in many circumstances, but it increases the expense and requires highly trained engineers to implement.[50] Paradoxically, failure to get rid of irrigation water properly once it has been provided may in the long run prove to be a bigger threat to world agriculture than not providing enough.

Flow requirements. The figures discussed so far have included withdrawals and consumption. They have not included the various uses for flow in stream channels that were identified earlier. Of these so-called *flow requirements,* the most demanding under most circumstances is for the dilution of wastes. The criterion generally used to determine the flow requirement for waste dilution is that the amount of dissolved oxygen in the water should not drop below 4 milligrams per liter (4 ppm, by weight).[51] This is the amount needed under most conditions to maintain a varied aquatic fauna.

Obviously, the amount of flow needed to dilute wastes to concentrations such that their bacterial or chemical decomposition does not deplete dissolved oxygen below this level depends directly on how much waste is discharged. The most commonly used quantitative measure of waste material in water is *biochemical oxygen demand* (BOD), which refers to the weight of oxygen needed to oxidize the wastes. A common unit of BOD is the *population equivalent* (the 0.113 kg, or 0.25 lb, of oxygen needed to oxidize the daily wastes of a "standard" urban person).[52] *Percentage of treatment* means the fraction of the BOD that is removed by waste-processing before the effluent is actually discharged to waterways.

If treatment of municipal wastes in the United States in 1960 averaged 70 percent and that of industrial wastes, 50 percent, the dilution requirement then would have been 2300 million cubic meters of water per day.[53] This compares to a daily flow (the annual total divided by 365) exceeded 9 years out of 10 of 2800 million cubic meters. Thus, counting both flow requirements and consumption (the latter about 300 million cubic meters per day), most of the reliable flow in the forty-eight contiguous states was already being used by society in 1960.

Most forecasts of future flow requirements for dilution of wastes assume extremely effective treatment—95 percent or more for both municipal and industrial wastes.[54] This means all wastes would receive tertiary treatment, which would require heavy investments in the construction of new treatment plants (see Chapter 10). Such forecasts must also estimate levels of population growth and economic growth, as well as the mix of industrial activities. Obviously, there are many possibilities, but all credible scenarios indicate substantial water deficits over most of the southwestern and south-central United States by the year 2020, even with 97-percent waste treatment

[46]University of California Food Task, *A hungry world,* p. 71.

[47]Ibid.

[48]See, for example, Eckholm, *Losing ground,* Chapter 7; Borgstrom, *Too many,* Chapter 8; see also Chapter 11 in this volume.

[49]V. Kovda, quoted in Eckholm, *Losing ground,* p. 124.

[50]For an interesting discussion of what seems possible in theory, see R. Revelle and V. Lakshminarayana, The Ganges water machine.

[51]Hunt, *Physiography,* p. 83; H. Landsberg, L. Fischman, and J. Fisher, *Resources in America's future.*

[52]An excellent discussion of water quality and waste treatment is N. Wollman and G. Bonem, *The outlook for water,* chapter 8. See also Metcalf and Eddy, Inc. *Wastewater engineering,* McGraw-Hill, New York, 1972, and Chapter 10 in this volume.

[53]Wollman and Bonem, *The outlook.* Accurate figures for what the average percentages of waste treatment actually were in 1960 do not seem to be available, but according to Wollman and Bonem they probably were no higher than those given here.

[54]See, for example, Ridker, *Future water needs.*

everywhere. High-growth scenarios extend the deficit region throughout the north-central region, as well.[55] Failure to achieve higher levels of treatment, if such failure is coupled with substantial economic growth, could cause national dilution requirements to exceed mean total runoff for the 48 contiguous states before the year 2000.[56]

Increasing the Supply

Several approaches to alleviating water shortages are possible: (1) One can redistribute the flow more evenly in time by building storage reservoirs or, in some circumstances, by revegetating denuded regions so that water is released more gradually. (Both of these strategies buy increased regularity of flow at the cost of a decreased total quantity of flow, owing to increased losses to evaporation.) (2) One can redistribute the water geographically by transferring it in pipelines or canals from one drainage basin to another. (3) One can try to move the people to the water—that is, to employ land-use planning tools to concentrate the population where the water is. (This approach is not considered further in this chapter; some discussion of land-use planning appears in Chapter 14.) (4) One can tap groundwater more extensively by means of wells. (5) One can render seawater or salty groundwater suitable for municipal, industrial, and agricultural use by desalting. (6) One can try to increase the efficiency with which water is used, for example, by minimizing the number of gallons needed to grow a given amount of cotton or to manufacture a given amount of steel.

Water projects. The extent to which water projects had increased the regularity of the flow of water in the United States had reached about 40 percent of the theoretically attainable figure by around 1970.[57] The construction of dams for this purpose (and others) is expensive and becomes increasingly so per unit of control gained, as the best sites are used first. Cost-benefit analysis to determine whether it is economical to build a large multipurpose dam (for flow regulation, flood control, hydropower generation, irrigation, recreation) is complicated. It is easily botched or misused by special interests, even independent of environmental issues and the difficulty of incorporating these into an economic framework.[58] Not surprisingly, then, cost-benefit analyses of water projects have generated many controversies.[59] (The environmental aspects of dams are considered briefly in connection with a discussion of hydropower in Chapter 8 and in more detail in Chapter 11.)

Diversion of water from regions of surplus to regions of deficit raises all the economic and environmental issues of flow-regulation projects, and more. Such inter-basin transfers are common in the western United States, with 20 percent of the population in the seventeen western states already being supplied by water moved 160 kilometers or more in 1968.[60] As the distances water is moved grow larger, the associated political difficulties often intensify. People in densely populated, water-short regions like southern California use the political power of their numbers to exert a claim on water from elsewhere (northern California, in this case), where the inhabitants see the environmental costs but receive few benefits of exporting water from their region. Few projects that transferred water across state lines existed in the United States as of the mid-1970s, but projects had been proposed (and were being taken seriously by some people) for moving water to arid parts of the United States from as far away as northern Canada.[61] The Soviet Union has long had plans to divert to the south the flow of several major rivers now emptying into the Arctic Ocean.[62] Those and other large-scale diversion schemes

[55]Ibid.

[56]This forecast is based on an average of 80-percent treatment of both industrial and municipal wastes and the high-growth scenario of Wollman and Bonem, *The outlook,* p. 69. The low-growth scenario with the same treatment levels produces the same result before 2020.

[57]Ridker, Future water needs, pp. 215–218. The theoretical maximum is expressed as a quantity of flow maintainable 98 percent of the time if all possible storage facilities are built.

[58]See, for example, Hirschleifer et al., *Water supply,* p. 23, for a good discussion.

[59]T. Parry and R. Norgaard, Wasting a river, and Julian McCaull, Dams of pork.

[60]Menard, *Geology,* p. 495.

[61]This scheme, the North American Water and Power Alliance, is described unenthusiastically in Menard, *Geology,* p. 496, and does not seem to have much support at this writing. See also Paul R. Ehrlich and John P. Holdren, Population and panaceas: A technological perspective; and W. Sewell, NAWAPA: a continental water system. Canadians view the scheme with considerable misgivings; see R. Bocking, *Canada's water: for sale?*

[62]P. Micklin, Soviet plans to reverse the flow of rivers; M. I. Goldman, *Environmental pollution in the Soviet Union.*

would be staggeringly expensive. (The estimate for the North American Water and Power Alliance—the scheme for transferring water from Canada, mentioned above—was $100 billion in the 1960s and would surely be much higher if reexamined in the light of more recent experience with construction costs.) The ecological effects might well extend to impact on continental and global climates (see Chapter 11).

Desalting. Some 700 desalting plants were in operation around the world in 1975, most of very modest size and almost none used to support irrigation of staple crops. The largest ones produced on the order of 35,000 cubic meters of fresh water per day, at a cost of around 15 cents per cubic meter.[63] In smaller plants, the cost was in the range of 25 to 50 cents per cubic meter. By contrast, farmers typically pay 1 to 2 cents per cubic meter for irrigation water. So, only for growing high-value crops such as tomatoes, avocados, and orchids can water from desalting be used economically for agriculture. It appears that desalting is too expensive by about a factor of 10 to permit its use for irrigating wheat, rice, or corn.[64]

Some desalting enthusiasts argue that a combination of lower future costs for desalting and reduced water requirements for staple crops (made possible by more refined irrigation schemes and by breeding more drought-resistant, water-efficient crop varieties) will soon change this verdict, opening an era in which the deserts will be made to bloom.[65] Most such analyses appear to rest on the hope of cheap nuclear power as a source of energy for the separation of salt from seawater. (The theoretical minimum amount of energy needed to remove the salt from a liter of seawater, which can be established using basic principles of thermodynamics, is a not too formidable 2.8 kilojoules. The most efficient plants actually constructed to date require about 170 kilojoules per liter for practical reasons not likely to be circumvented easily or soon.)[66] The price of nuclear energy has been rising, not falling, however, and other energy sources are becoming costlier, too (see Chapter 8). At one dollar per million kilojoules, a typical price for "low-cost" commercial fuel energy in 1975, the energy cost alone for desalting a cubic meter of seawater in an efficient plant was 17 cents.

Falling construction costs for large desalting plants were also rather widely predicted in the 1960s, but those have not materialized, either.[67] Moreover, if the water is to be used anywhere but on the seacoast (or directly adjacent to inland supplies of salty water), the costs of moving it and lifting it in elevation must be taken into account. Lifting costs alone are on the order of 1 cent per cubic meter per hundred meters of lift.[68] Under these conditions, one could scarcely afford to use seawater for irrigating staple crops on land above a few hundred meters elevation, even if the sea were fresh water to start with.

Water conservation and other strategies. The use of wells to develop groundwater supplies can in some instances be an economical alternative to dams and surface reservoirs for the purpose of flow regulation and storage,[69] but any situation in which withdrawals exceed natural recharge is obviously not a satisfactory long-term strategy.

As with so many other resource problems, close examination of the water situation suggests that the most economical and environmentally benign way to increase supplies beyond a certain point is really not to increase supplies at all, but rather to reduce consumption by more efficient use. A substantial fraction of municipal water use in the United States, for example, turns out to be the result of leaks, including dripping faucets, running toilets, and the like.[70] Furthermore, industrial water use could be significantly reduced by increasing recirculation at the expense of withdrawals.[71] There is genuine potential, as well, for reducing significantly the amount of water needed for productive irrigation.[72] At least one approach to this—the use of high-frequency irrigation (delivering small amounts of water at frequent intervals)

[63]Van Hylckama, Water resources, p. 161. The cost is based on energy prices before 1973 and could hardly be correct in 1977.

[64]M. Clawson, H. Landsberg, and L. Alexander, Desalted seawater for agriculture: Is it economic?

[65]See, for example, Gale Young, Dry lands and desalted water.

[66]J. Harte and R. Socolow, *Patient Earth*, p. 272. A more thorough introduction to standard desalting technology appears in Hirshleifer et al., *Water supply*, pp. 203–217.

[67]See, for example, Ehrlich and Holdren, Population and panaceas.

[68]Van Hylckama, Water resources, p. 161.

[69]See, for example, Revelle and Lakshminarayana, The Ganges.

[70]Water Resources Council, *The nation's water resources.*

[71]National Commission on Materials Policy, *Material needs*, chapter 8.

[72]See, for example, Young, Dry lands.

through pipes—is said by its supporters to be capable of increasing the efficiency of fertilizer uptake and increasing the variety of soils on which irrigation is possible.[73] Breeding crops more tolerant of salt is another way to reduce the use of fresh water in agriculture, but it is a time-consuming and as yet unpromising approach.

Naturally, the lengths to which society will go to use its water more efficiently depend in part on the price of water, and many economists believe that many present water problems in the United States—caused in large part by excessive consumption—could have been avoided if the price of water had not been kept artificially low by subsidies.[74] It is likely to prove necessary eventually, either by means of much higher prices or by other social restraints, to prevent people from moving into arid regions with the expectation that society will support their venture by making the necessary water available at negligible direct cost to the consumer.

FORESTS

With the disappearance of the forest, all is changed. At one season the earth parts with its warmth by radiation to an open sky—receives, at another, an immoderate heat from the unobstructed rays of the sun. Hence the climate becomes excessive and the soil is alternately parched by the fervors of summer and seared by the rigors of winter. Bleak winds sweep unresisted over its surface . . . . The face of the earth is no longer a sponge, but a dust heap, and the floods which the waters of the sky pour over it hurry swiftly along its slopes, carrying in suspension vast quantities of earthy particles which increase the abrading power and mechanical force of the current, and, augmented by the sand and gravel of falling banks, fill the beds of the streams, divert them into new channels, and obstruct their outlets.

—George Perkins Marsh,
Man and nature, 1864

Intimately related to freshwater supplies are another renewable resource—forests. Forests are not, of course, the same from place to place—as was seen in Chapter 4, the term *forest* has a multitude of meanings.[75] At the same time, diverse as they are, forests the world over tend to play similar roles in relation to human activities: maintenance of ecological diversity, preservation of watersheds and the prevention of erosion (and subsequent siltation of dams), moderation of climate, supplying wood for fuel and structures and paper, and providing hunting grounds and areas of aesthetic value for recreational purposes, to name a few.[75a] The multiple uses of forest land are often to one degree or another incompatible, but, for any or all of them to continue, preservation or regeneration of forests is necessary. Therefore, much of the discussion on the uses of forests tends to focus on what happens when they are destroyed—that is, on deforestation.

That deforestation results in heavy soil erosion, floods, and changes in local climate has been known—but not always heeded—for centuries. The annual floods that have plagued northern China since ancient times are a result of deforestation during the early dynasties.[76] The once-fertile hills of central Italy have been arid and subject to regular, occasionally devastating floods since the Middle Ages, when the trees were removed. It is interesting that medieval writers and many others since accurately predicted the results of deforestation without replanting or provision for reseeding and protection of seedlings and saplings. The ancient Greeks and Romans apparently were relatively conscientious in maintaining the forests and understood their value in protecting watersheds. But this understanding seems to have been partially lost during the Middle Ages, when the demands of growing populations for fuel, construction materials, and grazing land brought destruction of the forests in much of southern Europe. This destruction led the great naturalist Alexander von Humboldt to observe, in the middle of the nineteenth century, that the youthfulness of a civilization is proved by the existence of its woods.[77]

---

[73]S. L. Rawlins and P. A. C. Raats, Prospects for high-frequency irrigation.

[74]See, for example, Hirschleifer et al., *Water supply.*

[75]A fine introduction into the diversity and complexity of forests appears in S. H. Spurr and B. V. Barnes, *Forest ecology.*

[75a]For a splendid summary of the underappreciated values of forests to human society, see F. H. Bormann, An inseparable linkage.

[76]Borgstrom, *Too many,* p. 2.

[77]An excellent recent perspective on historical and contemporary forest problems around the world is given in Eckholm, *Losing ground,* chapter 2. For the consequences of deforestation in Italy, see Richard M. Klein, The Florence floods.

TABLE 6-10
World Forests

	Areas (million km²)				Timber Stocks (billion m³)			
	TOTAL TERRITORY	TOTAL FOREST LAND	CLOSED FOREST[a]	AREA COVERED BY 1973 REVIEW[b]	TOTAL IN AREA COVERED	CONIFEROUS PORTION	BROADLEAF PORTION	ESTIMATES FOR ALL FOREST LAND[c]
Africa	30.3	8.0	1.9	0.4	5.2	0.1	5.1	39
Asia (without USSR)	27.5	5.3	4.0	3.5	34.0	5.5	28.5	40
North America	21.5	6.3	6.3	3.9	36.0	26.5	9.5	59
Central America	2.7	0.7	0.6	0.2	2.2	0.7	1.5	6
South America	17.8	7.3	5.3	3.5	60.0	0.5	59.5	96
Australia and Oceania	8.5	1.9	0.8	0.4	1.3	0.3	1.0	9
Europe (without USSR)	4.9	1.7	1.4	1.3	12.0	8.0	4.0	13
USSR	22.4	9.2	7.7	6.9	73.3	61.3	12.0	79
World	135.6	40.3	28.0	20.1	224.0	102.9	121.1	341

[a]Land where crowns of trees cover more than 20% of area.
[b]Entirely within closed forests.
[c]Total of coniferous and broad-leaf, closed forest and other.
Source Reidar Persson, *World forest resources.*

World Forest Reserves

Today, similar demands are threatening forests around the world. Many irreplaceable tracts have disappeared entirely. Most of Europe, northern Asia, the eastern one-third of the United States, and vast areas of the American Northwest were once covered with forests. Only fractions of the forests of the eastern United States and of western Europe remain today, largely preserved through conscious conservation and reforestation policies, which were pioneered in Europe. Table 6-10 shows forested areas and estimated timber stocks for the world as of 1973.

The Soviet Union has the greatest remaining reserves of temperate and subarctic forest, including nearly half of the world's coniferous forest. About two-thirds is virgin, largely because it is relatively inaccessible. However, the best-quality trees for lumbering are in the European USSR, and as a result, those have been heavily exploited. Large reserves of coniferous forest also remain in North America, from Nova Scotia to Alaska. Forest management practices have, in theory, been established in most DCs, including the USSR and the United States, to preserve their forest for the future—but the success of such practices is in dispute. Interestingly, problems and conflicts over timber harvesting in the communist Soviet Union are quite similar to those that are so vexing in the capitalist United States.[78]

Australia and New Zealand in recent decades have also lost large tracts of forest, and much of what remains is being heavily exploited by intensive forestry. In addition, where replanting is done, native forest ecosystems are replaced with tree-farms of fast-growing, imported species harvested by broad-scale clearcutting.[78a]

Vast forest reserves also still exist in the tropics, especially in the Amazon valley, southeast Asia, and central Africa. Inaccessibility and economic factors have until recently protected those areas from destruction. Latin America, for example, harvested less than 4 percent of the wood produced worldwide in 1967–1969, despite having almost a third of the world's reserves.[79] Nevertheless, some of Latin America's more accessible forests have now vanished or have been selectively depleted of the most valuable species. The rate of clearing tropical rain forests has accelerated in the past decade or so to the point where many fear they will all but disappear by the end of the century.

It is important to recognize that the greatest cause of outright deforestation in the world today is almost

[78]Philip R. Pryde, *Conservation in the Soviet Union;* M. I. Goldman, *Environmental pollution in the Soviet Union.*
[78a]R. and V. Routley, *The fight for the forests.*
[79]E. P. Cliff, Timber—an old, renewable material.

certainly not large-scale commercial lumbering, but rather a combination of land-clearing for agricultural production and the gathering of wood by desperate peasants in need of fuel. While debates rage in the DCs about multiple-use and optimum harvesting practices, the very existence of forests is in jeopardy over large expanses of the world, where hunger and the need for warmth take precedence over more subtle concerns.[80]

TABLE 6-11
Annual Growth and Removal of Wood in the United States, 1952–2000

Year	*Softwoods* Growth	*Softwoods* Removals	*Hardwoods* Growth	*Hardwoods* Removals
GROWING STOCK (BILLION FT³)				
1952	7.8	7.8	6.1	4.1
1962	9.3	7.6	7.1	4.2
1970	10.7	9.6	7.9	4.4
1980	11.5	11.0	8.2	5.9
1990	11.8	11.6	8.2	7.0
2000	11.8	12.4	8.0	8.2
SAWTIMBER* (BILLION BOARD FT)				
1952	29.5	39.2	15.6	13.3
1962	34.7	37.7	17.6	12.6
1970	40.3	47.7	19.7	15.0
1980	43.8	50.4	20.9	16.2
1990	46.5	52.5	21.1	18.7
2000	47.9	55.4	20.9	21.2

Note: Figures for 1980, 1990, and 2000 are projections.

*This category is included in the other. Growing stock is trees 4 inches or more in diameter. Sawtimber is trees 12 inches or more in diameter. A board foot is 12 in. × 12 in. × 1 in.

Source: National Academy of Sciences, *Man, materials, and environment,* p. 135.

Forests in the United States

In the United States, lumber interests are accelerating their harvests, often at considerable expense to the forest environment, in their efforts to meet rising demand for construction wood and for paper. Table 6-11 shows both annual growth and annual removals of timber in the United States from 1952 to 1970, with projections to the year 2000. While growth has exceeded removals overall and may continue to do so, softwood sawtimber (coniferous trees more than 12 inches in diameter) has suffered serious deficits, which are expected to continue. Thus, the stock of those trees, which supply most of the wood for construction and pulping, is dwindling.[81] How much of the demand for wood in the United States (in the economic sense, the desire and ability to purchase it) is related to real needs is in dispute. For instance, if wood is cheap enough, the use of it as a structural material will increase and the demand for nonforest products (metals, concrete) that can meet the same needs will decrease. Much of the pressure generated by the industry for more logging in the national forests appears to have been created by a fear of loss of markets to other industries rather than by any genuine national need.[82] On the other hand, the United States has been a net importer of timber since 1941, and the fractional dependence on imports is growing.[83]

The U. S. lumber industry. Few subjects have been the source of more enduring environmental controversy in the United States than the needs and practices of the lumber industry. The controversy goes back to the middle of the nineteenth century, when the wholesale plundering of American forests was in full swing, due both to unscrupulous industry practices and to irresponsible farm clearing. A few voices protested—John Muir, Henry David Thoreau, Carl Schurz (President Hayes' Secretary of the Interior)—but the demolition of the forests continued.[84] In 1907 establishment of the Forest Service under Gifford Pinchot, a man who believed that exploitation and preservation of forests could be compatible, marked a turning point. The trend began toward sustained-yield forestry—harvesting trees like other crops—and toward consideration of nonlumbering uses of forest such as for wilderness, watershed preservation, and recreation.

That hopeful trend, however, has not led to any sort of equilibrium based on a comprehensive American forest policy. The timber industry, for instance, constantly pressures the Forest Service to open up more national

[80]Eckholm, *Losing ground,* chapter 6.

[81]National Academy of Sciences, *Man, materials, and environment,* chapter 5.

[82]N. Wood, *Clearcut,* p. 26.

[83]Cliff, *Timber;* see also National Commission on Materials Policy, *Material needs,* pp. 2–22.

[84]For a brief summary of the history of U.S. forests see Wood, *Clearcut,* p. 34 ff.

forest for harvesting—pressure that succeeds all too often.[85] At the same time pressures for recreational use are escalating, and the general public concern for conservation is increasing.

The degree of compatibility of different uses varies a great deal,[86] and decision-making in this area is complex, to say the least. In general, however, decisions by the Forest Service (and other government groups) have tended to favor the lumber interests, even though the Forest Service has not become a pawn of those interests to the extent that some other federal agencies (such as the Interstate Commerce Commission) have become subservient to the industries they are supposed to regulate. The political muscle of the lumber companies and the emergence of a generation of Forest Service officials trained to regard forests as crops have nonetheless kept timber harvesting at the top of the list of the multiple uses to which those forests are, according to law, to be put.

National forest policy. That one legitimate and important use of national forest land is supplying the United States with wood is not in dispute. But a series of related questions *are* in hot contention. They include:

1. How much of our national forest land should be assigned to growing crops of timber, and which areas should be put to that use?
2. How should demand for export be included in estimates of the need to cut on those lands?
3. To what extent should the intensive, high-yield forestry practices employed by industry on private lands be permitted on multiple-use public lands?
4. What methods of harvesting should be employed?

These questions are interrelated and can only be answered satisfactorily by a comprehensive forest-management policy. The way to proceed seems clear—toward a high-intensity, low-harvest-acreage policy similar to one suggested by Marion Clawson.[87] The concept is relatively simple. Growth of wood for extraction from our forests would be concentrated in the better forest sites (those producing the greatest yields and suited to rapid regeneration). Sites less suitable would be reserved for alternative uses or held for possible future harvests. The nation's wood would come from a much smaller area than if all of today's so-called commercial forests were harvested, and some prime timberland now seemingly doomed to be cleared could be set aside for wilderness.

Such a policy is desperately needed. The demand for forest products seems certain to rise over the next several decades; it will do so all the faster if we turn more to forests for fuel sources. In 1974 it was estimated that demand for wood would rise at a compound rate of perhaps 1.5 percent per annum between 1970 and 2000. The rise in recreational demand was projected to be much higher—perhaps 4 percent—meaning nearly a quadrupling of use by the end of the century.[88] Furthermore, it now seems likely that for economic reasons (for maintaining foreign exchange) the United States will want to expand its lumber exports to Japan and elsewhere.

If there is to be any chance of meeting those pressures on our forests without a national disaster, their exploitation must be more tightly controlled—not just at the expense of lumbering interests but also through such actions as equitable rationing of access to wilderness, since overuse by hikers and campers can destroy the very values conservation intends to preserve. As is so often the case, however, even when the direction in which policy should go seems clear, economic and political impediments to moving in that direction may be formidable. We return to that in Chapter 14.

Unsound practices. It is often more immediately profitable for a company to harvest timber in a way that essentially converts forest into a nonrenewable resource than to harvest in what may be the soundest method, taking the economic or environmental long view. In a sense, many forests have been treated as "terrestrial whales"—harvested with no consideration for maximum sustainable yield but rather with an eye on maximum return on capital (Chapter 7). For example, many areas

[85]See, for example, John Hart, Assault on the Siskiyous. For a more general discussion see the section on timber in Council on Environmental Quality, *Environmental quality, 1975,* pp. 220–230.

[86]For a good discussion of the relationships among uses see M. Clawson, *Forests: For whom and for what?*

[87]Conflicts, strategies and possibilities for consensus in forest land use and management.

[88]Demand estimates are based on L. L. Fischman, Future demand for U.S. forest resources.

have been subjected to the wrong kind of selective cutting. The most desirable species have been logged out, leaving only inferior trees to reseed. The result is an inferior forest, at least from the point of view of future harvests. This has been the fate of much hardwood forest in the eastern United States.[89]

This type of selective cutting is often disastrous, but the disaster is not as obvious as where there is clear-cutting (the wholesale removal of large tracts of mature forest). Done carefully, with appropriate care for aesthetics, placement of roads, removal of logs, and disposal of trash, and done in forest ecosystems with the appropriate capacity to regenerate (such as the Hubbard Brook forest discussed in Chapter 11), clear-cutting may be an appropriate way of harvesting timber. Unfortunately, much clear-cutting is done in inappropriate areas, that is, where the result is an impression of vast desolation in formerly scenic places, where placement of roads and dragging of logs play havoc with the soil, where silting of streams destroys valuable populations of game fishes, and where climatic and other factors make reforestation extremely slow or impossible.

Such activities have produced results that, through the dissemination of photographs such as those in Figure 6-10, have convinced much of the public that all lumbering is environmentally irresponsible. Similarly, the behavior of Georgia Pacific and Arcata Redwood companies in hurrying to harvest redwood stands that were "threatened" with inclusion in Redwood National Park was in the best tradition of the nineteenth-century "rape and pillage school" of forest management.[90] Indeed, the assistant to the chairman of Georgia Pacific was in favor of logging *within* national parks![91]

Unfortunately, even under appropriate conditions, clear-cutting and tree farming present problems that are analogous in some respects to those found in other forms of intensive agriculture. Use of pesticides, herbicides, and fertilizers on forest plots has caused off-site environmental problems, for example.[92] Tree farming also produces some of the liabilities of other kinds of monoculture.[93] For example, large stands of young trees are more susceptible to disease, pests, and fire than are forests containing trees of varied age.

Loggers defend the practice of clear-cutting large stands on the grounds that certain valuable species of trees need direct sunlight and space in which to grow—that is, cleared land. Presumably, some less destructive procedure can be used in many cases, such as clear-cutting small stands, if selective cutting and replanting individual trees is unsatisfactory. A great deal of research on appropriate harvesting procedures in various kinds of forest ecosystems is badly needed. At the rate forests are being cut in some areas, however, the forests may be gone before the research can be done.

Forests are threatened by more than a demand for lumber, fuel, and recreation. Much privately owned forested land (about 80 percent of the forest in the eastern United States) disappears each year under highways, housing subdivisions, airports, and other development projects. Strip-mining destroys thousands of acres in a process much more destructive of the soil than clear-cutting. In moist climates erosion and flooding are virtually inevitable after strip-mining and are accompanied by severe water pollution. Reforestation is often not attempted (although with care it frequently can be achieved). In publicly owned tracts in national forests, under the multiple-use policy, trees are cleared for recreational facilities (and many are damaged by the crowds of visitors), access roads, powerline cuts, mining activities, and sheep and cattle grazing. And in some areas, for example near Los Angeles, trees are being killed by smog.

Pressures on World Forests

The situation is far worse in many other countries. Half the trees cut down in the world are used for fuel, regardless of their potential value as lumber.[94] Clearing for agricultural land, especially in the tropics, is another great threat to this resource. Deforestation may be especially disastrous ecologically in the tropics. Because

[89]M. Clawson, *Forest policy for the future,* p. 183.
[90]Wood, *Clearcut,* p. 130.
[91]Ibid., p. 134.
[92]National Academy of Sciences, *Man, materials,* chapter 5.
[93]See, for example, Janick et al., *Plant science.*
[94]Eckholm, *Losing ground,* chapter 6.

A

FIGURE 6-10

A. Aerial view of the clear-cutting of redwoods near the Redwood National Park in Humboldt County, California. Heavy soil erosion and silting of streams usually follow such wholesale deforestation, especially on steep slopes like this. (Photo by Don Anthrop, courtesy of Friends of the Earth.) B. Another view of clear-cutting near the Redwood National Park in California, showing debris left by loggers and exposed soil. (Photo by Bruce Coleman, courtesy of Friends of the Earth.)

B

of poor transportation facilities and various economic factors, a great number of the felled trees (many of them valuable hardwoods) are not harvested and used as lumber, but are wasted or used for fuel. Brazil's forests once covered 80 percent of the country; by 1965 they covered only 58 percent.[95] A stretch through the Amazon forest is now being cleared for a transcontinental highway, which will open up vast areas of the forest for lumbering and agricultural clearing. Lumbering in Haiti's tropical forest has long since exterminated mahogany entirely, and that of Honduras is nearly gone. Replanting has seldom been practiced in tropical forests in the past, although a few countries are now introducing forest-management practices there. If tropical forests are not to vanish, as did temperate ones in Europe and the United States, conservation and management policies must be established.

A bright spot in the picture may be provided by the People's Republic of China. More than 30 percent of China's land area is said to be suitable for reforestation, and a reforestation program is in progress.[96]

Careful management of forests could assure humanity of the opportunity to benefit from forests more or less in perpetuity. Such management would include preservation of trees of mixed species and ages as much as possible, to discourage losses from pests, disease, and fire; careful selective logging in a long-term rotation scheme or intensive management of clear-cutting in appropriate areas; much more effort put into reforestation; and careful protection of the soil.

THE TAKEN-FOR-GRANTED RESOURCES

The resources we have discussed in this chapter—land, soil, water, forests—have for the most part not commanded the attention or the sense of urgency in the United States, either of the public at large or among dedicated environmentalists, that they deserve. Perhaps soil erosion and deforestation lack the glamour of the petroleum crisis or running out of tungsten, but the central role of the soil-water-forest complex in the support of industrial and agrarian societies alike means that high priority should be attached to understanding it and maintaining its integrity. If the United Nations conference on the environment in Stockholm in 1972 is any guide, the LDCs may understand this better than the DCs—for the lists of environmental problems raised by the poor countries at that meeting were heavy with threats to soil and forests. Sadly, the LDC governments that perceive the gravity of these threats generally are less well equipped to do anything about it than are the DC governments, where recognition is dimmer.

It is true that the wholesale loss of soil and forests is, as a general rule, proceeding faster in LDCs than elsewhere, and some might argue on this basis that the relative complacency of DCs about their own situations with respect to these resources is justified. It is not. Probably the main reason for overconfidence is lack of awareness of the complexity and subtlety of the soil-water-forest complex, and hence blissful ignorance of the ways it might be disrupted and the ways these disruptions could damage human well-being. It is important to recognize that soil is a chemical and biological system as well as a structural foundation for holding up plants; that what grows depends not just on adding water and fertilizer to any plot of land, but on widely varying characteristics of soils that are themselves the product of biogeochemical processes acting over millennia; and that these characteristics can be interfered with, perhaps irreversibly, by human activities operating over much shorter periods of time. (Some ways in which this could happen are described further in Chapter 11.) It is important to recognize, too, how tightly linked are the resources of soil and water and forest. Deforestation produces erosion and water pollution and makes runoff more erratic, reducing availability of water and causing more erosion. This process can become irreversible by altering the environment so drastically that reforestation is impossible.

Society ignores the complexity and fragility of these systems at its peril.

[95]Georg Borgstrom, *Hungry planet,* 2d ed. (Macmillan, New York, 1972), p. 347.

[96]S. Wortman, Agriculture in China.

Recommended for Further Reading

Clawson, M. 1975. *Forests: For whom and for what?* Resources for the Future, Washington, D.C. Excellent discussion of forest policy, highly recommended.

Eckholm, Eric. 1976. *Losing ground.* Norton, New York. An outstanding treatment of land, soil, water, and forests and the pressures they are being subjected to because of population growth and mismanagement.

Harte, J., and R. Socolow. 1971. *Patient Earth.* Holt, Rinehart and Winston, New York. An excellent collection of environmental case histories, covering land-use and water issues, among others.

Hunt, C. B., 1974. *Natural regions of the United States and Canada.* W. H. Freeman and Company, San Francisco. Detailed information on soils, water, vegetation, landforms.

Janick, J., R. W. Schery, F. W. Woods, and V.W. Ruttan. 1974. *Plant science.* 2d. ed. W. H. Freeman and Company, San Francisco. Contains thorough treatments of soils, soil chemistry, and their relation to plant productivity.

Leopold, Luna B. 1974. *Water: A primer.* W. H. Freeman and Company, San Francisco. Illuminating introductory treatment of surface and groundwater.

Persson, Reidar. 1974. *World forest resources.* Royal College of Forestry, Stockholm. This is the unofficial successor to the World Forest Inventory (WFI) of the Food and Agriculture Organization (FAO) of the United Nations. The last WFI was published in 1966 based on data gathered up to 1963. Persson, who worked in the FAO's forest division from 1968 to 1972, assembled this volume from data compiled through 1973 by himself and others at the FAO. It is the most comprehensive and up-to-date study of world forests we know of.

Additional References

Albrecht, W. A., 1956. Physical, chemical, and biochemical changes in the soil community. In *Man's role in changing the face of the earth,* Thomas, W. L., ed. University of Chicago Press, pp. 648–673. A study of the effects of long-term cultivation on midwestern soils.

Berwick, Stephen. 1976. The Gir forest: An endangered ecosystem. *American Scientist,* vol. 64, no. 1 (January-February), pp. 28–40. Excellent description of the problems of maintaining a semiarid forest ecosystem in the face of expanding human populations.

Bocking, Richard C. 1972. *Canada's water: for sale?* James Lewis and Samuel, Publishers, Toronto. Well-documented critique of plans for massive water transfers from Canada to the U.S., by a Canadian.

Borgstrom, Georg. 1969. *Too many.* Macmillan, Toronto. Good treatment of patterns of global land use.

Bormann, F. H. 1976. An inseparable linkage: Conservation of natural ecosystems and the conservation of fossil energy. *Bio Science,* vol. 26, no. 12 (December), pp. 754–759. Excellent summary of the values to society of forest ecosystems.

Brown, Lester R. 1975. The world food prospect. *Science,* vol. 190 (December 12), pp. 1053–1059. Tells how much land is used in the cultivation of various major crops.

California Land Use Task Force. 1975. *The California land.* Kaufmann, Los Altos, Calif., chapter 3. Trends and patterns of land use in a state where competing demands on land for agriculture, urbanization, and recreation are intense.

Carter, V. G., and T. Dale. 1974. *Topsoil and civilization.* University of Oklahoma Press, Norman, Okla. Historical and contemporary problems of erosion and desertification.

Clawson, M. 1974. Conflicts, strategies, and possibilities for consensus in forest land use and management. In *Forest policy for the future,* M. Clawson, ed. Resources for the Future, Washington, D.C., pp. 105–191. An interesting discussion of a high-intensity, low-harvest-acreage model of U.S. timber strategy.

———1976. The national forests. *Science,* vol. 191 (20 February), pp. 762–767. Defects in present management practices and some suggested remedies.

———ed. 1974. *Forest policy for the future.* Washington, D.C.: Resources for the Future. Very useful collection of articles.

———H. Landsberg and L. Alexander. 1969. Desalted seawater for agriculture: Is it economic? *Science,* vol. 165, pp. 1141–1148. This article shows desalting for large-scale staple-crop agriculture to be far from economic. Developments since 1969 have not altered this conclusion.

Cliff, E. P. 1975. Timber—an old renewable material. In *National materials policies,* National Academy of Sciences, Washington, D.C. Notes the continuing versatility of wood as a raw material.

Council on Environmental Quality (CEQ). 1975. *Environmental quality.* Government Printing Office, Washington, D.C. Extensive data and commentary on land, water, and timber.

Deevey, Edward. 1960. The human population. *Scientific American,* September. Reprinted in Ehrlich, Holdren, and Holm, eds., *Man and the ecosphere,* W. H. Freeman and Company, San Francisco, 1971, pp. 49–55. Contains classification of world land area by vegetation types.

Ehrlich, Paul R., and John P. Holdren. 1969. Population and panaceas: A technological perspective. *BioScience,* vol. 19, pp. 1065–1071. Discusses logistic and economic limitations on large-scale water movement and desalting.

Fischman, L. L. 1974. Future demand for U.S. forest resources. In *Forest policy for the future,* M. Clawson, ed., pp. 21–86.

Food and Agriculture Organization (FAO). 1960. *World forestry inventory.* United Nations, Rome. Standard reference, now somewhat dated.

Gerasimov, I. P.; D. L. Armand; and K. M. Yefron, eds. 1971. *Natural resources of the Soviet Union: Their use and renewal.* W. H. Freeman and Company, San Francisco. See the section on water, land, and vegetation.

Gieseking, John E., ed. 1975. *Soil components.* vol. 1, *Organic components* and vol. 2, *Inorganic components.* Springer-Verlag, New York. A comprehensive treatment of soil science for specialists.

Giessner, Klaus. 1971. Der mediterrane Wald im Maghreb. *Geographische Rundschau,* October 1971, pp. 390–400. Land use and deforestation in Tunisia, Morocco, and Algeria.

Goldman, M. I. 1972. *Environmental pollution in the Soviet Union.* The M.I.T. Press, Cambridge, Mass. Good coverage of forest practices, water-management projects, and other topics.

Groth, Edward, III. 1975. Increasing the harvest. *Environment,* vol. 17, no. 1 (January/February), pp. 28–39. Use of land and water in U.S. agriculture.

Haden-Guest, S.; J. K. Wright; and E. M. Techoff, eds. 1956. *A world geography of forest resources.* Ronald Press, New York. A comprehensive source book on such topics as principal commercial species, but very out-of-date on policy and exploitation.

Hart, John. 1975. Assault on the Siskiyous. *Cry California,* Fall, pp. 3–11. Deplores timber industry pressure to open scenic parts of national forests to lumbering.

Hirschleifer, J.; J. DeHaven; and J. Milliman. 1969. *Water supply.* University of Chicago Press. Good introduction to the economics of water projects for municipal supply and irrigation.

Hunt, Charles B. 1967. *Physiography of the United States.* W. H. Freeman and Company, San Francisco. Good treatment of soils, water, landforms.

Hylckama, T. Van, 1975. Water resources. In *Environment,* Murdoch, W., ed., Sinauer, Sunderland, Mass. pp. 147–165. Up-to-date survey of global water inventories and problems.

Judson, S. 1968. Erosion of the land. *American Scientist,* vol. 56, no. 4, pp. 356–374. Informative discussion of the history and present status of erosion around the world, based in part on loads of dissolved and suspended material in rivers.

Klein, Richard M. 1969. The Florence floods. *Natural history,* August/September, pp. 46–55. An historical account of the consequences of deforestation in Europe.

Landsberg, H.; L. Fischman; and J. Fisher. 1963. *Resources in America's future.* Johns Hopkins, Baltimore. An encyclopedia of quantitative information about resource supplies and patterns of use in the United States, noted here for its treatment of land, water, and forests. Somewhat dated but still very useful.

Marsh, George Perkins. 1864. *Man and nature.* Reprinted by Harvard University Press, Cambridge, Mass. 1965. The first true classic of the American conservation movement. Beautifully written.

McCaull, Julian. 1975. Dams of pork. *Environment,* vol. 17, no. 1 (January/February), pp. 11–27. Critique of construction of dams when not justified by other than short-term political expediency.

McHugh, J. L. 1966. Management of estuarine fisheries. In *A symposium on estuarine fisheries.* American Fisheries Society, Washington, D.C., special publication 3. Emphasizes importance of estuaries in marine food production, an important dimension of competing uses for coastal lands.

Menard, H. W. 1974. *Geology, resources and society.* W. H. Freeman and Company, San Francisco. Good introductory treatment of soils and the hydrologic cycle.

Metcalf and Eddy, Inc. 1972. *Wastewater engineering.* New York: McGraw-Hill. A useful, comprehensive text.

Micklin, P. 1971. Soviet plans to reverse the flow of rivers. In T. Detwyler, ed., *Man's Impact on Environment.* McGraw-Hill, New York, pp. 302–318.

Murray, C., and E. Reeves. 1972. *Estimated use of water in the United States in 1970.* United States Geological Survey circular 676, Government Printing Office, Washington, D.C.. Basic information on patterns of water consumption.

National Academy of Sciences (NAS). 1973. *Man, materials, and environment.* M.I.T. Press, Cambridge, Mass. Good treatment of environmental problems associated with forest products.

National Commission on Materials Policy. 1973. *Material needs and the environment today and tomorrow.* Government Printing Office, Washington, D.C.; June. Contains projections of future U.S. water use in homes, commerce, and industry.

Parry, T., and R. Norgaard. 1975. Wasting a river. *Environment,* vol. 17, no. 1 (January/February), pp. 11–27. Analytic critique of the cost-benefit analysis used by the Army Corps of Engineers to justify a dam on a California river.

Poland, J. F. 1973. Land subsidence in the western United States. In *Focus on environmental geology,* R. W. Tank, ed. Oxford University Press, New York.

President's Science Advisory Committee. 1967. *The world food problem.* 3 vols. Government Printing Office, Washington, D.C. Noted here for classification of world land area according to suitability for cultivation.

Pryde, Philip R. 1972. *Conservation in the Soviet Union.* Cambridge University Press, London. Contains chapters on land, water, and forests.

Rawlins, S. L., and P. A. C. Raats. 1975. Prospects for high-frequency irrigation. *Science,* vol. 188, pp. 604–610 (May 9). An approach to increasing the efficiency of water use in irrigation.

Revelle, R., and V. Lakshminarayana. 1975. The Ganges water machine. *Science,* vol. 188, pp. 611–616 (May 9). Use of wells and drainage systems to improve water management in the Ganges basin.

Richardson, S. D. 1966. *Forestry in communist China.* Johns Hopkins, Baltimore. Somewhat out-of-date, but still an important source, especially on such slowly changing subjects as soils and major tree species.

Ridker, R. G. 1972. Future water needs and supplies. In *Research reports,* vol. 3, R. Ridker, ed., Commission on Population Growth and the American future. Government Printing Office, Washington, D.C. Useful quantitative treatment of U.S. water situation, with projections to the year 2000.

Routley, R., and V. Routley, 1975. *The fight for the forests.* 3d ed. Research School of Social Sciences, Australian National University, Canberra.

Sanchez, P., and S. Buol. 1975. Soils of the tropics and the world food crisis. *Science,* vol. 188, pp. 598–603 (May 9). Problems and potential of tropical soils.

Sewell, W. 1967. NAWAPA: A continental water system. *Bulletin of the Atomic Scientists,* vol. 23, no. 7, pp. 8–13. Description of the dormant North American Water and Power Alliance.

Spurr, S. H., and B. V. Barnes. 1973. *Forest ecology.* 2d ed. Ronald, New York. Comprehensive—covers forests from genetics through physical factors, ecosystem characteristics, and historical development.

Strahler, A. N., and A. H. Strahler. 1973. *Environmental geoscience.* Hamilton, Santa Barbara, Calif. Contains a good introduction to soils and the hydrologic cycle.

Study of Man's Impact on Climate (SMIC). 1971. *Inadvertent climate modification.* M.I.T. Press, Cambridge, Mass. Contains estimates of flows in global hydrologic cycle.

University of California Food Task Force. 1974. *A hungry world: The challenge to agriculture.* Division of Agricultural Sciences, University of California, Berkeley. Use of land and water in world agriculture.

U.S. Department of Agriculture. 1974. *Foreign agricultural economic report,* 298. Government Printing Office, Washington, D.C. Useful data on land use in agriculture.

U.S. Department of Agriculture. 1973. *The outlook for timber in the United States.* Government Printing Office, Washington, D.C. Good data source.

U.S. Department of Commerce. 1975. *Statistical abstract of the United States.* Government Printing Office, Washington, D.C. Data on the uses and supplies of land and water.

U.S. Water Resources Council. 1968. *The nation's water resources.* Government Printing Office, Washington, D.C. Standard reference on water supply and use, now somewhat dated.

Vink, A. P. A. 1975. *Land use in advancing agriculture.* Springer-Verlag, New York. A detailed, technical discussion.

Wollman, N., and G. Bonem. 1971. *The outlook for water.* Johns Hopkins, Baltimore. Contains useful treatment of water quality and waste treatment.

Wood, N. 1971. *Clearcut.* Sierra Club, San Francisco. Survey of questionable practices in the timber industry, with emphasis on the West.

Wortman, S. 1975. Agriculture in China. *Scientific American,* June, pp. 13–21. Useful survey of a subject on which little information is available.

Young, Gale. 1970. Dry lands and desalted water. *Science,* vol. 167, pp. 339–343 (January 23). Expresses hope of desalting for large-scale agriculture, based on availability of cheap energy.

The human brain, so frail, so perishable,
so full of inexhaustible dreams and hungers,
burns by the power of the leaf.

–Loren Eiseley,
The Unexpected Universe, 1969

CHAPTER 7

A Hungry World

Photographs of Earth taken from the moon make the finite nature of our planet apparent in a way that no writing can. But knowing a vehicle is finite and knowing how many passengers it can carry are not the same thing. What is the actual capacity of Earth to support people? Unfortunately, there is no simple answer to this question, although certain theoretical limits may be calculated. Justus von Liebig's principle, known as the "law of the minimum," says, in essence, that the size of a population or the life of an individual will be limited by whatever requisite of life is in the shortest supply. It is not yet entirely clear what that requisite will be for the human population, which, as we have seen, is growing at an extraordinary rate. But the likeliest factor to limit Earth's capacity to support *Homo sapiens* is the supply of food, since this supply depends on the availability of so many other essential resources: land, water, nutrients, and energy.

Apart from the limits that may ultimately be posed by Earth's absolute capacity to support human beings, there are gross differences between groups of people with regard to their food supplies. The rich are abundantly, even wastefully fed; the poorest live perpetually on the brink of famine.

This chapter describes the present nutritional status of the human population and the outlook for meeting future

A

B

FIGURE 7-1

A. An example of slash-and-burn agriculture. The new clearing in second-growth forest contains many stumps of trees that have been cut high for use as props for growing plants. Some, although stripped of their leaves, will survive; along with invading tree seedlings they will slowly reforest the garden site. (Photo by Ray A. Rappaport.) B. An example of modern mechanized agriculture, which is characterized by high-energy inputs to maintain stability and high yields. These machines are wheat combines. (Photo by William A. Garnett.)

needs for food. It explores how the prognosis might be improved: ways in which food production might be increased, and how patterns of distribution might be changed to provide more food for the hungry millions. First, however, some description of the elements of food production is in order.

THE PRODUCTION OF FOOD

At the most basic level of all, human beings, like all other animals, have always been dependent on the process of photosynthesis for food. Whether primitive people ate berries, roots, fishes, reindeer, or whatever, the energy derived from food had the same ultimate source: the radiant energy of the sun.

Not until the agricultural revolution, however, did humanity begin to exercise some control over plant growth and attempt to concentrate and increase the yield from desirable food plants. (*Yield* refers to production per unit of land area, such as an acre or a hectare.) The earliest attempts at agriculture doubtless were based on the astute observation that certain accidental disturbances of the land by human activities increased the growth of some useful plants. Indeed, the "slash-and-burn" agriculture (*milpa* agriculture) practiced today in many humid tropical areas consists of little more than cutting and burning clearings in which seeds or cuttings of various desirable plants are then scattered. It would have been a small step from such a practice to the reduction of competition for the desired plants by simply hoeing weeds, protecting the crop from animals, and making use of the fertilizing effects of excreta and other organic wastes.[1]

Modern agriculture as practiced in most developed nations is, of course, completely different from milpa agriculture (see Figure 7-1). In many respects it is quite different even from traditional temperate-zone agriculture as still practiced in parts of Europe and many less

---

[1]Charles B. Heiser, Jr., *Seed to civilization: The story of man's food,* W.H. Freeman and Company, San Francisco, 1975; Jack R. Harlan, The plants and animals that nourish man. For some interesting ideas on the origin of milpa agriculture, see David R. Harris, The origins of agriculture in the tropics, *American Scientist,* vol. 60, pp. 180–193. It is possible that such cultivation, using cuttings rather than seeds, began in the tropical areas of Africa and South America as early as, or even earlier than, the first grain cultivation in Asia and Central America.

developed countries outside the tropics. The changes in temperate agriculture during the past few hundred years could quite fairly be considered a second agricultural revolution. The science of plant breeding has produced new crop varieties that are adapted to various growing conditions, high in yield, resistant to diseases, and so forth. Mechanical cultivation and harvesting, improved methods of fertilization and irrigation, the use of chemical and biological controls against plant and insect pests, weather forecasting, and many other technological advances have greatly increased the quantity of food that can be produced on a given area of land.

Some of these advances are mixed blessings, however. Many have unwelcome environmental side-effects, which will be discussed later in this chapter and further in Chapter 11. Some methods may contribute to higher productivity, but, if they are not used with care, their contribution is made at the expense of future production as soil depletion is accelerated.

Technology has also increased the quality of many crops, but not necessarily in all respects. For instance, high yields in grains have sometimes been gained at the cost of lowered pest resistance or other undesirable changes in characteristics. In general, high-yielding crops require considerably more support and attention than traditional strains in order to realize their full potential productivity.

Although human action can modify many of the conditions of plant growth, limits are imposed upon agricultural production by geographic variation in the amount of solar energy reaching the surface of Earth, temperatures of both soil and air, amount of soil moisture available, and so forth. And, because of the key role played by photosynthesis in agriculture, it is inevitable that farming will remain a highly dispersed human activity. Agriculture must remain spread over the face of Earth, because the energy of sunlight can only be utilized in photosynthesis at its point of arrival. Furthermore, especially when populations are large, agricultural production and the transport of agricultural goods will always remain intimately intertwined; food production cannot be considered in isolation from food distribution. It is not possible to concentrate agriculture in regions of need, as it is sometimes possible to concentrate production of other substances required by human beings.

FIGURE 7-2

An orange grove in Southern California being replaced by a subdivision. At lower left are undisturbed orange groves; at upper center is finished housing. At right is housing in various stages of completion; at lower right is a freshly cleared area with one orange tree remaining per lot. Since the photograph was taken (in the 1950s), the entire area has been developed. (Photo by William A. Garnett.)

Indeed, high and growing concentrations of human beings tend to be inimical to agriculture; food must be brought to them, and they occupy land that could produce it. As anyone knows who has lived in the country around Philadelphia, Chicago, or Los Angeles, for instance, farmland around cities is disappearing beneath pavement—each year about 250,000 hectares of prime agricultural land in the United States are "developed" into subdivisions and highways.[2] Between the early 1950s and early 1970s, some 11 million hectares were converted into airports, freeways, and suburbs—a total area larger than Ohio.[3] If less than first-class land is considered, the quantity that has been—and continues to be—lost rises to over 18 million hectares since 1945, with an annual loss of a million hectares in the early 1970s.[3a]

In recent decades, for each 1000 people added to the population of California, an average of 100 hectares of arable land has been covered by buildings and pavement.[4] Figure 7-2 graphically shows the process underway. Residents and industry also compete for freshwater

---

[2] *Time*, The world food crisis, November 11, 1974.

[3] D. Pimentel, et al., Energy and land constraints in food protein production.

[3a] Pimentel, et al., Land degradation: effects on food and energy resources.

[4] K. E. F. Watt, personal communication.

supplies, which are becoming increasingly scarce in many regions. (See Chapter 6 for more on conversion of land to urban uses and dwindling untapped water supplies.) Moreover, smog can reduce yields and even kill crops.

If farmland continued to be converted to urban use at the rates prevailing in the 1960s, California eventually would not be able to feed itself, let alone export food to other states and abroad as it does today. In dollar volume, California is the most important agricultural state. Fortunately, since 1970 immigration into California has slowed to a trickle, and rising farmland values, new protective tax laws, and actions of environmental groups have substantially reduced the rate of farmland conversion.

In general, it is important to remember that the agricultural system of a nation is an integral part of its socio-economic system, and that this often places constraints on how much food is produced.[5] For example, it is often overlooked in discussions of the world food problem that farmers, like plumbers, corporate executives, and university professors, expect economic rewards for their labors. They will not grow food to sell for less than it costs to grow it. Thus the economics of agroecosystems inevitably pervades realistic discussions of how much food can be grown in various places and how much can be stored and distributed in various patterns.

TABLE 7-1
Sources of Humanity's Food Energy

Food		*Percentage of energy supplied*
CEREALS		56
Rice	21	
Wheat	20	
Corn	5	
Other cereals	10	
ROOTS AND TUBERS		7
Potatoes and yams	5	
Cassava	2	
FRUITS, NUTS, AND VEGETABLES		10
SUGAR		7
FATS AND OILS		9
LIVESTOCK PRODUCTS AND FISH		11
total		100

Source: Lester R. Brown and Erik P. Eckholm, *By bread alone.*

Major Food Crops

Some 80 species of food plants have been domesticated, as opposed to only about two dozen kinds of animals. Over the centuries, most of them have been improved by selective breeding and/or by hybridization. Virtually all the original domestication of both plants and animals took place in prehistoric times.[6] But, in spite of the diversity of available food plants, a relatively small array of crops supplies the great bulk of the world's food. If one had to pick the three most important food plants in the world, the almost inevitable choice would be three species of grasses: rice, wheat, and corn. So important are these cereal grains that slightly more than one-half of the harvested land of the world is used to grow them. Wheat and rice together supply roughly 40 percent of humanity's food energy (Table 7-1). Altogether, cereal grains provide well over half of the calories consumed by the human population and nearly half of the protein.[7]

Rice is the most important crop of all; it is the staple food for over two billion people. As is shown in Figure 7-3, the People's Republic of China grows about 35 percent of the world's rice; India, Bangladesh, Indonesia, Japan, and Thailand account for another 43 percent. Most of the remaining 22 percent is grown in Southeast Asia and Latin America.[8] Total world production of rice (before milling) in 1974 was an estimated 323 million metric tons.

Wheat almost equals rice in importance to the diet of human beings. (Sometimes wheat production in tonnage exceeds that of rice, but some of it is used as feed for livestock.) In 1974 some 360 million metric tons of wheat were produced. Unlike rice, wheat does not grow well in the tropics, in part because one of its major diseases, wheat-rust fungus, thrives in warm, humid climates. Wheat is grown mostly where winters are cold and wet,

[5]Robert S. Loomis, Agricultural systems.

[6]Stuart Struever, ed., *Prehistoric agriculture.*

[7]Pimentel, et al., Energy and land constraints.

[8]United Nations Food and Agriculture Organization, *Production yearbook, 1974* (FAO, Rome, 1975); J. Janick et al., *Plant science.* These two are the main sources for what follows.

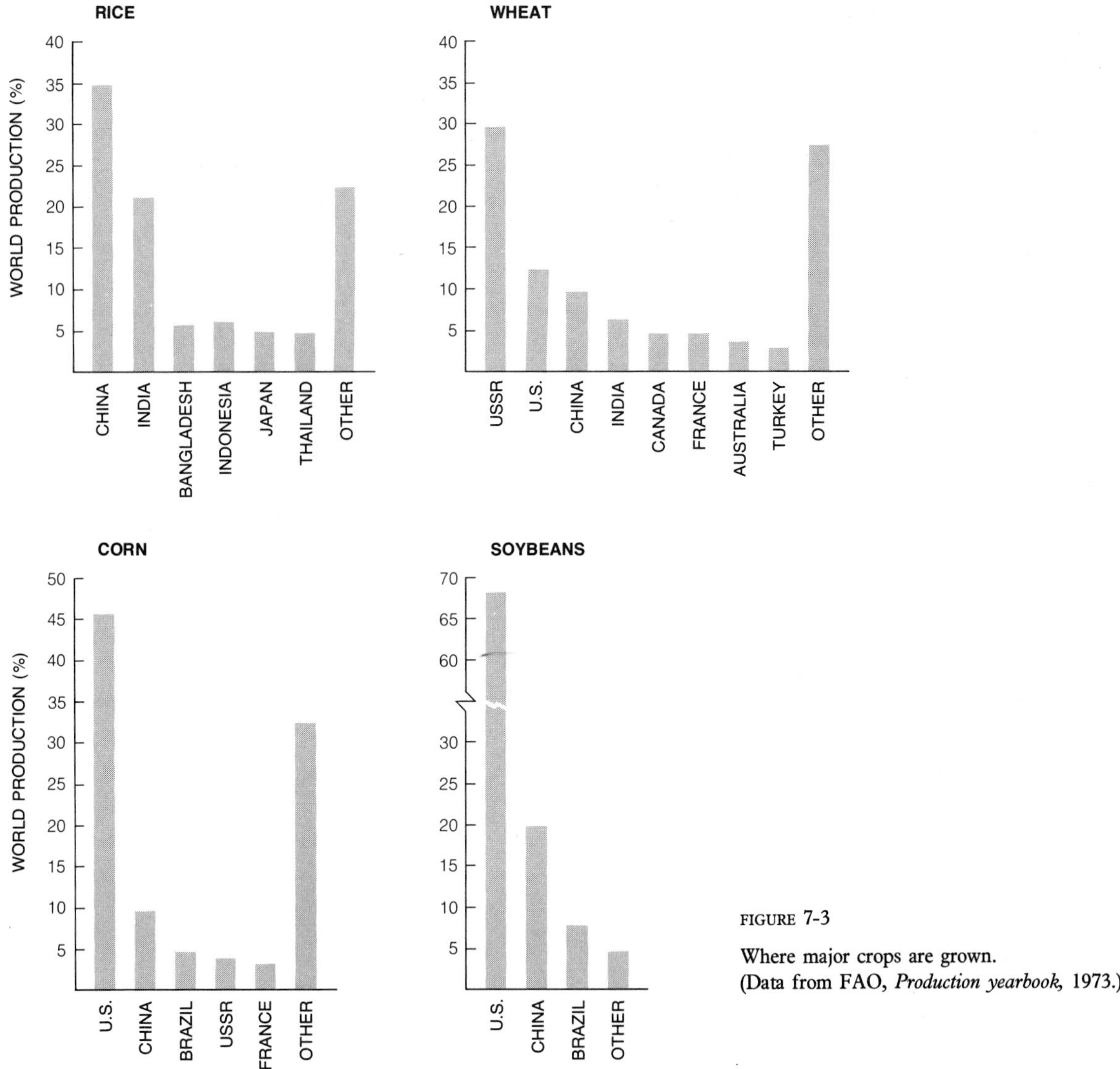

FIGURE 7-3

Where major crops are grown. (Data from FAO, *Production yearbook,* 1973.)

and summers hot and rather dry (although in the U.S. wheat belt most of the precipitation occurs in the summer). The Soviet Union produces nearly 30 percent of the world's wheat. Most of the rest is grown in such temperate areas as China, northern India, North America, Europe, and Australia.

Corn, or maize, is the third great cereal crop, with 1974 production being about 293 million metric tons. The long, warm, moist summers of the eastern half of the United States are ideal for corn production, and more than 45 percent of the world supply is grown there. It should be noted, though, that the bulk of American corn production is fed to livestock; human consumption of corn as a principal staple is mainly confined to Latin America and tropical Africa.

Rice, wheat, and corn together accounted for nearly one billion metric tons of grain in 1974. The rest of the world's cereal grain crop of about 1.2 billion metric tons was made up by other grains: barley, oats, rye, millet, and sorghum. Somewhat more than half the world's production of these grains come from the United States, the USSR, and Western Europe. These grains, together with corn, are commonly referred to as "coarse grains" (as contrasted with wheat and rice, the "small grains").

Roughly 300 million metric tons of potatoes are also grown annually, but the water content of the potato is so high (75 percent) that the food value of the total harvest is considerably less than that of any of the "big three" grains. (On a per-acre basis, however, the potato may be superior.) The potato is particularly well-adapted to cool climates. Fully one-third of the world's potato production comes from the Soviet Union, 16 percent comes from Poland, and over 11 percent from China. The United States and East and West Germany are also important producers. The rest of the world accounts for less than 30 percent, mostly European and Latin American countries.

The protein content of most modern grains ranges between 5 and 15 percent and is not complete protein (that is, it does not have an ideal balance of amino acids for human nutrition). In most grains the protein is too low in content of some essential amino acids, especially tryptophan and lysine. Grains and potatoes are all rich in protein, however, in comparison with some of the starchier staple crops commonly consumed in humid tropical countries: taro, cassava, yams, and plaintains.

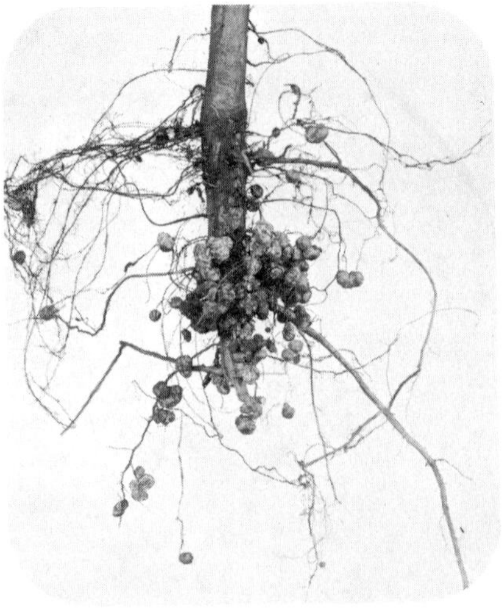

Legumes (a family of plants that includes peas, beans, peanuts, soybeans and several forage crops) cannot compete in volume with grains in world food production. They have two to four times the protein content of grains, however, and thus are critically important in human nutrition and for domestic animals as well. For the human population, legumes provide about 20 percent of the protein supply worldwide.[9] Bacteria associated with the roots of legumes have the ability to fix gaseous nitrogen from the atmosphere and convert it into a form that can be directly used by plants (See Figure 7-4). As a result, legumes also serve as fertilizer ("green manure") when planted in rotation or intercropped with other crops, and thereby also can contribute indirectly to the protein derived from other plants.

Two legumes, soybeans and peanuts (groundnuts), are grown mainly for use as oil sources and livestock feed. These two crops account for about two-thirds of the world's legume production of some 124 million metric tons; soybeans alone reached 63 mmt in 1973.[10] Both are excellent sources of protein, especially soybeans. The protein content of soybeans is some three times as high as that of wheat, for instance. Both soybean oil and peanut oil are used for making margarine, salad dressings, and shortenings, and are also used in various industrial processes. The high-protein material remaining after the oils are pressed out (presscake) is usually sold for livestock feed. Except in the Far East, relatively little of the soybean crop is directly consumed by people, although this is changing as inflation induces people in DCs to substitute cheaper foods for meat. Soy products are becoming increasingly popular with Americans. A significant portion of the peanut crop has long been eaten in the nut form or in candy or peanut butter around the world. Production of soybeans is concentrated in the United States and China, although production in Brazil was increasing rapidly in the 1970s. Peanuts are grown mainly in India and Africa.

The remaining legumes—beans and peas—are known collectively as pulses. There is a wide variety of these, including lima beans, string beans, white beans, kidney beans, scotch beans, peas, cow peas, garbanzos, and

FIGURE 7-4

Nitrogen-fixing bacteria inhabit the nodules of soybean roots in a mutualistic relationship. (Photo by J. C. Allen and Son.)

[9]Pimentel, et al., Energy and land constraints.

[10]Folke Dovring, Soybeans. This is an interesting account of the growth in importance of soybeans as a major food crop.

lentils. Because they are among the richest plant sources of protein, pulses provide a significant element in the human diet, especially in poor countries. Moreover, the proteins of pulses, although also incomplete, complement those of grains to furnish a complete protein meal when they are eaten together.

Unfortunately, annual world production of pulses has not increased significantly since 1962. In developed countries, they may have been replaced in part by increased consumption of meat and dairy products. But in rapidly growing less developed countries, the lack of increase in pulse production for more than a decade indicates a considerable reduction in per-capita supplies. Since the gap has mainly been filled by grains, the probable result is a deterioration of protein levels in diets, both in quantity and quality. In some countries, acreage planted to pulses has actually been *reduced* in favor of more profitable high-yield grains.[11]

Cereals and legumes are the worldwide mainstays of the human diet, but a vast variety of other plants is cultivated and consumed. Cassava, taro, sweet potatoes, and yams (all root crops) supply food energy to many people in the world, especially to the poor in humid tropical areas; people subsisting mainly on these starchy foods are relatively likely to suffer from protein deficiency. The roots of the sugar-beet plant and the stems of the cane-sugar plant (a grass) supply sugar to people around the world. The roots, stems, fruits, berries, and leaves of numerous other plants are important sources of energy, vitamins, and minerals in human diets.

Many plants are also used as forages—foods for domestic animals. Although ruminants (cattle, sheep, and goats) are often just turned loose on rangeland to graze and fend for themselves, many forage crops are grown in pastures or harvested and used for hay or silage (fermented fodder) specifically to feed them. In the United States, which consumes large quantities of meat per capita, the forage crop fed to animals in 1973 was only slightly less (as measured by nutritional equivalent) than the entire U.S. grain harvest for that year (and much of that was also fed to animals). Some 60 million acres of the world are planted in the legume *alfalfa* (called "lucerne" in Europe), which is among the most nutritious of all forage crops and is especially rich in protein. Some other legumes—for instance, clovers—are also grown as forage, as are a great variety of grasses.[12]

Food from Animals

The primary nutritional importance of domesticated animals in many cultures is as a source of high-quality protein. They are, of course, valued for other roles as well, especially in less developed countries where traditional techniques of agriculture still prevail. There the larger farm animals—cattle, horses, and water buffalo—are highly valued as draft animals and as transport. The dung of all livestock is valued everywhere as an important source of fertilizer and in some regions as fuel and building plaster. In some societies, the value of animals for food is almost incidental to their other uses.

The variety of animals that have been domesticated for food is considerably more limited than that of plants. Only nine species—cattle, pigs, sheep, goats, water buffalo, chickens, ducks, geese, and turkeys—account for nearly 100 percent of the world's production of protein from domesticated animals. Beef and pork together, in roughly equal amounts, account for some 90 percent of meat production (excluding poultry). Cows produce more than 90 percent of the milk consumed, water buffalo about 4 percent, and goats and sheep the remainder (ignoring tiny amounts from reindeer and some other minor domestic mammals).[13]

Although certain breeds of domestic animals are adapted to the tropics, animal husbandry is generally easier and more productive in temperate areas than in the tropics. It is primarily in the temperate zones that geneticists have produced animals capable of extraordinary yields of meat, milk, and eggs, given special care and intensive feeding of high-protein feedstuffs. The year-round high temperatures and possibly the high humidity of the tropics tend to slow growth and, in milk-producing animals, lower the production of milk and milk solids. Unfortunately, although forage may grow luxuriantly in many tropical areas, the native varieties are commonly

[11] J. D. Gavan and J. A. Dixon, India: A perspective on the food situation.

[12] H. J. Hodgson, Forage crops.

[13] H. H. Cole, ed., *Introduction to livestock production;* H. H. Cole and M. Ronning, eds., *Animal agriculture.*

low in nutrient value. High temperature and humidity also often provide ideal conditions for parasites and carriers of disease. For instance, in a large portion of Africa where rainfall and other conditions are suitable (about 37 percent of the continent) tsetse flies carry a serious disease, *nagana* (caused by single-celled organisms called trypanosomes), which makes cattle herding impossible.[14]

Domestic animals, especially cattle, are often more than mere meat or milk producers in LDCs. In the semiarid zones of East and West Africa, cattle are the basis of entire cultures. They are regularly tapped for blood as well as milk, and are intimately related to the social and economic life of certain groups. Cattle provide their owners with wealth and prestige, are used ceremonially, and have aesthetic value.

In India there is a large population of "sacred cattle," so called because of the Hindu taboo against slaughter. Visitors to India rather commonly conclude that the Indian food situtation could be ameliorated by slaughtering these "useless" animals. This judgment is based on a fundamental misunderstanding of the situation. Like so many folkways and taboos, the Indian taboo has a vital influence on the local ecology. Most of the cattle feed on forage and waste vegetation that are not human foods: they do not compete with people for food. The cattle *do* supply milk, and above all they supply power. Bullocks (castrated bulls) are the tractors of India; they are absolutely essential to her agricultural economy. Finally, the cattle also supply dung, which serves as the main cooking fuel of India, and which is also used as fertilizer and as plaster in houses. Of an estimated 800 million tons of dung produced each year, some 300 million were used as fuel in the 1960s. This fuel produced heat equivalent to that obtained from burning 35 million tons of coal (about half of India's coal production).[15]

The consumption of meat and poultry has grown very rapidly since World War II, especially in developed countries. World production in 1974 amounted to just under 116 million metric tons, of which the developed regions produced about 79 million metric tons and the less developed regions produced the remaining 37 million metric tons.[16] Meat clearly occupies a far less important position in the diets of people in LDCs, with the notable exception of herding societies such as the Masai, the people of the Sahel, and nomads in the Middle East and Central Asia.

[14]D. F. Owen, *Animal ecology in tropical Africa.*

[15]A. Leeds and A. P. Vayda, eds., *Man, culture, and animals.*

THE DIMENSIONS OF WORLD HUNGER

In 1967 the President's Science Advisory Committee Panel on the World Food Supply[17] estimated that 20 percent of the people in the less developed countries (which include two-thirds of the world's population) were undernourished (that is, were not receiving enough calories per day) and that perhaps 60 percent were malnourished (seriously lacking in one or more essential nutrients, most commonly protein). As many as a billion and a half people thus were described as either undernourished or malnourished. This may have been a conservative estimate; others have placed the number of "hungry" people during the mid-1960s at two billion or more.[18] The President's Panel further estimated that perhaps a half billion people were either chronically hungry or starving. (These numbers did not include the hungry and malnourished millions in the lower economic strata of developed countries such as the United States, or the numbers of people who could afford to eat well but were malnourished because of their ignorance of elementary nutrition.) Nor did this situation suddenly develop in the 1960s; chronic hunger had long existed among the poor around the world.

Recent History of Food Production

Between World War II and 1972, there was a steady, worldwide, upward trend in the amount of food produced for each person on Earth. This trend generally continued uninterrupted in the developed countries, with a few exceptions and setbacks, until the 1970s. In the less developed regions, however, the steady increase

[16]FAO, *Production yearbook,* 1974.

[17]*The world food problem,* vol. 2, p. 5.

[18]G. Borgstrom, *Too many.*

TABLE 7-2
Estimated Number of People with Insufficient Protein/Energy Supply by Regions (1970)

Region	*Population (in billions)*	*Percentage below lower limit*	*Number below lower limit (in millions)*
Developed regions	1.07	3	28
Developing regions excluding Asian centrally planned economies	1.75	25	434
Latin America	0.28	13	36
Far East	1.02	30	301
Near East	0.17	18	30
Africa	0.28	25	67
World (excluding Asian centrally planned economies)	2.83	16	462

Source: UN, *Assessment.*

in per-capita food production was halted sometime between 1956 and 1960, depending on the country. Because population growth in LDCs more or less equalled the growth in total food production, the available supply per person has fluctuated around the same level ever since. In 1970 the average country in Africa was producing *less* food per person than it had in the mid-1950s, while the average country in Latin America and the Far East had slightly improved its condition. Among less developed regions, only China and the near East significantly increased their food supplies per person between 1955 and 1970. This situation obtained in spite of substantial increases (roughly 30-35 percent) in *absolute food supplies* in all these areas during that period; population growth offset the gains.

There was widespread optimism in the late 1960s and early 1970s that improvements in agricultural techniques, especially in less developed nations (the Green Revolution), would allow food-production increases—at least for a few decades—to exceed the 2 percent annual growth of the world's population, which was then adding about 75 million hungry mouths every year. Between 1967 and 1972, food production did indeed rise more rapidly than population growth, most encouragingly in some of the hungriest nations in Asia. Even so, a large segment of the human population was not receiving sufficient daily bread.

The United Nations has very conservatively estimated that some 460 million people were "seriously undernourished" during those relatively food-abundant years just before 1972. Moreover, the UN conceded that, by less conservative criteria, the number of hungry people at that time actually might be *more than twice as great.* Because infants and young children are most likely to suffer when food supplies are inadequate, the UN further estimated that *perhaps one-half of all children under five years old in developing countries were inadequately nourished to some degree.*[19]

Table 7-2 shows the UN estimates of the distribution of undernourished people in the world by region in 1970. It should be noted that even in the generally well-fed developed regions, 3 percent, or 28 million people, were considered undernourished. Not a few of those were in the United States. Figure 7-5 shows where the hungry nations are located.

Since 1971, the prospects for raising nutritional levels in the poor countries have dimmed. The early 1970s, particularly 1972 and 1974, were marked by unusually adverse weather for agriculture in a broad array of regions, including densely populated Southern Asia, agriculturally important North America, much of tropical Africa, and parts of Southeast Asia, Brazil, the Soviet

[19]United Nations, *Assessment of the world food situation, present and future.* The estimate excluded China and other centrally planned countries in Asia because of insufficient data; China was not admitted to the United Nations until late 1971. It is worth noting, however, that the accumulating evidence, though not at all conclusive, indicates that the people of China and the other centrally planned Asian countries (North Vietnam and North Korea) have been fairly adequately fed in recent years. China responded to a poor harvest in 1972 by buying wheat from the United States. So far as anyone can tell, the Chinese people suffered no significant ill-effects from food shortage then.

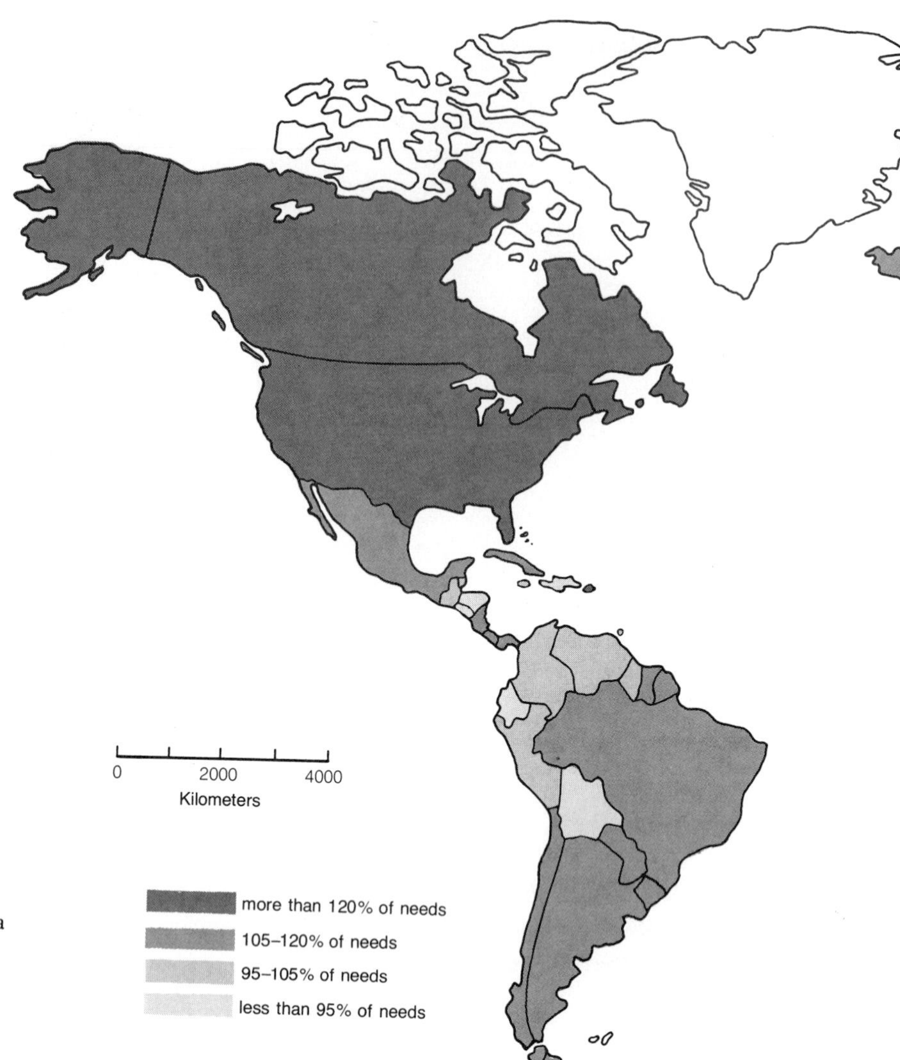

FIGURE 7-5

The geography of hunger, 1969–1971. (Data from *Assessment of the world food situation, present and future,* UN World Food Conference, 1974.)

Union, and China. These widespread weather changes, unanticipated by the agricultural community, manifested themselves mainly as floods, droughts, and sometimes both, at different times. The consequence of this series of weather changes, exacerbated in 1974 by the fourfold increase in oil prices and a severe shortfall in fertilizer production, was an unprecedented worldwide shortage of food by the end of that year.

In 1972, after a strong upward trend for 20 years, world food production declined. Production of grains—wheat, rice, and coarse grains—on which people in poor countries primarily depend for sustenance, fell 33 million metric tons below 1971 harvests, about 3 percent. To meet the growing demand, 25 million metric tons *more* than the 1971 total were needed. At that time adequate reserves existed; so most countries were able to obtain enough grain on the world market or from food aid to meet their needs, at least at prevailing inadequate standards.

The primary consequence of the 1972 shortfall in production was a worldwide steep rise in prices of basic foods, especially of grains. Higher food prices inevitably most affect the poorest people in every nation. The blame for the price-rise in grains has been attributed to speculation on the world market and to unusually large grain purchases in 1972 and 1973 by the USSR and China—some 30 million metric tons—mostly from the United States at low, government-subsidized prices. The basic cause, of course, was the production shortfall (and subsequently diminishing reserves), but this has often

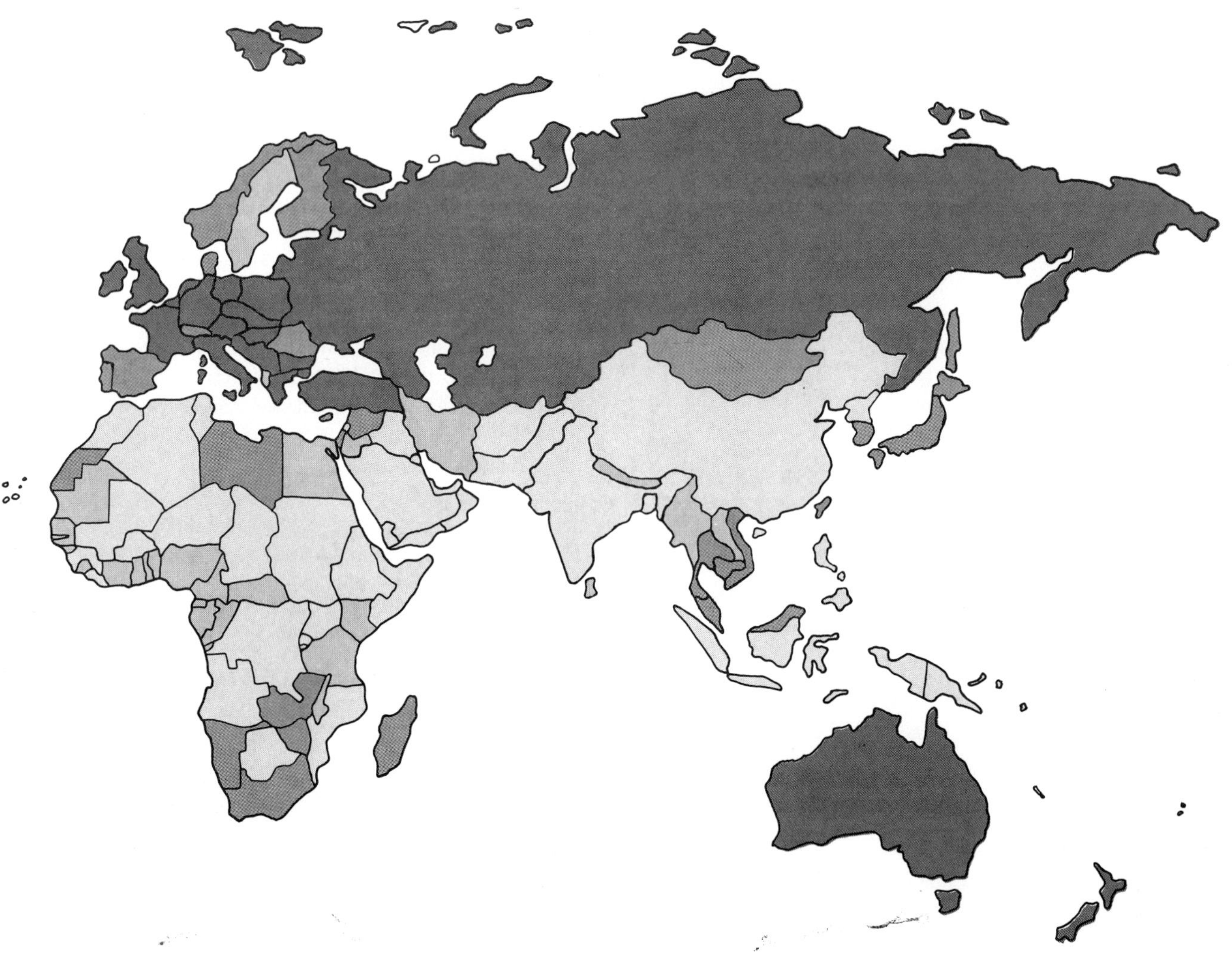

been overlooked, at least in the popular press. Between 1972 and 1974, world market prices for wheat, rice, corn (maize), and soybeans tripled or quadrupled. Later they declined somewhat, but generally have remained at about twice their 1972 levels.[20]

There was a partial recovery of food production in 1973, mainly in DCs, and per-capita grain production returned to "normal" levels on a worldwide average. Grain reserves continued to decline, however, as they were drawn down to compensate for the 1972 deficit.

Widespread bad weather struck again in 1974, coinciding with the energy crisis and a severe fertilizer shortage. This time the decline over the 1973 grain production amounted to some 50 million metric tons—even more than the decline of 1972, a drop of more than 4 percent. Per capita, of course, the decline was even greater: about 6 percent.

The world food picture in late 1974 was considerably gloomier than the unattractive situation described in detail by the President's Panel on the World Food Supply in 1967. World grain reserves (stored grain, mostly U.S. surplus, plus the potential production of idled land) in 1967 were equal to 55 days' supply, the low point for that decade. In 1974 reserves were down to a 33-day supply—essentially what exists in the "pipeline" of supply channels.[21]

[20]UN, *Assessment;* USDA Economic Research Service, *World agricultural situation,* WAS-12, December 1976.

[21]Lester R. Brown, The politics and responsibility of the North American breadbasket.

Large-scale famine was then occurring in the Sahel (the southern fringe of the Sahara desert, including parts of the nations of Chad, Gambia, Mali, Mauritania, Senegal, Upper Volta, and Niger), where drought had prevailed for six consecutive years.[22] Famine was also threatening India[23] and Bangladesh,[24] both of which had been struck by floods and at least partial monsoon failures in two of the previous three years. Other regions threatened with severe food shortages included some thirteen additional African countries, comprising virtually all of tropical Africa; four Central American and Caribbean nations; Pakistan, Sri Lanka, Laos, and Cambodia in Asia; and Yemen and South Yemen in the Middle East.

In October 1974, the United Nations' Food and Agriculture Organization (generally known as FAO) announced that no less than 32 nations, within which nearly three-quarters of a billion people were already marginally or inadequately nourished, were threatened with starvation and bankruptcy unless developed nations provided them with food and economic assistance.

On top of the widespread adverse weather in 1974, the oil embargo of fall 1973, followed by the quadrupling of oil prices by OPEC nations, caused serious problems for agriculture. Apart from the need for gasoline to operate farm machinery, petroleum and (especially) natural gas are needed for the manufacture of fertilizers. Manufactured fertilizers were already in short supply; the effect of the oil crisis was to worsen the shortage of fertilizers worldwide. And less developed countries, which have become increasingly dependent on fertilizers to raise their food production, were most hard hit. The UN estimated that the fertilizer shortage might have reduced grain production in LDCs in 1974 by 12 million metric tons.[25]

Almost simultaneously with the drops in world agricultural production, fisheries harvests, which had also risen steadily since World War II, began to decline. The peak, over 70 million metric tons of fish, was reached in 1971. In 1972 and 1973, the fish catch fell below 66 million metric tons.[26] Although fisheries production contributes only a small percentage of the calories in the world food budget, it is a vital source of protein, especially to protein-short LDCs.

Hopes were high that 1975 harvests would brighten the world food picture and allow some rebuilding of grain reserves. But total production barely exceeded the disastrous 1974 level. This time the poor harvests were centered mainly in the developed countries, especially the USSR. Because of bad weather again, the 1975 Soviet grain harvest fell some 55 million metric tons below that of the previous year. Meanwhile, the less developed nations enjoyed an average 5 percent increase in food production in 1975 after three consecutive poor years.[27]

The total world cereal crop for 1975/1976 was estimated by the U.S. Department of Agriculture at 1220 million metric tons, only 20 mmt above the previous year and still 34 mmt below the record of 1973/1974. Since most of the 1975/1976 shortfall occurred in DCs (especially the USSR), those countries absorbed it, largely through reduced meat consumption. Nevertheless, averaged worldwide, production of grain per capita, at 309 kilograms of grain per person, reached a ten-year low, and there was no improvement in the carryover supply.

The picture brightened somewhat in 1976/1977, when preliminary reports indicated a total grain harvest of over 1320 mmt.[27a] This increase of 100 mmt was achieved despite severe floods in Japan and parts of southeast Asia, drought in the north-central United States, and a drought in Western Europe unequalled in many centuries. Grain reserves, mostly of wheat, rose significantly

[22]Numerous popular articles have appeared in recent years on the Sahel tragedy. Among the more recent are: The drought revisited, *Time,* April 21, 1975; Sub-Sahara land hopeful on crops, *New York Times,* November 10, 1974, Disaster in the Sahel, *New Internationalist,* no. 16, June 1974. The ecological basis of the famine is discussed in Chapter 11.

[23]Vivid descriptions of the situation in India by fall of 1974 can be found in: Letter from New Delhi, *New Yorker,* October 14, 1974; India's grim famine: With luck only 30m will starve, *The National Times* (Australia), October 28–November 2, 1974; India: An unprecedented national crisis, by Marcus Franda, *Common Ground,* vol. 1, no. 1, pp. 63–76 (American Univ. Fieldstaff), Jan. 1975; Anguish of the hungry spreading across India, by Bernard Weinraub, *New York Times,* October 27, 1974.

[24]Kasturi Rangan, Bangladesh is faced with large-scale deaths from starvation, *New York Times,* October 11, 1974; Kasturi Rangan, Bangladesh fears thousands may be dead as famine spreads, *New York Times,* November 13, 1974; Kushwant Singh, Bangladesh, the international basket case, *New York Times Magazine,* January 26, 1975.

[25]United Nations, *Assessment.*

[26]United Nations, *Statistical yearbook,* 1974.

[27]USDA, WAS-9, WAS-10, and WAS-12.

[27a]USDA, WAS-12.

in 1977 for the first time since 1972 but were still far short of goals set by the 1974 World Food Conference.

The outlook for 1977/1978 was not encouraging. The disastrous winter of 1976/1977 in the United States alone, with record cold and snowfall in the East and severe drought in the West, could not fail to reduce agricultural production in the American granary. Once again, plans to build up world grain reserves as insurance against weather-caused reductions in grain production may be defeated by that same eventuality.

Agriculture's continuing dependence on weather thus has been emphatically brought home by the events of the 1970s. Moreover, the damage has not been limited to LDCs; such supposedly secure granaries as the United States, Europe, Australia, and the USSR have also suffered. Table 7-3 shows the U.S. Department of Agriculture estimates for the world's total grain production during the 1970s. Table 7-4 shows the decline in annual levels of the world's grain reserves since 1961.

Figure 7-6 shows the general trends of per-capita food production in developed and less developed areas (excluding the People's Republic of China) since 1955. Note that, like total production, *per-capita* food production in DCs has risen steadily, but in LDCs in 1975 it had barely recovered to the peak level achieved in 1970, not far above the level of the period 1961–1965. *This, of course, indicates an enormous increase in human misery.* Well over a *billion* people have been added to the populations of less developed nations since the early 1950s, and a large proportion of them are both very poor and chronically undernourished. Even though the average nutritional condition of the poverty-stricken of our planet may have remained about the same during those decades, both the *absolute numbers of the poor and their proportion of the total world population have increased rapidly.*

The worldwide nutritional situation that has characterized the past generation is totally unprecedented, in part because of the absolute numbers of people involved. Famines have occurred throughout history, but they have generally been temporary, if cataclysmic, events caused by weather or human conflicts and limited to relatively small, local populations. Such famines were undeniably tragic affairs that resulted in a great deal of human suffering, and chronic hunger has also been long

TABLE 7-3
*World Grain Production, 1969–1970 Through 1976–1977**

Year	*Grain production (million metric tons)*
1969/1970–1971/1972, averaged	1120
1972/1973	1102
1973/1974	1250
1974/1975	1201
1975/1976	1221
1976/1977	1321**

*Wheat, milled rice, and major coarse grains (corn, barley, rye, oats, and sorghum).
**Preliminary.
Source: USDA, *World agricultural situation,* WAS-12, December 1976, p. 18. 1972/1973 data from WAS-9, December 1975, p. 36.

TABLE 7-4
Index of World Food Security, 1961–1976 (figures are in million metric tons)

Year	*Reserve stocks of grain**	*Grain equivalent of idled U.S. cropland*	*Total reserves*	*Reserves as days of annual grain consumption*
1961	163	68	231	105
1962	176	81	257	105
1963	149	70	219	95
1964	153	70	223	87
1965	147	71	218	91
1966	151	78	229	84
1967	115	51	166	59
1968	144	61	205	71
1969	159	73	232	85
1970	188	71	259	89
1971	168	41	209	71
1972	130	78	208	69
1973	148	24	172	55
1974	108	0	108	33
1975	111	0	111	35
1976**	100	0	100	31

*Based on carry-over stocks of grain at beginning of crop year in individual countries for year shown.
**Preliminary estimates.
Source: Lester R. Brown, The politics and responsibility of the North American breadbasket. Worldwatch Institute.

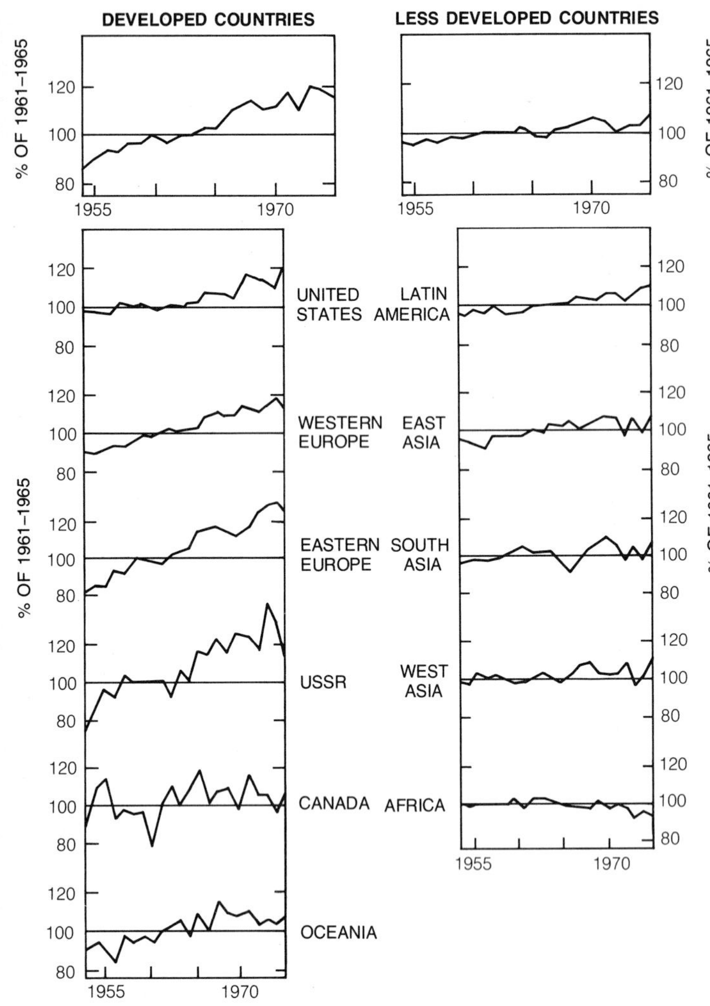

FIGURE 7-6

World food production per capita, 1954–1975. The developing countries have gained only 0.4 percent per year. In none of those regions has the index reached 110, and in Africa it has shown a downward trend since 1951. Per-capita food production trended upward 1.5 percent per year in the developed countries until the early 1970s. In each of those regions the index of per-capita food production has reached or exceeded 110 at least three times in the 22-year period. (Adapted from U.S. Department of Agriculture, *The world food situation and prospects to 1985,* Foreign Agricultural Economic Report No. 98, 1974; recent data from WAS-12.)

endemic in many areas. But the scale and ubiquity of hunger today is an entirely new phenomenon. Unceasing poverty-related privation, including hunger and malnutrition, is now endured by more than one billion people around the globe, and perhaps 400 million live on the brink of starvation.[28] This chronic hunger is also unprecedented because the multitudinous hungry have become increasingly aware of the dietary condition of the affluent few and have high hopes of emulating them, a situation that has grave political implications for the future.

This, then, is the fundamental reason that the human population reached such a precarious position with regard to its most basic resource—food—so suddenly in the mid-1970s: an already marginal situation was precipitated into a crisis by a series of weather-related bad harvests. The roots of the crisis lie: (1) in rapid population growth, which has necessitated an increase in food production of about 2 percent per year for the past generation just to maintain existing nutritional levels; (2) in the finite amounts of arable land, fresh water, and fertilizer available; (3) in the low productivity of traditional farming methods, especially in LDCs; (4) in environmental constraints; (5) in the lack of world investment (either monetary, social, or political) in increasing food production; and (6) in a political decision in the U.S. to eliminate government-held grain reserves. Underlying all the other factors, the world's economic system has created and perpetuates gross inequities in the distribution of food, as of other commodities. Thus a quarter of the human population have access to abundant food, while nearly half subsist on inadequate supplies and are tragically vulnerable to any disruption in that meager allotment.

Following the Rome Food Conference in November 1974, efforts were made to establish a worldwide food-information network, and to organize national and international food-reserve stockpiles to meet future deficits and to avert famine in the hungriest nations. A World Food Council, responsible to the UN Secretariat, was established to foster agricultural development in LDCs and to coordinate famine-relief efforts. A Consultative

[28] Jean Mayer, The dimensions of human hunger.

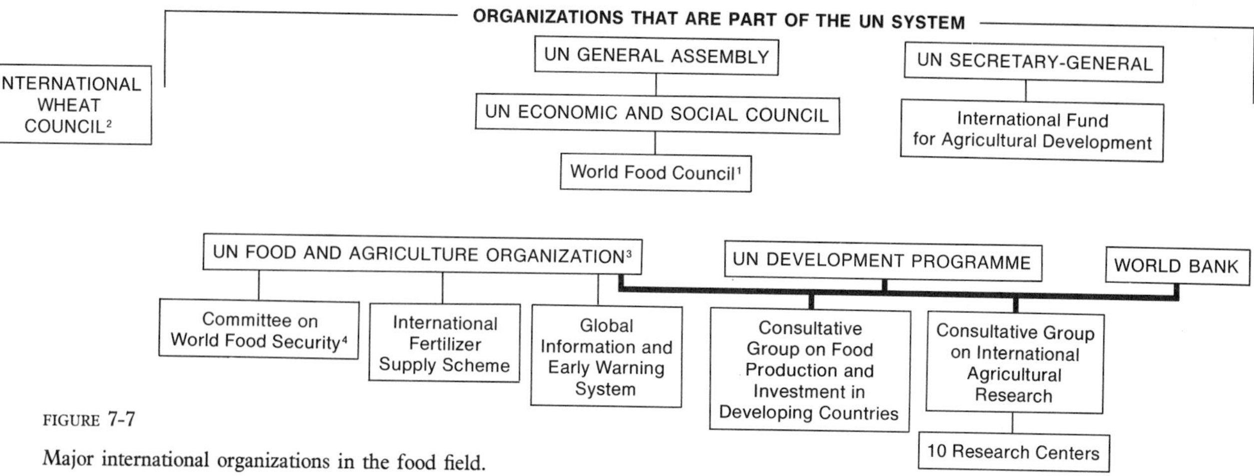

FIGURE 7-7

Major international organizations in the food field.

[1]Members of the World Food Council: Argentina, Australia, Bangladesh, Canada, Chad, Colombia, Cuba, Egypt, Federal Republic of Germany, France, Gabon, Guatemala, Guinea, Hungary, India, Indonesia, Iran, Iraq, Italy, Japan, Kenya, Libyan Arab Republic, Mali, Mexico, Pakistan, Rumania, Sri Lanka (Ceylon), Sweden, Togo, Trinidad and Tobago, United Kingdom, United States, USSR, Venezuela, Yugoslavia, and Zambia. [2]This loosely organized but important London-based consultative mechanism—which is outside the UN system of organizations and therefore has no official responsibility for implementing the recommendations of the World Food Conference—now involves some sixty countries, including the Soviet Union. It is the body within which international wheat agreements have been negotiated since the late 1940s. [3]The Soviet Union is not a member of the FAO. [4]Established by the FAO council in late November 1975 as a successor to the FAO Ad Hoc Working Party on World Food Security. (From McLaughlin, 1975, Overseas Development Council.)

Group on Food Production and Investment, connected with the World Bank, was set up to channel assistance funds into useful agricultural projects. Figure 7-7 shows the major international agencies involved with food, inside and outside the United Nations.

Thanks to a decline in demand for food in the rich countries, especially for feed grains, enough food was made available on the world food market and as food aid to head off large-scale famine in 1975. Some 36 million tons of grain were imported in 1973/1974 by LDCs (not including China), and 8.6 million tons were given to the neediest countries during 1974/1975.[29] The World Food Council has sought 10 million tons of food aid per year, but only about 9 million tons were donated in 1975/1976.[30] Importations of food by DCs declined to about 25 mmt in 1976/1977, the lowest in six years, thanks to good harvests that year.[30a] Nonetheless, while grain reserves remain at critically low levels, any significant problems in food production in 1977 and subsequent years are bound to have serious social, economic, and political repercussions. The possibility of a major famine that could bring population growth to a sudden, catastrophic halt has never been more real.[31]

THE DISTRIBUTION OF FOOD

Per-capita production figures are at best crude indicators of the food situation. They conceal gross differences that exist between countries, especially between the developed nations and the less developed nations. It is impossible to judge directly from per-capita food-production figures exactly what is happening to the average diet of individuals within each country, because the averaging process also conceals a great range of dietary differences between regions and income levels. The wealthiest urban classes in many LDCs eat very well, whereas the poorest—landless farm workers or urban shanty dwellers—live from hand to mouth. The prevailing economic system encourages production of food for the rich at the expense of food for the poor.[32]

[29]Martin M. McLaughlin, World food insecurity: Has anything happened since Rome?

[30]Jon McLin, Remember the World Food Conference?

[30a]USDA, WAS-12.

[31]Lester R. Brown, The world food prospect.

[32]Michael Lipton, Urban bias and food policy in poor countries.

Regional differences in diet may reflect different economic conditions or they may be the temporary result of good or bad harvests. For instance, in some areas of northern India, following the famine of the mid-1960s, which had necessitated the importation of nine million tons of grain from the U.S., wheat and rice were superabundant, and prices were dropping steadily. Yet, in spite of this surplus of food, seven million people were in danger of starvation in one province alone, and in northern India as a whole some 20 million people were described as being in "acute distress." This situation was due largely to local droughts in areas adjacent to those producing surpluses. The people were so poor that they could not create effective "demand" for food, producing the spectacle of surpluses and dropping prices in close proximity to starvation.

Even for an entire country, figures on food production may be unrevealing, since consumption equals production plus or minus trade. The trade positions of many less developed countries changed markedly between 1956 and 1975; many former grain exporters became heavy grain importers. At the same time, many of these hungry nations export food—including such high-protein foodstuffs as oilseed cakes and fishmeal—to the rich countries.[33]

The present failures of food distribution are the result of a host of interacting factors, including poverty, ignorance, cultural and economic patterns, and lack of transport systems. Although worldwide supplies of food today might theoretically be adequate to feed every human being if fairly distributed, the average diet within more than half of the less developed countries is below minimum standards of nutrition in calories alone. Distribution of specific nutrients, especially protein, is equally, if not more, inequitable, although less well documented.

Between the early 1950s and 1970s, food production in both developed and undeveloped regions increased at approximately the same average rate: around 3 percent per year. The difference is in the rates of population growth: less than 1.5 percent per year for DCs; 2 percent or more for most LDCs. Table 7-5 compares rates of population growth with growth in food production between 1952 and 1972. In LDCs, food production in 1952 was inadequate to feed the populations then existing. Since then, there has been a slight improvement overall, but in 34 out of 86 LDCs for which the United Nations had sufficient information, food production actually fell behind. If rising demand for food, which would be expected to accompany rising incomes, is considered, some 53 of these countries were failing to meet their food needs in 1972.[34]

In the developed world, by contrast, most populations were reasonably well-fed in 1952. Since population growth was much slower, increased affluence accounted for more than half the growth in food consumption between 1952 and 1972. Thus, whereas people in most non-communist poor countries were not significantly better-fed after twenty years of efforts to raise food production—indeed, many had lost ground—those in rich countries generally were enjoying much more sumptuous diets.[34a]

Levels of Nutrition

Some appreciation of the nutritional gap between rich and poor nations can be gained by comparing the availability of food energy and protein per capita. According to the United Nations Food and Agriculture Organization, some 3100 kilocalories (kcal) per day on the average were available to each person in developed countries in 1969–1971, some 23 percent above estimated needs. And an average of over 96 grams of protein were available per capita in DCs, also well above requirements. By contrast, in LDCs on the average only about 2200 kcal and less than 58 grams of protein per capita were available, about two-thirds of the amounts available in DCs and 5 percent below estimated needs.[35] Table 7-6 shows the estimated average food energy and protein supplies in 1969–1971 in different regions. A more detailed table comparing population growth rates and per-capita food supplies for individual countries in 1969–1971 can be found in Appendix 2.

Although individual needs for calories vary according to age, sex, body size, and activity, the FAO has

[33] UN, *Assessment.*

[34] Ibid.

[34a] See E. Eckholm and F. Record, The two faces of malnutrition, for a good overview of the world nutritional situation.

[35] UN, *Assessment.*

TABLE 7-5
Rate of Growth of Food Production in Relation to Population, World and Main Regions, 1952–1962 and 1962–1972 (in percent per year)

Region	1952–1962			1962–1972		
		Food production*			Food production*	
	Population	Total	Per capita	Population	Total	Per capita
DEVELOPED MARKET ECONOMIES**	1.2	2.5	1.3	1.0	2.4	1.4
Western Europe	0.8	2.9	2.1	0.8	2.2	1.4
North America	1.8	1.9	0.1	1.2	2.4	1.2
Oceania	2.2	3.1	0.9	2.0	2.7	0.7
EASTERN EUROPE AND USSR	1.5	4.5	3.0	1.0	3.5	2.5
Total developed countries	1.3	3.1	1.8	1.0	2.7	1.7
DEVELOPING MARKET ECONOMIES**	2.4	3.1	0.7	2.5	2.7	0.2
Africa	2.2	2.2	—	2.5	2.7	0.2
Far East	2.3	3.1	0.8	2.5	2.7	0.2
Latin America	2.8	3.2	0.4	2.9	3.1	0.2
Near East	2.6	3.4	0.8	2.8	3.0	0.2
ASIAN CENTRALLY PLANNED ECONOMIES	1.8	3.2	1.4	1.9	2.6	0.7
Total developing countries	2.4	3.1	0.7	2.4	2.7	0.3
World	2.0	3.1	1.1	1.9	2.7	0.8

*Trend rate of growth of food production, compound interest.
**Including countries in other regions not specified.
Source: UN, *Assessment.*

TABLE 7-6
*Average Daily Energy and Protein Supply, by Region**

Region	Energy (in kcal per capita)		Protein (in grams per capita)		Energy as percent of requirement	
	1961	1969–1971 (average)	1961	1969–1971 (average)	1961	1969–1971 (average)
DEVELOPED MARKET ECONOMIES	2950	3090	87.5	95.1	115	121
Western Europe	3020	3130	89.3	93.7	118	123
North America	3110	3320	92.3	105.2	118	126
Oceania	3210	3260	92.7	108.1	121	123
Other developed market economies	2420	2550	73.3	79.1	102	108
EASTERN EUROPE AND USSR	2990	3260	85.8	99.3	116	127
Total developed countries	2960	3150	87.0	96.4	116	123
DEVELOPING MARKET ECONOMIES	2130	2210	55.0	56.0	93	97
Africa	2120	2190	55.7	58.4	91	94
Far East	2050	2080	51.3	50.7	92	94
Latin America	2410	2530	63.7	65.0	100	105
Near East	2200	2500	62.3	69.3	89	102
ASIAN CENTRALLY PLANNED ECONOMIES	2020	2170	54.7	60.4	86	92
Total developing countries	2100	2200	54.9	57.4	91	95
World	2380	2480	65.2	69.0	100	104

*The figures give protein and energy content of the food available at the retail level after allowance for the storage and marketing losses and waste.
Source: UN, *Assessment.*

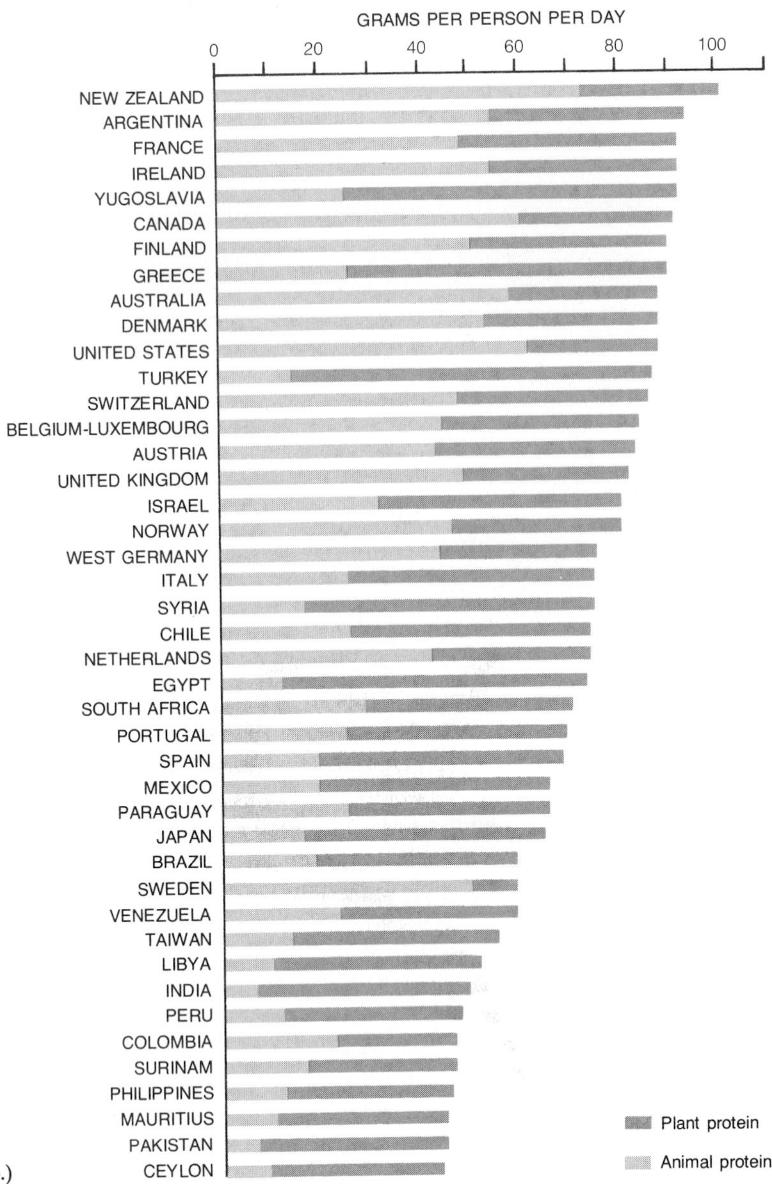

FIGURE 7-8

Daily per-capita total protein supplies in forty-three countries. (After Cole, 1966.)

established standard "reference" body weights and standard daily per-capita kilocalorie requirements for estimating a population's caloric food needs. Children's needs, which are higher than those of adults in proportion to their body weights, are standardized according to age groups. For adults, allowances are also made for pregnancies and differences in age and sex. Calculations, using these standardized average requirements, are then made for an entire population based on its age composition and vital rates. Recommended average daily allowances for calories and several other important nutrients for men, women, and children can also be found in Appendix 2.[36]

Individual protein requirements also vary with body

[36]See N. R. Scrimshaw and V. R. Young, The requirements of human nutrition, for a good summary of nutritional needs. For a useful discussion of how nutrients needed in human nutrition are derived from plants and from soil-air-water nutrient cycles, see J. Janick, C. H. Noller, and C. L. Rhykerd, The cycles of plant and animal nutrition.

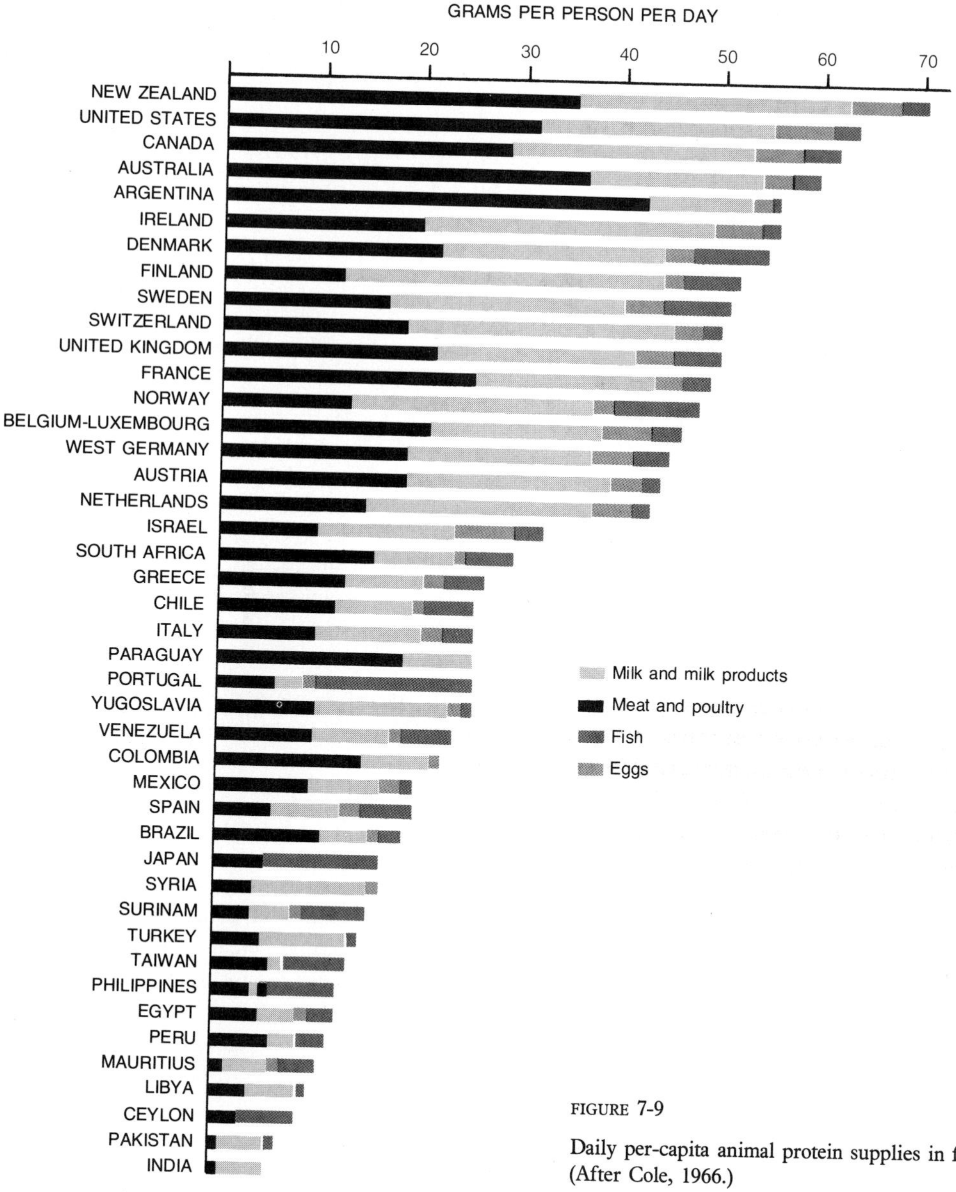

FIGURE 7-9

Daily per-capita animal protein supplies in forty-three countries. (After Cole, 1966.)

size and age, and are increased by pregnancy and lactation. Protein needs must also be calculated according to the quality of the sources; where animal foods are a rare element in the diet, more protein is needed to compensate for the generally lower quality of the protein in vegetable sources. Figures 7-8 and 7-9 show *per-capita* protein supplies for different countries in the 1960s. Since then, protein supplies, especially from animal sources, have increased in many DCs. In Japan, for instance, per-capita daily protein supplies from animal sources have risen from less than 20 to over 30 grams. Among developed regions, only Japan, the USSR, and Eastern Europe still obtain less than half their protein from animals, but the proportion is rising fast. Total protein supplies and plant/animal ratios have changed relatively little in most LDCs, however.

There has been a growing controversy in recent years about how much protein people actually need in their

TABLE 7-7
Recommended Daily Protein Allowances

Class	Age (in years)	Weight kg	Weight lbs	Protein (in grams) FAO	Protein (in grams) NAS/NRC	Protein (in grams) Canada
Infants	0–1	3–9	5–20	1.9/kg body weight	2 to 2.2/kg body weight	1.9 to 2.2/kg body weight
Children	1–9	10–30	21–81	14–25	20 to 39	18 to 37
Adolescents	10–19					
Male		31–65	81–135	36–38	40–54	38–54
Female		31–54	81–115	26–30	40–48	38–43
Adults	20–80					
Male		65–70	135–175	37	56	56
Female		55–58	115–128	29	46	41
Pregnant				38	76	61
Lactating				46	66	65

diets and whether a real protein shortage separate from simple food shortage exists in poor countries.[37] Standards for protein requirements have been steadily reduced since the 1950s as more precise measurements of needs have become possible.[38] The FAO's most recent calculations of protein needs were based on physiological tests of well-nourished individuals. Their calculations indicated that, for healthy people, a traditional, grain-based diet can provide sufficient protein if energy needs are met.

Some recent studies have cast doubt on the adequacy of these low standards, especially for people subsisting on diets that are only marginally adequate in other respects as well. When calories are insufficient, protein is utilized for energy rather than for growth or repair of body tissues. Protein needs also are considerably increased by infectious disease and parasitism, both of which are very common among impoverished, inadequately fed people. Finally, a tuber-based or grain-based diet is often too bulky for young children, who may not be able to eat enough to satisfy either their energy or protein needs.[39] Thus protein needs may often be higher for the hungry poor than for the well-fed, healthy rich. Moreover, the minimal standards set by the FAO may be inadequate even for otherwise well-nourished individuals. To ensure optimum health, protein intake probably should be considerably higher than the FAO minimum, even when calories are amply provided.

Appendix 2 contains more information on human nutritional requirements, and compares recommended nutrient allowances for people of different ages as set by: (1) FAO/WHO, (2) the U.S. National Academy of Sciences/National Research Council, and (3) the Canadian Bureau of Nutritional Sciences. The U.S. recommendations for protein, as well as for most other nutrients, are substantially higher than FAO's; Canada's recommended intakes are slightly lower than those of the U.S. Table 7-7 summarizes the different recommended protein-intake levels.

Conflicting accounts of the actual food situation sometimes result from different ways of comparing figures. Food-production figures in the past have often been quoted only in calories, taking no account of whether adequate protein or other nutrients were available. In addition, there is a vast difference between what is produced and what reaches the marketplace, and there are also losses between the market and the family table. Estimates of losses to insect and rodent pests and to spoilage before food reaches the market range from 10 percent to as high as 50 percent in some areas. These losses have not always been taken into account in official statistics. The FAO allowed for some losses of food before it reached the market in making the estimates of food supplies shown in Table 7-6, but not for losses between market and consumption. To allow for these and for differences in distribution between areas and income groups within countries, the UN noted that food energy supplies "should be at least 10 percent above aggregate requirements."

[37]Philip Payne, Protein deficiency or starvation?; J. C. Waterlow and P. R. Payne, The protein gap. See also the letter on Payne's article on protein deficiency by Henning Schroll in *New Scientist,* August 14, 1975, p. 397.

[38]John C. Abbott, The efficient use of world protein supplies, *UN, Assessment.*

[39]FAO, PAG statement no 20. See also Eckholm and Record, The two faces of malnutrition, p. 9, and references cited.

TABLE 7-8
Daily Energy Intake Per Capita by Income

Total income (Rs. per household per month)	Pakistan (1969–1970)				Bangladesh (1962–1963)			
	Urban		Rural		Urban		Rural	
	Percent of households	Kcal per capita/day	Percent of households	Kcal per capita/day	Percent of households	Kcal per capita/day	Percent of households	Kcal per capita/day
Less than 99	24	1620	14	1800	19	1550	44	2050
100–199	35	1690	50	1890	25	1750	34	2260
200–299	29	1670	23	2000	19	1720	14	2400
300–399	15	1700	8	2100	10	1810	4	2660
400–499	7	1730	3	2730	8	1800	2	2640
More than 500	10	1820	2	2270	19	1840	2	3060

Source: UN, *Assessment.*

As the table shows, the recommended level of food supply (with its 10-percent safety margin) was not reached in *any* developing region; and several regions—including some 57 nations—failed even to achieve the minimum requirement (100 percent of basic needs, with no safety margin). The UN concluded: "In view of the inevitable inequitable distribution in supplies, it is clear that all developing regions faced a serious energy-deficit problem in certain sections of the community." Although supplies of protein seemed adequate (by the low FAO standards) in virtually all countries, some of it doubtless was being used as energy to compensate for the calorie deficit. Therefore, the UN concluded that "the surplus of protein availability is more apparent than real."[40]

Given inadequate food supplies at the national level for 57 out of 97 less developed countries in 1970, and marginal supplies (less than a 10 percent margin of safety) in another 22, it can be assumed that the poorest segments of these populations were seriously undernourished. Very little direct research has been done on the subject, but a few limited surveys strongly support this conclusion. Table 7-8 shows two examples; similar results in some other LDCs are shown in tables in Appendix 2. In one province of India (Maharastra) in 1971, availability of food energy per person per day ranged from a grossly inadequate 940 kcal in the poorest 1 percent of households, to over 3000 kcal for the highest income groups.[41] Chronically undernourished people, who commonly also suffer from parasitism and disease, are typically apathetic, listless, and unproductive. In the past, well-fed Europeans and North Americans, seeing these symptoms among people in LDCs, but not understanding their cause, often concluded that natives of these areas were "lazy."

[40]UN, *Assessment.*
[41]UN, *Assessment.*

TABLE 7-9
Energy and Protein Intake of Schoolchildren in Hyderabad

Age group	Kilocalories		Protein (grams)	
	Low income	High income	Low income	High income
7–9	1429	2186	37.0	67.8
9–11	1411	2343	36.5	62.1
11–13	1292	2833	34.5	72.2
13–14	1374	2585	35.5	75.5
All age groups	1376	2485	35.9	69.4

Source: UN, *Assessment.*

Maldistribution of food supplies within households may be at least as serious as that between income levels. Children and pregnant and nursing women, who have the greatest nutritional needs in proportion to their sizes, are often left the smallest portions of food. Table 7-9 compares the caloric and protein intakes of children in high and low income groups in Hyderabad, India. After weaning, small children in poor countries are often fed starchy, bulky foods that fill them up without supplying enough calories, protein, and other nutrients to maintain health. Poor nutrition can lead to loss of appetite, further reducing their food intakes.

In many poor agricultural communities, when food supplies are insufficient, the men, who must be well-enough nourished to work and grow more food for their families, are deliberately fed first and best. Landless laborers are often fed by their employers, but their families are not. Many young children die of starvation as a result of such practices; others survive but may be permanently handicapped by extreme deprivation in the crucial early months of life (see next section). The health of women, who as mothers need extra protein and energy, may also suffer greatly.

Food shortages consequently show up in widespread malnutrition and hunger to an obvious degree among infants, preschool children (ages 1-4), and pregnant and nursing women. Deaths from starvation and malnutrition among young children in LDCs are commonplace. Of the 55 million deaths that occur worldwide each year, between 10 and 20 million have been estimated by French agronomists René Dumont and Bernard Rosier to be the result of starvation or malnutrition.[42] Most of these deaths are among children; nutritionist Alan Berg has estimated that some 15 million children die each year of malnutrition and associated diseases.[43] Box 7-1 describes some of the more prevalent nutritional-deficiency diseases.

In these cases, the cause of death usually is officially attributed to some infectious or parasitic disease, which only dealt the final blow. Diseases that ordinarily are only minor nuisances in well-nourished individuals are devastating to the malnourished, whose resistance is seriously impaired.[44] Even if the disease does not kill, it is likely to intensify the malnourishment by draining the individual's reserves. Diseases normally considered minor can precipitate a severe, previously unsuspected deficiency disorder; thus malnutrition encourages disease and in turn is exacerbated by it. Extremely poor sanitary conditions further complicate the picture; dysentery and infestations of various kinds of worms are commonplace among the poor in LDCs. Diarrhea, dangerous even in a well-fed baby, is disastrous to an ill-fed one. *For our purposes, any death that would not have occurred if the individual had been properly nourished may be considered as due to starvation, regardless of the ultimate agent.*

Research on nutrition and the poor in Latin America has begun to reveal a syndrome in which undernourished mothers, babies of low birth weights, high rates of infection in both mother and child, high infant mortality rates, and retarded psychomotor development in children are all associated. Supplemental feeding of pregnant women appears to be effective in reducing the incidence of low birth-weight babies and of infant mortality.[45] The interacting factors of malnutrition and disease are major causes of the high infant-mortality rates in the LDCs compared with those of the DCs (Table 7-10). In some countries infant mortality is eight or nine times as high as that in the United States (by no means the world's lowest).

Infants are significantly protected against both disease and severe nutritional deficiencies if they are breastfed. Mother's milk is extremely nourishing, does not transmit parasites, and indeed provides positive protection against infection, especially diarrheal disease.[46] Poor people in the LDCs (particularly those who migrate to cities and fill up the shantytowns) have begun to adopt from the wealthier urban classes (and from developed countries) the habits of bottle-feeding and early weaning. Consequently, in some areas, malnutrition and mortality rates among infants are on the increase. Unlike their affluent neighbors, low-income mothers can at best offer poor substitutes for their milk. The luckier infants receive formulas based on powdered or condensed milk. But powdered milk is expensive, so it is often "stretched" with extra water. Moreover, the water available for formulas and for washing the bottle is far from sterile, and without refrigeration the formulas may spoil rapidly. Thus the baby is exposed to dangerous infections. Even worse, out of combined ignorance and poverty, mothers may feed their babies barley flour, cornstarch, sago, or arrowroot gruels, perhaps with a tiny bit of milk added "for color."[47]

The weaning situation has been extensively studied in Chile, where it was found that the prevalence of breast-feeding for at least a year declined from 95 percent in the 1950s to 6 percent by 1969. By then only 20 percent of Chilean infants were nursed for even two months. Less

[42]René Dumont and Bernard Rosier, *The hungry future.*

[43]Nutrition, development, and population growth. See also Berg's *The nutrition factor: Its role in national development.*

[44]M. C. Latham, Nutrition and infection in national development; Gerald T. Keusch, Malnutrition and infection: Deadly allies.

[45]M. Katz et al., Symposium on malnutrition and infection during pregnancy.

[46]D. B. Jelliffe and E. F. P. Jelliffe, Human milk, nutrition, and the world resource crisis.

[47]Berg, Nutrition; Mike Muller, Money, milk, and marasmus.

TABLE 7-10
Infant Mortality Rates, Under One Year, 1972 (or most recent available figure)

Continent and country	*Rate per 1000 live births*
AFRICA	
Egypt	103.3 (1971)
Kenya	110.9
Liberia	159.2 (1971)
Madagascar	53.2
Mauritius	63.8
Réunion	44.5
Senegal	62.7
Tunisia	76.3 (1971)
NORTH AND CENTRAL AMERICA	
Barbados	30.9
Canada	17.1
Costa Rica	56.5 (1971)
Dominican Republic	45.2
Guatemala	79.0
Mexico	60.9
Puerto Rico	27.1
Trinidad and Tobago	26.2
United States	17.6
SOUTH AMERICA	
Argentina	58.3 (1967)
Chile	78.8 (1970)
Colombia	52.9 (1969)
Ecuador	78.5 (1971)
French Guiana	43.1
Peru	65.1 (1970)
Uruguay	40.4 (1971)
Venezuela	49.7 (1971)
OCEANIA	
Australia	16.7
Fiji	26.1
New Zealand	16.2 (1973)
ASIA	
Hong Kong	17.4
Indonesia	87.2 (1965)
Israel	22.1
Japan	11.7
Kuwait	38.5
Malaysia (West)	38.5 (1971)
Pakistan*	124.3 (1968)
Philippines	72.0 (1966)
Taiwan	19.0 (1968)
Thailand	22.5 (1971)
EUROPE	
Austria	25.2
Belgium	20.2
Bulgaria	26.2
Czechoslovakia	21.4
Denmark	13.5 (1971)
Finland	11.3
France	16.0
Germany, East	17.7
Germany, West	20.4
Greece	27.8
Hungary	35.1 (1971)
Ireland	17.7
Italy	27.0
Netherlands	11.7
Norway	11.3
Poland	28.5
Portugal	41.4
Spain	18.6
Sweden	10.8
Switzerland	13.1
United Kingdom— England and Wales	17.5
Yugoslavia	43.6

*Included Bangladesh.
Source: UN, *Demographic yearbook*, 1973.

extreme but significant declines have been observed in several other LDCs, including Mexico, the Philippines, Singapore, Kenya, and Nigeria.

Berg has calculated a conservative "cost" to LDCs of the switch to bottle-feeding, based on the value of the cow's milk that would be required to replace the mother's milk. Assuming that only 20 percent of the mothers who live in LDC cities do not nurse their children, the loss is $365 million. If half of the other 80 percent of urban babies are weaned by six months, the total loss is $780 million.[48] The real cost, of course, is far greater and probably cannot be measured in dollars. The greatest cost is the increased malnutrition and disease suffered by the children.

Chile has an excellent national health service, but it also has an embarrassingly high infant mortality rate, which seems to be associated with the recent shift in infant feeding practices. In Chilean villages, deaths among bottle-fed infants were found to be three times more frequent than among breast-fed babies. Interestingly, infant mortality has been found to be *rising* among families with incomes somewhat above poverty levels, evidently because more and more such families are weaning early.[49]

[48]Berg, Nutrition.

[49]Ibid.

BOX 7-1 Common Deficiency Diseases

The most commonly encountered deficiency diseases in LDCs are *marasmus* and *kwashiorkor* (Figure 7-10), both of which affect young children and have similar causes. Marasmus is probably indicative of overall undernourishment, but it is often referred to as a "protein-calorie deficiency." It seems to be related to early weaning or to a failure in breast-feeding, when inadequate substitutes for the mother's milk are provided, and it often appears following a bout of diarrhea or some other disease. Most victims are babies less than a year old. The child with marasmus is very thin and wasted, with wrinkled skin and enormous eyes.

Kwashiorkor is a West African word that means "the sickness the child develops when another baby is born." Kwashiorkor seems to be another form of protein-calorie starvation, resulting from inadequate supplementation for mother's milk after the age of six months or so. Sometimes it is precipitated by weaning, when the child of one or two years is offered only starchy, bulky foods to eat. In mild cases the child's physical growth is retarded, the hair and skin are discolored, and a pot-belly develops. There is also a loss of appetite. When the disease is more acute, the discoloration is more pronounced, hair is loosely rooted and pulls out in tufts, legs and feet swell with fluids, digestive problems arise, and the child becomes markedly apathetic. After this stage is reached, death will follow unless medical care can be quickly provided.

Vitamin-A deficiency often accompanies protein malnutrition and shows up in a drying of eye membranes (xerophthalmia) or softening of the cornea (kerotomalacia), which soon leads to blindness if not treated. Supplementing protein-deficient diets with high-protein foods without adding vitamin A may cause a previously unsuspected deficiency to appear in an acute form. This happened in early food-aid programs that distributed nonfat dry milk. Since 1965 American nonfat dry milk shipped overseas has been fortified with vitamin A. Vitamin-A deficiency is widespread in much of the less developed world, especially in South and Southeast Asia and parts of Latin America. Like many other nutritional problems, this one most often afflicts preschool children. The United Nations has estimated that as many as 100,000 children go blind each year in the Far East alone as a result of vitamin-A deficiency.*

Another prevalent form of malnutrition in LDCs, particularly among women and small children, is anemia, usually iron-deficiency anemia. Lack of protein, vitamin B_{12}, or folic acid can also play a part in anemia. During pregnancy, a fetus absorbs from the mother's stored reserves a large supply of iron, which it needs during the months after birth (mother's milk contains very little iron). Successive pregnancies can very quickly lead to exhaustion of a mother's reserve supply; if her diet does not replenish it, the result is anemia for both mother and child. This not only produces a lack of energy and low productiveness in the mother, but can also increase the likelihood of stillbirth and premature birth. The incidence of death from anemia ranges from 6 to 16 times higher in LDCs than in the United States. In Latin America, surveys have shown that between 5 and 15 percent of men have anemia and 10 to 30 percent of women do. Up to half the children in some areas are anemic.** It is common wherever poverty and poor sanitation prevail, and in these circumstances it is often aggravated by such parasitic infections as hookworm, which consume large amounts of blood.

Rickets and osteomalacia (softening of the bones) are due to lack of Vitamin D or calcium, or both. Vitamin D is synthesized in the skin when it is exposed to sunlight. Rickets first became a health problem for Europeans in smoky, congested cities during the Industrial Revolution, where children had only dim, narrow alleys for playgrounds and often were kept

*UN, *Assessment of the world food situation,* 1974.
**Ibid.

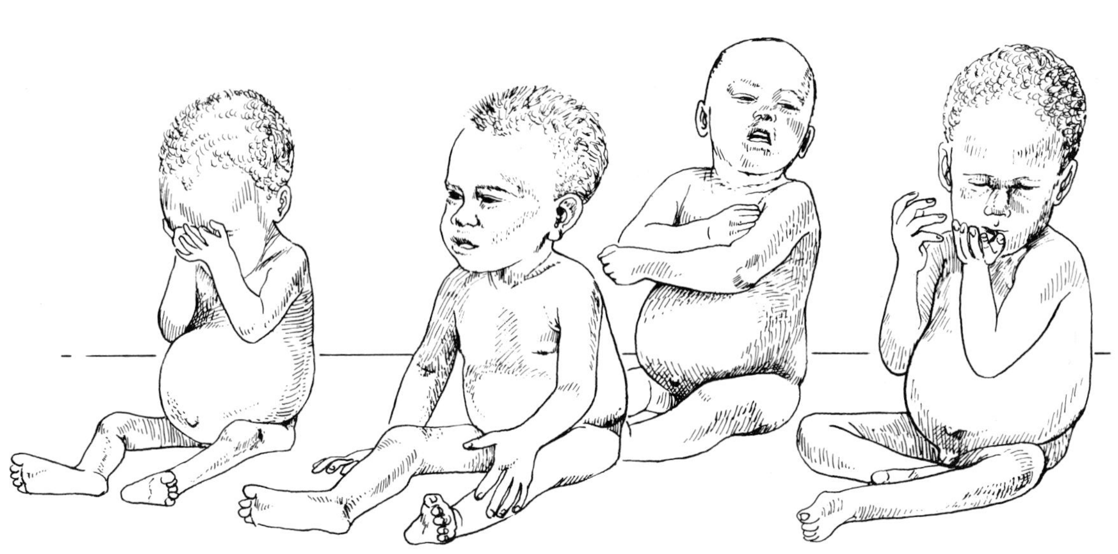

FIGURE 7-10

Symptoms of kwashiorkor (protein-calorie deficiency) in African children. (Drawn from a photograph by Eva D. Wilson.)

indoors to work.† Like many other deficiencies, this syndrome also affects both mother and child, for the calcium deprivation may begin in the prenatal period. During pregnancy, the fetus draws from the mother's body minerals and vitamins that may not be replenished by her food. Breast-feeding draws still greater amounts of calcium. Successive cycles of pregnancy and lactation may leave the mother virtually crippled by the drain on her bone structure, enforcing confinement to her house. Thus she is denied both the sunlight that would replenish her Vitamin D and the possibility of working to obtain better food.

Rickets, the childhood form of calcium deficiency, is not very common in tropical countries, where sunshine is abundant. Nevertheless, it does exist, more commonly in the cities and towns. It is found also in India, Pakistan, and parts of the Middle East. Customs of keeping children indoors and of keeping women secluded or heavily veiled undoubtedly contribute to the incidence of both diseases.

Lack of dietary iodine causes goiter, from which the UN estimates some 200 million people around the world suffer. Iodine is available from seafood and food grown in iodine-containing soils. Many regions of the world far inland from the sea have soils deficient in iodine. Iodine deficiency in mothers can cause cretinism—a form of dwarfing and severe mental retardation—in their children. But this can be entirely prevented simply by the use of iodized salt.

†W. F. Loomis, Rickets, *Scientific American*, December 1970.

Prolonged nursing, on the other hand, if accompanied by insufficient supplementary feeding, also can result in malnutrition for both child and mother. Mother's milk alone is adequate nourishment for a child for only the first four to six months after birth. Lactation can drain a woman's nutritional reserves if she is not adequately fed. Nevertheless, the extra food a nursing mother needs—as well as solid supplements for the baby after six months—can usually be supplied far more cheaply, easily, and safely than can safe and adequate substitutes for her milk.

It must also be mentioned that breastfeeding has an important demographic effect: it significantly delays the return of the woman's fertility after parturition and thus lengthens the period between births when birth control is not practiced.[50] The length of delay of the next pregnancy varies widely among income levels and countries, and is influenced by such factors as when and how much supplementary food is offered to the child and sexual customs associated with lactation. Conservatively, it can be said that the delay averages six months or more. Such increased birth spacing obviously benefits the health of mothers and children, and contributes as well to lower birth rates (Chapters 5 and 13).

Since breast-feeding is cheaper, more convenient, safer, and healthier for the child, and provides well-known emotional and psychological benefits for both mother and child, why is the vogue for bottle-feeding sweeping the cities of the less developed world? Various reasons have been proposed, including medical and health workers who encourage bottle-feeding, largely for reasons of convenience in health facilities. These people generally are unaware of the nutritional and health hazards of bottle-feeding for the poor. Often free powdered milk is distributed through health services, ostensibly for use as a supplement, but its availability encourages bottle-feeding. The baby-food and processed-milk industries have also been blamed for promoting their products among low-income groups who cannot afford them and who lack the facilities (safe water, refrigeration) to use them safely. An additional problem, especially for working mothers, is lack of privacy for nursing in public areas or workplaces. (That the nursing of a baby is a shocking sight is another peculiar Western notion that has been exported.) Underlying all these pressures is the prevalent idea among the poor that bottle-feeding must be superior because the rich do it. Because they know essentially nothing about nutrition or sanitation, illiterate poor mothers cannot understand that their adaptations of formula-feeding are vastly inferior to the traditional method, potentially fatally so.

Fortunately, the switch to the bottle is still largely limited to urban areas in LDCs; perhaps two-thirds of the infants in those countries are still breast-fed and thereby protected to a large extent against both malnutrition and disease. As awareness of the problem spreads among leaders in less developed nations, the trend may be reversed through the institution of educational programs to encourage breast-feeding, curbs on promotion of commercial baby foods, and provision of facilities for nursing in public places.

Because preschool-age children (1 to 5 years old) are no longer protected by breast-feeding against disease and malnutrition, it has been proposed that the mortality rate of this age-class is the best indicator of the nutritional level of a population (Table 7-11). In many parts of Latin America, Asia, and Africa, child mortality rates range from three to forty times higher than in the United States. Well over half the deaths among Latin American children under five in some countries have been attributed either directly or indirectly to malnutrition.[51] Although dependable statistics are hard to obtain, the mortality rate for children under four (including infants) in parts of India has been estimated to be as high as 250 per thousand. There is little question that most of these deaths also are basically due to malnutrition.

The President's Science Advisory Committee reported in 1967 that the high mortality rates of children 1 to 4 years old in LDCs "suggest that moderate protein-calorie malnutrition affects at least 50 percent of these children."[52] In 1974, the United Nations reached similar conclusions. Altogether, the UN cautiously estimated that, around 1970, perhaps ten million children under 5 years old in LDCs were severely malnourished, 80

[50]Berg, Nutrition; Robert Buchanan, Breast-feeding: Aid to infant health and fertility control.

[51]Pan American Health Organization, *Inter-American investigation of mortality in childhood, provisional report.*

[52]*World food problem*, p. 17.

TABLE 7-11
Child Mortality Rates, 1–4 Years, 1960–1962 (average annual)

Continent and country	*Rate per 1000 children*	*Continent and country*	*Rate per 1000 children*
AFRICA		EUROPE	
Mauritius	8.7	Austria	1.3
Réunion	9.6	Belgium	1.0
United Arab Republic	37.9	Bulgaria	2.4
		Czechoslovakia	1.2
NORTH AND CENTRAL AMERICA		Denmark	0.9
Barbados	3.7	Finland	1.1
Canada	1.1	France	1.0
Costa Rica	7.2	Germany, East	1.6
Dominican Republic	10.8	Germany, West	1.3
Guatemala	32.7	Greece	1.9
Mexico	13.8	Hungary	1.6
Puerto Rico	2.9	Ireland	1.2
Trinidad and Tobago	2.5	Italy	1.9
United States	1.0	Netherlands	1.1
		Norway	1.0
SOUTH AMERICA		Poland	1.6
Argentina	4.2	Portugal	8.0
Chile	8.0	Spain	2.0
Colombia	17.4	Sweden	0.8
Equador	22.1	Switzerland	1.2
Peru	17.4		
Venezuela	5.9	United Kingdom—England and Wales	0.9
		Yugoslavia	5.2
ASIA			
Ceylon	8.8		
China (Taiwan)	7.2	OCEANIA	
Hong Kong	4.4	Australia	1.1
Israel	1.8	Fiji Islands	3.7
Japan	2.2	New Zealand	1.2
Kuwait	3.6		
Philippines	8.4		
Syria	8.3		
Thailand	9.1		

Source: UN, *Statistical Series,* K/3, 1967.

million were moderately malnourished, and 120 million more suffered from milder forms of malnutrition.[53] How many millions more have been added to their ranks since 1972 can, as yet, only be guessed.

Implications of Severe Malnutrition in Children

The serious malnutrition prevalent in our overpopulated world causes incalculable suffering, waste of human life, and loss of human productivity. Malnourishment, especially protein deficiency, inhibits the development of protective antibodies and lowers resistance to diseases, thus contributing to higher death rates and loss of productivity in less developed countries. But even more alarming is the growing body of evidence that malnutrition in infants and young children may have essentially permanent effects. It has been known for a long time that severe undernourishment during the years of growth and development will result in a certain amount of dwarfing and delayed physical maturity, even if the deficiency is temporary and a normal diet is later restored. What is far more ominous is the evidence that malnourishment before birth and during the first two or three years afterwards may result in permanent impairment of the brain.

A child's body grows from 5 to 20 percent of its adult size in the first three years, but meanwhile the brain grows from 25 to 80 percent of its adult size. Recent

[53]UN, *Assessment,* p. 64.

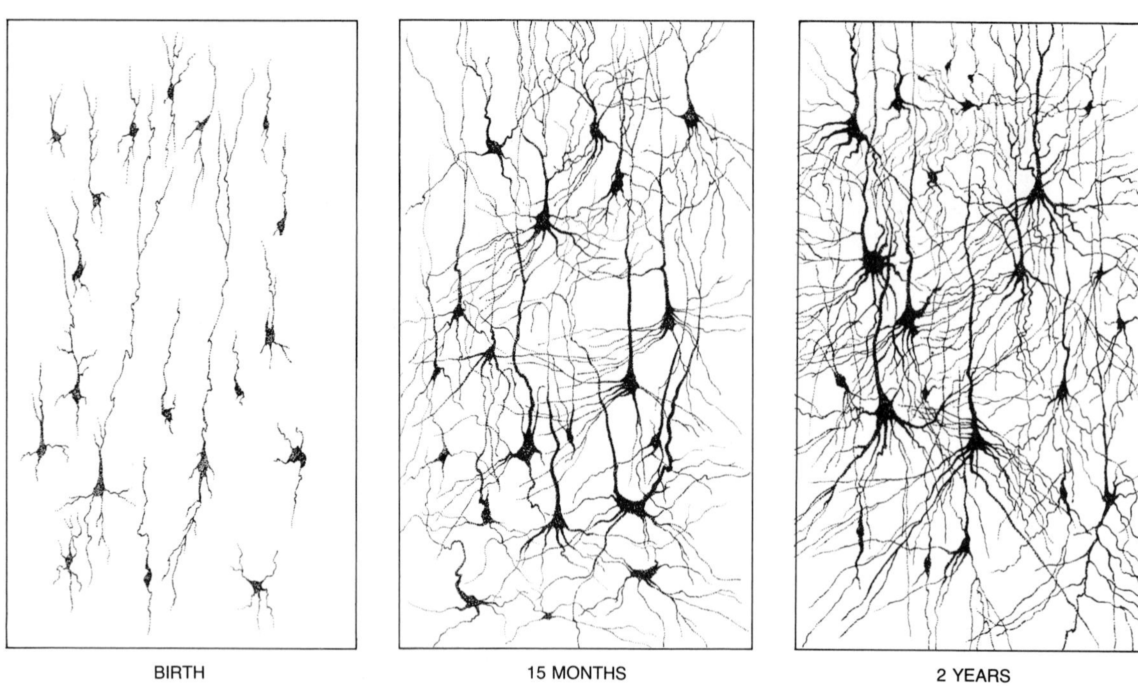

FIGURE 7-11

Development of neurons in the cerebral cortex of a young child. At birth all neurons are present but are immature. The drawings show stages of normal development of axons at birth, 15 months, and 2 years of age. (From Lewin, 1974.)

research has elucidated the normal growth pattern of the nervous system and the brain in human beings.[54] While the majority of *neurons* (nerve cells) are present in the brain of a developing fetus by 18 weeks after conception, they mature and establish their multiple interconnections much later. A second set of cells, known as *glia,* of which there are eight times as many as there are neurons, continue to multiply until the child is about two years old. The precise role of glia is not yet known, except that certain types of glial cells are responsible for the process of *myelination*—the creation of the insulating *myelin sheath*—around the *axons,* long fibers that extend from neurons and transmit messages from one neuron to another. Figure 7-11 shows the stages of normal development at birth, 15 months, and two years of age in the cerebral cortex. The myelin sheath is essential for the proper function of nervous tissue. Myelination goes on for at least four years after birth, but it is concentrated in the first two years. In addition, most of the development of the cerebellum, the part of the brain that, among other functions, controls coordination of the arms and legs, takes place between birth and age two.

Thus some 80 percent of human brain development takes place before birth and in the first two years afterwards. This extremely rapid brain growth must be supported with adequate food. If it is not, the brain essentially stops growing. Apparently, it may never regain the lost time if the deprivation is severe and prolonged. The sizes of both the head and the brain itself are reduced in individuals who were severely undernourished during those crucial early years.

Studies on rats have provided information on just what happens to a nutrient-deprived brain during its period of rapid growth. Of course, human implications must be inferred with care from research on laboratory animals. But the brain of a rat develops in essentially the same way as a human brain; only the timing is significantly

[54]Roger Lewin, The poverty of underñourished brains, and Starved brains. The second of these two articles is less technical and includes more recent studies.

different. It is now believed that hunger in human beings does not influence the number of neurons in the brain, which develop early in prenatal life, but practically everything else is affected. In malnourished animals, there are many fewer glial cells, and this doubtless is the primary reason for smaller brain-sizes in undernourished children. Myelination and axon development are reduced, and there are far fewer interconnections. One study of underfed young rats showed a reduction in connections of 38 percent, plus indications of damage to those that developed.[55] Such underdevelopment seems bound to have serious effects on reasoning ability, memory, and other functions in human beings. Finally, undernourishment results in underdevelopment of the cerebellum—an exception to the belief that neurons are generally protected from the effects of deprivation, as those of the cerebellum develop later than those in the rest of the brain. The consequence of impairment of the cerebellum is retarded development of motor coordination. Poor manual dexterity and clumsiness have long been observed as characteristic of undernourished children. Furthermore, these physical defects of the brain were produced in the laboratory animals not by extreme starvation, but by *moderate* levels of malnutrition.

Studies on rats also suggest that, when mothers are malnourished during pregnancy, their children and even grandchildren may suffer impairment of both brain development and the ability to form antibodies normally.[56] The mechanism affecting the second generation is unknown, although the cause for the first generation is fairly obvious. Whether or not this "second-generation effect" also applies to human beings is not known, although some of the findings of Guatemalan studies of maternal malnutrition are suggestive.[57] These studies indicate that mothers of small stature, who themselves exhibit signs of having suffered early malnourishment, are more likely to have babies of low birth weight. Such infants in LDCs (but not in developed countries, where other factors, such as cigarette smoking by mothers, seem to play larger roles in determining birth weights) are consistently more prone to disease, death, and retarded development.

An accumulating number of studies in various less developed countries have established a strong correlation between nutritional levels and physical and mental development in preschool and school-age children of poor families. Among impoverished youngsters in rural Guatemala and Mexico, height and mental achievement were positively correlated; all these children were near the lower end of both the height and mental-achievement scales for their ages, indicating that their development was affected by their nutrition. Among well-fed, middle-class children in the same societies, height and mental development showed no relationship.[58]

The development of a particular group of 22 children who had been virtually starved as infants was compared with that of other children in the same Mexican village, who were "normally" undernourished. The severely malnourished children showed signs of retarded language development by six months of age; at age three they were still below normal development for two-year-olds. Some catching up appeared by three and a half, as they showed signs of physical recovery from their early deprivation. But the trend suggests they will never fully catch up with their luckier peers.[59]

A study in Jamaica compared school-age children who had been severely malnourished before age two both with siblings who had no history of acute malnutrition and with neighbors or classmates of nearly the same age. The malnourished children scored significantly lower on IQ tests than the others did, although the sibs (who may also have been chronically malnourished early in life) performed slightly less well than did the unrelated controls. This failure to catch up occurred even though the acutely malnourished children had recovered in a hospital and had received special follow-up care for two years afterwards.[60]

In Chile, comparisons were made among Santiago slum children on adequate diets, other slum children receiving supplemented diets and medical care, and

[55]*New Scientist,* Starved brains fail to make the right connections.
[56]S. Zamenhof et al., DNA (cell number) in neonatal brain; W. J. Shoemaker and R. J. Wurtman, Prenatal undernutrition; R. K. Chandra, Antibody formation in first- and second-generation offspring of nutritionally deprived rats.
[57]Katz et al., *Symposium.*
[58]J. Cravioto et al., Nutrition, growth, and neurointegrative development.
[59]Lewin, Starved brains.
[60]M. E. Hertzig et al., Intellectual levels of school children severely malnourished during the first two years of life.

middle-class children. The slum children on supplemented diets more closely resembled the middle-class youngsters in physical and mental development than they did their neighbors with poor diets, although the two groups of slum children came from otherwise very similar environments. Of the malnourished children, only 51 percent reached the normal range of development, compared with 95 percent of the middle-class group. Another group of children, who had marasmus as infants and were subsequently given medical care and supplemental food, were all found to have intelligence considerably below normal three to six years later.[61]

Similar results have been obtained in studies conducted in the United States on severely malnourished children, comparing their later development with siblings and children of similar background who had no histories of malnutrition.[62] The malnourished children showed retarded growth and development, small head size, and poor language development.

An apparent exception to these and other findings is a study on young men who were conceived before and during an acute famine in the Netherlands during World War II.[63] Comparisons of their army-induction tests with men who were born in cities relatively unaffected by the famine revealed no significant differences in mental achievement. However, the acute phase of the famine lasted only about six months, and it occurred in a population that was quite adequately fed both before and afterward. Moreover, one can easily imagine that many adults donated some of their meager portions of food to expectant or nursing mothers and to babies.

The influence of malnutrition on mental and behavioral development is somewhat complicated by evidence that other environmental factors also play a part. A stimulating environment has been shown to have a direct role in the development of rat brains,[64] and recent research has shown that such effects can be found in human beings too. Since children who are deprived of food are very likely also to live in an impoverished environment in terms of social interaction and mental stimulation, it is not always easy or possible to separate these two causes of mental impairment. This is especially true when malnutrition begins in pregnancy or before, threatening the mother's ability even to feed and care for the child. Playing with the baby or otherwise providing the mental stimulation it needs may be quite beyond her capability, particularly if there are several other children. When the separate influences of environmental and nutritional deprivation have been studied, it was clear that the *combination* resulted in the greatest damage, but each had measurable effects.[65]

To what degree are early nutritional and/or environmental deprivation reversible? These matters are still being debated, but in general it can be said that at least some compensation is possible, but not easily achieved. In both rats and human children, environmental enrichment (in the form of varied, stimulating surroundings and plenty of social interaction) apparently can overcome the results of early deprivation if the deprivation was not too prolonged, and if the enrichment program is carried on for sufficient time.[66] The experience of the American Head Start Program for underprivileged children showed the consequences of giving up too soon. When the program was abandoned, children who had made substantial progress in educational achievement lost much of the ground they had gained.

It appears that nutritional enrichment likewise can eventually compensate to a large extent for early deprivation. A recent study of Korean orphans who had been adopted before the age of three by American middle-class families compared one subgroup that had been malnourished in infancy with "moderately nourished" and "well-nourished" subgroups and with American-born peers. Years later, when the adopted orphans were in grade school, their mean heights and weights had all exceeded those of Korean children of the same ages, although they were still below those of their American-born contemporaries. The mean IQs of all three sub-

[61]*Journal of American Medical Association,* Mental retardation from malnutrition: "Irreversible."

[62]H. P. Chase and H. P. Martin, Undernutrition and child development.

[63]Z. Stein et al., Nutrition and mental performance.

[64]S. Schapiro and K. R. Vukovich, Early experience effects upon cortical dendrites; M. R. Rosenzweig et al., Brain changes in response to experience; Patricia Wallace, Complex environments; D. A. Levitsky and R. H. Barnes, Nutrition and environmental interactions in the behavioral development of the rat.

[65]Lewin, Starved brains; for an explanation of how the interaction may operate, see D. A. Levitsky, Ill-nourished brains.

[66]Levitsky and Barnes, Nutrition and environmental interactions; for an explanation of how the interaction may operate, see D. A. Levitsky, Ill-nourished brains. Graham Chedd, Will the mind flourish despite neglect?

groups were comparable to those of American children. Differences persisted between the groups, however. The "malnourished" children on the average were smaller, lighter, and had significantly lower IQ scores than the well-fed children, and the "moderately nourished" group fell in between.[67]

This is a situation, of course, in which both nutritional and environmental enrichment have been amply provided and sustained. In other studies in which nutritional rehabilitation was provided temporarily and then the children returned to their impoverished homes, retardation of growth and development persisted. Such initially deprived youngsters never seem to catch up with adequately fed siblings or neighbors in the same environment in the absence of sustained special "enrichment" efforts.[68]

What does this mean in practical terms for the less developed regions? In a typical LDC, according to the UN, half of all children under five suffer some degree of undernutrition. Many die, but another fraction may survive with significant developmental retardation. Even though such handicaps might *eventually* be largely overcome through intensive, sustained rehabilitation, no poor country could afford such a program for a substantial portion of its child population.

At the very least, governments in all countries must be made aware of nutritional levels in their populations and what these levels can reasonably allow them to expect and demand of their people. The prevalence of hunger, especially among children in a large portion of the population, has grave implications for the future development plans of LDCs, including proposals for increasing food production. A government that expects elaborate development efforts to be carried out by a weakened, undernourished populace, a significant fraction of whom may be physically and mentally disadvantaged, is likely to be disappointed.

The exact mechanisms whereby undernutrition, infection, and an impoverished environment interact to produce high infant and child mortality, morbidity, and impaired development are not known. But more than enough is known to undertake a program of *prevention.* The goal would be simple: to ensure that every mother and her children are adequately fed during pregnancy and those crucial early years, and to provide them with basic medical care and sanitary living conditions. Such a program would be far easier and cheaper to institute than massive rehabilitation after the damage is done, and it would have broad benefits for the entire society. Unfortunately, achieving even such a relatively simple goal would require an enormous restructuring of priorities and reallocation of resources for most LDCs, and there is little sign of such change in most countries.[69]

The Other Side of the Coin

In stark contrast to the widespread hunger that prevails in many less developed areas, increased affluence has allowed a steady increase in nutritional levels in developed areas in past decades. Less than half of the growth in food consumption in DCs between 1952 and 1972 was due to population growth; the remainder was accounted for by affluence. This does not mean that people in rich countries directly consumed more kilocalories per person than they did twenty years earlier. Rather, they were eating far more meat, poultry, and dairy products, which today are produced in large part by feeding grains, oilseed cakes, and fishmeal to livestock.

Figure 7-12 shows the trend in per-capita beef and poultry consumption in the United States. Poultry consumption more than doubled, and that of beef nearly did between 1950 and 1972. Similar increases have taken place elsewhere, although people in most other DCs still consume less meat than Americans. This rising demand for meat has led to a rapidly growing demand for feedgrains and other feedstuffs in developed countries. By 1974, livestock were being fed *one-third* of the world's total production of grain.[70]

By 1972, people in DCs on the average consumed, directly and indirectly, four times as much food per

[67]M. Winick et al., Malnutrition and environmental enrichment by early adoption.

[68]Hertzig, *et al.,* Intellectual levels. For an excellent (if cautious) review of the confusing evidence on the role of malnutrition in mental development, see Michael C. Latham, Protein-calorie malnutrition in children and its relation to psychological development and behavior.

[69]That nutritional policies could or should be incorporated into development plans is a relatively new, almost radical idea, just beginning to gain acceptance. See particularly Berg, *The nutrition factor;* J. O. Field and F. J. Levinson, Nutrition and development; J. T. Dwyer and J. Mayer, Beyond economics and nutrition.

[70]Lester R. Brown and Erik P. Eckholm, *By bread alone.*

FIGURE 7-12

Per-capita consumption of poultry and beef in the United States, 1910–1973. (Adapted from Brown and Eckholm, *By bread alone.*)

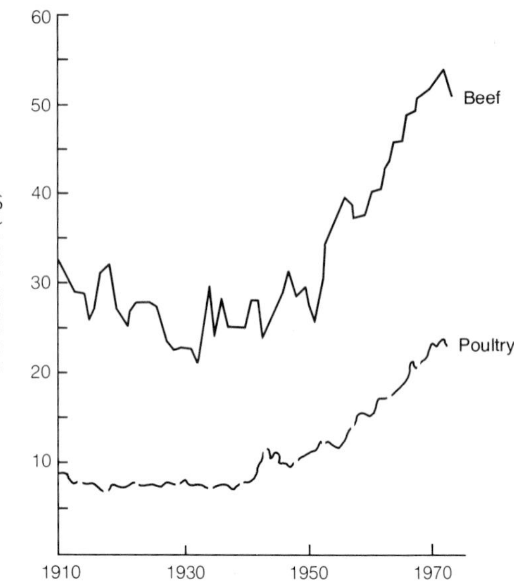

FIGURE 7-13
The relationship of direct and indirect grain consumption to per-capita income in selected countries. (From L. R. Brown, Population and affluence: Growing pressures on world food resources, *Population Bulletin,* vol. 29, no. 2. Courtesy of Population Reference Bureau, Inc., Washington, D.C.)

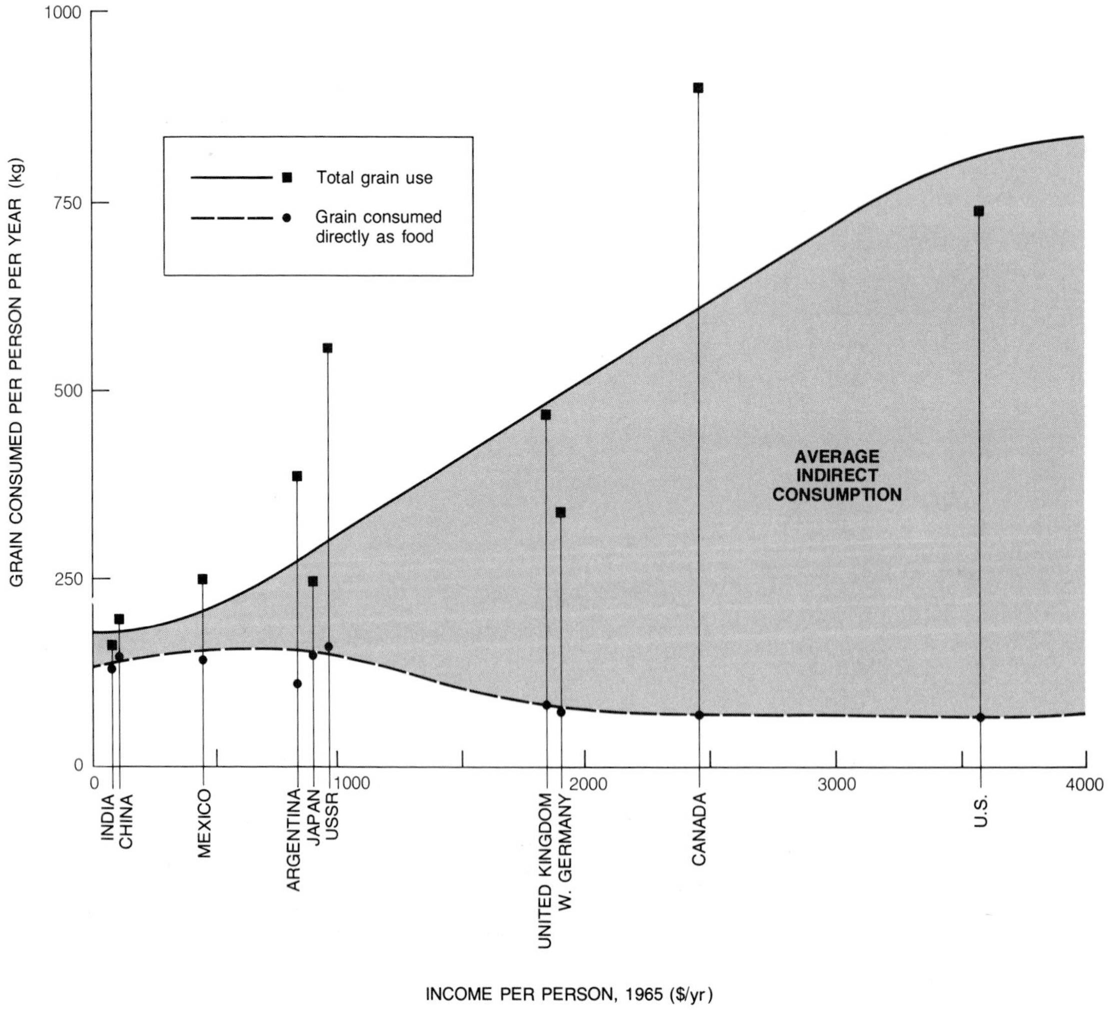

person as people in the LDCs.[71] A comparison among countries of grain consumption graphically shows the difference in diets between the rich and the poor (Figure 7-13). Three-fourths or more of the food energy in an Asian's diet comes directly from grain—135 to 180 kilograms (roughly 300 to 400 pounds) per year. An affluent American accounts for the consumption of nearly *a ton* of grain per year, but 80 percent of it is first fed to animals. Because Americans are thus feeding higher on the food chain (Chapter 4), most of the food value is lost to human nutrition. With American livestock-feeding methods, producing one kilogram of poultry requires two or three kilograms of grain, and producing one kilogram of beef on the feed lot requires ten or more kilograms of grain.[72] Other meats fall between these extremes of efficiency in conversion.

Cattle and sheep can be raised very successfully, if perhaps not so rapidly and abundantly, on forage grown on soils unsuitable for crops,[73] perhaps supplemented with agricultural by-products such as cornstalks. A relatively small grain supplement would result in quite satisfactory beef, especially if different cattle varieties were used that had been bred for efficient production of lean, tender meat. Present methods of beef production result in an animal with an excessive amount of fat.

Moreover, the fat in grainfed cattle appears to be of a different *quality* from that in range-fed animals. The latter contain abundant long-chain polyunsaturated fatty acids, needed nutritionally by human beings, particularly for building nervous tissue. Grain-fed animals, on the other hand, seem to be deficient in the long-chain polyunsaturates, but contain great amounts of nonessential saturated fat. Consumption of large amounts of saturated fat has been implicated as a contributing factor in cardiovascular disease, the leading cause of death in the United States and many other DCs.[74] The diets of citizens of affluent nations have been shown to have other adverse effects on health, also. Among the first of these is obesity, a contributing factor in several diseases. High protein, high fat diets have also been associated with some kinds of cancer that are relatively common in DCs.[74a]

Questions about the morality of feeding to livestock grains that could nourish hungry people have been raised in various quarters, especially since 1972.[75] Unfortunately, today's economic system once again is to blame. The poor and hungry people in other countries cannot afford the cereals and soybeans produced abundantly in the United States. The only "demand" for them is generated by livestock producers in the U.S. and other developed countries. Since 1973, rising costs of feedgrains—corn, sorghum, rye, barley, oats, etc.—due to increasing export demand, have led American farmers to reduce their grain-feeding of cattle and sheep. But the higher costs also put these grains even further out of reach of the poor in LDCs. Clearly, the only way to make the surplus grain produced in North America available to hungry people is to separate some of it from the commercial market and make it directly available to the LDCs either free or on special concessional terms. This, of course has been the aim of food aid programs; but as commercial demand grows, the temptation to reduce food aid programs also grows.

At least one developed country—Norway—has undertaken a national nutrition program aimed at improving diets and making the most efficient use of food resources.[76] Both by public education and by economic incentives and disincentives, people have been encouraged to demand, and farmers to produce, leaner meats, more grains and vegetables, and less sugar and livestock products. The result has reportedly been not only improved diets and health, but reductions in resources (land, water, energy, and fertilizer) used to produce the nation's food, and reductions in imports of feedgrains. The potential benefits of a nutrition policy are, it seems, not limited to LDCs.[77]

---

[71]UN, *Assessment.*

[72]Frances Moore Lappé, *Diet for a small planet;* Brown and Eckholm, *By bread alone.* The conversion varies according to how the animal is raised and at what age it is slaughtered. For a more detailed breakdown, see the University of California Food Task Force, *A hungry world,* p. 138.

[73]Hodgson, Forage Crops, and Forages, ruminant livestock, and food.

[74]Robert Allen, *Food for thought.*

[74a]Eckholm and Record, The two faces of malnutrition.

[75]Lappé, *Diet for a small planet,* and Fantasies of famine; Lester R. Brown, *In the human interest;* Brown and Eckholm, *By bread alone.*

[76]L. R. Brown and E. P. Eckholm, Next steps toward global food security.

[77]For suggestions and discussions of nutritional policies that might benefit the United States, see Jean Mayer, ed., *U.S. nutrition policies in the seventies.*

Hunger in America. It must be remembered, however, that not all Americans are overfed. Some 10 to 15 percent of the U.S. population have incomes too low to meet the most basic needs. People were shocked in 1968 when the extent of hunger, malnutrition, and clinical-deficiency diseases in the U.S. was first widely publicized. As in LDCs, this hunger and malnutrition appeared to be related to poverty and an accompanying syndrome of unemployment, displacement from the land, and appalling sanitary conditions, often accompanied by a high incidence of parasitism. Testimony before a Senate committee indicated that the nutritional level of a segment of the population examined in a Public Health Service survey in 1969 was as low as those found in many less developed countries. Investigation revealed that between *10 and 15 million* Americans were constantly and chronically hungry, including a large proportion of children. Another 10 to 15 million had incomes too low to provide a well-balanced diet.[78]

Among a random sample of 12,000 American men, women, and children from low-income areas in Texas, New York, Louisiana, and Kentucky, the survey found seven extremely severe cases of marasmus and kwashiorkor and eighteen cases of rickets, as well as many milder cases of malnutrition. There was also evidence of widespread goiter (caused by iodine deficiency), 17 percent of the 12,000 people had serious protein deficiencies, and a similar number were described nutritionally as "real risks." Most of the children were below average size for their ages, and 3.5 percent were definitely stunted. One-third of those under six were anemic, and nearly as many showed signs of being Vitamin-A deficient, many seriously so. Altogether, from 35 to 55 percent of all the people surveyed exhibited signs of serious nutritional deficiencies of various kinds.

The high incidence of deficiencies of Vitamins A and D and iodine found by the Public Health Survey is embarrassing, since they are all easily preventable. The need for the use of iodized salt may be forgotten or unknown among some of the poor; yet the government survey found that it was not even available in the markets in parts of Texas, a known goiter area.

The underlying causes of malnutrition and hunger in a country as rich as the United States resemble, in some respects, those in LDCs; they include inadequate food distribution, poverty, and ignorance. But in the United States they have existed mainly because of the lack of will on the part of the well-fed to do anything about them. U.S. government food-aid programs have clearly failed to achieve their supposed aims. Free surplus foods were distributed to the poor until the early 1970s by the U.S. Department of Agriculture. But that department's primary interest, unfortunately, seems to have been in the expeditious elimination of farm surpluses, rather than in the nutritional needs of the recipients. By the mid-1970s, the food-stamp program was the primary means of providing nutritional assistance to the poor, allowing them to buy food at reduced prices. But for the lowest-income groups, families with less than $1000 per year, even the stamps were too expensive. For a time many local governments declined to participate in the programs even when they had large eligible populations. Poor administration probably accounted for some of the failure as well. Free and low-cost school lunch programs have also had a long history of mismanagement of funds, and have been hampered by food-industry lobbying at the legislative level. But by 1975, they were reaching nearly 80 percent of the American school population.

In early 1969 Senator Ernest F. Hollings of South Carolina testified to the Senate Select Committee on Nutrition that, when he was governor of South Carolina from 1959 to 1963, he and other state officials deliberately concealed their state's hunger problem in an attempt to boost industrial development. They feared that knowledge of South Carolina's difficulties would discourage industry from locating there.

Public pressure has removed some of these problems, but they have been replaced by others. By 1975 some 19.5 million people were receiving food stamps at an annual cost to the federal government of five billion dollars.[79] The program has become a nightmare of overregulation and built-in inequity, but both Congress and the administration seem helplessly unable to improve it substantially. A better solution might be a comprehensive income-supplement system that would elminate the need for separate food programs.

[78]Ernest F. Holling, *The case against hunger;* Robert Sherrill, Why can't we just give them food?

[79]Kenneth Schlossberg, Funny money is serious.

Meanwhile the poor are not much better off than they were in 1968, despite the huge expansion of food programs. It has been estimated that perhaps 20 million additional people are eligible for food stamps but are not enrolled in the program. Inflation has effectively wiped out much of the benefit, especially for people living on small fixed incomes, as many elderly persons do. Rises in food prices between 1972 and 1975 disproportionately penalized the poor, because the cheapest foods (cheap cuts of meat, sugar, beans, etc.) escalated the most in price. At the height of some inflationary surges, the rumor circulated that millions of low-income Americans were subsisting on pet food.[80] This was hotly denied in many quarters, including some pet-food makers, but the rumor persisted.

In Spring 1974 the early results of a new national nutritional survey were released. This survey covered the entire population rather than concentrating on low-income areas.[81] Among the preliminary findings: about 95 percent of all preschool children and women of childbearing age had substandard intakes of iron, and 10 percent of the children were anemic; calcium-intake levels were low in black women; Vitamin A intake was low in poor white women; and many people seemed to be getting insufficient Vitamin C.

The overt starvation that was found in 1968 in the United States may since have been greatly reduced, but poor nutritional habits continue to exist at all income levels, and people in the lowest income levels still must struggle just to meet their minimum needs.

The World Trade System

Major elements in the distribution of food (and its inequities) around the world are the world trade system and the economic system of which it is a part. Unfortunately, food (like other commodities) goes to those who can pay for it, not necessarily to those who need it most, especially within and between capitalist economies. Distribution may be somewhat more equitable within communist and socialist countries, but on the world market capitalist rules prevail for them as well. Fortunately, there are programs that bypass this system and distribute donated food to the neediest or allow it to be purchased at lower cost, and there are indications that these programs may be expanded in the future.

The total volume of food that crosses national boundaries has always been a relatively small fraction of total production, but it has been growing even faster, at about 3.5 to 4 percent per year, than total food production and consumption. In 1973/1974, net exports of major grains traded amounted to an estimated 151 million metric tons, about 16 percent of world production of those grains for that year. (Rice is excluded from these figures, but only a small fraction of the rice crop is exported.) Among exported commodities, wheat is decidedly the leader; it accounts for more than a quarter of all food trade. Figure 7-14 shows the relative proportions by weight of important commodities traded. As the figure shows, more than half of them are grains. The growth in exports of grain worldwide is shown in Appendix 2.

There has been a substantial change in recent decades in the origin and destination of exported foods. Before World War II, many countries in Asia, Africa, and Latin America were important grain exporters. By the mid-1960s, those regions were importing grain in far greater quantities than they had ever exported it (Table 7-12). By 1970 the only net grain exporters of any significance among LDCs were Thailand, Burma, Mexico, and Argentina.[82] (Mexico has since reverted to being an importer.) While several LDCs were exporting rice in the early 1970s (notably the Philippines and China), they were simultaneously importing wheat, which was cheaper, and using the foreign exchange thus gained for other needed imports.

To picture the LDCs simply as net food importers would be a mistake, however. Although the DCs annually delivered some 2.5 million tons of gross protein to the LDCs during the 1960s, the LDCs sent the DCs about 3.5 million tons of higher quality protein in the form of fishmeal, soybeans, and presscakes of oilseeds. The DCs use nearly all of this to feed poultry, livestock, and pets. More than sixty countries, including Mexico, Panama, Surinam, Hong Kong, and India, supply the United States with shrimp, which could otherwise be a

[80]Dan Greenberg, Food for whom?

[81]*Science,* National nutrition.

[82]The FAO classifies Argentina as "less developed"; the United Nations includes it among the developed countries, at least with respect to its demographic characteristics.

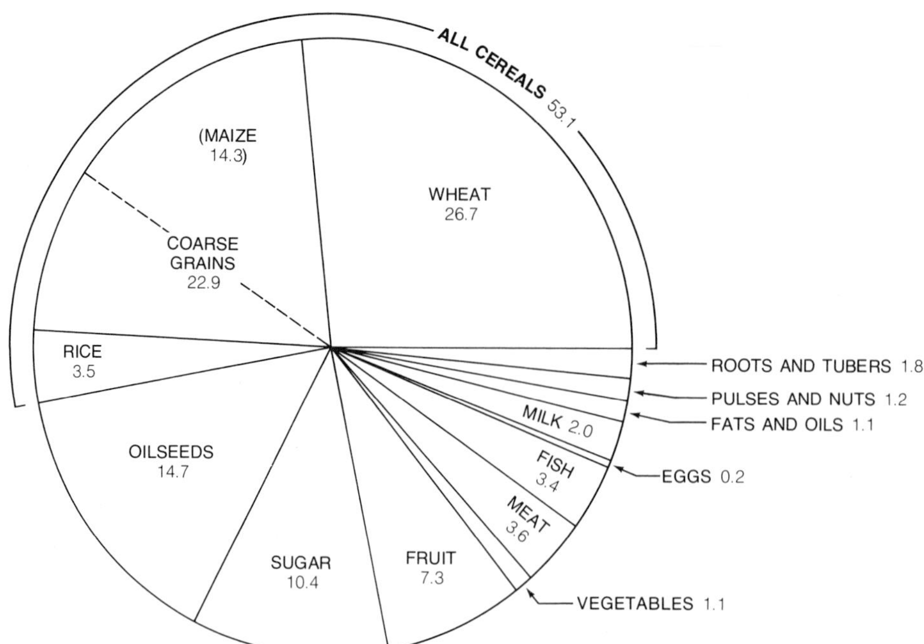

FIGURE 7-14

Distribution by commodity of world agricultural exports, 1970 (percentages of total metric tons). (From University of California Food Task Force, *A hungry world: The challenge to agriculture,* 1974.)

TABLE 7-12
*The Changing Pattern of World Grain Trade**

Region	*1934–1938*	*1948–1952*	*1960*	*1970*	*1976***
		Millions of metric tons			
North America	+5	+23	+39	+56	+94
Latin America	+9	+1	0	+4	−3
Western Europe	−24	−22	−25	−30	−17
Eastern Europe and USSR	+5	—	0	0	−27
Africa	+1	0	−2	−5	−10
Asia	+2	−6	−17	−37	−47
Australia and New Zealand	+3	+3	+6	+12	+8

*Plus sign indicates net exports: minus sign, net imports.
**Preliminary estimates of fiscal year data.
Source: Lester R. Brown, The politics and responsibility of the North American breadbasket. Worldwatch Institute.

life-saver for the protein-starved children of those countries. Peru has been exporting to the DCs most of its anchoveta catches, which potentially could relieve protein deficiencies in Latin America. Georg Borgstrom has described the advantage held by the rich countries of the world in the present pattern of protein flow as "an almost treacherous exchange."[83]

Many of these foods are beyond the means of the poor, so they are exported to earn needed foreign exchange. Some, such as anchoveta fishmeal and oilseed cakes, are not considered suitable for human consumption, and so are exported as feed, again for foreign exchange. Although political and commercial leaders in LDCs have willingly cooperated in promoting production of these commodities for export, their intentions were not necessarily evil. Some undoubtedly hoped to use the foreign exchange to purchase food and goods that might improve the prospects of their people, and some is spent that way. Unfortunately, the proceeds have often been squandered on luxuries for the wealthy urban elite or used for development projects that have no effect on the welfare of people outside the cities.

[83] *Too many,* pp. 237, 245, and 321.

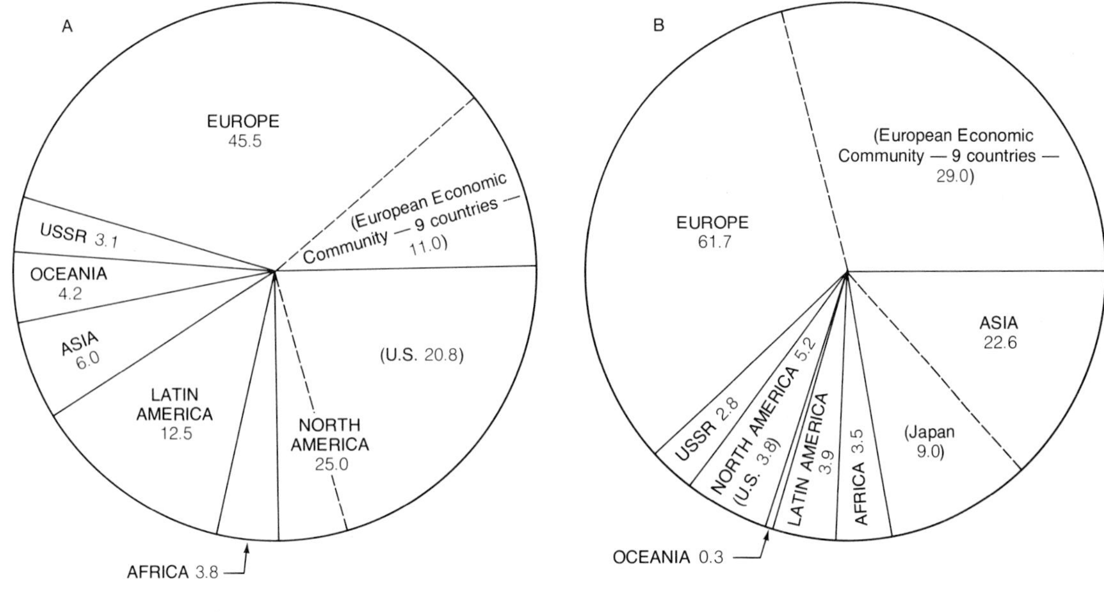

FIGURE 7-15

A. The distribution of world food exports by region, 1970 (percentages of total metric tons).
B. The distribution of world food imports by region, 1970 (percentages of total metric tons).
(From University of California Food Task Force, *A hungry world: The challenge to agriculture,* 1974.)

Although most Americans are far more conscious of U.S. food exported to LDCs, the vast majority of our exports go to DCs—indeed the overwhelming bulk of food trade occurs between developed countries. Figure 7-15 shows origins and destinations of food exports in 1970. All the less developed countries imported barely 21 percent of all imported food; indeed, they exported more than they imported in 1970. As the figure shows, Europe dominates both the export and especially the import scene; together with the USSR, in 1970 Europe took in nearly 65 percent of all imported food. (In several of the years since then, the Soviet share has been much larger.) Europe exports manufactured goods and high-quality protein foods in exchange for grain, feedstuffs, and other commodities. Most European countries are far more dependent on imports for their food than are the poor countries.

Japan is even more dependent on imports to feed its population than is Europe (Table 7-13). In 1970, Japan's 106 million people imported more than two-thirds as much food as did the nearly two billion people in the rest of Asia. Note that Japan's huge harvest from oceanic fisheries (labeled domestic production) is projected in the table to continue.

The United States and world trade. The United States is by far the world's leading exporter of food today, accounting for nearly half of all grain traded on the world market. Like other DCs, however, the U.S. is also a major importer of foods, especially oilseeds and fishmeal for livestock feed, seafood, meats, tropical fruits, sugar, coffee, and dairy products. These products come from all over the world, but our largest suppliers are Latin America (especially Brazil and Mexico), Asia (especially the Philippines), Europe, and Australia.

The biggest customers for U.S. exports in 1974, more or less in order of importance, were: Japan, several western European nations, Canada, the Soviet Union, and the People's Republic of China.[84] The last named two are by no means regular, longstanding buyers. In

[84]USDA, *Foreign agriculture,* February 23, 1976, p. 8.

TABLE 7-13
Japan: Summary Agriculture/Food Balance Sheet (1960, 1972, and projected 1985)

Commodity	*Domestic production* 1960	1972	1985	*Imports* 1960	1972	1985	*Total demand** 1960	1972	1985	*Food selfsufficiency* 1960	1972	1985
	Thousands of metric tons									*Percent*		
Rice	12,858	11,897	12,110	–	–	–	12,613	11,948	12,110	102	100	100
Wheat, total	1,531	284	553	2,384	5,088	5,346	3,965	5,372	5,899	39	5	9
(For feed)	–	–	–	–	–	–	(468)	(713)	(822)	–	–	–
Barley, total	2,301	324	890	–	1,518	1,612	2,141	1,842	2,502	108	18	36
(For feed)	–	–	–	–	–	–	(540)	(985)	(1,506)	–	–	–
Livestock Feed:												
Coarse grains**	3,773	5,628	5,837	1,898	9,888	14,772	5,671	15,516	20,609	–	30	28
Soybeans, total	418	127	427	1,128	3,369	4,580	1,517	3,496	5,007	–	4	9
Potatoes†	9,871	5,598	4,927	–	6	–	9,849	5,604	5,927	157	100	100
Peanuts	72	64	82	–	55	74	70	119	156	103	54	53
Pulses	429	268	218	59	110	162	488	378	380	88	71	57
Vegetables	11,742	15,837	20,136	–	204	–	11,742	16,041	20,136	100	99	100
Fruits	3,307	6,409	8,789	–	1,471	1,627	3,296	8,004	10,612	84	81	84
Milk products	1,939	4,944	7,680	237	775	462	2,176	5,719	8,142	89	86	94
All meats	517	1,730	2,747	87	417	446	604	2,147	3,193	–	81	86
Beef	141	290	508	–	77	117	147	367	625	96	79	81
Pork	149	793	1,325	–	90	10	155	883	1,335	96	90	99
Chicken	44	640	914	–	28	1	44	668	915	100	96	100
Other meats	183	7	–	–	222	318	58	229	318	–	3	–
Fish, total	5,803	10,376	11,953	–	876	2,801	5,383	10,472	13,903	101	101	95
Eggs	547	1,811	2,205	–	37	1	689	1,848	2,206	108	98	100
Sugar	–	621	1,064	1,243	2,456	2,787	1,419	3,077	3,851	–	20	28
Oils and fats, total	350	352	370	350	1,181	1,870	682	1,533	2,240	–	23	17

*Includes demand for food, food processing, seed, loss, and imports.
**Corn, sorghum, rye, oats, etc.
†Sweet and white potatoes.
Source: USDA, *Foreign agriculture,* October 6, 1975.

1975 the USSR, after suffering a severe setback in its wheat harvest, negotiated a purchase of some 20 million metric tons of American grain.[85]

Partly because much of the Soviet Union's productive land is relatively far north, and therefore more than usually susceptible to adverse weather such as early frost, and partly for other reasons, Soviet harvests can vary by as much as 30 percent from one year to the next.

The negotiations for the Soviet purchases in 1975 were accompanied by an uproar of protest by U.S. labor unions who anticipated a repetition of the grain-price escalation that followed the Soviet purchases in 1972.[86] The United States government then imposed a temporary embargo on grain exports to the USSR, which incensed wheat farmers[87] (and alarmed trading partners). Because the U.S. normally exports around two-thirds of its annual wheat crop and large portions of other grain crops (Figure 7-16), even very large Soviet purchases were unlikely to cause a domestic shortage or significant price changes unless the U.S. harvest had been well below normal levels or there were unusually great demand from other countries. Neither proved to be a problem in 1975. In order to avoid future crises caused by unanticipated purchases by the USSR, a special agreement was negotiated, whereby the USSR agreed to buy 6 million metric tons of grain from the U.S. each year from 1976 to 1981, with options to buy another 2 million metric tons as long as the American supply (stocks plus estimated production) was above 225 million metric tons.[88] Further purchases in any given year were also negotiable.

Probably the greatest cause of the unstable, wildly fluctuating grain prices on both the domestic and the world markets (Figure 7-17) since 1972 has been the

[85]For an interesting review of the history of and outlook for Soviet agriculture, see Alex Nove, Soviet grain, problems and prospects; or Will Russia ever feed itself?

[86]Food prices: Why they're going up again, *Time,* August 18, 1975.

[87]George Anthan, Washington farm policy makes few friends in Iowa, *New York Times,* August 24, 1975.

[88]USDA, WAS-9.

calculated elimination of U.S. grain reserves (which accounted for most of the world reserves) by the U.S. Department of Agriculture. Former Secretary of Agriculture Earl Butz and others in the USDA viewed recent worldwide food shortages as a bonanza for using up the surpluses of former years and meeting the nation's foreign-exchange balance of payments. In hot pursuit of a "free grain market," which supposedly would reward the productive American farmer, these individuals pursued policies that benefited neither American consumers nor the hungry abroad, but which made large amounts of money for their friends in big agribusiness corporations. As Lester Brown observed, Secretary Butz was opposed to the price-stabilization effect of sizable government-held grain reserves, "because he comes from an agribusiness background, and the more uncertainty there is, the more prices of grains fluctuate, the more money the traders who know what's happening [that is, the big grain traders] can make."[89]

Early indications from the Carter Administration were that the previous "agribusiness first" policy of the U.S. Department of Agriculture would be reversed. Indeed, even during the election campaign, President Carter had declared his support for reestablishment of grain reserves in the United States and also for establishment of a worldwide food reserve system as proposed by the U.N. World Food Conference in 1974 (see below).

The declines in worldwide grain harvests in 1972 and 1974 were not anticipated, nor were their effects on grain supplies and food prices. As a result of the unexpected shortages and the disappearance of reserves, far from being consistently rewarded for their efforts, American farmers have been subjected to various cost squeezes and unpredictable prices for their products.[90]

In recent years, the food-export business in the U.S. has boomed. Unfortunately, the boom was accompanied by a scandalous amount of cheating and corruption.[91] Some of this came to light when several LDCs, formerly recipients of free food, felt they had the right to complain

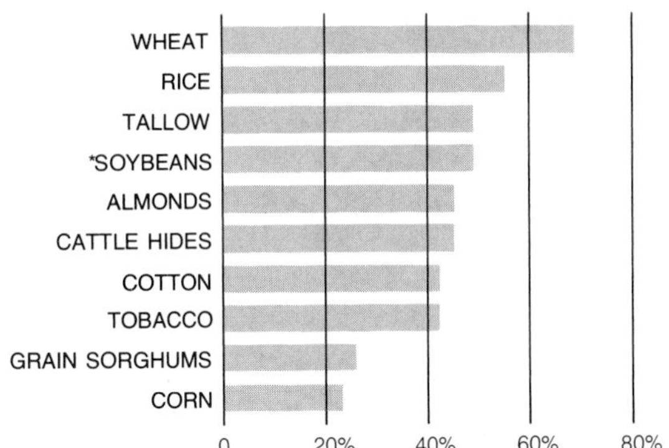

FIGURE 7-16

Leading U.S. agricultural exports as percentages of farm production, 1974 (year ending June 30). *Includes bean equivalent of meal. (Adapted from *Foreign agriculture,* U.S. Department of Agriculture, May 26, 1975.)

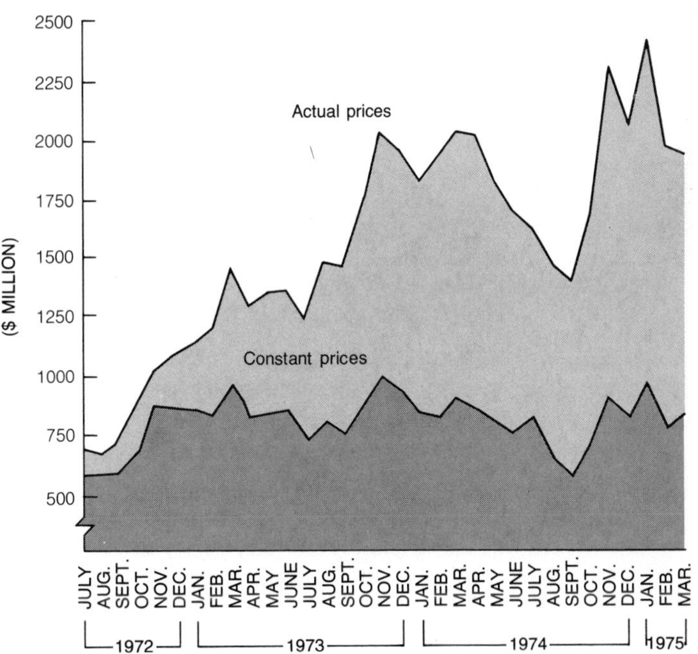

FIGURE 7-17

U.S. agricultural exports at actual and constant prices, July 1972–March 1975. (Adapted from *Foreign agriculture,* U.S. Department of Agriculture, May 19, 1975.)

[89] Quoted in Schneider and Mesirow, *The Genesis strategy,* p. 253.

[90] S. De Marco and S. Sechler, The marketplace of hunger. Excerpted from a full-length report by the Agribusiness Accountability Project, Washington, D.C. 20036. See also R. Morris and H. Sheets, Why leave it to Earl?

[91] Dirty grain, *Time,* June 30, 1975.

TABLE 7-14
Total Food Aid of Development Assistance Committee Countries at Both Current and 1968 Prices

	1964	*1965*	*1966*	*1967*	*1968*	*1969*	*1970*	*1971*	*1972*	*1973*
Food aid at current prices (million U.S. dollars)	1529.1	1311.3	1329.2	1124.8	1159.2	1174.0	1257.3	1217.1	1276.0	1129.7
Food price index* (1968 = 100)	110	97	104	105	100	95	93	101	113	231
Food aid at 1968 prices (million U.S. dollars)	1390.1	1351.9	1278.1	1071.2	1159.2	1235.8	1351.9	1205.1	1129.2	489.0

*Based on export price of U.S. wheat.
Source: FAO, *State of food and agriculture, 1974,* p. 27.

TABLE 7-15
U.S. Agricultural Exports, 1960–1974 (in millions of dollars)

	Public Law 480 (Food for Peace)				
	Title I (sales under special terms)	*Title II*	*Total*	*Total agricultural exports*	*Public Law 480 as percentage of total*
1960	1014	173	1304	4832	27
1961	879	244	1304	5024	26
1962	1048	259	1444	5034	29
1963	1213	259	1509	5834	27
1964	1330	248	1621	6348	26
1965	1051	253	1323	6229	21
1966	1054	211	1306	6881	19
1967	930	287	1230	6380	19
1968	924	251	1178	6228	19
1969	765	256	1021	5936	17
1970	766	255	1021	7693	13
1971	692	290	982	7693	13
1972	730	377	1107	9401	12
1973	541	209	750	17,677	4
1974	488	272	760	21,994	3

Source: Adapted from James W. Howe, *The U.S. and world development: agenda for action, 1975,* Overseas Development Council, Praeger, New York, 1975, pp. 246–247.

when their paid-for shipments arrived short-weighted and so contaminated that they were unfit for consumption. By 1976 some 26 nations, including the Soviet Union, had officially complained of contaminated, misgraded, and short-weighted shipments.[92] On investigation, the corruption proved to be very pervasive, and dozens of individuals—including grain inspectors, shippers, and grain dealers—were indicted in 1975.

Foreign aid: food. Just as the need for imported grains has grown in less developed countries since the 1950s, so for a while did food-aid programs. Between 30 and 45 percent of the food imported by LDCs between 1954 and 1969 was from one or another food-aid program. Most of this was U.S. surplus grain sold on concessional terms. During the 1960s United Nations multilateral programs also developed. Food-aid shipments reached a peak total of 18 million tons in 1964/1965. But they were scarcely half that volume in 1972/1973 and were even lower in the food-short period of 1973/1974. Table 7-14 shows the trend in international food aid from 1964 to 1973.

The decline in food aid was largely due to the disappearance of American surplus grain stocks, which until the early 1970s accounted for some 83 percent of the donated food. As grain prices rose, the U.S. government made no effort to increase the dollar commitment to Title II of Public Law 480 (the Food for Peace Act), the program that provided free food to poor nations, and the grain commitment shrank accordingly. In 1973 and 1974, the U.S. Administration even cut the program back. In those years, the poorest and neediest countries were receiving less than a fifth as much food as they had six to eight years earlier. In 1974, roughly half of all American food aid went to two countries, South Vietnam and Cambodia, neither of which was in acute distress.[93]

Table 7-15 shows the proportion of U.S. food exports that was devoted to aid programs over the years. Title I provided food under concessional terms: long-term, low-interest loans and publicly subsidized prices. Public and international pressures induced the U.S. government to increase shipments under both programs following the Rome World Food Conference. That it was not done sooner is no tribute to the leadership or sensitivity of the Nixon and Ford Administrations at a time when an unprecedented situation demanded new initiatives.

[92]United Press International, Massive grain-export scandal stains U.S. integrity worldwide, *San Francisco Chronicle,* February 8, 1976.

[93]Brown and Eckholm, Next step; Emma Rothschild, Food politics.

One reason for the decline in the volume of food aid in the early 1970s was the apparently rising per-capita production in many regions just before 1972. Several former recipients of free food had also become commercial buyers. This was especially true of India, whose government had deeply resented the strings attached by the U.S. to food donations in the 1960s. Among other demands, the U.S. had insisted on expansion of the Indian Family Planning Program.

In addition, public support for food aid (and foreign aid in general) seemed to be dwindling. Reports of widespread waste, corruption, and misappropriation of funds and materials in various famine and disaster-relief programs have undoubtedly contributed to this sentiment. In Bangladesh, following independence, much donated food was diverted to the black market, and some was smuggled into India where prices were higher.[94] Food was sent to the Sahel countries long after people began starving. When it finally arrived, much of it spoiled in storage before it could be moved by the region's inadequate transportation system to the needy, far inland. Even then, politics prevented most of it from reaching those most in need.[95]

In 1974/1975, Ethiopia quadrupled its exports of grain to other Red Sea nations. Meanwhile, perhaps a half million Ethiopians were starving, and the government had applied for free food from the U.S. Much of the food aid was resold, some was put in storage. When some of the food was released for the hungry, no airplanes were available to transport it to the hinterland; all aircraft were engaged in bombing the rebellious province of Eritrea.[96] For months the Ethiopian government had attempted to conceal the existence and extent of famine within the country. Officials of FAO and UNICEF were aware of the situation but apparently did not intervene.[97] Tales of failure in distributing donated food to victims of famine and other disasters are legion. Not all relief efforts are such dismal failures, however, and usually even in the worst cases, some of the food eventually finds its destination. Relief of the famine in the Indian province of Bihar in 1965-1966 is sometimes cited as one of the rare unqualified successes in averting disaster.

Although there have been direct transfers of food from DCs to LDCs, there have been very few programs for development assistance aimed at increasing LDC food production. Of the perhaps $20 billion of development assistance that was provided annually around 1972 from DCs to LDCs (mostly as loans, with some grants), only about $1 billion (5 percent) was earmarked for agriculture.[98] This is largely because until 1969, DC governments (especially food-exporting DCs such as the United States and Canada) were reluctant to encourage food production in LDCs, which might then compete on the world food market.[99] The slighting of agricultural development also may reflect the degree of commitment felt by the governments of hungry countries toward increasing food production to feed their people.

Since 1972, this long-neglected area has been somewhat revitalized, and United Nations agencies and the World Bank have belatedly concentrated far more effort on the agricultural sector. By 1974, commitments for agricultural development had increased to $3.6 billion. Among the proliferating agencies involved in food, in 1976 the newly created International Fund for Agricultural Development (IFAD) alone was pledged a starting fund of $1.2 billion in special drawing rights, mainly from DCs and OPEC nations. The fund will provide soft loans (long-term, low-interest) for agricultural development and nutritional improvement in LDCs, and recipient countries will have a majority vote in decisions about distribution. The fund is planned to expand to $5 billion annually by 1980.[100]

Agricultural research programs. The enormous increases in food production that will be required to feed the growing human population during the coming decades will also necessitate a substantial acceleration in agricultural research.[101] Unfortunately, for decades agriculture has been a neglected stepsister of the other sciences, even in developed countries. In most less

[94]Mike Muller, Aid, corruption and waste.

[95]Ibid.; Carnegie Endowment for International Peace, *Disaster in the desert*, New York, 1974; *New internationalist*, Disaster in the Sahel.

[96]CBS News, June 23, 1975.

[97]Jack Shepherd, *The politics of starvation*, Carnegie Endowment for International Peace, New York, 1975.

[98]FAO, *State of food and agriculture*, 1974.

[99]Sterling Wortman, Food and agriculture, p. 38.

[100]Tony Loftas, Green signal for UN's new billion dollar fund; Jon McLin, Remember the world food conference?

[101]S. H. Wittwer, Food production: Technology and the resource base.

TABLE 7-16
International Centers for Agricultural Research

Center and date founded	*Location*	*Research*	*Coverage*	*1975 budget (in thousands of dollars)*
International Rice Research Institute (IRRI), 1959	Los Banos, Philippines	Irrigated and upland rice; multiple-cropping systems	Worldwide, Asian emphasis	8520
International Center for the Improvement of Maize and Wheat (CIMMYT), 1964	El Batan, Mexico	Wheat, triticale, barley, maize	Worldwide	6834
International Institute of Tropical Agriculture (IITA), 1965	Ibadan, Nigeria	Various tropical crops (cereals, pulses, tubers); farming systems	Lowland tropics, African emphasis	7746
International Center for Tropical Agriculture (CIAT), 1968	Palmira, Colombia	Various tropical crops and livestock; farming systems	Lowland tropics, Latin American emphasis	5828
West African Rice Development Association (WARDA), 1971	Monrovia, Liberia	Rice	West Africa	575
International Potato Center (CIP), 1972	Lima, Peru	Potatoes, both tropical and temperate	Worldwide	2403
International Crops Research Institute for Semi-Arid Tropics (ICRISAT), 1972	Hyderabad, India	Sorghum, millet, various pulses, peanuts; farming systems	Worldwide, especially semi-arid tropics, nonirrigated farming	10,250
International Board for Plant Genetic Resources (IBPGR), 1973	FAO, Rome, Italy	Conservation of crop genetic material, especially cereals	Worldwide	555
International Laboratory for Research on Animal Diseases (ILRAD), 1974	Nairobi, Kenya	Trypanosomiasis, theileriasis (East Coast fever)	Africa	2170
International Livestock Center for Africa (ILCA), 1974	Addis Ababa, Ethiopia	Livestock production systems	Tropical Africa	1885
International Center for Agricultural Research in Dry Areas (ICARDA), to be established	Lebanon (?)	Probably mixed farming systems	Worldwide, especially semi-arid, winter rain-fall regions	–

Source: Adapted from N. Wade, International agricultural research, p. 587.

developed nations it has been virtually ignored.[102] Since the early 1960s, however, an international agricultural research structure has slowly evolved.

Leadership of the international effort is now centered in a consortium of governments and foundations called the Consultative Group on International Agricultural Research (CGIAR), which coordinates the efforts of the international research centers. The first two centers, established by the Ford and Rockefeller Foundations in 1959 and 1964, were the International Rice Research Institute (IRRI) in the Philippines and the International Maize and Wheat Improvement Center (CIMMYT) in Mexico. In addition to these, the consultative group is sponsoring six newer research centers and an International Board for Plant Genetic Resources.[103] These research units employed some 200 professional workers in 1975, and have been set up to cover most important crops and all major geographic areas. The group's budget was increased from $34 million in 1974 to $64 million in 1976. Table 7-16 shows locations and missions of the consultative group's research centers in the mid-1970s. In addition to this system, there are several other international agricultural research efforts sponsored outside of the CGIAR.

[102]A. Mayer and J. Mayer, Agriculture, the island empire.

[103]For a detailed description of the new centers for research, see Nicolas Wade, International agricultural research.

A major international effort is badly needed if the technical and biological problems attending new agricultural technology (discussed below) are to be solved. It must be realized, however, that instant solutions are not likely to materialize; the "miracle" that Norman Borlaug achieved in developing high-yield varieties (HYVs) of wheat followed decades of hard work and an intimate familiarity with the needs of farmers. Fancy facilities and high pay at these institutes cannot substitute for hard work, hard thinking, and knowledge of field conditions.

Perhaps the major research challenge now lies in the less developed countries themselves. In some LDCs, such as the Philippines, Taiwan, and India, impressive agricultural research is being done by national research institutions; but, overall, research in those nations has been neglected and poorly funded in comparison to that in DCs—about $240 million annually for all LDCs—although the amount is now increasing.[104] A serious obstacle to spreading new agricultural technology within LDCs has been the critical shortage of agricultural research workers, technicians, and extension workers. In 1960, a typical LDC had fewer than 15 agricultural workers per 100,000 population, whereas most DCs had as many as 150. There has been improvement since then, but there is still a long way to go.

Until recently, most agricultural assistance, whether composed of research methods, technologies, or donated foods themselves, has been Western-oriented. The result is that it has not always been suited to the recipients' social, economic, and cultural backgrounds. Locally grown, traditional foods of potential value, for instance, may be overlooked or neglected in favor of Western crops because they cannot be processed with Western technology. Unfamiliar donated foods also may be wasted because they are not widely accepted. Least appropriate of all is training LDC food specialists in sophisticated packaging and processing techniques that are economically useless for their home countries. Such problems can be avoided if research is conducted in the same regions where the results are needed, so that the technology can be adapted to local conditions and customs. Food specialists Brown and Pariser put it well: "The time is past when 'West is best' can be taken for granted; 'adapt and adopt' is surely less offensively arrogant and much more to the point."[105]

[104]Nicholas Wade, Green Revolution, part 1, and Green Revolution, part 2.

A final problem with agricultural research in both DCs and LDCs is that agriculturalists have long tended to do their work with little consideration of the crucial ecological and coevolutionary dimensions of the problems they were investigating (see Chapters 4 and 11). Growing awareness of the environmental side-effects of modern agricultural technology and of the inescapable ecological problems of agriculture in the tropics are changing this attitude in some quarters. But, in general, agricultural research is still paying a penalty for its long isolation from other life sciences.

There have been signs of renewed interest in agricultural research at national as well as international levels, including in the United States. In late 1975, the U.S. Congress passed a new International Development and Food Assistance Act, which authorized funds for agricultural development and research, including those pledged to IFAD; strengthened the Food for Peace Act (P.L. 480); and called on the President to push for establishment of a world food-reserve system.

In late 1975, the National Academy of Sciences published a recommended reorganization of the American agricultural-research establishment.[106] Among their recommendations were: (1) to make research one of the USDA's major missions; (2) to increase funding of research related to productivity; (3) to allocate funds to several specific areas of basic and applied research, including work on "photosynthesis, nitrogen fixation, genetic manipulation by DNA recombination and other techniques, alternatives to chemical pesticides, and alternative technologies which reduce consumption of energy;" (4) to establish a program of competitive grants; (5) to revitalize the Cooperative State Research Service, which channels funds to agricultural research stations; and (6) to establish a policy council for determining goals and policies, which would also coordinate activities with other agencies. Such a program, if implemented, might do much to revitalize the overbureaucratized

[105]N. L. Brown and E. R. Pariser, Food science in developing countries; see also Ross H. Hall, Feeding the hungry planet counterfeit chocolate and instant pop tarts.

[106]Nicholas Wade, Agriculture: Academy group suggests major shake-up to President Ford. The NAS report is titled *Enhancement of food production for the United States.*

TABLE 7-17
Projections of Food Demand, 1969–1971 to 1985 (medium population variant)

Region	*Compound growth rates*			*Total volume of demand in 1985*		
	*Zero income**	*Trend income***	*High income†*	*Zero income**	*Trend income***	*High income†*
	Percent per annum			*1969–1971 = 100*		
DEVELOPED COUNTRIES	0.9	1.5	–	115	126	–
Market economies	0.9	1.4	–	114	124	–
Eastern Europe and USSR	0.9	1.7	–	115	130	–
DEVELOPING MARKET ECONOMIES	2.7	3.6	4.0	150	170	180
Africa	2.9	3.8	4.1	153	176	183
Far East	2.6	3.4	4.0	148	166	180
Latin America	2.8	3.6	3.8	151	170	175
Near East	2.9	4.0	4.2	154	180	186
ASIAN CENTRALLY PLANNED ECONOMIES	1.6	3.1	3.5	127	158	168
ALL DEVELOPING COUNTRIES	2.4	3.4	3.8	143	166	176
WORLD	2.0	2.4	2.7	134	144	148

*Zero trend = no change in per-capita income.
**Trend income = increases in per capita-income commensurate with those of past two decades.
†High income = accelerated increases in per-capita income.
Source: UN, *Assessment.*

agricultural-research organizations and encourage development of more environmentally beneficial approaches to food production in the United States. Many of the research objectives, if realized, obviously would be equally helpful to other countries, especially LDCs.

The Future Outlook

Now that we have examined the unmet needs and demands for food today, it is necessary to consider those of the future. There are, of course, many potential and some unavoidable limitations on further increases in food production. These will be examined in later sections of this chapter. First, it would be wise to establish what the goals should be.

Because the world's population is still growing at close to 2 percent per year and can be expected to continue growing rapidly for at least the next several decades (barring a major catastrophe that raises the death rate), substantial increases in food production will be required merely to meet demand at the present per-capita level of consumption. Even if food distribution were made much more equitable at the same time, raising food production so that the undernourished billion or so people could be adequately fed represents an even greater challenge. Projections by the United Nations of increased food needs under these conditions just for the period between 1970 and 1985 are staggering.[107]

Table 7-17 shows projections of food demand, assuming population growth according to the United Nations "medium variant" projections, and compares three assumptions of change in demand. "Zero income" assumes no change in per-capita gross domestic product (GDP), hence no change in per-capita demand. "Trend income" assumes that per-capita GDP will continue past trends in growth. "High income" assumes an acceleration over past trends in per-capita GDP growth. Thus the world must raise total food production *at least a third* above 1970 levels by 1985 just to meet needs at the same per-capita level. If there is continued growth in affluence, demand for food in 1985 will be for nearly *50 percent more* than was consumed in 1970.

Several other groups besides the United Nations have made projections of food needs to 1985. Among these are Iowa State University, The U.S. Department of Agriculture,[108] and the University of California Food Task Force.[109] Although each group used slightly different assumptions in making their projections, their conclusions as to expected needs are basically similar.

[107]UN, *Assessment;* FAO, *The state of food and agriculture,* 1974.
[108]*The world food situation and prospects to 1985.*
[109]*A hungry world: The challenge to agriculture.*

When the projections are broken down by region, the expected needs in 1985 of the chronically food-short developing countries range from 48 percent to 86 percent above 1970 consumption, depending upon changes in per-capita demand. Even with a continuation of past trends in demand, less developed regions will need food increases ranging from 70 to 80 percent. Nearly doubling food production in those countries in fifteen short years would call for a virtual miracle. And some countries (Nigeria, Iran, Iraq, Saudi Arabia, and Thailand, for instance) will require *more than twice* as much food. China and other communist Asian countries have somewhat better prospects, largely because of their slower population growth. The developed countries, on the other hand, could get by with relatively modest increases (15 to 30 percent), although rising demand, especially in the Soviet Union, is likely to push "needs" considerably higher.

It should be noted, of course, that rising demand—at least that component due to greater affluence—will not apply equally to all kinds of food. Demand for some foods is expected to increase much more rapidly than for others. Production of protein and oil sources, such as meat, fish, dairy products (and, by implication, feed-grains), nuts, and pulses (beans and peas), must be increased at a much greater rate than production of starchy tubers, for example. The United Nations projections of increased demand for various commodities can be seen in Appendix 2. These projections, of course, do not take into account the effect that possible price changes would have in changing demand.

The projections are made by extrapolating the likely course of food-production increases for various regions, based on recent performance. Obviously, a great many factors can affect food production, from weather and climate changes to alterations in government policies and agricultural economics, including world trade. Such events are not taken into account, since they cannot be predicted.

Although the various groups who have made projections of future demand for food agree fairly closely on the expected demand, they part company on the subject of whether the increased demand can be successfully met. The U.S. Department of Agriculture report is relatively complacent about humanity's ability to feed itself in 1985. The USDA estimates, however, have been strongly attacked by knowledgeable critics. USDA scientists have claimed that their estimates indicate that it would be possible not only to keep food production ahead of population growth, but even to *increase* world grain production per capita.[110] Agronomist Louis Thompson, dean of agriculture at Iowa State University has declared that the optimism of the USDA "is not widely shared because their projections are based on coefficients developed from a period when weather was generally favorable, when there was a significant improvement in varieties of wheat and rice, and there was a significant uptrend in the use of nitrogen fertilizers on all cereal grains throughout the world."[111]

The United Nations in 1974 also estimated the ability of nations to increase food production fast enough to meet demand in 1985. When the UN extrapolated trend is compared with projected demand, a disturbing picture emerges: throughout the less developed world, *demand substantially outstrips production* (see Table 7-18). The trend of past decades, in which less developed countries switched from being food exporters to importers, appears to be accelerating. Indeed, except in the communist Asian countries, projected production increases largely fail even to keep pace with population growth. If demand for food worldwide can be met in 1985 (assuming the projections are borne out by events), it will therefore only be because of surplus production in developed countries—primarily North America.

The UN 1974 projections showed the total annual deficit of cereal grains in non-communist less developed nations increasing to 85 million metric tons in 1985.[112] If grain-exporters Argentina and Thailand were left out of the calculations, the deficit climbed to 100 mmt. If 1985 turned out to be another 1972, 1974, or 1975 in terms of reduced harvests, the estimated grain deficit could reach 120 million metric tons or higher. This shortfall in grain production in LDCs compares strikingly with average

[110]Anthony S. Rojko, Food production and demand prospects to 1985, a working paper presented to the Sterling Forest Conference on World Food Supply in a Changing Climate, 1974, dealing with the USDA report just cited. See Estimating future demand: Alternative grain projections for 1985, in *World economic conditions in relation to agricultural trade,* USDA, WEC-10, June 1976, pp. 31–41.

[111]L. M. Thompson, Weather variability, climatic change, and grain production.

[112]UN, *Assessment.*

TABLE 7-18
United Nations Projections of Food Demand and Production and Population Growth to 1985

Region	Volume growth rates			Volume indices	
	Demand for food	Production of food	Projected population growth	Demand for food	Production of food
	Percent per annum			1969–1971 = 100	
Developed countries	1.5	2.8	0.9	126	151
Market economies	1.4	2.4	0.9	124	143
Eastern Europe and USSR	1.7	3.5	0.9	130	168
Developing market economies	3.6	2.6	2.7	170	146
Africa	3.8	2.5	2.9	176	145
Far East	3.4	2.4	2.6	166	143
Latin America	3.6	2.9	3.1	170	152
Near East	4.0	3.1	2.9	180	157
Asian centrally planned economies	3.1	2.6	1.6	158	146
All developing countries	3.4	2.6	2.4	166	146
World	2.4	2.7	2.0	144	150

Source: UN, *Assessment.*

annual deficits in 1969–1971 of only 16 mmt, and even with that of 43 million metric tons in 1973/1974.[113]

In 1976 newer projections became available, and these were even more ominous. The World Food Council and FAO then estimated the probable 1985 food deficit in LDCs (if the weather is "normal" that year) to be 120 million metric tons.[114] The International Food Policy Research Institute has estimated the 1985/1986 deficit to be 100 million metric tons if average yearly food production increases can match the rate of the period 1960–1975. However, if the rate of increase is as slow as it has been since 1969, the deficit could reach a staggering 200 million metric tons.[115]

It is clearly expected that this anticipated huge deficit in food production—unless it can somehow be made up by greater-than-anticipated production increases within the LDCs—will be filled by the grain-exporting countries: the United States, Canada, Australia, Thailand, and Argentina. But there are some serious problems in the way of producing so much grain to help LDCs in addition to meeting increased demand both on the domestic market and from traditional trading partners. Nor is the assignment of transporting and properly distributing the grain in recipient nations an easy one. Transport facilities have been strained by the large grain transfers of the early 1970s; unless grain shipping facilities are expanded, the problem will be far worse in the early 1980s. Similarly, the problems that have plagued food-aid programs in the past will also worsen unless measures are taken to counteract them.

Finally, there will be some very tough decisions confronting both the importers and exporters if production should falter and the import needs fail to be met. These essentially political problems are explored more fully in Chapter 15.

EXPANDING THE HARVEST

Given the present precarious world food situation and the alarming outlook forecast by various groups, the important questions for the future are: can a continued expansion of food supplies be sustained? If so, for how long? And what are the best means of doing so that are consistent with improved human well-being?

Within the framework of any system of technology or any economic system, the environment imposes limits on agricultural production. As noted earlier, for the foreseeable future food production will depend on the availability of sunlight, fertile soil, water, and a growing season long enough for crops to mature. Unfortunately, these conditions are unevenly distributed over the Earth. For example, although many tropical forest areas have a

[113]USDA, WAS-9.
[114]Jon McLin, Remember the world food conference?
[115]Sterling Wortman, Food and agriculture.

year-round growing season and abundant rainfall, their soils are often extremely poor, making large-scale agriculture virtually impossible.[116] Vast portions of subtropical land lack adequate rainfall or nearby freshwater sources for irrigation. Most of the world's land that is suitable for growing crops is already being cultivated (Chapter 6). The best prospect of increasing food production therefore lies in raising yields (production per hectare) on that already cultivated land.

The Green Revolution

A great deal of publicity has been given to the so-called Green Revolution, a modernization of agricultural practices that some enthusiasts hoped would enable the less developed countries to keep agricultural production well ahead of population growth for several decades. Most of the Green Revolution's elements are already an integral part of agricultural systems in developed countries, where cereal yields have been consistently much higher than in LDCs (Figure 7-18). There are two general components to the Green Revolution: increased use of recently developed high-yield varieties of grain (primarily wheat and rice), and increased use of "inputs" (especially fertilizers and irrigation water, but also often pesticides), which are required to realize the potentially high yields of those crops.

Since the mid-1960s there has been a rapid expansion of acreage planted to high-yield crops in many LDCs. The area planted to new varieties of wheat and rice in Asia, Latin America, and Africa increased from about 59,000 hectares to over 32 million hectares between 1965 and 1975.[117] By 1975 it had reached 43 million hectares. Figure 7-19 shows the percentages of wheat and rice acreage planted in high-yield varieties in those years in several Asian countries. By 1972 HYVs occupied more than half the acreage planted to wheat in India and Pakistan, and half the acreage planted to rice in the Philippines. Since 1972, however, the rate of expansion of acreage planted to new crop varieties has slowed in several countries for reasons that are examined in the following sections.

[116]H. Ruthenberg, *Farming systems in the tropics.*

[117]Dana Dalrymple, *Development and spread of high-yielding varieties of wheat and rice in less developed countries.*

Miracle varieties. The new high-yield varieties of wheat and rice are capable of producing yields considerably greater than those of traditional strains. For instance, the first rice variety developed by the International Rice Research Institute in the Philippines, IR-8, can produce two or more times the harvest of traditional rice plants from a given area, *if handled correctly.* Some newer strains perform even better than IR-8 and have other improved qualities.

All the new grain varieties are extremely responsive to fertilizers. If conditions are suitable, and if a crop is fertilized at several times the level ordinarily used for traditional varieties, HYVs can use that fertilizer input much more efficiently in producing grain. If planted in good soil, given the large amounts of water that are a necessary accompaniment of heavy fertilizer inputs, and given protection from pests, the strong, short stalks of the new dwarf varieties can carry a truly miraculous load of grain.[118]

These new varieties also mature faster and are less sensitive to seasonal variations in day length than are traditional strains. Both characteristics increase the possibility of multiple cropping—that is, growing and harvesting more than one crop per year—when adequate water is available. In Mysore State in India, for example, farmers are growing three corn crops every fourteen months. Where there is a dry season with inadequate water available for growing rice, some farmers are growing new high-yielding grain sorghums (which require less water) in alternation with rice. In some areas of China, northern India, and Pakistan, farmers are planting rice in the summer and wheat in the winter.

It must be emphasized, however, that the *full potential* yields of the miracle grains can be realized *only if an entire complex of conditions is met,* especially the proper input of fertilizers, water, and pesticides. Without these, yields may be little higher than those of traditional varieties, and in some cases they may be less.

That the Green Revolution has considerable potential for increasing yields in many LDCs is beyond question. Early results of introducing the new seeds in several countries were very impressive. India's wheat harvest

[118]For a description of Green Revolution technology, see Lester R. Brown, *Seeds of change.*

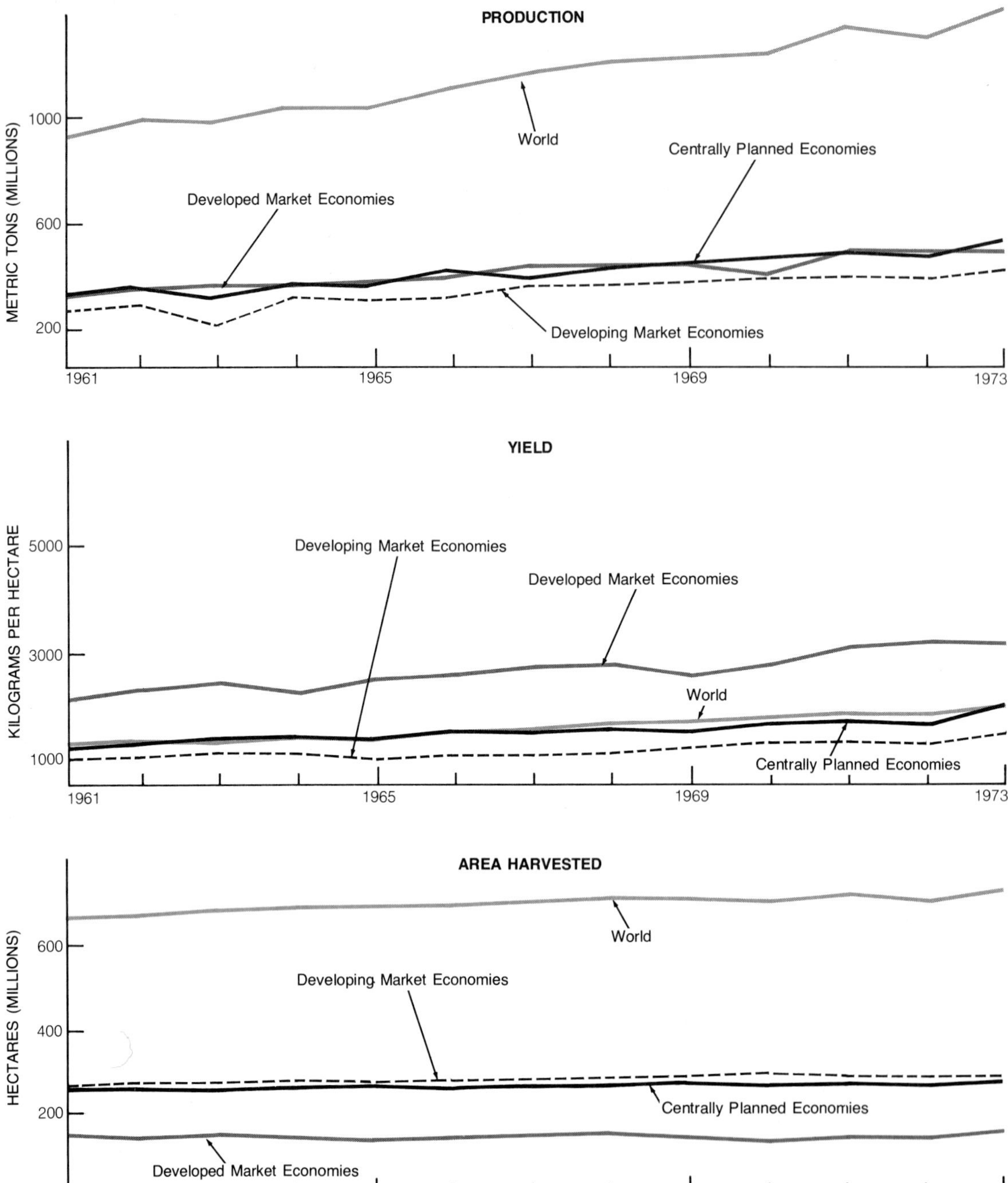

FIGURE 7-18

World grain production, yields, and areas, 1961–1973. Includes wheat, maize, rice (as paddy), minor and mixed grains. (Adapted from U.S. Department of Agriculture, *The world food situation and prospects to 1985*,. Foreign Agricultural Economic Report No. 98, 1974.)

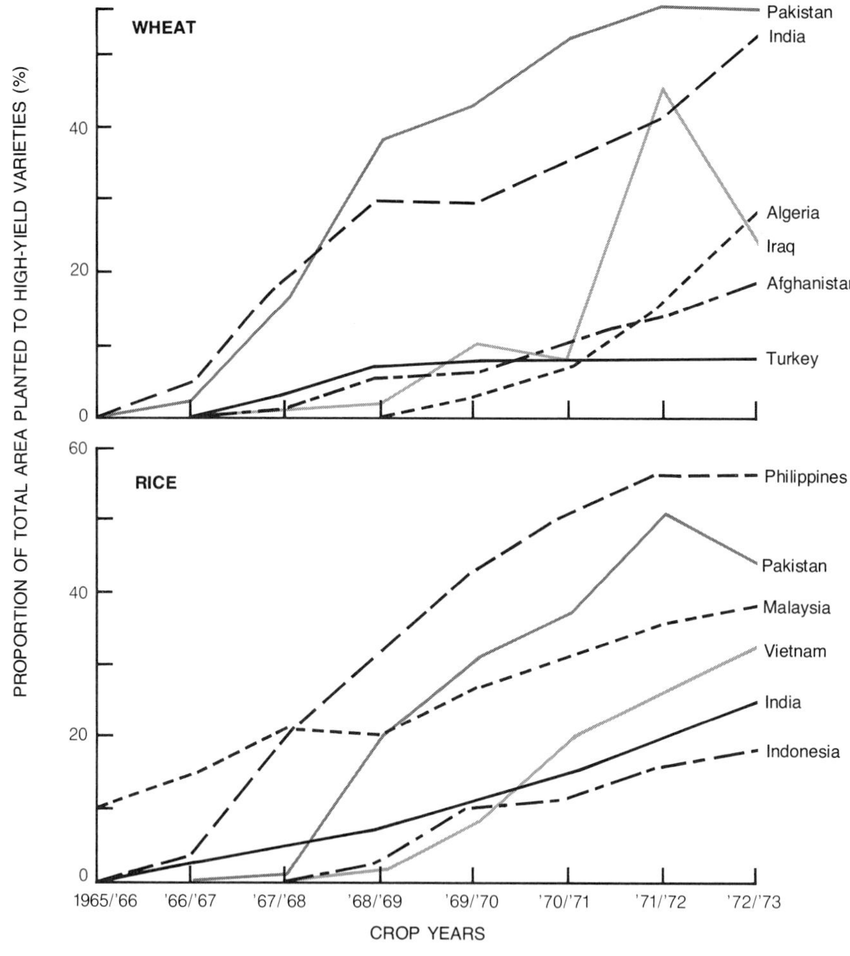

FIGURE 7-19

The proportion of total area planted to high-yielding varieties in Asia. (Adapted from U.S. Department of Agriculture, *Measuring the green revolution,* Foreign Agricultural Economic Report No. 106, 1975.)

more than doubled within six years (1965–1972), and the Pakistani crop in 1968 was 37 percent higher than in any previous year. There were also large gains in rice production in the Philippines and Ceylon between 1966 and 1968. All these gains were largely due to the new grain varieties.

According to Dana G. Dalrymple of the USDA, HYV and traditional strains could be directly compared by growing both on the same quality of irrigated land and adding equal amounts of fertilizer. In such a comparison, high-yield wheat might generally outperform traditional varieties by 50 to 100 percent in yield, and HYV rice might outperform the traditional varieties by 10 to 25 percent.[119] Significantly increased grain production is thus still *possible* in many LDCs where the HYVs have not yet replaced traditional varieties to any great extent. But those increases nevertheless would be modest in comparison with projected needs for just the next two decades. There are, in addition, many unanswered ques-

[119]Dana Dalrymple, *Measuring the Green Revolution: The impact of research on wheat and rice production,* pp. 25, 26, 35.

tions about various aspects of the Green Revolution—social, economic, environmental, and biological—that inevitably will influence its ultimate scale and duration.[120]

Economic and Social Factors

The Green Revolution extends far beyond the planting of new kinds of seeds, and it is beset by myriad economic headaches. Many of these problems are associated with the inputs required by the HYVs: the extra fertilizer, water, and in many cases farm machinery and pesticides needed to realize the full potential of the new seeds. The dependence of HYVs on heavy use of fertilizer, for example, made the fertilizer shortages and price inflation of 1974, aggravated by the energy crisis, a particularly serious problem for LDC agriculture.[121]

Fertilizers and other inputs. Natural fertilizers (manure, crop residues, etc.) could be used in place of manufactured ones, of course. In many ways they are preferable, especially for tropical soils.[122] The FAO has estimated that seven to eight times more nutrient elements were available in natural fertilizers that were not used in 1970–1971 in less developed regions than there were in the artificial fertilizers that were used.[123] Unfortunately, natural fertilizers are not always available at the right place and right time, and they are not easily collected. Moreover, there is often competition for them for other uses (for example in India where cow dung is widely used for fuel). So chemical fertilizers, even in very poor countries, are generally preferred and used.

The production of chemical fertilizers is straightforward, and a good deal is known about their effective application. Three principal elements, nitrogen, phosphorus, and potassium (in chemical shorthand, N, P, and K, respectively), are the basis of most fertilizer compounds. Supplies of some of the resources to make these fertilizers are limited (fossil fuels for nitrogen; phosphate deposits for phosphorus), and the problems associated with these limitations are discussed in Chapter 8 and Chapter 9. The HYVs now being deployed in many LDCs require 70–90 kilograms of fertilizer per hectare for optimum performance, but the average level of application in most LDCs is a fraction of that, ranging in 1973–1974 from 14 kilograms per hectare in Africa to 33 kilograms per hectare in South America.[124] Moreover, much of the fertilizer used in LDCs had to be imported.

There are staggering difficulties barring the implementation of fertilizer technology on the scale required to raise LDC grain yields to match those of DCs. The agricultural accomplishments of Japan and the Netherlands are often cited as offering hope to the LDCs, but, if India were to apply fertilizer as intensively as the Netherlands, India's fertilizer needs would amount to *one third the present world output.* Per-capita use in the Netherlands is more than ten times that of India. (But the Netherlands is nonetheless unable to feed itself).[125] Table 7-19 shows production and consumption of fertilizers in different regions of the world in 1973/1974.

If an LDC is to convert to fertilizer-intensive agriculture, the fertilizer must either be produced within the LDC or purchased from outside; and then it must be transported to the fields. Capital is required for fertilizer plants or for fertilizer purchases, and for transportation facilities. India, for example, had hoped to attain a fertilizer production of 2.4 million metric tons by 1971. But by 1974/1975, its production was only 1.3 million metric tons, only some 60 percent of the small amount used.[126] The difference had to be made up by imports. The energy crisis played a major role in the shortfall, as it did in other LDCs.[127] But that was not the sole cause of India's 1974 fertilizer shortfall; poor maintenance of equipment, shortages of raw materials, and problems

[120]For an early critique, see William C. Paddock, How green is the Green Revolution? A more recent summary of the problems associated with the Green Revolution is given in Wade, Green Revolution pt. 1, and Green Revolution, pt. 2.

[121]Michael Allaby, Fertilizers: The hole in the bag.

[122]S. P. Dhua, Need for organo-mineral fertilizer in tropical agriculture.

[123]FAO, *Ceres,* March/April 1975, p. 7.

[124]FAO, *Ceres,* May/June, 1975.

[125]The Netherlands in 1974/1975 used 50 kilograms per capita of nitrogen, phosphate, and potash fertilizers; India used 4.6 kilograms. (Note that this is up from about 2.5 kg in 1966–1967, however). The Netherlands, with slightly more than 2 percent of India's population, produced more nitrogen fertilizer and as much phosphate and potash. National Academy of Sciences (NAS), *Population and food, crucial issues,* p. 24; UN *Statistical Yearbook, 1975.*

[126]Ibid.

[127]UN *Assessment.*

TABLE 7-19
Preliminary Estimates of Production and Consumption of Commercial Fertilizers During 1973–1974

	Nitrogen		*Phosphate*		*Potash*		*Total NPK*	
	Production	*Consumption*	*Production*	*Consumption*	*Production*	*Consumption*	*Production*	*Consumption*
	Thousands of metric tons							
Africa	450	1,114	940	720	263	324	1,653	2,148
North and Central America	10,448	9,715	7,004	5,424	7,419	5,063	24,871	20,202
South America	423	868	478	1,048	19	662	920	2,578
Asia	7,938	9,276	3,018	4,046	815	2,086	11,771	15,408
Europe	14,051	11,320	8,965	8,684	7,810	8,635	30,826	28,639
Oceania	197	218	1,589	1,618	—	288	1,786	2,124
USSR	7,241	6,256	3,236	2,699	5,918	3,605	16,395	12,560
World total	40,748	38,767	25,230	24,239	22,244	20,663	88,222	83,669
Available world supply	38,930	—	24,420	—	21,003	—	84,353	—

Source: FAO, *Ceres,* May–June 1975. Available world supplies were calculated by subtracting from production figures the quantities used as a basis for other products as well as those lost during transport and handling.

with labor and transportation have plagued attempts to raise domestic production.

The energy crisis put a heavy burden on LDCs, many of which were short of foreign exchange and desperately needed to import both fertilizers and fossil fuels for manufacturing them. Fertilizer production within LDCs recently has been doubling about every five years, but it would have increased even faster if the cost of fertilizer (which is strongly affected by the price of oil) had not trebled between 1971 and 1974.[128] Figure 7-20 compares recent trends in fertilizer costs and consumption. Although LDC fertilizer production has been expected to continue rising rapidly, the rising capital requirements for production expansion and other problems may hold increases in production below increases in demand, especially after 1980. Chemical engineer and fertilizer specialist Raymond Ewell expects demand for fertilizers in LDCs to increase (in millions of metric tons) from 12.4 to 31 in 1980, 57 in 1990, and 92 in 2000.[129]

Whether such rapid rises in demand will indeed materialize is not clear; the price escalations of 1974 were naturally followed by a drop in demand, especially among the poorer farmers. Fertilizer prices declined

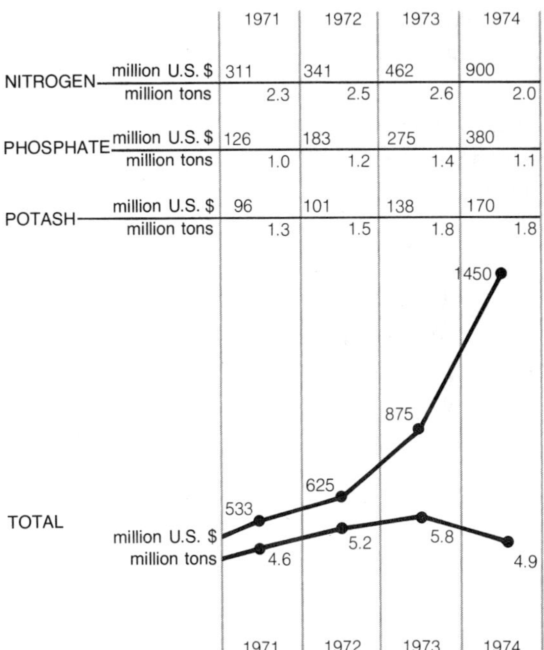

FIGURE 7-20

The cost of scarcity: The import of manufactured fertilizers by developing countries. The figures for 1972–1974 are estimates. (Adapted from *Ceres,* Food and Agriculture Organization, March–April 1975.)

[128]FAO, *State of food and agriculture, 1974.*

[129]Raymond Ewell, Food and fertilizer and the developing countries, 1975–2000.

dramatically in 1975 and 1976 as supplies expanded, but this apparently was not immediately translated into a resumption of rising demand in LDCs.[130] Unless the food-short countries can find the means both to expand their own production capacities and to subsidize fertilizer costs for poor farmers, the prospects of expanding the Green Revolution further will not be very bright.

In addition to fertilizers, abundant water is essential for fertilizer-responsive miracle grains; so there must be investment in large- or small-scale irrigation installations, such as dams, tube wells, pumps, and irrigation ditches. Pesticides are also necessary to get the most out of the new varieties, especially when they are planted in extensive monocultures. When timing is a problem, as for multiple-cropping, or when soil is extremely dry or heavy, mechanized planting and harvesting may be necessary. Roads, trucks, and railroads, which are required to bring inputs to the fields and take produce to markets, are often lacking in LDCs. Without access both to inputs and market outlets, there is little incentive for small farmers to adopt the new technology and expand their output. All the inputs and supporting facilities are expensive, and capital is in chronically short supply in most LDCs.

Poverty and related problems. Beyond the need to provide materials and transportation for farmers, there are serious economic problems resulting quite simply from poverty. The majority of farmers in LDCs are subsistence farmers; their farms are tiny and barely produce enough to support the farmer and his family. In many countries, progress in agricultural development is hindered by a lack of farm credit, which is simply unavailable or offered at usuriously high rates to small farmers.

New grains are typically introduced by "progressive" farmers, usually those with the largest, richest farms. They are in the best position to pay for the inputs of fertilizer, pesticides, irrigation water, and equipment. This advantage of large landholders over small farmers is intensified when the higher yields bring in more money, which can be further invested in more land and more fertilizer.[131] The result of this is to increase the income gap between rich and poor farmers, creating a two-tiered society. The rich farmers prosper, participate in, and benefit from some modernization of their country. The poor, on the other hand, are mostly left out of the development process; they remain stranded in destitution, their lives untouched, with little hope for a better life (see Chapter 15 for more on this subject).[132]

Moreover, when the larger farmers adopt the new technology, they often opt for a mechanized version of it. As a result, even though HYVs generally require considerably more work to produce their high yields, hired labor is displaced. In some areas this has significantly contributed to the flood of landless poor farm workers who are migrating to LDC cities (see Chapter 5).

If the small farmers are to participate in the Green Revolution, then, they must be provided with credit on reasonable terms and access to the seeds, fertilizer, water, and pest-control inputs. Then, when their crops have been harvested, they must be able to sell them for enough cash to pay their creditors and to invest in the inputs for the next crop. But in LDCs, even though local people may be hungry, they may not be able to buy food.

It is not unusual for agricultural economists to speak of helping hungry people by "increasing the demand for food." In some areas and in some years, farmers' yields may be increased by the new grains to the point where their marketable surplus is significantly expanded. This can produce a grain-glut that the local marketing system cannot immediately handle. Storage and transport facilities are inadequate for distribution, and there may not be sufficient "demand" for the food. There is virtually always a potential demand for increased food production, of course; but to become *effective demand,* desire must be matched with purchasing power. Destitute people, even though they may be starving, have essentially no purchasing power.

Increased grain production all too often means lower

[130]Dana G. Dalrymple, *The demand for fertilizer at the farm level in developing nations,* draft 3, Bureau for Program and Policy Coordination, AID, Washington, D.C., December 23, 1975; USDA, WAS-12.

[131]Some of these problems were discussed early by W. Ladejinsky (Ironies of India's Green Revolution), whose warnings have proven at least in part to be justified (Wade, International). For a vivid description of social problems associated with the Green Revolution in another country, see R. W. Franks, Miracle seeds and shattered dreams in Java.

[132]James B. Kocher, *Rural development, income distribution, and fertility decline,* an occasional paper of the Population Council, 1973.

grain prices. When this happens, the poor can afford to buy more food, but the farmer's incentive is reduced. If the low prices persist, they might result in *less* food being available. Governments in LDCs thus sometimes are forced into grain-price support programs they can ill afford. Striking a balance on food-price policy that puts food within the means of the urban poor without damaging the farmers' incentive is no easy task; not many LDC governments have wholly succeeded, although many have tried.

On the other hand, one problem with the Green Revolution appears to have been overestimated. Many observers, at the beginning, felt that small farmers in the LDCs could not be easily or quickly educated to use the new techniques. Experience in the late 1960s and early 1970s showed that in most cases, when incentives, supporting facilities, and credit were provided, acceptance was rapid: "Poor farmers, even those tens of millions who are either illiterate or barely literate, do indeed respond to new and profitable opportunities and can quickly adopt highly complicated production technologies with which they have had no prior experience."[133]

A final difficulty must be mentioned in connection with any change in food crops. In general, the hungriest people in the world are also those with the most conservative food habits. In South China, a local vitamin-B deficiency was caused because people refused to eat their rice unmilled. They objected to the additional cooking time required, they did not like the flavor, and it gave them upset stomachs. New varieties of grain often exhibit milling or cooking characteristics different from traditional ones. Even rather minor changes, such as going from a rice variety in which the cooked grains stick together to one in which the grains fall apart, may make a food unacceptable. It seems to be an unhappy problem of human nutrition that people would sometimes rather go hungry than eat a nutritious substance that they do not recognize or accept as food.[134]

Following the early successes of introducing the new technology in many less developed countries, various of these social and economic obstacles to its spread began to be felt. Once the better-off farmers with suitable land and access to irrigation water and other inputs had adopted the new technology, it proved relatively difficult to sustain the early rate of expansion. Practically speaking, the Green Revolution is not available to the small, poor farmers—who are the majority in most poor countries—without special supporting measures. Box 7-2 compares the quite different approaches to agricultural development taken by the two largest LDCs in the world, China and India.

In many ways the problem of revolutionizing LDC agriculture is inextricably tied up with the general problem of LDC "development." Shortages of capital, resources, and trained technicians exist along with lack of effective planning, the absence of adequate storage, transport, and marketing systems, and ineffective demand due to poor income distributions. When these are combined with high rates of population growth, malnutrition, and disease, they make any kind of development extremely difficult, and thus retard agricultural development in particular. It is a vicious cycle—one that will take much more than a new food-production technology to break.

Reduction of food losses. One area in which technology can greatly help to improve the food supply is in the reduction of losses in the field, in transit, and in storage. A conservative estimate of worldwide losses of crops, livestock, and forests to pests, diseases, and spoilage is about 30 percent. In less developed countries the percentage lost is often considerably higher.[135]

For example, the Indian Food and Agriculture Ministry estimated that in 1968 rats alone consumed almost 10 percent of India's grain production. Others think 12 percent may be more accurate. It would take a train almost 3000 miles long to haul the grain India's rats eat in a single year. And yet in 1968 India spent $265 million on importing fertilizers, about 800 *times* as much as was spent on rat control. Rats in two Philippine provinces in 1952–1954 consumed 90 percent of the rice, 20 to 80 percent of the maize, and more than 50 percent of the sugar cane.

[133] D. Gale Johnson, *World food problems and prospects,* p. 64.

[134] Igor De Garine, Food is not just something to eat; John McKenzie, Nutrition and the soft sell.

[135] W. B. Ennis, Jr., et al., Crop protection to increase food supplies.

BOX 7-2 India and China: Two Case Histories

The two most populous nations in the world are China (800 to 900 million) and India (over 600 million). Both are underdeveloped by the usual standards: low per-capita income or gross national product, and relatively little industry compared to developed nations. But between these two giants there are far more differences than similarities, and some of the more striking differences are to be found in their food and agricultural systems.

India

The story of India's agricultural system is in part a story of misplaced priorities, mismanagement, poor organization, ecological destruction, and inadequate use of limited resources. It is also a story of abject poverty and constant hunger in a large portion of the population. Available figures indicate that in the early 1970s there was enough food in India to meet needs at a minimal level, assuming an average per-capita requirement of 1955 kilocalories. If the actual population was 631 million (a high but generally accepted estimate derived from 1971 census data), an average of 1982 kcal and 59 grams of protein were available per person in 1974.[a] Scattered studies comparing average food intakes in households of various income levels in India over the years, however, have consistently shown consumption levels among the poor to be substantially below average for the nation and well below average needs (see Appendix 2 for United Nations figures on food).[b] The poorest 30 percent of the population has been estimated to receive 20 to 30 percent less kcal than the national average in normal times.

The urban poor are in a particularly precarious position; they are heavily dependent on food grain distributed by the government at low prices. This food is largely supplied from imports (including food aid) and surpluses in other regions. In times of shortage, farmers and grain dealers often hoard supplies, awaiting higher prices, and are especially reluctant to sell to the government. Unless imports are increased to compensate, the urban poor go hungry. Poor distribution of food supplies combined with economic problems also lead to hunger. More than once flood or drought in one province has caused a local famine while surpluses of grain piled up in the next one and government-supported prices held that grain beyond the reach of the poor.

India lived on the brink of starvation for decades until the Green Revolution in the late 1960s seemed to promise relief. Between 1966 and 1971, grain production, which supplies three-fourths of the calories in the Indian diet, rose an average of 4.5 percent per year, well above the population growth rate of 2.5 percent. By 1973, new high-yielding varieties (HYVs) accounted for 75 percent of India's total production of wheat and 36 percent of the rice. But after 1971, expansion of the Green Revolution lost momentum. Partly because of that and partly because of unfavorable weather, there was no increase in annual food-grain production between 1971 and 1975, although the population grew by about 54 million. Table 7-20 shows the record of India's food production since 1951, when the population was only about 363 million. It is worth noting that there has been *no* significant increase in production of pulses—a major source of protein—since 1951, although the population has increased by about 75 percent since then.

The problems attending the Green Revolution in India and elsewhere are described in the text. In general, however, the Green Revolution has tended to intensify existing social and economic differences between rural groups, differences that often affect a farmer's ability or incentive to increase production. These and other changes have led to a further displacement of landless farm workers, exacerbating an already enormous unemployment problem. The Green Revolution ran out of steam in India in the early 1970s partly because most of the farmers who could afford and had access to the necessary inputs (fertilizer, seed, irrigation, etc.) had already converted. An additional factor appears to have been an insufficient use of fertilizers. In the year 1973–1974, only a little more than half the amount recommended by the government (which was still below the economic optimum) was used on either HYVs or traditional varieties. This was partly due to short supplies, but there seems also to have been a lack of demand as well because of their higher prices and because small farmers were unfamiliar with their use.[c] It is estimated that increasing fertilizer application to recommended levels could alone increase grain production by 22 million tons.

[a] J. D. Gavan and J. A. Dixon, India: A perspective on the food situation. This is a major source for what follows. See also J. W. Mellor, *The agriculture of India.*

[b] Ibid.; PSAC, *The world food problem.*

[c] Gavan and Dixon, India.

TABLE 7-20
Food-Grain Production and Availability in India

Year	Production (million metric tons)*		Net imports (million metric tons)	Net available per capita (kg per year)
	Total	Pulses		
1950–1951	50.8	8.4	4.80	134.0
1955–1956	66.9	11.0	1.44	152.5
1960–1961	82.0	12.7	3.50	170.5
1964–1965	89.4	12.4	7.46	175.4
1965–1966	72.3	9.9	10.36	145.6
1966–1967	74.2	8.3	8.67	146.5
1967–1968	95.1	12.1	5.70	168.6
1968–1969	94.0	10.4	3.87	162.5
1969–1970	99.5	11.7	3.63	166.2
1970–1971	108.4	11.8	2.05	171.3
1971–1972	105.2	11.1	−0.48	172.8
1972–1973	97.0	9.9	4.12	153.1
1973–1974	103.6	9.8	6.10	167.0
1974–1975	(96–103)		8.0	(149–160)

*Rice, wheat, barley, maize, sorghum, millet, and pulses.
Source: Adapted from J. D. Gavan and J. A. Dixon, India: a perspective on the food situation, p. 542.

In 1975, the Indian government announced a massive land-reform program, combined with reform of the usurious farm-credit system, designed to extend the Green Revolution to the poor subsistence farmer.[d] Whether the program will be carried out successfully remains to be seen, but it is a long overdue step in the right direction. After years of neglecting agriculture and rural development in favor of industry, India may finally be shifting to a more realistic set of priorities.

But much more is needed than extension of Green Revolution techniques to the poorest farmers in order to make Indian agriculture a viable enterprise. Not only must it support today's 630 million, but also it must provide for several hundred million more Indians by the end of the century, regardless of the success or failure of population-control efforts (Chapter 13). To do this, the destructive effects of centuries of poor management must be reversed. A major factor in the disastrous floods and droughts so characteristic of India's history has been the disappearance of her once-abundant forests.[e] (For a discussion of this ecological relationship, see Chapter 6.) Forests have been steadily cleared throughout India's history to expand land area for crops and pasture. The wood has mainly been used for fuel and to some extent for construction. As the forests have been reduced to remnants in remote areas, wood for any use has become scarcer, whereas rates of water runoff and soil erosion have accelerated. Increasing dependence on cattle dung for fuel as a result has in turn restricted its availability for use as badly needed fertilizer.

Indian food production, of course, is heavily dependent on the monsoon—the seasonal rains of the summer months. Nearly all the rainfall for the most productive parts of the nation, especially the Northwest, comes with the monsoon. The winter crops of wheat and barley are indirectly dependent on monsoon rainwater brought by extensive irrigation; rice and other summer crops are directly dependent on them. Much of the monsoon water is lost through runoff, floods, and inefficient forms of irrigation, especially in years of abundant rainfall. In recent years, many thousands of tubewells have been sunk and millions of pumps installed to increase the amount and efficient use of irrigation water. This no doubt provided much of the impetus for the surge in wheat and rice production of the Green Revolution. Gavan and Dixon claim that a principal reason for the halt in production increases in the early 1970s was that the limits to

[d]William Borders, India tries again to reform farming, *New York Times,* August 23, 1975.
[e]Erik Eckholm, *Losing ground.*

(*Continued*)

BOX 7-2 (*Continued*)

expanding acreage planted to HYVs under present irrigation facilities had been reached.[f] Further expansion apparently must await more fundamental development of the hydrologic system. A first priority here should be development of a flood-control and storage system of reservoirs to accumulate water in years of good monsoons for use in years of monsoon failure and for alleviation of flooding. India already has plans for further expansion and improvement of the irrigation system, including a greater use of groundwater supplied by tubewells. What long-term effect this will have on the groundwater table is unclear, although there are methods whereby recharge can be induced during the monsoon.

More efficient utilization of India's limited water resources would, among other things, permit a significant increase in double- and triple-cropping (growing two or three crops per year on the same land). India already multiple-crops about 20 percent of its cultivated land, but the potential exists for a far higher percentage if sufficient water were available and if the time needed to harvest one crop and plow for the next were shortened, perhaps through increased mechanization.

An important long-range program that the Indian government has contemplated, but apparently has been unable to carry out, is large-scale reforestation. Such a program would provide immediate benefits by employing large numbers of people, and future benefits in building an important resource, contributing to flood control, reducing soil erosion, and restoring groundwater supplies. It might even have a stabilizing influence on the erratic monsoons. Such a program might be difficult and costly, and it might involve displacing large numbers of people, but the long-run benefits would surely outweigh the costs.

India's agricultural system thus has reached a momentous turning point. Most of the available easy measures to increase production—introduction of HYVs, increased production and use of fertilizers, and expansion of the archaic irrigation system—have already been exploited, although there is still some room for improvement through greater use of fertilizers and perhaps installation of more tube wells. At best, however, such extensions of past measures may buy a few more years of rapid population growth. Because they have mostly been imposed from outside, such efforts have often tended to damage, rather than strengthen, the underlying social and economic structure. Agricultural development in India since World War II has indeed been significant, and food production has certainly increased. But the average Indian is not much better off, and the lives of the poorest third of the population have remained basically untouched; they are as poor as ever, and there are many more of them.

If India is to survive even into the middle term, major investments must be made in capital, resources, and human effort to redevelop the agricultural system *from the bottom up.* This means that ways must be found to assist small farmers directly and to provide incentives for them to raise their production and become part of the national economy, and that new agricultural technology must be labor-intensive in order to provide employment for the rural poor, increase their purchasing power, and raise food production. Since most of the food would be consumed locally by the producers, this would also alleviate food-distribution problems.

Meaningful land reform, full exploitation of the potential of HYVs, achievement of control over the hydrological regime to allow full use of available water supplies without jeopardizing future supplies, improvement and conservation of arable soil, reforestation: realization of all these would permit considerable further expansion of India's agricultural production, perhaps a doubling of today's or more. India's *potential* for increased food production is thus very great; the perhaps equally great barriers to achieving it are mainly economic and political. If they can be surmounted, India's future could be relatively bright. But whether they will be overcome in time remains a matter for serious doubt.[g]

[f]Gavan and Dixon, "India."

[g]*The Ecologist* devoted a special issue to the problems of development in India, with emphasis on rural and agricultural development, in October 1975 (vol. 5, no. 8).

TABLE 7-21
Comparison of Factors of Agricultural Production Among Nations

Country	Yields (100 kg per hectare) Paddy rice	Wheat	NPK* fertilizer use (kg per hectare)	Multiple-cropping index (land multiple-cropped per year as percentage of total cultivated land)	Percent of cultivated land that is irrigated	Arable hectares per capita
United States	52.5	22.0	82.0	102	8	0.91
Japan	58.5	23.1	439.8	126	55	0.05
Taiwan	34.2	–	292.6	184	58	0.06
China	30.9	12.0	39.6	147	40	0.15
Burma	15.6	5.5	1.8	111	5	0.64
Pakistan	23.3	11.9	13.7	111	65	0.29
India	16.2	13.8	16.4	119	17	0.28

*Nitrogen, phosphate, potassium.
Source: Adapted from J. D. Gavan and J. A. Dixon, India: a perspective on the food situation, p. 545.

China

Judging from the limited available information, China appears to have made substantial progress since the 1949 Revolution in modernizing its agricultural and food-distribution systems and in providing adequate diets for its 1975 population of some 800–962 million.[h] The UN's estimated daily averages of 2170 kcal and 60 grams of protein available per person[i] are not much above India's, but they may be an underestimate. Moreover, supplies apparently are much more equitably distributed. Visitors to China from Western nations have uniformly commented on the absence of evident malnutrition and general deprivation among the Chinese people. Although everyone seems to live modestly, no one lacks the basic necessities of life. This, of course, is a radical change from conditions before the revolution, when extreme poverty, hardship, and starvation were commonplace. It is also very different from India today, where the existence of widespread poverty and malnutrition cannot be missed by any reasonably observant visitor.

Like the Indians, the Chinese depend mainly on cereals and pulses for their diets. But China's total food-grain production for 1971 (including potatoes and other tubers) was about 250 million metric tons, more than twice India's production that year.[j] This indicates that there was 50 to 60 percent more food available per person in China than in India. Furthermore, this food was produced on substantially *less* land; China has only about 107 million hectares of arable land—about 15 percent of its total land area—whereas India has over 140 million hectares. China's remarkable productivity is the result of using HYVs (many of them independently developed in China, especially rice)[k] and fertilizers, both natural and chemical, and of extensive multiple-cropping, intercropping (growing different crops together simultaneously), relay cropping (overlapping in time), and irrigation. (Table 7-21 shows comparisons of these factors among India, China, and several other countries.) There have

[h]Depending on whether one accepts China's figures, those of the United Nations, AID and the U.S. Census Bureau, or those of Robert Cook of the Environmental Fund.
[i]UN estimates, UN *Assessment.*

[j]Sterling Wortman, Agriculture in China. This and G. F. Sprague, Agriculture in China, are the primary sources for this section. Both articles are based on a visit to China by a group of American agronomists under the auspices of the National Academy of Sciences in 1974.
[k]For details of China's rice HYV program, see Dana G. Dalrymple, *Development and spread of high-yielding varieties,* pp. 90–92.

(*Continued*)

BOX 7-2 (*Continued*)

also been impressive programs of soil and water conservation and reforestation in China.

Rice is China's principal crop, accounting for almost half (44 percent) of the total grain production; wheat is second in importance, with about 17 percent of the total. Various other cereals and pulses, such as sorghum, millet, corn, barley, and soybeans, make up the rest. Acreage planted to rice is not very much greater than that planted to wheat, but rice is often double-cropped or even triple-cropped with another grain: for instance, rice-rice-wheat or rice-rice-barley.

Behind China's success in raising agricultural productivity lies its unique social and economic system, which has been designed to provide maximum incentive for production of food or factory output (and disincentive for large families; see Chapter 13). Both personal and community income are directly tied to productivity. With the exceptions of young children and the aged, everyone is expected to contribute to his or her production team's work. But rural families are also encouraged to have their own gardens and to raise a pig or two. The produce can be either consumed at home or—more often—sold for extra income.

Chinese agriculture is necessarily labor-intensive; some 80 to 85 percent of the population is engaged in agriculture or agriculture-related work. (By contrast, in the United States only about 2 percent of the population works in agriculture.) Therefore, although China has clearly embarked on a Green Revolution, it is quite different from the sort exported from the West, most markedly in the minimal dependence on heavy mechanization. The abundance of human labor has allowed the extensive use of intercropping, which is impractical where harvesting, weeding, and planting are all done by large machines. In order to free workers for other tasks, especially for small-scale rural industry, China is now striving to increase mechanization on the farm. But the mechanization is small to intermediate in scale, apparently resembling that of Japan and Taiwan.

Crop protection against pests and diseases is also labor-intensive. It is carried out by specialists who constantly check and survey crops in the field and spray only when an outbreak appears. Diseased plants and seeds are removed individually and destroyed. Broadcast spraying apparently is rarely done.[l] Some protection is also undoubtedly afforded indirectly by Chinese cultivation methods, especially intercropping, transplanting, and the use of fast-maturing strains of rice and wheat. Pest and disease resistance also are important goals in plant-breeding programs.[m]

Active plant-breeding programs have apparently been carried on in China since the Revolution. Chinese strains of high-yield, fast-maturing dwarf rice were being developed in the 1950s. Some work has also been done on hybrid corn, using American varieties imported before World War II, as well as on wheat, soybeans, sorghum, and millet. Most of the work today is carried on independently in communes, with help from provincial agricultural-research centers.

Visiting American agronomists have expressed concern that basic research in China is being neglected because academic agriculturalists are involved in the practical work and are not being replaced by younger, academically trained people. In the short run, this may not be too serious a problem, as long as the research is being done elsewhere and its results can be made available to the Chinese. But in the longer run it may prove a serious impediment to improvement of agricultural productivity. A complete lack of highly trained scientists might handicap the ability of the Chinese to utilize foreign technology, as well as destroy the domestic base for new research.

An advantage of the Chinese system, on the other hand, is that breeding experiments are being carried out independently in so many different places. This seems likely to result in many different improved varieties of each crop and the maintenance of a large pool of genetic variability.

[l]Sprague, Agriculture.

[m]For an environmentalist's view of Chinese agriculture, see Kieran P. Broadbent, The transformation of Chinese agriculture and its effects on the environment.

Chinese farmers have for centuries been efficient users of natural fertilizers: silt, human, and livestock wastes, and crop by-products, such as grainstalks, husks, and vegetable trimmings. All these are still in use, although crop by-products are also used as livestock feed. China clearly intends to increase the use of inorganic fertilizers and is building some 13 large chemical-fertilizer plants as well as importing fertilizers. By 1978, all needed fertilizer is expected to be produced domestically. In the early 1970s the level of fertilizer application in China was well above that in India, but apparently still below optimum.

As in India, China's potential food production is largely limited by available water. Most of the arable land is confined to three major river valleys, and over a third of it is irrigated by the largest irrigation system in the world.[n] China also has carried on for some years an extensive program of reforestation and restoration of eroded grasslands. After some early setbacks, there apparently has been steady progress for at least a decade in reforestation—or so visitors attest. Just how successful this has been is not known, but the frequent devastating floods of pre-Revolutionary China seem to have become a thing of the past.

Today, despite some setbacks and wrong turns, China's agricultural system appears to be on the whole an extraordinary success story, especially when compared with present conditions in most other LDCs or with conditions in China a generation ago. Whether or not one approves of the political measures taken to bring about the change, one cannot ignore the obvious results. Oft-heard comparisons with political systems in developed countries are inappropriate; it is far more pertinent to compare the lot of an average Chinese family with that of a low-income Indian or tropical African family whose traditions and way of life are much more similar. Even apart from the obviously greater economic security of the Chinese family, it can be argued that it also has a greater degree of control over its own destiny, despite the political restrictions.

But beyond the achievements of today, what are the prospects for further increases in Chinese food production? China's stringent population-control measures appear to have been more successful than India's so far, but the Chinese population is still growing by at least 1.6 percent annually, adding 14 to 18 million new mouths to feed each year. Food production hence must continue to rise at least as fast, and preferably faster, since the Chinese people have come to expect a steady increase in their standard of living. But the rapid rise in annual food production seen in the years before 1972 has apparently slackened (as in India), and Chinese agronomists reportedly are worried. Among other things, a serious food shortage might represent a threat to the present government.

It is a strange irony that the potential for further raising of food production is probably considerably less in China than in India, precisely because so much has already been accomplished. China has already gained substantial control of its hydrological system, although some further gains may yet be made there. No significant new land remains to be opened for growing crops unless huge investments were made in irrigation projects and soil improvement. The grassland-restoration program, however, may eventually result in the opening of grazing areas, and some expansion of multiple-cropping and inter-cropping may yet be possible. The greatest hope for increase probably lies in further replacement of traditional grains with HYVs, perhaps with some additional improvement of their yields through greater use of fertilizer and from results of ongoing crop-breeding programs. Maintaining momentum in the latter task, however, may require revitalization of basic scientific research.

China has a reasonable chance of winning the battle against its population explosion, but its success in raising food production to date is only half the story. The other half is population control (Chapter 13). Ultimately, success depends on winning on *both* fronts, especially as the remaining options for raising food production diminish.

[n]Mark Gayn, For water, the Chinese move mountains.

The FAO has estimated that in warm climates (like India's), rats may outnumber people by 3 to 1. Biologist Stephen C. Frantz studied a bandicoot rat population that subsisted on stored rice in a neighborhood of *godowns* (small warehouses) in Calcutta. Ordinarily, no effort was made by local people to prevent the rats from eating the grain. This one population in a small area consumed over 2 tons of grain per year and, by contamination caused a loss of 8 tons of rice per year—enough to support 30 people.[136] Such losses apparently are extremely common throughout the less developed world—yet they are largely preventable by such simple measures as building ratproof storehouses. Sometimes the problem is cultural. In South Asia, where people are accustomed to sharing food with rats and other competitors, they lack motivation to control pests—and this attitude is supported by religious beliefs.

Other pests besides rats also compete successfully for food produced by people. During the 1960s, birds in Africa destroyed crops worth more than $7 million annually. Insects in LDCs may destroy as much as 50 percent of a stock of grain in a year's storage period. Spoilage from molds, mildews, and bacteria also takes a heavy toll, even in DCs.[137] Since many LDCs are in the tropics and subtropics, where high temperatures and often high humidity encourage these organisms, their spoilage problems are even greater. Hence, the development of good storage and transport facilities alone might increase LDC food supplies at the market level by 20 percent or more.[138]

Problems with pests on crops in the field, like those with stored food, are also more severe in warm climates, where crops may be grown continuously year-round. Controlling populations of insect pests in fields and reducing losses due to them requires great care in order to avoid serious ecological problems. The same is true for controlling rats, birds, rusts, and other noninsect field pests. The ecological problems associated with control of pests in the field are discussed in Chapter 11.

Protection of foods once they are harvested, however, is much more straightforward and ordinarily involves much less ecological risk. Storage facilities may be refrigerated, made ratproof, and can be fumigated with nonpersistent pesticides that are not released into the environment until they have lost their toxicity. Transport systems can be improved so that more prompt movement, proper handling, refrigeration where necessary, and other measures greatly reduce spoilage en route. Perhaps the safest investment that could be made in LDCs toward improving the quantity and quality of food would be the improvement of methods of handling, shipping, and storing crops after the harvest.

Biological Problems

Perhaps even more important than the effects of the social and economic problems of agricultural development—including possible energy constraints—may be the potential effects of biological problems. Because biological problems usually take long periods of time to develop, early successes in the Green Revolution may have given the world a false impression of what rates of improvement in yields can be sustained.

For instance, in the 1960s the new grain varieties were rushed into production in places like Pakistan where the climate and irrigation conditions were favorable. They have sometimes been put into production without adequate field testing, which is very time-consuming, thus risking attack by insects and plant diseases.[139] Continuous breeding efforts, however, are being carried out in order to develop varieties suitable for different conditions. In general, though, when crops are selected for specific factors, such as high yield, something else may be sacrificed or overlooked, such as protein content or resistance to bacteria or insects.

The predictions[140] that pest problems would make serious inroads into the productivity of high-yield varieties have been borne out in several instances. For example, destruction of a substantial portion of the Indonesian rice crop in 1974–1975 has been blamed on the susceptibility of the IRRI strain planted to the insect

[136]Stephen C. Frantz, Rats in the granary.

[137]PSAC, *World food problem.*

[138]FAO, *State of food and agriculture, 1974;* Ennis, et al., Crop protection.

[139]W. C. Paddock, Phytopathology in a hungry world.

[140]Ibid.; P. R. Ehrlich and A. H. Ehrlich, *Population, resources, environment,* 1st ed., p. 99.

pest that carries grassy stunt virus.[141] Grassy stunt virus has also caused problems in the Philippines with a strain called IR-20. The latter had replaced IR-8 after it succumbed to another disease known as tungro. A third strain, IR-26, resisted all the local diseases and pests, but was too fragile to withstand strong winds.[142]

Simply planting extensive monocultures (a single strain of one crop) almost invites invasion by diseases and pests.[143] This practice is more common in DCs than in LDCs, but it has been increasing in LDCs as well. In addition, the new strains of rice are grown year-round in some tropical areas, providing a continuous habitat for pests and diseases, and the new short-stalked varieties with dense seed heads are vulnerable to attack by rats.[144]

Increased use of pesticides in developed countries has created a number of problems, which are discussed in detail in Chapter 11. Practicing more intensive agriculture and expanding the use of new crop varieties in LDCs almost certainly will require more input of pesticides with all of their deleterious ecological side-effects. Part of the price of agricultural development in those countries therefore may be an increase in environmental pollution and, possibly, a decrease in production of protein by fish-ponding and a decrease in food from the sea (see below). Besides the more obvious pollution problems caused by pesticides, the side-effects also include the development of resistance in pests and the extermination of their natural enemies.

Such untoward results in some areas have led to abandonment of pesticide use as farmers returned to traditional methods of pest control. In Sri Lanka, pesticides destroyed a species of ant that farmers by tradition had encouraged to control pests. Consequently, increasingly large quantities of chemicals were required to protect the crops. Unfortunately, as in this case, a failure in one element of the technological package (such as a severe pest outbreak) can lead to skepticism about the entire package.[145]

[141]The Indonesian situation is described by Jon Tinker, How the brown wereng did a red Khmer on the Green Revolution, *New Scientist,* (August 7, 1975).

[142]*Newsweek,* What comes naturally, Sept. 1, 1975.

[143]M. W. Adams, *et al.,* Biological conformity and disease epidemics.

[144]Tinker, How the brown wereng.

[145]A. B. Mendis, Sri Lankans question "modern farming" value, *Christian Science Monitor,* July 16, 1975.

One does not have to turn to Indonesia, Sri Lanka, or the Philippines, however, to see the decimation of modern crop strains by pests, especially where the crops are planted in huge monocultures. Americans were shocked into recognition of this problem when an epidemic attacked the U.S. corn crop in 1970. An estimated 710 million bushels, roughly 17 percent of the anticipated crop, was lost to southern corn-leaf blight. A new genetic strain of a fungus, *Helminthosporium maydis,* proved to be especially damaging to corn with "T cytoplasm," a type widely used in seed production. About 80 percent of the American corn crop was potentially susceptible to the disease.

It is hoped that measures being taken to replace the susceptible corn with resistant strains will prevent a repetition of the 1970 epidemic. The chance remains, however, that the fungus will evolve the ability to attack other strains; it has, after all, been coevolving with corn for many millennia.

L. A. Tatum of the Plant Science Research Division of the U.S. Department of Agriculture commented, "The corn blight epidemic is a dramatic demonstration that gains in crop production, especially from high yield varieties, may be short-lived unless supported by constant alertness and an aggressive research program. . . . The epidemic illustrates the vulnerability of our food crops to pests."[146] In 1972 a committee of the National Academy of Sciences found that "most major crops are impressively uniform genetically and impressively vulnerable."[147]

Genetic reserves. One of the most serious side-effects of the Green Revolution is the accelerating loss of reserves of genetic variability in crop plants, variability that is badly needed for continuing development of new strains.[148] A multitude of traditional crop varieties, which could potentially serve as reservoirs of variability, are rapidly being replaced by a relatively few high-yielding varieties throughout large areas. This process is

[146]The southern corn-leaf blight epidemic.

[147]NAS, *Genetic vulnerability of major crops.*

[148]O. H. Frankel et al., Genetic dangers in the Green Revolution; O. H. Frankel and E. Bennett, *Genetic resources in plants: Their exploration and conservation;* O. H. Frankel and J. G. Hawkes, eds, *Crop genetic resources for today and tomorrow.*

TABLE 7-22
Acreage and Farm Value of Major United States Crops and Extent to Which Small Numbers of Varieties Dominate Crop Acreage (1969 figures)

Crop	*Acreage (millions)*	*Value of crop (millions of dollars)*	*Total varieties*	*Major varieties*	*Acreage devoted to major varieties (percent)*
Bean, dry	1.4	143	25	2	60
Bean, snap	0.3	99	70	3	76
Cotton	11.2	1200	50	3	53
Corn*	66.3	5200	197**	6	71
Millet	2.0	?	—	3	100
Peanut	1.4	312	15	9	95
Peas	0.4	80	50	2	96
Potato	1.4	616	82	4	72
Rice	1.8	449	14	4	65
Sorghum	16.8	795	?	?	?
Soybean	42.4	2500	62	6	56
Sugar beet	1.4	367	16	2	42
Sweet potato	0.13	63	48	1	69
Wheat	44.3	1800	269	9	50

*Corn includes seeds, forage, and silage.
**Released public inbreds only.
Source: National Academy of Sciences, *Genetic vulnerability of major crops,* 1972, p. 287.

well advanced in developed countries where intensive plant breeding originated and modern crop strains are almost exclusively grown. Table 7-22 shows the degree to which American agriculture depends on a relatively few varieties of major crops.

Traditional varieties are now rapidly disappearing in LDCs as well, as farmers switch to new HYVs. Geneticist Reuben Olembo of the UN Environment Program expressed the problem vividly: "When farmers clear a field of primitive grain varieties, they throw away the key to our future. Eventually the new hybrid becomes so pure it cannot sustain itself."[149]

The introduction of a few new crop strains, of course, is not the only cause of the erosion of crop variability. Growing urban sprawl and extended cultivation continually wipe out populations of wild and semiwild ancestors of HYVs; famine in Biafra (and more recently in the Sahel) led to the loss of much potential crop diversity because everything that grew was consumed; the filling of Lake Nasser behind the Aswan dam drowned irreplaceable strains of feedgrains; and even the cleaning up of ruins in tourist areas of the Mediterranean basin has resulted in serious losses of plant genetic material.

Existing programs to create seed-stock reserves are woefully inadequate, both at the national and international levels. The National Seed Storage Laboratory at Fort Collins, Colorado, has been described as unevenly maintained, incomplete, and "shockingly deficient in some kinds of materials."[150]

Aside from nuclear war, there is probably no more serious environmental threat than the continued decay of the genetic variability of crops. Once the process has passed a certain point, humanity will have permanently lost the coevolutionary race with crop pests and diseases and will be no longer able to adapt crops to climatic change. The problem of genetic erosion is especially tragic because it could be solved at a cost miniscule compared to that squandered annually on weapons by DCs. The new International Board for Plant Genetic Resources of the Consultative Group on International Agricultural Research has begun to move in the right direction—establishing seed banks, and making material available for plant breeders.[151] Whether it moves rapidly enough and with the requisite safeguards remains to be seen.

Much more effort must be put into collecting and maintaining samples of traditional crop strains, and, wherever possible, into preserving crop strain diversity in the field. As noted in Chapter 4, merely saving small

[149]*Newsweek,* What come naturally.

[150]Jack P. Harlan, Genetics of disaster; and Our vanishing genetic resources. See also Judith Miller, Genetic erosion: Crop plants threatened by government neglect (an article from which some of the following material comes). Some idea of the size of the seed bank project is indicated in L. P. Reitz and J. C. Craddock, Diversity of germ plasm in small grain cereals.

[151]International Board for Plant Genetic Resources (FAO), The conservation of crop genetic resources.

samples of seed is not sufficient; and, because accidents have already destroyed some key collections,[152] it is important that duplicate collections be preserved in various parts of the world. Above all, programs should be under the careful supervision of plant geneticists who are knowledgeable in techniques of avoiding the decay of genetic variability.

Special problems of the tropics. Many of the poorest nations of the world, those with the most rapidly growing populations and most inadequate diets, are located in the Tropic Zone. In this region, agricultural productivity tends to be very low, but many agronomists hope that the potential for raising productivity is therefore great. Unfortunately, though, many of the biological problems that accompany the Green Revolution are intensified under the conditions of the humid tropics.

For example, it is not clear that breeding programs can keep ahead in the coevolutionary race against pests in the tropics. The life expectancy of new wheat strains in the northwestern United States is now reported to be only about five years.[153] Because, on the average, there are more generations of pests per year in the tropics, the rate at which they can penetrate strain resistance is likely to be even faster there. Hence, new crop strains need to be introduced perhaps every three years or so, unless pests can be effectively discouraged by other techniques, such as intercropping or rotation of crops.

If pesticides are employed, the heavy rains characteristic of equatorial regions may wash them quickly away, necessitating heavier or more frequent applications than are usual in temperate areas. The result, of course, would be amplification of the associated environmental consequences (see Chapter 11).

Similarly, the loss of organic matter from soils in the humid tropics, already serious because of heavy rains and thin soils, can be expected to increase as agriculture is intensified in those regions. Introduction of HYVs will necessarily be attended by increased use of fertilizers. But, if artificial fertilizers are used alone, the loss of organic matter from tropical soils may proceed even faster than it does in temperate areas.[154] There are likely to be other serious environmental problems if inorganic fertilizers are heavily used (Chapter 11). These problems, however, could be mitigated by favoring organic fertilizers over inorganic ones as much as possible. Knowledge of local soil characteristics (such as acidity or presence or absence of particular nutrients) can be a useful guide to appropriate fertilization and choice of crops.[155]

Today, the unavoidable (given rapid population growth) intensification of agriculture in the humid tropics generally takes one of two possible forms: (1) intensification of milpa farming, in which clearings are made larger and closer together, and regeneration times are shortened; or (2) imposition of large-scale, temperate-style agriculture, after clearing the forest. Either approach can lead to more or less permanent degeneration of the soil.[156]

Massive deforestation also seems to cause changes in local climate and exposes the land to severe flooding and erosion. Such destruction has occurred repeatedly in widely dispersed areas of the tropical world, from Nigeria and Zambia to Guatemala and the Amazon basin. Unfortunately, this trend is continuing, if not accelerating.

Large-scale agriculture may, indeed, not be possible in the humid tropics. But an approach that works—one grounded in large part in an understanding of tropical ecology—is beginning to emerge. This new agriculture also borrows heavily from milpa traditions in such practices as planting many different crops together (a milpa farmer may plant as many as 20 different species in his small clearing) in a small-scale, labor-intensive operation. Such small, family-run farms, often more efficient even in temperate agriculture than large-scale, highly mechanized operations, are still more so in many tropical settings.[157]

Experiments in mixed cropping are currently being carried out in several tropical areas in an effort to find the best kinds of mixtures for local conditions. Often adaptations of traditional practices prove fruitful. One variation is alternating forest growth with food crops (known as *agrisilviculture*). Sometimes trees are interplanted with shade-loving crops, rubber trees with coffee or peanuts,

[152] Wade, Green Revolution, pt. 1, and Green Revolution, pt. 2.
[153] Ibid.
[154] S. P. Dhua, Need for organo-mineral fertilizer.

[155] P. A. Sanchez and S. W. Buol, Soils of the tropics and the world food crisis.
[156] Erik P. Eckholm, *Losing ground;* E. P. Eckholm and K. Newland, No breadbasket in the jungle; Charles Posner, Agronomy to the rescue.
[157] Posner, Agronomy to the rescue.

for example. Mixed cropping frequently results both in higher yields and in reduced pest problems. (This is true both in tropical and in temperate areas.)[158]

An important principle in tropical farming is that the soil must always be covered (especially lateritic soil) to avoid sun-baking, leaching, and erosion. For additional protection, crop residues may be used as both mulch and fertilizer. In some tropical areas at least, minimal or no tillage of soil on slopes has proven helpful in reducing erosion without lowering yields.[159]

The lessons being learned in tropical agricultural research are vitally important for the futures of many tropical poor countries. The question now is whether they can be learned by agricultural establishments in those nations and the techniques can be transmitted to the farmers before the wrong approaches have destroyed the forest ecosystem beyond reclamation.

High-yield agriculture and climate. One potential drawback to the high-yielding crop varieties is that they have been bred to respond to a relatively narrow band of weather conditions—precipitation and temperature, particularly. Within the expected band of conditions they perform extremely well, but if rainfall or temperatures are too high or too low, yields may decline substantially. Generally, traditional varieties are less sensitive to stresses such as bad weather; under adverse conditions they may outperform HYVs.

A change in climate, if permanent and stable, can, of course, be compensated if necessary by breeding crop varieties that respond to the new set of conditions. But developing new strains in some situations might not even be necessary. For example, since the 1940s there has been a cooling trend in middle latitudes of the Northern Hemisphere, including the corn belt of the United States. If this trend continued to the year 2000, the resultant shorter growing seasons would be detrimental to corn and soybean crops at the northern edge of their range. Cooler weather would, however, be beneficial at the lower middle latitudes where the highest yields of these crops are obtained when average July and August temperatures are below normal.[160] As far as corn and soybeans are concerned, the overall effect of the continued cooling trend would probably be a gradual southward shift of the corn and soybean belts.

The most critical threat to crop yields is not a gradual change in overall climate, but an increase in its variability. For example, if the weather in the corn and soybean belts should be as variable in the last quarter of the twentieth century as it was in the first quarter, average yields of those crops would be reduced by about 3 percent.[161] If the U.S. is especially unlucky with the weather, the average could be reduced even further—hardly a cheering prospect for an era in which the world must count on constantly increasing yields of these crops.

A key point to remember is that the period of weather from 1940 to 1970, which is conventionally regarded as normal, was actually a period of *abnormally stable summer weather* for many of the world's granaries. The notion that good weather is normal weather is one important factor that has misled the U.S. Department of Agriculture to conclude, "Through the use of better varieties and improved cultivation and fertilization practices, man has reduced variation in [corn] yields in both good and bad weather."[162]

In recent years, the leadership of the USDA has persisted in the erroneous belief that modern technology has largely freed high-yield agriculture from the influence of weather. They have clung to this belief despite repeated warnings from many scientists concerned with the interactions between climate and agriculture, among whom are Reid Bryson, James McQuigg, Stephen H. Schneider, and Louis M. Thompson.[163] Thompson, an agronomist, and McQuigg, a climatologist, issued an important warning to the government in 1973.[164]

[158] R. B. Trenbath, Diversify or be damned? *The Ecologist,* vol. 5, no. 3, pp. 77–83.

[159] D. J. Greenland, Bringing the Green Revolution to the shifting cultivator. The author of this important paper is director of research at the International Institute of Tropical Agriculture in Nigeria.

[160] L. M. Thompson, Weather variability, climatic change, and grain production.

[161] Ibid.

[162] Report on the influence of weather and climate on United States grain production, U.S. Department of Agriculture, quoted in Thompson, Weather variability.

[163] By far the best presentation of the problem of climatic variability and its political implications can be found in S. H. Schneider and L. Mesirow, *The Genesis strategy.*

[164] Report to the National Oceanographic and Atmospheric Administration, The influence of weather and climate on United States grain yields: Bumper crops or drought, U.S. Department of Commerce, Washington, D.C., 1973.

Thompson had statistically analyzed yields of wheat, corn, and soybeans, and had shown that about half the variability in yields since 1900 could be explained by variability in the weather.[165] For example, in Missouri average corn yields increased from about 40 to about 80 bushels per acre between 1955 and 1973, and the variability of the yields decreased. Thompson's analysis showed that it was the abnormally favorable weather conditions for that period that reduced the absolute amount of yield variability, *not improved technology,* which appears to have reduced the percentage variability by increasing the total yield. McQuigg and Thompson argue strongly in their report that the consistently high grain yields of recent decades were basically caused by good luck with the weather and that it is "imperative that we not be lulled into a dangerous and unjustified expectation that such fortunate circumstances will continue." Their warning was prophetic in light of weather-related yield reductions in key United States crops in 1974, 1976 and 1977.

In fact, agriculturalists seem to be moving in directions that will reduce the chances of having good luck. One of the main elements of the technology of high-yield agriculture may make yields more vulnerable to variation than they were in traditional agroecosystems. Climatologist Stephen H. Schneider and his collaborator Lynne E. Mesirow argue in their fine book, *The Genesis strategy,* that HYVs, while producing higher absolute yields, tend to give *more variability* in absolute yield.[166] The essence of their argument is illustrated in Figure 7-21, which shows that HYVs, whether relatively sensitive or insensitive to environmental stresses, still are more variable in absolute yield than traditional varieties.

Climatic change therefore can have negative effects on agricultural yields in two different ways. One is through rapid directional change. Even if the change is toward "better" weather, there may be a depression of yields during the transition while farmers and the agroecosystems adjust. More important, increased variability in the weather could greatly enlarge the absolute difference between good and bad harvests. If humanity had superabundant food, this might make little difference, but even

[165]S. H. Schneider, personal communication based on a conversation with James McQuigg, August 26, 1976.

[166]Schneider and Mesirow, p. 263.

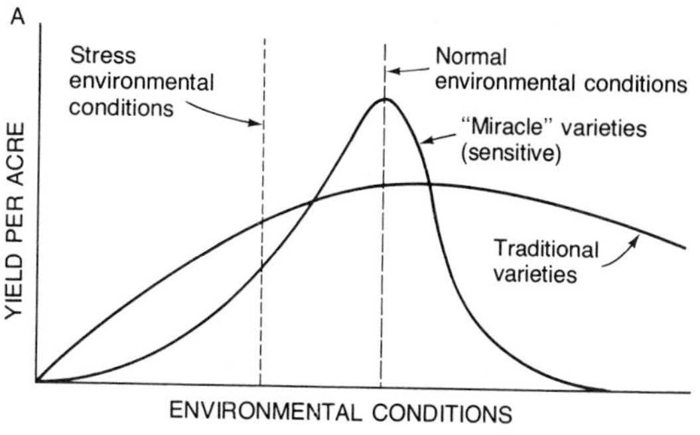

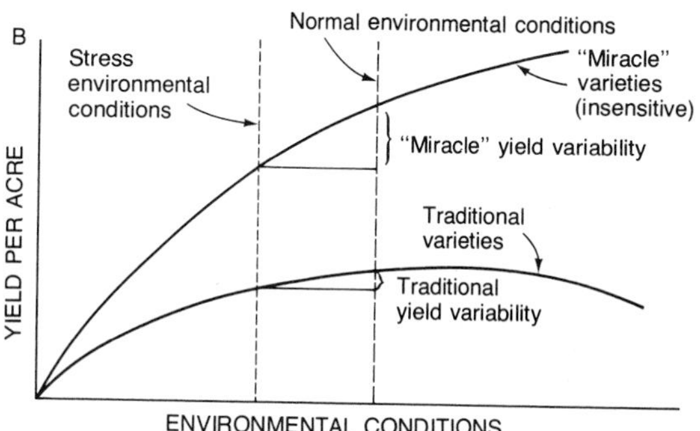

FIGURE 7-21

Part A shows how yield varies with environmental conditions for traditional varieties and for high-yield ("miracle") varieties that are particularly sensitive to such conditions. (Environmental conditions means some generalized aggregate of rainfall, humidity, fertilizer input, mean and extreme temperatures, etc.) Part B shows the same comparison between traditional varieties and a "better" set of high-yield varieties, which are relatively insensitive to environmental conditions and yield more than the traditional varieties no matter what the conditions. In both cases, *variability* in crop yield as a function of environmental factors is seen to be greater for miracle crops than conventional varieties. (From Schneider and Mesirow, *The genesis strategy.*)

now "world grain reserves are . . . roughly equivalent to (or smaller than) the difference between production in a favorable weather year worldwide and an unfavorable year."[167] When a few percentage points in global yield are all that stand between humanity and massive famines, it would seem prudent indeed to adopt Schneider's "Genesis strategy" and "store food in the fat years as a hedge against the lean."[168] Unhappily, the U.S. Department of Agriculture, largely for economic reasons, has preferred so far to keep its head in the sand.[169]

[167]James McQuigg at a workshop conference, World food supply in a changing climate, Sterling Forest, New York, 1974, quoted by S. H. Schneider and L. E. Mesirow, *The Genesis strategy,* p. 103.

[168]Specter at the feast, *The National Observer,* July 6, 1974, p. 18.

[169]See Chapter 8 of Schneider and Mesirow, *The Genesis strategy.* The Carter Administration, however, may take a different attitude.

High-Yield Agriculture and Resource Constraints

Modern, high-yield agriculture, as practiced in developed countries, can reasonably be described as a system that turns calories of fossil fuel into calories of food. Fossil fuels, of course, are used extensively in both the manufacture and the operation of farm machinery, in the production of pesticides and other materials used by farmers, and as both fuel and raw materials in the mining and manufacture of fertilizers.[170] Fossil fuels are also essential to the construction and operation of the systems that transport materials to the farm and carry farm produce to market. A significant portion of this energy must be used to stabilize otherwise unstable agricultural ecosystems; that is, to protect them from insect pests, plant diseases, winds, drought, floods, or the like.

As the use of manpower in North American and European agriculture has declined since 1900, fossil-fuel inputs have steadily increased. By 1970, less than 5 percent of the U.S. population lived on farms, compared to more than 23 percent in 1940. The reduction is less dramatic in most of Europe, where the small family farm is still the norm. Such reductions in human labor while food production increased substantially would have been impossible, of course, without great inputs of energy.

A study conducted in the 1960s indicated that, on the average, for each kilocalorie of food produced in the United States in 1960, some 1.5 kilocalories of fossil fuels were consumed directly by agriculture, and even more were consumed in related activities.[171] More detailed analyses of both American and British energy consumption in their food systems have since appeared. Biologist David Pimentel and his colleagues at Cornell University analyzed the energetics of producing corn, which was chosen as a typical crop.[172] They calculated that about 2.8 kilocalories of corn were obtained for each kilocalorie of energy input on U.S. farms in 1970. About half of the input replaced human labor, and the rest supported high productivity. This study covered only energy expended on the farm, although it did include the energy cost of manufacturing farm machinery, fertilizers, and pesticides. (In fact, corn, rather than being a "typical" crop, is among the more energetically efficient products in the U.S. food system.)[173]

Some other studies have been extended to include energy consumption by all elements of the food system: the farm and its inputs, food processing, packaging, distribution, storage, selling, and cooking. Steinhart and Steinhart estimated that the energy subsidy of the entire U.S. food system in 1970 amounted to an average of nearly 9 kilocalories for each kilocalorie obtained as food—and the subsidy has continued to rise in the 1970s.[174] Eric Hirst calculated that the U.S. food system accounted for about 12 percent of the national energy budget. About 40 percent of the energy in the food system was devoted to producing the food, and the rest was used in processing, distributing, and handling the food at home.

There are great variations, of course, in energy demand among crops. Corn, soybeans, sorghum, sugar cane, and wheat require relatively small inputs compared to caloric yields, for instance, whereas tomatoes, melons, and green vegetables rank high, and fruits, potatoes, rice, and peanuts fall in the middle. (These measurements can be somewhat misleading, however, because the energy-intensive crops are generally low in calories and are grown for other values such as vitamins, minerals, and fiber.)[175] The most energy-intensive of all foods are grain-fed animal products, when the energy subsidy of the feed crops is included.[176]

There are also very large variations in energy consumption among farming methods. Fossil-fuel inputs, for instance, are very low in LDCs compared to those in most industrialized nations. Figure 7-22 shows the energy subsidies, both for different crops and for different ways of obtaining food, from hunting and gathering and milpa (shifting) cultivation to intensive, high-yield crops and livestock production. It should be pointed out, however, that LDC agriculture is nonetheless quite energy-intensive—the difference is in the

[170]Michael J. Perelman, Farming with petroleum.

[171]H. L. Landsberg, et al., *Resources in America's future,* Johns Hopkins Press, Baltimore, 1963, p. 218.

[172]D. Pimentel, et al., Food production and the energy crisis. A British study (B. Pain and R. Phipps, The energy to grow maize, *New Scientist,* May 15, 1975, pp. 394–396) reached similar conclusions.

[173]D. Pimentel, et al., Energy and land constraints.

[174]J. S. Steinhart and C. E. Steinhart, Energy use in the U.S. food system; Eric Hirst, Food-related energy requirements.

[175]G. H. Heichel, Agricultural production and energy resources.

[176]D. Pimentel, et al., Energy and land constraints.

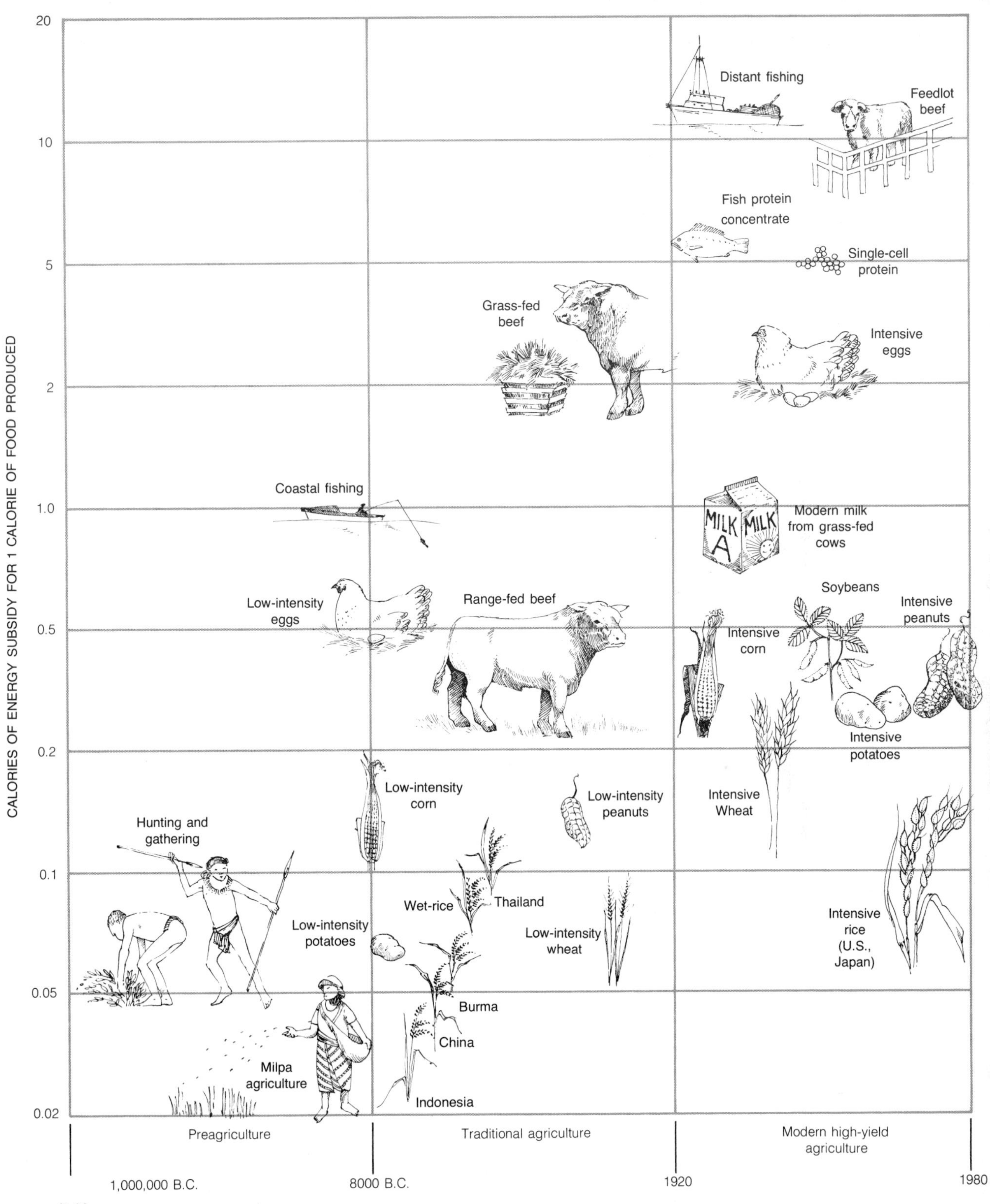

FIGURE 7-22

Energy subsidies for various food crops. (Data from J. S. Steinhart and C. E. Steinhart, Energy use in the U.S. food system, *Science,* vol. 184, April 19, 1974, p. 312.)

sources of energy and the efficiency of their utilization.[177] The main sources of energy for food production in most LDCs are wood, dung, crop wastes, draft animals, and human labor. In general, these sources are used very inefficiently.

What has all this to do with the Green Revolution? Most plans for modernizing agriculture in less-developed nations call for introducing energy-intensive practices similar to those used in North America and western Europe—greatly increased use of fertilizers and other farm chemicals, tractors and other machinery, irrigation, and supporting transportation networks—all of which require large inputs of fossil fuels. If systems of food production, processing, and distribution worldwide were "modernized" to the same degree as in the U.S. and the U.K., *the equivalent of 40 percent of the world's commercial fuel consumption in 1972 would be required to feed Earth's 4 billion people today.*[178] The likelihood that such high levels of energy use in the food system can or will be attained seems extremely remote, even though increased energy use in that system should have a high priority in the competition for resources.

It is becoming increasingly obvious that resource constraints—the limited amounts of arable land, fresh water (see Chapter 6), fossil-fuel energy and fossil-fuel-derived agricultural materials—are likely to circumscribe future agricultural development in LDCs. There are, however, many opportunities for increasing efficiency in the use of available energy sources[179] and for exploiting presently neglected potential resources, such as solar and wind energy, in both DCs and LDCs. (Such possibilities are discussed further in Chapter 8.)

It should be noted, moreover, that alternative farming methods that use far less fossil fuel than American-style agriculture requires, with no loss of productivity, are available. Both Japan and Taiwan, for example, attain yields similar to those of American farmers with lower fossil-fuel inputs. China has rapidly and successfully increased its food production in the past two decades with only a fraction of the energy cost typical of developed countries. The secret (and the price), of course, is much greater use of human labor and relatively less dependence on heavy machinery and manufactured fertilizers and pesticides.[180] Further increases in Chinese yields will undoubtedly require more energy, as fertilizer use increases and small-scale mechanization is introduced, but inputs seem likely to remain well below typical DC levels, at least for the foreseeable future. The approach that China has used is open to other LDCs, of course, and they would be wise to adopt those Chinese methods that suit their own situations.

Besides being less consumptive of diminishing energy resources, a more labor-intensive, less chemical-dependent agriculture causes far less environmental damage than does energy-intensive Western agriculture (see Chapter 11).[181] Western agricultural science may revolutionize food production in LDCs, but they in turn may be able to teach the West some techniques that will allow high yields to be maintained over the long term.

David Pimentel and his group have shown that, because of the limited supplies of arable land and energy, even today's human population of 4 billion could not be supported by a high-protein, American-style diet, in which 69 percent of the protein is derived from animals.[182] The outlook for feeding adequately (let alone bounteously) the 7 billion people expected in the year 2000, and still greater numbers after that, is decidedly gloomy. The Cornell group nevertheless has proposed a scenario in which adequate diets could be provided for the population of 2000 and beyond. In their scenario, people in rich countries would stop consuming grain-fed animals, depend more on vegetable sources of protein, and restrict their milk- and meat-eating to pasture- and range-fed animals. At the same time, people in poor countries could make greater use of animal protein by increasing and improving their flocks, herds, pastures, and rangeland.

Such a changeover could release enormous amounts of food resources and relieve pressures on energy supplies, even as diets for the poorer half of humanity were substantially improved. Without such a change, the

[177]A. Makhijani and A. Poole, *Energy and agriculture in the Third World.*

[178]G. Leach, Energy.

[179]W. J. Chancellor and J. R. Goss, Balancing energy and food production, 1975–2000.

[180]G. F. Sprague, Agriculture in China.

[181]For an excellent summary of American agriculture's abuse of the environment through profligate use of fossil fuels and farm chemicals, see Edward Groth, III, Increasing the harvest.

[182]Energy and land constraints.

Cornell group estimated that, to feed the population of 2000 at the same per-capita calorie and protein levels as in 1975, worldwide cereal production would have to be raised by 75 percent, legumes by 66 percent, and other vegetables by 100 percent. This assumes an increase of 30 percent in animal protein production also. If feedstuffs suitable for human consumption were diverted to the human supply and worldwide production of animal protein were reduced about 24 percent, however, it would be necessary to increase cereal production by the year 2000 by only 41 percent, legumes by 20 percent, and other vegetables by 50 percent. Obviously, if population growth slowed significantly in the next quarter-century, or if food production could be increased more rapidly, there would be an opportunity to improve the average human diet—preferably by providing an adequate one for the hungriest billion.

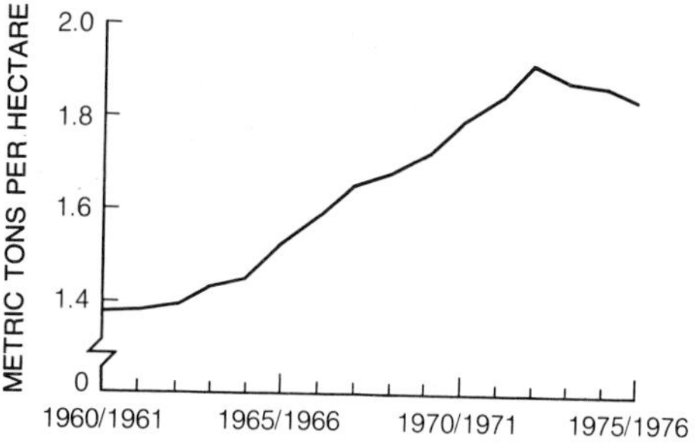

FIGURE 7-23

World grain yield per hectare, 1960–1976. Excludes rice; plotted as three-year sliding averages. (From Lester R. 1975, p. 1058.) Copyright 1975 by the American Association for the Advancement of Science.

Declining Yields and Proliferating Problems

One ominous element in the record of faltering grain production of the early 1970s was an overall decline in *average yield* (production per hectare) worldwide (Figure 7-23). This drop applied to all major cereals except rice, and reversed a long-estabished trend of steadily rising yields. Lester Brown, president of Worldwatch Institute, attributed the downturn primarily to five major factors, besides the weather:

> (1) the release for production of the 50 million acres of idled, below-average-fertility cropland in the United States that, added to the global cropland base, almost certainly reduced the average crop yield; (2) the high cost and tight supply of energy; (3) the high cost and tight supply of fertilizer; (4) the build-up of population pressures that reduce the fallow cycles of shifting [milpa] cultivators in large areas of West and East Africa, Central America, the Andean countries, and Southeast Asia to the point where fallow periods are now too short to allow soil fertility to regenerate; and (5) the growth of the demand for firewood in developing countries to such an extent that local forests could not keep pace and that more and more animal dung was used as fuel and less and less as an essential source of soil nutrients.[183]

Some additional factors, which like Brown's last two are directly related to population pressures (although they could be alleviated by better farming methods and resource management), could be added to this list. These include: irrigation with inadequate drainage, leading to accumulation of salts in the soil; increased soil erosion and accelerated silting-up of rivers and reservoirs caused by deforestation; expansion of cultivation into poor and unsuitable land, especially in mountainous regions; expansion of desert areas, largely because of overcultivation and overgrazing of the fragile desert-edge environment.[184]

By the mid-1970s, average yields from HYVs in many less-developed countries were also dropping. One reason was that the best land was planted first in these varieties, and less spectacular improvements in yield resulted from expansion onto poorer-quality land. In addition, some of the smaller farmers who were adopting the new technology may have been less able to provide all the necessary inputs in the right amounts and at the right time. In some areas, pest and crop diseases began to invade and to reduce harvests. Finally, the picture was clouded by the simultaneous occurrence of several years of unfavorable weather and the 1974 fertilizer shortage, both of which were discussed earlier.

These trends suggest that, although improved crop strains, better technology, and careful land and resource

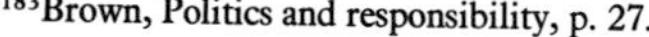

[183]Brown, Politics and responsibility, p. 27.

[184]Eckholm, *Losing ground.*

management might allow substantial increases in yield on good land where the Green Revolution has not yet been introduced, overall it will be increasingly difficult in the years ahead for food production in less developed regions to keep pace with population growth. The easier gains have already been made; successful exploitation of remaining opportunities will require proportionately much more effort, capital, energy, and care in avoiding untoward results.

As promising as high-yield agriculture may be, the funds, the personnel, the ecological expertise, and the necessary time to develop its full potential unfortunately may not be at humanity's disposal. Among other things, there is a serious *rate* problem. Even if research can create new technology quickly enough, there are apt to be considerable lags in getting the new technology into practice.[185] Revolutionizing agriculture, especially in the tropics, will be a time-consuming proposition, and population growth will not wait. Fulfillment of the Green Revolution's promise could come too late for many of the world's hungry, if it comes at all. Even its most enthusiastic boosters, including Norman Borlaug, who received the Nobel Peace Prize for developing the miracle wheats, have asserted that the Green Revolution cannot possibly keep food production abreast of population growth for more than two decades or so. Since a birth-control solution to the population explosion will inevitably take much longer than that, the prospects for avoiding massive deficits in food production in many less developed regions seem dim indeed. Unless food can be transferred from the rich nations on an unprecedented scale, the death rate from starvation in LDCs seems likely to rise in the next few decades.

FOOD FROM THE SEA

Perhaps the most pervasive myth of the population-food crisis is that humanity will be saved by harvesting the "immeasurable riches" of the sea. Unfortunately, the notion that vastly greater amounts of food can be extracted from the sea in the near future is an illusion. Biologists have carefully measured the riches of the sea, considered the means of harvesting them, and have found them wanting as a solution to the world food problem.

Fisheries Yields

The basis of the food-from-the-sea myth seems to be some theoretical estimates that fisheries' productivity might be increased to many times current yields. However, an analysis in 1969 by J. H. Ryther, of the Woods Hole Oceanographic Institution, put the maximum sustainable fish yield in the vicinity of 100 million metric tons, only about 43 percent more than the record 1971 harvest of just over 70 million metric tons (see Box 7-3).[186] Some marine biologists, more optimistic than Ryther, have estimated that a global fisheries yield of 150 million metric tons might be attained.[187] More recently, it has been suggested that even Ryther's estimates may be too high.[188]

In 1950, total world fisheries' production was about 21 million metric tons. For the next twenty years, production rose each year at an average rate of about 5 to 6 percent.[189] This rapid, sustained increase was largely due both to more intensive fishing and to the increasing use of technology, and probably also in part to more accurate and complete reporting.

In 1971, the rise in fisheries production came to a halt; in fact, the total catch of 70 million metric tons represented only a slight increase over the previous year. In 1972, there was an abrupt decline to less than 66 million tons. The catch in 1973 was about the same, and in 1974 it recovered slightly to 69 million tons (Figure 7-24).

For the growing human population, declines in the total catch of world fisheries mean even greater drops in per-capita yields (Figure 7-25). Since only about 2 percent of the world's calories come from the sea, one might easily draw the conclusion that a reduction of per-capita yield is not particularly important. On the contrary, it is extremely serious. Although food from the

[185]Wittwer, Food production.

[186]John H. Ryther, Photosynthesis and fish production in the sea.

[187]William E. Ricker, Food from the Sea; G. A. Rounsefell, Potential food from the sea; C. P. Idyll, The sea against hunger, and Anchovies, birds, and fishermen; and D. L. Alverson, et al., How much food from the sea?

[188]Brown, Politics and responsibility.

[189]Data from NAS, *Population and food.*

BOX 7-3 Productivity of the Sea

It is common for laymen to consider the oceans of the world a virtually limitless source of food. They would do well to heed the words of marine biologist J. H. Ryther, "The open sea—90 percent of the ocean and nearly three-fourths of the earth's surface—is essentially a biological desert. It produces a negligible fraction of the world's fish catch at present and has little or no potential for yielding more in the future." The upper layer of open seas, where there is enough light for photosynthesis, lacks the nutrients necessary for high productivity. The photosynthetic producer-organisms (phytoplankton) that live in this layer are extremely small in size. As a result very small herbivores and lower-order carnivores are able to function in food chains, and roughly five steps in the chains are interposed between the producers and human consumers. Thus not only are the basic mineral resources for the producers in short supply, but the energy losses in repeated transfers up the long food chains result in further reductions in the potential harvest.

Close to shore, and in certain offshore and coastal areas where powerful upwelling currents bring nutrients to the surface, productivity is 2 to 6 times higher; phytoplankton are larger, and food chains thus tend to be shorter. It is these areas that supply humanity with virtually all of its seafood. But the coastal areas are also the most subject to pollution. In many areas one-quarter to one-half of fishing production is dependent on estuaries, directly or indirectly—but people are busily destroying many of the world's estuaries.

The fisheries situation as viewed by Ryther is summarized in Table 7-23. Note that Ryther's productivity estimates are in the same ball park as those given in Table 4-6 when adjusted for the different classification of areas in that table, which were:

Area	*Percent of ocean*	*Average production*
Open ocean	92.0	57
Continental shelf	7.3	162
Upwelling zones	0.1	225
Algal bed and reef	0.2	900
Estuaries	0.4	810

The major differences in estimated maximum fisheries yields come from the multiplicative effects of variations in average productivity estimates (especially on the coastal zones), in the calculation of number of trophic levels (which depend primarily on assumptions about ecological and tissue-growth efficiencies), and in assumptions about the percentage of the production that can be harvested.*

*See William E. Ricker, Food from the sea.

TABLE 7-23
Productivity of the Ocean

Area	*Percent of ocean*	*Area (square kilometers)*	*Average productivity (grams of carbon per square meter per year)*	*Average number of trophic levels (approximate)*	*Annual fish production (millions of metric tons)*
Open ocean	90	326,000,000	50	5	1.6
Coastal zone*	9.9	36,000,000	100	3	120.0
Coastal upwelling areas	0.1	360,000	300	1.5	120.0
Total annual fish production					241.6
Amount available for sustained harvesting**					100.0
Fisheries yield in 1971, the largest catch so far					70.2

*Including certain offshore areas where hydrographic features bring nutrients to the surface.

**Not all the fishes can be taken; many must be left to reproduce or the fishery will be overexploited. Other predators, such as seabirds, also compete with us for the yield.

Source: After John H. Ryther, Photosynthesis and fish production in the sea.

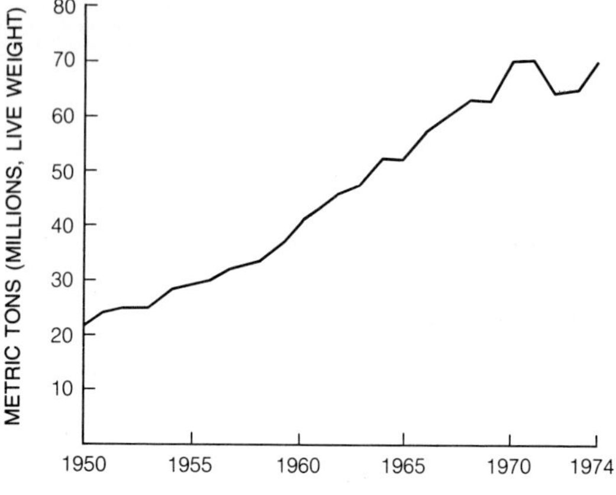

FIGURE 7-24

World fisheries production, 1950–1974. (Adapted from Brown and Eckholm, 1974; recent data from Lester R. Brown, *Worldwatch Paper 2,* 1975.)

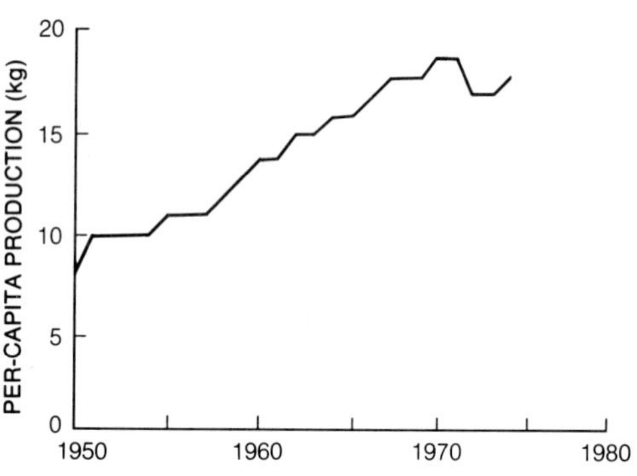

FIGURE 7-25

World fisheries production, per capita, 1950–1974. (Data from L. R. Brown, P. L. McGrath, and B. Stokes, Twenty-two dimensions of the population problem, *Worldwatch Paper 5,* March 1976.)

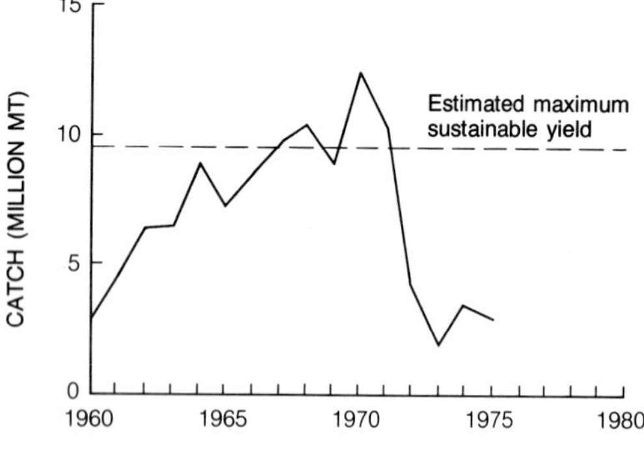

FIGURE 7-26

Peruvian anchovy catch, 1960–1975. (Adapted from L. R. Brown, P. L. McGrath, and B. Stokes, Twenty-two dimensions of the population problem, *Worldwatch Paper 5,* March 1976.)

sea provides comparatively few calories, it supplies about 14 percent of the world's animal protein directly, and a further portion indirectly as livestock feed. For some countries, especially for those where fishes provide a greater-than-average proportion of high-quality protein, the loss of this protein would be catastrophic. The Japanese, for instance, depend on seafood to provide somewhat more protein than is available to them as meat or poultry. Per-capita annual consumption of seafood in Japan is 71 pounds;[190] that of meat (most of which is imported, moreover) is only 51 pounds.

The anchoveta fishery. A major portion of the sudden 1972 decline in world fisheries yields and its subsequent fluctuations can be traced to changes in the Peruvian anchoveta fishery. In 1970, the yield from this fishery alone was almost 13 million tons; by 1973 it had declined to little more than 2 million tons, because of an interaction between people and nature. In 1972/73, warmer tropical waters invaded the cool, nutrient-rich Humboldt current that supports the fishery. Because they periodically recur around Christmas time, these inversions are known as El Niño (The Christ Child).[191] This natural event normally depresses the anchoveta population size; when applied to a population in which the adult stock was already badly depleted by overfishing, it triggered a catastrophic decline (Figure 7-26).[192] The Peruvian government imposed stringent regulations, but only a slight recovery was registered in 1974 and 1975.[193] It seems doubtful whether, even with careful management, sustained yields of anchovetas could ever exceed the 1970 level; the maximum sustainable yield has been estimated at about 9.5 million metric tons.[194]

Increasing the yields. Because the anchoveta fishery is potentially a significant element in the total harvest from the sea, it is difficult to predict future trends. If the anchovetas recover, worldwide yields may resume their

---

[190]Brown, *By bread alone.*

[191]K. Wyrtki, et al., Predicting and observing el Niño.

[192]John Gulland, The harvest of the sea; C. P. Idyll, The anchovy crisis.

[193]Brown, et al., Twenty-two dimensions; Pescaperu tries to solve its problems, the Lima *Times,* March 19, 1976.

[194]L. K. Boerema and J. A. Gulland, Stock assessment of the Peruvian anchovy *(Engraulis rigens)* and management of the fishery.

pre-1971 upward trend. Even if the global fish catch could be increased by the year 2000 to 100 million metric tons (Ryther's estimate of the maximum sustainable yield), however, there would still be less fish consumed per person than in 1970 (unless the human population growth rate decreases substantially in the meantime). Although such large increases in the fish catch would be desirable, the possibility cannot be dismissed that catches have now leveled off—and, indeed, that dramatic declines in many fish catches, similar to the anchoveta story, may soon occur.

To surpass the potential annual fish production of 70 to 150 million metric tons would require moving down the food chain from the large fish ordinarily found in fish markets to the harvesting of smaller animals or phytoplankton. All signs at the moment indicate that this will not be feasible or profitable in the near future, with the possible exception of some 25 to 50 million tons or more (some estimates range over 150 million metric tons) that might be harvested from populations of shrimplike krill in the Antarctic.[195] It has been speculated that in recent decades the supply of krill may have been greatly increased by the decimation of the populations of baleen whales that feed upon them (see the following section of text). But there is no evidence that the krill population has grown. Numerous other organisms also depend on them for food, including several kinds of fishes, seabirds, penguins, and seals. These may well have taken up any slack resulting from reduced whale predation.

Krill are a rich source of protein and apparently are reasonably palatable; they occur in dense, easily harvested swarms. Hence, they have attracted interest in several fishing nations. A paste made of krill and a krill/cheese product are already commercially available in the Soviet Union and reportedly are selling well. The Russians have also been using it as a livestock feed supplement. The Japanese, too, have been experimenting with foods based on krill.[196]

Adding krill or other plankton to the ocean harvest might increase the total fisheries yield, but it would not necessarily improve its quality or reduce its cost. The expenditure of money, fuel, and human energy required to harvest and process most kinds of plankton would be even greater than those demanded by distant fishing and would be colossal in relation to the yield. In many cases, the product would require considerable processing to be made palatable as human food. In addition, harvesting plankton in most areas would result in the depletion of stocks of larger fishes living farther up the food chain—fishes that could themselves be far more easily and cheaply harvested and that would be more welcome on the dinner table.

Two things stand between humanity and the future achievement by more conventional methods of even 100 million metric tons of fisheries yield. The first is overexploitation; the second is oceanic pollution (which is discussed in Chapter 11). The setbacks of the 1970s may mean that these two problems have already overtaken us.

Whaling

The story of the whale fisheries serves as a model of overexploitation.[197] It differs from other fisheries in that whales have been harvested primarily not for food but for whale oil, although they are now used extensively for food as well as for the production of a multitude of products from perfumes to fertilizer.

In 1933, a total of 28,907 whales were caught, producing 2,606,201 barrels of whale oil. In 1966, a third of a century later, 57,891 whales were killed, almost exactly twice as many as in 1933. But twice as many whales yielded only 1,546,904 barrels of oil—just about 60 percent of the 1933 yield. The reason can be seen in the charts of Figure 7-27. As the larger kinds of whales were driven toward extinction, the industry shifted to harvesting not only the young individuals of large species, but, with time, smaller and smaller species: first the gigantic blue whale, then the fin, the sei, and the sperm. By 1973, most of the whales caught were sperm or minke, a small species formerly considered beneath the whalers' notice.[198]

---

[195] I. Lyubimova et al., Prospects of the utilization of krill and other nonconventional resources of the world ocean.

[196] B. Bondar and P. J. Bobey, Should we eat krill?; Patti Hagan, The singular krill.

[197] Although whales are mammals, not fishes, the hunting of them is arbitrarily called a fishery.

[198] Victor B. Scheffer, The status of whales.

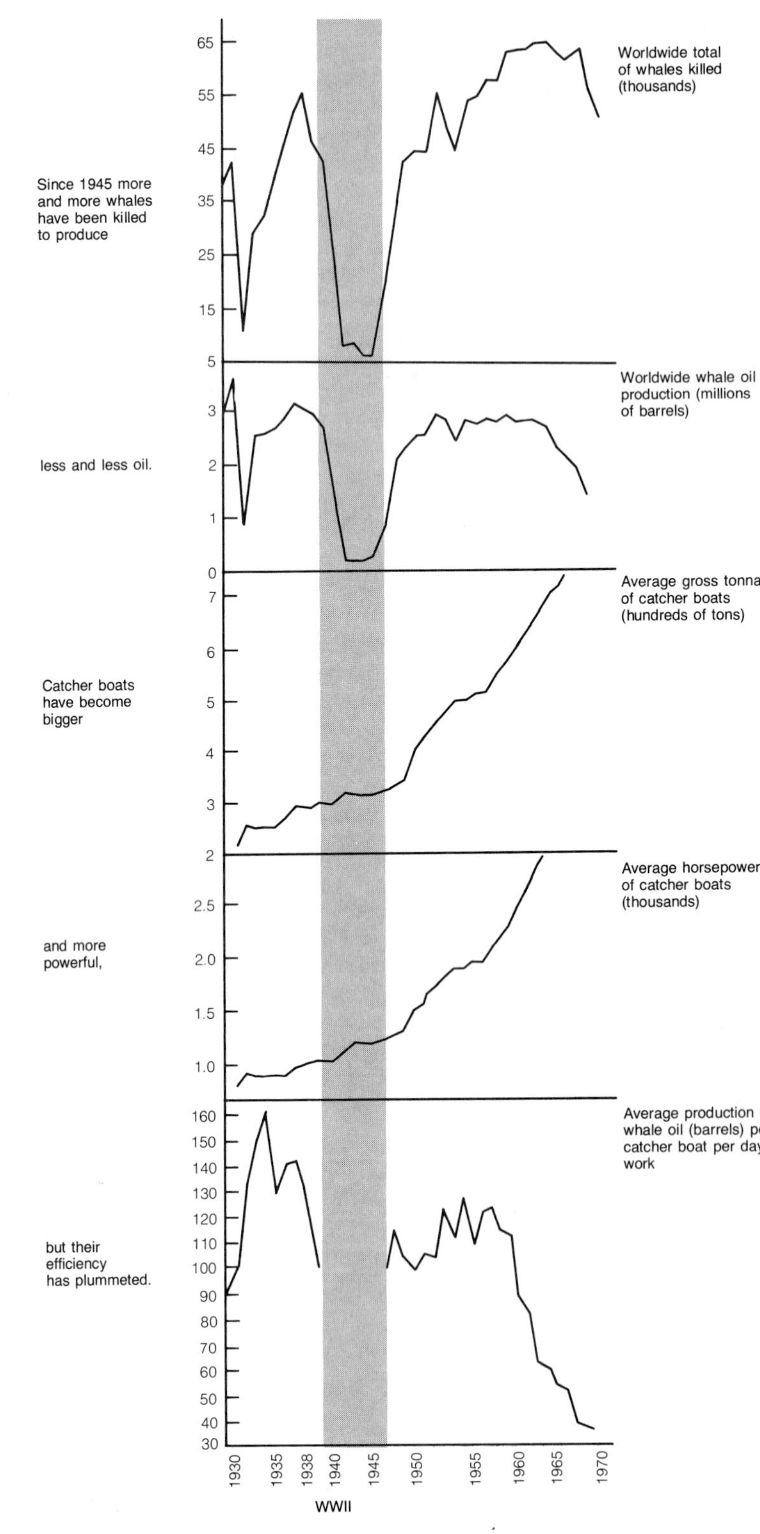

Since 1945 more and more whales have been killed to produce
less and less oil.
Catcher boats have become bigger
and more powerful,
but their efficiency has plummeted.
Worldwide total of whales killed (thousands)
Worldwide whale oil production (millions of barrels)
Average gross tonnage of catcher boats (hundreds of tons)
Average horsepower of catcher boats (thousands)
Average production of whale oil (barrels) per catcher boat per day's work
65
55
45
35
25
15
5
3
2
1
0
7
6
5
4
3
2
2.5
2.0
1.5
1.0
160
150
140
130
120
110
100
90
80
70
60
50
40
30
1930
1935
1938
1940
1945
1950
1955
1960
1965
1970
WWII

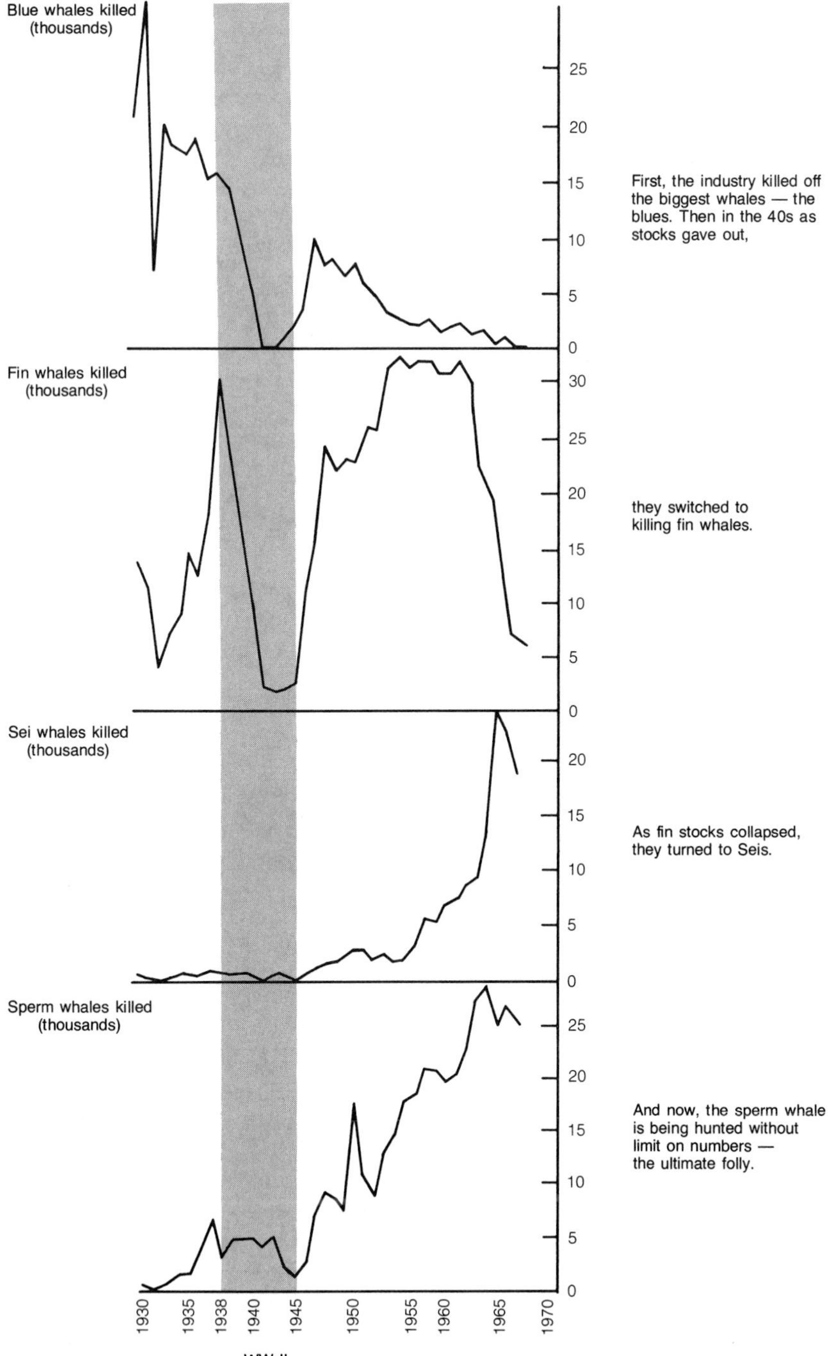

FIGURE 7-27

Overexploitation of whale fisheries. (After *New York Zoological Society Newsletter,* November 1968.)

TABLE 7-24
Effect of Whaling on Stocks of Ten Species of Whales

Species	*Virgin stock*	*1974 stock*	*Percent of virgin stock (1974)*
	Thousands		
Sperm, both sexes	922	641	69
male	461	212	45
female	461	429	93
Fin	448	101	22
Minke	361	325	90
Blue	215	13	6
Sei	200	76	38
Bryde	100	(40)?	?
Right*	(50)?	(2)?	?
Bowhead*	(10)?	(2)?	?
Humpback	50	7	14
Gray*	11	11	100
Total	2,367	1,218	51.4

*Not currently being hunted.
Source: Victor B. Scheffer, The status of whales, p. 3. *Pacific Discovery,* vol. 29, no. 1, 1976.

Overall, it has been estimated that whale stocks have been reduced by at least half through uncontrolled hunting during the past half century. Populations of the most heavily exploited species have been cut to a tiny fraction of their former sizes, whereas some of the smaller species have so far been relatively unaffected. Table 7-24 shows the depletion of ten important whale species. For the three species for which only fragmentary information exists, what there is suggests that they too have been reduced by half or more. It is disturbing to note that little or no recovery has been noted in stocks that have not been hunted for several decades, with the single exception of the California grey whale.

Technological "space-age" advances have greatly aided the whalers in this overexploitation. Ship-based helicopters locate whales and then guide killer boats to the quarry. The killer boats hunt by sonar, killing the quarry with an explosive harpoon head attached to a nylon line with an eighteen-ton test strength. The dead whale is inflated with compressed air so it will not sink, and a radio beacon is attached to the catch so that the towboat can find it and tow it to the factory ship, where it is quickly processed. Some attempts have been made to introduce more humane methods of killing the whales, but they seem not to have been accepted so far.

Efforts to curb the slaughter were remarkably unsuccessful until the 1970s, when public indignation began to be felt. Box 7-4 describes the history of international efforts to regulate whaling.

The killing of highly intelligent aquatic mammals is becoming even more common because of the recent escalation in the killing of small whales—belugas, porpoises, dolphins, and the like. Not only have these animals increasingly been candidates for hunting as the large whale species have been pushed toward commercial extinction,[199] but they are also being killed in large numbers in the course of commercial tuna fishing. For unknown reasons, porpoises are commonly associated with schools of yellowfin tuna (they do not feed on them) and are often trapped in the purse-seines of the tuna fishermen. Many of the trapped porpoises panic and dive, become entangled in the net, and drown. An estimated 200,000 to 500,000 per year were killed in that manner in the early 1970s.[200] By 1974, public concern over this slaughter had grown to the point that U.S. tuna vessels were required to incorporate a safety panel in their nets to aid the porpoises in escaping. The efficacy of this and other proposed measures remains to be seen—porpoises were still being needlessly killed in large numbers by tuna fishers in 1975 and 1976.[201] In early 1976, a court decision effectively banned U.S. tuna fishers from purse-seining tuna schools accompanied by porpoises. The result, however, may be a transfer of ownership of the tuna fleet to foreign registration rather than a change in fishing methods.[202]

So, not only are the giant blue and fin whales threatened (the largest animals that have ever lived—a blue whale weighs roughly 30 times as much as an elephant and is larger than the largest dinosaur), but so are the smaller whales whose intelligent behavior has

[199]John A. Burton, The future of small whales.

[200]George Reiger, First the whales, now the porpoises; Friends of the Earth, *Whale campaign manual.*

[201]Robert T. Orr, The tuna-dolphin problem; E. M. Leeper, Major research effort probes tuna-porpoise bond.

[202]Associated Press, Tuna net ban to save porpoises, Palo Alto *Times,* May 11, 1976.

received much publicity on television and in films and fascinated millions at marine parks. For even if the tuna-related slaughter of porpoises abates, commercial fishing of the small whales seems likely to increase.

Tragedy of the commons. It thus behooves us to ask, "For what?" What is gained by reducing the chances that future generations of people will be able to observe the behavior of these endlessly interesting animals and perhaps even communicate with them? For what does humanity risk silencing forever the fascinating songs of the humpback whale, which can range over 10 octaves, last for up to 30 minutes, and be repeated virtually verbatim? The answer is, for the profit of a few corporations, private and state.

Whale products are a trivial part of world commerce (worth about $170 million per year), and every single one of them has readily available substitutes from other sources. For sperm-whale oil, for instance, which has been claimed to be uniquely suited for automatic transmission fluid in cars and as an industrial lubricant, there has been found to be an analog produced by an obscure cactus, the *jojoba.*[203] Jojoba oil can be produced in large quantities at far lower cost than that of hunting whales. And, if cultivated, the plant would be in no danger of extinction. In short, whaling is not only cruel, but also, in the broad view, absurd.

Apart from these considerations, what can be said about the whaling industry's performance? Its drive toward self-destruction seems on the surface to contradict the commonly held notion that people will automatically change their behavior if they realize that it is against their own self-interest. Fully informed by biologists of the consequences of their behavior, the whaling industry has nonetheless continually operated against its own self-interest since 1963. Short-term self-interest, the lure of the "quick buck," clearly has been too strong to allow the long-run best interest of everyone to prevail. Those who own the industry apparently plan to make more money in the long run by forcing both the whales and the industry to extinction and then investing their ill-gotten gains elsewhere after the final collapse of the whale stocks.[204] Behavior that appears on the surface to be irrational thus turns out to have a perverse "rationality" in the context of the prevailing economic system.

As biologist Garrett Hardin pointed out, the sea is a "commons," analogous to a communal pasture open to all.[205] From the point of view of an individual herder exploiting such a pasture commons, there seems to be every reason to keep adding to his herd; although the grass is limited, he will get a larger share if he has a larger herd. If his animals do not eat the grass, someone else's will. Such reasoning, of course, is followed by each user of the commons. Individuals struggle to increase their herds until, at some point, the carrying capacity of the pasture is exceeded and it is destroyed by overgrazing.

Similarly, in the sea each individual, company, or country exploiting a whale or fish stock (equivalent to the grass of the pasture) strives to get a maximum share of the catch because each increment represents further immediate profit. Unless some strict agreement can be reached about how the fishery is to be used, maximum exploitation seems to be the best short-range strategy from the point of view of each user. After all, reason the Japanese, if we don't get the whales or the fish, the Russians will. The Russians take a similar view, as do the Norwegians, South Africans, and all the others. Unhappily, the end result of all these individual optimum strategies for dealing with the commons is disaster for all.

The whale story also illustrates the impotence of scientific advisory bodies in the face of entrenched economic interests—at least until public opinion is rallied on the side of the scientists. Sadly, it provides an example, too, of the willingness of many "captive" scientists to provide answers that suit the interest of their governmental or industrial employers. The Japanese scientists who essentially invented estimates of the stocks of blue whales in the Antarctic[206] provide an extreme example of this kind of behavior.

---

[203]Desert plant may replace sperm oil, *BioScience,* July 1975, p. 467.

[204]D. Pirages and P. Ehrlich, *Ark II,* W. H. Freeman and Company, San Francisco, 1974, p. 237.

[205]The tragedy of the commons.

[206]See, for instance, the Japan Whaling Association booklet, *Are the whales really threatened with extinction?* p. 8; see also *The Ecologist,* June 1974, p. 192.

BOX 7-4 International Regulation of Whaling: A Case History

After World War II, the 17 countries interested in whaling established the International Whaling Commission (IWC). This commission was charged with regulating the annual harvest, setting limits to the catch, and protecting whale species from extinction. In theory, commissioners from the various nations were to be responsible for ensuring the compliance of their nation's whalers with IWC decisions, but in fact their powers of inspection and enforcement were nonexistent. Instead of setting quotas on individual whale species, the IWC unfortunately established quotas on the basis of "blue-whale units." A blue-whale unit (bwu) is one blue whale or the equivalent in other species: two fin whales, two-and-a-half humpback whales, or six sei whales. Basing harvests on such units, of course, was ecological insanity. By making the mistake of lumping population units that was discussed in Chapter 4, the IWC guaranteed that disaster would occur. No rational conservation of stocks would be possible under such a system. The nations engaged in whaling in the Antarctic fishery were allowed a combined quota of 16,000 blue-whale units. Since the blue whales were the largest, they were the most sought after. Up until about 1950, blues continued to be taken, but their numbers declined sharply, which meant that the next largest, the fin whales, were hunted more vigorously.

In 1960 the Commission appointed a committee of biologists to investigate the stocks of Antarctic whales. Catches of blues and fins continued to decrease in the interval between establishment of the committee in 1960 and its report in 1963. The report detailed the overexploitation of the fisheries and warned that blues and humpbacks were in serious danger of extinction. It recommended that blues and humpbacks be totally protected and that the take of fins be strictly limited. It also urged abandonment of the system of blue whale units in favor of limits on individual species.

The committee also made some predictions. Their report stated that if unrestricted whaling continued in 1963-1964, no more than 8500 blue-whale units would be taken, and that 14,000 fins would be killed. Predictably, the warnings were ignored, and the limits were set at 10,000 bwu. The whalers killed 8429 bwu that season, and 13,870 fins were taken: the biologists' predictions proved uncannily accurate. An ominous note in these figures is that the catch of fin whales was about 35 percent of the estimated total population—probably three times the estimated *sustainable* yield.

When the results for 1963-64 were in, the biologists recommended a bwu total of 4000 for 1964-65, of 3000 bwu in 1965-66, and of 2000 bwu in 1966-67, in order to allow for recovery of the whale stocks. Again their advice was ignored. All four countries then engaged in Antarctic whaling—Japan, the Netherlands, Norway, and Russia—voted against accepting the recommendation, and instead agreed only to limit the 1964-65 season's catch to 8000 bwu, double the recommended number of units.

What happened in 1964-65? Only 7052 blue whale units were taken, well short of the 8000 quota. Furthermore, only 7308 fins were taken, and the majority of the remaining bwu consisted of almost 20,000 seis, well over a third of the total estimated population of that species. In both 1963-64 and 1964-65 the total Antarctic catch of whales was less than that from other areas of the world—an unprecedented situation. Meanwhile, the Netherlands had given up whaling and sold her fleet to Japan.

In an emergency session in May of 1965, the IWC decided to limit the 1965-66 catch to 4500 bwu, which again exceeded the biologists' recommendation. The IWC also tried unsuccessfully to give the now heavily fished sperm whales some protection. The whaling industry did not catch the 4500-bwu limit in 1965-66; the total was only 4089 units, and sei whales made up the majority. Meanwhile, whaling stations in Peru and Chile (not members of the IWC) killed 449 more blue whales, which were already dangerously near extinction.

Subsequent attempts to reach agreements to limit the take of fin, sei, and sperm whales in Antarctic and other waters failed. In 1966-67 there were four Japanese, two Norwegian, and three Russian antarctic whaling expeditions; the take was 3511 bwu (4 blues, 2893 fins, and 12,893 seis). Outside the Antarctic, seven factory ships and 24 land stations processed 29,536 whales, many of them sperms. In the calendar year 1967 a grand total of 52,046 whales were slaughtered, 25,911 of them sperm whales. In addition, Japan, hungry for protein, killed 20,000 porpoises. In

1968 Norway was forced out of the Antarctic whaling industry, leaving that field to Japan and Russia.

In 1968 the IWC failed to implement the International Observer Scheme that had been informally discussed in 1967. The scheme would have placed observers from other nations on whaling vessels to ensure that protected species or size classes were not harvested. In 1969 the Scientific Committee of the IWC again recommended the abolition of the pernicious blue whale unit system, but the IWC did not comply. In 1970 a small step forward was made when, although the bwu was retained for the Antarctic harvest, individual species limits were set for fin and sei whales in the North Pacific.

In 1972 the 24th meeting of the IWC met in a dramatically changed international atmosphere. In June 1972 the United Nations Conference on the Human Environment, held in Stockholm, Sweden, just two weeks before, had come out in favor of a ten-year moratorium on the commercial killing of whales; 53 nations had voted in favor of the moratorium, three had abstained, and none had opposed it. The supporters of the moratorium contended that it was necessary both to permit endangered stocks to begin recovering and to allow time for research to establish a basis for harvesting without depleting stocks after the moratorium.

Not unexpectedly for a child of the whaling industry, the IWC rejected the moratorium, claiming that "regulation by species and stocks was the only practical method of whale conservation." International pressure did, however, result in both the abandonment of the bwu and the implementation of the Observer Scheme. The latter, of course, led to the Japanese observing the Russians and vice-versa, rather like the fox and the coyote taking turns guarding the henhouse!

Pressure from conservation groups changed a number of IWC votes on the moratorium issue. It passed by a simple majority in the Scientific Committee, but fell short of the three-fourths majority required in the IWC Plenary Session. (There was, of course, no guarantee that either the Soviets or the Japanese would abide by the decision if a moratorium were voted; the IWC has no enforcement powers.)

In 1974 a watered-down version of the moratorium, called the New Management Procedure (NMP), was adopted by the Commission. It became effective in 1975 and automatically places on the protected list any population that the Scientific Committee considers to be below the population size providing an optimum sustainable yield (OSY), which in essence is the maximum sustainable yield (see Chapter 4) adjusted for economic, ecological, and sociopolitical factors. Thus, from 1976 on, the fin and blue whales should be totally protected, as should certain sei stocks.*

Two other categories were also established: "Initial Management Stocks," populations that can be reduced to the size providing optimum sustainable yields; and "Sustained Management Stocks," which are thought to be at about optimum size. If a stock drops significantly (about 10 percent) below OSY, it becomes protected.

It remains to be seen whether and how well the NMP will be observed, but there were some encouraging signs in 1975. The 1975 kill quotas were set about 20 percent below those of 1974 and included areas and shore stations not previously regulated. Rumors circulated that both Japan and the USSR had reduced their whaling fleets.

In addition to the tightening of IWC regulations, several nations have acted independently to discourage whaling. The U.S. government has put eight whale species on the Department of Interior's endangered species list, banned whaling by American companies or by foreign ships using American ports, and passed a law allowing economic pressure to be brought against another country that violates good fishery-management practice. The U.S. also no longer permits importation of whale products. Canada too has ended its whaling activities.

Ultimately the results of the ongoing Law of the Sea Conferences may determine the fate of the whales, but what the outcome will be is not yet clear. Several nations have extended their coastal territorial zones to a width of 200 miles, including the United States. If this becomes universal, over half the whale populations would be subject to protection by individual nations.

*The basic source of the post-1967 chronology is the Friends of the Earth, *Whale campaign manual;* post-1974 information is from V. B. Scheffer, The status of whales.

But in whaling controversies (or nuclear-power or pesticide controversies), the opinions of scientists employed by the special interests involved can be relatively easily detected and disregarded. More threatening and less understandable are those independent workers who, often on the basis of faulty assumptions or misinformation, give aid and comfort to exploiters. For instance, in 1972 marine biologist Ray Gambell argued against a whaling moratorium, basically on the grounds that maximum sustainable yields (MSY) and sustainable yields (SYs) for whale stocks could be accurately estimated.[207] But, as was explained earlier (Chapter 4), calculations of MSYs are based on certain assumptions about population units, density-dependent reproductive responses, lack of certain social structures, and genetic systems; assumptions that are likely not to be met by the whale populations. Gambell's discussion also was based on MSY in numbers rather than in weight, even though the latter would be more compatible with the long-term interests of humanity, the whales, *and* the industry (*if* the industry had any long-term interests).[208] Unfortunately, harvesting to maximize the weight of the catch would require stringent immediate conservation efforts to build up the population if it were to achieve beneficial results over the long term.

Only two major whaling nations remained by the 1970s: Japan and the USSR. The Soviets are less open than the Japanese about their intentions—although they seem to be in business on the same exploitative basis—and have not done much to defend their whaling activities. The Japanese, on the other hand, have been very active in justifying theirs. One claim is that whales are not really endangered, which defies all the evidence available.[209] A more prudent position would be to assume the worst rather than risk the irreversibility of extermination.

A second argument has been that most of the damage to whale stocks was done early in the game by Westerners, and it is therefore unfair to campaign against Japanese cruelty. Needless to say, the Japanese have no monopoly on cruelty or stupidity, and many nations have withdrawn from whaling on economic, *not* on compassionate grounds. But the Japanese whaling industry is nonetheless one of the two remaining major forces pushing the whales toward the brink of extinction today, and therefore it must be a target of those who are trying to save the whales.

A third argument is that the Japanese need the food. In the long run they might well need it, but at the moment whales supply only 0.8 percent of Japanese protein, and the consumption is decreasing.[210] Furthermore, the sperm whale accounts for some 40 percent by weight of the total catch now, and its meat is not suitable for human consumption.[211] If the Japanese whaling industry were truly concerned about the future diets of the Japanese people, it would be clamoring for a moratorium on whaling until stocks were built up to a verified MSY in weight.

There is no question that what progress has been made in retarding the all-out destruction of the whales has been achieved through aroused public pressure. The first reaction of the whaling interests seemed to be astonishment that anyone cared about the whales. But the technological age, which has provided more efficient means of exterminating whales, has also allowed scientists to study them. Their recordings and films in turn acquainted the public with the whale's extraordinary qualities. Why biologists—and poets—oppose unrestricted whaling was beautifully expressed by Victor Scheffer:

> Whales have become newly symbolic of real values in a world environment of which man is newly aware. They have become symbolic of life itself. I believe that we ought to stop killing them unless for human survival only, and then humanely. I see no need to extend this protective ethic to rabbits, or chickens, or fish. Whales are different. They live in families, they play in the moonlight, they talk to one another, and they care for one another in distress. They are awesome and mysterious. In their cold, wet, and forbid-

[207] Why all the fuss about whales?

[208] A specific critique of Gambell's position can be found in S. Holt, Whales: Conserving a resource; and a more general one in Friends of The Earth, *Whale campaign manual.*

[209] The Japanese arguments here and below are from the Japan Whaling Association booklet and Chinpei Comatsu, Monday comments, *Asahi Shinbun,* June 17, 1974; see also Norman Myers, The whaling controversy.

[210] Friends of The Earth, *Whale campaign manual.*

[211] Holt, Whales: Conserving a resource.

FIGURE 7-28

The Russian factory ship *Polar Star* lies hove to in the Barents Sea in June 1968, as two vessels from its fleet of trawlers unload their catch for processing. (Photo by Sovfoto.)

ding world they are complete and successful. They deserve to be saved, not as potential meatballs but as a source of encouragement to mankind.[212]

Overexploitation by Technology

The race to loot the sea of its protein is now in full swing. Japan, China, and the USSR took the lion's share of the world's fish catch in 1973, jointly landing over 40 percent of the total. Norway, the United States, and Peru came next, landing some 12 percent among them.[213] The remaining 48 percent of the seafood harvest went to all the other nations. Despite their relatively great need for cheap protein, less developed countries obtained only one-third of the catch.

Technological advances similar to those of the whaling industry are also being applied to other major fisheries around the world, even though many stocks are already overexploited and others evidently soon will be. Japan, the Soviet Union, and several eastern European nations have moved into big-time fishing with a vengeance. A single Rumanian factory ship equipped with modern devices caught in one day in New Zealand waters as many tons of fish as the whole New Zealand fleet of some 1500 vessels (see Figure 7-28).

Simrad Echo, a Norwegian periodical published by a manufacturer of sonar fishing equipment, boasted in 1966 that industrialized herring fishing had come to the Shetland Islands, where 300 sonar-equipped Norwegian and Icelandic purse-seiners had landed undreamed-of quantities of herring. An editorial in the magazine queried, "Will the British fishing industry turn . . . to purse-seining as a means of reversing the decline in the herring catch?" Another quotation from the same magazine gives further insight: "What then are the Shetlands going to do in the immediate future? Are they going to join and gather the bonanza while the going is good—or are they going to continue drifting and if seining is found to have an adverse effect on the herring stocks find their catches dwindling?" The answer is now clear. In January

---

212Scheffer, The status of whales.

213UN, *Statistical yearbook,* 1974.

1969, British newspapers announced that the country's east-coast herring industry had been wiped out. The purse-seiners took the immature herring that had escaped the British drifter's nets, which are of larger mesh, and the potential breeding stock was destroyed.

Other examples of overexploited stocks are east Asian and California sardines;[214] northwest Pacific and Atlantic salmon;[215] cod in many areas; menhaden; tuna in the Atlantic, Pacific, and Indian oceans; flatfish in the Bering Sea; plaice in the North Sea; halibut, hake, and haddock in the North Atlantic; and bottom fish in the western Pacific and eastern Atlantic oceans. Figure 7-29 shows the record of fish catches for three major overexploited fisheries in the North Atlantic. Figure 7-30 shows where and when depletion had occurred in overfished North Atlantic stocks by the late 1960s.

Some fish stocks, such as Pacific hake, South Atlantic herring, Yellow Sea bottom fish, anchovy off California, and clupeids in the Atlantic and Indian oceans, are as yet underexploited. It seems unlikely they will remain so for long, at least wherever they are not too mixed with other species or too dispersed for efficient fishing.

As more and more important fisheries have become depleted and yields have dropped, the pressures of competition have become more obvious. Soviet fishing boats have regularly made headlines by fishing close to both coasts of the United States and Canada. In American coastal waters (within 200 miles of the shore) in 1973, foreign fishing fleets (mainly Soviet and Japanese) caught more than 5 times as much seafood (3.6 million metric tons) as American fishermen did (635,000 metric tons).[216] One reason is that, except for the tuna fleet, American fishermen are still operating traditional, small fishing trawlers. In 1973, Japan sent 629 large trawlers, 23 enormous factory ships, and 60 support ships (for fueling the fishing fleet and carrying processed fishes back to Japan) to the Alaskan fishing grounds. Small wonder American fishermen are resentful. Efficient operations on that scale quickly drive small, independent fishermen out of business, especially once the fishery begins to be depleted.

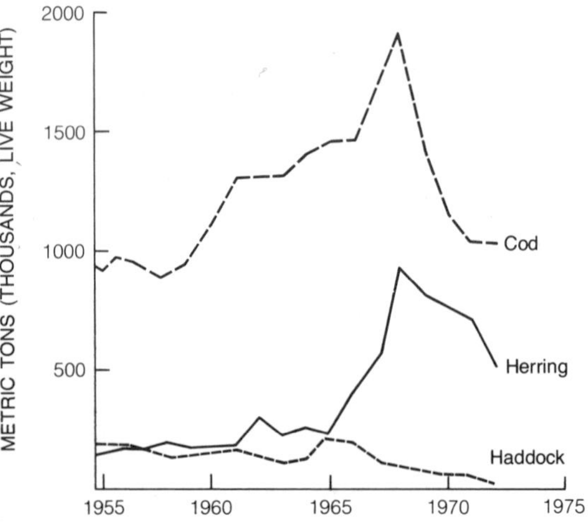

FIGURE 7-29

Annual catch of selected species in the northwest Atlantic, 1954–1972. (Adapted from Brown and Eckholm, *By bread alone.*)

In 1975, the U.S. Coast Guard seized 21 foreign vessels that were caught fishing inside the 12-mile territorial limit or had exceeded their negotiated quotas. Nearly $4 million in fines were collected and two vessels were confiscated. In early 1976, Congress passed a law extending U.S. jurisdiction over coastal waters to 200 miles, effective in March 1977. There is considerable alarm among American fisheries concerns over the state of diminishing fisheries. One government study indicated that, with proper management, 9 to 18 million metric tons of seafood a year might be harvested on a sustained basis from U.S. coastal waters.[217] But, even in the face of intensive effort, the total catch by both U.S. and foreign fishermen in 1973 was only 5.6 million metric tons.[218]

The competition for seafood resources is by no means limited to U.S. coastal waters. Between 1961 and 1971, the Peruvian government seized 30 United States tuna-fishing boats, and Ecuador had taken 70 others, in disagreements over the limits of territorial waters. For

---

[214] Garth J. Murphy, Population biology of the Pacific sardine (*Sardinops caerula*).

[215] Anthony Netboy, The unhappy fate of *Salmo salar*.

[216] William B. McCloskey, Board and seize.

[217] U.S. Department of Commerce, National plan for marine fisheries, October 1975.

[218] McCloskey, Board and seize.

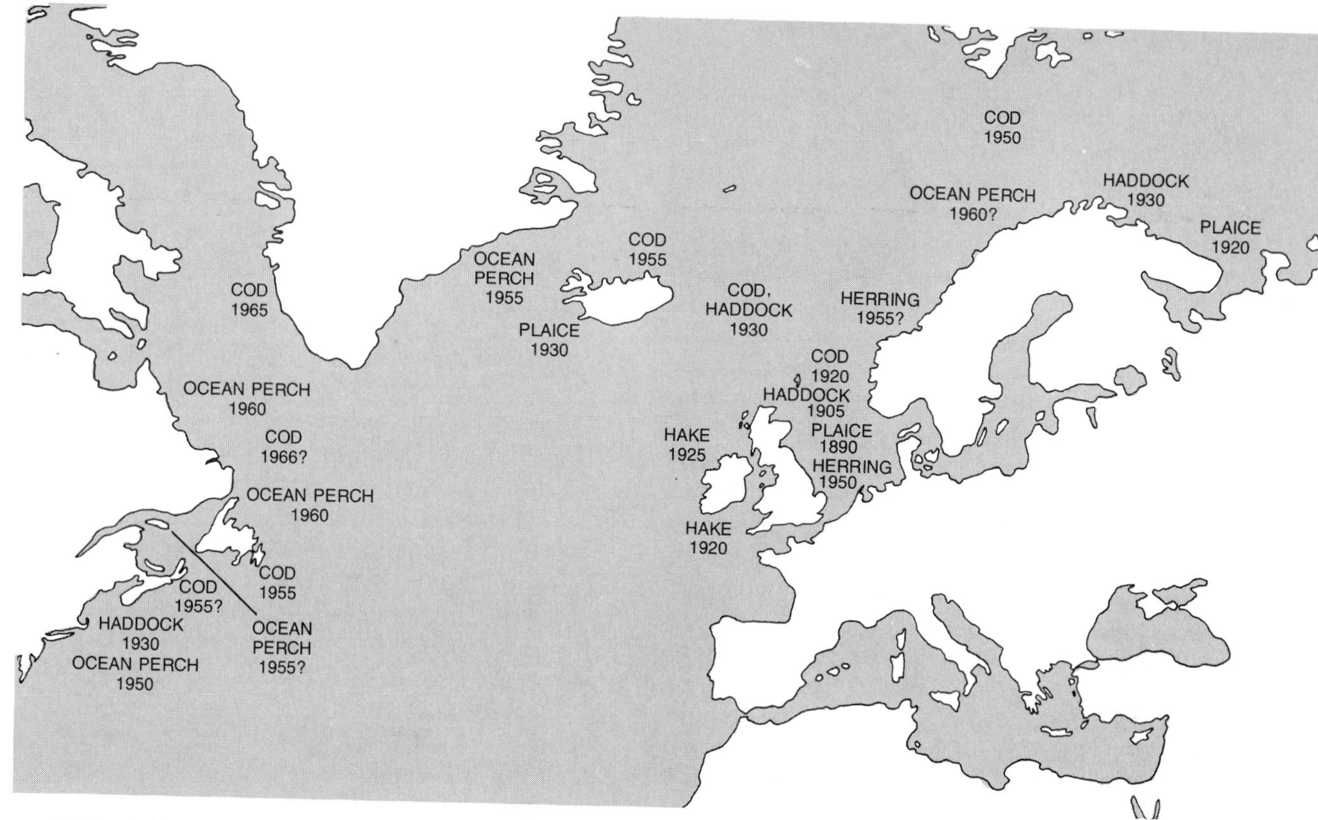

FIGURE 7-30

Overfishing in the North Atlantic and adjacent waters began in the 1890s in the North Sea, when further increases in fishing the plaice stock no longer produced an increase in the catch of that fish. By 1950 the same was true of North Sea cod, haddock, and herring; of cod, haddock, and plaice off the North Cape and in the Barents Sea; of plaice, haddock, and cod south and east of Iceland; and of ocean perch and haddock in the Gulf of Maine. Between 1956 and 1966 the same became true of ocean perch off Newfoundland and off Labrador, and cod west of Greenland. It may also be true of North Cape ocean perch and Labrador cod. (From S. J. Holt, The food resources of the ocean, *Scientific American,* Sept. 1969.

over a decade, Ecuador and Peru have claimed sovereignty over the ocean within 200 miles of their shores and have become increasingly tough in enforcing their claims. In 1975, the Ecuadorian government confiscated American tuna catches and even jailed the fishermen until their fines of $3 million were paid.

In the summer of 1973, Iceland and the United Kingdom seemed on the verge of war in their dispute over the North Atlantic cod fishery.[219] A settlement was negotiated, but proved to be short-lived; in late 1975 the argument flared up again. Iceland, heavily dependent on fishery exports for survival, in 1972 extended its territorial fishing jurisdiction to 50 miles from shore to protect the threatened cod fishery. In 1975, the limit was increased to 200 miles, and Iceland tried to persuade the United Kingdom to cut its codfish quota to barely half its 1974 catch. Meanwhile, Iceland had increased its fleet and begun fishing farther afield, including into North Sea herring. In December 1975, matters were so tense that Icelandic gunboats were patrolling; one was damaged in a collision, and a few weeks later it fired on a British ocean tug.[220] Ultimately, the U.K. agreed to a reduced codfish quota, and the dispute was settled—for the time being.

[219]Deborah Shapley, Science in the Great Cod War; *Time* and *Newsweek,* June 4, 1973; Ian Ashwell, The saga of the Cod War.

[220]*Time* magazine, The war for cod, December 29, 1975; *New Scientist,* Is the Cod War really a red herring?

Disputes can even arise within nations, it seems. In Cornwall, local day-fishermen, who still use poles and lines, have found their livelihoods threatened by large purse-seiners, which are wiping out the local mackerel population on which the day-fishermen depend.[221] Quotas were to be established from 1977 on, and the seiners were trying to push their 1975 and 1976 catches (on which quotas would be based) as high as possible. If the all-out fishing fails to destroy the stock, quotas set too high may later succeed. Judging from the fishing industry's past behavior toward the sea, one would suppose that if they were to go into the chicken-farming business, they would plan to eat up all the feed, all the eggs, all the chicks, and all the chickens simultaneously, while burning down the henhouses to keep themselves warm.

International fisheries management: too little too late? The list of fisheries conflicts keeps growing and will undoubtedly continue to do so until truly effective international regulation of the ocean commons becomes a reality. Just how and when this will be achieved cannot be predicted; it depends on the outcome of the Law of the Sea Conferences. (For more on these negotiations, see Chapter 15.)

Some progress has been made in that most major fishing nations now are aware that oceanic fisheries are endangered worldwide and that something must be done to protect these valuable resources if there is to be a significant harvest for future generations. There has been an increasing frequency of bilateral agreements between nations on fisheries management. A few regional international regulatory agencies have been established, such as the North West Atlantic and North East Atlantic fishery commissions (the latter has been involved in attempts to settle the Iceland-United Kingdom dispute, among others), and the General Fisheries Council for the Mediterranean. Although such commissions are gaining in strength, they still have no enforcement powers and must rely on individual nations to abide by decisions, agreements, and quotas. Like the United States, many nations have considered extending territorial limits to 200 miles, partly "in case" the Law of the Sea fails or is enacted too late to save major fish stocks, and partly to protect stocks already disappearing as other nations, not subscribing to regional commission regulations, "vacuum the sea."

[221]Michael Allaby, Cornwall's mackerel war.

As international regulation of fish resources becomes increasingly likely, the economic and national fishing interests have become more nervous and, evidently, more determined to get theirs while the getting is good. Japan, for instance, has figured that if all nations enforced 200-mile limits and excluded foreigners, Japanese fishing grounds (and yields) would be reduced by 45 percent. The jobs of half a million people employed in fishing (not including thousands employed in processing and canning) would be endangered, a major industry seriously damaged, and the diets of the Japanese people drastically changed. Even so, Japan has dropped its opposition to the 200-mile economic-zone policy (it is a major plank in Law of the Sea discussions and seems likely to be included), and apparently has resigned itself that international management of fish resources will be an inescapable part of the future.[222] But there has been no abatement of Japanese fishing activities so far. Once agreements are concluded and regulations established, Japan will probably be first in line applying for a large share of quotas and rights to fish in other nation's territories.

Aquaculture

What about "farming" the sea? Unfortunately, the impression that sea farming is here today or is just around the corner is illusory. For the most part, people still hunt the sea today or, in a relatively few cases, herd its animals (for example, oysters and a few kinds of fishes are herded). Indeed, the total annual world production from aquaculture of all kinds (salt, fresh, and brackish water) in the early 1970s was only about 5 million metric tons. This, however, amounted to half of all inland fisheries production. Moreover, the harvest from aquaculture supplies a substantial proportion of the fish and shellfish consumed in some nations—roughly 40 percent in China, 20 percent in Indonesia, and 6 percent in Japan.[223]

[222]Washington Post Service, Japanese fishermen fear "nightmare," Honolulu *Advertiser,* March 19, 1976.

[223]T. V. R. Pillay, The role of aquaculture in fishery development and management; FAO, *State of food and agriculture,* 1974.

Fish culture is a long-established practice in the Far East, where it is commonly integrated into the agricultural system in a closed-cycle resource chain. Farmers stock flooded rice fields with small fishes, whose wastes help fertilize the rice. The fishes feed on mosquito larvae and other aquatic pests, reducing the need for pesticides. When the fields are drained, fishes and rice are harvested together, and some of the fishes are saved for restocking in the next rice season.[224]

Not all present schemes for fish-farming are so frugal with nutrient resources, however. Fish have been raised in enclosures in the Po River estuary of Italy since Roman times, but today those fish are fed Peruvian anchovetas.[225] Similarly, many of the expanding aquacultural operations in the United States have concentrated on producing luxury seafoods such as lobster, shrimp, catfish, and salmon, largely by feeding them cheaper foods. Some of the fish farms and hatcheries run by American agribusiness corporations are located in poor Latin American countries, but the products are marketed in the United States.[226] This obviously contributes nothing to the food needs of those countries (although it may provide jobs and foreign exchange).

Not all American fish-farming attempts require extra resource inputs to support them, however. One small company in Chicago raises fishes in tanks on vegetable-produce wastes obtained from supermarkets; some others more nearly parallel the integrated systems of Asia, combining crops, bacteria, algae, and fish.[227]

Marine biologist John Ryther at Woods Hole Marine Laboratory has been experimenting with a project raising clams and mussels on algae grown on sewage sludge. Effluents from the shellfish also nourish sea worms and a sea plant called Irish moss. The sea worms are fed to flounder in separate tanks, and the Irish moss supports a colony of abalone. The cleaned-up municipal water can also be used again.[228] Similar experiments producing carp have also been carried out in Britain and some European countries with considerable success.[229] Such projects do present problems, of course: notably the possible transmission of diseases from the sewage to consumers of the shellfish, and the potential build-up of heavy metals from municipal wastes in the food chain (see Chapter 11); but these problems appear to be surmountable.[230]

Fish-farming may within a few years make a significant contribution to American diets. People in the business anticipate that the share from fish-farms of total U.S. seafood consumption may rise from 5 percent in 1974 to 15 percent in 1982.[231]

A more important question about aquaculture is whether and how much it potentially could enrich the scanty diets of the world's poor people. The answer depends on how effectively aquacultural technology can be introduced and utilized by the farmers, whether suitable water areas can be opened up without conflicting with land agriculture for resources (fertilizer, energy, etc.), and whether sufficient funds can be found for research and development. There is no question that, if established, aquaculture could produce high-quality protein at little cost for local consumption in many poor countries.

In Asia, where pond or rice-paddy fish-culture is part of tradition, expanding operations should be fairly easy if farmers are encouraged and provided with fry for stocking and markets for the fish produced. Indeed, pond-culture is now very widespread in China and is quickly becoming so in the Philippines, South Korea, and Indonesia. In Africa and Latin America, where no such tradition exists and the fishes themselves, as well as the technology, are unfamiliar, establishment of aquaculture may be somewhat more difficult.

But the potential exists, especially in regions where there are lakes, marshes, and ponds, all of which are naturally productive sites biologically. Fish-ponding can be carried on in combination with raising ducks or rice and other crops. (Of course, increased use of pesticides on crops may threaten such enterprises, although the fishes can contribute to pest control.) In Asia, duck- or livestock-fertilized ponds yield up to 2000 or 2500

[224]George Reiger, Aquaculture: Has it been oversold?
[225]Ibid.
[226]Liz R. Gallese, Aquatic harvest.
[227]Ibid.
[228]Reiger, Aquaculture.
[229]Reg Noble, Growing fish in sewage. See also the letter in response by Ron Edwards, *New Scientist*, August 14, 1975, p. 396.

[230]For a detailed study of aquaculture technology to date, see J. E. Bardach et al., *Aquaculture: The farming and husbandry of freshwater and marine organisms.*
[231]Gallese, Aquatic harvest.

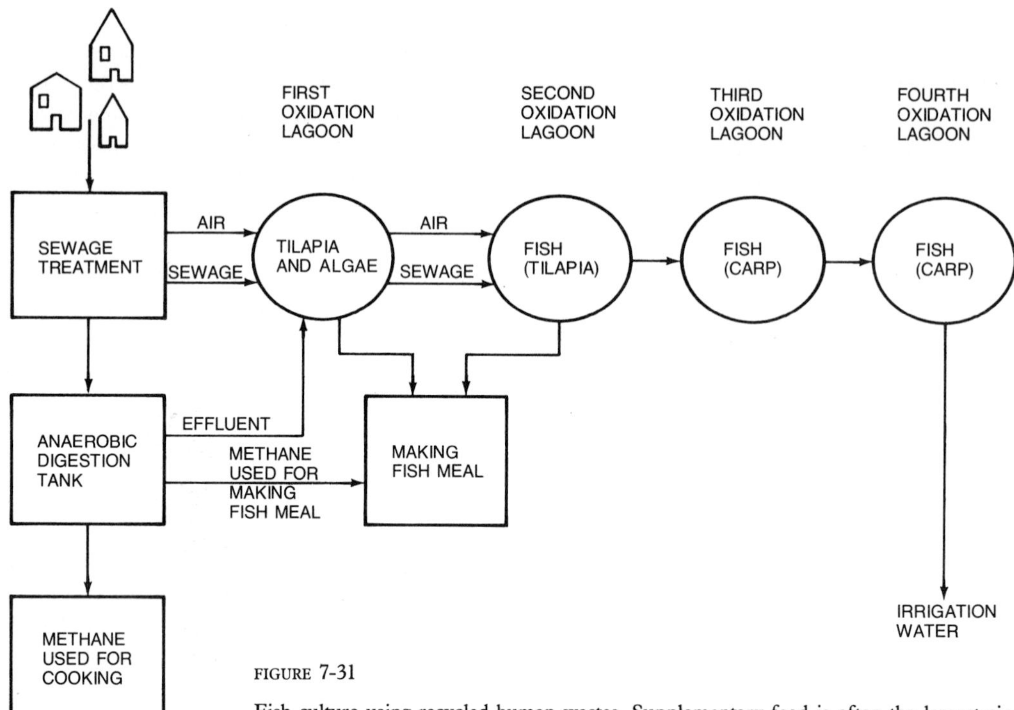

FIGURE 7-31

Fish culture using recycled human wastes. Supplementary feed is often the largest single operating expense in fish farming. Using sewage effluents avoids this cost and helps solve a sanitary problem as well. In this arrangement, air and treated sewage effluent pass through two oxidation lagoons where tilapia (or other rough fish) are grown. Such fish grow and reproduce rapidly and are harvested at a maximum sustained yield. Some of the tilapia is made into fish meal, using methane gas produced by anaerobic digestion of the sewage. The cleaner water passing through the third and fourth lagoons supports carp. After that it is used for irrigation. In an agricultural setting livestock wastes could be added to the effluent, and some of both the human and livestock effluents could be used to fertilize the land. (After *Ceres,* Food and Agriculture Organization, vol. 8, no. 3 (May/June 1975), p. 67.)

kilograms of fishes per hectare of water surface per year. (By contrast, the same land before flooding produced 11 kilograms of beef per hectare per year.[232]) Such projects generally use tilapia (mouth-breeding cichlid fishes) or carp. Figure 7-31 diagrams a fairly elaborate closed-cycle fish-culture scheme for raising both tilapia and carp by using sewage as fertilizer and producing methane gas as a by-product.

In 1967, the President's Science Advisory Committee postulated that a yield of some 15 million tons from pond-culture alone was possible by the year 2000.[233] More recent estimates by the FAO indicate that yields from all inland waters, including at least half from aquaculture, may reach 17 million metric tons by 1980, and that (if the necessary research and development are carried out, and increasing pollution does not defeat the effort) inland fisheries production worldwide could rise to 50 million metric tons by the end of the century. This would be a fairly impressive achievement, even though such a harvest would remain trivial compared to total world food needs (which by 2000 may include more than 2 billion metric tons of grain annually). Its value primarily would be as a source of crucially needed high-quality protein in many less developed regions. Again, it must be emphasized that this can be achieved

[232]H. L. Morales, The Blue Revolution; Ian Payne, Tilapia: A fish of culture.

[233]PSAC, *The world food problem,* vol. 2.

only if the requisite investments in research, development, and rural assistance to LDCs materialize.

Besides freshwater resources, brackish and saltwater lagoons and estuaries (also naturally abundantly productive) offer opportunities for aquaculture, although farming the open sea (mariculture) presents some formidable problems. The Japanese now "farm" the young of salmon, then release them to the ocean, from which they later return to spawn.[234] There are several "fish-farming" salmon projects in the United States, as well, but they are relatively new.[235] Expansion of such enterprises is possible, but may, like inland aquaculture, be limited by growing pollution of inshore waters, as well as by outright destruction of estuaries, drainage of swamps and marshes, and the like.

Apart from shellfish, crustaceans, and finfish, ocean waters produce aquatic plants, which are also potentially nutritious. These are not much exploited by the human population, except in Japan, where seaweed is cultured, sometimes in combination with fish-farming. Farming the seas' plant life would not be easy—just consider the difficulty of fertilizing and harvesting, for instance. Nonetheless, if the sea is emptied of its fishes and shellfishes by thoughtless human exploitation and pollution, perhaps some kind of phytoplankton (tiny marine plants) farming could be attempted (if the sea is not by then too badly poisoned by pollution). The crop would probably be relatively costly and not very tasty, but in desperation humanity might give it a try. For the immediate future, however, sea-farming of oceanic plants (unlike fish-culture) offers no hope at all of substantially affecting the world food problem.

Food from the Sea: The Outlook

The prospects of increasing the yield of food from the sea to support human life are decidedly not bright. Humanity apparently is very close to the limits of what can be harvested by methods now employed. Already, for example, in the North Sea "natural deaths are the exception among fishes of usable sizes."[236] Because of the predominance of the relatively sterile open ocean, the seas, which make up 70 percent of the planetary surface, account for only about a third of global net primary productivity (NPP). What potential there is for increasing the human food supply lies mainly on the 30 percent of Earth's surface that is land—where at least theoretical limits to productivity are somewhat more distant.

Indeed, far from being the answer to the food problem, the seas may not even be able to continue supporting the modest yield now being extracted from them. The setbacks of the early 1970s may have been the beginning of a long downward trend, even in the face of intensified fishing activity. Plans for increasing the yield from the sea generally have disregarded the effects of pollution on marine populations, especially those that are dependent on bays and estuaries for at least part of their life cycles. Unfortunately, even though some progress has been made toward protecting these ecosystems in developed countries, increasing use of farm chemicals (let alone growth of industrial effluents) in less developed countries by itself essentially guarantees a rise in oceanic pollution in coming decades. And the likely result will be reductions in the sizes of many fish populations.

Furthermore, expectations of higher fisheries yields have been based on the premise that fish stocks will be harvested rationally, but the history of fisheries so far gives little hope that rationality will prevail. Simultaneous attempts to harvest young and old of the same species, as well as both large species and the smaller species that the large ones eat to live, can be expected to continue, unless some kind of control can be imposed on the oceanic commons.

It is quite likely that the question of whether humanity will obtain a reasonable harvest from the sea and inland waters (equal to or better than that of 1971) at the end of this century will have been decided by the mid-1980s. Prompt establishment of a strong, effective Law of the Sea compact, or some other mechanism to protect oceanic and freshwater resources from environmental destruction and overexploitation, would allow humanity to continue enjoying their fruits. But if such cooperative management efforts are postponed into the 1980s, it may be too late—there may be precious little left to protect and conserve. And recovery, if it occurred at all, in many cases could take a very long time.

[234]Reiger, Aquaculture.
[235]Gallese, Aquatic harvest.
[236]Ricker, Food from the sea.

NEW AND UNCONVENTIONAL FOOD SOURCES

Efforts to increase food supplies for the growing human population in the next several decades will undoubtedly rest mainly on expanding supplies of traditional foods (albeit perhaps high-yielding versions) grown on presently cultivated land. There are nevertheless possibilities of enriching the diets of the poor or of making food-production systems more efficient by the use of unconventional foods. Such foods have sometimes been heralded in the popular press as "solutions" to the food problem, or at least as a means of filling the "protein gap." Such overstatements notwithstanding, some of these ideas (aquaculture, for example), if supported by research, development, and distribution, could make important contributions to human nutrition in some regions.

Protein Supplements

Some of the most unusual and most technologically sophisticated proposals have been in the realm of protein supplements.[237] Although totally "synthetic" food—a term occasionally still heard—has no reality (if it could be done, it would be far too costly in both money and energy to be useful), certain processed-food novelties do have potential as protein supplements.

Single-cell protein. Protein-rich material can be produced by culturing single-celled organisms on petroleum byproducts, sewage sludge, or other substrates. In theory, some of the protein deficit in LDCs could be made up with protein from such sources in the last two decades of this century. Knowledgeable people think it conceivable that such single-cell protein (SCP) could be made sufficiently pure for human consumption by 1980, although whether the purification costs would make it uneconomical is another question.[238]

Although it will be many years before SCP suitable for human food will be available, it already is beginning to make an indirect contribution as animal feed, especially in Europe and the USSR. It can, for instance, replace feeds such as corn, soybeans, and oilseed cakes, which alternatively can be fed to people. Obviously, SCP from petroleum hydrocarbons will be available only as long as supplies of petroleum last and are not prohibitively expensive. However, since the substrates usually are waste byproducts, SCP may have a role to fill temporarily, if all the technical, social, and economic problems can be worked out and if it can be produced without too great an energy subsidy.

Perhaps most difficult of all, people would have to be convinced that SCP is food. As has been mentioned before, people tend to be extremely conservative in their food habits.[239] The hungriest people are precisely those who recognize the fewest items as food because they have always existed on a diet of limited variety. Even though most Americans are used to an extremely varied diet, many would choose to starve to death rather than eat grasshoppers or snakes—which are perfectly nutritious, but are not generally acceptable as food in our culture.

A related project is the development of a protein supplement from algae grown especially for this purpose. A West German company is experimenting with a powder form that can be added to milk or other foods to raise protein content. It appears to have been beneficial in treating children with kwashiorkor and as a supplement for mothers on inadequate diets. It is expected that the product eventually can be made as cheaply as soy protein.[240] Unfortunately, the algal supplement suffers from many of the same drawbacks as SCP—particularly that of acceptability.

A high-quality protein and vitamin-rich concentrated food familiar to American health-food buffs is brewer's yeast, which also can be produced quite cheaply. However, it has not been seriously promoted as a food supplement, presumably because it is thought that the strong flavor might not be widely acceptable.

Perhaps the greatest disadvantages of these exotic proposals are that, because they involve fairly sophisticated manufacturing processes, they consume more

[237]For an overview of such proposals, see J. K. Loosli, New sources of protein for human and animal feeding.

[238]N. W. Pirie, *Food resources: Conventional and novel;* and Single-cell protein isn't chickenfeed; *New Scientist,* Single-cell protein comes of age.

[239]De Garine, Food is not just something to eat; McKenzie, Nutrition and the soft sell.

[240]Germans tap Third World's algal garden, *New Scientist,* January 16, 1975, p. 135.

energy (non-solar) than raising crops, and they are relatively expensive. The people who need them most are the least able to afford them. In addition, these products must be transported and distributed to the consumers, unlike foods they could grow themselves or obtain locally.[241]

Producing SCP from agricultural wastes by new, simple techniques may be a more practical approach for less developed countries. The product is a concentrated feed-supplement for pigs and poultry, and could be produced at the village level with a minimal energy input.[242] Even so, it might be more useful and efficient to use agricultural wastes as compost and fertilizer instead.

Research comparing the efficiencies (measured by total food produced and its nutritional value relative to energy and other inputs) of such alternative strategies is badly needed, but so far little has been done. Part of the difficulty is that one approach might for various reasons be suitable for one area, but not for another. For example, the reasons could be physical (soil, climate, amount of rainfall, etc.) or economic or social (costs of fertilizer, availability of farm labor, local food habits, or social organization).

Water hyacinths, FPC, leaf protein, and other ideas. Still other unorthodox sources of protein supplementation have been proposed, some of which are under preliminary investigation. One of the more interesting is the idea of converting water hyacinths and other aquatic weeds to cattle feed. But, although water hyacinths are abundant in the tropics (and pestiferous—they clog waterways) and contain protein that is high in the essential amino acid lysine (commonly lacking in cereals), their dry weight is only 5 percent of their wet weight, which presents a tremendous obstacle even to processing them into cattle feed. An attempt to herd manatees (walruslike animals), which eat the hyacinths, has proven unsuccessful.

Much has been written about fish-protein concentrate (FPC) as a valuable protein source.[243] It may help, but it is no panacea. Its chief advantage is that it might exploit fish stocks that are largely unexploited at present; but the corollary disadvantage is that these often supply food for stocks that are being fished. FPC harvesting is subject to all the problems of fishing in general, and the processing is relatively complex and demands an expensive factory. It also seems to be more costly, at least at the present stage of development, than protein concentrates from other sources. Finally, the acceptability of FPC presents the same problems that exist for SCP and other novel foods.

Leaf-protein extracts also present the same social and economic drawbacks that affect SCP and FPC. A technical difficulty is the extraction of the protein concentrate from the fiber content of the leaves, but this has been done successfully in small-scale projects and presumably could be done on a wider scale if the appropriate equipment were available to farmers.[244] The leaves of forage crops such as alfalfa and sorghum produce large proportions of high-quality protein. Alfalfa yields as much as 2,400 pounds of protein per acre—more than twice as much as soybeans. It has been estimated that, in an area equivalent to about 7 percent of all the land now under cultivation, enough alfalfa could be raised to provide the minimum protein needs of the world's population in 1970. The fibrous residue can be used as fodder for ruminant animals such as cattle, and the protein extract and other fractions can be fed to pigs and poultry, used as fertilizer, or made into a protein supplement for human consumption. Moreover, forages can be grown on soils too poor or hilly to support food grains. The advantages of leaf-protein appear to justify a reasonably large effort to develop it. But, even with substantial investment in research and development, it obviously will be many years before production can reach the point where it makes a significant contribution to the world food supply.

Still other ideas have been circulated, among which are making cattle-feed from wood and culturing algae in the fecal slime of sewage-treatment plants. The growing pressure for other needs on the world's forests (Chapter 6) makes the practicality of using them to feed cattle seem remote, to say the least. And the reaction of people in LDCs (or DCs for that matter) to proposals to feed them protein grown on sewage can well be imagined (although

---

[241] Colin Tudge, Why turn waste into protein?

[242] F. Imrie, Single-cell protein from agricultural wastes.

[243] J. E. Ramsey, FPC. See also N. W. Pirie, *Food resources;* and Orthodox and unorthodox methods of meeting world food needs.

[244] N. W. Pirie, Leaf protein as human food; Walter J. Bray, Green crop fractionation.

such algae would have some value as feed for livestock or fish-culture).

It is important, of course, to press ahead with the development of the most promising novel foods and to find ways of making them acceptable to diverse peoples. But it is reasonably clear that few of them will be major factors in the world food picture during the critical decade or two ahead. If the problems can be worked out, the most ecologically, economically, nutritionally, and aesthetically desirable of these processes eventually may be integrated into normal food supplies. Some may make their contributions indirectly as livestock feeds. Substituting SCP or leaf protein for foods acceptable to most people (such as soybeans and peanut meal) would release those foods for human consumption without reducing meat consumption by those who can afford it (and who seem less than eager to give it up).

New food combinations. The presscakes that remain after oil is squeezed out of soybeans, cottonseed, peanuts, and sesame seeds may be the most readily accessible, untapped source of protein for human consumption. Until recently, most presscakes were used as livestock feed or fertilizer; the rest were wasted. In DCs this situation is changing; as meat prices have risen, so have demand for and acceptance of soy products among consumers.[245]

Special foods have been created from conventional ones in some less developed countries by combining oilseed protein concentrates with cereals and sometimes with milk. The best known of these is *Incaparina,* developed by INCAP (Institute of Nutrition for Central America and Panama). It is a mixture of corn and cottonseed meal, enriched with vitamins *A* and *B.* Another product is CSM formula (corn, soya, milk), a mixture of 70 percent processed corn, 25 percent soy-protein concentrate, and 5 percent milk solids. A third is Vita-Soy, a high-protein soy-based beverage that has been marketed very successfully in Hong Kong. Another product using peanut meal and soy is being distributed in India to children, and a bun fortified with milk solids has been given to schoolchildren in the Philippines.[246]

[245]R. Leslie and A. Sutton, Why soya?

[246]Brown and Eckholm, By bread alone.

These and all similar products should be viewed more as future hopes than as current cures. As valuable protein and vitamin supplements, they hold considerable promise, but the economics of their production and distribution are not well worked out. In general, they seem best suited to urban areas, where distribution is less of a problem. They could be provided to children in schools and nurseries, for instance, and to pregnant and nursing mothers at health clinics. More important, the question of general acceptability remains open. Incaparina has been available in Central America for more than a decade, but its impact remains insignificant, in spite of determined efforts by private and commercial organizations to push its acceptance, and in spite of tremendous worldwide publicity. In 1973, the Quaker Oats Company gave up producing it. Other products seem to have been more successful, however, especially those in Asia.

A commonly wasted "by-product" of food processing is whey,[247] the residue from cheesemaking. In 1975, although some whey was being used as animal feed and was beginning to find other uses, a great deal of it was still discarded, to become a serious pollutant in rivers and streams. Within a few years, whey's usefulness as a protein, vitamin, and mineral supplement (in place of milk, for instance, in some products), as fertilizer, as a binding agent in pills, and as a livestock feed supplement, will probably end the pollution problems. There have even been successful attempts to make wine out of it! A product combining whey with soy milk is being tested in Latin America as a weaning food for babies.[248]

Increasing the Efficiency of Agriculture

Although novel foods may make at best a modest, and often only indirect, contribution to the human food budget in the next several decades, an avenue more likely to make a significant difference is that of improving the quality of traditional foods, while increasing their production. This approach minimizes acceptance problems and generally also involves the introduction of less elaborate and energy-consumptive new technologies.

[247]David Gumpert, Whey market grows fast . . . , *Wall Street Journal,* May 28, 1975.

[248]Brown and Eckholm, *By bread alone.*

Some of the more interesting agricultural research now underway is that being done on improvement of traditional staple crops.[249]

Crops: beyond HYVs. One of the goals of this research is to improve the protein quality of grains—that is, produce grains containing a better balance of the amino acids essential for human nutrition. This, of course, can be done fairly cheaply by enriching flour with processed amino acids (usually lysine, tryptophan, and methionine). Lysine-enriched wheat, for instance, has been shown to be beneficial both to laboratory rats and to human babies under carefully controlled conditions. Like other processed food supplements, however, such a solution may be of little use to the world's poorest and hungriest people, most of whom are subsistence farmers or farm laborers and purchase little or none of their food in markets. Even if they did, fortified grain or flour might be sufficiently more expensive than the ordinary kind to be out of their reach.[250]

An alternative to fortified grain is to breed new varieties with more complete protein balances or other desired characteristics. Increasing protein content or improving its quality in cereal strains can be achieved, but unfortunately such strains usually have higher energy and nitrogen requirements than those with standard protein content. Thus protein gains may be made at some cost in yield and/or significantly higher requirements for nitrogen fertilizer, either of which might make these strains economically unattractive to farmers.[250a] Such breeding programs in general take a good deal of time, but in the long run, successful ones may substantially contribute to the improvement of human diets. Some have already shown promise.

Using a naturally occurring mutant strain (known as Opaque-2 because the kernels are opaque), plant breeders have developed a strain of corn (maize) with digestible protein levels twice as high as those of ordinary corn and with adequate proportions of lysine and tryptophan. Opaque-2 corn has been shown to be nutritionally far superior in tests with farm animals and, subsequently, with malnourished Latin American children. But homozygous Opaque-2's softer, lighter kernels resulted in reduced yields, greater susceptibility to pests, and different milling characteristics. By interbreeding Opaque-2 with traditional strains, scientists at CIMMYT in Mexico have produced several new, improved-protein strains suitable for various climatic conditions. These were being field-tested around the world by 1976, and most appeared to yield as well as or better than traditional strains, and to retain both the traditional milling traits and the high-quality protein. The last major hurdle, if performance continues to fulfill its early promise, is to distribute seed to the farmers and the harvested grain to those who need it.[251]

A similar program is in progress to improve the quality of sorghum, which is the fourth most important grain in human diets, widely consumed in Asia and Africa, especially by the poor. Two strains of high-protein sorghum have been found in Ethiopia and are now the basis of a breeding program to develop a pest-resistant, high-yield variety. Such protein-improved corn, sorghum, and other cereals (if they are developed) no doubt can make important contributions to diet improvement among the poor, who subsist mainly on such foods.

Nutritionally speaking, though, one can question the wisdom of thereby encouraging large numbers of people to become even more dependent on a single food and further restricting the variety of foods eaten. Even if improved maize could be shown to provide an adequate supply of all known required nutrients (it does not), what of others that may exist, but are not yet discovered? And what if the local monoculture is wiped out by a drought or pest outbreak, as in the Irish potato famine?

Biologists are concerned about another possible pitfall to such improved crops. If they provide a nutritionally nearly complete food for people, they would also nourish pests very well. This is certainly true for rodent pests. Not enough is known about insect nutrition to say whether this applies to them as well, but the possibility clearly exists (see Chapter 4). Such hazards, of course, can be dealt with or avoided, and the benefits of developing and disseminating these new grains may

[249] P. S. Carlson and J. C. Polacco, Plant cell culture: Genetic aspects of crop improvement.

[250] Loosli, New sources of protein.

[250a] C. R. Bhatia and R. Rabson, Bioenergetic considerations in cereal breeding for protein improvement.

[251] Tony Wolff, Maize; "Super grain" of the future?

outweigh them. But it nevertheless seems wiser to us to encourage more production of pulses and other foods to supplement a grain-based diet than to try to make grains into an all-purpose food.

One of the more interesting developments in agricultural research is the cross-breeding of wheat and rye to produce a completely new grain called *triticale*, which gives promise of incorporating the best characteristics of each parent species. Among these characteristics are: (from wheat) high yield and high protein content for a cereal, and (from rye) higher proportion of lysine, ruggedness, resistance to disease, and adaptability to unfavorable climates and soils. In some respects, triticale may even outperform both parents. For instance, some strains rival the miracle wheats in yields.[252] In the mid-1970s, triticale was still being field-tested, but it is likely that, if a stable, fertile seed is developed, it will be widely grown by 1985.

Research is proceeding on developing for grains a nitrogen-fixing capacity, like that in the roots of legumes. The hope is that, if the procedure is successful, the need for nitrogen-containing fertilizers would be greatly reduced and protein content of crops might be boosted.[253] Nitrogen fertilizer manufacture consumes very large amounts of fossil fuel; on the farm it is often the single largest element of energy input.

Some preliminary research in which corn has been innoculated with a nitrogen-fixing bacterium, *Spirillum lipoferum*, is underway, but it is too early to know whether this approach will be fruitful.[254] Preliminary research also indicates that some species of *Rhizobium*, the bacterial genus that fixes nitrogen in symbiotic association with legumes, may be transferable to nonleguminous crops.[255] Another possibility is to induce the nitrogen-fixing ability in the crops themselves by selective breeding or cell-culture manipulation.[256] Or presently inept microorganisms may be given genes for nitrogen fixation by such genetic-engineering techniques (see Chapter 14).

[252]J. H. Hulse and D. Spurgeon, Triticale.

[253]R. W. F. Hardy and U. D. Havelka, Nitrogen-fixation research: A key to world food? See also J. J. Child, New developments in nitrogen fixation research.

[254]Nitrogen fixation in maize, *Science*.

[255]Research in agriculture produces encouraging results, *BioScience*, vol. 26, no. 1, p. 68.

[256]Hardy and Havelka, Nitrogen-fixation.

Cell-culturing also appears to be a means whereby botanists may produce new kinds of crops. Plants that cannot be cross-fertilized might be genetically combined or specific mutations introduced into a strain by cell culture. Desired genotypes also can be screened out in early stages and rapidly propagated by cloning—a procedure now commonly used in research on several crops.[257]

Research on nitrogen fixation and most potential applications for cell-culture technique is still in the early stages, and results are not yet predictable. The possibilities are exciting, however, and the research efforts clearly deserve support and encouragement. The same can be said of attempts to increase the photosynthetic efficiency of crops, another line of investigation just getting underway.[258]

Most of these unorthodox lines of research on crops are unlikely to pay practical dividends before the end of the century, unfortunately, which is no comfort for the hungry millions of today. The exceptions are triticale and improved-protein corn, which are in relatively advanced stages of development. But the built-in momentum to population growth guarantees that the "food problem" will not go away; hence long-term development projects are every bit as essential as those projects that will help augment food supplies within a few years.

One of the most encouraging trends in agricultural research is a renewed interest in, and appreciation for, what could best be called "ecological agriculture." Organic farmers in the United States and parts of Europe—long regarded as a lunatic fringe by the agricultural establishment—have stuck by this approach since the chemical age first reached the farm. Now agronomists are learning from their ideas and borrowing traditional, basically ecological techniques from peasants around the world.

Thus, the IRRI found a traditional "floating rice," crossed it with a dwarf, and created a high-yield floating rice that can survive productively in the frequent monsoon floods of India, Bangladesh, and Southeast Asia.[259]

[257]Carlson and Polacco, Plant cell culture; Jeremy Burgess, Towards novel plants.

[258]Israel Zelitch, Improving the efficiency of photosynthesis.

[259]Juan L. Mercado, High-yield, floating rice may help countries where food shortages are greatest.

And it has been discovered that paddy-rice yields can be enhanced by 50 to 100 percent when grown with a water fern *(Azolla)* that carries a symbiotic nitrogen-fixing alga *(Anabaena)*.[260] How to maintain the fragile water fern during the summer was once a closely guarded secret in two North Vietnamese villages; now the secret is out, and all Southeast Asia may benefit from higher rice yields without dependence on imported fertilizers.

These are only examples of innovations that can bring improvement in food supplies with relatively small changes and little social disruption. Aquaculture is another example in areas where some kind of fishing is part of the tradition. So are the varieties of intercropping and multiple-cropping that are being experimented with in many tropical and subtropical regions. The ecological approach produces less dramatically impressive increases than a switch from traditional to "miracle grains," but if widely adopted it could prove, when all the benefits are added up, to be a major contributor to future increases in the harvest. Indeed, as other chapters will explain, *failure* to adopt ecologically sound agricultural practices may foredoom other efforts to expand and maintain the food supply.

New sources of animal protein. Opportunities for making more efficient use of food resources also exist in animal husbandry, besides using animals that are productive on pasture and range and do not require feed-grains. It has been proposed, for example, that herding native antelope species in tropical Africa might prove more productive than herding cattle and would avoid several problems, especially that of the tsetse-borne cattle disease, *nagana.* The indigenous antelopes are naturally resistant to nagana, for instance, and they are well-adapted to exploitation of the local vegetation, which is often inadequate for cattle.

A recent study in the Serengeti Plains described an ecological association among migrating wildebeests and Thomson's gazelles and the grasslands on which they feed.[261] The huge herd of wildebeest appears to devastate the forage as it passes through. But, in actuality, the grazing seems to prevent senescence of the plants and to stimulate rapid new growth and increased productivity. When the gazelles arrive at the beginning of the dry season, a month after the wildebeests' passage, they graze the luxuriant new growth in preference to the dried-out old grass missed by the wildebeests. Such natural systems, if they are studied and knowledgeably exploited, rather than destroyed by imposing agricultural systems developed in other settings, probably could be adapted to support large numbers of human beings.

Some early experiments with antelope herding have indicated that several species can be successfully tamed and that many of them are much more productive, especially in the dryer areas, than cattle are. In addition, their grazing (or browsing) seems to be far less environmentally damaging. The oryx, particularly, may prove to be a superior animal for such dry areas as the Sahel, where overgrazing around wellheads by cattle and goats contributed heavily to the recent six-year famine. Oryx can survive on about one-tenth as much water as cattle, and will eat plants that cattle will not eat.[262]

Another promising animal is the eland (which we can attest produces very tasty meat). Because it is a browser rather than a grazer, eland can be fed on the same pasture with cattle without competing for the same food resources. Thus a given area's productivity of meat could be increased by a considerable amount.[263]

Although herding native antelopes instead of cattle might substantially improve meat yields from African plains, it may be practical only where cattle herding is not already practiced. Many African herders base their culture on an extraordinarily intricate relationship with their cattle. Their economy, their social structure, indeed, their entire lives revolve around their animals.[264] These groups might not take kindly to antelope herding.

An interest in indigenous meat animals has led to efforts to domesticate the North American buffalo (bison). Unfortunately, the once vast herds were nearly destroyed in the last century—a classic case of overexploitation. Interbreeding buffalo with cattle has also been attempted, but with little success until recently. In the 1960s, a California rancher succeeded in producing a

[260]Arthur W. Galston, The water fern-rice connection.
[261]S. J. McNaughton, Serengeti migratory wildebeest: Facilitation of energy flow by grazing.

[262]Andrew Jaffe, Ranching on the wild side.
[263]Ibid.
[264]R. Dyson-Hudson and N. Dyson-Hudson, Subsistance herding in Uganda.

fertile hybrid, which has been called *beefalo*.[265] Beefalo reportedly is very tasty and is leaner and more productive (faster-growing and requiring no grain feed) than beef, and the animals are hardier and easier to raise than cattle. If the public accepted it, beefalo could cause a minor revolution in American meat-eating habits and in the meat industry, with significant benefits to health, pocketbooks, and the world food situation. At the very least, beefalo could be an attractive alternative to beef, pork, and lamb.

Although the danger of losing genetic resources in crop plants has become fairly well recognized in recent years, little attention has been given to the same problem with domestic animals. There are numerous varieties of cattle, sheep, goats, and chickens that have become genetically adapted to different environments. But as with crops, modern (Western) animal husbandry tends to reduce stocks to one or two supposedly superior varieties. In the United States, for instance, the cattle industry is heavily based on Herefords and shorthorns for meat and Holsteins, Jerseys, and Guernseys for dairying.

In Britain, by contrast, there are some 60 varieties of sheep (the principal domestic animal). Many of these, even though domesticated, have in effect evolved for centuries in response to their local surroundings, including the climate, the soils, and especially the vegetation on which they feed.[266] Often a locally developed breed of sheep can be productive in a locale where introduction of other varieties has failed. Replacement of rare breeds with more conventional varieties may, especially in the harsher environments, create problems for farmers and even result in lower productivity.

Moreover, these indigenous varieties with their often special characteristics represent an invaluable pool of genetic variability for any future livestock-breeding programs. Their disappearance would be a permanent loss for humanity, like the loss of indigenous varieties of wheat, corn, or rice. And a large livestock monoculture, like a crop monoculture, has a built-in susceptibility to pests and disease epidemics.

In Britain there is now a movement to protect rare breeds of livestock. Elsewhere, although endangered wildlife is increasingly being protected, rare domestic breeds of animals are not. The United States seems to have few such breeds—partly because it was settled relatively recently and only a few breeds quickly became established—but it could join England in encouraging their preservation in long-established traditional societies. A given breed may seem to have no special value, but who knows when a change in climate, social customs, or the economics of feeding might make a particular characteristic of an obscure sheep, alpaca, or cow suddenly very valuable indeed?

[265]Carole Agus, When you say beefalo, mister, smile, *Newsday*. Reprinted in the San Francisco *Examiner and Chronicle*, October 5, 1975.
[266]G. L. H. Alderson, The value of rare breeds.

SHOULD WE BE PESSIMISTIC?

The world food situation during the mid-1970s was very precarious, mainly because reserves were so low and harvests failed to meet "normal" expectations in many areas. The outlook for achieving greater food security by the 1980s is not particularly bright, despite unquestionably great potential for increasing food production worldwide. This potential is greatest in less developed countries, but the obstacles to realizing it there are also very great. Their rapid population growth simultaneously makes expanding the food supply imperative and hinders progress toward it. The rich countries have more than enough food, and their needs for more are growing relatively slowly; even so, their capacity for expanding production may be approaching limits.

As must be apparent by now, we tend not to share the enthusiasm of many for some of the proposed "solutions" to the world food problem. Serious constraints and difficulties lie in the path of even the most practical general solution, that of increasing yields on land already under cultivation. Recent efforts have concentrated on the food-short LDCs; but agricultural programs such as the Green Revolution have usually been carried out with too little consideration for either their ecological or their social consequences. This neglect may have manifested itself as a contributing factor in the slackening spread of Green Revolution technology and the faltering food-production record of the 1970s. Regardless of whether this is so, it is clear that continued neglect of these vital factors could sooner or later effectively sabotage efforts to raise world food production.

Despite the hazards and difficulties, there is of course no choice but to push on with the most feasible agricultural programs. Among other things, some badly needed time might be bought to start bringing the population explosion to a halt. It is certainly evident that no conceivable increase in the food supply can keep up with current population growth rates indefinitely. In 1967 the Report of the President's Science Advisory Committee's Panel on the *World Food Problem* stated: "The solution to the problem that will exist after about 1985 *demands* that programs of population control be initiated now."[267] We emphatically agreed then, and the situation is even more urgent today.

But population growth is by no means the only factor that will influence whether or not the human population's food needs can be met during the rest of this century and beyond. The food problem cannot be solved—or even intelligently discussed—without consideration of resource (water, energy, etc.) constraints, land-use and tenure policies, environmental constraints, economics, social and cultural settings, and so forth. (Many of these interrelated problems are described in other chapters.)

For increasing food production, however, the key questions for the next decade or so seem to be:

1. Will the weather be favorable?
2. Can the Green Revolution begun in LDCs be expanded and converted into a real revolution in spite of the substantial problems associated with its achievement?
3. Will the ecological costs of the Green Revolution, especially the decay of genetic variability, prove too high?
4. Will environmental deterioration caused by overintensive farming, deforestation, overgrazing, and accelerated erosion nullify the positive impact of the Green Revolution by reducing yields in many areas?
5. Will the rich nations make a serious effort to help LDCs raise their food production?
6. Can international agreements for rational use of the sea be instituted before its food resources have been too far depleted?
7. Can a worldwide system of adequate food reserves be established and maintained?
8. Will all nations cooperate to establish and carry out a Global Food Strategy, as outlined at the Rome Food Conference in 1974?

The world food problem *can* be solved, but not easily. All the associated problems must be attacked simultaneously along with the task of producing more food. It will take a great deal of careful, committed effort in all nations and a considerable amount of luck as well. Obviously, the most prudent course is to work very hard for the best, but be prepared for the worst.

[267] PSAC, *World food problem*, vol. 1, p. 11.

Recommended for Further Reading

Berg, Alan. 1973. *The nutrition factor: Its role in national development.* The Brookings Institute, Washington, D.C. An important book on the relevance of nutrition to national policy in LDCs.

Brown, Lester R. 1975. The politics and responsibility of the North American breadbasket. October. *Worldwatch paper 2.* Worldwatch Institute, Washington, D.C. An excellent summary of the world food situation, outlook, and policy implications.

Brown, L., and E. P. Eckholm. 1974. *By bread alone.* Praeger, New York. Useful analysis of the food situation and its political, economic and social ramifications.

Eckholm, Erik P. 1976. *Losing ground: Environmental stress and world food prospects.* Norton, New York. A fine discussion of the environmental costs of efforts to raise food production.

Greenland, D. J. 1975. Bringing the Green Revolution to the shifting cultivator. *Science,* vol. 190, pp. 841–844 (November 28). An important paper on successful agricultural techniques for the humid tropics.

Groth, Edward III. 1975. Increasing the harvest. *Environment,* vol. 17, no. 1, pp. 28–39. Thorough summary of the environmental impact of United States agriculture.

Gulland, John. 1975. The harvest of the sea. In *Environment: Resources, pollution and society,* W. W. Murdoch, ed., Sinauer, Sunderland, Mass., pp. 167–189.

Heichel, G. H. 1976. Agricultural production and energy resources. *American Scientist,* vol. 64, pp. 64–72. Study of energy inputs in agriculture and possible ways of reducing them.

Latham, Michael C. 1974. Protein-calorie malnutrition in children and its relation to psychological development and behavior. *Physiological Reviews,* vol. 54, no. 3, pp. 541–565. An excellent review of the research on the association of malnutrition in children with retarded mental development.

Lipton, Michael. 1975. Urban bias and food policy in poor countries. *Food Policy,* vol. 1, no. 1, pp. 41–51. Interesting study on how the poorest people are left out of the food economy in developing countries.

Rothschild, Emma. 1976. Food politics. *Foreign Affairs,* January, pp. 285–307. Fascinating view of the politics and economics of the world food situation, especially the role of the U.S. government.

Schneider, S. H., and L. Mesirow. 1976. *The Genesis strategy.* Plenum, New York. A superb analysis by a climatologist and a journalist of the climate's role in how much food we will have in the future—and what social and political steps should be taken to avoid climate-induced catastrophes. This book must be read by everyone who eats.

United Nations. 1974. *Assessment of the world food situation, present and future.* World Food Conference, Rome. Best single source on the world's food problem. Comprehensive and concise.

Wade, N. 1974. Green revolution, pt. 1: A just technology, often unjust in use. Green revolution, pt. 2: Problems of adapting a Western technology. *Science,* vol. 186, pp. 1093–1096 and 1186–1192 (December 20 and 27).

Wortman, Sterling, 1976. Food and agriculture. *Scientific American,* September, pp. 30–39. An excellent (if somewhat optimistic) summary of the present food situation and how it might be improved in future decades. This article is an introduction to the *Scientific American*'s special issue on food and agriculture.

Additional References

Abbott, J. C. 1973. The efficient use of world protein supplies. Protein Advisory Group, FAO. *PAG Bulletin,* vol. 3, no. 1, pp. 25–35. On the FAO's protein standards and how distribution of food supplies might be improved.

Adams, M. W.; A. H. Ellingboe; and E. C. Rossman. 1971. Biological uniformity and disease epidemics. *BioScience,* vol. 21, pp. 1067–1070 (November 1). Emphasizes epidemic dangers arising from economic pressures for uniform crops.

Allaby, M. 1970. One jump ahead of Malthus. *The Ecologist,* vol. 1, no. 1 (July), pp. 24–28. Discussion of FAO's Indicative World Plan for agricultural development.

———. 1974. Fertilizers: the hole in the bag. *New Scientist,* Nov. 7, pp. 402–407. On the fertilizer shortage of 1974.

———. 1976. Cornwall's mackerel war. *New Scientist,* March 18, pp. 610–612. Interesting account of how mechanized fishing squeezes out old-fashioned fishermen—and destroys fish stocks.

Alderson, G. L. H. 1975. The value of rare breeds. *The Ecologist,* vol. 5, no. 2 (Feb.), pp. 39–41. On the need to preserve rare breeds of domestic animals.

Allen, R. J. 1975. Food for thought. *The Ecologist,* vol. 5, no. 1 (Jan.), pp. 4–7. On the beef produced by modern feeding methods and the possible dangers of the resultant high proportion of saturated fats.

Altman, P. L., and D. S. Dittmar, eds. 1968. *Metabolism.* Federation of American Societies for Experimental Biology. Bethesda, Md. Good source of detailed information on nutrition.

Altschul, A. M. 1969. Food: protein for humans. *Chemical and Engineering News,* vol. 47, Nov. 24, pp. 68–81. On possible sources of protein supplement.

——— and D. Rosenfield. 1970. Protein supplementation: satisfying man's food needs. *Unilever Quarterly,* vol. 54, no. 305 (March), pp. 26–84. On protein-fortified foods.

Alverson, D. L.; A. R. Longhurst; and J. A. Gulland. 1970. How much food from the sea? *Science,* vol. 168, pp. 503–505 (April 24). Discussion of Ryther's estimates on potential fish production and Ryther's reply.

American Universities Field Staff. 1975. *Common Ground,* vol. 1, no. 3 (July). Hanover, N. H. This entire issue is devoted to the food problem, primarily in LDCs. The journal is a useful one for information on less developed countries in general, as are the *Fieldstaff Reports* issued regularly on individual nations and their problems.

Ashwell, I. 1973. The saga of the cod war. *The Geographic Magazine,* vol. 45, no. 8, pp. 550–556 (May). On the fishery dispute between England and Iceland.

Bardach, J. 1968. *Harvest of the sea.* Harper & Row, New York. An overview of the oceans, reasonably optimistic.

Bardach, J. E.; J. R. Ryther; and W. O. McLerney. 1972. *Aquaculture: The farming and husbandry of freshwater and marine organisms.* Wiley, New York. On the present state of the art.

Berg, A. 1973. Nutrition, development, and population growth. *Population bulletin,* vol. 29, no. 1. Population Reference Bureau, Washington, D.C. On the food problem in LDCs. Condensed from *The Nutrition Factor* (see Recommended for Further Reading).

Bhatia, C. R., and R. Robson. 1976 Bioenergetic considerations in cereal breeding for protein improvement. *Science,* vol. 194, pp. 1418–1421 (December 24). Increasing or improving protein content of cereals may be achieved at some cost in yields or greater needs for fertilizer.

BioScience, 1975. Desert plant may replace sperm oil. Vol. 25, no. 7 (July), p. 467. On the jojoba cactus whose oil is chemically very similar to sperm whale oil.

———1976. Biology briefs: Research in agriculture produces encouraging results. Vol. 26, no. 1, p. 68. A brief summary of recent research in food production, including aquaculture, new strains of potatoes, algae for livestock feed, and nitrogen fixation in cereals.

Boerema, L. K., and J. A. Bulland. 1973. Stock assessment of the Peruvian anchovy *(Engraulis ringens)* and management of the fishery. *Journal of Fisheries Research Board, Canada,* vol. 30, pp. 2226-2235.

Boerma, A. H. 1970. A world agriculture plan. *Scientific American,* August, pp. 54–69. An optimistic view of the FAO's Indicative World Plan for agricultural development.

Bondar, B., and P. J. Bobey. 1974. Should we eat krill? *The Ecologist,* vol. 4, no. 7 (Aug./Sept.), pp. 265–266. On the possible ecological consequences of harvesting krill.

Borgstrom, G. 1967. *Hungry planet.* Collier-Macmillan, Toronto. See especially the discussion of fisheries.

———1969. *Too many.* Collier-MacMillan, Toronto. An interesting discussion of the limits of food production.

Borlaug, N. 1971. The green revolution, peace and humanity. *PRB Selection no. 35.* Population Reference Bureau, Washington, D.C. A condensation of Dr. Borlaug's speech on receiving the Nobel Prize in December 1970 for his work in developing high-yield varieties of wheat.

Boyko, H. 1967. Salt-water agriculture. *Scientific American,* March, pp. 89–96.

Bray, W. J. 1976. Green-crop fractionation. *New Scientist,*April 8, pp. 66–68. On the economics of leaf-protein extraction.

Broadbent, K. P. 1972. The transformation of Chinese agriculture and its effects on the environment. *International Relations,* April–June, pp. 38–51.

Brown, L. R. 1970. Human food production as a process in the biosphere. *Scientific American,* September, pp. 160–170. (*Scientific American* Offprint 1196, W. H. Freeman and Company, San Francisco.)

———1970. *Seeds of change: The green revolution and development in the 1970s.* Praeger, New York. An early, optimistic analysis of the Green Revolution and its impact on the various aspects of development strategy by an author eminently qualified to discuss the topic.

———1974. *In the human interest.* Norton, New York. Concise description of the human predicament and some suggestions for future action. Includes useful material on food situation.

———1975. The world food prospect. *Science,* vol. 190, pp. 1053–1059. (December 12). A condensed version of *Worldwatch Report 2* (See Recommended for Further Reading).

Brown, L. R. and E. P. Eckholm. 1975. Man, food and environment. In *Environment: resources, pollution, and society,* W. Murdoch, ed. Sinauer, Stamford, Conn., pp. 67–94. An excellent summary.

———1975. Next steps toward global food security. In *The U.S. and world development: Agenda for action 1975,* ed. James Howe. Overseas Development Council, Washington, D.C. Praeger, New York. A discussion of food policies based on the Rome Food Conference.

Brown, L. R.; P. L. McGrath; and B. Stokes. 1976. Twenty-two dimensions of the population problem. *Worldwatch Paper 5* (March). A general overview that includes much useful recent information on the food situation.

Brown, N. L., and E. R. Pariser. 1975. Food science in developing countries. *Science,* vol. 188, pp. 589–593 (May 9). On how food and agricultural development aid might be made more relevant to the needs of LDCs.

Brown, R. E., and J. D. Wray. 1974. The starving roots of population growth. *Natural History,* January, pp. 47–52. On the interaction among malnutrition and birth and death rates.

Buchanan, R. 1975. Breast-feeding: Aid to infant health and fertility control. *Population Reports,* Series J, No. 4 (July). George Washington University Medical Center. On the advantages of breast-feeding.

Burgess, J. 1974. Towards novel plants. *New Scientist,* October 24, pp. 242–247. On cell culture as a means of developing new crops.

Burton, J. A. 1975. The future of small whales. *New Scientist,* June 19, pp. 650–652. On the increased hunting of porpoises and dolphins.

Carefort, G. L., and E. R. Sprott. 1967. *Famine on the wind.* Rand-McNally, New York. Popular story of the battle against plant diseases.

Carlson, P. S., and J. C. Polacco. 1975. Plant-cell cultures: genetic aspects of crop improvement. *Science,* vol. 188, pp. 622–625 (May 9). A useful summary of recent research in crop genetics.

Chancellor, W. J. and J. R. Goss, 1976. Balancing energy and food production, 1975–2000. *Science,* vol. 192, pp. 213–218 (April 16.) Very worthwhile.

Chandra, R. K. 1975. Antibody formation in first and second generation offspring of nutritionally deprived rats. *Science,* vol. 190, pp. 289–290 (October 17). Research on effects of malnutrition.

Chao, K. 1970. *Agricultural production in communist China, 1949–1965.* Univ. of Wisconsin Press, Madison.

Chase, H. P., and H. P. Martin. 1970. Undernutrition and child development. *New England Journal of Medicine,* vol. 282, no. 17, pp. 933–939. An account of a U.S. study of infant malnutrition.

Chedd, G. 1970. Hidden peril of the green revolution. *New Scientist,* October 22, pp. 171–173. A discussion of the loss of genetic variability in crops.

———. 1973. Will the mind flourish despite neglect? *New Scientist,* January 11, pp. 71–72. On the need for environmental stimulation of young children.

Child, J. J. 1976. New developments in nitrogen fixation research. *BioScience,* vol. 26, no. 10, pp. 614–617 (October). On the possibility that nonleguminous crops may be enabled to fix nitrogen with a little help from friendly bacteria.

Christy, F. T., Jr., and A. Scott. 1965. *The common wealth in ocean fisheries.* Johns Hopkins Press, Baltimore. See especially the discussion of the productivity of the sea.

Cole, D. G., 1968. The myth of fertility dooms development plans. *National Observer,* April 22. A poignant account of efforts to farm in the tropics.

Cole, H. H., ed. 1966. *Introduction to livestock production, including dairy and poultry.* 2d ed. W. H. Freeman and Company, San Francisco. A basic source.

Cole, H. H., and M. Ronning, eds. 1974. *Animal agriculture.* W. H. Freeman and Company, San Francisco. Basic source.

Cravioto, J.; E. R. DeLicardie; and H. B. Birch. 1966. Nutrition, growth, and neurointegrative development: An experimental and ecological study. *Pediatrics* (supplement), vol. 38, no. 2, pt. 2 (August). Early study on effects of malnutrition on children.

Creech, J. L., and L. P. Reitz. 1971. Plant germ plasm now and for tomorrow. *Advances in Agronomy,* vol. 23, pp. 1–49. Reviews situation in United States relative to genetic resources for agriculture. Comprehensive.

Curwen, E. C., and G. Hatt. 1953. *Plough and pasture.* Schuman, New York. Deals with the early history of farming.

Dalrymple, D. 1975. *Measuring the green revolution: the impact of research on wheat and rice production.* USDA, Economic Research Service, Foreign Agricultural Economic Report, no. 106 (July). Washington, D.C. A report on performance of HYVs in LDCs.

———. 1976. *Development and spread of high-yielding varieties of wheat and rice in the less developed nations.* USDA Foreign Agricultural Report no. 95, Washington D.C. Useful information on development and adoption of HYVs in LDCs.

DeGarine, I. 1971. Food is not just something to eat. *Ceres,* vol. 4, no. 1 (January/February), pp. 46–51. A study of food habits in various cultures.

DeMarco, S., and S. Sechler. 1975. The marketplace of hunger. *Ramparts,* July. Exposé of American agribusiness and USDA policies.

Dhua, S. P. 1975. Need for organo-mineral fertilizer in tropical agriculture. *Ecologist,* vol. 5, pp. 153–157. On some of the special problems of agriculture in the tropics.

Dovring, F. 1974. Soybeans. *Scientific American,* Feb., pp. 14–21. All about one of the most valuable crops cultivated.

Duckham, A. N., and C. B. Masefield. 1970. *Farming systems of the world.* Chatto and Windus, London. Good basic source of information.

Dumont, R., and B. Rosier. 1969. *The hungry future.* Praeger, New York. See especially the discussion of agricultural problems in socialist countries.

Dwyer, J. T., and J. Mayer. 1975. Beyond economics and nutrition: the complex basis of food policy. *Science,* vol. 188, pp. 566–570 (May 9). A strategy for improving nutrition in LDCs.

Dyson-Hudson, R., and N. Dyson-Hudson. 1969. Subsistence herding in Uganda. *Scientific American,* February. On an African cattle culture.

Echols, J. R., 1976. Population vs. the environment: A crisis of too many people. *American Scientist,* vol. 64, pp. 165–173 (March/April). A rather gloomy view of the prospects for feeding the growing human population.

Eckholm, E. P., and F. Record. 1976. The two faces of malnutrition. *Worldwatch paper 9.* Worldwatch Institute, Washington D.C. Fine summary of nutrition in rich and poor countries.

———, and K. Newland. 1975. No breadbasket in the jungle. *Development Forum,* October. Good discussion of the problems of agriculture in the humid tropics.

Ehrlich, P. R., and J. P. Holdren. 1969. Population and panaceas: a technological perspective. *BioScience,* vol. 19, no. 12, pp. 1065–1071 (December). Reprinted in Holdren and Ehrlich, *Global Ecology* (see below). Discussion of limitations imposed by logistics, economics, and lead time on large-scale technological attempts to increase world food supply.

———, and R. W. Holm, eds. 1971. *Man and the ecosphere.* W. H. Freeman and Company, San Francisco. Important papers from *Scientific American* with critical commentaries.

Eichenwald, H. F., and P. C. Fry. 1969. Nutrition and learning. *Science,* vol. 163, pp. 644–648 (Feb 14). An early summary.

Ennis, W. B., Jr.; W. M. Dowler; and W. Klassen. 1975. Crop protection to increase food supplies. *Science,* vol. 188, pp. 593–598 (May 9). On increasing food supplies by control of pests and spoilage and by provision of adequate storage facilities.

Ewell, R. 1975. Food and fertilizer and the developing countries, 1975–2000. *BioScience,* vol. 25, no. 12 (Dec.), p. 771. On projected fertilizer demand in less developed countries from 1970 to 2000 and some of the problems that may prevent the achievement of the goal.

Fears, R. 1976. Pet foods and human nutrition. *New Scientist,* March 18, pp. 606–609. On the quantity and quality of food fed to pets in Great Britain.

Field, J. O., and F. J. Levinson. 1975. Nutrition and development: dynamics of political commitment. *Food Policy,* vol. 1, no. 1 (Nov.), pp. 53–61. On the need for development of nutrition policies in LDCs.

Food and Agriculture Organization of the United Nations. *Fisheries Yearbook.* FAO, Rome. Issued annually.

Food and Agriculture Organization of the United Nations. *Production Yearbook.* FAO, Rome. A basic source for agricultural data.

Food and Agriculture Organization of the United Nations. *Ceres.* A monthly journal on world agriculture.

Food and Agriculture Organization of the United Nations. *State of Food and Agriculture.* Annual volume.

Food and Agriculture Organization of the United Nations, Protein Advisory Group. 1973. PAG statement (no. 20) on the protein problem. *PAG Bulletin,* vol. 3, no. 1, pp. 4-10. A caveat on underestimating protein needs where food supplies are inadequate and among young children fed grain-based diets.

Foreign Agricultural Service. *Foreign Agriculture.* USDA, Washington, D.C. A monthly journal.

Frankel, O. H.; W. K. Agble; J. B. Harlan; and E. Bennett. 1969. Genetic dangers in the Green Revolution. *Ceres,* vol. 2, no. 5 (Sept./Oct.), pp. 35–37. Describes the loss of genetic variation in crops as new varieties replace diversity of older ones.

Frankel, O. H., and E. Bennett. 1970. *Genetic resources in plants: their exploration and conservation.* F. A. Davis, Philadelphia. A comprehensive source book.

Frankel, O. H., and J. G. Hawkes, eds. 1975. *Crop genetic resources for today and tomorrow.* Cambridge University Press, London. An important collection of rather technical papers on genetic reserves.

Franks, R. W. 1974. Miracle seeds and shattered dreams in Java. *Natural History,* January. Fine description of social problems associated with the Green Revolution.

Frantz, S. C. 1976. Rats in the granary. *Natural History,* February, pp. 10–21. A behavioral study of rats living on stored grain in Calcutta.

Friends of the Earth. 1974. *Whale Campaign Manual.* San Francisco.

Gallese, L. R. 1976. Aquatic harvest: U.S. firms are hoping to net big profits in rapidly expanding fish-farm industry. *Wall St. Journal,* Jan. 6. The title tells it all.

Galston, A. W. 1971. Crops without chemicals. *New Scientist,* June 3, pp. 577–580. How genetic manipulation may someday allow creation of nitrogen-fixing and disease-resistant plants.

———. 1975. The water fern-rice connection. *Natural History,* December. On how rice yields can be increased by growing it with a water fern.

Gambell, R. 1972. Why all the fuss about whales? *New Scientist,* June 22, p. 674. A defense of the whaling industry.

Gavan, J. D., and J. A. Dixon. 1975. India: a perspective on the food situation. *Science,* vol. 188, pp. 541–549 (May 9). On India's agriculture.

Gayn, M. 1972. For water the Chinese move mountains. *International Wildlife,* November/December, pp. 20–25. On China's remarkable irrigation system.

Goldsmith, E., ed. 1975. India. *The Ecologist,* vol. 5, no. 8. A special issue on the development problems confronting India, with emphasis on agriculture.

Hagan, P. 1975. The singular krill. *New York Times Magazine,* March 9, pp. 40–43. Discussion of the possibilities of harvesting krill, perhaps overly optimistic.

Hall, R. H. 1975. Feeding the hungry planet counterfeit chocolate and instant pop tarts. *Science Forum* (of Canada), October, pp. 3–6. On the relevance of modern food technology to the poor countries.

Hanson, J. A., ed. 1974. *Open sea mariculture.* Dowden, Hutchinson, and Ross, Stroudsburg, Penn. Possibilities and problems discussed in a way that makes it clear that the problems are so immense as to make any attempt questionable.

Hardin, Garrett. 1968. The tragedy of the commons. *Science,* vol. 162, pp. 1243–1248 (Dec. 13). Reprinted in Hardin, *Population, Evolution, and Birth Control,* W. H. Freeman and Company, San Francisco, and in Holdren and Ehrlich (see below).

Hardy, R. W. F., and U. D. Havelka. 1975. Nitrogen-fixation research: a key to world food? *Science,* vol. 188, pp. 633–643 (May 9).

Harlan, J. R. 1972. Genetics of disaster. *Journal of Environmental Quality,* vol. 1, pp. 212–215. On preservation of genetic reserves.

———. 1975. Our vanishing genetic resources. *Science,* vol. 188, pp. 617–622 (May 9).

———. 1976. The plants and animals that nourish man. *Scientific American,* September, pp. 88–97. Useful catalog of human food resources.

Harlan, J. R., and D. Zohary, 1966. Distribution of wild wheats and barley. *Science,* vol. 153, pp. 1074–1079 (September 2). About early agriculture.

Heady, Earl O. 1976. The agriculture of the U.S., *Scientific American,* September, pp. 106–127. Good summary of the United States food system.

Heiser, C. B., Jr. 1969. Some considerations of early plant domestication. *BioScience,* vol. 19, no. 3, pp. 228–231.

Hendricks, S. B. 1969. Food from the land. In *Resources and man,* P. E. Cloud, Jr., ed. W. H. Freeman and Company, San Francisco, Chapter 4. A hardheaded look at the food problem; the last section contains a good summary of what might be possible if an all-out effort to feed the world were undertaken.

Hertzig, M. E.; H. G. Birch; S. A. Richardson; and J. Tizard. 1972. Intellectual levels of schoolchildren severely malnourished during the first two years of life. *Pediatrics,* vol. 49, no. 6, pp. 814–824. Study on aftereffects of early malnutrition in children.

Hirst, E. 1974. Food-related energy requirements. *Science,* vol. 184, pp. 134–138 (April 12). Energy consumption in the United States food system.

Hodgson, H. J. 1976. Forage crops. *Scientific American,* February, pp. 61–75. Very interesting article on the value and extent of cultivation of forage crops.

———. 1976. Forages, ruminant livestock, and food. *BioScience,* vol. 26, no. 10 (October). A defense of meat in the diet and some ideas on how livestock production could be done with less demand on food resources directly usable by people.

Holdren, J. P., and P. R. Ehrlich, eds. 1971. *Global ecology.* Harcourt, Brace, and Jovanovich, New York. This collection contains several important papers on world food supplies, as well as many other aspects of the interaction of population with resources and environment.

Holt, S. 1974. Whales: Conserving a resource. *Nature,* vol. 251, pp. 366–367. A critique of Gambell's paper (see above).

Holling, E. F. 1970. *The case against hunger.* Cowles, New York. A moving account of hunger in the United States.

Hopper, W. David, 1976. The development of agriculture in developing countries. *Scientific American,* September, pp. 196–205. On the potential for raising food production in LDCs. Worthwhile, although it seriously underestimates environmental constraints.

Howe, E. E.; G. R. Jansen; and M. L. Anson. 1967. An approach toward the solution of the world food problem, with special emphasis on protein supply. *American Journal of Clinical Nutrition,* vol. 20, no. 10.

Hulse, J. H., and D. Spurgeon. 1974. Triticale. *Scientific American,* August, pp. 72–81. On a new grain bred from wheat and rye.

Hunter, J. R., and E. Camacho. 1961. Some observations on permanent mixed cropping in the humid tropics. *Turrialba,* vol. 11, no. 1, pp. 26–33.

Idyll, C. P. 1970. *The sea against hunger.* Crowell, New York.

———. 1973. The anchovy crisis. *Scientific American,* June, pp. 22–29. On the decline in the Peruvian anchoveta fishery in 1971.

Imrie, F. 1975. Single-cell protein from agricultural wastes. *New Scientist,* May 22, pp. 458–460.

International Board for Plant Genetic Resources. 1975. *The conservation of crop genetic resources.* FAO, Rome. On the new international organization charged with maintaining genetic variability in crops.

Jaffe, A. 1975. Ranching on the wild side. *International Wildlife,* vol. 5, no. 6, pp. 4–13. On an experimental ranch in Africa where antelopes are herded.

Janick, J.; R. W. Schery; F. W. Woods; and V. W. Ruttan. 1969 and 1974. *Plant science.* W. H. Freeman and Company, San Francisco. A fine survey covering all aspects of human use of plants.

Janick, J.; C. H. Noller; and C. L. Rhykerd, 1976. The cycles of plant and animal nutrition, *Scientific American,* September, pp. 74–86. On nutrient and energy cycles in natural and agricultural ecosystems.

Janzen, D. H. 1970. The unexploited tropics. *Bulletin of the Ecological Society of America,* September, pp. 4–7. A distinguished ecologist's view of agriculture in the tropics.

Jelliffe, D. B., and E. F. P. Jelliffe. 1975. Human milk, nutrition, and the world resource crisis. *Science,* vol. 188, pp. 557–561 (May 9). Important paper on the nutritional significance of the decline of breast-feeding in LDCs.

Jennings, Peter R. 1976. The amplification of agricultural production. *Scientific American,* September, pp. 180–194. On the Green Revolution technology, especially the high-yielding varieties of grain crops.

Johnson, D. G. 1974. *World food problems and prospects.* American Enterprise Institute for Public Policy Research, Washington, D.C. Useful analysis of world food situation by an experienced agricultural economist.

Journal of the American Medical Association. 1968. Mental retardation from malnutrition: irreversible. Vol. 206, no. 1, pp. 30–31. A report on the study of malnourished children in Chile.

Katz, M.; G. T. Keusch; and L. Mata, eds. 1975. *Symposium on malnutrition and infection during pregnancy.* In *American Journal of Diseases of Children,* vol. 124, no. 4 (April) and no. 5 (May). A major symposium on how malnutrition and infection during pregnancy contribute to mortality, morbidity, and impaired development in children of LDCs.

Keusch , G. T. 1975. Malnutrition and infection: Deadly allies. *Natural History,* November, pp. 27–34. On the interactions between malnutrition and infection in young children.

Ladejinsky, W. 1970. Ironies of India's green revolution. *Foreign Affairs,* July, pp. 758–768. An early discussion of difficulties.

Lappé, F. M. 1975. *Diet for a small planet.* 2d ed. Ballantine, New York. Explains clearly how DCs waste food resources in feeding livestock, and how one can obtain a high-quality protein diet by judiciously combining plant foods.

———. 1975. Fantasies of famine. *Harper's* (February), pp. 51–54, 87–90. On the maldistribution of the world's food, especially protein, and the waste of food resources.

Latham, M. C. 1975. Nutrition and infection in national development. *Science,* vol. 188, pp. 561–565 (May 9). On the interactions between disease and malnutrition.

Leach, G. 1975. Energy and food production. *Food Policy,* vol. 1, no. 1, pp. 62–73. Interesting study of energy inputs to food system, based mainly on United Kingdom data. Includes discussion of energy for food production in LDCs.

Leeds, A. and A. P. Vayda, eds. 1965. *Man, culture, and animals.* American Association for the Advancement of Science, Washington, D.C. See especially chapters on cattle herding in Africa and sacred cows of India.

Leeper, E. M. 1976. Major research effort probes tuna-porpoise bond. *BioScience,* vol. 26, no. 9, pp. 533–534 ff (September). Recent information on porpoises killed in tuna fishing. See also Gear innovations aid porpoise escape, p. 535.

Leslie, R., and A. Sutton. 1975. Why soya? *New Scientist,* December 18/25, pp. 734–737. On the probable future of soybeans as increasingly important protein sources in the future human diet, in DCs as well as LDCs.

Levitsky, D. A. 1976. Ill-nourished brains. *Natural History,* October, pp. 6–20. On the interaction between malnutrition and sensory deprivation.

———, and R. H. Barnes. 1972. Nutrition and environmental interaction in the behavioral development of the rat: Long-term effects. *Science,* vol. 176, pp. 68–71 (April 17). Effect of environmental enrichment in reversing effects of early malnutrition in rats.

Lewin, R. 1974. The poverty of undernourished brains. *New Scientist,* October 24, pp. 268–271.

———. 1975. Starved brains. *Psychology Today,* vol. 9, no. 4, pp. 29–33.

Loftas, T. 1976. Green signal for UN's new billion-dollar fund. *New Scientist,* February, p. 345. On the establishment of the International Fund for Agricultural Development (IFAD).

Loomis, Robert S. 1976. Agricultural systems. *Scientific American,* September, pp. 98–127. Compares various types of agricultural systems.

Loomis, W. F. 1970. Rickets. *Scientific American,* December. (*Scientific American* Offprint 1207, W. H. Freeman and Company, San Francisco.) History of the first appearance of rickets in Europe during the industrial revolution and the discovery of vitamin D.

Loosli, J. K. 1974. New sources of protein for human and animal feeding. *BioScience,* vol. 24, no. 1, pp. 26–31. Some novel food ideas.

Lyubimova, I.; A. G. Naumov; and L. L. Lagunov. 1973. Prospects of the utilization of krill and other nonconventional resources of the world ocean. *Journal of the Fisheries Research Board of Canada,* vol. 30, pp. 2196–2201.

Makhijani, A., and A. Poole. 1975. *Energy and agriculture in the Third World.* Ballinger, Cambridge, Mass. Includes information on how energy is obtained and used today, as well as proposals for providing more with greater efficiency.

Martin, P. S. 1970. Pleistocene niches for alien animals. *BioScience,* vol. 20, no. 4, pp. 218–221. Discussion of potential animal husbandry of so-far unexploited animals.

Mayer, A., and J. Mayer. 1974. Agriculture: The island empire. *Daedalus,* vol. 103, no. 3, pp. 83–95. Interesting discussion of the consequences of isolating agricultural research from other sciences.

Mayer, J. 1976. The dimensions of human hunger. *Scientific American,* September, pp. 40–49. On the extent of hunger and malnutrition worldwide, and suggestions for policies to relieve malnutrition.

Mayer, J., ed. 1973. *U.S. nutrition policies in the seventies.* W. H. Freeman and Company, San Francisco. Proposals and suggestions for national nutritional policies.

McCloskey, W. B. 1976. Board and seize. *New York Times Magazine* March 7, pp. 13, 81, 86. An interesting account of Coast Guard enforcement of American territorial jurisdiction within 12 miles of shore with regard to foreign fishing.

Mckenzie, J. 1968. Nutrition and the soft sell. *New Scientist,* November 21. On the difficulties of introducing unorthodox foods.

McLaughlin, M. F. 1975. World food insecurity: Has anything happened since Rome? Overseas Development Council, Washington, D.C., ODC *Communique* 27.

McLin, Jon, 1976. Remember the World Food Conference? *Fieldstaff Reports,* West Europe Series, vol. 11, no. 2. An update on international efforts to deal with the world food problem.

McNaughton, S. J. 1976. Serengeti migratory wildebeest: Facilitation of energy flow by grazing. *Science,* vol. 191, pp. 92–94 (January 9). On how wildebeest grazing stimulates new grass growth that supports Thomson's gazelles through the dry season.

Mellor, John W., 1976. The agriculture of India, *Scientific American,* September, pp. 154–163. On the past performance and future potential of Indian agriculture.

Mercado, J. 1975. High yield, "floating" rice may help countries where food shortages are greatest. *Science Forum* (Canada), vol. 47, October, pp. 10–11.

Miller, J. 1973. Genetic erosion: Crop plants threatened by government neglect. *Science,* vol. 182, pp. 1231–1233 (December 21).

Morales, H. L. 1975. The blue revolution. *Ceres,* July/August, pp. 46–48. On fish-farming.

Morris, I. 1970. Restraints on the big fish-in. *New Scientist,* December 3, pp. 373–375. Discussion of the limits on food from the sea.

Morris, R., and H. Sheets. 1974. Why leave it to Earl? *Washington Monthly,* November, pp. 12–19. Critique of USDA policies.

Muller, M. 1974. Money, milk, and marasmus. *New Scientist,* February 28, pp. 530–533. On the decline of breast-feeding in LDCs.

———. 1974. Aid, corruption, and waste. *New Scientist,* November 7, pp. 398–400. What happens to donated food on the way to the hungry in LDCs.

Murphy, G. J. 1966. Population biology of the Pacific sardine *(Sardinops caerula). Proceedings of the California Academy of Sciences,* vol. 34, no. 1, pp. 1–84. Another fishery overexploited essentially to extinction.

Myers, N. 1975. The whaling controversy. *American Scientist,* vol. 63, pp. 448–455 (July/August).

National Academy of Sciences. 1972. *Genetic vulnerability of major crops.* NAS, Washington, D.C. On some of the biological problems of high-yield grains.

———. 1975. *Population and food: Crucial issues,* NAS, Washington, D.C.

———. 1975. *Enhancement of food production for the United States.* NAS, Washington, D.C. Some stiff recommendations for strengthening agricultural research in the United States.

Netboy, A. 1973. The unhappy fate of *Salmo salar. The Ecologist,* December, pp. 468–470. On the North Atlantic salmon fishery.

New Internationalist. 1974. Disaster in the Sahel. June.

New Scientist. 1972. Starved brains fail to make the right connections. April 20, p. 121. About the effects of malnutrition on brain development.

———. 1974. Single-cell protein comes of age. November 28, pp. 634–639. On single-cell protein as a food supplement.

———. 1975. Is the cod war really a red herring? November 27, p. 500. On the new cod war and other fishery disputes between England and Iceland.

Noble, R. 1975. Growing fish in sewage. *New Scientist,* July 31, pp. 259–261. On fish-farming. See also the letter by Ron Edwards, *New Scientist,* August 14, 1975, p. 396.

Nove, A. 1975. Soviet grain: problems and prospects. *Food Policy,* vol. 1, no. 1 (Nov.), pp. 32–40. On agriculture in the USSR.

———. 1976. Will Russia ever feed itself? *New York Times Magazine,* February 1, p. 9. More on Russian agriculture.

Odum, H. T. 1971. *Environment, power, and society.* Wiley, New York. An interesting treatment of the energetics of ecosystems and human involvement in energy flows. See especially the material on the energy subsidy of agriculture.

Orr, R. T. 1976. The tuna-dolphin problem. *Pacific Discovery,* vol. 29, no. 1, p. 1. On the dolphins killed in the process of tuna fishing.

Owen, D. F. 1966. *Animal ecology in tropical Africa.* W. H. Freeman and Company, San Francisco.

Paddock, W. C. 1967. Phytopathology in a hungry world. *Annual Review of Phytopathology,* vol. 5, pp. 375–390. On some of the problems of the Green Revolution—specifically the susceptibility of monocultures to pests.

———. 1970. How green is the green revolution? *BioScience,* vol. 20, pp. 897–902 (August 15). An early warning.

Paddock, W., and P. Paddock. 1964. *Hungry nations.* Little, Brown, Boston. Good descriptions of conditions relating to LDC food production. A classic in its time, now somewhat out of date.

———. 1967. *Famine 1975!* Little, Brown, Boston. Discussion of the possibilities for revolutionizing LDC agriculture. Many considered the Paddocks overly pessimistic; unfortunately, events have borne out many of their predictions.

Pan American Health Organization. 1971. *Inter-American Investigation of Mortality in Childhood, Provisional Report.* Washington, D.C. On malnutrition and child mortality.

Paulik, G. J. 1971. Anchovies, birds and fishermen in the Peru Current. In *Environment: resources, pollution, and society,* W. W. Murdoch, ed. Sinauer, Stamford, Conn. A fine discussion of the oceanographic, economic, and sociological aspects of the Peruvian anchovy fishery by a distinguished figure in the field of mathematical analysis of resource management. Paulik's best conjecture of the potential production of all marine fish is 125 million tons per year.

Payne, I. 1975. Tilapia: A fish of culture. *New Scientist,* July 31, pp. 256–258. On fish-farming with tilapia (a cichlid fish).

Payne, P. 1974. Protein deficiency or starvation? *New Scientist,* Nov. 7, pp. 393–398. On the controversy over protein needs. See also the letter to the editor, *New Scientist,* August 14, 1975, p. 397.

Payne, P., and E. Wheeler. 1971. What protein gap? *New Scientist,* April 15, pp. 148–150. Discussion of complex factors affecting nutrition in LDCs.

Payne, R. 1968. Among wild whales. *New York Zoological Society Newsletter,* November. A good summary of the whaling situation. Reprinted in Holdren and Ehrlich (see above).

Perelman, M. J. 1972. Farming with petroleum. *Environment,* vol. 14, no. 8, pp. 8–13. On wasteful United States farming methods, particularly of fossil fuels.

Phillips, J. 1961. *The development of agriculture and forestry in the tropics.* Faber and Faber, London. Introduction to many of the problems faced by the LDCs.

Picardi, A. C., and W. W. Seifert. 1976. A tragedy of the commons in the Sahel. *Technology Review,* vol. 78, no. 6. An analysis of the causes of the Sahel famine.

Pillay, T. V. R. 1973. The role of aquaculture in fishery development and management. *Journal of the Fisheries Research Board of Canada,* vol. 30, pp. 2202–2217.

Pimentel, D.; W. Dritschilo; J. Krummel; and J. Kutzman. 1975. Energy and land constraints in food protein production. *Science,* vol. 190, pp. 754–761 (November 21). An interesting (and ominous) analysis of likely future constraints on food production.

Pimentel, D.; L. E. Hurd; A. C. Bellotti; M. J. Forster; I. N. Oka; O. D. Sholes; and R. J. Whitman. 1973. Food production and the energy crisis. *Science,* vol. 182, pp. 443–449 (November 2). Useful analysis of energy use in American agriculture.

Pimentel, D.; E. Terhune; R. Dyson-Hudson; S. Rochereau; R. Samis; E. A. Smith; D. Denman; D. Reifschneider; and M. Shepard. 1976. Land degradation: Effects on food and energy resources. *Science,* vol. 194, pp. 149–155 (October 8). On the loss of farmland to urbanization, highways, and soil erosion and the implications for future food production.

Pirie, N. W., 1966. Leaf protein as human food. *Science,* vol. 152, pp. 1701–1705 (June 24). On the potential of processed leaf protein as a food supplement.

———. 1967. Orthodox and unorthodox methods of meeting world food needs. *Scientific American,* February, pp. 27–35. (*Scientific American* Offprint 1068, W. H. Freeman and Company, San Francisco.)

———. 1969. *Food resources, conventional and novel.* Penguin, Baltimore. See especially the material on novel foods.

———. 1974. Single-cell protein isn't chickenfeed. *New Scientist,* September 26, p. 801. On single-cell protein as a food supplement.

Posner, C. 1975. Agronomy to the rescue. *New Scientist,* October 2, p. 31. A description of agriculture in Guatemala, including the ecological consequences of attempts at large-scale farming.

The President's Science Advisory Committee Panel on the World Food Supply. 1967. *The world food problem.* 3 vols. Washington, D.C. A very detailed basic source, now somewhat out of date. Summaries and individual papers.

Pyke, M. 1970. *Man and food.* McGraw-Hill, New York. Basic information on nutrition and food technology.

———. 1970. A taste of things to come. *New Scientist,* December 17. On synthetic food supplements; today vitamins, in the future amino acids and fatty acids.

Ramsey, James E. 1969. FPC. *Oceans,* vol. 2, no. 2, pp. 76–80. On fish-protein concentrate as a potential food supplement.

Ravenholt, A. 1971. Can one billion Chinese feed themselves? *Fieldstaff Reports,* East Asia Series, vol. 18, no. 2. American Universities Field Staff, Hanover, N.H. An interesting look at the population-food situation in China.

Reiger, G. 1975. Aquaculture: Has it been oversold? *International Wildlife,* January, pp. 21–24. Interesting survey of different approaches to fish-farming.

———. 1974. First the whales, now the porpoises. *National Wildlife* February/March, pp. 18–20. On the killing of porpoises by tuna fishermen.

Reitz, L. P., and J. C. Craddock. 1969. Diversity of germ plasm in small grain cereals. *Economic Botany,* vol. 23, pp. 315–323. On crop seed banks and the need to preserve genetic diversity in crops.

Revelle, Roger. 1976. The resources available for agriculture, *Scientific American,* September, pp. 164–178. A discussion of physical, biological, and social resources needed to increase food production and their limitations.

Rosenzweig, M. R.; E. L. Bennett; and M. C. Diamond. 1972. Brain changes in response to experience. *Scientific American,* February, pp. 22–99. On environmental stimulation.

Ricker, W. E. 1969. Food from the sea. In *Resources and man,* P. E. Cloud, ed. W. H. Freeman and Company, San Francisco (chapter 5). Slightly more optimistic than the estimates by Ryther.

Rounsefell, G. A. 1971. Potential food from the sea. *Journal of Marine Science,* vol. 1, no. 3. Good summary article.

Ruthenberg, H. 1971. *Farming systems in the tropics.* Clarendon Press, New York.

Ryther, J. H. 1969. Photosynthesis and fish production in the sea. *Science,* vol. 166, pp. 72–76. An excellent discussion of the potential maximum sustainable fish yield to human beings. Reprinted in Holdren and Ehrlich (see above).

Sanchez, P. A., and S. W. Buol. 1975. Soils of the tropics and the world food crisis. *Science,* vol. 188, pp. 598–603. On the problems and possibilities of agriculture in the tropics.

Schaeffer, M. B. 1965. The potential harvest of the sea. *Transactions of the American Fisheries Society,* vol. 94, no. 2, pp. 123–128. One of the more optimistic estimates of potential fish production.

Schapiro, S., and K. R. Vukovich. 1970. Early experience effects upon cortical dendrites: A proposed model for development. *Science,* vol. 167, pp. 292–294 (January 16). On environmental stimulation's effects on brain development.

Scheffer, V. B. 1976. The status of whales. *Pacific discovery,* vol. 29, no. 1, pp. 2–8. Recent progress in curbing uncontrolled whaling.

Schlossberg, K. 1975. Funny money is serious. *New York Times* September 28, pp. 12–13 ff. Details of the food-stamp program.

Science. 1974. National nutrition. Vol. 183, p. 1062 (March 15). A report on a U.S. national nutritional survey.

———. 1975. Nitrogen-fixation in maize. Vol. 189, p. 368 (August 1). On research toward making grains able to fix nitrogen as legumes do.

Scrimshaw, N. S., and J. E. Gordon. 1968. *Malnutrition, learning, and behavior.* MIT Press, Cambridge. A comprehensive, if slightly out of date, source of information on the effects of malnutrition.

Scrimshaw, N. S., and M. Behar. 1976. *Nutrition and agricultural development: Significance and potential for the tropics.* Plenum, New York. An information-rich compendium on the subject from a symposium held in December 1974.

Scrimshaw, N. S., and V. R. Young. 1976. The requirements of human nutrition. *Scientific American,* September, pp. 50–64. Interesting article on human nutritional needs, including some recent research results.

Shapley, D. 1972. Science in the Great Cod War. *New Scientist,* December 14, pp. 628–629. On the fishery dispute between England and Iceland.

Sherrill, R. 1970. Why can't we just give them food? *New York Times Magazine* (March 22). Feeding the hungry in the United States.

Shoemaker, W. J., and R. J. Wurtman. 1971. Perinatal undernutrition: Accumulation of catecholamines in rat brain. *Science,* vol. 171, pp. 1017–1019 (March 12). On the biochemical effects on rat brains of malnutrition before and after birth.

Slesser, M. 1973. How many can we feed? *Ecologist,* June, pp. 216–220. An interesting discussion of energy as a limitation on the Earth's food-producing capacity.

Sprague, G. F. 1975. Agriculture in China. *Science,* vol. 188, pp. 549–555 (May 9).

Stanton, W. R. 1964. Some social problems in tropical agriculture. *Tropical Science,* vol. 6, no. 4, pp. 180–186.

Stauls, W. J., and M. G. Blase. 1971. Genetic technology and agricultural development. *Science,* vol. 173 pp. 119–123 (July 9). On some of the problems of the Green Revolution.

Stein, Z.; M. Susser; G. Saenger; and F. Marolla. 1972. Nutrition and mental performance. *Science,* vol. 178, pp. 708–713 (November 17). A study of young men born during and after a World War II famine in Holland.

———. 1975. *The Dutch hunger winter of 1944–45.* Oxford University Press, London. A detailed presentation of the study on long-term results of famine during the perinatal period of development.

Steinhart, J. S., and C. E. Steinhart. 1974. Energy use in the U.S. food system. *Science,* vol. 184, pp. 307–316 (April 19). Detailed analysis.

Streuver, S., ed. 1971. *Prehistoric agriculture.* Natural History Press, Garden City, N.Y.

Sukhatme, P. V. 1966. The world's food supplies. *Royal Statistical Society Journal,* Series A, vol. 129, pp. 222–248. An important study in its time; slightly out of date, but the basic picture has not changed.

Tatum, L. A. 1971. The southern corn leaf blight epidemic. *Science,* vol. 171, pp. 1113–1116 (March 19). On the corn blight that ruined an estimated one-sixth of the 1970 U.S. corn crop.

Technology Review. 1970. Vol. 72, no. 4 (February). Special issue on nutritional problems in LDCs and their significance in development programs. Many interesting articles.

Thompson, L. M. 1975. Weather variability, climatic change, and grain production. *Science,* vol. 188, pp. 535–541 (May 9). On the sensitivity of grain crops to climate change. An excellent, information-packed article.

Tudge, Colin. 1975. Why turn waste into protein? *New Scientist,* April 17, pp. 138–139. On the practicality of SCP and other novel food projects.

United Nations. Annual. *Statistical yearbook.* New York. Full of information, including some on food and agriculture.

U.S. Department of Agriculture. 1975. *The world food situation and prospects to 1985.* Foreign Agricultural Economic Report no. 98. Probably overoptimistic–see, e.g., criticism by Thompson, 1975.

———, Economic Research Service. Quarterly. *World agricultural situation.* A useful report.

U.S. Department of Commerce. 1975. Draft outline for National Fisheries Plan. National Marine Fisheries Service.

University of California, Food Task Force. 1974. *A hungry world: The challenge to agriculture.* General Report and Summary Report. Division of Agricultural Sciences, Berkeley. Useful study; identifies areas where agriculture-related research should be concentrated in order to slow population growth and raise food production.

Wade, Nicholas. 1975. International agricultural research. *Science,* vol. 188, pp. 585–589 (May 9). Describes the international agricultural research centers.

———. 1975. Agriculture: Academy group suggests major shake-up to President Ford. *Science,* vol. 190, pp. 959–961 (December 5). On the National Academy of Sciences recommendations to improve agricultural research.

Wallace, P. 1974. Complex environments: Effects on brain development. *Science,* vol. 185, pp. 1035–1037 (September 20).

Waterlow, J. C., and P. R. Payne. 1975. The protein gap. *Nature,* vol. 258, pp. 113–117. More on the protein-needs controversy.

Watt, K. E. F. 1968. *Ecology and resource management.* McGraw-Hill, New York. See especially chapters 4 and 5 of this fine book.

Wellhausen, E. J., 1976. The agriculture of Mexico. *Scientific American,* September, pp. 128–150. On the impressive achievements of Mexican agriculture and the need for further rural development.

Went, F. W. 1957. Climate and agriculture. *Scientific American,* June. (*Scientific American* Offprint 852, W. H. Freeman and Company, San Francisco.) A classic on the importance of weather.

Wharton, C. R., Jr. 1969. The Green Revolution: Cornucopia or Pandora's box? *Foreign Affairs,* vol. 47, pp. 464–476. An excellent early summary of economic and social consequences of the Green Revolution.

Williams, G., and W. J. A. Payne. 1959. *An introduction to animal husbandry in the tropics.* Longmans, Green, London.

Williams, R. J. 1962. *Nutrition in a nutshell.* Dolphin, Garden City, N.Y. Popular summary of nutrition by a distinguished scientist.

Winick, M.; K. K. Meyer; and R. C. Harris. 1975. Malnutrition and environmental enrichment by early adoption. *Science,* vol. 190, pp. 1173–1175 (December 19). Results of a study of Korean orphans adopted by American families, some of whom had been malnourished in infancy.

Wittwer, S. H. 1975. Food production: Technnology and the resource base, *Science,* vol. 188, pp. 579–584 (May 9). On the need to expand agricultural research.

Wolff, T. 1976. Maize: "Supergrain" of the future? *War on Hunger,* (AID), March, pp. 15–18. On Opaque-2, a high-protein variety of corn.

Wyrtki, K.; E. Stroup; W. Pazert; R. Williams; and W. Quinn. 1976. Predicting and observing el Niño. *Science,* vol. 191, pp. 343–346 (January 30). On the warm current that occasionally appears off Peru, disrupting the anchoveta fishery.

Yarwood, C. E. 1970. Man-made plant diseases. *Science,* vol. 168, pp. 218–220 (April 10). How efficient agriculture can foster plant diseases.

Zamenhof, S.; E. van Marthens; and L. Granel. 1971. DNA (cell number) in neonatal brain: Second-generation (F_2) alteration by maternal (F_0) dietary-protein restriction. *Science,* vol. 172, pp. 850–851 (May 21). On the effects of malnutrition in pregnant rats on subsequent generations.

Zelitch, I. 1975. Improving the efficiency of photosynthesis. *Science,* vol. 188, pp. 626–633 (May 9). The possibilities for increasing crop productivity through more efficient photosynthesis.

SECTION

III

Energy and Materials

It seems clear that the first major penalty man will have to pay for his rapid consumption of the earth's nonrenewable resources will be that of having to live in a world where his thoughts and actions are ever more strongly limited, where social organization has become all pervasive, complex, and inflexible, and where the state completely dominates the actions of the individual.

—Harrison Brown, 1954

The material prosperity of modern industrial society has been built largely on a one-time windfall of rich, accessible fuels and metallic ores. These resources were formed and concentrated by biological and geologic processes operating over thousands of millennia. The natural subsidy provided for human enterprises by this situation has now nearly been used up. The most accessible, most concentrated deposits of coal, oil, natural gas, copper, iron, chromium, and tin have been found and exploited. They have built the buildings, bridges, railroads, highways, communication networks, and machinery of the industrial world. The processes that formed the windfall continue, but at so slow a pace that 10 million years would hardly suffice to build up again what society has extracted in the past decade.

Yet society is not running out of energy or raw materials in any absolute sense. Nuclear fuels, geothermal heat, and the continuing energy income from the sun represent enormous energy sources—enough to run a civilization even more energy-hungry than today's for millions of years and more. The metals remaining in Earth's crust in less concentrated form than the deposits exploited until now represent staggering tonnages of material, and even the metals already mined are not really gone but rather, at worst, dispersed. The essence of the situation, then, is not that resources of energy and materials, in general, are near exhaustion; it is that the cheap and easy ones are nearly gone.

In Chapter 8 we examine in detail the patterns of human energy use and the technical, economic, and environmental characteristics of energy sources available now and likely to become available in the next few decades. From the welter of detail a few clear messages emerge: the energy sources to which society must now turn will be substantially more costly than oil and gas have been; no energy source, old or new, is free of significant environmental liabilities; and using energy more efficiently can alleviate both the economic costs and the environmental risks that would be associated with continued rapid expansion of energy supply. The briefer review of patterns of materials supply and demand in Chapter 9 reveals many parallels with the energy situation and a similar prescription: whatever else is done, society must learn to use materials more efficiently in the future than it has in the past.

Some readers may wonder why we have chosen to devote quite so much attention to energy—Chapter 8 is the longest in the book. There are several reasons. First, energy has played a particularly fundamental role in shaping today's industrial economies, and virtually all published visions of the future of technological society are built around conceptions (or misconceptions) of what future energy sources will be like. Second, the extraction, conversion, and application of energy have been dominant ingredients of industrial society's assaults on the environment; to understand the environmental impact of energy is to grasp much of the environmental predicament as a whole. Third, there is an enormous variety of approaches to supplying energy. Since one of the central energy problems facing contemporary policy-makers is choosing from this menu of alternatives the least undesirable combination of sources, a text with any pretension to practical application must provide some detail about all of them. Moreover, because energy probably has been the most-studied resource, there is a good deal of relevant information to summarize. Finally, the energy situation can be thought of as a precursor of predicaments with other resources in the future: Energy is the first of technological society's "wells" to be perceived worldwide as threatening to run dry. And both the symptoms of this situation and the responses to it contain lessons that will apply to resource problems to come.

Chapters 8 and 9 deal only peripherally with implications for policy, concentrating instead on the somewhat less controversial technical, economic, and environmental aspects of energy and materials. Our own conclusions about the appropriate directions for energy policy and materials policy are summarized in Chapter 14 and Chapter 15. It may be useful, however, for the reader to have certain policy-related concerns in mind from the beginning.

Consider, for example, the implications for policy of the imminent depletion of the energy and materials windfall—that is, the deposits for which the subsidy by natural processes of concentration is very large and the additional investment of effort by society needed to obtain the resource in usable form is small. What would a society that must operate with much leaner resources be like? What technological choices would minimize such a society's vulnerability to interruption of its flows of energy and materials? Are there choices that could minimize the impact of depletion of the windfall on the prospects of poor countries for achieving a modicum of prosperity?

One particularly important concern, expressed by Harrison Brown in the passage that begins this introduction, is that the depletion of the windfall will lead to a loss of human freedoms. This may indeed be so. The usual reason for expecting this outcome is the supposition that government will have to impose tight restrictions on behavior in order to minimize inefficiency and waste. At least as threatening, however, are the centralization of authority and other constraints on human freedoms that might be associated with attempts to stave off scarcity by deploying complex, fragile, and unforgiving supply technologies. (Repressive measures that might be deemed necessary to protect electric power grids and nuclear fuel processing plants from sabotage come to mind.)

The last policy-related issue we will mention here is the desirability of diversity in energy and materials technologies. There is no single best energy source for all regions and all purposes or any way to obtain, say, fiber for clothing or construction material for buildings that is best in all circumstances. This would be true even if knowledge about society's needs and about the side effects of various ways to satisfy those needs were perfect: the mere fact of cultural and environmental diversity implies that technological diversity will be necessary to ensure good fits. But knowledge is not perfect, either about the nature of needs, technologies, and environments today or about future changes in any of them. In the face of incomplete information, technological diversity performs an additional function: it is the best insurance policy a society can buy against the unpredictable and the unexpected. (This is, of course, one of the functions of diversity in nature as well, as discussed in Chapter 4.)

Society must expect to pay for such insurance, of course. Diversity is not free. Payment is made when government spends money for investigation and development of energy and materials technologies that private enterprise is unwilling to support and when industry or government deploys for commercial operation technologies that are more expensive than the apparently cheapest alternative of the moment. (Consider an example: For many years before 1973 the cheapest way to generate electricity in some parts of the United States was to burn oil. Building only oil-fired generating plants then because it was cheapest would have proven to be a costly mistake when the price of oil suddenly quadrupled in 1973.) It should also be remembered that the general desirability of diversity does not mean society must or should embrace *all* alternatives. Part of the usefulness of diversity is having the option of rejecting alternatives that are found to be completely unsuitable.

No one is going to repeal the second law of thermodynamics, not even the Democrats.

—Kenneth Boulding, 1970

CHAPTER 8

Energy

Energy is the ultimate resource and, at the same time, the ultimate pollutant. The solar energy continuously intercepted by Earth drives the geophysical and ecological machinery that make the planet's surface habitable by human beings. The remarkable growth of the human population and the development of civilizations are attributable largely to the singular progress of our species in learning to harness natural flows and accumulations of energy and turn them to human ends. Human beings have learned to tame fire for warmth and light and protection; to organize (and later subsidize) photosynthesis as agriculture, thus allowing people to specialize and thereby promoting the growth of cities; to tap the energy of wind and running water for transportation and mechanical work; and to unlock the concentrated energy of coal and oil for extracting, concentrating, transporting, and applying the many other resources upon which society depends.

Yet, no means of harnessing energy—and no means of applying it—is completely free of adverse environmental

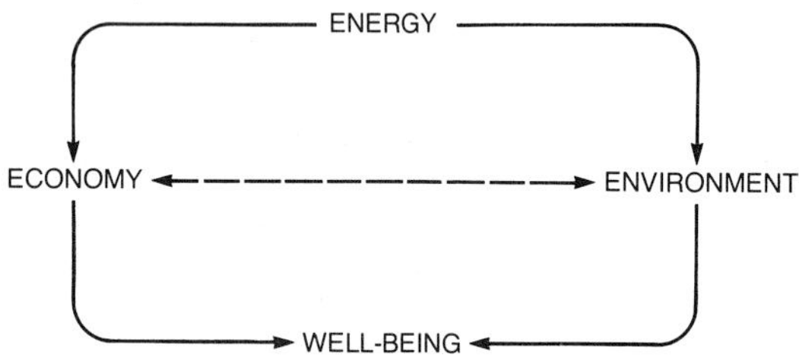

FIGURE 8-1

The relation between energy and well-being. Energy exerts its influences on well-being through the economy and through the environment. Energy's contribution to the production of goods and services in the economy exerts a largely positive effect on well-being. The adverse effects of the production and use of energy on the environment damage human health directly, as well as undermining environmental services that support the economy.

impacts. The impacts manifest themselves at all stages of energy-processing, from exploration to disposal of final wastes. Many of these impacts can be significantly controlled, at some expense in money and in energy itself. But, in consequence of the fundamental characteristics of energy and matter, reflected in the laws of thermodynamics (Box 2-3), the impact can never be averted entirely. All the energy people use ends up in the environment as heat; and energy, unlike other physical resources, cannot be recycled.

It is the dichotomy between energy's roles as ultimate resource and ultimate pollutant that generates the deepest of the several dilemmas that make up "the energy problem." Those two roles of energy—and the associated dilemmas—are represented schematically in Figure 8-1. The economy, which provides goods and services in support of human well-being, depends on energy and on raw materials supplied with the assistance of energy. But both the economy and the physical health of the population depend also on services provided by the nontechnological environment, and those services can be disrupted by the adverse effects of energy technology. In the expansion of any particular technology and in the expansion of civilization's energy use as a whole, a point must eventually be reached where the benefits to well-being of adding energy to the economic side of the relationship do not compensate for the damage to well-being caused by the environmental impact of making the extra energy available.

This conclusion leads directly to some crucial questions. Is it possible for modern economies to grow more rapidly (as measured by gross national product, GNP) than the energy supply grows? Or is it possible for them to grow at all if the rate of energy use is stationary or declining? Is it possible for human well-being to grow faster than GNP? If the links between energy and GNP and between GNP and well-being are as inflexible as many government officials and energy-industry spokespersons seem to believe, then the dilemma is sharp indeed: the economic imperative to expand energy use, driven in part by the legitimate needs of the poor, must confront the environmental imperative to limit energy use. This could be a crushing—indeed, catastrophic—collision. If, on the other hand, there is flexibility in the links between energy and GNP and between GNP and well-being, then the dilemma can be softened by *learning to do more good with less energy*. This is a more promising prospect, for the poor and for everyone.

Whether the rate of energy use is growing, constant, or shrinking, the question of what technologies are used to provide energy is critical. What are the choices, now and in the future? Which technologies are limited by finite resource supplies to the status of being interim measures, and which can serve for the long term? What are the environmental and social characteristics of the various options?

In this chapter, we review past, present, and possible future patterns of energy use, we survey the availability of major energy resources, and we discuss the characteristics of the various technological means of harnessing these resources. The special "resource" of energy conservation—that is, using energy more efficiently—is also treated here. The perhaps more controversial social and economic elements of the energy situation—the price of energy and its relation to broader problems of economics and equity; the organization of the energy industries; the character and quality of government planning, spending, and regulation in the energy field; the international politics of energy—are taken up in Chapter 14 and Chapter 15.

TABLE 8-1
Approximate Energy in Selected Fuels and Processes

	Energy produced or used (MJ)
Energy to feed 1 person for 1 day	10
Nonfood energy use per person per day, world average	200
Nonfood energy use per person per day, U.S. average	1,000
1 tank of gasoline (15 gal.)	2,000
1 barrel of oil (42 gal.)	5,900
1 metric ton of coal	29,000
Boeing 707 flight, San Francisco–New York	1,400,000
1 kilogram uranium-235, completely fissioned	79,000,000
Summer thunderstorm	160,000,000
Fuel input to 1000-Megawatt power plant, 1 day	260,000,000
Hydrogen bomb (1 Megaton)	4,000,000,000
Total human nonfood energy use per day	800,000,000,000
Sunlight striking top of atmosphere, 1 day	15,000,000,000,000,000

Note: 1 megajoule (MJ) = 948.4 British thermal units (Btu) = 239.0 kilocalories (kcal) = 0.2778 kilowatt-hours (kwh).

SIZE AND SOURCES OF CONTEMPORARY ENERGY USE

World energy use in 1975 amounted to roughly 260 trillion megajoules (see Box 2-1 and Table 8-1, concerning units of measure), not including energy in food and in dung, in wood, and in agricultural wastes burned for cooking and heating.[1] The latter, largely untabulated sources may amount to two-thirds or more of energy use in the poorest LDCs; they would add perhaps 15 to 20 percent to the global total.[2] Of the tabulated energy use, 45 percent was supplied by petroleum, 32 percent by coal, 19 percent by natural gas, 2 percent by hydropower, and 2 percent by nuclear energy. Sources of the energy used in the United States differ from those world averages mainly in that the proportions of coal and natural gas are reversed. The dominance of the fossil fuels—more than 95 percent of the total for the world and for the United States—is overwhelming. Equally striking is a comparison of energy use in DCs and LDCs: the former, with about 32 percent of the population, account for 83 percent of the world's use of energy.[3]

Data on energy use per person and GNP per person in selected countries appear in Table 8-2. (More complete figures appear in Appendix 1.) Although such data often are placed on a graph with a straight line "fitted" through the middle to support the contention that energy consumption and prosperity are tightly linked, the facts do not justify this view. It is obvious that poor countries use only a little energy per person and rich countries a lot, but within a given prosperity bracket the correlation is very weak. (This is so even if one ignores the notorious unreliability of GNP as a measure of comparative prosperity among countries.) Sweden, for example, has a higher GNP per person than the United States, but only about half the energy consumption per person. New Zealand has just over half the energy consumption per person of the United Kingdom, but a larger GNP per person. These examples show that there is substantial flexibility in the link between energy and GNP—flexibility that could reward further study of just how countries like Sweden, Switzerland, and New Zealand get so much apparent prosperity from so comparatively little energy.

Energy resources are distributed unevenly in the world, and the pattern of this distribution does not match the pattern of consumption. The imbalance in energy use reflected in the "annual energy consumption" column of Table 8-2 thus can be maintained only through substantial international flows of energy resources. The percentage of the dependence on energy imports in each country listed appears in the right-hand column of the table. The largest part of the international energy flows is in the form of petroleum, whose global patterns of production,

[1]International energy statistics in this chapter, unless otherwise attributed, are adapted from the United Nations, *Statistical yearbook.* U.S. energy statistics, unless otherwise attributed, are from U.S. Department of Commerce, *Statistical abstract of the United States.*

[2]Based on data in A. Makhijani and A. Poole, *Energy and agriculture in the Third World.* See also J. Darmstadter, *Energy in the world economy.*

[3]John P. Holdren, Energy and prosperity: Some elements of a global perspective.

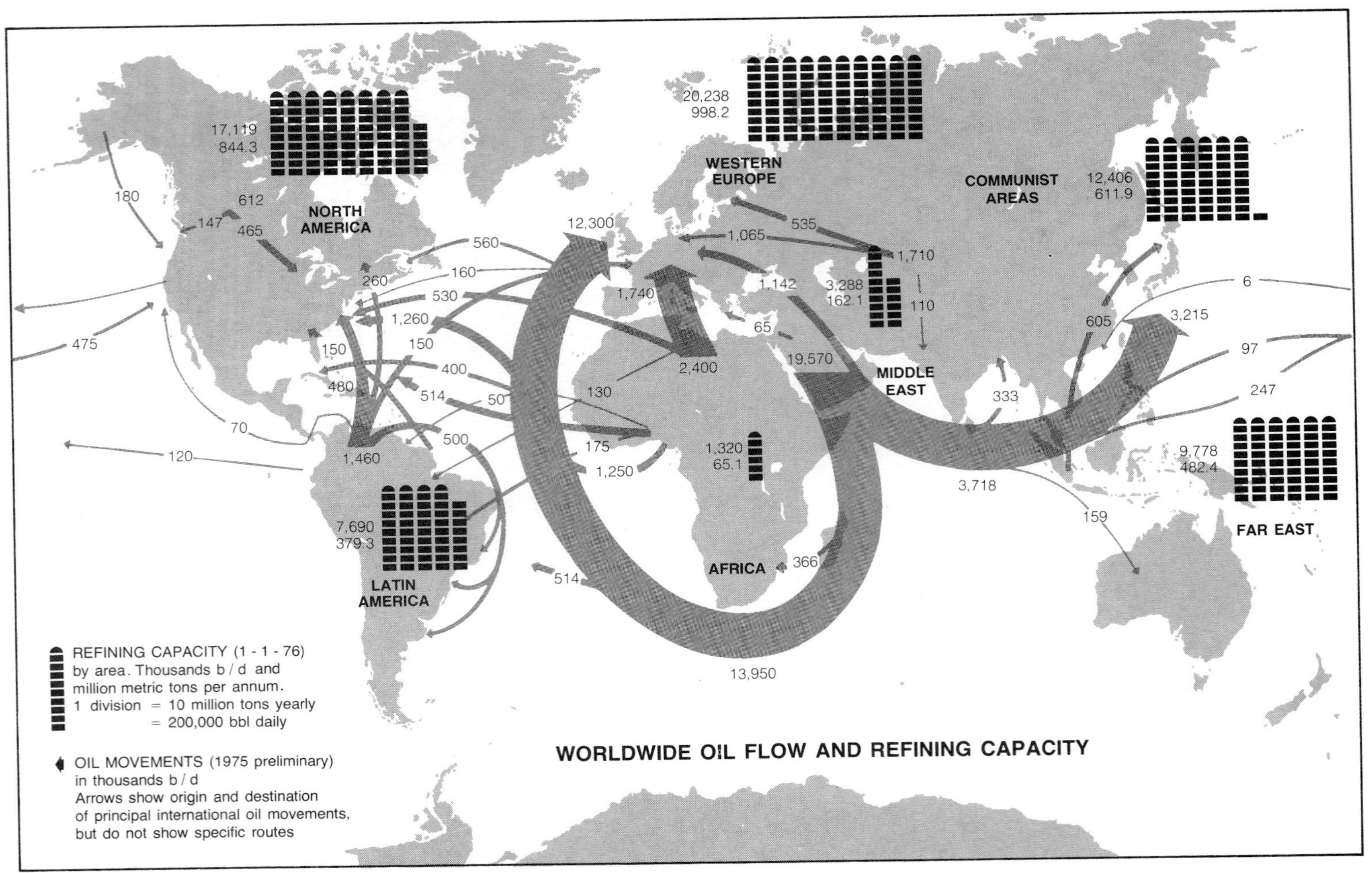

FIGURE 8-2

Global patterns of petroleum transportation. Arrows show origins and destinations of major international oil movements, although specific routes may differ from those shown. (After *International petroleum encyclopedia,* 1976, by permission of the publisher.)

TABLE 8-2
Energy and Prosperity. Energy Use and GNP in Selected Countries, 1973

Country	*Annual energy consumption per capita (MJ)*	*Equivalent GNP per capita ($U.S.)*	*MJ/$*	*Net imports of energy (% of consumption)**
United States	344,000	6200	55	11
Czechoslovakia	193,000	2870	67	19
East Germany	180,000	3000	60	22
Sweden	176,000	5910	30	90
United Kingdom	166,000	3060	54	47
West Germany	167,000	5320	31	50
Netherlands	175,000	4330	40	37
USSR	142,000	2030	70	NE**
Switzerland	108,000	6100	18	80
Japan	104,000	3630	29	98
New Zealand	92,900	3680	25	58
Argentina	55,000	1640	34	12
Mexico	39,000	890	44	3
China, People's Republic	16,300	270	60	2
Brazil	16,300	760	21	54
Egypt	8,500	250	34	NE
India	5,400	120	45	18
Indonesia	3,800	130	29	NE
Nigeria	1,900	210	9	NE

Note: Excludes wood, dung, agricultural residues, food.
*1971.
**NE = net exporter.
Sources: UN, *Statistical yearbook,* World Bank, *Atlas.*

consumption, and transportation are represented in Figure 8-2. Some of the international transactions in money and influence that accompany the energy flows are taken up in Chapter 15. It is enough to note here that for the industrialized minority to depend so heavily on energy resources not controlled by them is economically, politically, and even ethically precarious, for consumer and producer alike.

How is energy used in human society? The pattern of supply and use of energy in the United States in 1975 is shown in Figure 8-3. If we ascribe to each end use all of the primary energy that had to be supplied to make the end use possible (including losses in any transformation and transportation steps leading to that end use),[4] we conclude: about 25 percent of energy used in the United States is burned as fuel in transportation, 21 percent is used in residences, 14 percent is used in commercial buildings and enterprises, and 40 percent is used for industrial and other uses. (Transportation includes passengers and freight, civilian and military; commercial uses include government and private offices, stores, hospitals, and educational institutions; industrial uses include agriculture as well as manufacturing and other industrial activities.) The end uses of energy are treated in more detail at the end of the chapter, where we discuss the potential for energy conservation.

One-fourth of the U.S. primary energy supply is converted to electricity before being distributed for end use. With the exception of the hydroelectric component, this electricity is presently produced via a series of transformations of the form: potential energy of fuel (chemical or nuclear) → thermal energy → mechanical energy → electricity. The overall efficiency of this process, defined as the ratio of the electrical energy produced to the potential energy extracted from the fuel, averages only about 33 percent. The other two-thirds of the energy extracted from the fuel is discharged to the environment as thermal energy of very low availability (that is, the temperature of this thermal discharge is only slightly higher than that of its surroundings). The electricity, for which so high a price in fuel has been paid, is itself very high-grade energy and generally pays back

[4]The term *primary energy* refers to the basic energy sources—such as fossil and nuclear fuels, sunlight, the energy of falling water—from which *secondary energy* forms such as electricity and synthetic fuels can be made. *Losses* refers to that part of the energy that becomes degraded to unused or unusable forms (generally heat) in the course of processing and application (refer to Box 2-2).

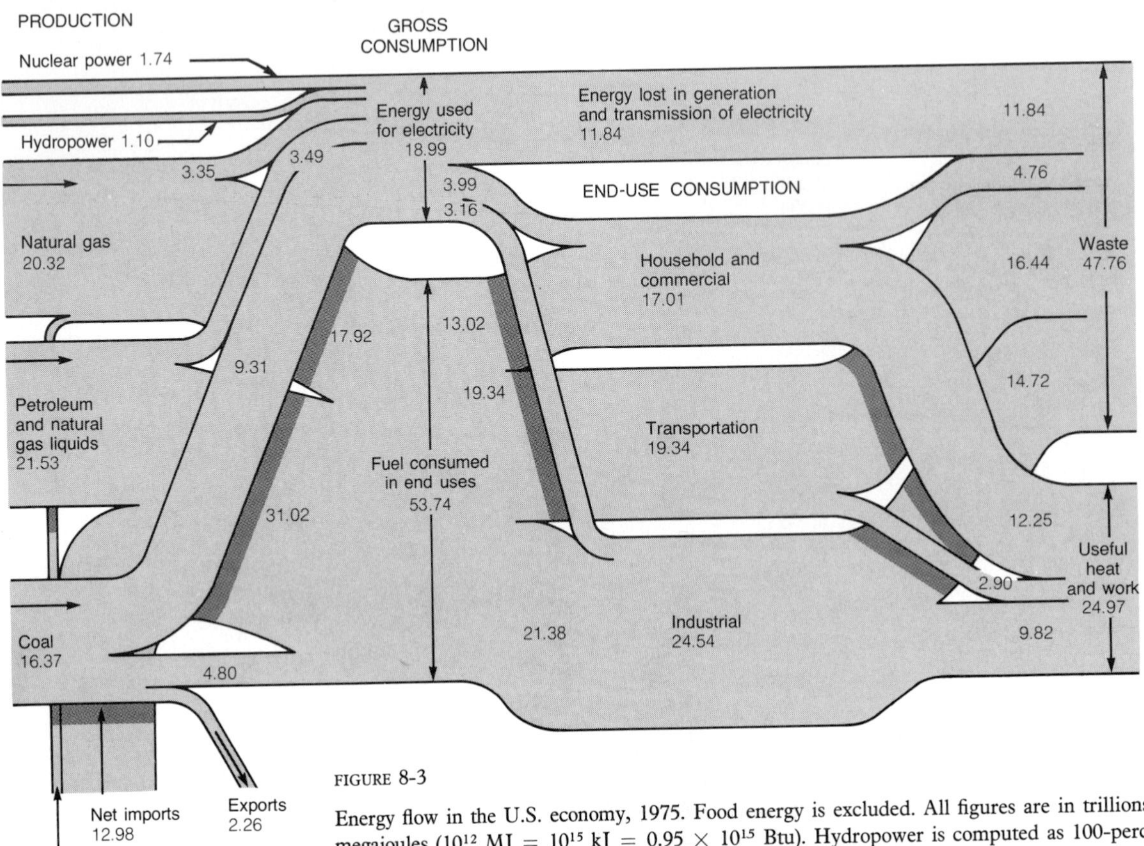

FIGURE 8-3

Energy flow in the U.S. economy, 1975. Food energy is excluded. All figures are in trillions of megajoules (10^{12} MJ = 10^{15} kJ = 0.95 × 10^{15} Btu). Hydropower is computed as 100-percent efficient. Changes in inventories (invariably relatively small) are lumped with net imports or exports. Industrial consumption includes nonfuel uses of energy resources (e.g., asphalt, petrochemicals). Efficiency figures used to disaggregate useful heat and work from waste are Cook's very rough estimates of first-law efficiency: household/commercial, 72 percent; transportation, 15 percent; industrial, 40 percent. Electric generation efficiency averages about 38 percent when hydro is included. (After Cook, 1976, updated using U.S. Bureau of Mines news release, 5 April 1976.)

some of the investment as high efficiency at the point of application. (The concept of efficiency is discussed further in Box 8-1.)

Energy use in the United States, as diagrammed in Figure 8-3, amounts to about a third of the world's total. The pattern in other DCs is similar to that in the United States, although typically a smaller fraction goes to transportation. In the Federal German Republic (West Germany), for example, transportation accounts for only about 15 percent of energy use; in Sweden, the figure is 16 percent.[5] Worldwide, about 25 percent of all primary energy used goes to generate electricity, as in the United States. Few reliable data are available on detailed patterns of energy consumption in LDCs.[6]

GROWTH AND CHANGE IN ENERGY FLOWS

Many of the most interesting and problematic aspects of the energy situation involve not merely the sizes that the energy flows within civilization have already attained, but the rates at which those flows are growing and the rates at which the patterns of supply behind them are changing. The growth of energy use in the United States between 1880 and 1975, broken down into the major

[5] W. Haefele, Energy choices that Europe faces; L. Schipper and A. Lichtenberg, Efficient energy use and well-being: The Swedish example.

[6] But see Makhijani and Poole, *Energy*, for the best available information on the subject.

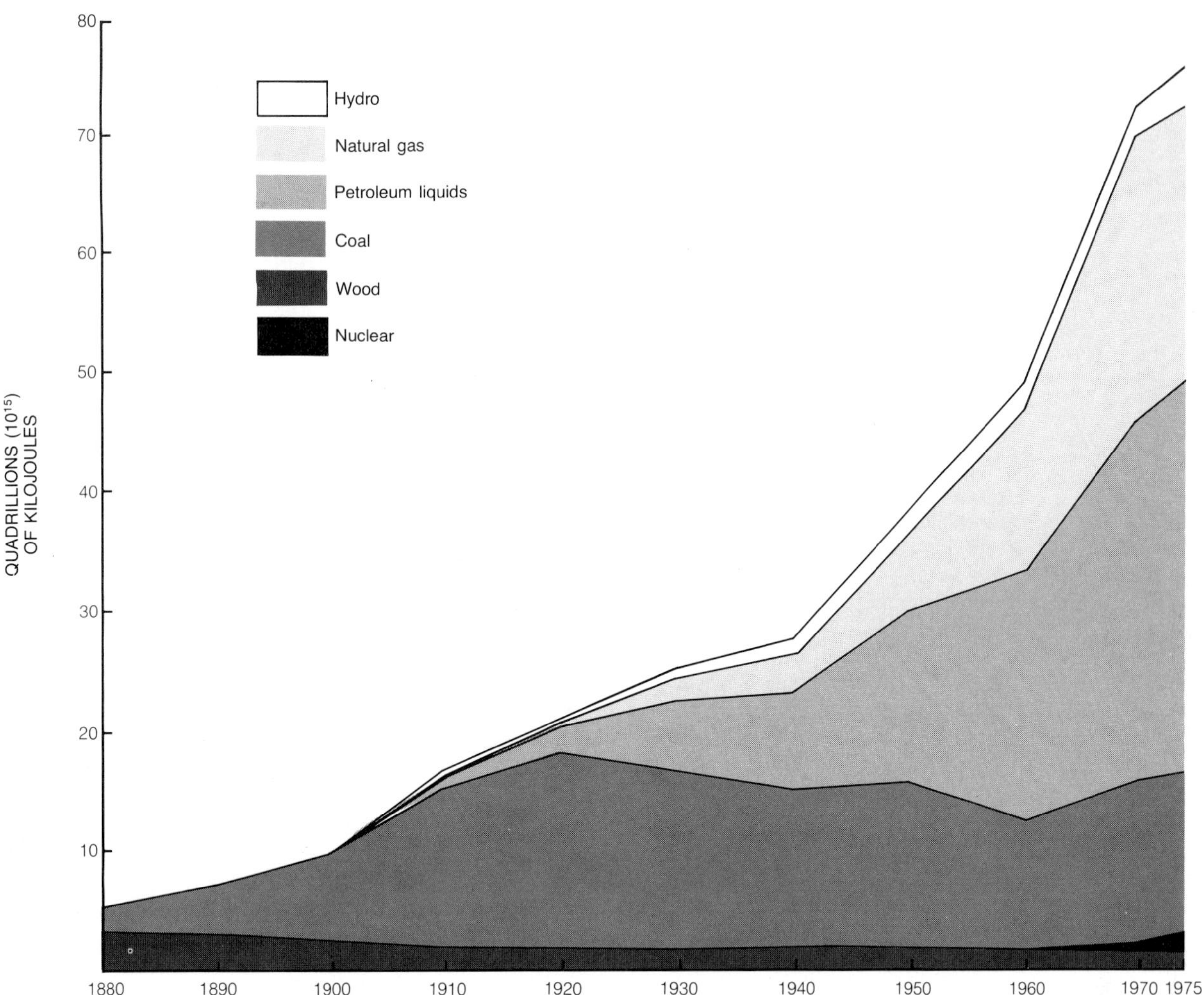

FIGURE 8-4

The evolution of energy use and sources of energy supply in the United States, 1880–1975. Note the continuing dominance of fossil fuels.

sources of supply, is shown in Figure 8-4. Note the decline in the importance of wood as a fuel, from 50 percent of the total supply in 1880 to perhaps 1 percent in 1975. Total U.S. energy use in 1975 was about 15 times what it was in 1880, with a U.S. population in 1975 that was 4.3 times what it was in 1880. Hence, energy use per person increased by a factor of 3.5 in that period. Thus we can say, as a crude first approximation, that population growth and energy use per person were about equally "responsible" for the increase in total energy use. The average annual rates of growth of energy use and population in the United States in different periods are indicated in Table 8-3.

In the global context, wood, dung, and agricultural

TABLE 8-3
Growth of Energy Use and Population in the United States

	Average annual rate of growth (%)		
	Population	*Energy use per person*	*Total energy use*
1880–1910	2.0	1.8	3.8
1910–1929	1.5	1.1	2.6
1929–1932	0.8	−9.3	−8.6
1932–1945	0.9	3.8	4.7
1945–1965	1.7	1.2	2.5
1965–1975	1.0	2.0	3.0

Sources: U.S. Department of Commerce, *Statistical abstract of the United States;* U.S. Department of Commerce, *Historical statistics of the United States.*

BOX 8-1 Efficiency

A definition of efficiency that is suitable for some purposes is:

$$\text{efficiency} = \frac{\begin{array}{c}\text{amount of energy delivered}\\ \text{in the form and replace desired}\end{array}}{\begin{array}{c}\text{amount of energy that must}\\ \text{be supplied to achieve the above}\end{array}}.$$

This efficiency takes no explicit account of the thermodynamic quality of the energy supplied, only the quantity, so it is called the *first-law efficiency.* (Recall from Box 2-2 and Box 2-3 that the first law of thermodynamics helps analysts keep track of the quantity of energy, while the second law helps them keep track of the quality of energy as well—that is, its availability for doing work.)

Applying the concept of first-law efficiency to the entire U.S. energy economy, Earl Cook has obtained the overall figure indicated on the right-hand side of Figure 8-3 (about 36 percent of the energy in the primary sources finally appears as useful heat and work).* The remaining 64 percent might be said to have been wasted, but that is an ambiguous term. Some of the energy was lost from the useful column because of imperfections in the energy technologies that were used, and some represented the toll that, according to the second law of thermodynamics, could not be avoided even by perfect technologies. The concept of first-law efficiency does not distinguish between these two kinds of waste.

*Earl Cook, *Man, energy, society.*

It is therefore useful to define another kind of efficiency that measures *by how much* the performance of a device or process falls short of what is theoretically attainable. To do this, one must keep track not of energy per se (which, according to the first law, is not used up at all) but rather of the availability of energy to do work (which is the important thing and *is* used up). The desired measure, called *second-law efficiency,* is the ratio

$$\frac{\begin{array}{c}\text{minimum amount of available work}\\ \text{needed to perform a desired function}\end{array}}{\begin{array}{c}\text{actual amount of available work}\\ \text{used to perform the function}\end{array}}.$$

The term *available work* is coming into widespread use as shorthand for "availability of energy to do work," which, again, is the value used up in all physical processes. The available work in a chemical fuel is approximately equal to its so-called *heat-of-combustion.* The available work in an object of mass m suspended a height h above the ground is equal to its gravitational potential energy ($m \times g \times h$, where g is the acceleration of gravity). The available work in a quantity of heat Q at temperature T_1 in an environment of temperature T_0 is $Q \times (1 - T_0/T_1)$, where the temperatures must be relative to absolute zero.**

**The best detailed exposition of the concepts of available work and second-law efficiency is American Physical Society, *Efficient use of energy,* pt. 1, *A physics perspective.*

wastes have remained somewhat more important energy sources than in the United States, but have declined from supplying 50 percent of worldwide energy use in 1880 to 20 percent in 1960 and perhaps to 15 percent in 1975. The growth in total energy use worldwide averaged 2.6 percent per year from 1880 to 1950 and about 3.5 percent per year from 1950 to 1975. The growth of population climbed steadily from 0.6 percent annually to perhaps 1.5 percent in the first period and averaged almost 2 percent per year between 1950 and 1975. Thus, the global rate of growth of energy use per person has stayed roughly in the range of 1 percent to 1.5 percent per year for essentially a century. Growth of the use of fossil fuels, which have supported most of the increase in world energy consumption since 1900, has recently been much more rapid—almost 5 percent per year between 1950 and 1972, compared to an average of 3.1 percent per year from 1880 to 1950. The per-capita growth rates in the use of fossil fuels during the spurt of growth since 1950 have ranged from 2.5 percent to more than 4 percent per year.

Many forecasts have projected enormous increases in U.S. and worldwide consumption of fossil and nuclear fuels over the next several decades, on the assumption that recent annual growth rates of 3 percent to 4 percent

The difference between first-law efficiency and second-law efficiency is made clearer by an example. Consider the task of heating a house, with the desired indoor temperature being 20° C (68° F) and the outdoor temperature being 0° C (32° F). An ordinary furnace operating under these conditions might manage to deliver to the rooms of the house 1 unit of energy as heat for every 1.5 units of energy extracted from its fuel. Its first-law efficiency would then be

$$\frac{\text{1 unit of heat in the rooms}}{\text{1.5 units of energy supplied from fuel}} \doteq 0.67 = 67 \text{ percent.}$$

Application of the second law of thermodynamics to the situation reveals that the minimum amount of available work required to deliver 1 unit of heat at 20° C to the inside of the house is only 0.07 units. (This is the amount of available work needed to operate the most efficient possible *heat pump* between the outside and inside temperatures specified, per unit of heat delivered. Heat pumps are further discussed later in this chapter.) Thus the second-law efficiency of the furnace in the application in question is

$$\frac{\text{0.07 units of available work (minimum needed to deliver 1 unit of heat)}}{\text{1.5 units of available work (heat of combustion of fuel actually used by furnace)}},$$

or about 4.7 percent.

Second-law efficiencies, we emphasize again, give a measure of how much improvement in performance is theoretically attainable (a low second-law efficiency means there is much potential for technological improvement). Widespread use of first-law efficiencies, which are usually much higher, may have led to the erroneous belief that potential gains in the efficiency of energy uses are small. In 1974, when a study group of the American Physical Society investigated the second-law efficiencies of the U.S. energy system, the figures they obtained were: industrial processes, 25 percent; space heating and cooling, 6 percent; transportation, 10 percent; and electricity generation, 30 percent.†

Obviously, there is a good deal of theoretical potential for improving efficiency of energy use before thermodynamics calls a halt. It must be remembered, however, that energy usefully applied, as well as the energy "lost" in the process, eventually ends up in the environment as low-grade heat. High efficiency reduces the total of that heat burden but cannot eliminate it.

†American Physical Society, *Efficient use of energy.*

per capita in the use of nonagricultural energy (rates we know are anomalous in historical terms) will be maintained. If such forecasts were accepted as descriptions of what the future should or must be like, there would be no choice but to embrace every available option for expanding energy supply—and quickly, with little time to deliberate about environmental and social impacts. Many people have suggested precisely this approach for U.S. and world energy policies. As a wise observer has remarked, however, trend is not destiny. Projections are not reliable as predictions; they merely give some idea what the future might be like under various sets of assumptions. If society does not like the picture of the future that some of the projections provide, it is at liberty to work to change the trends and assumptions that lead to those results.

To understand the implications of continuing recent trends in energy use—and to evaluate possibilities for modifying those trends—requires first of all a careful look at the technical side of the energy situation. In the next two sections of text, we investigate some of the main technical issues: the magnitude of energy resources, and the characteristics of the technologies available or under development for harnessing those resources.

ENERGY RESOURCES: SUPPLIES, DEPLETION, LIMITS

Among the major questions that arise in connection with present and projected patterns of energy use are those concerning the adequacy of the supplies of energy resources. Which resources are scarce and which abundant? What does it mean to run out, and how accurately can such eventualities be predicted? What is the potential for harnessing inexhaustible sources?

It is useful at the outset to distinguish between stock-limited, or *nonrenewable*, resources and flow-limited, or *renewable*, ones. The first category refers to fuels of which the Earth is endowed with fixed stocks; once the stocks are depleted, no more will be available on any time scale of practical interest. The main examples are the fossil fuels (principally coal, petroleum, natural gas, tar sands, and oil shales) and the nuclear fuels (principally uranium, thorium, deuterium, and lithium). The fossil fuels were accumulated over hundreds of millions of years, when plant material incorporating stored solar energy was separated from the energy cycle of the biosphere by biological and geophysical happenstance. The nuclear fuels are thought to have originated when the constituents that eventually became our sun and its planets were fused together from elemental hydrogen in more distant stars. How long the fixed stocks of fuel materials will last depends on how much is ever found in exploitable form (it is not obvious that all that exists will be found) and on the rate at which civilization chooses to exploit what is found.

Flow-limited resources, by contrast, are virtually inexhaustible in duration but limited in the amount of energy that is available per unit of time. The most important example is solar energy, including not only the incoming radiation from the sun but also the various other harnessable forms of energy into which sunlight is converted by natural processes: falling water, wind, waves, ocean currents, temperature differences in the oceans, and plant materials. A much smaller flow-limited source is the energy of the tides, which is derived from the kinetic and potential energy of the Earth-moon-sun system.

Geothermal energy is more difficult to classify as stock-limited or flow-limited, having some characteristics of both. At present, the exploitable form of geothermal energy consists of isolated pockets of hot water or steam. Those local stocks are depleted by use, but on a time scale of decades, or perhaps centuries, they can probably be replenished from the much larger stock of geothermal energy in the Earth's molten core. Future methods of tapping the geothermal energy stored in relatively deep dry rock will also be stock-limited in a short-term sense but flow-limited (by the rate at which heat flows from surrounding regions into the depleted rock) in the long term.

Analysis of the depletion of conventional stock-limited energy resources is itself a complicated enterprise. Much confusion is sometimes engendered in this connection by failure to distinguish clearly between reserves and resources. The term *reserves* generally refers to material whose location is known (proved reserves) or inferred from strong geologic evidence (probable reserves) and which can be extracted with known technology under present economic conditions (that is, at costs such that the material could be sold at or near prevailing prices). The *resources* of a substance include the reserves and, in addition, material whose location and quantity are less well established or which cannot be extracted under prevailing technological and economic conditions. The term *ultimately recoverable resources* describes an estimate of how much material will ever be found and extracted (implicitly including an assessment of how effective technology will ever become and how much civilization will ever be willing to pay for the material). Such estimates are necessarily very crude. The relation between reserves and resources is illustrated in Figure 8-5.

Probably the least sophisticated approach to the analysis of depletion is to estimate the lifetime of the supply by dividing present proved reserves by the present rate of consumption. This approach is the origin of the often-heard statements to the effect that, "We have *X* years' worth of petroleum left." The method errs because consumption is not likely to stay constant and because proved reserves often bear little relation to ultimately recoverable resources. Generally it doesn't pay to do the exploration and evaluation needed to establish new proved reserves when the material will not be extracted and turn a profit until fifteen or twenty years in the future; this is the main reason proved reserves rarely amount to more than a few decades' supply.

A somewhat more instructive way to assess the lifetime of a fuel is to divide available estimates of the ultimately recoverable resources by a level of consumption several times the present one (on the assumption that consumption will level off before too long) or a level of consumption continuing to grow as it has in the recent past. A shortcoming if a constant consumption is assumed is the sensitivity of the result to highly uncertain estimates of the resource and of the equilibrium level of consumption; if continuous growth is assumed, the result is not so sensitive to errors in the resource estimate but is very sensitive to the growth rate chosen.

The most realistic approach seems to be one devised by geologist M. King Hubbert.[7] He notes that the production cycle for any stock-limited resource is likely to be characterized by several phases: first, increasingly rapid growth in the rate of exploitation as demand rises, production becomes more efficient, and costs per unit of material fall; then a leveling-off of production as the resource becomes scarcer and starts to rise in price; and finally a continuous decline in the rate of exploitation, as increasing scarcity and declining quality proceed more rapidly than can be compensated for by improving technology, and as substitutes are brought fully to bear. Hubbert's approach incorporates explicitly the fact that society never really runs out of anything suddenly or completely; it merely uses the most concentrated and accessible supplies first and then gradually works its way into material of declining quality, until what remains is so dilute or so deep or so hard to find that it no longer pays to look for it and extract it.

A generalized illustration of Hubbert's production cycle appears in Figure 8-6. Note that the area under the production curve at any time represents the cumulative production up to that time and the amount under the "completed" curve represents the magnitude of the ultimately recoverable resources. The important measures of the lifetime of the fuel in this approach are the year in which the level of consumption reaches its peak (Y_p) and the year at which 90 percent of the ultimately recoverable resources has been extracted (Y_{90}).

[7]M. K. Hubbert, Energy resources. A recent update is M. K. Hubbert, *U.S. energy resources: A review as of 1972.*

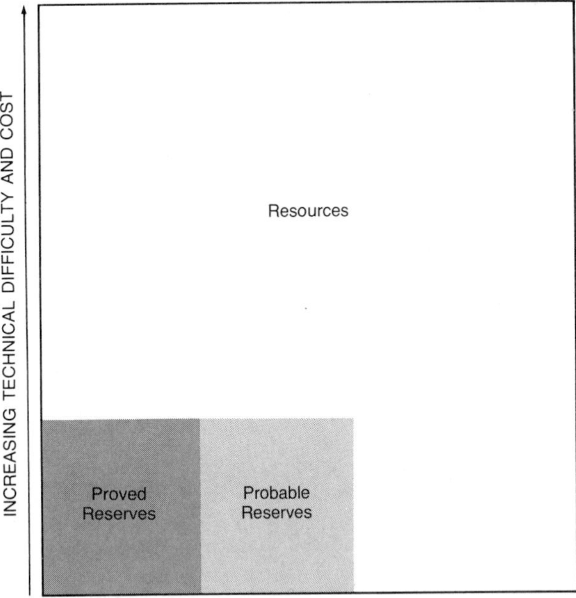

FIGURE 8-5

The relation between reserves and resources. Reserves comprise the part of the total resources that is extractable with present technology at or near present prices and the location and quality of which are well established. (Redrawn from J. Holdren, Energy resources, in *Environment,* 2d ed., W. Murdoch, ed., Sinauer Associates, Inc., by permission of the publisher.)

Conventional Fossil Fuels: Petroleum, Natural Gas, Coal

Summarized in Figure 8-7, for both the United States and the world, are values of recent annual consumption, proved reserves, and estimated remaining ultimately recoverable resources of the mainstays of today's energy use—petroleum, natural gas, and coal.[8] Note that the vertical scales in the figures are logarithmic, on which each major interval represents a multiplicative factor of 10. The difference between the low and high estimates of the remaining ultimately recoverable resources of petroleum liquids in the United States is more than a factor of 5. This point is the focus of a vigorous debate in the scientific community, reflecting varying interpretations

[8]The main sources of the data on reserves and resources are Cook, *Man, energy, society;* Hubbert, Energy resources; and *U.S. energy resources;* P. K. Theobald, S. P. Schweinfurth, and D. C. Duncan, *Energy resources of the United States;* National Academy of Sciences, *Mineral resources and the environment.*

FIGURE 8-6

The pattern of depletion of a finite resource. The rate of use increases exponentially at first as improved technology is brought to bear and economies of scale are exploited. Later, declining quantity and quality of the resource take over, and the rate of use levels off and then falls. Cumulative production up to any given time is represented by all the area under the curve to that time. (Redrawn from J. Holdren, Energy resources, in *Environment,* 2d ed., W. Murdoch, ed., Sinauer Associates, Inc., by permission of the publisher.)

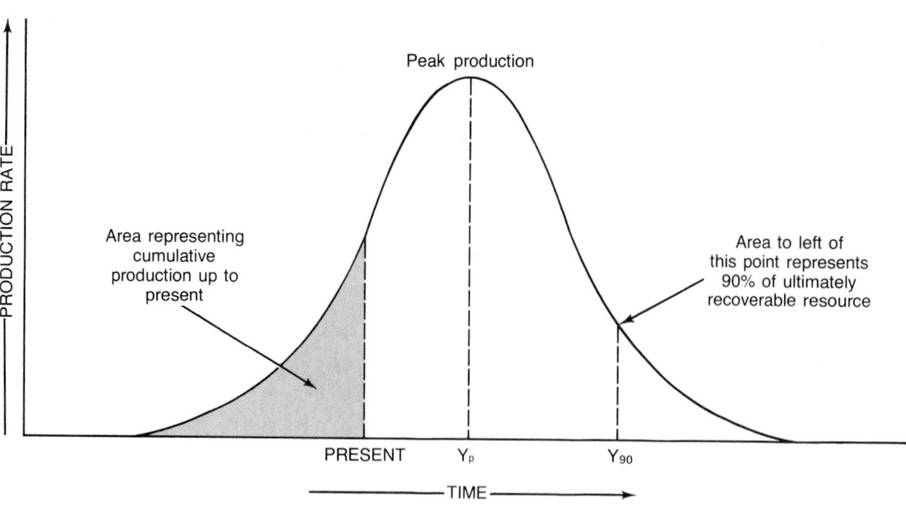

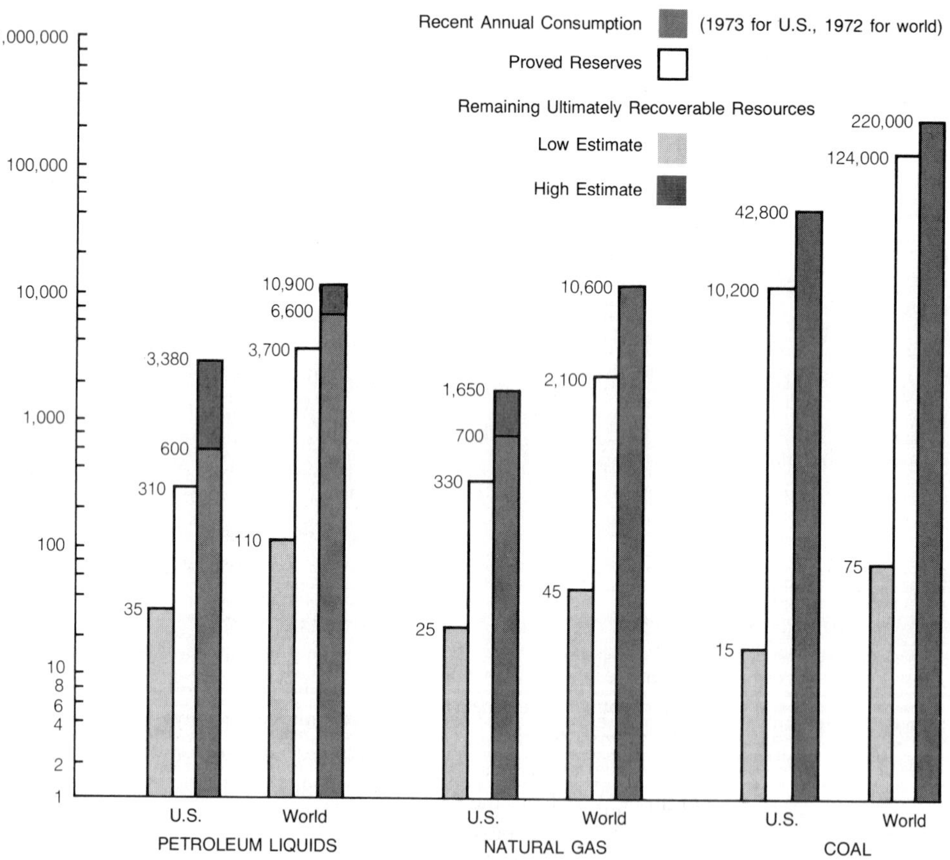

FIGURE 8-7

Reserves and resources of conventional fossil fuels (in trillions of megajoules). Estimates of reserves vary somewhat with the definitions used by the tabulating agency. Resource estimates vary even more widely. Note the logarithmic scale. (Various sources.)

TABLE 8-4
Lifetimes of Conventional Fossil-Fuel Resources

	At 1972/1973 rate of consumption (years)	*At 2.5%/yr increase in consumption*	*At 5%/yr increase in consumption*	*Date of* Y_p*	*Date of* Y_{90}*
UNITED STATES					
Petroleum liquids (lowest)	17	14	12	1970	2000
Petroleum liquids (highest)	97	49	35	2010	2050
Natural gas (lowest)	28	21	18	1980	2015
Coal	2800	171	99	2220	2450
WORLD					
Petroleum liquids (highest)	99	50	36	2000	2030
Coal	2900	172	100	2150	2400

*Hubbert's method.
Source: Based on data for ultimately recoverable resources in Figure 8-7.

of the geologic evidence and differing degrees of optimism about future extractive technologies.[9] While we suspect the lower estimates are more likely to prove correct, even the high estimates provide little leeway for continued growth in the consumption of oil and gas. This point is apparent in Table 8-4, which summarizes the results of applying various methods of analyzing depletion to the data of Figure 8-7.

Indeed, the clear message of Table 8-4 is that, by any method of analysis, U.S. supplies of petroleum and natural gas are severely limited. World supplies of those fuels, moreover, are almost as small in relation to projected demands as the U.S. supplies. Both for the United States and for the world, any significant increase in consumption of oil and gas will lead to the substantial depletion of the recoverable resources of those materials by early in the next century. And if the pessimists are correct, U.S. domestic production of petroleum was already near or even past its peak in 1974, with domestic natural gas not far behind.

U.S. and world supplies of coal are much larger—roughly 10 times the combined supplies of petroleum and natural gas. The coal resources could sustain consumption rates several times larger than today's for hundreds of years. As large as the supplies are, however, they could sustain a level of consumption that was growing continuously at 5 percent per year for only about a century—another example of the power (and danger) of high growth rates. The more realistic analysis by Hubbert suggests that coal consumption might peak around the year 2200 and that coal would be near the end of its importance as a major energy source some 200 years later.

A greatly expanded use of coal, which seems to be implied by the data on fuel supply, poses a number of problems. For coal to relieve the burden on petroleum and natural gas, it must be interchangeable with those fuels in a variety of applications. This interchangeability can be achieved by means of coal gasification and liquefaction, processes that are known to be technically feasible and capable of delivering 50 percent to 90 percent of the energy of the coal in the final gaseous or liquid synthetic fuel.[10] The facilities needed to accomplish these transformations are large, expensive industrial installations comparable in complexity to oil refineries (discussed below). The problem is not whether it can be done at all, but how quickly and at what cost in capital investment a significant transition from natural gas and petroleum to synthetic fuels from coal can be accomplished. This, along with the environmental liabilities of greatly increased reliance on coal, are discussed at greater length later.

Tar Sands and Oil Shale

Tar sands consist essentially of a mixture of sand and asphalt. The material is mined like rock and processed to convert the hydrocarbons into a synthetic crude petroleum. The principal known deposits are in Alberta,

[9]R. Gillette, Oil and gas resources: Academy calls USGS math misleading; S. F. Singer, Oil resource estimates; R. Gillette, Geological survey lowers its sights.

[10]See, for example, H. C. Hottel and J. B. Howard, *New energy technology: Some facts and assessments.*

Canada, and the energy recoverable from them amounts to about 1800 trillion megajoules.[11] (This is of the same order of magnitude as the remaining recoverable resources of petroleum in the United States.) A small commercial plant (about 50,000 barrels per day) has been in operation at the Athabasca tar sands since 1966, and several other commercial operations were scheduled for development in the late 1970s.

Oil shale consists of fine-grained sedimentary rock permeated by a rubbery solid hydrocarbon called *kerogen*. Oil shale is much more abundant than tar sands, but it is technologically more difficult to convert into synthetic crude oil. The Green River shales of Colorado, Utah, and Wyoming alone contain the equivalent of 2000 billion barrels of oil, or about 12,000 trillion megajoules, at concentrations of between 10 and 100 gallons of oil per ton of shale. Total U.S. resources at concentrations greater than 10 gallons per ton have been estimated at about 160,000 trillion megajoules. World resources of similar quality outside the United States have been estimated at 1,900,000 trillion megajoules.[12] How much of this vast amount of potential fuel can ever be extracted economically is completely uncertain at this time. Rising costs of conventional petroleum in the early 1970s sent major corporations scurrying to investigate the richer parts of the Green River shales. Whether substantial commercial operations develop there will depend for some time to come on investors' guesses about the price of petroleum in the future, as well as on future decisions concerning the environmental acceptability of oil shale operations. It is also possible that the oil shales will serve as the eventual source of hydrocarbons for lower-volume, recyclable uses for such activities as lubrication and the production of plastics, after the cheaper and more accessible sources have all been burned.

Nuclear Fuels: Fission

It has been rather widely assumed until recently that a shift to nuclear energy—first from fission and perhaps later from fusion—would provide the next major change in the composition of the world energy supply, augmenting and eventually supplanting the fossil fuels just as they earlier augmented and supplanted wood and agricultural wastes. Substitution of nuclear for fossil fuels is possible with today's technology only in the electricity-generation component of the energy economy, inasmuch as no commercial techniques exist for producing portable fuels in nuclear reactors or for using nuclear heat directly in industrial processes. Even so, nuclear energy production has been expanding at a rate that could quickly turn its 2-percent share of the world energy market in 1975 into a much larger one. A number of projections have suggested, for example, that the fraction of energy used in the United States to generate electricity will increase from 25 percent to 50 percent by the year 2000 and that nuclear reactors will then be providing half of that electrical half of the U.S. energy budget (or a quarter of the total). A variety of economic and environmental uncertainties that have arisen concerning nuclear fission now make forecasts of so large a role in the year 2000 seem questionable to many observers. One of the controversial issues has been the adequacy of the nuclear fuel supply under various circumstances; we consider that question here, deferring the others to a later section.

To understand discussions of nuclear fuel resources requires some knowledge of the way the fuels are used in fission reactors. This background is provided in Box 8-2. The essential conclusions are that uranium can actually deliver about 1 percent of its theoretical energy content in a contemporary converter reactor and perhaps 2 percent in an advanced converter reactor, and that uranium and thorium can deliver 40 percent to 70 percent of their theoretical energy contents in breeder reactors. Combining this information with estimates of domestic uranium resources published by the U.S. Energy Research and Development Administration (ERDA) and its predecessor, the U.S. Atomic Energy Commission (USAEC), gives the results shown in Table 8-5.[13] The resources are classified according to the so-called *forward cost* of uranium oxide (U_3O_8) from the

[11]Hubbert, Energy resources, and *U.S. energy resources.*

[12]Ibid; Theobald, Schweinfurth, and Duncan, *Energy resources.*

[13]In late 1974, part of the USAEC was merged with parts of other federal agencies dealing with energy development to form ERDA, and the other part of the USAEC became the Nuclear Regulatory Commission (NRC).

various deposits. The forward cost does not include certain parts of the uranium company's capital investment, nor does it make allowance for profit; it is therefore not to be confused with the *price* at which the uranium will be sold, which might be much higher. The quantities of uranium shown in Table 8-5 are sums of categories ERDA calls *identified resources* and *potential resources.*

The uncertainty in the estimates increases as the grade of ore decreases and the forward cost goes up. The resources in the range between \$66 and \$220 per kilogram are available only as by-products obtained when phosphorus, lignite, and other mineral products are mined and processed. The total quantity of uranium that can be recovered this way and the speed with which it can be recovered are highly uncertain and subject to factors outside the control of the uranium industry itself. The resources above \$220 per kilogram are from the Chattanooga shales of Tennessee and neighboring states. These shales contain only 60 to 70 parts per million (ppm) of U_3O_8 by weight, compared to 2000 ppm for the Colorado sandstones now being mined at a forward cost (in 1970 dollars) in the range of \$18 to \$22 per kilogram.

Controversy surrounds several aspects of the uranium-resource question. Some observers think that ERDA's estimate of the quantity of uranium ultimately recoverable at forward costs of \$66 per kilogram or less is as much as 3 times too high.[14] Others note that until 1972 the price of U_3O_8 was \$16 per kilogram or less, providing little incentive to explore for leaner, more expensive deposits. The price in 1976 had soared to \$80 per kilogram and more, prompting an expectation by many that more intensive (and successful) exploration for uranium in intermediate forward-cost categories would be stimulated.[15] And the size and precipitousness of the price rise worldwide led to suspicions, subsequently confirmed, of the existence of an international uranium cartel.[16]

Thorium supply is so far a much less controversial issue, in part because the lack of many commercial reactors designed to use it means there is little demand. Estimates of the thorium resource by the USAEC appear in Table 8-6.

The cost of electricity generated in nuclear reactors is so insensitive to the cost of raw uranium that the use of U_3O_8 costing \$110 per kilogram is not out of the question, even with the inefficient 1970 reactor technology.[17] (Should it prove *energetically* infeasible to use lean uranium ores in converter reactors—which seems quite unlikely—then this conclusion would have to be modified.) The U_3O_8 supplies listed at \$110 per kilogram or less in Table 8-5, if used in present-day converter reactors, could generate almost 300 times the 1975 U.S. electricity consumption. (Of course, the price reactor owners will have to pay for this uranium will be

TABLE 8-5
Recoverable U.S. Uranium Resources

Cost/kg U_3O_8 (1970 dollars)	*Quantity recoverable at this cost (million kg)*	*Energy in converter reactor* (trillion MJ)*	*Energy in breeder reactor** (trillion MJ)*
\$18 or less	745	588	35,000
\$18–\$22	445	351	21,000
\$22–\$33	691	546	33,000
\$33–\$66	1254	990	60,000
\$66–\$110†	4300	3400	204,000
\$110–\$220†	6700	5300	317,000
\$220–\$330†	4500+	3600+	215,000+

*1 percent of theoretical energy content.

**60 percent of theoretical energy content.

†Quantities in these categories are more uncertain than others.

Note: Compare 1975 U.S. energy use for electricity generation, 20 trillion MJ.

Sources: ERDA, *Report of the LMFBR program review group;* USAEC, *Potential nuclear power growth patterns.*

TABLE 8-6
U.S. Thorium Supplies and Their Energy Content

Cost/kg(\$)	*Kilograms recoverable at this cost*	*Energy content at 40% utilization (trillion MJ)*
33 or less	670	21,200
33–55	8,300	263,000
55–110	20,800	656,000

Source: USAEC, *Potential nuclear power growth patterns.*

[14]M. A. Lieberman, United States uranium resources: An analysis of historical data.

[15]For further discussions of the prospects in the leaner categories, see the uranium volume of National Academy of Sciences, *Mineral resources and the environment,* and U.S. Atomic Energy Commission, *Nuclear fuel resources and requirements.*

[16]It worked for the Arabs . . ., *Forbes,* January 15, 1975, pp. 19–21; Australian papers imply price-fixing cartel, *Nuclear News,* October 1976, p. 40.

[17]John P. Holdren, Uranium availability and the breeder decision.

BOX 8-2 Fission Reactors: Where the Energy Comes From

Nuclear fission is the splitting of certain heavy elements into lighter ones, thus releasing so much energy stored in the nuclear binding forces that the associated loss of mass is a detectable 0.1 percent (see also Box 2-2). Fission is induced when the nucleus of a suitable isotope is struck by a free neutron. (An *element* is characterized by the number of protons in the nucleus; different *isotopes* of the same element have the same number of protons but different numbers of neutrons in the nucleus.) Among the fragments from each fission event are some newly free neutrons—an average of about 2.5 per fission. The freeing of those neutrons makes possible a chain reaction: one or more of the newly free neutrons induces a new fission, which produces other free neutrons, which induce more fissions, and so on.

If a chain reaction grows very rapidly, the result is a fission bomb. In a 20-kiloton weapon, a kilogram of nuclear fuel is fissioned in a fraction of a millionth of a second, producing 999 grams of fission products and converting the other gram of the original mass into 79 million megajoules of heat, light, X-rays, and blast waves.* In a fission reactor, by contrast, the chain reaction is nurtured carefully to the desired level and then maintained there. In a large reactor generating electricity at a rate of 1000 electrical megawatts, it takes about seven hours to fission a kilogram of nuclear fuel. (Dividing the 79 million megajoules, almost all of which appears in the reactor as heat, by the number of seconds in seven hours gives a rate of 3000 megawatts. This *thermal power* is converted to electrical power at an efficiency of about one-third.) To obtain 79 million megajoules of thermal energy from the combustion of coal requires almost 3 million kilograms—a startling contrast to the equivalent 1 kilogram of fissioned material.

Isotopes that can sustain a fission chain reaction are called *fissile*. There are three important ones: uranium-235 ($_{92}U^{235}$), plutonium-239 ($_{94}Pu^{239}$), and uranium-233 ($_{92}U^{233}$). (The subscript tells the number of protons in the nucleus; the superscript tells the number of protons plus neutrons.) Of the fissile isotopes, only uranium-235 occurs in appreciable quantities naturally. It makes up 0.7 percent of the element uranium in nature. Plutonium-239 is produced by a series of nuclear transformations that may ensue after uranium-238 (the other 99.3 percent of natural uranium) is struck by a fast-moving neutron. Isotopes that can be transformed into fissile ones this way are called *fertile*. The other important fertile isotope is thorium-232 ($_{90}Th^{232}$), which upon being struck by a slow-moving neutron may undergo a series of transformations leading to fissile uranium-233. If struck by a particularly energetic neutron, the fertile isotopes uranium-238 and thorium-232 may also fission, but they are incapable of sustaining fission chain reactions on their own.

Most present-day nuclear fission reactors use uranium-235 as the primary nuclear fuel. A mixture of uranium-235 and uranium-238 is present in the reactor, and some of the neutrons released by the fission of uranium-235 strike uranium-238 nuclei to initiate the transformation to plutonium-239. Some of that plutonium is subsequently fissioned itself while still in the reactor, thus contributing to the chain reaction. (This process can be thought of as indirect fission of uranium-238.) Some plutonium remains when, after a year or so, the spent fuel is removed from the reactor. That plutonium, if recovered at a fuel reprocessing plant along with the unconverted and unfissioned uranium remaining in the fuel, may be recycled as fuel for the reactor that produced it; it may be saved for use in future reactors; or it may be used to manufacture nuclear bombs. The reactions in this nuclear fuel cycle and the similar one involving thorium are diagramed in Figure 8-8.

When all the details are taken into account, we find that a present-day commercial light-water-cooled reactor (LWR), recycling its plutonium, would fission about 10 grams of nuclear fuel (uranium or plutonium made from uranium) for

*About 79 million megajoules (in the form of heat, light, and blast waves) would be produced by detonating 20,000 tons of TNT; hence the "20-kiloton" rating of the bomb.

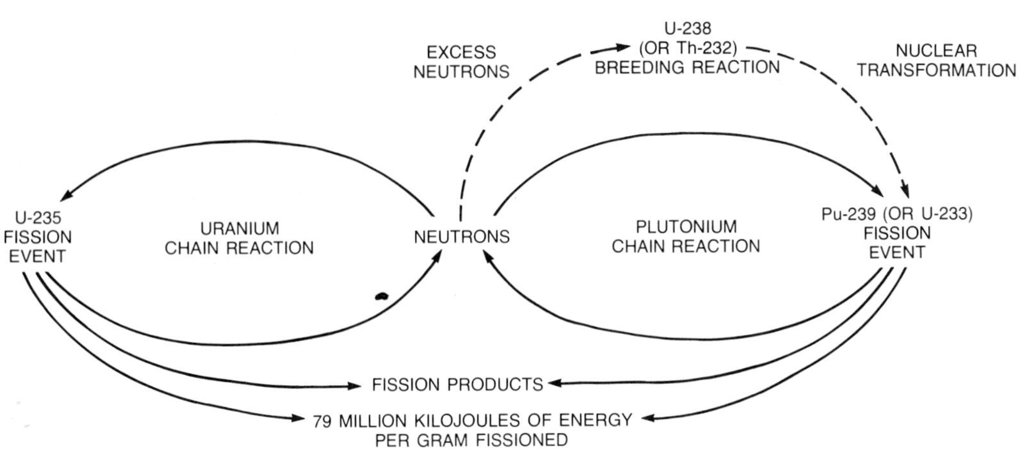

FIGURE 8-8

Nuclear reactions of uranium, thorium, and plutonium. A chain reaction occurs when one of the neutrons from each fission event initiates another fission event. Neutrons in excess of those needed to sustain the chain reaction may initiate transformations of fertile nuclei to fissile ones. In the "thorium cycle," the right-hand chain reaction runs on uranium-233 instead of plutonium. (Redrawn from J. Holdren, in *Environment,* 2d ed., Sinauer Associates, Inc., by permission of the publisher.)

every kilogram of natural uranium that is mined. This is a fuel-utilization efficiency of 1 percent, compared to the unattainable ideal in which every uranium nucleus mined is fissioned, directly or indirectly. If the plutonium is not recycled, the LWR's fuel utilization drops to 0.7 percent, or 7 grams fissioned per kilogram mined. A more advanced, high-temperature gas-cooled reactor (HTGR) relying on the Th-232 /U-233 conversion process may be able to achieve a fuel-utilization efficiency of about 2 percent, fissioning 20 grams of nuclear fuel for every kilogram of uranium mined. (For that type of reactor, uranium is the limiting resource even though some thorium is used; the fuel cycle requires the mining of only 1 kilogram of thorium for every 5 kilograms of uranium, and thorium is about 3 times as abundant in nature as uranium is.) One commercial-size demonstration plant of this type began operation in 1976 in the United States.

Water-cooled and gas-cooled reactors of the kinds just described are called *converters,* in reference to their ability to convert modest amounts of fertile material to fissile fuel. When the conversion ratio—the number of fertile to fissile conversions per fissile nucleus consumed—is low, the term *burner* is sometimes also used for such a reactor. By means of drastic changes in design, it is possible to build a reactor that converts fertile material to fissile fuel faster than the reactor consumes fissile fuel in its own chain reaction. Such a reactor is called a *breeder.* In terms of the fission reactions depicted in Figure 8-8, breeder reactors permit elimination of the loop that depends on scarce uranium-235. The fuel utilization of possible future breeder reactors could be perhaps 40 percent for fuel cycles based on the Th-232/U-233 conversion and 60 to 70 percent for fuel cycles based on the U-238/Pu-239 conversion (400 to 700 grams fissioned per kilogram of uranium or thorium mined).**

**For a more thorough treatment of the physics and technology of fission, see D. R. Inglis, *Nuclear energy: Its physics and its social challenge.*

somewhat higher than the cost given; but it is unlikely that uranium suppliers will try to charge more than operators of existing reactors can pay.) Breeder reactors could even use U_3O_8 priced at \$500 or \$1000 per kilogram without this expense's noticeably influencing the price of electricity; even prices much higher than forward costs for the leanest resources listed could be tolerated. Used in breeders, all the uranium resources listed amount to about 50,000 times the 1975 U.S. electricity consumption. The situation for thorium is similar: even the most expensive supplies listed in Table 8-6 could be utilized without noticeable impact on the price of electricity. Should our descendants choose to do so, they could probably also extract for use in breeder reactors the 4 trillion kilograms of uranium in the oceans and the even larger quantities of uranium and thorium dispersed in such common rocks as granite.

The rest of the world has been even less thoroughly explored for uranium and thorium than the United States. Estimated recoverable supplies of uranium outside the United States, below \$33 per kilogram of U_3O_8, amounted in 1973 to about 1.9 billion kilograms, or 50 percent more than the corresponding U.S. figure.[18] No meaningful figures are available above that cost range. The types of geologic formations that may contain significant concentrations of these fuels are widely distributed around the globe, however, and it is possible that uranium and thorium resources will be found on the various continents roughly in proportion to land area. This does not mean of course, that all countries are likely to be equally well endowed—or even endowed at all. In the mid-1970s the bulk of the world's identified uranium reserves were in relatively few countries (the United States, Canada, South Africa, France, Australia, Sweden, and Brazil), facilitating the formation of the cartel mentioned above.[19]

In the long term, however, it seems likely that the most serious difficulties with fission power, for the world as well as for the United States, will involve not the total supply or the cost of fuel but the other economic, environmental, and social aspects we discuss later.

[18] J. Cameron, A review of long term uranium resources, problems, and requirements in relation to demand 1975–2025.

[19] United States National Committee of the World Energy Conference, *World energy conference survey of energy resources, 1974.*

Nuclear Fuels: Fusion

The energy of the sun and of the hydrogen bomb comes from the fusing of light nuclei to form somewhat heavier ones, rather than from the fissioning of heavy nuclei. Harnessing fusion reactions in a nonexplosive way on the surface of Earth is far more difficult than harnessing fission. But controlled fusion—when it is at last achieved—could offer impressive advantages over fission with respect to safety, magnitude of long-lived radioactive wastes, and accessibility of an enormous fuel supply (fusion technology is considered in detail below).

The most suitable fuels for Earthbound fusion are the two heavy isotopes of hydrogen—*deuterium* and *tritium.* Deuterium (${}_1H^2$, usually abbreviated "D") is nonradioactive, and occurs in seawater in the ratio of 1 deuterium atom for every 6700 atoms of ordinary hydrogen. This does not sound like much, but it is a great deal; the deuterium in a gallon of seawater is equivalent in energy content to more than 300 gallons of gasoline. Tritium (${}_1H^3$, usually abbreviated "T") is radioactive with a half-life of 12.3 years and is almost nonexistent in nature; it can, however, be produced readily by bombarding lithium with neutrons. Lithium is thus a *fertile* material for fusion in much the same way that thorium-232 and uranium-238 are fertile materials for fission.

The principal fusion reactions are illustrated in Figure 8-9. The D-T reaction is significantly easier to achieve than the reactions involving deuterium alone, and early fusion reactors will almost unquestionably rely on it; hence, the tritium-producing reactions and the supply of lithium are of great importance. Lithium in its natural form consists of 92.6 percent lithium-7 and 7.4 percent lithium-6. Some calculations of the effective energy content of lithium as a fusion fuel have erroneously assumed that only the rarer lithium-6 could be used and thus have underestimated the energy available. The lithium-7 reaction consumes some energy, but far less than is obtained when the resulting tritium undergoes fusion. When the use of both lithium-7 and lithium-6 is taken into account, one finds that the net energy derived from converting a gram of natural lithium to tritium and then fusing the tritium with deuterium is between 45,000 and 90,000 megajoules, depending on the technology used. These figures are to be compared with the 30,000

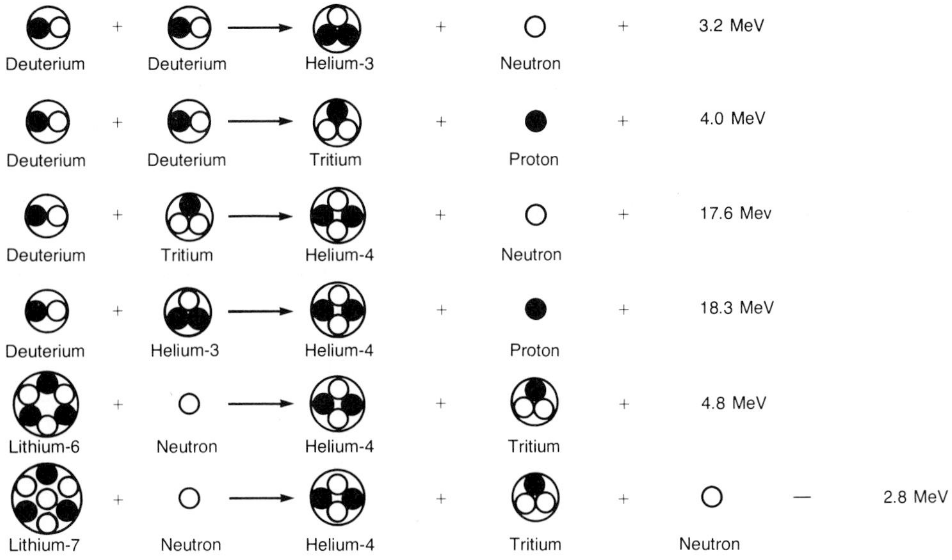

FIGURE 8-9

The most important reactions for terrestrial controlled fusion. The reaction that consumes tritium is the "easiest" to harness. The tritium consumed in this reaction must be produced from lithium by means of the two reactions at the bottom. Energy yields are in millions of electron volts (MeV) per reaction. (After Gough and Eastlund, 1971.)

megajoules one expects from a gram of natural lithium if only the contribution of the lithium-6 is considered. Lithium occurs in mineral ores called pegmatites, in heavy brines, and in seawater at a concentration of 0.17 grams per cubic meter (compared to 33 grams per cubic meter for deuterium).

Table 8-7 outlines the availability of the basic fusion fuels. Deuterium is so abundant as to be almost inexhaustible—it could supply a world energy demand much larger than today's for billions of years—and the technology for extracting it cheaply is already well established. Although lithium is less abundant, today's reserves and estimated resources[20] on land could support a greatly increased energy demand for centuries.[21] That should be long enough for technologists to make D-D fusion work or to learn to extract the lithium from the oceans. As with fission, limits on the use of fusion are much more likely to be based on environmental or social restraints than on availability of fuel.

[20] J. J. Norton, Lithium, cesium, and rubidium.

[21] John P. Holdren, Adequacy of lithium supplies as a fusion energy source.

TABLE 8-7
Fusion Fuels and Their Energy Content

Fuel	*Quality (billion kg)*	*Energy content (trillion MJ)*
LITHIUM		
U.S. reserves	4.0	360,000
U.S. estimated resources	2.9	260,000
Reserves outside the U.S.	0.4	36,000
Estimated resources outside the U.S.	2.7	240,000
Oceans	250,000	22,500,000,000
DEUTERIUM (IN OCEANS)	50,000,000	17,300,000,000,000

Sources: J. J. Norton, Lithium, cesium, and rubidium; John P. Holdren, Adequacy of lithium supplies as a fusion energy source.

Geothermal Energy

The size of geothermal energy resources is extraordinarily difficult to estimate, because the amount that can be recovered depends completely on the details of a technology that has only begun to be developed. A 1975 review by the U.S. Geological Survey (USGS) indicates identified resources of high-temperature geothermal energy in the United States, recoverable with existing technology, as about 270 trillion megajoules.[22] At an efficiency of conversion to electricity of about 10 percent (so low because of the low temperature associated with geothermal heat), this modest amount of energy could deliver electric power at a rate of 27,000 megawatts for only 30 years. This is equivalent to the production of 25 to 30 large fossil-fuel power plants. The only operating geothermal power plant in the United States, at The Geysers in northern California, had a capacity of about 500 electrical megawatts (Mwe) in 1976.

The United States has not been carefully explored for geothermal potential, however, and some experts believe that the potential of a single field in California's Imperial Valley exceeds the USGS figure for recoverable reserves in the entire United States. The USGS 1975 estimate for discovered and *undiscovered* high-temperature and intermediate-temperature geothermal resources in the ground in the United States was 12,000 trillion megajoules. In addition, the USGS estimated that there might be as much as 46,000 trillion megajoules available with present and near-future technology from geopressure areas, mostly off the Gulf coast of the southern United States.[23] If all these resources materialized, if 50 percent of the energy could be brought to the surface (compared to the 2 to 24 percent that is recoverable with existing technology), and if the energy were converted to electricity at 20 percent efficiency, it would amount to 970 times the 1970 U.S. consumption of electricity. Should it prove practical to tap the geothermal energy of deep, hot, dry rocks,[24] the accessible resource would be even larger. Obviously, the practical potential of geothermal energy depends very much on highly uncertain estimates about the size of the exploitable stock and the efficiency with which it can be harnessed. The *theoretical* potential is great enough that the problem is well worth pursuing.

Viewed as a widespread flow resource rather than a stock to be tapped in particularly favorable locations, geothermal energy is not encouraging. The rate of heat flow to the surface of the Earth, corresponding very roughly to the rate of heat generation by the nuclear disintegration of radioactive elements in the Earth's crust, is only about 0.063 watts per square meter of surface area (63 kilowatts per square kilometer). At a 20-percent conversion efficiency, a 1000-Mwe geothermal power plant relying on that flow would have to find a way to harness it over 80,000 square kilometers.

[22]D. E. White and D. L. Williams, eds., *Assessment of geothermal resources of the United States, 1975.*

[23]Ibid.

[24]A. L. Hammond, W. D. Metz, and T. H. Maugh, *Energy and the future.*

Solar Energy

Energy from the sun is a flow-limited resource: the energy income will continue for the lifetime of the sun (billions of years) but the rate of energy flow (that is, the *power,* and hence the amount of energy received in any given span of time) is fixed. This fixed flow amounts to 1400 watts per square meter, facing the sun at the top of the Earth's atmosphere. The average flow reaching the surface of the Earth (averaged over day and night, summer and winter, good and bad weather, and all latitudes) is about 170 watts per square meter, or 170 megawatts per square kilometer. The amount of solar energy falling annually on the surface of the forty-eight contiguous United States (where the average rate is 180 watts per square meter) is 42,000 trillion megajoules, or 650 times the total 1970 U.S. energy use. The important questions, then, are for what uses and with what technologies solar energy can be harnessed economically. The possibilities include not only the direct collection and harnessing of the sun's rays but the collection and use of solar energy stored in the hydrologic cycle, in wind and waves and ocean currents, in the temperature difference between deep and shallow ocean waters (ocean thermal gradients), and in plant material. The average global flows of thermal energy in some of those pathways are: hydrologic cycle, 40 billion megawatts; wind-waves-ocean currents, 0.25 billion to 2.5 billion megawatts; net photosynthesis, 100 million megawatts. Compared with worldwide energy use in the mid 1970s of 8 million megawatts, these are all impressive numbers. Actually harnessing a very sizable fraction of any of them would be a huge technological enterprise, however, and not without ecological risks. These aspects are discussed below.

Tidal Energy

Tidal energy is the least significant of the flow-limited energy sources. (See Table 8-8 for a summary of those we have discussed.) The total rate of tidal energy flows in shallow seas, where this energy is most accessible, is about 1.1 billion kilowatts, and only about 13 million kilowatts of that can be harnessed with existing technology.[25] Prospects for significant improvement in this amount are poor, on fundamental physical grounds.

TABLE 8-8
Power of Flow-Limited Energy Sources

Source	*Global power (million Mw)**
Solar power reaching Earth's surface	112,000
Solar power (1% of land area covered, 10% conversion efficiency)	25
Power in hydrologic cycle	39,000
Estimated exploitable hydropower	3
Power in wind, waves, ocean currents	2,500(?)
Estimated exploitable wind power	3(??)
Tidal power in shallow seas	1
Estimated exploitable tidal power	0.01
1975 human consumption (worldwide)**	8

*1 million Mw equals 31.5 trillion MJ per year.
**For comparison.
Sources: M. K. Hubbert, Energy resources; W. D. Sellers, *Physical climatology*.

ENERGY TECHNOLOGY

In this section of text we identify and briefly describe some of the most important energy technologies now in use or anticipated. Following descriptions of how those technologies work (including how most associated environmental problems arise) are comparisons of some of the economic and environmental characteristics of the various technologies. The paths by which energy finds its way from origin to application to disposal generally contain many steps, regardless of the energy source. These sequences of steps are called *fuel cycles,* even where no real cycling is involved. The major steps of most fuel cycles are listed in Table 8-9, with examples of specific activities that occur in each. Until relatively recently, public attention has focused mainly on what goes on at the harvesting and conversion steps—for example, in coal and uranium mining or in fossil-fuel and nuclear power plants. But complicated, expensive, and environmentally significant technologies are in operation at many of the other steps as well.

TABLE 8-9
The Cycle of Energy in Society

Stage	*Activity or device*
Exploration	Road-building, drilling, sampling
Harvesting	Mining, pumping, building dams
Concentration	Crushing, sorting, discarding
Refining	Cleaning, transforming chemically
Transportation*	Moving by train, truck, tanker, pipeline, transmission line
Storage*	Oil tanks, coal yards, batteries
Conversion**	Furnace, boiler, turbine, gasoline engine
Marketing*	Advertising, selling, bookkeeping
End use	Heating, cooling, materials-processing, moving vehicles, running appliances

*May occur more than once.
**Means changing the *form* of the energy (chemical to thermal, thermal to mechanical, mechanical to electrical, etc.).

Oil and Natural Gas

Exploration. The technology of exploiting petroleum and natural gas begins with exploration. The geology of these hydrocarbon materials, which forms the scientific underpinnings for the search, is a complex subject with a large literature.[26] A variety of analytic methods and instruments are used to locate the most promising regions. The presence of oil and gas generally can be confirmed only by actual drilling, however, and that is what makes exploration an expensive enterprise. In the United States alone, about 2.25 million wells have been drilled in the search for oil and gas since the first few successful wells in the mid-1800s. Of this considerable number of wells (averaging about 1000 meters in depth but ranging to as much as 8000 meters) only about

[25]Hubbert, Energy resources.
[26]For a brief introduction, see Cook, *Man, energy, society,* chapter 4. A more technical synopsis is T. H. McCulloh, Oil and gas.

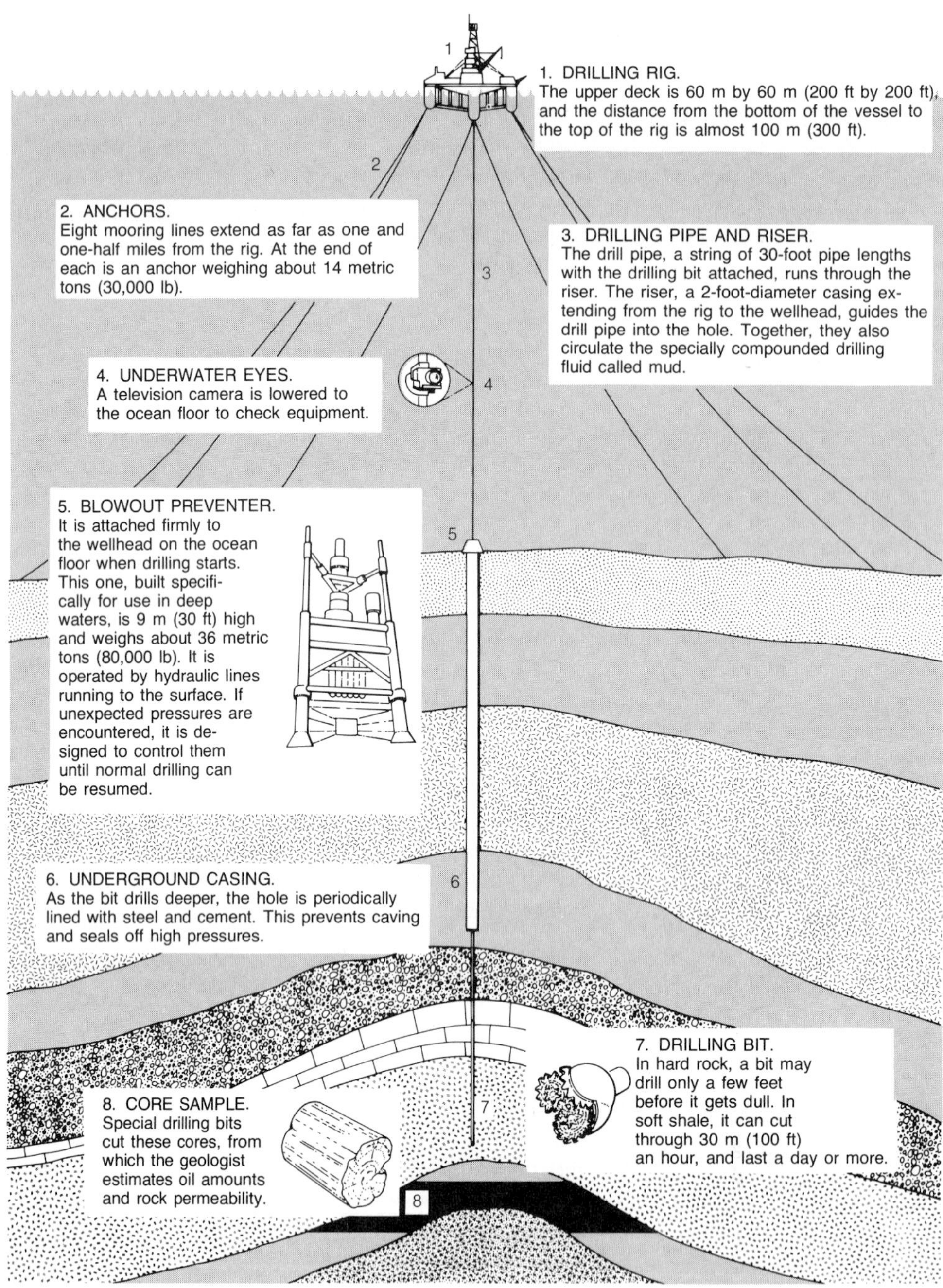

FIGURE 8-10

Diagram of offshore drilling rig. The complexity of this operation suggests one reason why the price of oil increases as society is forced to get it from less convenient locations. (From Press and Siever, *Earth*, W. H. Freeman and Co., San Francisco, 1974.)

1 exploratory well in 10 has found oil in sufficient quantities to justify production (that is, to pay for the additional costs of setting up equipment to extract oil once the well has been drilled).[27] Only 1 exploratory well in 50 has found enough oil to repay its total costs. (This is not to suggest, of course, that the oil business has not been profitable, but only that one must do a lot of exploratory drilling per good well.)

The complexity, the expense, and the environmental impact of exploratory drilling increase greatly as depletion of the most accessible deposits pushes the search for oil and gas into more remote and more hostile environments. Drilling from platforms offshore in such locations as the North Sea and the continental shelves of the United States is a much costlier operation than drilling onshore in most locations, and drilling in the deeper water of the continental slope will be costlier still (Figure 8-10). Environmentally, the heaviest costs of petroleum exploration are those incurred in the fragile arctic environment, where the scars of access roads and construction sites linger for decades.

Harvesting. Even after exploration is successful, the matter of getting the fuels out of the ground is still not entirely straightforward. This is so because the deposits are not underground lakes of oil capped by natural gas, but, rather, porous rock whose pores are filled (usually) with a mixture of oil, salty water, and natural gas (either dissolved or in separate pockets). Under the natural pressure associated with depth in Earth's crust, much of the gas and some of the oil and water flow up the pathway provided by the well to the surface. *How* much depends on the viscosity of the oil, which varies greatly, and on the porosity of the rock in which it exists. Often, pumping is necessary to bring much oil to the surface. The brine that comes with the oil—typically about 3 barrels of brine per barrel of oil—must be disposed of.

Although natural gas is itself a very useful fuel (today considered well worth finding and producing, even where it occurs separately from petroleum), it was once common practice in the United States to dispose of gas produced in conjunction with oil by flaring (burning it in an open flame at the wellhead). This was done because the cost of developing facilities to store and transport the gas to markets was too high in relation to the revenues its sale would bring. Today, major networks of gas pipelines link the producing fields of the United States and Canada with the major markets in those countries, but most of the gas produced in the Middle East, South America, and North Africa is still flared. It can be estimated that the energy content of the natural gas wasted annually in this way is equal to about 3 percent of the annual global consumption of energy in all forms.[28]

Whereas much of the gas that is produced never reaches the market, most of the oil that is discovered is never even produced. It clings tightly enough to the pores of the rock to resist even very elaborate schemes to wrest it out. These include injection of water or gas under high pressure down additional wells, to force the oil in the direction of the producing holes, and the use of detergents, solvents, and even underground combustion to scavenge the oil from rock. When these techniques are applied to oil fields that previously were worked using conventional techniques, the process is called *secondary recovery* or *tertiary recovery.* In modern practice, stimulated by higher oil prices, these techniques are often applied the first time a field is worked. Overall, the fraction of oil that has been extracted from discovered reservoirs (the *recovery factor*) has been only about 30 percent.[29] This figure is the basis for the estimates of recoverable petroleum resources cited earlier. Naturally, much interest and research has been devoted to the improvement of recovery techniques, in the hope of raising the low average recovery factor, but the most respected petroleum analysts are not yet counting on a higher figure in their projections.

The environmental impacts of oil and gas production fall into three main categories: (1) effects that are simply an expansion of the surface disruption and visual impact of exploration operations; (2) the release of petroleum and brine into the environment as a result of leaks of various kinds and blowouts (uncontrolled eruptions of

[27]R. R. Berg, J. C. Calhoun, R. L. Whiting, Prospects for expanded U.S. production of crude oil.

[28]Based on data in National Academy of Sciences, *Mineral resources and the environment,* p. 111.

[29]Berg, Calhoun, and Whiting, Prospects; Hubbert, Energy resources; and *U.S. energy resources.*

FIGURE 8-11

Supertanker of around 300,000 tons. U.S. imports of oil in 1975 amounted to the equivalent of unloading three such tankers per day.

gas, water, and oil under subterranean pressure); and (3) the often poorly planned growth in fragile areas of oil-handling facilities and the populations that operate them. These problems are most severe in the Arctic and in coastal regions, where other functions of the environment—as a wildlife habitat, as a commercial fishery, or as a recreational area—are particularly valuable and vulnerable.[30]

Transport. The transportation of oil over long distances poses similar hazards: accidental spills from tankers and pipelines; discharges of oil during routine operations (principally, cleaning tanks on the tankers); and preemption of land and the concomitant loss of other environmental services owing to the construction of pipelines and port facilities for tankers. The controversial trans-Alaska pipeline is expected initially to move 500,000 barrels of oil per day (almost 50 metric tons per minute) 1250 kilometers from Prudhoe Bay to Valdez through the hostile and generally fragile Alaskan environment. The eventual capacity is to be 2 million barrels per day. If there is a break in the pipeline—which could be caused by earthquakes, sagging with the melting of the permafrost underneath, embrittlement from extreme cold, destructive action by ice and current in the rivers the pipeline crosses, or combinations of these and other factors—the loss of hot oil (80° to 90° C) while the break was being isolated by valves would probably amount to between 15,000 and 50,000 barrels.[31]

More than half the oil produced worldwide moves by sea in tankers. The cost of shipping a barrel of oil is much lower in large tankers than in small ones (given present tanker construction), so the trend has been toward larger and larger ships. The 127,000-ton-supertanker *Torrey Canyon,* which went aground off the United Kingdom in 1967, was for that time a very large tanker. (The tonnage usually given for tankers is in *deadweight tons,* which refers to the ship's carrying capacity in short tons. *Displacement tons* means the weight of the water displaced by the fully loaded ship—that is, the deadweight tonnage plus the weight of the empty ship.) By the mid-1970s the jargon of tankers had expanded to include the terms VLCC (very large crude carrier—more than 200,000 deadweight tons) and ULCC (ultralarge crude carrier—more than 400,000 deadweight tons), and 800,000-ton tankers were on the drawing boards. A typical 300,000-ton VLCC is about 330 meters long (1100 feet) and 50 meters wide, holds more than 2 million barrels of oil, and draws 21 meters (69 feet) of water (Figure 8-11). This draft is too great for most U.S. ports, which typically are dredged to a depth of only about 12

[30]See, for example, Bosch, Hershner, and Milgram, Oil spills and the marine environment; Council on Environmental Quality, *Environmental Quality, 1974;* and Chapter 11 of this book.

[31]U.S. Department of the Interior, *Final environmental impact statement, proposed trans-Alaska pipeline.*

meters. The prospect of continuing heavy U.S. reliance on imported oil (which was around 7 million barrels per day in the mid-1970s), has raised the question of constructing new *deep-water ports.* Modifying most existing harbors for this purpose would be prohibitively expensive, and the most promising alternative seems to be installing deep-water mooring buoys for the big tankers, equipped with floating cargo hoses connected to underwater pipelines to shore.[32]

The large tankers claim one safety advantage over smaller ships: by reducing the number of ships needed to move a given amount of oil, they reduce congestion in sea lanes and harbors and hence should reduce the chance of collisions. On the other hand, they are considerably harder to maneuver or to stop, and the consequences of a single accident can be much more drastic. Whether the VLCCs and the ULCCs are structurally strong enough to endure for long the stresses produced by the interaction of their great weight with a violent ocean is debatable, and their record so far gives abundant cause for apprehension. Inasmuch as the basic purpose of supertankers is to provide cheap oil transportation, there is undeniably some incentive to cut corners. Almost without exception the big ships are each driven by a single propeller on a single shaft from a single steam turbine (some have two boilers feeding the turbine; most have only one). In most cases, then, just one major mechanical failure leaves the ship, with no backup system, at the mercy of the sea.[33] Furthermore, when oil begins moving out of the Arctic by tanker, the inherent hazards of tankers will be compounded by the chance of collisions with floating ice.[34]

In an attempt to bring to market some of the large amounts of natural gas now flared in the Middle East and elsewhere, increasing use of tankers that transport gas in liquefied form is likely. Liquefied natural gas (LNG) has 1/600 the volume of natural gas at normal temperature and pressure and must be kept in insulated refrigerated tanks at temperatures below the boiling point of methane (−161° C, or −260° F). Spilling small quantities of LNG onto water, which might occur in a minor accident involving an LNG tanker, could cause vapor explosions that might rupture adjacent compartments and create a much larger release. Whether a large explosion is possible in those circumstances is not certain, but a major fire or the spread of an asphyxiating cloud of unignited gas are genuine possibilities.[35] If such an event should occur in the harbor of, say, Boston or New York, the toll in life and property could be very high—tens of thousands or more dead and billions of dollars' worth of damage. The chemical energy stored in a large LNG tanker is roughly equivalent to a megaton of high explosive, or about 40 million gallons of gasoline.

Processing. Natural gas requires virtually no processing between extraction and use as a fuel, but this is not true of oil. Crude petroleum, as it comes from the ground, is a sticky, heavy, viscous mixture of thousands of hydrocarbon compounds; its properties vary significantly from one oil-producing region to another; it is hard to handle and actually rather difficult to burn. Conversion of this messy material into the array of petroleum products used in residences, commerce, and industry is the business of refineries.

Those large industrial complexes process the thousands of chemical constituents of crude petroleum in three general ways—sorting molecules into classes (distillation), breaking molecules apart (cracking), and reassembling them in new combinations (reforming, hydrogenation, and other processes). The partial removal of sulfur from fuel compounds for environmental reasons is becoming another important function of refineries. The product mix from a typical U.S. refinery is outlined in Table 8-10. Within limits, refineries can and do vary this composition from season to season, producing (for example) more heating oil in the fall for use in winter and more gasoline in the spring for use in summer. Among the nonenergy uses of petroleum hydrocarbons, subsumed under the term *petrochemicals,* are waxes, ointments, paints, plastics, detergents, synthetic pesticides, films, and fibers such as nylon and polyester.

The larger refineries have capacities of around 300,000 barrels of petroleum per day (corresponding to a chemi-

[32]Federal Energy Administration, *Fact sheet on deepwater ports,* Washington, D.C., August 1974, 20461.

[33]For an informative first-person account of the lore and problems of the supertankers, see Noel Mostert, *Supership.*

[34]Ramseier, Oil on ice.

[35]R. Wilson, Natural gas is a beautiful thing?

TABLE 8-10
What a Refinery Does with a Barrel of Crude Petroleum

Product	*Percentage of oil*
Gasoline	39
Distillate oils (diesel fuel and heating oil)	18
Residual fuel oil (for industry and power plants)	14
Lubricating oil, asphalt, petrochemicals	11
Propane, butane, and other gas products	8
Jet fuel	6
Consumed in refinery operation	4

Source: Forecast/Review 1976, *Oil and Gas Journal*, vol. 74, no. 4, pp. 101–120.

cal-energy flow of about 20,000 megawatts) and cost on the order of $500 million to construct.[36] Since petroleum products are readily stored, it is not necessary to tailor the output of refineries exactly to the pattern of demand at the moment, which permits the efficient situation in which refineries run almost 24 hours per day, 365 days per year near peak capacity. When demand is less than the refinery output, stocks of refined products are built up, and when demand exceeds refinery capacity, the stocks are drawn down. Stocks and flows in the U.S. petroleum industry in mid-1975 are indicated in Figure 8-12. Note that although stocks of refined products represent little more than thirty days' consumption, the buffer provided against a cutoff of imports is somewhat greater (the combined stocks of products and crude petroleum were equivalent in 1975 to about 120 days' worth of imports).[37]

Refineries themselves have significant effects on the environment. They emit substantial amounts of a wide variety of hydrocarbons to both air and water, which are variously odorous, unsightly, toxic, carcinogenic, or combine these features. Refineries and the associated storage facilities also represent a possibility of major fire, which, if combined with adverse weather conditions that confined the combustion products in a heavily populated area, could have serious public-health consequences.

[36]The biggest refinery in 1975 was Exxon's 450,000-bbl/day plant at Baton Rouge, Louisiana, which would probably cost almost $1 billion to duplicate (Council on Economic Priorities, *Cleaning up: The cost of refinery pollution control*).

[37]*Oil and Gas Journal*, 8 September 1975, p. 1.

Coal

The apparent limitations on the long-continued availability of oil and gas, brought so forcefully to public attention in the mid-1970s, caused a rapid intensification of interest in the technology of extracting and using the world's much more abundant supplies of coal. The use of oil and gas instead of coal in the first place was stimulated by the portability and versatility of the gaseous and liquid fuels. Now that the substitution must be reversed, it is natural that ways to overcome coal's disadvantages in those respects are being vigorously pursued. Inasmuch as coal mining has been dangerous to miners and/or particularly damaging to the physical environment, the prospect of expanded reliance on coal has focused much attention on these problems as well.

Mining. Coal deposits occur in nature in seams ranging in thickness from a few centimeters to many meters and lying at depths ranging from zero (outcroppings) to 1000 meters and more. Whether a given seam is considered minable at all, and whether surface mining or deep mining is the method of choice, depend on the thickness of the seam, the thickness of the overburden (the depth of the seam underground), the nature of the surface terrain, and the energy content and composition of the coal. Coals with different geologic histories differ markedly in composition and energy content and are classified on that basis into *ranks* (Table 8-11). A coal of high rank, such as bituminous coal, repays removing more overburden or tunneling deeper to get at a thin seam than does a coal of low rank, such as lignite.

The U.S. Geological Survey calls identified seams of bituminous and anthracite coal *reserves* if they are thicker than 70 centimeters and if they lie under less than 300 meters of overburden.[38] For lignite and subbituminous seams to qualify as reserves, they must be thicker than 150 centimeters. Coal seams down to 600 meters deep and thicker than 35 centimeters are considered part of the minable resource (that is, economically accessible at somewhat higher prices). As a rule, seams are only classified as surface-minable if they lie under less than 45 meters of overburden, although surface mining is

[38]P. Averitt, Coal.

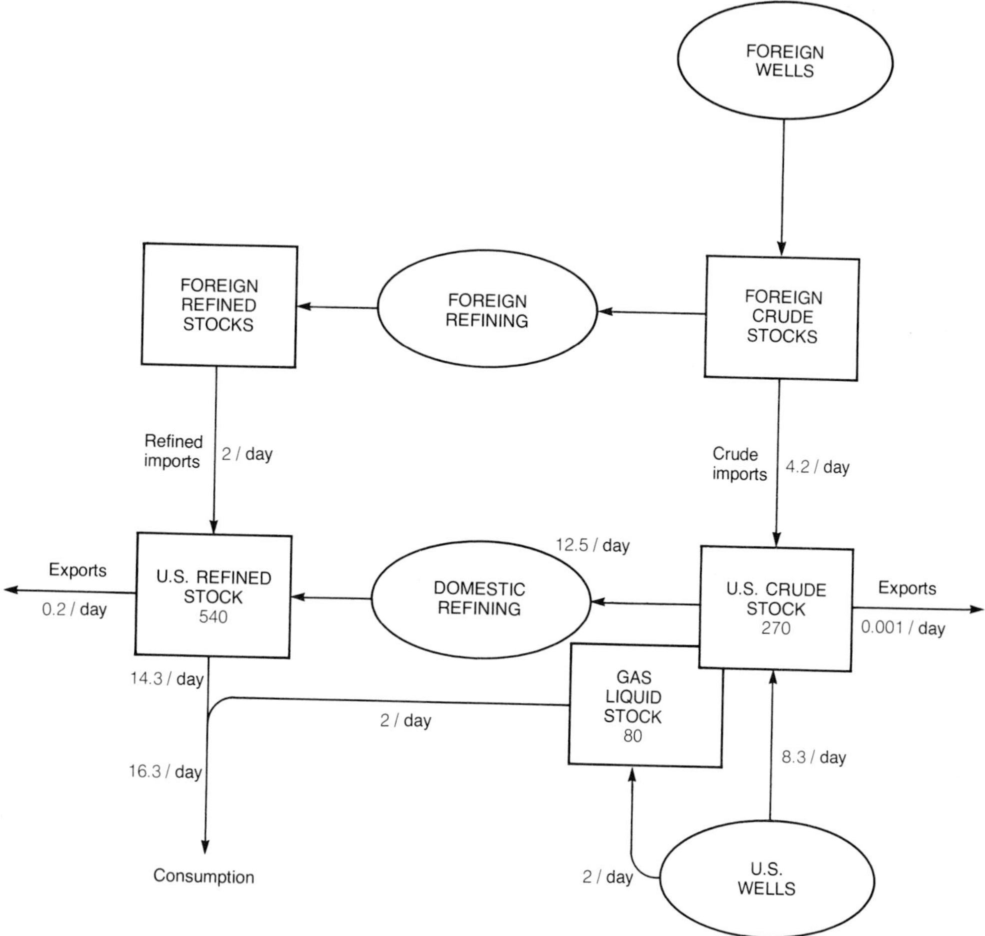

FIGURE 8-12

Stocks and flows in the U.S. petroleum industry in 1975 (millions of barrels). Each flow entails the possibility of a bottleneck, such as a strike or equipment shortage. Each stock represents a cushion against bottlenecks in the preceding flows. (Data from *Oil and Gas Journal.*)

TABLE 8-11
Composition and Energy Densities of Coals by Rank (ash-free basis)

Rank	Water content (%)	Fixed carbon content* (%)	Volatile matter** (%)	Energy content	
				Btu/lb	MJ/kg
Lignite	40–50	25–30	25–30	6,000–7,000	14–16
Subbituminous	20–30	35–45	30–40	8,500–11,000	20–26
Bituminous	5–15	45–75	20–40	12,000–15,000	28–35
Anthracite	3–6	85–90	3–10	13,000–15,000	30–35

*Fixed carbon is bound in a hexagonal pattern of carbon-carbon chemical bonds.
**Volatile matter consists of hydrocarbons that can be driven off at low temperatures.
Source: P. Averitt, Coal, pp. 133–142.

FIGURE 8-13

A bucket wheel excavator used for strip mining coal.

sometimes practiced through as much as 60 meters of overburden. Of particular importance in judging the feasibility of surface mining is the *stripping ratio,* which is the thickness of the overburden divided by the thickness of the seam. For economically viable mining, that ratio ranges up to 30/1 for bituminous coals and up to 18/1 for subbituminous coals and lignites.

Surface mining accounted for about half the U.S. coal production in the mid-1970s, but surface-minable coal makes up only 30 percent of the coal reserves and 10 percent of the estimated coal resources in place in the United States.[39] (The term *in place* means the amount of coal in the ground, some of which is not recoverable.) The main reason for harvesting surface-minable coal so far out of proportion to its representation in the reserves and resources in place is economic; coal can be extracted more cheaply by surface-mining techniques, which use very large machines and relatively little labor, than by deep mining.

Several kinds of surface mining are practiced, depending on terrain and the character of the seam. Open-pit strip mining is for thick, shallow coal beds on even terrain; area stripping removes the overburden from larger areas of flat-lying seams; contour strip mining exploits narrower seams that follow the contours of the land in hilly terrain. All these techniques employ large power shovels and bucket-wheel excavators (Figure 8-13). Auger mining bores into hillsides with augers up to 2 meters in diameter, generally beginning where contour mining has been carried out to the economic limit of overburden thickness. The recovery factor in surface mining (the fraction of the coal originally in place that is actually extracted) generally ranges from 80 to 90 percent.[40]

Hazards to life and limb in surface mining are modest compared to those of underground mining, but other environmental impacts are considerable. The removed overburden and exposed subsurface materials (and the land disrupted by access roads) are subject to erosion and gross down-slope motion, and cause siltation of local streams. In the eastern United States, where the coal and associated rocks are rich in pyrite, that mineral is oxidized to sulfate and sulfuric acid upon exposure to air, creating acid runoff and consequent soil acidification that kills stream life and renders revegetation difficult or impossible. In the western United States, some of the problems are ameliorated by flatter terrain and the very

[39]Theobald, Schweinfurth, and Duncan, *Energy resources.*

[40]For a particularly good discussion of the technology of coal mining, surface and underground, see E. A. Nephew, The challenge and promise of coal.

low sulfur content of the coal beds. On the other hand, reclamation in the West is made very difficult by the low and sporadic rainfall. Indeed, a major study by the U.S. National Academy of Sciences has argued that reclamation must be considered essentially impossible in those parts of the West where annual rainfall is less than 25 centimeters (10 inches) per year.[41]

Activities carried out under the banner of the "reclamation" of surface-mined land actually vary widely in aim, quality, and cost. The term *basic reclamation* describes attempts to minimize off-site damage, principally by arranging the displaced overburden in a stable configuration, with the best soil materials on top and the toxic and acid-forming substances on the bottom. Partial reclamation is an attempt to render the stripped land itself suitable for some productive use; this involves regrading of contours (not necessarily to the original shape), preservation or restoration of the original sequence of soil and rock strata, and several years of intensive management to render the soil productive again. Full reclamation, or restoration, means returning the land to its original contours and functions, which requires revegetation with native plant species in addition to the foregoing steps. This may be impossible in some areas—for example, where the amount of coal removed is a significant fraction of the total volume of material stripped.

The costs of reclamation range from around \$500 per acre for decent, basic reclamation to \$4000 per acre and more for full reclamation, where the latter is possible.[42] The costs increase sharply in steep terrain and in dry climates. Their contribution to the actual cost of coal depends, of course, on how much coal is extracted from each acre of stripped land—that is, on seam thickness. In the United States the seams are thickest in the West. A typical value for coal recovery in Western stripping is 1.5 million metric tons per square kilometer (6700 short tons/acre), and in Montana the average is about 4 times as high.[43] In the West, reclamation costs of \$6000/acre would contribute between 25 cents and \$1 per short ton to the cost of coal, to be compared to typical total costs of coal production in 1973 of between \$3 and \$5 per short ton. Eastern strippable seams yield an average of 730,000 metric tons per square kilometer (3300 short tons/acre); there, reclamation costs of \$3000/acre would add about \$1 per ton to the cost of coal.

Of the 8000 square kilometers that had been surface-mined for coal in the United States by the mid-1970s, hardly any had been fully reclaimed. Indeed, until the mid-1960s, even basic reclamation was the exception, not the rule. What passed for reclamation was largely a spotty and superficial effort that served the needs of coal-company public-relations people more than it served the land. One observer close to the subject has described reclamation of stripped land in Appalachia as "the small end of nothing, whittled down to a point."[44] The United Kingdom and the Federal German Republic (West Germany), major coal-mining countries in Europe, have better records of successfully practicing full reclamation in many areas. Many states in the United States now have laws requiring basic reclamation or more; how enforceable and effective they will be remains to be seen.[45]

Underground coal mining is more expensive and more hazardous to miners than surface mining, and it also has significant ecological effects. There are two basic techniques for underground mining. In *room-and-pillar mining,* a succession of underground rooms are cut into the coal seam and surrounding rock, and pillars of intact coal and rock are left standing to support the mine roof. In *continuous extraction,* the pillars are mined, temporary supports hold up the roof, and as the mining operation moves forward into the seam the roof is allowed to collapse behind it. In both approaches, the actual removal of the coal from the mine face can be done either by drilling and blasting or by cutting machines.

The most efficient method, where the character of the coal seam permits it, is a variety of continuous extraction called *longwall mining.* It uses a highly automated system of cutting machines, conveyors, and self-advancing roof supports and, accordingly, is more capital-intensive than room-and-pillar mining. Recovery factors and productivities in various methods of underground and surface mining are summarized in Table 8-12. The

[41]National Academy of Sciences, *Rehabilitation potential of Western coal lands.*

[42]E. A. Nephew, The challenge; E. A. Nephew and R. L. Spore, Coal mining and the environment.

[43]T. Pigford, M. J. Keaton, B. Mann, P. M. Cukor, G. Sessler, *Fuel cycles for electrical power generation,* Pt. 1.

[44]A. Miller, A coal miner looks at the energy crisis.

[45]See, for example, G. E. Dials and E. C. Moore, The cost of coal.

TABLE 8-12
Recovery Factors and Productivity in U.S. Coal Mining

Method	*Fraction of coal recovered (%)*	*Productivity (short tons/worker day)*
Room-and-pillar	50	2–5
Continuous extraction	60+	10–15
Auger	50	35–45
Contour, area stripping	80–90	35
Open-pit	near 100	near 80

Source: E. A. Nephew, The challenge and promise of coal.

average recovery factor for all underground mining in the United States in the early 1970s was around 57 percent.

Underground coal mining is widely known as an extraordinarily hazardous occupation, but not all of the hazard is inevitable. In fatal accidents (largely from falling roofs and methane explosions) per million worker hours between 1968 and 1971, there was a difference of a factor of 5 between the safest of the ten largest U.S. deep-mining enterprises and the least safe.[46] In the nonfatal injury rate in deep mines in the United States, the difference in the early 1970s between the safest company and the least safe company was about a factor of 10. The injury rate in the safest mines was less than the injury rates for the wholesale and retail trade, for real estate, and for higher education.[47] Evidently, underground coal mining *can* be made a reasonably accident-free occupation, and with existing technology.

A major hazard to underground coal miners in addition to accidents is black lung disease (called coal workers' pneumoconiosis, or CWP, in the technical literature). The disease impairs respiration by scarring and deforming lung tissue because of the inhalation of coal dust. There is no cure; the disease can be prevented only by reducing levels of coal dust in the mines—principally by better ventilation and water-spraying. In the mid-1970s there were about 125,000 identified cases of CWP in the United States and an estimated 3000 to 4000 deaths per year in which this disease was an underlying or contributing cause.[48] The 1969 U.S. Coal Mine Health and Safety Act and the 1972 Black Lung Law require the federal government to compensate victims of CWP and their dependents. The payments reached $1 billion in 1973 alone, and the annual expenditure by 1980 may be $8 billion.[49] In addition, the 1969 act established strict dust-level regulations for mines. If these regulations were enforced, black lung disease would be almost completely eliminated, judging by British experience and other medical evidence.[50]

Other major environmental burdens associated with underground coal mining are acid drainage from the mines (the result of the oxidation of exposed pyrites), subsidence of land that has been undermined (about 1 acre in 2 of undermined land subsides in the United States, damaging towns and farmland), and air pollution from slow-burning fires in abandoned mines and waste heaps.[51]

Processing. More than half the coal produced in the United States is cleaned before combustion or further processing in order to reduce the content of ash and inorganic sulfur. (That part of sulfur in coal that is bound into organic compounds, which usually amounts to more than half the sulfur present, cannot be removed this way.) The environmental disruption from cleaning coal includes significant atmospheric pollution in the form of particles, water pollution ("black water"), and the production of solid wastes.[52]

The motivation for processing coal further is twofold: (1) to remove the contained sulfur more completely, since it is a particularly dangerous pollutant if it reaches the atmosphere when coal is burned in electric power plants; and (2) to convert the coal into practical substitutes for petroleum and natural gas in applications other than electric-power generation. Gasification and liquefaction of coal are technologies that, in different variations, can

[46]Nephew, The challenge.
[47]Energy Policy Project, *A time to choose,* p. 182.
[48]Ibid., p. 184.
[49]NAS, *Mineral resources,* chapter 9.
[50]Ibid.
[51]For a quantitative discussion, see Council on Environmental Quality (CEQ), *Energy and environment: Electric power;* H. Perry, Environmental aspects of coal mining.
[52]Pigford et al., *Fuel cycles.*

serve either goal. *Solvent refining* is a technology not unrelated to liquefaction, but it has the sole purpose of producing a relatively clean fuel for generation of electricity.

Coal gasification has been practiced for many decades in Europe, where natural gas has been scarce and expensive. Indeed, coal gas was a major energy source in many U.S. cities until the 1920s. The basic concept behind gasification is not complicated. The coal is heated to drive off volatile substances [methane (CH_4) and more complex hydrocarbons], and then the remaining carbon is reacted with steam at high temperature to produce hydrogen and carbon monoxide ($C + H_2O \longrightarrow H_2 + CO$). The reaction is endothermic (energy-absorbing), and the required heat is generally supplied by the combustion of some of the carbon ($C + O_2 \longrightarrow CO_2$) and/or some of the products. The resulting mixture of H_2, CO, a little CH_4, and air has an energy content of 3.3 to 5.0 megajoules per cubic meter (100 to 150 Btu per cubic foot) and is called low-Btu gas or power gas.[53] This seems quite small compared to the 33 megajoules per cubic meter in natural gas, which is mostly methane, but the low-Btu gas is perfectly suitable as fuel for electric power plants that are near the gasification plant. (Because of its low energy density, it is not economical to transport low-Btu gas any significant distance.) The sulfur that was in the coal turns up in the gaseous product as H_2S, which lends itself to very complete removal (more than 99 percent) by reaction with lime or limestone in a desulfurization stage in the gasification plant.

For most industrial uses, a gas with higher energy content is required. The necessary 10 to 20 MJ/m^3 (300 Btu to 600 Btu per cubic foot) can be obtained by operating in oxygen rather than air (which does away with the nitrogen dilutant in the product) and by reacting some of the carbon monoxide with steam to produce more hydrogen. To drive the energy content still higher and produce a substitute for natural gas that can be distributed for domestic use in pipelines (called high-Btu gas, town gas, or pipeline gas), one must make more methane. This is done, starting with the medium-Btu product, by promoting the reaction $3H_2 + CO \longrightarrow CH_4 + H_2O$.

While the chemical reactions described here seem simple enough, the technology of bringing them about on a large scale is very complex. How completely and how rapidly the reactions take place depend strongly on temperature and pressure, which depend in turn on the progress of the reactions. Catalysts are needed at some steps, and ways to add and remove specific compounds selectively at specific stages can be very complicated. Controlling all these variables in a large network of pipes and vessels is a tricky business indeed.

The existing European technologies seem best suited to a scale of operations too small for the tasks envisioned for coal gasification in the United States. Consequently, the energy crunch of the early 1970s precipitated a belated rush in the U.S. energy-research community to find ways to adapt or replace those European technologies for bigger units.[54] A few large (250×10^6 MJ/day) gasification plants of both low- and high-Btu types are scheduled to begin operation in the United States in the late 1970s, but to replace any substantial fraction of U.S. natural gas use (about $66{,}000 \times 10^6$ MJ/day in the mid-1970s) in this way would take an enormous construction effort and corresponding investment.

Large gasification plants will not be without environmental impacts—although perhaps they would be less than those of oil refineries, which in many ways they will resemble. It does seem likely from recent assessments that gasification of coal will entail, overall, much less environmental damage than combustion of the coal directly.[55] The thermal efficiency of gasification technologies (the energy content of the product divided by the energy content of the coal input) is expected to range from around 50 percent to perhaps 90 percent.[56]

The idea of gasifying coal underground without even mining it—so called *in situ* (in place) gasification—goes

[53]The CH_4 comes from the reaction, $C + 2H_2 \longrightarrow CH_4$. For a more detailed discussion of gasification chemistry, see Hottel and Howard, *New energy;* or H. Perry, The gasification of coal.

[54]See, for example, A. M. Squires, Clean fuels from coal gasification; H. Perry, Coal conversion technology.

[55]Pigford et al., *Fuel cycles;* K. Smith, J. Weyant, and John P. Holdren, *Evaluation of conventional power systems.*

[56]Science and public policy program, University of Oklahoma, *Energy alternatives.*

back more than a century. The idea is to drill a number of holes into a coal seam and ignite a slow-burning underground combustion front, fed by air from one set of holes. The advancing front drives off low-Btu gas that can be collected at a second set of holes. This has been done commercially on a very small scale in the Soviet Union, and experiments were underway in the United States in the mid-1970s.[57] The intrinsic geologic and chemical-kinetic obstacles to widespread applicability or high efficiency for this approach seem large, however.

Like gasification, coal liquefaction has a history of several decades in Europe and other parts of the world, but only recently has attracted much interest in the United States. The idea is to produce liquid hydrocarbons that could replace petroleum as feedstock (input) for refineries or, alternatively, to produce directly a clean liquid fuel for use in electricity generating plants. The technology is similar to that of gasification. (Indeed, gasification is the first step in many of the processes existing or under development.) But higher pressures, the use of different catalysts, and other alterations in the process lead to a liquid rather than a gaseous product. Liquefaction is at least a few years behind gasification on the road to full-scale commercial operation in the United States. Eventually, the thermal efficiencies and costs are expected to be similar to those of gasification.[58]

Solvent refining is a means of extracting sulfur from coal to be used in power plants with less elaborate processing than gasification or liquefaction. The coal is crushed and dissolved in a solvent; then the product is filtered to remove ash and sulfur. The result is a solid fuel with a low melting point, having an energy density about 25 percent higher than the raw coal and a sulfur content about 4 times lower than the raw coal. Some observers believe that solvent refining will be of major importance in the late 1970s and early 1980s because it is easier than gasification and liquefaction.[59] It seems equally likely, however, that the percentage of sulfur that remains after solvent refining will be too high for future air-quality standards to be met if this fuel is used.

[57]Perry, Coal conversion technology.

[58]Ibid.

[59]C. Anderson et al., *An assessment of U.S. energy options for Project Independence.*

Oil Shales and Tar Sands

The problems of extracting oil shales and tar sands are very similar to those of mining coal. Both oil shales and tar sands are solid, occur in seams that vary in depth and thickness, and lend themselves (according to the ratio of depth and thickness) to deep mining or surface mining. The only commercial tar sand operation (Athabasca, in the province of Alberta, Canada) is an open-pit mine using bucket-wheel excavators. Commercial surface-mining operations for oil shale exist in Russia, Brazil, and Manchuria, but not, as of the mid-1970s, in the Green River shales of the western United States, which contain the world's largest identified oil-shale deposits.[60]

Both major North American deposits, the Athabasca sands and the Green River shales, will require deep mining to get at most of the resource. Where the deposits are surface-minable, moreover, they pose special difficulties in reclamation—in the first case because of the harsh northern climate and in the second because of steep terrain and minimal rainfall. The energy density of oil shale and tar sands in place is low—typically 2 to 4 megajoules per kilogram (about 2 to 4 million Btu per short ton) for oil shale and 3 to 6 megajoules per kilogram for tar sands, compared to 15 megajoules per kilogram for lignite and 30 megajoules per kilogram for bituminous coal.

Extracting hydrocarbon liquids from oil shales and tar sands requires elaborate technology. For the shales, the process is called *retorting* and involves crushing the shale and heating it to about 500° C (around 900° F) to drive off the liquid. The heating uses some of the contained carbon as an energy source. Attempts to carry out this simple-sounding procedure on a large scale in practice have encountered many difficulties.[61] Extracting the bitumen (a hydrocarbon mixture) from tar sands involves shaking, screening, heating, centrifuging, steam-treating, and some other steps. There, too, difficulties have been encountered in setting up a large operation, partly

[60]H. H. Hasiba, R. P. Trump, and A. David, *In-situ process options for the recovery of energy and synthetic fuels from coal, oil shale, and tar sands;* also United Nations, *Utilization of oil shale.*

[61]For a concise description of this and other aspects of oil shale, see G. U. Dinneen and G. L. Cook, Oil shale and the energy crisis.

because of the wide variation in the properties of the tar sands from even a single deposit.[62] The liquids that result from oil-shale retorting and tar-sands processing serve as synthetic crude petroleum, suitable for input into refineries.

The residue from the processing operations is called *spent shale* in the case of oil shale, and *tailings* in the case of tar sands. In each case, the volume of the residue considerably exceeds the volume of the raw material when it was in place. Thus, the residue more than fills the hole in the ground it came from, so disposal of spent shale and tar-sand tailings becomes a major problem. Significant aspects of the problem, aside from just finding a place to put the material, are the large amount of water required to stabilize it (that is, to keep it from blowing or sliding away) and the leaching of salts from the stabilized waste piles into ground and surface water. Leaching is especially troublesome in the Colorado River basin, where the Green River shales are found, because of preexisting difficulties with a high salt content in the Colorado.[63] One possible approach to the problem would exploit the minable quantities of certain other minerals contained in the spent shale. Extracting them could sufficiently reduce the volume that the residue could be returned to the underground rooms from which the shale was originally extracted (by room-and-pillar mining), and be sealed in, to prevent leaking.[64]

The troublesome aspects of extraction, processing, and residue management of oil shales and tar sands have kindled widespread interest in the possibility of processing these resources in situ. The basic approach is to drill a large number of holes into the seam, fracture the material by using conventional explosives to create permeability, ignite a combustion front and sustain it with compressed air forced down some of the holes, and tap the liquids driven off by the hot combustion gases at another set of wells.[65] This approach seems to solve the solid-residue problem, but its commercial feasibility and widespread applicability remain to be demonstrated. One traditional drawback of in-situ processes has been low fractional recovery of the resource. (For example, Allen estimates 20 to 30 percent for in-situ recovery of tar sands, compared to 50 to 60 percent from underground mining and 85 to 90 percent from open-pit mining.)[66]

[62]A. R. Allen, Coping with the oil sands.

[63]Environmental Impact Assessment Project, Institute of Ecology, *A scientific and policy review of the prototype oil shale leasing program: final environmental impact statement of the U.S. Department of the interior.*

[64]Ibid.

[65]Hasiba, Trump and David, *In-situ process;* Dineen and Cook, Oil shale; A. Lewis, The outlook for oil shale.

[66]Allen, Coping.

Electricity Generation with Fossil Fuels

Electricity generation accounted in the mid-1970s for about 70 percent of U.S. coal consumption, 15 percent of natural-gas consumption, and 10 percent of petroleum consumption. The technology with which a fossil fuel is used to generate electricity is the same in major respects, regardless of whether oil, gas, or coal is the fuel of choice. It is called the thermal generation of electricity because heat is deliberately produced as a step in the process.

Operation of thermal power plants. Most thermal-generating plants employ a steam cycle, which consists of the sequence of energy conversions indicated in Figure 8-14. Fuel and air are injected continuously into a furnace, where they are burned (coal has been pulverized first). The furnace is a metal box, which in a large electric power plant can be 30 meters on a side and more than 30 meters high. The box is lined with tubes that make up the boiler. Water flows through them and is heated and turned to steam by thermal energy transferred from the hot combustion products outside the tubes. The steam, which reaches pressures of 70 kilograms per square centimeter (1000 pounds per square inch) and temperatures above 500° C, is then directed into a steam turbine, usually in a series of stages—high pressure, medium pressure, and low pressure (Figure 8-15). A turbine is just a device that turns a fluid's internal energy (associated with temperature and pressure) into the mechanical energy of a rotating shaft. (The fluid can be a liquid, a gas, or a mixture; in a steam turbine it is mostly water vapor—a gas—with some liquid water appearing at the low-pressure end.) The conversion from internal to mechanical energy is accomplished by arranging blades

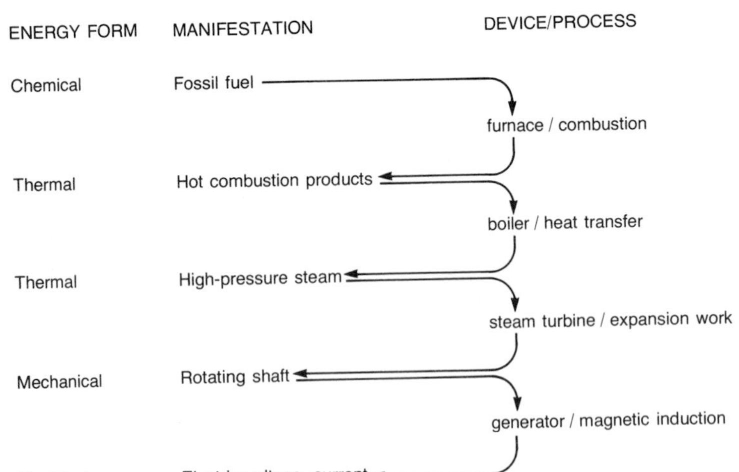

FIGURE 8-14

Energy conversions in thermal electricity generation with fossil fuels. The transformation from chemical to electrical energy takes place in stages, each of which exacts a toll in energy converted to waste heat.

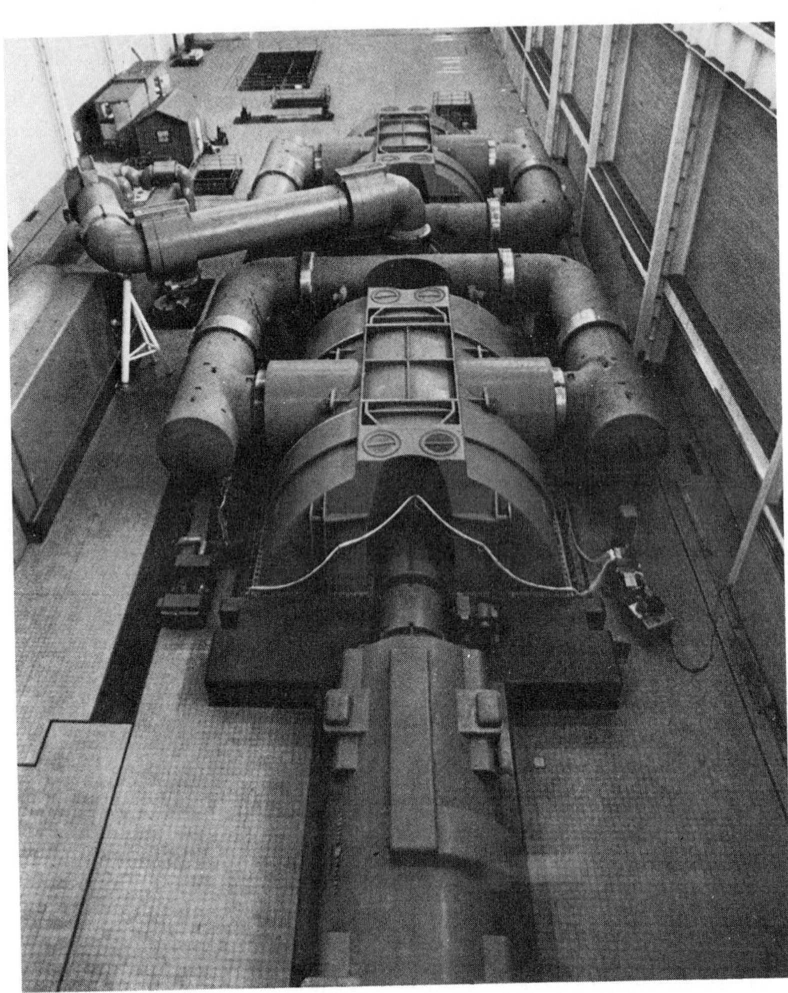

FIGURE 8-15

A compound steam-turbine-generator. The high-pressure turbine (at the left under the sharply angled duct) drives one generator, and the medium- and low-pressure turbines (center) drive another (foreground). The unit delivers electricity at a maximum rate of over 1 million kilowatts.

on a shaft in such a way that the working fluid is forced to turn them as it pushes its way from the high-pressure end of the device to the low-pressure end. Between the high-pressure stage and the medium- or low-pressure stage of the turbines in large thermal-power plants, the steam is usually returned to a special section of the boiler for *reheat.*[67]

The turbine shaft is connected to a generator shaft, which, as it spins, forces electric conductors to move through a magnetic field produced by electromagnets. The motion of a conductor through a magnetic field induces electric voltages, which, when connected to an external circuit, drive currents.[68] Generators used in typical power plants produce alternating current (the direction of the voltage and the current reverses repeatedly, going through about 60 complete cycles per second) at between 10,000 and 20,000 volts. The linked turbine and generator system is often called a *turbogenerator.*

The electricity is the desired output of a power plant, but there are also undesired (and in part unavoidable) outputs. One is waste heat. When the spent steam leaves the low-pressure turbine, it passes into a condenser, where it is returned to the liquid state so it can be returned readily to the boiler. In the process of being condensed to water, the steam gives up heat to a separate stream of water flowing through the condenser for that purpose. The warmed condenser water typically either is returned to the environment by direct flow into the ocean, lake, or river from which it came (once-through cooling), or it passes through a cooling tower, where the heat is transferred to the atmosphere.

That some of the heat produced by the combustion of fuel must be discharged from the steam cycle instead of being converted into electricity is a manifestation of the second law of thermodynamics. (Recall, from Box 2-4, that one of this law's many formulations says no process is possible whose sole result is the conversion of an amount of heat entirely into work. Turning a generator shaft is work.) Any device that converts heat into work is called a *heat engine.* The efficiency of any heat engine (that is, the fraction of the energy it handles that can be turned into work) cannot exceed $1 - T_{\text{low}}/T_{\text{high}}$. [$T_{\text{low}}$ is the lowest temperature at which the engine discharges heat (the temperature of the *heat sink*), and T_{high} is the temperature of the heat source, measured with respect to absolute zero.]

In a typical fossil-fuel-burning power plant, the *pertinent* value of T_{high} is the maximum steam temperature (around 800° kelvin), and the value of T_{low} is the temperature of the source of cooling water (say, 300° kelvin). Hence, the maximum theoretical efficiency is $1 - 300/800$, or 0.625. Practical power plants are necessarily far from ideal heat engines in many respects—approaching the theoretical ideal too closely in practice becomes prohibitively expensive. The average thermal efficiency (first-law efficiency) of fossil-fueled power plants in service in the United States in the mid-1970s (output of electricity divided by input of chemical energy) was only a bit over half the above figure—about 0.33, or 33 percent.[69] This means that two-thirds of the energy released by burning fossil fuels in electricity generating plants leaves the power plant as heat, not electricity. The most efficient conventional fossil-fueled power plants in operation are about 40 percent efficient, where 60 percent of the fuel's energy leaves the plant as heat. (The management of heat released from power plants is a problem common to all thermal generation of electricity, not just fossil fuels, so more detailed discussion of the associated problems is postponed to the section of text on general environmental problems of energy technology.)

Not all the heat discharged by fossil-fueled power plants leaves at the condenser; some leaves the furnace with the hot combustion products and is exhausted up the stack. Along with that heated air go various environmentally significant combustion products: sulfur dioxide (SO_2), produced by the combustion of sulfur present in the fuel as a contaminant; oxides of nitrogen (NO and NO_2, often labeled together as NO_x) produced when nitrogen in air and in the fuel combines with oxygen in

---

[67]An excellent introduction to the technology of energy conversion is W. C. Reynolds, *Energy: From nature to man;* see also C. Summers, The conversion of energy.

[68]See Reynolds, *Energy,* chapter 6, or any basic physics text.

[69]For a more thorough explanation of just how the second law exerts its toll in a steam power plant, see the very readable text by T. J. Healy, *Energy, electric power, and man,* chapter 5 (1974). For explanations of the inefficiencies beyond those described by the second law, see Summers, The conversion; and Reynolds, *Energy.*

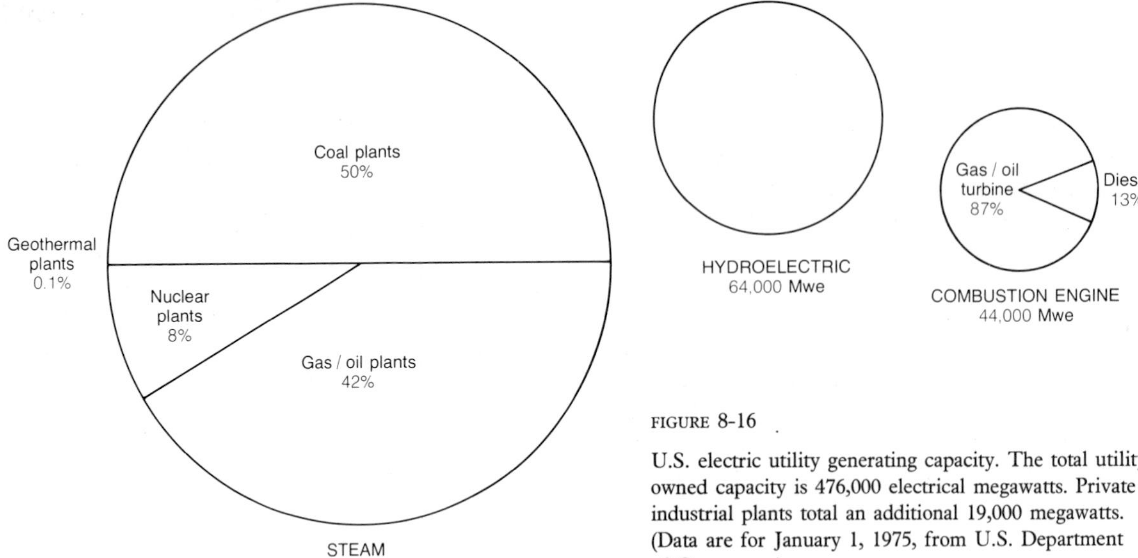

FIGURE 8-16

U.S. electric utility generating capacity. The total utility owned capacity is 476,000 electrical megawatts. Private industrial plants total an additional 19,000 megawatts. (Data are for January 1, 1975, from U.S. Department of Commerce.)

the hottest parts of the flame; solid particles (containing ash and such heavy metals as lead and cadmium); trace-element vapors (such as mercury); and carbon dioxide (CO_2) and water vapor (H_2O), the normal products of complete combustion of hydrocarbon fuels. Because power-plant furnaces are designed to give very complete combustion of the fuel, emission of pollutants arising from incomplete combustion—that is, carbon monoxide (CO) and unburnt hydrocarbons—is small. (This is not true of automobile engines.) The actual quantities and control of the effluents from fossil-fueled power plants are discussed in this chapter; their effects on human health and on the environment are considered in Chapter 10 and Chapter 11.

Two kinds of fossil-fueled thermal power plants other than those relying on steam cycles are in widespread use. One is the diesel generator, in which a diesel internal-combustion engine drives an electric generator. Because of their high capital costs, such units have not been able to compete economically with the steam cycle in very large sizes (more than a few megawatts), but they are very suitable for emergency power and for service in isolated and sparsely populated areas where electricity needs are not as large. The thermal efficiency of a modern diesel-electric unit is around 33 percent. Less expensive but also somewhat less efficient than diesels are gas turbines. Gas turbines for electric-power generation are very similar to those that power jet aircraft; the hot combustion products themselves turn the turbine, which is directly connected to a generator, and virtually all the waste heat is discharged directly into the atmosphere in the exhaust. These devices are also called *combustion turbines*—combustion gases turn the turbine, but the fuel can be liquid and often is. Even coal could be used, except that its dirty combustion products would erode the turbine blades too quickly. Gas turbines today are most widely used for *peak power*—that is, for helping meet demand for electricity at the hours of the day and on the days of the year when that demand is highest. Gas turbines are used this way because of both their rapid start-up and their low capital cost. Better gas-turbine design is improving the efficiency and operating lifetime of these devices, and their future substitution for steam turbines in large, baseload thermal-power plants has been envisioned.

The most promising avenue toward increasing the thermal efficiency of fossil-fueled power plants in the near future is to marry gas-turbine and steam-turbine technology in what is called a *combined cycle.* There, the hot exhaust of the gas turbine goes to a boiler where it raises steam for a steam turbine; in this role, the gas turbine is called a *topping cycle.* The system combines the good performance of gas turbines at very high temperatures with the ability of a steam cycle to extract energy down to low temperatures, resulting in overall thermal efficiencies of between 45 and 55 percent. Several such installations were planned or were under construction in the mid-1970s for commercial use by electric utilities.

The composition of the electricity-generating capacity in the United States in the mid-1970s is shown in Figure 8-16. The nuclear, geothermal, and hydroelectric components are discussed later in this chapter.

Air pollution control for power plants. Considerable ingenuity and expense have been applied to the task of reducing the air pollutants emitted by fossil-fuel-burning electric power plants. Inasmuch as coal is both the most abundant of the conventional fossil fuels and the worst polluter, it is treated most thoroughly here. Some comparisons with oil and gas are made at the end of the discussion.

The most visible air pollutant from coal-burning power plants is particulate matter. The simplest and least expensive methods for reducing particle emissions are settling chambers, in which the exhaust gas is slowed down enough to let heavy particles fall out by gravity; cyclone separators, in which swirling the exhaust gas throws particles to the edges of the separators for collection; and spray towers, in which water is sprayed head-on into the exhaust gases, from which it scrubs out some of the particles.[70] These techniques are not effective for removing particles smaller than about 10 microns in diameter (1 micron = 10^{-6} meter), which are the most troublesome environmentally. Increasingly tight emissions regulations have therefore required the widespread application of a more complicated and expensive technology, the *electrostatic* precipitator (Figure 8-17). In such a device, electrons are pulled off a central conductor by a very strong electric field. The electrons tend to be captured by gas molecules passing through the device in the exhaust stream, and the charged molecules in turn attach themselves to particles. So charged, the particles are attracted to the positively charged or grounded surrounding wall, on which they collect. Modern electrostatic precipitators under favorable circumstances can collect between 97 and 99.5 percent of the mass of particles in the stack gases from a coal-burning power plant, but the uncollected fraction consists mainly of the

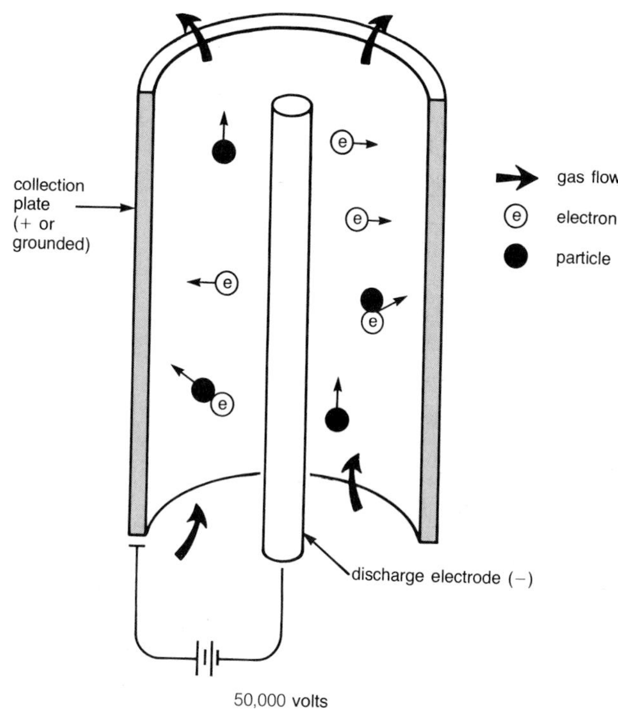

FIGURE 8-17

An electrostatic precipitator. Electrons drawn from the discharge electrode attach themselves to the particles, and the charged combination is drawn to the collector plate.

light and especially dangerous particles smaller than 1 micron in diameter. Breakdown of the precipitators, which is not infrequent, causes substantial additional emissions in practice.

The substance widely regarded as the most dangerous air pollutant emitted by coal-burning power plants is sulfur, in the form of sulfur dioxide (SO_2) and the more oxidized sulfur trioxide (SO_3). Many techniques have been tried in the attempt to reduce emissions of sulfur oxides. We summarize some of the more important approaches here.

It would be convenient to find coal that is naturally low enough in sulfur to meet emission standards. (The 1975 U.S. standard for new coal plants was 0.6 pounds of sulfur per million Btu of thermal energy, which corresponds to 0.7 percent sulfur in bituminous coal containing 12,000 Btu per pound or 0.4 percent sulfur in lignite

[70]For more detail on these and other pollution-control techniques, see G. M. Masters, *Introduction to environmental science and technology*, chapter 10.

containing 7000 Btu per pound.)[71] Unfortunately, only a small fraction of U.S. recoverable coal reserves contain so little sulfur—only about 16 billion out of 200 billion tons of recoverable reserves as of 1970, according to Rieber.[72] The amount of coal that could meet the 1975 standard after washing might be as high as 45 billion tons, but the amount would plummet to almost nothing if the standard were changed by the mid-1980s to 0.2 pounds of sulfur or less per million Btu. Such a change would certainly be desirable from the environmental point of view, and many think it will be made.[73]

An approach to sulfur control that has been especially popular in the United Kingdom is the use of unusually tall stacks to disperse the material more effectively. This, of course, is not really control at all; it merely alleviates acute problems near a plant by spreading out the damage. Scandinavians, who have reason to believe some of their problems with acidic rainfall (see Chapter 11) partly originate in sulfur oxides blowing over from the United Kingdom, do not perceive much merit in this approach, and they are right.

A large amount of effort has been invested, in the United States and elsewhere, in developing technology for removing sulfur oxides from stack gases before the gases reach the atmosphere. Indeed, the practicality of such technology for commercial application in electric utilities has been the subject of a prolonged and bitter controversy between the utilities and the U.S. Environmental Protection Agency in the early to mid-1970s.

The most highly developed of the technologies for cleaning stack gases is *wet scrubbing,* in which the exhaust gases are treated with a slurry of lime (CaO) or limestone ($CaCO_3$). (A slurry is a thick suspension of solid particles in water.) The oxides of sulfur react with the calcium to form insoluble calcium sulfites and sulfates, which are collected and eventually disposed of as a sludge. A definitive report on the subject in 1975 indicated that lime and limestone scrubbers on units up to 175 electrical megawatts had achieved 90-percent control of the sulfur oxides produced from low-sulfur coal (less than 1 percent sulfur).[74] For medium-to-high-sulfur coal, 90-percent control was reported on 100-megawatt units burning coal that was low in chlorine, but high-chlorine coal was posing problems. [The chlorine forms hydrochloric acid (HCl), which corrodes the equipment and makes the sludge acidic.]

The largest coal-fired units being built in the mid-1970s were about 750 electrical megawatts (a single power plant may have more than one unit). The report estimated installation costs of lime and limestone scrubbing at $60 to $130 (1974) per electrical kilowatt of capacity; equipping a 750-Mwe plant at $100 per kilowatt would cost $75 million—perhaps 20 percent of the cost of the power plant. Taking this expense and the costs of operating the scrubbers into account, the study computed an increase in electricity cost because of sulfur control of 0.3 to 0.6 cents per kilowatt hour, compared to total costs of electricity from coal in the range of 1.5 to 2.5 cents per kilowatt hour. When scrubbers are retrofitted to existing plants, rather than being built into new plants, the cost of sulfur control increases to 0.4 to 0.8 cents per kilowatt hour.

Aside from the expense and (according to U.S. utilities) the still-questionable reliability of the scrubbers, their most serious drawback is that they produce very large quantities of sludge. This can amount to more than a million metric tons per year for a 1000-Mwe plant, burning coal with 3 percent sulfur. The sludge is capable of causing serious water pollution, and disposing of the production of just one plant can consume around 1.5 square kilometers of land for sludge piles per year.[75] Using sludge for landfill or as foundation for highways has been suggested, but it is doubtful whether the United States (at least) really needs much more of either.

To avoid the waste problems of such throwaway stack-gas-control processes as wet scrubbing with lime and limestone, regenerative processes can be used. They produce sulfur or sulfuric acid, which can be sold, and recycle the catalysts (such as vanadium oxide) and scavengers (magnesium oxide, sodium sulfite) that are

[71]The notion that much "low-sulfur" Western coal does not deserve to be included among the reserves capable of meeting the 1975 standard, because its low energy content more than compensates for its low sulfur content, was slow to be appreciated. The paper most responsible for the awakening was Michael Rieber's Low sulfur coal: A revision of reserve and supply estimates. The English system of measure is used here because those are the official units used by the EPA.

[72]Ibid.

[73]See, for example, Hottel and Howard, *New energy.*

[74]National Academy of Sciences (NAS), *Air quality and stationary source emission control.*

[75]Ibid.

TABLE 8-13
Air Pollution from Fossil-Fuel Electricity Generating Plants (million kg pollutant/billion kwh generated)

	Sulfur oxides	*Particles*	*Nitrogen oxides*	*Hydrocarbons*
Uncontrolled coal*	16.0 (0.03)	6.7 (0.5)	3.0 (0.04)	0.39 (0.02)
Controlled coal (97% particles, 90% S)	1.6 (0.03)	0.2 (0.5)	3.0 (0.04)	0.39 (0.02)
Residual fuel oil (no controls)	6.5 (0.2)	0.22 (0.03)	2.9 (0.2)	0.53 (0.3)
Gasified coal (combined-cycle)	0.37 (0.03)	0.026 (0.5)	0.079 (0.04)	0.10 (0.02)
Natural gas	0.003 (0.1)	0.059 (0.002)	1.54 (0.3)	0.10 (0.002)

Note: A 1000-Mwe plant running at a typical average of 75 percent of its theoretical capacity generates 6.57 billion kilowatt hours per year. In each category, the first number is emissions from power plant itself. The number in parentheses represents the emissions from associated fuel-processing.

*2.6% sulfur, 12.5% ash, 28 MJ/kg.

Sources: Pigford et al., *Fuel cycles;* Smith et al., *Evaluation.*

used to extract the sulfur dioxide from the stack gas.[76] Regenerative processes have suffered from high costs and from the fact that their widespread implementation would quickly saturate the sulfur and sulfuric acid markets.

One other approach to sulfur control worth mentioning is drastic modification of the furnace and boiler in ways that would allow capturing the sulfur essentially at the time of combustion. The most promising technology of this type relies on gasifying the coal in a fluidized bed at the base of the boiler, instead of in a separate gasification plant.[77] Like the other forms of gasification, the fluidized-bed boiler may offer one of the better hopes for lowering sulfur emissions from coal combustion in the long term.

In practice, technologies for controlling sulfur and particles must be coordinated, not merely because the effects of the two pollutants on health are most severe when the two are present in combination (see Chapter 10), but also because one control technology may help or hinder the other. Some desulfurization steps require that very efficient particle control precede them or they do not work. Some electrostatic precipitators do not work well with low-sulfur coal. Some wet scrubbers extract particles as well as sulfur quite efficiently.

Unfortunately, the methods and combinations that succeed in controlling sulfur and particles do essentially nothing about nitrogen oxides. Those too, are dangerous to health and to the broader environment, but one hears little about nitrogen-oxide control for power plants because there are few promising techniques for doing it. Modifying burner and furnace design and operations to lower peak flame temperatures can provide an improvement of only around a factor of 2.[78] Burning in oxygen instead of air would not be worth its considerable cost, because there is enough nitrogen in most fossil fuels to keep emissions high despite this measure. Approaches like the catalytic converter, being used to control nitrogen oxides in automobiles, seem impractical or hopelessly expensive when applied to the sizable gas flows of a large electric power plant.

Carbon dioxide is produced in direct proportion to the carbon content of the fuel that is burned. Although it has no direct significance for health, the carbon dioxide can influence climatic processes globally. The quantities of carbon dioxide produced are much too large to catch and contain—2 to 3 tons of CO_2 per ton of coal. One report has proposed concentrating as much of the world's fossil-fuel conversion as possible at central coastal sites and discharging the carbon dioxide produced deep underwater to hasten uptake of some of it by the ocean.[79] This scheme is burdened with practical and economic difficulties so great that it cannot be considered a serious alternative for many decades, if ever.

Table 8-13 summarizes the air-emissions characteristics of the major fossil-fueled thermal technologies for electricity generation. The last one listed, natural gas, appears primarily as a yardstick. This cleanest of the fossil fuels is really too valuable to be burned in electric power plants and will almost certainly be reserved in the future for direct uses, where its portability and clean burning are essential.

[76]For details see Hottel and Howard, *New energy;* J. T. Dunham, Carl Rampacek, and T. A. Henrie, High-sulfur coal for generating electricity.

[77]See, for example, A. M. Squires, Clean power from dirty fuels.

[78]NAS, *Air quality,* p. 810.

[79]Marchetti, Carbon dioxide and the problem of geoengineering.

BOX 8-3 Abbreviations Frequently Encountered in the Nuclear Field

Technologies and Events

BWR	boiling-water reactor
CTR	controlled thermonuclear reactor
ECCS	emergency core-cooling system
HTGR	high-temperature gas-cooled reactor
HWR	heavy-water reactor
LMFBR	liquid metal fast breeder reactor
LOCA	loss-of-coolant accident
LWR	light-water reactor
MSBR	molten-salt breeder reactor
PWR	pressurized-water reactor

Organizations and Documents

CEQ*	Council on Environmental Quality
EPA*	Environmental Protection Agency
ERDA*	Energy Research and Development Administration
GAO*	General Accounting Office
IAEA	International Atomic Energy Agency
ICRP	International Council on Radiation Protection
NAS/NAE	National Academy of Sciences/ National Academy of Engineering
NFS	Nuclear Fuel Services, Incorporated
NPT	Nonproliferation Treaty
NRC*	Nuclear Regulatory Commission
NRDC	Natural Resources Defense Council
UCS	Union of Concerned Scientists
USAEC*	United States Atomic Energy Commission
WASH-740	1957 USAEC study of consequences of reactor accidents
WASH-1400	1974/1975 USAEC/NRC study of probability and consequences of accidents in LWRs.

Substances and Physical Units

Ci	curie
D	deuterium
MPC	maximum permissible concentration
MWD	megawatt day (virtually always thermal)
Mwe	megawatt (electrical)
Mwt	megawatt (thermal)
Pu-239	fissile isotope of plutonium, produced from U-238
RCG	radioactivity concentration guide (euphemism for MPC)
T	tritium
Th-232	naturally occurring fertile isotope of thorium
U-233	fissile isotope of uranium, produced from thorium
U-235	naturally occurring fissile isotope of uranium
U-238	naturally occurring fertile isotope of uranium

*Denotes federal agency.

Nuclear Fission

The physics of releasing energy from the fission of uranium, thorium, and plutonium is not terribly complicated, aside from some details (refer to Box 8-2), and it is now thoroughly understood by nuclear scientists. By contrast, the technology of harnessing this energy reliably, economically, and on a very large scale is very complicated, and there are some not-so-unimportant details that nuclear engineers and analysts have not yet worked out completely. Some of the important problems with nuclear fission, moreover, are not technological at all—or even environmental in a narrow sense—but social. In the space available here we can only touch on some of the main characteristics of fission technology and the questions that surround it, while guiding the reader to some of the larger and often more technical literature that exists on the subject. Abbreviations for quantities, units, technologies, and organizations mentioned frequently in this section and in the section on fusion, following, are summarized in Box 8-3.

Some basic information about radioactivity and radiation that will be useful in this discussion of nuclear technology appears in Box 8-4. The behavior of radioactivity in the environment and its effects on human health are considered in Chapters 10 and 11.

The nuclear fuel cycle associated with electricity production from fission is represented in Figure 8-18. Some reactors have fuel cycles different in certain respects from this one, which is for reactors using enriched uranium and plutonium as fuel. Those differences will be pointed out as we consider the stages of the fuel cycle individually.

Mining and milling. Uranium is mined on the surface in open-pit mines and underground by room-

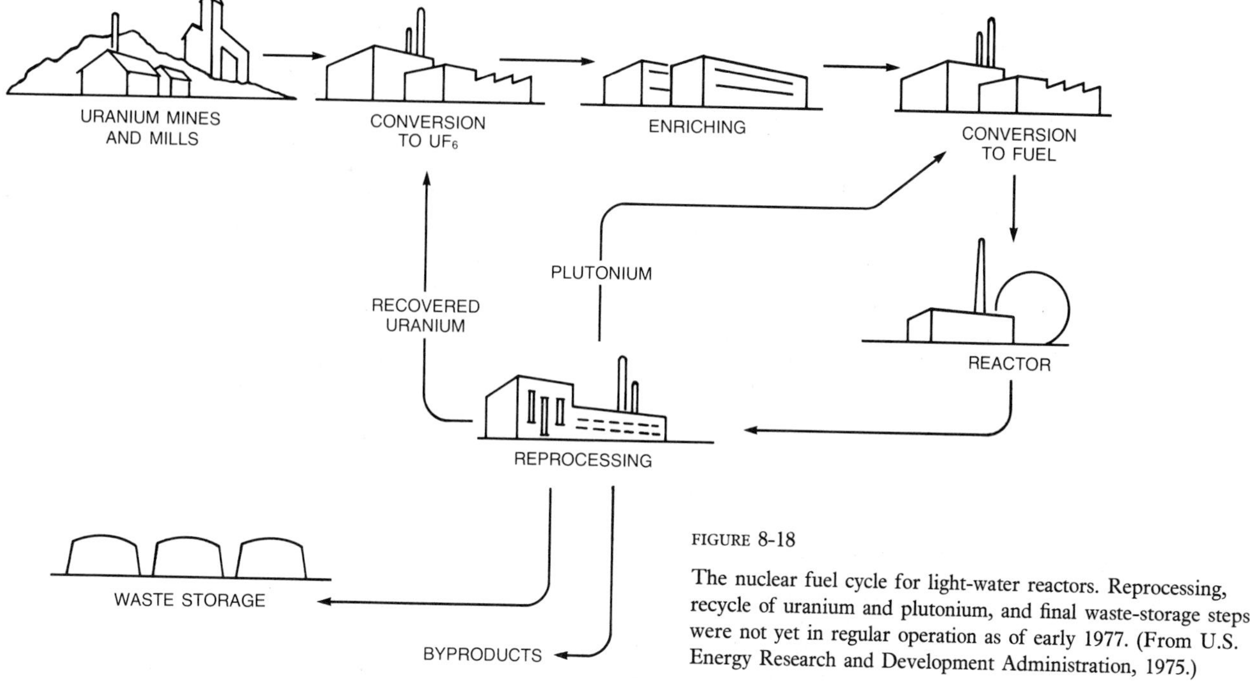

FIGURE 8-18

The nuclear fuel cycle for light-water reactors. Reprocessing, recycle of uranium and plutonium, and final waste-storage steps were not yet in regular operation as of early 1977. (From U.S. Energy Research and Development Administration, 1975.)

and-pillar methods. Production in the mid-1970s in the United States was split about half and half between surface and underground mining.[80] The problems in both cases are similar to those of coal mining: scarred landscapes, disposal of removed materials, revegetation in the dry climate of the Colorado plateau where the ore is found, poor working conditions and dangers in the underground mines. In place of the coal miner's exposure to black lung, the underground uranium miner is exposed to radon gas, a member of the radioactive decay chain leading from uranium-238. The radon seeps from the walls into the air in the mine, where it is inhaled. As a gas, it is exhaled again, but the radon atoms that happen to undergo radioactive decay while in the lungs deposit there the solid radioactive daughter polonium-218. Polonium-218 and its daughter lead-214 are both called radon daughters, and have been responsible for lung-cancer rates among uranium miners about 4 times higher than in the rest of the population.[81] Present U.S. standards for permissible exposure for uranium miners allow about twentyfold less exposure than those that prevailed when miners now dying of cancer were exposed. If the standards are complied with in practice—which involves good mine ventilation and strictly limiting miners' time underground—the risk will be much reduced. Whether the standards are yet strict enough is controversial.

In comparing all the problems of uranium mining with those of coal mining, it is important also to note that uranium requires considerably less material to be mined per electrical kilowatt hour actually generated. About 0.2 percent by weight of the sandstone ore mined in the Colorado plateau is recoverable uranium oxide (U_3O_8), 85 percent by weight of the U_3O_8 is uranium, and at most

[80]For technical details and descriptions of some of the environmental impacts of this and other stages of the nuclear fuel cycle (excepting reactors themselves), see U.S. Atomic Energy Commission, *Environmental survey of the nuclear fuel cycle.* An excellent critical review is D. Ford, et al., *The nuclear fuel cycle.*

[81]F. Lundin, et al., Mortality of uranium miners in relation to radiation exposure, hardrock mining and cigarette smoking 1950–1967. A most interesting part of the results reported is that the cancer rates of nonsmokers and the much higher cancer rates of smokers are *multiplied* by the same factor for the uranium miners—that is, the effects of smoking and radon are not simply additive. (See the discussion of synergism in Chapter 10.)

BOX 8-4 Radioactivity and Radiation

Radioactive atoms are atoms that undergo spontaneous transformations of the structure of their atomic nuclei. *Spontaneous* means the transformations take place without being stimulated by any event or force external to the atom. In the course of such a transformation, the nucleus emits energy. That energy is carried by particles that leave the nucleus or by electromagnetic radiation or both. The particles are generally either *alpha particles* (each a helium nucleus consisting of 2 protons and 2 neutrons) or *beta particles* (either electrons, arising from the disintegration of a neutron into a proton and an electron, or positrons, which are like electrons but positively charged and arise from the disintegration of a proton into a positron and a neutron). Less commonly, individual neutrons are emitted. The electromagnetic radiation emitted during nuclear transformations is called *gamma rays;* gamma rays are virtually identical to X-rays but often more energetic (hence, more penetrating). For reasons both historical and physical, the particles and the gamma rays are all termed *radiation.*

The spontaneous nuclear transformations that make up radioactivity always change the nuclear properties of the atoms involved and often change the chemical properties. If only the nuclear properties change, the atom involved becomes another isotope of the same element; if the chemical properties change, the atom involved becomes another element. Because the initial substance in any case is disappearing (by being changed into something else) the process is often termed *radioactive decay.*

Radioactive decay proceeds in such a way that a *fixed percentage* of the number of radioactive atoms present at the beginning of a specific period of time (a year, a day, a minute) undergo nuclear transformation during that period. Such a process (which also occurs with certain physical phenomena other than radioactivity) is the exact opposite of exponential growth, in which something increases by a fixed percentage of its initial value in a specified time. Whereas exponential growth at a given rate can be characterized by a doubling time, an exponential decay process such as radioactivity can be characterized by a *half-life*—the time required for half of a given initial quantity to disappear (or to be transformed into something else).

Suppose, for example, that we have a barrel of 1000 apples, which become rotten with a half-life of one week. This means that, after the first week, half of the 1000 apples have rotted, leaving 500 good ones. After another half-life—another week—half of the remaining 500 apples have rotted, leaving 250 good ones. After a total of three weeks—three half-lives—125 apples, or one-eighth of the initial 1000 remain in good condition.

The pattern for any exponential decay process is as follows:

Elapsed half-lives	*Fraction remaining*	*Elapsed half-lives*	*Fraction remaining*
0	1	4	1/16
1	1/2	10	1/1,024
2	1/4	20	1/1,048,576
3	1/8	N	$(\frac{1}{2})^N$

Each radioactive substance has its own unique and unchanging half-life (abbreviated $t_{1/2}$). For some substances the half-life is a fraction of a second; for others it is billions of years. A short half-life means the material is soon virtually gone, but nuclear transformations occur initially at a great rate. Broadly speaking, the associated hazard is short-lived but initially intense. A longer half-life means a proportionately slower initial rate of nuclear transformations. The associated hazard is initially less intense than that of a like number of atoms of a substance with a shorter half-life, but the hazard lasts much longer.

When we say a substance is highly radioactive, we mean many nuclear transformations occur within it each second. The yardstick by which radioactivity is measured is the radioactivity of 1 gram of radium-226, which undergoes about 37 billion nuclear transformations per second. That amount of radioactivity is called a curie (Ci). After radium's half-life of 1622 years, an initial gram will have diminished to half a gram, and the rate of nuclear transformations within the radium will be 18.5 billion per second, or half a curie.

For an isotope with a half-life much longer than radium (for example, uranium-235, with $t_{1/2} = 713$ million years), the amount needed to make a curie is much larger than a gram. It takes 476 kilograms of uranium-235 to produce the 37 billion disintegrations per second that make a curie.* For an isotope with a much shorter half-life than radium, a curie is a much smaller amount than a gram. Only 8 micrograms of iodine-131 ($t_{1/2} = 8.06$ days) make a curie.

The isotope formed by the radioactive decay of another may itself be radioactive. For example, the decay of radium-226 produces radon-222, a gas that is radioactive with a half-life of 3.83 days. The decay of the radon produces polonium-218, which is radioactive with a half life of 3.05 minutes. This is called a decay chain, and members of the chain are called *parents* and *daughters;* radium-226 is the parent of radon-222, which is the parent of polonium-218; polonium-218 is the daughter of radon-222. Radium is itself the sixth member down that particular chain, which begins with uranium-238 and ends with stable (nonradioactive) lead-206. Such chains are characteristic of the decay of radioactive isotopes higher than lead in the periodic table. Many isotopes lighter than lead produce stable daughters upon decay. For example, tritium, which is another name for hydrogen-3, decays to stable helium-3.**

Whereas curies measure the amount of radioactivity present, *rads* and *rems* measure the doses of radiation the radioactivity delivers. The rad is a measure of the amount of energy deposited per unit mass of absorbing material. (One rad equals 100 ergs of energy—10 millionths of a joule—deposited per gram of absorber.) Rems equal rads multiplied by a factor called relative biological effectiveness (RBE), which measures how effective the deposited energy is in doing damage. RBE is dependent on the particular biological system and effect being measured, as well as on the specific conditions of the exposure. The *quality factor* (QF) is a rough measure of the relative effectiveness of a particular type of radiation and is used for general discussions of radiation effects. It corresponds to the high end of the range of measured RBEs for a given type of radiation. The QF is 1.0 for gamma rays and most beta particles, but it is usually considered to be 10 for alpha particles. Doses most commonly encountered are measured in millirems. (One millirem equals 0.001 rem). For example, the average whole-body dose delivered to individuals in the United States from natural sources of radiation is between 100 and 200 millirems per year. (A whole-body dose means much more energy is deposited than if the dose were confined to a single part of the body, as sometimes happens; remember that the deposited energy is the product of the dose multiplied by the mass of tissue receiving that dose.)

The complicated connection between radiation dose and health is discussed more fully in Chapter 10. Here we mention only two figures to serve as yardsticks: (1) a whole-body dose of about 350 rems delivered suddenly would result in the deaths of half the people so exposed within thirty days (this is the $LD_{30}{}^{50}$);† (2) the whole-body dose—beyond that which comes from natural sources and medical exposures—that U.S. regulations deem permissible for individual members of the public is 500 millirems per year (3 to 5 times the dose from natural sources and about 0.001 of the acute $LD_{30}{}^{50}$. The maximum permissible concentrations (MPCs) of various radioactive substances in air and water to which the public is exposed are generally determined on the basis of this guideline of 500 millirems per year. MPCs are measured in microcuries per cubic centimeter ($\mu Ci/cm^3$), which is the same as curies per cubic meter (Ci/m^3).

*Note that there is no direct connection between the radioactive half-life of an isotope and whether the isotope is suitable fuel for fission or fusion. There are over 1400 radioactive isotopes, but only a few are fissile, and those that are have quite varied half-lives. Most of the fusion fuels are not radioactive at all. Indeed, radioactivity, on the one hand, and fission and fusion, on the other, represent quite different kinds of nuclear energy; fission and fusion release energy stored in what is known as the *strong nuclear force;* radioactivity releases energy stored in the *weak nuclear force.*

**One of the best introductions to radioactivity and radiation appears in John Harte and Robert H. Socolow, *Patient Earth.*

†$LD^{50}$is the most common statistic used in measuring lethal doses of anything (such as insecticides); its use is not confined to radiology.

1 percent by weight of the uranium can actually be fissioned (at 79,000 MJ/g) in the present-day nonbreeder reactors. Hence, one mines 1 kilogram of uranium ore to yield the same thermal energy at the power plant as about 50 kilograms of bituminous coal. This advantage would diminish to a ratio of 3 kilograms of uranium ore to 5 kilograms of coal if it became necessary to use the very low-grade uranium resources in the Chattanooga shales before the advent of more efficient reactors.

The *uranium mill* is the facility that extracts from each 1000 kilograms of sandstone ore its 2 kilograms or so of U_3O_8, producing in the process a large quantity of chemically toxic and mildly radioactive liquid wastes and a sandlike solid residue called tailings. The handling of the wastes through the early years of the nuclear industry (the 1950s and early 1960s) provides one of the examples of corporate and regulatory irresponsibility that have made informed citizens cynical about the management of nuclear energy. Liquid wastes were discharged into the streams of the Colorado plateau, producing higher than permissible concentrations of radioactivity in the drinking water of residents downstream. The tailings, which contained radium, were merely piled near the mills, exposed to leaching and erosion by rain and wind. Incredibly, some of the tailings eventually ended up as landfill in Grand Junction, Colorado, on which some 5000 homes and commercial buildings (including several schools) were built. Radon gas, produced by the decay of the radium in the tailings, diffuses readily through the porous concrete-slab foundations used in such construction. Uranium miners exposed to radon concentrations comparable to those found in buildings built over tailings show twice the normal incidence of lung cancer.[82] The tailings hazard in homes and commercial buildings was first discovered in 1966. In 1976 some of the affected buildings were still occupied, and many claims for compensation for lowered property values or repair work undertaken remained unsatisfied.

Piles of accumulated tailings in the United States amounted in 1975 to about 70 million cubic meters, with much of the material from uranium mined for bomb manufacture. Under United States Atomic Energy Commission (USAEC) projections of nuclear power growth, the accumulation would reach almost 500 million cubic meters in the year 2000.[83] Current regulations do not appear adequate to assure the safe management of those materials, although there is no obvious technical obstacle that would make that impossible.[84]

Fuel preparation. Most nuclear reactors cannot use natural uranium as fuel, because the fissile isotope uranium-235 is present at a concentration of only 0.71 percent. The uranium is therefore subjected to isotopic enrichment, in which the fraction of uranium-235 atoms present in the fuel is increased above its natural level and some of the uranium-238 atoms are discarded. This is an intrinsically difficult enterprise, because there is no chemical difference between uranium-235 and uranium-238 to aid in the separation. Most separation procedures therefore rely on the small difference in mass between the two isotopes (only about 1.3 percent) to distinguish them. The output of isotopic enrichment plants consists of one stream of uranium containing uranium-235 in an amount ranging from 2 to 94 percent, depending on the kind of reactor for which it is intended, and a tails stream, in which the uranium-235 content has been depleted to between 0.2 and 0.3 percent. The tails (not to be confused with tailings from uranium mills) are stored for anticipated use in breeder reactors, which will be able to convert the uranium-238 to fissile fuel.

The most widely used technique for isotope separation is *gaseous diffusion*, in which uranium in the form of gaseous uranium hexafluoride (UF_6) is made to pass under pressure through a series of thousands of porous barriers. Being slightly less massive, the UF_6 molecules that contain uranium-235 instead of uranium-238 diffuse through the barriers slightly more readily; after each stage, therefore, the concentration of uranium-235 is slightly enhanced in comparison to that of uranium-238.

[82]U.S. Congress, Joint Committee on Atomic Energy (JCAE), *Hearings on use of uranium mill tailings for construction purposes*, pp. 272–273.

[83]J. Blomeke, C. Kee, and J. Nichols, *Projections of radioactive wastes to be generated by the U.S. nuclear industry.*

[84]An excellent review of the whole tailings problem is T. C. Hollocher and James J. MacKenzie, Radiation hazards from the misuse of uranium mill tailings. For a discussion of the possible impact of emissions from tailings on future generations, see D. Comey, The legacy of uranium tailings.

Gaseous diffusion plants are enormous, very expensive industrial facilities. Being impractical in small sizes, they have been inaccessible to any but the largest industrial nations. (This inaccessibility has been considered a benefit by people preoccupied with avoiding a nuclear war, because the enriched uranium these plants produce can be used to make atomic bombs. The fewer nations with this capability, the better.) Gaseous diffusion plants also use large quantities of electric power, amounting to 3 to 5 percent of the quantity of electricity that nonbreeder reactors can deliver from the enriched uranium the plants produce.[85] The entire U.S. uranium-enrichment capacity in the mid-1970s consisted of three large gaseous-diffusion plants in Oak Ridge, Tennessee; Paducah, Kentucky; and Portsmouth, Ohio. These plants were constructed between 1943 and 1955 at a cost of $2.3 billion for the purpose of making enriched uranium for bombs. The enrichment capability of the three plants combined, operating at their full power consumption of about 6000 electrical megawatts, would feed about 120 water-cooled nuclear reactors of the kind in heavy use in the United States. Somewhat ironically, the power needs of the U.S. diffusion plants have been supplied in the past by plants burning strip-mined coal.

The production of gaseous UF_6 required by the diffusion plants from the U_3O_8 concentrate (yellow cake) produced at the mills takes place at separate *conversion plants.* Two were in operation in the United States in 1974. The environmental effects of these plants include routine discharge of small amounts of fluorine and uranium to the environment—apparently well within the levels permitted by regulations and less hazardous than emissions elsewhere in the nuclear fuel cycle.

Natural uranium is considerably less dangerous, gram for gram, than most other radioactive substances, because of the long half-lives and the correspondingly slow rates of emission of radiation of its constituents. In fact, of the roughly 100 radioisotopes for which maximum permissible concentrations (MPCs) are specified by national and international organizations, uranium is the only one whose chemical toxicity (as a kidney poison) exceeds its radiological toxicity. This is not to say, of course, that natural uranium is innocuous; but it is enough less hazardous than many other materials circulating in the nuclear fuel cycle that accidents and emissions at facilities handling only natural and low-enriched uranium are not of overriding concern in relation to other nuclear hazards. As recycling of uranium becomes more commonplace (that is, feeding conversion plants not only with freshly milled uranium but also with uranium recovered from spent reactor fuel at reprocessing plants) and as more complicated fuel cycles are developed, contaminants more dangerous than uranium-235 and uranium-238 (specifically, U-232, U-234, U-236) will appear in conversion and/or enrichment plants in growing quantities.[86] The hazards of those facilities must then be reexamined.

Alternatives to gaseous diffusion for isotope enrichment exist and are being used or tested around the world. The main ones are ultra-high-speed centrifuges, a related "nozzle" technique, and laser separation. The first two technologies rely on the tendency of gas molecules containing uranium-238 to be thrown more readily to the outside of a gas stream traversing a curved path than molecules containing the less massive uranium-235.[87] Centrifuge installations are in commercial use in Europe, are feasible in smaller sizes than gaseous-diffusion plants, and require only about one-tenth the energy per unit of separation performed. The nozzle technology is also feasible in installations of modest size but requires almost twice as much energy as gaseous diffusion.

Laser separation relies on an entirely different physical distinction between uranium-235 and uranium-238. In somewhat oversimplified terms, the idea is as follows. A carefully tuned laser, beamed through a gaseous compound of natural uranium, can add some energy to the uranium-235 atoms without adding any to the uranium-238 atoms. Provided with this head start in internal energy, the uranium-235 atoms can be ionized (stripped of an electron) by a second laser beam or by an electric

[85]For a more detailed description of the process and of the facilities in the United States, see USAEC, *Environmental survey;* V. Abajian and A. Fishman, Supplying enriched uranium; R. Levin, Conversion and enrichment in the nuclear fuel cycle.

[86]See, for example, the discussion in T. Pigford, Environmental aspects of nuclear energy production.

[87]See Abajian and Fishman, Supplying enriched uranium; R. Gillette, "Nozzle" enrichment for sale.

field too weak to ionize the uranium-238. Then the molecules containing the positively charged uranium-235 can be separated easily by electrical means from those containing the uncharged uranium-238.[88] This process, when perfected, may use less energy than even the centrifuge method.

Important details of all isotope-enrichment processes historically have been kept secret, because those technologies can be used to enrich uranium to make bombs. That the improvements in enrichment technology are making this capability accessible to many more nations is among the most serious adverse consequences of nuclear technology in general.[88a]

Breeder reactors produce their own fissile fuel (plutonium-239 and uranium-233) from abundant, fertile uranium-238 and thorium-232 (Box 8-2). They therefore do not need the isotopic enrichment of uranium-235 in natural uranium to provide them with the needed concentration of fissile material, except when not enough plutonium-239 or uranium-233 is available from stockpiles or other breeder reactors to provide for the initial loading of nuclear fuel. If most or all fission power came from breeder reactors, and if the total number of reactors were not growing too rapidly, the need for enrichment would be eliminated entirely. This could not eliminate the link between nuclear power and nuclear bombs, however, because the plutonium-239 and uranium-233 relied upon by breeder reactors are even more suitable as bomb material than uranium-235. Yet another kind of reactor, the nonbreeding heavy-water reactor (HWR), described below in the discussion of reactor technology, can use unenriched and unadulterated natural uranium as fuel. Like the breeder, then, the HWR bypasses the enrichment step of the fuel cycle; but because it unavoidably produces some plutonium-239, it too cannot entirely eliminate the link between electricity and bombs.

Once fissile material of suitable quality for the type of reactor in question is in hand, the next step in the nuclear fuel cycle is to fabricate the fuel. The fuel material may arrive at the fabrication plant as gaseous UF_6 from an enrichment plant, or as liquid plutonium nitrate or uranyl nitrate from a fuel reprocessing plant, or as the various solid uranium concentrates that come from uranium mills. The first step in fabrication is to convert those materials into solid oxides or carbides (for example, UO_2, PuO_2, UC). Those compounds are the raw material for the *fuel elements*, which take different forms, depending on the type of reactor. For contemporary LWRs, UO_2 is pressed into solid pellets about 13 millimeters (0.5 inch) long and 10 to 13 millimeters in diameter. The pellets are then loaded into thin, cylindrical, zirconium-alloy (Zircaloy) tubes, which are welded shut at the ends. About 3.7 meters (12 feet) of the length of the fuel rods is occupied by the pellets (the rods extend somewhat beyond the pellets).

The effluents associated with fuel-fabrication plants have been modest, and no operations likely to pose great risk of accident to the public have been involved. (Of course, in all manipulation of enriched uranium, care must be taken to avoid bringing togther the amount and configuration needed to initiate a nuclear chain reaction, but even if that happened the possible accidents could do little damage outside the plant.) Much more serious problems of public health and safety—and of occupational damage to the health of fuel-fabrication workers—may arise when and if the routine recycling of plutonium in reactor fuel commences. Plutonium is vastly more dangerous radiologically than uranium-235 and uranium-238, and even very small discharges of it cannot be tolerated (see Chapter 10). It could also be vulnerable in the fabrication plant to theft for use in bomb manufacture. The theft problem will also exist at fuel-fabrication plants serving reactors that use very highly enriched uranium, as does one type of reactor that seemed on the verge of commercialization in the mid 1970s.

Types of reactor. A typical nuclear-fueled electric power plant is similar in many respects to the fossil-fueled power plants already discussed. A heat source is used to produce steam at high pressure, which drives a steam turbine, which turns an electricity generator. The main difference is, of course, in the heat source, which can be any of several types of nuclear reactor.

The main components of the reactor itself are the fuel, the control rods, the coolant, and (depending on the type of reactor) the moderator.

The function of the moderator is to slow down

[88] R. N. Zare, Laser enrichment of isotopes.
[88a] B. M. Casper, Laser enrichment: A new path to proliferation.

neutrons released by the fissioning fuel nuclei. This is necessary in most reactors because of a fundamental property of fissile materials: an encounter between a fissile atom and a neutron is far more likely to cause the atom to fission if the neutron is moving slowly than if it is moving rapidly. Each fission event produces an average of about 2.5 neutrons, and, if the chain reaction is to be maintained, one of those neutrons must cause another fission event before it escapes or is absorbed unproductively (in a way that does not cause fission). In other words, sustaining a chain reaction requires a 40-percent (1/2.5) probability that a given neutron will cause a fission. But neutrons unavoidably start out with very high speeds—they are "born" that way—so they have only a small chance *per encounter* of producing another fission. The only ways to get the overall probability of fission up to 40 percent per neutron are (1) to slow the neutrons down (moderate them), thereby increasing the probability of fission per encounter with a fissile atom, and (2) to increase the density of fissile atoms (higher enrichment and/or more compact fuel), thereby increasing the number of encounters. Reactors employing strategy 1 are generally called *thermal reactors,* because they use a moderating material to slow the neutrons down to speeds corresponding to the temperature of their surroundings.[89] Reactors employing strategy 2 have no moderators and are called *fast reactors,* because the neutrons are fast. Thermal reactors are technically easier to design, to construct, and, in the view of most reactor experts, easier to operate than fast reactors. (Fast reactors share strategy 2 with bombs; a fast reactor is not the same as a bomb, but the separation in terms of physics is not as great as with thermal reactors.)[90]

To be a suitable moderator for a thermal reactor, a material should have low atomic weight (when a neutron hits a heavy nucleus, it bounces off without losing much speed), little tendency to absorb neutrons (a neutron absorbed by the moderator cannot cause a fission), and a reasonably high number of nuclei per unit of volume (gases are no good—they put too few moderator nuclei in a neutron's way). The best moderators are ordinary water and heavy water (D_2O, where *D* stands for deuterium, the stable heavy isotope of hydrogen with 1 proton and 1 neutron in the nucleus) and carbon in the form of graphite.

The materials for reactor control rods, by contrast, are chosen for their strong tendency to absorb neutrons. Cadmium and boron are widely used. To increase the power level in a reactor, the control rods are partly withdrawn from the *reactor core,* where the fuel and the moderator are interspersed, so that fewer neutrons are absorbed and more are available to cause fissions. To slow a reaction, the control rods are moved deeper into the core, making fewer neutrons available. In the event of a malfunction or a shutdown for maintenance, the control rods are pushed all the way into the core to quench the chain reaction by neutron starvation.

The function of the coolant is to carry the heat of fission and radioactive decay away from the core and deposit it where it can be used to generate electricity. Even when the chain reaction is shut down and no electricity is being generated, the coolant is needed to carry off the heat of radioactive decay of fission products in the core, which cannot be turned off. After a reactor has been operating for some time, the magnitude of the power associated with radioactive decay at the moment the chain reaction is shut down is 6 to 7 percent of the reactor's full rated power. Thus, a reactor rated at 3000 thermal megawatts (Mwt) would have a decay power at shutdown of as much as 210 Mwt.[91] (This is as much as the full power of fossil-fueled power plants considered large a few decades ago.) A full day after shutdown, the decay power is still a considerable 0.5 percent of full power, or 15 Mwt in a large plant (easily enough to melt the core if no coolant were present). The requirements on coolants and cooling systems are therefore not only high heat-removal capability during reactor operation but also high reliability long after the reactor has been turned off.

Reactors are generally classified and named according to the coolants and moderators they employ. Thus the

[89]From the branch of physics called statistical mechanics, one finds that the average speed, v, of a particle of mass, m, in equilibrium with surroundings at absolute temperature, T, is given by the relation $1/2mv^2 = 3/2kT$, where k is Boltzmann's constant.

[90]A good introduction for the material in this paragraph is Reynolds, *Energy,* chapter 7; for more detail, see D. R. Inglis, *Nuclear energy: Its physics and its social challenge;* a definitive technical text is S. Glasstone and A. Sesonske, *Nuclear reactor engineering.*

[91]See, for example, USAEC, *The safety of nuclear power reactors and related facilities,* National Technical Information Service, Springfield, Va., 1973 (WASH-1250).

light-water reactors (LWRs) in widespread commercial use in the United States and elsewhere are so named because ordinary water (light water, in contrast to heavy water) is used both as coolant and as moderator. Heavy-water reactors (HWRs) use heavy water as moderator, but generally light water or organic liquids as coolants because heavy water is expensive. (It is produced from seawater by isotope separation.) Most gas-cooled reactors (GCRs) use helium as a coolant, although some older designs use carbon dioxide; they are generally moderated with graphite. The liquid metal fast breeder reactor (LMFBR), of which there are many designs and a few operating prototypes, is cooled by liquid sodium; there is no moderator, and *fast* refers to the neutrons, not to the breeding (which may or may not be fast). Other kinds of breeder reactors being investigated are the gas-cooled fast breeder reactor (GCFBR) and molten-salt breeder reactor (MSBR).

An inventory of the world's power reactors as of late 1975 is given in Table 8-14. They accounted at that time for about 6 percent of the world's electricity generating capacity and 8.5 percent of that of the United States. Various studies have projected that the world's nuclear generating capacity will be between 2.5 and 3.5 million megawatts in the year 2000—more than 30 times the 1975 total in Table 8-14. Of course, this scenario is not inevitable.[92]

Our attention in the remainder of this section of text is confined mainly to four important types of reactor: the LWR of U.S. design, the Canadian HWR known as CANDU, the U.S. GCR known as the high-temperature gas reactor (HTGR), and the LMFBR under intensive investigation in the USSR, western Europe, and the United States. Some of the principal technical characteristics of these reactor types are summarized in Table 8-15.

LWRs of U.S. design are of two basic types: boiling-water reactors (BWRs) and pressurized-water reactors (PWRs). In a BWR the water serving as coolant and moderator is turned to steam in the reactor core, and the steam drives the steam turbine. In a PWR the water in the core is kept under such great pressure (about 150 atmospheres)[93] that it cannot boil and turn to steam; this hot, pressurized water instead is passed through a heat exchanger outside the reactor core, where its heat is used to make steam from water circulating in a separate closed cycle. The BWR and PWR steam cycles are presented schematically in Figure 8-19.

Indicated there are two of the main barriers against the release of the radioactive fission products from those reactors: the steel pressure vessel surrounding the core, and the steel-reinforced concrete containment structure surrounding the pressure vessel. The other main barriers are the solid matrix of the fuel pellets themselves, which contain most of the solid fission products, and the Zircaloy cladding that surrounds the fuel pellets. The core of a large LWR contains roughly 40,000 fuel rods encasing a total of about 100 tons of uranium oxide fuel. Enrichment is 2 to 4 percent uranium-235. About a third of the fuel is removed and replaced each year—a process that requires the reactor to be temporarily shut down. The steel pressure vessel of a PWR is about 13 meters high, 4 meters in diameter, and 20 centimeters (8 inches) thick. The pressure vessel of a BWR is about twice as large in outside dimensions, but with slightly thinner (15 cm to 18 cm) walls.[94]

LWRs of both types convert heat to electricity with an efficiency of about 32 percent—significantly less than the best fossil-fueled plants, although about equal to the national average for all thermal electricity generation. A second kind of efficiency sometimes discussed in regard to nuclear reactors is the fraction of the energy theoretically available in uranium that the reactor is capable of harnessing. This is between 0.5 percent and 1 percent for LWRs, 1 percent for HWRs, 1 to 2 percent for HTGRs, and probably 50 to 70 percent for LMFBRs.[95]

In addition to the safety questions discussed below, many of the large LWRs installed by utilities in the United States through the mid-1970s have been plagued by a variety of technical difficulties that have led to much poorer records of electricity production than expected.[96]

---

[92]For projections, see, for example, USAEC, *Nuclear power growth 1974–2000;* B. Spinrad, The role of nuclear power in meeting world energy needs.

[93]One atmosphere is 10.3 metric tons per square meter (14.7 pounds per square inch).

[94]For more detailed technical descriptions of LWRs, see USAEC, *The safety of nuclear power reactors;* or Nero, *A guidebook to nuclear reactors.*

[95]Holdren, Uranium availability, and the references therein.

[96]D. Comey, Will idle capacity kill nuclear power? D. Comey, Elastic statistics; C. Komanoff, *Power plant performance.*

TABLE 8-14

World Power Reactors (number of reactors over 100 Mwe in commercial operation as of late 1975)

	North America	*Western Europe*	*Eastern Europe/USSR*	*Japan*	*Other*	*Total*
LWR	52	23	12	9	2	98
GCR	0	25	0	1	0	26
HWR	5	0	0	0	3	8
LMFBR	0	2	1	0	0	3
OTHER	1	1	1	0	0	3
Total capacity (Gwe)	40.1	19.1	5.0	5.1	1.0	70.3

Source: World list of nuclear power plants, *Nuclear News,* vol. 18, no. 10, p. 63 (August 1975).

TABLE 8-15

Technical Characteristics of Reactors

	LWR	*HWR*	*HTGR*	*LMFBR*
Initial fuel*	3% U-235	0.7% U-235 (natural U)	94% U-235	40% U-235
Possible recycle fuel*	3% Pu/U-235	same as above	94% U-233/U-235	25% Pu
Annual consumption of natural uranium (1000 kg)	160	85–110	70	1.5
Pu or U-233 leaving reactor per year (kg)	220	270	190	500
Thermal efficiency	32%	29%	39%	39%
Power density in core (Mwt/m³)	50–90	5–9	8	400
Operating pressure in core (atmospheres)	70–150	100	45	1–2
Peak coolant temperature (°C)	320	310	750	540

Note: All reactors are assumed rated at 1000 Mwe, averaging 75 percent of that year-round.

*Percentage denotes mass fraction of fissile material in fuel.

Sources: USAEC, *Potential nuclear power growth patterns;* McIntyre, *Natural uranium heavy-water reactors;* Nero, *A guidebook to nuclear reactors.*

Whether the difficulties will be ironed out with more experience or whether they will worsen as the reactors grow older remains to be seen.

The heavy-water moderated CANDU reactor has not enjoyed the commercial success of LWRs, probably for reasons unrelated to technical merit. Among its advantages are its ability to use natural uranium as fuel, thus dispensing with the need for expensive, energy-consuming enrichment, and its ability to permit refueling without shutting the reactor down. The first feature results from the extraordinarily good properties of heavy water as a moderator; the second, from a design that has each fuel element in its own individual pressure tube, instead of having all fuel elements in one large pressure vessel. Ordinary water flows through the tubes, serving as the coolant, and the tubes are immersed in a large tank of the unpressurized heavy-water moderator. Many believe this design has important safety advantages.[97]

The HTGR is also widely held to have safety advantages over LWRs, mainly because of its low power density and the very large capacity of its graphite moderator to absorb excess heat in an emergency. The HTGR core consists of blocks of graphite with passages for the helium coolant and control rods, and compartments filled with fuel that looks like black sand [microspheres of highly enriched uranium carbide (UC_2) and thorium oxide (ThO_2), coated with graphite.] The HTGR fuel cycle uses the thorium-232–to–uranium-233 fertile/fissile conversion scheme (see Box 8-2). The core and the heat exchangers, where the hot helium is used to convert water to steam, are embedded in what amounts to a solid concrete tub laced with steel cables.

[97]McIntyre, Natural-uranium heavy-water reactors.

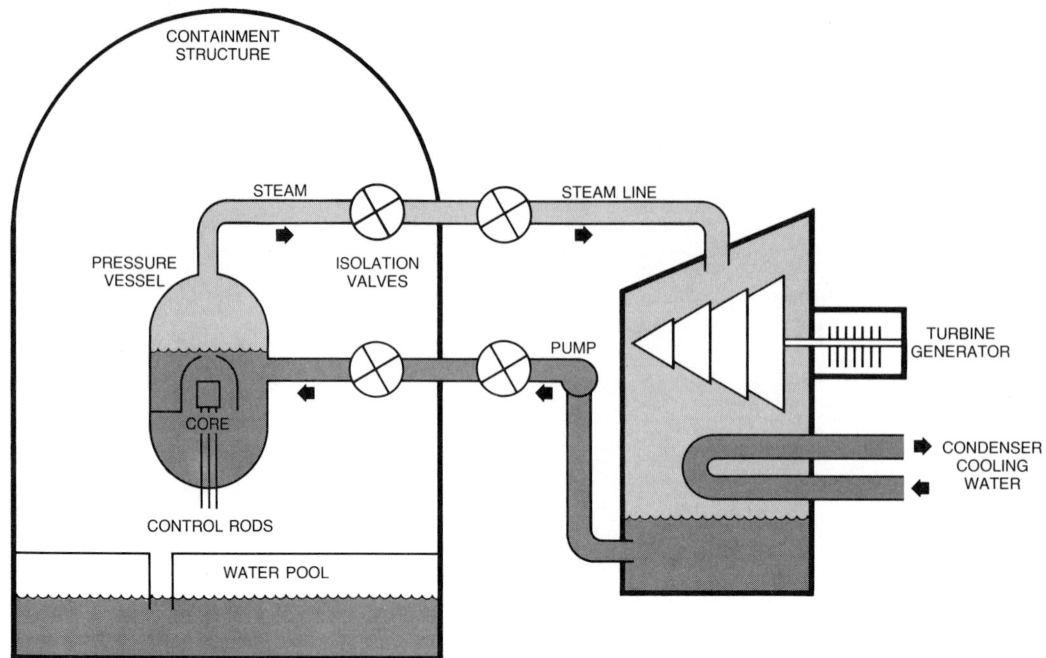

A. BOILING-WATER REACTOR (BWR)

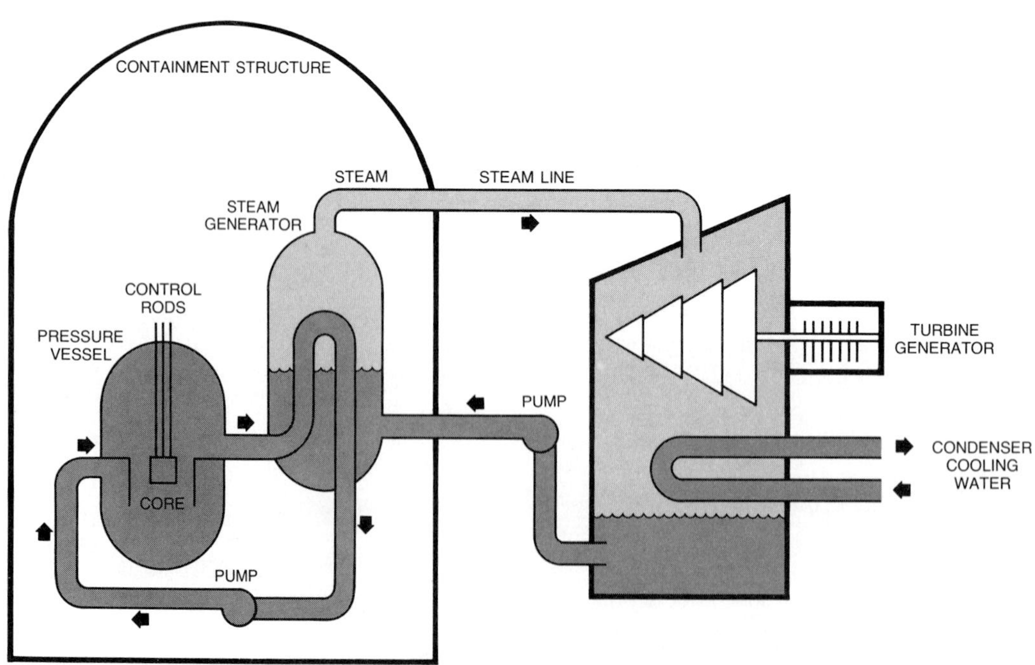

B. PRESSURIZED WATER REACTOR (PWR)

FIGURE 8-19

Schematic diagrams of boiling-water and pressurized-water reactors. The PWR core (B) is more compact and the pressure about twice as high as in the BWR (A). (From Science and Public Policy Program, University of Oklahoma, 1925.)

Among the advantages claimed for the HTGR are that it stretches uranium resources by relying partly on somewhat more abundant thorium, and that it has a thermal efficiency comparable to the best fossil-fueled plants—nearly 40 percent. It would lend itself to use with advanced gas turbines in place of or in addition to the steam cycle, to gain further increases in efficiency. There has also been considerable interest in using the high-temperature heat from HTGRs directly in industrial applications, without going through conversion to electricity.[98] This seems unlikely to see significant use before the 1990s, at the earliest. The only manufacturer of HTGRs in the United States announced in 1976 that it would not continue to market them, presumably because of slow sales and technical difficulties that plagued the demonstration plant at Fort Saint Vrain, Colorado.

If fission reactors were to become a mainstay of civilization's energy supply, breeder reactors would eventually be needed, because they can harness so much more of the potential energy in uranium and thorium than nonbreeders. It is worth emphasizing that a breeder does not get something for nothing—it does not create new fuel out of thin air, as certain advertisements might lead one to believe. It merely transforms a material that would not otherwise be usable as fuel (U-238 or Th-232) into usable (fissile) form. (This is not entirely unlike what a refinery does with crude petroleum.) All nuclear reactors actually perform this transformation to some extent, but, to be a breeder, a reactor must have the specific property that fertile-to-fissile conversions are taking place faster than fissions. Under those circumstances, the inventory of fissile material builds up as time goes on, and the excess can be drawn off to start new breeder reactors or to fuel nonbreeders. The time it takes a breeder reactor to produce an excess of fissile material equal to its initial inventory is called its *doubling time;* this quantity depends not only on the characteristics of the reactor itself but also on the losses of material and processing times elsewhere in the fuel cycle. The doubling time tells how rapidly breeder reactors could reproduce themselves if society wished to increase the number of such reactors, and it also tells (indirectly) what the ratio of breeders to nonbreeders would be in a steady-state situation, where fissile material was being consumed just as fast as it was being produced.[99]

On the assumption that breeders would be the surest way to secure a long-term energy supply, several of the world's most industrialized nations poured substantial fractions of their energy research efforts in the 1960s and 1970s into developing one particular kind of breeder, the sodium-cooled LMFBR.

The LMFBR is in many respects a much more difficult technology than the nonbreeding LWR, HWR, and HTGR. For one thing, to sustain a chain reaction using fast neutrons rather than slow (thermal) ones requires a very compact core with a high fraction of fissile material. This combination means a very high power density and very intense neutron flows in the core; the resulting high temperature and neutron damage make the weakening of fuel cladding and structural materials a difficult problem. The high power density also places severe demands on a coolant's ability to carry so much heat from so small a volume. Sodium has the advantage of being able to do this—even at low pressure (see Table 8-15). But sodium also has the disadvantages of becoming highly radioactive itself, of burning upon contact with air or water, and of being opaque (making maintenance especially difficult). To minimize the possibility of radioactive sodium's coming in contact with water, most LMFBR designs have an intermediate sodium loop to transfer the heat from the radioactive loop to the water loop, where steam is produced for the turbine (see Figure 8-20).

The doubling times of various LMFBR designs have been matters of some controversy. Proponents had hoped for a time not much longer than the historical doubling time of electricity consumption—say, 12 to 15 years. Some competent skeptics think a doubling time closer to 50 or 60 years is more likely.[100] This uncertainty has produced increased interest in alternative breeders: a gas-cooled fast breeder with a short doubling time

[98]*Nuclear News,* Nuclear process heat topical meeting.

[99]Studies of the "optimum" mixtures of breeder and nonbreeder reactors are reported in USAEC, *Potential nuclear power growth patterns,* and W. Haefele and A. Manne, Strategies for a transition from fossil to nuclear fuels. (This may well be a classic example of what philosopher/economist Kenneth Boulding has called suboptimization—determining the best way to do what should not be done at all).

[100]Cornell University, College of Engineering, *Report of the Cornell workshops on the major issues of a national energy research and development program.*

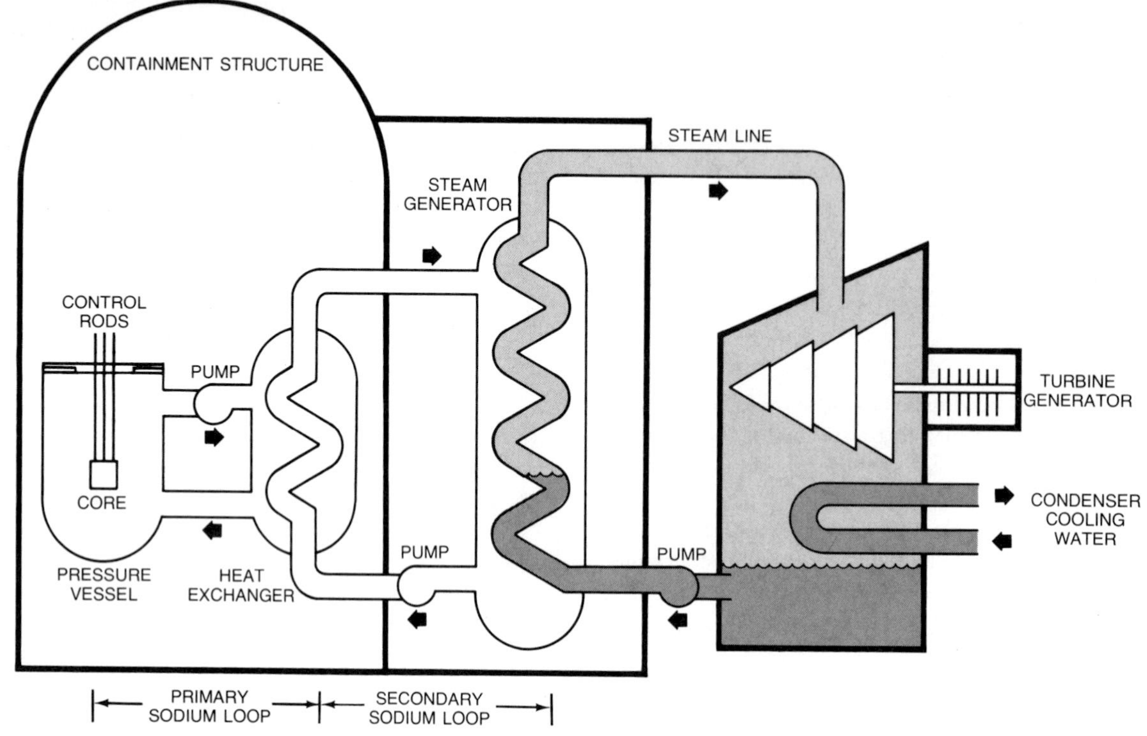

FIGURE 8-20

Schematic diagram of liquid metal fast-breeder reactor. The LMFBR core is smaller than that of a light-water reactor, and the power density is higher. Shown is the loop design favored by U.S. designers. (From Science and Public Policy Program, University of Oklahoma, 1975.)

(because the gas coolant gobbles up fewer neutrons, needed for breeding, than sodium), and a molten-salt-cooled breeder (in which the fuel is actually a constituent of the molten salt), using the thorium–to–uranium-233 conversion with thermal neutrons. The latter has a very long doubling time—perhaps it will barely breed at all—but it could have important safety advantages over the fast-neutron breeders.[101] A closely related question is: under what circumstances does deployment of LMFBRs make economic sense? It seems likely—even setting aside all issues of safety and environmental and social impact—that the answer is that such circumstances will not arise before 2015 or 2020, if ever.[102]

[101]A brief review of breeder options is found in Hammond, Metz, and Maugh, *Energy and the future,* chapter 7. See also D. J. Rose, Nuclear eclectic power; and Cornell University, *Report.*

[102]For an introduction to the two main sides of this convoluted controversy, see T. Cochran, *The LMFBR: An environmental and economic critique;* U.S. Energy Research and Development Administration, *Final environmental statement, liquid metal fast breeder reactor program.* Also I. C. Bupp, The breeder reactor in the U.S.: A new economic analysis.

Reactor hazards. Radiological hazards arising from the nuclear reactors themselves can be divided into three categories: (1) routine and accidental radiation doses to workers in nuclear power plants; (2) radiation doses to members of the public resulting from routine emissions of radioactivity from reactors in normal operation; (3) radiation doses to members of the public from accidents or sabotage at reactors.

Radiation doses to workers have received little public attention compared to the other two categories of hazard, but they are not negligible. The total occupational dose per nuclear power plant per year in the United States rose steadily from 188 person-rems in 1969 to 404 person-rems in 1973.[103] (The person-rem count is the result of adding the individual doses received by all persons exposed. Statistically, one would expect 1 cancer death to result from each 5000 to 10,000 person-rems—see Chapter 10.) Whether this increase is due to greater

[103]K. Z. Morgan, Effects of radiation on man: Now and in the future.

power-plant size, growing laxity of practices, growing requirement for maintenance with age, or some combination of these and other factors is not clear. Neither is it clear whether the trend will continue.

Following a vigorous controversy in the United States in the early 1970s concerning the consequences of low-dose radiation the public might receive from routine emissions in an expanded nuclear-power program, the USAEC tightened the guidelines for emissions from LWRs a hundredfold.[104] This had the effect of lowering the "design target" maximum dose delivered to a member of the public by routine emissions from an LWR of 5 millirem (mrem) per year. LWRs built after the mid-1960s apparently were able to meet the new guidelines handily.[105] In early 1977 the U.S. Environmental Protection Agency (which by then had secured jurisdiction over setting standards for radiation exposure) promulgated standards applicable not just to LWRs but to all reactor types and to other nuclear facilities as well, limiting exposure to any member of the public to 25 millirem per year.[105a] (See also Chapter 10.) This is a *regulation,* in contrast to the earlier 5 millirem "design guideline" for LWRs. It can be assumed that LWRs and probably other reactor types can meet the new standard more easily than, say, reprocessing plants (see below). To the extent that they can, routine emissions from the reactor become one of the least objectionable characteristics of fission power. It should be emphasized, however, that meeting such standards over the operating life of a reactor may prove more difficult than meeting them for the first few years, and that vigilant monitoring and enforcement will be required in any case to assure performance.

Accidents and attempted sabotage at nuclear power plants can have a wide range of consequences, from minor equipment damage and no release of radioactivity from the plant site, on one extreme, to a catastrophe with tens of thousands of people killed and tens of billions of dollars' worth of property damage, on the other. Since many people are rightly concerned about the worst thing that could happen as a result of putting a given reactor in a given location, we treat mainly the consequences and probabilities of the largest accidents here. The nuclear industry and its regulators call these Class IX accidents (the mildest accident is Class I). Their occurrence depends on a sequence of several equipment failures and/or errors, all deemed highly improbable (but see our discussion of probability, below).[106]

Deferring the question of probability for a moment, consider first the potential for harm in a very large accident. The main relevant questions are: (1) How much and what kinds of radioactive substances are inside a reactor? (2) How much could be released in the worst conceivable event? (3) Where would it go? (4) How many individuals and what kinds and quantities of territory would receive what doses as a result? (5) What pattern of deaths, injuries, and property damage would be caused by those doses? The amount of scientific uncertainty about the answers increases as one goes down the list, but reasonable estimates seem possible for all five. These questions have been studied in varying degrees for all the major reactor types, although probably most thoroughly for the LWRs.

A 1000-Mwe LWR after sustained operation contains about 12 billion curies of fission products, more than 3 billion curies of the heavy radioactive elements called actinides (the uranium fuel and its derivatives, including plutonium, thorium, and neptunium), and around 10 million curies of activation products (radioactive materials produced by the interaction of fission neutrons with the reactor structure).[107] Quantities of curies, by themselves, are not very enlightening measures of hazard (see Chapter 10), so it has become customary to define a crude measure of relative hazard as the number of curies of a given isotope divided by its maximum permissible concentration (MPC). The resulting number is the volume of air or water that would be required to dilute that material, uniformly mixed, down to the MPC. Also

[104]For various views of the controversy, see John P. Holdren and P. Herrera, *Energy,* pp. 62–67; JCAE, *Hearings on environmental effects of producing electric power;* J. W. Gofman and A. R. Tamplin, *Poisoned power.* See also Chapter 10.

[105]USAEC, *The safety of nuclear power reactors.*

[105a]*Nuclear News,* EPA limits dose to public, releases from fuel cycle, February 1977, p. 30.

[106]For descriptions of the first eight classes of accidents and an introduction to the measures provided to prevent or ameliorate them, see, for example, USAEC, *The safety of nuclear power reactors.*

[107]This and the subsequent discussion draw heavily on John P. Holdren, Hazards of the nuclear fuel cycle, and the references therein. See also Pigford, Environmental Aspects.

TABLE 8-16
Inventory of Radioactivity in a 1000 Mwe Light-Water Reactor at Shutdown (selected isotopes)

Isotope	*Half-life**	*Inventory (million Ci)*	*Maximum permissible concentration** (μCi/m³)*	*Air needed to dilute inventory to MPC (km³)*
Iodine-131	8.1 d	85	0.0001	850,000,000
Strontium-89	52 d	94	0.0003	310,000,000
Ruthenium-106	1 y	25	0.0002	130,000,000
Neptunium-239	2.4 y	1640	0.02†	80,000,000
Plutonium-238	89 y	0.057	0.000001†	57,000,000
Tellurium-132	3.3 d	120	0.004	30,000,000
Cesium-134	2.1 y	7.5	0.0004	19,000,000
Xenon-133	5.3 d	170	0.3	570,000

*d = days; y = years.
**MPC in air for continuous public exposure.
†MPC for insoluble form (soluble is stricter), since this is how material is found in reactors.
Sources: U.S. Nuclear Regulatory Commission, *Reactor safety study,* Code of Federal Regulations, Title 10, Chapter 1, Part 20, Standards for protection against radiation, Government Printing Office, December 1975.

relevant is the half-life of the isotope, which indicates how quickly the needed amount of dilution diminishes.

The inventories of a few of the most dangerous radioactive isotopes in an LWR at the instant the chain reaction is shut down appear in Table 8-16, along with their half-lives, their MPCs in air, and their relative hazards (measured in thousands of cubic kilometers). A somewhat more meaningful measure of potential hazard can be obtained by multiplying the inventory by the fraction of a material thought to be capable of becoming airborne in the worst conceivable accident, and then computing the volume of air required to dilute that smaller amount to the MPC. Such corrected relative hazards are tabulated in Table 8-17. The volumes are still very large; the releasable iodine-131 alone is sufficient at shutdown to contaminate the atmosphere over the forty-eight contiguous United States up to an altitude of 10 kilometers (the tropopause) to more than twice the MPC. (This is not to suggest that the material would actually be uniformly dispersed that way, but only to communicate some feeling for the magnitude of the problem.)

Potential contamination of surface water and groundwater by radioactivity released in a reactor accident is another measure of the hazard, and relative hazard figures analogous to those for air can be computed for water. For example, half the strontium-90 in a reactor at shutdown is enough to contaminate the annual freshwater runoff of the forty-eight contiguous states to 6 times the MPC (although, again, it would certainly not be distributed that way).

TABLE 8-17
Adjusted Relative Hazards of Radioactive Isotopes in a 1000-Mwe LWR at Shutdown

Isotope	*Fraction releasable**	*Adjusted relative hazard (km³)*
Iodine-131	0.70	600,000,000
Ruthenium-106	0.50	65,000,000
Strontium-89	0.10	31,000,000
Tellurium-132	0.70	21,000,000
Cesium-134	0.50	9,500,000
Xenon-133	1.00	570,000
Neptunium-239	0.005	400,000
Plutonium-238	0.005	290,000

*Fractions releasable to air in the worst-case accidents, according to U.S. Nuclear Regulatory Commission, *Reactor safety study.*

It is physically impossible for an LWR or any thermal-neutron reactor to blow up like a nuclear bomb. The only way a reactor could release to the environment the large amounts of radioactivity being discussed here is in an accident that caused much of the nuclear fuel to melt. Such a chain of events could involve steam explosions and releases of chemical energy that would break open the containment building above the ground; and almost certainly any large-scale fuel melting would lead to penetration by the molten mass through the steel and concrete layers into the ground below. These possibilities are mentioned further in the discussion of probability, below. For now, it suffices to emphasize that the concern is not with a reactor's blowing up like a bomb, but rather with its cracking open like an egg.

In some respects, however, such an event could be worse than a "typical" nuclear bomb. A large reactor's inventory of long-lived radioactivity is more than 1000 times that of the bomb dropped on Hiroshima. Moreover, the portion of the radioactivity that would issue from a cracked-open containment building would not be blown directly into the stratosphere—as was much of the bomb's radioactivity—but instead might be trapped by atmospheric conditions near the surface (where the people are).

The number of immediate and long-term human casualties and the amount of property damage resulting from a given release of radioactivity depend on the distribution of population around a site, the degree of evacuation that proves possible, and, especially, on weather conditions at the time. Several specific published estimates deserve mention. The first is a 1957 study conducted by the USAEC and commonly known by its document number, WASH-740.[108] It considered an LWR of about 500 Mwt (160 Mwe) about 30 miles from a major city, and concluded that the greatest consequences in the worst case would be about 3400 persons killed (to a distance of 15 miles), about 43,000 injured (to a distance of 45 miles), with maximum property damage around $7000 million. The report stated that, in most circumstances considered, the consequences would be considerably less than that (that is, "assumed losses would not exceed a few hundred million dollars"), and that the probability of any such major reactor accident was exceedingly low. At about the same time a less widely distributed study was published, concerning potential consequences of hypothetical accidents at a specific experimental LMFBR power plant—the 300-Mwt Fermi plant being built near Detroit.[109] It concluded that the worst event, which the authors termed "incredible," could kill as many as 133,000 persons.

The nuclear industry, the USAEC, and the Joint Committee on Atomic Energy (JCAE) of Congress were unhappy about the wide attention given to the maximum-casualty figures in WASH-740, and members of those groups increasingly disparaged that report, asserting that it used unduly pessimistic assumptions. In 1964 another study of LWR accidents was initiated by the USAEC and also performed at Brookhaven National Laboratory. The idea was to take into account the improved scientific information that had become available since 1957, and it was hoped that more realistic assumptions made possible by that information would more than compensate for the increased reactor size (up to 2000 Mwt, or about 600 Mwe) which by then had to be considered. After the preliminary results in 1965 indicated an *increase* in the potential consequences over those published in WASH-740, the project was canceled and the working papers locked up. They were released in 1973 as the result of a lawsuit brought under the Freedom-of-Information Act by conservationist organizations. The preliminary investigation had indicated, for the worst case, 45,000 short-term fatalities and land contamination in an area equal in size to Pennsylvania.[110] No attempt was made to assign a numerical probability to that event, but it was deemed highly unlikely.

The most recent and largest USAEC study of accidents in LWRs (WASH-1400) was released in draft form late in 1974 and in final form in October 1975.[111] It was performed over three years by USAEC staff (later part of the Nuclear Regulatory Commission) and outside consultants under the direction of a nuclear engineering professor at Massachusetts Institute of Technology, Norman Rasmussen. It is popularly known as the Rasmussen report. The report addressed itself to both the probability and the consequences of major accidents at LWR power plants. It did not address other types of reactors or other parts of the nuclear fuel cycle. The maximum accident considered, which was assigned a probability of one in a billion per reactor per year, would lead (in the study's estimation) to the consequences shown in Table 8-18. The uncertainty factors given in the table are those stated in the Rasmussen report itself. The multiplicative uncertainty of from 1/4 to 4 about the

[108]USAEC, *Theoretical possibilities and consequences of major accidents in large nuclear power plants.* The study was performed largely at the Brookhaven National Laboratory.

[109]Engineering Research Institute, *A report on the possible effects on the surrounding population of an assumed release of fission products into the atmosphere from a 300 megawatt nuclear reactor located at Laguna Beach, Michigan.*

[110]A. J. Court, F. P. Cowan, K. Downes, and B. H. Kuper, Exposure potentials and criteria for estimating the cost of major reactor accidents; and other documents in USAEC, WASH-740 update file.

[111]USAEC, *Reactor safety study* (draft); U.S. Nuclear Regulatory Commission, *Reactor safety study.*

TABLE 8-18
Consequences of Worst-Case Hypothetical LWR Accident as Estimated by the Rasmussen Report

Effect	*Rate or number*	*Duration*	*Total number, Rasmussen best estimate*	*Uncertainty range, multiplicative*	*Total number, Rasmussen low estimate*	*Total number, Rasmussen high estimate*
Prompt deaths	3,300	–	3,300	¼–4	825	13,200
Cancer deaths	1,500/yr	30–40 yr	45,000–60,000	⅙–3	7,500	180,000
Prompt illnesses	49,500	–	49,500	¼–4	12,375	198,000
Thyroid illnesses	8,000/yr	30–40 yr	240,000–320,000	⅓–3	80,000	960,000
Genetic effects	190/yr	many generations*	28,500	⅙–6	4,750	171,000
Property damage	$14 billion	–	$14 billion	⅕–2	$2.8 billion	$28 billion

*Equivalent to 150 years at constant rate.
Source: U.S. Nuclear Regulatory Commission, *Reactor safety study.*

"best estimate" of 3300 prompt deaths means that the actual value would fall in the range of from 825 to 13,200, in the view of the report's authors. The total of prompt deaths plus delayed cancer deaths has the very large range of from 8325 to 193,200. These deaths would take place in a total exposed population of 10 million people, according to the report.

The best-estimate casualty figures in the final draft of the Rasmussen report, as reproduced in Table 8-18, represent significant increases over the figures in the earlier draft. The upward revisions were made as the result of correcting a number of errors that were uncovered in several external and internal reviews of the report.[112] Specific responses to parts of these reviews are given in Appendix XI of the report's final draft.

It remains controversial whether the best-estimate casualty figures in the final draft now really represent the most realistic estimates that can be made. A critique of the final draft performed by the Environmental Protection Agency suggested that the Rasmussen best estimate of cancer deaths may still be too low by a factor of between 2 and 10.[113] This critique indicated that early deaths and illnesses were also underestimated in the final draft, but EPA was unable to estimate by how much because of inadequate documentation in the Rasmussen report's treatment of that topic. Other reviews of the calculations used by the Rasmussen group to estimate early casualties have revealed enough dubious assumptions and internal inconsistencies that it is clear the true uncertainty range is greater than indicated in Table 8-18.[113a]

No one disputes that extensive engineering precautions have been taken in an attempt to make reactor accidents of such magnitude very unlikely.[114] But how meaningful are the tiny probabilites computed in the Rasmussen study, representing the chance of a reactor accident that kills 1000 persons as being less than the chance of a catastrophe from a large meteorite's striking a city? It is difficult indeed to ascribe much credibility to such numerical values, for several reasons.

First of all, there are at least four categories of potential failure modes (in no implied order of likelihood):

1. human error and/or mechanical failure internal to an installation;
2. human error and/or mechanical failure external to the installation (such as a plane crash);
3. natural catastrophe (earthquake, tornado, tsunami);
4. malicious human activity (war, sabotage, terrorism).

The Rasmussen report's treatment of accident probability was based essentially exclusively on random internal mechanical failures—that is, on *some* of the failure modes in Category 1. It could *not* account for many kinds of

[112]See especially U.S. Environmental Protection Agency, *Reactor safety study: A review of the draft report;* H. Kendall and S. Moglower, *Preliminary review of the AEC reactor safety study;* American Physical Society, *Report of the APS study group on light water reactor safety;* H. Kendall, *Nuclear power risks: A review of the report of the APS study group.* The APS study goes well beyond a mere review of the Rasmussen report and is a major contribution to the nuclear safety debate in its own right.

[113]U.S. Environmental Protection Agency, *Reactor safety study: a review of the final report.*

[113a]J. P. Holdren, Zero-infinity dilemmas in nuclear power; J. Yellin, The Nuclear Regulatory Commission's Reactor Safety Study; F. von Hippel, Looking back on the Rasmussen report.

[114]See, for example, H. Lewis et al., Report of the APS study group on light-water reactor safety; and USAEC, *The safety of nuclear power reactors,* for extensive descriptions of these measures.

human error, for certain kinds of disasters such as large earthquakes, or for malice.

Reactor systems themselves are extraordinarily complex, and neither the probabilities of component failure nor the possible failure modes of the systems are known with sufficient assurance to permit a meaningful calculation even of the probability of a catastrophic event of Category 1, listed above. Although there has been no major accident to date (in loss of human life) at a commercial power reactor, there have been enough serious malfunctions to confound the calculators of such probabilities. For example, a fuel meltdown at the Fermi LMFBR in Detroit in 1965 exceeded the "maximum credible accident" for that installation.[115]

As of mid-1975, there had been little more than 1000 reactor years of power-reactor experience worldwide.[116] Therefore, *on the basis of experience alone,* no one can be sure that the probability of a catastrophic accident is not as high as 1/1000 per reactor-year (although so high a figure seems unlikely). Moreover, much of the early experience was with much smaller or otherwise much different reactors from, say, the very large LWRs that are coming into service today. It is not apparent, therefore, how much of the earlier experience is relevant to assessing accident probabilities now. Unfortunately, even the most careful theoretical analysis cannot entirely evade the pitfalls created by the lack of extensive operational experience—for example, uncertainty about the reliability of individual components of a system and the possibility of overlooking a combination of events more probable than those considered.

Moreover, an extended controversy in the early 1970s over emergency systems for LWRs in the United States revealed major gaps and apparent mismanagement in the USAEC reactor-safety program.[117] It is difficult to escape the impression that, in the event of a loss-of-coolant accident, the emergency core-cooling systems for contemporary pressurized-water reactors and boiling-water reactors of United States design might not be able to prevent the melting of a reactor core and a subsequent catastrophic release of radioactivity. The Rasmussen report *assumed* high reliability for those emergency systems; it did not prove it.

Notwithstanding this and other defects in the Rasmussen report's probability analysis, the study computed the probability of a complete core meltdown in an LWR of contemporary design (the event previously assumed to define a catastrophic accident) as 1 in 20,000 per reactor per year. This figure is much higher than any with which the USAEC had previously associated itself. It would indicate (if it still applied to the 1000 reactors widely projected to be in operation in the United States before the year 2000) a probability of 1 chance in 20 per year that such an accident would take place in this country. This result is only transformed into a reassuring one in the Rasmussen study by calculations and assumptions indicating that the consequences of a meltdown, once it occurred, would be much abated by retention of the radioactivity in soil and rock under the reactor, by meteorological factors, and by evacuation of the threatened population. This line of argument suddenly and drastically changed the official position—from "it won't happen" to "it's not so bad if it does." Those revised contentions in the Rasmussen report provide the basis for its disagreement with the two previous, more pessimistic USAEC-sponsored studies of the consequences of reactor accidents. The revised arguments therefore require the closest critical scrutiny. Reliance on evacuation seems particularly suspect.[118]

Of course, it may be possible in principle to design reactors that are inherently very safe against internal accidents, even if some present-day LWRs are not. Gas-cooled reactors may represent the direction in which such safe reactors are to be found, because the enormous heat capacity of the graphite moderator provides an extended period of grace following an accidental loss of coolant before the fuel begins to fail. (If the heat of radioactive decay after shutdown is not removed by primary or emergency coolant, the rate of heat generation

[115]Inglis, *Nuclear energy.* For a detailed description of this and other early reactor accidents in lay terms, see R. Fuller, *We almost lost Detroit.*

[116]*Nuclear News,* World list of nuclear power plants, vol. 8, no. 10 (August 1975), pp. 63–75.

[117]I. Forbes, D. Ford, H. Kendall, J. MacKenzie, Nuclear reactor safety: An evaluation of the new evidence; D. F. Ford, H. W. Kendall, and J. J. MacKenzie, A critique of the AEC's interim criteria for emergency core-cooling systems; R. Gillette, Nuclear safety: pt. 3, Critics charge conflicts of interest.

[118]See USEPA, *Reactor safety study: A review of the final report.*

is sufficient to initiate the melting of the fuel in an LWR within about 60 seconds.[119] In a high-temperature gas-cooled reactor, however, the graphite moderator can soak up the decay heat for well over an hour before the graphite coating of the fuel particles begins to sublime.)

Whether LMFBRs will prove to be significantly less safe than LWRs (or safer) is not entirely clear. The high power density and high enrichment of the fuel are negative features in terms of safety, as is the chemical reactivity of the sodium coolant. On the other hand, the low pressure of the coolant is an advantage for the LMFBR, and at least some designs have the characteristic that natural convection in the sodium can remove the decay heat fast enough to prevent core melting, even if all the coolant pumps should fail. One of the most important questions is how much energy could be released in a "nuclear excursion" in an LMFBR—the sort of near-bomb behavior that is strictly limited to fizzles in LWRs by the basic properties of the fuel. Some reactor experts believe that properly designed LMFBRs will not be capable of much more than a fizzle, either; they assert that the maximum possible nuclear-energy release is small enough to be contained within the layers of steel and concrete surrounding the core. Other equally qualified specialists insist that the possibility of excursions too large to be contained cannot be ruled out.[120]

Although some of the engineering approaches to assuring reactor safety against internal accidents apply also in some measure to external events (Categories 2–4, above) there are important differences. To an even greater extent than is true of internal accidents, for example, it is possible for the cause of an externally imposed disruption to disable the emergency systems as well as the primary reactor functions. The nature of natural catastrophes such as earthquakes is such that it is virtually impossible to guarantee the integrity of a system against the strongest conceivable event, although it may be possible to reduce the probability of failure to a very low level by careful construction and siting. Society may find it difficult, however, to decide on what is an acceptably low probability for an almost completely unacceptable event.

It is possible, although not yet certain, that the probability and/or magnitude of major releases of radioactivity that might be associated with events of Categories 1–3 at reactors can be reduced to tolerable levels by siting the reactors under several hundred feet of rock or earth fill. Preliminary studies indicate that the construction-cost penalty of this approach would not exceed 10 percent.[121] Thus, isolation from events of Category 2 would be virtually assured, and in Category 3 only earthquakes would still be of consequence. The degree of containment against major releases of radioactivity by any catastrophes that might befall an underground reactor remains to be thoroughly investigated. Placing reactors underground, however, would seem to have considerable advantage over surface siting.

Perhaps the most troublesome events of all, potentially, are those in Category 4—the malicious disruption of reactor systems through acts of war, insurrection, sabotage, or terrorism. The possibilities are obvious, and we will not dwell on them in detail. Suffice it to say that in the event that a determined and knowledgeable saboteur gains access to a nuclear power plant, all theoretical calculations concerning reactor reliability become meaningless. A study by the General Accounting Office of the U.S. government in 1974 confirmed the reality of that possibility.[122]

Spent fuel. Neither the technology nor the environmental impact of nuclear energy ends with the generation of electricity at the reactor. The nuclear fuel must eventually be removed from the reactor core—not so much because the fissile component would be used up but because the accumulating fission products "poison" the chain reaction by absorbing neutrons. Most reactors are operated on a three- or four-year cycle; that is, once a year, one-fourth to one-third of the fuel is removed and replaced with a fresh batch. The material removed is called spent fuel. It is first stored at the reactor site so

[119] W. K. Ergen (chairman), *Emergency core cooling: Report of advisory task force committee on power reactor emergency cooling.*

[120] For elements of this controversy, see Cochran, *The LMFBR*, chapter 7 and appendixes C and G; F. R. Farmer, ed., *Nuclear reactor safety.*

[121] M. Watson, W. Kammer, N. Langley, L. Selzer, R. Beck, *Underground nuclear power plant siting;* G. Yadigaroglu and S. O. Anderson, Novel siting solutions for nuclear power plants.

[122] R. Gillette, GAO calls security lax at nuclear plants.

some of the most intense but short-lived radioactivity can decay before further handling. Then the fuel is shipped to a reprocessing plant, where as much as is practical of the useful uranium and plutonium isotopes are separated from the fission products and other radioactive wastes. The uranium and plutonium are then stored or recycled, and the wastes are stored, pending adoption of a plan for their permanent management or disposal. All these steps together are often called the "back end" of the nuclear fuel cycle. They present some of the greatest technical and environmental problems associated with nuclear power.

Cooling the spent fuel elements immediately after removal from the reactor core takes place in pools of water provided for that purpose at the reactor site but outside the main containment building. At that point, then, the barriers against the release of radioactivity that were provided in the reactor by the reactor vessel and by the main concrete-and-steel containment building are no longer present. In these respects, the spent fuel is more vulnerable to dispersal by external events, such as sabotage or earthquakes, than the fuel in the reactor core. However, probably less radioactivity could be widely dispersed by such events than by the meltdown of a reactor core. During the 150-day cooling-off period that is customary for LWR fuel, the radioactivity in a 40-ton annual batch of spent fuel drops from about 5 billion curies to 135 million curies. (The complete lack of commercial fuel-reprocessing plants in the mid-1970s in the United States has led to the retention of fuel in storage pools for much longer than 150 days, creating the problem for reactor operators of where to put the overflow.[123]) The economics of the LMFBR fuel cycle will require that the spent fuel be discharged more frequently and in smaller batches, which will be cooled for only 30 days.[124] The shorter cooling period means that radioactivity about 3 times greater than that of LWR fuel will have to be handled in shipment and processing, posing significant additional problems.

Shipment of the intact spent-fuel elements from the storage pool to the reprocessing plant takes place in heavily shielded casks. The heat of radioactive decay after 150 days of cooling amounts to about 20 kilowatts per metric ton of fuel, requiring continuous cooling in the cask to prevent the fuel from melting. Spent-fuel casks shipped by truck weigh up to 35 metric tons; those shipped by rail, as much as 100 metric tons.[125] The casks are designed and tested to withstand severe impacts, fire, and immersion in water. The main question is the probability of there being a shipping accident severe enough to rupture such a cask. (The chance would seem to be low if the casks are as good as claimed.) There will be ample opportunity to learn the answer by experience; the largest casks must make about 10 trips a year to service a 1000-Mwe LWR. This means there will be more than 1000 cask-trips per year for the 100 reactors expected to exist in the United States before 1985.

Once at the reprocessing plant, the fuel elements are chopped into pieces and the contents dissolved in acid for chemical separation. At that point the barriers between the concentrated radioactive material and the environment are at their lowest, for then the protection afforded by the metal cladding and the ceramic matrix of the individual solid fuel elements is gone. Virtually all of the operations at the reprocessing plant must be conducted by remote control because of the intense radiation emanating from the wastes. Many of the gaseous and liquid effluents are controlled by using scaled-up versions of the systems used at reactors. (A single, large reprocessing plant of the future may serve as many as fifty reactors, so the amount of radioactivity handled will be very large indeed—about 7 billion curies per year after the 150-day cooling periods.) Under present practices, all of the radioactive gas krypton-85 ($t_{1/2} = 10.8$ years) goes up the reprocessing-plant stack, and all of the tritium ($t_{1/2} = 12.3$ years) is released to air or water. Traces of other radioactive isotopes are released, but most are concentrated in the residual liquid high-level waste—some 1200 liters of it per metric ton of spent fuel processed (around 40,000 liters per reactor per year), containing 12,000 curies of fission products per gallon.[126]

[123] *Nuclear News,* Ten reactors currently do not have enough fuel storage.

[124] Pigford, et al., *Fuel cycles,* chapter 10.

[125] For more detail, see Pigford, Environmental aspects, pp. 536–537; USAEC, *The safety of nuclear power reactors,* sections 1.5 and 4.2; C. Smith, Shipment and reprocessing of irradiated power reactor fuels.

[126] Pigford, Environmental aspects, p. 525.

BOX 8-5 Radioactive Wastes: An Aspirin Tablet per Person?

It is not uncommon to hear from the public-relations arm of the nuclear industry that the radioactive wastes from nuclear power are equivalent in size to only an aspirin tablet per year for every person whose electricity is provided by nuclear plants.* Probably the most misleading aspect of this analogy is that *toxicity,* not volume, is the important characteristic of those wastes. If a tablet were to be an apt comparison, it would have to be a cyanide tablet—and even that would not do justice to the actual toxicity of the fission products.

It turns out, moreover, that 1 tablet per person is far from a correct figure, even in respect to volume. If the high-level radioactive wastes from a reprocessing plant were to be solidified in their most concentrated form (the form to which the aspirin-tablet view presumably refers), the resulting volume per 1000-Mwe LWR per year would be 2.5 to 3 cubic meters.** Since such a plant, running at a generous average of 75 percent of full capacity, could meet the full electricity demand of 750,000 Americans in 1975 (this includes not only their homes but also the associated commerce and industry), the volume of high-level solid waste per person served would be 3.3 to 4 cubic centimeters. The volume of an aspirin tablet is about 0.4 cubic centimeters, so the solidified high-level wastes would be about the size of 10 aspirin tablets per person.

That, however, is only the tip of the iceberg. Most high-level wastes have not been solidified yet, and federal law requires only that such solidification take place within 10 years of the creation of the wastes. The volume of the liquid form before solidification is 10 times greater than that of the solid (therefore, we would have 100 aspirin tablets per person). Additionally, there are the highly radioactive remains of the fuel cladding (2 cubic meters per reactor year, or 5 more aspirin tablets per person).

There is still more. The reprocessing plant also produces annually for every 1000-Mwe reactor about 25 cubic meters of intermediate-level liquid wastes (contaminated to between 10,000 and 1 million times the maximum permissible concentration) and 1200 cubic meters of low-level liquid wastes (10 to 10,000 times the MPC). Those wastes would amount to 60 and 3000 additional aspirin tablets per person, respectively. Low-level solid wastes from the reprocessing plant and from the reactor itself amount to between 80 and 160 cubic meters per year (200 to 400 more aspirin tablets per person). Those wastes contain alpha-emitting radioisotopes of very long half-life.

All this adds up to a volume equal to that of between 3300 and 3600 aspirin tablets per year per person served. If the Nuclear Regulatory Commission (NRC) were to approve the routine recycling of plutonium in LWRs, an additional 340 cubic meters of plutonium-contaminated wastes per reactor per year would appear at the fuel-fabrication plants—another 850 aspirin tablets per person served. Dismantling the reactor and other radioactive fuel-cycle facilities at the ends of their operating lifetimes would add more waste to the total, amounting to perhaps 500 cubic meters per year of operation, or 1250 aspirin tablets per person.† The total would still perhaps not be an overwhelming volume, around 2000 cm^3 of waste per person per year. But remember, the toxicity of this material is what is really important.

It is disquieting, in any case, to find persons in the nuclear industry—so quick to complain about what its representatives consider to be irresponsible statements from environmentalists—glibly dispensing information that is both qualitatively misleading and quantitatively wrong by a factor of thousands.

*See, for example, General Electric Co., *Nuclear power: The best alternative.*

**Most data in this box are from USAEC, *The safety of nuclear power reactors and related facilities,* p. 4-89; T. H. Pigford, Environmental aspects of nuclear energy production, p. 525.

†ERDA, *Alternatives for managing wastes from reactors and post-fission operations in the LWR fuel cycle.*

TABLE 8-19

Radioactive Wastes in Storage After Various Decay Periods (selected isotopes)

Isotope	Half-life (years)	Maximum permissible concentration in water (Ci/m³)	Curies per 1000-Mw reactor year after decay of t years			
			t = 10	t = 100	t = 1000	t = 10,000
Cesium-137	30	2×10^{-5}	5,000,000	630,000	5×10^{-4}	–
Strontium-90	28	3×10^{-7}	3,600,000	400,000	10^{-4}	–
Technetium-99	210,000	2×10^{-4}	450	450	450	430
Zirconium-93	900,000	8×10^{-4}	110	110	110	109
Plutonium-239	24,400	3×10^{-4}	51	55*	60	108
Neptunium-237	2,100,000	3×10^{-4}	18	18	18	18

*Pu-239 increases for a time because it is being produced by the radioactive decay of other isotopes.

Sources: T. Hollocher, in D. Ford et al., *The nuclear fuel cycle,* chapter 1; USAEC, *The safety of nuclear power reactors.*

Less intensely radioactive, but still dangerous wastes are also produced as intermediate- and low-level liquids and solids (see Box 8-5).

The release of tritium and krypton at reprocessing plants is the largest routine emission of radioactivity in the nuclear fuel cycle. Krypton eventually becomes thoroughly mixed with the global atmosphere, and tritium with atmospheric and surface water[127] At that point, their contribution to human exposure to radiation is small compared to those of natural sources of radiation (this is not to say it is entirely harmless—see Chapter 10). This will remain true even if the use of nuclear power grows rapidly for another thirty years. The increasing releases, especially of tritium, could cause relatively severe local problems before then, however, and they would presumably have to be controlled if such nuclear power growth materialized.

The only commercial fuel-reprocessing plant to operate in the United States before 1977 was the Nuclear Fuel Services, Inc. (NFS), plant near Buffalo, New York, which was in service from 1966 to 1971 before being shut down for expansion and repairs. Its peak rated capacity was around 300 tons of fuel per year, corresponding to the output of fewer than ten large reactors. Emissions from the plant have been studied by several groups; the plant occasionally operated very close to the permissible limits and could not have come close to the much tighter emissions guidelines that have since been applied to the reactors themselves.[128] (Reprocessing plants were excluded from those revised guidelines.) What this plant's emissions might be if it came back into service at 3 times the old rated capacity—originally scheduled for 1978—remains to be seen. The plant's operators announced in 1976 that it might not reopen at all. A second commercial reprocessing plant built by the General Electric Company near Morris, Illinois, was to have come into service in 1974. It did not work and was shut down without reprocessing any fuel, after an investment of about $65 million.[129] A reprocessing plant large enough to serve almost fifty large reactors was scheduled to begin commercial operations near Barnwell, South Carolina, in 1977 or 1978, but has been delayed.

It has been claimed that the technology exists, and will be implemented, to make routine emissions very modest, even at such large reprocessing plants.[130] This may prove to be true. If it does, the serious question that will remain about such plants, with their large inventories of radioactive poisons and the relative paucity of solid barriers against the release of those poisons, is their vulnerability to such hard-to-predict disruptions as fires, earthquakes, tornadoes, and the intervention of saboteurs.

As with operations at the reactors and the reprocessing plants, the need for actual long-term management of radioactive wastes from reprocessing plants confronts society with a situation in which the routine impact perhaps can be made very small, but the consequences of conceivable nonroutine events are very great. In the case of managing the wastes, moreover, the necessity for ironclad safeguards extends far beyond the life of the reactors, the people who build them, and the people who

[127]National Council on Radiation Production and Measurements, *Krypton-85 in the atmosphere;* M. Eisenbud, *Environmental radioactivity.*

[128]An excellent review of the NFS experience is D. Ford et al., *The nuclear fuel cycle,* chapter 6.

[129]Marvin Resnikoff, Expensive enrichment.

[130]See, for example, USAEC, *Environmental survey,* section F.

TABLE 8-20
Relative Hazard of Radioactive Wastes Accumulated in the U.S. Through the Year 2000

Time	*Inhalation hazard (air) (million km³)*	*Ingestion hazard (water) (1000 km³)*
The year 2000	7,300,000	50,000.0
100 years later	1,900,000	3,600.0
1,000 years later	150,000	5.5
10,000 years later	50,000	2.4
100,000 years later	6,200	1.4
1,000,000 years later	4,000	0.7

Note: Units are volumes needed to dilute to MPCs.
Source: USAEC, *High-level radioactive waste management alternatives,* p. A-9.

use the electricity they produce. Table 8-19 lists the half-lives of some of the most dangerous long-lived radioactive wastes, along with the number of curies of each that would be present for each year of operation of one large LWR, after various periods of decay. The amount of waste produced annually in an economy of 1000 large reactors, of course, would be 1000 times as much of each of the isotopes listed, in addition to others not in the table.

A 1974 study of waste-management alternatives published by the USAEC calculated the hazard of the total waste inventory the USAEC expected to have accumulated in the United States by the year 2000. That is, the study divided the anticipated inventory of each isotope by its MPCs in air and water, to obtain what were termed an inhalation hazard and an ingestion hazard.[131] The magnitude of those hazards at intervals up to 1 million years later (counting only wastes produced in the United States until 2000) were then computed. The results are summarized in Table 8-20. The huge volumes of air and water that would be required to dilute the waste material down to the MPCs, even tens and hundreds of thousands of years after it was produced, testify to the degree of control that must be achieved.

Many proposals have been put forward for providing such safeguards for radioactive waste materials. The suggestions include burial in salt deposits, in deep bedrock, in the deep trenches on the ocean floor, at the bottom of the Antarctic ice cap, and in underground cavities blasted for the purpose with nuclear explosives. They include ejecting the wastes from the solar system in rockets, letting them ride into Earth's interior at subduction zones where tectonic plates collide, or merely storing them in concrete-and-steel bunkers under surveillance until someone thinks of a better way.[132] Some of the schemes have defects that are easily identified (waste-bearing rockets could blow up on the launching pad) and other have defects that have been pointed out by specialists in the fields involved (the future of the Antarctic ice cap is too uncertain for us to rely on it, and even now there is evidence of significant melting and of fast pathways to the open ocean at its base).[133] Some have promise. The option of separating out the long-lived actinides and breaking them up into shorter-lived fission products by bombarding them with fast neutrons, either in a fast breeder reactor or a fusion reactor, may have merit as a way of changing a million-year problem into a thousand-year problem.[134] Whether this is really practical is not known. Indeed, no scheme yet proposed is free of substantive uncertainties and/or controversy within the technical community. Certainly, any approaches that require maintenance or continuing surveillance of storage facilities must be regarded as temporary expedients and not solutions, since the continuity of society even over 500 years can hardly be guaranteed. And, whereas some existing or future proposal involving fission *may* be satisfactory, it is hard to be complacent about the use of fission with no solution actually in hand.[134a]

The record of the handling of radioactive wastes produced so far, moreover, is not especially encouraging. Pending the beginning of U.S. commercial operations to solidify high-level waste, it is still being stored as liquid in steel tanks at the reprocessing plants. This is the method used by the USAEC to manage the radioactive wastes from its bomb-building programs, from which

[131] USAEC, *High-level radioactive waste management alternatives,* p. A-9.

[132] Notable surveys of the high-level waste problem and various proposed solutions are T. Hollocher, Storage and disposal of high level wastes; A. S. Kubo and D. J. Rose, Disposal of nuclear wastes; USAEC, *High-level radioactive waste.*

[133] C. Bull, Radioactive waste disposal.

[134] Kubo and Rose, Disposal; W. Wolkenhauer et al., *Transmutation of high-level radioactive wastes with a controlled thermonuclear reactor.*

[134a] For a provocative and insightful study of ethical as well as technical dimensions of the problem, see G. I. Rochlin, Nuclear waste disposal: two social criteria.

there have been several leaks totaling hundreds of thousands of gallons of high-level liquids at both the Hanford, Washington, and Savannah River, Georgia, sites.[135] It is believed that essentially all the radioactivity from those spills has been confined by absorption by soil particles in the immediate vicinity of the tanks.

In the early 1970s, the USAEC announced that a solution had been chosen—burial in abandoned salt mines, as in fact is practiced in both the Federal German Republic (West Germany) and the Democratic Republic of Germany. Unfortunately, the USAEC picked a particular mine in Lyons, Kansas, that was quite literally full of holes (from drilling for oil and gas decades before). The agency abandoned its plans for this "national repository" after the Kansas Geological Survey identified the site's defects.[136] In 1974, the USAEC announced that a new official solution was to be retrievable surface storage facilities—an interim plan until something better came along, of course—and that three potential sites in the western United States were under scrutiny. The draft environmental impact statement for the project reflected so slipshod an approach that complaints were received from utilities and manufacturers of nuclear equipment, as well as environmentalists, and that plan was shelved.[137] USAEC's successor, ERDA, in 1975 was investigating salt deposits again, that time in New Mexico.

Management of intermediate- and low-level wastes has received less scrutiny by the technical community at large, but it also poses significant problems (see Box 8-5). Those materials typically have been placed in oil drums and stacked on the surface on government sites or buried under a few meters of earth at those sites and at various commercial burial grounds. A study by the National Academy of Sciences of radioactive-waste management in the late 1960s concluded that management practices were "barely tolerable . . . on the present scale of operations" and "would become intolerable with much increase in the use of nuclear power."[138] At the Hanford, Washington, government nuclear facility, so much liquid waste contaminated with plutonium was dumped into a single trench over a period of twenty-two years that a genuine and serious danger of an explosive nuclear chain reaction arose (it was estimated that 100 kg of plutonium was contained in about 50 m^3 of soil).[139]

A final waste problem is the question of what to do with the reactors themselves (and, for that matter, the reprocessing plant) after their twenty- to forty-year service lives are over. The facilities are intensely radioactive and are not as easy to chop up and dissolve in acid as individual fuel elements. So far, only a few small plants have been decommissioned, and neither the costs nor adequate techniques for large ones are known with certainty.[140]

The weapons connection. Perhaps the most troublesome of all the environmental and social risks of nuclear power is the connection between nuclear-power systems and nuclear weapons—specifically, the possible diversion of fissionable and toxic material, produced in civilian power programs, for illegitimate and destructive uses.

The knowledge needed to construct fission bombs (popularly called atomic bombs), for example, is relatively widespread and accessible.[141] The principal obstacle to bomb-building until now has been the restricted availability of suitable fissile materials, which only large industrial nations have had the technical resources to obtain. The spread of fission reactors is now changing this situation, because *all* such reactors produce materials suitable for bomb-making, and some reactors even require such materials as input. The idea has been widely propagated that the form of plutonium produced in LWRs is not usable in making bombs, but that is

[135]See, for example, Hollocher, in Ford et al., *The nuclear fuel cycle.*

[136]W. W. Hambleton, The unsolved problem of nuclear wastes. Hambleton was director of the Kansas Geological Survey during the Lyons controversy.

[137]USAEC, *Management of commercial high-level and transuranium contaminated radioactive waste.* The most comprehensive and telling critique was T. Lash and J. Bryson, *Comments of the Natural Resources Defense Council, Inc., and the Sierra Club on the USAEC WASH-1539.*

[138]Summarized in National Academy of Sciences/National Research Council, *Resources and man,* p. 8.

[139]USAEC, *Contaminated Soil Removal Facility: Richland, Washington.*

[140]One of the few relevant official documents is USAEC, *Elk River dismantling: Environmental statement.* See also S. Harwood et al., The cost of turning it off.

[141]A good popular introduction to the problem is J. McPhee, *The curve of binding energy.* The book is built around a biographical sketch of T. B. Taylor, formerly an accomplished designer of fission bombs, who is as responsible as any individual for calling wide attention to the risk of clandestine bomb production.

incorrect. Use of LWR plutonium presents some additional difficulties in design and renders the explosive yield somewhat unpredictable, but devastating nuclear explosives *can* be made with it.[142]

The problem has both international and national components. Internationally, the main concern is nuclear proliferation—the spread of nuclear weapons into the hands of governments that did not previously possess such weapons. The Nonproliferation Treaty, signed in 1968 and officially reviewed in 1975, was aimed at ameliorating this threat, but it has many defects: Many nations have not signed it; the safeguards provided by the treaty and administered by the International Atomic Energy Agency (IAEA) may be able to detect governmental diversion of fissile material from peaceful uses into weapons programs, but they cannot physically prevent it; and the sanctions that can be invoked against governments that are detected violating the treaty are weak.[143] India's nuclear explosion in May 1974, which brought the official membership of the "nuclear club" to six (the others: U.S., USSR, United Kingdom, France, China), was accomplished with the aid of materials from a reactor supplied by Canada. It is widely surmised that Israel has fission bombs or the capacity to assemble some quickly—again, with raw materials from reactors. The Federal Republic of (West) Germany agreed in 1975 to sell Brazil a complete nuclear fuel-cycle "package," including the reprocessing technology needed to extract plutonium from spent fuel.[144] Brazil has not signed the Nuclear Nonproliferation Treaty.

Perhaps as threatening as international proliferation of nuclear weapons is the possibility of the theft and misuse of nuclear materials by subnational groups—terrorists, blackmailers, or organized or individual black marketeers who would sell to the highest bidder. (Fissile material is worth about $10,000 per kilogram as nuclear fuel; what it might bring on the black market for use in weapons is anyone's guess.) The bidders, of course, might include governments still lacking their own nuclear facilities or wishing to avoid the risk of being caught at diversion by IAEA safeguards. The theft of nuclear materials by subnational groups could be done by stealth or by force, and of course the possibility of an inside job is especially difficult to exclude.[145] The explosion of a "homemade" nuclear bomb of the sort within the reach of small, technically literate groups could kill tens of thousands of people—in the worst case, hundreds of thousands—and injure even more if it took place in a major city. Even a fizzle by such a bomb could be devastating.[146]

All this is not to suggest that it would be easy to steal fissile material and manufacture a fission bomb with it. In fact, it would be quite difficult and extremely dangerous for the conspirators. But it does not have to be easy; if it is possible at all—and it is—this is a risk from nuclear power that needs far more public attention. How many nuclear explosions in major cities are too many? One per decade? One per century? One ever? How can one compare this sort of risk with the impacts of fossil fuels? These questions must be answered by society as a whole, not by technologists alone.

The problem of the theft of fissile materials—especially plutonium and secondarily uranium-233—is compounded by the great radiological toxicity of those materials. Bungled attempts at theft, leading to dispersal of the materials, could have serious consequences for public health. Table 8-21 lists the MPCs for the main fissile isotopes and tells how many grams of each makes a curie. The mixtures of plutonium isotopes that come from reactors are about 5 times as dangerous, gram for gram, as pure plutonium-239. The most dangerous pathway for plutonium intake is inhalation. The amount needed to produce a 50-percent chance of lung cancer when deposited in the lung following inhalation is somewhat controversial, but it is probably in the range of from 10 to 100 micrograms of plutonium-239, or one-

[142]Authoritative references on this important point are D. B. Hall, Adaptability of fissile materials to nuclear explosives; T. B. Taylor, Diversion by non-governmental organizations, p. 181.

[143]See, for example, T. A. Halsted, The spread of nuclear weapons—is the dam about to burst? Mason Willrich, ed., *International safeguards and nuclear industry.*

[144]R. Gillette, Nuclear proliferation: India, Germany may accelerate the process.

[145]The best study of the theft problem to date is M. Willrich and T. Taylor, *Nuclear theft: Risks and safeguards.*

[146]For frightening descriptions of the possibilities, see J. McPhee, *The curve of binding energy;* Willrich and Taylor, *Nuclear theft;* C. V. Chester, Estimates of threats to the public from terrorist acts against nuclear facilities.

TABLE 8-21
Properties of Fissionable Materials

Isotope	*Maximum permissible concentration in air* (Ci/m^3)	*Maximum permissible concentration in water* (Ci/m^3)	*g/Ci*	*Critical mass (kg)**
Plutonium-239	6×10^{-14}	5×10^{-6}	16	4–8
Uranium-235	4×10^{-12}	3×10^{-5}	470,000	11–25
Uranium-233	4×10^{-12}	3×10^{-5}	105	5–9

*For a spherical mass of material in metallic form. Different neutron-reflector materials give the ranges of values shown. Critical masses for oxides (instead of metals) are about 50 percent greater.
Source: M. Willrich and T. Taylor, *Nuclear theft: Risks and safeguards.*

fifth as much reactor-grade plutonium.[147] This enormous toxicity suggests the possibility of large-scale radiological terrorism using plutonium—an enterprise that may be considerably easier than manufacturing a clandestine bomb.[148]

The full magnitude of the problem becomes apparent when one compares the quantities of fissile material involved in nuclear fuel cycles with the amounts needed for nuclear malevolence. The critical masses of fissile material needed to make nuclear bombs are listed in the right-hand column of Table 8-21; they range from 4 to 25 kilograms. Even smaller amounts might be used effectively for radiological terrorism. As indicated in Table 8-15, a single large power reactor produces an annual output of fissile material in the range of hundreds of kilograms. (Some of the material produces fissions in the reactor before the fuel is removed for reprocessing and so is not counted as output.) In a reactor economy of 1000 large plants, the flow of fissile material would amount to hundreds of thousands of kilograms per year. Historically, the nuclear industry has been unable to keep track of its fissile materials with an accuracy of better than about 99 percent per year.[149] The missing 1 percent or so, known as material unaccounted for (MUF) might only be mixed up with various radioactive wastes; the point is, there is no way to be sure.

The vulnerability of fissile material to theft varies greatly from point to point in the fuel cycle. Spent reactor fuel is not very vulnerable because there the fissile isotopes are mixed up with fission products whose penetrating radiation makes the mixture impossible to handle without the most elaborate equipment. Fresh reactor fuel is not very radioactive, but for most reactors the fissile material is mixed up with fertile or inert material and is too bulky for convenient theft. The greatest points of vulnerability are probably at the reprocessing plant after the fissile material has been separated from the fission products, at the fuel-fabrication plant before the fuel elements are assembled, and in any transportation and storage links between those two steps. A study by the government General Accounting Office in 1973 showed that theft of multibomb quantities of fissile material from U.S. storage facilities would not have been difficult.[150] Safeguards have been tightened up since then, but by what means is classified and by how much is impossible to assess.

One proposal for reducing the risk of nuclear theft is to consolidate the facilities of the commercial nuclear fuel cycle into fewer sites. This could consist of merely putting reprocessing and fabrication plants together, or of adding ten or more large reactors to a reprocessing-fabrication complex in a well-guarded "nuclear park" or "nuclear energy center."[151] If adopted, the latter strategy would require substantial reorganization in the utility industry to organize, finance, and otherwise cope with

[147]Notable in the large literature of this subject, which incorporates but is not limited to the hot-particle controversy, are: National Academy of Sciences, *The effects on populations of low levels of ionizing radiation;* USAEC, *Generic environmental impact statement: Mixed-oxide fuel;* A. Tamplin and T. Cochran, *Radiation standards for hot particles;* W. J. Bair, and R. C. Thompson, Plutonium: Biomedical research; International Atomic Agency, *Inhalation risks from radioactive contaminants.* See also Chapter 10.

[148]L. DeNike, Radioactive malevolence.

[149]Deborah Shapley, Plutonium: Reactor proliferation threatens a black market.

[150]R. Gillette, Nuclear safeguards: Holes in the fence; see also USAEC, A special safeguards study (the Rosenbaum report).

[151]USAEC, *Evaluation of nuclear energy centers,* Government Printing Office, Washington, D.C., 1973, WASH-1288; Nuclear Regulatory Commission, *Nuclear energy center site survey.*

the generation of 10,000 Mwe or more at a single site. Concentrating the environmental impacts of so much activity at one site might also pose problems.

The idea that the way to guard against nuclear theft is to use more guards, more thorough investigation of industry employees, more surveillance, and so on, has been challenged as a major threat to civil liberties.[152] And the nuclear industry has vigorously opposed many proposed safeguard methods as causing unwarranted expense and disruption of their activities.

Nuclear Fusion

The difficulty in harnessing fusion as a practical energy source is associated with three conditions essential to the process: (1) the fusion fuel must be heated to a temperature of tens of millions to billions of degrees; (2) the fuel must be dense enough to yield a significant reaction rate; (3) the fuel must be confined under those conditions for a time long enough that the energy output from fusion reactions exceeds the energy input for heating and confinement. A quarter-century of research on fusion has developed many ingenious approaches to the problem, but none has yet attained the combination of conditions needed for a fusion reactor to produce more energy than it consumes. If this break-even set of conditions is achieved in the late 1970s or early 1980s, as many scientists now think likely, the first commercial fusion reactors might be ready for service around the year 2000.

At the temperatures where fusion can take place, all substances are in the fourth state of matter, or plasma. That is, if solid iron (for example) is heated to 1535° C, it becomes a liquid; if it is heated further, to 3000° C, the liquid boils and becomes vapor—literally, a gas consisting of iron atoms. If the gas is heated still further, to 10,000° C and more, the increasingly energetic collisions between the iron atoms begin to knock electrons loose. When there are enough free electrons flying around in the gas of iron atoms that the gas begins to display electrical properties (for example, becoming a good conductor of electricity), the mixture is called a plasma. Atoms that have lost one or more of their electrons are called ions, and a plasma that is hot enough will consist entirely of electrons and ions; no neutral atoms will remain. Although relatively rare on Earth's surface, plasma is by far the most common state of matter in the universe—the sun and all other stars are made of it.

The reason the fusion reactions that fuel the stars run only at the very high temperatures where plasma prevails is simple; two light nuclei can fuse into a heavier one only if they are brought extremely close together. At ordinary temperatures, nuclei are held far apart by the shell of electrons that surrounds each of them. With the electrons gone, as in a "low-temperature" plasma of a few tens of thousands of degrees Celsius, two nuclei still cannot be made to come together because, being both positively charged, they repel each other with enormous force. Temperatures of tens of millions of degrees and more are needed to give the nuclei the tremendous speed required for them to crash together despite their strong electrical repulsion. Fission reactions, by contrast, are initiated by neutrons; a neutron penetrates an intact electron shell and crashes into the nucleus inside without encountering any electrical force at all, so fission can work at room temperature.

In the sun and other stars, the fusion plasma is held together by the gravitational force of its own tremendous mass. This will not work on Earth's surface. Nor can one hold the fusion plasma with any conventional container. Either the plasma would melt the container, or the container would cool the plasma to well below the kindling temperature of fusion. (Usually it is the latter—the container cools the plasma; the plasma, although hot, is too dilute to melt through much metal.)

There are two approaches capable of releasing fusion energy on Earth's surface. One is to heat the fuel so rapidly to fusion temperatures that fusion reactions take place before the hot gas has time to blow itself apart. This is called *inertial confinement,* because inertia holds the atoms together for the fraction of a second needed to get a substantial amount of fusion energy. An extreme case of inertial confinement is what happens in a hydrogen

[152]J. G. Speth, A. R. Tamplin, T. B. Cochran, Plutonium Recycle: The fateful step; R. W. Ayres, Policing plutonium: The civil liberties fallout. For a discussion in the British context, see Sir Brian Flowers, Chairman, Royal Commission on Environmental Pollution, *Nuclear power and the environment.*

bomb. It may also be possible to make a fusion reactor this way, using lasers or intense beams of electrons or heavy ions as the initial energy source. (In a hydrogen bomb, a fission bomb serves as the trigger that provides the initial heating.)

The second approach is to take advantage of the electrical properties of the plasma to heat it and confine it, using electromagnetic fields. This approach is called *magnetic confinement.* This has had the longer history of the two approaches in the controlled-fusion field (bombs, although intentional, are uncontrolled in this terminology), and we therefore treat it first.

Magnetic confinement. The heart of the matter is that electrically charged particles—namely the electrons and positively charged ions—cannot move very far perpendicular to the direction of a strong magnetic field. The stronger the magnetic field, the more tightly the particles are constrained. One can think of magnetic fields, in fact, as exerting a pressure on plasma; and by arranging magnets cleverly it is possible to produce a set of magnetic fields that push in on a plasma from virtually every direction. Such an arrangement is often called a "magnetic bottle." Of course, Newton's laws should remind us that if the magnetic field is pushing on the plasma, the plasma must be pushing back. It does, and the magnetic field transmits its push to the magnet's structure. Thus the system "knows" it is containing something, but the hot plasma itself is held away from the magnets and all material structure.

Unfortunately, it is not quite so easy in practice. Roughly twenty-five years of effort in laboratories around the world have revealed a dismaying tendency for the plasma to leak from the magnetic bottles faster than anticipated. (The enterprise has been compared to trying to hold watery Jello in a cage of rubber bands.) There are two main ways in which the plasma escapes. One is when collisions among ions knock them across the magnetic field and eventually into the walls or otherwise out of the machine. (Remember, particles that hit the wall lose most of their energy and with it the capacity to react.) The motion by interparticle collisions is called *classical diffusion,* and it is slow enough that a fusion reactor can work in spite of it. The second escape mechanism is called *instabilities.* These may involve large-scale, coherent motion of the plasma (macroinstabilities), in which the magnetic field is systematically deformed by the plasma itself in ways that bring the plasma into contact with the walls. Alternatively, instabilities can take the form of interactions of certain groups of ions and electrons (that is, those in a particular speed range) with each other and with the magnetic field in such a way that the rate of diffusion of plasma across the magnetic field is greatly enhanced. These are called microinstabilities. Most of the effort in controlled-fusion research has been devoted to cataloging, analyzing, and trying to circumvent those instabilities.

Three types of magnetic bottle have received most of the attention in recent fusion research and are widely believed to represent the best hopes for success among the many approaches to magnetic confinement that have been invented. The three are the theta pinch, the mirror machine, and the tokamak. They are illustrated schematically in Figure 8-21.

In the theta pinch, the plasma takes the shape of a long rod. It is held away from its tubular container by a magnetic field whose direction is parallel to the axis of the rod. The plasma is compressed to high density and temperature by suddenly increasing the strength of that magnetic field. A fusion reactor using the theta pinch would operate in pulses, since the very strong field required cannot be maintained for long. To reduce or eliminate the escape of plasma out the ends of the rod, the theta pinch must either be made very long (a kilometer or more for a reactor) or bent into a doughnut shape (torus) that closes upon itself.

Mirror machines operate with the plasma at somewhat lower densities and would be capable, in theory, of running more or less steadily, rather than in pulses. The name *mirror* comes from the tendency of the moving charged particles to reverse direction (hence, "reflect") if they move into a region where the strength of the magnetic field increases very sharply. The earliest mirror machines contained basically cylindrical plasmas and looked like a section of a theta pinch but with very strong fields at the ends forming the "mirrors." Those plasmas were unstable, and ways were subsequently found to produce more complicated magnetic-field shapes with the basic desirable properties of mirrors but without the strongest instabilities. The high temperatures achieved

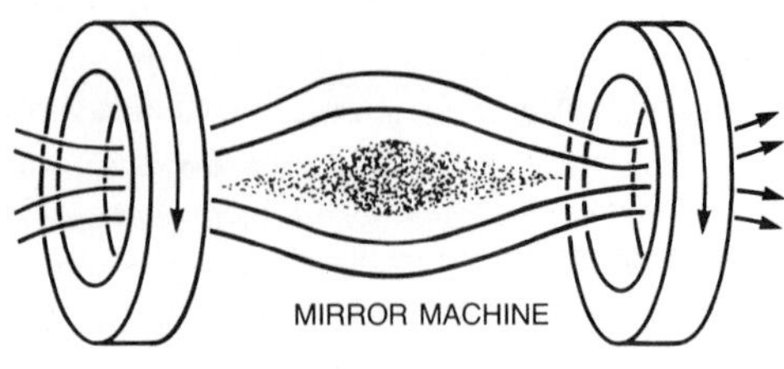

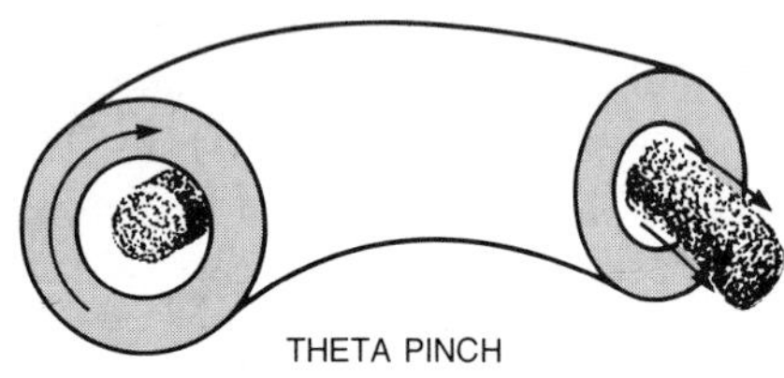

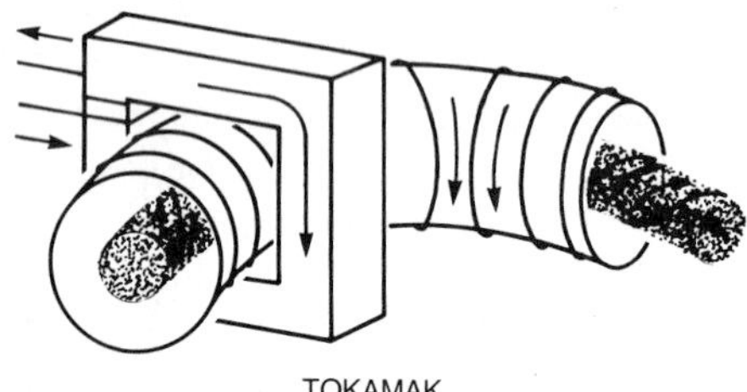

FIGURE 8-21

Schematic diagrams of three concepts for fusion reactors. From bottom to top are the tokamak, the theta pinch, and the mirror machine. The tokamak and theta pinch diagrams show one-quarter of the full toroidal device. (After Gough and Eastlund, 1971.)

in modern mirror machines are produced by injecting high-energy beams of neutral fuel atoms across the magnetic field and into the plasma.The atoms in the beam ionize as soon as they hit the plasma, they become part of it, and they deposit their energy there.

Tokamaks are toroidal (doughnut-shaped) devices of medium plasma density, in which a strong current is made to flow along the tube of plasma itself. This current heats the plasma and produces a magnetic field that helps to suppress instabilities. Tokamaks surged to a position of dominance in world fusion research after important successes were achieved in the USSR with this approach in 1969. (Magnetic-confinement fusion research was declassified by international agreement in 1958, and the field has been a model of international scientific information-sharing ever since.) Large tokamaks that are expected to approach fusion break-even conditions are scheduled for operation in the late 1970s in several parts of the world. Sad experience in the fusion field, however, makes most experts wisely reluctant to count those chickens before they hatch.

The elusive break-even point, which would conclusively demonstrate the scientific feasibility of fusion—although by no means the engineering practicality—is the achievement of plasma density and average time of confinement such that the product of those quantities (with density measured in ions per cubic centimeter and time in seconds) equals 10^{14}. This must be done while the plasma temperature is 50 million° C or more. This set of requirements is known as the Lawson condition, after the British physicist who showed in 1957 that its achievement would permit a fusion machine running on the deuterium-tritium (D-T) reaction to produce more electricity than it consumed. The performance of past and future fusion machines is compared to the Lawson condition in Table 8-22.[153] Note that the break-even conditions for the D-D reaction are considerably more difficult to attain.

TABLE 8-22
How Close Is Magnetic Confinement to Energy Break-Even?

Device, country	n*(sec)* × τ*(ions/cm³)*	*Temperature (million° C)*
Mirror (U.S., 1975)	10^{11}	100
Theta-pinch (U.S., 1972)	3×10^{11}	20
Tokamak (USSR, U.S., 1972)	10^{12}	5
Advanced tokamak (USSR, U.S., 1977?)	10^{13}–10^{14}	10–100
Lawson condition (D-T plasma)	10^{14}	50
Lawson condition (D-D plasma)	10^{16}	500

Source: R. Hirsch and W. Rice, Nuclear fusion power and the environment.

[153]Particularly good expanded coverage of the material treated here is offered by W. Gough and B. Eastland, The prospects of fusion power; R. F. Post and F. L. Ribe, Fusion reactors as future energy sources; R. Hirsch and W. Rice, Nuclear fusion power and the environment. For readers with strong technical backgrounds, the basic physical principles are well covered in the classic D. J. Rose and M. Clark, *Plasmas and controlled fusion.*

Laser fusion. Although it was conceived in 1961, the idea of using lasers to produce fusion miniexplosions in pellets of fusion fuel had to await the development of the very powerful lasers of the late 1960s and early 1970s before experimentation could begin in earnest. In the late 1970s, the performance of lasers (and of high-energy beams of electrons or ions, which could serve the same function) remain the principal limitation holding back this approach to controlled fusion.

In laser fusion, the Lawson condition still applies, but the aim is to meet the condition the same way a fusion bomb does—not by confining a low density for a long time, but by creating enormously high densities in a plasma held together for the tiniest fraction of a second by its own inertia. In magnetic confinement, the highest densities that can be considered are around 10^{16} ions per cubic centimeter (around 1000 times less dense than the air we breathe), requiring confinement times of about a hundredth of a second for energy break-even. (The limit on density comes from the maximum pressure the magnet structure can withstand; at 100 million° C, 10^{16} particles/cm^3 exert a pressure of about 130 atmospheres—a ton per square inch.) By contrast, the break-even conditions for laser fusion are a density of 10^{26} particles per cubic centimeter and a confinement time of 10^{-12} (a millionth of a millionth) second. This density is from 1000 to 10,000 times that of normal liquids and solids, and the process by which it is achieved is *implosion.*[154]

To produce implosion, tiny fuel pellets must be irradiated symmetrically from all sides by precisely synchronized, precisely focused laser beams. These beams are pulsed; that is, they deliver their energy in bursts, each of very short duration. Probably, the required spherical symmetry will be obtained by splitting a single powerful laser beam with mirrors and then focusing the components of the beam on the fusion combustion chamber. To build a successful laser-fusion reactor based on the D-T reaction would require a laser that could deliver a pulse of 1 nanosecond duration containing 0.3 megajoule of energy (1 nanosecond = 10^{-9} second). The laser must also have an efficiency of 10 percent in converting electric energy to laser energy. The best lasers available in 1974 had energies around 0.001 megajoules per pulse and efficiencies between 0.1 and 2 percent. Nevertheless, the science and technology of lasers is changing rapidly, and it is not inconceivable that the improvements needed to make laser fusion break even energetically will be made. A laser capable of delivering 0.01 to 0.05 joules in a pulse of less than a nanosecond is scheduled for operation in 1977.[155]

Assuming that a suitable laser were available, a laser-fusion reactor of 100-Mwe generating capacity would operate by detonating about 100 pellets of D-T fuel per second. Each of those implosions would produce about 30 megajoules—100 times as much energy as the laser deposits in the pellet to detonate it. (Thirty megajoules is about the amount of energy released in the explosion of 7 kilograms of TNT.) The high repetition rate needed for a large plant might be accomplished by using several split-beam lasers, each with its own combustion chamber. The combustion chambers would have to be lined with materials capable of withstanding the rapid-fire explosions inside and of transferring the energy outward in a form suitable for conversion to electricity. A diagram of a laser-fusion power plant is shown in Figure 8-22.

Engineering aspects. Whether controlled fusion is accomplished with magnetic confinement or with lasers, the transition from a demonstration of scientific feasibility to a practical power plant will require the solution of some difficult engineering problems. This could easily require ten or fifteen years of intensive (and expensive) work—and with bad luck, even more.

In either scheme, for example, the D-T fusion reactions produce about 80 percent of their energy in the form of extremely fast neutrons. These are several times as energetic as the neutrons that create the very difficult materials problems in fission breeder reactors. As many of the neutrons as possible must be made to deposit their energy as heat in a solid or liquid "blanket," from which

[154]An excellent and detailed description of the entire laser-fusion problem by some of the pioneers of the field is J. Emmett, J. Nuckolls, and L. Wood, Fusion power by laser implosion. A shorter and less technical description appears in Chapter 14 of Hammond, Metz, and Maugh, *Energy and the future.*

[155]Emmett, Nuckolls, and Wood, Fusion power, p. 31.

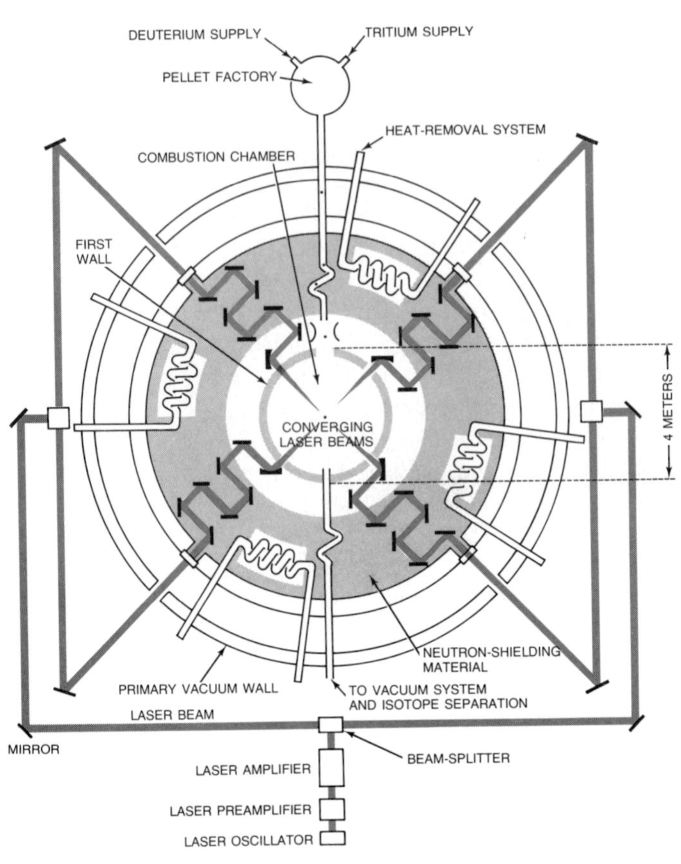

FIGURE 8-22

Schematic diagram of a laser fusion power plant. (From Emmett et al., 1974.)

the heat can be extracted for generating electricity. It is desirable that the neutrons end up being absorbed by lithium, which thereby breeds tritium to replace that which reacts. Neutrons that get absorbed in structural materials instead of in lithium do great damage and convert the elements that absorb them into radioactive isotopes, many with long half-lives. Under fusion conditions, large quantities of X-rays and stray ions of various kinds are also produced, and they, too, bombard the inner structure of the reactor.

Even if a laser with the required performance for laser fusion can be built, making laser components that will *last* under the stresses of handling huge pulses of energy many times a second for years on end will be extremely difficult, perhaps impossible. The lenses and mirrors that handle the laser beam close to the combustion chamber will be especially hard to protect from neutrons and X-rays.

In magnetic-confinement fusion, the magnets are like the lasers in laser fusion: they are the cornerstone of the system, very expensive, and vulnerable to damage by overheating from their own circulating energy or from energy deposited by neutrons and X-rays. The problem is especially difficult because most magnetic-confinement schemes appear feasible only with superconducting magnets—special materials whose resistance to electric current drops to zero when they are cooled to the temperature of liquid helium, a few degrees above absolute zero. These magnets must be very close to the fusion plasma they are containing; if they were far away, the confining field would be too weak. Thus, the fusion engineer faces the remarkable task of maintaining a temperature of about 4 degrees above absolute zero, at most a meter or so away from a fusion plasma of 100 million degrees Celsius, releasing energy at a rate of thousands of megawatts. When all the machinery needed to create, confine, heat, shield, and replenish the fusion plasma is taken into account, together with the devices needed to convert its energy into electricity, a fusion-reactor system will be a very complicated enterprise.

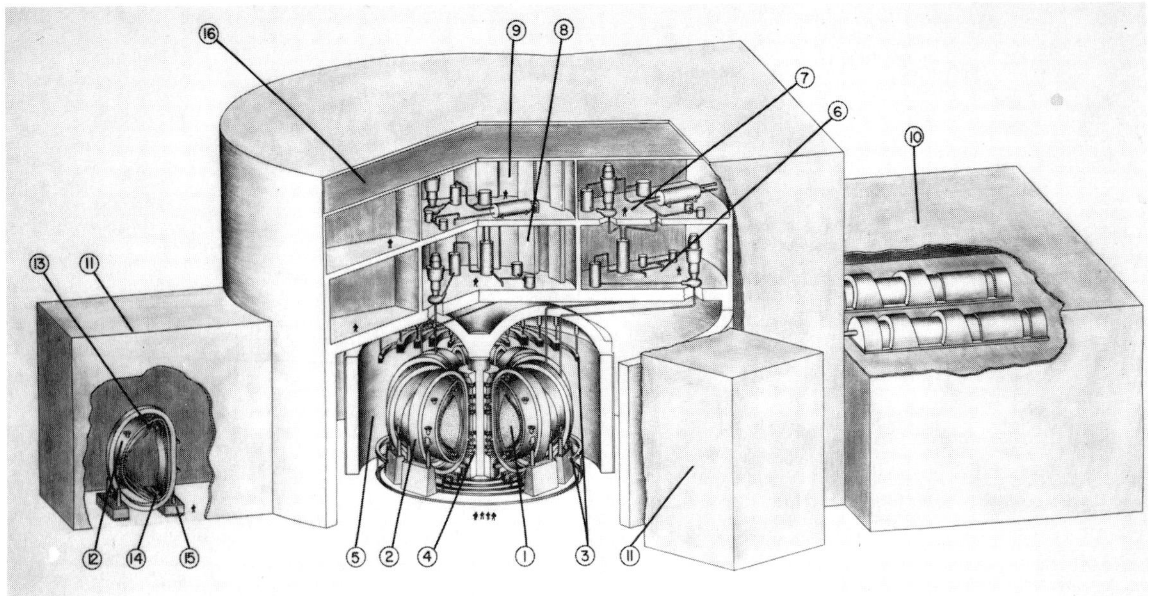

FIGURE 8-23

Conceptual design of a tokamak fusion reactor. The great complexity likely to characterize fusion reactors means they will not be cheap. 1, Plasma; 2, Toroidal field coil (12); 3, Retractable divertor coil (8); 4, Transformer coil (10); 5, Evacuated primary containment building; 6, Li primary system (one for each of 12 modules); 7, Na secondary system (one for each of 12 modules); 8, Divertor Li primary system; 9, Divertor Na secondary system; 10, Turbine-generator building; 11, Hot cell repair area; 12; Magnet shield; 13, Blanket; 14, Divertor collection area; 15, Motorized module support vehicle; 16, Auxiliary equipment area. (From Badger, et al., 1975.)

This is illustrated for magnetic confinement by the conceptual tokamak-reactor power plant presented in Figure 8-23.

Environmental aspects. Fusion offers the potential for significant environmental and safety advantages, compared to fission, in three main respects. First, the fuels and reaction products of fusion are nonradioactive, except for tritium. Being a fuel, it can be burned up and need not become a waste-management problem. Second, there is no chance of a runaway reaction that could release more energy than intended. The conditions under which fusion flourishes are so extreme and so difficult to attain that any malfunction merely causes a departure from those conditions and thereby quenches the reaction. (A good deal of the essence of this situation has been summed up in the only partly humorous statement, "Fusion must be safe, because it doesn't work.") Third, fusion does not automatically produce materials needed to make nuclear explosives; hence, the problem of nuclear theft need not arise with fusion.

None of the foregoing potential advantages is absolute, and it would be possible to design fusion reactors with so little concern for their environmental characteristics that the advantages over fission would be minimal. This can be avoided only if optimizing the environmental characteristics of fusion reactors is given high priority and intensive effort throughout the process of reactor development and design.

The inventory of tritium in a 1000-Mwe D-T fusion reactor, for example, varies between 10 megacuries and 500 megacuries in different conceptual designs.[156] (The term *conceptual design* indicates that these are not designs for plants actually to be built. Designs for real plants will have to await more progress in basic fusion physics.) The lower figure represents a relative hazard (inventory divided by MPC) about 20,000 times less than the radioactive iodine in a fission reactor of the same size, and

[156]Most data in this section are from John P. Holdren, T. K. Fowler, and R. F. Post, Fusion power and the environment; G. Kulcinski, Fusion power: An assessment of its potential impact in the USA; Hirsch and Rice, Nuclear fusion power.

the second figure a relative hazard 400 times less than the radioactive iodine. [This calculation assumes all the tritium (T) is incorporated into water, forming HTO instead of H_2O by replacing normal hydrogen; this HTO is much more dangerous than tritium gas and has a lower MPC. Radioactive iodine is the most dangerous substance easily releasable from a fission reactor in gaseous form.] If ingenious design can actually keep the tritium inventory near 10 megacuries or less—about three days' fuel consumption in a 1000-Mwe fusion system—then even successful sabotage probably could not cause a release that would lead to fatal acute radiation exposure outside the reactor site. Great care will have to be taken in any case to minimize routine emissions of tritium, which at high temperatures is capable of diffusing rather readily through steel.

The second radiological hazard of fusion is the material in the reactor structure that becomes radioactive because of bombardment by neutrons. The size of this inventory of activation products depends on what material is used for the inner structure of the reactor. Niobium, which is a good structural material for fusion reactors in other respects, has activation products whose total relative hazard at reactor shutdown would be only 10 to 100 times less than that of the fission products in a fission reactor of the same size. If vanadium can be used instead of niobium, the initial relative hazard would be about 1000 times less than that of fission products. After a year, the margin becomes much larger—a factor of 1 million or more—because the half-lives of most activation products of vanadium are short.

The environmental promise of fusion relative to fission is even greater if one considers the possibility of clever designs that minimize the opportunities for neutrons to come into contact with structural materials, and the possibility of harnessing fusion reactions more difficult than D-T, which produce fewer neutrons.

That fusion reactors are incapable of nuclear excursions does not make them absolutely safe against release of whatever radioactive materials are inside, because other sources of energy may be available to break reactors open. Most conceptual fusion-reactor designs embody a great deal of liquid lithium, for example, which serves both as a coolant and as the means for breeding tritium fuel. Lithium, like the sodium used to cool the fission LMFBR, is chemically reactive; a large lithium fire is probably the maximum conceivable accident for a fusion reactor. Much attention is now being given in the conceptual design of fusion reactors to the possibility of using coolants other than lithium and incorporating the lithium needed to breed tritium in molten salt or a solid.

A few people have suggested that controlled fusion might accelerate the spread of nuclear weapons (including into terrorist hands) just as fission might, because the tritium could be diverted or stolen to make fusion bombs.[157] The analogy is inept in two respects. First, as far as is known, no one has ever succeeded in making a fusion bomb without using a fission bomb for a trigger.[158] Thus, it is the availability of *fissile* materials that limits the manufacture of nuclear bombs of all kinds. Second, the further limit on fusion bombs is lack of knowledge and technical sophistication, not lack of usable fusion fuels. A group with the knowledge to make a fusion bomb would not need tritium from a fusion reactor to do it.[159] One must ask, of course, whether the dissemination of fusion-power technology will spread the knowledge needed to make fusion bombs. The knowledge relevant to magnetic confinement is not relevant to the design of bombs, so the answer there is no. Some parts of laser-fusion research were still classified at this writing, apparently because that knowledge is related to the problem of making a fusion bomb.[159a] This connection to nuclear weaponry seems to us to be a serious drawback of laser fusion.

Fusion-Fission Hybrids

As early as the beginning of controlled-fusion research in the 1950s, the idea occurred to some people to combine fusion and fission technology in a hybrid power system. The idea kindled renewed interest in the 1970s, both in the Soviet Union and the United States. The essence of

[157]W. Haefele and C. Starr, A perspective on fission and fusion breeders; for detailed counterarguments, see the responses by F. von Hippel and by J. Holdren (Comments on fission and fusion breeders) in the same journal, April 1975.

[158]Willrich and Taylor, *Nuclear theft.*

[159]See, for example, the discussion of fusion bombs in Inglis, *Nuclear Energy,* pp. 183–187.

[159a]See, for example, W. Metz, Energy research: Accelerator builders eager to aid fusion work; ERDA, *Final report of the special laser fusion advisory panel.*

the concept is to wrap a subcritical fission blanket around a sub-break-even fusion reactor core. (Subcritical means that the fission part has a composition and configuration such that it cannot sustain a chain reaction by itself.) The fusion neutrons then cause fissions in the blanket, from which about 10 times as much energy per fusion neutron is produced as in a pure fusion reactor. This relieves the Lawson condition for energy break-even—the plasma containment in the fusion core can be almost 10 times less effective in a hybrid than in a pure fusion reactor and still permit the machine to produce a net energy output.

Suitably designed fusion-fission hybrids could also be used mainly to make fission fuel by arranging for the fusion neutrons to cause fertile-to-fissile conversions in the blanket. The fuel thus produced could be used in pure fission reactors elsewhere. This approach has been proposed in case pure fission breeder reactors don't work very well. Furthermore, hybrids could be used to fission the long-half-life heavy elements (actinides) produced in pure fission reactors, thus reducing their half-lives to those of fission products. The energetic fusion-reactor neutrons would be much more effective at fissioning actinides than are fission-reactor neutrons.[160]

Environmentally, fusion-fission hybrids have some of the worst characteristics of both parents. They would have somewhat fewer neutron-activation products than a pure fusion system, but almost as large a quantity of fission products as a pure fission system. There would be less tritium than in a pure fusion reactor, but still a lot, and there would be essentially the same risk of nuclear theft as in a pure fission system. The principal advantage would seem to be a much smaller chance of an accident than in a pure fission breeder reactor, *if* it is shown that breeder reactors are as dangerous as some of their critics think. It seems unlikely that hybrids will be as attractive as pure fusion systems, once those work; and, because hybrids combine the considerable complexity of both fusion and fission technology, they could easily be extremely expensive.[161]

[160]A good, although technical, review of hybrid possibilities is L. M. Lidsky, Fission-fusion systems: Hybrid, symbiotic, and Augean; see also U.S. Energy Research and Development Administration, *DCTR fusion-fission energy systems meeting.*

[161]For a more detailed examination of the environmental and cost questions, see J. P. Holdren, The relevance of environmental concerns in contemplating development of fission-fusion hybrids, in ERDA, *DCTR.*

Geothermal Technology

The character and environmental impact of geothermal energy technology depend strongly on the kind of deposit being tapped. The five main kinds are: (1) vapor-dominated (dry) steam, in which little or no liquid water comes to the surface with the steam; (2) hot water and wet steam, in which the resource is actually hot water under high pressure, some of which "flashes" to steam as the water is brought to the surface; (3) hot, dry rock, in which the water that serves a heat-transfer medium must be pumped in from the surface; (4) "geopressure" resources, consisting of hot brines present in combination with methane gas under pressure; (5) magma (see Chapter 2), for which no harvesting technology has yet been worked out. Harvesting technologies corresponding to the first three categories are illustrated schematically in Figure 8-24.

The technology of dry-steam geothermal fields is the simplest. Wells are dug into steam reservoirs, typically at depths of 200 to 3000 meters.[162] The dry-steam electricity generating plant at The Geysers, California, requires about fourteen such wells, each supplying 150,000 pounds of steam per hour, for each of its 110-Mwe units. The steam comes up the well under its own pressure and is directed through valves and pipes to a low-pressure turbine. The steam enters the turbine at about 175° C and 7 atmospheres pressure. Those values, much lower than those for fossil-fueled or nuclear generating plants, lead to a turbine efficiency of about 22 percent. The overall plant efficiency is about 15 percent. The steam passes from the turbine to a condenser, and then about three-fourths of the water produced there from the steam (condensate) is evaporated into the atmosphere in a wet cooling tower. The remainder of the water is reinjected into the steam-bearing underground formation.

Hot-water technology differs from that for dry steam in requiring separation of the hot water from the associated steam before the steam enters the turbine. The hot brine, whose salinity may approach 100 times that of seawater, meets one of three fates: it may be discharged at the surface to mix with fresh water runoff (as happens in

[162]Most data in this section are from Science and Public Policy Program, University of Oklahoma, *Energy alternatives: A comparative analysis.* A shorter review is Hammond, Metz, and Maugh, chapter 9.

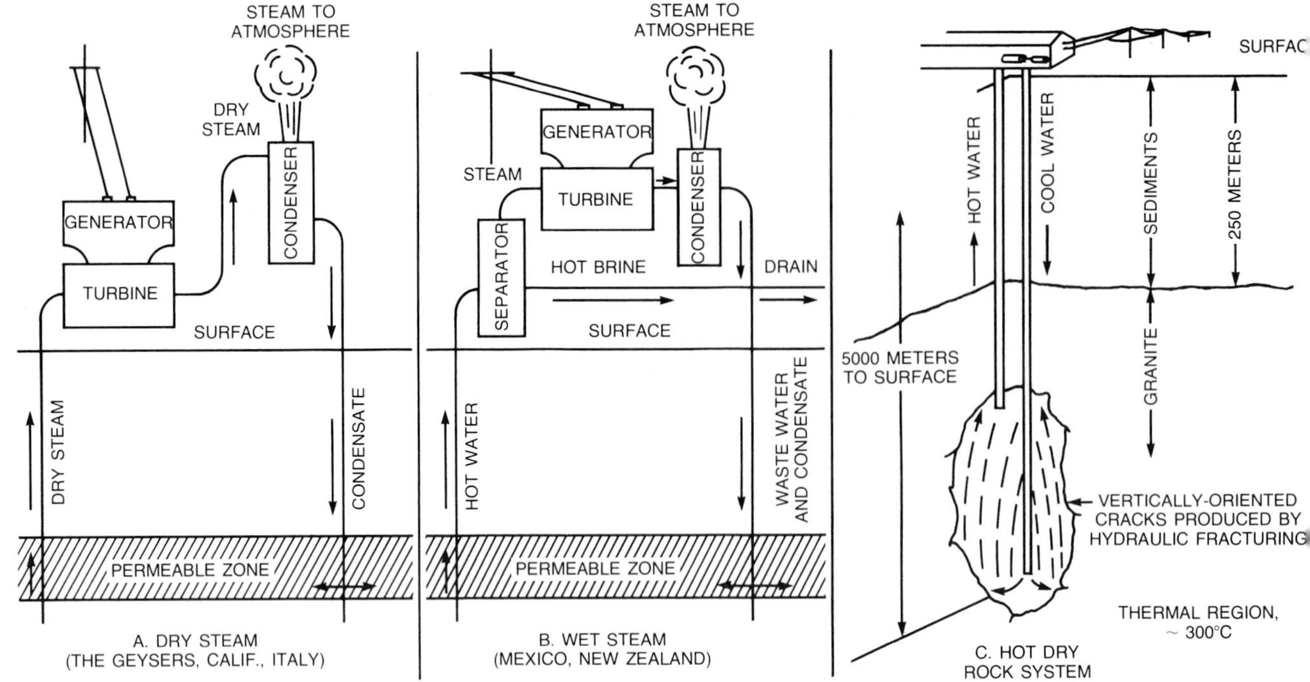

FIGURE 8-24

Three ways to harness geothermal energy. (After Science and Public Policy Program, 1975.)

the hot-water fields in New Zealand);[163] it may be reinjected into the ground (Japan); or it may be treated to remove the minerals for possible sale, rendering the water usable for agricultural or other use (as planned for some future installations in southern California and elsewhere). As with dry-steam systems, much of the condensate is evaporated in cooling towers. Advanced hot-water power plants will probably eventually use a closed cycle, in which the hot water transfers its energy to an organic fluid such as isobutane and then is reinjected into the ground. The organic fluid is vaporized in the heat exchanger, drives a turbine, is recondensed, and then returns to the heat exchanger. (Turbines that use organic fluids are more efficient at temperatures below 200° C than steam turbines, but there is an energy loss in the water-to-organic-fluid heat exchanger.) The overall steam-to-electricity efficiency of hot-water plants is only around 11 percent.

Technology for harnessing the geothermal energy in hot, dry rock had not been perfected as of the mid-1970s, but encouraging experiments were underway.[164] The basic idea is to drill to depths between 2000 and 10,000 meters, where rock temperatures between 300° and 700° C are encountered (depending in detail on the proximity of upward intrusions of magma from deeper in Earth, as described in Chapter 2). Water is pumped down the well under great pressure to fracture the hot rock at the bottom, producing a large cracked volume in which the rock can give up its heat to water that is subsequently circulated. A second well is drilled into each fractured area to complete the path for this circulation; the circulating water flashes to steam when it reaches the lower pressures near the surface, and the steam drives a turbine. As in the other schemes, there must be a condenser and a means of discharging the waste heat at the surface.

At a few locations around the world, geothermal steam is available in close proximity to human settlements and is used directly for heating buildings and greenhouses, rather than for producing electricity. Such applications will probably remain of strictly local importance.

[163] R. Axtmann, Environmental impact of a geothermal power plant.

[164] A. L. Hammond, Dry geothermal wells.

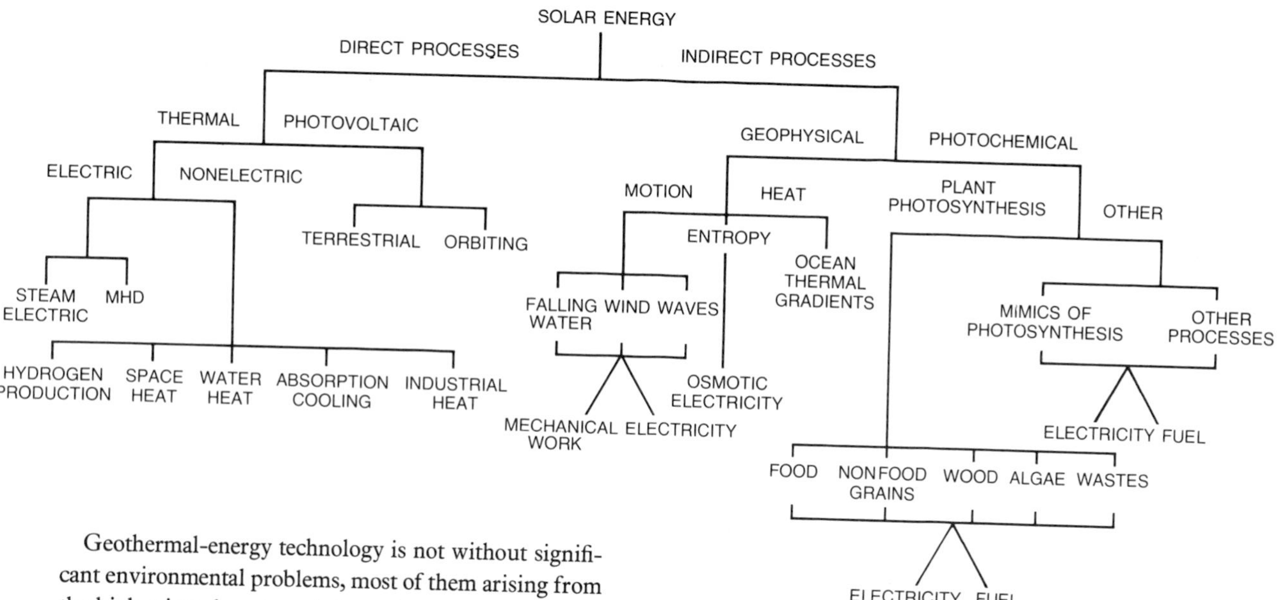

FIGURE 8-25

Options for harnessing solar energy. There are many possibilities. Excluded here are fossil fuels, which are solar energy stored in chemical form over millions of years. MHD = magnetohydrodynamics.

Geothermal-energy technology is not without significant environmental problems, most of them arising from the high mineral content of the underground deposits of steam and hot water. The contaminants include sulfur, arsenic, mercury, fluorides, ammonia, radon gas, and a variety of salts that corrode equipment and that can pollute surface water if the brines are not reinjected into the underground deposits. Sulfur emissions (in the form of odorous hydrogen sulfide) from The Geysers dry-steam plant are roughly equal to the sulfur emissions from a fossil-fueled plant of the same size burning low-sulfur oil.[165] Sulfur emissions from open-cycle hot-water plants may even exceed those from uncontrolled burning of high-sulfur coal. Reduction of those emissions is one strong motivation for using the more expensive closed cycle with organic working fluid in these plants.

Emissions of radon gas probably vary considerably from one geothermal reservoir to the next. No definitive data are available; it is possible that the most serious associated problem will be the exposure of workers to accumulations of radon gas in geothermal-plant buildings.[166]

Because of the low thermal efficiency, the waste heat discharged to the environment at geothermal installations is several times that at fossil-fueled or nuclear power plants of like generating capacity. Additional environmental liabilities of geothermal technology (mostly of only local influence) are ground subsidence, noise, and the possibility that fluid injection may trigger earthquakes.

Notwithstanding the technical and environmental problems that must be overcome or ameliorated, geothermal energy possibly has the potential to be producing 30,000 Mwe of electrical power in the United States by 1985; 100,000 Mwe by 1990; and 200,000 Mwe (about half the U.S. 1970 installed capacity) by the year 2000, according to a major study conducted by the National Science Foundation for the Federal Energy Administration.[167]

Direct Uses of Solar Energy

The abundance and long duration of the solar resource are not in doubt. The important questions are for what uses and with what technologies solar energy can be harnessed economically. There are a great many options, most of which are identified in Figure 8-25. They are

[165]M. Goldsmith, Geothermal resources in California.

[166]Science and Public Policy Program, *Energy alternatives;* T. Gesell, J. Adams, L. Church, Letters: Geothermal power plants—environmental impact.

[167]FEA, *Geothermal energy task force report.* See also, P. Kruger and C. Otte, eds., *Geothermal energy: Resources, production, stimulation.*

TABLE 8-23
Distribution of Solar Energy in the United States (MJ/m²-day)

	December	*March*	*June*	*September*	*Annual average*
Burlington, Vt.	5.1	12.3	20.0	13.6	12.6
Seattle	2.6	12.1	23.4	13.8	13.1
Omaha	6.8	14.6	24.6	14.5	15.3
Atlanta	8.1	14.6	21.0	18.1	15.8
Tucson	9.9	19.9	27.8	19.7	19.8

Note: Figures are average amounts of energy incident on a flat horizontal surface, in megajoules per square meter per day (MJ/m^2-day). Multiply by 11.6 to get w/m^2, or by 88.1 to get Btu/ft^2-day.
Source: U.S. Department of Commerce, *Climatological data: National summary.*

divided somewhat arbitrarily there into direct and indirect applications of solar energy. By direct we mean technologies wherein incident sunlight is converted directly into a desired form—heat or electricity—for essentially immediate application. By indirect we refer to processes wherein the solar energy is converted into intermediate forms—wind, falling water, chemical energy stored by photosynthesis—before being used. We consider the direct uses first.

Important in all such uses is the intensity of incoming solar energy and the variation of that intensity with time. At noon on a clear day on Earth's surface, a collector perpendicular to the rays receives around 1000 watts per square meter (w/m^2). As indicated earlier, the average on a continuous basis in the United States is about 180 w/m^2. (The latter, in units still commonly used in the United States, is 1370 Btu per square foot per day.) The distribution of incident sunlight in the United States in differing regions and times of year is given in Table 8-23.[168]

Those energy densities are lower than values typically encountered in "high-technology" energy systems—for example, the several hundred thousand watts per square meter of heat-transfer surface in a fossil-fueled boiler. They are not low, however, compared to many kinds of needs. The rate of residential energy use in the United States in 1975 averaged 2500 thermal watts per person, which corresponds to the solar input on 14 square meters of average territory in this country.

Heat and cold. Among direct uses of solar energy, the oldest and most widespread applications have been those that used sunlight as heat: drying crops, distilling water, warming water for domestic use, warming dwellings, cooking in reflector-ovens.[169]

Solar collectors for heating domestic water have been manufactured commercially and used widely for many years in Australia, Israel, India, the USSR, and Japan. Such systems were used in Florida in the 1930s, before cheap natural gas was introduced there, and in the mid-1970s they were coming back onto the market in many parts of the United States in response to soaring prices of electricity and natural gas. Water heating is probably the simplest solar technology with the potential for replacing significant amounts of fossil fuel and electricity in this country, as it requires only a flat-plate collector and some rather simple plumbing.

Flat-plate collectors are presented schematically in Figure 8-26. Water flows in tubes, either attached to or part of a sheet of black metal or plastic. Sunlight is absorbed by the black surface as heat warms the water, which is stored in an insulated tank. If a glass plate (or two) is placed over the collection plate to keep the wind from cooling it and to trap some of the heat that would otherwise be radiated away, and if the back of the plate is insulated to reduce heat losses there, water temperatures around 60° C (140° F) are readily attained. This is sufficient for domestic purposes. Such collectors were being marketed for about \$70 to \$100 per square meter

[168]More detail on the distribution of incident solar energy in the United States can be found in J. I. Yellot's Solar radiation and its uses on Earth.

[169]The classic text, indispensable for the history of these and other uses worldwide, is F. Daniels, *Direct use of the sun's energy.* See also J. R. Williams, *Solar energy: Technology and applications.*

($10 per square foot) in the United States in 1975. Seven to ten square meters are required to meet *most* of the hot-water needs of a typical dwelling in the United States. (In times of prolonged bad weather, some augmentation with gas or electricity is required.)[170]

For heating swimming pools, a substantial energy-user in the United States and some other countries, the glass plates and insulation on the flat-plate collectors can be dispensed with because lower temperatures suffice. Low-temperature collectors for pool heating were being sold for around $40 per square meter in 1975 (about half the area of the swimming pool in collectors is required).

Most dwellings get a significant part of their space-heating in winter from solar energy automatically—that is, from sunlight entering through the windows. When special attention is paid to maximizing the winter input of sunlight and minimizing summer input, through the orientation, design, and construction of a building, this form of solar heating can greatly reduce fossil-fuel and electricity use without the purchase of special solar collectors.[171] In most climates, this basic use of solar energy cannot meet all heating needs of typical dwellings; for many years, experimenters interested in further reducing the use of fossil fuels and electricity have been constructing heating systems using solar collectors of various kinds. Most of them have used flat-plate collectors of the sort described above for water heating.[172] Use of the heated water for warming interior spaces is a more demanding enterprise than water heating for other domestic uses, however, requiring significantly more collector area for a typical dwelling (between 60 and 120 square meters). The high initial cost of such a venture, with collectors costing nearly $100 per square meter, has discouraged commercialization.[173]

Many experts believe that the price of a collector suitable for space-heating will come down to around $65 per square meter ($6 per square foot) if large quantities are produced. At that price solar systems can compete with resistive electric heating (conversion of electricity to heat by running it through suitable wires) in some parts of the United States, and with direct use of natural gas and fuel oil if those become expensive enough. There will nevertheless be many institutional and economic barriers to the rapid spread of solar-heating technology; among them: the high initial costs, which seem to be an obstacle even where the economics over the life of the device are favorable; uncertainty among consumers

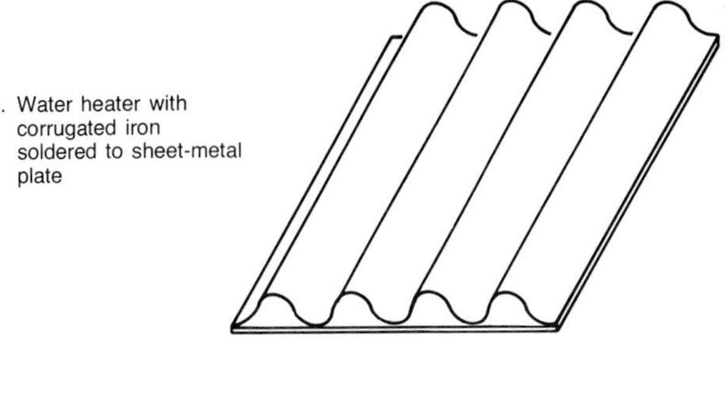

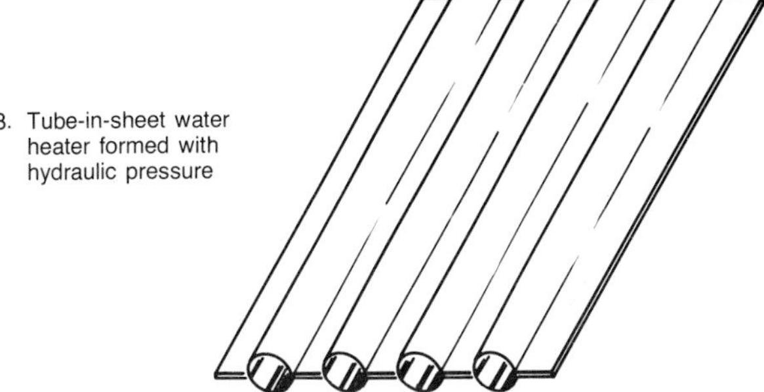

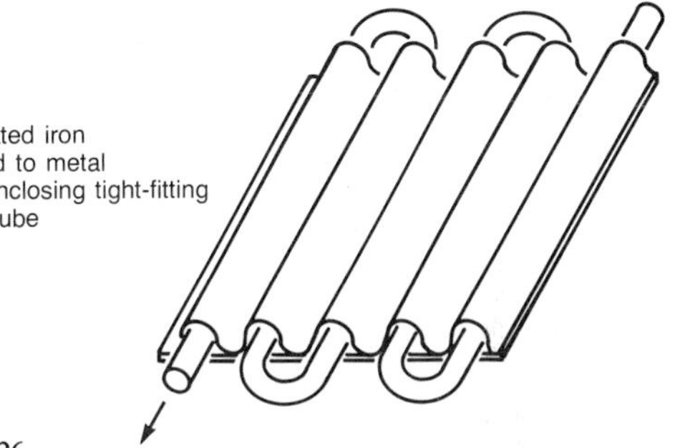

FIGURE 8-26

Flat-plate solar collectors. There are many approaches to the design of flat-plate collectors, suggested by the three represented here. Economy of construction and durability are essential goals. Sheets of plastic or glass may be added to top and layers of insulation to bottom to reduce losses. (After Daniels, *Direct use of the sun's energy.*)

[170] A well-documented reference for these and many subsequent points in this section is P. Steadman, *Energy, environment, and building.*

[171] American Physical Society, *Efficient use of energy.*

[172] Detailed descriptions of many of the pioneering "solar houses" are in Steadman, *Energy.*

[173] A definitive study of the economics of solar heating in different climates, as of 1970, is R. Tybout and G. Löf, Solar house heating.

about the long-term reliability of solar systems; the thousands of building codes in the United States, many with quite different requirements that solar systems would have to meet.[174] A variety of incentive programs and demonstration projects—including some large government buildings heated with solar energy—were being undertaken by the U.S. government in the mid-1970s to try to overcome those barriers.[175]

In climates where air conditioning is also a significant energy-user, solar cooling can be considered, too. This is not really paradoxical—any air conditioner requires an energy source, and there are technologies for which that source is heat, not electricity. They are called *absorption air conditioners,* and traditionally they have been designed to use natural gas as an energy source. Versions modified to run on solar energy require water temperatures of 80° to 95° C (170° to 200° F.) or more; therefore, they need better collectors than suffice for ordinary water and space heating.

The most economical way to achieve the higher temperatures needed is probably to coat the collector plate and tubes with a *selective surface.* Such coatings absorb sunlight in the visible wavelengths very efficiently but radiate energy away very inefficiently. (Ordinary black paint radiates energy away in the infrared wavelengths just as effectively as it absorbs incident visible radiation; it is *nonselective.* This sets a limit on the temperature that can be achieved, because the rate of energy loss by radiation goes up as the fourth power of the collector temperature.) Several such coatings were available on commercial flat-plate collectors in the $100/m^2 range in the mid-1970s.[176] The efficiency of flat-plate collectors—that is, the fraction of incident sunlight they deliver as heat—is usually between 40 percent and 50 percent. Precisely opposite to a heat engine, a given flat-plate collector becomes *less* efficient as the water temperature rises, because all the losses increase with temperature. This is a price that must be paid if high-temperature water is needed, as for air conditioning.

In addition to using selective coatings, more glass cover plates, and more insulation on the back, one can also obtain higher temperatures in solar collectors by using adjustable mounts that track the sun or curved collectors that focus the collected energy on a small area. Sun-tracking and -focusing collectors may be suitable for electricity generation and specialized industrial applications, but they seem too expensive for space-heating and air conditioning. But possibly innovation and mass production will change this verdict.

The most effective use of an investment in solar collectors for residences or small commercial buildings is in a system that serves waterheating, spaceheating, and air-conditioning needs together. Such a combination is illustrated schematically in Figure 8-27. To maximize the amount of sunlight collected for such combined summer and winter use, the collector should be tilted toward the equator at an angle from the horizontal equal to the latitude. For winter heating only, the optimum angle is latitude plus 15 degrees.[177] Energy storage for a solar heating system for a typical residence is most economically provided by several thousand gallons of water in an insulated tank. Less storage is required for cooling systems, since the heaviest demand occurs at times when the sun is shining brightly (or was a few hours earlier). The cost of storage using hot water, or alternatively, hot rocks, is around $1000 for a few days' winter reserve for a residence—a modest fraction of the cost of the collectors.[178] It seems likely that combined solar systems like the one depicted in Figure 8-27 will be widely available in the United States in the first half of the 1980s.

In addition to its use in residences and commercial buildings, solar heat has also found application in high-temperature furnaces, which use mirrors to focus the sunlight collected over a large area onto a small volume. Temperatures greater than 3000° C have been obtained. The largest such furnace, completed at Odeillo, France, in 1970, can focus a megawatt of solar energy on a small target.[179] The potential applications

[174]A major study of these barriers is R. Schoen, A. S. Hirshberg, J. Weingart, and J. Stein, *New energy technology for buildings.*

[175]U.S. Energy Research and Development Administration, *National plan for solar heating and cooling: Interim report.*

[176]A good discussion of coatings is found in Meinel and Meinel, *Applied solar energy.*

[177]For more about the interesting geometry of the solar-collector, see Daniels, *Direct use;* Steadman, *Energy;* Meinel and Meinel, *Applied solar energy.*

[178]See, for example, W. Morrow, Solar energy: Its time is near.

[179]Steadman, *Energy.*

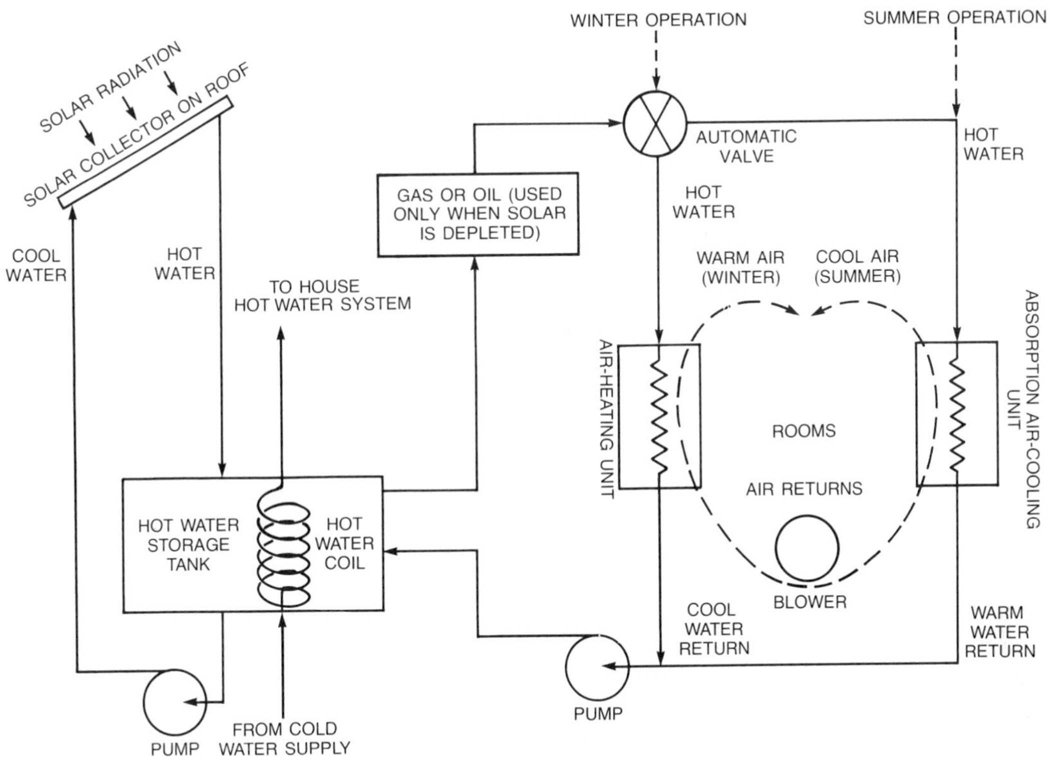

FIGURE 8-27

Solar energy system for heating, cooling, and water heating. Such multipurpose systems offer the greatest economy.

for these expensive, special-purpose devices do not make up a significant fraction of industrial energy use. Of greater interest are the possibilities for making solar energy available cheaply for processes where low-temperature heat suffices. Relatively little work was done in this area before the mid-1970s, because the economics looked unattractive in an era of cheap fuels.[180]

Thermal-electric systems. The dispersed uses of solar heat discussed above are especially attractive because they reduce dependence on complex, centralized systems with expensive distribution networks—the sun does the distribution. There is also interest in applying solar energy to central-station generation of electricity, however, largely because of the soaring costs and the less and less acceptable environmental impacts of other methods of generating electricity.

[180]A few recent efforts are W. Dickenson and R. Neifert, *Parametric performance and cost analysis of the proposed Sohio solar process heat facility;* W. Read, A. Choda, P. Cooper, Solar timber kiln.

One way to generate electricity with sunlight is to let solar heat replace fossil or nuclear fuels as the heat source in a more-or-less conventional steam cycle. This requires collectors more sophisticated than the flat-plate collectors discussed above, since temperatures of at least 200° C are needed to make the heat-to-electricity conversion efficiency high enough to be attractive. There are at least two particularly promising approaches. One is to use steerable collectors shaped like parabolic troughs, focusing the sunlight on pipes carrying a heat-transfer fluid such as liquid sodium to a central boiler and steam turbine plant. In a version of this scheme developed by A. B. Meinel and M. P. Meinel of the University of Arizona, the design of the collector and selectively coated central pipe allows a sodium temperature of 550° C to be achieved. Energy storage for operation at night and in cloudy weather requires 20 million cubic meters of rock for a plant with average capacity of 1000 megawatts. The total plant area would be 30 square kilometers, with an actual collector area about 16 kilometers, corresponding

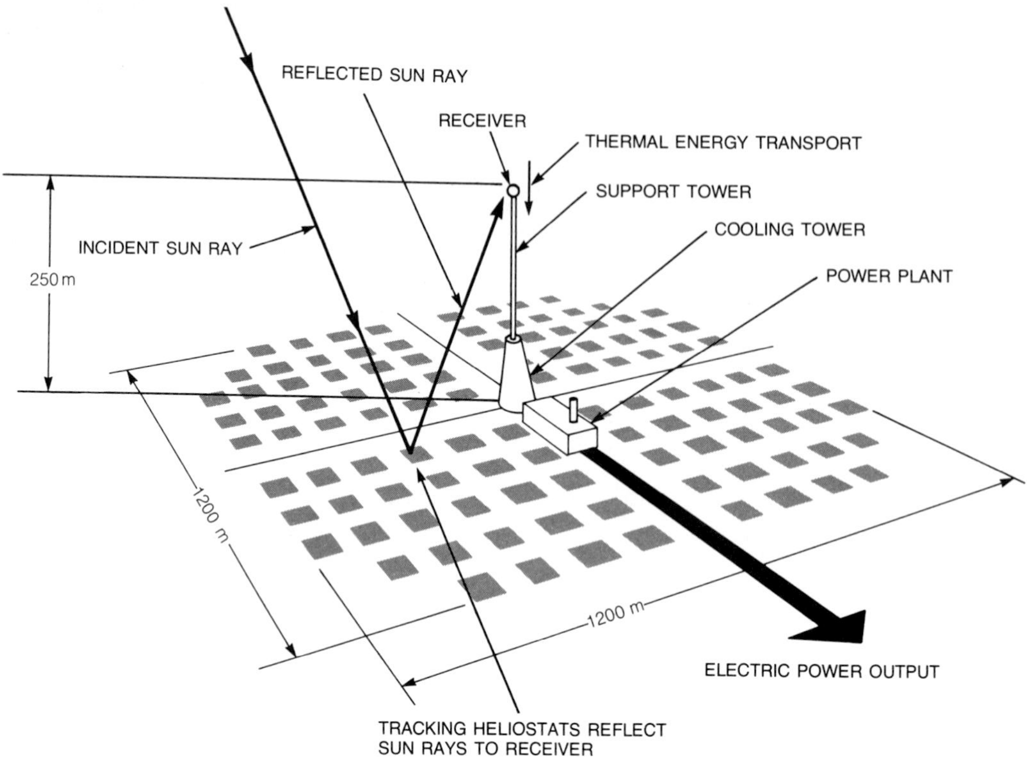

FIGURE 8-28

Solar thermal-electric plant. The central tower in a field of sun-tracking mirrors (heliostats) may be the first solar electricity-generating scheme to become economically attractive. (After JPL, *Program review.*)

to a ratio of electric energy to solar energy incident on the collectors of about 25 percent.[181] A variety of studies have placed the cost of such a plant in the range of $1000 to $2000 per electrical kilowatt.[182]

The second approach uses a field of steerable mirrors (called heliostats) focused on a single central receiver on a tower (see Figure 8-28). The central-receiver approach has an advantage over the trough-and-pipe system in that the energy travels as sunlight to the central location with little loss and no pumping. Focusing many mirrors on a small boiler can produce high temperatures, and hence high thermal-to-electric conversion efficiency. The overall plant efficiency might easily match that of a fossil-fueled power plant—say, 35 to 40 percent. Cost estimates again fall in the range $1000 to $2000 per average electrical kilowatt,[183] as opposed to $300 to $500 for fossil-fueled and $600 to $1000 for nuclear plants. Combined systems, where the waste heat from generating electricity is used for space-heating, water-heating, and air conditioning, have been suggested for large commercial and industrial complexes. Use of high-temperature heat from focusing solar collectors for direct production of hydrogen has also been suggested.[184]

Photovoltaic conversion. The direct production of electricity from sunlight by means of photovoltaic cells is well understood. The technology has had extensive application in the space program. The advantage of the process is its simplicity: the cells, which look like wafers of glass or plastic, are self-contained electricity generators that need only be hooked up to a load (in series, to obtain the desired voltage)—no pipes, no liquid metals or steam, no rotating machinery. The disadvantages are low efficiency, which is limited by the physics of the process

[181]A. B. Meinel and M. P. Meinel, Physics looks at solar energy.
[182]Morrow, Solar energy; Jet Propulsion Laboratory, *Program review: Comparative assessment of orbital and terrestrial central power stations.*
[183]Ibid.

[184]Morrow, Solar energy.

to a theoretical maximum around 22 percent and which more commonly has been 10 percent or less, and high cost, which has been $100,000 per electrical kilowatt or more for the space applications.[185]

Photovoltaic cells used in the space program have usually been made of silicon. Silicon is abundant, but difficult to produce in the purity and single-crystal form needed to make a solar cell. Photovoltaic cells have also been made with cadmium sulfide (cheaper to make than silicon cells, but less durable and less efficient) and gallium arsenide (efficient, but gallium is scarce). Significant progress was being made in the mid-1970s on techniques of mass producing silicon cells much more cheaply than previously possible.[186] Development of a gallium arsenide cell capable of converting sunlight concentrated a thousandfold at efficiency around 15 percent (making possible great reductions in the cell area needed for a given power output) was announced in 1975 by Varian Corporation of Palo Alto, California.[187] These advances hold out the hope that the cost of electricity generation with photovoltaic cells could fall to the range of a few thousand dollars per average electrical kilowatt in the 1980s.

If solar cells become cheap enough—say, $500 per peak kilowatt—they will probably be used in combined systems on individual roofs, with the energy that is not converted to electricity being harnessed for heating and cooling. Such a system could produce enough extra electricity above household needs to run an electric commuter vehicle.[188]

The idea of placing large arrays of photovoltaic cells in synchronous Earth orbit to take advantage of sunlight undiluted by Earth's geometry and atmosphere has been pursued persistently by P. Glaser and colleagues at the Arthur D. Little Company, Cambridge, Massachusetts.[189] (In a synchronous orbit a satellite remains over the same spot on Earth all the time; its orbital period is synchronized with the period of Earth's rotation.) There are significant technological difficulties with this approach, not least of which are those associated with beaming the electric power produced down to Earth using microwaves—difficulties that include endangering people and other organisms if the beam should drift. It seems likely that one of the methods of producing electricity from sunlight on Earth's surface will turn out to be more economical and less risky.

Environmental effects. The environmental characteristics of direct uses of solar energy seem preferable to those of other technologies, but the solar option will not be entirely free of significant impacts. For example, materials requirements for covering large areas with collectors will be significant; extracting and processing those materials will produce some environmental disruption. Extensive land use itself, pre-empting other uses, is a significant effect. Installation of large solar-electric plants in the sunny Southwest would probably encourage extensive industrial and residential development of fragile and scenic desert areas there. And there will be waste heat! Although much of the solar energy collected would have been converted to heat at Earth's surface by natural processes, solar technology increases the heat burden somewhat because a collector absorbs more and reflects less than the natural surface. Also, there would be a redistribution of energy insofar as energy was collected, say, in the desert and then used in cities elsewhere.

Indirect Solar Energy

Solar energy makes itself available in a variety of indirect forms as well as in the form of light striking Earth's surface. Those forms include the chemical energy stored via photosynthesis in plants, the energy of the hydrologic cycle, the energy of wind and of waves and ocean currents, and the energy represented by the temperature difference between deep and shallow ocean waters (ocean thermal gradients).

Photosynthesis. The first energy technologies, fire and agriculture, harnessed energy stored by photosynthesis. Agriculture and burning wood are still important energy technologies today, of course, but they by no

[185] J. Weingart, Solar energy; Hammond, Metz, and Maugh, *Energy*, chapter 11; a comprehensive listing of the extensive literature of this and other aspects of solar energy is U.S. Atomic Energy Commission, *Solar energy: A bibliography.*
[186] Weingart, Solar energy.
[187] L. W. James and R. L. Moon, GaAs concentrator solar cell.
[188] J. Weingart, Solar energy.
[189] P. Glaser, Power from the sun; and Solar power from satellites.

means exhaust the potential of photosynthesis. The annual net photosynthetic production of the biosphere (the amount of solar energy stored in chemical bonds by plants and not consumed by the plants' metabolic processes) is around 10 times the annual commercial energy use of civilization.[190] An estimated 5 percent of this amount takes place in agricultural ecosystems;[191] the photosynthetic energy that reaches the human population as food is only a tenth of that 5 percent, or 0.5 percent of net photosynthesis (for a fuller discussion, see Chapter 3 and Chapter 7).

The agricultural "energy system" is not only a producer of energy in the uniquely useful form of food, but it is also a consumer of commercial energy forms—mostly fossil fuels—that subsidize the production, processing, and delivery of solar energy as food (see Box 8-6). If more of the solar energy actually captured in agriculture could be harnessed—specifically, by using the energy in the uneaten or inedible plant parts now called *agricultural wastes*—it is possible that agriculture could start augmenting commercial energy supplies rather than draining them.

In the United States in the early 1970s, agricultural and food wastes and manure were estimated by the U.S. Bureau of Mines to be almost 600 million metric tons of dry organic matter per year; it was estimated that only about 8 percent of this was "readily collectable."[192] (Calculations based on net photosynthesis would suggest that 600 million metric tons is much too low a figure, but we will use it here as an official minimum estimate.) The average energy content of this material is about 10 megajoules per kilogram. Most of the energy is made available as heat if the dried waste is burned directly as boiler fuel; conversion of the waste to more conventional liquid, gaseous, and solid fuels yields 60 to 70 percent of the original energy in the final product.[193] Taking an average figure of 65 percent conversion, the readily collectable fraction of U.S. agricultural and food wastes could have yielded about 300 billion megajoules per year in the early 1970s, or 0.4 percent of total U.S. energy use at that time. If modification of agricultural practices permitted collecting as much as 50 percent of the Bureau of Mines estimate, then the energy recoverable at 65 percent conversion would roughly equal the recent commercial energy *inputs* to U.S. food-growing (but not food processing, transportation, and so on) as discussed in Box 8-6.

Organic wastes from sources other than agriculture (urban refuse, sewage, logging wastes, industrial wastes) amounted to about 300 million metric tons in the United States in the early 1970s, of which about 30 percent was estimated to be readily collectable.[194] At 65-percent conversion, that would total 600 million megajoules per year, or 0.8 percent of the total U.S. energy use at the time. It does not seem unreasonable to suppose that, with effort, the collectable fraction of those nonagricultural organic wastes might be doubled.

The simplest and cheapest way to harness the energy of organic wastes is by direct combustion. This is now being done in devices ranging from the electric-utility boilers in St. Louis, which burn municipal wastes mixed with coal and gas,[195] to open fires and simple stoves for cooking and heating in the villages of India, where cow dung, crop residues, and wood are burned. The total energy embodied in these noncommercial fuels in India is apparently considerable. According to Makhijani and Poole, it is equal to all commercial energy use in that country.[196] Unfortunately, the efficiency with which the noncommercial energy forms are converted into useful heat and work in India and other LDCs is very low—Makhijani's estimate is 5 percent.[197] This problem could

[190]Commercial energy use means consumption of fuels and electricity that are sold, and excludes food and other plant and animal matter gathered by the user. The global rate of commercial energy use in 1975 was around 8.4 million megawatts (that is, 265 trillion megajoules per year—*New Scientist,* July 22, 1976, p. 181) compared to net photosynthesis around 100 million megawatts (G. Woodwell and E. Pecan, eds., *Carbon and the biosphere,* National Technical Information Service, Springfield Va., 1973, USAEC CONF-720510, p. 369).

[191]R. Whittaker and G. Likens, Carbon in the biota.

[192]L. Anderson, *Energy potential from organic wastes: A review of the quantities and sources;* see also A. Poole, The potential for energy recovery from organic wastes.

[193]Science and Public Policy Program, *Energy alternatives,* chapter 10; Makhijani and Poole, *Energy and agriculture.*

[194]Anderson, *Energy potential*

[195]Science and Public Policy program, *Energy alternatives,* chapter 10.

[196]Makhijani and Poole, *Energy and agriculture,* p. 23. When plant material that "fuels" work animals is counted in, the noncommercial organic materials outweigh commercial energy in India 2 to 1, the authors say.

[197]A. Makhijani, Solar energy and rural development for the Third World.

BOX 8-6 Energy and Food: "Helping" the Sun

It has been said that Americans eat potatoes made mostly of petroleum. The statement refers to the heavy infusions of fossil fuels that are used in operating the many phases of the United States food industry—agriculture, processing, packaging, transport, marketing, storage, and preparation. Detailed studies have shown that the amount of nonsolar energy used in all those activities in the United States was almost 10 times greater than the energy content of the food consumed in 1970 (having increased from around 6 in 1960, 2 in 1930, and 1 in 1910).[a]

Where was all the energy going in 1970? About a fourth of the total for the food system was used on the farm (tractor fuel, electricity for irrigation pumps) or to manufacture things used on the farm (fertilizers, pesticides, tractors, other machinery).[b] Almost 40 percent was used to process, package, and transport the food (including the energy costs of cans, bottles, and paper wrappings). The remainder was used mainly for refrigeration and cooking in homes and businesses.

Although the food system is, strictly speaking, an energy technology, it is one with a negative energy balance—far more commercial energy goes in than food energy comes out. This works economically because food energy fetches so high a price. Bread at 40 cents a pound represents an "energy price" of about $75 per gigajoule (1000 megajoules), whereas gasoline at 60 cents a gallon is less than $5 per gigajoule. The massive subsidization of U.S. agriculture and food processing with cheap fossil fuel cannot be duplicated in developing countries, where under the U.S. pattern more energy would be required for the food system than is available for all purposes combined; and the prospects that such quantities could be made available in the forseeable future are decidedly dim.[c] Indeed, as the real costs of the fossil fuels and the environmental costs of the energy-intensive agricultural practices themselves become increasingly apparent, there is more and more reason to break away from this pattern even in the United States and other DCs. The amount of solar energy captured by plants on farms and then wasted, as commercial energy pours in from elsewhere, suggests the possibility of restoring sunlight to its original position as the *main* driving force of agriculture—and perhaps even of exporting some nonfood fuel to the rest of society as well.

Some experimentation along these lines has been started in the United States and several other developed countries, notably the United Kingdom and Australia. Perhaps the best-known and most comprehensive such project in the United States is that of the New Alchemy Institute in Massachusetts.[d] This organization, which was founded in 1969 by two marine biologists, operates a small farm on Cape Cod and another in California and plans to start a third in Canada. For energy, the Massachusetts farm is dependent mainly on windmills and solar heaters. The solar heat is stored in greenhouse-covered fish ponds, which also produce edible fishes and fertilizer for crops. Since all crops are produced by "organic" methods (no synthetic fertilizers, pesticides, or other chemicals), the energy costs of the chemicals are also saved. The New Alchemy Institute's water-pumping windmill design has already been exported to India; many of its other energy-saving methods and technical inventions might also be adaptable to LDC agriculture (as well as to that in DCs).

Some farmers in the United States have practiced organic farming for decades, believing that the food produced in this way is nutritionally superior and that the method preserves and builds up the quality of soil (see Chapter 7 and Chapter 11). Because no synthetic chemicals are used and mechanization is minimal, organic farms on the average use only about 35 percent as much energy as conventional farms in the United States do.[e]

---

[a]J. Steinhart and C. Steinhart, Energy use in the U.S. food system; E. Hirst, Food-related energy requirements.

[b]See also D. Pimentel, L. Hurd, A. Bellotti, M. Forster, I. Oka, O. Sholes, and R. Whitman, Food production and the energy crisis.

[c]D. Pimentel, et al., Energy and land constraints in food protein production.

[d]Nicholas Wade, New Alchemy Institute: Search for an alternative agriculture, *Science,* vol. 187, pp. 727–729 (February 28, 1975).

[e]Nicholas Wade, Boost for credit rating of organic farmers, *Science,* vol. 189, p. 777 (September 5, 1975).

be somewhat ameliorated by the use of improved—but still simple—stoves for burning these materials.

Unless large boilers are at hand that can burn organic wastes and capture the heat efficiently to produce steam (which makes little sense in rural India and is not necessarily the best use of the materials or the energy in the United States), the way to increase the efficiency of applying the energy in such materials is to convert them into more compact fuels. One way to do this, which was in the pilot-plant stage of development in the United States in the mid-1970s, is to produce fuel oil from the wastes by *hydrogenation*. Hydrogenation consists of treating the waste material with steam and carbon monoxide under high pressure. Complicated and sophisticated facilities are required, and the yield is about 1.4 barrels of low-sulfur fuel oil per metric ton of dry organic matter, representing a conversion efficiency around 63 percent.[198]

Less elaborate technology suffices for *pyrolysis*, which means decomposition without combustion. This is accomplished by heating the material in the absence of air. The process produces a charcoal-like solid fuel (char), a medium-energy gas (10 to 18 MJ/m^3), and combustible liquids. The efficiency is around 70 percent. Small pilot plants were subjecting municipal waste to pyrolysis at several locations in the United States in the mid-1970s, and larger installations were planned.[199] Either aproach may prove a useful way to deal with municipal waste (primarily garbage, much of which is paper) in developed countries, but this is probably not the best use of agricultural wastes anywhere.

More attractive in many respects than any of the foregoing approaches is *biogasification*, which refers to the breakdown of organic matter by anaerobic bacteria, producing methane gas (CH_4) and carbon dioxide (CO_2). The process takes place in enclosed volumes of various designs, called digesters, which can be small and cheap to serve the needs of small living groups and villages, or much larger and more elaborate to handle efficiently the larger volumes of wastes from towns, livestock feedlots, and so on. The gas, as produced, has an energy content around 20 megajoules per cubic meter, but the CO_2 can be removed with straightforward technology to produce nearly pure methane with an energy content of 38 megajoules per cubic meter. Not only is this fuel suitable for cooking, heating, and electricity generation in units of many kinds and sizes, but farm machinery can be modified to burn it in place of gasoline.[200]

Biogasification has the further great advantage that the nutrients in the waste material—nitrogen, phosphorous, and others—are not wasted but are retained in a compact residue much more suitable for use as fertilizer than the original material. The economics and technology of putting biogasification units into rural villages in Asia, Africa, and Latin America to provide fuel, electricity, and fertilizer have been summarized by Makhijani and Poole. A schematic diagram of one of the very promising combined-use systems appears in Figure 8-29. In the mid-1970s in the United States, at least one commercial firm was proceeding with plans for a large biogasification plant running on the wastes of cattle feedlots in Colorado, with the product to be sold to a gas pipeline company.[201]

All the techniques described here for extracting energy from organic waste can also be applied to organic material grown explicitly for that purpose. Serious proposals have been put forward for using fast-growing trees (pines, eucalyptus) to supply wood for electric-utility boilers;[202] grain can be fermented to produce alcohol for use as fuel; and the idea of culturing algae in ponds for use directly as fuel or as fodder for biogasification has stimulated considerable research in the past few decades.[203] The same basic difficulties confront all these schemes: (1) the efficiency with which plants convert solar energy to stored chemical energy is low—rarely more than 0.5 percent (although a few percent has been claimed for some kinds of algae)— so the required land area is large; (2) water needs are high for most of the schemes; (3) the energy cost of maintaining suitable growing conditions, supplying nutrients, and harvesting

[198]Hammond, Metz, and Maugh, *Energy*, chapter 12; Science and Public Policy Program, *Energy alternatives*, chapter 10.

[199]W. Kasper, Power from trash; A. Poole, The potential.

[200]See especially Makhijani and Poole, *Energy and agriculture;* Steadman, *Energy*.

[201]Makhijani and Poole, *Energy and agriculture.*

[202]Science and Public Policy Program, *Energy alternatives*, chapter 11; G. Szego and C. Kemp, Energy forests and fuel plantations.

[203]See, for example, C. Golueke and W. Oswald, Power from solar energy via algae-produced methane; Hammond, Metz, and Maugh, *Energy*, chapter 12.

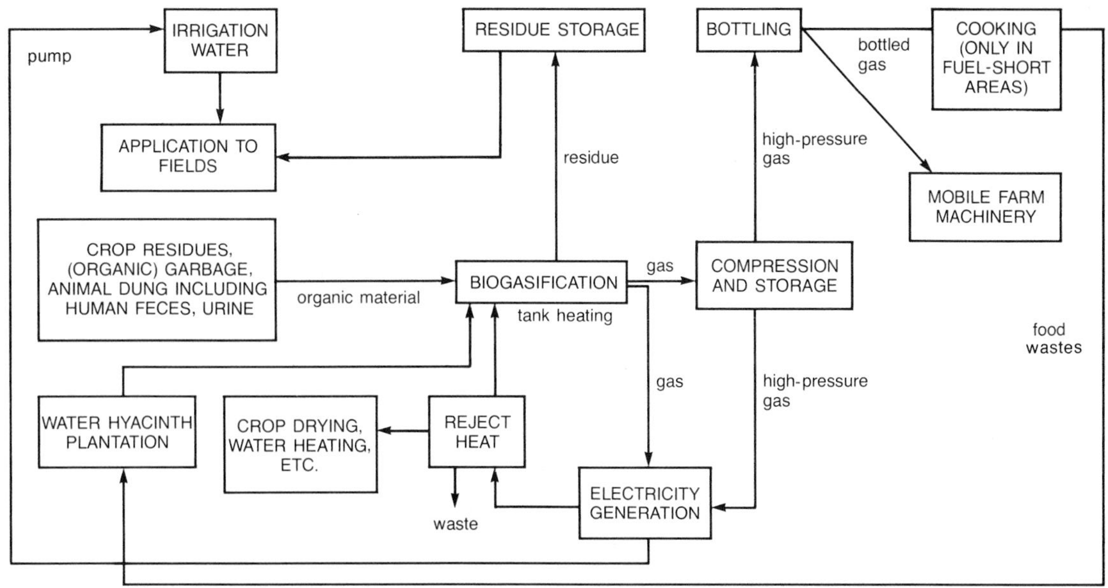

FIGURE 8-29

Village biogasification and electricity system. Energy technology tailored to the needs of developing countries is urgently needed. (After Makhijani and Poole, 1975.)

a crop can be high, so the net energy profit may not be large; (4) the economic pressure to produce high yields can lead to the same ecological problems that have been associated with high-yield agriculture and high-yield timber production (see Chapter 11); (5) photosynthetic products are likely to be more valuable as food, feed, fertilizer, or industrial raw materials than as fuels. Nevertheless, the possibility of a successful energy plantation based on a high yielding plant or alga of some kind cannot be entirely ruled out.

The use of photosynthetic materials to replace hydrocarbons from fossil fuels as raw materials for the chemical industry is of interest in itself.[204] About 6 percent of U.S. fossil-fuel use in the 1970s was for such nonfuel uses. Petrochemicals have largely replaced such photosynthetic materials as alcohol from molasses and grain, and rubber from the rubber plant *Hevea,* for strictly economic reasons;[205] that revolution could likewise be reversed for economic reasons—namely, the soaring costs of fossil fuels.

[204]Although the energy in fossil fuels was stored by photosynthesis hundreds of millions of years ago, *photosynthetic materials* in the present context means plant matter of more recent origin.

[205]Melvin Calvin, Solar energy by photosynthesis.

Finally, there is a possibility to use photosynthesis by imitating it. More specifically, some researchers hope that, by gaining sufficiently detailed understanding of the biochemical machinery of photosynthesis, they can devise nonbiological systems that use similar reactions to convert solar energy into chemical energy (in the form of hydrogen) or electrical energy, but at higher efficiency than that attained by green plants.[206] Part of the basis of their hope for higher efficiency is that plants must spend a substantial part of the energy they handle to maintain their own life-support systems and to propagate themselves. The nonbiological mimic need not perform such functions, or so it seems at first. However, all the energy costs of building such a system and maintaining it—analogous to the plant's energy expenditures in supporting and propagating itself—must be charged against its net efficiency.

Hydropower. Of the nonbiological processes that provide opportunities for indirect harnessing of solar energy, by far the most heavily used is the hydrologic cycle. Developed hydroelectric capacity worldwide in

[206]Ibid.

1974 was 307,000 electrical megawatts (Mwe), compared to an estimated potential of about 2,300,000 Mwe.[207] (U.S. hydro capacity in 1975 was 66,000 Mwe compared to a potential of 172,000 Mwe and a total electrical capacity in all forms of 505,000 Mwe.[208]) Most of the undeveloped hydro capacity is in Asia, Africa, and South America. Although the flow of rivers can be expected to be roughly constant over many millennia, much of the potential of specific hydroelectric sites is typically destroyed within one to three centuries when the reservoirs fill with silt. No real solution for this problem is yet known.[209]

Hydropower is harnessed by building a dam with water turbines and generators installed at the base. The energy that would have been dissipated as the water descended over the streambed is then stored as potential energy in the form of water that builds up behind the dam. When electricity is needed, tunnels through the dam are opened and the stored energy—the pressure of a column of water tens to 100 or more meters high—drives water through them and into the turbines with great force. The generators turned by the turbines are essentially identical to those in steam-electric plants. The efficiency with which hydroelectric plants convert the potential energy of the water to electricity is high—about 90 percent in the best installations, and an average of 75 to 80 percent.[210]

Some hydroelectric installations have capacities equal to or larger than the largest fossil-fueled and nuclear power stations: there are several hydro plants of around 2000 Mwe in the United States, two of more than 4000 Mwe in the Soviet Union, and even larger plants under construction. One of them, the Itaipu Dam, which is a joint project of Brazil and Paraguay, is expected to have an eventual generating capacity of more than 10,000 Mwe.[211]

Hydroelectric plants are not without adverse environmental and social impacts. The spawning grounds of migratory fishes of commercial and recreational importance, such as salmon, are often destroyed by hydroelectric facilities, or the fishes are prevented from reaching them. Other wildlife habitat and valuable farmland may be destroyed, and long-time human residents forced to move. Seepage from reservoirs can raise a water table and bring subsurface salts with it, impairing the fertility of the soil. Stream conditions downstream from dams can be greatly altered, and estuaries and the associated fisheries can be affected. Rapid fluctuations of river levels with the intermittent operation of hydro plants—which are especially cherished by utilities for their ability to start rapidly when the need arises—can be especially disruptive.[212]

The reservoirs behind dams lose water by evaporation in proportion to their surface area; in dry climates this can aggravate water shortages by reducing the average flow and can increase the concentration of dissolved minerals in the water remaining. In some instances, the filling of large reservoirs has triggered earthquakes because the weight of the accumulating water has shifted the balance of stresses in the underlying crust (see Chapter 11). Perhaps more important than causing small earthquakes, however, is the vulnerability of dams to destruction in large ones. If a major dam upstream from a densely populated region should give way suddenly, tens of thousands of people could be killed.[213]

A second form of hydropower is sometimes mentioned. The source of that energy is the work done by the sun in evaporating fresh water from the surface of the salty ocean (as distinguished from the work done in lifting the evaporated water to high altitudes, which is the source of the energy tapped by conventional hydropower installations). That *desalination energy* ordinarily is dissipated as heat in the zones near the mouths of rivers, where fresh and salt water mix. It is possible in principle to tap this energy by means of technology based on semipermeable membranes; one analyst has suggested that an efficiency of conversion to electricity of 25 percent is attainable, at costs per kilowatt hour about 10 times higher than for producing electricity from coal.[214] The analyst has noted, however, that this technology

[207]U.S. Department of the Interior, *Energy perspectives 2,* p. 38. Hubbert, Energy resources, gives 2,900,000 Mwe as the potential.

[208]Ibid. pp. 127, 143.

[209]I. Nisbet, Hydroelectric power: A nonrenewable resource?

[210]Science and Public Policy Program, *Energy alternatives,* chapter 9.

[211]A. Golenpaul, ed., *Information please almanac,* p. 332.

[212]A good survey of ecological effects of hydroelectric installations is given by R. Hagan and E. Roberts, Ecological impacts of water storage and diversion projects; see also G. Garvey, *Energy, ecology, economy,* and K. Lagler, Ecological effects of hydroelectric dams.

[213]D. Okrent et al., *Estimates of risks associated with dam failure.*

[214]R. Norman, Water salination: A source of energy.

would be environmentally disastrous for estuaries and so could not be tolerated on a large scale.

Wind and waves. Windmills have been used to pump water and turn grindstones for centuries, and they are still in extensive use for pumping in many parts of the world today. Over the past several decades, windmills of various sizes and designs also have been used to generate electricity, generally on a one-of-a-kind basis. The peak output of such devices has ranged from around 1 electrical kilowatt, for adaptations of the pumping machines of the sort typically seen on American farms, to the 1250 electrical kilowatts of the famous Smith-Putnam machine that operated from 1941 to 1945 on Grandpa's Knob in Vermont. The blades of the latter machine swept a circle 53 meters (175 feet) in diameter.[215]

The total energy in the winds is large. Estimates for the globe fall in the range of 250 million to 2500 million megawatts of average continuous power. It seems unlikely that as much as 1 percent of the total could actually be harnessed, but even that small fraction represents a great deal of energy—3 times the world's 1975 use of commercial energy, if we take the lower extreme of the range of estimates of total wind power. A study under the auspices of the National Science Foundation and the National Aeronautics and Space Administration (NASA) concluded in 1972 that wind power in the United States could deliver about 5 trillion (5×10^{12}) megajoules of electrical energy by the year 2000.[216] This is close to the *total* U.S. demand for electricity in 1972.

Why, then, has wind power not been harnessed more extensively to date? One reason is that the wind is unpredictable from hour to hour and day to day, although the average energy delivered annually in a given location is generally very consistent. Meeting electricity needs that cannot be timed to coincide with periods when the wind is blowing therefore requires a means of storing electricity, which is difficult and expensive. A second obstacle has been the high cost of building a windmill in relation to the average amount of power it can deliver and the cost of power in the past from more conventional sources. These factors have confined the use of wind power for electricity generation to locations far from electric-utility grids selling cheap power from fossil fuels or hydro dams, and to applications where a little power can be used very effectively (as for communications and lighting).[217]

The power that a windmill can produce is proportional to the area swept by its blades and to the cube of the wind speed. In other words, for a given blade, the available power goes up eightfold for every twofold increase in wind speed. Economic feasibility, therefore, depends strongly on the frequency and steadiness of high winds at a given site. At least 12 miles per hour is needed for most applications—a fact that makes islands, coastal sites, and hilltops particularly attractive places for windmills. Since the wind speed increases with height above the ground, there is also incentive to place windmills on tall towers; this, of course, increases costs, as does designing the equipment to withstand high winds without breaking.

For basic physical reasons, windmills cannot extract all the energy that passes through the swept area. The theoretical maximum is about 60 percent for windmills with horizontal axes, and only a fraction of that theoretical limit can actually be attained by existing machines. An efficient two-blade propeller-type windmill can get about 330 watts per square meter of swept area from a wind blowing 11 meters per second (25 mph). This is 37 percent of the power in the wind and 62 percent of the amount theoretically extractable. Conversion of the mechanical energy of the spinning shaft to electricity with a good generator can be nearly 100 percent efficient. Three types of windmills are illustrated in Figure 8-30.

Ambitious schemes have been put forward for the construction of large arrays of wind generators on seacoasts, offshore on anchored floating platforms, and over highway and railroad rights-of-way.[218] The construction costs for such installations have been estimated

[215]Good surveys of the history and technical characteristics of windmills are to be found in Steadman, *Energy*, pp. 185–211; J. McCaull, Windmills; Marshal Merriam, Wind energy for human needs; and Windmills for less developed countries. (Steadman and Merriam include lists of manufacturers.)

[216]NSF/NASA Solar Energy Panel, *An assessment of solar energy as a national energy resource.*

[217]See especially Merriam's discussion on this point (in Windmills).

[218]W. Heronemus, Wind power: A near-term partial solution to the energy crisis; Science and Public Policy Program, *Energy alternatives,* chapter 11. An important study of large-scale wind systems in Denmark is B. Sørenson, Energy and resources.

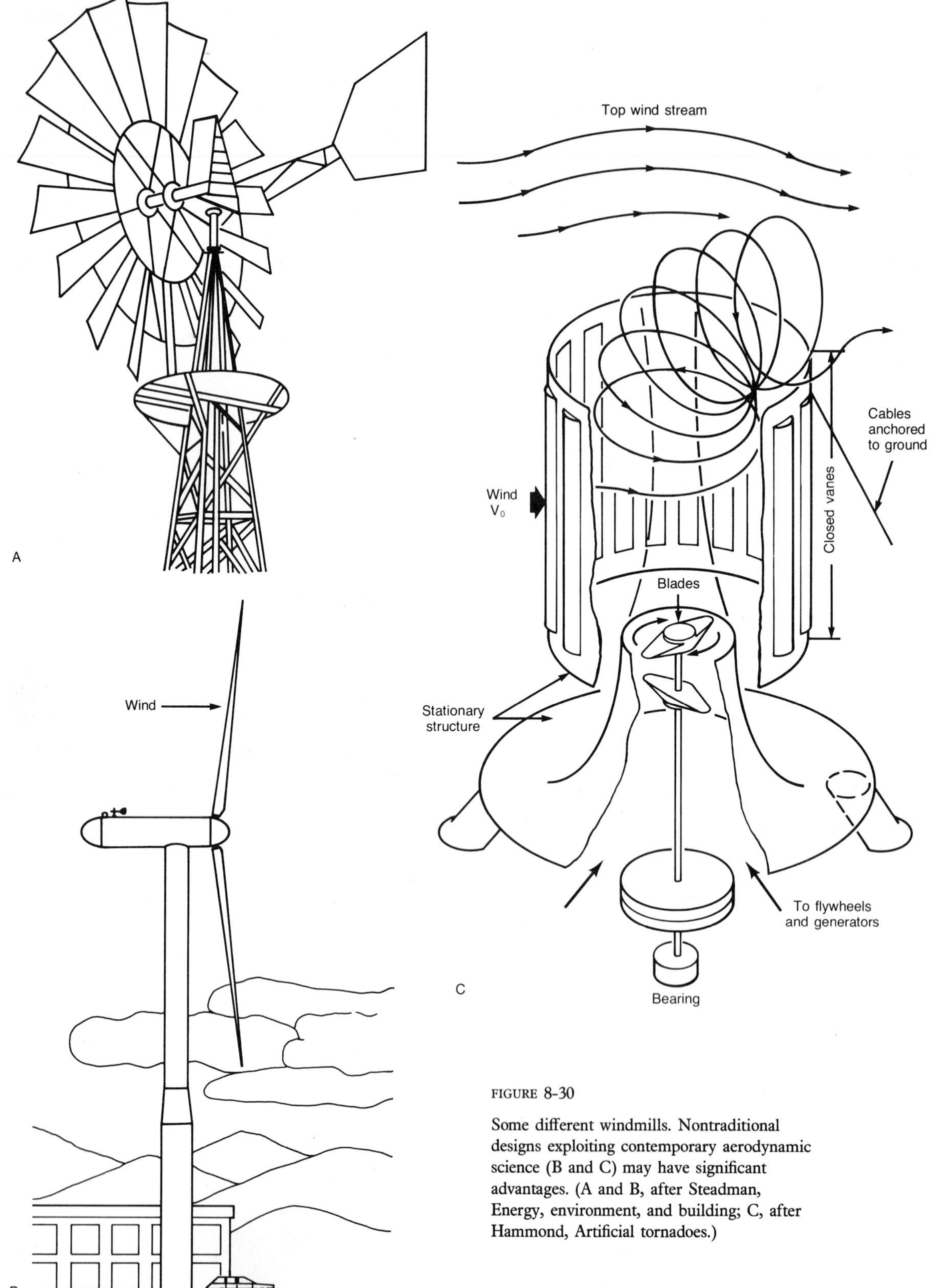

FIGURE 8-30

Some different windmills. Nontraditional designs exploiting contemporary aerodynamic science (B and C) may have significant advantages. (A and B, after Steadman, Energy, environment, and building; C, after Hammond, Artificial tornadoes.)

to be in the range of $200 per electrical kilowatt, which is much lower than achieved for smaller mass-produced windmills and larger experimental ones to date. Even if those costs are underestimates, however, harnessing the wind may prove to be a significant and attractive way to produce electricity. Adverse environmental effects would be mainly the aesthetic impact of the windmills and destruction of birds, until the amount of wind harnessed became large enough to present the possibility of large-scale climatic impact. Sensible restraint can prevent the last problem, and the others are perhaps a small price to pay in comparison to the impacts of most alternatives.

When the wind blows over large expanses of water, a substantial part of its energy is transferred to waves. They can carry the energy far from the place it was supplied. There are many coastlines in the world (as well as regions far from shores) where the reliability of energy flow in waves is considerably greater than that of the wind. Over the years several kinds of devices have been constructed in attempts to harness wave power, both in deep water and in shallow. Many obstacles remain to be overcome, not least of which is the tremendous battering that wave-power systems receive in storms. Nevertheless, the possibility of successful and economical systems cannot be ruled out.[219]

Ocean thermal gradients. Solar energy is also stored in the oceans in the form of the temperature difference between warm surface water and the colder layers 750 meters to 1000 meters below. In many parts of the world, that temperature difference is between 20° and 25° C. That is enough to support the operation of a heat engine converting thermal energy to mechanical work with a maximum theoretical efficiency of around 3 percent. The efficiency likely to be attainable in practice is 1 to 2 percent.[220]

The reservoir of energy is so large that, in this respect, such low efficiency is not a serious drawback. The heat transported by the Gulf Stream alone,[221] converted to electricity at 1-percent efficiency, corresponds to an average power of 21 million electrical megawatts—about 100 times the average electric power use in the United States in 1975. The problem with low efficiency is that enormous volumes of water and energy must be handled per unit of useful energy delivered, which makes the equipment unwieldy and expensive. Particularly troublesome in that respect would be the huge intake pipes for sucking up cold water from the deeps, and the turbines, which would have to be very large to extract significant amounts of energy at low temperature and low pressure. And, somehow, the huge structures would have to be designed to withstand the battering of the sometimes hostile ocean.

Those obstacles notwithstanding, the advocates of drawing power from ocean thermal gradients believe that it can be practical and economical—and, like most forms of using solar energy, relatively benign environmentally. Systems that evaporate the seawater itself to provide the vapor for the turbines could produce fresh water from the condensers as a desirable side product. Other designs use an organic working fluid, such as propane, in a closed cycle. A study for the Federal Energy Administration in 1974 indicated that large sea-thermal power plants could be constructed for around $600 per electrical kilowatt of generating capacity.[222] If this were an underestimate by a factor of 3, or even 5, the approach would still be economically interesting.

Advanced Conversion: MHD and Fuel Cells

Magnetohydrodynamics (MHD) and fuel cells are not primary energy sources; they are technologies of energy conversion that may make existing and future primary sources—such as fossil fuels, fission, fusion, or solar energy—more efficient or more versatile.

Magnetohydrodynamics. MHD generation is a means of converting the thermal and kinetic energy of a flow of hot gas or liquid metal directly to electricity, bypassing the intermediate stage of the mechanical energy of rotating machinery. The most common approach is to seed hot combustion gases, from burning a

---

[219]See, for example, M. Wooley and J. Platts, Energy on the crest of a wave.

[220]See, for example, D. Othmer and O. Roels, Power, fresh water, and food from cold, deep sea water; C. Zener, Solar sea power.

[221]Computed as 2200 km^3/day at a temperature 20° C warmer than the deep water below it.

[222]U.S. Federal Energy Administration, *Solar energy task force report.*

fossil fuel, with a material such as potassium or cesium that is easily ionized (stripped of electrons) at those temperatures. The free electrons make the combustion products conduct electricity. The hot, electrically conducting gas is then expanded through a nozzle to increase its velocity and passed through a channel to which a strong magnetic field is applied. Just as in mechanical generators, the motion of a conducting medium through a magnetic field produces an electric voltage. In an MHD generator, the current is drawn off from electrodes lining the channel.

Many small experimental MHD generators have been built in various countries, but a variety of technical problems remain to be worked out before this technology is commercially available.[223] The first commercial plants will probably use MHD as a topping cycle in combination with a conventional steam cycle. A pilot plant of that kind, producing 25 electrical megawatts from an MHD generator and 50 electrical megawatts from a steam cycle, began operation in the Soviet Union around 1971. Such plants may have difficulty competing economically with gas-turbine combined-cycle plants, which yield overall plant efficiencies in the same range—45 to 55 percent. (The efficiency of the USSR prototype is only about 30 percent.) Pure MHD plants of the future possibly could achieve efficiencies of 60 percent or more, and there are ways to combine MHD conversion with nuclear fission and solar energy sources as well as with fossil fuels.[224] A technology closely related to MHD might be used to convert the energy of charged particles in fusion plasmas directly to electricity.[225]

Fuel cells. Fuel cells are devices for converting the stored chemical energy in natural gas, hydrogen, or other chemical fuels directly to electricity, at efficiencies as high as 60 percent or more. A fuel cell operates on the identical principle as an ordinary battery: a chemical reaction yielding electrons (oxidation) takes place at one electrode and a reaction consuming electrons (reduction) takes place at the other. The resulting deficiency of electrons at one electrode and excess at the other causes a voltage between them. The fuel cell differs from a battery only in that the reactants are continuously supplied from outside the fuel cell itself, and the reaction products are continuously removed. Fuel cells may eventually be important as electricity generators, in both centralized and dispersed applications (perhaps, for example, in individual homes and in automobiles), and as part of a hydrogen economy—if one materializes (that concept is discussed below). First, however, the technology must overcome present obstacles of short operating lifetime, reliance on scarce materials as catalysts, and efficiences far lower in practice than in theory.[226]

Realization of practical fuel cells for electricity generation would have considerable environmental advantages over combustion of fossil fuels—emissions of oxides of nitrogen would be significantly reduced, and the higher efficiency would mean a much smaller burden of waste heat.

Energy Storage and Transmission

Energy is easy to store in the form of fossil fuels, and its transportation by various means—train, barge, pipeline, tanker, truck—is generally technologically straightforward, if not always cheap or environmentally benign. Electricity is generally more expensive to transmit than moving the amount of fuel required to make the electricity, and electricity is much more difficult to store.[227]

A distinction is made in the electricity industry between transmission and distribution: The former refers to moving electricity from generating centers to consumption centers, involving relatively long distances and high voltages (138 kilovolts or more). Distribution refers to moving electricity to individual users through networks of shorter, lower-voltage lines. Most transmission is done with overhead lines. Increasingly, distribution systems are being installed underground. One reason more transmission lines are not placed underground is that soil and rock are less able than air to carry

[223]See Hammond, Metz, and Maugh, *Energy*, chapter 4; Dicks, Magnetohydrodynamic central power.

[224]Science and Public Policy Program, *Energy alternatives*, chapter 12.

[225]Post and Ribe, Fusion reactors.

[226]T. Aaronson, The black box; Hammond, Metz, and Maugh, *Energy*, chapter 17; Science and Public Policy Program, *Energy alternatives*, chapter 12.

[227]For a concise treatment of transportation costs, see Hottel and Howard, *New energy*, pp. 44–46.

away the concentrated heat load imposed by transmission lines carrying large amounts of power. Technologies for underground transmission that could circumvent this problem are under intensive investigation: cables insulated with compressed gas; cryogenic cables running at the temperature of liquid nitrogen (80° kelvin), where electric resistance is 10 times lower than at normal temperatures; and superconducting cables running at the temperature of liquid helium (4° kelvin), where electrical resistance in certain materials is zero. All are expensive and probably can become economical only for the transmission of very large amounts of power.[228]

The environmental impacts of overhead transmission are the use of significant amounts of land, the unsightliness of towers and wires in scenic areas, and the effects of the strong electric fields that high-voltage lines produce in their vicinity. Some 28,000 square kilometers were dedicated to transmission lines in the United States as of the early 1970s, and some projections for the year 2000 envision twice that.[229] The health effects of exposure to the electric fields that exist under high-voltage lines are not well established, and more research is needed.[230] It is somewhat unsettling to discover that those fields are strong enough to light an unconnected fluorescent bulb at a distance of 50 meters from a 765-kilovolt line.

A number of improvements in energy systems would be made possible by the development of better means of energy storage. Direct use of sunlight for heating and cooling, for example, requires less supplemental fuel as more heat storage is available. The most economical methods for storing energy so far are insulated tanks of water or bins of rocks. Substances whose melting points are in the right temperature range for the application (60° to 100° C for heating, 200° C or more for thermal power plants or high-temperature industrial applications) could store significant amounts of energy as latent heat of melting. But various practical difficulties with this approach have so far resisted solution, despite research over several decades.[231] Characteristics of various means of heat storage are presented in Table 8-24.

TABLE 8-24
Thermal Energy Storage

Material and method	*Energy densities* MJ/m^3	KJ/kg
Water heated 20°C	47	47
Rocks (30% void space) heated 20°C	19	10
Sodium metal melting at 98°C	93	98
Ferric chloride melting at 304°C	770	265
Gasoline chemical energy*	34,000	51,000

*For comparison.
Source: H. C. Hottel and J. B. Howard, *New energy technology: Some facts and assessments,* p. 96.

Electricity is extremely difficult to store *as* electricity. Small amounts are stored for use in scientific experiments in devices called capacitor banks, which accumulate electric charges on oppositely charged plates separated by insulators. But those devices store only small amounts of energy and are exceedingly expensive. Substantial amounts of electrical energy can be stored in the magnetic fields of large superconducting magnets (perhaps 10 to 50 MJ/m^3). Such magnets were still an experimental technology in the mid-1970s, but the possibility of storing commercial electricity that way was under investigation.[232]

Most "electricity storage" actually stores some other kind of energy that is readily produced from electricity and readily converted back to it. Batteries, for example, store electricity as chemical energy (see the description of fuel cells, above). Batteries tend to be heavy, bulky, and expensive, however, compared to equipment for storing and converting like amounts of energy with, say, gasoline. The familiar lead-acid automobile battery stores about 120 kilojoules of electrical energy (33 watt hours) per kilogram, nickel-zinc batteries about twice as much, and high-temperature sodium-sulfur batteries 10 times as much (about 1200 kJ/kg).[233] The overall efficiency of charging and discharging (that is, electricity out divided by electricity in) in such batteries is 65 to 80 percent. So far, batteries have been much too expensive for use in storing the large amounts of electricity needed to supply peak loads in electric-utility systems, although they are

[228]See Hammond, Metz, and Maugh, *Energy,* chapter 16.
[229]Ibid.
[230]For an introduction to this controversy, see L. Young and H. Young, Pollution by electrical transmission, and the rebuttal and rejoinder in *Bulletin of the Atomic Scientists,* vol. 31, no. 7, pp. 31–53.
[231]See Hottel and Howard, *New energy,* pp. 94–100.
[232]R. Hein, Superconductivity: Large scale applications.
[233]Hottel and Howard, *New energy,* pp. 91–93, 306–310.

used sometimes to store electricity produced by small windmills.

The principal method of electricity storage by utilities in the United States is pumped storage, wherein the energy is actually stored as the potential energy of water pumped uphill. Pumped-storage systems consist of two reservoirs, one high and one low, connected by pipes containing dual-purpose pump-turbines. During periods of low demand, such as late at night, electricity from the primary source (fossil fuels, fission, perhaps solar energy in the future) is used to pump water from the lower reservoir to the higher one. At times of high demand, the water is allowed to fall back to the lower reservoir, thus spinning the turbines and generating electricity. The overall efficiency of the exchange is near 70 percent.[234] Some environmental disruption is generally involved in the construction of the upper reservoir (the lower one is usually a natural body of water). There are few enough satisfactory sites that pumped storage is unlikely ever to amount to more than a small percentage of total generating capacity in the United States. Thus, it can meet only a little of the need for peaking and backup power.

Flywheels provide another means of storing energy, as mechanical energy of rotation of massive, rapidly spinning discs. The energy storable in flywheels is limited by the strength of materials—as speed of rotation (and stored energy) increases, at some point the stresses in the wheel become too great and the material fractures and flies apart. Flywheels made of conventional steels are limited to the range of energy storage per kilogram characterizing lead-acid and nickel-zinc batteries. New high-strength materials and novel flywheel designs that exploit the special properties of those materials may be able to increase the performance roughly tenfold.[235] That would make flywheels potentially attractive for energy storage in electric-utility systems and perhaps also, if safety can be assured, as the means by which energy is stored in electric automobiles.

Hydrogen is a portable chemical fuel that can be manufactured by dissociating water using any of several processes, given a primary energy source. It can also be manufactured from fossil fuels. Hydrogen is relatively clean burning, producing only water as a combustion product and oxides of nitrogen as a side product if it is burned in air. It is generally cheaper to transport hydrogen in pipelines than to transmit an equivalent amount of electricity. Hydrogen offers a means of storing and transporting energy obtained from intermittent sources such as sunlight, and it could offer a way for electricity from nuclear fission and nuclear fusion to serve as the energy source for aircraft and other applications requiring portability, long after the fossil fuels are gone. An important drawback of hydrogen produced by using electricity is the low overall efficiency of the process—typically less than 60 percent. Thermochemical processes for the production of hydrogen are under intensive investigation; they consist of a series of chemical reactions at various temperatures, in which water is decomposed and all the other reactants are recycled. The primary energy source could be sunlight or some more conventional source.[236]

The energy stored in liquid hydrogen is three times that in an equal amount of gasoline by weight but one-third that in an equal amount of gasoline by volume. The low volumetric energy content and relative difficulty of maintaining hydrogen as a liquid (which requires very low temperatures) have led to interest in storing hydrogen as solid metal hydrides for use in automobiles. Such hydrides have twice the volumetric energy content of liquid hydrogen, or about two-thirds that of gasoline. They would appear also to be somewhat safer than using liquid or gaseous hydrogen in cars (although it is possible that gasoline is more dangerous than hydrogen in any case). Another approach is to combine hydrogen and carbon monoxide to produce the liquid fuel methanol ($2H_2 + CO \longrightarrow CH_3OH$). Much research and development remains to be done before hydrogen and its derivatives see widespread use as fuel, but enthusiasts see such advantages that they already have coined the term *the hydrogen economy* to describe a hydrogen-centered energy system of the future.[237]

[234] Science and Public Policy, *Energy alternatives,* chapter 9.

[235] R. Post and S. Post, Flywheels. See also Post et al., Letters.

[236] An excellent review article covering hydrogen production, properties, and prospects is C. Bamberger and J. Braunstein, Hydrogen: A versatile element. See also C. Marchetti, Hydrogen and energy.

[237] D. Gregory, The hydrogen economy; J. O'M. Bockris, A hydrogen economy.

"Waste" Heat

Because it is not possible to convert heat entirely to work (see the discussion of the second law of thermodynamics in Box 2-3), all thermal power plants deliver heat as well as electricity. This is so whether the original energy source is the combustion of fossil fuel, fission, fusion, geothermal energy, or sunlight. Most commonly, the heat is considered a waste product and is delivered not to a customer, as the electricity is, but to the environment. The reasons for this lie in thermodynamics and economics: Thermodynamically, the energy discharged is of low quality (that is, it is not much warmer than the environment, and so its heat is not easy to put to use). Economically, it has been cheaper to burn more fuel to meet energy needs than to invest in equipment that could harness some of the low-quality energy being discharged from power plants.

This has not been true everywhere, however, and it will not necessarily be true in the future. Particularly in Europe, where fuel has been more expensive than in the United States, the technology of using heat discharged from electric power plants to heat buildings and supply energy for low-temperature industrial processes has been applied extensively. Sometimes this involves lowering somewhat the fraction of fuel energy that is converted to electricity, in order to increase the temperature and hence the usefulness of the discharged heat. In Sweden, the fraction of the fuel's energy converted to electricity in power plants averages 29 percent (compared to 32 percent in the United States), but the Swedes utilize another 24 percent of the fuel's energy as heat; they waste only 47 percent. In the United States, 68 percent is wasted.[238] Recognition in the United States, too, that economic and environmental constraints mean energy must be used more carefully, should lead to the siting of more industrial plants that use low-temperature heat next to power plants that can supply that heat very cheaply.

One must pay to get rid of most of the heat that is not used. That is, failure to remove heat from the condenser of a steam cycle and deposit it somewhere else would disrupt the system as effectively as a clogged drain disrupts a sink. The methods for removing the heat and discharging it somewhere in the environment all cost money and energy in varying degrees.

The simplest approach is once-through cooling—taking cool water from a river, lake, bay, or ocean, passing it through a condenser where it picks up the waste heat, and discharging it to the original source some 8° to 10° C (15° to 18° F) warmer than when it began. A fossil-fueled electric power plant running at 1000 electrical megawatts with an efficiency of 40 percent warms about 32 cubic meters of water per second (500,000 gallons per minute) by 8° C. A nuclear plant delivering the same amount of electricity at 32 percent efficiency (the figure for an LWR) causes the same temperature rise in 53 cubic meters of water per second. (That corresponds to the entire flow of a moderate-size stream.) The thermal discharge to water from the nuclear plant is higher not only because the efficiency of operation is lower, but also because the fossil-fueled plant discharges about 15 percent of its waste heat directly to the atmosphere via the stack.

Ecological effects of once-through cooling include: direct effects on aquatic organisms due to warmer water or rapid changes in temperature when the plant goes on and off; reduction in the water's capacity to assimilate wastes, because its oxygen content is lower; increased evaporation from the water surface, reducing the availability of water downstream and increasing its salinity; destruction of organisms, particularly juveniles, which pass through the intakes and condensers; and water pollution by chemical compounds added to condenser water to suppress slime and scale. There is a large literature concerning these effects; how harmful they are in a given situation is often controversial.[239] In any case, once-through cooling is rarely considered acceptable for new power plants except at ocean sites, which are increasingly scarce because of competition for that land. Even in oceanside facilities, it is often deemed necessary to construct expensive outfalls that spread the warmed water over large areas or into deeper water offshore.

One alternative to once-through cooling that is possible in a few locations is to construct *cooling ponds*. They

[238]L. Schipper and A. Lichtenberg, Efficient energy use and well-being: The Swedish example.

[239]F. Parker and P. Krenkel, *Physical and engineering aspects of thermal pollution;* see also Chapter 10 here.

require 4 to 8 square kilometers (1000 to 2000 acres) of land per 1000 electrical megawatts of generating capacity, and a source of water to replace that which evaporates. The ponds might be usable for other purposes, such as aquaculture or algae farming.[240]

Coming into much wider use are *wet-cooling towers*, in which heated cooling water from the power plant condenser falls through an upward-moving stream of air to be cooled mainly by evaporation. The air may be forced through the tower by fans (in mechanical-draft towers) or by forces arising from the shape of the tower and the humidity inside (natural-draft towers). The first requires energy to operate; the second is large and expensive to build—as much as 180 meters in diameter at the base and 150 meters high. Both kinds of wet tower consume significant amounts of water by evaporation—10 million cubic meters (8300 acre feet) per year for a 1000-megawatt fossil-fueled plant averaging 75 percent of peak capacity, 17 million cubic meters per year for an LWR of the same size and capacity factor. The total water consumption is about 60 percent higher than those figures, because it is necessary to discharge some water laden with dissolved salts that are not removed in the evaporation process. This discharge is called blowdown. A modest amount of water is also lost as drift (droplets blown out of the tower as liquid without evaporating). Both drift and blowdown water are laden with chemicals that have been added to the circulating water to control corrosion, scale, and slime—they include sulfuric acid, chromates, copper compounds, and chlorine.[241]

Dry-cooling towers avoid the problems of water consumption and water pollution of wet towers by circulating the water through an elaborate array of closed passages so none is lost; the heat is transferred to air flowing over and around the passages much as in the radiator of an automobile. Dry towers, however, are expensive both to construct and to operate. Existing designs increase fuel consumption for a given net electricity output by about 4 percent.[242] They have been used only in small power plants.

[240]W. Oswald, Ecological management of thermal discharges.

[241]An introduction to cooling technology is R. Woodson, Cooling towers; a more complete and more technical description is in Pigford, et al., *Fuel cycles,* chapter 6.

[242]Woodson, Cooling towers; Pigford, Keaton, and Cukor, *Fuel cycles.*

Comparing Costs and Impacts of Energy Technologies

A major reason for the particularly rapid growth of energy use per capita in the past two decades was that energy was cheaper than what it replaced—human labor and time, for example. More than this, it was so cheap in the United States in relation to the other expenditures of the middle and upper classes that there was little incentive for those people not to waste it with abandon. Two kinds of previously hidden costs have now become apparent. First, the cost of depleting the richest, most accessible fossil fuels must now be paid in the form of rapidly rising expenses for locating, extracting, and processing the leaner and more remote deposits that remain, and for developing and deploying sophisticated technologies to harness less limited substitutes. Second, as the combination of population growth and rising energy use per person has driven the sheer size of energy operations upward, the environmental and social costs of energy—once ignorable—have become pervasive and painful. Rising demand for other commodities (water, coastal land, investment capital), whose availability may be diminished by growing energy systems, has intensified the relatively new sensation of the high cost of energy.

Economic costs. The economic costs of energy technology can be broken down into capital costs (construction and interest during construction) and operating costs (fuel, water, wages, maintenance, insurance, and so forth, in operation). High capital costs cause special difficulties because the money must be spent, and interest paid on amounts borrowed, well before the facilities start to operate. This situation is exacerbated by high rates of growth, because the ratio of facilities under construction to facilities in operation is high during such periods. Summarized in Table 8-25 are the capital costs associated in the mid-1970s with energy facilities of various kinds.[243] Those amounts are roughly what one would have to pay (in 1974 dollars) to build or buy such facilities in the mid-1970s per kilowatt of energy flow

[243]Partly adapted from Anderson, et al. *An assessment.*

handled. The numbers illustrate the differences in cost between shallow, rich deposits and deep, lean ones (Persian Gulf compared to U.S onshore oil), and the still higher costs associated with synthetic fuels (coal liquefaction) and less exhaustible sources (solar, nuclear). The numbers also suggest that merely replacing the present thermal electricity generating plants in the United States (439 million electrical kilowatts in 1975) as they wear out will cost 150 billion to 200 billion 1974 dollars. One study performed for the federal government indicated that the investment in the U.S. energy industry between 1974 and 1985 would have to be 585 billion 1974 dollars in order to maintain an average annual growth of energy supply of 3.6 percent while reducing reliance on imports.[244] The Energy Policy Project of the Ford Foundation estimated that a capital investment of 2150 billion 1974 dollars would be required to maintain a total energy growth of 3.4 percent per year in the United States between 1975 and 2000.[245]

In each of the investment figures cited, electricity-generation facilities account for about 43 percent. The especially heavy capital burden associated with electricity is due not only to the technical complexity of generating plants, but also to the historical necessity of building facilities with about twice as much electricity-generating capacity as the average demand requires. The reasons for this situation and some of its ramifications are explored in Box 8-7.

The costs of construction, interest, taxes, labor, and other inputs (and, of course, profits) at each stage of energy processing determine the price of the energy form as it emerges from that stage. Recent prices of various energy forms in 1975 dollars are listed in Table 8-26. Note the large increases in cost that are associated with extensive processing.

Because nuclear plants are the most expensive to build of the presently available technologies for electricity generation, and because their fuel is relatively cheap, it becomes especially important economically that those plants be run near their full capacity as many hours per

[244]Anderson et al., *An assessment.*

[245]Energy Policy Project, Ford Foundation, *A time to choose,* Ballinger, Cambridge, Mass., 1974, p. 470. (We have converted the reference's 1970 dollars to 1974 dollars, with an inflation factor of 1.27.)

TABLE 8-25
Capital Costs for Energy Technologies (1974 dollars)

Fuel and heat	*Dollars per thermal kilowatt of flow (24-hour average)*
Oil well, Persian Gulf	4
Oil well, U.S. onshore	100
Oil well, U.S. offshore	200
Oil pipeline (1500 km)	12
Tanker from Persian Gulf	20
Oil refinery	30
Coal strip mine	20
Coal underground mine	40
Coal train (1500 km)	4
Coal slurry pipeline (1500 km)	25
Coal liquefaction or gasification	180
Oil shale extraction and processing	200
Solar home heating	600
Electricity	***Dollars per electrical kilowatt***
Geothermal dry-steam plant	200
Hydro dam and power plant	300
Coal-fired plant	450
Fission reactor (light-water cooled)	600
Uranium mining and milling*	3
Uranium enrichment*	23
Solar thermal electric plant**	1200(??)
Fusion reactor	1200(??)
Transmission and distribution of electricity	200

*Cost normalized to peak electrical kilowatts of reactor capacity.
**Cost is not based on peak power but on yearly production in kwh divided by 6100 hours. This puts the capital cost on a comparable basis with a nuclear or fossil-fueled plant with an annual load factor of 70 percent.

TABLE 8-26
Prices of Energy Forms (1975 dollars)

Energy form	*Price ($/GJ)**
Bituminous coal ($20/short ton, to electric utilities)	0.79
Natural gas ($1/1000 ft^3 to California residence)	1.00
Crude petroleum ($11/bbl, to refinery)	1.86
Jet fuel ($0.40/gal, to airlines)	3.03
Gasoline ($0.65/gal, retail)	4.92
Electricity ($0.03/kwh, to California residence)	8.33
Bread ($0.50/lb, retail)	92.50

*1 gigajoule *(GJ)* = 1000 *MJ* = 0.95×10^6 Btu.

BOX 8-7 Producing Electricity on Demand

Because no economical means for storing large quantities of electricity is available, and because electricity travels through wires at essentially the speed of light, a power company must generate the electricity it sells at virtually the instant its customers demand it. If 500,000 New Yorkers happen to turn on their 200-watt television sets to watch the evening news at the same moment, the load on Consolidated Edison's generating system instantaneously increases by 100 megawatts—almost 40 percent of the capacity of the Indian Point nuclear generating plant. As this example suggests, of course, the amount of electricity demanded by customers, individually and in the aggregate, varies from minute to minute, from hour to hour, and indeed from season to season. The highest demands are called *peak loads:* the daily peak is associated with lights, television, electric ranges, and so forth being turned on in the evening; the yearly peaks are in the coldest part of winter (heating) and the hottest part of summer (air conditioning—the larger demand of the two). The minimum demand on the system is called the *baseload.*

The newest, most efficient generating plants in a power company's inventory are baseloaded—they are kept running close to their full capacity as much of the time as their need for routine maintenance and freedom from breakdowns permit. Additional plants are brought on line to meet daily peaks, and others may stand by for most of the year waiting for those coldest and hottest days (or for the baseloaded plants to break down). The *load factor*—for a single plant or for a whole system of plants—is the amount of electric energy actually generated in a specified period divided by the amount that could have been generated in that period if all plants had worked at full capacity the whole time. The load factor of the U.S. utility system in 1974 was about 45 percent. All that expensive generating capacity standing unused, of course, must still be paid for, and there is no one but consumers to pay (or taxpayers, if floundering utilities have to be rescued from bankruptcy by government).

A traditional approach has been to offer large manufacturing companies substantial discounts for buying large amounts of electricity late at night (in off-peak hours), thus permitting generating capacity that would otherwise not be used at that time to earn some revenue. An approach that has been suggested as being more likely to encourage conservation as well as raising the load factor would be peak pricing—charging a surcharge for electricity consumed during peak periods, to encourage people to move discretionary uses of electricity (for example, the operation of clothes washers and dryers) away from the peak times. This would require special meters—doubtless worth it.

year as possible. That is, since a plant, once built, must be paid for whether it is running or not, and since the cost of nuclear fuel to run it is small compared to the plant's construction cost, the way to achieve a low cost per kilowatt hour of electricity is to produce as much electricity per plant per year as possible—that is, to achieve a high capacity factor. (For this reason, power companies try to use their nuclear plants to meet the baseload and use other kinds of generating capacity to match the rises and falls associated with the peaks.) If the large nuclear power plants that first came into commercial operation in the late 1960s and early 1970s should prove incapable of maintaining high capacity factors over long operating lifetimes—say, 20 to 25 years each—then the cost of electricity from fission would turn out to be much higher than has been advertised. The long-term reliability of large nuclear power plants is still unknown (the first one larger than 500 electrical megawatts began commercial operation only in 1968), but the operating record as of the mid-1970s is disturbing. The average capacity factor of nuclear plants has been 50 to 60 percent, rather than the predicted 70 to 80 percent.[246]

Resource requirements. Part of the economic cost of energy technology is the value of physical resources, other than fuels, that are used in the construction or operation of energy facilities. Land, water, and nonfuel mineral resources are three such resources on which present and future energy technologies can make heavy demands. It is not obvious that the apparent economic

[246]Comey, Elastic statistics; C. Komanoff, *Power plant performance.*

TABLE 8-27
Land Use in Fuel Cycles for Electricity Generation

Fuel	*Inventory (km²/plant)**	*Temporary commitment (km² yr/plant yr)***	*Permanent commitment (km²/plant yr)*
Deep-mined coal	12–15	10–29	small
Surface-mined coal	12–15	20–240	small
Oil	3–14	small	small
Surface-mined uranium for LWR	1	1–2	0.001
Solar-thermal†	56	small	small

*Includes facilities for processing and transportation, but not transmission.
**Ten-year mean time for restoration to other use.
†Plant capable of delivering 1000-Mwe-yr per yr at 100% load factor (18 Mwe average per km²).
Source: R. Budnitz and J. Holdren, Social and environmental costs of energy systems.

TABLE 8-28
Use of Water in Fuel Cycles for Electricity Generation (million m³/plant yr)

Fuel	*Evaporated in wet towers at power plant*	*Blowdown water in plant cooling towers**	*Fuel-processing water use***	*Waste-management water use***
Standard coal†	11.0	6.6	0.3	1.7
Coal gasification/Combined-cycle††	6.6	4.0	0.5	small
Oil (residual fuel oil)	10.0	6.0	1.5	small
Uranium (LWR)	17.0	10.0	0.5	0.01

*Returned to surface polluted.
**Some evaporated; some returned.
†Wet-lime scrubbing for SO_2 removal.
††Combined-cycle power plant efficiency is 47 percent; fuel-cycle thermal efficiency is 37 percent.
Source: R. Budnitz and J. Holdren, Social and environmental costs of energy systems.

value of those resources—the price energy companies must pay to use them—is an adequate measure of the real cost to society of making the resources unavailable for other uses now or in the future. It is therefore important to look at the actual quantities of resources involved, and not just at the present economic cost of those resources. Land and water requirements for a variety of energy technologies are indicated in Tables 8-27 and 8-28.

Requirements of various energy technologies for materials other than fuel and water need closer attention. Although the materials demands of such future technologies as controlled nuclear fusion are highly uncertain, because no one yet knows just what those systems will look like, it is apparent that demands on alloying elements and special-purpose materials such as vanadium, chromium, nickel, and beryllium could be significant if very large generating capacities are envisioned.[247] Heavy materials demands may be an important liability of the widespread use of some kinds of solar-energy technology, although solar systems are not likely to require as exotic materials as fusion will.

The construction and operation of energy facilities themselves requires some energy. In other words, it takes energy to get energy. It is a characteristic of rich energy resources, such as thick coal beds right at the surface of the ground, that only a small amount of energy must be invested in exploration and harvesting in order to reap a large energy reward. If the resource is deeper or leaner, or if it must be processed extensively before use, the necessary investment in energy increases along with the economic one. It is possible in principle to envision an energy resource so lean or so intractable that more energy

[247]Kulcinski, Fusion power.

must be spent to obtain and process the fuel than it contains. Only if the fuel had some very special properties could that be considered a viable enterprise. (Food is an example of a fuel with such properties—namely, it is suitable for running the bodily machinery of human beings. The U.S. system of food production and processing invests 6 to 60 kilocalories of other fuels for every kilocalorie of food energy consumed, as outlined in Box 8-6.)

The study of the energy investments needed to get energy has acquired the name *net energy analysis.* In such analysis one should distinguish among three general kinds of investments and/or losses: (1) the part of the resource that is dispersed or left in the ground in nonretrievable form in the course of extraction and processing operations; (2) the part of the resource that is actually used as energy to support extraction and processing operations; (3) the inputs of other energy forms (fuel, electricity) needed to support those operations.

Accurate figures for energy investment during construction are difficult to obtain. But those energy inputs cannot be neglected in net energy analysis, and they are especially important where an energy system is growing rapidly. In that situation, significant inputs of energy are being made to a large number of facilities under construction that will not yield energy outputs until they are completed. One analysis has indicated that light-water-cooled nuclear reactors as a system become net consumers of energy if the system grows with a doubling time shorter than 4.5 years, even though each such reactor is a substantial net producer of energy over its operating lifetime.[248] This result, if confirmed, is a major setback for the view that dependence on fossil fuels can be reduced rapidly by means of the very rapid growth of nuclear power.

Assaults on people and ecosystems. Beyond the use of scarce resources, the environmental impact of energy technology and energy use can best be discussed by distinguishing between two aspects of the situation: what energy technology does *to* or puts *into* the environment, and what the consequences of those actions or inputs are (that is, how the environment responds to what is done to it or put into it). The inputs can be classified as effluents, accidents, and other environmental transformations. By *effluents* we mean routine discharges to the environment—air, water, and land—that are associated with the normal operation of energy systems (as distinguished from accidents). We define accidents broadly to include not only malfunctions caused by defective equipment or human error, but also disruptions caused by natural events (storms, earthquakes, tsunamis) and by malicious human intervention (sabotage, terrorism, acts of war). A summary of some of the main types of accidents, effluents, and environmental transformations associated with various energy technologies appears in Table 8-29.

The consequences of these inputs fall into four categories: (1) human death and disease as direct results; (2) direct damage to economic goods and services (for example, crops, domestic animals, property, tourism); (3) disruption of natural biological and geophysical processes, with consequent risk or damage to the "free" goods and services those processes provide; (4) aesthetic impact (litter, cluttered landscape, impaired visibility). Note that a single input may produce consequences of all four kinds. Oxides of nitrogen produced by combustion, for example, cause or aggravate respiratory disease, damage crops, alter the acidity of rainfall, and contribute to photochemical smog that impairs visibility. The effects on health, property and ecological systems that result from pollution and other disruptions—not only from energy technology but from other activities producing similar inputs to the environment—are the subject of detailed treatments in Chapter 10 and Chapter 11.

Impact on social systems. Adverse impacts of energy technology on human well-being can manifest themselves not only in the form of direct economic costs and damages to the physical environment but also as disruptions of the fabric of social systems. These can result, for example, from the kinds and physical scales of technologies that are chosen, from the geographical patterns of location of energy facilities, and from the degree of centralization and interconnectedness in energy systems.[248a] Impacts of particular concern include:

[248]P. F. Chapman, The ins and outs of nuclear power. See also ERDA 76-1, Appendix B, Net energy analysis of nuclear power production.

[248a]An extended discussion of the social consequences of alternative energy futures for the United States is given by A. Lovins, Energy strategy: The road not taken. See also R. Budnitz and J. Holdren, Social and environmental costs of energy systems; and E. Cook, *Man, energy, society.*

TABLE 8-29
Some Negative Impacts of Energy Production and Use

ACCIDENTS
- Roof collapse or gas explosion in mine
- Tanker fire or explosion (oil or liquefied natural gas)
- Dam failure
- Refinery fire
- Core meltdown and breach of containment of nuclear reactor
- Leakage of radioactive waste from storage facility
- Fire in nuclear fabrication or reprocessing
- Electrical fire
- Gas explosion in building
- Automobile crash

EFFLUENTS
- Unburned or incompletely burned fuel: hydrocarbons, carbon monoxide, plutonium
- "Combustion" products and side products: carbon dioxide, water vapor, nitrogen oxides, sulfur oxides, lead compounds (from gasoline additives), fission products, tritium (fission and fusion)
- Activation products (from neutrons in fusion and fission)
- Trace contaminants: ash particles, mercury and other heavy metals (in coal and petroleum), radon (in uranium ore, coal, and geothermal steam), hydrogen sulfide (in geothermal steam), salts and brines (in geothermal steam or hot water, wastes from harvesting fossil and nuclear fuels)
- Stray electromagnetic fields and ionizing radiation: fields (from microwave and overhead transmission systems), neutrons and X-rays (from fission and fusion reactors)
- Noise
- Heat

ENVIRONMENTAL TRANSFORMATIONS
- Subsidence of ground (extraction of fossil fuels, geothermal steam)
- Loss of soil and vegetation, alteration of topography (unreclaimed surface mining)
- Alteration of river flows and evaporation patterns by hydro projects
- Suburbanization from use of automobiles
- Landscape clutter with transmission lines, oil derricks, other facilities

aggravation of inequity; redistribution of population; facilitation of military developments; and increased vulnerabilities (*of* the energy sector or society as a whole, *to* disruptions of natural or human origins). Some examples related to specific aspects of energy technology appear in Table 8-30. More extensive discussions of some of these matters will be found in Chapters 14 and 15.

Of perhaps equal importance are the adverse effects of society's *responses* to impacts or threats of impacts. These responses may take the form of uneasiness and mistrust at the level of the individual, and centralization of authority and misuse of power (leading in turn to loss of public participation in decision making and even loss of civil liberties) at the level of governments. Conceivably the most serious liability of such energy sources as fission and fusion is that, in the forms now in use or envisioned, they lend themselves to economic application only in units so large as to foster excessive centralization.

ENERGY USE AND CONSERVATION

Increasing the availability of energy by means of expanding reliance on old technologies and developing and deploying new ones is a costly and risky enterprise, economically as well as environmentally. Minimizing environmental and social risk should be elevated to the top of the list of criteria governing the choice of which technologies are to be relied upon most heavily. But it seems likely that the energy sources best able to meet that criterion will be both expensive economically and slow to be fully developed and deployed. For the United States and other industrial nations, there is no mix of technologies available or in prospect that can make ten to thirty years of further energy growth at 4, 3, or even 2 percent per year look appealing.

It is essential therefore, to examine the possibility of avoiding such growth by rational conservation of energy. By this we mean not doing without energy, or "going

TABLE 8-30
Some Social Impacts of Energy Technology

AGGRAVATION OF INEQUITY	
Fossil fuels	Create worst air pollution in central cities from which poor cannot escape
Nuclear fission and fusion	Steers rich-country research and development into channels with little direct early benefit for poor countries
End-use	Energy-intensive mechanization and automation may eliminate unskilled jobs
REDISTRIBUTION OF POPULATION AND ECONOMIC ACTIVITY	
Hydropower	Displacement of valley residents
Offshore oil, imported oil, and gas	Coastal urbanization around support facilities
Western coal	Haphazard development on the High Plains
Solar	Development in the Southwest desert
FACILITATION OF MILITARY DEVELOPMENTS	
Fission	International proliferation of nuclear weapons
Imported oil	Oil revenues fund armaments for exporting nations
Laser fusion	Links to military lasers and design of fusion bombs
OTHER ALTERED VULNERABILITIES	
Hydropower	Dam failure from earthquake or sabotage
Fission	Vulnerability to terrorist nuclear bombs or radiological weapons
Imported oil	Political blackmail by exporters
All-electric economy	Dependence on central authority; regional blackout from central-system accident or sabotage

Source: J. Holdren, Costs of energy as potential limits to growth.

TABLE 8-31
Approaches to Energy Conservation in the Short and Middle Terms

	Short term (5 years)	*Middle term (5–15 years)*
LEAK-PLUGGING	More insulation in buildings More efficient air conditioners Use of heat pumps for heating	More efficient cars More efficient building design More efficient power plants
MODE-MIXING	Switch freight to rail Dress more appropriately for weather Switch containers to glass returnables	Increase durability of goods (more repair, less manufacture) Reliable, convenient urban transit Switch intercity passengers to fast rail carriers
OUTPUT-JUGGLING	More sailboats, fewer motorboats More backpacks, fewer trail bikes More books, fewer movies	More communication, less business travel More education, art, music, less motorized recreation More health services, less heavy manufacturing
BELT-TIGHTENING	Car pools, lower speed limit, less pleasure driving Houses cooler in winter, warmer in summer	Live closer to work Smaller dwellings

back to caves and candles" but, rather, doing better with the energy that is available—increasing the amount of human well-being extracted from each bit of energy use. It is helpful in this context to distinguish among four classes of energy conservation measures:

1. "leak-plugging" or the "technical fix," whereby ways are found to perform exactly the same services for less energy, by improving technology or operating procedures or both—essentially no difference is noticed by the consumer;

2. "mode-mixing," whereby the same general functions and services of energy are performed, but with significant differences in approach—the consumer perceives some difference, but does not feel worse off;

3. "output juggling," whereby the mix of goods and services in the economy is changed to emphasize those areas that deliver the highest contributions to income and employment per unit of energy use—the consumer perceives significant differences, but most do not feel worse off;

4. "belt-tightening," whereby changes in behavior or expectations are required that many consumers regard as disruptive and detracting from well-being.

Examples of measures in the four categories are given in Table 8-31 for short-term (next five years) and middle-term (five to fifteen years) periods, in which significant impact of the various conservation measures could begin to be felt. Neither with respect to time nor with respect to the categories themselves are the boundaries always sharply defined. Major effort could accelerate the impact of some measures or neglect could delay the impact of any of them. One person might consider, say, bicycling to work a case of mode-mixing that actually made him/her better off, while another would consider bicycling a clear case of belt-tightening. Obviously, conservation based on the first three categories will be easiest to implement; they are the first things a rational society will do when it perceives the need for conservation in time. Of course, modest forms of belt-tightening may also be undertaken willingly by a rational society interested in gaining economic and environmental benefits tomorrow in exchange for restraint today. The most severe forms of belt-tightening, enforced by rationing, long gasoline lines, brownouts, and so on, are the result of discounting the need for rational conservation and failing to act in time.

Several careful studies have shown that the energy-saving potential of rational conservation in the United States is enormous.[249] Their conclusions have been based on sector-by-sector breakdowns of energy use in the United States and examinations of the opportunities for conservation in each sector. Such a breakdown for 1973 is shown in Table 8-32. One insight that has emerged is that the same mix of goods and services enjoyed by the U.S. population in the early 1970s *could* have been provided at a level of energy use around 60 percent of that which actually prevailed. (Makhijani and Lichtenberg arrived at 62 percent, considering only measures in the leak-plugging and mode-mixing categories; using more recent information about attainable efficiencies, Ross and Williams calculated a figure of 57 percent with leak-plugging measures alone.)

A somewhat more instructive (but also more difficult) approach is to take into account population growth, economic growth, and difficulties in implementing conservation measures in order to calculate the realistically attainable effect of conservation in slowing energy growth at various times in the future. An admittedly rough cut at this approach by the Office of Emergency Preparedness in the Executive Office of the President of the United States concluded in 1972 that measures of modest economic and social impact (mostly leak-plugging plus a little mode-mixing) could cut *in half* the growth in use of energy expected under business-as-usual growth forecasts for the period between 1971 and 1985.

A more thorough study of overall conservation potential was made by the Energy Policy Project of the Ford Foundation, which analyzed and described three scenarios: (1) Historical growth—a continuation of the 1950–1970 trend; (2) Technical Fix—accounting for

[249]Among the most important of these are A. Makhijani and A. Lichtenberg, *An assessment of energy and materials utilization in the U.S.A.;* Office of Emergency Preparedness (OEP), *The potential for energy conservation;* Energy Policy Project, *A time to choose;* American Physical Society, *Efficient use;* Marc Ross and Robert Williams, The potential for fuel conservation; L. Schipper, Raising the productivity of energy utilization.

TABLE 8-32
Uses of Energy in the United States in 1973

	Energy used (trillion MJ)	*Percent of total energy used*
RESIDENTIAL		
Space heating	7.59	9.6
Water heating	2.25	2.9
Refrigeration	1.24	1.6
Air conditioning	1.06	1.3
Lighting	0.87	1.1
Cooking	0.66	0.8
Drying clothes	0.36	0.5
Other electric	0.82	1.0
Subtotal	14.85	18.8
COMMERCIAL		
Space heating	4.51	5.7
Lighting	3.44	4.4
Air conditioning	1.72	2.2
Refrigeration	0.92	1.2
Water heating	0.64	0.8
Cooking	0.16	0.2
Asphalt or road oil	1.33	1.7
Subtotal	12.72	16.2
INDUSTRIAL		
Process steam	11.47	14.6
Direct heat	7.48	9.5
Electric drive	6.84	8.7
Feedstocks	4.21	5.3
Electrolytic processes	0.99	1.3
Other electric	0.30	0.4
Subtotal	31.29	39.8
TRANSPORTATION		
Autos	10.35	13.1
Trucks	4.11	5.2
Pipelines	1.91	2.4
Airplanes	1.36	1.7
Rail	0.66	0.8
Ships	0.27	0.3
Buses	0.17	0.2
Other	1.16	1.5
Subtotal	19.99	25.2
Total	78.85	100

Note: Some figures are uncertain to ±20 percent.
Source: Ross and Williams, The potential for fuel conservation.

attainable rates of implementation of measures in the leak-plugging and mode-mixing categories but no output-juggling or belt-tightening; and (3) Zero Energy Growth—in which output-juggling and lifestyle changes that some would consider belt-tightening were added to the Technical-Fix measures. (Energy use in this "Zero Growth" scenario actually only levels off in the year 2000, at a value about a third larger than the 1975 figure.)

The Ford results and those of several other forecasts with and without conservation are summarized in Table 8-33.

The remarkably consistent conclusion of the independent evaluations outlined in Table 8-33 is that increases in efficiency alone could be saving 13 trillion to 25 trillion megajoules per year by 1985 and 66 trillion megajoules per year by the year 2000, compared to forecasted energy use in the absence of conservation measures. (The largest figure mentioned is nearly equal to *total* U.S. energy use in 1970; a trillion megajoules is 0.95 quadrillion Btu.) Promoting some output juggling and lifestyle changes in addition to the increases in efficiency could raise the savings to as much as 90 trillion megajoules in the year 2000.

A major two-year energy study being conducted for ERDA by the National Academy of Sciences indicated in its interim report in January 1977 that the range of scenarios being considered for the United States in the year 2010 spanned a range of total energy use from 74 trillion to 220 trillion megajoules.[249a] The lower figure is about the same as U.S. energy use in 1975, and represents a drastic downward revision in the low end of the range of energy futures given credibility by major organizations. Obviously, very large efforts at increasing the efficiency of energy use would be required to bring about this low-growth future, but the flavor of the Academy's report suggested this might be achieved without great economic disruption.[249b]

Before considering more closely the economic implications of such major programs of energy conservation, it is useful to look more closely at some of the methods by which the savings could be achieved.

Energy in Buildings

According to Table 8-32, almost 20 percent of all energy use in the United States goes for heating and air conditioning dwellings and commercial buildings. Such buildings are, for the most part, poorly insulated, overventilated (more than enough air changes per hour, for

[249a]National Academy of Sciences, *Interim Report of the National Research Council Committee on Nuclear and Alternative Energy Systems.*

[249b]See also P. M. Boffey, Academy study finds low energy growth won't be painful, *Science,* vol. 195, p. 380 (January 28).

each of which a buildingful of outside air must be heated or cooled to the desired inside temperature), and not designed to take advantage of the outside environment when it is suitable (for example, admitting sunlight through south-facing windows in winter).[250] This is in addition to the strange penchant of Americans—much rarer where energy has been more expensive—for heating the same buildings in winter (to 24° C, or 75° F) that they overcool in summer (to 20° C, or 68° F). Even the very large buildings operated by major firms, from which one might expect thriftier practices, are often operated in needlessly wasteful fashion—for example, without reducing furnace thermostat settings drastically when the buildings are unoccupied.[251]

Such shortcomings in energy management in buildings are compounded by two others: the widespread use, especially in dwellings, of heating and cooling units that are much less efficient than is possible and desirable, and excessive lighting in commercial buildings, which is an inefficient way to heat in winter and adds a heavy burden on the air-conditioning system in the summer. Heating with electrically driven heat pumps (which move heat from the outside to the inside), on the market in the 1970s, delivers 2 or 3 times as much heat energy per unit of fuel consumed as the more frequently encountered resistive electrical heating (which merely converts electricity into heat); and that factor could rather easily be increased to at least 4.[252] There was a difference of a factor of 2.5 in efficiency between the most efficient room air conditioner on the market in the early 1970s and the least efficient one—that is, one required 2.5 times less electricity than the other to perform the same amount of cooling.[253] And the illumination levels in most commercial buildings almost certainly exceed what is needed for good vision and comfort by at least a factor of 2.[254]

A 1975 study by the American Institute of Architects concluded that achievable energy conservation measures that would remedy the foregoing defects and others in buildings in the United States could save 25 trillion megajoules per year by 1990. That is the equivalent of 12 million barrels of oil per day—twice the amount of imports to the United States in 1975—and somewhat more energy than nuclear power could deliver in 1990 even if the crash program of expansion recommended by some were undertaken.[255]

TABLE 8-33
Projections of U.S. Annual Energy Use With and Without Conservation (trillion MJ)

Projections	*Use in 1985*	*Use in 2000*
ERDA (1975) "no new initiatives"	113	174
EPP (1974) "historical growth"	122	197
OEP (1972) "business-as-usual"	122	—
EPP (1974) "technical fix"	97	131
OEP (1972) "maximum conservation"	97	—
ERDA (1975) "improved end-use efficiencies"	100	127
EPP (1974) "zero energy growth"	93	106
CEQ (1974) "half and half"	—	128
IEA (1976) "low growth"	—	107

Note: In 1975 the actual total of energy used in the United States was 75 trillion megajoules.

Sources: Energy Research and Development Administration, *A national plan for energy research development and demonstration: Creating energy choices for the future;* Energy Policy Project, *A time to choose;* OEP, Office of Emergency Preparedness, *The potential for energy conservation;* Council on Environmental Quality, *Environmental quality,* 1974; Institute of Energy Analysis, *Economic and environmental implications of a U.S. nuclear moratorium.*

Industry

Industry accounted for about 40 percent of U.S. energy use in the 1970s (Table 8-32). The energy squeeze of 1973 and 1974 led to almost immediate energy savings of 15 to 30 percent (without loss of output) by many large firms, simply by plugging obvious energy leaks in their processes.[256]

More substantial changes can produce significantly larger savings. One of the most promising avenues is

[250]See, for example, Steadman, *Energy;* R. Stein, A matter of design.

[251]Contrary to a widespread misconception, basic physics guarantees that energy will be saved if the temperature is lowered overnight, notwithstanding the fact that the furnace must run vigorously for a while to warm the building again when it is turned on in the morning. See American Physical Society, *Efficient use.*

[252]Ibid.

[253]E. Hirst and J. Moyers, Efficiency of energy use in the United States.

[254]Stein, A matter of design; J. Appel and J. MacKenzie, How much light do we really need?

[255]American Institute of Architects, *A nation of energy-efficient buildings by 1990.*

[256]C. Berg, Conservation in industry; Schipper, Raising the productivity.

TABLE 8-34
Energy Savings in Recycling

Material	Energy costs (1000 MJ/MT) Virgin	Energy costs (1000 MJ/MT) Scrap	U.S. annual consumption (MT)	Percent annual consumption lost in municipal wastes
Finished steel	50	26	81,000,000	12
Aluminum	255	8	4,100,000	25
Copper	60	7	2,100,000	10
Paper	24	15	46,000,000	70
Glass	25	25	14,000,000	80
Plastics	162	NA	11,000,000	35

Note: NA = not available.
Sources: W. Franklin, D. Bendersky, W. Park, and R. Hunt, Potential energy conservation from recycling metals in urban solid wastes; P. F. Chapman, The energy cost of materials.

heavier reliance on *cogeneration* of electricity and process steam or process heat. The term means generating electicity within large industrial facilities and applying the part of the fuel's energy not converted into electricity to process needs on the spot. The overall efficiency can be much higher than when electricity is purchased from a utility and fuel for direct heat and steam generation is purchased separately.[257]

A substantial part of industrial energy use is for the production and refining of basic raw materials: iron and steel, aluminum, plastics, glass, paper, cement. Significant fractions of each year's production of all of those materials, except the last, disappear each year into municipal waste-disposal systems. In many cases, substantial energy savings can be realized by recycling such materials, not to mention the desirable reduction in pressure on the dwindling supplies of virgin raw materials.[258] Some examples of this are suggested in Table 8-34. (The reader handy with arithmetic might notice that the energy saved by recycling a metric ton of paper happens not to be much different from the energy one could recover by burning the waste paper as fuel instead; one cannot do both, and counting the savings both ways must be avoided in making projections.) There is no energy savings in recycling glass—that is, consuming old glass and remelting it to make new—but there is a large savings in switching to returnable bottles.[259] In general, in fact, making a product more durable yields a much bigger energy gain than recycling it.[260] Recyclability is not a substitute for durability but should complement it.

To the extent that part of the consumption of raw materials such as steel and aluminum must continue to come from virgin materials, energy can be saved by changes in the processes that are used for producing finished metal from ore. The basic-oxygen process for steel production uses almost 4 times less energy per ton of product than the open-hearth process, but in 1970 that process still was used in producing only half of the United States output.[261] A new process for producing aluminum uses 43 percent less energy than the standard electrolysis method. The aluminum industry in the early 1970s was using 2.8 percent of all electricity from utilities in the United States.[262]

Transportation

Of the quarter of United States energy use that occurs in the transportation sector, more than half is used in automobiles. Actually, this computation counts only fuel burned in moving freight and people. If one were to assign to the transportation sector those energy expenditures in the industrial and commercial sectors that are part of transportation activities—manufacturing cars and planes, building railroads and highways, refining lubricating oil, and so on—then transportation as a whole would account for 35 to 40 percent of all U.S. energy use, and the automobile at least 21 percent.[263]

[257]E. Gyftopolous, L. Lazaridis, T. Widmer, *Potential fuel effectiveness in industry;* F. von Hippel and R. Williams, Energy waste and nuclear power growth.

[258]See, for example, W. Franklin, D. Bendersky, W. Park, and R. Hunt, Potential energy conservation from recycling metals in urban solid wastes.

[259]B. Hannon, Systems energy and recyling: A study of the beverage industry; and Bottles, cans, energy.

[260]R. Berry and M. Fels, The energy cost of automobiles; R. T. Lund, Making products live longer.

[261]Office of Emergency Preparedness, *The potential.*

[262]M. Rubin, Plugging the energy sieve.

[263]E. Hirst and R. Herendeen, Total energy demand for automobiles.

TABLE 8-35
Fuel Used in Various Modes of Transportation in the United States, 1970

Mode of transportation	*Percentage of total transportation fuel use*
Urban passenger (auto, bus, subway)	35
Intercity passenger (auto, plane, bus, train)	26
Urban freight (truck)	14
Intercity freight (truck, plane, train, waterway, pipeline)	15
Military aviation	3.6
General aviation (private aircraft)	0.6
Other (other military, passenger and pleasure boats, etc.)	6

Source: E. Hirst, *Energy consumption for transportation in the United States.*

A breakdown of U.S. fuel use in transportation by function is given in Table 8-35. Of the part used for urban passenger transport, automobiles account for 97 percent, and of the energy used for intercity passenger transport they use 77 percent; of the energy used for intercity freight, trucks use about 48 percent.[264] These statistics, however, do not accurately reflect the number of passenger miles and ton miles carried by the different modes, because the efficiences in passenger miles per gallon and ton miles per gallon of fuel differ so drastically from one kind of transportation to another. (We bow to convention and familiarity in this section and use the English units of measure; the reader can convert at 132 megajoules per gallon.) Of course, the transportation efficiency depends not only on the technical characteristics of the vehicle (technical efficiency) but also on how full it is compared to its capacity (load factor). Efficiencies of various modes of freight and passenger transportation are detailed in Table 8-36.

[264]E. Hirst, *Energy consumption for transportation in the U.S.*

TABLE 8-36
Transportation Efficiencies, 1970 Technology

Passengers	*Technical efficiency (seat mi/gal)*	*Average load factor (passengers/seat)*	*Transportation efficiency (passenger mi/gal)**
Two-deck suburban train	400	0.50	200
Intercity bus	220	0.57	125
Commuter train	200	0.50	100
Cross-country train	144	0.56	80
New York subway	150	0.50	75
Average U.S. auto traveling between cities (5 seats)	70	0.48	34
Average U.S. auto traveling within one city (5 seats)	70	0.28	20
Boeing 747 jet airplane	40	0.55	22
Boeing 707 jet airplane	34	0.62	21
Proposed U.S. supersonic transport	23	0.62	14
Helicopter	13	0.62	8
Freight			*Ton mi/gal*
100,000-ton tanker			930
Large pipeline			500
Freight train (200 cars)			420
Freight train (100 cars)			250
Container ship			150
Forty-ton truck			50
Air freight			11

*Divide by 132 to get miles/megajoule.
Source: R. Rice, System energy and future transportation.

Clearly, four basic strategies are available for reducing energy use in transportation: (1) increase the technical efficiency of a given kind of vehicle (for example, reduce speed, increase engine efficiency, improve streamlining); (2) increase the load factor (car pools, less duplication in airline schedules); (3) switch traffic to more efficient modes (cars to buses, trucks to trains); (4) reduce the amount of motorized transportation (plan errands better, replace trips with telecommunication, bicycle or walk for short trips.)

The most obvious target for increased technical efficiency is the automobile, both because it is inefficient now and because it is so heavily used. There are abundant opportunities for improvement. For example, small electric cars would be much more efficient in urban traffic than conventional autos, notwithstanding the inefficiency of electricity generation, because they do not idle and because they can recover energy spent accelerating by using the electric motor in reverse as a generator while braking. (This is called regenerative braking.) Charging could be done at night when other electricity demands are low, so no increase in electricity-generating capacity would be required.[265]

Improving automobiles powered by combustion engines is also possible. Lighter cars, low-loss tires, more efficient transmissions, and better streamlining could reduce automotive consumption of fuel by at least 15 to 35 percent without changing the basic engine at all.[266] Among those the biggest energy-saver is reducing vehicle weight. With modest improvements, the spark-ignition, Otto-cycle (intermittent combustion) gasoline engine that powers most cars in America today can meet stricter emission standards and get significantly better mileage than the vehicles of the early 1970s, according to a study completed in 1975 by the Jet Propulsion Laboratory (JPL) of the California Institute of Technology in Pasadena.[267] The improvement would be about 22 percent without use of the stratified-charge concept pioneered by Honda, and about 33 percent with the stratified charge.[268] [In a stratified-charge engine, burning begins in a small region inside the cylinder where the fuel-to-air ratio is high and then spreads into the rest of the cylinder where the ratio is low; the result is good combustion of a mixture that on the average is leaner (contains a lower ratio of fuel to air) than a conventional engine can burn. This produces better mileage and lower emissions of pollutants.]

Further improvements in economy could be obtained by more drastic engine changes. A diesel engine could provide almost a 40-percent improvement in mileage over 1974 Otto-cycle engines, a gas turbine engine a 62 percent improvement, and a Stirling-cycle continuous-combustion engine an improvement of 80 percent, according to the JPL results. (These calculations of improvement do not include the gains to be made by reducing vehicle weight and other changes.) Gas-turbine engines (also called Brayton-cycle engines) have been powering experimental automobiles for many years. The Stirling-cycle engine is in many respects similar to steam engines (Rankine-cycle), but its "working fluid" is a noncondensable pressurized gas, such as hydrogen or helium, instead of water. It appears to be superior to the steam engine for automotive applications. Both the gas-turbine and the Stirling-cycle engines are more expensive than conventional Otto-cycle engines and for fundamental reasons will probably remain so, but a concerted development effort and mass production probably could reduce the cost penalty to around $200.

It does not seem unreasonable, then, to expect, and indeed to require by law, that the technical efficiency of automobiles be steadily and significantly increased over the next ten years. A 40-percent decrease in automotive fuel consumption from the 1974 level, which is achievable by 1980 without major engine changes and without decreasing miles driven, would save 2 million barrels of oil per day.[269] Large additional savings in the same period could be achieved by more car-pooling, by reducing reliance on the automobile for very short trips, and by improving bus service to attract commuters away

[265]For a discussion of electric cars, see National Academy of Sciences, *An evaluation of alternative power sources for low-emission automobiles.*

[266]See, for example, J. Pierce, The fuel consumption of automobiles; and American Physical Society, *Efficient use.*

[267]Jet Propulsion Laboratory, *Should we have a new engine: An automobile power systems evaluation.*

[268]These percentages were obtained in the JPL study for engines of equivalent performance. Naturally, sacrificing some performance could lead to even bigger gains in mileage.

[269]Pierce, The fuel consumption.

from their cars. In the middle term, introduction of the more radical engine changes and of better urban transit systems could continue the drop in fuel consumed per passenger mile.

Large savings in transportation energy are also possible by switching intercity passengers from cars and planes into fast, comfortable trains on routes up to 1000 kilometers or so. Switching long-distance freight transport from trucks onto trains should be encouraged, too. A detailed study by transportation specialist Richard Rice of what could be done by the year 2000 indicated that the United States might have 117 percent more passenger traffic and 47 percent more freight traffic in that year than in 1970 (measured in passenger miles and ton miles) while using 13 percent *less* transportation fuel.[270]

Economic and Social Impact of Conservation

The view that energy conservation should be the cornerstone of a rational U.S. energy policy has been attacked by many in the energy industry, who appear to believe that conservation will have dire economic consequences. Loss of jobs, economic stagnation, and thwarting the legitimate aspirations of the poor are generally mentioned as the specific consequences of saving energy. There is much evidence to suggest, however, that that view is incorrect. Energy conservation does not merely make sense environmentally; it also makes sense economically.

First of all, slowing the growth of energy consumption by means of rational conservation measures can save a great deal of money. For, although technological improvements to increase energy efficiency often require some additional capital investment over conventional practice, that investment is usually less than the investment that would be needed to produce from new sources (offshore oil, nuclear fission, geothermal development) an amount of energy equal to that saved. In this sense, conservation is the cheapest new energy source. The Ford Foundation Energy Policy Project's Technical Fix scenario reduces energy-related capital investment (the sum of the investment for supply and for conservation) by 285 billion 1970 dollars between 1975 and 2000, compared to the Historical Growth scenario.[271] The investment capital saved by conservation, of course, would in principle be available to support this country's many other pressing needs—better health care, nutrition, educational facilities, environmental cleanup, and so on.

Direct savings to consumers in the form of money not spent on energy is another side of the same coin. Many consumer investments in energy conservation, such as buying extra insulation, pay off very quickly. The value of the energy saved exceeds the expenditure in a short time, or, in the case of financed purchases, lower fuel bills more than compensate for increased loan payments immediately.[272] Money saved in this way can be spent in ways that contribute directly to the consumer's sense of well-being (which expenditures on energy wasted because of poor insulation and needlessly inefficient appliances and automobiles do not).

Furthermore, less energy can actually mean more employment. The energy-producing industries make up the most capital-intensive major sector of the U.S. economy and one of the least labor-intensive.[273] This means that each dollar of investment capital taken out of energy production and invested elsewhere, and each dollar saved by an individual because of reduced energy use and spent elsewhere in the economy, is likely to benefit employment.

In summary, the link between energy use and economic prosperity is not firm, but flexible. The notion that there is a one-to-one correspondence between energy consumption and economic prosperity is probably the most dangerous delusion in the energy-policy arena. It is true that very poor countries use only a little energy per person, and that rich countries use much more, but within a given prosperity bracket there is enormous variation in energy used per dollar of GNP. In 1974, three western European countries—Sweden, Denmark and Switzerland—had per-capita GNPs *higher* than that of the United States, despite their using only around half the energy per person (see Table 8-2.) How do those countries produce so much more GNP per unit of energy

[270] R. Rice, Toward more transportation with less energy.

[271] Energy Policy Project, *A time to choose.*

[272] Schipper, Raising the productivity.

[273] See ibid., and references therein.

used than the U.S.? The answer is complex, of course, and has partly to do with the fact that those countries have a somewhat larger fraction of their economic activities in services (such as health care and education), which are less energy-intensive per dollar and per job than manufacturing, than does the United States. Those peoples are also more careful with their energy than we are.[274] It is clear from such comparisons between countries, as well as from comparisons of different sectors within the U.S. economy, that the United States could change the *pattern* of its economic growth in ways that would greatly reduce the growth in its energy consumption without a corresponding cost in prosperity.[275]

PERSPECTIVES ON THE ENERGY PROBLEM

Why worry about energy? What has gone wrong or is likely to? The many people who are deeply troubled by the energy situation in the United States can be divided, to a great extent, into two groups, according to their perceptions of the general nature of the situation: those who believe this country is in danger of having too little energy, too late, and those who believe that the threat is too much energy, too soon.

The specific problems envisioned by the too-little-too-late school have been widely articulated: running out of cheap domestic energy resources, dependence on unstable foreign sources, high prices, economic stagnation, and the perpetuation of poverty. The too-much-too-soon camp is most troubled by the prospect of excessive growth in energy use, stimulating premature transitions to untested technologies accompanied by undesirable or even unbearable costs to human health, ecosystems, and human values.

Not surprisingly, the two camps have rather different views of the role of new energy technology, as well as of the nontechnological dimensions of the energy problem. The goal of new technology in the eyes of the too-little-too-late school is to restore the era of abundant, cheap energy. According to the too-much-too-soon group, the first priority in shaping and choosing new energy technologies should be to minimize the social and environmental impacts of obtaining energy and of using it. The principal nontechnological concern of the too-little-too-late people is that environmentalists and others may block progress toward the desired goal of abundant, cheap energy. The nontechnological dimensions of the energy problem perceived by the too-much-too-soon group include coming to grips with limits and redistributing the finite economic pie that limits must eventually imply.

The strategies of the two groups for dealing with the energy situation, then, are almost diametrically opposed. The too-little-too-late group favors crash programs to develop and deploy all resources and technologies, with priority to whatever promises to be cheapest. The too-much-too-soon group wants to slow down, buy time by maximizing the efficiency of energy use, and use that time to select a mix of energy technologies that is as benign environmentally and socially as money and ingenuity can make it.

The two perspectives sketched out here are in some sense caricatures of a broader and more complex spectrum of opinion, of course, and the situation is complicated further when the focus of concern is broadened to include the diversity of countries beyond the United States. Nevertheless, the dangers facing the industrial nations are rather neatly summed up by the Scylla of too-little-too-late and the Charybdis of too-much-too-soon. Readers may draw their own conclusions from the material here and in Chapters 10–12, as to which danger is the more real. Energy policy, being a matter of steering a course that gives the widest margin of safety against the greatest hazard, is a highly controversial subject that we defer until Chapters 14 and 15.

[274]Schipper and Lichtenberg, Efficient energy use.

[275]In addition to Energy Policy Project, *A time to choose,* and Schipper, Raising the productivity, see especially B. Hannon, Options for energy conservation.

Recommended for Further Reading

Brobst, D. A., and W. P. Pratt, eds. 1973. *United States mineral resources.* Government Printing Office, Washington, D.C., United States Geological Survey paper 820. An indispensable reference book covering fossil and nuclear fuels, as well as other mineral resources. The reader should only be warned that more recent USGS publications take a considerably more pessimistic view of the quantity of U.S. oil likely to be recoverable.

Clark, Wilson. 1975. *Energy for survival.* Doubleday, Garden City, N.Y. An enormous, well-written, and up-to-date compendium covering supply and demand sides of the energy equation.

Cook, Earl. 1976. *Man, energy, society.* W. H. Freeman and Company, San Francisco. Brilliant introduction to energy technology, its social functions, and associated problems. The book's ambivalence about positive and negative roles of energy in relation to human well-being reflects the central dilemma of the energy situation. Unsurpassed in its treatment of historical development of the energy-society interface. Rich in quantitative information.

Energy Policy Project. 1974. *A time to choose: The report of the Energy Policy Project of the Ford Foundation.* Ballinger, Cambridge, Mass. A thoughtful and data-rich examination of alternative pathways for U.S. energy policy. Strong on economic and social aspects, thinner on technology and environment. Its powerful case for low growth was pooh-poohed by many influential advocates of the status quo, and it received less attention than it deserved.

Hollander, J. M., and Simmons, M. K., eds. 1976. *Annual review of energy.* Vol. 1. Annual Reviews, Inc., Palo Alto, Calif. Twenty-eight articles by some of the most prominent energy specialists in the U.S., covering energy supply and distribution, conservation, economics, environmental impacts, and policy. The articles vary in depth and sophistication, but there are some gems. Unsurpassed for up-to-date, extensive bibliographies on most aspects of energy technology.

Hubbert, M. K. 1969. Energy resources. In *Resources and man,* National Academy of Sciences/National Research Council. W. H. Freeman and Company, San Francisco. Classic quantitative treatment of depletion of fossil fuels by the distinguished geophysicist who predicted correctly in the early 1950s that U.S. domestic petroleum production would peak around 1970.

Lovins, Amory. 1975. *World energy strategies.* Ballinger, Cambridge, Mass. A wide-ranging, provocative, brilliantly written essay arguing for restraint in energy growth and diversity and "gentleness" in new sources of supply.

Lovins, Amory. 1977. *Soft energy paths: Toward a durable peace.* Friends of the Earth/Ballinger, Cambridge, Mass. An eloquent and penetrating investigation of alternatives to centralization and reliance on nuclear power in DCs and LDCs alike.

Makhijani, A., and A. Poole. 1975. *Energy and agriculture in the Third World.* Ballinger, Cambridge, Mass. This was prepared for the Energy Policy Project of the Ford Foundation. The most careful and useful look to date at the uses of energy in agricultural societies, where wood, dung, and agricultural residues are major sources. Excellent treatment of biogasification and other approaches to more efficient use of indigenous sources.

Nuclear Energy Policy Study Group. 1977. *Nuclear power issues and choices.* Ballinger, Cambridge, Mass. The best book to date on nuclear power.

Schipper, Lee. 1976. Raising the productivity of energy utilization. In *Annual review of energy,* Hollander and Simmons, eds. An extraordinarily perceptive and well-documented essay on the potential for energy conservation.

Steadman, P. 1975. *Energy, environment, and building.* Cambridge University Press, London. A splendid, if somewhat disorganized, handbook of diagrams, data, and references on energy conservation in buildings, solar heating, wind power, methane digesters, and related topics.

Steinhart, J., and C. Steinhart. 1974. *Energy.* Duxbury Press, North Scituate, Mass. An outstanding introductory text on technology, environmental impact, and policy.

Additional References

Aaronson, T. 1971. The black box. *Environment,* vol. 13, no. 10 (December), pp. 10–18. Useful introductory discussion of fuel cells.

Abajian, V., and A. Fishman, 1973. Supplying enriched uranium. *Physics Today,* vol. 26, no. 8, pp. 23–29.

Ahern, W.; R. Doctor; W. Harris; A. Lipson; D. Morris; and R. Nehring. 1975. Energy alternatives for California: Paths to the future. Rand Corporation, Santa Monica, Calif., R-1793-CSA/RF. A systematic and data-rich study of the options open to California.

Allen, A. R. 1975. Coping with the oil sands. In *Perspectives on energy,* L. C. Ruedisili and M. W. Firebaugh, eds. Oxford University Press, New York. Prospects and problems of this largely Canadian resource.

American Institute of Architects (AIA). 1975. *A nation of energy-efficient buildings by 1990.* AIA, Washington, D.C. Indicates energy-efficient buildings could save more energy by 1990 than nuclear power could provide.

American Physical Society (APS). 1975. *Efficient use of energy:* Pt. 1, *A physics perspective.* American Institute of Physics, New York, AIP Conference proceedings 25. The most definitive and deepest work to date on the technical aspects of energy conservation and efficiency.

Anderson, C.; E. Behrin; E. Green; G. Higgins; W. Ramsey; B. Rubin; and G. Werth. 1974. *An assessment of U.S. energy options for Project Independence.* Lawrence Livermore Laboratory, Livermore, Calif., UCRL-51638. Useful compilation of data and projections, emphasizing economic costs of new supply technologies.

Anderson, L. 1972. *Energy potential from organic wastes: A review on the quantities and sources.* Government Printing Office, Washington, D.C., U.S. Bureau of Mines information circular 8549. A standard reference on the energy potential of agricultural and municipal wastes.

Appel, J., and J. MacKenzie. 1974. How much light do we really need? *Bulletin of the Atomic Scientists,* vol. 30, no. 10, pp. 18–24. Indicates potential for significant energy savings by more rational use of interior and exterior lighting.

APS. *See* American Physical Society.

Averitt, P. 1973. Coal. In *United States mineral resources,* Brobst and Pratt, eds. Standard work on geology, characteristics, and occurrence of coal.

Axtmann, R. 1975. Environmental impact of a geothermal power plant. *Science,* vol. 187, pp. 795–803 (March 7). Case study of the Waireki, New Zealand, wet-steam geothermal plant.

Ayres, R. W. 1975. Policing plutonium: The civil liberties fallout. *Harvard Civil Rights/Civil Liberties Law Review,* vol. 10, pp. 369–443 (Spring). Dismaying examination of potential social costs of a plutonium economy.

Bair, W. J., and R. C. Thompson. 1974. Plutonium: Biomedical research. *Science,* vol. 183, pp. 715–722 (February 22). Reviews experiments on retention, dosimetry, and effects of plutonium.

Balzani, V.; L. Moggi; M. Manfrin; F. Bolleta; and M. Gleria. 1975. Solar energy conversion by water photo-dissociation. *Science,* vol. 189, pp. 852–856 (September 12). Technical review of the chemistry of direct and catalytic dissociation of water by sunlight.

Bamberger, C., and J. Braunstein. 1975. Hydrogen: A versatile element. *American Scientist,* vol. 63, pp. 438–447 (July/August). Excellent technical introduction to the literature of the production and applications of hydrogen.

Berg, C. 1975. Conservation in industry. *Science,* vol. 184, pp. 264–270 (April 12). Summary of potential for more-efficient energy use in selected major industries.

Berg, R. R.; J. C. Calhoun; and R. L. Whiting. 1974. Prospects for expanded U.S. production of crude oil. *Science,* vol. 184, pp. 331–336 (April 19). A sober look at an uncertain situation.

Berkowitz, D., and A. Squires, eds. 1970. *Power generation and environmental change.* M.I.T. Press, Cambridge, Mass. A collection of papers from a 1969 American Association for the Advancement of Science symposium. Dated in some respects, but contains some useful insights on coal and hydropower.

Berry, R. Stephen, and M. Fels. 1973. The energy cost of automobiles. *Bulletin of the Atomic Scientists* vol. 39, no. 10 (Dec.), p. 11. Instructive early example of an energy analysis of a major economic sector.

Berry, R. Stephen, and Hiro Makino. 1974. Energy thrift in packaging and marketing. *Technology Review,* vol. 76, no. 4 (Feb.), pp. 33–43. Potential energy savings available from wiser use of packaging materials.

Blomeke, J.; C. Kee; and J. Nichols. 1974. *Projections of radioactive wastes to be generated by the U.S. nuclear industry.* National Technical Information Service, Springfield, Va., ORNL-TM-3965.

Bockris, J. O'M. 1972. A hydrogen economy. *Science,* vol. 176, p. 1326 (June 23). Oversimplified and overoptimistic prescription for replacing portable fossil fuels with hydrogen.

Boesch, D. F.; C. H. Hershner; and J. H. Milgrim. 1974. *Oil spills and the marine environment.* Ballinger, Cambridge, Mass.

Bolin, B. R. 1977. The impact of production and use of energy on the global environment. *Annual Review of Energy,* vol. 2.

Broda, E. 1976. Solar power—the photochemical alternative. *Bulletin of the Atomic Scientists,* vol. 32, no. 3 (March), pp. 49–52. A distinguished Austrian biochemist calls for an international effort to learn to "mimic" photosynthesis.

Brookings Institution. 1975. *Energy and U.S. foreign policy.* Ballinger, Cambridge, Mass. One of a number of distinguished outside studies contracted for by the Energy Policy Project of the Ford Foundation.

Brown, T. 1971. *Oil on ice.* Sierra Club Books, San Francisco. Popular treatment of the hazards of Arctic oil development.

Budnitz, R.; and John P. Holdren. 1976. Social and environmental costs of energy systems. *Annual review of energy,* J. M. Hollander and M. K. Simmons, eds., vol. 1, pp. 553–580. Develops a systematic framework for the examination of energy's social and environmental impacts, and illustrates the difficulties of various approaches with examples.

Bull, C. 1975. Radioactive waste disposal. *Science,* vol. 189, p. 596 (August 22). Useful survey.

Bupp, I. C. 1974. The breeder reactor in the U.S.: A new economic analysis. *Technology Review,* vol. 76, no. 8, pp. 26–36. Indicates that the economic viability of the liquid metal fast breeder reactor in the United States is less certain than industry and government analyses have indicated.

———, J. Derian, M. Donsimoni, and R. Treitel. 1975. The economics of nuclear power. *Technology Review,* vol. 77, no. 4 (Feb.), pp. 14–25. The most cogent analysis we have seen of the confused economics of commercial nuclear power.

Calder, William A., III. 1976. Energy crisis of the hummingbird. *Natural History,* vol. 85, no. 5 (May), pp. 24–29. Simultaneously an interesting technical report and a suggestive message for society, noting how hummingbirds attain "energy balance through conservation" under conditions of scarcity, and commending this approach to humans.

Casper, B. M. 1977. Laser enrichment: A new path to proliferation. *Bulletin of the Atomic Scientists,* vol. 33, no. 1, pp. 28–41.

Calvin, Melvin. 1974. Solar energy by photosynthesis. *Science,* vol. 184, pp. 375–81 (April 19). Technical description of the possibilities of using or mimicking photosynthesis.

———. 1976. Photosynthesis as a resource for energy and materials. *American Scientist,* vol. 64, no. 3 (May/June), pp. 270–278. Good technical discussion of photosynthetic energy conversion and photochemical mimics of this process, with a good bibliography.

Cameron, J. 1975. A review of long term uranium resources, problems and requirements in relation to demand 1975–2025. In *Proceedings, Workshop on Energy Resources,* International Institute for Applied Systems Analysis, Laxenburg, Austria. Very useful update on the uranium situation by an independent (nongovernment) expert.

CEQ. *See* Council on Environmental Quality.

Chapman, P. F. 1975. The energy cost of materials. *Energy Policy,* March, pp. 47–57. One of several surveys to be consulted for data on the energy investments made to produce metals, plastics, and other basic materials.

———. 1974. The ins and outs of nuclear power. *New Scientist,* vol. 64, pp. 866–869 (December 19). Controversial examination of the net energy yield of nuclear power programs. Makes the valid point that a doubling time of less than about four years in nuclear capacity leads to a situation in which all the output of operating plants is consumed in the construction of others not yet on line.

Chester, C. V. 1976. Estimates of threats to the public from terrorist acts against nuclear facilities. *Nuclear Safety,* vol. 17, no. 6 (November–December), pp. 659–665.

Cochran, T. 1974. *The LMFBR: An environmental and economic critique.* Johns Hopkins Press, Baltimore. A comprehensive and competent attack on the official view of breeder economics and safety.

Cohn, C. E. 1975. Improved fuel economy for automobiles. *Technology Review,* vol. 77, no. 4, pp. 44–52. Energy losses in the internal combustion engine and ways to reduce them.

Comey, D. 1974. Will idle capacity kill nuclear power? *Bulletin of the Atomic Scientists,* vol. 30, no. 9, pp. 23–28. Uses official statistics to conclude that U.S. nuclear power plants are falling far short of the availability and capacity factors predicted by the manufacturers.

———. 1975. Elastic statistics. *Bulletin of the Atomic Scientists,* vol. 31, no. 3 (May), p. 3. Another contribution to the debate over capacity factors of nuclear reactors.

———. 1975. The legacy of uranium tailings. *Bulletin of the Atomic Scientists,* vol. 31, no. 7 (Sept.), pp. 43–45. Argues that radioactive material escaping from tailings piles at uranium mills will produce enough cancer deaths over the next several tens of thousands of years to offset the alleged health advantage of fission over coal—a controversial conclusion.

Commoner, Barry. 1976. *The poverty of power.* Knopf, New York. Lucid description of the laws of thermodynamics and powerful presentation of the case for matching quality of energy sources to the requirements of specific end uses. Unfortunately, the book is marred by serious misinterpretation of M. K. Hubbert's work on depletion of petroleum, with the result that Commoner bases much of his policy stance on a large overestimate of how much petroleum is likely to be available in the future.

Conference Board. 1974. *Energy consumption in manufacturing.* Ballinger, Cambridge, Mass. Authoritative and extensive quantitative survey prepared for the Energy Policy Project of the Ford Foundation.

Cornell University, College of Engineering. 1972. *Report of the Cornell workshops on the major issues of a national energy research and development program.* Ithaca, N.Y. Useful critical discussion of the U.S. breeder reactor program and some other aspects of energy technology.

Council on Economic Priorities. 1972. *The price of power: Electric utilities and the environment.* M.I.T. Press, Cambridge, Mass. Thorough study of pollution control practices in the United States utility industry with profiles of sixteen giant utilities.

———. 1975. *Cleaning up: The cost of refinery pollution control.* New York. Actually a quite comprehensive treatment of the oil-refining business in the United States, not restricted to the cost of pollution control.

Council on Environmental Quality (CEQ). 1973. *Energy and environment: Electric power.* Government Printing Office, Washington, D.C. One of the first systematic compendia of the quantifiable impacts of electric power generation by various means. Includes water consumption, land use, occupational deaths and injuries, emissions, and net energy characteristics of nuclear and fossil technologies.

———. 1974. *Environmental quality.* Government Printing Office, Washington, D.C. The annual report of the CEQ is always rich in reporting of recent events and controversies in air pollution, water pollution, solid waste, and so on. This one has particularly strong coverage on economic costs of pollution control.

Court, A. J.; F. P. Cowan; K. Downes; and B. H. Kuper. 1965. Exposure potentials and criteria for estimating the cost of major reactor accidents. Brookhaven National Laboratory, Upton, N.Y. (unpublished). This work was to have been part of the USAEC 1965 update of its 1957 reactor-safety study (WASH-740). The update was aborted when the preliminary results proved too pessimistic, but the working papers for it were made available in 1973 (in the USAEC's public documents room in Washington, D.C.) under threat of a Freedom of Information Act lawsuit.

Craig, P.; J. Darmstadter; and S. Rattien. 1976. Social and institutional factors in energy conservation. In *Annual review of energy,* Hollander and Simmons, eds. Perceptive discussion of one of the central issues in contemporary energy policy.

Daniels, F. 1964. *Direct use of the sun's energy.* Yale University Press, New Haven. The classic treatise on solar energy. Still indispensable for the serious student of the subject.

Darmstadter, J. 1968. *Energy in the world economy.* Johns Hopkins Press, Baltimore. A useful compendium of international statistics, together with interpretations and speculations by the author.

———. 1975. *Conserving energy.* Johns Hopkins Press, Baltimore. Discussion of the long-term outlook for slowing energy growth in the New York region.

DeNike, L. 1974. Radioactive malevolence. *Bulletin of the Atomic Scientists,* vol. 30, no. 2 (Feb.), p. 16. Frightening but realistic survey of the possibilities for sabotage and terrorism via the commercial nuclear fuel cycle, by a Ph.D. in one of the most relevant disciplines—psychology.

Dials, G. E., and E. C. Moore. 1974. The cost of coal. *Environment,* vol. 16, no. 7 (Sept.), pp. 18–37. Thorough discussion of technical and policy aspects of cleaning up coal, including mine reclamation. Computes dollar cost of cleaning up and finds coal would still be competitive with other energy sources if this price were paid.

Dickenson, W., and R. Neifert. 1975. *Parametric performance and cost analysis of the proposed Sohio solar process heat facility.* University of California, Lawrence Livermore Laboratory, Livermore, UCRL-51783. Technical analysis of one of the first specific proposals in a crucial area of solar-energy application—industrial process heat.

Dicks, J. B. 1975. Magnetohydrodynamic central power: A status report. In *Perspectives on energy,* Ruedisili and Firebaugh, eds. (See below.)

Dickson, E. M.; J. W. Ryan; and M. Smulyan. 1976. *The hydrogen economy: A preliminary technology assessment.* Stanford Research Institute, Menlo Park, Calif. Technology, economics, safety, institutional factors.

Dinneen, G. U., and G. L. Cook. 1974. Oil shale and the energy crisis. *Technology Review,* vol. 76, no. 3 (Jan.), pp. 26–33. Useful survey article on the technology and prospects of exploiting oil shale.

Doyle, W. S. 1976. *Strip mining of coal: Environmental solutions.* Noyes Data Corporation, Park Ridge, N.J. Comprehensive, technical summary of reclamation methods and costs.

Duffie, J. A., and W. A. Beckman. 1974. *Solar energy thermal processes.* Wiley, New York. An engineering text.

———. 1976. Solar heating and cooling. *Science,* vol. 191, pp. 143–149 (January 16). Useful progress report on solar technology for heating and cooling buildings.

Dunham, J. T.; Carl Rampacek; and T. A. Henrie. 1974. High-sulfur coal for generating electricity. *Science,* vol. 184, pp. 346–351 (April 19). Surveys methods of sulfur control available in the early 1970s.

Eckholm, Erik P. 1975. The other energy crisis: Firewood. *Worldwatch Institute,* Washington, D.C. Informative treatment of pressure on forest resources to supply energy needs in poor countries.

Eisenbud, Merril. 1973. *Environmental radioactivity,* 2d ed. Academic Press, New York. Useful collection of quantitative information and references on behavior of radioactive isotopes in the environment.

Elliott, D.; and L. Weaver, eds. 1972. *Education and research in the nuclear fuel cycle.* University of Oklahoma Press, Norman. Contains good coverage of the technologies of uranium enrichment and fuel reprocessing, as they stood in the late 1960s.

Emmett, J.; J. Nuckolls; and L. Wood. 1974. Fusion power by laser implosion. *Scientific American,* June, pp. 24–37. The best available general article on laser fusion.

Energy Research and Development Administration (ERDA). *See* U.S. Energy Research and Development Administration.

Engineering Research Institute. 1957. *A report on the possible effects on the surrounding population of an assumed release of fission products into the atmosphere from a 300 megawatt nuclear reactor located at Laguna Beach, Michigan.* University of Michigan, Ann Arbor. An obscure study conducted for the USAEC in connection with the construction of the Fermi experimental liquid metal fast breeder reactor. Indicated that a severe accident under adverse weather conditions could kill 188,000 people in nearby Detroit.

Environmental Protection Agency (EPA). *See* U.S. Environmental Protection Agency.

Ergen, W. K., et al. 1967. *Emergency core cooling: Report of advisory task force committee on power reactor emergency cooling.* USAEC, Washington, D.C. An important official study of a critical element of the safety of light-water reactors, much cited in later work.

Farmer, F. R., ed. 1977. *Nuclear reactor safety.* Academic Press, New York. Useful coverage at a technical level of safety issues surrounding the LMFBR, as well as other reactor types.

Feiveson, H. A., and T. B. Taylor. 1976. Security implications of alternative fission futures. *Bulletin of the Atomic Scientists,* vol. 32, no. 10 (Dec.), pp. 14ff. Suggests that a thorium/uranium-233 fuel cycle could have significant advantages over uranium-235/plutonium with respect to safeguards against diversion for weapons.

Finney, B. C.; R. E. Blanco; R. C. Dahlmann; F. G. Kitts; and J. P. Witherspoon. 1975. *Nuclear fuel reprocessing,* National Technical Information Service, Springfield, Va., ORNL-IM-4901. Good, up-to-date survey of technology and expected environmental impacts of nuclear fuel reprocessing.

Fletcher, K; and M. Baldwin. 1973. *A scientific and policy review of the prototype oil shale leasing program final environmental impact statement of the U.S. Department of the Interior.* Environmental Impact Assessment Project, Washington, D.C. Good treatment of water requirements of oil shale development and of the problem of disposing of spent shale.

Flowers, Sir Brian (Chairman). 1976. *Nuclear power and the environment.* Sixth report of the Royal Commission on Environmental Pollution. Her Majesty's Stationery Office, London. Very thorough and scholarly review of the pros and cons of nuclear power. Recommends that "a major commitment to fission power and a plutonium economy should be postponed as long as possible."

Forbes, I.; D. Ford; H. Kendall; and J. MacKenzie. 1971. Nuclear reactor safety: An evaluation of the new evidence. *Nuclear News,* September, pp. 32–40. The paper by four members of the Massachusetts-based Union of Concerned Scientists that initiated a prolonged controversy about the adequacy of emergency core-cooling systems for light-water reactors.

Ford, D. F.; H. W. Kendall; and J. J. MacKenzie. 1972. A critique of the AEC's interim criteria for emergency core-cooling systems (ECCS). *Nuclear News,* January, p. 28. Another important piece of the ECCS controversy (see Forbes, Ford, and MacKenzie).

———; T. Hollocher, H. Kendall, J. MacKenzie, L. Scheinman, and A. Schurgin. 1975. *The nuclear fuel cycle.* M.I.T. Press, Cambridge, Mass. Excellent reviews of hazards in uranium mining and milling, fuel reprocessing, and waste management, together with a short summary of the light-water-reactor safety controversy. Highly recommended.

Fox, R. W. (Chairman). 1976. *Ranger uranium environmental inquiry.* Australian Government Publishing Service, Canberra. Detailed review of nuclear technology and associated issues, undertaken in connection with Australia's deliberations about exporting her uranium.

Franklin, W.; D. Bendersky; W. Park; and R. Hunt. 1975. Potential energy conservation from recycling metals in urban solid wastes. In *The energy conservation papers,* R. Williams, ed.

Fuller, R. 1975. *We almost lost Detroit.* Reader's Digest Press, Garden City, N.Y. Notwithstanding the sensational title, a generally sober and accurate popular account of the 1965 accident at the Fermi breeder reactor near Detroit, as well as other reactor accidents around the world.

Garvey, G. 1972. *Energy, ecology, economy.* Norton, New York. A perceptive statement by a Princeton University political scientist, emphasizing the difficulty and importance of bringing ecological insights into cost-benefit analysis of energy technology.

General Electric Co. 1975. *Nuclear power: The best alternative.* GEZ-6301.4A. San Jose, Calif. A piece of industry propaganda, illustrating not only the standard arguments for all-out nuclear development but also what seems to be an astonishing degree of contempt for the intelligence of the intended audience.

Gesell, T.; J. Adams; and L. Church. 1975. Letters: Geothermal power plants—environmental impact. *Science,* vol. 189, p. 328 (August 1). Raises the issue of radon gas released in geothermal operations.

Gillette, R. 1972. Nuclear safety. (Pt. 3), Critics charge conflicts of interest. *Science,* vol. 177, no. 4053, p. 970 (September 15). One in a series of articles by this reliable and objective reporter on the light-water reactor safety controversy.

———. 1973. Nuclear safeguards: Holes in the fence. *Science,* vol. 182, pp. 1112–1114 (December 14). Reports the laxity of safeguards in effect against theft of bomb-grade nuclear materials in the United States in the early 1970s, as determined by an investigation by the General Accounting Office.

———. 1974. GAO calls security lax at nuclear plants. *Science,* vol. 186, pp. 906–907 (December 6). Reports a General Accounting Office finding that sabotaging a nuclear power reactor would not be as difficult as is commonly supposed.

———. 1975. Geological survey lowers its sights. *Science,* vol. 189, p. 200 (July 18). Reports a drop by a factor of 3 in USGS estimates of undiscovered recoverable U.S. oil and gas, a major concession to M. K. Hubbert and other critics of the higher earlier estimates.

———. 1975. "Nozzle" enrichment for sale. *Science,* vol. 188, p. 912 (May 30). Description of the Becker process for enriching uranium and the impact the marketing of this process by the Federal Republic of Germany (West Germany) and others may have on the world situation.

———. 1975. Nuclear proliferation: India, Germany may accelerate the process. *Science,* vol. 188, pp. 911–914 (May 30). Spread of nuclear weapons through experimental and commercial reactors and supporting facilities made available through international "cooperation."

———. 1975. Oil and gas resources: Academy calls USGS math misleading. *Science,* vol. 187, pp. 723–727 (February 28). The dispute between optimists (at the U.S. Geological Survey) and pessimists (advising the National Academy of Sciences) over the amount of domestic gas and oil remaining to be found in the United States.

Glaser, P. 1974. Power from the sun. *Unesco Courier,* vol. 27, pp. 16–21. Popular discussion of solar electricity production using satellites.

———. 1977. Solar power from satellites. *Physics Today,* vol. 30, no. 2 (February), pp. 30–38. Argues that satellite power stations could be built for $1500 per kilowatt.

Glasstone, S., and A. Sesonske. 1963. *Nuclear reactor engineering.* Van Nostrand, Princeton, N.J. Standard reference work for the physics and technology of fission reactors.

Gofman, J. W.; and A. R. Tamplin. 1971. *Poisoned power.* Rodale Press, Emmaus, Pa. Two early critics of nuclear power state their case. Emphasis is on routine emissions.

Goldsmith, M. 1971. *Geothermal resources in California: Potentials and problems.* California Institute of Technology Environmental Quality Laboratory, Pasadena, Report 5. Sober look at geothermal's prospects by an observer with no axe to grind.

Goldstein, I. S. 1975. Potential for converting wood into plastics. *Science,* vol. 189, pp. 847–852 (September 12). Fulfillment of all plastic needs from wood does not seem impossible, technically or economically.

Golenpaul, A., ed. 1975. *Information please almanac.* 29th ed. Dan Golenpaul Associates, New York.

Golueke, C., and W. Oswald. 1963. Power from solar energy via algae-produced methane. *Solar Energy,* vol. 7, no. 3, pp. 86–92. An early description of one possible approach to bioconversion of solar energy.

Gough, W., and B. Eastland. 1971. The prospects of fusion power. *Scientific American,* February, pp. 50–64. Excellent survey of progress toward harnessing fusion. Still a useful introduction in 1976.

Greenburg, William. 1973. Chewing it up at 200 tons a bite: Strip mining. *Technology Review,* vol. 75, no. 4, pp. 46–55. Well-illustrated documentation of damage in Appalachian strip-mining.

Gregory, D. 1973. The hydrogen economy. *Scientific American,* January, pp. 13–21. Possibility of replacing hydrocarbons as portable fuel.

Grooms, D. W. 1976. *Nuclear materials safeguards: A title bibliography.* Vol. 1, *1964–1974.* National Technical Information Service, Springfield, Va. A very useful guide to literature that is otherwise hard to find.

Gruen, Victor. 1975. Atomenergie und "Des Kaisers neue Kleider." *Die Zukunft* (Austria), vol. 12, end of June, pp. 15–19. A noted environmental planner and author uses the fable of the emperor's new clothes as a vehicle to express his critique of nuclear power.

Gyftopolous, E.; L. Lazaridis; and T. Widmer. 1974. *Potential fuel effectiveness in industry.* Ballinger, Cambridge, Mass. Prepared by the Energy Policy Project of the Ford Foundation, this report documents the potential for large energy savings in U.S. industry.

Haefele, W. 1974. Energy choices that Europe faces. *Science,* vol. 184, pp. 360–367 (April 19). Useful survey of Europe's options by the head of the energy project at the International Institute for Applied Systems Analysis in Austria.

——— and A. Manne. 1974. *Strategies for a transition from fossil to nuclear fuels.* International Institute for Applied Systems Analysis, Laxenburg, Austria, Report RR-74-7.

Haefele, W., and C. Starr. 1974. A perspective on fission and fusion breeders. *Journal of the British Nuclear Energy Society,* vol. 13, no. 2 (April), pp. 131–139. Two strong advocates of fission argue that fusion's potential advantages are small. (See the rebuttals in the April 1975 issue of the same journal by Holdren and von Hippel.)

Haefele, W.; J. Holdren; G. Kessler; and G. Kulcinski; with contributions from A. Belostotsky, R. Grigoriants, M. Styrikovich, and N. Vasiliev. 1977. *Fusion and fast breeder reactors.* International Institute for Applied Systems Analysis, Laxenburg, Austria. Book-length report of a major cooperative study, with collaborators from the U.S., the Federal Republic of Germany, and the U.S.S.R., comparing technical, resource, and environmental aspects of fusion reactors and LMFBRs.

Hagan, R. M., and E. B. Roberts. 1973. Ecological impacts of water storage and diversion projects. In *Environmental quality and water development,* C. R. Goldman; J. McEvoy, III; and P. J. Richardson, eds. W. H. Freeman and Company, San Francisco, pp. 196–215. Very thorough and well-documented treatment.

Hall, D. B. 1971. Adaptability of fissile materials to nuclear explosives. In *Proceedings of symposium on implementing nuclear safeguards* (Kansas State University, October 25–27, 1971). Praeger, New York. Definitive statement by an expert on the usability of oxide and contaminated forms of fissile materials for nuclear explosives.

Halsted, T. A. 1975. The spread of nuclear weapons—is the dam about to burst? *Bulletin of the Atomic Scientists,* vol. 31, no. 5, pp. 8–11. A discussion of the status of the Nonproliferation Treaty just before the review conference of 1975.

Hambleton, W. W. 1972. The unsolved problem of nuclear wastes. *Technology Review,* vol. 74, no. 5 (March/April), pp. 15–19. The individual most responsible for stopping the USAEC's ill-advised commitment to waste storage in a Lyons, Kansas, salt mine explains the difficulties.

Hammond, A. L. 1973. Dry geothermal wells: Promising experimental results. *Science,* vol. 182, pp. 43–44 (October 5). Progress report on the hot-dry-rock approach.

———. 1975. Artificial tornadoes: A novel wind energy concept. *Science,* vol. 190, pp. 257–258 (October 17). A clever exploitation of aerodynamics to extract wind energy from an area larger than the generator itself.

———. 1976. Nuclear proliferation: Warnings from the arms control community. *Science* vol. 193, pp. 126–130 (July 9). Inadequacy of existing safeguards against the spread of weapons via commercial nuclear power.

———, W. D. Metz, and T. H. Maugh, II. 1973. *Energy and the future.* American Association for the Advancement of Science, Washington, D.C. Surveys advances in the technologies of fission, fusion, MHD, fossil-fuel conversion, and energy transmission and storage.

Hammond, O. H., and R. E. Baron. 1976. Synthetic fuels: Prices, prospects, and prior art. *American Scientist,* vol. 64, pp. 407–417 (July/August). Excellent survey of technology for oil shale, tar sands, and liquefaction and gasification of coal.

Hannon, B. 1972. Systems energy and recycling: A study of the beverage industry. *Environment,* vol. 14, no. 2, pp. 11–21. Indicates the substantial amount of energy used for beverage containers and how that amount could be reduced by recycling.

———. 1974. Options for energy conservation. *Technology Review,* vol. 76, no. 4, pp. 24–31. Useful survey of evident possibilities for increased energy efficiency, together with some insights into its effects on employment and GNP.

Harte, J., and R. H. Socolow. 1971. *Patient Earth.* Holt, Rinehart and Winston, New York. Case studies in management of resources and environment, together with instructive introductions to the basics of energy, water, radiation, population growth. Highly recommended.

Harwood, S.; K. May; M. Resnikoff; B. Schlessinger; and P. Tames. 1976. The cost of turning it off. *Environment,* vol. 18, no. 10 (December), pp. 17–26. The problems of decommissioning nuclear reactors after they wear out.

Hasiba, H. H.; R. P. Trump; and A. David. 1973. *In-situ process options for the recovery of energy and synthetic fuels from coal, oil shale, and tar sands.* American Institute of Mining, Metallurgical and Petroleum Engineers, Inc., New York, AIME paper SPE 4710.

Healy, T. J. 1974. *Energy, electric power, and man.* Boyd and Fraser, San Francisco. A good undergraduate text with emphasis on generation, applications, and regulation of electricity.

Hein, R. 1974. Superconductivity: Large scale applications. *Science,* vol. 185, p. 221–222 (July 19). Potential of superconduction technology in energy production, storage, transmission, and end use.

Herendeen, R. 1974. Energy and affluence. *Mechanical Engineer,* October. Shows how direct and indirect energy use vary with income class.

——— and A. Sebald. 1975. Energy, employment, and dollar impact of certain consumer options. In *The energy conservation papers,* Robert H. Williams, ed. Use of energy analysis to show the way toward less energy-intensive life-styles.

Heronemus, W. E. 1975. Wind power: A near-term partial solution to the energy crisis. In *Perspectives on energy,* L. C. Ruedisili and M. W. Firebaugh, eds. Systematic look at large-scale use of wind power in electric utility systems.

Hirsch, R. and W. Rice. 1974. Nuclear fusion power and the environment. *Environmental Conservation,* vol. 1, Winter, pp. 251–262. Progress toward fusion and a brief discussion of the environmental implications of success.

Hirst, E. 1972. *Energy consumption for transportation in the U.S.* National Technical Information Service, Springfield, Va., ORNL-NSF-EP-15. [A shorter version appeared as Transportation energy use and conservation potential, *Bulletin of the Atomic Scientists,* vol. 29, no. 9, p. 36–42.] A thorough study assembling much useful data about how energy is used in moving people and freight in autos, trucks, aircraft, buses, and so on.

———. 1974. Food-related energy requirements. *Science,* vol. 184, pp. 134–138 (April 12). Shows that food production, processing, delivery, marketing, storage, and preparation account for about 12 percent of total U.S. energy use.

———. 1976. Transportation energy conservation policies. *Science,* vol. 192, pp. 15–20 (April 2). Advocates higher gasoline taxes and tight fuel-economy standards for new automobiles.

———. 1976. Residential energy use alternatives: 1976 to 2000. *Science,* vol. 194, pp. 1247–1252 (December 17). Potential for large energy savings through increased efficiency.

——— and R. Herendeen. 1973. Total energy demand for automobiles. Society of Automotive Engineers, New York. (Reprinted in U.S. Senate Committee on Interior and Insular Affairs, *Energy Conservation:* Hearings on S.2176, 93d Cong., 1st sess., August 1973.) Finds that energy used in manufacturing, in servicing, and in otherwise supporting automobiles is half as great as the energy autos use directly as fuel.

——— and J. Moyers. 1973. Efficiency of energy use in the United States. *Science,* vol. 179, p. 1299–1304 (March 30). Surveys possibilities of energy conservation in buildings, transportation, and industry, identifying large potential savings.

Hocevar, C. J. 1975. *Nuclear reactor licensing—a critique of the computer safety prediction methods.* Union of Concerned Scientists, Cambridge, Mass. Detailed technical critique by an expert on computer analysis of reactor safety who resigned from the USAEC's principal contractor for safety analysis.

Holdren, J. P. 1971. Adequacy of lithium supplies as a fusion energy source. In *Controlled thermonuclear research.* U.S. Congress, Joint Committee on Atomic Energy. Government Printing Office, Washington, D.C. Shows that availability of lithium is unlikely to limit the use of deuterium-tritium fusion.

———. 1974. Hazards of the nuclear fuel cycle. *Bulletin of the Atomic Scientists,* vol. 30, no. 8 (October), pp. 14–23. Surveys risks of routine emissions, accidents, sabotage, and theft and diversion of nuclear materials for weapons at reactors and other fuel-cycle facilities.

———. 1975. Energy and prosperity: Some elements of a global perspective. *Bulletin of the Atomic Scientists,* vol. 30, no. 1 (January), pp. 26–28. Presents a scenario combining lowered population growth and a shift of the bulk of energy growth from rich countries to poor ones.

———. 1975. The relevance of environmental concerns in contemplating development of fission-fusion hybrids: A personal view. In *DCTR fusion-fission energy systems meeting,* U.S. Energy Research and Development Administration, pp. 209–216. Argues that hybrids may sacrifice the potential environmental advantages that make fusion desirable.

———. 1975. Uranium availability and the breeder decision. *Energy systems and policy,* vol. 1, no. 3. Uses USAEC and USGS data to show that nonbreeder reactors could economically meet forseeable nuclear generating requirements through the year 2020 using low-grade uranium. This suggests high priority on the breeder reactor is unjustified.

———. 1976. Auswirkungen der Energieprobleme auf die Unternehmung. *Journal für Betriebswirtschaft* (Austria), vol. 1/76. pp. 29–33. Argues that reductions in the growth rate of energy use need not adversely affect industrial economies.

———. 1976. Zero-infinity dilemmas in nuclear power. In Committee on Insular and Interior Affairs, U.S. House of Representatives, *Reactor safety study (Rasmussen report),* Serial No. 94-61, Government Printing Office, Washington, D.C., pp. 357–364. Shortcomings of methodology and presentation in the Rasmussen Report, together with other ingredients of the decision-makers' dilemma surrounding nuclear power.

———. 1977. Costs of energy as potential limits to growth. In *The sustainable society: Social and political implications,* D. Pirages, ed., Praeger, New York. Rising economic, environmental and social costs of energy supply—systematic assessment and implications.

———; T. K. Fowler; and R. F. Post. 1976. Fusion power and the environment. In *Energy and the environment: Cost-benefit analysis,* R. A. Karam and K. Z. Morgan, eds., Pergamon, New York. Elucidates the magnitude of the potential environmental advantages of fusion over fission, while emphasizing the effort that would be necessary to translate the potential into reality.

——— and P. Herrera. 1971. *Energy.* Sierra Club Books, New York. A pre-embargo introduction to the energy dilemma, emphasizing the environmental liabilities of supply technologies and the underexploited potential of energy conservation.

Hollocher, T. C. 1973. Storage and disposal of high level wastes. In D. F. Ford, et al., *The nuclear fuel cycle.* One of the best introductions to the nuclear-waste problem.

——— and J. J. MacKenzie. 1975. Radiation hazards from the misuse of uranium mill tailings. In *The nuclear fuel cycle,* Ford, D. F., et al. The best survey of the tailings problem in Grand Junction and elsewhere on the Colorado plateau.

Hottel, H. C., and J. B. Howard. 1971. *New energy technology: Some facts and assessments.* M.I.T. Press, Cambridge. Heavily technical coverage of coal gasification and liquefaction, with briefer treatment of oil shale, sulfur control, nuclear fission, and solar energy. Dated in important respects.

Hubbert, M. K. 1974. *U.S. energy resources: A review as of 1972.* Senate Committee on Interior and Insular Affairs, Washington, D.C., 93–40 (92–75). Useful update of Hubbert's earlier work on resource estimation.

Huettner, D. A. 1976. Net energy analysis: An economic assessment. *Science,* vol. 192, pp. 101–104 (April 9). Focuses on the limitations of net energy analysis as a major basis for policy decisions.

Inglis, D. R. 1973. *Nuclear energy: Its physics and its social challenge.* Addison-Wesley, Reading, Mass. Even-handed introduction to the physics, applications, and problems of nuclear energy by a distinguished veteran of the field's early years.

Institute for Energy Analysis. 1976. *Economic and environmental implications of a U.S. nuclear moratorium.* Oak Ridge Associated Universities, Oak Ridge, Tennessee. Suggests that doing without nuclear power is possible, but expresses reservations about the high use of coal that would result.

International Atomic Energy Agency (IAEA). 1970. *Environmental aspects of nuclear power stations.* IAEA, Vienna. Conference proceedings containing a variety of useful papers on radiation, thermal pollution, and other topics.

International Institute for Applied Systems Analysis (IIASA). 1975. *Proceedings: Workshop on energy resources.* IIASA, Laxenburg, Austria. Up-to-date review of global energy resources, emphasizing fossil and nuclear fuels.

James, L. W., and R. L. Moon. 1975. GaAs concentrator solar cell. *Applied Physics Letters,* vol. 26, p. 467–470 (April 15). A breakthrough in solar-cell technology, permitting 1000-fold concentration of the incident sunlight (with mirrors) without the loss of efficiency that characterizes other cells under those circumstances.

JCAE. *See* U.S. Congress, Joint Committee on Atomic Energy.

Jet Propulsion Laboratory (JPL). 1975. *Program review: Comparative assessment of orbital and terrestrial central power stations.* Jet Propulsion Laboratory, Pasadena. An extensive NASA-sponsored study emphasizing the economics of solar generation of electricity as measured against conventional systems.

———. 1975. *Should we have a new engine? An automobile power systems evaluation.* 2 vols. JPL, Pasadena. Very thorough study of engine options–turbines, steam engines, diesels, and others–comparing performance, economics, and emissions.

Kansas State University. 1972. *Proceedings of symposium on implementing nuclear safeguards.* Praeger, New York. Authoritative papers on the risks of nuclear theft and diversion.

Karam, R. A., and K. Z. Morgan, eds. 1976. *Energy and the environment: Cost benefit analysis.* Pergamon, New York. Proceedings of a symposium, emphasizing the fission-coal comparison.

Kasper, W. 1974. Power from trash. *Environment,* vol. 16, no. 2 (March), pp. 34–38. Potential for using municipal waste for electricity production.

Kelley, J. H., and E. A. Laumann, eds. 1975. *Hydrogen tomorrow: Demands and technology requirements.* Jet Propulsion Laboratory, Pasadena. A substantive technical assessment with an extensive bibliography.

Kendall, H. W. 1975. *Nuclear power risks: A review of the report of the APS study group on light water reactor safety.* Union of Concerned Scientists, Cambridge, Mass. A prominent physicist and nuclear critic cuts through the waffling language of the American Physical Society report, to underline that document's disturbing conclusions about reactor safety.

——— and S. Moglewer. 1974. Preliminary review of the AEC reactor safety study. Sierra Club, San Francisco, and Union of Concerned Scientists, Cambridge, Mass. Identifies major shortcomings in the reactor-safety study and concludes accident probabilities and consequences are underestimated.

Komanoff, Charles. 1976. *Power plant performance.* Council on Economic Priorities, New York. A detailed examination of the reliability of coal-fired and nuclear power plants suggests nuclear's presumed cost advantage is illusory.

Krieger, David. 1975. Terrorists and nuclear technology. *Bulletin of the Atomic Scientists,* vol. 31, no. 6 (June), pp. 28–34. A sobering evaluation of perhaps the greatest social/environmental hazard of nuclear power.

Kruger, P., and C. Otte, eds. 1973. *Geothermal energy: Resources, production, stimulation.* Stanford University Press, Calif. Good introduction to the field.

Kubo, A. S., and D. J. Rose. 1973. Disposal of nuclear wastes. *Science,* vol. 182, p. 1205 (December 21). A brief but systematic treatment of the options for managing high-level nuclear wastes. Good introduction to the subject.

Kulcinski, G. 1974. Fusion power: An assessment of its potential impact in the USA. *Energy Policy,* vol. 2, p. 104. Very comprehensive and useful treatment of the technological side of fusion, including impact on the resources that will be needed to build fusion reactors.

Lagler, K. 1971. Ecological effects of hydroelectric dams. In *Power generation and environmental change,* D. Berkowitz and A. Squires, eds. One of the few available popular treatments of this subject. Mainly a listing, with little elaboration.

Lash, T., and J. Bryson. 1974. *Comments of the Natural Resources Defense Council, Inc. and the Sierra Club on the USAEC WASH-1539.* Natural Resources Defense Council, Palo Alto, Calif. Systematically demolishes a very unsatisfactory environmental-impact statement prepared by the USAEC on retrievable surface storage of radioactive wastes.

Lave, L. B., and L. P. Silverman. 1976. Economic costs of energy-related environmental pollution. In *Annual review of energy,* J. M. Hollander and M. K. Simmons, eds. Lave continues to do the best work available on economic quantification of energy's environmental impacts.

Levin, R. 1972. Conversion and enrichment in the nuclear fuel cycle. In *Education and research in the nuclear fuel cycle,* D. Elliott and L. Weaver, eds. Explains in unusual detail the technology of uranium enrichment by gaseous diffusion.

Lewis, A. 1974. The outlook for oil shale. University of California, Lawrence Livermore Laboratory, Livermore, UCRL-75242. Economic costs and technological obstacles are surveyed.

Lewis, H. W., et al. 1975. Report to the American Physical Society by the study group on light-water reactor safety. *Reviews of modern physics,* vol. 47, supplement 1 (summer). An exceedingly thorough and careful examination of the status of light-water reactor safety by an independent group of physicists. Unfortunately, some disturbing conclusions are buried in the rhetoric of a complacency not justified by the substantive content.

Lewis, R. 1972. *The nuclear power rebellion: Citizens versus the atomic industrial establishment.* Viking, New York. A history of the USAEC and the Joint Committee on Atomic Energy, emhasizing controversies and conflicts with independent scientists and citizen groups.

Lidsky, L. M. 1975. Fission-fusion systems: Hybrid, symbiotic, and Augean. *Nuclear Fusion,* vol. 15, pp. 151–173. The most comprehensive survey paper on hybrids.

Lieberman, M. A. 1976. United States uranium resources: An analysis of historical data. *Science,* vol. 192, pp. 431–436 (April 30). Argues on the basis of drilling and discovery rates that much less high-grade uranium remains to be discovered than official projections indicate.

Livingston, R. S., and B. McNeill. 1975. *Beyond petroleum.* vol. 1, *Biomass energy chains.* Stanford University, Energy Information Center, Stanford, Calif. A careful look at the use of bioconversion as a large-scale substitute for fossil fuels. Eucalyptus trees are found attractive for this purpose.

Lovins, A. 1976. Energy strategy: the road not taken. *Foreign Affairs,* October, pp. 55–96. Compelling case for low energy growth and reliance on "soft" technologies. Emphasizes evils of large scale and centralization.

———, and John Price. 1975. *Non-nuclear futures: The case for an ethical energy strategy.* Ballinger, Cambridge, Mass. An eloquent and thoughtful exposition of some drawbacks of nuclear power.

Lund, R. T. 1977. Making products live longer. *Technology Review,* vol. 79, no. 3 (January), pp. 49–55. Potential savings in energy and materials are significant, but there are some obstacles.

Lundin, F.; J. Lloyd; J. Smith; E. Archer; and D. Holaday. 1969. Mortality of uranium miners in relation to radiation exposure, hardrock mining and cigarette smoking 1950–1967. *Health Physics,* vol. 16, pp. 571–578.

Makhijani, A. 1976. Solar energy and rural development for the Third World. *Bulletin of the Atomic Scientists,* vol. 32, no. 6 (June), pp. 14–24. A scientist now working in Indian villages describes possibilities for tailoring solar technologies to local needs.

———; and A. Lichtenberg. 1971. *An assessment of energy and materials utilization in the U.S.A.* University of California, Electronic Research Laboratory, Berkeley, ERL-M310, revised. [Also published in slightly abridged form under the title, Energy and well-being, *Environment,* vol. 14, no. 5 (September 1972).] A pioneering disaggregation of energy end uses in the United States, showing how much energy goes for major raw materials and for specific goods and services.

Marchetti, C. 1973. Hydrogen and energy. In *Proceedings of IIASA planning conference on energy systems.* International Institute for Applied Systems Analysis, Laxenburg, Austria, Report PC-3. Useful survey of possible applications of hydrogen by an innovative advocate of the hydrogen economy.

———. 1977. Carbon dioxide and the problem of geoengineering. *Climatic Change,* vol. 1, no. 1.

Martin, J. E.; E. D. Harward; and D. T. Oakley. 1971. Radiation doses from fossil-fuel and nuclear power plants. In *Power generation and environmental change,* D. Berkowitz and A. Squires, eds. M.I.T. Press, Cambridge, Mass. Study showing the radiation dose from a modern coal plant is 5 times greater than the dose from a pressurized-water reactor but 10,000 times less than that from a boiling-water reactor.

Masters, G. M. 1974. *Introduction to environmental science and technology.* Wiley, New York. Readable introductory text surveying population, mineral resources, energy, food, and air pollution. Coverage is strongest on technologies for pollution control.

Maugh, T. H., II. 1976. Natural gas: United States has it if the price is right. *Science,* vol. 191, pp. 549–550 (February 13). Unconventional deposits would become exploitable if the price went up.

McCaull, J. 1973. Windmills. *Environment,* vol. 15, no. 1, (January/February) pp. 6–17. History and contemporary prospects, dated somewhat by developments in a rapidly moving field.

McCulloh, T. H. 1973. Oil and gas. In *United States mineral resources,* D. A. Brobst and W. P. Pratt, eds. Government Printing Office, Washington, D.C., Geological Survey paper 820. Solid treatment of geology and availability of oil and gas, written before the U.S. Geological Survey revised its estimates of U.S. resources downward.

McIntyre, H. C. 1975. Natural uranium heavy-water reactors. *Scientific American,* October, pp. 17–27. Good description of heavy-water reactor technology.

McPhee, J. 1974. *The curve of binding energy.* Farrar, Straus, and Giroux, New York. A brilliant and frightening introduction to the link between nuclear power and nuclear bombs, written around a biographical sketch of one-time preeminent bomb designer Theodore Taylor.

Meinel, A. B., and M. P. Meinel. 1972. Physics looks at solar energy. *Physics Today,* February, pp. 44–50. Introductory article emphasizing electric power generation.

———. 1976. *Applied solar energy.* Addison-Wesley, Reading Mass. A detailed and thorough engineering text, covering availability of the resource, optics, and heat transfer with the comprehensiveness appropriate for those intending to become specialists in solar-system design.

Merriam, Marshal. 1972. Windmills for less developed countries. *Technos,* April/June, pp. 2–23. Excellent discussion of applications of windmills where they are most needed.

———. 1977. Wind energy for human needs. *Technology Review,* vol. 79, no. 3 (January), pp. 28–39.

Merrigan, J. A. 1975. *Sunlight to electricity.* M.I.T. Press, Cambridge, Mass. Good short text on photovoltaics.

Metz, W. D. 1976. Fusion research: What is the program buying the country? *Science,* vol. 192, pp. 1320–1323 (June 25). A perceptive progress report and critique of the U.S. fusion-research program.

———. 1976. Laser enrichment: Time clarifies the difficulty. *Science,* vol. 19, pp. 1162–1163, 1193 (March 19). The laser approach appears more difficult and expensive than overoptimistic early estimates indicated.

———. 1976. Energy research: Accelerator builders eager to aid fusion work. *Science,* vol. 194, pp. 307–309 (October 15). Possible use of heavy-ion beams in place of lasers or electron beams to initiate fusion microexplosions. Also mentions link between classified inertial-confinement fusion work and fusion weapons design.

Metzger, P. 1972. *The atomic establishment.* Simon and Schuster, New York. Well written, critical history of the USAEC and the Joint Committee on Atomic Energy.

Miller, A. 1973. A coal miner looks at the energy crisis. *The Center Magazine,* November/December, pp. 35–45. The head of the United Mine Workers expresses some perceptive views about strip-mining, reclamation, and other topics.

Morgan, K. Z. 1976. Effects of radiation on man: Now and in the future. In *Energy and the environment: Cost benefit analysis.* R. A. Karam and K. Z. Morgan, eds. Pergamon, New York. One of the preeminent radiation health physicists in the world discusses reasons for continuing concern about radiation exposure in medicine and the nuclear industry.

Morrow, W. 1973. Solar energy: Its time is near. *Technology Review,* vol. 76, no. 2, pp. 31–42. Excellent survey article covering thermal and electric applications of solar energy.

Morse, F. H., and M. K. Simmons. 1976. Solar energy. In *Annual review of energy,* J. M. Hollander and M. K. Simmons, eds. Good status report on the various approaches. Excellent bibliography.

Mostert, Noel. 1974. *Supership.* Knopf, New York. Highly readable account of the hazards of supertankers by a talented journalist and environmentalist, who spent a long voyage researching the topic.

Moumoni, Abdou. 1973. Energy needs and prospects in the Sahelian and Sudanese zones in Africa: Prospects of solar power. *Ambio,* vol. 2, no. 6, pp. 203–213. Useful example of analysis aimed at tailoring energy technologies to local resources and needs.

Naill, R. F.; D. L. Meadows; and J. Stanley-Miller. 1975. The transition to coal. *Technology Review,* vol. 78, no. 1 (Oct./Nov.), pp. 18–29. Application of systems-dynamics computer modeling to explore U.S. energy options.

National Academy of Sciences (NAS). 1969. *Resources and man.* W. H. Freeman and Company, San Francisco. A sober and articulate analysis of the resource side of the human predicament—food, energy, materials—with a refreshing lack of waffling.

———. 1972. *The effects on populations of low levels of ionizing radiation.* NAS, Washington, D.C. Still the most competent and comprehensive major study of effects on humans of prolonged exposure to low-level radiation.

———. 1973. *An evaluation of alternative power sources for low-emission automobiles.* NAS, Washington, D.C. Part of the bookshelf of any specialist on the topic of alternative engines.

———. 1974. *Rehabilitation potential of western coal lands.* Ballinger, Cambridge, Mass. This report to the Energy Policy Project of the Ford Foundation indicates that strip-mined lands in regions receiving an average of less than 10 inches of rainfall probably cannot be reclaimed at all.

———. 1975. *Mineral resources and the environment.* NAS, Washington, D.C. A major NAS study focusing most heavily on mineral fuels—oil, gas, coal, and uranium. Several important appendix volumes and a summary volume are available.

———. 1975. *Air quality and stationary source emission control.* Committee on Public Works, U.S. Senate/Goverment Printing Office, Washington, D.C. Superb review of state-of-the-art of pollution control for power plants.

———. 1976. *Energy for rural development: Renewable resources and alternative technologies for developing countries.* NAS, Washington, D.C. Very useful survey of technologies, suppliers, and research organizations, covering wind, hydropower, biomass, solar heat, solar-electric systems, geothermal energy, and energy storage.

———. 1977. *Interim Report of the National Research Council Committee on Nuclear and Alternative Energy Systems.* NAS, Washington, D.C. Useful discussion of the characteristics of the U.S. energy problem, plus the suggestion that energy use as low as 74 trillion megajoules (70 quadrillion Btu) is conceivable for the U.S. in 2010.

National Council on Radiation Protection and Measurement. 1975. *Krypton-85 in the atmosphere: Accumulation, biological significance, and control technology.* NCRP Publications, Washington, D.C. July.

Nephew, E. A. 1973. The challenge and promise of coal. *Technology Review,* vol. 76, no. 2 (Dec.), pp. 21–29. The best short survey article on the technology and environmental impacts of coal mining.

——— and R. L. Spore. 1974. Coal mining and the environment. In *Energy conservation and the environment.* Oak Ridge National Laboratory, Tenn., ORNL-NSF-EP-77. Research summary emphasizing results of a major study of economic costs of reclaiming surface mined land in Appalachia.

Nero, Anthony V., Jr. 1976. *A guidebook to nuclear reactors.* University of California, Lawrence Berkeley Laboratory, report LBL-5206. Very useful compilation of reactor characteristics and specifications, accessible to the nonspecialist.

Newton, G. C., Jr. 1976. Energy and the refrigerator. *Technology Review,* vol. 78, no. 3 (Jan.), pp. 56–63. Detailed look at refrigerator technology and the means available for increasing the efficiency of that appliance.

Nisbet, I. 1974. Hydroelectric power: A nonrenewable resource? *Technology Review,* vol. 76, no. 7 (June), p. 5. Addresses the worldwide problem of the silting up of reservoirs.

Norman, R. 1974. Water salination: A source of energy. *Science,* vol. 186, pp. 350–352 (October 25). Considers recovery of that part of the energy in the hydrologic cycle that is spent by the sun in evaporating fresh water from the ocean. Concludes the energy would be expensive and the environmental impact in estuarine regions high.

Norton, J. J. 1973. Lithium, cesium, and rubidium. In D. A. Brobst and W. P. Pratt, eds. *United States mineral resources.* Government Printing Office, Washington, D.C. One of only a few documents giving data on lithium resources (needed for deuterium-tritium fusion reactors).

NSF-NASA Solar Energy Panel. 1972. *An assessment of solar energy as a national energy resource.* National Technical Information Service, Springfield, Va. The first high-powered "official" study to conclude that solar energy could meet a significant fraction of the U.S. energy needs in the period 2000 to 2020.

Nuclear News. 1975. World list of nuclear power plants. Vol. 18, no. 10 (Aug.), p. 63. Locations, types, sizes, and start-up dates of plants in operation and under construction.

———. 1974. Nuclear process heat topical meeting. *Nuclear News,* vol. 17, no. 15 (Dec.), pp. 81–83. Surveys prospects for nonelectric industrial applications of the heat generated in nuclear reactors and finds them unencouraging for the near future.

———. 1975. Ten reactors currently do not have enough fuel storage. Vol. 18, no. 6 (mid-April), p. 64A.

Nuclear Regulatory Commission. See U.S. Nuclear Regulatory Commission.

Odum, H. T. 1971. *Environment, power, and society.* Wiley, New York. Ambitious attempt to view ecology and society in the same energy-centered framework. Ranges from obscure and overdrawn to brilliant.

Office of Emergency Preparedness (OEP), Executive Office of the President of the United States. 1972. *The potential for energy conservation.* Government Printing Office, Washington, D.C. Solid, persuasive study by many talented contributors, showing how increased end-use efficiency could cut the energy growth anticipated between 1972 and 1985 in half. The OEP was disbanded by President Richard M. Nixon not long after this study was published.

Okrent, D., et al. 1974. *Estimates of risk associated with dam failure.* University of California, Los Angeles, report UCLA-ENG-7423. Suggests that sudden failure of dams upstream of major cities could cause thousands to hundreds of thousands of deaths per incident.

ORNL-NSF Environmental Program. 1974. *Energy conservation and the environment.* Oak Ridge National Laboratory, Tenn., ORNL-NSF-EP-77.

Oswald, W. 1973. Ecological management of thermal discharges. *Journal of Environmental Quality,* vol. 2 (April/June), pp. 203–207. Use of the heat in power-plant discharges for agriculture.

Othmer, D., and O. Roels. 1973. Power, fresh water, and food from cold, deep sea water. *Science,* vol. 182, pp. 121–125 (October 12). Potential harnessing of ocean thermal gradients.

Parker, F., and P. Krenkel. 1970. *Physical and engineering aspects of thermal pollution.* CRC Press, Cleveland. Detailed technical treatment for specialists.

Patterson, Walter C. 1976. *Nuclear power.* Penguin, Harmondsworth, UK. The best "environmentalist" introduction to nuclear power.

Perry, A. M., and A. M. Weinberg. 1972. Thermal breeder reactors. *Annual review of nuclear science,* vol. 22, p. 317ff. Breeding and near-breeding in various thermal reactor designs.

Perry, H. 1970. Environmental aspects of coal mining. In *Power generation and environmental change,* D. Berkowitz and A. Squires, eds. Introductory survey by a prominent specialist in fossil fuels.

———. 1974. Coal conversion technology. *Chemical Engineering,* vol. 81, no. 15 (July 22), pp. 88–102. Technical problems and potential of gasification and liquefaction of coal.

———. 1974. The gasification of coal. *Scientific American,* March, pp. 19–25. Readable introduction to gasification for power generation and industrial and domestic uses, with *Scientific American*'s usual good diagrams.

Pierce, J. 1975. The fuel consumption of automobiles. *Scientific American,* January, pp. 34–44. Excellent treatment of where the energy goes in an automobile–rolling friction, flexing tires, air drag, and so on–together with the prospects for improvements.

Pigford, T. 1974. Environmental aspects of nuclear energy production. *Annual Review of Nuclear Science,* vol. 24, pp. 515–559. Quantitative look at the emissions from nuclear fuel cycles by a nuclear engineer who is highly respected both by critics and proponents of using nuclear power.

———; M. J. Keaton; B. Mann; P. M. Cukor; and G. Sessler. 1974. *Fuel cycles for electrical power generation,* Pt. 1. Teknekron, Inc., Berkeley, Calif., Report EED 103. One of the major comparative studies of environmental impacts of electricity generation alternatives. Superb fuel-cycle diagrams.

Pimentel, D.; W. Dritschilo; J. Krummel; and J. Kutzman. 1975. Energy and land constraints in food protein production. *Science,* vol. 190, pp. 754–761 (November 21). Argues that interlocking problems of land, water, energy, and environmental disruption severely limit the amount of protein that can be produced, making population control essential.

Pimentel, D.; L. Hurd; A. Bellotti; M. Forster; I. Oka; O. Sholes; and R. Whitman. 1973. Food production and the energy crisis. *Science,* vol. 182, p. 443–449 (November 2). Traces energy use in U.S. production of corn in detail, and shows energy implications of adopting this style of agriculture in developing countries.

Poole, A. 1975. The potential for energy recovery from organic wastes. In *The energy conservation papers,* R. H. Williams, ed., Ballinger, Cambridge, Mass. Authoritative and up to date.

Portola Institute. 1974. *Energy primer.* Portola Institute, Menlo Park, Calif. A splendid large-format guide to the literature of solar energy and energy conservation.

Post, R. F.; J. R. Morris; and F. J. Hooven. 1974. Letters. *Scientific American,* March, pp. 8–10. Continuation of the flywheel discussions. (See below.)

Post, R. F.; and S. Post. 1973. Flywheels. *Scientific American,* December, pp. 17–23. An intriguing look at how recent advances in high-strength materials may make an old idea for energy storage newly practical in transportation and electric-utility applications.

Post, R. F., and F. L. Ribe. 1974. Fusion reactors as future energy sources. *Science,* vol. 186, p. 397–407 (Nov. 1). An optimistic progress report by prominent fusion researchers at the Livermore and Los Alamos laboratories.

Primack, J.; F. Finlayson; N. Rasmussen; R. Weatherwax; H. Kouts; F. von Hippel; and H. Bethe. 1975. Nuclear reactor safety. *Bulletin of the Atomic Scientists,* vol. 31, no. 7 (September), pp. 15–41. Views of critics and supporters of the Rasmussen report on reactor safety.

Pugwash Conference on Science and World Affairs. 1973. Report of the working group on energy of the 23d conference. *Pugwash Newsletter,* Fall. [Reprinted in *Congressional Record,* Senate, vol. 119, pp. S18727-S8730 (October) and in *Perspectives on energy.* L. C. Ruedisili and M. W. Firebaugh, eds.] The Pugwash conferences are held annually by an international group of distinguished and influential scientists. A major topic of the 1973 meeting was nuclear energy. The summary report states "grave concern" over unresolved questions of reactor safety, radioactive waste management, and use of nuclear materials for bombs by countries or terrorists.

Ramseier, R. 1974. Oil on ice. *Environment,* vol. 16, no. 4 (May), pp. 6–14. Possibility of oil spills in the Arctic and their effects on climate.

Rattein, S., and D. Eaton. 1976. Oil shale: The prospects and problems of an emerging energy industry. In *Annual review of energy,* J. M. Hollander and M. K. Simmons, eds. Excellent coverage of environmental effects and economic obstacles.

Read, W.; A. Choda; and P. Cooper. 1974. Solar timber kiln. *Solar Energy,* vol. 15, no. 4, pp. 309–316. One of many possible industrial applications of solar energy.

Resnikoff, M. 1975. Expensive enrichment. *Environment,* vol. 17, no. 5 (July/Aug.), pp. 28–35. Notwithstanding the title (cryptically substituted for the author's descriptive one by the magazine's editors), this article deals with reprocessing of nuclear fuels–the technical difficulties, the economic costs, the environmental impacts.

Resources for the Future. 1968. *U.S. energy policies: An agenda for research.* Johns Hopkins Press, Baltimore. Although dated in some respects by the events of the 1970s, this book offers a useful compilation of information about state and federal policies related to coal, oil, gas, uranium, and electricity, as they evolved from the 1930s through the 1960s.

Revelle, R. 1976. Energy use in rural India. *Science,* vol. 192, pp. 969–975 (June 4). Villagers provide themselves far more energy from biological sources than they buy, but they use it ineffectively.

Reynolds, W. C. 1974. *Energy: From nature to man.* McGraw-Hill, New York. A well-written and absorbing introduction to energy technology aimed at college undergraduates outside engineering.

Rice, R. 1972. System energy and future transportation. *Technology Review,* vol. 74, no. 1 (January), pp. 31–37. Energy intensity of alternative modes of moving people and freight. One of the basic references in the field.

———. 1974. Toward more transportation with less energy. *Technology Review,* vol. 76, no. 4 (Nov.), pp. 44–53. Outlines a scenario for the year 2000 in which the United States obtains far more passenger miles and ton miles than in the 1960s with less energy.

Rieber, M. 1973. Low sulfur coal: A revision of reserve and supply estimates. *Center for Advanced Computation, Document 88.* University of Illinois, Champaign-Urbana. Revises downward the accepted estimates of U.S. reserves of low-sulfur coal by correcting for the low energy content per pound of many Western coals.

Rochlin, G. I. 1977. Nuclear waste disposal: Two social criteria. *Science,* vol. 195, pp. 23–31 (January 7). A penetrating look at questions of irreversibility and other aspects of the technical/ethical dilemma of radioactive wastes.

Rose, D. J. 1974. Nuclear electric power. *Science,* vol. 184, pp. 351–359 (April 19). The case for a major role for nuclear fission by an articulate proponent.

——— and M. Clark. 1961. *Plasmas and controlled fusion.* M.I.T. Press, Cambridge, Mass. Classic text on harnessing fusion by means of magnetic confinement.

——— and M. Feiertag. 1976. The prospect for fusion. *Technology review,* vol. 79, no. 2 (December), pp. 20–43. A critical review.

Ross, M., and R. Williams. 1977. The potential for fuel conservation. *Technology Review,* vol. 79, no. 4 (February), pp. 48–57. A useful summary of recent patterns of energy use in the United States and of the potential for greater efficiency.

Rotty, R. M.; A. M. Perry; and D. B. Reiser. 1975. *Net energy from nuclear power.* Institute for Energy Analysis, Oak Ridge, Tenn., IEA report 75-3. Probably the most comprehensive study to date of this question; concludes even light-water reactors using Chattanooga shales turn an energy profit.

Rubin, M. 1974. Plugging the energy sieve. *Bulletin of the Atomic Scientists,* vol. 30, no. 10 (December), pp. 7–17. Survey of potential for more-efficient end use of energy.

Ruedisili, L. C., and M. W. Firebaugh, eds. 1975. *Perspectives on energy.* Oxford University Press, New York. Collection of articles emphasizing sources of energy supply. A mixed bag, useful for its variety of viewpoints and a considerable number of good pieces resurrected from obscure publications.

Scherer, H. N., and B. J. Ware. 1975. The impact of high voltage lines. *Bulletin of the Atomic Scientists,* vol. 31, no. 7 (Sept.), pp. 51–52.

Schipper, L. 1975. *Energy conservation: Its nature, hidden benefits and hidden barriers.* Energy and Resources Group, University of California, Berkeley, ERG 75-2. Excellent introduction to the potential of more efficient energy use.

——— and A. Lichtenberg. 1975. Efficient energy use and well-being: The Swedish example. *Science,* vol. 194, pp. 1001–1013. Careful analysis of energy use in the U.S. and Swedish economies, showing exactly where greater efficiencies enable Swedes to extract more well-being per unit of energy than do Americans.

Schoen, R.; A. S. Hirshberg; J. M. Weingart; and J. Stein. 1975. *New energy technology for buildings.* Ballinger, Cambridge, Mass. Prepared for the Energy Policy Project of the Ford Foundation, this report emphasizes solar technology for buildings and the economic and institutional barriers to its implementation.

Schumacher, E. F. 1973. Western Europe's energy crisis: Problem of life-styles. *Ambio,* vol. 2, no. 6, pp. 228–232. The guru of intermediate technology applies his thinking to Europe's energy dilemma.

———. 1976. Patterns of human settlement. *Ambio,* vol. 5, no. 3, pp. 91–97. Connection between settlement patterns and energy use.

Science and Public Policy Program, University of Oklahoma. 1975. *Energy alternatives: A comparative analysis.* Government Printing Office, Washington, D.C. Comprehensive although somewhat unwieldy comparison of energy-supply alternatives, with extensive bibliographies.

Scientific American. 1971. *Energy and power.* Freeman and Company, San Francisco. Collection of articles from the September 1971 *Scientific American.* The best are those by Hubbert, Cook, Summers, Luten, and Tribus and McIrvine.

Seaborg, G. T. 1970. *Nuclear milestones.* W. H. Freeman and Company, San Francisco. A personal history of the nuclear age; by its nature uneven in coverage, but still informative.

Sellers, W. D. 1965. *Physical climatology.* University of Chicago Press. Good basic text.

Shapley, Deborah. 1971. Plutonium: Reactor proliferation threatens a black market. *Science,* vol. 172, pp. 143–146 (April 9). Short discussion of the growing threat of theft of fissile material for bombs as reactors spread.

Shurcliff, W. A. 1976. Active-type solar heating systems for houses: A technology in ferment. *Bulletin of the Atomic Scientists,* vol. 32, no. 2 (Feb.), pp. 30–40. Up-to-date survey.

Singer, S. F. 1975. Oil resource estimates. *Science,* vol. 188, p. 401 (May 2). A critique of the estimation procedures employed by M. K. Hubbert and the Committee on Mineral Resources and the Environment of the National Academy of Sciences.

Smith, C. 1972. Shipment and reprocessing of irradiated power reactor fuels. In *Education and research in the nuclear fuel cycle,* D. Elliott and L. Weaver, eds. Good technical description of the reprocessing technology in place in the 1960s.

Smith, K.; J. Weyant; and J. P. Holdren. 1975. *Evaluation of conventional power systems.* University of California, Berkeley, Report ERG-75-7. Detailed survey of economic and environmental costs of electricity generation with coal, oil, gas, and nuclear fission.

Socolow, R. H. 1977. The coming age of conservation. *Annual Review of Energy,* vol. 2. An international perspective on prospects for conservation.

Sørenson, B. 1975. Energy and resources. *Science,* vol. 180, p. 255–260 (July 25). A scenario for supplying Denmark's energy needs with wind and sunlight.

Speth, J. G.; A. R. Tamplin; and T. B. Cochran. 1974. Plutonium recycle: The fateful step. *Bulletin of the Atomic Scientists,* vol. 30, no. 9, pp. 15–22. The case against permitting the recycle of plutonium as fuel for light-water reactors.

Spinrad, B. 1971. The role of nuclear power in meeting world energy needs. In *Environmental aspects of nuclear power stations,* International Atomic Energy Agency, Vienna. Forecasts high global growth of electricity use and a dominant role for nuclear energy in providing the electricity.

Squires, A. M. 1974. Clean fuels from coal gasification. *Science,* vol. 184, pp. 340–346 (April 19). Good review article by a prominent coal enthusiast.

———. 1972. Clean power from dirty fuels. *Scientific American,* October, pp. 26–35. Emphasizes use of coal in gas turbine/steam turbine combined-cycle power stations.

Stauffer, T. 1974. Oil money and world money: Conflict or confluence? *Science,* vol. 184, p. 321–325 (April 19). This assessment of the economic impact of the 1973/1974 oil embargo finds it smaller than many accounts.

Stein, R. 1972. A matter of design. *Environment,* vol. 14, no. 8 (October), pp. 16–29. Identifies significant opportunities for energy conservation in the construction and operation of commercial buildings.

Steinhart, J. 1975. The impact of technical advice on the choice for nuclear power. In *Perspectives on energy,* L. C. Ruedisili and M. W. Firebaugh, eds. A critical and penetrating analysis that deserves much wider readership.

——— and Steinhart, C. 1974. Energy use in the U.S. food system. *Science,* vol. 184, pp. 307–316 (April 19). History of increasing use of energy in the growing and processing of food.

Stewart, R. J. 1976. Oil spills and offshore petroleum. *Technology Review,* vol. 78, no. 4 (February), pp. 46–59. Data and analysis of experience and prospects with respect to oil spills.

Summers, C. 1971. The conversion of energy. *Scientific American,* September, pp. 148–160. (Reprinted in *Energy and power, Scientific American,* ed., W. H. Freeman and Company, San Francisco, 1971.) Capsule introduction to technological aspects of energy conversion.

Szego, G.; and C. Kemp. 1973. Energy forests and fuel plantations. *Chemtech,* May, pp. 275–284. Proposal to use fast-growing pine or eucalyptus trees as fuel for power-plant boilers.

Tamplin, A., and T. Cochran. 1974. *Radiation standards for hot particles.* National Resources Defense Council, Washington, D.C. Proposes lowering the standard for the permissible lung burden of plutonium particles by roughly 100,000 times, based on the hypothesis that doses delivered locally by small "hot" particles are more dangerous than uniformly-distributed doses of equal energy.

Taylor, T. B. 1973. Diversion by non-governmental organizations. In *International safeguards and nuclear industry,* M. Willrich, ed. Johns Hopkins Press, Baltimore. A look at nuclear theft by subnational groups, by a preeminent authority on nuclear weapons.

Taylor, T. B. 1975. Nuclear Safeguards. *Annual Review of Nuclear Science,* vol. 25, pp. 407–421. The best short treatment of the technical basis for concern that small groups could produce nuclear bombs with stolen nuclear materials.

Theobald, P. K.; S. P. Schweinfurth; and D. C. Duncan. 1972. *Energy resources of the United States.* Government Printing Office, Washington, D.C., Geological Survey circular 650. Summary of the U.S. Geological Survey position before its estimates of U.S. gas and oil were revised sharply downward in 1975.

Thorndike, E. H. 1976. *Energy and environment: A primer for scientists and engineers.* Addison-Wesley, Reading, Mass. Good intermediate-level text.

Total Environmental Action. 1975. *Solar energy home design in four climates.* Total Environmental Action, Harrisville, N.H. A guide for the serious builder.

Tybout, R. and Löf, G. 1970. Solar house heating. *Natural Resources Journal,* vol. 10, no. 2 (April), pp. 268–326. A classic paper in the contemporary literature of solar energy, showing that solar heat could compete with electric resistive heating in sunny parts of the United States.

United Nations. Annual. *Statistical yearbook.* U.N. Publications, New York. This is the basic reference for our international energy-use statistics.

———. 1967. *Utilization of oil shale.* U.N. Publications, New York. Summarizes early experience in oil-shale utilization in the USSR and elsewhere.

U.S. Atomic Energy Commission (USAEC) Annual. *The nuclear industry.* Government Printing Office, Washington, D.C., WASH 1174-73. The 1973 volume, in particular, is useful for its treatment of the status of the uranium industry and for updates on other unglamorous aspects of the fuel cycle.

———. 1957. *Theoretical possibilities and consequences of major accidents in large nuclear power plants.* Government Printing Office, Washington, D.C., WASH-740. Much-quoted early study of the consequences of a hypothetical accident at a small power reactor. Gives a worst case of 3400 early fatalities, an event the study deems to have low but unspecified probability.

———. 1964/1965. WASH-740 update file. USAEC, Public Documents Room, Washington, D.C. An update of the 1957 reactor-safety study was begun in 1964 but aborted after preliminary results had indicated higher casualty estimates than the earlier study.

———. 1970. *Potential nuclear power growth patterns.* Government Printing Office, Washington, D.C., WASH-1098. Dated forecasts, but useful for the detailed descriptions of the characteristics of various reactor designs and fuel mixes, and for estimates of low-grade uranium resources.

———. 1972. *Contaminated soil removal facility: Richland, Washington.* National Technical Information Service, Springfield, Va., WASH-1520. Describes some of the problems that have developed in the handling of radioactive wastes from military programs.

———. 1972. *Elk River dismantling: Environmental statement.* National Technical Information Service, Springfield, Va., WASH-1516. One of the few available documents that deals with decommissioning nuclear reactors at the end of their operating lifetimes.

———. 1973. *Nuclear fuel resources and requirements.* Government Printing Office, Washington, D.C., WASH-1243.

———. 1973. *The safety of nuclear power reactors and related facilities.* National Technical Information Service, Springfield, Va., WASH-1250. An uneven but in some respects very useful compendium of information about light-water reactors, radiation, waste-handling, regulations, and related topics.

———. 1974. *Environmental impact statement on the liquid metal fast breeder reactor program.* Government Printing Office, Washington, D.C., WASH-1535. Prepared after a successful environmentalist lawsuit demanded a programmatic (as opposed to reactor-by-reactor) impact statement, this controversial document slights plutonium problems and unresolved questions about breeder safety, but contains considerable valuable information about nonnuclear alternatives.

———. 1974. *Environmental survey of the nuclear fuel cycle.* National Technical Information Service, Springfield, Va., WASH-1248. An official look at emissions, water use, land use, and so on, emphasizing steps in the fuel cycle other than the reactor itself.

———. 1974. *Generic environmental impact statement: Mixed-oxide fuel.* National Technical Information Service, Springfield, Va., WASH-1327, draft. Controversial, and certainly incomplete, discussion of the consequences of plutonium recycle for light-water reactors.

———. 1974. *High-level radioactive waste management alternatives.* National Technical Information Service, Springfield, Va., WASH-1297. A generally even-handed and data-rich assessment of the known options for managing nuclear wastes.

———. 1974. *Management of commercial high-level and transuranium contaminated radioactive waste.* USAEC Washington, D.C., WASH-1539 draft. Scandalously incomplete and incompetent environmental impact statement, deplored publicly by environmentalists and privately by nuclear industry trade associations.

———. 1974. *Nuclear power growth 1974–2000.* Government Printing Office, Washington, D.C., WASH-1139(74). Forecast of an expanding role for nuclear power through the year 2000, although at a slower rate than euphoric earlier forecasts.

———. 1974. *Reactor safety study,* 12 vols. Government Printing Office, Washington, D.C., WASH-1400 draft. Draft of the so-called Rasmussen report on the safety of light-water reactors. Badly organized, carelessly printed, needlessly tedious, and systematically overoptimistic. Some of the errors were remedied in the final draft (see U.S. Nuclear Regulatory Commission, *Reactor safety study*), but new errors were introduced.

———. 1974. *Solar energy: A bibliography.* National Technical Information Service, Springfield, Va. Very useful and comprehensive guide to the literature.

———. 1974. A special safeguards study (the Rosenbaum report). *Congressional Record,* April 30, 1974, pp. S 6621–6630. High-level study revealing shocking gaps in U.S. safeguards against theft of nuclear materials.

U.S. Congress, House of Representatives, Committee on Science and Technology. 1975. *ERDA Authorization Hearings:* Part 1, *1976 and transition period conservation.* Government Printing Office, Washington, D.C. Notable for its inclusion in full of the American Physical Society study, *Efficient use of energy,* pt. 1.

U.S. Congress, Joint Committee on Atomic Energy (JCAE). 1969 and 1970. *Hearings on environmental effects of producing electric power,* pts. 1 and 2. Government Printing Office, Washington, D.C. Extensive coverage of environmental effects of coal and nuclear fission.

———. 1971. *Controlled thermonuclear research.* Government Printing Office, Washington, D.C.

———. 1971. *Hearings on use of uranium mill tailings for construction purposes.* 92d Congress, 1st Session. Government Printing Office, Washington, D.C.

U.S. Congress, Office of Technology Assessment. 1975. *An analysis of the ERDA plan and program.* Government Printing Office, Washington, D.C. A distinguished group of consultants deliver a biting 300-page critique of the Energy Research and Development Administration program, finding overemphasis on high-technology, centralized sources of supply and underemphasis on diversity and conservation.

U.S. Department of Commerce. Annual. *Statistical abstract of the United States.* Government Printing Office, Washington, D.C. An indispensible storehouse of information about energy use—and almost every other activity—in the United States.

———. 1960. *Historical statistics of the United States, colonial times to 1957.* Government Printing Office, Washington, D.C.

———. 1970. *Climatological data: National summary.* Government Printing Office, Washington, D.C. Gives distribution of incident solar energy in the United States.

U.S. Department of the Interior. 1972. *Final environmental impact statement, proposed trans-Alaska pipeline.* Vol. 1. Government Printing Office, Washington, D.C. An uneven but useful document, largely ignored in the final congressional vote.

———. 1976. *Energy perspectives 2.* Government Printing Office, Washington, D.C. Very useful compilation of data on energy resources and reserves in the U.S. and worldwide.

U.S. Energy Research and Development Administration (ERDA). 1975. *A national plan for energy research development and demonstration: creating energy choices for the future.* Government Printing Office, Washington, D.C., ERDA-48. Widely criticized by environmentalists and academic energy experts for lack of vision, failure to grasp essential difficulties, and underemphasis on more efficient end-use of energy.

———.1975. *DCTR fusion-fission energy systems meeting.* Government Printing Office, Washington, D.C., ERDA-4. Motivation, preliminary designs, and potential problems of fission-fusion hybrid reactors.

———. 1975. *Final report of the special laser fusion advisory panel.* National Technical Information Service, Springfield, Va. ERDA-28. Good review of status of laser-fusion research, with some discussion of relevance to fusion-bomb technology.

———. 1975. *Final environmental statement, liquid metal fast breeder reactor program. 10 vols.* (7 of them, the *Proposed final environmental statement,* USAEC, December 1974, WASH-1535). ERDA, Washington, D.C., ERDA-1535. Updated material on uranium resources and other aspects of LMFBR economics and impacts.

———. 1975. *National plan for solar heating and cooling: Interim report.* ERDA Technical Information Center, Oak Ridge, Tenn., ERDA-23. Outlines a reasonably ambitious plan for deploying solar technology. Whether ERDA is serious about carrying it out remains an open question.

———. 1975. *Nuclear fuel cycle: A report by the fuel-cycle task force.* National Technical Information Service, Springfield, Va., ERDA-33. Identifies difficulties in reprocessing and in waste management.

———. 1975. *Report of the liquid metal fast breeder reactor program review group.* Government Printing Office, Washington, D.C., ERDA-1. Recent data on uranium resources and the government view of breeder reactor economics.

———. 1976. *A national plan for energy research development and demonstration: Creating energy choices for the future.* Government Printing Office, Washington, D.C., ERDA 76-1. Updated and somewhat improved version of ERDA-48.

———. 1976. *Alternatives for managing wastes from reactors and post-fission operations in the nuclear fuel cycle.* Government Printing Office, Washington, D.C. ERDA 76-43. More technical detail about processes and low-level and intermediate-level wastes than available in most other studies.

U.S. Environmental Protection Agency (EPA). 1975. *Reactor safety study: A review of the draft report.* National Technical Information Service, Springfield, Va., EPA-520/3-75-012. Telling critique of the USAEC Rasmussen report on safety of light-water reactors.

———. 1976. *Reactor safety study (WASH-1400): A review of the final report.* EPA, Washington, D.C., EPA-520/3-76-009. Uncovers many remaining defects in the final draft of the Rasmussen report and indicates that its estimate of cancer deaths is low by a factor of 2 to 10.

U.S. Federal Energy Administration, 1974. *Fact sheet on deepwater ports.* Government Printing Office, Washington, D.C. An abbreviated treatment.

———. 1974. *Geothermal energy task force report.* Government Printing Office, Washington, D.C. This was prepared by an interagency task force on geothermal energy under the direction of the National Science Foundation, for the Project Independence Blueprint. Optimistic and data-rich treatment of the potential of geothermal development in the United States.

———. 1974. *Solar energy task force report.* Government Printing Office, Washington, D.C. This report was prepared for the Project Independence Blueprint by an interagency task force on solar energy under the direction of the National Science Foundation. It indicates that solar energy could be supplying roughly 40 quadrillion Btu of commercial energy in the United States by the year 2000 if a crash program were implemented.

U.S. National Committee of the World Energy Conference. 1974. *World energy conferenc survey of energy resources, 1974.* New York. Detailed survey of distribution of fossil and nuclear fuels, with briefer attention to geothermal and solar sources.

U.S. Nuclear Regulatory Commission (NRC). 1975. *Nuclear energy center site survey.* NUREG-75/018. Government Printing Office, Washington, D.C. Considers potential and difficulties of clustering several nuclear reactors along with their fuel reprocessing and fabrication facilities.

———. 1975. *Reactor safety study: An assessment of accident risks in U.S. commercial nuclear power plants.* WASH-1400, NUREG-75/014. National Technical Information Service, Springfield, Va. An enormous quantity of information related to probabilities and consequences of nuclear-reactor accidents. Marred by clumsy, careless, and occasionally seriously misleading exposition, as well as many questionable assumptions and some outright errors. Popularly known as "The Rasmussen Report."

von Hippel, F. 1977. Looking back on the Rasmussen report. *Bulletin of the Atomic Scientists,* vol. 33, no. 2, pp. 42–47. A telling overview of shortcomings in the Nuclear Regulatory Commission's study of light-water reactor safety.

von Hippel, F., and J. P. Holdren. 1975. Discussion of "A perspective on fusion and fission breeders." *Journal of the British Nuclear Energy Society,* vol. 14, no. 2, pp. 119–122. Independent rebuttals to an article asserting that fusion has few if any environmental advantages over fission.

von Hippel, F. and R. H. Williams. 1975. Solar technologies. *Bulletin of the Atomic Scientists,* vol. 31, no. 9 (Nov.), pp. 25–31. A survey emphasizing the environmental liabilities of various possibilities.

———. 1976. Energy waste and nuclear power growth. *Bulletin of the Atomic Scientists,* vol. 32, no. 10 (December), pp. 18ff. Well argued case against an early commitment to the breeder reactor.

Watson, M.; W. Kammer; N. Langley; L. Selzer; R. Beck. 1972. *Underground nuclear power siting.* California Institute of Technology, Pasadena, Environmental Quality Laboratory report 6. Indi-

Young, L., and H. Young. 1974. Pollution by electrical transmission. *Bulletin of the Atomic Scientists,* vol. 30, no. 10 (Dec.), pp. 34–38. Argues that the electric fields produced by high-voltage electric transmission lines may be harmful to health.

Zare, R. N. 1977. Laser separation of isotopes. *Scientific American,* February, pp. 86–98. Survey of the technical possibilities.

Zener, C. 1973. Solar sea power. *Physics today,* January, pp. 48–53. An early enthusiast of harnessing ocean thermal gradients outlines the possibilities.

———. 1976. Solar sea power. *Bulletin of the Atomic Scientists,* vol. 32, no. 1 (Jan.), pp. 17–24. Thoughtful update of earlier work, suggesting that a 100-Mwe plant could be built and tested by 1983.

cates nuclear plants could be located under a few hundred feet of solid rock at an increase in construction cost of about 10 percent.

Weingart, J. 1975. Solar energy. In *McGraw-Hill Encyclopedia of Science and Technology.* McGraw-Hill, New York. Useful, concise review article.

White, D. E., and D. L. Williams, eds. 1975. *Assessment of geothermal resources of the United States, 1975.* Government Printing Office, Washington, D.C., Geological Survey circular 726.

Whittaker, R., and G. Likens. 1973. Carbon in the biota. in *Carbon in the biosphere,* G. Woodwell and E. Pecan, eds., National Technical Information Service, Springfield, Va., USAEC CONF-720510.

Williams, J. R. 1974. *Solar energy: Technology and applications.* Ann Arbor Science Publishers, Ann Arbor Mich. A useful text.

Williams, R. H., ed. 1975. *The energy conservation papers.* Ballinger, Cambridge, Mass. Prepared for the Energy Policy Project of the Ford Foundation, this very useful collection covers recycling, the energy needs of pollution control, the employment impact of conservation, and other topics.

Willrich, M., ed. 1973. *International safeguards and nuclear industry.* Johns Hopkins Press, Baltimore. Good background reading on proliferation and diversion.

Willrich, M., and T. Taylor. 1974. *Nuclear theft: Risks and safeguards.* Ballinger, Cambridge, Mass. Prepared for the Energy Policy Project of the Ford Foundation, this is the most comprehensive and authoritative treatment of misuse of nuclear material by subnational groups.

Wilson, R., 1973. Natural gas is a beautiful thing? *Bulletin of the Atomic Scientists,* vol. 24, no. 7 (Sept.), pp. 35–40. Enumerates hazards of storing and transporting natural gas, focusing on liquified natural gas tankers.

Wolf, M. 1976. Photovoltaic solar energy conversion. *Bulletin of the Atomic Scientists,* vol. 32, no. 4 (April), pp. 26–33. An optimistic report on progress toward economically attractive solar cells.

Wolkenhauer, W., et al. 1973. *Transmutation of high-level radioactive wastes with a controlled thermonuclear reactor.* Springfield, Va., National Technical Information Service, Battelle, Pacific Northwest Laboratories Report BNWL-1722. Preliminary study of using neutrons from a fusion reactor to shorten the lifetimes of radioactive wastes from fission.

Woodson, R. 1971. Cooling towers. *Scientific American,* May, pp.70–78. Various approaches to cooling large power plants, with estimates of the economic costs of each approach.

Wooley, M., and J. Platts. 1975. Energy on the crest of a wave. *New Scientist,* May 1, pp. 241–243. Possibility of harnessing the energy in ocean waves for production of electricity.

World Bank. Annual. *World Bank atlas.* Washington, D.C. Convenient collection of data on population, GNP, and their growth rates for all countries.

Yadigaroglu, G., and S. O. Anderson. 1974. Novel siting solutions for nuclear power plants. *Nuclear Safety,* vol. 15, November/December, pp. 651–664. Technical and safety characteristics of floating and underground power plants.

Yellin, Joel. 1976. The Nuclear Regulatory Commission's reactor safety study. *Bell Journal of Economics,* vol. 7, no. 1, pp. 317–339. A devastating technical critique.

Yellot, J. I. 1974. Solar radiation and its uses on Earth. In *The energy primer,* Portola Institute, ed. Portola Institute, Menlo Park, Calif. pp. 4–24. An excellent introduction to solar heating, cooling and cooking.

The idea that we are moving into a world of absolutely secure and effortless abundance is nonsense.

—Kenneth Boulding, 1970

CHAPTER 9

Materials

Materials discussed in this chapter include nonfuel mineral resources, forest products, natural and artificial fibers, and some other chemicals; excluded (except for occasional purposes of comparison) are fuels, foods, and drugs.

The world situation with respect to materials has many similarities to the energy situation. The near-term difficulties arise not so much from "running out" in an absolute sense as from the rising environmental costs of mobilizing and using ever larger quantities, from the economic and social dislocations that result from substituting one class of resources for another, and from the political ramifications of the nonuniform geographical distribution of resources and the capacity to exploit them.

In the longer term, the question of scarcity looms larger. It is sometimes asserted that, since our planet is quite literally made of materials, and since, with negligible exceptions, these do not leave the planet but remain here even after use, civilization can never run out of them. Although this assertion is true in a narrow sense, it misses the real issues. For "nonrenewable" resources, such as chromium and mercury, exhaustion occurs in the practical sense when the remaining unexploited material and the dispersed used material are so dilute that concentrating them simply costs too much in dollars, energy, or environmental disruption. "Too much" in this context means that the benefits of having the concentrated material do not match the costs of getting it.[1] For "renewable" resources, such as wood or cotton, the question is what levels of population and consumption per person can be supported by the sustainable yield. A

[1]An excellent exposition of this point is given by Earl Cook, Limits to exploitation of nonrenewable resources.

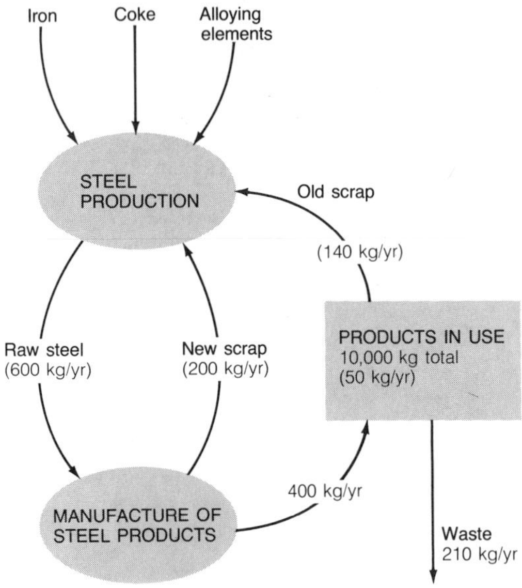

FIGURE 9-1

Stock and flow of steel in the United States, per capita. There is an annual increase in the stock corresponding to about 0.5 percent. The average residence time of steel in the economy is about 29 years. (After Garrels et al, 1975.)

TABLE 9-1
Amount and Value of Materials Flows in the United States in 1972, per Inhabitant

Material	*Flow (kilograms per person per year)*	*Value (dollars per person per year)*
Sand and gravel	4100	5.47
Stone	3900	5.94
Petroleum	3500	85.10
Natural gas	2300	18.97
Coal	2300	17.07
Forest products	1250	20.00
Iron and steel	550	24.43
Cement	360	6.55
Clays	270	1.26
Salt	200	1.66
Natural fibers and oils	23	15.00
Aluminum	23	12.40
Copper	11	8.06
Lead	7	1.26
Zinc	7	2.07
Natural rubber	5	1.40
All other metals	16	7.69
All other nonmetals	550	1.57
Totals	19,300	236.75

Note: Fuels are included for comparison. Values are 1972 prices in 1972 dollars.
Source: National Commission on Materials Policy, *Material needs and the environment today and tomorrow.*

"sustainable" yield must be consistent with other demands on land, water, sunlight, human labor and the other inputs to production; and the level of environmental disruption it entails must be neither intolerable nor growing.

It needs to be emphasized that achievable and sustainable levels of renewable materials production are different concepts. What might be achieved only with the assistance of nonrenewable inputs (say, concentrated phosphate inputs for high-yield crop production) is, in the long term, not sustainable.

MATERIALS USE: FLOWS AND STOCKS

Most data published on use of materials refer to annual production or flow—for example, tons of iron per year or cubic meters of wood per year. Less frequently tabulated but very important is the stock of material in service—for example, the total tonnage of steel tied up in the artifacts of civilization (buildings, vehicles, railways, etc.). As with materials balances encountered in other applications, the flow equals the stock divided by the average lifetime of the material in use ("residence time"), if the stock is constant in size.

The relation between stock and flow for steel in the United States is indicated schematically in Figure 9-1. The stock of steel in products in use is about 17 times the annual production and about 25 times the actual annual increase in the stock. The difference between production and input to stock is "new scrap": trimmings, shavings, and so on, which are recycled as feed to the steel-production process. "Old scrap" is material recycled for the production of new steel following use as manufactured products.

Patterns of Supply and Use in the United States

Table 9-1 shows the amounts of materials mobilized per person (flows) in the United States in 1972, together with the value of these materials in 1972 dollars. Fuels are included for comparision, and amount to 42 percent

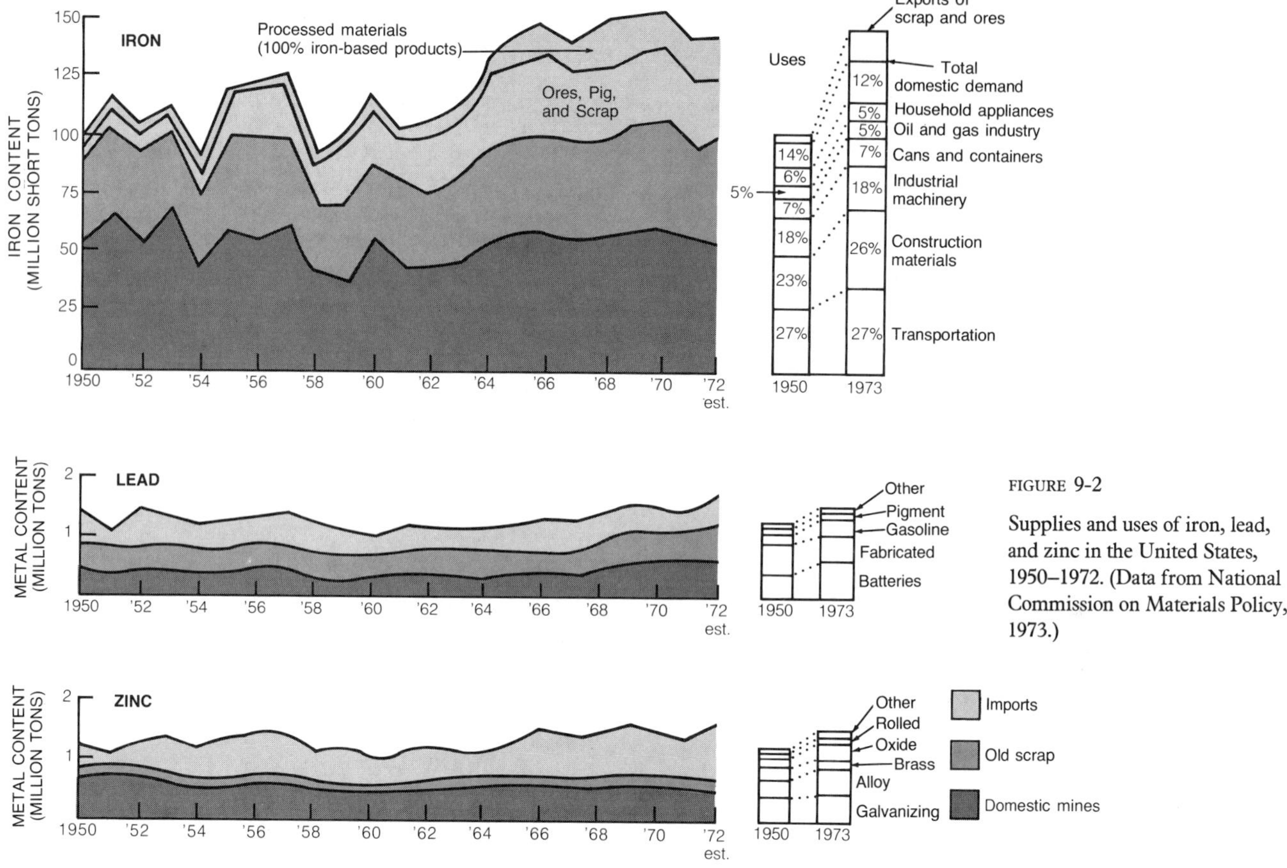

FIGURE 9-2

Supplies and uses of iron, lead, and zinc in the United States, 1950–1972. (Data from National Commission on Materials Policy, 1973.)

of the mass and 51 percent of the value of the totals shown. (Note that the prices are pre-oil-embargo: the figure given in Table 9-1 for petroleum corresponds to \$3.33 per barrel, roughly a fourth of the price three years later. The increase between 1972 and 1975 in the "value" of the oil alone exceeds the total value in 1972 for all the materials shown).

About a fourth of the value of the materials mobilized in the U.S. in 1972 was accounted for by metals.[2] The history of the sources and uses of the five most important ones—iron and steel (counted as one), aluminum, copper, lead, and zinc—from 1950 to 1972 is depicted graphically in Figures 9-2 and 9-3. Except for aluminum, the upward trend in annual use has been gradual. The impression that much of the industrial growth taking place in this period has been based on the use of newer, lighter materials in place of the traditional metals is reinforced by the data for plastics shown in Figure 9-4. Note that the mass of plastics being produced in the early 1970s already exceeded that of aluminum, copper, lead, and zinc combined. The continuing dominant role of iron and steel among industrial materials should not be underestimated, however. The *growth* between 1950 and 1972 in the tonnage of iron flowing into the U.S. economy (from 100 to 140 million tons per year) exceeds by a factor of more than two the *total* tonnage of flow of aluminum and plastic combined in 1972.

Use of the traditional construction materials, sand, gravel, and crushed stone, more than tripled in the United States between 1950 and 1972, as shown in Figure 9-5. These represent ten times the bulk of all the metals used, and hence are among the best indicators of the size of society's large-scale environmental transformations. Supplies of fertilizers, an index of the size of perturbations in natural nutrient cycles, are shown for the U.S. between 1950 and 1972 in Figure 9-6.

[2]National Commission on Materials Policy, *Material needs and the environment today and tomorrow.*

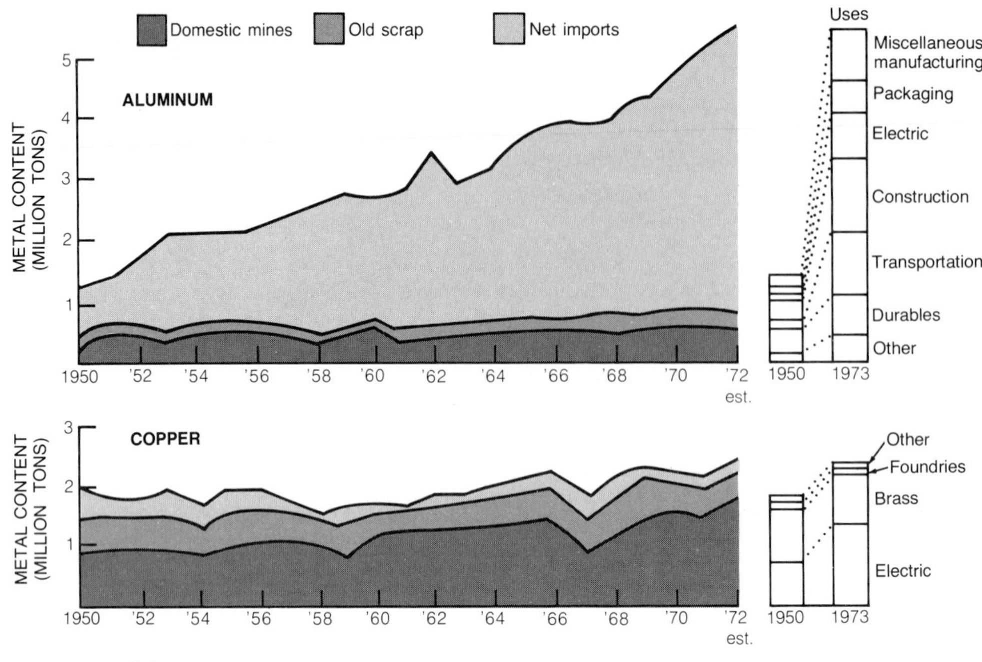

FIGURE 9-3

Supplies and uses of aluminum and copper in the United States, 1950–1972. Aluminum substitutes for copper in many electric applications, and for steel in construction, transportation, and packaging. (Data from National Commission on Materials Policy, 1973.)

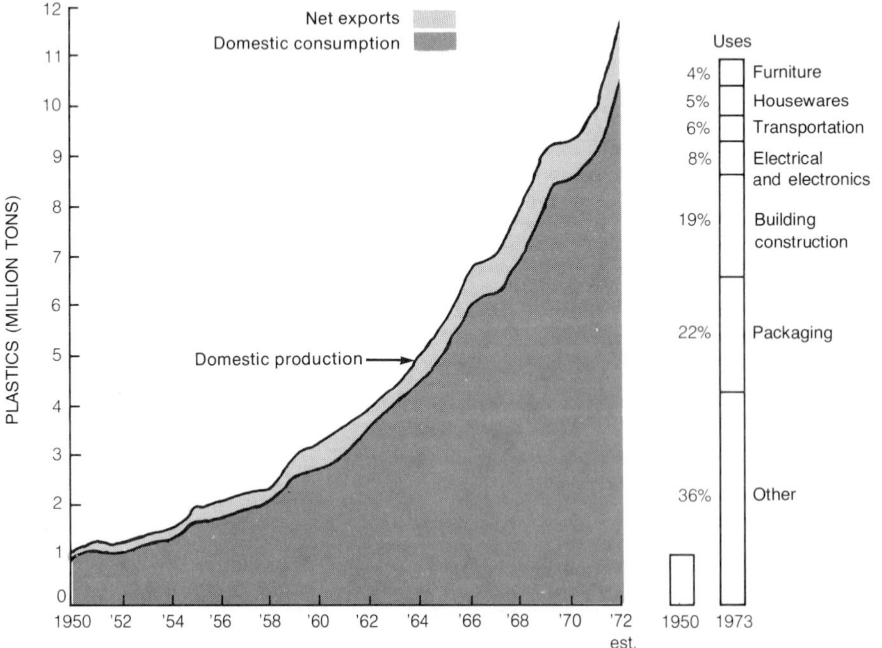

FIGURE 9-4

Supplies and uses of plastics in the United States, 1952–1972. Most plastics are derived from natural gas or petroleum. (Data from National Commission on Materials Policy, 1973.)

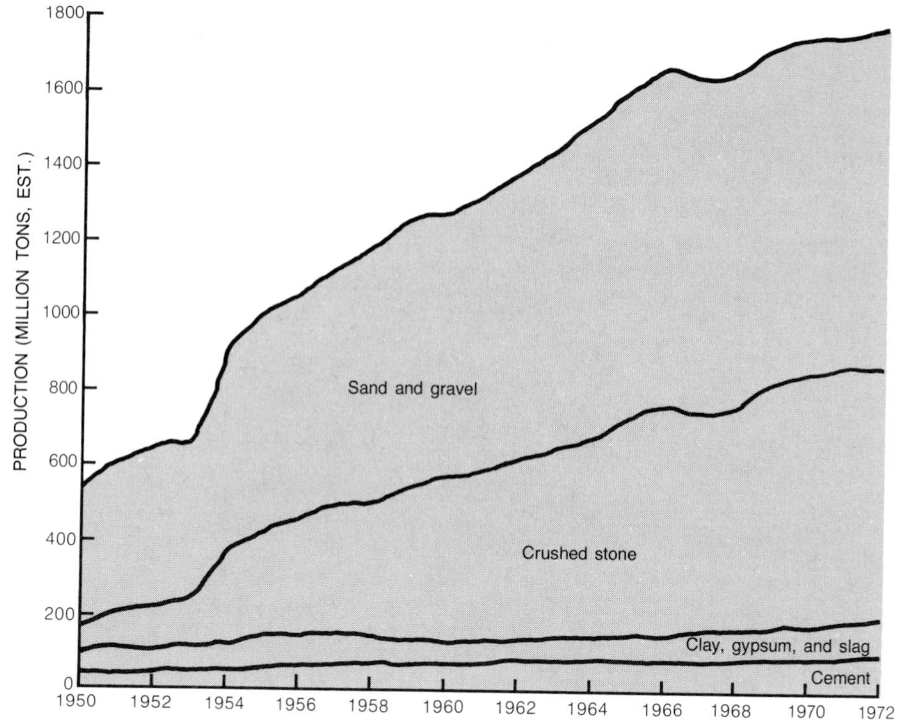

FIGURE 9-5

Supplies of nonmetallic construction materials in the United States, 1950–1972. (Data from National Commission on Materials Policy, 1973.)

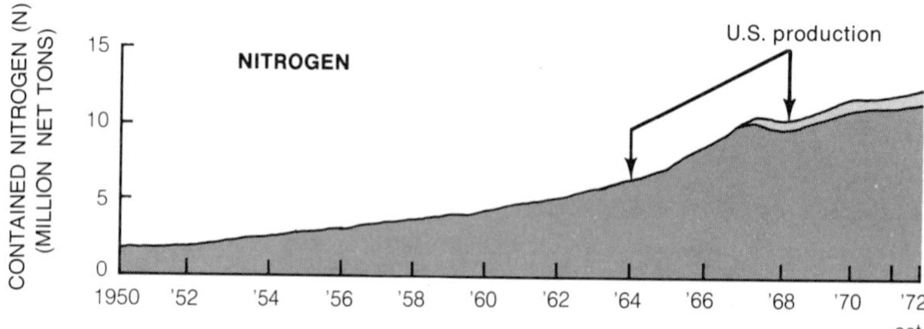

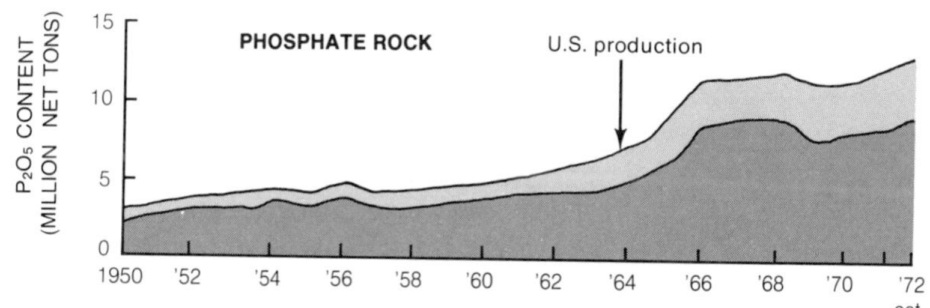

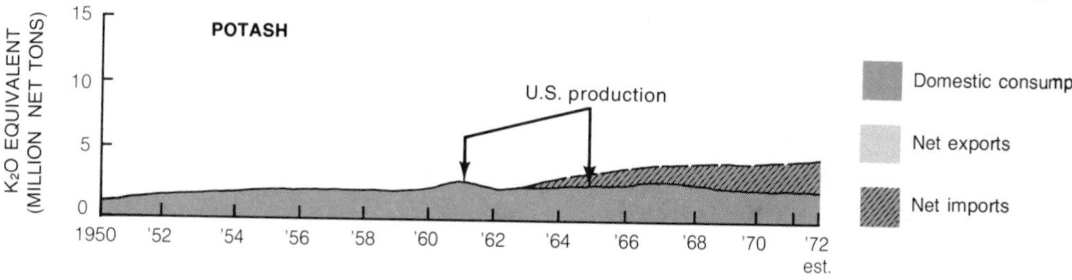

FIGURE 9-6

Supplies of fertilizers in the United States, 1950–1972. (Data from National Commission on Materials Policy, 1973.)

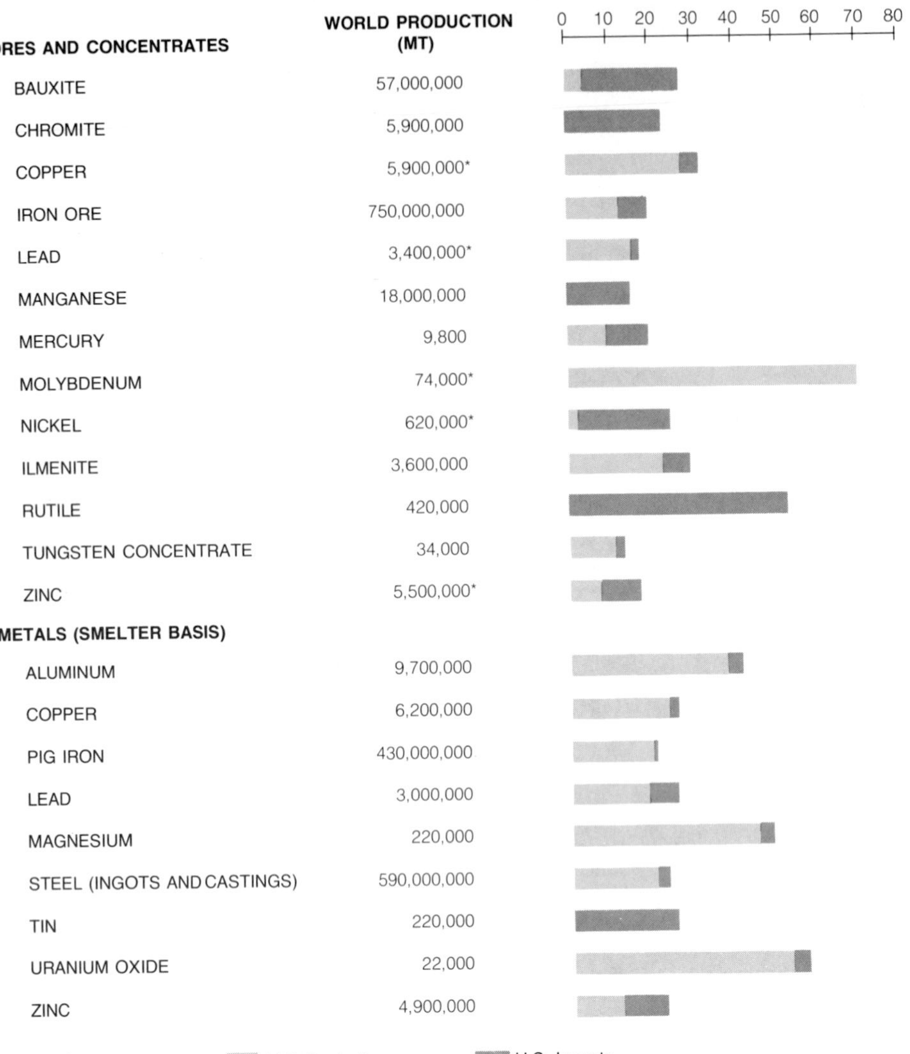

FIGURE 9-7

U.S. production and imports as a fraction of world production for selected materials, 1970. (Data from National Commission on Materials Policy, 1973.)

Materials Supply Worldwide

The share of worldwide use of materials accounted for by the United States, based on an index of 31 of the most important metals, nonmetals, and mineral fuels, fell from nearly 50 percent to around 32 percent between 1950 and 1972.[3] This decline in U.S. dominance was due not to the poor countries gaining in affluence and increasing their use of materials, but rather to medium-rich regions—eastern and western Europe, the Soviet Union, Japan—growing richer.

[3]Ibid., pp. 2–15.

The sizes of U.S. material production and imports as fractions of world production are indicated for some important minerals in Figure 9-7. If figures for consumption in Europe, the Soviet Union, and Japan are added to the U.S. figures for these materials, the total in most cases would reach 85 or 90 percent. The extent of U.S. dependence on imports for its supply of a larger variety of materials is shown in Figure 9-8, together with the countries from which the bulk of the imports come.

What do these data mean? Concern about the size of the U.S. share of world consumption and about the fraction of this share that is imported takes several forms.

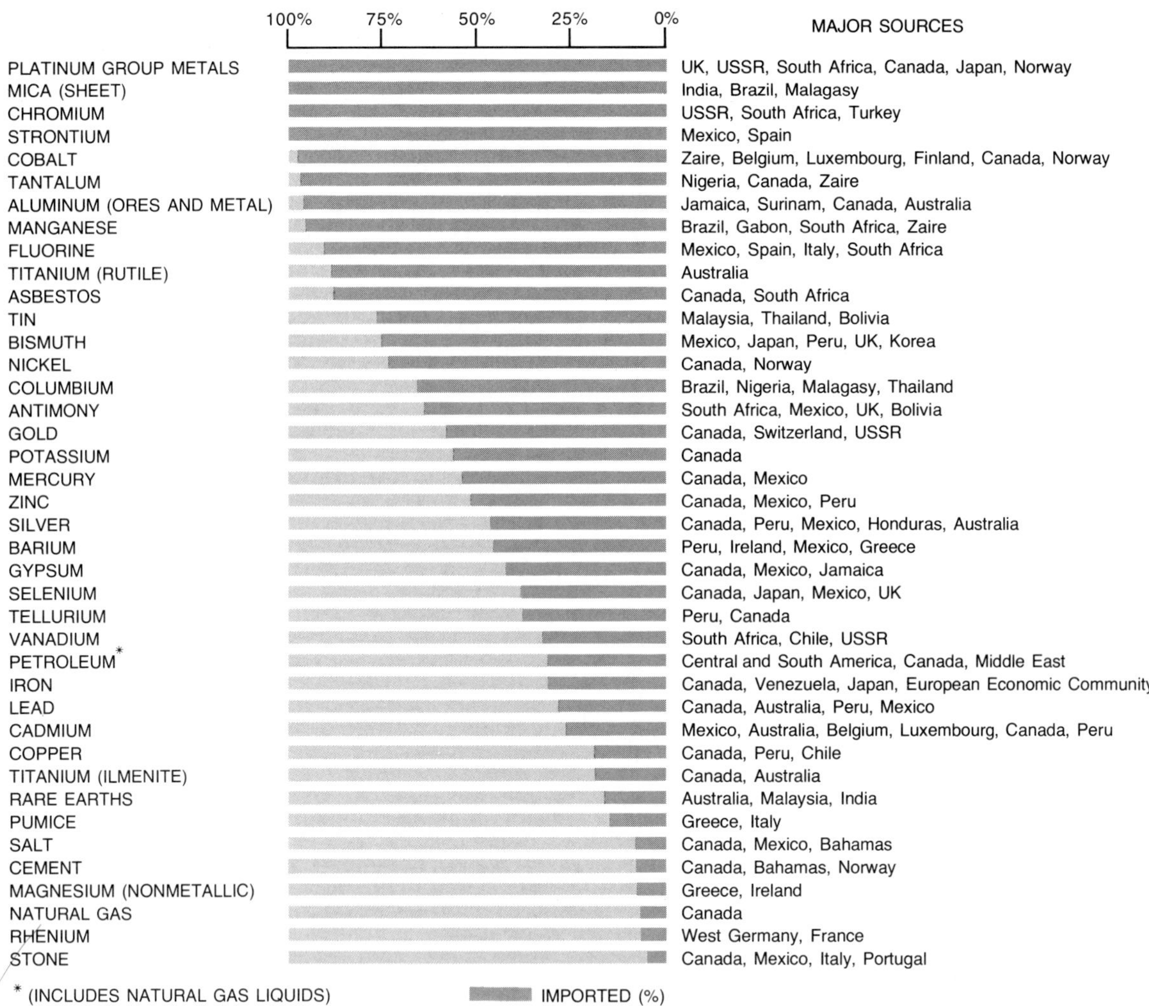

FIGURE 9-8

Percentage of U.S. mineral requirements imported in 1972. (Data from National Commission on Materials Policy, 1973.)

Is it equitable for so small a fraction of the world's population to consume so much? Are the aspirations of the poor countries compromised by the outflow of their richest mineral resources, or would they be compromised even more by a reduction of the flow of money (or the goods they buy with it) in the opposite direction? Can the United States (or other developed countries) afford the dollar outflow associated with rising dependence on imports? At what degree of dependence on imports does a nation's vulnerability to politically motivated embargos become too high a price to pay?

Most economists would argue that there is no problem of equity as long as the United States pays for what it uses; other countries sell what they have and use the proceeds to buy what they need (such as food from the U.S.). Such interdependence need be neither unfair nor threatening. Indeed, interdependence may be stabilizing. A counterargument is that until recently the world market prices of raw materials produced in the poor countries were held unduly low by means of the economic and political power of the DC consumers. The economies of the rich countries flourished on the cheap raw materials provided by the poor countries, who had little to show for the transaction. Regardless of one's

TABLE 9-2
Requirements for 4 Billion Newcomers at U.S. per capita Stock of Metals

Metal	1970 U.S. stock per capita (kilograms)*	Requirement for 4 billion people (million MT)	1972 world production (million MT)**
Steel	10,000	40,000	625
Copper	150	600	5.9
Lead	150	600	3.4
Aluminum	125	500	9.7
Zinc	100	400	4.9

*Harrison Brown, *Human materials.*
**U.S. National Commission on Materials Policy, *Material needs.*

viewpoint on the history of this situation, it is clear that LDC holders of mineral resources of various kinds are watching with intense interest the results of the OPEC experiment in drastically raising the price of oil.[4]

A longer view of the resource situation in international terms must take account of the fact that the real costs of resource extraction will increase as the deposits of highest quality become depleted. If the high-grade deposits possessed by countries now poor are sold to rich countries in exchange for short-term cash flow, these poor countries may find in a few decades that materials-intensive industrial development in a world of sharply increased materials costs is simply beyond their economic reach, regardless of how cleverly they have invested the funds won from the sale of the last low-cost materials on Earth.

The strictly physical aspects of the dynamics of the rich-poor gap in use of energy and materials have been examined by Harrison Brown, whose intriguing diagram illustrating the development of that gap is reproduced in Figure 15-1.[5] Brown has emphasized elsewhere that the gap between rich and poor countries in stocks of materials is a more realistic measure of the differences in prosperity than are the flows on which most comparisons rest.[6] That is, for example, the 10,000 kilograms of steel per person in use in the United States is a better index of prosperity than the 600 kilograms per person per year that is added to the stock and replaces losses. Brown calculates that raising the 1970 world population to the 1970 per-capita stock of major metals characteristic of the ten richest nations would require more than 60 years' output of the world's mines (at 1970 production levels), ignoring continuing demands in the rich countries and all losses everywhere.

Let us look at the problem another way. How much material would it take to provide the *next* 4 billion inhabitants of the world with the per-capita stock of steel, copper, lead, aluminum, and zinc that the U.S. had around 1970? The numbers are given and compared with recent world production of these metals in Table 9-2. These are enormous quantities—perhaps *four times* the cumulative amounts that have ever been mined.[7] There is no doubt that this much material exists; however, the economic, energetic, and environmental costs of extracting it are likely to be formidable.

There is little reason to suppose, moreover, that the bulk of the world's mineral production in the coming decades will be used to build up the per-capita stock in the parts of the world that are now poorest and where most of the population growth is expected. Rather, it will probably continue to go for replacement of losses and enlargement of stocks in countries already rich.

PROSPECTS FOR NEW MINERAL SUPPLIES

What is the potential for future exploitation of the "nonrenewable" materials in Earth's crust? Evaluation of this issue requires knowledge of the geological features that govern the existence and distribution of various minerals, together with information about the technology, economics, energetics, and environmental impact of extracting minerals and converting them to useful forms.

[4]For further discussion on these points, see, for example, E. R. Fried, International trade in raw material: myths and realities; H. H. Landsberg, Materials: some recent trends and issues, *Science,* Vol. 191, pp. 637–641 (February 20, 1976); E. N. Cameron, The contribution of the United States to national and world mineral supplies.

[5]Harrison Brown, The fissioning of human society.

[6]Harrison Brown, Human materials production as a process in the biosphere.

[7]This figure follows from the assumption that the U.S. has about one-third of the existing world stocks (in proportion to its share of GNP), and that the stocks represent about two-thirds of the cumulative amount ever mined (the latter figure based on an estimate for steel in H. Brown, Human materials).

Geologic Factors

The resources of the Earth's crust are very unevenly distributed—a result of the uneven distribution of the processes that led to their deposition and concentration. Consequently, some areas of Earth (and thus some nations) are richly endowed with mineral wealth, while others are depauperate. The distribution of coal, for instance, presumably represents the pattern of distribution of certain types of swamp plant communities that existed several million years ago. Some minerals have been formed by weathering and sedimentation; others have been concentrated at local fractures or other discontinuities in Earth's crust; still others have been formed and concentrated by the violent processes occurring at the intersections of tectonic plates.[8]

The concentration of some minerals varies more or less continuously from very high-grade ores to concentrations below the average abundance of the element in the crust. Certain types of copper ores exhibit this pattern of deposition, as do the ores of other important metals, such as iron and aluminum. Many others, including ores of lead, zinc, tin, nickel, tungsten, mercury, manganese, cobalt, precious metals, and molybdenum, do not. They show sharp discontinuities in concentration.

The frequently discontinuous distribution of ores, as well as other factors, make untenable the views of certain economists who think that only economic considerations determine the availability of mineral resources. They have the idea that, as demand increases, mining will simply move to poorer and poorer ores, which are assumed to be progressively more and more abundant. These economists have misinterpreted a principle called the "arithmetic-geometric ratio" (A/G ratio)—a principle developed by mineral economist Sam Lasky for application to certain types of ore deposits within certain limits. It is valid only for those ores (such as porphyry-copper deposits) and only within those limits. The idea is that, as the grade of ore decreases arithmetically, its abundance will increase geometrically until the average abundance in Earth's crust is reached. Often it is assumed that the additional cost of mining the low-grade ores can easily be absorbed, since the dollar value of mineral resources is at present only a small part of the gross national product. But, as noted above, the geological facts of mineral distribution do not support this proposition as a general view. Although some ores approximate a distribution where the A/G ratio may be applied, most do not.[9]

Resource Estimation

Just as with the nonrenewable energy resources treated in the preceding chapter, in discussions of nonfuel minerals, one must distinguish between *reserves* (material whose location is established and which is known to be extractable with present technology near present prices) and *resources* (material whose location is known or suspected, but whose quality is such that it requires new technology and/or substantially higher prices for exploitation to be feasible).

Several techniques are widely used to estimate the adequacy of mineral resources for the future. The simplest (but least informative) is to calculate how long present reserves will last at present consumption rates. The number of years obtained by dividing reserves by the present consumption rate is sometimes called the "static reserve index." Often reserves stand at only 20 to 50 years' supply, simply because there is little incentive to spend money to establish additional reserves when that much material is already at hand. For many materials, at least, more supplies will be discovered in the future when the effort is made. On the other hand, the static reserve index does not account for future increases in consumption. In this respect, the static reserve index is an overgenerous indicator of adequacy, partly compensating, or perhaps overcompensating, for the underestimate that results from using only present reserves.

More sophisticated analyses may use detailed information about past patterns of exploration and about the size of unexplored areas that offer geological promise of holding the ores in question to estimate the "ultimately recoverable" quantities. These ultimately recoverable amounts can then be compared with regional and global cumulative consumption figures obtained from economic

[8]See, for example, P. A. Rona, Plate tectonics and mineral resources; P. W. Guild, Discovery of natural resources, and Chapter 2 of this book.

[9]See Thomas S. Lovering, Mineral resources from the land; and Preston Cloud, Mineral resources today and tomorrow.

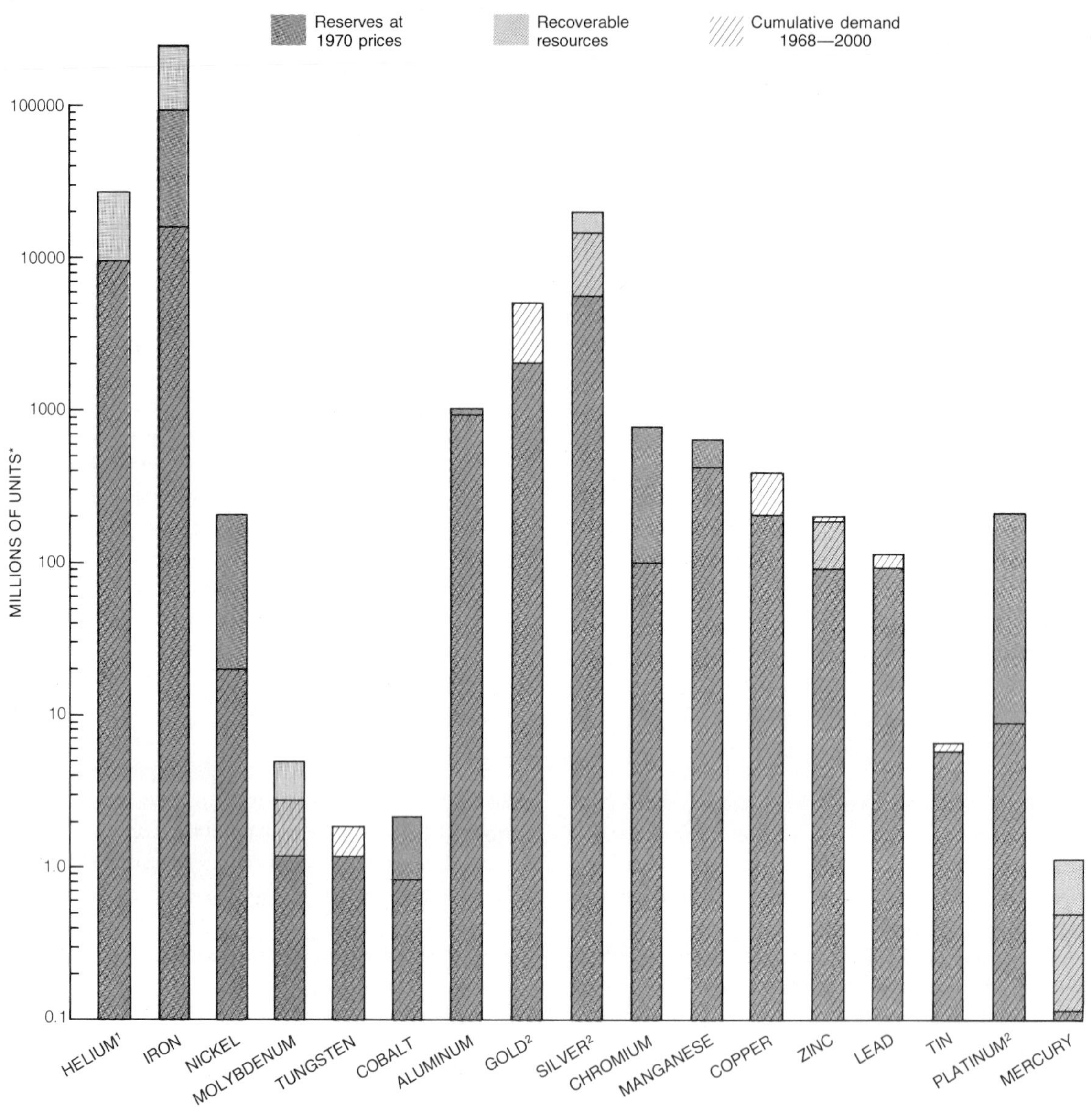

FIGURE 9-9

Global supplies of selected minerals compared with cumulative demand. The scale is logarithmic. (After Cloud, 1975.)

models based on various assumptions about patterns of development. These calculations may not be much more reliable *as predictions* than the static reserve index, so sensitive are they to the economic assumptions and to assumptions about what ores may be exploitable with unknown future technologies. They should be regarded, therefore, not as predictions but rather as possible outcomes if certain specified assumptions turn out to be correct.[10]

In this spirit, we present in Figure 9-9 some estimates derived by Cloud[11] largely from figures compiled by the U.S. Bureau of Mines.[12] There the forecasted cumulative global demand from 1968 to 2000 for various minerals is compared to the reserves at 1970 prices and, in some cases, to the recoverable resources at specified higher prices. Forecasted demand exceeds the estimated supply for copper, zinc, lead, tin, gold, and tungsten. The higher demands that would result from establishing a rich-country level of materials stock for the present and projected population of the world, as discussed above, would make the picture even more pessimistic.

The United States situation for reserves and resources of the principal mineral commodities is summarized in Table 9-3.

AUGMENTING RESOURCES: RECYCLING, SUBSTITUTION, LOW-GRADE ORES

Besides the discovery of new supplies of mineral wealth, there are three approaches available to forestall or alleviate shortages of specific materials. One is to increase the fraction of economic needs met by recycling material that was previously incorporated into products and used, or by capturing and reusing process ingredients not embodied in final products (for instance, certain chemicals). The second is substitution, which itself takes many forms: substitution of abundant or renewable materials for scarce and/or nonrenewable ores in specific products; substitution of resource-conserving product designs for resource-intensive ones; substitution of resource-conserving functions and activities for resource-intensive ones. The third approach is to exploit "ores" in which the concentration of the desired material is very low; in the vision of the future enjoyed by some technologists, these "ores" include sea water and common rock.

Recycling

In principle, recycling is capable of greatly reducing the ratio of virgin material to total material in the inputs to industrial civilization. There are physical limits to how far this ratio can be reduced, however, which arise in two ways: (a) some irretrievable dispersal of material in use is inevitable; and (b) if the stock of material in use is not constant but growing, all of the growth must be supplied from virgin material (unless a one-time windfall is available in the form of a stockpile of scrap accumulated before recycling was being practiced to the maximum feasible extent).

There are also engineering-economic limitations on the degree of recycling; these arise from the difficulties of producing a product of sufficient purity for certain applications at a price competitive with virgin materials. Naturally, as the price of virgin materials rises, more elaborate technologies for recycling become economically attractive. Even where price alone might seem to make recycling appropriate, however, institutional obstacles sometimes intervene. These may take the form of freight rates, tax policies, regulations, existing capital equipment, or practices embedded in tradition. All of these have the effect of encouraging the use of virgin materials at the expense of recycling.[13]

Table 9-4 shows the fractions of consumption of various materials obtained from recycling old scrap in the United States around 1970. The amounts that are theoretically recyclable—that is, the fractions of consumption that could be met by theoretically available scrap—are generally much higher; for example, 70 to 80

[10]For good discussion and detailed examples, see National Academy of Sciences, *Mineral resources and the environment;* and Skinner, A second iron age ahead?

[11]Mineral resources today and tomorrow.

[12]U.S. Bureau of Mines, *Mineral facts and problems, 4th ed.*

[13]A good discussion is given by Frank Austin Smith, Waste material recovery and reuse, *in* R. Ridker, ed., *Population, resources, and the environment.* For the economic aspects, see Toby Page, *An economic basis for materials policy.*

TABLE 9-3
U.S. Reserves and Resources of Selected Mineral Commodities

Commodity	Units[a]	Probable cumulative primary mineral demand 1971–2000[b]	Reserves at 1971 prices	Identified resources[c]	Hypothetical resources[d]
Aluminum	Million S.T.	370	13	Very large	KDI
Antimony	Thousand S.T.	822	110	Small	Small
Arsenic	Thousand S.T.	800	700	–	–
Asbestos	Million S.T.	43	9	Small	Insignificant
Barium	Million S.T.	31	45	Very large	Very large
Beryllium	Thousand S.T.	28	28	Very large	Huge
Bismuth	Million lb.	81	10	–	–
Boron	Million S.T.	5	40	Very large	Huge
Bromine	Billion lb.	12	17	Huge	Huge
Cadmium	Million lb.	560	264	–	–
Cesium	Thousand lb.	350	–	–	–
Chlorine	Million S.T.	645	Adequate	Huge	Huge
Chromium	Million S.T.	19	–	Insignificant	Insignificant
Cobalt	Million lb.	540	56	–	–
Columbium	Million lb.	288	–	–	–
Copper	Million S.T.	93	81	Large	Large
Fluorine	Million S.T.	39	6	Small	Small
Gallium	Metric Tons	281	Adequate	–	–
Germanium	Thousand lb.	1,600	900	–	–
Gold	Million tr. oz.	293	82	Large	KDI
Graphite	Million S.T.	2	–	Very large	KDI
Hafnium	Short Tons	1,280	Adequate	–	–
Indium	Million tr. oz.	19	11	–	–
Iodine	Million lb.	269	225	Very large	Huge
Iron	Billion S.T.	3	2	Very large	Huge
Kyanite	Million S.T.	9	15	Huge	Huge
Lead	Million S.T.	34	17	Large	Moderate
Lithium	Thousand S.T.	183	2,767	Huge	Huge
Magnesium	Million S.T.	52	Adequate	Huge	Huge
Manganese	Million S.T.	50	–	Large	KDI
Mercury	Thousand flasks[e]	1,730	75	Small	KDI
Molybdenum	Billion lb.	3	6	Huge	Huge
Nickel	Billion lb.	14	–[f]	Large	KDI
Phosphorus	Million S.T.	208	39	Very large	Huge
Platinum	Million tr. oz.	16	1	Moderate	Large
Potassium	Million S.T.	216	50	Very large	Huge
Rare earths	Thousand S.T.	452	5,045	Huge	KDI
Rhenium	Thousand lb.	360	400	–	–
Sodium	Million S.T.	1,160	Adequate	Huge	Huge
Silver	Million tr. oz.	4,400	1,300	Moderate	Large
Strontium	Thousand S.T.	771	–	Huge	Huge
Sulfur	Million L.T.	514	75	Huge	Huge
Titanium	Million S.T.	32	33	Very large	Very large
Tungsten	Million lb.	1,000	175	Moderate	Moderate
Vanadium	Thousand S.T.	471	115	Very large	KDI
Zinc	Million S.T.	62	30	Very large	Very large
Zirconium	Million S.T.	4	4	Large	KDI

[a]S.T. = short ton = 2000 lb = 0.9072 MT; L.T. = long ton = 2240 lb = 1.016 MT; tr. oz. = troy ounce = 31.10 grams.

[b]As estimated by U.S. Bureau of Mines, 1973.

[c]Identified resources are defined as including reserves and materials other than reserves which are essentially well known as to location, extent, and grade and which may be exploitable in the future under more favorable economic conditions or with improvements in technology.

[d]Hypothetical resources are undiscovered, but geologically predictable, deposits of materials similar to identified resources.

[e]76 lb. flasks.

[f]Less than one unit.

Resource appraisal terms: Huge—Domestic resources (of the category shown) are greater than ten times the minimum anticipated cumulative demand (MACD) between the years 1971 and 2000. Very large—Domestic resources are 2 to 10 times the MACD. Large—Domestic resources are approximately 75 percent to twice the MACD. Moderate—Domestic resources are approximately 35 percent to 75 percent of the MACD. Small—Domestic resources are approximately 10 percent to 35 percent of the MACD. Insignificant—Domestic resources are less than 10 percent of the MACD. KDI—Known Data Insufficient; resources not estimated because of insufficient geological knowledge of surface or subsurface area.

Source: National Commission on Materials Policy, *Material needs.*

percent for copper and aluminum and 27 percent for magnesium. Notwithstanding this potential, between 1950 and 1970 the fraction of consumption actually provided by recycling was decreasing in the United States for most materials.[14]

Urban solid wastes in the United States in 1971 comprised 230 million tons of paper, plastics, rubber, metals, organic material, and other debris. Three-quarters of this amount was collected, but only a small fraction was recycled. Most was disposed of by incineration and landfill (see also Chapter 10). The Environmental Protection Agency estimated the amounts that *could* have been recovered as 34 million tons of paper, 13 million tons of glass, and 15 million tons of ferrous metals.[15]

TABLE 9-4
Fraction of Consumption from Recycling in the United States Around 1970

Material	*Old scrap as percentage of consumption*
Antimony	60
Lead	35
Silver	33
Iron	30
Rubber	26
Gold	25
Mercury	25
Tin	18
Paper	18
Copper	17
Chromium	15
Glass	5
Aluminum	4
Zinc	4
Textiles	4
Magnesium	3

Source: National Commission on Materials Policy, *Material needs,* Chapter 4D.

Substitution

Substitution of one type of material for another is a venerable tradition in human history (think of the Stone Age, followed by the Bronze Age, and then the Iron Age) and is done for many reasons. The rapid growth of the use of aluminum and plastics in the past three decades has been at least in part the result of substituting these materials in applications that otherwise would have been served by wood or steel. These substitutions were made, not so much because of scarcity or high prices of iron and wood, but rather because of the superior properties of plastic and aluminum (e.g., strength-to-weight ratio, durability, ease of fabrication) in the desired applications. The substitution of synthetic fibers for cotton and wool has apparently been due to a combination of price and the more desirable properties of the substitutes from some points of view. On the other hand, the replacement of materials derived from contemporary plants (distillation products of wood, alcohol from molasses and grain) by petroleum as the basis for much of the organic chemical synthesis industry was very largely a matter of price.[16]

A return to photosynthetic material as the basis for production of plastics and other synthetics would not be enormously expensive; in some cases plant products might be competitive with oil at the latter's 1976 price of about $12 per barrel. Use of wood or other crops grown for this raw-material function might also prove to be more benign environmentally than reliance on low-grade fossil resources such as oil shale. In the short to middle term, however, it seems more likely that industrial civilization will rely increasingly for its hydrocarbon feedstocks on coal, the supplies of which are much greater than those of gas and oil, and the cost of which will probably remain for some time below that of fresh photosynthetic material.[17]

For the long term, the extent to which the need for materials can be met by renewable (photosynthetic) substances will depend on the size of the global population and, of course, on the amount of material required per person. The size of U.S. wood-product consumption around 1970, at roughly 240 million metric tons, exceeded that of all synthetic polymers by 13-fold. This means that meeting the needs of the present U.S.

[14]National Commission on Materials Policy, *Materials needs.*
[15]Ibid.
[16]Melvin Calvin, Solar energy by photosynthesis; K. V. Sarkanen, Renewable resources for the production of fuels and chemicals.

[17]See, for example, A. M. Squires, Chemicals from coal.

population for synthetics from wood-based materials, assuming a wood-to-synthesis conversion efficiency of 33 percent,[18] would require increasing U.S. wood-product production by 25 percent. (The actual processes, efficiencies, and energy requirements for doing this require much closer investigation.) On a global basis, the number would certainly be less encouraging than for the United States, and the unexploited part of Earth's photosynthetic potential may be needed more for food production than for raw material for plastics.[19] The versatility of photosynthetic material—usable as food, fuel, chemical feedstock, construction material, paper—is both an asset and a liability. It is a liability because there are so many competing uses for a finite photosynthetic potential. Again, this is one of the more obvious reasons that there is an inverse connection between population size and the material standard of living that can be sustained in the long term.

Possibilities for substitution among the major industrial metals have been the subject of much discussion.[20] Optimists argue that there are more abundant substitutes for almost everything that is scarce or potentially scarce, and this is at least partly true. Aluminum, iron, magnesium, and titanium are among the most abundant elements in Earth's crust (see Chapter 2), and these could replace many scarcer materials.

One problem is that the substitutes often are distinctly inferior in some important properties: tungsten's high melting point is unequalled by other metals; platinum's efficiency as a catalyst is unparalleled; gold's properties in electrical contacts cannot be duplicated by other materials; stainless steel cannot be made without chromium; and mercury has physical and chemical properties that (in important respects) are unique. It must also be recognized that some often-cited substitutes are themselves not very abundant. The main substitutes for mercury in advanced batteries, for example, are cadmium and silver. These are in fact also scarce. The main substitute for tungsten in most applications is molybdenum, which is also scarce.

Another defect in the optimistic view is the possibility that technologies not yet invented, but eventually needed, will make large demands on particularly scarce resources. It is possible, for example, that controlled nuclear fusion would make heavy demands on beryllium, niobium, chromium, and lead.[21] It is also possible that efficient solar cells would require large amounts of gallium.

Nevertheless, it is hard to disagree with the optimists to this limited extent: no metals that are scarce enough to be exhausted in the next hundred years or so seem to be so vital to civilization that their exhaustion demonstrably would mean large-scale catastrophe. Unfortunately, the complacency about materials supply that such a statement tends to generate is unwarranted, for two reasons beyond the obvious uncertainties. First, the rising costs and lowered technical efficiency associated with an increasing general scarcity of useful metals and with the substitution of inferior alternatives significantly steepens the path to material prosperity that today's less developed countries must climb. Substitution may only make the rich a little poorer, but it could make the poor much less likely to get richer. Second, as has been recognized by many for a long time, the tightest limits on civilization's expanding use of materials of all kinds are probably not raw supply or even economic costs but, rather, the environmental impact of extraction, processing, and use.[22]

In the long term, a possible exception to even the limited optimism about material supply expressed here is phosphorus, for this is one element that is neither very abundant in Earth's crust nor replaceable. Concern that the world could not support more than 2 billion people without the use of phosphate fertilizer, and that resources of phosphate rock could be exhausted before the end of the twenty-first century, were expressed in a major study

[18]The efficiency corresponds to that of existing wood-to-chemical cellulose processes. See Sarkanen, Renewable resources.

[19]For a discussion of the potential of agricultural residues as raw materials, see J. E. Atchison, Agricultural residues and other nonwood plant fibers.

[20]For a very optimistic view, see H. E. Goeller and Alvin M. Weinberg, The age of substitutability. On the other side, see, for example, C. F. Park, *Earthbound.*

[21]See, for example, J. P. Holdren, T. K. Fowler, and R. F. Post, Fusion power and the environment, and references therein.

[22]See, for example, National Academy of Sciences, *Man, materials, and environment;* J. P. Holdren and P. R. Ehrlich, Human population and the global environment.

sponsored by the Institute of Ecology in 1972.[23] This alarming conclusion was criticized elsewhere as unduly pessimistic, because the static reserve indices of phosphate rock, based on the sum of identified and hypothetical reserves, range from several hundred to one thousand years, both for the United States and for the world. The Institute of Ecology's work assumed a continuation of the exponential growth rate in phosphorus use that has prevailed for the past few decades, however, and their results are correct only if this assumption holds.[24] It seems overwhelmingly likely that other factors will stop the expansion of world agriculture before minable phosphorus supplies run out. Nevertheless, if a stabilized phosphate consumption should be as much as five times that of the early 1970s, world supplies might be gone in two hundred years. As a long-term problem, then, this is a very serious matter. The question of how civilization might manage in a world without high-grade phosphorus resources does not seem to have been carefully addressed.

One obvious way to ameliorate supply problems for phosphorus and other potentially scarce materials is to learn to use them more efficiently—that is, to get more of the desired output per unit of input. It is not at all clear how to do this for phosphorus. What is needed is a way to increase the fraction of the phosphorus applied to the soil that plants take up. For many other materials, raising the efficiency of use is not so difficult. The amount of metal used in automobiles can be reduced by making them smaller, for example, and the flow of metals through automobiles can be reduced by making them more durable. (Making a product more durable is almost always preferable to recycling in terms of energy inputs.[25]) More drastic changes for the better than simply making the same device smaller or more durable can also be envisioned. An example is the replacement of heavy, cumbersome, noisy, slow, mechanical calculating machines (they were about the size and weight of today's office electric typewriters and several times as expensive) with tiny, light, silent, fast, efficient, and relatively inexpensive hand-held calculators. This is a splendid demonstration that progress and economic growth can be based on extracting a greatly increased amount of service from each unit of energy and material.

Even more fundamental substitutions are those where the function is changed, but the overall service performed is similar. An example of this sort (already mentioned in the foregoing chapter, but as relevant for saving materials as for saving energy) is the substitution of communication for transportation.

Low-Grade Ores and the Energetics of Materials

It is all but inevitable that the highest-quality ores—those closest to the surface, or having the highest concentration of metals compared to waste materials—are the first to be exploited. The progression toward lower-quality material can be slowed by ingenuity and frugality in design, substitution, and recycling, but, across the entire range of nonrenewable materials, it cannot be stopped. As the quality of ore diminishes, all else being equal, both the amount of waste material and the energy used to separate metal from waste must increase. The viability of the cornucopian vision—the vision of a world where a population several times today's is supported in material abundance by materials obtained either from renewable sources or from the nearly inexhaustible principal constituents of sea water and Earth's crust—depends strongly on whether the energy use and waste production associated with the nearly inexhaustible materials are manageable.

Some insight into the difficulties that this hypothetical future world would entail can be gleaned from Table 9-5, which compares the lowest grade of minable ores in 1975 with the grade characteristic of common rock. For aluminum, iron, and titanium, it is possible that "common rock" will be mined, although at sharply increasing multiples of present impact. For minerals above copper in the table, the mining of common rock seems unlikely ever to occur. The energetics of extracting copper from its ores as a function of grade are illustrated in Figure 9-10. One would expect qualitatively similar curves to prevail for other metals.

[23]The Institute of Ecology, *Man in the living environment.*

[24]See, for example, the review by David Laing, The phosphate connection.

[25]R. S. Berry and M. Fels, Production and consumption of automobiles; R. T. Lund, Making products live longer.

TABLE 9-5
Ratio of Cutoff Grade (Lowest Concentration Economically Recoverable in 1975) to Crustal Abundance for Selected Elements

Element	*Crustal abundance (ppm)*	*Cutoff grade (ppm)*	*Ratio*
Mercury	0.089	1,000	11,200
Tungsten	1.1	4,500	4,000
Lead	12	40,000	3,300
Chromium	110	230,000	2,100
Tin	1.7	3,500	2,000
Silver	0.075	100	1,330
Gold	0.0035	3.5	1,000
Molybdenum	1.3	1,000	770
Zinc	94	35,000	370
Uranium	1.7	700	350
Carbon	320	100,000	310
Lithium	21	5,000	240
Manganese	1,300	250,000	190
Nickel	89	9,000	100
Cobalt	25	2,000	80
Phosphorus	1,200	88,000	70
Copper	63	3,500	56
Titanium	6,400	100,000	16
Iron	58,000	200,000	3.4
Aluminum	83,000	185,000	2.2

Source: Earl Cook, Limits to exploitation of nonrenewable resources.

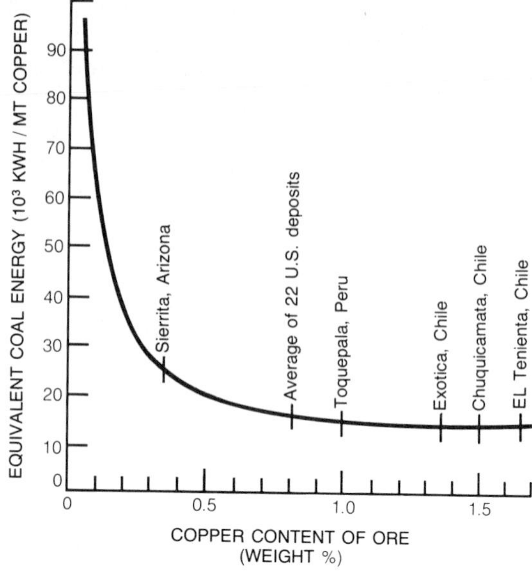

FIGURE 9-10

Energy requirements for different grades of sulfide copper ores. (From Cook, 1975. Copyright 1975 by the American Association for the Advancement of Science.)

TABLE 9-6
Energy Intensity of Various Materials

Product	*Energy requirement (MJ/kg)*
Asphalt	6
Lumber	6–7
Cement	8
Glass	17
Iron and steel	24–42
Petroleum-based plastics	45–135
Zinc	65
Chromium	60–125
Aluminum	200
Magnesium	350
Titanium	400

Note: Ores and processes appear as of early 1970s. Savings possible in plant materials by using associated scrap as an energy source has not been counted. Chemical energy embodied in feedstocks is an additional 40 megajoules per kilogram for petroleum products and 16 megajoules per kilogram for wood products.

Source: E. T. Hayes, Energy implications of materials processing; E. C. John and S. B. Preston, Timber: More effective utilization.

Some further comparisons of the energy intensity of various materials are presented in Table 9-6. Evidently, substituting the light, abundant metals for the heavier, scarce ones will carry a heavy energy cost. Substituting titanium for stainless steel (which requires chromium) would be especially expensive in energy consumed, unless ways are found to reduce greatly the amount of material of this type now used in industrial society.

CONCLUSIONS

The materials situation has much in common with the energy situation in its structure and characteristics, and, in fact, the two are tightly linked by the energy requirements of obtaining materials and the materials requirements of obtaining energy.

Like energy resources, materials resources can be divided usefully into nonrenewable and renewable kinds—stocks and flows. The dividing line is not quite as sharp for materials as for energy, however, inasmuch as energy's capacity to do useful work can be used only once, whereas materials can be recycled. Dispersed "nonrenewable" material resources can in principle be made "renewable" by the application of sufficient energy to reconcentrate the dispersed matter, but in many cases the energy cost is so high as to make the renewable-nonrenewable distinction quite clear in practical terms.

Like the energy situation, the problem with materials is not running out in the absolute sense. In the short to middle term, humanity is running out of some particular forms of materials, such as tungsten and mercury, which society is accustomed to having and in this sense is dependent upon (analogous to oil and natural gas). But there are replacements with somewhat different characteristics (such as titanium and aluminum), which are vastly more abundant and with which it appears possible (at first glance, at least) to fashion a substantially similar, if not identical, material standard of living (analogous to oil shale, low-grade uranium in breeder reactors, and fusion fuels on the energy side).

The difficulties, then, are somewhat more subtle than just plain "running out." They include:

1. Managing a smooth transition (technically, economically, socially) from a system based on scarce materials to a system based on more abundant ones—in other words, the problem of "getting from here to there."
2. Avoiding the imposition of unbearable environmental and/or social burdens that may attend some of the technologies of abundance.
3. Preventing the prospects of people now poor from plummeting as the real economic costs of the material basis of prosperity rise.

Those who view with optimism, or even complacency, the prospects of dealing with these difficulties generally assume: that energy will be cheap in the future; that substitutes for the scarcest materials will always turn up on time; that management will be skillful; that the market mechanism will allocate the real costs of scarcities efficiently; and that environmental problems will be nuisances rather than deep threats to human welfare. We believe that the weight of the evidence on all these questions supports a much more pessimistic conclusion, and that deliberate large-scale changes in the pattern of "business-as-usual" with respect to materials production and use will be necessary.

Specifically, by far the most attractive option appears to be to learn how to derive more well-being out of each kilogram of material that flows through society—by recycling, by paring down oversized artifacts, by increasing durability, by substituting among alternative processes that meet the same human goals in ways that reduce the use of materials. Choices among alternative materials to meet the same needs should be made with more emphasis on minimizing environmental disruption in extraction, processing, and use; and the energy intensity of materials should become a major criterion (the smaller the better). The potential of much heavier reliance on renewable sources of materials as a means of reducing both energy intensity and environmental impact should be investigated and compared with the use of low-grade nonrenewable resources.

Only if the rich countries alter their consumptive behavior in these directions (which they can afford to do, and which also would in all probability ease their unemployment problems), can the depletable, relatively inexpensive, high-grade resources that remain be preserved for what we believe should be their highest-priority use—the construction of an affordable bridge to a modest level of prosperity for people in less developed countries who are now desperately poor.

Recommended for Further Reading

Brobst, D. A., and W. P. Pratt, eds. 1973. *United States mineral resources.* Geological survey paper 820. Government Printing Office, Washington, D.C. As indispensible for information on origins, occurrence, resources, and uses of nonfuel materials as it is for energy resources.

Cloud, Preston. 1975. Mineral resources today and tomorrow. In *Environment,* William Murdoch, ed. Sinauer, Sunderland, Mass. Cogent exposition of the "pessimist's" view of mineral supply.

Cook, Earl. 1976. Limits to exploitation of nonrenewable resources. *Science,* vol. 191, pp. 677–682 (February 20). Concise and penetrating analysis of the meaning of depletion.

Landsberg, Hans H.; Leonard L. Fischman; and Joseph L. Fisher. 1963. *Resources in America's future.* Johns Hopkins Press, Baltimore. A classic compendium that remains a useful introduction to concepts and terminology, despite dated statistics.

U.S. Bureau of Mines. 1970. *Mineral facts and problems,* 4th ed. Government Printing Office, Washington, D.C. Another compendious and useful product by the government resource specialists.

U.S. National Commission on Materials Policy. 1973. *Material needs and the environment today and tomorrow.* Government Printing Office, Washington, D.C. Tremendous amount of quantitative information about renewable and nonrenewable materials crammed into one document, together with a large number of far-reaching policy recommendations.

U.S. National Commission on Supplies and Shortages. 1976. *Government and the nation's resources.* Government Printing Office, Washington, D.C. While it makes a number of useful suggestions for improving government's capacity to anticipate and moderate shortages, this report is most notable for its dogmatic adherence to a cornucopian view of substitutability and smooth operation of the market—a view almost completely unencumbered by recognition of the difficulties posed by rising economic and environmental costs and the limitations of substitution, as discussed in this chapter. As one example of the depth of analysis on these points, we note that a table of "substitutes" on pp. 21–22 lists tungsten as the only substitute for molybdenum in tool steel, and, elsewhere in the table, molybdenum as the only substitute for tungsten in the same application. The table also lists natural gas as a substitute for coal.

Additional References

Atchison, J. E. 1976. Agricultural residues and other nonwood plant fibers. *Science,* vol. 191, pp. 768–772. (February 20). Potential of photosynthethic matter as a renewable materials resource.

Berry, R. S., and M. Fels. 1973. Production and consumption of automobiles. *Bulletin of the Atomic Scientists,* vol. 27, no. 8 (Sept.) p. 11. Shows materials and energy savings are generally greater if durability of consumer goods is increased than if they are recycled frequently.

Brown, Harrison. 1970. Human materials production as a process in the biosphere. *Scientific American,* September, pp. 194–208. Concise and cogent introduction to society's materials problems.

———. 1975. The fissioning of human society. *Quarterly Review of Economics,* vol. 89, pp. 236–246 (May). Shows the historical development of a rich-poor gap in the use of steel and, by implication, other materials.

———, James Bonner, and John Weir. 1957. *The next hundred years.* Viking, New York. A classic, insightful introduction to the interlocking problems of food, population, and mineral resources.

Calvin, Melvin. 1974. Solar energy by photosynthesis. *Science,* vol. 184, pp. 375–381 (April 19). Potential of photosynthesis as a means of producing raw materials for purposes other than food and fuel.

Cameron, E. N. 1973. The contribution of the United States to national and world mineral supplies. In *The mineral position of the United States,* 1975–2000, E. N. Cameron, ed., University of Wisconsin Press, Madison, pp. 9–27. An introduction to minerals problems based on a symposium of the Geological Society of America.

Fried, E. R. 1976. International trade in raw materials: Myths and realities. *Science,* vol. 191, pp. 641–646 (February 20).

Garrels, R. M.; F. T. Mackenzie; and C. Hunt. 1975. *Chemical cycles and the global environment.* Kaufmann, Los Altos, Calif.

Goeller, H. E., and Alvin M. Weinberg. 1976. The age of substitutability. *Science,* vol. 191, pp. 683–689. (February 20). An exposition of the view that serious economic and social consequences of depletion can be avoided by timely substitution of abundant materials and/or ingenuity for scarcer substances.

Guild, P. W. 1976. Discovery of natural resources. *Science,* vol. 191, pp. 709–713 (February 20). Geology and exploration.

Hayes, E. T. 1976. Energy implications of materials processing. *Science,* vol. 191, p. 661 (February 20). Useful contribution to the growing literature on energy requirements for materials extraction, processing, and fabrication.

Holdren, John P., and Paul R. Ehrlich. 1974. Human population and the global environment. *American Scientist,* vol. 62 (May/June), pp. 282–292. Discusses environmental "limits" that are likely to set in before a limit to growth is reached because of depletion of mineral resources.

Holdren, John P.; T. K. Fowler; and R. F. Post. 1976. Fusion power and the environment. In *Energy and the environment—cost benefit analysis,* R. A. Karam and K. Z. Morgan, eds. Pergamon, New York. Includes discussion of materials requirements of fusion.

Institute of Ecology, The (TIE). 1972. *Man in the living environment.* University of Wisconsin Press, Madison. Discussion of depletion of phosphate rock if recent exponential growth in fertilizer use were to persist another century.

John, E. C., and S. B. Preston. 1976. Timber: More effective utilization. *Science,* vol. 191, p. 757 (February 20).

Kneese, A. V. 1976. Natural resources policy, 1976–86. In U.S. Congress, Joint Economic Committee, *U.S. economic growth,* pp. 122–160. Specific insightful proposals toward more rational resource policies.

Laing, David. 1975. The phosphate connection. *The Ecologist,* vol. 5, pp. 240–241. Elucidation of the controversy over the timing of depletion of phosphorous resources.

Long, T. V., II, and L. Schipper. 1976. Resource and energy substitution. In U.S. Congress, Joint Economic Committee, *U.S. economic growth,* pp. 94–121. Excellent discussion of potentials and problems of substitution.

Lovering, Thomas S. 1969. Mineral resources from the land. In *Resources and man,* National Academy of Sciences, pp. 109–134. Sober view of limitations on exploitation of mineral resources.

Lund, R. T. 1977. Making products live longer. *Technology Review,* vol. 79, no. 3 (January), pp. 49–55. Merits of durability and obstacles in the way of increasing it.

McHale, J. 1976. Resource availability and growth. In U.S. Congress, Joint Economic Committee, *U.S. economic growth,* pp. 1–50. Wide-ranging treatment, emphasising prospects for technological change to extract more well-being from each unit of resources.

National Academy of Sciences (NAS). 1969. *Resources and man: A study and recommendations by the Committee on Resources and Man of the National Academy of Sciences/National Research Council,* W. H. Freeman and Company, San Francisco. Superb chapters by eminent authors on the pressure of human populations on food and material resources.

———. 1973. *Man, materials, and environment.* M.I.T. Press, Cambridge, Mass. Excellent, data-rich survey of environmental impacts of materials extraction and processing.

———. 1975. *Mineral resources and the environment.* NAS, Washington, D.C. A major academy study covering nonfuel materials as well as energy resources, with an especially comprehensive case study of copper.

———. 1975. *National materials policy.* NAS, Washington, D.C. Proceedings of a symposium with short papers by a wide variety of prominent specialists on renewable and nonrenewable resources.

Page, Toby. 1976. *An economic basis for materials policy.* Johns Hopkins Press, Baltimore. A perceptive discussion of the economics of recycling, among other topics.

Park, C. F. 1975. *Earthbound.* Freeman-Cooper, San Francisco, Calif. A prominent geologist elucidates his pessimism about the future of minerals supply.

Ridker, R., ed. 1972. *Population, resources, and the environment.* Vol. 3 of *Research reports of the Commission on Population Growth and the American Future.* Government Printing Office, Washington, D.C. Generally sanguine view of resource availability in the United States through the year 2020, with some caveats about the need for recycling and about environmental liabilities.

Rona, P. A. 1973. Plate tectonics and mineral resources. *Scientific American,* January, pp. 86–95. Relation of new geophysical knowledge to a growing understanding of how and where mineral deposits are formed.

Sarkanen, K. V. 1976. Renewable resources for the production of fuels and chemicals. *Science,* vol. 191, pp. 773–776 (February 20).

Skinner, Brian J. 1976. A second iron age ahead? *American Scientist,* vol. 64 (May/June), pp. 258–269. Problems and prospects of relying on relatively abundant metals after scarce ones are depleted.

Smith, Frank Austin. 1972. Waste material recovery and reuse. In *Population, resources, and the environment,* R. Ridker, ed. Good introduction to the nature and potential of recycling.

Squires, A. M. 1976. Chemicals from coal. *Science,* vol. 191, pp. 689–700 (February 20). Our most abundant conventional fossil fuel as a basis of chemical synthesis.

TIE. *See* Institute of Ecology.

United Nations. Annual. *Statistical yearbook.* UN Publications, New York. World data on materials production and use.

United States Congress, Joint Economic Committee. 1976. *U.S. economic growth from 1976 to 1986: Prospects, problems, and patterns,* vol. 4, *Resources and Energy.* Joint Committee Print 78-653, Government Printing Office, Washington, D.C. Good collection of essays on resource depletion, substitution, and policy.

U.S. Council on International Economic Policy. 1974. *Special report: Critical imported materials.* Government Printing Office, Washington, D.C. Concise, data-rich discussion of national origins, supplies, prices, and uses of critical materials.

U.S. Department of Commerce. Annual *Statistical abstract of the United States.* Government Printing Office, Washington, D.C. Contains information on patterns of United States and international materials use, and appears more promptly than the more comprehensive *Minerals yearbook,* published by the Department of the Interior.

U.S. Department of Interior. Annual. *Minerals yearbook.* Government Printing Office, Washington, D.C. A compendium of information about state, national, and international minerals industries—reserves, production, sales, exploration, major new facilities.

SECTION

IV

Understanding Environmental Disruption

But our inability to assign definite values to these causes of the disturbance of natural arrangements is not a reason for ignoring the existence of such causes in any general view of the relations between man and nature, and we are never justified in assuming a force to be insignificant because its measure is unknown, or even because no physical effect can be traced to it as its origin.

—George Perkins Marsh, 1864

There is only one solution. Man must recognize the necessity of cooperating with nature. He must temper his demands and use and conserve the natural living resources of this earth in a manner that alone can provide for the continuation of his civilization.

—Fairfield Osborn, 1948

As the human population grows and the quantity of energy and materials used by each person increases, it is becoming apparent that the resource whose sufficiency is most in doubt is neither space, nor energy, nor metallic ores, but rather the capacity of natural processes to maintain a hospitable environment. These processes include dispersal and detoxification of wastes, cycling of nutrients, natural controls on crop pests and agents of human disease, management of water flows, and regulation of climate. How these functions are accomplished was described in Chapter 2 through Chapter 4. We now consider how they can be overloaded or undermined by the activities of human society, and outline what the consequences for human welfare are or may be.

The subject of environmental problems is large and diverse, and it is easier to deal with when viewed in some logical framework. We find it useful, as the basis for such a framework, to distinguish among three steps in environmental disruption: (1) what society does to the environment (the *insult*); (2) what the environment does as a consequence of what is done to it (the *response*); and (3) the resulting damage to human well-being (the *environmental cost*).

Insults include: the discharge of material effluents to air, water, and the land surface; the production of heat, noise, and electromagnetic radiation; removal of plants and animals; and physical transformations such as drilling, damming, dredging, filling, mining, pumping, paving, and erecting structures. Some of these impacts occur as accidents as well as intentionally, and some are produced by the interaction of human activities and natural events.

Environmental responses to the insults include: accumulation of materials in undesirable forms, concentrations, and locations; changes in the diversity, abundance, and distribution of organisms; reduction of primary productivity; changes in host-parasite and predator-prey relationships; loss of water storage and control of water flow; loss of nutrient storage capability; geologic events such as erosion, subsidence, slides, and earthquakes; alteration of flows of solar and terrestrial radiation through the atmosphere; and changes in patterns of atmospheric and marine circulation and of humidity and rainfall. Often several such responses are simultaneous and interconnected.

The human costs of environmental disruption fall for the most part into the following categories: death, disease, and malformation from exposure to harmful substances and radiations (including but not limited to cancer, birth defects, and genetic effects); epidemic and parasitic disease; hunger, starvation, and impoverishment owing to loss of terrestrial and marine productivity; death, injury, and impoverishment from floods, slides, and other meteorological or geological events arising from society's impacts; other damages to property such as by air and water pollution; irretrievable loss of genetic information and potential services with the extinction of species; aesthetic degradation and denial of recreational resources; and economic costs of replacing or supplementing diminished natural services with technology. These costs may manifest themselves in a sudden and drastic increase, they may creep up gradually over a long span of time, or some of them may appear in the form of increased fluctuations (that is, variability) in such processes as food production and epidemic disease.

We have chosen somewhat arbitrarily to divide our coverage of environmental disruption into two categories, according to the nature of the pathway between insult and cost. We deal in Chapter 10 with what we have called direct assaults on human health—namely, phenomena in which the pathway between insult and human costs does not depend on disruption of ecological systems as an intermediate link. In Chapter 11, we discuss indirect assaults on human well-being, wherein the disruption of an ecological system is the essential link between the insult and the human cost. Obviously, the same impact can lead to costs via both pathways: water pollution as a health hazard to people who ingest the water represents a direct assault and therefore is treated in Chapter 10; water pollution can also lead to adverse effects on aquatic and terrestrial ecosystems resulting in subsequent costs to society, and those pathways are treated mainly in Chapter 11.

Three important themes apply with equal force to the issues treated in both chapters, so we introduce them here: (1) the importance of not neglecting dispersed, chronic hazards while dealing with concentrated, acute ones; (2) the special dangers arising from time lags between the initiation of an insult and the appearance of the resulting cost; and (3) the nature of uncertainty in environmental assessment and its implications for policy-making.

It is a truism that people's attention is captured by spectacular events—disastrous smogs, massive oil spills from blowouts or tanker wrecks, and epidemics of acute poisoning from mercury or cadmium or pesticides. Similarly, the threats most likely to be taken seriously are those to which spectacular or otherwise compelling images can be attached—the SST, the whales as endangered species, suggestions for putting dams in the Grand Canyon. These are all important matters, and we are grateful for the attention they have attracted to environmental concerns. But it is essential that environmentalists and environmental scientists avoid pouring all their resources into winning a few spectacular battles while losing the war. For every ton of oil spilled into the oceans in accidents, twenty tons are discharged unnoticed in routine operations. For every coal miner who dies in a cave-in, making headlines, ten people may die because of air pollution from burning coal, unheralded. For every hectare of spectacular landscape saved from despoilation in national parks, a hundred hectares of more ordinary land remain at risk. Struggles to stave off extinctions, species by species, cannot succeed if habitat throughout the world is disappearing under pavement and plow. Somehow, society must learn to recognize and combat the subtle threats as well as the spectacular ones, or it will find itself nickel-and-dimed into environmental impoverishment.

Time lags between insults to the environment and the unmistakable appearance of the consequences compound the predicament with respect to hazards both subtle and spectacular, because they postpone recognition of the need for corrective action. A variety of lags may be important: the time required for contaminants to be transported horizontally or vertically in ocean or atmosphere or over or under the land; the time it takes for such materials to find their ways up food chains; the time associated with the rates of certain chemical reactions, such as those responsible for the formation of photochemical smog; the ill-understood phenomena responsible for the latency period between many carcinogenic insults and the actual appearance of the cancers; the lag between mutagenic insults and the appearance of genetic disorders in subsequent generations. Besides these physical phenomena, there is often an analysis lag—that is, the time it takes to understand theoretically and/or establish with measurements just what is happening. The threat posed by fluorocarbons to atmospheric ozone is a good example of lags of several kinds: the rate of diffusion of the fluorocarbons up to the stratosphere, where the ozone is, is slow; the reactions that lead to the destruction of the ozone are slow; and slowest of all was the development of scientific understanding of the existence of a threat and the details of its operation.

To the time lags already mentioned must be added the time lags of societal response: inventing solutions and getting them in place. What the lags add up to, all too often, is a situation in which corrective action is too little and too late. By the time the symptoms are unmistakable and the cause isolated, the damage may be irreversible. Species that have been eradicated cannot be restored. The radioactive debris of atmospheric bomb tests cannot be reconcentrated and isolated from the environment, nor can the chlorinated-hydrocarbon pesticides that have spread through the biosphere. Radiation exposure cannot be undone.

Clearly, if problems that are potentially irreversible are to be caught in time, society must be prepared to act on imperfect information. Tremendous gaps exist in scientific understanding of environmentally induced diseases, of the operation of ecosystems, even of the simpler nonbiological processes that govern such aspects of the environment as climate. It is customary in the scientific community, when confronted with a possible environmental threat of one kind or another, to refer to these gaps in understanding and call for more research to reduce the uncertainties before taking any action. But the fact is that the uncertainty usually cannot be removed—and often cannot even be reduced—within the time in which a decision must be made. Policy-makers must accept a degree of scientific uncertainty as an irremovable component of their decision-making predicament. Given that decision-making in the face of uncertainty means some mistakes are sure to be made, the most reasonable policy is one that errs on the side of avoiding those mistakes that are irreversible. Another way of saying this is: the greater the degree of irreversibility potentially associated with a given course of action (or inaction), the heavier should be the burden of proof upon those advocating this course to show that the irreversible harm will not in fact materialize.

He will manage the cure best who forsees what is to happen from the present condition of the patient.

—Hippocrates, ca. 460–377 B.C.

Don't drink the water and don't breathe the air.

—Tom Lehrer, Pollution, 1965

CHAPTER 10

Direct Assaults on Well-Being

In some respects the activities of humanity over the past several centuries have made the environment more hospitable. Some parts of the countryside in places as diverse as Europe and China are undoubtedly more productive, more pleasant, more varied in flora and fauna than they were in prehistoric times. In terms of freedom from epidemic disease, cities are much healthier places than they once were. But the activities of human society have also created some new threats to life and health and made some old threats worse. These threats arise from insults—effluents, accidents, and environmental transformations—generated by the activities of societies both industrial and agricultural.

Deaths and illnesses ascribable directly to such insults understandably have received much of the attention that the public and policy-makers have given to environmental matters. Respiratory ailments from air pollution, hepatitis from polluted water, cancer from a host of environmental contaminants—all have a clear and compelling claim on the public consciousness. These direct threats to life and health, and corollary threats to economic goods and services, are the subject of this chapter. Many of the insults discussed here also undermine human well-being by disrupting the natural functioning of geophysical and ecological processes. These often subtle and unpublicized indirect assaults on human well-being are taken up in Chapter 11.

The term *pollution* describes the class of environmental insults with which most people are most familiar. The dictionary defines it as "a state of being impure or unclean, or the process of producing that state."[1] A *pollutant* is an agent—for example, chemicals, noise,

[1] *Webster's Third New International Dictionary,* Springfield, Mass., G. & C. Merriam, 1966.

radiation—that produces the state of pollution. What is meant by *impure* or *unclean* needs to be clarified, however. For the purposes of this book, we interpret impure and unclean to imply the presence of agents added to the environment by society in kinds and quantities potentially damaging to human welfare or to organisms other than people. By this definition, pollution is a man-made phenomenon. This is not to deny that agents naturally present in the environment can be harmful. Natural ionizing radiation doubtless does biological damage, a variety of plant pollens cause respiratory disease, hydrocarbons emitted by trees can contribute to the formation of photochemical smog, particulate matter from volcanoes influences climate, and so on. But we believe it useful to preserve a distinction between these nonhuman natural phenomena and pollution as a process or condition having human origins. Two further definitions are useful in this connection. We define *qualitative pollutants* as agents produced and released only by human activities and not otherwise present in nature. We define *quantitative pollutants* as contributions made by society to the environmental pools of agents that would be present even in the absence of human influences.

Within the category of quantitative pollutants, there are three distinct criteria by which a human contribution may be judged significant: (1) Humanity can perturb a natural cycle with a large amount of a substance ordinarily considered innocuous, either by overloading part of the cycle (nitrogen, Chapter 11), by destabilizing a finely tuned balance (CO_2, Chapter 11), or by swamping the natural cycle completely (heat, in the very long term, Chapter 11). (2) An amount of material that is negligible when compared to natural flows of the same thing can produce an important disruption if released in a sensitive spot, within a small area, or suddenly (oil, Chapter 11). (3) *Any* addition of a substance that is dangerous even at its natural concentrations is significant (mercury and many radioactive substances, Chapter 10).

For synthetic pollutants, of course, the situation is even more clear-cut. There can be no question of the potential for harm from biologically active substances with which organisms have had no prior evolutionary experience (synthetic organic pesticides, PCBs, and herbicides, Chapters 10 and 11).

AIR POLLUTION

"The air nimbly and sweetly recommends itself unto our gentle senses," wrote William Shakespeare in *Macbeth.* Perhaps he was referring to the air in the countryside, for even in Shakespeare's day the air in London would hardly have inspired such sentiments. It was smoky, and it stank. The nature of air pollution has changed somewhat since then, but it remains the most obvious form of pollution worldwide. It can be felt when it burns the eyes and irritates the lungs. Virtually every major metropolis of the world has serious air-pollution problems. Travelers know how often their first sight of a city can be spoiled by the pall of smog. Today, however, it is not only the air over cities that is polluted. Large regions are now afflicted to some degree. Humanity is taxing the capacity of the atmosphere to absorb, and to transport away from areas of high population density, the enormous amounts of waste exhausted into it. Air pollution is now recognized not only as a phenomenon that rots nylon stockings and windshield-wiper blades, that corrodes paint and steel, and that blackens skies and the wash on the clothesline; it is recognized as a killer of people.

Types and Sources of Air Pollutants

There are many different ways to sort and classify air pollutants: by source, by chemical composition, by types of reactions undergone, by type of effect on health, and so on. The main categories monitored nationally are sulfur oxides, nitrogen oxides, hydrocarbons, carbon monoxide, and particulate matter. Estimates of emissions of these pollutants in 1974 in the United States are given in Table 10-1.[2]

The first two source categories in Table 10-1 represent the combustion of fossil fuels. Sulfur oxides result from the presence of sulfur in coal and fuel oil as a natural contaminant. Emissions are almost entirely in the form of sulfur dioxide gas (SO_2), mixed with 1 to 3 percent sulfur

[2]Council on Environmental Quality, *Environmental Quality, 1975.* More detail on the emissions characteristics of various sources of pollutants is given in U.S. Environmental Protection Agency (EPA), *Compilation of air pollutant emission factors.*

TABLE 10-1

Emissions of Air Pollutants in the U.S., by Source (million tons/yr, 1974)

Source	*Sulfur oxides*	*Nitrogen oxides*	*Hydrocarbons*	*Carbon monoxide*	*Particulates*
Transportation	0.8	10.7	12.8	73.5	1.3
Stationary fuel combustion	24.3	11.0	1.7	0.9	5.9
Industrial processes	6.2	0.6	3.1	12.7	11.0
Solid waste disposal	0.0	0.1	0.6	2.4	0.5
Miscellaneous*	0.1	0.1	12.2	5.1	0.8
Total	31.4	22.5	30.4	94.6	19.5

*Includes oil and gasoline production.

Source: Environmental Protection Agency, in Council on Environmental Quality, *Environmental quality, 1975,* p. 440.

trioxide (SO_3), also gaseous. Once in the atmosphere, SO_2 can be oxidized to SO_3; the SO_3 reacts with water vapor or dissolves in water droplets to form sulfuric acid, H_2SO_4. The sulfur dioxide can also form the weak acid H_2SO_3 directly, and the sulfate ion (SO_4^-) appears in a variety of solid and liquid particulates in addition to H_2SO_4.[3] The rate at which SO_2 is oxidized to the much more dangerous sulfuric acid and other sulfates is greatly increased when significant numbers of suspended particles are present, because these provide surfaces that facilitate the reactions. Atmospheric concentrations of sulfur oxides are generally measured in parts per million (ppm) by volume of SO_2; 1 ppm of SO_2 by volume is 2.2 ppm by weight or 2.7 milligrams per cubic meter of air at sea level.

The oxides of nitrogen of interest in most air-pollution contexts are nitric oxide (NO) and nitrogen dioxide (NO_2). Emissions are usually calculated as grams or tons of NO; a concentration of 1 ppm NO by volume is also about 1 ppm by weight, or 1.2 milligrams per cubic meter. The colorless nitric oxide is slowly oxidized in air to orangish-brown NO_2, a process that is much faster in badly polluted atmospheres. Nitrogen dioxide reacts readily with water vapor to form nitric acid, HNO_3. Formation of nitric oxide from nitrogen and oxygen takes place at the high temperatures (and sometimes pressures) produced in the combustion of fossil fuels. The nitrogen comes not only from the air, but is also present as a contaminant in significant quantities in coal, oil, and natural gas.[4] This means that nitrogen-oxide pollution could not be eliminated by burning fuel in pure oxygen rather than air, as has sometimes been suggested.

A great variety of hydrocarbons are emitted in fossil-fuel combustion when the fuel does not burn completely. (Complete combustion of hydrocarbon fuels would give H_2O and CO_2). Those of greatest interest are the "reactive" ones, which participate in the formation of photochemical smog, and others known or suspected to be carcinogenic (cancer-causing). The bulk of the emissions of hydrocarbons in the United States is methane (CH_4), which falls in neither of these categories.

Another product of incomplete combustion is carbon monoxide (CO). The bulk of the emissions of this compound comes from engines used in transportation. Concentrations are usually measured in parts per million by volume; 1 ppm by volume of CO is about equal to 1 ppm by weight, or 1.2 milligrams per cubic meter.

Particulate matter in polluted air occurs in a tremendous variety of sizes and chemical compositions. Many particles contain heavy metals such as cadmium, mercury, and lead, which are either natural contaminants of the original fuel or (like lead) have been added deliberately to improve fuel performance. "Suspended particulates" are those 10 microns (thousandths of a millimeter) or smaller in aerodynamic equivalent diameter, that is, the diameter of a sphere with the same air resistance as the particle. Below the 10-micron range, the settling velocity is low enough so that atmospheric mixing tends to keep the particles suspended. Particles of a micron or less have the longest residence times in the atmosphere and are the most difficult for pollution-control equipment to remove from gaseous effluent. As already noted, some atmospheric particles are formed from substances emitted as gases or vapors.

[3]For an extended discussion, see P. P. Gaspar, *Sulfur in the atmosphere,* chapter 2.

[4]National Academy of Sciences, *Air quality and stationary source emission control,* chapter 14.

The term photochemical smog describes a variable mixture of compounds, including ozone (O_3) and other more complex reactive chemicals formed by the action of sunlight on nitrogen oxides and hydrocarbons. Ozone and other chemicals that readily give up an oxygen atom in chemical reactions are often lumped together under the term *oxidants.*[5] The most common oxidant other than ozone is peroxyacetl nitrate (PAN).

Important sources of pollutants other than fuel combustion include the smelting of ores, petroleum refining, pulp and paper mills, chemical plants, and trash burning.

Impacts on Health

Death rates are above normal when and where air pollution occurs at significant concentrations. The demise of the very young, the very old, and those with respiratory ailments is accelerated.[6] Perhaps the most dramatic case ever recorded was the London smog disaster of 1952 (see Box 10-1). But such disasters have still been less significant to public health than have the less spectacular, but ultimately more far-reaching, effects that day-to-day exposure has had on people living in seriously polluted localities. In 1968, sixty faculty members of the Medical School of the University of California at Los Angeles made a recommendation to the residents of southern California's smoggy areas. Their statement read, in part: "air pollution has now become a major health hazard to most of this community during much of the year," and they advised "anyone who does not have compelling reasons to remain to move out of smoggy portions of Los

[5]A good introductory discussion is D. A. Lynn, *Air pollution: Threat and response,* chapter 3.

[6]An excellent introduction to the impacts of pollutants on health and the methods used to discover these impacts in large populations is Samuel S. Epstein and Dale Hattis, Pollution and human health. For a discussion of air pollution's effects on children, who are more susceptible than adults because of their size and relatively high levels of metabolism and activity, see Dorothy Noyes Kane, Bad air for children.

FIGURE 10-1

Air pollution is a worldwide problem. *Top.* An early morning inversion blankets the Los Angeles basin in smog, while the higher Hollywood Hills in the foreground remain clear. This picture was taken in 1949. (Photo by William A Garnett.) *Center.* Air pollution from a plant near Alvik, Norway, in July 1972. (Photo by Robert E. Van Vuren.) *Bottom.* Steel mills in an industrial area south of Sydney, Australia, in 1962. (Photo by William A. Garnett.)

BOX 10-1 Air Pollution Disasters

Donora, Pennsylvania, is a small town in the steep valley of the Monongahela River; in 1948 it had a population of 12,300. Because of the steepnesss of the surrounding hills, it tends to be even smokier than other mill towns. In the autumn, fog is often added to the smoke, making the mixture smog (smog equals smoke plus fog in the strict sense of the word, but air pollution not involving fog, such as that found in Los Angeles, is now commonly called smog). On Tuesday, October 26, 1948, a thermal inversion (a layer of warm air above a layer of cold air; see Figure 10-3) trapped fog and smoke producing a lethal situation. The red, black, and yellow smoke from Donora's huge wire factory, zinc and sulfuric acid plants, and steel factory lingered for days over the grimy town, and the upper layer of fog absorbed the sun's heat, creating more warm air above the cold and intensifying the inversion. The smog persisted through Sunday, and 6,000 people, nearly half the people in the area, were made ill as a result. Fifteen men and five women died, and the lives of many others may have been shortened.

A similar smog occured in London in 1952; the combination of fog and thermal inversion was accompanied by severe cold weather. London's homes were heated by coal, and the cold greatly increased fuel consumption and the production of smoke. The atmospheric content of sulfur dioxide rose to double its usual level. The episode started on Friday, December 5, and by Sunday the smog had reduced visibility to only one yard in parts of London, and created multitudes of incredible situations. For example, so much smog seeped into theaters that only people in the first four rows could see the cinema screen. People inadvertently walked off of quays along the Thames and fell into the river. A pilot trying to taxi to the terminal at London Airport after an instrument landing got lost, as did the party sent to search for him. The consensus was that about 4,000 deaths were directly attributable to the London smog.*

There have, of course, been other smog disasters, as well as many close calls. Two often-cited cases occurred in the Meuse Valley of Belgium in 1930 and at Poza Rica Near Mexico City in 1950. When the next smog "disaster" will come, no one knows. But in August 1969 citizens of both Los Angeles and St. Louis were warned by doctors not to play golf, jog, or do anything that involved deep breathing because of the air-pollution hazards that prevailed. The activities of school children in the Los Angeles basin are curtailed on doctors' orders with increasing frequency, and attrition of the health of asthmatics and others with respiratory or cardiovascular problems continues.

*Mortality figures on Donora and London are from U.S. Department of Health, Education and Welfare, *Air quality criteria for sulphur oxides.*

Angeles, San Bernardino, and Riverside counties to avoid chronic respiratory diseases like bronchitis and emphysema."[7]

What are the general effects of individual air pollutants on health?

Carbon monoxide combines with the pigment hemoglobin in blood more efficiently and more tightly than oxygen does, displacing the oxygen that hemoglobin normally transports. Thus carbon monoxide tends to cause suffocation by occupying the high-speed transport system that in the human organism normally guarantees a steady renewal of the supply of oxygen necessary to maintain metabolism in the cells. When oxygen supply to the cells is reduced, the heart must work harder, as must the respiratory mechanism. These effects may produce a critical strain in people with heart and lung diseases. When a person lives for eight hours in an atmosphere containing 80 parts per million (ppm) of carbon monoxide, the oxygen-carrying capacity of the circulatory system is diminished by about 15 percent. (That is, the "saturation" of oxygen-transport sites with carbon monoxide—the carboxyhemoglobin level—is 15 percent.) This has about the same effect as the loss of more than a pint of blood. Observable effects on human performance appear to set in at around 3 percent carboxyhemoglobin in the blood.[8]

[7] *New York Times,* Sept. 15, 1968.

[8] Lynn, *Air pollution,* chapter 4; G. Wright et al., Carbon monoxide in the urban atmosphere.

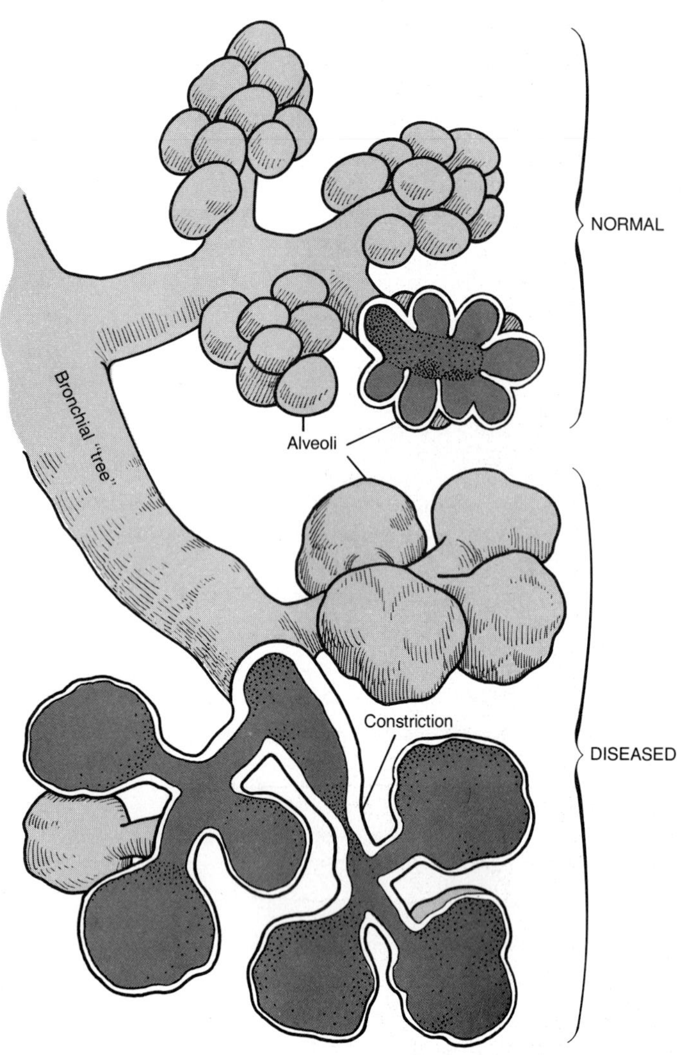

FIGURE 10-2

Bronchitis-emphysema, a disease caused or aggravated by air pollution. In the normal lung the bronchial tubes branch into millions of tiny chambers (alveoli), where transfer of oxygen to blood takes place. In the diseased lung the alveoli coalesce, reducing the amount of surface available for oxygen transfer. Furthermore, the "twigs" of the bronchial tree are constricted, reducing the rate at which air is exchanged. (After McDermott, 1961.)

When traffic is badly snarled, the carbon-monoxide content of the air may approach 400 ppm. Symptoms of acute poisoning, often experienced by people in traffic jams and on freeways, include headache, loss of vision, decreased muscular coordination, nausea, and abdominal pain. If exposure to concentrations in the hundreds of ppm is prolonged, unconsciousness, convulsions, and death follow. Cases of chronic carbon-monoxide poisoning have been reported, and an association between high concentrations of atmospheric carbon monoxide with higher mortality in Los Angeles County has been demonstrated for the years 1962 to 1965.[9]

Sulfur oxides have been implicated in the increased rates of acute and chronic asthma, bronchitis, and emphysema observed in people exposed to concentrations encountered in many cities in the U.S.[10] Indirect and limited evidence suggests there may also be some association between sulfur oxides and lung cancer.[11]

Asthma is an allergic supersensitivity of the bronchial tree, the set of branching tubes that carry air from the trachea to the lungs. An asthmatic attack causes the muscles that encircle the "twigs" of the bronchial tree to contract and narrow the tubes. The victim is able to inhale air, but is unable to exhale with sufficient force to clear the lungs. The result is a distension of the lungs: input exceeds output. Carbon dioxide builds up in the lungs, and the victim also suffers oxygen deprivation. Asthma attacks kill several hundred Americans a year; even attacks that are not lethal often last for long periods, and may lead to more or less permanent changes in the breathing apparatus.

Bronchitis, inflammation of the bronchial tree, leads to difficulty in expelling foreign matter from the lungs by coughing. The muscles surrounding the bronchial tubes weaken, and mucus accumulates. There is a progressive loss of breathing ability. Bronchitis is often accompanied by emphysema, a disease of the air sacs in the lungs (Figure 10-2). These air sacs tend to fuse, essentially coalescing from clusters of small pouches to form larger

[9]A. C. Hexter and J. R. Goldsmith, Carbon monoxide: Association of community air pollution with mortality.

[10]An exceedingly useful review is National Academy of Sciences (NAS), *Air quality*, chapter 4, Health effects of sulfur oxides; see also J. French et al., The effect of sulfur dioxide and suspended sulfates on acute respiratory disease; L. Lave and E. Seskin, Air pollution and human health; D. P. Rall, Review of health effects of sulfur oxides.

[11]NAS, *Air quality*.

ones. This is accompanied by a narrowing of the finer branches of the bronchial tree. The combined results are a reduction of total surface area for the exchange of oxygen between air and blood stream and a reduction of the amount of air flow through the lungs. This process takes place gradually over a period of years, while the lungs become progressively less capable of providing oxygen for activity. The victim of fatal emphysema dies of suffocation.[12]

The available evidence suggests that sulfur dioxide alone, at concentrations commonly encountered in urban air, would not be able to cause the observed increases in bronchitis and emphysema; rather, there is a *synergism* between SO_2 and suspended particulate matter. This synergism probably involves the tendency of SO_2 adsorbed onto small particles to penetrate farther into the lung than SO_2 gas alone, and also involves the faster conversion of SO_2 into more dangerous sulfates in the presence of particles.[13]

Of the oxides of nitrogen, the most active biologically is NO_2. Its effects include reduction of the oxygen-carrying capacity of the blood (like CO), bronchial and other lung damage (like SO_2), and acute pulmonary edema (accumulation of excess fluid in the lung, also caused by ozone).[14] Although atmospheric levels of NO_2 rarely reach concentrations at which these direct effects can be demonstrated to occur, a major study of school children in Chattanooga, Tennessee, demonstrated an increase in respiratory infections at a concentration of NO_2 that is regularly exceeded in 85 percent of all U.S. cities of over 500,000 population.[15]

Most of the many kinds of hydrocarbons emitted into the atmosphere have not been shown by themselves to be harmful to human health at levels usually encountered in urban air (1 to 4 ppm in most cities). The lowest demonstrated effect is irritation of mucous membranes by benzene at around 100 ppm.[16] The concentration at which hydrocarbons strongly suspected to be carcinogens, such as benzpyrene, may be harmful is not known.

[12]See, for example, Lynn, *Air pollution,* chapter 4, for more detailed discussion.

[13]NAS, 1975, *Air quality.*

[14]Lynn, *Air pollution.*

[15]C. M. Shy et al., The Chattanooga school children study, pp. 582–588.

[16]Lynn, *Air pollution.*

Much of the concern about adverse effects on health of hydrocarbons and nitrogen oxides stems from the photochemical smog these two classes of pollutants combine to produce under the influence of sunlight. The main ingredient of such smog is ozone, which kills experimental animals by damaging the respiratory tract at concentrations in the tens of parts per million, which causes similar damage (but without mortality) at 5 to 10 parts per million, and which produces symptoms of bronchitis and emphysema (again, in animals) under long-term exposure at around 1 ppm. Statistical evidence in Los Angeles, with the worst photochemical smog in the country (see below), reveals no mortality or morbidity (disease) effects, but does reveal some correlation of oxidant levels with reduced lung function in respiratory patients and with impairment of athletic performance. Constituents of photochemical smog other than ozone produce eye irritation whenever total oxidant concentrations exceed about 0.10 ppm.[17]

The disease effects of particulates take several forms: synergistic effects with other pollutants, as discussed above; the direct effects of sulfate particulates (increasingly well-studied in recent years and also mentioned above); and causation of cancer or other ailments by specific toxic ingredients, such as cadmium, lead, mercury, beryllium, and asbestos. The latter effects are treated below.

Unfortunately, it is difficult to make definitive statements about the precise health effects of air pollution, for reasons explained in Box 10-2. In spite of these problems, the evidence pointing to the severity of air pollution as a definite hazard is now massive. Consider these sample findings. Cigarette smokers from smoggy St. Louis, Missouri, have roughly 4 times the incidence of emphysema as smokers from relatively smog-free Winnipeg, Manitoba. At certain times, air pollution increases the frequency of head colds. Ten years after a smog disaster in Donora, Pennsylvania, in 1948, those residents who had reported severe effects during the smog showed the highest death rates. (This, of course, does not prove that the smog hurried them toward their graves—perhaps only previously weakened people suffered severe effects.) Pneumonia deaths are more frequent in areas of

[17]Lynn, *Air pollution,* pp. 104 ff. See also J. Kagawa and T. Toyama, Photochemical air pollution.

BOX 10-2 Assaying the Hazards of Pollutants

A hint of the difficulty of relating specific adverse effects on health to specific pollutants is provided by the example of cigarette-smoking. From the analyst's point of view, assaying the health hazards of smoking should be far easier than is the case for most contaminants. In smoking, the source of the pollutant is relatively uniform in character (although the number of potentially hazardous substances in tobacco smoke is large), and the intensity and duration of exposure are known with reasonable accuracy for a large number of individuals. Even with these advantages, it took many years to do the research required to demonstrate convincingly a close association between smoking and heart disease and lung cancer. (Whether the smoking public even today is convinced is arguable).

The difficulties facing toxicologists and epidemiologists in most other cases are much greater. We summarize some of the most important of these difficulties here. (Some apply to the smoking problem, too, but many do not.)

1. Pollutants are numerous and varied, and many of them are difficult to detect. Their concentrations vary geographically. In many areas, techniques for monitoring pollutants are highly inadequate, and long-term records are unavailable. Yet long periods of study are usually needed to reveal delayed and chronic effects.
2. It is often impossible to determine with precision the degree of exposure of a given individual to specific pollutants.
3. Which pollutant among many candidates is actually responsible for the suspected damage is often unknown. In many if not most cases, the agent doing the damage is a "secondary" substance produced by the chemical or radioactive transformation of the "primary" pollutant produced by human activity.
4. The preceding difficulty is multiplied many times over by the importance of *synergisms,* wherein the effect of two agents acting in concert exceeds the sum of the effects to be expected if the two acted individually. One or both agents in a synergism might be secondary substances produced from pollutants, one might be a naturally occurring agent, or there might be more than two actors involved.
5. Persons being studied for effects of pollutants may differ in many respects besides their degree of exposure to the suspected agent—for example, in socioeconomic class, sex, age, physiological susceptibility to certain contaminants, occupational exposure to pollutants, and smoking habits. Variation of many factors at once in the sample population makes it easy to be misled about what is causing what.
6. Official records of incidence of disease and causes of death are somewhat unreliable, for two main reasons: first, diagnostic procedures, nomenclature, and the knowledge of the average physician vary with time and probably, to some extent, regionally as well; second, final causes of death are often different from the malady that brought death near, and the primary maladies are often not listed on the death certificate.
7. Controlled experiments with laboratory animals are of limited usefulness because of differences in physiology between the experimental animals and humans. Effects with a long latency period between insult and symptoms may not appear at all in animals whose natural lifespan is short. For these reasons, the extent to which animal data can be used to infer effects of pollutants on humans is often controversial. The animals that most resemble humans physiologically—the large primates—are so expensive (and, in some cases, endangered as species) that experiments involving substantial numbers are impracticable.
8. Very large sample populations (of animals or people) are needed to investigate effects at low doses of pollutants, where only a small percentage of those exposed will manifest the suspected effect even if the cause-effect relationship is genuine. It cannot be assumed that the dose-response relation is linear with dose, that is, that effects occur in the same direct proportion to dose from low doses to high ones. For some agents, low doses may produce more damage per unit of exposure than high doses; for others, there may be a threshold in dose below which no ill effect occurs. It has been customary in regulation of pollution to assume that evidence obtained at high doses can be extrapolated linearly to low ones; this will be overcautious in some cases and not cautious enough in others.

high pollution. Chronic bronchitis is more serious among British postmen who work in areas of high air pollution than in those who serve in relatively smog-free areas. Emphysema death rates have skyrocketed as urban air pollution has increased (although incidence of this disease is also high in rural areas, where dust is probably the culprit). The United Kingdom has higher overall rates of air pollution than the United States, and death from lung cancer is more than twice as common among British men as it is among American men. The lung-cancer death rates in the United Kingdom are correlated with the density of atmospheric smoke. The lung-cancer rate for men over 45 in the smoggiest part of Staten Island, New York, is 55 per 100,000. In a less smoggy area just a few miles away, the rate is 40 per 100,000.[18]

Some of the effects just described are still the subject of controversy within the scientific community, undoubtedly because of the sorts of difficulties described in Box 10-2. However, much of the debate resembles the cigarette-smoking-and-cancer arguments of a few years ago—the evidence is "only statistical," but to those knowledgeable in statistics, it is already persuasive and is becoming overwhelming. In short, air pollution kills. Since it usually kills slowly and unobtrusively, however, the resulting deaths are not dramatically called to the attention of the public. Estimates of the annual American financial loss resulting from air pollution's effects on health run as high as 14 to 29 billion dollars. A 1970 study put the *lower limit* on the annual savings in medical care and lost income that a 50-percent reduction in air pollution in major urban regions would provide at slightly more than 2 billion dollars.[19]

Standards

Standards imposed by federal and state agencies for permissable degrees of air pollution by major contaminants fall into two basic categories. *Ambient air-quality standards* specify the concentrations of various pollutants permitted to exist in the lower level of the atmosphere where people, other organisms, and property can be exposed to them; these standards are generally given in parts per million (by volume) or micrograms of contaminant per cubic meter of air. *Emission standards* specify what quantities of different contaminants may be released per unit of time or per unit of activity (e.g., miles driven in an automobile) by various pollutant sources.

Operationally, the setting and enforcement of emission standards are the principal tools for seeing that ambient air standards are met. It is exceedingly difficult, however, to relate emissions to concentrations in an exact quantitative way. One knows, of course, that higher emissions mean higher ambient concentrations, all else being equal; but the precise relation depends on the geographical distribution of a tremendous variety of sources (from automobiles to dry-cleaning establishments to refineries and electric-power plants), on the interaction of these with meteorological conditions that change not only from day to day but sometimes from minute to minute, and on complex chemical and photochemical reactions the pollutants undergo with each other and with other atmospheric constituents. This clearly is a case where statistical correlation of emissions and ambient air quality would be a useful approach. But this, too, is difficult because (1) there generally are not enough measuring stations to get an accurate picture of the spatial distribution of ambient air quality, and (2) it is hard to know what total emissions were in a given region on a given day. Even if one knows the emission characteristics of all sources, one must also know the intensity with which all those sources were in use on the day in question.[20]

Emission standards are set, then, partly on the basis of incomplete analytic models of the processes relating emissions to ambient air quality, partly on the basis of an incomplete body of statistical data, and partly by the outcome of competing political pressures generated by people in favor of clean air, on the one hand, and the pollution-producing industries and manufacturers of

[18]See, for example, NAS, *Air quality*, chapter 4; W. Winkelstein and R. Gay, suspended particulate air pollution; Lave and Seskin, *Air pollution*. See also S. Epstein and D. Hattis, Pollution and human health.

[19]Lave and Seskin, Air pollution. See also Lave and Silverman, Economic costs of energy-related environmental pollution.

[20]For useful summaries of the work that has been done on this set of questions, see John Trijonis, The relationship of sulfur oxide emissions to sulfur dioxide and sulfate air quality, in *Air quality*, NAS; and National Academy of Sciences, *Air quality and automobile emissions control*, vol. 3, *The relationship of emissions to ambient air quality*.

TABLE 10-2
U.S. Ambient Air Quality Standards

Pollutant	*Standard*	*Micrograms per cubic meter*	*Parts per million by volume*
Total suspended particulates (TSP)	Primary: annual mean*	75	—
	24-hour**	260	—
	Secondary: annual mean	60	—
	24-hour	150	—
Sulfur dioxide (SO_2)	Primary:† annual mean	80	0.03
	24-hour	365	0.14
Carbon monoxide (CO)	Primary: 8-hour	10,000	9.0
	1-hour	40,000	35.0
Nitrogen dioxide (NO_2)	Primary: annual mean	100	0.05
Nonmethane hydrocarbons (HC)	Primary: 3-hour††	160	0.24
Photochemical oxidants (O_x)	Primary: 1-hour	160	0.08

*Annual mean is geometric mean for particulates, arithmetic mean for all others.
**Averages for specified number of hours not to be exceeded more than once per year.
†Where no separate secondary standard is given, it is to be assumed to be identical to primary standard.
††6 A.M. to 9 A.M.
Source: CEQ, *Environmental quality, 1975,* pp. 300–303.

pollution-producing devices on the other. Ambient air-quality standards are supposed to be set to protect public health and property, although, again, the data and theory needed to do this properly are incomplete, and political pressures and value judgments cannot help entering into the process. As an example of the latter: should standards be set to protect the "average" member of the public or the most sensitive member of the public—the asthmatic, the very old, the very young?

Emissions standards, once set, can be enforced by spot-checking individual sources (for example, automobiles or power plants) for compliance and by fining or shutting down violators. Ambient standards as such cannot be enforced, but it is not uncommon to try to alleviate the worst conditions by requiring or encouraging reduced use of major sources (even if they meet established emission standards) on days when meteorological conditions threaten to make ambient air quality especially bad.

The ambient air-quality standards in force in the United States in 1975 are summarized in Table 10-2. "Primary standards" are designed to protect public health and "secondary standards" to protect public welfare (meaning property and aesthetics). Amendments to the Clean Air Act passed by Congress in 1970 set mid-1975 as the deadline for achieving the primary standards, but the deadline was not met; at the deadline, the standards were being violated for one or more pollutants in 156 of the nation's 247 air quality control regions.[21] Although it is sometimes suggested that the ambient standards incorporate large margins of safety between the specified concentrations and those at which actual adverse effects on health would be expected, major reviews by the National Academy of Sciences have affirmed repeatedly that evidence for such margins is absent and that no scientific basis existed at the time of these reviews for revising the standards.[22] (Interestingly, there are no standards at all for indoor air quality in homes and public buildings—see Box 10-3.)

The emissions standards for automobiles that have been developed as part of the attempt to improve ambient air quality have had a complex history. The Clean Air Act Amendments of 1970 established specific goals for reducing emissions from autos, but they also permitted the Environmental Protection Agency (EPA) considerable leeway in extending the amount of time allowed for automobile manufacturers to comply. An extension of one year was made by the administrator of EPA in April 1973 for 1975 standards, with interim standards to be enforced in place of the statutory requirements. Under the pressure of the "energy crisis" in 1974, and responding to the questionable assertion that tight emission control and good fuel economy are incompatible, Congress entered the arena once more with amendments to

[21]Council on Environmental Quality (CEQ), *Environmental quality, 1975,* pp. 299 ff.

[22]NAS, *Air quality;* NAS, *Air quality and automobile emission control,* vol. 3.

the Clean Air Act that extended the interim standards for hydrocarbons and carbon monoxide and replaced the statutory standard for nitrogen oxides with a new one.[23] All the while, the state of California has consistently imposed standards stricter than the federal ones. The history of automotive emission standards and their possible status through 1981 are summarized in Table 10-3.

Emission standards to be applied to stationary sources of air pollution have also been characterized by change, confusion, and controversy. Most visible has been the debate about the efficacy and reliability of stack-gas scrubbers to remove sulfur dioxide from the effluent of coal-burning and oil-burning electric-power plants (see also Chapter 8). Electric utilities have argued that these devices are inordinately expensive and not reliable; the Environmental Protection Agency has insisted that scrubbers are a proven technology and should be applied.[24] The industry favors the use of tall stacks to disperse the effluent and "intermittent controls," meaning curtailment of operations or switching to low-sulfur fuels during adverse meteorological conditions. Emissions standards in force in 1976 for new fossil-fuel-burning steam-electric-power plants are summarized in Table 10-4.

[23]For more detail in this convoluted history, see, for example, Lynn, *Air pollution*, chapter 9; CEQ *Environmental Quality, 1975*, pp. 52–59.
[24]CEQ, *Environmental quality, 1975*, p. 46.

TABLE 10-3
Automobile Emission Standards (grams per mile)

	HC	*CO*	*NO_x*
Uncontrolled cars (pre-1968)[a]	8.7	87.0	3.5
1970–1971 federal standards[b]	4.1	34.0	
1972–1974 federal standards[b]	3.0	28.0	3.1
1975[c] and 1976[d]			
Federal 49-state standards	1.5	15.0	3.1
California standards	0.9	9.0	2.0
1977[e] federal 50-state standards	1.5	15.0	2.0
1978 statutory standards	0.41	3.4	0.4
Administration bill (January 1975)			
1977–1981 50-state standards	0.9	9.0	3.1
Post-1981 50-state standards	[f]	[f]	[f]
EPA recommendation (March 1975)			
1977–1979	1.5	15.0	2.0
1980–1981	0.9	9.0	2.0
Post-1981	0.41	3.4	[f]
Revised administration proposal (June 1975)			
Through 1981	1.5	15.0	3.1
Post-1981	[f]	[f]	[f]

[a]On the basis of 1975 test procedures.
[b]Imposed administratively by EPA.
[c]Imposed by EPA as interim standards after suspension of statutory standards, except for California's HC and NO_x standards, which were set by the state.
[d]Imposed by Congress in Public Law 93–319, except for California's NO_x standards, which were set by the state[f].
[e]Imposed by EPA as interim standards after suspension of statutory standards, except for NO_x standards, which were imposed by the Congress (Public Law 93–319).
[f]Administrative discretion.
Source: CEQ, *Environmental quality, 1975*, p. 53.

TABLE 10-4
New Source Standards of Performance for Fossil-Fuel-Fired Steam Generators

Pollutant	*Standard*
Particulate matter	0.10 lb. per million Btu heat input, maximum two-hour average
	20 percent opacity (except that 40 percent opacity is permissible for not more than two minutes in any hour)
Sulfur dioxide	0.80 lb. per million Btu heat input, maximum two-hour average when liquid fossil fuel is burned
	1.2 lbs. per million Btu heat input, maximum two-hour average when solid fuel is burned
Nitrogen oxides	0.20 lb. per million Btu heat input, maximum two-hour average, expressed as NO_2, when gaseous fossil fuel is burned
	0.30 lb. per million Btu heat input, maximum two-hour average, expressed as NO_2, when liquid fossil fuel is burned
	0.70 lb. per million Btu heat input, maximum two-hour average, expressed as NO_2, when solid fossil fuel (except lignite) is burned

Source: NAS, *Air quality and stationary-source emission control*, p. xliv.

BOX 10-3 Air Quality Indoors

There are standards for air quality outdoors and in industrial workplaces, but most people spend most of their time in places where air quality is neither monitored nor regulated—in homes, offices, classrooms, stores, cars, buses, planes, and other enclosed places. Ironically, the concentrations of air pollutants in these heavily used indoor environments often exceed those that are permitted outdoors.

The few studies that have been done of air pollution in homes have identified several potentially important sources of harmful contaminants. Gas stoves, for example, emit nitrogen dioxide, nitric oxide, and carbon monoxide. In homes tested in a study for the Environmental Protection Agency, nitrogen dioxide concentrations often exceed 100 $\mu g/m^3$ in the kitchen and sometimes approached that concentration throughout the house; carbon monoxide concentrations sometimes approached 10,000 $\mu g/m^3$.[a] Presumably, improperly vented gas water heaters and furnaces can also contribute significantly to indoor concentrations of these combustion products.

Other indoor air contaminants are dispensed intentionally from aerosol cans of all varieties—deodorants, hair sprays, cleaning agents, and insecticides, among others. Of concern are not only the products themselves, but the fluorocarbon propellants found in many of them. Concentrations of the latter in some circumstances exceed the Threshold Limit Values applied in industry.[b]

The most pervasive form of air pollution indoors, however, almost certainly is tobacco smoke. The health risk that smokers impose upon themselves has been suspected for a long time and established beyond any reasonable doubt since the 1960s. The plight of some millions of American nonsmokers who are clinically allergic to tobacco smoke is well known to the victims and to the medical profession, but it has not been widely publicized. Also well established medically is the special threat that tobacco smoke represents for nonsmoking victims of asthma, bronchitis, emphysema, and heart disease.[c]

More recently, attention has turned belatedly to the possibility that tobacco smoke at concentrations commonly encountered indoors is hazardous to otherwise healthy, nonallergic nonsmokers. The risk to nonsmokers (more accurately, passive smokers, that is, people who inhale smoke *involuntarily* from their environment) should hardly come as a surprise in view of the large number of carcinogenic and otherwise toxic substances that have been identified in tobacco smoke. They include cadmium, oxides of nitrogen, benzo(a)pyrene and other hydrocarbons, carbon monoxide, and particulate matter. Probably many passive smokers have consoled themselves with the belief that the voluntary smokers sucking the smoldering tobacco are inhaling and absorbing most of the pollutants themselves. Unfortunately, studies have shown that the sidestream smoke—that which drifts off the tip of the cigarette—contains several times as much of the main pollutants as the mainstream smoke inhaled by the voluntary smoker.[d]

Obviously, the sidestream smoke is diluted by surrounding air before being inhaled by the passive smoker, but the dosage can still be substantial. Concentrations of particulate matter in excess of 3000 $\mu g/m^3$ have been measured in smoke-filled rooms at parties, or 40 times the U.S. standard for outside air. In public places, concentrations of particulate matter from tobacco smoke have been measured at up to 400 $\mu g/m^3$.[e] Carbon monoxide concentrations in smoke-filled rooms reach at least 40,000 $\mu g/m^3$ and prolonged smoking in enclosed automobiles has produced CO concentrations of 100,000

[a] U.S. Environmental Protection Agency, *A study of indoor air quality.*

[b] Ibid.

[c] See, for example, I. Schmeltz, D. Hoffmann, and E. L. Wynder, The influence of tobacco smoke on indoor atmospheres; and W. S. Aronow, Effects of carbon monoxide on coronary heart disease.

[d] On this and subsequent points, an especially good review article is Jon Tinker, Should public smoking be banned?

[e] In addition to Tinker, see W. C. Hinds and M. W. First, Concentrations of nicotine and tobacco smoke in public places.

$\mu g/m^3$. Studies of the carboxyhemoglobin content in the blood of voluntary and passive smokers indicate that the passive smoker in unusually smoky conditions receives the equivalent of smoking one to two cigarettes per hour, and under conditions common in homes, offices, bars, and theaters receives the equivalent of smoking a cigarette a day.

Demonstrating conclusively that these kinds of exposures actually can cause disease (as distinguished from aggravating preexisting disease or allergy) among nonsmokers is difficult for many of the reasons enumerated in Box 10-2: A large population of subjects must be kept track of over an extended period if a statistically significant effect is to be discerned, many other kinds of insults will be operating in the same population at the same time, some of the other insults may interact synergistically with passive smoking, and so on. The most informative studies of which we are aware investigated the incidence of bronchitis, pneumonia, and other respiratory ailments among young children whose parents were heavy smokers; the children had a significantly higher incidence of the ailments than the children of nonsmoking parents.[f] It is conceivable, of course, that the same part of the genetic makeup of certain persons predisposes them to respiratory ailments and also predisposes them to take up smoking; if this were true, there would be a correlation between smoking and respiratory disease in the smokers and their children, but it could not be said that the smoking "caused" the disease. Most authorities consider this hypothesis of a common genetic origin of smoking and respiratory disease to be inconsistent with the medical evidence.[g]

Whether there is a threshold in level of exposure to cigarette smoke, below which no lasting harm occurs, is not known and would be very difficult to establish. The appropriately cautious approach taken by most regulatory authorities in dealing with other insults, such as radiation, has been to assume for purposes of analysis that no threshold exists. If, on this assumption, the data for lung-cancer risk versus exposure to tobacco smoke among active smokers is extrapolated into the range of exposure suffered by passive smokers, the conclusion is that passive smokers exposed to the equivalent of one to two cigarettes per day may suffer a doubled risk of dying of lung cancer as a result of this exposure.[h] At five cigarettes per day, the active smoker suffers a roughly fivefold increase in risk of dying from lung cancer, compared to the "spontaneous" incidence.

The likelihood that otherwise healthy nonsmokers are being damaged by inhaling other people's smoke, coupled with the certainty that passive smoking is harmful to persons unfortunate enough to be allergic to tobacco smoke or suffering from a variety of preexisting diseases, make society's tolerance for public smoking in an era of growing environmental concern an ever more striking anomaly. As of 1976, the state of California, New York City, and a few other major political entities had passed laws restricting smoking in public buildings and public transportation systems. These measures are a good beginning, but there is ample reason to go much further. In situations where nonsmokers literally have no escape (such as on buses and aircraft, whose ventilation systems are incapable of maintaining a real distinction between smoking and no-smoking zones), smoking should long ago have been banned outright.

There is no doubt, of course, that voluntary smoking provides a great many people with a great deal of pleasure. But it seems to us that this activity should be legally confined, as certain other pleasurable (and considerably less dangerous) activities are, to consenting adults in private.

[f] S. Gilder, The passive smoker; J. Colley, W. Holland, R. Corkhill, Influence of passive smoking and parental phlegm on pneumonia and bronchitis in early childhood.

[g] For the arguments on both sides of the genetic predisposition issue, see P. Burch, Does smoking cause lung cancer? and R. Doll, Smoking, lung cancer, and Occam's razor.

[h] Tinker, Should public smoking be banned?

It has become evident in the 1970s that in some regions the ambient air-quality standards cannot be met within the foreseeable future solely by progressively tightening emissions standards. The emissions characteristics of vehicles and other fuel-burners now in existence can be modified only so far by the addition of retrofitted control devices. The cleanest fuels—low-sulfur coal, low-sulfur oil, and natural gas—are those in shortest supply (see Chapter 8). The rate at which new, cleaner engines and power plants replace old ones is limited, and further drastic reduction of new-source emission standards will require time-consuming technical transitions (e.g., to radically different automobile engines and to gasification or liquefaction prior to combustion of coal).[25]

Several control strategies other than emissions standards have been discussed by government agencies, and some have been tried. They include: (1) "transportation control" schemes to reduce automobile use in urban areas, for example, by making parking more expensive or by making alternative transportation available; and (2) control by land-use regulations of the siting of indirect sources—facilities such as shopping centers, stadiums, and airports—which attract large numbers of vehicles and thus induce air-pollution problems.

A particularly vigorous controversy was underway in the mid-1970s on the issue of "significant deterioration" of air quality. Court decisions in 1972 and 1973 held that, under the Clean Air Act, no state could permit significant deterioration of air quality in areas where it was already cleaner than required by ambient standards. Industry spokespersons argued that this ruling amounted to arbitrary and capricious land-use regulations, effectively prohibiting further industrial development. Regulations issued by EPA in 1974 to comply with the court ruling were a compromise, identifying three classifications of areas: Class I, where air quality would be protected at existing levels; Class II, where moderate increases in pollution levels would be permitted; and Class III, where growth could proceed until air pollution reached national standards. Governors could determine how regions within their states were to be classified. These regulations have been challenged both by industrialists as too severe and by environmentalists as too lenient.[26]

Urban Air Pollution: A Case History

Four centuries ago, Juan Rodriguez Cabrillo recorded in his diary that smoke from Indian fires in the Los Angeles basin rose for a few hundred feet and then spread to blanket the valley with haze. Because of this phenomenon, he named what is today called San Pedro Bay, the Bay of Smokes. Cabrillo was observing the effect of a thermal inversion. Normally, the temperature of the atmosphere decreases steadily with increased altitude, but during an inversion a layer of warm air overlies cooler air below and severely limits the vertical mixing of the atmosphere, and pollutants accumulate in the layer of air trapped near Earth's surface (Figure 10-3; see also Chapter 2). Because of the wind patterns in the eastern Pacific and the ring of mountains surrounding the Los Angeles basin, it is an ideal place for the formation of inversions, usually at about 2000 feet above the floor of the basin. In the basin, they occur on about 7 out of every 16 days.

Los Angeles has abundant sunshine, another climatic feature that contributes to its air-pollution problems. Sunlight acts on a mixture of oxygen, nitrogen oxides, and hydrocarbons to produce photochemical smog. Combustion products from well over 3 million cars are expelled into the atmosphere of the Los Angeles basin in addition to the wastes discharged by oil refineries and other industries. As a result, the air breathed by residents of Los Angeles contains far more than the usual mixture of nitrogen, oxygen, and carbon dioxide—it also contains carbon monoxide, ozone, aldehydes, ketones, alcohols, acids, ethers, peroxyacetyl nitrates and nitrites, alkyl nitrates and nitrites, benzpyrene, and many other dangerous chemicals.

Smog first became prominent in Los Angeles during World War II. Since then the Los Angeles County Air

[25]See, for example, Lees et al. *Smog;* Jet Propulsion Laboratory, *Should we have a new engine? An automobile power systems evaluation.*

[26]For more complete discussion, see CEQ, *Environmental quality, 1975,* pp. 50–52.

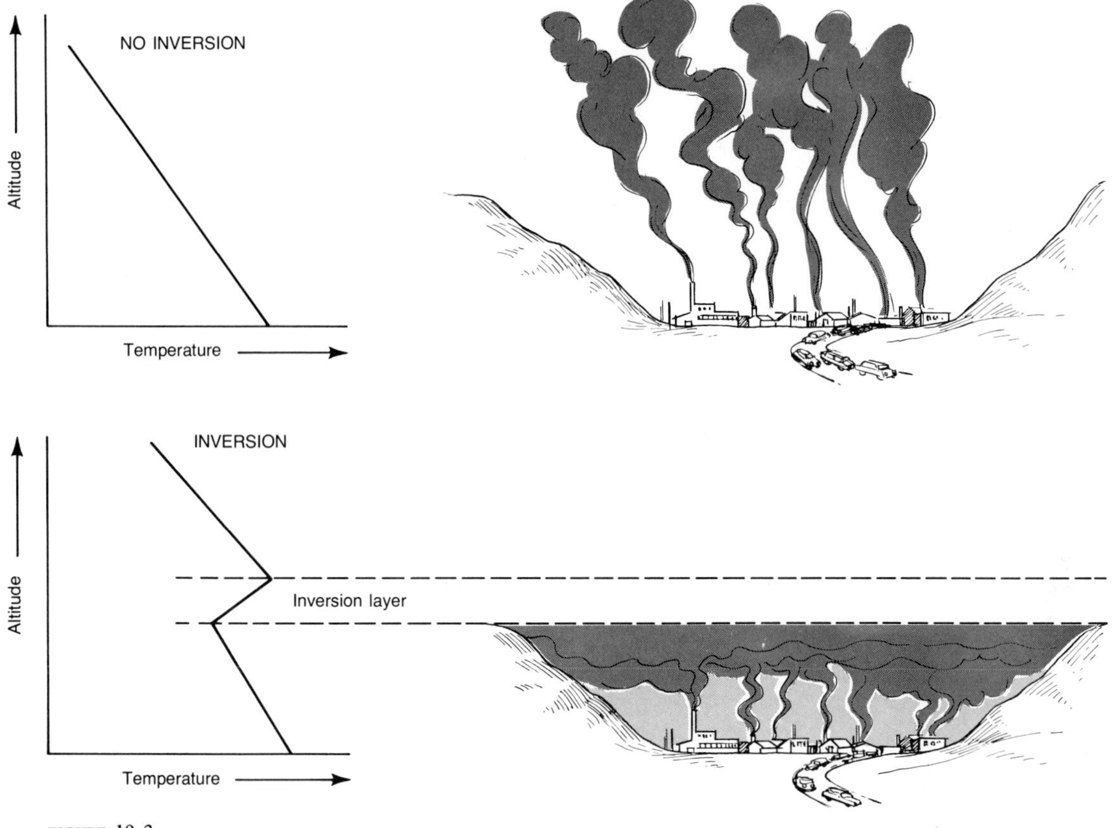

FIGURE 10-3

Temperature inversion, in which a layer of warm air overlies a layer of cooler air, trapping air pollution close to the ground.

Pollution Control District (APCD) has pursued a vigorous policy of smog abatement. The district has imposed strict controls on industry, setting rigid emission standards for power plants, refineries, and other sources of pollution. Some 1.5 million domestic incinerators, a dozen large municipal incinerators, 57 open-burning dumps, and incinerators in commercial buildings have been eliminated. Coal-burning has been made illegal, and so has (for most of the year) the burning of oil with a high sulfur content. Control is exercised over the escape of vapors from petroleum storage tanks and gasoline-loading facilities. Also controlled are commercial processes that require organic solvents, the olefin content of gasoline sold in Los Angeles County, and many other contributors to air pollution. Furthermore, all cars sold in California were required to have smog-control devices designed to reduce crankcase emissions of hydrocarbons before the devices were required nationwide.[27]

The Los Angeles area also has partially "controlled" its smog by generating a portion of its electricity in areas of low population in New Mexico and Nevada, using low-quality coal that would not be tolerated under the air-quality laws of California or Arizona. This is roughly equivalent to throwing garbage in a neighbor's yard because his yard is larger and he is powerless to prevent it. It is worth pondering whether the "necessity" of exporting pollution this way from areas of high population density and affluence might not indicate something about the desirability of further growth in those areas.

[27]For details on the history and prospects of the Los Angeles situation, see, for example, Lees et al. *Smog.*

WATER POLLUTION

Water pollutants take many forms. One useful classification follows:

1. *Disease-causing organisms*—specifically parasites, bacteria, and viruses, which often enter water with human sewage;[28]
2. *Synthetic organic compounds* in the form of industrial, household, and agricultural chemicals, as well as water-treatment chemicals added deliberately and the products formed by the reaction of these with other contaminants;
3. *Inorganic compounds and mineral substances,* including acids, mineral fibers such as asbestos, and heavy metals, discharged directly into water by certain mining and industrial operations and also entering water as fallout or in precipitation from the atmosphere;
4. *Radioactive substances* from commercial and military applications of nuclear energy;
5. *Oxygen-demanding wastes*—namely, organic compounds contained in sewage and some industrial effluents, whose biological or chemical degradation depletes dissolved oxygen;
6. *Plant nutrients,* such as nitrogen and phosphorous, from sewage and agricultural runoff;
7. *Sediments* from erosion caused by agriculture or construction;
8. *Thermal discharges* from power plants and certain industrial facilities.

Water pollutants also can be classified by their effects: direct impact on health in the form of bacterial or viral disease; production of cancer, genetic defects, and birth defects; other varieties of acute and chronic toxicity to people;[29] and effects on ecosystems, through which an impact on human beings may subsequently be felt.

This section of text gives an overview of sources, degree, and treatment of water pollution. Pesticides, radioactivity, fluorides, and heavy metals (which occur in air and soil as well as in water) are treated in more detail later in this chapter. These and other water pollutants receive further attention in the discussions of carcinogens and mutagens. Effects on ecosystems, especially the impacts of Items 5 through 8 in the above list, are discussed in Chapter 11.

Sources and Degrees of Water Pollution

Approximately one-third of waste water in the United States comes from households and two-thirds from commerce and industry.[30] The most commonly used index of pollution is *biochemical oxygen demand* (BOD), which refers to the quantity of oxygen required by bacteria to oxidize organic waste aerobically to carbon dioxide and water. A standard measure of BOD in practice is the amount of oxygen used in the first five days of decomposition at 20° C; this is called BOD_5. Domestic sewage typically has a BOD_5 of around 200 milligrams of oxygen per liter, and that for industrial waste may reach several thousand milligrams per liter.[31] A BOD of 0.17 pound, or 77 grams, is sometimes called a *population equivalent,* being roughly equal to the daily requirement for the domestic wastes of one person. When commercial and industrial wastes are added in, there are about 3 population equivalents of BOD actually produced per person in the United States—that is, a requirement of 0.5 pound, or 230 grams, of dissolved oxygen per person per day. The capacity of a sewage treatment plant is generally measured in population equivalents per day.

Contamination of water by sewage is the principal cause of water-borne disease, including cholera, typhoid and paratyphoid fever, dysentery, and infectious hepatitis. The cause-and-effect relation became evident gradually in the course of a series of major epidemics of cholera and typhoid fever in England, Germany, and the United States between 1850 and 1900. In each of these, certain cities or parts of cities were struck heavily while adjacent areas escaped relatively lightly. Invariably the epidemic-stricken areas obtained their water from different wells or different stretches of river than the areas that escaped, so

[28]Modified slightly from G. M. Masters, *Introduction to environmental science and technology,* chapter 5.

[29]It is worth noting that *absence* of certain contaminants in water may also be harmful. Persons whose drinking water is soft (low in dissolved minerals) have a higher incidence of cardiovascular disease than persons who drink hard water. (See H. Hudson and F. Gilcreas, Health and economic aspects of water hardness and corrosiveness; L. C. Neri et al., Health aspects of hard and soft waters.)

[30]W. T. Edmondson, Fresh water pollution.

[31]Masters, *Introduction to environmental science,* chapter 5.

TABLE 10-5
U.S. Water Quality Trends, 1963–1972

Indicator	Standard	Basis	Percent of reaches exceeding standards 1963–1967	Percent of reaches exceeding standards 1968–1972
Fecal coliforms	2,000/100 ml	Recreation	17	43
Total coliforms	10,000/100ml	Recreation	23	20
Suspended solids	80 mg/1	Aquatic life	26	14
Ammonia	0.89 mg/1	Aquatic life	16	6
Dissolved solids	500 mg/1	Water supply	25	18
Sulfates	250 mg/1	Water supply	12	12
Phenols	0.001 mg/1	Water supply	86	71
Nitrite and nitrate	0.9 mg/1	Nutrient	18	26
Total phosphate	0.3 mg/1	Nutrient	30	41

Source: CEQ, *Environmental quality, 1974,* p. 366.

the evidence that the crucial difference was contamination with sewage eventually became overwhelming.[32]

BOD, although a rough measure of the quality of waste, does not accurately indicate the risk of disease; for that, more specific indices are required. One of the most common is the number of coliform bacteria (sometimes, more specifically, fecal coliforms—intestinal bacteria, especially of the genus *Escherichia,* found in feces) per unit volume of water. Although the bacteria are themselves relatively harmless, their presence in large numbers indicates that pathogens are probably present as well; conversely, their absence is a good, although not perfect, indication that pathogens are absent. United States Public Health Service (USPHS) drinking-water standards for coliform organisms specify that the most probable number (MPN) shall not exceed 1 coliform organism per 100 milliliters of water. (The MPN is determined by culturing a series of samples from the water supply in a medium favorable to the growth of coliform bacteria.) Standards recommended by the Environmental Protection Agency for water-contact recreational activities specify MPNs of 10,000 total coliforms or 2000 fecal coliforms per 100 milliliters.[33] The latter coliform criteria are those typically used when a beach is closed because of pollution.

Table 10-5 shows water-quality trends in the United States between 1963 and 1972, measured against standards of coliform bacteria and other indicators, for a sample of "reaches" covering major parts of the inland waters of the country. As the table indicates, water quality in the United States in this period was improving in some respects but deteriorating in others.

Even after processing in municipal water-treatment plants, the water supplied for drinking in cities in the United States is not always safe. There is some evidence, for example, that a high content of organic matter in water can somehow protect viruses from the disinfective effects of the chlorine heavily used in municipal water treatment.[34] Infectious hepatitis is spreading at an alarming rate in the United States, and a major suspect for the route of transmission is the "toilet-to-mouth pipeline" of water systems not made safe by chlorination.[35] The total incidence of water-borne diseases in the United States dropped steadily from the 1930s to the mid-1960s but then started to rise again; the reasons for the upturn are not known in detail.[36]

The safety of chlorine itself as an ingredient of water treatment has been questioned on the grounds that it may interact with other chemicals in water to form mutagenic and carcinogenic compounds.[37] Whatever the cause, there are suspicious correlations between drinking-water sources and cancer deaths.[38]

Another direct health hazard is nitrate pollution. The heavy use of inorganic fertilizers in agriculture results in

[32]C. ReVelle and R. ReVelle, *Sourcebook on the environment,* pp. 33–36.

[33]CEQ, *Environmental quality,* 1974. p. 366.

[34]See, for example, J. Crossland and V. Brodine, Drinking water.

[35]An example of the failure of chlorination to control the hepatitis virus in India is described in Masters, *Introduction to environmental science,* p. 150.

[36]G. F. Kraun; L. J. McCabe; and J. M. Hughes, Waterborne disease outbreaks in the U.S.: 1971 through 1974.

[37]See, for example, R. Tardiff and M. Deinzer, *Toxicity of organic compounds in drinking water;* J. L. Marx, Drinking water: another source of carcinogens?; and the sections on carcinogens and mutagens below.

[38]Page et al., Drinking water and cancer mortality in Louisiana.

the flow of a heavy load of nitrates into water supplies; nitrates also accumulate in high concentrations in crops. Nitrates themselves are not especially dangerous, but when certain bacteria are present in the digestive tract, they may convert the nitrates into highly toxic nitrites. Farm animals and human infants are particularly likely to have in their digestive tracts these types of bacteria as well as the appropriate conditions for the conversion of nitrate to nitrite. In addition, conversion of nitrates to nitrites can occur in any opened container of food, even if it is subsequently refrigerated. Nitrate water pollution in lakes, streams, and wells probably is most dangerous in the Central Valley of California, where it is a severe public-health hazard and where doctors often recommend that infants be given only pure bottled water. It is also serious, however, in such other states as Illinois, Wisconsin, and Missouri.[39]

Treatment of Water and Sewage

Water-treatment plants are those used to bring "raw" water (e.g., from rivers and reservoirs) up to drinking-water quality. Sewage-treatment plants are intended to bring domestic and industrial waste up to a quality suitable for discharge into rivers, lakes, or coastal waters.

The main steps in typical water-treatment plants are coagulation, settling, and filtration to remove suspended particles, aeration to remove the volatile substances most responsible for taste and odor, and chlorination to kill pathogenic organisms. The coagulant, often alum $[Al_2(SO_4)_3 \cdot 18H_2O]$, enables colloidal particles to stick together when they encounter one another; *flocculation* refers to the agglomeration of submicroscopic coagulated particles into larger ones that settle out or that can be readily filtered. The filter is generally sand and gravel. These treatment processes are ineffective for removing dissolved solids, which exceed the recommended concentration of 500 milligrams per liter in many American communities.[40] These can be partly removed by more expensive chemical techniques (water softening) or by physical desalting processes. The latter are very expensive and are not widely employed (see also Chapter 6).

There is a wide variety of possibilities for the treatment of sewage. In 1970, about 73 percent of the population of the United States was served by sanitary sewer systems; the remaining 27 percent relied on cesspools and septic tanks.[41] Of the roughly 150 million people served by sewers, the output of about 10 million people was discharged to the environment untreated (raw sewage); the output of 40 million received what is called primary treatment; and that of 100 million received primary and secondary treatment.

Primary treatment consists of mechanical filtration, screening, and settling, followed by chlorination. It removes 50 to 65 percent of the suspended solids and 25 to 40 percent of the 5-day BOD. The products are a solid sludge and a liquid effluent that is not suitable for any direct reuse; only where the receptacle is the open ocean can primary treatment alone possibly be considered adequate. The cost of such treatment is 4 to 5 cents per 1000 gallons (including the construction cost of the facilities), and the electricity cost of operation is in the range of 10 to 20 kilowatt hours per year per population equivalent of capacity.[42]

Secondary treatment adds to primary treatment (minus the chlorination) a set of biological processes similar to the decomposition processes that occur in nature; that is, the organic wastes are transformed by bacteria in the treatment plant, where oxygen is provided by aeration, instead of depleting dissolved oxygen in the receiving waters. The sludge from this process, consisting largely of bacterial masses, is concentrated and processed further in an anaerobic digester. Here most of the material is converted into carbon dioxide and methane (CH_4), the latter being collectible for use as fuel in the sewage plant or elsewhere (see also Chapter 8). The remaining solids are dried and can be used for fertilizer or landfill. Secondary treatment removes about 90 percent each of the 5-day BOD and the suspended solids. The liquid effluent is suitable for industrial reuse and, in some circumstances, for irrigation. The cost of treatment up to

[39] See, for example, N. Gruener and R. Toeplitz, The effect of changes in nitrate concentration in drinking water on methemoglobin levels in infants; and National Academy of Sciences, *Accumulation of nitrate.*

[40] Masters, *Introduction to environmental science,* p. 151.

[41] These and succeeding data in this paragraph are from U.S. Environmental Protection Agency, *The economics of clean water, summary.*

[42] See, for example, American Chemical Society, *Cleaning our environment: The chemical basis for action;* or Eric Hirst, The energy cost of pollution control.

the secondary level (including the primary step) is 8 to 15 cents per 1000 gallons, and the electricity consumption is 30 to 70 kilowatt hours per year per population equivalent. A major defect of secondary treatment is the low degree of removal of nutrients, which is typically around 50 percent of the nitrogen and 30 percent of the phosphorus. The high nutrient concentrations remaining in the effluent from secondary treatment contribute heavily to the eutrophication problems described in Chapter 11.

Tertiary treatment of sewage was in use in the early 1970s for only a tiny fraction of the U.S. population, but it is receiving increased attention because of growing interest in eutrophication and in direct reuse of waste water. The idea is to remove 97 to 99 percent or more of the BOD, 90 percent or more of the phosphorus, and as much as possible of complex organics and nitrogen. There is an enormous variety of tertiary-treatment technologies addressed to those goals, including physical, chemical, and biological processes.[43] Among the tertiary processes used in different combinations in different plants are distillation, reverse osmosis, electrodialysis, chemical precipitation, ion exchange, and carbon adsorption. Tertiary treatment is expensive (17 to 54 cents per 1000 gallons) and electricity-intensive (66 kilowatt hours per year per population equivalent in the most well-known operative plant, at South Lake Tahoe, California). The effluent from successful tertiary treatment can be used for irrigating food crops, for recreation, and perhaps (say the advocates of some processes) for direct human consumption. Lack of understanding of the circumstances in which pathogenic viruses and toxic chemicals survive treatment makes it difficult to rely on producing pure drinking water this way, however.[43a]

Relation to Population

Water pollution from sewage provides one of the classic examples of the diseconomies of scale accompanying population growth. If a few people per mile live along a large river, their sewage may be dumped directly into the river and natural purification will occur. But if the population increases, the waste-degrading ability of the river becomes strained, and either the sewage or the intake water must be treated if the river water is to be safe for drinking. Should the population along the river increase further, more and more elaborate and expensive treatment will be required to keep the water safe for human use and to maintain desirable fishes and shellfishes in the river. In general, the more people there are living in a watershed, the higher are the per-capita costs of avoiding water pollution.

As the populations of many municipalities grow, their sewage-treatment facilities, though once adequate, may be outgrown. Funds for new sewage facilities can be obtained only at the expense of funds needed for more and better schools, police departments, water systems, roads, and other public services. Inevitably, it seems, the available funds are insufficient to meet all of these needs, which are created, in part, by increases in population. The sewage problem is increased by lax inspection and lax enforcement of public-health standards, which permit construction of septic tanks too close together or in unsuitable soils in many of the rural and suburban areas where there are no general sewage facilities.

Novel Approaches

The expense in dollars and energy to cope with expanding sewage-treatment needs with ever-more-sophisticated tertiary-treatment facilities has led some people to think seriously about and to develop alternative approaches. One that is widely regarded in the conventional sewage-treatment fraternity as heresy, but that has achieved notable success in several major installations, is "land treatment." The three basic varieties of this approach are rapid infiltration through porous surface layers into deeper aquifers, crop irrigation by overland flow, and crop irrigation by slow infiltration. In all three, one starts with the effluent from secondary treatment, and the idea is to let natural processes (rather than expensive technological replacements) do the rest. Of course, there are many circumstances where the population is so dense or the particular chemical pollutants so refractory that natural processes could not handle the

[43]For details, see, for example, ACS, *Cleaning;* and Masters, *Introduction to environmental science,* pp. 160–163.

[43a]M. D. Sobsey, Enteric viruses and drinking-water supplies.

load. It has been argued that the high cost of tertiary treatment points up the disadvantages of so overburdening natural processes that they must be replaced completely by technology.[44] We agree.

An alternative approach to sewage treatment that is already in use in the United States and several other countries is ponding with algae. The waste water is introduced into large, shallow ponds, where bacteria populations maintained for the purpose ingest the dissolved organic material and convert it to carbon dioxide and water. Algae in the ponds use the carbon dioxide together with nutrients present in the waste water to produce biomass, which may be harvested and dried for use as animal feed or fuel. The oxygen produced by the algae as a product of photosynthesis is utilized by the bacteria in metabolizing the waste materials, completing the symbiosis.[45] A disadvantage shared by this approach and land treatment is their relatively large requirement for land area.

Yet another approach to the sewage problem is to mount an attack closer to the source. The average American family flushes about 35,000 gallons per year down its toilet, which is both a drain on municipal water supplies and a strain on municipal sewage treatment.[46] A variety of improvements has been suggested, from reducing the water use by placing bricks in the tank (only a partial solution to part of the problem) to several novel toilets that incinerate or compost what they collect. The one receiving the most attention is the Swedish *clivus multrum,* which composts wastes without water, electricity, or chemicals, wafts odors out a chimney on the roof, and needs little maintenance.

Perhaps it is time, in view of recent developments in composting toilets, land treatment and ponding for sewage-plant effluent, and biogasification (see Chapter 8) to rethink the entire sewage system.

Beyond Sewage

Even complete and effective treatment of sewage, if that could be achieved, would leave many water-pollution problems untouched. Many industries discharge wastes directly into waterways; such discharges must be controlled on a plant-by-plant basis. Runoff from agricultural lands carries the residues of pesticides and fertilizers. Storm sewers not connected to sewage-treatment systems carry a heavy burden of hydrocarbons and heavy metals washed from city streets into waterways. Such so-called area sources (as distinct from point sources) are especially difficult to control. As far as at least the heavy metals are concerned, the best control would seem to be to prevent their emission in the first place; a major step toward this is the elimination of tetraethyl lead in gasoline. Many water pollutants other than heavy metals also originate as air pollutants. Nitrates and sulfates, for example, fall in the rain, having been emitted as oxides of nitrogen and sulfur. In this instance, water pollution control means air pollution control. Some other very serious forms of water pollution have their origins in solid wastes accumulating on the land: for example, tailings from mines of various kinds, and sludges from industrial processes (including some air-pollution control measures that produce sludges). Finding ways to stabilize these solids so they do not contaminate water supplies is difficult. The problem of acid drainage from coal mines is particularly serious and widespread, and apparently destined to increase substantially as reliance on coal as an energy source grows (see also Chapter 8).

Regulation of Water Pollution

The history of water-pollution abatement in the United States has resembled that of air pollution—generally too little effort applied too late. Prior to 1972, the federal approach to control of water pollution was defined by the Federal Water Pollution Control Act (FWPCA) of 1948 and the Refuse Act of 1899. Under the FWPCA, enforcement of regulations was so slow and cumbersome as to be almost nonexistent. A Supreme Court interpretation of the Refuse Act in 1960 improved matters somewhat, holding that the government could sue industries to stop their discharges into navigable waterways. A national system of discharge permits was later set up under the jurisdiction of the Army Corps of

[44]For a good discussion of "land treatment" in this context, see Jeff Stansbury, Of human waste and human folly.

[45]W. J. Oswald, Engineering applications; Metcalf and Eddy, Inc., *Wastewater engineering.*

[46]Sam Love, An idea in need of rethinking: the flush toilet.

Engineers and the Environmental Protection Agency, but it was never fully implemented.[47]

In 1972, Congress passed amendments to the FWPCA, requiring that all polluters obtain "permits" from the EPA that limit amounts and constituents of material to be discharged. Progressively tightened emission standards for industrial and municipal discharges were called for, with important deadlines in 1977 and 1983. The 1972 amendments also provided for an increase in federal aid to local governments for the construction of municipal waste-treatment plants ($18 billion was authorized over a 3-year period). Effluent guidelines set up under the amendments since 1972 have been challenged in many lawsuits by the industries affected, while some environmentalists have complained that the discharge permits in practice are simply "licenses to pollute" that do not serve the spirit of the law.[48] There had nevertheless been some improvement in water quality in many areas by 1977. The establishment of standards with deadlines has simplified the problems both of polluters in controlling their effluents and of government agencies in carrying out regulatory functions.[48a]

Prior to 1974, the monitoring of municipal water supplies for drinking safety was in the hands of the Public Health Service, which was empowered only to set standards to prevent the introduction and spread of disease organisms. The myriad of dangerous and possibly dangerous chemicals appearing in increasing quantities in U.S. drinking-water supplies went largely unregulated. The Safe Drinking Water Act, which became effective in December of 1974, requires that EPA promulgate primary drinking-water standards (regulating substances with adverse impact on human health) and secondary standards (regulating nonhealth effects, such as taste and odor). Primary standards were to be in effect in interim form by December 1976 and in final form by September 1977. Enforcement authority will be mainly in the hands of individual states. Another provision of the 1974 act gives the administration of EPA authority to block underground waste-disposal practices that threaten aquifers used for drinking water and to stop federal funding of any other projects that may threaten such aquifers.[49]

The Ocean Dumping Act of 1972 regulates dumping by American ships and other ships leaving U.S. ports. Jurisdiction is divided among EPA, the Secretary of the Army, and the Coast Guard. Sewage sludge was a major component of the material being dumped in the mid-1970s, most of it accounted for by the activities of Philadelphia and New York City off the Atlantic coast. If the EPA succeeds in halting this dumping, it will aggravate an already difficult problem of on-land disposal for rising amounts of sludge.

PESTICIDES AND RELATED COMPOUNDS

Prevalence

The public is exposed to some substances, such as chlorinated hydrocarbons, lead, mercury, and fluorides, in so many ways that these must be considered general pollutants. Chlorinated hydrocarbons are among the most ubiquitous manufactured chemicals in the environment. Of these, dichlorodiphenyltrichloroethane[50] or DDT (Figure 10-4) has been employed the longest, having been put into mass use late in World War II. It is the most commonly used and most thoroughly studied of all synthetic insecticides. DDT, together with its breakdown products DDE and DDD (TDE), often occurs in concentrations of more than 12 parts per million (ppm) in human fat, and as high as 5 ppm in human milk (though the usual range is some 0.05 to 0.26 parts per million).[51]

[47]For details in this and subsequent paragraphs, see CEQ, *Environmental quality, 1975,* pp. 59–82.

[48]C. G. Trump, Public eye on pollution.

[48a]John R. Quarles, National water quality: Assessing the mid-course correction.

[49]CEQ, *Environmental quality, 1975,* pp. 76–77.

[50]DDT is *d*ichloro*d*iphenyl*t*richloro-ethane. DDT is often metabolized to DDE, *d*ichloro-*d*iphenyl-dichloro-*e*thylene, and DDD (TDE), *d*ichloro-*d*iphenyl-*d*ichloro-ethane. DDT, DDE, and DDD are often lumped together in residue studies as DDT-R or "total DDT." These compounds are very similar in structure to other pesticides such as methoxychlor and kelthane (see Appendix 3; R. D. O'Brien, *Insecticides: Action and metabolism;* and J. Capizzi and J. M. Wite, eds., *Pesticides, pest control, and safety on forest and range lands.)*

[51]See, for example, for fat, James E. Burns, Organochlorine pesticide and polychlorinated biphenyl residues in biopsied human adipose tissue, Texas, 1969–1972; and National Academy of Sciences (NAS), *Contemporary pest control practices and prospects: The report of the executive committee.* For milk, see E. P. Savage et al., Organochlorine pesticide residues and polychlorinated biphenyls in human milk, Colorado, 1971–1972, and references therein.

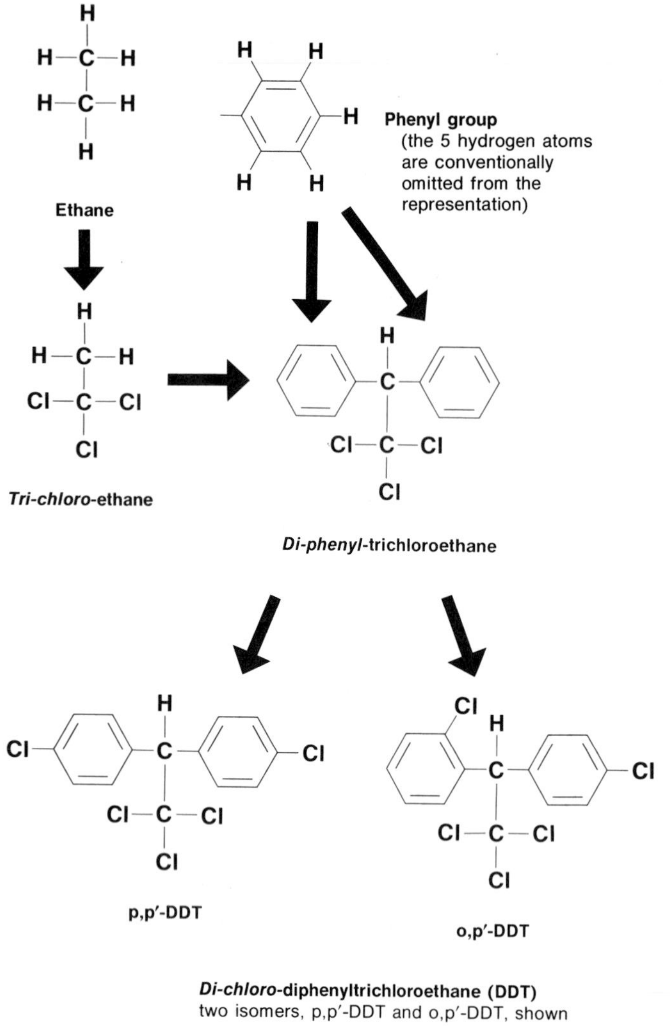

Ethane

Phenyl group
(the 5 hydrogen atoms are conventionally omitted from the representation)

Tri-chloro-ethane

Di-phenyl-trichloroethane

p,p′-DDT

o,p′-DDT

***Di-chloro*-diphenyltrichloroethane (DDT)**
two isomers, p,p′-DDT and o,p′-DDT, shown

FIGURE 10-4

The structure and name of DDT. The long, complex name indicates the structure of the molecule based on the simple two-carbon organic compound ethane (C_2H_6) found in natural gas. Three chlorine atoms are substituted for the three hydrogens bonded to one carbon atom, and two phenyl groups (C_6H_5 radicals, benzene minus one hydrogen) are bonded to the other carbon of ethane. Chlorine atoms substitute for one hydrogen of each phenyl group. Two isomers (molecules composed of the same number and kinds of atoms but arranged differently) of DDT are shown. The p, p′ isomer has both chlorines in the "para" position, opposite the ethane carbon. The o, p′ isomer has one chlorine in the "ortho" position, adjacent to the carbon. Not shown is a ring with the chlorine in the *m* (meta) position, with one hydrogen between the carbon and the chlorine. (For a brief view of biological chemistry, see White, 1970.)

In the early 1970s most mother's milk in the United States contained so much DDT that it would have been declared illegal in interstate commerce; the permissible level in cow's milk is set by the FDA at 0.05 parts per million. Other chlorinated hydrocarbon insecticides, including aldrin, dieldrin, and benzene hexachloride (hexachlorobenzene—HCB), have also been found in human milk.

Recently there has been some tendency for total DDT levels (as well as those of other chlorinated hydrocarbons) to decline in human adipose (fat) tissues in the United States (Table 10-6), although there is great variation from study to study.[52] With the banning of almost all uses of DDT in 1972 and regulatory action against other chlorinated hydrocarbons following soon thereafter, it seems likely that residues of these chemicals in human tissues and milk will decline substantially in the late 1970s in the U.S. and in other nations that have reduced their use.

Another class of chlorinated hydrocarbon compounds, polychlorinated biphenyls (PCBs), has also been found to be a serious pollutant, showing up in human fat and milk.[53] These compounds are used in a variety of industrial processes and are released into the environment in a variety of ways. They vaporize from storage containers, are emitted from factory smokestacks, are dumped into rivers and lakes with industrial wastes, and, along with a variety of other hydrocarbons, are added to the load of particulate atmospheric pollutants as automobile tires are worn down. They get into food products through contact with paint and plastics, and through accidental contamination. For example, a shipment of 60,000 chicken eggs contaminated with PCBs reached consumers in 1971, after the hens had consumed contaminated fish meal.[54] The most serious food-contamination episode involving PCBs was the Kanemi rice-oil (Yusho) disaster in Japan. More than 1000 people were stricken with horrible acne-like skin lesions (chloracne) and an array of other symptoms including vomiting, diarrhea, headaches, and visual disturbances,

[52]For example, Burns, Organochlorine; S. L. Warnick, Organochlorine pesticide levels in human serum and adipose tissue, Utah, fiscal years 1967–1971.

[53]For example, Burns, Organochlorine; Savage et al., Organochlorine.

[54]Joe Pichirallo, PCB's: leaks of toxic substances raise issue of effects, regulation.

TABLE 10-6
*Chlorinated Hydrocarbon Pesticides in Human Adipose Tissue, U.S., FY 1970–1974**

Pesticide	*Concentration in lipid (arithmetic mean, ppm)*				
	FY 1970	*FY 1971*	*FY 1972*	*FY 1973*	*FY 1974*
Total DDT equivalent	11.65	11.55	9.91	8.91	7.83
HCB (benzene hexachloride)	0.60	0.48	0.40	0.37	0.32
Dieldrin	0.27	0.29	0.24	0.24	0.20
Heptachlor epoxide	0.17	0.12	0.12	0.12	0.10
Oxychlordane*	–	–	0.15	0.15	0.15
Sample size	1412	1612	1916	1092	898

*First full year in which oxychlordane was analyzed was FY 1972 (FY = fiscal year).
Source: U.S. Environmental Protection Agency, 1974.

after a heat-exchanger leaked PCBs into oil used in frying foods.[55]

Chlorinated hydrocarbons and other pesticides are present in very low concentrations in drinking water, in fruits and vegetables, and even in the air. Greater amounts are present in meat, fish, and poultry.[56] A summary of the average pesticide contents of foods tested between 1965 and 1970 is shown in Table 10-7. Averages, however, are not the whole story. At times the dosage is direct and high. Farmers sometimes far exceed legal residue levels of insecticides on their crops and get away with it, because inspection is inadequate. Some ill-informed grocers spray their produce to kill fruit flies. In the summer of 1968, our research group found leaking cans of chlordane dust (a chlorinated hydrocarbon insecticide) on a narrow shelf above the onion bin in a supermarket. The dust was present on the produce. The manager, on being informed, took prompt corrective action, but not before some of his customers had added to their loads of chlorinated hydrocarbons. By the summer of 1969, the pesticides had reappeared on the shelf over the produce, and complaints had to be renewed. Obviously, the sale of all pesticides should be prohibited in food stores.

A colleague of ours has observed massive antiroach spraying (presumably of chlordane) in a restaurant kitchen, where the spray drifted over exposed food. Some restaurants formerly used lindane vaporizers; fortunately these have now been banned. Regardless of whether such practices and the resultant heavy doses are common or not, continuous "light" exposure is virtually unavoidable.

[55]M. Kuratsune et al., Epidemiological study of Yusho, a poisoning caused by ingestion of rice oil contaminated with a commercial brand of polychlorinated biphenyls; Jun Ui, *Polluted Japan.*

[56]R. E. Duggan and J. R. Weatherwax, Dietary intake of pesticide chemicals.

Effects

Can low-level exposure be dangerous? Because of the variety of problems enumerated in Box 10-2, and others that we deal with below in the section on carcinogenesis, it has been very difficult to evaluate the long-term and chronic effects of pesticides. Biologists have long been warning that there is no evidence that DDT, even though its effects may not be immediately obvious, might not have subtle or long-term effects. In fact, there is every reason to believe that the biologically active molecules of DDT are dangerous. In 1962 Rachel Carson wrote, "For the population as a whole, we must be more concerned with the delayed effects of absorbing small amounts of the pesticides that invisibly contaminate our world."[56a] But often the possibility of subtle, chronic effects has been discounted by industry, ignored by the government, and forgotten by the public. That DDT has very low immediate toxicity to mammals, including human beings, has been known since it was first put in use, and this has never been questioned. Promoters of pesticides have even resorted to the dangerous extreme of eating spoonfuls of pure DDT in an effort to prove how harmless it is, but such actions in no way demonstrate

[56a]*Silent spring.*

TABLE 10-7
*Pesticide Chemicals in Food**

Compound	Daily intake (mg)						6-year average
	*FY*** 1965*	*FY 1966*	*FY 1967*	*FY 1968*	*FY 1969*	*FY 1970*	
Organochlorine insecticides							
DDT	0.031	0.041	0.026	0.019	0.016	0.015	0.025
DDE	0.018	0.028	0.017	0.015	0.011	0.010	0.017
DDD (TDE)	0.013	0.018	0.013	0.011	0.005	0.004	0.011
subtotal	0.062	0.087	0.056	0.045	0.032	0.029	0.053
Dieldrin	0.005	0.007	0.004	0.004	0.005	0.005	0.005
Lindane	0.004	0.004	0.005	0.003	0.001	0.001	0.003
Heptachlor epoxide	0.002	0.003	0.001	0.002	0.002	0.001	0.002
HCB (Benzene hexachloride)	0.002	0.004	0.002	0.003	0.001	0.001	0.002
Aldrin	0.001	0.002	0.001	T	T	T	0.001
Dicofol (kelthane)	0.003	0.002	0.012	0.010	0.007	0.004	0.006
Endrin	T	T	T	0.001	T	T	0.000
Methoxychlor	–	T	0.001	0.001	T	0.001	0.001
Heptachlor	T	–	T	T	T	T	T
Toxaphene	–	0.002	–	0.002	0.004	0.001	0.002
Perthane	T	0.001	–	0.001	0.004	–	0.001
Endosulfan	–	T	T	T	0.001	0.001	0.000
Organophosphate insecticides							
Malathion	–	0.009	0.010	0.003	0.012	0.013	0.008
Diazinon	–	0.001	T	T	T	0.001	0.000
Parathion	–	T	0.001	T	T	T	0.000
Ethion	–	T	0.002	0.001	0.003	0.004	0.002
Carbamate insecticide							
Carbaryl	0.150	0.026	0.007	–	0.003	–	0.031
Herbicide							
2,4-D	0.005	0.002	0.001	0.001	T	T	0.002
Fungicide							
PCP	T	0.006	0.001	0.001	0.002	–	0.002

*Values are determined from analyses of foods prepared from "market basket" samples collected in five major U.S. cities and designed to simulate the diet of a 16 to 19-year-old male. T (trace) indicates an amount less than 0.001 mg.

**Fiscal year.

Source: R. E. Duggan and P. E. Corneliussen, *Pesticide Monitoring Journal,* vol. 5, pp. 331–341.

that DDT is safe for human consumption over the long run.

People can understand acute poisoning, but they find subtle and cumulative physiological changes difficult to grasp. Why should it matter if high concentrations of chlorinated hydrocarbons are being stored in their bodies? Years ago, a study of workers in a DDT plant and another done with convicts purported to show that no ill effects resulted from heavy exposure.[57] But those two studies were poorly designed and utterly inadequate to assure the long-term safety of DDT when introduced into the *entire human population.* Both were done with people whose first exposure occurred as *adults,* and the convict study followed individuals for *less than two years.* The study of exposed workers did not investigate what had happened to workers who were no longer employed. The effects on the delicate developmental systems of fetuses and infants were not investigated; nor were there any women or children in the study. No attempt was made to investigate the possible effects of DDT exposure on large populations over several decades, and the causes of death in large numbers of people with high and low exposures were not statistically compared.

Biologists have just started to get an inkling of what that "harmless" chlorinated hydrocarbon load may be doing to people over the long run. Animal studies give some clues. In high doses, DDT and some other chlorinated hydrocarbons—aldrin, dieldrin and endrin—have

[57]W. J. Hayes et al., The effects of known repeated oral doses of chlorophenothane (DDT) in man; E. R. Laws et al., Men with intensive occupational exposure to DDT. A more recent study by E. R. Laws, et al., Long-term occupational exposure to DDT, deals with a very small group of men (35), but does indicate at least that DDT is not as potent a carcinogen as some other known causes of occupational cancers.

been shown to increase the incidence of cancers, especially liver cancers, in mice. This indicated that they might also be carcinogenic in human beings. However, these chemicals at some doses stimulate enzyme systems (mixed-function oxidizing enzymes) which metabolize not only the chlorinated hydrocarbons but also other carcinogens. Thus, their relationship to cancer may be very complex, and studies to date cannot be considered conclusive.[58] But, overall it seems clear that human contact with the pesticides should be minimized.

It must be made clear that only a small minority of the pesticides tested are in any way implicated in carcinogenesis. In studies of 120 different compounds, 11 pesticides were judged carcinogenic, but 89 (73 pesticides) showed no significant indications of carcinogenicity (20 compounds were questionable).[59] Since the compounds tested were chosen as likely carcinogens *a priori* on the basis of their chemical structure or other prior indications of possible carcinogenicity, the findings are conservative. The National Academy of Sciences 1976 study of pest-control practices estimates that an upper limit on the proportion of currently used pesticides that may cause cancers in human beings is about 25 percent.[60] This is not necessarily much cause for cheer, since DDT and other widespread compounds have been implicated—and a generation of people that have been exposed to DDT and its relatives since before they were born is now maturing.[61]

Other investigations have produced ominous results. One study, in which data were obtained by autopsies, showed a correlation between DDT levels in fat tissue and cause of death. Concentrations of DDT and its breakdown products, DDE and DDD, as well as dieldrin (another chlorinated-hydrocarbon pesticide), were significantly higher in the fat of patients who died of softening of the brain, cerebral hemorrhage, hypertension, portal cirrhosis of the liver, and various cancers than in groups of patients who died of infectious diseases. The histories of the patients in the study showed that concentrations of DDT and its breakdown products in their fat were strongly correlated with home use of pesticides, heavy users having much higher concentrations than light or moderate users.[62]

More conclusive investigations of these effects are urgently needed, but in the light of what is known about the deleterious effects of chlorinated hydrocarbons on laboratory animals, the results of this study alone leave little room for complacency. Neurophysiologists have established that DDT has irreversible effects on impulse conduction in nerve cells. It is not surprising, therefore, that several studies implicate DDT in the disturbance of nervous-system function. Effects on EEG (brain wave) patterns have been shown; trout exposed to 20 parts per *billion* DDT showed a loss of learning ability.[63] Finally, the behavior of larval marine crustaceans (locomotion, etc.,) is significantly affected at concentrations below 200 parts per trillion (ppt).[64]

As indicated above, there is evidence that the amount of DDT stored in human tissues has not increased for the past decade or so in the United States, and may be declining. At a given exposure level, it apparently takes about one year for an equilibrium to be established between intake and loss through excretion and breakdown, after which continued exposure produces no increase in DDT storage.[65] The mean concentration of DDT in human populations varies widely from one geographic location to another, both within and between countries. It also varies with diet, race, age, and undetermined individual differences. For reasons that are not entirely clear, the black population has a much higher average level of DDT concentration in the blood than does the white population. It is possible that this is a "poverty effect" due to greater home use in attempts to control roaches; it might also be a dietary effect. Above-average DDT levels in blacks includes those who live in cities, as well as farm workers who might be expected to have more than average exposure to insecticides. Table 10-8 shows the DDT concentrations that have been

[58]Carcinogenicity of pesticides is thoroughly reviewed by Kingsley Kay in Occupational cancer risks for pesticide workers.

[59]J. R. M. Innes et al., Bioassay of pesticides and industrial chemicals for tumorigenicity in mice; a preliminary note.

[60]NAS, *Contemporary pest control practices and prospects,* p. 66.

[61]V. Fiserova-Bergerova et al., Levels of chlorinated hydrocarbon pesticides in human tissues.

[62]J. L. Radomski et al., Pesticide concentrations in the liver, brain, and adipose tissues of terminal patients.

[63]J. M. Anderson and M. R. Peterson, DDT: sublethal effects on brook trout nervous system. *Science,* vol. 164, 1969, pp. 440–441.

[64]R. Burnet, unpublished.

[65]Hayes et al., The effects. W. S. Hoffman et al., The pesticide content of human fat tissue.

TABLE 10-8
Mean Concentration of DDT in Human Body Fat*

Population	*Year*	*Number in sample*	*DDT (ppm)*
United States	1942	10	0
United States	1950	75	5.3
United States	1955	49	19.9
United States	1954–1956	61	11.7
United States	1961–1962	130	12.6
United States	1961–1962	30	10.71
United States	1962–1963	282	10.3
U.S. (all areas)	1964	64	7.0
U.S. (New Orleans)	1964	25	10.3
U.S. (white, over 6 yrs.)	1968	90	8.4
U.S. (nonwhite, over 6 yrs.)	1968	35	16.7
U.S. (all areas)	1970	1,412	11.65
Alaskan Eskimo	1960	20	3.0
Canada	1959–1960	62	4.9
Canada	1966	27	3.8
United Kingdom	1961–1962	131	2.2**
United Kingdom	1963–1964	65	3.3
United Kingdom	1964	100	3.3**
Germany	1958–1959	60	2.2
Hungary	1960	50	12.4
France	1961	10	5.2
Israel	1963–1964	254	19.2
India (Delhi)	1964	67	26.0

*DDT is expressed as DDT plus its breakdown product DDE converted into equivalent DDT units. Some figures include minor amounts of other breakdown products.

**Geometric mean.

Source: See Wassermann et al., 1965.

found in a series of studies done at different times and places.

Generally, people in the most northern countries, where growing seasons are short and insects are not a year-round problem, have substantially smaller DDT burdens than people in the United States. Intensive agriculture in Israel, as well as increased household use of pesticides, is probably responsible for the high levels found there. Unfortunately, reports of DDT loads from other countries with intensive agriculture, such as Japan and the Netherlands, are not available. High levels in Delhi, India, may be related to the use of DDT to preserve stored food.

In a study of individuals from Dade County, Florida, a significantly lower DDT-DDE concentration was found in children under 5 years of age, suggesting that they had not yet reached their equilibrium levels. Six stillbirths and fetuses were examined and found to have loads more closely reflecting concentrations in their mothers' tissues. Passage of DDT across the placental membrane into the fetus has now been demonstrated to take place as early as the 22nd week of pregnancy, and may occur well in advance of that.[66]

Studies in dogs show that DDT storage concentrations rise dramatically if aldrin, another chlorinated-hydrocarbon insecticide, is also ingested.[67] This is another example of synergism between pollutants, about which too little is known. Whether aldrin also affects DDT storage concentrations in human beings is not known, but it is certainly possible.

Other studies have shown that certain anticonvulsant drugs can act to reduce DDT concentrations in blood and fat tissues of people.[68] Nothing is known about how this occurs or what long-term side effects may follow the use of these drugs for DDT reduction. As long as DDT is ubiquitous, the treatment would be only temporary, unless the drugs were taken frequently or continuously.

It is difficult at this juncture to evaluate the magnitude of the direct threat to human health represented by present levels of chlorinated-hydrocarbon contamination. Most analyses have dealt with DDT, although human beings are also being exposed to a wide range of related compounds, some of which have considerably higher immediate toxicity. There are indications that dieldrin, perhaps four times as toxic as DDT, may be involved in portal cirrhosis of the liver, and that benzene hexachloride may contribute to liver cancer. Furthermore, almost nothing is known about synergistic interactions between chlorinated hydrocarbons, or between these chemicals and other drugs and environmental contaminants.[69] The critical question, we reiterate, is not immediate toxicity, but *long-term effects.* The oldest people who have been exposed to high concentrations of DDT since conception reached the age of thirty in 1976. It is possible that their life expectancies already have been greatly reduced; it is also possible that there will be no significant reduction. No one will know until more time has passed.

At any rate, humanity will eventually find out what the overall effects of the chlorinated-hydrocarbon load are,

[66]Fiserova-Bergerova et al., Levels of chlorinated hydrocarbons.

[67]W. B. Deichmann et al., DDT tissue retention: sudden rise induced by the addition of aldrin to a fixed DDT intake.

[68]J. E. Davies et al., Effects of anticonvulsant drugs on dicophene (DDT) residues in man, *Lancet,* July 5, 1969; pp. 7–9.

[69]See, for example, A. H. Connery and J. J. Burns, Metabolic interactions among environmental chemicals and drugs.

since the persistence of these compounds guarantees decades of further exposure even after their use has been discontinued. The continued release of chlorinated hydrocarbons into the environment is tantamount to a reckless global experiment, and all human beings—as well as all other animals that live on Earth—are playing the role of guinea pigs.

In 1972, a ban on DDT for almost all uses in the United States was imposed by the U.S. Environmental Protection Agency. (The regulation of pesticides is discussed in detail in Chapter 14 as a case study of the interaction of economics and environment in the political arena.) Concern has been expressed that banning of chlorinated hydrocarbons would lead to increased immediate mortality from pesticides, because the organophosphate compounds that would be used to replace DDT, although they are much less persistent and presumably present a relatively small long-term risk, have a higher acute toxicity. But around 1969 occupational deaths from pesticides (mainly organophosphates) ran about 12 per year nationally, and there has been no sign of an increase.[70]

In the most spectacular recent episode of acute toxicity involving a pesticide in the United States, the guilty agent was a complex chlorinated hydrocarbon, kepone. Thirty persons working in the plant producing this insecticide-fungicide were hospitalized with tremors, blurred vision, loss of memory, and a threat of such long-term effects as sterility and cancer.[71]

One organophosphate, leptophos, which has not been approved by the EPA for use in the U.S. but is marketed abroad, apparently causes delayed neurological damage rather than immediate illness. Victims of organophosphate poisoning, if they survive, usually recover completely. The delayed neuropathy caused by leptophos, however, induces possibly permanent paralysis, and seems to have affected at least a dozen employees of the Velsicol plant in Texas that manufactures it.[71a]

Another potential direct threat to human health posed by pesticides involves the possible teratogenicity, mutagenicity, or carcinogenicity of herbicides such as 2,4-D, 2,4,5-T, picloram, and cacodylic acid. Some of the toxicity reported in early studies of 2,4,5-T was due to contamination of the herbicide with the exceedingly toxic chlorinated hydrocarbon, dioxin.[72] The degree of risk to people posed by uncontaminated herbicides is in dispute,[73] but in view of the enormous increase in the use of these chemicals, caution is indicated.

For both chlorinated hydrocarbons and herbicides, the direct threat to humanity, as noted above, is difficult to assess. At present, however, it would appear that, as alarming as the direct threat may be, the *indirect threat* is much more serious. These compounds have the potential for irreversibly damaging the capacity of ecological systems to supply those essential services without which civilization cannot persist (Chapter 11).

TRACE METALS

A variety of trace metals are naturally present in the biosphere at low concentrations, cycling through atmosphere, surface water, soil, living creatures, oceans, and sediments in much the same ways as the nutrients discussed in Chapter 3. The same metals exist in ore deposits and in technological society in much greater concentrations, but in the context of the behavior of their dispersed forms in the biosphere they are called trace metals. Some are themselves micronutrients; some are toxic to people even at environmental concentrations that occur naturally; others have had their natural concentrations augmented by human activities to levels at which they become harmful. Among the trace metals of greatest health interest are lead, mercury, cadmium, arsenic, beryllium, nickel, chromium, selenium, vanadium, molybdenum, copper, and zinc.[74]

All of these metals are mined for industrial applications. Part of what is mined reaches the biosphere in the form of losses at various stages of processing; some

---

[70]NAS, *Contemporary pest control practices,* pp. 89–90. See also Chapter 11 and Appendix 3 here.

[71]B. A. Franklin, A crippler called kepone.

[71a]Kevin Shea, Profile of a deadly pesticide.

[72]ReVelle and ReVelle, *Sourcebook,* pp. 129–132; Lawrence McGinty, The graveyard on Milan's doorstep. It was the massive release of dioxin in an explosion in a chemical plant that required the evacuation of the town of Seveso, near Milan, Italy, in 1976.

[73]For example, see A. W. Galston, Some implications of the widespread use of herbicides.

[74]A good introduction to trace metals in the environment is R. M. Garrels, F. T. Mackenzie, and C. Hunt, *Chemical cycles and the global environment.*

TABLE 10-9
Comparison of Flows of Trace Metals for Human Activities and Natural Processes (10^6 kg per year)

Element	Mining	Emission to air	Natural rainout	Natural stream load
Zinc	5000	730	1000	370
Lead	3000	400	310	180
Chromium	2000	50	120	7
Arsenic	60	50	190	15
Cadmium	14	4	NA	<40
Mercury	9	10	1	3

Note: NA = not available.
Source: Garrels et al., *Chemical cycles,* p. 111; H. J. M. Bowen, *Trace elements in biochemistry.*

reaches the biosphere as the result of wear during the use of manufactured products; some gets there through disposal of worn-out products. Some of the metals are used in forms in which dispersal in the biosphere is intentional—for example, drugs, gasoline additives, and agricultural chemicals. Virtually all of the metals tested above are present as contaminants in fossil fuels, particularly coal and petroleum; combustion of these fuels releases substantial quantities of the trace metals to the biosphere, either as particulates in the exhaust gases or in ash that is later incorporated into soil and surface water.[75] Even such human activities as cultivation and deforestation, which disrupt large areas of Earth's surface, may increase the rates at which trace metals are mobilized by outgassing and leaching.

Although it is sometimes mistakenly asserted that the contribution of human activities to producing the concentrations of trace metals found in the biosphere has been minor compared to that of natural processes, accumulating evidence on the global geochemistry of these elements leads to the opposite conclusion.[76] Table 10-9 shows the rates of mobilization by mining, emission to the atmosphere by human activities, estimated rainout from an unpolluted (prehuman) atmosphere, and natural flux to the oceans in rivers. The artificial flows approach or exceed the natural ones in almost every case.

The physical pathways and chemical transformations that govern the details of trace-metal hazards to people are complex and often ill-understood.[77] Some chemical and physical forms of a given element are much more toxic than others (e.g., the methyl-mercury complex, CH_3Hg—, compared to metallic mercury); chemical transformations occur in both directions both with and without mediation of organisms; and low environmental concentrations can be turned into high ones by food chains. Some concentration factors in marine organisms are shown in Table 10-10.

The toxicity of trace metals to humans is generally clear at high concentrations and less obvious at low ones. The levels known to be dangerous vary widely; lead and cadmium are toxic at the same concentrations at which iron and zinc are beneficial, for example. Kinds of effects also vary: lead and methyl mercury damage the central nervous system; cadmium, arsenic, and selenium are known to be carcinogenic in animals, and the first two are directly toxic in other ways; beryllium is both carcinogenic and poisonous.[78]

In the following subsections we look more closely at lead, mercury, and cadmium as illustrative and relatively well-studied examples of the hazards of trace metals.

Lead

The effects of ingestion of lead in large quantities are well known. Symptoms of lead poisoning include loss of appetite, weakness, awkwardness, apathy, and miscarriage; it causes lesions of the neuromuscular system, circulatory system, brain, and gastrointestinal tract.[79] The most serious causes of acute lead poisoning in the United States today are the ingestion of chips of lead-based paint by small children and the contaminated moonshine whiskey made in lead-soldered automobile radiators. Painters, foundry and smelter workers, and typographers risk acute lead poisoning occupationally.

[75]K. K. Bertine and E. D. Goldberg, Fossil fuel combustion and the major sedimentary cycle; D. H. Klein, Heavy metals: Fallout around a power plant.

[76]See, for example, J. J. Morgan, Trace metals in the environment; and Garrels, Mackenzie, and Hunt, *Chemical cycles.*

[77]See, for example, J. M. Wood, Biological cycles for toxic cycles in the environment.

[78]A good overview is T. H. Maugh, Trace elements: A growing appreciation of their effects on man. See also H. A. Schroeder, Trace elements in the human environment; National Academy of Sciences, *Geochemistry and the environment.*

[79]U.S. Environmental Protection Agency, *Environmental lead and public health.*

TABLE 10-10
Concentration Factors of Trace Elements in Marine Organisms

	Copper	*Nickel*	*Lead*	*Cobalt*	*Zinc*
Seaweed	–	550–2,000	–	–	900
Plankton	400–90,000	<20–8,000	30–12,000	<100–16,000	–
Anchoveta	80	–	10,000	–	400
Yellowfin tuna	200	–	–	–	700

Source: E. D. Goldberg, *Chemical oceanography,* p. 185.

Overexposure to lead may have been a factor in the decline of both the Greek and Roman civilizations.[80] The Romans lined their bronze cooking, eating, and wine-storage vessels with lead. They thus avoided the characteristic unpleasant taste of copper and the obvious symptoms of copper poisoning, trading them for the pleasant flavor of lead and the more subtle symptoms of lead poisoning. Even in more recent times, lead poisoning due to drinking acidic beverages from pewter mugs was not uncommon ("modern" pewter no longer contains lead).

Contemporary industrial societies have largely eliminated the lead-lined pipes and vessels that probably made acute lead poisoning rather common in earlier times. On the other hand, contemporary industrial activities are mobilizing and dispersing far larger quantities of lead on a global scale than previously was the case, and the fate of this lead in the environment and the possibility of chronic insults to human health as a result have become topics of legitimate concern.

The quantity of lead mined worldwide in the early 1970s was around 3 million metric tons annually, about 10 times more than is mobilized annually by the natural weathering of crustal rocks.[81] The largest single use of the lead that is mined is in storage batteries, followed by fabricated items such as shotgun pellets, bullets, radiation shields, and lead weights. Somewhat more than 10 percent of the lead mined was being used in the early 1970s as a gasoline additive in the form of tetraethyl lead, a compound considerably more mobile in the biosphere and perhaps three times more toxic than elemental lead.[82]

[80]S. C. Gilfillan, Lead poisoning and the fall of Rome.
[81]Garrels, Mackenzie and Hunt, *Chemical cycles,* p. 127.
[82]See, for example, National Academy of Sciences, *Airborne lead in perspective,* H. E. Christensen, ed., *The toxic substances list.*

Emissions of tetraethyl lead to the atmosphere around 1970 were estimated at 400,000 metric tons annually; the amount added by combustion of coal and oil containing lead as a trace contaminant was about 100 times smaller.[83]

The pattern of increase in the lead contamination of the atmosphere has been revealed by studies of the lead content of the Greenland ice cap. The ice cap "lead load" increased about fivefold between 1750 and 1940, and twentyfold between 1750 and 1967. By comparison, studies show that the content of sea salts in the Greenland ice cap have not changed since 1750, indicating that changes in the overall pattern of deposition of materials in the ice is not the cause of the lead increase.[84] That similar patterns of lead contamination are not found in the Antarctic ice cap lends strong support to the thesis that atmospheric lead pollution originated first with lead smelting and then more recently with the combustion of gasoline, two sources of contamination that are concentrated in the Northern Hemisphere. The spread of pollution to the Southern Hemisphere is largely blocked by the hemispheric restriction of atmospheric circulation patterns (see Chapter 2).

Another indication of the scale of civilization's impact on environmental lead concentrations is that the lead content of the open ocean has increased threefold to fivefold since the introduction of lead-based gasoline additives.[85] Lead is the only heavy metal whose open-ocean concentrations had been measurably influenced by civilization as of the early 1970s.

[83]Garrels et al. *Chemical cycles,* p. 127; see also T. J. Chow and J. L Earl, Lead aerosols in the atmosphere: increasing concentrations.
[84]M. Murozumi, et al., Chemical concentrations of pollutant lead aerosols, terrestrial dusts, and sea salts in Greenland and Antarctic snow strata; Z. Jaworowski, Stable lead in fossil ice and bones.
[85]E. D. Goldberg and K. K. Bertine, Marine pollution.

TABLE 10-11
Lead Concentrations in the Environment

Location	*Concentration (ppb, by weight)*
"Clean air"	0.0003–0.011[a]
Global atmospheric average	0.003[a]
Deep ocean water	0.01–0.03[a,b]
Surface ocean water	0.07[b]
Average U.S. rural air	0.5[c]
Average U.S. urban air	1–4[a,c]
Average U.S. drinking water	4[a]
"Permissible" in urban air	7[a]
Air at 45th St., New York City	8[a]
"Permissible" in drinking water	50[a]
Maximum in U.S. drinking water	70[a]
Typical plants	2,000[a]
Sedimentary rocks	16,000[a]
Typical soil	20,000[a]
Urban plants	60,000–300,000[d]
Soil beside highways	>100,000[a,d]

Sources: [a]Garrels et al., *Chemical cycles,* ch. 10. [b]Goldberg and Bertine, Marine pollution, [c]J. J. Chisolm, Lead poisoning. [d]G. Bini, Lead in the rural environment.

Table 10-11 shows lead concentrations that have been measured in various parts of the human environment, together with "permissible" standards for air and drinking water set by agencies in the United States. The numbers in the table suggest—and research has confirmed—that plants do not readily take up metallic lead from the soil, but they extract tetraethyl lead (probably directly from the air as well as soil) much more efficiently.[86] The latter concentration effect is one of the factors that now make ingestion of lead in the diet a more significant pathway for human exposure than breathing of it.

How much lead are residents of the United States getting and what are the consequences? The average intake of lead in the American diet is 0.3 to 0.4 milligrams per day, of which less than 10 percent is absorbed and the remainder promptly excreted.[87] This intake is about 20 times larger than that to be expected in a natural environment (i.e., one uncontaminated by industrial activities). Intake from breathing urban air typically is in the range of 0.02 milligrams per day, but the fraction absorbed is perhaps 40 percent. The typical body burden of lead in industrial countries is roughly 100 times the natural figure.

Typical human exposures to lead in industrial society, then, are far higher than exposure in an uncontaminated environment. On the other hand, they are lower by factors of 3 to 10 than exposures that have been associated with obvious symptoms of severe lead poisoning. A vigorous controversy rages about whether lead intake at the levels now being experienced by the large populations of urban regions are actually damaging to health.

It is known that lead interferes with the production or operation of a variety of enzymes that play important roles in the human body. Changes in enzyme levels are detectable when blood levels of lead reach 30 micrograms per 100 milliliters of whole blood (0.3 ppm—parts per million); typical blood levels in urban environments are 0.1 to 0.2 ppm and individuals occupationally exposed to heavy automobile traffic often exceed 0.3 ppm.[88] Clinical symptoms of lead poisoning first appear at blood levels of 0.5 ppm in children and 0.8 ppm in adults, and some observers consider the demonstrated interference with enzymes below these levels inconclusive as evidence of real harm.[89] Experiments have demonstrated impairment of learning in lambs produced by ewes with lead levels in blood of 0.34 ppm, however, and correlations of hyperactivity and mental retardation with blood levels in children suggest that 0.25 ppm may already represent the danger level.[90] It is possible, of course, that high lead levels in blood are coexisting symptoms of certain physiological disturbances, rather than the causes of these, but it seems imprudent to assume this without real evidence. If the pessimists are correct, there is no margin of safety between harmful levels of lead and those experienced by many members of urban populations.

[86]Bini, Lead in the rural environment.

[87]Data in this paragraph are from Clair C. Patterson, Contaminated and natural lead environments of man.

[88]S. Hernberg et al., δ-Aminolevulinic acid dehydrase as a measure of lead exposure; Lynn, *Air pollution;* J. R. Goldsmith and A. J. Hexter, Respiratory exposures to lead: epidemiological and experimental dose-response relationships.

[89]J. J. Chisolm, Lead poisoning.

[90]T. Carson et al., Slowed learning in lambs prenatally exposed to lead; O. David et al., Lead and hyperactivity; *New Scientist,* Mental deficiency and lead linked in new survey. Neurological effects of lead are discussed at length in D. Bruce-Smith and H. A. Waldron, Lead, behavior, and criminality.

Ironically, the most significant steps taken in recent years to reduce the amount of lead in the human environment have been motivated not by concern about lead's toxicity but rather by laws restricting emissions of other pollutants. Specifically, the catalytic converters used by most American automobile manufacturers to meet the emissions standards mandated by the Clean Air Act of 1970 for hydrocarbons, carbon monoxide, and nitrogen oxides are fouled and rendered inoperative by the tetraethyl lead in gasoline. As a result, the Environmental Protection Agency in late 1973 promulgated a schedule for the reduction of the lead content of gasoline and required all retailers above a specified volume of business to make available a lead-free gasoline after July 1, 1974.[91] Before these regulations went into effect, the lead content in gasoline actually had been rising somewhat, from 2.3 grams of lead per gallon in 1963 to 2.6 grams of lead per gallon in 1970.[92] The EPA schedule required that the average lead content of gasolines offered for sale not exceed 1.7 grams per gallon after January 1, 1975, and 0.5 grams per gallon after January 1, 1979. The latter figure was successfully challenged as being "without scientific basis," in a lawsuit brought by the Ethyl Corporation in 1974; the EPA has appealed.[93]

Mercury

Mercury is a heavy, silvery metal that is liquid at room temperature. It is used in the production of chlorine (which in turn is used in large quantities in the production of plastics) and of caustic soda (which has many industrial uses), as well as in the manufacture of electrical equipment. Smaller quantities are used in paints, agricultural fungicides, and dental amalgams, in the pulp and paper industry, in medicines (so-called mercurials), and in thermometers. World production of mercury in 1970 was about 10,000 metric tons, of which about 25 percent was used in the United States.[94]

A detailed study of the fate of commercial mercury in the United States around 1970 indicated that 76 percent was for applications where the mercury is recyclable in principle (e.g., chlorine-caustic soda manufacturing, electrical equipment) and 24 percent was for dissipative uses (e.g., paint, fungicides, pharmaceuticals).[95] Losses to the environment in the *potentially* recyclable chlorine-caustic soda application amounted to 23 percent of the total U.S. mercury use, however. In total, then, at least half of the 2500 tons of mercury used annually in the United States reaches the biosphere in one form or another (sometimes, as with paints, after a long delay).

Other sources of mercury added to the environment by the activities of civilization are the roasting of sulfide ores of other metals (possibly contributing as much as 2000 metric tons of mercury per year worldwide[96]) and the combustion of fossil fuels containing mercury as a trace contaminant.

The mercury content of coal varies widely, with published values for different coals ranging from 0.01 ppm to 33 ppm by weight.[97] If the average value worldwide should be as high as 1 ppm, then mercury mobilized by coal combustion would be about 3000 metric tons annually. It was shown in tests on one large United States coal-fired power plant that more than 90 percent of the mercury in the coal goes up the stack and less than 10 percent remains in the bottom ash.[98] Other work has shown that the mercury and other trace-metal contaminants of coal are preferentially concentrated in the particles at the small end of the size-range produced by combustion; these particles are the most likely to escape stack-gas controls, the most persistent in the atmosphere, and the most likely to penetrate to the lungs upon inhalation.[99] Unfortunately, it cannot be assumed even that the mercury remaining in particles large enough to be collected by control devices or in bottom ash stays out of the environment; it is subject to outgassing and leaching from ash storage piles.

[91]CEQ, *Environmental quality, 1974,* p. 155.

[92]See, for example, C. ReVelle and P. ReVelle, *Sourcebook on the environment,* pp. 134–146.

[93]CEQ, *Environmental quality, 1974,* p. 155, CEQ, *Environmental quality, 1975,* p. 105.

[94]National Commission on Materials Policy, *Material needs and the environment today.*

[95]R. A. Wallace, et al., *Mercury in the environment.*

[96]H. V. Weiss, et al., Mercury in a Greenland ice sheet: evidence of recent input by man.

[97]Bertine and Goldberg, Fossil fuel; O. Joensu, Fossil fuels as a source of mercury pollution. Joensu found a mean value of 3.3 ppm of mercury in U.S. coals sampled, but suggested a figure of 1 ppm for world coal production.

[98]C. E. Billings and W. R. Matson, Mercury emmissions from coal combustion.

[99]D. Natusch, et al., Toxic trace elements: preferential concentration in respirable particles.

TABLE 10-12
Mercury Concentrations in the Environment

Location	Concentration (ppb, by weight)
"Clean air"	0.001 to 0.010[a,b]
Suburban air	0.003[c]
Polluted urban air	0.01 to 0.2[a]
Dissolved in oceans	0.03 to 0.15[d]
Dissolved in streams	0.07[d]
Air in painted rooms*	0.07 to 1.5[c]
Air in doctor/dentist offices	1 to 5[c]
Polluted water	2 to 5[a]
Beef	3[e]
Shrimp	14[e]
Soil	50[d]
Rocks	50 to 200[d]
Most marine fish	150[a]
Leaves of urban trees	150 to 1000[e,f]
Swordfish, tuna	180 to 2400[a]
Fish from polluted waters	up to 10,000[a]
Feathers of seed-eating birds	20,000[a]

*Varies with type of paint and interval since painting.
Sources: [a]Wallace et al., *Mercury in the environment.* [b]Weiss et al., Mercury in a Greenland ice sheet. [c]R. S. Foote, Mercury vapor concentrations inside buildings. [d]Garrels et al., *Chemical cycles.* [e]W. H. Smith, Lead and mercury burden of urban woody plants. [f]J. T. Tanner et al., Mercury content of common foods determined by neutron activation analysis.

The mercury content of petroleum is even less well-measured than that of coal. It was found to be 10 ppm in one (probably exceptional) circumstance.[100] If it averages 1 ppm worldwide, the mercury entering the atmosphere as a result of oil combustion could be approximately 3000 metric tons.

By how much have the activities of civilization altered the natural flows of mercury through the environment? The prehuman rate of mercury mobilization by weathering has been estimated as about 1000 metric tons per year.[101] The precivilization flow of mercury from the surface to the atmosphere by outgassing from land and oceans was perhaps 25,000 metric tons per year.[102] A reasonable estimate would seem to be that civilization (as of 1970) has increased the amount of mercury that is flowing in rivers from land to oceans to about 4 times the natural value, and the flow of mercury from surface to atmosphere by roughly 50 percent.[103] (Possibly the increase of natural outgassing by surface-modifying activities of civilization is as important as direct human inputs of mercury.) The uncertainty in these figures is large (at least a factor of 2 up or down) but they are consistent with a doubling in the mercury content of precipitation in the last several decades as suggested by ice samples from the Greeland ice sheet.[104]

Some concentrations of mercury that have been measured in various parts of the natural and "man-made" environment are summarized in Table 10-12. It is important, in pondering the significance of these levels, to distinguish between the different chemical forms in which mercury occurs.

Inorganic mercury can be either the metallic form, encountered environmentally principally as the vapor, or any of a variety of inorganic salts and complexes in which the mercury has oxidation numbers of +2 (mercuric compounds) or +1 (mercurous compounds). Inorganic mercury compounds are toxic, but not extremely so, and they are not concentrated in food webs. The form most commonly encountered in the Earth's crust is insoluble mercuric sulfide (HgS), which under oxidizing conditions is converted to more soluble $HgSO_4$. Mercury compounds reaching Earth's surface generally degrade to the metallic form, which volatilizes under the action of sunlight.[105]

Organic mercury occurs most commonly as phenyl mercury ($C_6H_5Hg^+$), methyl mercury (CH_3Hg^+), and methoxyethyl mercury ($CH_3OCH_2CH_2Hg^+$), the first form in paints and pulp and paper operations, and the latter two forms in agricultural chemicals. These forms are much more toxic than inorganic mercury, and are concentrated in food webs. It was discovered in 1969 that microorganisms widespread in sediments are capable of forming methyl mercury and dimethyl mercury from inorganic mercury compounds.[106] It is this phenomenon that has made mercury poisoning from high levels of methyl mercury in fish so serious a threat.

The symptoms of chronic poisoning by inorganic mercury have been known for a long time. They include headache, fatigue, irritability, tremors, and other nervous

[100]Bertine and Goldberg, *Fossil fuel.*

[101]Garrels et al., *Chemical cycles;* Bertine and Goldberg, Fossil fuel, Table 3, last column.

[102]Garrels et al., *Chemical cycles.* See also Weiss, et al., Mercury in the Greenland ice sheet.

[103]Garrels et al., *Chemical cycles.*

[104]Ibid. These results have been questioned by E. M. Dickson, Mercury and lead in the Greenland ice sheet: A reexamination of the data, and by R. A. Carr and P. E. Wilkniss, Mercury in the Greenland ice sheet: Further data.

[105]Wallace et al., *Mercury.*

[106]Ibid.

disorders. Chronic mercury poisoning from the processing of felt used for hats was the origin of the phrase "mad as a hatter."[107] A U.S. standard based on early experience in the felt-hat and electronics industries allows 100 micrograms of inorganic mercury per cubic meter of air for an eight-hour working day; an international symposium has suggested a value half as high for the elemental form; and studies of animals exposed continuously to mercury vapor have led the Russians to establish a 24-hour limit of 0.3 micrograms per cubic meter.[108] (One microgram per cubic meter is roughly 1 part per billion by weight.) There is some evidence of mercury poisoning among people occupationally exposed to mercury vapor at 10 to 30 micrograms per cubic meter.[109] About three-quarters of any metallic mercury vapor inhaled is absorbed, and once in the body, inorganic mercury concentrates preferentially in the kidney, liver, and brain.[110] A tentative standard for mercury in drinking water has been set by the U.S. Public Health Service at 5 parts per billion.[111]

Among organic forms of mercury, phenyl mercury is converted rapidly in the body to inorganic forms and is not considered more dangerous than these. Methyl and ethyl mercury (often termed alkyl mercury compounds) are similar to each other and much more dangerous than the phenyl and inorganic forms.[112] Methyl mercury concentrates in the body in red blood cells and in the nervous system, and it selectively attacks nerve cells. Its biological half-life in human beings is about 70 days.[113] Symptoms of methyl mercury poisoning may first appear weeks to months after exposure to toxic concentrations; they include "numbness and tingling of the lips or hands and feet, ataxia (lack of motor coordination), disturbances of speech, concentric constriction of the visual fields, impairment of hearing, and emotional disturbances."[114] This type of poisoning is sometimes called Minimata disease, because the first recorded epidemic of the sort occurred in the Minimata district of Japan (Box 10-4). Cases of fatal poisoning from ingestion of grain treated with organic mercurial fungicides have been documented in Iraq, Pakistan, Guatemala, and the United States.[115]

The United States standard for airborne organic mercury compounds is 10 micrograms of Hg per cubic meter, or 10 times less than the inorganic standard. Breathing this concentration for an eight-hour work day (10 m^3 of air inhaled) would produce a daily intake of 100 micrograms of Hg, an average blood concentration of 60 micrograms of Hg per liter of whole blood (60 ppb), and a brain concentration of 1,000 ppb.[116] The blood level at which chromosome damage has been observed is about 200 ppb, overt symptoms of mercury poisoning occur between 400 and 1,000 ppb Hg in blood, and the blood level associated with inevitable injury and death is variously stated as 1000 to 1400 ppb.[117]

The United States Food and Drug Administration standard for methyl mercury in fish is 500 ppb Hg on a wet-weight basis. To receive a daily intake of methyl mercury equal to that permitted by the occupational air standard (100 micrograms per day) would require the consumption of only 200 grams of fish per day (a bit under half a pound) contaminated to the 500 ppb permitted by the standard. Blood levels of methyl mercury corresponding to chromosome damage could be reached by consuming about 600 grams of fish per day contaminated at this level; such heavy fish consumption is most unusual in the U.S. diet. In the early 1970s, there were fishing restrictions in force in the U.S. in 18 states because of mercury contamination.[118] The recovery time for contaminated waters is very slow, ranging from tens to perhaps hundreds of years.[119]

Cadmium

Cadmium is physically and chemically similar to zinc, and the two metals always occur together in nature. Whereas zinc is essential to life, however, cadmium is

[107]ReVelle and ReVelle, *Sourcebook on the environment*, p. 153.
[108]Ibid.
[109]M. H. Berlin et al., Maximum allowable concentrations of mercury compounds: Report of an international committee.
[110]Berlin et al., Maximum allowable; P. C. Stein et al., Mercury in man.
[111]Wallace et al., *Mercury*.
[112]Ibid.
[113]Berlin et al., Maximum allowable.
[114]Ibid.

[115]F. Bakir et al., Methyl mercury poisoning in Iraq; A. Curley et al., Organic mercury identified as the cause of poisoning in humans and hogs.
[116]Berlin et al., Maximum allowable.
[117]Neville Grant, Mercury in man; Berlin et al., Maximum allowable.
[118]ReVelle and ReVelle, *Sourcebook on the environment*, p. 154.
[119]Ibid.

BOX 10-4 The Minimata Incident

In Minimata, Japan, a small city on the west coast of Kyushu, the economy is dominated by the chemical plants of Chisso Corporation.* Pollution problems affecting local fishermen have been occurring for half a century, but the problem that was to make Minimata world famous first showed up in the early 1950s. In 1953, "Birds seemed to be losing their sense of coordination, often falling from their perches or flying into buildings and trees. Cats, too, were acting oddly. They walked with a strange rolling gait, frequently stumbling over their own legs. Many suddenly went mad, running in circles and foaming at the mouth until they fell—or were thrown—into the sea and drowned."** This "disease of the dancing cats," as it was known to the local fishermen, soon spread to fishermen and their families, with horrifying results. Severe trembling and mental confusion were followed by numbness, disturbed vision and speech, general loss of control of bodily functions, violent thrashing unconsciousness, and, in some 40 percent of the victims, death. By July 1970, the number of officially recognized cases had climbed to 121, with 46 deaths—and only the more severe cases are officially recognized.†

*Much of the following material on Minimata is based on N. Huddle et al., *Island of dreams: Environmental crisis in Japan.*
**Ibid., p. 107.
†Ken Otani and Jun Ui, Minimata disease.

Although Chisso Corporation (with some governmental cooperation) did everything possible to prevent the blame from being laid at its door, by 1959 an independent study had shown that Minimata disease was methyl mercury poisoning and that Chisso's effluents were the "likely source." Soon thereafter Chisso offered minimal compensation, the start of a long battle for financial aid for victims at Minimata and other sufferers of methyl mercury poisoning who began to appear at Niigata on western Honshu in the mid-1960s.‡ It was not until 1968 that the government of Japan recognized officially that mercury was the cause of Minimata disease, and not until 1973 that Chisso finally was forced to admit its culpability and to agree to pay reasonable compensation.

By 1975, careful health surveys had resulted in the uncovering of some 3500 victims of Minimata disease, and an estimated 10,000 additional people may still develop symptoms. Chisso, meanwhile, is in financial trouble because of the costs of indemnifying victims and has resorted to financial stratagems to avoid payment—including spinning off profitable subsidiaries to open the possibility of Chisso itself declaring bankruptcy.

‡The history of this dispute is in Huddle et al., *Island of dreams.*

inimical to life. Even in small quantities it causes kidney dysfunction and bone demineralization, the latter especially if combined with a calcium deficiency. If inhaled, it causes fibrosis of the lungs and probably emphysema, and there is some evidence from animal studies that it may be teratogenic and carcinogenic.[120]

World production of cadmium in the early 1970s was around 17,000 metric tons annually.[121] The principal uses were electroplating, in stabilizers for plastics, and in pigments, alloys, and batteries; most of these uses are dissipative and nonrecyclable. A significant amount may reach the atmosphere through smelting and reclamation of steel scrap and incineration of plastics. The content of cadmium in fossil fuels is not well established, but a modest number of measurements indicate that it may be around 0.5 ppm in oil and may average 1 ppm in coal. Were this the case, emissions to the global environment from burning fossil fuels would be in the range of 5,000 metric tons per year. The natural rate of flow for cadmium through the environment as a result of weathering has been estimated, from oceanic sedimentation rates, at 500 metric tons per year.[122] The flow from mining alone is more than 30 times larger. Cadmium provides one of the most impressive examples of a human perturbation dwarfing the "natural background."

The principal human intake of cadmium among nonsmokers in relatively unpolluted areas appears to be in food; 20 to 50 micrograms per day is ingested and, of

[120]An excellent review is V. Hiatt and J. E. Huff, The environmental impact of cadmium: an overview. Data in this section are from Hiatt and Huff unless otherwise noted.

[121]U.S. Department of Commerce, *Statistical abstract of the United States, 1974,* p. 668.

[122]Bertine and Goldberg, Fossil-fuel combustion, table 3.

this, perhaps 2 micrograms is retained. Smokers may absorb 0.2 micrograms per cigarette, making a pack per day equivalent to twice the absorption in the diet. An intake of 5 parts per million cadmium in air for 8 hours delivers a lethal dose, and 1 part per million for 8 hours is dangerous. The recommended Threshold Limit Value (recommended not to be exceeded in work environments) in the United States is 100 parts per billion (0.1 ppm), although it is unlikely that this level is harmless. Part of the cadmium problem is that the fraction not excreted immediately has an exceedingly long half-life in the body—around several hundred days—so that low doses received over a long period can lead to accumulation of a high body-burden. The U.S. drinking water standard for cadmium is 10 parts per billion, a level that is not infrequently exceeded.

Major toxic effects due to cadmium poisoning have been documented in industrial workers and in villages in Japan whose water supply was contaminated with drainage from a cadmium mine. Acute cadmium poisoning received the name *Itai-Itai* or "ouch-ouch" disease in Japan, because of the painfulness of the associated bone and muscle abnormalities. Effects on people at lower dose rates are still undocumented, but are suspected.

There is every reason to believe that cadmium is accumulating steadily in the environment, and its known characteristics as a persistent cumulative poison in the body give much reason for concern.[123]

FLUORIDES

Fluoridation of public water supplies for partial protection against tooth decay is an emotion-charged subject. The scientific evidence supporting the efficacy and safety of mass fluoridation at the generally recommended level of 1 milligram per liter of water (1 ppm) is not as good as it ought to be, but neither is there convincing evidence that it is harmful.[124] Although there are certainly some cranks in the antifluoridation school, there are also some serious and competent scientists and responsible laymen who have been unmercifully abused because of the position they have taken on this controversial issue. Perhaps the strongest argument against mass fluoridation of drinking water is that individual treatment with fluoride is simple and can be supplied cheaply on public funds for those wishing to use it.

There is no question that fluoride is toxic in high concentrations, and fluoride pollution from a variety of industrial activities is a significant problem. Fluorides are discharged into the air from steel, aluminum, phosphate, pottery, glass, and brick works. These sources together emit perhaps 150,000 tons of hydrogen fluoride annually, and the same activities emit some tens of thousands of tons of fluorides annually into waterways.[125] Intentional addition of fluorides in fluoridation programs makes a modest but not negligible contribution of perhaps 20,000 tons per year to the human-caused fluoride inputs to the environment.

The main problems encountered in trying to evaluate health threats from fluoride pollution are familiar ones: the boundary between safe and unsafe levels is a fuzzy one; some individuals are more sensitive than others; and fluorides may act in combination with other pollutants to do damage at concentrations where the fluorides alone would not be harmful.

Fluorides have been shown to concentrate in food chains, and evidence suggesting a potential for significant ecological effects is accumulating.[126] Harm to terrestrial plants and algae at concentrations encountered in polluted environments has been documented, and the ability of certain plants and microorganisms to synthesize particularly toxic organic fluorides has been demonstrated. The toxicity of inorganic and organic fluorides to soil organisms is essentially unexplored and is a potential danger point.

CHEMICAL MUTAGENS

Many chemicals found in the environment are considered hazardous because they, like ionizing radiation (discussed in the following section), are able to cause

[123]For a discussion of the difficulties of dealing in an economic framework with cadmium and pollutants with similar characteristics of accumulation and longevity, see C. L. Nobbs and D. W. Pierce, The economics of stock pollutants: The example of cadmium.

[124]NAS, *Fluorides;* World Health Organization, *Fluoride and human health.*

[125]Edward Groth III, Fluoride pollution.

[126]Ibid.

mutations. Mutations are sudden, inheritable changes in the makeup or arrangement of the genetic information that is coded into the structure of giant molecules of deoxyribonucleic acid (DNA).[127] These changes in the genes are important to us for two basic reasons—because they affect the genetic composition of future generations and because they appear to be involved in the production of cancers (carcinogenesis is discussed below).

Individual mutations are thought to be random events, so that one cannot specify which gene or genes will be affected when an organism is exposed to a *mutagen* (mutation-causing agent). Similarly, when a mutation is detected, it is ordinarily impossible to identify the mutagenic agent. Mutations are also rare events—in most animals (including *Homo sapiens*) an average rate would be around 1 mutation per 1 million genes per generation—the rate varying from gene to gene.[128] Mutations are an important source of the variability that is essential to the evolutionary process. It is generally agreed by evolutionists, however, that spontaneous mutation rates and other evolutionary properties of human populations provide more than sufficient genetic variability to allow humanity to evolve in response to current or foreseeable selection pressures. Spontaneous mutations are those that occur naturally. About 10 percent of them are thought to be caused by "background" radiation (see following text), and the remainder by unavoidable errors in the cells' manipulations of the genetic information and by unknown chemical mutagens.[129]

[127]*Deoxyribonucleic acid* is the repository of genetic information in the cells of all higher organisms (in a few viruses a very similar compound, RNA, is used). These are giant molecules (macromolecules) made up of two long sequences of subunits called *nucleotides.* Four kinds of nucleotides are found in DNA, each having a different nitrogenous base that can pair with just one of the other bases. The base pairs hold the long sequences together like the rungs of a long, twisted ladder—the famed double helix. The genetic information is coded into the sequence of the base pair "rungs." For a simple review of the biochemical basis of heredity, see P. R. Ehrlich, R. W. Holm, and I. Brown, *Biology and society.* A biochemical explanation of kinds of mutations can be found in J. D. Watson, *Molecular biology of the gene,* 3d ed. Benjamin, New York, 1976, or any other modern text in biochemical genetics.

[128]Technically the rate is given per locus. For further general discussion of mutation and its evolutionary significance, see P. R. Ehrlich, R. W. Holm and D. R. Parnell, *The process of evolution,* especially chapter 3 and in particular the section on chromosomal alterations, which we have included here under "mutations." A comprehensive discussion of mutation in human populations may be found in L. L. Cavalli-Sforza and W. F. Bodmer, *The genetics of human populations.*

[129]W. F. Bodmer and L. L. Cavalli-Sforza, *Genetics, evolution, and man,* p. 694.

Mutations may be thought of as small, random changes in an extremely complex mechanism. It is not surprising, then, that most of them are harmful to an organism—or, in the jargon of the geneticist, *deleterious.* The chance of a mutation's being beneficial is small, for the same kind of reason that a random change in the circuitry of a TV set or computer is unlikely to improve its functioning. Deleterious mutations—which means 95 percent or more of *all* mutations—are normally weeded out of the gene pool of a population by natural selection (Chapter 4). In human populations, however, medical advances have made it possible for individuals carrying deleterious mutations to survive and breed, thus limiting the action of selection. For example, some human groups may be accumulating deleterious mutants that cause nearsightedeness or farsightedness because widespread use of eyeglasses has lessened the selective pressures against such genes.[130] For this reason many geneticists are concerned about long-term deterioration of the quality of the human gene pool and a corresponding decrease in the quality of life.[131] Even though, for example, nearsighted people and certain diabetics may be perfectly viable in the environment of a highly technological society today, and people carrying genetic defects such as that which causes Tay-Sachs disease may be made normal in an environment of the future, increase in the genes associated with these disorders is not to be taken lightly. Treatment of such genetic disorders involves a social cost, and one that future societies might be unwilling or unable to bear.

There is every reason, then, to avoid increasing the human mutation rate by the exposure of people to man-made chemical mutagens. The first problem in so doing is to determine which of the hundreds of thousands of synthetic chemicals released into the environment are mutagenic. The problems of screening chemicals for mutagenicity (mutagenetic activity) are numerous.[132] The test system must be very sensitive to detect a rare mutation with a small effect, and the results of the test must be highly reproducible. The test must be able to

[130]Ibid., p. 661.

[131]See, for example, Committee of the Council of the Environmental Mutagen Society, Environmental mutagenic hazards.

[132]Much of the material here is taken from the committee report cited in the preceding note.

TABLE 10-13
Mutagen Screening Systems

Test system	*Time to run test*	*Operating costs**	*Initial investment costs*	*Relative ease of detection***	
				Gene mutations	*Chromosome alterations*
Microorganisms with metabolic activation:					
Bacteria	2 to 3 days	Very low	Low	Excellent	
Yeasts	3 to 5 days	Very low	Low	Good	Unknown
Neurospora crassa	1 to 3 weeks	Moderate	Moderate	Very good	Good
Cultured mammalian cells with metabolic activation	2 to 5 weeks	Moderate to high	Moderate	Excellent to fair	Unknown
Host-mediated assay with:					
Microorganisms	2 to 7 days	Low to moderate	Low to moderate	Good	
Mammalian cells	2 to 5 weeks	Moderate to high	Moderate	Unknown	Good
Body fluid analysis	Variable	Variable	Low to moderate	Variable	
Plants:					
Vicia faba (broad bean)	3 to 8 days	Low	Low		Relevance unclear
Tradescantia paludosa (spiderwort)	2 to 5 weeks	Low to moderate	Moderate	Potentially excellent	
Insect:					
Drosophila melanogaster (fruit fly)	2 to 7 weeks	Moderate	Moderate	Good to excellent	Good to excellent
Mammals:					
Dominant lethal mutations	2 to 4 months	Moderate to high	Moderate		Unknown
Blood or bone marrow cell genetics	1 to 5 weeks	Moderate	Moderate		Potentially good
Specific gene mutations	2 to 3 months	High to very high	High to very high	Unknown	

*Operating costs vary widely, depending upon the exact procedure and the number of substances tested simultaneously. Very low is approximately $1000; low is $1000 to $5000; moderate is $3000 to $10,000; high is $10,000 to $20,000; and very high is $25,000 upward.
**Since most of these test systems do not detect all classes of gene mutation or chromosomal alterations, these columns refer only to the detectable effects.
Source: Data from Council of the Environmental Mutagen Society, Committee on Environmental Mutagenic Hazards.

detect the variety of biochemical and microstructural events that are lumped under the rubric *mutation.* (A microstructural event is a change in chromosome[133] structure or number.)

The test system should have metabolic properties similar to those found in human beings. Many examples are known of chemicals that are not mutagenic until they are altered into another chemical form by the life processes of an organism. Similarly, various mutagens have been shown to be promptly metabolized into inactive forms in some organisms so that they cannot cause mutations in them. An ideal test system would, then, perfectly simulate our life processes. Related to this problem is that of the interaction of mutagens. Two substances may interact so that the mutagenicity of one of them is enhanced. For example caffeine, which inhibits DNA repair processes, may increase the rate of mutation-induction by various mutagens.

A variety of mutagen screening systems have been developed. These include bacterial systems that can detect biochemical mutations but not microstructural alterations (in chromosomes), and systems using fungi, higher organisms or mammalian cells in cell culture, that can detect both mutations and some chromosomal changes.

The properties of a variety of these systems are shown in Table 10-13. With the exception of the plant systems and *Drosophila,* the nonmammalian test systems shown include an activation system so that inactive compounds may be converted to mutagens if that would occur in a mammal. (*Drosophila* possesses at least one enzyme system that activates some mutagens in a manner similar to a system found in the liver of mammals.) One procedure for activation involves the addition of metabolically functional mammalian tissue extracts to the test system along with the suspected mutagen. In a second activation procedure an intact mammal (either *Homo sapiens* or a rodent) is exposed to the suspected mutagen and tissue extracts from the mammal are added to the test system. In a so-called host-mediated assay the microorganisms or mammalian cells used in the test system are introduced into the body cavity of a rodent, which is then

[133]Chromosomes are the organelles (tiny organs) of the cell nucleus, with which most of the nuclear DNA is associated.

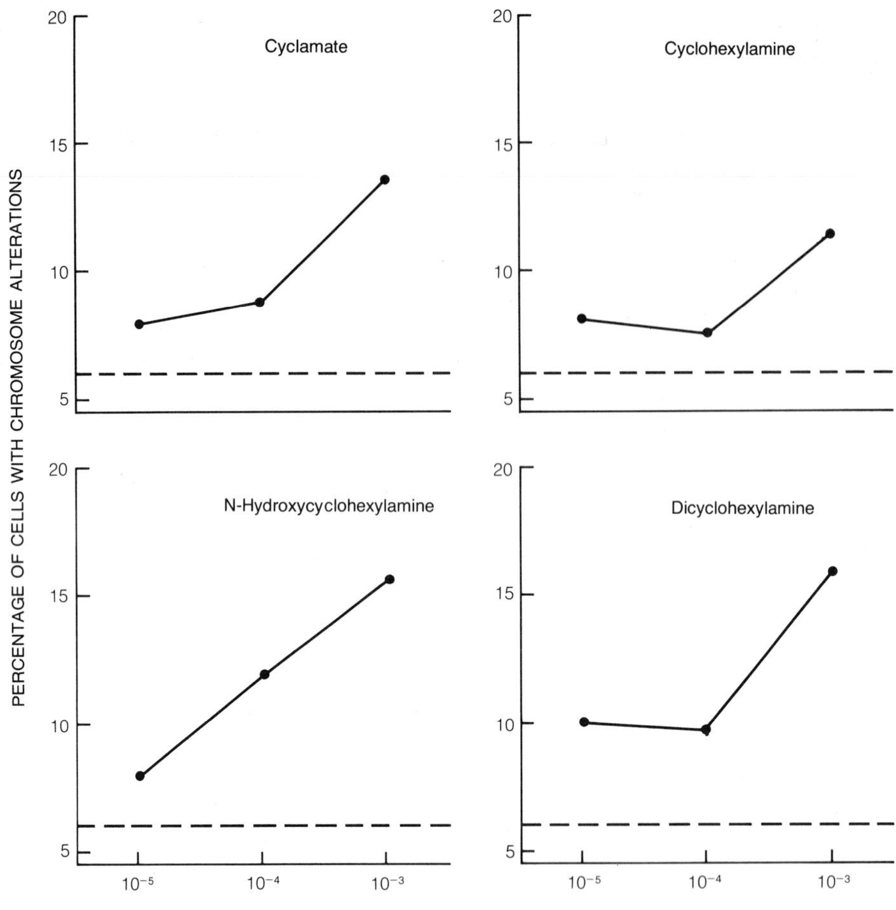

FIGURE 10-5

Chromosomal alterations in tissue-cultured human white blood cells as a function of doses of a cyclamate and three related chemicals. Exposure was for 25 hours. Concentrations are given in moles per liter (a mole is the weight in grams of a compound numerically equal to its molecular weight). Each point represents analysis of 100 cells. (Data from Stoltz et al., 1970.)

TABLE 10-14
A Sample of Mutagens

Mutagen	*Use or occurrence*
Acridine orange	Dye
Aflatoxin	Fungal toxin which may contaminate foods
Benzidine	Manufacture of dyes
Benzo[a]pyrene	Air pollution resulting from incomplete combustion
Captan	Agricultural fungicide; antibacterial agent in soaps
Chloramphenicol	Antibiotic
Cigarette smoke concentrate	Smokers' lungs
Cyclamate	Artificial sweetener
Dichlorvos (vapona)	Shell No-Pest Strip insecticide
Ethidium bromide	By veterinarians: against trypanosomal infections of cattle
N-methyl-N′-nitro-N-nitrosoguanidine (MNNG)	Industrial alkylating agent
Proflavine	Antiseptic
Sodium nitrite	Many industrial, medical, and veterinary uses
Trimethyl phosphate (TMP)	Gasoline additive, flame retardant, solvent for paints, catalyst for preparation of plastic materials
Uracil mustard	Anticancer drug
Vinyl chloride	Manufacture of plastics; as refrigerant, aerosol propellant

Sources: McCann et al., Detection of carcinogens as mutagens; Epstein and Hattis, Pollution and human health; Matsumura, Toxicology of insecticides; Stoltz et al., Cytogenetic studies with cyclamate; Sanders, Chemical Mutagens; Merck Index.

exposed to the suspected mutagen. The test microbes or cells are later recovered and checked for mutations.

The results of one series of mutagenicity tests using cultures of human white blood cells are shown in Figure 10-5. The four suspected mutagens tested were: cyclamate, an artificial sweetener; cyclohexylamine and N-hydroxycyclohexylamine, both breakdown products of cyclamate; and dicyclohexylamine sulfate, an occasional contaminant of cyclamate. As can be seen in the figure, a 25-hour exposure to high concentration of any of these compounds caused a rise in the percentage of cells in the test culture with chromosomal alterations.[134]

An enormous number of compounds have already been reported to be mutagenic in one or more test systems (Table 10-14). They include pesticides, dyes, refrigerants, anticancer drugs, drugs used in veterinary medicine, air pollutants, fuel additives, tranquilizers, chemicals used in the plastics industry, antibiotics, and a variety of industrial akylating agents (chemicals used in industrial processes to introduce alkyl—that is, ethyl, propyl, and such—radicals into organic molecules).[135]

Identifying a chemical as a mutagen is, however, only the first step in evaluating the hazard it poses. One must also know, among other things, if the test results can properly be extrapolated from the test system to *Homo sapiens*, what patterns of susceptibility there will be in the human population, how much of the chemical is loose in the environment and how it is distributed, the current and projected levels of production, and the persistence of the compound. All these factors must be integrated into a difficult cost-benefit analysis for which, at the moment, there are no satisfactory guidelines. The basic problems are similar to those discussed below in the evaluation of the hazards of radiation. One can attempt to place a value on the total future cost of one individual's being exposed to a given dose (concentration multiplied by time) of a mutagen, just as attempts have been made to estimate the dollar cost of one person-rem of radiation exposure.[136] But the assumptions that must be made in order to do this border on the ludicrous.

The overall risk to humanity from mutagenic chemicals seems great, but for the reasons indicated above, difficult to evaluate. As the distinguished geneticist James F. Crow put it, "There is reason to fear that some chemicals may constitute as important a risk as radiation, possibly a more serious one . . . . To consider only radiation hazards may be to ignore the submerged part of the iceberg."[137] The wise course would seem to be to reduce public exposure immediately to suspected mutagens to the greatest possible extent, tolerating unavoidable exposure only where the benefits seem great. But doing this can be extremely difficult. The case of cyclamate is an instructive one. In August 1970, cyclamates were banned by the U.S. Food and Drug Administration after a long battle with commercial interests. The argument for allowing their use was that they were important to diabetics and also saved lives by helping prevent obesity. This was countered with arguments that cyclamate-sweetened products were not particularly effective in weight reduction. Suggestions that products sweetened with cyclamates could be dispensed only to those with medical need (by prescription) led to counterarguments that the volume of business would be insufficient to keep an adequate variety of products available. In the end we think the right decision was made, but the decision-making process was long and agonizing.[138]

When one considers that the diet of most people in developed countries contains thousands of synthetic colors, flavors, thickeners, preservatives, emulsifiers, antibiotics, pesticides, and contaminants from packages, many of which may be mutagenic (and carcinogenic), one can begin to appreciate the magnitude of the problem.

IONIZING RADIATION

The year 1896 marked the discovery of two kinds of penetrating radiation, different in origin, but subsequently recognized to be related in character. The first of the two radiations was man-made, produced by a cathode-ray tube (then a technological curiosity), and was named X-rays by its discoverer, Wilhelm Roentgen. A scant few months later, Henri Becquerel discovered penetrating radiation emanating spontaneously from a

[134]D. R. Stoltz et al., Cytogenetic studies with cyclamate.
[135]H. J. Sanders, Chemical mutagens.
[136]Committee, Environmental mutagenic hazards.
[137]Chemical risk to future generations.
[138]See, for example, J. S. Turner, *The chemical feast; Time*, August 26, 1974, p. 67.

compound of uranium, a phenomenon shortly thereafter given the name "radioactivity" by Pierre and Marie Curie.[139]

X-rays were subsequently shown to be energetic electromagnetic waves produced when fast-moving electrons were decelerated in encountering a "target" material (hence the German term *Bremstrahlung,* meaning "braking radiation"). Early studies of radioactivity showed that its emissions were of three kinds, which were named *alpha, beta,* and *gamma* radiation. Later it was shown that alpha and beta radiation were actually energetic particles, and that gamma radiation consisted of electromagnetic waves identical in some cases to X-rays but in other cases even more energetic. All these emissions (and some others since discovered) are today characterized as *ionizing radiation,* because the particles or waves involved are energetic enough to break electrons loose from atoms they encounter.

Although the phenomenon was not discovered until 1876, and its ubiquity was not recognized for some time thereafter, humanity lives and has always lived in a virtual sea of ionizing radiation. It comes from naturally radioactive rocks in Earth's crust, from naturally occurring radioactive materials that circulate in the biosphere, and from cosmic rays arriving from space. These natural sources of ionizing radiation have been augmented in the twentieth century by various medical, military, and commercial uses of radioactive materials and X-rays.

The long history and universality of exposure to ionizing radiation does not mean that it is harmless. The ionizing property—the ejection of electrons from the outer shells of atoms—is the key to the harm. Such ionization can destroy a chemical bond, and if the bond destroyed is in a molecule crucial to the function of a living cell, then harm to the organism may result. Some cells are dispensable to an organism made up of billions of them, but there are points of special vulnerability: death of a few cells in a fetus at certain stages can produce congenital abnormalities; mutations in germ cells can produce genetic effects that manifest themselves only in future generations; and damage to the DNA in other cells can produce cancer. There is reason to believe that a burden of such effects is, and always has been, associated with natural ionizing radiation. Obviously, the size of this burden has not been such as to imperil the survival of the human race, but neither can it be supposed to be negligible.

Radioactivity and ionizing radiation have been intensely studied since their discovery eighty years ago. Indeed, the often-heard statement that radioactivity is the most studied and best-understood major "pollutant" is almost certainly true. This is not to say, however, that understanding is adequate; it may be *less inadequate* than for other pollutants, such as heavy metals or nitrogen oxides, but many important uncertainties about ionizing radiation and specific radioactive materials remain unresolved. We treat some of them in the discussion that follows. Suffice it to say here that it would be foolish to view with complacency the significant additions to natural radiation exposure that contemporary civilization has already produced and any that it might contemplate producing in the future.

Properties and Pathways

The physical characteristics of radioactive transformations and the associated terminology are summarized in Box 8-3. Here we discuss the characteristics of different forms of ionizing radiation and how these characteristics affect the pathways that govern human exposure.

Particulate forms of ionizing radiation (alpha particles, beta particles, and neutrons) penetrate matter to distances that depend in part on their energies. Alpha particles consist of two neutrons and two protons, and thus are relatively massive. They travel only a short distance in air and generally cannot penetrate the dead protective layer of human skin. An alpha particle must have an energy of 7.5 million electron volts (MeV) to penetrate this layer, and few radioactive substances emit such energetic alphas. Thus, isotopes that emit alpha particles and nothing else (plutonium-239 is such an isotope) generally are dangerous only if they have access to the inside of the body; then the alpha particle can deposit its energy in living tissue, and, indeed, the massive particle does great

[139]See, for example, Merrill Eisenbud, *Environmental radioactivity.*

damage over the short pathway where its energy is deposited. Alpha particles are called high-LET (for high linear energy transfer) radiation because of this property.

Beta particles, being electrons or positrons and hence very light, are more penetrating than alpha particles of the same energy. The range of a negative beta particle in air is about four meters for every MeV of energy it starts out with; typical energies of beta particles are between a few hundredths of an MeV and a few MeV. To penetrate the dead protective layer of skin, a beta particle needs 0.07 MeV. Beta particles from krypton-85 and strontium-90 have more than enough energy to do this, but beta particles from tritium (hydrogen-3) do not.[140] Thus, tritium is of significance only as an *internal emitter*—irradiating cells from within the body. Krypton-85, a noble gas, is not absorbed by the body to any appreciable extent and so is of significance mainly as an *external emitter.* Strontium-90 is important as both an external and internal emitter.

The most penetrating forms of ionizing radiation are neutrons and gamma rays. Relatively few radioactive isotopes emit neutrons, but neutrons are produced in abundance in nuclear fission and nuclear fusion. Reactors of both kinds must be heavily shielded with lead, steel, and concrete to protect operating personnel from the neutrons produced. Gamma rays undergo attenuation in matter according to an exponential law of the form

$$I = I_o e^{-\lambda x},$$

where I is intensity, I_o is the initial intensity, x is distance traversed, and λ is a constant that depends on the material being penetrated and the energy of the gamma rays.[141] For gamma rays of energies commonly encountered, attenuation passing through building walls reduces exposures to people inside by 10 to 70 percent for homes, and 70 to 90 percent for large commercial buildings.[142]

In summary, alpha particles are dangerous only if emitted within the body; beta particles are most dangerous when emitted within the body, but energetic ones can penetrate several meters of air and the skin; and gamma rays and neutrons travel tens to hundreds of meters or more in air and can penetrate solid walls.

In addition to the type and energy of radiation emitted, radioactive substances can be distinguished according to their different radioactive half-lives (Box 8-3), their different behaviors in the physical environment, and their different behaviors in organisms.

A short half-life means that the amount of radioactivity declines rapidly. (Recall that radioactivity is measured in curies, where 1 curie equals 37 billion disintegrations per second.) If one starts with one curie of an isotope with a half-life of one minute (sodium-25 is such an isotope), it will have decayed to one trillionth (10^{-12}) of a curie after only 40 minutes. An initial curie of an isotope with a long half-life, such as the 4.5 billion years of uranium-238, is still essentially a curie a million years later—its activity changes only imperceptibly in time periods that are short compared to the half-life.

Directly related to differences in half-life are large differences in *specific activity*—that is, the number of curies per gram of an isotope. One gram of iodine-131 (an isotope with a half-life of 8.05 days) represents 123,000 curies; but it takes over 6 kilograms of iodine-129, with a half-life of 17 million years, to make a single curie.[143] A curie of strontium-89 (51-day half-life) would fit on the head of a pin; a curie of thorium-232 (14-billion-year half-life) weighs 10 tons.

Generally speaking, isotopes of intermediate half-life and specific activity are considered the most dangerous. Isotopes of very short half-life (minutes or less) decay away before they can move very far in the environment; those of very long half-life (millions of years or more) have such low specific activities that it takes large quantities to produce a high dose rate.

Summarized in Table 10-15 are the radiation types, half-lives, and specific activities of some of the most important natural and artificial radioactive isotopes.

The behavior of these isotopes in the environment varies widely with their chemical properties. Tritium is a

[140]For energies of the radioactive emissions of all known isotopes, see R. C. Weast, ed., *Handbook of chemistry and physics.*

[141]For values for common materials over the range of energies encountered, see U.S. Department of Health, Education and Welfare, *Radiological health handbook.*

[142]U.S. Nuclear Regulatory Commission, *Reactor Safety Study,* WASH-1400/NUREG-75-014, appendix 6, pp. 11–22.

[143]The formula relating specific activity to half-life is: curies/gram = $358{,}000/At_{1/2}$, where A is the isotope's atomic weight and $t_{1/2}$ is the half-life in years.

TABLE 10-15
Physical Characteristics of Important Radioactive Isotopes

Name	*Radiation**	*Half-life***	*Specific activity (Ci/gram)*
Tritium	$\beta^-(0.02)$	12y	9700
Carbon-14	$\beta^-(0.16)$	5800y	4.6
Phosphorus-32	$\beta^-(1.7)$	14d	2.8×10^5
Potassium-40	$\beta^-(1.3)$, $\gamma(1.5)$	1.3×10^9y	6.9×10^{-6}
Iron-59	$\beta^-(1.6)$	45d	4.9×10^4
Cobalt-60	$\beta^-(1.5)$, $\gamma(2.2)$	5.3y	1.1×10^3
Zinc-65	$\beta^+(0.33)$, $\gamma(1.1)$	245d	8.2×10^3
Krypton-85	$\beta^-(0.67)$, $\gamma(0.52)$	11y	390
Strontium-90	$\beta^-(0.54)$	29y	140
Technetium-99	$\beta^-(0.29)$	2.1×10^5y	1.7×10^{-2}
Iodine-129	$\beta^-(0.15)$, $\gamma(0.04)$	1.7×10^7y	1.6×10^{-4}
Iodine-131	$\beta^-(0.81)$, $\gamma(0.72)$	8.1d	1.23×10^5
Tellurium-132	$\beta^-(0.22)$, $\gamma(0.22)$	3.3d	3.0×10^5
Cesium-137	$\beta^-(0.18)$, $\gamma(0.66)$	30y	87
Radon-222	$\alpha(5.0)$, $\gamma(0.51)$	3.8d	1.6×10^5
Radium-226	$\alpha(4.8)$, $\gamma(0.64)$	1600y	1.0
Thorium-232	$\alpha(4.0)$, $\gamma(0.06)$	1.4×10^{10}y	1.1×10^{-7}
Uranium-233	$\alpha(4.8)$, $\gamma(0.1)$	1.6×10^5y	9.6×10^{-2}
Uranium-235	$\alpha(4.6)$, $\gamma(0.39)$	7.1×10^8y	2.1×10^{-6}
Uranium-238	$\alpha(4.2)$, $\gamma(0.05)$	4.5×10^9y	3.3×10^{-7}
Plutonium-239	$\alpha(5.1)$	2.4×10^4y	0.06

Note: Data are rounded to two significant figures.
*β^- = negative beta particle, β^+ = positron, α = alpha particle, γ = gamma ray, number in parentheses is maximum energy in MeV.
**y = years, d = days.
Source: Weast, *Handbook.*

form of hydrogen: as hydrogen gas, it diffuses rapidly in the atmosphere; as a constituent of water, it follows the hydrologic cycle; it moves throughout living matter but does not concentrate along food chains or in particular organs. Strontium imitates calcium in nutrient cycles and organisms; it concentrates in bone and is called a "bone-seeker." Iodine concentrates in the thyroid gland; it reaches human beings very efficiently by the pathway: fallout on grass → cows → milk → people. Krypton is a noble gas and is not taken up appreciably by organisms; it diffuses throughout the atmosphere, from which it delivers an external dose to people and other organisms. Cesium is tightly bound to soil, staying near the surface and delivering an external dose of gamma radiation to passersby for years after being deposited; it also concentrates heavily in aquatic food chains.[144]

The biological half-life of an isotope refers to the time in which an organism excretes half of a given initial amount. Other things being equal, the longer the biological half-life of a radioactive isotope, the more dangerous it is; for the longer the material stays in the body, the more radioactive disintegrations take place. Tritium incorporated into the body in water is one of the more innocuous radioisotopes in this respect, being excreted with a biological half-life of around 10 days; strontium, in contrast, has a biological half-life in human beings of about 50 years.

Sources and Doses

Recall from Box 8-3 that the absorbed dose of radiation is measured in *rads* (where 1 rad means 100 ergs of energy deposited in each gram of absorbing material) or *rem* (where rem are obtained by multiplying rads by a *quality factor* or *Relative Biological Effectiveness,* which measures the efficiency of the energy in doing biological damage). Modest doses are usually measured in millirem (1 millirem = 10^{-3} rem).

Human doses from the natural background sources range in the United States from 100 to 250 millirem per year, with an average near 150 millirem per year. This

[144]See, for example, Eisenbud, *Environmental radioactivity.*

dose comes from cosmic rays[145] (40 to 160 millirem per year, increasing with elevation); from uranium and thorium and their decay chains, and from potassium-40 in Earth's crust (30 to 115 millirem per year, depending on location); from potassium-40 in food and water (17 millirem per year average); and from the decay products of radium—especially radon gas—in granite blocks and bricks (about 8 millirem per year average, with wide variations depending on building materials used).[146] These are the *whole-body doses;* doses to individual organs are higher in some instances.

The principal source of artificial radiation exposure is medical X-rays. A chest X-ray delivers about 9 millirem, a gastrointestinal tract X-ray about 200. The average medical and dental radiation exposure to members of the population of the United States is roughly 70 millirem per year, or about half the natural background.[147] A round-trip, cross-country airline flight adds about 4 millirem from extra cosmic radiation; fallout from nuclear-weapons tests worldwide delivers about 4 millirem per year (the figure was a few times higher at the peak of the testing in the early 1960s); and an hour per day of television viewing delivers about 0.15 millirem per year in the form of X-rays.[148] The average dose to members of the U.S. public from the nuclear-power industry around 1970 was 0.01 millirem per year.[149] Most of the exposure from nuclear operations was due to the routine release of tritium and krypton-85.

Health Impacts and Standards

High doses of radiation delivered within a short period of time can produce acute illness or death within hours to weeks after the exposure. Such doses, in the range of 100 rem (100,000 millirem) to 1000 rem or more, could be experienced by individuals near the detonation of a nuclear weapon, or in the pattern of most intense fallout from such a weapon, or by individuals downwind of a major accident at a nuclear reactor or fuel-reprocessing plant, or by workers in severe industrial accidents involving mishandling of radioactivity.

At whole-body doses of 100 to 200 rem, the effects are mainly vomiting, fatigue, temporary sterility in males, and likely aborting of pregnancies of less than two months' duration. At doses of more than 200 rem, some early deaths (in the first 60 days) occur in the more sensitive members of the population, and the $LD_{50/60}$ (dose killing 50 percent of the exposed persons within 60 days of exposure) is generally taken to be 250 to 450 rem.[150] One report has argued that intensive medical care, including bone-marrow transplants, could increase the LD_{50} to 500 rem or more.[151] (The cause of death in the dose range below 1000 rem is infection and internal bleeding resulting from destruction of blood-forming cells in the bone marrow.) At doses above 1000 rem, death generally occurs within a week because of destruction of the lining of the gastrointestinal tract.

Delayed effects of large radiation exposures observed in survivors of the nuclear-bomb attacks on Japan in 1945 were most obvious among children who were *in utero* at the time of the explosion and were exposed to 10 to 150 rem; they suffered from a high incidence of microcephaly (small head circumference) and mental retardation.[152] The "emergency dose limit" promulgated by the International Council on Radiation Protection is 25 rem once in a lifetime. It is difficult to understand what operational significance this limit is intended to have.

The evidence is overwhelming that doses of radiation too small to produce the acute and early effects described above do produce a burden of extra cancers and genetic defects that is statistically predictable. The evidence on this point is of five kinds: (1) studies of the survivors of Hiroshima and Nagasaki; (2) studies of patients treated by radiation for nonmalignant diseases; (3) studies of

[145]Cosmic rays are mainly high energy protons and helium nuclei; these interact with nuclei in the atmosphere to form "secondary" particles and electromagnetic waves energetic enough to be ionizing radiation.

[146]Eisenbud, *Environmental radioactivity.*

[147]See, for example, United Nations Scientific Committee on the Effects of Atomic Radiation (UNSCEAR), *Ionizing radiation: levels and effects,* vol. 1, *Levels.*

[148]Ibid; NAS, *The effects on populations of exposure to low levels of ionizing radiation.*

[149]Ibid.

[150]See, for example, Eisenbud, *Environmental radioactivity,* pp. 20–22; Nuclear Regulatory Commission, *Reactor Safety;* UNSCEAR, *Ionizing radiation;* A. Casarett, *Radiation biology.*

[151]Nuclear Regulatory Commission, *Reactor safety.*

[152]R. W. Miller, Delayed radiation effects in atomic bomb survivors.

groups occupationally exposed to radiation, such as uranium miners and painters of radium dials on wrist watches; (4) studies of children whose mothers were X-rayed during pregnancy; (5) experimental studies on a wide variety of animals at varying doses and dose rates.

Induction of cancer in a population exposed to radiation is characterized by a latency period, during which no effect is evident, followed by a plateau period of elevated risk and then (for some cancers) a return to normal, spontaneous level of incidence.[153] For leukemia, the latency period may be as short as two years and the plateau of increased risk lasts about 25 years. For other cancers, the latency period may be 10 to 25 years, and studies of irradiated human populations have not yet revealed a termination of the plateau period.

The increase in cancer incidence due to radiation exposure is usually expressed as extra deaths per rem per million people exposed, or extra deaths per year per rem per million people exposed. The best estimate of the National Academy of Sciences 1972 review of these matters was an extra 200 cancer deaths (including those from leukemia) per million adults per rem.[154] This would represent an increase of about 2 percent in the "spontaneous" cancer rate. The percentage increase is much higher for children than for adults, and an important and, as yet, unresolved question is whether this *percentage* elevation of the cancer risk of an exposed child is maintained throughout life, as the spontaneous risk increases. The greatest sensitivity to development of cancer per unit of radiation dose is when the individual is exposed *in utero.*

Accounting for the age structure of the population, the NAS study estimated that increasing the background radiation exposure in the United States by 100 millirem per year would produce 3000 to 4000 additional cancer deaths per year and an equal number of nonfatal cancers. The uncertainty range given on their result spanned about a factor of 2, larger or smaller.

The assumption used by NAS and by all national and international standard-setting bodies is that the degree of elevation of risk of cancer is proportional to dose, down to the smallest doses and dose rates—the *linear hypothesis.* Some authorities believe that low doses and dose rates are less effective than higher ones at inducing cancer and that the linear hypothesis therefore represents an upper boundary on consequences.[155] Other experts have put forward arguments to suggest that the linear hypothesis could *underestimate* the risk at low doses.[156] A very useful property of the linear hypothesis in estimating potential effects of radiation exposure is that the distribution of a given number of "person-rem" does not matter; that is, 1 million person-rem is expected to produce the same number of cancers, whether it is delivered as 1 rem to each of a million people, or as 10 rem to each of 100,000 people, or in any other combination adding up to 1 million person-rem (as long as individual doses do not exceed the 200-rem threshold for early effects).

Concerning genetic effects of radiation, there is again some controversy about whether the linear hypothesis gives the best estimate of expected effects. There is evidence of the existence of biological mechanisms that can repair some kinds of genetic damage, and one might conclude, therefore, that there is a dose-rate threshold, below which the repair mechanisms could "keep up." On the other hand, it is likely that the repair mechanisms are imperfect—sometimes a "mistake" is made—and animal experiments exposing large populations to low doses of radiation have not been able to demonstrate the existence of a threshold. The NAS review estimated that an increase of 100 millirem per year in average radiation exposure to the U.S. population would produce at equilibrium (assuming a steady 3.6 million births per year) between 600 and 15,000 additional serious genetic effects per year, compared to a "natural" total of about 200,000.

Standards for permissible radiation exposure have been set by the responsible national and international bodies at levels where it is supposed that the benefits from the activities producing the exposure outweigh the harm done by the exposure. Of course, no rigorous calculation of such a balance is possible, and none has been seriously attempted. The standards in widespread

[153]NAS, *The effects.*
[154]Ibid.

[155]Nuclear Regulatory Commission, *Reactor safety.*
[156]See, for example, Karl Z. Morgan, Suggested reduction of permissible exposure to plutonium and other transuranium elements; J. Martin Brown, Linearity vs. nonlinearity of dose response for radiation carcinogenesis.

use are 5 rem per year (whole-body) for workers over 18 years of age occupationally exposed to radiation (no occupational exposure is permitted under 18), 10 times less (500 millirem per year) to individual members of the public, and 170 millirem per year average to large populations. These limits are for artificial radiation exposure exclusive of medical radiation, an omission many experts would like to see remedied.

A controversy initiated in the early 1970s by John Gofman and Arthur Tamplin of the University of California and Lawrence Livermore Laboratory accelerated a trend in the direction of tighter guidelines. Not long after these scientists began urging a drastic tightening in the standards, based on estimates of the substantial number of extra cancers that would result if 170 millirem per year were actually received on the average in the United States, the U.S. Atomic Energy Commission proposed as a "design objective" that doses to persons in unrestricted areas (i.e., outside the plant boundary) be kept "as low as is reasonably achievable." It was made clear that this would be interpreted to mean 5 millirem per year whole-body dose from gaseous effluents and 3 millirem per year from liquid effluents in the case of commercial light-water reactors—that is, a reduction of about 100-fold from previously accepted standards. The successor to the USAEC's regulatory responsibilities, the Nuclear Regulatory Commission, in 1975 adopted substantially similar design objectives for light-water reactors: 5 millirems to the whole body or to any organ from liquid effluents, 5 millirems to the whole body or 15 millirems to the skin from gaseous effluents.[157] In early 1977, the Environmental Protection Agency exercised its statutory authority to issue standards (which, unlike "design objectives," are unambiguously binding) applicable to *all* types of power reactors and other fuel-cycle facilities (e.g., uranium mills, reprocessing plants). These standards restrict the dose to members of the public from any facility to 75 millirems per year to the thyroid gland and 25 millirems per year to any other organ or the whole body.[157a]

[157]U.S. General Services Administration, *Code of Federal Regulations*, title 10, *Energy*, Part 50, Appendix I.

[157a]*Nuclear News*, EPA limits dose to public, releases from fuel cycle, February 1977, p. 30. The figures given are the limit for the sum of all exposure pathways: gases, liquids, particulates, and direct radiation.

TABLE 10-16
Maximum Permissible Concentrations for Some Important Isotopes

Isotope	*Ci/m³ in air*	*Ci/m³ in water*
Tritium	2×10^{-7}	3×10^{-3}
Carbon-14	1×10^{-7}	8×10^{-4}
Krypton-85	3×10^{-7}	not applicable
Strontium-90	3×10^{-11}	3×10^{-7}
Iodine-131	1×10^{-10}	3×10^{-7}
Cesium-137	5×10^{-10}	2×10^{-5}
Radon-222	3×10^{-9}	not applicable
Radium-226	2×10^{-12}	3×10^{-8}
Uranium-235	4×10^{-12}	3×10^{-5}
Uranium-238	3×10^{-12}	4×10^{-5}
Plutonium-239	6×10^{-14}	5×10^{-6}

Note: Figures are curies per cubic meter in air and water for public exposure. Where a distinction is made in the regulations between soluble and insoluble forms, the lower concentration is used here.

Source: U.S. General Services Administration, *Code of Federal Regulations.*

Maximum permissible concentrations (MPCs) of individual isotopes in air and water are published in the U.S. Code of Federal Regulations[158] for both occupational and public exposure. They have been based, for the most part, on an occupational dose of 5 rem per year and an individual public dose of 500 millirem per year. That is, the MPC for a given isotope in air in a nuclear-industry workplace is calculated so that a worker could not receive more than 5 rem per year from that isotope; the MPC for the same isotope in air breathed by the public would be smaller, both to account for full-time exposure and to produce the smaller maximum dose of 500 millirem per year. The MPCs account for the physical characteristics of the isotopes, including radioactive and biological half-lives and nature of the radiation, but not (in general) the possibility of concentration in food chains. Also, when more than one isotope is present at a time, as is usually the case, the concentrations must, of course, be kept below the single-isotope MPCs to keep the dose rate to the 5 rem per year or 500 millirem per year levels. The MPCs as of mid-1976 for some important isotopes are listed in Table 10-16.[159] The EPA's 1977 standards mean that nuclear power facilities will have to be operated in such a way that the average

[158]*Code of Federal Regulations,* title 10, part 20.

[159]Notice that to transform these standards to the mass basis generally used for conventional air and water pollutants—that is, micrograms per cubic meter in air or parts per million in water—one must apply the specific activity values in Table 10-15. For example, for tritium, 2×10^{-7} Ci/m³ ÷ 9700 Ci/gram = 2×10^{-11} grams/m³, or 0.00002 micrograms per cubic meter.

concentrations beyond the facility boundary are considerably lower than the MPC values given in the table.

A key unresolved issue in radiation standards at this writing is whether plutonium and perhaps certain other alpha emitters are more dangerous to health than was assumed in the derivation of the presently established MPCs for these isotopes. One element of the uncertainty has to do with the "hot particle" question—essentially, whether the nonuniform irradiation of tissue that results from the short range of alpha particles is more effective in producing cancer than uniform deposition of the same amount of energy.[160] Another issue is whether the ICRP model of the way the lung clears itself of foreign particles, which was used to derive the present standards, is valid.[161] The few experiences of accidental exposure of humans to known doses of plutonium cannot yet resolve the question of insoluble plutonium's toxicity: in one case (Los Alamos, 1944/1945), only 3 people were exposed to the insoluble form; the other case (Rocky Flats, Colo., 1965) was too recent for most of the cancers that may eventually appear to have done so by 1976.[162] Although it seems likely as of late 1976 that the most pessimistic version of the hot-particle hypothesis will not turn out to be correct, informed opinion seems to be converging on the view that plutonium is 5 to 200 times more dangerous than the existing MPCs imply.[163] If this is the case, the difficulties of a nuclear power economy based on recycling plutonium and perhaps other alpha emitters will be significantly magnified.

It is important to emphasize that radiation standards and the corresponding MPCs are established with the goal of protecting *human* health, primarily against the delayed effects (cancer and genetic defects) expected to occur even at low doses and dose rates. Although radiation of course affects organisms other than human beings, no plant or other animal is known to be significantly more sensitive. Some reasons why this is so for cancer and genetic defects are clear enough. For radiation-induced cancer, with its typically long latency period, rather few nonhuman organisms survive the other rigors of existence long enough for an extra cancer risk caused by radiation to express itself. For genetic defects, as noted in the previous section, human ethics and medical technology see to it that many defects are preserved and propagated in the population; in nonhuman organisms, most mutations are removed by selection.

Finally, it may be observed that radioactive materials are often deemed dangerous (if the standards are any guide) in physical quantities far smaller than those characteristic of most other toxic compounds. The relatively good record of a small nuclear industry in containing these materials so far (see Chapter 8 for more discussion and some exceptions) must be tempered with recognition of the difficulty of maintaining the nearly flawless containment desired as the size of the nuclear enterprise grows.

THE ENVIRONMENT AND CANCER

While we spend our life asking questions about the nature of cancer and how to prevent it, society merrily produces oncogenic substances and permeates the environment with them. Society does not seem prepared to accept the sacrifices required for effective prevention of cancer.

—Renato Dulbecco,
1975, on receipt of the Nobel Prize in medicine for his cancer research.

Cancer is the disease that most strikes fear into the heart of the average American, and cancers now are responsible for almost one-fifth of all deaths in the United States (Figure 10-6). This is less than half the toll now taken by arterial diseases, but the long, slow death frequently associated with cancer and the seemingly random way it selects its victims gives cancer a special horror. As biologist John Cairns, an expert on carcinogenesis, has said, "For some reason heart attacks and

---

[160]The hypothesis that nonuniform irradiation by insoluble particles of plutonium oxide in the lung can be much more effective at inducing cancer than uniform irradiation, and that the present standards (based on a uniform irradiation model) accordingly are several orders of magnitude too loose, was put forward by A. R. Tamplin and T. B. Cochran, *Radiation standards for hot particles,* and rebutted by W. J. Bair, et al., *A radiobiological assessment of the spacial distribution of radiation dose from inhaled plutonium.* See also the discussion of plutonium toxicity in Chapter 8.

[161]A critique of the ICRP model is J. W. Gofman, *The cancer hazard from inhaled plutonium.*

[162]J. Martin Brown, Health, safety, and social issues of nuclear power.

[163]K. Z. Morgan, Suggested reduction; Brown, Health, safety and social issues; J. T. Edsall, Toxicity of plutonium and other actinides; R. C. Thompson, Transuranium element toxicity.

strokes tend to be thought of as natural hazards of age, and either a normal end to a satisfactorily long life or, when they occur in middle-aged men, the wages of overeating and lack of exercise. In contrast, cancer is thought of as an unpredictable disease that strikes indiscriminately at rich and poor, fat and thin, old and middle-aged as if it usually owed nothing to external causes."[164]

It has, in fact, been almost exactly two centuries since external causes were first associated with cancer. In 1775 Sir Percival Pott published "Chirurgical observations relative to the cataract, the polypus of the nose, the cancer of the scrotum, the different kinds of ruptures, and the mortification of the toes and feet," in which he accurately noted that chimney sweeps were likely to contract cancer of the scrotum. It was a century later in 1875 that the next association was observed of an environmental factor with human cancer, when the induction of skin cancer was related to occupational exposure to coal tar (a substance chemically related to soot).[165] Many other examples of occupational carcinogenesis associated with such diverse substances as lubricating oils, dyestuffs, and radium paint were identified in the late nineteenth and early twentieth centuries.[166] And more recently cadmium, arsenic, asbestos, vinyl chloride, hair dyes, various pesticides, plutonium, and other materials to which those employed in certain industries are heavily exposed have been implicated (Box 10-5).

The degree of risk associated with occupational exposure to carcinogens can be quite spectacular. One-quarter of 366 males who worked in a coal tar dye plant in the United States between 1912 and 1962 contracted bladder cancer.[167] Considering how potent some chemical carcinogens appear to be, it is not surprising that the counties of the United States where the chemical industry is more highly concentrated show excessive rates of bladder, lung, liver, and certain other cancers among males.[168]

[164]The cancer problem, *Scientific American,* November 1975, p. 64.
[165]I. Berenblum, *Carcinogenesis as a biological problem,* chapter 1.
[166]E. Boyland, Cancer at work, *Nature,* September 18, 1975, pp. 170–171.
[167]C. J. Goldwater, A. J. Rosso, and M. Kleinfeld, Bladder tumours in a coal tar dye plant.
[168]R. Hoover and J. F. Fraumeni, Jr., Cancer mortality in U.S. counties with chemical industries.

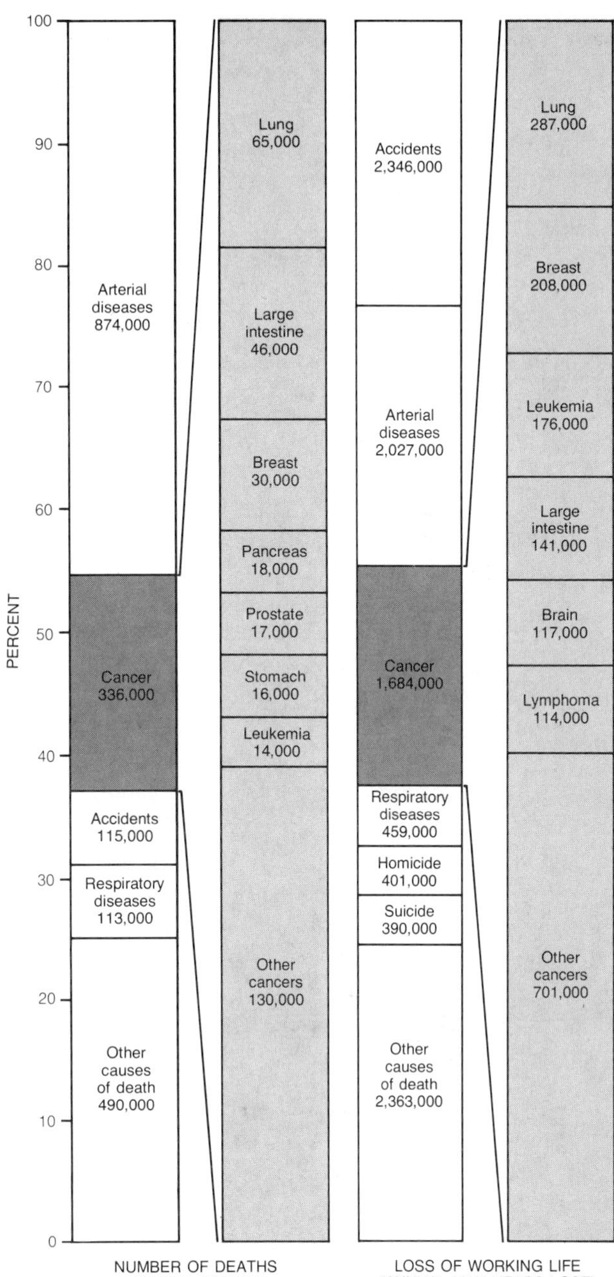

FIGURE 10-6

Deaths from cancer now make up almost a fifth of all deaths in the United States. Of the deaths attributed to cancer, more than 60 percent are caused by a few common forms of the disease. The remainder are distributed among more than 100 other cancers. The impact of each kind of cancer can also be judged from the shortening of life span it causes, measured here in lost working years, with working life assumed to extend from age 20 to age 65. Among all causes of death, the principal effect of considering shortening of life span instead of simple mortality is to increase the importance of accidents; among cancers, it emphasizes the relatively high incidence of leukemia in young people. Lung cancer, however, is still predominant. (After J. Cairns, 1975.)

BOX 10-5 A Potpourri of Chemical Carcinogens

A number of chemical carcinogens have already been discussed in the sections on air pollution, pesticides, and so on. There are, however, numerous other chemical carcinogens and suspected chemical carcinogens that are not readily classified by structure, mode of contact, or pattern of utilization of the compound (see Figure 10-7). Some of the more important of these are discussed here.

Carcinogens in Tobacco Smoke

In the 1964 Report of the Advisory Committee to the Surgeon General of the U.S. Public Health Service, a long series of epidemiological studies were cited that clearly associated lung cancer with smoking.[a] Although a very few scientists still claim that there is no causation in the correlation (i.e., that some common factors make people both prone to smoking and prone to lung cancer, but that the first does not cause the second), most differences of opinion focus on the nature of the carcinogens in the smoke. The majority of scientists are sure they are chemical carcinogens (thousands of different chemicals are produced by incomplete burning of the tobacco). The particular culprits might be polycyclic hydrocarbons (organic compounds having several fused rings—see Figure 10-7). Cigarette smoke condensate and various chemical fractions of it are quite mutagenic[b] and cause malignant transformation in tissue culture.[c] One researcher has argued, however, that the carcinogenicity of tobacco smoke is due to radioactive polonium, which collects on tobacco leaves.[d]

Asbestos

A rare form of cancer, mesothelioma, developing in the "skin" membranes lining chest and abdominal cavities, is strongly correlated with exposure to asbestos.[e] This substance is also implicated in cancer of the larynx, lung, and gastrointestinal tract.[f] About one-half of asbestos workers die of cancer, and the risks extend to the workers' wives and families, who are exposed to asbestos dust and fibers on workclothes. Furthermore, there is evidence from studies of asbestos workers that smoking and asbestos exposure act synergistically in producing cancer; that is, the risk of cancer to those exposed to both asbestos and smoking is very much greater than the sum of the risks of those exposed to one or the other.[g]

The general public is exposed to asbestos fibers in the air from brake drums, insulation, and the like, and in food and water from diverse sources. One of the most publicized pollution cases of the 1970s involved the contamination of Lake Superior with asbestos or asbestos-like fibers from taconite tailings being dumped in the lake by the Reserve Mining Company.[h]

Arsenic

Long known to be poisonous, arsenic has now been shown to be almost certainly involved in producing both respiratory and skin cancers in human beings. Male smelter workers show a strong correlation between degree of exposure to arsenic and incidence of respiratory cancers, although sulphur dioxide cannot be eliminated as a possible cause.[i]

In a local area of the southwest coast of Taiwan, water from artesian wells contains a high concentration of arsenic. Again, "the prevalence rate for skin cancer showed an ascending gradient according to the arsenic content of the well water, that is, the higher the arsenic content, the more patients with skin cancer."[j]

Nitrosamines

Nitrites are widely distributed in the environment and are commonly used in curing meat and fish. Nitrates are also common in soils and plants, as are microorganisms capable of reducing nitrates to nitrites. Secondary amines[k] may be present in a variety of foods, including cereals, mushrooms, various vegetables and fruits, fish, cheese, tea, wine, and beer. They are also found in some drugs. These amines have been shown to react with nitrite to form nitrosamines, some of which are potent carcinogens. Human beings may take in nitrosamines directly from the environment, or they may be synthesized from

[a] U.S. Department of Health, Education and Welfare, *Smoking and health;* a key study was E. C. Hammon and D. Horn, Smoking and death rates.

[b] L. D. Kier, E. Yamasaki, and B. N. Ames, Detection of mutagenic activity in cigarette smoke condensates.

[c] W. F. Benedict et al., Malignant transformations of mouse cells by cigarette smoke condensate.

[d] E. A. Martell, Tobacco radioactivity and cancer in smokers.

[e] R. J. C. Harris, Cancer and the environment.

[f] See references in P. T. Shettigara and R. W. Morgan, Asbestos, smoking and laryngial carcinoma.

[g] I. J. Selikoff et al., Asbestos exposure, smoking and neoplasia.

[h] See Luther J. Carter, Pollution and public health: taconite case poses major test.

[i] A. M. Lee and J. F. Fraumeni, Jr., Arsenic and respiratory cancer in man: An occupational study.

[j] W. P. Tseng et al., Prevalence of skin cancer in an endemic area of chronic arsenicism in Taiwan.

[k] Amines can be considered compounds derived from ammonia (NH_3) by substitution of organic radicals (R) such as CH_3 for one or more hydrogens. Primary amines have the formula RNH_2, secondary amines RRNH.

A.

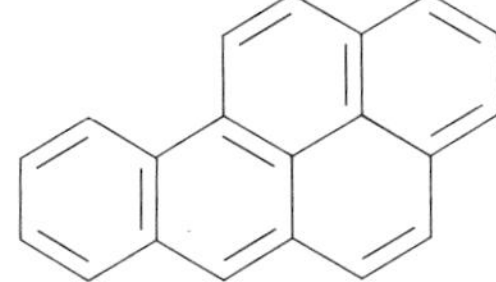

BENZPYRENE
(also called benzopyrene;
3,4-benzpyrene; benzo(a)pyrene),

A POLYCYCLIC AROMATIC HYDROCARBON

B.

BUTTER YELLOW
(4-dimethylaminoazobenzene, or DAB)

A CARCINOGENIC AZO COMPOUND

C.

$(CH_3)_2N-N=O$

DIMETHYLNITROSAMINE
(N-nitrosadimethylamine, DMN)

A NITROSAMINE (an alkylating agent)

D.

$R-N(CH_2-CH_2Cl)_2$

NITROGEN MUSTARD (an alkylating agent)

FIGURE 10-7

Chemical structures of four carcinogenic compounds. A and B are aromatic (containing benzenelike rings). Azo compounds have the N-N configuration. Alkylating agents are rather simple, highly reactive compounds that can combine with certain functional parts of key molecules in living cells. For details on what is known of the relationship between chemical structure and carcinogenesis, see Berenblum (1974) and references to the Ames group.

nitrite and secondary amines in the digestive tract. The degree of risk from nitrosamines is not certain at the moment, but a program at least to reduce the levels of their precursors in the diet would seem prudent.[l] Individuals can do this, for instance, by restricting their intake of cured meats, which contain large amounts of nitrates. Taking Vitamin C along with foods high in nitrites may help; there is some evidence that Vitamin C can block the synthesis of nitrosamines in the digestive tract.[m]

Hormones in Animal Products and Other Food Additives

Something on the order of 2500 different substances are being purposely added to the U.S. food supply. Most are added directly, but some are added indirectly by injection or implantation, or in animal feed. These substances include hormones and antibiotics which are used to promote growth and health in animals, and flavorings, colorings, preservatives, emulsifiers, stabilizers, and so on, added to processed foods.[n] Several of these substances have been implicated as carcinogens. For instance, diethylstilbestrol (DES), formerly fed to up to three-quarters of the cattle slaughtered in the United States, was connected with a rare kind of vaginal cancer affecting the *daughters* of women treated with DES to prevent threatened miscarriage. DES had also been shown to cause tumors in mice as early as 1964. These discoveries led to a regulatory mess that Nicholas Wade of *Science* magazine described in 1972 as follows: "The history of the attempt to control DES is a record that includes negligence, deception, and suppression by the USDA (U.S. Department of Agriculture) and prevarication by the FDA (Food and Drug Administration)."[o] The FDA did eventually ban DES, but the ban was reversed by the U.S. Court of Appeals in January 1974. Subsequently, the FDA revoked approved methods of identifying DES in meat, effectively banning it again.[p] The issue of the safety of estrogenic hormones as feed additives and implanted pellets is extremely complex, especially since similar hormones are present in human beings. The entire issue remains unresolved.[q]

Controversy has also marked the banning of other carcinogenic food additives, from cyclamates to red dye no. 2.[r] Much of the debate has centered on the Delaney clause. The clause, part of the U.S. Food, Drug, and Cosmetic Act of 1958, was named after its sponsor, Congressman James J. Delaney of New York. It states "no (food) additive shall be deemed to be safe if it is found to induce cancer when ingested by man or

[l]Material on nitrosamines from W. Lizinsky and S. S. Epstein, Nitrosamines as environmental carcinogens; P. N. Magee, Toxicity of nitrosamines: Their possible human health hazards; Nitrosamines: Ubiquitous Carcinogens? William Lijinsky, How nitrosamines cause cancer.

[m]Sidney S. Mirvish et al., Ascorbate-nitrite reaction: Possible means of blocking the formation of carcinogenic N-nitroso compounds.

[n]G. O. Kermode, Food additives.

[o]N. Wade, DES: A case study of regulatory abdication.

[p]*Environment,* September 1974.

[q]See, for example, H. H. Cole et al., On the safety of estrogenic hormone residues in edible animal products.

[r]For example, S. S. Epstein et al., Wisdom of cyclamate ban; P. M. Boffey, Color additives: Botched experiment leads to banning of red dye no. 2.

(*Continued*)

BOX 10-5 (*Continued*)

animal or if it is found, after tests which are appropriate for the evaluation of the safety of food additives, to induce cancer in man or animal." The food industry, with an enormous financial stake in many additives, and some scientists have argued that the Delaney clause is "unscientific"—largely because it leads to the banning of substances that have been shown to cause cancer after experiments in which animals were exposed to extremely high doses. The basis of this criticism is the hypothesis that there is a threshold dose below which the chemical will be noncarcinogenic. This hypothesis is rejected by most experts in the field, who support the Delaney clause as a necessary conservative bulwark against cancer caused by food additives.[s] Another common claim is that virtually anything in high enough doses will cause cancer—a claim that is simply false.

We conclude this sampling of the problems of chemical induction of cancers with the observation that they are not caused only by chemicals that human beings manufacture or deliberately expose themselves to. The high incidence of liver cancer in Africa and certain other tropical areas is associated with a product produced by the fungus *Aspergillus flavus.* The substance, *aflatoxin,* is an extremely potent carcinogen. The fungus grows on grain and root crops stored in humid conditions. The carcinogenic properties of aflatoxin were first suspected when a large number of turkeys died in Great Britain after being fed peanuts contaminated with *Aspergillus flavus.*[t]

[s]For example, Nicholas Wade, Delaney anti-cancer clause: Scientists debate on article of faith; Edward Edelson, Food laws should be even tougher.

[t]Harris, Cancer and the environment, p. 60; Denis P. Burkitt, Cancer and environment.

FIGURE 10-8

Geography of a cancer suggests a probable cause of the disease. The incidence of cancer of the large intestine among women in twenty-three countries is closely related to per-capita meat consumption in those countries. The data are adjusted to eliminate differences in age composition of the populations. An alternative explanation attributes cancer of the large intestine to a low consumption of cereals. The two hypotheses are hard to distinguish because high meat consumption and low cereal consumption tend to go together. (After J. Cairns, 1975.)

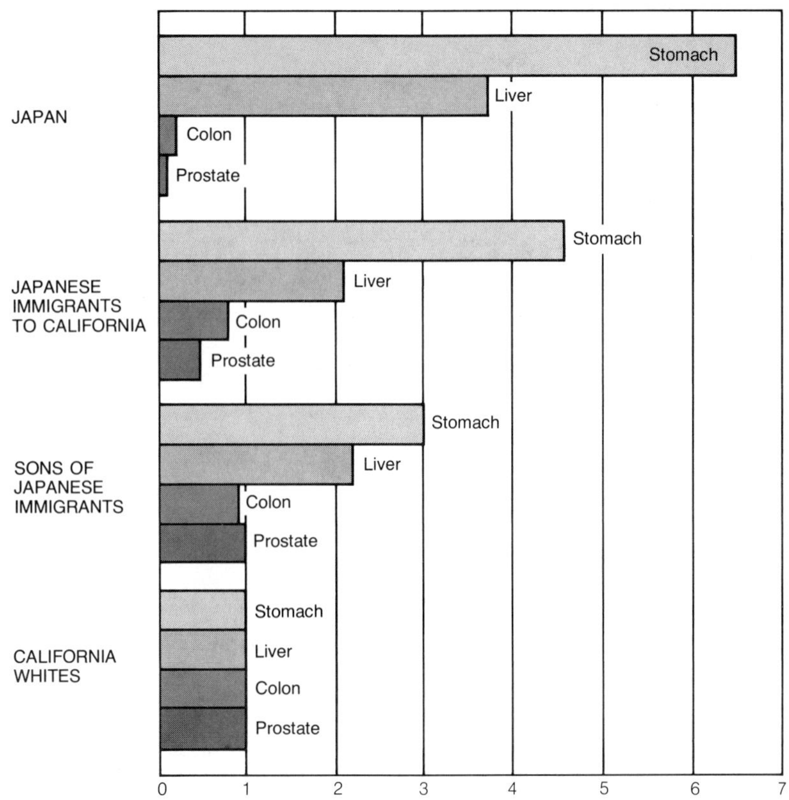

FIGURE 10-9

Change in the incidence of various cancers with migration from Japan to the United States provides evidence that the cancers are caused by components of the environment that differ in the two countries. The incidence of each kind of cancer is expressed as the ratio of the death rate in the population being compared to that in a hypothetical population of California whites with the same age distribution; the death rates for whites are thus defined as 1. The death rates among immigrants and their children tend consistently toward California norms, but the change requires more than a generation, suggesting that causative agents are factors influenced by culture rather than hazards to which all are exposed equally. (After J. Cairns, 1975.)

It was the uneven geographic distribution of many cancers that provided a major clue to their environmental origin. For example, Kangri cancer occurs in the abdominal wall of the Kangris of Tibet; the Kangris carry pots of heated charcoal under their clothes for warmth. Stomach cancer is much more common in Japan than in most other nations, and the incidence is high also in Iceland and Finland. The reasons for these foci are still obscure. Burkett's lymphoma is found commonly only in warm, moist areas, especially Africa and New Guinea, and seems to be associated with chronic malaria. Skin cancers are caused by ultraviolet radiation and are more common in sunny climes. Cancer of the bowel is the second most common cancer in most of Europe, North America, and New Zealand, but is rare in LDCs. It is thought that it is related to eating a great deal of animal fat, or possibly to low consumption of cereals (Figure 10-8). The list of geographic correlations is a long one, which we have only sampled.[169]

Further evidence of the environmental origins of various cancers is found in data on migrants. For example, when Japanese move to the United States, the high level of stomach cancer among them tends to disappear, and the frequency of other cancers tends to converge with that of white Americans (Figure 10-9). The patterns can be explained by gradual changes in such cultural factors as diet.

Despite the early and extensive association of cancers with exposure of workers to various chemicals and to radiation, and despite the extensive geographic correlations, only recently has the environmental induction of nearly all cancers been widely recognized. It is now generally accepted that *at least three-quarters of human cancers are "environmental" in origin* (that is, not caused

[169]For further examples, see R. J. C. Harris, Cancer and the environment; and D. P. Burkitt, Cancer and environment.

by viruses, spontaneous breakdown of immune mechanisms, and the like).[170]

The exact mechanism of carcinogenesis remains a mystery, though much recent evidence supports the old theory that mutation within a body cell may be the key initiating event in most environmental carcinogenesis.[171] This evidence shows that carcinogens function by mutating the genetic apparatus (DNA) of a cell, altering its hereditary properties in ways that lead to its uncontrolled proliferation. Almost all chemical carcinogens appear to interact directly with the base pairs of DNA molecules or to be metabolized by the body to active forms that interact with the DNA.[172] There are different types of these mutagenic active forms that can produce frameshift mutations or base-pair substitutions, which alter the genetic message coded into the base sequence of the molecules.[173]

The picture of carcinogenicity that is gradually emerging is one in which somatic mutations (those occurring in body cells other than those that produce sperm or eggs) lead to the production of new lines of genetically identical cells (clones) that are "fitter" than other lines. That is, the new clones are able to outreproduce other clones and, freed of the normal constraints on cell reproduction, invade other adjacent tissues.[174] The lethality of cancers is, however, strongly associated with the ability of cancerous clones not only to invade neighboring tissues, but also to colonize distant tissues—that is, to *metastasize.* Therefore, whatever genetic changes occur in the cell must also produce the ability of cells swept into blood or lymphatic circulation to found cell colonies in alien tissues where cell-cell interactions are unlike those of the tissue where the cancer clone got its start. There does not seem to be any universal metastatic ability (cancers normally colonize rather specific tissues). For instance, lung cancers tend to move to adrenal glands and brain, prostate cancers to the bones, and brain cancers normally are not metastatic.[175]

One theory of carcinogenesis holds that each cell is prevented from becoming cancerous by a series of genes. What is required for a cancer to start up, according to this model, is a series of mutational steps. First a normal cell must be subject to a mutational event that alters one of the restraining genes but that does not so damage the cell that it cannot reproduce. This cell carrying the somatic mutation then gives rise by cell division to a clone of mutant cells, each lacking one restraining gene. In turn, a viable mutation in the new line may lead to a clone lacking two of the restraints. Repeats of this process eventually lead to a precancerous state (perhaps a benign growth) and then a full-blown malignancy. This hypothetical process is diagramed in Figure 10-10.

Models of carcinogenesis, in which a sequence of subcellular events culminates in cancer, have great appeal because they lead to an explanation of two of the most important features of cancers. One is the common pattern of increased incidence with age (there are a few exceptions to this) and the other the long latent period (often 20 years or more) that seems frequently to occur between first exposure to carcinogens and the clinical appearance of the disease. A striking example is cancer of the penis, a rare cancer found only in elderly men. It can be prevented by circumcision in the first few days of life, but may occur if circumcision is delayed for only a few years.[176] The carcinogenic process in this case must be initiated early in life—perhaps some substance that accumulates under the foreskins of babies is capable of causing an "initiating" mutation that alters a key restraining gene or otherwise makes the tissue susceptible to a later "precipitating" step or steps, which produce the actual cancer.[177]

Whatever the actual mechanism of carcinogenesis, it is clear that one must not search for the cause of a particular cancer only in the immediate past environment of its

[170]For example, S. S. Epstein, Environmental determinants of human cancer.

[171]Cairns, The cancer problem; M. McCann, et al., Detection of carcinogens as mutagens; McCann and Ames, Detection of carcinogens.

[172]McCann and Ames, Detection of carcinogens.

[173]B. N. Ames, W. E. Durston, E. Yamasaki, and F. D. Lee, Carcinogens are mutagens: A simple test system combining liver homogenates for activation and bacteria for detection. There has been criticism of the equating of mutagenesis and carcinogenesis (for example, H. Rubin, Carcinogenicity tests), but the weight of evidence tends to support the hypothesis (B. N. Ames, Carcinogenicity tests).

[174]For example, John Cairns, Mutation selection and natural history of cancer; Sir Macfarlane Burnet, The biology of cancer, in J. German, ed., *Chromosomes and cancer.*

[175]Cairns, The cancer problem.

[176]Ibid, p. 67.

[177]Harris Busch, Introduction, in *The molecular biology of cancer,* Harris Busch, ed., p. 18.

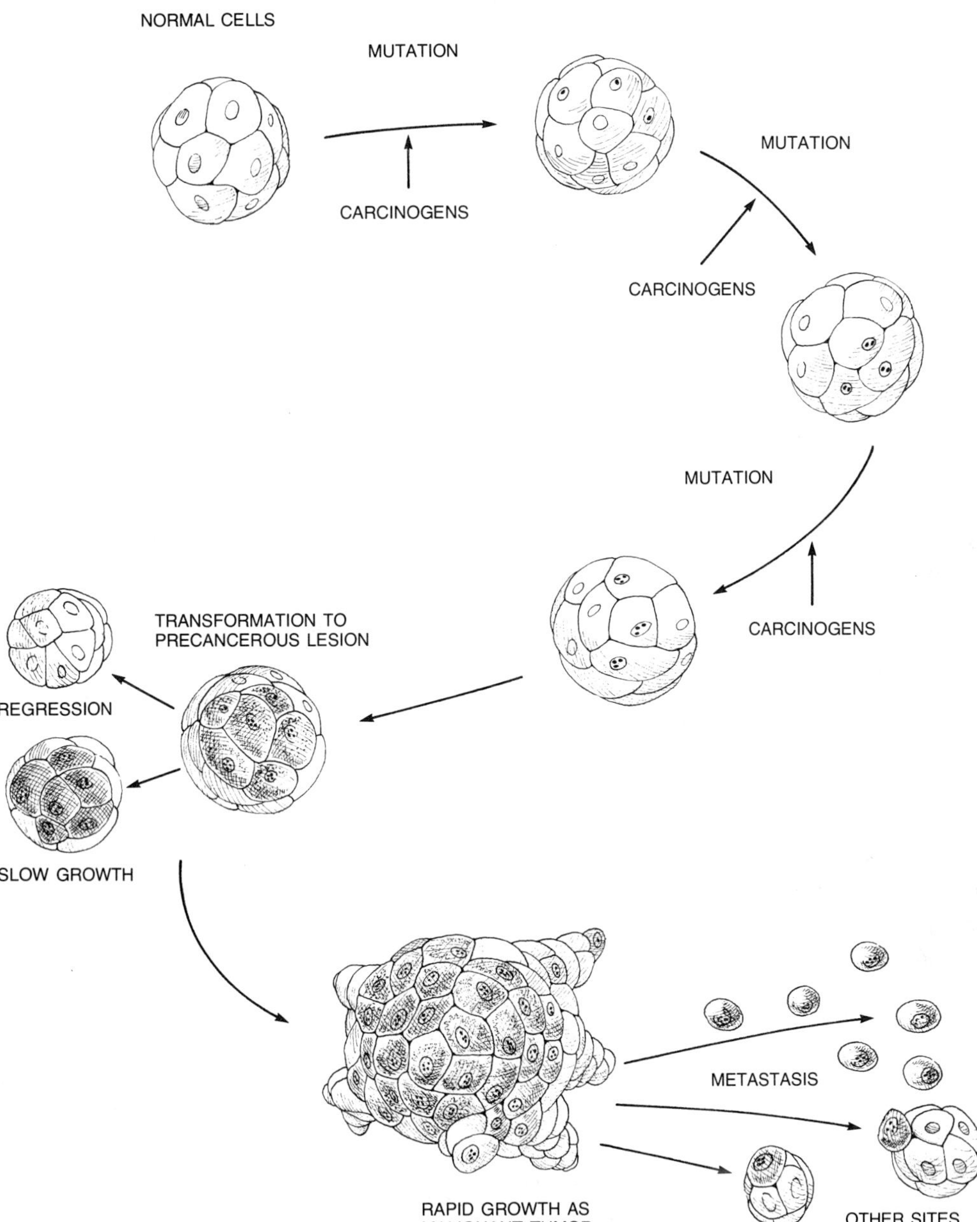

FIGURE 10-10

One theory of carcinogenesis states that cells are restrained from becoming cancerous by several independent genes and that tumors develop only when mutations accumulate in all those genes within a single line of cells. The mutations (black dots within cell nuclei) are seldom spontaneous but are apparently caused by carcinogenic factors in the environment. Once a precancerous lesion has formed, it must in many cases regress or grow very slowly; only a few lesions progress to an invasive, metastasizing tumor. (After J. Cairns, 1975.)

victims. For example, in several nations the occurrence of lung cancer is correlated not with present smoking habits but with cigarette consumption 20 years ago.[178] Equally, if a new carcinogen is introduced into the environment today, it may be two or three decades before the cancers it causes begin to show up in the mortality tables.

The problem of the latent period thus greatly enhances the difficulty of evaluating the carcinogenic hazards of various environmental factors. In retrospective studies it is often difficult to determine exposure levels in the distant past. In prospective studies it may be necessary to wait 30 or more years for definitive results. For these reasons scientists have tended to move toward studies of carcinogenesis in nonhuman organisms, where short life histories greatly reduce the problem of the latent period, and careful experimental exposures to suspected carcinogens are possible.

Almost all tests of carcinogenicity are done in rats and mice, although some suspected carcinogens have been tested in studies with dogs (notably beagles, in the case of plutonium). When tumors are induced in the experimental animals, it is clear only that the test substance can produce cancer in the experimental system. The question of carcinogenicity in human beings remains open. In general, if a substance is carcinogenic in one mammal, it will be in another, although exceptions are known. For example, 2-napthylamine is a potent inducer of bladder cancer in dogs, monkeys, and people, but not in mice, rats, guinea pigs, or rabbits.[179]

A further complication of animal tests is the need to use very high doses of the substance being screened—the usual recommendation being that the maximally tolerated dose (MTD) be administered. (The MTD is that dose producing neither weight loss nor increased noncancer mortality.) The use of the MTD is necessary because of the small numbers of animals used in tests (often around 50). For example, if a carcinogen produced one cancer in each of 100 human beings exposed (more than 2 million cancers if the entire U.S. population were exposed), the chances of detecting carcinogenicity in an experimental group of 50 mice with the same equivalent dose and susceptibility are essentially zero. Indeed, some 8000 mice would have to be treated (with 8000 controls) to produce a reasonably certain demonstration[180] that the material could induce cancer if there were the usual number of tumors in the controls. (The numbers given are based on a 10 percent incidence of tumors in the controls, which is common.)

When animal tests do reveal a substance to be carcinogenic, attempts to halt its use or restrict exposures are often protested on the grounds that mouse cancers are not human cancers and that the doses used in the experiments were unreasonably large ("a 165-pound man would have to eat 45,000 pounds of bacon a day every day for 600 days to get the same effect").[181] But there is no way to demonstrate that an animal carcinogen will not produce human cancers at some dose level or in some human groups or in combination with some other substance. The high experimental doses, of course, are required to permit detection of carcinogenesis in small test groups of animals. Furthermore, it is just as likely that people would be even more susceptible to the carcinogen than the test animals as that they would be less so. For these and related reasons it is impossible to determine a safe dose of a known carcinogen—which is the *raison d'être* of the 1958 Delaney Amendment, which establishes a "zero tolerance" for food additives that produce cancers in any test animals (Box 10-5).

The properties of carcinogenic materials (structure of chemical compounds, type of ionizing radiation emitted) are obviously related to their ability to intervene in cellular machinery. As noted in the discussion of radiation, it is already possible to make a reasonable prediction about the dangers of a radiation source on the basis of the kind and energy of the emission (alpha, beta, gamma, neutron, and so on) and where inside or outside the body the emission takes place. Similarly, members of certain groups of chemical compounds such as polycyclic hydrocarbons (organic compounds with a multiple ring structure—benzpyrene, benzanthracene, and the like) are always suspect because of the kinds of reactions to which

[178]Ibid.

[179]Epstein, Environmental determinants, p. 2427. Material in the following paragraph is also derived largely from this source.

[180]Probability would be less than 0.05 that the observed difference between treated and control mice was due to chance alone.

[181]Dr. William Sherman of the National Livestock and Meat Board, commenting on tests on rats of the carcinogenicity of nitrates—compounds used in curing bacon (Palo Alto *Times*, February 13, 1976).

their structure makes them prone. The identification of chemical carcinogens is complicated, however, by accumulating evidence that noncarcinogenic environmental pollutants are often transformed into carcinogens by the machinery of the body and that it is these end products that share the key chemical properties.[182] This is not surprising, considering the phenomenon of activation of chemical mutagens discussed previously and the apparent relationship between mutagenesis and carcinogenesis. This activation phenomenon may be one of the reasons for those differences in susceptibility to the same compound among different species. In the tissues of a fruit fly a given compound may be broken down into harmless metabolites; in the tissues of a human being they may be converted into a potent cancer-inducing agent.

One of the most hopeful signs in the battle against chemical carcinogens has been the recent development of the Ames test. Biochemist Bruce Ames of the University of California at Berkeley and his colleagues have invented a system that employs a set of strains of the bacterium *Salmonella typhimurium* to test a chemical for mutagenicity. The strains are especially sensitive to mutagens for several reasons. One is that a repair system (present in all normal living things) that monitors DNA and corrects most but not all of the damage has been eliminated in the test bacteria.[183] The mutant strains cannot grow normally because they are unable to synthesize the amino acid histidine. When the billion or more bacteria in a test plate are exposed to a mutagen, however, there is a good chance that the defective DNA code sequence of at least one bacterium will be changed back into a sequence that properly codes for the manufacture of histidine. Such a "reverted" mutant bacterium will then be the founder of a normally growing colony on the plate. The level of activity of a given mutagen will be related to the number of reverted colonies per test plate. The test combines on a single Petri plate these bacteria and a rat (or human autopsy) liver homogenate, which provides the mammalian metabolism that converts precarcinogens to their active mutagenic forms.

The success of the Ames test has itself added to the evidence that cancers are initiated by somatic mutations. In initial studies, eighteen known polycyclic chemical carcinogens were shown by Ames and his colleagues[184] to be potent mutagens after they were "activated" (converted to mutagenic form) by liver enzymes from rats and human beings. Subsequent studies proved 157 (90 percent) of 175 known carcinogens mutagenic, while of 108 "noncarcinogens" only 14 gave positive test results, and many of these may be due to the statistical limitations of animal cancer tests for showing noncarcinogenicity. Japan for eight years permitted use of furylfuramide as a food additive after it had been "cleared" of carcinogenicity in two sets of animal experiments. After it was later shown to be mutagenic in bacteria it was reevaluated and found to be a carcinogen in another animal test.[185]

The great advantages of the Ames test as a tool for detecting environmental carcinogens are its sensitivity and speed and the low cost of screening a compound. A standard test by the National Cancer Institute (NCI) using mice or rats costs roughly $100,000 and takes three years.[186] A test with the Ames screen costs roughly $200 and takes three days![187]

That the enormously expensive War on Cancer has been a catastrophic failure has been widely recognized. Most of the statistical progress in cancer survival rates apparently has not come from that war but from reduced death rates on operating tables attributable to improved surgical techniques and use of antibiotics to stem postsurgical infections.[188]

Two factors have been responsible for the failure. First, eager politicians have poured vast amounts of money into seeking a "cure," on the unlikely assumption that cancer was a single disease amenable to treatment with a single miracle drug. This trend was opposed by

[182]T. H. Maugh, Chemical carcinogenesis: A long-neglected field blossoms; J. Miller and E. C. Miller, Chemical carcinogenesis: Mechanisms and approaches to its control.

[183]B. N. Ames, F. D. Lee, and W. E. Durston. An improved bacterial test system for the detection and classification of mutagens and carcinogens.

[184]Ames et al., Carcinogens are mutagens.

[185]J. McCann, E. Choi, E. Yamasaki, and B. N. Ames, Detection of carcinogens as mutagens in the *Salmonella*/microsome test: Assay of 300 chemicals; R. Lewin, Bacteria to be used to detect cancer-causing chemicals; McCann and Ames, Detection of carcinogens.

[186]National Academy of Sciences, Contemporary pest-control practices and prospects: The report of the executive committee, p. 64.

[187]R. Lewin, Cancer hazards in the environment, p. 168.

[188]D. S. Greenberg, Stalemate in cancer treatment.

knowledgeable molecular biologists who understood that information about the basic mechanisms of cancer was inadequate to justify such an effort. Among biologists, the "war" was often compared to trying to send men to the moon before the discovery of Newton's laws of motion.

The second factor was a lack of recognition that cancers are largely environmentally caused, with a resultant distortion of research priorities toward cure rather than prevention—and toward "high-powered" science. The scientists most involved in the "war" were largely recruited from the ranks of surgeons, biochemists, radiologists, and virologists—mostly people with little interest in studying the release of carcinogens into the environment or the possible nutritive factors involved in the induction of cancers. This has led, for example, to a continued expenditure of more than $50 million annually into the unsuccessful and unpromising search for human cancer viruses, compared to only $3 million spent on nutritional investigation. As the distinguished science reporter Daniel Greenberg, put it, "A partial explanation is that nutrition is a low prestige field, and easily evokes the image of high school cafeteria dieticians, whereas virology wins Nobel prizes."[189]

Cancer researcher Dr. Philippe Shubik recently summed up the situation in a statement to the National Cancer Advisory Board: "It is a universal opinion that cancer can be attributed to environmental factors in the main. . . . Cancer is largely a preventable disease."[190] Whether his words will be heeded remains an open question. In the mid-1970s it appeared likely that billions of dollars will be spent during the rest of this century, attempting to cure people whose sickness could have been prevented.

NOISE POLLUTION

Noise pollution as a widespread phenomenon is as old as the industrial age. The problem recently has been thrown into sharp focus by the discovery that some teenagers were suffering permanent hearing loss following long exposures to amplified rock music, and by public concern about the effects of sonic booms caused by supersonic transports (SST). But noise pollution is much more pervasive than these extreme examples indicate. Studies of nonindustrialized peoples in Africa and India have indicated that progressive loss of hearing with age, which is universal in industrial societies, is not a natural part of aging but a consequence of the noisy modern environment.[191]

TABLE 10-17
Noise Levels (in decibels)

Threshold of hearing	1
Normal breathing	10
Leaves rustling in breeze	20
Whispering	30
Quiet office	40
Homes	45
Quiet restaurant	50
Conversation	60
Automobile	70
Food blender	80
Niagara Falls at base	90
Heavy automobile traffic, or jet aircraft passing overhead	100
Jet aircraft taking off, or machine gun at close range	120

Noise is usually measured in decibels (abbreviated *db*). A tenfold increase in the strength of a sound adds 10 units on the decibel scale; a 100-fold increase adds 20. Silence, defined somewhat arbitrarily as the average human threshold of hearing, is represented as zero decibels. The formal definition of the decibel scale is

$$\text{decibels} = 10 \log_{10}\left(\frac{\text{measured intensity}}{\text{average human hearing threshold intensity}}\right).$$

Table 10-17 gives the decibel values of some representative sounds. Actually, the human ear responds differently to different sound frequencies; high-frequency sounds are perceived as louder than low-frequency sounds of the same actual intensity. Accordingly, many investigations of noise pollution employ a weighted scale that accounts for the sensitivity of the human ear. It is called the "A-weighted scale of sound levels," and its units are abbreviated "db(A)."

Even a brief exposure to intense noise can cause temporary loss of hearing acuity. Permanent loss of hearing follows chronic exposure to high noise levels. Noise levels as low as 50 to 55 decibels may delay or

[189]Stalemate, p. 25.
[190]Quoted by Lewin, Bacteria to be used.

[191]ReVelle and ReVelle, *Sourcebook*,. p. 162.

interfere with sleep and result in a feeling of fatigue on awakening. Recently there has been growing evidence that noise in the 90-decibel range may cause irreversible changes in the autonomic nervous system. Noise may be a factor in many stress-related diseases, such as peptic ulcer and hypertension, although present evidence is only circumstantial.[192] Not surprisingly, noise can also cause stress and other physiological disturbances in animals other than people, including reproductive problems and altered predator-prey relations.[193]

Noise pollution is clearly a growing threat to health and happiness. Even if the biosphere is not subjected to the booms of large-scale commercial use of the SST, the need for noise abatement will continue to be serious. Unless action is taken against the proliferation of motorcycles, "tote-goats," power lawnmowers, motorboats, noisy appliances, and the like, they will make aural tranquility, even in the wilderness, a thing of the past. Possibly, however, this problem will prove to be more readily solvable with technology, imagination, and determination than most pollution problems.

THE WORK ENVIRONMENT

Serious as the general environmental levels of chemical pollutants, radiation, and noise may be, exposure to such insults in the work environment is usually much more intense. This is cause for great concern for a number of reasons. The first, of course, is concern for the lives of the individuals exposed to the hazard, even when those exposed are a tiny fraction of the population (as, for example, in the case of the uranium miners discussed in Chapter 8). Second, very large numbers of people are occupationally assaulted by high concentrations of some dangerous substances (e.g., asbestos, vinyl chloride, benzpyrene). Third, the effects of occupational exposure extend beyond the working population. Asbestos fibers on workmen's clothes threaten their families and friends; mutated genes in workers exposed to radiological or chemical mutagens are spread into the population outside of the workplace. And fourth, inadequate standards for the confinement of dangerous substances in the workplace make them a focus for contamination of adjacent areas or for accidental contact with nonworkers. A woman living downwind from a plant using vinyl chloride died of *hemangiosarcoma*,[194] a rare cancer associated with this chemical.[195] A child who dipped one finger into an open can of TEPP (tetraethylpyrophosphate, an extremely toxic pesticide—see Appendix 3) later sucked the finger and died.[196]

Every year some 100,000 to 200,000 new synthetic chemicals are made available to industry and about 500 go into commercial use.[197] But to date, the hazards associated with only about 500 chemicals altogether have been evaluated and some sorts of exposure standards established. Society in essence is playing Russian roulette with the untested chemicals now in use and the largely untested annual flood of new ones.

The problems of protecting workers and the general public are exemplified by the vinyl chloride (VC) story. VC, a chlorinated hydrocarbon, is not a rare chemical found only in a few laboratories or one to which only a few workers are exposed. VC itself is used as an aerosol propellant for solvents. More importantly, it is a key component of the pervasive plastic polyvinyl chloride (PVC), from which the VC frequently escapes. PVC is found almost everywhere—in records, boots, furniture, wrapping paper, electrical insulation, pipes, and films. It is estimated to contribute $12 billion to the U.S. gross national product annually. Worldwide, plants producing VC and PVC employ an estimated 70,000 workers, and millions work in plants where VC and PVC are used. Perhaps one-third of humanity is daily exposed to PVC in one form or another.[198]

The economic stakes involved with VC are clearly enormous. It is therefore not surprising that the giant chemical corporations involved in production of 12 million tons of it per year[199] were slow to accept the evidence that it was carcinogenic. In the face of building

[192]Aage R. Møller, Noise as a health hazard; How good are work noise standards?

[193]Ibid.

[194]Hemangiosarcoma is a mixture of a *hemangioma*, a tumor consisting of blood vessels, and a *sarcoma*, a cancer arising from bone, muscle, or other connective tissue. The term *angiosarcoma*, often found in the literature on vinyl chloride, means the same thing.

[195]C. Levinson, The malevolent workplace, p. 26.

[196]D. P. Sachs, Work at your own risk.

[197]Levinson, The malevolent workplace.

[198]Data from Levinson, ibid., which is the source for much of the material on VC that follows.

[199]C. Maltoni, The value of predictive experimental bioassays in occupational and environmental carcinogenesis.

TABLE 10-18
Work Environment Standards in Different Countries

	USA-OSHA 1974	*Federal Republic of Germany 1974*	*German Democratic Republic 1973*	*Sweden 1975*	*Czechoslovakia 1969*	*USSR 1972*
	(mg/m^3)	*(mg/m^3)*	*(mg/m^3)*	*(mg/m^3)*	*(mg/m^3)*	*(mg/m^3**)*
Acetic acid	25	25	20	25	–	5
Acetone	2400	2400	1000	1200	800	200
Ammonia	35	35	25	18	40	20
Aniline	19	19	10	19	5	0.1
Antimony and compounds (as Sb)	0.5	0.5	0.5	0.5	–	0.3–2
Arsenic and compounds	0.5	0	0.3	0.05	0.3	0.3
Benzene	30	0	50	30	50	5
Beryllium	0.002	0	0.002	0.002	–	0.001
1,3-Butadiene	2200	2200	500	–	500	100
Butyl alcohol	300	300	200	150	100	10
Cadmium (metal dust and soluble salts)	0.2	–	0.1*	0.05	–	0.1
Carbaryl (Sevin)	5	5	–	–	–	1
Carbon disulfide	60	60	50	30	30	10
Carbon monoxide	55	55	55	40	30	20
Carbon tetrachloride	65	65	50	65	50	20
Chlorine	3	1.5	1	3**	3	1
Cobalt, metal fume and dust	0.1	0.5	0.1	0.1	0.1	0.5
Cyclohexane	1050	1050	–	–	–	80
2,4-D	10	10	–	–	–	1
DDT	1	1	1	–	–	0.1
p-Dichlorobenzene	450	450	200	–	–	20
Dichlorvos (DDVP)	1	1	–	–	–	0.2
Dieldrin	0.25	0.25	–	–	–	0.01
Diethylamine	75	75	50	–	–	30
Dinitrobenzene	1	1	1	–	1	1
Dioxane	360	360	200	90	–	10
Ethyl acetate	1400	1400	500	1100	400	200
Ethyl alcohol	1900	1900	1000	1900	1000	1000
Ethyl amine	18	18	20	–	–	1
Ethyl chloride	2600	2600	2000	–	–	50
Ethyl ether	1200	1200	500	1200	300	300
Ethylene imine	1	1	1	0	–	0.02
Fluoride (as F)	2.5	2.5	–	2.5	1	1
Formaldehyde	3	1.2	2	3**	2	0.5
Furfural	20	20	10	–	–	10
Hydrogen cyanide	11	11	5	11	3	0.3

evidence that the compound could have serious health effects, they pressed to retain old standards that allowed workers to be exposed to VC at concentrations of 1500 milligrams per cubic meter (mg/m^3) of air. In April 1974 the Occupational Safety and Health Administration (OSHA), in response to the deaths of four workers from hemangiosarcoma, issued a temporary emergency standard of 150 mg/m^3. In October of the same year, a permanent standard of 3 mg/m^3 (1 ppm of vinyl chloride gas) was established. The final standard was established only after legal appeals by the industry had been struck down in court.[200] Industry argued, among other things, that they could not refine their measuring techniques sufficiently to meet the new standards. This statement was patently false. Indeed, "In many cases the same corporations who testified that the technology is not available were the same corporations which have contracted with the Department of Defense to develop these monitoring devices."[201]

[200]Council on Environmental Quality, *Environmental quality, 1975,* p. 104.

[201]Levinson, The malevolent workplace, p. 27.

TABLE 10-18 (*Continued*)

	USA-OSHA 1974	Federal Republic of Germany 1974	German Democratic Republic 1973	Sweden 1975	Czechoslovakia 1969	USSR 1972
	(mg/m³)	(mg/m³)	(mg/m³)	(mg/m³)	(mg/m³)	(mg/m³**)
Hydrogen fluoride	2	2	1	2**	1	0.5
Hydrogen sulfide	30**	15	15	15	10	10
Lead, inorganic fumes and dusts	0.2	0.2	0.15	0.1	0.05	0.01
Lindane	0.5	0.5	0.2	–	–	0.05
Manganese and compounds (as Mn)	5**	5	5	2.5	2	0.3
Mercury, metal	0.1**	0.1	0.1	0.05	0.05	0.01
Methyl alcohol	260	260	100	260	100	5
Methylene chloride	1740	1750	500	350	500	50
Molybdenum, insoluble compounds	15	15	10	–	–	6
Naphtha (coal tar)	400	–	–	–	200	100
Naphthalene	50	50	20	–	–	20
Nickel carbonyl	0.007	0.7	–	0.007	–	0.0005
Nickel, metal	1	0	0.5	0.01	–	0.5
p-Nitrochlorbenzene	1	1	1	–	1	1
Ozone	0.2	0.2	0.2	0.2	0.1	0.1
Phenol	19	19	20	19	20	5
Phosgene	0.4	0.4	0.5	0.2**	0.4	0.5
Pyridine	15	15	10	15	5	5
Selenium compounds	0.2	0.1	0.1	0.1	–	0.1
Sodium hydroxide	2	2	2	2**	–	0.5
Styrene	420	420	200	210	200	5
Sulfur dioxide	13	13	10	5	10	10
Sulfuric acid	1	1	1	1	1	1
Tetraethyl lead (as Pb)	0.075	0.075	0.05	0.075	–	0.005
Toluene	750	750	300	375	200	50
Trichloroethylene	535	260	250	160	250	10
Trinitrotoluene	1.5	1.5	1.5	–	1	1
Turpentine	560	560	300	560	–	300
Uranium, soluble compounds (as U)	0.05	0.05	–	–	–	0.015
Uranium, insoluble compounds (as U)	0.25	0.25	–	–	–	0.075
Vinyl chloride	3	–	500	3	–	30
Xylene	435	870	200	435	200	50
Zinc oxide fume	5	5	5	5	5	6

*As CdO.
**Ceiling value.
Source: Margareta Winell, An international comparison of hygienic standards for chemicals in the work environment.

The problems of protecting people from chemical, radiological, and physical[202] insult in the workplace are very complex. Society, for example, has clearly decided that conditions within the workplace 10 to 100 times worse than those encountered outside of it are tolerable—as differing standards set by the Environmental Protection Agency (EPA) and OSHA show. For example, it is permissible for a worker in the United States to be exposed for eight hours daily to 13 mg/m³ of sulfur dioxide, whereas EPA limits for the general public are exceeded if the concentration goes above 1.3 mg/m³ for three hours once a year.[203] Even accepting this assumption, it remains extremely difficult to assess the actual hazards associated with exposure to the level allowed.

Although nations that establish standards for exposure presumably all have the same goal, those standards vary a great deal from country to country (Table 10-18). For example, standards tend to be much more rigorous in the

[202]See, for example, I. Ostrand et al., Heat stress in occupational work.

[203]B. Commoner, Workplace burden.

Soviet Union than in the United States, especially for substances like chlorinated hydrocarbons, which affect the central nervous system, and alkylating agents such as ethylene imine, which generally are mutagenic.[204] In a less developed country like India, concentrations of many substances above the OSHA limits are regularly encountered.[205] In the latter case, deleterious effects may be exacerbated by the general poor health and nutrition of the workers.

An especially vexing problem is that of carcinogenesis in the workplace, which may even differentially affect workers in different parts of the same industrial plant.[206] A major difficulty with cancer prevention is, of course, the latent period—the time between first exposure to an occupational carcinogen and the first clinical evidence of cancer. This period is usually 20 to 35 years, although it may be as short as 10 years or as long as 50 or more.[207] Until satisfactory screening procedures are developed (and the Ames test should be a big help here) and are coupled with rigorous controls, workers will continue to play the role of guinea pigs.

It is very important that unions become even more deeply involved in these problems—especially in seeing that more research on health hazards is done, coordinated internationally, and carried out by agencies other than corporations, which may have a vested interest in the results. They can also work to see that physicians are better informed on the hazards peculiar to various work environments and also, through political action, see to it that standards are set conservatively and are enforced rigorously.

If the unions do not get the job done, it won't be done, because the initiative clearly will not come from government or industry. Charles Levinson, secretary general of the International Federation of Chemical and General Workers Union, the union that led the worldwide fight to improve VC standards, put it very well:

> The battles to control already known hazards, such as asbestos, vinyl chloride and arsenic have yet to be won by the workers. The latency period for effective legislation to control industrial cancers appears to be longer than the latency period of the disease. The key to the problem is not in the scientific lag, but rather the economic and political lag. The familiar slogan "Safety Pays" is really a cruel joke. Safety does not pay, it costs. It costs corporations money to be safe; it takes money to finance studies on occupation diseases; it costs in down-time when a noxious or lethal substance floods the workplace; it costs in efficiency when workers have to wear respirators at their jobs. These costs do not add a penny to the balance sheets. The profit-motivated allocation of resources within a company does not often permit a high priority for industrial safety.[208]

GEOLOGICAL HAZARDS

Geological hazards, such as landslides—or even earthquakes—are sometimes caused by human activities. These include changing the contours of land for housing or industrial construction or building large dams to meet the needs of growing populations for additional supplies of fresh water.

When Lake Mead was filled (1939) following the completion of Hoover Dam, thousands of seismic events—the largest of which was an earthquake with a magnitude of 5 on the Richter scale—were recorded in that previously inactive area. Large dams in other usually inactive regions of the world have caused numerous earthquakes with magnitudes greater than 6, large enough to do substantial damage to urban areas. An earthquake that registered 6.4 on the Richter scale was triggered by the filling of the Kogna Dam in India in 1967, causing 200 deaths.[209] Some geologists suspect that the lowering of water tables, now a worldwide occurrence, could have similar effects.

In 1967 the consequences of four years of pumping fluid chemical wastes into an underground reservoir near Denver became clear. A series of earthquakes occurred, the three largest of which had magnitudes of about 5; slight damage was reported in Denver. The amount of

[204] M. Winell, An international comparison of hygienic standards for chemicals in the work environment.

[205] N. L. Ramanathan and S. Kashyap, Occupational environment and health in India.

[206] See, for example, C. K. Redmond, et al. Long-term mortality of steelworkers. pt. 4, Mortality from malignant neoplasms among coke-oven workers.

[207] I. J. Selikoff, Recent perspectives in occupational cancer.

[208] The malevolent workplace, p. 25.

[209] G. J. F. MacDonald, The modification of the planet Earth by man.

energy released in the series of earthquakes was slightly greater than that released by a 1-kiloton atomic bomb, more energy than was expended in pumping the fluid into the reservoir. The remaining energy had been stored in the Earth's crust by geologic processes, and its release was triggered by the injection of fluid into the underground reservoir.[210]

In 1963, the bottom of the Baldwin Hills reservoir in the Los Angeles area ruptured, causing water to burst through the dam, flooding suburbs below. Fortunately, there was enough warning that the inhabitants could be evacuated in time. The cause of the reservoir failure was eventually traced to the fact that it had been situated over ancient faults, which evidently were reactivated by fluid injection in nearby oil fields for oil recovery and waste disposal.[211]

Underground nuclear explosions also have the potential for releasing such stored energy. Although the widely discussed Amchitka test in 1971 did not induce a major quake, that in no way guarantees that future tests will not serve as triggers to set off earthquakes that may be far more serious than any yet caused by human intervention in the dynamics of the Earth's crust. On the other hand, knowledge gained from underground injections and explosions may permit use of them to relieve stresses that, if allowed to accumulate, could lead to major earthquakes.

Another human-induced geological hazard is ground subsidence. The problem here is the destruction of homes and other structures when the surface sinks due to the removal of water, oil, or large quantities of ore from beneath.[211a]

In addition to humanity's capability of triggering geological misfortunes, poor planning, partly abetted by rapid population growth, increases the impact of natural geological phenomena. Thus homes and apartment buildings have been built on potentially unstable landfill in the earthquake-prone San Francisco Bay area, schools and homes sit virtually astride the infamous San Andreas fault in the same vicinity, and residences cover steep hills subject to downhill creep and mudslides in the wet season. An equally absurd situation is heavy settlement in floodplains. (How, then, can the inevitable flood be called a natural disaster?) This problem has often been compounded by clear-cut logging of associated watersheds, which destroys the ability of the land to retain water and thus intensifies flooding (see also Chapter 6).

[210] J. H. Healy et al., The Denver earthquakes.

[211] D. H. Hamilton and R. L. Meeham, Ground rupture in the Baldwin Hills.

[211a] For a much more thorough discussion of subsidence, as well as of landslides, see H. W. Menard, *Geology, resources, and society,* chapter 14, and P. T. Flawn, *Environmental geology.*

THE HUMAN ENVIRONMENT

In addition to the physical consequences to human beings of environmental deterioration, it is useful to consider what kind of environment they are best adapted to. What size groups does a person feel most comfortable in? How important is solitude for the well-being of the human psyche? Is the color green, which is known to have a soothing effect, an important component of the human environment? Have human beings evolved to feel most comfortable in a certain kind of environment, and, if so, can evolution rapidly adapt *Homo sapiens* to a new one? Such questions have been the subject of extensive speculation, but they are exceedingly difficult to answer. In theory, for instance, natural selection could change certain human characteristics dramatically in six to eight generations—in only about 200 years (although this would involve a very large portion of the population's not reproducing in each generation). But other characteristics may be so ingrained in the human genetic-developmental system that they would be impossible to change without much longer periods of genetic readjustment, or the changes might even be so traumatic as to lead to extinction.

To give an analogy, one may, by selection, experimentally create a strain of fruit flies that is resistant to DDT in six to eight generations, presumably as a result of some minor changes in enzyme systems or behavior. It seems unlikely, however, that any number of generations of selection would produce a fruit fly able to fly with one wing; in fact, an attempt to produce such a change by artificial selection would probably lead to extinction of the experimental population.

Some biologists feel that humanity's evolutionary history has been such that the present environments to which people are being subjected figuratively amount to flying with one wing. This general viewpoint has been expressed by three biologists at the University of Wisconsin, who believe that mankind's genetic endowment has been shaped by evolution to require "natural" surroundings for optimum mental health:

> Unique as we may think we are, we are nevertheless as likely to be genetically programmed to a natural habitat of clean air and a varied green landscape as any other mammal. To be relaxed and feel healthy usually means simply allowing our bodies to react in the way for which one hundred millions of years of evolution has equipped us. Physically and genetically, we appear best adapted to a tropical savanna, but as a cultural animal we utilize learned adaptations to cities and towns. For thousands of years we have tried in our houses to imitate not only the climate, but the setting of our evolutionary past: warm, humid air, green plants, and even animal companions. Today, if we can afford it, we may even build a greenhouse or swimming pool next to our living room, buy a place in the country, or at least take our children vacationing on the seashore. The specific physiological reactions to natural beauty and diversity, to the shapes and colors of nature (especially to green), to the motions and sounds of other animals, such as birds, we as yet do not comprehend. But it is evident that nature in our daily life should be thought of as a part of the biological need. It cannot be neglected in the discussions of resource policy for man.[212]

There is little consensus among cultures, or even within our own culture, on what sort of an environment best provides an optimal quality of life. In addition, there is very little experimental evidence on how varying such factors as the density of the population, the level of noise, or the amount of green in the environment may alter human behavior.

It is known from the systematic observations of anthropologist Edward T. Hall that peoples of different cultures have different perceptions of "personal space."[213] It is not clear, however, how much such differences are attributable to the *perception* of crowding as opposed to *tolerance* of crowding. For instance, do the residents of Tokyo feel uncrowded at densities that might make residents of Los Angeles feel intolerably crowded, or are the Japanese somehow better able to tolerate the crowding, even though their perceptions of it may be essentially the same?

There is almost no information on the levels of crowding at which people feel most happy and comfortable and can perform various tasks with the greatest efficiency. It is not known whether high density during one part of the daily routine (at work, for example) coupled with low density at another (at home) would have the same effects as medium density throughout the day. It is not known exactly what role high density may play in mental health and the incidence of stress diseases[214] nor whether density alone can be a contributing cause to riots. People have many opinions about such questions, but there is little solid information on which to base conclusions.

Some experimental work on the effects of crowding on human beings has been done by psychologist Jonathan Freedman and his associates in collaboration with one of us.[215] In short-term experiments, no differences were found between crowded and uncrowded groups in performance of a series of tasks. When games were played that permitted competitive or cooperative strategies to be adopted, or when other measures of social interaction were used, the results were more interesting. In all-male groups a crowded situation produced significantly higher levels of competitiveness. In all-female groups the result was reversed; the women in crowded circumstances were more cooperative, while those in less crowded conditions were more competitive. In mixed groups (both sexes present) crowding had no detectable effect.

These results must be interpreted with much caution. They suggest that all-male juries should be avoided, as well as groups of men making world-shaking decisions in crowded rooms. But the results do not reveal much about the more general effects of crowding in human populations, except to reinforce the notion that human beings can adapt readily to what *a priori* might seem to be difficult conditions—at least, as far as task-performance is concerned.

[212]H. H. Iltis, P. Andrews, and O. L. Loucks, Criteria for an optimum human environment.

[213]*The hidden dimension;* see also Robert Sommer, *Personal space.*

[214]John Cassel, Health consequences of population density and crowding.

[215]P. R. Ehrlich and J. Freedman, Population, crowding, and human behavior; J. L. Freedman, *Crowding and behavior.*

Much of the discussion of effects of crowding on human beings has been based on extrapolation from the results of behaviorist John Calhoun's classic studies of crowded rats.[216] The assumption is sometimes made that the kinds of social and physical pathologies he observed in crowded rats will sooner or later turn up in populations of people if they become too crowded. What studies exist on human populations have provided conflicting or ambiguous results. The chief difficulty is to untangle density effects from other social factors such as poverty, unemployment, lack of education, and rates of migration.[217] Even if high density does lead to social pathology in people, it is clear that many other limiting factors would come into play before the human population grew to the point where density itself set a limit. After all, people living in the most crowded cities, such as Manhattan and Tokyo, have not shown social pathologies to a degree sufficient to halt population growth. If only one-fourth of the land surface of Earth were populated to the density of Tokyo, the world population would be about 600 billion people. Clearly, something besides density itself—famine, plague, war—will stop the growth of the human population long before that point is reached.

Due to the lack of data, we must resort to speculation in further discussion of the psychological and social effects of human crowding. In dealing with a high population density, the Japanese seem to have developed a variety of cultural devices to alleviate the stress. It has been suggested that their very formal and elaborate etiquette may be one mechanism for self-protection against the inevitable frictions of constant human encounter. The Japanese have been relatively crowded for a long time; by 1870 Japan had 82 people per square kilometer. Thus, a century ago, Japan had almost four times the population density of the United States today.

In contrast to the Japanese and the Europeans, who also have had high population densities for several generations, people from currently or recently low-density countries (such as the United States or Australia) are likely to have reputations of being informal and easygoing, or even bumptious and rude. The Japanese are famous for their interest in aesthetic values, which they demonstrate in their arts and their lovely gardens. They also successfully create an illusion of space where there is very little in their homes and buildings, a talent that possibly contributes much to domestic serenity.

People generally are unaware of the influence that population size and density have upon their ways of life and their perceptions of the world. After all, these factors usually do not change drastically in times on the order of a generation or less. When they do change rapidly, as they are today in many less developed countries, the result seems more likely to produce disruption than gradual social change. Around 1910 the United States had about half the number of people it has today. Society then differed from today's in ways that cannot be entirely explained by the processes of industrialization and urbanization or by such historical events as two world wars, a depression, and two "limited" wars. Such qualities as friendliness and neighborliness, once common in this country and generally esteemed, now seem to exist primarily in rural areas, small towns, and occasionally in enclaves in big cities. In myriad ways the lives of Americans have become more regulated and regimented, a trend that is at least partly due to population growth. Few would claim that such changes contribute positively to the quality of American life.

The Urban Environment

The deterioration of the U.S. environment, both physically and aesthetically, is most apparent in cities. The dehumanizing effect of life in the slums and ghettoes particularly, where there is little hope for improving conditions (Figure 10-11), have often been cited as causes contributing to urban rioting and disturbances. Crime rates usually reach their zenith in these neighborhoods. Such symptoms of general psychological maladjustment suggest that modern cities provide a less than ideal environment for human beings.

There seems to be abundant evidence that traditional cultural patterns break down in cities, and also that the high numbers of contacts with individuals not part of one's circle of regular social acquaintances may lead to

[216]Population density and social pathology.
[217]O. R. Galle, W. R. Gove, and V. M. McPherson, Population density and pathology: What are the relationships for man?

FIGURE 10-11

Attempts at urban renewal to provide housing for the poor are not always successful. This huge project in St. Louis was so badly designed that some buildings had been abandoned and were scheduled for demolition only fifteen years after they were built. (Photo by William A. Garnett.)

mental disturbance (defined here merely as behavior generally considered disturbed by the majority of the society). It is important to note that antisocial behavior and mental illness are found in all cultures, and that indeed the same disorders recognized by psychiatrists in the West are found even in primitive peoples. Therefore, it seems reasonably certain that lack of a natural environment (where *natural* refers to the sort of environment in which *Homo sapiens* evolved) is not the sole cause of such behavior. Nevertheless, that lack may well serve to aggravate the problems of people living in our most crowded, smoggy, and impersonal metropolises.

Crime rates are some 5 times as high in urban as in rural areas. Though some of this difference may be due to disparities in reporting, not all of it can be explained on this basis. Such factors as unemployment, poverty, and a poor social environment undoubtedly contribute, as well. Some studies have shown rates of violent crimes to be positively correlated with actual population densities in American cities.[218] As urban population densities have risen in the past generation, so have crime rates.

However, none of these studies show that crowding alone causes crime. Indeed, careful statistical studies show that density itself is not positively correlated with crime rates or other social pathologies.[219] Jay Forrester has suggested that the rate of migration into a city is more highly correlated with crime rates.[220] More recent work indicates that crowding *per se* is neither good nor bad but merely tends to intensify each individual's reaction to a given situation.[221] The only exception is that crowding may have a slight association with minor mental disturbances.[222]

The environmental deterioration of American cities is most obvious to the poor who live in them. For them, environmental deterioration has nothing to do with the disappearance of fish and wildlife in national forests or litter in campgrounds. Their concern is ghetto ecology, including the wildlife in their homes—rats, mice, and cockroaches. Air pollution reaches its highest levels in city centers; here also are there most likely to be inadequate sewage and solid-waste disposal systems. Heat in winter is often insufficient, space is at a premium, crime rates and vandalism are high, food is often inadequate, medical care is poor at best, opportunities for recreation are virtually nil, schools are at their worst, and public transportation is expensive and inconvenient. In short, all the problems and disadvantages of cities are greatly intensified for the poor. This environmental syndrome is reflected by higher death rates among the poor (especially infant and child mortalities) than for the general population.

---

[218]Crime rate vs. population density in United States cities: A model, R. L. Kyllonen.

[219]I. Pressman and A. Carol, Crime as a diseconomy of scale; O. R. Galle, J. D. McCarthy, and W. Gove, Population density and pathology; Irving Hoch, City size effects, trends, and policies.

[220]Jay W. Forrester, Counterintuitive behavior of social systems.

[221]Ehrlich and Freedman, Population, crowding, and human behavior; J. Freedman, *Crowding and behavior.*

[222]Freedman, *Crowding and behavior,* p. 142.

FIGURE 10-12

Many urban problems are largely the result of unplanned, haphazard development. Planning could avoid the serious problems of congestion, transportation, and destruction of valuable land that accompany urban sprawl, as exemplified here. Mass-production techniques are used to cover huge areas in the Los Angeles basin with houses in a few months. *Upper left.* Land cleared for building. *Upper right.* Foundations poured and lumber stacked neatly for each unit. *Lower left.* Siding and roofs in place. *Lower right.* The result. (Photos by William A. Garnett.)

Of course, many, if not most, of the present hazards and discomforts of city life could be eliminated or mitigated by more creative design of houses and neighborhoods (Figure 10-12), by the development of alternative, less-polluting means of transportation, by finding solutions to the problems of racial minorities and the poor in general, and by more efficient and equitable forms of administration. If urban areas were planned and developed so people could live near their places of employment, many problems related to transportation would be alleviated, including congestion and pollution from automobiles. Making the vicinities of factories pleasantly habitable would present some problems but would result in considerable pollution abatement. Similarly, the social problems created by the separate existence both of suburban bedroom communities and city-center ghettoes might also be relieved. Of course, all of this requires vast infusions of time, imagination, and money, all of which are in short supply.

Aesthetic Considerations

Some destitute mountain folk from the Appalachians, who were moved to New York where jobs were available, promptly fled back to the mountains, preferring poverty amid pleasant surroundings to life in such a horrible place. The aesthetic poverty of U.S. cities and suburbs has reached such a degree that most citizens are aware of it. Newspapers are replete with stories describing slums, ghettos, rats, trash, and garbage. This is one of the reasons why weekends and holidays invariably bring on a mass exodus from the cities. Unfortunately, frontier habits of thoughtless littering and defacement seem likely to reduce attractive rural areas and state and national parks to similar levels of ugliness.

Studies with young animals and indirect evidence from young children indicate that the richness of the sensory environment early in life influences the extent of later mental development. Sensory stimulation in young rats resulted in measurably larger brain sizes in adulthood than in their sensorily deprived litter-mates, and it affected their learning and problem-solving abilities as well. Children who have been exposed to a variety of sights, sounds, and experiences when they are very young may learn faster and later on be more likely to develop attitudes of inquiry and exploration.

Yet cities, once a rich source of varied sensory experiences, are becoming more monotonous and dismal. Modern urban development programs flatten blocks at a time—blocks that once included a mixture of buildings of different ages and styles—and then replace them with concrete monoliths that lack aesthetic quality. The variety of sounds, at least some of which were pleasing to hear, in smaller towns and on farms, is also coming to be replaced by an incessant din of traffic and construction.

A zoologist with an interest in environmental psychology, A. E. Parr of the American Museum of Natural History, has written that city children of a generation or two ago spent much of their time exploring and participating in the activities of the city, while today children are confined to dreary schoolrooms, their homes, and the local park. Poorer ones may play in the streets, and in this respect perhaps they are luckier. But many of today's city children are being deprived of firsthand knowledge about the city they live in and how the social organizations within it function, which creates a sort of alienation from their surroundings. At the same time their surroundings are becoming more and more monotonous and less attractive. Children's urges toward inquisitiveness, exploration, and ingenuity (qualities that will be desperately needed in the next generation) may thus be stifled outside the schools as well as in them.[223]

Suburbs are often better than the cities in aesthetic qualities and sensory stimulation, but not invariably so. Although the environment is usually more natural and includes trees and gardens, many suburbs tend to reduce everything to a common denominator. All the houses in a given area are similar, if not identical, and so are the gardens, parks, and shopping centers. Each modern real-estate development is generally inhabited by people of about the same age, educational level, type of employment, and economic status. There is not much opportunity for children to meet people whose points of view differ from their own or those of their parents. Although the children may be freer to explore in the suburbs than in the city, there is sometimes even less of interest to find there. The absence of men most of the time may result in an even greater alienation of youngsters (and wives as well) from the functioning society. Of course, television may compensate somewhat for the lack of sensory and social variety in children's lives, but it does not encourage inquisitiveness or offer opportunities for exploration, ingenuity, or direct experience. On the contrary, it may foster passiveness and a tendency to regard life as a spectator sport.

THE EPIDEMIOLOGICAL ENVIRONMENT

Today the population of *Homo sapiens* is the largest in the history of the species, it has the highest average density, and it contains a record number of undernourished and malnourished people. The population, or rather a small but important segment of it, is also unprecedentedly mobile. People are in continual motion around the globe, and they are able to move from continent to continent in hours. The potential for a worldwide epidemic (pandemic) has never been greater, but people's awareness of this threat has probably never been smaller. Contrary to popular belief, "medical science" has definitely not conquered epidemic disease, as recent experience with

[223] A. E. Parr, The five ages of urbanity.

influenza, cholera, typhoid, yellow fever, and Lassa fever have shown.[224]

The behavior of viruses is not completely understood, but it is known that the spontaneous development of highly lethal strains of human viruses and the invasion of humanity by extremely dangerous animal viruses are possible. It is also known that crowding increases the chances for development of a virus epidemic. Should, say, an especially virulent strain of flu appear, it is doubtful that the United States and other developed countries could produce enough vaccine fast enough to save most of their populations. Needless to say, the problem would be even more severe in the LDCs. Certainly, little effort could be made to save most of humanity. Consider, for example, the difficulty the United States had in coping with the mild Asian flu epidemic of 1968. It was not possible to manufacture enough vaccine to protect most of the population, and the influenza death rate in 1968 was more than 4 times as high as that of 1967. Only 613 deaths were attributed to flu, but society paid a high price for the disease in extra medical care and loss of working hours. That the number of deaths was not higher was due primarily to the relatively mild character of the virus, rather than to modern medicine. More recently, the swine flu fiasco of 1976–1977 certainly did not build confidence that public health machinery will be able to cope competently with future epidemic threats.

In 1967 an outbreak of a previously unknown disease occurred among a shipment of vervet monkeys that had been imported into laboratories in Marburg, Germany, and in Yugoslavia. This severe, hemorrhagic disease infected 25 laboratory workers who came into contact with the monkeys and their tissues. Seven of those people died. Five secondary infections occurred in individuals who came into contact with the blood of the original patients; all of those individuals survived. Humanity was extremely fortunate that the first infections of *Homo sapiens* by Marburg virus occurred around laboratories where the nature of the threat was quickly recognized, and the disease contained (it was not susceptible to antibiotics). If it had escaped into the human population at large, and if the disease had retained its virulence as it passed from person to person, an epidemic resulting in hundreds of millions or even billions of deaths might have occurred. Among well-fed laboratory workers with expert medical care, 7 out of 30 patients died.[225] Among hungry people with little or no medical care, mortality would be much higher. The infected monkeys passed through London airport in transit to the laboratories. If the virus had infected airport personnel, it could have spread around the world before anyone realized what was happening. In addition, it is hardly reassuring that infection of laboratory workers with viruses is a rather common occurrence, and the potential virulence of possible "escapees" from labs is increasing.[226]

The highly mechanized society of the United States is also extremely vulnerable to disruption by such events as power failures, floods, and snowstorms. What would happen if the nation were confronted with an epidemic that kept masses of sick people from work and caused the uninfected to stay home or flee the cities because of their fear of infection? This might slow or even stop the spread of the disease, but hunger, cold (in the winter), and many other problems would soon develop as the services of society ceased to operate. Almost total breakdown has been known to occur in much less complex societies than the U.S. in the face of the black death–breakdown that occurred among people far more accustomed to a short life, hardship, disease, and death than the population of the Western world today.[227] The panic may well be imagined if Americans were to discover that "modern medical science" either had no cure for a disease of epidemic proportions, or had insufficient doses of the cure for everyone. The disease itself would almost certainly impede the application of any ameliorating

---

[224]L. K. Altman, Hong Kong flu is affecting millions in wide areas around world, *New York Times,* January 18, 1970; H. Schwartz, Influenza: Yes you really had it; and H. Schwartz, Cholera now spreading to remote regions: Eruption is the most widespread since 1899 pandemic, *New York Times,* September 26, 1971; B. Dixon, Typhoid bacilli learn a new trick; J. Lederberg, Yellow fever still is a menace, J. G. Fuller, *Fever: The hunt for a new killer virus;* T. Monath et al., Lassa virus isolation from *Mastomys natalensis* rodents during an epidemic in Sierra Leone.

[225]R. E. Kissling et al. Agent of disease contracted from green monkeys. More recent cases contracted in parts of Africa (outside laboratories) have been reported, including several hundred deaths. (New outbreak of Marburg disease, *New Scientist,* October 28, 1976, p. 199.)

[226]For example, R. P. Hanson, et al., Arbovirus infections of laboratory workers; N. Wade, Microbiology: Hazardous profession faces new uncertainties.

[227]W. L. Langer, The black death.

measures. Distribution of vaccines, for instance, would be difficult if airlines, trains, and trucks were not running.

In many parts of the world, public-health conditions are developing that have a high potential for disaster. The rats that live on stored grain in India have renewed the specter of a major outbreak of bubonic plague. Nitrate pollution of water is creating conditions in which dangerous soil organisms are brought into contact with human beings for the first time. The organism that has recently caused cases of a fatal meningitis has been identified as a soil-dwelling amoeba.[228] It may be just the first of many such agents to appear seemingly from nowhere.

Irrigation projects in the tropics and subtropics around the world are spreading the conditions that promote the parasitic disease *schistosomiasis (bilharzia),* which, together with malaria, is one of the two most prevalent serious diseases on Earth.[229] The broadcast use of chemotherapy and antibiotics has created a serious medical problem through the introduction of resistance in bacteria and other parasites. Modification of the climate would also inevitably influence disease patterns; for example, the length of time viruses remain infectious is in part a function of humidity. A trend toward drying would encourage some, whereas others would thrive in increased moisture. It is suspected, in addition, that weather changes can trigger epidemics.[230]

As if the threat of a natural pandemic were not gruesome enough, there is always the threat of biological warfare or of an accidental escape of lethal agents from a biological warfare laboratory or, conceivably, from a laboratory engaged in genetic engineering experiments (see material on recombinant DNA research in Chapter 14). Although most laypeople have long been afraid of thermonuclear war, they are just beginning to grasp the colossal hazard posed by chemical and biological warfare (CBW). Any country with one or two well-trained microbiologists and even a modest budget can build its own biological doomsday weapons. Constructing lethal viruses against which there is little or no resistance in human populations can easily be done in theory; it may already have been done in practice. There were at one time rumors of the development by the American CBW establishment of a pneumonic rabies, one that, instead of being transmitted by bite, is transmitted in the same way as the common cold: from person to person via exhaled droplets. This is certainly possible, since under special conditions (such as those that sometimes occur in caves full of rabid rats) rabies appears to have been transmitted through the air. Such a disease would be a disastrously effective weapon if it were transmitted by infected individuals before symptoms appear, since once they do appear, rabies is (with one notable recent exception) 100 percent fatal. Other possibilities for lethal agents are many—for example, anthrax, which even in its "natural" state can be transmitted by contaminated aerosols, plague, tularemia, Q-fever, and encephalitis, to name a few[231]—disseminated in their natural forms or in the form of special "hot" strains that are drug-resistant or superlethal. Besides direct assaults on human beings, overt or covert attacks on a nation's food supply might be made by introducing plant diseases. The more crowded a population is, and the smaller its per-capita food supplies, the better a target it would be for a biological warfare attack.

Why would nations develop such weapons? For the same reason they develop others. They hope to immunize or otherwise protect their own populations and thus avoid a biological backlash. These weapons have a special appeal for small and poor powers, which see themselves threatened by larger, richer ones and which lack the funds or the expertise to develop nuclear weapons.[232]

Chemical-biological weapons may never be used, but that does not rule out the possibility of an accident. Virus laboratories, especially, are notoriously unsafe. By 1967, some 2700 laboratory workers had become accidentally infected with viruses transmitted by insects, and 107 had died.[233] Their deaths were caused by just one group

[228] J. H. Callicott, Amebic meningo encephalitis.

[229] K. S. Warren, Precarious odyssey of an unconquered parasite; N. Ansari, *Epidemiology and control of schistosomiasis.*

[230] K. E. F. Watt, *Ecology and resource management,* McGraw-Hill, New York, 1968, p. 162 ff.

[231] F. M. LaForce et al, Epidemiologic study of a fatal case of inhalation anthrax; J. Lederberg, Swift biological advance can be bent to genocide.

[232] M. Meselson, Behind the Nixon policy for chemical and biological warfare.

[233] Hanson, et al., Arbovirus infections.

of viruses. Fatal accidents occur in laboratories where work is done on other kinds of viruses, as well as other microorganisms. The inability of government CBW agencies to avoid accidents was made clear by the Skull Valley, Utah, CBW disaster of 1968, in which many thousands of sheep were poisoned when a chemical agent "escaped,"[234] and by the possible escape of Venezuelan Equine Encephalitis from the Dugway, Utah, proving ground in 1967. Congressman Richard D. McCarthy of New York announced in 1969 that CBW agents were being transported around the country in small containers *on commercial airliners!*

In 1969, President Nixon announced the unilateral renunciation by the United States of the use of biological warfare, even in retaliation.[235] He directed that the stocks of biological agents be destroyed and that further work on defenses against biological weapons be transferred from the Department of Defense to the Department of Health, Education and Welfare. Destruction of U.S. biological warfare materials was systematically carried out in 1970 and 1971, although in 1975 it was discovered that the Central Intelligence Agency had not destroyed some toxins in its possession.

[234]P. M. Boffey, 6000 sheep stricken near CBW center.
[235]M. Meselson, Chemical and biological weapons, *Scientific American,* May 1970.

Some level of research might be continuing clandestinely in the United States (although the possibility seems remote), and it would be a simple matter for a future administration quickly to reestablish biological warfare capability. Indeed, with the rapidly increasing ability of biologists to manipulate the genetics of microorganisms, the possibilities for creating deadly agents seem endless.[235] Furthermore, there is little sign that the U.S. action has led to the end of work on biological weapons elsewhere. Biological warfare laboratories are potential sources of a man-made "solution" to the population explosion. It is essential that some way be found to block all further work on biological weapons—the risk for humanity is simply too great.

It should be clear now that humanity is creating an enormous array of hazards that directly threaten the health and welfare of all people. Unfortunately many of these hazards are poorly understood, and many undoubtedly remain unrecognized at present. The next chapter shows that the level of *indirect* threats to human welfare is just as high and the level of understanding just as low.

[236]P. Berg et al., Potential biohazards of recombining DNA molecules.

Recommended for Further Reading

Cairns, John. 1975. The cancer problem. *Scientific American,* November. A superb semi-popular review of environmental carcinogenesis.

Council on Environmental Quality (CEQ). Annual. *Environmental quality.* Government Printing Office, Washington, D.C. Extensive data and discussion on recent measured levels of air and water pollution across the United States, as well as special topics in energy, land use, transportation, radiation, and environmental legislation and regulation.

Huddle, N.; M. Reich; and N. Stiskin. 1975. *Island of dreams: Environmental crisis in Japan.* Autumn Press, New York. Well-documented and illustrated survey of the serious environmental problems of one of the world's most intensely industrial nations.

Jet Propulsion Laboratory (JPL). 1975. *Should we have a new engine? An automobile power systems evaluation.* California Institute of Technology, Pasadena. The most comprehensive study we have seen of alternative automobile engines.

Lynn, D. A. 1976. *Air pollution: Threat and response.* Addison-Wesley, Reading, Mass. Excellent introductory text.

Murdoch, William W., ed. 1975. *Environment.* Sinauer, Sunderland, Mass. An outstanding, well-integrated set of chapters covering air pollution, freshwater pollution, marine pollution, pesticides, and legal remedies, among other topics.

National Academy of Sciences (NAS). 1975. *Air quality and stationary-source emission control.* Washington, D.C. Superb reference on health and ecological effects of sulfur oxides, and on control technologies for sulfur oxides and nitrogen oxides from stationary sources. Good bibliography.

ReVelle, C., and P. ReVelle. 1974. *Sourcebook on the environment.* Houghton Mifflin, Boston. Good, concise coverage of many of the direct threats to human health covered in this chapter.

Shaw, E. A. G. 1975. Noise pollution: What can be done? *Physics Today,* vol. 28, no. 1, pp. 46–58. Excellent review article.

Additional References

Ahmed, A. Karim; D. F. MacLeod; and J. Carmody. 1972. Control for asbestos. *Environment,* vol. 14, pp. 16–29. Describes setting of standards for asbestos exposure.

Allen, J. R., and D. H. Norback. 1973. Polychlorinated biphenyl- and triphenyl-induced gastric mucosol hyperplosion in primates. *Science,* vol. 179, pp. 498–499 (February 2). Rhesus monkeys show possible precancerous changes after being fed PCBs.

American Chemical Society. 1969. *Cleaning our environment: The chemical basis for action.* ACS Publications, New York. Dated in many respects, but still a useful introduction to essential concepts and terminology in air and water pollution.

Ames, B. N. 1976. Carcinogenicity tests. *Science,* vol. 191, pp. 241–245 (January 23). An effective reply to H. Ruben's 1976 criticism.

———; F. D. Lee; and W. E. Durston. 1973. An improved bacterial test system for the detection and classification of mutagens and carcinogens. *Proceedings of the National Academy of Sciences,* vol. 70, pp. 782–786. Describes Ames test.

———; W. E. Durston; E. Yamasaki; and F. D. Lee. 1973. Carcinogens are mutagens: A simple test system combining liver homogenates for activation and bacteria for detection. *Proceedings of the National Academy of Sciences,* vol. 70, pp. 2281–2285. An extremely important paper demonstrating that cancer-causing chemicals also cause mutations and can thus be detected by their mutagenic activity in bacterial systems. This discovery opened the possibility of using bacterial cultures to screen chemicals for carcinogenic properties.

———; H. O. Kammen; and E. Yamasaki. 1975. Hair dyes are mutagens: Identification of a variety of mutagenic ingredients. *Proceedings of the National Academy of Sciences,* vol. 72, pp. 2423–2427. Mutagenic compounds found in all permanent hair dyes tested. This means that 30 percent of American women have probably been exposed to cancer from this source, especially beauticians.

Ansari, N. 1973. *Epidemiology and control of schistosomiasis.* University Park Press, Baltimore. Comprehensive and technical monograph.

Åstrand, I.; O. Axelson; V. Eriksson; and L. Olander. 1975. Heat stress in occupational work. *Ambio,* vol. 4, no. 1, pp. 37–42. General review.

Aronow, W. S. 1974. Effects of carbon monoxide on coronary heart disease. *Geriatrics,* vol. 29, no. 10, pp. 141–146. Indicates restrictions on cigarette smoking in public places may be necessary to protect heart patients from high carbon-monoxide levels produced by smoking.

Babu, S. P., ed. 1975. *Trace elements in fuel.* American Chemical Society, Washington, D.C. Quantities of trace contaminants in coal and oil, pathways for escape to the environment, and physiological effects.

Bache, C. A.; W. H. Gutenmann; and D. J. Lisk. 1971. Residues of total mercury and methyl mercuric salts in lake trout as a function of age. *Science,* vol. 172, pp. 951–952 (May 28). Shows buildup of mercury concentrations as fish grow bigger.

Bakir, F., et al. 1973. Methyl mercury poisoning in Iraq. *Science,* vol. 181, pp. 230–241 (July 20). Fatal poisoning from consumption of grain treated with mercury fungicide.

Bates, Marston. 1968. Crowded people. *Natural history,* October.

Benedict, W. F.; N. Rucker; J. Faust; and R. E. Kouri. 1975. Malignant transformation of mouse cells by cigarette smoke condensate. *Cancer Research,* vol. 35, pp. 857–860.

Benson, W. W.; and J. Gabica. 1972. Total mercury in hair from 1,000 Idaho residents, 1971. *Pesticides Monitoring Journal,* vol. 6, pp. 80–83. Maximum levels found in older age groups approached the 150-ppm level, which is considered dangerous.

Berelson, B., and G. A. Steiner. 1964. *Human behavior: An inventory of scientific findings.* Harcourt, New York. An invaluable source of information on subjects ranging from perception to mental illness and cultural change.

Berenblum, I. 1974. *Carcinogenesis as a biological problem.* American Elsevier, New York. Technical. Chapters 1 and 2 contain a useful review of studies of carcinogenesis.

Berg, P.; D. Baltimore; H. W. Boyer; S. N. Cohen; R. W. Davis; D. S. Hogness; D. Nathans; R. Roblin; J. D. Watson; S. Weissman; and N. D. Zinder. 1974. Potential biohazards of recombinant DNA molecules. *Science,* vol. 185, p. 303 (July 26). The start of the violent and enduring controversy on experimentally combining DNA from different organisms.

Berlin, M. H.; T. W. Clarkson; L. T. Friberg; J. C. Gage; L. G. Goldwater; A. Jernelov; G. Kasantzis; L. Magos; G. F. Nordberg; E. P. Radford; C. Ramel; S. Skerfving; R. G. Smith; T. Suzuki; A. Swensson; S. Tejning; R. Truhaut; and J. Vostal. 1969. Maximum allowable concentrations of mercury compounds. *Archives of Environmental Health,* vol. 19, pp. 891–905. A detailed technical discussion.

Bertine, K. K., and E. D. Goldberg. 1971. Fossil-fuel combustion and the major sedimentary cycle. *Science,* vol. 173 (July 16), pp. 233–235. Significant quantities of trace elements enter the environment as effluents from the combustion of fossil fuels.

Billings, C. E., and W. R. Matson. 1972. Mercury emissions from coal combustion. *Science,* vol. 176, pp. 1232–1233 (June 16). Indicates 90 percent of mercury in coal reaches the environment through the stack.

Bini, G. 1973. Lead in the rural environment. *International Journal of Environmental Studies,* vol. 5, pp. 59–61. Useful review article.

Blum, Arlene, and B. N. Ames. 1977. Flame-retardant additives as possible cancer hazards. *Science,* vol. 195, pp. 17–23 (January 7). The main flame retardant used in children's pajamas is a mutagen and may be a carcinogen.

Bodmer, W. F., and L. L. Cavalli-Sforza. 1976. *Genetics, evolution and man.* W. H. Freeman and Company, San Francisco. Good, brief discussion of mutagenesis in *Homo sapiens.*

Boffey, P. M. 1968. 6000 sheep stricken near CBW center. *Science,* vol. 159, p. 1442 (March 29). Early report on major CBW "near miss" (no human lives were lost). The army later admitted a nerve-gas release was the cause (*New York Times,* May 22, 1969). For further details, see Brodine, Gaspar, and Pallmann, The wind from Dugway.

———. 1976. Color additives: Botched experiment leads to banning of red dye no. 2. *Science,* vol. 191, pp. 450–451 (February 6). Insight into the realities of regulation.

Bogland, E. 1975. Cancer at work. *Nature,* vol. 257, pp. 170–171. A brief review of the early history of occupational cancers.

Bowen, H. J. M. 1966. *Trace elements in biochemistry.* Academic Press, New York. Excellent text.

Brodine, V.; P. P. Gaspar; and A. J. Pallmann. 1969. The wind from Dugway. *Environment,* January/February. Details of the sheep-kill–chemical-warfare disaster.

Brown, J. Martin. 1976. Health, safety and social issues of nuclear power and the nuclear initiative. In *The California nuclear initiative,* W. C. Reynolds, ed. Institute for Energy studies, Stanford University, Palo Alto. A brilliant review, especially illuminating on plutonium toxicity and other biomedical aspects of nuclear power.

———. 1976. Linearity vs. nolinearity of dose response for radiation carcinogenesis. *Health Physics,* vol. 31, pp. 231–245 (September). The best available discussion of the linear hypothesis.

Brown, J. R. 1967. Organochlorine pesticide residues in human depot fat. *Canadian Medical Association Journal,* vol. 97, pp. 367–373. Data on Canadian populations.

Brown, S. M.; M. G. Marmot; S. T. Sacks; and L. W. Kwok. 1975. Effect on mortality of the 1974 fuel crisis. *Nature,* vol. 257, pp. 306–307. Reduction in the use of gasoline in the San Francisco Bay area in the first quarter of 1974 was accompanied by a sharp drop in death rates from cardiovascular disease and chronic lung disease, compared to the same quarter in 1970–1973.

Bruce-Smith, D., and H. A. Waldron. 1974. Lead, behavior, and criminality. *Ecologist,* vol. 4, no. 10, pp. 367–377. Possible neurological effects of lead.

Bryan, G. T., and E. Erturk. 1970. Production of mouse urinary-bladder carcinomas by sodium cyclamate. *Science,* vol. 167, pp. 996–998 (February 13). Key study leading to banning of cyclamates.

Bryan, G. T.; E. Erturk; and O. Yoshida. 1970. Production of urinary-bladder carcinomas in mice by sodium saccharin. *Science,* vol. 168, pp. 1238–1240 (June 5). Saccharin shown capable of causing cancer.

Bryan, G. W. 1976. Heavy metal contamination in the sea. In R. Johnston, ed., *Marine pollution,* p. 185. Comprehensive, data-rich, with a good bibliography. Concludes that with the exception of Minamata disease heavy metals have not caused permanent poisoning yet, but the threat is not trivial.

Burch, Phillip. 1974. Does smoking cause lung cancer? *New Scientist,* vol. 63, February 21, pp. 458–463. Argues in favor of the hypothesis that genes that predispose to heavy smoking also predispose to various diseases, including lung cancer—that is, that both smoking and lung cancer are caused by a common genetic factor rather than smoking itself causing cancer. See also the rebuttal by Richard Doll, Smoking, lung cancer, and Occam's razor.

Burkitt, Denis P. 1971. Cancer and environment. *International Journal of Environmental Studies,* vol. 1, pp. 275–279. Good material on geographic distribution of cancers.

Burnet, Sir Macfarlane. 1974. The biology of cancer. In *Chromosomes and cancer,* J. Germon, ed. Wiley, New York, pp. 21–38.

Burns, E. Hames. 1974. Organochlorine pesticide and polychlorinated biphenyl residues in biopsied human adipose tissue—Texas 1969–1972. *Pesticides Monitoring Journal,* vol. 7 pp. 122–126. High levels of DDT found in Mexican-Americans. No decrease in storage levels detected.

Busch, Harris ed. 1974. *The molecular biology of cancer.* Academic Press, New York. A collection of technical papers on the molecular mechanisms underlying the cellular processes that must be altered to produce cancers.

Cairns, J. 1975. Mutation selection and the natural history of cancer. *Nature,* vol. 255, pp. 197–200. Discusses mechanisms that may protect rapidly-renewing tissues of mammals from the appearance of cancerous clones of cells.

Cairns, John Jr. 1974. Indicator species vs. the concept of community structure as an index of pollution. *Water Resources Bulletin,* vol. 10, pp. 338–346. A general discussion.

———; J. W. Hall; E. L. Morgan; R. E. Sparks; W. T. Waller; and G. F. Westlake. 1973. *The development of an automated biological monitoring system for water quality.* Virginia Water Resources Research Center, Blacksburg, bulletin 51. Describes a system that continuously monitors breathing and swimming activity of fishes exposed to effluent.

———; G. R. Lanza; and B. C. Parker. 1972. Pollution-related structural and functional changes in aquatic communities with emphasis on freshwater algae and protozoa. *Proceedings of the Academy of Natural Sciences of Philadelphia,* vol. 124, pp. 79–127. A comprehensive review with a fine bibliography.

———; R. E. Sparks; and W. T. Waller. 1973. The use of fish as sensors in industrial waste lines to prevent fish kills. *Hydrobiologia*, vol. 41, pp. 151–167. Cairns and his group have done much pioneering work on the biological monitoring of water pollution, of which this paper is just one example. See also R. E. Sparks, John Cairns, Jr., and A. G. Heath, The use of bluegill breathing rates to detect zinc.

Calhoun, John B. 1962. Population density and social pathology. *Scientific American*, February. Studies of crowding in rats. (*Scientific American* Offprint 506, W. H. Freeman and Company, San Francisco).

Callicott, J. H. 1968. Amebic meningioencephalitis due to free-living amebas of the Hartmanella (acanthamoeba) Naegleria group. *American Journal of Clinical Pathology*, vol. 49, p. 84.

Capizzi, J., and J. M. Wite. 1971. *Pesticides, pest control, and safety on forest and range lands*. Continuing Education, Corvallis, Oregon. See especially Wite's chapter, A chemical classification of pesticides.

Carlisle, David. 1972. An inconsistent ban: DES. *New Scientist*, vol. 56, p. 315. Critical of agricultural banning in face of extensive medical use. See also comment by Colin Tudge on same page.

Carr, R. A.; and P. E. Wilkniss. 1973. Mercury in the Greenland ice sheet: Further data. *Science*, vol. 181, pp. 843–844 (August 31).

Carson, Rachel. 1962. *Silent spring*. Houghton Mifflin, Boston. The classic early warning on pesticides.

Carson, T.; G. Van Gelder; G. Karas; and W. Buck. 1974. Slowed learning in lambs prenatally exposed to lead. *Archives of Environmental Health*, vol. 29, pp. 154–156.

Carter, Luther J. 1974. Pollution and public health: Taconite case poses major test. *Science*, vol. 186, pp. 31–36 (October 4). Describes court battles over dumping of material containing asbestos in Lake Superior (see Cook, Glass, and Tucker, Asbestiform amphibole minerals).

Casarett, A. P. 1968. *Radiation biology*. Prentice-Hall, Englewood Cliffs, N.J. Readable textbook.

Cassel, John. 1971. Health consequences of population density and crowding. In *Rapid population growth: consequences and policy implications*, R. Revelle, ed. Johns Hopkins Press, Baltimore.

Cavalli-Sforza, L. L., and W. F. Bodmer. 1971. *The genetics of human populations*. W. H. Freeman and Company, San Francisco. Comprehensive source on mutation in human populations.

Chisolm, J. J. 1971. Lead poisoning. *Scientific American*, February, pp. 15–23. Focuses on acute effects that manifest themselves at high doses.

Chow, T. J., and J. L. Earl. 1970. Lead aerosols in the atmosphere: Increasing concentrations. *Science*, vol. 169, pp. 577–580 (August 7). Evidence that automobile gasoline additives are a major source of atmospheric lead.

Christensen, H. E. 1973. *The toxic substances list*. U.S. Department of Health Education and Welfare, Government Printing Office, Washington, D.C. A basic reference for the specialist.

Cole, H. H.; G. H. Gass; R. J. Gerrits; H. D. Hofs; W. H. Hole; R. C. Preston; and L. C. Ulberg. 1975. On the safety of estrogenic hormone residues in edible animal products. *Bioscience*, vol. 25, pp. 19–25. Shows complexity of evaluating cancer risks in residues of DES and similar products.

Colley, J. R. T.; W. W. Holland; and R. T. Corkhill. 1974. Influence of passive smoking and parental phlegm on pneumonia and bronchitis in early childhood. *Lancet*, vol. 2, pp. 1031–1034 (November 2).

Committee of the Council of the Environmental Mutagen Society. 1975. Environmental mutagenic hazards. *Science*, vol. 187, pp. 503–514 (February 14). Key paper on screening for mutagenicity and evaluating hazards.

Commoner, B. 1973. Workplace burden. *Environment*, vol. 15, no. 6, pp. 15–20. Job exposure to PCBs; comparison of environmental and occupational standards.

Connery, A. H.; and J. J. Burns. 1972. Metabolic interactions among environmental chemicals and drugs. *Science*, vol. 178, pp. 576–586 (November 11). Focuses on the alteration of microsomal enzyme systems of the liver that are involved in detoxification and may be reduced by various chemicals.

Cook, Philip M.; G. E. Glass; and J. H. Tucker. 1974. Asbestiform amphibole minerals: Detection and measurement of high concentrations in municipal water supplies. *Science*, vol. 185, pp. 853–855 (September 6). Estimates fiber count in Duluth water supply (see Carter, Pollution and public health).

Cowell, E. B. 1976. Oil pollution of the sea. In R. Johnston, ed., *Marine pollution*, pp. 353–401. Concludes that added cancer risks from oil in seafoods must be very low, and that ecosystemic effects are likely to be much less than those of other pollutants such as heavy metals and chlorinated hydrocarbons.

Craig, R. E. 1976. Dispersion in estuaries and inshore waters. In R. Johnston, ed., *Marine pollution*, pp. 159–183. A mathematical treatment of a topic key to the appraisal of the pollution situations.

Crossland, J., and V. Brodine. 1973. Drinking water. *Environment*, vol. 15, no. 3, pp. 11–19. Excellent treatment of chemical, bacterial, and viral pollution of drinking-water supplies, including problems and limitations of chlorination.

Crow, J. T. 1968. Chemical risk to future generations. *Scientist and Citizen*, June/July, pp. 113–117. A distinguished geneticist considers the risks of chemical mutagenicity may be as serious as those from radiation.

Curley, A., and R. Kembrough. 1969. Chlorinated hydrocarbon insecticides in plasma and milk of pregnant and lactating women. *Archives of Environmental Health*, vol. 18, pp. 156–164. Showed an average of 0.06 to 0.08 parts per million DDT-R in first three months after delivery, with a range of 0.04 to 0.16 parts per million.

Curley, A.; V. Sedlak; E. Girling; R. Hawk; W. Barthel; P. Pierce; and W. Likosky. 1971. Organic mercury identified as the cause of poisoning in humans and hogs. *Science*, vol. 172, pp. 65–66 (April 2).

Dale, W. E.; M. F. Copeland; and W. J. Hayes, Jr. 1965. Chlorinated insecticides in the body fat of people in India. *Bulletin of World Health Organization*, vol. 33, pp. 471–477. Source of Indian data.

David, O.; J. Clark; and K. Voeller. 1972. Lead and hyperactivity. *Lancet*, October, pp. 900–903.

Deichmann, W. B.; W. E. MacDonald; and D. A. Cubit. 1971. DDT tissue retention: Sudden rise induced by the addition of aldrin to a fixed DDT intake. *Science*, vol. 172, pp. 275–276 (April 16). A disturbing synergism.

Deitz, V. R., ed. 1975. *Removal of trace contaminants from the air*. American Chemical Society, Washington, D.C. Technical treatise covering a wide variety of contaminants from combustion products to pesticides.

Dickson, E. M. 1972. Mercury and lead in the Greenland ice sheet: A reexamination of the data. *Science*, vol. 177, pp. 536–538 (August 11).

Dixon, B. 1972. Typhoid bacilli learn a new trick. *New Scientist*, vol. 55, pp. 571–580. Some strains of this deadly bacterium have become resistant to the "drug of choice," chloramphenicol.

Doll, Richard. 1974. Smoking, lung cancer, and Occam's razor. *New Scientist,* vol. 63, February 21, pp. 463–467. A persuasive rebuttal to Phillip Burch's position that smoking doesn't actually cause lung cancer. Doll explains why most authorities believe there is a causal relationship.

Dubos, René. 1965. *Man adapting.* Yale University Press, New Haven. Deals with many of the problems covered in this chapter.

Duggan, R. E., and J. R. Weatherwax. 1967. Dietary intake of pesticide chemicals. *Science,* vol. 157, pp. 1006–1010 (September 1). Highest residues in meat, fish, and poultry.

Edelson, Edward. 1973. Food laws should be even tougher. *New Scientist,* vol. 57, pp. 315–316. Brief overview of Delaney clause controversy.

Edmondson, W. T. 1975. Fresh water pollution. In *Environment,* William W. Murdoch, ed. Useful survey.

Edsall, J. T. 1976. Toxicity of plutonium and some other actinides. *Bulletin of the Atomic Scientists,* vol. 32, no. 7 (September), pp. 27–37. Good review article, citing several kinds of evidence for the view that plutonium is more dangerous than present standards imply.

Edvarson, K. 1975. Radioecological effects of nuclear warfare. *Ambio,* vol. 4, no. 5/6, pp. 209–210. Estimates of radiation doses to people and the associated delayed casualties from hemispheric fallout after a large nuclear war.

Ehrlich, Paul R., and J. L. Freedman. 1971. Population, crowding, and human behaviour. *New Scientist,* April 1. General discussion, reporting results of first experimental work on crowding in human beings.

Ehrlich, Paul R.; John P. Holdren; and Richard W. Holm, eds. 1971. *Man and the ecosphere.* W. H. Freeman and Company, San Francisco. Important papers from *Scientific American,* with critical commentaries.

Ehrlich, Paul R.; Richard W. Holm; and I. L. Brown. 1976. *Biology and society.* McGraw-Hill, New York. Contains a lay overview of molecular genetics and also of the biology of various environmental problems.

Ehrlich, Paul R.; R. W. Holm; and D. R. Parnell. 1974. *The process of evolution.* 2d ed. McGraw-Hill, New York. See especially the discussion of chromosomal alterations which in the present text are included under the rubric *mutation.*

Eisenbud, Merril. 1973. *Environmental radioactivity,* 2d ed. Wiley, New York. A wide-ranging introduction with an extensive bibliography. Includes details of techniques for computing maximum permissible concentrations and doses by various pathways.

Epstein, S. S. 1973. The Delaney amendment. *Ecologist,* vol. 3, pp. 424–431. A spirited defense of the Delaney clause by a distinguished cancer researcher.

———. 1974. Environmental determinants of human cancer. *Cancer Research,* vol. 34, pp. 2425–2435. A key review article.

———, and D. Hattis. 1975. Pollution and human health. In *Environment,* William W. Murdoch, ed. Good introduction to the epidemiological aspects of pollution.

———, A. Hollaender, J. Lederberg, M. Legator, H. Richardson, and H. H. Wolff. 1969. Wisdom of cyclamate ban. *Science,* vol. 166 p. 1575 (December 26). Useful discussion of why the ban should be supported.

Fiserova-Bergerova, V.; J. L. Radomski; J. E. Davis; and J. H. Davis. 1967. Levels of chlorinated hydrocarbon pesticides in human tissues. *Industrial Medicine and Surgery,* vol. 36, pp. 65–70.

Flawn, P. T. 1970. *Environmental geology.* Harper & Row, New York. Excellent material on earthquakes, subsidence, man as a geological agent, and so forth.

Foote, R. S. 1972. Mercury-vapor concentrations inside buildings. *Science,* vol. 177, pp. 513–514 (August 11).

Forrester, Jay W. 1971. Counterintuitive behavior of social systems. *Technology Review,* vol. 73, no. 3, pp. 52–68. Preliminary report of "Limits to Growth" study, with discussion of the relation of population density to crime rates.

Franklin, B. A. 1976. A crippler called Kepone. *This World* (San Francisco *Examiner* and *Chronicle*), February 15.

Freedman, J. L. 1975. *Crowding and behavior.* W. H. Freeman and Company, San Francisco. Review by a psychologist who is one of the pioneers in research on crowding.

French, J.; G. Lourimore; W. Nelson; J. Finklea; T. English; and M. Hertz. 1973. The effect on sulfur dioxide and suspended sulfates on acute respiratory disease. *Archives of Environmental Health,* vol. 27, pp. 129–133.

Friedman, I., and N. Peterson. 1971. Fossil fuels as a source of mercury pollution. *Science,* vol. 172, pp. 1027–1028 (June 4). Mercury pollution from fossil fuels is shown to be comparable to that from industrial waste.

Fuller, J. G. 1974. *Fever! The hunt for a new killer virus.* Ballantine, New York. Popular account of Lassa fever.

Galle, O. R.; W. R. Gove; and V. M. McPherson. 1972. Population density and pathology: What are the relationships for man? *Science,* vol. 176, pp. 23–30 (April 7). Untangling variables is difficult.

Galle, O. R.; J. D. McCarthy; and W. Gove. 1974. *Population density and pathology.* Paper presented at the annual meeting of the Population Association of America in New York, 1974. No positive correlation found between crowding and alcoholism, suicide, or homicide—and a *negative* one with the latter two.

Galston, A. W. 1971. Some implications of the widespread use of herbicides. *BioScience,* vol. 21, pp. 891–892. See also papers by Johnson and by Westing in the same issue.

Gamberale, Francesco. 1975. Behavioral toxicology: A new field of job health research. *Ambio,* vol. 4, no. 1, pp. 43–46. Performance may be affected by exposure to certain substances, and irreversible effects on the central nervous system are possible.

Garrels, R. M.; F. T. Mackenzie; and C. Hunt. 1975. *Chemical cycles and the global environment.* Kaufmann, Los Altos, Calif. Contains useful information on flows and toxicity of trace metals.

Gaspar, P. P. 1975. Sulfur in the atmosphere. In *Sulfur in the environment,* Missouri Botanical Garden. St. Louis. Excellent survey of sulfur's reactions in the atmosphere.

German, James, ed. 1974. *Chromosomes and cancer.* Wiley, New York. A collection of technical papers on the changes associated with cancer in the gene-bearing organelles of the cell. See especially the article by Burnet, The biology of cancer.

Gilbert, R. G.; R. C. Rice; H. Bouwer; C. P. Gerba; C. Wallis; and J. L. Melnick. 1976. Waste water renovation and reuse: Virus removal by soil filtration. *Science,* vol. 192, pp. 1004–1005 (June 4). Encouraging evidence that human viral pathogens are effectively removed by filtration of viruses through soil.

Gilder, S. S. B. 1973. The passive smoker. *Canadian Medical Association Journal,* vol. 109, no. 11, pp. 1084–1089 (December 1). Shows nonsmokers in a room with smokers reach a CO blood level equal to that of smokers smoking 1 cigarette per hour. Also correlates children's respiratory illness with parents' smoking.

Gilfillan, S. C. 1965. Lead poisoning and the fall of Rome. *Journal of Occupational Medicine,* February, pp. 53–60. Detailed historical case study. Fascinating.

Gofman, J. W. 1975. The cancer hazard from inhaled plutonium. Committee for Nuclear Responsibility, Dublin, Calif.

——— and A. R. Tamplin. 1971. *Poisoned power.* Rodale, Emmaus, Pa. Scientists from the Lawrence Radiation Laboratory present their case on radiation and the hazards of nuclear power.

Goldberg, E. D. 1965. In *Chemical oceanography,* J. P. Riley and G. Skirrow, eds. Academic Press, New York. pp. 163–196.

———, and K. K. Bertine. 1975. Marine pollution. In *Environment,* William W. Murdoch, ed. Excellent material on trace metals.

Goldsmith, J. R., and A. I. Hexter. 1967. Respiratory exposures to lead: Epidemiological and experimental dose-response relationship. *Science,* vol. 158, pp. 132–134 (October 6).

Goldwater, C. J.; A. J. Rosso; and M. Kleinfeld. 1965. Bladder tumours in a coal tar dye plant. *Archives of Environmental Health,* vol. 11, pp. 814–817. High rates of induction recorded.

Gordon, J. E., and N. S. Scrimshaw. 1973. Cholera morbus revisited. *International Journal of Environmental Studies,* vol. 4, pp. 291–298. Good overview of cholera.

Grant, Neville. 1971. Mercury in man. *Environment,* vol. 13, no. 4, pp. 8–15. Useful introductory article.

Greenberg, D. S. 1975. Stalemate in cancer treatment. *Environment,* April/May, pp. 19–20, 25. (Reprinted from *Science and Government Report,* Dec. 1, 1974.) Describes in statistical detail the failure of the War on Cancer boondoggle.

Groth, Edward, III. 1975. Fluoride pollution. *Environment,* vol. 17, no. 3, pp. 29–38. Very comprehensive and even-handed review.

Gruener, N., and R. Toeplitz. 1975. The effect of changes in nitrate concentration in drinking water on methemoglobin levels in infants. *International Journal of Environmental Studies,* vol. 7, pp. 161–163.

Hall, E. T. 1966. *The hidden dimension.* Doubleday, Garden City, N.Y. Basic source on human use of personal space.

Hamilton, D. H., and R. L. Meeham. 1971. Ground rupture in the Baldwin Hills. *Science,* vol. 172, pp. 333–344 (April 23). Dam failure traced to fluid injection in nearby oil fields.

Hammond, A. S., and J. E. Huff. 1974. Asbestos: World concern, involvement, and culpability. *International Journal of Environmental Studies,* vol. 6, pp. 247–252. Review of worldwide exposure.

Hammond, E. C., and D. Horn. 1958. Smoking and death rates: Report on forty-four months of follow-up of 187,783 men: pt. 1, Total mortality; pt. 2, Death rates by cause. *Journal of the American Medical Association,* vol. 166, pp. 1159–1172, 1294–1308. Huge epidemiological study showing clear relationship of smoking to coronary disease, lung cancer, and other cancers.

Hanson, R. P.; S. E. Sulkin; E. L. Buescher; W. McD. Hammon; R. W. McKinney; and T. H. Work. 1967. Arbovirus infections of laboratory workers. *Science,* vol. 158, pp. 1283–1286 (December 8). Describes incidence of laboratory accidents with arthropod-borne viruses.

Harris, R. J. C. 1970. Cancer and the environment. *International Journal of Environmental Studies,* vol. 1, pp. 59–65. See especially sections on cultural cancers. Useful bibliography.

Hayes, W. J., Jr.; W. E. Dale; and C. I. Perkle. 1971. Evidence of safety of long-term high, oral doses of DDT for man. *Archives of Environmental Health,* vol. 22, pp. 119–135. Short-term study showing the undisputed lack of acute toxicity of DDT; it does not speak to human carcinogenesis or other long-term safety.

Hayes, W. J., Jr.; W. F. Durham; and C. Cueto. 1956. The effects of known repeated oral doses of chlorophenothane (DDT) in man. *Journal of the American Medical Association,* vol. 162, pp. 890–897. Poorly designed study purporting to show DDT harmless to humans.

Healy, J. H.; W. W. Rubey; D. T. Griggs; and C. B. Raleigh. 1968. The Denver earthquakes. *Science,* vol. 161, pp. 1301–1310 (September 27). Injection of fluid wastes near Denver triggered earthquakes.

Hernberg, S.; J. Nikkanen; G. Mellin; and H. Lilius. 1970. δ-Aminolevulinic acid dehydrase as a measure of lead exposure. *Archives of Environmental Health,* vol. 21, pp. 140–145.

Hexter, A. C., and J. R. Goldsmith. 1971. Carbon monoxide: Association of community air pollution with mortality. *Science,* vol. 172, pp. 265–267 (April 16). One of a relatively few major community studies relating air pollution to higher mortality.

Hiatt, V., and J. E. Huff. 1975. The environmental impact of cadmium: An overview. *International Journal of Environmental Studies,* vol. 7, no. 4, pp. 277–285. Splendid review article.

Hinds, W. C., and M. W. First. 1975. Concentrations of nicotine and tobacco smoke in public places. *New England Journal of Medicine,* vol. 292, no. 16, pp. 844–845 (April 17).

Hirschhorn, N., and W. B. Greenough, III. 1971. Cholera. *Scientific American,* August. Map of recent pandemic, details on treatment, toxin, etc.

Hirst, Eric. 1973. The energy cost of pollution control. *Environment,* vol. 15, no. 8, pp. 37–44. Indicates that control of air pollution, water pollution, solid waste, and thermal pollution to the extent and with the technologies envisioned in the early 1970s would use not more than a few percent of the United States energy budget at that time.

Hoffman, W. S.; W. I. Fishbein; and M. B. Andelman. 1964. The pesticide content of human fat tissue. *Archives of Environmental Health,* vol. 9, pp. 387–394. Discusses establishment of equilibrium concentrations of DDT.

Holdren, John P., and Paul R. Ehrlich, eds. 1971. *Global ecology.* Harcourt Brace Jovanovich, New York. Includes basic papers on several classes of environmental hazards.

Holmberg, B. 1975. Biological aspects of chemical and biological weapons. *Ambio,* vol. 4, no. 5, pp. 211–215. Excellent survey of effects on humans and the environment.

———. 1975. The inhuman factor. *Ambio* vol. 4, no. 1, pp. 1–5. An overview of occupational health with suggestions for improving it.

Hoover, R., and J. F. Fraumeni, Jr. 1975. Cancer mortality in U.S. counties with chemical industries. *Environmental Research,* vol. 9, pp. 196–207. High mortality is associated with presence of chemical industries.

Hudson, H. E., and F. W. Gilcreas, 1976. Health and economic aspects of water hardness and corrosiveness. *Journal of the American Waterworks Association,* vol. 68, pp. 201–204. Mortality rate from cardiovascular disease is 24 percent higher in communities with low total water hardness than in communities with high hardness.

Hueper, W. C. 1972. Environmental cancer hazards. *Journal of Occupational Medicine,* vol. 14, pp. 149–153. Details on occupational carcinogenesis.

Hurn, R. W., ed. *Approaches to automotive-emissions control.* American Chemical Society, Washington, D.C. Detailed and technical.

Iltis, H. H.; O. L. Loucks; and P. Andrews. 1970. Criteria for an optimum human environment. *Bulletin of the Atomic Scientists,* vol. 26, no. 1, pp. 2–6. Discusses some of the less obvious requisites of human existence. Reprinted in Holdren and Ehrlich, *Global ecology*.

Innes, J. R. M.; B. M. Ullard; M. G. Valerir; L. Petrucelli; L. Fishbein; E. R. Hart; A. J. Pallotta; R. R. Bates; H. L. Falk; J. J. Gart; M. Klein; I. Mitchell; and J. Peters. 1969. Bioassay of pesticides and industrial chemicals for tumorigenicity in mice: a preliminary note. *Journal of the National Cancer Institute*, vol. 42, no. 6, pp. 1101–1114. Study of cancer induction in mice by a variety of chemicals, including DDT and several other pesticides.

Jahns, Richard H. 1968. Geological jeopardy. *Texas Quarterly*, vol. 11, no. 2, pp. 69–83. (Reprinted in Holdren and Ehrlich, *Global ecology*.) A survey of geologic environmental hazards.

Jaworowski, Z. 1968. Stable lead in fossil ice and bones. *Nature*, vol. 217, pp. 152–153.

Joensu, O. 1971. Fossil fuels as a source of mercury pollution. *Science*, vol. 172, pp. 1027–1028 (June 4). Suggests a mean value of 1 part per million for average mercury content of coals worldwide.

Johnston, R. 1976. Mechanisms and problems of marine pollution in relation to commercial fisheries. In R. Johnston, ed., *Marine pollution*, pp. 3–156. Covers a vast range of topics—see especially material on North Sea oil and gas operations.

———, ed. 1976. *Marine pollution*. Academic Press, New York. Up to date and comprehensive.

Jones, R. M., and R. Fagan, 1975. Carboxyhemoglobin in nonsmokers: A mathematical model. *Archives of Environmental Health*, vol. 30, no. 4, pp. 184–189.

Kagawa, J., and T. Toyama. 1975. Photochemical air pollution. *Archives of Environmental Health*, vol. 30, pp. 117–122. Relates ambient concentrations of oxidants to physiological effects.

Kane, D. N. 1976. Bad air for children, *Environment*, vol. 18, no. 9 (November), pp. 26–34. On children's special sensitivity to air pollution.

Kay, Kingsley. 1974. Occupational cancer risks for pesticide workers. *Environmental Research*, vol 7, pp. 243–271. A thorough review. Bibliography covers 175 papers.

Kermode, G. O. 1972. Food additives. *Scientific American*, March. A general survey of the types and uses of additives (excluding those given to live animals).

Kier, L. D.; E. Yamasaki; and B. N. Ames. 1974. Detection of mutagenic activity in cigarette smoke condensates. *Proceedings of the National Academy of Sciences*, vol. 71, pp. 4159–4163. Ames test detects mutagenic activity in condensate and several fractions thereof; shows great promise for further investigations.

Kissling, R. E.; R. Q. Robinson; F. A. Murphy; and S. G. Whitfield. 1968. Agent of disease contracted from green monkeys. *Science*, vol. 160, pp. 888–890 (February 20). Source on Marburgvirus.

Knox, J. F.; S. Holmes; R. Doll; and I. D. Hill. 1968. Mortality from lung cancer and other causes among workers in an asbestos textile factory. *British Journal of Industrial Medicine*, vol. 25, pp. 293–303. Occupational lung cancers caused by asbestos.

Knudson, A. G. 1973. Mutation and human cancer. *Advances in Cancer Research*, vol. 17, pp. 317–352. Presents two-or-more-mutational-step models of carcinogenesis in which, in hereditary disposition to cancer, the first step occurs before the egg is fertilized (that is, it is mutation-inherited from a parent).

Kothny, E. L, ed. 1973. *Trace elements in the environment*. American Chemical Society, Washington, D.C. Nine chapters covering the main metals of health concern plus various dusts and aerosols.

Kraun, G. F.; L. J. McCabe; and J. M. Hughes, 1976. Waterborne disease outbreaks in the U.S.: 1971 through 1974. *Journal of the American Waterworks Association*, vol. 68, pp. 420–424. Also includes discussion of historical trends.

Kryter, K. D. 1970. *The effects of noise on man*. Academic Press, New York. Useful for detailed information.

Kuratsune, M., et al. 1972. Epidemiological study of Yusho, a poisoning caused by ingestion of rice oil contaminated with a commercial brand of polychlorinated biphenyls. *Environmental health perspectives*, experimental issue no. 1, April.

Kyllonen, R. L. 1967. Crime rate vs. population density in United States cities: A model. *Yearbook of the Society for General Systems Research*, vol. 12, pp. 137–145.

La Force, F. M.; F. H. Bumford; J. C. Feeley; S. L. Stokes; and D. B. Snow. 1969. Epidemiologic study of a fatal case of inhalation anthrax. *Archives of Environmental Health*, vol. 18, pp. 798–805. This deadly disease can be transmitted through the air.

Langer, W. L. 1964. The black death. *Scientific American*, February. See especially psychosocial effects.

Lave, L., and E. Seskin. 1970. Air pollution and human health. *Science*, vol. 169, pp. 723–733 (August 21). Good review of the evidence as of 1970. Estimates that a 50 percent reduction in air pollution would save 2 billion dollars in health care costs annually in the U.S.

Lave, L. B., and L. P. Silverman. 1976. Economic costs of energy-related environmental pollution. In *Annual review of energy*, J. Hollander and M. Simmons, eds., vol. 1, Annual Reviews Inc., Palo Alto, Calif. Good survey of kinds of economic costs of pollution and methods of estimating them.

Laws, E. R., Jr.; A. Curley; and E. F. Biros. 1967. Men with intensive occupational exposure to DDT. *Archives of Environmental Health*, vol. 15, pp. 766–775. This study tends to indicate little or no toxicity of DDT to adults during periods of a decade or more. It says nothing about the effects of exposure during longer stretches, especially when exposure begins before birth. Information on the causes of death of men who have worked for chlorinated hydrocarbon manufacturers would be of greater interest on the subject of adult toxicity than this sort of study.

Laws, E. R.; W. C. Maddrey; A. Curley; and V. W. Burse. 1973. Long-term occupational exposure to DDT. *Archives of Environmental Health*, vol. 27, pp. 318–321. Thirty-five men heavily exposed to DDT for an average of 25 years did not show liver disease.

Lederberg, J. 1968. Swift biological advance can be bent to genocide. *Washington Post*, August 17. A distinguished molecular biologist speculates on biological warfare possibilities.

———. 1970. Yellow fever is still a menace. *San Francisco Sunday Examiner and Chronicle*, March 22. The threat to Asia seems especially severe.

———. 1971. Biological warfare: A global threat. *American Scientist*, vol. 59, pp. 195–197. An overview dealing also with the potential for natural epidemics.

Lee, A. M., and J. F. Fraumeni, Jr. 1969. Arsenic and respiratory cancer in man: An occupational study. *Journal of the National Cancer Institute*, Vol. 42, pp. 1045–1052. Supports hypothesis that inhaled arsenic produces cancers of respiratory system, but other concomitant factors such as high concentrations of SO_2 cannot be ruled out.

Lees, L., et al. 1972. *Smog: A report to the people*. Ward Ritchie, Los Angeles.

Levinson, C. 1975. The malevolent workplace. *Ambio*, vol. 4, no. 1, pp. 24–29. Survey of hazardous conditions and lax enforcement of standards around the world. Especially fine discussion of vinyl chloride.

Lewin, R. 1976. Bacteria to be used to detect cancer-causing chemicals. *New Scientist,* January 22, p. 179. An excellent brief summary of the Ames screen.

———. 1976. Cancer hazards in the environment. *New Scientist,* January 22, pp. 168–169.

Lijinsky, W. 1973. Nitrites in foods. *Science,* vol. 182, pp. 1194–1196 (December 21). Supports Schuck and Wellford, Botulism and nitrites.

———. 1976. Health problems associated with nitrites and nitrosamines. *Ambio,* vol. 5, no. 2, pp. 67–72. Good summary of chemistry and carcinogenic potential of nitrites used in processing of meat and fish.

———, and S. S. Epstein. 1970. Nitrosamines as environmental carcinogens. *Nature,* vol. 225, pp. 21–23. Suggests that cancers might be caused by nitrosamines formed in digestive tract from ingested nitrites and secondary amines.

Likosky, W. 1971. Organic mercury identified as the cause of poisoning in humans and hogs. *Science,* vol. 172, pp. 65–66 (April 2). Ingestion of grain treated with organic mercury fungicides.

———. 1977. How nitrosamines cause cancer. *New Scientist,* January 27, pp. 216–217. Tells how altering molecular structure helps in understanding carcinogenetic activity.

Love, S. 1975. An idea in need of rethinking: the flush toilet. *Smithsonian,* May, pp. 61–66.

Lowrance, W. W. 1976. *Of acceptable risk.* Kaufmann, Los Altos, Calif. An interesting exploration of the concepts of risk, safety, and acceptability, with instructive examples.

Lumsden, M. 1975. "Conventional" war and human ecology. *Ambio,* vol. 4, no. 5–6, pp. 223–228. Discussion of effects of World War II and Vietnam war on urban and rural environments.

MacDonald, G. J. F. 1969. The modification of the planet Earth by man. *Technology Review,* vol. 72, no. 1, pp. 26–35. See especially the section on man-made earthquakes.

Magee, P. 1971. Toxicity of nitrosamines: Their possible human health hazards. *Food and Cosmetics Toxicology,* vol. 9, pp. 207–218. Concludes hazard is difficult to assess.

———. 1973. Nitrosamines: Ubiquitous carcinogens? *New Scientist,* August 25, pp. 432–434. Semipopular review, no bibliography.

Maltoni, Cesare. 1975. The value of predictive experimental bioassays in occupational and environmental carcinogenesis—an example: vinyl chloride. *Ambio,* vol. 4, no. 1, pp. 18–23. Underscores the need for screening industrial compounds *before* they go into widespread use.

Martell, E. A. 1974. Radioactivity of tobacco trichomes and insoluble cigarette particles. *Nature,* vol. 249, pp. 215–217. Shows that radioactive polonium taken up from the environment by tobacco plants shows up in smoke from cigarettes.

———. 1975. Tobacco radioactivity and cancer in smokers. *American Scientist,* vol. 63, no. 4, pp. 404–412. Argues that mechanism by which cigarette smoke causes cancer and arteriosclerosis is radioactivity taken up by the tobacco plant.

Marx, J. L. 1974. Drinking water: Another source of carcinogens? *Science,* vol. 186, pp. 809–811 (November 29).

Mason, T. J., and F. N. McKay. 1974. *U.S. cancer mortality by county: 1950–1969.* Department of Health, Education and Welfare, Washington, D.C., publication NIH 74–615.

Masters, G. M. 1974. *Introduction to environmental science and technology.* Wiley, New York. Good introductory text, with concise coverage of population, food, energy, and pollution control.

Maugh, T. H. 1973. Trace elements: A growing appreciation of their effects on man. *Science,* vol. 181, pp. 253–254 (July 20). Excellent short overview.

———. 1974. Chemical carcinogenesis: A long-neglected field blossoms. *Science,* vol. 183, pp. 940–944 (March 8). An informative review by a science journalist.

McCann, J., and B. N. Ames. 1976. Detection of carcinogens as mutagens in the *Salmonella*/microsome test: Assay of 300 chemicals—discussion. *Proceedings of the National Academy of Sciences,* vol. 73, pp. 950–954. Of 175 carcinogens, 157 (90 percent) were mutagenic. Discusses evidence that both chemical carcinogens and radiation cause cancer by damaging DNA.

McCann, J.; E. Choi; E. Yamasaki; and B. N. Ames. 1975. Detection of carcinogens as mutagens in the Salmonella/microsome test: Assay of 300 chemicals. *Proceedings of the National Academy of Sciences,* vol. 72, pp. 5135–5139. Further evidence of the high correlation between carcinogenicity and mutagenicity. Lists chemicals. Both DDE and dieldrin were negative by the Ames test.

McCann, J.; N. E. Spingarn; J. Kobori; and B. N. Ames. 1975. Detection of carcinogens as mutagens: Bacterial tester strains with R factor plasmids. *Proceedings of the National Academcy of Sciences,* vol. 72, pp. 979–983. New strains that increase sensitivity of Ames test.

McDermott, W. 1961. Air pollution and public health. *Scientific American,* October. A perceptive early statement of the likely dangers.

McGinty, Lawrence. 1976. The graveyard on Milan's doorstep. *New Scientist,* August 19, 1976, pp. 383–385. On the toxicity of dioxin, a chlorinated hydrocarbon that can contaminate 2,4,5-T.

McMichael, W. C. 1973. Tobacco smoke and energy conservation. *Building systems design,* vol. 70, October/November, pp. 17–18. Smokers at convention increase energy requirements for air-conditioning six-fold.

Menard, H. W. 1974. *Geology, resources, and society.* W. H. Freeman, San Francisco. Chapter 14 is an excellent treatment of ground subsidence and landslides caused by various human activities.

Merless, R. R. 1971. Talc-treated rice and Japanese stomach cancer. *Science,* vol. 173, pp. 1140–1141 (September 17). Presents evidence that asbestos-contaminated talc on rice in the diet is the carcinogen or cocarcinogen responsible for the high incidence of stomach cancer in Japan.

Meselson, M. 1970. Behind the Nixon policy for chemical and biological warfare. *Bulletin of the Atomic Scientists,* January. Indicates nations lacking nuclear capability need these weapons more than the United States does.

———. 1970. Chemical and biological warfare. *Scientific American,* May. General survey of the subject.

Metcalf and Eddy, Inc. 1972. *Wastewater engineering.* McGraw-Hill, New York. A technical handbook of water treatment methods.

Miller J., and E. C. Miller. 1971. Chemical carcinogenesis: Mechanisms and approaches to its control. *Journal of the National Cancer Institute,* vol. 47, pp. v–xiv. Contains an important summary of the mechanism of activation (changing noncarcinogens into carcinogens).

Miller, R. W. 1969. Delayed radiation effects in atomic-bomb survivors. *Science,* vol. 166, pp. 569–574 (October 31). Summary of observations on the survivors of Hiroshima and Nagasaki.

Miller, Stanton, S., ed. 1974. *Water pollution.* American Chemical Society, Washington, D.C. One hundred six articles from the journal *Environmental Science and Technology,* strong on monitoring and control.

Mirvish, S. S.; L. Walleave; M. Eagen; and P. Shubeck. 1972. Ascorbate-nitrite reaction: Possible means of blocking the formation of carcinogenic N-nitroso compounds. *Science,* vol. 177, pp. 65–68 (July 7). Salts of ascorbic acid (Vitamin C) may block formation of nitrosamines in the digestive tract.

Møller, A. R. 1975. Noise as a health hazard. *Ambio,* vol. 4, no. 1, pp. 6–13. Excellent introduction to physiological basis of hearing impairment from noise, emphasizing individual variation in susceptibility.

———. 1977. How good are the work noise standards? *New Scientist,* January 27, pp. 192–194. Noise influences organs other than ears.

Monath, T. P.; V. F. Newhouse; G. E. Kemp; H. W. Setzer; and A. Cappiapuoti. 1974. Lassa virus isolation from *Mastomys natalensis* rodents during an epidemic in Sierra Leone. *Science,* vol. 185, pp. 263–265 (July 19). Extrahuman cycle demonstrated in a rodent inhabiting houses.

Morgan, J. J. 1972. Trace metals in the environment. In *Science, scientists, and society,* W. Beranek, Jr., ed. Bogden and Quigley, New York. Useful compilation of data and discussion.

Morgan, Karl Z. 1975. Suggested reduction of permissible exposure to plutonium and other transuranium elements. *American Industrial Hygiene Association Journal,* August, pp. 567–575. An eminent health physicist suggests that the linear hypothesis may underestimate effects at low doses.

Murozumi, M.; T. S. Chow; and C. Patterson. 1969. Chemical concentrations of pollutant lead aerosols, terrestrial dusts and sea salts in Greenland and Antarctic snow strata. *Geochimica et Cosmochimica Acta,* vol. 33, p. 1247.

National Academy of Sciences (NAS). 1971. *Fluorides.* NAS, Washington, D.C. A review of the evidence.

———. 1972. *Accumulation of nitrate.* NAS, Washington, D.C. Nitrate water pollution and its effects on human health.

———. 1972. *Airborne lead in perspective.* NAS, Washington, D.C.

———. 1972. *The effects on populations of exposure to low levels of ionizing radiation* (BEIR Report). NAS, Washington, D.C. Estimates number of cancer deaths and genetic defects in the U.S. population due to low-dose radiation, based on linear hypothesis of effects versus dose.

———. 1974. *Air quality and automobile emissions control.* vol. 3, *The relationship of emissions to ambient air quality.* NAS, Washington D.C. A detailed and very useful document, with an extensive bibliography.

———. 1974. *Geochemistry and the environment.* NAS, Washington, D.C.

———. 1976. *Contemporary pest-control practices and prospects: The report of the executive committee.* NAS, Washington, D.C. Contains a good summary of the problem of detecting carcinogenic chemicals.

National Clearinghouse for smoking and health. Annual. *Bibliography of smoking and health.* Center for Disease control, U.S. Department of Health, Education and Welfare, Atlanta. Abstracts of international literature on smoking and health, including effects of smoking on nonsmokers.

Natusch, D.; J. Wallace; and C. Evans. 1974. Toxic trace elements: Preferential concentration in respirable particles. *Science,* vol. 183, pp. 202–204 (January 18). Shows most of the heavy metals concentrate in the smallest particles emitted from fuel combustion.

Neri, L. C.; D. Hewitt; G. B. Schreiber; T. W. Anderson; J. S. Mandel; and A. Zdrojewsky. 1975. Health aspects of hard and soft waters. *Journal of the American Water Works Association,* August, pp. 403–409. Detailed technical treatment of correlation of disease and water softness.

Nero, A. V., and Y. C. Wong. 1977. *Radiological health and related standards for nuclear power plants.* Lawrence Berkeley Laboratory, University of California. LBL-5285. Excellent job of sorting out various national and international standards and presenting them in readable form.

New Scientist. 1975. Mental deficiency and lead linked in new survey. March 20, p. 692.

———. 1976. U.S. bans commonest red food colour. January 29, p. 215.

Newton, K. G., and N. C. Greene. 1972. Organochlorine pesticide residue levels in human milk, Victoria, Australia, 1970. *Pesticides Monitoring Journal,* vol. 6, pp. 4–8. DDT-R averaged 0.139 parts per million for rural and 0.145 parts per million for urban mothers. Gives FDA tolerance for cow's milk.

Nobbs, C. L., and D. W. Pierce. 1976. The economics of stock pollutants: The example of cadmium. *International Journal of Environmental Studies,* vol. 8, pp. 245–255. Difficulties of conventional cost-benefit analysis in dealing with persistent pollutants.

Nordberg, G. F. 1974. Health hazards of environmental cadmium pollution. *Ambio,* vol. 3, no. 2, pp. 55–66. Excellent review article.

Norwood, W. D.; and C. E. Newton, Jr. 1975. U.S. transuranium registry study of thirty autopsies. *Health Physics,* vol. 28, pp. 669–675. Discusses how plutonium distributes itself in the human body, and notes that the number of deaths that have occurred to date among workers exposed to plutonium and among unexposed but otherwise similar control groups is inadequate to permit conclusions concerning what body burden of plutonium is sufficient to cause cancer.

Nottingham, J. 1972. The dangers of chemical and biological warfare (CBW). *Ecologist,* February, pp. 4–6. An overview of the threat.

O'Brien, R. D. 1967. *Insecticides:* Action and metabolism. Academic Press, New York. Information on chemistry and metabolism of DDT and other pesticides.

Oswald, W. J. 1976. Engineering applications. In *Handbook of microbiology,* 2d edition. CRC Press, Cleveland. Novel approaches to waste treatment using bacteria, algae, and solar energy.

Otani, K., and J. Ui. 1972. Minimata disease. In *Polluted Japan,* J. Ui. ed., pp. 14–16.

Page, T.; R. H. Harris; and S. S. Epstein. 1976. Drinking water and cancer mortality in Louisana. *Science,* vol. 193, pp. 55–57 (July 2). Statistical analysis indicates a relationship between cancer mortality rates and drinking water from the Mississippi River.

Parr, A. E. 1968. The five ages of urbanity. *Landscape,* vol. 17, no. 3. Describes the impact of modern city life on people of different ages.

Patterson, C. C. 1965. Contaminated and natural lead environments of man. *Archives of Environmental Health,* vol. 11, pp. 344–360. Still the best survey of the lead problem.

Perkins, E. J., 1976. The evaluation of biological response by toxicity and water quality assessments. In R. Johnston, ed., *Marine pollution,* pp. 505–585. Examines in detail how the effects of insults to marine ecosystems are determined.

Perlmutter, M., and M. Lieber. 1970. *U.S. geological survey, water supply paper 1879 G.* Washington, D.C. Discusses chromium and cadmium pollution of Long Island ground water.

Pichirnallo, J. 1971. PCB's: Leaks of toxic substances raises issue of effects, regulation. *Science,* vol. 173, pp. 899–902 (September 3). Details of egg-contamination episodes.

Polunin, Nicholas, ed. 1972. *The environmental future.* Macmillan, London. Contains many sections relevant to this chapter.

Pott, Sir Percival. 1775. *Chirugical observations relative to the cataract, the polypus of the nose, the cancer of the scrotum, the different kinds of ruptures, and the mortification of the toes and feet.* Hawes and Collins, London. (Reprinted in *National Cancer Journal Monograph,* vol. 10, pp. 7–13.) Pott made the first link between an environmental factor (chimney soot) and cancer.

President's Science Advisory committee (PSAC). 1973. *Chemicals and health.* Government Printing Office, Washington, D.C. An important source of summary data on chemicals in the environment.

Pressman, J., and A. Carol. 1971. Crime as a diseconomy of scale. *Review of Social Economy,* vol. 29, pp. 227–236. No relationship found between crime and crowding.

Quarles, John R. 1977. National water quality: assessing the mid-course correction. *Sierra Club Bulletin,* February, pp. 14–17. Acting administrator of the EPA reports on progress in controlling water pollution.

Radomski, J. L.; W. B. Deichmann; E. E. Clizer; and A. Rey. 1968. Pesticide concentrations in the liver, brain, and adipose tissues of terminal patients. *Food and Cosmetic Toxicology,* vol. 6, pp. 209–220. Correlation of home use of pesticides, pesticide concentrations in fat, and various causes of death.

Rall, David P. 1974. Review of health effects of sulfur oxides. *Environmental Health Perspectives,* August, p. 97ff.

Ramanathan, N. L., and S. Kashyap. 1975. Occupational environment and health in India. *Ambio,* vol. 4, no. 1, pp. 60–65. An overview.

Redmond, C. K.; A. Ciocco; J. W. Lloyd; and H. W. Rush. 1972. Long-term mortality study of steelworkers: pt 6, Mortality from malignant neoplasms among coke oven workers. *Journal of Occupational Medicine,* vol. 14, pp. 621–629. Workers in the vicinity of coke ovens suffer greatly increased cancer load in comparison with those in other parts of steel plant. Useful bibliography.

Reeves, A. L.; H. E. Puro; and R. G. Smith. 1974. Inhalation carcinogenesis from various forms of asbestos. *Environmental Research,* vol. 8, pp. 178–202. Animal tests and review of hypotheses about two main types of cancer caused by asbestos.

Rubin, H. 1976. Carcinogenicity tests. *Science,* vol. 191, p. 241. Criticizes view that cancers originate as mutations in body cells (see Ames, Carcenogenicity tests).

Sachs, D. P. 1970. Work at your own risk. *Saturday Review,* June 6, pp. 64–65. Reports death of a child who sucked finger after putting it into a can of TEPP.

Sander, J., and F. Seif. 1969. Bakterielle Reduktion von Nitrat im Magen des Menschen als Ursache einer Nitrosamin-Bildung. *Arzneimittellehre Forschung,* vol. 19, p. 1091. Sodium nitrate and a secondary amine (diphenylamine) were given to thirty-one human subjects and nitrosdiphenylamine was later detected in the stomach contents.

Sanders, H. J. 1969. Chemical mutagens: pt. 1, The road to genetic disaster; pt. 2, An expanding roster of suspects. *Chemical and Engineering News,* May/June. An excellent popular summary, somewhat dated but still valuable.

Savage, E. P.; J. D. Tessari; J. N. Malberg; H. W. Wheeler; and J. R. Bagby. 1973. Organochlorine pesticide residues and polychlorinated biphenyls in human milk, Colorado, 1971–1972. *Pesticide Monitoring Journal,* vol. 7, p. 15. Total organochlorines and PCBs ranged from 27 to 521 parts per billion.

Schild, G. 1970. Hong Kong "flu": Problems of prediction. *New Scientist,* October 29, p. 222. The causes of epidemics, both the immunological and other biological properties of the virus and extrinsic factors like the weather, are still poorly understood.

Schmeltz, I.; D. Hoffman; and E. L. Wynder. 1975. The influence of tobacco smoke in indoor atmospheres: pt. 1, An overview. *Preventive Medicine,* vol. 4, no. 1, pp. 66–82. Good literature review of studies of contaminant concentrations and possible effects on nonsmokers.

Schmidt, F. 1974. Tabakrauch als wichtigste Luftverschmutzung in Innenraumen und als pathogenische Noxe für Passivräucher. *Medizinische Welt,* vol. 25, no. 44. Good review article on the effects of passive smoking, including cancer risk, allergic reactions, and sensitivity of children.

Schroeder, H. A. 1971. Trace elements in the human environment. *Ecologist,* May, pp. 15–19. Good review article.

Schuck, P. H., and H. Wellford. 1973. Botulism and nitrites. *Science,* vol. 180, p. 1322 (June 29). Disagrees with Wolff and Wasserman, Nitrates, nitrites and nitrosamines (see their reply adjacent, and Lijinsky, Nitrites in foods).

Schwartz, H. 1972. Influenza: yes, you really had it. *New York Times,* February 13. Graph of epidemics from September 1969 to February 1972.

Selikoff, I. J. 1975. Recent perspectives in occupational cancer. *Ambio,* vol. 4, no. 1, pp. 14–17. Survey of recent experience emphasizing the difficulties in evaluation and prevention that arise from long latency period between insult and incidence of disease.

Selikoff, I. J.; R. A. Bader; M. E. Bader; J. Churg; and E. C. Hammond. 1967. Asbestos and neoplasia. *American Journal of Medicine,* vol. 42, pp. 487–496. Good summary of the massive threat of asbestos-induced cancer; bibliography of early literature.

Selikoff, I. J.; E. C. Hammond; and J. Churg. 1968. Asbestos exposure, smoking, and neoplasia. *Journal of the American Medical Association,* vol. 204, pp. 106–112. Synergism involving asbestos fibers and tobacco smoke.

Shea, Kevin P. 1973. PCB: The worldwide pollutant that nobody noticed. *Environment,* vol. 15, November, pp. 25–28. A general review.

———. 1977. Profile of a deadly pesticide. *Environment,* vol. 19, January/February, pp. 6–12. Deals with the neurotoxic organophosphate Phosvel (leptophos) which may be able to cause crippling disease.

Shettigara, P., and R. W. Morgan. 1975. Asbestos, smoking, and laryngeal carcinoma. *Archives of Environmental Health,* vol. 30, pp. 517–519. Bibliography gives access to literature on cancers caused by asbestos.

Shy, C. M.; J. P. Creason; N. E. Pearlman; C. E. McClain; F. B. Benson; and M. M. Young. 1970. The Chattanooga school children study: Effects of community exposure to nitrogen dioxide, pts. 1 and 2. *Journal of the Air Pollution Control Association,* vol. 20, p. 539–545 (August) and pp. 582–588 (Sept.).

Smith, C. E. G.; D. I. H. Simpson; E. T. W. Bowen; and I. Zlotnik. 1967. Fatal human disease from vervet monkeys. *Lancet,* vol. 2, no. 7526, pp. 1119–1121. (See also pp. 1129–1130 of the same issue.) Source on Marburgvirus.

Smith, W. H. 1972. Lead and mercury burden of urban woody plants. *Science,* vol. 176, p. 1237–1239 (June 16).

Sobsey, M. D. 1975. Enteric viruses and drinking-water supplies. *Journal of the American Water Works Association,* August, pp. 414–417. Problems of detection and surveillance.

Sommer, R. 1969. *Personal space.* Prentice-Hall, Englewood Cliffs, N.J. Special emphasis on design of buildings to fit peculiarities of human space requirements.

Sparks, R. E.; J. Cairns, Jr.; and A. G. Heath. 1972. The use of bluegill breathing rates to detect zinc. *Water Research,* vol. 6, pp. 895–911. A bioassay for a nonlethal toxicant.

Stecker, Paul G., ed. 1968. *The Merck Index: An encyclopedia of chemicals and drugs.* 8th ed. A standard reference work describing an enormous array of chemicals (some 42,000 in this edition) and giving structural formulas for about 10 percent of them. Information on synthesis, characteristics, uses, and toxicity.

Stein, P. C.; E. E. Campbell; W. D. Moss; and P. Trujillo. 1974. Mercury in man. *Archives of Environmental Health,* vol. 29 (July), pp. 25–27. Good reference on the fate of mercury once in the body.

Stoltz, D. R.; K. S. Khera; R. Bendall; and S. W. Gunner. 1970. Cytogenetic studies with cyclamate and related compounds. *Science,* vol. 167, pp. 1501–1502 (March 13). Tests with human leucocyte cultures shows these compounds cause chromosome damage.

Tamplin, A. R., and T. B. Cochran. 1974. *Radiation standards for hot particles.* Natural Resources Defense Council, Washington, D.C. Argues that under some circumstances plutonium can be 100,000 times more hazardous than existing standards imply—a factor too large for most other authorities to swallow.

Tanner, J. T.; M. H. Friedman; D. N. Lincoln; L. A. Ford; and M. Jaffee. 1972. Mercury content of common foods determined by neutron activation analysis. *Science,* vol. 177, pp. 1102–1103 (September 22).

Tardiff, R., and M. Deinzer. 1973. *Toxicity of organic compounds in drinking water.* EPA Water Supply Research Laboratory, Cincinnati. Chlorination of water supplies may itself be a source of carcinogens.

Thompson, R. C. 1975. Transuranium element toxicity—dose response relationships at low exposure levels. Summary and speculative interpretation relative to exposure limits. In *Radiation Research,* O. Nygaard, H. Adler, and W. Sinclair, eds., Academic Press, New York, pp. 1278–1284. Support for the view that plutonium is perhaps 5 times more hazardous than existing MPCs suggest.

Tinker, J. 1973. PCBs at Maendy: Scare or disaster? *New Scientist,* June 21, pp. 760–762. Alarming PCB pollution at one location in Wales.

———, 1973. Should public smoking be banned? *New Scientist,* August 9, pp. 313–315. Excellent concise review of the evidence concerning harmfulness of tobacco smoke to nonsmokers.

Topping, G. 1976. Sewage and the sea. In R. Johnston, ed., *Marine pollution,* pp. 303–351. Calls for action now before the situation gets out of hand.

Trijonis, J. 1975. The relationship of sulfur-oxide emissions to sulfur dioxide and sulfate air quality. In *Air quality and stationary-source emission control,* NAS. The best work on a difficult technical problem.

Trump, C. G. 1974. Public eye on pollution. *Environment,* vol. 16, no. 10, pp. 13–16. Critique of government practices in regulating water pollution.

Tsing, W. P.; H. M. Chu; S. W. How; J. M. Fong; C. S. Lin; and Shu Yeh. 1968. Prevalence of skin cancer in an endemic area of chronic arsenicism in Taiwan. *Journal of the National Cancer Institute,* vol. 40, pp. 453–463. Relates high arsenic content of water to skin cancer.

Turner, J. S. 1970. *The chemical feast.* Grossman, New York. Report of Ralph Nader's study group on the U.S. Food and Drug Administration; see especially material on cyclamates.

Ui, J., ed. 1972. *Polluted Japan.* Jishu Koza Citizens Movement, Tokyo. A shocking, often angry set of articles documenting in words, statistics, and photographs the intense industrial pollution in Japan.

United Nations Scientific Committee on the Effects of Atomic Radiation (UNSCEAR). 1972. *Ionizing radiation: Levels and effects.* 2 vol. United Nations, New York. Very detailed review of the evidence. UNSCEAR refuses to extrapolate evidence obtained at high doses to estimate low-dose effects, however.

U.S. Department of Commerce. Annual. *Statistical abstract of the United States.* U.S. Government Printing Office, Washington, D.C.

U.S. Department of Health, Education and Welfare. 1964. *Smoking and health.* Government Printing Office, Washington, D.C. The summary of why those who claimed cigarettes to be the equivalent of coffin nails were correct.

———. 1969. *Air quality criteria for sulphur oxides.* Government Printing Office, Washington, D.C. Somewhat dated but still useful compendium of information on effects and bases for early standards.

———. 1970. *Radiological health handbook.* Government Printing Office, Washington, D.C. Useful tabulations of energies of radioactive emissions and shielding factors for various materials.

U.S. Environmental Protection Agency (EPA). 1971. *Effects of noise on people.* NTID 300.7. National Technical Information Service, Springfield, Va. Valuable basic reference.

———. 1971. *Environmental lead and public health.* Report AP-90. Air Pollution Control Office, Research Triangle Park, North Carolina.

———. 1971. *Fundamentals of noise: Measurement, rating schemes and standards.* National Technical Information Service, Springfield, Va., NTID 300.15.

———. 1972. *The economics of clean water, summary.* Government Printing Office, Washington, D.C. Extent of various degrees of sewage treatment in the U.S., among other topics.

———. 1973. *Compilation of air pollutant emission factors.* 2d ed. EPA, Washington, D.C.

———. 1975. *DDT: A review of scientific and economic aspects of the decision to ban its use as a pesticide.* EPA, Washington, D.C., EPA-540/1-75-022. Self-justifying but full of useful information.

———. 1975. *A study of indoor air quality.* EPA-USO/4-74-02. EPA, Washington, D.C. Presents measurements of concentrations of oxides of nitrogen and carbon monoxide in homes due mainly to operation of gas stoves.

U.S. Federal Water Pollution Control Administration. 1968. *Cost of clean water,* vol. 3. Government Printing Office, Washington, D.C. Character and origins of the plight of Lake Erie.

U.S. General Services Administration. 1976. *Code of federal regulations,* title 10, *Energy,* parts 20 and 50. Standards for protection against radiation.

U.S. National Commission on Materials Policy. 1974. *Material needs and the environment today and tomorrow.* Government Printing Office, Washington, D.C. Contains useful material on civilization's flows of heavy metals.

U.S. National Council on Radiation Protection and Measurements. 1975. *Natural background radiation in the United States,* NCRP Publications, Washington, D.C., report 45. Very thorough discussion of contributions of cosmic rays and naturally occuring isotopes to doses in the U.S., with an appendix on fallout from weapons tests.

U.S. Nuclear Regulatory Commission. 1975. *Reactor safety study.* Government Printing Office, Washington, D.C., WASH 1400/NUREG-75-14. Many details of shielding, pathway, and dosimetry calculations.

Vallentyne, J. R. 1972. Freshwater supplies and pollution: Effects of the demophoric explosion on water and man. *The environmental future,* N. Polunin, ed., Macmillan, London, pp. 181–199. An excellent overview. Coins the word *demophoric* to "encompass all aspects of the biology of human populations and technological production-consumption." Thus, we are undergoing a demophoric explosion.

van der Leeden, Frits. 1975. *Water resources of the world: Selected statistics.* Water Information Center, Port Washington, N.Y. Extensive information on water-quality standards and extent of water pollution around the world.

Wade, N. 1972. DES: A case study of regulatory abdication. *Science,* vol. 177, pp. 335–337 (July 29). Another USDA-FDA foul-up discussed.

———. 1972. Delaney anti-cancer clause: Scientists debate on article of faith. *Science,* vol. 177, pp. 588–591 (August 18).

———. 1972. FDA invents more tales about DES. *Science,* vol. 177, p. 503 (August 11). Follows up on above.

———. 1973. Microbiology: Hazardous profession faces new uncertainties. *Science,* vol. 182, pp. 566–567 (November 9). See especially material on the possibility of a man-made influenza pandemic.

———. 1977. Dicing with nature: Three narrow escapes. *Science,* vol. 195, p. 378 (January 28). Some potentially dangerous experiments involving recombinant DNA that were carried out in two cases and seriously contemplated in a third.

Wagner, J. C.; C. A. Sleggs; and P. Marchand. 1960. Diffuse pleural mesothelioma and asbestos exposure on the northwestern Cape Province. *British Journal of Industrial Medicine,* vol. 17, pp. 260–271. First strong association of asbestos and mesothelioma found in studies in asbestos hills of South Africa.

Wallace, R. A.; W. Fullarson; W. Shults; and W. S. Lyon. 1971. *Mercury in the environment.* National Technical Information Service, Springfield, Va., ORNL-NSF-EP-1. Outstanding review paper covering all aspects of the subject.

Warnick, S. L. 1972. Organochlorine pesticide levels in human serum and adipose tissue, Utah, Fiscal Year 1967–1971. *Pesticides Monitoring Journal,* vol. 6, pp. 9–13. Tendency for storage levels to increase.

Warren, C. E. 1971. Suspended particulate air pollution. *Archives of Environmental Health,* vol. 22, January, pp. 174–177. Indicates that particulate air pollution may act directly or synergistically to cause cirrhosis of the liver.

Warren, K. S. 1974. Precarious odyssey of an unconquered parasite. *Natural History,* May, pp. 47–52. Discusses spread of schistosomiasis (bilharzia) with irrigation.

Wassermann, M.; M. Gon; D. Wassermann; and L. Zellermazer. 1965. DDT and DDE in the body fat of people in Israel. *Archives of Environmental Health,* vol. 11, pp. 375–379. Source of much of the data in the table of DDT concentrations in various nations, sources in the bibliography.

Watson, J. D. 1976. *The molecular biology of the gene.* 3d ed. Benjamin, Boston. A fine summary of the chemical bases of heredity.

Watt, K. E. F. 1968. *Ecology and resource management.* McGraw-Hill, New York. See section 6.3 (p. 156ff) on the dynamics of epidemic and epizotic waves.

Weast, R. C., ed. 1976. *Handbook of chemistry and physics.* Chemical Rubber Co., Cleveland. Indispensable for its tabulation of all radioactive isotopes.

Weichart, G. 1973. Pollution of the North Sea. *Ambio,* vol. 2, no. 4, pp. 97–106. Case study of one of the more intense cases of regional industrial water pollution.

Weish, P., and E. Gruber. 1975. *Radioaktivität und Umwelt.* Gustav-Fischer Verlag, Stuttgart. Those who don't read German should hope for a translation; this is a better introduction to radioactivity and the environment than any we know of in English.

Weiss, H. V.; M. Koide; and E. D. Goldberg. 1971. Mercury in a Greenland ice sheet: Evidence of recent input by man. *Science,* vol. 174, pp. 692–694 (November 12). Includes comparisons of natural and man-made sources.

White, E. H. 1970. *Chemical background for the biological sciences.* 2d ed. Prentice-Hall, Englewood Cliffs, N.J. Useful review of biological chemistry relevant to pesticide material in this chapter.

Winell, Margarita. 1975. An international comparison of hygienic standards for chemicals in the work environment. *Ambio,* vol. 4, no. 1, pp. 34–36. Information on some 160 substances.

Winkelstein, W., and R. Gay. 1971. Suspended particulate air pollution. *Archives of Environmental Health,* January, pp. 174–177.

Wogan, G. N. 1967. Naturally occurring carcinogens in foods. *Progress in Experimental Tumor Research,* vol. 11, pp. 134–162. Survey of carcinogenic hazards of contaminants introduced into food by biological processes (e.g. metabolic products of fungi) and compounds naturally present in foods (e.g. pyrrolizidine alkaloids). Extensive bibliography.

Wolff, I. A., and A. E. Wasserman. 1972. Nitrates, nitrites and nitrosamines. *Science,* vol. 177, pp. 15–19 (July 7). Reviews nitrosamine carcinogenesis hazard and opposes immediate reduction of nitrite and nitrate in cured meats because of possibility of food poisoning (but see Schuck and Wellford, Botulism and nitrites, and Lijinski, Nitrites in foods).

Wood, J. M. 1974. Biological cycles for toxic cycles in the environment. *Science,* vol. 183, pp. 1049–1052 (March 15). Indicates complexity of pathways to humans.

World Health Organization (WHO). 1970. *Fluoride and human health.* WHO, Geneva, monograph 59.

Wright, G.; S. Jewczyk; J. Onrot; and P. Tomlinson. 1975. Carbon monoxide in the urban atmosphere. *Archives of Environmental Health,* vol. 30, March, pp. 123–129. Relates atmospheric concentration of carbon monoxide to level of carboxyhemoglobin in blood and consequent physiological effects.

Zeidberg, L. D.; R. A. Prindle; and E. Landau. 1964. The Nashville air pollution study, III: morbidity in relation to air pollution. *American Journal of Public Health,* vol 54, no. 1, pp. 85–97.

I suggest that the earth's biota is our single, most important resource. While protecting it will not assure wealth and grace for man, its decimation will assure increasing hardship for all.

—G. M. Woodwell
Success, Succession, and Adam Smith, 1974

CHAPTER 11

Disruption of Ecological Systems

The direct effects of pollution on property, on human health, and on the quality of life are varied and important, but they may ultimately prove to be less critical for society as a whole than the less obvious effects of pollution and other human activities on the ecological systems that sustain human life.

Crucial to these systems are the green plants that are the basic energy source for all other forms of life on Earth, and green plants are provided with the material ingredients of growth by the nutrient cycles of the biosphere. Those cycles do routinely what human society as yet cannot do—convert wastes completely into resources, using energy from the sun. The crops of civilization are watered, nourished, and protected from potential pests with considerable help from natural processes, which include the formation and preservation of soil itself. The agents and carriers of human disease, like crop pests, are controlled more often by natural enemies or by environmental conditions than by human action. Climate and the composition of the atmosphere itself are regulated by geophysical and biological processes that may be susceptible to human interference.

These and other "public services" of the global ecosystem cannot be replaced by technology now or in the foreseeable future. This is so in many instances because a process is not understood scientifically. And, even where scientific knowledge might be adequate, the sheer magnitude of the tasks performed by natural

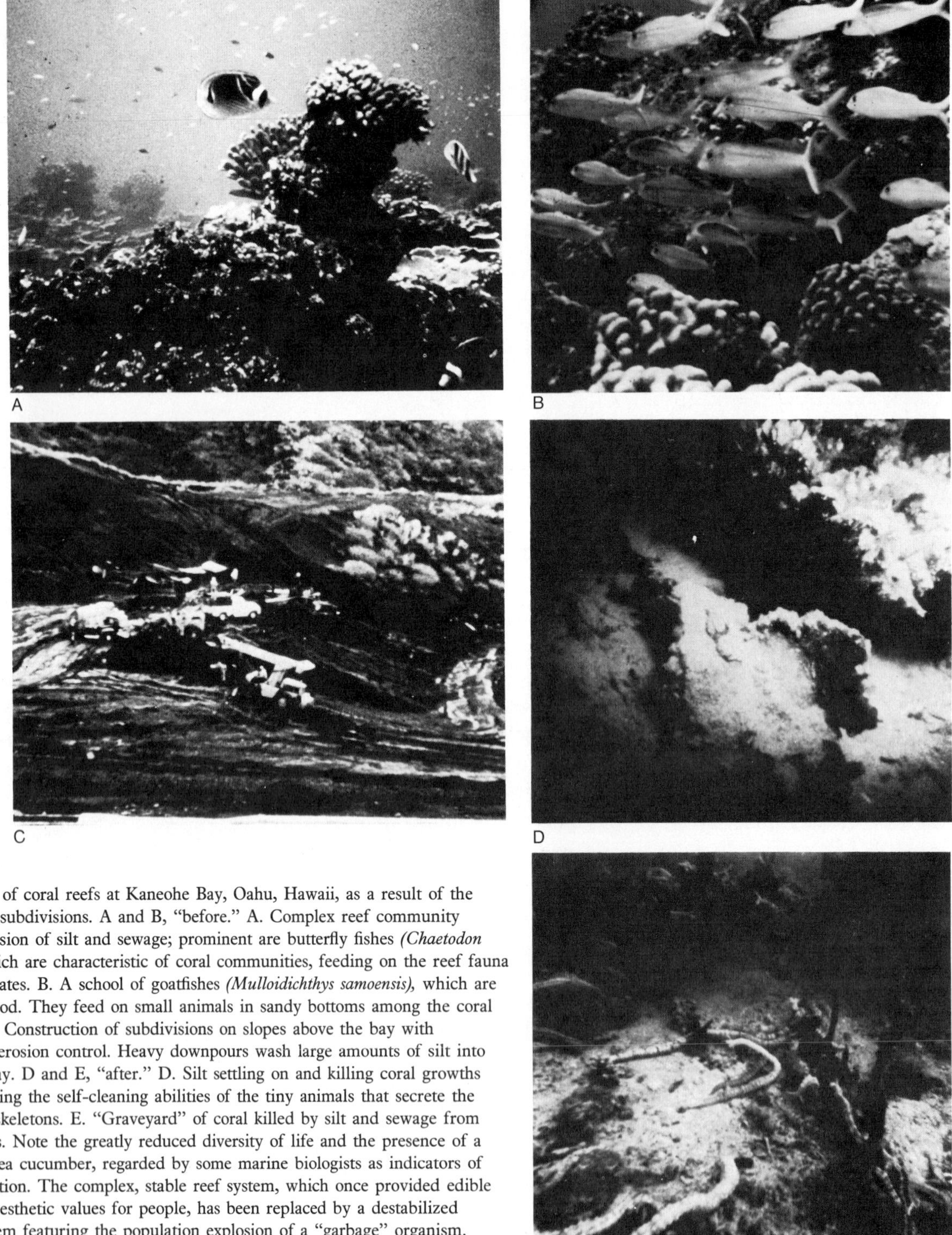

FIGURE 11-1

Destruction of coral reefs at Kaneohe Bay, Oahu, Hawaii, as a result of the building of subdivisions. A and B, "before." A. Complex reef community before intrusion of silt and sewage; prominent are butterfly fishes *(Chaetodon lunula),* which are characteristic of coral communities, feeding on the reef fauna of invertebrates. B. A school of goatfishes *(Mulloidichthys samoensis),* which are prized as food. They feed on small animals in sandy bottoms among the coral growths. C. Construction of subdivisions on slopes above the bay with inadequate erosion control. Heavy downpours wash large amounts of silt into Kaneohe Bay. D and E, "after." D. Silt settling on and killing coral growths by overloading the self-cleaning abilities of the tiny animals that secrete the hard coral skeletons. E. "Graveyard" of coral killed by silt and sewage from subdivisions. Note the greatly reduced diversity of life and the presence of a species of sea cucumber, regarded by some marine biologists as indicators of heavy pollution. The complex, stable reef system, which once provided edible fishes and aesthetic values for people, has been replaced by a destabilized simple system featuring the population explosion of a "garbage" organism. (From the film *Cloud Over the Coral Reef* by Dr. Lee Tepley and Dr. R. E. Johannes.)

ecosystems dwarfs civilization's capacity to finance, produce, and deploy the technology necessary to replace them.

Since the support provided for human life by ecosystems is indispensable and irreplaceable, it is essential that the mechanisms behind those vital functions—and the potential for disrupting them through pollution and other human activities—be carefully studied.[1] The mechanisms were discussed in chapters 2, 3, and 4. This chapter is an introduction to the disruptions.

MODIFYING ECOSYSTEMS

Like any other creatures, human beings have always had some effect on the ecological systems of which they were a part, but the history of deliberate and significant modification of ecosystems doubtless began with the development of agriculture.[1a] Since then, human influence has reached to the remotest areas of the planet and has been intensified by increasing numbers of people and the development of modern technology.

What are some of the ways in which humanity modifies ecological systems? Obviously, some ecosystems are destroyed outright by such diverse activities as clearing land to plant crops, starting fires, building dams, applying defoliants to jungles, constructing buildings, and laying pavement. (See Figure 11-1 for an example of how activities on land can damage an ecosystem in an adjacent bay.) Forests are chopped down for structural wood and firewood.[2] Estuaries are dredged, filled, or altered by bulkheads.[3] And, as discussed later in Box 11-3, ecosystems can be destroyed as a part of military strategy.

The effects of such assaults are diverse. Paved areas are normally removed from natural systems for long periods—and their rapid reclamation is both costly and difficult. Dams take land out of terrestrial systems for long periods, but as noted earlier, dams are temporary structures, and enriched land will eventually be returned. Strip-mined areas in developed countries (some 1.6 million hectares in the United States and 2.2 million hectares in the USSR by 1974)[4] often have not been reclaimed; the practicability of doing so at all is a function of both economics and ecology.[5] When prairie is converted to cornfield, an unstable ecosystem replaces a stable one. Attempts to stabilize such systems artifically can lead to further destabilization and bring about changes elsewhere as well.

Physical assaults on ecosystems often interact with overexploitation and pollution to threaten species with extinction. For example, industrial and harbor development encroaching on breeding areas is combining with oil pollution and competition from the fishing industry to deplete South African jackass penguin populations already reduced in size by overexploitation of the bird's eggs and disruption (since halted) of their breeding activities.[6]

Now that ecologists are gaining a more detailed understanding of the factors that threaten ecosystems, they are beginning to examine carefully strategies for preserving natural diversity. Especially interesting have been attempts to develop a guideline for location, number, size, and configuration of natural reserves, based on the theory of island biogeography.[7] Few topics are more worthy of investigation, although, of course, application of the principles uncovered will require a commitment to conservation and a halt to human expansion while there are significant wild areas left to conserve.

Deforestation

The values to human society of healthy forest ecosystems extend far beyond the obvious ones of timber, wood products, and recreational resources. Forest ecologist F. H. Bormann has summarized these additional less-appreciated, but perhaps ultimately more important

[1]The subtleties of the interactions that can be discovered by such studies, even when a pastoral society is involved, are illustrated by Stephen Berwick, The Gir forest: An endangered ecosystem.

[1a]For an absorbing account of the ecological impact of past civilizations, see J. Donald Hughes, *Ecology of ancient civilizations.*

[2]See Chapter 6, and Erik Eckholm, *Losing ground.*

[3]W. E. Odum, Insidious alteration of the estuarine environment.

[4]*Report of the national commission on Materials Policy,* Government Printing Office, Washington, D.C., 1974, p. 7-7; Norman Precoda, Left behind: Soviet mine wastes.

[5]For example, T. W. Box, R. F. Hadley, and M. G. Wolman, ed., *Rehabilitation potential of western coal lands.*

[6]P. G. H. Frost, W. R. Siegfried, and J. Cooper, Conservation of the jackass penguin [*Spheniscus demersus* (L.)].

[7]Jared M. Diamond, The island dilemma: Lessons of modern biogeographic studies for the design of natural reserves; A. L. Sullivan and M. L. Shaffer, Biogeography of the megazoo.

values: "Forest ecosystems . . . exercise considerable control over patterns of climate, hydrology, circulation of nutrients, erosion, and the cleansing functions of air and water, as well as over the status of streams, lakes, and underground water supplies."[7a] Moreover, tropical forests especially represent a vast reservoir of genetic diversity of plants, animals, and microorganisms, any of which potentially could be of direct benefit to humanity, and all of which play their parts in maintaining the ecosystem.[7b]

Wholesale logging of forests creates extreme changes that effectively destroy the forest ecosystem. Numerous animals that depend on the trees for food and shelter disappear. Many of the smaller forest plants depend on the trees for shade; they and the animals they support also disappear.

Removal of temperate-zone forests also results in heavy losses of nutrients from the soil. These losses may overload streams with nutrients and, if prolonged, may limit the ability of succession to restore the forest ecosystem. If disruption of a forest floor is severe, widespread erosion losses may become serious. If such disruption is avoided, the potential for recovery remains high if the successional process can begin within a year or two of cutting, since early successional species are adapted to take advantage of the increased abundance of water and nutrients in such areas.[8] In time, if reforestation is not carried out, a deforested area is invaded by pioneer weedy plants that often have far fewer desirable characteristics for human use than did the forest that was removed. As discussed in Chapter 4, areas from which tropical forests have been removed may have much less potential for successional recovery, particularly where soils are lateritic.

Loss of plant cover and topsoil reduces the capacity of an area to retain water, diminishes the supply of fresh water, causes silting behind dams, and has other serious consequences for human beings. The flooding along many of the world's rivers, from the Ganges in India to the Eel River in California, has been greatly aggravated by heavy deforestation in their watersheds.

[7a]F. H. Bormann, An inseparable linkage: conservation of natural ecosystems and the conservation of fossil energy, p.754.

[7b]Peter Gwynne, Doomed jungles?

[8]F. H. Bormann et al., The export of nutrients and recovery of stable conditions following deforestation at Hubbard Brook.

Deforestation also significantly reduces the amount of water transferred from ground to air by transpiration by trees, which in turn affects climate, at least locally. Downwind of a deforested area, weather is made more arid and subject to greater extremes of temperature. Removal of tropical rainforests also reduces the absorption of incident sunlight. As tropical forests are progressively cleared during the rest of this century, the result may be unanticipated changes in climate, perhaps on a global scale. Indeed, some changes attributable to tropical deforestation have been noted already.[8a]

Human activities have already substantially reduced the world's forests and produced a great increase in the amount of desert and wasteland, as noted in Chapters 4 and 6. Such destructive activities have accelerated as the human population has increased, and in many cases complex interactions between human beings and the environment have led, or have threatened to lead, to *ecocatastrophes* (dramatic failure of the life-support capability of an ecosystem).

Slash-and-Burn Agriculture

One of the clearest examples of how overpopulation can lead to environmental deterioration can be seen in one kind of nonmechanized farming. In tropical forests, people for centuries have practiced what is known variously as slash-and-burn or milpa or swidden agriculture.[9] In that method a clearing is cut in a forest during the driest part of the year and the felled trees left in place. After they have dried, they are burned. The fire not only provides fertile ash, it also kills insects and the seeds of weeds. The farmer plants a crop as rain commences and then injects additional energy into the system in the form of labor—fighting weeds with hoe and machete.

After the harvest the inedible parts of the crop plants are chopped down, allowed to dry in the field, and burned. Since the mass of plant material is smaller than that of the previous year when the forest was first cleared,

[8a]Reasearch findings by G. Potter, H. Ellsaesser, M. McCracken, and F. Luther (of the Lawrence Livermore Laboratory of the University of California) on this point were reported in *World Issues,* vol. II, no. 1 (February–March 1977), p. 18.

[9]D. H. Janzen, The unexploited tropics.

the fire is not so hot and there is less ash. As a result the soil is less thoroughly fertilized and the pest kill is less complete. The downhill spiral continues for a year or two until it is no longer profitable to farm that clearing. The milpa farmer then moves on, creates a new clearing, and repeats the whole process. Meanwhile the forest gradually reclaims the original clearing. Tens or hundreds of years later, the original clearing may once again be farmed.[9a]

Because the tropical forest is a tightly closed system as far as nutrient cycles are concerned (Chapter 3), the small, widely spaced clearings of swidden farmers do little damage to that system. Adjacent trees help protect a clearing from the torrential tropical rains, and their roots, extending into the clearing, recapture nutrients. When a clearing is abandoned, the forest can reinvade it. But what happens when human population growth forces farmers to return to previously farmed plots before the forest has totally reclaimed them? Or when clearings are made larger in order to support more people?

When a sizable chunk of forest is cleared for agriculture (or defoliated for military purposes), the continuous recycling of nutrients is interrupted. The surrounding forest no longer breaks the force of the rain, and tree roots penetrate only the periphery of the clearing. Heavy rains wash away the thin supply of soil nutrients, of which the last to go (where they are present) are iron and aluminum oxides. When certain iron-rich lateritic soils, which underly perhaps 5 to 10 percent of tropical forests, are eroded and exposed to sun and oxygen, a series of complex chemical changes may take place, resulting in the formation of a rocklike substance called laterite (from *later,* the Latin word for brick). Laterization has occurred over wide areas of the tropics, starting long ago and continuing in recent years. Those who have been fortunate enough to visit Angkor Wat in Cambodia (Figure 11-2) have seen magnificent cities and temples built by the Khmers 800 to 1000 years ago. The construction materials were sandstone and laterite, and laterization may have been a principal reason for the disappearance of the Khmer civilization shortly after its greatest monuments were constructed. After laterization, unfortunately, the forest normally is unable to reinvade a clearing successfully. Even without laterization, a cleared area will rapidly lose the nutrients required for satisfactory agricultural yields—nutrients that can only be restored by forest regrowth or by careful fertilization.

FIGURE 11-2

Laterite construction in the temple of Angkor Wat near Ankor Thom, a major city of the ancient Khmer civilization in what is now Cambodia. Laterite on exposure to air turns into a bricklike form of rock still widely used for construction. (Photo by United Nations.)

Catastrophic loss of soil fertility is thus a natural consequence of increased population density among slash-and-burn agriculturalists. In order to support more people, the age-old patterns of movement are accelerated.[10] Sites of previous clearings are revisited before the

[9a]For an interesting description of swidden agriculture in New Guinea, where farmers show clear understanding of local ecology and work with it rather than against it, see Roy A. Rappaport, Forests and man.

[10]The cultural consequences are discussed in A. P. Vayda, ed., *Environment and cultural behavior.* See especially the paper by Vayda, Expansion and warfare among swidden agriculturalists.

forest has totally reclaimed them. As a result, the fires are less hot, the ash less abundant, and soil fertility decreased. Clearings must be abandoned ever more often, and, to compensate, larger clearings are made. The road to soil deterioration is open.

The general pattern described has been repeated in many tropical areas when and where the human population has increased. It has been hypothesized that overintensive tropical agriculture contributed to the collapse of both the Khmer and the classic Mayan civilizations—although it seems likely that both of those societies had advanced to permanent, rather than milpa cultivation before laterization and other problems overtook them.[11]

Farming the Tropics

A traveler in the tropics today cannot help being impressed by the poor quality of much of the land cleared of forest there. At best, a great deal of that land can serve only as second-rate pasture. Silting of rivers is also easily observed, but subtle changes in climate resulting from removal of forest are less obvious.

Tropical forests are usually able to reinvade small clearings where soils are subject to laterization before the process is complete. Whether large areas that have been kept cleared for substantial periods of time can be reforested after laterization is an open question. Reforestation has been successful in some areas where the soil crust has been carefully broken up, fertilizers applied, and the entire system carefully cultivated. But natural reforestation (and, especially, reestablishment of a semblance of the original diversity) seems unlikely. Even most of the attempts supported by human activity have failed. Laterization is continuing in various parts of the tropics and will doubtless proceed more rapidly as people become increasingly desperate for food. According to one geologist, Mary McNeil, "The ambitious plans to increase food production in the tropics to meet the pressure of the rapid rise of population have given too little consideration to the laterization problem and the measures that will have to be undertaken to overcome it."[12] She points to one fiasco at Iata in the Amazon basin, where the government of Brazil once attempted to found a farming community. Laterization destroyed the project, when "in less than five years the cleared fields became virtually pavements of rock."

The degree of threat to tropical agriculture posed by lateritic soils is a matter of controversy.[13] Unfortunately, tropical soils are not well understood, so prediction of the consequences of clearing tropical forests for agricultural purposes is difficult.

Some things can be said with assurance, however. First of all, the term *the tropics* covers a multitude of sins. Far from being uniform, the tropics are more diverse ecologically than the temperate regions. Therefore, the ecological and agricultural situation for each location must be evaluated separately. And, furthermore, that evaluation may not provide quick and easy solutions to the problems of agricultural development. For instance, much of the Amazon Basin presents a severe challenge to agriculture. With great effort and care, successful agricultural programs could be developed to farm the so-called *terra firme*—land above the floodplains that are periodically inundated (and thus fertilized) by the Amazon. Such programs would involve the interlocking of farming with animal husbandry, to make manure available for fertilizer (it tends to be much more satisfactory under tropical conditions than inorganic fertilizers). The constraints on agriculture in Amazonia, moreover, are such as to make difficult the continual adjustments necessary to meet changing local and international market conditions.[14]

The Trans-Amazonian Highway

In 1970, Brazil began a crash program of highway constuction in the Amazon basin. The central project is the Trans-Amazonian Highway. When completed, the highway is to connect such Atlantic coast ports as Belem and Recife with points in Peru and Bolivia, through

[11]Although it has been widely stated that the classic Maya were primarily milpa agriculturalists, some recent work indicates otherwise. See B. L. Turner, II, Prehistoric intensive agriculture in the Mayan lowlands.

[12]Lateritic soils. See also McNeil's Lateritic soils in distinct tropical environments: Southern Sudan and Brazil.

[13]See, for example, P. W. Richards, *The tropical rainforest,* University Press, Cambridge, 1964; C. N. Williams and K. T. Joseph, *Climate, soil and crop production in the humid tropics;* Betty J. Meggers, Amazonia: Man and culture in a counterfeit paradise; and, especially, P. H. Sanchez and S. W. Buol, Soils of the tropics and the world food crisis.

[14]Harold Sioli, Recent human activities in the Brazilian Amazon region and their ecological effects. See also B. J. Meggers' article in the same volume.

which countries they may someday be linked by road to the Pacific. The route of the Trans-Amazonian Highway runs roughly parallel to the river itself, about 320 kilometers to the south. The highway is planned to tie in with an extensive additional network of roads crisscrossing the basin.[15]

The program was initiated by President Emilio Médici after he had visited the drought-devastated northeast of Brazil in 1969, in order "to carry the landless population of the Northeast to the unpopulated lands of the Amazon." An agritown of forty-eight to sixty families is planned for every 10 kilometers along the 4800-kilometer length of the highway. The government has expropriated all land within 50 miles of the road network (an area of almost 2.3 million square kilometers—much larger than Mexico), on which it plans to establish colonists on 100-hectare (250-acre) parcels.[16]

Some 8000 Amazonian Indians are to be resettled from the development area onto reservations in a move reminiscent of United States policy in the nineteenth century. Although eighty-four Brazilian social scientists signed a protest against the plan for the Indians, it is clear that the development project will be permitted to move ahead.[17] The great Amazonian rain forest, complete with its rich array of animals and peoples, appears destined to follow the tall-grass prairies of North America to extinction. But the tragedy of the Amazon will be even greater. The European successors of the North American Indians at least were able to extract great wealth on a continuing basis from the lands they appropriated. But the current efforts of the Brazilians will, in all probability, merely net them a few harvests at the cost of irreversible destruction of the region. Amazonia could be turned into the world's largest parking lot.

The tragedy is all the greater because there have been ample warnings for Brazilians—warnings from home, not just from foreign ecologists. The failure of the agricultural colony set up at Iata was one portent. But the Brazilian government, like other governments, seems to find it hard to learn from experience. And, like other governments, it also may turn a deaf ear to expertise when politics and special interests are involved. Scientific reports published by a government agency, Instituto Brasileiro de Geografia, pointed out the pitfalls of the development program, warning that "a disaster of enormous proportions" would occur[18] if the policy were carried through.

The key to the situation could be the rumor that groups behind the development were actually interested in opening the Amazon basin for oil and other mineral exploration—that agriculture was a secondary concern, more of an excuse than anything else. But it is not certain that the forest covers a mineral bonanza.

It is possible that Brazilians do not really want to know the truth about Amazonia, for that would force them to confront the true dimensions of their country. Gone would be myths of untold abundance, of limitless resources, of future world power. Brazilians would have to recognize the biological and physical limits within which their nation must operate in order to survive—much as citizens of the United States in the 1970s have had to face the limitations to their power. But the Brazilians have a tougher job, since they must confront reality *before* they have had their fling at being overdeveloped. And there is little sign that they are ready for that confrontation.[19]

In Brazil today, one sees a striking example of a ubiquitous phenomenon—the inability of social systems to respond effectively to imperatives arising from the laws of nature. Since the laws of nature are unlikely to be repealed, it would behoove humanity to see whether the "laws" of social behavior are equally fixed (Chapters 14 and 15). If they prove to be, as some social scientists seem to think, then the outlook for *Homo sapiens* is bleak indeed.

Desertification and the Sahel Famine

Another dramatic example of the interaction of human population size with natural systems is seen in the Sahel famine. (The Sahel is the region of Africa on the southern fringe of the Sahara.) The climatic events

[15]*Time,* September 13, 1971.

[16]Quoted by Affonso Henriques in The awakening Amazon giant, *Americas,* February 1972; *Time,* September 13, 1971.

[17]*Time,* September 13, 1971.

[18]Meggers, Amazonia, p. 154.

[19]See, for instance, Para SEMA, Ehrlich revela meisa-verdades, *O Estado de Sao Paulo,* January 15, 1975. For a general review of the Brazilian situation, see J. C. Jahoda and D. L. O'Hearn, The reluctant Amazon basin.

triggering the famine are discussed later in this chapter, but people themselves played a major role in creating conditions in which famine could be triggered. In some areas, for instance, colonial officials misinterpreted the ecologically sound pastoral systems of nomads living in the arid region as inefficient and wasteful. They limited the nomads' movements (the better to govern and tax them) and attempted to commercialize the economy so that meat could be sold. Following the drilling of thousands of wells, the building of storage tanks for water, and the introduction of veterinary medicine, the herds of cattle in the area were greatly increased.

The inevitable result was overgrazing, soil erosion, and desertification—since the removal of vegetation greatly increases the rate of runoff and thus reduces the beneficial results of rain.[20] As ecologist J. L. Cloudsley-Thompson wrote, "Man cannot escape responsibility for having created a large part of the Sahara desert. In regions where the needs of the vegetation are delicately balanced by precarious rainfall, overgrazing and the utilization of firewood can have a disastrous and irreversible effect."[21]

The populations of human beings and domestic animals in the Sahel were outstripping the area's ability to produce food and forage before the drought of the late 1960s and 1970s. The repeated failures of the monsoon in the early 1970s were the final blow. The herds of many pastoralists were virtually wiped out. Hundreds of thousands—perhaps as many as 1.5 million people had died of hunger by the end of 1974. Because the population is scattered and government figures untrustworthy, the true dimensions of the disaster will probably never be known. In Ethiopia, for instance, deliberate attempts were made to cover up the famines.[22]

The way of life of many of the pastoral peoples seems to have been destroyed. Nomadic peoples like the Tuareg, the fabled "blue men" of the desert, have crowded into hideous slums on the margins of poverty-stricken towns in the southern Sahel. There, on relief, they are turning to farming to supplement their meager rations.

[20]For an overview, see E. P. Eckholm, Desertification: A world problem.

[21]J. L. Cloudsley-Thompson, The expanding Sahara, p. 9.

[22]Ethiopia says famine was covered up, New York *Times*, November 18, 1973.

Suggested cures for the problem indicate that no lessons have been learned. The president of Niger has urged, for instance, that international aid be supplied to drill 2500 wells, averaging 300 meters deep, across that country. The cost would be almost a quarter of a billion dollars, and successful completion of the project would almost certainly result in an acceleration of desertification through overgrazing.[23]

Agriculture and Instabilities

Even where overpopulation, the quality of soils, lack of rain, erosion, or salt accumulation do not pose special problems, the practice of agriculture alone may cause ecological difficulties. The most basic one is that agriculture is a simplifier of ecosystems, replacing relatively complex natural biological communities with relatively simple man-made ones based on a few strains of crops. Agricultural communities thus tend to be less stable than their natural counterparts: they are vulnerable to invasions by weeds, insect pests, and plant diseases, and they are particularly sensitive to extremes of weather and variations in climate. Historically, humanity has attempted to defend agricultural communities against the instabilities to which they are susceptible by means of vigilance and the application of "energy subsidies" (for example, by hoeing weeds, and more recently by using pesticides and mechanical cultivation). The effort has not always been successful.

Any monoculture is highly vulnerable to plant pests and diseases. An insect pest, a fungus, or a strain of bacteria can sweep through the entire plant population. A classic example of the destruction of a monoculture is provided by one of the first Green Revolutions—the introduction of the potato into Ireland in the eighteenth century. The potato provided the basis for an increase in the Irish population from 3 million people living in poverty to 8 million living in poverty. In such situations, expansion of the food supply does not necessarily lead to an increase in the standard of living; more frequently, it leads only to more people living at the same low standard. Between 1845 and 1848, a fungal blight invaded the fields, producing one of history's great disasters—the

[23]R. Baker, Famine: The cost of development?

Irish potato famine. The unstable potato ecosystem collapsed and with it the artificially augmented carrying capacity of the land. In four years of crop failures, 1.5 million people starved to death, 2 million emigrated, and millions of others underwent great suffering through semistarvation.[24]

Advances in agricultural technology in the past hundred years have not resolved the ecological dilemma of agriculture; they have aggravated it. The dilemma can be summarized in this way: agriculture tries to manage ecosystems in such a way as to maximize productivity; nature "manages" ecosystems in such a way as to maximize stability. The two goals are incompatible. In short, in agriculture productivity is achieved at the expense of stability.

Of course, humanity must practice agriculture to support even a fraction of the existing human population. A degree of instability in agricultural ecosystems must therefore be accepted and, where possible, compensated for by technology. However, the trends in modern agriculture, associated in part with the urgent need to cope with unprecedented population growth and in part with the desire to maximize yields (the amount of harvest per hectare) for strictly economic reasons, are especially worrisome ecologically. The three major liabilities are:

1. As larger and larger land areas are given over to farming, the unexploited tracts available to serve as reservoirs of species diversity and to carry out the public service functions of natural ecosystems become smaller and fewer.

2. Even in parts of the world where land area under agriculture is constant or (for economic reasons) dwindling, attempts to maximize yields have led to dramatic increases in the use of pesticides and inorganic fertilizers—increases that have far-reaching ecological consequences themselves.

3. The quest for high yields has led also to the replacement of myriad traditional crop varieties around the world with a few, specially bred, high-yielding strains. Areas of unprecedented size are now planted to single varieties of wheat or rice. Because of this enormous expansion of monoculture, the chances are much greater for an epidemic crop failure from insects or disease—one that might occur over an area far greater than any crop failure in the past.

[24] G. L. Carefoot and E. R. Sprott, *Famine on the wind.*

POLLUTANTS IN ECOSYSTEMS

The expansion and intensification of agriculture has been accompanied by a continuing Industrial Revolution that has multiplied many times over both the magnitude and the variety of the substances introduced into the biological environment by human beings. In the last chapter we classified these substances as either *qualitative pollutants* (synthetic substances produced and released only by human action) or *quantitative pollutants* (substances naturally present in the environment but released in significant additional amounts by human activities).

Well-known qualitative pollutants include the chlorinated hydrocarbon pesticides such as DDT, the related class of industrial chemicals called PCBs, and some herbicides. These substances are biologically active in the sense that they stimulate physiological changes. But, because organisms have had no experience with them over evolutionary time, the substances are usually not biodegradable. Indeed, some, like the pesticides kepone and mirex, are among the most stable molecules ever synthesized by chemists. Thus, they may persist in the environment for years, and even decades, after being introduced, and be transported around the globe by wind and water. Their long-term effects will be discovered only by experience.

As noted in Chapter 10, the significance of quantitative pollutants in a given situation must be judged according to whether the natural abundance of the agent is altered slightly or substantially, locally or globally, suddenly or gradually, and according to how harmful the agent is at its naturally occurring concentrations.

Concentration of Toxic Substances in Ecosystems

Nowhere is human ecological naiveté more evident than in popular assumptions about the capacity of the atmosphere, soils, rivers, and oceans to absorb pollution. Those assumptions all too often take the following form:

if 1 liter of poison is added to 1 billion liters of water, then the highest concentration of poison to which anything will be exposed is about one part per billion. This might be approximately true if complete mixing by diffusion took place rapidly (which it often does not) and *if only physical systems were involved.* But because *biological systems* are involved, the situation is radically different. Ignorance of this point is not confined to laymen. For instance, Sir Robert Robinson, Nobel laureate in organic chemistry, made the following classic blunder. In a letter to the London *Times* (February 4, 1971) discounting the threat of leaded compounds to oceanic plankton, he began: "Neither our 'Prophets of Doom', nor the legislators who are so easily frightened by them, are particularly fond of arithmetic . . . " and then went on to do some "simple arithmetic" (as he described it) to show that the dilution of lead in the oceans would be so great that the lead would remain biologically negligible. Of course, his whole exercise completely missed the point, because of—among other things—the phenomenon of biological amplification.

Filter-feeding animals, for example, may concentrate poisons to levels far higher than those found in the surrounding medium. Oysters capture food by constantly filtering the water they inhabit, and they live in shallow water near the shore, where pollution is heaviest. Consequently, their bodies often contain much higher concentrations of radioactive substances or dangerous chemicals than the water in which they live. For instance, oysters have been found to accumulate up to 70,000 times the concentration of chlorinated hydrocarbon insectides that exists in their environment.[25] Food chains may also lead to concentration of toxic substances; they act as a kind of biological amplifier. The diagram of a Long Island estuary food web in Figure 4-25 shows how the concentrations of DDT and its derivatives tend to increase in food chains from one trophic level to another. That tendency is especially marked for the chlorinated hydrocarbons because of their high solubility in fatty substances and their low solubility in water. Although the clam and the mud snail are at the same trophic level, the filter-feeding clam accumulates more than half again as much DDT as the mud snail because of the difference in their food-capturing habits.

[25]P. A. Butler, The significance of DDT residues in estuarine fauna. Concentration factors (residue in organism divided by that in environment) as high as 1 million have been recorded for DDT residues in sea squirts (E. E. Kenaga, Factors related to bioconcentration of pesticides).

The mechanism of concentration in food chains is simple. One would expect from the second law of thermodynamics (Chapter 2) that the mass of herbivores normally is not as great as the mass of plants they feed on. With each step upward in a food chain the biomass is reduced. Energy present in the chemical bonds of organisms at one level does not all end up as bond energy at the next level, because much of the energy is degraded to heat at each step. In contrast, losses of DDT and related compounds along a food chain are small compared to the amounts that are transferred upward through the chain because they tend to be neither degraded nor eliminated from the organisms. As a result, the concentration of DDT increases at each level (Figure 11-3). Concentrations in the birds at the end of the food chain are from tens to many hundreds of times as great as in the animals farther down the chain.

Food chain concentration in aquatic environments is not as frequently observed as in terrestrial ones because of the tendency at each trophic level for the concentrations of compounds to equilibrate between organism and water—the equilibrium being roughly the same at all levels. Concentration will only occur if movement from level to level is fast enough to prevent the reaching of equilibrium at each level.[26]

Insecticides in Ecosystems

Besides being direct threats to human health, synthetic insecticides[27] are among society's most potent tools for

[26]See, for example, R. W. Risebrough, E. Huschenbeth, S. Jensen, and J. E. Portmann, Halogenated hydrocarbons. Technical papers providing the background for this conclusion include J. L. Hamelink, R. C. Waybrant, and R. C. Ball, A proposal: Exchange equilibria dominate the degree chlorinated hydrocarbons are biologically magnified in lentic environments; H. O. Saunders and J. H. Chandler, Biological magnification of a polychlorinated biphenyl (Aroctor^{R} 1254) from water by aquatic invertebrates; R. E. Reinert, Accumulation of dieldrin in an alga *(Scenedesmus obliquus), Daphnia magna,* and the guppy *(Poecilia reticulata);* G. R. Harvey et al., Observations on the distribution of chlorinated hydrocarbons in Atlantic Ocean organisms.

[27]Insecticides are chemicals designed to kill insects, miticides are to kill mites, and herbicides are to kill weeds. All are pesticides. Pesticides are sometimes referred to as biocides; miticides are often lumped in with insecticides, as they are here. Other pesticides are used against rodents (rodenticides), roundworms (nematocides), fungi (fungicides), bacteria (antibiotics), and so on.

simplifying and thus destabilizing ecosystems (they are discussed in Box 11-1). The increase in the concentration of the most persistent of those compounds with each upward step in a food chain exposes the populations least able to survive poisoning to the highest concentrations.

There are several reasons why the organisms near the upper ends of food chains are less able to cope with the poisons than are, for example, herbivores. The first traces back again to the second law of thermodynamics. Because of the loss of available energy at each transfer, the higher a given population occurs in a food chain, the smaller that population is (everything else being equal). This means that if a poison were applied that would kill most of the predators and herbivores in an area, it would be more likely to exterminate the population of predators than the population of herbivores, simply because there would be fewer predators to begin with. Purely by chance, some members of the larger population would be more likely to survive. It is not even necessary to kill all individuals of any one species of predator to force it to extinction. If survivors were too scattered or weakened for the sexes to find one another and produce offspring, extinction would surely follow. Or, if survivors were few, loss of genetic variability might cause the population to dwindle to zero. (See also Chapter 4.)

Another reason that small populations of animals high on a food chain are more vulnerable is that smaller populations tend to have less genetic variability. Suppose, for instance, that 1 individual per 100,000 in each of two species of insects by chance carries a mutant gene that makes it naturally resistant to a certain pesticide. Assume that one species is a herbivore (a pest, for our purposes) and its population in a field consists of 1 million individuals, while the second species is a predator of the first, with a population of 100,000 individuals. If the field is thoroughly treated with the pesticide, killing all susceptible insects, 10 individuals of the pest species will survive, but only 1 of the predator species will survive, each of the survivors being naturally resistant mutants. In this oversimplified example, the consequences are obvious. The small group of resistant pest insects can quickly reproduce a large population, free from attack by its predator. But because most individuals in the replacement pest population will be resistant, the next treatment with insecticide will have

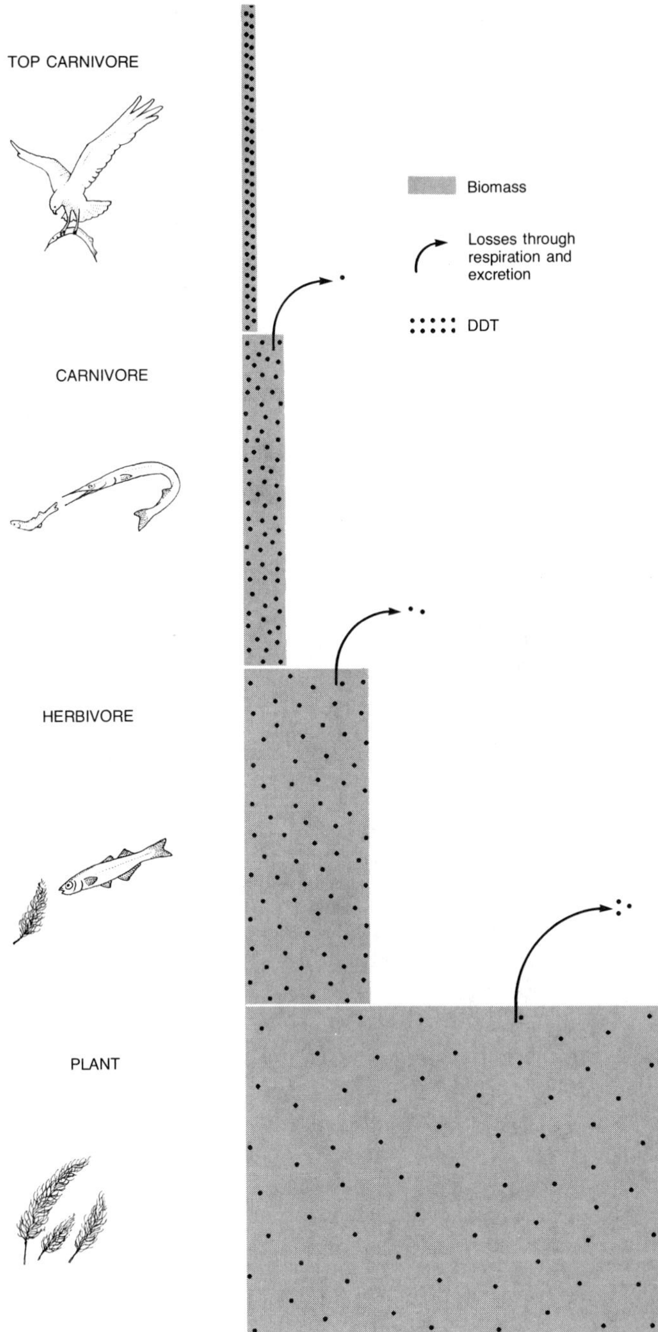

FIGURE 11-3

Concentration of DDT along a simple food chain. As living material is passed from one link to another, more than half of it is consumed by respiration or excreted (arrows). The losses of DDT residue along the chain, on the other hand, are small in proportion to the amount transferred, leading to the high concentrations in carnivores. (After Woodwell, 1967.)

BOX 11-1 Synthetic Insecticides

The majority of synthetic insecticides belong to three groups of compounds: chlorinated hydrocarbons, organophosphates, and carbamates.

Chlorinated Hydrocarbons

Chlorinated hydrocarbons include DDT, benzene hexachloride (BHC), dieldrin, endrin, aldrin, chlordane, lindane, isodrin, toxophene, and similar compounds designed to kill insects. DDT is the most thoroughly studied of the chlorinated hydrocarbons, and much of the following discussion is based on what is known about it. In its behavior it is more or less typical of the group, although other chlorinated hydrocarbons may be more soluble in water, more toxic, less persistent, and so forth. In insects and other animals these compounds act primarily on the central nervous system in ways that are not well understood, but the effects range from hyperexcitability to death following convulsions and paralysis. There is evidence that DDT interferes with the movements of ions through the membranes of nerve cells—movements that must occur for nerve impulses to be propagated. Effects of DDT outside the nervous system also seem linked to processes involving cell membranes, as, for instance, in the membranous energy-mobilizing apparatus of the mitochondria (the power plants of cells).[a] Chronic effects on vertebrates include infiltration of fat into heart muscle and fatty degeneration of the liver, which is often fatal. Fishes and other aquatic animals seem to be especially sensitive to chlorinated hydrocarbons. Their oxygen uptake is somehow blocked at the gills, causing death from suffocation. That chlorinated hydrocarbons apparently can influence the production of enzymes may account for their wide range of effects.

Chlorinated hydrocarbons tend to be highly soluble in fats and fatty tissues. In animals this means that they may be stored at sites remote from the primary active site in the nervous system and thus rendered relatively harmless. These compounds are more toxic to insects than to mammals, primarily because they are absorbed more easily through insect cuticle than through mammalian skin. Chlorinated hydrocarbons vary greatly in their toxicity to plants. They are able, at least in experimental situations, to slow the rate of photosynthesis—almost certainly by operating on the membranes of the photosynthetic organelles (the chloroplasts).[b]

Four properties make chlorinated hydrocarbons a particular threat to ecosystems:

1. Chlorinated hydrocarbons have a wide range of biological activity; they are broad-spectrum poisons, affecting many different organisms in many different ways. They are toxic to one degree or another to essentially all animals.
2. They have great stability. It is not clear, however, just how long DDT persists in ecosystems. Fifty percent of the DDT sprayed in a single treatment, for example, might still be found in a field ten years later. This would not mean, however, that the other 50 percent had been degraded to biologically inactive molecules; it might only have gone elsewhere. Probably DDT (including its biologically active breakdown product DDE) has an average half-life (the time required before 50 percent has been degraded) of much more than a decade. Indeed, DDE may be virtually immortal.[c]
3. Chlorinated hydrocarbons are very mobile. For example, the chemical properties of DDT cause it to adhere to dust particles, on which it can be blown around the world. Four different chlorinated hydrocarbons have been detected in dust filtered from the air over Barbados, apparently having been transported there across the Atlantic;[d] frog populations in unsprayed areas high in the Sierra Nevada of California are polluted with DDT.[e] Furthermore, DDT codistills with water (when water evaporates and enters the atmosphere, DDT goes with it). Chlorinated hydrocarbons thus travel in the air and in surface waters.
4. The high solubility of chlorinated hydrocarbons in fats amounts to an affinity for organisms. These pesticides move continually from the nonliving part of the environment into living systems. To attempt to monitor DDT levels merely by testing water (as has frequently been done) is ridiculous. Water is saturated with DDT (that is, it can dissolve no more) when it has dissolved 1.2 parts per billion, but the chemical does not remain for long in water;

[a] J. R. Corbett, *The biochemical mode of action of pesticides,* Academic Press, London, 1974.

[b] J. R. Corbett, *The biochemical mode of action of pesticides,* pp. 170, 178.

[c] A useful quantitative review of physical properties and mobility of DDT is G. M. Woodwell et al., DDT in the biosphere: where does it go?

[d] Risebrough et al., Pesticides: Transatlantic movements.

[e] L. Cory, P. Fjeld, and W. Serat, Distribution patterns of DDT residues in the Sierra Nevada mountains.

it is quickly removed by any organisms that live there.

It is these four properties—an extreme range of biological activity, stability, mobility, and affinity for living systems—that cause biologists to fear that DDT and its relatives are degrading the life-support systems of our planet. If any one of the four properties was lacking, the situation would be much less serious, but in combination they pose a deadly threat.

Organophosphates

Organophosphates include parathion, EPN, malathion, Azodrin, diazinon, dichlorvos, TEPP, phosdrin, and numerous others. These poisons are descendants of the nerve gas Tabun (ethyl N-dimethylphosphoramidocyanidate), developed in Nazi Germany during World War II. The majority of them are cholinesterase inhibitors; they inactivate the enzyme responsible for breaking down a nerve "transmitter substance," acetylcholine. The result in acute cases of poisoning is a blockade of synapses (connections between nerve cells) that use acetylcholine as a transmitter—often with lethal effect. Unlike chlorinated hydrocarbons, organophosphates tend to be unstable and nonpersistent; hence, they tend not to produce chronic effects in ecosystems or to accumulate in food chains.[f] They often, however, are extraordinarily toxic. For example, the LD_{50} (dose required to kill 50 percent of a group of test animals) of TEPP when administered orally to white rats is only from 1 to a few milligrams per kilogram of body weight.[g] It is so toxic it is not marketed today.

Organophosphates inhibit other enzymes as well as cholinesterase. Indeed, some of the ones that show relatively great toxicity for insects and little toxicity for mammals do so because they poison an esterase that is more critical to the functioning of insect than of mammalian nervous systems. Malathion, which is violently poisonous to insects, is relatively nontoxic to mammals (acute oral LD_{50} in rats 900–5800 mg/kg) because mammalian liver and, to a lesser degree, other tissues contain the enzyme carboxyesterase, which destroys malathion. But relatively high toxicity to mammals can occur when malathion is used in combination with some other organophosphates (such as EPN) that apparently inhibit carboxyesterase. For example, in dogs one-fortieth of the LD_{50} of malathion administered with one-fiftieth of the LD_{50} of EPN killed *all* the experimental animals—a classic example of a synergistic effect.[h]

While most organophosphate pesticides produce acute poisoning, with transient loss of muscular strength and coordination due to their inhibition of cholinesterase, a few of these compounds have a delayed neurotoxic effect. For example, one organophosphate, Phosvel (leptophos), has a very low acute oral toxicity in chickens (4700 mg/kg), but after receiving doses ranging from 180 to 3000 mg/kg, which did not cause immediate symptoms, individuals developed irreversible, lethal neurological problems. The symptoms of this nerve poisoning appeared only after a delay of 8 to 13 days. Phosvel has been implicated in a kill of some 1300 water buffalo in the Nile delta in 1971,[i] and employees of a Phosvel manufacturing plant have developed delayed neurological symptoms (see Chapter 10).

Carbamates[j]

Insecticides of the carbamate group include Sevin (carbaryl), zectran, baygon, dimetilan, pyrolan, and Temik (aldicarb). Chemically, these are esters of a derivative of carbamic acid. Attention originally was called to this group of compounds in the nineteenth century because one of them, eserine (physostigmine), proved to be the active ingredient in a poisonous plant, *Physostigma venenosum,* used in trials by ordeal by West Africans. Synthetic analogues of eserine were used in medicine, but they had no insecticidal properties. Synthetics with insecticidal properties were first developed by Geigy Company in Switzerland in 1947.[k]

Like organophosphates, carbamates inhibit cholinesterase, and some have very high acute toxicity (for example, aldicarb is in the same class as TEPP).[l] They were introduced in many instances as substitutes for chlorinated hydrocarbons when insects developed resistance to the latter. They are quite selective in their action, as some insects are highly susceptible to these poisons and others are quite resistant. They also show variation in their degree of persistence in the environment,[m] but generally they are much less persistent than chlorinated hydrocarbons.

[f]See, however, J. Katan, T. W. Fuhreman, and C. P. Lichtenstein, Binding of [^{14}C] parathion in soil.

[g]Fumio Matsumura, *Toxicology of insecticides,* p. 65. (LD_{50} stands for *L*ethal *D*ose 50 percent.)

[h]R. D. O'Brien, *Insecticides, action and metabolism,* Academic Press, London, 1967.

[i]Information on Phosvel from M. B. Abou-Donia et al., Neurotoxic effect of leptophos.

[j]For a detailed discussion, see R. J. Kuhr and H. W. Dorough, *Carbamate insecticides: Chemistry, biochemistry, and toxicology,* CRC Press, Cleveland, Ohio, 1976.

[k]O'Brien, *Insecticides.*

[l]Matsumura, *Toxicology,* p. 85.

[m]For example, Osman M. Aly and M. A. El-Deb, Studies of the persistence of some carbamate insecticides in the aquatic environment, *Advances in Chemistry,* vol. 3, pp. 210–243.

little effect. If dosage of the insecticide is increased, the pest species will respond by becoming more and more resistant with each generation. Not only herbivorous pests but other large populations can easily evolve such resistance; for example, resistance to DDT has developed in many mosquito populations, which has hampered malaria-control programs.

Artificial poisons tend to be much more effective against predators and parasites than against herbivores for another reason—the long coevolutionary experience herbivores have with plant poisons. Herbivores that were not adept at circumventing poisons are mostly long since extinct. Small wonder that the evolutionary "winners" now being assaulted by mankind's poisons have so often managed to evolve resistance to them rapidly. Indeed, applications of pesticides often lead to *higher* concentrations of pests rather than lower, either because they directly poison the natural enemies of the pest or because they indirectly decrease the efficiency of those enemies as control agents. They accomplish the latter in several ways. One is through the very success of the pesticide in reducing the target pest population. This may deprive the pest's natural enemies of their prey and thus reduce the predator or parasite population to a level where it is ineffective as a control when the pest population resurges. Similarly, the natural enemies of the pest may be decimated if the pesticide kills off another species preyed on by the same predator or parasite. Such an alternate host may be necessary to keep the predator population going all year round; if it is destroyed, the natural control is destroyed also.[28]

There are, of course, many actual cases in which differential kill of predators has released some prey species from their natural restraints. It is fair to say, for instance, that mites, as pests, are a creation of the pesticide industry. Careless overuse of DDT and other pesticides has promoted many of these little insectlike relatives of spiders to pest status by killing the insects that previously kept them under control. The emergence of the European red mite as a major pest in apple orchards followed the use of DDT to control the codling moth.[29] This is only one of the many examples in which pesticides intended for one pest have led others to flourish. A common response by the pesticide industry to such situations is to recommend the use of heavier doses of the original pesticide or to develop more potent poisons, which then create another array of pollution problems.[30]

In such cases one or more pests were being held in check by natural biological controls, which were upset by the introduction of the chemical. That so many organisms can be "promoted" to pest status by the killing of predators and parasites with pesticides is itself a powerful testimonial for reliance on biological controls, instead. Such controls are constantly at work suppressing potential pests at no economic cost.

Effects of Insecticides on Nontarget Organisms

Of all the synthetic organic pesticides, probably more is known about DDT than any other. It is the oldest and most widely used chlorinated hydrocarbon insecticide. Although there has been an almost total ban on the use of DDT in the United States since 1972 and its use has been prohibited in some other countries, worldwide use in the mid-1970s was probably as great as in the mid-1960s.[31] DDT is found everywhere—not only where it has been applied, but all over the Earth.[32]

Virtually every kind of animal on Earth has been exposed to it. As noted earlier (Table 10-6), concentrations in the fat deposits of people in the United States average about 12 ppm, and in the people of India and Israel they are much higher. More startling and significant in some ways has been the discovery of DDT

[28] C. B. Huffaker, The ecology of pesticide interference with insect populations (Upsets and resurgences in insect populations). See also the discussion of the Volterra principle in chapter 22 of J. Roughgarden's *Theory of population genetics and evolutionary ecology, an introduction,* for another reason why pest control programs may lead to bigger pest problems.

[29] For a detailed discussion of the role of pesticides and predators in the control of plant-eating mites, see C. B. Huffaker, M. van den Vrie, and J. A. McMurtry, The ecology of tetranychid mites and their natural control; J. A. McMurtry, C. B. Huffaker, and M. van den Vrie, Ecology of tetranychid mites and their natural enemies: A review.

[30] Numerous examples of promotion of nonpests to pests by pesticide misuse are given in Paul De Bach, *Biological control by natural enemies.*

[31] Ecologist G. M. Woodwell, quoted in the *New York Times,* February 14, 1975. World use in 1973 was estimated at about 150,000 metric tons.

[32] T. J. Peterle, DDT in Antarctic snow, *Nature,* vol. 224, p. 620 (November 8, 1969). His estimates of the quantity of DDT are now thought to be much too high (R. Risebrough, personal communication.)

FIGURE 11-4

A crushed egg in the nest of a brown pelican off the California coast. This egg had such a thin shell that the weight of the nesting parent's body destroyed it. The concentration of DDE in the eggs of this 300-pair colony reached 2500 parts per million; no eggs hatched. (Photo by Joseph R. Jehl, Jr.)

residues in the fat deposits of Eskimos and in those of Antarctic penguins and seals.[33] Seals from the east coast of Scotland have been found to have concentrations of DDT as great as 23 ppm in their blubber, and both DDT and DDE contaminate fishes living 2500 meters deep in the ocean.[34] Pesticide pollution is truly a worldwide problem.

The impact of chlorinated hydrocarbons on birds. Because DDT breaks down so slowly, it lasts for decades in soils. For instance, in the Long Island estuary studied by Woodwell and his colleagues (Figure 4-25), the marsh had been sprayed for twenty years for mosquito control. Up to 32 pounds per acre of DDT were found in the upper layer of mud there. Such concentrations in U.S. soils are not unusual. As a result of the progressive concentration of DDT as it moves up food chains, the danger to the lives and reproductive capacities of fish-eating birds became extreme in the 1960s. Nesting failures among bald eagles attributable to DDT reached proportions that brought the survival of the species into severe jeopardy. In addition, reproductive difficulties in populations of such diverse birds as the peregrine falcon and the brown pelican have been traced to residues of DDT. DDE, a breakdown product of DDT, interferes with the birds' ability to transport calcium, which results in their laying eggs whose shells are so thin that they are crushed by the weight of the incubating parents (Figure 11-4). Similar effects have been caused experimentally by polychlorinated biphenyls (PCBs), which are chlorinated hydrocarbons used extensively in industry and which are closely related to the insecticides, as well as by mercury compounds.[35] If they reach high enough levels in the environment they could cause problems for bird populations.

The evidence against DDT in the case of birds' eggs is now overwhelming.[36] Studies have been made of the thickness of the eggshells of raptorial birds in museum collections. Among the eggs of those species investigated that feed high on food chains, there was in virtually all

[33]W. T. L. Sladen, C. M. Menzee, and W. L. Rechel, DDT residues in Adélie penguins and a crabeater seal from Antarctica; R. W. Risebrough et al., Transfer of chlorinated biphenyls to Antarctica. The latter study also recorded PCBs in Antarctic fauna.

[34]Reported incidentally in R. Barber, A. Vijakumar, and F. Cross, Mercury concentrations in recent and ninety-year-old benthopalagic fish.

[35]For an excellent review of eggshell-thinning, including some of the controversy surrounding it, see A. S. Cooke, Shell thinning in avian eggs by environmental pollutants.

[36]See, for example, J. L. Lincer, DDE-induced eggshell-thinning in the American kestrel: A comparison of the field situation and laboratory results.

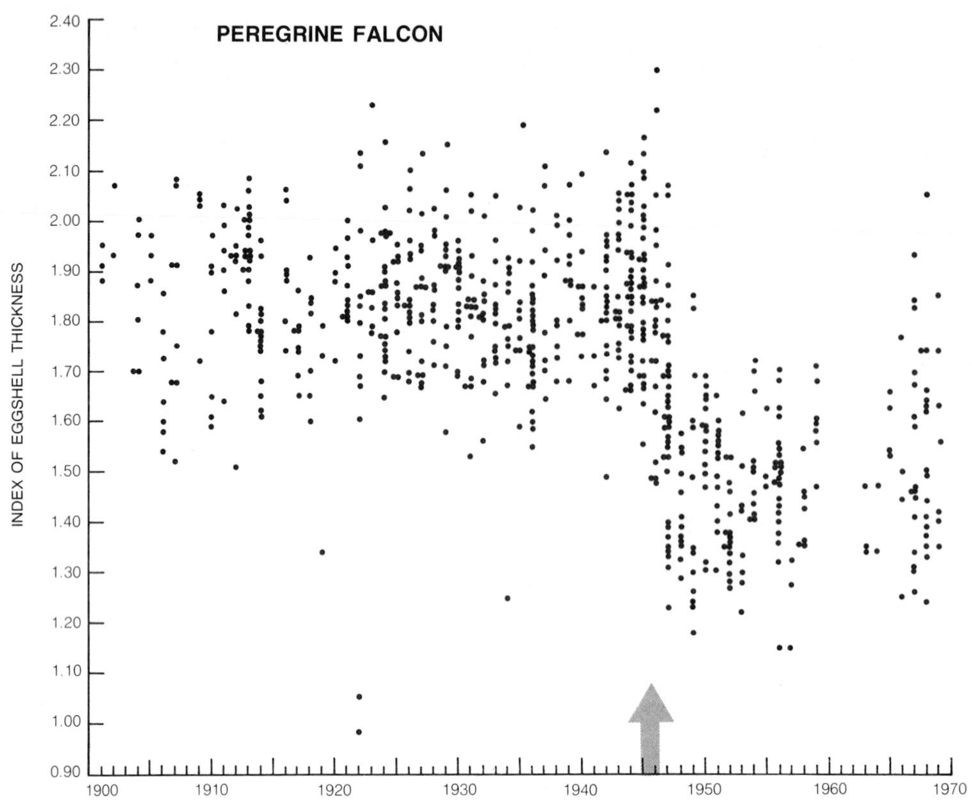

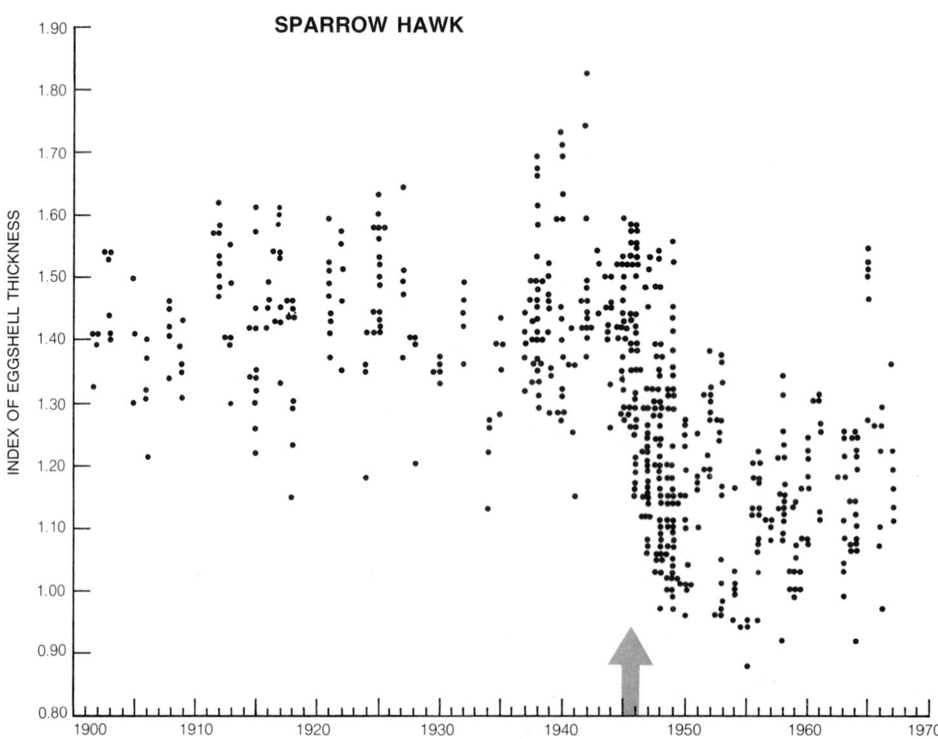

FIGURE 11-5

Changes in the thickness of the eggshells of the peregrine falcon and the sparrow hawk in Britain. Arrows indicate the first widespread use of DDT. (After Ratcliffe, 1970.)

cases a sharp decrease in the thickness of shells between 1945 and 1947, when DDT was generally introduced (Figure 11-5). DDT has been directly implicated in eggshell thinning as early as 1948.[37] In the United Kingdom a strong correlation has also been shown between the level of chlorinated-hydrocarbon contamination in various geographical regions and the thickness of eggshells of peregrine falcons, sparrow hawks, and golden eagles nesting in those regions. The exceptions make the case even more convincing. The shells of one Florida population of bald eagles first thinned in 1943, not between 1945 and 1947. Investigations disclosed that that population lived in a county where large-scale DDT testing took place in 1943. One pair of peregrines on the coast of California was an exception to the general rule of nesting failure. Examination of their nests revealed that they were feeding inland on mourning doves. Mourning doves are herbivores; therefore the peregrines were feeding much lower in the food chain than if they had been feeding on fish-eating seabirds. They picked up less DDT and were therefore able to reproduce successfully.

Experimental feedings of DDT to mallard ducks, American sparrow hawks, and Japanese quail all produced thin eggshells and reduced hatch rates. DDE, a widely distributed, stable breakdown product of DDT, has also been shown to reduce the thickness of mallard eggshells and to reduce hatchability. Sensitivity to DDE varies greatly from species to species. Brown pelicans, cormorants, and raptors show high sensitivity; ducks, gulls, and ringdoves, moderate sensitivity; and quail, chickens, and Bengalese finches, low sensitivity.

At one time it was thought that the thin eggshell phenomenon was produced by alterations in estrogen levels, which are involved in the storage of calcium in birds. However, biologist D. B. Peakall of Cornell University did a series of experiments in which DDE was injected into ringdoves shortly before they laid eggs. The eggs, when laid, had thin shells. The DDE greatly reduced the activity of carbonic anhydrase, an enzyme that plays a critical role in providing calcium for eggshell production. It is now thought that inhibition of that enzyme and ATPases involved in transporting calcium from blood to eggshell is the basic mechanism that produces the thinning.[38]

Dieldrin injected shortly before eggs are laid does not cause thinning of the eggshells. It and other chlorinated hydrocarbons (especially PCBs) do, however, lower the estrogen level, which in turn delays breeding. DDT does not have as great an estrogen effect as dieldrin, nor is it apparently as potent an inducer of liver enzymes. Late breeding is an important component of observed declines in the numbers of predatory birds, since breeding is normally timed to coincide with optimal food supplies for the young. Interestingly, some of the most spectacular declines in the populations of these birds occurred years after thin eggshells first appeared—about the time that dieldrin was introduced.

There was, fortunately, a steady decrease in the amount of DDT used in the United States during the 1960s, use at the end of the decade being on the order of 25 percent what it was at the start.[39] At the end of 1972 its use was almost totally banned. Few reductions in DDT (or other organochlorine pesticides) residues were reported before 1970,[40] but by 1974 a steady decline in the concentrations of DDT and its breakdown products DDD and DDE had been detected in migratory songbirds and in the eggs of brown pelicans.[41]

In the United Kingdom, where use of organochlorines had been restricted, investigators were able to show an increase in the breeding success of Scottish golden eagles that was associated with a decline in the DDE and dieldrin content of their eggs, and they also recorded a decrease in the organochlorine content of cormorant (shag) eggs.[42]

Shell-thinning is not the only way in which DDT can affect birds. For instance, it can also influence behavior

[37]D. B. Peakall, DDE: Its presence in peregrine eggs in 1948.

[38]D. B. Peakall, Pesticides and the reproduction of birds; and Physiological effects of chlorinated hydrocarbons on avian species.

[39]D. W. Johnston, Decline of DDT residues in migratory songbirds.

[40]For example, R. F. Reidinger, Jr., and D. G. Crabtree, Organochlorine residues in golden eagles, United States, March 1964–July 1971; W. E. Martin and P. R. Nickerson, Organochlorine residues in starlings—1970, *Pesticides Monitoring Journal,* vol. 6, pp. 33–40.

[41]David W. Johnston, Decline; D. W. Anderson et al., Brown pelicans: Improved reproduction off the Southern California coast.

[42]J. D. Lockie, D. A. Ratcliffe, and R. Balharry, Breeding success and organo-chlorine residues in golden eagles in west Scotland; J. C. Coulson, J. R. Deans, G. R. Potts, J. Robinson, and A. N. Crabtree, Changes in organochlorine contamination of the marine environment of eastern Britain monitored by shag eggs.

associated with migration.[43] Such effects should decrease if the use of this dangerous chemical were phased out. Thus, if the use of organochlorines declines, there seems to be every reason for optimism that the effects of those poisons on the ecosystem will abate.

The impact of chlorinated hydrocarbons on aquatic organisms. Birds are not the only organisms that have suffered from chlorinated hydrocarbons. Coho salmon in Lake Michigan, which also feed at high trophic levels, have been laying eggs that contain DDT residues. In 1968 almost 700,000 young salmon died as they absorbed the last DDT-rich drop of oil from their yolk sacs. Trout have had similar problems, and DDT has been found in such commercially important marine fishes as tuna, mackerel, and hake.

One spectacular example of the destruction of nontarget organisms by pesticides was described in detail by reporter Frank Graham, Jr.,[44] who recounted the story of a great Mississippi fish kill in the early 1960s. Rough estimates gave the total loss in the four years from 1960 to 1963 as between 10 million and 15 million fishes in the lower Mississippi and its bypass, the Atchafalaya. The fishes killed included several kinds of catfish, menhaden, mullet, sea trout, drumfish, shad, and buffalo fish. The die-offs were ruinous to the local fishing industry. A thorough investigation by government (U.S. Public Health Service) and private laboratories placed the blame primarily on the highly toxic chlorinated hydrocarbon insecticide endrin and one of its derivatives. They were found not only in the blood and tissues of dying fishes and water birds but also in the mud in areas where fishes were dying. In experiments, extracts made both from the mud and from the tissues of dying fishes killed healthy fishes. It was found that fish kills were greatest in 1960 and 1963, when endrin was used commonly to treat cotton and cane crops in the lower Mississippi valley, and that fish kills were smallest in 1961 and 1962, when very little endrin was used.

The Public Health Service found that runoff from agricultural lands following dusting and spraying was one major source of endrin. The other source was the Memphis plant of the Velsicol Chemical Corporation; waste endrin from the manufacturing process was getting into the river. Graham described the reaction of the Velsicol Corporation:

"Velsicol, under fire, shot back. Bernard Lorant, the company's vice-president in charge of research, issued strong denials. In a statement to the press, he said that endrin had nothing to do with the Mississippi fish kill, that the symptoms of the dying fish were not those of endrin poisoning, and that Velsicol's test proved that the fish had died of dropsy." Unfortunately for the Velsicol defense, dropsy happens to be a disease that is *never epidemic* in fishes.[45]

At a May 1964 conference in New Orleans on the Mississippi fish kill,[46] a theme promoted by the pesticide industry was that only communist sympathizers would criticize the extravagant way pesticides are used. Their approach was exemplified by a statement made well before the conference by Parke C. Brinkley, then president of the National Agricultural Chemicals Association: "Two of the biggest battles in this war [against communism] are the battle against starvation and the battle against disease. No two things make people more ripe for Communism. The most effective tool in the hands of the farmer and in the hands of the public health official as they fight these battles is pesticides."[47] This kind of response is found all too often in industries whose products are found to be dangerous. Finding ways to avoid the introduction and wide deployment of such products is a great social challenge. Once a great deal of money is committed to them, their producers tend to defend them vigorously, regardless of the risks to themselves or society (see our discussion of ozone depletion below).

In June 1969 a vast fish kill occurred in the Rhine River. Preliminary investigations indicated that containers holding at least 90 kilograms of the chlorinated hydrocarbon insecticide Endosulfan, which had dropped off a barge, were responsible. The increase in public

[43]J. J. Mahoney, Jr., DDT and DDE effects on migratory condition in whitethroated sparrows, *Journal of Wildlife Management*, vol. 39, pp. 520–527.

[44]*Disaster by default: Politics and water pollution.*

[45]Endrin is still killing fishes in the South (see R. P. Clark, Case-study of pesticide-related fish kills in Alabama, *Environmental Conservation*, vol. 1, p. 309). Mosquito fishes there have become resistant to endrin and are toxic to predators (P. Rosato and D. E. Ferguson, The toxicity of endrin-resistant mosquito fish to eleven species of vertebrates).

[46]Sponsored by the U.S. Secretary of Health, Education and Welfare (see Frank Graham, Jr., *Disaster by default*, pp. 128–130).

[47]Ibid, p. 130.

understanding between 1964 and 1969 of the ecological dangers of pesticides was perhaps indicated by the refreshing absence on that occasion of comments from the pesticide industry about either dropsy or Communists.

Some of the most devastating effects of pesticides in aquatic systems come from releases in manufacture and transport. Just as the Velsicol plant appears to have been a major source of endrin in the Mississippi, so wastes from the Montrose Chemical plant in Los Angeles County, the sole producer of DDT in the United States, appear to have been the major source of residual DDT concentrations in organisms in the coastal waters of California in 1969-70.[48] Sand crabs *(Emerita analoga)* near the sewage outfall carrying the Montrose discharge showed DDT concentrations over 45 times as great as they did near major agricultural drainage areas. This is encouraging, since measures to prevent accidental releases from factories are much more readily devised than measures to prevent the movement of pesticides from the fields where they are applied.

Another example will illustrate how complex, subtle, and far-reaching the effects of pesticide pollution may be. Ecologist L. B. Slobodkin, of the State University of New York, has described a plan to block the seaward ends of lochs in western Scotland and use them as ponds for raising fishes.[49] One of the problems was to find ways to raise the young fishes in the laboratory so they could be "planted" in the ponds. It was discovered that newly hatched brine shrimp would serve as a satisfactory food for the kinds of fishes that would be raised. The shrimp could be obtained from brine-shrimp eggs gathered commercially in the United States and sold to tropical-fish fanciers for feeding young tropical fishes. The supplies came from two places: San Francisco Bay and the Great Salt Lake. But sufficient eggs for the project could no longer be obtained from San Francisco Bay because of the demands of local aquarists and because large areas of former brine shrimp habitat had been transformed into residential subdivisions. Unfortunately, the Utah supply was of no use to the project either, because brine shrimp hatched from Utah eggs killed the young fishes in the United Kingdom. The Utah shrimp had absorbed the insecticides that drained into the Great Salt Lake from surrounding farmlands. Thus, insecticide pollution in Utah hampered fish production in Scotland!

The list of nontarget animals affected by insecticides is now of encyclopedic proportions. The amazing diversity of organisms involved, besides many beneficial insects, includes robins, amphipods, planarians, whitefish, earthworms, old-squaw ducks, warblers, rabbits, quail, lake trout, mosquito fish, bluegills, foxes, opossums, mice, ospreys, muskrats, pheasants, turkeys, gulls, fiddler crabs, salmon, frogs, toads, snakes, big-game mammals, and various plants. Poisoning of these or any other organisms, of course, always affects the ecosystems in which they function.[50]

Insecticides, plankton, and marine food chains. The effects of insecticides in water are not confined to aquatic animals. Perhaps the most disturbing ecological news of 1968 was contained in the short paper "DDT reduces photosynthesis by marine phytoplankton." The author, environmental scientist Charles F. Wurster of the State University of New York, reported that DDT reduced photosynthesis in both experimental cultures and natural communities of marine phytoplankton (such as algae and diatoms), the tiny green plants that float free in the waters of the oceans. Effects were noted at DDT concentrations of only a few parts per billion, quantities commonly suspended in waters near land sites treated with DDT. Water at a distance from treatment sites, however, ordinarily has DDT concentrations averaging less than one part per billion.

Similar results have been confirmed for DDT, dieldrin, and the related chlorinated hydrocarbon pollutants, PCBs. Dieldrin has been shown not only to inhibit growth in dinoflagellates but to cause cell disintegration at concentrations of 100 ppb.[51] Moreover, the size reductions persisted for several generations after removal from

[48]Robin Burnett, DDT residues: Distribution of concentrations in *Emerita analoga* (Stimpson) along coastal California.

[49]Aspects of the future of ecology.

[50]See D. Pimentel, *Ecological effects of pesticides on non-target species,* and O. B. Cope, Interactions between pesticides and wildlife.

[51]For example, J. L. Mosser, N. S. Fisher, T. Teng and C. F. Wurster, Polychlorinated biphenyls: Toxicity to certain phytoplankters; C. D. Powers; R. G. Rowland; and C. F. Wurster, Dieldrin-induced destruction of marine algal cells with concomitant decrease in size of survivors and their progeny.

dieldrin exposure. The vulnerability of phytoplankters to chlorinated hydrocarbons varies with environmental factors such as temperature, light intensity, and interspecific competition, as well as with geographical location.[52] Recent work has indicated that it is not the photosynthetic process of the phytoplankton that is affected by the chlorinated hydrocarbons but the rate of division of the plant cells.[53]

The possible effects of DDT on phytoplankton in nature are difficult to evaluate. Phytoplankton are the primary producers responsible for most of the food taken from the sea. If photosynthesis by marine phytoplankton were significantly reduced, the amount of life in the seas would be reduced; if marine photosynthesis ceased, virtually all sea life would die. But there is no sign that chlorinated hydrocarbons would ever reach a level in the marine environment that would pose any threat to the phytoplankton community as a whole. In response to chlorinated-hydrocarbon pollution, significant qualitative changes in the phytoplankton community seem more probable than large quantitative changes. Phytoplankton populations are differentially susceptible to chlorinated hydrocarbons; even extremely low concentrations might result in shifts of dominance, leading to huge blooms of one or a few species. Indeed, changes in dominance relations have been recorded at chlorinated-hydrocarbon concentrations that had no detectable effect on single-species cultures.[54] Such shifts could, in turn, produce serious consequences throughout the oceanic food webs.

One possibility is that phytoplankton less acceptable to large herbivores would dominate, so that larger animals would be affected. This shortening of food chains might leave only microscopic plants and animals as sources of food from the sea. Another possibility is that phytoplankton communities near shore could become dominated by smaller species, thereby lengthening food chains and dramatically reducing the sizes of populations of fishes at the upper trophic levels. All of this is, of course, purely speculative, especially since levels of pollution found to cause shifts in photosynthetic rates have so far been found only extremely rarely in marine environments. As use of these pollutants declines, this once seemingly serious threat to the oceans may prove to be a nonproblem.

Similarly, the problems besetting inland waters could be aggravated by the effects of DDT on freshwater phytoplankton. On the other hand, DDT or other insecticides may actually cause phytoplankton blooms because zooplankters, which normally limit the phytoplankters by grazing on them, may be even more susceptible to the pesticides.[55] As C. F. Wurster wrote, "Such effects are insidious and their cause may be obscure, yet they may be ecologically more important than the obvious, direct mortality of larger organisms that is so often reported."[55a]

Insecticides and soils. The effects of pollutants on soils are difficult to evaluate. Soils are not just collections of crushed rock; they are extraordinarily complex ecosystems. The animals of the soil are extremely numerous and varied (Figure 11-6). In forest communities of North Carolina, for example, an estimated 300 million small invertebrates live in each hectare of soil, about 30,000 per square meter. Some 70 percent of them are mites, a group of arthropods that may eventually be found to be as diverse as insects. In a study of pasture soils in Denmark, as many as 45,000 small oligochaete worms, 10 million nematodes (roundworms), and 48,000 small arthropods (insects and mites) were found in each square meter.[56] Even more abundant are the microflora of the soil. More than a million bacteria of one type may be found in a gram (0.035 ounce) of forest soil, as well as almost 100,000 yeast cells and about 50,000 bits of fungus mycelium. A gram of fertile agricultural soil has yielded over 2.5 billion bacteria, 400,000 fungi, 50,000 algae, and 30,000 protozoa.

In most natural situations, the plants, animals, and microorganisms of the soil are absolutely essential for its fertility. The roles some of those organisms play in the ecology of soil were indicated in our discussion of the

[52]Fisher, N. S., Effects of PCB on interspecific competition in natural and gnotobiotic phytoplankton communities in continuous and batch cultures, *Microbial Ecology,* vol. 1, pp. 39–50, 1974. This paper, dealing with temperature, contains references to the literature on the other interactions.

[53]Fisher, N. S., Chlorinated hydrocarbon pollutants and photosynthesis of marine phytoplankton: A reassessment, *Science,* vol. 189, pp. 463–464 (August 8, 1975).

[54]Mosser, Fisher, Wurster, Polychlorinated biphenyls.

[55]S. Hurlbert, M. Mulla, and H. Wilson, Effects of an organophosphorus insecticide on the phytoplankton, zooplankton, and insect populations of fresh-water ponds.

[55a]DDT reduces photosynthesis.

[56]C. Overgaard-Nielsen, Studies on enchytraeidae 2: Field studies, *Natura Jutlandica,* vol. 4 (1955), pp. 5–58.

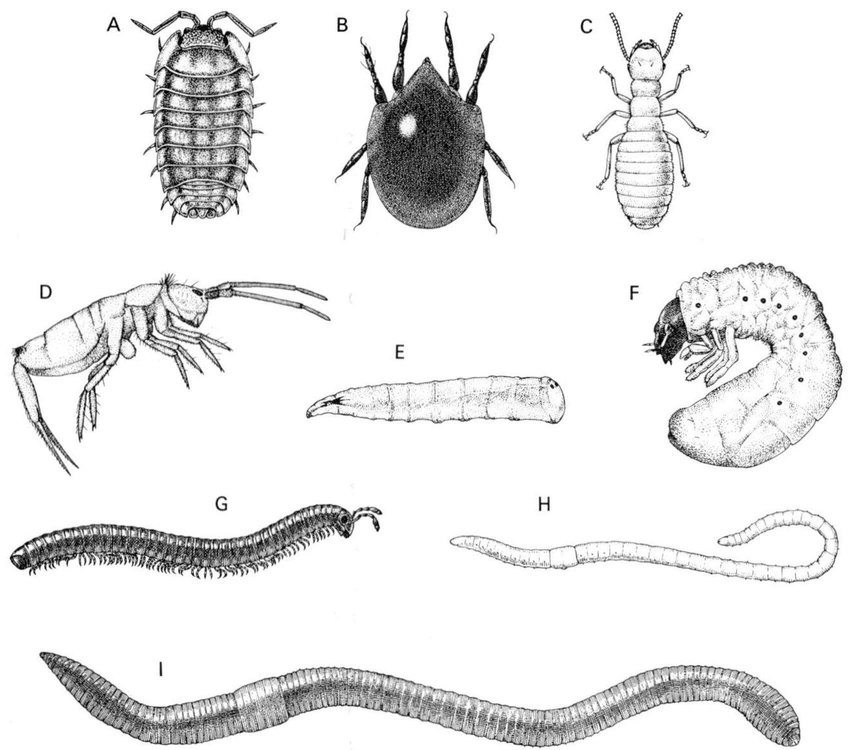

FIGURE 11-6

Nine soil-dwelling animals representative of groups that are the chief consumers of plant debris and are primarily responsible for the fertility of the soil. Seven of them belong to the phylum Arthropoda; they are (A) the wood louse, a crustacean; (B) the oribatid mite, an arachnid; (C) a termite, (D) a springtail, (E) a fly larva, and (F) a beetle larva, all insects; and (G) a millipede, a myriapod. The other two are worms of the phylum Annelida, (H) an enchytraeid worm; and (I) the common earthworm, the largest animal in the community. (From Edwards, 1969.)

nitrogen cycle (Chapter 3). The beneficial effects of earthworms are well known, but most people are unaware of the myriad other complex (and in many cases still poorly understood) ecological relationships within the soil that make it suitable for the growth of oak trees, sagebrush, corn, or any other plants. The soil contains microorganisms that are responsible for the conversion of nitrogen, phosphorus, and sulfur to forms available to the plants. And many trees have been found to depend on associations with fungi. The fungi get carbohydrates and other essential substances from the roots, and the root-fungus complex is able to extract from the soil minerals that could not be extracted by the root alone. Such mycorrhizal associations are just beginning to be understood, but it is clear that in many areas the visible plant community would be drastically altered if the mycorrhizal fungi were absent from the soil.

Recognizing, as they do, that most of the complex physical and chemical processes responsible for soil fertility are dependent upon soil organisms, environmental biologists are opposed to the continuing treatment of soils with heavy dosages of deadly and persistent poisons. Consider, for instance, a study of the persistence of ten different chlorinated hydrocarbons in a sandy loam soil at an experimental station. Table 11-1 summarizes the results, which, because of the conditions of the study, may be close to the upper limits for persistence. Half of these insecticides had more than one-third of the amounts applied remaining in the soil fourteen or more years after treatment. Under normal agricultural conditions, chlorinated hydrocarbons seem to persist for three

TABLE 11-1
Persistence of Insecticides in Soils

Insecticide	*Years since treatment*	*Percent remaining*
Aldrin	14	40
Chlordane	14	40
Endrin	14	41
Heptachlor	14	16
Dilan	14	23
Isodrin	14	15
Benzene hexachloride	14	10
Toxaphene	14	45
Dieldrin	15	31
DDT	17	39

Source: R. G. Nash and E. H. Woolson, Persistence of chlorinated hydrocarbon insecticides in soils. Copyright 1967 by the American Association for the Advancement of Science.

to five years, whereas organophosphates and carbamates are gone in one to three months or less.

Considerable evidence already exists that the use of insecticides may reduce soil fertility, especially in woodland soils, which are subject to spraying but not artificial cultivation. Populations of earthworms, soil mites, and insects are dramatically changed, and they in turn affect the soil fungi, which are their principal food. Even if bacteria were not affected directly, there is no question that the general effects on the soil ecosystem would carry over to them and to other microorganisms. But it would be unwarranted to assume that the bacteria were not directly affected. It is known that a few microorganisms can degrade DDT to DDD under the proper conditions; a few can degrade dieldrin to aldrin and several other breakdown products of unknown toxicity. Our ignorance of the interactions of insecticides, herbicides (discussed later in this chapter), and other environmental poisons with soil microorganisms is immense.

Agriculture, Ecology, and Pest Control

Pest-control, especially insect-pest control, in agriculture today is an ecological disaster. Agronomists understandably breed out of plants some of their natural chemical defenses against the pests. Various herbivore poisons also poison people and most taste unpleasant, although some spices, which are used in small quantities, are produced by plants as pesticides. Farmers plant crops in tight, simple monocultures, inviting pest outbreaks, to which they then respond with synthetic pesticides, often killing a higher proportion of some nontarget populations than of the target population of pests. Because synthetic pesticides, whether intended for pest animals or pest plants, have toxic effects on so many nontarget organisms, they are more accurately called *biocides.* And, because those nontarget populations often include predators and parasites of pests or potential pests, the pesticides often make pest problems worse.

Pesticides and crop losses. There are a few signs that ecologically sound agricultural practices may eventually be adopted, but so far the general trend has been in the opposite direction. The percentage of crop losses to insects in the United States seems not to have been reduced since 1945, despite the enormously increased use of powerful pesticides. In 1948, William Vogt noted in his book *Road to survival*[57] that "one-tenth of all crop plants are destroyed by insects in the U.S. every year." Vogt based his comment on statistics published by the U.S. Department of Agriculture. Georg Borgstrom, also using Department of Agriculture figures, observed that crop losses due to insects in the 1960s amounted to the yield from about one-fifth of the total acreage, or about one-sixth of the cash value of the total crop production in the United States.[58] When the storage-loss component was subtracted, the field losses amounted to slightly more than one-tenth of total production—about the same as 1948. The President's Science Advisory Committee panel on the World Food Problem estimated insect losses in the field during the 1950s as between 4 and 14 percent, depending on the crop.

In 1948, according to zoologist Robert L. Rudd of the University of California, DDT, benzene hexachloride, and lead arsenate were the only insecticides of any significance used.[59] By 1958, production of DDT and other chlorinated hydrocarbon insecticides (some of which was exported) in the United States amounted to nearly 12 times the 1948 production of DDT. Overall, pesticide usage in the United States more than doubled between 1960 and 1970, with about 500 million kilograms being used in 1972.[60] Rudd pointed out that it is difficult to get accurate estimates of pest losses and that standards of pest damage have changed through time.[61] Nevertheless, the consistency of estimates of losses caused by pests between the 1940s and 1960s was rather striking. Indeed, since 1965 the percentages of many major crops lost to pests may have been *rising.*[62] Thus, despite huge inputs of biocides, insects and diseases have been claiming a constant or growing share of the American farmers' greatly increased agricultural production.

---

[57]Sloane, New York.
[58]*Too many,* Macmillan, New York, 1969.
[59]*Pesticides and the living landscape.*
[60]U.S. Department of Agriculture, *The pesticide review,* 1973.
[61]*Pesticides.*
[62]See D. Pimentel, Extent of pesticide use, food supply, and pollution; and E. Groth, III, Increasing the harvest.

What proportion of that increased production can be attributed to the use of synthetic pesticides? Certainly not as much as the pesticide industry would like us to believe, but synthetic pesticides may play a more significant role than is indicated in those rather dismal percentage-loss figures. High-yield strains of crops, heavily fertilized, probably require more protection per acre than lower-yield strains. That is, one might expect even greater percentages of some crops to be lost to pests today if we were still using the control techniques of 1940.

But on others the use of synthetic pesticides has decreased crop yields. According to University of California entomologist Robert van den Bosch (one of the nation's outstanding insect ecologists and an expert on ecologically sound control measures), in some California cotton fields harvests *increase* when pesticides are withdrawn. Pest problems on that state's important citrus crops are now about 3 times as severe as they were in the 1940s.[63] Ten percent of the world's insecticide load is applied to 5.7 million hectares of irrigated California land, and the state is rapidly becoming an insecticide disaster area. Of the 25 most serious insect pests in the state (each causing more than $1 million in damage), about 85 percent are resistant to one or more insecticides and all are involved in pesticide-aggravated problems—that is, they commonly have resurged following pesticide application, or they were not pests until insecticides changed the ecological situation, or pesticides applied to control them engendered outbreaks of other pests.[64]

Uncertainties about losses relative to the intensity of today's control practices make it difficult to evaluate the success of these practices, even ignoring the key questions of the undesirable side effects of pesticides or whether alternative strategies adopted decades ago would have provided superior control.[65] Could, for instance, similar or greater yields have been achieved since World War II with control methods that were more ecologically sophisticated than current pesticide practices? It is the opinion of systems ecologist K. E. F. Watt of the University of California that, when measured against successful biological and integrated control programs, "most pesticide projects have been failures." It is worth noting here that the Chinese have independently arrived at the same conclusion and have been actively developing other modes of pest control.[65a] We are convinced that the pest-control procedures in use in the 1950s and 1960s will eventually be seen as one of humanity's most tragic blunders and that when the total accounting is done, it will reveal that other methods of control would have provided higher yields at less direct cost and with fewer deleterious consequences for human beings.

Case histories of insecticide failures. Pesticides, especially the persistent ones, simplify the ecosystems to which they are applied and those into which they are transported by wind and water. The results of direct application are all too often the same: pests are freed from natural restraints. A pest, at first seemingly controlled, is soon back in even larger numbers than before. This destabilizing effect is so common that it is often cited in the scientific literature as evidence that ecosystem simplification leads to instability. Unfortunately, things do not end there in agricultural practice, and higher doses of pesticides are applied, thus aggravating the situation still further.

The history of attempts to control cotton pests in the coastal Cañete Valley of Peru has been reported by entomologist Ray F. Smith of the University of California. Against the advice of entomologists who recommended the use of cultural-control methods (such as destroying weeds which harbor pests) and inorganic and botanical insecticides, synthetic organic pesticides were widely introduced in that valley in 1949. At first the use of the pesticides, principally the chlorinated hydrocarbons DDT, BHC, and toxaphene, was very successful.

[63]Information on the California situation from R. van den Bosch, *Bug bomb* (manuscript in preparation) and seminar, Stanford University, May 3, 1976.

[64]R. T. Luck, R. van den Bosch, and R. Garcia, Chemical insect control: A troubled pest management strategy, *Bioscience*, in press.

[65]A key recommendation of the *Report of the executive committee, Study on problems of pest control*, National Academy of Sciences, Washington, D.C., 1976, was that research to resolve this uncertainty have top priority. It should have been done years before, but the vested interests of the agricultural chemicals industry and the pro-pesticide attitudes of the U.S. Department of Agriculture prevented it.

[65a]National Academy of Sciences, Insect control in China: Trip report of the Committee on Scholarly Communication with the People's Republic of China, Insect Control Delegation, NAS, Washington, D.C., 1976. See also Robert L. Metcalf, China unleashes its ducks, *Environment*, vol. 18, no. 9 (November 1976), pp. 14–17.

Cotton yields increased from 494 kilograms per hectare (440 lbs/acre) in 1950 to 728 kilograms per hectare (648 lbs/acre) in 1954. The cotton farmers concluded that if more pesticide were applied, more cotton would grow. Insecticides "were applied like a blanket over the entire valley. Trees were cut down to make it easier for the airplanes to treat the fields. The birds that nested in these trees disappeared. Other beneficial animal forms, such as insect parasites and predators, disappeared. As the years went by, the number of treatments was increased; also, each year the treatments were started earlier because of the earlier attacks of the pests."[66]

Trouble started in 1952, when BHC proved no longer to be effective against aphids. In 1954 toxaphene failed against the tobacco leafworm. Boll weevil infestation reached extremely high levels in 1955/1956, and at least six new pests had appeared, pests that were not found in similar nearby valleys that had not been sprayed with organic pesticides. In addition, the numbers of an old pest, larvae of the moth *Heliothis virescens,* exploded to new heights, and showed a high level of DDT-resistance. Synthetic organic phosphates were substituted for the chlorinated hydrocarbons, and the interval between treatments was shortened from one or two weeks down to three days. In 1955/1956, cotton yields dropped to 332 kilograms per hectare, despite the tremendous amounts of insecticide applied. Economic disaster overtook the valley. In 1957 an ecologically rational integrated-control program was initiated, in which biological, cultural, and chemical controls were combined. Conditions improved immensely, and yields rose to new highs.

This example should not be taken to mean that ecologically unsound pesticide programs have been instituted only in other places and in former times. Many examples can be cited of mistakes made here in the United States. For example, in both California and Arizona, profit margins have been dropping for cotton farmers because of insect attacks and the rising costs of chemical pesticide applications. In an attempt to evaluate the control measures used by agriculturalists, biologists uncovered some astounding information. The programs designed to control cotton pests in those states were reviewed by Kevin Shea, scientific director of the U.S.-based Committee for Environmental Information.[67] Shea reported, "controlled experiments on small plots suggest that cotton growers in California may have spent thousands of dollars to fight an insect, the lygus bug, that has no appreciable effect on the final production per acre." Reduction of the number of lygus bugs per acre *did not lead to increased yields,* apparently because the bugs fed on "surplus" squares (flower buds) of cotton, which would not ripen in any case. Spraying for lygus bugs in mid-season with some pesticides not only did not help yields, but lowered them by killing the insect predators of the bollworm, which caused outbreaks of bollworms and other pest caterpillars. In fact, by the mid-1970s the bollworm had virtually disappeared as a pest of cotton in the San Joaquin Valley. This had occurred because of adjustments in the lygus spray program (that is, sprays have been limited to restricted acreages in the early part of the season).[68]

Most disturbing of all is the Azodrin story. Azodrin is a broad-spectrum organophosphate insecticide manufactured by the Shell Chemical Company (a subsidiary of the Shell Oil Company). Azodrin kills most of the insect populations in a field, but like other organophosphates (and unlike the cholorinated hydrocarbons) it is not persistent. Its effects are devastating to populations of predatory insects. Therefore, when a field is reinvaded by pests, or when pest survivors make a comeback, their natural enemies are often absent, and pest-population booms may occur. Experiments by van den Bosch and his colleagues clearly indicated that, rather than controlling bollworms, Azodrin applications, through their effect on the bollworms' natural enemies, actually *increased* bollworm populations in treated fields. Figure 11-7 summarizes the experimental results.

Other Azodrin experiments, and the similar results obtained with the use of other broad-spectrum pesticides, make it clear that the control procedure, rather than helping the farmer, often has precisely the opposite effect. One might reasonably expect the pesticide manu-

[66]Quote is from R. F. Smith, The new and old in pest control, Memorie della Reale Acadademia Nazionale dei Lincei (Rome), Mimeographed, 1969. Further material on the Cañete disaster, including complete records of yields from 1943 to 1963 can be found in T. B. Barducci, Ecological consequences of pesticides used for the control of cotton insects in Cañete Valley, Peru, in *The careless technology; Ecology and international development,* M. T. Farvar and J. P. Milton, eds.

[67]Kevin P. Shea, Cotton and chemicals.

[68]R. van den Bosch, personal communication, June 1, 1976.

facturer to withdraw the product, or at least warn customers and advise them how to avoid the disastrous effects. However, Shea wrote: "Shell Chemical Company, manufacturer of Azodrin, was aware of the University's findings through publications and from a seminar given at the Shell Research Center in Modesto. Nevertheless, the Company decided to promote the material for use on cotton pests in the San Joaquin Valley. Shell mounted a massive sales campaign. Radio, television, billboards, bumper stickers, and trade journal ads were employed to move Azodrin out of the warehouses and into the fields. Azodrin was heralded as being unmatched in its ability to kill every major insect likely to damage cotton." The Modesto seminar was given by van den Bosch, who has said, "our own experiments indicate considerable odds against significant economic gains resulting from the use of Azodrin."[69]

Shell further has been promoting the use of Azodrin on a fixed schedule, whether pests are present or not. But fixed-schedule spraying unnecessarily damages nontarget organisms, destabilizes the agricultural ecosystem, and creates pest problems that otherwise would not arise. Aside from enhancing those effects, such programs, of course, promote the development of resistant strains of pests and the destruction of natural enemies. This guarantees the "need" for heavier and heavier doses of Azodrin. As one Azodrin advertisement put it, "even if an overpowering migration *(sic)* develops, the flexibility of Azodrin lets you regain control fast. Just increase the dosage according to label recommendations." The pesticide manufacturer is clearly the only beneficiary of such practices. It is ironic that Shell in 1975 was heavily promoting Azodrin in the Cañete Valley of Peru, as indicated by Figure 11-8!

A similar problem is the heavy use of pesticides in attempts to control so-called cosmetic pests—insects whose damage to crops is limited largely or wholly to the appearance of the produce. Growers often suffer genuine economic losses from such pests because consumers have been conditioned by advertising to associate blemish-free appearance with high quality. A well documented

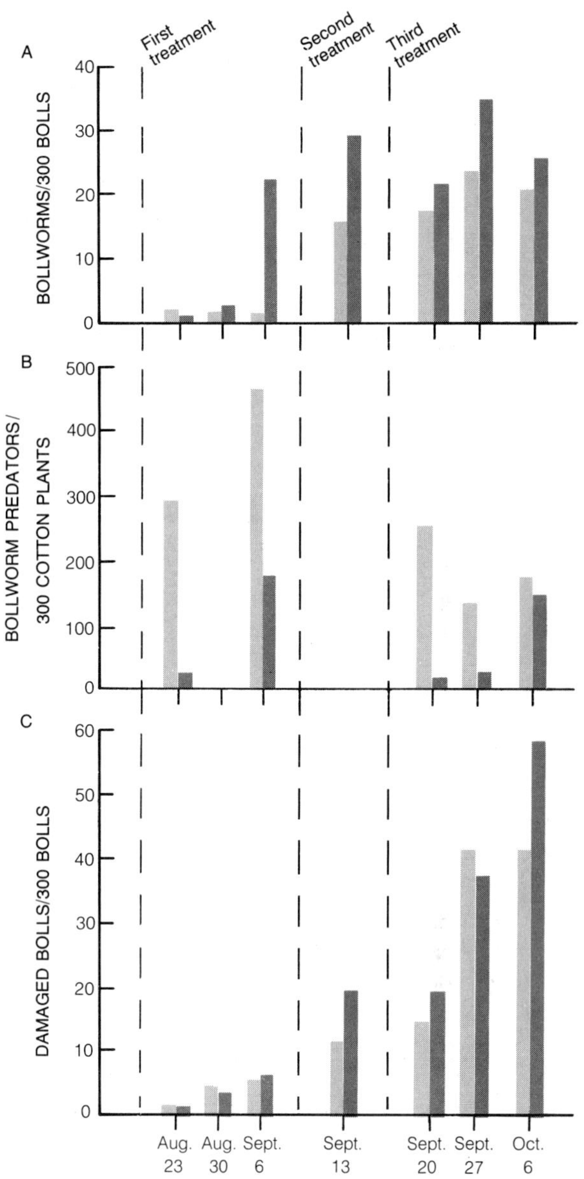

FIGURE 11-7

The results of an experiment using Azodrin to "control" bollworms. A. The number of bollworms in the untreated control plot compared with the number found in the plot treated with Azodrin. B. The number of bollworm predators in the control plot and the plot treated with Azodrin. C. The number of damaged cotton bolls in the control plot and the plot treated with Azodrin. These results indicate that Azodrin is more effective against bollworm predators than against bollworms, so the pesticide treatment *increases* the damage to the crop. (Data from R. van den Bosch et al., *Pest and disease control program for cotton,* University of California Agricultural Experiment Station, 1968.)

[69]Van den Bosch's view of the Azodrin situation can be found in The toxicity problem: Comments by an applied insect ecologist, in *Chemical fallout: Current resarch on persistent pesticides,* M. W. Miller and G. G. Berg, eds.

FIGURE 11-8

A sign advertising Azodrin in the Cañete Valley of Peru, January 1975. (Photo by P. R. Ehrlich.)

example of pesticide abuses in connection with cosmetic pests is the case of the citrus thrips, which scars some oranges grown in California but does not significantly influence yield or damage trees.[70]

Van den Bosch has stated that it is his conservative estimate that in California twice as much insecticide is used as is actually needed.[71] Since the insecticide market in California probably amounts to some $125 million to $150 million a year, one can understand the reluctance of the petrochemical industry to see a sensible pattern of use emerge that would reduce that market by at least 50 percent.

Pesticides and the Department of Agriculture. It would be unfair to blame the petrochemical industry alone for the misuse of pesticides. The U.S. Department of Agriculture (USDA) has also contributed heavily to environmental deterioration resulting from such misuse. That agency has long uncritically promoted pesticides, often displaying a distressing degree of ignorance of ecology in the process. An outstanding example can be found in the history of the fire-ant program, in which the USDA in the late 1950s attempted to "exterminate" that insect over a large portion of the United States by spraying with the chlorinated hydrocarbons dieldrin and heptachlor. Many independent biologists protested the program, asserting that extermination of the ants would be virtually impossible and that the unwanted side effects would be horrendous. Undaunted, the USDA forged ahead, but by 1960 it was clear that the program was a fiasco, as predicted. The disaster is examined in detail in Appendix 3.

With respect to the fire ant, however, the USDA apparently was incapable of learning. Armed with a new chlorinated-hydrocarbon insecticide, mirex, the department announced plans in 1970 to spray bait pellets over some 4.5 million hectares in the South. During the previous eight years, mirex had already been used over large areas on an experimental basis against the fire ant. It was at first touted as the perfect pesticide for the program, because virtually all the bait found its way into the ants' nests, leaving very little to poison nontarget organisms, and it appeared to be generally less toxic than other chlorinated hydrocarbons such as dieldrin or heptachlor. But, as time and research went on, it was discovered that mirex was not so harmless, after all. Like other chlorinated hydrocarbons, it is persistent and tends to be concentrated in food chains.[72] In laboratory tests, it has been found to be highly toxic to shrimp, crabs, and crayfish, as well as to insects other than the fire ant. It is also somewhat toxic to at least some birds and mammals and is carcinogenic in mice. Because of overtreatment (repeated applications after most of the ant nests had been poisoned), enough mirex escaped into the environment to cause problems.

When the USDA announced the new program, the Environmental Defense Fund, together with several other conservation groups, filed suit against it. In April 1971, their motion for a preliminary injunction against the fire-ant program was denied, and the program was initiated immediately. However, the action had served to delay its start. Moreover, perhaps partly because of the suit and partly because some states failed to produce their shares of the funds for it, the originally planned program was considerably curtailed.

[70]M. Brown, An orange is an orange. For some insight into the political problems of opposing the pesticide industry, see the account of van den Bosch's efforts to produce a report for the EPA on the benefits and costs of cosmetic pesticide application in Robert Wuliger, The cosmetics of agribusiness.

[71]Personal communication, June 1, 1976.

[72]P. W. Borthwick; T. W. Duke; A. J. Wilson, Jr.; J. I. Lowe; J. M. Patrick, Jr.; and J. C. Oberheu, Accumulation and movement of mirex in selected estuaries of South Carolina, 1969–71.

A number of other government agencies became interested in mirex. The Department of the Interior put mirex on its list of restricted pesticides, and the Department of Health, Education and Welfare disapproved of mirex because of its carcinogenic properties. The Council on Environmental Quality also recommended against the use of mirex, and the Environmental Protection Agency (EPA) in 1972 limited mirex applications to once a year and to areas away from forests and waterways (three times a year without spatial restriction had been the practice). In 1975 the USDA at last abandoned the goal of eradicating the fire ant. Secretary of Agriculture Earl L. Butz gave as the reason the EPA restrictions, which he said would turn USDA operations "into a control program of living with the ants rather than working toward an eradication program to wipe them out."[73] In late 1976, the USDA and the EPA settled the six-year-old battle over mirex with an 18-month phase-out program.[73a] But it is likely that the USDA will continue the attack on fire ants with some new compound. Although *no* widespread insect pest has ever been eradicated by pesticides, and none is ever likely to be, this news has yet to penetrate the appropriate recesses of the USDA. In 1974, for instance, the department seriously recommended a scheme to "eradicate" the boll weevil. Whether or not that program will be attempted remains to be seen.[74] Whether it would be successful is less in doubt.

Not all pest-control programs initiated by the USDA have been so incompetent. Some ecologically sophisticated programs have been initiated within the department. Perhaps the most brilliant was that against the screwworm, a fly whose larvae (maggots) can be an extremely serious pest on cattle. Annual losses in livestock because of that pest were estimated to have been as much as $40 million a year in the early 1960s. Under the leadership of entomologist E. F. Knipling, the USDA embarked on a massive program of sterilizing male screwworm flies by irradiation and then releasing them in infested areas. The female screwworm only mates once. By flooding infested areas with sterile males, the screwworm was essentially eradicated from the southeastern United States. The effectiveness of that biological-control program makes an interesting contrast with the futile and destructive fire-ant program.

Alternative Methods of Controlling Populations of Insects and Mites

There are three main reasons why the broadcast use of synthetic poisons is a generally undesirable way of controlling the sizes of pest populations. The first, demonstrated in Chapter 10, is that it exposes human beings to compounds that often have high acute toxicity and to others that may have long-term effects on health, including the induction of cancers. The second is that, by affecting nontarget organisms, synthetic poisons may disrupt the crucial service functions of ecosystems upon which human beings depend. One of those functions is, ironically, the control of some 98 or 99 percent of the potential pests.[75] When that function is disrupted by the use of pesticides, the result, as in the Cañete Valley, is the promotion of organisms that have been released from natural controls to pest status.

The third reason the broadcast use of synthetic poisons is undesirable is that such use encourages the development in pests of resistance to the pesticides. This problem is so serious that it has been described as a "primary obstacle to successful pest control today."[76] Some major insect pests are now resistant to nearly all the insecticides registered by the U.S. government for their control.

These failings mean that not only does broadcast spraying represent both direct and indirect hazards to human beings, but that very often the spraying does not control the pest—and even exacerbates pest problems. Nevertheless, we could gain the impression from pesticide industry propaganda that only current patterns of chemical control stand between us and death from insect-borne disease or starvation. Nothing could be further from the truth. There are, in many cases, alternatives to broadcast use of pesticides that are more

[73] *New York Times,* April 20, 1975.

[73a] Constance Holden, Mirex: Persistent pesticide on its way out.

[74] Kevin P. Shea, The last boll weevil, *Environment,* vol. 16, no. 5 (June 1974).

[75] Paul De Bach, *Biological control by natural enemies,* pp. 59–64.

[76] The quote and following material in the paragraph are from G. P. Georghiou, Resistance of insects and mites to insecticides and acaricides and the future of pesticide chemicals.

effective in controlling pests and that pose little or no threat to people or ecosystems.

Biological control by predators and parasites. Perhaps the best known of those alternatives is biological control using predators and parasites.[77] In essence, this is employing the same technique "used" by natural ecosystems to achieve near-perfect control of potential pests. When a pest problem arises, organisms that attack the pest are introduced, and nature takes its course.

The first (and still most famous) case of biological control is the saga of the cottony-cushion scale. This scale insect, *Icerya purchasi,* a native of Australia, was discovered in California in 1868 and by the mid-1880s was in the process of destroying the California citrus industry. A parasitic fly and a predatory beetle were imported from Australia, where those and other natural enemies kept *Icerya* from becoming a pest. The importations occurred in 1888 and 1889 and achieved spectacular success. By the end of 1889 *Icerya* had ceased to be a problem in California. The beetle (the Australian ladybird or vedalia beetle) achieved the first great success, spreading rapidly, but it is clear that the fly would have been equally successful, and today it is the primary control factor in coastal areas.[78]

There is an interesting footnote to that biological-control success story. In 1945 and 1947 DDT was first widely used on citrus in California. The spraying decimated populations of the vedalia beetle and caused a catastrophic population explosion of the cottony-cushion scale, which had been demoted to a nonpest status for more than half a century. Severe economic damage was done in just a few years until the spray programs were discontinued and biological control reestablished.[79]

There are many other biological-control success stories, but they are little known to the public. At small expense and effort a pest problem can thus be solved once and for all. The continuing, expensive effort—often with ever-increasing failure of control and harmful side effects—that characterizes many chemical-control programs, is absent. Only monitoring is required to make sure the biological control continues to work. By importing predators or parasites some degree of permanent control has been achieved on some 130 insect pest species. About one-third of them have been completely controlled, one-third substantially controlled, and one-third partially controlled. Some of the insects have been the targets of control programs in more than one country—all told, there have been worldwide some 275 successful biological-control projects.[80]

All in all, there appears to be about a 50-percent chance of achieving significant control of an insect pest by importing natural enemies to attack it. Nevertheless, of some 5000 recorded species of insect pests around the world, attempts have been made to find and import natural enemies of fewer than 5 percent.[81] But, of course, there is no profit for the petrochemical industry if pests are controlled by natural enemies (and relatively little profit even if chemical controls themselves work!).

Another type of biological control with the potential for being as effective as the use of arthropod enemies of insects is the dispersing of bacterial, fungal, and viral parasites that also attack the insects. Although up to 1959 there were only two such microbial insecticides on the market, by 1975 nearly fifty had been given trade names and were in commercial or experimental use. It has been estimated that, for example, the successful use of the pathogen *Baculovirus heliothis* to control pink bollworms on cotton could reduce the use of synthetic pesticides by at least 8 million kilograms annually.[82]

The importation of natural enemies is not without risk, it must be noted. For example, the introduction of mongooses into Jamaica to control rats led to an ecocatastrophe in which the native fauna of birds and small land animals was decimated. Today, however, importing agencies have established extremely careful protocols to screen out such "bad actors," doing careful pre-importation experiments in special fail-safe quarantine facilities.

Biological control by genetic methods. Other forms of biological control have also been successful.

[77]Beautifully summarized in De Bach, *Biological control by natural enemies.*

[78]For details of the history of the *Icerya* control program, see ibid., pp. 92–100.

[79]Paul De Bach and B. R. Bartlett, Effects of insecticides on biological control of insect pests of citrus, *Journal of Economic Entomology,* vol. 44, pp. 372–383, 1951.

[80]De Bach, *Biological control by natural enemies,* pp. 191–192.

[81]Ibid.

[82]C. M. Ignoffo, Entomopathogens and insecticides.

The sterile-male technique has already been discussed in connection with the screwworm program in the southeastern United States. That biological-control programs once successful may not be permanently successful is shown by the history of attempts to control screwworms along the border between the United States and Mexico. Conditions there were not as favorable to the technique, and initial successes in the mid-1960s were followed by a resurgence of screwworms in the early 1970s—a resurgence made more serious because ranches then lacked the skilled cowboys, trained horses, and necessary facilities to reinstitute older methods of control.[83] One of the problems was that in the sustained program necessary to prevent reinfestation by screwworms from Mexico (in contrast to the "quick fix" in the southeast) maintaining the genetic quality of the stocks used for release required genetic monitoring, which was not done properly.

Unfortunately, it appears that the selection pressures inadvertently applied in the laboratory produced a strain in which the males could not compete with wild males. This led to a collapse of control.[84] The USDA is now attempting to remedy these problems. Among other things, it is contracting for extensive genetic research.[85] The crucial point is that no pest-control program, biological or chemical, can ever really be considered a *permanent* success—monitoring and backup plans in case of resurgence or reinfestation should always follow any successful program.

The success of the screwworm program has led to intensive investigations of other methods of *genetic control* of pest populations.[86] A great deal of attention has been paid, for instance, to the use of natural sterility produced by chromosomal rearrangements, and other techniques such as inducing sex-ratio distortion have been considered. So far, successes have been limited to pilot studies,[87] but there is every reason to believe that there will be future successes of the kind achieved with the initial screwworm program.

Biological control by cultural and hormonal methods. Another form of biological control is so-called *cultural control,* in which conditions in the crop ecosystem are modified to the detriment of the pests or to the advantage of their natural enemies. Weeds or crop remains that harbor pests can be destroyed, planting or harvesting dates modified, crops rotated, several crops planted together, and so on. Perhaps the most promising form of cultural control has already been discussed in Chapter 4—the genetic enhancement of plant defenses to produce strains resistant to pests, to aid crops in their coevolutionary races with the organisms that attack them. Research is also being carried out with a view to isolating and making use of plants' natural chemical defenses against insects and plant diseases.[88a] For instance, one group of chemicals seems to inhibit the juvenile hormones of insects, thus disrupting their development. Another substance appears to elicit in plants a generalized response to diseases.

The use of attractants, especially of pheromones (hormones that operate outside the body—in this case, sex lures used by insects to attract mates),[88] has had limited but important success in pest control. It has been especially effective against tephritid fruit flies, which often do major damage in orchards and melon fields. An artificial sex pheromone, methyl eugenol, has achieved several local eradications of *Dacus dorsalis,* the oriental fruit fly, and eugenol is used as the lure in traps that are monitored to detect importations of that important pest.[89]

[83]The screw worm strikes back, *Nature,* vol. 242, pp. 493–494 (April 20, 1973); R. C. Bushland, Screwworm eradication program, *Science,* vol. 184, pp. 1010–1011 (May 31, 1974).

[84]The problems of preventing mass-reared laboratory strains from diverging from wild strains are severe and related to those of maintaining genetic variability in seed banks. See G. L. Bush, Genetic variation in natural insect populations and its bearing on mass rearing programmes; G. L. Bush and R. W. Neck, Ecological genetics of the screwworm fly, *Cochliomya hominivorax* (Diptera: Calliphoridae) and its bearing on the quality control of mass reared insects; G. L. Bush, R. W. Neck, and G. B. Kitto, Screwworm eradication: inadvertent selection for noncompetitive ecotypes during mass rearing.

[85]Bushland, Screwworm eradication.

[86]G. G. Foster, et al., Chromosomal rearrangements for the control of insect pests, *Science,* vol. 176, pp. 875–880 (May 26, 1972); R. H. Smith and R. C. von Borstel, Genetic control of insect populations, *Science,* vol. 178, pp. 1164–1174 (December 15, 1972); G. Davidson, *Genetic control of insect pests;* R. Pal and M. J. Whitten, *The use of genetics in insect control;* Alan S. Robinson, Progress in the use of chromosomal translocations for the control of insect pests.

[87]For example, H. Laven, J. Cousserans, and G. Guille, Eradicating mosquitoes using translocations: A first field experiment.

[88]M. Beroza, Insect sex attractants, *American Scientist,* vol. 59, pp. 320–325, 1971.

[88a]Thomas H. Maugh II, Plant biochemistry: two new ways to fight pests.

[89]De Bach, *Biological control by natural enemies,* p. 264–265; D. L. Chambers et al., Pest control by attractants: A case study demonstrating economy, specificity, and environmental acceptability.

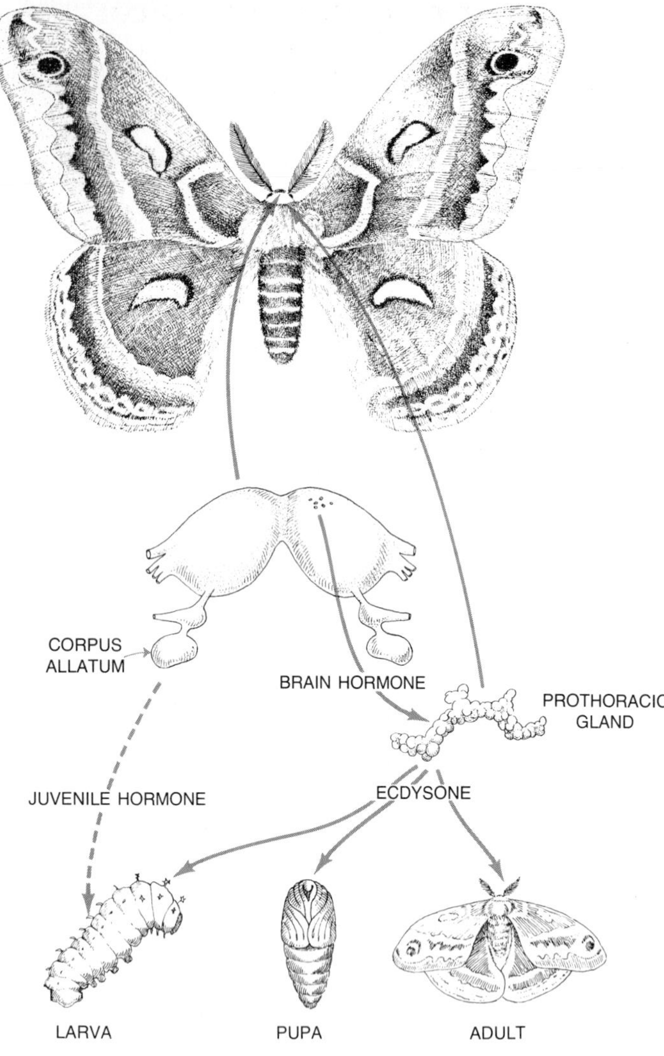

FIGURE 11-9

Hormonal activity in the Cecropia moth, the animal used for much of the early experimental work on the control of insect growth and metamorphosis. Juvenile hormone (broken line) comes from the corpora allata, tiny glands just behind the brain. A second substance, brain hormone, stimulates the prothoracic gland to secrete ecdysone, which initiates the shedding of the external skeleton as the caterpillar grows. The caterpillar stage is controlled by a balance of juvenile hormone and ecdysone. In the normal course of development the flow of juvenile hormone is stopped when the caterpillar is full grown, permitting metamorphosis into the pupa (the resting stage in which the adult structure is formed.) If more juvenile hormone is applied after its natural production ends, development is deranged; the hormone then acts as an insecticide. (After Williams, 1967.)

Besides using external hormones to lure insects to their deaths or to disrupt their mating behavior,[90] internal hormones can be used to disrupt their development (which is controlled by a balance of juvenile hormones and those causing metamorphosis, Figure 11-9). Such so-called third-generation insecticides[91] are now undergoing field testing. How great a problem the evolution of resistance to them will present is still unknown. In theory, insects can evolve behavioral mechanisms to avoid exposure, barriers to prevent absorption, or tolerance to greater variability in hormone levels, but whether such changes will occur in practice is an open question.

Integrated control. There obviously is no single panacea to replace the broadcast spraying of pesticides. What is required is a shift to ecological pest management[92]—that is, to what is often called *integrated control.* Integrated control has as its goal the maintenance of potential pest populations below the levels at which they cause serious health hazards or economic damage. It does not attempt to exterminate pests—which, as stated earlier, has never been accomplished by the broadcast spraying of pesticides. Integrated control involves using one or more techniques appropriate to the particular pest situation. Mosquitoes may be controlled by draining swamps in which larvae live, stocking lakes with mosquito-eating fishes, or applying hormonal insecticides, or perhaps directly applying toxic nonpersistent insecticides to any standing water that will not support fishes and cannot be drained. Similarly, a crop could be protected by practices such as planting it in mixed cultures with other crops, destroying pest reservoirs adjacent to fields, introducing and encouraging appropriate predators and parasites, enhancing the natural defenses of crop populations, luring pests from fields with baits, and using nonpersistent insecticides. These and other practices may be combined to achieve both high levels of desirable control and a minimum of damage to the ecosystems of the world. Sometimes, as in

[90]W. Roelofs, Manipulating sex pheromones for insect suppression.

[91]Carroll M. Williams, Third generation pesticides. For a more recent review see J. J. Menn and F. M. Pallas, Development of morphogenetic agents in insect control.

[92]See, for example, R. L. Giese, R. M. Peart, and R. T. Huber, Pest management.

the successful screwworm program, no chemical control will be necessary; at other times chemical methods may play major roles.

Integrated control programs have been enormously successful where they have been tried. An outstanding example is a program in cotton in California. Robert van den Bosch and his co-authors wrote[93] about the control of pests on cotton in California's Central Valley, "Existing pest control practices are both inefficient and expensive, and because of this they are directly contributing to the economic crisis [among cotton growers]. Accumulating evidence indicates that integrated control is much more efficient and less expensive, and the hard-pressed growers are beginning to realize this."

Another successful integrated control program has been established in three California cities (Berkeley, Palo Alto, and San Jose) to protect street trees.[93a] Since this protection is mainly for cosmetic purposes, the customary heavy use of poisons is even less justifiable than it is on farm produce. Once established, the urban integrated control program appears to be less costly to taxpayers as well as far less of a threat to their health.

The transition away from the relatively simple chemical techniques will require planning and training, and will perhaps produce some temporary economic stress. One county agricultural extension service entomologist, faced with a successful integrated-control program, said, "Your damn pest management program is ruining my business. I can't get pilots who are willing to work for me when there is so little insecticide being used."[94] Such attitudes are, quite naturally, widespread in the insecticide industry, where profits depend on the avoidance of permanent solutions to pest problems—other than perpetual spraying.

Since banning the chlorinated hydrocarbons should not be delayed, more expensive methods of control may have to be used temporarily. But there is no reason the transition should have serious consequences for human health or nutrition. The step would be necessary, however, even if such consequences *were* foreseen as serious, since continued use of persistent insecticides risks an unprecedented catastrophe for the entire planet. In fact, positive benefits would be immediate in many areas, where the development of DDT-resistant mosquitoes is already reducing the effectiveness of mosquito-control programs. It is important to remember, above all, that avoiding unhappy side effects from any control program, integrated or not, depends on intelligent surveillance and periodic reevaluation. *Any* tinkering with ecosystems may have unforeseen and deleterious consequences.

Herbicides in Ecosystems

In recent years there has been an enormous upsurge in the use of herbicides as a substitute for farm machinery and labor in cultivating crops to increase productivity of range and pastureland;[95] for keeping roadsides, railroad rights-of-way, and powerline cuts free of shrubs; and as military defoliants during the Vietnam war. The rate of increase in herbicide use has far outstripped that of synthetic insecticides, and annual sales of herbicides are now larger.[96] Several kinds of herbicides are in wide use (Box 11-2). Members of one group (2,4-D; 2,4,5-T; picloram; and so on) are similar to plant hormones and cause metabolic changes in the plant that lead to death or leaf drop. Members of another group (simazin, monuron, and the like) interfere with a critical process in photosynthesis, causing the plant to die from lack of energy. The way others disrupt plant metabolism is less well understood. Although their direct toxicity to animals is low, herbicides have great impact on animal populations, since all animals depend on plants for food, at least indirectly. Furthermore, as a result of the coevolutionary interactions discussed earlier, most herbivorous animals are specialized to feed on one kind or on just a few kinds of plants.

[93]R. van den Bosch, T. F. Leigh, L. A. Falcon, V. M. Stern, D. Gonzales, and K. S. Hagen, The developing program of integrated control of cotton pests in California, in C. B. Huffaker, ed., *Biological control,* p. 377.

[93a]W. Olkowski, H. Olkowski, R. van den Bosch, and R. Hom, Ecosystem management: A framework for urban pest control.

[94]L. Dale Newsom, Pest management: Concept to practice, in *Insects, science and society,* D. Pimentel, ed., p. 273.

[95]K. C. Barrons, Some ecological benefits of woody plant control with herbicides, *Science,* vol. 165, pp. 465–468 (August 1, 1969), but see critiques, Controversial uses of herbicides, *Science,* vol. 166, pp. 310–311 (October 17, 1969).

[96]U.S. Dept. of Agriculture, *The Pesticide Review,* 1974.

BOX 11-2 Some Synthetic Herbicides

Herbicides That Mimic Indoleacetic Acid

This group of herbicides includes 2,4-D, 2,4,5-T, picloram, and several others. The compounds are chemically similar to the growth-regulating substance indoleacetic acid. That plant hormone (an auxin) controls such diverse activities as shoot growth, root growth, apical dominance, and phototropism. Herbicides in this hormone-like group function by causing uncontrolled growth and metabolism—the plant, in essence, grows itself to death.*

Indoleacetic acid does not function as a growth substance in animals, and therefore it is not surprising that these herbicides have essentially no direct effect on animals. Differential toxicity to broad-leaved plants (in contrast to narrow-leaved grasses) is a function of the greater ease with which the compounds are absorbed by the broad-leaved plants. Some of the herbicides, such as 2,4-D, are rapidly metabolized in woody plants, which usually localize the damage (they are defoliated but not killed). Other herbicides, such as picloram, remain active for long periods in trees and ecosystems.

*For more details, see J. Van Overbeek, Survey of mechanisms of herbicide action, in *The physiology and biochemistry of herbicides,* L. J. Audis, ed., Academic Press, New York, 1969.

Symmetrical Triazines and Substituted Ureas

These two classes of compounds include atrazine, simazine, fenuron, diuron, and monuron. Both kinds of compound block a critical step in photosynthesis, known as the Hill reaction. The plant, in essence, starves to death. Since animals do not photosynthesize, they are not directly affected by these compounds, with the exception of possible mutagenic effects from the triazines.

Others

A wide variety of other synthetic compounds, including chlorinated aliphatic acids (dalapon, TCA), phenols (DNBP), acetamides (propanil) and thiocarbamates, can act as herbicides. Their modes of action are varied, and many are poorly understood. For instance, the carbamate sulfoxides interfere with plant metabolism and growth and are often highly selective, but the precise mechanism for their action has not been discovered. They are, however, highly biodegradable—and the mechanism of their metabolic destruction is fairly clear.**

**J. E. Casida, R. A. Gray, and H. Tilles, Thiocarbamate sulfoxides: Potent, selective, and biodegradable herbicides.

In the light of these considerations, it is possible to evaluate the statements made by many United States government officials concerning the lack of danger to animals or the uncertainty of effects on animals of our defoliation activities in Vietnam (Box 11-3). Defoliation of tropical jungles inevitably leads to the local extinction of many populations of insects, birds, arboreal reptiles, and arboreal mammals. But, of course, *animals* in official statements can all too often be translated "elephants, tigers, and other large mammals." In temperate forests there is generally a less distinct canopy fauna, but changes in animal populations in response to large-scale defoliation would certainly be tremendous.

Little is known about the direct effects of herbicides on soil microorganisms. Research in Sweden indicates that herbicides destroy bacteria that are symbiotic with legumes, although the bacteria apparently are capable of developing some resistance.[97] Some herbicides, such as 2,4-D, are quickly degraded by bacteria and persist for only a few weeks or months; others (2,4,5-T and, presumably, picloram) are more persistent. Soil microorganisms (primarily bacteria and fungi) do not photosynthesize; they are consumers, not producers. Therefore, they probably will not be affected by herbicides that block photosynthetic processes, although there could, of course, be other metabolic effects. Herbicides that function as simulated plant hormones are unlikely to disturb the growth processes of the soil flora, since there is no evidence that the plant hormone simulated by those substances functions in bacteria or fungi. Those herbicides may, of course, have other physiological effects, since, as noted, some are metabolized by soil bacteria.

[97]Does killing weeds destroy the soil? *New Scientist and Science Journal,* March 25, 1971, p. 663.

BOX 11-3 Ecocide in Indochina

The practice of genocide, unhappily, has a long history in human affairs. Ecocide (the deliberate destruction of ecosystems) is for practical reasons a rather recent development. Destruction of enemy crops has frequently occurred in warfare, and the near-extermination of the bison was a decisive factor in America's conquest of the Plains Indians (the slaughter was not a purposeful military strategy, but its effects were known at the time). But, until recently, humanity has not been able to destroy the entire life-support system over substantial portions of the surface of Earth in a short space of time. Now, however, synthetic herbicides, insecticides, weather-modification technology, and nuclear weapons have given people a greatly increased capability of committing ecocide. If the widespread use of biocides continues, despite growing knowledge of the probable consequences, civilization may destroy much of the carrying capacity of this planet for human life. If that occurs, however, survivors will be able to explain what happened as a result of greed and stupidity—after all, no one really wanted the unhappy side effects of synthetic biocides.

But no such excuse can be made for the practice of ecocide by the armed forces of the United States in the Vietnam war.[a] In that war the United States attempted to win by substituting firepower for manpower. It managed to retain control of the main cities, so the vast majority of its firepower was concentrated on the countryside, rather than on population centers. The people in rural areas and agricultural and natural ecosystems bore the brunt of the assault both with "conventional" weapons and with herbicides and other technologies for ecosystem alteration and destruction.

According to a report of the National Academy of Science (NAS), through 1971—when spraying stopped—some 1.5 million hectares of South Vietnam, 10 percent of the country had been treated with about 20 million gallons of herbicides,[b] applied at an average of 13 times the dose recommended by the U.S. Department of Agriculture for domestic use. Most of the spraying was done in forests in an unsuccessful attempt to expose the enemy and secure the area (as indicated in Table 11-2). At such dosages some of the trees, especially mangroves, can be not just defoliated but killed by a single application (see Figure 11-10). Multiple applications kill other kinds of trees. The American Association for the Advancement of Science Herbicide-Assessment Commission (AAAS-HAC) reported that perhaps half the trees in the mature hardwood forests north of Saigon were damaged. One of the herbicides widely used in Vietnam was picloram, which is both potent and (like DDT) persistent. It is so dangerous that the Department of Agriculture has not licensed it for use in the cultivation of any American crop.

By the end of 1971 at least 100,000 hectares of cropland in South Vietnam had been sprayed with herbicides (Table 11-2) with the stated purpose of denying food to enemy soldiers. This was done in an attempt also to starve civilian populations sympathetic to the National Liberation Front and to force people to move from the countryside into cities, where they would be easier to control. As our military was well aware, the first to suffer when food becomes scarce in wartime are not soldiers, but children, old people, and pregnant and nursing women. The AAAS-HAC reported that virtually all the crops destroyed would have supplied food to civilians, especially to the Montagnard tribesmen of the central highlands.

The general effect of the herbicide programs was to degrade Vietnamese ecosystems. Forests attacked with herbicides have been invaded by bamboo, and some areas may have undergone laterization. The danger of laterization is especially severe in farmland attacked with herbicides. Large areas of mangrove forest, which grows along waterways and plays a critical role in the maintenance of economically important fisheries, have also been destroyed. According to the NAS report, about 36 percent of the mangroves in South Vietnam (0.6 percent of the country's area) have been killed, and the forests will not recover for perhaps a century.[c] The long-term consequences of the programs are incalculable, since they have also certainly had a profound effect on the fauna of the area (and animals, in turn, are important to the plants for pollination and seed dispersal) and probably also on the organisms of the soil, which are essential to its fertility. Very often in Vietnam plant succession in repeatedly defoliated areas has resulted in the establishment of an impoverished community dominated by bamboo or low grasses of no use to the Vietnamese.

[a]Some of the material here is from the Stanford Biology Study Group, The destruction of Indochina.

[b]National Academy of Sciences, *Effects of herbicides in South Vietnam:* pt. A *Summary and conclusions.*

[c]Ibid.

(*Continued*)

BOX 11-3 (*Continued*)

Herbiciding operations also may have left the Vietnamese with a legacy of birth defects, as some of the constituents of herbicides are teratogenic.[d] Due in large part to the AAAS-HAC report and other pressures from the American scientific community, the use of herbicides as a military weapon in Vietnam was discontinued in May of 1971.

Herbicides were not the only ecocidal weapon used in Indochina. In 1967/1968 alone, more than 3.5 million 500-to-750-lb (225–340 kg) bombs were dropped on Vietnam, each creating a crater as much as 14 meters across and 9 meters deep. If those craters were placed in a line, they would stretch for some 50,000 kilometers, a distance longer than the circumference of Earth. They occupy 40,000 hectares.

From 1965 to 1973 the U.S. military detonated 7 million metric tons of high explosives in South Vietnam, the equivalent to the explosive power of 400 Hiroshima-size atomic bombs—almost half a ton of munitions for each hectare of South Vietnam's land area. The area of craters created in South Vietnam by bombs and shells was some 150,000 hectares (almost 1 percent of the land), 2 billion cubic meters of soil were displaced, and millions of additional hectares were contaminated with missile fragments.[e] In many areas of Vietnam, peasants are afraid to reoccupy bombed fields because of the danger from unexploded ordnance.

[d]See, for example, H. A. Rose and S. P. R. Rose, Chemical spraying as reported by refugees from South Vietnam, *Science*, vol. 177, pp. 710–712 (August 25, 1972.)

[e]For information on damage by munitions see A. H. Westing and E. W. Pfeiffer, The cratering of Indochina; and A. H. Westing, Environmental consequences of the second Indochina war: A case study. The recent statistics are from the latter.

FIGURE 11-10

These aerial photos show the extent of damage to South Vietnamese mangrove forests from U.S. military herbicide spraying. *Top.* An unsprayed mangrove forest about 60 miles from Saigon. *Center.* In 1970, a once-similar forest five years after spraying. Dark spots are surviving trees. *Bottom.* A herbicide-damaged rubber plantation about 40 miles north of Saigon. The dead trees in the foreground have been cut down. In the background, among other dead rubber trees is a plantation workers' resettlement. (Wide World Photos.)

TABLE 11-2
*Land Sprayed with Herbicides One or More Times in Vietnam, 1965–1971 (estimated)**

	Total area in 1953		*Number of times sprayed August 1965–March 1971 in millions of hectares*				*Total sprayed one or more times*	
*Type of vegetation***	*Millions of hectares*	*% of total*	*1*	*2*	*3*	*4+*	*Millions of hectares*	*% of type*
Inland forest	10.49	62.4	0.69	0.25	0.089	0.045	1.08	10.3
Cultivated land	3.16	18.8	0.08	0.02	0.005	0.000	0.10	3.2
Mangrove forest	0.29	1.7	0.06	0.03	0.012	0.008	0.11	36.1
Other	2.86	17.1	0.13	0.03	0.008	0.000	0.16	5.5

*Does not include the effects of missions before August 1965 (4.8 million liters) and missions after that date for which location information is incomplete (4.2 million liters), representing about 12.5 percent of the total volume of herbicides accounted for.

**"Inland forests" includes dense forest, secondary forest, swidden zones, bamboo forests, open dipterocarp, *Lagerstroemia* and Leguminosae forests. "Other" includes pine forests, savanna and degraded forests, grasslands and steppes in higher elevations, dunes and brushland, grass and sedge swamps, and areas of no vegetation (urban areas, roads, water courses, and so forth).

Source: National Academy of Sciences, *Effects of herbicides in South Vietnam,* pt. A.

Many of the bomb craters pocking the surface of Indochina are permanently filled with water. From our observations of World War II bomb craters in New Guinea and the Solomon Islands in 1965, we believe it is reasonable to expect natural recovery of many such cratered areas to take at least a century.

Another ecocidal device that was used by the U.S. in Indochina was the BLU-82B multipurpose bomb, the so-called daisy-cutter. That 15,000-pound (6800-kg) concussion weapon cleared an area the size of a football field to make an "instant landing zone" for helicopters. It was also used as an antipersonnel weapon, as it could kill all plant and animal life within a radius of some 65 meters (an area of more than 1.3 hectares), and the zone of death and injury extended some 400 meters (an area of 50 hectares). Hundreds of those devices were used in Vietnam.[f] Also used for clearing landing areas as well as against troops was the CBU-55 fire air explosive. It produces an exceedingly powerful blast by spraying an aerosol cloud of fuel over the target area and then detonating it. Blast overpressures of about 20 kilograms per square centimeter are produced over a circle of 15 meters in diameter.[g] The bomb was introduced into the Vietnam war in 1971 by U.S. forces and was used after their departure by South Vietnam. According to the United States Department of Defense, 2000 of them were dropped by the South Vietnamese air force between 1972 and 1975. They were also used by Cambodian government forces in Cambodia. Information on the scale and permanence of the damage done in either country is not available.

Perhaps the crudest tool the United States used to destroy the ecology of Indochina was the Rome plow. This is a heavily armored D7E caterpillar bulldozer weighing 33 tons and carrying a blade designed to cut down a tree of any size. Rome plows were first used in 1966 to clear several hundred yards on both sides of all main roads in South Vietnam. In 1968 they were distributed to "land-clearing companies," each with thirty plows, to mow down any Vietnamese forests thought advantageous to the enemy. Each company had the capability of clearing 40 hectares per day of fully developed upland forest or 160 hectares per day of light jungle. About 350,000 hectares of South Vietnamese forest (3 percent of South Vietnam's forests, 2 percent of its land area) were plowed as were thousands of hectares of rubber plantations, orchards and farms.[h] The immediate ecological damage caused by exposing and abrading the soil surface over such huge areas is colossal, and the subsequent establishment of undesirable plant communities all too common.

Ecocide in Indochina was not limited to combat operations. A clandestine raid in April 1969 defoliated 70,000 hectares in eastern Cambodia and damaged about a third of the rubber trees then in production in Cambodia. The damage was concentrated in an area with the highest yield per acre in Cambodia. In addition to that serious blow to the rubber crop (which is the underpinning of that nation's economy), damage to local food production was severe. The operation was carried out before the Cambodian

[f]A. H. Westing, The super bomb, *American Report,* vol. 2, n. 3.

[g]Clarence A. Robinson, Jr., Special report: Fuel air explosives, *Aviation Week and Space Technology,* February 19, 1973.

[h]Westing, The super bomb.

(*Continued*)

BOX 11-3 (*Continued*)

invasion in order to put pressure on the Sihanouk government, and the raid may have been flown by persons employed by the U.S. Central Intelligence Agency.[i]

Although ecocide is not formally a war crime, it contributed much "wanton destruction" and "devastation," which are considered both war crimes and crimes against humanity under the charter of the International Military Tribunal at Nuremberg. The use of herbicides (and tear gases) is against the Geneva Protocol of 1925, as interpreted in 1969 by the main political committee of the U.N. General Assembly. The vote on that was 58 to 3, with 35 abstentions. The only nations to vote no with the United States were Australia, which allied itself with the United States in Vietnam, and Portugal, which employed those weapons in its own wars in Africa.[j]

[i]A. H. Westing, Herbicidal Damage to Cambodia, in *Harvest of death: Chemical warfare in Vietnam and Cambodia,* J. B. Neilands, G. H. Orians, E. W. Pfeiffer, A. Vennema, and A. H. Westing, Free Press, New York, 1972.

[j]A. Humbaraci, *Threats to the ecology of southern Africa,* Zambian Information Office, Rome, 1971.

The effects of herbicides on soil are not necessarily all negative, however. The principal reason for plowing is to destroy weeds, and the process of removing crop debris, leaving fields bare, and then plowing them is a major source of soil erosion. Erosion is an extremely serious problem—as much as one-third of the topsoil in parts of the United States has been lost to it in the past century.[97a] With the massive use of herbicides, a "zero-tillage" system can be established, in which herbicides substitute for plowing and the land is subject to far less erosion. Such a system has been in use in the southeastern United States on 1 million hectares for several years.[98] Whether that benefit of the massive use of herbicides outweighs the costs remains to be seen; we are doubtful—especially in view of their possible direct effects on people, discussed in Chapter 10. Some combination of minimum tillage with other methods of weed control may prove superior from the ecological/soil-conservation point of view.

Herbicides have also been adopted by other organisms than human beings. A flightless grasshopper has been discovered to secrete 2,5-dichlorophenol, apparently derived from 2,4-D, along with other naturally occurring disagreeable substances derived from plants, in its defensive fluid. This unusual ingredient appears to be very successful in discouraging predatory ants; thus, in attacking weeds, human beings inadvertently encourage a herbivore.[99] The subtlety of the effects of biocides is difficult to overestimate. For example, herbicides can serve as synergists of insecticides, and the nature of the synergism is itself influenced by such other environmental factors as soil type.[100]

Too little is known also about the effects of herbicides on aquatic life, but the evidence is mounting that they are substantial. Members of the group including 2,4-D are particularly toxic to fishes, although less so than most insecticides, and they have also been found toxic to freshwater crustacea.[101]

The runoff of herbicides, especially those that interfere with photosynthesis, into inland and coastal waters could be more serious than the effects of herbicides on soil fertility. The photosynthetic processes of phytoplankton, as well as the growth of other plants, could be disturbed. Again, it is important to remember that changes in basic producer populations will inevitably affect populations higher up in the food chains. The need for comprehensive studies of the effects of herbicides in aquatic ecosystems is escalating as those chemicals not

[97a]D. Pimentel et al., Land degradation: Effects on food and energy resources.

[98]Brian Gardner, Environmental paradox, *New Scientist,* November 29, 1973, pp. 641–642. G. B. Triplett, Jr. and D. M. van Doren, Jr., Agriculture without tillage.

[99]T. Eisner, L. B. Hendry, D. B. Peakall, and J. Meinwald, 2,5-dichlorophenol (from ingested herbicide?) in defensive secretion of grasshopper. See also I. N. Oka and D. Pimentel, Herbicide (2,4-D) increases insect and pathogen pests on corn.

[100]T. L. Liang and E. P. Lichtenstein, Synergism of insecticides by herbicides: Effect of environmental factors.

[101]For comprehensive coverage of herbicide effects, see Pimentel, *Ecological effects;* for the crustaceans, Herman O. Sanders, Toxicities of some herbicides to six species of freshwater crustaceans.

only enter aquatic systems as runoff but are applied directly for aquatic weed-control.[102]

Even with the small amount of information that exists, it is hard to be complacent about widespread indiscriminate use of herbicides under any circumstances. The spraying of potent biocides over large areas because it is easier and quicker than careful cultivating or weeding is a practice ecologists can only deplore. The herbicide story may turn out to be a repetition of the insecticide story, but the case for dependence on chemicals seems even weaker for weed-killers. Like insecticides, they should be used with discretion and only when necessary. Otherwise, problems such as development of resistance in weeds may be added to the growing concern over direct effects (Chapter 10) and the effects of these compounds on the ecosystem. Some weeds have developed resistance to herbicides, as have some crops.[103] The latter may be an important advantage if crop strains can be developed that will permit the action of herbicides to be more selective.

More attention should be paid to developing integrated-control methods for weeds, and in recalcitrant cases where those methods or mechanical weeding proves infeasible, a return to weeding by human effort should be considered. Adjustment of the economic system so that more labor can be employed profitably in agriculture might possibly help solve social and economic problems ranging from unemployment to overurbanization.

Quantitative Pollutants with Known Ecosystemic Effects

Most attention to the impacts of pollutants on natural ecological systems has been directed at pesticides. And, with the exception of radiological pollutants (see below), detailed studies of the effects of a given pollutant on an entire terrestrial ecosystem have been confined very largely to synthetic insecticides.[104] It is clear that many other qualitative pollutants (such as the PCBs) must have ecosystemic effects but they have at most been guessed at.

We now turn to a consideration of some of the quantitative pollutants—petroleum, mercury, nitrates, phosphates, and radiation. Ecological systems have had to deal with all of them for eons, but now they may be present in quantities that constitute overloads for the systems in which they occur.

Petroleum pollution. One ocean pollutant that has received a great deal of publicity—much of it the result of spectacular supertanker accidents—is oil. In 1970, when Thor Heyerdahl sailed a papyrus raft across the Atlantic Ocean, he reported, "Clots of oil are polluting the mid-stream current of the Atlantic Ocean, from horizon to horizon."[105] Oil has reached the sea in a variety of ways. Among them are the massive accidental spills from tankers that have received so much publicity, as well as many smaller spills. Those probably account for less than 0.1 percent of the total amount of oil transported at sea. But the volume is so huge (about 1.2 billion metric tons per year, or 60 percent of all sea-transported goods) that the spills and oil purposely flushed from tankers amount to a considerable influx.[105a] Another source is fuel oil spilled from ships not involved in transporting oil, especially in connection with their refueling operations. In addition to shipping spills, there have been accidents in the extraction of oil from the seafloor, of which the 1969 Santa Barbara leak is the most widely known example. Some oil reaches the sea in sewage as wastes from automobile crankcases and from industry (including refineries). There is also the natural influx of oil into the oceans from submarine seeps. Those may be important locally, but on a global scale the input from seeps appears to be about 10 times smaller than human contributions.[106] Estimates of the magnitudes of major

[102]For insight into some of the complexities of herbicide effects, see R. L. Simpson and D. Pimentel, Ecological effects of the aquatic herbicide fenac on small ponds.

[103]R. G. Ryan, Resistance of common groundsel to simazine and atrazine; M. J. Pinthus, Y. Eshel, and Y. Shohori, Field and vegetable crop mutants with increased resistance to herbicides.

[104]For example, G. W. Barrett, The effects of an acute insecticide stress on a semienclosed grassland ecosystem; C. R. Malone, Effects of diazinon contamination on an old-field ecosystem; D. J. Shure, Insecticide effects on early succession in an old field ecosystem.

[105]His observations (reported in Atlantic ocean pollution and biota observed by the *Ra* expeditions) have been confirmed quantitatively (B. F. Morris, Petroleum: Tar quantities floating in the northwestern Atlantic taken with a new quantitative neuston net; C. S. Wong, D. R. Green, and W. J. Cretney, Quantitative tar and plastic waste distributions in the Pacific Ocean).

[105a]Gene Coan, Oil pollution. See also W. B. Travers and P. R. Luney, Drilling, tankers, and oil spills on the Atlantic outer continental shelf.

[106]M. Blumer, Submarine seeps: Are they a major source of open ocean oil pollution?; National Academy of Sciences, *Petroleum in the marine environment.*

TABLE 11-3
Sources of Petroleum in the Ocean

Source	Flow (million MT/yr)
Marine transportation	2.1
Coastal oil refining	0.2
Offshore oil production	0.1
Industrial wastes	0.3
Municipal waste & urban runoff	0.6
Atmospheric rainout*	0.6
Natural seeps	0.1–0.6

*From hydrocarbons evaporated on continents, mostly anthropogenic.
Sources: Study of Critical Environmental Problems, *Man's impact on the global environment;* National Academy of Sciences, *Petroleum in the marine environment;* R. M. Garrels, F. T. Mackenzie, and C. Hunt, *Chemical cycles and the global environment.*

sources of petroleum in the oceans are given in Table 11-3.

The effects of oil pollution on oceanic ecosystems, beyond the immediate and obvious decimation of populations of fishes, shellfishes, and seabirds at the site of a spill (Figure 11-11), are now being discovered, thanks in part to a relatively small spill that occurred in 1969 near the Woods Hole Oceanographic Institute in Massachusetts. Effects vary with the type of oil, how far from shore it is spilled, and how long it can "weather" (be degraded by microorganisms, dissolve, and evaporate) before reaching shore, and what organisms live in the affected areas. Some components of oil are toxic; others are known carcinogens. Weathering can reduce their toxicity, but the carcinogenic components are long-lasting. Oil washed to shore lingers on rocks and sand for months or years, but the marine life may need a decade or more to recover, even after the oil is no longer obvious.[107]

Populations of some seabirds, especially the diving birds (such as ducks and puffins in the English Channel), which are most susceptible, have been drastically reduced in recent years, probably largely because of oil contamination.[108] Besides killing thousands of birds directly, oil toxins have been shown experimentally to affect their reproduction and to reduce the viability of their eggs when applied directly to them. Other effects are more subtle but nonetheless cause for concern—such as the altering of feeding behavior in lobsters.[109]

Detergents used to clean up oil spills have been found to make the situation worse in many cases.[110] Not only are the detergents themselves toxic to many forms of life but they disperse the oil and spread it into new areas. They may also render it more easily absorbable by small marine organisms by breaking it up into droplets.

Immediately after the Massachusetts spill, there was a 95-percent mortality of fish, shellfish, worms, and other sea animals in the immediate area. Nine months later, repopulation had still not taken place. Surviving mussels failed to reproduce. Some constituents of the oil were still present and killing bottom-dwelling organisms eight months later. Surviving shellfish and oysters took in enough oil to be inedible and retained it even months after having been transplanted at a distance. According to marine biologist Max Blumer, there is a possibility that the carcinogenic constituents of oil, which are absorbed unchanged by those and other small organisms, may in time be incorporated into and contaminate entire food chains.[111] Although large amounts would probably spoil the taste and smell of conventional foods, toxic and carcinogenic effects are certainly possible at levels of contamination too low to taste or smell. It has also been suggested that higher levels of contamination might go undetected in fish-protein concentrates,[112] which some people consider to be a potential future source of protein for human beings. To the extent, however, that the carcinogens in oil would accumulate mostly in the fat of fishes rather than in muscle, the carcinogenicity problem in fish-protein concentrates would be minimized.

Some effort is being made to develop bacterial strains that can quickly degrade spilled oil; more efficient technical means of collecting it before it reaches shore are also being developed.[113] In view of the amount of oil

[107]There has been some controversy over the effects of oil spills on ecosystems, especially because of differing results obtained by groups studying the 1969 Santa Barbara spill and the Woods Hole group. This controversy is dealt with in D. F. Boesche, C. H. Herschner, and J. H. Milgram, *Oil spills and the marine environment.* The bibliography of this report to the Ford Foundation Energy Policy Project gives entry to the significant literature on ecosystemic effects of oil spills. See also the National Academy of Sciences, *Petroleum in the marine environment.*

[108]Wesley Marx, *Oilspill,* p. 26ff.

[109]J. Atema and L. Stein, Effects of crude oil on the feeding behavior of the lobster *Homarus americanus, Environmental Pollution,* vol. 6, pp. 77–86, 1974.

[110]See, for example, O. Linden, Acute effects of oil and oil/dispersant mixture on larvae of Baltic herring.

[111]W. Sullivan, Oil called peril to food supply in sea, *New York Times,* June 16, 1970.

[112]Tony Loftas, The unseen dangers of oil.

[113]These are summarized well in Boesche, Herschner, and Milgram, *Oil spills.*

A

B

C

FIGURE 11-11

A. An aerial photograph of the 1971 oil spill from a tanker collision in San Francisco Bay. Some of the oil has already washed out the Golden Gate, at the left. One tanker is in the center of the picture, Sausalito at the upper left, Angel Island and the Richmond–San Rafael Bridge at the upper right, and Alcatraz Island at the lower right. B. Volunteers cleaning a beach fouled by the spilled oil. C. Some of the birds that were killed. (Photo A courtesy of Western Aerial Photos, Inc.; photo B by Klink, Photofind, San Francisco; photo C by Robert Schen, Photofind, San Francisco.)

already polluting the oceans and the increasing potential for further spills represented by the rising volume of oil being transported by sea and the increasing size of tankers, efforts to deal with such accidents should be vigorously pursued. At the same time, much can be done in the area of prevention without further research. Oil can and should be removed from sewage; safety regulations for both drilling platforms and tankers can be tightened and enforced; the flushing of tankers can be prohibited; and other ships can be forbidden to waste or discard oil products of any kind. Legislation covering some of these points has been enacted in the United States, but, with the exception of tracing one tanker responsible for a spill and prosecuting its captain,[114] enforcement before the end of 1976 was virtually nil.[114a]

Mercury and other heavy metals. Mercury, in organic forms such as methyl mercury, has been found experimentally to reduce photosynthesis in marine and freshwater phytoplankton. Photosynthesis was significantly inhibited at concentrations in water of 0.1 parts per billion (one-fiftieth the amount now tolerated by U.S. public-health standards—5 ppb). When concentrations of mercury reached 50 parts per billion, growth stopped almost completely.[115] Mercury's effects on phytoplankton resemble those of DDT; like the chlorinated hydrocarbons, it also tends to be concentrated in food chains.[116] Thus, its *potential* impact on oceanic food webs may be serious and similar to that of DDT. The key question in both is whether environmental concentrations of these chemicals, singly or in combination, will ever be high enough to have a significant effect. Like DDT, enough inorganic mercury has already accumulated on lake- and streambeds in North America to provide a serious threat (if the mercury is converted to the soluble organic form)[117] to freshwater and estuarine life for decades to come, unless a way is found to remove it. San Francisco Bay, alone, was estimated by the U.S. Geological Survey in 1971 to have some 52 metric tons of mercury on its bottom, with concentrations ranging from 0.25 to 6.4 parts per *million* in bottom sediment.

What effect mercury has high in oceanic food chains is not clear, however. High levels of mercury in oceanic fishes such as tuna and swordfish may well arise through food-chain amplification of natural oceanic mercury levels, independent of pollution contributions,[118] but that does not necessarily mean that ecological effects from anthropogenic increments of mercury will be absent. It is certainly possible that mercury could have deleterious effects on terrestrial food chains. It has been shown, for instance, that mercuric chloride can be responsible for eggshell-thinning in birds;[119] but high concentrations would appear to be necessary to elicit that effect,[120] and it has been demonstrated *only* for mercuric chloride, not methyl mercury, which is the predominant form in the environment.

There is evidence that mercury may influence community structure by affecting plants and insects as well as higher vertebrates. Laboratory experiments have been done using tomatoes, corn, and beans grown in hydroponic solution with aphids feeding on the plants and lacewings feeding on the aphids. Concentrations as low as 0.006 parts per million (ppm) of methyl mercury hydroxide in the hydroponic solution led to reductions in biomass of the tomatoes, while corn and beans were about a half and a tenth as sensitive respectively. The aphids concentrated mercury to a level about 1700 times the concentration in treatment solutions and suffered a

[114]*New York Times,* November 8, 1975. The ship was identified by "fingerprinting" the oil—carefully checking its chemical composition, which is unique for each shipload.

[114a]December 1976 saw a rash of tanker accidents, which cost 9 lives, 50 injuries, and spilled nearly 30 million liters of oil. All five ships involved were chartered in Liberia, and ownership was difficult to determine. One result was renewed discussion of how such accidents could be prevented and safety regulations imposed on foreign-registered ships. Some international mechanism of control is clearly required. (See Ducking liability at sea, *Environment,* vol. 19, no. 1, January/February 1977, pp. 25ff.)

[115]R. C. Harriss, D. B. White, and R. B. McFarlane, Mercury compounds reduce photosynthesis by plankton.

[116]For example, N. Fimreite, W. Holsworth, J. Keith, P. Pearce, and I. Gruchy, Mercury in fish and fish-eating birds near sites of industrial contamination in Canada; K. Henriksson, E. Karppanen, and M. Helminen, High residue of mercury in Finnish white-tailed eagles; A. Haney and R. Lipsey, Accumulation and effects of methyl mercury hydroxide in a terrestrial food chain under laboratory conditions.

[117]B. Olson and R. Cooper, Comparison of aerobic and anaerobic methylation of mercuric chloride by San Francisco Bay sediments.

[118]See Barber, Vijayakumar, and Cross, Mercury concentrations; and the comments on it, *Science,* vol. 178, p. 133 (April 13, 1973). There has also been controversy over whether concentration in fishes increases with age, for example, G. West, Methylmercury as percentage of total mercury in flesh and viscera of salmon and sea trout of various ages, *Science,* vol. 181, pp. 567–568 (August 10, 1973).

[119]G. Stoewsand et al., Eggshell thinning in Japanese quail fed mercuric chloride, *Science,* vol. 173, pp. 1030–1031 (September 10, 1971).

[120]Cooke, Shell-thinning.

significant decrease in fecundity and lengthened development time when the concentration in the treatment solution was 0.02 ppm. The lacewings concentrated mercury to 4200 times that in the hydroponic solution.[121]

The long-term ecological effects in terrestrial food chains and in the seas of other heavy metals (those with density 5 times that of water or more), such as lead, cadmium, chromium, nickel, and thallium, are not known. But, since they are known to be toxic to many forms of life,[122] it would be unreasonable to assume their effects to be negligible. Some, for example, can be potent inhibitors of photosynthesis.[123]

Air pollution and ecosystems. Air pollution assaults humanity indirectly, as well as directly. The ecological systems of Earth clearly are degraded by the quantitative and qualitative pollutants that are injected into the atmosphere, although we are just beginning to understand some of their effects in detail. Many others are unknown or, at best, guessed at.[124]

In some cases damage is dramatically obvious. For instance, in northern Ontario, Canada, sulfur dioxide pollution has virtually destroyed the natural forest ecosystem for 8 kilometers downwind of an iron-sintering plant and has severely damaged it 16 kilometers or more away. Damage can be detected from the air 30 kilometers from the site (Figure 11-12).[125]

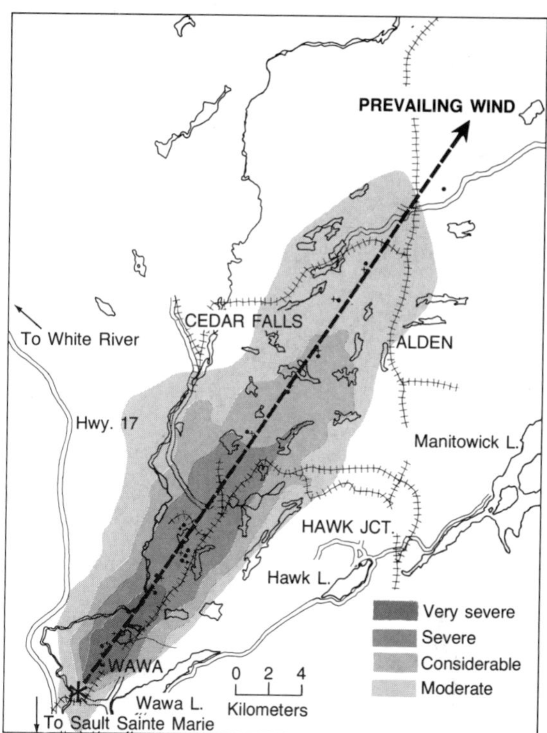

FIGURE 11-12

The extent of damage caused by Wawa, Ontario, iron-sintering plant. Darkest area, very severe; ground vegetation nearly all gone. Next area, severe; all trees gone, most shrubs gone. Next area, considerable; most trees killed. Next area, moderate; trees damaged but little damage to ground flora. (Data from Gordon and Gorham, 1963.)

Other damage, less obvious but more important because of the area involved, is done by acid rains falling over a large portion of Europe and the northeastern United States. Sulfur oxides and nitrogen oxides are, as described earlier, injected into the atmosphere in large quantities by the burning of fossil fuels. Those oxides change in chemical reactions in the atmosphere into strong acids—sulfuric and nitric, respectively. Unless they are neutralized in reactions with alkaline compounds in the atmosphere, those acids eventually return to Earth in rain. Rainfall in unpolluted areas is normally slightly acid (pH usually is between 5.5 and 6.5) because water and carbon dioxide combine in the atmosphere to form carbonic acid, a weak acid. In the 1970s, the pH of rain over much of the northeastern United States was less than 4, values from 3 to 3.5 were not unusual, and one rain with a measured pH of 2.1 was recorded.[126] (Recall that a drop of 1 pH unit represents a tenfold increase in acidity.) Values of rain pH below 4 have been recorded over much of northern Europe, where the location and

[121]Haney and Lipsey, Accumulation.

[122]For lead, see W. Coello, Z. A. Saleem, and M. A. Q. Khan, Ecological effects of lead in auto-exhaust; for a general discussion and access to the literature, see M. Waldichuk, Some biological concerns in heavy metals pollution, in *Pollution and physiology of marine organisms,* F. J. Vernberg and W. B. Vernberg, eds.

[123]F. R. Bazzaz, R. W. Carlson, and G. L. Rolfe, The effect of heavy metals on plants, pt. 1.

[124]See W. H. Smith's review, Air pollution: Effects on the structure and function of the temperate forest ecosystem.

[125]A. G. Gordon and E. Gorham, Ecological aspects of air pollution from an iron-sintering plant at Wawa, Ontario. For a more general discussion and other examples, see W. Knabe, Effects of sulfur dioxide on terrestrial vegetation.

[126]Much of the information in this section is from National Academy of Sciences, *Air quality and stationary source emissions control,* chapter 5 and chapter 7; see also A. Holt-Jensen, Acid rains in Scandinavia; G. E. Likens and F. H. Bormann, Acid rain: A serious regional environmental problem; N. Malmer, Acid precipitation: Chemical changes in the soil.

FIGURE 11-13

The map charts the acidity of rainfall in the United States in the two-week period from March 15 to March 31, 1973. Measurements were made by schoolchildren with a technique accurate to ± 0.2 pH and tabulated by the National Oceanic and Atmospheric Administration. The results show significant acidification of all rain falling east of the Mississippi River. (From Strong, 1974.)

spread of the regions affected are well correlated with major sources of sulfur emissions, the growth of those sources, and established patterns of atmospheric dispersion. The pH of rain falling on the United States in two weeks in March 1973, as measured in an experiment involving schoolchildren across the country using a technique with an accuracy of pH ± 0.2, appears in Figure 11-13.[127] The spread of acid rain in Europe from 1956 to 1966 is represented in Figure 11-14.

The overall effects of acid rains on ecosystems are not well understood, but they have the potential for serious damage. The rains may modify rates at which nutrients are leached from soils and foliage; they can reduce or exterminate fish populations by acidifying streams; they can affect soil microorganisms, especially those responsible for nitrogen fixation; they can influence the behavior of bacterial and fungal pathogens; they can enhance uptake of the toxic heavy metal cadmium from the soil; and they may interact synergistically with herbicides and other synthetic compounds.

Acid rains were one of the first environmental phenomena to attract attention because of their international implications. Sweden made them the topic of a case study for a United Nations Conference on the Human Environment in Stockholm in 1972. Sweden's forests have suffered a reduction in growth rates starting in the 1950s, thought to be due to acid rains, and salmon and trout have disappeared from Swedish streams and lakes where the pH has fallen much below 5.[128] The sulfur that rains down on Sweden apparently originates in northwest Europe, especially in the United Kingdom. (Besides the potentially serious ecosystemic effects, Sweden was concerned about the corrosion of structural materials by the

[127]The project is described in C. L. Strong, The amateur scientist.

[128]C. O. Tamm, Acid precipitation: Biological effects in soil and on forest vegetation; C. L. Schofield, Acid precipitation: Effects on fish; B. Almer et al., Effects of acidification on Swedish lakes.

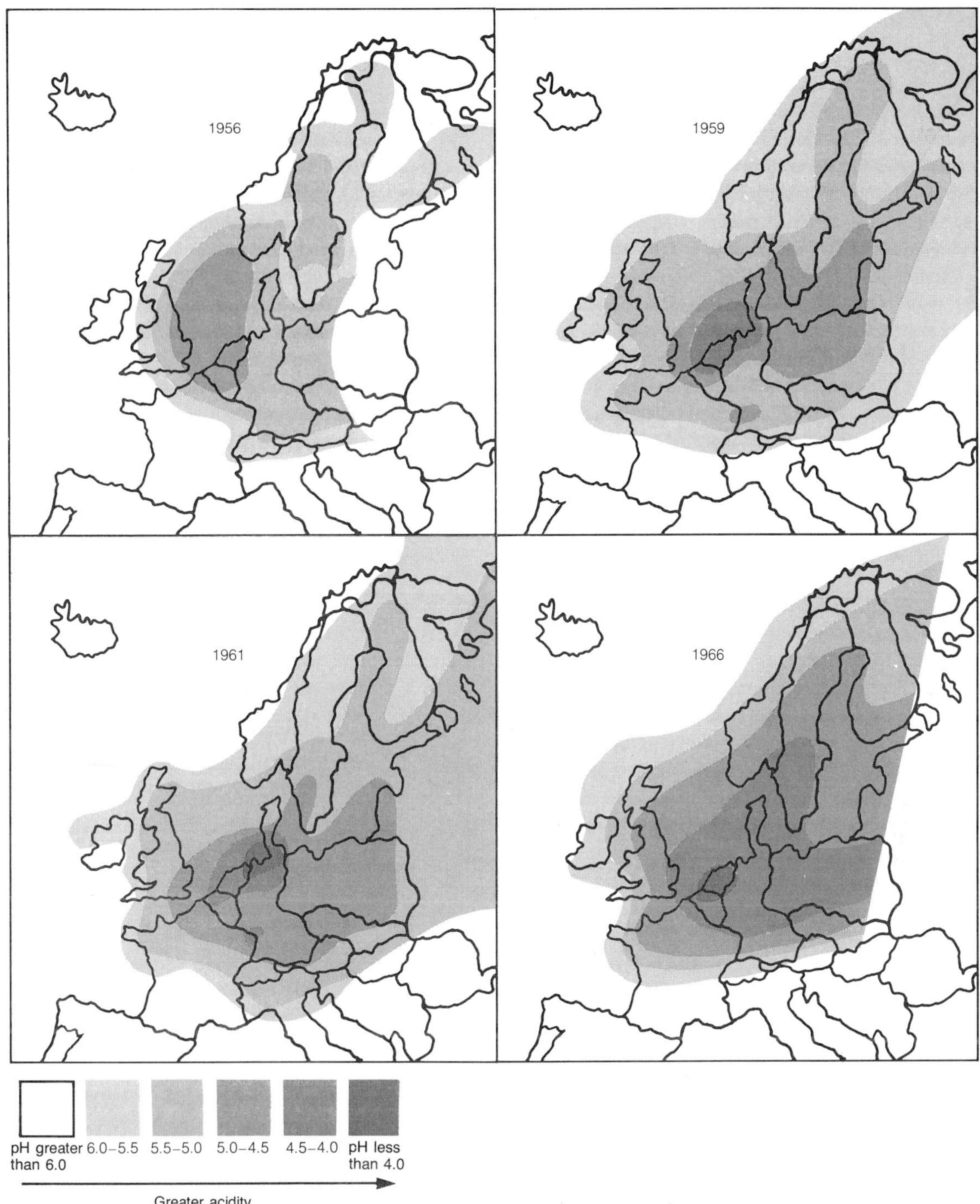

FIGURE 11-14

The steady spread of acid rain in northern Europe from 1956 to 1966 is shown in this sequence of maps. The region of greatest acidity, around Belgium and the Netherlands, reflects both heavy emissions of oxides of sulfur and nitrogen and prevalent meteorological conditions in the region. (From S. Oden, Nederbordens forsurning-ett generellt hot mot ekosystemen. In I. Mysterud, ed., *Forurensning og biologisk milijovern,* Univeritetsforlaget, Oslo, 1971, pp. 63–98.)

rains—especially damage to limestone buildings. In Sweden alone the economic value of the damage amounted to $500,000 annually.)

Air pollution can have direct deleterious effects on ecosystems, in addition to causing acid rains. Ozone, which plays such a crucial and positive ecological role in the stratosphere, is extremely damaging to plants. It enters leaves through the pores (stomata) used for normal gas exchange and is thought to alter the permeability of the membranes of cells there. This causes nutrient and electrolyte imbalances and the cells die. Chronic exposure to ozone may weaken plants and make them more susceptible to disease, or it may age them prematurely (cutting yields in crops like citrus)—all without outward signs of injury. Sensitivity in plants is such that a year or two of exposure to relatively low concentrations [15 parts per hundred million (pphm) can significantly alter the composition of a community—with results that could be deleterious].[129]

Ozone is an important component of photochemical smog (Chapter 10), which contains other oxidants damaging to plants—peroxyacetyl nitrate (PAN) and nitrogen dioxide. PAN is very phytotoxic, more so than ozone, but ozone normally occurs in much greater concentrations.[130]

Photochemical smog originating in Los Angeles (with ozone concentrations of as much as 70 pphm) has had a dramatic impact on the ecosystems of southern California. Some 125 kilometers east of the city two-thirds of the 65,000-hectare San Bernardino National Forest has been affected, and within the affected area 50 percent of the trees have been moderately or severely damaged.[131] In the northeastern United States there is also extensive forest damage from photochemical smog, and concern over ozone damage is growing in the United Kingdom.[132] In those areas the ozone concentration is only one-third or less that of the Los Angeles basin, but ozone is more damaging to the plants in those more humid areas.

[129]M. Harward and M. Treshow, Impact of ozone on the growth and reproduction of understory plants in the aspen zone of western U.S.A.

[130]J. L. Marx, Air pollution: Effects on plants, is the source for much of the information in this and the following paragraph.

[131]Edwards Hay, Smog, the quiet killer.

[132]P. D. Moore, Ozone over Britain.

The effects of air pollutants on plants can be both complex and subtle. Sulfur dioxide damages plants directly (and differentially) in addition to contributing to acid rain.[133] In the United Kingdom in the summer, however, there is a problem with sulfur-deficiency on nitrate-rich fertilized farmland. The sulfur-dioxide pollution helps to overcome that deficiency, thus stimulating plant growth. There is evidence, however, that this benefit is more than balanced by deleterious effects of the sulfur dioxide on winter growth.[134] Much investigation needs to be done to elucidate such interactions and to determine what effects pollutants have on mutation rates and on the production and germination of seeds. It is also important to identify the ultimate impact of air pollution not just on the plants but on all components of an ecosystem. For instance, fluoride is directly injurious to plants and is also concentrated by them.[135] Under conditions of severe pollution, forage can be so contaminated as to produce fatal fluorosis in cattle,[136] but the effect of lower levels of fluoride pollution on herbivores is unknown. It seems likely that such fluoride pollution would have local ecosystemic effects at most.[137]

Nitrogen, phosphorus, and eutrophication. Nitrogen and phosphorus are nutrients required in large quantities for the growth of terrestrial and aquatic plants. (The natural cycles of both elements and the magnitudes of some of the perturbations imposed by civilization on those cycles are described in Chapter 3.) The heavy use of nitrogen and phosphorus fertilizers has arisen because the availability of the two elements to plants is often the factor that determines how much plant material can be grown. That is, if sunlight, water, and carbon dioxide are available in abundance, adding nitrogen or phosphorus (whichever is limiting in the given situation), or both, can

[133]For example, J. A. O'Conner, D. G. Parberg, and W. Strauss, The effects of phytotoxic gases on native Australian species, pt. 1, Acute effects of sulphur dioxide, *Environmental Pollution*, vol. 7, pp. 7–23, 1974.

[134]Ozone and sulphur dioxide are damaging UK plants, *New Scientist*, January 23, 1975.

[135]S. B. McLaughlin, Jr., and R. L. Barnes, Effects of fluoride on photosynthesis and respiration of some south-east American forest trees; and J. B. Davis and R. L. Barnes, Effects of soil-applied fluoride and lead on growth of loblolly pine and red maple.

[136]Marx, Air pollution.

[137]For example, D. A. Wright and A. W. Davison, The accumulation of fluoride by marine and intertidal animals.

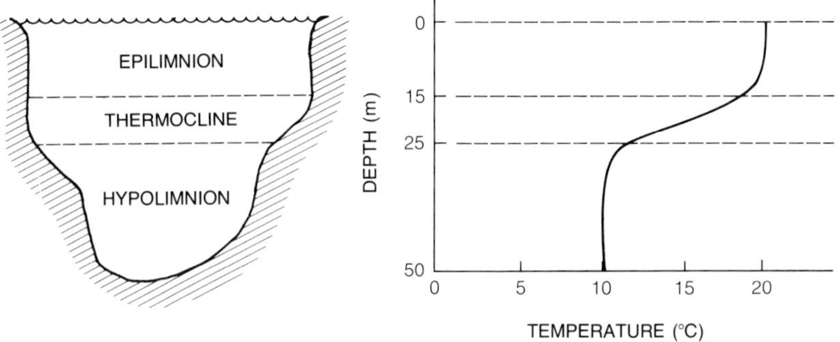

FIGURE 11-15

Thermal stratification in a temperate-zone lake in summer.

increase the yield. (Of course, there are circumstances in which other nutrients—for example, calcium or iron—are limiting.) This situation becomes a liability when extra phosphorus and nitrogen are made available inadvertently to ecosystems in which extra plant growth is undesirable.

The most important example of that phenomenon is in aquatic ecosystems—rivers, lakes, and coastal waters. There, overfertilization can produce overgrowth of aquatic weeds that interfere with recreational uses of the affected bodies of water. More seriously, overfertilization can lead to rapid growth of various algae, which can have several undesirable consequences: reduced transparency of the water, cutting off bottom plants from sunlight; formation of surface scums that are unsightly, smell bad, and discourage recreation; the generation of unappealing taste and odor in drinking water; the creation of a concentration of dissolved organic material conducive to the support of various disease organisms that would not prosper in less rich waters; the alteration of the *relative* abundance of the various algal species present, with adverse effects on food chains established under the previous conditions; and the depletion of dissolved oxygen, with resulting loss of fish life when the algal overgrowths or blooms die off and decompose.[138]

How can oxygen-depletion arise from the overgrowth of plants, inasmuch as they must have produced as much oxygen in their lifetimes as is needed for their decomposition (see Chapter 3)? The answer is twofold. First, oxygen is continuously exchanged between water bodies and the atmosphere, and under many circumstances that exchange depletes dissolved oxygen to less than what it would otherwise be (not all the oxygen produced in the water stays in the water, and what leaves may not be completely replaced from the atmosphere). Second, dead algae often sink and, as they decompose, deplete the oxygen content of deeper layers of water where the oxygen content already tends to be lower than that of the surface layer. (There is more oxygen near the surface because that is where most of the photosynthesis goes on and where oxygen enters from the atmosphere.)

The oxygen depletion is aggravated in many temperate-zone lakes by a phenomenon called *thermal stratification.* As discussed in Chapter 4, there is a warm layer of water at the surface in summer called the epilimnion, which is well mixed by the action of wind and waves and in which the temperature is almost uniform. Below the epilimnion is a layer called the thermocline, in which the temperature decreases 1° C or more for every meter of depth. The lowest layer contains the coldest water, is almost uniform in temperature, and is called the hypolimnion. (See Figure 11-15.) There is almost no vertical mixing in the thermocline and hypolimnion. The stratification is maintained because the density of water varies with temperature and the maximum density occurs at 4° C. Thus, as long as the coldest water in the lake is not less than 4° C, the coldest water will be on the bottom, slightly less cold (and hence less dense) water just above it, and so on.

A temperate-zone lake that is stratified this way gets

[138]For discussion of these effects, see American Chemical Society, *Cleaning our environment: The chemical basis for action;* W. T. Edmondson, Fresh water pollution, in *Environment,* W. Murdoch, ed., Sinauer, Sunderland, Mass., 1975, pp. 251–271.

thoroughly mixed vertically twice a year. In the autumn, surface temperatures start to drop, eventually falling below the temperature of the deeper layers. Having thus become denser than the underlying layers, the surface water sinks. In freezing climates, the turnover process continues until the thoroughly mixed lake has been uniformly cooled to 4° C; as the surface water cools further, it no longer sinks because it then becomes *less* dense than the 4° C water below. The eventual result is a winter stratification with ice on top and water slightly above freezing below. Then, in the spring, the warming of the surface layer to the density maximum at 4° C causes that water to sink into the slightly cooler and less dense water below, and the lake turns over again.

Summer thermal stratification keeps oxygen-rich water at the surface from mixing into deeper layers; sustaining animal life in the deep water therefore depends on whether the supply of oxygen provided by turnover in the spring lasts until the next turnover in the autumn. If a lake is clear enough, some light penetrates to the hypolimnion so that the oxygen provided by the turnovers may be supplemented by photosynthesis there. Such oligotrophic lakes are clear, deep, and relatively low in plant life. Maintaining this condition depends on a shortage of nutrients. In eutrophic lakes, which have an abundance of nutrients, algal growth cuts off sunlight near the surface, and the decomposition of the dead organic matter raining down from above depletes oxygen in the hypolimnion, which can be replaced neither by photosynthesis (because there is no light) nor by mixing (because of stratification). As noted in Chapter 4, eutrophic lakes therefore cannot support populations of those species of fishes that require cold water, because in summer the deep, cold water contains no oxygen.

Natural processes cause all lakes to undergo the transition from oligotrophic to eutrophic over a long period of time. Specifically, the transition is brought about by the flow of nutrients in streams that drain the surrounding area, with the effect not only of enriching the organic content of the lake water but also of filling the lake gradually with dead organic matter that settles on the bottom. This natural transition is called eutrophication. The same term has been given to the acceleration of the process that takes place when the activities of civilization lead to substantial increases in the flow of nutrients into a lake. In everyday usage the term has become synonymous with *overfertilization* of any body of water—lake, river, estuary, bay, or near-shore ocean waters. The specialist's term for overfertilization of a body of water due to human activity is *cultural eutrophication.*

Several anthropogenic pathways to water exist for both nitrogen and phosphorus (see also Chapter 3). Both substances are applied to fields in inorganic form in fertilizer,[139] and both are present in sewage and in the wastes from livestock feedlots. Nitrates originating in vehicle exhausts fall in the rain, and phosphates added to detergents to improve their "cleaning power" become ingredients of municipal waste water. Neither nitrates nor phosphates are removed effectively from sewage by primary or secondary treatment plants.[140]

Phosphorus is the limiting nutrient in the growth of aquatic plants in far more circumstances than nitrogen is. One reason for this is that some aquatic plants (including blue-green algae) can convert atmospheric nitrogen that has become dissolved in the water into usable chemical form. The growth of those plants is unlikely to be limited by lack of nitrogen. The other major reason is that nitrogen compounds are in general much more soluble than phosphorus compounds, so the former migrate much more readily through soil and into waterways. The higher mobility of nitrogen compounds leads to much greater concentrations of nitrogen than of phosphorus in most natural bodies of water—enough so that phosphorus is the limiting nutrient for plant growth.

Because phosphorus compounds are so tightly bound to the soil, even very heavy fertilization does not lead to the leaching of much phosphorus into groundwater and surface water. Fertilizer phosphorus that reaches waterways does so almost entirely by being carried along in eroded soil particles. Even in the water, most of that phosphorus remains in suspension (not in solution) so it is not readily accessible for use by aquatic plants. By far the largest source of soluble phosphorus in waterways is municipal sewage, which contains phosphorus both from excrement and from detergents.[141]

[139]Frank G. Viets, Jr. Water quality in relation to farm use of fertilizers.

[140]American Chemical Society, *Cleaning our environment.*

[141]SCEP, *Man's impact on the global environment,* p. 146.

Many examples of the cultural eutrophication of lakes, due mainly to phosphorus additions in sewage, have been documented.[142] Some of them, such as Lake Washington in Seattle, some of the lakes around Madison, Wisconsin, and Lake Onondaga in New York, have made dramatic recoveries when citizen action has stopped the sewage discharges or restricted the use of phosphate detergents.[143]

The most famous example of advanced cultural eutrophication, Lake Erie, has been less fortunate. The streams that feed Lake Erie drain a large area that is heavily populated, highly industrialized, and intensively cultivated. Controlling the sources of phosphorus over such an area would be an enormous undertaking. The lake itself is relatively shallow (66 meters maximum depth, compared to between 230 and 406 meters in the other Great Lakes), and a thick layer of muck on the bottom contains vast quantities of nutrients that under appropriate conditions might redissolve into the lake. Large algal blooms are so common in Lake Erie, that only a few days after the onset of thermal stratification in the summer the oxygen in the hypolimnion is essentially gone.[144] The relative abundance of fishes in the lake has undergone a drastic transition over the past fifty years, characterized by replacement of species highly valued by people as food (lake trout, walleye, blue pike) with species considered less desirable (alewife, carp, sheepshead). Some of the changes in fish populations have been brought about not by cultural eutrophication alone, of course, but by the combined effects of eutrophication, the introduction by people of the sea lamprey and the alewife, and the heavy pollution of the lake with pesticides, industrial chemicals, and heavy metals.[145] Lake Erie is not dead, but it clearly is suffering from premature old age combined with a case of chronic poisoning. Unless it somehow proves possible to prevent permanently the resuspension of the inventory of toxins and nutrients in Lake Erie's bottom sediments, its condition—unlike those of smaller lakes—will not be reversible.

Although the best known and probably most serious examples of cultural eutrophication are lakes, rivers and estuaries are not immune to the problem. In a major ten-year survey of the twenty-two most important rivers and harbors in the United States (ranked by length and volume for rivers and by size of adjacent populations for harbors), 84 percent of the sections sampled exceeded phosphorus and phosphate concentrations associated with potential eutrophication, and 54 percent showed an increase in those concentrations between the period from 1963 to 1967 and the period from 1968 to 1972.[146] Nitrate concentrations exceeded those associated with potential eutrophication in 25 percent of the sections sampled and had increased between the two periods in 74 percent of the sections. Contrary to a fairly widespread impression, the circulation patterns in typical estuaries, and even those along open ocean coastlines, are not conducive to rapid mixing of pollutants into the deeper water offshore; therefore, cultural eutrophication of those ecologically crucial regions is not a problem that can be ignored safely.[147]

Even though phosphorus rather than nitrogen is most often the governing nutrient in cultural eutrophication, overuse of inorganic nitrogen fertilizers may prove to be the greater environmental hazard for other reasons. One reason is that runoff of nitrates into surface- and groundwater supplies can lead to concentrations great enough to pose a direct toxic danger to the health of animals and human beings, both as methemoglobinemia and as a potential carcinogen (see Chapter 10). Secondly, the accelerated release of nitrous oxide (N_2O) into the atmosphere may in time adversely affect the ozone layer (as discussed below) with implications for human health and future food production. A further reason for concern about the prevalent pattern of using nitrogen fertilizer is the effect of those practices on soil humus, which is essential to the natural nitrogen cycle (see Chapter 6).

[142]Edmondson, Fresh water pollution; W. T. Edmondson, Lake Washington, in *Environmental quality and water development;* C. R. Goldman; J. McEvoy, III; P. J. Richerson, eds., W. H. Freeman and Company, 1973.

[143]Ibid; C. B. Murphy, Jr., Effect of restricted use of phosphate-based detergents on Onondaga Lake.

[144]Federal Water Pollution Control Administration, *Cost of clean water,* vol. 3, Government Printing Office, Washington, D.C. 1968. Other good accounts of the plight of Lake Erie are A. Beeton, Man's effects on the Great Lakes, in *Environmental quality,* Goldman, McEvoy, and Richerson, eds.; C. F. Powers and A. Robertson, The aging Great Lakes, *Scientific American,* November 1966; N. M. Burns et al., Processes within Lake Erie.

[145]J. H. Leach and S. J. Nepszy, The fish community in Lake Erie.

[146]Council on Environmental Quality, *Environmental quality, 1974,* pp. 282–289.

[147]SCEP, *Man's impact,* pp. 146–148.

Humus, the organic matter in soil, is a poorly understood complex of compounds of high molecular weight. In natural soils inorganic nitrogen normally constitutes less than 2 percent of the nitrogen present. Most of the nitrogen is tied up in the large organic molecules of humus, which are derived from such varied sources as the fibrous remains of woody plant tissues, insect skeletons, and animal manure. The presence of humus makes the soil a favorable medium for the complicated chemical reactions and mineral transport needed for the growth of higher plants. Bacteria in the soil decompose humus to form nitrates and various other nutrient substances required by plant roots.

Roots require oxygen in order to take up nitrates and other nutrients, but oxygen is not available if the soil is tightly compacted, nor is water absorbed well. Thus one important function of humus is to maintain the porosity of soil, which permits oxygen to penetrate to the roots of plants and promotes the retention of water. Greater capacity to absorb and hold water reduces runoff and soil erosion after heavy rain and prolongs the retention of soil moisture during times of drought. On several counts, then, humus is essential for the healthy growth of plants, and particularly (as experienced farmers know) for good crops.

In natural soil systems the nitrogen cycle is tight; not much nitrogen escapes to the atmosphere or is removed from the soil by leaching or surface runoff. It has been shown experimentally (as well as by centuries of farming experience) that by maintaining the supply of humus the fertility of soil can be perpetuated. This is not possible when fertilizers containing inorganic nitrogen are employed, unless organic carbon (in such forms as crop residues, sawdust, or straw) is supplied to the microorganisms in the soil. The undesirable decline of humus, which often occurs under heavy inorganic fertilization, is due to the failure of farmers to return crop residues (and thus carbon) to the fields. The decline is not caused by any deficiency in the fertilizers themselves. Indeed, if carbon is supplied in the proper proportion to inorganic nitrogen, the supply of humus can be increased and the quality of the soil improved.

If attempts are made to maintain soil fertility by continued applications of inorganic nitrogen fertilizers alone, the capacity of soil to retain nitrogen is reduced as its humus content drops. In humus, nitrogen is combined into nonsoluble forms that are not leached from the soil by rainwater. Depletion of humus "loosens" the soil cycles and permits large amounts of nitrate to be flushed readily out of the soil. Only about 50 to 60 percent of the applied nitrogen is incorporated into the crops.[148] This loss plus depletion of the original humus leads to the need for more and more fertilizer, in a vicious circle.

The serious consequences of such human interventions in the nitrogen and phosphorus cycles call for strong remedial measures. The only successful steps against phosphorus pollution that had been taken in the United States as of 1975 were restrictions on the phosphorus content of detergents, a few local bans on the sale of phosphorus-containing detergents, and diversion of sewage and industrial wastes from a number of acutely suffering lakes.[149] With specific regard to nitrogen, there are only restrictions on the nitrate levels in foods. Much more systematic measures are required, the most important of which would be closing the open nitrogen and phosphorus cycles of agriculture by returning the organic "wastes"—now contributing to the pollution problem—to the soil.

Human excrement, for instance, is considerably richer in both nitrogen and phosphorus than cattle manure. In the People's Republic of China, human waste is carefully collected and used largely untreated, along with manure and agricultural wastes. These organic fertilizers still comprised about half of China's total fertilizer applications in the early 1970s.[150]

The direct use of human (or livestock) waste as fertilizer presents opportunities for the transmission of many diseases and parasites. Some methods of treatment, such as aerobic or anaerobic digestion by bacteria, however, appear to prevent this, at least for most fertilizing purposes. Treated sewage water and sludge (the concentrated residue that settles out of sewage water) is used successfully as fertilizer in many parts of the world, including the United Kingdom, Australia, Fed-

[148]G. Stanford, C. England, and A. Taylor, *Fertilizer use and water quality.*

[149]An account of the national brouhaha over detergents in the early 1970s (from a predominantly probusiness viewpoint) can be found in William S. Rukeyser, Fact and foam in the row over phosphates.

[150]Jon Sigurdson, Resources and environment in China, *Ambio,* vol. 4, no. 3, pp. 112–119, 1975.

eral Republic of Germany, and a few places in the United States.[151] At least one operating plant in the United Kingdom, run by the local water authority, sells recovered water to industry and treated liquid and dried-sludge fertilizer to local farmers. It uses the sludge gas produced by the digestion process to generate electricity that runs the plant, a nearby sewage pumping station, and an incinerator, and cooks meals for a group of senior citizens. "Waste" heat from the generators is used for the digesters.[152] Although the costs of collecting, treating, and distributing sewage have been a major obstacle to using it as fertilizer, this system apparently costs little more than conventional sewage-disposal methods.

In the United States, the manure of cattle produced on feedlots alone far exceeds in volume that produced by the human population, even though phosphorus and nitrogen concentrations are lower.[153] The nutrients in that material, as well as manure from similarly managed chickens and pigs, also could and should be returned to the soil. Some 80 to 90 percent of these animals are in feedlots for part or all their lives. In the past, huge volumes of feedlot sewage were discharged into rivers, causing severe pollution. The EPA has made reduction of pollution from that source to zero by the mid-1980s a goal, which should provide incentive for alternative uses. If all feedlot sewage in the United States were used for fertilizer, it would provide more than enough for all U.S. acreage planted in corn.[154] If augmented with municipal sewage, garbage, and other wastes, it would, of course, go even farther.

Other potential sources of organic fertilizing nutrients include agricultural wastes (some of which can also be used as livestock fodder), treated garbage, and food-processing wastes. Most of these presently are wasted: they are discharged in waterways, put in landfill, or burned in incinerators. The values of these materials as fertilizer must, of course, be balanced against their values for other uses, such as supplementary livestock feed and energy sources, taking into consideration the energy and other costs of the alternatives. But it is clear that merely throwing them away and then cleaning up the mess (both costly and energy-consuming exercises) is the *least* intelligent solution.

The most promising method of recovering and recycling the nutrients from manure, human sewage, crop residues, and other organic wastes—while deriving energy as well—is with biogasification plants like the one described above (also discussed in Chapter 8). Such facilities, which can range in size from backyard digesters to large factories, have the dual advantage of producing needed fuel from the hydrocarbon content of the wastes and leaving the nitrogen, phosphorus, and other nutrients behind in a residue much more compact than the original wastes. Thus, transportation costs and handling problems associated with using those residues as fertilizer should be less than those of using the uncompacted raw material. The prospects that this approach can compete economically with using inorganic fertilizers are improved by the rising cost of the latter, particularly the very energy-intensive inorganic nitrogen fertilizer whose cost is closely tied to the cost of energy. Even if fertilizer from organic wastes should turn out to be more expensive at first than inorganic fertilizers, however, its use should be strongly encouraged by regulations and subsidies, in recognition of its ecological advantages.

The U. S. National Aeronautics and Space Administration (NASA) has recently been conducting experiments using water hyacinths to purify waste water. These aquatic plants, generally considered a pest in warm regions around the world, have proven remarkably efficient at absorbing nutrients and other pollutants from sewage water. The dried plants then can be used to make biogas and/or for fertilizer or livestock feed.[154a]

Naturally, care must be taken to control the new problems that innovative approaches to old problems often bring. (When phosphorus was discredited on ecological grounds as an ingredient in detergents, for example, one of the first substitutes that was tried was NTA—nitrilotriacetic acid. Then evidence appeared that

[151]John Coldrick, Sewage as a resource, *New Scientist,* October 30, 1975; Lawrence D. Hills, Putting waste water to work, *The Ecologist,* vol. 5, no. 9, pp. 344–346, 1975; Sam Love, An idea in need of rethinking: The flush toilet, *Smithsonian,* May 1975, pp. 61–65.

[152]J. Coldrick, Sewage.

[153]E. Groth III, Increasing the harvest.

[154]D. Pimentel, L. Hurd, A. Bellotti, M. Forster, I. Oka, O. Sholes, and R. Whitman, Food production and the energy crisis, *Science,* vol. 182, pp. 443–449 (November 2, 1973).

[154a]Bill Wolverton, Don't waste water-weeds, *New Scientist,* August 12, 1976, pp.318–320.

that compound was a potent mutagen, and its use was discontinued.[155]) The precise effects on soil organisms of fertilizing with various kinds of manure are not yet known, although they are being investigated. Results of comparing yields under different fertilizing regimes—all organic, all inorganic, or a combination—in small, controlled studies indicate that the mixed approach may be best for many crops.[156]

Perhaps the most serious potential problem associated with continuously recycling nutrients by means of biogasification and application of the residues as fertilizer is accumulation of toxic heavy metals, whose concentration could increase at each cycle. While trace amounts of many of these—copper, cadmium, cobalt, for instance—are essential to life, high concentrations accumulated in soil and concentrated by crops can be deadly. Some experimental schemes for processing urban sludge are attempting to remove these and other toxic substances to be recycled in industry. Better yet, the industries themselves should be encouraged to remove such toxins before discharging them into waste water. In LDCs, most people still live in rural areas, which would minimize both the problem of transporting their wastes to farms and the likelihood of significant pollution with heavy metals or other toxic materials.

Thermal pollution. The term *thermal pollution* is most commonly used to describe the discharge of waste heat from thermal generation of electric power or from industrial processes into natural bodies of water. The ultimate fate of this energy—and of all other energy mobilized by human activity—is to find its way into the atmosphere and from there into space. The atmospheric aspects of this more general "heat problem" are considered later; here we consider only the effects of heat deposited directly into aquatic ecosystems.

Aquatic thermal pollution has been the focus of much research and considerable controversy. Some of the controversy has arisen because the effects are so different at different sites. Even very large power plants can discharge their heat to the ocean with minimal effect where deep water lies close to shore and where the local surface and underwater topography permit good mixing of heated effluent with colder water. Undoubtedly, there are even circumstances where the heated effluent can be beneficial—for example, in accelerating the growth of shellfish.[157] On the other hand, large discharges of waste heat in bays or estuaries where mixing is poor can produce serious problems, as is also often the case in rivers and lakes. Documentation of the adverse effects has led to the widespread use by power plants of cooling towers to transfer the waste heat directly to the atmosphere (see Chapter 8).

Among the most important adverse effects of a temperature increase that affects a substantial part of a natural body of water are:[158]

1. The dissolved oxygen content of the water falls, reducing the capacity of organisms in the water to detoxify chemical wastes.

2. The diminished oxygen content places a stress on aquatic organisms, which is compounded because the elevated temperature raises their metabolic rate and hence their need for oxygen. (As a rough average, metabolic rate doubles for every 10° C rise in temperature.)[159]

3. A large temperature increase can kill some organisms outright, while producing biochemical changes that prevent others from reproducing or increase their susceptibility to toxic substances.[160] Temperature changes due to repair, refueling, or normal cycling of a power plant can greatly reduce the possibility of a biota's adapting to a new temperature regime.

4. Species of fishes and plants most tolerant to heat often are the least desirable from the human point of view, such as rough fishes and the blue-green algae most responsible for taste and odor problems in municipal water supplies. The role of temperature in determining what species are present is suggested by the data in Figure 11-16.

---

[155]Samuel S. Epstein, Toxicological and environmental implications of the use of nitrilotriacetic acid as a detergent builder, pts. 1 and 2. For a less technical report, see Epstein's NTA.

[156]Hills, Putting waste water to work.

[157]Joseph Priest, *Problems of our physical environment,* p. 106.

[158]A good survey is C. A. Carlson, Jr., Impact of waste heat on aquatic ecology. See also John R. Clark, Thermal pollution and aquatic life.

[159]G. Masters, *Introduction to environmental science and technology,* Wiley, New York, 1974.

[160]Effects at high temperatures are illustrated in J. W. Gibbons and R. R. Sharitz, eds., Thermal alteration of aquatic ecosystems.

Other effects that may be significant in some circumstances are alteration of the thermal stratification and time of turnover of thermally stratified water in lakes (which can affect productivity and species composition), and increased rates of evaporation from heated bodies of water. The Environmental Protection Agency recommends, in order to minimize the magnitude of adverse effects, that waste-heat discharges from such facilities be managed in such a way that the maximum temperature rise after mixing not exceed 5° F in streams, 3° F in lakes, 4° F in coastal marine environments in winter, and 1.5° F in coastal marine environments in summer.[161]

Radiation and the structure of ecosystems. Ecosystemic effects of radiation have been investigated through the use of chronic irradiation as a perturbing influence in experiments on natural ecosystems. The experiments employed powerful sources of radiation (9500 Ci cesium-137, 3000–4000 Ci cobalt-60) that exposed adjacent parts of an ecosystem to thousands of roentgens per day and areas progressively farther from the source to doses that declined roughly as the square of the distance.[162] The general results of such experiments in oak-pine forest, the lichen flora of that forest, and the herbaceous flora of an old field produced the following generalities. The structure of the community changed as upright plant forms were differentially damaged and prostrate forms were placed at a relative advantage. Dominant forms replaced one another along the gradient of radiation dosage as they do along natural environmental gradients, diversity declined with increasing dosage, and usually (but not always) net production decreased with increased dosage.[163] These changes are quite similar to those produced by other gradients of environmental stress, such as increasing altitude on mountains, approach to the spray zone on seashores, decreasing rainfall as the edge of the desert nears, or nearness to an iron-sintering plant (as described in the

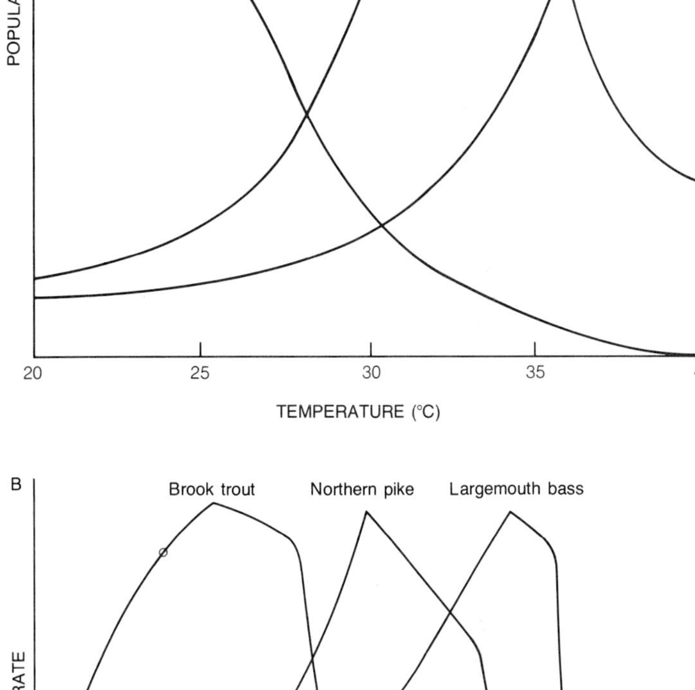

FIGURE 11-16

Change in species composition with temperature. A. The effect of temperature on phytoplankton (After J. Cairns, Jr., 1956, cited in Masters, below). B. The effect of temperature on three species of fish. Spawning temperatures are circled. (After G. Masters, *Introduction to environmental science and technology,* Wiley, New York, 1974.)

[161]Environmental Protection Agency, *Water quality criteria required by the federal Water Pollution Control Act amendments of 1972.* Government Printing Office, Washington, D.C., 1973.

[162]G. M. Woodwell, Radiation and the patterns of nature. For a more recent review, see F. W. Whicher and L. Fowley, Jr., Effects of ionizing radiation on terrestrial plant communities, *Advances in Radiation Biology,* vol. 4, pp. 317–366, 1974.

[163]G. M. Woodwell and R. H. Whittaker, Effects of chronic gamma irradiation on plant communities.

preceding text). The reasons for these patterns are not completely understood, but they seem to be related to changes in the production/respiration ratio in various segments of the community. For instance, trees are limited in size because, as they grow, the proportion of bark, which contributes heavily to respiration, increases compared to that of photosynthetic leaves. Stresses tend to decrease photosynthesis rather than respiration; therefore they affect trees more than smaller plants, which do proportionately less respiring.[164]

Structural changes in vegetation also change nutrient patterns and inevitably have a dramatic impact on the fauna. Like other pollutants, radioisotopes are concentrated by food chains—for instance, cesium-137 has been found to double in concentration with each step in Alaskan lichen → caribou → wolf (or Eskimo) food chains, and plutonium concentrations in algae of 1000 to 6000 times that of their environment have been measured.[165]

In general, ecologists tend to feel that genetic disturbances from radiation exposure in nonhuman populations of both plants and animals are not serious; they assume that selection will compensate for them. Effects of radiation on animals are diverse, but some generalizations are possible. For animal populations, the major stress seems to be effects on reproductive processes rather than shortened lifespans. Long-lived species are more sensitive to radiation than short-lived ones; therefore, since predators are generally longer-lived than herbivores, they would be differentially removed from irradiated ecosystems.[166] In this way, radiation effects may be very similar to those of pesticides.

It would appear that potential levels of radiation releases from nuclear-power enterprises, which are of great concern because of their direct effects on humanity, would probably have little serious effect on other components of ecosystems. On the other hand, in the aftermath of thermonuclear war, radiation could be one of the major stresses on Earth's ecological systems.

[164]G. M. Woodwell, Effects of pollution on the structure and physiology of ecosystems.

[165]W. C. Hanson, Cesium-137 in Alaskan lichens, caribou and Eskimos; W. R. Schell and R. L. Watters, Plutonium in aqueous systems.

[166]F. B. Turner, Effects of continuous irradiation on animal populations, *Advances in Radiation Biology*, vol. 5, pp. 83–144, 1975.

ATMOSPHERE AND CLIMATE

The complicated geophysical machinery that governs weather and climate is described in Chapter 2. The more carefully this machinery has been studied, the more intricate and, in many instances, delicately balanced it has seemed to be. The complexity and possible fragility of atmospheric and related climatic phenomena mean that the possible avenues of significant human intervention are many. They include changing the abundance of atmospheric constituents that govern the atmosphere's transparency to solar and terrestrial radiation (for example, by adding carbon dioxide, particles, water droplets and water vapor, and by destroying ozone), altering the characteristics of the interface between the atmosphere and land or sea (for example, by agriculture, urbanization, deforestation, desertification, and oil spills), and perturbing natural energy flows with the release of heat from industrial activities.

It cannot yet be said that atmospheric processes, weather, and climate are thoroughly understood, even exclusive of the growing perturbations caused by the activities of civilization. Not surprisingly, then, the actual magnitude and present and future consequences of such human perturbations cannot be accurately and unambiguously stated even as individual effects, much less in combination. It is not even known whether all the important potential effects have been identified—not to mention quantified. The sudden emergence in 1974 and 1975 of the probable role of spray-can propellants as a threat to the ozone layer is indicative of the sorts of further surprises that may yet be in store.

Clearly, the fact that knowledge of the possibilities is incomplete is anything but grounds for complacency. Enough is already known to make plain that civilization has become a force large enough *in theory* to disrupt atmospheric processes and climate not only on regional but on hemispheric and even global scales. That technological civilization has reached a level of activity that implies significant potential influence over global processes so crucial to well-being, without commensurate understanding or control, should appall any thoughtful person. In the following text we survey some of the more important mechanisms for human intervention in atmosphere and climate, beginning with the threats to the ozone layer that became really credible only in the mid-1970s.[167]

Threats to the Ozone Layer

In the atmosphere at sea level, only about 1 molecule of 100 million is ozone (chemical formula O_3). Most of the small atmospheric pool of this compound is concentrated, however, in the part of the stratosphere lying between 15 and 40 kilometers altitude. In that region the molecular concentration of ozone reaches about 15 parts per million.[168] That is still only a trace, but it is enough to play a crucial role in the interaction of the atmosphere with incoming sunlight. In particular, atmospheric ozone is the only effective shield of Earth's surface against ultraviolet solar radiation in the range of wavelengths that are damaging to plants and to animals, as discussed further below. Moreover, the absorption of this radiation in the stratosphere and consequent heat production there are responsible for the stratospheric temperature inversion that suppresses mixing of the lower atmosphere (troposphere) with the air at the higher altitudes. This fact, and the mere circumstance that the absorbed energy does not reach Earth's surface, certainly have some effect on world climate.

The stratospheric pool of ozone is the result of a balance between continuous processes that produce and destroy this substance. (The size of the pool varies with latitude and with time in response to a variety of natural factors.) Production takes place when molecular oxygen (O_2) is split by ultraviolet solar radiation and the resulting oxygen atoms (O) attach themselves to other oxygen (O_2) molecules:

$$O_2 \longrightarrow O + O,$$
$$O + O_2 \longrightarrow O_3.$$

Destruction takes place by means of several different reactions, in which the net results are either

$$O + O_3 \longrightarrow O_2 + O_2$$

or

$$2O_3 \longrightarrow 3O_2.$$

The destruction reactions proceed most rapidly in the presence of certain catalysts: the hydroxyl radical HO (which comes from water vapor in the stratosphere), nitric oxide (NO), and atomic chlorine (Cl).[169] All of them are scarce in the natural stratosphere, although crucial to its chemistry. Activities of civilization that change the stratospheric concentrations of these catalysts also change the rate at which ozone is destroyed, thereby altering the production-destruction equilibrium and possibly reducing the stratospheric pool of ozone.

SSTs and nuclear war. The first specific threat to the ozone layer to be taken seriously by people in the technical community was the proposed operation of a fleet of supersonic transports (SSTs). An early concern was that the water vapor introduced into the stratosphere in the exhausts of those aircraft would cause a reduction in ozone by increasing the stratospheric concentration of HO.[170] This particular concern subsequently proved to be misplaced; the real hazard to ozone in SST exhausts is nitric oxide, which is a much more effective catalyst for the ozone-destruction reactions than HO. A paper published by chemist Harold Johnston of the University of California at Berkeley in 1971 indicated that the nitric oxide emitted by a fleet of 500 SSTs of the U.S. design could reduce the stratospheric ozone concentration by an average of 20 percent, with local peak reductions up to 50 percent.[171] This finding was strongly attacked by SST proponents, but a combination of further research and exhaustive reviews by panels of experts under the

[167]An excellent reference—authoritative but aimed at the intelligent lay person rather than at the specialist—providing more extended discussion of the entire set of issues surrounding human intervention in atmosphere and climate is S. H. Schneider with L. E. Mesirow, *The genesis strategy.*

[168]A good review of the data on the natural distribution of ozone is given in H. S. Johnston, Photochemistry in the stratosphere—with applications to supersonic transports.

[169]A much more comprehensive treatment of ozone chemistry is P. J. Crutzen, Estimates of possible variations in total ozone due to natural causes and human activities. See also C. E. Kolb, The depletion of stratospheric ozone.

[170]The direct effects of the added water vapor on the transmission of radiation by the stratosphere also have to be considered. See below, and SCEP, *Man's impact,* pp. 64–74.

[171]H. S. Johnston, Reduction of stratospheric ozone by nitrogen oxide catalysts from SST exhaust. The other pioneer in the identification of this threat was P. J. Crutzen (see, for example, his The influence of nitrogen oxides on the atmospheric ozone content.)

auspices of the National Academy of Sciences and the United States Department of Transportation completely substantiated Johnston's work. One of the reviews, by the Climatic Impact Assessment Program (CIAP) of the Department of Transportation, produced a final report written so obscurely that some journalists misread it as a refutation of Johnston's results; and a few made fools of themselves in nationally syndicated columns decrying the "environmental hysteria" that had stopped the SST.[172] Most of the confusion caused by the CIAP report was caused by the prominence it gave to the conclusion that a somewhat smaller fleet of the lower-flying, smaller-engined Concorde SSTs would *not* significantly disrupt the ozone layer, while it buried the confirmation of Johnston's conclusion about 500 U.S. SSTs in the fine print.[173]

Nuclear bombs offer an additional avenue by which significant amounts of nitrogen oxides can be added to the stratosphere. The high temperature in nuclear fireballs produces nitrogen oxides in abundance from atmospheric nitrogen and oxygen, and much of that material is deposited in the stratosphere. Although there is some controversy about the issue, several investigators believe that ozone depletion by atmospheric bomb tests conducted in the early 1960s was great enough (around 5 percent) to show up in the relatively crude historical data that are available for stratospheric ozone concentrations.[174] Although depletion of ozone may seem at first glance to be the least of humanity's worries if a large nuclear war ever took place, that is not really so obvious. In some circumstances, the global depletion of ozone might have a greater effect on noncombatant nations distant from the conflict than would radioactive fallout.[175]

Chlorofluorocarbons. It was known as early as 1973 that free chlorine in the stratosphere would be an even more efficient catalyst than nitric oxide for destruction of ozone, but since no source of free chlorine that could reach the stratosphere was known at that time, little concern was expressed about this phenomenon. It was shown in 1974, however, that a class of compounds variously known as chlorofluorocarbons, fluorocarbons, and Freons could be dissociated by wavelengths of sunlight present only in the stratosphere, to release free chlorine.[176] Those compounds have been used very widely as refrigerants and as propellants in some aerosol spray cans. The most common ones have the chemical formulas $CFCl_3$ and CF_2Cl_2. They are essentially inert to chemical reaction and relatively insoluble in water. The result of these properties is that virtually the total amount put into the atmosphere remains there, chemically intact, until it reaches the stratosphere.

The amount of chlorofluorocarbons thought to have reached the stratosphere by late 1974 was only enough to have caused about a 1 percent decrease in the ozone—a change too small to be detected by existing techniques. Production of those compounds has been growing rapidly, however; in this situation, a large fraction of the amount *ever* produced has been produced only recently and has not had time to diffuse up to the stratosphere. (Recall from Chapter 2 that the mixing time between troposphere and stratosphere is a few years.) Some calculations have indicated that ozone depletion due to catalytic destruction by chlorine from chlorofluoromethanes could reach 5 percent by 1990, even if production of those compounds had been halted at the end of 1975, and around 15 percent by the year 2000 if production continued to grow at 10 percent per year.[177]

There are many approximations in such calculations, and more precise analyses and measurements were underway as this text was being written. The available information gives ample cause for serious concern, however, a position underlined by a federal scientific task force that reviewed the issue in mid-1975.[178] Assertions

[172]The CIAP report itself is A. Grobecker, S. Coroniti, and R. Cannon, *The effects of stratospheric pollution by aircraft.* The more forthright of the two major scientific reviews of the question in the United States is National Academy of Sciences, *Environmental impact of stratospheric flight.*

[173]See the exchange of letters by T. Donahue and A. Grobecker in *Science,* vol. 187, pp. 1142–1145 (March 28, 1975).

[174]A good concise review of the subject is A. L. Hammond and T. H. Maugh, II, Stratospheric pollution: Multiple threats to Earth's ozone.

[175]National Academy of Sciences, *Long-term worldwide effects of multiple nuclear-weapons detonations.*

[176]The original paper is M. J. Molina and F. S. Rowland, Stratospheric sink for chlorofluoromethanes: Chlorine atom catalyzed. Good accounts of the implications are given in Hammond and Maugh, Stratospheric pollution; and Crutzen, Estimates.

[177]Hammond and Maugh, Stratospheric pollution. Subsequent research has generally confirmed these findings (T. H. Maugh II, The ozone layer: The threat from aerosol cans is real).

[178]Interagency Task Force on Inadvertent Modification of the Stratosphere, *Fluorocarbons and the environment.*

by the industries producing chlorofluorocarbons that no action should be taken to curtail production until proof of harm is persuasive *to them,* are so irresponsible as to defy imagination.

Nitrogen fertilizer. The man-made threats to ozone discussed so far—SSTs, nuclear bombs, and aerosol propellants and refrigerants—share the characteristic that human well-being does not depend in any fundamental sense on the use of the offending products. SSTs are not economically necessary, harmless substitutes can be found for most applications of chlorofluoromethanes (modifications of the finger-operated spray pump familiar in window-cleaner bottles could handle most aerosol-can applications), and it should be plain that nuclear bombs are a product the world can do without. Thus, the future magnitude of those threats *could* be limited without serious social cost merely by the exercise of good sense—that is, by not producing or using them any longer. An intrinsically more difficult problem is posed by the possibility that nitrogen fertilizer is the source of yet another threat to ozone. As Orville Freeman, former U.S. Secretary of Agriculture, has pointed out: "A world without fertilizer would be a world without the capacity to sustain a billion of our fellow human beings."[179]

The danger is that nitrous oxide (N_2O) produced from nitrates and nitrites in soil or water by denitrifying bacteria (see above in this chapter and Chapter 3) is oxidized in the upper atmosphere to ozone-destroying nitric oxide. Applying more nitrogen fertilizer may add more nitrous oxide to the atmosphere, which means more nitric oxide in the stratosphere, which means less ozone. The intrinsic difficulty is the apparent reliance of immediate prospects for increased food production on greater use of nitrogen fertilizer. This threat to the ozone is less certain at this writing than the others discussed here, because of uncertainties in the atmospheric chemistry of N_2O and in the magnitude of flows in the natural nitrogen cycle.[180] Some models of the processes at work suggest that ozone depletion from this cause is likely to be small and gradual.

If the worst proves to be true, however, forecasted increases in the use of nitrogen fertilizer could produce a *15-percent reduction* in stratospheric ozone by the year 2025. That prospect would pose an agonizing dilemma; unlike its relationships to SSTs, bombs, and spray cans, civilization is *really* hooked on nitrogen fertilizer. At the very least it is another argument in favor of using nitrogen fertilizers so they are maximally effective and minimally wasted, and for relying as much as possible on natural fertilizers (from which relatively little nitrogen "leaks" to the atmosphere.)

Other threats to ozone. There may be other compounds as dangerous to the ozone layer as those already mentioned, or more so. Carbon tetrachloride (CCl_4), for one, is added to the lower atmosphere by processes both natural and human. There is evidence that human activity is the principal source, and that a significant quantity of the carbon tetrachloride reaches the stratosphere.[181] It is conceivable that chlorination of drinking water and of sewage are important sources that have some effect on ozone. Bromine is known to be an even more efficient catalyst for the destruction of ozone than chlorine; bromides are used in gasoline additives, agricultural chemicals, and flame-retardants. Pathways to the stratosphere for bromides have not yet been evaluated. Alkali metals such as sodium and potassium might destroy ozone if added to the stratosphere by nuclear explosions over oceans or by intentional seeding as a chemical/climatological weapon.[182] Many of these possibilities may prove to be false alarms, but, as in Russian roulette, only one "loaded" possibility may be too many.

Consequences of ozone depletion. The existing ozone layer screens out more than 99 percent of incoming solar energy in the wavelength region between 0.23 and 0.32 microns; radiation of those wavelengths is harmful to most forms of terrestrial life, and the small fraction that gets through is known to cause sunburn, skin cancer, and eye damage in human beings, as well as various kinds

---

179Quoted in *Chemical and Engineering News,* June 17, 1974, p. 13.

180See, for example, Crutzen, Estimates; Council for Agricultural Science and Technology, *Effect of increased nitrogen fixation on stratospheric ozone;* H. S. Johnston, *Analysis of the independent variables in the perturbation of stratospheric ozone by nitrogen fertilizers;* M. B. McElroy et al., sources and sinks for atmospheric N_2O.

181H. B. Singh et al., Atmospheric carbon tetrachloride.

182See Kolb, The depletion; Schneider and Mesirow, *The genesis strategy,* chapter 6.

of damage to other animals and plants.[183] Most scientists agree that terrestrial life did not evolve until the ozone layer was established. The special effectiveness of ultraviolet radiation in damaging living systems is due to the sensitivity of the genetic material DNA and of proteins to those wavelengths. DNA exhibits a resonance—the capacity to absorb radiant energy very efficiently—at wavelengths around 0.265 microns. Proteins typically have resonances in the range of 0.275 to 0.285 microns. The energy absorbed when radiation of those wavelengths strikes the DNA and protein molecules damages them, causing the many disruptive effects now known, and probably others as well.

Analytic and computer models of varying degrees of sophistication have been used to estimate what increase in the ultraviolet radiation reaching the surface would be associated with different degrees of depletion of the stratospheric ozone.[184] Although the relation between ozone depletion and increased ultraviolet at the surface varies with latitude and other factors, a rough average is that a 5-percent decrease in ozone produces a 10-percent increase in radiation. The best-studied effect of such an increase is an increase in the incidence of human skin cancers, the magnitude of which is estimated to be about equal to the percentage change in radiation. Thus a 5-percent decrease in ozone and a 10-percent increase in ultraviolet radiation would produce 20,000 to 60,000 additional skin cancers per year in the United States alone, and perhaps 5 times as many worldwide. (Incidence of skin cancer is higher among light-skinned people than among dark-skinned.)[185] About 5 percent of the skin cancers would be fatal. A 30-percent reduction in ozone would be expected to produce on the order of 1 million additional skin cancers per year worldwide, of which perhaps 50,000 would be fatal.

Although an increase in skin cancer is the best understood of the effects of ozone depletion, it is by no means the only and not necessarily even the most serious such effect. Laboratory tests have indicated that increased ultraviolet radiation impairs the growth of certain crop plants and adversely affects a wide variety of organisms from bacteria to vertebrates. Phytoplankton, the primary producers at the base of oceanic food webs, may prove especially vulnerable if the light-receptors that trigger the protective dive response to excess radiation are not sufficiently sensitive to ultraviolet light. Furthermore, many insects "see" ultraviolet light and rely on it for navigation; interference with their pollination function is but one of several conceivable consequences for insects of an increase in ultraviolet intensity. Acceleration of the mutation rate of microorganisms because of DNA's sensitivity to ultraviolet could have adverse effects on human beings through disease, causing more frequent development of strains of microorganisms against which people would have no resistance and of strains resistant to antibiotics. The consequences for ecosystems of differential susceptibility among different organisms to increased ultraviolet radiation cannot be predicted with any accuracy, but such differential susceptibility is known to exist and the possibility of its resulting in serious instability cannot be excluded.[186]

Nonbiological damage from increased ultraviolet radiation is likely to include faster deterioration of paints, fabrics, plastics, and other materials. The magnitude and economic cost of such effects is uncertain—and dependent on the amount of increased radiation—but it would surely be significant.

Probably least certain of all is the impact of ozone depletion on climate. The situation is extremely complicated: ozone absorbs and reradiates radiant energy in the infrared part of the spectrum of wavelengths as well as in the ultraviolet part; so do products of some of the reactions that consume ozone, and so do most of the catalysts for the ozone-destroying reactions and their precursors (chlorine is such a catalyst, the chlorofluorocarbons are its precursors). One recent study based on a relatively simple model found it possible that continued growth of chlorofluorocarbon production could produce

[183]National Academy of Sciences, *Biological impacts of increased intensities of solar ultraviolet radiation;* see also Hammond and Maugh, Stratospheric pollution; Crutzen, Estimates.

[184]See, for example, M. B. McElroy, S. C. Wofsy, J. E. Penner, J. C. McConnell, Atmospheric ozone: Possible impact of stratospheric aviation; F. Alyea, D. Cunnold, R. Prinn, Stratospheric ozone destruction by aircraft-induced nitrogen oxides; National Academy of Sciences, *Environmental impact of stratospheric flight.*

[185]National Academy of Sciences, *Environmental impact of stratospheric flight;* A. Karim Ahmed, Unshielding the sun . . . human effects.

[186]For discussions of the nonhuman biological effects of increased ultraviolet radiation, see especially National Academy of Sciences, *Environmental impact of stratospheric flight,* and J. Eigner, Unshielding the sun . . . environmental effects.

a significant global warming by the year 2000, independent of the effect on ozone, merely because of a greenhouse effect in which those compounds would block outgoing infrared radiation.[187] Changes in the radiation-absorbing and -emitting properties of the atmosphere not only change the direct radiation flows at Earth's surface, however; they also change the vertical temperature distribution in the troposphere and the stratosphere, which in turn changes the rate of vertical circulation.[188] All of this could influence climate in ways that as yet defy detailed prediction.

TABLE 11-4
Average Changes in Aspects of Local Climate Caused by Cities

Aspect	*Comparison with rural environment*
Cloud cover	5%–10% more
Winter fog	100% more
Summer fog	30% more
Precipitation	5%–10% more
Summer relative humidity	8% less
Winter relative humidity	2% less
Total radiation	15%–20% less
Ultraviolet radiation	5%–30% less
Annual mean temperature	0.5°–1°C more
Average winter minimum temperature	1°–2°C more
Mean wind speed	20%–30% less

Source: H. E. Landsberg, Man-made climate changes, *Science,* vol. 170, pp. 1265–1274 (December 18, 1970).

Climate Change Through Surface Modification

Whereas the importance to climate of processes high in the stratosphere has been appreciated only relatively recently, the relevance to climate of the condition of Earth's surface is more obvious. The most important features are: (1) presence or absence of water, (2) reflectivity, or albedo, (3) ability to transfer water to the atmosphere, (4) capacity to store heat, and (5) topography and texture. These interrelated features determine how much of the incident radiant energy is captured, how it is apportioned between surface and atmosphere, how the surface interacts with the winds, and how the shoreline interacts with ocean currents. Civilization can influence the surface conditions by changing or removing vegetation, by damming and diverting rivers to form reservoirs and irrigation projects, by "reclaiming" land from shallow seas and bays, by covering land with pavement and buildings, by spilling oil on water, snow, and ice, and by releasing previously stored energy as heat.

Cities and heat. The most obvious and also the most localized such effects are those associated with cities. The differences in various aspects of climate between urban areas and adjacent rural environments are summarized in Table 11-4. The changes in climate are caused by urban heat, snow removal, accelerated runoff, altered albedo and heat-storage capacity resulting from replacing forests and fields with concrete and buildings, and the greater surface roughness.[189] The differences indicated in Table 11-4 have not necessarily all been bad, in the sense of causing harm; some may even have been beneficial. What is interesting is that they provide concrete evidence of quite dramatic human influence on local climates—influences that could become adverse in terms of (for example) agriculture, as urban settlements expand and exert their effects over larger areas.

Especially careful attention must be paid to the heat released in urban regions as both populations and energy use per person grow. This is the ultimate form of thermal pollution—not just waste heat but the inevitable conversion of virtually all useful energy to an equal amount of heat, as predicted by the laws of thermodyamics (Box 2-3). The heat released by human activities in Manhattan—more than 600 watts per square meter—is about 6 times the natural net radiation balance in that region.[190] (The net radiation balance is incoming radiation minus outgoing radiation, a figure of particular climatic significance, as discussed in Chapter 2.) Over the much larger area of Los Angeles County—about 10,000 square kilometers—the heat being released by human activities around 1970 was about 6 percent of the natural net radiation balance.

Various combinations of area covered and power density produced by human activities, both actual and hypothetical, are represented graphically in Figure 11-17. It is clear there that human energy use averaged over

[187]V. Ramanathan, Greenhouse effect due to chlorofluorocarbons: Climatic implications.

[188]R. A. Reck, Stratospheric ozone effects on temperature.

[189]H. E. Landsberg, Man-made climatic changes, *Science,* vol. 170, pp. 1265–1274 (December 18, 1970); Study of Man's Impact on Climate, *Inadvertent climate modification,* chapter 7; W. P. Lowry, The climate of cities.

[190]H. Flohn, as reported in SMIC, *Inadvertent,* p. 58.

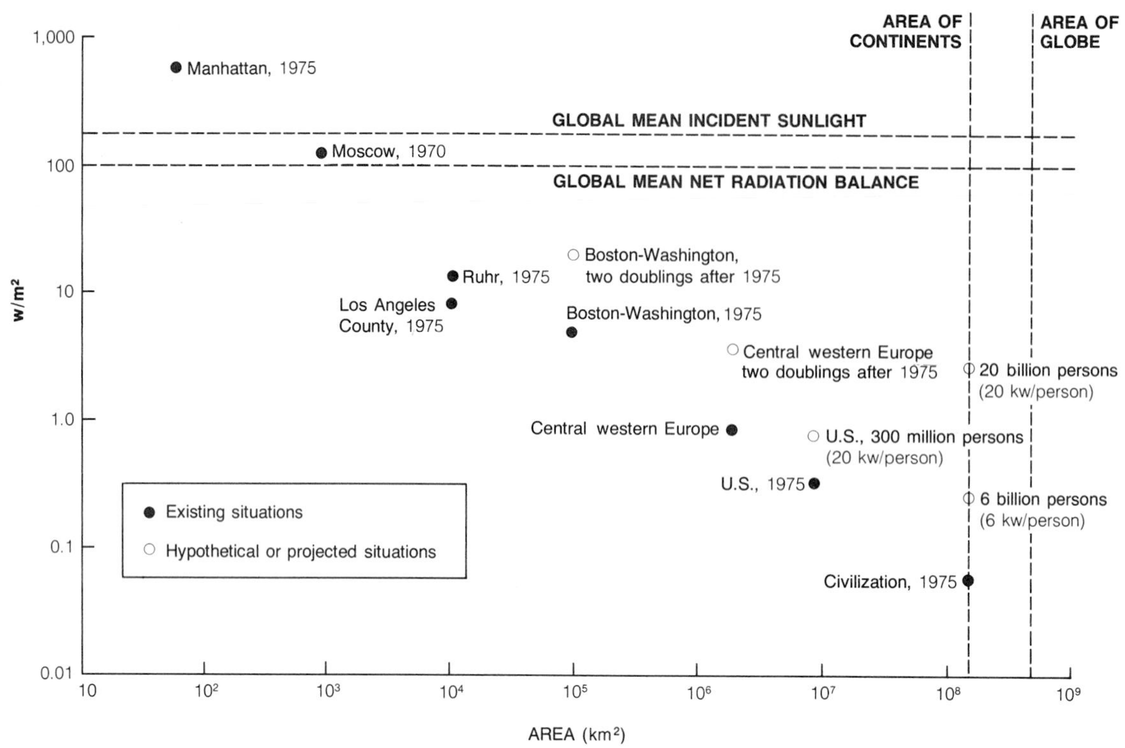

FIGURE 11-17

Man-made power densities and area. Ten percent of the net radiation balance has been reached over areas of 10,000 square kilometers and 1 percent over areas exceeding 1,000,000 square kilometers. (After National Center for Atmospheric Research, *Atmospheric implications of energy alternatives.*)

all the continents is still more than 1000 times smaller than the natural radiation balance. However, a population of 6 billion people using energy at the rate per capita in Sweden in 1975 would be equivalent to almost 0.4 percent of the natural radiation balance on the continents, and a hypothetical society of 20 billion people using energy at the rate of 20 thermal kilowatts per person, as envisioned by A. M. Weinberg and P. Hammond,[191] would reach 2.6 percent of the radiation balance on the continents. Even if the latter energy use were evenly distributed over the land surface, it could probably produce significant changes in global climate; conceivably even the smaller amount could do so.

How does one reach this conclusion? The simplest models assume that human heat input is equivalent to a fractional increase in solar input, distributed over a uniform Earth. Straightforward calculation for this enormously oversimplified situation suggests that an increment of 1 percent of the average solar energy flow at the top of the atmosphere (that is, 3.4 watts per square meter, averaged over the whole globe) would produce an increase of about 0.7° C in mean global surface temperature.[192] (This model is described in Box 11-4.) Weinberg and Hammond were reassured by this sort of result, since their 400-billion-kilowatt civilization averaged out to only about 0.8 watts per square meter of land and sea. Unfortunately the outlook is not really reassuring. Making the model slightly more realistic by accounting for some of the important effects of the atmosphere (instead of doing the calculations just for a solid body) increases the apparent sensitivity of global surface temperature to heat input by a factor of roughly from 2 to 4—that is, instead of 0.7° C from an increment of 3.4 watts per

[191]A. M. Weinberg and P. Hammond, Limits to the use of energy.

[192]See, for example, J. P. Holdren, Global thermal pollution, in *Global Ecology: Readings toward a rational strategy for man,* John P. Holdren and Paul R. Ehrlich, eds.

BOX 11-4 Simplified Global Energy Balance and Civilization's Contribution

The simplest calculation represents Earth as a blackbody radiating heat into space at a rate corresponding to its mean surface temperature (T). The energy-balance formula corresponding to that assumption is

$$SC + M = SC\alpha + 4C\epsilon\sigma T^4.$$

The left-hand side of the equation represents the rate of input of energy to Earth—the solar constant S multiplied by the cross section (C) that Earth presents to the sun, plus miscellaneous energy inputs (M), including tides, geothermal energy, and heat dissipation from human activities. The right-hand side represents the rate of output of energy from Earth; α represents the albedo, so $SC\alpha$ stands for the reflected sunlight; σ stands for the constant in the Stefan-Boltzmann radiation law; and ϵ represents the effective emissivity (basically a "fudge factor" that corrects for neglecting the effects of the atmosphere, which really does most of the Earth-atmosphere system's radiating to space, at a temperature of about 24° C lower than the average surface temperature, as described in Chapter 2). The factor of 4 in the radiation term is there because the total global surface area, which radiates, is 4 times the cross-sectional area (C).

The values of these parameters are as follows: $SC = 1.74 \times 10^{17}$ watts, $M = 3.0 \times 10^{13}$ watts (of which about 0.8×10^{13} watts was civilization's contribution, as of 1975), $\alpha = 30$ percent, and $\sigma = 5.67 \times 10^{-8}$ if T is measured in degrees kelvin and C in square meters. Then, setting $\epsilon = 0.61$ gives the observed surface temperature of 288° K, or 15° C.

The sensitivity of the temperature in the model to changes in the energy input can be obtained readily by elementary calculus. Let the amount of heat that must be radiated away, $SC(1 - \alpha) + M$, be denoted R. For temperature changes (ΔT) that are much less than the temperature's initial value of 288° K, one finds

$$\Delta T/T = 0.25\ \Delta R/R,$$

where ΔR is the change in the amount of heat that must be radiated away. This means that a 1-percent increase in the amount of heat to be radiated away produces an increase of 0.25 percent in surface temperature. That is,

$$\Delta T/T = 0.25\ (0.01) = 0.0025,$$

$$\Delta T = 0.0025\ (288°\ \text{K}) = 0.72°\ \text{K}.$$

Such an increase in average global surface temperature could be quite significant. The corresponding 1-percent change in the present value of R (1.22×10^{17} watts) would amount to an increase in the 1975 human energy use by a factor of about 150. That amounts to just over 7 doublings, a feat that would require about a century at a growth rate of 5 percent per year. Each doubling thereafter would double the temperature increment, so that to reach an unquestionably intolerable global average increase of $16 \times 0.72 = 11.5°$ K (11.5° C, or 21° F) would require only an additional 4 doublings—56 years at 5 percent per year.

Calculations with so oversimplified a model are satisfactory for showing the impossibility on climatic grounds of long-continued exponential growth of human energy use. However, as noted in the text, the complexities of the atmosphere and the fact that human energy use is not evenly distributed over Earth's surface suggest that serious thermal disruption could occur much sooner than this simplest of energy-balance models indicates.

square meter, one might get 1.2° to 2.6° C.[193] Moreover, the complexities of atmospheric circulation are such that one would expect an average increase of, say, 1 degree, to be associated with much greater temperature changes in certain regions, such as near the poles. Wind and rainfall patterns could change drastically as a result.

What makes thermal disruption of climate an even more imminent possibility than the foregoing considerations suggest, however, is that civilization's heat inputs are distributed very unevenly over the land surface—not uniformly, as all the simple models assume. A graphic illustration of this fact is provided in Figure 11-18, a satellite photograph of the central and eastern United States at night. Large, concentrated sources of heat can influence the atmospheric long waves that determine

[193]These results and an excellent discussion of the entire problem are in S. H. Schneider and R. Dennett, Climatic barriers to long-term energy growth.

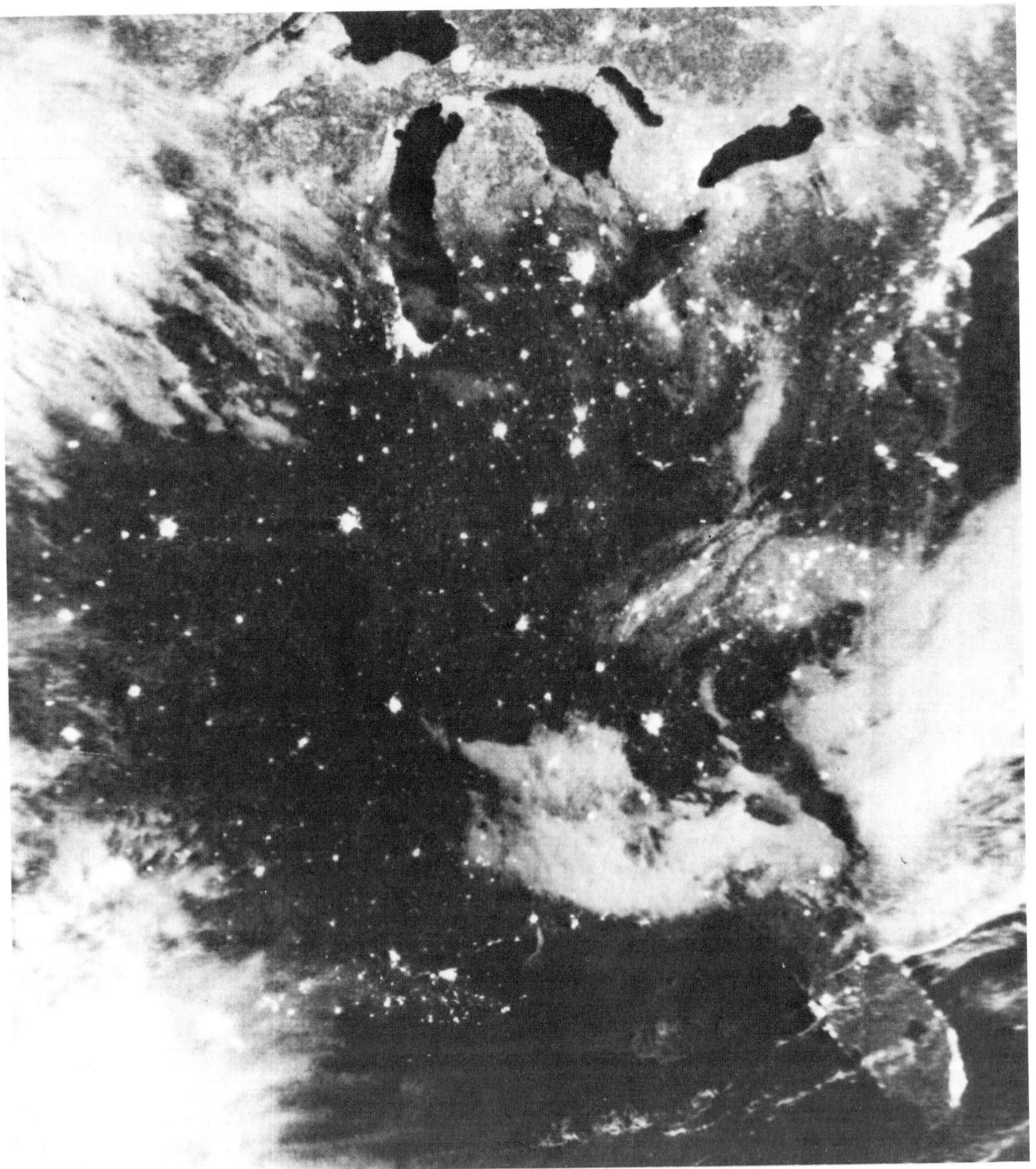

FIGURE 11-18

Urban regions of central and eastern United States at night. Bright areas produced by the lights in urban regions show up in this satellite photograph. Note especially the Boston–Washington corridor, the industrial centers around the Great Lakes, and the Palm Beach–Miami corridor in southeastern Florida. (Photo courtesy NASA.)

many climatic features long before global average warming becomes significant.[194] Computer models available in the mid-1970s were not sophisticated enough to represent the consequences of scattered human heat sources realistically. It seems likely on a variety of grounds, however, that another one or two doublings in energy consumption would place several of the world's most industrialized regions at a heat-source level capable of influencing climate over millions to tens of millions of square kilometers.

TABLE 11-5
Scale of Climate-Related Alterations Associated with Agriculture (around 1970)

Alteration	*Magnitude*
Conversion of forest to fields and grasslands	18 to 20% of area of continents (albedo changed from 0.12–0.18 to 0.20)
Subsequent conversion of fields and grasslands to desert	5% of area of continents (albedo changed from 0.20 to 0.28)
Area under irrigation	1.5% of area of continents
Reduction of continental runoff by irrigation	5%
Increase in continental evaporation due to irrigation	2%
Increase in evaporation from irrigated areas	100 to 1000%
Area covered by artificial reservoirs	0.2% of area of continents

Source: Study of Man's Impact on Climate, *Inadvertent climate modification.*

Agriculture and desertification. The earliest significant human influence on climate was undoubtedly that of vegetation changes brought about by human use of fire, deforestation, cultivation, and grazing. Subsequently, changes brought about by irrigation projects joined this category of climatic impacts associated with the provision of food and fiber. The scale of some of the modifications is suggested by the figures in Table 11-5, which represent significant changes both in energy balance and in water budget. (Note, for example, that an albedo increase of 0.02 over 10 percent of the continental land area produces a reduction of 51 million megawatts in the rate at which solar energy is absorbed at Earth's surface; this is about *6 times* the rate of commercial energy use in 1975.)

As far as is known, the actual changes in climate associated with such surface alterations have been mainly regional, rather than global. (Neither measurements nor models have been good enough to be sure.) One reason for this may be that some human activities, such as irrigation of arid lands, actually decrease albedo, which compensates to some degree for man-made increases in the albedo elsewhere.

Regional changes can themselves be devastating. There has been particular interest in possible climatological explanations of the prolonged drought of the late 1960s and early 1970s in sub-Saharan Africa, mentioned earlier. One observer has suggested that the drought could have been brought on, or at least aggravated by, the following chain of events: overgrazing bared high-albedo soils, a resulting drop in the absorption of solar energy at the surface reduced the heating of near-surface air, and the reduction of updrafts resulting from that phenomenon inhibited cloud formation and rainfall, producing drought.[195] (The increased albedo that can result from overgrazing is apparent in the satellite photo in Figure 11-19). A superficially similar plant-cover–albedo–rainfall feedback mechanism has been described by J. Charney, P. Stone, and W. Quirk; it seems more consistent than the first model with the large area of the effect observed in the Sahel, and its plausibility has been confirmed by incorporating the mechanism into a computer model of the global atmosphere that can account for interaction of the Sahel with other regions.[196]

Oil and ice. Oil slicks on the ocean surface change the albedo, the roughness (hence the energy transfer from surface to atmosphere), and the evaporation rate. Data on the sizes of oil slicks and their persistence is not as yet adequate to determine whether they influence meteorological conditions in more than a temporary and highly local fashion.[197]

It has been suggested that spills associated with oil production and transportation activities in the Arctic could have serious climatic effects there, because of the following combination of circumstances: under Arctic

[194]See Schneider and Dennett, Climatic barriers; and Marie Boyko, Climatic effects of thermal pollution, in *Atmospheric implications of energy alternatives,* National Center for Atmospheric Research.

[195]Joseph Otterman, Baring high-albedo soils by overgrazing: A hypothesized desertification mechanism. Subsequent argumentation pro and con can be found in R. D. Jackson, S. B. Idso, and J. Otterman, Surface albedo and desertification.

[196]J. Charney, P. Stone, and W. Quirk, Drought in the Sahara: A biogeophysical feedback mechanism.

[197]G. J. F. MacDonald, Man, weather, and climate; SMIC, *Inadvertent,* pp. 164–165.

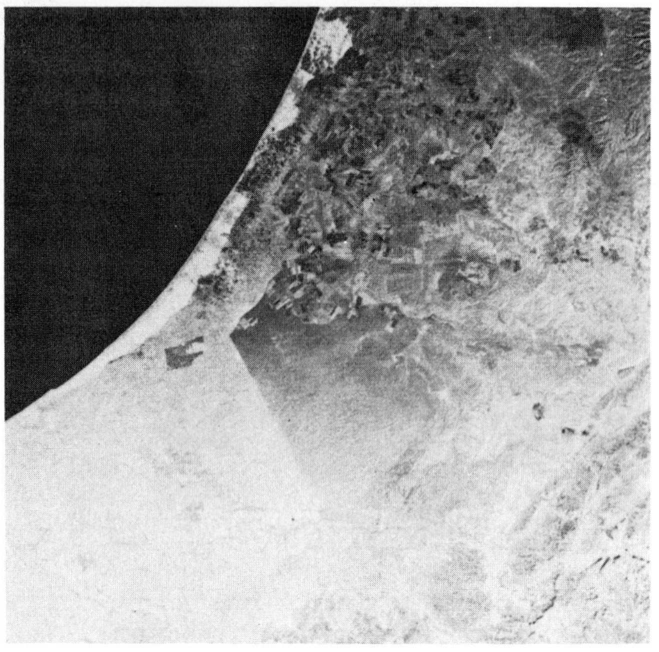

FIGURE 11-19

Change in albedo from overgrazing in the Middle East. Note the sharp demarkation between overgrazed light areas and vegetated dark areas. (Photo courtesy National Center for Atmospheric Research.)

conditions, biological degradation of spilled oil is very slow; the dynamics of the Arctic pack ice provides several mechanisms by which the oil can be spread over very large areas and then find its way to the surface of the ice, drastically reducing the albedo. The climate of the entire Northern Hemisphere is very sensitive to the heat balance in the Arctic.[198] Changes in albedo are particularly important there because of the very large amount of sunlight received in the polar summer (see Chapter 2) and the associated possibility of its completely melting the sea ice. Whether the ice would reform, once melted, is not known; dramatic changes in climate could be expected if it did not.[199] Whether oil spills really could cover enough area to raise this possibility is controversial: critics of the hypothesis claim that a 2-million-barrel spill could not cover more than 100 square kilometers of ice, compared to the 10 million square kilometers maximum extent of the sea ice; proponents say the coverage of such a spill could range from 240 to 800,000 square kilometers.[200]

Another possible threat to Arctic sea ice is a Soviet scheme for diverting major rivers now flowing into the Arctic Ocean. The project, underway in the mid-1970s, is expected to shift the flow southward for the purpose of irrigating parts of the Soviet Union previously too arid for cultivation; the residue is to flow into the Caspian Sea. The loss of the substantial freshwater flow of those rivers into the Arctic Ocean can be expected to increase the salinity of the surface layer, making it more difficult to freeze and possibly significantly reducing the area covered by sea ice.[201]

Modifying the Troposphere

The activities of civilization certainly have modified Earth's surface significantly, and they appear to be modifying the stratosphere. What of the troposphere, where most of the mass of the atmosphere resides and most of the motion that "produces" climate takes place? Aside from the influences already mentioned, civilization's direct impact on the troposphere is mainly of three kinds: an increase in the concentration of carbon dioxide, which is worldwide and uniformly distributed; an increase in the concentration of particles in the atmosphere over large regions (but little if any increase in other regions); and the production of high-altitude clouds initiated as jet aircraft contrails at the tropopause. The principal impact of all these phenomena occurs through the interaction of the contaminants with incoming solar radiation and outgoing terrestrial radiation.

Carbon dioxide. Combustion of fossil fuels at the 1975 rate would add carbon dioxide to the atmosphere at a rate sufficient to increase the atmospheric concentration of this gas by about 3 parts per million per year if it all remained in the atmosphere (see Chapter 3). In fact,

[198]W. J. Campbell and S. Martin, Oil and ice in the Arctic Ocean: Possible large-scale interactions. See also Chapter 2 for an expanded discussion of the sensitivity of hemispheric climate to Arctic conditions, and W. W. Kellogg, Climatic feedback mechanisms involving the polar regions.

[199]SMIC, *Inadvertent*, pp. 159–162.

[200]R. Ayers, Jr.; H. O. Jahns; and J. Glaeser, Oil spills in the Arctic Ocean, and comments by S. Martin and W. J. Campbell.

[201]W. W. Kellogg and S. H. Schneider, Climate stabilization: For better or for worse.

however, it appears that only about 50 percent of the carbon dioxide that has been produced since heavy reliance on fossil fuels began toward the end of the nineteenth century has remained in the atmosphere, and that a similar fraction of what is now being injected is remaining there.[202] The remainder of the carbon dioxide presumably is being absorbed in the mixed layer of the oceans and, conceivably, part of it is appearing as an increase in terrestrial and oceanic biomass.

The part that remains in the atmosphere is of considerable climatic significance because of the crucial role played by carbon dioxide in Earth's energy balance through its greenhouse effect (Chapter 2). The atmospheric concentration of carbon dioxide increased by more than 10 percent (from about 290 ppm to 320 ppm) between 1880 and 1975, a finding supported by a number of independent measurements.[203] If all other factors had been constant, the enhanced greenhouse effect associated with this increase could have increased the average global surface temperature about 0.3° C.[204] If the use of fossil fuels continues to grow at 3 to 4 percent per year, available models suggest an atmospheric concentration of carbon dioxide of between 365 and 385 parts per million in the year 2000 and, all other factors being constant, a corresponding temperature increase between 1975 and 2000 of 0.3° to 0.6° C.[205]

Significantly, moreover, Earth's climatic machinery is such that the effect of warming due to carbon dioxide is expected to be several times as great near the poles as on the average.[206] This means that a 0.5° C global average warming could cause significant changes in atmospheric circulation, extensive melting of sea ice, and perhaps the initiation of melting from the Greenland and Antarctic ice sheets with a concomitant increase in sea level.

Some complications must be mentioned, however. First, many factors other than fossil-fuel combustion are capable in principle of influencing the atmospheric concentration of carbon dioxide. They include, among others, the rate of uptake of carbon dioxide in ocean surface layers and the size of the planetary biomass. Some of these factors have been taken into account in the models used to arrive at the projections of future carbon-dioxide concentrations quoted above, but it is possible that important effects have either been left out or incorrectly modeled. This means the carbon-dioxide concentration could grow more rapidly than the models predict, or more slowly. Second, the warming associated with an increase in carbon dioxide could bring feedback loops into play that would either accelerate the warming trend (positive feedback) or slow it (negative feedback). An example of the former would be increased ocean-surface temperatures driving more carbon dioxide out of solution and into the atmosphere; an example of the latter would be increased evaporation (because of the warmer surface temperature) producing increased cloud cover, which would cool the surface. Third, other, largely independent modifications of the troposphere are taking place that could further complicate the response to rising carbon-dioxide concentrations (chief among them are particles and aircraft contrails), as well as the other natural and human influences on climate discussed earlier in this chapter and in Chapter 2.

Particles and contrails. Particles in the atmosphere are of many sizes and compositions, corresponding to the diversity of their origins: smoke from forest fires, agricultural burning, and the combustion of fossil fuels; solid and liquid particles that began as gaseous emissions from combustion and natural processes; sea salt; dust from volcanic explosions and from agricultural activity. (The term *aerosol* is often used interchangeably with *particles* in the literature of climate, although technically *aerosol* refers to particles of less than 1 micron in diameter together with the gas in which they are suspended.) The exact magnitudes of the various sources of particles are in most cases uncertain, by significant amounts. A tabulation of estimates collected by the Study of Man's Impact on Climate[207] in 1971 appears in Table 11-6. The fraction of the total that is man-made probably falls somewhere between 10 percent and 30 percent.

[202]SMIC, *Inadvertent;* NCAR, *Atmospheric implications,* pp. 15–17.

[203]A good review is J. M. Mitchell, A reassessment of atmospheric pollution as a cause of long-term changes of global temperature. See also L. Machta, Prediction of CO_2 in the atmosphere.

[204]S. Manabe, Estimates of future change of climate due to the increase of carbon dioxide concentration in the air; S. H. Schneider, On the carbon dioxide-climate confusion.

[205]Mitchell, A reassessment; SMIC, *Inadvertent,* pp. 233–240.

[206]See, for example, Kellogg and Schneider, Climate stabilization; Schneider and Dennett, Climatic barriers. Schneider, On the carbon dioxide–climate confusion.

[207]Jointly sponsored by M.I.T. and the Royal Swedish Academy of Sciences.

TABLE 11-6
Particles Less Than 20 Microns in Radius Emitted into or Formed in the Atmosphere

Particles	*Amount emitted into or formed in atmosphere (million MT)*
ANTHROPOGENIC PARTICLES	
Direct emissions of particles	10–90
Particles formed from SO_2 emissions	130–200
Particles formed from NO_X emissions	30–35
Particles formed from hydrocarbon emissions	15–90
NATURAL PARTICLES	
Volcanic debris	25–150
Sea salt	300
Particles formed from H_2S emissions	130–200
Particles formed from NH_3 emissions	80–270
Particles formed from NO_X emissions	60–430
Particles formed from hydrocarbon emissions	75–200
PARTICLES OF MIXED ORIGINS	
Soil and rock debris	100–500
Forest fires and slash burning	3–150
Rounded Totals	1000–2600

Source: Study of Man's Impact on Climate, *Inadvertent climate modification,* p. 189.

Even if the fraction were more accurately known, its meaning would be difficult to ascertain. Unlike carbon dioxide, particles generally do not become uniformly mixed in the atmosphere; their life expectancy before falling out is too short. Therefore, the concentration of particles in the atmosphere tends to be high for some distance downwind of the major sources and low elsewhere.[208] The smallest particles remain in the atmosphere longest and therefore have the biggest effects; this means that sources of small particles, whose contribution to emissions may not be very large by weight, make a disproportionate contribution in terms of climatic impact.

There is no doubt that major volcanic eruptions, when they occur, are the single greatest source of atmospheric particles; such eruptions put a considerable quantity of debris into the stratosphere, where it remains long enough to spread over an entire hemisphere. Climatic records indicate that uncommonly cold years have followed some of the major volcanic eruptions of the past 200 years, presumably because the particles have screened out some sunlight.[209]

[208]NCAR, *Atmospheric implications.*
[209]Mitchell, A reassessment, SMIC, *Inadvertent,* p. 283.

It has been widely surmised that the growing influence of civilization's particle production between volcanic eruptions has had a similar cooling effect, and, indeed, that this might be responsible for the apparent worldwide cooling trend observed between 1940 and 1965.[210] (A widespread conjecture has been that an apparent global warming between 1900 and 1940 was caused by the buildup of carbon dioxide from the combustion of fossil fuels, after which the cooling effect of particles became dominant and reversed the trend.)

Considerable doubt has been cast on this point of view by growing understanding of the complexity of the interaction of atmospheric particles with radiation, and by a lack of evidence that increases in particles have been more than regional in extent. With respect to the first point, it is now known that under some circumstances particles can have a net heating effect rather than a cooling effect; what happens depends on the size and composition of the particles, on their altitude, on the reflectivity of underlying clouds, and on the reflectivity of Earth's surface.[211] Concerning the areal extent of increases in particles from human activities, coverage has been much greater in the Northern Hemisphere than in the Southern; the climatic influence of this may have been appreciable, but its effect is surely more complicated than a uniform cooling.

As noted in Chapter 2, particles play another important role in climatic processes by serving as condensation centers for the formation of water droplets or ice crystals when the relative humidity exceeds 100 percent. Although there is virtually always a surplus of atmospheric particles that could serve as condensation nuclei if the relative humidity were very high, the actual dynamics of cloud formation is governed by that class of particles whose properties permit condensation when the relative humidity first barely exceeds 100 percent. That class of particles, called *cloud nuclei,* is defined as particles that are active condensation centers below 101 percent relative humidity.[212] Particles that have the property of initiating freezing in a droplet that contains them are

[210]See, for example, R. A. Bryson and W. M. Wendland, Climatic effects of atmospheric pollution.
[211]SMIC, *Inadvertent,* pp. 215–220; B. C. Weare, R. L. Temkin, F. M. Snell, Aerosol and climate: Some further considerations; P. Chýlek and J. Coakley, Aerosols and climate.
[212]SMIC, *Inadvertent,* pp. 220–223.

called *ice nuclei.* Under many circumstances, an increase in the atmospheric concentration of cloud nuclei can increase cloud cover but decrease rainfall, because more but smaller droplets are formed, and small droplets do not fall as readily as large ones. Man-made particles can also have the effects of increasing rainfall and decreasing cloud cover—this is what is done intentionally in cloud-seeding programs to stimulate rainfall—but those phenomena seem to be rarer than those with the opposite effect (decreasing rainfall, increasing cloud cover). Present data are inadequate to discern any long-term global trend in cloud cover that might be occurring because of particle pollution. There is some local evidence, however, of an increase in the albedo of clouds to which extra cloud nuclei have been added by human activities.[213]

In the upper troposphere and lower stratosphere, where subsonic jet airliners cruise, the natural humidity tends to be very low. There, the availability of water vapor, more than the properties of condensation nuclei, governs the formation of the cirrus clouds that can exist at those altitudes. The white contrails often visible from the ground behind high-flying jet planes are ice clouds formed from the water vapor supplied by the aircraft's exhausts. Water vapor added to the atmosphere near the tropopause could be sufficient to trigger increased high cloud cover over very large areas of the globe by the 1980s; since 1965 an increase in high cloud cover over the United States, which *might* be due to aircraft operations, has been measured.[214] The effect of high cloudiness in areas where there is no low cloud cover below is to cool the surface during the day and to warm it somewhat at night, the latter produced by an enhanced greenhouse effect. Which is the stronger effect depends on the detailed properties of the clouds, which vary widely.[215]

What's Happening, and Why Does It Matter?

A principal message of the foregoing discussion of civilization and climate is that climate is very complicated and imperfectly understood, as are the human interventions in various aspects of the climatic machinery. What can be stated with assurance is that human modification of Earth's vegetation has had significant (if gradual) effects on the climates of large regions, that densely populated urban centers in industrialized countries have had quite extreme climatic effects extending over areas on the order of 10,000 square kilometers each, and that continuation of exponential growth in energy use would *eventually* lead to intolerable global climatic change from the effects of heat dissipation alone. With almost as much certainty we can say that the buildup of atmospheric carbon dioxide in the past seventy-five years has been due mainly to the combustion of fossil fuels, and that one effect of that buildup *would* have been (in the absence of other changing factors) a modest increase in average global surface temperature. Finally, we can say that the magnitudes of other human interventions in processes that influence climate—such as catalyzing the destruction of atmospheric ozone, alteration of the coverage of Arctic sea ice, modification of the atmospheric-particulate load over large regions, and augmentation of high cirrus clouds with water vapor from jet exhausts—already are or soon will be great enough to raise the *possibility* of significant disruption of climate in ways whose details still cannot be predicted with any confidence.

Role of civilization in observed climatic changes. The relative responsibility of man-made and natural processes for the variations in climate that actually have taken place in this century is controversial (see Box 11-5). The case for the importance of human influences to date—particularly the combination of carbon dioxide and particles—has been presented urgently and in many forums by meteorologist Reid Bryson.[216] He has put forward the hypothesis that the persistent failure of the summer monsoons in sub-Saharan Africa in the late 1960s and early 1970s, which produced severe drought in that region, could have been caused by a change in circulation patterns understandable as the combined effect of carbon dioxide and particles. Basically, his argument is that man-made particles cool the middle to high latitudes more than the equatorial latitudes, increasing the strength of the circumpolar vortex that is

[213]Ibid.

[214]Ibid, pp. 246–250.

[215]S. Manabe and R. T. Weatherald, Thermal equilibrium of the atmosphere with a given distribution of relative humidity; SMIC, *Inadvertent,* pp. 245–246.

[216]See, for example, Bryson and Wendland, Climatic effects; R. A. Bryson, A perspective on climatic change.

BOX 11-5 Some Anomalies in Regional and Global Climates in the 1960s and 1970s

Climate has always been changing, and the details of the changes have always been to a great extent unpredictable. Whether any given short-term change represents a turning point in a long-term pattern rather than a mere fluctuation is impossible to say at the time the change is experienced. Climatologists define normal climate as the average of a recent thirty-year period—in the early to mid-1970s the period in use was 1930 to 1960. Departures from the norm can take the form of *trends* in the average value of such indicators as temperature or rainfall, or else the *variability* of those quantities from year to year can change whether or not the several-year average is changing.

The historical evidence makes it quite clear that the world's climate from 1930 to 1960—today's defined norm—was representative of one of the warmer periods in the last hundred millennia (see Chapter 2). It is reasonably clear that a cooling trend began to set in between 1940 and 1945, at least in the Northern Hemisphere, although the data for the Southern Hemisphere are scantier and not indicative of cooling. Many observers have speculated that the cooling could be the beginning of a long and persistent trend in that direction—that is, an inevitable departure from an abnormally warm period in climatic history.

There would be enormous uncertainty in arguing that the middle of the twentieth century will prove to be such a turning point, however, even without the possibility that civilization itself may be influencing the climatic machinery to be other than it would have been by itself. At the same time, the evidence is sufficient to show that the least that has been happening in the 1960s and 1970s is a considerable increase in the variability of climate compared to the earlier part of the century.

There is evidence, for example, that the growing seasons in Canada, Iceland, and England have shortened by a few weeks for a number of years in this period and that rainfall has decreased significantly in southern England. The winter of 1962/1963 was one of record-breaking cold throughout Europe. The year 1972 was characterized by unusual floods in the midwestern United States, warming of the coastal waters off Peru, an extension of a drought that had commenced a few years earlier in sub-Saharan Africa, delayed onset of the monsoon in India, and a severe drought in the USSR. In 1974 the United States and Canada experienced excessive spring rainfall, intense drought in July, and early fall frosts, while Brazil suffered the worst floods in history.* The USSR had a wheat-crop failure in 1975 because of drought. In 1976, western Europe suffered unprecedented heat and drought during the summer months. The winter of 1976–1977 was one of the driest on record in the western United States and one of the snowiest in the eastern U.S. Regardless of whether all these events are parts of a consistent trend and whether human activities have yet influenced these phenomena, the very fact of increased climatic variability is bad news in a world with decreasing leeway for adjusting to surprises.

*For a good review of these events, see Schneider and Mesirow, *The Genesis strategy*.

driven by that gradient (Chapter 2). At the same time, says Bryson, the effect of carbon dioxide in changing the vertical temperature profile of the lower atmosphere is more important than its overall warming effect, and the weakening in subtropical circulation patterns induced by this altered vertical temperature profile reinforces the effect of the strengthening of the circumpolar vortex. The net result may have been to push the summer position of the intertropical convergence southward, keeping the monsoons and their rainfall out of the Sahel.

Various aspects of Bryson's view have been disputed. Mitchell argues, for example, that until now natural sources (particularly volcanoes) have contributed more particles than have human activities.[217] Schneider and Mass have argued that much of the global climate variation of the past 400 years possibly could be explained by variations in solar output (correlated with sunspot cycles) together with changes in the amount of volcanic dust in the atmosphere.[218] Some others appear

[217]Mitchell, A reassessment.

[218]S. H. Schneider and C. Mass, Volcanic dusts, sunspots, and temperature trends: Climatic theories in search of verification.

to believe that our knowledge of climate is still so inadequate that any speculation about the cause of a particular change is premature. Regardless of the extent to which Bryson's view and other such hypotheses prove right or wrong in detail, however, those kinds of analysis have served a useful function in calling attention to the idea that alteration of circulation patterns is a more significant and more imminent form of climatic change than changes in average surface temperature.

The only real certainty about climate change is that *it will happen.* Even without the inadvertent influences of civilization, the natural forces that have produced rather drastic variations in climate throughout Earth's history will continue to produce them. In the long term, the expected natural trend in the absence of human influences is a cooling from the unusually warm conditions that have prevailed over the past hundred years.[218a] The likelihood of cooling on a time scale of hundreds to thousands of years, however, does not rule out the possibility of shorter periods of warming superimposed on the long-term trend; if the correlation between sunspot cycles and climate proves out, this combined with accumulating CO_2 could produce such a short-term warming beginning around 1980.[219]

If there is any consensus on the likely overall direction of human influences on climate in the future, it is a shaky one to the effect that the dominant influence is or soon will be in the direction of global warming. The bases for this view are that the increase in carbon dioxide from human activities is global and consistently produces a warming effect, whereas the man-made increase in particles is regional and produces cooling *or* warming, depending on circumstances. That changes in patterns of circulation and the accompanying changes in precipitation and extremes of temperature are more important than changes in mean global temperature cannot be emphasized enough, however. This is why there can be scant consolation in the idea that a man-made warming trend might cancel out a natural cooling trend. Since the different factors producing the two trends do so by influencing different parts of Earth's complicated climatic machinery, it is most unlikely that the associated effects on circulation patterns would cancel each other.

[218a]This conclusion follows not only from casual examination of the place of today's conditions in the pattern of climatic variation over the past million years (see Chapter 2), but it has gained recent support from a very thorough study of the effect on climate of variations in Earth's orbit taking place over time periods of tens of thousands of years (J. D. Hays, J. Imbrie, and N. J. Shackleton, Variations in Earth's orbit: Pacemaker of the ice ages).

[219]Schneider and Mass, Volcanic dusts.

Consequences of climatic change. If climate change is a historical fact and a future inevitability, why worry? The argument is often put forward that people have survived climate change in the past and will continue to do so. Moreover, the argument goes on, if civilization adds its own influences to natural climatic trends, how do we know the result won't be an improvement?

The response to this has several parts. First, to talk merely of survival as a species is to evade the issue of the degree of social disruption and human suffering that have attended regional climatic change in recent history and, presumably, at times in the more distant past. That the drought-induced famine in the Sahel in the early 1970s did not threaten to extinguish the human race is no consolation to the thousands who died. The problems besetting prehistoric human populations in the Northern Hemisphere during the probably rapid onset of the latest ice age can only be imagined, but they must have been severe.

Today, moreover, the absolute magnitude of the human misery that could be caused by climate change is much larger than it ever was because the human populations in virtually all regions of the world are much larger than they were before. Far more people would be affected by any given regional climatic change, and there is not likely to be any room in adjacent regions into which they could flee.

The part of the ecosphere most sensitive to climatic change—that is, the element most easily disrupted to the point of directly influencing human well-being—is agriculture.[220] Farmers know very well that a year's crop can be ruined by rain that comes too early or too late, or in too great quantity or too little, by too much hot weather or too much cold, by early frosts, and by other vagaries of weather. And a small change in average conditions can change the extremes enough (for example) to change the

[220]S. B. Idso, in *Man's impact,* Matthews, Kellogg, and Robinson, eds., pp. 184–191.

length of the growing season substantially. Not surprisingly, then, there is a strong and well-documented connection between weather and agricultural production nationally and worldwide–"good" weather means high yields; "bad" weather means low yields. Furthermore, increased *variability* in weather can be as disruptive of agriculture as changes in mean conditions.[221]

This phenomenon is the reason that *no* rapid change in climate is likely to be an improvement; the crops grown in a given region generally are quite closely adapted to the typical weather pattern—the climate—in that region. Therefore, any significant change tends to be, from the standpoint of growing a particular crop, a change from good weather to bad. Farming practices—time of planting, in particular—are also based on expected weather patterns. Naturally, patterns of agriculture could be modified to follow at least some kinds of climatic change, if the change were gradual enough. Artificially induced climatic change might be quite rapid, however, as indeed some natural changes apparently have been in the past. As discussed in Chapter 7, there is no leeway in the world food situation to absorb a significant climate-induced drop in production over broad areas of the world. Whatever adjustments in crop characteristics and cultivation patterns might *eventually* be made in response to rapid climate change would come too late to save hundreds of millions from famine.

Another, somewhat more speculative respect in which climate change could lead to great increases in human misery is by altering the abundance and the geographical distribution of various disease-producing organisms. As is the case with crops, the degree to which such organisms and the other organisms that transport them (vectors) thrive is governed by such environmental conditions as temperature and moisture, in terms of both averages and extremes. Changes in climatic patterns therefore might give certain of those organisms access to human populations that have no prior evolutionary experience with them and hence little or no resistance to them. Alternatively, such changes might remove checks on the abundance of organisms preexisting in an area, to the extent that a previously minor hazard becomes a plague. (This is true of pathogens that attack crops and trees, as well as those that attack people.)[222]

It is obvious, of course, that sustained climatic change either in the form of a new glaciation or a prolonged warming that involved substantial melting of the Greenland and Antarctic ice sheets would change the pattern of human settlement as well as that of agriculture. The melting of half the volume of present ice sheets would raise sea level by about 40 meters, enough to flood most coastal cities and cover many fertile coastal plains. Such extensive melting would require enormous amounts of energy, however, and so could not occur overnight. If climate changed so drastically that an additional 5 percent of all the solar energy now reaching Earth's surface were absorbed in the melting of ice (compared to the fraction of a percent presently absorbed in summer melting of ice that is restored in winter), sea level would rise about 1.1 meters per year.[223] A climate change great enough to produce this result would damage world agriculture so severely that the effect of the initial change in sea level would hardly be noticed by comparison.

Intentional Modification of Weather and Climate

The idea of influencing the weather intentionally dates back to the rain dances and related rituals of many nontechnological civilizations. Modifying the weather by technological means, however, had its real beginnings in 1946, when it was demonstrated that seeding clouds with dry ice or silver iodide could produce precipitation when none would have occurred naturally. Thirty years later, rainmaking was rather widely practiced in some parts of the world, but many details of its effectiveness and side effects remained controversial. Rainmaking works under some meteorological conditions but not under others; sometimes the attempt may actually pro-

[221]For more extensive discussion and more reviews of recent statistics, see Chapter 7 and Schneider and Mesirow, *The genesis strategy.*

[222]See J. M. May, Influence of environmental transformation in changing the map of disease, in *The careless technology,* Farvar and Milton, eds.; G. H. Hepting, Climate and forest diseases, in *Man's impact,* Matthews, Kellogg, and Robinson, eds., pp. 203–226.

[223]This figure is readily obtained from the following data: heat of melting of ice, 330 megajoules per cubic meter of water produced; area of oceans, 360×10^{12} square meters; solar energy reaching Earth's surface, 2.7×10^{18} megajoules per year.

duce less precipitation than would have occurred naturally. How far downwind of the seeding activity the effects persist is not known, and the genuine possibility of decreasing needed rainfall on neighboring regions (including neighboring nations) poses serious political problems.[224]

Seeding has been used not only to produce rain, but also, under varying circumstances, to dissipate cold fog (by initiating formation of ice crystals that fall out), to suppress hail (by fostering formation of many small particles rather than fewer large ones), and to steer hurricanes and/or weaken the winds associated with them. These measures, too, have the potential for inadvertent side effects and for transferring bad weather to one's neighbors. Indeed, Honduras blamed its disastrous hurricane (Fifi) of 1974 on just such activity by the United States, although there is no evidence to support the claim and the United States weather bureau denied it.

The practice of altering hurricanes contains the remarkable possibility that intentional weather modification on one scale will lead to unintentional climate modification on another. This is so because those tropical storms play a crucial role in the global climatic balance by transporting energy from the warm tropics into the cooler middle latitudes. Systematic disruption of that function would unquestionably produce significant alterations of climate over large regions, in forms not now predictable in detail.

Intentionally modifying not merely the local phenomena that make up the weather, but also the climate over large regions, has been discussed for years. We might hope that the rather primitive state of knowledge concerning climatic machinery and how civilization may unintentionally be modifying it would discourage all groups from any deliberate intervention for a long time to come, but governments and other bodies have all too often shown themselves incapable of sensible restraint. Among the schemes that have been mentioned are: sprinkling soot on the Arctic sea ice to melt it, causing warmer but probably more snowy winters in the Arctic region; damming the Bering Strait, another way of causing the Arctic sea ice to melt; damming the Gulf Stream between Florida and Cuba; and creating a layer of stratospheric dust to counteract global warming due to carbon-dioxide buildup.[225] In all these cases, present knowledge is inadequate to show that the unintended consequences would not exceed the intended ones.

Naturally, the possibility of using weather modification as a weapon has not escaped the notice of military planners. The only known instance of actual use of such techniques, as of 1977, was the use of cloud seeding by the United States in Vietnam between 1967 and 1972. The aim of those operations was to inhibit the movement of troops and supplies along the Ho Chi Minh Trail. The actual physical effect was probably minimal: 5 or 6 centimeters may have been added to the typical monsoon rainfall of about 50 cm.[226] The international political impact of the precedent of American use of weather as a weapon may be much greater.

As understanding of climatic processes increases, the possibilities of misusing the new knowledge for weaponry become more awesome. The possibility of using chemicals to poke holes deliberately in another nation's ozone shield is now obvious enough, and intentional manipulation of storms and droughts does not seem entirely farfetched. Geophysicist Gordon MacDonald has emphasized the possibility that environmental warfare using climate modification could be carried out covertly over a period of years without the victims' being aware of the cause of their misfortunes.[227]

The potential for destruction, both intentional and inadvertent, associated with climatic warfare is second only to that of biological and nuclear war (and even this ranking may eventually prove to be questionable). It is therefore of the greatest importance to outlaw the use of weather- and climate-modification weapons by international agreement, notwithstanding the obvious difficulties of monitoring and enforcement. The Soviet Union and the United States submitted a joint proposal for a

[224]For good introductions to the subject of weather modification, see National Academy of Sciences, *Weather and climate modification: Problems and prospects,* 1966, and *Weather and climate modification: Problems and progress,* 1973, Washington, D.C.

[225]See Kellogg and Schneider, Climate stabilization.

[226]The Vietnam operations and other important elements of military weather modification are described in G. J. F. MacDonald, Weather as a weapon, *Technology Review,* vol. 78, no. 1 (Oct./Nov. 1975), pp. 57–63.

[227]Ibid.

pact prohibiting environmental warfare to the Geneva disarmament talks in August 1975. The pact would rule out "military or other hostile use of environmental modification techniques having widespread, long-lasting or severe effects as the means of destruction, damage, or injury to another state."[228] This wording would preclude not only modification of weather and climate for military purposes, but also the intentional production of earthquakes, tidal waves, and ecological imbalances of various kinds.

THERMONUCLEAR WARFARE

Much has been written, especially by military theoretician Herman Kahn, on the effects of thermonuclear warfare, the possibilities of limited thermonuclear warfare, and so on.[229] Since modern societies seem bent on continuing to prepare for such conflicts, we have little sympathy for those of Kahn's critics who feel that it is immoral to try to analyze the possible results. It would be pleasant (but probably incorrect) to assume that if everyone were aware of the terrible magnitude of the devastation that could result from a nuclear war, the stockpiles of fission and fusion weapons would soon be dismantled. This does not mean that Kahn's analysis is sound—quite the contrary. It has the major flaw of grossly underrating the possible environmental consequences of those projected wars. In addition to the instantaneous slaughter of millions of people and the demolition of property, the effects of any large thermonuclear exchange would inevitably constitute an enormous ecological and genetic disaster—especially for a world already on the edge of nutritional and environmental catastrophe.

Consider the effects that even a rather limited nuclear exchange among the United States, USSR, China, and various European powers would have on the world food supply. Suddenly, international trade would be greatly reduced, and the developed world would be in no position to supply either food or technological aid to the less developed. No more high-yield seed, no more fertilizers, no more grain shipments, no more tractors, no more pumps and well-drilling equipment, trucks, other manufactured products or machines would be delivered. Similarly, the LDCs would not be able to send DCs minerals, petroleum, and food products. The world could be pitched into chaos and massive famine almost immediately, even if most countries were themselves untouched by the nuclear explosions.

But of course no country would be left unscathed. All over the world radiation levels would rise, possibly preventing cultivation of crops in many areas. Blast effects and huge fires burning in the Northern Hemisphere would send large amounts of debris into the atmosphere, conceivably dwarfing the volcanic and pollution effects previously discussed.[230] The entire climate of the Earth could be altered, especially since large holes would probably be punched in the ozone layer. In many areas, where the supply of combustible materials was sufficient, huge fire storms would be generated, some of them covering many hundreds of square kilometers in heavily forested or metropolitan areas.

Something is known about such storms from experience during World War II. On the night of July 27, 1943, Lancaster and Halifax heavy bombers of the British Royal Air Force dropped 2200 metric tons of incendiary and high-explosive bombs on the city of Hamburg. Thousands of individual fires coalesced into a fire storm covering about 15 square kilometers. Flames reached 4500 meters into the atmosphere, and smoke and gases rose to 12,000 meters. Winds, created by huge updrafts and blowing in toward the center of the fire, reached a velocity of more than 240 kilometers per hour. The temperature in the fire exceeded 787° C, high enough to melt aluminum and lead. Air in underground shelters was heated to a point where, when they were opened and oxygen was admitted, flammable materials and even corpses burst into flame. The shelters had to cool for *ten days to two weeks* before rescuers could enter.

Anyone interested in further details of what a *small* fire storm is like is referred to Martin Caidin's excellent book, *The night Hamburg died.*[231] From his account, we

[228]Ibid., p. 63.

[229]Herman Kahn, *On thermonuclear war;* and *On escalation.*

[230]The extent of fires is a matter of some controversy—see W. S. Osburn, Jr., Forecasting long-range ecological recovery from nuclear attack.

[231]Ballantine, New York, 1960. For a literary view, see Kurt Vonnegut's *Slaughterhouse five,* which describes the results of a similar raid on Dresden (Dell, New York, 1971).

can imagine the ecological consequences of generating numerous fire storms and burning off a substantial portion of the Northern Hemisphere. In areas where conditions led to the development of fire storms, the removal of all vegetation would not be the only effect; the soil might be partly or completely sterilized, as well. There would be few plant communities nearby to donate the seeds for rapid repopulation, and rains would wash away the topsoil. Picture what now happens on defoliated California hills during the winter rains, and then imagine the vast loads of silt and radioactive debris being washed from immense bare areas of northern continents into offshore waters, the site of most of the ocean's productivity. Consider the fate of aquatic life, which is especially sensitive to the turbidity of the water, and think of the many offshore oil wells and supertankers that would be destroyed by blast in the vicinity of large cities and left to pour their loads of crude oil into the ocean. Think of the runoff of solvents, fuels, and other chemicals from ruptured storage tanks and pipelines. And radioactivity from nuclear reactors, fuel reprocessing plants, and other nuclear-power facilities would be added to that of the bombs themselves.

Ecosystems would be assaulted as they are assaulted in peacetime (as we have seen, radiation stresses do not differ greatly from others), but the scale of the assault and its rapidity would be unprecedented. Recovery would inevitably be much slower than from other kinds of ecocatastrophes.[232]

The human survivors of any large-scale thermonuclear war would face a severely devastated environment. If a full-scale war were waged in which a substantial portion of United States and Soviet weapons were detonated, most of the survivors would be in the Southern Hemisphere. They would lack many of the tools needed to maintain a modern civilization, since much technology would be irretrievably lost. If the technological structure of society were destroyed, it would be almost impossible for survivors to rebuild it because of resource depletion. Most high-grade ores and rich and accessible fossil-fuel deposits have long since been used up. Technology itself is necessary for access to what remains. Only if enough scrap metals and stored fuel remained available would there be a hope of reconstruction, which would have to begin promptly before those stocks rusted, drained away, or were lost in other ways. Even more serious, banks of plant genetic material would certainly be destroyed or lost through lack of care, making the regeneration of high-yield agriculture difficult or impossible. From what is known of past large disasters, it seems unlikely that survivors, without outside assistance, would be able psychologically to start rapid reconstruction.[233]

If there were extensive use of nuclear weapons in both hemispheres, or if chemical or biological weapons were used simultaneously, the survivors would probably consist of scattered, isolated groups. Such groups would face genetic problems, since each would possess only a small part of humanity's genetic variability and would be subject to a further loss of variability through inbreeding. Studies of human populations have shown that inbreeding increases infant mortality. In addition, it appears that prenatal damage increases linearly with the degree of inbreeding.[234] In such a situation it is problematical whether culturally and genetically deprived groups of survivors could persist in the face of much harsher environmental conditions than they had faced previously. In short, it would not be necessary to kill every individual with blast, fire, radiation, nerve gas, and pathogens in order to force *Homo sapiens* into extinction.

ECOLOGICAL ACCOUNTING

Many existing and potential forms of ecological disruption have been described in this chapter, sometimes in rather technical detail. It may be helpful at this point to summarize the relevance of these considerations to human welfare. In other words, just what could an ecological catastrophe mean for human beings?

The various ways in which the biosphere supports human life were outlined at the beginning of the chapter.

[232]E. P. Odum, Summary, in *Ecological effects of nuclear war,* G. M. Woodwell, ed., pp. 69–72. See also NAS, *Long-term,* which is incomplete and has poorly-thought-through conclusions but contains useful data and bibliographies.

[233]There is a fascinating literature on reactions to and recovery from catastrophes. See A. H. Barton, *Communities in disaster: A sociological analysis of collective stress situations,* especially the last chapter.

[234]L. L. Cavalli-Sforza and W. F. Bodmer, *The genetics of human populations,* W. H. Freeman and Company, San Francisco, 1971.

The loss of one or more of those vital services would kill or seriously impair the health of a significant fraction of the human population. Such a loss could result from any large-scale ecological breakdown, but there are relatively few forms that its human consequences can take. Probably the most likely would be a widespread shortage of food. Such a shortage could result from the disruption of oceanic food webs, from progressive loss of soil fertility or of soil itself, from outbreaks of crop pests brought about by misuse of pesticides, from crop failures initiated by changed climatic conditions or plant diseases attacking vast monocultures, or from a combination of such factors.

Perhaps the second most likely event would be a deterioration of public health resulting from an accumulation of toxic or disease-harboring substances at overloaded links in nutrient cycles (for instance, surface waters overloaded with organic matter or the accumulation of nitrites in groundwater and soil), and including the possibility of epidemic disease.

A third might be a dramatic rise in the incidence of birth defects and cancers, brought about by the individual or combined effects of the array of persistent mutagens and carcinogens that society continues to disperse in the biosphere.

The role of population size and distribution in generating ecological problems has been touched upon here already and is treated more systematically in Chapter 12. A point that should be obvious but that is often overlooked is that population factors can also govern the seriousness of a disruption, once one is underway. For example, it is largely because the growing population has stretched food production to its limits that there is little reserve against temporary crop failures caused by pests, plant disease, or weather variations. The sheer size and density of the human population in many parts of the world helps to make external aid almost impossible in time of local famine or other disaster. Epidemic diseases, on the other hand, can spread more readily through dense populations, especially when malnourishment has made resistance low.

Moreover, as a population grows, a larger portion of its people tend to live in hazardous locations. Biologists have long recognized that the size of a population relative to the area supporting it almost always influences the death rate when disaster strikes. As ecologists H. G. Andrewartha and L. C. Birch state in their classic book, *The distribution and abundance of animals:*

> It is difficult to imagine an area so uniform that all the places where animals may live provide equal protection from the elements, and it is certain that the proportion of animals living in more favorable places would vary with the density of the population. A smaller number is likely to be better protected than a larger number in the same area.[235]

Human beings are no exception. For instance, since the famous 1906 earthquake, a growing proportion of the rapidly increasing population of the San Francisco Bay area has been housed on landfill, on sea cliffs, and even along the fault itself (Figure 11-20). Most of the buildings on landfill and other geologically unstable substrates have not been built to withstand the extraordinary shaking to which such structures are subjected in an earthquake. Geologist R. H. Jahns, discussing this situation, wrote, "The oft-used analogy of a block of Jello on a vibrating platter is grossly simplified but nonetheless reasonable, and assuredly a structure that in effect is built upon the Jello must be designed to accommodate greater dynamic stresses if it is to survive the shaking as effectively as a comparable structure built upon a platter."[236] When the next big earthquake occurs in that overpopulated area, a great many people are likely to die simply because they are living in geologically marginal locations.

On the Ganges delta of Bangladesh, a large, mostly destitute population lives exposed on flat lowland, despite the ever-present danger of climatic disaster for which the region is famous. They live on the delta because there is no room for them elsewhere in grossly overpopulated Bangladesh. In November 1970, some 300,000 people perished when a huge tidal wave driven by a cyclone swept over the delta. Most of the victims would not have died if their land had not been overpopulated. Because of the poverty and overcrowding, evacuation following the flood was impossible. And, because the region was already nutritionally marginal, people

[235]University of Chicago Press, 1954, p. 18.
[236]Geologic jeopardy.

FIGURE 11-20

Development near the San Andreas Fault on the San Francisco Peninsula. The broken white line shows the approximate location of the fault. A manifestation of excessive population density, lack of adequate zoning regulations, and the irresponsibility of developers in the location of homes and schools virtually astride major earthquake faults and on coastal bluffs subject to periodic slides *(left foreground)*. Note homes placed between areas where slides have already occurred. (Photo by William A. Garnett.)

were starving immediately after the disaster. This cataclysm was described as the greatest documented natural disaster in history.[237]

Governmental and other decision-makers, whose job it is to weigh the costs and benefits of alternative courses of action, have rarely given much weight to the considerations discussed in this chapter. In the past, the environmental consequences of human activities have usually not been linked in the minds of policy-makers to the specific kinds of actions (or lack of them) that caused the problems. As environmentalists now strive to bring such costs into society's balance sheets, they find themselves bearing a heavy burden of proof.

After all, say the defenders of the status quo, environmentalists cannot show exactly when or how an ecological disaster will take place, or how many human lives will be lost. Without solid evidence, how is one to act? This point of view is leading society to treat grave risks that are poorly understood as if they were no risks at all. In any balance sheet of costs and benefits, this is faulty accounting. One does not need to know the date of a future flood to avoid building residential developments on floodplains, or the exact magnitude of a possible earthquake to keep nuclear reactors away from major faults. If a risk entails the potential for major impact on human welfare and if actions that increase the risks are identifiable, then it is only prudent to avoid or restrain such actions as far as possible, even when knowledge concerning the risk is incomplete.

Ecological disruption clearly entails such risks, and it is time to shift the burden of proof. Where, for example, are the *benefits* of population growth that justify the ecological risks accompanying it? Despite social, economic, and political barriers to proper ecological accounting, it is urgent and imperative for human society to get the books in order.

[237]Garrett Hardin, Nobody ever dies of overpopulation.

Recommended for Further Reading

Bormann, F. H. 1976. An inseparable linkage: Conservation of natural ecosystems and the conservation of fossil energy. *BioScience,* vol. 26, no. 12 (December), pp. 754–760. A clear, concise statement on the unsung values to society of natural ecosystems and the costs of impairing their functions or destroying them outright. The discussion focuses on forest ecosystems, but the principles involved are much more widely applicable.

De Bach, Paul. 1974. *Biological control by natural enemies.* Cambridge University Press, London. A superb, up-to-date summary. Highly recommended.

Ehrlich, Paul R., John P. Holdren, and Richard W. Holm. *Man and the ecosphere.* W. H. Freeman and Company, San Francisco. Most articles are pertinent to this chapter.

Graham, Frank, Jr. 1970. *Since silent spring.* Fawcett, New York. Details of pesticide controversies.

Marsh, George P. 1874. *The earth as modified by human action.* Scribner's, New York. A great classic.

Rudd, Robert L. 1975. Pesticides. In W. W. Murdoch, ed., *Environment: Resources, pollution and society,* 2d Ed. Sinauer, Sunderland, Mass. A fine summary article.

Schneider, S. H. and L. E. Mesirow. 1976. *The genesis strategy.* Plenum, New York. Excellent discussion of the effects of civilization on climate and how changes thus induced may affect humanity's attempts to support a growing population.

Study of Critical Environmental Problems (SCEP). 1970. *Man's impact on the global environment,* M.I.T. Press, Cambridge, Mass. Good summary, as of 1970, of the state of knowledge of human impact on terrestrial, oceanic, and atmospheric systems, measured against the scale of natural processes.

Woodwell, G. M. 1970. Effects of pollution on the structure and physiology of ecosystems. *Science,* vol. 168, pp. 429–433 (April 24). A classic paper.

———. 1974. Success, succession and Adam Smith. *Bioscience,* February, pp. 81–87. This superb article is a "must" for anyone interested in ecology and the future of humanity.

Additional References

Abel, A. L. 1954. The rotation of weed killers. *Proceedings of British Weed Control Conference,* vol. 2, pp. 249–255. Early report of herbicide resistance.

Abou-Donia, M. B.; M. A. Othman; G. Tantawy; A. Zaki Khalil; and M. F. Shawer. 1974. Neurotoxic effect of leptophos. *Experientia,* vol. 30, pp. 63–64.

Acree, F., Jr.; M. Beroza; and M. C. Borman. 1963. Codistillation of DDT with water. *Agricultural and food chemistry,* vol. 11, pp. 278–280. Important paper about the mobility of DDT.

Ahmed, A. Karim. 1975. Unshielding the sun . . . human effects. *Environment,* vol. 17, pp. 6–14 (April/May).

Almer, B.; W. Dickson; and U. Miller. 1974. Effects of acidification on Swedish lakes. *Ambio,* vol. 3, no. 1, pp. 30–36. Documents the decline in pH in Swedish lakes and the extermination of certain phytoplankton, zooplankton, and fish populations.

Alyea, F.; D. Connold; and R. Prinn. 1975. Stratospheric ozone destruction by aircraft-induced nitrogen oxides. *Science,* vol. 188, pp. 117–127 (April 11).

American Chemical Society. 1969. *Cleaning our environment: The chemical basis for action.* Washington, D.C. Includes good discussion and an extensive bibliography on eutrophication.

Anderson, D. W.; J. R. Jehl, Jr.; R. W. Risebrough; L. H. Woods, Jr.; L. R. Deweese; and W. G. Edgecomb. 1975. Brown pelicans: Improved reproduction off the southern California coast. *Science,* vol. 190, pp. 806–808 (November 21). Breeding improvement related to a decline of DDE in anchovies and therefore in pelican eggs.

Antommari, P.; M. Corn; and L. De Mair. 1965. Airborne particulates in Pittsburgh, association with p,p-DDT. *Science,* vol. 150, pp. 1476–1477 (December 10). Early paper showing presence of DDT in the atmosphere of a city.

Ashton, F. M., and A. S. Crafts. 1973. *Mode of action of herbicides.* Wiley, New York. Up-to-date summary, good bibliographies, technical.

Atkins, E. L.; R. L. Macdonald; and E. A. Greywood-Hale. 1975. Repellant additives to reduce pesticide hazards to honey bees: Field tests. *Environmental Entomology,* vol. 4, pp. 207–210. Describes progress at keeping bees out of treated fields.

Ayers, R. C., Jr.; H. O. Jahns; and J. L. Glaeser. 1974. Oil spills in the Arctic Ocean: Extent of spreading and possibility of large-scale thermal effects. *Science,* vol. 186, pp. 843–844 (November 29). See also comments by S. Martin and W. J. Campbell, immediately following (under same title) on pp. 845–846.

Baker, K. F., and R. J. Cook. 1974. *Biological control of plant pathogens.* W. H. Freeman and Company, San Francisco. The impression is widespread that biological control is useful only against insects. This fine text shows how erroneous that notion is.

Baker, R. 1974. Famine: The cost of development? *The Ecologist,* vol. 4, pp. 170–175 (June). Shows how inappropriate development can accelerate the deterioration of arid lands.

Barber, R.; A Vijayakumar; and F. Cross. 1972. Mercury concentrations in recent and ninety-year-old benthopelagic fish. *Science,* vol. 178, pp. 636–639 (November 10). Gives entry to the literature on mercury in deep-sea fishes and also reports DDT and DDE in those fishes.

Barrett, G. W. 1968. The effects of an acute insecticide stress on a semienclosed grassland ecosystem. *Ecology,* vol. 49, pp. 1014–1035. Although the carbamate used became inactive in a few days, long-term effects on the decomposition of litter, the density and diversity of arthropods, and reproduction in mammals were reported.

Barton, A. H. 1969. *Communities in disaster: A sociological analysis of collective stress situations.* Doubleday, Garden City, N.Y. Analyses of individual and social responses to disasters such as the Irish potato famine, Hiroshima, the 1953 Dutch flood, and tornadoes.

Battan, E. S. 1966. *The effects of nuclear war on the weather and climate.* The Rand Corp., Santa Monica, Calif., RM-4989-TAB. Says enough is not known for accurate prediction of effects—a situation that still prevails.

Bazzaz, F. A.; R. W. Carlson; and G. L. Rolfe. 1974. The effect of heavy metals on plants. Pt. 1, Inhibition of gas exchange in sunflowers by Pb, Ca, Mi, and T1. *Environmental Pollution,* vol. 7, pp. 241–246. Lead, cadmium, nickel, and thallium inhibit photosynthesis in detached sunflower leaves.

Beamish, R. J.; W. L. Lockhart; J. C. Van Loon; and H. H. Harvey. 1975. Long-term acidification of a lake and resulting effects on fishes. *Ambio,* vol. 4, pp. 98–102. Documents the reproductive failure of some species and the complete disappearance of others in a Canadian lake, coincident with a steady drop in the lake's pH.

Beeton, A. M. 1973. Man's effects on the Great Lakes. In *Environmental quality and water development,* C. R. Goldman; J. McEvoy, III; and P. J. Richerson, eds. W. H. Freeman and Company, San Francisco, pp. 250–280. Comprehensive review of eutrophication and other problems in the Great Lakes.

Bennington, S. L.; P. G. Connors; C. W. Connors; and R. W. Risebrough. 1975. Patterns of chlorinated hydrocarbon contamination in New Zealand, sub-Antarctic, and coastal marine birds. *Environmental Pollution,* vol. 8, pp. 135–147. DDE concentration in a falcon egg from the sub-Antarctic, sufficiently high to cause shell-thinning.

Berger, R., and W. F. Libby. 1969. Equilibration of atmospheric carbon dioxide with sea water: Possible enzymatic control of the rate. *Science,* vol. 164, pp. 1395–1397 (June 20). Illustrates the complexity of the role played by the ocean in regulating the carbon dioxide content of the atmosphere.

Berwick, Stephen. 1976. The Gir forest: An endangered ecosystem. *American Scientist,* vol. 64, pp. 28–40. An exceptionally interesting article describing the intricate problems involving people, domestic animals, and wild animals that must be solved if this important semiarid ecosystem is to be preserved (it is the last redoubt of the Asian lion).

Bitman, J.; H. C. Cecil; S. J. Harris; and G. F. Frees. 1969. DDT induces a decrease in eggshell calcium. *Nature,* vol. 224, pp. 44–46. Experiments with Japanese quail.

Black, C. A. 1968. *Soil-plant relationships,* 2d ed. Wiley, New York. Technical and comprehensive.

Blumer, M. 1972. Submarine seeps: Are they a major source of open ocean oil pollution? *Science,* vol. 176, pp. 1257–1258 (June 16).

Blus, L. J.; B. S. Neely, Jr.; A. A. Belisle; and R. M. Prouty. 1974. Organochlorine residues in brown pelican eggs: Relation to reproductive success. *Environmental Pollution,* vol. 7, pp. 81–91. DDE seemed primarily responsible for nest failure, but the effects were confounded with those from dieldrin.

Boeck, W. L.; D. T. Shaw; B. Vonnegut. 1975. Possible consequences of global dispersion of ^{85}Kr. *Bulletin of the American Meteorological Society,* vol. 56, pp. 527ff (May). Accumulation of krypton-85 in the atmosphere due to nuclear power operations could reduce resistance between ocean and atmosphere by 15 percent by the year 2025, as a result of increased ionization. This might cause changes in climate.

Boesch, D. F.; C. H. Herschner; and J. H. Milgram. 1974. *Oil spills and marine environment.* Ballinger, Cambridge, Mass. This useful summary provides access to most of the pertinent literature.

Boffey, Philip M. 1975. Nuclear war: Federation disputes Academy on how bad effects would be. *Science,* vol. 190, pp. 248–250 (October 17). Critique of National Academy of Sciences, *Long-term world-wide effects of multiple nuclear-weapons detonations.*

Bormann, F. H.; G. E. Likens; D. W. Fisher; and R. S. Pierce. 1968. Nutrient loss accelerated by clear-cutting of a forest ecosystem. *Science,* vol. 159, pp. 882–884 (February 23). Shows an accelerated nutrient loss in cutover ecosystems.

Bormann, F. H; G. E. Likens; T. Siccama; R. Pierce; and J. Eaton. 1974. The export of nutrients and the recovery of stable conditions following deforestation at Hubbard Brook. *Ecological Monographs,* vol. 44, pp. 255–277.

Borthwick, P. W.; T. W. Duke; A. J. Wilson, Jr.; J. I. Lowe; J. M. Patrick, Jr.; and J. C. Oberheu. 1973. Accumulation and movement of Mirex in selected estuaries of South Carolina, 1969–71. *Pesticides Monitoring Journal,* vol. 7, pp. 6–26.

Bourne, W. R. P. 1976. Seabirds and pollution. In R. Johnston, ed., *Marine pollution,* pp. 403–502. Data on types of pollution and their effects in different areas and on different types of birds. Includes interesting accounts of individual pollution incidents.

Box, T. W.; R. F. Hadley; and M. G. Wolman, eds. 1974. *Rehabilitation potential of western coal lands.* Ballinger, Cambridge, Mass. Comprehensive and up-to-date.

Brown, M. 1975. An orange is an orange. *Environment,* vol. 17, July/August, pp. 6–11. Pesticide abuses in a campaign against cosmetic pests of California oranges, the citrus thrips.

Brown, W. L., Jr. 1961. Mass insect control programs: Four case histories. *Psyche,* vol. 68, pp. 75–111. A distinguished entomologist and population biologist evaluates attempts to control the fire ant, the gypsy moth, the Mediterranean fruit fly, and the screwworm.

Bryson, R. A. 1973. Drought in Sahelia: Who or what is to blame? *The Ecologist,* vol. 3, (October), pp. 366–371. Popular summary of Bryson's theory of the meteorological factors contributing to the failure of the monsoons in the late 1960s and early 1970s.

———. 1974. A perspective on climatic change. *Science,* vol. 184, pp. 753–760 (May 17). Significant changes in climate can result from small changes in the governing variables. The role of man-made atmospheric particles and carbon dioxide is reviewed and found significant.

———, and T. J. Murray. 1977. *Climates of hunger.* University of Wisconsin Press, Madison. An important overview of climatic change.

——— and W. M. Wendland. 1975. Climatic effects of atmospheric pollution. In *The changing global environment,* S. F. Singer, ed. Reidel, Dordrecht, Netherlands, pp. 139–147. Summarizes the case for believing man-made carbon dioxide and particles to be important factors in climate variations since 1940.

Budyko, M. I. 1974. *Climate and life.* Academic Press, New York. Outstanding text by one of the world's most respected figures in climatology.

Burgess, H. D., and N. W. Hussey, eds. 1971. *Microbial control of insects and mites.* Academic Press, New York. Comprehensive, technical. A wide range of subjects, including resistance, interactions between pathogens, propogation, and economics.

Burnett, Robin. 1971. DDT residues: Distribution of concentrations in *Emerita analoga* (Stimpson) along coastal California. *Science,* vol. 174, pp. 606–608 (November 5). Shows a concentration much higher near the outfall of a DDT-manufacturing plant than in an agricultural runoff area.

Burns, N. M.; J.-M. Jaquet; A. L. W. Kemp; D. C. L. Lam; J. H. Leach; M. Munawar; T. J. Simons; P. G. Sly; R. L. Thomas; N. H. F. Watson; and J. D. H. Williams. 1976. Processes within Lake Erie. *Journal of the Fisheries Research Board of Canada,* vol. 33, pp. 639–643 (March). Summarizes an issue devoted entirely to the condition of Lake Erie.

Bush, G. L. 1975. Genetic variation in natural insect populations and its bearing on mass-rearing programmes. In *Controlling fruit flies by the sterile-insect technique.* International Atomic Energy Agency, Vienna, pp. 9–17, IAEA-PL-582/2. Describes large genetic changes due to domestication of the flies.

——— and R. W. Neck. 1976. Ecological genetics of the screwworm fly, *Cochliomya hominivorax* (Diptera: Calliphoridae) and its bearing on the quality control of mass reared insects. *Journal of Environmental Entomology,* in press. Up-to-date report on genetic differences between mass-reared and wild strains, showing important differences in loci involved in producing enzymes critical to flight activity.

———; R. W. Neck; and G. B. Kitto. 1976. Screwworm eradication: Inadvertent selection for noncompetitive ecotypes during mass rearing. *Science,* vol. 193, pp. 491–493 (August 6). More on the problems of rearing sterile males to compete with wild ones.

Butler, P. A. 1969. The significance of DDT residues in estuarine fauna. In *Chemical fallout: Current research on persistent pesticides,* W. M. Miller and G. G. Berg, eds, Charles C. Thomas, Springfield, Ill., pp. 205–218. Contains information on ability of oysters to concentrate DDT.

——— and P. T. Spruger. 1963. Pesticides: A new factor in coastal environments. In *Transactions of the twenty-eighth North American wildlife and natural resources conference,* pp. 378–390. Summary, with good bibliography of papers.

Byerly, T. C. 1975. Nitrogen compounds used in crop production. In *The changing global environment,* S. F. Singer, ed. Reidel, Dordrecht, Netherlands, pp. 377–382. Reprint of 1970 analysis with short update.

Cade, T. J.; J. L. Lincer; C. M. White; D. G. Rosenau; and L. G. Swartz. 1971. DDE residues and eggshell changes in Alaskan falcons and hawks. *Science,* vol. 172, pp. 955–957 (May 28). Shows a strong relationship between DDE content and eggshell-thinning.

Cairns, John, Jr. 1974. Indicator species vs. the concept of community structure as an index of pollution. *Water Resources Bulletin,* vol. 10, pp. 338–346. A general discussion.

———, J. W. Hall, E. L. Morgan, R. E. Sparks, W. T. Waller, and G. F. Westlake. 1973. *The development of an automated biological monitoring system for water quality.* Virginia Water Resources Research Center, Blacksburg, bulletin 51. Describes a system that continuously monitors breathing and swimming activity of fishes exposed to effluent.

Cairns, J. Jr.; G. R. Lanza; and B. C. Parker. 1972. Pollution related structural and functional changes in aquatic communities with emphasis on freshwater algae and protozoa. *Proceedings of the Academy of Natural Sciences of Philadelphia,* vol. 124, pp. 79–127. A comprehensive review with a fine bibliography.

Cairns, J. Jr.; R. E. Sparks; and W. T. Waller. 1973. The use of fish as sensors in industrial waste lines to prevent fish kills. *Hydrobiologia,* vol. 41, pp. 151–167. Cairns and his group have done much pioneering work on the biological monitoring of water pollution, of which this paper is just one example. See also R. E. Sparks; J. Cairns, Jr.; and A. G. Heath, The use of bluegill breathing rates to detect zinc.

Calder, Nigel, ed. 1968. *Unless peace comes.* Viking, New York. Effects of future weapons systems.

Campbell, Ian. 1974. Human mismanagement as a major factor in the Sahelian drought tragedy: Diagnosis of a famine. *The Ecologist,* vol. 4, pp. 164–169 (June). Discusses how "even before the drought took its toll the animal and human population of the Sahel was outstripping its food production."

Campbell, W. J., and S. Martin. 1973. Oil and ice in the Arctic Ocean: Possible large-scale interactions. *Science,* vol. 181, pp. 56–58 (July 6). Slow rate of biodegradation gives oil time to spread over large areas, reducing the reflectivity of sea ice.

Carefoot, G. L., and E. R. Sprott. 1967. *Famine on the wind.* Rand McNally, Chicago. On plant diseases (see especially material on the Irish potato famine).

Carlson, C. A., Jr. 1971. Impact of waste heat on aquatic ecology. In *Power generation and environmental change,* D. A. Berkowitz and A. M. Squires, eds. M.I.T. Press, Cambridge, Mass., pp. 351–364. Good survey of the effects of waste heat discharged to water.

Carson, Rachel. 1962. *Silent spring.* Houghton Mifflin, Boston. This classic, thought to be alarmist by many when it was published, now appears to have understated the pesticide problem in some respects.

Casida, J. E., R. A. Gray, H. Tilles. 1974. Thiocarbamate sulfoxides: potent, selective, and biodegradable herbicides. *Science,* vol. 184, pp. 573–574 (3 May).

CEQ. *See* Council on Environmental Quality.

Chambers, D. L., R. T. Cunningham, R. W. Lichty, and R. B. Thrailkill, 1974. Pest control by attractants: a case study demonstrating economy, specificity, and environmental acceptability. *BioScience,* vol. 24, pp. 150–152. Describes work on fruit flies (Tephritidae), with emphasis on the oriental fruit fy, *Dacus dorsalis.*

Charney, J., P. H. Stone, and W. J. Quirk. 1975. Drought in the Sahara: A biogeophysical feedback mechanism. *Science,* vol. 187, pp. 434–435 (February 7).

Chýlek, P., and J. Coakley. 1974. Aerosols and climate. *Science,* vol. 183, pp. 75–77 (January 11). Demonstrates that particles can cause atmospheric heating as well as cooling.

Cicerone, R. J.; R. S. Stolarski; and S. Waters. 1974. Stratospheric ozone destruction by man-made chlorofluoromethanes. *Science,* vol. 185, pp. 1165–1167 (September 27). Establishes importance of chlorofluorocarbons as a threat to ozone.

Clark, John R. 1969. Thermal pollution and aquatic life. *Scientific American,* March. (*Scientific American* offprint 1135, W. H. Freeman and Company, San Francisco.)

Cloudsley-Thompson, J. L. 1974. The expanding Sahara. *Environmental Conservation,* vol. 1, spring, pp. 5–13. Interesting ecological summary article emphasizing role of human impact in expansion.

Coan, Gene. 1971. Oil pollution. *Sierra Club Bulletin,* March, pp. 13–16. Discussion of the immediate and long-term effects of oil pollution on marine life by a marine biologist. Good bibliography.

Coello, W.; Z. A. Saleem; and M. A. Q. Khan. 1974. Ecological effects of lead in auto-exhaust. In *Survival in toxic environments,* M. Khan and J. Bederka, eds. Academic Press, New York. Details on concentrations and toxicities.

Cole, LaMont C. 1966. Complexity of pest control in the environment. In *Scientific aspects of pest control.* National Academy of Sciences-National Research Council, Washington, D.C., publication 1402.

Colton, J. B., Jr.; F. D. Knopp; and B. R. Burns. 1974. Plastic particles in surface waters of the northwestern Atlantic. *Science,* vol. 185, pp. 491–497 (August 9). Detailed review. At the moment, the threat from plastics appears to be minor compared to that from other pollutants.

Commoner, Barry. 1967. *Science and survival.* Viking, New York. Technology and survival (see especially the material on the ecological effects of thermonuclear war).

———. 1975. Threats to the integrity of the nitrogen cycle: Nitrogen compounds in soil, water, atmosphere, and precipitation. In *The changing global environment,* S. F. Singer, ed. Reidel, Dordrecht, Netherlands, pp. 340–366. Somewhat controversial assessment, reprinted without change from 1970 version.

Connor, J. A.; D. G. Parberg; and W. Strauss. 1974. The effects of phytotoxic gases on native Australian plant species. Pt. 1, Acute effects of sulphur dioxide. *Environmental Pollution,* vol. 7, pp. 7–23. Sensitivity varies from species to species.

Constable, J. D.; R. E. Cosk; M. Meselson; and A. H. Westing. 1974. AAAS and NAS herbicide reports. *Science,* vol. 186, pp. 584–585 (November 15). Points out great similarities, although the American Association for the Advancement of Science thought damage to inland forests was greater.

Cooke, A. S. 1973. Shell-thinning in avian eggs by environmental pollutants. *Environmental Pollution,* vol. 4, pp. 85–157. A fine review with a superb bibliography (see especially the "note added in proof" on a recent controversy about the source of shell-thinning).

Cooper, D. F., and W. C. Jolly. 1969. *Ecological effects of weather modification.* University of Michigan, School of Natural Resources, Ann Arbor. This report, sponsored by the United States Department of the Interior, is an excellent, balanced summary of possible consequences of purposeful weather modification and contains much material related to the effects of gradual climatic change. Good bibliography.

Cope, O. B. 1971. Interactions between pesticides and wildlife. *Annual Review of Entomology,* vol. 16, pp. 325–364. Complementary to D. Pimentel, *Ecological effects of pesticides on non-target species.* Arrangement is according to effects.

Corbett, J. R. 1974. *The biochemical mode of action of pesticides.* Academic Press, London and New York. An excellent source for pesticide structures and physiological effects—technical but readable.

Cory, L.; P. Fjeld; and W. Serat. 1970. Distribution patterns of DDT residues in the Sierra Nevada mountains. *Pesticides monitoring journal,* vol. 3, pp. 204–211. Pollution far from sources.

Cottam, Clarence. 1965. The ecologist's role in problems of pesticide pollution. *BioScience,* vol. 15, pp. 457–462.

Coulson, J. C.; J. R. Deans; G. R. Potts; J. Robinson; and A. N. Crabtree. 1972. Changes in organochlorine contamination of the marine environment of eastern Britain monitored by shag eggs. *Nature,* vol. 236, pp. 454–456 (April 28). Shows reduction.

Council for Agricultural Science and Technology. 1976. *Effect of increased nitrogen fixation on stratospheric ozone.* Report no 53. Iowa State University, Ames, Iowa. Report of an interdisciplinary scientific task force, containing critical review of magnitude of anthropogenic nitrogen fixation compared to natural processes and alternative estimates of ozone depletion from increased atmospheric N_2O.

Council on Environmental Quality (CEQ). 1970. Ocean dumping. Report to the president, Government Printing Office, Washington, D.C. Analyzes present and anticipated trends in ocean dumping of wastes and recommends the formulation of a national policy for regulation.

———. 1971. *Environmental quality: Second annual report.* Government Printing Office, Washington, D.C. This report concentrates on the costs of environmental protection—what is spent now and what will be needed in the future. Subsequent annual volumes are goldmines of information on topics covered in this chapter.

Cowell, E. B. 1976 Oil pollution of the sea. In R. Johnston, ed., *Marine pollution,* pp. 353–401. Concludes that added cancer risks from oil in seafoods must be very low, and that ecosystemic effects are likely to be much less than those of other pollutants such as heavy metals and chlorinated hydrocarbons.

Cox, James L. 1970. DDT residues in marine phytoplankton: Increase from 1955 to 1969. *Science,* vol. 170, pp. 71–73 (October 2).

Crutzen, P. J. 1970. The influence of nitrogen oxides on the atmospheric ozone content. *Quarterly Journal of the British Meteorological Society,* vol. 96, pp. 320–325. One of the pioneering papers in uncovering the threat to ozone.

———. 1974. Estimates of possible variations in total ozone due to natural causes and human activities. *Ambio,* vol. 3, no. 2, pp. 201–210. Quantitative results for ozone reduction caused by nuclear war, SSTs, Freons, and nitrogen fertilizer. An important and thorough paper.

Davidson, G. 1974. *Genetic control of insect pests.* Academic Press, New York. A good, brief review.

Davis, J. B., and R. L. Barnes. 1973. Effects of soil-applied fluoride and lead on growth of loblolly pine and red maple. *Environmental Pollution,* vol. 5, pp. 35–44. Both toxins reduced growth of seedlings.

De Bach, Paul, ed. 1964. *Biological control of insect pests and weeds.* Reinhold, New York. Covers one of the components of integrated control.

Diamond, Jared M. 1975. The island dilemma: Lessons of modern biogeographic studies for the design of natural reserves. *Biological Conservation,* vol. 7, pp. 129–146. Applies the theory of island biogeography to understanding the number of species a system of reserves can support, what will happen with various patterns of habitat destruction, and what geometrical patterns of reserves would maximize the preservation of species.

Doane, Robert R. 1957. *World Balance Sheet.* Harper, New York. Source of data on land classification.

Dochinger, L. S., and C. E. Seliskar. 1970. Air pollution and the chlorotic dwarf disease of Eastern white pine. *Forest Science,* vol. 16, pp. 46–55. This serious disorder is caused by ozone and sulfur dioxide, singly and in combination.

Dorst, Jean. 1970. *Before nature dies.* Wm. Collins Sons, London. A very interesting popular treatment of many of the topics discussed in this chapter.

Dugan, P. R. 1972. *Biochemical ecology of water pollution.* Plenum, New York. Brief, highly readable, well done. (Available in paperback, 1975).

Eckholm, E. P. 1975. Desertification: A world problem. *Ambio,* vol. 4, no. 4, pp. 137–145. Calls for a radical transformation of life in the edges of deserts.

———. 1976. *Losing ground: Environmental stress and world food prospects.* Norton, New York. A fine popular treatment, indicative of a growing awareness of the ecological constraints on agriculture among nonecologists. Chapter 4 on desertification is especially relevant to this chapter.

Edwards, Clive A. 1969. Soil pollutants and soil animals. *Scientific American,* April. (*Scientific American* offprint 1138, W. H. Freeman and Company, San Francisco.)

Egler, F. E. 1964. Pesticides—in our ecosystem. *American Scientist,* vol. 52, pp. 110–136. An outspoken ecologist discusses the problems of getting ecologically sophisticated control of pests.

——— and S. R. Foote. 1975. *The plight of the rightofway domain.* 2 vols. Futura Media Service, Mt. Kisco, N.Y. Offbeat but most interesting discussion of the mismanagement of the vegetation on more than 200 million hectares in the United States along the sides of highways and railheads, under electric transmission lines, and the like. Notes the "six principles of intelligent management."

Ehrlich, Paul R., and L. E. Gilbert. 1973. Population structure and dynamics of the tropical butterfly *Heliconius ethilla. Biotropica,* vol. 5, pp. 69–82. Shows how relatively large areas of forest are necessary for the persistence of some insect populations.

Eigner, Joseph. 1975. Unshielding the sun . . . environmental effects. *Environment,* vol. 17 (April/May), pp. 15–18. Potential effects of ozone depletion on phytoplankton, insects, DNA.

Eisner, T.; L. B. Hendry; D. B. Peakall; and J. Meinwald. 1971. 2,5-Dichlorophenol (from ingested herbicide?) in defensive secretion of grasshopper. *Science,* vol. 172, pp. 277–278 (April 16). Evidence that grasshoppers ingest herbicide and use it to defend themselves against other insects.

Epstein, Samuel S. 1970. NTA. *Environment,* vol. 12, no. 7, pp. 3–11. On nitrilotriacetic acid as a substitute for phosphorus in detergents.

———. 1972. Toxicological and environmental implications of the use of nitrilotriacetic acid as a detergent builder. 2 pts. *International Journal of Environmental Studies,* vol. 2, pp. 291–300, and vol. 3, pp. 13–21. More on NTA.

Fabacher, D. L., and H. Chambers. 1974. Resistance to herbicides in insecticide resistant mosquitofish, *Gambusia affinis. Environmental Letters,* vol. 7, pp. 15–20. First instance of fishes' becoming resistant to herbicides entering water from treated fields.

Farvar, M. T., and J. P. Milton, eds. 1972. *The careless technology: Ecology and international development.* Natural History Press, Garden City, N.Y. A wide diversity of articles on human assaults on ecosystems in LDCs. Some articles now dated (they are based on conference papers given in 1968).

Fimreite, N.; W. Holsworth; J. Keith; P. Pearce; and I. Gruchy. 1971. Mercury in fish and fish-eating birds near sites of industrial contamination in Canada. *Canadian Field Naturalist,* vol. 85, pp. 211–220. Mercury concentrations in fishes and fish-eating birds positively correlated with trophic level.

Fisher, J.; N. Simon; and J. Vincent. 1969. *Wildlife in danger.* Viking, New York. A comprehensive summary of the state of endangered species of vertebrate animals and plants. Readable and well illustrated.

Fisher, N. S.; E. J. Carpenter; C. C. Remsen; and C. F. Wurster. 1974. Effects of PCB on interspecific competition in natural and gnotobiotic phytoplankton communities in continuous and batch cultures. *Microbial Ecology,* vol. 1, pp. 39–50. Toxicity of PCBs to a diatom greatest when it was in competition with other species.

Fletcher, W. W. 1974. *The pest war.* Wiley, New York. Despite its ecological naiveté, this book contains some useful information.

Flohn, Hermann. 1969. *Climate and weather.* McGraw-Hill, New York. A fine summary.

Foster, G. G.; M. J.Whitten; T. Prout; and R. Gill. 1972. Chromosome rearrangements for the control of insect pests. *Science,* vol. 176, pp. 875–880 (May 26). Describes possible use of insect strains with compound chromosomes (artificially produced chromosomes with two homologous arms attached to the same centromere) to control pest populations.

Frink, C. 1967. Nutrient budget: Rational analysis of eutrophication in a Connecticut lake. *Environmental Science Technology,* vol. 1, p. 425. Technical investigation of nitrogen and phosphorus concentrations in bottom sediments.

Frost, Justin. 1969. Earth, air, water. *Environment,* vol. 11, pp. 14–33. Discusses the major role of the atmosphere in distributing chlorinated hydrocarbons.

Frost, P. G. H.; W. R. Siegfried; and J. Cooper. 1976. Conservation of the jackass penguin [*Spheniscus demersus* (L.)]. *Biological Conservation,* vol. 9, pp. 79–99. Oil pollution is just one of several factors leading to decline of this species.

Garrels, R. M.; F. T. Mackenzie; and C. Hunt. 1975. *Chemical cycles and the global environment,* Kaufmann, Los Altos, Calif. Concise, quantitative treatment of origins and fates of chlorinated hydrocarbons and petroleum in the global environment.

Georghiou, G. P. 1971. Resistance of insects and mites to insecticides and acaricides and the future of pesticide chemicals. In *Agricultural chemicals,* J. E. Swift, ed. University of California, Division of Agricultural Sciences, Berkeley, pp. 112–124.

Gibbons, J. W., and R. R. Sharitz. 1974. Thermal alteration of aquatic ecosystems. *American Scientist,* vol. 62, pp. 660–670 (November/December). Response of aquatic communities to particularly intense thermal loadings.

———, (eds.) 1974. *Thermal ecology.* USAEC, Technical Information Center, Springfield, Va. A wide-ranging symposium on the responses of organisms and communities to thermal stress. See especially papers by McKenny and Dean and Thatcher on combinations of thermal and heavy-metals stresses, and Stearney et al. on the effects of thermal stress on nonaquatic elements of each.

Giese, R. L.; R. M. Peart; and R. T. Huber. 1975. Pest management. *Science,* vol. 187, pp. 1040–1052 (March 21). Useful introductory discussion and description of systems approach to control of alfalfa pest.

Gilmour, C. M., and O. N. Allen, eds. 1965. *Microbiology and soil fertility.* Oregon State University Press, Corvallis.

Glass, Bentley. 1962. The biology of nuclear war. *American Biology Teacher,* vol. 24, pp. 407–425 (October). An early evaluation of the possible results of nuclear war.

Goldberg, E. G. 1972. *A guide to marine pollution.* Gordon and Breach, New York. Chapters on halogenated hydrocarbons, petroleum, organic and inorganic chemicals, nutrients, suspended solids, radioactivity, test organisms and monitoring systems.

Goodland, R. J. A., and H. S. Irwin. 1975. *Amazon jungle: Green hell to red desert.* American Elsevier, New York. Summarizes history, biota, ecology, ethnology of Amazonia and possible repercussions of its development.

Gordon, A. G., and E. Gorham. 1963. Ecological aspects of air pollution from an iron-sintering plant at Wawa, Ontario. *Canadian Journal of Botany,* vol. 41, pp. 1063–1078. Detailed study of a severe localized air pollution problem.

Graham, Frank, Jr. 1966. *Disaster by default: Politics and water pollution.* M. Evans, New York.

Grobecker, A.; S. Coroniti; and R. Cannon. 1974. *The effects of stratospheric pollution by aircraft.* Technical Information Service, Department of Transportation, Springfield, Va., DOT-TST-75-50. Written obscurely enough to be widely misinterpreted as reassuring on the effects of a fleet of SSTs. It actually confirms the seriousness of the threat to ozone by a large fleet.

Groth, E. III. 1975. Increasing the harvest. *Environment,* January/February. A fine review article with much material on the ecological cost of agriculture. The bibliography is most useful, especially the references on crop losses.

Gruener, N., and R. Toeplitz. 1975. The effect of changes in nitrate concentration in drinking water on methemoglobin levels in infants. *International Journal of Environmental Studies,* vol. 7, pp. 161–163.

Guenzi, W. D., ed. 1974. *Pesticides in soil and water.* Soil Science Society of America, Madison, Wis. Deals with many technical aspects of pesticide behavior in soil and surface water.

Gwynne, Peter. 1976. Doomed jungles? *International Wildlife,* July/August, pp. 36–47. Fine article on the values of tropical forests, now rapidly being destroyed.

Hallsworth, E. G., and W. A. Adams. 1973. The heavy metal content of rainfall in the East Midlands. *Environmental Pollution,* vol. 4, pp. 231–235. Soils of England's midlands are receiving regular additions of lead, vanadium, manganese, chromium, nickel, copper, and molybdenum from rain.

Hamelink, J. L.; R. C. Waybrant; and R. C. Ball. 1971. A proposal: Exchange equilibria control the degree chlorinated hydrocarbons are biologically magnified in lentic environments. *Transactions, American Fisheries Society,* vol. 100, pp. 207–214. Describes exchanges between water and fat.

Hammond, Allen, L. 1971. Phosphate replacements: problems with the washday miracle. *Science,* vol. 172, pp. 361–363 (April 23).

——— and T. H. Maugh, II. 1974. Stratospheric pollution: Multiple threats to Earth's ozone. *Science,* vol. 186, pp. 335–338 (October 25). Concise summary of relevant reactions and potential consequences.

Haney, A., and R. L. Lipsey. 1973. Accumulation and effects of methyl mercury hydroxide in a terrestrial food chain under laboratory conditions. *Environmental Pollution,* vol. 5, pp. 305–316. Significant effects on both plants and the aphids feeding on them; high concentrations.

Hanson, W. C. 1967. Cesium-137 in Alaskan lichens, caribou and eskimos. *Health Physics,* vol. 13, pp. 383–389. Classic paper showing concentration by food chains.

Haque, R., and V. H. Freed, eds. 1975. *Environmental dynamics of pesticides.* Plenum, New York. Contains a number of important review articles. Highly technical.

Hardin, Garrett. 1971. Nobody ever dies of overpopulation. *Science,* vol. 171, p. 527 (February 12). A hard-hitting editorial pointing out the relationship of large population size with high death rates.

Harper, J. 1956. Ecological aspects of weed control. *Outlook on agriculture,* vol. 1, pp. 197–205. An early paper predicting the development of resistance to herbicides by weeds.

———. 1956. The evolution of weeds in relation to herbicides. *Proc. British Weed Control Conference,* vol. 3, pp. 179–188. A basic source on the potential for the evolution of herbicide-resistance.

Harriss, R. C.; D. B. White; and R. B. McFarlane. 1970. Mercury compounds reduce photosynthesis by plankton. *Science,* vol. 170, pp. 736–737 (November 13).

Hart, C. W., Jr., and S. L. H. Fuller, eds. 1974. *Pollution ecology of freshwater invertebrates.* Academic Press, New York. Arranged by organism; technical.

Harvey, G. R.; H. P. Miklas; V. T. Bowen; and W. G. Steinhauer. 1974. Observations on the distribution of chlorinated hydrocarbons in Atlantic Ocean organisms. *Journal of Marine Research,* vol. 32, pp. 103–118. Data do not support food-chain magnification.

Harward, M., and M. Treshow. 1975. Impact of ozone on the growth and reproduction of understory plants in the aspen zone of western U.S.A. *Environmental Conservation,* vol. 2, pp. 17–23. Significant effects found at 15 pphm and lower.

Harwood, R. F. 1975. Economics, esthetics, environment and entomologists: The tussock moth dilemma. *Environmental Entomology,* vol. 4, pp. 171–174. Interesting account of the battle over the use of DDT.

Hasler, Arthur, D. 1975. Man-induced eutrophication of lakes. In *The changing global environment,* S. F. Singer, ed. Reidel, Dordrecht, Netherlands, pp. 383–399. Reprint of an excellent 1970 survey.

Hay, Edwards. 1970. Smog, the quiet killer. *American Forests,* vol. 76, April, pp. 16–19. Contains statistics on smog damage to San Bernardino National Forest.

Hays, J. D.; John Imbrie; and N. J. Shackleton. 1976. Variations in the Earth's orbit: Pacemaker of the ice ages. *Science,* vol. 194, pp. 1121–1132 (10 December). Studies of ocean floor sediments laid down over a period of almost half a million years reveal that much of the climatic variation during this span of time took place in phase with changes in Earth's orbit having periods of 23,000, 42,000 and 100,000 years. The prognosis, based on these orbital changes and ignoring anthropogenic influences, is for extensive Northern Hemisphere glaciation in the next several thousand years.

Hazeltine, W. 1972. Disagreement on why brown pelican eggs are thin. *Nature,* vol. 239, pp. 410–411. Incorrectly disputes relationship between DDT and breeding failures in birds. (See also J. L. Lincer, DDD-induced eggshell-thinning in the American kestrel.)

Heath, R. G.; J. W. Sparn; and J. F. Kreitzer. 1969. Marked DDE impairment of mallard reproduction in controlled studies. *Nature,* vol. 224, pp. 47–48.

Hedgpeth, J. W. 1973. Protection of environmental quality in estuaries. In *Environmental quality and water development,* C. R. Goldman; J. McEvoy, III; and P. J. Richerson, eds. W. H. Freeman and Company, San Francisco, pp. 233–249. Thermal, chemical, and landfill effects.

Hendry, Peter. 1970. Who's afraid of advanced technology? *Ceres,* July/August, pp. 45–48. On integrated pest-control.

Henriksson, K.; E. Karppanen; and M. Helminen. 1966. High residue of mercury in Finnish white-tailed eagles. *Ornis Fennica,* vol. 43, pp. 38–45. High levels reported in this and the following paper strongly indicate food-chain concentration.

———. 1969. The amounts of mercury in seals from lakes and seas. *Nordisk Hygienisk Tidskrift,* vol. 50, pp. 54–59.

Hess, W. N., ed. 1974. *Weather and climate modification.* Wiley, New York. Good survey articles.

Heyerdahl, Thor. 1971. Atlantic ocean pollution and biota observed by the *Ra* expeditions. *Biological Conservation,* vol. 3, pp. 164–167. These are the more detailed observations on which Heyerdahl's valuable publicizing of oceanic pollution were based.

———. 1975. How to kill an ocean. *Saturday Review,* November 29, 1975, pp. 12–18. A popular overview of the threat to the marine environment.

Hickey, J., and D. Anderson. 1968. Chlorinated hydrocarbons and eggshell changes in raptorial and fish-eating birds. *Science,* vol. 162, pp. 271–273 (October 11). Correlation of eggshell change with presence of chlorinated-hydrocarbon residue.

Hill, Dennis S. 1975. *Agricultural insect pests of the tropics and their control.* Cambridge University Press, London. Extensive bibliography.

Hills, Lawrence D. 1969. Farming with free fertility for profit. *Journal of the Soil Association,* October. How treated sewage can be successfully used as fertilizer.

Holden, Constance. 1976. Mirex: Persistent pesticide on its way out. *Science,* vol. 194, pp. 301–303 (October 15). Recent paper on the fire-ant-mirex controversy.

Holdren, John P. 1971. Global thermal pollution. In *Global ecology,* John P. Holdren and Paul R. Ehrlich, eds. Calculation of ultimate thermal limits using the crudest model of Earth's heat balance.

——— and Paul R. Ehrlich, eds. 1971. *Global ecology: Readings toward a rational strategy for man.* Harcourt Brace, Jovanovich, New York. Numerous papers in this collection elaborate on points discussed in this chapter.

Holdren, John P., and P. Herrera. 1972. *Energy.* Sierra Club Books, New York. Contains good discussion of local, regional, and global thermal pollution.

Hollin, John T. 1965. Wilson's theory of ice ages. *Nature,* vol. 208, pp. 12–16 (October 2). Describes a partial check of Wilson's ice-age theory.

Holt-Jensen, A. 1973. Acid rains in Scandinavia. *Ecologist,* vol. 3, pp. 378–382 (October). Review article with good maps.

Holton, J. R. 1972. *An introduction to dynamic meteorology.* Academic Press, New York. Good text for the serious and mathematically inclined student of meteorology/climatology.

Hudson, Norman. 1971. *Soil conservation.* Cornell University Press, Ithaca, N.Y. A comprehensive text on erosion and its prevention.

Huffaker, C. B. 1970. Summary of a pest management conference: A critique. In *Concepts of pest management,* R. L. Rabb and J. E. Guthrie. North Carolina State University Press, Raleigh.

———. 1971. The ecology of pesticide interference with insect populations (upsets and resurgences in insect populations). In *Agricultural chemicals, harmony or discord for food, people, environment,* J. E. Swift, ed., University of California Division of Agricultural Sciences, Berkeley, pp. 92–104. A fine discussion of how pesticides upset the "balance of nature."

———. 1971. Biological control and a remodeled pest control technology. *Technology Review,* vol. 73, June, pp. 30–37. An excellent summary paper.

———, ed. 1971. *Biological control.* Plenum, New York. A comprehensive bible of ecologically sane pest-control practices. Ought to be read by everyone interested in alternatives to today's disastrous pesticide practices.

———, M. van den Vrie, and J. A. McMurtry. 1969. The ecology of tetranychid mites and their natural control. *Annual Review of Entomology,* vol. 14, pp. 125–174. See especially the comparison of the reproductive-stimulation and predator-inhibition hypothesis.

———. 1970. Ecology of tetranychid mites and their natural enemies: A review. Pt. 2, Tetranychid populations and their possible control by predators: An evaluation. *Hilgardia,* vol. 40, pp. 391–458.

Hughes, J. D. 1975. *Ecology of ancient civilizations,* Univ. of New Mexico Press. Fascinating study of the environmental impact of early civilizations.

Hunt, Eldridge G. 1966. Biological magnification of pesticides, *Symposium on scientific aspects of pest control.* National Academy of Sciences-National Research Council, Washington, D.C., pp. 252–261. Information on the buildup of pesticides in food chains.

Hurlbert, S.; M. Mulla; and H. Wilson. 1972. Effects of an organophosphorus insecticide on phytoplankton, zooplankton, and insect populations of fresh-water ponds. *Ecological Monographs,* vol. 42, pp. 269–299. Discusses differential susceptibility of phytoplankton and zooplankton; useful bibliography.

Hutnik, R. J., and G. Davis, eds. 1973. *Ecology and reclamation of devastated land.* 2 vols. Gordon and Breach, New York. Technical papers on properties and repair of land subject to strip-mining, polluted with mine tailings, and so forth. Technical.

Ignoffo, C. M. 1975. Entomopathogens as Insecticides. In *Insecticides of the future,* M. Jacobson, ed. Dekker, New York, pp. 23–40. Discusses potential of microbial pathogens as insecticides.

IMOS. *See* Interagency Task Force on Inadvertent Modification of the Stratosphere.

Institute of Ecology (TIE). 1972. *Man in the living environment.* Report of the Workshop of Global Ecological Problems. University of Wisconsin Press, Madison. Much important material on the relationship of population growth to environmental problems. The material on depletion of phosphorus supplies has since been shown to be overly pessimistic.

Interagency Task Force on Inadvertent Modification of the Stratosphere (IMOS). 1975. *Fluorocarbons and the environment.* Government Printing Office, Washington, D.C., NSF 75-403. Federal scientific task force finds "legitimate cause for concern" that fluorocarbon aerosol propellants and refrigerants are damaging Earth's ozone shield, with potentially serious effects on health, ecological systems, and climate.

Jackson, R. D.; S. B. Idso; and J. Otterman. 1975. Surface albedo and desertification. *Science,* vol. 189, pp. 1012–1015 (September 19). Controversy over the relations among vegetation, surface albedo, and surface temperature.

Jacobson, M., ed. 1975. *Insecticides of the future.* Dekker, New York. See especially articles on microbial insecticides and manipulation of sex pheromones and growth and development hormones.

Jahns, R. H. 1968. Geologic jeopardy. *Texas quarterly,* vol. 11, no. 2, pp. 69–83. Deals with geological hazards whose impact may be intensified by overpopulation. (Reprinted in John P. Holdren and Paul R. Ehrlich, eds., *Global ecology.*)

Jahoda, J. C., and D. L. O'Hearn. 1975. The reluctant Amazon basin. *Environment,* October. A good review of the potential for development and disaster.

Janzen, D. H. 1970. The unexploited tropics. *Bulletin of the Ecological Society of America,* September, pp. 4–7. A brief classic on the ecology of tropical agriculture.

———. 1973. Tropical agroecosystems. *Science,* vol. 182, pp. 1212–1214 (December 21). A brilliant summary of the problems of tropical agriculture and what temperate-zone nations do to exacerbate them. Good bibliography.

Johnston, D. W. 1974. Decline of DDT residues in migratory songbirds. *Science,* vol. 186, pp. 841–842 (November 29).

Johnston, H. S. 1971. Reduction of stratospheric ozone by nitrogen oxide catalysts from SST exhaust. *Science,* vol. 173, pp. 517–522 (August 6). The original paper showing the plausibility of a nitrogen-oxide threat to the ozone layer. Its distinguished author was strongly criticized and even ridiculed by SST proponents, but subsequent reviews by impartial bodies completely upheld his results.

———. 1974. Photochemistry in the stratosphere—with applications to supersonic transports. *Acta Astronautica,* vol. 1, pp. 135–136 (January/February). Excellent technical introduction to the ozone-SST problem by the pioneer in the field.

———. 1976. *Analysis of the independent variables in the perturbation of stratospheric ozone by nitrogen fertilizers.* University of California Lawrence Berkeley Laboratory Report LBL-5488. Discusses ranges of uncertainties in crucial parameters governing ozone depletion due to increases in fertilizer use.

———, G. Whittier, and J. Birks. 1973. Effect of nuclear explosions on stratospheric nitric oxides and ozone. *Journal of Geophysical Research,* vol. 78, p. 6107.

Johnston, R., ed. 1976. *Marine pollution.* Academic Press, New York. Up to date and comprehensive.

Jones, D. P., and M. E. Solomon, eds. 1974. *Biology in pest and disease control.* Wiley, New York. This symposium volume covers a vast diversity of topics from plant breeding for resistance to genetic and behavioral control of insects—including such offbeat topics as biological control of pests in greenhouses.

Kahn, Herman. 1962. *Thinking about the unthinkable.* Horizon, New York. A good reply to those who attacked Kahn personally over *On thermonuclear war* rather than exposing the book's many flaws.

———. 1968. *On escalation.* 2d ed. Penguin, Baltimore. An interesting analysis that reveals much about the thinking of military planners at the height of the Cold War.

———. 1969. *On thermonuclear war.* 2d ed. Free Press, New York. The original "it wouldn't be so bad" book, first published in 1960 and hopelessly flawed by—among other things—the author's ignorance of ecology.

——— and A. J. Weiner. 1967. *The year 2000.* Macmillan, New York. An outstanding example of futurism that discounts problems of population, resources, and environment. The words *ecology* and *environment* do not appear in the index, which may explain in part why Kahn seems to view the possibility of thermonuclear war with relative equanimity.

Kassas, M. 1970. Desertification versus potential for recovery in circum-Saharan territories. In *Arid lands in transition,* American Association for the Advancement of Science, Washington, D.C. Short discussion of the human role in enlarging the Sahara and an extensive bibliography of the scientific literature on the subject.

Katan, J.; T. W. Fuhremann; and C. P. Lichtenstein. 1976. Binding of [^{14}C] parathion in soil: A reassessment of pesticide persistence. *Science,* vol. 193, pp. 891–894 (September 3). A decrease of extractable residue in soils was accompanied by an increase of unextractable (bound) residues, indicating that the whole notion that organophosphates are nonpersistent should be reevaluated.

Kearney, P. C.; R. G. Marsh; and A. R. Isensee. 1969. Persistence of pesticide residues in soils. In *Chemical fallout,* M. W. Miller and G. G. Berg, eds., pp. 54–67. This is a basic source of estimates on persistence of pesticides under normal agricultural conditions.

Keeney, D. R., and W. R. Gardner. 1975. The dynamics of nitrogen transformations in the soil. In *The changing global environment,* S. F. Singer, ed. Reidel, Dordrecht, Holland, pp. 367–375.

Kellogg, W. W. 1974. Climatic feedback mechanisms involving the polar regions. In *Proceedings of Climate of the Arctic.* University of Alaska, College Press, Fairbanks. Discussion of sensitivity of global climate to conditions in polar regions, and survey of phenomena that influence those conditions.

——— and S. H. Schneider. 1974. Climate stabilization: For better or for worse? *Science,* vol. 186, pp. 1163–1172 (December 27). Prospects for modifying climate both intentionally and inadvertently, and discussion of associated political problems.

Kenaga, E. E. 1972. Factors related to bioconcentration of pesticides. In *Environmental toxicology of pesticides,* F. Matsumura, G. M. Boush and T. Misuto, eds., Academic Press, New York. Levels and mechanisms discussed.

Ketchum, Bostwick H., ed. 1972. *The water's edge: Critical problems of the coastal zone.* M.I.T. Press, Cambridge, Mass. Proceedings of a workship on human impacts on fragile coastal ecosystems and on legal and management aspects.

Khan, M. A. Q., and J. P. Bedurka, eds. 1974. *Survival in toxic environments.* Academic Press, New York. Rather technical papers—see especially those of Hodgson and of Plapp on mechanisms of pesticide-resistance in insects.

Klechkovskii, V.; G. Polikarpov; and R. Aleksakhin, eds. 1973. *Radioecology.* Wiley, New York. Translation of a Soviet symposium with papers on terrestrial and aquatic systems.

Knabe, W. 1976. Effects of sulfur dioxide on terrestrial vegetation. *Ambio,* vol. 5, no. 5-6, p. 213–218. Mechanisms for SO_2 effects on ecosystems and concentrations at which various effects manifest themselves.

Kohl, D. H.; G. B. Shearer; B. Commoner. 1971. Fertilizer nitrogen contribution to nitrate in surface water in a cornbelt watershed. *Science,* vol. 174, pp. 1331–1334 (October 24).

Kolb, C. E. 1975. The depletion of stratospheric ozone. *Technology Review,* vol. 78, no. 1, pp. 39–47. Good, concise review.

Kondratyev, K. Ya. 1965. *Radiative heat exchange in the atmosphere.* Pergamon, London. Essential for the serious student of physical climatology.

Kontogiannis, J. E., and J. C. Barnett. 1973. The effect of oil pollution on survival of the tidal pool copepod, *Tigriopus californicus. Environmental Pollution,* vol. 4, pp. 69–79. Oil lowers survival rate both through direct toxicity and by acting as a barrier to oxygen transfer between air and water.

Kouyoumjian, H. H., and R. F. Uglow. 1974. Some aspects of the toxicity of p,p′-DDT, p,p′-DDE, and p,p′-DDD to the freshwater planarian *Polycelis felina* (Tricladida). *Environmental Pollution,* vol. 7, pp. 103–109. Nervous-system effects observed.

Kuhr, R. J., and H. W. Dorough. 1976. *Carbamate insecticides: Chemistry, biochemistry and toxicology.* CRC Press, Cleveland. Comprehensive and technical.

Lamb, H. H. 1972. *Climate: Past, present, and future.* Methuen, London.

Laven, H.; J. Cousserans; and G. Guille. 1972. Eradicating mosquitoes using translocations: A first field experiment. *Nature,* vol. 236, pp. 456–457 (April 28). Reports successful test of introduced genetic semisterility to control a natural population.

Leach, J. H., and S. J. Nepszy. 1976. The fish community in Lake Erie. *Journal of the Fisheries Research Board of Canada,* vol. 33, no. 3, pp. 622–638. Detailed discussion of roles of overfishing, eutrophication, and other factors in changing species composition.

Liang, T., and E. P. Lichtenstein. 1974. Synergism of insecticides by herbicides: Effect of environmental factors. *Science,* vol. 186, pp. 1128–1130 (December 20). Synergism of DDT and parathion by the herbicide atrazine varied with soil type. (For the original work on synergisms see Lichtenstein, Liang, and Anderegg, 1973. Synergism of insecticides by herbicides.)

Lichtenstein, E. P.; T. Liang; and B. Anderegg. 1973. Synergism of insecticides by herbicides. *Science,* vol. 181, pp. 847–849 (August 31). This is the original paper. For more recent work, see Liang and Lichtenstein, Synergism of insecticides by herbicides.

Lichtenstein, E. P.; K. R. Schultz; T. W. Fuhrmann; and T. T. Liang. 1969. Biological interaction between plasticizers and insecticides. *Journal of Economic Entomology,* vol. 62, pp. 761–765. Demonstrates toxicity of PCBs to insects and shows that those compounds may increase the toxicity of dieldrin and DDT.

Likens, G. E., ed. 1972. *Nutrients and eutrophication: The limiting nutrient controversy.* Special symposium, vol. 1, American Society of Limnology and Oceanography. Allen Press, Lawrence, Kans.

——— and F. H. Bormann. 1974. Acid rain: A serious regional environmental problem. *Science,* vol. 184, pp. 1176–1179 (June 14). An excellent recent technical review.

———, and N. M. Johnson. 1969. Nitrification: Importance to nutrient losses from a cutover forested ecosystem. *Science,* vol. 163, pp. 1205–1206. Large increase in loss of nitrates documented for deforested area.

———. 1972. Acid rain. *Environment,* vol. 14, pp. 33–40 (March). A good review article for the layman.

———, D. W. Fisher, and R. S. Pierce. 1970. Effects of forest cutting and herbicide treatment on nutrient budgets in the Hubbard Brook watershed-ecosystem. *Ecological Monographs,* vol. 40, pp. 23–47. Detailed evaluation of the biogeochemical effects of deforestation.

Lincer, J. L. 1975. DDE-induced eggshell-thinning in the American kestrel: A comparison of the field situation and laboratory results. *Journal of Applied Ecology,* vol. 12, pp. 781–793. Shows that the correlative relationship between DDE in the egg and eggshell-thinning is the same for both captive experimental birds and the wild population. Good bibliography for eggshell-thinning controversy (which no longer exists; see Hazeltine, Disagreement on why brown pelican eggs are thin).

Lincoln, C.; W. P. Boyer; and F. D. Miner. 1975. The evolution of insect pest management in cotton and soybeans: Past experience, present status, and future outlook in Arkansas. *Environmental Entomology,* vol. 4, pp. 1–7. Good history of control practices and problems.

Linden, O. 1975. Acute effects of oil and oil/dispersant mixture on larvae of Baltic herring. *Ambio,* vol. 4, no. 3, pp. 130–133. Use of dispersant increases toxicity 50 to 100 times and greatly slows rate of diminution of toxicity.

Lockie, J. D.; D. A. Ratcliffe; and R. Balharry. 1969. Breeding success and organo-chlorine residues in golden eagles in West Scotland. *Journal of Applied Ecology,* vol. 6, pp. 381–389. Shows increased breeding success correlated with a decline in organochlorine residues.

Loftas, Tony. 1971. The unseen dangers of oil. *New Scientist,* February 4, p. 228. Concise account of the effects of oil pollution on marine ecology.

Lowry, W. P. 1967. The climate of cities. *Scientific American,* August. Good introduction to the subject, well illustrated.

MacDonald, G. J. F. 1968. How to wreck the environment. In *Unless peace comes,* N. Calder, ed. Viking, New York, pp. 181–205. Describes weather modification for military purposes.

———. 1975. Man, weather, and climate. *In Environment,* W. W. Murdoch, ed., 2d ed. Sinauer, Sunderland, Mass., pp. 381–396. Readable concise survey of human influences on climate.

McElroy, M. B.; S. C. Wofsy; J. E. Penner, and J. C. McConnell. 1974. Atmospheric ozone: Possible impact of stratospheric aviation. *Journal of Atmospheric Sciences,* vol. 31, pp. 287–303. Another analysis confirming the seriousness of the threat to ozone by SSTs.

McElroy, M. B.; J. W. Elkins; S. C. Wofsy; and Y. L. Yung. 1976. Sources and sinks for atmospheric N_2O. *Review of Geophysics and Space Physics,* vol. 14, pp. 143–150. Estimates of effects of fertilizer use on ozone.

MacFarlane, R. B.; W. A. Glooschenko; and R. C. Harriss. 1972. The interaction of light intensity and DDT concentration upon the marine diatom, *Nitzschia delicatissima* Cleve. *Hydrobiologia,* vol. 39, pp. 373–382. Strongest effects of DDT occurred at highest light intensities—just one of the complexities of pesticide-plankton interaction.

Machta, Lester. 1973. Prediction of CO_2 in the atmosphere. In *Carbon and the biosphere,* G. M. Woodwell and E. V. Pecan, eds. National Technical Information Service, Springfield, Va., USAEC CONF-720510. Mathematical models and correlation with measurements.

McLaughlin, S. B., Jr., and R. L. Barnes. 1975. Effects of fluoride on photosynthesis and respiration of some south-east American forest trees. *Environmental Pollution,* vol. 8, pp. 91–95. Pines are more sensitive than hardwoods.

McMurtry, J. A.; C. B. Huffaker; and M. Van den Vrie. 1970. Ecology of tetranychid mites and their natural enemies: A review. Pt. 1, Tetranychid enemies: their biological characters and the impact of spray practices. *Hilgardia,* vol. 40, pp. 331–390. Insecticide spraying promotes spider mites to the status of major pests.

McNeil, M. 1964. Lateritic soils. *Scientific American,* November. Author's pessimism about laterization and tropical agriculture is disputed by P. H. Sanchez and S. W. Buol, Soils of the tropics and the world food crisis.

———. 1972. Lateritic soils in disturbed tropical environments: Southern Sudan and Brazil. In *The careless technology,* M. T. Farvar and J. P. Milton, eds. Natural History Press, Garden City, N.Y. pp. 591–608.

Malmer, N. 1976. Acid precipitation: Chemical changes in the soil. *Ambio,* vol. 5, no. 5–6, p. 231–234, Increases in leaching as influenced by acid rain and detailed soil properties. Potential for synergistic effects.

Malone, C. R. 1969. Effects of diazinon contamination on an old-field ecosystem. *American Midland Naturalist,* vol. 82, pp. 1–27. Primary effects were on vegetation, not on insects!

Manabe, S. 1971. Estimates of future change of climate due to the increase of carbon dioxide concentration in the air. In *Man's impact on climate,* W. H. Matthews, W. W. Kellogg, and G. D. Robinson, eds., pp. 249–264. Significant temperature increases by the year 2000 could result from continued rapid growth in the use of fossil fuels.

——— and R. T. Weatherald. 1967. Thermal equilibrium of the atmosphere with a given distribution of relative humidity. *Journal of Atmospheric Sciences,* vol. 24, pp. 241–259.

Marks, P. L., and F. H. Bormann. 1972. Revegetation following forest cutting: mechanisms for return to steady-state nutrient cycling. *Science,* vol. 176, pp. 914–915 (May 26). Succession tends to minimize loss of nutrients from cutover systems.

Martin, J. H., and W. W. Broenkow. 1975. Cadmium in plankton: Elevated concentrations off Baja California. *Science,* vol. 190, pp. 884–885 (November 28). Plankton concentration carried to approximately 3 times the levels found elsewhere, reasons unknown.

Martin, H., and C. R. Worthing. 1974. *Pesticide manual: Basic information on the chemicals used in active components of pesticides.* 4th ed. British Crop Protection Council. Alphabetically organized summary of structure, production, use, side effects, and so forth, of more than 500 compounds.

Martin, R. D., ed. 1975. *Breeding endangered species in captivity.* Academic Press, New York. A diversity of papers focusing on different species from Galapagos tortoises to Indian rhinos.

Marx, J. L. 1975. Air pollution: Effects on plants. *Science,* vol. 187, pp. 731–733 (February 28). A good summary on ozone and other oxidants.

Marx, Wesley. 1967. *The frail ocean.* Coward, McCann, New York. On human assaults on oceanic ecosystems.

———. 1971. *Oilspill.* Sierra Club, San Francisco. A good overview for the layman.

Matsumura, Fumio. 1975. *Toxicology of insecticides.* Plenum, New York. Comprehensive, technical, good bibliographies.

——— and G. M. Boush. 1967. Dieldrin: Degradation by soil microorganisms. *Science,* vol. 156, pp. 959–961 (May 19). Shows that a few microorganisms can break down dieldrin in the soil.

———. 1968. Breakdown of dieldrin in soil by a microorganism. *Nature,* vol. 219, pp. 965–967. Identifies some of the products of dieldrin breakdown.

——— and T. Misato, eds. 1972. *Environmental toxicology of pesticides.* Academic Press, New York. Rather technical papers; considerable information on the situation in Japan.

Matthews, W. H.; W. W. Kellogg; and G. D. Robinson, eds. 1971. *Man's impact on climate.* M.I.T. Press, Cambridge, Mass. Background papers for the Study of Critical Environmental Problems (SCEP). Good introductions to major aspects of climate change.

Maugh, T. H. II. 1976. Plant biochemistry: Two new ways to fight pests. *Science,* vol. 192, pp. 874–876 (May 28). Report on research aimed at using plants' natural defenses to protect crops against pests and diseases.

———. 1976. The ozone layer: The threat from aerosol cans is real. *Science,* vol. 194, pp. 170–172. (October 8). Confirmation of earlier studies on ozone destruction by chlorofluorocarbons.

Meggers, B. J. 1971. Amazonia: Man and culture in a counterfeit paradise. Aldine-Atherton, Chicago. A fine synthesis of culture and ecology.

———. 1973. Some problems of cultural adaptation in Amazonia, with emphasis on the pre-European period. In *Tropical forest ecosystems in Africa and South America: A comparative review,* B. J. Meggers, E. S. Ayensu, and W. D. Duckworth, eds., pp. 311–320. Smithsonian Institution, Washington, D.C. Excellent on several aspects of agriculture in tropical rain forest regions.

Menn, J. J., and F. M. Pallas. 1975. Development of morphogenetic agents in insect control. In *Insecticides of the future,* M. Jacobson, ed. Dekker, New York, pp. 71–88. Recent advances in the development of juvenile-hormone-type insecticides.

Metcalf, R. L., and W. H. Luckman, eds. 1975. *Introduction to insect pest management.* Wiley, New York. A first-class volume dealing with principles, techniques, and examples, with integration much superior to most multi-author volumes.

Miller, Albert. 1966. *Meteorology.* Merrill, Columbus, Ohio. Lucid introductory text with especially good treatment of energy balance.

Miller, M. W., and G. G. Berg, eds. 1969. *Chemical fallout: Current research on persistent pesticides.* Thomas, Springfield, Ill. An excellent volume containing a number of important papers.

Mitchell, H. H. 1961. *Ecological problems and postwar recuperation: A preliminary survey from the civil defense viewpoint.* U.S. Air Force project and research memorandum. A pioneering document, somewhat overoptimistic and now out-of-date.

Mitchell, J. M. 1975. A reassessment of atmospheric pollution as a cause of long-term changes of global temperature. In *The changing global environment,* S. F. Singer, ed., pp. 149–173. Argues that long-term warming is more likely than cooling, in consideration of combined effects of man-made carbon dioxide and particulate additions to the atmosphere. Also contends that the cooling trend that began in the 1940s must have had natural not human origin.

Molina, M. J., and F. S. Rowland. 1974. Stratospheric sink for chlorofluoromethanes: Chlorine atom catalyzed destruction of ozone. *Nature,* vol. 249, p. 810. The original paper showing that chlorofluorocarbons could be a threat to ozone.

Moll, K. D.; J. H. Cline; and P. D. Marr. 1960. *Postattack farm problems.* Pt. 1, *The influence of major inputs on farm production.* Prepared for Office of Civil Defense Mobilization under the auspices of Stanford Research Institute (SRI), Menlo Park, Calif. Limited circulation (200 copies). One of the few attempts to investigate the consequences of a nuclear attack systematically. Others by SRI include studies of the effects of a nuclear attack on railroad transport and the petroleum industry.

Moore, N. W., ed. 1966. Pesticides in the environment and their effects on wildlife. *Journal of Applied Ecology,* vol. 3, June, supplement. This supplement contains many other interesting papers on pesticide ecology.

Moore, P. D. 1975. Ozone over Britain. *Nature,* vol. 256, p. 537 (August 14). Short summary.

Moriarty, F., ed. 1975. *Organochlorine insecticides: Persistent organic pollutants.* Academic Press, New York. Monitoring, residues, economic analysis, and so forth. Technical.

Morris, B. F. 1971. Petroleum: Tar quantities floating in the northwestern Atlantic taken with a new quantitative neuston net. *Science,* vol. 173, pp. 430–432 (July 30). Suggests that previous estimates of ocean pollution were too low.

Mosser, J. L.; N. S. Fisher; T. Teng; and C. F. Wurster. 1972. Polychlorinated biphenyls: Toxicity to certain phyto-plankters. *Science,* vol. 175, pp. 191–192 (January 14). Shows differential susceptibility.

Mudd, J. B., and T. T. Kozlowski, eds. 1975. *Responses of plants to air pollution.* Academic Press, New York. A comprehensive set of up-to-date technical papers, good bibliographies.

Mulla, M. S., and L. W. Isaak. 1961. Field studies on the toxicity of insecticides to the mosquito fish, *Gambusia affinis. Journal of Economic Entomology,* vol. 54, pp. 1237–1242. Reports high toxicity to mosquito-eating fishes of pesticides used in mosquito-abatement programs.

Murphy, C. B., Jr. 1973. Effect of restricted use of phosphate-based detergents on Onondaga Lake, *Science,* vol. 182, pp. 379–381, (October 26).

NAS. *See* National Academy of Sciences.

Nash, R. G., and E. H. Woolson. 1967. Persistence of chlorinated hydrocarbon insecticides in soils. *Science,* vol. 157, pp. 924–927 (August 25). Gives long-term limits on persistence through studies in which pesticides were mixed uniformly into loam in experimental plots.

National Academy of Sciences (NAS). 1972. *Accumulation of nitrate.* NAS, Washington, D.C. Useful overview with extensive bibliography.

———. 1973. *Biological impacts of increased intensities of solar ultraviolet radiation.* NAS, Washington, D.C. Good introduction and survey as of 1973, but already somewhat dated.

———. 1974. *Effects of herbicides in South Vietnam.* Pt. A, *Summary and conclusions.* NAS, Washington, D.C. This report may underestimate the damage to inland forests (see dissents at end) but otherwise represents a consensus of the scientific community (see Constable et al., AAAS and NAS herbicide reports).

———. 1975. *Air quality and stationary source emissions control.* Government Printing Office, Washington, D.C. Thorough survey of the production and consequences of acid rain, the effects of oxides of nitrogen and sulfur on ecosystems, and other topics, prepared for Senate Committee on Public Works.

———. 1975. *Environmental impact of stratospheric flight: Biological and climatic effects of aircraft emissions in the stratosphere.* Washington, D.C. Documents seriousness of hazards to life that could result from heavy use of supersonic transports.

———. 1975. *Understanding climatic change.* NAS, Washington, D.C. Good survey.

———. 1975. *Long-term worldwide effects of multiple nuclear-weapons detonations.* NAS, Washington, D.C. A badly flawed effort which still contains some useful information. Note also the report's letter of transmittal in which NAS president Philip Handler finds the report "encouraging" because it indicates that humanity (but not necessarily civilization) would survive a nuclear war! See also Philip M. Boffey, Nuclear war: Federation disputes Academy on how bad effects could be.

———. 1975. *Petroleum in the marine environment.* NAS, Washington, D.C. Comprehensive discussion of sources and effects.

National Center for Atmospheric Research (NCAR). 1975. *Atmospheric implications of energy alternatives.* NCAR, Boulder, Colo. Proceedings of a symposium containing up-to-date discussions of effects of heat, carbon dioxide, and particles.

Neilands, J. B.; G. H. Orians; E. W. Pfeiffer; A Vennema; and A. H. Westing. 1972. *Harvest of death: Chemical warfare in Vietnam and Cambodia.* Free Press, New York. See especially the chapter by Westing on Cambodia. Comprehensive coverage of the use of poison gases and herbicides. Highly recommended.

New Scientist. 1971. Does killing weeds destroy the soil? March 25, p. 663. On the effects of herbicides on soil bacteria.

Nuorteva, P., and Erkki Hasanen. 1972. Transfer of mercury from fishes to sarcosaprophagous flies. *Annales Zoologici Fennici,* vol. 9, pp. 23–27. Bioaccumulation occurs at levels of concentration in fishes that are higher than natural (0.17 ppm).

Odum, W. E. 1970. Insidious alteration of the estuarine environment. *Transactions of the American Fisheries Society,* vol. 4, pp. 836–847. Summary of ecology of estuaries and how they are threatened. Good bibliography.

Oka, I. N., and D. Pimentel. 1976. Herbicide (2,4-D) increases insect and pathogen pests on corn. *Science,* vol. 193, pp. 239–240 (July 16).

Olkowski, W.; H. Olkowski; R. van den Bosch; and R. Hom. 1976. Ecosystem management: A framework for urban pest control. *BioScience,* vol. 26, no. 6 (June), pp. 384–389. Describes a program for protecting urban trees against pests, using integrated control methods.

Olson, B., and R. Cooper. 1976. Comparison of aerobic and anaerobic methylation of mercuric chloride by San Francisco Bay sediments. *Water research,* in press. Conversion of mercury to organic form.

Osburn, W. S., Jr. 1968. Forecasting long-range ecological recovery from nuclear attack. In *Proceedings of the symposium on post-attack recovery from nuclear war.* National Academy of Sciences-National Academy of Engineering-National Research Council, Washington, D.C. Good source of information and references, but like many establishment documents on this subject, overoptimistic because of its "one-at-a-time" approach to effects. (Updated in V. Schultz and F. Wicker, eds., *Ecological aspects of the nuclear age: Selected readings in radiation ecology.*)

Otterman, Joseph. 1974. Baring high-albedo soils by overgrazing: A hypothesized desertification mechanism. *Science,* vol. 186, pp. 531–533 (November 8). Denuding by overgrazing bares high-albedo soils, cooling surface, decreasing lift of air for cloud formation and precipitation, and giving regional climatic desertification.

Pal, B., and M. J. Whitten, eds. 1974. *The use of genetics in insect control.* American Elsevier Pub. Co., New York. A diverse collection of rather technical papers with heavy emphasis on mosquitoes, and a chapter on spider mites (which are not insects). Bibliographies give good access to the technical literature.

Peakall, D. B. 1967. Pesticide-induced enzyme breakdown on steroids in birds. *Nature,* vol. 216, pp. 505–506. Indicates that DDT and dieldrin can change hormone metabolism and upset breeding.

———. 1970. Pesticides and the reproduction of birds. *Scientific American,* April, pp. 73–74. Semipopular account of the way chlorinated hydrocarbons affect breeding behavior and viability of eggs in birds. (For a more up-to-date and somewhat more technical treatment see D. B. Peakall, Physiological effects of chlorinated hydrocarbons on avian species.)

———. 1974. DDE: Its presence in peregrine eggs in 1948. *Science,* vol. 183, pp. 673–674 (February 15). An important paper showing an association of DDT with thinning of eggshells as early as 1948.

———. 1975. Physiological effects of chlorinated hydrocarbons on avian species. In *Environmental dynamics of pesticides,* R. Haque and V. Freed, eds. Plenum, New York, pp. 343–360. An excellent technical summary.

Pell, E. J., and E. Brennan. 1975. Economic impact of air pollution on vegetation in New Jersey and an interpretation of its annual variability. *Environmental Pollution,* vol. 8, pp. 23–33. Describes great year-to-year variation in susceptibility of vegetation, possibly due to rainfall difference.

Perkins, E. J. 1976. The evaluation of biological response by toxicity and water quality assessments. In R. Johnston, ed., *Marine pollution,* pp. 505–585. Examines in detail how the effects of insults to marine ecosystems are determined.

Peterle, T. J. 1969. DDT in Antarctic snow. *Nature,* vol. 224, pp. 620 (November 8). Tests indicate as much as 2400 MT of DDT could have accumulated in Antarctic snow by 1967.

Pfeiffer, E. W. 1973. Post-war Vietnam. *Environment,* vol. 15, November, pp. 29–43. Describes attempts to recover from effects of war.

Pimentel, D. 1971. *Ecological effects of pesticides on non-target species.* Office of Science and Technology, Executive Office of the President, Washington, D.C. Comprehensive coverage of the literature to 1970, arranged chemical by chemical. See also O. B. Cope, Interactions between pesticides and wildlife, which has complementary arrangement of the information.

———. 1973. Extent of pesticide use, food supply, and pollution. *Journal of the New York Entomological Society,* vol. 81, pp. 13–33. Reports increases in crop losses in spite of increased pesticide use, due in part to "the practice of substituting insecticides for sound bioenvironmental pest control (for example, crop rotation and sanitation) and also to higher consumer standards."

———, ed. 1975. *Insects, science, and society.* Academic Press, New York. See especially the article on pest management by L. D. Newsome, which has an informative discussion of integrated controls for soybean and cotton crops.

———; E. C. Terhune; R. D. Dyson-Hudson; S. Rochereau; R. Samis; E. A. Smith; D. Denman; D. Reifschneider; and M. Shepard. 1976. Land degradation: Effects on food and energy resources. *Science,* vol. 194, pp. 149–155 (October 8). Details losses of valuable U.S. topsoil to erosion and how they might be reduced.

Pinthus, M.; Y. Eshel; and Y. Shohori. 1972. Field and vegetable crop mutants with increased resistance to herbicides. *Science,* vol. 177, pp. 715–716 (August 25). Mutants of both wheat and tomato were found that were resistant to a triazine and an acetamide herbicide.

Polunin, Nicholas, ed. 1972. *The environmental future.* Macmillan, London. Contains many sections relevant to this chapter.

Porricelli, J. D.; V. F. Keith; and R. L. Storch. 1971. Tankers and the ecology. *Transactions of the Society of Naval Architects and Marine Engineers,* vol. 79, pp. 169–221. Contains much useful data on tanker incidents and accidents, traffic controls, terminals, and the like, in spite of the inappropriate "the" in the title!

Porter, R. D., and S. N. Wiemeyer. 1969. Dieldrin and DDT: Effects on sparrow hawk eggshells and reproduction. *Science,* vol. 165, pp. 199–200 (July 11). Controlled feeding experiments.

Powell, N. A.; C. S. Sayce; and D. F. Tufts. 1970. Hyperplasia in an estuarine bryozoan attributable to coal tar derivatives. *Journal of the Fisheries Research Board of Canada,* vol. 27, pp. 2095–2096. Study of abnormal growth in a small marine animal induced by oil pollution.

Powers, C. D.; R. G. Rowland; and C. F. Wurster. 1977. Dieldrin-induced destruction of marine algal cells with concomitant decrease in size of survivors and their progeny. *Environmental pollution,* vol. 12, pp. 17–25. More on the effects of chlorinated hydrocarbon insecticides on marine phytoplankton.

Precoda, Norman. 1975. Left behind: Soviet mine wastes. *Environment,* vol. 17, no. 8, pp. 14–20. Results of strip-mining in the USSR–nearly 40,000 hectares per year being devastated.

Priest, Joseph. 1973. *Problems of our physical environment.* Addison-Wesley, Reading, Mass. Good introductory text to physical aspects of energy and environmental problems.

Ramanathan, V. 1975. Greenhouse effect due to chlorofluorocarbons: Climatic implications. *Science,* vol. 190, pp. 50–51 (October 3). Simplified model shows mean global surface temperature could increase 0.9° K by year 2000, because of the direct effect of chlorofluorocarbons in blocking outgoing terrestrial radiation.

Rappaport, Roy A. 1976. Forests and man. *The ecologist,* vol. 6, no. 7 (August-September), pp. 240–246. An anthropologist describes the ecologically conscious behavior of swidden agriculturalists in New Guinea and makes some pertinent observations on how technological societies have lost this awareness.

Rasool, S. I., ed. 1973. *Chemistry of the lower atmosphere.* Plenum, New York. Good discussion of climate modification by atmospheric pollution.

——— and S. H. Schneider. 1971. Atmospheric carbon dioxide and aerosols: Effects of large increases on global climate. *Science,* vol. 173, pp. 138–141 (July 9). An increase of aerosol concentration by a factor of 4 could reduce surface temperature by as much as 3.5° K, enough to trigger an ice age, if sustained.

Ratcliffe, D. A. 1967. Decrease in eggshell weight in certain birds of prey. *Nature,* vol. 215, pp. 208–210. Demonstrates rapid synchronous decline of eggshell thickness at the time chlorinated hydrocarbon pesticides were introduced. This was key evidence in establishing the role of these substances in the decline of bird populations.

———. 1970. Changes attributable to pesticides in egg breakage frequency and eggshell thickness in some British birds. *Journal of Applied Ecology,* vol. 7, pp. 67–115. Expands and updates a 1967 paper, giving more information on the temporal and geographic correlations between eggshell strength and use of chlorinated hydrocarbons. Extensive bibliography.

Reck, R. A. 1976. Stratospheric ozone effects on temperature. *Science,* vol. 192, pp. 557–559 (May 7). The temperature inversion at the stratopause could be weakened by substantial ozone depletion.

Reidinger, R. T., Jr., and D. G. Crabtree. 1974. Organochlorine residues in golden eagles, United States, March 1964–July 1971. *Pesticides Monitoring Journal,* vol. 8, pp. 37–43. Suggests level of organochlorine poisoning remained rather constant between 1965 and 1970.

Reinert, Robert E. 1972. Accumulation of dieldrin in an alga *(Scenedesmus obliquus), Daphnia magna,* and the guppy *(Poecilia reticulata). Journal of the Fisheries Research Board of Canada,* vol. 29, pp. 1413–1418. Concentration factors directly from water were 1282 for the alga, 13,954 for *D. magna* and 49,307 for the guppy.

Revelle, R., and H. E. Suess. 1967. Carbon dioxide between atmosphere and ocean and the question of an increase of atmospheric CO_2 during the past decades. *Tellus,* vol. 9, no. 1, pp. 18–27.

Risebrough, R. W.; R. J. Huggett; J. J. Griffin; and E. D.Goldberg. 1968. Pesticides: Transatlantic movements in the northeast trades. *Science,* vol. 159, pp. 1233–1236 (March 15). Important paper on aerial transport of chlorinated hydrocarbons.

Risebrough, R. W.; E. Huschenbeth; S. Jensen; and J. E. Portmann. 1972. Halogenated hydrocarbons in *A guide to marine pollution,* E. G. Goldberg, ed., Gordon and Breach, New York, pp. 1–17. Provides access to the literature on biconcentration (or the lack of it) by marine food chains.

Risebrough, R. W.; W. Walker II; T. T. Schmidt; B. W. de Lappe; and C. W. Connors. 1976. Transfer of chlorinated biphenyls to Antarctica. *Nature,* vol. 264, pp. 738–739 (December 23/30). DDT and PCBs found in Antarctic snow and in penguin eggs.

Robinson, Alan S. 1976. Progress in the use of chromosomal translocations for the control of insect pests. *Biological Reviews,* vol. 51, pp. 1–24. Good review, extensive bibliography.

Roe, Frank G. 1951. *The North American buffalo.* University of Toronto Press. Classic on destruction of a major element of an ecosystem.

Roelofs, Wendell. 1975. Manipulating sex pheromones for insect suppression. In *Insecticides of the future,* M. Jacobson, ed. Dekker, New York, pp. 41–59. Reviews various ways in which pheromones may be used to control insect populations.

Rosato, P., and D. E. Fergusson. 1968. The toxicity of endrin-resistant mosquito fish to eleven species of vertebrates. *BioScience,* vol. 18, pp. 783–784.

Roughgarden, J. 1978. *Theory of population genetics and evolutionary ecology; an introduction.* Macmillan, New York. Chapter 22 on predation is highly pertinent to understanding the failure of many pesticide programs.

Rudd, Robert L. 1964. *Pesticides and the living landscape.* University of Wisconsin Press, Madison. The classic on ecological effects of pesticides.

Rukeyser, William S. 1972. Fact and foam in the row over phosphates. *Fortune,* January. A business view of pollution from detergents and its regulation.

Ryan, R. G. 1970. Resistance of common groundsel to simazine and atrazine. *Weed Science,* vol. 18, pp. 614–615. Resistance developed in a nursery where the herbicides had been in use for a decade.

Sabloff, J. 1971. The collapse of the classic Mayan civilization. In *Patient Earth,* J. Harte and R. H. Socolow, eds. Holt, Rinehart and Winston, New York, pp. 16–27. Blames collapse on overintensive milpa agriculture (see also B. L. Turner, Prehistoric intensive agriculture in the Mayan lowlands).

Sanchez, P. H., and S. W. Buol. 1975. Soils of the tropics and the world food crisis. *Science,* vol. 188, pp. 598–602 (May 9). Tends to minimize problems of laterization.

Sanders, H. O. 1970. Toxicities of some herbicides to six species of freshwater crustaceans. *Water Pollution Control Federation Journal,* vol. 42, no. 1, pp. 1544–1550.

——— and J. H. Chandler. 1972. Biological magnification of a polychlorinated biphenyl (Aroclor[R]1254) from water by aquatic invertebrates. *Bulletin of Environmental Contamination and Toxicology,* vol. 7, pp. 257–263. Accumulation may be very rapid.

Schell, W. R., and R. L. Watters. 1975. Plutonium in aqueous systems. *Health Physics,* vol. 29, pp. 589–597.

Schneider, S. H. 1974. The population explosion: Can it shake climate? *Ambio,* vol. 3, pp. 150–155. Readable survey of issues in human modification of climate.

———. 1975. On the carbon dioxide-climate confusion. *Journal of Atmospheric Sciences,* vol. 32, pp. 2060–2066 (November). Excellent review article, reconciling different estimates of effects of CO_2 based on different models and assumptions.

——— and R. Dennett. 1975. Climatic barriers to long-term energy growth. *Ambio,* vol. 4, no. 2, pp. 65–74. Good summary of potential effects of carbon dioxide, particles, and heat released from human activities.

———, and R. E. Dickinson. 1974. Climate modeling. *Reviews of Geophysics and Space Physics,* vol. 12, no. 3, pp. 447–493. Superbly comprehensive and authoritative review of the goals, techniques, and early results of climate modeling and correlation with experimental measurements. More than 200 references.

———, and C. Mass. 1975. Volcanic dusts, sunspots, and temperature trends: Climatic theories in search of verification. *Science,* vol. 190, pp. 741–746 (November 21). Much of the observed climatic variation of the past 400 years may possibly be explained by variations in the sun's output, combined with changes in amounts of volcanic dust in the atmosphere.

Schofield, C. L. 1976. Acid precipitation: Effects on fish. *Ambio,* vol. 5, no. 5-6, pp. 228–230. Documents depletion of fish stocks as a consequence of acidification.

Schultz, V., and F. Wicker, eds. 1972. *Ecological aspects of the nuclear age: Selected reading in radiation ecology.* Technical Information Center, Oak Ridge, Tenn. Reprints important papers on radioisotope cycling, effects of ionizing radiation, and nuclear war, among others.

Scott, J. M.; J. H. Wiens; and R. R. Claeys. 1975. Organochlorine levels associated with a common murre die-off in Oregon. *Journal of Wildlife Management,* vol. 39, pp. 310–320. High levels may have interacted with nutritional stress to cause an unusually high mortality level.

Scotto, J.; A. Kopf; and F. Urbach. 1974. Nonmelanoma skin cancer among Caucasians in four areas of the United States. *Cancer,* vol. 34, p. 349. Major contribution to establishing the quantitative correlation between levels of ultraviolet radiation and skin cancer.

Scoville, Herbert. 1974. Nuclear explosives: Potential for ecological catastrophe. In *Air, water, earth, fire,* Sierra Club. Sierra Club, San Francisco, pp. 27–37.

Sears, Paul. 1971. An empire of dust. In *Patient Earth,* J. Harte and R. H. Socolow, eds. Holt, Rinehart and Winston, New York, pp. 2–15. A classic on the dust bowl.

Sellers, W. D. 1973. A new global climate model. *Journal of Atmospheric Sciences,* vol. 12, pp. 241–254.

Seshachar, B. R. 1971. Problems of environment in India. In *Proceedings of joint colloquium on international environmental science.* Government Printing Office, Washington, D.C., 63–562. Documents human influence in expansion of Rajasthan (Thar) desert.

Seymour, A. H., ed. 1971. *Radioactivity in the marine environment.* National Academy of Sciences, Washington, D.C. A set of highly technical papers.

Shapley, Deborah. 1971. Mirex and the fire ant: Decline in fortunes of "perfect" pesticide. *Science,* vol. 172, pp. 358–360 (April 23).

Shea, Kevin P. 1968. Cotton and chemicals. *Scientist and Citizen,* November. Gives details of the Azodrin situation.

Shell, W. R., and R. L. Watters. 1975. Plutonium in aqueous systems. *Health Physics,* vol. 29, October, pp. 589–597. This entire issue of *Health Physics* is devoted to plutonium.

Shepard, P., and D. McKinley, eds. 1969. *The subversive science.* Houghton Mifflin, Boston. Selected readings in ecology. Excellent, but now somewhat out-of-date.

Shure, D. J. 1971. Insecticide effects on early successsion in an old field ecosystem. *Ecology,* vol. 52, pp. 275–279. The major effect of diazinon on vegetation seems to depend on soil moisture.

Simon, N., and P. Geroudet. 1970. *Last survivors: Natural history of 48 animals in danger of extinction.* World, New York. A handsome volume on some vanishing passengers of Spaceship Earth. Highly recommended.

Singer, S. F., ed. 1975. *The changing global environment.* Reidel, Dordrecht, Netherlands. Interesting collection of papers by the editor and many others, emphasizing climate change and interference in nitrogen cycle (many were written before 1971 and have been only slightly updated).

Singh, H. B.; D. P. Fowler; and T. O. Peyton. 1976. Atmospheric carbon tetrachloride: Another man-made pollutant. *Science,* vol. 192, pp. 1231–1234 (June 18). Strong evidence that human activity is the principal source of atmospheric CCl_4; like the fluorocarbons, a probable precursor of ozone destruction.

Sioli, Harold. 1973. Recent human activities in the Brazilian Amazon region and their ecological effects. In *Tropical forest ecosystems in Africa and South America: A comparative review,* B. J. Meggers, E. S. Ayensu, and W. D. Duckworth, eds. Smithsonian Institution, Washington, D.C. Important source on farming the tropics.

Sladen, W. T. L.; C. M. Menzee; and W. L. Rechel. 1966. DDT residues in Adélie penguins and a crabeater seal from Antarctica: Ecological implications. *Nature,* vol. 210, pp. 670–673.

Slobodkin, L. B. 1968. Aspects of the future of ecology. *BioScience,* vol. 18, pp. 16–23. Source on insecticide–brine-shrimp–fish-farming sequence.

Smagorinsky, J. 1974. Global atmospheric modeling and the numerical simulation of climate. In *Weather and climate modification,* W. N. Hess, ed. Wiley, New York.

SMIC. *See* Study of Man's Impact on Climate.

Smith, J. W. 1975. Spider mites: Population suppression by interspecific hybridization. *Environmental Entomology,* vol. 4, pp. 588–590. Indicates feasibility of using inundations of males of one species to suppress a population of another.

Smith, R. F. 1970. Pesticides: Their use and limitations in pest management. In *Concepts of pest management,* R. C. Rabb and F. E. Guthrie, eds. North Carolina State University Press, Raleigh. General discussion of the problems of pesticide use.

Smith, R. H., and R. C. von Borstel. 1972. Genetic control of insect populations. *Science,* vol. 178, pp. 1164–1174 (December 15). An overview with a very useful bibliography.

Smith, W. H. 1974. Air pollution: Effects on the structure and function of the temperate forest ecosystem. *Environmental Pollution,* vol. 6, pp. 111–129. Review with extensive bibliography.

Snyder, N. F.; H. A. Snyder; J. L. Lincer; and R. T. Reynolds. 1973. Organochlorines, heavy metals, and the biology of North American Accipiters. *BioScience,* vol. 23, pp. 300–305. Heavy-metal contamination relatively slight and only one, cadmium, positively correlated with eggshell thinning.

Southwood, T. R. E., and M. J. Way. 1970. Ecological background to pest management. In *Concepts of pest management,* R. L. Rabb and F. E. Guthrie, eds. North Carolina State University, Raleigh. An interesting general discussion.

Sparks, R. E.; J. Cairns, Jr.; and A. G. Heath. 1972. The use of bluegill breathing rates to detect zinc. *Water Research,* vol. 6, pp. 895–911. A bioassay for a nonlethal toxicant.

Stanford Biology Study Group. 1970. The destruction of Indochina. (Reprinted in John P. Holdren and Paul R. Ehrlich, *Global ecology: Readings toward a rational strategy for man.*) On ecocide.

Stanford, G.; C. England; and A. Taylor. 1970. *Fertilizer use and water quality.* United States Department of Agriculture, Washington, D.C., Agricultural Research Service report 41–168. Good overview.

Stockholm International Peace Research Institute (SIPRI). 1976. *Ecological consequences of the second Indochina war.* Almqvist and Wiksell, Stockholm. An excellent, data-rich summary with comprehensive references. This monograph was prepared by Arthur H. Westing.

Stoewsand, G. S., J. L. Anderson, W. H. Gutenmann, C. A. Bache, and D. J. Lisk, 1971. Eggshell thinning in Japanese quail fed mercuric chloride. *Science,* vol. 173, pp. 1030–1031, 10 September. A suggestive study which, however, does not employ the form of mercury most common in the environment.

Stonier, Tom. 1963. *Nuclear disaster.* Meridian, Cleveland. Describes ecological effects of thermonuclear war; some material outdated by recent ecological work but well worth reading.

Strong, C. L. 1974. The amateur scientist. *Scientific American,* June. Describes a project in which acid rain was measured throughout the United States by schoolchildren.

Study of Man's Impact on Climate (SMIC). 1971. *Inadvertent climate modification.* M.I.T. Press, Cambridge, Mass. Authoritative review, as of 1971, of the potential for human disruption of climate. Excellent bibliography.

Sullivan, A. L., and M. L. Shaffer. 1975. Biogeography of the megazoo. *Science,* vol. 189, pp. 13–17 (July 4). A discussion of the factors that should be considered in designing a system of wildland reserves to preserve a diversity of plant and animal species as human settlements expand.

Swift, J. E., ed. 1971. *Agricultural chemicals: Harmony or discord for food, people, environment.* University of California, Division of agricultural sciences, Berkeley, vol. 1, p. 151. Interesting articles on such diverse topics as nitrogen fertilizer use (Stout) and pesticide resistance (Georghiou).

Tamm, C. O. 1976. Acid precipitation: Biological effects in soil and on forest vegetation. *Ambio,* vol. 5, no. 5-6, pp. 235–238. Possible mechanisms by which acid inputs could affect forest growth.

———; H. Holmen; B. Popovíc; and G. Wiklander. 1974. Leaching of plant nutrients from forest soils as a consequence of forestry operations. *Ambio,* vol. 3, no. 6, pp. 211–221. Modern forestry practices increase leaching of nutrients, causing elevated concentrations of nitrogen and sometimes phosphorus in streams and groundwater.

Thomas, W. A., ed. 1972. *Indicators of environmental quality.* Plenum, New York. Papers dealing with methodology for quantifying ecological problems. Useful but uneven in quality.

Thomas, William L., Jr., ed. 1956. *Man's role in changing the face of the earth.* University of Chicago Press. An international symposium edited with the collaboration of Carl O. Sauer, Marston Bates, and Lewis Mumford. Comprehensive and still very useful despite its age.

TIE. *See* Institute of Ecology.

Tinker, Jon. 1971. 1969 Seabird wreck: PCBs probably guilty. *New Scientist,* April 8, p. 69. Report on PCBs and their lethal effect on seabirds under stress.

———. 1971. One flower in ten faces extinction. *New Scientist,* May 13, pp. 408–413. More on the loss of stocks for potential food plants and other valuable plants.

———. 1971. The PCB story: Seagulls aren't funny any more. *New Scientist,* April 1, pp. 16–18. On how PCBs affect seabirds and how one manufacturer has treated the matter responsibly.

Travers, W. B., and P. R. Luney. 1976. Drilling, tankers and oil spills on the Atlantic outer continental shelf. *Science,* vol. 194, pp. 791–796 (November 19). A geologist and an attorney in the Department of Interior make a good case for drilling off the U.S. East Coast as environmentally much safer than importing oil via tankers. Includes some good data on oil spills.

Triplett, G. B., Jr., and D. M. van Doren, Jr. 1977. Agriculture without tillage. *Scientific American,* January, pp. 28–33. On the advantages (principally in drastically reducing soil erosion) of a zero-tillage system of agriculture. Unfortunately, the system requires heavy inputs of herbicides.

Tucker, A. 1972. *The toxic metals.* Earth Island, London. Good, popular description of heavy-metal pollution.

Turner, B. L., II. 1974. Prehistoric intensive agriculture in the Mayan lowlands. *Science,* vol. 185, pp. 118–123 (July 12). States that the classic Maya practiced intensive agriculture.

Turner, F. B. 1975. Effects of continuous irradiation on animal populations. *Advances in Radiation Biology,* vol. 5, pp. 83–144. A fine review of the literature, good comparison with other environmental insults.

Ulfstrand, S.; A. Södergren; and J. Raböl. 1971. Effect of PCB on nocturnal activity in caged robins, *Erithacus rubecula L. Nature,* vol. 213, pp. 467–468 (June 18).

U.S. Department of Agriculture. 1975. *The pesticide review, 1974.* Agricultural Stabilization and Conservation Service, Washington, D.C. Late figures on volume and value of production.

Vallentyne, J. R. 1972. Freshwater supplies and pollution: Effects of the demophoric explosion and water and man. In *The environmental future,* N. Polunin, ed., Macmillan, London, pp. 181–199. An excellent overview. Coins the word *demophoric* to "encompass all aspects of the biology of human populations and technological production-consumption." Thus, we are undergoing a demophoric explosion.

van den Bosch, Robert. 1969. The significance of DDT residues in estuarine fauna. In *Chemical fallout: Current research on persistent pesticides,* Miller and Berg, eds., pp. 205–220. Information on the ability of oysters to concentrate DDT.

———. 1969. The toxicity problem: Comments by an applied insect ecologist. In *Chemical fallout,* M. W. Miller and G. G. Berg, eds. Charles C. Thomas, Springfield, Ill., pp. 97–109.

———. 1971. Biological control of insects. *Annual Review of Ecology and Systematics,* vol. 2, pp. 45–66. Good survey of literature through 1970.

———. In press. *Bug bomb.* Doubleday, New York. A devastating insider's view of the disastrous consequences for agriculture of dependence on broadcast use of synthetic organic pesticides.

Vayda, A. P., ed. 1969. *Environment and cultural behavior.* Natural History Press, Garden City, N.Y. See especially Vayda's paper, Expansion and warfare among swidden agriculturalists, pp. 202–220.

Vernberg, F. J., and W. B. Vernberg. 1974. *Pollution and physiology of marine organisms.* Academic Press, New York. Mostly technical papers on heavy metals, pesticides, oil, and synergisms. Papers by Waldichuk on heavy metals and Duke and Dumas on pesticides in coastal environments are of the most general interest.

Viets, Frank G., Jr. 1971. Water quality in relation to farm use of fertilizers. *BioScience,* vol. 21, no. 10, pp. 460–467.

Vostal, J. J., ed. 1971. *Biologic effects of atmospheric pollutants: Fluorides.* National Academy of Sciences, Washington, D.C. Effects on ecosystems deemed localized.

Warren, Charles E. 1971. *Biology and water pollution control.* Saunders, Philadelphia. A thorough introduction to water-pollution ecology.

Washington, W. M. 1972. Numerical climate-change experiments: The effect of man's production of thermal energy. *Journal of Applied Meteorology,* vol. 11, pp. 768–772. A first rough attempt to include civilization's heat discharge in global climate models.

Wasserman, Larry Paul. 1969. Sweetwater pollution. *Science and Technology,* June, pp. 20–27. Ecological aspects of water pollution.

Weare, B.; R. L. Temkin; and F. M. Snell. 1974. Aerosol and climate: Some further considerations. *Science,* vol. 186, pp. 827–828 (November 29). Whether added aerosol produces net heating or cooling of Earth-atmosphere systems depends not only on properties of aerosol but on its location in the atmosphere, on cloud reflection, and on surface reflectivity.

Weinberg, A. M., and P. Hammond. 1970. Limits to the use of energy. *American Scientist,* vol. 58, p. 412 (July/August). Argues that abundant energy could permit support of populations much larger than today's in comfort. Underestimates climatological effects of such energy use.

Weisberg, Barry, ed. 1970. *Ecocide in Indochina.* Canfield, San Francisco. A radical view.

Weiss, Edith Brown. 1974. Weather as a weapon. In *Air, water, earth, fire,* Sierra Club, ed. Sierra Club, San Francisco, pp. 51–62.

Westing, Arthur H. 1971. Ecological effects of military defoliation on the forests of South Vietnam. *BioScience,* vol. 21, no. 17, pp. 893–898. A fine early discussion.

———. 1972. Herbicides in war: Current status and future doubt. *Biological Conservation,* vol. 4, pp. 322–327. A good summary.

———. 1975. Environmental consequences of the second Indochina war: A case study. *Ambio,* vol. 4, pp. 216–222. The best recent overview.

———, and E. W. Pfeiffer. 1972. The cratering of Indochina. *Scientific American,* May. The effects of high explosives on the land of Vietnam described by two of the scientists prominent in bringing the practice of ecocide to the attention of the public.

Westöö, G. 1973. Methylmercury as percentage of total mercury in flesh and viscera of salmon and sea trout of various ages. *Science,* vol. 181, pp. 567–568 (August 10). Found no age dependence.

Whicher, F. W., and L. Fowley, Jr. 1974. Effects of ionizing radiation on terrestrial plant communities. *Advances in Radiation Biology,* vol. 4, pp. 317–366. An excellent review.

Whiteside, Thomas. 1970. *Defoliation.* Ballantine, New York. On the dangers of herbicides, especially as used in Indochina.

Whitten, Jamie L. 1966. *That we may live.* Van Nostrand, Toronto. A clever piece of propesticide propaganda by a U.S. congressman. It attempts to give the impression that its conclusions are endorsed by scientists, although at least four of the most distinguished scientists interviewed in the course of its preparation disagree totally with its conclusions. Read this if you want to know your enemy. Whitten does not confine his activities to promoting pesticides. U.S. Representative Richard Bolling (D, Missouri) has written, "Study the unpardonable problem of malnutrition and even starvation in this country and you'll encounter Representative Jamie Whitten of Mississippi, Chairman of the Appropriations Subcommittee on Agriculture and lord of certain operations of the Agriculture Department," *Playboy,* November 1969, p. 255.

Widstrand, Carl Gösta. 1975. The rationale of nomad economy. *Ambio,* vol. 4, pp. 146–153. An anthropological view of settling the peoples of the Sahel.

Wigglesworth, V. B. 1968. *The life of insects.* New American Library, New York. A good paperback introduction to the terrestrial animals most important to humanity.

Wilde, Jan de. 1975. Insect population management and integrated pest control. *Ambio,* vol. 4, pp. 105–111. An overview of pest management.

Williams, Carroll M. 1967. Third generation pesticides. *Scientific American,* July. (Reprinted in Paul R. Ehrlich, John P. Holdren, and Richard W. Holm, *Man and the ecosphere.*) General discussion of hormonal insecticides.

Williams, C. N., and K. T. Joseph. 1970. *Climate, soil and crop production in the humid tropics.* Oxford University Press, Kuala Lumpur. See especially section on laterization.

Wilson, A. T. 1964. Origin of ice ages: An ice shelf theory for Pleistocene glaciation. *Nature,* vol. 201, pp. 147–149. The basic source of the Antarctic ice-cap-slump theory of glacial periods.

Wofsy, S. C.; M. B. McElroy; and N. D. Sze. 1975. Freon consumption: Implications for stratospheric ozone. *Science,* vol. 187, pp. 535–537 (February 14). Finds ozone reduction of 16 percent by 2000 if production of chlorofluorine gases continues to grow at 10 percent per year.

Wong, C. S.; D. R. Green; and W. J. Cretney. 1974. Quantitative tar and plastic waste distributions in the Pacific Ocean. *Nature,* vol. 247, pp. 30–32. Tar and plastic wastes shown to be widespread in surface waters of the Pacific.

Woodwell, G. M. 1967. Radiation and the patterns of nature. *Science,* vol. 156, pp. 461–470. Fits radiation damage sensitivity into general ecological patterns.

———. 1967. Toxic substances and ecological cycles. *Scientific American,* March. (*Scientific American* offprint 1066, W. H. Freeman and Company, San Francisco.) Excellent summary. (Reprinted in Paul R. Ehrlich, John P. Holdren, and Richard W. Holm, *Man and the ecosphere.*

———, ed. 1965. *Ecological effects of nuclear war.* National Technical Information Service, Springfield, Va., USAEC report BNL-917 (C43).

———, P. P. Craig, and H. A. Johnson. 1971. DDT in the biosphere: Where does it go? *Science,* vol. 174, pp. 1101–1107 (December 10). Very useful review of data and speculations about DDT in soils, in the oceans, in the atmosphere, and in the biota.

Woodwell, G. M., and R. H. Whittaker. 1968. Effects of chronic gamma irradiation on plant communities. *Quarterly Review of Biology,* vol. 43, pp. 42–55. Describes and interprets key experiments.

Wright, D. A., and A. W. Davison. 1975. The accumulation of fluoride by marine and intertidal animals. *Environmental Pollution,* vol. 8, pp. 1–13. Even in fluoride-polluted waters, tissue concentrations apparently are not increased—accumulation in both vertebrates and invertebrates occurs largely in skeletal parts.

Wuliger, Robert. 1977. The cosmetics of agribusiness. *The nation,* January 8, pp. 17–20. Provides some interesting insight into the political problems of doing research on pest control.

Wurster, Charles, F., Jr. 1968. DDT reduces photosynthesis by marine phytoplankton. *Science,* vol. 159, pp. 1474–1475 (March 29). An important paper; the ultimate significance of its findings is still unknown. See also Powers, et al, Dieldrin-induced destruction.

———. 1971. Persistent insecticides and their regulation by the federal government. Testimony before the Senate Committee on Agriculture and Forestry, March 25. Government Printing Office, Washington, D.C.

——— and D. B. Wingate. 1968. DDT residues and declining reproduction in the Bermuda petrel. *Science,* vol. 159, pp. 979–981 (March 1). Shows the effects of DDT on a bird of the open ocean. See also the exchange of letters between the authors of this paper and Lewis A. McLean of Velsicol Chemical Corp., a company that manufactures pesticides (*Science,* vol. 161, p. 387.).

Wurster, D. H.; C. F. Wurster; and W. N. Strickland. 1965. Bird mortality following DDT spray for Dutch Elm disease. *Ecology,* vol. 46, pp. 488–489. Good bibliography of related papers.

SECTION

V

The Human Predicament: Finding a Way Out

We have presented a survey of the "hard" sciences associated with the human predicament in the first eleven chapters of this book; the final section considers various aspects of societal response to that predicament. Chapter 12 is relatively brief and transitional. In it are examined the difficult question of how optimum population size might be defined and the ways in which population growth, increasing affluence, and faulty technologies interact to generate environmental impact. The conclusion that all of these causes are inextricably intertwined—that responsibility for the predicament cannot be ascribed to any one of them in isolation—provides fundamental background for the chapters that follow. Given this "web of responsibility," how can the world society change its collective behavior in order to permit civilization to persist into the indefinite future? What changes now can assure that in the future people will live reasonably secure and happy lives, supported by properly functioning ecological and social systems?

One step is obvious. The necessity of restraining the growth of the human population has long been evident to thoughtful people. Chapter 13 deals with ways in which this has been attempted in the past, how it might be dealt with in the future, and the current controversy about population control and development. Questions of technology (how effective and safe are contraceptives?), motivation (how can people be persuaded to use contraceptives, sterilization, or abortion?), and morality (should they?) are strongly interconnected. And these issues are not divorced from others equally knotty—poverty, racial discrimination and political power, to mention a few. While achieving population control rapidly would be very difficult if only for the numerical reasons given in Chapter 5, the difficulty is compounded by various social problems discussed in Chapter 13.

Chapter 14 focuses on American society and its institutions. The United States serves as a model for all developed countries—the one that in most respects has developed farthest, for better or for worse. If developed countries are to exercise leadership in a revolution of human attitudes and behavior, the most appropriate source for such leadership is the United States. And if such a revolution is to occur, it must involve virtually all parts of the sociopolitical system because of the pervasive nature of the crisis now building. Institutions that help individuals to relate to their environments—religion, science, medicine, education, and the law—all are sorely in need of modification to reflect the new realities of existence in the last part of the twentieth century. And the economic and political systems through which individuals have their major impact on the environment require equally drastic revision.

Similarly, as discussed in Chapter 15, the international system as presently constituted offers little hope of resolving the human predicament. A world divided by a vast and widening gap in wealth and income seems even less capable of solving serious problems than is a nation divided into rich and poor—especially while the poverty-stricken vastly outnumber the wealthy. Some possibilities for reorganizing the world, first to reduce and then to eliminate the gap between rich and poor, is the theme of that chapter. Our conclusion is that the only hope for closing the gap involves changing the ways of life of both the affluent and the hungry. The affluent must recognize that their futures are heavily dependent on the fate of the poor; the poor must accept new goals if their condition is to improve rather than deteriorate.

Ever present in any consideration of the international situation is the threat of nuclear Armageddon. A thermonuclear war is one event that would make almost all the issues and arguments raised in this book academic. Sadly, the probability of such a denouement may well be increasing—and this adds special urgency to the need for changing the ways in which nations interact.

In Chapter 14 and Chapter 15 especially, we frequently leave the solid ground of facts and venture into the quicksand of opinion and speculation. To do otherwise would be to omit topics that we feel may hold the key to the survival of society. No one can demonstrate "scientifically" that a given modification of the legal system of the United States or of the development goals of Kenya or Brazil will lead to an improvement in the prognosis for humanity, but we do not consider this a valid reason for not discussing such changes. We hope that at the very least our ideas in these and similar areas will stimulate discussion, which in turn may lead to action. For, as should be obvious, we are not sanguine about the prospects for civilization if it continues down its present path.

Maximum welfare, not maximum population, is our human objective.

—Arnold Toynbee, *Man and hunger,* 1963

CHAPTER 12

Humanity at the Crossroads

The maximum size the human population can attain is determined by the physical capacity of Earth to support people. This capacity, as discussed earlier, is determined by such diverse factors as land area; availability of resources such as energy, minerals, and water; levels of technology; potential for food production; and ability of biological systems to absorb civilization's wastes without breakdowns that would deprive mankind of essential environmental services. Of course, no one knows exactly what the maximum carrying capacity of Earth is; it would certainly vary from time to time in any case. Presumably, the capacity would be sustainable at a very high level for a short period by means of rapid consumption of nonrenewable resources. In the longer term, a lower capacity would be determined by the rate of replenishment of renewable resources and the accomplishments of technology in employing very common materials. Whatever the maximum sustainable human population may be, however, few thoughtful people would argue that the maximum population could be the same as the *optimum.* The maximum implies the barest level of subsistence for all. Unless sheer *quantity* of human beings is seen as the ultimate good, this situation certainly cannot be considered optimal.

The minimum size of the human population, on the other hand, is that of the smallest group that can reproduce itself. Like the maximum, the minimum size is also not the optimum. It would be too small to permit the many benefits of specialization and division of labor, of economies of scale in the use of technology, of cultural diversity, and so on. The optimum population size, then, lies somewhere between the minimum and maximum possible sizes.

THE OPTIMUM POPULATION

Biochemist H. R. Hulett has made some interesting calculations bearing on the subject of an optimum population. He assumed that the average United States citizen would not consider the resources available to him or her excessive, and he then divided estimates of the world production of those resources by the American per-capita consumption. On this basis, Hulett concluded: ". . . it appears that (about) a billion people is the maximum population supportable by the present agricultural and industrial system of the world at U.S. levels of affluence."[1] By Hulett's criteria, then, even ignoring depletion of nonrenewable resources and environmental deterioration, the population of the Earth is already 3 billion people above the present optimum.

Since decisions that determine population size are made, consciously and unconsciously, by the people alive at a given time, it seems reasonable to define the optimum size in terms of their interests. Accordingly, one might define the optimum as the population size below which well-being per person is increased by further growth and above which well-being per person is decreased by further growth.

Like most definitions of elusive concepts, this one raises more questions than it answers. How is well-being to be measured? How does one deal with the uneven *distribution* of well-being and particularly with the fact that population growth may increase the well-being of some people while decreasing that of others? What if a region is overpopulated in terms of one aspect of well-being but underpopulated in terms of another? What about the well-being of future generations? One cannot define an optimum population for any part of the world at any time without reference to the situation in all other parts of the world and in the future.

No complete answers are possible, but it is time that such questions be seriously addressed. The following observations are intended mainly to stimulate further discussion.

Priorities

The physical necessities—food, water, clothing, shelter, a healthful environment—are indispensable ingredients of well-being. A population too large and too poor to be supplied adequately with them has exceeded the optimum, regardless of whatever other aspects of well-being might, in theory, be enhanced by further growth. Similarly, a population so large that it can be supplied with physical necessities only by the rapid consumption of nonrenewable resources or by activities that irreversibly degrade the environment has also exceeded the optimum, for it is reducing Earth's carrying capacity for future generations. If an increase in population decreases the well-being of a substantial number of people in terms of necessities while increasing that of others in terms of luxuries, the population has exceeded the optimum for the existing sociopolitical system. The same is true when population increase leads to a larger *absolute* number of people being denied the necessities—even if the fraction of the population so denied remains constant (or even shrinks).

It is frequently claimed that the human population is not now above the optimum because if the available food (and other necessities) were in some way equitably distributed there would be enough for everyone.[2] But it is only sensible to evaluate optimum population size in terms of the organisms in the population under consideration, not in terms of hypothetical organisms. Thus, if an area of Africa has more lions than the local prey can support and the lions are starving, then there is an overpopulation of lions even though all the lions could have enough to eat *if* they evolved the capacity to eat grass.

Grossly unequal distribution of food and other goods is characteristic of contemporary *Homo sapiens* just as

[1]Optimum world population. Note that there is a large volume of conventional economic literature in existence that focuses on a narrowly defined economic optimum. This literature is of little interest to the discussion here (see, e.g., Spengler, Optimum population theory).

[2]For example, Barry Commoner, How poverty breeds overpopulation (and not the other way around), *Ramparts,* August/September 1975.

meat eating is of *Panthera leo.* Cultural evolution might lead toward greater equity (is China showing the way?), and might even produce a species of saints to replace *Homo sapiens* some time in the future. But until that occurs, it would seem wise to consider population optima in terms of human beings *as they now behave* and to strive for a world where everyone has the requisites of life *in spite of* unequal distribution of goods. At the same time, efforts should be made to reduce the inequities, and if they were successful the improved distribution could reduce the *degree* of overpopulation *without a reduction in population size.*

Density

It is popular among leaders of LDCs to compare their relatively low population densities with the much higher densities of European nations and infer that LDCs can accomodate several times more people per square kilometer than they now have. Population density in itself, however, is a poor measure of overpopulation or underpopulation.[3] Shortages of many resources other than physical space—for instance, fresh water, fertile soils, suitable climate, or minerals—may make it difficult to supply even a sparse population in a given area with the necessities of existence. Large parts of Africa, North and South America, and Australia are or could quickly become overpopulated in this respect despite their low densities because over large areas they lack sufficient dependable water, good soils, or a moderate climate.

The suggestion that all land areas can be made to support population densities as great as those of some European countries is misleading for two reasons. First, Europe is blessed with very favorable soils and climate; and second, Europe is by no means self-sufficient, even in food. For instance, Denmark, an exporter of dairy products, eggs, and meat, imports huge quantities of oil-seed cakes and grain to feed its livestock. In the late 1960s, Denmark imported more protein per person than any other country—240 pounds per year. This is three times the average annual protein consumption of each Dane!

The favorite example for showing that the world as a whole is underpopulated (averaging 28 people per square kilometer in 1972) is the prosperous Netherlands, which has 326 people per square kilometer.[4] This "Netherlands Fallacy" is an example of what is known in philosophy as the *fallacy of composition*—that what is true for a part must be true for the whole. The Netherlands can support 326 people per square kilometer only because the rest of the world does not. It ranks second in the world behind Denmark in imports of protein per person, a large portion of which, again, is fed to livestock. Much of the Netherlands' food, most of its fiber, and nearly all the metals needed in industry—iron, antimony, bauxite, copper, tin, and so on—are imported. Until the 1970s, when a large natural gas field in the northern part of the country was found and tapped, the Dutch imported nearly half their energy. Now their exports of gas more than compensate for oil imports.[5]

The Netherlands is an extreme example of the general situation of Western Europe. Measured against food demand and production, Europe is already overpopulated. In addition, the continent is a consumer of nonrenewable resources that are largely imported from other areas, and it also has serious population-related environmental problems.

Regardless of the great differences in population densities and degrees of over or underpopulation among nations, it is clear that discussion of population problems must focus on the Earth as a whole, because it has become a single, closed-loop feedback system as far as human activities are concerned. Air pollution is a global problem, resource depletion is a global problem, food shortage is a global problem, chlorinated hydrocarbon pollution is a global problem; thus an excessive population in one area of the world creates problems for all other areas.

Human Values

The concept of an optimum population size must also account for human values beyond physical necessities and economic purchasing power. Such values include an environment that is psychologically as well as physio-

[3]For an excellent discussion, see A. T. Day and L. H. Day, Cross-national comparison of population density.

[4]Figures from the United Nations' *Statistical Yearbook* for 1973.

[5]Paul Kemezis, Dutch devise wary energy policy, *New York Times,* January 26, 1975.

logically agreeable, a satisfying degree of contact with other people, a variety of educational opportunities, freedom from crime and excessive external restraints on personal behavior, and access to means of resolving conflicts and distributing justice. Many questions can be raised concerning these aspects of the human environment. What degree of contact is satisfying and what amount of interference excessive? How important is solitude for psychological well-being? There is little experimental evidence on most of these questions and little consensus among cultures or even within some cultures on what constitutes an agreeable environment. These uncertainties and lack of consensus suggest that a population size can be considered optimum only if it is far enough below physical limits to permit a good deal of environmental, social, and cultural diversity. Near the limits, diversity must be sacrificed in order to maximize production of physical necessities. As has been discussed in several earlier chapters, productivity and diversity may also conflict in agricultural and other biological systems. More generally, as soon as population growth begins to close more options that it opens, one can say that the population size has exceeded the optimum.

In today's world, many "way of life" options are being rapidly foreclosed. One of the major social consequences of the population explosion—the seductive technology of the West and the resource exploitation and neocolonialism it has helped to engender—is what might be described as a decay of cultural variability. Under the pressure of agricultural and tourist development, the ancient way of life of the Hawaiians is rapidly disappearing. It is now difficult to see a genuine hula in the 50th state, and the Hawaiian language is dying out. In Alaska the Eskimo culture has crumpled under the attraction of jobs on the DEW line (Distant Early Warning radar net) and in oil exploration and development. Snowmobiles are replacing dogsleds and old skills and customs are fast disappearing. At opposite ends of the world, the bucolic lifestyles of the Scottish Islanders and the Falkland Islanders are being threatened by oil development. The Indians of Paraguay are being systematically exterminated to make way for "progress."[6] Indian tribes in the Amazon Basin are being pushed aside or killed in conflicts over territory and food supplies, again for the sake of progress.[7]

The last nomadic human cultures are almost gone. The Tuaregs were all but destroyed by the Sahelian drought; the American plains Indians have long since been herded into reservations. Even in the absence of land-grabbing and other economic motivation, nomadism is dying. Less than 1000 of the 30,000 !Kung bushmen are still nomadic; the rest have settled down as poor farmers adjacent to Bantu settlements, where their nomadic culture is quickly forgotten. Births are no longer widely spaced, and the bushmen consequently are having a population explosion. Women are losing their once nearly equal status with the men because they are no longer major providers and because the Bantus refuse to deal with them. And their children are becoming aggressive, a trait almost completely suppressed among the nomadic bushmen.[8] Similarly, all but a few of the nomadic Australian aborigines are now settled, and their fabled bark paintings are losing their power as they are bowdlerized for trade. Soon this ancient art form may disappear altogether as the old male artists die off and young men refuse to continue the tradition.

The reasons for the conversion of the bushmen and aborigines to a sedentary life are complex, but one factor certainly is the difficulty that governments have in controlling nomads. In Australia, a significant element has been the desire of various missionary groups to control the lives of the nomads and replace their symbol-rich, naturalistic mythology with a considerably duller one of Western invention.

Certain values may be inconsistent with large numbers of people, although numbers themselves may be considered a value by such people as businessmen (who see bigger markets), politicians (who see more political power), or those who want large families. People who promote quantity of human beings as a value in itself, however, may be overlooking the cheapness such abundance often brings. One form of the conflict between values and numbers arises in the choice between having many children who are deprived or having fewer who can

[6]See, for example, John Hillaby, Genocide in Paraguay, *New Scientist*, January 16, 1975, p. 153.

[7]George Hawrylyshyn, No match for progress, *International Wildife*, March/April 1976, pp. 41–47; personal communication with oil company employees in Peru, 1975.

[8]G. B. Kolata, !Kung hunter-gatherers: feminism, diet, and birth control, *Science*, vol. 185, pp. 932–934, 1974.

be raised with the best care, education, and opportunity for successful adulthood. The dilemma applies to a society as well as to a family. It is apparently no accident that a disproportionate number of the most successful individuals are first or only children; nor that children of large families (particularly with more than four children), whatever their economic status, on the average perform less well in school and show lower I.Q. scores than their peers from small families.[9]

Although human beings are capable of adapting themselves to a wide variety of environments, it is plain that they do much better in some sets of circumstances than others. A vitally important point is how success of a society is measured—whether by the number of individuals who can barely survive in a given area, or by the number who can live healthy, productive, reasonably happy, and comfortable lives.

The Time Factor

The optimum population concept is of course a dynamic quantity, not a static one, and the concepts of overpopulation and underpopulation, therefore, are also dynamic. With the passage of time, both technological change and cultural evolution will inevitably change what would be regarded as optimum population sizes. In the face of such changing conditions, the world's governments should be ready to encourage appropriate population trends, just as they now attempt to produce desired economic trends. While the size of the human population must be brought under rational control, it should not be done with the idea of establishing and conforming to some permanently frozen "optimum" number.

In facing the prospects for the near future, it must be remembered that optimum means "optimum under existing social and technological conditions." As indicated above, to argue that a region is not overpopulated by pointing out that certain *hypothetical* social and technological changes might relieve the stresses is to misunderstand the biological meaning of overpopulation. In this context, the conclusion is inescapable that, in terms of present patterns of human behavior and the current level of technology, *the planet Earth as a whole is overpopulated.*

[9]R. B. Zajonc, Family configuration and intelligence; William D. Altus, Birth order and its sequelae; L. Belmont and F. A. Marolla, Birth order, family size, and intelligence. See also Roger Revelle et al., *Rapid population growth; Consequences and policy implications.* It includes several articles on the advantages to children of being first born or in small families.

UNDERSTANDING THE WEB OF RESPONSIBILITY: THE FIRST STEP TO SOLUTIONS

Pressures related to the size of the human population are already large and are growing rapidly. There is pressure on physical resources—land, food, water, forests, metals. There is pressure on the biological environment, whose ability to remove and recycle human wastes and to provide other vital services, from pest control to fish production, is being sorely taxed. There is pressure on society's ability to dispense services—education, medical care, the administration of justice. Indeed, there is even pressure on such important values as privacy, freedom from restrictive regulations, and the opportunity to choose from a variety of life styles.

Population size is not the only cause of these pressures. The consumption of materials and energy per person are also important factors. So is the type of technology that people employ to make the consumption possible, as well as the economic, political, and social forces that influence personal and institutional decision making. Can these factors be disentangled? Can one or another be identified as the dominant culprit in creating the present human predicament? It would be convenient if the answer were yes, for this would imply that a simple-minded, single-faceted solution exists.

Unfortunately, the answer is no. All the factors are important, and often they are inextricably linked by an array of cause-and-effect connections. Humanity's predicament has deepened so rapidly because a number of the contributing factors—population, consumption per person, the careless use of technology—*have been growing simultaneously,* and the ability of individuals and governments to adapt their behavior to ever more rapidly changing conditions and problems has not kept pace. Obviously, in considering the causes of humanity's plight, one is confronted not by a single culprit but by a complex and tightly woven web of responsibility. If human society is to find adequate and rational solutions, it is essential to investigate all the factors that interact to cause these problems and to discover the nature and consequences of the interactions. Although some of the more subjective aspects of the human predicament, such as pressures on values, are perhaps equally important, the problems of resources and the environment are easier to describe quantitatively. We shall therefore use these latter problems to illustrate in more detail what we mean by a "web of responsibility."

Multiplicative Factors

The most fundamental point is that the factors that contribute to growing resource consumption and environmental degradation are multiplicative rather than additive. This idea is expressed by a simple equation,

$$\text{resource consumption} = \text{population} \times \text{consumption per person}, \quad (1)$$

and by the slightly more complicated one,

$$\text{environmental impact} = \text{population} \times \text{consumption of goods per person} \times \text{environmental impact per quantity of goods consumed}. \quad (2)$$

Since consumption of goods per person is a measure of affluence, and since environmental impact per unit of goods consumed depends on the technologies of production, Equation 2 has sometimes been abbreviated as "impact equals population times affluence times technology." Note also that there is a distinction between consumption of resources and consumption of goods. Producing a good such as food may require large or small amounts of a resource such as phosphate fertilizer, depending on the form of agricultural technology being employed.

For problems described by multiplicative relations like Equations 1 and 2, no factor can be considered unimportant. The consequences of the growth of each factor are amplified in proportion to the size and the rate of growth of each of the others. Rising consumption per person has greater impact in a large population than in a small one—and greater impact in a growing population than in a stationary one. A given environmentally disruptive technology, such as the gasoline-powered automobile, is more damaging in a large, rich population (many people own cars and drive them often) than in a small, poor one (few people own cars and drive them less). A given level of total consumption (population times consumption per person) is more damaging if it is provided by means of a disruptive technology, such as persistent pesticides, than if provided by means of a relatively nondisruptive one, such as integrated pest control.

Quantitatively, the important point about Equations 1 and 2 is that slowly growing factors, when they multiply each other, lead to rapidly growing totals. Consider the following example for the resource equation. Suppose we wish to know whether population growth or rising consumption per capita played a greater role in the growth of total energy consumption in the United States between 1880 and 1966. In this period, total energy consumption increased about twelvefold, and the population increased fourfold.[10] It may therefore appear that consumption per capita was a more important factor than population growth. It was not. Consumption per capita increased threefold, versus fourfold for population. The twelvefold increase in the total consumption of energy arose as the *product,* not the sum, of the fourfold increase in population and the threefold increase in consumption per capita.

The results may be even more deceptive when there are three contributing factors, as there are in the environment equation. In a hypothetical case where population, per capita consumption of some commodity, and the impact of technology per unit of consumption all increase threefold, the total impact increases *27-fold.* The contributing factors here are equally important, but each seems quite small compared to the total.

Needless to say, the numerical quantities in the

[10] These and most other statistics in Chapter 12 are from *Historical statistics of the United States, colonial times to 1957,* U.S. Dept. of Commerce, U.S. Gov't Printing Office, 1957; and *Statistical abstract of the United States, 1976,* U.S. Dept. of Commerce, U.S. Gov't Printing Office, 1976.

resource and environment equations will vary greatly depending on the problem under scrutiny. For example, there are many different kinds of environmental impact, and different forms of consumption and technology are relevant to each. The population factor itself may refer to the population of a city, a region, a country, or the world, depending on the problem being considered. Our formulas, then, represent not just two calculations but many. We shall give a number of examples below—but first a few comments about the individual factors are in order.

TABLE 12-1
United States Total and Urban Population in Selected Years

Year	*Total population*	*Urban population*
1900	76,094,000	30,160,000
1910	92,407,000	41,999,000
1940	132,122,000	74,424,000
1946	141,389,000	–
1968	201,177,000	–
1970	205,200,000	149,279,000
1975	213,540,000	–

Source: Statistical abstract of the United States, 1976.

TABLE 12-2
United States GNP Per Person in 1958 Dollars

Year	*GNP per person*
1900	$ 940
1910	$1150
1940	$1740
1946	$2240
1968	$3515
1970	$3525
1975	$3820

Source: Statistical abstract of the United States, 1976; and Historical statisics of the United States: colonial times to 1957.

Population. The U.S. and world population situations have already been discussed in detail in Chapter 5. For the purposes of elucidating the role of population growth and the other factors in the web of blame, we shall focus on the United States over various time periods in the span from 1900 to 1975. The total population and urban population of the United States for several years in this period are given in Table 12-1. The table shows that the U.S. population in 1970 was 2.7 times as large as in 1900 and 1.55 times as large as in 1940. The urban population has increased even faster: in 1970 it was 4.95 times as large as in 1900 and 2 times as large as in 1940.

TABLE 12-3
Flows of Basic Resources in the United States

Year	*Annual steel production (lbs/person)*	*Annual energy consumption (million Btu/person)*	*Daily water use (gal/person)*
1900	300	96	–
1910	635	154	875
1940	1020	181	1030
1946	941	205	1170
1970	1285	328	1600
1975	1092	333	1800

Source: Statistical abstract of the United States, 1976; and Historical statistics of the United States: colonial times to 1957.

Affluence and consumption. How does one measure affluence? This is certainly a more difficult task than counting people. A conventional but much criticized measure of affluence is Gross National Product per capita. Gross National Product (GNP) consists of expenditures by consumers and government for goods and services, plus investment. So that figures for different years can be meaningfully compared in spite of inflation, they are usually converted to their equivalent in the dollars of some reference year. GNP per capita in the United States, measured in 1958 dollars, is given for selected years between 1900 and 1975 in Table 12-2. GNP per person, corrected for inflation, was 4.06 times as large in 1975 as in 1900 and 2.2 times as large as in 1940.

As is detailed in Chapter 14, it is easy to find fault with GNP as a meaningful index of affluence. In one sense it includes too much. Dollars spent on catching and prosecuting a growing number of violators of a growing number of laws contribute to GNP, as do the costs of wars and the costs of attempts to clean up pollution. Since these expenditures reflect or are necessitated by a declining rather than an improving quality of life, they should hardly be regarded as an indication of affluence. In another sense, GNP takes too little into account. Perhaps the "cost" of decaying cities, now being paid not in dollars but in the misery of those who must live and work there, should somehow be *subtracted* from GNP.

Despite the shortcomings of GNP as a measure of affluence, no alternative measures have yet gained wide acceptance. One possible approach is to use production or consumption of certain basic materials as an indicator. Typically, steel and energy are chosen as representative commodities, simply because large quantities of both are essential to running an industrial civilization. Another critical material in this connection is water. Figures for steel, energy, and water are given in Table 12-3. Note

TABLE 12-4
Stock of Consumer Durables in the United States

Item	1940s	1970s
Automobiles in use per capita	0.21 in 1940	0.59 in 1973
Refrigerators in use per capita	0.15 in 1946	0.27 in 1973
Clothes dryers in use per capita	0.001 in 1949	0.16 in 1973
Percentage of households with air conditioners	0.2% in 1948	48.6% in 1973

Source: Landsberg, Fischman, and Fisher, Resources in America's future, Johns Hopkins Press, Baltimore, 1963; Statistical abstract of the United States, 1975.

TABLE 12-5
Annual Per Capita Expenditures on Necessities in the United States in 1958 Dollars

Year	Food	Housing (rent or equivalent)	Clothing
1910	$175	$131	$ 87
1940	$231	$104	$ 87
1946	$346	$ 95	$133
1970	$440	$328	$214
1975	$452	$378	$206

Source: Statistical abstract of the United States, 1976; Historical statistics of the United States: colonial times to 1957.

that the per capita use or production of these commodities in the United States has increased between twofold and fourfold since 1900. The figures are not entirely unrelated, of course. It takes water and energy to produce steel; steel and water to make energy available; steel and energy to make water available.

Using flows of materials as an index of affluence has the drawback that it is often not *flow* that measures well-being but rather the stock of goods maintained by the flow. Owning a refrigerator is an indication of affluence; having to replace it frequently is not. Thus the amount of steel or the number of refrigerators and automobiles in existence in a society are better measures of affluence than the annual consumption or sales of these things. The quantity of goods, machinery, and materials owned or in existence is often referred to as *capital stock;* the annual consumption, or *throughput* as it is sometimes called, measures additions to the stock itself and replacement of losses (for example, junked automobiles that are not reclaimed). To the extent that a part of GNP is just flows of goods and materials measured in dollars, GNP shares the defect of focusing on throughput rather than on capital stock.

Changes over the last few decades in the capital stock of a number of goods known as *consumer durables* are shown in Table 12-4. Such figures are rather good indicators of rising affluence.

In some instances, of course, a flow rather than a stock is the appropriate measure of affluence. This seems to be the case for the necessities of existence—food, clothing, and shelter. In the case of food, kilocalories and grams of protein per day measure adequacy; beyond that, annual dollar expenditures on food measure variety and quality. To some extent, rising expenditures on food may also reflect increasing costs of production (to be discussed below). On the average, diets have been adequate in terms of quantity in the United States throughout this century. But increasing affluence, as reflected in expenditures on food, is very apparent in Table 12-5. Since clothing wears out rather rapidly, annual expenditure (a flow) is a reasonable measure of the quality of the stock. In the case of shelter, annual per capita expenditure in the form of rent or mortgage payments is probably a reasonable index of quality, after correction has been made for inflation. Statistics like "housing units" per capita do not help much; they measure the size of living groups, but they do not distinguish between one-room apartments and palatial mansions. Clothing and housing expenditures are shown along with those for food in Table 12-5.

Obviously, there are many ways to define and measure affluence, none of them completely satisfactory. Nevertheless, the picture that emerges from all the admittedly imperfect measures is a consistent one: affluence, by *any* reasonable definition, has increased dramatically in the United States in this century and especially in the last 30 years.

Technology. As noted above, society's emphasis on throughput in economic accounting sometimes leads to oversimplifying the connection between consumption and affluence. The factor most responsible for the real complexity of this connection is the character of the technology used to transform flows into benefits.

The relations among consumption, affluence, and

technology are well illustrated by the example of energy. Some of our energy consumption provides direct benefits in the form of heat for cooking and for heating water and space (homes, offices, etc.). Even in space heating, however, the real benefit is the "stock" of heat maintained inside, and the flow of energy is needed only to replace losses through walls, windows, and so on. The amount of energy flow needed to maintain a given temperature depends on technology, particularly the efficiency with which fuel is converted to heat and the quality of the insulation in the buildings being heated.

Another substantial part of society's energy consumption is needed simply to make possible the large throughput of other materials in our economy—steel, water, glass, plastics, and paper, to name some important ones. For given rates of consumption of these materials, the amount of energy required again depends on the technology used: the details of mechanical and chemical processing; whether or not recycling is employed; whether the process uses electricity or direct combustion of fuel; and so on. Transportation is yet another component of affluence in which energy consumption depends strongly on the sort of technology employed—small cars or large ones, trains or planes, gasoline engines or electric motors, and so on.

Technology is constantly changing. Such changes are stimulated largely by economic factors, such as the desirability of cheaper methods of production of existing kinds of goods; the profitability of inventing and marketing new kinds of goods; and the need to find substitutes for materials made scarce by heavy demands. Partly because ecological values have not been properly accounted for in our economic system, the changes in technology stimulated by that system have sometimes been profoundly disruptive of the environment.

The rapidly rising reliance on plastics in American manufacturing is a technological change that can be attributed partly to the quest for cheapness, partly to the desire for durability (which is admirable as long as the plastic is not being used in throwaway goods), and perhaps partly to scarcity of alternate materials such as certain kinds of wood. Of course, if the economic system is functioning "properly," scarcity leads to rising prices, so the cheapness of plastic and scarcity of the alternative reinforce each other.

Increasingly heavy use of fertilizers and synthetic organic pesticides in agriculture is a technological change stimulated partly by increased total demand for food and partly by economic forces that dictate *how* a greater demand will be met. In this case, alternatives would have been to bring more land into production, to promote labor-intensive rather than capital-intensive, high-yield agriculture, or to use integrated pest control.

Environmental impact. Only in a relatively few cases is it easy to assign an exact numerical value to the third factor in Equation 2—the environmental impact associated with a particular amount of consumption. It is possible to record the emissions of lead and oxides of nitrogen per vehicle mile, the pounds of sulfur dioxide released per kilowatt-hour of electricity generated, and other similar data. Even when such numbers are available, however, really good analysis is made difficult by several factors:

1. Most forms of consumption give rise to many different forms of environmental impact. For example, electricity production from coal causes air pollution, water pollution, solid waste, defacement of the landscape, and disruption of local ecosystems. Changes in technology may reduce some aspects of impact while increasing others.
2. The different kinds of impact associated with alternative technologies to meet the same need are hard to compare. For example, how does one compare the environmental impact of oil spills with that of coal mining?
3. Most of our knowledge concerns what people put into the environment, but not how the environment responds. This accounts for much of the difficulty associated with the previous two points. It is not enough to know how much lead is emitted by human activities; it is necessary to know how to put numerical values on the human health effects in the short and long term, on any impairment in the functioning of individual species of plants and animals, and on the general ecological effects resulting from the simultaneous action of lead on many organisms at once. It is not enough to know how much nitrogen is applied to fields; it is also necessary to know in detail what the health effects and ecological effects are

after it gets there. In short, it is *response,* not *input,* that really defines environmental impact. In almost every case, society's knowledge is far from adequate to assess this response quantitatively.

All this is not to say that society is too ignorant to take corrective action. The evidence of damage is overwhelming, and many of the basic causes are clear. But one must be cautious about using selected numbers to draw sweeping conclusions about the numerical increase in environmental damage over a given time span, and about the assignment of responsibility among the many factors that play a role.

The United States Since World War II

The pitfalls of underestimating the complexity of the web of responsibility are well illustrated by the statement frequently heard that "faulty technology" developed since World War II has been the principal culprit generating the environmental crisis in the United States.[11] Examination of this hypothesis is a useful way to look more deeply and specifically into some of the points raised above.

The main evidence offered to show that technology has been the dominant environmental villain is the observation that some indices of pollution in the United States have increased by 200 percent or more since World War II, while the population and affluence were growing much more slowly. Among the usual examples of dramatically increasing sources of pollution in the postwar period are emissions of lead and nitrogen oxides in auto exhausts, the use of synthetic pesticides and nitrogen fertilizer in agriculture, and the use of phosphates in detergents. But these examples would prove the hypothesis only if *all* of the following conditions were met:

1. The calculations for these examples showed that population growth and rising affluence have been minor contributors to the total increase, arithmetically speaking.

[11]The most vigorous exponent of the "faulty technology" hypothesis has been biologist Barry Commoner, whose book *The Closing Circle* contains a number of the specific fallacies we describe in this chapter.

2. The changes in technology that led to rapid growth in these indices of pollution were not sometimes *caused* by increases in total demand (population times consumption per capita) that could not be met by earlier technology.
3. The examples represented a valid sampling of all important kinds of environmental impact.

In actuality, *none* of these conditions is met by examples that have been said to demonstrate a dominant role for faulty technology.

Arithmetic of growth. Because the contributing factors—population growth, per capita consumption, and technology—are multiplicative, each factor is important no matter how fast the other factors have grown. According to Table 12-1, the U.S. population grew 45 percent between 1946 and 1970. In purely arithmetic terms (ignoring all possible cause-and-effect connections between population growth and the other factors), this says that our impact would only have been about two-thirds as large in 1970 as it actually was if the population had not grown in this interval. (The ratio of the 1946 population to that in 1970 is $1/1.45 = 0.69$, or slightly over two-thirds). Of the large total increase in impact, the one-third that is "explained" by population growth is an important contribution.

Table 12-2 shows that by one measure, GNP per person corrected for inflation, affluence grew 57 percent between 1946 and 1970. If GNP per capita were in fact a valid measure of the contribution of affluence to environmental impact, these figures would indicate that the 1970 impact would have been only 64 percent as large as it actually was if affluence had not grown in the 1946–1970 interval, again ignoring cause-and-effect connections among the factors. (The ratio of the 1946 per capita GNP to that in 1970 is $1/1.57 = 0.64$.) If neither population nor affluence had grown since World War II, the total environmental impact in 1970 would have been only 44 percent ($.69 \times .64$) of that actually experienced (within the limitations of GNP per person as a measure of the contribution of affluence to environmental impact, and ignoring cause-and-effect connections among the factors).

BOX 12-1 Automotive Lead: A Case Study

The emissions of lead from automobile exhausts increased 415 percent in the period between 1946 and 1968. Does this mean that the 42 percent increase in the population was responsible for only one-tenth of the increase in emissions? Not at all, because the contributing factors are multiplicative, not additive. Let us rewrite the equation given in the text symbolically (using $\cdot$ as a multiplication sign):

$$I = P \cdot C \cdot T,$$

where I denotes environmental impact, P is population, C is consumption per person, and T is the technological impact per unit of consumption. If, in a given time period, the increases in the various quantities are denoted ΔI, ΔP, ΔC, and ΔT, then the equation for the later time is

$$I + \Delta I = (P + \Delta P) \cdot (C + \Delta C) \cdot (T + \Delta T).$$

Percentages emerge when the equation is rewritten in the form

$$1 + \frac{\Delta I}{I} = \left(1 + \frac{\Delta P}{P}\right) \cdot \left(1 + \frac{\Delta C}{C}\right) \cdot \left(1 + \frac{\Delta T}{T}\right),$$

where $\Delta I/I$ times 100 is the percentage increase in environmental impact, $\Delta P/P$ times 100 is the percentage increase in population, and so on. (Note that an increase of 100 percent means a doubling of the initial quantity, an increase of 200 percent a tripling, and so on.)

The 42 percent increase in population between 1946 and 1968 means that $\Delta P/P$ for this period is 0.42 and the population factor, $1 + \Delta P/P$, is 1.42. In considering automotive emissions, the quantity "consumed" is vehicle miles per capita, which doubled in the period in question. Thus $\Delta C/C = 1.00$, $1 + \Delta C/C = 2.00$. The complete impact equation for lead emissions from automobiles therefore is

$$\begin{aligned} 1 + \frac{\Delta I}{I} &= 1 + 4.15 = 5.15 \\ &= \left(1 + \frac{\Delta P}{P}\right) \cdot \left(1 + \frac{\Delta C}{C}\right) \cdot \left(1 + \frac{\Delta T}{T}\right) \\ &= 1.42 \cdot 2.00 \cdot 1.81. \end{aligned}$$

In this example, the technology factor, emissions of lead per vehicle mile, is intermediate in importance between the population factor and the consumption factor. Population is not unimportant (without population growth, the total increase would have been 252 percent rather than 415 percent); technology is not dominant. This is so even though the emission of lead by automobiles is one of the *best* available examples of faulty technology in the post-war period.

The point here is not that the relative impact of technology has not grown substantially since World War II; in some cases, it has. But *especially* in such cases the total impact has been made that much greater because population and affluence were growing too. Some arithmetic calculations pertaining to growing environmental impact are shown in full detail in Box 12-1, using the actual example of automotive lead emissions since World War II.

Cause-and-Effect Relations

Increases in total consumption, brought about by population growth and rising affluence, can cause changes in the technology factor in several ways. Consider the use of man-made fibers such as nylon in clothing. The rapidly growing synthetic fiber industry is often cited as an example of an ecologically faulty technology, since these materials require large quantities of energy in their production and degrade only slowly in the biosphere. However, providing today's total U.S. demand for fiber *without* the synthetics would have required nearly a doubling in production of cotton and wool by 1972 over the 1945 levels (which were higher than some more recent ones). Whether this would have been practical at all is questionable. And, if it had been done, what would have been the ecological costs in terms of pounds of fertilizer and pesticides applied to cotton fields, the side effects of irrigation projects, and the erosion of farmland resulting from overgrazing? What about the loss of acreage to food production given over to cotton and flax? Clearly, technology changes with demand, and it is meaningless to consider the environmental and economic impacts of one kind of technology without also considering the impacts of alternative technologies that would permit the same material consumption.

Aluminum is another material whose consumption is increasing rapidly and which requires a great deal of energy to obtain from ore. Its use in cans is certainly a faulty technology unrelated to population growth or real affluence, but containers comprise only 10 percent of U.S. aluminum use. Fourteen percent is used in the electrical industry, where aluminum has been substituted for copper, which has been made scarce by heavy demands. Twenty-two percent is used in building and construction, partly to replace wood in siding, window frames, awnings, and so on. Nineteen percent is used in the manufacture of vehicles—automobiles, trucks, aircraft—where its light weight in comparison to alternative metals leads to substantial fuel energy savings in operation.[12] Meeting the demands of a growing population for better housing with wood alone would put additional pressure on forests, some of which are already being too intensely exploited. Substitutions of one material for another—nylon for cotton, aluminum for copper, aluminum and plastics for wood—are inevitable as a growing, increasingly affluent population presses on a finite resource base. Obviously, any additional environmental impact that results from such substitutions cannot justifiably be blamed on "faulty technology" alone.

Another way in which population growth and rising per capita consumption cause increases in technological impact is through the *law of diminishing returns.* This refers to a situation in which, in the jargon of the economist, the additional output resulting from each additional unit of input becomes less and less. Here "output" refers to a desired good (such as a food or metal), and "input" refers to what must be supplied (say, fertilizer, or energy, or raw ore) to obtain the output. Suppose that consumption of goods per person is to be held constant while the population increases. If the law of diminishing returns prevails, the per-capita consumption of inputs needed to provide the fixed per-capita level of goods will increase. Since environmental impact is generated by the inputs (such as energy) as well as by the use and disposal of the goods themselves, the per-capita impact will also increase.

To see how the law of diminishing returns operates in a specific example, consider the problem of providing nonrenewable resources such as minerals and fossil fuels to a growing population, even at unchanging levels of per-capita consumption. More people means more demand, and thus more rapid depletion of resources. As the richest supplies of these resources and those nearest to centers of use are consumed, it becomes necessary to use lower-grade ores, to drill deeper, and to extend supply networks. All these activities increase the *per capita* use of energy and hence the *per capita* impact on the environment. In the case of partly renewable resources such as water (which is effectively nonrenewable when groundwater supplies are mined at rates far exceeding natural replenishment), per-capita costs and environmental impact escalate enormously when the human population demands more than is locally available. Here the loss of free-flowing rivers and other economic, aesthetic, and ecological costs of massive water-movement projects represent increased per-capita penalties directly connected to population growth. Of course, these effects would also eventually overtake a stationary population that demands more than the environment can supply on a perpetual basis; growth simply speeds up the process and allows less time to deal with the problems created.

The law of diminishing returns is also at work when society tries to increase food production to meet the needs of growing populations. Typically, attempts are made both to overproduce on land already farmed and to extend agriculture to marginal land. Overproduction requires increased energy use out of proportion to the gain in yield, through the processes of obtaining and distributing water, fertilizer, and pesticides. Farming marginal land also increases per-capita energy use, since the amount of energy invested per unit of yield increases as less desirable land is cultivated. Both activities often "consume" the fertility built into the natural soil structure. Similarly, as the richest fisheries stocks are depleted, the yield per unit of effort drops, and more and more

---

[12]Figures on aluminum use are from National Commission on Materials Policy, *Material Needs and the Environment Today and Tomorrow,* Government Printing Office, Washington, D.C., 1974.

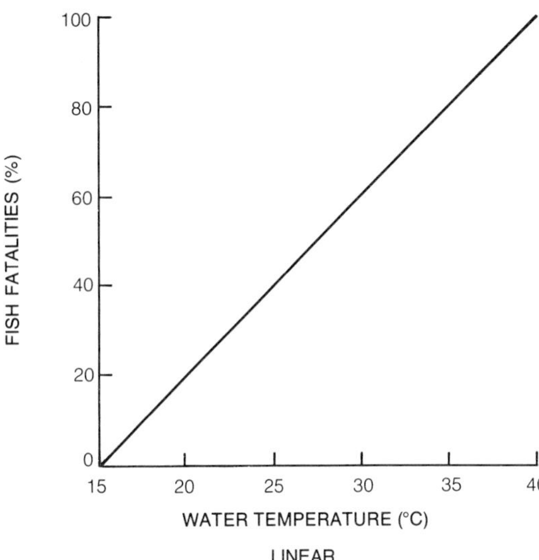

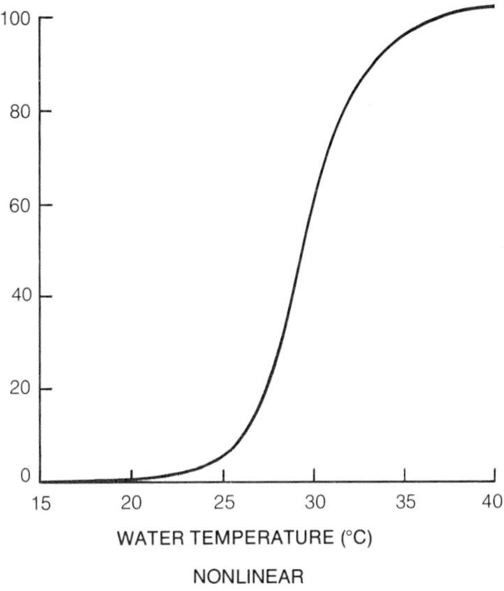

FIGURE 12-1

Idealized linear and nonlinear dose-response relations. In the real world, graphs like that on the right usually apply.

energy per capita is required to maintain the supply. Once a stock is depleted beyond a certain point it may not recover–it may be effectively nonrenewable.

Substitutions and diminishing returns are examples of the way in which population growth and rising consumption generate disproportionate increases in the *input* side of environmental impact–in what mankind *does to* the environment. Mankind's environmental predicament is also greatly aggravated by situations where relatively small changes in inputs may cause dramatic changes in the environment's *response.*

Threshold effects are one such type of situation. For example, below a certain level of pollution, trees will survive in smog. But when a small increment in the local human population produces a small increment in smog, living trees become dead trees. Perhaps 500 people can live around a certain lake and dump their raw sewage into it, and its natural systems will be able to break down the sewage and keep the lake from undergoing rapid ecological change. But 505 people may overload the system and result in a polluted or eutrophic lake.

Such thresholds characterize the responses of many organisms or groups of organisms to many different kinds of environmental changes: fish die when water temperature exceeds a certain threshold or when dissolved oxygen content falls below a certain threshold; different crops have different thresholds for tolerance of dissolved salts in irrigation water; carbon monoxide is fatal to people at high concentrations, but, as far as is known, causes only reversible effects at low concentrations. Scientists describe such situations as displaying a *nonlinear dose-response relation.* Nonlinear in this context means that a graph plotting response (say, percentage of deaths in a population of fish) versus dose (say, temperature in the habitat) will not be a straight line. The difference between linear and nonlinear dose-response relations is shown schematically in Figure 12-1.

Another form of nonlinear behavior in dose-response relationships is *synergism.* Here one is concerned with the simultaneous interacting effects of two or more kinds of input, where each kind of input acts to intensify the effects of others. For example, sulfur dioxide and various kinds of particulate matter are found at the same time in city air and for hundreds of miles downwind, and the combination appears to cause measurable adverse effects on health when the concentrations of both pollutants are well below the levels where one is dangerous individually.[12a] (One possible explanation is that sulfur dioxide adsorbed onto fine particles penetrates further into the lungs than the pure gas can; another is that the particles accelerate the transformation of sulfur dioxide into more dangerous sulfates.) Thus the joint effect is *synergistic:* it exceeds the sum of the individual effects expected if sulfur dioxide and particles had been present separately.

Synergisms also occur in environmental systems that

[12a]See, for example, David A. Lynn, *Air pollution,* Addison-Wesley, Reading, Mass., 1976, p. 97, and Chapter 10 here.

influence human health less directly than the incidence of disease. A particularly disturbing example is the combined effect of DDT and oil spills in coastal waters. DDT is not very soluble in sea water, so the concentrations to which marine organisms are ordinarily exposed are small. However, DDT is very soluble in oil. Oil spills therefore have the effect of concentrating DDT in the surface layer of the ocean, where much of the oil remains, and where many marine organisms spend part of their time. These organisms are thus exposed to far higher concentrations of DDT than would otherwise be possible. As a result, the combined effects of oil and DDT probably far exceed the individual effects.[12b] Many other synergisms in environmental systems are possible. Investigation of such effects is one of the most difficult (and neglected) areas of environmental analysis.

Other forms of impact. It is possible to get the impression from some of today's discussions of environmental problems that society's troubles began with the advent of the internal combustion engine, DDT, and nuclear fission. Although these are significant problems, we have shown in previous chapters that they are far from the whole story. Loss of good land to erosion, to faulty irrigation practices, and to overgrazing dates back thousands of years.[12c] Scattered over Earth are the remains of past ecocatastrophes, from Angkor Wat to the Tigris and Euphrates valleys to deforested southern Europe and the Middle East. Serious environmental deterioration was caused and is still being caused by preindustrial societies—especially by their agricultural practices.[13] The southward spread of the Sahara and contributions of dust to atmospheric pollution made by subsistence farmers are cases in point.

In addition, overexploitation of commercially valuable species of plants and animals has driven some to extinction and threatens many others—whales, a dozen species of fishes, several kinds of wild cats, birds, hardwood trees, and so on. Ocean fisheries are threatened by destruction of breeding grounds through dredging and filling operations in estuaries and marshes, as well as by overfishing and pollution. The extension of monocultures of a few, selected high-yield varieties of grain over large areas is increasing the vulnerability of world agriculture to disruption. In the United States, some of the best agricultural land is continually disappearing under suburbs, airports and highways. In short, there is a great deal more to environmental deterioration than pollution.

No single index can measure these numerous forms of environmental impact. For many of them, even statistics are lacking from which some allocation of responsibility among population growth and the other contributing factors could be derived. Many observers agree, however, that use of energy is the best single measure available of human impact on natural surroundings. The use of energy is central to most of the activities in question, and it is a direct contributor to many of the most obvious environmental problems.[13a] Moreover, as noted above, energy consumption per capita combines within a single statistic a measure both of affluence and of the impact of the technology that provides the affluence. It may not be possible to unravel the numerous connections *between* population size and per capita energy consumption. Nevertheless, it is useful to weigh the purely arithmetic contributions of these two factors to the recent growth of *total* energy consumption.

In an earlier example, we showed that population growth was a greater contributor than rising consumption of energy per capita to the increase in total U.S. energy consumption over the past 95 years. During a more recent period, 1940 to 1975, the population increased by 62 percent while energy consumption per capita increased by 83 percent. Worldwide, energy consumption during the 1960s and early 1970s was increasing at about 5 percent per year—about 2 percent per year due to population growth and 3 percent per year due to rising consumption per capita. Obviously, if energy consumption is a good measure of environmental

[12b]R. Revelle, E. Wenk, B. Ketchum, and E. Corino, Ocean pollution by petroleum hydrocarbons, in *Man's impact on terrestrial and oceanic ecosystems,* W. Matthews, F. Smith, and E. Goldberg, eds., M.I.T. Press, Cambridge, Mass., p. 313.

[12c]J. Donald Hughes, *Ecology of ancient civilizations,* University of New Mexico Press, 1975.

[13]For example, Erik Eckholm, *Losing ground; environmental stress and world food prospects.*

[13a]Of eleven global environmental problems identified as potentially serious in the landmark Study of Critical Environmental Problems (SCEP, *Man's impact on the global environment,* M.I.T. Press, Cambridge, Mass., 1970), six stem directly from energy production and two more from the use of fuels in high-flying jet aircraft.

impact, population growth has continued to be an important contributor to that impact, both in the United States and in the world as a whole.

Perfect Technologies and Shifting Impact

It is sometimes claimed that dramatic improvements in technology will compensate for continued growth in population and consumption per person. That is, if the per-capita impact on the environment due to technology can be sufficiently reduced, growth in population and consumption per capita need not lead to increased environmental degradation. This is certainly true for some kinds of activites and for a limited time. Some kinds of air pollution in the Los Angeles Basin, such as hydrocarbons and carbon monoxide, were decreasing in the early 1970s, even though both the population and the consumption of fuels were increasing. Installation of sewage treatment facilities in the late 1960s subsequently improved water quality in Seattle's Lake Washington and Wisconsin's Lake Mendota despite growing populations in these areas.

Such technological improvements should certainly be sought and applied, but they are not complete cures. One reason is that many technological "fixes" for environmental problems simply shift the impact to somewhere else, rather than removing it. Incinerating garbage pollutes the air, and available techniques for removing oxides of sulfur from power plant exhaust gases generate either solid wastes or water pollution. Switching from internal combustion engines to electric automobiles simply shifts part of transportation's pollution burden from the air over highways to air over power plants. Removing the lead from gasoline has apparently increased particulate emissions and may have increased the proportion of emitted hydrocarbons that are carcinogenic as well.

Even the approaches that successfully relieve one problem without creating another one are nevertheless imperfect. There is no such thing as "zero emissions." As percentages of contaminants per unit volume of effluent (say, treated water or stack gases from power plants) are reduced to very small levels, the costs of the control measures in dollars and energy become very large. In fact, reducing contaminant concentrations to zero would require an infinite amount of energy. Long before it could be achieved, of course, the environmental impact associated with supplying the energy for pollution control would exceed the impact of the pollution itself. This is the law of diminishing returns at its worst.

A good example is the economics of sewage treatment. The cost of removing 80 to 90 percent of the biochemical and chemical oxygen demand (standard indices of pollutants in water), 90 percent of the suspended solids, and 60 percent of the resistant organic material by means of secondary treatment in the late 1960s was about 8 cents per thousand gallons in a large plant. But if there is so much sewage that its nutrient content creates a serious eutrophication problem (as is the case in much of the United States today), or if water is in such short supply that sewage water must be reused for industry, agriculture, or ground-water recharge, advanced treatment is necessary. The cost ranges from 2 to 4 times as much as for secondary treatment (17 cents per 1000 gallons for irrigation of food crops, 34 cents per 1000 gallons to yield a drinkable supply).[14] This story could be repeated for many other forms of environmental impact.

There is good reason to believe, therefore, that an increasing fraction of national income will have to be spent during the next few decades to hold pollution to tolerable levels. Even then, some important aspects of the problem may go unnoticed until irreversible damage has been done, and other aspects may worsen for the lack of available technology to deal with them at any price. At the moment, for instance, no technology has been developed to control emissions of nitrogen oxides from electric power plants, and it is not practical to control emissions of carbon dioxide from all combustion of fossil fuels because the volume of the effluent is so great. Tilling the soil and mining operations may accelerate the rate at which mercury is removed from Earth's crust and injected into the ecosystem.[15] More mercury may be released to the environment this way than by industrial processes, and no remedy is known.

As noted in earlier chapters, the ultimate pollutant is

[14]Figures on cost of sewage treatment are from *Cleaning our environment: the chemical basis for action*, Washington D.C., American Chemical Society, 1969.

[15]See K. K. Bertine and E. D. Goldberg, Fossil fuel combustion and the major sedimentary cycle, *Science*, vol. 173, p. 233, 1971.

heat. All recycling and other forms of pollution control require energy, and all the energy people use ultimately turns up in the environment as waste heat. More efficient generation and utilization of energy can relieve this problem somewhat, but they cannot eliminate it. If, miraculously, all other environmental defects of our technology could be remedied, this one would remain.

It must be concluded that improving technology to reduce its contribution to total environmental impact is worthwhile but is not the entire answer. Under any set of technological conditions, there will be some impact associated with each unit of consumption, and, therefore, at some level of population size and consumption per person, the total impact will become unsustainable.

THE PROSPECTS

The tightly interlocked and simultaneously growing factors that comprise what we have called the web of responsibility must *all* be attacked if humanity is to avoid future environmental breakdowns or mass famines. A strategy that treats only *some* of the factors is bound to fail. The interrelated consequences of various policies have been sharply illustrated by *The Limits to Growth*[16] (sponsored by the Club of Rome and further described in Box 12-2), which suggested that only by controlling *all* the interacting factors could future catastrophe be averted.

[16]D. H. Meadows et al., *The limits to growth.*

BOX 12-2 Computer Models and the Limits to Growth

The appearance in 1972 of the book *The Limits to Growth* generated an international storm of controversy. The book describes the results of a project carried out at the Massachusetts Institute of Technology on "the predicament of mankind"—the interlocking problems of population, food, raw materials, pollution, and economic growth. The principal conclusions of the project were that the trends characterizing these elements of the human condition in the twentieth century could not be sustained for long into the future, and that if the growth of population, industrial production, and pollution were not stopped by enlightened social action, then they would be stopped by one or more kinds of physical catastrophe—famine, resource exhaustion, or epidemic disease. Figure 12-2 shows the projected results of present trends if they continue with no interference from society.

In addition, the model demonstrated that controlling only one or two of the major interacting influences on the world system—population, resource depletion, environmental deterioration—would produce at least equally disastrous results. To take just one example, if a program of reducing demands on exhaustible resources (by finding abundant substitutes, recycling, and so forth) were established without controlling the other factors, the consequences would be worse than a future in which resources were exhausted. To quote Jay W. Forrester of M.I.T., who published early results of the study in 1971, on the results of a computer run in which it was assumed that technology could circumvent resource limits:

> By not running out of resources, population and capital investment are allowed to rise until a pollution crisis is created. Pollution then acts directly to reduce birth rate, increase death rate, and to depress food production. Population, which, according to this sample model, peaks at the year 2030, has fallen to one-sixth of the peak population within an interval of 20 years—a world-wide catastrophe of a magnitude never before experienced.[a]

Forrester's and the Meadows' analyses (and those of subsequent workers such as Mesarovic and Pestel[b]) projected the collective results of various trends in this way, in each case controlling or altering different interacting factors.

[a]Jay W. Forrester, Counterintuitive behavior of social systems.
[b]M. Mesarovic and E. Pestel, *Mankind at the turning point.*

Their results showed that some form of disaster lies ahead unless *all* the factors are controlled: population growth, pollution, resource consumption, and the rate of capital investment (industrialization).

This was hardly a new conclusion in 1972. Indeed, the argumentation and evidence for this general world-view had been accumulating steadily since the time of Malthus (see Box 13-2), and a rash of books drawing substantially similar conclusions had appeared in the decades following World War II.[c] What accounts, then, for the extraordinary response—both disparaging and laudatory—that these views elicited when they appeared in *Limits to Growth* in 1972?

Several factors contributed: first, the status of M.I.T. as virtually a worldwide synonym for careful scientific analysis; second, the sponsorship of the project by the vaguely mysterious Club of Rome, an international collection of influential academicians, industrialists, and public figures; third, the extraordinarily direct and lucid style with which the authors presented their conclusions; and fourth, the major role played in the underlying analysis by a "computer model" of the world.

Of these factors, the last was almost certainly the most important. The book appeared at a time when the capabilities of large computers had already become part of public conventional wisdom (or folklore), but when the idea that computer results are no better than the information fed into them was not so widespread. Thus the notion that a computer had certified the bankruptcy of growth gave the conclusion public credibility, and at the same time provided a target for indignant economists and others who saw the outcome as an illustration of the syndrome known in the computing trade as "garbage in, garbage out."[d]

How do computer models in general, and the *Limits* model in particular, actually work? The idea behind computer modeling is to simulate in a general way the behavior of complicated physical systems. The technique is used when the situation of interest is too complicated to analyze with equations solvable with pencil and paper, or with laboratory or field experiments on a reasonable scale; and when it is too time-consuming or too risky simply to observe the real system and see what happens. Systems or processes that meet these conditions and that accordingly have been studied with computer models include the global meteorological system, various ecosystems, the safety systems of nuclear reactors, the growth of cities, and the evolution of galaxies.

In all such cases, models are constructed by identifying what seem to be the most important

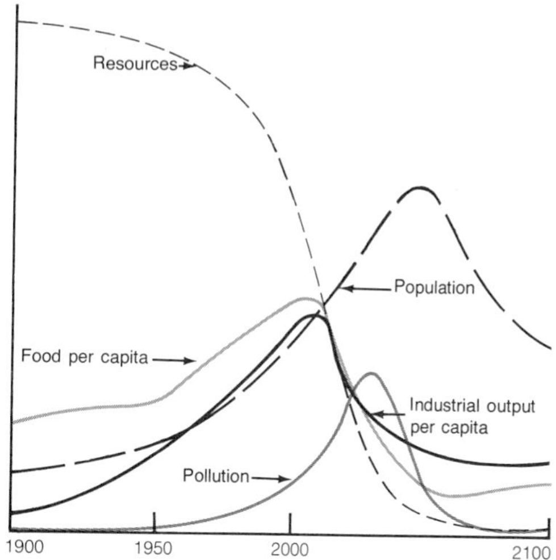

FIGURE 12-2

The "standard" world model run assumes no major change in the physical, economic, or social relationships that have historically governed the development of the world system. All variables plotted here follow historical values from 1900 to 1970. Food, industrial output, and population grow exponentially until the rapidly diminishing resource base forces a slowdown in industrial growth. Because of natural delays in the system, both population and pollution continue to increase for some time after the peak of industrialization. Population growth is finally halted by a rise in the death rate due to decreased food and medical services. (After Meadows et al., 1972.)

[c]For example, William Vogt, *Road to survival;* Fairfield Osborne, *Our plundered planet;* Harrison Brown, *The challenge of man's future;* Georg Borgstrom, *The hungry planet,* Macmillan, New York, 1965; Paul Ehrlich, *The population bomb,* Ballantine, New York, 1968; Preston Cloud, ed., *Resources and man,* W. H. Freeman, San Francisco, 1969; P. R. Ehrlich and A. H. Ehrlich, *Population resources, environment,* W. H. Freeman, San Francisco, 1970.

[d]See, for example, K. Kaysen, The computer that printed out W*O*L*F, *Foreign Affairs,* 1972, which tries but fails to stick the "garbage" label on *Limits to Growth,* missing the point in major respects.

(Continued)

components of the system under study and by writing down in mathematical form what seem to be the main cause-and-effect relationships linking these components. The components are characterized by the values of associated "state variables"—for example, the surface temperature of the ocean, the pressure in a reactor core, the population of a city. Sometimes the relationships between different variables are known exactly from physical laws, but more often these links must be represented in very approximate or even hypothetical form, consistent with whatever limited data may be available from the "real world."

The computer model used in the *Limits to Growth* work evolved from a simpler one devised by Forrester, who had earlier devised structurally similar models of corporations and of cities.[e] Major subdivisions of the *Limits* model include capital investment, pollution, resources, population, and agriculture. In many instances, the feedback loops linking variables in these subdivisions incorporate time delays reflecting lags between environmental change and response, which are common in both biological and social systems. Thus, for example, capital investment in the health-service sector of the economy leads after a time lag to improved health care, which—along with factors related to crowding, nutrition, and pollution—influences life expectancies and hence population size.

When supplied with conditions at some starting point in time, the *Limits* computer model traces out the subsequent behavior of the major system variables—population, resources, pollution, and some others—based on the assumptions in the model. The resulting output takes the form of graphs displaying the rise and fall of the system variables as time goes by. As they appear in *Limits to Growth,* these graphs are dated only at rather wide intervals—1900, 2000, 2100. This is perfectly reasonable, since the results are intended simply to be indicative of the sorts of behavior the world system is prone to, rather than predictions of exactly what the state of the system will be on a specific date. It could hardly be otherwise, since considerations of computer capacity and running time (to say nothing of uncertainties concerning the way the world works) dictate that much detail be omitted.

Contrary to some of the criticisms of *Limits to Growth* that have been published, however, such simplification does not invalidate the results. Indeed, those who construct mathematical models of all kinds consciously *avoid* reproducing the system being studied in all its details; if they did not, the model would be as difficult to deal with as the real world. The essence of modeling is to include in the model only those variables and interconnections that are truly critical, thus yielding the central features of the behavior of the system without an impenetrable array of details.

Of course, it is possible to err on the side of simplifying too much. The *Limits* model considered only one class of generalized pollutants and one class of generalized resources, each having properties thought to be representative of the most important items in the actual categories. There is also only one population, whose characteristics in the model represent in some sense an average of all the world's different populations. These are major approximations, and it may reasonably be asked whether what has been left out of the model, such as the interaction between different societies responding very differently to the same sorts of environmental change, is not just as important as what has been included. The authors of *Limits to Growth* recognized the need to investigate this question. They and others encouraged by them have devoted much effort to developing more detailed models and to testing the sensitivity of the results to the various assumptions used.[f]

On the question of sensitivity to assumptions, many technologists have claimed that a different (and cheerier) result can be obtained from the *Limits* model by making modest changes in assumptions. The work that is generally quoted in support of this contention, however, deals not with the *Limits* model but with Forrester's earlier one, and it does not in fact support the contention at all.[g] The investigator was able to make the original Forrester model reach a utopian result only by assuming that a sixfold increase in technology over the 1970 levels would lead to an eightfold increase in food production, and that a fourfold increase in

[e]See Jay W. Forrester, *World dynamics; Urban dynamics,* M.I.T. Press, Cambridge, Mass., 1969; *Industrial dynamics,* M.I.T. Press, Cambridge, Mass., 1961.

[f]See, for example, D. L. Meadows and D. H. Meadows, eds., *Toward global equilibrium.*

[g]R. Boyd, World dynamics: a note. *Science,* vol. 177, pp. 516–519, 1972.

technology would reduce resource input and pollutant output per unit of material standard of living to zero.

The first assumption is contrary to all recent experience; doublings of agricultural productivity have required triplings and quadruplings of technological inputs. The second assumption is impossible in principle since it violates the second law of thermodynamics, one of the most thoroughly verified laws of nature. All one could safely conclude from this work is that Forrester's model is "sensitive" to the introduction of miracles into the assumptions. Presumably, the more sophisticated model in *Limits to Growth* would also be "sensitive" in this way, but that is hardly a defect.

The most detailed critique of the *Limits* model was performed by a group at the University of Sussex, England, and was published together with a reply by the authors of *Limits of Growth* in a book called *Models of Doom.*[h] The Sussex critics accused the *Limits* group of leaving out economics and social change, of underestimating the power of technology, and of daring to make policy recommendations on the basis of a flawed model. The response of the *Limits* group was that their model probably overestimated the effectiveness of the price mechanism rather than underestimated it, that evidence of the limitations of technology has been accumulating rapidly, that in the absence of any perfect models one must make policy recommendations with the best ones available, and that social change (which is hard to model) is precisely what they were trying to stimulate by their recommendations. On the issue of whether the model overstated or understated the imminence of disaster, we might add that the simplistic treatment of environmental risks probably understated the danger more than other flaws overstated it.

Probably the most imposing attempt to construct a more realistic model than that in *Limits* was described in 1974 in *Mankind at the Turning Point: The Second Report to the Club of Rome,* by M. Mesarovic and E. Pestel. This model divided the world into ten political/geographical regions, modeling each of these on five "strata": (1) physical environment; (2) technology; (3) economic systems; (4) institutional and social responses; and (5) individual needs and responses.

Notwithstanding *Turning Point's* occasional gratuitous disparagement of the oversimplification in *Limits to Growth* (difficult to understand in view of its obvious debt to the earlier work), the conclusions were strikingly similar: continuation of recent trends in population growth, industrialization, and environmental disruption will lead to disaster; deliberate and massive social and economic change will be necessary to avoid this outcome. The added sophistication of *Turning Point's* regional disaggregation, showing the problems that can arise from such interactions as competition among regions for scarce resources, should be welcomed. At the same time, it seems fair to say that the net effect of this added degree of detail is to make the prognosis *more* pessimistic than that in *Limits,* not less so. Basically, regional disaster or negative interactions leading to wars seem more imminent than a uniform global disaster, which was the only kind the aggregated model in *Limits* could reveal. (This, of course, is another conclusion that many analysts have reached over the years without benefit of computer modeling).

Obviously, the model in *Turning Point* is still far from perfect. Certainly neither it nor other computer models can be used to predict the future in detail. Nevertheless, computer modeling seems a useful way to acquire or communicate insights about the implications of present trends, and it has the great advantage of requiring that assumptions about relevant relationships be made explicit. Surely this is an improvement over the situation most likely to prevail when people think about the future of a complicated world—the "models" in their heads are full of assumptions that are not only unstated but perhaps even unrecognized. In short, those critics who believe the world cannot be modeled should stop thinking about the future entirely, for implicitly all who do are modeling in their heads.

The purpose of caring at all where humanity is going, of course, whether one finds out with or without the aid of a computer, is not prediction for its own sake. It is, rather, that if we do not like the projected consequences of present trends and values, we can take conscious action to change course.

[h]H. Cole, C. Freeman, M. Jahoda, K. Pravitt, eds., *Models of doom,* Universe Books, New York, 1973.

It has been claimed that the technology factor should be tackled first because it is the easiest to deal with. As should be clear from the preceding analysis, this is a completely misleading idea. If that approach alone were carried out, it would serve only to deepen the human predicament; even the most dramatic improvements in technology would ultimately be canceled by rising population and consumption levels.

The momentum inherent in population growth commits *Homo sapiens* to many decades of further increase under even the most optimistic assumptions. And the momentum of economic growth makes it unlikely that growth in consumption per person in rich nations can quickly be halted, either—particularly as long as economic growth is erroneously perceived as a substitute for eliminating the gross inequities in the distribution of wealth. Since it seems both inevitable and just that the poor nations will press for growth in *their* economies, the misappropriation of the world's resources by rich countries must soon be confronted along with the more general problem of poverty in LDCs. If humanity ignores population growth, overconsumption, and maldistribution of wealth now because these problems are tough and chooses instead to deal only with the relatively easy technological questions, the prospects twenty or thirty years hence will be gloomy indeed. The momentum of population and consumption trends will still be committing world society to even more growth, but most of the easy technological tricks to soften its environmental impact will by then have been exploited. Moreover, the prospects for eventual prosperity in the LDCs, already slim, will be hopeless if the rich countries are permitted to go on looting the world's high-grade resources for their own extravagant consumption for a few more decades.

It is also clear that attacking each of the other factors in isolation—growth of population or material consumption—would be an equally futile exercise. The most draconian control of population growth will be of no avail if technology and consumption are not controlled as well. Suppressing growth of material consumption without providing technological improvement or population control—the most unlikely eventuality—might retard environmental damage, but at the cost of impoverishing all of humanity.

Obviously, the time is long past for quibbling about which factor in the human predicament is "most important." They are *all* important. Failure to come to grips with all the factors—*simultaneously, now*—will surely sabotage the future for people now alive and for generations to come. The following chapters explore some of the avenues by which humanity might avoid some of the more serious pitfalls ahead, starting with the knotty issue of population control.

Recommended for Further Reading

Ehrlich, Paul R., and John P. Holdren. 1971. Impact of population growth. *Science,* vol. 171, pp. 1212–1217 (26 March). A discussion of the impact of population growth on the environment.

Iltis, H. H.; O. L. Loucks; and P. Andrews. 1970. Criteria for an optimum human environment. *Bulletin of the Atomic Scientists,* vol. 26, January, pp. 2–6. On an optimum environment for human beings.

Meadows, Donella H.; D. L. Meadows; J. Randers; and W. W. Behrens III. 1972. *The limits to growth.* Universe Books, Washington, D.C. The famous study of the Club of Rome, showing that control of *all* factors—population, economic growth, and environmental deterioration—is necessary to avoid catastrophe some time in the future.

Spengler, Joseph J. 1975. *Population and America's future.* W. H. Freeman and Company, San Francisco. A detailed study of the impact of population growth on the U.S., especially economic and social impact.

United States Commission of Population Growth and the American Future. ·1972. *Population and the American future.* Signet Books, New York. Summary of the National Commission's Report, in which no advantages were seen in further U.S. population growth, but many advantages were seen in stopping growth.

Additional References

Altus, William D. 1966. Birth order and its sequelae. *Science* vol. 151, pp. 44–49 (January 7). Evidence that first-born children are more likely than others to achieve eminence or educational attainment.

Belmont, L. and F. A. Marolla. 1973. Birth order, family size and intelligence. *Science* vol. 182, pp. 1096–1101. (December 14) More evidence that first-born children are achievers.

Brown, Harrison. 1954. *The challenge of man's future.* Viking, New York. An excellent early warning on the population and resource problems.

Coale, Ansley J. 1970. Man and his environment. *Science* vol. 170, pp. 132–136 (October 9). A naive view of the relationship between population, resources, and environment. Undocumented, but an excellent source for examples of various fallacies.

Commoner, Barry. 1971. *The closing circle.* Knopf, New York. Strongly argues that faulty technology is to blame for most of the human predicament.

Day, A. T. and L. H. Day, 1973. Cross-national comparison of population density. *Science,* vol. 181, pp. 1016–1023 (14 Sept.). Excellent critique of the fallacies often associated with discussions of population density.

Eckholm, Erik P. 1976. *Losing ground; environmental stress and world food prospects.* W. W. Norton, Inc., New York. Excellent up to date treatment of agriculture's side effects.

Ehrlich, P. R., and J. P. Holdren. 1972. One-dimensional ecology. *Bulletin of the Atomic Scientists* vol. 28, April. A detailed, documented refutation of Barry Commoner's contention that population growth and affluence do not play significant roles in causing environmental deterioration.

Enke, Stephen. 1970. Zero U. S. population growth—when, how, and why. *Tempo.* January. General Electric Co., Santa Barbara, California. Includes discussion of the economic impact of population growth in the U.S.

Forrester, Jay W. 1971. Counterintuitive behavior of social systems. *Technology Review* vol. 73, no. 3. Early report on the "Limits to Growth" study.

———. 1971. *World dynamics.* Wright-Allen Press, Cambridge, Mass. A computer model study of the world system.

Goldsmith, Edward, et al. 1972. *Blueprint for survival.* Houghton-Mifflin Co., New York. Paperback ed., Signet, 1974. A plan for escaping from humanity's predicament.

Holdren, John. 1973. Population and the American predicament: the case against complacency. *Daedalus,* vol. 102, no. 4, pp. 31–44. Reasons for believing the U.S. has exceeded its optimum population size.

Hulett, H. R. 1970. Optimum world population. *BioScience,* vol. 20, no. 3. A pioneering attempt at estimating its size.

Meadows, D. L. and D. H. Meadows., eds. 1973. *Toward global equilibrium.* Wright-Allen Press, Cambridge, Mass. An elaboration of the *Limits to growth* study.

Mesarovic, M., and E. Pestel. 1974. *Mankind at the turning point: the second report to the Club of Rome.* E. P. Dutton, New York. Use of a regionally disaggregated model yields generally similar conclusions to those in *Limits to growth.*

Morris, Desmond. 1967. *The naked ape.* McGraw-Hill, New York. In spite of some errors of fact and interpretation, this is an excellent book for putting humanity in perspective.

Odum, Eugene, P. 1971. The optimum population for Georgia. *The Ecologist,* vol. 1, no. 9, pp. 14–15. An analysis of how optimum population might be determined, using the state of Georgia as a model.

Osborne, Fairfield. 1948. *Our plundered planet.* Little, Brown & Co., Boston. An early warning on the population-resource-environment crunch.

Revelle, Roger (chairman). 1971. *Rapid population growth: consequences and policy implications.* Report of a National Academy of Sciences Study Committee. Johns Hopkins Press, Baltimore. A cautious report that enormously underestimates both the role of population growth in inducing environmental deterioration and the environment's role as a limitation on population growth. Contains a number of interesting papers on social and economic aspects of population growth.

Spengler, Joseph J. 1968. Optimum population theory. *International encyclopedia of the social sciences,* vol. 12, pp. 358–362. Macmillan Co., New York. A concise introduction to conventional economic thinking on the subject.

Vogt, William. 1948. *Road to survival.* Sloane, New York. One of the classic "early warnings", like Osborne's *Our plundered planet.*

Ward, Barbara. 1966. *Spaceship Earth.* Columbia University Press, New York. An analysis of the developing human predicament by a distinguished economist.

Wray, Joel. 1971. Population pressures on families: family size and child spacing. In Revelle, *Rapid population growth.* A comprehensive treatment of the relationship of family size to the family's health, nutrition, welfare and I.Q., in both DCs and LDCs.

Zajonc, R. B. 1976. Family configuration and intelligence. *Science,* vol. 129, pp. 227–236 (April 16). A recent study confirming that children in large families tend to perform less well scholastically.

Of all things people are the most precious.

—Mao Tse Tung

CHAPTER 13

Population Policies

Any set of programs that is to be successful in alleviating the set of problems described in the foregoing chapters must include measures to control the growth of the human population. The potential goals of such measures in order of possible achievement are:

1. Reduce the *rate* of growth of the population, although not necessarily to zero.
2. Stabilize the *size* of the population; that is, achieve a zero rate of growth.
3. Achieve a negative rate of growth in order to *reduce* the size of the population.

Presumably, most people would agree that the only humane means of achieving any of these goals on a global basis is by reducing the birth rate. The alternative is to permit the death rate to increase, which, of course, will inevitably occur by the agonizing "natural" processes already described if mankind does not rationally reduce its birth rate in time.

Even given a consensus that curbing population growth is necessary and that limiting births is the best approach, however, there is much less agreement as to how far and how fast population limitation should proceed. Acceptance of the first goal listed above requires only that one recognize the obvious adverse consequences of rapid population growth—for example, dilution of economic progress in less developed countries, and aggravation of environmental and social problems in both developed and less developed countries. Economists and demographers, many of whom will not accept the third goal at all and ascribe no urgency to the second, generally do espouse the first one (at least for the LDCs).

Accepting the second goal simply means recognizing that Earth's capacity to support human beings is limited and that, even short of the limits, many problems are related to population size itself rather than only to its rate of growth. Accepting the idea that stabilizing the size of the population is urgently necessary requires recognizing that the limits are already being approached and that, although technological and cultural change may eventually push the limits back somewhat, the prudent course is to halt population growth until existing problems can be solved. Virtually all physical and natural scientists accept the ultimate inevitability of halting population growth, and most of them accept the urgency of this goal. Much of the first part of this book has been an exposition of why the "inevitable and urgent" position is reasonable.

The most controversial goal is the third one listed above—reducing the size of the human population. Accepting this goal implies a belief that there is an optimum population size and that this optimum has already been exceeded (or will have been exceeded by the time population growth can be stopped). It also implies that each society has a right—indeed a responsibility—to regulate its population size in reference to the agreed-upon optimum. In a world where the right (and the responsibility) of married couples to determine their own family size has become a widely accepted notion only in the past generation or two, the idea that nations have such a right or obligation is a truly radical one. Unfortunately, humanity cannot afford to wait another quarter century for the idea to gain complete acceptance.

Given the threat to the environment posed by today's population in combination with today's technology, and given the menace this situation represents to an already faltering ability to provide enough food for the people now alive, it is clear that the human population is already above the optimum size. (How *far* above the optimum is more difficult to determine; see Chapter 12). It is, of course, conceivable that technological and social change will push up the optimum in the time it takes to bring population growth to zero. More probably, however, the population size will have to be reduced eventually to *below today's level* if a decent life is to be assured for everyone.

Whether this view of long-term necessity is accepted or not, of course, the goal of any sensible population policy for the immediate future is the same—to gain control over growth. This chapter describes the recent evolution of population policies, explores some potential (but still largely unexploited) means of achieving such control over population growth, and discusses the interacting effects of other policies (especially development policies) on population growth.

FAMILY PLANNING

An essential feature of any humane program to regulate the size of the human population must be provision of effective means for individuals to control the number and timing of births. This approach is commonly termed "family planning," and family planning programs have been introduced in many LDCs in the past two decades with the goal of providing the means of birth control to the people. These are the main population policies now in existence.

The family planning movement, however, historically has been oriented to the needs of individuals and families, not of societies. Although birth control is essential for achieving population control, *family planning and population control are not synonymous.* Before proceeding to an examination of the important difference between the two, some historical perspective on the practice of birth control and the family planning movement is in order.

Birth Control

Many birth control practices are at least as old as recorded history. The Old Testament contains obvious references to the practice of withdrawal, or *coitus interruptus* (removal of the penis from the woman's vagina before ejaculation). The ancient Egyptians used crude barriers to the cervix made from leaves or cloth, and even blocked the cervical canal with cotton fibers. The ancient Greeks practiced population control through their social system as well as through contraception; they discouraged marriage and encouraged homosexual rela-

BOX 13-1 Institutionalized Infanticide in the Eighteenth Century*

Where the Number of lusty Batchelors is large, many are the merry-begotten Babes: On these Occasions, if the Father is an honest Fellow and a true Church of England-Man, the new-born Infant is baptized by an indigent Priest, and the Father provides for the Child: But the Dissenters, Papists, Jews, and other Sects send their Bastards to the Foundling Hospital; if they are not admitted, there are Men and Women, that for a certain Sum of Money will take them, and the Fathers never hear what becomes of their Children afterwards . . . in and about London a prodigious Number of Infants are cruelly murdered unchristened, by those Infernals, called Nurses; these detestable Monsters throw a Spoonful of Gin, Spirits of Wine, or Hungary-Water down a Child's Throat, which instantly strangles the Babe; when the Searchers come to inspect the Body, and enquire what Distemper caused the Death, it is answered, Convulsions, this occasions the Article of Convulsions in the Bills of Mortality so much to exceed all others. The price of destroying and interring a Child is but Two Guineas; and these are the Causes that near a Third die under the Age of Two Years, and not unlikely under two Months.

I have been informed by a Man now living, that the Officers of one Parish in Westminster, received Money for more than Five Hundred Bastards, and reared but One out of the whole Number. How surprizing and shocking must this dismal Relation appear, to all that are not hardened in Sin? Will it not strike every one, but the Causers and Perpetrators with Dread and Horror? Let it be considered what a heinous and detestable Crime Child-murder is, in the Sight of the Almighty, and how much it ought to be abhorred and prevented by all good people.

*This material is quoted from George Burrington's pamphlet "An answer to Dr. William Brakenridge's letter concerning the number of inhabitants, with the London bills of mortality," London, J. Scott (1757).

tionships, especially for men. The condom, or penis sheath, dates back at least to the Middle Ages. Douching, the practice of flushing out the vagina with water or a solution immediately after intercourse, has had a similarly long history. Abortion is a very ancient practice and is believed to have been the single most common form of birth control in the world throughout history, even during the past century when it was illegal in most countries. The simplest, most effective, and perhaps the oldest method of birth control is abstention; but this method seems to have been favored mainly by older men, particularly unmarried members of the clergy.

Infanticide, which is viewed with horror today by prosperous people in industrialized societies, has probably always been practiced by societies lacking effective contraceptive methods.[1] It was a rather common practice among the ancient Greeks, and the Chinese and Japanese are known to have used it for centuries, especially in times of famine. In agrarian or warlike societies, female infanticide has often been practiced to provide a greater proportion of men or to consolidate upper classes. Only a century or two ago, infanticide was widely practiced in Europe in an institutionalized, although socially disapproved system sometimes called "baby farming" (Box 13-1).[2]

Infanticide rarely takes the form of outright murder. Usually it consists of deliberate neglect or exposure to the elements. Among the Eskimos and other primitive peoples who live in harsh environments where food is often scarce, infanticide was, until recently, a common practice, as greater importance was placed on the survival of the group than on the survival of an additional child. There is a strong suspicion that female infanticide persists in parts of rural India. It exists even in our own society, especially among the overburdened poor, although intent might be hard to prove. Certainly "masked infanticide" is extremely common among the poor and hungry in less developed countries, where women often neglect ill children, refuse to take them to medical facilities, and may even show resentment toward anyone who attempts treatment. According to Dr. Sumner Kalman of the Stanford University Medical Center, the average poor mother in Colombia—where 80 percent or more of a large family's income may be needed to provide

[1]Mildred Dickeman, Demographic consequences of infanticide in man.

[2]William L. Langer, Checks on population growth: 1750–1850.

FIGURE 13-1

This machine makes oral contraceptive pills at the rate of 10,000 tablets per minute. The operator wears a protective mask to avoid inhaling steroids, which could cause hormonal changes. (Photo courtesy of Syntex Laboratories, Inc.)

food alone—goes through a progression of attempts to limit the number of her children. She starts with ineffective native forms of contraception and moves on to quack abortion, infanticide, frigidity, and all too often to suicide.[3]

The development of modern methods of contraception and the spread of family planning have eliminated the need for such desperate measures as infanticide and self-induced abortion in most developed nations and among the wealthier classes of most less developed countries. But modern methods of birth control are still by no means available to every potential parent in the world. The most effective contraceptives—oral contraceptives (Figure 13-1), IUDs, and safe, simple sterilization— have been available even to the affluent only since the early 1960s. A description of the modern methods of birth control most used today and others still under development can be found in Appendix 4 in the back of this book.

[3]Modern methods of contraception. *Bulletin of the Santa Clara County (Calif.) Medical Association,* March 1967.

Family Planning: A Short History

During the Industrial Revolution in England, an early advocate of limiting the size of families through contraception was labor leader Francis Place. Realizing that a limited labor pool would be likelier to win high wages and better working conditions from employers than would a plentiful supply of workers, in 1822, Place published a treatise, *Illustrations and Proofs of the Principle of Population,* which reached large numbers of people.[4] This was followed by a series of handbills that urged birth control in the interest of better economic and physical health and also described various contraceptive methods. Additional books on birth control appeared both in England and the United States during the 1830s and continued to circulate until the 1870s, when legal attempts were made to suppress them in both countries. The attempt failed in England, but in the United States the "Comstock Law" was passed by Congress in 1873. It forbade the dissemination by mail of birth control information, classing it as "obscene literature." Many states also passed laws against birth control literature, known as "little Comstock laws," and in 1890 importation of such literature was outlawed.[5]

America's heroine in the family planning movement was Margaret Sanger, a nurse. Her main objective was to free women from the bondage of unlimited childbearing through birth control, and her efforts thus were a part of the women's emancipation movement. In 1916 Mrs. Sanger opened the first birth control clinic in Brooklyn, for which she was arrested and jailed. As a result of her case, however, court decisions subsequently permitted physicians to prescribe birth control in New York for health reasons.

These were the first of many such decisions and changes in state laws that ultimately permitted the sale and advertisement of contraceptive materials and the dissemination of information about birth control. But the change was slow. The last such court decision was made in 1965, when the U.S. Supreme Court ruled that the Connecticut statute forbidding the use of contraceptives was an unconstitutional invasion of privacy. In 1966 the

[4]Reprinted in 1930 by Houghton Mifflin Co., Boston.

[5]W. Best and L. Dupré, Birth control. Much of the historical material in this section is based on this source.

Massachusetts legislature repealed the last of the state Comstock Laws. Margaret Sanger and others who joined her rapidly growing birth control movement (first known as the Birth Control League, later as the Planned Parenthood Federation) after World War I led the fight for these legal changes and for support from medical, educational, health, and religious organizations.

Counterparts to Margaret Sanger existed in many other countries, especially in northern and western Europe, and planned parenthood movements became independently established in several nations. Their founders, like Mrs. Sanger, were motivated primarily by concern for the health and welfare of mothers and children, and their campaigns emphasized these considerations.

Concurrently, intellectual organizations concerned primarily with population growth, known as Malthusian Leagues, were also promoting birth control. These, of course, were intellectual descendants of Robert Malthus, who first put forth warnings about the dangers of overpopulation (see Box 13-2). They were active in several European countries; but after World War I, when European birth rates had reached quite low levels, Malthusian concerns seemed to lose relevance and the movement died out.

The birth control movement in the United States was at first opposed by the medical profession. As the health and welfare benefits of family planning became apparent, the medical profession moved to a position of neutrality. In 1937 the American Medical Association (AMA) finally called for instruction on contraception in medical schools and medical supervision in family planning clinics. But it was not until 1964 that the AMA recognized matters of reproduction, "including the need for population control," as subjects for responsible medical concern.[6]

Religious opposition to the birth-control movement was initially even stronger than medical opposition. The Roman Catholic church still opposes "artificial" methods of birth control, but Planned Parenthood clinics cooperate in teaching the rhythm method to Catholics who request it. Acceptance of birth control came gradually from the various Protestant and Jewish groups after initial opposition. Official sanction was given by the Anglican (Episcopal) Communion in England and the United States in 1958, by the Central Conference of American Rabbis (Reform) in 1960, and by the National Council of Churches in 1961.

Birth rates in America and Europe had already begun to decline long before the first birth-control clinics were established (Chapter 5). Nevertheless, the family-planning movement, particularly in the United States, probably deserves some credit for today's relatively low birth rates. It certainly played a great role in increasing the availability of contraceptives and birth control information. This was accomplished not so much through Planned Parenthood clinics, which never have reached more than a small fraction of the total population, but through the removal of restrictive laws, the development of medical and religious support, and the creation of a social climate in which birth control information could circulate freely. Since passage of the U.S. Family Planning Act in 1970, Planned Parenthood clinics have been a major provider of free and low-cost contraceptive services to low-income people through government grants.

Throughout its history, the emphasis and primary concern of the family planning movement has been the welfare of the family; it has stressed the economic, educational, and health advantages of well-spaced, limited numbers of children.[7] Its policy has been to provide information and materials for birth control in volunteer-staffed clinics, serving any interested client, but primarily the poor who could not afford treatment by a private physician. Once the movement was established in the United States, little effort was made to recruit clients, beyond the routine promotion that accompanied the opening of a new clinic. For the United States this policy was apparently adequate; this nation is now overwhelmingly committed to the idea of family planning and the practice of birth control.

Contraceptive practice in the United States. By 1965, survey results showed that some 85 percent of married women in the United States had used some method of birth control. Most by then favored the more effective methods such as the pill. Among older couples,

[6]Best and Dupré, Birth control.

[7]These advantages are very real, as the World Health Organization has recently confirmed. See Dr. Abdel R. Omran, Health benefits for mother and child.

BOX 13-2 Thomas Robert Malthus, 1766–1834

The name Malthus and the terms Malthusian and neo-Malthusian are so completely identified with concern about population pressure that a note about the man seems appropriate. Robert Malthus enjoyed what was certainly one of the happiest personal situations ever devised by man; he was an eighteenth-century English country gentleman of independent means. His youth and early manhood were spent in the last years of the Enlightenment, the Age of Reason, a time when learned and wise men saw themselves on the threshold of a world of concord among men and nations in which want and oppression would not exist. Man's imminent entry into this paradise was to be achieved through his discovery of the immutable Laws of Nature which were thought to be such that they could be understood by the human faculty of Reason. All discord, want, and cruelty were held to result from an ignorance of these Laws, which led man to their disobedience. It was an age of very great hope when Nature and Reason were enshrined.

Malthus' father, Daniel, the very embodiment of these values, was well connected in the intellectual and philosophical circles of the time, being a close associate of David Hume and a correspondent, friend, and finally, an executor of Jean Jacques Rousseau.

In 1784, after a preparation through home tutoring, Malthus entered Cambridge, where in 1788 he graduated with first-class honors in mathematics. With graduation he took Holy Orders in the Church of England but remained at Cambridge, where he achieved his M.A. in 1791 and became a Fellow of his College in 1793. In 1796 he became curate of the church at Albury, where his father resided, and settled down to country life.

These were the years of the French Revolution, years that Dickens called "the best of times, the worst of times." Neither the Revolution's war, internal and external, nor even its Terror yet dampened the ambience of optimism that characterized the world of thought. In 1793 William Godwin published his *Enquiry Concerning Political Justice* and the next year saw the appearance of the Marquis de Condorcet's *Essay on the Progress of the Human Spirit,* both of which sought to demonstrate that man's progress from darkness, superstition, and cruelty into the light of Concord through Reason was almost complete. Daniel Malthus, like most of the thoughtful men of the time, was much taken by these writings, but Robert could not share his enthusiasm. Cambridge had not, as he put it, given him "that command over his understanding which would enable him to believe what he wished without evidence." The concern that haunted Robert was population growth. How could a perfect society be achieved, let alone maintained, if population was constantly pressing against resources? Finally, Robert committed his misgivings to writing so he could present them systematically to his father. Daniel was so impressed with the arguments that he encouraged his son to publish them, which he did anonymously in 1798, under the title, *An Essay on the Principle of Population as it Affects the Future Improvement of Society With Remarks on the Speculations of Mr. Godwin, M. Condorcet and Other Writers.* His speculations centered on the proposition that man's "power of population is indefinitely greater than the power in the earth to produce subsistence. . . ." This he propounded with strict immutability and mathematical regularity characteristic of the Natural

sterilization had become the single most popular method. By 1970 one-quarter of American women over 30 either were sterilized or their husbands were; by 1973, 23 percent of married couples of all ages relied on sterilization for birth control. Most of the women not using birth control in the 1965 and 1970 surveys were subfertile, pregnant, or planning to use contraceptives only when their families were complete. Moreover, despite the official position of the Roman Catholic church, Catholic women in these surveys showed a level of use of "artificial" contraceptives nearly as high as that of non-Catholic women.[8]

How much of recent U.S. population growth was due to unwanted births has been a matter for debate among demographers. The National Fertility Study of 1965 indicated that 17 percent of all births between 1960 and

[8]Charles F. Westoff, Changes in contraceptive practices among married couples, in Westoff, ed. *Toward the end of growth, population in America;* C. F. Westoff and L. Bumpass, The revolution in birth control practices of U.S. Roman Catholics.

Laws of the Age of Reason as "population, when unchecked, increases in a geometrical ratio. Subsistence increases only in an arithmetical ratio . . . " The first *Essay* challenged the visions of an age and the reactions were immediate and predictably hostile, though many listened. The controversy led to the publication in 1803 of an enlarged, less speculative, more documented, but equally dampening second essay. This one was signed and bore the title, *An Essay on the Principle of Population or a View of its Past and Present Effects on Human Happiness with an Inquiry into our Prospects Respecting the Future Removal or Mitigation of the Evils it Occasions.** Malthus added to and modified the *Essay* in subsequent editions, but it stood substantially unchanged.

In 1804 he accepted a post at the East India Company's college at Haileybury which prepared young men for the rule of India, where he remained until his death. His marriage, in the same year, ultimately produced three children.

The ironies in Malthus' life are obvious. He was one of eight children. He occupied a position of comfort in an intellectual atmosphere of optimism, but was compelled by the rigor of his intellect to argue that nature condemned the bulk of humanity to live in the margin between barely enough and too little. Finally, his message as a teacher fell on the ears of future colonial bureaucrats who would guide or preside over the destinies of India.

Since the conversations between Robert Malthus and his father almost two centuries ago, two sets of factors which were beyond their ken have emerged. The first set combined to put elements into a population-subsistence relationship that Malthus could not have foreseen. On one hand, the introduction of massive death control procedures—immunization, purification of drinking water, the control of disease-carrying organisms, improved sanitation, etc.—have removed many of the checks that Malthus assumed as "natural." On the other hand, developments in agriculture—high-yield plant strains, the powering of equipment with fossil fuels, the use of new techniques of fertilization and pest control—have massively increased food production.

The second set of factors has become widely significant only in the last quarter century and evident to most laymen only in the last decade. These are the deleterious effects on the biosphere resulting from agriculture and industry. With our planet's population bloated by death control and sustained only poorly through an agriculture based on nonrenewable resources and techniques which buy short-run, high yields at the expense of long-run, permanent damage to the "Earth's power to produce subsistence," we face a prospect inconceivable in the Age of Reason. Malthus looked into a dismal future of "vice and misery" begot of an uncontrolled, and, to his mind, uncontrollable population growth. We look into one where the dismal is compounded with peril, not because humanity cannot control its population, but because it *will* not.**

*Reprinted with numerous other articles on the same topic in Philip Appleman, ed., *An essay on the principle of population.*

**This box is a modification of an essay supplied to us by historian D. L. Bilderback. For further reading about Malthus, see particularly John Maynard Keynes, *Essays in biography;* J. Bonar, *Malthus and his work,* 2d ed., 1924; G. F. McCleary, *The Malthusian population theory;* and, of course, Malthus' First and Second Essays.

1965 were not wanted by both parents and 22 percent were not wanted by at least one parent. The incidence of unwanted births was found, not unexpectedly, to be highest among the poor, to whom birth control and safe abortion were least available. Demographer Charles Westoff estimated that eliminating such a high proportion of unwanted births might reduce the U.S. rate of natural increase by as much as 35 to 45 percent.[9]

However, another distinguished demographer, Judith Blake, pointed out that the high incidence of unwanted births calculated by Westoff for the U.S. during 1960–1965 was caused in large part by births occurring disproportionately to women who already had several children.[10] During those six years, there were unusually small proportions of first and second children born and unusually large proportions of births of higher orders (which are more likely to be unwanted). Hence, due to

[9]L. A. Westoff and C. F. Westoff, *From now to zero: fertility, contraception and abortion in America.*

[10]Reproductive motivation and population policy.

the age composition of the population, the *total* proportion of unwanted births in the U.S. was higher for those years than it has been at other times.

During the late 1960s, such changes as the increasing use of the pill and IUDs and relaxation of restrictions against voluntary sterilization substantially reduced the incidence of unwanted births of all orders. Results of the 1970 National Fertility Study confirmed this change, indicating that only about 14 percent of births between 1965 and 1970 were unwanted.[11] Most of the reduction in fertility in that period was due to reductions in unwanted and unplanned births. Since 1970, the extension of family planning services to the poor and the reversal of abortion laws (see below) have evidently further extended the trend, as attested by record low fertility rates.

There is no question that providing better contraceptives and simplified sterilization procedures, legalizing abortion, and ensuring that all are easily available to all members of the population reduces the incidence of unwanted pregnancy—a socially desirable end in itself. But even if a perfect contraceptive were available, the contraceptive-using population probably never will be perfect. People forget, are careless, and take chances. They are also often willing to live with their mistakes when the mistakes are babies. The complete elimination of unwanted births therefore is probably not possible. Nor does that alone account for the dramatic drop in the U.S. birth rate in the early 1970s. Rather, it appears that a significant change in family-size goals took place around that time, especially among young people who were just starting their families.[12]

Changing attitudes in the United States. Public surveys taken between 1965 and 1972 revealed a growing awareness of the population problem on the part of the American public. In 1965, about half of the people interviewed in a Gallup Poll thought that U.S. population growth might be a serious problem; in 1971, 87 percent thought that it was a problem now or would be by the year 2000. In January 1971 only 23 percent of adults polled thought four or more children constituted the ideal family size, in contrast to 40 percent in 1967. One of the three most commonly given reasons for favoring small families in 1971 was concern about crowding and overpopulation; the others were the cost of living and uncertainty about the future.

In October 1971, a survey sponsored by the U.S. Commission on Population Growth and the American Future disclosed a still greater level of concern about the population explosion among Americans. Specifically, it was discovered that:

1. Over 90 percent of Americans viewed U.S. population growth as a problem; 65 percent saw it as a *serious* problem.
2. Over 50 percent favored government efforts to slow population growth and promote population redistribution.
3. Well over 50 percent favored family limitation even if a family could afford more children.
4. About 56 percent favored adoption after births of two biological children if more were desired.
5. Only 19 percent felt that four or more children were the ideal number for a family; 45 percent favored two or less. The mean was 2.33.
6. Only 8 percent thought the U.S. population should be larger than its current size.

Concurrent with the rise in public concern about population growth, Zero Population Growth, Inc., was founded in late 1968 to promote an end to U.S. population growth through lowered birth rates as soon as possible and, secondarily, to encourage the same goal for world population. The organization hoped to achieve this by educating the public to the dangers of uncontrolled population growth and its relation to resource depletion, environmental deterioration, and various social problems; and by lobbying and taking other political action to encourage the development of antinatalist policies in the government. Since its founding, ZPG has taken an active role in promoting access to birth control for all citizens, legalized abortion, women's rights, and environmental protection. More recently it has begun to explore changes in U.S. immigration policies. ZPG has clearly been a factor in changing attitudes toward family size and population control.

[11]Charles F. Westoff, The modernization of U.S. contraceptive practice; Trends in contraceptive practice: 1965–1973; The decline of unplanned births in the United States.

[12]U.S. Bureau of the Census, Fertility history and prospects of American women: June 1975.

The growth of the women's liberation movement in the U.S. since 1965 has almost certainly been another important influence on attitudes (and thus on birthrates) through its emphasis on opportunities for women to fulfill themselves in roles other than motherhood. Many young women today are refreshingly honest about their personal lack of interest in having children and their concern for obtaining opportunities and pay equal to those of men. Such attitudes were virtually unthinkable in the United States before 1965.

The women's movement was a potent force behind the liberalization of U.S. abortion laws, and has also actively campaigned for the establishment of low cost day-care centers for children and tax deductions for the costs of child care and household work. Such facilities and policies lighten the costs of childbearing, but they also encourage mothers to find work outside the home. The experience of many societies suggests that outside employment of mothers discourages large families more than the existence of child-care facilities encourages them.

Both the growing concern about the population problem and the ideas of women's liberation doubtless contributed to changing attitudes toward family size in the 1970s. The economic uncertainty of the period may also have been a factor. While it may never be possible to determine the causes exactly, the achievement of subreplacement fertility in the United States is one of the most encouraging developments since 1970.

POPULATION POLICIES IN DEVELOPED COUNTRIES

Although birth control in some form is almost universally practiced in developed countries, very few have formulated any explicit national policies on population growth other than regulation of migration. Some European countries still have officially pronatalist policies left over from before World War II, when low birth rates led to concern about population decline.

Of course, many laws and regulations enacted for economic, health, or welfare reasons have demographic effects: for instance, those governing the availability of contraceptives, sterilization, and abortion; marriage and divorce; income taxes and family allowances; and immigration regulations.

The United States

The United States has no specific population policy, although various laws, including those regulating immigration and the administration of income taxes, have always had demographic consequences. Most tax and other laws were until recently implicitly pronatalist in effect. In the late 1960s this situation began to change as state laws restricting the distribution of contraceptive materials and information were repealed and as abortion laws were relaxed in several states. In 1970 Congress passed the Family Planning Services and Population Research Act, established the Commission on Population Growth and the American Future, and passed the Housing and Urban Development Act, which authorized urban redevelopment and the building of new towns. In 1972, an amendment to the Constitution affirming equal rights for women passed Congress, but as of 1977 it was not yet ratified by the required number of states.

The Family Planning Services and Population Research Act of 1970 had the goal of extending family planning counselling and services to all who needed them, particularly the poor. It also provided funds for research on human reproduction. Some 3.8 million women were being provided with family planning services by 1975, 90 percent of whom had low or marginal incomes. Another 1.9 million were being served by private physicians. But it has been estimated that another 3.6 million eligible women (including about 2.5 million sexually active teenagers) were still not receiving needed help in the mid-1970s. Particularly neglected were women in rural areas and small towns. Government-subsidized services have been provided through local health departments, hospitals, and private agencies (primarily Planned Parenthood), most of which are located in urban areas. A leveling-off of increases in clients in 1974 and 1975 over previous years has been attributed mainly to lack of increased funding by the government rather than to lack of need.[13]

[13]Marsha Corey, U.S. organized family planning programs in F 1974; Joy G. Dryfoos, The United States national family planning program, 1968–74; The Alan Guttmacher Institute, Organized family planning services in the United States: FY 1975; T. H. Firpo and D. A. Lewis, Family planning needs and services in nonmetropolitan areas.

Since 1967, the U.S. Agency for International Development (AID) has been permitted to include family planning assistance in its programs. Funding for overseas family planning assistance has been steadily increasing since then, and by fiscal 1976 had reached a level of $201.5 million.[14]

The U.S. Commission on Population Growth and the American Future presented its findings and recommendations in 1972 in the areas of demographic development, resource utilization, and the probable effects of population growth on governmental activities.[15] After two years of study, the Commission concluded that there were no substantial benefits to be gained from continued population growth, and indeed that there were many serious disadvantages. Besides recommending the liberalization of abortion laws and numerous other population-related policies, the report strongly recommended that contraceptives be made available to all who needed them, including minors; that hospital restrictions on voluntary sterilization be relaxed; that sex education be universally available; and that health services related to fertility be covered by health insurance. It also recommended policies to deal with immigration, population distribution, and land use. Perhaps most important, the Commission stated:

> Recognizing that our population cannot grow indefinitely, and appreciating the advantages of moving now toward the stabilization of population, the Commission recommends that the nation welcome and plan for a stabilized population.[16]

Unfortunately, apart from expressing strong disagreement with the recommendations on abortion, President Nixon took no action on the Commission's report, nor did President Ford show any inclination to do so. The abortion question was made moot by the Supreme Court's decision in 1973 (see section on abortion below). Congress has contented itself mainly with expanding federal family planning services. Thus, although the United States has not hesitated to advocate the establishment of official antinatalist population policies in less developed countries, it has not established one for itself.

The current low fertility of American women seems to have taken the urgency from the zero population growth movement—even though that fertility trend could easily reverse itself at any time. Given its present age composition, the U.S. still could reach the higher population projections of the Census Bureau (Chapter 5) if another baby boom occurred. In the mid-1970s, however, no consensus for immediate ZPG existed, and interest in population problems has been focused on aspects other than the birth rate—primarily on distribution and immigration.

Social objections to ZPG. The proposal to stop population growth naturally aroused considerable opposition on religious, social, and economic grounds. The role of religion in determining attitudes toward population growth, as well as toward the environment and resource limitation, is discussed in more detail in Chapter 14.

The primary social argument that has been raised against halting U.S. population growth is that it would substantially change the nation's age composition.[17] As the population stabilized, the median age would increase from about 28 to about 37. Less than 20 percent of the population would then be under 15, and about the same percentage would be over 65 years old. At present, about 25 percent of the population is under 15, and 11 percent is over 65. It is assumed that such an old population would present serious social problems. Figure 5-15 (Chapter 5) shows the age compositions of the U.S. in 1900 and 1970 and how it would look in a future stationary population.

It is true that old people tend to be more conservative than young people, and they seem to have difficulty adjusting to a fast-changing, complex world. In an older population there would be relatively less opportunity for advancement in authority (there would be nearly as many 60 year-olds as 30 year-olds—so the number of potential

[14]AID in an Interdependent World, *War on hunger* special supplement, June 1975; see Phyllis T. Piotrow, *World population crisis: The United States response* for an historical account of U.S. involvement in overseas population programs.

[15]*Population and the American future.*

[16]*Population and the American future.* By a "stabilized population," the Commission meant a stationary one.

[17]Ansley J. Coale, Man and his environment, *Science,* vol. 170, pp. 132–136 (9 Oct. 1970).

chiefs would be about the same as the number of Indians). There would also be many more retired people, a group already considered a burden on society.

But even those who raise this argument must realize its fundamental fallacy. In the relatively near future, growth of the human population *will* stop. It would be far better for it to stop gradually through birth limitation than by the premature deaths of billions of people. (In the latter case, there would be other, much more serious problems to worry about). Therefore, if this generation does not initiate population control, we simply will be postponing the age composition problems, leaving them to be dealt with by our grandchildren or great grandchildren. Our descendants will be forced to wrestle with these problems in a world even more overcrowded, resource-poor, and environmentally degraded than today's.

Moreover, the assumption that an older population must be much less desirable than a younger one is questionable in this society. Today, chronic underemployment and high unemployment are exacerbated by a labor pool constantly replenished by growing numbers of young people, which forces early retirement of the old, making them dependents on society. Many of our current social problems, including the recently skyrocketing crime rates and serious drug problems, are associated with the younger members of the population. If population growth stopped, the pressure of young people entering the labor pool would decline, while crime and unemployment problems could be expected to abate, as would the need for forced retirement of older workers.

Old people today are obsolete to a distressing degree. But this is the fault of our social structure and especially of our educational system. The problem with old people is not that there are or will be so many of them, but that they have been so neglected. If underemployment were reduced, outside interests encouraged during the middle years, and education continued throughout adult life (as suggested in Chapter 14), older people would be able to continue making valuable contributions to society well into their advanced years. Maintaining the habits of active interest in society and learning new, useful skills might effectively prevent obsolescence and the tendency to become conservative and inflexible with advancing age.

Thus, although there may be some disadvantages to an older population, there are also some definite advantages. While the proportion of dependent retired people grew, that of young children would shrink. The ever-rising taxes demanded in recent decades to support expanding school systems and higher educational facilities would cease to be such a burden; indeed, that has begun to happen already. The same is true of resources now devoted to crime control and other problems primarily of young people. Some of that money could be diverted instead to programs to help the aged. Moreover, the growth in the proportion of senior citizens (the numbers will not change; they are already born) will be far more gradual than the decline in numbers of babies and small children that has already occurred, allowing ample time for society to adjust to the change.

In the meantime, if birth rates remain low, the overall dependency ratio of the population will decline. In 1970 there were 138 dependents for every 100 workers in the United States; by 1980 the ratio will drop to about 118 and may be 112 or less by 1990.[18] Even after the numbers of the aged begin to rise in the population, the dependency ratio will remain relatively low. As Kingsley Davis pointed out, the highest proportion (about 75 percent) of people in productive ages (15–65) is found in a population that is making the transition from growth to ZPG. The proportion is nearly as high in a stationary population (about 63 percent).[19] And if years of productivity were extended to 70 and beyond, the proportion would be even higher, of course. By contrast, in very rapidly growing LDC populations, the proportion of people in their productive years (15 to 65) can be 50 percent or less.

Economic objections to ZPG. The economic objections to ZPG are based upon the realization that a nongrowing population implies at least a much more slowly growing economy, if not a nongrowing one. This thought strikes fear in the breasts of most businessmen and economists, even though a perpetually growing economy is no more sustainable than a perpetually growing population. The implications of a steady-state economy are discussed in Chapter 14; here we limit

[18]U.S. Bureau of the Census, *Population of the United States: Trends and prospects 1950–1990.*

[19]Zero population growth: the goal and the means.
no. 4, 1973, pp. 15–30.

ourselves to some of the aspects more obviously related to population growth.[20]

In 1971, economist J. J. Spengler noted the economic advantages and disadvantages of ZPG.[21] One of the advantages is increased productivity per person, partly because of greater capital available for investment, and partly because of a reduced dependency ratio. Other advantages include stabilized demand for goods and services; increased family stability as a result of there being fewer unwanted children; reduction of costs of environmental side effects; and opportunities to minimize the effects of population maldistribution. On the minus side, Spengler mentioned the problems associated with the changed age structure and pointed out that there would be a relative lack of mobility for workers and less flexibility in the economy because there would be fewer entrants into the labor force. He was also concerned that there might be a tendency toward inflation, due in part to increases in the service sector and in part to pressure to raise wages more than rising productivity justified. Recent events, as population growth has slowed (though there is not yet a decline in growth of the labor pool), suggest that Spengler may be right about the inflation pressures, although many other influences clearly are involved too. And certainly there are ways to compensate for those pressures.

The question of labor shortage for an expanding economy in a stationary population has also been raised. But, as economist Alan Sweezy has pointed out, workers (and their families) are the main consumers as well as the producers.[22] And, as mentioned above, the productive portion of a population is largest in stationary and transitional populations.

There was speculation by economists during the 1930s and 1940s that consumption patterns would be drastically, and presumably adversely, changed if population growth stopped. But a recent study comparing consumption patterns in the U.S. population of 1960/1961 (when it was growing relatively fast) with those of a projected stationary population indicated that the changes would be surprisingly minor.[23] The most notable difference was that there would be proportionally more households (called *spending units* by economists) in an older stationary population; families would be smaller but more numerous. Many of the changes in actual spending patterns would balance each other; in a stationary population there would be a greater demand for housing, for instance, but a lower demand for clothing and transportation. In no case were the changes more than a few percent.

Differential reproduction and genetic quality. A common concern about population control is that it will in some way lead to a reduction in the genetic quality of *Homo sapiens.*[24] This concern is often expressed in such questions as "if the smart and responsible people limit their families while the stupid and irresponsible do not, couldn't that lead to a decline of intelligence and responsibility in humanity as a whole?" The technically correct answer is "no one knows"; the practical answer is "there is no point in worrying."

No one knows, because it is not at all clear what, if any, portion of the variation in traits like "intelligence" or "responsibility" (however defined, and definition is difficult and controversial) is influenced by genetics. The most intensively studied example of such "mental" traits is performance on various so-called intelligence tests, and it has not been possible to demonstrate unambiguously that genes make any significant contribution to an individual's scores.[25]

There is no point in worrying about it because, even if these traits had a substantial genetic component and people with "bad" genes greatly outproduced people with "good" ones, it would take a great many generations (hundreds of years at a minimum) for the differential reproduction to produce a socially significant effect. Moreover, if such an effect were discovered, it could then

[20]For a further discussion, see U.S. Commission on Population Growth, *Population and the American future,* vol. 2.

[21]Economic growth in a stationary population, *PRB selection* no. 38, Population Reference Bureau, Inc., Washington, D.C., July 1971; see also Spengler, *Population and American future.*

[22]Labor shortage and population policy.

[23]D. Eilenstine and J. P. Cunningham, Projected consumption patterns for a stationary population.

[24]For discussion of this question, see papers in C. J. Bajema (ed), *Natural selection in human populations.*

[25]See especially Leon J. Kamin, *The science and politics of IQ* for a critique of the twin data on which most of the evidence for the heritability of IQ rests.

be reversed either by reversing the selective pressures (for example, encouraging reproduction of those with high IQ test scores) or, more likely, by modifying the social environment in order to improve the performance of those with poor scores ("bad" genes).

Note that we have put quotation marks around "good" and "bad." It is common for nonbiologists to think that heredity is a fixed endowment that rigidly establishes or limits skills, abilities, attitudes, or even social class. In fact, heredity is at most one of two sets of interacting factors, the other being the cultural and physical environment. When heredity does play a significant role (and it often may not), it is the *product* of this interaction that is of interest, and that product may be modified very effectively by changing the environment.[26] There is therefore no need for deep concern about the possible genetic effects of population control.

Another related issue that seems to encourage a pronatalist attitude in many people is the question of the *differential reproduction* of social or ethnic groups. Many people seem to be possessed by fear that their group may be outbred by other groups. White Americans and South Africans are worried there will be too many blacks, and vice versa. The Jews in Israel are disturbed by the high birth rates of Israeli Arabs, Protestants are worried about Catholics, and Ibos about Hausas. Obviously, if everyone tries to outbreed everyone else, the result will be catastrophe for all. This is another case of the "tragedy of the commons," wherein the "commons" is the planet Earth.[26a] Fortunately, it appears that, at least in the DCs, virtually all groups are exercising reproductive restraint.

For example, in the United States fertility in the black population has consistently been higher than white fertility (black mortality has also been higher). Since birth control materials and information began to be made available to low-income people in the late 1960s, black fertility has been declining even more rapidly than white fertility. By 1974, black women under 25 expected to have essentially the same number of children as white women their age: an average of 2.2 (see Box 13-3).[27]

The ideal situation, in our opinion, would be for all peoples to place a high value on diversity. The advantages of cultural diversity are discussed in Chapter 15; the reasons for avoiding a genetic monoculture in *Homo sapiens* are essentially the same as those for avoiding one in a crop plant—to maintain resistance to disease and a genetic reservoir for potential adaptation to changed environments in the future. The advantages also include the possibility of aesthetic enjoyment of physical diversity.[28] Some day we hope that whites will become distressed if blacks have too few children, and that, in general, humanity will strive to maximize its diversity while also maximizing the harmony in which diverse groups coexist.

Distribution and mobility. Obscuring the population controversy in the United States in the late 1960s was the tendency of some demographers and government officials to blame population-related problems on population maldistribution. The claim was that pollution and urban social problems are the result of an uneven distribution of people, that troubled cities may be overpopulated, while in other areas of the country the population has declined.[29] The cure promulgated in the 1960s was the creation of "new cities" to absorb the 80 million or so people then expected to be added to the U.S. population between 1970 and 2000.

It is of course true that there is a distribution problem in the United States. Some parts of the country are economically depressed and have been losing population—often the most talented, productive, and capable elements—while other areas have been growing so rapidly that they are nearly overwhelmed. Patterns of migration and settlement are such that residential areas have become racially and economically segregated to an

[26]A detailed explanation for the layman of the complex issues of the inheritance of intelligence can be found in P. Ehrlich and S. Feldman, *Race bomb.* See also F. Osborn and C. J. Bajema, The eugenic hypothesis, for an optimistic evaluation of the genetic consequences of population control.

[26a]Garrett Hardin, The tragedy of the commons.

[27]Frederick S. Jaffe, Low-income families: fertility changes in the 1960s; Population Reference Bureau, Family Size and the Black American.

[28]There is more genetic variation *within* groups of human beings than between them, but some of the inter-group variation may be biologically important (and is more widely recognized by lay persons).

[29]For instance, demographer Conrad Taeuber, who supervised the 1970 U.S. Census, in a speech delivered at Mount Holyoke College in January 1971 (quoted in the *New York Times,* Jan. 14, 1971).

BOX 13-3 Poverty, Race, and Birth Control in the United States*

The entrance of the United States government into the field of birth control through the extension of family planning services to the poor aroused a controversy quite out of proportion to its potential effect on the national birth rate, particularly in the black community, some members of which perceived it as a policy of "genocide" against racial minorities.

In the United States, birth rates have long been higher among the poor and among nonwhites (blacks, orientals, and native Americans) than among the nonpoor and among whites. High birth rates are generally associated with low economic and educational levels in most countries, including the United States. At the same time, the poor and nonwhites also have had consistently higher death rates, especially among infants and children. Above the poverty level, the birth rate difference between races diminishes, and college-educated nonwhites have *fewer* children than their white peers. In recent years (especially since the national family planning program was established) the birth rates of the poor and nonwhites have been declining even more rapidly than those of the population as a whole.**

Although there is conflicting evidence regarding desired family size among the poor, several surveys conducted in the 1960s indicated that poor couples wished to have only slightly more children than middle-class couples, and nonwhite couples in most socioeconomic classes wanted *fewer* children than comparable whites did. This was especially true among the younger couples in their prime childbearing years.

At the same time, the incidence of unwanted children among the poor and near-poor in the early 1960s was estimated to be as high as 40 percent. For nonpoor couples the incidence was about 14 percent.† The reasons for this disparity between desires and actual reproductive performance appear to have lain less in the lack of knowledge of contraceptives than in the unavailability of effective ones. The poor who used birth control tended to use cheaper and less reliable methods than did members of the middle class. Because poor people simply could not afford the more effective contraceptives, and because no family planning information or services were provided through welfare health services until the late 1960s, most low-income people were until then deprived of effective methods of birth control.

Between 1965 and 1970, fertility among the poor and near-poor declined by 21 percent, doubtless due in part to the new services that by 1970 were reaching an estimated 1.5 million women. The greatest fertility decline occurred among nonwhite women below the poverty level. As family planning services have expanded, nonwhite fertility has continued to drop rapidly.

Despite the tendency of black militants to regard the provision of birth control information and services to the poor as a policy of "genocide" against blacks, and although the potential for abuse exists, it should be emphasized that the government's present program is basically intended to benefit the poor, and poor children in particular. In this connection it is unfortunate that the government chose to label its policy as a "population control" measure, which it is not; rather it was a logical and long overdue extension both of the family planning movement and of the welfare program.

Fears of discrimination have been aroused in areas where middle-class social workers of people operating birth control clinics in poor neighborhoods have put pressure on women to accept birth control services. There have also been cases of black women being sterilized without informed consent, and laws have been proposed for compulsory sterilization of welfare mothers. Hence black fears of genocide are not altogether unfounded. The recent decline in black fertility, however, may have defused much of the white prejudice against "black welfare mothers." The best way to avoid either the appearance or the actuality of discrimination in administration of birth control services is to have the services administered by residents of the same neighborhoods they serve as far as possible.

Although many middle-class Americans favor population control for others, especially the poor, they must realize that it is really their own excessive reproduction that accounts for most of the U.S. population growth rate. Furthermore, the middle class and the wealthy are responsible for the high rate of consumption and pollution, which are the most obvious symptoms of overpopulation in the United States.

**Source:* Population Reference Bureau, Family size and the black American; Robert G. Weisbord, *Genocide? birth control and the black American,* Greenwood, Westport, Conn., 1975. For a discussion of the social and biological meanings of race, see Ehrlich and Feldman, *Race bomb.*

**P. Cutright and F. S. Jaffe, Family planning program effects on the fertility of low-income U.S. women.

†L. A. Westoff and C. F. Westoff, *From now to zero.*

extreme degree. This trend could be expected to have many undesirable social consequences (one has been the school-busing controversy). Central cities are being economically strangled and abandoned, while industry and members of the taxpaying middle class flee to the suburbs. But some social scientists have advanced the notion that, rather than being the cause of our social problems, maldistribution and migration might be symptoms of a deeper, more general malady.[30]

Population maldistribution is different from, although related to, the problem of absolute growth, and it demands a different set of solutions. Nevertheless, the distribution situation would certainly be exacerbated by a continuation of rapid population growth.

Unfortunately, the proposal to create new cities has several drawbacks. The scale of the project alone is dismaying. New cities would have to be built at the improbable rate of one the size of Spokane (Figure 13-2), Washington, *per month* until the end of the century just in order to absorb the population growth that in the late 1960s was projected for that period. In order to provide space alone for that many more people, the United States would have to sacrifice substantial amounts of land now in agricultural production. Three hundred Spokanes would occupy about 10 million acres, which is equivalent to the land producing the entire U.S. cotton crop. Wasteland or grazing land could be used instead, but most people would not find such areas desirable places to live, and shortage of water might also be a limiting factor.

Furthermore, new cities would not necessarily reduce pollution; rather, they would provide additional foci of environmental deterioration. Thus the net effect on *total* environmental impact nationwide, aside from redistributing it, would be beneficial only if careful planning were used to minimize commuting and other destructive activities in the new communities.

Peter Morrison of the Rand Corporation has pointed out several social and economic disadvantages of new cities.[31] The first difficulty is the enormous cost of building each new city, including the creation of a solid economic base to attract immigrants, in competition with older cities. The populations of new cities, unless controlled by explicit resettling policies, might be even more homogenous than that of today's suburbs and would tend to be even more mobile. Thus new cities would be quite unstable and would tend to intensify, rather than relieve, the problems of social segregation.

FIGURE 13-2

An aerial view of Spokane, Washington. If the population of the United States had continued to grow as fast as it did in the late 1960s, a city of this size would have to be built each month between 1970 and the end of the century to accommodate the additions to the population. (Photo courtesy of Spokane Chamber of Commerce.)

Morrison suggested that a better solution to distribution problems would be to revitalize existing cities and form policies that encouraged migration in desired directions. People who move to new areas are usually attracted to better job opportunities or higher wages. Most go where they already have friends or relatives, a factor that militates against the successful establishment of new cities. Most migration in the United States occurs between urban areas; relatively few people now move from rural to urban areas. Such policies as local tax situations that encourage or discourage the development of industries, and differences among states in welfare benefits have considerable potential influence on migration.

Since passage of the Population Act in 1970, the government has encouraged the development of new

[30]Peter Morrison, Urban growth, new cities, and the population problem.
[31]Ibid; U.S. Commission on Population Growth, *Population and the American future,* vol. 5.

cities by providing funds and guaranteeing loans to developers. Some new communities have been developed within old cities—Roosevelt Island in New York and Cedar-Riverside in Minneapolis, for example—but most are built some distance from older centers. The new community program was plagued with funding problems in the early 1970s, partly because of President Nixon's penchant for impoundment of funds, and partly because of HUD's fondness for red tape and failure to come through with promised technical and planning assistance or aid in starting transportation and school systems. Despite these obstacles, several new towns have come into being. The best of them incorporate housing for all income levels and try to attract minority groups. At least one new town, Woodlands, Texas, was planned by ecological architect Ian McHarg with an eye to preserving the local forest and recycling the water supply.[32]

The issue of new cities has faded somewhat since 1970, possibly because it has become increasingly difficult just to finance the maintenance of existing cities and suburbs, without taking on the even greater burden of building new ones. Another limiting factor may have been the 1973/1974 energy crisis, which starkly illuminated many of the faults of today's settlement and commuting patterns. Lowering population growth rates and some abatement of internal migration may also have caused politicians to view the need as less urgent than it seemed a few years earlier. Nevertheless, the problem remains of accomodating the tens of millions of people who will be added to the U.S. population by the end of the century.

In addition, the numerous social difficulties caused by present and past movements of people must be solved and efforts made to prevent their being intensified in the future. Between 1950 and 1970, one American in five moved each year, about 22 percent of these to a different state. Disproportionate numbers of the people who move are young couples in their twenties and their children. The destructive effects of such mobility on people and on communities have been vividly described by Vance Packard.[33] People are not inclined to develop loyalty or civic concern toward a town in which they feel themselves temporary residents. The community thereby loses potential support from many of its most active and talented citizens. High mobility may be hardest on children. When children cannot establish community roots, it is not surprising that they grow up alienated from older generations and from society at large.

As a result of undirected migration since World War II, many urban areas in the United States have experienced severe problems. Some cities have grown enormously while others have lost population. Peter Morrison has described the demographic effects of rapid growth on one city, San Jose, California, which tripled its population between 1950 and 1970, and population decline on another, St. Louis, Missouri.[34] San Jose's mostly young, extremely mobile population provides the advantages of a highly flexible job market and a low rate of dependency (retirees and jobless poor). But the city's population has grown almost faster than urban services such as sewers, schools, and streets could be provided for it. No time was available for planning; developers put up houses wherever land was available. In the early 1970s, San Jose looked at itself and was appalled: a classic example of unplanned urban sprawl—"slurbia" it is called in the vernacular.

St. Louis, by contrast, is an acute example of central city decay. The central city's population declined by 17 percent during the 1960s, while the surrounding suburbs grew by 29 percent. Those who moved out were predominantly young families, leaving behind a rising proportion of aging and retired people and disadvantaged minorities, especially blacks. High and middle-income families, both black and white, departed for suburbs or other cities, leaving the city of St. Louis to support a high proportion of low-income people on an inadequate tax base.

One approach to ameliorating the problems of overburdened cities is to encourage people to return to rural areas and small towns and cities. Such a policy, however, might require considerable revamping of American agricultural and industrial employment systems, as well as of local welfare policies that inadvertently stimulate migration from rural areas to cities. Such explicit policy

[32]New towns in trouble, *Time,* March 24, 1975.

[33]*A nation of strangers;* see also Urie Bronfenbrenner, The origins of alienation.

[34]Urban growth and decline: San Jose and St. Louis in the 1960s. Another recent study, in which many of the economic, social and environmental effects of unplanned urban growth are examined, is Irving Hoch, City size effects, trends, and policies.

changes, although there are many powerful arguments in their favor, have only begun to appear, and those have come mainly from the private sector as business firms relocated in smaller cities and towns. There has been considerable discussion of reorganizing welfare policies on a federal standard so that no locality will provide more attractive benefits than any other, but to date the discussion has not been turned into action.

Even without policy changes, however, a reversal of the centuries-long trend toward urbanization in the U.S. may now have occurred spontaneously.[35] Fed up with the growing disadvantages of life in large cities—rising crime rates and declining levels of services and amenities—millions of Americans have moved from cities to rural areas and small towns. A surprisingly large number of them have taken up farming, but with varied success. Some of this back-to-the-farm movement derives from the earlier hippie movement and from a growing desire among young, well-educated people for a more self-sufficient, independent way of life than is possible in a large city. Eventually, this change in life-style and personal goals may influence large companies and the government to develop policies that encourage decentralization and discourage unnecessary mobility.

Policies and Practices in Other Developed Countries

Explicit population policies are the exception rather than the rule in most developed countries.[36] Where laws affecting demographic trends have existed, they have generally been indirect, most commonly regulating or prohibiting abortion or the distribution of contraceptive information and materials. As in the United States, most such laws until recently have been pronatalist in intent. Nevertheless, a predominant social trend throughout the twentieth century has been the growth in acceptance of the idea of family limitation.

Canada. Canada's population policies have generally followed the same lines as those in the United States, with the exception that family allowances—small allotments to subsidize support of children—have been provided for decades. Prohibitions on distribution of contraceptive devices or information were repealed in 1969, and soon afterwards a government family planning program was launched. Regulation of abortion was also liberalized somewhat in 1969, but the new law has been applied very conservatively. Easy access to abortion is by no means a reality in Canada.[37]

The Canadian birth rate is slightly higher (15.7 in 1975) than that of the United States and has also been dropping rapidly. A major factor in Canadian population growth has been immigration, which in the 1960s made up about one-third of the nation's annual growth. In the early 1970s immigration increased as fertility declined. Traditionally liberal immigration policies are currently being reevaluated with a view to tightening restrictions and reducing the inflow.[38]

Western Europe. Western European countries generally have no official population policies other than pronatalist policies left over from before World War II when birth rates were very low.[39] Many of these countries still have family allowances to help support children in large families. Predominantly Catholic European countries still banned or restricted contraceptives and abortion as late as the 1970s.

In Europe, widespread practice of *coitus interruptus* has been given the major credit for lowering birth rates during the nineteenth and early twentieth centuries, with illegal abortion also playing an important role. In most of Western Europe by the 1970s, *coitus interruptus* and the condom were still the most used contraceptive methods, followed by the pill and the rhythm method. Among Western European countries, only in England and Scandinavia are other contraceptive devices as well known and readily available as they are in the United States. The condom is still the most commonly used device, however, and withdrawal is much more widely practiced than it is in America. However, use of the pill is increasing.[40]

[35] Roy Reed, Rural areas' population gains now outpacing urban regions; Americans on the move, *Time*, March 15, 1976.

[36] Bernard Berelson, ed., *Population policy in developed countries.*

[37] Margot Zimmerman, Abortion law and practice—a status report.

[38] Wendy Dobson, National population objectives are slowly taking shape.

[39] Much of the information on current policies come from Richard C. Shroeder, Policies on population around the world.

[40] Norman B. Ryder, The family in developed countries.

Sweden is an exception among European countries in that it has had an official population policy since the 1930s. This policy provided for sex education (including birth control) in schools, permitted abortion in some circumstances, and offered family planning services as part of the national health organization. In addition, Sweden was the first country to have a program to assist other family planning programs abroad.

England, since 1974, has provided contraceptives and abortions through its National Health Service, and Parliament has begun discussion of developing an antinatalist policy. England also provides some family planning assistance to LDCs, mostly its former colonies.

Even though birth control has been illegal to some degree in most Catholic countries, late marriage, high rates of illegal abortion, and the use of withdrawal and the rhythm method have helped keep birth rates down. Planned parenthood groups have long existed in France, Belgium, and the Netherlands in a quasi-legal status, but until recently they were hampered by laws restricting the dissemination of information and materials. When France legalized contraceptives in the late 1960s, family allowances were also increased. Birth control devices are still entirely illegal in Ireland, although a movement for change has begun. They are also essentially illegal in Spain and Portugal. Italy has legalized the pill for "medical purposes" (presumably to combat the extremely high illegal abortion rate—see next section), and condoms are available "for disease prevention." In 1971, Italian laws prohibiting the dissemination of birth control information were declared unconstitutional, thus opening the way for much greater access to contraceptives. In 1975 a new law authorized local governments to establish "family centers" to counsel citizens on family matters, including family planning.[41]

Immigration policies are also being reevaluated in several Western European countries. In recent years, much of the labor force (11 percent in France and West Germany, 7 percent in Britain, and 37 percent in Switzerland) has been composed of "guest workers"—temporary migrants from poorer countries in Southern Europe, Northern and Central Africa, and the Middle East.[42] The worldwide economic recession in the mid-1970s led to an intensification of the controversy, especially in Switzerland, which has twice considered outright deportation of all immigrants (thus throwing many firms, dependent on migrants, into panic).[43] So far such proposals have been rejected, although many social problems continue to be blamed on the foreigners in most of these countries. Should economic conditions seriously worsen, such xenophobic policies could be revived and even implemented.

Eastern Europe and USSR. In the Soviet Union and Eastern European countries, the substantial post-World War II declines in fertility were achieved mostly through abortion, which is provided by their national health services. These countries now also distribute contraceptives, including the pill, partly in an effort to reduce the abortion rate. This policy seems to be succeeding in some countries, although abortion is still the primary means of birth control. Discouragement of early marriage, an emphasis on training, education, and the full outside employment of women also undoubtedly strongly encourage the small family trend.

Extremely low birth rates in Eastern European countries have caused a reversion to more pronatalist policies—especially a tightening of abortion laws—in response, apparently, to concern about future labor supplies. Communist ideology officially calls for a pronatalist posture, and the Soviet government periodically exhorts its people to have more children. Interestingly, however, the Russians have cautiously begun to recommend lower fertility in rapidly growing less developed countries.[44]

Oceania. Australia and New Zealand have historically regarded themselves as underpopulated. Consequently their policies until recently were pronatalist and pro-immigration. These policies are currently being reevaluated as the public becomes aware of the world population problem, and neither country any longer

[41]Brenda Vumbaco, Recent law and policy changes in fertility control.

[42]Clyde H. Farnsworth, The doors are closing to world's immigrants, *New York Times,* December 22, 1974.

[43]A bout of xenophobia, *Time,* October 28, 1974.

[44]Boris Urlanis, The hour of decision, *Unesco Courier,* July/August 1974, pp. 26–29. The author is described as "the USSR's leading demographer."

subsidizes the transport costs of immigrants. A Zero Population Growth movement was founded in Australia in 1971. As former English colonies, both countries have long had family planning organizations and access to contraceptives. Their birth rates have been well within the usual DC range, although their growth rates have been inflated by high immigration rates. As in many European countries and the United States, the birth rates in Australia and New Zealand have been declining toward replacement levels since 1970.

Japan. Japan, the only fully industrialized country in Asia, reduced its birth rate rapidly to DC levels after World War II, largely by legalizing abortion. A policy of encouraging the use of contraceptives has since reduced the abortion rate without changing the birth rate, even though Japan has been slow to legalize the pill and the IUD. The social policy on population, which was promoted through massive educational and communications programs in the 1950s, very strongly discouraged having a family with more than 2 children. Accordingly, fertility has been close to replacement levels since then. Around 1970, alarmed by an apparent labor shortage, Japanese industry began campaigning for more births. The crude birth rate rose during the mid-1970s, but the rise was essentially an artifact of age composition; the postwar baby boom children born before legalized abortion halved the birth rate (1945–1955) were then in their twenties—the prime reproductive years. The recession of 1974 effectively seems to have silenced the campaign for higher fertility. At the same time, the growth of both environmental concern and a women's liberation movement in Japan may have a fertility-reducing effect in future years.

Abortion

The most controversial method of birth control without question is abortion, which is surrounded by legal, ethical, and moral dilemmas. Despite this, it seems to have been practiced in all societies and is probably still the commonest method of birth control today, especially in LDCs. Until the early 1970s, abortion was illegal in most countries, including the United States (see Box 13-4). Disapproval of the practice probably originated with the Judeo-Christian ethic, yet it was not made illegal until the nineteenth century. Then it was outlawed on the grounds that it was dangerous to the mother—which it was before sterile techniques were developed. When performed today under appropriate medical circumstances by a qualified physician, however, abortion is much safer than a full-term pregnancy. The death rate in the United States for legal abortion in the first trimester (first three months of pregnancy) is less than 2 in 100,000. For second-trimester abortions the rate rises to 12 per 100,000, still only half the maternal death rate for childbirth.[45]

But danger to the mother escalates alarmingly when the abortion is illegal, as it still is in many countries. The amount of risk varies according to the circumstances, which may range from self-inducement with a knitting needle or, almost equally hazardous, unsterile help from untrained people, to reasonably safe treatment by a physician in a hotel or clandestine clinic.

Changing abortion laws in DCs. Before abortion was legalized in the United States, bungled illegal abortions were the greatest single cause of maternal deaths, accounting for a conservatively estimated 300 or more deaths per year.[46] They still are in those countries where abortion remains illegal or not yet widely available. In Italy, for example, contraceptives were entirely banned until 1971, and the illegal abortion rate at that time was estimated to be equal to or higher than the birth rate—800,000 to 1.5 million per year—and costing as many as 3000 lives per year.[47] Most of these abortions were self-inflicted or accomplished with the aid of a sympathetic but untrained friend. When a woman with a hemorrhage was brought to a hospital, she was automatically given tetanus and penicillin shots. She never

[45]*Family planning perspectives,* Abortion-related deaths down 40 percent. . . . See also C. Tietze and S. Lewit, Legal abortion, whose figures for abortion mortality, derived from the U.S. and the U.K., show abortion mortality risks approximately equal to childbirth between the twelfth and sixteenth weeks, and somewhat higher thereafter. Both sources agree on the low risks of first trimester abortions.

[46]Christopher Tietze, The effect of legalization of abortion on population growth and public health. For an excellent overview of the changing legality of abortion worldwide and related social issues, see Tietze and Lewit, Legal abortion.

[47]Reported by David Burrington for *NBC News,* February 5, 1975.

BOX 13-4 Abortion in the United States

Before 1967, abortion was illegal in the United States except when the mother's life was endangered by continuing the pregnancy. Only six years later, the situation had been completely reversed, legally if not everywhere in practice. Yet the change was not effected overnight; it was the result of changed public attitudes in response to a growing reform movement.

By the end of 1970, 15 of the 50 states had at least partially moderated their abortion laws. Most of these new laws permitted abortion only in cases where bearing the child presented a grave risk to the mental or physical health of the mother, where the pregnancy was a result of incest or rape, and where (except in California) there was a substantial likelihood that the child would be physically or mentally defective. To obtain an abortion, a woman usually had to submit her case to a hospital reviewing board of physicians, a time-consuming and expensive process. Although the laws ostensibly were relaxed to reduce the problem of illegal abortions, hospital boards at first interpreted the changes in the law so conservatively that they had little effect. The number of illegal abortions per year in the U.S. during the 1960s has been variously estimated at between 200,000 and 2 million, with 1 million being the most often quoted figure. This amounted to more than one abortion for every four births. At that time, there were estimated to be 120,000 illegal abortions per year in California; in the first year after the passage of California's "liberalized" law there were just over 2,000 legal ones. The figures were similar for the other states.

In 1970 Hawaii, Alaska, and New York passed new laws essentially permitting abortion on request, and Washington State legalized abortion on request not by legislation but by referendum. Meanwhile, several other states began to interpret their relatively restrictive laws much more liberally, and the legal abortion rate rose considerably. These changes in state laws were preceded and accompanied by an erosion of public opposition to abortion. Table 13-1 shows the changes in public disapproval as revealed in polls taken between 1962 and 1969 for demographer Judith Blake.

A poll taken early in 1970 asked: Should an abortion be available to any woman who requests one? In apparent contradiction to the earlier opinions, more than half of those interviewed said yes. Although most respondents did not approve of abortion except for the more serious reasons, the majority apparently felt that mothers should be free to make their own decisions.

Continuing this trend, a poll conducted in 1971 for the U.S. Commission on Population Growth and the American Future found that 50 percent of the adults interviewed felt that the decision to have an abortion should be made by the woman and her doctor, 41 percent would permit abortions under certain circumstances, and only 6 percent opposed abortion under all circumstances. Similar results have been obtained in subsequent surveys.[a]

In January 1973, the U.S. Supreme Court announced its decision on an abortion case which in effect legalized abortion on request nationwide, at least for the first trimester (13 weeks), with restrictions on the second trimester being permitted in the interest of protecting women's health. Only in the last ten weeks of pregnancy, (when the child, if born, had a chance of survival) the court ruled, could states prohibit abortion except "to preserve the life or health of the mother."[b]

The number of legal abortions performed in 1972 (before the Supreme Court decision) was about 600,000; in 1975 it was about one million—approximately the estimated previous number of illegal abortions. At least two-thirds of these abortions probably would have been obtained illegally if legal abortions had been unavailable.[c] Nor had illegal abortions entirely disappeared—25 of the 47 deaths from abortions in 1973 were from illegal ones (those not performed under proper medical supervision)—although the incidence of such deaths clearly had been drastically reduced by 1975.[d]

Yet, three years after the Supreme Court decision, there were still large discrepancies from one region to another and between medical facilities in providing abortion services. An ongoing national study by the Guttmacher Institute[e] in 1975 concluded that between 260,000 and 770,000 women who needed abortions in 1975—20 to 40 percent of the women in need—

[a]W. R. Arney and W. H. Trescher, Trends in Attitudes toward abortion, 1972–1975.

[b]For a lively account of the campaign to change U.S. abortion laws, see Lawrence Lader, *Abortion II: making the revolution.*

[c]Edward Weinstock, et al., Legal abortions in the United States since the 1973 Supreme Court decisions; Abortion need and services in the United States, 1974–1975, *Family Planning Perspectives,* vol. 8, no. 2, March 1976.

[d]Richard Lincoln, The Institute of Medicine reports on legalized abortion and the public health.

[e]Part of the Planned Parenthood Federation of America. The 1976 Study was titled: *Provisional estimates of abortion need and services in the year following the Supreme Court decisions: United States, each state and metropolitan area.* The 1976 Study was *Abortion 1974–1975—need and services in the United States, each state and metropolitan area.*

were still unable to obtain them. More than half of all abortions after 1973 were carried out in specialized clinics, while public hospitals (which provide most medical services to the poor) were lagging even behind private hospitals in providing services. Only one in five U.S. public hospitals reported performing any abortions in 1975. Thus in many areas it was substantially more difficult for poor women to obtain abortions than for middle-class or wealthy women, even though government funds were available to cover the costs. Teenagers, who account for about one-third of the need for abortion services and for a large and growing portion of the illegitimate birth rate, also seem to have poor access to safe abortions. Finally, abortion services were found to be generally less available in the southern and central regions of the U.S. than on either coast.

In the United States, the majority of abortion recipients are young and/or unmarried. There is some debate over the degree to which legal abortion has affected American fertility overall, but it seems to have had a significant effect on the rate of illegitimate births. In 1971 reductions in illegitimate births in states with legal abortion ranged as high as 19 percent, while in most states without legal abortion they continued to increase.[f] Following the Supreme Court decision, the rising rate of illegitimacy halted briefly, then began again. The rise was accounted for by an increase in teenage pregnancy.

There is no evidence that abortion has replaced contraceptives to any significant degree, despite the apprehensions of antiabortion groups on this score. Most women seeking abortion have a history of little or no contraceptive practice, and many are essentially ignorant of other means of birth control. Those who return for subsequent abortions have been found to be still ignorant of facts of reproduction, using contraceptives improperly, or to have been poorly guided by their physicians.[g]

Paralleling the trend toward liberalized abortion policies in the U.S. has been the growth of right-to-life groups who are adamantly opposed to abortion. These groups have lobbied actively against reform of state laws and, since the Supreme Court decision, have tried to persuade Congress to reimpose sanctions against abortion through Constitutional amendments. Under their pressure, Congress has removed funds for

[f]J. Sklar and B. Berkov, Abortion, illegitimacy, and the American birth rate.

[g]Blame MD mismanagement for contraceptive failure, *Family Planning Perspectives,* vol. 8, no. 2, March/April 1976, pp. 72–76.

TABLE 13-1
Change in Disapproval of Abortion (all white respondents)

	Percentage of disapproval			
Reason for abortion	*1962*	*1965*	*1968*	*1969*
Mother's health endangered	16	15	10	13
Child may be deformed	29	31	25	25
Can't afford child	74	74	72	68
No more children wanted	–	–	85	79

Source: Judith Blake, Abortion and public opinion.

abortion services from Foreign Aid grants to LDCs. In 1976, Congress also passed a law forbidding federal assistance for abortions in the U.S., a move that denies these services to low-income women—precisely the group whose chances for a decent and productive life are most likely to be jeopardized by an unwanted child. Whether the courts will consider such a discriminatory law constitutional is another question. Right-to-life groups have also played a part in harassing clinics, hospitals, and other organizations that provide abortion. This activity often embarrasses clients and possibly has also discouraged other institutions from providing abortion services.

Action by right-to-life groups in Boston resulted in the trial and conviction for manslaughter in early 1975 of physician Kenneth Edelin following a late-term abortion (about 20 weeks). The prosecution maintained that the fetus might have survived if given life-supporting treatment. (The conviction was overturned in December 1976 by the Massachusetts Supreme Judicial Court.)[h] The consequence of the original verdict nevertheless was to discourage late second-trimester abortions (31 states already had laws against them except to protect the mother's life or health; in most states abortion by choice was available only through the 20th week). Unfortunately, this change also will affect mainly the poor and/or very young women, who through ignorance or fear are more likely to delay seeking an abortion until the second trimester.

In 1976, a Right-to-Life political party was formed, centering on the abortion issue. Its candidate, Ellen McCormack, entered primaries in several states, but never succeeded in winning more than 5 percent of the vote. Most Americans, it appears, accept the present legal situation at least as the lesser of evils.

[h]*Time* and *Newsweek,* March 3, 1975. Both magazines covered the trial and the issues it raised in some detail. See also Barbara Culliton's thoughtful article, Edelin trial; jury not persuaded, and Edelin conviction overturned, *Science,* vol. 195, January 7, 1977, pp. 36–37.

admitted having had an abortion; under Italian law she had committed a crime and could be sent to prison. Some years ago in a confidential survey of 4000 married women of all classes, all admitted to having had abortions, most of them many times.[48]

A movement is now underway to loosen the laws against abortion in Italy, following the limited legalization of the pill in 1971, despite strong opposition from the Vatican and conservative political elements. The Italian constitutional court in early 1975 ruled that abortion is legal if doctors determine that the pregnancy threatens the physical or mental health of the mother.

Before the 1970s, variations on the Italian abortion tragedy prevailed in several other Western European countries. In France, contraceptives were available but not openly, and the illegal abortion rate and attendant rates of death and injury nearly matched those of Italy. In late 1974, abortion was legalized in France, shortly after a new law was passed greatly increasing public access to contraceptive devices and information.

Similar reversals have occurred in many DCs since 1965. West Germany, Denmark, and Austria legalized abortion on request between 1973 and 1975, although its status in Germany was changed by a court decision and remains to be reestablished by legislation. In 1975 Sweden changed its already moderately liberal law to allow abortion up to the twelfth week as a decision for the woman alone to make. Finland, Norway, and Iceland have long had liberal policies, but they fall short of availability on request. Laws against abortion in Greece and the Netherlands have been neither observed nor enforced and soon may be reversed. The same was formerly true of Switzerland, which in 1975 moved to liberalize its abortion laws. Great Britain has in effect permitted abortion on request since 1967. Spain, Portugal, Belgium, and Ireland still had very restrictive laws in 1976.[49]

In most of Eastern Europe, abortion has long been legal and usually subsidized by the state. Abortion has been legal since 1920 in the Soviet Union, and in most Eastern European countries (except Albania) since the 1950s. Abortion brought birth rates so low that Bulgaria, Czechoslovakia, and Hungary tightened their regulations in 1973. Romania severely restricted access to abortion in 1966, with the result that its birth rate virtually doubled the following year. Since then, the birth rate has declined toward the 1966 level, indicating an increase in illegal abortions. The rates of hospitalizations and deaths from abortion complications have also risen substantially. Meanwhile the huge cohort of children born in 1967 has caused havoc in the Romanian school systems.[50]

Canada has relaxed its abortion law somewhat; practice is considerably short of "on request," but widely liberal interpretation of the new law might make it close. Canadians denied abortions often go to the United States. Australia is moving toward liberal policies, although access varies by state. New Zealand remains restrictive, but discussion of change has begun.

Abortion in LDCs. The tragedy of illegal abortion thus is rapidly becoming a thing of the past in most of the developed world, but change is coming more slowly in much of the less developed world. In some countries the problem of illegal abortion is increasing because the need for abortion seems to be rising. There are important exceptions, particularly China, where abortion has been liberally provided by medical services since 1957. In India abortion was legalized in 1972, but there was so little publicity that even large segments of the medical community as well as the public were unaware of it for the first few years. For those who knew, high costs and excessive red tape were effective deterrents. For at least the first three years, the number of legal abortions was extremely low (41,000 in the first five months), while the number of nonmedical illegal abortions was appallingly high (at least 4 million a year).[51]

Elsewhere in Asia, abortion has been legalized in South Korea (1973), North Vietnam (1971), Hong Kong (1972), and Singapore (1969, further liberalized in 1974). Abortion is firmly illegal in Taiwan, but apparently easily obtainable from medical practitioners, nonetheless. Laws are still restrictive in Indonesia, Pakistan, Sri Lanka, Thailand, and the Philippines, but there are signs

[48]L. Zanetti, The shame of Italy.

[49]Zimmerman, Abortion, law and practice; C. Tietze and M. C. Murstein, Induced abortion: a factbook, 1975. These two are the major sources for what follows.

[50]Teitze and Murstein, Induced abortion; Charles F. Westoff, The populations of the developed countries.

[51]The abortion dilemma, *Atlas,* November 1974, pp. 16–18.

that they may soon be changed in several of these countries.

In the Middle East and North Africa, laws are generally very restrictive, except in Tunisia (which has had abortion on request in the first trimester since 1973) and Cyprus, which partially liberalized its law in 1974. Israel's tough anti-abortion law was weakened by a challenging court decision in 1952 and is seldom observed today. Abortions reportedly are also available through medical facilities in Egypt despite a strict anti-abortion law.

In Africa south of the Sahara, abortion is generally prohibited (the exceptions being Zambia since 1972 and some liberalization in South Africa). Ironically, these restrictive laws are holdovers from colonial times; they are not rooted in local culture.[52]

Abortion is still illegal in most Latin American countries, although laws have recently been relaxed to permit it under certain circumstances in El Salvador, Guatemala, Mexico, Panama, Brazil, Chile, Argentina, Ecuador, and Peru. Abortion essentially on request is available only in Uruguay and Cuba (since 1968 in both cases).

Illegal abortion is rampant in Latin America. Contraceptives are legally available in most Latin American countries, but in practice only accessible to the rich. The illiterate poor, who make up a large share of the Latin American population are generally unaware of the existence of birth control other than by ancient folk methods, and could not afford modern methods even if they knew of them. There are exceptions where governments and volunteer organizations such as Planned Parenthood have established free birth control clinics (see next section). Although these can help, they as yet reach only a small fraction of the population, mainly in cities. In rural areas where hunger and malnutrition are often widespread, a failure of primitive birth control methods leaves women with no alternative but to practice equally crude forms of abortion.

In the 1960s bungled abortions were estimated to account for more than 40 percent of hospital admissions in Santiago, Chile. In that country, an estimated one-third of all pregnancies end in abortion. In Mexico, 400,000 women per year are treated in hospitals for illegal abortions; the abortion rate is conservatively estimated at one-fourth the birth rate.[53] For South America as a whole, some authorities believe that one-fourth of all pregnancies end in abortion; others estimate that abortions outnumber births.

Liberalizing abortion laws in various countries has been shown to have two important effects. The first is a very large decline in maternal deaths and morbidity (illness) associated with illegal abortion. The degree of reduction of death and illness depends on the degree of change in the law, the previous rate of illegal abortions, and how they were usually performed (i.e., self-inflicted under unsanitary circumstances or performed clandestinely by medical personnel). The number of annual abortion deaths in the U.S. dropped from over 150 per year before 1970 to 47 (25 of which were from illegal abortions) in 1973; in England the decline was from 60 before 1968 to 11 in 1974.[54] Declines in many European countries and LDCs, where crude self-abortion has been more common, will probably be much greater. Conversely, the number of deaths in Romania, where abortion regulations were tightened, rose from about 70 in 1965 to over 370 in 1971.[55]

The other result of liberalizing abortion laws is to provide such services safely to low-income women. When abortion is illegal, the rich can usually still obtain a safe illegal procedure or can afford to travel to another country where legal abortion is available. The poor have no such options; it is they who suffer most either from the burdens of large families or from dangerously unsafe illegal abortions.

The moral issue. The greatest obstacles to freely available, medically safe abortion in many developed countries and in Latin America are the Roman Catholic Church and other religious groups that consider abortion immoral. The crux of the Catholic argument is that the embryo is, from the moment of conception, a complete individual with a soul. In the Catholic view, induced abortion amounts to murder. Some Catholics also oppose

[52]Sue Tuckwell, Abortion, the hidden plague.

[53]*Atlas*, The abortion dilemma; Tuckwell, Abortion, p. 20.

[54]C. Tietze and M. C. Murstein, Induced Abortion: a factbook. The rate of abortion deaths was declining during the 1960s, especially after 1967 when several states relaxed laws to permit more legal abortions.

[55]Ibid.

abortion on the grounds that it will encourage promiscuity—exactly the same reason given in Japan for banning the pill and the IUD. There is no evidence to support either point of view on promiscuity, but, even if there were an increase, it would seem a small price to pay for a chance to ameliorate the mass misery of unwanted pregnancies—especially since the main ostensible reason for social disapproval of promiscuity is the production of unwanted children.

Many Protestant theologians hold that the time when a child acquires a soul is unknown and perhaps unimportant. They see no difficulty in establishing it at the time of "quickening," when movements of the fetus first become discernible to the mother; or at the time, around 28 weeks, when the infant, if prematurely born, might survive outside its mother's body. To them, the evil of abortion is far outweighed by the evil of bringing into the world an unwanted child under less than ideal circumstances.

To a biologist the question of when life begins for a human child is almost meaningless, since life is continuous and has been since it first began on Earth several billion years ago. The precursors of the egg and sperm cells that create the next generation have been present in the parents since they were embryos themselves. To most biologists, an embryo or a fetus is no more a complete human being than a blueprint is a complete building.[55a] The fetus, given the opportunity to develop properly before birth, and given the essential early socializing experiences and sufficient nourishing food during the crucial early years after birth, will ultimately develop into a human being. Where any of these is lacking, the resultant individual will be deficient in some respect. From this point of view, a fetus is only a *potential* human being, with no particular rights. Historically, the law has dated most rights and privileges from the moment of birth, and legal scholars generally agree that a fetus is not a "person" within the meaning of the U.S. Constitution until it is born and living independent of its mother.

From the standpoint of a terminated fetus, it makes no difference whether the mother had an induced or a spontaneous abortion. On the other hand, it subsequently makes a great deal of difference to the child if an abortion is denied and the mother, contrary to her wishes, is forced to devote her body and life to the production and care of the child. In Sweden, a study was made to determine what eventually happened to children born to mothers whose requests for abortions had been turned down. When compared to a group of children from similar backgrounds who had been wanted, more than twice as many of the unwanted youngsters grew up in undesirable circumstances (illegitimate, in broken homes, or in institutions); more than twice as many had records of delinquency, or were deemed unfit for military service; almost twice as many had needed psychiatric care; and nearly five times as many had been on public assistance during their teens.[56]

In a 1975 study in Czechoslovakia, nine-year old children whose mothers had been denied abortions were compared with carefully matched "controls."[57] The unwanted children tended to have more problems of health and social adjustment and to perform less well in school than did their peers who had been wanted. Further, it appeared that the disadvantages of being unwanted—initially, at least—affected boys more strongly than girls.

There seems little doubt that the forced bearing of unwanted children has undesirable consequences not only for the children and their families, but for society as well, apart from the problems of overpopulation. The latter factor, however, adds further urgency to the need for alleviating the other situations. An abortion is clearly preferable to adding one more child to an overburdened family or an overburdened society, where the chances that it will realize its full potential are slight. The argument that a decision is being made for an unborn person who "has no say" is often raised by those opposing abortion. But unthinking actions of the very same people help to commit future unheard generations to misery and early death on an overcrowded planet. One can also challenge the notion that older men, be they medical doctors, legislators, or celibate clergymen, have the right to make decisions whose consequences are borne largely by young women and their families.

There are those who claim that free access to abortion

[55a]Garrett Hardin, Abortion—compulsory pregnancy?

[56]Lars Huldt, Outcome of pregnancy when legal abortion is readily available.

[57]Z. Dytrych, et al., Children born to women denied abortion.

will lead to genocide. It is hard to see how this could happen if the decision is left to the mother. A mother who takes the moral view that abortion is equivalent to murder is free to bear her child. If she cannot care for it, placement for adoption is still possible in most societies.

Few people would claim that abortion is preferable to contraception, not only because of moral questions, but also because the risk of subsequent health problems for the mother may be greater. Death rates for first-trimester, medically supervised abortions are a fraction of those for pregnancy and childbirth but considerably higher in later months.[58] Large and rapidly growing numbers of people nevertheless feel that abortion is vastly preferable to the births of unwanted children, especially in an overpopulated world. Until more effective forms of contraception than now exist are developed, and until people become more conscientious in use of contraceptives, abortion will remain a needed back-up method of birth control when contraception fails.

Attitudes on abortion have changed in most countries in recent years, and they can reasonably be expected to change more in the future. The female part of the world's population has long since cast its silent vote. Every year over one million women in the United States, and an estimated 30 to 55 million more elsewhere, have made their desires abundantly clear by seeking and obtaining abortions. Until the 1970s, these women were forced to seek their abortions more often than not in the face of their societies' disapproval and of very real dangers and difficulties. Millions still must do so.

There is little question that legalized abortion can contribute to a reduction in birth rates. Wherever liberal laws have been enacted, they have been followed by lowered fertility. Longstanding evidence is available from Japan and Eastern Europe, where abortion was the primary effective form of birth control available for some years after liberalization, and where the decline in fertility was substantial. The extent of decline is bound to be related to the availability of other birth control methods; but even in the United States and England, where contraceptives have been widely available, the decline in fertility after reversal of abortion policies was significant.

[58]Tietze and Murstein, Induced abortion.

According to at least one study, availability of abortion (legal or illegal) may be necessary in order for a population to reach and maintain fertility near replacement level, given current contraceptive technology and patterns of sexual behavior.[59] Liberalization of abortion policies in those countries where it is still largely or entirely illegal is therefore justifiable both on humanitarian and health grounds and as an aid to population control.

POPULATION POLICIES IN LESS DEVELOPED NATIONS

In response to rising alarm during the 1950s over the population explosion in less developed countries, both private and governmental organizations in the United States and other nations began to be involved in population research and overseas family planning programs. First among these, naturally, was the International Planned Parenthood Federation, which grew out of the established national groups. By 1975 there were Planned Parenthood organizations in 84 countries, supported by their own governments, private donations, government grants from developed countries, or some combination of these sources.[60]

Various other private and governmental organizations followed Planned Parenthood into the field, including the Ford and Rockefeller Foundations, the Population Council, the U.S. Agency for International development (AID), and agencies of several other DC governments. International organizations such as the World Bank and various UN agencies, particularly the UN Fund for Population Activities, had joined by 1970. The 1960s brought a great proliferation of family planning programs in LDCs, which were assisted or administered by one or another of these groups. Most assistance from DCs was provided through one of the international or private organizations. In 1960 some $2 million was spent by developed countries (and the U.S. was not then among them) to assist LDC family planning programs; by 1974

[59]C. Tietze and J. Bongaarts, Fertility rates and abortion rates: simulations of family limitation, *Studies in family planning,* vol. 6, no. 5, May 1975, p. 119.

[60]Population Reference Bureau, *World population growth and response,* pp. 243–248.

TABLE 13-2
Family Planning in LDCs

Population (millions, 1975)	*Have an official policy to reduce population growth rate*	*Have official support of family planning for other reasons*	*Neither have policy nor support family planning*
400+	People's Republic of China (1962) India (1952, reorganized 1965)	–	–
100–400	Indonesia (1968)	Brazil (1974)	–
50–100	Mexico (1974) Pakistan (1960, reorganized 1965) Bangladesh (1971)	Nigeria (1970)	–
25–50	Turkey (1965) Egypt (1965) Iran (1967) Philippines (1970) Thailand (1970) South Korea (1961) Vietnam (1962 in North)	Zaire (1973)	Burma Ethiopa Argentina
15–25	Morocco (1968) Taiwan (1968) Colombia (1970)	Tanzania (1970) South Africa (1966) Afghanistan (1970) Sudan (1970) Algeria (1971)	North Korea Peru
10–15	Nepal (1966) Sri Lanka (Ceylon) (1965) Malaysia (1966) Kenya (1966)	Venezuela (1968) Chile (1966) Iraq (1972) Uganda (1972)	
Less than 10	Tunisia (1964) Barbados (1967) Dominican Republic (1968) Singapore (1965) Hong Kong (1973) Jamaica (1966) Trinidad and Tobago (1967) Laos (1972, possibly discontinued) Ghana (1969) Mauritius (1965) Puerto Rico (1970) Botswana (1970) Fiji (1962) El Salvador (1968) Gilbert and Ellice Islands (1970) Guatemala (1975) Grenada (1974) Bolivia (1968, reorganized 1973) Costa Rica (1968) El Salvador (1968)	Cuba (early 1960s) Nicaragua (1967) Syria (1974) Panama (1969) Honduras (1966) Dahomey (1969) Gambia (1969) Rhodesia (1968) Senegal (1970) Ecuador (1968) Honduras (1965) Benin (early 1970s) Haiti (1971) Papua-New Guinea (1969) Paraguay (1972) Liberia (1973) Lesotho (1974) Western Samoa (1971) Madagascar (1974) Sierra Leone (early 1970s) Swaziland (1969) Togo (early 1970s) Zambia (early 1970s) Cambodia (1972, possibly discontinued) Guyana (1975) Surinam (1974) Uruguay (1971) Other small Caribbean countries (1960s)	Cameroon Angola Malawi Jordan Lebanon Saudi Arabia Syria Yemen Mali Upper Volta Mozambique Burundi Central African Republic Chad Comoros Congo Equatorial Guinea Guinea-Bisseau Ivory Coast Libya Mauritania Niger Rwanda Seychelles Somalia Namibia Israel

Sources: Berelson, Population control programs; Nortman, Population and family planning programs, 1975; Population Reference Bureau, *World population growth and response.*

the amount was over $200 million, more than half of it from USAID. Yet less than two percent of all foreign assistance goes to LDC family planning programs, and most LDCs allot less than one percent of their budgets to it.[61]

During the 1960s national family planning programs were established in some 25 LDCs, while 17 other governments began supporting or assisting the activities of private Planned Parenthood organizations. The early 1970s saw a further proliferation of these programs until by 1975, 34 less developed countries officially favored the reduction of population growth, and 32 more supported family planning activities for other reasons. Some 55 additional LDCs still did not support family planning, or in a few cases opposed it. But the combined 1973 populations of the pro-family planning countries were nearly 2.5 billion, whereas the total combined population of the anti-family planning nations was only about 250 million.[62] Table 13-2 shows details.

Government Policies in LDCs

So far family planning programs are the primary policies that have been brought into action against the population explosion in most LDCs. Outstanding exceptions are the People's Republic of China,[63] Indonesia, India, Pakistan, South Korea, Singapore, Tunisia, Egypt, and a few other countries where other social and economic policies have been adopted to supplement family planning.[64] However, many family planning programs have been established and are even being supported by governments for reasons other than reduction of population growth, usually to protect the health and welfare of mothers and children. Although no country has yet adopted attainment of ZPG as a goal, many have aimed at an ultimate reduction of growth rates to DC levels—around 1 percent per year or less. A few countries, by contrast, still want to increase their usually already rapid growth. Many others are beginning to reevaluate their pronatalist policies as consequences of rapid growth become increasingly evident. The following discussion sums up these various approaches by continent.[65]

Africa. Africa, an extremely diverse continent, growing at about 2.6 percent per year, includes some of the world's poorest and most rapidly growing nations. Because high mortalities, especially of infants, are also commonly found in these countries, concern over rapid growth and action to curb it have developed only relatively recently in most of them. Indeed, some African governments remain staunchly pronatalist.

The belief that more people are needed for development is common among African nations south of the Sahara. Policies in Cameroon, Malawi, and Upper Volta still frankly favor growth, while Zambia and the Malagasy Republic have only recently reversed their positions (in 1975). Concern about poorly controlled migration is greater in many of these countries than concern about high birth rates.

In general, family planning on a private basis has long been available in former African colonies of England, but not in those of such Catholic countries as France, Belgium, Spain, Italy, and Portugal. Former English colonies were among the first to establish national family planning policies, although emphasis in some cases is put on health and family welfare justifications. Kenya and Ghana have two of the oldest and strongest family planning programs in subSaharan Africa, and both have goals of reducing population growth. Interest in family planning at least for health reasons is growing in most former English colonies, although a few such as Malawi still discourage or ignore the activities of private family planning organizations. Nigeria, the most populous and one of the richest (in terms of resource endowment) African countries, was only beginning to show interest in family planning for health reasons in 1976, despite rapid growth.

[61] Dorothy Nortman, Population and family planning programs: A factbook, 1974. Population Reference Bureau, *World population growth and response.*

[62] D. Nortman, Population and family planning programs, 1974 and 1975.

[63] See Edgar Snow, Report from China—III: population care and control, for an early report on China. More recent reports have generally confirmed that first impression: for example, Pi-Chao Chen, China: population program at the grass roots, in *Population: perspective 1973,* H. Brown, J. Holdren, A. Sweezy, B. West, eds.

[64] Vumbaco, Recent law and policy changes.

[65] For country-by-country details of policies and recent demographic trends, Population Reference Bureau, *World population growth and response,* prepared with the assistance of the U.S. Agency for International Development, is invaluable.Schroeder and Vumbaco each provide useful summaries, as does the more recent D. Nortman and E. Hofstatter, Population and family planning programs: a factbook, 1976.

In South Africa and Rhodesia, the dominant European populations have traditionally practiced birth control. These countries are now trying to extend family planning services to their African populations. South Africa's family planning is offered through its Planned Parenthood affiliate and funded by the government; Rhodesia's services are government-supported, but operated by several private international groups.

Former French colonies have begun to relax their prohibitions to allow the commercial sale of contraceptives and to support some family planning activities. The first family planning clinics in French-speaking continental Africa have been established in Senegal, whose government is beginning to show interest in family planning. Most former French colonies, however, remain complacent about their rates of population growth. An exception is Mauritius, an island nation with one of the highest population densities in the world (see Chapter 5). Mauritius has a vigorous and comparatively successful family planning program. Since the 1950s, the growth rate has been reduced to about 2.1, despite an unusually low death rate of 7 per 1000 population.

The Portuguese colonies, Mozambique and Angola, remained pronatalist and strongly opposed to birth control until they achieved independence in 1975. Establishment of population programs must await the stabilization of the new governments.

Some North African countries have initiated family planning programs; Egypt, Tunisia, and Morocco have fairly strong, antinatalist policies. Tunisia, in particular, has ventured beyond family planning to legalize sterilization (considered immoral and against Moslem law in most Islamic countries) and abortion, to limit financial allowances for children to four per family, raise the legal marriage age, and ban polygamy. In addition, women's rights, usually very restricted in Moslem societies, are being promoted. Some other North African countries—Algeria, Libya, Mauritania—remain pronatalist or uninterested.

Many African countries still have death rates above 20 per thousand, and some even more than 30. A number of demographers and family planning officials believe that interest in population control will remain low in those countries until the death rates have been substantially reduced, especially among infants and children. It is vitally important to change this point of view so that efforts can be made to lower birth rates *along with* death rates; that most family planning efforts have begun in African countries as a part of maternal and child health services is an encouraging sign.

Latin America. Latin America as a region, despite having some of the highest population growth rates in the world (about 2.9 percent for the entire region), has also been very reluctant to accept a need for population control. This is probably due in part to the influence of the Roman Catholic Church, but there is also a widespread belief, at least in South America, that the continent still contains vast untapped resources of land and minerals, that the answer to all problems is development, and that more people are needed for development. Latin American politicians, moreover, tend to view proposals originating in the United States for birth control with understandable suspicion. Some seem to believe the U.S. is trying to impose a new and subtle form of imperialism.[66] In some countries, this reaction has even had the effect of inhibiting the teaching of demography and family planning in universities.

Latin American economists and politicians have come to accept family planning (often referred to as "responsible parenthood") mainly on health and welfare grounds and as a means of reducing the horrendous illegal abortion rate. Some leaders are beginning to realize, however, that the galloping population growth rate is swallowing all the economic progress each year, leaving a per-capita rate of progress of zero or less. A few countries have established essentially, though not always explicitly, antinatalist policies as a result—notably Chile, Colombia, several Caribbean countries, and all of the Central American countries. The efforts of some family planning programs in the Caribbean (mainly former British colonies) have been counted among the most successful, especially those of Barbados and Trinidad and Tobago. Birth rates have declined there since the early 1960s, and have declined as well in Chile, Colombia, Costa Rica, Nicaragua, Panama and Venezuela.

[66]National Academy of Sciences, *In search of population policy: views from the developing world;* Population policy in Latin America.

At the other extreme, Brazil and Argentina have policies generally promoting growth. Brazil does permit private family planning groups to operate, however, especially in the poverty-stricken Northeast. Argentina, having a relatively low birth rate and feeling threatened by rapidly growing Brazil, in 1974 banned dissemination of birth control information and closed family planning clinics. Since the practice of birth control is well established in the Argentine population, the action is not likely to have great effect except perhaps to raise the already high abortion rate, mostly illegal.

Asia. Asia includes over half of the human population and is growing at about 2.3 percent per year. Both mortality and birth rates are generally lower than those in Africa, and both have been declining in several countries.

Asia presents a widely varied picture in regard to population policies. At one extreme, China, India, Thailand, Indonesia, Sri Lanka, Hong Kong, Singapore, Taiwan, and South Korea are pursuing strong family planning policies, in several cases reinforced by social and economic measures, some of which are described below. All of these countries have recorded declines in birth rates, some of them quite substantial. Family planning programs have also been established in Pakistan, Bangladesh, Nepal, Malaysia, and the Philippines, but the impact, if any, on birth rates is negligible so far.

A few rapidly growing countries, notably Cambodia and Burma, currently are pursuing pronatalist population policies, although family planning is privately available in the latter country. Other "centrally planned" countries in Southeast Asia seem to be following China's example in population policies; North Vietnam has had a family planning program for some time, which presumably was extended to South Vietnam when the nation was unified. Policies in North Korea are unknown.

Middle Eastern nations are still largely pronatalist in their outlook, with the exceptions of Turkey and Iran which have national family planning programs. Several countries, including Afghanistan, Bahrain, Cyprus, Iraq, Jordan, Lebanon, and Syria, are interested in establishing family planning services for health and welfare reasons. The remaining countries favor continued growth, although they may tolerate family planning activity in the private sector. Among these is Israel, for obvious reasons. At the furthest extreme is Saudi Arabia, which has outlawed importation of contraceptives. Nearly all Middle Eastern countries are growing rapidly with relatively high, although declining death rates.

The United Nations. For many years, the United Nations limited its participation in population policies to the gathering of demographic data. This, however, was instrumental in developing awareness of the need for population policies, especially among LDCs, whose governments often had no other information about their population growth. Since the late 1960s the UN has taken an active role in coordinating assistance for and directly participating in family planning programs of various member nations, while continuing the demographic studies. A special body, the UN Fund for Population Activities (UNFPA), advises governments on policies and programs, coordinates private donors and contributions from DC governments, and sometimes directly provides supplies, equipment, and personnel through other UN agencies.

In 1967 the UN Declaration on Social Progress and Development stated that "parents have the exclusive right to determine freely and responsibly the number and spacing of their children."[67] The statement affirmed the UN's increasing involvement in making family planning available to all peoples everywhere and contained an implicit criticism of any government policy that might deny family planning to people who wanted it. The statement has sometimes been interpreted as a stand against compulsory governmental policies to control births; however, the right to choose whether or not to have children is specifically limited to "responsible" choices. Thus, the Declaration also provides governments with the right to control irresponsible choices.

In 1974 the United Nations' World Population Conference, the first worldwide, government-participating forum on the subject, was convened in Bucharest. Publicity attending the event gave an impression of enormous disagreement among participating groups. But in fact it provided a valuable forum for an exchange of

[67]Declaration on Population, Teheran, 1968, *Studies in Family Planning,* no. 16, January, 1967.

ideas and information and seems to have stimulated interest in population problems among many less developed nations that had previously shown no interest at all. The conference is discussed in more detail later in this chapter.

Family Planning Programs

Studies conducted in LDCs when family planning programs are initiated have typically revealed that knowledge of birth control is very limited in these populations, especially outside the cities and the educated classes. The practice of birth control is even more limited. A major difficulty is that people in the LDCs generally want more children than do people in DCs, for various reasons that are discussed below in the section on *Motivation.*

Family planning programs in LDCs are usually carried out either through independent clinics or in cooperation with maternal and child health agencies, or both. In some countries, mobile units are used to carry workers and equipment to remote villages. Unlike traditional planned parenthood organizations in DCs, these programs actively recruit clients, employing specially trained field workers for this purpose and utilizing whatever forms of mass communication and promotion seem effective and appropriate. These may include pamphlets and circulars, advertisements in public transportation, billboards, radio and newspaper announcements, or plays and skits produced by traveling troupes. In India an elephant has been taken from village to village and used to pass out pamphlets and contraceptives. The primary emphasis in most programs has been on preventing the "unwanted child." Initially at least, the greatest effort has been made to reach women who already had at least three children, because they are usually most receptive to the idea of birth control.[68] The hope is that, as family planning gains acceptance, younger women with fewer children will begin to practice birth control. In countries with well-established, strong programs, this has happened.

Family planning programs generally offer a choice of birth control methods, sometimes including sterilization, although before the mid-1970s this method was only used or promoted on a large scale in India, Pakistan, and Bangladesh. The most popular method in Asia has been the IUD, although it has proven to be less ideal than it first seemed. Barely 50 percent of the women fitted with IUDs still wear them two years later. Malnutrition may contribute to this high discontinuance rate by increasing the tendency to bleed after insertion (which in turn worsens the malnutrition—especially iron deficiency anemia). This is just one example of how conditions partly caused by overpopulation can hinder efforts to establish population control.

The use of other methods, especially the contraceptive pill, has been increasing in recent years. Some countries are now permitting distribution of the pill without prescription by family planning workers. These workers interview clients beforehand with a questionnaire designed to eliminate women whose medical histories indicate that the pill might have dangerous side effects for them. Since in most LDCs, the danger of pregnancy and childbirth are several times greater than in DCs and far outweigh the health risks of the pill, this approach seems to be working quite successfully in Thailand and Pakistan, among other countries.[69] The pill is proving considerably more successful than the IUD had been in both countries.

Distribution of condoms has become an important element of the family planning program in India, Pakistan, and several other countries. Other traditional methods, such as diaphragms, jellies and foams, are also increasingly being offered. Abortion was widely available only in China among LDCs before the mid-1970s, but if recent changes in abortion laws are implemented, and if abortion services are integrated into the family planning structure, the situation could change dramatically in several countries.

Clinic staffs include doctors (usually gynecologists), nurses, midwives, and occasionally social workers. A few programs also employ anthropologists to advise the staff

[68]Most of the information on how family planning programs are organized comes from various issues of *Studies in Family Planning* and other periodicals published by The Population Council, Inc. For a general overview, see W. B. Watson and R. J. Lapham (eds.), Family planning programs: world review 1974; or Population Reference Bureau, *World population growth and response.* In addition, the July/August 1974 issue of *Unesco Courier* contained several articles on family planning programs and population policies in LDCs.

[69]Freedman and Berelson, The record of family planning programs; Milton Viorst, Population control: Pakistan tries a major new experiment.

personnel on the best approach to villagers. Midwives are often used as field workers and/or medical workers in clinics, although some problems have resulted from employing them. Midwives sometimes see family planning as a threat to their incomes from child delivery, as well as from illegal abortion, in which they may be profitably involved. Some of the newer programs are recruiting teachers or other respected community leaders to act as distributors of contraceptives, usually condoms or pills.

There is, of course, a great deal of variation among programs in terms of services offered, means of distributing materials and information, recruitment methods, and so forth. The approaches that have been used in India, and their results under difficult circumstances, are described in Box 13-5. India's family planning program, although derived from Western aid programs, is by no means typical. Even though many of the problems it faces are shared by other LDCs, in some respects, including the sheer magnitude and diversity of the population itself, it is essentially unique. Indonesia, Pakistan, and Bangladesh present some of the same logistic difficulties as India, but each of those has a population only a fraction as large. China's population is larger than India's, but possibly less diverse, and its political organization allows policies to be imposed from the top (see Box 13-6 for a detailed discussion of China's population policies). Its totally indigenous population program is different in several important respects from that of any other country.

Besides offering contraceptives, family planning programs in many LDCs, like the older organizations in DCs, provide counseling services for marriage, parenthood, and child spacing, and assistance for subfertile and sterile couples. Women's discussion groups are often organized in villages to interest wives in birth control. Advice on nutrition and child care may be included in the discussions, partly because these subjects may attract women to the family planning program, and partly because dissemination of this information contributes to the program's child welfare goals.

Some hope of increased effectiveness in reaching younger women early in their reproductive lives lies in introducing family planning to them immediately after the birth of their first child. Pilot studies of this approach in both DCs and LDCs have brought promising results, although to be effective it may require special personnel in the hospital who do nothing else. Attempts to have hospital staff members add to their other duties the teaching of family planning to maternity patients have often failed, however. Doctors and nurses in such hospitals are generally overworked already; and they often have not been particularly motivated in favor of family planning. Moreover, in the poorest LDCs (where birth rates are apt to be highest) children are seldom born in a hospital except among the wealthy urban classes, who are likely to be using birth control already.

With the exception of India (and perhaps China), no LDC had an official family planning program prior to 1960, and most have been established since 1965. Because they are so new, it is difficult to evaluate the potential value of most of these programs.

For example, one of the most active among newer family planning programs is Indonesia's (1968), which quickly outran the World Bank's estimates of what could be accomplished within three years after the organization was set up.[70] By 1974 about 32 percent of women of reproductive age in Bali and perhaps a similar proportion in East Java were using contraceptives, mostly as a result of the program's efforts. Nationwide, about 14 percent were using birth control. Many other LDCs have been unable to match that performance even in a considerably longer period of time. It is still too early for results to show in the nation's birth rate, however, and whether the early momentum in recruitment can be maintained remains to be seen.

Some of the earlier and stronger family planning programs have made considerable progress in terms of reaching a large proportion of the reproductive population.[71] Around 1973, for instance, contraceptive users as a percentage of women of reproductive age had exceeded 60 percent in Singapore, not far below the rate commonly found in developed countries. In Taiwan and Hong Kong, acceptance rates were well over 50 percent, and in South Korea and Colombia they had reached 30 percent.

[70]Jon Tinker, Java: birth control battlefield; Freedman and Berelson, The record of family planning programs.

[71]Watson and Lapham, Family planning programs; Nortman, Family planning programs: a factbook, 1974 and 1975; Berelson, An evaluation of the effects; Freedman and Berelson, The record of family planning programs.

BOX 13-5 India: A History of Frustration

Once poverty caused overpopulation, but it is now overpopulation that is causing poverty.

–Karan Singh
Minister for Health and Family Planning in India

India's family planning program began in 1952, when the country had a population of over 360 million and was growing at about 2 percent per year. For the first decade the program was not strongly supported, but in 1965 it was overhauled and a better organized and supported effort ensued. But the modest reduction in the birth rate between 1965 and 1975 from 41 per thousand population to about 35 (according to Indian demographers) was matched by the decline in mortality. In 1975 the population was over 600 million and still growing at close to 2 percent. If the birth rate cannot be further reduced substantially, (and the death rate does not rise), the population will reach one billion by the end of the century.[a]

India's family planning measures have included the establishment of clinics (associated with maternal health facilities where possible), temporary camps, and mobile units (Figure 13-3), all accompanied by an active education campaign both within and outside the schools to promote small families. By 1975 there were some 1900 urban family planning centers, 5000 rural centers, and 33,000 subcenters throughout the country. Vasectomy and the IUD have been the most used methods, although female sterilization, condoms, and other contraceptives have been made increasingly available. Men who accept vasectomies, and any individual who persuades a man to have one, are paid small fees. Railway stations have been used as vasectomy clinics in place of hospitals, partly because they attract large numbers of people and partly because Indians traditionally regard hospitals as a place to die. In addition, a program of active research and development of new contraceptive methods, including investigations of folk methods and reversible vasectomy, has been carried on.

During the 1960s India ran into some problems with its family planning policies, particularly in rural areas. Aside from the monumental logistic difficulty of taking family planning to every one of 500,000 villages, a good deal of overt resistance has been met in some places, which has even led occasionally to riots and the destruction of camps and mobile units. This resistance resulted in part from the existence of three active medical traditions in India besides Western medicine–ayurvedic, unani, and homeopathic. The family planning program originally was implemented only through Western medicine, a circumstance that naturally resulted in resentment and opposition from the others.[b] Resistance has also come from religious and ethnic minority groups who may have perceived family planning as discrimination. Perhaps most fundamental, family planning may be perceived by rural peasants as directly contrary to their economic interests (see section on motivation). In the late 1960s, this opposition showed itself in a drop in vasectomy and contraceptive acceptance rates.[c]

In an effort to expand the effectiveness of the program, India began experimenting with "family planning festivals." In one district during July 1971, over 60,000 vasectomies were performed at one festival. IUDs, condoms, and female sterilizations were also available. Greater than usual incentive payments and gifts were offered both to recipients and to recruiters. The festival also included entertainment and cultural events. There was a great deal of publicity, and entertainers toured the surrounding countryside beforehand to attract people to the festival. Cooperation and support were secured from local voluntary organizations, government officials, professional groups, and labor unions, which probably contributed much to the success of the campaign.[d] Altogether, by 1975 some 14 million Indian people had been sterilized, many of them in such special festival camps.

Expansion of family planning activities in

[a]A. B. Wadia, India's painful struggle toward the small family norm. For an overview of the situation in India, see P. Visaria and A. K. Jain, India.

[b]John Lorraine, Population patterns in the mid 1970s.

[c]Joseph Lelyveld, Birth curb drive slowing in India. *New York Times,* April 20, 1969.

[d]K. K. Lurien, A world record for Ernakulam, S. Krishnakumar, Kerala's pioneering experiment in massive vasectomy camps; V. H. Thakor and V. M. Patel, The Gujarat State massive vasectomy campaign.

India was forced to a halt in late 1973 and 1974 by a governmental financial crisis, which was followed by the oil crisis that quadrupled India's costs for vitally needed oil imports. The family planning budget for 1974 was cut to half the originally planned amount. In response to consternation expressed by other nations over that action, some of the funds were later restored, but only enough to allow the continuation of already established activities.

In late 1974, possibly spurred by the example of China's apparent success and by India's deteriorating food situation (Chapter 7), India announced another reorganization of the family planning program.[e] Funding for the five-year period 1974–1979 was increased more than 80 percent over 1969–1974. It was planned to broaden the availability of Copper-T IUDs, oral contraceptives, and abortion, none of which had been generally available through the program before. Educational and motivational efforts also were to be increased. In addition, family planning workers were being retrained as general health workers in an effort to raise public health standards throughout the country while also providing information and the means of birth control. The corps of family-planning/health workers is projected to expand from 80,000 to 130,000 over time. This is clearly a worthwhile plan on all counts, provided the health services are adequate and the birth control drive is not diluted by the additional duties of the workers.

In early 1976, India took an even more radical step in its population policies, requiring government employees in New Delhi with more than two children to be sterilized and denying public housing and other benefits. Incentives were provided for those who restricted their families to no more than two children. The federal government also encouraged states to enact similar compulsory laws. The state of Punjab passed a law imposing a prison sentence, a fine, or mandatory sterilization for couples who bear a third or subsequent child, with some broad exceptions. Maharashtra state passed a similar law affecting

FIGURE 13-3

A mobile vasectomy clinic in Bombay, India. This bus brings birth control information and materials to people in remote villages. (Photo courtesy of Carl Purcell, Agency for International Development.)

couples with more than three children, and West Bengal was considering such a law.[f]

The compulsory sterilization policy proved to be a major factor in the defeat of Indira Gandhi's government in March 1977. The new government's Minister of Health and Family Planning promptly announced a reversal of the policy and a return to emphasis on contraceptives rather than sterilization in the family planning program.[g]

---

[e] W. B. Watson and R. J. Lapham, eds. Family planning programs; Marcus F. Franda, Shifts in emphasis in India's population policy.

[f] Vumbaco, Recent law; India: ban on births, *Time,* March 8, 1976; Forced sterilization: a tough bid to cut India's birth rate, San Francisco *Sunday Examiner and Chronicle,* April 11, 1976; William D. Hartley, Indian state may force sterilization on families in desperate attempt to control its population, *Wall St. Journal,* July 7, 1976. See also the editorial and group of articles on the subject in IPPF, *People,* vol. 3, no. 4, 1976.

[g] William Borders, India will moderate birth-curb program, *New York Times,* April 3, 1977.

BOX 13-6 China: An Apparent Success Story

Any brief treatment of Chinese society is difficult and necessarily contains elements of overgeneralization. First of all, the huge geographical expanse and the vastness of the population—nearly a billion people—are difficult to envision. Second, the Chinese people possess a cultural diversity possibly as rich as that of Europe, and even older traditions. Finally, it seems that there is no overall, systematic keeping of vital statistics and population figures in China, and those statistics that do exist are not readily available to outsiders. The Chinese are traditionally xenophobic, and the Western intrusion of the last century and a quarter—from the Opium Wars through the United States debacle in Vietnam and Soviet pressure on northern Chinese borders—have only heightened this traditional aloofness. The available information is therefore fragmentary and has to some extent been filtered by a highly centralized and autocratic regime. Still, the accounts of foreign travellers in China and the release of official statements and figures allow some conclusions to be drawn about the nature of population policy in the People's Republic.[a]

Superficially, the expressed population policies of the People's Republic of China seem slightly schizophrenic. Official rhetoric preached abroad roundly condemns Malthusian ideas: "The poor countries have not always been poor. Nor are they poor because they have too many people. They are poor because they are plundered and exploited by imperialism."[b] The same article goes on to blame "relative overpopulation and widespread poverty" in the United States and the Soviet Union on "ruthless oppression and exploitation which the superpowers practice at home."

But, despite assertions that there is no such thing as overpopulation, China admits to having a policy of "planned population growth," with this rationale:

> We do not believe in anarchy in material production, and we do not believe in anarchy in human reproduction. Man must control nature, and he must also control his numbers. . . .
>
> We believe China's policy benefits many aspects of life—national construction, the emancipation of women, protection of mothers and women and children, proper bringing up of the young, better health for the people and prosperity for the nation. It is, in other words, in the interests of the masses of the people.[c]

In recent years, as China has begun to open up to the outside world, it has become increasingly clear not only that "birth planning," as it is called, is seriously advocated and supported by the government, but that it has begun to reap results. Exactly how successful the policy has been overall is impossible to say because there are no reliable nationwide population statistics. The last reasonably comprehensive census was conducted in 1953 (when a total mainland population of about 583 million was found), and estimates of vital rates since then are basically guesswork.[d] Hence the estimates of total population in 1975 range from below 800 million to 962 million.[e] China specialist Leo Orleans has proposed a set of estimates and projections of China's population from 1954 to 1980, and his arguments in support of them are convincing. He suggests that the 1975 population was about 850 million, with a birth rate of 27 per thousand, a death rate of 12 per thousand, and a natural increase of 1.5 percent. These figures are slightly above those of the UN.

China's efforts to curb population growth began in the 1950s following the release of the census results and a period of heated discussions of the pros and cons of birth control. An organized campaign implemented by the Ministry of Public Health was launched in 1957 but then was suspended in 1958 during the Great Leap Forward, an intensive effort at economic development. The period 1959–1961 was one of food shortage and economic crises, and, although established birth control clinics continued to

[a]For a recent overview, see International Planned Parenthood Federation, China 1976: a new perspective.

[b]China on the Population Question, *China Reconstructs*.

[c]Ibid.

[d]Leo A. Orleans, China: Population in the People's Republic. This is an excellent source for historical background, although otherwise somewhat out of date.

[e]Orleans, China's population figures: Can the contradictions be resolved? The lowest are based on casual statements by Chinese officials at the UN; the highest are from the *World Population Estimates* of the Environmental Fund, which bases its estimates on the figures of John Aird, a demographer in the U.S. Department of Commerce Foreign Demographic Analysis Division.

function, there was no official encouragement for their use.

While China was recovering from this crisis period, the government again began advocating "birth planning" to protect the health of mothers and children. An important part of this campaign was promotion of late marriage (23 to 25 for women, 25 to 28 for men) and the two-child family spaced by 3 to 5 years.[f] Both abortion and sterilization were legal from the start, but the middle 1960s were a period of active expansion of facilities (along with expansion of health care in general) and experimentation in improved techniques. It was then that the Chinese developed the vacuum technique for abortion, which has made the procedure much safer than before, and which has since been adopted around the world. Active research was also carried out on simplified sterilization procedures. It appears, for instance, that the Chinese may have been the first to do female sterilizations with very small incisions.[g]

China has all along manufactured all its own contraceptive devices and pharmaceuticals, unlike other LDCs. The latest invention is the "paper pill," sheets of water-soluble paper impregnated with oral contraceptives, which are easy to transport, store, and distribute.[h] Each sheet contains a month's supply of "pills" in perforated squares that dissolve in the mouth when eaten. This development is expected to increase use of oral contraceptives considerably, especially in remote rural areas where the pills have been less accepted than in the cities.

Virtually every method of birth control is being actively used in China: sterilization, abortion, the combined steroid pill and the progestin mini-pill, long-term injections, IUDs (the Chinese developed their own, a stainless steel ring), condoms, diaphragms, foams, and jellies.

The various forms of birth control have long been available to the people in the major cities and their suburbs. During the 1960s, health care, including birth control services, was increasingly extended to more remote rural areas. As an indication of the success of the health care programs, the death rate for the entire country is estimated to have dropped from nearly 35 per 1000 population in 1949 to about 17 per 1000 in 1970[i] and perhaps 13 in 1974.[j] Infant mortality, which fairly accurately reflects levels of both health care and nutrition, is thought to have been between 20 and 30 per 1000 births in 1974.[k] In some urban communes (which apparently do keep careful demographic statistics), the crude death rate is 5 or less, and an infant mortality rate of 8.8 per 1000 live births has been claimed for the city of Shanghai.[l]

China's unique health care system, together with greatly improved distribution of the food supply, can claim credit for this remarkable change. At the time of the Revolution, a grossly inadequate corps of trained medical personnel existed, mainly concentrated in the large cities. While actively training thousands of doctors, paramedics, and nurses and establishing hospitals and health centers in smaller cities, the Chinese also promptly tackled sanitation and hygiene at the grass-roots level through educational campaigns.

More recently, selected people have been given four to six months' basic medical training and assigned part-time to care for basic health needs in their production brigades. These individuals are called "native doctors" in the cities and "barefoot doctors" in the country. Their responsibilities include giving injections and innoculations, administering first aid and simple treatments for diseases, supervising sanitation measures, teaching hygiene in schools, and distributing contraceptive materials. For medical treatment beyond their competence (including abortions and sterilizations), the barefoot doctors refer patients to the nearest regional hospital. Barefoot doctors in turn are assisted by part-time volunteer health aides, usually housewives, whom they train themselves.[m]

It now appears that China is attempting to upgrade the quality of grass-roots health care by sending fully trained medical personnel from city hospitals on rotation to rural health centers, where, among other things, they provide additional training for local health workers. Some barefoot doctors have thereby become qualified to do abortions, IUD insertions, and steriliza-

[f]Pi-Chao Chen, China's population program at the grass-roots level.

[g]Orleans, Family planning developments in China, 1960–1966: abstracts from medical journals.

[h]Carl Djerassi, Fertility limitation through contraceptive steroids in the People's Republic of China.

[i]Orleans, China: Population in the People's Republic.

[j]Norman Myers, Of all things people are the most precious.

[k]Ibid.

[l]Joe Wray, How China is achieving the unbelievable.

[m]Pi-Chao Chen, China's population program at the grass-roots level; V. W. Sidel and R. Sidel, The delivery of medical care in China.

(*Continued*)

tions, as well as other minor operations.[n]

Both child bearing and birth control are fully supported and helped in China. Paid maternity leave, time off for breast-feeding, free nursery care, and all needed medical attention are provided for mothers. Paid leave is also given for abortion, sterilization, and IUD insertions, and all birth control services are essentially free.

While the means of birth control are provided through the health care system in China, primary responsibility for motivating couples to make use of them rests with the Revolutionary Committee (or governing council) of the production brigade or commune. Usually one member of the committee is the "responsible member" for birth planning.[o] In rural areas, "women's cadres"—married women with children, who are known and respected by their neighbors—carry contraceptives and the pro-birth control message house to house.[p]

In some of the cities, low birth rates have been so enthusiastically adopted as a goal that neighborhoods collectively decide how many births will be allowed each year and award the privilege of having babies to "deserving couples."[q] Priority is given to newlyweds, then to couples with only one child who have waited the favored period of time for the second birth.[r] The result has been phenomenally low birth rates for these neighborhoods, ranging from 4 to 7 per 1000 population. The center city of Shanghai reportedly had a 1972 birth rate of 6.4, while that for the city plus suburbs was 10.8.[s] The 1972 birth rate for Peking was reported by Joe Wray to have been about 14 per 1000 population; Myers placed it at 18.8 for city and suburbs combined.

Joe Wray has speculated that these low rates may have been helped by a relatively low proportion of women in their child-bearing years. Given the recent Chinese policy of sending urban young people to rural areas to work, this may be so, even though China's demographic history would indicate a relatively large and growing proportion of people in their teens and twenties for the country as a whole by 1975.

Exiling young people "temporarily" to rural communes probably was done for political reasons. Large numbers of urban youth are a potential source of insurgent trouble, especially if insufficient jobs are available. Scattering the young people in the countryside could effectively defuse that threat. Moreover, the relatively well-educated city youth could help spread the ideology of the central government to remote rural areas. But it appears that the policy may also have had demographic effects. Most of the city children are not happy down on the farm; consequently, they are reluctant to marry, settle, and raise families there. Nor are rural young people eager to marry the sophisticated city people with their strange ways.[t]

The official Chinese position on birth planning—an ideal of late marriage and a small, well-spaced family of two children—appears to have been overwhelmingly accepted in cities and is rapidly gaining acceptance in rural areas, according to reports from foreign visitors.[u] The prevailing attitude is that early marriage and having more than two children are prime examples of irresponsible behavior. Nevertheless, there is still resistance from older generations, especially mothers-in-law, who by tradition have long wielded considerable power within families and apparently still do.

Besides official encouragement to limit families, there are other incentives built into the social and economic system as well. Emancipation of women and their incorporation as full working members of society was an early, important goal of the Revolution. It has apparently been realized to a great extent, especially among younger women, and undoubtedly exerts a powerful influence on childbearing.

Pi-Chao Chen has pointed out disincentives to family limitation in the per capita grain allowance, which augments a family's supply when a child is added, and in the addition of another worker (preferably a boy who will remain in the family) to contribute to family income.[v] But it has also been observed that, even though another worker may help increase a family's total income, that income must still be divided among all family members. Additional members reduce the share available per person.[w] Furthermore, since

[n] Chen, China's population program.
[o] Wray, How China is achieving the unbelievable.
[p] Han Suyin, The Chinese experiment.
[q] Wray, Achieving the unbelievable; Han, Chinese experiment.
[r] Freedman and Berelson, The record of family planning programs.
[s] Wray, Achieving the unbelievable; Myers, People are the most precious.
[t] Joseph Lelyveld, The great leap farmward.
[u] Tameyoshi Katagiri, A report on the family planning program in the People's Republic of China; Sidel and Sidel, Medical care; Han, Chinese experiment; Myers, People are the most precious; Chen, China's population program; Wray, Achieving the unbelievable.
[v] Chen, China's population program.
[w] Sterling Wortman, Agriculture in China.

compulsory primary education is rapidly becoming the rule in China, children's productivity is inevitably deferred at least until the teenage years.

While there is no question whatever about the Chinese leadership's position on birth planning, coercion does not appear to be a part of the program beyond the extensive use of peer pressure and the dissemination of propaganda on all levels. There were reports of curtailed maternal benefits, reduced grain rations, and discriminatory housing and employment assignments for parents of three or more children in some areas during the 1960s, but these measures seem to have been largely abandoned. Possibly they aroused more resentment than cooperation and were found to be less than beneficial to the children.

By the mid-1970s, China's far-reaching population program evidently had been extended to the far corners of the nation—no mean trick in itself. What the results have been is impossible to assess with accuracy, but it is becoming increasingly clear that they are significant indeed. The remarkable vital rates prevailing in major cities have already been cited, but those of rural communes for which data exist, while higher than the cities', show significant reductions from pre-revolutionary levels (birth rate about 45, death rate 34 to 40, infant mortality above 200).[x] Reported birth rates for rural districts in the early 1970s range from as low as 14 in an area near Shanghai[y] to 20–24 in communes near Peking[z] and some others in more remote provinces.[aa] These areas generally report very low death rates also. Levels of contraceptive usage in urban and rural areas are compared in Figure 13-4. Certainly the communes visited by outsiders are among the most successful by Chinese standards, and so their birth and death rates should not be taken as representative of the entire country. But they may represent the leading edge of an established trend. That the policy has been so successful in many areas, especially where it is long established, indicates that similar success can be expected elsewhere in time.

[x]Orleans, China: Population in the People's Republic.
[y]Katagiri, A report.
[z]Sidel and Sidel, Medical care.
[aa]Chen, China's population program.

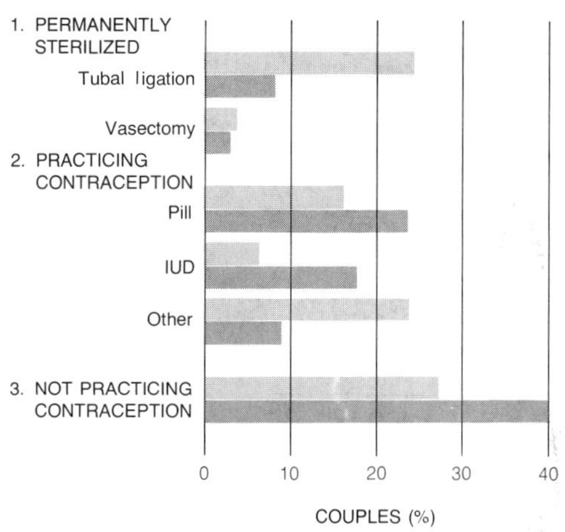

FIGURE 13-4

Contraceptive practices in an urban area (*light grey*) and in a rural area (*dark grey*) in China are compared; the urban sample is from the city of Hangchow, a provincial capital, and the rural sample is from a commune outside Peking. Sterilization is nearly three times commoner in the urban than in the rural sample, and substantially fewer rural males use contraceptives. The bias seems to be reflected in the difference between urban and rural birth rates: below 10 per 1000 in some urban areas and above 20 per 1000 in some rural ones. (From Sidel and Sidel, 1974.)

If available estimates of vital rates for all of China reflect reality, there has already been a substantial reduction in birth and death rates. Norman Myers of the FAO quotes birth rate estimates for large cities of between 10 and 19 per 1000 population, for medium-sized cities, 14 to 23, and for rural areas 20 to 35. He put the national 1974 birth rate at 29 and the death rate at 13, giving a natural increase of 1.6 percent per year. Comparison of these estimates with those of other Asian nations at similar levels of development is striking, to say the least. And no doubt other less developed countries—and perhaps some developed countries as well—can learn a great deal from the Chinese experience.[bb]

[bb]Chen, Lessons from the Chinese experience: China's planned birth program and its transferability.

TABLE 13-3
Family Planning Effects Measured Against Goals

Country	Program begun	Birth rate per 1000 Goal*	Birth rate per 1000 1976**	Growth rate (%) Goal*	Growth rate (%) 1976**	Population of married couples Target† (millions)	Population of married couples Protected by 1974 (%)
India	1952, 1965	40–25 (in 10 years)	35	–	2.0	102	15.1
S. Korea	1961	–	29	2.9–1.5 (by 1976)	2.0	4.5	30.5
Taiwan	1964	36–24 (by 1973)	23	3.02–1.86 (1965–1973)	1.9	1.8	55
Sri Lanka (Ceylon)	1965	33–25 (in 8–10 years)	28	1.6 (by 1976)	2.0	1.7	–
Turkey	1965	–	39	3.0–2.0 (by 1972)	2.6	5.6	2.5
Singapore	1965	30–under 20 (in 5 years)	20	–	1.6	0.3	60.1
Malaysia	1966	–	39	3.0–2.0 (by 1985)	2.9	1.6	9.3
Morocco	1965	50 to 45 (by 1973)	46	–	2.9	2.6	6.2
Dominican Republic	1967	48–40 (by 1972) –28 (by 1977)	46	3.4–2.7 (by 1972)	3.0	–	–
Trinidad and Tobago	1967	38 to 20 (by 1977)	26	–	1.5††	–	–

*Data on birth and growth rate goals that have been set by the national family planning programs are from Berelson, *Studies in family planning*, no. 39 (supp.), 1969. Where two numbers are given under goals, the first is the starting point.

**Data for 1976 birth and growth rates are from the Population Reference Bureau, Inc.

†The target population is the number of married couples in the reproductive ages (15–44). The protected population refers to the percentage of the target population which is sterilized or using some form of contraception, whether provided by a government program or through private services. Data from Dorothy Nortman, Population and family planning: a factbook.

††Natural increase in Trinidad and Tobago is close to 2.0. The difference is accounted for by massive emigration.

Many other countries, on the other hand, even with relatively long-established family planning programs, have made discouragingly little progress toward fulfilling their own short-term goals of birth rate and growth rate reduction (Table 13-3), some of which may however have been unrealistically optimistic. In seeking reasons for the apparent lack of success of many family planning programs, the people associated with them have naturally looked to drawbacks of the programs themselves or to ways in which governments implement them.[72] Some correlation between the availability of a variety of birth control methods—as one indication of a strong program—and decline in birth rate can be seen in Table 13-4. A surprising number of programs rely on only one or two contraceptive methods, and relatively few make use of two of the most effective methods—abortion and sterilization.

The strength of the family planning program, however, is clearly not the whole story. Taiwan and South Korea, for instance, have shown considerable drops in birth rates since their relatively early and strong programs were initiated, but birth rates in both countries had begun to decline even before then, indicating a preexisting desire for smaller families in much of the population. How much of the recent decline is directly due to the family planning program is practically impossible to determine, as the administrators of the programs themselves admit. Presumably, the activities of the family planning program facilitated and accelerated the developing trend toward smaller families.

Recently, several other small less developed nations—Hong Kong, Singapore, Costa Rica, Barbados, Trinidad and Tobago, Fiji, and Mauritius—have dramatically reduced their birth rates (see Table 13-4). No doubt the relatively strong family planning programs in many of these nations can claim some of the credit for the rapid changes, but other social and economic factors ap-

[72]W. Parker Mauldin, Family planning programs and fertility declines in developing countries; Berelson, An evaluation of the effects; and Freedman and Berelson, The record of family planning programs.

TABLE 13-4
Availability of Fertility Control Methods in 33 Countries, 1973; Crude Birthrates, 1960 and ca. 1973; and Percentage Decline in Crude Birthrate, 1960–1973; by Country

Country	*Availability of methods**					*Crude birthrate*		*% decline in birthrate*
	ORALS	IUDS	CONVENTIONALS	STERILIZATION	LEGAL ABORTION	1960	CA. 1973	*1960–1973*
China	+	+	+	+	+	–**	33	–**
South Korea	+	+	+	+	+	45	28	37
Puerto Rico	+	+	+	+	–	32	24	26
Singapore	+	+	+	+	~	39	22	43
Taiwan	+	+	+	+	~	40	24	39
Thailand	+	+	+	+	–	45–50	41	14
Barbados	+	+	+	~	–	29–32	20	33
Colombia	+	+	+	~	–	48	40	17
Egypt	+	+	+	~	–	43	34–36	19
Hong Kong	+	+	+	~	–	36	20	45
Jamaica	+	+	+	–	–	39–40	32	20
Philippines	+	+	+	~	–	45–50	42–45	8
Sri Lanka	+	+	+	~	–	37	30	19
Trinidad/Tobago	+	+	+	~	–	37–39	25	34
Venezuela	+	+	+	–	–	46–48	38	17
Dominican Rep.	+	~	+	–	–	45–48	45–50	–
El Salvador	+	+	~	~	–	47–49	41	15
India	~	~	+	+	~	42	37–39	10
Indonesia	+	+	~	~	–	43	†	†
Nepal	+	~	+	~	–	48	40	17
Pakistan	~	+	~	+	–	48	45–50	–
Tunisia	+	+	~	~	~	44	38	13
West Malaysia	+	~	~	+	–	41	33	20
Guatemala	+	~	~	–	–	46–48	39	17
Iran	+	~	~	–	–	48	48	–
Mauritius	+	~	~	~	–	39	25	35
Mexico	+	~	~	~	–	44–45	43–45	–
Morocco	+	~	~	–	–	50	50	–
Bangladesh	~	~	~	~	~	45–50	45–50	–
Ghana	~	~	~	~	–	47–52	47–50	–
Kenya	~	~	~	~	–	50	50	–
Laos	~	~	~	~	–	47	47	–
Turkey	~	~	~	–	–	43	33	23

*+ = general availability; ~ = limited availability; – = not available.
**Recent reports from visitors to China indicate significant birthrate declines, at least in some areas. However, firm data are not available.
†Recent demographic surveys indicate substantial declines in total fertility rates in recent years, but firm figures on the levels of the crude birthrates are not available.
Source: Adapted from Mauldin, Family planning programs and fertility declines in developing countries.

parently have played a precipitating role in changing people's attitudes toward family size. What these external factors may be has begun to emerge from comparisons of the few countries in which birth rates have dropped with others that have shown no significant reductions. These socioeconomic influences are discussed later in this chapter.

Studies in various countries with different levels of development and different population densities have indicated that people tend to have the number of children they say they want, although reproductive ideals, of course, may change through time.[73] Surveys have shown that the average number of children wanted per family in recent decades has varied from 2.0 to 3.3 in European countries; in the U.S. it was about 3.3 during the early 1960s and approximately 2.3 in the early 1970s.

By contrast, the average in most LDCs ranges between 3.5 and 5.5, and higher fertility reflects these desires. People in LDCs also seem to prefer overshooting to

[73]Freedman and Berelson, The record of family planning programs; Freedman and Hermalin, Do statements about desired family size predict fertility?

undershooting their ideals, given higher infant and child mortality rates. Because of those rates, replacement fertility in those countries would be about 2.8 children per woman—somewhat above the 2.1 needed in DCs where mortality is lower. Obviously, therefore, wherever average desired family sizes are above three, population growth in LDCs cannot be stopped merely by preventing "unwanted" births, although that is certainly a desirable first step.

MOTIVATION

Unquestionably the single most important factor in a country's reproductive rate is the motivation of the people toward the regulation of family size. The strength of the desire for a small family is critical. If a couple is determined not to have more than two children, they usually will not, regardless of whether or not there is a birth control clinic down the street. Conversely, if motivation is weak, the practice of birth control is likely to be a sometime thing—although the motivation may grow with the number of children in the family.

The overriding importance of motivation is made clear by the example of Europe, where the family planning movement has had relatively little influence, particularly in Catholic countries. The continent as a whole has the lowest birth rates of any major region in the world, and many European countries have had low birth rates for at least two generations. The population of Europe is growing at considerably less than 1 percent per year (0.6 percent); only Albania and Iceland have growth rates that exceed 1.2 percent. Moreover, several countries—both Germanies, Malta, Portugal, and Luxembourg—now have achieved negative growth rates; that is, their populations are now declining very slightly or fluctuating around a zero rate of growth.

This remarkable record has been accomplished largely in the absence of modern contraceptives. The dissemination of both information and devices until recently has been completely banned in several countries and seriously restricted in others. Yet the birth rates have been just as low in these countries as in neighboring countries where information and devices were generally available and in moderately wide use. *Coitus interruptus* is known and practiced everywhere, especially where contraceptives have been restricted, and is generally backed up by abortion, either legal or illegal, depending on the country. In one way or another, most Europeans have managed to avoid having children they do not want, and today they commonly want no more than two.

Motivation in LDCs

In many less developed countries, the opposite situation obtains: people say they want larger families and often end up with even more children than they had originally desired.[74] Although people may show interest in birth control, when modern contraceptives are offered they are frequently spurned. Why haven't Indian peasants, for instance, eagerly accepted birth control devices? One explanation is that, among other things, to do so may be directly against the peasants' economic interests as they perceive them.

Many observers have theorized that prospective parents rationally base their family size decisions on the advantages and disadvantages of children. In developed countries, the costs of raising, supporting, and educating each child are considerable, competing for other desired purchasable "goods" and for time in which the mother could earn income. The benefits, on the other hand, are largely confined to the emotional rewards and satisfaction of the desire for immortality. Economic returns come only after the children are adults, if ever.

Among the poor in traditional societies, the cost/benefit structure is quite different: children contribute to the family economy from an early age and represent old-age insurance to boot. Costs are comparatively small, limited to food (on a farm the children help produce the food), clothing, and shelter.[75]

Another factor often cited as an important influence on birth rates is the infant mortality rate.[76] In many poor countries such as India, Pakistan, Bangladesh, and much of tropical Africa, infant mortality is still very high. It is

[74]Freedman and Hermalin, Do statements about desired family size predict fertility?

[75]This view is almost conventional wisdom in development literature. A good description and references to other works on the subject can be found in James E. Kocher, Rural development, income distribution, and fertility decline, p. 60.

[76]Harald Fredrickson, Feedback in economic and demographic transition.

estimated at about 140 per 1000 live births in India nationwide, for instance, and doubtless is even higher among the rural poor.[77] Preschool child mortality also is high. In these countries, therefore, one out of every four or five children dies by the age of five. For the poorer half of the population, the number may be closer to one out of three. Hence, to have reasonable assurance that at least one son—and preferably two for extra security—will survive to adulthood, couples must bear an average of six children.

Some family planning specialists have suggested that couples who have lost children may overcompensate and bear more than one child to replace each one lost.[78] The connection between high fertility (especially closely spaced births) and child mortality does not seem to be generally recognized in illiterate poor populations (Box 13-7).

Indian writer Mahmood Mamdani has described the situation in the village of Manupur in the state of Punjab, site of an early experimental attempt to introduce family planning which had disappointing results.[79] The problem of land fragmentation is a major one at Manupur—large families mean that many sons eventually must divide up the family farm—but such fragmentation has been going on for a long time. The potential user of birth control is very often a victim of land fragmentation, struggling to wrest a living from a piece or pieces of land marginal in size or quality or both. But according to Mamdani, the problem of future fragmentation is seen as just that—a *future* problem. The task of making a living and assuring support in old age is a pressing one for today.

In the struggle to make ends meet today, sons (and to a lesser extent daughters) are considered a necessity. Without sons a farmer may be unable to farm his land; he must rent it out, which is a considerably less desirable alternative. Sons either work the farm in place of hired laborers, or they work in the city and, if they can, send money back to the farm. In either case they may add substantially to the family's income, but only marginally to costs.

There were, of course, other factors that militated against small families in Manupur, among them a strong pronatalistic tradition. In India a woman is judged primarily by her fertility: "May you have many sons" is a standard greeting to a woman. Barrenness is considered a disgrace, a bad omen. Some villagers believe that a barren wife is a "witch" who can place children and others under evil spells. The childless woman is barred from attending childbirths and from many celebrations. She is likely to be divorced or to be the reason for her husband to take an additional wife.

Small wonder, then, according to Mamdani, that Manupur villagers, who politely told the family planning workers they would practice birth control and accepted devices, seldom ever used them. Those who did were merely replacing inefficient methods with better ones. There was some decline in the birth rate (from 40 to 35 per thousand between 1957 and 1968) during the birth control campaign, but Mamdani claimed that it was mainly due to a rise in the age of marriage associated with technological and social change in the village. Only the Brahmins, whose social dominance and way of life were being undermined by those changes and who traditionally value education and scorn farming and other physical labor, saw much advantage in family planning. Of the majority of villagers, ". . . in Manupur, those who had few resources responded to adversity not by decreasing their numbers but by increasing them. In numbers they found security and the only opportunity for prosperity."[80]

Some critics have wondered, however, why the villagers should have been less polite and more candid to Mamdani, a relatively casual visitor from the city, than to the missionary medical workers who lived in the area for several years and ministered to the village families.[81] The authors of the Khanna study were quite aware of the social and traditional barriers to contraceptive acceptance and the need for social and economic change to

[77]A. B. Wadia, India's painful struggle.

[78]James E. Kocher, Rural development income distribution and fertility decline, p. 60. See also C. E. Taylor, J. E. Newman, and N. U. Kelly, The child survival hypothesis.

[79]*The myth of population control: family, caste, and class in an Indian village.* This work is primarily a critique of the Khanna Study (see J. B. Wyon and J. E. Gordon, *The Khanna study: population problems in the rural punjab,* Harvard Univ. Press, Cambridge, Mass., 1971). In spite of occasional shooting at straw men and a lack of perspective on population problems, Mamdani gives an informative picture of the economic and social dynamics of an Indian village.

[80]Mamdani, *Myth of population control,* p. 127.

[81]See, for instance, the review of Mamdani's book written by an Indian who was familiar with the Khanna study: P. Visaria, *Population Studies.*

BOX 13-7 Fertility, Maternal and Infant Health, and Mother's Milk

Typifying the interconnections between rapid population growth, and poverty, poor nutrition, and poor health is the infant mortality-fertility syndrome.[a] It is widely believed that an important factor motivating couples living in poverty—especially in LDCs—to have large families is high infant and preschool child mortality.[b] But it seems to be less widely recognized that high fertility itself contributes to these high death rates.

Studies in many countries, both developed and less developed, for decades have shown that generally the risks of stillbirth, prematurity, and infant and child mortality increase with each birth after the fourth. The exception is the first birth, which is attended by a higher risk (presumably for biological reasons).[c] Rapid childbearing also leads to higher mortality, especially if the interval between births is less than a year. In this case, all the children in the family may be at risk: older siblings because of the general burden of supporting the larger family; the next youngest child who may have been weaned too early; and the new baby because of the mother's burdens, which may include nutritional stress.

[a]Joe Wray, The starving roots of population growth, *Natural History*, January 1974. See also Erik Eckholm and Kathleen Newland, Health; The family planning factor, for a good general discussion.

[b]Harald Fredrickson, Feedback; Kocher, Rural development; C. E. Taylor, J. S. Newman and N. U. Kelly, Interactions between health and population.

[c]Taylor, et al. Interactions. This paper provides an entree to the very extensive literature on this subject.

That children in large families are relatively disadvantaged, even in comfortably-off families in DCs where nutrition and medical services are quite adequate, is fairly well known. Not only are infant and child death rates higher in large families, but the children tend to be less healthy, smaller for their ages, and to perform less well in school and on IQ tests. These tendencies also increase with birth order.[d]

Early and late childbearing also result in higher infant mortality rates. In both developed and less developed countries, mortality ranges from 75 to 100 percent higher for infants born to women under 20 than to women aged 25–29. In most poor countries, 10 to 20 percent of all births are to teenagers. In the United States 20 percent of births are to teenagers. This is a high proportion for a developed country, and it may be a factor in the relatively high infant mortality rate in the U.S. Childbearing after 34 also carries increasing risks for the children; the danger here tends to be proportionally greater in poor countries where general health conditions are poorer and medical facilities are less adequate.

Less well studied, but clearly established is the relationship of maternal deaths to fertility. Again excepting first births, the mother's risks of death and serious disease or injury from pregnancy and childbirth increase with each birth after the third and with the shortness of birth interval.[e] Higher rates of maternal mortality and complications are

[d]Ibid.; see also Chapter 12 of this book.

[e]Robert Buchanan, Effects of childbearing on maternal health.

precede a change in attitudes. What the study (and Mamdani's critique) showed was the large and growing discrepancy between the peasants' perceptions of advantageous reproductive behavior and where their real advantages lay.

Land fragmentation by now is acute, but employment in a city is also an increasingly less viable alternative (see Chapter 15 on the problem of unemployment in India and other LDCs). When the current crop of babies reaches adulthood, this problem is likely to be much worse. As better-off rural couples limit their families, they are in a position to consolidate their affluence; the multiplying poor are losing ground.

The situation described by Mamdani and the attendant attitudes are by no means confined to Indian peasants; they prevail among the rural poor throughout Asia, Africa, and Latin America with minor differences. Tradition, usually reinforced by religious teaching, is strongly pronatalist, and interference with the reproductive process is commonly considered immoral.[81a] Furthermore, displaced—whether temporarily or permanently—urban migrants generally share the

[81a]Alan Sweezy believes that the influence of traditional morals relating to reproduction is often overlooked or underestimated by social scientists trying to explain resistance to family planning, perhaps in large part because it is difficult to quantify. (Sweezy, Economic development and fertility change.)

also associated with childbearing before the age of 20 and after 30, especially after 34.

These trends are consistent in all countries and social levels where they have been studied. The main difference is that among the poorer classes in poor countries, the mortality rates are many times higher than in developed countries. Maternal mortality ranges up to 50 times higher in some LDCs than in DCs. The usually cited reasons are the prevalence of malnutrition, poor sanitation and health practices, and the lack of medical services in LDCs. Malnutrition, which most affects children under five, is endemic in many LDCs (see Chapter 7 for a fuller discussion). In recent years this has been exacerbated by the trend toward abandonment of breast-feeding in favor of commercial formulas. Most poor families cannot afford to use formulas in full strength, and the lack of sanitary facilities, including safe water, makes their use extremely hazardous. Adequate medical care, also, is unavailable to the poor in most LDCs, especially in rural areas.

To these fairly obvious factors in high infant, child, and maternal mortalities in LDCs could be added high fertility and early and late childbearing. About 40 percent of women in LDCs have four or more children, whereas in DCs only 6 or 7 percent do. In poor countries women commonly marry and begin having children as young as 15 or 16, and they often continue bearing children up to the age of 40 or more. The irony that reducing high infant and child mortalities in LDCs (and thereby increasing population growth) may be a necessary prerequisite to acceptance of family limitation among the poor (apart from being imperative on humanitarian grounds) has often been remarked on; the idea that the use of birth control may be one important means of saving the lives of children and mothers is only beginning to be widely appreciated.

Improving nutrition is another vitally important way of saving lives and improving the health, well-being, and productivity of people in general. One of the best—and least costly—ways to improve nutrition of infants is to encourage breast-feeding, especially for the first six months of life. Here again, the relationship is not a simple one, for breast-feeding tends to suppress fertility in the mother and thus extends the important interval between births.[f] Lactation does not reliably prevent conception, however. Providing contraceptives to a nursing mother therefore can ensure that premature weaning is not forced by the occurrence of another pregnancy, which would endanger the lives of both children and of the mother. The abandonment of breast-feeding leads both to higher birth rates and higher infant mortalities; reinstating it as a general practice would tend to reduce both, and might as a result lead to lower family-size aspirations as well.

[f]Buchanan, Breast-feeding—aid to infant health and fertility control.

economic and social viewpoint of their rural cousins—and their reproductive goals. Many urban poor families grow their own food in their shantytowns, and children are valued as helpers in the gardens and as income earners in the streets. In such situations, wherever children are perceived (correctly or not) by their parents more as blessings than burdens, it is probable that large families will continue to prevail.

The impact of colonialism. Anthropologist Mildred Dickeman has suggested that a personal, short-term perception of the advantage of a large family has come to take precedence over the long-term disadvantage to society because of a "breakdown in social integration," which she regards as "a failure in one of the most fundamental ecological functions of human social systems."[82] This social breakdown, she claims, was caused by Western colonialism, which interfered with traditional societies' perceptions of their food supplies, resource limitations, and demographic situations.

Nearly all societies encompass seemingly contradictory attitudes and ideologies regarding natality. Dickeman discusses the practice of infanticide in particular, but such phenomena as birth control, abortion, and marriage

[82]Dickeman, Infanticide.

customs are also subject to varying attitudes and mores. These conflicting attitudes allow societies to fine-tune their responses to external changes without having to change the basic ideological structure itself. Thus, when overpopulation threatens food supplies, for example, antinatalist behavior can be encouraged, and when epidemics or war have decimated a population, antinatalism can again be discouraged. Pronatalist attitudes are very strong in traditional societies because through most of humanity's evolutionary history they have been needed to maintain populations and to allow a moderate amount of growth when warranted.

The sudden introduction of death control, Western morality, and access to communications and other resources, as Western technology impinged upon the underdeveloped world in the wake of the colonial era and World War II, disrupted social perceptions of the consequences of high birth rates in those areas. The impact was characterized by "rapid and fluctuating changes in agricultural productivity, labor demand, urbanization, emigration, and military expansion, often coupled with introduced epidemic disease."[83] Because most of these disturbed societies have adopted Western ideology, their traditional methods of controlling population have been abandoned and unfortunately replaced by less efficient and less desirable ones, mainly self-induced abortion and disguised infanticide through neglect, abuse, and even starvation. Dickeman concludes that the world population can only be controlled when less developed societies are socially stabilized and integrated and the people can realistically assess their actual resource and ecological position. Then, she feels, the people will make reasonable family-size choices in accordance with that position.

The Demographic Transition

A great many social and economic factors have been associated in the past with declining fertility in various societies. Among them are the general level of education, the availability and quality of health care, the degree of urbanization, the social and economic status of women and the opportunities open to them for education and employment outside the home, the provision of social security for old age, and the costs to families of raising and educating each child. The more extensive each of these factors is, the lower fertility generally will be. In addition, later marriage, lower tolerance for illegitimacy, low infant mortality, and extended breast-feeding all operate directly to reduce fertility. In most LDCs, levels of health care, education, and women's status remain low for the poor majority, while marriage comes early and infant mortality rates are high.

Most family planning programs in the 1960s made little effort to influence any of these factors, as demographer Kingsley Davis pointed out in 1967.[84] Those that tried to influence people at all confined themselves to emphasizing the economic and health advantages of small families to parents and their children.

In the 1950s and 1960s, government officials, economic advisors, and many demographers believed that the process of economic development would automatically bring about the higher levels of education and urbanization in LDCs that have elsewhere been associated with declines in fertility, and thus would cause a "demographic transition" in LDCs. These people favored family planning because they thought it would facilitate the supposedly inevitable demographic transition, although they believed that no significant reduction in fertility could occur until the prerequisite (but unknown) degree of development had been reached.

Numerous studies have established quite clearly that population growth is *in itself* a major barrier to economic development. Economist Goran Ohlin wrote in 1967:

> The simple and incontestable case against rapid population growth in poor countries is that it absorbs very large amounts of resources which may otherwise be used both for increased consumption and above all, for development . . . The stress and strain caused by rapid demographic growth in the developing world is actually so tangible that there are few, and least of all planners and economists of the countries, who doubt that per capita incomes would be increased faster if fertility and growth rates were lower . . . .[85]

[83]Ibid.

[84]Population policy: will current programs succeed? See also Davis, Zero population growth: The Goal and the Means.

[85]*Population control and economic development,* p. 53.

The potential value of population control in aid programs to LDCs has also been studied intensively. The late economist Stephen Enke did much of the analysis, and his conclusions may be summarized in three points: (1) channeling economic resources into population control rather than into increasing production "could be 100 or so times more effective in raising *per capita* incomes in many LDCs"; (2) an effective birth control program might cost only 30 cents per capita per year, about 3 percent of current development programs; and (3) the use of bonuses to promote population control is "obvious in countries where the 'worth' of permanently preventing a birth is roughly twice the income per head."[86]

Enke's results were strongly supported by computer simulation work by systems analyst Douglas Daetz, who examined the effects of various kinds of aid in a labor-limited, nonmechanized agricultural society.[87] His results brought into sharp question the desirability of aid programs not coupled with population control programs. They might provide temporary increases in the standard of living, but these would soon be eaten up by population expansion. In many circumstances, population growth and aid inputs may interact to cause the standard of living to *decline below* the pre-aid level.

As a result of studies like Ohlin's, Enke's, and Daetz', family planning began to be incorporated into assistance programs for LDCs in the 1960s. But the purpose in most cases was only to reduce growth rates to more "manageable" levels by eliminating "unwanted births." This great faith of economists and demographers in the potential of industrial development to bring about a spontaneous demographic transition, which, aided by family planning, would reduce population growth and accelerate the development process, encouraged LDC governments to relax under the illusion that *all* their social and economic problems were being solved. Unfortunately, their faith was misplaced.

Reliance on a demographic transition was misplaced for many reasons, not the least of which is uncertainty as to exactly what caused the original one in nineteenth-century Europe.[88] And, as was pointed out in Chapter 5, conditions in contemporary LDCs in many ways are markedly different from those in Europe and North America one to two centuries ago when fertility began to decline there.

By the mid-1960s, although several LDCs had apparently reached quite advanced degrees of industrial development, there was little sign of a general decline in fertility. Birth rates dropped in some countries, but they remained high, or in a few cases even rose, in other, supposedly eligible countries. Because of this unexpected result, there has been some argument among demographers whether the theory of the demographic transition can even be applied to LDCs and whether there is good reason to hope that it will occur in most of them.

An analysis of fertility trends in some Latin American countries (often cited as prime examples of nonconformity to demographic transition theory) by demographer Stephen Beaver indicates that a demographic transition has begun or is at least incipient in the countries he examined.[89] But, he suggests, cultural and economic factors can cause time lags in the process. A considerably broader spectrum of factors may influence fertility than just reduced mortality (especially of infants), increasing urbanization, and industrialization, which are classically believed to be the primary causes of declining fertility.

It is becoming increasingly clear that industrialization—the style of development undertaken by most developing countries—is not conducive to a demographic transition. This seems to be so because industry in most LDCs employs and benefits only a fraction of the population, creating a two-tiered society in which the majority are left untouched by modernization.[90] Such unequal distribution of the benefits of modernization (access to adequate food, clothing, decent shelter, education, full-time employment, medical and health care, etc.) is most pronounced in rural areas, where some 70 percent of the population of LDCs live.

[86]Birth control for economic development.

[87]*Energy utilization and aid effectiveness in non-mechanized agriculture: a computer simulation of a socioeconomic system.* PhD. diss., University of California, 1968.

[88]Michael S. Teitelbaum, Relevance of demographic transition theory for developing countries; Alan Sweezy, Recent light on the relation between socioeconomic development and fertility decline.

[89]*Demographic transition theory reinterpreted.*

[90]James E. Kocher, Rural development; and James P. Grant, Development: the end of trickle down?

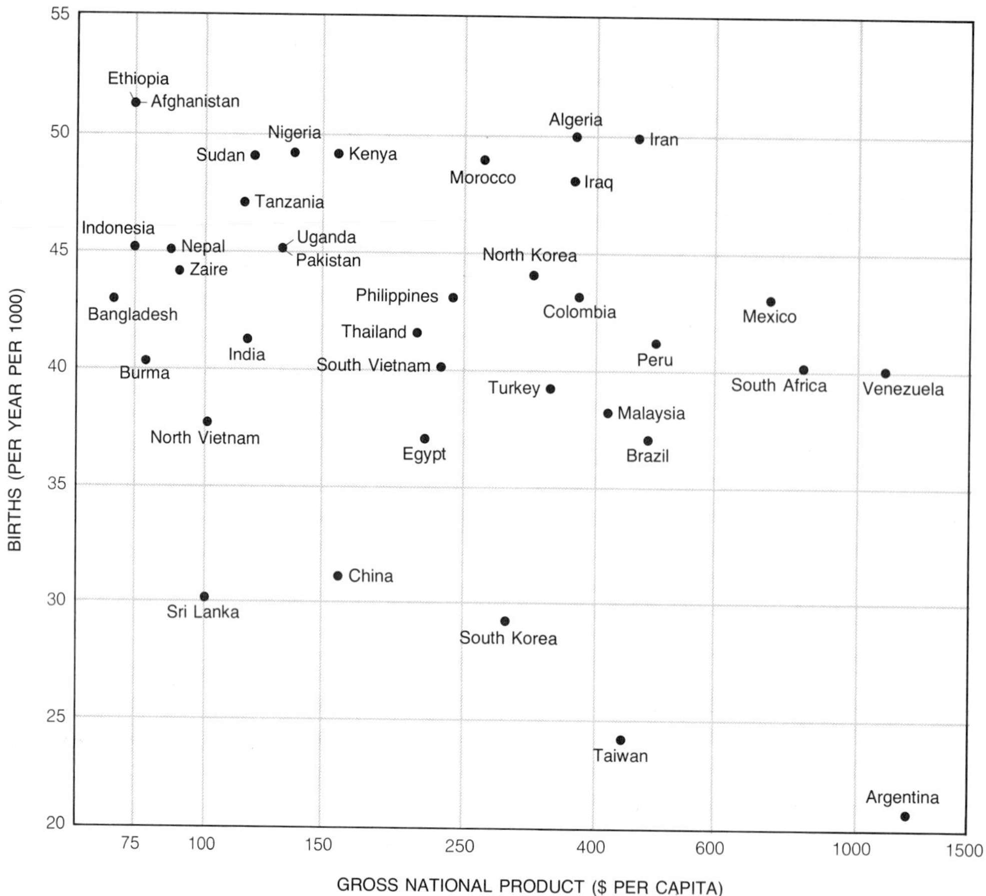

FIGURE 13-5

There is an absence of any clear relation between the birth rate and the level of development (as measured by per-capital GNP) in the less developed countries with more than 10 million population. A decline in birth rates has occurred recently in a number of these nations. (From Demeny, 1974.)

Per capita Gross National Product is a statistic often used to measure the extent of "development" that has taken place in a given country; per-capita GNP, however, is an averaged figure that may conceal very large differences among income groups. And the correlation of degrees of development as measured by per-capita GNP with reduction in fertility is extremely mixed, to say the least (Figure 13-5). One explanation is that, in strongly two-tiered societies, birth control may be adopted by the affluent, educated minority, but not by the majority still living in poverty. The conclusion from this is that fertility will decline significantly only when the benefits of modernization are extended to all economic levels.

Economist Alan Sweezy has pointed out that, while this explanation may account for fertility declines in some instances, the expected declines have not occurred in some countries—notably in Latin America—even among the affluent and middle classes.[90a] He suggests that lingering strong traditions, including pro-natalist attitudes, may be a reason. In Latin America such traditions are supported by the Roman Catholic Church, which still officially opposes "artificial" methods of birth control and abortion.

If a demographic transition should take place in

[90a]Economic development and fertility change.

LDCs, a decline from present high fertility to replacement level alone would require considerable time, probably at least a generation. And time is running very short. If appropriate kinds of development and vigorous family planning programs had been initiated just after World War II, when death control and the ideas of economic assistance were first introduced in LDCs, the population problem might be of more manageable dimensions today. But plainly it would still be with us. Without such a history, even if the strongest feasible population control measures were everywhere in force today, the time lag before runaway population growth could be appreciably slowed, let alone arrested, would still be discouragingly long. For most LDCs it will be *at least* four generations before their populations cease to expand—unless catastrophe intervenes—because of the age composition of their populations. Even if replacement reproduction were attained by 2005, most LDC populations would at least double their 1970 populations, and some would increase *3.5-fold.*[91]

This built-in momentum virtually guarantees that, for many less developed countries, shortage of resources and the environmental and social effects of overpopulation will combine to prevent sufficient "development" to induce a demographic transition. Complacently counting on either a spontaneous demographic transition or on voluntary family planning programs—or even a combination—to reduce population growth and thereby ensure successful development would therefore be a serious mistake. The establishment of family planning programs may make it easier to improve social conditions in poor countries, but it is no substitute for appropriate development; and it is also clear that development alone cannot lead to a reduction of population growth on the needed scale.

POPULATION CONTROL: DIRECT MEASURES

Before any really effective population control can be established, the political leaders, economists, national planners, and others who determine such policies must be convinced of its necessity. Most governments have been reluctant to try measures beyond traditional family planning that might be effective because they considered them too strong, too restrictive, and too much against traditional attitudes. They are also, reasonably enough, concerned about resistance from political opponents or the populace at large. In many countries such measures may never be considered until massive famines, political unrest, or ecological disasters make their initiation imperative. In such emergencies, whatever measures are economically and technologically expedient will be likeliest to be imposed, regardless of their political or social acceptability. A case in point was the sudden imposition in 1976 of compulsory sterilization in some Indian states and for government employees in Delhi, following two decades of discouraging results from voluntary family planning.

People should long ago have begun exploring, developing, and discussing all possible means of population control. But they did not, and time has nearly run out. Policies that may seem totally unacceptable today to the majority of people at large or to their national leaders may be seen as very much the lesser of evils only a few years from now. The decade 1965–1975 witnessed a virtual revolution in attitudes toward curbing population growth among LDC leaders, if not necessarily among their people. Even family planning, easily justified on health and welfare grounds alone and economically feasible for even the poorest of countries, was widely considered totally unacceptable as a government policy as recently as 1960.

Among objections to population control measures cited by demographer Bernard Berelson in 1969 were the need for improved contraceptive technology; lack of funds and trained personnel to carry out all proposed programs; doubt about effectiveness of some measures, leading to failure to implement them; and moral objections to some proposals such as abortion, sterilization, various social measures, and especially to any kind of compulsion.[92]

Most objections to population control policies, how-

[91] Thomas Frejka, *The future of population growth: alternative paths to equilibrium.*

[92] See Berelson's Beyond family planning, for a conservative view of potential measures for population control. Since 1969, Berelson has found many formerly unacceptable measures to have become much more acceptable: for instance, An evaluation of the effects of population control programs; and Freedman and Berelson, The record of family planning programs, published in 1974 and 1975 respectively.

ever, can be overcome or are likely to disappear with time and changing conditions; indeed many of them already have. Contraceptive technology has been improved in recent years (see Appendix 4). Promising methods of birth control that are not now technologically possible should also be developed, so that they can be made available.[92a] Further generous assistance from developed countries could remove remaining economic and lack of personnel barriers to population-control programs in LDCs. The effectiveness of a measure can only be evaluated after it has been tried. Moral acceptability is very likely to change as social and economic conditions change in most societies, as demonstrated by the reversal of abortion policies in many countries between 1967 and 1975.

The struggle for economic development in the LDCs is producing considerable social upheaval, which will particularly affect such basic elements of society as family structure. Radical changes in family structure and relationships are inevitable, whether population control is instituted or not. Inaction, attended by a steady deterioration in living conditions for the poor majority, will bring changes everywhere that no one could consider beneficial. Thus, it is beside the point to object to population-control measures simply on the grounds that they might change the social structure or family relationships.

Among proposed general approaches to population control are family planning, the use of socioeconomic pressures, and compulsory fertility control. Maximum freedom of choice is provided by traditional family planning; but family planning alone should not be regarded as "population control" when it includes no consideration of optimum population size for the society and makes no attempt to influence parental goals.

The use of abortion and voluntary sterilization to supplement other forms of birth control can quite properly be included as part of family planning and made available at costs everyone can afford. This, of course, has been done in a few countries with considerable apparent success (Table 13-4). Moreover, there is still a good deal of room for expansion of family planning services in LDCs, where they are not yet available to more than a fraction of most populations. Family planning programs not only provide the means of contraception, but, through their activities and educational campaigns, they spread the idea of birth control among the people. *These programs should be expanded and supported throughout the world as rapidly and as fully as possible, but other measures should be instituted immediately as well.* Given the family size aspirations of people everywhere, additional measures beyond family planning will unquestionably be required in order to halt the population explosion—quite possibly in many DCs as well as LDCs.

Socioeconomic Measures

Population control through the use of socioeconomic pressures to encourage or discourage reproduction is the approach advocated by, among others, demographer Kingsley Davis, who originated many of the following suggestions.[93] The objective of this approach would be to influence the attitudes and motivations of individual couples. An important aspect would be a large-scale educational program through schools and communications media to persuade people of the advantages of small families to themselves and to their society. Information on birth control, of course, must accompany such educational efforts. This is one of the first measures that can be adopted, and it has been increasingly employed in many of the more active family planning programs in LDCs. It has also been used in some DCs, notably the U.S. and England, mainly, but not entirely, by private groups such as Planned Parenthood and ZPG.

As United States taxpayers know, income tax laws have long implicitly encouraged marriage and childbearing, although recent changes have reduced the effect somewhat. Such a pronatalist bias of course is no longer appropriate. In countries that are affluent enough for the majority of citizens to pay taxes, tax laws could be adjusted to favor (instead of penalize) single people,

[92a]Unfortunately, this area is still being seriously neglected. It has been estimated that funds could fruitfully be tripled over 1974 levels to take advantage of existing knowledge and trained personnel in research on reproduction and development of new contraceptives. (M. A. Koblinsky, F. S. Jaffe, and R. O. Greep, Funding for reproductive research: The status and the needs.) See also Barbara J. Culliton, Birth control: Report argues new leads are neglected (*Science,* vol. 194, pp. 921–922, November 26, 1976) for a discussion of a forthcoming Ford Foundation Report, *Reproduction and human welfare.*

[93]Davis, Population policy.

working wives, and small families. Other tax measures might also include high marriage fees, taxes on luxury baby goods and toys, and removal of family allowances where they exist.

Other possibilities include the limitation of maternal or educational benefits to two children per family. These proposals, however, have the potential disadvantage of heavily penalizing children (and in the long run society as well). The same criticism may be made of some other tax plans, unless they can be carefully adjusted to avoid denying at least minimum care for poor families, regardless of the number of children they may have.

A somewhat different approach might be to provide incentives for late marriage and childlessness, such as paying bonuses to first-time brides who are over 25, to couples after five childless years, or to men who accept vasectomies after their wives have had a given number of children.[94] Lotteries open only to childless adults have also been proposed. The savings in environmental deterioration, education, and other costs would probably justify the expenditure. All of these measures, of course, suffer the drawback of influencing the poor to a greater degree than the rich. That would be unfortunate, since the addition of a child to an affluent family (which has a disproportionate impact on resources and environment) is in many ways more harmful to society than the addition of a child to a poor family.

Adoption to supplement small families for couples who especially enjoy children can be encouraged through subsidies and simplified procedures. It can also be a way to satisfy couples who have a definite desire for a son or daughter; further research on sex determination should be pursued for the same reason. A special kind of social-security pension or bond could be provided for aging adults who have few or no children to support them in their old age.

The latter idea, proposed in detail by economist Ronald Ridker, has been tried with some success on tea estates in southern India.[95] As implemented, the plan made monthly deposits in a pension fund for each female worker enrolled in the plan as long as she spaced her children at least three years apart and had no more than three. If more children were born, the payments were reduced. Since managers of the tea estates were already paying maternity and health benefits, the costs of the pension fund were at least partially offset by savings from those. A large majority of the women signed up for the program, and within the first four years there were substantial drops not only in fertility, but in infant mortality and in worker absenteeism.[96] The first pilot project included only about 700 women; it remains to be seen whether implementation of the pension plan on other tea estates and in other situations in India will be equally successful.

There are many possibilities in the sphere of family structure, sexual mores, and the status of women that can be explored.[97] With some exceptions, women have traditionally been allowed to fulfill only the roles of wife and mother. Although this has changed in most DCs in recent decades, it is still the prevailing situation in most LDCs, particularly among the poor and uneducated. Anything that can be done to diminish the emphasis upon these traditional roles and provide women with equal opportunities in education, employment, and other areas is likely to reduce the birth rate. Measures that postpone marriage and then delay the first child's birth also help to encourage a reduction in birth rates. The later that marriage and the first child occur, the more time the woman will have to develop other interests. One of the most important potential measures for delaying marriage, and directly influencing childbearing goals as well, is educating and providing employment for women.

Women can be encouraged to develop interests outside the family other than employment, and social life could be centered around these outside interests or the couple's work, rather than exclusively within the neighborhood and family. Adequate care for pre-school children should be provided at low cost (which, moreover, could provide an important new source of employment). Provision of child care seems more likely to encourage employment outside the home, with concomitant low reproduction, than to encourage reproduction. Women represent a

[94] A study has been made of the economic feasibility of such a policy for the United States by Larry D. Barnett (Population policy: payments for fertility limitation in the U.S.).

[95] Synopsis of a proposal for a family planning bond; and Saving accounts for family planning, an illustration from the tea estates of India.

[96] V. I. Chacko, Family planners earn retirement bonus on plantations in India.

[97] Judith Blake, Demographic science and the redirection of population policy; Reproductive motivation; Alice Taylor Day, Population control and personal freedom: are they compatible?

large, relatively untapped pool of intellectual and technical talent; tapping that pool effectively could help reduce population growth and also would provide many other direct benefits to any society.

Social pressures on both men and women to marry and have children must be removed. As former Secretary of Interior Stewart Udall observed, "All lives are not enhanced by marital union; parenthood is not necessarily a fulfillment for every married couple."[98] If society were convinced of the need for low birth rates, no doubt the stigma that has customarily been assigned to bachelors, spinsters, and childless couples would soon disappear. But alternative lifestyles should be open to single people, and perhaps the institution of an informal, easily dissolved "marriage" for the childless is one possibility. Indeed, many DC societies now seem to be evolving in this direction as women's liberation gains momentum.[99] It is possible that fully developed societies may produce such arrangements naturally, and their association with lower fertility is becoming increasingly clear. In LDCs a childless or single lifestyle might be encouraged deliberately as the status of women approaches parity with that of men.

Although free and easy association of the sexes might be tolerated in such a society, responsible parenthood ought to be encouraged and illegitimate childbearing could be strongly discouraged. One way to carry out this disapproval might be to insist that all illegitimate babies be put up for adoption—especially those born to minors, who generally are not capable of caring properly for a child alone.[100] If a single mother really wished to keep her baby, she might be obliged to go through adoption proceedings and demonstrate her ability to support and care for it. Adoption proceedings probably should remain more difficult for single people than for married couples, in recognition of the relative difficulty of raising children alone. It would even be possible to require pregnant single women to marry or have abortions, perhaps as an alternative to placement for adoption, depending on the society.

Somewhat more repressive measures for discouraging large families have also been proposed, such as assigning public housing without regard for family size and removing dependency allowances from student grants or military pay. Some of these have been implemented in crowded Singapore, whose population program has been counted as one of the most successful.

All socioeconomic measures are derived from knowledge of social conditions that have been associated with low birth rates in the past. The more repressive suggestions are based on observations that people have voluntarily controlled their reproduction most stringently during periods of great social and economic stress and insecurity, such as the Depression of the 1930s.[101] In a sense, all such proposals are shots in the dark. Not enough is known about fertility motivation to predict the effectiveness of such policies. Studies by demographer Judith Blake[102] and by economist Alan Sweezy[103] for instance, have cast serious doubt on the belief that economic considerations are of the greatest importance in determining fertility trends. Sweezy has shown that the decline of fertility in the 1930s in the United States was merely a continuation of an earlier trend. If their views are correct, then severely repressive economic measures might prove to be both ineffective and unnecessary as a vehicle for population control, as well as socially undesirable. At the very least, they should be considered only if milder measures fail completely.

Involuntary Fertility Control

The third approach to population limitation is that of involuntary fertility control. Several coercive proposals deserve discussion, mainly because some countries may ultimately have to resort to them unless current trends in birth rates are rapidly reversed by other means.[104] Some

[98] *1976: Agenda for tomorrow.*

[99] Judith Blake, The changing status of women in developed countries; E. Peck and J. Senderowitz (eds.), *Pronatalism, the myth of mom and apple pie;* Ellen Peck, *The baby trap.*

[100] The tragedy of teenage single mothers in the U.S. is described by Leslie Aldridge Westoff in Kids with kids. The adverse health and social effects of teenage child-bearing in an affluent society have recently been documented by several studies. One good sample can be found in a special issue of *Family planning perspectives,* Teenagers, USA.

[101] Richard A. Easterlin, *Population, labor force, and long swings in economic growth.* Further discussion of Easterlin's ideas can be found in Deborah Freedman, ed., Fertility, aspirations and resources: A symposium on the Easterlin hypothesis.

[102] Are babies consumer durables? and Reproductive motivation.

[103] The economic explanation of fertility changes in the U.S.

[104] Edgar R. Chasteen, *The case for compulsory birth control.*

involuntary measures could be less repressive or discriminatory, in fact, than some of the socioeconomic measures suggested.

In the 1960s it was proposed to vasectomize all fathers of three or more children in India. The proposal was defeated then not only on moral grounds but on practical ones as well; there simply were not enough medical personnel available even to start on the eligible candidates, let alone to deal with the new recruits added each day! Massive assistance from the developed world in the form of medical and paramedical personnel and/or a training program for local people nevertheless might have put the policy within the realm of possibility. India in the mid-1970s not only entertained the idea of compulsory sterilization, but moved toward implementing it, perhaps fearing that famine, war, or disease might otherwise take the problem out of its hands. This decision was greeted with dismay abroad, but Indira Gandhi's government felt it had little other choice. There is too little time left to experiment further with educational programs and hope that social change will generate a spontaneous fertility decline, and most of the Indian population is too poor for direct economic pressures (especially penalties) to be effective.

A program of sterilizing women after their second or third child, despite the relatively greater difficulty of the operation than vasectomy, might be easier to implement than trying to sterilize men. This of course would be feasible only in countries where the majority of births are medically assisted. Unfortunately, such a program therefore is not practical for most less developed countries (although in China mothers of three children are commonly "expected" to undergo sterilization).

The development of a long-term sterilizing capsule that could be implanted under the skin and removed when pregnancy is desired opens additional possibilities for coercive fertility control. The capsule could be implanted at puberty and might be removable, with official permission, for a limited number of births. No capsule that would last that long (30 years or more) has yet been developed, but it is technically within the realm of possibility.

Various approaches to administering such a system have been offered, including one by economist Kenneth Boulding.[105] His proposal was to issue to each woman at maturity a marketable license that would entitle her to a given number of children—say, 2.2 in order to have an NRR = 1. Under such a system the number could be two if the society desired to reduce the population size slowly. To maintain a steady size, some couples might be allowed to have a third child if they purchased "decichild" units from the government or from other women who had decided not to have their full allotments of children or who found they had a greater need for the money. Others have elaborated on Boulding's idea, discussing possible ways of regulating the license scheme and alternative ways of alloting the third children.[106] One such idea is that permission to have a third child might be granted to a limited number of couples by lottery. This system would allow governments to regulate more or less exactly the number of births over a given period of time.

Social scientist David Heer has compared the social effects of marketable license schemes with some of the more repressive economic incentives that have been proposed and with straightforward quota systems.[107] His conclusions are shown in Table 13-5.

Of course, a government might require only implantation of the contraceptive capsule, leaving its removal to the individual's discretion but requiring reimplantation after childbirth. Since having a child would require positive action (removal of the capsule), many more births would be prevented than in the reverse situation. Certainly unwanted births and the problem of abortion would both be entirely avoided. The disadvantages (apart from the obvious moral objections) include the questionable desirability of keeping the entire female population on a continuous steroid dosage with the contingent health risks, and the logistics of implanting capsules in 50 percent of the population between the ages of 15 and 50.

Adding a sterilant to drinking water or staple foods is a suggestion that seems to horrify people more than most proposals for involuntary fertility control. Indeed, this

[105] *The meaning of the 20th century*, pp. 135–136.

[106] Bruce M. Russett, Licensing: for cars and babies; David M. Heer, Marketing licenses for babies; Boulding's proposal revisited.

[107] Ibid.

TABLE 13-5
Evaluation of Some Relatively Coercive Measures for Fertility Reduction

Effect	*Marketable license systems*		*Financial incentive systems*			*Quota systems*
	Boulding proposal for baby licenses	*Baby licenses that may be sold or lent at interest to the government*	*Monthly subsidy to persons with no more than two children*	*Monthly tax on persons with more than two children*	*One-time tax for excess babies over two*	*Identical quota for all couples*
Restriction on individual liberty	Moderately severe	Moderately severe	Moderately severe	Moderately severe	Moderately severe	Very severe
Effect on quality of children's financial support	Probably beneficial	Probably beneficial	Unknown	Unknown	Probably beneficial	Slightly beneficial
Effectiveness and acceptability of enforcement mechanisms	Effective enforcement at possible price of depriving some children of a family environment	Effective enforcement at possible price of depriving some children of a family environment	Fairly effective enforcement	Fairly effective enforcement	Effective enforcement at possible price of depriving some children of a family environment	Effective enforcement at possible price of depriving some children of a family environment
Effectiveness for precise regulation of the birth rate	Moderate	High	Low	Low	Low	Moderate

Source: Adapted from David Heer, Marketing licenses.

would pose some very difficult political, legal, and social questions, to say nothing of the technical problems. No such sterilant exists today, nor does one appear to be under development. To be acceptable, such a substance would have to meet some rather stiff requirements: it must be uniformly effective, despite widely varying doses received by individuals, and despite varying degrees of fertility and sensitivity among individuals; it must be free of dangerous or unpleasant side effects; and it must have no effect on members of the opposite sex, children, old people, pets, or livestock.

Physiologist Melvin Ketchel, of the Tufts University School of Medicine, suggested that a sterilant could be developed that would have a very specific action—for example, preventing implantation of the fertilized ovum.[108] He proposed that it be used to reduce fertility levels by adjustable amounts, anywhere from 5 to 75 percent, rather than to sterilize the whole population completely. In this way, fertility could be adjusted from time to time to meet a society's changing needs, and there would be no need to provide an antidote. Contraceptives would still be needed for couples who were highly motivated to have small families. Subfertile and functionally sterile couples who strongly desired children would be medically assisted, as they are now, or encouraged to adopt. Again, there is no sign of such an agent on the horizon. And the risk of serious, unforeseen side effects would, in our opinion, militate against the use of *any* such agent, even though this plan has the advantage of avoiding the need for socioeconomic pressures that might tend to discriminate against particular groups or penalize children.

Most of the population control measures beyond family planning discussed above have never been tried. Some are as yet technically impossible and others are and probably will remain unacceptable to most societies (although, of course, the *potential* effectiveness of those least acceptable measures may be great).

Compulsory control of family size is an unpalatable idea, but the alternatives may be much more horrifying. As those alternatives become clearer to an increasing number of people in the 1980s, they may begin *demanding* such control. A far better choice, in our view, is to expand the use of milder methods of influencing family size preferences, while redoubling efforts to ensure that the means of birth control, including abortion and

[108]Fertility control agents as a possible solution to the world population problem, pp. 687–703.

sterilization, are accessible to every human being on Earth within the shortest possible time. If effective action is taken promptly against population growth, perhaps the need for the more extreme involuntary or repressive measures can be averted in most countries.

POPULATION CONTROL AND DEVELOPMENT

Population control cannot be achieved in a social or economic vacuum, of course. To formulate effective population control measures, much greater understanding is needed about all peoples' attitudes toward reproduction, and how these attitudes are affected by various living conditions, including some that seem virtually intolerable to people in developed countries. Even more, it is essential to know what influences and conditions will lead to changes in attitudes in favor of smaller families.

The economists and demographers who believed that urbanization and industrialization of LDCs would automatically induce a demographic transition in those societies seem to have been disastrously wrong. While they waited for the birth rate to fall, one billion people were added to the human population. At the very least, it is obvious that the causes of demographic transitions are far more complex than was once believed. But the social scientists may have been wrong mainly in their approach. Many aspects of modernization may indeed have important influences on reproductive behavior.

Such influences, of course, fall outside the purview of population programs; they are an integral part of development as it affects—or fails to affect—each member of a society. When development is the kind that improves the living conditions of everyone down to the poorest farm worker, development that starts *at the grass roots level*, then there is hope that poverty, hunger, disease, and hopelessness might be reduced—and along with them the desire for many children.[109]

The general problems of LDC development are discussed in detail in Chapter 15, but its indirect effects on fertility are worth mentioning here. While no one factor of development can be singled out as ever having "triggered" a decline in fertility—no particular level of infant mortality or per-capita GNP, for instance—*a constellation of factors* does often seem to be associated with such declines. Among these are rural development and land reform favoring small, family-owned farms; availability of adequate food, basic health care, and education (especially of women) to the entire population; industries favoring labor-intensive, rather than capital-intensive, means of production; and a relatively small income gap between the richest and poorest segments of the population.[110]

Table 13-6 compares some of these interrelated factors in nine less developed nations, four of which have shown significant drops in fertility since 1960 and five of which have not. While each of the nine countries, like nearly all LDCs, exhibits some of the salient factors listed above, those with substantially reduced fertility much more commonly manifest them. Understanding of the important influences on reproductive behavior and how they operate is so far sketchy at best. Achieving a solid base for population policy may be one of the most important—and perhaps most difficult—research assignments for the next decade.

Since the goals of both development and population control are supposedly identical—an improvement in the well-being of all human beings in this and future generations—it seems only reasonable to plan each to reinforce the other. Emphasis accordingly should be placed on policies that would further the goals of *both* family limitation and development—for example, rural development and land tenure reform; increased agricultural output; universal primary education for children; old-age support schemes; and improved health care and nutrition, especially for mothers and children.

Survival of human society nevertheless seems likely to require the imposition of direct population control measures beyond family planning in most LDCs. There is no guarantee that processes of modernization can quickly enough induce the necessary changes in attitudes that might bring growth to a halt. High priority should be given to stimulating those attitude changes and counteracting the effects of pronatalist traditions.

[109]William Rich, Smaller families through social and economic progress; Kocher, *Rural development;* Grant, Development.

[110]Ibid. See also Freedman and Berelson, The record of family planning programs.

TABLE 13-6

Comparison of LDCs with Different Modes of Development

Indicators	Taiwan	Korea	Costa Rica	China	Philippines	Mexico	Brazil	Central African Republic	India
Per capita GNP: 1960	$176	$138			$169	$441	$268		
1973	$490 (1972)	$340	$710	$270	$280	$890	$760	$160	$120
GNP growth rates 1965–1972	6.9%	8.5%	4.1%	4.6%	2.6%	2.8%	6.0%	1.0%	1.5%
Primary school enrollment, %	♂ 91 ♀ 90	♂ 98 ♀ 98	94	Presumably high	93	55	100(?)	NA	♂ 81 ♀ 49
Unemployment and gross underemployment	10% (1963) 4% (1968)	8.1% (1963) 4.5% (1972)	NA	Virtually zero	14.5% (1961) 15.0% (1968)	Significant and rising	10–12% (1970)	NA	>15% (1970)
Ratio of income controlled by top 20% to bottom 20%	15:1 (1953) 5:1 (1964)	5:1	11:1 (1969)	NA**	12:1 (1956) 16:1 (1965)	10:1 (1950) 16:1 (1969)	22:1 (1960) 25:1 (1970)	NA	5:1 (1957)
Income improvement of poorest 20% from 1952–1974*	200%	>100%	NA	NA	Negligible	Negligible	Negligible	Negligible	Negligible
Exports ($ million): 1960	$ 164	$ 5.2			560	831	1269	39	2958
1973	1428	835.2	$339		961	1402	2310		
Effective land reform	Yes	Yes	Some	Yes	No	No	No	NA	No
Agricultural workers per 100 hectares	195	197	NA	NA	71	35*	43	NA	NA
Percentage of farmers belonging to farmer's cooperatives (late 1960s)	Virtually 100	Virtually 100	NA	NA	17%	5%	28%	NA	NA
Yield per acre (lbs) food grains 1972	3510	2850	NA	NA	1145	1225	1280	NA	NA
Literacy rate, %	85	71	84	25	72	78	61	5–10	28
Life expectancy (years)	69	61	68	62	58	63	61	41	50
Infant mortality per 1000 births	28	60	54	55	78	61		190	139
Per-capita energy consumption (kg coal equivalent) 1971	NA	860	446	561	298	1270	500	60	186
Population growth rates									
1958–1963	3.5	2.8	4.5	NA	3.2	3.2	3.1	2.3	2.3
1970–1975	1.9	2.0	2.8	1.7	3.3	3.2	2.8	2.1	2.4
Crude birth rate, 1976	23	29	28	27	41	46	37	43	35
Death rate, 1976	5.0	8.8	5.9	10	11	8	9	22	15

*Approximate figures.
**NA = not available.

Source: Adapted from James P. Grant, Growth from below: a people-oriented development strategy; Data from Grant, James W. Howe, et al., *The U.S. and world development: agenda for action 1975,* Praeger, New York, 1975; *1975 and 1976 World population data sheets,* Population Reference Bureau, Inc., Washington, D.C.; *World population estimates, 1975,* The Environmental Fund, Inc., Washington, D.C.; Nortman, Population and family planning programs, *Reports on population and family planning,* Population Council, no. 2, 6th ed., Dec. 1974; *World Bank Atlas, 1975,* December, Washington, D.C.

But while some people seek the best means of achieving population control, in other quarters the debate continues as to whether it is necessary—or even desirable.

Population Politics

I am not sure that the dictatorship of the proletariat, especially if led by an elite, will solve the problem of social justice; I am certain starvation will not solve the problem of overpopulation.

—Tom O'Brien,
Marrying Malthus and Marx

Family planning programs have spread throughout the less developed world and are now established in the majority of less developed countries. Many countries, especially those with long-established programs that have been frustrated by lack of success in reducing birth rates simply through making means of birth control available, have progressed to measures beyond family planning. As could be expected, this has aroused opposition, informed and uninformed, from many quarters. Some groups see threats to their personal liberties; even more commonly, people see threats to their economic or political interests. In addition, there are many proponents of population control who strongly disagree on the most appropriate approach.[111] By 1974, when the United Nations World Population Conference took place in Bucharest, the chorus of clashing viewpoints was almost deafening.[112] Most press reports and coverage of the Conference by special groups conveyed an impression of enormous confusion and prevailing disagreement,[113] despite the ultimate ratification of a World Population Plan of Action and 21 resolutions.[114]

A very useful summary of all the various views of the population problem and how (or whether) to deal with it has been compiled by demographer Michael S. Teitelbaum.[115] Because it is the best listing we have seen, we are borrowing Teitelbaum's outline for the framework of the following discussion.[116]

Positions Against Special Population Programs and Policies

Pronatalist. This viewpoint favors rapid population growth to boost economic growth and an expanding labor supply, as well as to increase opportunities for economies of scale in small countries. Pronatalists believe there is strength in numbers (both political and military) and are more concerned about competition with rapidly growing neighboring countries or among segments of their own populations than about the disadvantages of rapid growth. This group now seems to be a diminishing minority.

Revolutionist. Revolutionaries oppose population programs because they may alleviate the social and political injustices that might otherwise lead to the revolution they seek. This view is particularly common in Latin America.[117] (Conversely, many politicians support family planning in the hope that it will dampen the revolutionary fires.)

Anti-colonial and genocide positions. This group is very suspicious of the motives of Western population control advocates. Some believe that effective population programs would retard development and maintain LDCs in economic subservience to DCs. Others see population

[111]National Academy of Sciences, *In search of population policy.*

[112]J. Mayone Stycos, Demographic chic at the UN.

[113]The list of accounts is very long, even leaving out a plethora of anticipatory books and articles. Here is a partial one: Anthony Astrachan, People are the most precious; Donald Gould, Population polarized; P. T. Piotrow, World plan of action and health strategy approved at population conferences; Conrad Taeuber, Policies on population around the world; Brian Johnson, The recycling of Count Malthus; M. Carder and B. Park, Bombast in Bucharest; D. B. Brooks and L. Douglas, Population, resources, environment: the view from the UN; W. P. Mauldin, et al., A report on Bucharest; Marcus P. Franda, Reactions to America at Bucharest; *Concerned Demography,* Emerging population alternatives; International Planned Parenthood Federation, (IPPF) *People,* special issue, vol. 1, no. 3, 1974; in addition, IPPF published a daily newspaper called *Planet* during the conference.

[114]United Nations, *Report of the UN World Population Conference, 1974.*

[115]Population and development: is a consensus possible?

[116]Bernard Berelson has also described the conflicting views on population in the *Population Council Annual Report* 1973, pp. 19–27, and The great debate on population policy. The latter was written as a dialog among three "voices," representing the family planning advocates, those who see "development" as the important issue, and academic critics of the family planning approach to population control. The dialog is informative, often witty, but unfortunately leaves the reader with an impression of much greater consensus than probably exists among the viewpoints.

[117]J. Mayone Stycos, Family planning: reform and revolution.

programs as an effort by DCs to "buy development cheaply." The most extreme position is taken by those who regard population control as a racist or genocidal plot against nonwhite citizens of LDCs. Holders of this position blame resource shortage and environmental problems exclusively on the greediness of rich countries. To the extent that high fertility in LDCs is a problem, they emphasize that it is due to their poverty, which in turn is caused by overconsumption in DCs.[118]

Accommodationist. This viewpoint is basically anti-Malthusian: because history shows that Earth is capable of supporting far more people than Malthus thought, he was wrong; these people believe that further improvements in agriculture and technology will permit accommodation of a much larger population than today's. To them what is called overpopulation is really underemployment; restructuring the economic system will allow societies to provide jobs and meet the basic needs of everyone, no matter how many. The slogan adopted by the *New Internationalist* for the Population Conference—"Look after the people and population will look after itself"—epitomizes this position.[119]

The problem-is-population-distribution. Some people holding this view simplistically compare population densities of different regions without regard to available resources and means of support. They also focus on the serious problem of urban migration in LDCs and conclude that policies should concentrate on population redistribution rather than on birth control.[120]

Mortality and social security. This view concentrates on the significance of infant and child mortality in motivating reproductive behavior; if infant mortality were reduced, fertility would automatically decline. This view is also held in varying degrees by many pro-population control advocates as well as those against it. Barry Commoner[121] subscribes to it, but he quotes a formula devised by AID. Whether the relationship is as clear as is commonly believed has been called into question by Alan Sweezy, among others.[122]

The other side of this coin is social security—the need for children, especially sons, to support parents in old age.[123]

Status and roles of women. Social pressures defining the role of women as wives and mothers, with status attached primarily to that role, are a major cause of high fertility, according to this view. Large families are likely to prevail until alternative roles are made available to all women.[124]

The religious doctrinal position. There are two distinct, but not necessarily mutually exclusive views here. One is essentially fatalistic: "Be fruitful and multiply, God will provide." This view is common among both Western and Eastern religions. The other (mainly the Roman Catholic Church) sees population growth as a problem, but regards most forms of birth control as more or less immoral.[125]

Medical risk. People holding this view are more impressed by the risks that attend the use of contraceptives such as the pill and the IUD, and surgical procedures such as abortion and sterilization than by the risks run by *not* using them. (The risk of death from childbearing alone is considerably higher, especially among the poor in LDCs, than any of these, and both maternal and infant mortality are known to be reduced substantially by the use of birth control for birth spacing.)[126] A milder version of this view is held by large segments of the medical profession who oppose the distribution of the pill without prescription and the insertion of IUDs by paramedical personnel, despite the established safety of both procedures compared to the consequences of not using them.[127]

---

[118]This perspective has been put forth by Barry Commoner, How poverty breeds overpopulation (and not the other way around); and Pierre Pradervand, The Malthusian man. Pradervand and Commoner, among others, also oppose present population programs on anticolonialist grounds.

[119]Peter Adamson, A population policy and a development policy are one and the same thing.

[120]Maaza Bekele, False prophets of doom. This article expresses this and the above three viewpoints clearly.

[121]Commoner, How poverty breeds overpopulation.

[122]Recent light.

[123]Mamdani, *Myth of population control.*

[124]Blake, Reproductive motivation; Day, Population control and personal freedom; *Ceres,* Women: a long-silent majority.

[125]Pope Paul VI, *Humanae Vitae.*

[126]A. Omran, Health benefits; Buchanan, Effects of childbearing; Eckholm and Newland, Health.

[127]Mauldin, Family planning programs and fertility declines.

Holistic development. Holders of this view are "demographic transition" believers who are convinced that social and economic development are responsible for whatever declines in fertility have occurred in LDCs, not family planning programs, which they consider a waste of effort and funds that should be put into development.[128]

Social justice. This position emphasizes redistribution of wealth within and among nations to improve the condition of the poor.[129] It is related to the idea of grassroots development, but is somewhat more extreme in that many of its proponents feel that redistribution of wealth is the *only* policy that will reduce population growth and solve other problems as well.

Positions Supporting the Need for Population Programs and Policies

Population hawks. Teitelbaum sums up this position as follows:

> . . . Unrestrained population growth is the principal cause of poverty, malnutrition, and environmental disruption, and other social problems. Indeed we are faced with impending catastrophe on food and environmental fronts.[130]
> . . . Such a desperate situation necessitates draconian action to restrain population growth, even if coercion is required. "Mutual coercion, mutually agreed upon."[131]
> . . . Population programs are fine as far as they go, but they are wholly insufficient in scope and strength to meet the desperate situation.[132]

Provision of services. This viewpoint holds that family planning programs are essential for reducing birth rates and that there is still a great unmet demand for birth control in LDCs; what is needed is to expand family planning services to meet the demand.[133] Part of the failure of family planning is due to provision of inadequate contraceptive technologies.[134] This position is held most strongly by administrators and associates of family planning programs and their donor agencies.

Human rights. This position, held by virtually everyone who is in favor of family planning or other population control policies, derives from the idea that there is a fundamental human right for each person responsibly to determine the size of his or her family.[135]

Another right that has been recognized in many countries including the United States[136] is that of women to control their bodies. This is especially relevant to the issue of abortion, but applies also to contraception and sterilization. Family planning also contributes to health, especially of women and children; and one more human right is that to health care.

Population programs plus development. Here again we quote Teitelbaum, who expressed it well:

> . . . Social and economic development are necessary but not sufficient to bring about a new equilibrium of population at low mortality and fertility levels. Special population programs are also required.[137]

---

[128]Bekele, False prophets; Commoner, How poverty breeds overpopulation. A more sophisticated form is Adamson's (A population policy)—at least he advocates development at the grass-roots level (see Social Justice section).

[129]Pradervand, Malthusian man; some writers for *Concerned Demography.*

[130]We, along with some colleagues, are considered among the principal proponents of this position (see especially P. Ehrlich, *The population bomb,* which is the most commonly cited source). Like most of the statements in this summary, this one is both exaggerated and oversimplified. We would not, for example, blame poverty or malnutrition principally on overpopulation, although it certainly contributes to their perpetuation. Likewise, population growth is one of three interacting causes of environmental deterioration; the others are misused technology and increasing affluence (see Chapter 12). As an aside, it is interesting that the first edition of the *Population bomb,* written almost a decade before this book, is still often cited both as if it reflected the situation in the mid-1970s and as if we still held precisely the same views today as we did then.

[131]Garrett Hardin, The tragedy of the commons.

[132]Davis, Population policy; P. R. Ehrlich and A. H. Ehrlich, *Population resources environment,* W. H. Freeman and Company, San Francisco, 1970 and 1972, chapter 10.

[133]Stycos, Demographic chic; Berelson, Effects of Population Control Programs.

[134]Mauldin, Family planning programs and fertility declines.

[135]UN Declaration on Population, Tehran, 1968, printed in *Studies in Family Planning,* no. 16, January 1967 and no. 26, January 1968. Teitelbaum omitted the important word "responsibly" in his discussion.

[136]Supreme Court decision on abortion, 1973.

[137]Advocates of this include Rich, Smaller families; James E. Kocher, Rural development; Grant, Development; and Lester R. Brown, *In the human interest.*

While we are usually classified by others as "population hawks," we agree more closely with this position in terms of what should be done. What follows, however, is far too mild a statement on the urgency of ending population growth; Teitelbaum discusses only the social aspects and completely leaves out environmental and resource constraints on population growth:

> Too rapid population growth is a serious intensifier of other social and economic problems, and is one, though only one, of a number of factors behind lagging social and economic progress in many countries.
>
> Some countries might benefit from larger populations, but would be better served by moderate rates of growth over a long period than by very rapid rates of growth over a shorter period.
>
> An effective population program therefore is an essential component of any sensible development program.

This general position (including the portion just quoted) is widely held by social scientists, politicians, economists, and quite likely by Teitelbaum himself.

Like the blind men with the elephant, each viewpoint grasps a piece of the truth, but none encompasses all of it. As should be evident, the above positions are by no means mutually exclusive, and probably none is held monolithically by anyone. Rather, most people argue from several related positions at once. Some apparently violent disagreements, when analyzed, turn out to be only a matter of emphasis or of leaving something out of the picture.

Teitelbaum, Berelson, and others see the germ of a consensus emerging from the debate. If so, and if the consensus produces an effective approach to the population problem that all can more or less agree on, the controversy will have been worthwhile. But to the extent that population policies are connected to the larger confrontation between the rich developed world and the poor less developed world (with waters frequently muddied by China and the Soviet Union who say one thing about population control and practice another), consensus may prove to be elusive. Even more important, LDCs are unlikely to take very seriously population goals and policies recommended by DCs that do not impose such goals and policies upon their own people.

World Population Plan of Action

In view of the diversity of opinions held by various individuals and groups on population control, it is not surprising that the United Nations' *World Population Plan of Action* turned out to be a bulky, nearly unreadable document some 50 pages long.[138] Summing it up is almost impossible; the 20 resolutions and numerous recommendations covered virtually every subject that might affect or be affected by population growth. In the initial statement of "Principles and Objectives," the *Plan* declared:

> The principal aim of social, economic and cultural development, of which population goals and policies are integral parts, is to improve levels of living and the quality of life of the people. Of all things in the world, people are the most precious. . . .

It then proceeded to affirm the rights of nations to formulate their own population policies, of couples and individuals to plan their families, and of women to participate fully in the development process. It condemned racial and ethnic discrimination, colonialism, foreign domination, and war. And it also expressed concern for preserving environmental quality, for maintaining supplies and distribution of resources, and for increasing food production to meet growing needs.

More specifically with regard to population policies, the following recommendations were made:[139]

- Governments should develop national policies on population growth and distribution, and should incorporate demographic factors into their development planning.
- Developed countries should also develop policies on population, investment, and consumption with an eye to increasing international equity.
- Nations should strive for low rather than high birth and death rates.
- Reducing death rates should be a priority goal, aiming for an average life expectancy in all

[138] United Nations, *Report of the UN World Population Conference*, 1974.

[139] Adapted from a summary by Piotrow, World Plan of Action.

countries of 62 by 1985 and 74 by 2000, and an infant mortality rate below 120 by 2000.

- All nations should ensure the rights of parents "to determine in a free, informed and responsible manner the number and spacing of their children," and provide the information and means for doing so.
- Family planning programs should be coordinated with health and other social services, and the poor in rural and urban areas should receive special attention.
- Efforts should be made to reduce LDC birth rates from an average of 38 in 1974 to 30 per 1000 by 1985.
- Nations are encouraged to set their own birth rate goals for 1985 and to implement policies to reach them.
- Nations should make special efforts to assist families as the basic social unit.
- Equality of opportunity for women in education, employment and social and political spheres should be ensured.
- Undesired migration, especially to cities, should be discouraged, principally by concentrating development in rural areas and small towns, but without restricting people's rights to move within their nation.
- International agreements are needed to protect rights and welfare of migrant workers between countries and to decrease the "brain drain."
- Demographic information should be collected, including censuses, in all countries.
- More research is needed on the relation of population to various institutions and to social and economic trends and policies; on improving health; on better contraceptive technologies; on the relation of health, nutrition, and reproduction; and on ways to improve delivery of social services (including family planning).
- Education programs in population should be strengthened.
- Population assistance from international, governmental, and private agencies should be increased.
- The Plan of Action should be coordinated with the UN's Second Development Decade strategy, reviewed every five years, and appropriately modified.

Unfortunately, a sense of urgency about reducing population growth, which had been present in the draft Plan, was lost in the final version under the pressure of political disagreement. The environmental and resource constraints on population growth were essentially left out of conference discussions and hence omitted from the Plan of Action.[140] Also, the value of family planning programs tended to be downgraded in favor of an overwhelming emphasis on "development" as the way to reduce birth rates.

The conference may not have blazed any radically new trails in its recommendations, but it still cannot be accused of taking a strictly narrow view of the population problem. Its neglect of environmental and resource aspects and the political problems that will accrue to those limitations is deplorable, but social and economic aspects were fully explored. Probably the conference's greatest value was to expose participants (many of whom did hold narrow views or were uninformed about some of the issues) to the information and viewpoints of others. And the mere existence of a world conference helped draw world attention to the population issue and emphasized that nations have a responsibility to manage their populations. Before the conference most national governments still seemed to believe that population problems were neither their concern nor within their ability to control.

The final Plan of Action was adopted by consensus of the 136 member nations (with reservations by the Vatican). Whether the resolutions and recommendations will be taken with the seriousness the problem warrants remains to be seen. For many countries it will not be easy, given the overwhelming problems their governments face. But on the answer hangs the future of humanity.

It was repeatedly emphasized at Bucharest that population control is no panacea for solving the problems of development or social and economic justice. This is perfectly true, of course; but unless the runaway human

[140]W. P. Mauldin et al., A report on Bucharest.

population is brought under control—and soon—the result will be catastrophe. *What kind* of catastrophe cannot be predicted, but numerous candidates have been discussed in this book: ecological collapses of various kinds, large-scale crop failures due to ecological stress or changes in climate and leading to mass famine; severe resource shortages, which could lead either to crop failures or to social problems or both; epidemic diseases; wars over diminishing resources; perhaps even thermonuclear war. The list of possibilities is long, and overpopulation enhances the probability that any one of them will occur. Population control may be no panacea, but without it there is no way to win.

Recommended for Further Reading

Blake, Judith. 1971. Reproductive motivation and population policy. *BioScience,* vol. 21, no. 5, pp. 215–220. An analysis of what sorts of policies might lower U.S. birth rate.

Berelson, Bernard. 1974. An evaluation of the effects of population control programs. *Studies in Family Planning,* vol. 5, no. 1. An important contribution to the controversy by a distinguished demographer active in the family planning field.

Chen, Pi-Chao. 1973. China's population program at the grass-roots level. *Studies in Family Planning,* vol. 4, no. 8, pp. 219–227. Also published in *Population perspective: 1973,* Brown, Holdren, Sweezy, and West, eds. Excellent summary.

Davis, Kingsley. 1973. Zero population growth: The goal and the means. *Daedalus,* vol. 102, no. 4, pp. 15–30. Useful critique of population policies, actual and proposed, especially of the United States.

Katchadourian, H. A., and D. T. Lunde. 1975. *Fundamentals of human sexuality.* 2nd ed. Holt, New York. A superb text for sex education; useful for birth control information also.

Kocher, James E. 1973. *Rural development, income distribution and fertility decline.* Population Council Occasional Papers. An important work on the connection between grass-roots development and fertility.

Population Reference Bureau, Inc. 1975. Family size and the black American. *Population Bulletin* vol. 30, no. 4. A study of black reproductive behavior and attitudes in the U.S.

———. 1976. *World population growth and response 1965–1975: A decade of global action.* A compendium on recent demographic trends and the evolution of population policies around the world.

Revelle, Roger. 1971. *Rapid population growth: Consequences and policy implications.* Report of a study committee, National Academy of Sciences. Johns Hopkins Press, Baltimore. Contains a number of interesting papers on social and economic effects of population growth, but weak on environmental and resource aspects.

Teitelbaum, Michael S. 1974. Population and development: Is a consensus possible? *Foreign Affairs,* July, pp. 742–760. An excellent discussion of the myriad viewpoints on population control.

Tietze, C., and M. C. Murstein. 1975. Induced abortion: A factbook. *Reports on Population/Family Planning,* 14 (2d ed.), December. Recent information on abortion worldwide.

United States Commission on Population Growth and the American Future. 1972. *Population and the American future,* 6 vols. Government Printing Office, Washington, D.C. (A paperback edition of the summary and recommendations was published by Signet, New York.)

Additional References

Adams, E. Sherman. 1969. Unwanted births and poverty in the United States. *The Conference Board Record,* vol. 6, no. 4, pp. 10–17. Somewhat out of date, but useful.

Adamson, Peter. 1974. A population policy and a development policy are one and the same thing. *New Internationalist,* May, pp. 7–9. An interesting article based on the work of William Rich and James Grant (see below), but considerably more antiMalthusian in its approach.

American Universities Field Staff. *Fieldstaff Reports.* These useful reports, several issued each month, focus on population related issues on a country-by-country basis.

Appleman, Philip, ed. 1976. *An essay on the principle of population.* Norton, New York. A reprinting of Malthus' famous essay along with many other essays and articles on the same general subject from Malthus' time to the present.

Arney, W. R., and W. H. Trescher. 1976. Trends in attitudes toward abortion, 1972–1975. *Family Planning Perspectives,* vol. 8, no. 3, pp. 117–124. On U.S. public opinion on abortion.

Association for Voluntary Sterilization (14 W. 40th St., New York, N.Y.). Excellent source of much information on sterilization, including how and where to obtain one.

Astrachan, Anthony. 1974. People are the most precious. *SR/World,* October 19. An account of the Bucharest Conference on World Population.

Ayala, F. J., and C. T. Falk. 1971. Sex of children and family size. *Journal of Heredity,* vol. 62, no. 1, pp. 57–59. Study indicating that desire for children of a particular sex may have little influence on family size in the U.S.

Bajema, C. J. 1971. Estimates of the direction and intensity of natural selection in relation to human intelligence by means of the intrinsic rate of natural increase. In Bajema, ed. *Natural selection in human populations.* Wiley, New York, pp. 276–291. Concludes that fertility has become positively correlated with IQ.

———. 1971. The genetic implications of American life styles in reproduction and population control. In *Natural selection in human populations,* Bajema, ed. Wiley, New York, pp. 359–368. See especially discussion of genetic consequences of compulsory population control.

———, ed. 1971. *Natural selection in human populations.* Wiley, New York. A diverse collection—see especially the section on natural selection and the future genetic composition of human populations.

Baldini, R., et al. 1974. The abortion dilemma. *Atlas,* November. Twelve reports on abortion policies around the world.

Barnett, Larry D. 1969. Population policy: Payments for fertility limitation in the U.S. *Social Biology,* vol. 16, no. 4. An analysis of the economics of such a program.

Beaver, Steven E. 1975. *Demographic transition theory reinterpreted.* Lexington Books, Lexington, Mass. A detailed analysis that indicates what the important social factors that induce a demographic transition may be.

Behrman, S. J., L. Corsa, Jr., and R. Freedman, eds. 1969. *Fertility and family planning; a world view.* University of Michigan Press, Ann Arbor. A basic source on family planning.

Bekele, Maaza. 1974. False prophets of doom. *Unesco Courier,* July/August. An anti-Malthusian viewpoint, stressing poverty, distribution, and overurbanization as problems and denying that overpopulation exists.

Belsky, Raymond. 1975. Vaginal contraceptives: a time for reappraisal? *Population Reports,* series H, no. 3. On the problems, history, efficacy, and recent improvements of contraceptive foams, jellies, creams, suppositories, and so forth.

Berelson, Bernard, 1969. Beyond family planning. *Science,* vol. 163, pp. 533–543. An evaluation of proposed means of population control and an affirmation of the value of family planning programs. (Reprinted in Holdren and Ehrlich, *Global ecology.*)

———. 1975. The great debate on population policy; an instructive entertainment. An occasional paper of the Population Council. An informative and witty "dialog" among holders of different views on population control.

———, ed. 1974. *Population policy in developed countries.* McGraw-Hill, New York. Discusses past and present policies in each country individually; useful.

——— et al. 1966. *Family planning and population programs.* University of Chicago Press, Chicago. A classic study of early family planning programs.

Best, Winfield, and Louis Dupré, 1967. Birth control. *Encyclopedia Britannica.* Interesting account of the history of the planned parenthood movement.

Blake, Judith. 1965. Demographic science and the redirection of population policy. *Journal of chronic disease* vol. 18, pp. 1181–1200. On implicit policies contained in social attitudes towards marriage, families, and women's role in society.

———. 1968. Are babies consumer durables? *Population Studies,* vol. 22, no. 1, pp. 5–25. An examination of economic factors motivating family planning.

———. 1971. Abortion and public opinion: the 1960–1970 decade. *Science,* vol. 171, pp. 540–549. Documents change in American attitudes toward abortion during the 1960s.

———. 1974. The changing status of women in developed countries. *Scientific American,* September, pp. 136–147.

Boulding, Kenneth. 1964. *The meaning of the 20th century.* Harper and Row, New York. Contains a distinguished economist's proposal of a baby-licensing scheme.

Bronfenbrenner, Urie. 1974. The origins of alienation. *Scientific American,* August. On the failure of Americans to establish community roots and its social consequences.

Brooks, D. B., and L. Douglas. 1975. Population, resources, environment: The view from the U.N. *Canadian Forum,* January. A Canadian report on the World Population Conference; one of the authors is a resource economist.

Brown, H.; J. P. Holdren; A. Sweezy; and B. West, eds. 1974. *Population perspective: 1973.* Freeman-Cooper, San Francisco. Excellent collection of readings on the population situation.

Brown, Lester R. 1974. *In the human interest.* Norton, New York. This book was written for the delegates to the UN World Population Conference and includes a good discussion of grass-roots development—especially rural development—and population control.

———, P. L. McGrath, and B. Stokes. 1976. Twenty-two dimensions of the population problem. *Worldwatch Paper 5,* March. Worldwatch Institute, Washington, D.C.

Buchanan, Robert. 1975. Breast-feeding—aid to infant health and fertility control. *Population Reports,* Series J, no. 4. On the interactions among nutrition, birth-spacing, breast-feeding, and infant mortality.

———. 1975. Effects of childbearing on maternal health. *Population Reports,* series J, no. 8, November.

Bumpass, L., and C. F. Westoff. 1970. The "perfect contraceptive" population. *Science,* vol. 169, pp. 1177–1182. Discussion of incidence of unwanted births in the U.S. during the 1960s.

Calderone, Mary S. 1970. *Manual of family planning and contraceptive practice.* William & Wilkins Co., Baltimore. This book includes material on the U.S. family planning movement and the medical, health, social, and educational aspects of birth control. Much more useful than just as a guide.

Carder, M. and B. Park. 1975. Bombast in Bucharest. *Science for the People,* January. An American radical left view of the World Population Conference.

Carvalho, J. A. M. 1974. Regional trends in fertility and mortality in Brazil. *Population Studies,* vol. 28, no. 3, pp. 401–421. Documents the demographic effects of a two-tiered society.

Ceres. 1975. Women: A long silent majority. March/April. UN Food and Agriculture Organization. A special issue on women's roles and status, especially in LDCs.

Chacko, V. I. 1975. Family planners earn retirement bonus on plantations in India. *Population Dynamics Quarterly,* vol. 3, no. 3. Early results of a "social security" program to encourage family limitation.

Chandrasekhar, S. 1972. *Infant mortality, population growth and family planning in India.* University of North Carolina Press, Chapel Hill, N.C. This book by India's former family planning minister, examines India's recent demographic history and describes the family planning program.

Chasteen, Edgar R. 1971. *The case for compulsory birth control.* Prentice-Hall, Englewood Cliffs, New Jersey.

Chen, Pi-Chao. 1975. Lessons from the Chinese experience: China's planned birth program and its transferability. *Studies in Family Planning,* vol. 6, no. 10, pp. 354–366. On how some of China's population policies might be adapted to fit situations in other LDCs.

China Reconstructs. 1974. China on the population question. Vol. 23, no. 11. How the Chinese government officially views it. This journal is published for foreign readers in English and several other languages by the China Welfare Institute.

Chowdbury, A. K. M. A.; A. R. Kahn; and L. C. Chen. 1976. The effect of child mortality experience on subsequent fertility: in Pakistan and Bangladesh. *Population studies,* vol. 30, no. 2, pp. 249–261 (July). Concludes that in non-contracepting populations the effect of losing a child increases fertility largely by biological means—by shortening the period of breast-feeding and post partum infertility.

Commoner, Barry. 1975. How poverty breeds overpopulation (and not the other way around). *Ramparts,* August/September. Presents a simplistic view of overpopulation, popular among Third World spokesmen, that blames development problems primarily on over-consumption and greediness of DCs.

Concerned Demography. 1974. Emerging population alternatives, vol. 4, no. 2. Winter. Special issue on the World Population Conference by a leftist radical organization of demographers.

Consumer Reports. 1971. Voluntary sterilization. June, pp. 384–386. A good review of both male and female sterilization.

Cook, Robert. *World population estimates.* The Environmental Fund, Inc., Washington, D.C. An annually produced data sheet whose demographic estimates are a matter of controversy.

Corey, Marsha. 1975. U.S. organized family planning programs in FY 1974. *Family Planning Perspectives* vol. 7, no. 3.

Culliton, Barbara J. 1975. Edelin trial: jury not persuaded by scientists for the defense. *Science,* vol. 187, pp. 814–816. A thoughtful article on the trial of a doctor for manslaughter after performance of a late-term abortion.

Cutright, P. and F. S. Jaffe, 1976. Family planning program effects on the fertility of low-income U.S. women. *Family Planning Perspectives,* vol. 8, no. 3 (May/June), pp. 100–110.

Darity, W. A., C. B. Turner, and H. J. Thiebaux. 1971. Race consciousness and fears of black genocide as barriers to family planning. *Perspectives from the Black Community, PRB Selection no. 37* (June). Population Reference Bureau, Inc. An analysis of genocide fears and attitudes toward birth control in the black population of the U.S.

Davis, Kingsley. 1967. Population policy: will current programs succeed? *Science,* vol. 158, pp. 730–739. One of the most important papers on socioeconomic approaches to population control; excellent. Reprinted in Holdren and Ehrlich, *Global Ecology.*

———. 1973. Zero population growth: The goal and the means. *Daedalus,* vol. 102, no. 4, pp. 15–30. A splendid follow-up to the earlier paper (above).

Day, Alice Taylor. 1968. Population control and personal freedom: are they compatible? *The Humanist,* November/December. Contains some fine ideas in the socioeconomic realm of population control measures.

Demeny, Paul. 1974. The populations of the underdeveloped countries. *Scientific American,* September, pp. 149–159. Includes some discussion of possible population control policies.

Dickeman, Mildred. 1975. Demographic consequences of infanticide in man. *Annual Review of Ecology and Systematics,* vol. 6. Annual Reviews, Inc., Palo Alto, Calif. A wide-ranging article that explores many aspects of ways in which societies regulate their numbers.

Djerassi, Carl. 1969. Prognosis for the development of new birth-control agents. *Science,* vol. 166, pp. 468–473. (Reprinted in Holdren and Ehrlich, *Global ecology.*)

———. 1970. Birth control after 1984. *Science,* vol. 169, pp. 941–951. Discussion of the state of contraceptive development and suggestions of how the U.S. government might facilitate such development. Still useful.

———. 1974. Fertility limitation through contraceptive steroids in the People's Republic of China. *Studies in Family Planning,* vol. 5, pp. 13–30. Discussion of China's use of the pill, including a description of the new "paper pill."

Dobson, Wendy. 1975. National population objectives are slowly taking shape, now we need policies. *Science Forum* (Canada), vol. 48, pp. 24–27. On population policies in Canada.

Dryfoos, Joy G. 1976. The United States national family planning program, 1968–1974. *Studies in Family Planning,* vol. 7, no. 3, pp. 80–91. A review of the growth and accomplishments of the U.S. family planning program.

Dytrych, Z., et al. 1975. Children born to women denied abortion. *Family Planning Perspectives,* vol. 7, no. 4, pp. 165–171. A Czechoslovakian study showing that denial of abortion tends to result in disadvantaged children.

Easterlin, Richard A. 1968. *Population, labor force, and long swings in economic growth.* Columbia University Press, New York. A detailed and scholarly treatment attempting to demonstrate that American fertility patterns are primarily determined by economic factors.

Eckholm, E., and K. Newland. 1977. Health: The family planning factor. *Worldwatch paper 10,* Worldwatch Institute, Washington, D.C. A concise summary of the interactions between birth control and health and the safety of contraceptives.

Ehrlich, Paul R. 1968. *The population bomb.* 2nd ed., 1971. Ballantine, New York. Describes the links of overpopulation with environmental deterioration and resource depletion, and advocates population control for those as well as social reasons.

——— and S. Feldman. 1977. *The Race bomb,* Quadrangle, New York. A debunking of popular myths about race and intelligence, with a discussion of black attitudes toward population control.

Eilenstine, D., and J. P. Cunningham. 1972. Projected consumption patterns for a stationary population. *Population Studies,* vol. 26, pp. 223–231. On some of the economic characteristics of a stationary population.

Enke, Stephen. 1966. The economic aspects of slowing population growth. *The Economic Journal,* vol. 76, no. 301, pp. 44–56.

———. 1969. Birth control for economic development. *Science,* vol. 164, pp. 798–801. A cost-benefit analysis concluding that investments in birth control would benefit a less developed country economically by a ratio of as much as 80 to 1. Reprinted in Holdren and Ehrlich, *Global Ecology.*

———. 1971. The economics of slowing population growth. *Tempo.* General Electric Co. Center for Advanced Studies, Santa Barbara, Calif. Basically a cost-benefit analysis, showing that the costs of slowing population growth would be far outweighed by the benefits.

——— and R. G. Zind. 1969. Effects of fewer births on average income. *Journal of Biological Sciences,* vol. 1, pp. 41–55.

Family Planning Perspectives. 1971. P. L. 91–572, milestone U.S. family planning legislation, signed into law. Vol. 3, no. 1, pp. 2–3. Details of the 1970 Family Planning Act.

———. 1975. Abortion-related deaths down 40 percent . . . . Vol. 7, no. 2, p. 54.

———. 1976. Special issue: Teenagers, USA. Vol 8, no. 4. Series of studies on contraceptive practices of American teenagers and the social consequences of teenage childbearing.

Firpo, T. H., and D. A. Lewis. 1976. Family planning needs and services in nonmetropolitan areas. *Family planning perspectives,* vol. 8, no. 5, pp. 231–240.

Franda, Marcus. 1974. Shifts in emphasis in India's population policy. *Fieldstaff Reports* vol. 18, no. 7.

———. 1974. Reactions to America at Bucharest. *Fieldstaff Reports,* vol. 21, no. 3. A report on the World Population Conference.

Freedman, Deborah, ed. 1976. Fertility, aspirations, and resources: A symposium on the Easterlin hypothesis. *Population and development review,* vol. 2, nos. 3 and 4. Discussion of motivational factors in reproductive behavior.

Frederiksen, Harald. 1969. Feedback in economic and demographic transition. *Science,* vol. 166, pp. 837–847. An overly optimistic discussion of the possible benefits of death control in motivating people to have smaller families in LDCs.

Freedman, R., and B. Berelson. 1976. The record of family planning programs. *Studies in Family Planning,* vol. 7, no. 1. An assessment of family planning programs by the family planning establishment.

Freedman, R., and A. J. Hermalin. 1975. Do statements about desired family size predict fertility? The case of Taiwan. *Demography,* vol. 12, no. 3, pp. 407–416.

Frejka, Tomas. 1973. *The future of population growth: alternative paths to equilibrium.* Wiley, New York. Detailed projections of population growth assuming eventual attainment of ZPG.

Gould, Donald. 1974. Population polarized. *New Scientist,* September 5. An account of the Bucharest World Population Conference.

Grant, James P. 1973. Development: the end of trickle down? *Foreign Policy,* no. 12, Fall, pp. 43–65. Also issued as *Overseas Development Council Development Paper 16* under the title: Growth from below; a people-oriented development strategy. On grass-roots development and its probable effect on fertility; very thought provoking.

Guttmacher, Alan F. 1966. *The complete book of birth control.* Ballantine, New York. Revised. Clear description of all presently used methods of birth control.

Guttmacher Institute. 1975. *Provisional estimates of abortion need and services in the year following the Supreme Court decisions: United States, each state and metropolitan area.* A detailed survey that concluded that many medical facilities were failing to provide abortion services to women who needed them in 1974.

———. 1976. Organized family planning services in the United States: FY 1975. *Family planning perspectives,* vol. 8, no. 6, pp. 269–274. Latest report on the U.S. family planning program.

Han, Suyin. 1974. The Chinese experiment. *Unesco Courier,* July/August, pp. 52–55. A relatively personalized account of China's population policies.

Hardin, Garrett. 1966. The history and future of birth control. *Perspectives in Biology and Medicine,* vol. 10, no. 1. Contains some interesting historical data.

———. 1968. Abortion—compulsory pregnancy? *Journal of Marriage and Family,* vol. 30, no. 2. Discussion of abortion from a biologist's point of view.

———. 1968. The tragedy of the commons. *Science,* vol. 162, pp. 1243–1248. A classic paper, urging population control through "mutual coercion, mutually agreed upon."

———. 1970. *Birth control.* Pegasus, New York. Excellent up-to-date discussion.

Hauser, Philip M. 1967. Family planning and population programs. *Demography,* vol. 4, no. 1. Critical review of Berelson's book on family planning, raising some pertinent questions on the approach of family planning as a solution to the population problem.

Heer, David M. 1975. Marketing licenses for babies; Boulding's proposal revisited. *Social Biology,* vol. 22, pp. 1–16. On baby licensing, variations on the theme, and other compulsory population control measures.

Hoch, Irving. 1976. City size effects, trends, and policies. *Science,* vol. 193, pp. 856–863 (September 3). On many of the problems that attend urban growth, especially unplanned growth.

Holdren, J. P. and P. R. Ehrlich, eds. 1971. *Global ecology: readings toward a rational strategy for man.* Harcourt, Brace, Jovanovich, New York. Reprints Enke, Birth control; Davis, Population policy; Berelson, Beyond family planning; and Djerassi, Prognosis.

Huber, S. C. et al. 1975. IUDs reassessed—a decade of experience. *Population Reports,* Series B, no. 2, January.

Huldt, Lars. 1968. Outcome of pregnancy when legal abortion is readily available. *Current Medical Digest,* vol. 35, no. 5, pp. 586–594. An account of the Swedish study of young people whose mothers had been denied abortions.

International Planned Parenthood Federation (IPPF). *People.* A quarterly journal published in London. Volume 1 (1974), no. 3, was a special issue on the Bucharest World Population Conference. IPPF also published a daily newspaper, *Planet,* during the conference.

———. 1976. China 1976: A new perspective. *People,* vol. 3, no. 3. A special issue on China, especially its population policies.

———. 1976. India: A sterile solution? *People,* vol. 3, no. 4. A special issue on India's population policies. The editorial is the source of the quote from Karan Singh.

Jaffe, Frederick S. 1972. Low-income families: fertility changes in the 1960s. *Family Planning Perspectives,* vol. 4, no. 1, pp. 43–47. Documents the rapidly declining fertility among American poor families.

Johnson, Brian. 1974. The recycling of Count Malthus. *The Ecologist,* vol. 4, no. 10. A well written report on the Bucharest World Population Conference by a British population activist.

Johnson, Stanley. 1970. *Life without birth.* Little, Brown, Boston. A personal and vivid exploration of the population explosion and family planning programs in LDCs around the world.

Kalman, Sumner M. 1967. Modern methods of contraception. *Bulletin of the Santa Clara County [California] Medical Society,* March.

Kamin, Leon J. 1974. *The science and politics of IQ.* Wiley, New York. Includes a critique of studies of twins on which most of the evidence for IQ heritability rest.

Kangas, Lerni W. 1970. Integrated incentives for fertility control. *Science,* vol. 169, pp. 1278–1283. Suggestions for improving family planning programs in LDCs.

Katagiri, Tameyoshi. 1973. A report on the family p anning program in the People's Republic of China. *Family Planning Perspectives,* vol. 4, no. 8. The author of this report is a distinguished family planning expert in Japan.

Ketchel, Melvin M. 1968. Fertility control agents as a possible solution to the world population problem. *Perspectives in Biology and Medicine,* vol. 11, no. 4. Discussion of fertility-reducing agents that could be administered impartially to all members of a society.

Koblinsky, M. A.; F. S. Jaffe; and R. O. Greep. 1976. Funding for reproductive research: The status and the needs. *Family planning perspectives,* vol. 8, no. 5, pp. 212–225. Research on reproduction and new contraceptive agents is still being neglected.

Krishnakumar, S. 1972. Kerala's Pioneering experiment in massive vasectomy camps. *Studies in Family Planning,* vol. 3, no. 8, pp. 177–185. On one of India's family planning festivals.

Lader, Lawrence. 1966. *Abortion.* Beacon, Boston.

———. 1969. Non-hospital abortions. *Look,* January 21. On the horrors of illegal abortion.

———. 1973. *Abortion II: making the revolution.* Beacon, Boston. A lively history of the battle to change U.S. abortion laws.

Langer, William L. 1972. Checks on population growth: 1750–1850. *Scientific American,* February. Fascinating account of demography in industrializing Europe, including the important role of infanticide.

Lelyveld, Joseph. 1974. The great leap farmward. *New York Times Magazine,* July 28, pp. 6 ff. An interesting account of China's deurbanization policy and its probable political and demographic consequences.

Lincoln, Richard. 1975. The Institute of Medicine reports on legalized abortion and the public health. *Family Planning Perspectives,* vol. 7, no. 4.

Lorraine, J. A. 1970. *Sex and the population crisis,* Wm. Heinemann Medical Books, Ltd., Surrey, England. A book on contraception in the context of the population explosion.

———. 1976. Population patterns in the mid-1970s. *New Scientist,* January 8, pp. 81–83. A concise description of the population situation and many of the problems of family planning programs.

Lurien, K. A. 1971. A world record for Ernakulam. *Hindustan Times,* August 29. An account of one of India's massive family planning festivals.

McElroy, William D. 1969. Biomedical aspects of population control. *BioScience,* vol. 19, no. 1, pp. 19–23. More on the population control controversy; another strong vote for more effective action.

Mamdani, Mahmood. 1972. *The myth of population control: family, caste, and class in an Indian village.* Monthly Review Press, New York. A critique of Wyon and Gordon's *Khanna Study* and an attempt to explain why India's family planning efforts have been unsuccessful.

Marigh, T. H. 1974. 5-Thio-D-Glucose: a unique male contraceptive. *Science* vol. 186, p. 431.

Matsunaga, Ei. 1971. Possible genetic consequences of family planning. In Bajema, ed. *Natural selection,* pp. 328–344. One conclusion is "because of the lack of our knowledge on many important points, it is difficult to evaluate the extent of the assumed dysgenic effect upon some mental traits that are correlated with social stratification."

Mauldin, W. Parker. 1975. Family planning programs and fertility declines in developing countries. *Family Planning Perspectives,* vol. 7, no. 1. A critique of family planning programs by a program administrator.

——— et al. 1974. A report on Bucharest. *Studies in Family Planning,* vol. 5, no. 12. The World Population Conference as viewed by the family planning establishment.

Meek, Ronald L., ed. 1971. *Marx and Engels on the population bomb.* Ramparts Press, Berkeley. Reprints the attacks of Marx and Engels on Malthus; contains a most interesting introductory essay by New Left theorist Steve Weissman.

Moody, Howard. 1968. Protest. *Glamour,* April. A Protestant view of abortion.

Morrison, Peter. 1970. *Urban growth, new cities, "the population problem."* Rand Corporation P-4515-1. December. An analysis of population distribution and migration patterns in the U.S. and the new cities approach to dealing with them.

———. 1974. Urban growth and decline: San Jose and St. Louis in the 1960s. *Science,* vol. 185, pp. 575–762. This study shows the effects of the mobile society on a rapidly growing city and one that is losing population.

Myers, Norman. 1975. Of all things people are the most precious. *New Scientist,* January 9, pp. 56–59. Description of China's population program and its achievements by an FAO scientist.

National Academy of Sciences. 1974. *In search of population policy: views from the developing world.* U.S. Government Printing Office, Washington, D.C.

Newman, Lucille F. 1968. *Family planning: an anthropological approach.* Paper presented at the International Congress of Anthropological and Ethnological Sciences, Tokyo, September 6. Raises some pertinent points relative to attitudes and reproductive behavior.

New Scientist. 1974. Reversible sterilization by fallopian blocking. March 28, p. 800. A new technique for female sterilization that may be reversible.

———. 1974. Hormone mixture makes a male pill. December 19, p. 860.

Nortman, Dorothy. 1974 and 1975. Population and family planning programs: a factbook. *Reports on Population/Family Planning* no. 2. Population Council, New York. Useful summaries.

———, and Ellen Hofstatter, 1976. Population and family planning programs: A factbook. *Reports on population/family planning,* no. 2, 8th ed. Population Council, New York. The latest and evidently the last of the series.

O'Brien, Fr. John A. 1968. *Family planning in an exploding population.* Hawthorne, New York. A progressive Catholic point of view.

O'Brien, Tom. 1975. Marrying Malthus and Marx. *Environmental Action,* August 30, pp. 3–11. A splendid synthesis of Marxist and Malthusian ideas in the context of the present human predicament.

Ohlin, Goran. 1967. *Population control and economic development.* Development Centre of the Organization for Economic Cooperation and Development (OECD), Paris. A classic analysis of the effect of rapid population growth in retarding development.

Okorafor, Apia E. 1970. Dialog: Africa's population problems. *Africa Report,* June, pp. 22–23.

Omran, Abdel R. 1974. Health Benefits for mother and child. *World Health,* January. The World Health Organization's conclusions on the benefits of family planning to maternal and child health.

Orleans, Leo A. 1971. China: Population in the People's Republic. *Population Bulletin,* vol. 27, no. 6. An excellent historical account of Chinese population growth and policies.

———. 1973. Family planning developments in China, 1960–1966: abstracts from medical journals. *Studies in Family Planning,* vol. 4, no. 8. A fascinating glimpse of family planning activity and research in China during the 1960s.

———. 1976. China's population figures: can the contradictions be resolved? *Studies in Family Planning,* vol. 7, no. 2. Helpful comparisons of differing estimates of China's population size today and in the near future. Orleans proposes his own estimates, which fall between the extremes of the Chinese government estimates and those of a China expert in the U.S. Bureau of Economic Analysis.

Osborn, F., and C. J. Bajema. 1975. The eugenic hypothesis. *Social Biology,* vol. 19, pp. 337–345. An optimistic evaluation of the genetic consequences of population control.

Packard, Vance. 1972 and 1974. *A nation of strangers.* Pocket Books, New York. Describes the destructive consequences of a mobile society to people and communities.

Parsons, Jack. 1971. *Population versus liberty.* Pemberton Books, London. Argues effectively that the loss of liberty due to overpopulation is greater than that needed to reduce the number of births.

Peck, Ellen. 1971. *The baby trap.* Bernard Geis Associates, New York. An attack on the traditional pronatalist image of motherhood and an exploration of alternative life styles.

——— and J. Senderowitz, eds. 1974. *Pronatalism: the myth of mom and apple pie.* Crowell, New York. Interesting papers on women's changing attitudes toward motherhood.

Pilpel, Harriet. 1969. The right of abortion. *Atlantic,* June. Ethical and legal problems of abortion.

Piotrow, Phyllis Tilson. 1973. *World population crisis: The United States response.* Praeger, New York. An historical study of U.S. overseas population assistance programs.

———, ed. 1976. Voluntary sterilization. The Draper World Population Fund Report, no. 3, Autumn-Winter. Reports on sterilization policies and practices around the world.

———. 1974. World plan of action and health strategy approved at Population Conference. *Population Reports,* series E, no. 2. A report on the Bucharest conference by an American demographer.

Pope, Carl. 1972. *Sahib: An American misadventure in India.* Liveright, New York. A vivid personal account by a former Peace Corps volunteer of the family planning program in India.

Pope Paul VI. 1968. *Humanae Vitae.* The papal encyclical that reaffirmed the Roman Catholic church's view that contraceptives are immoral.

Population Council, New York. *Studies in Family Planning.* A monthly series. An excellent account of family planning programs around the world.

———. *Population and development review.* A quarterly journal on population-related development issues published by the Population Council, New York.

Population Reference Bureau, Inc. (Washington, D.C.). Their *Population Bulletin* and other publications often cover population policies around the world. The annual *Population Data Sheet,* based mainly on U.N. estimates, is a useful and convenient source of information.

Population Reports. A series of reports issued by the Department of Medical and Public Affairs, George Washington University Medical Center, Washington, D.C. The reports are mainly on various contraceptive methods, abortion, sterilization, and research on new methods, drugs, or devices.

Potts, Malcolm, et al. 1975. Advantages of orals outweigh disadvantages. *Population Reports,* series A, no. 2. A comprehensive report on oral contraceptives and their side-effects.

Pradervand, Pierre. 1970. International aspects of population control. *Concerned Demography,* vol. 2, no. 2, pp. 1–16. A discussion of some of the political problems associated with population issues, especially in Latin America.

———. 1974. The Malthusian man. *New Internationalist,* May, pp. 10–13ff. A leftist view that tends to blame problems of overpopulation in LDCs on neocolonialism and overconsumption in DCs.

Ransil, Bernard J. 1969. *Abortion.* Paulist Press Deus Books, New York. Serious discussion of the moral aspects of abortion, written by a Catholic M.D.

Reed, Roy. 1975. Rural areas' population gains now outpacing urban regions. *New York Times,* May 18. On the recent reversal of rural-urban migration in the U.S.

Rich, William. 1973. Smaller families through social and economic progress. *Overseas Development Council,* Monograph no. 7. Another article on grass-roots development and how it affects fertility.

Ridker, Ronald. 1969. Synopsis of a proposal for a family planning bond. *Studies in Family Planning, no. 43,* June, pp. 11–16. Plan for a "social security" program for workers on a tea estate in India.

———. 1971. Saving accounts for family planning, an illustration from the tea estates of India. *Studies in Family Planning,* vol. 2, no. 7, pp. 150–152.

Rinehart, Ward, 1975. Minipill—a limited alternative for certain women. *Population Reports,* series A, no. 3. On the oral contraceptive containing progestin only.

——— and J. Winter. 1975. Injectable progestogens—officials debate but use increases. *Population Reports,* series K, no. 1.

Russett, Bruce M. 1970. Licensing: For cars and babies. *Bulletin of the Atomic Scientists,* November, pp. 15–19. An elaboration of Boulding's scheme.

Ryder, Norman. 1973. Contraceptive failure in the United States. *Family Planning Perspectives,* vol. 5, no. 3, pp. 133–142. A comparative study of the effectiveness of various birth control methods.

———. 1974. The family in developed countries. *Scientific American,* September, pp. 122–135.

Salisbury, G. W., and R. G. Hart. 1975. Functional integrity of spermatozoa after storage. *BioScience,* vol. 25, no. 3, pp. 159–165. On the possibility of storing sperm samples before sterilization.

Science, 1976. Special issue on the Habitat Conference, vol. 192, June 4. Contains many articles on urbanization in both DCs and LDCs.

Schroeder, Richard C. 1974. Policies on population around the world. *Population Bulletin,* vol. 29, no. 6.

Schwartz, Herman. 1967. The parent or the fetus? *Humanist,* July/August. A discussion of legal and ethical aspects of abortion.

Segal, Sheldon J. 1974. The physiology of human reproduction, *Scientific American,* September. Brief description of human reproduction including how present day contraceptives work and how future ones might work.

Shalita, Ronald. 1975. Prostaglandins promise more effective fertility control. *Population Reports,* series G., no. 6.

Short, R. V., and D. T. Baird, eds. 1976. A discussion on contraceptives of the future. *Proceedings of the Royal Society of London,* B. Biological sciences. vol. 195, pp. 1–224, 10 December. A symposium on contraceptive and reproductive research.

Sidel, V. W., and R. Sidel. 1974. The delivery of medical care in China. *Scientific American,* April, pp. 19–27. Interesting description of China's medical care system.

Sklar, J., and B. Berkov. 1974. Abortion, illegitimacy, and the American birth rate. *Science* vol. 185, pp. 909–914. On the effect on legitimate and illegitimate birth rates of legalized abortion.

Snow, Edgar. 1971. Report from China—III: Population care and control. *The New Republic,* May 1. An interesting early report.

Spengler, Joseph J. 1971. Economic growth in a stationary population. *PRB Selection* no. 38. Population Reference Bureau. Washington, D.C. An early paper on the economic consequences of a stationary population.

———. 1975. *Population and America's Future.* W. H. Freeman and Co., San Francisco. Economic aspects of population growth in the U.S. and the probable benefits of ending population growth.

Stycos, J. Mayone. 1971. Family planning: Reform and revolution. *Family Planning Perspectives,* vol. 3, no. 1, pp. 49–50. On the relevance of family planning to development and politics in LCDs, especially in Latin America.

———. 1971. Opinion, ideology, and population problems: Some sources of domestic and foreign opposition to birth control. In Revelle, *Rapid population growth.*

———. 1974. Demographic chic at the U.N. *Family Planning Perspectives,* vol. 6, no. 3, pp. 160–164. Good article on the population debate that preceded the UN Conference on World Population.

Sweezy, Alan. 1971. The economic explanation of fertility changes in the U.S. *Population Studies,* vol. 25, no. 2, pp. 255–267. Presents evidence that assumptions that American fertility trends are primarily determined by economic factors are false.

———. 1973. Labor shortage and population policy. *Caltech Population Program Occasional Papers,* series 1, no. 6. A critique of the argument that ending population growth will cause labor shortages.

———. 1973. Recent light on the relation between socioeconomic development and fertility decline. *Caltech Population Program Occasional Papers,* series 1, no. 1. Interesting study showing that fertility declines have occurred in many European areas with little or no industrial development.

———. 1976. Economic development and fertility change. *New perspectives on the demographic transition, Occasional monograph series,* no. 4, Interdisciplinary Communications Program, Smithsonian Institution. An analysis of possible causes of demographic transition, suggesting that traditions may carry more influence against birth control than is commonly supposed. Excellent.

Taeuber, Conrad. 1974. Policies on population around the world. *Population Bulletin,* vol. 26, no. 6. Includes an account of the Population Conference in Bucharest; a "population establishment" view.

Taylor, C. E.; J. E. Newman; and N. U. Kelly. 1976. The child survival hypothesis. *Population Studies,* vol. 30, no. 2, pp. 263–278. On the relation between infant mortality and fertility.

———. 1976. Interactions between health and population. *Studies in Family Planning,* vol. 7, no. 4, pp. 93–100. On how health influences fertility and vice-versa.

Teitelbaum, Michael S. 1975. Relevance of demographic transition theory for developing countries. *Science,* vol. 188, pp. 420–425. Interesting paper showing that causes of the demographic transition in DCs are unclear and may not be applicable to LDCs at all.

Terry, Geraldine B. 1975. Rival explanations in the work-fertility relationship. *Population Studies,* vol. 29, no. 2, pp. 191–203. Explores factors affecting the tendency of working women to have smaller families.

Thakor, V. H., and V. M. Patel. 1972. The Gujarat State massive vasectomy campaign. *Studies in Family Planning,* vol. 3, no. 8, pp. 186–192. An account of one of India's family planning festivals.

Tietze, Christopher. 1975. The effect of legalization of abortion on population growth and public health. *Family Planning Perspectives,* vol. 7, no. 3. On how abortion services are being provided in the U.S.

——— and Sarah Lewit. 1977. Abortion. *Scientific American,* January. Good general discussion of the recent changes in abortion policies around the world.

Tinker, Jon. 1974. Java: Birth control battlefield. *New Scientist,* February 21, pp. 483–486. How one LDC decided to run its own program rather than depend on foreign specialists.

Tuckwell, Sue. 1974. Abortion, The hidden plague. *New Internationalist,* May. Contains some serious errors in fact (e.g., claiming U.S. abortion deaths were as high as a quarter of a million before legalization), but also some interesting information on abortion in LDCs.

Udall, Stewart. 1968. *1976: Agenda for tomorrow.* Harcourt, Brace and World, New York. Anticipating the Bicentennial, a noted environmentalist and former Secretary of the Interior called for changed attitudes among Americans toward their environmental resources and their family sizes.

Unesco Courier. 1974. Population policy in Latin America. July/August.

United Nations. 1975. *Report of the U.N. World Population Conference, 1974.* E/Conf. 60/19, Bucharest, 19–30 August, 1974. U.N., New York.The final official report of the World Population Conference, including the World Plan of Action and 21 resolutions adopted by the delegates.

U.S. Bureau of the Census. 1974. *Population of the United States: Trends and prospects 1950–1990.* Series P-23, no. 49. A useful analysis of U.S. demographic trends.

———. 1976. Fertility history and prospects of American Women: June 1975. *Current Population Reports: Population Characteristics.* Series P-20, no. 288.

Urlanis, Boris. 1974. The hour of decision. *Unesco Courier,* July/August, pp. 26–29. The USSR's leading demographer cautiously advocates population control for rapidly growing LDCs.

Viorst, M. 1976. Population control: Pakistan tries a major new experiment. *Science,* vol. 191, pp. 52–53.

Visaria, P. 1975. Book Reviews: The myth of population control. *Population Studies* vol. 29, no. 2, pp. 323–327. A review of Mamdani, *Myth of population control.*

——— and A. K. Jain, 1976. India. *Country Profiles* (Population Council), May. A study of India with emphasis on demography and its family planning program.

Vumbaco, Brenda J. 1976. Recent law and policy changes in fertility control. *Population Reports,* Series E, no. 4.

Wadia, A. B. 1974. India's painful struggle toward the small family norm. *Bulletin of the Atomic Scientists,* June, pp. 25–28. A somewhat optimistic report by the head of India's Planned Parenthood organization.

War on Hunger. 1975. AID in an interdependent world. Special supplement, June. Information on U.S. population assistance programs.

Watson, W. B., and R. J. Lapham, eds. 1975. Family planning programs: world review 1974. *Studies in Family Planning,* vol. 6, no. 8. A useful summary.

Weiner, Myron. 1971. Political demography: An inquiry into the political consequences of population change. In Revelle, *Rapid population growth.*

Weinstock, Edward, et al. 1975. Legal abortions in the U ited States since the 1973 Supreme Court decisions. *Family Planning Perspectives,* vol. 7, no. 1.

Weisbord, Robert G. 1973. Birth control and the black American: a matter of genocide? *Demography,* vol. 10, no. 4, pp. 571–590. Good discussion of a sensitive issue.

Westoff, Charles F. 1972. The modernization of U.S. contraceptive practice. *Family Planning Perspectives,* vol. 4, no. 3, pp. 9–14. Family planning attitudes and practices in the U.S., based on 1965 National Fertility Study.

———. 1974. The populations of the developed countries. *Scientific American,* September, p. 115. Fine summary of recent demographic trends.

———. 1976. The decline of unplanned births in the United States. *Science* vol. 191, pp. 38–41. Good discussion of recent fertility trends in U.S., indicating that much of the recent reduction in fertility was due to fewer unwanted births.

———. 1976. Trends in contraceptive practice: 1965–1973. *Family Planning Perspectives,* vol. 8, no. 2, pp. 54–57. On recent contraceptive practice among Americans.

———. ed., 1973. *Toward the end of growth; population in America.* Prentice-Hall, Englewood Cliffs, N.J. Useful collection of articles on population in U.S.

——— and L. Bumpass. 1973. The revolution in birth control practices of U.S. Roman Catholics. *Science,* vol. 79, pp. 41–44.

Westoff, Leslie Aldridge. 1976. Kids with kids. *New York Times Magazine,* February 22. On the increase in illegitimate births to teenage girls.

——— and C. F. Westoff. 1971. *From now to zero: Fertility, contraception and abortion in America.* Little, Brown, Boston. Excellent, comprehensive account of demographic structure and population policies in the U.S. Includes an interesting discussion of fertility in the black po ulation and the impact of population policies on it.

Willie, Charles V. 1971. A position paper. Perspectives from the black community. *PRB Selection no. 37.* Population Reference Bureau. Discussion of the black community's views on family planning programs and the issue of genocide.

Willing, Martha Kent. 1971. *Beyond conception: our children's children.* Gambit, Boston. A woman biologist's view of the population explosion and the future.

Wood, H. Curtis, Jr. 1967. *Sex without babies.* Whitmore, Philadelphia. A complete review of voluntary sterilization.

World Health Organization. 1967. Biology of fertility control by periodic abstinence. *Technical Report, no. 360.* A study of the rhythm method.

Wortman, Judith. 1974. Female sterilization by mini-laparotomy, *Population Reports,* Series C, no. 5.

———. 1975. Female sterilization using the culdoscope. *Population Reports,* Series C, no. 6. On the vaginal approach to sterilization.

———. 1975. Vasectomy—What are the problems? *Population Reports,* Series D, no. 2.

Wortman, Sterling. 1975. Agriculture in China. *Scientific American,* June, p. 21. Contains some interesting observations on small family motivation in China.

Wray, Joe. 1974. How China is achieving the unbelievable. *People* (I.P.P.F.), vol. 1, no. 4. Another account of China's population program.

Zanetti, L. 1966. The shame of Italy. *Atlas,* August. On the abortion problem in Italy.

Zimmerman, Margot. 1976. Abortion law and practice—a status report. *Population Reports,* Series E, no. 3.

The ecological constraints on population and technological growth will inevitably lead to social and economic systems different from the ones in which we live today.

In order to survive, mankind will have to develop what might be called a steady state.

The steady state formula is so different from the philosophy of endless quantitative growth, which has so far governed Western civilization, that it may cause widespread public alarm.

—René Dubos, 1969

Mistrust of technology is an attitude that ought to be taken seriously. It has positive value in avoiding grave disasters.

—Roberto Vacca, 1974

CHAPTER 14

Changing American Institutions

Changing individual attitudes on population size in general and family size in particular is only part of the problem facing humanity today. This chapter and the next examine the need for institutional changes to meet the population-resource-environment crisis. Here we focus primarily on the institutions of the most influential country in the world. It is the United States that in the past few decades has been the leader in humanity's reckless exploitation of Earth; it was also in the United States that the resistance to that exploitation first became well organized. It seems unlikely to us that disaster can be averted without dramatic changes in the structure of many American institutions—changes that could support and consolidate gains in such areas as family size, resource conservation and environmental awareness that have already been made on the basis of transformed individual attitudes.

Many of the institutional problems discussed here also have relevance to other nations, especially other DCs that since World War II have emulated the United States in many respects. Readers in other countries, therefore, may find some of this text directly relevant, even though the focus is on the United States. In Chapter 15 we expand our outlook to examine international institutions. All these institutions must be altered—and soon—or they and society as we know it will not survive. Whether significant changes in attitudes can occur fast enough to affect humanity's destiny is an open question. In our discussion we have held to one overriding principle: today's problems cannot be solved by destroying the existing institutions; there is neither the time nor the leadership to dismantle them completely and replace them with others. Today's institutions must be bent and reshaped but not destroyed.

No one is more acutely aware than we are of the difficulties and hazards of trying to criticize and comment constructively on such broad areas as religion, education, economics, legal and political systems, and the psychology of individuals and societies. We believe, however, that in order for people to translate into effective and constructive political action what is now known about the roots of the crisis, new, far-reaching and positive programs must be undertaken *immediately.*

In this chapter and the next, we therefore depart from the realm of relatively hard data in the physical, biological, and social sciences to embark on an exploration of the many other areas of human endeavor that are critically important to a solution of our problems.[1] In doing so we are making the assumption that many reforms are essential. The dangers of making the opposite assumption are beautifully set forth in the following quotation from biologist Garrett Hardin's article, "The Tragedy of the Commons":

> It is one of the peculiarities of the warfare between reform and the status quo that it is thoughtlessly governed by a double standard. Whenever a reform measure is proposed it is often defeated when its opponents triumphantly discover a flaw in it. As Kingsley Davis has pointed out, worshippers of the status quo sometimes imply that no reform is possible without unanimous agreement, an implication contrary to historical fact. As nearly as I can make out, automatic rejection of proposed reforms is based on one of two unconscious assumptions: (i) that the status quo is perfect; or (ii) that the choice we face is between reform and no action; if the proposed reform is imperfect, we presumably should take no action at all, while we wait for a perfect proposal.
>
> But we can never do nothing. That which we have done for thousands of years is also action. It also produces evils. Once we are aware that the status quo is action, we can then compare its discoverable advantages and disadvantages with the predicted advantages and disadvantages of the proposed reform, discounting as best we can for our lack of experience. On the basis of such a comparison, we can make a rational decision which will not involve the unworkable assumption that only perfect systems are tolerable.

[1]Many of these topics are treated in greater depth in Dennis C. Pirages and Paul R. Ehrlich, *Ark II: Social response to environmental imperatives;* its footnotes and bibliographies provide further access to the pertinent literature, especially in political science.

RELIGION

Religion, broadly defined, would include all the belief systems that allow *Homo sapiens* to achieve a sense of transcendence of self and a sense of the possession of a right and proper place in the universe and a right and proper way of life. In short, everyone wants to feel important and in tune with a right-ordered world. The attempt to achieve a sense of well-being in these terms is so pervasive among human cultures that it may be counted as a necessity of human life. With religion so broadly defined, political parties, labor unions, nation states, academic disciplines, and the organized structure of the environment-ecology movement would have to be counted among our religious institutions. Certainly, representatives of all those groups have struggled to protect and propagate their views as assiduously (and sometimes as fiercely) in our time as Genghis Khan, the Christian Crusaders, or the Protestant Christian missionaries did in theirs. In this discussion, however, we limit our attention to those groups customarily called the world's great religions, the traditions of belief and practice belonging to members of the Judeo-Christian, Moslem, Buddhist, and Hindu traditions.

Religion must always be viewed in its two parts: the first and more readily evident element being the formal structure of authority and administration that in our Western tradition is called "the church;" and the second, more elusive, and in the long run more important element, the system of attitudes called, in the Western manner, "the faith." In our treatment of the two parts, we concentrate upon the relationship between organized religion and population control because that is the area where contemporary social needs and imperatives have most clearly come into conflict with cherished traditional values usually promulgated and supported by religions. Moreover, humane population control calls for the integration of contraceptive techniques into culturally accepted sexual practices, and sexual practice is the area of human activity that is typically most extensively regulated by taboo. Thus, the acceptance or rejection of birth control and various methods of carrying it out have been important issues in organized Western religion for several decades.

Our treatment of religious attitudes also focuses upon perceptions of the environment, because how an individual perceives and treats the world is determined by his or her overall view of his or her place in that world. The Christian concept of life in this world, as voiced by Saint Paul, that "here we have no abiding city," for example, conceivably could help explain why some people show rather little concern for the long-term future of the global environment or for the well-being of future generations.

Most of our attention is on the Western, Judeo-Christian religious tradition because it is primarily within that tradition that the population-resource-environment crisis has been engendered.

Organized Religious Groups and Population Control

Within the theological community in the Western world, there has recently been a heartening revolution in thought and action on such varied social concerns as the quality of life in urban areas, civil rights for minority groups, and the war in Vietnam. Since the late 1960s, environmental deterioration and the population explosion have become important concerns. Protestant, Catholic, and Jewish clergy have come more and more to the forefront of public activities in these areas, often at considerable personal sacrifice and risk.

Conspicuous among clergy who have risked their careers have been Catholic theologians who opposed the official pronatalist position of the Vatican. For example, Father John A. O'Brien, a distinguished professor of theology at Notre Dame University in Indiana, edited the excellent book *Family planning in an exploding population* in 1968. He also was a leader in criticizing Pope Paul VI's 1968 encyclical, *Humanae Vitae,* which reiterated the church's condemnation of contraceptives. Commenting on the encyclical, Father O'Brien wrote, "Since the decision is bound to be reversed by his [Pope Paul's] successor, it would be far more honorable, proper and just for the Pope to rescind it himself."[2] Ivan Illich, who renounced his priesthood after a controversy over birth control in Puerto Rico, wrote that the encyclical "lacks courage, is in bad taste, and takes the initiative away from Rome in the attempt to lead modern man in Christian humanism."[3] Thousands of others, from cardinals to lay people, have also spoken out. Since its publication, the encyclical has caused immense anguish among Catholics, millions of whom have followed their consciences and used contraceptives, often after a period of intense soul-searching.[4] Indeed, clergyman sociologist Father Andrew Greeley attributes the recent substantial erosion in religious practices and church support among American Catholics almost entirely to *Humanae Vitae.*[5]

Adamant opposition to birth control by the Roman Catholic Church and other conservative religious groups for many years helped delay the reversal in developed countries (including the United States) of laws restricting access to contraceptives and the extension of family-planning assistance to LDCs. Support of outdated dogma among Catholic spokespeople still sometimes hinders effective attacks on the population problem in Catholic countries and in international agencies that support family-planning programs. Thus, as late as 1969, elderly Catholic economist Colin Clark claimed on a television program that India would, in a decade, be the most powerful country in the world because of its growing population! He also wrote, "Population growth, however strange and unwelcome some of its consequences may appear at the time, must be regarded, I think, as one of the instruments of Divine Providence, which we should welcome, not oppose."[6]

By the mid-1970s, however, the influence of such persons was on the wane—so much so that a reaffirmation by Pope Paul of his anti-population-control dogma at the 1974 World Food Conference in Rome was greeted by almost universal ridicule. Within the church, Pope

[2] *Reader's Digest,* January 1969.

[3] *Celebration of awareness.*

[4] F. X. Murphy and J. F. Erhart, Catholic perspectives on population issues, *Population Bulletin,* vol. 30 (1975), no. 6.

[5] *Catholic schools in a declining church,* Sheed & Ward, Mission, Kans., 1976.

[6] *Los Angeles Times,* November 9, 1969.

Paul's influence seems likely to decline as older members of the hierarchy are replaced by administrators more in touch with humanity and modern times. Growing numbers of priests and other clerics in the lower ranks of the hierarchy no longer condemn the use of contraceptives—some even condone abortion under some circumstances, although the hierarchy is, if anything, even more rigidly opposed to that. A great many Catholic laymen are ahead of the Church in changing their attitudes; by the mid-1970s more than 80 percent of Catholics in the United States approved of the use of contraceptives.[7]

The new look in attitudes is typified by those of Catholic biologist John H. Thomas of Stanford University, who in 1968 wrote to San Francisco's Archbishop Joseph T. McGucken:

> The Church must affirm that the birth rate must soon be brought in line with the death rate—i.e., a growth rate of zero. This is the responsibility of all people regardless of race or religion. The Church must recognize and state that all means of birth control are licit . . . (it) must put its concern for people, their welfare, and their happiness above its concern for doctrine, dogma, and canon law . . . It is time that the Church stop being like a reluctant little child, always needing to be dragged into the present.

John Thomas was also a prime mover in promoting the *Scientists' statement against the birth-control encyclical*, which within five weeks in 1968 was signed by more than 2600 scientists.[8] He was joined by two other Catholic biologists, Dennis R. Parnell (California State University at Hayward) and Brother Lawrence Corey (St. Mary's College, Moraga, California) in mailing the statement with their endorsement to the approximately 150 Roman Catholic bishops in the United States.

Furthermore, it should not be forgotten that physician John Rock, who played a leading role in developing the contraceptive pill, is a Catholic. He also participated in the theological debate on the morality of birth control until the encyclical was issued, effectively squelching the debate.

Except for the Roman Catholic church, all major Western religious groups had by 1970 officially sanctioned "artificial" contraception, although some continued to oppose liberal abortion policies. Religious leaders of various faiths in the United States have helped overcome ancient cultural taboos related to reproduction by emphasizing the quality of human life rather than its quantity. Protestant, Catholic, and Jewish theologians, for example, have been active in promoting sex education in schools, and many Protestant and Jewish theologians and lay people have supported liberal abortion policies. Bishop C. Kilmer Myers, of the Episcopal diocese of California, for example, in the late 1960s established the Ad Hoc Metropolitan Planning Group, which has been deeply concerned with the problems of population and environment. The Social Ministry of the Lutheran Church in America promulgated a highly enlightened policy on population in the 1960s; Methodist groups were in the forefront of abortion-law reform in the United States. Thus, there is good reason to hope that organized Western religious groups may become a powerful force in working toward population control worldwide, especially as the human suffering caused by overpopulation becomes more widely recognized.

Non-Western religions. The possible roles of non-Western religious institutions in the population crisis are more problematical than that of Western religions. For example, within Islamic religion there is no organized, deep involvement in social problems, although Islamic scholars have tried to find religious justification for practicing birth control in some countries hard-pressed by exploding populations. There are at least 500 million Moslems in the world (roughly half the number of Christians), more than 95 percent of whom live in Africa and Asia, with high concentrations in such problem regions as Indonesia and the Indian subcontinent. Pakistan, by establishing a government-supported family-planning program as early as 1960, made it clear that Moslem countries can attempt to solve their population problems without religious conflict.[9] Several other Moslem countries have since established family-planning programs and/or changed their laws to permit broader access to birth control. In the foreseeable future, however, it seems unlikely that Islam itself will become a positive force for population control.

[7]Greeley, *Catholic schools.*

[8]J. J. W. Baker, Three modes of protest action.

[9]M. Viorst, Population control: Pakistan tries a major new experiment.

Much the same can be said of Buddhism, which—if those who also subscribe to Shinto, Taoism, and Confucianism are also counted as Buddhists—has perhaps 700 million adherents, most of them in Asia. The barriers to population control in Asia and the potential for accepting it both seem to be connected much more with social conditions than with religion. Therefore, it seems unlikely that changes in the religion would have any substantial effect on establishment of population policy, although religious support for small families might encourage acceptance of family planning.

Similarly, it is hard to picture Hinduism, as an entity, becoming a force in population control. More than 99 percent of the 450 million or so Hindus live in Asia, mostly in India. Like Buddhism, it is a rather heterogeneous, relatively noninstitutionalized religion. There is still considerable opposition to population control among Hindus, perhaps based more on medical beliefs, local superstitions, and a sense of fatalism than on anything inherent in the religious structure.

For Westerners who favor population control, one of the best courses of action seems to lie in working with the already established religious groups to change people's attitudes toward population growth. In the rest of the world, the relative fragmentation of religious groups, their lack of hierarchic organization, and their psychosocial traditions would seem to limit their capacity to influence population control efforts.

Religious Attitudes and the Environment

In the United States, the unorthodox but constructive and quasi-religious attitudes first expressed widely in the 1960s by members of the whole-Earth, hippie movement may well help save the environment. The initial phase of the hippie movement was characterized by a groping and testing that produced, among other things, the dangerous macrobiotic diet and the horror of the Manson family. Aside from such excesses, however, the hippies borrowed many religious ideas from the East, particularly Zen Buddhism, combined them with the collectivist, passivist element from Christian tradition, and attempted to forge a code based on close personal relationships, spiritual values, a reverence for life, group self-reliance, and an abhorrence of violence. By the mid-1970s this code had become well established in a more mature and praiseworthy form that might be called the independence movement. People in that movement are attempting to find simpler, more ecologically sound modes of existence, and to reduce their dependence on fancy, nonessential, and vulnerable technological gimmickry. Their unofficial publications such as *Mother Earth News* and *CoEvolution Quarterly* abound with suggestions for disconnecting oneself from the "effluent society." If any one idea binds members of the movement together, it is the belief—essentially religious—that human beings must cooperate with nature and not attempt to subdue nature with brute force.

Many people in our society are unhappy with these attitudes, which go against long-cherished and religiously sanctioned political and economic beliefs. They feel that turning away from a consumer orientation has grave implications for the future of the economy. Others see in the independence movement the vanguard of a new social revolution that could lead to a very different, far better society.

Lynn White, Jr., professor emeritus of history at the University of California, Los Angeles, and past president of the American Historical Association, has suggested that the basic cause of Western society's destructive attitude toward nature lies in the Judeo-Christian tradition. He pointed out, for instance, that before the Christian era, people believed trees, springs, hills, streams, and other objects of nature had guardian spirits. Those spirits had to be approached and placated before one could safely invade their territories: "By destroying pagan animism, Christianity made it possible to exploit nature in a mood of indifference to the feelings of natural objects."[10] Christianity fostered the basic ideas of "progress" and of time as something linear, nonseparating, and absolute, flowing from a fixed point in the past to an end point in the future. Such ideas were foreign to the Greeks and Romans, who had a cyclical concept of time and did not envision the world as having a beginning. Although a modern physicist's concept of time might be somewhat closer to that of the Greeks than to that of the

[10]The historical roots of our ecological crisis.

Christians, the Christian view is nevertheless the prevalent one in the Western world: God designed and started the universe for the benefit of mankind; the world is our oyster, made for human society to dominate and exploit. Western science and technology thus can be seen to have their historical roots in the Christian dogma of humanity's separation from and rightful mastery over nature.

Europeans held and developed those attitudes long before the opportunity to exploit the Western hemisphere arrived. The frontier or cowboy economy that has characterized the United States seems to be a natural extension of that Christian world view. Therefore, White claimed, it may be in vain that so many look to science and technology to solve our present ecological crisis:

> Both our present science and our present technology are so tinctured with orthodox Christian arrogance toward nature that no solution for our ecologic crises can be expected from them alone. Since the roots of our trouble are so largely religious, the remedy must also be essentially religious, whether we call it that or not.

A number of anthropologists and others have taken issue with White's thesis, pointing out that environmental abuse is by no means unique to Western culture, and that animism had disappeared, at least in western Europe, before Christianity was introduced. As examples they cite evidence of ancient and prehistoric environmental destruction, such as the human-induced extinction of Pleistocene mammals and the destruction of the fertility of the Near East by early agricultural activity, as well as the behavior of non-Western cultures today.

Geographer Yi-Fu Tuan of the University of Minnesota observed that there is often a large gap between attitudes toward the environment expressed in a religion or philosophy and the actual practices of the people who profess those attitudes.[11] While Chinese religions, for example, stressed the view that man was a part of nature (rather than lord of it) and should live in harmony with it, the Chinese did not always live by that belief. Concern for the environment, especially preserving forests and protecting soils, were expressed throughout Chinese history, but Yi-Fu Tuan suggests that this may often have been in response to destruction that had already taken place. The fact that China was a complex civilization complete with a bureaucracy and a large population doubtless militated against fulfillment of those ideals. By the twentieth century, China's once-plentiful forests had been nearly destroyed to build cities and clear land for agriculture. All that remained in most areas were small patches preserved around temples. Ironically, the present government, which explicitly rejects the traditional religions, has attempted to restore the forests on a large scale.[12]

Lewis W. Moncrief of North Carolina State University, who might be described as an environmental anthropologist, feels that the religious tradition of the West is only one of several factors that have contributed to the environmental crisis.[13] Along with some other anthropologists, he has suggested that an urge to improve one's status in society is probably a universal human characteristic and that expressing this urge through material acquisitiveness and consumption of resources is, if not universal, at least common to a great variety of cultures. Perhaps what is unique about Western culture in this regard is the degree of its success.

Moncrief postulated several factors that he felt were just as influential as the Judeo-Christian outlook in determining European and North American behavior toward the environment. The first were the development of democracy and the Industrial Revolution, which together provided individual control over resources (if only a family farm) for a far greater proportion of the population than before and simultaneously provided the means to exploit those resources more efficiently. The existence of a vast frontier fostered the belief in North America that resources were infinite; all of our wasteful habits derive from that. Moncrief thinks it is no accident that the first conservation movement appeared just as the frontier was closing; Americans suddenly and for the first time began to realize that their resources were, after all, finite.

In 1893, moved by a remark from the 1890 census

[11]Our treatment of the environment in ideal and actuality.

[12]For an overview of present Chinese attitudes, see L. A. Orleans and R. P. Suttmeier, the mass ethic and environmental quality, *Science,* vol. 170, pp. 1173–1176 (December 11, 1970); a related account of Japanese attitudes toward the environment is Masao Watanabe, The conception of nature in Japanese culture.

[13]The cultural basis for our environmental crisis.

about the disappearance of public land and the consequent disappearance of the frontier, Frederick Jackson Turner, then at the University of Wisconsin and subsequently at Harvard, observed:

> American social development has been continually beginning over again on the frontier. This perennial rebirth, this fluidity of American life, this expansion westward with its new opportunities . . . furnish the forces dominating American character.[14]

A generation earlier, E. L. Godkin, editor of the *Nation*, had written that the American frontier population had "spread itself thinly over a vast area of soil, of such extraordinary fertility that a very slight amount of toil expended on it affords returns that might have satisfied even the dreams of Spanish avarice."[15]

Traditional North American (and, to some extent, European) attitudes toward the environment thus are not exclusively products of our religious heritage, although that doubtless played an important part. These attitudes may just spring from ordinary human nature, which in Western culture was provided with extraordinary social, political, technical, and physical opportunities, particularly connected with the nineteenth-century American frontier. Such opportunities were bound to engender optimism, confidence in the future, and faith in the abundance of resources and the bounty of nature. That they also produced habits of wastefulness and profligacy was not noticed. Past institutions in the United States rarely dealt with environmental problems; if they were recognized at all, they were usually considered to be someone else's responsibility.

In the twentieth century, as the growing population became increasingly urban and industrialized, the environmental effects multiplied, and the nation was rather suddenly confronted with a crisis. How today's Americans ultimately resolve the environmental crisis will depend on much more than changes in philosophical outlook, but such changes unquestionably must precede or at least accompany whatever measures are taken. Individual conduct is clearly capable of being modified and directed by an appropriate social environment—the change in reproductive habits in the United States testifies to that, as does the great increase in environmental consciousness. Unfortunately, the environmental problem may prove more difficult because it requires changing more than the attitudes and behavior of individuals: those of firmly established, powerful institutions—primarily business and governmental organizations—must also be changed.

How large a role organized religion may play in guiding the needed changes in individual attitudes toward the environment or in influencing the behavior of other institutions is still uncertain. Many religious groups have already shown leadership, including some already mentioned in connection with population-related issues. A particularly hopeful sign was the concern expressed in January 1976 by the National Council of Churches about the ethics of using and spreading the technology of nuclear power, and the discussion promoted by the World Council of Churches on the nuclear issue and on the relation of energy policy to the prospects for a "just and sustainable" world.[16]

Ecological Ethics

Many persons believe that an entirely new philosophy must now be developed—one based on ecological realities. Such a philosophy—and the ethics based upon it—would be antihumanist and against Judeo-Christian tradition in the sense that it would not focus on an anthropocentric universe.[17] Instead, it would focus on human beings as an integral part of nature, as just one part of a much more comprehensive system.

This is not really a new perspective. In one sense, Western philosophy has been a continuous attempt to establish the position of *Homo sapiens* in the universe, and the extreme anthropocentrism of thinkers like Karl Marx and John Dewey has been strongly attacked by, among others, Bertrand Russell.[18] Russell, for example,

[14]The significance of the frontier in American history, in *The early writings of Frederick Jackson Turner,* ed. F. J. Turner.

[15]Aristocratic opinions of democracy.

[16]See The plutonium economy: A statement of concern, *Bulletin of the Atomic Scientists,* January 1976, pp. 48–49; P. M. Boffey, Plutonium: its morality questioned by National Council of Churches, *Science,* vol. 192, pp. 356–359 (April 23, 1976); Paul Abrecht, ed., Facing up to nuclear power, *Anticipation,* no. 21, October 1975, pp. 1–47.

[17]See Frank E. Egler, *The way of science: A philosophy of ecology for the layman;* and George S. Sessions, Anthropocentrism and the environmental crisis. The latter is a good, brief summary with a useful bibliography.

[18]*A history of Western philosophy;* the debate is summarized in Sessions, Anthropocentrism.

pointed out Marx's philosophical closeness to classical Judeo-Christian thought:

> His purview is confined to this planet, and, within this planet, to Man. Since Copernicus, it has been evident that Man has not the cosmic importance which he formerly arrogated to himself . . . There goes with this limitation to terrestrial affairs a readiness to believe in progress as a universal law . . . Marx professed himself an atheist, but retained a cosmic optimism which only theism could justify.[19]

The concern of ecological ethics is not primarily that of considering the human position in the cosmos, but rather of considering the roles played by human beings in the ecosphere. It takes a view diametrically opposed to the position expressed by Aristotle 2300 years ago: "Now if Nature makes nothing incomplete, and nothing in vain, the inference must be that she has made all animals for the sake of man."[20]

From the standpoint of ecological ethics, the world is thus seen to be not humanity's oyster but a complex system that supports us, of which we are a part, and toward which we have moral responsibilities. Ethical theorist Joseph Margolis has written:

> But it may well be that the ethical visions of the future—assuming the earth has a future—will be discarded as beneath debate if they do not include, centrally, an account of the ethics of the human use of the inanimate and non-human world. Such a discipline . . . might be called moral ecology. . . .[21]

Whether or not such a philosophy is incorporated into religious dogma is immaterial. What counts is that something like it has influenced many Americans and Europeans already, and may come to be accepted in other places as well. (In some cultures, of course—some native American world views and some aspects of Hinduism come to mind—the idea of humanity as a part of nature has always predominated.) The sooner an ethic based on respect for the natural world can be adopted, the better. The beneficiaries will be not only ourselves but our children and grandchildren.

[19]Quoted in Sessions (ibid).
[20]*Politics* 1, 88.
[21]Joseph Margolis, *Values and conduct,* p. 212.

The Conservation Movement

The fascination and profound emotions—essentially religious feelings—aroused in many people by wilderness areas, wildlife, and beautiful natural scenery are not easily explained to those who do not share them. Disparate beliefs and attitudes are obvious every time conservationists find themselves defending aesthetic values against people who are equally dedicated to "progress." This divergence of views was elegantly summarized by the brilliant French anthropologist Claude Levi-Strauss, who noted that any species of bug that people spray with pesticides is "an irreplaceable marvel, equal to the works of art which we religiously preserve in museums."[22]

For many years now, people in the conservation movement have fought individually and in groups to halt the extinction of animal species and the destruction of the last vestiges of the primitive areas of Earth. Some of the campaigns conducted by such organizations as the Sierra Club, the Audubon Society, the Defenders of Wildlife, the Wilderness Society, and the Nature Conservancy in the United States, and by the World Wildlife Fund and similar organizations in other countries,[22a] have been successful. It is becoming clear, however, that in the long run the conservation movement as a whole has been fighting a losing battle.

Perhaps the most obvious reason the battle is being lost is that conservation is a one-way street: each organism or place conserved essentially remains in perpetual jeopardy. Each gain is temporary, but every loss is permanent. Species cannot be resurrected; places cannot be restored to their primitive state. Consequently, even if the conservationists were evenly matched against the destroyers, the battle would probably remain a losing one. But, of course, the battle has been far from even. Powerful economic interests and government agencies, pushed by population pressures, have promoted the development of every possible inch of the United States by building dams in desert canyons, driving roads through the remaining wilderness areas, cutting the last

[22]Discussion of the Special Commission on Internal Pollution, London, October 1975.
[22a]For an interesting history of the parallel (but quite different) growth of the conservation movement in the U.K., see Max Nicholson, The ecological breakthrough.

of the primeval forests, drilling for oil on the northern slope of Alaska, and so on. It is a tribute to the conservationists, past and present, that any of our primitive areas remain relatively unspoiled. Political and financial power tend to be arrayed against conservation, and, as people increase and resources dwindle, the situation seems bound to deteriorate further. In many parts of the world the situation is worse than in the United States; in a few it is better.

There are encouraging signs that a new thrust is appearing in the conservation movement. Growing numbers of people have realized that conservation is a global problem, that in the long run it is not enough to preserve such isolated treasures as a grove of redwood trees. If global pollution causes a rapid climatic change, the grove cannot long survive. Many conservationists now recognize that if the growth of the human population is not stopped, and the deterioration of the planetary environment is not arrested, *nothing* of value will be conserved.

This understanding and the growing general public awareness of the problems of the environment have given rise to a number of new organizations. Some of them, like Friends of the Earth (FOE), are more militant offshoots of older conservation groups. Others, including Environmental Action (which grew from the organization that sponsored the first Earth Day in 1970) and Ecology Action, are new. Zero Population Growth (ZPG) is primarily concerned with the population problem but is also interested in the environmental consequences of it. ZPG, one branch of the Sierra Club, Environmental Action, and FOE have foregone the tax advantages of an apolitical posture in order to campaign and lobby for their goals, frequently combining their efforts on issues of common concern. They also cooperate in environmentalist lawsuits (see "The Legal System," below) through organizations such as The Environmental Defense Fund (EDF) and the Natural Resources Defense Council (NRDC). Such organizations generally differ from many of the older conservation groups in being more oriented to humanity as an endangered species than to preserving wilderness and wildlife only for their aesthetic and recreational values. Sister organizations of FOE, as well as ZPG, have been established in other countries.

In Europe, Australia, and New Zealand, the environmental movement has established its own political parties, known in Britain as the Ecology Party, in France as Ecologie et Survie, in New Zealand as the Values Party, etc. These parties have succeeded in winning seats in Britain's Parliament and gaining significant percentages of the vote in several countries.[22b] In March 1977, the ecology party in France won a nationwide average of 10 percent of the vote in municipal elections. In some towns in Alsace (where the party originated) they won 60 percent.[22c]

It seems likely that conservationist and environmental organizations will become still more militant and more united—especially in their global concerns. While important local battles must continue to be fought, more general programs of public education and political action should become predominant. Obviously, it is no longer necessary to plead for conservation only on aesthetic or compassionate grounds, since the preservation of the diversity of life and the integrity of the ecological systems of Earth is absolutely essential for the survival of civilization.

SCIENCE AND TECHNOLOGY

For many people, science and technology have taken on the aspect of a religion. How often one hears statements beginning, "any society that can send a man to the moon can. . . ." and ending with some problem—usually immensely more complex and difficult than space travel—that science and technology are expected to solve![23] The population-food imbalance is a common candidate; others are various types of pollution or other ecological problems.

Three things are generally wrong with these statements of faith. First, science and technology have not yet reached the point relative to those problems that they had reached relative to the man-on-the-moon project by

[22b]Edward Goldsmith, Ecology—the new political force.

[22c]Ecologists emerge as a potent force in French election, *New York Times*, March 20, 1977.

[23]One book on the human predicament written from this point of view (but in which the science is often very weak) is John Maddox's *The doomsday syndrome.* See the retrospective review written three years later by John Woodcock, Doomsday revisited.

1955. The general outlines of a solution are not clear to all competent scientists in the pertinent disciplines. Second, and equally important, there is no sign of a societal commitment to a crash program to solve those nonspace problems. Third, any solutions to those problems would spell significant changes in the ways of life of millions of people, which the space program did not.

The public, indeed, has developed a touching but misplaced faith in the ability of science and technology to pull humanity's chestnuts out of the fire. There is not the slightest question that with clever and cautious use of scientific and technological resources, a great deal of good could be accomplished. But can the required amount of cleverness and caution be found? Despite enormous scientific advances during the past thirty years, it is perfectly clear that the *absolute amount* of human misery has increased (because of the enormous growth in the numbers of poverty-stricken human beings), while the chances that civilization will persist have decreased. There has been an abundance of science and technology, but they have been unbalanced and out of control.

Priorities and Planning

It has been estimated that more than 400,000 scientists and engineers—about half the technical community of the world—are working on weapons of war. Each year, military research and development worldwide cost about $25 billion, some 4 times what is spent on medical research (and perhaps 1000 times that spent on ecological research).[24] Medicine and public-health measures have attacked the death rate with vigor but for a long time ignored the birth rate, in the process threatening humanity with unprecedented catastrophe. Physics has produced nuclear and thermonuclear weapons, a legacy so weighty on the minus side of the balance that it is difficult to think of any serious pluses with which to counter it. Biology has provided weapons for biological warfare and has seen many millions of dollars poured into molecular genetics, a field offering little immediate improvement in human welfare but possessing great potential for curing or preventing inborn defects or for curing cancer, and the like. The greatest contribution of molecular genetics to human welfare has been the Ames test (Chapter 10), which, ironically, will help protect humanity from the "triumphs" of organic chemistry! Meanwhile, support for environmental studies has been relatively insignificant, despite repeated warnings by ecologists for more than a quarter of a century that human action was threatening to destroy the life-support systems of the planet. The behavioral sciences—still in their infancy—have also languished despite their potential value in helping to solve human problems.

Most of the great "advances" in technology, from DDT and X-rays to automobiles and jet aircraft, have caused serious problems for humanity. Some of those problems would have been difficult to anticipate (Box 14-1), but most were foreseen, were warned against, and could have been avoided or ameliorated with sensible societal planning. The question now is, how can such planning be done in the future so as to minimize the unfortunate consequences of technological "advances" made thus far—to say nothing of those yet to come?

It is clear from the records of organizations such as the American Medical Association and the AEC (now the Nuclear Regulatory Commission, NRC), and from statements by technological optimists and scientific politicians that scientists (like other groups in our population) cannot be relied upon to police themselves. Some way must be found to foster greater participation by other segments of society in the major decison-making processes affecting science and technology. This is essential, of course, to the survival of society, but it is also important as protection for scientists themselves. Burdens of guilt, like those borne by the physicists involved in developing atomic weapons, must be avoided wherever possible, or at least more broadly shared.

Controls

We are not in a position here to propose a detailed structure for controlling science and technology, but we can suggest some general directions. Government agencies such as the National Science Foundation and

[24]See Stockholm International Peace Research Institute, Why arms control fails. Of course, the causes of the lack of balance and control are complex, and we do not have space to discuss them here. For an introduction to the subject, see Robin Roy, Myths about technological change, *New Scientist,* May 6, 1976, pp. 281–282.

BOX 14-1 Risks, Benefits, and New Technologies

As previously indicated, it is common for unforeseen difficulties to arise with new technologies, and the more grandiose the technological enterprise, the greater the problems seem to be. Supertankers provide a classic example of the difficulties encountered in scaling up an already hazardous technology.* Oil tankers have always been prone to accident, but the frequency (and environmental consequences) of accidents have escalated dramatically as their size has increased. In 1945 the largest oil tankers were 18,000 deadweight tons (dwt). In the early 1960s the maximum size had risen to 100,000 dwt and by the end of that decade had exceeded 300,000 dwt. In the 1970s planners were looking forward to constructing tankers in the megaton range.

Both the stresses imposed upon the structures of the larger ships and their different handling characteristics were unanticipated. Supertankers sometimes crack when being loaded and show a distressing tendency to disintegrate spontaneously at sea. The huge cleaning machines used to wash out their tanks after unloading apparently create minithunderstorms in the cavernous spaces. These thunderstorms even produce lightning, which can detonate oil fumes if the fume-air mixture is neither too rich nor too lean, blowing the tank or the ship apart.

The hydrodynamic properties of the huge ships are such that they must begin "putting on the brakes" three miles before reaching a full stop. They are difficult to maneuver and their captains require special training. Yet because of their great draft they are often operated in waters where their keels extend to within two feet of the charted bottom. This is a dangerous practice both because hydrodynamic factors reduce maneuverability in shallow water and because in some areas the depth of the bottom is continuously changing. These factors, among others, have led to a rash of collisions and groundings, often with disastrous results. For example, in 1970 the relatively small supertanker *Polycommander* ran aground near the Spanish coast and ignited. Some 16,000 tons of oil burned, generating a fire storm whose updrafts carried oil high into the atmosphere and created a black rain along the coast, doing extensive damage to crops, livestock, homes, and gardens.

Some of the difficulties with supertankers can be blamed on dangerous economies undertaken by the owners. Ships can be designed that are stronger, more maneuverable, and more resistant to explosion than most of those now in service. And personnel on many ships could be much better trained; many officers running ships registered under flags of convenience such as Panama and Liberia are not properly certified, and some have proven hopelessly incompetent. There is little doubt, either, that the Intergovernmental Maritime Consultative Organization (IMCO), a specialized United Nations agency, has proven ineffective as a regulatory body.

But the familiar saga of profits-before-safety-or-environment, so characteristic of the energy industry, is not the whole story. The unanticipated characteristics of the big ships threaten both safety and profits, since the disaster rate has pushed insurance premiums toward uneconomic levels. What will happen as these ships age (they were designed to be written off after ten years) remains to be seen. The prospects are not cheering.

One does not, however, have to turn to such exotica as the supertankers to see the impact of the unexpected in new technologies. The heavily regulated safety-oriented aviation industry provides more than enough examples. A classic was the series of fatal crashes of De Havilland Comet jets, caused by unanticipated fatigue failures of the cabin under pressurization, that lost the United Kingdom its lead in the race to develop passenger jet aircraft. The success of the United States industry (and its fine safety record) was due in no small degree to the Boeing 707, which, unlike the Comet, was not a novel design but had behind it a long operating history with military jet tankers of similar size and configuration.

Design flaws have often led to one or more fatal crashes of new transport aircraft. Gas leaking into heating systems during transfer from one tank to another destroyed a Douglas DC-6 with the loss of fifty-two people, and it nearly destroyed another before the problem was identified and corrected. Unexpected stresses transmitted from propeller to wing caused the disintegration in midair of two Lockheed Electra propjets.** After correction of the problem, the aircraft had a fine safety record in civil and

*The discussion of tankers is based on N. Mostert's fascinating *Supership* and D. F. Boesch et al., *Oil spills and the marine environment*, Ballinger, Cambridge, Mass., 1974.

**Stephen Barlay, *The search for air safety*. The following material on T-tail jets is largely from this source also. For a balanced, readable account of aviation accidents in the prejet age, see Robert J. Serling, *The probable cause*.

(*Continued*)

military service. More recently, insufficient strength in the cabin floor, which buckled during decompression after an improperly secured baggage door opened, led to the fatal crash of one of the new wide-bodied jet airbuses, and the near-crash of another. The buckling of the floor rendered control cables running beneath it inoperable.

As with the supertankers, the human factor often enters into disasters associated with new aviation technology. The introduction of T-tailed short-haul jets such as the Boeing 727, the Douglas DC-9, the BAC 111, and the Hawker-Siddeley Trident brought into service aircraft with high sink rates, designed for short-field operations. A series of Boeing 727 accidents at first caused doubts about its fundamental airworthiness, but careful analysis of the accidents and the aircraft's subsequent excellent record for safe operation indicated that some pilots just were not able to make the transition to handling the new jets. It was also discovered that some design characteristics of 727s, such as weakness in the fuel lines that run under the floor, had increased the lethality of "survivable" crashes. New training standards and structural modifications helped solve the problems.

Similarly, the safety record of the highly regulated nuclear power industry shows clearly how the unexpected must be expected when dealing with novel technologies. Although no vast disasters have yet occurred in the use of fission reactors to generate power, there has been an enormous number of minor accidents and near-misses—many arising from totally unanticipated sources. Workers make improper welds, inspectors set fires while using candles to detect air leaks, cooling systems fail to perform as they are supposed to, and parts added to increase safety tear loose to cause accidents that endanger the lives of hundreds of thousands of people. (For a more extensive discussion, see Chapter 8.)

Experience with complex technologies, including those in the extremely safety-conscious aviation and nuclear power industries, gives a message loud and clear. The application of top engineering experience, the use of redundant systems, limiting operations to highly trained professionals, and strict government regulation are not enough to prevent accidents. No "fault tree" analysis can foresee all possible branches of the tree, all the conceivable "common-mode" failures. No regulatory body can ride herd on every operator day and night, discover his or her mental quirks, monitor his or her levels of boredom, stress, dissatisfaction, physical and mental health—all of which are factors in determining how safe the operator's performance will be.

We must face it—unsinkable Titanics sink, earthquake-proof overpasses guaranteed to Force 8 on the Richter scale collapse in earthquakes orders of magnitude less severe; foolproof rapid-transit control computers get fooled; and cable-car cables that engineers say don't snap, do snap.† Perfect safety is a myth. Therefore, when any massive new technology is introduced, its presumed benefits must be weighed against possible risks. And, when the risks are evaluated, they can never be presumed zero.

When looking at risks, many complex factors other than scale must be considered:

1. Concentrated versus distributed deaths and injuries. It appears, for instance, that roughly 50,000 distributed deaths on U.S. highways is a risk acceptable to the public. But 50,000 deaths annually concentrated in a single nuclear power plant accident seemingly would not be. Other factors, such as perceived availability of alternatives and degree of personal control, may well enter here also.
2. Immediate toxicity versus long-term toxicity. How does society balance 100 deaths from acute poisoning against the induction of 500 cancers that will kill twenty years later, or 5000 birth defects in future generations?
3. Direct effects versus indirect effects. How, for example, should society evaluate the impact of pollution of a river by an industrial plant on the water supply of a town downstream compared to its effect on the food supply of that town through reduction of the fisheries productivity of the sea?
4. Irreversibility. How much should the reversibility of events be weighed in a risk-benefit analysis? Many forms of air pollution are reversible; if injection of material into the atmosphere were stopped, the atmosphere would soon cleanse itself. Some other pollutants are readily degraded

†Engineer Arturo Tanesini, commenting on a cable car accident in Italy that killed forty-two people after a supporting cable snapped, said, "supporting cables just don't snap," Honolulu *Advertiser*, March 11, 1976.

by ecological systems. On the other hand, strip mining often permanently destroys the land, many pollutants are extremely slow to degrade, and the toxic effects of a nuclear power plant accident could persist for half a million years.

5. Uncertainty. How does one evaluate the unknowns?

We do not pretend to have answers to these complex questions, of course, especially when both benefits and risks tend to be hard to identify, let alone quantify early in the development of a technology. We do suggest, however, that the tendency to develop and deploy technologies helter-skelter with little or no public airing—at least until capital and other commitments are such that the economics of an industry become a part of the issue—should be controlled somehow. In particular, the benefits should be most carefully considered, since in certain situations the maximum benefits may be rather clear while the maximum risks may be utterly unanticipated. A good example is the use of aerosol cans with fluorocarbon propellants to spray underarm deodorants. The risks of inhaling a fine mist of deodorant are not clear (but in our opinion it is not a good idea to inhale regularly a fine mist of anything except, perhaps, water), and the risks to the ozone layer are, at this writing, in some dispute. But it seems unlikely that the benefits of this sort of deodorant application (in comparison to many others) would be considered by a normal person to be worth *any* risk to life or health or to the integrity of Earth's ecological systems.[††]

[††]The whole question of the evaluation of hazards is considered in an important book by W. W. Lowrance, *Of acceptable risk: Science and the determination of safety* (Kaufmann, Los Altos, Calif., 1976.)

National Institutes of Health regularly employ ad hoc committees and panels of scientists to evaluate research programs and individual research projects. Universities also on occasion use such groups to evaluate programs or departments. Ad hoc panels of nonscientists might be integrated into these systems, drawn perhaps from citizens serving their sabbaticals (see "Education" below). Such panels could both advise agencies directly and report to a paragovernmental central body (perhaps elected), empowered to intervene whenever it was felt that the public interest was endangered. This power would extend to research under *any* auspices—government, military, university, or industry. The central body could also be charged with continually informing both government and the public of pertinent trends in science and technology.

Increased awareness and scrutiny of science and technology will not, in themselves, suffice. Although laymen can become very knowledgeable about science and technology, as the performances of several congressmen involved in appropriations for scientific and technical projects have demonstrated, it is often very difficult or impossible for individuals, whether scientists or not, to foresee the consequences of certain trends. A second element is therefore required in the control system: an apparatus—possibly in the form of research institutes—concerned solely with such assessment and reporting to the central body suggested above, as well as to the general public. Perhaps a set percentage of all funds used in government, university, and industrial research should be assessed for the support of those organizations, which should be kept strictly independent of each of those three interests.

Some of the work that might be done by such institutes would be an extension of the sort of programs now being run by systems ecologist K. E. F. Watt's group at the University of California at Davis, by systems analysts Jay W. Forrester of the Massachusetts Institute of Technology, and Dennis and Donella Meadows of Dartmouth. Watt has forecast the dismal consequences of continuing various prevailing strategies of resource management and social policies. The Meadows, Forrester, and their colleagues have shown most convincingly that many of the various proposed courses of action may have unexpected—and often very undesirable—results. The studies of this group were made familiar to the world by the publication of *Limits to Growth*[25] (see Box 12-2).

In addition to such broad-scope evaluations as those,

[25]Potomac Associates, Washington, D.C., 1972.

some research institutes need to be investigating and reporting on much more detailed questions. For example, is medical research being done with adequate attention to the needs of all segments of the population and to birth control as well as death control? Are the benefits and risks of the breeder reactor being studied in proper depth? What are the possible dangerous consequences of further investigating the properties of a given virus or biocidal compound?

These questions have been settled largely by the scientific community in the past, with results that can most charitably be described as mixed.[26] For a long time the thrust in research was that whatever could be tried should be tried. Physicists exploded the first atomic bomb after Germany had been defeated and Japan's defeat was a certainty, *although some of them apparently thought at the time there was a nonzero chance that the explosion would destroy all life on Earth.*[27] It is difficult to find parallels, outside nuclear weaponry, displaying quite this degree of willingness to risk total environmental disaster, but traces of it arguably are present in proposals to "wait and see" what the consequences of assaulting the ozone layer with fluorocarbons or SST fleets will be.

On the bright side, microbiologists Paul Berg and Stanley Cohen of Stanford and Herbert Boyer of the University of California in mid-1974 called on their colleagues to bring to a halt research on recombinant DNA, studies involving transfers of genetic material from one species to another.[28] They recognized that hybrid microorganisms could cause extraordinarily virulent infectious disease and that the experimental work could conceivably lead to the spread of resistance to antibiotics or to the escape of bacterial strains carrying oncogenic (cancer-inducing) viruses. A distinguished molecular biologist, Robert Sinsheimer, has written:

> Could an *Escherichia coli* strain [a variety of a ubiquitous bacterial resident on the human digestive tract] carrying all or part of an oncogenic virus become resistant in the human intestine? Could it thereby become a possible source of malignancy? Could such a strain spread throughout a human population? What would be the consequence if even an insulin-secreting strain became an intestinal resident? Not to mention the more malign or just plain stupid scenarios such as those which depict the insertion of the gene for botulinus toxin into *Escherichia coli*?[29]

In early 1975 an international scientific meeting established a set of safety principles under which such research could be continued. The scientists at the meeting concluded that the more dangerous experiments should be deferred until special "crippled" strains of organisms could be developed—that is, strains with a very low probability of surviving outside the laboratory (experience has shown that there is no such thing as an "escape-proof" microbiological laboratory). Some of the scientists, however, argued against social control of the experiments, claiming an absolute right to free inquiry. Since that meeting, various attempts have been made to draft rules that would permit doing this dangerous research, and there has been continuing controversy.[30]

In these cases, scientists themselves have assessed the risks and then "voted" for all of humanity. With regard to the atomic bomb, the possible savings in American (and Japanese) lives by shortening World War II may have come into the calculus, and perhaps also the thought that sooner or later someone else would blow up an A-bomb without knowing *for sure* that it would not destroy the planet. But would the people of the planet (to say nothing of the other living organisms) have voted yes to taking, say, a one-in-a-million chance on oblivion in order to speed victory for the United States in World War II? (That the chances of killing all life on the planet turned out to be zero is beside the point—the scientists involved were not sure of that at the time.)

[26]See, for example, the contrasting views of F. J. Dyson, The hidden cost of saying "no!"; and P. R. Ehrlich, The benefits of saying "yes."

[27]N. P. Davis, *Lawrence and Oppenheimer.* There is no doubt, in light of present knowledge of nuclear reactions, that the chance of igniting the atmosphere with a nuclear bomb and thereby extinguishing all life on Earth is truly zero. A completely persuasive case on the point is made by H. A. Bethe, Ultimate catastrophe? *Bulletin of the Atomic Scientist,* June 1976, pp. 36–37. Bethe's further contention, however, that the scientists on the nuclear bomb project were completely sure of this in 1945, is not persuasive.

[28]P. Berg, et al., Potential biohazards of recombinant DNA molecules.

[29]Troubled dawn for genetic engineering. The article also contains a good, brief, layperson's introduction to the technology of DNA manipulation.

[30]Sinsheimer, Troubled dawn; Nicholas Wade, Recombinant DNA: NIH Group Stirs storm by drafting laxer rules; Bernard Dixon, Recombinant DNA: Rules without enforcement?

Similarly, in the case of recombinant DNA, although scientists seem to be acting much more responsibly, we must still ask whether they are the appropriate ones to make the decision. No laboratory safeguards can guarantee that an accidental escape will never occur. Are the possible benefits to medicine and agriculture of this research worth any risk of releasing a serious plague or cancer-inducing organism? We do not know the answer, but we think the franchise on the decision should be extended to include at least representatives of those who will be taking the risks and (perhaps) receiving the benefits.

The Science Court

One danger in allowing scientists to decide an issue for society is that often the specialists in a field disagree violently on the proper course of action for society to take, even though they may have no serious disagreement on the known salient facts. For example, qualified scientists have been assembled on both sides of issues such as whether to develop the SST, ban the use of pesticides and aerosols, or develop nuclear power, to name a few. As Stephen Schneider and Lynne Mesirow observed regarding the SST battle:

> An interesting point here is that most of the bitter scientific antagonists in the SST debate were probably in far greater agreement on what was known and unknown scientifically, and on the odds that state-of-the-art estimates would be correct, than they were over whether the evidence justified opposition to the planes. That is, the interpretation of the weight of the evidence that guided their opposition or support was based not only on the scientists' technical knowledge of the issues, but also on their *personal* philosophies—on whether or not they wanted the SSTs and on whether they thought the benefits of the project were worth the risks of ignoring the worst possibilities. This is not to suggest that most testimony was deliberately misleading, but rather that scientists, like most people, shade to some extent their perception of the merits of conflicting evidence with the shadow of their personal philosophy . . . . The issues facing future generations are too critical to permit the technical components to be obscured in attacks on the personal philosophies of experts. . . .[31]

As they pointed out, some mechanism is needed so the public and decision-makers can separate the technical opinions of scientists from their political opinions.

One suggestion for opening up the process of ethical decision-making in science has been put forward by physicist Arthur Kantrowitz.[32] He proposed that in science policy disputes (such as those over SSTs and ozone, DDT and ecosystems, the risks and benefits of recombinant DNA research) the technical aspects of the cases be, in essence, tried in a scientific court. The first step would be to separate the scientific from the moral and political questions. What *might* be done with genetic engineering technology is a disputable scientific question, in principle soluble by experiment; what *should* be done is a political-moral question not in principle amenable to experimental solution.

Once the separation had been accomplished, then advocates of the different scientific points of view would "try" them before scientific judges. Thus, scientists convinced that DDT posed a serious threat to ecosystems could present their case, and the scientific advocates of the ecosystemic safety of DDT could present theirs. Each side could cross-examine the other. The judges would be selected for their neutrality on the issue, but would have the benefit of scientific training to help them evaluate the opposing views. The final step would be publication (within the limits of national security) of the opinions of the scientific judges.

It is easy for anyone familiar with scientific disputes to attack these proposals. In some cases the separation of scientific from moral and political questions is difficult. Is the question "Are blacks genetically less intelligent than whites?" scientific or moral? We would claim that the very posing of the question is a political act about which a moral judgment can be made—but *in theory* it is a question amenable to experimental investigation.

A thornier problem would be selection of judges. In many cases today, disputes concern the negative direct or indirect effects of technology on humanity or on the

[31] *The genesis strategy*, pp. 188–189.

[32] See, for example, Controlling technology democratically.

ecosphere. The split within the scientific community on this is deep and bitter, and finding judges satisfactory to both technologists and environmentalists (for want of better terms) might often prove exceedingly difficult.

In spite of the difficulties, we support Kantrowitz's proposal for the test establishment of an institution for making scientific judgments as described above. The present methods of making such judgments are so bad that any promising alternative or modification deserves a chance. Installation of such a system will, as Kantrowitz points out, take place only over strong objections. It would threaten the vested interests of the politicians who wish to make politically expedient decisions supported by "facts" provided by their pet science advisers. And those scientists who have made lucrative careers and gained much personal power by telling politicians what they want to hear would not be pleased by the prospective dilution of their influence.[33]

Of course, even the most sophisticated scientific assessment apparatus could not avert all mistakes, but if it were backed by a growing feeling of social responsibility among scientists, it should be possible to improve the record greatly. In addition, ways must be found to increase public participation in technological decision-making—a need that is being increasingly recognized.[34]

The remainder of the solution of learning to live with science and technology is to leave plenty of margin for error. For safety, we must learn to operate somewhat below our capability: not to push ourselves and Earth's ecosystems to the absolute limit, and not to do research in areas where a single slip can produce catastrophe.

Scientific Societies

Is there any way that scientific societies can improve the process of technology assessment? Unfortunately, scientists, like other professionals, have been slow to approach their social responsibilities corporately. For instance, the paramount scientific organization in the United States is the quasigovernmental National Academy of Sciences (NAS). Being elected to that organization is a high honor for a research scientist, and committees operating under its aegis often perform excellent studies on topics of broad interest to both scientists and society as a whole. Unfortunately, however, the NAS suffers from a number of difficulties that make some of its work suspect and often give the public an erroneous impression of its conclusions.[35]

First of all, the NAS, under its charter, is advisory to the government, and as a result its studies are often funded by government agencies. This has at times led to results being colored or suppressed. Similarly, the NAS also accepts funds from industry, another questionable procedure if results are to be unbiased. Since, however, the NAS must have funds if studies are to be done, its choices appear to be limited, and in fairness we might say that the objectivity of NAS studies has been fairly respectable, considering the constraints under which it operates. But, as Ralph Nader has stated, its "prestigious talents are all too often subverted from working in pursuit of the public interest."[36]

Perhaps a more fundamental problem is that, admittance being honorary, the NAS membership is generally elderly (the median age of its 866 members in 1970 was 62) and therefore likely to contain a rather conservative, status-quo-oriented sample of the universe of scientists. Worse yet, many of the most talented scientists among NAS members remain immersed in their own research, leaving those with a talent for politics to exercise the academy's influence, sometimes against the public good.

Although periodically some interest is shown in "reforming" the NAS, it seems highly unlikely that any real progress will be made in that direction. Instead, other scientific organizations are gaining prominence that have open memberships, are member-supported, and are independent of government and big business; and they are beginning to give science a respected voice on social issues. Prominent among them is the Federation of

[33]Ibid., p. 508.

[34]For example, see John P. Holdren, The nuclear controversy and the limitations of decision-making by experts.

[35]For a detailed critique, see P. Boffey, *The brain bank of America.* This commentary has been described as harsh by some academy members, but its fundamental validity seems indisputable to anyone who has observed the functioning of the NAS for any period.

[36]Introduction to Boffey, *The brain bank,* p. xxiii. See also Harold Green's analysis of NAS president Philip Handler's defense of DDT, The risk-benefit calculus in safety determination; and Handler's reply, A rebuttal: The need for a sufficient scientific base for government regulation.

American Scientists (FAS), which has about 7000 members (compared to the NAS 1000), including half of America's Nobel laureates. The FAS declines, rather than relies upon, government contracts, which may explain why its budget is only one five-hundredth as large as that of the NAS. But its voice is already more persuasive to many because of its independence.

Outer Space and the Environmental Crisis

Repeatedly, since it has become clear that population growth was moving humanity into an ever-worsening crisis, the suggestion has been made that *Homo sapiens* seek relief from the pressures it was generating by migrating away from Earth. That this is an unsatisfactory long-term solution follows immediately from arithmetic. Under any scenario of exponential growth at rates close to those on Earth today, everything in the visible universe would have to be converted into human flesh in a few thousand years, and a cosmic ball of people would soon thereafter be expanding with the speed of light. At a more mundane level, biologist Garrett Hardin in 1959 published some simple calculations demonstrating the utter impracticality of launching spaceships from Earth on a large enough scale to solve human population problems by interstellar migration.[37] Soon thereafter, physicist John Fremlin pointed out that, at then current growth rates, any time humanity wished to "solve" the population problem by extraterrestrial migration, it would take only about a half-century to populate Venus, Mercury, Mars, the moon, and the moons of Jupiter and Saturn to the same population density as Earth—since the surface areas of these planets and moons are not 3 times that of Earth, they would reach the Earth population density in less than two doubling times.[38]

Recently a new and rather different approach to solving human problems in outer space has been proposed, not by science fiction writers but by a respected professor of physics, Gerard K. O'Neill of Princeton University. The basic idea is to colonize not planetary surfaces but space itself, drawing energy from the sun and materials first from the moon and then from the asteroid belt. O'Neill and his colleagues have done extensive preliminary calculations and conclude that, without the development of radically new technologies:

1. We *can* colonize space, and do so without robbing or harming anyone and without polluting anything.
2. If work is begun soon, nearly all our industrial activity could be moved away from Earth's fragile biosphere within less than a century from now.
3. The technical imperatives of this kind of migration of people and industry into space are likely to encourage self-sufficiency, small-scale governmental units, cultural diversity and a high degree of independence.
4. The ultimate size limit for the human race on the newly available frontier is at least 20,000 times its present value [about 500 years of growth at present rates].[39]

The general plans for O'Neill Colonies have been widely discussed and need not concern us in detail here.[40] An ingenious plan has been devised for propelling materials excavated from the moon's surface to the assembly sites of the first colonies where the materials would be processed on the spot. The processing would take advantage of the abundant solar energy, convenient heat sink, and zero gravity of space. The colonies would be both self-replicating and virtually entirely self-sustaining. Oxygen, for instance, would be recovered from the lunar soil—although hydrogen to be combined into water would be one of the few imports from Earth. The first colony might well be a space manufacturing facility (SMF) established at Lagrange 5 (L5), a point in space that follows the Earth and the moon, has zero gravity, and about which thousands of colonies could move in quasielliptical orbits.

The first products of the SMF could be huge solar power plants (Satellite Solar Powered Stations, SSPS)

[37]Interstellar migration and the population problem, *Heredity,* vol. 50 (1959), pp. 68–70.

[38]How many people can the world support? *New Scientist,* October 29, 1964.

[39]O'Neill, The colonization of space.

[40]For example, O'Neill, The colonization of space; Colonies in orbit, *New York Times Magazine,* January 18, 1976; and *The high frontier;* Colonizing space, *Time,* May 26, 1975; Issac Asimov, Colonizing the heavens, *Saturday Review,* June 28, 1975; Gwyneth Cravens, The garden of feasibility, *Harpers,* August 1975; Graham Chedd, Colonization at Lagrangea, *New Scientist,* October 24, 1974, pp. 247–249.

which would beam low-density microwaves to Earth where they would be received by antenna arrays, converted to electricity, and fed into power lines.[41] Subsequently, colonies could be built as space habitats of what at first seem to be daunting dimensions—for instance, cylinders of up to 16 miles in length and 4 miles in diameter, as in O'Neill's earlier plans, or perhaps spheres of similar volume, which he now thinks superior.[42] The colonies would be shielded from cosmic radiation, would receive day-length sunlight with a system of mirrors, and would rotate to produce normal gravity on their inner surfaces. Within the colony, O'Neill envisions a very pleasant environment for up to 10,000 people, including large areas of "natural" environment with trees, grass, birds, bees, butterflies, and bodies of water. A wide variety of sports and diversions would be available, enhanced by the options of pursuing them at normal gravity on the inner surface of the station or at zero gravity at the rotational axis. Industry would be carried on largely at zero gravity, which provides great benefits;[43] agriculture would be assigned to separate chambers where it could take advantage of an infinite variety of light regimes, gravities, atmospheres (including high CO_2), and so on.

The prospect of colonizing space presented by O'Neill and his associates has had wide appeal, especially to young people who see it opening a new horizon for humanity. The possible advantages of the venture are many and not to be taken lightly. In theory, many of humanity's most environmentally destructive activities could be removed from the ecosphere entirely; the population density of the Earth could be reduced; and a high quality of life could be provided to all *Homo sapiens.* It might even make war obsolete.

What can one say on the negative side about this seeming panacea? At the moment the physical technology exists largely on paper, and cost estimates depend in part on numbers from the National Aeronautics and Space Administration (NASA)—not necessarily a dependable source.[44] There appear to us, however, to be no more technical barriers inherent in the further development of the O'Neill technology than in others in which society has committed itself to large, open-ended and highly speculative investments—fusion power technology being a prime current example, the atomic bomb one from the relatively recent past.

On the biological side, things are not so rosy. The question of atmospheric composition may prove more vexing than O'Neill imagines, and the problems of maintaining complex artificial ecosystems within the capsule—or anywhere—are far from solved. The microorganisms necessary for the nitrogen cycle and the diverse organisms involved in decay food chains would have to be established, as would a variety of other microorganisms necessary to the flourishing of some plants. "Unwanted" microorganisms would inevitably be included or would evolve from "desirable" ones purposely introduced. Furthermore, in many cases the appropriate desirable organisms for introduction are not even known. Whatever type of system were introduced, there would almost certainly be serious problems with its stability. Biologists simply have no idea how to create a large, stable artificial ecosystem. For a long time it is likely that the aesthetic senses of space colonists would have to be satisfied by artificial plants, perhaps supplemented with specimen trees and flower beds.

The problems in the agricultural modules might be easier to solve but are far from trivial. Since, according to O'Neill, agricultural surface is relatively cheap to construct, it seems likely that early stations should have perhaps 4 times as much as is required to sustain the colony, and that it should be rather highly compartmented and diverse to minimize the chances for a disaster to propagate. A great deal of research will have to go into developing appropriate stable agricultural systems for space. The challenge is fascinating—especially because of the variety of climatic regimes possible, the potential for excluding many pests, and the availability of abundant energy.

We can say, then, that although there appear to be no absolute physical barriers to the implementation of the O'Neill program, potentially serious biological barriers remain to be investigated. What about psychological, social, and political barriers? The question of whether *Homo sapiens* can adapt to the proposed space station environment seems virtually answered. Six thousand

---

[41] O'Neill, Space colonies and energy supply to the Earth.
[42] O'Neill, personal communication, February 1, 1976.
[43] See, for example, Harry C. Gatos, Materials processing in space.
[44] For example, Les Aspin, The space shuttle: Who needs it?

men live for long periods on a navy supercarrier orders of magnitude smaller than a proposed space habitat, without women and without numerous amenities of life envisioned by O'Neill. Many city dwellers pass their lives in similarly circumscribed areas and in much less interesting surroundings (travel among stations and occasionally back to Earth is envisioned). There is little reason to doubt that most people would adapt to the strange situation of access to different levels of gravity. Whether or not society will support the venture is another matter. Much may depend on whether O'Neill's calculations[45] on the profitability of the solar-power generating enterprise stand up under closer scrutiny and limited experiment.

The strongest objections that will be raised against space colonization are that it cannot help humanity with the problems of the next crucial decades; that it will divert attention, funds, and expertise from needed projects on Earth; and that it is basically just one more technological circus like nuclear power or the SST. That space colonies will have no immediate impact is recognized by O'Neill, but he argues that society should look to medium-range as well as short-range solutions. Diversion of funds and expertise also do not seem to be extremely serious objections. There is, for instance, no sign that capital diverted from, say, a boondoggle like the B-1 bomber would necessarily be put to "good" use. Equally, it does not follow that money for space colonies must be diverted from desirable programs. The expertise needed is superabundant—many trained aerospace engineers, for example, were unable to find appropriate employment in the mid-1970s.

The possibility of diverting attention from immediate problems like population control is much more serious and can only be avoided by assiduous care on the part of O'Neill and other promoters of the project. Some of O'Neill's associates have done his cause grave harm by not realizing this. At every stage people must be reminded that, for the potential of space even to be explored, a functioning society and economy must be maintained for the next three decades.

Environmentalists, including us, had a strong negative reaction to O'Neill's proposals when first presented with them.[46] The proposals smack of a vision of human beings continually striving to solve problems with more and bigger technology, always turning away from learning to live in harmony with nature and each other and forever dodging the question of What is a human being for? But, again, O'Neill's vision shares many elements with that of most environmentalists: a high-quality environment for all peoples, a relatively less populated Earth on which a vast diversity of other organisms can thrive in an unpolluted environment with much wilderness, a wide range of options for individuals, and perhaps time to consider those philosophical questions. The price of this would, of course, be a decision that a substantial portion of humanity would no longer dwell on Earth.

Environmentalists often accuse politicians of taking too short-term a view of the human predicament. By prematurely rejecting the idea of space colonies, they could be making the same mistake.

MEDICINE

By the 1970s members of the medical profession in the United States and elsewhere were becoming aware of the seriousness of the population problem and the role that medicine has played in creating it, as well as the role that profession must play if the problem is to be solved. More and more physicians now realize that medical intervention in lowering death rates must be balanced by intervention in lowering birth rates. In the United States, courageous doctors openly defied antique abortion laws and risked grave financial loss by performing vasectomies before the legal climate became favorable to those procedures. Interest in the problems of environmental medicine has been rising also, and medical doctors have been at the forefront in sounding warnings (often ignored) about the hazards of air pollution, water pollution, and other environmental threats to public health.

On the debit side, the medical profession as a whole was tardy in backing even such elementary programs as the repeal of laws limiting sex education, the distribution of contraceptive information, and the establishment of

[45]Space colonies and energy supply.

[46]See, for example, *Coevolution Quarterly*, Spring 1976.

family-planning services for the poor. Furthermore, medical training has militated against abortion except under extremely limited circumstances, and the record of the profession (in contrast to those of some courageous individual physicians) in the area of abortion reform was atrocious. For some time after a so-called liberal abortion law was enacted in California, a substantial portion of the abortions in that state continued to be performed by a single group of doctors. Even two years after abortion was legalized nationwide in 1973, only 17 percent of public hospitals and a pitifully small number of private clinics offered abortion services.[47] The medical profession should have taken the lead in abolishing not only the abortion laws but all of the pseudolegal hospital rituals attendant to performing abortions.

The history of the medical profession's attitude toward voluntary sterilization in the past also has generally been reactionary and moralistic. For example, "quotas" based on a woman's age and the number of living children she had were commonly used to determine whether that woman could obtain voluntary sterilization in many United States hospitals during the 1960s.[48] The doctor has the responsibility of establishing that a patient fully understands the consequences of sterilization and any possible temporary side effects, and that he or she would not be physically harmed by the operation. But the doctor should have no right to make the ultimate decision whether an adult should be voluntarily sterilized.

The American Medical Association is an extremely powerful organization and an enormous potential force for good. But, as in many other areas of social reform, such as in providing decent health care to all Americans, the AMA has conspicuously dragged its feet on the population controversy. Rather than leading the crusade for population-control measures, particularly those that pertain to medical practice, the AMA finally went on record as supporting these policies only after pressure was applied from outside by the public and from within by the younger members.

Whether the medical profession in the United States will become a strong force for population control remains to be seen. It has a great potential for helping to solve the population problem, both at home and through technical aid to other countries. Many medical professionals in the United States, for instance, have actively assisted in training programs for understaffed family-planning and general public-health services in less developed countries. Such activities could be expanded and encouraged within the profession.

In addition, the medical profession can be taken to task for concentrating far too little effort on "health care" and far too much on "disease care." Again with outstanding exceptions among individual physicians, organized medicine has, for example, failed to take any lead in questioning the public-health consequences of the large-scale technologies used in agriculture, power generation, transportation, and other sectors of modern life. While medical and biological scientists have wasted billions of dollars in ill-conceived searches for cancer cures, the AMA has been largely silent about the environmental causes of the vast majority of cancers (see Chapter 10). It is high time that the medical profession as a whole threw its enormous prestige into the battle against environmental deterioration, particularly those aspects that threaten public health.

Finally, we must note that the entire pattern of modern health care has been strongly attacked by that prince of intellectual iconoclasts, Ivan Illich. Illich claimed that modern medicine is destroying our health, turning us into "slaves of a monopolist international medical industry"—consumers of a product called health.[49] As with Illich's devastating critique of education (see "Education"), his opinions deserve careful attention even if they are extremely heterodox, and even if his suggestions for change seem impractically individualistic.[50]

EDUCATION

In the United States and around the world there clearly has been an almost total failure to prepare people to understand and make decisions relating to the population-resource-environment crisis. The universities, which

[47]Guttmacher Institute, *Provisional estimates of abortion need and services in the year following the Supreme Court decision*, New York, 1975.

[48]Paul R. Ehrlich and Anne H. Ehrlich, *Population, resources, environment*, 2 ed., W. H. Freeman and Company, San Francisco, 1972, chapter 9.

[49]*Medical nemesis: The expropriation of health.*

[50]Other critiques of the medical system include René Dubos, *The mirage of health;* and Rick Carlson, *The end of medicine.*

should be leading the way in education, have been too conservative and too compartmentalized. Unfortunately, most human problems do not fall neatly into such academic categories as sociology, history, economics, demography, psychology, or biology. The solutions to these problems require the simultaneous application of the best ideas from many academic disciplines. The failure to provide a multidisciplinary education partially explains the optimism of many physical scientists, economists, technologists, and others relative to the environmental crisis. Their kind of optimism is exemplified by a statement by physicist Gerald Feinberg, who wrote in 1968, "Most of our immediate problems will be solved in a relatively short time by the march of technology and the worldwide spread of those aspects of Western culture that are responsible for our high living standards."[51]

Consequences of Overspecialization

There are many examples of such naive optimism mixed with cultural chauvinism that testify to the failure of schools to provide a broad appreciation of science and technology and to place them in a sociopolitical context. The illusion that the Green Revolution would save humanity from starvation, common in the early 1970s, illustrated a faith in science and technology characteristic of the "well-informed" layman. That faith is all too often shared by academicians who have acquired little insight into biology and into what is involved in raising crop yields or in establishing agricultural development in poor countries. Ignorance of the environmental consequences of population expansion leads many social scientists to underrate the significance of population growth in the DCs and the immediacy of the environmental threat.

Such narrowness of outlook is not exclusive to any particular group of scientists. For example, an oceanographer, ridiculing some of the ecological problems associated with agriculture, once told an audience at the University of California at Berkeley that, with modern fertilizing techniques, soil only serves to prop plants up. The president of the United States National Academy of Sciences, writing in the journal *Science,* at various times has attacked scientists who were trying to have DDT banned and has downplayed the health effects of air pollution and the probable overall impact of nuclear war. Many of the solutions put forth by technological optimists are based on ignorance of ecology, demography, anthropology, sociology, and other nontechnological fields. Those who see a panacea in nuclear agroindustrial complexes, for instance, are simultaneously required to ignore (among other things) economics, the scale of the food problem, the state of reactor technology, the potential ecological damage, and an entire spectrum of political and social complexities. Those few technologists who still propose migration (to Australia or to other planets) as a solution to the population problem, or who would accommodate surplus people in concrete cities floated on the sea, simply need remedial work in arithmetic. Even projects that *might* be technically feasible can provide no amelioration of the dilemmas of the near future, because *rate problems* guarantee too great a lag-time.

When highly trained and presumably knowledgeable people are so uninformed, it is hardly surprising that the average person has difficulty evaluating the situation. Not only do most citizens of the United States and other developed countries lack even a skeleton of the necessary technical background, but many do not feel confident enough of their analytic abilities to do even the elementary "back-of-the-envelope" calculations that might permit them to decide which of two "experts" is correct on a given question. For instance, exposing as fraudulent the notion that the Alaskan oil field would be a panacea for American energy needs would require only dividing U.S. annual consumption of oil (6 billion bbl) into known and estimated Alaskan reserves (9 billion and 45 billion bbl, respectively). Unfortunately, few people think of making such checks for themselves. Those who might, often would not know where to find the information on comsumption and reserves—high schools and universities turn out few students well versed in the use of libraries.

The fast-approaching problems of the future will require a citizenry equipped to make difficult choices and to evaluate the qualities of leaders, whether in politics or business. Too few graduates of any educational level (high school to Ph.D.) today have the broad backgrounds

[51]Quoted in Ehrlich and Ehrlich, *Population, resources, environment,* p. 357.

necessary to make such choices intelligently. Too few citizens understand the workings of the political and economic systems well enough to begin making appropriate changes in those systems—such lessons are not taught in school.

New Priorities for Education

The goals of the educational system in the United States need to be reexamined, and new priorities need to be set. At present, the system is largely failing to meet even the old stated goals. But such an overhaul of the educational system will require the cooperation of some elements of society who may see in it a threat to their own interests—from the small group of the ultra-rich, who control much of the power in the United States and who want no changes in the system, to entrenched university professors whose doctrinaire defense of rigid boundaries between their separate disciplines is one more obstacle to solving the world's problems.

One would think that many of the needed educational reforms could be introduced relatively easily at the university level. Unfortunately, like all other mature institutions, universities are quite resistant to changes in their antiquated structures. Nevertheless, the possibility does exist of loosening the rigid departmental organization in order to provide some exchange of information and ideas among disciplines, even though the rate of movement is still very slow. Stanford University, with the help of the Ford Foundation in 1970, developed an interdisciplinary undergraduate curriculum in "Human Biology," with the express purposes of avoiding the trap of disciplinary myopia and of preparing students to engage pressing human problems. By 1975 the program included 350 undergraduate students and was the third most popular major on campus. In 1973, the University of California at Berkeley instituted a campuswide interdisciplinary graduate program in Energy and Resources, which now has tenured faculty not assigned to any department—a significant break with tradition.

Many other colleges and universities have also instituted interdisciplinary programs of various sorts, while courses dealing with the problems of the survival of civilization are proliferating on lower educational levels as well. Such reforms, however, must continue to accelerate if the educational system is to contribute in any significant degree to improving civilization's chances. Without a growing cadre of well-educated people, the kinds of citizen-participation programs we suggest later in this chapter will not constitute much of an improvement over the present political system.

The Role of Students

Perhaps the greatest hope for action in our universities and colleges lies with the students. Although the activism of the late 1960s has faded, students in the mid-1970s as a group are still much more socially aware than were the students of the 1950s and early 1960s. Many seem determined to change our society for the better and are actively working for political and social change. In our opinion and that of many colleagues, the majority of the most exciting and progressive changes in higher education during the 1960s had their roots in student activism. We hope that those former students, who are now beginning to take responsible roles in business and the professions, may in the 1970s and 1980s produce equally salutary changes in other institutions as well.

To a large extent, recent college graduates and students today have more realistic views of the world than their parents because they do not see it through the rose-colored glasses that were constructed for earlier generations by society and its educational system. Those who matured just before World War II were young during a time when personal financial insecurity was an overriding consideration for much of the population. Since World War II, students have grown up in an era when, for most, financial security could be taken for granted, so other social issues could claim their attention. The period was also one of unprecedented change. The world was brought into students' homes through the medium of television, and they were forced into a global outlook by global threats to their personal safety. Many of these young people are change-oriented and concerned about other people, and they think about subtle problems that involve all of humanity. That they show such concern should not be viewed as anything but a hopeful sign.

Although the educational system below the college level is in some ways less resistant to change than colleges and universities, it is similarly inadequate in preparing people for the realities of the world crisis. In some of the better school systems, however, there have been changes—sometimes at the initiative of students. Elementary and junior high school students in many areas have in various ways demonstrated their concern about environmental deterioration. Many teachers have encouraged interest in population growth and the environment, with or without administrative support. Since Earth Day 1970, in particular, there has been a widespread effort to introduce environmental concern into schools at virtually every level. Programs to encourage environmental and population education in schools have also been established at the federal level in the Department of Health, Education and Welfare.

Sex Education

A lack of adequate sex education is still a serious problem in the United States and many other countries. We face both a population problem and a venereal disease epidemic in the United States, and yet powerful groups are determined to keep the "facts of life" from our young people. No subject is more likely to bring out a mob of angry parents than the thought of introducing the most innocuous sex-education curriculum into a school, even if the program is endorsed by educators, psychiatrists, and clerics of many faiths. Some parents in our sex-saturated society even claim that a straight-foward description of sexual intercourse, of the sort that should be perfectly acceptable reading for any child, is part of a communist plot to destroy our youth! This is a vicious cycle, with a minority of ignorant or disturbed parents fighting to guarantee that their children grow up equally ignorant or disturbed.

There are, of course, formidable barriers to reasonable sex education in schools, churches, and in the home. One is a lack of training for potential teachers, who must have a thorough understanding of the subject. The second is the nearly ubiquitous feeling that sex education must be tied up with moral judgments. In the face of massive ignorance and our current population crisis, however, it is difficult to construct an argument against teaching about three basic aspects of sex in the schools. First, children must be thoroughly informed about the anatomy of sex organs and the physiology of sex and reproduction. Second, they must be taught the difference between "sex" and reproduction and about the methods of contraception. Third, they should be informed of the dangers of venereal disease.

These straightforward factual matters are easy. Introducing the student to the role sex plays in society, the attitudes toward it in different religious and social groups, attitudes toward contraception, illegitimacy, marriage, divorce, virginity, and sex-as-just-plain-fun must be handled with great care and by specially trained teachers. But the cycle of the blind leading the blind, that of embarrassed and uninformed parents "educating" their children, must be broken somehow. The experience of Planned Parenthood and other organizations that help teenagers with sexual problems (often unwanted pregnancies) is that keeping youngsters ignorant does not prevent early experimentation with sex, as is usually the intention. On the contrary, informed youngsters seem much less likely to engage in sexual adventures before they are emotionally ready and are even less likely to find themselves incipient parents.

One way in which school systems have successfully introduced sex-education programs is by giving parents a preview of the material. The parents are invited to evaluate the program—in fact, one purpose is to educate *them.* Such preparation of the adult population would seem essential to avoid perpetuating ignorance. A sex-education program has even been initiated in West Germany for grandparents, who often care for children while parents work. Perhaps sex education should be promoted for all parents of preschool children in the United States.

In recent years, at least, several frank and competent books have become available for those interested enough to educate themselves. For preadolescents, the book *Where did I come from?* by Peter Mayle is excellent, and for young women, *Our bodies, ourselves* by the Boston Women's Health Book Collective has produced a revolution of understanding. At a more comprehensive and intellectual level, we can recommend *Fundamentals of human sexuality* by psychiatrists Herant Katchadourian and Donald Lunde, which has enjoyed great success as a college text and is highly recommended for any adolescent or adult who wants to understand his or her sexuality.

The Brain Drain

Our educational system is failing to produce not only those competent to teach sex education, but also the ecologists, agricultural scientists and technicians, social scientists, paramedical personnel, and various other specialists needed to help solve the pressing problems of the world—especially in the less developed countries. Indeed, for decades there has been a brain drain. Trained personnel from the LDCs, especially medical doctors, are understandably attracted to the United States and other DCs, where they can earn a good living. Ironically, this often happens because, despite their great needs for trained people, LDCs may have no jobs for them. That many individuals from the LDCs who are educated in the DCs do not wish to return to their homelands is even sadder. Although some DCs, notably the Soviet Union, virtually force a return to the homeland, most do not. One relatively simple and humane solution would be for the DCs to establish and help staff more training centers *within* the LDCs. This should have the additional benefits of training local people to work on problems of local significance and of familiarizing visiting faculty members from the DCs with those problems.

Changing the Educational Structure

While a great deal can be done to improve the educational system within the general framework now recognized, more fundamental changes will probably be required if large technological societies are to discover ways to govern themselves satisfactorily while solving or preventing the social and environmental problems that now threaten to destroy them. Ivan Illich has suggested the abolition of formal education and the making of educational materials and institutions available to all on a cafeteria basis.[52] To those struggling in the present system, the idea has considerable appeal; but even Illich recognizes the enormous drawbacks inherent in such an unstructured approach.

We would suggest another strategy, one that expands on ideas already current in education. First of all, we think that a major effort should be made to extend education throughout the life span, rather than attempting to cram all education into the first fifteen to twenty-five years. It is becoming widely recognized that maturity and experience are often a benefit in learning. Students who have dropped out, worked, and then returned to school generally do so with renewed vigor and increased performance. Experience in the real world can lead students to avoid much wasted effort in the educational world. A program of encouraging interruption of education, perhaps for one or two years during or directly after high school and another two years after receiving an undergraduate degree might be a good start. For example, a student interested in becoming a physician might spend two years after high school doing clerical work in a hospital or doctor's office or serving as an orderly. When his or her undergraduate education was completed, two additional years could be spent working with a doctor as a paramedic. Similarly, individuals going into business, government, science, bricklaying, plumbing, or what-have-you should have a chance to try out their chosen professions and trades at the bottom before completing their educations.[53]

The benefits of the program would be many, including better understanding of the problems faced by associates (a doctor who has been an orderly should have more insight into the situation of the orderlies), and fewer cases of people committing themselves to careers too early, with too little knowledge of what the commitment involves, and discovering the error too late to make another choice. Students who, on completing high school, were unsure of what their futures should be, could try out several possibilities.

What about youngsters who have no desire to go beyond high school or vocational school? Should their educations end at that point? In the United States, for instance, nearly 1 adult in 5 reportedly lacks "those skills and knowledges which are requisite to adult compe-

[52] *Deschooling society.*

[53] For a more detailed discussion of restructuring our educational system, see Dennis C. Pirages and Paul R. Ehrlich, *Ark II: Social response to environmental imperatives,* chapter 6.

tence."[54] We believe that a technological society, especially a democracy, cannot afford such a large proportion of poorly educated citizens.

Every citizen should be drawn into the problems of societal decision-making. We would suggest that *all* people be required to take sabbatical leaves every seventh year, which could be financed in various ways depending on the choice of activity (this and the employment "problems" created by such a program are considered under "Economic and Political Change"). Each person would be required to spend the year bettering society and himself or herself in a way *approved by the individual's immediate colleagues.* A physician might petition his or her county medical society for permission to study new surgical techniques or anthropology. A garbage collector might petition coworkers to permit him or her to take a year's course in sanitary engineering or recycling techniques at a university. A secretary might apply to the government for a grant to spend a sabbatical serving on an ad hoc citizens' committee to evaluate the direction of research in high-energy physics. A business executive might apply for one of the open sabbatical chairs that could be established on the city council (as well as in all other legislative bodies). A flight instructor might persuade the local pilot's association to appoint him or her to one of the exchange positions in the local Federal Aviation Administration office, with an FAA counterpart being required (if qualified) to take over the instructor's job for a year. *All* bureaucrats should be required to take some of their sabbaticals as nongovernmental workers in the areas they administer and all professors to take some of theirs outside the groves of academe—or at least outside their own fields.

The details of such a program would be complicated, but its benefits, we believe, would far outweigh its costs. A growing rigidity of roles in our society must be broken, and virtually everyone must be brought into its decision-making processes. Indeed, the discontent expressed today by many groups is based on their feeling of being cut off from participation in important decisions that affect their lives.

Some moves in this general direction have been made in the People's Republic of China, where city people and academics have been forced to join rural communes and participate in completely different work from what they had done before. It would be interesting to know what success the Chinese have had. We would certainly not advocate forcing people to change their occupations against their wishes, any more than we would advocate adopting the Chinese communist system of government. But the basic idea behind this policy seems valuable, and an adaptation of it that fit our political system might well be worth exploring.

As an example of how citizen participation in political decision-making can work, a group of scientists led by ecologist C. S. Holling at the University of British Columbia have involved local businessmen, politicians, and private citizens in a computer simulation of a prospective development project, as an experiment in the results of citizen decision-making.[55] Everyone contributed to the assumptions of the model, and all were satisfied with the model created. Then various people were allowed to try out their pet development plans on the model. When a politician found that his or her plan led to environmental disaster, the politician had to acknowledge the error. The politician could not blame the model because he or she had been involved in building what was believed to be a realistic one.

We believe that it is possible, at least in theory, to get away from a we-they system of running the country, to give everyone a chance to participate. Grave problems would unquestionably accompany the attempt, but since we are both morally committed to some form of democracy and intellectually convinced that the present system is both undemocratic and lethally ineffectual, we see no choice but to try a change.

THE LEGAL SYSTEM

Perhaps the greatest potential for reversing environmental deterioration in the United States and for bringing our population growth under control lies in the effective utilization of our legal system.[56] A law may be defined as

[54]Based on a U.S. Office of Education study, reported in *Time,* November 10, 1975, p. 6.

[55]Personal communication.

[56]Much of this section is based on discussions with attorney Johnson C. Montgomery, whose death in December 1974 was a loss deeply felt by people in the ZPG movement.

a "rule of conduct for a community, prescribed by a governing authority and enforced by sanction." The sanction enforcing a law may be either a reward or a punishment. For instance, to control agricultural production, the government might pay a subsidy for not raising crops on part of his land (a reward) or jail a farmer who raises crops (a punishment). Where a government wishes to induce an affirmative action, a promised reward is often more effective than the threat of punishment. In the United States, constitutional questions involving due process, equal protection, and so forth are more likely to arise where punishment, rather than reward, is involved. Bonuses for not having children would certainly raise fewer constitutional questions than jail for overreproducers, for example.

Law is also sometimes defined as codified custom. In a sense, legislators, police officers, and judges are merely social instruments for enforcing customary behavior. Historically they have also helped to create custom by defining acceptable conduct. This has been especially true of legislators and is becoming increasingly true of judges. When the new problems of local and global overpopulation and environmental deterioration arose, they clearly demanded the establishment of new rules of conduct and new customs—in short, new laws. Just as the ancient laws relating to trespass had to be modified by the courts and by the legislatures to handle the new circumstances created by automobiles and airplanes, new devices are now being developed for dealing with pollution and population pressure. The laws of the free-enterprise system were failing to meet the needs of everyone everywhere as long as they permitted—let alone encouraged—unrestricted reproduction and pollution.

Environmental Law and Lawsuits

Many aspects of environmental deterioration can be curbed or controlled through legal means. Probably the easiest form to control is pollution, whether caused by industry in the processes of mining and manufacturing or by individuals in their ordinary lives (air pollution from automobiles and home heating, for instance). Before 1965, there was relatively little control by law of pollution, and the existing regulatory mechanisms were quickly becoming obsolete and inadequate as the volume and variety of pollutants multiplied. Fortunately, there are many legal precedents that have permitted society to oppose polluters legally. Two examples are the legal precepts of *nuisance* and *trespass.*

Nuisance. Under common law (the law generally applicable in the United Kingdom and former British colonies) and under civil law (the law generally applicable in the rest of the Western world), the concept of nuisance has for centuries permitted governments to bring some of their coercive powers to bear on those who create excessive smoke, noise, odor, filth, and the like. In some jurisdictions access to sunlight and even an attractive view are among the aesthetic values protected by public administrators. Public administrators, however, in general have not been noted for their diligence in complaining about local businesses. Nuisances have more often been successfully stopped by individual citizens who have obtained injunctions to stop them. (Private citizens may receive money damages for injuries caused them by a nuisance.)

Existing nuisance laws have presented a number of difficulties, however. First, the nuisance doctrine generally serves only to protect rights associated with real property. As matters now stand, a private nuisance can be stopped only by a person occupying adjacent or nearby property. Even in the most enlightened jurisdictions, little if anything can be done to protect people in the vicinity who do not own or occupy property.

Second, the nuisance doctrine requires that a complainant show a causal relationship between the condition he or she is complaining about—for example, smoke or noise—and a direct injury to himself. Generally he has to show that the condition is *the* cause of injury. Obviously, if each of several polluters contributes a little to the overall problem, the nuisance doctrine is not much help. On the other hand, there is growing authority for the proposition that if a suit is filed against all the persons who are contributing to a nuisance, it is up to them to show to what extent each has contributed. Thus there have been successful cases involving river pollution in which *all* upstream contributors have been sued.

Third, the nuisance doctrine is applied only if in the eyes of the court the polluter is causing more harm than good. Unfortunately, it has been held by many courts that a so-called lawful business (paint manufacturing, for example) cannot constitute a nuisance. Today there is an increasing public tendency to recognize the dangers from pollution, however, and, in balancing them against economic considerations, to require businesses to do whatever a court or an administrative agency may think is economically reasonable. For instance, in the case of *Boomer* versus *Atlantic Cement Company,*[57] individual plaintiffs were awarded damages for cement dust falling on their property, but the court refused to issue an injunction that would halt the plant's operations, even though it found those operations created a nuisance. The court reasoned that the economic activities of the company were too valuable to the area and too many other people would be harmed if the plant were closed down.

That the economic interests of the polluters are taken into consideration by government authorities, however, often leads to spurious arguments based on the notion that restrictions would foster unfair competition: "We can't compete with the Jones Company if we can't spray our crops with DDT." The answer to this argument of course is: "We will stop the Jones Company too." Often the best way of avoiding unfair-competition arguments is to pass legislation that affects an entire industry. For example, if a law were passed prohibiting the manufacture of *all* persistent insecticides (for instance, all those with half-lives of more than one week under average field conditions), the chemical companies would very quickly increase production of those that met the requirements and would develop new ones that would also break down rapidly.

The serious defects in the existing nuisance laws might make it appear that they cannot really assist in controlling pollution, but that is not so. With relatively minor adjustments, those laws could be made very effective. These are among the changes that must be made: (1) expand the nuisance doctrine to include people who are hurt by the pollution but who do not occupy nearby property; (2) permit individuals to bring actions not only on their own behalf, but also on behalf of all other individuals in similar circumstances who are being damaged by pollution; (3) permit recovery of punitive damages (damages in excess of the dollar value of the injury suffered) in cases where the polluter could have avoided some or all of the pollution; (4) organize public-spirited scientists so that they might become a more readily available source of testimony. The real value of the nuisance laws is that they provide an existing framework within which to elaborate newer and more restrictive rules of conduct without also requiring the development of previously unrecognized rights and duties.

Trespass. Another ancient legal doctrine, that of trespass, can also assist in stopping pollution. According to law, if you hit another person with your fist or with your automobile, or if you hike over another person's land, you have committed a trespass. Trespass is both a crime (a public offense) and a tort (an individual, private injury).

For many years there have been metaphysical arguments concerning what constitutes a trespass—for example, whether it is necessary to be able to see whatever hits you or falls on your land. It has been said that rays of light cannot constitute a trespass, and in the past not even smoke could constitute a trespass. However, the old idea that it was necessary to be able to see, feel, and even weigh the offensive object is going out of style. The decision in one California case permitted recovery of substantial damages for lung injuries sustained by a motorist who drove through invisible chemical fumes emitted by a factory.

One serious defect in applying the trespass laws to the control of pollution is that the most an individual can recover are the damages to that individual, which are generally limited to the monetary value of the private injuries. In one case, however, the Oregon Supreme Court permitted a private individual to collect punitive damages in addition to his actual personal damages. The court reasoned that some private wrongs are so evil that the wrongdoer should be punished as well as being forced to pay for the actual injury to the complainant. Punitive damages have long been recognized in our legal systems. If industries guilty of pollution are assessed for punitive damages, private individuals will have some incentive to initiate lawsuits against them. Recently, this possibility has induced some industries to curtail their

---

[57] 1970. 26 N.Y. 2d 219, 257 N.E. 2d 870, 309 N.Y.S. 2d 312.

pollution. It has also induced some insurance companies to withdraw insurance against such suits, and a few states have contemplated the prohibition of insurance for pollution liability.

Like nuisance laws, the trespass laws could be made much more effective merely by permitting an individual to sue for the value of the injuries sustained by *all* individuals similarly situated. Such suits are called *class actions,* and the individual represents not only himself or herself, but also all others similarly situated or in the same class. There exists ample authority for class actions in other circumstances. For example, a stockholder has long been able to bring a class action on behalf of all stockholders against a corporation or its officers or directors. Today, there is evidence that trespass laws will increasingly be used in what are essentially class actions against polluters. The suits against the Union Oil Company by the State of California and by individuals in connection with the 1969 oil leak in the Santa Barbara Channel were class actions. In 1973, however, the class-action approach to legal intervention to improve environmental quality received a setback. The United States Supreme Court declared that each member of a class must suffer damages of more than $10,000 (rather than pooled damages amounting to that much) before a federal court could hear an environmental lawsuit.[58] Since such individual damage is rarely demonstrable, environmental class actions successfully prosecuted in federal courts will become relatively rare.

Suits and interventions by public-interest groups. Perhaps the most impressive success story in the legal battle for the environment has been the rising influence of a relatively few organized public-interest groups that have been using the lawsuit and other forms of legal intervention in a persistent and systematic way. A pioneer in this respect has been the Environmental Defense Fund (EDF). This organization, composed of scientists, lawyers, and other citizens, has been going into the courts and appearing before government regulatory agencies since the late 1960s in its efforts to protect the environment. It started in 1966 by using the courts to stop spraying with DDT in Suffolk County, Long Island. As a result of the publicity accompanying the EDF suit, the state of Michigan rigidly restricted the use of DDT. Then, in an adversary-style hearing before the Wisconsin Department of Resources between December 1965 and May 1969, EDF was able to demolish the flimsy case of those attempting to defend continued use of DDT.[59] Faced with the certainty of cross-examination, many of the scientists who usually defended the petrochemical industry were noticeably absent from the witness chair (although not from the public press).

As a result of those hearings, DDT was banned in Wisconsin. EDF then carried its battle to the federal level, where it played a major role in persuading the Environmental Protection Agency to declare a virtually complete ban on use of DDT in the United States at the end of 1972 (see below).[60] Originally a shoestring operation, EDF has gained considerable admiration and support from scientists and others aware of such environmental threats. Other groups, such as the National Resources Defense Council (NRDC, founded in 1970), have also become very active in taking environmental issues to court. In 1975 NRDC had a staff of four scientists and fourteen attorneys, and had on its docket more than 100 lawsuits and other legal actions of national significance. Environmental groups like Friends of the Earth and the Sierra Club have also been involved, alone or in coalition with other groups, in many such actions in defense of the environment, frequently in cooperation with the legal staffs of EDF or NRDC. Some of the most notable accomplishments of the legal actions undertaken by the growing and increasingly sophisticated collection of environmental public-interest groups are discussed in the sections that follow.

Legislation and Administrative Agencies

Both the need for and the effectiveness of legal action by individuals and citizen groups are linked to the larger

[58]Zahn versus International Paper Company, 42 U.S.L.W. 4087.

[59]The story of the EDF at Madison is told in a very lively fashion by H. Henkin, M. Merta, and J. Staples, *The environment, the establishment, and the law.*

[60]The ban was lifted in 1974 so that DDT could be used against the tussock moth in the Northwest, a very unfortunate decision. See Robert F. Harwood, Economics, esthetics, environment, and entomologists: The tussock moth dilemma.

framework of existing laws and the agencies that administer them. In some sense the easiest route to improvements in environmental protection would seem to be the passage of more comprehensive controls and the establishment of streamlined procedures for administering them. Almost certainly, the courts would have no constitutional objections to any reasonable legislative limitations on the activities of polluting industries—for example, requirements that effluents be purified, reduced, or eliminated. The courts could even sustain statutes that would put certain corporations out of business.

There are two major difficulties in getting effective legislative action. First is the notion that if a higher government authority (for example, the United States Congress) enacts a law regulating a certain activity, it may have preempted the field so that a lesser government authority (for example, a state) cannot enact legislation dealing with the same subject. This has led the tobacco and automobile industries to push for federal regulation in order to avoid the enactment of possibly more-restrictive state laws. Inconsistencies in laws of different jurisdictions create a problem for industry, and there is no easy answer. A national economy does require national standards; it would be extremely difficult for the automobile manufacturers to satisfy fifty different statutory schemes to regulate automobile pollution. Yet some local problems are so severe that they require more drastic solutions than need be applied to the country at large. Thus California (and only California) is permitted tougher automobile emission standards than those established by the Environmental Protection Agency for the rest of the nation.

The second difficulty with legislative action is that legislators are often not cognizant of new problems, and some are notoriously at the beck and call of established pressure groups, such as the automobile manufacturers and the oil industry. Furthermore, in those situations where a legislature has taken action, the action has generally consisted of setting up regulatory agencies like the Food and Drug Administration, the Federal Trade Commission, or the Federal Communications Commission. Such agencies in time have tended to become dominated by the industries they are intended to regulate—ultimately the foxes wind up minding the chickens.[61] Nevertheless, as public pressure has grown, the public has already seen and can expect to see more results from legislation and from regulatory agencies than it has in the past.

In the early 1970s steps were taken in the United States toward placing stricter controls on the release of pollutants into air and water. The Clean Air Act (as amended in 1970) and the Federal Water Pollution Control Act amendments (1972) set national pollution standards for air and water.[62] As we discussed in Chapter 11, however, it was clear by the mid-1970s that the high expectations of environmentalists were not to be realized—at least not as rapidly as they had hoped. There remains a need for establishing and implementing a nationwide (to say nothing of worldwide) program drastically limiting emissions of harmful materials from industry, automobiles, homes, and other sources.

National Environmental Policy Act. A major landmark in the fight for environmental quality in the United States was the passage of the National Environmental Policy Act (familiarly known as NEPA)[63], which became law on January 1, 1970. The bill was modeled in large part after the Employment Act of 1946, which "declared a responsibility in the Federal Government to maintain a prosperous and stable national economy."[64] In a similar vein, NEPA declared a responsibility in the federal government to restore and maintain environmental quality.

NEPA created in the Executive Office of the President a three-member Council on Environmental Quality (CEQ), which was charged with assisting and advising the president in the preparation of the annual *Environmental Quality Report* and with carrying out a number of other survey and advisory capacities for monitoring the quality of the environment and the influence of government agencies and actions on it.

---

[61]For a fascinating description of industry-government "cooperation" on air pollution, see J. C. Esposito, *Vanishing air,* which, although somewhat out of date, gives the flavor of interactions among politicians, agencies, and businessmen.

[62]For a useful citizen's guide to these acts, see J. Cannon, *A clear view.*

[63]The National Environmental Policy Act of 1969, public law 91-190, January 1, 1970 (42 U.S.C. 4321-4347).

[64]Council on Environmental Quality, *Environmental Quality, 1972,* p.222.

The key provision of NEPA, however, is its famous Section 102(C):

> The Congress authorizes and directs that, to the fullest extent possible: (1) the policies, regulations, and public laws of the United States shall be interpreted and administered in accordance with the policies set forth in this act and (2) all agencies of the Federal Government shall–
>
> (C) Include in every recommendation or report on proposals for legislation and other major Federal actions significantly affecting the quality of the human environment, a detailed statement by the responsible official on–
>
> (i) The environmental impact of the proposed action,
>
> (ii) Any adverse environmental effects which cannot be avoided should the proposal be implemented,
>
> (iii) Alternatives to the proposed action,
>
> (iv) The relationship between local short-term uses of man's environment and on the maintenance and enhancement of long-term productivity, and
>
> (v) Any irreversible and irretrievable commitments of resources which would be involved in the proposed action should it be implemented. Prior to making any detailed statement, the responsible Federal official shall consult with and obtain comments of any Federal agency which has jurisdiction by law or special expertise with respect to any environmental impact involved. Copies of such statement and the comments and views of the appropriate Federal, State, and local agencies, which are authorized to develop and enforce environmental standards, shall be made available to the President, the Council on Environmental Quality and to the public as provided by section 552 of title 5, United States Code, and shall accompany the proposal through the existing agency review processes.

This is the section of NEPA that established the Environmental Impact Statement (EIS), which provided a crucial legal lever for public intervention on the side of the environment. The vast majority of environmental suits have been in the area of public law (concerning the relationship of citizens to the government) in contrast to private law (which deals with the relationship of citizens with one another). An early instance was the famous Storm King case,[65] a lawsuit brought by an environmental group against the Federal Power Commission, which had granted Consolidated Edison of New York a permit to build a pumped-storage hydroelectric plant below scenic Storm King Mountain on the Hudson River. The 1965 decision in the Storm King case helped establish the standing (a position from which to assert legal rights or duties) of individuals or groups with records of concern for the environment–in other words, it established that environmentalists could sue to protect environmental values from the adverse effects of administrative decisions.

That legal step forward was followed by a half-step back in another public law case (the Mineral King case), in which the Sierra Club sued to prevent Walt Disney Productions from turning a lovely part of the Sierra Nevada into a plastic wonderland.[66] In the Mineral King case, the United States Supreme Court held that members of the Sierra Club had to *use* the area in question in order to gain standing; the interest of the club members in preserving the wilderness was not sufficient cause to stop the Disney project. (For a novel approach to the question of standing–an approach that would have served the environment well in the Mineral King case–see Box 14-2.)

In the context of concerned groups having standing in environmental cases, NEPA's requirement of environmental impact statements (and the required public airing of the EIS) has proven to be a godsend. A series of cases brought by groups such as the Committee for Nuclear Responsibility, the Environmental Defense Fund, the Sierra Club, and the Natural Resources Defense Council have determined that an EIS is to provide "full disclosure" of the environmental implications of any impending decision, that it must set forth opposing views on significant environmental issues raised by the proposal, that it must contain a full analysis of costs and impacts of alternatives, and that it must balance adverse environ-

---

[65]Scenic Hudson Preservation Conference versus Federal Power Commission, 1965. 354 F 2d 608. For a brief discussion of the case, see J. Holdren and P. Herrera, *Energy*, pp. 181–183.

[66]Sierra Club versus Morton, 1972, U.S.L.W. 4397. For good discussions of the question of standing and environmental law in general, see J. E. Krier, Environmental law and its administration; and C. D. Stone, *Should trees have standing? Toward legal rights for natural objects.*

BOX 14-2 A Note on Standing

The legal machinery and the basic legal notions needed to control pollution are already in existence. Slight changes in the legal notions and diligent application of the legal machinery are all that are necessary to induce a great reduction in pollution in the United States. One change in those notions that would have a most salubrious effect on the quality of the environment has been proposed by law professor Christopher D. Stone in his celebrated monograph, *Should trees have Standing?** In that tightly reasoned essay, Stone points out the obvious advantages of giving natural objects standing, just as such inanimate objects as corporations, trusts, and ships are now held to have legal rights and duties. If this were done, questions such as that of the standing of the Sierra Club in the Mineral King case, mentioned earlier, would disappear—for, as Justice William O. Douglas pointed out in his dissenting opinion in that case, *Sierra Club versus Morton* would "be more properly labeled as *Mineral King v. Morton.*"

*Originally published in 1972 in the *Southern California Law Review;* available as a book, which also reprints the U.S. Supreme Court's opinions in Sierra Club versus Morton (the Mineral King controversy).

mental effects against the benefits of the proposal.[67] Failure to conform fully to the requirements has been the basis of numerous successful lawsuits in which projects have been stopped until proper environmental impact statements were prepared.

The strength of NEPA lies in the formal commitment of the government to environmental quality and the required public airing of potential impacts by the EIS procedures. In the five years 1970 through 1974, more than 6000 impact statements were filed. In the opinion of the CEQ, by 1974 NEPA had "succeeded in its objective of incorporating an environmental perspective into the decision-making process of Federal agencies."[68] This statement seems accurate to us, both because it agrees with our impressions and because, when it was made, Russell W. Peterson, one of the brightest and most straightforward of Washington bureaucrats, was chairman of the CEQ.[68a] In addition, the general approach of NEPA has been adopted by local and state governments. By 1974 twenty-one states and Puerto Rico had adopted the EIS process, as had governments in such nations as Australia, Canada, and Israel.[69] One of the most impressive of the state acts is California's 1970 Environmental Quality Act (amended), which requires impact statements on all projects, private or government, that will significantly affect the environment. In the mid-1970s some 6000 statements were being filed annually.[70]

As far-reaching and successful as NEPA has been in this context, some weaknesses are also evident. While it has raised consciousness of the environment in government agencies and in the business community, concrete results in terms of prevention and repair of environmental deterioration have been less apparent. Thus far, NEPA has been mainly an instrument for disseminating information rather than one for guiding policy. It cannot, in itself, lead to the cancellation of a project—even though citizens groups have repeatedly employed it to delay projects where EIS provisions have not been meticulously followed. Indeed, a key flaw in the act as first applied was that its enforcement depended entirely upon the public, and the public could use it only to delay, not to halt, projects that would have massive negative impacts on the environment.[71] As far as NEPA was concerned, the Army Corps of Engineers legally could plow the United States under, or the Nuclear Regulatory Commission could permit the country to be totally contaminated with lethal amounts of radioactive wastes, as long as the EIS requirements of the law were followed scrupulously. In applying NEPA, the courts seem to be moving toward substantive rather than procedural re-

[67]CEQ Environmental Quality, 1972, pp. 242–246.

[68]CEQ, Environmental Quality, 1974, p. 372. This report has a good brief historical account of the evolution of NEPA (pp. 372–413).

[68a]In 1976 he resigned and in 1977 was succeeded by Charles Warren, a California State legislator with a thorough understanding of environmental issues. President Carter's appointment of Warren continues the tradition of excellence in this position.

[69]Ibid., pp. 399–413.

[70]In California they are technically known as environmental impact reports (EIR).

[71]D. W. Fischer, Environmental impact assessment as an instrument of public policy for controlling economic growth. The appendix to the article contains an informative critique of NEPA.

view, however. This means that projects may be halted for reasons other than failure to follow the EIS provision meticulously.[72]

Several landmark court cases have clarified the obligations of government agencies under NEPA. In *Calvert Cliff's coordinating committee* versus *AEC* (1971), the United States Court of Appeals for the District of Columbia held that the Atomic Energy Commission could not exclude water quality considerations from its environmental impact statement merely because the power plant in question had already received a certificate of compliance with federal water quality regulations from the state. The court found that the "crabbed interpretation" of NEPA by the AEC would prevent the AEC from making a balanced determination of the best course of action. In *Scientists' Institute for Public Information* versus *AEC* (1973), the District of Columbia Court of Appeals ruled in connection with the liquid metal fast breeder reactor (LMFBR) that comprehensive environmental impact statements must be prepared for acknowledged programs, not merely for individual facilities; that is, the combined impact of many LMFBRs and the associated facilities had to be examined in advance since the AEC had acknowledged that it had a program and not a single facility in mind. In *Sierra Club* versus *Morton* (1974), involving fossil-fuel development on the Great Plains, the District of Columbia Court of Appeals defined requirements for a programmatic environmental impact statement in certain circumstances even where an agency had not recognized its actions as a program.

NEPA was one important step in the right direction, and it may become a prime weapon in the fight for environmental quality. But it will prove inadequate unless ways are found to introduce comprehensive environmental planning throughout the nation, in which legal standards for balancing environmental values against other values are applied to all projects with significant impact, government or private. How this might be accomplished—and some existing legislation is leading in this direction—is discussed further in "Economics and Political Change." That section also discusses the possibility that relatively simple legislation dealing with the consumption of resources might eventually replace much of the cumbersome ad hoc system that is now evolving for the control of environmental impact.

[72]J. E. Krier, personal communication.

Environmental Protection Agency. Contrary to a rather widespread misimpression, the Environmental Protection Agency was not created by NEPA but rather by an administrative reorganization that took place in December 1970. It consolidated the Federal Water Quality Administration (formerly in the Department of Interior); the National Air Pollution Control Administration (formerly in the Department of Health, Education and Welfare, HEW); the pesticide registration, research, and standard-setting programs of the Department of Agriculture and the Food and Drug Administration; the solid-waste management programs of HEW; and some of the functions of the Federal Radiation Council and the Atomic Energy Commission for setting standards for radiation exposure. The EPA was given all the functions and responsibilities necessary to carry out the Clean Air Act and the Federal Water Pollution Control Act; and under its first administrator, William D. Ruckelshaus, it made a reasonably rapid start at doing so.[73] His successor, Russell E. Train, continued to build an increasingly effective organization in an often difficult political environment.

Unlike CEQ, which is a small advisory group in the Executive Office of the President, the EPA is a large operating agency with a staff in 1976 of 8800 people and estimated budget outlays in that year of $3 billion. It maintains research laboratories in several parts of the country. The best concise record of the accomplishments as well as the shortcomings of the EPA are the CEQ's annual reports on the state of the nation's environment.

Occupational Safety and Health Act. As noted in Chapter 10, workers are often exposed to much higher concentrations of dangerous substances than are considered acceptable for the population at large. The main legal protection for workers is provided under the Occupational Safety and Health Act of 1970, which authorized the Labor Department to establish standards for exposure of workers to hazardous pollutants, to

[73] See CEQ, *Environmental quality, 1970* and *1971.*

provide training programs, and to set up a system for reporting occupational illness and injury. These duties are carried out by the Occupational Safety and Health Administration (OSHA). The National Institute of Occupational Safety and Health (NIOSH) does research for and recommends standards to OSHA.

Three types of standards for exposure to pollutants can be set by OSHA: consensus standards adopted from a list provided by a group of government and industrial scientists, permanent standards, and temporary emergency standards. Permanent standards generally include, in addition to the eight-hour limits for worker exposure provided by consensus standards, regulations covering work practices, monitoring, and medical surveillance. Temporary standards are effective only for a six-month period, an interim during which permanent standards are developed.

By 1975, consensus standards had been set for about 400 chemicals, and OSHA and NIOSH were moving to change them to permanent standards. Permanent standards had already been established for asbestos, vinyl chloride, and a group of fourteen carcinogens; and permanent standards have been proposed for arsenic, coke-oven emissions, and noise. Some groups feel that those standards are not strict enough; for example, a chemical workers union unsuccessfully challenged in court those established for the fourteen carcinogens.

It seems certain that a constant tug-of-war will ensue between consideration of the costs (real or imagined) to industry of lowering workers' exposure to hazards and consideration of the legitimate desires of workers to protect their health. In view of the large numbers of people directly or indirectly involved (remember, hazardous materials like asbestos and plutonium can be taken home inadvertently by workers, placing their families and friends at risk), it seems clear that OSHA's activities are a long-overdue step in the right direction.

Population Law

The impact of laws and policies on population size and growth has, until very recently, largely been ignored by the legal profession. The first comprehensive treatment of population law was that of the late Johnson C. Montgomery,[74] an attorney who was president of Zero Population Growth, and whose ideas are the basis of much of the following discussion.

To date, there has been no serious attempt in Western countries to use laws to control excessive population growth, although there exists ample authority under which population growth could be regulated. For example, under the United States Constitution, effective population-control programs could be enacted under the clauses that empower Congress to appropriate funds to provide for the general welfare and to regulate commerce, or under the equal-protection clause of the Fourteenth Amendment.[75] Such laws constitutionally could be very broad. Indeed, it has been concluded that compulsory population-control laws, even including laws requiring compulsory abortion, could be sustained under the existing Constitution if the population crisis became sufficiently severe to endanger the society. Few today consider the situation in the United States serious enough to justify compulsion, however.

The most compelling arguments that might be used to justify government regulation of reproduction are based upon the rapid population growth relative to the capacity of environmental and social systems to absorb the associated impacts. To provide a high quality of life for all, there must be fewer people. But there are other sound reasons that support the use of law to regulate reproduction.

It is accepted that the law has as its proper function the protection of each person and each group of people. A legal restriction on the right to have more than a given number of children could easily be based on the needs of the first children. Studies have indicated that the larger the family, the less healthy the children are likely to be and the less likely they are to realize their potential levels of achievement.[76] Certainly there is no question that children of a small family can be cared for better and can

[74]Population explosion and United States law.

[75]"No state shall make or enforce any law which shall abridge the privileges or immunities of citizens of the United States, nor shall any State deprive any person of life, liberty, or property, without due process of law; nor deny to any person within its jurisdiction the equal protection of the laws."

[76]Joe D. Wray, Population pressure on families: Family size and child-spacing, in Roger Revelle, ed., *Rapid population growth: Consequences and policy implications,* Johns Hopkins Press, Baltimore, 1971; R. B. Zajonc, Family configuration and intelligence, *Science,* vol. 192, pp. 227–236 (April 16, 1976).

be educated better than children of a large family, income and other things being equal. The law could properly say to a mother that, in order to protect the children she already has, she could have no more. (Presumably, regulations on the sizes of adopted families would have to be the same.)

A legal restriction on the right to have children could also be based on a right not to be disadvantaged by excessive numbers of children produced by others. Differing rates of reproduction among groups can give rise to serious social problems. For example, differential rates of reproduction between ethnic, racial, religious, or economic groups might result in increased competition for resources and political power and thereby undermine social order. If some individuals contribute to general social deterioration by overproducing children, and if the need is compelling, they can be required by law to exercise reproductive responsibility—just as they can be required to excercise responsibility in their resource-consumption patterns—*providing they are not denied equal protection.*

Individual rights. Individual rights must be balanced against the power of the government to control human reproduction. Some people—respected legislators, judges, and lawyers included—have viewed the right to have children as a fundamental and inalienable right. Yet neither the Declaration of Independence nor the Constitution mentions a right to reproduce. Nor does the UN Charter describe such a right, although a resolution of the United Nations affirms the "right *responsibly* to choose" the number and spacing of children (our emphasis). In the United States, individuals have a constitutional right to privacy and it has been held that the right to privacy includes the right to choose whether or not to have children, at least to the extent that a woman has a right to choose *not* to have children. But the right is not unlimited. Where the society has a "compelling, subordinating interest" in regulating population size, the right of the individual may be curtailed. If society's survival depended on having more children, women could be required to bear children, just as men can constitutionally be required to serve in the armed forces. Similarly, given a crisis caused by overpopulation, reasonably necessary laws to control excessive reproduction could be enacted.

It is often argued that the right to have children is so personal that the government should not regulate it. In an ideal society, no doubt the state should leave family size and composition solely to the desires of the parents. In today's world, however, the number of children in a family is a matter of profound public concern. The law regulates other highly personal matters. For example, no one may lawfully have more than one spouse at a time. Why should the law not be able to prevent a person from having more than two children?

The legal argument has been made that the First Amendment provision for separation of church and state prevents the United States government from regulating family size. The notion is that family size is God's affair and no business of the state. But the same argument has been made against the taxation of church property, prohibition of polygamy, compulsory education of and medical treatment for children, and many similar measures that have been enacted. From a legal standpoint, the First Amendment argument against family-size regulation is devoid of merit.

There are two valid constitutional limitations on the kinds of population-control policies that could be enacted. First, any enactments must satisfy the requirements of due process of law; they must be reasonably designed to meet real problems, and they must not be arbitrary. Second, any enactments must ensure that equal protection under the law is afforded to every person; they must not be permitted to discriminate against any particular group or person. This should be as true of laws giving economic encouragement to small families as it would be of laws directly regulating the number of children a person may have. This does not mean that the impact of the laws must be exactly the same on everyone. A law limiting each couple to two children obviously would have a greater impact on persons who desire large families than it would on persons who do not. Thus, while the due-process and equal-protection limitations preclude the passage of capricious or discriminatory laws, neither guarantees anyone the right to have more than his or her fair share of children, if such a right is shown to conflict with other rights and freedoms.

It is often argued that a fetus or an embryo is a person who has a right to life, and therefore abortion as a birth-control measure must be rejected. Supporters of this argument point out that certain rights of a fetus have been legally recognized. For example, some states permit a fetus to recover money damages for personal injuries sustained before birth. Under some circumstances the common law has permitted a fetus, if subsequently born alive, to inherit property. The intentional killing of a fetus (through injury to the mother) has been declared by statute to constitute murder, although under the statute the fetus is not defined as a human being.

Although some rights of the fetus after quickening have been protected in some states, most of those states require that the infant be born and living before the rights vested prior to birth actually are recognized and enforced. Most jurisdictions afford no protection to property rights or personal rights of the unquickened fetus, and no jurisdiction has protected the rights of embryos. Furthermore, analysis of the situations in which rights of the fetus have been recognized disclose that it is generally not the fetus's rights, but rather the rights of its parents or others that are being protected. For example, when a fetus did receive money damages for prenatal injuries, in reality it was the parents' and the society's economic interests that were being protected.

Those who argue that a fetus has a right to life usually proceed from the assumption that life begins at or soon after conception. As stated elsewhere, the question, When does life begin? is misleading. Life does not begin; it began. The real question, from a legal as well as from religious, moral, and ethical points of view, is as follows: in what forms, at what stages, and for what purposes should society protect human life? Obviously overweight people regard their fat cells differently from their brain cells. A wandering sperm cell is not the same thing as a fertilized egg; nor is a fetus a child. Yet a fat cell, a sperm cell, a fetus, a child, an adult, and even a group of people are all human life.

The common law and the drafters of the U.S. Constitution did not consider a fetus a human being. Feticide was not murder in common law because the fetus was not considered to be a human being, and for purposes of the Constitution a fetus is probably not a "person" within the meaning of the Fourteenth Amendment. Thus, under the Constitution, abortion is apparently not unlawful, although infanticide obviously is. This is a very important distinction, particularly since most rights, privileges, and duties in our society are dated from birth and not from some earlier point in time. Capacity to contract, to vote, to be drafted, to obtain Social Security rights, drivers' licenses, and the like, are all dated from birth, which is a very convenient, relatively definite point in time from which to date most rights. Certainly, the moment of birth is easier to ascertain than the moment of conception, implantation, or quickening. Such an easily ascertainable point in time is a sensible point from which to date Constitutional rights, which should not depend upon imprecisions.

The fact that a fetus is probably not a "person" with Constitutional rights does not, however, mean that society has no interest in the fetus. Society does have an interest in ensuring that an appropriate number of healthy children are born. To protect the health of the mother, some regulation of abortion is still necessary and appropriate. For example, laws requiring that abortions be performed only by qualified medical personnel in appropriately licensed institutions now exist in most states, and there are regulations governing eligibility for insurance or other financial aid.

Legal reform. In predecessors of this book, we recommended a series of reasonable, constitutional, and desirable legal changes in the United States to discourage population growth:

1. A federal statute could be enacted that would prohibit any restrictions on safe, voluntary contraception, sterilization, and abortion, and the dissemination of information about them.

2. State and federal governments could subsidize voluntary contraception, sterilization, and abortion. Laws could require that birth-control clinics be opened at public expense in all suitable locations. They could also require that group and individual health insurance policies cover the costs of abortion and sterilization.

3. Tax laws could be revised, and new laws could be passed that would provide incentives for late marriage,

small families, and alternative roles for women. The tax disadvantage to single, childless persons could be eliminated.

4. State and federal laws could make sex education, including instruction about contraception, mandatory in all schools, and the government could sponsor public education programs designed to encourage people to want fewer children.

5. Federal support and encouragement for the development of more effective birth-control drugs and devices could be greatly increased.

We are pleased to report that between 1970 and 1975 all of these changes took place, at least to some degree. Much of what remains to be done consists of extending or more fully implementing programs that now exist. The only real exception is mandatory sex education, but even on a voluntary basis the trend is toward expansion, and there is support and encouragement both from the Department of Health, Education and Welfare and from private organizations such as the Sex Information and Education Council of the United States (SIECUS).

If these relatively uncoercive policies should fail to maintain a low American birth rate, more coercive laws might well be written (see Chapter 13 for examples). At the moment, there might be little justification or public support for such laws, but if the resource and environmental situations are allowed to deteriorate, popular support might develop rapidly. There has been considerable talk in some quarters at times of forcibly suppressing reproduction among welfare recipients (perhaps by requiring the use of contraceptives or even by involuntary sterilization). This may sadly foreshadow what our society might do if the human predicament gets out of hand. We hope that population growth can be controlled in the United States without resorting to such discriminatory and socially disruptive measures. That, in fact, has been one purpose of this and our previous books—to stimulate population control by the *least* coercive means before it is too late. The decline in birth rates in the United States and other developed countries since 1970 is a most hopeful sign that population control can be easily achieved in those countries, but we must reiterate that the United States and most other DCs are still a long way from zero population growth.

BUSINESS, LABOR, AND ADVERTISING

Although legal and legislative action are essential to the solution of pollution problems in the United States, it is to be hoped that American industries will not wait to be coerced into responsible behavior. In fact, a few industries took the initiative for cleaning up their effluents before it was legally required, and some found it possible to make profits from pollution by-products. Such unexpected bonuses are not possible in all cases, of course. Tax incentives and government subsidies for cleaning up pollution may be applied when costs are high, but in the long run abating pollution will best be achieved as a part of a complete overhaul of our tottering economic system.

Meanwhile, many industrial organizations are exploring technological methods for dealing with various kinds of pollution; indeed, new companies have appeared whose entire business is pollution abatement or waste disposal of one sort or another. On the preventive side of the coin, environmental consulting firms have begun to appear. Their business is to advise communities and businesses in planning development with the least possible damage to the environment and the most benefit to the human inhabitants. Many of them are involved in writing the environmental impact statements required by the NEPA and several states. These trends and others, such as research on recyclable or biodegradable containers, should certainly be encouraged.

Labor

Labor also has an important role to play in easing the pressure on the environment. In the United States an unfortunate "jobs versus the environment" attitude was promoted as the mid-1970s recession developed. Many business and labor leaders, believing that the only solution to problems of unemployment was to fire up the old ecologically destructive economic machine once again, lobbied for the relaxation of measures to protect the environment. The basic message of environmentalists that not only were many jobs threatened by the continuing rape of the environment, but that many lives, and indeed the persistence of civilization, were threatened also, obviously had not penetrated.

Environmental protection in reality has proven to be

far more a creator of jobs than a destroyer. The Council on Environmental Quality in 1975 estimated that through 1974 fewer than 14,000 workers had lost their jobs as a result of environmental controls, most of them through closure of plants that were obsolescent, inefficient, and already only marginally profitable. In most cases environmental controls only hastened the inevitable. But, although a precise estimate would be difficult to make, it is clear that thousands more jobs have been created by environmental protection. Building and modernizing urban sewage systems alone provides perhaps 85,000 jobs for each $1 billion spent. People are needed to administer and enforce environmental programs and to build, install, operate, and maintain pollution abatement equipment, and so forth.[77]

Labor should be among the leaders in the movement to maintain environmental quality, even though workers, along with the rest of society, will have to pay part of the costs. Many more working people are exposed to environmental hazards, from poor safety standards in workplaces to smog, than are industrialists and bankers who work in plush, air-conditioned offices and can afford to live beyond the smog belt.

In Australia, labor has moved into the forefront, battling against development of Australia's uranium deposits and against other projects deemed socially or environmentally injurious. Led by Jack Mundey, a leader in the building trades in New South Wales, "Green Bans" have been instituted, in which union members simply refuse to work on such projects.[78] In 1974 many millions of dollars' worth of construction work was being held up by Green Bans in Sydney alone. If only such a sense of social responsibility pervaded the labor movement everywhere!

There is every reason to believe that in years to come environmentalists and workers (two groups whose interests already greatly overlap) more and more will find their interests becoming congruent. For example, environmentalists are increasingly concerned about the energy-intensiveness of our economic system—as are many people in the labor movement as they see energy being substituted for workers. The important idea that improvements in energy efficiency not only spare the environment (by reducing energy requirements) but also increase employment is well illustrated in the following discussion by Schipper:

> Compare, for example, two air conditioners of equal capacity, operating in similar homes under similar loads in the same climatic region, one requiring half the power of the other. If a consumer buys the more efficient unit, some of the money otherwise spent on energy is used for extra materials and labor, and this expenditure results in a more carefully constructed, more efficient air conditioner. Since manufacturing is generally more labor-intensive than electric utilities, the redirection of spending—from paying for electricity to investment in a more efficient unit— raises the total demand for labor per unit of air conditioning and still provides for the consumer's desire for comfort. [Moreover] when the consumer spends the money saved by energy conservation, the new purchase will require increased labor in comparison to buying electricity. The result is more goods or services and more employment, with less energy consumed.[79]

Higher energy costs, which are now resulting from the appearance in the balance sheets of the costs of depletion and pollution, increase the potential savings and employment benefits derivable from greater energy efficiency (see also Chapter 8).

A reorientation of business, labor, and consumer values is obviously in order. Resources of all kinds are limited, but Americans behave as though they were not. The neglected virtues of economy and thrift must be restored to the pedestals that they once occupied in this country.

Advertising

Advertising plays a leading role in perpetuating the American system of consumerism. Whether the blame for this lies largely with industry or with the consumers is difficult to determine and probably does not much matter. What does seem evident is that advertising does not *have* to be mostly antienvironmental. In the late 1960s many advertisements began to appear featuring various companies' efforts at pollution abatement. Such

[77]*Environmental quality–1975,* pp. 533–536. See also Patrick Heffernan, Jobs and the environment.

[78]M. Hardmann and P. Manning, *Green bans;* The Green Bans, *Sierra Club Bulletin,* April 1975, p. 18; R. Roddewig and J. S. Rosenberg, In Australia, unions strike for the environment.

[79]Lee Schipper, Raising the productivity of energy use.

concern over the corporate image with respect to pollution was no doubt a necessary first step, but more than advertising of environmental protection is required.

Environmentalists have been increasingly irritated by self-serving ads showing how Company XX has always been deeply involved in protecting the environment. Those emanating from oil companies—among the greatest destroyers of the environment—are especially galling. Ads from pollutors posing as environmentalists have been christened "ecopornography." Much more acceptable are ads that offer useful information to consumers on how they can cooperate with business in environmentally beneficial projects, such as energy conservation or recycling materials. While we certainly do not condone heavy promotion of new versions of products whose environmental contribution is negligible or questionable, such as certain gasoline additives or disposable flashlights, we welcome ads that feature genuine improvements, such as unleaded gasolines or non-aerosol spray containers. Admittedly, the line dividing such cases is not always easy to draw.

The advertising industry can do much more than it has so far to encourage its clients to promote products by stressing such qualities as durability, economy, and versatility. For example, automobile advertising should emphasize economy of purchase and operation, especially low gasoline consumption, durability, compactness, comfort (but not massiveness—interior room can be maintained even as weight is greatly trimmed), engine efficiency, safety, and low pollution emissions. For a time after the energy crisis of 1974 the trend was in that direction, but by 1976 there was a move back toward the bad old days. Advertising that stresses large size and high power in cars should be permanently discontinued.

Beyond cooperating with clients in antipollution promotions, advertising companies could by agreement refuse to design ads promoting wasteful or polluting products—for example, ads featuring throwaway products, food in throwaway cans and bottles, or goods wrapped in unnecessary layers of packaging. Above all, every effort should be made to expunge from advertising the idea that the quality of life is closely related to the rate at which new products are purchased or energy is consumed.

Advertising agencies can also make a contribution to the population situation by refusing to produce ads featuring large families. Under pressure from population and women's organizations, some of the obvious changes have already been made in ads for many products. Other ways have been found to promote heavy-duty washing machines than as an item for large families—dormitories, hospitals, and other institutions use them also, for instance. Families with three or more children have lately been depicted as large families, and the two-child family appears the norm. Women are increasingly featured playing roles other than homemaker and mother, and the convenience of many goods is being stressed more as a value for working women than for the overburdened mother, as they once were exclusively. This trend should be encouraged.

The critical problem, of course, is to find a way to swing both advertising clients and agencies in the right direction. While public utilities, for example, could and should be prohibited from promoting greater use of electric power through advertising, similar legal controls over all advertising would undoubtedly prove too cumbersome.

A court decision in August 1971[80] held that, under the fairness doctrine, radio and television stations that carry advertising for big, high-horsepower cars also must broadcast information about the environmental threat such cars represent. The suit had been brought by Friends of the Earth and the Environmental Defense Fund after the Federal Communications Commission had ruled against such a policy. If it were widely applied, this interpretation of the fairness doctrine might discourage manufacturers and advertisers from promoting socially and environmentally undesirable products; to date, unfortunately, it has not been widely applied.

The late 1970s and early 1980s will be crucial years for everyone. The business community in the United States and around the world is faced with a particularly difficult choice. It can continue to pursue the economic goals of the past decades until either an environmental disaster overtakes civilization or until governments and the public compel a change; or it can actively initiate novel approaches to production and industry, with a view to protecting the environment, preserving limited resources, and truly benefiting humanity.

[80]Washington, D.C. Court of Appeals.

ECONOMIC AND POLITICAL CHANGE

Practical men, who believe themselves to be quite exempt from any intellectual influences, are usually slaves to some defunct economist. Madmen in authority, who hear voices in the air, are distilling their frenzy from some academic scribbler of a few years back.

—John Maynard Keynes, 1936

In relation to the population-resources-environment crisis, economics[81] and politics can usually be viewed as two sides of a single coin. A very large number of political decisions are made on an economic basis, especially those relating to environmental and resource problems. Illustrating the influence of economics, Lord Keynes wrote (in the lines just preceding the epigraph of this chapter): "The ideas of economists and political philosophers, both when they are right and when they are wrong, are more powerful than is commonly understood. Indeed the world is ruled by little else."[82] If anything, his statement is even more true today than it was then.

Economics nevertheless is sometimes wrongly blamed for political problems. Although the major political division of the developed world—that between capitalist and communist nations—is thought to be based on differences in economic ideology, the actual differences are relatively few. A major cause of humanity's current plight lies not in the economic differences between those two political spheres but in the economic attitudes that they hold *in common.*

Gross National Product and Economic Growthmanship

Economists are not unanimous in their views of economic growth. Some have perceived that perpetual economic growth is as impossible to sustain as perpetual population growth. Herman Daly in 1975 told a Congressional committee:

> In 1936 John Maynard Keynes remarked that "The part played by orthodox economists, whose common sense has been insufficient to check their faulty logic, has been disastrous to the latest act." The same words ring true in 1975. It is easy to be trapped by the excessive rigidity of our own values and goals. The South Indian Monkey Trap, for example, works solely on the basis of rigid goals. A hollowed-out coconut is filled with rice and fastened by a chain to a stake in the ground. There is a hole in the coconut just large enough to allow the monkey to insert its extended hand, but not large enough to permit withdrawal of his clenched fist full of rice. The monkey is trapped by nothing more than his refusal to let go of the rice, to reorder his goals, and to realize that in the given circumstances his freedom is more important than the fistful of rice. We seem to be trapped in a growth-dominated economic system that is causing growing depletion, pollution, and disamenity, as well as increasing the probability of ecological catastrophe. We must open our collective fist and let go of the doctrine of perpetual growth, or else we will be caught by the consequences.[83]

In the 1967 edition of his classic economics text, by contrast, Paul A. Samuelson of M.I.T. wrote: "The ghost of Carlyle should be relieved to know that economics, after all, has not been a dismal science. It has been the cheerful, but impatient, science of growth."[84] In 1976, viewing the prospects for continued economic growth in the United States and the rest of the world, he still found them cheering.[85] The majority of economic theorists agree with Samuelson, as do most businessmen and politicians. Some economists besides Daly have questioned the growth ethic, however. For example, E. J. Mishan stated in 1967:

> The skilled economist, immersed for the greater part of the day in pages of formulae and statistics, does occasionally glance at the world about him and, if

[81]For a general review of orthodox economics, we recommend the latest edition of Paul A. Samuelson's fine text, *Economics* (latest edition at this writing, the tenth, 1976). For a more detailed treatment of environmental economics, see Richard Lecomber, *Economic growth versus the environment.* For the latter, familiarity with economic concepts such as indifference curves and inferior goods (explained in Samuelson) is required.

[82]*The general theory of employment, interest, and money,* Harcourt, New York, 1964 (originally published in 1936).

[83]Herman E. Daly, in testimony before the Joint Economic Committee of Congress, hearings on economic growth, October 23, 1975.

[84]*Economics: An introductory analysis,* McGraw-Hill, New York, 1967.

[85]Limits to growth: What lies ahead? *Honolulu Advertiser,* March 15, 1976. In fairness to Samuelson, part of his cheer was engendered by the declining rate of population growth in the United States.

> perceptive, does occasionally feel a twinge of doubt about the relevance of his contribution. . . . For a moment, perhaps, he will dare wonder whether it is really worth it. Like the rest of us, however, the economist must keep moving, and since such misgivings about the overall value of economic growth cannot be formalized or numerically expressed, they are not permitted seriously to modify his practical recommendations.[86]

GNP. In much of the world—indeed, in all countries with any aspirations toward modernization, progress, or development—a general economic index of advancement is growth of the gross national product (GNP). The GNP is the total national output of goods and services valued at market prices. Stated another way, it consists of the sum of personal and government expenditure on goods and services, plus the value of net exports (exports minus imports) and private expenditure on investment. It can be a very useful economic indicator.

More important than what the GNP is, however, is what it *is not:* it is not a measure of the degree of freedom of the people of a nation; it is not a measure of the health of a population; it is not a measure of the equity of distribution of wealth; it is not a measure of the state of depletion of natural resources; it is not a measure of the stability of the environmental systems upon which life depends; it is not a measure of security from the threat of war. It is not, in sum, a comprehensive measure of the *quality* of life, although, unhappily, it is often believed to be.

When the standards of living of two nations are compared, it is customary to examine their *per-capita* GNPs. Per-capita GNP is an especially unfortunate statistic. First of all, it is the ratio of two statistics that are at best crude estimates, especially in the LDCs where neither GNP nor population size is known with any accuracy. More important, comparisons of per-capita GNP overestimate many kinds of differences. For instance, a comparison of per-capita GNPs would lead to the conclusion that the average person in the United States lives almost 10 times as well as the average Portuguese and some 60 times as well as the average Burmese. This, of course, is meaningless, since virtually all services and some goods are much cheaper in the LDCs, and GNP calculates only what enters the recorded money economy. Americans pay perhaps 5 or 10 times as much for farm labor, domestic help, haircuts, carpentry, plumbing, and so forth as do people in the LDCs, and the services in the United States may be of inferior quality. And yet, because of the accounting system, those services contribute between 5 and 10 times as much to our GNP as the same services do to the GNPs of, say, Burma or India.

Furthermore, figures on the increase of per-capita GNP in LDCs do not take into account such things as rise in literacy rate, and thus may underrate the amount of progress a country has made toward modernization. Nor does the GNP measure many negative aspects of the standard of living. Although the average Burmese unquestionably lives much less well than the average person in the United States, the average American may cause 100 times as much ecological destruction to the planet.

Another problem with GNP and per-capita GNP reckoning is that they are measures devised by and for DCs, in which accurate government record-keeping is an established tradition and virtually all of a society's productive activity enters the money economy, where it is recorded and can be totaled. Yet even in the United States, agricultural, dairy, and livestock production consumed on the farm either is ignored or loosely estimated in the calculation of our total food production. This does not significantly affect decisions based on food production because production for consumption on the farm represents only a small part of overall United States food production (even though it would still account for millions of dollars' worth of food). In an LDC, where subsistence agriculture, home manufacture of household items, barter, and money transactions too small and casual to be noted are the rule, an analysis of the overall situation by government-published production records can and commonly does lead to very serious misjudgements about the real condition of an economy and society.

Finally, it must be remembered that the per-capita GNP statistic can and often does conceal gross inequities *within* countries in the distribution of goods and services. This makes it an even more fallible index of well-being.

[86] *The costs of economic growth,* pp. *ix–x,* Praeger, New York.

Growthmanship. A serious criticism that can be leveled at the majority of economists applies equally to most people and societies: they accept a doctrine of economic determinism. The myths of cornucopian economics, as opposed to the realities of geology and biology, have already been discussed, but the problem is much more pervasive than that. Economic growth has become *the* standard for progress, *the* benefit for which almost any social cost is to be paid.

This prejudice in economic thought can be fully appreciated by a perusal of Samuelson's *Economics.* The book, of course, is oriented toward economic growth. The increasing scarcity of nonrenewable resources is presented in it only briefly as a problem of less developed countries. The eventual physical constraint placed on material growth by the conversion to heat of all the energy people consume is not discussed in the text, nor are the more imminent environmental constraints considered in our earlier chapters. Implicit in Samuelson's treatment of economic development is the idea that it is possible for 5 billion to 7 billion people to achieve a standard of living similar to that of the average American of the 1960s. Excessive technological optimism is explicit or implicit throughout the book.

Nevertheless, Samuelson's text reveals more understanding of problems related to population size and environmental quality than the writings of many other economists. He does realize that growth of GNP must be "qualified by data on leisure, population size, relative distribution, quality, and noneconomic factors." In the 1970 edition, Samuelson added two chapters dealing with economic inequality, the quality of life, and problems of race, cities, and pollution. Furthermore, in 1969 Samuelson wrote:

> Most of us are poorer than we realize. Hidden costs are accruing all the time; and because we tend to ignore them, we overstate our incomes. Thomas Hobbes said that in the state of nature the life of man was nasty, brutish and short. In the state of modern civilization it has become nasty, brutish and long.[87]

Most economists subscribe to the "bigger and more is better" philosophy: the growing mixed economy is something to analyze, improve, and by all means to keep growing. In an article that appeared in the *New York Review of Books,* Nobel laureate economist Wassily Leontief of Harvard remarked, "If the 'external costs' of growth clearly seem to pose dangers to the quality of life, there is as yet no discernible tendency among economists or economic managers to divert their attention from this single-minded pursuit of economic growth."[88]

Indeed, when those external costs (various kinds of environmental and social deterioration) do come to the attention of economists, *growth* is seen as the way to deal with them. Walter Heller, once chairman of the President's Council of Economic Advisers, has stated, "I cannot conceive a successful economy without growth."[89] Accordingly, he urges expansion of the United States economy so that resources will become available to fight pollution. Heller, like many other economists, confuses more of the disease with the cure!

That economists have clung to their "growthmania" is not surprising, however. After all, natural scientists often cling to outmoded ideas that have produced far less palpable benefits than the growing mixed economies of the Western world in the twentieth century. The question of whether a different economic system might have produced a more equitable *distribution* of benefits is not one that Western economists like to dwell on. Furthermore, the idea of perpetual growth is congruent with the conventional wisdom of most of the businessmen of the world; indeed, of most of the world's population.

The people of the LDCs naturally wish to emulate the economic growth of the West, and they long for "development" with all its shiny accoutrements. Why should they be expected to know that it is physically and ecologically impossible for them to catch up with the United States when many of the "best informed" Americans are still unaware of that fact? Before attempting to pursue the Western pattern of development, perhaps they should contemplate Heller's belief that the best

[87]*Newsweek,* October 6, 1969.

[88]Quoted in Ehrlich and Ehrlich, *Population, resources, environment,* 2nd ed., p. 382.

[89]Undoubtedly an accurate statement. This quote and some of his other views are cited in E. F. Schumacher, *Small is beautiful; Economics as if people mattered,* pp. 111–112. For direct access to the views of Heller and other modern growthmen, see his *Perspectives on economic growth.* See also William Nordhaus and James Tobin who conclude in Is growth obsolete? that it is not, and that GNP is a pretty good measure of "secular progress." For a wonderful (if unintentional) parody of the writing of an uninformed economist, see Norman Macrae, America's third century.

hope for pulling the United States out of its environmental difficulties is yet more growth—even though the United States already co-opts some 30 percent of the world's resource use. Under that prescription, even catching up would not suffice.

New approaches to the national product. It is by now abundantly clear that the GNP cannot grow forever. Why should it? Why should we not strive for zero economic growth (ZEG) as well as zero population growth? As John Kenneth Galbraith pointed out in *The new industrial state,* it would be entirely logical to set limits on the amount of product a nation needs and then to strive to reduce the amount of work required to produce such a product (and, we might add, to see that the product is much more equitably distributed than it is today). Of course, such a program would be a threat to some of the most dearly held beliefs of this society. It would attack the Protestant work ethic, which insists that one must be kept busy on the job for forty hours a week. It is even better to work several more hours moonlighting, so that the money can be earned to buy all those wonderful automobiles, detergents, appliances, and assorted gimcracks that *must* be bought if the economy is to continue to grow. But this tradition is outmoded; the only hope for civilization in the future is to work for *quality* in the context of a nongrowing economy, or at least an economy in which growth is carefully restricted to certain activities.[90]

A number of interesting suggestions about GNP have been made by economist Edwin G. Dolan in his fine little 1969 book, *TANSTAAFL: The economic strategy for environmental crisis.* TANSTAAFL (which stands for **T**here **A**in't **N**o **S**uch **T**hing **A**s **A** **F**ree **L**unch) contains a lucid consideration of population-environment economics, and we recommend it, even though we differ with the author on some points. Dolan, along with some other economists, would rename the GNP the gross national cost (GNC).[91]

More important, Dolan would distinguish between two types of GNC. Type I GNC would measure that fraction of GNC produced with renewable resources and recycling of wastes. Type II GNC would be that depending on the depletion of nonrenewable resources and the production of indestructible wastes. The problems of discrimination might be difficult (consider, for instance, calculating the energy component involved in the production of Type I GNC), but the basic aim is sound. As Dolan says, "Politicians and economists would then design their policies to maximize Type I and minimize Type II. In the eyes of world opinion a high Type I component would be a source of national pride, while high production of the Type II variety would be a source of shame."

In a more technical vein, economists William Nordhaus and James Tobin, recognizing the problems inherent in GNP as a measure of what people value, have suggested some tentative (and sensible) modifications in GNP to produce a measure of economic welfare (MEW).[92] Their discussion gives hope that better *economic measures* can and should be developed—even though it is obvious to them and other thoughtful economists that *no* single measure of economic welfare is ever going to be fully satisfactory.[93]

The problem of finding even a partially satisfactory measure of total welfare, or quality of life (QOL), is infinitely more difficult.[93a] Beyond the question of refining the concept of GNP as a measure (or perhaps, more realistically, of disseminating the limitations of its usefulness throughout the economic, business, and political communities, which all too often act as though maximizing GNP were the ultimate human value), lies a more important issue. That is the perception by many people that the relationship between GNP and QOL has become negative; as GNP rises, QOL declines.[94]

Since there is no agreed-upon measure of QOL, this perception is unlikely to be tested by classical economic methods—but that does not mean that the phenomenon is not real. Perhaps the attempts by economists to refine the

[90]For an informative, brief discussion of work, leisure, and ZEG, see Paul W. Barkley and David W. Seckler, *Economic growth and environmental decay: The solution becomes the problem.* See also Chapter 3 of Pirages and Ehrlich, *Ark II.;* Herman Daly, The economics of the steady state; and Fred Hirsch, *Social limits to growth.*

[91]Kenneth E. Boulding has long championed that name change. See also the chapter on "GNP-Fetishism" in Victor A. Weisskopf's *Alienation and economics.*

[92]Is growth obsolete?

[93]See, for example, Arthur M. Okun, Social welfare has no price tag.

[93a]An extensive discussion of the problem of defining QOL is contained in Peter W. House, *The quest for completeness: Comprehensive analysis in modeling, indicators, gaming, planning and management.*

[94]P. R. Ehrlich and R. Harriman, *How to be a survivor: A plan to save Spaceship Earth.*

concept of GNP or to define QOL[95] eventually will permit a more precise tracking of the relationship, but it seems unlikely that human social systems or the ecological systems of the planet can afford to wait. We suspect that the era of indiscriminate growth will come to an end soon—preferably through political action generated by subjective perceptions of declining QOL by large numbers of people—but if not, by the intervention of ecocatastrophes. Hints of the former could be seen in such phenomena as the popularity in 1976 of California governor Jerry Brown's "limits to growth" campaign for the presidency.

Cost-benefit analyses. One of the problems with growthmania is that for too long the penalties of growth have been ignored by the economic system. Cost-benefit calculations until very recently were done with too narrow an outlook and over too short a time span.

For example, consider the history of a contemporary housing development. A developer carves up a southern California hillside, builds houses on it, and sells them, reaping the benefits in a very short time. Then society starts to pay the costs. The houses have been built in an area where the native plant community is chaparral (Chapter 4). Chaparral, known to plant ecologists as a "fire climax," would not exist as a stable vegetation type unless the area burned over occasionally. When it does, the homes are destroyed, and the buyers and the public start paying hidden costs in the form of increased insurance rates and emergency relief.

Of course, there are hidden costs even in the absence of such a catastrophe. A housing development puts a further load on the water supply and probably will be a contributing political factor in the ultimate flooding of distant farmland to make a reservoir. Perhaps wind patterns cause smog to be especially thick in the area of the development, and as it begins to affect the inhabitants they and society pay additional costs in hospital bills and high life-insurance premiums. And, of course, by helping to attract more people into the area, the development helps to increase the general smog burden.

[95]See, for example, Lowdon Wingo, The quality of life: Toward a microeconomic definition. See also the discussions in Chapter 12 and below of the connections between quality of life and diversity of personal options, and Richard Easterlin's fascinating Does economic growth improve the human lot?

Then there are the problems of additional roads, schools, sewage-treatment plants, and other community requirements created by the subdivision. While the builder may have put the roads in the subdivision, increased taxes must pay for increased upkeep on roads in the subdivision area, and eventually for new roads demanded by increasing congestion. Among the saddest phenomena of our time are the attempts by politicians and chambers of commerce to attract industry and developers to their areas to "broaden the tax base." The usual result, when the dust has settled, is that the people who previously lived in the area have a degraded environment and *higher* taxes.

In short, the benefits are easily calculated and quickly reaped by a select few; the costs, on the other hand, are diffuse, spread over time, and difficult to calculate. For example, how would one assess the cost of weather modification by pollution, which might result in the deaths of millions from starvation? What is the value of an ecological system destroyed by chlorinated hydrocarbons? What is the value of one life lost to emphysema?

The disparity between the few elements accounted for in present methods of cost-benefit analysis and the real costs borne by society is even more obvious when the problem of industrial pollution is considered. Here the benefit is usually the absence of a cost. Garbage is spewed into the environment, rather than being retained and reclaimed. The industry avoids real or imagined financial loss by this process. The term *imagined loss* is used because some industries have found that reclaiming pollutants has more than paid for the cost of retaining them. More often than not, however, the industry benefits from pollution, and the public pays the short- and long-term costs. Air pollutants damage crops, ruin paint, soil clothes, dissolve nylon stockings, etch glass, rot windshield-wiper blades, and so on. Pollutants must be removed, often at considerable expense, from water supplies. People with emphysema, lung cancer, liver cancer, and hepatitis must be given expensive hospitalization. Insurance costs go up. In these, and in myriad other ways, *everyone* pays.

Perhaps the most subtle and least appreciated costs are those society must shoulder when it damages or destroys ecosystems that formerly performed essential free services. For example, destruction of natural areas, especially forests, can change climate locally, often resulting in greater frequency and intensity of floods and droughts and a need for water management projects. Soil erosion can be greatly accelerated, leading to silting of streams and lakes, with damage to fisheries and polluted water supplies. With the loss of the air purifying functions of ecosystems, air pollution is increased.[95a]

These costs are what accountants euphemistically call external diseconomies, because they are external to the accounting system of the polluter. A persuasive case can be made that, at an advanced stage of industrialization, the diseconomies far outweigh the benefits of growth. Such a case was made in detail by economist Ezra Mishan some years ago and refined since.[96]

That the costs to society of pollution and environmental destruction far exceed those of abatement or prevention is no longer in serious doubt. U.S. national pollution-control expenditures for 1972, both public and private, amounted to $19 billion; the annual costs of just air and water pollution were variously estimated (so far as they could be) in a range from $10 billion to $50 billion around 1970.[97] And those estimates probably left out many of the indirect costs, which are often impossible to sort out from other causes, and some for which there is no price tag, such as aesthetic value.

The simplest way to attack external diseconomies directly is to require industry to internalize them. Companies can be forced by law to absorb the costs of greatly reducing the release of pollutants. Profits would then be added on after *all* costs were paid. Clearly, the most sensible solution in most cases is for society to insist on pollution abatement *at the source.* It is cheaper in every way to curtail it there, rather than attempt to ameliorate the complex problems pollutants cause after they are released into the environment.

Society, having permitted the pollution situation to develop, should also shoulder some of the burden of its correction. As a theoretical example, Steel Company X, located on the shores of Lake Michigan, is pouring filth into the lake at a horrendous rate. A study shows that it would cost two dollars per share of common stock to build the necessary apparatus for retaining and processing the waste. Should the company be forced to stop polluting and pay the price?

Certainly it must be forced to stop, but it seems fair that society should pay some of the cost. When Company X located on the lake, everyone knew that it would spew pollutants into the lake, but no one objected. The local people wanted to encourage industry. Now, finally, society has changed its mind, and the pollution must stop. But should Company X be forced into bankruptcy by pollution regulations, penalizing stockholders and putting its employees out of work? Should the local politicians who lured the company into locating there and the citizens who encouraged them not pay a cent? Clearly society should order the pollution stopped *and pick up at least part of the bill.* It would be a bargain in the long run; society is already paying a much higher cost for the pollution.

Such a situation actually occurred in 1971. Congress refused to vote funds for the continuance of the SST project, in part because of environmental considerations. As mentioned earlier, the decision cost thousands of existing jobs and even more potential jobs. Society must find mechanisms to compensate people who lost jobs in such a way, and it must retrain and, if necessary, relocate them. Such dislocations are certain to occur more often and on a larger scale as polluting, energy-wasting, and socially dangerous industries and projects are phased out. Fortunately, time should be available to smooth the transitions in most situations.

It has become obvious that one needed change in the economic system is to adopt a new method of cost-accounting that fully incorporates such items as resource depletion and environmental degradation, even though such a change might involve grave political repercussions.

Economics, Resources, and the Environment

The Bucky Fulfilling dreams of technologically based abundance of the sixties now seem adolescent and remote.

—Hazel Henderson,
Planning Review, April/May 1974

[95a]F. H. Bormann, An inseparable linkage: Conservation of natural ecosystems and the conservation of fossil energy.

[96]*The costs of economic growth;* Ills, bads, and disamenities: The wages of growth.

[97]CEQ, *Environmental quality, 1975,* pp. 496–543.

Economist Kenneth Boulding once described the present economic system of the United States as a *cowboy economy.*[98] The cowboy metaphor refers to a reckless, exploitive philosophy based on two premises: more resources are waiting just over the horizon, and nature has a boundless capacity to absorb garbage. For practical purposes, those premises were valid in the days of the American frontier. In that world it made some sense to seek rapid improvements in human welfare strictly through economic growth, with little regard for what *kind* of growth or for the sorts of waste that accompanied it.

But today the old premises are wrong. It is now clear that physical resources are limited and that humanity is straining the capacity of the biological environment to absorb abuse on a global scale. The blind growth of a cowboy economy is no longer a viable proposition—even though, as noted above, an astonishing number of economists (and others) still cling to the belief that it is.

The accepted measure of success in a cowboy economy is a large throughput. *Throughput* refers to the rate at which dollars flow through the economy and, insofar as dollar flow depends on the sale of physical goods rather than services, to the speed with which natural resources are converted into artifacts and rubbish. A conventional indicator of throughput is the GNP.

Boulding has described a rational alternative to the GNP-oriented cowboy economy, calling this alternative the *spaceman economy,* in harmony with the concept of Spaceship Earth. Consistent with the finiteness of this planet's supply of resources and the fragility of the biological processes that support human life, such an economy would be nongrowing in terms of the size of the human population, the quantity of physical resources in use, and human impact on the biological environment. The spaceman economy need not be stagnant, however; human ingenuity would be constantly at work increasing the amount of actual prosperity and well-being derivable from the fixed amount of resources in use.

Quite the opposite of the cowboy economy, which thrives on throughput, the spaceman economy would seek to minimize the throughput needed to maintain its stable stock of goods. This is an obvious goal for any economy as regards population. A given population size can be maintained by a high birth rate balanced by a high death rate (high throughput) or by a low birth rate balanced by a low death rate (low throughput). Most people would agree that the low-throughput situation is preferable. Applying this to material goods, the "birth rate" is the production rate and the "death rate" is the rate at which the goods wear out or become obsolete. A given level of affluence, measured in terms of the stock of goods per person, can be maintained by very different levels of resource flow. Thus, a society with one refrigerator for every three people can maintain this level of affluence with refrigerators that need replacement every ten years (high throughput) or every forty years (low throughput).

Quality of life in a spaceman economy. Could people's desires for material comforts and a high quality of life be met in a spaceman economy? There are good reasons to believe the answer is yes. With an unchanging number of people, society's efforts can be devoted entirely to improving conditions for the population that exists, rather than to struggling to provide the necessities of existence for new additions. Moreover, focusing attention on the *quality* of a fixed stock of goods in a spaceman economy is in many respects a more direct route to prosperity than emphasizing throughput in a cowboy economy. This is so because, as Boulding has argued, *quality* of stock is often a better measure of well-being than throughput. Most people would rather own one Rolls Royce than a succession of Fords.

Furthermore, once a good diet, adequate housing, clean water, sanitation facilities, and a certain basic level of well-made material goods have been provided, quality of life becomes largely a matter of the availability of services and personal options. Services include education, medical care, entertainment and recreation, fire and police protection, and the administration of justice. Services do involve the use of material resources and do affect the environment. For example, commercial office space, much of it associated with the provision of services, is a major consumer of electricity for lighting, heating, and air conditioning. Nevertheless, there is great potential for improving and extending services while reducing the associated material, energy, and environmental demands.

[98]The economics of the coming Spaceship Earth.

Personal options consist of access to a variety of landscapes, living accommodations, career possibilities, cultural environments, recreational opportunities, interpersonal relationships, degrees of privacy, and so forth. Personal options are an important part of the quality of an individual's life even when they are not exercised—it pleases us to know we *could* live in the country, even though we may choose to live in cities. Options also have value beyond the preferences of the majority of people in any given society. If the majority of citizens preferred an urban environment, that would not be sufficient reason to transform all living areas of the planet into urban environments—this is tyranny of the majority. Even those who enjoy neither canoeing nor golf should concede that a society with room for golf courses and free-flowing rivers is preferable to a society without those options. It is even reasonable to suppose that in human society diversity on a small scale (individual choice) promotes stability on a large scale (society as a whole).

Insofar as personal options are part of quality of life, the spaceman economy is a clear choice over the cowboy economy. Population growth and the transformation of an ever larger fraction of the biosphere to maintain the growth of throughput are destroying options in the United States now and for the future. By stabilizing the population and reducing the level of environmentally disruptive activities associated with throughput of resources, the spaceman economy would preserve remaining options; by focusing on services and finding new ways that "people can live more gently on the Earth,"[99] it would create new ones.

Converting to a spaceman economy. How can the world society make the transition from a cowboy economy to a spaceman economy? How do we get from here to there? Population control, of course, is absolutely essential, with an eventual target of a *smaller* population than today's.[100] Another task that must be faced squarely is the redistribution of wealth within and between nations. Otherwise, fixing the quantity of physical goods in use would freeze the majority of human beings in a state of poverty.

Within rich countries such as the United States, the problem could be alleviated by a relatively moderate amount of redistribution. Economist Herman Daly has called for the establishment of a *distributist institution,* which would limit the range of financial inequity in the United States. He suggests establishing maximum and minimum incomes, arguing, "Most people are not so stupid as to believe that an income in excess of say $100,000 per year has any real functional justification . . . especially . . . when the high paid jobs are also usually the most interesting and pleasant." He would also limit personal and corporate wealth and then "put responsible social limits on the exercise of monopoly power by labor unions, since the countervailing monopoly power of corporations will have been limited."[101]

The critical question, of course, is how to get around the extraordinary power interests that would be unalterably opposed to maximum income limits and (if possible) even more opposed to direct taxation of wealth. Greed and the desire for power are extraordinarily strong forces against any serious attempts to curb income and wealth, and many conventional economists (with their hands firmly clenched on Daly's symbolic rice) would oppose such limitation on the grounds that it would kill the incentive system that keeps the economy growing. Daly suggests gradual implementation as a strategy—and perhaps that could be made to work, since the *principles* of progressive income taxation and some sort of "floor" under individual income are rather well established in our society. The real sticky wicket would be direct taxation of wealth, since that would threaten the entrenched power of the Rockefellers, Carnegies, Fords, Kennedys, and countless other beneficiaries of enterprising and acquisitive ancestors. But once some system of further redistribution were established in the United States, it would then be justifiable to implement a transition to a spaceman economy as quickly as possible.

In the poor countries, a degree of careful expansion of productive activities—that is, continued economic growth sufficient to raise per-capita living standards—as

---

[99]See S. Page, Jr., and W. Clark, The new alchemy: How to survive in your spare time.

[100]See, for example, Emile Benoit, A dynamic equilibrium economy, *Bulletin of the Atomic Scientists,* February 1976; Ehrlich and Ehrlich, *Population, resources, environment, 1st ed.,* p. 322.

[101]Testimony before the Joint Economic Committee of Congress, October 23, 1975, pp. 10 and 11; see also the book he edited, *Toward a steady-state economy.*

well as massive transfers of goods and technical assistance from the rich countries (see Chapter 15) will be necessary before the notion of a spaceman economy can be seriously entertained. It is clear that redistribution alone would be insufficient to give all human beings an acceptable standard of living—at least, acceptable by today's DC standards. That would mean a per-capita GNP of only about $1000, even if population size were also frozen at 4 billion.

Reducing throughput. The strategy of converting productive capacity from frivolous and wasteful enterprises to legitimate social needs should be accompanied, even in the short term, by efforts to minimize the throughput of resources associated with production. Herman Daly has suggested a specific mechanism for accomplishing such a reduction: putting strict *depletion quotas* on the natural resources of the United States.[102] That is, limits would be placed on the total amount of each resource that could be extracted or imported by the United States each year. This would not only directly reduce the pressure Americans place on the resources of the planet, but would also automatically generate a trend toward recycling and pollution abatement. With resources scarce (and thus expensive), a premium would be placed on the durability of goods, recycling, and the restriction of effluents (which often contain "resources" not now economically recoverable). Environmental deterioration from the processes of resource extraction and transport would be reduced, as would that resulting from manufacturing resources into finished goods. Less energy is usually required to recycle materials than to start anew from basic resources. And depletion quotas on fossil fuels and fissionable materials would encourage the frugal use of energy.

Limiting the amount of energy available would, of course, also tend to limit the weight and number of automobiles, encourage the use of mass transit, and promote the substitution of efficient high-speed trains for energetically wasteful short- and medium-haul jet airplanes. As Daly notes, a basic system of depletion quotas would have to be supplemented to some degree with such devices as taxes on effluents, but we agree with him that operating at the resource rather than the rubbish end of the system is fundamentally the better approach. It requires controls at many fewer points and thus would be simpler to institute, because it tackles the system where the materials are still concentrated rather than dispersed.

One of the most difficult problems in implementing the Daly system would be dealing with imports. Obviously, quotas would have to be established on imported raw materials, or the primary result of the system would be merely to shift pressure from U.S. resources to the resources of the rest of the world. If American manufacturers alone were strictly rationed, there would surely be an upsurge in manufactured imports. Restrictions therefore would have to be placed on the import of manufactured goods, perhaps based on their "resource content." Those restrictions might best be put only on imports from other developed countries to encourage them to establish depletion quotas also. Restrictions could be omitted for certain manufactured goods from less developed countries wherever it seemed that access to United States markets would be a genuine economic help to the exporter.

Another suggestion for a government system that could be employed to limit throughput has been put forward by two ecologists (described in Box 14-3). It is a more complex system than Daly's, but has the big advantage of making the public aware of the environmental impact of human activities.

Daly claims that cornucopians should make no objection to schemes that limit resource depletion, for they are eternally assuring us that technological progress (such as substitutions for depleted resources) would be encouraged by rising resource prices, and that such advances would make resource supplies virtually infinite.[103] Since depletion quotas would increase the price incentives, they could be viewed as a test of the faith of the technological optimists—a test that would simulta-depletion quotas would increase the price incentives, they could be viewed as a test of the faith of the technological optimists—a test that would simultaneously conserve our resource heritage in case not enough technological rabbits appear from the hat.

[102]The stationary state economy. See also his *Toward a steady-state economy,* for expansion of these ideas.

[103]See, for example, H. E. Goeller and A. Weinberg, The age of substitutability.

BOX 14-3 A Novel Scheme for Limiting Environmental Deterioration

Two Australian ecologists, Walter E. Westman and Roger M. Gifford, have put forth a novel suggestion for maintaining the quality of the environment at any level desired by society.* They propose establishing a money-independent "price" on every activity that has a clear environmental impact. The basic nonmonetary unit would be the natural resource unit (NRU). NRUs would be distributed equally among individuals and by special means to business firms, government entities, and nonprofit organizations.

The overall level of environmental impact would be regulated by government establishment of both the total yearly allocation of NRUs and the price in NRUs of every good, service, and activity of environmental significance. This would lead in effect to a "rationing" of rights to pollute, destroy habitats, add to population pressure, or extract natural resources.

The advantages of such a system are numerous. Open, rather than covert, decisions on the quality of the environment would be made. Since NRUs would not be transferable, the system would be equitable—the rich would not be allowed greater per-capita impact than the poor. Individuals, however, would be able to accumulate NRUs throughout their lives and could determine how to spend them free of arbitrary government decision-making. It might be possible, for instance, for an individual to have a second child or to fly a light aircraft 100 hours per year, but not both. Or one might decide to have an air-conditioned house, but if so, an overseas vacation might be possible only once every ten years. Instead of direct constraints being placed by society on activities, each person's life-style would be partially determined by a series of environmental trade-offs of his or her own choosing.

On the debit side would be the enormous bureaucratic problem of setting up the equivalent of a second monetary system, the great problem of assigning reasonable values to goods and activities, and the inevitable corruption and scheming that institution of such a plan would induce. Its authors present a most interesting discussion of its details and offer it in the full knowledge that it is not politically feasible at present. But it is hard to disagree with one of their major conclusions: "Although involving more planning and more governmental regulation than is currently deemed feasible or acceptable, we believe the mechanism would lead to less restriction of personal freedom in a steady-state society than would the current trend toward unsystematic imposition of governmental regulations."

*Environmental impact: Controlling the overall level.

Daly summarized his distributive and throughput-limiting proposals as follows:

> In spite of their somewhat radical implications, these proposals are based on impeccably respectable conservative premises: private property and the free market. If private property is good, then everyone should share in it; and, making allowances for a range of legitimate inequality, no one should be allowed to hog too much of it, lest it become the instrument of exploitation rather than the barrier to exploitation that was its classical justification. Even orthodox economic theory has long recognized that the market fails to deal adequately with depletion, pollution, and distribution. These proposals supplement the market at its weak points, allowing it to allocate resources within imposed ethical and ecological limits.[104]

Much additional effort by economists and others will be required to work out details of the changes required in order to minimize throughput in the economic system. One further step, however, is already clear. Both before and after depletion quotas are established, ways must be found to control advertising. Advertising plays a key role in promoting growthmania in the DCs. In those nations the basic human needs for food, clothing, shelter, medical care, and education are being met for perhaps 90 percent of the populations. In order to keep those economies growing, therefore, new "needs" must be created. E. F. Schumacher has written, "The cultivation

[104]1975 testimony, p. 12.

and expansion of needs is the antithesis of wisdom. It is also the antithesis of freedom and peace. Every increase of needs tends to increase one's dependence on outside forces over which one cannot have control, and therefore creates existential fear. Only by a reduction of needs can one promote a genuine reduction in those tensions which are the ultimate cause of strife and war."[105]

The employment problem. Redirecting production into more useful channels and reducing the throughput associated with production will entail considerable retraining and temporary unemployment in the work force. These problems will be all the more difficult in the United States because of the unemployment problem that already exists. The 4 to 10 percent unemployment figures commonly quoted as the economy cycles between boom and recession do not reveal the true seriousness of the problem. First of all, this overt unemployment is very unevenly distributed in the population. Racial minorities, young workers, women, and, above all, young minority workers suffer disproportionately. The pressure of unemployment at the younger end of the labor pool is probably a major reason that American society has been so rigid about retirement around the age of 65. Many talented people are removed from the labor force even though they may still be capable of ten years or more of productive work and do not wish to be "put out to pasture." The enforced separation of older people from their economic lives also clearly contributes to their general problems.

Added to these components of the employment picture is disguised unemployment: people doing jobs that are either unnecessary or detrimental to society, or both. Anyone familiar with government, big business, universities, the military, or any large bureaucracy, knows how many people are just doing busywork or pushing paper. When those people are combined with workers who are engaged in such fundamentally counterproductive activities as building freeways, producing oversized cars and unneeded appliances, devising deceptive advertising, or manufacturing superfluous weapons systems, the number of people who are unemployed, underemployed, or misemployed is seen to make up a substantial portion of the work force.

[105]*Small is beautiful,* p. 31.

Of course, the whole employment problem would be badly aggravated if society attempted to discontinue too abruptly those jobs that are unnecessary or socially and environmentally destructive. Maintaining some of those activities is probably necessary in the short run while changes in employment patterns are worked out. But now is the time to start planning and maneuvering to phase out both disguised unemployment and destructive products without damaging society and without creating enormous levels of overt unemployment.

The transition should be greatly assisted by the obvious potential for expanded employment in services such as health care and education (including adult education); in developing energetically efficient transportation systems for people and freight; in perfecting and deploying solar and other environmentally desirable energy technologies; in recycling and pollution-control industries; in environmental improvement activities such as reclamation of strip-mined land, reforestation, and the construction of urban parks; in converting the food production system to more wholesome, less wasteful and energy-consumptive practices; and in the development, production, and distribution of better contraceptives.[106] The transition should also be eased somewhat because the numbers of new young job-seekers will begin to decline after 1980, because of the smaller number of births in the United States in the 1960s compared to the 1950s. And, if the trend of past decades in which workers have been increasingly replaced by fuel-burning machinery is reversed, the result obviously will be more jobs.

In the longer term, even with greater use of labor instead of machines in some areas of the economy, the solution to the employment problem may well require a reduction in the amount of work done by each worker in order to create more jobs. Gradually shortening the work week (ultimately to twenty-five hours or less) or decreasing the number of work weeks per year (companies could have different spring-summer and fall-winter shifts) would accomplish this. There would be more time for leisure, which might be better enjoyed by a more educated population. There would also be more time for people both to obtain that education and to put it to good

[106]See, for example, Patrick Heffernan, Jobs and the environment.

use participating in running society (see "Education"). There should be few but positive consequences from such a reduction in working time. Pay might have to be reduced, but so would many expenses if material goods were built to endure and there were no longer social pressures to consume for the sake of consuming. If people could be diverted from the high-speed, mechanized forms of leisure activity now promoted by advertising, the pace of life would undoubtedly slow down, with attendant psychological and physical benefits. If a stable economic system could be achieved, life would indeed by different from—and conceivably much improved over—what it is today.

Economics and pesticides: a case history of environmental politics. The profound changes necessary to save the environment and society will not be made easily, however. Powerful opposition can be expected from economic interests. Such opposition has long been mounted by the petrochemical industry, whose behavior foreshadowed that of other industries. It is worthwhile to examine this behavior in some detail at this point as an example of the kinds of barriers that may obstruct any attempts to establish a spaceman economy in the United States.

The giant petrochemical industry has applied constant political pressure (through friends in Congress and such agencies as the USDA) and has resorted to outright lies about the safety of pesticides in order to avoid regulation, particularly since the publication in 1962 of Rachel Carson's book, *Silent spring,* which was addressed to the public at large. The industry has attempted to discredit responsible scientists who have nothing to sell, but who oppose modern patterns of pesticide usage because they have learned through careful and patient study that DDT and related pesticides are not mere killers of insects, but threaten the capacity of Earth to support human life. Desperately worried biologists have attempted, through public education and by going to court, to keep more of these poisons from entering the environment, and concerned conservationists have done what they could. But until 1969 the petrochemical industry was almost completely successful in forestalling any effective regulation of its activities. Since the Wisconsin hearings on DDT in that year, the industry has been losing battles, but not gracefully.

The industry's early tactics were typified by an editorial that appeared in the journal *Farm chemicals* (January 1968), which not only labeled every biologist critical of current pesticide practice as a member of a "cult" and a "professional agitator," but also claimed that "scientists themselves literally ostracized Rachel Carson, and they will come to grips with this eroding force within their own ranks. Of course, it is not unusual that the character of the scientific community is changing. It may be a sign of the times. The age of opportunism!" This editorial appeared four years after Rachel Carson's death, yet the ghost of this remarkably sensitive and extremely capable marine biologist apparently still haunted those whose products she had found were dangerously polluting the environment.

Unquestionably, some chemists and entomologists attempted to discredit Rachel Carson. Most of those who did, however, were either employed by the petrochemical industry or were too narrowly trained (as many entomologists still are) to appreciate the dangers in the use of such powerful chemicals. Scientists in other disciplines disagreed with her too, but for the wrong reasons: some argued that she was speaking outside her field of expertise; others charged her with emotionalism. Thousands of biologists, however, admired her tremendously for her breadth of view and for awakening the general public to the hazards posed by the use of dangerous chemicals in attempts to increase the production of food.

It is true that there were a few factual errors in *Silent spring,* but in many ways Rachel Carson *underestimated* the hazards of DDT and certain other chlorinated hydrocarbons. Nevertheless, she succeeded in awakening the public—and did so in a way that a more technical and highly documented book like Robert L. Rudd's *Pesticides and the living landscape* could not. Rudd, a zoologist, came to many of the same conclusions that were presented in *Silent spring,* but because his book was not addressed to the general public it did not engender the level of attack that was directed toward the Carson book. In our opinion, no biologist has made a greater contribution to humanity in this century than Rachel Carson. And recent events and government decisions have fully justified her position.

The petrochemical industry is now on the defensive because, as we described earlier in this chapter, scientists and other citizens have discovered that there are legal remedies against environmental degradation and health hazards and have been using them.

It seems unlikely that the reaction of the industry was based on the DDT or chlorinated hydrocarbon issue alone. A more likely reason was apprehension about the precedents that would be set if any or all of those chemicals were banned or restricted in use. The industry would prefer to account primarily to the friendly and compliant USDA, not to the EPA or to groups of scientists who are worried about the ecological effects and long-term dangers to human well-being caused by their activities.

Soon after the Environmental Protection Agency was created in 1970, it was given responsibility for the registration and regulation of pesticides. Litigation by the Environmental Defense Fund produced a court order early in 1971 for EPA to issue public notices of cancellation of registration of DDT and to review DDT for suspension. Cancellation stops sales after thirty days, provided that the manufacturers do not appeal, a process that can go on for years. Suspension, on the other hand, takes effect at once, even as appeal proceeds. The notices of cancellation for DDT, as well as aldrin, dieldrin, mirex, and the herbicide 2,4,5-T were, of course, appealed.

After lengthy hearings, EPA banned DDT for almost all uses in 1972. It found that DDT "posed an unacceptable risk to man and the environment."[107] Restrictions were also placed on the use of mirex, a pesticide mainly used against the fire ant (Appendix 4). The proceedings against 2,4,5-T were confused by the discovery that tetrachlorodioxin (TCDD) impurities were the major toxic threat from that herbicide.

Between 1972 and 1974 restrictions were placed on aldrin and dieldrin, and in October 1974 an immediately effective ban was placed on their production. EPA administrator Russell E. Train's decision was made because those compounds represented an "imminent hazard"[108] because of their capacity to induce tumors in mice (indicating a direction in the EPA similar to the Delaney amendment's zero tolerance for food additives found carcinogenic in test animals, described in Chapter 10). In July 1975 two other chlorinated hydrocarbons, chlordane and heptachlor, were also banned because of their carcinogenicity in laboratory tests. All of these bans are under appeal as this is written, but the trend toward much more careful regulation of pesticides had been clearly established a decade after Rachel Carson's death from cancer in 1964, and the EPA was showing signs of increasing toughness.

In 1972 the old Federal Insecticide, Fungicide, and Rodenticide Act (FIFRA) was amended by the Federal Environmental Pesticide Control Act (FEPCA), expanding the EPA's authority to classify pesticides for general or restricted use, regulate the way they are used, and specify labeling—authority that was quickly employed to improve record-keeping on amounts and disposition of all pesticides produced. In October 1974 the EPA announced proposed regulations for registering new pesticides and reregistering those already on the market. In a critical provision, those regulations established a "presumption against new or continued registration of any pesticide with extremely high acute toxicity characteristics *or which produces in laboratory or field situations any evidence of oncogenicity* [*tumor induction*], *teratogenicity, or multitest evidence of mutagenicity. . . .*"[109]

The presumption could be rebutted, but the burden of proof would be on the company applying for registration. To say the least, the pesticide industry is "concerned" about the tough new regulations—and, if only from an economic point of view, they should be, since there is strong evidence that the cost of developing new products and keeping them registered is increasing rapidly.[110]

A comprehensive study of the problems of pest-control by a committee of the National Academy of Sciences concluded that regulation could be improved, but that provided little comfort to the petrochemical industry. The study found that considerations entirely

[107]CEQ, *Environmental Quality—1972.*

[108]L. J. Carter, Controversy over new pesticide regulations.

[109]Quoted by Carter (his emphasis).

[110]National Academy of Sciences, *Study on problems of pest control.*

within the agricultural sector—namely, the declining efficacy of pesticides with the development of resistance in pests—demanded greater attention to alternative methods of pest control. The committee was especially concerned with the impact of regulation on the development of new technologies to replace the conventional broad-spectrum chemicals that have dominated the pest-control scene since 1950. It is clear, of course, that the required technologies are unlikely to be generated within the chemical industry. The NAS report went on to point out:

> The products produced by the chemical industry appear admirably to meet the economic goals that we assume dominate the decision-making processes in private industry. Unfortunately, the sole example of overlap between the properties desired by the industry and those of the most promising alternatives would seem to be the observation that the industry favors short persistence over long by a wide margin. Conversely, however, industry favors a broad spectrum of biological activity over a narrow spectrum by almost the same margin.[111]

In short, a compound that must be repeatedly applied, that kills natural enemies, and produces rapid evolution of resistance is preferred by pesticide manufacturers—merely because, in the process of not working, it can be recommended in ever-increasing doses and eventually can be replaced by another ecological sledgehammer marketed by the same industry. Pest-control techniques that were truly effective, of course, would be a disaster for the pesticide industry.

Implementation of one regulatory recommendation of the NAS study, that the availability of alternatives should influence registration judgements, would be another serious blow for the industry, as well as a major step toward protecting humanity from its activities. Tougher regulations quite likely would cause some decline in traditional firms involved in manufacturing pesticides. Fortunately, as noted in Chapter 11, ecologically sound pest management (which would include sparing use of chemicals integrated with other techniques) would be more labor-intensive than the present broadcast-spray system. At least in theory, then, a transition to such management could be accomplished with a net gain of jobs in the economy, although many individuals would certainly have to be retrained.

[111]Ibid., vol. 1, p. 139.

Economics versus environmental reality. Defensive reactions have also come from other industries whose activities contribute heavily to pollution. Representatives of the inorganic-nitrogen-fertilizer industry have given extensive testimony before Congress, most of which confirmed the belief of many biologists that the industry just cannot (or does not want to) grasp the dimensions of the problems that result from failure to maintain an adequate supply of humus in the soil. Manufacturers of fluorocarbons and aerosol cans have vigorously lobbied against restrictive legislation. Makers of nonreturnable containers and poisonous food additives have fought to continue marketing their products. The list is both interminable and understandable; no person or corporation likes to see income or economic survival threatened.

It is most difficult to protect the environment when economists, industries, and government agencies team up to wreak havoc, as they did, in effect, in the case of the supersonic transport. Building and marketing a commercial SST was "justified" in the United States largely on the grounds that it was needed economically to protect the balance of payments. President Richard M. Nixon, in endorsing the nation's SST program in 1969, stated, "I want the United States to continue to lead the world in air transport." The economic penalties that would be incurred from damage caused by sonic booms were probably not included in the administration's consideration of whether to proceed with the project, nor were the psychological and emotional damages people would suffer, nor the possible effects on the world's climate (which themselves might cause heavy economic damage) from the operation of these high-altitude jets. Indeed, even the lethal possibility of reducing Earth's ozone shield took second place to the balance of payments.

Fortunately, a combination of factors, including intensive lobbying on the adverse side effects of the SST by environmental organizations and testimony by several distinguished economists that it was an economic boondoggle, convinced Congress that the SST's disadvantages outweighed its very questionable advantages, and the U.S. program was killed in 1971.

In 1975 the debate began anew when rights to land in the United States were requested for the Anglo-French SST, Concorde. The issue is still in doubt, but several things are apparent—the Concorde is extremely noisy, fuel-inefficient, and probably uneconomical. If it remains in service, it will be as a monument to government stupidity and the momentum of technological circuses.

Government Planning

The fragmentation of responsibility among government agencies in the United States makes a reasonable response to problems extremely difficult and planning to avert them virtually impossible. The lack of overall control of environmental matters and the virtual impossibility of dealing with problems in any coordinated way are illustrated by the area of urban affairs, aspects of which now come under the jurisdictions of the Department of Housing and Urban Development, the Department of Health, Education and Welfare, as well as the Departments of Labor, Commerce, Interior, Justice, and Transportation, to name just the major ones. It is clear that the executive branch of the federal government badly needs reorganizing.

Such coordinated planning as takes place in the federal government is largely confined to the preparation and review of the annual federal budget. It is fair to say that the time horizons considered in this process are typically short and the emphasis on conventional economic indicators heavy. Resource and environmental matters accordingly receive less attention than they deserve.[111a]

Some detailed suggestions on reforming the political structure of the United States to make it more responsive to the requirements of the population-resource-environment situation may be found in the book *Ark II.*[112] We discuss only one such reform here: the institutionalization of government planning.

The Center for the Study of Democratic Institutions has an ongoing project under the direction of R. G. Tugwell, designed to produce a modern constitution for the United States. The proposed constitution, now in its thirty-third draft, deserves wide circulation and study. One of the features of the Tugwell constitution is a planning branch of the government, with the mission of doing long-range planning. As should be apparent from the preceding discussion, without planning we believe there is little chance of saving civilization from a downward spiral of deepening social and environmental disruptions and political conflicts. Human societies have shown little aptitude for planning so far, but it is a skill that must soon be developed.[112a]

A private organization, California Tomorrow, sponsored a group of planners who produced a document that might serve as a preliminary model for the kind of planning that can be done. *The California tomorrow plan: A first sketch* presents a skeletal plan for the future of the state of California.[113] It describes "California zero," the California of today, and two alternative futures: California I is a "current-trends-continue" projection; California II is a projection in which various alternative courses of action are followed.

The plan considers twenty-two major problem areas, including population growth and various kinds of environmental deterioration, and looks at both the causes of the problems and policies to ameliorate them. California I is compared with California II, and suggestions for phasing into the California II projection are given. The details of the plan need not concern us here, but the subjects of concern in the plan are roughly those of this book. What is encouraging is that a private organization could put together a comprehensive vision of the future of one of the largest political entities in the world, proving that intelligent, broad-spectrum planning can be done.

[111a]A sense of the planning inputs to and implications of the federal budgeting process is conveyed in the series of volumes, *Setting national priorities*, published annually by the Brookings Institution since 1970. The 1976 volume, edited by Henry Owen and Charles L. Schultze, takes a longer-range perspective (10 years) on issues raised by the budget, and examines the problems of coordinated long-range planning in a government of divided powers.

[112]Pirages and Ehrlich.

[112a]A series of important books on the tools and prospects for comprehensive governmental planning appeared in 1976 and 1977 under the authorship of social scientist and modeler Peter W. House and colleagues: House, *The quest for completeness;* House and Williams, *The carrying capacity of a nation;* House and McLeod, *Large scale models for policy evaluation;* House, *Trading-off environment, economics, and energy.*

[113]Alfred Heller, ed., *The California tomorrow plan.*

The next question is, how can "USA Zero" be started toward "USA II"? It may well be necessary to form a new political party founded on the principles of population control, environmental quality, a stabilized economy, and dedication to careful long-range planning. Such a party should be national and international in its orientation, rather than basing its power on parochial issues as the current parties do. In 1854 the Republican party was created de novo, founded on the platform of opposition to the extension of slavery. It seems probable that in the 1980s and 1990s the environmental issue will become even more prominent than the slavery issue was in the 1850s, and a powerful new ecology party might be established, as has occurred in several other countries. It could, indeed, grow out of such political organizations as Zero Population Growth and Friends of the Earth.

Obviously, such changes as those briefly proposed above will threaten not only numerous politicians of both major parties, but many economic institutions and practices. They are likely to be opposed by vast segments of the industrial state: by much of the oil and petrochemical industry, the steel industry, the automobile industry, the nuclear power industry, the construction industry, and by some labor unions, land developers, the Army Corps of Engineers, the USDA, the Nuclear Regulatory Commission, and the chambers of commerce, to name only a few.

Even a cursory knowledge of the pervasiveness of and the degree of political control by these interests leads to the conclusion that the necessary changes in attitudes and behavior are extremely unlikely to occur among the individuals and organizations where it would be most helpful. But what is at stake is survival of a society and a way of life. If these are to be preserved in recognizable form, cooperation of all elements of society, regardless of personal interests, will be required. Some social scientists believe such cooperation can be obtained by the systematic application of social and political sanctions.[113a] We tend to agree, but doubt that even sanctions will work unless there is also a common goal—a realistic view of a desirable and attainable future—that all can strive toward.

[113a] L. D. Nelson and J. A. Honnold, Planning for resource scarcity.

SOME TARGETS FOR EARLY CHANGE

Institutions are shaped by issues, and issues in turn are shaped and evolve in response to the character of the institutions that identify and grapple with them. Accordingly, our discussion of American institutions so far has been framed in the context of the broad issues in population and environment that we believe are central to the human predicament. It is useful now to add to the discussion some rather more specific problem areas—energy policy, transportation and communications, and land use—which need early attention, which will test the ability of institutional change to redirect technology and social energies in pursuit of saner ends, and which, in being grappled with, may serve to reshape further the institutions themselves. Along with population policy and pollution control, which have already received detailed attention in this and the preceding chapters, we view these problems as high-priority targets for early change.

Energy Policy

Who should make energy policy? How should it be carried out? What should be its goals? These are the principal questions on the policy side of energy, and they are interdependent. As unfortunately sometimes is forgotten, it is fruitless to try to answer the first two questions without already having some semblance of an answer for the third.

The United States had an energy policy during the first two-thirds of the twentieth century, but it was rarely articulated in public. In any event, the public was not paying much attention. The policy was the result of the goals of two groups—a few interested politicians and their appointees, whose goal was to see that energy was made available as cheaply as possible to meet whatever demand might materialize, and the owners and operators of energy companies (oil companies, coal companies, energy-equipment manufacturers, electric utilities, and so on), whose goal was to expand their businesses and their profits as rapidly as possible. The goals of the two groups coincided nicely.

That the interests of private enterprise and of public

TABLE 14-1
Diversification in the Oil Industry
(involvement of oil companies with other fuels)

Petroleum company	*Rank in assets*	*Gas*	*Oil shale*	*Coal*	*Uranium*	*Tar sands*
Standard Oil of New Jersey (Exxon)	1	X	X	X	X	X
Texaco	2	X	X	X	X	–
Gulf	3	X	X	X	X	X
Mobil	4	X	X	–	X	–
Standard Oil of California	5	X	X	–	–	–
Standard Oil of Indiana	6	X	X	–	X	X
Shell	7	X	X	X	X	X
Atlantic Richfield	8	X	X	X	X	X
Phillips Petroleum	9	X	X	–	X	X
Continental Oil	10	X	X	X	X	–

Source: N. Medvin, *The energy cartel.*

policy coincide is not necessarily a bad thing. As Adam Smith expounded the idea in his famous metaphor of the invisible hand, this is the way a free-market economy full of entrepreneurs is supposed to work. Unfortunately, the history of U.S. energy policy is one of the most telling available examples of what can go wrong with this ideal situation: the consolidation of economic interests into oligopoly and monopoly; the tightening influence of the economic interests over the policy-makers and regulators, and indeed the infiltration of the latter by the former; the resulting vigorous pursuit of policies that still serve private interests but have long since lost their relevance to the public interest.

This complicated set of issues has been the focus of many analyses much more extensive than we can provide here.[114] What follows is a brief overview of some of the most important topics: the character of the U.S. energy industry, government activity in energy, and energy prices and the poor. International aspects of energy policy are considered in Chapter 15.

U.S. energy industry. The energy industry is an important sector of the U.S. economy by any measure: according to one tabulation, it accounts for 3 percent of the total employment, 4 percent of the national income, and 27 percent of the annual business investment in new plants and equipment.[115] A different way of counting, which includes taxes and other items missed in the figures just given, is to add up all the money spent on energy by consumers. Such a tabulation must include both *direct purchases* (gasoline, electricity, natural gas, heating oil) and *indirect purchases* of energy (for example, the fraction of an airline ticket's price that pays for jet fuel, the part of the price of an automobile that pays for the energy needed to build it, the energy to run the hair drier at the beauty parlor, and so forth). The total computed this way was around 10 percent of the gross national product at pre-embargo (1973) energy prices.

The greatest concentration of economic and political power in the energy industry is found in the large oil companies. Ten of the top twenty companies on *Fortune* magazine's 1975 list of the largest industrial corporations in the United States were oil companies, and the assets of those ten alone topped $154 billion. Their 1974 sales were $116 billion.[116] Those companies have become large both by vertical integration and by diversification. The first term means that a single company is involved in many stages of processing an energy source—for example, exploration, production, refining, marketing. Diversification refers to involvement of a single company with several different resources—for example, oil, coal, uranium, oil shale. (Naturally, diversification can go beyond energy resources—some oil companies own movie theaters, for example.) A glance at Table 14-1 reveals that the major oil companies are really energy companies, as all of them are involved with three or more different resources.

As big as the major energy companies are, the concentration of the energy business in the few largest organizations does not quite qualify for the label *anticompetitive* under the usual rule of thumb, which is that 70 percent of the business be concentrated in the largest eight firms.[117] The degree of concentration in various sectors of the U.S. energy industry is shown in Table

[114]Especially recommended as introductions to the subject are: David Freeman et al, *A time to choose: The report of the Energy Policy Project of the Ford Foundation,* chapters 5–7, 9–11; J. Steinhart and C. Steinhart, *Energy,* chapters 13 and 14; N. Medvin, *The energy cartel;* Resources for the Future, *U.S. energy policies: An agenda for research.*

[115]David Freeman et al., *A time to choose,* p. 142. Included are production and processing of coal, oil, and natural gas, gas and electric utilities, pipeline transport, and wholesale and retail trade. *Not* included are manufacturers of energy-handling equipment, such as electricity generators and nuclear reactors.

[116]Fortune directory of the 500 largest industrial corporations, *Fortune,* vol. 91, no. 5 (May 1975), pp. 210–211.

[117]Freeman et al., *A time to choose,* p. 231.

TABLE 14-2
Concentration in the United States Energy Industries (around 1970)

Industry	*Percentage of total activity in 8 largest firms*
Crude-oil production	50
Petroleum refining	59
Gasoline sales	52
Interstate natural gas sales	43
Coal production	40
Uranium mining and milling	79
Electric generating equipment	100

Source: David Freeman et al., *A time to choose,* p. 231.

14-2. The *effective* degree of concentration is probably higher than the figures reflect, however, because of the large number of joint ventures linking the major companies in collaborative enterprises. These include jointly owned or operated oil fields, pipelines, refineries, and a bewildering variety of other arrangements. Among the ten or fifteen largest oil companies, almost all of the possible two-company combinations in joint ventures are actually in existence.[118]

The political power of the major energy companies in practice is reflected in the special treatment by the government they have gained and largely preserved for themselves in the forms of the depletion allowance, foreign tax credits, and other tax dodges.[118a] (The depletion allowance for all but the smallest producers was at last repealed in 1975.) Between 1962 and 1971 the five largest U.S. oil companies paid an average of 5.2 percent income tax on their profits, compared to an average corporate income tax for all industries of about 42 percent. The difference could be regarded as a raid on the U.S. Treasury by those five companies in the amount of about $17 billion.[119] (These five companies were all in the top ten U.S. corporations in profitability in 1976. Their after-tax profits totalled $6.2 billion.[119a])

It may be argued, of course, that developing and marketing energy resources is an increasingly complicated and expensive business that only very large and financially vigorous corporations can handle. Indeed, this is precisely what the energy companies do argue. Yet it is not entirely clear what the American people as a whole gain by leaving those very profitable and also very crucial activities in the hands of private enterprise. Increasingly, the same corporations that swear by the free-market system in some respects have shown themselves more than willing to abandon it selectively, campaigning for all manner of special subsidies, tax incentives, and privileges, while expecting the government to undertake the riskiest and most difficult parts of the energy enterprise. Thus the federal government finds itself providing most of the liability insurance for nuclear reactors, trying (without much success as of 1976) to persuade private industry to get into the uranium-enrichment business, underwriting most of the cost of a demonstration breeder reactor for the utilities, paying to bring the technology of sulfur control for coal and oil to a state of development deemed economically viable by the utilities, and so on.

On the other hand, the idea of letting the government take over the energy business entirely is not particularly appetizing. The experiences of other nations where the energy industry has been nationalized shows that this is no guarantee against bungling and exploitation, as does the U.S. experience with government enterprises in other fields. At the same time, it seems clear that the goals of the energy companies have become increasingly removed from the public interest in the 1970s. More energy for its own sake (or for profit's sake) can no longer serve as the goal of national energy policy, and it is apparent that much tighter control over the energy industry by government is the minimum prescription for steering away from this outmoded view.

Government's role. The response of government to the growing complexity of energy issues over the past few decades has been piecemeal and uncoordinated. Each emerging set of problems, it seems, has led to creation of a new agency or assignment of responsibility to an existing one, without regard for the way pieces of the energy problem interact with each other. The result is overlapping jurisdiction in some cases—in which conflicts arise among federal, state and local governmental entities—and no jurisdiction at all in others. Some of the principal federal agencies involved in energy are listed in Box 14-4, along with synopses of their responsibilities that suggest some of the potential conflicts and ambiguities. Operating sometimes in collaboration with,

[118]See Medvin, *The energy cartel,* chapter 5 and Appendix 1.

[118a]See, for example, A. J. Lichtenberg and R. D. Norgaard, Energy policy and the taxation of oil and gas income.

[119]The figures are from Steinhart and Steinhart, *Energy,* p. 282.

[119a]Milt Moskowitz, The top ten money earners, *San Francisco Chronicle,* April 2, 1977, p. 31.

BOX 14-4 Some Federal Agencies Involved in Energy

Council on Environmental Quality (CEQ)
- Consults with other federal agencies on environmental impacts of their actions
- Receives and evaluates environmental impact statements on energy facilities

Energy Research and Development Administration (ERDA)
- Develops and demonstrates new sources of energy supply
- Analyzes and encourages energy conservation
- Makes forecasts of energy needs and proposes strategies to meet them
- Operates certain energy facilities (such as uranium-enrichment plants)

Environmental Protection Agency (EPA)
- Devises and enforces standards for air and water quality, bearing on operation of power plants and automobiles

Department of Commerce (DOC)
- Devises and implements programs and standards for industrial energy conservation

Department of Housing and Urban Development (HUD)
- Devises and implements standards for energy conservation in buildings

Department of the Interior (DOI)
- Controls energy development (for example, oil drilling, coal mining) on federal lands, including offshore
- Maintains statistics on reserves and production of mineral energy resources
- Produces and markets electric power through four regional administrations (Bonneville, Alaska, Southwest, Southeast)

Federal Energy Administration (FEA)
- Collects and verifies information about availability of energy to consumers
- Regulates the mix of products from refineries
- Allocates energy supplies in times of shortage
- Makes forecasts and devises strategies

Federal Power Commission (FPC)
- Controls prices and standards of service for sales of electricity and natural gas across state lines
- Licenses hydropower facilities on navigable waterways

Interstate Commerce Commission (ICC)
- Regulates interstate oil and coal-slurry pipelines

Nuclear Regulatory Commission (NRC)
- Devises and enforces standards for safety of nuclear-energy facilities

Securities and Exchange Commission (SEC)
- Regulates management practices of electric utilities

sometimes at odds with these agencies is a host of congressional committees, themselves engaged in almost continuous jockeying with each other for jurisdiction and influence.

In early 1977 President Carter proposed a sweeping reorganization of energy-related functions in the Executive Branch, centered around a new Department of Energy equal in status to Commerce, Interior, Treasury, and so on. Upon approval by Congress, the Department of Energy will replace the Energy Research and Development Administration, the Federal Power Commission, as well as assuming most of the energy-related responsibilities of the Department of Interior, the Department of Commerce, the Department of Housing and Urban Development, the Interstate Commerce Commission, and the Securities and Exchange Commission. Two new administrations would be created within the Department: the Energy Information Administration, collecting and distributing information about energy supplies and uses, and the Energy Regulatory Commission, covering economic regulation only. The Nuclear Regulatory Commission, the Environmental Protection Agency, and the Council on Environmental Quality would retain their powers as listed in Box 14-4.

The confusion in Washington (which one may hope the Carter reorganization will reduce) is compounded, of course, by the existence of public utilities commissions in forty-six of the fifty states, with widely varying responsibilities in the energy field. About half of them control both public and investor-owned utilities (electricity and natural gas, plus nonenergy activities); the other half control only the investor-owned utilities. Most set the rates charged for electricity and gas, to protect the consumer from the monopoly that the nature of distribution systems for gas and electricity makes almost inevitable. They are also generally responsible for assuring the safety of systems under their jurisdiction, one of several overlaps with other agencies.

Government action in the energy field is not only encumbered by this enormous organizational complexity, but it has often been enfeebled as well by internal conflicts of interest. These have arisen from the standard problem of infiltration of regulatory agencies by committed representatives of the regulated organizations, and also sometimes from the incorporation of promotional and regulatory functions within the same agencies. Perhaps the most visible example of the pitfalls of the latter situation was the Atomic Energy Commission, which from its creation in 1946 was empowered both to regulate and to promote the peaceful and military applications of nuclear energy. Some of the difficulties that nuclear fission as an energy source faces in the late 1970s can be attributed to mistakes that arose from this inherent conflict and from the cozy relationship that evolved between the AEC and its supposed congressional watchdog, the Joint Committee on Atomic Energy, (JCAE).[120]

The AEC-JCAE combination for many years was the most active and visible agency connected with energy in Washington, and its vigorous promotion of nuclear fission to the near-exclusion of research on other energy sources left the United States in the 1970s with far fewer energy options than it could and should have had. The AEC was split in late 1974 into the Nuclear Regulatory Commission, on the one hand, and several divisions of the Energy Research and Development Administration on the other (see Box 14-4). The JCAE was stripped of its power in a Congressional committee reorganization in early 1977.

Energy prices and the poor. If it is obvious that energy in the United States has been underpriced, encouraging overexploitation and waste, it is equally apparent that sharp price increases cause a disproportionate burden on the poor. The poor spend a larger fraction of their incomes on direct energy purchases than do higher-income groups, they are less able to cut back on energy consumption because a larger part of their consumption is for essential rather than discretionary uses, and they are less able to invest money in insulation and other improvements that will reduce energy expenditures in the long run.[121]

Increases in energy prices are not *quite* as regressive as they seem at first glance, however, because total energy expenditures (for direct purchases plus the "indirect" energy embodied in other goods and services) increase almost in direct proportion to income.[122] Even so, the plight of the poor requires that special measures be taken to reduce the impact of higher energy prices on them. Such measures should include changing the rate structure for purchases of electricity and natural gas, so that small users pay less per unit of energy rather than more (compared with large users), as is now generally the case. Subsidies for the purchase of insulation and similar improvements could easily be paid for out of increased taxes on the profits of energy companies. It would not be difficult to design an energy tax and rebate system that actually served as an income redistribution device favoring the poor while discouraging heavy energy consumption in higher-income groups.

In short, the special problems of the poor must be taken into account as energy prices rise, and they can be. Indeed, the nation would have to face up to the problems of the poor whether energy prices were rising or not. It would be doubly absurd if the government were to take the position, having failed to deal adequately with the problem of poverty directly, that its energy policy must revolve around holding energy prices low for everyone in order to deal with poverty indirectly. At the same time, there is no reason whatever that higher prices for energy, which are needed to help promote conservation and to pay for ameliorating energy's environmental damages,

[120]Good critical histories are R. Lewis, *The nuclear power rebellion: Citizens versus the atomic industrial establishment;* P. Metzger, *The atomic establishment.*

[121]According to Freeman et al., chapter 5, poor Americans spent 15 percent of their income on natural gas, electricity, and gasoline in the early 1970s, compared to 7 percent, 6 percent, and 4 percent for the lower middle class, upper middle class, and the well-off segments of the population.

[122]R. Herendeen, Energy and affluence.

must mean higher profits for the energy companies. Preventing this is a straightforward matter of tax policy.

Directions for a rational energy policy. The main questions that energy policy must confront can be summarized: (1) How much energy should be supplied? (2) With what technologies should it be supplied? (3) Who should pay the associated costs? At issue under the first question are the costs and benefits to society of various levels of energy consumption and various rates of change in those levels (growth or decline). The second question – which should be viewed not as a search for the ideal energy source but as a search for the least undesirable mixture of sources – is important regardless of the answer to the first; a stabilized or even a reduced level of energy use would not absolve society from making difficult choices about how best to supply that level. Similarly, the third question – involving how prices, taxes, and regulation are employed to distribute the direct and indirect costs of energy use – is crucial no matter how the first two questions are answered.

Still, the three questions are far from independent. If the answer to the question "How much?" is a great deal, the range of choice under "What technology?" diminishes; society may have to choose all the options at once, at great expense. And the greater the costs, the trickier is the question "Who pays?"

On the question of how much should be supplied, our view is that the United States is threatened far more by the hazards of too much energy, too soon, than by the hazards of too little, too late. That the contrary view is so widely held seems to be the result of two factors: (1) The economic, environmental, and social costs of today's level of energy use, and of rapid growth in this level, have been seriously underestimated by most observers. (2) The economic and social costs of slower growth have been just as seriously overestimated. The underpinnings for these assertions are found in Chapters 8, 10, and 11.[122a] We reiterate here in capsule form the relevant conclusions that we draw from that material.[122b]

[122a]A particularly cogent and eloquent formulation of the arguments for both points was recently published by Amory Lovins, Energy Strategy: The road not taken.

[122b]These arguments were first published in slightly abbreviated form in John P. Holdren, Too much energy, too soon, *New York Times,* Op-Ed page, July 23, 1975.

Rapid growth in energy use fosters expensive mistakes. Especially where the existing level of energy use is already high, rapid growth forces exploitation of high-cost energy sources as well as low-cost ones, it strains available supplies of investment capital, and it encourages gambles on inadequately tested technologies. The pressure of growth favors streamlining of assessment and licensing processes, further enlarging the probability that some of the gambles will fail – at great economic, environmental, or social cost.

Even at slower growth rates, increases in energy use may do more harm than good. While the productive application of energy fosters prosperity through the operation of the economic system, the environmental and social effects of the same energy flows undermine prosperity by means of direct damage to health, property, and human values, and by disrupting "public-service" functions of natural systems. Clearly, the benefits to well-being obtained through the economic side of the relationship by means of increased energy use could in some circumstances be completely cancelled by the associated damage to well-being through the environmental side. Not only has this outcome probably already occurred for some energy sources in some locations, but under continued growth it is eventually inevitable overall, irrespective of the energy sources chosen.

Conservation of energy means doing better, not doing without. Fortunately, the slowing of energy growth, and even the eventual reduction of the total level of energy use, need not mean a life of economic privation for the public. The essence of conservation is the art of extracting more well-being out of each gallon of fuel and each kilowatt hour of electricity. Much progress in this direction can be made through changes that increase efficiency in industrial processes and electricity generation, and in energy-consuming devices in homes, commerce, and transportation. Of course, some kinds of energy conservation will require changes in individual behavior, and critics of conservation are quick to suggest that this implies a return to primitive existence. In a society whose members use 5000-pound automobiles for half-mile round trips to the market to fetch six-packs of beer, consume the beer in underinsulated buildings that are overcooled in summer and overheated in winter, and then throw the aluminum cans away at an energy loss equivalent to one-third of a gallon of gasoline per six-pack, the primitive-existence argument strikes us as the most offensive kind of nonsense.

Saving a barrel of oil is generally cheaper than producing a barrel. Slowing the growth of energy consumption by means of rational conservation measures can actually save a great deal of money. For, although technological improvements to increase energy efficiency often require some additional capital investment over conventional practice, this investment is usually less than the investment that would be needed to produce from new sources (offshore oil, nuclear fission, geothermal development) an amount of energy equal to that saved. In this sense, conservation is the cheapest new energy source. The money saved by conservation, of course, would in principle be available for some of this country's many other pressing needs.

Less energy can mean more employment. The energy-producing industries comprise the most capital-intensive and least labor-intensive major sector of the U.S. economy. Accordingly, each dollar of investment capital taken out of energy production and invested in another activity, and each dollar saved by an individual by reduced energy use and spent elsewhere in the economy, is likely to benefit employment.

We conclude therefore that the high rates of growth of energy use and electricity generation traditionally anticipated for the period between 1975 and 2000 are *neither desirable nor necessary.* They are not desirable because the economic, environmental, and social costs of such growth are likely to be severe; they are not necessary because the application of a modicum of technological and economic ingenuity can produce continued—indeed, growing—prosperity without them.

Both in the short term and thereafter, then, the mainstay of a rational energy policy for this country should be learning to *do more with less.* Some efforts at more efficient use of energy will come about automatically through the impact of higher energy prices. Even without industry price-gouging, these are inevitable because of the technical intractability, in various respects, of the energy sources that remain. Price is likely not to be a sufficient incentive to wring from the socioeconomic system all the increased efficiency that is possible and desirable, however, primarily because of certain differences in perceived interests of industries and consumers; regulations such as efficiency standards for appliances, automobiles, and buildings should therefore be used to supplement the price mechanism. And "lifeline" rates and other subsidies to the poor should be instituted to alleviate the impact of higher prices on those least able to make energy-saving adjustments.

Environmentally, the first step is to clean up the mainstays of the present energy budget, the fossil fuels. Special attention must be given to finding environmentally tolerable ways to exploit the abundant resources of coal and possibly of oil shale. The environmental and social risks of fission, including the threat of terrorism and sabotage, either at the facilities or elsewhere by using stolen nuclear materials, deserve the most searching reevaluation before a national commitment is made to expand reliance on this source. In our own view, the threat posed by fission power to the fabric of the social and political system through the spread of radiological and explosive nuclear weapons—a threat that is a virtually inevitable concomitant of this energy technology—is *qualitatively* different from the risks of other energy technologies, and indeed a price not worth paying for the benefits of fission power. But the choice is more a social and political one than a technical one, and it should be made not by scientists but by the broader public.

The many forms of solar energy deserve vigorous investigation to find the ones most benign environmentally and most practical technically. Attention should be focused not merely on centralized electric power stations but on the myriad possibilities for dispersed applications. Fusion and geothermal power also deserve further investigation to learn whether they can meet, in a practical way and at an affordable price, the conditions of low environmental impact so essential in any long-term energy source.

It should be recognized by now that there is value in diversity in technological systems as well as in biological ones. Diversity is insurance against uncertainty, and for insurance one should be prepared to pay something. Society should not build only the cheapest energy technologies, nor even only the ones that seem on today's analysis most benign environmentally. If threats overlooked or underrated today turn out to be important, altering a mix of energy technologies will be easier and less disruptive than abandoning a monoculture. At the same time, one should not conclude from an exaggerated preoccupation with diversity that society must develop *all* possibilities; the very value of diversity is to secure the flexibility to say no to those possibilities that clearly are unsuitable.

Transportation

Fuel burned for transportation in industrial nations accounts for 15 to 25 percent of all energy used by such countries. Including the energy used to manufacture and maintain the transportation systems would raise that figure to 25 to 40 percent of the total energy use (refer to Chapter 8 for details). Transportation's contribution to pollution may be taken at a first approximation to be proportional to its share of energy use; its impact on nonfuel resources is also large. Perhaps most important, transportation systems are major forces in determining the use of land and shaping the human environment. What have been the forces that have influenced this system, and how might they be changed for the better?

The automobile. The introduction of annual automobile model changes by General Motors in 1923 quickly pushed most competitors out of business, reducing the number of automobile manufacturers in the United States from eighty-eight in 1921 to ten in 1935. Only four of any economic significance remain today. A few companies therefore have been able to manipulate both demand and quality in a way that has resulted in a continual high output of overpowered, overstyled, underengineered, quickly obsolescent, and relatively fragile automobiles. These characteristics of the automobile, together with the dominance of this form of personal mobility over many more sensible alternatives, are responsible for a remarkable array of demands on resources and environmental problems. For example, immediate relief from a major portion of our air-pollution problems and a substantial reduction in the demand for steel, lead, glass, rubber, and other materials would result from the replacement of existing automobiles with small, low-horsepower, long-lasting cars designed for recycling. And, of course, the savings in petroleum would be spectacular. If the average size of the American cars on the road in 1970 were reduced to that of European cars, the gasoline saved would have run the cars of Europe for that year!

To facilitate a shift to smaller cars, the U.S. government might remove tariffs and import restrictions on automobiles that meet strict exhaust-emission standards, so that small foreign cars would become even more attractive to American buyers. Heavy excise taxes on large Detroit products and reduced taxes on small, gas-economical ones would help shift buying habits in the domestic market. Gasoline consumption, exhaust emissions, and the components of air pollution produced by the wear of tires on asphalt and from the asbestos of brake linings would all be reduced by the use of smaller, lighter cars. Recycling old automobiles and building longer-lasting ones would reduce both the consumption and the environmental impact of obtaining resources, as well as reducing the pollution directly associated with automobile production. The rewards of such a program would not be limited to pollution abatement and the saving of petroleum and other resources. Because small cars need less room on the highway and in parking lots, transportation would *through that change alone* become pleasanter, safer, and more efficient.

Of course, there would be several adverse consequences of even such a mild program of "automobile control." Between 10 and 20 percent of the American population derives its living directly or indirectly from the automobile: its construction, fueling, servicing, selling, and the provision of roads and other facilities for it. Not all of these jobs would be affected by conversion to smaller, more durable automobiles and to other forms of transportation, but many would be. In the long run, workers displaced from auto production could be employed in ways that would reduce reliance on environmentally destructive technological processes in other industries.

Unless there were careful planning to ameliorate the consequences, such a conversion could have extremely disruptive effects on the national economy. The economy, however, is demonstrably capable of accommodating itself to very far-reaching changes. Even without extensive planning, for example, the United States economy converted almost 50 percent of its productive capacity from war-related products to peacetime products between 1946 and 1948. The flexibility of our economic institutions is often grossly underestimated.

Public transportation. One of the great difficulties with conversion from automobiles to public transportation has been the tendency to seek flashy, expensive, "space-age" solutions to America's transport problems.[123] In case after case, aerospace companies and contractors have promoted such technological circuses, and in several instances they have succeeded in having them produced. The crowning blunder may be BART, San Francisco's Bay Area Rapid Transit system. That system is a double tragedy—not only has it not accomplished what it set out to do, but it has tended to give new ventures in mass transit an undeservedly bad reputation (Box 14-5). BART cost a fortune to build and has proven inordinately expensive to run. Since its delayed opening, it has been constantly plagued with malfunctions. Perhaps most discouraging, despite carrying full loads in rush hours, BART has not appreciably diminished automobile traffic in the Bay Area.

It is clear that much more sensible urban planning must be done if cheap, reliable, and efficient mass transport is to replace a significant portion of the automobile traffic in cities and suburbs—as it seemingly must if Americans are to retain much of their mobility into the twenty-first century.[124] It may well be that what *Consumer Reports* called the "moonshoot mentality" has moved planners too far toward a pattern of expensive new rail systems "that offer riders sleek cars with 'space-age' features." The way of the future—at least for urban areas—may be more in the direction of buses, perhaps in some cases powered by flywheel systems.[125]

In the meantime, paratransit—a mix of partial solutions including special bus lanes on freeways, well-organized car-pooling, reform of taxi regulations, and expansion of bus service—might be a big help.[126] Many such schemes were introduced in early 1974, stimulated by the energy crisis. But when gasoline was again plentiful, if no longer so cheap, many of the car-pooling arrangements were abandoned and bus and train use again declined. Little-used "diamond" lanes reserved for buses and car-pools on California freeways, rather than encouraging car-pooling, became a source of considerable resentment by commuters crowded into the remaining lanes. Eventually, they were abolished. Apparently, one of the greatest obstacles to establishing a sensible transport system is the addiction of the American public to fast personal cars.

Railroads. Whatever the ultimate solutions to urban transport problems in the United States may be, it is evident that they should be integrated with a restored and revitalized national rail network. Federal funds should not be committed, for instance, to any rail projects that are not standard gauge (and thus cannot be integrated into the existing network). It goes without saying that an enormous effort will be required to reestablish decent passenger train service accessible to most people. The Amtrak program has fallen far short of this goal.[127] This is tragic, since railroads not only are by far the most energy-efficient transporters of people, they are much less disruptive of the landscape than superhighways, and their terminals do not gobble land as jetports do.[128]

Much more money, including all gasoline taxes not needed for highway maintenance should be allocated to rebuilding the railroads. Moreover, planners must redesign the system so that, unlike the present Amtrak (and, of course, the Interstate Highway system), it does not promote the growth of cities at the expense of rural areas. Amtrak routes are designed much like airline routes, focusing on schedules between relatively large and distant cities. Intermediate areas have no service, or have service at extremely inconvenient hours. BART-type

[123]Actually, the United States at one time had quite good urban electrified rail transit systems. They were dismantled following short-sighted decisions promoted by, among others, General Motors. See John E. Ullman, Getting the rails back.

[124]As long as fuel remains relatively cheap and automobile use relatively unrestricted, it looks as if *no* system of mass transit would make much of a dent in energy use or traffic congestion. See Robert Lindsey, Mass transit, little mass.

[125]R. F. Post and S. F. Post, Flywheels.

[126]Para-transit, *Consumer Reports,* April 1975.

[127]William A. Peterman, The myth of Amtrak.

[128]For an incisive discussion of the economics of railroads in the United Kingdom, see J. Ogilvie and B. Johnson, Railways: Accounting for disaster.

BOX 14-5 Bay Area Rapid Transit: A Case History

In 1957, when the California legislature created the Bay Area Rapid Transit District (BART), electric trains of the existing Key System joined San Francisco with cities on the other side of San Francisco Bay. The Key System used part of the lower deck of the Oakland Bay Bridge, and consisted of five lines with 55.9 miles of track.* Because of declining patronage in the 1950s, the system was said to be losing $350,000 annually and in need of $4.5 million to renovate its tracks. In 1958 the Key System was closed down.

In 1962 voters in three Bay Area counties, after a propaganda campaign financed in large part by contractors and others hoping to profit from the building of BART, voted a $792-million bond issue for its construction. The system was to provide fast, convenient commuting to San Francisco, and relieve the glut of automobiles that was choking the city and befouling the air in an area once renowned for its beauty. A first blow was dealt to those aims when counties both north and south of the city voted not to join the system, which was then constructed with 25 of its 34 stations in the East Bay (east across the bay), where only 17 percent of the commuters who worked in San Francisco lived (60 percent of those who work in downtown San Francisco live in the city itself).

In late 1974 BART was finally in "full" service—well behind schedule and at a cost of $1.6 billion rather than the programed $1 billion. It thus cost 350 times as much to build as it would have cost to repair the Key System (230 times, if corrected for inflation). In 1975 it was losing about $20 million per year, or 60 times as much as the Key System. But even at that cost, service was far from satisfactory. The space-age design featured, among other things, streamlined cars and fully computerized controls for what was described by promoters as a "modern 'supported duorail' system" (English translation: train on train track).

In a surpassing bit of folly, the "supported duorails" were not made standard gauge, so standard railroad cars cannot be run on them, and the system cannot be hooked into existing rail lines. The flashy looking BART trains have cars slanted at one end at front and rear. Consequently, cars can only be removed from or added to the center of the train, vastly complicating the process of changing the length of trains between rush and nonrush hours. The cars, purchased from an aerospace company, have been plagued with troubles, exacerbated by the total absence of test track in the original system plan.

The ultimate fiasco, however, was the fail-safe automatic train-control system designed by Westinghouse (which also builds "fail-safe" nuclear power reactors) so that human operators would be unnecessary. Trains roared past stations; doors opened between stations and refused to open at stations; phantom trains were "detected" and real trains were lost by computers, each time causing the whole system to grind to a halt; trains ran at erratic speeds. Chaos ruled. For months a train was not allowed to leave a station until notified by a BART employee over the telephone from the next station that it was safe to proceed. Eventually a traditionally designed signal system had to be installed at additional cost.

Whether the automated system will ever function properly and reliably is questionable. What is clear is that BART has made no significant difference in the automotive congestion in San Francisco. The majority of its riders have switched to BART from commuter bus lines and car pools, and a substantial number seem to be shoppers who used to shop in the East Bay.

After two years of operation, some of the most annoying malfunctions of BART had been conquered, and a rapid ride in the clean, comfortable cars provided a striking contrast to the average subway or commuter train. Nevertheless, BART appeared to be the wrong system in the wrong place—hugely expensive and not designed to serve the real transit needs of the area. It was intended as a service for commuters from wealthy bedroom communities, not for people of the city (especially the poor). It thus subsidized both urban sprawl and the rich. Whether, in an era of increasingly expensive gasoline and, it is hoped, of increasing restrictions on automotive commuting, BART will even fulfill that mission remains to be seen.

*Information on the Key and BART systems is taken from Trouble in mass transit: Why can't the people who put a man on the moon get you downtown? *Consumer Reports.*

systems may make it simpler for the wealthy to live outside decaying cities; Amtrak makes it less desirable to live and work in small towns and rural areas. Such patchwork solutions will not work; the planning of our national transportation system must be comprehensive because of the massive social impact of that system.

Stimuli for change. Despite the obviously growing need for an overhaul of the transport system in the United States, it seems unlikely it will be changed significantly for the better until the public becomes sufficiently fed up with smog, noise, delays, and danger that it is willing to forego further growth in both the automobile population and the gross national product. Emissions from automobiles have been lowered and certainly will be reduced even further, but until the public rebels against cars, their numbers will probably increase rapidly enough to keep the overall smog level dangerously high and gas consumption rising, as more and more land disappears under freeways. The problem is worst in the United States, but a similar trend exists in other DCs.

Growing energy problems may eventually provide the needed catalyst for a rebellion against cars. One cheering sign by the mid-1970s was a dramatic increase in bicyling, leading even to the designation of bike lanes in the streets of some municipalities. Whatever can be done to stimulate a bicycle cult to rival the big-car cult should be done. If and when a transition can be made to a nongrowing population and economy, both the need for business travel and the pressure to build more vehicles and more goods should be reduced; perhaps then a rational and comprehensive land, air, and water transport[129] system for the nation can be developed.

The kinds of transport problems that now plague the DCs (the United States in particular) can (and we hope will) be totally avoided in most LDCs, where there is still an opportunity to build systems based primarily on a mix of low-cost mass transit and bicycles.[130]

[129]In some areas, canals and other inland waterways can be very efficient in moving freight. See M. G. Miller, The case for water transport.

[130]See Ivan Illich, *Energy and equity;* and Allan K. Meier, Becaks, bemos, lambros, and productive pandemonium, *Technology Review,* Jan. 1977, pp. 56–63.

Communications

Unlike most other institutions, the communications system may have great potential for instituting positive change in individual attitudes and the direction of society.[131] Television and radio seem to have universal appeal and with relatively little expenditure could have virtually universal coverage. If human problems are to be solved on a worldwide basis, some means of intercommunication among the peoples of the world must be employed. One possibility is for the DCs to supply LDCs with large numbers of small, transistorized TV sets for communal viewing in villages. Such sets could provide the information channels for reaching the largely rural populations of the less developed world. These channels could provide both a route for supplying technical aid and a means of reinforcing the idea that the people are members of a global community. Such a project is already underway in Indonesia,[132] and a satellite-beamed program was used experimentally with great success in India until the satellite service was terminated in 1977.[132a]

Isaac Asimov has described the potentialities of electronic communications as a "fourth revolution" on a par with the developments of speech, writing, and printing.[133] Considering the enormous influence of radio and television in Western countries, their future impact in largely illiterate societies can hardly fail to be even greater. But that revolution will not realize its full potential until electronic communications are as widespread and commonplace as the printed word now is, and until ways are found to provide feedback from the viewing public into the communications network.

Communications satellites. The first small commercial communications satellite station was launched in 1965, with one channel for television and 240 relays for voice transmissions. A much more sophisticated system, INTELSAT IV, was initiated in 1971 with the launch-

[131]*Scientific American,* September 1973, was a special issue on communications that included several articles pertinent to this discussion.

[132]Cynthia Parsons, Indonesia studies best use of TV, Honolulu *Advertiser,* March 11, 1975.

[132a]India, however, planned to continue much of the rural program using ground stations (Yash Pal, A visitor to the village, *Bulletin of the Atomic Scientists,* January 1977, pp. 55–56).

[133]The fourth revolution.

ing of two satellites. By 1975 the INTELSAT IV system was complete with seven satellites in place, three over the Atlantic Ocean and two each over the Pacific and Indian oceans. Eighty-six member nations were being served by 80 Earth stations with 103 antennas in 58 countries.[134]

The system has permitted a number of countries that previously had had virtually no contact to communicate with each other by satellite. An interesting example is Chile and Argentina; the Andes were once too great a barrier. INTELSAT transmits data, transoceanic telephone and teletype messages, television broadcasts, and facsimilies of letters, newspapers, or photographs. Distributional satellites are also being established to relay messages within countries as a supplement to the international INTELSATs. Eventually, the hope is to develop a system for broadcasting directly to each home. This is not expected to become a reality before the 1980s, however, and even then many think it will be limited to the sort of service described above—programs beamed to schools, community centers, and villages, especially in LDCs.

The potential for creating a true "global village" through such a communications network should not be ignored. Even apart from the opportunity to bring diverse peoples together for exchange of ideas and information, there is a great opportunity for a general lowering of hostilities. Familiarity breeds friendship far more often than contempt.

Programming and propaganda. There remains, of course, the substantial danger that a worldwide communications network will not be used for the benefit of humanity or will further erode cultural diversity. If, like the television system in the United States, it is employed to promote the ideas and interests of a controlling minority, the world would be better off without it.[135] If it is used to create a global desire for plastic junk and the Los Angelization of Earth, it would be a catastrophe. Concerns over this and related programming problems have already been raised at the United Nations. One delegate, for instance, correctly pointed out that "Films considered the acme of art in one country [might be] judged pornographic in another."[136] The problems of supplying channels for information are thus easily solved in comparison with the problems of determining what information should flow along those channels and in what format.

Much programming ought to be informational, even if presented as entertainment. People in the LDCs need help in increasing agricultural production and improving public health, as well as information on the need for population control and the ways it may be achieved. Programming should be carefully designed by social scientists and communications experts thoroughly familiar with the needs and attitudes of the audiences in each country or locality. This is particularly important in the LDCs, where it will be especially difficult because of the lack of trained people and the radical change in attitudes that is required. Control of the communications media obviously should be public, with maximum safeguard against abuses and against the problems of "cultural homogenization." The problem of controlling "Big Brother" will be ever present in all societies.

Educating people in the developed nations to the problems of population and environment is not too difficult, assuming time and space can be obtained in the media. Material can be more straightforward, since in most DCs there is already rather widespread awareness of many environmental problems. In the United States a great step could be taken merely by requiring that both radio and television assign some of their commercial time to short public-service "spots" calling attention to the problems of population, resources, and environment. This could be justified under the equal-time doctrine that put the antismoking message sponsored by the American Heart Association and the American Cancer Society on TV (see "Advertising" section). The FCC might be empowered to require that networks donate time for ads to awaken people to the population-resource-environment crisis. Such spots, sponsored by voluntary organizations like Planned Parenthood, ZPG, and the Sierra Club, have been moderately effective in drawing public

[134]Information on INTELSAT is from Hughes Aircraft Company, *Intelsat IV case history:* vol. 2, *The international satellite communications system: Intelsat IV,* Hughes Aircraft Company, El Segundo, Calif., December 1974. A more recent source is Burton I. Edelson, Global satellite communications. *Scientific American,* February 1977, pp. 58–73.

[135]Pirages and Ehrlich, *Ark II,* pp. 200ff.

[136]Paul Hofmann, Curb on world TV is debated at UN, *New York Times,* November 3, 1974.

attention to the problems. Unfortunately, the advertising budgets available to these groups are puny compared to those of General Motors or Exxon. Long documentary specials, whether prepared by the networks or by educational stations, seem relatively ineffective in initiating awareness of a problem, although they are useful in providing detailed information. For the most part, they reach only those who are already aware that a particular problem exists. Most people want to be entertained; they do not want to hear bad news.

Moving information instead of people. In the longer term, more ambitious exploitation of the potential of communications systems may help to relieve pressure on energy supplies and other resources. Specifically, it is far less costly in terms of energy to move information than to move people and things. Computer terminals coupled to television sets (for graphic display and face-to-face conversations) and to telephone lines (for data transmission) could eliminate the need for commuting to and from work in many kinds of jobs. Newspapers, which today are responsible for the consumption of great quantities of wood pulp, could be displayed a page at a time, under the control of the reader, on the computer-television hookup. Scientific and business meetings, each of which now entails hundreds of thousands of passenger miles of fuel-gobbling jet travel, could be managed on closed-circuit television for a tiny fraction of the impact on resources.

Of course, there are problems to be surmounted before such schemes can be implemented, not the least of which is the protection of privacy and confidential communications. Such difficulties can, in principle, be solved, and it seems clear that the communication–information-processing area is one field in which technological innovation can make important contributions to alleviating the resource-environment crunch.

Land Use

Land use has become a catch phrase in the contemporary environmental debate, but the term calls forth very different images and priorities in the minds of different groups of people. This is so because so many of the compelling social and environmental issues of the day are tied rather directly to how the land is used. Urban decay, the existence of ghettos, lack of access to decent low-cost housing, and the problem of busing of schoolchildren can all be viewed as interrelated consequences of prevailing patterns of urban land use. Another aspect of the pattern is suburbanization and the energy-intensive long commutes to work that go with it. The loss of prime agricultural land and recreational open space under settlements, industrial parks, transportation systems, and energy facilities is yet another dimension. And certainly the conflict of development of land versus continued provision of essential services by natural and lightly exploited ecosystems (perhaps most strikingly apparent today in the destruction of estuaries and wetlands) is a central ingredient of the human predicament in the long term.

Increasingly, the opinions of thoughtful policy-makers and observers are converging on the view that the resolution of the problems just enumerated will require a degree of comprehensiveness in land-use planning that exceeds anything contemplated previously in the United States. (Some other Western countries—the United Kingdom and Sweden, for example—have been flirting with comprehensive planning for longer.[137]) Here *comprehensive* means integrating systematically society's social and environmental goals with the pattern of land use on regional and national scales. It is clear, of course, that such comprehensive planning, even if successful, is not a *sufficient* condition for the solution of social and environmental problems, but a strong case can be made that it is a *necessary* one. In the remainder of this section of text, we first discuss some goals of land-use planning and policy and, second, the tools for pursuing those goals and the obstacles that make the task a difficult one.

Goals. The planner's easiest task is setting down desirable goals (easy, at least as long as one does not inquire too closely about making them all compatible with each other). Here is our own partial list.

[137]Peter Heimburger, *Land policy in Sweden,* Ministry of Housing and Physical Planning, Stockholm, 1976. On this and many other points raised here, see also the excellent book by William H. Whyte, *The last landscape,* Doubleday, Garden City, N.Y., 1970.

1. Central cities should be restored to attractiveness and economic viability. In respect to location, absence of competing uses, value of existing structures, and potential for cultural and racial integration, they are much too valuable to waste.

2. Housing developments should be planned in ways that integrate low-cost and higher-cost units and that provide for community open space and resource-conserving community recreational facilities (instead of private)—swimming pools, workshops, darkrooms, and so on.

3. Settlement patterns and transportation systems should be integrated in ways that minimize commuting distances and reliance on the private automobile.

4. Construction of settlements should avoid areas especially prone to flood, fire, landslide, and earthquake.

5. Prime agricultural land should be defended absolutely against encroachment by all other potential uses. The world food situation and the high environmental impact of bringing marginal land under cultivation dictate this highest priority for good land already under agricultural use.

6. Land areas that have remained in wilderness or near-wilderness condition until now should be preserved as such, permitting them to serve aesthetic and ecological functions inconsistent with exploitation or development. More intelligent and efficient use of land already being exploited is preferable to further encroachments on wilderness.

7. Nonwilderness areas where ecological processes perform particularly crucial services in support of civilization should be identified, the extent and value of their services clarified, and the land withdrawn from uses of lesser value that are incompatible with the continued provision of the natural services. Filling of wetlands and estuaries for residential development is an example where even on present knowledge a complete prohibition clearly is justified.

Tools and obstacles. On the assumption that the foregoing or some other set of goals were agreed upon by policy-makers, the question would remain what tools are available with which the goals might effectively be pursued. Among those that have been used or contemplated for land-use management in the United States are: zoning ordinances; preferential tax assessment of different types of land; government purchases of open space; selective siting of facilities owned or substantially supported by government; control of building permits to establish local growth ceilings, moratoria, or timed development contingent on meeting specified conditions; use of the environmental impact statement to force consideration of adverse impacts and alternatives; and government-funded urban renewal projects.[138]

The use of zoning as a tool for land-use planning and management has suffered from three difficulties. The first is fragmentation among the decision-making entities, rendering comprehensive planning or results impossible. In California alone, more than 1400 government entities are involved in zoning.[139] Special-purpose agencies dealing with housing, air pollution, water pollution, energy development, and fish and game (to continue with the California example) separately pursue interests that should influence zoning decisions, but there is no general mechanism for exerting such influence and no effective machinery for coordinating the goals of the agencies. The result of this partial vacuum is fragmented control of zoning by local communities, most of which do so in pursuit of a perceived interest in local growth.[140]

A second difficulty with the zoning tool is the questionable constitutionality of zoning ordinances that are discriminatory in practice, even if not in intent. Keeping density down by zoning the land remaining in a community for single-family dwellings on two-acre lots may succeed in preserving a status quo that the current inhabitants cherish, but it excludes low-income people and thus preserves a residential stratification that is undesirable for society as a whole. The likelihood that zoning ordinances having this effect will eventually be found unconstitutional places in jeopardy other, more

[138]A more extensive discussion of these tools than space permits here can be found in CEQ, *Environmental quality–1974.* See also Elaine Moss, ed., *Land use controls in the United States.*

[139]On this and other aspects of land-use planning in California, see the very useful study by the Planning and Conservation Foundation, *The California land: Planning for people,* Kaufmann, Los Altos, Calif., 1975.

[140]The dynamics of this process and the fallacies underlying the belief that such growth necessarily will be beneficial are examined perceptively by Harvey L. Molotch, The urban growth machine, in *Environment,* William Murdoch, ed., Sinauer, Sunderland, Mass., 1975.

enlightened uses of the zoning tool, as well perhaps as other land-use controls.[141]

A third difficulty with zoning that also carries over into the other forms of control is the question of what forms of regulation really are legally a "taking," requiring compensation of the landowner. Involved here is the basic conflict between the rights of a holder of private property—one of the most cherished American traditions—and the public's interest in sound and coordinated management of land.[142]

Close to zoning in influence on land use is taxation, although the influence of taxes on use may be inadvertent more often than it is used as a tool. Certainly one of the major driving forces behind the development of prime agricultural land in the United States has been the almost universal practice of assessing land for taxation on the basis of the land's most valuable potential use. Unfortunately, agricultural land has lower market value than developed land. Thus the spread of suburbs has led to assessment of adjacent agricultural land at the value it would have if subdivided for residential or commercial development. This leads of course to taxes that the agricultural revenues from the land cannot support and forces the farmer to sell out. In this way, assessment of the land as a potential subdivision leads inevitably to realization of the potential. Some states have begun to experiment with legislation permitting agricultural lands to escape such discriminatory and crippling taxation. California's Williamson Act, one of the more widely publicized examples, has proven too narrow and restrictive to be of great value, however, and more comprehensive measures are needed.[143]

The imposition of ceilings or moratoria on local growth by a few communities around the United States—Petaluma and Pleasanton, California, and Mount Laurel, New Jersey, for example—has attracted much attention. These decisions have been implemented through control of building permits, made contingent in some cases upon achieving in the community some specified level of adequacy of sewage systems, schools, water supply, or other factors. Like zoning practices, this approach has come under sharp legal scrutiny to determine its constitutionality.[144]

Possibly as important as all the tools that have been used by policy-makers to influence patterns of land use intentionally have been the inadvertent effects of government investments in certain kinds of growth-shaping facilities. Transportation systems—most notably the interstate highway system, but also airports, ports, and mass-transit systems—have been especially influential. So have water projects, sewage lines, and water-treatment plants, and centers of government research and bureaucracies.[145] Unless these influences are thoroughly understood and taken into account deliberately and comprehensively, other approaches to land-use planning have little chance to succeed.

All of the foregoing difficulties underline the necessity for a more coordinated approach to land use in the United States than any that has been implemented up until now. Balancing priorities among competing uses is at the core of the problem, and this can only be done in a sensible way on a regional (collections of counties or a state or states) or national level. An example of what might be accomplished if the political obstacles were overcome is offered by the remarkable *California tomorrow plan,* already discussed.[146] The plan describes how trends now underway in California would lead, if unchecked, to significant disruptions in the well-being of the people of the state before the year 2000, and it describes a more sensible alternative future based upon a state zoning plan. The goals of the land-use plan are very similar to those listed above.

Perhaps the most comprehensive approach to planning that has a reasonable chance of being enacted in the near future is the California Coastal Plan, produced on the mandate of a statewide ballot initiative in 1972 and delivered to the legislature in December 1975. The plan covers the 1600-kilometer California coastline in a strip extending inland to the coastal mountains, an average

[141]Some recent court decisions are described in CEQ, *Environmental Quality, 1975,* pp. 186–187.

[142]An extended discussion of this point is found in Planning and Conservation Foundation, *The California land.*

[143]Planning and Conservation Foundation, *The California land,* p. 49. For a more general discussion, see CEQ, *The impact of differential assessment of farm and open land,* Government Printing Office, Washington, D.C., 1976.

[144]See, for example, CEQ, *Environmental quality, 1975,* and Molotch, The urban growth machine.

[145]CEQ, *The growth shapers: Land-use impacts of infrastructure investments,* Government Printing Office, Washington, D.C., 1976.

[146]Alfred Heller, ed., *The California tomorrow plan.*

width of perhaps 8 kilometers. It takes account of the competing pressures of energy development, residential use, transportation, recreation, and ecological values, and offers guidelines and machinery for resolving the conflicts in a systematic way.

As with all ambitious undertakings, it is no doubt possible to find flaws in the *California tomorrow plan* and in the much more detailed California Coastal Plan. The question, however, is not whether they are flawed but whether they represent a substantial improvement over the status quo. We believe that they do, and indeed that they are illustrative of the sort of thoughtful and systematic approach that must find application around the country if planning for the rational use of land is to emerge from the disarray that has characterized land use in the United States until now.

A QUESTION OF GOALS

It is fitting to close this chapter with some reflections on the long-range goals of Western society. Can they be, as English economist Wilfred Beckerman apparently thinks, economic growth for the next 2500 years?[147] Beckerman reasons that since growth has occurred since "the days of Pericles," there is "no reason to suppose that it cannot continue for another 2500 years." It turns out that he is wrong on both counts. Careful studies of economic conditions in England for the past 600 years or so, for example, show average growth rates on the order of 0.5 percent per year—one-tenth of the 5 percent envisioned by most growthmen for "healthy" economies.

Social scientist Jack Parsons has done some interesting extrapolations that put long-continued economic growth in perspective. He extrapolated economic growth in England *backward* at the conservative rate of 1 percent per year. At the time of Pericles (490–424 B.C.), at that rate the annual income of the average household would have been 1.5 ten-millionths of a penny. Hence, even Beckerman's history is bad—growth cannot have gone on since the time of Pericles at even the "low" rate of 1 percent per annum. Careful historical analysis indicates that fluctuation rather than constant growth has been the fundamental characteristic of Western culture's economic history. The purchasing power of builders' wages in southern England reached a peak between 1450 and 1500 that was not attained again until the late years of the nineteenth century.[148]

Economic boom clearly is not and cannot be a long-term phenomenon. Until about 1950, economic growth rates of more than 2 percent per annum were very unusual. The 4, 5, or even 6 percent growth rates that economists now seem to regard as the norm are in fact a phenomenon in which a few countries are exploiting much more than could conceivably be considered their fair share of the planet's resources over a time span of a quarter of a century. Assuming conservatively that human beings have had a 1-million-year tenure on Earth, it is clear that human societies have existed in what Beckerman would undoubtedly consider economic stagnation for 99.99 percent of that tenure.

Economic growth—that is, per-capita increases in the availability of goods and services—throughout recorded history has been engendered by two sets of circumstances and/or a combination of them. The first such set is the development of widescale economic integration, which allows for the development of more efficient organization of resources, human and natural. The Hellenistic world, from Alexander the Great until the birth of Christ, was an example of such a set.[149] So were the uniting of former British colonies into the United States and, later, the European Economic Community.

The second and more common set of circumstances has been one in which some group on the periphery of a central cultural zone has managed to gain control over the exploitation of some vast hinterland and then serve as the broker between that resource-rich frontier and the high-consuming metropolis. For example, the rich and attractive Minoan culture on the island of Crete controlled the trade from Egypt and western Asia to the Greek lands to the north in the middle of the second millennium B.C. The Hanseatic League of the high Middle Ages had outposts from London to Novgorod

[147]Beckerman's views are cited by Jack Parsons in The economic transition, from which most of our figures on growth, past and future, are taken.

[148]Phelps Brown and J. Hopkins, Seven centuries of the prices of consumables, compared with builders' wage rates, *Economica*, NS vol. 23 (1956), November, pp. 296–314.

[149]See Mikhail Rostovtzeff, *Social and economic history of the Hellenistic world.*

that plucked herring, furs, lumber, and all manner of resources from the North Sea and Baltic basins and sold them to medieval Europeans, while ornamenting the cities of Hamburg, Bremen, and Lübeck with an elegance and prestige still visible. The Dutch monopoly on the spice trade in the seventeenth century supported the artistic flowering that is best known to us in the work of Rembrandt van Rijn. Finally, the race for empire of recent centuries, characterized above all by British majesty and wealth before 1945, sponsored the most recent expansion, which allowed the citizens of the DCs to enjoy a now-declining affluence.[150]

Systems of economic integration are always very fragile, and the pattern of economic growth based on the hegemony of exploiters over the resource-rich frontier seems to carry the seeds of its own destruction. In order to exploit an area, it is necessary to organize it, either by organizing the indigenous population or by sending forth emigrants from the metropolis. What starts out as an organization for economic exploitation consistently tends to become an organization for political resistance to the metropolis and finally a cadre for political and economic independence. The Ariadne legend in Greek literature, retold in a sagacious reconstruction of its historical context by Mary Renault in *The King Must Die*, tells a story of the Greeks breaking the economic hold of the Minoans on their culture. The *Iliad* was probably the story of a postdecolonization war fought over control of the pottery trade, rather than over the beautiful Helen. The disintegration of the British Empire and the other European overseas empires of the recent past began even before the empires were fully formed.

The loss of mastery over an erstwhile dependency does not necessarily mean that the resources of that area are lost to the metropolis as a whole. But it usually does mean comparatively hard times for the previous proprietors of the resources and a better deal for the new owners. Minoan culture was completely obscured until its rediscovery in the early years of this century. The development of Baltic powers reduced Hamburg, Bremen, and Lübeck to places of only local significance as Europe moved into the modern period. Casual perusal of current daily newspapers will illustrate the cost to Britain of inflexibility in the face of change.

Economic growth since the days of Pericles has been spastic and dependent rather than inexorable and self-generating as Beckerman would have it. When a society has achieved a transient economic integration or gained control over some neglected bonanza, its economy has grown. The bonanzas of our planet have pretty well been found by now, and those remaining are slipping ever more surely into the hands of proprietors resident in the lands where they occur—the OPEC nations, for example. Americans and Europeans will have to settle down to a lifestyle set against the background of a declining resource base. While today's technological sophistication may put us in a better position to ameliorate the effects of the end of the boom than were, say, the Minoans, it also gives us the means to destroy civilization in the process of squabbling over the tail end of the resources. Furthermore, those past booms did not end with the entire planet overpopulated and severe ecological constraints limiting what new technologies could be adopted—something invariably ignored by economic Pollyannas whose "historical perspective" rarely extends beyond the beginnings of the most recent boom.[151]

What are the prospects for the future? Setting aside the physical and biological constraints that were already beginning to limit growth by the mid-1970s, could sustained growth reasonably be expected for the next 2500 years? A simple calculation by Parsons shows Beckerman's view of the future to be as preposterous as his view of the past is fallacious. Again Parsons uses a modest 1 percent per annum growth rate. This gives a doubling time of 70 years—a lifespan—so that on the average each person is about twice as well off at death as at birth. At this rate a person's wages for an hour of work reach 1 million pounds (about $2 million) an hour in a little more than 1500 years, and at the end of Beckerman's 2500 years of growth, "a small child's pocket money, at say, 0.5 percent of the GNP per capita per week (one shilling and sixpence a week in 1970) would be five thousand million pounds."

[150]For a masterful account of the impact of the West's most recent resource capture, see Walter Prescott Webb, *The great frontier*. The historical discussion in this section owes much to historian D. L. Bilderback.

[151]For example, see Glenn Hueckel, A historical approach to future economic growth. Hueckel's "historical" perspective extends about 200 years, not even to the beginning of the Western boom. Needless to say, the article shows a characteristically blissful ignorance of ecology.

To emphasize the absurdity of there being 2500 more years of economic growth in England, Parsons describes what he calls the "millionaire barrier." At the 1 percent growth rate, the average person would have the living standard of a millionaire (income of £100,000 per year) just before 2400 A.D. At a "normal" growth rate of 5 percent per year, the millionaire barrier would be reached in 85 years. Parsons then asks the logical question: once everyone is a millionaire, who will generate the goods and services that everybody wants to consume?

Our long-range goal, then, cannot be continued economic growth. Indeed, the main justifications for growth given by economists—that it will generate the economic power needed to "clean up the environment" and improve the lot of the poor—imply that the consequences of growth in the future will be precisely the opposite of what they have been in the past.

We have already described the devastating effects of economic growth on the environment and the continuing efforts of growthmanic politicians and industrialists to destroy it with ever more energy use and ever more "development." The case for improving the lot of the poor through growth is equally preposterous. Although there has been considerable material improvement in the lot of the poor in industrial nations during the last century, the gap between poor and rich has not closed appreciably; indeed, in most countries (including the United States) it has widened over the past two decades.[152] And, since poverty is a relative concept and there has been a revolution of rising expectations, "in the minds of persons with low incomes . . . a $4000 income for a family of four might be less tolerable in today's society than the pittance received by the poor in sixteenth-century England."[153]

Furthermore, the gap between rich and poor nations has grown during the recent period of rapid economic growth in the DCs. This gap is even greater than that indicated by national per-capita GNP statistics because the gap between the rich and the poor within LDCs has been growing very rapidly in many of those nations showing the most "development." Thus between 1950 and 1970 the ratio between the average income of the richest 20 percent of the Brazilian population and that of the poorest 20 percent increased from 15/1 to 25/1.[154] Similar increases in inequity of income distribution have occurred alongside economic growth in Mexico, Pakistan, the Philippines, and Ghana, to name a few.

[152]Pirages and Ehrlich, *Ark II,* pp. 270–274.

[153]Ibid, p. 272.

What, then, if not growth, should the long-range goals of society be? Haven't the economists explained that the opposite of growth is stagnation? The answer, of course, is that in noncancerous biological systems the opposite of growth is *maturity.* What a mature society should be like ought to be (but is not) a matter of wide discussion, and we are willing to make some suggestions. It will have a "dynamic equilibrium economy"[155] in which pressures on nonrenewable resources will be very nearly nonexistent, and, of course, the population will be essentially stationary. Some mechanism will have been found to escape from bigness—perhaps through decentralization of government and industry or political fragmentation or reduction in population size or some combination of these.

There seems to be a growing consensus that bigness is basic to our problems—that Americans may have gone to the point of social diseconomies of scale as well as material ones.[156] According to some observers, hunting and gathering societies could be counted as truly affluent because individuals could fully supply their simple needs with a few hours of work each day.[157] But, perhaps more important, groups were small enough that each member of a hunting-and-gathering society was a repository for virtually all the nongenetic information—the culture—of that society. Each person knew who he or she was and where he or she fit in society. Alienation was not a problem. Work was not an onerous diversion from pleasure, but a fulfilling part of life itself.

In our conception of a mature society, there would be a considerably more equitable distribution of wealth and income than is found in most contemporary societies. Possibly this would be achieved by some formal mechanism.[158] On the other hand, perhaps it could be achieved

[154]James P. Grant, Development: The end of trickle down? *Foreign Policy,* fall 1973.

[155]The term (though not the idea) was invented by Emile Benoit.

[156]Pirages and Ehrlich, *Ark II,* p. 59.

[157]For example, Marshall Sahlins, *Stone age economics.*

[158]Such as the national council for the regulation of differential wages proposed by Wilfred Brown in *The earnings conflict,* Halsted Press, New York, 1973.

automatically as the society shifted away from the pursuit of bigness and the maximization of various indices developed by economists suffering from "physics envy," and moved toward maximizing things not amenable to statistical treatment, such as individual satisfaction and the quality of life. In a mature society the economic problem would in essence be solved.

Can a transition to a mature society be achieved in the United States? The question is obviously open. But we reiterate that a central question is that of *scale.* Can society escape the modern massiveness that threatens both the human environment and the human psyche today? It is probably no coincidence that the most intellectually stimulating book written by an economist in the 1970s was entitled *Small is beautiful.*[159]

[159]Schumacher.

Recommended for Further Reading

Boffey, P. 1975. *The brain bank of America.* McGraw-Hill, New York. Critique of the National Academy of Sciences. Slightly too negative, but generally accurate.

Bonjean, Charles M., ed. 1976. Scarcity and society, *Social science quarterly,* vol. 57, no. 2, September. This collection of essays by social scientists contains many articles pertinent to the issues raised in this chapter.

Boulding, Kenneth E. 1966. The economics of the coming Spaceship Earth. In *Environmental quality in a growing economy,* H. Jarrett, ed. Johns Hopkins Press, Baltimore. A superb article about making the transition from a cowboy economy to a spaceman economy.

Daly, Herman, ed. 1973. *Toward a steady-state economy.* W. H. Freeman and Company, San Francisco. A fine collection—see especially Daly's contributions.

Ehrlich, Paul R., and Anne H. Ehrlich. 1974. *The end of affluence.* Ballantine, New York. Discusses many facets of the ending of economic growth.

Hardin, Garrett. 1968. The tragedy of the commons. *Science,* vol. 162 (December 13), pp. 1243–1248. A classic article.

Heilbroner, R. L. 1974. *An inquiry into the human prospect.* Norton, New York. A distinguished economist looks at the human predicament, with special emphasis on political implications. Brief and highly recommended.

Hirsch, Fred. 1976. Social limits to growth. Harvard Press, Cambridge, Mass. Argues that affluence breeds social dissatisfaction, generating socio-political limits on economic growth. Note especially the treatment of positional goals. Thought provoking.

Holdren, John P. 1976. The nuclear controversy and the limitations of decision-making by experts. *Bulletin of the Atomic Scientists,* March, pp. 20–22. What to do when expert consensus is impossible.

Illich, Ivan. 1971. *Deschooling society,* Harper and Row, New York. A provocative book of interest to all those concerned with the future of the educational system.

Krier, J. E. 1975. Environmental law and its administration. In *Environment: Resources, pollution, and society,* W. W. Murdoch, ed., 2d ed. Sinauer, Sunderland, Mass., pp. 413–436. An excellent treatment.

Lovins, Amory. 1976. Energy strategy: The road not taken? *Foreign Affairs,* October. A brilliant essay dealing with the social choices required to move society off its present disastrous course.

Lowrance, W. W. 1976. *Of accepted risk: Science and the determination of safety.* Kaufmann, Los Altos, Calif. The best overview of the evaluation of hazards created by technologies.

Mishan, Ezra J. 1967. *The costs of economic growth.* Praeger, New York. A pioneering discussion.

Pirages, Dennis C., and Paul R. Ehrlich. 1974. *Ark II: Social response to environmental imperatives.* W. H. Freeman and Company, San Francisco. An analysis of changes in society that might help forestall the fate predicted by Roberto Vacca, *The coming dark age.* Notes and bibliography give access to much of the pertinent literature of economics, political science, sociology, and the like.

Schumacher, E. F. 1973. *Small is beautiful: Economics as if people mattered.* Harper and Row, New York. One of the most important economic books of the 1970s—a must.

Stone, C. D. 1974. *Should trees have standing? Toward legal rights for natural objects.* Kaufmann, Los Altos, Calif. Originally published in the *Southern California law review* (1972), this beautifully written essay is a must for anyone interested in the law and the environment.

Watt, K. E. F. 1974. *The Titanic effect: Planning for the unthinkable.* Sinauer, Stamford, Conn. An analysis by an ecologist showing the economic problems created by shortsighted emphasis on growth of the GNP.

Additional References

Arrow, K. J., and A. C. Fisher. 1974. Environmental preservation, uncertainty, and irreversibility. *The Quarterly Journal of Economics,* vol. 88, pp. 312–319 (May). Application of economic formalism to the problem of irreversible risk.

Asimov, Isaac. 1970. The fourth revolution. *Saturday Review,* October 24, pp. 17–20. On the potentialities of electronic communications to revolutionize world society.

Aspin, Les. 1972. The space shuttle: Who needs it? *Washington Monthly,* September. A congressman looks at NASA's maneuvering for dollars.

Ayres, Edward. 1970. *What's good for GM.* Aurora, Nashville. An indictment of the degree to which the United States is run for the automobile. Full of useful information such as, "In 1969, as a result of auto and highway clout, the federal government spent $50 on highways for every dollar it spent on mass transit."

Baker, J. J. W. 1975. Three modes of protest action. *Bulletin of the Atomic Scientists,* February, pp. 8–15. Describes scientists' statement against the birth-control encyclical of Pope Paul VI.

Barber, Richard. 1970. *The American corporation.* Dutton, New York. Gives information on concentration of power.

Barkley, P. W., and D. W. Seckler. 1972. *Economic growth and environmental decay: The solution becomes the problem.* Harcourt Brace Jovanovich, New York. An incisive book by two economists. Highly recommended.

Barlay, Stephen. 1970. *The search for air safety.* Morrow, New York. Detailed analysis of aviation accidents.

Barnet, Richard. 1972. *Roots of war.* Atheneum, New York. A controversial treatment of the domestic roots of America's foreign interventions.

Beckerman, Wilfred. 1974. *Two cheers for the affluent society.* St. Martin's, New York. An economist displays candidly how nearly total ignorance of physics and biology can lead to an optimistic view of economic growth. See especially the confusion of pollution with environmental deterioration and the quaint acceptance of the "natural pollutants" fallacy on page 11.

Bell, D., and H. Perloff, eds. 1971. *The future of the United States government: Toward the year 2000.* Braziller, New York. Essays speculating on the problems of government organization and public policy in the year 2000.

Benoit, Emile. 1976. The coming age of shortages, A dynamic equilibrium economy, and First steps to survival. *Bulletin of the Atomic Scientists,* January, pp. 6–16; February, pp. 47–55; and March, pp. 41–48. An economist joins the ecologists in examining the human predicament and proposes some interesting solutions in a series of three articles.

Berg, P.; D. Baltimore; H. W. Boyer; S. N. Cohen; R. W. Davis; D. S. Hogness; D. Nathans; R. Roblin; J. D. Watson; S. Weissman, and N. D. Zinder. 1974. Potential biohazards of recombinant DNA molecules. *Science,* vol. 185, p. 303 (July 26). Calls for voluntary controls on dangerous genetic research.

Berle, A. A., Jr. 1968. What GNP doesn't tell us. *Saturday Review,* August 31. A brief, lively discussion. Reprinted in John P. Holdren and Paul R. Ehrlich, *Global ecology: Readings Towards a Rational Strategy for Man.*

Birch, Charles. 1975. *Confronting the future.* Penguin books, Harmondsworth, Middlesex, England. A lively, hopeful book on the human predicament by a distinguished Australian population biologist.

Boffey, P. M. 1976. Plutonium: Its morality questioned by National Council of Churches. *Science,* vol. 192, pp. 356–359 (April 23).

Bolling, Richard. 1965. *House out of order.* Dutton, New York. Critique of the House of Representatives by a congressman. Reforms still fall well short of Bolling's recommendations.

Boston Women's Health Book Collective. 1976. *Our bodies, our selves.* 2d ed. Simon and Schuster, New York. Excellent layperson's guide to health problems of women, including information on sexual behavior and reproduction.

Bormann, F. H. 1976. An inseparable linkage: Conservation of natural ecosystems and the conservation of fossil energy. *BioScience,* vol. 26, no. 12 (December), pp. 754–760. On the economic costs of damaging or destroying natural ecosystems.

Boulding, Kenneth E. 1973. The shadow of the stationary state. *Daedalus,* fall, pp. 84–101. A mildly optimistic article in which one of the most imaginative economists says our fate will depend in large part on how clever we are at political invention.

———. 1974. What went wrong, if anything, since Copernicus? *Bulletin of the Atomic Scientists,* January. A "thought piece" by one of our best thinkers.

Bronfenbrenner, U. 1970. *Two worlds of childhood: U.S. and USSR.* Russell Sage Foundation, New York. Shows how concern for society can be instilled in children; largely anecdotal and therefore must be read with caution.

Brooks, Harvey. 1973. The technology of zero growth. *Daedalus,* fall, pp. 139–152. Points out, correctly in our opinion, that while some of today's technologies will decline in a zero growth world, others will flower.

Brush, Stephen G. 1976. Can science come out of the laboratory now? *Bulletin of the Atomic Scientists,* April. Criticizes standard (Baconian) view of scientific enterprise, emphasizes need for brilliant intuition, and discusses how misunderstanding about how science works has helped poison science-society relationships.

Cannon, J. 1975. *A clear view.* Inform, Inc., New York. A citizen's guide to the abatement of pollution.

Carlson, Rick. 1975. *The end of medicine.* Wiley, New York. A critique.

Carter, L. J. 1974. Controversy over new pesticide regulations. *Science,* vol. 186, p. 904 (December 6). On EPA banning of dieldrin and aldrin. CEQ. *See* United States.

Chamberlain, Neil. 1970. *Beyond Malthus.* Basic Books, New York. Population growth and the distribution of power between and within nations.

Cipolla, Carlo M. 1965. *The economic history of world population.* Penguin, Baltimore.

Cirino, Robert. 1971. *Don't blame the people.* Diversity Press, Los Angeles. A systematic description of the way the news media filter and distort the information that reaches the American public.

Clark, Colin. 1967. *Population growth and land use.* Macmillan, London. The author of this book once claimed on a television show that India would be the richest country in the world in ten years or so *because* of population growth! Read his book, paying careful attention to Clark's treatment of environmental problems.

Clark, Joseph S. 1964. *Congress: The sapless branch.* Harper and Row, New York. Senator Clark criticizing our moribund legislature.

Coale, Ansley. 1970. Man and his environment. *Science,* vol. 170, pp. 132–136 (October 9). A simplistic and undocumented view of the relationship between population, resources, and environment.

Colwell, Thomas B. 1972. Ecology and philosophy. In *Philosophical issues,* J. Rachels and F. A. Tillman, eds., Harper and Row, New York.

Consumer Reports. 1975. Trouble in mass transit: Why can't the people who put a man on the moon get you downtown? March. Source of information on BART.

———. 1975. Para-transit. April. Describes a mix of stop gap measures to help with the urban transportation crisis.

Cottle, T. J. 1975. Show me a scientist who's helped poor folks and I'll kiss her hand. In *Science and society,* N. H. Steneck, ed. University of Michigan Press, Ann Arbor, pp. 216–227. A scathing denunciation of the priorities of science.

Council on Environmental Quality (CEQ). Annual. *Environmental quality.* Government Printing Office, Washington, D.C. These annual volumes began to appear in 1970. They are gold mines of information on environmental matters.

———. *See also* United States Council on Environmental Quality.

Dales, J. H. 1968. *Pollution, property, and prices.* University of Toronto Press. One economist's suggestions for cleaning up our environment.

Dalkey, Norman C. 1972. *Studies in the quality of life: Delphi and decision-making.* Heath, Lexington, Mass. Controlled interrogation as a technique for evaluating quality of life.

Daly, Herman. 1971. *The stationary state economy.* Distinguished Lectures, 2. University of Alabama. A seminal contribution, putting forth the notion of placing depletion quotas on resources. (Reprinted in H. Daly, ed., *Toward a steady-state economy.*)

———. 1974. The economics of the steady state. *The American Economic Review,* vol. 64, pp. 15–21 (May). Good discussion of the concept of "ultimate efficiency," defined as the ratio of service (the desired end) to throughput (which is not a benefit but a cost).

———, 1977. *Steady state economics: The economics of biophysical equilibrium and moral growth.* W. H. Freeman and Co., San Francisco.

The world's foremost steady state economist explains the functioning of a spaceship economy and the defects of the current economics of growth. Every economist should study this volume.

Davis, Nuel P. 1968. *Lawrence and Oppenheimer.* Simon and Schuster, New York. Describes risks that were thought to accompany detonation of first A-bomb.

Dixon, Bernard. 1976. Recombinant DNA: Rules without enforcement? *New Scientist,* January 29, p. 218. States, "Sir John Kendrew has called for an international commission to monitor potential dangers behind contemporary research trends in biology. For some of this work to be carried out beneath a cloak of military or commercial security, he believes, would be dangerous. Precisely that situation is now developing. And despite the plethora of committees, we still have no assurance that any commission or other authoritative international body is doing or can do, anything about it. Sooner or later, legislation may be the only answer."

Dolan, Edwin, G. 1969. *TANSTAAFL: The economic strategy for environment crisis.* Holt, Rinehart and Winston, New York. Brief and highly recommended.

Domhoff, G. W. 1967. *Who rules America?* Prentice-Hall, Englewood Cliffs, N.J. An analysis of power in the tradition of C. Wright Mills. Important reading although somewhat dated.

Dubos, René. 1971. *The mirage of health.* Harper and Row, New York. A critique of the health system.

Dyson, F. J. 1975. The hidden cost of saying "no"! *Bulletin of the Atomic Scientists,* June. High praise for technological circuses. (See Paul R. Ehrlich, The benefits of saying "yes.")

Easterlin, Richard A. 1974. Does economic growth improve the human lot? Some critical evidence. In P. A. David and M. W. Reder, eds. *Nations and households in economic growth.* Academic Press, New York, pp. 89–125. Reaches the depressing conclusion that "the growth process itself engenders ever-growing wants that lead it ever onward."

Egler, Frank E. 1970. *The way of science: A philosophy of ecology for the layman.* Hafner, New York. An ecologist's attempt to create a philosophy of ecology.

Ehrlich, Paul R. 1975. The benefits of saying "yes"! *Bulletin of the Atomic Scientists,* September. A reply to F. J. Dyson, The hidden cost of saying "no."

——— and R. L. Harriman. 1971. *How to be a survivor: A plan to save Spaceship Earth.* Ballantine, New York. Covers many of the problems discussed in this chapter. Contains the text of the Tugwell Constitution.

——— and J. P. Holdren. 1969. Population and panaceas: A technological perspective. *BioScience,* vol. 19, pp. 1065–1071. Discusses the limits of technological fixes to food supply problems and concludes that many such solutions would lead to catastrophe.

———. 1972. The hysteria against the case. *London Times,* June 26. Reprinted in *Equilibrium* (ZPG), October 1972, and *Current Affairs Bulletin,* vol. 49, no. 10 (March 1973). A review of Maddox, *The doomsday syndrome.*

Epstein, Edward. 1973. *News from nowhere.* Random House, New York. How what is news is determined.

Esposito, J. C. 1970. *Vanishing air.* Grossman, New York. Report of the Nader task force on air pollution.

Fagley, Richard M. 1960. *The population explosion and Christian responsibility.* Oxford University Press, New York. A Protestant perspective on the population explosion and a good source of information on religious attitudes toward population control.

Fischer, A. C., and F. M. Peterson. 1976. The environment in economics: A survey. *Journal of Economic Literature,* vol. 14, pp. 1–33 (March). Comprehensive review of the ways economists have dealt with environmental problems.

Fischer, D. W. 1974. Environmental impact assessment as an instrument of public policy for controlling economic growth. *International Journal of Environmental Studies,* vol. 6, pp. 233–242.

Frank, Jerome. 1966. Galloping technology, a new social disease. *Journal of Social Issues,* no. 4. Source of the descriptive phrase for one of the most serious problems we face.

Freeman, David; Pamela Baldwin; Monte Canfield, Jr.; Steven Carhart; John Davidson; Joy Dunkerley; Charles Eddy; Katherine Gillman; Arjun Makhijani; Kenneth Saulter; David Sheridan; and Robert Williams. 1974. *A time to choose: The report of the Energy Policy Project of the Ford Foundation.* Ballinger, Cambridge, Mass. A thoughtful, data-rich examination of alternative pathways for United States energy policy. Its powerful case for low growth in energy use was pooh-poohed by many influential advocates of the status quo, and it received less attention than it deserved.

Friedman, Milton. 1970. The social responsibility of business is to increase its profits. *New York Times Magazine,* September 13. Argues that as long as businessmen operate within the law, it is an unfair tax on stockholders to devote resources to anything but maximizing profits (neglecting the role businessmen play in determining the passage and administration of those laws).

Fuller, John G. 1975. *We almost lost Detroit.* Reader's Digest Press, New York. Documents how the AEC pressed on with Fermi fast breeder, even though a string of accidents had indicated how little could be predicted about nuclear technologies.

Galbraith, John K. 1967. *The new industrial state.* Signet, New York. A most interesting, logical, and controversial thesis about the nature of the military-industrial-university-government complex.

———. 1973. *Economics and the public purpose.* Houghton Mifflin, Boston. Calls, possibly in vain, for a reorientation of the concerns of economists.

Gatos, Harry C. Undated. *Materials processing in space.* Statement before Subcommittee on Manned Space Flight, Committee on Science and Astronautics, U.S. House of Representatives. Details the advantages of zero gravity processing.

Georgesçu-Roegen, N. 1971. *The entropy law and the economic process.* Harvard University Press, Cambridge, Mass. An economic analysis *beginning* with the laws of thermodynamics. Technical. For an amusing contrast, see Richard Zeckhauser, The risks of growth.

Godkin, E. L. 1865. Aristocratic opinions of democracy. *North American Review,* January.

Goeller, H. E., and A. Weinberg. 1976. The age of substitutability. *Science,* vol. 191, pp. 683–689 (February 20).

Goldsmith, Edward. 1976. Ecology—the new political force. *The Ecologist,* vol. 6, no. 9, pp. 310–311. The ecology movement in Europe has evolved into increasingly successful political parties.

Graham, Frank Jr. 1970. *Since silent spring.* Fawcett-Crest, Greenwich, Conn. Details of the pesticide controversies.

Graubard, S. R., ed. 1973. The no-growth society. *Daedalus,* fall. Several important articles.

Greeley, Fr. Andrew. 1976. *Catholic schools in a declining church.* Sheed and Ward, Mission, Kans. A survey of Catholic attitudes, showing that the decline in church participation among Catholics is largely due to the papal encyclical condemning birth control.

Green, Harold P. 1975. The risk-benefit calculus in safety determination.

The George Washington Law Review, vol. 43, pp. 791–807. A dissection of an article by Philip Handler, president of the National Academy of Sciences. See Handler, 1975.

Hamilton, W. F., II; and D. K. Nance. 1969. Systems analysis of urban transportation. *Scientific American,* July. Problems of urban transport and some possible solutions.

Hammond, George S. 1976. The value system in the scientific subculture. *Bulletin of the Atomic Scientists,* December, pp. 36–40. Perceptive analysis of how pure science has become a new religion.

Handler, Philip. 1975. A rebuttal: The need for a sufficient scientific base for government regulation. *The George Washington Law Review,* vol. 43, pp. 808–813. A rebuttal to Harold P. Green, The risk-benefit calculus in safety determination. Among other amazing statements, Handler says, "[the charge that] DDT 'can impair reproduction of birds' . . . rests exclusively on the behavior of the brown pelicans of Anacapa Island, which lay in the effluent stream from a factory which manufactured DDT, and it is equally possible that the thinning of eggshell formation in that colony was occasioned by a variety of other external phenomena" (p. 812) (See Chapter 11 here for the diverse evidence that makes his statement nonsense.)

Hardin, Garrett, ed. 1969. *Population, evolution, and birth control.* 2d ed. W. H. Freeman and Company, San Francisco. A fine collection of readings edited by one of the best writers among biologists.

———, and John Baden, eds. 1977. *Managing the Commons,* W. H. Freeman, San Francisco. A stimulating collection of essays covering social and ethical dimensions of dealing with scarcity and public goods.

Hardmann, M., and P. Manning. 1975. *Green bans.* Australian Conservation Foundation. Describes how workers in Australia have withheld their labor from socially or environmentally undesirable projects.

Harvard Law Review Association. 1971. Legal analysis and population control: The problem of coercion. *Harvard Law Review,* vol. 84, no. 8, pp. 1856–1911.

Harwood, Robert F. 1975. Economics, esthetics, environment, and entomologists: the tussock moth dilemma. *Environmental Entomology,* vol. 4, pp. 171–174. Discussion of the decision to lift the DDT ban so it could be used against a tussock moth outbreak in the northwestern United States.

Hayes, Denis. 1971. Can we bust the highway trust? *Saturday Review,* June 5, pp. 48–53.

Heffernan, Patrick. 1975. Jobs and the environment. *Sierra Club Bulletin,* April, pp. 25–30. Gives data supporting the view that "environmental standards and programs, rather than eliminating jobs, are currently significant sources of employment."

Heilbroner, Robert L. 1972. *The worldly philosophers: The lives, times and ideas of the great economic thinkers.* 4th ed. Simon and Schuster, New York. This classic, written by one of the most outstanding and ecologically aware modern economists, is a must for all interested in the development of economic thought.

Heller, Alfred, ed. 1971. *The California tomorrow plan.* Kaufmann, Los Altos, Calif. A classic—shows how much can be accomplished with low-budget planning.

Heller, Walter, ed. 1968. *Perspectives on economic growth.* Random House, New York. A compendium of the conventional wisdom of economic growth. These views can still be found among economists today, but see E. F. Schumacher, *Small is beautiful: Economics as if people mattered,* for an informed economist's perspective.

Henderson, Hazel. 1974. The entropy state. *Planning Review,* vol. 2, April/May, pp. 1–4. A fascinating brief article from an outstanding futurist. You might wish to read the profile of Ms. Henderson by Constance Holden in *Science,* vol. 190, pp. 862–864 (November 28, 1975).

Henkin, H.; M. Merta; and J. Staples. 1971. *The environment, the establishment, and the law.* Houghton Mifflin, Boston. An excellent recounting of the landmark DDT hearing in Wisconsin 1968/1969 with much quoted testimony.

Herendeen, R. 1974. Energy and affluence. *Mechanical Engineer,* October. Shows how direct and indirect energy use vary with income.

Holdren, John P. and Paul R. Ehrlich, eds. 1971. *Global ecology: Readings towards a rational strategy for man.* Harcourt Brace Jovanovich, New York. Reprints Berle's What GNP doesn't tell us; Boulding's Economics of the coming Spaceship Earth; and Ehrlich and Holdren's Population and panaceas.

Holdren, John and P. Herrera. 1971. *Energy.* Sierra Club, San Francisco. See discussion of Storm King case and similar battles.

Holliday, Robin. 1977. Should genetic engineers be contained? *New Scientist,* February 17, pp. 399–400. Considers chance of disaster very remote on the basis of approximate (and generally conservative) probability calculations.

Hooker, C. A. 1975. Has the scientist any future in the brave new world? In *Science and society,* N. Steneck, ed. University of Michigan Press, Ann Arbor, pp. 306–356. See especially the material on the scientific establishment. Useful bibliographic notes.

House, Peter W. 1976. *The quest for completeness: Comprehensive analysis in modeling, indicators, gaming, planning and management.* D. C. Heath and Co, Lexington, Mass. Strategies for long-range, comprehensive planning, incorporating environmental concerns. Contains a useful discussion of measures of quality of life.

———. 1977. *Trading-off environment, economics and energy: A case study of EPA's Strategic Environmental Assessment System.* D. C. Heath and Co., Lexington, Mass. Discusses a computer-based system for developing long-range analyses of the impacts of energy alternatives—one ingredient of comprehensive planning.

———, and J. McLeod. 1977. *Large-scale models for policy evaluation.* Wiley-Interscience, Somerset, N.J.

———, and Edward R. Williams. 1976. *The carrying capacity of a nation.* Heath and Co., Lexington, Mass. Develops a planning model incorporating environmental resources as well as labor and capital.

Hueckel, Glenn. 1975. A historical approach to future economic growth. *Science,* vol. 187, pp. 925–931 (March 14). Dramatizes the need for training economists in history and environmental sciences.

Illich, Ivan. 1970. *Celebration of awareness.* Doubleday, Garden City, N.Y. Brilliant critique of social institutions by one of today's most imaginative thinkers.

———. 1973. *Tools for conviviality.* Harper and Row, New York. A devastating critique of society. Illich argues, "survival in justice is possible only at the cost of those sacrifices implicit in the adoption of a convivial mode of production and the universal renunciation of unlimited progeny, affluence, and power on the part of both individuals and groups."

———. 1974. *Energy and equity.* Harper and Row, New York. Another critical work by a man who has been described as the twentieth century's leading Luddite.

———. 1976. *Medical nemesis: The expropriation of health.* Random House, New York. A hard-hitting critique, claiming, among other things, that the medical system has convinced people "society has a supply of *health* locked away that can be mined and marketed." Highly recommended.

Istock, Conrad E. 1971. Modern environmental deterioration as a natural process. *International Journal of Environmental Studies,* vol. 1, pp. 151–155. A concise and important article that should be read by all economists.

Johnson, W. R. 1973. Should the poor buy no growth? *Daedalus,* fall, pp. 165–189. Suggests that alliances of the very poor and the middle class to wrest more from the super-rich hold the best hope for more equity.

Kahn, H., and A. J. Wiener. 1967. *The year 2000.* Macmillan, New York. A monument to the technological optimists' inability even to come close in forecasting the future. The words *ecology, environment,* and *pollution* do not appear in the index—and Japan is seen as a potential superpower!

Kantrowitz, Arthur. 1975. Controlling technology democratically. *American Scientist,* vol. 63, pp. 505–509. Proposes the use of scientific advocates before scientific judges to settle scientific aspects of policy disputes.

Katchadourian, H., and D. Lunde. 1975. *Fundamentals of human sexuality.* 2d ed. Holt, Rinehart and Winston, New York. A superb treatment by two psychiatrists, easy to read and authoritative.

Kelso, L. O., and M. J. Adler. 1958. *The capitalist manifesto.* Random House, New York. The original exposition of Kelso's theory of universal capitalism, a proposal for capitalist rather than socialist redistribution of wealth.

Kelso, L. O., and P. Hetter. 1967. *Two-factor theory: The economics of reality.* Random House, New York. A revolutionary book by capitalists. The authors point out that *fewer than 1 percent of United States households are capitalist* and set out proposals to change all that.

Kozol, Jonathan. 1967. *Death at an early age.* Houghton Mifflin, Boston. A devastating examination of one of our educational system's major failures.

Landau, N.J., and P. G. Rheingold. 1971. *The environmental law handbook.* Ballantine, New York. How to fight pollution in the courts.

Lecomber, Richard. 1975. *Economic growth versus the environment.* Wiley, New York, A brief, informative book. Those unfamiliar with elementary economics will need to read it with a basic economics text like Paul A. Samuelson, *Economics* at hand.

Leonard, George B. 1968. *Education and ecstasy.* Delacorte, New York. A most thoughtful and original book on education.

Lewis, R. 1972. *The nuclear power rebellion: Citizens versus the atomic industrial establishment.* Viking, New York. A history of the Atomic Energy Commission and the Joint Committee on Atomic Energy, emphasizing controversies and conflicts with independent scientists and citizen groups.

Lichtenberg, A. J., and R. D. Norgaard. 1974. Energy policy and the taxation of oil and gas income. *Natural Resources Journal,* vol. 14, pp. 501–518. Discusses the depletion allowance, foreign tax credits, and other aspects of tax treatment of the oil industry.

Lindsey, Robert. 1975. Mass transit, little mass. *New York Times Magazine,* October 19. If cars remain unrestricted and gasoline cheap, mass transit won't help much with congestion or energy conservation.

Loebl, Eugen. 1976. *Humanomics: How we can make the economy serve us—not destroy us.* Random House, New York. A critique of standard capitalist and Marxist economics by a professor of economics who has served in several key economic positions in communist Czechoslovakia. He starts from the premise, "Conventional economics has become, despite its remarkable degree of sophistication, not only a useless tool, but a dangerous one. Its deceptive application has created a crisis which threatens the very foundation of our civilization."

Lundberg, Ferdinand. 1968. *The rich and the super-rich.* Bantam, New York. An eye-opening book for those bedazzled by "people's capitalism" and the high-school-civics-class versions of how our government functions.

McCaull, Julian. 1976. Energy and jobs, *Environment,* January/February, pp. 18–20. Reports on relationship of energy use to employment.

Macrae, Norman. 1975. America's third century. *The Economist,* October 25. Read this to discover what happens when an economist "raid(s) the fertile mind of Herman Kahn."

Maddox, John. 1972. *The doomsday syndrome.* McGraw-Hill, New York. A curious mixture of incompetent analysis and technology-as-religion. Maddox has great faith in the rationality of the scientific-industrial system. For a refutation, see Ehrlich and Holdren, the hysteria against the case; and John Woodcock, Doomsday revisited.

Margolis, Joseph. 1971. *Values and conduct.* Oxford University Press, New York. An important book by a well-known ethical theorist—an introduction to moral philosophy.

Marx, Leo. 1970. American institutions and ecological ideals. *Science,* vol. 170, pp. 945–952 (November 27). A thoughtful discussion of the profound changes in our institutions that really cleaning up the environment will require.

Mayle, Peter. 1973. *Where did I come from?* Lyle Stuart, Secaucus, N.J. Good book for preteens on sex and reproduction.

Means, Richard L. 1970. *The ethical imperative: The crisis in American values.* Doubleday, Garden City, N.Y. Excellent.

Medvin, N. 1974. *The energy cartel.* Random House, New York. Useful for the history of vertical and horizontal integration of the United States energy industry.

Meier, Richard L. 1976. A stable urban ecosystem. *Science,* vol. 192, pp. 962–968 (June 4). A vision of stationary population and resource-conserving cities.

Metzger, P. 1972. *The atomic establishment.* Simon and Schuster, New York. Well written critical history of the Atomic Energy Commission and the Joint Committee on Atomic Energy.

Miller, M. G. 1975. The case for water transport. *Ecologist,* vol. 5, pp. 259–261. "A waterway can carry freight more economically than the equivalent area of road or rail, causing less disruption to the environment, using less energy and generating less pollution."

Mintz, M., and J. S. Cohen. 1971. *America, inc.: Who owns and operates the United States.* Dial, New York. A very important book dealing with the evils of concentrated economic power and possible ways of diffusing it. See especially the material on big oil companies, and then think about events since the book was published.

Mishan, Ezra J. 1970. *Technology and growth: The price we pay.* Praeger, New York. A more popular version of *The costs of economic growth.*

———. 1973. Ills, bads, and disamenities: The wages of growth. *Daedalus,* vol. 102, no. 4 (Fall), pp. 63–87.

Moncrief, Lewis W. 1970. The cultural basis for our environmental crisis. *Science,* vol. 170, pp. 508–512 (October 30).

Montefiore, Hugh. 1975. Population control: An ethical and theological perspective. *International Journal of Environmental Studies,* vol. 8, pp. 53–58. A worthwhile discussion, giving insight into the moral concerns of a well informed Anglican bishop.

Montgomery, Johnson C. 1971. The population explosion and United States law. *Hastings Law Journal,* vol. 22, no. 3, pp. 629–659. First definitive treatment of this subject.

Moore, Gerald, 1976. Legal aspects of marine pollution control. In R. Johnston, ed., *Marine pollution,* Academic Press, New York, pp. 589–679. Examines international level and controls at the national level in the USA and UK. Detailed and highly documented.

Moss, Elaine, ed. 1976, *Land use controls in the United States.* Dial Press for the Natural Resources Defense Council, New York. A handbook for public-interest groups.

Mostert, Noel. 1974. *Supership.* Knopf, New York. Well written description of the economics and hazards of these giant ships.

National Academy of Sciences (NAS). 1976. *Study on problems of pest control.* NAS, Washington, D.C. One of the best efforts of the NAS. Deals with many of the economic and political aspects of the functioning of the pesticide system. See especially volume 1, *Contemporary pest control practices and prospects.*

Nelson, L. D., and Julie A. Honnold. 1976. Planning for resource scarcity: A critique of prevalent proposals. In C. M. Bonjean, ed., *Scarcity and Society* (see Recommended Reading). Claims various proposals, such as educational reform and long-term planning, made by the authors of this book and other environmentalists, may be dangerous. The environmentalists' proposals may delay movement to systems of sanctions social scientists think are necessary. An important paper.

Nicholson, Max. 1976. The ecological breakthrough. *New Scientist,* November 25, pp. 460–463. A history of the development of ecology, once an obscure branch of "pure" science, into a subject of worldwide political importance. The focus is on the U.K., long a leading center of professional ecology.

Nordhaus, William, and James Tobin. 1972. Is growth obsolete? *Fiftieth Anniversary Colloquium, National Bureau of Economic Research,* Columbia University, New York. A thoughtful article within the traditional economic paradigm, attempting to produce a measure for economic welfare (MEW). Environmentalists should read this. (See also Arthur M. Okun, Social welfare has no price tag.)

O'Brien, Fr. John A., ed. 1968. *Family planning in an exploding population.* Hawthorne, New York. Statements by scholars within and outside the Catholic church, edited by an outstanding Catholic theologian who has strongly disagreed with that church's stand on birth control.

Ogilvie, J., and B. Johnson. 1975. Railways: Accounting for disaster. *New Scientist,* October 23. Economics of British railways—well done.

Okun, Arthur M. 1971. Social welfare has no price tag. *Survey of Current Business,* July, pp. 128–133. Speaking against revision of the GNP, the author says it never has and never will measure social welfare and warns against attempts to formulate alternatives like that of Nordhaus and Tobin (above).

Olson, M.; H. H. Landsberg; and J. L. Fisher. 1973. Epilogue. *Daedalus,* fall, pp. 224–241. Even though we disagree to some extent, this is interesting reading on the no-growth society.

O'Neill, Gerard K. 1974. The colonization of space. *Physics Today,* September. The original article on space colonies.

———. 1975. Space colonies and energy supply to the Earth. *Science,* vol. 190, pp. 943–947 (December 5). Describes construction of satellite solar-power stations by a space manufacturing facility.

———. 1977. *The high frontier: Human colonies in space.* Wm. Morrow, New York. Details O'Neill's space-colony scheme. Fascinating reading.

Ophuls, William. 1973. *Prologue to a political theory of the steady-state.* Ph.D. Dissertation, Yale University. Integrates political theory and environmental concerns; excellent.

———. 1977. *Ecology and the politics of scarcity.* W. H. Freeman, San Francisco. A useful, well-argued text, covering the nature of the environmental predicament and a political scientist's perspective on solutions.

Owen, Henry, and Charles L. Schultze, eds. 1976. *Setting national priorities: The next ten years.* Brookings Institution, Washington D.C. One in a series of volumes with this title, published annually by Brookings since 1970. Most deal rather narrowly with the annual federal budget, but this one takes a longer view of issues in defense, inflation, interdependence, energy, environment, and other issues touched by the budget but in need of longer-range, more systematic planning.

Page, S., Jr., and W. Clark. 1975. The new alchemy: How to survive in your spare time. *Smithsonian,* February, pp. 82–88. Describes the activities of the New Alchemy Institute, focused on small-scale, low-energy, and nonchemical farming.

Parsons, Jack. 1975. The economic transition. *Conservation Trust.* The ultimate demolition of the main myths of growth.

———. 1977. *Population fallacies.* Elek/Pemberton, London. A penetrating analysis of fallacies concerning population growth and its relationship to socio-economic and other factors.

Patterson, Walter C. 1976. *Nuclear power.* Penguin, Baltimore. A fine overview for the layman with an especially useful and clear discussion of the complexities of reactor technology.

Pearson, D., and J. Anderson, 1968. *The case against Congress.* Simon and Schuster, New York. Pre-Watergate description of the mess in our legislation. Much is still pertinent in the late 1970s.

Peterman, W. A. 1974. The myth of Amtrak. *Environment,* vol. 16, November.

Pirages, Dennis C. 1975. The unbalanced revolution. In *Science and Society,* N. H. Steneck, ed. University of Michigan Press, Ann Arbor, pp. 231–249. Discusses bringing science back under the control of society.

———, ed. 1971. *Seeing beyond: Personal, social and political alternatives.* Addison-Wesley, Reading, Mass. A fine collection of readings bringing together a wide variety of articles dealing with contemporary human problems.

———, ed. 1977. *The sustainable society: Social and political implications.* Praeger, New York. A useful collection of articles, combining technological, economic, and political viewpoints.

Platt, John. 1969. What we must do. *Science,* vol. 166, pp. 1115–1121 (November 28). A classification of the urgency of our multiplicity of crises and suggestions on how we might meet them.

Post, R. F., and S. F. Post. 1973. Flywheels, *Scientific American,* December, pp. 17–23. On one mode of conserving energy in transportation.

Primack, Joel, and Frank von Hippel. 1974. *Advice and dissent.* Basic Books, New York. A readable discussion of the role of scientists in the political arena. Case studies include the SST, the antiballistic missile, pesticides, chemical and biological warfare, and nuclear power.

Resources for the Future. 1968. *U. S. energy policies: An agenda for research.* Johns Hopkins Press, Baltimore. Although a little out-of-date, this book offers a useful compilation of information on state and federal policies regarding coal, oil, gas, and uranium since 1930.

Roddewig, R., and J. S. Rosenberg. 1975. In Australia, unions strike for the environment. *Conservation Foundation Letter,* Washington, D.C., November. On the green bans against environmentally damaging projects.

Rostovtzeff, Mikhail. 1941. *Social and economic history of the Hellenistic world.* 3 vols. Oxford University Press, New York.

Russell, Bertrand. 1945. *A history of western philosophy.* Simon and Schuster, New York. A classic by one of the greatest thinkers of the twentieth century. See especially the material on anthropocentrism.

Sahlins, Marshall. 1972. *Stone age economics.* Aldine, Chicago. Primitive people had few possessions but were not poor: ". . . it was not until culture neared the height of its material achievements that it erected a shrine to the Unattainable: Infinite Needs."

Samuelson, Paul A. 1976. *Economics.* 10th ed. McGraw-Hill, New York. *The* standard economics text.

Schipper, Lee. 1976. Raising the productivity of energy use. *Annual Review of Energy,* vol. 1, pp. 455–517. Well-documented discussion of potential for increasing employment and real economic well-being through saving energy.

Schneider, S. H., and L. E. Mesirow. 1976. *The genesis strategy.* Plenum, New York. Contains some useful ideas on the science-policy interface.

Serling, Robert J. 1960. *The probable cause.* Doubleday, Garden City, N.Y. Somewhat out-of-date but still interesting description of aviation accidents in the golden age of prop transport.

Sessions, George S. 1974. Anthropocentrism and the environmental crisis. *Humboldt Journal of Social Relations,* vol. 2, pp. 1–12. Overview with good bibliography.

Sierra Club Bulletin. 1975. The green ban. April, pp. 18–19. On the actions of organized labor against environmentally damaging projects in Australia.

Sinsheimer, Robert. 1975. Troubled dawn for genetic engineering. *New Scientist,* October 16, pp. 148–151. Contains a good summary of the technology, risks, and benefits of recombinant DNA experiments.

———. 1977. An evolutionary perspective for genetic engineering. *New Scientist,* January 10, pp. 150–152. A distinguished biologist expresses concern that National institutes of Health guidelines for recombinant DNA research are "too narrowly conceived" and "inadequate."

Skinner, B. F. 1971. *Beyond freedom and dignity.* Knopf, New York. Skinner finally says it in terms understandable even to those who have not followed his work—individuals can neither be blamed for their failures nor credited with their accomplishments. The book caused an uproar even before publication. Must reading, even if you disagree.

Spengler, Joseph J. 1960. Population and world economic development. *Science,* vol. 131, pp. 1497–1502 (May 20). Old but worthwhile.

Steinhart, J., and C. Steinhart, 1974. *Energy.* Duxbury, North Scituate, Mass. An outstanding introductory text on technology, environmental impact, and policy.

Steneck, N. H., ed. 1975. *Science and society.* University of Michigan Press, Ann Arbor. A diverse collection—see especially the articles by Pirages, Cottle, Hooker, and Toulmin.

Stockholm International Peace Research Institute (SIPRI). 1976. Why arms control fails. *Atlas World Press Review,* February, pp. 11–13. Statistics on numbers of scientists involved in war research (about half of them).

Stone, Tabor R. 1971. *Beyond the automobile: Reshaping the transportation environment.* Prentice-Hall, Englewood Cliffs, N.J. An interesting book that explores some new directions for transportation in the United States.

Todd, John. 1976. Pioneering for the 21st century: A New Alchemist's perspective. *The Ecologist,* vol.6, no. 7, pp. 252–257. More on the self-sufficient, low-impact lifestyle of the New Alchemy Institute.

Toulmin, S. E. 1975. The twin moralities of science. In *Science and Society,* N. H. Steneck, ed. University of Michigan Press, Ann Arbor, pp. 111–124. Claims "the very *success* of modern science is the greatest obstacle to its own *continuance,"* and questions whether those tested in purely disciplinary forums are suited for giving advice on social welfare or national policy. Beautifully written and thought-provoking.

Train, Russell E. 1974. The quality of growth. *Science,* vol. 184, pp. 1050–1053 (June 7). An overview by the former administrator of the EPA. Calls for developing effective democratic government institutions "to direct and regulate growth."

Tuan, Yi-Fu. 1970. Our treatment of the environment in ideal and actuality. *American Scientist,* vol. 58, May/June, pp. 244–249.

Tugwell, R. 1970. *Model for a new constitution.* Freel, Palo Alto, Calif. This model is intended as a vehicle for generating discussion of constitutional reform.

Tunney, John. 1975. *The changing dream.* Doubleday, Garden City, N.Y. A U.S. senator comes to grips with the population-resources-environment crisis.

Turner, Frederick J., ed. 1938. *The early writings of Frederick Jackson Turner.* Books for Libraries, Plainview, N.Y. On the American frontier and the attitudes it engendered.

Udall, Stewart L. 1968. *1976: Agenda for tomorrow.* Harcourt, Brace and World, New York. See especially Chapter 8, "The renewal of politics." Many cogent points made on population, environment, and the quality of life, but the agenda, sadly, was not adopted.

Ullman, John E. 1975. Getting the rails back. *Environment,* December, pp. 32–36. A look at the trolley systems that used to be.

United States Council on Environmental Quality (CEQ), Environmental Protection Agency (EPA), and Department of Housing and Urban Development (HUD). 1975. *The costs of sprawl.* Government Printing Office, Washington, D.C. A detailed report comparing uncontrolled sprawl with planned high-density clusters and finding that clustering saves space, money, and energy.

Vacca, Roberto, 1974. *The coming dark age.* Doubleday, Garden City, N.Y. A frightening description of the accelerating breakdown of social organization.

Viorst, M. 1976. Population control: Pakistan tries a major new experiment. *Science,* vol. 191, pp. 52–53 (January 9).

Wade, Nicholas. 1975. Recombinant DNA: NIH group stirs storm by drafting laxer rules. *Science,* vol. 190, pp. 767–769 (November 21). Describes dispute over first attempt of National Institutes of Health to set regulations on genetic engineering experiments. (See Robert Sinsheimer, Troubled dawn for genetic engineering, or N. Wade, Recombinant DNA: NIH sets strict rules to launch new technology.)

———. 1975. Recombinant DNA: NIH sets strict rules to launch new technology. *Science,* vol. 190, pp. 1175–1179 (December 19). Gives NIH committee containment guidelines for experiments.

Wagar, J. Alan. 1970. Growth versus the quality of life. *Science,* vol. 168, pp. 1179–1184 (June 5). A critique of the cult of growth with an interesting "simplified calculus for the good life."

Watanabe, Masao. 1974. The conception of nature in Japanese culture. *Science,* vol. 183, pp. 279–282 (January 25). Observes that traditional Japanese love of nature "has not yet been completely replaced by the idea of man and his relation to nature which underlies Western science. Still immersed in nature itself, the Japanese people do not quite realize what is happening to nature and to themselves, and are thus exposed more directly to and are more helpless in, the current environmental crisis."

Webb, Walter Prescott. 1951. *The great frontier.* University of Texas Press, Austin. Views the era of world wars as a consequence of readjustment following the closing of the frontier, which was opened in 1492.

Weisskopf, Walter. 1971. *Alienation and economics.* Dutton, New York. Economics of scarcity.

Westman, W. E., and R. M. Gifford. 1973. Environmental impact: Controlling the overall level. *Science,* vol. 181, pp. 819–825 (August 31). A heterodox plan for establishing a price in money-independent units for activities, including childbirth, that cause environmental impact.

Wheeler, Harvey. 1971. *The politics of revolution.* Glendessary, Berkeley, Calif. Outlines the kinds of revolutionary thinking required by recent environmental trends. Well written.

White, Lynn, Jr. 1967. The historical roots of our ecological crisis. *Science,* vol. 155, pp. 1203–1207 (March 10). A classic paper.

Wingo, Lowdon. 1973. The quality of life: Toward a microeconomic definition. *Urban Studies,* vol. 10, pp. 3–18. An important analysis, but sometimes couched in the oppressive jargon that so often poisons the social science literature. For example: "The complex interactions between external conditions and the psychophysiological preference apparatus, or 'utility generator' of the individual is the basic element in the economist's interpretation of the world." Translation: "Economists study the choices people make in various conditions."

Woodcock, John. 1975. Doomsday revisited. *Quarterly Review of Biology,* vol. 50, pp. 425–428. A devastating analysis of John Maddox, *The doomsday syndrome.*

Woodward, Herbert. 1976. *Capitalism can survive in a no-growth economy.* Brookdale/Walker, Stamford, Conn. Argues cogently that it can survive and thrive. Well worth reading.

Zeckhauser, Richard. 1973. The risks of growth. *Daedalus,* vol. 102, no. 4, pp. 103–118. An article noteworthy only because it shows how ignorance of the physical world can warp an economist's conclusions. Zeckhauser shows he is unfamiliar with the second law of thermodynamics by his statement (p. 117), "Recycling is not the solution for oil, because the alternate technology of nuclear power generation is cheaper."

A planet cannot, any more than a country, survive half slave, half free, half engulfed in misery, half careening along toward the supposed joys of almost unlimited consumption. Neither our ecology nor our morality could survive such contrasts. And we have perhaps ten years to begin to correct the imbalance and to do so in time.

—Lester Pearson, 1969

CHAPTER 15

Rich Nations, Poor Nations, and International Conflict

Throughout this book we have been referring to developed and less developed countries—the rich and the poor nations—because this is the fundamental division of humanity today. In our view, it supersedes the more recognized political-economic division between capitalism and communism. The growing gulf between rich and poor nations is fairly recent. For most of the history of industrial civilization (and before), there was a continuum from the poor to the rich; and most nations and their peoples were poor. Then, as geochemist Harrison Brown of the California Institute of Technology described it, since World War II, "a striking pattern has evolved amounting to no less than a fissioning of human society into two quite separate and distinct cultures—the culture of the rich and the culture of the poor, with very few people living in between these two extremes."[1] That fissioning between nations can be seen quite clearly, for example, in trends of per-capita energy consumption and per-capita steel consumption (see Figure 15-1). But many other differences exist, most of which have been enumerated in previous chapters: rates of population growth; levels of nutrition, health, education, and general well-being.

If current trends were to continue, by the year 2020 there would be about 10.5 billion people, of whom 1.4 billion would be rich, 8.5 billion poor, and 0.6 billion in

[1]Population growth and affluence: The fissioning of human society.

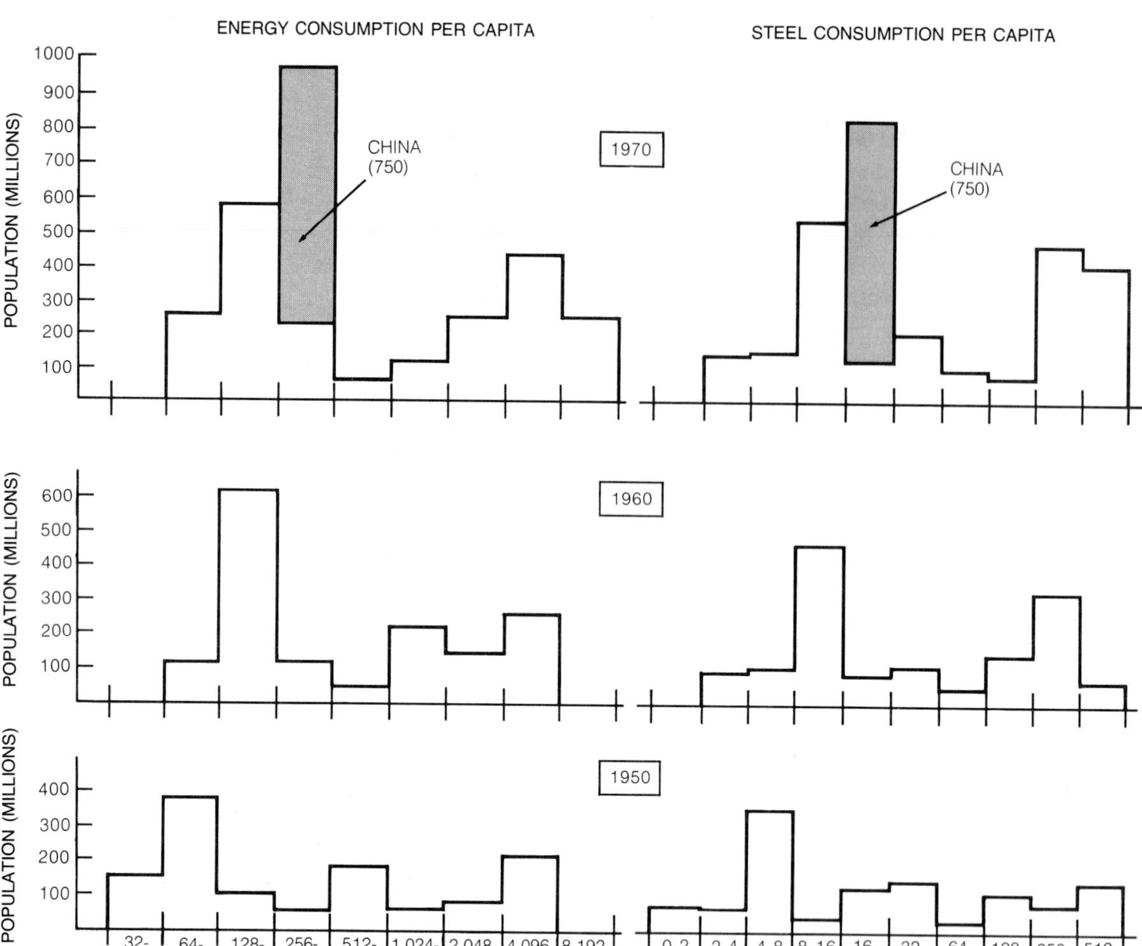

FIGURE 15-1

The evolution of the rich-poor gap in the use of energy and materials. Note that information on China was available only for 1970. (From H. Brown, 1975.)

between. The ratio of the per-capita energy consumption between the rich and the poor would have climbed from 20.5 to 39.9—that is, the gap would virtually have doubled. The environmental implications of such an overall rate of energy consumption are discussed in Chapter 8, but there would be grave political implications as well. If the world were to continue on that route, it is not unlikely that much of the energy used would be generated by nuclear power plants. As Brown warned, "The potential instabilities in a system composed of an affluent minority coexisting with a crowded, hungry, and discontented majority, which has access to nuclear fuels, are awesome to contemplate."[2]

The consequences of the gap between rich and poor nations, and possibilities for healing it before it leads to a nuclear Armageddon, are the basic subject of this chapter. It is vital to avoid the awesome situation Brown described, and the urgency is great since the international situation grows more threatening daily. Before considering corrective action, however, we examine some of the elements of the existing situation, with particular con-

[2]Ibid., p. 242.

sideration of why, after nearly two decades of effort to develop poorer nations, most of them are even poorer than before in comparison with the rich nations.

RICH WORLD, POOR WORLD

In recent years a widely used international taxonomy has developed by which politicians could avoid using such descriptive terms as *the poor nations, the have-nots,* or as one historian put it (sadly, but perhaps accurately), *the ain't-gonna-gets.* The code[3] classifies nations into various "worlds."

1. The First World: These are the noncommunist DCs, such as Australia, Denmark, Japan, Portugal, the United Kingdom, the United States, and West Germany. Many, but not all, are democracies. Economically also, the First World is a mixed bag. Portugal, although rich compared to Haiti, is poor compared to the United States. The United Kingdom still had a high per-capita income in 1976, but its economic prospects were bleak; and although Japan was doing better than the UK, its long-term prospects were dreadful.[4]

2. The Second World: This is the group of the communist countries—another mixed bag, including Albania, China, Cuba, North Korea, Poland, the USSR, and Yugoslavia, among others. Some—the USSR and most eastern European countries—are highly industrialized; the Asian communist countries and Albania are not.

3. The Third World: These are the poor nations thought by some to have a chance of getting rich, or at least of developing to a substantial degree without a great deal of external aid, generally because of their resource bases. The group includes the Organization of Petroleum Exporting Countries (OPEC), Argentina (agricultural products), Malaysia (lumber, rubber, tin), Morocco (phosphates), Zaire (copper), Zambia (copper), and countries like Brazil, Mexico, Taiwan, and South Korea, which have attracted outside capital and which have relatively well-developed industries. The prospects of many of these nations hinge on how effectively they can institute population control; that of Brazil is also heavily tied to whether it ceases the destruction of Amazonia before it is complete.[5]

4. The Fourth World: This is a group of LDCs that might become economically self-sustaining with moderate outside help. It includes Colombia, Egypt, Ghana, India, Indonesia, Peru, the Philippines, Turkey, and Vietnam.

5. The Fifth World: These are the international "basket cases"—nations that for the foreseeable future can only persist with substantial outside aid. They have difficulty feeding themselves and have little to offer for export. Grossly overpopulated Bangladesh is the largest, but others include Chad, Ethiopia, Guinea, Somalia, Rwanda, and Upper Volta. They are generally characterized by extreme poverty; several are in the Sahel region of Africa that was disastrously stricken by drought between 1968 and 1975. Most of the thirty-two nations listed by the United Nations in 1974 as most in need of help are in this category.

In some classifications, the Third and Fourth worlds are lumped into the Third World, and the Fifth World is called the Fourth.[6] Occasionally, an older classification is used in which all LDCs (including China) are called the Third World. Sometimes *North* and *South* or *high-income* and *low-income* are used as synonyms for *rich* and *poor.*[7]

Whatever classifications are used, it should be remembered that the key divisions are based on wealth and that most persons live in countries and in circumstances that, compared with the United States, can only be considered poor. In 1973, 61 percent of the world's population lived in countries where per-capita annual incomes were less than \$500,[8] and 20 percent had less than \$50 income per person. In contrast, fewer than 10 percent lived in countries where per-capita incomes were greater than \$5000, and more than half of those were Americans.

---

[3]See for example, *Time,* Poor vs. rich: A new global conflict, December 22, 1975.

[4]See Paul R. Ehrlich and A. H. Ehrlich, *The end of affluence,* chapter 4.

[5]Ibid.; see also J. C. Jahoda and D. L. O'Hearn, The reluctant Amazon basin.

[6]For example, The world's economic division, *New York Times,* January 25, 1976. See also Nathan Keyfitz, World resources and the world middle class. Keyfitz lists his groups of nations as capital-rich countries, resource-rich countries, developing countries, and poor countries. Keyfitz cites differential rates of population growth as a major cause of the growth in the income gap.

[7]For example, Roger D. Hansen, A "new international economic order"? An outline for a constructive U.S. response.

[8]*World Bank Atlas,* 1975, Washington, D.C. Preliminary figures.

TABLE 15-1
Income Distribution Within Selected Less Developed and Developed Countries

	Percentage of national income received by population groups				
	Richest 20%	*Second 20%*	*Third 20%*	*Fourth 20%*	*Poorest 20%*
LESS DEVELOPED COUNTRIES					
Argentina (1961)	52.0	17.6	13.1	10.3	7.0
Ecuador (1970)	73.5	14.5	5.6	3.9	2.5
Egypt (1964–1965)	47.0	23.5	15.5	9.8	4.2
India (1963–1964)	52.0	19.0	13.0	11.0	5.0
Kenya (1969)	68.0	13.5	8.5	6.2	3.8
Korea, Rep. of (1970)	45.0	22.0	15.0	11.0	7.0
Mexico (1969)	64.0	16.0	9.5	6.5	4.0
Sri Lanka (1969–1970)	46.0	20.5	16.5	11.0	6.0
Tanzania (1967)	57.0	17.0	12.0	9.0	5.0
DEVELOPED COUNTRIES					
Australia (1967–1968)	38.7	23.4	17.8	13.5	6.6
France (1962)	53.7	22.8	14.0	7.6	1.9
Germany, Dem. Rep. (1970)	30.7	23.3	19.8	15.8	10.4
Germany, Fed. Rep. (1970)	45.6	22.5	15.6	10.4	5.9
Hungary (1967)	33.5	23.5	19.0	15.5	8.5
Japan (1968)	43.8	23.4	16.8	11.3	4.6
Sweden (1970)	42.5	24.6	17.6	9.9	5.4
United Kingdom (1968)	39.2	23.8	18.2	12.8	6.0
United States (1970)	38.8	24.1	17.4	13.0	6.7

Notes: Income distribution data are incomplete and deficient, and inter-country comparisons should be made with caution. A completely equal distribution of national income would show the richest 20 percent and the poorest 20 percent of the population (as well as all other quintiles) each receiving 20 percent of that country's income.

Source: J. W. Sewell, ed. *The United States and World development agenda,* 1977. Overseas Development Council, Praeger, New York.

Sixty-seven percent of the world's wealth is controlled by 17 percent of the population.

The statistics on disparities in *average* incomes between rich countries and poor countries, as shocking as they are, do not reveal the true magnitude of the rich-poor gap. That magnitude becomes fully apparent only when the uneven distribution of income *within* countries is taken into account. The nature of this distribution in most countries is such that a great many people have incomes far below the average. Income distributions for 44 LDCs around 1970 are shown in Table 15-1.

The growing disparity in wealth and access to high living standards has not gone unnoticed by the poor majority. Not only is this gap now the most significant economic division between nations, it is rapidly becoming a political issue of overwhelming importance. Defusing the rich-poor confrontation may be humanity's most urgent political task in the next decade or two.

Trade and Foreign Aid: An International Shell Game

Inequality and injustice within countries are matched only by inequality and injustice between countries. These are the two obscenities of world development. And they are obviously linked.

—Louis Emmerji,
Director of the World Employment Programme, International Labour Organization, 1975

When one reads the literature on DC-LDC relationships—especially that dealing with the economic aspects—it is sometimes difficult to believe that the writers are all describing the same situation. Consider the question of whether developed countries exploit LDCs (or, as is often stated, do the DCs practice neocolonialism or economic imperialism?). On one side, in connection with the extraction of raw materials from LDCs, economist Ansley Coale in 1970 declared: "The most effective forms of assistance that the developed countries (including the United States) give to the less developed countries are the purchases they make from the less developed countries in international trade."[9]

On the other hand, socialist economist Pierre Jalée wrote in 1968 that LDCs "are not poor because of a curse of nature, that they are not lacking in natural wealth, least of all in raw materials for heavy industry. They are poor only because . . . this natural wealth has been, and still is being, plundered by imperialism for the needs of its own industrialization, at the expense of those countries from which it flows away in its raw state."[10]

Which, if either, of these views is correct?

It is quite true that great damage would be done to LDC economies if DCs reduced their purchases of commodities. LDC economies have been set up to supply commodities to DCs, and generally are not in a position to use those commodities themselves. But one must question why less developed nations are in such a position; that is, what historical events channeled their economic development into such narrow pathways? One must also ask who or what determines the prices paid for the commodities? And, perhaps most important, one must ask who (that is, what group) within an LDC benefits from the trade in commodities? Is it the mass of the people or is it a small ruling elite? If the latter, are the DC commodity consumers in any way involved in keeping those elites in power? No special economic expertise is needed to find a partial answer to these questions.

The shortcomings of the Coale position do not, however, wholly validate Jalée's. There is no reason to believe that present-day LDCs would have developed their natural wealth by now if it were not for the rapacious interference (or at least influence) of the DCs. The cultural conditions for an Industrial Revolution were hardly universal. After all, the Chinese did not undergo such a revolution even though they were civilized long before western Europe. Nor did the Arabs, who also possessed a rich civilization, find or utilize their vast oil resources. Without the stimulus of Western resource-tapping and the example of Western materialism, would the Third World even be interested in industrial development or its presumed fruits?

The truth is probably closer to Jalée's view than Coale's. Whether or not the LDCs would eventually have found and utilized their resources for themselves, with or without nonexploitive help from DCs, is beside the point. In recent years the resource flow has been predominantly from LDCs to DCs. The rich have been getting steadily richer and most of the poor have been lucky to stay even.

A third view of the situation presented by writer Tom O'Brien seems to us more accurate than that of either Coale or Jalée:

> I am not suggesting the underdevelopment of the Third World is a result of intentional efforts by the developed world, but neither is it the result of misguided benevolent intentions leading to unintentionally negative results. The intention of capital is profit, which, even when it includes the benevolent belief that profit-for-some can be profit-for-all, nevertheless means without some political mechanism for redistribution, an ever-widening gap between those who have more capital and those who have less. There has been no conscious conspiracy to depress the Third World; the unconscious operation of the market has been enough.[11]

In view of the comparatively great wealth of the developed nations, there should be a great deal the United States and other affluent nations might do to help improve conditions for people in the less developed world. To date, however, the rich world has generally done more to worsen the situation of the poor than to improve it—and the United States has been a leader in that performance, despite its record of foreign assistance.

Since World War II, United States economic interests have expanded to the far corners of Earth, investing many billions of dollars to develop a trade network designed to serve our national self-interest. Like other powerful nations, the United States has consistently used economic, political, and military means to maintain this trade network. American foreign-aid programs have been far more economic and political in orientation than humanitarian (despite the beliefs of most Americans that

[9] Man and his environment.

[10] *The pillage of the Third World.*

[11] Marrying Malthus and Marx.

the programs were selfless); American resources have been devoted mainly to providing additional material goods for ourselves and to an expensive and dangerous arms race, rather than to improving the lot of our fellow human beings.

Latin America and the United States: Problems of Paternalism

The pattern of relationships among DCs and LDCs prevailing until recently is exemplified by the behavior of the United States toward Latin America in this century. The United States has long claimed a special relationship with its neighbors to the south, but this more often than not has meant a desire for exclusive exploitation rights. The one-sidedness of the agreement has not gone unnoticed by Latin Americans.

When Sol Linowitz resigned in 1969 as U.S. ambassador to the Organization of American States, he warned of the possibility of "a series of Vietnams" in Latin America. The same year Nelson A. Rockefeller, then governor of New York, was sent on a fact-finding tour south of the border for President Nixon. He was greeted with a violence that underlined the Linowitz warning. Rockefeller was, of course, an especially ironic choice since his family's association with Standard Oil is so much a symbol of U.S. economic imperialism. But one does not have to look far for more fundamental reasons for his hostile reception.

Population growth in Latin America was proceeding at an average of 2.9 percent per year during the first eight years of the Alliance for Progress, while per-capita economic growth only averaged about 1.5 percent per year, a full percentage point below the Alliance target. A large portion of the Latin American population was then—and still is—for the most part living in appalling poverty. For millions, diets were inadequate, infant and child mortality sky-high, and decent housing often nonexistent. If 10,000 houses had been built *per day* in Latin America between 1969 and 1979, something on the order of 100 million of our southern neighbors (more than one-fourth of the expected population there) would still not be adequately housed. Although land reform has begun in some countries—most recently in Peru—10 percent of the people in Latin America still owned 90 percent of the land in 1976. And in most Latin American countries, progress toward an equitable distribution of income has been slow, especially for the rural populations.

Development in most of Latin America has scarcely touched the poor. The rich-poor gap has widened in many countries, especially the richer ones such as Brazil and Mexico, and national economies have tended to become two-tiered. The upper tier consists of large landholders and the urban upper and middle classes, especially in such industrial centers as São Paulo and Mexico City. In the lower tier are the urban poor and peasants, bypassed by modernization. In Mexico City, for example, a skilled worker in 1976 earned more than \$500 a month, including benefits. But outside the city, minimum wages for farm workers were \$5 a day, and because of underemployment many earned as little as \$100 per year.[12]

In several countries, notably Brazil, Peru, and Paraguay, there is a third, even lower tier—primitive Indians, who are being systematically exterminated as roadblocks in the path of progress. In Paraguay, which is heavily under U.S. influence, there have been charges of United States Central Intelligence Agency (CIA) complicity in those programs.[13] True or not, that such charges are widely believed south of the border says something about U.S.–Latin American relations.

Latin America's political instability is legendary (Figure 15-2). Between 1961 and mid-1976 political changes were made by military force in Argentina, Bolivia, Brazil, Chile, Dominican Republic, Ecuador, El Salvador, Guatemala, Honduras, Panama, and Peru—in some countries more than once. This political turmoil cannot all be blamed on the United States, but American behavior in Latin America has done little to foster stability there. Although the days when United States corporations directly controlled small countries are over, a huge reservoir of ill will remains from those days, when those corporations openly took what they wanted of the mineral and agricultural wealth of the continent. This

[12]A no-nonsense mood takes hold in Mexico, *U.S. News and World Report*, June 21, 1976, pp. 63–66. For a description of the situation in Brazil, see Robert Harvey, Brazil: The next nuclear power?

[13]John Hillaby, Genocide in Paraguay.

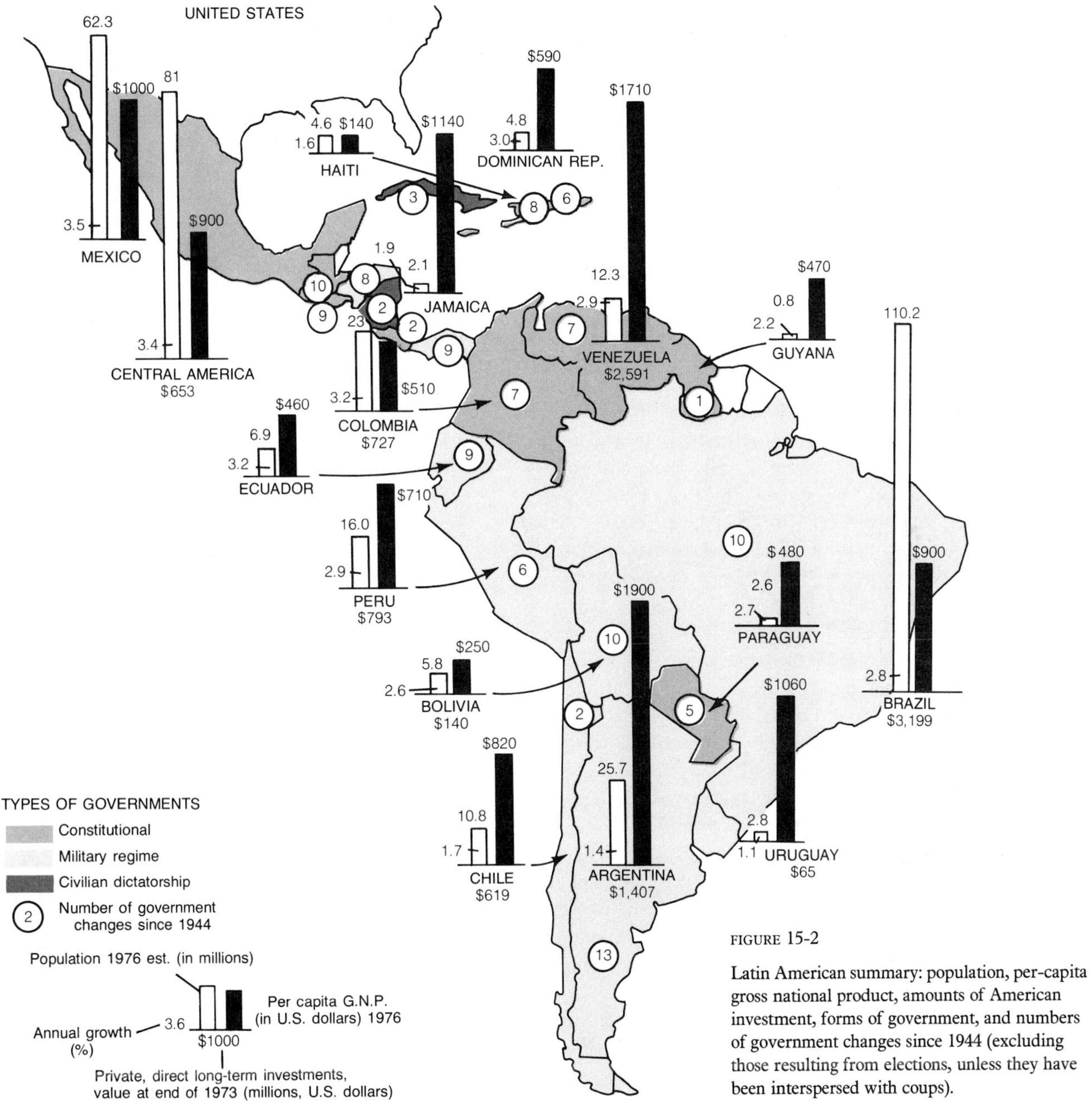

FIGURE 15-2

Latin American summary: population, per-capita gross national product, amounts of American investment, forms of government, and numbers of government changes since 1944 (excluding those resulting from elections, unless they have been interspersed with coups).

widespread resentment was deepened by revelation of CIA involvement in Chile before the 1974 coup that overthrew the Allende government in Chile. Moreover, North American economic exploitation of Latin America is even now far from finished. While some United States multinational companies are now so well-behaved that they can serve as examples of benevolence, having made significant contributions to their host nations, they still drain vast amounts of natural-resource capital from those nations. And the actions of some other United States multinational firms have had dramatically undesirable effects, especially on the poorest segments of the populations.[14]

[14]For example, see R. J. Barnet and R. E. Müller, *Global reach: The power of the multinational corporations,* chapter 7; and Robert J. Ledogar, *Hungry for profits: U.S. food and drug multinationals in Latin America.*

Since World War II, Latin American attitudes on DC-LDC relationships have been deeply influenced by the United Nations Economic Commission for Latin America (ECLA), and especially by one man, Dr. Raúl Prebisch of Argentina. Prebisch directed ECLA from 1950 to 1962 and became probably the best known economist in the LDCs in 1964 when he chaired the first meeting of UNCTAD (the United Nations Conferences on Trade and Development). Prebisch in 1950 promulgated the idea that the trade relations between DCs and LDCs were not working in favor of the LDCs as classical theory claimed, but *against* the LDCs.[15] He contended that the long-range terms of trade would always favor industrial over agricultural products and proposed a series of remedial steps including development of industrial capacity to manufacture products that traditionally had been imported. The Prebisch thesis that the rich exploit the poor through unfavorable conditions of trade has become a given in the approach of Latin Americans in their dealings with the United States—and indeed in the views of informed people in most of the less developed world toward the developed world.

In 1969, Latin American governments, meeting at Viña del Mar, Chile, presented a program for improving economic relations with the United States. They requested the United States to lower tariff barriers against Latin American goods and asked for a preferential market for their manufactured products. Basically, they were seeking redress for the economic imbalance in which Latin America still gave the United States more than it received in return. American aid to Latin America amounted to $11 billion in the first eight years of the Alliance for Progress. But profits extracted by U.S corporations operating in Latin America, interest on loans, and arrangements in which aid funds were required to be spent for goods on the expensive markets in the United States (and shipped on U.S. ships) more than compensated for the aid.

Following Viña del Mar and Governor Rockefeller's 1969 trip, there was disappointingly little change in U.S. policies toward Latin America. Rockefeller recommended establishment of more equitable economic relations, to be fostered through tariff changes and other means, and abandonment of the policy of economic "punishment" for governments that nationalized such local industries as copper without satisfactorily compensating the United States companies that had developed them (known as the Hickenlooper amendment). Rockefeller also recommended, however, that the United States continue to support all foreign governments that happened to be in power (whether we approved of them or not) and that it sell arms and military equipment to them on request, a policy that has only contributed to the volatility of Latin American politics. Such recommendations, together with some of the CIA's activities, have shown clearly that the United States still places its economic interests in Latin America ahead of the vital interests of the Latin American people.

There is little question that U.S. economic interests will be a source of continuing potential trouble with Latin America, even if aid, trade, and investment reforms are instituted. There is, however, a growing move away from dependency on the United States. More and more Latin American states are trading with each other and with distant parts of the world. Mexico is shipping its newly discovered oil to Brazil, Uruguay, Cuba, Israel, and the Philippines.[16] Brazil is sending its manufactured goods and produce not only to its neighbors, but to China, Japan, the Soviet bloc, and African nations.[17]

The OPEC revolution. Resentment of exploitation by DCs and efforts to adjust the balance began in Latin America, but have spread to other less developed regions as well. Less developed countries are demanding full participation in the industrialization of the world and a full chance to consume their own resources. For example, the Lima Declaration of the U.N. Industrial Development Organization in 1975 set a goal in which 25 percent of the world's industrial production would come from LDCs by 2000, in contrast to 7 or 8 percent in 1975.[18] Nevertheless, given the world's ecology-resource situation, it is questionable whether the wisest course for

[15]E. J. Williams and F. J. Wright, *Latin American politics: A developmental approach,* p. 109.

[16]Alan Riding, Mexico becomes oil exporter, *New York Times,* January 26, 1975.

[17]*New York Times,* January 26, 1975.

[18]Hansen, A "new international economic order."

most LDCs now would be to turn away entirely from their roles as commodity-suppliers, even if that were economically possible. It would seem foolish to invest wealth in an attempt to compete with DCs in processing what remains of most industrial resources, escalating environmental destruction in the process.

A much more intelligent strategy for the LDCs would appear to be to strive toward obtaining more stable prices and a much higher return on their commodities, especially their irreplaceable mineral wealth. A start in this direction was made in 1971 when oil-rich nonindustrial countries first banded together in the Organization of Petroleum Exporting Countries to bargain successfully as a group for higher prices for their oil. But the rise of about 20 percent in prices achieved then was virtually nothing compared to the nearly 300 percent (from $3 per barrel to almost $12 per barrel) achieved as a result of the Arab oil embargo between October 1973 and January 1974.

That embargo and the increase in the price of oil shook the industrial world to its foundations and changed forever the relationship between the rich (including OPEC) and the poor nations. It created enormous financial problems for DCs hell-bent on continued economic growth, and it threatened the very existence of some LDCs (as discussed in Chapter 7), *which generally applauded the price increase, nonetheless.* The change in oil prices inevitably will continue to have profound, far-reaching, and in many cases unexpected consequences for both developed and less developed economies.

The DCs, as has been noted, built their present prosperity on a foundation of cheap energy. Their economies have been geared to run on cheap energy, and old-style economic growth (which is still the stated goal of most politicians and economists) depends on cheap energy. During this century, the industrialized countries have shifted more and more to using petroleum as the source of that energy, despite repeated warnings that the supply of inexpensive, pumpable petroleum was bound to be exhausted shortly after the year 2000. Economists, determined to keep both physical constraints and human behavior out of their calculus, figured in 1961 that only half of the European Common Market's coal production would be profitable in 1970.[19] Planners therefore cut the capacity of the western European and British coal industries virtually in half between 1960 and 1970. Dependence on imported fuels in the Common Market consequently rose from 30 percent to more than 60 percent, and in the United Kingdom from 25 percent to 44 percent.

How could such a shortsighted course of action be taken? Simple. The politicians, economists, and industrialists running the show were confident that the Arabs would never be able to get together with Africans and Latin Americans to jack up the price of petroleum. Oil had always been cheap in the past; therefore, oil would be cheap in the future. Oil would take care of short- and mid-term energy needs. And, if oil supplies really could not be expanded infinitely (or recycled, as one economist has thought possible!),[20] then nuclear power or some other convenient scientific miracle would bail them out in the long term. In their opinion, it would certainly be wrong to maintain a coal industry that had prospects of becoming uneconomic. So the industrial countries now must buy oil from OPEC—and some of them must buy it regardless of the price.

The United States was in principle in a much better position to tolerate the increase in oil prices than many other nations. In late 1973 the United States was importing about 35 percent of its total petroleum consumption (6 million of the 17 million barrels consumed per day), with a third of those imports coming from Arab states. As a fraction of the *total* energy use in the United States, the imports amounted to around 16 percent. By contrast, Japan and some European countries were dependent on imported oil for 80 to 90 percent of their total energy use. For those countries, a prolonged and effective embargo would have produced complete economic catastrophe; as it was, they were saved by their modest stockpiles of petroleum, by the leakiness of the embargo, and by drastic conservation measures. Clearly, the Arab states did not want to produce catastrophe among their customers; but they did want to exercise

[19]E. F. Schumacher, *Small is beautiful: Economics as if people mattered,* pp. 116–117.

[20]Richard Zeckhauser, The risks of growth, p. 117. The fall 1973 issue of *Daedalus* is devoted to articles about the no-growth society.

TABLE 15-2
Oil Production and Reserves in OPEC Nations and Others in 1975

	Production, (million bbl/day)	*Reserves (billion bbl)*
OPEC producers		
Saudi Arabia	6.8	148.6
Iran	5.4	64.5
Venezuela	2.3	17.7
Nigeria	1.8	20.2
Libya	1.5	26.1
Kuwait	1.8	68.0
Iraq	2.2	34.3
United Arab Emirates*	2.0	32.3
Algeria	0.9	7.4
Indonesia	1.3	14.0
Qatar	0.4	5.9
Ecuador	0.2	2.5
Gabon (associate member)	0.2	2.2
Subtotal	26.8	443.7
Other producers		
USSR	9.8	80.4
United States	8.4	33.0
Canada	1.4	7.1
China	1.6	20.0
Others	5.1	76.5
Subtotal	26.3	217.0

*Abu Dhabi, Dubai, Sharjah, Ajman, Um al Quwain, Ras al Khaimah, and Fujairah.
Source: 1976 International petroleum encyclopedia.

their political muscle and begin to reap the economic rewards to which the world's dependence on their oil entitled them.[21] The extent of that dependence and some hint of its future extent are indicated in Table 15-2.

The immediate effect of the increased oil price on all the industrialized countries was to produce massive trade deficits[22] and to threaten their economies by destabilizing the international monetary system. A veritable flood of money started moving from the DCs to the OPEC nations, primarily to those in the Middle East. In 1974 alone, this flood amounted to some $75 billion more than would have been transferred under the earlier price structure, and it left the nations of the oil cartel with an estimated cash surplus of $65 billion.[23] This does not include increases in the prices of other energy forms, imported and domestic, that were stimulated at least in part by the oil situation. (The average price of coal delivered to U.S. utilities, for example, rose from around $8 per ton to about $20 per ton in the months immediately following the oil embargo.)

Notwithstanding a great deal of earnest handwringing in the industrial nations about whether the OPEC countries could "productively" absorb so much money so rapidly, they appear to have plenty of ideas on how to spend it. A sizeable amount was promptly reinvested in the industrial economies ("recyling petrodollars"), mainly in stocks of large corporations. (This seemed a clear enough signal that the OPEC countries had little desire to destroy the economies of the industrial world, but the outrage of many staunch supporters of free enterprise at the notion of the Arabs' owning substantial pieces of U.S. business was a bit amusing.) They have also invested heavily in the industrialization of their own countries, and, significantly, they have begun importing much greater amounts of food, primarily from the United States. Some of their funds have been set aside as foreign aid to poor countries.

Two aspects of the flow of petrodollars are less benign. One is that so little of the money is flowing in the direction of the poorest countries—those that have neither industry nor resources. They were hit extremely hard by the increase in oil prices—their expenditures on imported energy went up $15 billion, and their expenditures on imported food and fertilizer went up $5.5 billion between 1973 and 1974.[24] The second negative aspect is that so much of the money is being spent on weapons (see "Population, Resources, and War").

But, of course, one country's surplus is another's debt. Added to an already marginal economic situation (for which OPEC was in no way to blame), the financial hemorrhaging, as it has been called, could eventually lead to the bankruptcy of some of the weaker industrial nations, such as Italy. The Organization for Economic Cooperation and Development (OECD) estimated conservatively that by 1980 the members of the oil cartel would have about $300 billion in petrodollars.[25] And the petroleum-importing nations would have accumulated trading deficits equal to that amount. Where might the

[21]For extensive discussions of the history and politics of the international oil trade, see M. A. Adelman, *The world petroleum market;* Brookings Institution, *Energy and U.S. foreign policy;* M. A. Adelman et al., The U.S. and the world oil market.

[22]*New York Times,* January 26, 1975.

[23]Paul Lewis, Getting even. See also T. Stauffer, Oil money and world money: Conflict or confluence.

[24]David Freeman, et al., *A time to choose: The report of the Energy Policy Project of the Ford Foundation,* p. 164.

[25]Lewis, Getting even.

industrial states, burdened by this enormous debt, find the funds to meet their own needs for foreign exchange? And how would they pay the debts themselves?

As the new realities began to sink in, a search for solutions to various energy-related financial problems ensued. Among the early responses were: large increases in expenditures for research and development of alternative energy sources; increased interest in energy conservation and in ways to stockpile oil; and considerable attention to how oil-importing nations might counter the OPEC cartel. Eighteen oil-importing nations formed the International Energy Agency (IEA) in November 1974, with stated objectives of providing security against another oil embargo by means of sharing oil, sharing "equitably among industrial nations the burden of conservation" (whatever that meant), and coordinating measures to stimulate development of alternative sources.[26]

In the United States, the federal government hastily launched Project Independence, which was intended to free the nation from dependence on OPEC oil by the 1980s. In terms of standard thinking about economic growth and the resultant "needs" of the United States, that project was doomed to failure from the start.[27] Serious conservation efforts were discussed but not instituted. In the European Common Market there was talk of cutting reliance on oil imports from 63 percent to 50 percent by 1985 by slowing the growth of energy consumption, rebuilding the coal industry, increasing natural gas production, and accelerating programs to build nuclear power plants.[28]

But, of course, such long-range plans, even if they were effective in reducing oil consumption, could not solve the pressing financial problems of the West. The United States approach to the situation in 1975 fundamentally was to find some way to break the cartel's power and drive prices down again. Such action, at the very least, required unity among the consumers, but that unity proved highly elusive. The basic idea was that, if each nation cut back some on oil imports (one suggestion was for a 3 million bbl/day cutback by all DCs combined, with one-third of the cutback to occur in the United States), then the excess capacity of the OPEC producers (capacity to produce more oil than could be sold at the prevailing price) would become large enough to tempt one of them to break the cartel.

It is even possible that the United States government alone, by interposing itself between buyers and sellers, could break the cartel, as Christopher D. Stone and Jack McNamara of the University of Southern California Law Center have suggested.[28a] The basic idea, in essence, would be to create a new major buyer in the international market—one interested in lower prices rather than the high prices desired by the multinational oil companies that now control the situation. Furthermore, the use of a bidding system would encourage secrecy, allowing some of the more cash-hungry OPEC nations like Nigeria and Indonesia to cut their prices on the sly. Implementing such a plan, however, would require great political courage, since powerful interests have a huge stake in keeping oil prices high. The billions invested in the Alaskan oil enterprise and Britain's commitment to North Sea oil are just two examples.

The French approach, on the other hand, was that the major consumers, OPEC countries, and the other LDCs should enter trilateral negotiations aimed at reconciling the long-term needs of each group: energy for the West, and capital and aid in industrializing for the OPEC countries and the other LDCs.

Serious difficulties attend all of these approaches. There is no guarantee, for instance, that lowering demand would break the cartel—and indeed that ploy failed. Far from being hurt by reduced demand, the Arab nations, which have the most abundant supplies, might well prefer to keep their production low in the knowledge that their oil in the ground is going to be even more valuable in the future—a much more secure nest egg than most of the prospects for investing their petrodollars. They are not fools—they *know* that petroleum supplies are not infinite, and they are not hard pressed for cash as are some OPEC countries. Moreover, many DC economies have already been weakened in the 1970s by both inflation and recession—hardly putting the DCs in a

[26]U.S. Department of State, International energy program, news release, Bureau of Public Affairs, Washington, D.C., July 14, 1975.

[27]National Academy of Engineering, U.S. energy prospects: An engineering viewpoint, Washington, D.C., 1975.

[28]*Time,* December 30, 1974.

[28a]How to take on OPEC.

strong position to do economic battle with the oil suppliers. Even though the abrupt rise in oil prices contributed to these economic problems, it is not at all clear that reducing them again would be economically beneficial, especially in the long run.

The French approach to OPEC is more sensible in the long run, and the United States has gradually come around to it, in principle if not entirely in practice. Unhappily, at least through 1976, most effort in the West has gone toward finding ways of temporarily cushioning the blow of the petrodollar drain. The basic palliative has been to find ways to recycle about $60 billion annually in OPEC's surplus oil revenues to consumer nations in financial difficulty so that, in turn, they can buy more oil with it. Several plans have been suggested, all involving direct or indirect borrowing from the OPEC nations. This, of course, would increase the dependence of the consumers on the producers—but in many ways that seems more attractive than such alternatives as spending dollar and gold reserves (they would be exhausted in a year or so) or gradually selling their countries to the oil cartel.

Meanwhile, the world monetary system has been threatened by a crisis of confidence. Will nations attempt to pay their oil bills by simply printing money, or by restricting imports from OPEC and increasing exports to compensate for the effect of petroleum prices on their trade balances? Nations that managed to do the latter would, in effect, be exporting their deficits to other nations—opening the prospects of a trade war and worldwide depression. The industrial nations in 1974 pledged themselves against such a course of action, but whether the pledge will hold remains to be seen. Recycling petrodollars could lead to the bankruptcy of many states and the diversion of petrodollar investments into fiscally hardy nations like the United States and West Germany to whatever extent those states are willing to permit foreign investment.

It appears to us that the dilemmas raised by the success of the OPEC cartel (and any successful attempts by LDCs to follow OPEC's example with copper, bauxite, tin, or other commodities) will only be solved by dramatic changes in attitude, especially in the United States and other DCs, that would permit serious negotiations between rich, oil-rich, and poor countries to take place. The situation can only get worse unless some equitable, long-term plan for allocating the world's resources—including money—can be developed.

But arranging rational transfers of wealth would require careful planning, patience, and a degree of international cooperation and good will heretofore unknown. The DCs would have to move consciously to retreat from overdevelopment, most of them foregoing further growth in material consumption (although not necessarily in perceived well-being). The OPEC nations, on the other hand, would have to view at least part of their oil wealth as being held in trust for all LDCs, which they have shown little inclination to do so far. In addition, OPEC would have to show great restraint in dealing with the West for fear of destroying the economies in which they wish to invest their petrodollars and from which they hope to gain assistance in development. One encouraging sign is that the OPEC nations know that oil extraction will not go on forever and that they must look to a time when their nations will be integrated into an international economic system on some basis other than as commodity suppliers.

So far, unfortunately, the developed countries have appeared determined to continue their pursuit of material growth and seem little inclined to participate in any kind of redistribution. As long as DCs agonize over the effect on food prices if the poor should get the money to buy it, or over reduced standards of living in DCs if petrodollars are used by LDCs to absorb goods and services from them,[29] then a rational solution is unlikely to be found. Sad to report, the prospect of military action to break the OPEC cartel was even bandied about[30] and sanctioned as an extreme recourse by Secretary of State Henry A. Kissinger.[31] If this were the path eventually taken by the Western world, then, even if it were "successful," the future would be bleak indeed. For such action would mean that even the barest fundamentals of the global situation, in which all people are increasingly interdependent, have not been grasped by Western leaders. But whatever the outcome of this fast-changing situation, the OPEC revolution has transformed the

[29]Fred Banks, Copper is not oil, *New Scientist,* August 1, 1974.

[30]Robert W. Tucker, Oil: The issue of American intervention; Miles Ignotus, Seizing Arab oil.

[31]*Time,* January 20, 1975.

power structure of the world dramatically and perhaps permanently.

From the above discussion, it should be clear that a program of raising commodity prices in general, even if successful, would not necessarily help solve the problems of the poor nations—especially since such price increases would inevitably include the prices of foodstuffs, which many LDCs must import.[32] Poverty is not concentrated where the valuable natural resources are. For instance, Saudi Arabia, which has the world's largest oil reserves (some 175 billion barrels) is inhabited by less than 0.25 percent of the human population. All the OPEC nations together include only 15 percent of the world's population; and nearly half those people live in Indonesia, which is far from being the most richly endowed with oil.

Furthermore, as noted above, the successes of some less developed countries in raising commodity prices may mean disaster for others. As petroleum prices increased in 1974, for instance, India's plight substantially worsened. In the early 1970s India did not consume very much oil (about 200 million bbl/year). But 70 percent of that oil was imported, and 85 percent of it was needed for activities related to development, including irrigation and the production and transport of fertilizer. In 1974 India was forced to spend about 80 percent of its export earnings on oil alone. Whereas in 1970 India's oil imports cost only $140 million, in 1974 they exceeded the $1 billion in foreign aid that had been pledged to India that year by other nations![33]

Economic problems in the DCs also may have a heavy impact on the poorer LDCs. In 1974 Japan's severe energy shortage resulted in a drop in fertilizer production there, which caused a reduction in Japan's exports to nations like India, Indonesia, and the Philippines, all of which badly needed fertilizer. Similarly, enormous imports of wheat by the Soviet Union in 1972 and 1973 drove prices of that vital commodity up and reduced the supplies that were available to poor countries either through purchase or aid programs.[34]

There is still considerable debate among economists on technical points of tariff and trade policies in general. LDCs have been arguing strongly for measures to raise prices of their commodities, to obtain trade preferences, and generally to increase transfers of resources from DCs to LDCs.[35] Such changes until the mid-1970s were generally opposed by the DCs, and the United Nations Conferences on Trade and Development (UNCTAD) have increasingly seen confrontations along DC-LDC lines since the promulgation of the Prebisch thesis. Most LDCs accept Prebisch's belief that there is a built-in bias in world trade and finance in favor of the DCs, and they have seen in UNCTAD an opportunity to eliminate or even to reverse that bias.

A complicating factor in a system of trade preferences is the power of multinational corporations, which may generate 50 percent or more of the manufactured exports of some LDCs. Some opponents of trade preferences claim that they would largely be a "giveaway" to big business.[36] Once again, the already rich and powerful would benefit, not the poor.

If trade preferences and higher prices on commodities (when imposed suddenly, at least) may cause more problems than they solve, what kind of policies might enable poor nations to improve the lot of *all* of their people (rather than just a small elite)? The answer seems to lie primarily in changing the goals of development and, as a corollary to that, changing the form in which the necessary aid flows from the rich countries to the poor.

Development Assistance: A Grand Plan Gone Awry

Since 1950 and before, the United States in particular and more recently other developed nations have provided funds in the form of grants or low-cost loans to less developed countries in an effort to help them. Most Americans indeed are far more conscious of the foreign-aid budget than they are of the exploitive activities of United States businesses or of the unfairness of U.S. trade policies to LDCs. Surveys even in the mid-1970s

[32]William Schneider, Jr., Agricultural exports as an instrument of diplomacy.

[33]Data on impact of increased oil costs on India are from *New York Times,* December 13, 1973, and January 20, 1974, and from M. F. Franda, India and the energy crunch.

[34]Lester R. Brown, *In the human interest,* pp. 36 and 42.

[35]For more details on LDC demands in international trade, aid, foreign investment, technology transfer, and the international monetary system, see Hansen, A new international economic order; Barbara Ward, The Cocoyoe Declaration.

[36]Guy F. Erb, The developing countries in the Tokyo round, pp. 89–90.

indicated that most people in the United States still supported foreign aid out of generosity, not because it was profitable.[37] Yet, because of the political behavior of Third World nations in recent years (often perceived by uninformed Americans as ingratitude), public support for foreign aid has declined. With that decline, the United States has provided a dwindling share of the total amount of assistance from Western DCs (from well over half to about one-third), and the percentage of the United States GNP thus employed has also decreased (from 0.59 percent in 1963 to 0.29 percent in 1972).

Disillusionment with foreign aid is not limited to the United States; some other donor nations (France, West Germany, and the United Kingdom) have also cut back their assistance, at least as percentages of their GNPs.[38] On the other hand, aid from other countries—notably the Scandinavian countries, Australia, Canada, China, the Soviet Union, and lately Japan and OPEC countries—has increased since 1960. In 1974 several OPEC countries were far outperforming the West as aid-givers, measured as a percentage of their GNPs. Saudi Arabia, Kuwait, United Arab Emirates, and Iraq gave 3 or 4 percent of their GNPs; tiny Qatar gave a whopping 11 percent.[39]

Total aid commitments from members of the Organization for Economic Cooperation and Development from governmental and private sources reached $25.5 billion in 1975.[40] Of that only $13.5 billion came from governments (more than half of it being loaned, not given, though at low-interest, long-term rates). Much of the remainder ($9.5 billion) had to be spent on goods from the donor country (often at higher cost) or for salaries and repatriation bonuses for Western administrators and technical experts. When all such "catches" were accounted for, the LDCs were left with about $5.3 billion in 1975.[41]

While many LDCs have become somewhat dependent upon foreign aid to keep their economies alive (and in many cases to feed their people), there is a widespread feeling that the United Nations Development Decade of the 1960s and its successor, the Second Development Decade, have failed to accomplish their mission of significantly improving the condition of the LDCs. LDCs also often feel degraded by the strings that have been attached to aid projects and ensnared by seemingly multiplying interest payments. Some recipient countries have at times declined development aid for reasons of politics or pride—India and Tanzania, among others—although, as a result of economic buffeting by the energy crisis and the world recession, they of necessity have been returning for help.

Traditional Western attitudes toward less developed countries have often seriously complicated DC efforts to help the rest of humanity. Developed countries, both capitalist and communist, have long assumed that they knew what was best for the nations of the Third World. And many Third World leaders, educated in DCs, have accepted that view. An unspoken assumption of all such aid seems to have been that the best hope for the LDCs lay in emulating the path followed by the DCs, that by applying the ideas of Marx, Malthus, or perhaps Henry Ford, the LDCs could pull themselves out of the mire of poverty.

The hubris of this view has been lost on most citizens of the DCs, but it has become glaringly obvious to many inhabitants of the Third World. The peoples of Indochina developed, among others, the culture that produced Angkor Wat. The Chinese had a venerable civilization when the British still lived in caves and painted themselves blue, and the civilization of India is nearly as old. Africans built Zimbabwe and produced the incomparable Benin bronzes long before Europeans "discovered" them in the nineteenth century. The proud people of Asia, Latin America, and Africa do not appreciate being considered somehow backward and in need of charity.

The original purpose of foreign aid, of course, was to help the underdeveloped world develop in essentially the same ways that Western countries—and later, the Soviet bloc—had. This was to be accomplished by concentrating investment in the creation of a modern sector in each developing country—a core of industrialization in cities, which would provide employment for the growing population and generate a rise in personal incomes and

[37]C. R. Frank, Jr., and M. Baird, Foreign aid: Its speckled past and future prospects.

[38]Ibid.

[39]The Arab's turn now, *New Internationalist,* January 1976, pp. 8–9.

[40]*World Bank report for 1975.* World Bank, Washington, D.C.

[41]For an interesting breakdown, see The heart of the matter, *New Internationalist,* January 1976, pp. 4–5.

national GNP. The benefits of that growth were expected to "trickle down" to the poorer strata of society, which were not directly involved in the development effort.

It was an ambitious and, in its purported aims, a rather noble plan, conceived in the expansively optimistic years before 1960. Unfortunately, it did not work. Louis Emmerji, director of the World Employment Programme of the International Labour Organization (ILO) clearly expressed the dismal results of the United Nations Development Decade:

> One look at the cities of the Third World today with their inner circles of steel and glass and their outer circles of poverty and junk, tells us that it hasn't worked. The heart of the "modern sector" is an enclave of privilege where a few people receive incomes far above the countries' average whilst the people of the slums and shanty towns lack basic necessities . . . .
>
> The failure of economic growth to "trickle down" led to rising inequalities and the resulting unemployment and poverty. And all the time agriculture languished in low priority—contributing to the food problem as we know it.[42]

One fatal flaw in the theory was that it overlooked the historical pattern of industrialization in Europe and North America. There, rural development, including small-scale rural industry, preceded urban industry. Indeed, the first inventions and factories fashioned agriculture-related tools and machines. Cities were mainly trading centers; only later was manufacturing located near cities, when nonagricultural consumer goods became the primary output. Even today in DCs, many agricultural items are manufactured in smaller cities in agricultural regions—an example is the headquarters of Massey-Ferguson, manufacturer of huge tractors and combines, in Des Moines, Iowa. The example for LDCs—where 50 to 80 percent of the populations are still rural—should have been obvious. But for urban-oriented economists, planners, and officials, the lesson was somehow overlooked.

The blame for such poor judgement (at least as seen in 20-20 hindsight) cannot all be put on aid donors; much of it lies at the doorstep of decision-makers (government or business) in the LDCs who accepted the assistance and helped to determine the kinds of development that were undertaken. Some of them have been victims of bad advice, however. Perhaps a large share of blame should be pinned on the economists and other development experts who designed aid programs and projects and who promulgated the trickle-down theory. In addition, private investors from DCs—especially multinational corporations—have also contributed heavily to the unbalanced pattern of LDC development.

[42]Workless of the world, *New Internationalist*, October 1975, p. 8.

Development and the Environment

One particularly unhappy aspect of some development programs has been their ecological incompetence, a direct consequence of the environmental nearsightedness that has so long afflicted the politicians and technologists of the developed nations. Western technology exported to the LDCs has certainly been a mixed blessing, whether or not that technology has been part of a formal aid program. The consequences of the export of death-control technology to the demographic situation have been examined earlier, as have such problems as were created by the disastrous export of Western pesticide technology to places like the Cañete Valley of Peru. The list, however, runs far beyond this; it includes misuse of pesticides in Malaysia and the encouragement of schistosomal parasites in Africa. In addition, with or without aid and technology from DCs, there has been acceleration of deforestation, soil deterioration, and erosion in Indonesia, India, and Pakistan and in much of Africa and Latin America. In almost every case, great problems could have been avoided or ameliorated if ecologically sound approaches had been taken.[43]

What is perhaps the classic example of misplaced aid in development has been supplied by the Soviet Union. That was the construction of the Aswân High Dam, which may well prove to be the ultimate disaster for Egypt. As has been characteristic of much foreign aid, the ecological consequences and social alternatives were not considered in advance. Irrigation from the dam project, completed in 1970, cannot increase food pro-

[43]For examples, see M. T. Farvar and J. P. Milton, eds., *The careless technology;* Jon Tinker, Is technology neocolonist?; Erik Eckholm, *Losing ground: Environmental stress and world food prospects.*

duction enough to feed the number of people that were added to the Egyptian population even during the dam's construction period. This is not a criticism of the dam itself, except insofar as it absorbed resources that might better have been put into population control and agricultural development.

Furthermore, as had been predicted beforehand, the conversion of some 500 miles of Nile floodplain from a one-crop system of irrigation to a four-crop rotation system has had deleterious effects on the health of that population. Perennial irrigation creates ideal conditions for the spread of certain snails which are the intermediate hosts of the blood flukes that cause the serious parasitic disease schistosomiasis (also called bilharzia). Parasitologists expected the Aswân Dam to be the ultimate cause of an explosive outbreak of this disease, and their expectations have been met. The average incidence of schistosomiasis along the Nile between Cairo and Aswân was about 5 percent in 1937. In 1972, following completion of the dam, it had risen to 35 percent, a sevenfold increase.[44]

In addition, the change in the flow of the Nile has had deleterious effects on fisheries in the eastern Mediterranean. It will also have a negative impact on the fertility of the soil of the Nile delta, since the Aswân Dam will restrain nutrients that were previously deposited there annually by the Nile flood. This potential soil depletion will be exacerbated by the growing of several crops rather than one a year. Attempts to solve the problem will undoubtedly include an accelerating use of inorganic fertilizers, with attendant ecological complications.

On the plus side, new fisheries may become established in the Mediterranean and in Lake Nasser (formed behind the dam); it is conceivable that new drugs will help control schistosomiasis, and technology may be able to maintain yields on the newly irrigated land. But, even if most of the problems created by the dam can be solved, two important principles will not have been changed. The first is that *all* major development projects are bound to have ecological consequences, which should be carefully evaluated *at the time of planning,* not dealt with haphazardly after the deed is done. The second is that if an effort equal to that involved in the Aswân Dam project had been channeled into population control, rural development, and agricultural production, it could have benefited Egypt far beyond the rewards of even a totally problem-free dam—especially since in the long run the reservoir behind the dam will silt up and thus become useless.

Bringing land under cultivation through irrigation has long been recognized as no permanent solution to population-food imbalances. Two decades before the completion of the Aswân High Dam, Charles Galton Darwin pointed out that the Sukkur barrage on the Indus River, a dam diverting water to irrigate 2.4 million hectares of India, did not result in adequate diets for people who had previously gone hungry. As he put it, "After a few years the effect was only to have a large number of people on the verge of starvation instead of a small number."[45]

Population can easily increase enough to overstrain any resource, which is precisely what is happening in Egypt today. In the mid-1970s the birth rate in Egypt was estimated to be around 38, the death rate 14, and the growth rate 2.4 percent (doubling time, 29 years). In this context, the Aswân High Dam, which required more than a decade to construct and added to the arable pool of land an equivalent of 800,000 hectares (one-third of the previously cultivated land), is a small project indeed. Egypt would have to complete the equivalent of four more Aswân High Dams before the end of the century just to maintain its present inadequate level of nutrition, if there were no change in yields. Worst of all, the propaganda associated with the dam lulled many Egyptians and others into a false sense of security, so that little was done either to curb the growth of the population of Egypt or to improve its stagnant agricultural system. When the dam was completed, its inadequacy for solving Egypt's food and development problems became evident. Since then, the government has been supporting a national family-planning program and agricultural improvement efforts with considerably more enthusiasm than before.

Roadblocks to development. Disillusionment with development has become widespread, not only because large investments of resources and effort have yielded

[44]Henry Van der Schalie, Aswan Dam revisited.

[45]*The next million years,* p. 37.

BOX 15-1 The Manpower Explosion in LDCs

One of the unhappy consequences of the rapid increase in the rates of LDC population growth in the 1950s and 1960s is that the children born during that period are now entering the labor pool in large numbers. Some 350,000 more young people are entering the labor force than old people retire *each week* in south Asia alone. If population growth continues at current rates, the increment will rise to 750,000 per week by the year 2000. This means that about 18 million new jobs are needed per year to provide for these young people and their families.* Needless to say, the cities and budding industries of south Asia cannot begin to meet the need.

These statistics are particularly staggering when considering that unemployment and underemployment have been creating enormous problems throughout these economies for some time already and that competition for jobs was being described as cutthroat before 1970. Furthermore, no successes in birth control, regardless of how spectacular, could affect the statistics for at least the next fifteen years, since the people involved have already been born. The situation in south Asia is more or less characteristic of that in other LDCs, in most of which 20 to 30 percent of the eligible working populations are either unemployed or severely underemployed.

*Mesarovic and Pestel, *Mankind at the turning point.*

The worker explosion will require dramatic efforts to provide jobs in both urban and rural sectors of LDC economies. Much might be accomplished by concentrating on labor-intensive agricultural methods and introducing Social Security-type programs that would permit old or otherwise marginal workers to withdraw from the labor pool without tragic results. Similarly, development in general can produce more jobs if it is carefully planned so that unnecessary mechanization is sharply limited.

If the labor problem is not solved, unemployment and associated disruption may themselves present serious barriers to development. When peasants are forced off the land and can find no jobs elsewhere, they often turn to militant revolutionary groups (such as the Naxalite movement in India in the 1960s and various guerrilla groups in Latin America active in this decade). Land grabs, terrorist activity, and general social disruption have become increasingly common in LDCs in the 1970s, and the link with high rates of unemployment is hardly tenuous.

unexpected and undesired results, but also because various social obstacles have severely impeded progress. Among them, of course, has been the largely unanticipated acceleration of population growth in most LDCs since 1950.

The necessity for population control to permit even limited development of LDCs is plain from practical experience (per-capita income gains being small in the face of record population growth) as well as from economic analysis and computer simulations.[46] Unhappily, population control has proven more difficult to achieve in many LDCs than was originally anticipated for various social and economic reasons (Chapter 13). Moreover, the less developed world today has an unfavorable demographic situation that differs markedly from what prevailed in the DCs during their industrialization. In particular, LDCs are hampered by high dependency ratios (the ratio of economically unproductive to productive people in the population) and explosively growing labor pools (see Box 15-1).

Obstacles to development go far beyond those generated by rapid population growth, however. LDCs would face competition from the DCs if they attempted to compete in international markets by producing manufactured goods. Europe and North America did not have vastly more advanced nations to compete with when they were developing. This is one factor that keeps LDCs in the role of commodity-producers, concentrating on the production of agricultural goods and minerals. The LDCs do, however, have the advantage (or potential advantage) of access to the technological expertise of the DCs.[47]

[46]Goran Ohlin, *Population control and economic development;* Douglas Daetz, Energy utilization and aid effectiveness in nonmechanized agriculture; Stephen Enke, Birth control for economic development. See also Nathan Keyfitz, World resources.

[47]Gunnar Myrdal, The transfer of technology to underdeveloped countries.

BOX 15-2 The Soft State

Viewed in the Western cultural context, many LDCs are not unified political units, equivalent in that sense to most DCs. Most LDCs face grave problems of internal equity and social organization, and those problems present formidable barriers in the path of development. Among the most critical difficulties is the prevalence of graft.

Economist Gunnar Myrdal has suggested that the problems of *soft states* are in part an unfortunate legacy of anarchic attitudes that arose during colonial times.* The patterns of civil disobedience, noncooperation, and overt rebellion that developed during the struggles for independence persist and are now operating to the detriment of the indigenous governments. This is not very surprising, especially in countries where elites trained by colonial powers have, on gaining independence, merely continued the operation of the government apparatuses as they inherited them—and have adopted many of the attitudes of the colonial rulers, as well.

The anarchic patterns flourish along with the corruption that has historically characterized many LDC governments and that is almost invariably a corollary of an illiterate, ill-informed, or misled populace. Graft has long been a way of life in most LDCs and is recognized as such by the citizens of those countries themselves. For example, in 1968 Indian Minister for Foreign Affairs and Labor, S. Rajaratnoam, described government by graft as "kleptocracy." He said:

> It is amazing how otherwise excellent studies on development problems in Asia and Africa avoid any serious reference to the fact of corruption. It is not that the writers do not know of its existence but its relevance to the question of political stability and rapid economic development appears not to have been fully appreciated. It may also be that a serious probing of the subject has been avoided lest it should offend the sensibilities of Asians.**

Most LDCs are traditional societies in which "connections," large-scale graft, and petty bribery (with little loyalty to community or nation) have thrived as an acceptable form of transaction in both business and government. Jon Tinker has vividly described how the system works in the Indonesian family-planning program, where it operates largely to further the program rather than as an obstacle to its implementation:

> Family planning staff are not well paid, and as often as not their salaries are mislaid on the lengthy journey from Jakarta via province,

* *The challenge of world poverty.*

**Quoted in Myrdal, ibid., p. 229.

At present, though, there are serious barriers to the transfer of technology inherent in patent laws, license fees, and royalties, and in the tendency of industries to keep their processes and techniques secret. The problems of transferring technology have been accentuated by a lack of scientific and technical traditions in LDC societies or in their educational institutions, most of which were originally established by colonial powers. The consequence is often that, even when a technology might be available, people in LDCs may not appreciate its value or have the necessary background for adapting it to their own use. As Pakistani physicist Abdus Salam described it, "it is not just know-how which the developing countries need; it is also the *know-why.*"[48]

[48]Abdus Salam, Ideals and realities.

At least initially, LDCs also have an advantage in their large pools of cheap labor. This has already been exploited in several countries by multinational corporations, which, for example, have set up factories in Taiwan, South Korea, and Southeast Asia for manufacturing clothing and assembling electronic devices.

Additional obstacles to progress are the burdens of colonial history and traditions, the character of present political decision-making apparatus, the failure of governments to institute land reform, and a wide array of government economic policies. Unfortunately, a narrow focus on economics characterizes discussions about these problems. For instance, economists often point out that the coffee trade has "enriched" Brazil, ignoring the ecological effects of what Georg Borgstrom describes as the "almost predatory exploitations by the coffee plant-

regency and district governments to the village clinic. So an illegal charge is made both for a visit to a clinic and for the contraceptive device . . . . Indonesians do not normally accept money to do something they should not do, but instead make a charge for what they ought to do anyway. These payments finance a complex welfare system, both inside each government office and extending outside to the children and grandmothers and cousins of the staff. The corrupt and bloated Indonesian general with his Swiss bank account may genuinely exist for all I know, but he should not be confused with the subtle network of claims and obligations which fans outwards from every Indonesian in a government job.[†]

Such a system can be described as corrupt or irrational only in a context of Western values, of course. Unfortunately, in many areas the system is far less benign.

Although DCs are not wholly free from graft, the populace in those nations generally recognizes graft as an evil, and it is seldom as open and pervasive as in many LDCs. Circumstances compel us to accept this culture-bound Western value judgment. Western medicine and public-health procedures have been a key factor in promoting overpopulation; Western economic goals are accepted by LDC governments, educational systems, and large segments of LDC populations. As far as we can see, Western-style organizational solutions at this time may be the only kind that offers substantial hope of ameliorating the crises that now face the world society. Therefore, culture-bound as it appears—and is—our discussion must be within that framework.

Whatever its origins, corruption undoubtedly increased when partial vacuums were created by the withdrawal of colonial administrations. In general, it has tended to increase since independence and has helped to block many needed social changes, including land and tenancy reforms (for instance, giving tenant farmers a reasonable return on their labors). It often prevents foreign aid from reaching its intended recipients. It greatly weakens local respect for government and for planning and thus indirectly blocks programs to improve standards of living. It also makes more difficult the kind of coordinated international actions required if efforts like the World Food Program are to achieve maximum success. In short, responsibility for the dismal state of world efforts to help the needy may lie largely at the doorstep of the DCs, but not entirely so.

[†]Java: Birth control battlefield.

ers."[49] Dependence on that commodity has not only ruined much of Brazil's soil but is also a major reason why many Brazilians are inadequately fed today.

Furthermore, the LDCs generally lack the cultural traditions that originally led to industrialization in the DCs. As economist Neil Jacoby of the University of California wrote, "development requires a people to choose a new set of philosophical values."[50] The cultural differences show up in various ways. One of them is the pervasive corruption—especially in government—that characterizes many LDCs, inducing Gunnar Myrdal to call them "soft states" (see Box 15-2).

DCs have often failed to recognize the strong psychological need of the LDCs for independence. As Deputy Administrator I. G. Patel of the United Nations Development Program put it:

> Most of the developing countries have bitter memories of colonial exploitation and racial and other forms of discrimination. Hence, beneath the desire for economic progress is the need to obliterate past hurts and humiliations, to regain dignity and self-respect, which they enjoyed for long centuries but lost during the brief period of Western domination. . . . It is no exaggeration to describe the goals of the developing world today as more psychological than economic, and to perceive that independence is more cherished than economic progress.[51]

The economic and political aspects of development

[49]*The hungry planet,* 2d ed., Macmillan, New York, 1972, p. 336.
[50]The progress of peoples.

[51]What the developing countries really want.

and DC-LDC relationships are extremely complex.[52] But, whatever the "answers" are to the disputed points of policy and questions of who is at fault, it has become abundantly clear that no solution to the general problem can be found until, in effect, the rules of the game are changed.

There is growing agreement that past development policies that focused solely on achieving an industrial takeoff have failed miserably to pull the poorest 25 percent of the world's people out of poverty. As we have mentioned, this is partly because the numbers of the poorest have been increasing much more rapidly than the efforts to help them.[53] Growth in that segment of the population is very rapid and generally is accelerating as death rates fall. But another important reason is that very little has been done directly to help the groups with the lowest incomes in most LDCs.

Recognizing this, both the United States in its bilateral aid program and the World Bank in its multilateral programs have recently shifted their emphases from urban-industrial to rural-agricultural development. In essence, an attempt is to be made to redress the inequities fostered by the previous GNP-is-everything approach, to try to bring the benefits of development to the bottom tiers of two-tiered economies. Efforts are to be made to tackle the problems of the poor directly, instead of depending on "trickle-down" to help them.

As should be apparent by now, the problems of development are a very complex mix of population, food, resource, energy, environmental, social, political, and economic factors. Because of the growing constraints imposed by the various elements of this mix, it is becoming clear that most LDCs cannot and should not be industrialized along DC lines. The most impressive constraints may the the environmental ones. As one biologist put it, "Just think what would happen to the atmosphere if 700 million Chinese started driving big automobiles!"

But it also has become evident that the depletion of high-grade nonrenewable resources would not permit more than a very modest industrial development of most LDCs (unless, of course, there were some sort of massive deindustrialization of most DCs).[53a] Even if the resources of Earth could be mobilized rapidly enough to meet the demands that fully industrializing all LDCs would create, *essential ecological systems would collapse under the added stress.* Whether or not economists and politicians wish to recognize it, growth as occurred in DCs during the past few decades is over,[54] and it will never occur in the majority of LDCs. In an era in which energy costs and capital scarcity are increasing and will clearly continue to do so, only a fool would attempt to push the capital- and energy-intensive United States model of development upon societies already suffering from rampant unemployment.

If large-scale industrialization is not to occur in the LDCs, how, then, are they to develop? Some other course must be found, and we predict it will increasingly resemble the labor-intensive Chinese model. And well it might, for the People's Republic of China is the only large LDC that has made significant strides toward solving its population and food problems and substantially raising standards of living and health for its people. For countries like India and Indonesia, the Chinese model of development offers some hope; the standard United States model (complete with an overmechanized Green Revolution) offers none. The key to successful development also lies partially in the DC-LDC relationship. Without drastic changes in DC attitudes and aid patterns, the LDCs probably will not develop in any sense; rather, many are likely to collapse into chaos.

Aid and International Politics

The problems of foreign aid and development cannot, of course, be divorced from the problems of international politics. Because of their own backgrounds and capabili-

[52]For example, see Robert O. Keohane and Van Doorn Ooms, The multinational firm and international regulation; and Frank and Baird, Foreign aid.

[53]John G. Sommer, U.S. voluntary aid to the Third World: What is its future?

[53a]Some of the obstacles to extending a DC lifestyle to the world's growing number of poor people are described in Nathan Keyfitz, World resources. Keyfitz believes that the affluent fraction of the world's population—those above the poverty level—might be increased from 15 percent in 1975 to 28 percent in 2000 and nearly half by 2025. But even though the population escaping from poverty is projected to increase more rapidly than the total population, or even the population of LDCs, the absolute numbers of the poor would still be greater than today. Keyfitz questions whether resources and technology can be mobilized fast enough to maintain this growth of material affluence without environmental destruction, and we are even more doubtful.

[54]Ehrlich and Ehrlich, *The end of affluence.*

ties, the two most powerful DCs, the United States and USSR, have approached aid differently. The United States, with a vast store of capital to draw on, has seen the problems of the LDCs primarily in terms of a shortage of capital. The Soviets, on the other hand, because of their relatively recent history of revolution and the more recent successful revolutions in two LDCs—China and Cuba—tend to emphasize the export not of capital but of political change, of revolution.

Unhappily, many nations threw off the yoke of colonial exploiters after World War II only to have it replaced by home-grown repressive governments. Political scientist Harlan Cleveland put it succinctly: "Nor did freedom for nations lead directly to freedom for individuals. Colonial rule was often supplanted by military rule, Czars were succeeded by commissars, white domination gave way to black dictatorships, extraterritoriality was pushed out by totalitarianism."[55]

The need for dramatic political change in many countries is obvious—but most recent changes have been in the wrong direction. Haiti (with a per-capita GNP of $70 in 1972) had no chance while it was under dictator François Duvalier, and its present prospects seem no better. The assumption of "emergency powers" by Prime Minister Indira Gandhi of India in 1975, including suppression of dissent, did not encourage optimism for the political future of that troubled country. The autocratic regimes, military or civilian, in many Latin American and African nations, many of them beset by terrorism and revolutionary activity, seem barely able to keep the peace and their seats in power, let alone do much to improve the lives of their peoples. Tales of severe repression and torture of dissidents in Brazil and Chile—both countries that ostensibly have a great deal going for them—horrify outsiders and frighten off tourists (if not foreign investors).

Democracy is a fragile form of government, especially where it is not backed by appropriate traditions and some degree of economic equity. Economic equity may be especially important, and a fundamental aspect of equity is landholding. In many nominal democracies, land reform unquestionably is sorely needed to give the people incentive to improve their agricultural practices and a chance to participate in the modernization process. Revolution is one potentially effective way to achieve land reform.

Both the capitalist and revolutionary points of view on aid have a certain validity, but both are also sadly deficient. If real progress in helping LDCs is to be made, both superpowers will have to change their ways. The United States must stop supporting assorted dictators around the world merely because they claim to be anticommunist. It must accept that in many countries most of the people might well be better off under regimes that the U.S. perceives as communist than under their present regimes. In Latin America, in particular, the need for social justice as a first step toward economic development has been widely recognized (but rarely implemented). If badly needed reforms do not take place peacefully, they will sooner or later be attempted by revolution. It is imperative that U.S. officials in LDCs realize that their contacts within those countries are all too often unrepresentative of the people as a whole. The attitudes of the governing classes in the capitol cities are unlikely to resemble those of peasants or of the masses in urban slums.

There is, of course, no doubt that corporate interests, sensitive to the resource limits of the United States and motivated by the desire for profits, play a substantial role in shaping American foreign policy. The interlocking directorates of the government and various industrial giants are well known. Executives move freely from big business into administrative positions in the government, while high-level bureaucrats and military leaders are welcomed into executive positions with corporations doing business with the government. In 1969, for instance, each of the top twenty defense contractors in the United States employed an average of 65 retired military men of the rank of colonel, navy captain, or higher.[56] The military-industrial complex, among other things, wishes to assure the United States control over the resources it deems essential—and in the process often has attempted to control the destinies of LDCs.

It is evident that the LDCs can undertake and would profit from having control over their own resources and destinies. The contrary view has often been held in the

[55]Our coming foreign policy crisis, p. 11.

[56]Dennis C. Pirages and Paul R. Ehrlich, *Ark II: Social response to environmental imperatives.*

past as doctrine by the DCs. For example, there were dire (and erroneous) warnings that the Egyptians would be unable to run the Suez Canal when they took it over from the British in 1956. The success of OPEC surely has put that fairy tale to rest once and for all!

Nonetheless, it seems unlikely that there is much to be gained in attempting to shatter the power of international corporations, many of which, among other things, are heavily engaged in the exploitation of LDC resources. A primary reason is that it probably would be impossible in the absence of supporting changes in attitude in DC societies. As long as economic standards reign supreme, economic power will tend to become concentrated; only more fundamental changes will suffice. And those changes must be made with great care. International corporations supply planning, coordination, capital, and expertise in their operations within LDCs; considerable economic hardship could result from a sudden dissolution of those giants. But they could be quickly stopped from draining capital away from the LDCs; after all, the extraction of capital goes against the West's conventional wisdom of what is required to eliminate poverty in those nations.

Russia should face the facts of life, too. The Soviets blame most of the problems of the world on capitalist imperialism, but that just is not supported by the evidence. Revolution is at best a partial answer; it cannot remove the biological and physical constraints upon development, although it may well remove some of the social and economic barriers. At worst, as noted above, revolution only replaces one despotism with another. Furthermore, the Soviet Union's intervention in other countries in defense of what it perceives as its vital interests has been fully as blatant and brutal as that of the capitalist imperialists, as the Soviet invasion of Czechoslovakia in 1968 so clearly demonstrated. It is ironic that the USSR, in Angola and elsewhere, now seems to be emulating the grand imperialism pioneered in the nineteenth century by western European powers and the United States.

But the differing approaches of the United States (as well as other Western nations) and the USSR, which dominated international politics in the first two decades after World War II, must now share the stage with the policies of the LDCs themselves, which are increasingly determined to narrow the gap between the rich and the poor. The OPEC revolution has shown that traditional international politicoeconomic relationships *can* be dramatically and profoundly altered. And even if, as some claim, the case of oil is unique, the self-interest of the rich nations is clearly tied to the condition of the poor. As Harlan Cleveland has written, "If two-thirds of the world simply failed to cooperate in international arrangements that require general consent—nuclear safeguards, weather watch, crop forecasting, public health, narcotics control, environmental monitoring, and measures against hijacking and terrorism—everybody would lose, but the world powers would likely lose the most."[57]

In short, for the world commons to operate for the benefit of all people requires it to be administered cooperatively—and the poor can demand a price for their cooperation. More positively, there is general agreement among the rich that poverty *should* be wiped out—and that consensus would make selfishness a more difficult course (although one that certainly might yet be taken).

International politics in the near future will most likely be focused on the question of whether the rich and the poor can strike a new *planetary bargain,* to use Harlan Cleveland's term. Can the developed countries show the necessary self-restraint and the less developed countries the necessary changes in attitudes and organization to rearrange the relationships among nations successfully? There are some hopeful signs.

A group consisting of most Third World nations, calling themselves the Group of 77, in 1974 presented a case to the United Nations for a New International Order. In May 1974 the United Nations General Assembly adopted by consensus a Declaration on the Establishment of a New Economic Order, whose stated aims include: "to correct inequalities and redress existing injustices and ensure steadily accelerating economic development, peace and justice for present and future generations."[58]

The Declaration called for stabilization of commodity prices and markets for them and for establishment of a link between those prices and prices paid for manufactured products imported from DCs. It also called for

[57]Our coming foreign policy crisis, p. 13.

[58]The new economic order, *New Internationalist,* October 1975 (a special issue on this subject).

restraint of research into synthetic substitutes for commodities, which have already damaged markets for some products, such as sisal, jute, and rubber. (Higher prices and diminishing resources of petroleum will eventually undermine this activity, but that is little comfort to LDCs today.) Finally, the New Economic Order would encourage the development of producer associations and trade unions among LDCs in order to negotiate favorable trade terms more effectively. Such trade associations, while not having the clout of OPEC (where conditions were uniquely suitable for setting up a cartel), have already been established for several commodities, including bananas, cocoa, coffee, copper, phosphates, tea, and tin.[59]

The reaction to the New Economic Order among DCs, especially at first, was generally negative, and the United States was the most recalcitrant. But it soon became obvious that the demands of the Group of 77 could not be ignored. United Nations Secretary General Kurt Waldheim told a later United Nations conference in Lima, Peru: "the New Economic Order is the price of peace."[60]

In September 1975, in an address before the United Nations by Secretary of State Henry Kissinger, the United States officially took a stand favoring new bargains, including a "fundamental structural improvement in the relationship of the developing countries to the world trading system . . . such as preferences, favorable concessions, and exceptions which reflect their economic status."[61] Kissinger also urged the world community to address the basic problems of access of LDCs to capital markets, the transfer of technology, and "the principles to guide the beneficial operation of transnational enterprises." He pointed out the need for controlling population growth, for increasing food reserves, and for reducing food wastage, and he pledged the United States to contribute to a program of action if all nations "met in a spirit of common endeavor." The speech ended with some interesting rhetoric:

> My government does not offer these propositions as an act of charity, nor should they be received as if due. We know that the world economy nourishes us all, we know that we live on a shrinking planet. Materially as well as morally, our destinies are intertwined. . . .
>
> There remain enormous things for us to do. We can say once more to the new nations: We have heard your voices. We embrace your hopes. We will join your efforts. We commit ourselves to our common success.

Although the speech did not indicate awareness of many of the concerns of this chapter, it did indicate a growing power within the United States government of persons who realize the degree to which all nations are interdependent and understand that the future of the United States depends on how well the entire world deals with the population-resource-environment crisis. No doubt the success of the OPEC cartel's embargo and raising of oil prices also had much to do with the United States change of heart toward the aspirations of poor countries. History makes it difficult to believe that the change in attitude could have been accomplished without the bludgeon of OPEC oil or some similar weapon in the control of the nonindustrial nations.

How much action will follow the rhetoric remains to be seen. And how ready the LDCs are to put aside their own rhetoric and join in common solutions to common problems also is in doubt. Unfortunately, less than three months after the Kissinger speech, the use of the United Nations as a forum for divisive propaganda on the part of the Eastern and Third World blocks reached an extreme with the unfortunate "Zionism is racism"[62] declaration. That declaration strengthened, at a critical time, isolationist forces in the United States who already considered both the United Nations and foreign aid utterly useless. The declaration was followed a few months later by a failure of Third World and communist nations to join the Western nations in a worldwide condemnation of international terrorism or to agree to oppose it and refuse cooperation with extortionists.

There is a real danger that the past colossal failures of both the United Nations and foreign-assistance efforts will lead to a withdrawal of the United States from efforts to help solve vital international problems. It would behoove all governments to remember that, with-

[59]"New Internationalist" guide to UNCTAD IV, *New Internationalist,* April 1976, pp. 6–7.

[60]The New Economic Order, *New Internationalist,* 1975.

[61]Address by Secretary of State Henry A. Kissinger (delivered by Ambassador Daniel P. Moynihan), seventh special session of the United Nations General Assembly, New York, September 1, 1975. Reprinted in the *New York Times,* September 2, 1975, p. 20.

[62]*Time,* November 24, 1975.

out the wholehearted collaboration of the United States, western Europe, the USSR, and the People's Republic of China, *any* resolution of world problems is extremely unlikely. And failure to resolve them will most likely lead to war.

POPULATION, RESOURCES, AND WAR

Desmond Morris some years ago observed, ". . . the best solution for ensuring world peace is the widespread promotion of contraception and abortion . . . moralizing factions that oppose it must face the fact that they are engaged in dangerous war mongering."[63] As he suggested, population-related problems may be increasing the probability of a thermonuclear Armageddon. Avoiding such a denouement for civilization is the most pressing political-economic problem of our time.

In 1969 the world saw in a microcosm what may be in store: Two grossly overpopulated Central American countries, El Salvador and Honduras, went to war against each other. El Salvador had an estimated population of 3.3 million, a population density of 160 people per square kilometer, with a doubling time of 21 years. Honduras had a population of 2.5 million, a density of only 22 per square kilometer, and the same doubling time as El Salvador. More significant statistics have been provided by the Latin American Demographic Center; they show that in El Salvador the population density per square kilometer of *arable* land was 300 persons, while in Honduras it was only 60 persons.

Almost 300,000 Salvadorans had moved into Honduras in search of land and jobs because of overpopulation and resulting unemployment at home. Friction developed among the immigrants and the Honduran natives; El Salvador accused Honduras of maltreating the Salvadorans; and the problem escalated into a brief but nasty war. The conflict was ended by the intervention of the Organization of American States (OAS). In a precedent-shattering move, the OAS recognized demographic factors in its formula for settling the dispute—an international body acknowledged that population pressure was a root cause of a war.[64]

[63] *The naked ape,* McGraw-Hill, New York, 1967.
[64] *Population Bulletin,* December 1969, pp. 134–135.

Systematic analyses of the role of population pressures in generating wars, carried out by political scientist Robert C. North and his colleagues at Stanford University, have supported earlier conclusions based on anecdotal evidence. Statistical studies of the involvement of major European powers in wars in modern times have revealed very high correlations among rates of population growth, rising GNP, expanding military budgets, and involvement in wars, although technical considerations make drawing conclusions about causes and effects hazardous. In more detailed multivariate analyses, Professor North found a complex causal chain involving population growth in relation to static or slowly growing resources, technological development, a tendency to invest energy beyond previous boundaries of society, and increases in the presumed needs and demands of a populace.

Writing about the root causes of World War I, North and political scientist Nazli Choucri of the Massachusetts Institute of Technology concluded:

> Our most important finding is that domestic growth (as measured by population density and national income per capita) is generally a strong determinant of national expansion. Our investigations have identified strong linkages from domestic growth and national expansion to military expenditures, to alliances, and to international interactions with a relatively high potential for violence.[65]

In ancient times such tendencies were somewhat buffered by oceans, mountain ranges, deserts, vast distances, and slow means of travel. Rome could raze Carthage but not China or the cities of South American and Central American Indians. Today, however, with vast increases of population and unprecedented developments in technology, transportation, and communications, the peoples of the world are cheek by jowl, and there is little geographical buffering left. North pointed out that states in nonaggressive phases, like modern Sweden, tend to share certain characteristics: "A relatively small and stable population, a relatively high and steadily developing technology, and good access to

[65] *Nations in conflict: National growth and international violence.*

resources (either domestic or acquired through favorable trade)."[66]

Finite resources in a world of expanding populations and increasing per-capita demands create a situation ripe for international violence. The perceived need to control resources has been a major factor in U.S. military and paramilitary involvements around the globe since World War II.

The role of resources in motivating United States intervention in Southeast Asia, for example, has been stated explicitly by many American political leaders. Richard M. Nixon said in 1953, when he was vice president: "If Indo-China falls, Thailand is put in an almost impossible situation. The same is true of Malaya with its rubber and tin." President Dwight D. Eisenhower wrote in 1963: "The loss of all Vietnam together with Laos in the west and Cambodia on the southwest . . . would have spelled the loss of valuable deposits of tin and prodigious supplies of rubber and rice." In a magazine interview in 1954, President Eisenhower also mentioned tungsten as being an important resource found in Indochina.[67] The same magazine was headlined, "Why U.S. Risks War in Indo-China." A paragraph below the title of the article was: "One of the world's richest areas is open to the winner in Indo-China. That's behind the growing U.S. concern. Communists are fighting for the wealth of the Indies. Tin, rubber, rice, key strategic raw materials are what the war is really about. U.S. sees it as a place to hold—at any cost." A listing in the article of the components of "the big prize: Southeast Asia" included tin, rice, rubber, oil, minerals (tungsten, iron, zinc, manganese, coal, and antimony), and foodstuffs.

The view of United States politicians was not changed by active entry of the nation into the Vietnam war in the mid-1960s, despite a great deal of propaganda about saving the people from communist control. President Lyndon B. Johnson in 1966 bluntly told soldiers at Camp Stanley in Korea: "They want what we've got and we're not going to give it to them." Greatly increased oil exploration in Southeast Asia and the mapping-out of oil leases in the waters off South Vietnam in 1970 added credibility to the importance of resources as a factor in the United States involvement. Ironically, once the war was "lost" in 1975, American oil companies resumed their exploration activities with permission of the new regime, unhindered by dangerous military activity.

The United States thus has shown itself to be willing to fight under some circumstances to protect its resource base and to deny resources to others. It also has been willing to attempt intervention in the internal affairs of LDCs to assure that governments friendly to United States investors and sympathetic to our resource needs remained in power, as CIA activities before the Allende coup in Chile and earlier against Castro in Cuba demonstrated.

This approach clearly is still a factor in United States foreign policy, and it will continue to be if the business community has its way, although business has become somewhat more sophisticated in its perceptions of resource realities. For example, in 1971 before the Vietnam war was over, an article in *Forbes* magazine complained about the growing U.S. dependence on foreign sources for raw materials: "Unfortunately, all this is happening at a time when the Vietnam war and the world balance of power make it almost impossible for the U.S. to defend its overseas supply sources. When we practiced gunboat diplomacy, we really didn't need it. Now, when we need it, we can't use it."[68]

In late 1974, when American troops were no longer fighting in Vietnam, the Arab oil embargo aroused new talk of gunboat diplomacy. Although the embargo lasted only a few months, the subject continued to be debated in the press and academic literature, while the U.S. army carried out desert maneuvers.[69] There was even a reflexive urge in the U.S. government to join the fighting in Angola against the USSR in 1975, even though U.S. resource interests in that poverty-stricken country were trivial at most. Indeed, the reasons for Soviet intervention there remain something of a mystery, given the previous lack of success of the Soviets in establishing a lasting sphere of political influence in Africa.

If the rich countries insist on continued expansion of their cowboy economies, accelerating competition over

[66]Rates of population growth, rates of technological growth and tendencies toward large scale violence, *Studies in International Conflict and Integration,* Stanford University, Calif., June 2, 1969 (mimeo draft).

[67]*U.S. News and World Report,* April 16, 1954.

[68]*Forbes,* August 1, 1971.

[69]For example, Ignotus, Seizing Arab oil; Tucker, Oil.

the dwindling resources of the planet can be expected. Moreover, if nations fail to establish rational control of the oceans, squabbles over rights to shrinking fishery yields or to seabed resources may also precipitate serious conflicts. Since, even if nations should move in the right direction, competition for resources is almost bound to become increasingly intense for some time, it is crucial that legal devices quickly be developed for the resolution of such international conflicts.

International Conflict in the Nuclear Age

Indeed, it is in the area of international conflict above all that the old rules must be changed.[69a] Most national leaders still view war as "continuation of politics by other means," as Clausewitz described it in the early nineteenth century. Politicians still seem not to have learned that thermonuclear war *itself* is a far more deadly enemy than any other nation. They still talk of winning, when in reality only losing is possible. In the United States in 1975, there actually was some consideration of "first use" of nuclear weapons. Secretary of Defense James R. Schlesinger stated, "The first use of . . . nuclear force, even in very limited ways, carries grave risks of escalation *and should be considered only when the consequences of conventional defeat would be even more serious*" (our emphasis).[70] We find it difficult to imagine a situation in which "the consequences of conventional defeat" could be worse than those of a nuclear exchange, especially since confinement to a "very limited" force seems highly unlikely.

The conclusion seems inevitable that if nations continue to build and distribute nuclear arms and biological weapons, sooner or later World War III will occur. And it *will* be the war that ends all wars—at least all world wars—for a very long time, if not forever.

Unfortunately, a great deal of United States policy with regard to national defense is founded on the idea of a *balance of terror,* a concept created by a group of scientists specializing in what is known as the *theory of nuclear deterrence.* What the politicians apparently do not know (or refuse to believe) is that this theory is based on assumptions that have been demonstrated to be untenable, analyses that are inapplicable, and nonexistent or irrelevant data.[71] A similar foundation has been developed in parallel by the Soviet Union for its military policy.

Why would presumably intelligent people be taken in by transparent theorizing? Because the "analysis" of the military situation can be conveniently arranged to produce desired results; the answers are engineered to fit precisely the expectations of the appropriate government officials. Leaders of nations naturally believe that their nations must be strong if they are to survive. Nuclear weapons fit right into a pattern that has prevailed throughout human history, one that dictates arming against an enemy in order to avoid attack. In the past, the stronger society in a conflict always won. But nations have not been able to adjust to the new rules of the game: *with thermonuclear weapons, regardless of which side is stronger and which attacks, both sides will lose.* A National Academy of Sciences report released in 1975 painted such a grim picture of the probable consequences of a nuclear war that Philip Handler, president of the academy, said he could only be "encouraged" by its conclusion that some people would survive somewhere.[72]

Four elements make recognition of the new rules and acting upon them difficult. First, there are always scientists who will tell politicians that nuclear or chemical-biological wars can be won. If the other side is utterly destroyed and 20 million Americans survive the conflict, is that not victory? Even if the U.S. had just two survivors and the other side had none, that would spell victory to some politicians. The late Senator Richard Russell, for example, said in 1969, "If we have to start over again with another Adam and Eve, I want them to be Americans."

[69a]A crucial source on the analysis of international relations is Robert Jervis, *Perception and misperception in international politics.*

[70]From Report to Congress on nuclear force posture in Europe under P. L. 93-365, May, 1975. See also Frank Barnaby, Changing nuclear myths.

[71]Details may be found in Philip Green's *Deadly logic.* See also the Stockholm International Peace Research Institute paper, Why arms control fails; The myth of deterrence lulls world opinion.

[72]See, for example, Bernard T. Feld, The consequences of nuclear war; National Academy of Sciences (NAS), *Long-term worldwide effects of multiple nuclear weapons detonations.* The report, by the way, neglected many of the worst ecological and social consequences of a nuclear conflict. See the amusing comment of "Adriadne" on the NAS report in *New Scientist,* October 23, 1975; and the Federation of American Scientists press release, The National Academy of Sciences seems to lack public policy sense, October 4, 1975.

Deterrence and the balance of terror. A second element is the notion that stockpiled weapons will not be used, that the balance of terror will be a stable one. This notion has been examined in detail by behavioral scientists, and few of them seem anxious to bet on it.

Most Americans, however, seem to feel that the chances of thermonuclear war are remote. Many, for instance, apparently believe that the limited test-ban treaty negotiated during the 1960s greatly diminished the chances of thermonuclear war. Their confidence stands in sharp contrast to the apprehension of those most concerned with the arms race. In 1964, for instance, a survey of experts at Rand Corporation (a military-industrial think tank) revealed the following subjective estimates of the probability of thermonuclear war: 1 chance in 10 in 10 years, 1 chance in 4 in 25 years.

Other knowledgeable people do not seem to consider World War III any less likely to occur. Professor Bernard T. Feld, former Director-General of the Pugwash Conferences on Science and World Affairs, wrote late in 1974:

> The world is entering upon perilous times—perhaps the most dangerous period in its entire history. It is my judgement that the odds are around one in three that a nuclear weapon will be used in a conflict situation before the year 1984; and that the chances are greater than fifty-fifty for nuclear war to occur in the 26 years remaining in this century.[73]

Disagreements among arms-race experts culminated in the anti-ballistic missile (ABM) controversy of the early 1970s. Well-informed people realized that the deployment of multiple independently targeted reentry vehicles (MIRVs) and ABMs promised to destabilize the balance of terror. A missile equipped with a MIRV can strike at a series of targets. The payload is a vehicle known as a bus, which drops off a series of warheads aimed independently at different targets. An ABM is a system for destroying incoming enemy missiles.

The combination would greatly increase the advantages of making a first (preemptive) strike. Each missile with a MIRV is a single target in its silo, but it would become a salvo once launched. A preemptive counterforce strike against an enemy's missiles might, with the multiplicative advantage of MIRVs, saturate the enemy ABM capability and destroy much of the opponent's strike capability. The aggressor could launch a preemptive strike and then hope to use its ABMs to shoot down most or all of its enemy's weakened second strike. The aggressor could thus hope to escape with little or no damage. (The ecological and radiation dangers to the entire planet rarely are considered major factors in military-governmental war scenarios.) The principle of *mutually assured destruction* (appropriately labeled MAD) upon which peace is supposed to be based will have been violated.[74]

Although strict limitations were placed on the deployment of ABM systems in the United States and the Soviet Union (see Box 15-3 for a chronology and description of international arms-control agreements since World War II), both nations are now engaged in a race to improve the accuracy of their MIRVed missiles and to move on to MARVs (maneuvering reentry vehicles), which are even more difficult to intercept and which are equipped with multiple warheads that can be sent Earthward in different directions and at different speeds. United States ICBMs could hit within 350 meters of a target at a range of more than 10,000 kilometers in 1975. In the near future, accuracy should improve three- to tenfold.[75]

Further improvement in accuracy is also possible through the use of self-guided cruise missiles. Cruise missiles are essentially pilotless jet airplanes carrying warheads. Recent technological developments permit such missiles to be fitted with computers for terrain-matching and recognition, which allows them to determine their positions in flight with an accuracy of within 7 to 10 meters anywhere on Earth—thus allowing virtual pinpoint delivery of nuclear warheads.[76]

The Strategic Arms Limitation Talk (SALT) negotiations between Secretary General Leonid Brezhnev and President Gerald R. Ford in Vladivostok in autumn 1974 appear to have set a limit of 2400 delivery vehicles for nuclear weapons for each nation. That number, with

[73]Doves of the world unite!

[74]A helpful guide to the jargon of nuclear war is the United States Arms Control and Disarmament Agency's *SALT lexicon.*

[75]Barnaby, Changing nuclear myths. Technically, accuracy is described in terms of a circular error probability (CEP). With a CEP of 100 meters, at least one-half the missiles launched will land 100 meters or less from the target.

[76]Kosta Tsipis, The long range cruise missile.

BOX 15-3 Arms Control Agreements

Since World War II, the nations of the world have made sporadic attempts to reduce the threat of Armageddon by entering into agreements on the use of the ever-more-potent weapons developed by their scientists. To say that those agreements are inadequate would be an extreme understatement. Aside from biological weapons, they have not led to the destruction of a single arm, not even a pistol, let alone an ICBM. The arms agreements do, however, represent some stumbling steps, often in the right direction, and they are symbolic of the healthy respect that society in general has for the new weapons.

There have been several multilateral agreements:

- 1959, *Antarctic Treaty.* Prohibits all military activity in the Antarctic area and makes the area the first zone to be kept free of nuclear bombs. In force by 1961, it had seventeen signatories by the end of 1973. Disarmament advocate Philip Noel Baker said of this treaty, "While disarming Antarctica we put 7000 nuclear weapons in Europe. We should have disarmed Europe and put those weapons in Antarctica."
- 1963, *Partial Test-Ban Treaty.* Prohibits detonation of nuclear bombs in the atmosphere, under water, and in outer space but not underground. In force by 1963, this had 106 signatories by 1973. The Stockholm International Peace Research Institute (SIPRI) regarded it mainly as an antipollution measure: "The first modern international treaty to control the contamination of our environment."
- 1967, *Outer-Space Treaty.* Prohibits all military activity in outer space, including launching of nuclear weapons into Earth orbit. In force by 1967, the treaty had seventy-one signatories by 1973.
- 1967, *Treat of Ttatelolco.* Makes Latin America a second zone free of nuclear weapons. In force in 1967, the treaty had eighteen signatories by 1973. Unfortunately, Brazil and Argentina, the two outstanding candidates for the nuclear club in the area, have not fully accepted the treaty. Without them it is worthless.
- 1968, *Nuclear Nonproliferation Treaty (NPT).* Prohibits the obtaining of nuclear weapons by nations not already possessing them. Signatories with nuclear weapons promise not to give them to others or assist others in making them. In force in 1970, the treaty had ninety-seven signatories by 1976. France, India, Israel, and China, among the nuclear powers, have never signed, nor have South Africa and Argentina, either of which could quickly build bombs. Pakistan, Brazil, and Spain are among other nonsignatories with the capacity of building bombs within perhaps five years, and signatories Canada, Iran, South Korea, and West Germany could quickly join the nuclear club if they wished to withdraw from the NPT. Article 6 of the NPT pledged the nuclear powers to "pursue negotiations in good faith on effective measures relating to cessation of the nuclear arms race at an early date and to nuclear disarmament." The failure of some signatories to keep that pledge could be used as an excuse for others to renounce the treaty.
- 1971, *Seabed Treaty.* Prohibited weapons of mass destruction on the ocean floor. It was put in force in 1972 and had fifty-seven signatories by the end of 1973.

highly accurate MIRVing (or MARVing) and/or the use of cruise missiles, would permit the deployment by the Soviet Union and by the United States individually of *2 to 3 times* the number of warheads believed necessary for a successful counterforce strike against the other nation's ICBMs.[77]

Thus, even without extensive ABM deployment, the temptation to make a first strike on the enemy's nuclear forces might be too much for military minds to forego in a time of extreme tension. There is no certainty that the remaining undamaged missiles would be launched at the aggressor's cities, since this would invite retaliation in kind. But either the United States or the USSR would have more than ample warheads to destroy the other nation completely *after having either launched or received* a successful counterforce strike. In 1974, for instance, the United States at well below the Vladivostok limits could deliver some 8000 nuclear warheads; both the United

[77]L. J. Carter, Strategic arms limitation; pt. 2, "Leveling up" to symmetry.

- 1972, *Biological Weapons Convention.* Prohibited the development, production, and stockpiling of bacteriological and toxin weapons and requires destruction of existing stocks. It was not in force by 1974, but there were thirty-one signatories in 1973.

In addition to the multilateral agreements, eight bilateral agreements have been made between the United States and the Soviet Union, each of which went into force the year it was signed. And three SALT II agreements had been reached in 1974 that had not yet been ratified by Congress in early 1975.

The bilateral agreements are:

- 1963, *"Hot-Line" Agreement.* Established direct telephone and telegraph connection between the two governments for use in emergencies. (The facilities have been used.)
- 1971, *"Hot-Line" Modernization Agreement.* Added two satellite communications circuits to the system to increase its reliability.
- 1971, *Nuclear Accidents Agreement.* Specified procedures to reduce risk of accidental war by notification and exchange of information in case of accidental or unauthorized explosion of a nuclear bomb.
- 1972, *High Seas Agreement.* Designed to prevent dangerous incidents involving ships or aircraft on or over the oceans.
- 1972, *SALT I ABM Treaty.* Limited deployment of ABMs to a maximum of 100 missiles and launchers at each of two specified sites in each country.
- 1972, *SALT I Interim Offensive Arms Agreement.* Provided a five-year freeze on the aggregate number of ICBMs and SLBMs (submarine-launched ballistic missiles), on each side, but did not restrict the numbers of strategic bombers.
- 1973, *Protocol to High Seas Agreement.* Prohibited simulated attacks by each country on nonmilitary ships of the other.
- 1973, *Nuclear-War-Prevention Agreement.* Provided for consultations when it appears there is a risk of war between the two nations and moved a short distance in direction of a "no-first-use" agreement.
- 1974, *SALT II ABM Treaty.* Reduced deployment of ABMs to one site in each country (USSR chose Moscow, and the United States, a Minuteman ICBM site; both ABM systems are questionably effective).
- 1974, *SALT II Threshold Nuclear-Test-Ban Treaty.* Outlawed underground tests of nuclear bombs with yields in excess of 150 kilotons. This was intended to be in force in 1976.
- 1974, *SALT II Interim Offensive Arms Agreement.* Committed United States and USSR to negotiate extention of the SALT I Interim Offensive Arms Agreement through 1985.
- 1974, *Vladivostok Accord.* Agreement reached by President Gerald Ford and Leonid Brezhnev that for the next ten years each nation would be limited to 2400 strategic missile launchers, of which no more than 1320 would be armed with MIRVed missiles.

Sources: Alva Myrdal, The international control of disarmament, 1974; Bernard T. Feld, Doves of the world unite!; International Atomic Energy Agency, *A short history of nonproliferation;* Stockholm International Peace Research Institute (SIPRI), Why arms control fails. See also Ramsdell Gurney, Arms and the men; Paul H. Nitze, Assuring strategic stability; *Time,* April 11, 1977.

States and the USSR are considered to have *fewer than 100 cities that would make worthwhile targets.*[78] Fewer than 2 percent of the warheads therefore would have to survive the first strike. We must also note in passing that even a strictly counterforce strike aimed only at missile sites would kill many millions of people outright, enormously increase the human load of cancers and mutations, and produce untold ecological consequences.

Hence there has developed a trend away from the basic idea of deterrence: MAD, the possession of invulnerable nuclear weapons by both sides so that attack and retaliation would perforce be aimed against population centers (and therefore presumably be unthinkable).[79] In place of such deterrence, the situation could be one in which a nation receiving a counterforce strike must

[78]Frank Barnaby, The Ford-Brezhnev agreement assessed.

[79]There has been discussion of moving back toward this posture with a land-based mobile ICBM system (Kim Willanston and Lloyd H. Norman, Missiles on the move, *Newsweek,* February 16, 1976.

choose to retaliate against its opponent's cities in the sure knowledge that it is committing suicide in so doing. The significance of this change is difficult to judge. The United States has officially added a counterforce option to its deterrence strategy, a step that may simply be an attempt to make limited nuclear wars thinkable—part of the "if you've got the hardware, you ought to use it" philosophy that so often seems to characterize military "thinking."

Whether or not these new trends weaken the balance of terror may, however, be beside the point, for deterrence theory itself is fundamentally flawed. The underlying assumption of deterrence theory—that leaders will behave rationally—is not only weak, but has been repeatedly contradicted by history. Scientists may make guesses about the probability of a thermonuclear war, but their guesses are really no better than the guesses of any informed person.[80] We agree with those who feel that the nuclear arms race, ostensibly intended to deter aggression and increase national safety, has in actuality greatly *reduced* the security of the United States.

Nuclear proliferation. The larger the number of nations that possess nuclear weapons, the greater the likelihood of nuclear war would seem to be. This conclusion seems obvious enough: countries that do not have nuclear bombs cannot use them in whatever conflicts they are involved in; for a given number of conflicts, the bigger the fraction in which one or more parties have nuclear arms, the bigger the chance that such weapons will be used. The counterargument has been advanced that, in a world where many countries have nuclear weapons, everyone will be more careful and there will be fewer conflicts altogether, but we and many others find this view unconvincing.

The spread of nuclear weapons to more nations is called proliferation. (Among specialists the term *horizontal proliferation* is often used; *vertical proliferation* means an increase in number or sophistication of weapons within a nation.) Countries known to have exploded nuclear weapons prior to 1974 were the United States, the Soviet Union, France, the United Kingdom, and the People's Republic of China. In 1974 India became the sixth member of the "nuclear club" by exploding a nuclear device underground in the Rajasthan desert. India claimed this device was a "peaceful nuclear explosive" (abbreviated PNE in most arms-control discussions), but in fact there is no practical difference between such a device and a weapon.

The Nonproliferation Treaty (NPT), which went into force in March 1970 upon ratification by forty-three signatory nations, was intended to prevent the spread of nuclear weapons beyond the five nations that had them then.[81] Obviously, it did not stop India, nor has it stopped Israel, which has not yet exploded a nuclear weapon but is acknowledged in the intelligence community to possess them.[82]

The biggest weakness of the NPT is that not everyone subscribes to it. More than a third of the nations of the world were not party to the treaty as of December 1975: forty-two nations, including India and Israel, had not signed; another fourteen had signed but not ratified it; and ninety-seven nations were parties to the treaty. Among the holdouts were nuclear-weapon states France and China, together with a number of countries having the capability and perhaps some incentive to acquire nuclear weapons: Pakistan, Brazil, Argentina, Chile, Egypt, Indonesia, South Africa, and Spain, for example.[83]

The NPT's stipulations are in any case not particularly strict. Party states that have nuclear weapons agree not to transfer these to any states that do not have nuclear weapons or to assist or encourage such states to acquire nuclear weapons. Party states that do not have nuclear weapons agree not to acquire them, either for military or peaceful purposes. The parties without nuclear weapons also agree to a set of safeguards applied by the Interna-

[80]A good introduction to this problem is to read the three books by Herman Kahn listed in the bibliography of this chapter, followed by Green's *Deadly logic,* Jerome D. Frank's *Sanity and survival,* and Herbert F. York's *Race to oblivion* and *Arms control,* Plate's *Understanding doomsday,* and finally Robert F. Kennedy's *Thirteen days,* Norton, New York, 1969. These will provide the reader with some background for making his or her own predictions.

[81]Good background on the NPT, including the full text of the treaty and a synopsis of the NPT Review Conference of 1975, is available in International Atomic Energy Agency, *A short history of proliferation.*

[82]See, for example, CIA estimates that "Israel has 10 to 20 nuclear weapons available for use," *New York Times,* March 15, 1976, p. 1.

[83]See William Epstein, the proliferation of nuclear weapons; and Norman Gall, Atoms for Brazil, dangers for all.

tional Atomic Energy Agency to ensure compliance with the treaty. The safeguards all have to do with accounting for the whereabouts of special nuclear material used and produced in the peaceful nuclear energy programs of these countries. (Special nuclear material refers to that which is suitable, without further isotopic separation, for making nuclear explosives.) Even if the safeguards work perfectly, however, they can only *detect* the diversion of special nuclear material for explosive purposes; they cannot prevent it. It is possible that a country determined to evade even detection could do so, and the only sure penalty for detection would be some measure of international outrage—a price many a nation has paid before in its perceived self-interest. Any party to the NPT can withdraw from it openly with three months' notice to the United Nations Security Council.

The NPT has been further weakened by the behavior of the weapons states that signed it. Their obligations under the treaty include pursuing negotiations in good faith toward cessation of the nuclear arms race and toward complete disarmament; the nonweapons states believe—rightly in our view—that these obligations have not been met. The NPT also calls for mutual assistance in securing the benefits of peaceful nuclear technology for all parties to the treaty. But the United States has been freer in its transfers of nuclear technology to certain DC nonparties to the treaty (for example, Spain and South Africa) than to LDCs that are parties to the treaty. This has made the LDCs wonder aloud just what benefits they are receiving by adhering to the NPT.

The principal real barriers to proliferation have been good intentions (as exemplified by but not restricted to the NPT) and lack of easy access to the special nuclear materials needed to make nuclear weapons. Lack of knowledge of how to make a nuclear weapon has *not* been an important barrier, because even most poor countries could mobilize the modest amount of scientific and technical talent required to design and fabricate a fission bomb, given information available in the unclassified literature. (Making a fusion bomb—a hydrogen bomb in popular parlance—is much more difficult.)

Access to special nuclear material is now becoming easier, as a result of four factors: (1) the spread of small nuclear reactors designed for research but capable of producing modest quantities of plutonium usable for bombs; (2) the spread of commercial power reactors that produce large quantities of plutonium (enough for 10 or 20 bombs per reactor per year); (3) the spread of fuel reprocessing plants that can extract the plutonium from spent reactor fuel; and (4) the spread of uranium enrichment technology capable of producing bomb-quality material from natural uranium. (See also the discussions of these technologies in Chapter 8.)

The possibility of building a "research" reactor for the purpose of making plutonium for bombs is open to virtually any LDC that can persuade a DC to supply it with slightly enriched uranium for fuel (or with heavy water that permits the use of natural uranium as fuel—this is apparently what India did). Fuel reprocessing technology good enough to extract a few bombs' worth of plutonium per year from the output of such reactors is not very difficult for even a small country to build. For small countries planning in advance to acquire a small nuclear weapons capability, the combination of a research reactor and small-scale reprocessing capability will probably remain the easiest route for some years to come.

The spread of commercial nuclear power reactors and related technology (mainly large enrichment and reprocessing plants) poses a somewhat different threat. These facilities provide countries not necessarily planning in advance to acquire nuclear weapons with an opportunity to do so very quickly if they should so decide. That a country embarks on a peaceful nuclear power program with the best of intentions is no guarantee that it will not take advantage of the nuclear weapons "fringe benefit" of its power program if circumstances change to make this seem advantageous. It seems certain that the spread of commercial nuclear power technology will accelerate the spread of nuclear weapons in this way; perhaps many recipient countries will not exercise the option to acquire weapons, but some surely will.[84]

Ownership of a large enrichment plant or large commercial reprocessing plant provides the greatest access to bomb-grade materials. Germany's sale of a reprocessing plant and an enrichment plant to Brazil and France's sale of a reprocessing plant to Pakistan therefore

[84]A good, concise discussion of the link between commercial nuclear power and proliferation is Allen L. Hammond, Nuclear proliferation, pt. 1, Warnings from the arms control community.

have justifiably generated a good deal of international concern, and much of the thinking about how to stem proliferation has focused on these two kinds of facilities.[85] One suggestion that has been made is to seek an agreement among the major industrial nations to expand enrichment capacity in cooperatively owned and operated facilities in the DCs; these consortia would offer low-enriched uranium (suitable for reactor fuel but not for bombs) to the members and to LDCs at prices too good to refuse, in exchange for plutonium-bearing spent fuel. The spent fuel would not be reprocessed anywhere for the time being, but instead would be stored at a few central locations in DCs, possibly to be recycled later in nuclear-energy centers having breeder reactors and a reprocessing plant clustered at a single well-guarded site.[86] Because France and West Germany expect to make a good deal of money exporting enrichment and reprocessing plants, they probably would not agree to this scheme unless it were accompanied by some sort of plan to divide up more equitably the world reactor market, which is now dominated by the United States. An even bigger obstacle is that the LDCs can hardly be expected to be more enthusiastic about complete dependence on DCs for uranium fuel than DCs are about dependence on OPEC for oil; one of the main ostensible reasons for wanting nuclear power, after all, is energy independence.

Of course, LDCs eventually will be able to build their own commercial fuel-reprocessing plants and uranium enrichment plants, and it is sometimes argued that this means it doesn't matter much what the United States or other DCs try to do now about proliferation. We disagree. It is true that all countries that want nuclear bombs *eventually* will get them, but it is essential to slow the process as much as possible, in order to give the world political community as much time as possible to work out institutions and measures that will make the use of nuclear bombs less likely.

We are encouraged to note that recent major studies of the nuclear power question in the United Kingdom, Australia, and the United States have placed heavy emphasis on the weapons connection as the most serious liability of nuclear power. The September 1976 report of the U.K.'s Royal Commission on Environmental Pollution (known as the Flowers Report after its chairman, Sir Brian Flowers) held that:

> . . . the spread of nuclear power will inevitably facilitate the spread of the ability to make nuclear weapons and, we fear, the construction of these weapons. . . . It has been argued that the possession of these weapons by the U.S.A. and the U.S.S.R. has been a powerful force for mutual toleration, but however true this is it would be folly to suppose that proliferation would necessarily lead to a similar balance and restraint in relations between other nations. Indeed, we see no reason to trust in the stability of any nation of any political persuasion for centuries ahead.[86a]

The Flowers report concluded, with strong emphasis on the potential for misuse of plutonium by subnational groups as well as for proliferation, that the U.K. "should not rely for energy supply on a process that produces such a hazardous substance as plutonium unless there is no reasonable alternative."

The Ranger Uranium Environmental Inquiry, convened by the Australian government to consider the wisdom of mining and exporting the substantial quantities of uranium at the Ranger site in that country's Northern Territory, concluded in its October 1976 report: "The nuclear power industry is unintentionally contributing to an increased risk of nuclear war. This is the most serious hazard associated with the industry."[86b] The Ranger report recommended that the decision to mine and sell uranium from the Northern Territory be postponed, that Australian policy should seek to limit or restrict expansion of the production of nuclear energy, and that no sales of Australian uranium should take place to any country not party to the NPT.

Finally, the March 1977 report of the Nuclear Energy Policy Study Group of the Ford Foundation in the U.S. observed that:

---

[85]See James J. Glackin, The dangerous drift in uranium enrichment; and Allen L. Hammond, Nuclear proliferation.

[86]For details of this and other proposals, see Abraham A. Ribicoff, A market-sharing approach to the world nuclear sales problem.

[86a]Sir Brian Flowers et al., *Nuclear power and the environment.*

[86b]R. W. Fox, G. G. Kelleher, C. B. Kerr, *Ranger uranium environmental inquiry.*

> In our view, the most serious risk associated with nuclear power is the attendant increase in the number of countries that have access to technology, materials, and facilities leading to a nuclear weapons capability. . . . If widespread proliferation actually occurs, it will prove an extremely serious danger to U.S. security and to world peace and stability in general.[86c]

The Ford group recommended that the U.S. defer the recycle of plutonium and the commercialization of the breeder reactor and that it seek "common supplier action to ban the export of such technology." It recommended also that the U.S. and other supplier nations provide assured supplies of slightly enriched uranium to other countries at favorable prices, a plan whose drawbacks we have already mentioned above. In April 1977, President Carter announced a nuclear policy for his administration essentially congruent with the Ford Study's recommendation.

While we applaud the progress represented by the positions taken by the Flowers, Ranger, and Ford reports and by the Carter administration's position, our own preference is for a stronger stance. We believe there should be an absolute embargo on the export of enrichment and reprocessing technology by any nation.[86d] The United States should cajole and, if necessary, coerce its allies into compliance, using every incentive and/or peaceful sanction at its disposal. (The possibilities are considerable, not least of which is the fact that West Germany and France will be dependent on U.S. enriched uranium for their own nuclear power programs into the 1980s.) Since the Soviets are also intensely concerned about proliferation, there is a chance that they would cooperate. Countries that have power reactors but no enrichment or reprocessing capability could be supplied with low-enriched uranium by the sort of consortium mentioned above, but there is reason to question whether any *additional* power reactors should be exported by anyone. A universal embargo on reactor exports may seem a drastic measure—certainly drastic enough to require rewriting the NPT—but lowering the probability of a nuclear holocaust is a desperately important task. The sort of pussyfooting that characterized attempts to stem proliferation before 1977 was not merely a scandal but a threat to the survival of civilization.

[86c]Spurgeon Keeny et al., *Nuclear power issues and choices.*

[86d]See also the chapter on proliferation in A. Lovins, *Soft energy paths: Toward a durable peace.*

Chemical, biological, and environmental weapons. Even if humanity does manage to stop the proliferation of nuclear weapons, it still must deal with the ever-increasing deadliness of conventional weapons and the prospective horrors of chemical and biological warfare (CBW) and environmental warfare. Biological and chemical weapons, which could be nearly as destructive of lives as nuclear arms, seem to have some prospects of being eventually considered "conventional."[87] Environmental warfare is newer and potentially perhaps even more threatening.[88]

Achieving disarmament. The third element of difficulty in changing the rules of international relations is uncertainty about the best way to achieve disarmament and security in a world where in the past security has usually been provided by brute force, either threatened or overtly exercised. Unfortunately, the effort going into the study of peaceful means to world security has been infinitesimal compared with that going into military research, although almost no area needs greater immediate attention. The basic requirement is evident: once again it is a change in human attitudes so that the in-group against which aggression is forbidden expands to include *all* human beings.

If this could be accomplished, security might be provided by an armed international organization, a global analogue of a police force. Many people have recognized this as a goal, but the way to reach it remains obscure in a world where factionalism seems, if anything, to be increasing. The first step necessarily involves partial surrender of sovereignty to an international organization. But it seems probable that, as long as most people fail to comprehend the magnitude of the danger, that step will be impossible. At the very least, societies

[87]J. P. Perry Robinson, The special case of chemical and biological weapons; see also Bo Holmberg, Biological aspects of chemical and biological weapons.

[88]For example, see Chapter 11 and Frank Barnaby, The spread of the capability to do violence: An introduction to environmental warfare; Jozef Goldblat, The prohibition of environmental warfare; and Bhupendra M. Jasani, Environmental modification: New weapons of war?

must learn to weigh the risks inherent in attempting to achieve controlled disarmament against the risks of continuing the arms race. An attempt at disarmament could lead to a war, or to the destruction or domination of the United States through Chinese or Soviet "cheating." But, if disarmament were successfully carried out, and if an international police force were established, the reward would be a very much safer world in which resources would be freed for raising the standard of living for all people.[89] No problem deserves more intensive study and international discussion.

The dynamics of disarmament appear to be even more complex than those of arms races. Nevertheless, in 1970 the Arms Control and Disarmament Agency (ACDA), the only United States agency charged with planning in this area, had a budget of only a few million dollars (contrasted with $80 billion for "defense"). Representative John F. Seiberling of Ohio put it succinctly: "The Pentagon has 3000 people working on arms sales to other countries while the Arms Control and Disarmament Agency has 12 people monitoring arms sales. That gives you an idea of where the executive branch priorities are."[90] Moreover, the ACDA is heavily influenced by the Department of State bureaucracy, still a stronghold of cold-war thinking.

It has been suggested that an important step toward disarmament could be taken by the establishment of an international disarmament control organization, which would serve as a clearinghouse for informtion on the quantity and quality of weapons in various nations and would thus help to detect cheating on international agreements.[91] As a semi-independent United Nations agency, such an organization could play a vital role—but so far there has been no significant effort to establish one.

Diverting the military to peaceful purposes. The fourth element of difficulty involves economics and the military establishment. Although this will be discussed in terms of the United States, there is every reason to believe that an analogous situation exists in the Soviet Union, the other military superpower. Civilians should realize that peace and freedom from tension are not viewed as an ideal situation by many members of the military-industrial-government complex. By and large, professional military officers, especially field grade and higher, hope for an end to international tensions about as fervently as farmers hope for drought. When there is an atmosphere of national security, military budgets are usually small, military power minimal, and military promotions slow. The founders of the United States recognized that the military services were unlikely to work against their own interests, so they carefully established ultimate civilian control over the army and navy. It worked rather well for a long time.

But times have changed. Wars are no longer fought with simple, understandable weapons like axes, swords, and cannon. Now a nation needs weapons systems with complex and often arcane components, such as acquisition radar, VTOL fighters, Doppler navigators, MIRVs, cruise missiles, and nuclear submarines. Such systems cannot be produced rapidly, on demand, by a few government contractors. Long-term planning is required, involving not only the military services but also a large number of industrial organizations that supply various components.

Those organizations, not unnaturally, often hire retired military officers to help them in their negotiations with the government, where decisions on appropriations for armaments are made. The necessary intimacy of the military and industry in development and procurement of weapons led Dwight D. Eisenhower to coin the term *military-industrial complex.* The term *military-industrial-labor-government* complex sometimes seems more accurate. In his heavily documented 1970 book, *Pentagon capitalism,* industrial engineer Seymour Melman of Columbia University showed that even that term is inadequate to describe the Frankenstein's monster that has been created.[92]

This complex seems to have an aversion to peace, but it

[89]See, for example, Ronald Huisken, The consumption of raw materials for military purposes; and Ruth L. Sivard, Let them eat bullets! The military budgets of the United States and USSR in 1973 were greater than the combined annual income of more than 1 billion people in thirty-three of the poorest nations and almost 20 times the value of all foreign aid from all sources.

[90]Quoted in San Francisco *Chronicle and Examiner,* November 9, 1975.

[91]Alva Myrdal, The international control of disarmament.

[92]See especially Melman's chapter 7.

is not composed of a group of evil, conspiring people determined to napalm babies and keep the world poised on the edge of thermonuclear disaster. Rather, it is composed of people who, because of their personal histories and associations, are convinced that the only hope for survival of democracy lies in confronting the Soviet Union with overwhelming strength. On the other side, of course, their Soviet counterparts see Soviet preparedness as the only force preventing an attack by the capitalists, who want to destroy the Soviet way of life. The Soviets tend to forget that Americans did not attempt to destroy them when we enjoyed a nuclear monopoly. People in the United States, on the other hand, tend not to appreciate the valid roots of Soviet anti-Western paranoia. Members of both complexes are generally not long on introspection. Even though perpetuating the cold war adds to their own prestige and power, they do not see this as a major factor in their behavior. Indeed, many undoubtedly go to their jobs without thinking about why they are doing them at all. In individual instances, however, it must be difficult even for members of the complex to avoid admitting the truth to themselves.

With the United States military budget now in the vicinity of $100 billion annually, it is not hard to find a quick $50 billion a year or so that might instead be used by the United States to try to save itself and the rest of the world. Melman, for example, showed how more than $50 billion could have been trimmed from the 1970 military budget without compromising national security.[93] Naturally, if huge cuts were suddenly made in military budgets, substantial economic dislocations and unemployment would occur, even if very careful planning preceded the cuts. Furthermore, it is probably politically unrealistic to expect the funds necessary for dealing with the world predicament to be diverted in great amounts from the U.S. military budget. Perhaps we should take Samuel Day's approach and, rather than cutting military budgets, give the army, navy, and air force new battles to fight. Day suggests declaring war on environmental deterioration and assigning the air force to police air quality, the navy to fight water pollution, and the army to "direct its martial spirit and organizational talents" to preserving the land—perhaps by developing new energy technologies.[94]

The problem of breaking the power of the U.S. military-industrial-labor complex (and its analogues in other nations) and the related problem of finding a way to world peace are, obviously, among several major obstacles that must be overcome if civilization is to survive.

Two French scientists, Marcel Fetizon and Michel Magat, succinctly summarized the dilemma of modern warfare: "We must either eliminate science or eliminate war. We cannot have both."[95] One might go even further. Science and technology are incompatible with present human attitudes. Either the attitudes must change or science and technology will disappear, and one way or another most of *Homo sapiens* will go with them.

Conventional Arms

One of the unhappy facts of today's military situation is that while attention is focused on the nuclear arms race, a spectacular conventional-arms race has been going on relatively unheralded. The DCs in general and the United States and USSR in particular have been culpable in supplying vast amounts of arms to other nations. India and Pakistan, for instance, fought bloody wars in 1964 and 1973 with arms supplied by the United States to both sides. Needless to say, our military aid hardly helped those two LDCs toward development (although if the arms had not been obtained from the United States, the USSR, the United Kingdom, or France would gladly have supplied them).

George Thayer some years ago made a detailed study of the conventional arms trade.[96] His treatment was clearly not anti-American (or procommunist), and yet he felt constrained to state:

> Still, today's arms trade is essentially an American problem. No nation talks more loudly about peace, yet no nation distributes as many weapons of war. No nation has spoken so passionately in favor of nuclear

[93]Melman, Appendix C; also Plate, *Understanding doomsday,* Appendix D.

[94]Let's put the troops to work.

[95]The toxic arsenal, in *Unless peace comes,* Nigel Calder, ed., p. 146.

[96]*The war business:* The international trade in armaments, p. 376.

controls, yet no nation has been so silent on the subject of conventional arms controls. Nor has any nation been as vocal in its desire to eradicate hunger, poverty, and disease, yet no nation has so obstructed the fight against these ills through its insistence that poor countries waste their money on expensive and useless arms.

Although military expenditures have peaked in the DCs, they are still skyrocketing in the LDCs—among them, the countries least able to afford arms. If the DCs really believe their rhetoric about helping the LDCs, they should halt the flow of arms from DCs to LDCs. After Thayer's book was written, the Pentagon maintained that it had stopped vigorously promoting arms sales. Yet in 1974, U.S. sales were *8 times* the level Thayer had described, and double that of the Soviet Union.[97] The Soviet Union, France, and the United Kingdom have also been heavily involved in peddling weapons to LDCs.[98]

In addition there has been a trend toward supplying not obsolete but the most up-to-date arms, especially to oil-rich Middle Eastern countries, in an attempt to repatriate petrodollars. Iran, in particular, is being converted into a major military power. Another economic reason for the hucksterism is that the unit cost of procuring weapons systems drops with the size of the production run. For instance, the Pentagon hopes to sell as many as 3000 new YF-16 air-superiority fighter planes to other countries, thereby reducing the cost of their production to the United States Air Force and ringing up some $20 billion in sales (and needed foreign exchange). Should the United States be stupid enough to try to seize Middle Eastern oil fields, it might well end up fighting military forces equipped with the finest weapons its own technologists can develop!

As long as the excuse can be given that, if the United States refrains from selling the weapons, the French, the Swedes, or the Soviets will sell them, and as long as such sales are believed to be needed to counterbalance the petrodollar drain, the Pentagon will probably continue to sell arms. The rewards for doing so appear too much greater than those of striving for multilateral controls or, heaven forbid, unilaterally refusing to accept blood money on the basis of principle. Presumably, the Pentagon is confident of its ability to cope with any potential danger to the United States posed by unstable Third World countries that are armed to the teeth.

HELPING THE POOR: A PROBLEM IN ETHICS

Assuming human society for the next quarter-century somehow manages to avoid a nuclear conflagration—whether by disarming, by containing nuclear proliferation, or just by committing itself to peace through negotiation—all the other elements of the human predicament remain. It is becoming clear that human beings, and particularly thoughtful people in the rich nations, are now faced with some long-avoided ethical questions that can no longer be ignored. They concern such matters as the distribution of wealth, the exploitation of one group of people by another, the responsibility of those now living for the acts of their forebears and for the legacy of their descendants, and the duties of the provident toward the improvident.

Perhaps the most difficult of all are the questions about what might be called intergenerational equity. Is it ethical, for example, for this generation to create radioactive materials that future generations must guard or beware of? Can people alive today ethically risk the capacity of the planet to support future generations in order to provide themselves with highly affluent lives? Is there any way that actual deprivation today can be balanced against hypothetical deprivation in the future? What are the ethics that govern life-and-death decisions in the face of uncertainty? Unfortunately, traditional human value systems, which evolved in a relatively steady-state world, provide little guidance in questions of intergenerational equity.

Such ethical issues and how this generation resolves them (or fails to resolve them) will have profound consequences for our future and those of generations to come. We cannot provide definitive answers to these

[97] J. W. Finney, Arms Sales, a real growth industry. An even more recent source shows no decline in the pace of arms peddling by the Pentagon (Michael T. Klare, The political economy of arms sales). President Carter has expressed concern over the problem, but whether his administration will succeed in reversing the trend against powerful economic interests remains to be seen.

[98] Anne H. Cahn, Have arms, will sell.

questions, of course; they must be debated and discussed widely. But we feel that people must be made aware not only of the ethical meanings of the judgements they make but of their practical consequences and implications. At the same time, defining an ethical position—whether as an individual or as a nation—is essential to identifying attainable goals. If this generation can reach an informed consensus on the kind of world society it hopes to have a century or two centuries hence, it can meet its problems with a coordinated response rather than simply lurching from crisis to crisis and fighting among groups over the solution to each one. As we have pointed out, failure to institute reform when it is needed is also action that has consequences.

The issues of wealth, exploitation, responsibility to future generations, and many others as well, are all related to philosophical questions that have long puzzled human beings. The most fundamental of those questions probably is, What is the value (or purpose) of human life? Some people, believing that human life in itself has enormous value, would like to maximize the number of human beings alive at any given time. A Brazilian economist at a United Nations meeting in late 1973 stated explicitly that he thought humanity's goal should be to have the maximum number of people existing at the minimum standard of living. (To his credit, he did not fall into the common logical trap of simultaneously attempting to maximize both numbers and living standards!) He also stated his reason for promulgating that goal: "Because I was glad to be born."[99]

Our view is that it would be better to have half a billion people leading comfortable and secure lives than 20 billion living at the fringes of existence. But our view—that human life has whatever value people give to it—is no more defensible scientifically than that Brazilian's view. Society could promote the existence of the maximum number of people, or it could strive for the maximum standard of living (however measured) for each person. About all that one can say with assurance is that attempting to do either in one generation would have profound consequences for future generations.

Questions about the value of human life are made more complex by the genetic, social, political, and economic diversity of *Homo sapiens*. Just ask the following questions of some of your close friends and see how different the answers are even within a single group: "How much social and personal effort should go into equalizing incomes, opportunities, and attitudes within and among nations?" Or, to put it another way, "Would the world be better off if everyone were the same height, color, and personality, and if they all had the same income and social status?"

Some people might answer the second version yes, because they think uniformity would do away with class distinctions, racism, and war. We would say no—in part because *Homo sapiens* shows a strong tendency to invent differences where natural ones do not exist, but, more important, because we believe that biological and cultural diversity, in addition to adding interest to human life, provide humanity with the flexibility necessary to adjust to changed conditions and thus avoid disaster. Of course, diversity of income is easy for the affluent to espouse, and extolling genetic diversity could be an excuse for maintaining a supply of underdogs to do menial tasks. One of the critical questions facing humanity may be whether or not a satisfactory balance can be struck between equality and diversity.

With those philosophical issues in mind, let us turn to two practical issues coming into sharp focus as the age of scarcity commences: *lifeboat ethics* and *triage.*

Lifeboat Ethics

The ethics of aid-giving have been examined by Garrett Hardin with the logical rigor that those who know the other writings of that outstanding biologist have come to expect and cherish. Moving on from his classic analysis of the "Tragedy of the commons," Hardin examined the options open to the rich nations with respect to sharing with the poor and compared each rich nation metaphorically to a lifeboat with a load of comparatively rich people.[100]

> The poor of the world are in other, much more crowded lifeboats. Continuously, so to speak, the poor fall out of their lifeboats and swim for a while in the

[99]We immediately asked him if he would have been sorry if he had not been born!

[100]Living in a lifeboat.

water outside, hoping to be admitted to a rich lifeboat, or in some other way to benefit from the "goodies" on board. What should the passengers on a rich lifeboat do? This is the central problem of the "ethics of a lifeboat."

Hardin then examines what the passengers of a lifeboat of limited carrying capacity (and perhaps filled to 80 percent of its capacity) can do about those still swimming. One option is to take aboard all of the needy—until the lifeboat is swamped and all drown: "Complete justice, complete catastrophe." A second option is to take on enough people to fill the remaining carrying capacity, sacrificing any safety factor represented by that excess capacity. But then the critical problem of how to choose those to be saved rears its ugly head. A third option is to admit no more to the boat, preserve the safety factor, guard against boarding parties, and assure the survival of the passengers.

That the last option is unjust, Hardin admits. Those who feel guilty, he points out, can change places with those in the water. Those willing to climb aboard obviously would have no such qualms, so the lifeboat would automatically purge itself of guilt as the conscience-stricken surrendered their places.

Hardin does not, of course, restrict himself to the metaphorical analysis. He dwells on the finite nature of Earth and of the resources of each nation (the limited carrying capacity of the lifeboats), the much more rapid population growth among the poor than the rich, and the suspect motivations and dismal results of aid programs so far attempted. He claims, "Every life saved this year in a poor country diminishes the quality of life for subsequent generations," a claim that may well be correct. He argues strongly that "well-meant sharing of food in a world of irresponsible reproduction" promotes catastrophe, and he suggests that the United States reduce immigration to the point where births plus immigrants balance deaths plus emigrants (that is, to ZPG). He concludes that, in the absence of a world government capable of controlling human reproduction worldwide, survival with dignity demands that we practice the ethics of the lifeboat.

We share with Hardin the sense that assistance to nations without population control may do no good and may do great harm. We do believe that it is possible, however, to supply assistance that will both improve the lot of the recipients and help to depress birth rates, although we admit to being extremely pessimistic about whether such aid will ever be given or whether in many areas it can be given in time to avoid further disaster.

Our greatest disagreement with Hardin comes not in the analysis of lifeboat ethics within his framework, but with the metaphor itself. In order for it to be sufficiently realistic to apply to today's situation, some changes would have to be made in the image. For instance, there would have to be a flow of rations between the lifeboats, in which the rich lifeboats regularly took more than they gave. And the rich lifeboats would have to be dependent on the poor for all sorts of materials they needed to maintain their affluence, materials not found among their own original provisions. Furthermore, the rich passengers on the lifeboats would have to be engaged in wasting their survival rations, while the poor would have none to waste. (Hardin's statement about saving lives in poor countries is even more applicable to the rich. Every life preserved in the United States threatens the resources and environment of the planet many times more than a life preserved in, say, Bangladesh). And finally, the people in the poor lifeboats should be energetically arming themselves with nuclear and biological weapons in an effort to present a credible threat to the rich.[101]

We think, therefore, that there are strong practical as well as ethical reasons for changing behavior in the rich lifeboats before adoption of a strict lifeboat ethic should even be considered. At the very least, elimination of resource waste and of dependence on poor countries for raw materials seem to be required before the metaphor could be applied. It seems likely, however, that the rich nations will be forced to cut down their waste of resources and perhaps to reduce their imports from the LDCs, whether they want to or not. Even so, the fundamental interdependence of nations is unlikely to disappear. Nor is the peril of nuclear or chemical-biological conflict, the chances for which would surely be enhanced by a refusal of rich nations to assist nations in need. Finally, there is no evidence that the American

[101]For another critique of lifeboat ethics, see W. W. Murdoch and A. Oaten, Population and food: Metaphors and the reality. Further discussion of these issues can be found in Comments, *The Ecologist*, vol. 8, nos. 6 and 8 (August and October), 1976.

public is yet hardhearted enough to watch children starve on their television news programs without offering help. C. P. Snow predicted such news stories in 1968 and they came to pass in the early 1970s during the Sahel famine. The impact on the conscience of the United States public was considerable and doubtless helped accelerate American aid efforts.

Triage

If it is granted that the rich countries must make some effort to help poor countries (whether on moral or practial grounds), then the issue becomes one of deciding how to allocate the funds, food, or whatever is needed. This is particularly a problem if there is not enough to go around.

William and Paul Paddock, in their 1967 book *Famine—1975!* predicted a deteriorating world food situation in the 1970s and considered the difficult question of how the United States might allocate the limited food that would be available for foreign aid. They proposed a policy based on the concept of *triage,* a term borrowed from military medicine. Briefly, the idea is this: when casualties crowd a dressing station to the point where all cannot be cared for by a limited medical staff, some decisions must be made on who will be treated. All incoming casualties are placed in one of three classes. In the first category are those who will survive regardless of treatment; in the second are those who can be saved, but only if they are given prompt treatment; and in the third group are those who will die regardless of treatment. When medical aid is severely limited, it is concentrated on the second group alone; the others are not treated.

The Paddocks suggested that the United States devise a similar system for classifying nations in need of help. Some countries would be able to maintain self-sufficiency without enormous outside aid. They would be ones with abundant resources to trade for foreign purchases (OPEC nations, for example) or with efficient governments, strong population-control programs, and strong agricultural development programs. Although our aid might help them, they could get along without it. The Paddocks suggested that Libya was probably such a country because it had the resources, in the form of oil, that would allow it to purchase food as its population expanded.

Some nations, on the other hand, might become self-sufficient if they were given some food to tide them over. The Paddocks thought that Pakistan—at least West Pakistan—might have been such a country. Considering the recent history of that nation, however, we wonder if they were not too optimistic.

Then there is the last, tragic category: those countries so far behind in the population-food race that there is no hope that limited food donations could see them through to self-sufficiency. The Paddocks felt that India, among others, was probably in this category. Bangladesh is today a more clear-cut example.[102]

In a situation where LDC needs for free or low-cost food imports might greatly exceed what was available, the Paddocks recommended giving food only to those countries it would really help—the second category. The first group might suffer a few lean months or have to sacrifice foreign exchange to buy food but would be in no danger of starvation. The third group would suffer greatly from famine, but giving aid needed just as badly elsewhere would only postpone the inevitable in such hopeless cases.

When the book was published, many people declared the Paddocks' proposal immoral, while others ridiculed their prediction of famine in the mid-1970s. After all, the Green Revolution was going to banish famine forever!

That the Paddocks' predictions on famine were accurate is now history, and the onset of famine on the Indian subcontinent in 1974, following on the heels of several years of famine in the Sahel, brought renewed attention to the idea of triage.[103] By then, however, the question seemed largely moot. The United States no longer had vast grain surpluses it was willing to give away, and it was allocating its food aid not on the basis of recipients' needs, but mainly on the basis of what the United States government perceived as its own political interests. Hence, the bulk of American food aid went to the U.S.-supported regimes in South Vietnam and Cambodia in 1974 and the beginning of 1975.

Although the precise situation in which the Paddocks envisioned triage's being applied no longer holds, ethical

[102]Kushwant Singh, The international basket case.
[103]Wade Green, Triage.

questions associated with the allotment of limited aid seem certain to be raised repeatedly in the future. Assuming that rich nations will (and should) transfer food and other aid to the poor, and further assuming that such transfers may not be sufficient to meet all the needs of the poor, the rich nations—especially the food-exporting ones—are confronted with some rather unpalatable alternatives.[104]

First, they could continue to do what they have been doing: allot aid largely on the basis of perceived self-interest with a little humanitarianism blended in. This is the course of least resistance. It has accomplished little in the past except to create enmity among recipients, and it promises little more for the future.

Second, they could attempt to spread their aid "evenly" among all the needy (whose numbers are rapidly increasing), realizing that it is doing no good but appeasing those who consider this the only ethical course.

Third, they could practice some form of triage, based purely on perception of need and potential for attaining self-sufficiency. This would be an immoral policy in the view of some observers, who would say, "What gives the United States (or Canada, or Australia) the right to decide who lives and who dies?" Of course, since the ethical questions surrounding triage start with the assumption that available aid is inadequate to help everyone but could help some, any of the above approaches would amount to playing God; the only difference would be in the outcome.

Finally, the rich countries can avoid the dilemma by donating their assistance funds or commodities to international "banks," leaving the distribution to committees of the whole composed of the potential recipients. This course has considerable merit, and indeed aid is increasingly being allocated in this way. The World Food Council is a case in point, as its allocations of donated food are determined by a mixed committee of donor and recipient countries, in which the recipients are the majority. Similarly, bilateral assistance is being replaced by funding both direct assistance and loans through the World Bank and various regional development banks.

[104]For a discussion of such alternatives and the food producers' responsibilities, see Lester R. Brown, The politics and responsibility of the North American breadbasket.

Representatives of recipient nations have been gaining greater voice in determining allocation in recent years. Whether this change will result in the aid's going where it will do the most good remains to be seen; past performance of people from LDCs in positions of power suggests they are no more generously endowed with wisdom or fairness than are people from DCs. But at least the developed countries cannot be blamed for administrative failures if the decisions have been made by people from LDCs. Although donors of foreign aid understandably do not wish to see their assistance wasted, they must learn to take that chance (after all, a not inconsiderable amount has been wasted when they controlled the purse strings). If a recipient country blatantly abuses aid in the view of its peers in a development agency, future assistance funds can be denied.

Regardless of how development resources are allocated, care must be taken to keep large bureaucratic organizations such as the U.S. Agency for International Development (AID) and the World Bank under continuous scrutiny. Like all such institutions, they have vested interests in "success" and in their own perpetuation. The record of AID in the past, for instance, has been mixed, to say the least.[105] The abuses found in 1975 and 1976 in the grain shipping business in the United States—including shipment of short weighted and contaminated grain—are another example. Careful oversight and independent evaluation of all national and international agencies and assistance programs are needed now. And if the amount of development assistance is increased in future years, as it clearly should be, it will become even more essential to safeguard the implementing organizations against abuses and inefficiency.

INVENTING A BETTER FUTURE

The orientation of hope is toward the future; even in the darkest hours forces emerge which make a new future possible. We have not reached the point of no return. What holds men back is not the pressure of reality but the absence of dreams. If enough people could come to see

[105]For critiques, see W. and E. Paddock, *We don't know how: An independent audit of what they call success in foreign assistance;* and Karen De Young, Selling the Sahel.

their present predicament and the possibility of a new way into the future we could make the first step into the new world. We need in practice the moral equivalent of war to direct our purposes and mobilize our endeavours just to make the next step one that is in the right direction.

One sort of world is dying. Another is struggling to be born. We may not be able to predict the future. We can invent it.

—Charles Birch,
Confronting the Future, 1975

If it is generally agreed that all nations on Earth are becoming increasingly interdependent and must cooperate to create what has been called a human community,[106] how is this to be accomplished? We have examined many of the dangers that lie ahead, inevitable or potential, and discussed some of the wrong choices that have been made in the past. What new, realistic goals can now be held up that all humanity can agree on and strive toward? What choices—in development policy, in managing the world resource commons, in narrowing the rich-poor gap—will help humanity attain those goals?

Obviously these are questions that must be decided by an informed consensus among all nations, but we will add to the dialogue some suggestions of our own. In our opinion, major changes must occur in the three intertwined areas of foreign aid, development goals, and international politics.

What Rich Countries Can Do

The rich must live more simply so the poor may simply live.

—Charles Birch,
Confronting the Future, 1975

All the rich nations must by now recognize that their fates are inextricably bound up with those of the LDCs—the OPEC oil cartel and the Indian A-bomb should have made this crystal clear. They must further recognize that their accustomed patterns of using resources cannot continue much longer—if depletion and rising prices fail to force a change, militant LDCs may succeed. Political and economic realism and any sense of fair play dictate that measures must be taken to effect some form of redistribution of the wealth of the world. In other words, rather than abandoning efforts to help poor countries, the overdeveloped rich world should be *increasing* those efforts.

Transferring wealth. Two scientists, Lord Snow of the United Kingdom and Andrei D. Sakharov of the USSR, made rather similar proposals along this line some years ago. Sakharov, "father of the Russian hydrogen bomb" and one of the youngest men ever elected to the Soviet Academy of Sciences, in 1968 expressed his views in an extraordinary document entitled, "Progress, Coexistence, and Intellectual Freedom," which was not published in the USSR. Among his many proposals was that, after the United States and the USSR have "overcome their alienations," they should collaborate in a massive attempt to save the LDCs. This attempt would be financed by contributions to the effort from the DCs of 20 percent of their national incomes over a fifteen-year period.

Lord Snow, an eminent physicist and novelist, supported Sakharov's suggestion. He recommended that the rich nations devote 20 percent of their GNPs for ten or fifteen years to the task of population control and development of the poor countries.[107]

Both proposals called for a transfer of wealth roughly *10 times greater* than that represented by the oil price increase and traditional foreign aid combined.[108] We believe an effort of this magnitude is not only justified but essential. By the scale of the effort, and by its no-strings-attached nature (a substantial portion should be channeled through international agencies under control of LDCs), the people of the less developed world might be convinced that those in the developed countries *do* care. Though there is much suffering today in the LDCs (and more is clearly unavoidable), a substantial lowering of DC-LDC tensions could occur if the LDCs

[106]John Richardson, Jr., Preparing for a human community, news release, U.S. Department of State, Washington, D.C., May 18, 1976.

[107]Lecture given at Westminster College, Fulton, Missouri, November 12, 1968. Reprinted in the *New York Times,* November 13, 1968.

[108]Foreign aid from DC governments and OPEC amounted in 1973 to about $15 billion out of a world product of perhaps $5000 billion. Another $1.4 billion went through private agencies, of which about $1 billion was spent in the United States (Sommer, U.S. voluntary aid).

felt that help was really on the way. And, of course, the joint DC effort could help to bring about that community of feeling generally regarded as essential to the abolition of war.

This brings us to the question of what changes in the DCs might be made to permit such a transfer of wealth? Some people seem to believe that all that would be required is for the rich to change their lifestyle and consume only as much as the average human being. Then the wealth saved could be transferred to the poor, raising them to the average. But income is closely tied to productivity. As Nathan Keyfitz observed, "If, starting tomorrow, Americans were all to live like Indians, then their higher incomes would simply disappear. There would be nothing to transfer. How much is transferable depends on the extent to which Americans could consume like Indians while continuing to produce like Americans."[108a] Some way therefore must be found to free wealth and transfer it without breaking the close link between production and consumption.

De-development of Overdeveloped Countries

The proper object of economic activity is to have enough *bread, not infinite bread, not a world turned into bread, not even vast store houses full of bread. The infinite hunger of man, his moral and spiritual hunger, is not to be satisfied, is indeed exacerbated, by the current demonic madness of producing more and more things for more and more people. Afflicted with an infinite itch, modern man is scratching in the wrong place, and his frenetic clawing is drawing blood from the life-sustaining circulatory systems of his spaceship, the biosphere.*

–H. E. Daly, 1973

In a sustainable world with a more just distribution of wealth, a nation is over developed when the citizens of that nation consume resources and pollute the common environment at a rate which is greater than would be possible for all the people in the world.

–Charles Birch,
Confronting the Future, 1975

[108a]Nathan Keyfitz, World resources.

The most critical change of all must be a change in goals; all people, rich and poor alike, must come to recognize that being a citizen of a giant, smoggy, freeway-strangled industrial state is not necessary to being a happy, healthy, fulfilled human being. For by Birch's definition and several other criteria, the industrial nations, which the world has become accustomed to calling DCs, are really *overdeveloped countries* (ODCs).

Today the trinkets of industrial civilization have the strongest appeal to the naive, both within and outside industrial society. If DCs continue to train their own people to think of the power lawn mower and automatic icemaker as the finest achievements of humanity, it seems unlikely that the rising expectations of the LDCs will rise above them either. But if we in the United States (and Europeans, Soviets, Japanese, Canadians, and Australians) can learn to recognize and attempt to correct our own errors, then perhaps people in the LDCs will see their way clear to establishing new goals—development within resource limitations and with careful attention to the *quality* of life.

It is therefore apparent that one key to saving world society lies in a measured and orderly retreat from overdevelopment in today's ODCs—a process we will label, for want of a better word, *de-development.* If the ODCs can successfully move toward spaceman economies, systematically eliminate the wasteful, frivolous, and ecologically harmful aspects of their behavior, shift the economic emphasis to Type I GNC (Chapter 14), and divert their excess productivity and technological expertise into helping the poorer people of the world rather than exploiting them, then perhaps the citizens of the poor countries will accept a different kind of development—what we call *grass-roots development*—as their most desirable goal. On the other hand, if the ODCs continue to loot the world of its high-grade resources, use their technology to produce doomsday weapons and senseless gadgets for superconsumers, and permit the gap between the rich and the poor to continue to widen, it seems certain that the people of the LDCs will continue to strive toward overdevelopment themselves.

As we see it, de-development of the ODCs should be given the top priority. Only when that course is firmly established, will there be any real hope for all of humanity to generate a worldwide spirit of cooperation rather than competition and to plan the development of our spaceship with the holistic perspective that is so essential to the survival of civilization. Only then can consumption in the LDCs be linked both psychologically and physically to production in the ODCs and a substantial transfer of wealth accomplished.

In short, the DCs must not only give unprecedented aid to the LDCs, they must help the LDCs avoid the mistakes made by the DCs. Something like this message must come across:

> By making the fundamental error of basing our standard of progress on expansion of material throughput, we have created a vast industrial complex and great mental, moral, and aesthetic poverty. Our cities are disaster areas, our air often unbreathable, our people increasingly regimented, and our spirit increasingly domitable. We require far too large a slice of the world's resources to maintain our way of life. We, in short are not developed, we are *overdeveloped.* We now realize that our current patterns of consumption and resource exploitation cannot and should not be sustained. While we are correcting our mistakes and de-developing, we want to help you develop your nation—not in our image, but in whatever way is most appropriate for your culture. And we hope that this development will start at the grass roots level to improve the quality of life for your poorest people.

It must be clearly recognized that *development* in the minds of a great many people means the industrialization of the globe, and that the material culture of the West seems to have a nearly irresistible appeal to most human beings. Whatever value judgements one might wish to make about this are probably immaterial—since the planet almost certainly cannot support even 4 billion people with the material throughput per person associated with, say, the United States or West Germany today. The task thus becomes one of diverting people from pursuing that material-intensive and environmentally unsustainable lifestyle. The only way to divert the rush in the LDCs to mimic overdevelopment is to change the model—to trim from the lifestyle and supporting technology of the ODCs their energetic and material profligacy while increasing the quality of life. That is the essence of de-development.

Harnessing technology. The whole idea of de-development has met with considerable misunderstanding and resistance, and will undoubtedly meet with much more. Some people have mistakenly assumed that the idea of de-development is basically antitechnological. The emotion that accompanies resistance to de-development is exemplified by the reaction of physicist Alvin M. Weinberg, who wrote that the de-development message was "we should destroy technology since technology got us into this dilemma, and this will set things right."[109]

This is certainly not what we mean by de-development. Instead, technology must be brought under control and turned to the service of humanity. Technology is essential to de-development, but as de-development proceeds, society must be more discriminating in the use of technology and much more cautious about its potentially disastrous side effects. Emphasis should be shifted to maximizing efficiency, learning to get more from less. Technology should be used to further human goals other than satisfaction of the desire for material growth. Technologists must learn the physical and biological limitations of their discipline and be prepared to put social limitations on its use.

But to turn away from technology itself would be to condemn to death many hundreds of millions of people now living on this overpopulated planet. The fullest use of technological expertise will be needed to maximize agricultural production, while minimizing the destructive effects of agriculture on the ecosystems of the planet. New technologies must be developed for recycling materials, for controlling pollutants, for efficient transport systems, and for population control. Efficiency in power generation from fossil fuels must be increased in order to buy time for developing new technologies for the generation of power. Technologies will be needed at all stages to help in the transition from a cowboy to a spaceman economy; technology will play a key role in the processes of both grass-roots development and de-development.

Angry opposition to de-development can be expected from some technologists who are used to having their schemes for progress accepted without question by a dazzled public. SSTs, space colonies, thermonuclear weapons and delivery systems, geodesic domes over

[109]*BioScience,* April 1, 1971.

cities, fission power, giant automobiles, plastic wrappings, genetic engineering, disposable packages and containers, synthetic pesticides, and the like are supposed to be accepted as self-evidently desirable. However, many technologists now correctly perceive that, if the ODCs are to be de-developed and civilization is to persist, the halcyon days of unquestioning public acceptance of technological "progress" must disappear forever.

Energy and prosperity. Civilization is not running out of energy; but it is running out of cheap energy, out of environmental tolerance for disruptive energy technologies, and out of time in which to do something about it.[110]

The global dilemma that is emerging from this situation has three main elements.

1. Energy is an indispensible (necessary but not sufficient) ingredient of prosperity. The prospects for prosperity of nations presently poor, and of the poorer segments of rich nations, are threatened as the price of this indispensible commodity rises.

2. The technologies of energy supply, conversion, and application are dominant ingredients of civilization's disruption of the global environment. (Chapter 8, Chapter 10, Chapter 11).

3. High rates of growth of energy use in the rich countries, where total use is already very high, compound the foregoing problems. Rapid growth on top of an already large base becomes increasingly troublesome economically as the base gets ever larger:

   a. Supplies of capital for building new facilities are strained, so capital itself becomes more expensive.
   b. Such cheap energy resources as remain do not suffice, so more expensive ones are tapped.
   c. The world market price of even the cheaply extractable resources rises to equal that of the expensive supplements, so poor countries can no longer afford to pay even for their present pathetic share of the world energy supply, and rich countries experience serious problems of inflation and balance of payments.
   d. In desperate attempts to sustain rapid growth and increase self-sufficiency, firms and nations gamble ever larger stakes on unproven energy technologies, some likely to fail expensively. The same hasty technological gambles, forced by a high growth rate on a large base, greatly increase the chance and probable magnitude of serious environmental mistakes.

No policy or combination of policies can deal successfully with these problems unless it incorporates as a central element a sharply reduced rate of growth of global energy use. Overconsumption in the richest countries and the legitimate needs of the poor countries dictate that this reduction be accomplished by an even sharper slowdown in growth of energy use in the rich countries, where most use now takes place.

Table 15-3 compares the rates of energy use in the United States, other ODCs, and LDCs. The lower part of the table shows annual growth rates in population and energy use in the early 1970s. Some hint of the problems implied by continuation of these trends may be obtained, for example, by extending the 5-percent annual rate of growth in total energy use through the year 2020, accompanied by population growth rates of 1 percent per year in the rich countries and 2.5 percent per year in the poor ones. The result is 8.3 billion people in LDCs, with an average annual energy use of 1.66 thermal kilowatts per capita and 1.9 billion people in ODCs with an average annual per-capita use of 34.3 thermal kilowatts. The worldwide total annual energy use would be 80 billion thermal kilowatts, more than 10 times the 1972 figure.

An even worse outcome would ensue if attempts were made to raise the energy consumption of the LDCs to match the moving target of rapidly increasing energy consumption by the ODCs. Not only would the gap between them not be closed, but the world economy and the environment would be wrecked in the attempt.

But there is an alternative. It is easily shown that a dramatic slowdown in the growth of energy use in the rich countries would permit, in principle, an *acceleration* of the growth of per-capita energy use in the poor countries within a context of *slackening global growth.* In this way the wide rich-poor gap in energy use, which

[110]This section is based on John P. Holdren, Energy and prosperity: Some elements of a global perspective.

roughly parallels the rich-poor gap in well-being, could begin to be narrowed. (As we have noted, of course, much attention must also be given to the other aspects of socioeconomic development, without which energy alone cannot produce prosperity.) The slower rate of growth in total global energy use, and the much slower growth in the rich countries, where certain environmental impacts of energy technology are now most severe, would significantly reduce the grave environmental risks that accompany continuation of past trends.

The success of such a scheme would depend heavily on the success of population control. Only if population growth rates were very much reduced could the high growth in per-capita energy use needed and desired in the LDCs be achieved within an economically and environmentally sustainable rate of total growth. In the rich countries, the effect of multiplying even quite small population increments by the very high per-capita energy use already prevailing there makes it essential for them to approach zero population growth as soon as possible.

A specific scenario illustrating how the bulk of growth in energy use might be diverted from rich to poor countries, while population growth is slowed, is outlined in Table 15-4.

The rates of population growth and per-capita energy use indicated in the four intervals of time are optimistic but not physically impossible. Until 1980 the growth of per-capita energy use in both rich countries and poor ones represents only a moderate reduction from recent trends, and the average rates of population growth in this period are unchanged from recent values.

The steady decline of ODC population growth to zero over the subsequent two decades seems not entirely implausible, in view of declining fertility rates already being experienced in the United States, Europe, and elsewhere. The reductions shown in population growth in the poor countries between 1980 and 2020 would require consensus and enormous effort, as we have emphasized earlier, but it may be possible.

There is no question that growth rates in per-capita energy use as large as those shown in the table for the LDCs between 1990 and 2020 are possible in individual countries for limited spans of time. But achieving those *averages* throughout the less developed world for thirty years would be a formidable task, requiring a transfer of technical resources and capital from the rich countries to the poor ones of the magnitude envisioned by Sakharov and Snow.

If such a transfer of wealth could be effected, by whatever means,[110a] the results would be quite remark-

TABLE 15-3
Global Energy Use (1972) and Rates of Change (late 1960s and early 1970s)

	United States	*Other ODCs*	*LDCs*
DISTRIBUTION			
Population (billions)	0.2	1.0	2.5
Per-capita energy use (kwt)	12.0	3.7	0.5
Total energy use (billion kwt)	2.4	3.7	1.3
% of global energy use	33.0	50.0	17.0
ANNUAL GROWTH RATE (%)			
Population	0.7	1.0	2.5
Total energy use	5.0	5.0	5.5
Per-capita energy use	4.3	4.0	3.0

Note: Energy consumption is given as the equivalent continuous rate, in thermal kilowatts (kwt), excluding food, dung, and some wood used for fuel. (A consumption of 24 thermal kilowatt hours per day corresponds to the equivalent continuous rate of 1 thermal kilowatt.)
Sources: United Nations statistical yearbook, 1974; United States Department of Commerce, *Statistical abstract of the United States,* 1975.

TABLE 15-4
A Scenario for Redistribution of Growth in Energy Use

	ODCs		*LDCs*	
	Population	*Per-capita energy use*	*Population*	*Per-capita energy use*
POSTULATED AVERAGE GROWTH RATES IN SPECIFIED PERIODS (%)				
1972–1980*	1.0	3.0	2.5	2.5
1980–1990	0.7	1.0	2.0	3.5
1990–2000	0.3	0.5	1.5	4.5
2000–2020	0.0	0.2	1.0	4.5
VALUES AT SPECIFIED TIMES (POPULATION IN BILLIONS, PER-CAPITA ENERGY USE IN KWT)				
mid-1972	1.20	5.25	2.50	0.50
mid-1980	1.30	6.65	3.05	0.61
mid-1990	1.39	7.35	3.72	0.86
mid-2000	1.44	7.72	4.31	1.33
mid-2020	1.44	8.03	5.26	3.20

Total energy use in 2020 = 28.4 billion kwt.
Total population in 2020 = 6.7 billion.
Average annual rate of growth in total energy use, 1972–2020 = 2.8%.
*Measured from midyear to midyear.
Source: John P. Holdren, Energy and prosperity.

[110a]One possibility that has been proposed is to tax nonrenewable resources exported from LDCs to ODCs, including fossil fuels (Julian Lessey, Taxes for conservation). This would have the effect simultaneously of reducing consumption in ODCs and providing funds for development in LDCs.

able. The total rate of energy use by a world population of 6.7 billion people in 2020 would be about 28 billion thermal kilowatts, or 4 times the 1972 rate instead of more than 10 times. Average per-capita energy use among the 5.3 billion people in LDCs would roughly equal the 1972 rate for Japan or Austria, and the average per-capita energy use of the 1.4 billion people in all ODCs would be about that of the United States in the early 1960s.

It is far from certain, of course, that 4 times the 1972 rate of energy use could be managed in 2020 without grave environmental problems, just as it is not clear that 6.7 billion people could be fed and provided with other raw materials for a decent existence without undermining essential environmental services. Nevertheless, there is perhaps a chance for success, particularly with the degree of international cooperation that might emerge from a substantial narrowing of the rich-poor gap. There is *no* chance if past trends continue.

Success will require, in addition to the sort of drastic reallocation of growth just described, great emphasis on promoting those technologies of energy and materials supply that generate the least environmental disruption, and on phasing out those that pose the greatest threats of irreversible ecological or social harm. Solar energy has great promise in the first category, for instance; whereas nuclear fission deserves careful scrutiny as to whether it belongs in the second.

A final essential ingredient of this scenario would be a major, coordinated, worldwide campaign of research, development, and implementation aimed at increasing the amount of prosperity derived from each unit of energy (and, indeed, from each unit of other raw materials). (See Chapter 8 and Chapter 9.)

Tailoring technologies of energy supply and application to specific regional conditions might avoid in the LDCs much of the needless energy waste that now prevails in the ODCs.[110b] By maximizing the benefit derived from each increment of energy use, while minimizing the undesirable side effects, prosperity in the poor countries surely could be increased faster than the rate of growth of energy use itself. Even in rich countries, where a drastic slowing of growth in energy use is clearly called for, ingenuity could reduce the impact of rising energy costs and environmental destruction and brighten the prospects for an increase in actual well-being. Such transitions would unavoidably pose some economic problems, but they are likely to be much less severe and more temporary than the growing economic problems of maintaining the status quo. Indeed, the evidence is mounting that proceeding along the present course is *physically* impractical as well as socially unacceptable and politically perilous. Viewed in that context, the above scenario, utopian as it may seem at first, appears as plain common sense.

[110b]Such an approach is apparently being taken in China: Vaclav Smil, Intermediate energy technology in China.

What Poor Countries Can Do

The man who holds that every human right is secondary to his profit must now give way to the advocate of human welfare.

—Theodore Roosevelt

No race can prosper till it learns that there is as much dignity in tilling a field as in writing a poem.

—Booker T. Washington

A large-scale effort on the part of the ODCs to transfer wealth and resources to LDCs will not suffice, however, unless there are basic changes in the value systems related to development. If industrialization of the entire world is neither possible nor desirable, new standards of value will have to be established that permit *all* peoples access to the means of filling the basic human needs for adequate food, shelter, clothing, employment, education, and medical care, regardless of the economic value of their productivity. Future development programs that do not face up to the problem of assuring relatively equitable use of the aid *within* a given country, are unlikely to be very successful, since the political liabilities they produce are likely to swamp any economic benefits.

Recognizing the necessity of reducing inequities within LDCs, the first question asked of any aid project should be: Will it benefit the people, or will it benefit only the government or some special-interest group in the recipient country? If the project benefits only the smaller groups, it should be rejected unless it can be proved that it will ultimately benefit the general population in some real and measurable way. By this standard, a steel mill might be a poor project for an LDC, for instance, even though it could provide employment for a few hundred people and would contribute to the economy. A steel mill might be justified if the country had rich deposits of iron ore that could most efficiently be processed nearby, and if export earnings seemed likely to make the investment worthwhile.

A fertilizer plant, on the other hand, would also provide employment and benefit the LDC's economy. Beyond that, the fertilizer it produced would enhance the country's ability to increase its food production and feed its population adequately. It would also allow the country to produce for itself a needed commodity that would otherwise have to be imported.

New priorities: grass-roots development. Perhaps the most urgent task for most less developed countries is to establish ecologically sensible agricultural development, with supporting facilities for distribution, storage, and marketing of food. But, as noted in Chapter 7, agricultural development is necessarily connected with general economic improvement in rural areas: road-building; production of fertilizer, farm implements, and machinery; and increased demand for food are all essential ingredients.

Even before they can be provided, many countries will have to institute meaningful reform in land ownership and tenure patterns, which largely determine the distribution of rural income and wealth. Land reform is no easy task, large landholders are usually an entrenched, conservative lot who wield considerable power. But such change *can be* accomplished, as witness the achievements of Japan (just after World War II—and doubtless a key to Japan's successful postwar recovery), China, Taiwan, South Korea, and to some extent Mexico. [111] The last four countries are usually counted among the more successful developing nations, and their attention to land tenure and rural development has clearly been a significant factor in their success.

Development planned to help the poorest people, not aimed primarily at massive industrialization and growth of the GNP, we have called *grass-roots development.*[112]

What grass-roots development would mean in practice might, of course, vary in detail from area to area, but some needs may prove nearly universal. Ecologically sound agricultural development, rather than industrialization, should receive priority virtually everywhere, and most LDCs also have other requirements that must be met. They include medical and educational services, sanitation facilities, roads, electrification, and communications adequate to the demands of an agrarian society—in other words, the infrastructure of modern life. In attempting to fill those needs, finding appropriate means should be the first consideration: *how to make the limited resources do the most good with the least destruction of other values* (cultural and environmental values and general well-being).

A country undergoing grass-roots development thus would move only partway along the narrow road that was taken in the past by today's overdeveloped nations, while at the same time broadening its goals and outlook. Such a nation, we hope, would learn from the mistakes of the DCs: it would create no horrors like Los Angeles; it would not base its economy on the continuing rape of the world's nonrenewable resources; it would create, in E. S. Schumacher's words, "technology with a human face."[113] Although the emphasis of grass-roots development would tend to be on agriculture, the blessings of appropriate technology in other areas would also be available, partly through indigenous manufacture and partly through cooperation and trade with ODCs and other LDCs.

Intermediate technology. One essential ingredient of grass-roots development would be deployment of what Schumacher has called *intermediate technology.*[114] This kind of technology, as he describes it, "is vastly superior to the primitive technology of bygone ages but at the same time much simpler, cheaper and freer than the supertechnology of the rich." The essence of intermediate technology is to create work places at much lower levels of capital investment than has been considered

[111]James E. Kocher, *Rural development, income distribution, and fertility decline.*

[112]This was called *semi-development* in Ehrlich and Ehrlich, *Population, resources, environment,* but the image seemed wrong, and people wisely ignored the term. Live and learn.

[113]*Small is beautiful.*

[114]Ibid., p. 145.

normal in the ODCs or hertofore in the "modernized" sectors of most LDC economies. As we have mentioned (see Box 15-1), jobs are essential to helping the poor. Even if population-control measures should be successful beyond our wildest dreams, the need for millions of additional jobs every year in LDCs will persist beyond the end of the century.

The basic knowledge needed to create intermediate technologies already exists, but a large-scale effort to develop specific technologies appropriate to various situations in the poor nations has thus far been lacking. Low-cost, labor-intensive methods are urgently needed for housing and road construction, irrigation, food processing and storage, transportation, power generation, light industry, sanitation, and health-care delivery in LDCs, to name a few potential applications. Some progress is being made in developing such technologies; China has pioneered in several, including irrigation, local small-scale manufacturing, and rural health services, for instance. What has been lacking are coordinated efforts to develop such technologies, to disseminate information about them among countries, and to supply feedback on technical problems from workers in the field in LDCs to facilities in either the LDCs or the ODCs that are equipped to solve them.[115]

Energy technologies are especially critical in determining the patterns of future development in less developed countries. Policy-makers are convinced that LDCs must have access to reasonably priced energy if they are to develop at all, but they seem not to have considered the *appropriateness* of the energy technologies now being exported by industrial nations to nonindustrial ones. The energy technology being promoted most vigorously on the international market in the mid-1970s was nuclear reactors, yet one could hardly imagine a technology less well suited to the conditions in most poor countries. The economies of scale in nuclear plants make them unattractive in small sizes; malfunctions are costly and difficult to repair; and most poor countries that choose to use nuclear plants for generating energy will end up as dependent on industrial nations for their supplies of enriched uranium and for fuel-reprocessing services as they now are on OPEC nations for oil. (Less developed countries that can afford their own reprocessing plants, of course, obtain the capacity to fuel a nuclear-weapons program along with this element of independence.)[116]

How much more useful and sensible it would be to develop and export technologies that would help the nonindustrial nations to harness the flow resources—hydroelectric, plant material, sun, and wind—which so many of them have in special abundance, which lend themselves to small, durable installations, and which would foster independence rather than dependence. Sun and wind power, in particular, have begun to show great promise for small-scale application in LDCs.[117] And they clearly could be used that way in ODCs as well.

What sorts of projects might LDCs concentrate on developing, and how does intermediate technology fit in? A prime need in many LDCs is an adequate road network; lack of roads is a great hindrance to development efforts and may be a major factor in the urban bias of development. Roads, however, can be built without the sort of heavy machine-equipment used in ODCs. Instead, simpler techniques, resembling those used by DCs several decades ago, would probably be more efficient in poor countries and would certainly provide more employment for unskilled labor.

The same is true for extending electrification and electronic communications to poor and remote rural areas. The first goal could be to provide a single power supply, refrigeration unit, television receiver, and telephone to each village, to be used communally. This makes more sense than attempting to provide all of them at once to each home (which would be impossible anyway, at least in the foreseeable future). Once each village was supplied with the basic services, further expansion of the system could be undertaken.

[115]A relatively interesting, low-cost scheme for increasing scientific and technological interactions between ODCs and LDCs has been suggested by chemist Carl Djerassi, A modest proposal for increased north-south interaction among scientists. See also G. S. Hammond and W. M. Todd, Technical assistance and foreign policy.

[116]Reservations about these and other aspects of nuclear fission, placed in the international context, were expressed in the report of the twenty-third Pugwash conference on science and world affairs—some 100 scientists from 29 countries—in Finland in 1973. The relevant parts of the report are reprinted in L. Ruedisili and M. Firebaugh, eds., *Perspectives on energy,* Oxford University Press, New York, 1975, pp. 279–285. See also the section on proliferation, above.

[117]See, for instance, Abdou Moumoni, Energy needs and prospects in the Sahelian and Sudanese zones in Africa: Prospects of solar power; A. Makhijani and A. Poole, *Energy and agriculture in the Third World;* A. Makhijani, Solar energy and rural development for the Third World.

Transportation should certainly not be designed along ODC lines. Buses, whether imported or locally manufactured, are far more practical than cars in countries where only a fraction of the population can afford cars and where roads capable of accommodating cars by the million do not exist. Moreover, air pollution problems and energy constraints would render attempting to create an auto-centered transport system throughout the less developed world ill-advised, even if the other resources existed to do it. A special vehicle should be designed for LDC farmers, low-powered, economical, and sturdy. Owners of several small neighboring farms might own one communally. Alternatively, a local farmers' cooperative or the government might provide for the transport of agricultural produce to market on a pickup-and-delivery basis, and for the distribution of seed and fertilizer at appropriate times.

Farm machinery need not be highly mechanized to be efficient. Japan and Taiwan, for example, have developed very efficient agricultural systems without heavy mechanization. Economist Bruce F. Johnston has written, "simple, inexpensive farm equipment that is well suited to local manufacture in small- and medium-scale rural workshops" would be far more beneficial to the economies of LDCs and more practical than the use of heavy machinery.[118] Not the least benefit of such a system would be its dependence upon abundant farm labor.

Irrigation systems (necessary for modern high-yield grain crops in many regions) need not be based on grand-scale, elaborate concrete dams of the sort that attract tourists in the western United States. Even where large dams are built, the projects can be labor-intensive, as some have been in India.[119] China reportedly has developed the world's largest irrigation system without use of energy- and material-consuming pumps just by using gravity to control the water flow.

Ideas for useful development projects using intermediate technology abound; the difficulty frequently lies in having them implemented. On government priority lists, modest projects that would nevertheless benefit many people, such as road-building or irrigation projects, may be outweighed by the glamor of a steel mill or a national airline. In industrial countries, small projects are usually accomplished (planned, funded, and built) locally; in LDCs the necessary resources (administrators, funds, materials, and building organizations) are generally lacking at the local level, so people must depend on the central government to supply them. A large part of the problem is the need to generate these essential resources *at the grass-roots level:* to disseminate the needed skills; to utilize the unemployed and off-season farm labor, possibly through rural cooperatives; to find the funds, either locally or outside; to mobilize the needed materials; and perhaps above all, to develop local organizational talent.

Grass-roots development and economic growth. Economist James Kocher has described how (in theory, at least) grass-roots rural development could, through various positive feedbacks, become self-reinforcing, improving the lives of the people and allowing them to make further improvements.[120] An essential part of the picture is that such development would provide motivation for family limitation, which in turn would further enable families to invest in other things (better food and housing, farm equipment, small consumer products such as sewing machines, bicycles, household items). Those goods preferably would be locally produced, thus providing employment and generating local income. Figure 15-3 shows the effects of development efforts as they have often been applied in the past: the already better-off segment of the population benefits, modernizes, and practices birth control; the impoverished majority benefits only slightly at best; and the income gap between the groups widens. Figure 15-4 shows some of the feedback effects of grass-roots development, in which generally increased well-being leads to further increases in well-being.

Kocher postulates that a necessary precondition for egalitarian rural development is the introduction of new agricultural technology. He cautions, however, that the new technology must suit the local resource endowment (physical and human). If a technology demanding a high level of mechanization, for example, is introduced in an area where a high level of underemployment already exists, the result will be the opposite of that intended—the labor will be displaced and the income gap will be widened.[121]

[118]Unemployment and underemployment.
[119]Myrdal, The transfer of technology.

[120]*Rural development.*
[121]Ibid.

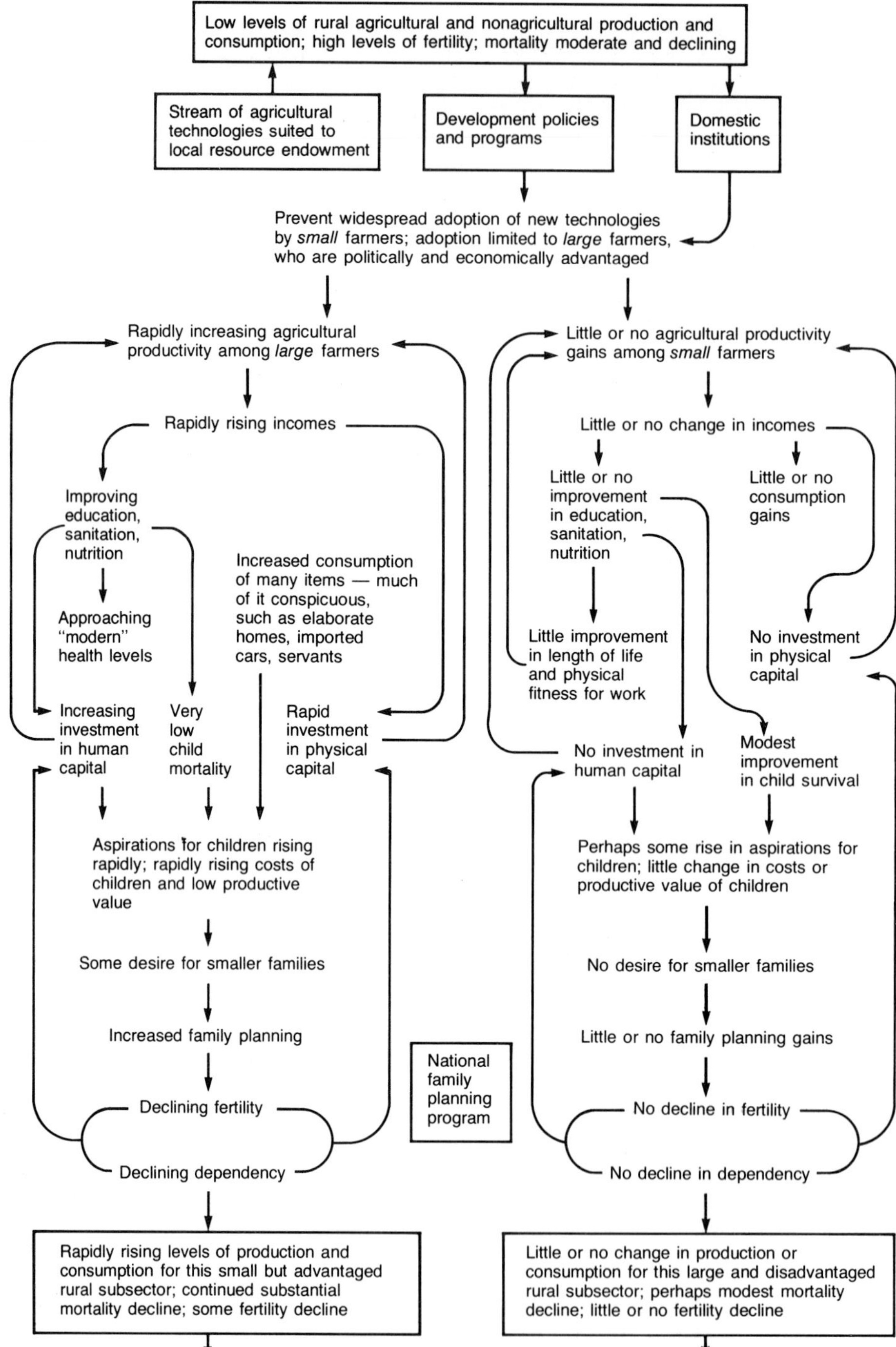

FIGURE 15-3

An example of a two-tiered rural society in which there is growth in agricultural productivity, but the benefits are mainly restricted to those who operate large farms. Widespread rural development does not take place, and there is no decline in fertility among the majority of the population. Usually, unemployment increases and generates migration to the cities. (Adapted from J. Kocher, 1973.)

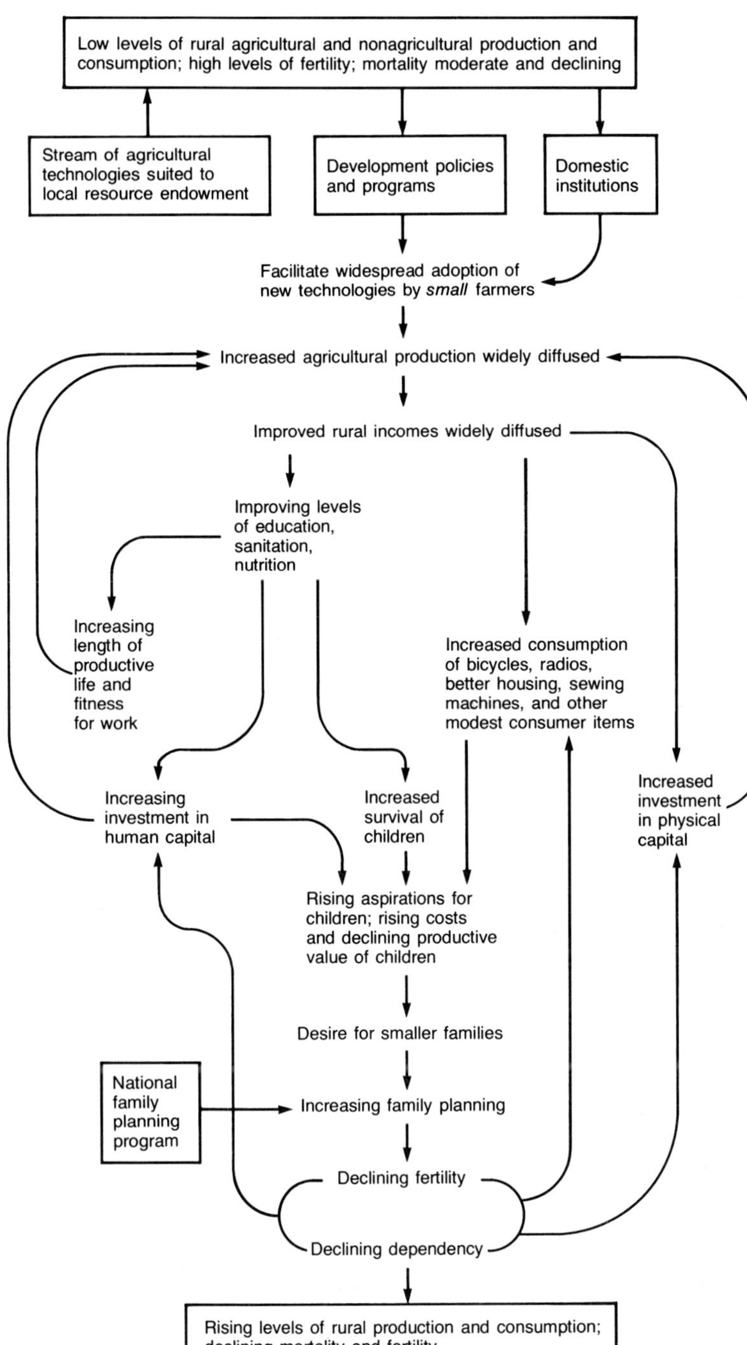

FIGURE 15-4

An example of successful grass-roots rural development, in which agricultural productivity increases among operators of both large and small farms. Consumption of food and other products rises, as does the standard of living. Labor-intensive farming, support activities, and demand for locally produced goods combine to provide employment and to stem migration to cities. Education and other costs of raising children (along with lowered infant mortality) generate incentive for smaller families, and fertility declines. (Adapted from J. Kocher, 1973.)

Some economists and others have expressed concern that a grass-roots approach to development would result in much slower economic growth than would concentration on an industrial sector. But this does not appear to be the case. James Grant has pointed out that investment in relatively egalitarian societies (where appropriate technologies have been used, education and health care are widely available, and the income gap between the highest and lowest 20 percent of the population has *decreased* since 1950), such as Taiwan and South Korea, has produced significantly more growth in per-capita GNP than has investment in less egalitarian countries, such as Brazil, Mexico, and the Philippines. Grant concludes:

> Contrary to the assumptions of the 1960s, the development record of these countries indicates that policies which enhance social equity need not deter, and may even accelerate, over-all economic growth . . . [E]quity can be more efficient than inequity and "trickle-down" in advancing growth in both rich and poor countries.[122]

There is, of course, no guarantee that grass-roots development will work—that it will lift the poor majority out of poverty, end their chronic hunger, reduce fertility, and fulfill their hopes for a better life before the consequences of overpopulation overtake humanity. The evidence that the grass-roots approach can succeed is fragmentary and tentative at best. (Here, again, we wish dependable information existed for China, where the grass-roots approach almost in extreme form seems to be the rule. But the rest of the world must rely on what little information the Chinese government releases and on the perceptions and testimony of foreign visitors.) But, as we see it, there are no viable alternatives, and arguments in favor of grass-roots development (aside from the probability of its success) are compelling: it represents a serious, direct effort to help the world's poorest, most disadvantaged people—especially the children, who suffer most. We see no choice but to try it.

Providing social services. The grass-roots approach to social services would assure provision of basic services to an entire population *before* the sophisticated, luxurious forms were added on for the rich minority. Unfortunately, this approach has seldom been taken.

[122]James P. Grant, Development: The end of trickle-down?

Education is an obvious case in point. In most LDCs, educational systems mimicking those of ODCs (where universal primary education is well established) have been set up. Every LDC has at least one institution of higher learning to serve the country's elite, but most LDCs have too few primary schools. The result is that large portions of the young population are excluded from any education, because the LDC government cannot afford to extend the system to everyone. Today, over a third of the world's adults lack the skills of reading and writing; in LDCs the proportion is even higher. And, although the proportion of illiterate adults in the world declined between 1950 and 1970 (from 44 to 34 percent of the adult human population), the *absolute number* of illiterates rose (from 700 million to 800 million).[123]

One unfortunate aspect of this is that two-thirds of the illiterate adults are women. As Lester Brown, Patricia McGrath, and Bruce Stokes expressed it, while young men are being educated to participate in modern life, "Women's minds, on the other hand, are being bound as cruelly as once their feet were."[124] Yet educating women is clearly vital both for reducing fertility and for furthering the goals of development.

Moreover, education in LDCs, rather than being tailored to the needs of local cultures, often seems designed to destroy those cultures. One of the great tragedies of Latin America, for instance, is the university system that has evolved there. Latin American universities produce many attorneys, philosophers, poets, and "pure" scientists, but not the agriculturalists, ecologists, paramedics, and public-health specialists that area so desperately needs. Educational problems in India and other Asian countries are similar.

A particularly difficult question is what sort of educational system (if any) should be offered to groups that are still somewhat isolated from industrial society. We think education for Eskimos or Kalahari Bushmen should be

[123]L. R. Brown, P. L. McGrath, and B. Stokes, Twenty-two dimensions of the population problem; Population Reference Bureau, *Literacy and world population.*

[124]Brown, McGrath, and Stokes; Twenty-two dimensions; see also Patricia L. McGrath, The unfinished assignment: Equal education for women.

designed to produce first-class Eskimos or Bushmen, not caricatures of North Americans, Englishmen, or Russians (although the option to acquire technical or academic educations should remain open to those who may desire them).

Education is particularly an area where innovations in methods and approaches are sorely needed. Mass education in traditional Western style of the rapidly growing population of children is simply beyond the means of most poor countries. It has been suggested that basic education of the masses be deferred to adulthood (or possibly adolescence), when it can be accomplished far more economically in terms of both time and money (an adult can acquire in a year the equivalent of an entire grade-school education). If effort were now concentrated on adults, especially mothers, they could then begin to teach their own children. Some educational resources might profitably be devoted to producing and distributing locally designed versions of the toys and games that prepare children in Western societies to learn in school. Satellite television broadcasting also can substitute economically for much of the educational apparatus, especially if each school or village is equipped with a receiver. Such a system has great potential for eradicating illiteracy and generally informing large segments of any population who have a common language, while requiring a minimum of trained people. A single teacher, for instance, could direct a course in basic arithmetic to the entire population of a country in a few weeks.

Medicine is another essential social service that has been inappropriately developed in many poor countries. Glittering modern hospitals can be found in most LDC capital cities, where they provide the wealthy with the best of care. But a farmer's pregnant wife may never see a doctor before, during, or after the birth of her baby—only a poorly trained, though experienced, midwife. Too often young doctors from less developed countries go to ODCs for advanced training in esoteric specialties. Since too few jobs exist in the home countries for their specialties, many remain in the ODCs—despite the desperate need for competent medical care in LDCs.

Some countries are trying to change this situation. Costa Rica, Cuba, and Sri Lanka (perhaps taking a cue from China's success), for instance, have extended health services to the poor through rural clinics and with extensive use of paramedics, with the result that infant mortality rates have declined substantially. India has begun to move toward such a program also. Mexico now requires young medical doctors whose educations have been paid for by state scholarships to give a year's service each in rural clinics.

Grass-roots health care is clearly the best approach to improving the general well-being of a people. China has shown the way: start by bringing basic sanitation, hygiene, and nutrition to all the people through a network of minimally trained health-care workers backed up by paramedics, nurses, and doctors. When the basics are established, the training of health-care workers (barefoot doctors) can be progressively upgraded. This is what China has done, and it evidently works there. (See the more extensive discussion in Chapter 13.) Efforts to introduce similar programs in some other LDCs have had mixed results, however. In some places, fees are charged for services, which discourages their use. Even very low fees are a deterrent to destitute peasants. Moreover, unless birth control is included, health care for infants may not always be appreciated.[124a]

Self-sufficiency and other goals. Among development goals, that of achieving self-sufficiency is frequently mentioned. Such a goal is certainly admirable, especially if it means reaching a stage where foreign aid from ODCs is no longer needed just to keep a populace from starving and an economy from collapsing. But self-sufficiency in the sense of autonomy—supporting a population with resources found entirely within national borders—is in many ways undesirable and, for most LDCs, impractical.

In recent decades, the world economy has been characterized by a growing interdependence among nations. In general, despite the abuses of exploitation, this is a good thing. Perhaps its greatest value is as a deterrent to warfare, a value that may often be overlooked. But interdependence also provides people (at least potentially) with otherwise unavailable goods from distant parts of the globe. As the system has evolved,

---

[124a]Paul Harrison, Basic health delivery in the Third World.

unfortunately, there has been too much exploitive trade between ODCs and LDCs and too little of any kind between LDCs. But the system needs to be adjusted, not abolished.

Autonomy is impractical for the majority of LDCs, in part because they are small. Relative self-sufficiency may be possible for China or perhaps for India, but not for Malawi or Uruguay—just as the United States can be more self-sufficient in this sense than the United Kingdom or the Netherlands. Not all regions can be made productive in economic terms. Some areas within Western countries today are maintained at economic expense because they supply other values—certain parts of the United States are maintained as parks or wilderness, for instance, whereas others are heavily industrial. Similarly, some parts of the world may have to be maintained at economic expense in the future because they supply other values: natural beauty, biological or cultural diversity, survival and happiness for fellow human beings, and, in the long run, survival for everyone.

There is no reason why LDCs could not be developed differentially. Some might have considerable industry and others be limited almost entirely to agricultural development or even left partly undeveloped. Unfortunately, this option is already rapidly being foreclosed in many places, and for some areas the loss will far outweigh any long-term gains (the destruction of the Amazon basin forest is a case in point). Large industrial complexes quite reasonably could be built near rich deposits of resources: for instance, near the copper deposits in Zambia, the bauxite in Jamaica, or the oil in Nigeria, Indonesia, and the Middle East. Disparate economic entities, including concentrations of agriculture and of industry, could perhaps be loosely federated in regional economic associations similar to the European Common Market. Such associations have indeed been formed in areas such as East Africa and Central America, and they have begun to generate increased trade and specialization in products among their members.

As examples of possible alternative paths of development, Kenya and Tanzania might undergo grass-roots development while remaining primarily agricultural and recreational areas. Tanzania has been moving this way for some time; Kenya is still too much oriented toward Western-style development and has suffered as a result from problems caused by a two-tiered economy. Tanzania, Kenya, and some other African nations could supply the world with a priceless asset: a window on the past, when vast herds of large animals roamed the Earth. They could also provide one of the many living stocks of organic diversity, stocks that may prove of immeasurable value as humanity attempts to replenish the deteriorated ecosystems of the planet and seeks new foods, drugs, fibers, or other naturally-derived products. Those African nations and similar areas could serve as rest-and-rehabilitation centers for people from the more frantic industrial parts of the planet—including areas of Africa, such as Nigeria and Zambia, that are richly endowed with mineral or energy resources and might develop into highly industrial areas.

Many less developed countries could also serve as guarantors of cultural diversity, areas specifically reserved to permit peoples to maintain their traditional ways of life. One of the grim dangers facing *Homo sapiens* is the continued homogenizing of cultures, the erosion of humanity's spectacular array of cultural differences. Urbanization, mass communications, and the explosive spread of Western technology and Judeo-Christian attitudes have already irretrievably reduced this diversity. But who is to say that one world view is better than another, that a British scientist's way of structuring the world is superior to that of a Hopi Indian, that a militant Christianity is superior to a gentle Oriental religion, or that the Australian aboriginal view of kinship is inferior to that of a jet-set sophisticate?

Preserving this diversity will require nothing less than a restructuring of Western ideals and values, which have unfortunately become predominant almost wordwide. A demand must be created for the cultural resources that Australian aboriginals, Eskimos, Kenyans, and Amazonian Indians can supply. Those priceless resources are in short supply, they are dwindling rapidly, and they are nonrenewable. A way must be found to permit such people access to more of the fruits of industrial societies without turning them into factory workers. This will require considerably more thought than has heretofore gone into development. How, for instance, can the benefits of modern health care be brought to, say, the

African Masai or the newly discovered Tasaday people of the Philippines without irreparably damaging their cultures? We believe ways could be found to transfer some Western technical benefits to other cultures without destroying those cultures, but it would take a major commitment on both sides.

It is encouraging to us in this context that people in less developed countries have recently become much more concerned with making their own decisions about their paths of national development. Those peoples should know best what suits their cultures and resource endowments. Unfortunately, they are still too much influenced by Western material ambitions and habits of consumption; but there are signs that this, too, is beginning to change.

The time has come for both the ODCs and the LDCs to recognize that each has a great deal of value to offer the other. Human dignity and inventiveness are certainly not the sole possession of any human group. It is possible, for instance, that LDC governments seriously interested in helping their citizens might do better to look to Peking or Havana for new ideas than to Washington, London, or Moscow. Indeed, it is quite likely that both the Americans and the Soviets could also learn from both China and Cuba. Americans might learn a lot from both countries about delivering adequate food and medical care to all their people. The Soviets might learn from the Chinese how to improve their perpetually faltering communal agriculture, and Americans might rediscover from them a sense of national purpose. The world at large has already learned something about population control from the Chinese.

That is not to say that both Cuba and China cannot in turn learn from the United States and the USSR. Both Cuba and China are much in need of the kinds of technical expertise that the ODCs have developed in so many areas, but they are certainly in the best position to judge their own needs. Fundamentally, *all* countries must reevaluate a long series of assumptions about such things as carrying capacity, population growth, food production, environmental deterioration, energy needs, economics, progress, equity of material distribution, and the quality of life. Perhaps the biggest step of all toward creation of genuine human community would be a recognition that what is required is not a process in which ODCs teach LDCs, communists teach capitalists (or vice versa), or scientists teach peasants, but a process of mutual learning.

INTERNATIONAL CONTROLS: THE GLOBAL COMMONS

Mutual coercion, mutually agreed upon.
—Garrett Hardin, 1968

It has been apparent for some time that the nations of this planet cannot long survive without a system of worldwide controls for dealing with the ecosphere, the world economic system, and world population growth. Such a system must above all be capable of resolving national differences. This is the basic conclusion, for instance, of Professor of international law Richard A. Falk's analysis of the situation, as exemplified by his projections of alternate future scenarios (Box 15-4).

In our opinion, one of the areas where international controls could be established most easily is over what may be called the global commons. All human beings must extract needed materials from the soil, the atmosphere, and the waters of Earth, and the hydrologic and biogeochemical cycles bind the three together into an indivisible entity. Although nations vary greatly in their mineral and fossil fuel endowments, it would clearly be wise (if not yet politically feasible) to consider *all* such supplies of nonrenewable resources as a commons also.

Idealistically, we might enter a plea here for surrendering some national sovereignty to a world government, but it is apparent that any movement in that direction will be extremely slow at best. Valuable as the United Nations has been in many respects,[125] it is clear that it will not become a supernational government in the foreseeable future. There does seem to be, however, some chance that humanity might be able to move much more rapidly than it has in the past toward international agreements on the control of the world commons. Treaties have been successfully worked out to control the

[125]See, for example, Benjamin M. Becker, The United Nations after thirty years.

BOX 15-4 The Falk Projections

In his 1971 book, *This endangered planet,* professor of international law Richard A. Falk of Princeton University presented two fundamental scenarios for the possible course of politics in a world threatened by ecological catastrophe. In the first scenario, he envisioned that the 1970s would see the "politics of despair." People would come to recognize that governments cannot deal with the problems of society. The gap between rich and poor nations would continue to widen, ecocatastrophes would become more common, the arms race and technological circuses would continue, while governments would persist in their pursuit of growth of GNP. The world system would face crisis after crisis, but no organized attempts would be made to attack underlying causes. Government repression would become more commonplace, and "people will increasingly doubt whether life is worth living." By 1976 this scenario seemed frighteningly accurate.

As the first scenario proceeds, the decade of the 1980s would feature the "politics of desperation." Governments would realize their helplessness in the face of human problems, but the elites who ran them would turn more and more to repression to maintain their privileges. The suffering people of the world would become increasingly hostile toward the fortunate few living in islands of affluence. LDCs might develop nuclear or biological warfare capability in attempts to force redistribution of resources on the ODCs. Realignments of power among ODCs and token concessions to the LDCs would be inadequate to halt this drive, so ODCs might recolonize some LDCs in order to enforce "peace" and maintain the world trade system that favored them. The United States would find itself powerless to intercede, even if it were so inclined.

"The politics of catastrophe" would take over in the 1990s. In that decade an immense disaster, ecological or thermonuclear, would overtake humanity. The reorganization (if any) of the world after the catastrophe would depend on the exact form of the disaster and who survived. The reorganization would most likely be world-oriented rather than nation-state-oriented. If, by chance, the outmoded world-order system were not irremediably damaged in the 1990s, then it certainly would be in the twenty-first century, which Falk labeled the "era of annihilation."

Falk's second scenario is more optimistic. It envisions a rapid recognition that the world system based on sovereign states cannot possibly deal effectively with the problems of the endangered planet. In this scenario, the 1970s would be the "decade of awareness," in which people in general faced squarely the nature of the emergency that engulfs human society. (By 1976, although such awareness had actually grown, it was still restricted to a miniscule portion of the world population.)

The 1980s would be the "decade of mobilization," in which awareness would be converted into action that would move people away from accepting the primacy of the sovereign state. A new worldwide political movement, based on transnational thinking, would overwhelm the conservative forces dedicated to maintaining the status quo.

The 1990s would be the "decade of transformation," in which humanity moved in the direction of stability in both population and economic systems: "A new political man will emerge from such a climate of opinion and change. The planet will be governed as a system that needs to guard against relapse and reversion, and regards the diversities within itself as a source of vitality and vigor." That decade would lead to the twenty-first century as the "era of world harmony"—based on ecological humanism and human beings living in harmony with nature.

Obviously, we find Falk's first scenario more probable, and events of the 1970s have tended more in that direction. His second one seems wildly optimistic, especially in light of the growth-potential built into the age structure of the human population, the rapidly rising constraints on that growth, and the potential for conflict they engender. But it surely is a noble target at which to aim!

uses of outer space and Antarctica. More recently, there have been extensive negotiations on a treaty to control the use of oceans.

Law of the Sea. What has been described as "the greatest international conference ever held"[126] met in Caracas in summer 1974 to begin work on a treaty dealing with the control of the oceans. The second session of the third United Nations Conference on the Law of the Sea (UNCLOS)[127] reached no final agreements, but in its tortuous proceedings several trends could be discerned. The emphasis was on dividing up the pie—on how to allocate rights to exploit the oceans rather than how to protect their vital functioning in the ecosystems of Earth. The less developed nations were anxious to "augment their meager natural resources with none of the unpleasant connotations of economic aid."[128] The overdeveloped countries, on the other hand, were primarily trying to retain as much as possible of their hegemony over the seas (which they, far more than the LDCs, have the ability to exploit).

A dominant trend has been toward establishing a 200-mile economic zone, which would effectively balkanize most of the oceans' known wealth. One view is that this would lead to having humanity's common heritage decimated piecemeal as individual nations exercised dominion over all living and nonliving resources within their zones. About the only good thing that can be said about the 200-mile zone is that its establishment might lead eventually to more rational use of those resources since their individual ownership by nations would at least tend to avoid the problems involved in multilateral exploitation of a commons.

Other topics discussed in detail at the ongoing conference have been rights of passage through straits, the rights of landlocked nations to a share of oceanic resources, the establishment of an international authority for the mining of seabed minerals outside the economic zones, the responsibility of nations to control pollution originating from their shores and to protect the marine environment, and the establishment of means of settling disputes and enforcing agreements.

A third eight-week session of UNCLOS in Geneva in May 1975 produced a draft treaty, which was not voted on by the participating nations but was instead considered the basis for further negotiation.[129] The draft extended the territorial waters of all nations to 12 miles from shore, provided for a 200-mile economic zone, specified means to control polluting activities, and encouraged the transfer of technology from rich to poor nations. The most controversial provision was for an International Seabed Authority, controlled de facto by the LDCs (who would be a majority in the agency), that would regulate deep-sea mining. The United States has held out for "private initiative" to share in managing the seabed resource.

Further negotiations are scheduled for 1977. In part, their success will depend on what unilateral actions are taken by nations in the meantime. The United States, for example, has extended its jurisdiction over fisheries up to 200 miles from shore, which conforms with the draft treaty. Several other countries, including Mexico and Canada, have followed suit. But legislation being considered by Congress on deep-sea mining does not conform to the draft treaty. This places U.S. negotiators, who have tried to dissuade other nations from taking unilateral action, in an awkward position. If Congress passes such legislation, it could have a less than salubrious effect on future negotiations—especially if American firms are permitted to begin deep-sea mining before the treaty is finally passed and ratified. On the other hand, these unilateral actions may be pushing negotiators to examine other alternatives. By 1977, Elizabeth Mann-Borgese was envisioning a third possibility for the Seabed Authority as "a comprehensive and flexible system of joint ventures, acceptable to states and companies under the control of the [A]uthority and for the benefit of all countries, especially the poorer ones. . . ."[129a]

[126]Elizabeth Mann Borgese, Report from Caracas, the law of the sea, *Center Magazine,* November/December, 1974.

[127]The first session in New York in 1973 dealt only with procedures; the first and second conferences in 1958 and 1960 had accomplished little but reveal the complexities of the problems and the diverse positions of states and blocs (see Edward Wenk, Jr., *The politics of the ocean,* chapter 6).

[128]C. R. Pinto of Sri Lanka, quoted in *Time,* July 29, 1974. It has been suggested that "The uses of international commons should be taxed for the benefit of the poorest strata of the poor countries" (Barbara Ward, The Cocoyoc Declaration), but there is thus far little sign that this will occur.

[129]Material in this paragraph is based primarily on Deborah Shapley, Now, a draft sea law treaty: But what comes after?

[129a]Quoted in Claiborne Pell, The most complex treaty ever negotiated in history, *World Issues,* vol II, no. 1 (February/March), 1977.

The complexity and comprehensiveness of the treaty account for the lengthiness of the negotiations. But, unfortunately, even a definitive treaty may fail to provide the kind of apparatus required to administer, conserve, and distribute the resources of the seas in a way that is equitable and that fully protects the vitally important ecosystems of the oceans, just because an exploitative view of the environment continues to dominate all such discussions.

U.N. Environment Program. The exploitative view of the environment first surfaced explicitly at the international level at the United Nations Conference on the Human Environment at Stockholm in 1972. That gathering featured platitudes from the ODCs, who are busily engaged in looting the planet and destroying its ecological systems, and demands from the LDCs that they get a piece of the action. One could only take heart that the world's nations even took the condition of the environment seriously enough to attend such a conference. That they did was a tribute to the brilliance, persuasiveness, and persistance of one man, Canadian businessman Maurice Strong, secretary general of the conference.

Strong became the first executive director of the United Nations Environment Program (UNEP), the major positive result of the Stockholm conference. UNEP was given only a small budget, and its headquarters was tucked away in Nairobi, perhaps in the hope that it would not make waves. Under Strong's leadership, it nevertheless began to serve several vital functions. For instance, it has established the Earth Watch monitoring system to serve as an international clearinghouse for environmental information. Earth Watch is explicitly designed also to help bridge the gap between scientists and technologists on one hand and political decision-makers on the other.[130] The kinds of information to be collected include an international register of toxic chemicals, which list properties of those chemicals, their uses, their effects, and their known or inferred pathways in the environment.

UNEP's very location in Nairobi (the first such United Nations agency headquartered in an LDC) has resulted in its first major contribution—an enormous and growing interest and concern in poor nations about environmental problems.[131] This concern was already well established in some areas among the people[132] but had been notably absent in most LDC governments.

Under Strong's leadership a list of high-priority areas was established at UNEP: (1) human settlement, health, habitat, and well-being; (2) land, water, and desertification; (3) trade, economics, technology, and the transfer of technology; (4) oceans; (5) conservation of nature, wildlife, and genetic resources; (6) energy.

A program has been started in each area, and by early 1975 more than 200 projects had been initiated, projects that according to Strong were designed "to create a leverage to move the programme towards our priorities."[133] Unfortunately for UNEP, Maurice Strong left the agency in 1975; whether the acorn of UNEP will ever grow into the great oak of an international environmental protection organization, so desperately needed, will depend on many things—not least of which will be the quality of its leadership.

Toward a Planetary Regime

International attempts to tackle global problems—or at least to start a dialogue among nations—have proliferated in recent years. Besides the UNCTAD, Law of the Sea, and Environmental conferences, the United Nations has sponsored World Population and World Food conferences (discussed earlier) in 1974, a conference on the Status of Women in 1975, the Habitat Conference of 1976 (dealing with the problems of cities), and a conference on Water Resources in 1977. A Conference on Science and Technology is scheduled for 1978, and it is expected to create a new agency for World Science and Technology Development. The agency's mission will be to facilitate the transfer of needed technologies to LDCs and to foster development of indigenous scientific and technological education and research in those countries.[134]

[130]Maurice Strong, A global imperative for the environment.

[131]Roger Lewin, Environment in a developing world; Jon Sigurdson, Resources and environment in China; Conor Reilly, Environmental action in Zambia.

[132]For example, see Amil Agarwal, Ghandi's ghost saves the Himalayan trees.

[133]Lewin, Environment in a developing world, p. 632.

[134]Salam, Ideals and realities.

Superficially, it usually appears that such conferences do little more than highlight the political differences between rich and poor countries, but in fact they can lead to constructive action on the problems discussed. Because of the diversity of interests and viewpoints of individual nations, and because of the inequities of the world economy, it seems to take an unconscionably long time to reach a consensus on dealing with each problem. But an important step often is to obtain agreement that *a problem exists,* first of all, and, second, that international action is appropriate and necessary. Each of the conferences named has been the culmination of this process; but what counts for the future is whether agreement can be reached on solutions to the problems and whether controls can be established before it is too late.

Regulation of one vital global commons has not yet been seriously discussed—that commons is the atmosphere. Even more than the resources of the oceans, the atmosphere is shared by all human beings—and other organisms as well. It is crucial to preserve the atmosphere's quality and the stability of global climate.[135] But that these are now threatened and should be protected by international agreement is only beginning to be recognized in a few quarters.

Should a Law of the Sea be successfully established, it could serve as a model for a future Law of the Atmosphere to regulate the use of airspace, to monitor climate change, and to control atmospheric pollution. Perhaps those agencies, combined with UNEP and the United Nations population agencies, might eventually be developed into a Planetary Regime—sort of an international superagency for population, resources, and environment. Such a comprehensive Planetary Regime could control the development, administration, conservation, and distribution of *all* natural resources, renewable or nonrenewable, at least insofar as international implications exist. Thus, the Regime could have the power to control pollution not only in the atmosphere and the oceans, but also in such freshwater bodies as rivers and lakes that cross international boundaries or that discharge into the oceans. The Regime might also be a logical central agency for regulating all international trade, perhaps including assistance from DCs to LDCs, and including all food on the international market.

[135] S. H. Schneider and L. E. Mesirow, *The genesis strategy.*

The Planetary Regime might be given responsibility for determining the optimum population for the world and for each region and for arbitrating various countries' shares within their regional limits. Control of population size might remain the responsibility of each government, but the Regime should have some power to enforce the agreed limits. As with the Law of the Sea and other international agreements, all agreements for regulating population sizes, resource development, and pollution should be subject to revision and modification in accordance with changing conditions.

The Planetary Regime might have the advantage over earlier proposed world government schemes in not being primarily political in its emphasis—even though politics would inevitably be a part of all discussions, implicitly or explicitly. Since most of the areas the Regime would control are not now being regulated or controlled by nations or anyone else, establishment of the Regime would involve far less surrendering of national power. Nevertheless, it might function powerfully to suppress international conflict simply because the interrelated global resource-environment structure would not permit such an outdated luxury.

What the Human Community Can Do

Humanity has reached a critical point in its history. Either the fissioning of societies into two distinct groups—rich and poor—will proceed, leading inevitably to conflict and possibly to economic collapse of some regions, at least; or serious efforts will be made to bring the two groups closer together. With regard to the latter course, as we have discussed at some length, there are plenty of ideas on how to go about it. The main obstacles are, as usual, social, political, and economic. Too few people in ODCs are convinced of the absolute necessity of reducing their consumption of material and environmental resources—of de-development. Too few people in all countries appreciate the environmental and resource constraints within which society must operate. And too many people with power oppose changing the present course because, for the time being, they are profiting from the status quo. And it may not be possible to change the course of human society until those powerful people are fully convinced that their benefits will vanish unless they do.

Assuming that the formidable obstacles can nevertheless be overcome and the two separate "worlds" started on the appropriate paths—the rich world begins to de-develop, and the poor world undertakes grass-roots development—full cooperation between the two groups will be required to make it work. Biologist Charles Birch, paraphrasing Garrett Hardin, described such cooperation as "mutual concern mutually agreed upon."[136] The LDCs cannot succeed without substantial assistance from ODCs, and the ODCs will continue to need commodities and resources from LDCs to maintain their industrial structures, even if those structures are made vastly more efficient and are partially transferred to LDCs. The most crucial decades are those just ahead, in which there must be a transition to a size-controlled (eventually declining) population, an internationally regulated Planetary Regime for the global commons, and something resembling the "dynamic equilibrium economy" espoused by Herman Daly and Emile Benoit.

Certain guiding principles for national behavior have been proposed by many individuals as being essential to the establishment of a genuine world community in which such cooperative measures could be carried out. As outlined by United States Assistant Secretary of State John Richardson, Jr., a consensus is emerging:

1. Governments ought to promote the general welfare of those they govern, not merely enlarge their own and the nation's power;
2. Starvation anywhere is unacceptable;
3. Torture by governments anywhere is unacceptable;
4. The use of nuclear and biological weapons is unacceptable; and
5. Political, cultural, and ideological diversity—within some limits—ought to be tolerated.[138]

Managing the transition to what some people have called a sustainable world[139] without a major catastrophe of some kind (war, mass famine, pandemic, ecological disaster, or economic collapse), will require far more than good luck. It will require careful planning and hedging against such unpredictable eventualities: Schneider and Mesirow's "Genesis strategy." (The Genesis strategy is based on the biblical story in which Joseph warned the pharaoh of Egypt that seven fat years would be followed by seven lean years, and he advised the pharaoh to store up grain during the fat years to tide the population over when famine came.) Thus, high priorities must be given by the international community to building up food reserves, to preventing and repairing major environmental damage, to protecting the ocean and atmospheric commons, to preventing high casualties from natural disasters (earthquakes, volcanic explosions, hurricanes, and such), to protecting populations against disease, to avoiding conflict between nations, and to that essential concomitant of all of these—population control. There is movement toward these precautionary measures, but so far the movement is dishearteningly slow.

Humanity cannot afford to muddle through the rest of the twentieth century; the risks are too great, and the stakes are too high. This may be the last opportunity to choose our own and our descendants' destiny. Failing to choose or making the wrong choices may lead to catastrophe. But it must never be forgotten that the right choices could lead to a much better world.

[136]*Confronting the future,* p. 348.

[138]Preparing for a human community, Department of State News Release, May 18, 1976.

[139]Birch, *Confronting the future;* Dennis Pirages, *A sustainable society: Social and political implications.*

Recommended for Further Reading

Barnet, R. J. and R. E. Müller. 1974. *Global reach: The power of the multinational corporations.* Simon & Schuster, New York. A scathing indictment.

Birch, Charles. 1975. *Confronting the future.* Penguin, Harmondsworth, UK. A lively, hopeful book on the human predicament by a distinguished Australian population biologist.

Brown, Lester R. 1974. *In the human interest.* Norton, New York. An excellent overview of the world dilemma, including some useful proposals for action.

Choucri, N., and R. C. North. 1975. *Nations in conflict: National growth and international violence.* W. H. Freeman and Company, San Francisco. A quantitative approach to the causes of war—including population growth.

Ehrlich, Paul R., and R. L. Harriman. 1971. *How to be a survivor: A plan to save Spaceship Earth.* Ballantine, New York. A concise description of a strategy that might get humanity through the crisis now developing.

Frank, Jerome D. 1967. *Sanity and survival.* Random House, New York. The psychology of war and peace. Excellent.

Jervis, Robert. 1976. *Perception and misperception in international politics.* Princeton University Press, Princeton, New Jersey. Superb analysis of how decision-makers' perceptions of their environments shape policy, with numerous instructive examples. Jervis shows that perceptions diverge systematically from reality and indicates ways that being alert to perceptions and misperceptions can enhance understanding of international relations. An extremely important book.

Kocher, James E. 1973. *Rural development, income distribution, and fertility decline.* Population Council, New York, occasional paper. Very important paper on development, showing advantages of grass-roots development that involves and benefits an entire population, not just an urban elite.

Laslo, Ervin (project coordinator). 1977. *Goals for mankind: A report to the Club of Rome on the new horizons of global community.* Dutton, New York. An atlas of contemporary goals, both national and transnational. A most useful compendium for those who would like to set new goals for humanity.

Lovins, Amory. 1977. *Soft energy paths: Toward a durable peace.* Ballinger, Cambridge, Mass. Eloquent and innovative discussion of alternative energy futures, emphasizing appropriate technology and the avoidance of nuclear proliferation.

Myrdal, Gunnar. 1970. *The challenge of world poverty: A world anti-poverty program in outline.* Pantheon, New York. Based on *Asian drama,* this is much shorter but goes beyond it. A "must" for those interested in the problems of development.

Paddock, W., and E. Paddock. 1973. *We don't know how: An independent audit of what they call success in foreign assistance.* Iowa State University Press, Ames. A critique that emphasizes, among other things, the failure of headquarters bureaucracies to learn in response to experience in the field.

Schneider, S. H., and L. E. Mesirow. 1976. *The Genesis strategy.* Plenum, New York. On the human predicament with an emphasis on the role of climate. This book also contains some shrewd and sensible suggestions for avoiding global disaster, at the heart of which is the Genesis strategy itself.

Schumacher, E. F. 1973. *Small is beautiful: Economics as if people mattered.* Harper and Row, New York. Perhaps the most important economic book of the 1970s, with ideas especially pertinent to LDC development.

York, Herbert F. 1970. *Race to oblivion: A participant's view of the arms race.* Simon & Schuster, New York. Merciless examination of the military-industrial complex and its "ideas." From an impeccable source.

Additional References

Adelman, M. A. 1972. *The world petroleum market.* Johns Hopkins Press, Baltimore. On the international history and politics of oil.

———; R. E. Hall; K. F. Hansen; J. H. Holloman; H. D. Jacoby; P. L. Joskow; P. W. MacAvoy; H. P. Meissner; D. C. White; and M. B. Zimmerman. 1974. The U.S. and the world oil market. *Technology Review,* vol. 76, no. 6, pp. 47–52.

Agarwal, Anil. 1975. Gandhi's ghost saves the Himalayan trees. *New Scientist,* August 14, pp. 386–387. Describes an Indian peasant movement to keep the timber industry from destroying forests.

Aron, Raymond. 1957. *On war.* Norton, New York. A European view of the influence on international relations of nuclear armaments and planetary politics.

Barber Associates, Inc. 1975. *LDC nuclear power prospects, 1975–1990: Commercial, economic, and security implications.* ERDA-52. National Technical Information Service, Springfield, Va. An important and detailed analysis, indicating that the potential usefulness of nuclear power in LDCs has been widely overestimated.

Barnaby, Frank. 1974. The Ford-Brezhnev agreement assessed. *New Scientist,* December 5, pp. 734–736. Information on Vladivostok SALT negotiation.

———. 1975. The spread of the capability to do violence: An introduction to environmental warfare. *Ambio,* vol. 4, pp. 178–185. An overview. Contains useful tables of weapons.

———. 1976. Changing nuclear myths. *New Scientist,* January 15. Discusses consequences of efforts to achieve first-strike capability.

———. 1976. World armament and disarmament. *Bulletin of the Atomic Scientists,* June, pp. 25–32. Up-to-date information on the arms race.

Barnet, R. J., and R. D. Falk, eds. 1965. *Security in disarmament.* Princeton University Press, N.J. A collection of essays dealing with such subjects as systems of inspection, violations of arms-control agreements, and supernational versus international models for disarmament.

Becker, Benjamin M. 1975. The United Nations after 30 years. *Bulletin of the Atomic Scientists,* November, pp. 31–35. An interesting overview.

Beitz, C. R., and T. Herman, eds. 1973. *Peace and war.* W. H. Freeman and Company, San Francisco. A broad sampling of thirty articles from authors as diverse as Thomas Schelling, who writes on the "art of coercion, of intimidation and deterrence," and Mohandas Gandhi.

Berg, Alan. 1973. *The nutrition factor: Its role in national development.* The Brookings Institute, Washington, D.C. On the relevance of nutrition to development policies in LDCs.

Berry, R. Stephen. 1975. Crises of resource scarcity. *Bulletin of the Atomic Scientists,* January, pp. 31–36. A chemist looks at the changing international resource picture and, among other things, recommends utilizing a multiplicity of energy technologies to "hedge our bets."

Betts, R. J. 1977. Paranoids, pygmies, pariahs, and nonproliferation. *Foreign Policy,* no. 26 (Spring), pp. 157–183. A pithy, cogent argument to the effect that, in proliferation, "there are no simple solutions that are feasible, no feasible solutions that are simple, and no solutions at all that are applicable across the board." We disagree only insofar as we believe some simple, if drastic approaches are at least worth trying.

Blair, John M. 1976. *The control of oil.* Pantheon, New York. Cogent, well documented case against the concentration of economic and political power wielded by the "seven sisters" of the international oil business—Exxon, Mobil, Standard of California, Texaco, Gulf, Royal Dutch Shell, and British Petroleum.

Boot, J. C. G. 1974. *Common globe or global commons: Population regulation and income distribution.* Marcel Dekker, New York. A provocative and wide-ranging discussion of approaches to global management of population size and the distribution of income.

Boulding, Kenneth E. 1962. *Conflict and defense.* Harper and Row, New York. A pioneering attempt to create a general theory of conflict.

Brookings Institution. 1975. *Energy and U.S. foreign policy.* Ballinger, Cambridge, Mass. On the history and politics of oil.

Brown, Harrison. 1975. Population growth and affluence: The fissioning of human society. *Quarterly Journal of Economics,* vol. 84, pp. 236–246. Gives statistics on evolution of rich-poor division.

Brown, Lester R. 1972. *World without borders.* Random House, New York. Generally excellent treatment on international aspects of the planetary ecological crisis; it is perhaps too sanguine about the role of multinational corporations. The emphasis is on food.

———. 1975. The politics and responsibility of the North American breadbasket. Worldwatch Institute, Washington, D.C., paper 2. An excellent summary of the world food situation, outlook, and policy implications.

——— and E. P. Eckholm. 1975. Next steps toward global food security. In *The U.S. and world development: Agenda for action 1975,* J. W. Howe, ed. Good discussion based on 1974 World Food Conference.

———; P. L. McGrath; and B. Stokes. 1976. Twenty-two dimensions of the population problem. Worldwatch Institute, Washington, D.C., Paper 5. A concise overview.

Bulletin of the Atomic Scientists. 1975. The Cocoyoc declaration. March, pp. 6–10. A call for reform of the international economic order by an international group of natural and social scientists.

Cahn, Anne. 1975. Have arms, will sell. *Bulletin of the Atomic Scientists,* April, pp. 10–12. Describes fierce competition among arms-suppliers to sell ever-more-sophisticated weapons to those who don't need them.

Calder, Nigel, ed. 1968. *Unless peace comes.* Viking, New York. A description of future weapons systems.

Carter, L. J. 1975. Strategic arms limitation (II): "leveling up" to symmetry. *Science,* vol. 187, pp. 627–632, February 21. Details on SALT talks.

Choucri, Nazli. 1972. Population, resources and technology: Political implications of the environmental crisis. *International Organization,* vol. 26, pp. 175–212. A key discussion by a political scientist.

Clarice, Robin. 1972. *The science of war and peace,* McGraw-Hill, New York. Contains much useful information but is now partly out of date.

Cleveland, Harlan. 1975. Our coming foreign policy crisis. *Saturday Review,* September 6. An excellent, thought-provoking article, marred only by a nonsensical statement about human ability to provide for a growing population.

Coale, A. J. 1970. Man and his environment. *Science,* vol. 170, pp. 132–136 (October 9). The traditional DC view of international trade is expressed here.

——— and E. M. Hoover. 1958. *Population growth and economic development in low-income countries.* Princeton University Press, N.J. A pioneering work.

Coombs, P. H.; A. Pearse; J. Hutchinson; L. T. Khoi; T. P. Llaurado; R. Colin; and P. Freire. 1971. Seven articles on education in LDCs in *Ceres,* vol. 4, no. 3, pp. 23–51.

Culbertson, John M. 1971. *Economic development: An ecological approach.* Knopf, New York. Outlines a theory of economic development that, to quote the author, "indicates that the pessimistic warnings that present day civilization may come to an early end merit serious consideration. It also explains why the optimistic theories of economic development are believed, although they are false—or because they are false."

Daetz, Douglas. 1968. Energy utilization and aid effectiveness in non-mechanized agriculture: A computer simulation of a socioeconomic system. University of California, Berkeley, Ph.D. dissertation.

Darwin, C. G. 1952. *The next million years.* Hart-Davis, London. A prophetic book.

Day, Samuel H. 1975. Let's put the troops to work. *Bulletin of the Atomic Scientists,* April, pp. 4–5. An interesting suggestion for peaceful uses of the military.

De Young, Karen. 1975. Selling the Sahel. *Washington Monthly,* September, pp. 31–40. Attacks AID motives in pushing Sahel relief.

Development Dialogue. A biannual journal on development issues published by the Dag Hammerskjöld Foundation, Ovre Slottsgatan 2, S-752 20, Uppsala, Sweden. Useful for anyone concerned with international development problems.

Djerassi, Carl. 1976. A modest proposal for increased north-south interaction among scientists. *Bulletin of the Atomic Scientists,* February, pp. 56–60. Suggests sponsoring of DC scientists by professional organizations for involvement with research groups funded within LDCs by the LDCs.

Eckholm, E. P. 1976. *Losing ground: Environmental stress and world food prospects.* Norton, New York. On the environmental problems attending efforts to raise food production.

Edwards, E. O., ed. 1974. *Employment in developing nations.* Columbia, New York. A diverse group of rather technical papers on everything from unemployment statistics to appropriate technologies.

Ehrlich, Paul R., and Anne H. Ehrlich. 1970. *Population, resources, environment: Issues in human ecology.* W. H. Freeman and Company, San Francisco. Source of terms *de-development* and *semidevelopment.*

———. 1974. *The end of affluence.* Ballantine, New York. Discusses various aspects of the world predicament, especially economics and resource scarcity.

Elliott, Charles. 1975. *Patterns of poverty in the Third World.* Praeger, New York. A detailed study of how poverty is perpetuated and wealth consolidated in world economics.

Enke, Stephen. 1969. Birth control for economic development. *Science,* vol. 164. pp. 798–802 (May 16).

Epstein, William. 1975. The proliferation of nuclear weapons. *Scientific American,* April, pp. 18–33. Details the spread of these weapons and indicates which nations are likely to be the next to go nuclear.

———. 1975. Nuclear-free zones. *Scientific American,* November, pp. 25–35. A possibly overoptimistic evaluation of the role such zones could play in preventing the spread of nuclear weapons.

———. 1976. *The last chance: Nuclear proliferation and arms control.* Free Press, New York. History, present situation and prospects analyzed—a good overview.

Erb, G. F. 1974. The developing countries in the Tokyo round. In *The U.S. and the developing world.* Praeger, New York, pp. 89–90. Describes how multinational corporations make giving trade preferences to LDCs difficult.

———. 1975. Trade initiatives and resource bargaining. In *The U.S. and world development: Agenda for action 1975.* J. W. Howe, ed., pp. 87–102. Focus is on commodity policy.

Falk, Richard A. 1971. *This endangered planet.* Random House, New York. A thought-provoking view of the global crisis.

———. 1975. *A study of future worlds.* Free Press, New York. Proposes a system of global institutions to solve global problems but recognizes the vast impediments to implementation. By a distinguished international lawyer.

——— and S. H. Mendlovitz, eds. 1973. *Regional politics and world order.* W. H. Freeman and Co., San Francisco. A series of basic papers on regionalism, covering topics such as the UN regional economic commissions and various theories of the relationships of power blocs to world order.

Farvar, M. T., and J. P. Milton, eds. 1972. *The careless technology.* Natural History Press, Garden City, N.Y. International aspects of environmental problems.

Federation of American Scientists (FAS). 1975. How one decision maker triggered the end of the world. *F.A.S. Public Interest Report,* vol. 28, no. 9 (November), Washington, D.C. Scenario on how easily first use of nuclear weapons could lead to Armageddon.

Feld, Bernard T. 1974. Doves of the world unite! *New Scientist,* December 26. Contains a pessimistic prediction on the probability of nuclear war and accounts of arms agreements.

———. 1976. The consequences of nuclear war. *Bulletin of the Atomic Scientists,* June. At best, civilization would be crippled; at worst, annihilated. Actually an optimistic evaluation since some important ecological consequences are not included.

Finney, J. W. 1975. Arms sales, a real growth industry. New York *Times,* January 26. An update on George Thayer, *The war business.*

Fitzgerald, H. Ernest. 1972. *The high priests of waste.* Norton, New York. Why the arms race is incredibly expensive in addition to being incredibly dangerous.

Fox, R. W.; G. G. Kelleher; and C. B. Kerr. 1976. *Ranger uranium environmental inquiry: First report.* Australian Government Printing Office, Canberra. A review of the implications of the widespread use of nuclear power, carried out to assist the Australian government in devising a policy on the use of its uranium resources. Highlights proliferation risks and recommends against uranium sales to countries not party to the NPT.

Flowers, Sir Brian, Chairman. 1976. *Nuclear power and the environment.* Sixth report of the Royal Commission on Environmental Pollution. Her Majesty's Stationery Office, London. Sober and even-handed review of the potentials and risks associated with the use of nuclear power in the United Kingdom. Concludes that "a major commitment to fission power and a plutonium economy should be postponed as long as possible."

Franda, M. F. 1974. India and the energy crunch. *Fieldstaff Reports.* Hanover, N.H. Deals with the problems created in India and other LDCs by increased energy costs.

Frank, C. R., Jr., and M. Baird. 1975. Foreign aid: Its speckled past and future prospects. *International Organization,* vol. 29, no. 1, pp. 133–167.

Frank, Jerome D. 1976. Psychological aspects of the nuclear arms race. *Bulletin of the Atomic Scientists,* April, pp. 22–24. Brief summary paper, claims that habit and unwillingness to look far ahead prevent politicians from dealing with nuclear weapons as a unique threat. Frank suggests limited (symbolic) unilateral disarmament by United States as a way of starting toward general nuclear disarmament.

Gall, Norman. 1976. Atoms for Brazil, danger for all. *Bulletin of the Atomic Scientists,* June. Turning Brazil into a nuclear power constitutes an important step toward nuclear war.

Garner, Fradley. 1975. The Mediterranean lives. *Environment,* vol. 17, no. 3, pp. 40–41. An overview of the pollution problems of the Mediterranean.

Glacken, James J. 1976. The dangerous drift in uranium enrichment. *Bulletin of the Atomic Scientists,* February, pp. 22–29. Describes why "the major powers no longer enjoy a monopoly in making weapons-grade material."

Goldblat, Jozef. 1975. The prohibition of environmental warfare. *Ambio,* vol. 4, pp. 186–190. United States-Soviet draft agreement de-

Grant, James P. 1973. Development: The end of trickle-down? *Foreign Policy,* no. 12 (Fall). A good source contrasting the effects of two-tiered development and grass-roots development, especially on population growth.

———. 1975. The OPEC nations: Partners or competitors? In *The U.S. and world development: Agenda for action 1975,* J. W. Howe, ed., pp. 135–148. Hopes DCs and OPEC will find common goals.

———and R. H. Johnson. 1975. Systems overloads and world transformations. In *The U.S. and World Development; Agenda for action 1975,* J. W. Howe, ed., pp. 148–156. Considers problem less one of physical limits than of institutional breakdowns.

Greene, Philip. 1968. *Deadly logic.* Schocken, New York. An analysis of deterrence theory—a critically important work.

Green, Wade. 1975. Triage. *New York Times Magazine,* January 5, pp. 9 ff. On allocating limited food aid resources.

Greene, Felix. 1971. *The enemy: What every American should know about imperialism.* Random House, New York. A classical Marxist analysis of the role of the West in the world of today and yesterday. Read this to know what intelligent critics of the capitalist system say, based on a world view entirely different from that of the average American. Note his acceptance of the labor theory of value. Some of the "facts" cited are highly questionable.

Gurney, Ramsdell. 1975. Arms and the men. *Bulletin of the Atomic Scientists,* December, pp. 23–43. A review of disarmament negotiations since World War II.

Haines, W. W. 1974. Dark days in Ankara. *Environment,* vol. 16, no. 8, pp. 6–13. Extreme air pollution in an LDC city where "rising affluence and increased industrialization will only worsen the already intolerable situation."

Hammond, Allen L. 1976. Nuclear proliferation (I): warnings from the arms control community. *Science,* vol. 193, pp. 126–130 (July 9). Concise discussion of the outlook for reactor related proliferation of nuclear weapons, with emphasis on the role of reprocessing fuel for plutonium recycle.

Hammond, G. S., and W. M. Todd. 1975. Technical assistance and foreign policy. *Science,* vol. 184, pp. 1057–1059 (September 26). Discusses, among other things, joint United States-LDC programs. (See Carl Djerassi, A modest proposal for increased north-south interaction among scientists.)

Hansen, Roger D. 1975. A "new international economic order"? An outline for a constructive U.S. response. Overseas Development Council, paper 19. Washington, D.C. Details LDC demands and suggests how they should be met.

———. 1975. The emerging challenge: Global distribution of income and economic opportunity. In *The U.S. and world development: Agenda for action 1975,* J. W. Howe, ed., pp. 157–187. A general discussion of poverty and redistribution.

———. 1975. U.S.-Latin American economic policy: Bilateral, regional or global? Overseas Development Council, Washington, D.C., paper 18. Argues for a multilateral approach with a tilt toward Latin America, preserving some degree of special relationship. Contains useful economic summary data.

Hardin, Garrett. 1968. The tragedy of the commons. *Science,* vol. 162, pp. 1243–1248 (13 December). A key paper for thinking about global problems.

———. 1974. Living in a lifeboat. *BioScience,* October, pp. 561–568. Highly controversial article on the ethics of aid. Hardin's brilliant prose once again has served as the focus for an extensive debate.

Harrison, Paul. 1976. Basic health delivery in the Third World. *New Scientist,* February 17, 1977, pp. 411–413. On some "barefoot doctor" experiments in Latin America.

Harvey, Robert. 1977. Brazil: The next nuclear power? *Atlas World Press Review,* March. Good overview of Brazil, including its disastrous attempts to develop Amazonia, its political and economic situation and growing military power.

Hedberg, Hollis D. 1976. Ocean boundaries and petroleum resources. *Science,* vol. 191, pp. 1009–1018. Discusses what different undersea boundaries would mean to United States. Argues for natural "base of slope" boundary rather than artificial 200-mile limit.

Heilbroner, R. L. 1959. *The future as history.* Harper and Row, New York. A classic, recommended.

———. 1974. *An inquiry into the human prospect.* Norton, New York. A somewhat pessimistic exploration of humanity's likely future. Excellent.

Hersh, Seymour M. 1969. *Chemical and biological warfare.* Doubleday, Garden City, N.Y.

Hertzog, Arthur. 1965. *The war-peace establishment.* Harper and Row, New York. An introduction to the views of those researchers concerned with our military-foreign policy stance.

Hillaby, John. 1975. Genocide in Paraguay. *New Scientist,* January 16. Describes attempts to destroy Indians.

Hoagland, Hudson. 1969. Technology, adaptation and evolution. *Bulletin of the Atomic Scientists,* January, pp. 27–30. A well-known biologist looks at, among other things, war and overpopulation.

Holdren, John P. 1975. Energy and prosperity: Some elements of a global perspective. *Bulletin of Atomic Scientists,* vol. 30, no. 1, pp. 26–28. A scenario illustrating possibilities attendant upon redistributing energy use between rich and poor countries.

——— and Paul R. Ehrlich, eds. 1971. *Global ecology: Readings toward a rational strategy for man.* Harcourt Brace Jovanovich, New York. Reprints Hardin's "Tragedy of the Commons" and Illich's "Outwitting the 'Developed' Countries."

Hollick, A. L., and R. E. Osgood. 1974. *New era of ocean politics.* Johns Hopkins Press, Baltimore. Discusses issues relating to international ocean regimes. Interesting section on United States security interests.

Holmberg, Bo. 1975. Biological aspects of chemical and biological weapons, *Ambio,* vol. 4, pp. 211–215. An overview concentrating mostly on chemical weapons.

Holsti, P. R., and R. C. North. 1966. Comparative data from content analysis: Perceptions of hostility and economic variables in the 1914 crisis. In *Comparing nations,* R. L. Merritt and S. Rokkan, eds. Yale University Press, New Haven, pp. 169–190. Shows value of "perceptions" abstracted from newspapers and other documents in the analysis of international conflict.

Howe, James W., ed. 1975. *The U.S. and world development: Agenda for action 1975.* Praeger, New York. A timely and useful compendium on development problems. Some useful tables in the back.

——— and J. W. Sewell. 1975. Triage and other challenges to helping the poor countries develop. In *The U.S. and world development: Agenda for action 1975,* J. W. Howe, ed., pp. 55–71. Claims, "the evidence of human *progress* has been lost from sight altogether."

Huisken, Ronald. 1975. The consumption of raw materials for military purposes. *Ambio,* vol. 4, pp. 229–233. Useful data on this colossal waste of Earth's resources.

Ignotus, Miles. 1975. Seizing Arab oil. *Harpers,* March, pp. 54–62. This article, written under a pseudonym by a "professor and defense consultant with intimate links to high level U.S. policy-makers" was widely viewed as an administration trial balloon. See also Robert W. Tucker, Oil: The issue of American intervention.

Illich, Ivan. 1969. Outwitting the "developed" countries. *New York Review of Books,* November 6. On some unconventional development strategies. Illich's recommendations are in the same spirit as E. F. Schumacher's in *Small is beautiful.*

———. 1970. *Celebration of awareness.* Doubleday, Garden City, N.Y. Brilliant book by one of today's most imaginative thinkers. See especially Chapter 10, "Sexual Power and Political Potency," in which Illich discusses the population situation in Latin America.

International Atomic Energy Agency (IAEA). 1976. *A short history of nonproliferation.* IAEA, Vienna. Very useful summary of the origins of the Nonproliferation Treaty and its implementation. Includes full text of the treaty and list of signers and nonsigners as of February 1976.

Jacoby, Neil H. 1969. The progress of peoples. *Center Occasional Papers,* vol. 2, no. 4. Center for the Study of Democratic Institutions, Santa Barbara, Calif. An interesting discussion of the problems of development.

Jahoda, J. C., and D. L. O'Hearn. 1975. The reluctant Amazon basin. *Environment,* October. Summarizes problems of development.

Jalée, Pierre. 1968. *The pillage of the Third World.* Modern Reader, New York. A leftist view of neocolonialism.

Jarrett, Henry, ed. 1966. *Environmental quality in a growing economy.* Johns Hopkins Press, Baltimore. An interesting collection. See especially the article by Boulding, "The economics of the coming Spaceship Earth."

Jasani, Bhupendra M. 1975. Environmental modifications: New weapons of war? *Ambio,* vol. 4, pp. 191–198. A review of the possibilities.

Jensen, C. E.; D. W. Brown; and J. A. Mirabito. 1975. Earthwatch, *Science,* vol. 190, pp. 432–438 (October 31). An ambitious (and acronym-loaded) discussion of what a global environmental assessment program operated by UNEP could be like.

Johnson, B. 1976. International environmental conventions. *Ambio,* vol. 5, no. 2, pp. 55–65. An excellent overview.

Johnston, B. F. 1972. Unemployment and underemployment. In *Are our descendents doomed?* H. Brown and E. Hutchings, Jr., eds. Viking, New York. Recommends intermediate technology for LDC farms.

Kahn, Herman. 1960. *On thermonuclear war.* Princeton University Press, N.J. This book brought much unfair personal criticism of Kahn. It is the subject of devastating professional analysis by Philip Green in *Deadly logic.*

———. 1962. *Thinking about the unthinkable.* Horizon, New York. An able reply to the personal attacks made on Kahn after *On thermonuclear war* was published.

———. 1965. *On escalation.* Penguin, Baltimore. The most recent work by the best known of the deterrence theorists.

Keeny, Spurgeon M., Jr., Chairman. 1977. *Nuclear power issues and choices.* Report of the Nuclear Energy Policy Study Group of the Ford Foundation. Ballinger, Cambridge, Mass. A thoughtful and largely evenhanded review of the technical, economic, environmental, and political issues surrounding nuclear power, with heavy emphasis on proliferation. Recommends deferral of plutonium recycle and commercialization of the liquid metal fast breeder reactor in the U.S., with continued reliance on light water reactors.

Keohane, R. O., and Van Doorn Ooms. 1975. The multinational firm and international regulation. *International Organization,* vol. 29, pp. 169–209.

Keyfitz, Nathan. 1976. World resources and the world middle class. *Scientific American.* July, pp. 28–35. An important article on the prospects of improving the well-being of the world's poor majority.

Kissinger, Henry. 1975. Speech before United Nations General Assembly, September 2. Reprinted in the New York *Times,* September 2, p. 20. This was the speech in which the United States pledged to help LDCs through increased aid and improved trade agreements.

Klare, Michael T. 1976. The political economy of arms sales. *Bulletin of the Atomic Scientists.* November, pp. 11–18. The U.S. is still the world's leading arms peddler, and the trade is flourishing.

Kratzer, Myron B. 1975. International cooperation in nuclear energy and nonproliferation. *Current Policy, The Department of State,* vol. 7, November. He does not believe proliferation is inevitable; he is overly optimistic about such things as the IAEA safeguards.

Ledogar, Robert J. 1975. *Hungry for profits: U.S. food and drug multinationals in Latin America,* IDOC/North America, New York. Claims that in the Latin American milieu of minimal regulation and self-medication United States drug companies have often made their profits at the expense of the health of the local people. Says that the activities of the food companies, especially the substitution of cash crops for subsistence crops, has often resulted in lower quality diets for the hungriest people.

Lewin, Roger. 1975. Environment in a developing world. *New Scientist,* March 13, pp. 632–633. A brief description of the first years of UNEP.

———. 1975. International attack on insect pests. *New Scientist,* April 17, pp. 124–125. Describes functioning of International Centre of Insect Physiology and Ecology (ICIPE) in Nairobi.

Lessey, Julian. 1976. Taxes for conservation. *New Scientist,* October 7, p. 30. A proposal to tax nonrenewable resources imported by DCs from LDCs, to encourage conservation and benefit LDC economies.

Lewis, Paul. 1974. Getting even. *New York Times Magazine,* December 15. Interesting discussion of the OPEC revolution. Points out that by 1974 Arab "development aid is already up to the target set by the United Nations—something which cannot be said for the rest of the industrial world and particularly for the United States, which is not only the world's richest nation but also its meanest."

Lipton, Michael. 1975. Urban bias and food policy in poor countries. *Food Policy,* vol. 1, no. 1, pp. 41–51. How the poorest people are left out of the food economy in LDCs.

Lovins, Amory, and John H. Price. 1975. *Non-nuclear futures: The case for an ethical energy strategy,* Lippincott, Philadelphia. Eloquent, thoughtful exploration of alternative energy futures for the world.

Lockwood, Lee. 1967. *Castro's Cuba, Cuba's Fidel.* Random House, New York. Contains an interview in which Castro describes his approach to Cuban grass-roots development.

Low, H. C., and J. W. Howe. 1975. Focus on the Fourth World. In *U.S. and world development: Agenda for action 1975,* J. W. Howe, ed. Problems of the poorest group of LDCs.

McGrath, Patricia L. 1976. The unfinished assignment: Equal education for women. *Worldwatch paper 7,* Worldwatch Institute, Washington, D.C.

Makhijani, A. 1976. Solar energy and rural development for the Third World. *Bulletin of the Atomic Scientists,* June. Pleads for decision-makers not to emulate industrial nations but to spread small solar technologies to benefit poor. A good example of grass-roots development.

——— and A. Poole. 1975. *Energy and agriculture in the Third World.* Ballinger, Cambridge, Mass. On appropriate energy technology for LDCs. Excellent.

Mazrui, Ali A., 1975. The new interdependence: from hierarchy to symmetry. In *The U.S. and world development: Agenda for action 1975,* J. W. Howe, ed., pp. 118–134. A rather optimistic view.

Melko, Matthew. 1975. Peace: A subject worth studying. *Bulletin of the Atomic Scientists,* April, pp. 31–34. Gives a list of peaceful societies and suggests investigating why they are peaceful.

Melman, Seymour. 1962. *Disarmament, its politics and economics.* American Academy of Arts and Sciences, Boston, Mass.

———. 1970. *Pentagon capitalism: The political economy of war.* McGraw-Hill, New York. See especially Chapter 7 for a summary of myths about the military establishment. Melman sees it as independent of real United States needs, defense or economic.

Mesarovic, M., and E. Pestel. 1974. *Mankind at the turning point.* A second report from the Club of Rome that criticizes *The limits to growth,* Meadows et al., but hardly presents a more encouraging view of the "problematique."

Moumoni, Abdou. 1973. Energy needs and prospects in the Sahelian and Sudanese zones in Africa: Prospects of solar power. *Ambio,* vol. 2, no. 6, pp. 203–213. On sensible kinds of energy development for LDCs.

Muller, Mike. 1974. Aid, corruption and waste. *New Scientist,* November 7, pp. 398–401. Points out the key role in preventing famine played by preventing hoarding by maintaining confidence in the market system. Claims this has been a major achievement of United Nations Disaster Relief Organization.

Murdoch, W. W., and A. Oaten. 1975. Population and food: Metaphors and the reality. *BioScience,* vol. 25, September, pp. 561–567. A critique of Hardin's lifeboat ethics.

Myrdal, Alva. 1974. The international control of disarmament. *Scientific American,* October. Source of information on arms-control agreements.

Myrdal, Gunnar. 1968. *Asian drama.* 3 vols. Pantheon, New York. A monument on politics, economics, planning, and population in Asia. Comprehensive and rather depressing.

———. 1974. The transfer of technology to underdeveloped countries. *Scientific American,* September, pp. 173–182. On the existing barriers to the transfer of technology and how they might be overcome.

National Academy of Sciences (NAS). 1975. *Long-term worldwide effects of multiple nuclear-weapons detonations.* NAS, Washington, D.C. Although some of the individual sections are competent, the overall conclusions are not. The letter of transmittal by Philip Handler was especially unfortunate.

New Internationalist. 1976. The world is your shopping basket: trade special, who sells what, where, and who makes the money. Vol. 38, April. A key issue of an important journal. See especially the UNCTAD IV supplement in this issue.

Newland, Kathleen. 1975. Women in politics: A global review. Worldwatch Institute, Washington, D.C., *Worldwatch paper 3.* Data on voting and literacy rates by sex, women in national legislative bodies, and so forth.

Nitze, Paul H. 1976. Assuring strategic stability in an era of détente. *Foreign Affairs,* vol. 54, no. 2 (January), pp. 207–232. A knowledgeable hawk argues that SALT agreements may be leading to instability of the nuclear deterrence system.

O'Brien, Tom. 1975. Marrying Malthus and Marx. *Environmental Action,* August 30, pp. 3–11. A splendid synthesis of Marxist and Malthusian ideas in the context of the present human predicament.

Ohlin, Goran. 1967. *Population control and economic development.* Organization for Economic Co-Operation and Development, Paris. An important early analysis on the interactions of growth and development.

Paddock, W., and P. Paddock. 1967. *Famine, 1975!* Little, Brown, Boston. The classic application of the triage principle to food aid for hungry nations.

Patel, I. G. 1976. What the developing countries really want. *Atlas World Press Review,* February, pp. 22–23. Food and shelter are not their only aspirations.

Pearson, Lester B. 1969. *Partners in development.* Praeger, New York. Report to the World Bank by the Commission on International Development.

Peccei, Aurelio. 1969. *The chasm ahead.* Macmillan, London. A distinguished Italian industrialist and member of the Club of Rome examines the human predicament and reaches conclusions startlingly close to those of many ecologists.

Pincus, John A., ed. 1968. *Reshaping the world economy.* Prentice-Hall, Englewood Cliffs, N.J. Especially useful source on wórld trade problems.

Pirages, Dennis C. ed. 1977. *The sustainable society: Social and political implications.* Praeger, New York. A collection of articles with technological, economic, and political viewpoints pertinent to this chapter.

———, and Paul R. Ehrlich. 1974. *Ark II: Social response to environmental imperatives.* W. H. Freeman and Company, San Francisco. A detailed examination of many of the subjects of this chapter.

Plate, Thomas G. 1971. *Understanding doomsday.* Simon & Schuster, New York. A gold mine of information on the arms race.

Platt, John. 1969. What we must do. *Science,* vol. 166, pp. 1115–1121 (November 28). A classification of our multiplicity of crises and suggestions on how we might meet them.

Population Reference Bureau. 1975. Literacy and world population. *Population Bulletin,* vol. 30, no. 2. Illiteracy and the need for population-control information go hand in hand.

Pugwash Conference. 1973. Twenty-third conference report. *Congressional Record,* Senate, vol. 119, pp. S18727-S8730, October 8. The conference's working group on energy expressed reservations about the proliferation of nuclear plants and fuel-reprocessing facilities in LDCs.

Rand, C. T. 1975. *Making democracy safe for oil.* Little, Brown, Boston. Describes the role of the oil industry in the Arab oil embargo.

Rathjens, George W. 1969. *The future of the strategic arms race: Options for the 1970's.* Carnegie Endowment for International Peace. Old but good.

Reilly, Conor. 1975. Environmental action in Zambia. *Environment,* October, pp. 31–35. Zambia is starting to face up to the problems of rapid industrialization and exploitation of natural resources.

Renshaw, E. F. 1976. *The end of progress: Adjusting to a no-growth economy.* Duxbury Press, North Scituate, Mass. Superb overview of the global predicament and the prospects for evasive action in the form of a transition to a sustainable state.

Ribicoff, Abraham A. 1976. A market-sharing approach to the world nuclear sales problem. *Foreign Affairs,* vol. 54, pp. 763–787. Proposes a variety of national and international measures to stop the export of nuclear fuel reprocessing facilities, with the aim of slowing proliferation of nuclear weapons.

Robinson, J. P. Perry. 1975. The special case of chemical and biological weapons. *Bulletin of the Atomic Scientists,* May, pp. 17–23. Expresses concern that these might evolve into being thought of as conventional weapons.

Rose, William M. 1975. Submarine vs. anti-submarine: The billion dollar merry-go-round. *Bulletin of the Atomic Scientists,* April, pp. 27–30. Discusses the Trident SLBM system—another military boondoggle.

Rothschild, Emma. 1976. Food politics. *Foreign Affairs,* January, pp. 285–307. On the role of food in international economics and politics.

Roy, Robin. 1976. Myths about technological change. *New Scientist,* May 6, pp. 281–282. Brief overview of various theories about relationships of society to galloping technology.

Sakharov, Andrei D. 1968. *Progress, coexistence and intellectual freedom.* Norton, New York. Heroic statement by the brilliant physicist called the father of the Russian H-bomb.

Salam, Abdus. 1976. Ideals and realities. *Bulletin of the Atomic Scientists,* vol. 32, no. 7, pp. 9–15. A Pakistani scientist examines the rich-poor confrontation.

Sampson, Anthony. 1975. *The seven sisters: The great oil companies and the world they shaped.* Viking, New York. A "biography" of the organizations that play such a crucial role in the energy situation, providing insights into the international control of petroleum.

Sanders, Sol. 1969. *A sense of Asia.* Scribner's, New York.

Schelling, Thomas C. 1968. *The strategy of conflict.* Oxford University Press, Oxford. Well worth reading. Schelling is one of the brightest of the deterrence theorists.

Schneider, William Jr. 1975. Agricultural exports as an instrument of diplomacy. *Food Policy,* vol. 1, no. 1. Concludes that U.S ability to export food (or withhold it) could be a useful tool in economic warfare.

Sewell, J. W. ed. 1977. *The United States and world development agenda 1977.* Praeger, N.Y. The Overseas Development Council's fifth annual assessment of U.S. relations with the LDCs. Very useful discussions of food, population, technology transfer, arms sales, income distribution, and other important topics, backed up with extensive tabulations of recent statistical data.

Shapley, Deborah. 1975. Now, a draft sea law treaty: But what comes after? *Science,* vol. 188, p. 918 (May 30).

Sherwood, Martin J. 1975. *A world destroyed.* Knopf, New York. A brilliant overview of the origins of United States atomic policy, much of it based on recently declassified information. Emphasizes early attempts to make A-bombs a United States-UK monopoly.

Sigurdson, Jon. 1975. Resources and environment in China. *Ambio,* vol. 4, pp. 112–119. Environmental considerations enter into Chinese development plans, which include decentralized industrialization, delayed urbanization, and a concern for fundamental human needs. A "friendly" overview.

Singer, J. D., and M. Small. 1972. *The wages of war, 1816–1965: A statistical handbook.* Wiley, New York. A compendium of data on wars: periodicity, seasonal factors, who was involved (how disposed nations and regions are to war), severity, battle deaths, and so forth.

Singh, Kushwant. 1975. The international basket case. *New York Times Magazine,* January 26. Describes conditions in Bangladesh.

Sivard, Ruth L. 1975. Let them eat bullets! *Bulletin of the Atomic Scientists,* April, pp. 6–10. Discusses the impact of the world's spending $30 million *per hour* on armed forces and armaments.

Smil, Vaclav. 1977. Intermediate energy technology in China. *Bulletin of the Atomic Scientists.* February, pp. 25–31. Interesting view of how China is tapping energy resources on a small-scale, local basis for rural industry and household use. Among sources being used are coal, hydropower, biogas, and solar heat.

Sommer, John G. 1975. U.S. voluntary aid to the Third World: What is its future? Overseas Development Council, development paper 20, Washington, D.C. An interesting summary of the pitfalls of various aid programs.

Springell, Peter. 1975. Some observations on the Australian environmental scene. *Ecologist,* February, pp. 42–47. See especially the section on the trade unions.

Sprout, H., and M. Sprout. 1971. *Toward a politics of the planet Earth.* Van Nostrand Reinhold, New York. Political scientists take a comprehensive look at the human dilemma. Chapter 11 is especially interesting.

Stauffer, T. 1974. Oil money and world money: Conflict or confluence. *Science,* vol. 184, pp. 321–325 (April 19). On recycling petrodollars.

Stavrianos, L. S. 1976. *The promise of the coming dark age.* W. H. Freeman and Company, San Francisco. A weirdly optimistic tour de force by an author who could use further education in ecology.

Stockholm International Peace Research Institute (SIPRI). 1976. Why arms control fails: The myth of "deterrence" lulls world opinion. *Atlas World Press Review,* February, pp. 11–13. Contains data on overkill and weapons systems and discusses the failure to disarm.

Stolnitz, George J. 1974. Population and labor force in less developed regions: Some main facts, theory, and research needs. In *Employment in developing nations,* E. O. Edwards, ed. Columbia University Press, New York. pp. 235–245. A good overview.

Stone, Christopher D., and Jack McNamara. 1976. How to take on OPEC. *New York Times Magazine,* December 12, pp. 38ff. Describes a plan by which U.S. government might break the cartel.

Strong, Maurice. 1974. A global imperative for the environment. *Natural History,* March. Description of UNEP by its "creator."

Thayer, George. 1969. *The war business: The international trade in armaments.* Avon, New York. A detailed description of the conventional arms trade.

Time. 1975. Poor vs. rich: A new global conflict. December 22. A popular review defining the first-through-fifth-world terminology.

Tinker, Jon. 1974. Java: Birth control battlefield. *New Scientist,* February 21. Describes how corruption permeates the social and political system in one LDC.

———. 1974. Is technology neocolonist? *New Scientist,* May 9, pp. 302–305. A fascinating review of Indonesian environmental problems as seen by Mocktar Lubis, environmentalist and editor of a Jakarta newspaper.

Tsipis, Kosta. 1975. The long range cruise missile. *Bulletin of the Atomic Scientists,* April, pp. 15–26. The technology and implications of this frightening new development are discussed.

Tucker, Robert W. 1975. Oil: The issue of American intervention. *Commentary,* January, pp. 21–31. Possibly another trial balloon. Despairs of success in recycling petrodollars and the possibility of the Arabs' acting reasonably.

United Nations. Annual. *Statistical yearbook.* Statistical Office of the United Nations, New York. A gold mine of information on population, manufacturing, agriculture, trade, consumption, and so forth.

United States Arms Control and Disarmament Agency (ACDH). 1975. *SALT lexicon.* Rev. ACDH, Washington, D.C. A useful guide for translating the jargon-riddled literature on nuclear war. Sample: "Crisis Stability: A strategic force relationship in which neither side has any incentive to initiate the use of strategic nuclear forces in a crisis situation."

Van der Schalie, H. 1974. Aswan dam revisited. *Environment,* vol. 16, no. 9. Describes increase of schistosomiasis.

Vermeer, Donald E., 1976. Food, farming and the future: The role of traditional agriculture in developing areas of the world. *Social Science Quarterly,* vol. 57, pp. 383–396. An important paper indicating the crucial role that traditional agriculture *must* play in solving the world food problem.

Voevodsky, John. 1969. Quantitative behavior of warring nations. *Journal of Psychology,* vol. 72, pp. 269–292. Shows that there is considerable orderliness in numbers of troops engaged, battle deaths, and other statistics of modern wars.

Ward, Barbara (chairperson). 1975. The Cocoyoc declaration. *Bulletin of the Atomic Scientists,* March, pp. 6–10. This is an excerpt of the statement produced by an international meeting of social and natural scientists at Cocoyoc, Mexico, in October 1974, sponsored jointly by UNCTAD and UNEP. The declaration calls for a new international economic order.

Wenk, Edward Jr. 1972. *The politics of the ocean.* University of Washington Press, Seattle. Becoming out of date but still a useful source on the complexities of controlling the oceanic commons.

Williams, E. J., and F. J. Wright. 1975. *Latin American politics: A developmental approach.* Mayfield, Palo Alto, Calif. An excellent survey of the political actors in the region and the historic and economic dimensions of their stage.

Wright, Quinsy. 1965. *A study of war.* 2d ed. University of Chicago Press. A huge volume, dealing primarily with wars prior to 1941 (first edition). Wright has a four-factor theory of the origins of war, these being technology, law, social organization, and distribution of opinions about basic values. A rich source of information. See especially the appended commentary on war since 1942.

York, Herbert F., ed. 1973. *Arms control: Readings from Scientific American.* W. H. Freeman and Company, San Francisco. A wide-ranging collection.

———. 1976 *The advisors: Teller, Oppenheimer, and the superbomb.* W. H. Freeman, San Francisco. An insightful history of the decisions leading to the development of the U.S. and Soviet hydrogen bombs, by an insider on the U.S. side. Must reading for those interested in the psychology of the arms race.

Zeckhauser, Richard. 1973. The risks of growth. *Daedalus,* fall, pp. 103–178. States, "recycling is not the solution for oil, because the alternate technology of nuclear power generation is cheaper," (p. 117). This paper helps demonstrate how ignorance of the physical world keeps many economists from coming to grips with the international situation.

The future is purchased by the present.

–Samuel Johnson, *The rambler*

CHAPTER 16

Summary

At the end of Chapter 1 we contrasted two possible views of the present human condition and the prospects for the future. Obviously, the spectrum of opinion on this most important of issues is continuous and not confined to two well-defined camps. Nevertheless, it is helpful, after struggling with the enormous body of principles, data, estimates, and arguments considered in the intervening chapters, to try to summarize some of the essential points by referring again to two distinct camps. We call them cornucopians and neo-Malthusians.

CORNUCOPIANS VERSUS NEO-MALTHUSIANS

Cornucopians are often preoccupied with the apparent theoretical capacity of Earth to supply a large (but fixed) population with basic raw materials over long spans of time. They refer to the vast stores of minerals available at low concentration in seawater and in the first few miles of Earth's crust, and they argue that cheap and abundant energy from fission breeder reactors or controlled thermonuclear fusion will make those dilute mineral resources economically accessible (as well as permitting large-scale desalting of seawater with which to make the deserts bloom with food crops). Even ardent cornucopians do not postulate continued population growth beyond a few more doublings, however, for that many people could not be sustained under any assumptions.

The neo-Malthusians reject the hypothetical steady-state scenario as largely irrelevant. They focus on rates—the dynamic character of the problem—arguing that (1) technology does not provide adequately for the *present* world population, (2) technology and resources cannot be mobilized (or paid for) quickly enough to provide adequately for the much larger population to which humanity seems imminently committed, and (3) serious environmental errors are being made and will continue to be made in the hasty attempts to mobilize technology and resources quickly enough. In short, the neo-Malthusians perceive not an "equilibrium problem" (can a world be imagined in which 20 billion people, 5 times the present population, could be supported?) but rather what a mathematician would call an "initial-value problem" (how can we get from here to there, and especially with such a bad start?). Some observers on both sides have asked reflectively whether anyone would *like* a world with 10 or 20 billion people in it, but that is another matter.

When cornucopians do come to grips with the dynamic aspects of the problems, their argument generally relies on the timely and smooth operation of the price mechanism to bring about substitution and technological innovation as required. They view continued economic growth as the path by which the poor will acquire the means to participate in the price mechanism.

The neo-Malthusian view fears "stickiness" in the price mechanism, dramatic price rises for raw materials that will prevent the poor from achieving prosperity, and nonlinear mechanisms (such as diminishing returns, thresholds, synergisms) that will cause moderate increases in population and resource demand to generate disproportionate economic, social, and environmental costs. According to this position, it is likely that human demands and impact at some point in the future will exceed a (possibly dynamic) limit as it stands *at that time,* leading to a large increase in the human death rate or in the incidence of poverty. The neo-Malthusian view proposes conscious accommodation to the perceived limits to material growth via population limitation and redistribution of wealth, in order to prevent the "overshoot" phenomenon.

On these points we find ourselves firmly in the neo-Malthusian camp. We hold this view not because we believe the world to be running out of materials in an absolute sense, but rather because the barriers to continued material growth, in the form of problems of economics, logistics, management, and environmental impact, are so formidable.

DEFECTS IN THE CORNUCOPIAN VISION

Of the defects in the cornucopian argument, the gravest are these:

1. The presumption that advanced technology will make energy very cheap;
2. The presumption that abundant, cheap energy—if available—would prove to be a sufficient condition for abundance of all kinds;
3. The serious underestimation of the degree of environmental degradation that would be generated by the proposed cornucopian technologies;
4. The even more serious underestimation of the impact on human well-being that major environmental disruption portends.

First, there is little reason to believe that energy will get cheaper. The advanced energy technologies with the greatest potential in terms of abundance—solar energy, controlled fusion, and fission breeder reactors—are all characterized by raw fuel that is free, or nearly so; but the high capital costs likely to be associated with those technologies will lead to high overall energy costs despite free fuel.

Cheap energy, even if it should miraculously materialize, is not enough. Food, shelter, clothing, education, and opportunity for the billions will certainly require energy, but they will also require other raw materials, social organization and cooperation, and much help from the already beleaguered processes of the biosphere. The processes by which energy can be "converted" into the other needed raw materials are often difficult, usually environmentally disruptive, and almost always expensive. Social stresses arising from competition for energy and materials make organization and cooperation more difficult, not easier. And the side effects of the escalating flows of energy and materials through civilization are diminishing the capacity of the biosphere to support human activities at a time when the need for such support is expanding.

The widespread tendency to underestimate the future environmental damages of the energy and materials technologies has two facets—an overconfidence in technology's capacity to "clean up" the environment, and a narrow view of environmental disruption that includes direct assaults on health via emission of pollutants but not the systematic damage to life-supporting ecosystems via, for example, habitat destruction, overexploitation of plant and animal species, erosion, and alteration of the chemical environment in soil and surface water.

With respect to technology's capacity to clean up, it is true, of course, that the environmental impact of many of today's energy and materials technologies can and should be dramatically reduced. For each proposed technical fix, however, it is important to ask: How fast can it be implemented? How much of the hazard will it abate? What will society do for an encore after those gains have been erased by further growth? How much will it cost, and who will pay? Will it produce new negative impacts in exchange for the ones abated?

For some environmental impacts of energy and materials technologies, no fix is in sight: Carbon dioxide, for example, is produced by combustion of fossil fuels in quantities too large to contain, and it may already be influencing climate. Particles less than 1 micron in diameter (emitted by combustion of fossil fuels and to a lesser extent by mining operations and agriculture) mostly escape available controls; unfortunately, the sizes smaller than 1 micron are precisely the most serious in terms of both human health and the disruption of climate. The human factor may make it impossible to design foolproof safeguards against nuclear-fission disaster. Finally, heat is the ultimate pollutant. In the unlikely event that nothing else stops the growth of energy use first, heat will stop it by generating major climatic disruption. This outcome is predictable from the laws of thermodynamics; it can be postponed somewhat by clever reliance on solar energy, but it cannot be averted.

The gravest threat to human well-being arising from the environmental impact of energy and materials technology is probably not direct poisoning by the emissions, but rather the loss of natural services now provided by biogeochemical processes. Contrary to popular belief, such natural services cannot be replaced by technology now or in the foreseeable future. Not only do we not know how to do it, but if we did, we couldn't afford it. What is alarming is that civilization, while unable to replace the natural services upon which its survival depends, has become a great enough disruptive force to undermine them. The available evidence is insufficient to prove conclusively that disaster is upon us, but it indicates we are playing in a league where environmental balances on regional and global scales hinge on human actions.

ALTERNATIVE APPROACHES TO TECHNOLOGY AND WELL-BEING

This summary so far, consistent with the material in the foregoing chapters, has presented a pessimistic view of the human predicament and the prospects that current trends will improve it. We believe that a realistic prognosis would now include continuing worldwide inflation; further widening of the prosperity gap between rich and poor; increased incidence of famine and quite possibly other environmentally-related increases in death rates; heightened social unrest characterized by strikes, riots, and terrorism; more frequent international confrontations over resources; a rising level of international tension aggravated by all these factors, with a probability of nuclear conflict that increases not only in proportion to this level of tension but also in some (perhaps nonlinear) relation with the growing number of possessors of nuclear weapons. What, then, can we advocate?

It is clear, first of all, that no combination of policies and technologies can significantly ameliorate the predicament unless it overcomes the nontechnological roots of the problem: population growth, competitive nationalism, racism, the maldistribution of wealth and opportunity, the illusion that economic throughput and material well-being are directly proportional, and the hubris that supposes civilizations to be self-supporting without help from natural ecosystems. The highest priority must therefore be given to measures that directly attack these driving forces.

The cornerstone of a rational program should be a great reduction in the growth of throughput of energy and materials in the rich countries. Such a reduction would permit, in principle, an *acceleration* of the application of energy and materials to meet the genuine needs of the poor countries, *within a context of slackening global growth.* In this way, the gap in prosperity between rich and poor could begin to close—a prospect that supporters of rapid overall growth have often held out to the poor but never delivered. At the same time, the slower growth in the rate at which energy and materials are mobilized worldwide, and the even slower growth in the rich countries, where certain environmental impacts of energy and materials technologies are now most severe, would significantly reduce the grave environmental risks that accompany continuation of recent trends.

The success of such a scheme, of course, depends strongly on the success of programs to limit the growth of populations. Only at lowered rates of population growth can the relatively high increase in the use of energy and materials per person that is needed in the poor countries be achieved within an economically and environmentally sustainable rate of global growth. In the rich countries, the effect of multiplying even small population increments by the very high levels of resource use and environmental impact per person already prevailing there makes it essential to approach a zero rate of population growth as soon as possible.

Another essential ingredient of the approach we advocate is a massive, coordinated worldwide campaign of research, development, and implementation aimed at increasing the well-being actually delivered for each unit of energy and raw-materials throughput, while decreasing the amount of adverse environmental impact per unit of throughput. This proposal should be recognized as a prescription not for *less* technology but for *better* technology—more frugal, better focused on the most compelling needs, more compatible with the fabric of the physical and social environments.

The potential of increased technological efficiency notwithstanding, the pursuit of efficient technologies must be tempered by two concerns. The first is that even the most efficient technology must be applied and expanded cautiously, lest the environmental impact of its throughput disrupt environmental services or social relationships of greater importance than the services the technology provides. The second concern is to avoid the pitfall of trading away too much diversity in the single-minded pursuit of efficiency. One must generally pay something extra in throughput for diversity. In this sense, diversity is inefficient, but many natural ecosystems seem to demonstrate that diversity is good insurance against uncertainty about the future, and civilization would probably do well to learn from the example. Just how much of this insurance civilization should buy and what it will cost are questions that need further study.

Within these constraints, the potential for favorably altering the ratio of service to throughput by a major directed effort means that prosperity in the poor countries can be increased at a rate greater than the rate at which resource use is growing. And it means that, even in rich countries where a drastic slowing of growth in energy use is called for, ingenuity can reduce the impacts on the economy and on the prospects for increases in actual well-being. This possibility, together with increased awareness in the rich countries that their own well-being is imperiled by the social, economic, and environmental consequences of continuing present trends, provide the only real basis for believing that the technological changes and rich-poor reallocations envisioned here can actually take place.

Obviously, the best approaches to increasing the ratio of service to throughput will not be identical for all regions. It seems clear from the difficulties enumerated in Chapter 15 that new technology for the developing regions must be tailored to specific local conditions rather than transferred wholesale from industrial nations. Rather than centralization, technical complexity, standardization, and interdependence, the characteristics of new technologies for developing regions should be, insofar as possible, dispersal, simplicity, diversity, and independence. Durability and reliability, which often go hand in hand with simplicity, are also essential. It is evident that the technologies of industrial nations, as well, should in many instances evolve away from complexity and centralization, and in all instances they should move away from reliance on a standard of perfection in manufacture, maintenance, and operation that is simply not attainable in practice.

Industrial nations, rich as they may seem to be, must also recognize that they are not rich enough to do what must be done while wasting resources on entirely frivolous economic fiascoes. Supersonic transports, overproduction of subsonic air buses, a proliferation of unfillable luxury hotels and vacation condominiums—all are economic blunders that will cause some well-deserved bankruptcies but, unfortunately, only after desperately needed technical and economic resources have been wasted.

Military expenditures are in a category by themselves. No one can afford them, the poor even less than the rich. But most countries make them—to a total of almost $300 billion worth per year worldwide. This cannot be considered merely a waste, inasmuch as the expenditures profoundly threaten human well-being through what is bought even more than through what is not bought. The most powerful single lever at the disposal of industrial nations for narrowing the prosperity gap is to shut off all sales and gifts of military hardware to the poor countries uniformly, replacing them with offerings of technologies selected for their abilities to contribute to genuine increases in well-being. Naturally, the gesture will be a hollow one if the industrial nations do not at the same time divert their own expenditures on weaponry to productive purposes.

EPILOGUE

We are regularly informed in all solemnity that the sorts of drastic changes proposed here are economically, politically, and socially impractical or unrealistic. No one has yet devised a plausible scheme, for example, to see that reductions in throughputs of resources in the rich countries (if they could actually be achieved) are translated into increased availability of resources for rational development in the poor countries. Little real progress has been made on global disarmament by the superpowers, and extensive proliferation of nuclear weapons is widely (if quietly) held to be inevitable. The seriousness of population growth continues to be widely underestimated or misperceived by scholars and governments alike. We believe it is past time for the social-science community to devote its full attention to the removal of these sociopolitical obstacles to societal survival, just as the physical-science and engineering communities must devote theirs to the transformation of technology. For the alternative of proceeding along the present course is not only even less practical economically, politically, and socially than the demanding changes that are required, it is also impractical *physically*. The real question, for those concerned about realistic solutions, is whether scholars and decision-makers of all varieties can devise ways to bring human behavior into harmony with physical reality in time.

APPENDIX 1

World Demography

Most of the figures for Table A1-1 are from the 1976 *World Population Data Sheet* of the Population Reference Bureau, Inc., Washington D.C. The exception is per-capita energy consumption figures, which are from the Environmental Fund's *Population Estimates, 1974* (see below).

Estimates for many countries undoubtedly contain a large margin of error. In many cases census data are extremely unreliable; in others undetected changes in birth or death rates since the latest census may introduce considerable error into extrapolations. And, of course, in some instances the figures may represent faulty extrapolations from incorrect census data.

The approximate character of available world demographic data was underlined by the appearance since 1974 of similar data sheets produced by the Environmental Fund, Washington, D.C., showing strikingly different figures for many countries (including the United States) from those of the U.N. or the U.S. Bureau of the Census. Their explanations for the discrepancies are not implausible and may in many cases be correct. For example, the Environmental Fund includes an estimate of illegal immigrants in its U.S. figures, whereas the Census Bureau and most other organizations do not include them.

On the whole, we believe the figures we are presenting here are the best estimates available. Most of them, of course, should be considered to represent rough magnitudes. A difference of a point or two in birth rates between two countries may have no significance whatever. The most accurate census data come from the DCs; those of many LDCs are extremely suspect. The per-capita gross national product figures should be used with special caution; since population figures and total GNP are both only approximate at best, per-capita GNP figures, a ratio of the two, are especially liable to error. The major features of the current world demographic picture are clear in these data, but in using them their limitations should always be kept in mind.

Table A1-2 shows the population projections of demographer Tomas Frejka in detail (see Chapter 5), demonstrating population momentum.

TABLE A1-1 *World Demographic and Related Statistics*

Region or country[a]	*Population estimate, mid-1976 (millions)*[b]	*Birth rate*[c]	*Death rate*[c]	*Rate of population growth (annual, percent)*[d]	*Number of years to double population*[e]	*Population projection to 2000 (millions)*[f]	*Infant mortality rate*[g]	*Population under 15 years (percent)*	*Median age (years)*	*Life expectancy at birth (years)*	*Urban population (percent)*[h]	*Per-capita gross national product (US $)*[i]	*Per-capita energy consumption, 1972*[j]
WORLD	**4,019**	**30**	**12**	**1.8**	**38**	**6,214**	**105**	**36**	**22.9**	**59**	**38**	**1,360**	**1,984**
AFRICA	**413**	**46**	**20**	**2.6**	**27**	**815**	**152**	**44**	**18.0**	**45**	**23**	**340**	**363**
Northern Africa	**100**	**43**	**16**	**2.6**	**27**	**190**	**124**	**44**	**18.0**	**52**	**37**	**440**	**–**
Algeria	17.3	49	15	3.2	22	36.7	126	48	16.0	53	50	650	533
Egypt	38.1	38	15	2.3	30	64.0	98	41	19.4	52	43	280	324
Libya	2.5	45	15	3.7	19	5.1	130	44	17.8	53	29	3,360	4,407
Morocco	17.9	46	16	2.9	24	35.6	130	44	18.2	53	37	430	223
Sudan	18.2	48	18	2.5	28	37.9	141	45	17.2	49	13	150	119
Tunisia	5.9	38	13	2.4	29	10.9	128	44	17.4	54	40	550	349
Western Africa	**120**	**49**	**23**	**2.6**	**27**	**242**	**175**	**45**	**17.7**	**41**	**17**	**230**	**–**
Benin (Dahomey)	3.2	50	23	2.7	26	6.0	185	45	17.3	41	13	120	32
Cape Verde Islands	0.3	33	10	2.3	30	0.4	91	44	17.7	50	6	340	116
Gambia	0.5	43	24	1.9	36	0.9	165	41	20.3	40	14	170	82
Ghana	10.1	49	22	2.7	26	21.2	156	47	16.7	44	29	350	152
Guinea	4.5	47	23	2.4	29	8.5	175	43	18.5	41	16	120	96
Guinea-Bissau	0.5	40	25	1.5	46	0.8	208	37	22.1	38	20	330	94
Ivory Coast	6.8	46	21	2.5	28	13.1	164	43	18.5	44	28	420	309
Liberia	1.6	50	21	2.9	24	3.0	159	42	19.8	45	28	330	368
Mali	5.8	50	26	2.4	29	11.1	188	44	18.0	38	12	70	23
Mauritania	1.3	39	25	1.4	50	2.3	187	42	19.0	38	10	230	100
Niger	4.7	52	25	2.7	26	9.6	200	46	17.2	38	8	100	28
Nigeria	64.7	49	23	2.7	26	135.1	180	45	17.4	41	16	240	66
Senegal	4.5	48	24	2.4	29	8.1	159	43	18.3	40	30	320	156
Sierra Leone	3.1	45	21	2.4	29	5.8	136	43	18.6	44	13	180	135
Togo	2.3	51	23	2.7	26	4.6	127	46	17.2	41	15	210	63
Upper Volta	6.2	49	26	2.3	30	11.0	182	43	18.3	38	7	80	12
Eastern Africa	**117**	**48**	**21**	**2.8**	**25**	**238**	**152**	**45**	**17.6**	**44**	**12**	**200**	**–**
Burundi	3.9	48	25	2.4	29	7.3	150	45	18.4	39	3	80	10
Comoro Islands	0.3	44	20	2.4	29	0.5	160	43	18.4	42	5	170	49
Ethiopia	28.6	49	26	2.6	27	53.6	181	44	18.2	38	11	90	35
Kenya	13.8	49	16	3.4	20	31.3	119	46	16.7	50	10	200	165
Malagasy Republic	7.7	50	21	2.9	24	16.7	102	45	17.3	44	14	170	69
Malawi	5.1	48	24	2.4	29	9.7	148	45	17.5	41	4	130	53
Mauritius	0.9	28	7	1.2	58	1.2	46	38	20.1	66	44	480	151
Mozambique	9.3	43	20	2.3	30	17.4	165	43	18.8	44	10	420	144
Reunion	0.5	28	7	2.1	33	0.7	47	43	18.6	63	43	1,210	348
Rhodesia	6.5	48	14	3.4	20	15.2	122	46	16.9	52	19	480	582
Rwanda	4.4	50	24	2.8	25	8.8	133	44	17.9	41	3	80	12
Somalia	3.2	47	22	2.5	28	6.5	177	45	17.2	41	26	80	33
Tanzania	15.6	50	22	2.7	26	33.4	162	47	16.6	44	7	140	72
Uganda	11.9	45	16	3.3	21	24.6	160	44	17.7	50	8	160	66
Zambia	5.1	51	20	3.1	22	11.3	160	46	17.4	44	34	480	508
Middle Africa	**47**	**44**	**21**	**2.4**	**29**	**88**	**165**	**43**	**18.6**	**42**	**22**	**250**	**–**
Angola	6.4	47	24	1.6	43	12.3	203	42	18.8	38	15	580	205
Cameroon	6.5	40	22	1.8	38	11.6	137	40	19.6	41	20	260	100
Central African Republic	1.8	43	22	2.1	33	3.4	190	42	19.0	41	27	200	54
Chad	4.1	44	24	2.0	35	6.9	160	41	19.1	38	12	90	20
Congo (People's Rep. of)	1.4	45	21	2.4	29	2.7	180	42	18.8	44	37	380	219
Equatorial Guinea	0.3	37	20	1.7	41	0.5	165	37	23.3	44	9	260	180
Gabon	0.5	32	22	1.0	69	0.7	178	32	29.8	41	17	1,560	888
Sao Tome e Principe	0.1	45	11	2.0	35	0.1	64	33	–	–	23	470	–
Zaire	25.6	45	20	2.8	25	50.3	160	44	17.8	44	25	150	86

TABLE A1-1 (*Continued*)

Region or country[a]	Population estimate, mid-1976 (millions)[b]	Birth rate[c]	Death rate[c]	Rate of population growth (annual, percent)[d]	Number of years to double population[e]	Population projection to 2000 (millions)[f]	Infant mortality rate[g]	Population under 15 years (percent)	Median age (years)	Life expectancy at birth (years)	Urban population (percent)[h]	Per-capita gross national product (US $)[i]	Per-capita energy consumption, 1972[j]
Southern Africa	**29**	**43**	**17**	**2.7**	**26**	**56**	**119**	**41**	**19.5**	**51**	**44**	**1,120**	**–**
Botswana	0.7	46	23	2.3	30	1.4	97	46	17.0	44	13	270	–
Lesotho	1.1	39	20	2.1	33	1.8	114	38	21.1	46	5	120	–
Namibia	0.9	46	23	2.2	32	1.6	177	41	19.7	41	23		–
South Africa	25.6	43	16	2.7	26	50.6	117	41	19.5	52	48	1,200	2,770
Swaziland	0.5	49	22	3.2	22	1.0	149	46	16.7	44	8	400	–
ASIA	**2,287**	**33**	**13**	**2.0**	**35**	**3,612**	**121**	**38**	**21.1**	**56**	**25**	**450**	**–**
Southwest Asia	**87**	**43**	**14**	**2.9**	**24**	**166**	**114**	**44**	**18.2**	**55**	**41**	**1,050**	**–**
Bahrain	0.2	44	15	2.9	24	0.5	78	44	17.8	61	78	2,250	5,117
Cyprus	0.7	18	10	0.8	87	0.8	28	32	24.7	71	43	1,380	1,705
Gaza	0.4	50	16	3.4	20	0.9	–	49	–	52	79	–	–
Iraq	11.4	48	15	3.3	21	24.3	99	48	16.0	53	61	970	642
Israel	3.5	28	7	2.9	24	5.5	23	33	25.1	71	86	3,380	2,712
Jordan	2.8	48	15	3.3	21	5.9	97	48	16.2	53	43	400	331
Kuwait	1.1	45	8	5.9	12	3.0	44	43	19.1	69	22	11,640	10,441
Lebanon	2.7	40	10	3.0	23	5.7	59	43	18.6	63	61	1,080	889
Oman	0.8	50	19	3.1	22	1.6	138	–	–	–	–	1,250	182
Qatar	0.1	50	19	3.1	22	0.2	138	–	–	–	–	5,830	–
Saudi Arabia	6.4	49	20	2.9	24	12.9	152	45	17.6	45	18	2,080	900
Syria	7.6	45	15	3.0	23	16.0	93	49	15.4	54	44	490	455
Turkey	40.2	39	12	2.6	27	71.3	119	42	19.0	57	39	690	564
United Arab Emirates	0.2	50	19	3.1	22	0.5	138	34	21.3	–	65	13,500	–
Yemen Arab Republic	6.9	50	21	2.9	24	13.8	152	45	17.6	45	7	120	13
Yemen (People's Republic of)	1.7	50	21	2.9	24	3.4	152	45	17.6	45	26	120	423
Middle South Asia	**851**	**37**	**16**	**2.2**	**32**	**1,493**	**137**	**41**	**19.2**	**49**	**20**	**160**	**–**
Afghanistan	19.5	43	21	2.2	32	36.3	182	44	17.9	40	15	100	38
Bangladesh	76.1	47	20	2.7	26	144.8	132	46	16.7	43	9	100	32
Bhutan	1.2	44	21	2.3	30	2.2	–	42	18.9	44	3	70	–
India	620.7	35	15	2.0	35	1,051.4	139	40	19.6	50	20	130	186
Iran	34.1	45	16	3.0	23	67.0	139	47	16.4	51	43	1,060	954
Maldive Islands	0.1	50	23	3.3	21	0.2	–	44	–	–	11	90	–
Nepal	12.9	43	20	2.3	30	23.2	169	40	20.3	44	4	110	15
Pakistan	72.5	44	15	2.9	24	146.4	124	46	16.6	50	26	130	158
Sikkim	0.2	–	–	2.0	35	0.4	208	40	19.5	–	5	90	–
Sri Lanka	14.0	28	8	2.0	35	21.0	45	39	19.9	68	22	130	146
Southeast Asia	**327**	**38**	**15**	**2.4**	**29**	**583**	**108**	**43**	**18.3**	**51**	**20**	**220**	**–**
Burma	31.2	40	16	2.4	29	53.5	126	41	19.6	50	19	90	58
Indonesia	134.7	38	17	2.1	33	230.3	125	44	18.1	48	18	150	133
Khmer Republic	8.3	47	19	2.8	25	15.8	127	45	17.2	45	19	–	25
Laos	3.4	45	23	2.4	29	5.7	123	42	18.9	40	15	–	79
Malaysia	12.4	39	10	2.9	24	22.0	75	44	17.7	59	27	660	492
Philippines	44.0	41	11	3.0	23	86.3	74	43	18.4	58	32	310	311
Portuguese Timor	0.7	44	23	2.1	33	1.1	184	42	18.9	40	10	130	10
Singapore	2.3	20	5	1.6	43	3.1	16	39	19.7	67	100	2,120	885
Thailand	43.3	36	11	2.5	28	86.0	81	45	17.3	58	13	300	305
Vietnam (Dem. Republic of)	24.8	32	14	1.8	38	44.1	–	41	19.1	48	12	130	140
Vietnam (Republic of)	21.6	42	16	2.6	27	34.9	–	41	19.3	40	19	170	287
East Asia	**1,023**	**26**	**9**	**1.7**	**41**	**1,369**	**23**	**33**	**23.9**	**63**	**30**	**710**	**–**
China (People's Republic of)	836.8	27	10	1.7	41	1,126.0	–	33	23.5	62	23	300	567
Hong Kong	4.4	19	5	2.1	33	5.8	18	36	22.0	71	90	1,540	1,034
Japan	112.3	19	6	1.2	58	132.7	11	24	29.6	73	72	3,880	3,251

(*Continued*)

TABLE A1-1 (*Continued*)

Region or country[a]	*Population estimate, mid-1976 (millions)*[b]	*Birth rate*[c]	*Death rate*[c]	*Rate of population growth (annual, percent)*[d]	*Number of years to double population*[e]	*Population projection to 2000 (millions)*[f]	*Infant mortality rate*[g]	*Population under 15 years (percent)*	*Median age (years)*	*Life expectancy at birth (years)*	*Urban population (percent)*[h]	*Per-capita gross national product (US $)*[i]	*Per-capita energy consumption, 1972*[j]
Korea (Dem. People's Rep. of)	16.3	36	9	2.7	26	27.5	–	42	18.5	61	38	390	2,161
Korea (Republic of)	34.8	29	9	2.0	35	52.3	47	40	19.6	61	41	470	827
Macau	0.3	25	7	1.8	38	0.4	78	38	18.9	–	97	270	305
Mongolia	1.5	40	10	3.0	23	2.7	–	44	18.1	61	46	620	963
Taiwan (Republic of China)[k]	16.3	23	5	1.9	36	22.0	26	43	18.2	69	63	720	–
NORTH AMERICA	**239**	**15**	**9**	**0.8**	**87**	**294**	**16**	**27**	**27.9**	**71**	**74**	**6,580**	**11,256**
Canada	23.1	15	7	1.3	53	31.6	16	29	26.5	73	76	6,080	10,757
United States	215.3	15	9	0.8	87	262.5	17	27	28.1	71	74	6,640	11,611
LATIN AMERICA	**326**	**37**	**9**	**2.8**	**25**	**606**	**75**	**42**	**18.9**	**62**	**59**	**940**	–
Middle America	**81**	**45**	**9**	**3.4**	**20**	**172**	**65**	**46**	**16.9**	**62**	**56**	**900**	–
Costa Rica	2.0	28	5	2.3	30	3.6	45	42	18.2	69	41	790	478
El Salvador	4.2	40	8	3.2	22	8.8	54	46	16.9	58	39	390	199
Guatemala	5.7	43	15	2.8	25	11.1	79	44	17.6	53	34	570	260
Honduras	2.8	49	14	3.5	20	6.2	117	47	16.5	54	28	340	231
Mexico	62.3	46	8	3.5	20	134.4	61	46	16.8	63	61	1,000	1,318
Nicaragua	2.2	48	14	3.3	21	4.8	123	48	15.7	53	49	650	408
Panama	1.7	31	5	2.6	27	3.2	44	43	18.2	66	49	1,010	848
Caribbean	**27**	**31**	**9**	**2.1**	**33**	**44**	**71**	**41**	**19.9**	**64**	**43**	**820**	–
Bahamas	0.2	22	6	4.2	16	0.3	32	44	18.7	66	58	2,460	4,965
Barbados	0.2	21	9	0.8	87	0.3	38	34	22.3	69	4	1,110	1,113
Cuba	9.4	25	6	1.8	38	14.9	29	37	22.4	70	60	640	1,168
Dominican Republic	4.8	46	11	3.0	23	10.8	98	48	16.1	58	40	590	261
Grenada	0.1	26	8	0.4	173	0.1	32	47	–	63	8	300	–
Guadeloupe	0.4	28	7	1.5	46	0.5	44	40	19.2	69	9	1,050	548
Haiti	4.6	36	16	1.6	43	7.1	150	41	18.8	50	20	140	28
Jamaica	2.1	31	7	1.9	36	2.8	26	46	17.3	68	37	1,140	1,568
Martinique	0.3	22	7	0.5	139	0.5	32	41	19.0	69	33	1,330	728
Netherlands Antilles	0.2	25	7	1.8	38	0.4	28	38	–	73	32	1,530	–
Puerto Rico	3.2	23	6	2.4	29	4.0	23	37	21.6	72	58	2,400	4,191
Trinidad and Tobago	1.1	26	7	1.5	46	1.4	26	40	19.3	66	12	1,490	4,201
Tropical South America	**178**	**38**	**9**	**2.9**	**24**	**338**	**82**	**43**	**18.1**	**60**	**58**	**840**	–
Bolivia	5.8	44	18	2.6	27	10.6	108	43	18.3	47	35	250	210
Brazil	110.2	37	9	2.8	25	207.5	82	42	18.6	61	58	900	532
Colombia	23.0	41	9	3.2	22	44.3	76	46	16.9	61	64	510	610
Ecuador	6.9	42	10	3.2	22	14.0	78	47	16.3	60	39	460	296
Guyana	0.8	36	6	2.2	32	1.2	40	44	17.2	68	40	470	1,012
Paraguay	2.6	40	9	2.7	26	5.1	65	45	16.6	62	38	480	119
Peru	16.0	41	12	2.9	24	30.9	110	44	17.6	56	60	710	622
Surinam	0.4	41	7	3.2	22	0.9	30	50	15.1	66	49	870	2,211
Venezuela	12.3	36	7	2.9	24	23.1	54	44	17.4	65	75	1,710	2,473
Temperate South America	**39**	**24**	**9**	**1.5**	**46**	**52**	**67**	**32**	**25.7**	**67**	**80**	**1,540**	–
Argentina	25.7	22	9	1.4	50	32.9	64	29	27.4	68	81	1,900	1,728
Chile	10.8	28	8	1.7	41	15.9	78	39	20.5	63	76	820	1,516
Uruguay	2.8	21	10	1.1	63	3.4	45	28	29.4	70	80	1,060	906
EUROPE	**476**	**15**	**10**	**0.6**	**116**	**540**	**22**	**24**	**32.2**	**71**	**64**	**3,680**	–
Northern Europe	**82**	**13**	**12**	**0.2**	**347**	**91**	**15**	**24**	**33.4**	**72**	**73**	**3,960**	–
Denmark	5.1	14	10	0.4	173	5.4	12	23	32.5	73	80	5,820	5,567
Finland	4.7	13	10	0.4	173	4.8	10	24	30.1	69	58	4,130	4,928
Iceland	0.2	20	7	1.3	53	0.3	11	32	24.7	74	86	5,550	4,182
Ireland	3.1	22	11	0.7	99	4.0	17	31	26.8	72	52	2,370	3,303

TABLE A1-1 (*Continued*)

Region or country[a]	Population estimate, mid-1976 (millions)[b]	Birth rate[c]	Death rate[c]	Rate of population growth (annual, percent)[d]	Number of years to double population[e]	Population projection to 2000 (millions)[f]	Infant mortality rate[g]	Population under 15 years (percent)	Median age (years)	Life expectancy at birth (years)	Urban population (percent)[h]	Per-capita gross national product (US $)[i]	Per-capita energy consumption, 1972[j]
Norway	4.0	15	10	0.6	116	4.5	12	24	32.4	74	45	5,280	4,639
Sweden	8.2	13	11	0.4	173	9.3	9	21	35.3	75	81	6,720	5,739
United Kingdom	56.1	13	12	0.1	693	62.3	16	24	34.0	72	76	3,360	5,398
Western Europe	**153**	**13**	**11**	**0.5**	**139**	**171**	**16**	**24**	**33.1**	**72**	**77**	**5,460**	**–**
Austria	7.5	13	12	0.1	693	8.1	23	24	33.7	71	52	4,050	3,608
Belgium	9.8	13	12	0.3	231	10.7	16	23	34.3	71	87	5,210	6,468
France	53.1	15	10	0.8	87	61.9	12	24	32.6	73	70	5,190	4,153
Germany (Federal Republic of)	62.1	10	12	0.2	347	66.5	21	23	34.4	71	88	5,890	5,396
Luxembourg	0.4	11	12	0.7	99	0.4	14	21	35.2	71	68	5,690	6,468
Netherlands	13.8	14	8	0.9	77	16.1	11	27	28.9	74	77	4,880	5,711
Switzerland	6.5	13	9	0.7	99	7.3	13	24	32.1	73	55	6,650	3,620
Eastern Europe	**107**	**17**	**10**	**0.7**	**99**	**122**	**26**	**23**	**31.4**	**70**	**55**	**2,670**	**–**
Bulgaria	8.8	17	10	0.7	99	10.0	25	22	33.5	72	59	1,770	4,130
Czechoslovakia	14.9	20	12	0.8	87	16.9	20	23	31.8	70	56	3,220	6,844
Germany (Dem. Republic of)	16.8	11	14	−0.3	–	17.9	16	23	34.5	71	75	3,430	5,995
Hungary	10.6	18	12	0.6	116	11.1	34	20	34.2	70	49	2,140	3,279
Poland	34.4	18	8	1.0	69	40.1	24	25	28.4	70	55	2,450	4,556
Rumania	21.5	20	9	1.0	69	25.8	35	25	31.0	69	42	–	3,150
Southern Europe	**134**	**18**	**9**	**0.8**	**87**	**156**	**26**	**26**	**31.1**	**71**	**51**	**2,130**	**–**
Albania	2.5	30	8	2.4	29	4.1	87	40	19.2	71	34	530	667
Greece	9.0	16	8	0.4	173	9.7	24	25	33.4	72	53	1,970	1,607
Italy	56.3	16	10	0.8	87	61.7	23	24	32.7	72	53	2,770	2,796
Malta	0.3	18	9	0.4	173	0.3	21	26	27.1	70	94	1,060	1,305
Portugal	8.5	19	11	−0.4	–	9.6	38	28	29.4	68	26	1,540	908
Spain	36.0	19	8	1.1	63	45.1	14	28	30.2	72	61	1,960	1,765
Yugoslavia	21.5	18	8	0.9	77	25.7	40	27	28.8	68	39	1,250	1,610
USSR	**257**	**18**	**9**	**0.9**	**77**	**314**	**28**	**28**	**29.7**	**70**	**60**	**2,300**	**4,767**
OCEANIA	**22**	**22**	**10**	**1.8**	**38**	**33**	**53**	**33**	**25.7**	**68**	**71**	**3,800**	**4,275**
Australia	13.8	18	9	1.5	46	20.0	16	29	27.6	72	86	4,760	5,701
Fiji	0.6	28	5	1.9	36	0.8	21	41	18.9	70	33	720	518
New Zealand	3.2	19	8	2.2	32	4.4	16	32	25.8	72	81	4,100	2,887
Papua-New Guinea	2.8	41	17	2.6	27	5.1	159	45	17.8	48	11	440	188

[a]Included are all United Nations members and all geopolitical entities with populations larger than 200,000.

[b]Based on the U.S. Bureau of Census estimate for mid-1974 or on the most recent official country or United Nations estimate (for most countries the latter estimate was for mid-1974) and updated to mid-1976.

[c]For the developed countries, with complete or nearly complete registration of births and deaths, nearly all the rates shown pertain to 1973 or 1974. For nearly all the developing countries, with incomplete registration, the rates refer to the 1970–1975 period and are taken from the United Nations medium-variant estimates and projections as assessed in 1973. These figures should be considered as rough approximations only.

[d]Based on population changes during part or all of the period since 1970. For most countries these rates are the same as those for natural increase, but because the time periods to which the two rates pertain are different and because the birth and death rates as well as the population estimates for the less developed countries are generally rough approximations only, small differences between the two rates should not be considered as precise estimates of net immigration or net emigration. Larger differences between them do indicate that migration has been a factor in population change.

[e]Based on the rate of population growth shown and assuming no change in the rate.

[f]Except for the United States, based on the application of the percentage increase in the population 1975–2000 implied by the United Nations medium-variant projections to the population total as estimated for mid-1975. For the United States, the figure shown is the Series II projection of the U.S. Bureau of the Census.

[g]Rates pertain to 1973 or 1974 or latest available estimates, generally obtained from the sources cited above.

[h]The percentage of the total population living in areas defined as urban by each country.

[i]Data from *World Bank atlas,* 1975.

[j]In kilograms of coal equivalent (derived from U.N. data).

[k]The United Nations does not show figures for Taiwan. These figures were estimated separately. The population of Taiwan was assumed to increase to the year 2000 at the same rate as that of the People's Republic of China.

Source: Population Reference Bureau, *1976 World population data sheet;* per-capita energy consumption from The Environmental Fund, *World population estimates 1974.*

TABLE A1-2
Projected Population Size, by Paths to a Nongrowing Population, Selected Countries, 1970–2150

Area	Path to a nongrowing population*	Population (millions) 1970	2000	2050	2100	2150	Percent increase 1970–2150
WORLD	**Rapid**	**3,645.0**	**5,922.5**	**8,172.2**	**8,388.6**	**8,382.0**	**129**
	Slow	**3,645.0**	**6,669.8**	**13,024.7**	**15,102.4**	**15,148.0**	**315**
East Asia	**Rapid**	**940.8**	**1,485.0**	**2,001.7**	**2,062.3**	**2,060.4**	**119**
	Slow	**940.8**	**1,645.5**	**3,010.9**	**3,448.4**	**3,456.4**	**267**
Hong Kong	Rapid	4.0	6.6	9.1	9.2	9.2	132
	Slow	4.0	7.4	13.8	15.7	15.8	296
Japan	Immediate	105.8	130.6	138.1	138.5	138.4	31
	Rapid	105.8	130.9	138.8	139.2	139.1	31
Republic of Korea	Rapid	31.9	56.8	78.9	80.6	80.4	152
(South Korea)	Slow	31.9	64.7	128.1	148.0	148.3	365
Republic of China	Rapid	13.7	25.8	37.2	38.0	38.0	177
(Taiwan)	Slow	13.7	29.0	58.9	68.6	69.0	402
South Asia	**Rapid**	**1,102.7**	**2,079.3**	**3,076.6**	**3,166.2**	**3,163.2**	**186**
	Slow	**1,102.7**	**2,468.9**	**5,915.8**	**7,169.6**	**7,196.5**	**552**
India	Rapid	534.3	948.3	1,365.5	1,407.0	1,402.6	163
	Slow	534.3	1,100.2	2,431.8	2,897.0	2,900.2	443
Bangladesh	Rapid	69.2	151.0	239.7	247.2	246.7	257
	Slow	69.2	186.4	528.3	664.6	667.5	865
Pakistan	Rapid	57.0	108.8	160.4	164.1	163.6	187
	Slow	57.0	129.9	311.0	373.9	374.3	557
Iran	Rapid	27.9	56.2	85.9	88.5	88.4	217
	Slow	27.9	68.4	179.8	222.4	223.5	700
Ceylon	Rapid	12.1	21.8	30.2	30.7	30.6	152
	Slow	12.1	24.5	47.3	54.1	54.1	346
Philippines	Rapid	37.8	78.6	118.6	122.5	122.3	223
	Slow	37.8	95.2	239.7	293.7	294.6	679
Thailand	Rapid	36.6	72.1	105.5	107.8	107.5	194
	Slow	36.6	86.0	202.2	241.8	242.0	562
West Malaysia	Rapid	9.4	18.3	26.8	27.5	27.4	193
	Slow	9.4	21.3	47.3	56.1	56.3	502
Singapore	Rapid	2.1	3.9	5.5	5.6	5.6	159
	Slow	2.1	4.3	8.2	9.3	9.3	335
Turkey	Rapid	34.5	61.6	88.4	91.3	91.2	164
	Slow	34.5	70.9	151.4	179.2	179.8	421
Israel	Rapid	2.8	4.4	6.0	6.1	6.1	118
	Slow	2.8	4.9	8.8	10.0	10.0	258
Europe	**Immediate**	**474.0**	**527.1**	**565.2**	**566.3**	**565.9**	**19**
	Rapid	**474.0**	**560.6**	**640.7**	**645.4**	**645.0**	**36**
West Germany	Immediate	63.2	64.8	67.1	67.2	67.2	6
(Federal Republic)	Rapid	63.2	67.6	73.4	73.8	73.7	17
France	Immediate	51.2	56.7	60.2	60.3	60.2	18
	Rapid	51.2	60.3	68.3	68.7	68.7	34
Netherlands	Immediate	13.1	15.8	17.2	17.2	17.2	32
	Rapid	13.1	17.1	20.2	20.3	20.3	55
Belgium	Immediate	9.8	10.4	10.9	10.9	10.9	12
	Rapid	9.8	10.7	11.7	11.7	11.7	20
Austria	Immediate	7.8	8.1	8.5	8.5	8.5	9
	Rapid	7.8	8.5	9.6	9.6	9.6	23
Italy	Immediate	55.9	63.4	66.9	67.0	67.0	20
	Rapid	55.9	65.5	71.5	71.9	71.9	29

TABLE A1-2 (*continued*)

Area	Path to a nongrowing population*	Population (millions)					Percent increase 1970–2150
		1970	2000	2050	2100	2150	
Yugoslavia	Immediate	20.9	25.6	28.2	28.5	28.5	37
	Rapid	20.9	26.5	30.1	30.6	30.6	47
Greece	Immediate	9.2	10.7	11.2	11.2	11.2	22
	Rapid	9.2	10.8	11.5	11.5	11.5	25
Poland	Immediate	33.7	41.0	44.9	45.0	44.9	33
	Rapid	33.7	41.8	46.8	46.9	46.9	39
Czechoslovakia	Immediate	14.8	16.7	17.8	17.8	17.8	20
	Rapid	14.8	16.6	17.5	17.5	17.5	18
Hungary	Immediate	10.6	11.4	11.8	11.9	11.9	11
	Rapid	10.6	11.2	11.3	11.3	11.3	6
England and Wales	Immediate	50.2	53.2	55.8	55.9	55.8	11
	Rapid	50.2	56.4	63.0	63.4	63.4	26
Sweden	Immediate	7.9	8.3	8.6	8.6	8.6	8
	Rapid	7.9	8.5	8.9	9.0	9.0	13
Denmark	Immediate	5.0	5.6	6.0	6.0	6.0	19
	Rapid	5.0	6.0	6.7	6.8	6.8	36
USSR	**Immediate**	**260.1**	**302.5**	**326.9**	**327.6**	**327.3**	**26**
	Rapid	**260.1**	**314.2**	**353.3**	**355.3**	**355.0**	**37**
Africa	**Rapid**	**344.2**	**620.2**	**899.2**	**934.3**	**933.2**	**171**
	Slow	**344.2**	**729.1**	**1,663.6**	**2,003.3**	**2,008.3**	**483**
Nigeria	Rapid	64.7	129.2	197.8	204.9	204.7	216
	Slow	64.7	157.2	422.5	527.1	529.2	718
Ghana	Rapid	9.0	16.8	24.8	25.5	25.4	183
	Slow	9.0	20.2	49.8	60.3	60.4	573
Ivory Coast	Rapid	4.4	7.6	10.7	10.9	10.7	144
	Slow	4.4	8.9	19.9	23.5	23.1	427
Liberia	Rapid	1.5	2.7	3.8	3.9	3.9	150
	Slow	1.5	3.2	7.2	8.5	8.5	450
Tanzania	Rapid	13.2	24.4	35.9	36.9	36.7	178
	Slow	13.2	29.2	71.8	87.1	87.1	558
Kenya	Rapid	10.9	20.7	30.3	31.1	31.0	183
	Slow	10.9	24.8	59.7	71.9	71.9	557
Mauritius	Rapid	0.8	1.5	2.1	2.2	2.2	163
	Slow	0.8	1.7	3.4	3.9	3.9	379
United Arab Republic	Rapid	33.5	62.4	91.7	94.1	93.7	180
	Slow	33.5	74.0	176.3	212.9	213.0	536
Morocco	Rapid	15.8	33.4	51.9	53.6	53.6	239
	Slow	15.8	41.4	116.1	145.8	146.5	828
Algeria	Rapid	13.8	28.6	44.2	45.7	45.6	231
	Slow	13.8	35.2	95.9	119.7	120.2	772
Tunisia	Rapid	5.0	9.9	14.7	15.1	15.1	201
	Slow	5.0	12.0	29.5	35.8	35.8	615
Swaziland	Rapid	0.4	0.8	1.2	1.2	1.2	177
	Slow	0.4	1.0	2.3	2.8	2.8	547
North America	**Immediate**	**227.7**	**276.7**	**311.6**	**312.6**	**312.4**	**37**
	Rapid	**227.7**	**301.6**	**368.2**	**371.9**	**371.7**	**63**
United States	Immediate	205.7	250.4	279.2	279.8	279.6	36
	Rapid	205.7	264.7	311.8	314.0	313.9	53
Canada	Immediate	20.5	26.2	29.3	29.4	29.4	44
	Rapid	20.5	27.7	32.8	33.0	33.0	61

(*Continued*)

TABLE A1-2 (*Continued*)

Area	Path to a nongrowing population*	Population (millions)					Percent increase 1970–2150
		1970	2000	2050	2100	2150	
Latin America	**Rapid**	**283.2**	**539.7**	**797.3**	**823.4**	**823.8**	**190**
	Slow	**283.2**	**625.9**	**1,396.4**	**1,683.3**	**1,695.6**	**498**
Brazil	Rapid	94.0	180.9	265.9	274.3	274.4	192
	Slow	94.0	209.3	459.3	550.8	554.4	490
Colombia	Rapid	21.1	41.2	60.3	62.0	61.9	193
	Slow	21.1	47.7	104.8	125.0	125.6	494
Peru	Rapid	13.5	27.7	42.0	43.3	43.2	219
	Slow	13.5	33.2	81.3	99.6	100.1	639
Venezuela	Rapid	10.1	21.6	33.2	34.1	34.1	236
	Slow	10.1	25.7	63.8	78.5	79.2	681
Mexico	Rapid	50.7	108.7	167.9	173.5	173.4	242
	Slow	50.7	131.3	335.4	416.4	419.4	727
El Salvador	Rapid	3.4	7.2	11.2	11.6	11.6	239
	Slow	3.4	8.6	22.3	27.9	28.1	723
Honduras	Rapid	2.7	6.0	9.3	9.6	9.6	253
	Slow	2.7	7.2	18.6	23.2	23.4	759
Costa Rica	Rapid	1.7	3.7	5.7	5.9	5.9	238
	Slow	1.7	4.4	10.8	13.3	13.4	672
Argentina	Immediate	24.0	29.9	33.5	33.8	33.7	41
	Rapid	24.0	32.4	39.1	39.7	39.7	66
Chile	Immediate	9.6	13.3	15.7	16.0	15.9	66
	Rapid	9.6	15.4	20.5	21.0	21.0	119
Cuba	Rapid	8.0	14.2	20.2	20.7	20.7	158
	Slow	8.0	15.9	32.1	37.9	38.2	375
Dominican Republic	Rapid	4.3	9.7	15.4	16.0	16.0	271
	Slow	4.3	12.0	33.3	42.2	42.6	886
Puerto Rico	Immediate	2.9	4.1	4.8	4.9	4.9	65
	Rapid	2.9	4.7	6.2	6.3	6.3	113
Trinidad and Tobago	Immediate	1.1	1.6	1.9	1.9	1.9	79
	Rapid	1.1	1.9	2.6	2.7	2.7	145
Oceania	**Immediate**	**18.5**	**23.4**	**26.9**	**27.2**	**27.2**	**46**
	Rapid	**18.5**	**27.0**	**35.1**	**35.8**	**35.8**	**92**
Australia	Immediate	11.9	14.6	16.2	16.2	16.2	36
	Rapid	11.9	16.2	19.6	19.8	19.8	66

*Paths were chosen to represent reasonable estimates of when an NRR of 1.0 might be reached. For countries with NRRs in 1970 of 1.75 or more, the rapid and slow paths were used; countries with 1970 NRRs below 1.75 were expected to grow along the lines of the immediate and rapid paths.

Source: Thomas Frejka, *Population Bulletin,* vol. 29, no. 5, 1974. Courtesy of Population Reference Bureau, Inc., Washington, D.C.

APPENDIX 2

Food and Nutrition

Despite the emphasis on the need for a balanced diet that has been a part of school curricula and general public information in the United States since the 1920s and 1930s, some Americans are still convinced that a typical Asian can live happily and healthily on one bowl of rice per day. The truth is that an Asian's nutritional requirements are just the same as those of an American, although the total amounts an Asian may need of some nutrients may be less, because of the Asian's smaller size (itself doubtless the result of poorer nutrition during the years of growth). The Asian, however, meets his or her nutritional needs through a quite different assortment of foods from those an American would choose.

The traditional diets of various peoples of the world differ tremendously, from the East African Masai diet of berries, grain, vegetables, milk, blood from cattle, and some sheep or goat meat, to the Polynesian diet of coconut, fish, breadfruit, taro, tropical fruits, and occasional pork or poultry. American and European diets—once based on relatively few foods, such as beef, mutton, poultry, dairy products, eggs, wheat and other cereals, potatoes (more recently), pulses, vegetables, and fruits—have grown in the past generation to include a fantastic array of foods from all parts of the world. Nevertheless, the relatively limited traditional diets of most of the people in less developed countries, where undernutrition and malnutrition are today very widespread, could be basically adequate to meet their needs.

The existing nutritional deficiencies result mainly from insufficient supplies of some or all of those foods. Lack of sufficient food may be a result of being too poor to buy it or ignorance of the best choices, or both. (The inexcusably poor diets of many Americans are more often due to ignorance of nutrition or to indifference than to poverty.) Table A2-1 shows available food energy and protein supplies per capita in the world averaged over 1969 through 1971. Diets of lower-income groups in less developed countries are often seriously deficient in kilocalories (and, accordingly, in other nutrients as well). Surveys in several LDCs have shown very clearly the discrepancies in food intake per person between highest and lowest income families (Tables A2-2 and A2-3).

As rapid population growth in LDCs has strained efforts to maintain food supplies, demand for imported food has increased dramatically, especially since 1972. This trend is shown in Table A2-4, comparing the quantities of grain exported (traded between countries) with total production and consumption. The bulk of exported grain goes to developed countries, but the share exported to LDCs has been rising rapidly in recent years. Table A2-5 shows United Nation's projections of expected increases in worldwide demand for various kinds of food between 1970 and 1985.

TABLE A2-1

Population, Food Supply, and Demand for Food in Individual Countries, 1969–1971

Country	Population	Food production[a]	Domestic demand for food[b, c]	Dietary energy supply[c, d]: Kilocalories per capita per day	Dietary energy supply[c, d]: Percentage of requirements[f]	Protein supply[c,d]: Grams per capita per day
	Percentage rate of growth per year[e]					
Developed Countries						
Albania	2.8	3.6	4.6	2390	99	74
Australia	2.1	3.7	2.4	3280	123	108
Austria	0.4	2.5	1.1	3310	126	90
Belgium-Luxembourg	0.6	2.1	1.2	3380	128	95
Bulgaria	0.8	4.3	2.8	3290	132	100
Canada	2.2	2.2	2.5	3180	129	101
Czechoslovakia	0.9	1.8	1.9	3180	129	94
Denmark	0.7	1.6	1.3	3240	120	93
Finland	0.8	2.4	1.1	3050	113	93
France	1.0	3.0	2.0	3210	127	105
Germany, East	−0.3	1.6	0.8	3290	126	87
Germany, West	1.0	2.5	1.9	3220	121	89
Greece	0.8	4.0	2.3	3190	128	113
Hungary	0.5	3.0	1.9	3280	125	100
Ireland	0.1	1.7	0.3	3410	136	103
Israel	3.4	7.7	4.9	2960	115	93
Italy	0.7	2.9	2.3	3180	126	100
Japan	1.1	4.3	3.7	2510	107	79
Malta	0.1	3.2	1.2	2820	114	89
Netherlands	1.3	3.0	1.7	3320	123	87
New Zealand	2.1	2.7	2.0	3200	121	109
Norway	0.9	1.3	1.3	2960	110	90
Poland	1.4	3.0	2.3	3280	125	101
Portugal	0.6	1.7	2.3	2900	118	85
Rumania	1.1	3.2	2.7	3140	118	90
South Africa	2.4	3.9	3.2	2740	112	78
Spain	0.9	3.4	3.0	2600	106	81
Sweden	0.7	0.9	1.0	2810	104	86
Switzerland	1.5	1.7	1.9	3190	119	91
United States	1.5	2.0	1.6	3330	126	106
USSR	1.5	3.9	3.0	3280	131	101
United Kingdom	0.5	2.8	0.7	3190	126	92
Yugoslavia	1.2	4.5	2.4	3190	125	94
Less Developed Countries						
Afghanistan	1.9	1.7	2.2	1970	81	58
Algeria	2.4	−0.8	3.4	1730	72	46
Angola	1.8	2.7	3.0	2000	85	42
Argentina	1.7	1.8	2.0	3060	115	100
Bangladesh	3.5[g]	1.6[g]	–	1840	80	40
Barbados	0.6	−0.1	–	–	–	–
Bolivia	2.3	5.0	2.7	1900	79	46
Botswana	2.0	2.3	–	2040	87	65
Brazil	3.0	4.4	4.0	2620	110	65
Burma	2.2	2.4	3.3	2210	102	50
Burundi	2.0	2.4	2.4	2040	88	62
Cameroon	1.8	3.3	2.5	2410	104	64
Central African Republic	1.8	2.8	1.1	2200	98	49
Chad	2.1	0.9	1.2	2110	89	75
Chile	2.5	2.2	3.3	2670	109	77
China	1.7	2.3	–	2170	91	60
Colombia	3.3	3.1	3.9	2200	95	51
Congo	1.9	2.2	3.7	2260	102	44
Costa Rica	3.8	5.4	4.8	2610	116	66
Cuba	2.2	1.1	2.0	2700	117	63
Cyprus	1.1	5.4	2.3	2670	108	–

TABLE A2-1 (*Continued*)

Country	Population	Food production[a]	Domestic demand for food[b, c]	Dietary energy supply[c, d]: Kilocalories per capita per day	Dietary energy supply[c, d]: Percentage of requirements[f]	Protein supply[c,d]: Grams per capita per day
	Percentage rate of growth per year[e]					
Dahomey	2.3	1.5	0.1	2260	98	56
Dominican Republic	3.3	2.2	3.6	2120	94	48
Ecuador	3.3	5.4	4.0	2010	88	47
Egypt	2.6	3.4	3.8	2500	100	69
El Salvador	3.0	3.6	4.1	1930	84	52
Ethiopia	1.8	2.3	3.0	2160	93	72
Gabon	0.6	3.6	2.4	2220	95	57
Gambia	1.8	4.4	—	2490	104	64
Ghana	2.9	3.9	3.2	2320	101	49
Guatemala	3.0	4.1	4.2	2130	97	59
Guinea	2.0	2.0	3.4	2020	88	45
Guyana	3.0	2.5	3.6	2390	105	58
Haiti	2.3	1.0	2.2	1730	77	39
Honduras	3.3	4.0	4.2	2140	94	56
India	2.1	2.4	3.0	2070	94	52
Indonesia	2.5	2.0	2.6	1790	83	38
Iran	2.8	3.3	5.4	2300	96	60
Iraq	3.3	2.8	5.2	2160	90	60
Ivory Coast	2.2	4.9	2.6	2430	105	56
Jamaica	1.9	1.9	3.3	2360	105	63
Jordan	3.2	1.8	6.6	2430	99	65
Kenya	3.0	2.6	4.7	2360	102	67
Khmer Republic	2.8	3.5	4.3	2430	109	55
Korea, North	2.7	—	—	2240	89	73
Korea, South	2.7	4.8	4.7	2520	107	68
Laos	2.4	3.7	3.7	2110	95	49
Lebanon	2.8	5.0	3.1	2280	92	63
Lesotho	1.6	0.5	—	—	—	—
Liberia	1.5	1.1	1.8	2170	94	39
Libyan Arab Republic	3.6	5.3	—	2570	109	62
Madagascar	2.4	2.8	2.1	2530	111	58
Malawi	2.5	4.7	3.7	2210	95	63
Malaysia (West)	3.0	5.2	4.3	2460	110	54
Mali	2.1	1.6	4.3	2060	88	64
Mauritania	2.0	2.4	3.0	1970	85	68
Mauritius	2.6	1.3	3.0	2360	104	48
Mexico	3.4	5.3	4.3	2580	111	62
Mongolia	2.9	—	—	2380	106	—
Morocco	3.0	2.8	3.3	2220	92	62
Mozambique	1.7	2.7	3.2	2050	88	41
Nepal	1.8	0.1	2.1	2080	95	49
Nicaragua	3.0	4.9	3.9	2450	109	71
Niger	2.8	4.1	2.2	2080	89	74
Nigeria	2.4	2.0	3.1	2270	96	63
Pakistan	3.0	3.0	4.2	2160	93	56
Panama	3.2	4.3	4.8	2580	112	61
Paraguay	3.1	2.6	3.4	2740	119	73
Peru	2.9	2.9	3.9	2320	99	60
Philippines	3.2	3.2	4.2	1940	86	47
Rhodesia	3.4	3.9	4.1	2660	111	76
Rwanda	2.6	1.8	1.9	1960	84	58
Saudi Arabia	2.4	2.9	5.0	2270	94	62
Senegal	2.2	3.3	1.2	2370	100	65
Sierra Leone	2.0	2.4	3.9	2280	99	51
Somalia	2.2	1.1	1.5	1830	79	56
Sri Lanka	2.5	3.6	3.1	2170	98	48

(*Continued*)

TABLE A2-1 (*Continued*)

Country	Population	Food production[a]	Domestic demand for food[b, c]	Dietary energy supply[c, d]: Kilocalories per capita per day	Dietary energy supply[c, d]: Percentage of requirements[f]	Protein supply[c,d]: Grams per capita per day
	Percentage rate of growth per year[e]					
Sudan	2.9	4.3	3.9	2160	92	63
Surinam	3.1	–	4.0	2450	109	59
Syrian Arab Republic	3.0	1.8	4.6	2650	107	75
Tanzania	2.4	3.1	3.0	2260	98	63
Thailand	3.1	5.3	4.6	2560	115	56
Togo	2.3	5.4	2.4	2330	101	56
Trinidad and Tobago	2.5	1.9	4.8	2380	98	64
Tunisia	2.9	0.8	4.3	2250	94	67
Turkey	2.7	3.0	3.8	3250	129	91
Uganda	2.4	1.8	3.2	2130	91	61
Upper Volta	1.8	4.7	1.2	1710	72	59
Uruguay	1.3	0.8	1.2	2880	108	100
Venezuela	3.5	6.1	4.0	2430	98	63
Vietnam, North	2.7	–	–	2350	114	53
Vietnam, South	2.5	4.3	3.2	2320	107	53
Yemen Arab Republic	2.4	−0.2	3.9	2040	84	61
Yemen, Democratic Republic	2.4	1.6	−1.0	2070	86	57
Zaire	2.0	0.2	2.3	2060	93	33
Zambia	2.9	4.3	4.8	2590	112	68

[a]Food component of crop and livestock production only (excludes fish production).
[b]Calculated on basis of growth of population and per-capita income.
[c]Total food, including fish.
[d]1969–1971 average.
[e]Exponential trend 1952–1972.
[f]Revised standards of average requirements (physiological requirements plus 10 percent for waste at household level).
[g]1962–1972.
Source: Assessment of the world food situation, present and future, UN World Food Conference, 1974.

TABLE A2-2
Daily Per-Capita Energy Intake in Rural Madagascar, 1962, and Rural Tunisia, 1965–1968, by Income

Madagascar: Income per household, FMG per year	Madagascar: Percent of households	Madagascar: Kcals per capita per day	Tunisia: Total expenditure Dinars per capita per year	Tunisia: Percent of households	Tunisia: Kcals per capita per day
1–20	55	2150	Under 20	8	1780
20–40	28	2290	20–27	8	2120
40–80	11	2250	27–32	8	2190
80–130	4	2360	32–45	20	2430
130–190	2	2350	45–53	11	2620
190–390	1	2340	53–64	12	2750
390–590	0.3	2360	64–102	20	2900
Other	0.2	–	102–150	9	3180
			150–200	2	3250
			Over 200	2	3150

Source: Assessment of the world food situation, present and future, UN World Food Conference, 1974.

TABLE A2-3
Daily Per-Capita Energy Intake in Brazil, 1960, by income

	Northeast			
	Urban		*Rural*	
Cruz. per household per year	*Percent of households*	*Kcals per capita per day*	*Percent of households*	*Kcals per capita per day*
Under 100	9	1240	18	1500
100–149	13	1500	14	1810
150–249	26	2000	25	2140
250–349	17	2320	13	1820
350–499	14	2420	10	2280
500–799	11	2860	11	2370
800–1199	5	3310	5	3380
1200–2499	4	4040	3	2870
Over 2500	1	4290	1	2900

	East			
	Urban		*Rural*	
Cruz. per household per year	*Percent of households*	*Kcals per capita per day*	*Percent of households*	*Kcals per capita per day*
Under 100	5	1180	7	1420
100–149	5	1530	10	2100
150–249	17	1880	20	2210
250–349	14	2090	15	2720
350–499	17	2220	13	2670
500–799	20	2630	13	2920
800–1199	11	2820	8	3060
1200–2499	9	3270	11	3040
Over 2500	2	3750	3	4100

	South			
	Urban		*Rural*	
Cruz. per household per year	*Percent of households*	*Kcals per capita per day*	*Percent of households*	*Kcals per capita per day*
Under 100	1	1480	4	2380
100–149	3	1740	4	2900
150–249	11	1970	16	2500
250–349	13	2050	15	2860
350–499	20	2360	18	2970
500–799	22	2470	21	3000
800–1199	14	2780	9	3780
1200–2499	12	3080	10	4160
Over 2500	4	3170	3	4770

Source: Assessment of the world food situation, present and future, UN World Food Conference, 1974.

TABLE A2-4
World Grain Supply and Proportion Exported (million MT)

Marketing year	*Production*	*Total exports*	*Consumption total*
1960–1961	657.0	69.9	640.6
1961–1962	624.2	80.8	648.1
1962–1963	671.3	78.0	664.8
1963–1964	661.7	94.1	664.5
1964–1965	696.3	92.4	686.0
1965–1966	701.9	108.1	734.7
1966–1967	771.1	100.0	744.1
1967–1968	785.6	97.4	767.4
1968–1969	822.4	89.7	794.4
1969–1970	825.7	102.1	839.3
1970–1971	823.7	109.2	855.5
1971–1972	911.4	111.2	892.8
1972–1973	888.1	141.8	925.4
1973–1974	970.4	151.0	959.5

Note: Includes wheat, rye, barley, oats, corn, and sorghum, but not rice.
Source: Adapted from Foreign Agricultural Service and Economic Research Service, *Grain data base,* November 1974.

TABLE A2-5
Projected Increase in World Demand for Food by Major Commodity Groups
(assuming "medium" population growth projection and "trend" growth in per-capita gross domestic product)

	Consumption (million MT)	Projected demand (million MT)	Total increase (percent)	Growth rates (percent p.a. compound)
	1969–1971	1985	1985/1970	1970–1985
Cereals[a]	1207	1725	42.9	2.4
Wheat[a]	332	447	43.8	2.0
Rice, paddy[a]	310	447	44.3	2.5
Coarse grains[a]	565	831	46.9	2.6
Starchy roots	279	342	22.3	1.4
Sugar (raw basis)	70	107	54.1	2.9
Pulses, nuts and oilseeds	52	79	51.2	2.8
Vegetables	223	330	48.0	2.6
Fruits	158	250	58.2	3.1
Meat[b]	107	168	57.3	3.1
Beef and veal	39	60	54.7	3.0
Mutton and lamb	7	12	69.1	3.6
Pig meat	36	53	48.3	2.7
Poultry meat	16	29	83.5	4.1
Eggs	19	29	50.8	2.8
Fish	41	68	64.6	3.4
Whole milk, including butter[c]	389	532	36.9	2.1
Cheese	9	14	51.7	2.8
Fats and oils[d]	33	49	47.9	2.6
Butter (fat content)	5	7	33.9	2.0
Vegetable oils	22	35	55.1	3.0

Note: All data are rounded.
[a]Including feed and nonfood demand, in primary commodity equivalent.
[b]Including offals.
[c]Including milk products in liquid milk equivalent.
[d]Including animal fats.
Source: Assessment of the world food situation, present and future, UN World Food Conference, 1974.

THE ESSENTIAL NUTRIENTS

Some knowledge of basic nutrition is important, both for understanding the world food situation and for optimizing one's own health through better nourishment. Some forty-five compounds and elements found in foods are considered essential nutrients, necessary for life and health in human beings. These nutrients fall into five general categories: *carbohydrates, fats, proteins, vitamins,* and *minerals.* Each nutrient can be found in a wide variety of foods, although no one food contains all of them. Each performs some particular function or functions within the body, providing energy, building and repairing tissue, or maintaining the physiological processes of life.[1]

[1]For a detailed summary of the nutrient contents of a wide variety of foods, see The Department of Agriculture handbook 8, *Composition of foods,* Washington, D.C., 1963, also published as *Handbook of the nutritional contents of foods,* Dover Publications, New York, 1975. Bernice K. Watt and Annabel L. Merrill, eds.

Carbohydrates and Fats

Energy for the life processes and for activity is obtained through "burning" food in the process known as *metabolism.* Usually this energy is provided by carbohydrates and fats, although if those elements are undersupplied, proteins may be utilized to make up the deficit. The potential energy from food is measured in *kilocalories.* One kilocalorie (kcal) is the amount of energy (in the form of heat) required to raise the temperature of 1 kilogram of water 1°C.

Carbohydrates are sugars and starches. They are both made of the same elements—carbon, hydrogen, and oxygen. In digestion, starch (which is a structurally more complicated molecule) is broken down to simple sugars. These sugars may then be metabolized at once or stored for future needs.

Sugars are found most abundantly in fruits, and to a smaller extent in vegetables, milk, and milk products.

Refined sugars, which are used in cooking, baking, and preserving, come from sugar cane or sugar beets. Starches are found in cereals and vegetables, especially pulses and root vegetables such as potatoes and yams.

Fats are present in both plant and animal foods, as well as eggs and dairy products. Besides being a source of energy, whether used directly or stored as a reserve, fats are important structural constituents of cell membranes. They also provide the sheaths that surround nerves, help to support internal organs, and assist in the utilization of fat-soluble vitamins.

When insufficient supplies of carbohydrates and fats are eaten, the stored reserves are consumed and weight is lost. There is usually an accompanying curtailment of physical activity. If the weight loss continues until the reserves are gone, the individual starves. Food-energy starvation is often hard to distinguish from other deficiencies. Even if enough protein is provided in the diet to meet protein needs, it is instead metabolized for its caloric value, so protein deficiency results. Vitamins and minerals are also likely to be undersupplied when intake of carbohydrates and fats is too low.

A diet deficient in fats is likely to produce irritability and possibly deficiencies in the fat-soluble vitamins.

Needs for food energy are related to body size, age, and level of activity. Children and pregnant or nursing mothers need proportionately more kilocalories relative to their body weights than other adults, to support growth. A man engaged in extremely heavy work may need nearly twice as much food energy as a man with a sedentary job. Table A2-6 shows the National Academy of Sciences–National Research Council recommended dietary allowances for most nutrients, including kilocalories.

Proteins

Proteins are the structural materials of life, including human life. They also serve in many other roles, as enzymes (biological catalysts) and as oxygen transport compounds (hemoglobin). Most parts of the body—muscles, bones, skin, even hair and blood—are made up largely of proteins. Whereas there are millions of different proteins, all of them are built from about twenty *amino acids.* The differences are in the arrangements and proportions of the amino acids. These subunits, in turn, are composed primarily of carbon, nitrogen, oxygen, and hydrogen. When eaten, the complicated protein molecules are broken down in digestion into their constituent amino acids, which are then reassembled in the body to meet protein needs. Eight of the amino acids are essential in our diets; the others can be synthesized from simple precursors.

Proteins are essential for growth and development, for tissue maintenance and repair, and for healing and recovery from disease. They also play a part in regulating the metabolism of sugar. To support growth, infants and children need higher proportions of protein relative to their body weights than adults. So, for the same reason, do pregnant and lactating (nursing) women. Physical activity does not affect protein needs, although severe illness or injury does increase those needs temporarily.

Proteins are found in virtually all foods, but in enormously differing quantities and qualities. Complete-protein foods—those that contain all of the essential amino acids—are primarily animal foods: meat, fish, poultry, eggs, and dairy products. Nuts and pulses also provide substantial amounts of protein, and cereals have moderate amounts, but all of these are of lower quality. This means that the essential amino acids in these foods do not occur in ideal proportions for meeting nutritional needs. Protein of the highest quality (except for mother's milk) is found in eggs, and that of the next best quality is found in cow's milk.

Foods containing lower-quality protein can, however, be combined to make meals with high-quality protein. One of the best is to combine a pulse with a cereal. Thus, many traditional mixtures from various cuisines—Mexican tortillas and beans; Chinese mixtures of rice, beans, and nuts; New England's baked beans and brown bread—actually are high-quality protein meals.

Small amounts of animal protein such as milk or meat can also greatly enhance the quality of vegetable proteins. Here again, the combination is superior in quality to each component taken separately. It should be emphasized, though, that the separate components must be consumed *at the same time* in order to work; having rice for breakfast and beans for lunch will not do the job.[2]

[2]For a detailed description of protein combinations plus recipes, see Frances Moore Lappé's *Diet for a small planet,* 2d ed., Ballantine, New York, 1975.

TABLE A2-6
Recommended Daily Dietary Allowances

	Age (years)	Weight (kg)	Weight (lbs)	Height (cm)	Height (in)	Energy (kcal)	Protein (g)	Fat-soluble vitamins: Vitamin A (IU)	Vitamin D (IU)	Vitamin E (IU)
Infants	0.0–0.5	6	14	60	24	kg × 117	kg × 2.2	1,400	400	4
	0.5–1.0	9	20	71	28	kg × 108	kg × 2.0	2,000	400	5
Children	1–3	13	28	86	34	1300	23	2,000	400	7
	4–6	20	44	110	44	1800	30	2,500	400	9
	7–10	30	66	135	54	2400	36	3,300	400	10
Males	11–14	44	97	158	63	2800	44	5,000	400	12
	15–18	61	134	172	69	3000	54	5,000	400	15
	19–22	67	147	172	69	3000	52	5,000	400	15
	23–50	70	154	172	69	2700	56	5,000	400	15
	51+	70	154	172	69	2400	56	5,000	400	15
Females	11–14	44	97	155	62	2400	44	4,000	400	12
	15–18	54	119	162	65	2100	48	4,000	400	12
	19–22	58	128	162	65	2100	46	4,000	400	12
	23–50	58	128	162	65	2000	46	4,000	400	12
	51+	58	128	162	65	1800	46	4,000	400	12
Pregnant						+300	+30	5,000	400	15
Lactating						+500	+20	6,000	400	15

Note: The allowances are intended to provide for individual variations among most normal persons as they live in the United States under usual environmental stresses. Diets should be based on a variety of common foods in order to provide other nutrients for which human requirements have been less well defined. See text

A diet deficient in protein results in a lack of energy, stamina, and resistance to disease. In children the result is retarded growth and development. If the deficiency is severe and continues over a long period of time, even if the child survives to adulthood, he or she may never fully recover (see Chapter 7).

Vitamins

Vitamins are essential nutrients needed in minute amounts compared with carbohydrates, fats, and proteins. They fill a variety of needs in the regulation of life processes. The lack of any of the thirteen or more essential vitamins leads to problems of cellular metabolism, which may lead to a serious deficiency disease and ultimately to death. Many vitamins are depleted or destroyed by exposure to light, air, heat, or alkaline conditions. They are therefore often lost from food through improper storage or cooking methods.

Vitamins fall into two general classes: fat-soluble (vitamins A, D, E, and K) and water-soluble (B complex and C). The fat-soluble vitamins can be absorbed only in the presence of bile salts, which are brought into the digestive system by fat in the diet.

Vitamin A exists in vegetables and fruits in a precursor form known as *carotene,* which is converted in the liver to Vitamin A. It is found as Vitamin A most abundantly in liver, eggs, and dairy foods. It is needed for normal vision, healthy skin, gums, and soft tissues, and for resistance to respiratory illnesses. Vitamin A is a precursor of *retinene,* which together with a protein makes up visual purple, the photosensitive substance of the retina.

A lack of Vitamin A first shows up in night blindness, skin problems, and susceptibility to colds. When it is more extreme, the visual and skin problems intensify, and blindness may result *(xerophthalmia).* Blindness from Vitamin A deficiency is a major health problem in some LDCs.

TABLE A2-6 (*Continued*)

Water-soluble vitamins							Minerals					
Ascorbic Acid (mg)	*Folacin (µg)*	*Niacin (mg)*	*Riboflavin (mg)*	*Thiamine (mg)*	*Vitamin* B_6 *(mg)*	*Vitamin* B_{12} *(µg)*	*Calcium (mg)*	*Phosphorus (mg)*	*Iodine (µg)*	*Iron (mg)*	*Magnesium (mg)*	*Zinc (mg)*
35	50	5	0.4	0.3	0.3	0.3	360	240	35	10	60	3
35	50	8	0.6	0.5	0.4	0.3	540	400	45	15	70	5
40	100	9	0.8	0.7	0.6	1.0	800	800	60	15	150	10
40	200	12	1.1	0.9	0.9	1.5	800	800	80	10	200	10
40	300	16	1.2	1.2	1.2	2.0	800	800	110	10	250	10
45	400	18	1.5	1.4	1.6	3.0	1200	1200	130	18	350	15
45	400	20	1.8	1.5	2.0	2.0	1200	1200	150	18	400	15
45	400	20	1.8	1.5	2.0	3.0	800	800	140	10	350	15
45	400	18	1.6	1.4	2.0	3.0	800	800	130	10	350	15
45	400	16	1.5	1.2	2.0	3.0	800	800	110	10	350	15
45	400	16	1.3	1.2	1.6	3.0	1200	1200	115	18	300	15
45	400	14	1.4	1.1	2.0	3.0	1200	1200	115	18	300	15
45	400	14	1.4	1.1	2.0	3.0	800	800	100	18	300	15
45	400	13	1.2	1.0	2.0	3.0	800	800	100	18	300	15
45	400	12	1.1	1.0	2.0	3.0	800	800	80	10	300	15
60	800	+2	+0.3	+0.3	2.5	4.0	1200	1200	125	18+	450	20
80	600	+4	+0.5	+0.3	2.5	4.0	1200	1200	150	16	450	25

for more detailed discussion of allowances and of nutrients not tabulated. IU = international units.
Source: Food and Nutrition Board, National Academy of Sciences–National Research Council, 1973.

The Vitamin B complex consists of at least eight vitamins, which were originally thought to be only one when first discovered. These vitamins are necessary for efficient metabolism. Although they perform different functions, they seem to act somewhat synergistically, and they often occur together in foods. The richest sources of the entire complex are liver, whole grains, yeast, and unpolished rice. Deficiencies involving several B vitamins simultaneously are fairly common. The lack of one also may impair the action of the others.

Thiamine (Vitamin B_1), besides having an important role in carbohydrate metabolism, is necessary in regulating growth and in maintaining the health and functions of the circulatory, digestive, and nervous systems. Its absence leads to the disease known as *beriberi,* whose symptoms are lack of energy, nervous and emotional disorders, and digestive and circulatory disturbances.

Beriberi often accompanies a high-carbohydrate diet, usually one based on polished rice. The thiamine in rice is in or just under the outer skin of the grain, which is removed in milling. Where rice is hand-pounded, undermilled, or parboiled (soaked and partly cooked) before milling, at least some of the thiamine is preserved. But polished rice is preferred in many countries for its keeping qualities and because the product of milling (the polishings or husks) may be used as livestock feed. Infantile beriberi, an acute form of the disease caused by deficiency in the mother during pregnancy, strikes breast-fed infants and soon leads to death unless it is treated promptly.

Beriberi was for a time widespread in Southeast Asia and the Philippines. This was partly because of the introduction of modern community rice mills, which eliminated the need for hand-pounding, formerly done at home. Pregnant and nursing women in those areas by tradition were restricted to very limited diets, which further curtailed their intake of thiamine as well as other vitamins and protein. Specific nutritional programs have recently reduced the incidence of beriberi in Southeast Asia.

Riboflavin (Vitamin B_2) is also involved in carbohydrate metabolism, functioning as a coenzyme. Deficiency leads to problems with eyes, the central nervous system, and the skin *(ariboflavinosis).* This deficiency frequently appears together with Vitamin A deficiency. Riboflavin is found in the usual B-vitamin foods, plus milk and eggs.

Pyridoxine (Vitamin B_6) also functions as a coenzyme involved in protein and fat metabolism. It is needed for healthy skin, nerves, and muscles.

Vitamin B_{12}, unlike the other B vitamins, is not found in vegetable sources; it is obtained mainly from milk and liver. It is used therapeutically for treatment of pernicious anemia and probably normally prevents its occurrence. (Strict vegetarians, who avoid even milk and eggs, run a risk of developing pernicious anemia.)

Niacin (nicotinic acid) participates in a wide variety of metabolic processes as part of the NAD $\rightleftharpoons$ NADP electron-transfer system. It is essential for normal function of the nervous system, soft tissues, skin, and liver. The symptoms of deficiency include mental disorders, skin problems, and swollen gums and tongue. The severe deficiency disease *pellagra* is characterized by the "three Ds"—diarrhea, dermatosis, dementia. This disease often is found among people whose staple food is corn. In Latin America it somehow seems to be avoided through the practice of soaking corn in limewater before grinding it. Pellagra was a serious problem among poor families in the southeastern United States before World War II.

Choline is essential for normal functioning of the liver, the kidneys, and several glands, as well as for fat metabolism.

Pantothenic acid functions as a component of *coenzyme A,* involved in carbohydrate, fat, and protein metabolism. It is needed for growth, for the health of the skin, the digestive tract, and the adrenal gland.

Folic acid is involved in the regulation of red blood cells and the function of the liver and glands. Deficiency may lead to liver and digestive disturbances.

Biotin is essential to cellular metabolism and functions, among other places, in the Krebs cycle. Deficiency produces an anemia, skin and heart disorders, sleeplessness, and muscular pain.

Other B vitamins are *para-aminobenzoic acid* (PABA) and *inositol.* PABA is an intermediate in folic acid synthesis, and inositol is involved in the metabolism of fats.

Vitamin C (ascorbic acid) is essential for healthy skin, gums, and blood vessels. It is also built into cell walls and is necessary for their continuing strength. Vitamin C also is an important factor in resistance to stress and infection. This vitamin is widely found in fruits, peppers, leafy green vegetables, and potatoes, the richest sources being peppers and citrus fruits. It is relatively unstable, being quickly destroyed by heat, and cannot be stored in the body for more than a few days.

Symptoms of Vitamin-C deficiency include bleeding gums, a tendency for small blood vessels to break and hemorrhage, and low resistance to infection. Extreme deficiency is the familiar disease of sailors and explorers, *scurvy.* Scurvy still appears occasionally in arid countries during drought or famine. Mild cases have been found among the urban poor, especially the elderly, even in developed countries.

There is growing evidence that official recommended daily allowances of Vitamin C are much too low, being barely enough to prevent the appearance of severe deficiency symptoms. Everyone interested in nutrition should read Linus Pauling's provocative *Vitamin C, the common cold, and the flu.*[3] The book is controversial, but we and many of our colleagues have increased our Vitamin C intake to hundreds or thousands of milligrams per day. Read this book and decide for yourself.

Vitamin D is sometimes known as the sunshine vitamin. The precursor *ergosterol,* which is obtained from green plants, is changed to Vitamin D in the skin when it is exposed to sunlight. In developed countries today, most commercially sold milk is enriched with Vitamin D through irradiation. The only satisfactory source of converted Vitamin D, if sunshine and irradiated milk are unavailable, is fish liver oils. It is quite likely that the thick blanket of smog hanging over American cities interfers with the manufacture of Vitamin D in urban populations, which has implications for adults who do not drink fortified milk.

Vitamin D is intimately involved in the absorption and utilization of calcium and phosphorus (see below), and

[3]W. H. Freeman and Co., San Francisco, 1976.

consequently in the growth and maintenance of the bone structure. *Rickets* is a disease of children who lack Vitamin D and/or calcium and phosphorus. In these children the growth and development of the bones is disturbed and retarded. The children may be permanently stunted and have more or less malformed bone structure. The corresponding disease in adults is *osteomalacia,* in which the bones become brittle and are easily broken. This occurs when calcium is drawn from the bones to meet daily needs and is not sufficiently replaced in the diet over a long period of time.

Vitamin E seems to be involved in reproductive functions; lack of it may lead to repeated miscarriage. It is obtained from nuts and vegetable oils, particularly wheatgerm oil.

Vitamin K is essential to normal blood-clotting activity. This vitamin is ordinarily manufactured by intestinal bacteria and is also found in green leaves, fat, and egg yolks. The intestinal supply may be cut off temporarily following an antibiotic regime, especially one that is orally administered.

Minerals

Seventeen of the essential nutrients are minerals. Many of them are required only in minute amounts.

Bones and teeth are composed primarily of *calcium* and *phosphorous.* Calcium also plays a part in the regulation of nerves and muscles and is necessary for healthy skin and for blood-clotting. The best source of calcium is milk, followed by yellow cheeses. It can also be obtained from the bones of fish and other animals and from green vegetables, shellfish, and lime, which is sometimes used in the preparation of food. Hard water used for drinking or in cooking also contributes calcium.

Phosphorus is closely involved with calcium in bone-building and nerve and muscle regulation. It is also important in sugar metabolism and the utilization of vitamins, and it is critically involved in transfers of energy in living systems. Phosphorous is abundant in dairy foods, poultry, eggs, and meat and occurs in moderate amounts in most vegetables. Deficiency is therefore relatively uncommon.

Iron is an essential component of hemoglobin, the protein in red blood cells that carries oxygen to the cells of the body. *Iron-deficiency anemia* is the commonest kind of anemia. Its symptoms include lack of energy and stamina. It is more common among women, whose iron needs are higher due to blood loss in menstruation and the demands of pregnancy. Anemic women are susceptible to stillbirth and miscarriage and are likely to produce anemic children. Iron is most abundant in liver, other organ meats, eggs, molasses, oysters, and apricots. Smaller amounts are found in meat and green vegetables.

Sulfur is necessary for the building of some proteins in the body and must be ingested in amino acids. It is found in many high-protein foods, both plant and animal.

Sodium chloride—ordinary table salt—is essential to life, although toxic in too large doses. It occurs naturally in seafoods, meat, and a few fruits and vegetables. It is also found in processed foods such as cheese, bread, and canned foods. Vegetarians may have difficulty getting enough salt; otherwise deficiency is unlikely except where there is danger of heat prostration.

Potassium is a widely available mineral found in meat, fruits, and vegetables. Together with sodium, potassium helps to regulate the body's fluid balance. Too much of either can cause a deficiency of the other. Potassium also is essential for metabolism of sugar in muscle cells. It is needed most during periods of rapid growth.

Iodine is an essential component of thyroid hormones that regulate growth, development, and metabolic activities. It is found in seafood and in crops grown in iodine-rich soil. Its lack results in *goiter,* characterized by a swelling of the thyroid gland in the neck. In extreme forms of this disease, cretinism or deaf-mutism may be produced in children. Before World War II goiter was relatively common in the interior of the United States, where seafood was unavailable and the soils lack iodine. Since then iodized salt has been available, use of which prevents goiter.

Zinc is a component of insulin and therefore involved in the body's utilization of carbohydrates and protein. It is found in pulses, organ meats, and green vegetables. Recent research indicates that it may be more important than was believed earlier and that contemporary fertilizing methods may result in crops being deficient in zinc.

Magnesium is necessary for the utilization of both

calcium and Vitamin C. It is found in a wide variety of foods.

Manganese is necessary for lactation and some other glandular functions. It is obtained from a variety of nuts and vegetables.

Some other trace elements that are necessary for health are: *chromium, cobalt, copper, molybdenum,* and *selenium.* Deficiencies in these minerals have rarely, if ever, been seen.

It is quite possible that other essential nutrients exist that have not yet been isolated. The importance of trace elements cannot be overemphasized. Because they are often required in such minute amounts, and perhaps because there seems to be considerable individual variation in requirements, there is some tendency to overlook them. The wisest course to follow if one cares about maintaining health is to eat as wide a variety of foods as possible, preferably from different geographical areas, choosing from among each of the major food groups every day: protein foods (meat, poultry, fish, eggs, beans, or nuts), dairy foods, cereals or tubers, vegetables, and fruits. To ensure the least loss of fragile vitamins, one should choose fresh food in preference to processed foods and cook it minimally.

APPENDIX 3

Pesticides

THE FIRE ANT PROGRAM: AN ECOLOGICAL CASE STUDY

The red fire ant *(Solenopsis invicta)* is a nasty, but not-too-serious pest in the southeastern United States. Its nests form mounds that interfere with the working of fields. Its stings may cause severe illness or death in sensitive people, but it is a considerably smaller menace in this regard than are bees and wasps. The ant is best described as a major nuisance. After limited and inadequate research on the biology of the fire ant, the USDA in 1957 came up with the astonishing idea of carrying out a massive aerial spray campaign, covering several states, against the ant. Along with other biologists, including those most familiar with the fire ant, one of us (P.R.E.) protested the planned program, pointing out, among other things, that the fire ant would be one of the *last* things seriously affected by a broadcast spray program. A quote from a letter he wrote concerning the problem to Ezra Taft Benson, then Secretary of Agriculture, follows:

> To any trained biologist a scorched-earth policy involving the treatment of 20 million acres with a highly potent poison such as dieldrin should be considered as a last ditch stand, one resorted to only after all of the possible alternatives have been investigated. In addition such a dangerous program should not even be considered unless the pest involved is an extremely serious threat to *life* and property.
>
> Is the Department of Agriculture aware that there are other consequences of such a program aside from the immediate death of vast numbers of animals? Are they aware that even poisoning the soil in a carefully planned strip system is bound to upset the ecological balance in the area? We are all too ignorant of the possible sequelae of such a program. Has it been pointed out that an adaptable and widespread organism such as the Fire Ant is one of the least likely of the insects in the treated area to be exterminated? It is also highly likely that, considering its large population size, the Fire Ant will have the reserve of genetic variability to permit the survival of resistant strains.
>
> I would strongly recommend that the program be suspended: 1) until the biology of the ant can be thoroughly investigated with a view toward biological control, baiting, or some other control method superior to broadcast poisoning, and 2) until trained ecologists can do the field studies necessary to give a reasonable evaluation of the chances of success, and the concomitant damage to the human population, wildlife, and the biotic community in general of *any* contemplated control program.

> I hope that the United States will learn from the disastrous Canadian Spruce Budworm program and hesitate before carrying out a program whose consequences may be a biological calamity.

This reply came from C. F. Curl, then Acting Director of the USDA Plant Pest Control Division. Note the emphasis on eradication in this excerpt:

> Surveys do indicate that the imported fire ant infests approximately 20,000,000 acres in our southern states. This does not mean, however, that the eradication program is embarked on a "scorched earth policy." The infestation is not continuous and the insecticide is applied only to areas where it is known to exist. The small outlying areas are being treated first to prevent further spread and of the large generally infested areas only a portion is treated in any one year.
>
> The method of eradication, namely, the application in granular form of two pounds of either dieldrin or heptachlor per acre is based on an analysis of research information compiled from State and Federal sources. Use experience on other control programs such as the white-fringed beetle and Japanese beetle was also taken into consideration before the final decisions were made. All the data indicated that a program could be developed which would be safe and would present a minimum of hazard to the ecological balance in the areas to be treated.
>
> To date approximately 130,000 acres have been treated. This includes a block of 12,000 acres at El Dorado, Arkansas, treated nearly a year ago. Reports indicate the program is successful in eradicating the ants. No active mounds have been found in the El Dorado area and the results look equally good in other locations treated to date. Observers vitally interested in the impact of this program to other forms of life have not reported serious disturbances in the area as a whole.
>
> Close liaison has been established with the Fish and Wildlife Service to continue their observations and to keep us informed currently as to the effect this program may have on fish and wildlife in the area. Experience to date indicates that a successful program can be carried out with a minimum hazard to the beneficial forms of life present.
>
> We believe that the points mentioned in your letter were given ample consideration before the initiation of the fire ant eradication program. We recognize of course that in any program where insecticides are used, certain precautions are necessary. Our experience has shown that insecticides can be applied successfully using very definite guidelines which can be established to minimize the hazard to fish and wildlife and to preclude any hazard to domestic animals and human health. Such guidelines are being followed in the operation of all control and eradication programs in which the U.S. Department of Agriculture participates.

In order to permit you to judge for yourself who was right, here are parts of an article on the results of the program by William L. Brown, Jr., of the Department of Entomology of Cornell University, an outstanding biologist and a world authority on ants:

> With astonishing swiftness, and over the mounting protests of conservation and other groups alarmed at the prospect of another airborne 'spray' program, the first insecticides were laid down in November, 1957. The rate of application was two pounds of dieldrin or heptachlor per acre . . . Dieldrin and heptachlor are extremely toxic substances – about 4–15 times as toxic to wildlife as is DDT. Many wildlife experts and conservationists as well as entomologists both basic and economic, felt a sense of forboding at the start of a program that would deposit poisons with 8–30 times the killing power of the common forest dosage of DDT (one pound per acre in gypsy moth control).
>
> . . . The misgivings of the wildlife people seem to have been justified, since the kill of wildlife in sample treated areas appears to have been high in most of those that have been adequately checked. The USDA disputes many of the claims of damage, but their own statements often tend to be vague and general.
>
> . . . Although the USDA claims that the evidence is inconclusive in some cases, there does exist contrary information indicating that stock losses from ant poisons may sometimes be significant.
>
> . . . A serious blow was dealt the program in late 1958, when treatments were only one year old; Senator Sparkman and Congressman Boykin of Alabama asked that the fire ant campaign be suspended until the benefits and dangers could be evaluated properly. Then, in the beginning of 1960, the Food and Drug Administration of the Department of Health, Education, and Welfare lowered the tolerance for heptachlor residues on harvested crops to zero, following the discovery that heptachlor was transformed by weathering into

a persistent and highly toxic derivative, heptachlor epoxide, residues of which turn up in milk and meat when fed to stock. Some state entomologists now definitely advise farmers against the use of heptachlor on pastures or forage.

. . . The original plan set forth in 1957 called for eradication of the ant on the North American continent, by rolling back the infestation from its borders, applying eradication measures to more control foci in the main infestation, and instituting an effective program of treatment of especially dangerous sources of spread, such as nurseries. Nearly four years and perhaps 15 million dollars after the plan was announced, the fire ant is still turning up in new counties, and is being rediscovered in counties thought to have been freed of the pest in Arkansas, Louisiana, Florida, and North Carolina.

Subsequently a bait was found that allowed effective fire-ant control. It was claimed that the insecticide in the bait, Mirex (a chlorinated hydrocarbon), was virtually harmless to vertebrates and bees. Starting in 1962 Mirex was sprayed by aircraft over large areas with three applications per year. Then in 1972, when it was discovered that Mirex was killing juvenile shrimp and crabs, the Environmental Protection Agency (EPA) forbade spraying near waterways and limited applications to once a year. Subsequently Mirex was shown to be a weak carcinogen.[1] In 1976 it was agreed that all forms of Mirex were not to be used after June 1978.[1a]

In 1975 the USDA decided to give up its fire ant campaign, and Secretary of Agriculture Earl Butz blamed the EPA restrictions for the failure of the program. The EPA responded, quite correctly, that a decade of unrestricted Mirex use had failed even to contain the fire ant, let alone exterminate it. As Brown commented, "[*S. invicta*] . . . is very well-named, for it truly is unconquerable."[2] Ecologist Edward O. Wilson of Harvard University, famous as the author of *Sociobiology*,[3] is also *the* authority on ant behavior and ecology. He responded to the USDA decision by pointing out that a program to exterminate the fire ant was questionable even if the only undesirable side effect was to kill other ants: "Ants occupy one of the middle links in the food chain—they consume other small insects and are scavengers that recycle nutrients from decomposing material in fields and woodlands—and no one has ever examined the long-range consequences of killing off lots of ants."

The USDA and state governments spent almost $150 million on the fire-ant fiasco, almost none of it on research that might have led to appropriate controls. The program, of course, had strong political support in the South, since the ant is an annoying pest and because a lot of federal money was spent locally in futile attempts to exterminate it. Ed Wilson wrote an appropriate epitaph for this classic boondoggle: "The fire ant control program in the South is the Vietnam of entomology."

SOME IMPORTANT PESTICIDES[4]

The left-hand column in Table A3-1 gives the commonest names for the insecticides, other names by which they are known, and the chemical designations. (Sometimes on labels a chemical designation may be simplified. For instance, aldrin will sometimes be listed simply as "hexachlorohexahydro-*endo, exo*-dimethanonaphthalene.) The second column gives the general uses of the chemicals, coded as follows:

Acar. = acaracide (used against mites)
Ins. = insecticide (used against insects)
Syn. = synergist (makes insecticide more potent)
MP = moth-proofer
C. fum. = commodity or space fumigant
S. fum. = soil fumigant
Sys. = systemic insecticide (taken up by plant)
Nem. = nematocide (kills roundworms)

The right-hand column indicates mammalian toxicity judged by experiments on rats (no symbol), rabbits (Rb), white mice (M), or dogs (D). They are mostly given as LD_{50}—that is, the dose level that killed 50 percent of the experimental animals. The doses used in studying acute toxicity are in parts per million of live animal

[1]Jane E. Brody, Agriculture Department to abandon campaign against fire ant, *New York Times*, April 20, 1975.

[1a]Constance Holden, Mirex: Persistent pesticide on its way out. *Science*, vol. 194 (15 October 1976), pp. 301–303.

[2]Most of the material in this and the following paragraph is also from Brody, Agriculture Department.

[3]Harvard University Press, Cambridge, Mass., 1975.

[4]Adapted from *Bulletin of Entomological Society of America*, 1969, vol. 15, pp. 85–135.

weight. AO = acute oral toxicity; AD = acute dermal (skin application) toxicity. Chronic oral toxicity (CO) is the highest level (parts per million in diet) at which no effect is seen in 90 days or more.

Fumigant toxicities: VA = acute vapor toxicity, the highest level in ppm thought not to be dangerous to human beings with 60 minutes exposure; VC = chronic vapor toxicity, same for 8 hours per day, 5 days per week.

For example, chlordane killed 50 percent of rats tested in different experiments at oral doses of 283–590 milligrams per kilogram (mg/kg) of body weight. When chlordane was applied to the skin, 50 percent of the rats died at doses of 580 mg/kg in at least one experiment, but in another, a dose of 1600 mg/kg did not produce 50 percent deaths. In rabbits more than 50 percent were killed with a skin dose of 780 mg/kg. In rat experiments diets with greater than 25 or less than 150 ppm did not produce symptoms in 90 days or more.

As a general rule there will be a reasonable correlation between other mammals and human beings in the toxicity of these compounds. Thus TEPP, with an AO of 0.5–2 in rats is exceedingly toxic to people. An amount equal to about one-millionth of your body weight will kill you. DDT, on the other hand, is much safer as far as acute exposure is concerned.

Note that chlorinated hydrocarbons appear in several groups: "Chlorinated aryl hydrocarbons," "DDT relatives," and "fumigants" (paradichlorobenzene). The chemical structures of a sample of insecticides and one herbicide are shown in Figure A3-1.

TABLE A3-1
Some Important Pesticides

Common and technical names	*Use*	*Mammalian toxicity*
ACTIVATORS OR SYNERGISTS FOR INSECTICIDES		
Piperonyl butoxide (Butacide[R]) α-[2-(2-butoxyethoxy)-ethoxy]-4,5-methylenedioxy-2-propyltoluene	Ins. Syn.	AO > 7500, M3800 D > 7500 Rb > 7500 AD Rb > 1880 CO 1000, D700
BOTANICALS		
Rotene powder and resins (derris) (cubé) 1,2,12,12α,tetrahydro-2-iso-propenyl-8,9-dimethoxy-[1]benzopyrano-[3,4-b]furo[2,3-b][1] benzopyran-6 (6aH)one	Ins.	AO 60–1500, M350 AD Rb > 1000–3000 CO 25, D > 400
Pyrethrins (cinerin) Pyrethrum (principally from plant species *Chrysanthemum cinariaefolium*)	Ins.	AO 200–2600 AD > 1800 CO 1000
Allethrin (synthetic pyrethrins) 2-allyl-4-hydroxy-3-methyl-2-cyclopenten-1-one ester of 2,2-dimethyl-3-(2-methylpropenyl)-cyclopropanecarboxylic acid	Ins.	AO 680–1000 M480, Rb4290 AD > 11200 CO 5000, D 4000
Nicotine (sulfate) Black Leaf 40[R] *l*-1-methyl-2-(3-pyridyl)-pyrrolidine	Ins.	AO 50–91, M24 AD 140, Rb50
CHLORINATED ARYL HYDROCARBONS (containing 6 or more chlorines)		
Benzene hexachloride (BHC, HCB) 1,2,3,4,5,6-hexachloro-cyclohexane, mixed isomers and a specified percentage of gamma	Ins.	AO 600–1250 CO 10 (Toxicity depends on ratio of isomers)

TABLE A3-1 (*Continued*)

Common and technical names	*Use*	*Mammalian toxicity*
Lindane (gamma BHC) 1,2,3,4,5,6-hexachlorocyclo-hexane, 99% or more gamma isomer	Ins.	AO 76–200, M86 Rb60–200, D40 AD 500–1200 Rb300–4000 CO 50, 25 D > 15
Chlordane 1,2,4,5,6,7,8,8-octachloro-3α,4,7,7α-tetrahydro-4,7-methanoindane	Ins.	AO 283–590 AD 580–> 1600 Rb < 780 CO > 25–< 150
Heptachlor 1,4,5,6,7,8,8-heptachloro-3α,4,7,7α-tetrahydro-4,7-methanoindene	Ins.	A040–188, M68 AD 119–320 Rb2000 CO 0.5–> 5 D4–5
Aldrin Not less than 95% of 1,2,3,4,10,10-hexachloro-1,4,4α,5,8,8α-hexahydro-1,4-endoexo, 5,8-dimethano-naphthalene	Ins.	AO39–60, M44 D65–90, Rb50–80 AD 80–> 200 Rb < 150 CO 0.5, 25, D1
Dieldrin Not less than 85% of 1,2,3,4,10,10-hexachloro-6,7-epoxy-1,4,4α,5,6,7,8α-octahydro-1,4-endo-exo-5,8-dimethanonaphthalene	Ins.	A040–100 D65–95, M38 Rb45–50 AD 52–117, Rb250–360 CO 0.5, Dcal
Endrin 1,2,3,4,10,10-hexachloro-6,7-expoxy-1,4,4α,5,6,7,8,8α-octahydro-1,4-endo-endo-5,8-dimethano-naphthalene	Ins.	AO 3–45, Rb7–10 AD 12–19, Rb60–120 CO > 1–< 25
Endosulfan (Thiodan[R]) 6,7,8,9,10,10-hexachloro-1,5,5α,6,9,9α-hexahydro-6,9-methano-2,4,3-benzodioxathiepin 3-oxide	Acar. Ins.	AO 30–110 AD 74–130, Rb360 CO 30, D30
Toxaphene Chlorinated camphene containing 67–69% chlorine	Ins.	AO 40–283, M112 D15, Rb < 780 AD 600–1613 Rb780–4000 CO 10, 25 Dca400
Mirex Dodecachlorooctahydro-1,3,4-methano-2H-cyclobuta[cd]pentalene	Ins.	AO 235–702 AD Rb800
Kepone Decachlorooctahydro-1,3,4-methano-2H-cyclobuta[cd]pentalene	Ins.	AO 95
DDT Relatives (Diphenyl Aliphatics)		
DDT (dichloro diphenyl trichloro-ethane) 1,1,1-trichloro-2,2-bis-(p-chlorophenyl) ethane	Ins. MP	AO 87–500 M150–400 Rb250–400 AD 1931–3263 Rb2820 CO 5, 1, D400

(*Continued*)

TABLE A3-1 (*Continued*)

Common and technical names	*Use*	*Mammalian toxicity*
DDD (TDE) Dichlorodiphenyl dichloro-ethane 1,1-dichloro-2,2-bis-(p-chlorophenyl) ethane	Ins.	AO 400–3400 M2500 AD Rb 4000–> 5000 CO ca100–900
Kelthane[R] (dicofol) 4,4′-dichloro-α-(tri-chloromethyl)-benzhydrol	Acar.	AO 575–1331 D > 4000 Rb1810 AD 1000–1230 Rb2100 CO 20–100, D300 D100
Methoxychlor 1,1,1-trichloro-2,2-bis-(p-methoxyphenyl) ethane	Ins.	AO 5000–7000 M1850, Rb > 6000 AD > 2820–> 6000 CO 100, >200 D > 4000
FUMIGANTS		
Methyl bromide Bromomethane	C. fum. S. fum.	VA 200 VC 20
Cyanide (prussic acid) (HCN) Hydrocyanic acid	C. fum. S. fum.	AO Rb4 CO > 300 VA 40 VC 10
Paradichlorobenzene (PDB) p-dichlorobenzene	C. fum. MP	AO 500–5000 M2950 AD Rb > 2000 VA 500 VC 75
Naphthalene	C. fum. MP	VC 10
Carbon disulfide	C. fum.	VA 200 VC 20
Vapam[R] Sodium methyldithio-carbamate	Nem. S. fum.	AO 820, M285 AD Rb800
ALIPHATIC DERIVATIVES OF PHOSPHORUS COMPOUNDS		
Tepp (TEPP) Tetraethyl pyrophosphate	Ins.	AO 0.5–2, M1–7 AD 2–20, Rb5
Dipterex[R] (trichlorfon) Dimethyl (2,2,2-trichloro-1-hydroxyethyl) phosphonate	Ins.	AO 450–699 M300–500 AD > 2800, Rb5000 CO < 100–125
DIBROM[R] (naled) 1,2-dibromo-2,2-dichloroethyl dimethyl phosphate	Acar. Ins.	AO 430 AD Rb1100 CO D7.5 mg/kg
Vapona[R] (dichlorvos) 2,2-dichlorovinyl dimethyl phosphate	C. fum. Ins.	AO 25–170 AD 59–900, RB107 CO < 50
Phosdrin[R] (mevinphos) Methyl 3-hydroxy-alpha-crotonate, dimethyl phosphate	Ins. Sys.	AO 3–7, M8–200 AD 3–90, Rb13–55 CO 0.8, D1

TABLE A3-1 (*Continued*)

Common and technical names	*Use*	*Mammalian toxicity*
Azodrin[R]	Ins.	AO 21
3-hydroxy-N-methyl-cis-crotonamide dimethyl	Sys.	AD Rb354
phosphate	Acar.	CO 1.5
Systox (demeton)	Acar.	AO 2–12
Mixture of 0,0-diethyl S-(and 0)-2-[(ethylthio)ethyl]	Ins.	AD 8–200, Rb24
phosphorothioates	Sys.	CO 1, D1, D2
Malathion	Ins.	AO 885–2800
Diethyl mercaptosuccinate, S-ester with 0,0-		M720–4060
dimethyl phosphorodithioate		AD > 4000–> 4444
		Rb4100
		CO 100–1000, D100
ARYL (PHENYL) DERIVATIVES OF PHOSPHORUS COMPOUNDS		
Methyl parathion	Ins.	AO 9–42, M32
0,0-dimethyl 0-p-nitrophenyl		AD 63–72, Rb1270
phosphorothioate		
Parathion	Acar.	AO 3–30, M6–25
0,0-diethyl 0-p-nitrophenyl	Ins.	Rb10, D3
phosphorothioate		AD 4–200 Rb40–870
		CO 1, 50, D1
EPN	Acar.	AO 8–36
0-ethyl 0-p-nitrophenyl	Ins.	
phenylphosphonothioate		
HETEROCYCLIC DERIVATIVES OF PHOSPHORUS COMPOUNDS		
Diazinon	Acar.	AO 66–600
0,0-diethyl 0-(2-isopropyl-	Ins.	M80–135
4-methyl-6-pyrimidyl)		Rb130–143
phosphorothioate		AD 379–1200
		Rb 4000
		CO 1, D 0.75
SULFONATES		
Mitin FF[R]	MP	AO 750–1380
Sodium 5-chloro-2-(4-chloro-2-(3-(3,4-		
dichlorophenyl)-ureido)phenoxy)benzenesulfonate		
CARBAMATES		
Baygon[R]	Ins.	AO 95–175
0-isopropyoxyphenyl		AD > 1000
methylcarbamate		CO 800
SEVIN[R]	Ins.	AO 307–986
Carbaryl		D > 759, Rb710
1-naphthyl methylcarbamate		AD > 500–> 4000
		Rb > 2000
		CO 200, D200–400
Temik[R] (aldicarb)	Acar.	AO 1–30
2-methyl-2-(methylthio)propionaldehyde	Ins.	
0-(methylcarbamoyl)oxine	Nem.	

p,p′–DDT

$Cl-C_6H_4-C(H)(CCl_3)-C_6H_4-Cl$

Lindane
(gamma isomer
of benzene hexachloride)

ClH_2, ClH_2, ClH_2, ClH_2, H_2Cl, H_2Cl

Chlordane

CCl, ClC, CH, CHCl, CCl_2, ClC, CH, CHCl, CCl, CH_2

DDE

$Cl-C_6H_4-C(=CCl_2)-C_6H_4-Cl$

Heptachlor

Cl, Cl, Cl, CCl_2, Cl, Cl

Aldrin

Cl, Cl, CH_2, CCl_2, Cl, Cl

DDD (TDE)

$Cl-C_6H_4-C(H)(HCCl_2)-C_6H_4-Cl$

Dicofol (Kelthane)

$Cl-C_6H_4-C(OH)(CCl_3)-C_6H_4-Cl$

Dieldrin

Cl, Cl, O, CH_2, CCl_2, Cl, Cl

Endrin

Cl, Cl, O, CH_2, Cl–Cl, Cl, Cl

Methoxychlor

$CH_3O-C_6H_4-C(H)(CCl_3)-C_6H_4-OCH_3$

Endosulfan

CCl, ClC, $CHCH_2$–O, CCl_2, S=O, ClC, $CHCH_2$–O, CCl

Mirex

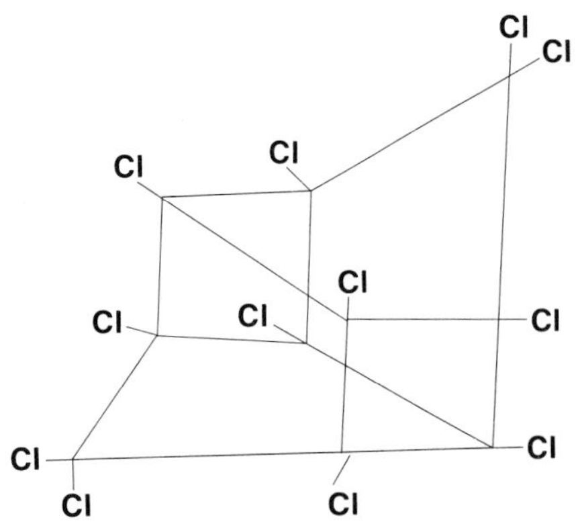

Paradichlorobenzene

$Cl-C_6H_4-Cl$

2,4-D (herbicide)

Cl (positions 2 and 4) $-C_6H_3-O-CH_2COOH$ (position 1); ring positions 1, 2, 3, 4, 5, 6

CHLORINATED HYDROCARBONS

Parathion

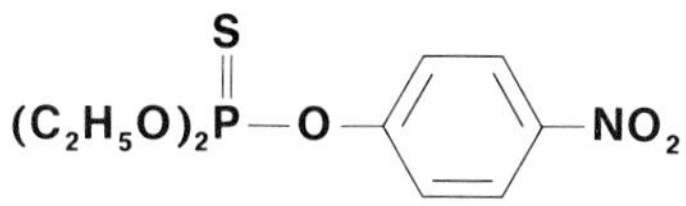

$(C_2H_5O)_2P(S)$—O—C_6H_4—NO_2

Methyl parathion

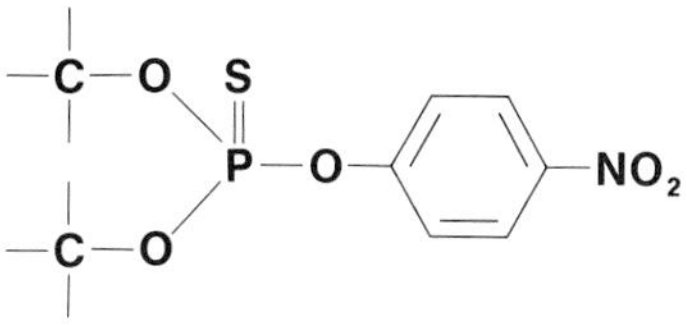

Malathion

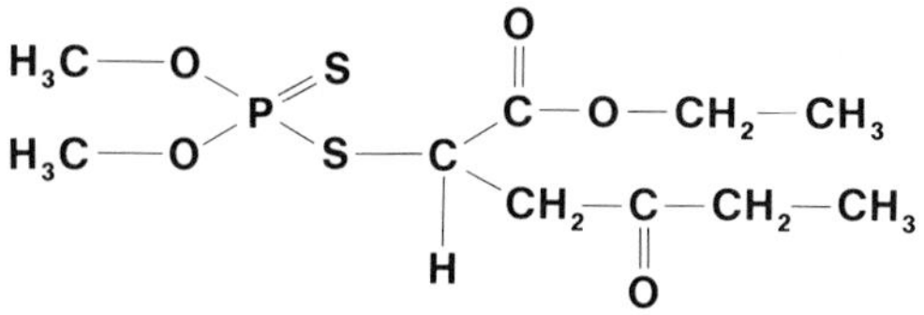

Tepp
(Tetraethyl pyrophosphate)

$(C_2H_5O)_2P(O)OP(O)(OC_2H_5)_2$

Dichlorvos
(Dichlorovinyl dimethyl phosphate)

$(CH_3O)_2P(O)OCH{=}CCl_2$

Diazinone

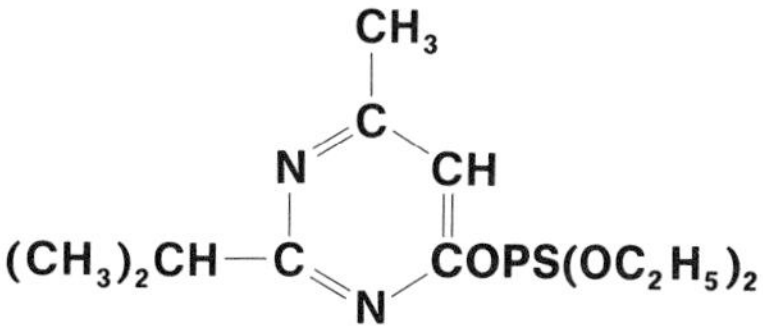

ORGANOPHOSPHATE INSECTICIDES

Sevin
(Carbaryl)

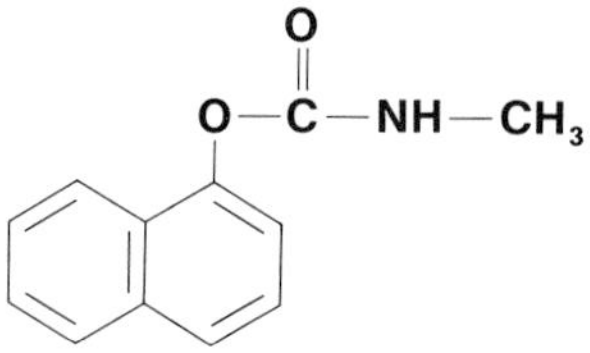

Zectran

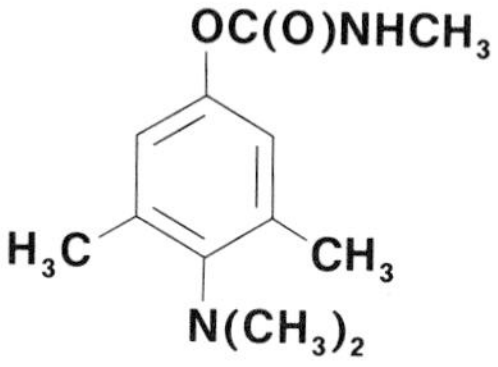

OC(O)NHCH$_3$

H_3C CH_3 $N(CH_3)_2$

CARBAMATE INSECTICIDES

FIGURE A3-1

The chemical structures of insecticides and one herbicide. Three general classes are shown: chlorinated hydrocarbons, organophosphates, and carbamates. The herbicide 2,4-D (2,4-dichlorophenoxy acetic acid) is also a chlorinated hydrocarbon and is shown for comparison. The herbicide 2,4,5-T (2,4,5-trichlorophenoxy acetic acid) has the same structure as 2,4-D, except that it has three chlorine atoms on the phenyl ring, the additional one in the 5 position.

APPENDIX 4

Reproduction and Birth Control

REPRODUCTIVE ANATOMY AND PHYSIOLOGY

According to those who have been involved in the Planned Parenthood movement, the two greatest obstacles to successful birth control are ignorance and prudery. In fact, the two often go together. Women who have been raised to fear and dislike sex will often resist learning the facts of reproduction and be very reluctant to discuss any aspect of the subject, including birth control, with their doctors or anyone else. Regardless of such psychological problems, women who are ignorant of their own anatomy and the significance of the menstrual cycle are very likely to have failures in their birth control programs, simply because they do not understand how they work or why. Here is one more argument for good sex education programs in schools, churches, and in the home.[1] A sound understanding of the reproductive process is essential to the effective use of at least the conventional methods of birth control. There is even enough uncertainty among educated persons about human reproductive biology and contraception to make a brief review appropriate here.[2]

Conception occurs when a *spermatozoon* (sperm cell) from a man meets and fertilizes an *ovum* (egg cell) within a woman's body. The various forms of contraception are designed to prevent that occurrence in a number of ways, either by erecting a physical or chemical barrier between sperm and egg or through adjustment of the hormone system (see next section of text).

Spermatozoa are manufactured continuously by the millions daily in a man's testes. This goes on from the age of puberty (around fourteen) until very old age. Each spermatozoon contains the genetic information that the man passes on to the child in the event conception takes place. But unless it meets and fertilizes an egg cell, it dies within a few days. These microscopic, active cells, which resemble minute tadpoles, are emitted in the hundreds of millions each time a man ejaculates. The testes are also the source of production of the male hormone, *testosterone*, which is released to the bloodstream and is responsible for sexual activity and for the development of a man's secondary sexual

[1]A superb college-level text is H. A. Katchadourian and D. T. Lunde, *Fundamentals of Human Sexuality*, 2d ed., Holt, Rinehart and Winston, New York, 1975.

[2]Sheldon J. Segal, The physiology of human reproduction, *Scientific American*, September 1974.

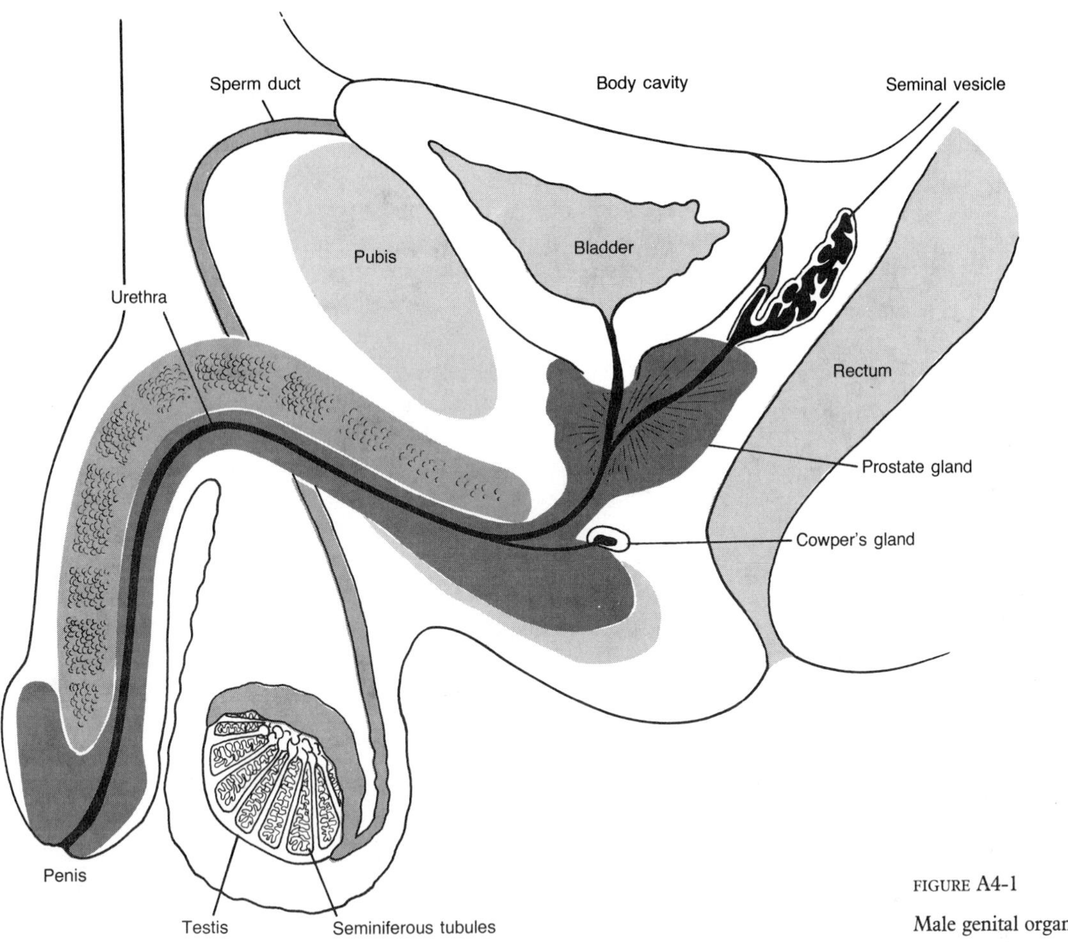

FIGURE A4-1

Male genital organs.

characteristics such as a deep voice, a beard, and typical male body structure.

When the spermatozoa are mature, they are moved upward through one of a pair of sperm ducts (*vas deferens*) to the *seminal vesicle* (Figure A4-1). This acts as a reservoir for storage until the man ejaculates. Each vas deferens opens into the urethra, a tube that extends the length of the penis. During intercourse when the man experiences his climax, or orgasm, a series of muscular contractions force the sperm cells in a fluid matrix known as semen through the urethra, injecting it into the vagina. The semen is a mixture produced in several glands including the prostate. It provides the spermatozoa with protection after they are deposited in the vagina, which is a relatively hostile environment.

The woman's reproductive cells (ova) are present in immature form in her ovaries from birth (Figure A4-2). From puberty (around 13) until she reaches menopause, somewhere around the age of 45 or 50, one egg cell or ovum (or occasionally two or more, which may result in multiple births, usually twins or triplets) is brought to maturity approximately every 28 days. A single ovum is so small it would be visible to the naked eye only as a tiny speck, yet it is many thousands of times larger than a spermatozoan. Besides the mother's genetic contribution to the potential child, the egg cell contains nourishment to support the early development of the embryo, should the ovum be fertilized.

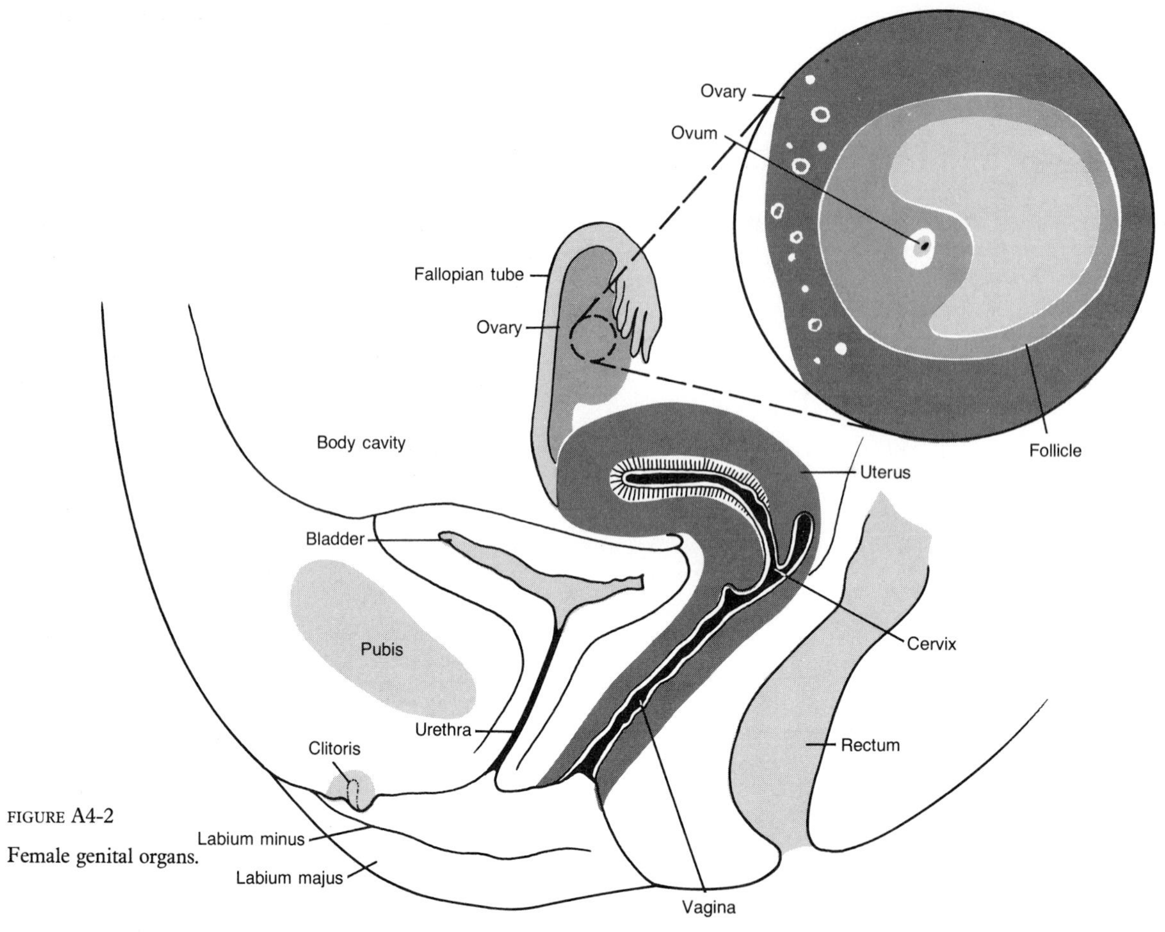

FIGURE A4-2
Female genital organs.

Besides being the source of ova, the ovaries also secrete the female hormones, which, along with certain pituitary hormones, regulate the woman's menstrual cycle and the successful completion of a pregnancy. *Estrogen,* which is also responsible for the secondary sexual characteristics of a woman, such as the developed breasts and the pelvic bone structure adapted to the bearing of children, initiates the maturation of the ovum and the preparation of the uterus for pregnancy. In one of the two ovaries each month, an ovum, which is surrounded by a group of cells called a follicle, ripens and is released (ovulation). It enters the adjacent flared end of a trumpet-shaped structure known as a fallopian tube and travels slowly down it toward the uterus (womb). If fertilization does not take place during the one or two days of this journey, the ovum begins to deteriorate and eventually dissolves.

After the ovum is discharged from the follicle, the latter develops into a structure called a *corpus luteum,* which begins to secrete the other female hormones, including *progesterone.* Progesterone further stimulates the buildup of a lining of cells and extra blood vessels in the uterus, in preparation to receive a developing embryo for implantation. If conception (fertilization) does not occur, the corpus luteum degenerates and ceases to produce progesterone. In the absence of fertilization, about 14 days after ovulation the lining of the uterus is sloughed away through the vagina over a period of 5 or 6 days in the process of menstruation. Then the cycle begins again.

Spermatozoa that have been deposited in the vagina during coitus still have a long way to go relative to their size and vulnerability before fertilization can take place. The mucus lining of the vagina is acid, and the sperm cells cannot live long in such an environment. They must find their way into and through the thick mucus filling the cervical canal of the uterus. They are equipped with an enzyme capable of dissolving the mucus, but apparently it requires large numbers of them to dissolve enough to allow them to reach the uterus. Many, of course, are lost along the way. The uterus provides a favorable, alkaline environment, but the spermatozoa must still find their way from there into the fallopian tubes. If an ovum is descending one of the fallopian tubes as the remaining several thousand spermatozoa swim up it, one of the spermatozoa may succeed in penetrating the capsule of the egg cell. Once one has penetrated, the fertilized ovum is impervious to all the others. The ovum continues to descend the tube, undergoing cell division as it goes. When it reaches the uterus and is implanted in the uterus wall, it is a rapidly developing embryo. At this early stage it is already producing a hormone, a gonadotropin that stimulates the corpus luteum to continue producing progesterone, thus preventing menstruation.

Within five weeks, the growing embryo has established its *placenta*, the organ through which food and oxygen from the mother and wastes and carbon dioxide from the fetus (as it is called after the third month) are exchanged. Throughout the rest of the pregnancy the placenta also secretes progesterone, which protects the implantation of the fetus and suppresses ovulation and menstruation. Nine months from conception, the infant is born. With powerful contractions from the uterus, the child is forced through the cervix and vagina, which expand to accommodate it. During lactation (the period when the mother is producing milk) menstruation usually continues to be suppressed, although ovulation may or may not occur.

METHODS OF BIRTH CONTROL

For individuals or couples who wish to avoid having children, either temporarily or permanently, a wide variety of methods exist from which to choose. Since one person's ideal contraceptive may be completely unsuitable for one reason or another for someone else, it is prudent to be familiar with all the possibilities and with the advantages and disadvantages of each.

Conventional Methods

Among the so-called conventional methods and devices for birth control are the condom, the diaphragm, and the cervical cap; various creams, jellies, and foams; the douche; and the rhythm system. All of these are intended to prevent the meeting of sperm and ovum. More recent additions to the arsenal include the contraceptive pill and the intrauterine device (IUD). Some of these methods and devices are more effective than others, and each has advantages and disadvantages that may make it more or less suitable for a couple at a particular stage of life. Beyond these contraceptives, for a couple whose family is complete, there is sterilization. When contraceptives fail, as they occasionally do, the unwanted pregnancy may be ended by abortion.

In addition to the conventional methods of birth control, there are certain folk methods, used mainly in the United States by ingenious teenagers, including douches with soft drinks and condoms devised from plastic wrapping materials. Despite the ingenuity they reflect, they cannot be recommended—especially the douche. Their effectiveness is unknown, although that of the plastic condom may be quite high.

New methods of birth control are now being developed and tested in laboratories, and some of them may become available to the public within the next few years.

The condom. Many men have learned about the condom in the armed forces, where it is presented to them as a means of avoiding veneral disease. It is also one of the most popular and most effective means of birth control. Usually made of rubber, the condom is a very thin sheath that fits tightly over the penis during intercourse and retains the semen after ejaculation. Its advantages lie in its simplicity of use and its availability. The failure rate is low, especially if the man has been instructed in its proper use. Care is especially required to insure against spillage of semen at the time of withdrawal. Defective condoms are seldom encountered and can be guarded against by inspection before use. Unlike other devices, condoms require no fitting or prescription by a doctor; but many men complain that they interfere with the enjoyment of intercourse by reducing sensation and by causing an interruption of foreplay in order to apply them.

The diaphragm. This device, essentially a rubber cup with a rubberclad rim of flexible spring steel, is designed to fit over the cervix, where it acts as a barrier to sperm. It is inserted into the vagina before intercourse, and is left in place for several hours afterward. Before insertion it is coated on the edges and underside with a spermicidal jelly or cream to prevent any sperm from getting through underneath. A well-fitted, properly used diaphragm is a highly effective contraceptive,[3] but it is relatively complicated to use compared to the condom and some other methods. To ensure a proper fit, it must be prescribed by a doctor, who also instructs the woman about its placement and use. When in position, it cannot be felt, and its use does not in any way interfere with either partner's enjoyment of sexual relations.

The cervical cap. Like the diaphragm, the cervical cap bars entrance of sperm into the uterus. It is made of plastic or metal, fits tightly over the cervix, and may be left in place for long periods of time. It need be removed only for menstruation. If properly fitted, the cap is extremely effective. Its main disadvantage lies in the difficulty of placing it correctly.

Spermicidal agents. A variety of spermicidal jellies and creams are available that can be deposited in the upper vagina with special applicators. Although these agents are less effective than the devices discussed above, they have the advantage of being easier to use than mechanical contrivances, and they require neither fitting nor prescription by a doctor.

Foam tablets, aerosols, and suppositories are similar to the jellies and creams, and operate on the same principles. The foam varieties may be more effective than the others, perhaps because they are more thoroughly dispersed in the vagina.

Rhythm. Also referred to as periodic abstention, rhythm is the only method of birth control now sanctioned by the Roman Catholic church. The basic idea is to abstain from sexual relations during the several days each month when a woman might be capable of conceiving. The difficulty is that this period is often hard to determine, particularly in women with irregular menstrual cycles. To avoid conception, the couple must abstain from coitus for at least two days before and one-half day after ovulation. Unfortunately the occurrence of ovulation can only be determined after the event, and not too accurately even then. When ovulation has taken place, the woman's temperature rises about half a degree and drops again when her menstrual period begins. The time of ovulation must be predicted on the basis of carefully kept records of her previous menstrual and temperature cycles. To allow an adequate safety margin, several additional days should be included both before and after the estimated fertile period. Thus, the period of abstention amounts to a considerable fraction of the month, to the inevitable detriment of the conjugal relationship, especially since the fertile period usually is a time when the woman is relatively more receptive to sexual relations. What is worse, the rhythm method is one of the least effective of birth-control methods. Approximately one woman in six has a cycle so irregular that the system will not work at all for her. But the church claims this is the only natural form of birth control, since it requires no mechanical devices or chemical solutions—a claim that neglects the necessary preoccupation with calendars, clocks, thermometers, pencils, and graphs.

The pill. The modern steroid oral contraceptive, generally known as "the pill," is the most effective means of birth control generally available today, except for sterilization and abortion. When taken without fail according to instructions, it is virtually 100 percent effective.

The pill is composed of the female hormone estrogen and of progestin, a synthetic substance that is chemically similar to the natural progesterone produced by a woman's ovaries. This combination is believed to act by suppressing ovulation. The pill is taken daily for 20 or 21 days of the 28-day cycle, beginning on the fifth day after the onset of the menstrual period. The steroids may be administered sequentially or in a combined form. In the sequential system, the estrogen is

[3]Judith Wortman, The diaphragm and other intravaginal barriers—a review. *Population Reports,* series H, no. 4, January 1976.

administered alone during the early part of the cycle, with the progestin added only during the latter part. The pills have the effect of regularizing the menstrual cycle to exactly 28 days, even in women who have never had regular cycles before. Moreover, menstrual flow is noticeably reduced, or even occasionally suppressed altogether. Most women consider these effects advantageous.

As is inevitable with any drug, particularly a hormonal drug, there may be undesirable side effects. Most of these, however, wear off within a few months or can be dealt with by adjusting the dosage or changing brands. Many of them resemble the symptoms of pregnancy, which in a sense is hormonally simulated in the woman's body by the progestin. The most common side-effects are tenderness and swelling of the breasts, weight gain and retention of fluid, nausea, headaches, depression, nervousness and irritability, changes in complexion, and bleeding. About one in four or five women taking the pill experiences one or more of these symptoms.

The advantages of an oral contraceptive are obvious, even apart from the advantage offered by its effectiveness. Its use is far removed in time from the act of intercourse, and there are no mechanical devices or chemicals except the pill to deal with. On the other hand, the woman must remember to take it each day, which requires a fairly high degree of motivation. The chances of pregnancy increase with each forgotten pill.

Apart from the relatively common minor side effects of the pill, there is a small risk of more serious consequences. Research published in the United Kingdom in 1968 revealed that women over the age of 35 who were using the pill had a significantly higher chance (8 per 200,000) of dying of thrombophlebitis (inflammation of veins together with blood clots) or pulmonary embolism (blood clots in the blood vessels of the lungs) than women of the same age who were not using the pill (1 in 200,000). The risk is less than one-half as high in either case for women under 35. Up to the age of 40 the risk of death from thromboembolic disease while using the pill is considerably less than that of death resulting from pregnancy. Demographer Charles Westoff has calculated that the risk of death from complications of pregnancy and childbirth to a population of women who switched from the pill to other, less effective forms of birth control, would be about three and a half times as great as the risk of death from thromboembolism incurred from using the pill.[4] The estrogen component of the pill appears to be responsible for development of the thromboembolic disorders. Subsequent research in both the United Kingdom and the United States has generally supported these findings[5] and also discovered that women on the pill have a similarly higher risk of suffering strokes or developing gall bladder disease. Less serious but more common is the increased incidence of bladder infection (20 to 30 percent higher) among pill takers. In 1975 another British study was published indicating that women over 40 who take the pill have about 5 times as great a probability of having heart attacks as nonusers.[6]

Because of the thromboembolic and stroke risks, the United States Food and Drug Administration (FDA) for several years has required that the labels of the Pills warn of possible hazard to women with histories of venous disorders, high blood pressure, and cardiac problems and has strongly recommended that doctors prescribe only low-estrogen pills. Since 1976, prescribing instructions have been required to warn that they are unacceptable for women over 40.[7]

Newer versions of the pill contain far lower doses of steroids—one-tenth as much or less as early versions on which most research on side effects is based. These low-dose pills appear to cause a somewhat lower incidence of thrombosis and other dangerous side effects, although how much cannot be determined until they have been in use for a decade or two.

On the plus side, it has long been known that the pill acts to regularize and moderate menstrual periods. The result of this is a considerable reduction in iron-deficiency anemia, a circumstance potentially of considerable benefit to women in LDCs, where anemia

[4]L. A. Westoff and C. F. Westoff, *From now to zero*, Little, Brown, Boston, 1971.

[5]British doctors give the Pill its strongest vote of confidence so far, *People*, vol. 1, no. 4, pp. 25–28; *Family Planning Perspectives*, 7-year prospective study of 17,000 women using the pill, IUD, and diaphragm shows benefits of each outweighs risks, vol. 8, no. 5 (Sept./Oct. 1976), pp. 241–245.

[6]J. I. Mann, et al., Myocardial infarction in young women with special reference to oral contraceptive practice, *British Medical Journal*, vol. 4, p. 253 (May 3, 1975).

[7]FDA planning to rewrite "pill" label, *Intercom* (Population Reference Bureau), vol. 3, no. 11 (December 1975).

is very common among women of child-bearing age. Association of the pill with breast cancer remains inconclusive. A British study indicated that the pill may reduce the incidence of abnormalities in the breasts and thus may act to prevent breast cancer.[8] But a California study in 1975 suggested that women who use the pill before child-bearing may run a higher risk of having breast cancer later in life.[9] And a small study in Colorado indicated that the sequential pill—in which the two steroids are taken in sequence rather than simultaneously—may increase the risk of uterine cancer.[10]

While these dangerous side effects are alarming, it must be remembered that the risks are of very low level, indeed. Even for women over 40, the risk of heart attack is about 55 per 100,000. Moreover, heart attack has usually occurred where other predisposing factors, such as heavy smoking, high blood pressure, obesity, or a family history of heart disease, also were present. For younger women the risks of heart attack or other hazards are far smaller.[10a]

With the possible exception of aspirin (which also has potentially dangerous side effects), no other drug has been taken by tens of millions of people regularly over extended periods of time. This phenomenon both increases the likelihood that such side effects will show up and makes it possible for them to be detected at such statistically low levels. But much more time will have to pass and much more data will have to be gathered before definite statements can be made about long-term risks associated with the use of oral contraceptives. Society is in somewhat the same position in regard to the pill as it was when DDT first came into use. The risks must be weighed against the benefits, and the long-term risks are still unknown. From what we know now, it appears that for most women the benefits still outweigh the risks; the latter can be minimized through close supervision by an alert physician. Obviously, continued monitoring of the long-term effects of the pill (or any other hormonal contraceptives) is essential.

Despite the frequency of minor side effects and the low, but genuine risk of very serious ones, the pill is currently the most popular modern method of contraception around the world. Over 50 million women are using it, some 9 million in the United States alone.

The IUD. The intrauterine device, or IUD, as it is generally known, is a plastic or metal object that is placed inside the uterus and left there for as long as contraception is desired. It comes in a variety of shapes, each having advantages and disadvantages relative to the others. The most commonly used today include the Lippes loop, the ring, and the Dalkon shield (Figure A4-3), although new styles are continually being developed.

That the presence of a foreign body in the uterus would act to prevent pregnancy has been known for a long time, but until modern antibiotics and sterilization techniques were available, they were unsafe to use. Exactly how these devices work is uncertain, but the likeliest possibility is that they prevent the implantation of the fertilized egg after conception. Recent research indicates that in human beings IUDs prevent implantation by changing the condition of the endometrium (lining of the uterus), making the interior of the uterus in various ways inhospitable both to the fertilized egg and to spermatozoa.

The newest IUDs are models made of or incorporating active substances that directly prevent pregnancy. Two of these, the Cu7 and the Copper T, are made of copper. A third version contains progesterone in minute amounts, which acts locally essentially as the pill does in inhibiting ovulation.[11]

The advantages of an IUD for the user are several: the primary one is that once in place it can be forgotten (except for the copper and hormone-releasing versions, which must be replaced after a couple of years). There are no pills to remember, no contraceptive materials to deal with. This is a great advantage for an individual whose lack of motivation, educational background, or financial resources would make other forms of birth

[8] *People*, British doctors; Study finds Pill may cut breast cancer risk, *Family Planning Perspectives*, vol. 7, no. 5 (September–October 1975).

[9] *Newsweek*, November 17, 1975.

[10] Dangerous sequence? *Time*, January 5, 1976.

[10a] For a good general discussion of the safety of various contraceptives, including the pill, see Erik Eckholm and Kathleen Newland, Health: The family planning factor, Worldwatch Institute, Washington, D.C., January 1977. For an overview of the safety of the pill, see Paul Vaughan, The pill turns twenty, *New York Times Magazine*, June 13, 1976, pp. 9 ff.

[11] IUDs reassessed: A decade of experience, *Population Reports*, series B, no. 2 (January 1975).

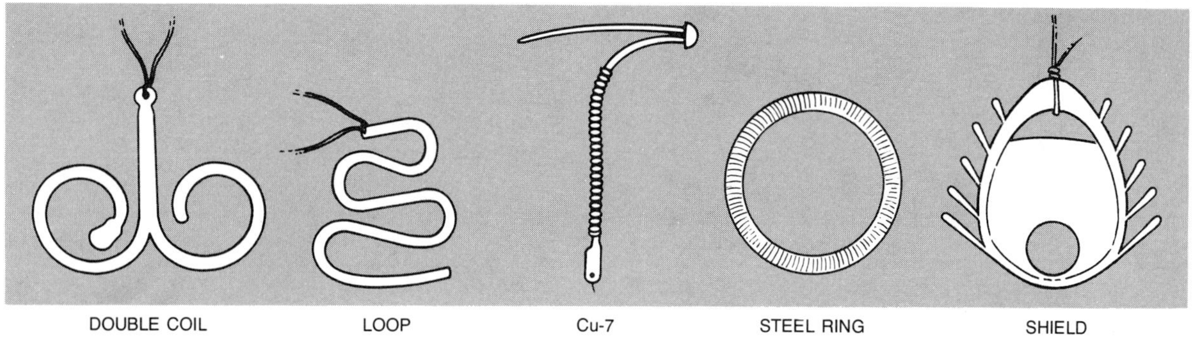

FIGURE A4-3

Various forms of IUDs.

control unreliable or too expensive. The device costs only a few cents. It must be inserted and subsequently checked at least once, perhaps a month later, by a physician or a paramedical person. These advantages have made IUDs especially popular with family-planning programs in less developed nations, where about half of the 15 million IUDs currently in use are being worn.

About 10 percent of women spontaneously expel the device, sometimes without knowing that they have. This tendency varies greatly with age and also with the number of children previously borne. Young women with no children are most likely to expel it; women over 35 with several children are least likely. Expulsion is most likely to occur during the first year of use, and becomes less and less likely thereafter.

For the woman who can successfully retain the IUD, it is a highly effective contraceptive, exceeded only by the pill and sterilization. The pregnancy rate varies somewhat with size and type of IUD and is higher among young women (as it is under any conditions). The risk of pregnancy drops considerably after the first year of use and continues to drop for succeeding years.

Many women have to remove the IUD because of such side effects as bleeding and pain. Some bleeding and discomfort are usual for a short time after insertion, and an increased menstrual flow is common; but when these symptoms continue or are excessive, it is best to remove the IUD. Such problems usually disappear immediately after the device is taken out. There is no evidence that IUDs lead to the development of cancer. The IUD may rarely be associated with pelvic inflammation, though there is some question whether the device is primarily responsible or only aggravates a preexisting condition. In very rare cases perforation of the uterus occurs, and there is considerable evidence that this happens during insertion. Even given these rare but dangerous side effects, the death rate for IUD users is quite low: 1 to 10 per 1 million woman years of use in the United States.

In 1974 the Dalkon shield was discovered to be associated with severe infections in pregnancy, which led to several deaths. The distribution of the device was suspended for six months while investigation proceeded. It appeared that the construction of the tail (which normally protrudes from the uterus) caused it to act as a "wick" for bacteria to invade the uterus, which can be especially dangerous if the wearer is pregnant. The FDA allowed the shield to be distributed again in the United States under a careful program of medical supervision and reporting, but the Agency for International Development (AID) and Planned Parenthood have suspended its use, at least until the "wick" problem is solved.

Most differences in performance among IUDs probably are smaller than differences in the quality of care from one clinic to another. When the IUD is fitted by well-trained and experienced people, and reassurance and support are given to patients who experience side effects, failure rates are generally lower, regardless of the type of device used. In general, the IUD is probably most suitable for women over 30 who have had at least one or two children; they are least likely to have a birth-control failure, to have problems with side effects, or to expel the IUD.

TABLE A4-1
Twelve-Month Failure Rates of Contraceptive Methods (pregnancies per 100 woman years of use)

Method	*Among couples intending to delay their next pregnancy*	*Among couples intending to prevent further pregnancies*
Pill	7	4
IUD	15	5
Condom	21	10
Diaphragm	25	17
Foam	36	22
Rhythm	38	21
Douche	47	40
Overall rates all methods	26	14

Source: Norman Ryder, Contraceptive failure in the United States, *Family Planning Perspectives,* vol. 5, no. 3, pp. 133–142.

Effectiveness of methods. Table A4-1 gives information on the effectiveness of various methods of birth control. Effectiveness is calculated on the basis of 100 woman years—that is, the number of women per 100 women using a given method who become pregnant in a one-year period. Among 100 women using no contraception, 80 can expect to be pregnant by the end of one year. The failure rates are based on actual results from the United States 1970 National Fertility Survey. No distinction is made between failure of the method itself or carelessness in its use. The results make it clear, however, that a stronger motivation for preventing further pregnancy (rather than spacing or delaying births) results in a lower failure rate even with such effective methods as the pill or the IUD.

Sterilization. For couples whose families are complete and who wish to rid themselves of concern about contraceptives, sterilization is often the best solution. This procedure can be performed on either partner, but it is much simpler for the male. A vasectomy takes only fifteen or twenty minutes in a doctor's office. The procedure consists of cutting and tying off the vas deferens, thus making it impossible for sperm to be included in the ejaculate (although the absence of the sperm may only be detected by microscopic examination).

The female's operation until recently has been much more complicated, involving an internal surgical operation with the usual attendant risks. The abdomen was opened under anesthesia and a section of the fallopian tubes cut and removed so that the ova could not pass through. This operation was usually done right after the birth of a baby, a time when the tubes are in a relatively accessible position. A new method, involving an approach through the vagina is now being used by some doctors and may prove to be simpler and safer. Perhaps even better than the vaginal approach is the new "minilaparotomy," which has been tested in several countries including the United States, Thailand, and the Philippines. This method involves a tiny incision—only about an inch long—and can be done with only local anesthetic. Because the procedure is simpler and the recovery time so much shorter, the minilaparotomy can be done on an outpatient basis. Needless to say, this also reduces the costs to the patient.[12]

Contary to the beliefs of many people, sterilization does not in any sense end one's sex life. Vasectomy is *not* castration. The hormonal system is left intact, and sperm are still manufactured by the body; they are just prevented from leaving it. Sexual performance, including orgasm and ejaculation, is normally unchanged. Complications are rare; when they occur, they usually are minor and temporary.[13] In the few cases in which psychological problems develop, they usually are found to have grown out of previously existing disturbances. In many cases, psychological improvement is reported as worry over unwanted children ends.

The same is generally true for the female; her hormones still circulate, ova are still brought to maturity and released, the menstrual cycle goes on. All that is changed is that her ova never reach the uterus, nor can sperm travel up the fallopian tubes. Complications from the newer, simplified procedures appear to be infrequent, although they can be relatively serious. Adverse psychological reactions to sterilization among women are extremely rare.

[12]Female sterilization by mini-laparotomy, *Population Reports,* series C, no. 5 (November 1974); for a review of all current tubal sterilization methods, see Judith Wortman, Tubal Sterilization: Review of methods, Population Reports, series C, no. 7 (May, 1976).

[13]Vasectomy: What are the problems? *Population Reports,* series D, no. 2 (January 1975).

Some individuals hesitate to take so final a step as sterilization. Although in actual practice only a very small percentage of sterilized people ever ask to have the operation reversed, many want some assurance beforehand that it can be done. For men, successful reversal of the operation is achieved in less than 30 percent of cases on the average. New methods of sterilization, notably one in which plastic plugs are inserted into the vas deferens, show promise of being virtually 100 percent reversible, but this alternative is not yet available.[14] The woman's operation can be reversed in 25 to 66 percent of the cases, but women have been even less likely than men to request restoration of fertility.

For men who still have lingering doubts about taking the final step of sterilization, it is now possible to preserve a sample of sperm in a frozen sperm bank for up to ten years. In the future this period can probably be extended. Thus, if a second wife years later wishes children, they can be provided by artificial insemination. Another possibility is that live sperm might be removed from the father's testes and used for insemination, although this has not yet been attempted, as far as we know.

Abortion. Abortion is the arrest of a pregnancy. The medically approved method of inducing abortion in the early stages today is through a fairly simple procedure known as vacuum aspiration, which removes and destroys the embryo. This procedure can be done any time during the first twelve weeks of pregnancy on an outpatient basis; over 85 percent of abortions in the United States are now done this way. After the thirteenth week, an abortion becomes considerably more complicated and hazardous, the usual method being saline injection.

Until around 1970, abortion was illegal in the United States and most other countries of the world. Since then, laws have been changed in a growing number of countries. Illegal abortion is extremely dangerous, whereas legal abortion, practiced in appropriate medical circumstances in the early months of pregnancy, is safer than pregnancy and childbirth. The legal changes and moral issues surrounding abortion are discussed in Chapter 13.

Possibilities for the Future

Many possible ways of interfering with the reproductive process have yet to be explored; some of the most promising of these are under investigation in laboratories or are being tested clinically in human beings. Within the next decade or two a variety of new methods of birth control should become available for general use. Some of the methods currently being developed show considerable promise as practical approaches for population control in less developed countries, where the simplest and cheapest methods are most useful in family-planning programs. Most of the new contraceptives are designed for women; some are extensions of the research that produced the Pill.[14a]

Progestins Among the developments most likely to prove useful soon are various forms of low, continuous dosages of the steroid progestin. Like the higher dosage of progestin combined with estrogen in the present pill, the low progestin dosages also suppress ovulation. This method seems to be slightly less effective than the combined-hormone pill, but the use of progestin alone has the advantage of avoiding some of the more dangerous aspects of the pill, such as the increased risks of thromboembolism, heart attack, and stroke that seem to be associated with the estrogen component. But some side effects do appear. Some women have complained of headaches and dizziness. A more serious drawback seems to be a tendency toward irregular bleeding and amenorrhea (absence of menstruation).

Very large study programs involving thousands of women around the world have been carried out with two forms of low-dose progestins: a minipill, taken daily with no "time off" to keep track of; and intramuscular injections at three-month or six-month intervals. The minipill by 1975 was being used by several hundred thousand

[14] Lois E. Bradshaw, Vasectomy reversibility: A status report, *Population Reports,* series D, no. 3 (May 1976). More recently, a method using microsurgery has proven relatively successful in cases in which reversal was attempted within 10 years after the vasectomy: *Family Planning Perspectives,* Microsurgery is promising for vasectomy reversals, vol. 8, no. 5 (Sept./Oct. 1976), p. 246.

[14a] Recent research on contraceptive technology and reproduction is reported in R. V. Short and D. T. Baird, A discussion on contraceptives of the future, *Proceedings of the Royal Society of London, B. Biological Sciences,* vol. 195, pp. 1–224, 10 December 1976.

women around the world. For the most part, it is used by women who are lactating (which is disrupted by estrogen) or who for other reasons should avoid the estrogen component of the combined pill.[15]

The three-month injections of progestins are now in use in clinical studies by the International Planned Parenthood Federation in over fifty countries around the world, including the United States. This method of birth control appears to be particularly useful as a postpartum contraceptive to provide spacing between children, as it does not interfere with lactation. Several LDCs, particularly Egypt, are interested in the method for this reason.

Both the minipill and injections produce the side effects of irregular bleeding and amenorrhea, which is disturbing to some women, although the bleeding usually disappears after a few months. These side effects may be controlled by administering very small doses of estrogen for a few days each month. Potentially more serious, the effect of the injections may not be immediately reversed after the injections are stopped.

Another way of administering progestin is the "time capsule," which can be implanted under the skin by a hypodermic needle. The material of which the capsule is made—a silicone rubber known as Silastic or a lactate polymer—releases the steroid at a constant rate over a long period of time, potentially 25 or 30 years. Its effect is completely reversible by removal. Time capsules for shorter periods (a year or less) are now being clinically tested and should be generally available within a few years if they prove successful.

Another version of the continuous low-dosage progestin is the vaginal ring. This device fits over the cervix like a diaphragm, but, rather than blocking the entrance, it slowly releases progestin into the surrounding tissues. It needs replacement only once a month.

Progestin administered in low dosages in any of the ways discussed above shares with the progestin-estrogen pill the advantages of relatively high effectiveness and convenience and has the additional advantages of being far less complicated to use (especially the implanted capsule) and of avoiding the hazards of estrogen. It is quite likely that all these forms will be considerably less expensive, at least by the time they can be used in large quantities. If long-term testing does not turn up some new and unanticipated difficulty, progestin holds considerable promise as an effective mode of birth control.

[15]Minipill: A limited alternative for certain women, Ward Rinehart, *Population Reports,* series A, no. 3 (September 1975).

The morning-after pill. Morning-after birth control usually consists in taking a substantial oral dose of an estrogen (in the United States, most often it is diethylstilbestrol, or DES) within a few days after coitus.[16] Pregnancy is prevented, but the woman usually feels quite sick for a day or two. In early 1975, the Food and Drug Administration authorized the use of DES as a postcoital contraceptive by the general public, despite considerable evidence that it may cause cancer. Many young women whose mothers a generation ago took DES to prevent threatened miscarriages have developed cancer of the vagina or the cervix. DES is known to be carcinogenic in other circumstances as well.

In view of this link with cancer and the discomfort associated with its use, we certainly do not recommend the DES morning-after pills. Other hormonal compounds are also being investigated, but they may present similar or other hazards. A far better—and safer—move is to obtain an early abortion. In the earliest weeks, this is a very simple procedure, sometimes euphemistically called "period extraction." The best of all choices, of course, is to use effective contraceptives.

Prostaglandins. A few years ago the discovery of prostaglandins, a group of hormonelike substances related to fatty acids and found in many mammalian tissues, sparked hope that a new abortifacient agent might be developed. Prostaglandins are now being used successfully in some second-trimester abortions, and newer, still-experimental methods are expected to reduce side-effects and shorten the period between induction and abortion (now up to forty-eight hours). Unfortunately, research results for the early weeks of pregnancy so far have been disappointing, however, largely because of side effects and incomplete abortion. Newer ways of using prostaglandins combined with other drugs in early pregnancy may avoid these problems.[17]

[16]Ward Rinehart, Postcoital contraception: An appraisal, *Population Reports,* series J, no. 9 (January 1976).

[17]Ronald Shalita, Prostaglandins promise more effective fertility control, *Population Reports,* series G, no. 6 (September 1975).

Methods for men. Attempts to find steroid or other chemical forms of contraceptives for men have until recently been remarkably unsuccessful. Usually they are aimed at reducing or interfering with spermatogenesis. Several of the early compounds proved to be incompatible with the consumption of alcoholic drinks, a serious drawback in many societies. When progestins were administered to volunteers, spermatogenesis was suppressed, but so was the production of the male sex hormone testosterone, which led to impotence and a loss of libido. These effects might be avoided by adding the male hormone androgen to the progestins, but such a mixture has been thought likely to cause side effects as the pills for women do.

An Australian research team in late 1974 announced the results of a successful early test on an estrogen-androgen combination that had for fifteen years been used as a treatment for osteoporosis and for symptoms of "male menopause" without the appearance of serious side effects. The only side effect found was mild nausea in some patients at the beginning of the treatment. The only disadvantages were that the drug took effect slowly —from 12 to 18 weeks—and wore off slowly (up to 9 months) after discontinuation.[18]

Another new possibility, so far tested only in mice, is the use of a compound known as 5-thio-D-glucose, which appears to prevent spermatogenesis by interfering with the testes' sugar metabolism. This method capitalizes on the fact that only the testes (and some tumors) depend on a particular sugar, D-glucose, for energy. Administering 5-thio-D-glucose to mice induces a mild diabeteslike condition (which may reduce appetite and thus be useful in weight control) and atrophy of the testes. The latter effect appears to be completely reversible within eight weeks in mice with no effect on subsequent offspring for two generations.[19]

In addition to these promising chemical approaches to male contraception, two removable mechanical devices still in the experimental stage are being developed as means of reversible sterilization. One, invented by an Indian physician, consists of a clip that can be attached to the vas deferens. The other is a plastic or silicone plug that can be inserted in the vas deferens. Not only could these new devices be used as temporary contraceptives but they also would satisfy the objections to sterilization from those who fear taking an irreversible step. Unfortunately, sometimes the vas remains permanently closed if the clip is removed after a long period of time. The plugs sometimes have the opposite drawback. The vas may expand so that sperm can pass through, or the plug may eventually deteriorate. The technique shows promise, however, and the plugs are being tested in human volunteers by the Association for Voluntary Sterilization.

Other new methods. A variety of chemicals are being tested on laboratory animals, in the hope of finding some that will not have the drawbacks of the steroid compounds. But since many seem to act by influencing some part of the natural hormone system, it is not too surprising that similar side effects have been associated with some of them. Nevertheless, these possibilities, which have only begun to be investigated, deserve careful examination.

At least one folk method of contraception is being looked into. A South American weed, *Stevia rebaudiana*, has traditionally been used by the Indians in Paraguay as a contraceptive. Each day the women drink a cup of water in which the powdered weed has been boiled. Experiments with rats indicated a reduction in fertility of from 57 to 79 percent compared with a control group, with low fertility lasting up to two months after withdrawal of the drug. Undoubtedly many such folk methods are known in various human cultures. Some of them may be quite effective and might prove adaptable to the urgent need for population control, particularly in less developed countries.

Some other ideas being tested in laboratories are more sophisticated versions of contraceptives already in use. These include long-lasting spermicidal creams, removable blocks for the fallopian tubes,[20] and a version of the vaginal ring that releases a spermicide. There are also experiments on immunizing a woman against her husband's sperm and others on enzymes or chemicals that decapacitate sperm. Whereas many of these ideas may

[18]Hormone mixture makes a male pill, *New Scientist*, December 19, 1974, p. 860.

[19]T. H. Marigh, 5-Thio-D-Glucose: A unique male contraceptive, *Science*, vol. 186, p. 431 (November 1, 1974).

[20]Reversible sterilization by fallopian blocking, *New Scientist*, March 28, 1974, p. 800.

prove impractical for one reason or another, others may ultimately be developed into useful additions to the contraceptive arsenal.

Research on male contraceptives is also proceeding along some lines parallel with that for contraceptives for women. Immunizing men against their own sperm would theoretically be a way to halt sperm production. However, this possibility will require many years to develop, if it is even feasible. Another idea is to give men a hormone implant that would suppress sperm production over a period of time.

Despite these interesting lines of research, it appears that the present emphasis on contraceptives for the female will continue for some time, since research on male methods is so far behind in development.

Research and development. In the light of the current world-population situation, it is clear that research on means of birth control has been neglected for too long. Although some potentially valuable possibilities for birth control have come out of recent research, obviously we are still many years away from having an ideal contraceptive—one that is cheap, easy to use, effective, and free from unpleasant or dangerous side effects. In the United States, a *minimum* of 8 to 10 years of testing is required by law before a new contraceptive agent can be released to the general public.[21] Since contraceptive chemicals, unlike most other drugs, are intended for continuous or regular use over long periods of time, perhaps decades, by large numbers of people, the need for exhaustive testing is genuine. But there is no question that it requires a great deal of time and increasing quantities of money. Unless some incentives, including government support, are soon established to encourage research and development in the birth-control field, new contraceptive agents may be delayed in their appearance on the market even beyond the middle 1980s. In view of the world's great need for cheap, simple, and effective means of birth control, the United States and other DCs have an obligation to make positive efforts to encourage their development.

[21]See Carl Djerassi, Birth control after 1985, *Science,* vol. 169, pp. 941–951, Sept. 4, 1970, for a detailed discussion of the problems of contraceptive research and development. Since Djerassi's paper was published, disappointingly little has been done to encourage expansion of this area of research: M. A. Koblinsky, F. S. Jaffe, and R. O. Greep, Funding for reproductive research: The status and the needs, *Family Planning Perspectives,* vol. 8, no. 5 (Sept./Oct. 1976), pp. 212–224. The Ford Foundation seems to have reached similar conclusions, as reported by B. J. Culliton, Birth control: Report argues new leads are neglected, *Science,* vol. 194, pp. 921–922, November 26, 1976.

Acknowledgments

In attempting to deal with a topic as broad and pervasive as the population-resource-environment situation, it was inevitable that we would often cover topics outside our fields of competence. Study of the literature can only partially correct for this; critiques by knowledgeable reviewers are also essential. We, of course, remain indebted to all who helped with the two editions of *Population, Resources, Environment,* for that book served as a starting point for this one. A large number of busy people have been kind enough to read all, or substantial sections of the *Ecoscience* manuscript. These people are listed below with brief indications of their fields of expertise when this is not clear from their institutional affiliations.

Bruce Ames, Department of Biochemistry, University of California at Berkeley (carcinogenesis); D. L. Bilderback, Department of History, Fresno State University; L. C. Birch, School of Biological Sciences, University of Sydney (ecology); Robert van den Bosch, College of Natural Resources, Division of Biological Control, University of California at Berkeley (ecology of agroecosystems, integrated control); Earl Cook, Dean of Geological Sciences, Texas A & M University (energy and mineral resources); Dana Dalrymple, Foreign Economic Service, U.S. Department of Agriculture, Washington, D.C.; Erik P. Eckholm, Senior Researcher, Worldwatch Institute, Washington, D.C. (agriculture and ecology); Gail Finsterbusch, Cabin John, Md. (agriculture); Cynthia Green, Zero Population Growth, Washington, D.C.; Denis Hayes, Worldwatch Institute, Washington, D.C. (science policy); Donald Kennedy, Department of Biological Sciences, Stanford University (neurophysiology, pesticides, science policy); Nathan Keyfitz, School of Public Health, Harvard University (demography); James Krier, School of Law, University of California at Los Angeles (environmental law, law and economics); Harold Mooney, Department of Biological Sciences, Stanford University (community ecology); Richard Norgaard, Department of Agricultural Economics, University of California at Berkeley; Robert E. Ricklefs, Department of Biology, University of Pennsylvania (population biology); Robert Risebrough, Bodega Marine Laboratory, University of California at Berkeley (ecology, pesticides); Jonathan Roughgarden, Department of Biological Sciences, Stanford University (population biology); Stephen Schneider, Deputy Head, Climate Project, National Center for Atmospheric Research, Boulder, Colo.; Kirk Smith, Environmental Health Sciences, University of

California at Berkeley (energy and health); Alan Sweezy, Division of Humanities and Social Sciences, California Institute of Technology (economics, demography); John H. Thomas, Department of Biological Sciences, Stanford University (population control, theology).

In addition, the following faculty with experience in using *Population, Resources, Environment* as a text have reviewed the entire manuscript and made many helpful comments: George Lawrence, Department of Life Sciences, Bakersfield College; Larry O. Spreer, Department of Chemistry, University of the Pacific; Matthew Tuohey, Department of Sociology, Azusa Pacific College. We have also benefited greatly from the hundreds of cards and letters commenting on *Population, Resources, Environment* sent to W. H. Freeman and Company by others using the book.

In any enterprise of this scale, one inevitably asks and receives numerous favors of colleagues and friends—the loan of a photograph or document, a bit of technical information, or simply some advice. From others we have shamelessly pirated ideas. We appreciated all of these numerous "assists" and would like specifically to thank: Hannes Alfvén, University of California at San Diego and Royal Institute of Technocracy, Stockholm; Katie Armitage, University of Kansas; C. K. Birdsall, Department of Electrical Engineering, University of California at Berkeley; Justin Blackwelder, Environmental Fund, Washington, D.C.; David Brower, Friends of the Earth, San Francisco; Harrison Brown, California Institute of Technology, Division of Geological Sciences; Lester Brown, Worldwatch Institute, Washington, D.C.; Reid Bryson, Department of Meteorology, University of Wisconsin; Robert Budnitz, Lawrence Berkeley Laboratory; Chester B. Dugdale, Department of Biological Sciences, Fairleigh Dickinson University; Marcus Feldman, Department of Biological Sciences, Stanford University; Dan Ford, Union of Concerned Scientists; T. K. Fowler, Lawrence Livermore Laboratory; Paul Growald, Economic and Social Opportunities Food Bank, San Jose, Calif.; Victor Gruen, Victor Gruen Center for Environmental Planning, Los Angeles and Vienna; Ernst Haas, Department of Political Science, University of California at Berkeley; Charles A. S. Hall, Woods Hole Biological Laboratory; Bruce Hannon, Center for Advanced Computation, University of Illinois; John Harte, Lawrence Berkeley Laboratory; Frank von Hippel, Center for Environmental Studies, Princeton University; Eric Hirst, Oak Ridge National Laboratory; Jack Hollander, Lawrence Berkeley Laboratory and National Academy of Sciences; C. S. Holling, University of British Columbia; Richard W. Holm, Department of Biological Sciences, Stanford University; Peter Kapitsa, Moscow; Henry Kendall, Union of Concerned Scientists; Richard Lamm, State Capitol, Denver; Lester Lees, California Institute of Technology; Allan J. Lichtenberg, Department of Electrical Engineering, University of California at Berkeley; Amory Lovins, Friends of the Earth, London; Donald Lunde, Department of Psychiatry and Law School, Stanford University; Dan Luten, Department of Geography, University of California at Berkeley; Bruce Lusignan, Department of Electrical Engineering, Stanford University; Guy Pauker, Rand Corporation; David Pesonen of Dreyfus, McTernan, Brotsky, Herndon and Pesonen, San Francisco; Dennis Pirages, Department of Political Science, University of Maryland; Richard F. Post, Lawrence Livermore Laboratory; E. W. Pfeiffer, Department of Zoology, University of Montana; Peter H. Raven, Missouri Botanical Garden, St. Louis; R. T. Ravenholt, Office of Population, AID; Trish Sarr, Friends of the Earth; Lee Schipper, Energy and Resources Group, University of California at Berkeley; Judith Senderowitz, Population Institute, Washington, D.C.; Robert Socolow, Center for Environmental Studies, Princeton University; Frank Talbot, Environmental Studies Program, Macquarie University, Sydney; Tom Turner, Friends of the Earth, San Francisco; Kenneth E. F. Watt, Department of Zoology, University of California at Davis; Ward B. Watt, Department of Biological Sciences, Stanford University; Jerome Weingart, University of California at Berkeley and International Institute for Applied Systems Analysis, Vienna; Arthur H. Westing, Department of Biology, Windham College; Robert Williams, Center for Environmental Studies, Princeton University; George Woodwell, Woods Hole Biological Laboratory.

Loy Bilderback and Don Kennedy have both gone far beyond the normal role of reviewers, having been closely involved with both editions of *Population, Resources, Environment* as well as with *Ecoscience*. Their ideas have influenced us greatly and (along with bits of their prose) have often slipped into the work uncredited. Their assistance has been extraordinary. The help of our good friend and attorney, Johnson C. Montgomery, was sorely missed after his death in December 1974. Much of the material on legal matters still bears the stamp of his thinking—especially his pioneering work on the legal aspects of population control.

Peggy Craig, Claire Shoens, and other staff members of the Falconer Biology Library at Stanford have once more been of enormous assistance to us. Their highly competent and cheerfully given help has time and again permitted us to solve difficult bibliographic problems. Reuben Pennant has patiently Xeroxed reference materials and several drafts of manuscript. Thanks for invaluable reference work are also due Mari Wilson, librarian for the Energy and Resources Information Center at the University of California at Berkeley.

Typing chores for this edition have been handled expertly by Darryl Wheye at Stanford and Sue Black, Linda Elliott, Linda Marczak, George Moon, Becky New, Debbie Tyber, and Denise Wior at Berkeley. Seemingly endless proofreading of galleys was accomplished with the able assistance of Robert Wise and Kim Binette (in Hawaii), and Susan Mann, Glenn Lunde, Jennifer Montgomery, and Julia Kennedy (all of Palo Alto and Stanford). We are especially grateful to Julie, who devoted many hours of spare time for six weeks to the job. Julie, Jenny, and Glenn also helped in assembling the chapter bibliographies. Jane Lawson Bavelas at Stanford once again helped us with myriad aspects of the work.

Judith Quinn, our project editor, has done a superb job of polishing the manuscript, dealing cheerfully with the numerous crises inevitable in the final stages of a project of this scale. Her skill and patience have made our task much easier. The reader doubtless will appreciate the skill and attention to detail that Jean McIntosh devoted to the indices, as we appreciated her good humor in the face of preposterous time pressures.

Finally we would like to express our deep appreciation to Cheri Holdren, who put up with many "social" evenings that were long working sessions on the manuscript of this book. She cheerfully gave us aid and comfort while continuing to balance with great success the needs of her children and the initial stages of her own career as a research biologist. We hope now that the book is in hand she will think the effort worth it.

Index of Subjects

abortion, 216–217, 753–761, 837, 839, 997
historical, 186, 739
fertility rate and, 212, 216–217, 755, 758, 761
religious groups on, 808
medical profession and, 824
acaracide, 981
accidents, in energy production, 488, 489
acidity
soil, 89, 92, 254
of rainfall, 89, 92, 661–662, 663
sulfur reaction and, 89
of water, 263
adenosine triphosphate (ATP), 72, 73
adoption, 785, 786
advertising, 841–842
aerosols
natural, 42
in propellants, 552, 597, 674–675
affluence, and consumption, 721–722
Afghanistan, 331, 968
demography of, 201, 762, 765, 782, 961
Africa. *See also* Sahel *and countries by name*
geography of, 13, 31, 250, 260, 273
monsoons of, 57, 685–686
demography of, 179, 185, 198, 199, 200, 208, 222–231 *passim*, 305, 309, 776–777, 960–961, 965
urbanization of, 237, 238, 239
food supply in, 287–299 *passim*, 326, 328, 329, 342, 375
in world trade, 317, 318, 319, 394, 521
fertilizer use in, 332, 333
petroleum and, 394, 413
cancer in, 590, 591
family planning in, 759, 762, 763, 808
age composition, 98, 106–115, 197, 202–208, 218, 746–747
of countries, 960–963
Agency for International Development (AID) U.S., 746, 761, 763, 924, 995
agriculture. *See also* food supply
resource use by, 2, 3, 264, 265, 473
ecosystem effect of, 48, 284–285, 623–629
model system for, 171
population and, 186, 192, 193, 208–209, 231, 348
effect of technology on, 193, 285, 335, 338, 340
land use and, 235, 248, 252, 276, 872
milpa, 284, 345, 349, 624–626
research in, 323–326, 340
climate and, 681, 687–688
in less developed countries, 931, 933, 934, 935
Agriculture Revolution, population and, 182, 183, 185–186, 189, 198, 235
agrisilviculture, 345–346
air, 32–33, 36
air conditioning, 468, 469, 492–493, 722
aircraft, transport, 685, 815–816
supersonic, 673–674, 819, 856–857
air pollution, 542–555, 661–664
standard for, 427–429, 549–555
radioactive, 443–444, 452
trace metals in, 568
from automobiles, 865
Alaska, 414, 825
Albania, 776, 887, 963, 968
albedo, 42–43, 61, 62, 681–682
aldrin, 564, 566, 641, 855, 981, 983
Aleutian low, 55
algae, 71, 138, 163, 560, 665, 671
in nitrogen cycle, 82, 83, 85, 375, 666
in soil, 253, 640
as protein supplement, 370, 371–372
oxygen balance and, 665, 667
Algeria, 331, 894, 968
demography of, 762, 764, 782, 960, 965
Alliance for Progress, 890, 892
alpha particles, 580–581
altitudinal gradients, in biomes, 157, 159
alum, in water treatment, 558
aluminum, 19, 20, 87, 726
in soil, 254–255, 256
supplies of, 516–530 *passim*
Amazon basin, 31, 142, 260, 626–627, 718
forests of, 157, 273, 278, 345, 626
American Medical Association (AMA), 741, 824
Ames, Bruce, mutagenicity test by, 595, 814
amino acids, 73, 82, 83, 128, 973
amino group (NH_2^+), 81
ammonia (NH_3), 68, 81–87, 557, 598, 684
ammonification, 82, 83, 86
ammonium ion (NH_4^+), 81, 84, 86, 87
ammonium nitrate, 84
ammonium sulfate, 84, 91
Amtrak, 866, 868
Anabaena algae, 375
anchovies, 354–355, 569
Andes mountains, 17
anemia, 306, 316, 976, 977, 993
Angola, 909, 960, 968
population policy in, 762, 764
animals. *See also by type*
in nutrient cycles, 77–91 *passim*
in food chains, 128–129
in biomes, 149–158 *passim*
as food, 289–290
husbandry of, 289, 375–376
as test organisms, 577–579, 594
pesticide effects on, 634–642
anions. *See also by name*
in nutrient cycles, 73
Antarctica, 166–170, 355, 359, 360–361, 635, 912
geography of, 13, 25–28
antelopes, 375
anthracite, 78, 416

anthropocentrism, 811–812
antibiotics, 192n
antibody production, malnutrition and, 309, 311
antimony, 521, 526, 527, 598
Appalachia, 419
aquaculture, 366–369
aquatic organisms. *See also* fish
  chlorinated hydrocarbons in, 638–639
  oil pollution and, 658
aquifers, 31
Arabs, the, 217, 893–895
Arcata Redwood Company, 276
arctic ecosystems, 140, 148, 149. *See also* tundra
Arctic region, 13, 25, 28, 148, 149, 689
  oil in, 414, 681–682
Argentina, 241, 395, 886, 887, 888, 890, 891
  demography of, 200, 220, 305, 309, 782, 962
  food and nutrition in, 300, 301, 314, 317, 327, 328, 966, 968
  family planning in, 759, 762, 765
  arms control and, 912, 914
argon, in air, 33
Ariadne legend, 874
Aristotle, 812
arms control, 911–913, 917–918
Arms Control and Disarmament Agency (ACDA), U.S., 918
Army Corps of Engineers, 560–561
arsenic, 526, 568, 588, 598
asbestos, 521, 526, 588
ascorbic acid, 976
Asia. *See also* centrally planned economies; South Asia; *and countries by name*
  geography of, 31, 57, 260
  land use in, 82, 250, 257, 268, 273
  demography of, 179, 189–201 *passim,* 222–224, 226, 228–231, 305, 309, 901, 961–962, 964
  urbanization of, 237, 238, 240
  food consumption in, 291, 294, 306, 315, 327, 372
  food production in, 296, 329, 333, 342, 364, 367–368
  in world trade, 317, 318, 319
  population policy in, 758, 762, 765, 808, 809
Aspergillus fungus, 590
asthenosphere, 12, 14, 17, 18
asthma, 546
Aswân Dam, 261, 344, 899–900
Atacama desert, 56
Athabasca tar sands, 404, 422
atmosphere, 12, 14, 32–33, 36–63, 69, 672–690, 943
  gases of, 13, 32–33, 39, 42
  heat in, 14, 425
  water transport in, 29, 30, 69, 70
  circulation of, 51–55
  nutrients in, 79–80, 81, 84–87
  sulfur cycle and, 89, 90, 91
  trace elements in, 570, 572
Atomic Energy Commission (AEC), U.S., 404n, 443, 445, 447, 452–453, 585, 836, 862
atomic mass unit, 72
Audubon Society, 812
Australia, 237, 466, 668–669, 813, 835, 841, 888
  geography of, 31, 250, 260
  community ecology of, 118, 119, 145, 273
  demography of, 199, 215, 216, 222, 227, 230, 305, 309, 963, 966
  aborigines of, 231, 718
  migration to, 230, 234
  agriculture and diet in, 287, 295, 300, 301, 473, 968
  in world trade, 318, 319, 328, 521
  in international affairs, 656, 887, 898, 916
  population policy of, 754–755, 758
Australopithecus hominids, 184
Austria
  demography of, 200, 217, 305, 309, 757, 963, 964
  diet in, 300, 301, 968
automobiles
  energy use by, 492, 494, 496–497
  emissions from, 550–551, 569–570, 725
  stock of, 722
  policy for, 865–866
autotrophs, 129
Avogadro's number, 72
Azodrin, 644–645, 646, 985
Azolla fern, 375
Azotobacter bacteria, 82, 83

babies, low birth-weight, 304, 311
bacteria
  photosynthesis by, 71–72
  decomposition by, 77–78, 134, 474, 558, 560, 658
  in nutrient cycles, 82–83, 86, 88, 89–90, 288, 668
  disease and, 192, 608
  in soil, 253, 255, 640, 642, 652
  and food loss, 342
  in water pollution and treatment, 556–557, 558, 668
  in mutagenicity test, 577
Baculovirus pathogen, 648
Bahamas, the, 521, 962
Bahrain, 765, 961
Baja California, plant community of, 148
Bangladesh, 303, 887
  demography of, 179, 208, 692–693, 775, 776–777, 782, 961, 964
  food and nutrition in, 286, 287, 294, 323, 923, 968
  family planning in, 762, 765, 766, 767, 775
Barbados, 235, 762, 764, 775, 968
  demography of, 305, 309, 775, 962
barium, 521, 526
barley, 287, 320
basaltic crust, Earth's, 12, 17, 19–20
Batesian mimicry, 125
batteries, for electricity storage, 481–482
bauxite, 520
Bay Area Rapid Transit (BART), 866, 867
baygon, 985
Becquerel, Henri, 579
beef, 289, 290, 320, 321, 572
  consumption of, 313–315, 972
  energy subsidy to, 265, 315, 439
beefalo, 375–376
Belgium, 521, 545
  demography of, 205, 216, 305, 309, 963, 964
  diet in, 300, 301, 968
  family planning in, 754, 758
Benin, 762, 960
Benson, Ezra Taft, 979
benzene hexachloride (BHC), 563, 564, 641, 643–644, 982
Berg, Paul, 818
beriberi, 975–976
beryllium, 526, 568, 598
beta particles, 581

Bhutan, 961
Biafra, famine in, 344
bicarbonate ion (HCO_3), in water, 262
biochemical oxygen demand (BOD), 160–161, 269, 556
biochemical plant defenses, 126
bioclimatic regions, 248–249
biogasification, 474–475, 669
biological warfare, 608–609, 913, 917
biomass, 78–80, 85, 87
 of various ecosystems, 131–134, 137, 146
biomes, 144–159
biosphere, 11–13, 691–693
 assaults on, 541–620, 621–709
biotin, 976
birds
 DDT in, 635–638
 pollution effect on, 658, 659, 660
Birth Control League, 741
birth control movement. *See* family planning
birth defects, 576–577, 586, 654
birth rate, 1, 183–186, 190–212 *passim*, 222–223
 in population dynamics, 98, 99, 100, 105, 108–109
 family planning and, 741, 743, 767, 774–775
 urban/rural, 773
 infant mortality and, 776–777
 of selected countries, 790, 959–963
births, unplanned, 742–744, 750, 760–761, 766
bismuth, 521, 526
bituminous coal, 78, 416–418, 485
blackbody, 41, 44
Black Lung Law (1972), 420
blacks
 DDT in, 565
 reproduction rate of, 749
bogs, soils of, 256
Bohemia, famine in, 188
Bolivia, 200, 521, 762, 890, 891, 962, 968
bombs
 nuclear, 456–457, 462, 674
 in Vietnam, 654–655
Boomer vs. *Atlantic Cement Company*, 831
boreal region, 249
Borlaug, Norman, 325, 352
boron, 22, 526
Boston Women's Health Book Collective, 827
botanical pesticides, 982
Botswana, 762, 961, 968
Boyer, Herbert, 818
brain drain, 828
brain size, culture and, 184–185
Brazil. *See also* Amazon basin
 demography of, 200, 782, 790, 891, 962, 966
 urbanization of, 239, 241
 agriculture and diet in, 287, 288, 291, 300, 301, 686, 968, 971
 in world trade, 319, 521, 892
 energy use and development in, 395, 422, 454, 476, 521
 population policy in, 759, 762, 765
 development of, 790, 875, 887, 890, 891, 902–903, 905
 arms control and, 912, 914, 915
breastfeeding, 304–305, 306, 307, 772, 779
breeder reactors, 404, 405, 407, 408, 434–449 *passim*, 836
brewer's yeast, 370
Brezhnev, Leonid, 911, 913
British thermal unit (Btu), 16
bromine, 22, 526, 675
bronchitis, 546–547, 549
Brookhaven National Laboratory, 445
Brown, Jerry, 847
bubonic plague, 182, 186–187, 189, 607, 608
Buddhism, on population control, 809
buffalo, interbreeding of, 375–376
Bulgaria, 216, 305, 309, 758, 963, 968
Burma
 food and nutrition in, 317, 339, 349, 968
 demography in, 762, 765, 782, 961
Burundi, 762, 960, 968
business, as an institution, 840
butterflies
 population structure of, 115–120, 138, 142–143
 in coevolution, 126–127
 in various biomes, 155, 157
Butz, Earl, 321, 981

Cabrillo, Juan Rodriguez, 554
Cactoblastis moth, 143
cadmium, 521, 526, 568, 573–575, 598
Calandra oryzae, 102n
calcification, 255, 256
calcium, 20, 637
 in water, 22, 24, 92, 262, 263
 as nutrient, 68, 73, 92–93, 306–307, 976, 977
calcium ions (Ca^+), 73, 87, 254
calcium carbonate ($CaCO_3$), 255, 256, 263
calcium phosphate ($Ca_3(PO_4)_2$), 89, 519, 528–529
California, 241, 270, 624, 660, 835
 land use in, 252, 285, 872–873
 food production in, 285–286, 364, 642, 648, 651
 geothermal development in, 410, 463, 464, 465
 air pollution in, 237, 276, 544–545, 546, 551, 553, 554–555, 664, 833, 835
 abortion in, 756, 824
California Coastal Plan, 872–873
Calvert Cliff's coordinating committee vs. *AEC*, 836
Cambodia, 235, 294, 322, 624, 655–656, 762, 765, 923
Cameroon, 762, 763, 960, 968
Canada
 demography of, 199, 200, 215, 216, 224–231 *passim*, 305, 309, 753, 962, 965
 migration and, 233, 234, 235, 753
 urbanization of, 237, 238
 water supply in, 260, 270, 271
 food and nutrition in, 287, 296, 300, 301, 302, 314, 361, 686, 968
 in international affairs, 270, 271, 319, 323, 328, 454, 521, 898, 912
 power development in, 403–404, 413, 438, 454, 894
 pollutants in, 566, 590, 661, 835
 population policies in, 753, 758
cancer, 586–596, 994, 998
cane sugar, production of, 289
Cape Verde Islands, 960
carbamates, 564, 633, 641, 985, 987
carbohydrates (CH_2O)
 plant, 75, 77–78
 in food chains, 129
 as nutrient, 972–973
carbon
 sources of, 20, 22, 32, 70, 530
 as nutrient, 67, 70, 71, 74–80

carbon (*continued*)
fixed, 78–79, 162, 417
isotope of, 80, 582, 585
carbonate ion (CO_3^-), 79, 262
carbon dioxide, 33, 36, 69, 70, 80, 81, 254, 262, 474
radiation and, 42, 45, 46, 47
from fossil fuel combustion, 69, 78–81, 84, 91, 682–683
in nutrient cycles, 71, 77–81, 84
in food chains, 128–129
in electricity generation, 426, 429
climate effects and, 682–683, 685–686
carbon monoxide
from decomposition, 78, 80, 81
from volcanoes, 79
in air pollution, 543, 545–546, 550, 552
standards for, 551, 598
carbon tetrachloride (CCl_4), 598, 675
carcinogenesis, 588–590, 592–959, 600
by air pollution, 542
by pesticides, 564–565, 981
from radiation, 583–584, 586
from oil contamination, 658
cardiac diseases, 993–994
Caribbean area, 233, 235, 294, 762, 764. *See also countries by name*
demography of, 199, 222, 962
carnivores, 77, 128–131, 133, 134
carrying capacity, 99
Carter Administration (U.S.), 321, 347n, 861, 917
catalytic converter, 429
cattle, "sacred," 290. *See also* beef
Ceanothus, in chaparral, 159
celibacy, 190, 191, 739
cell-culturing, in crop development, 374
Center for the Improvement of Maize and Wheat (CIMMYT), International, 324
Center for Tropical Agriculture (CIAT), International, 324
Central African Republic, 200, 762, 790, 960, 968
Central America, 143, 239, 333, 521, 891. *See also countries by name*
biogeography of, 13, 155–157, 250, 260, 273
demography of, 199, 222, 305, 307, 891, 962
food consumption in, 294, 372
family planning in, 762, 764
Central Intelligence Agency, U.S., 609, 656, 890, 891, 909
centrally planned economics (Asian)
food production and distribution in, 291, 299, 326, 328, 330
family planning in, 765
cereals, 286–287, 294, 351, 972. *See also* grains *and cereals by name*
cervical cap, 991, 992
cesium, 22, 526
isotopes of, 444, 451, 582, 585, 671, 672
Ceylon. *See* Sri Lanka.
Chad, 762, 887, 960, 968. *See also* Sahel
chaparral, 144–145, 157–158, 159
chemical and biological warfare (CBW), 608–609, 913, 917
chemical energy, 15, 33
chernozem, soil of, 256
child labor, 205, 206
child spacing, 184–185, 212, 308, 741, 767, 772
children
nutrition of, 303–304, 309–313, 316, 974–975
mortality rate of, 309, 777
unwanted, 739, 742–744, 750, 760–761, 766
right to, 837–839
Chile, 521, 590, 890–891, 905, 914
demography of, 200, 305, 309, 962
food and nutrition in, 300, 301, 304–305, 311–312, 360, 966, 968
family planning in, 759, 762, 764
China, ancient, 115, 187–190, 272, 739, 810
China, People's Republic of
demography of, 179, 198–199, 201, 225, 230, 770–775 *passim,* 782, 790, 961, 963
migration from, 233, 240
development of, 241, 887, 904, 931, 932, 933
irrigation in, 268, 933
food and agriculture in, 286–292 *passim,* 314, 327, 329, 335, 339–341, 349, 350, 363–367 *passim,* 968
in international affairs, 292, 317, 319, 869, 898, 912, 914
energy use in, 349, 350, 395, 886
family planning in, 758, 762–775 *passim,* 787
health care in, 771–772, 937
oil in, 894
chlordane, 563, 641, 982, 983
chloride ion, 73, 262, 263
chlorinated hydrocarbons, 561–567, 597, 630, 632–642, 854, 855, 981–984, 986
chlorine, 22, 68, 526, 598
Chlorobium bacteria, 90
chlorofluorocarbons, 674–675, 676–677
chlorophyll, 73
choline, 976
Choristoneura budworm, 153
Chromatium bacteria, 90
chromite, 520
chromium, 20, 315, 521–530 *passim,* 568
cities
migration to, 235, 239, 240, 752
dehumanization in, 603–606
and heat, 677–681
"new," 749, 751–752
central, 871
citrus crops, 143, 643, 646, 648
Cladophora algae, 138
Clark, Colin, 225
class action suits, 832
Clean Air Act, 550–551, 554, 571, 833, 836
clear-cutting, 276, 277
climate, 32–33, 36–63, 346–348
changes in, 672–690
climax community, 135–137, 847
Clive, Robert, 190
clivus multrum dry toilet, 560
Clostridium bacteria, 82
clothing, 722, 725
clouds, 90, 677
radiation and, 42, 45, 46, 47, 61
seeding of, 684–685, 688–689
coal, 78, 79, 264
energy from, 393, 396, 397
stocks and flow of, 402, 403, 516
gasification and liquefaction of, 403, 420–422, 429
fuel cycle of, 416–422
electricity generation from, 423, 426, 485, 487
air pollution from, 427–429
trace metals in, 568, 571, 574

and world trade, 893, 894
Coal Mine Health and Safety Act, U.S. (1969), 420
coal workers' pneumoconiosis (CWP), 420
cobalt, 569, 598
as nutrient, 68, 977
supplies of, 521, 524, 526, 530
isotope of, 582, 671
Cocoyoc Declaration, 897n
cod, 364, 365
coevolution, 124–128, 155
Cohen, Stanley, 818
Colombia, 233, 590, 887, 891
urbanization of, 239, 241
food and nutrition in, 300, 301, 324, 966, 968
demography of, 305, 309, 775, 782, 962
family planning in, 739–740, 762, 764, 767, 775
colonialism, 779–780, 905
Colorado River, 261, 262, 264
basin of, 423
columbium, 521, 526
combustion engine, 426
combustion turbine, 426
commensalism, 125
Commercial Revolution, 187, 189
commercial uses of energy and materials, 266, 395, 396, 492, 556
commons
tragedy of the, 359, 806
globe as, 939–944
communications industry, 868–870, 932
community ecology, 128–145
Comoro Islands, 762, 960
competition, in population dynamics, 99, 106, 125
"Comstock Laws," 740–741
condensation nuclei, 36, 684–685
condom, 739, 991–992, 996
conduction, 24, 40, 45, 46
Congo, People's Republic of, 200, 762, 960, 968
conservation movement, 491–493, 497–498, 812–813, 863–865
Consultative Group on International Agricultural Research (CGIAR), 324
continental drift, 17
continental shelf, 27, 76, 132, 166
contraceptives, 991–1000. *See also* sterilization
oral, 740, 766, 773, 991, 992–994, 996
research on, 997–1000
convection, 24, 40, 51
convergence zones, intertropical, 55
converter reactor, 404, 405, 408
cooling ponds and towers, 483–484
Cooperative State Research Service, 325
copper, 22, 24, 68, 530, 569, 994
stocks and flow of, 516–530 *passim*
coral reefs, 163–166
core, Earth's 12, 13, 14
Corey, Lawrence, 808
Coriolis deflection, 52–53, 54, 55
corn, 293, 343, 346–349, 373
importance of, 189, 286, 287
in world trade, 318, 321
corn, soya, milk formula (CSM), 372
cornucopianism, 953–955
Costa Rica, 762, 764, 790, 937, 966, 968
demography of, 205, 305, 309, 790, 962
cotton, 127–128, 321, 344, 515
pest control for, 127, 643–645, 648, 651
Council on Environmental Quality (CEQ), 647, 833, 861
cretinism, 307
crime rates, 604
crops, 93, 133, 189, 286–289, 343–345, 660–661. *See also* grains *and crops by name*
land for, 14, 251–252, 295
high-yield varieties (HYV), 325, 329–352 *passim*, 629, 643
multiple, 338, 339, 345–346
monocultures of, 343, 628–629
pests and yields of, 642, 643–644
crowding, 602–603, 604, 607
Crusades, the, 228
crust, Earth's, 12, 14, 17–20, 69
Cuba, 887, 937, 966, 968
demography of, 200, 962
migration from, 232, 233
family planning in, 759, 762
culture, growth of, 183, 184–185
curie (ci), 432
Curie, Marie, 580
Curie, Pierre, 580
cyanide, 984
cyclonic circulation, 52, 53
Cyprus, 759, 765, 961, 968
Czechoslovakia, 395, 598–599, 758, 760, 968
demography of, 200, 216, 305, 309, 963, 965

Dacus fruit fly, 649
Dahorney, 762, 960, 969
dairy products, 313, 349, 972
in world trade, 318, 319, 320
dams, 261, 270, 600–601
Danaus butterfly, 126
death rate, 183–202 *passim*, 208–210
in population dynamics, 1, 98, 99, 100, 105
age-specific, 107, 108–109, 112–114, 203–205
from nuclear accident, 446
air pollution and, 544–545
from cancer, 587, 591
abortion and, 755, 756, 759, 761
and health care, 764, 771
high fertility and, 778–779
in selected countries, 790, 959–963
decomposition. *See also* bacteria
in nutrient cycles, 77–78, 80, 81
biomass and, 134, 137
de-development of overdeveloped countries, 926–930, 956
Deevey, Edward S., Jr., 71, 75
Defenders of Wildlife, 812
defoliation, military, 653–656
deforestation, 78, 272, 276–278, 337–338, 345, 568, 623–624, 848
Delaney Amendment (1958), 589–590, 594
democracy, 810, 829
demography, 98, 181–246, 959–966. *See also* birth rate; death rate; population
transition in, 780–783, 790
denitrification, 83, 84, 85–86
Denmark, 497–498, 590, 640, 717, 758, 887
demography of, 192, 195, 217, 305, 309, 962, 965
diet in, 300, 301, 968
density, atmospheric, 37
density dependence, in populations, 119

deoxyribonucleic acid (DNA), 73, 576, 592, 676
recombinant, 818–819
dependency ratio, 204, 205, 206, 209, 747
Depression, age composition and, 208, 211, 212
desalination, 271
energy of, 476–477
desert, 132, 144–149, 627–628
percent of land in, 248, 249, 252
soil type in, 255, 256
Desulforvibrio bacteria, 90
Desulfotomaculum bacteria, 90
detergents, phosphorus in, 89
deuterium, 408–409, 458, 459, 461
developed countries (DCs). *See also countries by name*
resource use in, 2–3, 273, 278, 393, 521–522, 886, 887, 888, 929–930
demography of, 107, 108, 179, 197–200, 204, 210, 215–219, 224–231 *passim,* 885
migration and, 232
urbanization of, 237–240
agriculture and diet in, 288–298 *passim,* 313–317, 326, 328, 330, 343, 968
in world trade, 297, 317, 319, 323, 888–889, 892–897
population policies in, 745–761
and less developed countries, 897–904, 925–926, 929–930
arms and, 915–916, 919–920
development, economic, 897–904, 925–926
population growth and, 780–783, 790
grass-roots, 926, 931–936
Dewey, John, 811
dew point, 37
diaphragm, 991, 992, 993, 996
diarrhea, 304
diazinon, 564, 985, 987
dichlorodiphenyl trichloroethane (DDT), 562, 632, 642, 980, 982, 983–984, 986
in food chain, 139, 630, 631
malaria and, 197, 634
pollution from, 561–567, 634–642
regulation of, 598, 832, 854–855
oil spill, synergism with, 728
dichlorvos, 987
dieldrin, 563, 564, 565, 566, 598, 637, 639–640, 641, 646, 855, 979–981, 983, 986
diesel generator, 426
diet
variation in, 297–298, 335, 370, 372, 967
deficiencies in, 300–309 *passim,* 316, 972–978
diethylstilbestrol (DES), 589, 998
diffusion, gaseous, 434–435
dilan, 641
diminishing returns, law of, 726–727
disarmament, 911–913, 917–918
disclimax, 135, 137
diseases. *See also by name*
infectious, 190, 192, 197, 198, 302, 303, 304, 556–557, 608
deficiency, 306–307, 316, 972–978
from nuclear accident, 446
from air pollution, 544–549
from trace metals, 567–575 *passim*
threat of epidemic, 606–609
climate and, 688
cardiac, 993–994
dispersal, 117
dispersion, 117
dissolved oxygen concentration (DO), 160
dissolved solids, in water, 262–263, 264, 265
distribution and movement, in population structure, 115–117, 227–243, 749–753
disulfide ion ($S_2^{=}$), 90
diversity
stability and, 141, 390, 628–629, 921, 938–939, 956
radiation and, 671
in technological systems, 864–865
doldrums, low-pressure, 55
domestic use
of resources, 266, 267, 268, 421, 517, 518
of energy, 395, 396, 492
waste from, 556
Dominican Republic, 233, 762, 890, 891, 969
demography of, 200, 305, 309, 774, 775, 962, 966
doubling time, in population dynamics, 101–102, 114, 182–184, 200–202
douche, 739, 991, 996
drought, 2, 187, 292, 294, 296, 337, 685–686
drugs, from plants, 126
dung
as fuel, 290, 332, 337, 351, 397–398, 472
as soil nutrient, 350, 351
dust storms, 150, 151

earthquakes, 2, 14, 17, 21
nuclear accidents and, 448
dams and, 476, 600–601
fault lines of, 692, 693
Earth Watch, 942
Eastern Hemisphere. *See continents by name*
ecology
population dynamics and, 98
community, 128–161
ethics of, 811–812
Ecology Action, 813
Economic Commission for Latin America (ECLA), U.N., 892
economics
growth rate of, 843–853, 873–876
and political change, 843–858
ecosystems, 97, 132, 138
modification of, 623–629
pollutants in, 629–672
Ecuador, 233, 888, 890, 891, 894
demography of, 305, 309, 962
food and nutrition in, 364–365, 969
population policy of, 759, 762
Edelin, Kenneth, 757
education
as institution, 824–829
in LDCs, 936–937
efficiency, 398–399
effluents. *See also* water pollution
from energy production, 488, 489
regulation of, 561
Egypt, ancient, 235
Egypt, 268, 395, 887, 888, 900, 906, 914
demography of, 200, 305, 775, 782, 960
Aswân Dam, 261, 344, 899–900
diet in, 300, 301, 969
family planning in, 759, 762, 763, 764, 775, 900

Einstein, Albert, 16
Eisenhower, Dwight D., 909, 918
electric power
  water use for, 265–268
  energy supply through, 395–396, 399
  efficiency in generation of, 399, 438, 441, 471, 476, 477
  from resources, 423–429, 438, 441, 463, 464, 465, 469–471, 475–477, 479–480
  in water treatment, 558, 559
electromagnetic radiation, 15–16, 39–45, 580
  infrared, 16, 40, 42, 44–46, 61
  ultraviolet, 40, 42, 84, 676–677
electrostatic precipitator, 427, 429
element, 406
elephant seal population, 124
El Salvador, 890, 908, 962, 966, 969
  family planning in, 759, 762, 775
emission standards, 549–551, 554
employment, 853–854, 864
  urbanization and, 238, 239
  in agriculture, 348
  in automobile industry, 865
endangered species, 142
endosulfan, 564, 983, 986
endrin, 564, 638, 641, 983
energy, 391–513. *See also* thermodynamics, laws of, *and energy sources and resources by name*
  food situation and, 3, 292, 293, 348–351, 393, 473, 485, 488
  of physical systems, 14–16, 23, 33–35, 75
  atmospheric, 39, 46–48, 51
  consumption of, 101, 393–396, 398, 402, 466, 489–497, 721–722, 728, 790, 886, 927, 929, 959–963
  world trade of, 393–396
  conversion loss of, 395, 396, 398, 399, 425, 483–484, 670–671, 730
  transmission of, 480–482
  cost of, 484–489, 490, 862–863, 954–955
  policy for, 858–865
  prosperity and, 928–930
Energy Research and Development Administration (ERDA), U.S., 404n, 453, 861, 862
England
  famine in, 188
  London fire, 189
  demography of, 191–195 *passim,* 216, 238–239, 305, 309, 376, 873
  family planning in, 191–192, 740, 753, 754, 759, 761, 784
  migration from 192, 232
  growth of, 241, 686
  pollution in, 544, 545, 556
English channel, 133–134, 658
entropy, 34
environment
  concern about, 1–9, 826–827, 942
  energy technology effect on, 461–462, 471, 476, 479, 480, 483, 488, 489
  cancer and, 586–596
  legal protection of, 829–840
  and LDC development, 899–904
Environmental Action, 813
Environmental Defense Fund (EDF), 646, 813, 832, 834, 842, 855
environmental impact
  calculation of, 720–721, 723–724, 726, 727, 728, 729
  reports on, 834–836
Environmental Impact Statement (EIS), 834–836
Environmental Pesticide Control Act, Federal (FEPCA), 855
Environmental Protection Agency (EPA), U.S., 836, 861;
  on air quality, 428, 550, 551, 554, 571
  nuclear power regulation by, 443, 585–586
  on water quality, 561, 669
  on pesticides, 567, 647, 832, 885, 981
Environmental Quality Act (California), 835
enzymes, 72, 632, 633
epidemics, threat of, 606–607
epilimnion, 160, 665–666
EPN, 985
Equatorial Guinea, 762, 960
equilibrium, 23
  of physical systems, 22, 29, 43–44, 60
Erebia butterfly, 115, 157
  erosion, 17–20, 69, 150, 153, 257, 258, 656
  from deforestation, 272, 276–278, 624
Escherichia bacteria, 556
eserine, 633
Eskimos, 154, 231, 566, 635, 718, 739
estrogen, 990, 992–993, 997–998
ethics, of decisions, 920–924
Ethiopia, 233, 762, 782, 887, 960
  food and agriculture in, 323, 324, 373, 628, 969
Ethyl Corporation, 571
Euler's formula, 110
Euphausia krill, 167, 169
euphotic zone, 160, 163
Euphydryas butterfly, 115, 118–119, 138
Europe. *See also countries by name*
  agriculture in, 2, 268, 284, 333, 634
  geography of, 31, 260
  land use in, 147, 250, 272, 273
  demography of, 179, 189–200 *passim,* 208, 216–218, 222–229, 231, 305, 309, 717, 962–965
  bubonic plague in, 186–187
  famine and drought in, 188, 191, 294, 295
  migration and, 228–229, 231–233, 234
  urbanization of, 237, 238–239
  food production in, 287, 288, 296, 299, 300, 301, 326, 328, 363, 367, 370
  in world trade, 318, 319, 394, 893
  energy use in, 438, 439, 483, 520
  cancer in, 590, 591
  pollution in, 634, 661–662, 663, 678, 686
  population policies in, 739, 741, 745, 753–754, 758, 761, 776
  environmental movement in, 810, 813
European Common Market, 319, 521, 893, 985. *See also countries by name*
eutrophication, 160, 559, 666–667
evaporation, in hydrologic cycle, 29–30, 32, 69
evapotranspiration, in hydrologic cycle, 29–30
evolution, 122–128
exchange capacity, of soil, 254
excrement. *See* wastes, organic
exponential growth, 100–104
extinction, 142–143

fallout, dry
  of nutrients, 91, 93
family planning, *See also* abortion; contraceptives
  by child spacing, 184–185, 212, 308, 741, 767, 772
  history of, 185–186, 192, 193, 212, 232, 737–745
  by infanticide, 186, 188, 191–192, 739
  by delayed marriage, 225, 771, 772, 785, 839
  migration and, 230, 234–235
  as policy, 737–738, 789–796
  religion and, 741, 759–760, 768, 806–813
  in developed countries, 745–761
  in less developed countries, 761–776, 934, 935
  motivation for, 776–783, 837–838
  direct measures for, 783–789
  politics of, 791–796
  the law on, 837–840
Family Planning Act (1970), 741
Family Planning Services and Population Research Act (1970), 745
famine, 187, 188, 294–297, 344
  potato, 190–191, 232, 628–629
  in Sahel, 627–628
Far East. *See also countries by name*
  food production in, 291, 299, 326, 328, 367
  petroleum in, 394
fats and oils
  dietary, 286, 972–973
  world trade, 318, 320
  pesticides in, 562, 563, 566, 632, 728
Federal Energy Administration (FEA), U.S., 861
Federal Power Commission (FPC), U.S., 861
Federation of American Scientists (FAS), 821
feed
  grain as, 313–315, 320
  world trade in, 318, 319, 320
  fish as, 354, 355
  protein supplements as, 370, 371–372
feedback mechanisms, 60
  in global climate, 59–61, 62
  in population dynamics, 119
feldspar, weathering of, 70
Fermi LMFBR, Detroit, 445, 447
fertility rate, 206, 778–779
  in selected countries, 210–212, 216–218
  abortion and, 212, 216–217, 755, 758, 761
  transition in, 780–783, 789
  involuntary control of, 783, 786–789
fertilizers
  nutrient cycles and, 84–93 *passim,* 254, 333, 519, 664–668, 674
  supply of, 272, 293, 294, 519, 897
  high-yield crop varieties and, 329, 332–334, 336, 339, 345
  natural and chemical compared, 332, 345
  use of, 339, 341
fetus, legal rights of, 757, 839
Fiji Islands, 305, 309, 762, 963
Finland, 521, 590, 591, 758
  demography of, 217, 305, 309, 962
  diet in, 300, 301, 968
fire-ant program, 646–647, 979–981
fish
  consumption of, 286, 972
  production of, 294, 352–369
  in world trade, 317–320
  energy subsidy to, 349
  pollution and, 572, 635, 638–642, 656, 658, 660, 667
fish-protein concentrate, 371, 658
fission, nuclear, 404–408, 430–456, 864
  bomb, 393, 406, 434, 436
  reactors, 405–407, 485
flat-plate solar collectors, 466–467, 468
floods, 2, 187, 272, 292, 294, 296, 337, 341
flow, 23
  in hydrologic cycle, 29
Flowers, Sir Brian, 916
fluorides, 575, 598, 664
fluorine, 22, 68, 521, 526
fluorocarbon propellants, 552, 597, 674–675
flux, solar, 46, 48–51
flywheels, for electricity storage, 482
folic acid, 976
Food and Agriculture Organization of the United Nations (FAO), 297
food aid programs
  foreign, 315, 322–323, 922–924;
  domestic, 316–317
Food and Drug Administration (FDA), U.S., 573, 579, 589, 970, 993
food chains, 128–131, 137, 138, 168
  pollutants in, 630–631, 640, 658, 660, 672
Food for Peace Act, 325
Food Production and Investment, Consultative Group on, 297
food supply, 283–385, 967–978. *See also types of food by name*
  production of, 1–4, 180, 189, 283–290, 328–352, 968–971
  consumption of, 290–297, 335, 370–376; 967–978
  distribution of, 297–328
  loss of, 335, 342–343, 345, 561–564, 642–644
  energy subsidy to, 348–351, 393, 473, 485, 488
  expenditure for, 722
Ford, Gerald, 322, 746, 911, 913
Ford Foundation, 324, 761
foreign aid, 890, 892, 897–899, 904–908. *See also* Agency for International Development
  of food, 315, 322–323, 922–924
  by OPEC, 894
forests, 75, 76, 93, 131–147 *passim,* 158, 249, 252, 272–278, 337, 624. *See also* deforestation; tropics
  soil of, 256, 640
  milpa agriculture in, 284, 345, 349, 624–626
  products of, 516
  herbicides in, 653
  plowing of, 655
  air pollution and, 661, 664, 684
Forest Service, U.S., 274–275
Forrester, Jay W., 817
fossil fuels, 348, 393, 398, 400–404, 864
  carbon dioxide from combustion of, 69, 78–81, 84, 91, 682–683
  in carbon cycle, 78, 80, 81
  electricity generation with, 423–429, 483, 484
  air pollution from combustion of, 542–543, 568, 571, 574, 661
  trace metals in, 568, 571, 574
Fourteenth Amendment, 837
France, 241, 566, 813, 888
  food and nutrition in, 188, 287, 300, 301, 968

demography of, 191, 193, 194, 195, 216, 305, 309, 963, 964
in international affairs, 521, 754, 895–896, 898, 912, 914–917, 920
family planning in, 754, 758
French Guiana, 305
frequency dependence, in natural selection, 127
freshwater, 13, 14, 22, 27, 132, 249, 160–161, 265
flow of, 29, 30, 69, 85, 86, 88, 259, 260
groundwater and, 29, 30, 31, 69, 262–264, 266, 267, 444, 451
runoff of, 29–31, 69, 258–262, 267, 278
surface water of, 87, 89, 92–93, 252, 264, 266–267, 444
temperature of, 160–161, 665–666
use of, 264–267
aquaculture in, 366–369
trace metals in, 568, 572, 660
eutrophication of, 666–667
friction, atmospheric circulation and, 52, 53–54
Friends of the Earth (FOE), 813, 832, 842
fruit flies, 577, 649
fruits, nuts, vegetables, 286, 318–321, 344, 972
fuel
cost of, 485
uses of, 495
energy use in, 865
fuel cells, 480
fumigants, 981, 982, 984
Fundamentals of Human Sexuality, 827–828
fungi, 86, 134, 343, 590
in soil, 253, 255, 640–641, 642
fusion, 408–409, 456–462, 485
fusion-fission hybrids, 462–463

Gabon, 521, 894, 960, 969
gallium, 526
Gallup Poll, on population growth, 744
Gambia, 762, 960, 969. *See also* Sahel
gamma rays, 581
Gandhi, Indira, 769, 787
gases
atmospheric, 13, 32–33, 39, 42
perfect, equation for, 37
in soil formation, 252
diffusion of, 434–435
gas turbine, 426
Gaza, 961
gene pool, 122–123
General Electric Co., 451
General Fisheries Council, 366
General Motors, 865
generation time, 110–111
Genesis strategy, 944
genetic defects, 576–577, 586, 654
genetic drift, 124
genetic feedback, 119
genetic variability, 343–345, 376, 576, 631, 634, 748–749
Geneva disarmament talks (1975), 690
Geneva Protocol (1925), 656
genital organs (human), 989, 990
Georgia Pacific Company, 276
geothermal energy, 19, 20, 400, 409–410
electricity generation from, 426, 463–465, 485
German Democratic Republic, 233, 395, 453, 566, 590, 598–599, 888
demography of, 200, 217, 218, 230, 305, 309, 776, 963
food and nutrition in, 288, 968
germanium, 526
German (pre-war), 191, 232, 556
Germany, Federal Republic of (West)
demography of, 200, 217, 218, 230, 305, 309, 776, 963, 964
migration and, 233, 754
diet and nutrition in, 288, 300, 301, 314, 370, 968
energy use in, 395, 396
energy technology in, 419, 453, 454, 521, 668–669
pesticides in, 566, 638–639
health in, 590, 598–599, 607, 758, 827
development of, 887, 888, 898
arms control and, 912, 915, 916, 917
Geysers, The, 410,463, 464, 465
Ghana, 239, 875, 887, 960, 965, 969
family planning in, 762, 763, 775
Gilbert and Ellice Islands, 762
glaciers. *See* ice and glaciers
Glaser, P., 471
glass
recycled, 527
energy intensity of, 530
Glaucopsyche butterfly, 126–127
gleization, 255, 256
Gloeocapsa bacteria, 83
glucose
from photosynthesis, 71, 128
in food chains, 128–129
goats, 289
Gofman, John, 585
goiter, 307, 316, 977
gold, 22, 24, 521, 524, 526, 527, 530
government. *See also* United States *and specific units by name*
land owned by, 251
environmental planning by, 857–858, 860–862
types of, 887, 890–891
grains. *See also crops by name*
production of, 287, 292–295, 298, 327–328, 971
consumption of, 289, 313–315, 336–341 *passim*, 373, 972
reserves of, 292–296, 321, 322
in world trade, 292, 315, 317–322, 967, 971
prices of, 292, 320–321, 322, 334–335
as feed, 313–315, 320
high-yield varieties (HYV), 325, 329–352 *passim*, 629, 643
granitic crust, Earth's 12, 17, 19
Grapes of Wrath, The (Steinbeck), 150
graphite, 526
grassland, 132–135, 137, 144–145, 149–151, 249
gravity, atmosphere and, 52
Great Britain. *See also countries by name*
famine in, 187
food production in, 189, 363–364, 367, 376
migration and, 233, 754
abortion in, 758
Great Salt Lake, dissolved solids in, 264
Greece, ancient, 272, 569, 739
Greece, 232, 233, 300, 301, 521, 758, 968
demography of, 216, 305, 309, 963, 965
greenhouse effect, 45, 683

Greenland, ice sheet of, 27–28, 569
Greenland shark, 25
Green Revolution, 291, 329–332, 332–352 *passim*
Green River oil shales, 404, 422
Grenada, 762, 962
gross national cost (GNC), 846
gross national product (GNP)
  consumption and, 393, 395, 721–722, 724
  birth rate and, 782
  development and, 790, 843–844, 846–847, 891
  of selected countries, 959–963
gross primary production (GPP), 74, 131, 133, 135, 137, 162
groundwater, 29, 30, 31, 69, 262–264, 266, 267
  radioactivity in, 444, 451
growth rate
  exponential, 100–104
  economic, 843–853, 873–876
Guadeloupe, 962
Guatemala, 311, 345, 573, 890, 969
  demography of, 305, 309, 962
  family planning in, 759, 762, 775
Guinea, 887, 960, 969
Guinea-Bissau, 762, 960
Gulf Stream, 26
Guyana, 233, 762, 891, 962, 969
Gymnorhina magpie, 120
gypsum ($CaSO_4 \cdot H_2O$), 91, 92, 262, 264
gypsy moth, 980
gyres, 25–26

Haber and Bosch process, 84
haddock, 364, 365
Hadley cells, 55–56
hafnium, 526
Haiti, 233, 278, 762, 891, 905, 962, 969
half-life, 432, 444, 451, 581, 582
Hanseatic League, 873–874
Hawaii, 143, 622, 718
Head Start Program, 312n
heat, 15, 33, 398, 399. *See also* space heating and cooling; water
  in energy conversion, 395, 399, 425, 483–484, 670–671, 730
  from human activities, 677–681
heat engines, 425
heat pump, 399
Heliconius butterfly, 115–120 *passim*, 138, 142–143
helium, 33, 524
Helminthosporium fungus, 343
hemangiosarcoma, 597, 598
hemoglobin, 73
hepatitis, infectious, 557
heptachlor, 564, 641, 646, 980–981, 983, 986
heptachlor epoxide, 563, 564, 981
herbicides, 564, 567, 651–657, 986, 987
herbivores, 77, 125, 128–131, 133, 134
herring, 364, 365
hexachloride benzene (HCB), 563, 564, 641, 643–644, 982
Hickenlooper amendment, 892
high-yield crop varieties (HYV), 325, 329-352 *passim*, 629, 643
Hinduism, on population control, 809
hippie movement, 809
Hitler, Adolf, 230
Hollings, Ernest F., 316
Homo sapiens
  effect on physical systems of, 92–93, 149, 166, 677–686
  population dynamics of, 98, 106, 116
  other organisms and, 117, 142–143
  in food chain, 129–131
  development of, 185, 309–311
  migration of, 230–232
  mutations in, 576, 579
  environment and, 601–606, 809–812
  power of, 677–681
homosphere, 39
Honduras, 278, 521, 689, 762, 969
  demography of, 200, 962, 966
  politics of, 890, 908
Hong Kong, 240, 317
  demography of, 198, 201, 205, 208, 305, 309, 775, 961, 964
  family planning in, 758, 762, 765, 767, 775
hormones, 988–991, 992–994, 996, 998, 999, 1000
  additives of, 589
housing, 238, 243, 722
Housing and Urban Development Act (1970), 745
Hubbard Brook Forest, 276
Hubbert, M. King, 401
Humanae Vitae, 807
Human Environment, United Nations Conference on the (Stockholm, 1972), 5, 277, 361, 662, 942
humidity, 36, 61, 289–290, 677
humus, 147, 150, 157, 253–257, 667–668
Hundred Years' War, 187
Hungary, 556, 590, 758, 888, 968
  demography of, 191, 193, 194, 200, 216, 305, 309, 963, 965
hunting and gathering societies, 186, 208–209, 235, 349
hydrocarbons, 78, 422–423, 551, 684. *See also* chlorinated hydrocarbons
  emission of, 416, 684
  in air pollution, 543, 547, 550, 554
  polycyclic, 594–595
hydrogen, 20, 32, 33, 465, 470, 482
  as nutrient, 67, 71, 74–80
hydrogenation, 474
hydrogen ion (H^+), 70, 254, 263. *See also* acidity
hydrogen sulfide (H_2S), 68, 72, 90, 91, 599, 684
hydrologic cycle, 29–32, 410, 411, 475, 476
hydropower, 393, 396, 397, 411, 426, 465, 475–477, 485
hydrosphere, 21–32
hydrosulfide ion (HS^-), 90
hydroxyl ion (OH^-), 70
hypolimnion, 160–161, 665–666

ice and glaciers, 22, 27–29, 30, 62–63, 69
  amount of, 13, 14, 248, 249
  temperature and 59, 144, 683
  biomass and, 132
  and soil, 252
Iceland, 55, 365, 686, 758, 776, 962
  cancer in, 590, 591
Icerya insect, 648
igneous rocks, 19–20
illegitimacy, 757, 786
illness. *See* diseases
Illustrations and Proofs of the Principle of Population (Place), 740
ilmenite, 520, 521
immigration. *See* migration
implosion, 459
inbreeding, 691
Incaparina, 372
income distribution, 887–888
India
  agriculture in, 2, 286, 287, 288, 290, 324, 325, 332–333, 335–339, 342
  nuclear power in, 3, 454, 914, 915

population dynamics in, 100–101, 179, 190, 198, 201, 204, 208, 218, 308, 768, 776–777, 790, 961
geography of, 149, 150, 686
famines in, 187, 188, 190, 294, 298
birth rate in, 198, 768, 775, 776–778, 782, 790
population projections for, 220, 221, 225–226, 964
migration from, 232, 233
urbanization of, 240, 241, 242–243
health care in, 242–243, 608, 769, 937
irrigation in, 268, 269, 900, 933
diet and nutrition in, 300, 301, 303, 307, 314, 372, 969
in world trade, 317, 521, 897
aid to, 323, 898, 923
family planning in, 323, 739, 758, 762–769, 775, 783, 785, 787, 808, 809
high-yield crops in, 329, 331, 332–333, 336
energy use in, 395, 466, 472
as developing country, 790, 868, 887, 901, 905
weapons and, 912, 914, 915, 919

Indian tribes
American, 251
South American, 231, 718, 890

indium, 526

Indochina, 653–656, 909. *See also countries by name*

Indonesia, 395, 868, 887, 897, 914
food and agriculture in, 2, 268, 286, 287, 331, 342–343, 349, 366, 367, 968
demography of, 201, 305, 775, 782, 897, 961
urbanization of, 240, 241
family planning in, 758, 762, 763, 765, 767, 775, 902–903
oil in, 894, 895

industrialization, 1, 232, 740, 810, 894. *See also* developed countries (DCs)
population and, 183, 184, 192–193, 196, 197, 731.

industry
nutrient cycles in, 87–87, 89
water use by, 266, 267, 268, 271
energy use by, 395, 396, 399, 421, 468–469, 492–494, 517, 865
pollution from, 543, 556, 840, 847
metals in, 568, 570, 571
employment hazards in, 597–600
energy, 858–860
in less developed countries, 931

inertial confinement (fusion), 456–457

infanticide, 186, 188, 191–192, 739

infant mortality, 304, 305, 776–779, 790, 960–963

influenza epidemic (1918), 210

inositol, 976

input/output analysis, 23

insecticides, 153, 562, 564, 630–646, 979–987

isolation, 46

Institute of Nutrition for Central America and Panama (INCAP), 372

institutions, on environmental deterioration, 805–884

INTELSAT satellite, 868–869

Intergovernmental Maritime Consultative Organization (IMCO), 815

International Atomic Energy Agency (IAEA), 454, 914–915

International Board for Plant Genetic Resources (IBPGR), 324

International Center for Agricultural Research in Dry Areas (ICARDA), 324

International Crops Research Institute for Semi-Arid Tropics (ICRISAT), 324

International Development and Food Assistance Act (U.S.), 325

International Energy Agency (IEA), 895

International Fund for Agricultural Development (IFAD), U.N., 323, 325

International Institute of Tropical Agriculture (IITA), 324

International Laboratory for Research on Animal Diseases (ILRAD), 324

International Livestock Center for Africa (ILCA), 324

International Military Tribunal, Nuremberg, 656

International Rice Research Institute (IRRI), 324, 329, 342–343, 374

International Seabed Authority, 941

International Whaling Commission (IWC), 360–361

International Wheat Council, 297

Interstate Commerce Commission (ICC), U.S., 861

intrauterine device (IUD), 991, 993, 994–995, 996

inversion, atmospheric, 48

iodine
supplies of, 22, 526
as nutrient, 68, 307, 316, 977
isotope of, 444, 581, 582, 585

ionizing radiation, 579–586

ionosphere, 12, 39

Iran, 233, 241, 268, 327, 894, 912, 969
demography of, 201, 775, 782, 961, 964
family planning in, 762, 765, 775

Iraq, 241, 573, 762, 765, 894, 898
food and agriculture in, 268, 269, 327, 331, 969
demography of, 782, 961

Ireland, 232, 521, 754, 758
food and nutrition in, 188, 190–191, 194, 195, 300, 301, 628–629, 968
demography of, 191, 195, 200, 216, 305, 309, 962

iron
stock and flow of, 14, 17, 20, 516–530 *passim*
in nutrient cycles, 68, 73, 87, 317, 977
oxides of, 79
soil pH and, 254–255, 256
in water, 262, 264
isotope of, 582

iron sulfide (FeS_2), 91, 92

irrigation, 341, 681, 899–900, 933
water use for, 266–269, 271–272
high-yield crop varieties and, 334, 338, 339

Islam, on population control, 808

isodrin, 641

isotopes, 406. *See also specific elements*
half-life of, 432, 444, 451, 581, 582
maximum permissible concentration (MPC), 433, 444, 451, 585–586
properties of, 580–582

Israel, 3, 466, 566, 590, 835, 912
demography of, 217, 305, 309, 961, 964
diet in, 300, 301, 968
nuclear weapons in, 454, 914
population policy in, 759, 762, 765

Italy, 272, 324, 367, 464, 521, 894

Italy (*continued*)
demography of 200, 216, 305, 309, 963, 964
migration from, 232, 233
diet in, 300, 301, 968
population policy in, 574, 758
Ivory Coast, 239, 762, 960, 965, 969

Jamaica, 233, 311, 521, 590, 648, 762, 891, 969
demography of, 197, 775, 891, 962
Japan, 395, 520, 887, 888, 898, 931
agricultural food production in, 2, 268, 286, 287, 294, 339, 349, 350, 933
in world trade, 3, 275, 319, 320, 521, 893, 897
population pressure in, 179, 227, 230, 241, 243, 602, 603
death rate in, 198, 305, 309, 961
population of, 199, 201, 204, 208, 217, 218, 220, 222–223, 230, 961, 964
nutrition in, 300, 301, 314, 968
food from sea in, 354, 355, 360–369 *passim*
energy technology in, 439, 464, 466
pollution in, 562–563, 574, 575, 583
cancer in, 590, 591, 595
population policy in, 739, 755, 760, 761
Jasper Ridge butterfly populations, 118–119
jet streams, circumpolar, 56
Johnson, Lyndon B., 909
Joint Committee on Atomic Energy (JCAE), U.S., 445, 862
jojoba cactus, 359
Jordan, 762, 765, 961, 969
joule (J), 16
Judeo-Christian religious tradition, 807, 809–810

Kalahari Desert, 56, 231
kelthane, 984, 986
Kenya, 239, 305, 324, 888, 938, 969
demography of, 200, 305, 775, 782, 960, 965
family planning in, 762, 763, 775
kepone, 983
Khmer civilization, ancient, 625–626
Khmer Republic, 961, 969
kilocalorie (kcal), 16, 972
Knipling, E. F., 647
Korea, Democratic People's Republic of (North), 268, 291n, 762, 782, 887, 962, 969
Korea, Republic of (South), 233, 268, 312–313, 367, 521, 969
demography of, 198, 201, 774, 775, 782, 790, 962, 964
development of, 241, 887, 888, 902, 912, 936
family planning in, 758, 762, 763, 765, 767
krill, 355
krypton, 33, 451
isotope of, 449, 581, 582, 583, 585
!Kung bushmen, 185, 186, 718
Kuwait, 201, 305, 309, 894, 898, 961
kwashiorkor, 306, 307, 316, 370
kyanite, 526

labor groups, 840–841
lakes and rivers. *See* freshwater
land, 247–257. *See also* agriculture
in nutrient cycles, 70, 80, 81, 85–92 *passim*
production on, 74–76, 132, 138, 248–251
use of, 285–286, 487, 559–60, 870–873.
langley, 46
Laos
food situation in, 294, 969
family planning and demography in, 762, 775, 961
laser fusion, 459–460
laser separation, of isotopes, 435–436
Lasky, Sam, 523
latent heat. *See* vaporization, heat of
lateritization, 255, 256, 625–626, 653
Latin America, 268, 273, 306, 394, 890. *See also* Central America; South America
demography of, 179, 195–201, *passim*, 208, 222, 224–227, 231, 305, 962, 964, 966
United States and, 232, 233, 890–892
urbanization of, 237, 238, 239, 241
food and nutrition in, 286, 288, 291, 296, 299, 304, 326, 328, 329, 372
in world trade, 317, 318, 319
population policy in, 759, 762, 764–765, 791
as developing country, 890, 901, 905, 912, 936
Latin American Demographic Center, 908
latitude, 48–51, 54–56, 61
Law of the Sea, U.N. Conferences on the (UNCLOS), 5, 361, 366, 941–942
Lawson condition, 458, 459
leaching, 70
lead, 22, 568–571, 599
isotope of, 431
supplies of, 516–530 *passim*, 569
tetraethyl, 560, 569–570, 599, 725, 729
leaf-protein extracts, 371
Lebanon, 324, 762, 765, 961, 969
legal system, 829–840
legumes, 82, 86, 288–289, 344
pulses, 289, 318, 320, 972
Leopold, Aldo, 145, 247
Lesotho, 762, 961, 969
less developed countries (LDCs). *See also countries by name*
energy and resource use by, 2–3, 274, 278, 393, 521–522, 886, 927
in international politics, 3, 5, 904–908, 915, 916, 919–920
demography of, 107, 179, 196–210 *passim*, 218–231 *passim*, 304, 717, 747, 885
migration and, 232, 234–235
urbanization of, 237–243
agriculture in, 250, 284–285, 325, 348–350, 933, 934, 935
nutrition in, 290–299 *passim*, 303–309, 311, 313, 968–970
food production in, 290–299 *passim*, 342
aid to, 296–297, 897–899
in world trade, 317–318, 323, 888–889, 892–897
projected food demand in, 326–328
fertilizer use in, 332–335, 344
population policies in, 738–740, 755, 758–759, 761–784, 789–796
development in, 789–796, 828, 844, 887, 888, 897–904, 925–926, 929–939
mass communications in, 868, 869, 932
lethal dose (LD), 433, 981
Liberia, 305, 324, 762, 960, 965, 969

Libya, 762, 764, 894, 923, 960
  diet in, 300, 301, 969
Liebig, Justus von, law of the minimum, 73, 283
lifeboat ethics, 921–923
life expectancy, 109, 112–114, 185, 208, 209, 790
  in selected countries, 960–963
life table, 108–109, 112–114
lighting, energy for, 492, 493
lightning, nitrogen fixation and, 84, 85, 86
lignite, 78, 416
lime (CaO), 428
limestone ($CaCO_3$), 70, 262, 264, 428
Limits to Growth, 817
limpets, 163
lindane, 564, 983, 986
Lindeman's efficiency, 133
liquefied natural gas (LNG), 415
literacy, 936
lithium, 22, 24, 408–409, 462, 526, 530
Lithops stone plant, 126
lithosphere, 12, 14, 17–19
Little, Arthur D., Company, 471
littoral zone, 160
Littorina snail, 163
livestock, 286, 375–376
locust plague, 150
logarithmic growth, 100–104
lumber industry, 274–275
lupines, in coevolution, 126–127
Lutheran Church in America, Social Ministry of, 808
Luxembourg, 218, 521, 776, 963
  diet in, 300, 301, 968
lysine, 128, 373–374

Macan, 962
Madagascar. *See* Malagasy Republic
magma, 17, 19, 20
magnesium
  supplies of, 20, 520, 521, 526, 527, 530
  in water, 22, 24, 92, 262, 263, 264
  as nutrient, 68, 92–93, 977
  ions of, 73, 254
magnetic confinement (fusion), 457–458, 460–461
magnetic field, 14
magnetohydrodynamics (MHD), 465, 479–480
magpie populations, 118, 119, 120
maize. *See* corn
Malagasy Republic, 521, 762, 763, 969, 970
  demography of, 200, 305, 960
malaria, 197
malathion, 564, 633, 985
Malawi, 762, 763, 960, 969
Malaya, 198
Malaysia, 331, 521, 887
  demography of, 201, 305, 774, 775, 782, 961
  family planning in, 762, 765, 774
Malaysia, West, 964, 969
Mali, 762, 960, 969. *See also* Sahel
Maldive Islands, 961
malnourishment, 290
malnutrition, 298, 300–313
  diseases of, 306–307, 316, 972–978
Malta, 776, 963, 968
Malthus, Thomas Robert, 741, 742–743
Malthusian Leagues, 741
Malthusian rate of increase, 102, 104
Manchuria, mining in, 422
manganese, 254, 262, 599
  as nutrient, 68, 977
  supplies of, 520, 521, 524, 526, 530
mankind. *See Homo sapiens*
mantle, Earth's, 12, 13, 14, 17, 18
manure, 668, 669
marasmus, 306, 316
Marburg virus, 607
marriage, delayed, 225, 771, 772, 785, 839
Martinique, 962
Marx, Karl, 811–812
Massachusetts Institute of Technology (MIT), 730, 731
mass balance, 23
mass fraction, 33, 36
mass media, 868
mass transit, 238, 866, 867
materials. *See also by name*
  stocks and flows of, 515–522, 530–531
  supplies of, 522–531
mating preferences, 115
Mauritania, 762, 764, 960, 969. *See also* Sahel
Mauritius, 300, 301, 762, 764, 775, 969
  demography of, 204, 206, 305, 309, 775, 960, 965
maximally tolerated dose (MTD), 594
maximum permissible concentrations (MPCS), 433, 444, 451, 455
maximum sustainable yield (MSY), 121–122
Mayan civilization, 235, 626
Mayle, Peter, 827
McCormack, Ellen, 757
McHarg, Ian, 752
meat, 289–290, 313, 590, 972. *See also types by name*
  in world trade, 318, 319, 320
Médici, Emilio, 627
medicine, 183, 191, 192, 823–824, 937
Mediterranean lands, 63, 143, 145, 366. *See also countries by name*
Meinel, A. B., 469
Meinel, M. P., 469
Melanesia, 199, 222
menstruation, 990, 992, 993
mercury
  supplies and uses of, 22, 515, 520, 521, 524, 526, 527, 530, 571
  contamination with, 568, 571–573, 599, 660–661
Mesopotamia, 235
mesosphere, 12, 39
metabolism, 77–78, 972
metals
  trace, 68, 567–575, 670
  flow and value of, 516, 517, 520
  pollution by, 660, 661, 670
methane (CH_4), 33, 84, 474, 543, 558
  in carbon cycle, 78, 80, 81
methoxychlor, 564, 984, 986
methylbromide, 984
methylparathion, 985, 987
Metropolitan Planning Group, Ad Hoc, 808
Mexico, 241, 264, 268, 545, 887, 891, 937
  demography of, 196–205 *passim,* 220, 221, 305, 309, 775, 782, 790, 891, 962, 966
  migration from, 233, 234–235, 237
  food and diet in, 300, 301, 305, 311, 314, 324, 969
  in world trade, 317, 319, 521, 892
  energy use in, 395, 790
  family planning in, 759, 762, 775
  income distribution in, 875, 888, 890
mica, 521
micron, 40
micronesia, 199, 222

microorganisms, 252, 253, 577, 640–642, 652. *See also by type*
Mid-Atlantic Ridge, 17
Middle Ages, 191, 231–232, 739, 873–874
Middle East, 201, 233, 307, 521, 920. *See also countries by name*
  petroleum in, 3, 394, 413, 894
  food and agriculture in, 185, 291, 294, 299, 326, 328, 810
  family planning in, 759, 762, 765
midwives, 766, 767
migration
  population dynamics and, 98, 124, 192–197 *passim*, 227–235, 763
  urbanization and, 192, 235, 239, 240, 604, 752
militant revolutionaries, 901
military, the, land use by, 252
military-industrial complex, 905, 918–919
milk, 265, 289, 561–562, 972
millibar, 37
milpa agriculture, 284, 345, 349, 624–626
Mineral King lawsuit, 834, 835
minerals
  as nutrient, 21, 67, 68, 975, 977–978
  mining for, 24, 89, 252, 416–420, 431, 487, 517, 518, 529–530, 568
  world trade in, 521
minilaparotomy, 996
Minimata disease, 573, 574
minimum law of the, 73, 283
Minoan culture, 873, 874
Mirex, 981, 983, 986
Mitin, 985
models, mathematical, 170–172, 731–732
Moho discontinuity, 12
mole, 36, 72
molecular fraction, 32, 33, 36
molybdenum, 22, 68, 599, 977
  supplies of, 520, 524, 526, 530
Mongolia, 962, 969
mongoose, 143
monkey trap, South Indian, 843
monsoons, summer, 57, 158, 337, 685–686
Montrose chemical plant, 639
morning-after pill, 998
Morocco, 188, 887, 969
  demography of, 200, 774, 960, 965
  family planning in, 762, 764, 774, 775, 782
mortality. *See also* death rate
  infant, 305
  child, 309, 604, 778–779
Moslem countries, 808. *See also by name*
Moslem law, family planning and, 764
moth proofer, 981, 983, 984, 985
mountains, 13, 17, 144–145, 248, 256
Mozambique, 762, 764, 960, 969
Muir, John, 274
Mullerian mimicry, 125
multi-species population systems, 120–121
Mundey, Jack, 841
Murphy, R. C., 167
mutation
  in population evolution, 124
  chemically induced, 575–579, 595
  carcinogenesis by, 592–593, 595
  radiation and, 676
mutualism, 125
mutually assured destruction (MAD), 911, 913
Myers, Bishop C. Kilmer, 808

Nagana, 375
Namibia, 762, 961
naphthalene, 984
natality. *See* birth rate
National Academy of Sciences (NAS), 325, 820
National Aeronautics and Space Administration (NASA), U.S., 669
National Cancer Institute (NCI), 595
National Council of Churches, on nuclear power, 811
National Environmental Policy Act (NEPA), 833–836. *See also* Council on Environmental Quality (CEQ)
National Institute of Occupational Safety and Health (NIOSH), 837
National Institutes of Health (NIH), 817
National Science Foundation, 814
National Seed Storage Laboratory, 344
natural gas, 78, 79, 393, 396, 397, 413, 429
  stock and flow of, 402, 403, 516, 521
  fuel cycle of, 411–416
  electricity generation from, 423, 426, 485
natural gas liquids, 396
Natural Resources Defense Council (NRDC), 813, 832, 834
natural selection, 122–128
Nature Conservancy, 812
nematocide, 981
Neo-Malthusianism, 953–954
neon, 33
Nepal, 775, 782, 961, 969
  family planning in, 762, 765, 775
neptunium, 329, 444, 541
net community production (NCP), 132, 133–135, 137
net primary production (NPP), 74–76
  in communities, 131–133
  marine, 162
Netherlands, the, 332, 360, 395, 590, 717, 754, 758
  demography of, 216, 305, 309, 717, 963, 964
  food and nutrition in, 300, 301, 312, 968
neutrons, 581
New Alchemy Institute, 473
New Economic Order, Declaration on the Establishment of a U.N., 906–907
New Guinea, 187, 591. *See also* Papua New Guinea
newton (n), 16
New Zealand, 234, 237, 250, 273, 463, 464, 813
  demography of, 199, 215, 216, 222, 305, 963
  food production and consumption in, 300, 301, 318, 363, 968
  energy use by, 393, 395
  cancer in, 590, 591
  population policy in, 754–755, 758
Nicaragua, 762, 764, 962, 969
nickel, 14, 17, 20, 22, 569, 599
  supplies of, 520, 521, 524, 526, 530
nicotinamide adenine dinucleotide phosphate (NADP), 72, 73
nicotine sulfate, 982
Niger, 628, 762, 960, 969. *See also* Sahel
Nigeria, 233, 345, 395, 521, 590
  demography of, 200, 220, 221, 782, 960, 965
  urbanization of, 239, 241

food production and consumption in, 305, 324, 327, 969
family planning in, 762, 763
oil production in, 894, 895
nitrates (NO_3), 72, 81–86, 608, 666
in water, 557–558, 560, 666, 667
nitric acid, 84, 254
nitrification, 82, 83, 85
Nitrobacter bacteria, 82, 83
nitrogen, 36, 80–87, 664–670
atmospheric, 32, 33, 42, 70, 72
as nutrient, 67, 70–73, 93, 664–665
in soil, 70, 87, 254, 668
fixation of, 82–87, 288, 374, 666
in fertilizer, 84, 86, 333, 519, 666, 667, 668
in water, 558–559
nitrogen base in nucleotides, 73
nitrogen oxides, 81–87 *passim*, 425, 429, 672
in air, 33, 543, 547–554 *passim*, 661, 664, 674, 675, 684
in water, 557, 558
nitrosamines, 588–589
Nitrosomonas bacteria, 82, 83
Nixon, Richard, 322, 609, 746, 752, 856, 909
nomads, 718
North America, 145, 232, 238, 250, 273, 394, 439. *See also* Canada; United States
geography of, 13, 31, 260
demography of, 192–200 *passim*, 222, 224, 225, 226, 305, 309, 962, 965
food and agriculture in, 287, 291, 299, 318, 319, 333
cancer in, 590, 591
North American Water and Power Alliance (NAWAPA), 270–271
North Atlantic Fishery Commissions, 366
Northern Hemisphere, geography of, 49–50, 53–55, 62, 682, 686. *See also continents by name*
North Pole ice pack, 28
Norway, 521, 590, 758
demography of, 192, 195, 217, 305, 309, 963
food and nutrition in, 300, 301, 315, 360–361, 363, 968
Notestein, Frank, 225
Nothofagus beech, 153
nuclear energy, 271, 393, 396, 397, 400, 404, 601, 816, 862. *See also* fission; fusion; reactors, nuclear
electricity generation from, 426, 442–453, 483–487, 916
weapons from, 453–457, 462, 674, 690–691, 910–919
Nuclear Fuel Services, Inc. (NFS), 451
Nuclear Nonproliferation Treaty (NPT), 454, 912, 914–915
Nuclear Regulatory Commission (NRC), 404n, 445, 450, 585, 861, 862
Nuclear Responsibility, Committee for, 834
nucleic acids, 73
nucleotides, 73, 576n. *See also* ADP; NADP
nuisance law, 830–831
nutrient cycles, 67–95, 145–157
nutrition, 967–978. *See also* diet; malnutrition

Occupational Safety and Health Administration (OSHA), 598–599, 836–837
Ocean Dumping Act (1972), 561
Oceania, 13, 273, 754–755. *See also countries by name*
demography of, 195, 199, 222–231 *passim*, 305, 309, 963, 966
urbanization of, 237, 238
food and agriculture in, 268, 296, 299, 319, 333.
oceans, 13, 14, 17, 21–30 *passim*, 51, 263, 264, 267, 369, 471. *See also* Law of the Sea
salts in, 21–22, 24, 25, 71
pollution of, 24, 657–658, 660
currents in, 25–26, 69, 410, 411
weather and, 61–62
biomass in, 74–76, 132, 133, 134
and nutrient cycles, 79, 80, 81, 85–88, 90, 91, 92
habitats of, 161–170
utilities' use of, 264–265
food from, 352–366, 369
trace elements in, 569, 570, 572
arms control for, 912, 913.
offshore drilling, 412, 413
oil. *See* petroleum
oil companies, diversification of, 859–860
oilseed presscakes, 317, 318, 319, 372
oil shale, 78, 79, 264, 404, 422–423, 485
Oman, 961
Opuntia cactus, 143
organic matter. *See also* humus; wastes, organic
dead, 68–69, 75–91 *passim*
in soil, 253, 254
in eutrophication, 665, 666
Organization for Economic Cooperation and Development (OECD), 894, 898
Organization of American States (OAS), 908
Organization of Petroleum Exporting Countries (OPEC) 3, 887, 892–897, 898, 906, 907
organophosphates, 564, 633, 641, 644, 984–985, 987. *See also compounds by name*
osteomalacia, 306–307, 976
outgassing, 84, 85, 91
overdeveloped countries (ODCs), 926–930
overgrazing, 681, 682, 728
overpopulation, 227, 716–719, 760
awareness of, 212, 791–796
ovulation, 990, 992
oxidants, 544, 547, 550
oxidative metabolism. *See* respiration
oxychlordane, 563
oxygen, 20, 68, 90, 92, 160, 665, 667
atmospheric, 32, 33, 42, 70, 78–79
as nutrient, 67, 71, 74–80
in food chains, 128–129
dissolved, in water, 263, 269, 270
ozone (O_3), 33–47 *passim*, 84, 90, 673–676
in smog, 544, 547, 599, 664

Pacific Ocean, 17, 162
packaging, materials used in, 517, 518
Pakistan, 232, 241, 307, 573, 875
demography of, 179, 201, 305, 775, 776–777, 782, 961, 964
food and agriculture in, 268, 269, 294, 300, 301, 303, 329, 331, 339, 923, 969
family planning in, 758, 762–767 *passim*, 775, 808
arms control in, 912, 914, 915, 919

Panama, 317, 759, 762, 764, 890, 962, 969
  tropical forest of, 133, 134
Pangaea, 17
pantothenic acid, 976
paper, recycled, 527
Papilio butterfly, 143
Papua New Guinea, 762, 963
para-aminobenzoic acid (PABA), 976
paradichlorobenzene, 598, 982, 984, 986 (fig.)
Paraguay, 300, 301, 476, 762, 891, 962, 969
  Indians of, 718, 890, 999
Paramecium aurelia, 104
Parasitism, 125
  nutrition and, 302, 303, 304, 306, 316
  pest control by, 648
parathion, 564, 985, 987
parks and wildlife refuges, land use by, 252
Parnell, Dennis R., 808
particulate matter, 427, 543, 547, 551, 552, 683–686
pasture, land use by, 252
Patella limpet, 163
Paul VI, Pope, 807–808
peanuts, 189, 288, 320, 344, 349
peat, source of, 78
pellagra, 976
penguins, 623
permafrost, 153, 155, 248
Permian period, 92
peroxyacetyl nitrate (PAN), 544, 664
Peru, 147–149, 360, 626–627, 686, 887, 890, 891
  demography of, 107, 200, 305, 309, 962, 966
  urbanization of, 239, 241
  food production and consumption in, 300, 301, 318, 324, 354, 363, 364–365, 969
  in world trade, 318, 521
  pesticide use in, 643–644, 645, 646
  population policy of, 759, 762, 782
pesticides, 642, 854–856, 979–987. *See also* fungicides *and compounds by name*
  effect of community of, 138, 343, 345
  insecticides, 153, 562, 564, 630–646
  crop yields and, 334, 642–644
  pollution from, 560–567, 642–647
  resistance to, 634, 644, 647
  alternatives to, 647–651.
pests
  food loss to, 335, 342–343, 345, 373, 642, 643–644
  control of, 647–651
Peterson, Russel W., 835
petrochemicals, 415, 416, 475, 854–855
petroleum, 78, 79, 201, 393, 396, 865
  in world trade, 3, 294, 393–395, 415, 893, 909
  cost of, 3, 485, 893–894
  refining of, 265, 415–416, 417
  fuel cycle of, 411–416
  electricity generation from, 423, 426, 485, 487
  stock and flow of, 516–517, 521, 894
  trace elements in, 568, 572, 574
  pollution from, 657–660, 681–682, 728
petroleum liquids, 397, 401–403
pH. *See* acidity
phenols, 557, 599
pheromones, 649
Philippines, the, 233, 875, 887, 897
  demography of, 198, 201, 305, 309, 775, 782, 790, 961, 964
  agriculture in, 268, 317, 319, 324, 325, 329, 331, 335, 343, 367
  food and nutrition in, 300, 301, 305, 372, 969
  family planning in, 758, 762, 765, 775
phosdrin, 984
phosphate rock, 89, 519, 528–529
phosphates, 73, 87–88, 333
  in water, 557, 666, 667, 668
  organophosphates, 564, 633, 641, 644, 984–985, 987
phosphorus
  supplies of, 22, 526, 528–529, 530
  as nutrient, 68, 71, 73, 87–89, 93, 664–666, 976, 977
  in wastes and water treatment, 559, 666–667
  isotope of, 582
phosvel, 633
photosynthesis, 472, 527–528
  energy in, 14, 33, 76, 284
  in nutrient cycles, 69, 71, 74, 78, 80, 81
  in food chain, 128–132
  solar energy use by, 128, 129, 130, 285, 410, 465, 471–475
  mimicry of, 465, 475
  pollutants and, 639, 652, 660
photovoltaic conversion, 465, 470–471
Phylloxera grape pest, 143
phytomass, 71, 74–76
phytoplankton, 133–134, 160, 161, 676
  Antarctic, 166, 167, 169
  in food chain, 353, 355
  pollutants in, 569, 639–640, 660
Pinchot, Gifford, 274
Place, Francis, 740
planetary regime, 943
Planned Parenthood Federation, International, 741, 759, 761, 763, 764, 784, 827, 988
Plant Genetic Resources, International Board for, 324, 344
plant breeding, 285, 340, 344, 373. *See also* high-yield crop varieties
plants. *See also* crops
  in nutrient cycles, 82, 86, 88, 90, 91, 92
  coevolution of, 125–127
  in food chain, 128, 131–134, 369
  of various biomes, 144–168
  pollutants and, 570, 664.
plasma, high-energy, 456
plastic flow, 13n
plastics, supplies and uses of, 517, 518, 527, 530
plate boundaries, Earth's, 17, 18
platinum, 521, 524, 526
Plectonema bacteria, 83
Pleistocene glaciation, 62, 142, 810
plutonium
  recycling of, 406–407, 431, 436, 449, 586
  isotopes of, 406, 407, 444, 451, 454–455, 580, 582, 585, 586
  hazards of, 453, 454, 672, 916
podzolization, 254–255, 256
Poland, 288, 590, 887, 968
  demography of, 216, 305, 309, 963, 965
polar regions, 55–56, 62, 249
political refugees, 232
politics, 3, 843–858, 890–891, 902–910
pollution, 541–542. *See also* air pollution; wastes; water; *and contaminants by name*
  noise, 596–597
  concentration of, 629–631

residence time, 22–25, 29–30, 69–70, 87
residential energy use. *See* domestic energy use
resources. *See also by type*
  consumption of, 1, 2, 484–489, 719–734
  defined, 179, 400, 401
  supplies of, 515, 522–525
respiration (R)
  chemistry of, 71–72, 74, 81
  cellular, 129
  community, 133, 135, 137
  plant, and radiation, 672
reunion, 305, 309, 960
rhenium, 521, 526
rhinoceros, population structure of, 115
Rhizobium bacteria, 82, 83, 374
Rhodesia, 762, 764, 960, 969
rhythm system, 991, 992
ribonucleic acid (RNA), 73
rice, 265, 286, 293, 340, 349, 367, 972
  production of, 287, 339, 344
  in world trade, 317, 318, 320, 321
  high-yield varieties (HYVs), 329, 331, 336
  pest susceptibility of, 342–343
rickets, 306–307, 316, 976
right-to-life groups, 757, 839
Rock, John, 808
Rockefeller, Nelson A., 890, 892
Rockefeller Foundation, 324, 761
rocks
  types of, 19, 79, 87, 92, 252, 570
  in nutrient cycle, 70
  trace metals in, 570, 572
Roentgen, Wilhelm, 579
Roman Catholic Church, population policy of, 741, 742, 753, 759–760, 764, 782, 792, 807–808, 992
Roman Empire, 187, 188, 208, 231, 272, 569
roots and tubers, 286, 288, 289, 318, 344
rubber, consumption of, 516, 527
Ruckelshaus, William D., 836
Rumania, 216–217, 363, 590, 963, 968
runoff, 29–31, 69, 258–262, 267, 278
rural areas
  energy intake in, 303
  urban climate compared, 677
Russia, 188, 189
ruthenium, 106, 444
rutile, 520, 521
Rwanda, 762, 887, 960, 969

sabotage, nuclear disaster by, 442, 443, 446, 448, 454
Safe Drinking Water Act, 561
Sahara Desert, 56, 63, 149
Sahel, 290, 294, 323, 344, 375, 627–628, 681, 685–686, 718, 887
Salmonella bacteria, 595
salts, 14, 262–263, 264, 266, 521
  ocean, 21–22, 24, 25, 71
  phosphate, 87–88
  in soil, 255, 256
  as nutrient, 977
Samoa, Western, 762
San Andreas Fault, 17
sand and gravel, 516, 519
Sanger, Margaret, 740–741
sanitation, 190, 191, 192, 242
Sao Tome e Principe, 960
satellites, communications, 868–869
saturation, of air, 36
Saudi Arabia, 327, 762, 765, 894, 898, 969
  demography of, 201, 897, 961
savanna, 76, 132, 144–145, 146, 150, 158
sawtimber, 274
Scandinavia, 217, 232, 428, 753, 898. *See also countries by name*
Scenic Hudson Preservation Conference vs. *Federal Power Commission* (1965), 834n
schistosomiasis, 608, 899–900
Schurz, Carl, 274
Scientists' Institute for Public Information vs. *AEC*, 836
Scotland, 216, 635, 637
screwworm flies, 647, 649
scurvy, 976
sea cucumber, 622
seafloor spreading, 17
sea ice. *See* ice and glaciers
sea level, glaciation and, 28–29, 62, 63
seasons, solar flux and, 49–50
Securities and Exchange Commission (SEC), U.S., 861
sedimentation, 19, 20
  in nutrient cycles, 70–71, 81, 85, 87, 88, 91, 92
selective agents, in natural selection, 123–124
selerium, 68, 521, 568, 599, 977
Senegal, 305, 762, 764, 960, 969. *See also* Sahel
sensible heat, 45, 46, 47, 51, 61
sere, 135
sevin, 985, 987
sewage treatment, 557, 558–560, 668–669, 729, 841
sex education, 827–828, 840, 988
Sex Information and Education Council of the United States (SIECUS), 840
sex ratio, human, 202
Seychelles, 762
shantytowns, 239, 240–241, 242, 304, 779
sheep, 289, 315
Shell Chemical Company, 644, 645
Sierra Club, 812, 832, 834
Sierra Club vs. *Morton*, 834, 835, 836
Sierra Leone, 762, 960, 969
sikkim, 961
silica (SiO_2), in water, 262, 264
silicates, weathering of, 70
silicon, 19, 20, 22, 24, 68, 471
silver, 22, 24, 521, 524, 526, 527, 530
Singapore, 240, 305, 758
  demography of, 201, 205, 208, 774, 775, 961, 964
  family planning in, 762, 763, 765, 767, 775, 786
slavery, migration and, 231, 232
smallpox, 190, 192
Smith-Putnam windmill, 477
smog, 276, 286, 543, 544, 547, 550, 554, 664
smoke, tobacco, 588, 594
snow blitz, 63
soap, 190, 191
social organization, 1, 8, 488–491
sodium, 20, 22, 24, 68, 73, 254, 262, 441, 526
  isotope of, 581
soil, 93, 179–180, 252–257, 656, 684
  moisture of, 29, 30, 31
  acidity of, 89, 92, 254
  microorganisms in, 252, 253, 640–642, 652
  trace metals in, 570–572
Soil Conservation Service, 257
solar constant, 46
solar energy, 19, 20, 32, 33, 39, 42–51, 61, 284, 393

in ecosystems, 629–672
as limit to growth, 730–731
laws on, 830–835
costs of, 847–848
polonium, 218, 431
polychlorinated bipheryls (PCBs), 562–563, 634, 637, 639
Polynesia, 186, 199, 222
polyvinyl chloride, 597
pond culture, 367, 560
population, 1–9, 181–246, 956. *See also* demography
world, 2, 5, 100, 101, 102, 104, 195, 199–202, 221–222, 715–719, 901, 960–963
in population dynamics, 23, 97–122
in less developed countries, 218–222, 291, 717, 790, 885–886, 927, 960–963
projections of, 221–227, 959–966
density of, 227–231, 247–248, 251, 602–604, 717
distribution and movement of, 227–243, 749, 751
food production and, 291, 296, 298, 299, 328, 968–970
resource consumption and, 397, 398, 720–734
of United States, 721, 724
policies for, 737–803, 839–840
Population Act (1970), 751
population control and policies. *See* family planning
Population Council, 761
pork, 289, 320, 972
porpoises, 356, 360
Portugal, 232, 233, 521, 656, 754, 758, 887
demography of, 216, 305, 309, 776, 963
diet in, 300, 301, 968
postwar baby boom, 207, 211, 215, 216, 225, 755
potash, in fertilizer, 333, 519
potassium, 20, 73, 254, 262
isotope of, 20, 582, 583
in seawater, 22, 24, 92
as nutrient, 68, 92–93, 977
supplies of, 521, 526
Potato Center International (CIP), 324
potatoes, 93, 189, 190, 286, 288, 344, 349
famine, 190–191, 232, 628–629
poultry, 313, 314, 315, 320, 972
poverty, 316, 334–335, 604–606, 750, 778–779
power, 15, 16
Prebisch, Dr. Raúl, 892, 897
precipitation, 144, 146, 677
in hydrologic cycle, 29–30, 61, 69
predator-prey systems, 120, 124–125, 138, 648
pregnancy
nutrition and, 303–304, 311, 974–975
unplanned, 739, 742–744, 750, 757, 760–761, 766
presscakes, oilseed, 317, 318, 319, 372
pressure, atmospheric, 37, 38, 52
profundal zone, 160
progesterone, 990, 994
progestin, 992–993, 997–998, 999
Project Independence, 895
prostaglandins, 998
protein, 72–73, 288, 300–303, 354
in nitrogen cycle, 82, 83, 86
plant, 289, 300, 973;
supplies of, 298–300, 967–970
deficiency diseases of, 306, 309, 316
single-cell (SCP), 349, 370–371
supplements for, 370–372
protozoa, in soil, 640
Pseudomonas bacteria, 83
Puerto Rico, 235, 237, 590, 762, 775, 835
demography of, 197, 305, 309, 775, 962, 966
pulses, 289, 318, 320, 972
Punapedaloides butterfly, 157
pyrethrins, 982
pyridoxine, 976
pyrolysis, 474

Quatar, 894, 898, 961
Quaker Oats Company, 372
Quality Factor (QF), 433

Race
immigration bias and, 230
birth rate and, 749, 750
rad, 433, 582
radiation. *See also* electromagnetic radiation; radioactivity; solar energy
ozone and, 33–47, 675–676
terrestrial, 44–47, 50, 6
ionizing, 579–586
and ecosystems, 671–67
urban/rural, 677
radioactivity, 20, 432–433,
579–585, 672. *See also*
hazards from, 442–448, 46
583–584
radium, 226, 582, 585
radon, 222, 582, 585
radon gas, 431, 433, 434, 465,
railroads, 866, 868
rainfall, 84, 86, 89, 91, 92–93, 5
in soil formation, 252, 254
acid, 661–662, 663
Ranger Uranium Environmental Inquiry, 916
Rasmussen report, 445–447
rate of increase
in population dynamics, 99–100
instantaneous (IRI), 99–100, 105
intrinsic, 100, 104, 110–111
reactors, nuclear, 404–408, 430–450, 483, 484, 487, 488, 585, 836
in world trade, 3–4, 5, 915, 917, 932
hazards of, 442–448
spent fuel from, 448–453
fusion, 456–458, 461
reclamation, land, after mining, 419
recommended daily allowances, 300, 974–975
recycling
of nuclear fuels, 406–407, 431, 435, 436, 449, 586
energy savings in, 494, 525, 527
Redwood National Park, 276, 277
refineries, oil, 415–416
Refuse Act, 560
relative biological effectiveness (RBE), 433, 582
religion, 806–813. *See also* Roman Catholic Church
birth control and, 741, 768
abortion and, 759–760
rem, 433, 582
reproduction, anatomy of, 988–991
reproductive potential, of populations, 98
reproductive rate, 99, 209
net (NRR), 99, 108–109, 114, 208, 209–210, 213–214, 218–221
reserves, defined, 400–401
estimation of, 523, 524

fixing of, 128–129
as resource, 284, 400, 410, 411
uses of, 465–479, 485, 487
collectors for, 466–467, 468, 470
solvent refining, 421, 422
Somalia, 762, 887, 960, 969
Sonoran Desert, 56
sorghum, 287, 321, 329, 344, 371, 373
South Africa, 521, 623
demography of, 199, 200, 782, 961
diet in, 300, 301, 968
family planning in, 759, 762, 764
arms control in, 912, 914, 915
South America, 234, 273, 332, 333, 413, 521, 718. *See also countries by name*
geography of, 13, 17, 31, 250, 260
demography of, 199, 222, 305, 307, 962, 966
urbanization of, 237, 239
population policy of, 759, 764
Southeast Asia, 115, 240, 765, 902, 961. *See also countries by name*
food production in, 286, 294
United States in, 909
Southern Hemisphere, 49, 53–55. *See also continents by name*
soybeans, 293, 346, 347, 349
production of, 287, 288, 344
in world trade, 317, 320, 321
space, outer, colonization of, 821–823
space heating and cooling, 399, 467–469, 471, 485, 492–493
space manufacturing facility (SMF), 821–822
Spaceship Earth, economy for, 849–854
Spain, 232, 268, 521, 754, 758
demography of, 200, 216, 305, 309, 963
diet in, 300, 301, 968
arms control in, 912, 914, 915
species, worldwide number of, 97
specific activity, isotopic, 581, 582
spermatozoa, 988–991, 996, 999
Spirillum bacteria, 374
Sri Lanka (Ceylon), 343, 888, 937
demography of, 196–198, 205, 309, 774, 775, 782, 961, 964
food and nutrition in, 294, 300, 301, 331, 969
family planning in, 758, 762, 765, 774, 775
Stanford University, 826
starvation, 304, 311. *See also* famine; malnutrition
steam engine, 423–425, 426
steam turbines, 423–425
steel, 265, 516, 520, 522, 721–722, 886
Stefan-Boltzmann constant, 44
Steinbeck, John, 150
steppes, 93, 248
sterilization, 740, 742, 764–773 *passim,* 784, 823, 824, 839, 991, 996–997, 999
for pest control, 649
compulsory, 783, 787, 840
Stevia weed, 999
stocks, 23
stone plants, mimicry by, 126
Storm King lawsuit, 834
Strategic Arms Limitation Talk (SALT), 911–912, 913
stratopause, 12, 38–39
stratosphere, 12, 38–39, 47, 48, 84
strip mining, 276, 418, 623
Strong, Maurice, 942
strontium, 22, 521, 526
isotopes of, 444, 451, 581, 582, 585
student activism, 826–827
subbituminous coal, 78, 416–418
subboreal regions, 249
subduction zones, 17
subtropics, 249, 255
suburbanization, 238, 606, 872
succession, 135–137
Sudan, 762, 782, 960, 970
Suess effect, 80
Suez Canal, 906
sugar, 972
as nutrient, 286, 972–973
in world trade, 318, 319, 320
sugar beets, 93, 289, 344
sulfa drugs, 191, 192n
sulfates ($SO_4^=$), 73, 79, 84, 89–92, 542
in water, 262, 557, 560
sulfides ($S^=$), 90
ores of, 571
sulfur, 20, 22, 70, 254, 465, 526
as nutrient, 68, 71, 79, 89–93, 977
isotopes of, 92
in coal, 420–421, 422, 427–429
sulfur acids, 90, 91, 92, 254, 543, 599
sulfur oxides, 90, 91, 425, 684
as air pollutant, 427, 542–551 *passim,* 599, 661, 664
sun. *See* solar energy
superconducting magnets, 461
supersonic transports, 673–674, 819, 856–857
supertankers, 414–415, 815
surface water, 87, 89, 92–93, 252, 264, 266–267, 444
Surinam
demography of, 200, 762, 962
diet in, 300, 301, 970
in world trade, 317, 521
survivorship curve, 107, 108
Swaziland, 762, 961, 965
Sweden, 483, 590, 598–599, 652, 662–664, 678, 888
demography of, 191–197 *passim,* 203, 205, 217, 305, 309, 963, 965
diet in, 300, 301, 968
energy use in, 393, 395, 396, 497–498
population policy in, 754, 758, 760
swidden agriculture. *See* milpa agriculture
Switzerland, 521, 754, 758
demography of, 217, 305, 309, 963
diet in, 300, 301, 968
energy use in, 395, 497–498
symbiosis, 82, 83, 85, 125
synergism
in air pollution effects, 547, 548, 727
of pollutants, 566, 633, 656, 727–728, 981, 982
synthetic polymers, 527–528
Syria, 300, 301, 309, 961, 970
population policy in, 762, 765
systox, 985

taiga, 144–145, 146, 152–153, 249
Taiwan, 300, 301, 588, 887, 902, 936
demography of, 197–198, 201, 208, 220, 221, 305, 774, 775, 782, 790, 962, 963, 964
agriculture in, 325, 339, 350, 933;
family planning in, 758, 762, 765, 767, 775
tallow, in world trade, 321
Tamplin, Arthur, 585
tantalum, 521
Tanzania, 762, 782, 888, 898, 938, 960, 965, 970
tar sands, 78, 403–404, 422–423

taxation, as policy tool, 872
technetium, 99, 451, 582
technology, 1–2, 4–5, 35, 927–928, 942, 955
  sea overexploitation by, 363–366
  and environmental impact, 720, 722–725, 729–730, 734
  "faulty," 724–726
  and science, as institution, 813–823
  faith in, 813–814, 825
  in less developed countries, 901–902, 931–933
tectonic plates, 17, 18, 20
tellurium, 444, 521, 582
temperate forest biome, 93, 132, 133, 134, 140, 144–147, 249, 250, 273, 624
temperature, 34, 41, 42, 60, 289–290, 468, 677. *See also* thermal energy
  absolute, 37
  atmospheric, 37, 38, 39, 51
  and climate, 59, 61, 62, 144, 146
  gradients of, in water, 161, 479, 665–666
  soil types and, 254–255
  species composition and, 670, 671
Tepp, 982, 984
terrestrial radiation, 44–47, 50, 60
territory, 116
testosterone, 988, 999
textiles, recycled, 527
Thailand, 241, 521, 758
  food and agriculture in, 268, 286, 297, 317, 327, 328, 349, 970
  demography of, 305, 309, 775, 782, 961, 964
  family planning in, 762, 765, 766, 775
thermal energy. *See also* heat; thermodynamics, laws of
  circulation of, 24n, 52
  gradients of, 161, 479, 665–666
  pollution with, 670–671
thermal power plants, 423–427
thermocline
  ocean, 24, 25
  freshwater, 160–161, 665, 666
thermodynamics, laws of, 32–35, 391–392
  in food chains, 129–131, 133, 630, 631
  efficiency and, 398–399, 425
thermosphere, 12, 39
Thiobacillus bacteria, 83, 90
Third World, 887, 898, 906
Thirty Years' War, 187
Thomas, John H., 808
Thoreau, Henry David, 274
thorium, 22, 405, 407, 408
  isotope of, 20, 406–407, 581, 582
  in fission reactors, 404, 439, 441, 442
threshold effects, 727
Tibet, 591
tides, energy in, 14, 411
Tierra del Fuego Indians, 231
Timor Portuguese, 961
tin, 68, 520, 521, 524, 527, 530
tissue-growth efficiency, 133
titanium, 20, 521, 526, 530
tobacco, 127n, 321
  smoke from, 588, 594
Togo, 762, 960, 970
Townshend, Lord Charles, 189
toxaphene, 564, 641, 643–644, 983
trace elements, 67, 68, 567–575, 670, 977–978. *See also by name*
trade, world, 317–326, 888–897. *See also commodities and countries by name*
  of petroleum, 3, 294, 393–395, 415, 893, 909
  of grain, 292, 297, 298, 315
  of materials, 517–520
Train, Russell E., 836, 855
Trans-Amazonian Highway, 626–627
transformation, chemical, in nutrient cycling, 68–69
transpiration, in hydrologic cycle, 29
transport, physical, 29, 68
transportation, 192, 543, 865–868, 933
  mass public, 238, 866, 867
  efficiencies in, 335, 342, 399, 495
  energy use by, 395, 396, 399, 492, 494–497, 865
  of oil, 414–415
  materials use by, 517, 518
tree farming, 276
trespass law, 831–832
triage, 923–924
Tribolium flour beetles, 120–121
Trinidad and Tobago, 970
  demography of, 205, 305, 309, 774, 775, 962, 966
  migration from, 233, 235, 774n
  family planning in, 762, 764, 775
Triticale, 374
tritium, 408–409, 433, 449, 451, 461–462, 581–582, 583, 585
trophic levels, 129–131, 133, 160
tropics, 55–56, 249, 255, 284
  forests of, 75, 76, 93, 132, 133, 134, 138–146 *passim*, 155–158, 276, 278, 624
  food production in, 289–290, 345–346
tropopause, 12, 38
troposphere, 12, 37–38, 46–48, 52, 55–56, 84
  modification of, 682–685
tsetse fly, 290, 375
tundra, 144–145, 146, 153–155, 157
  amount of, 248, 249, 252
  soil of, 256
tungsten, 520, 524, 526, 530
Tunisia, 305, 775, 960, 965, 970
  family planning in, 759, 762, 763, 764, 775
turbines, 423, 427, 464, 476
Turkey, 521, 887
  food and agriculture in, 150, 268, 287, 300, 301, 331, 970
  family planning in, 762, 765, 774, 775
  demography of, 774, 775, 782, 961, 964
2, 4-D, 564, 652, 656, 986
2, 4, 5-T, 652, 987

Uganda, 171, 762, 782, 960, 970
underdeveloped areas. *See* less developed countries (LDCs)
undernourishment, 290–292
unemployment rate, 316, 853–854
  demography and, 212, 747
  urbanization and, 238, 239
  of selected countries, 336, 790, 901
Union Oil Company, 832
Union of Soviet Socialist Republics (USSR)
  biogeography of, 145, 146, 150, 248, 250, 260, 268–273 *passim*, 682, 686
  demography of, 195, 199, 200, 216–231 *passim*, 963, 965
  urbanization of, 237, 238, 241
  food production in, 287–292 *passim*, 296, 301, 326, 328, 333, 355, 360–364, 370, 968
  grains in, 292, 294, 295, 314,

319–322, 897
in world trade, 292, 318–322, 521, 897
energy and materials use in, 395, 520
energy technology in, 422, 438, 439, 458, 466, 476, 480, 894
pollution in, 573, 598–600
military and war in, 689–690, 909–914, 917, 919, 920
population policies in, 754, 758
and less developed countries, 898, 905–906, 925
United Arab Emirates, 894, 898, 961
United Arab Republic, 309, 965. *See also* Egypt
United Kingdom. *See also countries by name*
demography of, 204, 205, 218, 305, 309, 963, 965
migration and, 234
food and diet in, 300, 301, 314, 365, 473, 968
energy technology in, 393, 395, 419, 428, 473, 623, 668–669
in world trade, 521, 893
pollution in, 549, 566, 636, 637, 664
cancer in, 590
environmental movement in, 813, 830
development of, 887, 888, 898
on weapons, 914, 916, 920
United Nations
population policies of, 225, 765–766
food-aid programs of, 322, 323
agencies and conferences of, 942–943; Conference on the Law of the Sea (UNCLOS), 941; Conferences on Trade and Development (UNCTAD), 892, 897; Development Decades, 898; Environment Program (UNEP), 942; Fund for Population Activities (UNFPA), 761, 765; UNICEF, 323; Industrial Development Organization, 892; International Geophysical Year, 169; Social Progress and Development, Declaration on, 765; World Food Conference, 5, 295, 296–297, 321, 322, 807; World Population Conference, 5, 765, 791, 794–795
United States
food production in, 2, 287, 288, 289, 295, 296, 325, 339–349 *passim*, 361–369 *passim*, 376, 473, 968
in world trade, 3, 292, 315, 319–322, 323, 328, 415, 417, 889–890, 892–893
fossil fuels in, 3, 393, 401–404, 411–428 *passim*, 894–896
demography of, 107–114 *passim*, 179, 183–184, 192, 193, 195, 199–220 *passim*, 224–231 *passim*, 305, 309, 721, 778, 929, 962, 965
land use in, 147, 150, 248, 251–252, 273–276, 285, 623
water use in, 166, 265–272
migration and, 192, 232–234
urbanization of, 235–238, 240, 241, 677, 678
pollution in, 237, 241, 276, 544–575 *passim*, 582–585, 661, 662, 664, 981
biogeography of, 257–265, 656, 667, 685, 686
nutrition in, 291–292, 300, 301, 312, 314–317, 968
energy and materials use in, 393, 395–396, 466, 473, 482, 483, 485, 491–494, 497–498, 516–522, 526, 527, 927
nuclear power in, 409, 431, 435, 438–458 *passim*, 582–585, 909–919
geothermal energy in, 410, 465
solar energy in, 466–468
organic wastes in, 472, 474, 668–669
hydroelectric generation in, 476
pesticides in, 562, 563, 565, 566, 634–646 *passim*
medicine and health in, 586–590, 598–600, 607–609, 823–824
military in, 653–656, 689–690, 909–919, 941
development of, 721, 722, 887, 888, 922–923
population policies in, 740–753, 755–757, 761, 784, 837–840
institutions in, 805–884
and less developed countries, 890–892, 897–899, 904–907, 922–925
agencies and departments of: Coast Guard, 364; Code of Federal Regulations, 585; Commission on Population Growth and the American Future, 745, 746; Department of Agriculture, 251, 316, 325, 646–647, 979–981; Department of Commerce, 861; Department of Defense, 251; Department of Energy, 861; Department of Health, Education and Welfare, 647, 827, 840, 980; Department of Housing and Urban Development (HUD), 752, 861; Department of the Interior, 251, 361, 647, 861; Fish and Wildlife Service, 980; Food, Drug, and Cosmetic Act (1958), 589–590; Public Health Service (USPHS), 561. *See also specific governmental units by name*
University of California, Berkeley, 826
uplifting, 91, 252
Upper Volta, 762, 763, 887, 960, 970. *See also* Sahel
uranium, 22, 599, 915
isotopes of, 20, 393, 406–407, 431, 433–435, 438, 454, 455, 581, 582, 585
in fission reactors, 404, 406–407, 439
resources of, 405, 408, 530
mining of, 430–431, 434, 487
recycling of, 431, 435, 449
uranium hexaflouride (UF_6), 431, 434
uranium oxide (U_3O_8), 404–405, 408, 431, 434, 435, 520
urban areas, 252, 303, 603–605, 677–681
migration and, 185, 235–243, 752–753
population of, 721, 960–963
new cities, 749, 751–752
urea, 82, 84
Uruguay, 200, 305, 759, 762, 891, 962, 970

vagility, 117
vanadium, 68, 521, 526
Vapona, 984
vaporization, heat of, 32, 33, 45, 46, 47, 51, 55–56
variability, genetic, 124, 718

Varian Corporation, 471
vasectomy, 996–997, 999
vegetation, 248–251
  soil types and, 255, 256
Velsical Chemical Corporation, 638
Venezuela, 239, 521, 609, 891, 894
  diet in, 300, 301, 970
  demography of, 305, 309, 775, 782, 891, 962, 966
  family planning in, 762, 764, 775
Vietnam, 232, 233, 887
  food and agriculture in, 268, 291n, 322, 331, 375, 923, 970
  war in, 653–656, 689, 909
  family planning in, 758, 762, 765
  demography of, 782, 961
vinyl chloride (VC), 597–598, 599
viruses, as public health threat, 607–609
vitamins
  deficiencies in, 306–307, 316, 317, 335
  daily allowances for, 974–977
volcanoes, 14, 17, 19, 684
  in nutrient cycles, 69, 79, 84, 85, 86, 91
vortex, circumpolar, 56

Wales, demography of, 191, 194, 195, 216, 305, 309
war, 1, 908–920. *See also* weapons
  population and, 186, 187
  chemical and biological, 608–609, 913, 917
  environmental, 689–690, 917
  thermonuclear, 690, 914–917
wastes, organic
  in nutrient cycles, 77, 82, 88, 91
  in water, 269, 556–557, 558
  food culture and, 367, 368, 370, 371–372
  as energy source, 397–398, 465, 472, 474
  agricultural, 397–398, 472, 669
  for fertilizer, 668–669; radioactive, 434, 448–453; solid, 527, 543, 556–557, 558, 560
water, 257–272. *See also* freshwater; hydropower; hydrosphere; oceans
  in physical systems, 22, 69, 258–264
  in nutrient cycles, 70–71, 73, 76–78, 92–93
  in food chains, 128–129
  in soil formation, 252, 253
  quality of, 263–264
  use of, 264–271, 487, 721–722
  pollution of, 278, 428, 444, 451, 556–561, 570, 572, 575, 668–669
  in electricity generation, 425, 426, 483–484, 487, 670–671
  heating of, 465, 466–467, 469, 492
water buffalo, 289
water hyacinths, 271, 669
Water Pollution Control Act, Federal (FWPCA), 560–561, 833, 836
water projects, 270–271. *See also* dams; irrigation
water table, 31, 263, 600
water vapor, 36–37, 38, 42, 84, 90
  terrestrial radiation and, 45, 46, 47, 61
Watt, K. E. F., 817
watt (W), defined, 16
wave power, 465, 479
weapons, 3, 689, 814, 911–912, 913, 957
  nuclear, 453–457, 462, 674, 690–691, 910–919
  in Vietnam, 654, 655
  control of, 911–913, 917–918
  conventional, 919–920
weather, 57–63, 291–296, 346–348, 608, 688–690
weathering, geologic, 17, 19, 20, 70–71, 88, 91, 93, 252
West African Rice Development Association (WARDA), 324
Western Hemisphere, 185, 189, 228–230. *See also continents by name*
  migration to, 192, 231–232
wet scrubbing, 428–429
whales, 154, 166–169, 355–363
  oil from, 355, 356, 359
wheat, 93, 265, 286–287, 293, 340, 349, 972
  world trade in, 317–321, 897
  high-yield varieties (HYVs), 325, 329, 331, 334, 336, 345
  production of, 339, 344, 347
Where Did I Come From? (Mayle), 827
whey, 372
Wilderness Society, 812
Williamson Act (California), 872
wind, 20, 52, 54–56, 61, 69, 677
  power in, 411, 465, 477–479
windmills, 473, 477–479
Wisconsin glaciation, 62–63
women's liberation movement, and fertility rate, 212, 745, 755
wood, 274–275, 397, 515, 527–528
Woods Hole Oceanographic Institute, 658
work, defined, 15
work conditions. *See also* unemployment rate
  hazards of, 597–600
  standards for, 836–837
  for nongrowth, 853–854.
World Bank, 297, 323, 761, 767, 904, 924
World Council of Churches, on nuclear power, 811
World Food Conference (Rome, 1974), U.N., 5, 295, 296–297, 321, 322, 807
World Food Council, 296–297, 924
World Population Conference (Bucharest, 1974), U.N., 5, 765, 791, 794–795
World War I, birth rate and, 210
World War II
  birth rate and, 207, 212
  fire storm of, 690
  nuclear explosion in, 818
World Wildlife Fund, 812

X-rays, 579, 580, 583
xenon, 133, 144
xerophthalmia, 974

yams. *See* roots and tubers
Yemen, 294, 762, 961, 970
yields, agricultural. *See also* high-yield crop varieties *and crops by name*
  defined, 284
  by country, 339
  declining, 350–351
Yugoslavia, 232, 233, 590, 607, 887
  demography of, 200, 216, 305, 309, 963, 965
  diet in, 300, 301, 968

Zahn versus *International Paper Company,* 832n

Zaire, 521, 762, 782, 887, 960, 970
Zambia, 200, 239, 345, 887, 960, 970
Zectran, 987
zero population growth (ZPG), 109, 115, 197, 209, 234, 744, 755, 784, 813, 922, 927
  U.S. potential for, 212–215
  three paths to, 218, 219–222
  U.N. expectation of, 225
  objections to, 746–748
zinc
  as nutrient, 68, 977
  supplies of, 516–530 *passim*
  contamination by, 568, 569
  isotope of, 582
zirconium, 451, 526
zoning, 871–872

Index of Names

Aaronson, T., 480n, 500
Abajian, V., 435n, 500
Abbott, John C., 302n, 379
Abel, A. L., 694
Abele, L. G., 174
Abon-Donia, M. B., 633n, 694
Abrecht, Paul, 811n
Acree, F., Jr., 694
Adalakha, A., 226n, 244
Adams, E. Sherman, 797
Adams, J., 465n, 503
Adams, M. W., 343n, 379
Adams, Robert M., 235, 244
Adams, W. A., 699
Adamson, Peter, 792n, 793n, 797
Adelberg, E. A., 72n, 82n
Adelman, M. A., 894n, 946
Adler, M. J., 881
Agarwal, Amil, 942n, 946
Agble, W. K., 343n, 381
Agency for International Development (AID), U.S., 199, 202, 223, 339n
Agus, Carole, 376n
Ahern, W., 500
Ahmed, A. Karim, 610, 694
Aird, John S., 199
Albrecht, W. A., 257n, 279
Alderson, G. L. H., 376n, 379
Aleksakhin, R., 701
Alexander, G., 90
Alexander, L., 271n, 279
Alderson, G. L., 379
Allaby, Michael, 332n, 366n, 379
Allee, W. C., 145n, 173
Allen, A. R., 423, 500
Allen, E., 90n, 95
Allen, J. R., 610
Allen, O. N., 699
Allen, Robert J., 315n, 379
Allgren, C. E., 174
Almer, B., 662n, 694
Almqvist, E., 87n, 94
Altman, L. K., 607n
Altman, P. L., 379
Altschul, A. M., 379
Altus, William D., 719n, 735
Alverson, D. L., 352n, 379
Aly, Osman M., 633n
Alyea, F., 676n, 694
American Association for the Advancement of Science (AAAS), 351; Herbicide-Assessment Commission (HAC), 653, 654. *See also Science*
American Chemical Society, 558n, 559n, 610, 665n, 666n, 694, 729n
American Institute of Architects, 493, 500
American Physical Society, 398n, 399, 446n, 467n, 491n, 493n, 496n, 500
American Universities Field Staff, 379, 797
Ames, Bruce N., 588n, 592n, 595n, 596n, 610, 611, 615, 616
Andelman, M. B., 614
Anderegg, B., 702
Anderson, C., 422n, 484n, 485n, 500
Anderson, D. W., 637n, 695, 700
Anderson, J. L., 660n, 707
Anderson, J. M., 565n
Anderson, Jack, 882
Anderson, L., 472n, 500
Anderson, S. O., 448n
Anderson, T. W., 556n, 617
Andrewartha, H. G., 104n, 119n, 173, 692
Andrews, P., 602n, 614
Annual Reviews, 173
Ansari, N., 610
Anson, M. L., 382
Anthan, George, 320n
Antommari, P., 695
Appel, J., 493n, 500
Appleman, Philip, 743n, 797
Archer, E., 431n, 506
Aristotle, 812n
Ark II, 857
Armand, D. L., 260n, 280
Arney, W. R., 756n, 797
Aronow, W. S., 552n, 610
Arrow, K. J., 877
Ashton, F. M., 695
Ashwell, Ian, 365, 379
Asimov, Isaac, 821n, 868, 877
Aspin, Les, 822n, 877
Associated Press, 358n
Association for Voluntary Sterilization, 797, 999n
Astrachan, Anthony, 791n, 797
Astrand, I., 610
Atchison, J. E., 528n, 533
Atema, J., 658n
Atkins, E. L., 695
Atlas report, 239n, 242n, 244, 395, 759, 790n, 887n, 898n
Atomic Energy Commission (AEC), U.S., 404, 405n, 431n, 434, 435n, 437n, 438n, 439, 441, 443n, 445, 446n, 449n, 450n, 451n, 452, 453n, 455n, 471n, 502, 511
Aurelius, Marcus, 67
Averitt, P., 78n, 94, 416n, 417n, 500
Avon, Raymond, 946
Axelson, O., 610
Axtmann, R., 463n, 500
Ayala, F. J., 797
Ayers, R. C., Jr., 682n, 695
Ayres, Edward, 877
Ayres, R. W., 456n, 500

Babb, T. A., 155n
Babu, S. P., 610
Bacastow, R., 80n, 94
Bache, C. A., 610, 660n, 707
Baden, John, 880
Bader, M. E., 618
Bader, R. A., 618
Badger, B., 461
Bagby, J. R., 561n, 562n, 618
Bair, W. J., 455n, 500, 586n
Baird, D. T., 802, 997n
Baird, M., 898n, 904n, 948
Bajema, C. J., 748n, 749n, 797, 801
Baker, H. G., 173
Baker, J. J. W., 808n, 877

Baker, K. F., 695
Baker, Noel, 912
Baker, R., 628n, 695
Bakir, F., 573n, 610
Baldini, R., 797
Baldwin, M., 502
Baldwin, Pamela, 879
Balharry, R., 637n, 702
Ball, R. C., 630n, 699
Baltimore, D., 609, 611, 878
Balzani, V., 500
Bamberger, C., 482n, 500
Banks, Fred, 896n
Barber Associates, Inc., 946
Barber, Richard, 635n, 660n, 695, 877
Bardach, J. E., 367n, 379
Barducci, T. B., 644n
Barkley, Paul W., 846n, 877
Barlay, Stephen, 815n, 877
Barnaby, Frank, 910n, 911n, 913n, 917n, 946
Barnes, B. V., 175, 272n, 281
Barnes, R. H., 312n, 382
Barnes, R. L., 664n, 698, 702
Barnet, Richard J., 877, 891n, 945, 946
Barnett, J. C., 702
Barnett, Larry D., 785n, 797
Baron, R. E., 504
Barrett, G. W., 140n, 657n, 695
Barrons, K. C., 651n
Barthel, W., 573n, 612
Bartlett, B. R., 648n
Bartlett, M. S., 173
Barton, A. H., 691n, 695
Bates, Marston, 610
Bates, R. R., 565n, 615
Batschelet, E., 100n
Battan, E. S., 695
Bazilevich, N. I., 74n, 76n, 95, 132n, 174, 249n
Bazzaz, F. R., 661n, 695
Beamish, R. J., 695
Beaver, Steven, 781, 797
Beck, R., 448n
Becker, Benjamin M., 939n, 946
Beckerman, Wilfred, 5n, 873, 878
Beckman, W. A., 502
Bedurka, J. P., 701
Beeton, A. M., 667n, 695
Behar, M., 384
Behrens, W. W., 170n, 730n, 731n, 734, 945
Behrin, E., 422n, 484n, 485n, 500
Behrman, S. J., 244, 797
Beier, George F., 239n, 245
Beitz, C. R., 946
Bekele, Maaza, 792n, 793n, 797
Belisle, A. A., 695
Bell, D., 878
Bellotti, A. C., 348n, 384, 473n, 509, 669n
Belmont, L., 719n, 735
Belsky, Raymond, 797
Bendall, R., 578n, 579n, 619
Bendersky, D., 494n, 503
Benedict, W. F., 588n, 610
Bennett, E. L., 312n, 343n, 381, 384
Bennington, S. L., 695
Benoit, Emile, 850n, 875n, 878
Benson, F. B., 547n, 619
Benson, W. W., 610
Berelson, Bernard, 203, 244, 610, 753n, 762n, 766n, 767n, 772n, 774n, 775n, 783, 789, 791n, 794, 796, 797, 799
Berenblum, I., 587n, 611
Berg, Alan, 304, 305, 308n, 313n, 378, 379, 946
Berg, C., 493n, 500
Berg, G. G., 703
Berg, P., 609n, 611, 818n, 878
Berg, R. R., 413n, 500
Berger, R., 695
Berkov, B., 212, 246, 757n, 802
Berkowitz, D., 500
Berle, A. A., Jr., 878
Berlin, M. H., 573n, 611
Beroza, M., 649n, 694
Berry, R. Stephen, 494n, 500, 529n, 533, 946
Bertine, K. K., 568n, 569n, 570n, 571n, 572n, 574n, 611, 614, 729n
Berwick, Stephen, 279, 623n, 695
Best, Winfield, 740n, 741n, 797
Bethe, Hans, 818n, 509
Betts, R. J., 946
Beverton, R. J. N., 121n
Bhatia, C. R., 373n, 379
Bible, the, 11, 944
Bilderback, D. L., 230, 743n, 874n
Billings, C. E., 571n, 610
Bini, G., 570n, 611
BioScience, 359n, 374n, 379
Birch, H. B., 311n, 380
Birch, H. G., 311n, 313n, 381
Birch, L. Charles, 73n, 95, 102n, 104n, 119n, 173, 692, 878, 924–925, 926, 944, 945
Birdsell, J. B., 186n, 245
Birks, J., 701
Biros, E. F., 615
Bitman, J., 695
Black, C. A., 695
Blair, John M., 946
Blake, Judith, 212n, 743, 756, 785n, 786, 792n, 796, 797
Blanco, R. E., 502
Blase, M. G., 385
Bliss, L. C., 155n
Blomeke, J., 434n, 500
Blum, Arlene, 611
Blumer, Max, 657n, 658, 695
Blus, L. J., 695
Bobey, P. J., 355n, 379
Bocking, Richard C., 270n, 279
Bockris, J. O., 482n, 501
Bodmer, W. F., 173, 245, 576n, 611, 612, 691n
Boeck, W. L., 695
Boer, P. J. den, 173
Boerema, L. K., 354n, 379
Boerma, A. H., 379
Boesch, D. F., 414n, 501, 658n, 695, 815n
Boffey, P. M., 492n, 589n, 609n, 611, 695, 811n, 820n, 876, 878
Boggs, M. D., 233n, 246
Bogland, E., 611
Bogue, D. J., 244
Bolin, Bert, 58n, 64, 74n, 94, 501
Bolleta, F., 500
Bolling, Richard, 708, 878
Bonar, J., 743n
Bondar, B., 355n, 379
Bonem, G., 269n, 270n, 281
Bongaarts, J., 761n
Bonjean, Charles M., 876
Bonnell, M. L., 124n
Bonner, James, 533
Bonner, W. D., 36n, 39n, 42n, 43n, 45n, 53n, 54n, 55n, 57n, 64
Boot, J. C. G., 946
Borders, William, 337n, 769
Borgstrom, Georg, 150, 248n, 251n, 264n, 265n, 268, 269n, 272n, 278n, 279, 290n, 318, 379, 642n, 731n, 903
Borlaug, Norman, 352, 379
Borman, M. C., 694
Bormann, F. H., 93n, 94, 272, 279, 623–624, 661n, 694, 695, 702, 703, 848n, 878
Borthwick, P. W., 646n, 695
Bossert, W. H., 98n

Boston Women's Health Book Collective, 878
Boulding, Kenneth, 391, 441n, 456, 515, 787, 788, 798, 846n, 849, 876, 878, 946
Bourne, W. R. P., 695
Boush, G. M., 703
Bouwer, H., 613
Bouvier, Leon, F., 215n, 245
Bowen, E. T. W., 618
Bowen, H. J. M., 94, 568n, 611
Bowen, V. T., 630n, 699
Box, T. W., 623, 696
Boyd, R., 732n
Boyer, H. W., 609n, 611, 818n, 878
Boyer, W. P., 702
Boyko, H., 379
Boyko, Marie, 681n
Boyland, E., 586n
Brackett, J. W., 199n, 245
Bradshaw, Lois, E., 997n
Braidwood, R. J., 185n, 245
Braunstein, J., 484n, 500
Bray, Walter J., 371n, 379
Breedlove, Dennis E., 126n, 127n
Brennan, E., 705
Bretherton, F., 26n, 64
Brigham, A. R., 90n, 94
Brigham, A. U., 90n, 94
Brinkley, Parke C., 638
Broadbent, Kieran P., 340n, 379
Brobst, D. A., 94, 95, 499, 532
Broda, E., 501
Brodine, V., 557n, 611, 612
Brody, Jane E., 981n
Broenkow, W. W., 703
Bronfenbrenner, Urie, 752n, 798, 878
Brookhaven National Laboratory, 445n, 502
Brookings Institution, 501, 857n, 946
Brooks, D. B., 791n, 798
Brooks, Harvey, 878
Brower, David R., 8
Brower, L. P., 126n
Brown, D. W., 949
Brown, Harrison, 1, 6, 245, 388, 389, 522, 533, 730n, 735, 798, 885, 886, 946
Brown, Irene, 576n, 613
Brown, J. Martin, 584n, 586n, 611
Brown, J. R., 611
Brown, Lester R., 128n, 184n, 199, 245, 251n, 279, 286n, 293n, 295n, 297n, 313n, 314, 315n, 318, 321, 322n, 329n, 351, 352n, 354, 378, 379, 380, 372n, 793n, 798, 897n, 924n, 936, 945, 946
Brown, M., 646n, 696
Brown, N. L., 325n, 380
Brown, Phelps, 873n
Brown, R. E., 380
Brown, R. G., 190, 192n, 193n, 194, 195, 246
Brown, S. M., 611
Brown, T., 501
Brown, Wilfred, 875n
Brown, William L., Jr., 696, 980–981
Bruce-Smith, D., 570n, 611
Brush, Stephen G., 878
Brussard, P. F., 115n
Bryan, G. T., 611
Bryan, G. W., 611
Bryson, J., 453n, 506
Bryson, Reid A., 346, 684, 685–687, 696
Buchanan, Robert, 308n, 380, 778n, 779n, 792n, 798
Buck, W., 570n, 612
Budnitz, R., 487n, 488n, 501
Budyko, M. I., 30n, 31n, 51n, 64, 696
Buescher, E. L., 607n, 608n, 614
Bulan, C. A., 140n
Bull, C., 452n, 501
Bulland, J. A., 379
Bulletin of the Atomic Scientists, 481n, 811n, 946
Bulletin of Entomological Society of America, 981n
Bumford, F. H., 608n, 615
Bumpass, L., 798, 803
Buol, S. W., 253n, 281, 345n, 384, 626n, 706
Bupp, I. C., 442n, 501
Burch, Phillip, 553n, 611
Burgess, H. D., 696
Burgess, Jeremy, 374n, 380
Burkitt, Denis P., 590n, 591n, 611
Burnet, Sir Macfarlane, 592n, 611
Burnett, Robin, 565n, 639n, 696
Burns, B. R., 697
Burns, J. J., 566n, 612
Burns, James E., 561n, 562n, 611
Burns, N. M., 696
Burns, R. C., 82n, 83n, 85n, 86n, 87n, 94
Burrington, David, 755n
Burrington, George, 739n
Burse, V. W., 615
Burton, John A., 358n, 380
Busch, Harris, 592n, 611
Bush, G. L., 649n, 696
Bushland, R. C., 649n
Butler, P. A., 630n, 696
Butz, Earl L., 647
Byerly, T. C., 696

Cade, T. J., 696
Cadle, R., 90n, 95
Cahn, Anne H., 920n, 946
Caidin, Martin, 690
Cairns, John, 586–587, 590, 591, 592n, 593, 609, 611, 612, 619, 671, 696, 707
Calder, Nigel, 63n, 64, 696, 919n, 947
Calder, William A., III, 501
Calderone, Mary S., 798
Calhoun, John B., 603, 612
Calhoun, John C., 413n, 500
California Land Use Task Force, 279
California Tomorrow, 857
California Tomorrow Plan: A First Sketch, The, 857, 872, 873
Callicott, J. H., 608n, 612
Calvin, Melvin, 475n, 501, 527n, 533
Camacho, E., 382
Cameron, E. N., 522n, 533
Cameron, J., 408n, 501
Campbell, E. E., 573n, 619
Campbell, Ian, 696
Campbell, W. J., 682n, 696
Canfield, Monte, Jr., 879
Cannon, J., 833n, 878
Cannon, R., 674n, 699
Capizzi, J., 561n, 612
Cappiapuoti, A., 607n, 617
Carder, M., 791n, 798
Carefort, G. L., 380, 629n, 696
Carhart, Steven, 879
Carlisle, David, 612
Carlson, C. A., Jr., 670n, 696
Carlson, P. S., 373n, 374n, 380
Carlson, R. W., 661n, 695
Carlson, Rick, 824n, 878
Carmody, J., 610
Carnegie Endowment for International Peace, 323n
Carol, A., 604n, 618
Carpenter, E. J., 640n, 698
Carr, R. A., 572n
Carr-Saunders, A. M., 195n, 245
Carson, Rachel, 563, 612, 696, 854
Carson, T., 570n, 612

Carter, Luther J., 588n, 612, 855n, 878, 912n, 947
Carter, V. G., 279
Carvalho, J. A. M., 798
Casarett, A. P., 583n, 612
Casida, J. E., 652n, 697
Casper, B. M., 436n, 501
Cassel, John, 602n, 612
Cathcart, J. B., 89n, 94
Cavalli-Sforza, L. L., 173, 245, 576n, 611, 612, 691n
CBS News, 323n
Cecil, H. C., 695
Center for the Study of Democratic Institutions, 857
Ceres, 792n, 798
Cervantes, Miguel de, 181
Chacko, V. I., 785n, 798
Chamberlain, Neil, 878
Chambers, D. L., 649n, 697
Chambers, H., 698
Chambers, K. L., 173
Chancellor, W. J., 350n, 380
Chandler, J. H., 630n, 706
Chandra, R. K., 380
Chandrasekhar, S., 798
Chao, K., 380
Chapman, P. F., 488n, 494n, 501
Charney, J., 681, 697
Chase, H. P., 312n, 380
Chasteen, Edgar R., 786n, 798
Chedd, Graham, 312n, 380, 821n
Chen, L. C., 798
Chen, Pi-Chao, 763n, 771n, 772–773, 796, 798
Chester, C. V., 454n, 501
Chilarov, M. S., 155n
Child, J. J., 374n, 380
China Reconstructs, 770n, 798
Chisholm, J. J., 570n, 612
Choda, A., 469n, 509
Choi, E., 595n, 616
Choucri, Nazli, 908, 945n, 947
Chow, T. J., 569n, 612, 617
Chowdbury, A. K. M. A., 798
Christensen, H. E., 569n, 612
Christiansen, F., 141n
Christy, F. T., Jr., 380
Chu, H. M., 588n, 619
Church, L., 465n, 503
Churg, J., 588n, 618
Chylek, P., 684n, 697
Cicerone, R. J., 697
Ciocco, A., 600n, 618
Cipolla, Carlo M., 878
Cirino, Robert, 878
Claeys, R. R., 706
Clark, Colin, 807, 878
Clark, John R., 670n, 697
Clark, Joseph S., 570n, 612, 878
Clark, M., 458n, 509
Clark, R. P., 638n
Clark, Wilson, 499, 850n, 882
Clarkson, T. W., 573n, 611
Clausewitz, Karl von, 910
Clawson, Marion, 271n, 275, 276n, 279
Cleveland, Harlan, 905, 906, 947
Cliff, E. P., 273n, 274n, 280
Cline, J. H., 703
Clizer, E. E., 565n, 618
Cloud, Preston, 36n, 63, 64, 72n, 78n, 79n, 94, 523n, 524, 525, 532, 731n
Cloudsley-Thompson, J. L., 173, 628, 697
Club of Rome, 730, 731, 945
Coakley, J., 684n, 697
Coale, Ansley J., 190n, 193n, 244, 735, 746n, 878, 889, 947
Coan, Gene, 657n, 697
Cochran, T. B., 442n, 448n, 455n, 456n, 501, 510, 586n, 619
Coello, W., 661n, 697
Coevolution Quarterly, 823n
Cohen, J. S., 881
Cohen, S. N., 609n, 611, 818n, 878
Cohn, C. E., 501
Coldrick, John, 669n
Cole, D. G., 380
Cole, H. H., 289n, 300, 301, 380, 589n, 612, 733n
Cole, LaMont C., 697
Colin, R., 947
Colley, J. R. T., 553n, 612
Collier, B. D., 172
Colton, J. B., Jr., 697
Colwell, Thomas B., 878
Comatsu, Chinpei, 362n
Comey, D., 434n, 438n, 486n, 501
Commoner, Barry, 501, 599n, 612, 692, 701, 716n, 724n, 735, 792, 793n, 798
Concerned Demography, 793n, 798
Conference Board, 501
Connery, A. H., 566n, 612
Connors, C. W., 635n, 695, 706
Connors, P. G., 695
Constable, J. D., 697
Consumer Reports, 798, 866, 867n, 878
Cook, Earl, 396, 398n, 401n, 411n, 488n, 499, 515n, 530, 532
Cook, G. L., 422n, 502
Cook, Philip M., 612
Cook, R. J., 695
Cook, Robert C., 198–199, 234, 339n, 798
Cooke, A. S., 635n, 660n, 697
Coombs, P. H., 947
Cooper, D. F., 697
Cooper, J., 623n, 698
Cooper, P., 469n, 509
Cooper, R., 660n, 704
Cooper, Thomas, 193
Cope, O. B., 639n, 697
Copeland, M. F., 612
Corbett, J. R., 632n, 697
Corey, Marsha, 745n, 798
Corino, E., 728n
Corkhill, R. T., 553n, 612
Corn, M., 695
Corneliussen, P. E., 564n
Cornell University, 441n, 442n, 501
Coroniti, S., 674n, 699
Corsa, L., Jr., 244, 797
Cory, L., 632n, 697
Cosk, R. E., 697
Cottam, Clarence, 697
Cottle, T. J., 878
Coulson, J. C., 631n, 697
Council for Agricultural Science and Technology, 675n, 697
Council on Economic Priorities, 416n, 501
Council on Environmental Quality (CEQ), 275n, 280, 414n, 420n, 493n, 501, 502, 542n, 543n, 550n, 551, 554n, 557n, 561n, 571n, 598n, 609, 667n, 833n, 835, 836n, 841n, 848n, 855n, 871n, 872n, 878, 883
Court, A. J., 445n, 502
Cousserans, J., 649n, 702
Cowan, F. P., 445n, 502
Cowell, E. B., 612, 697
Cowles, H. H. C., 135
Cox, G. W., 172
Cox, James L., 697
Crabtree, A. N., 637n, 697
Crabtree, D. G., 637n, 705
Craddock, J. C., 344n, 384
Crafts, A. S., 695
Craig, P. P., 502, 609, 632n

Craig, R. E., 612
Cravens, Gwgneth, 821n
Cravioto, J., 380
Creason, J. P., 547n, 619
Creech, J. L., 380
Creed, R., 173
Cretney, W. J., 657n, 709
Cross, F., 635n, 660n, 695
Crossland, J., 557n, 612
Crow, James F., 579, 612
Crutchfield, J. A., 122n, 173
Crutzen, P. J., 84n, 94, 673n, 674n, 675n, 697
Cubit, D. A., 566n, 612
Cueto, C., 614
Cukor, P. M., 419n, 420n, 421n, 429n, 449n, 482n, 484n, 509
Culbertson, John M., 947
Culliton, Barbara J., 757n, 784n, 798, 1000n
Cunningham, J. P., 748n, 799
Cunningham, R. T., 649n, 697
Cunnold, D., 676n, 694
Curl, C. F., 980
Curley, A., 573n, 612, 615
Curtis, H., 129n, 145n, 174
Curwen, E. C., 245, 380
Cutright, P., 750n, 798

Daetz, Douglas, 781, 901n, 947
Dahlmann, R. C., 502
Dale, T., 279
Dale, W. E., 564n, 565n, 612, 614
Dales, J. H., 878
Dalkey, Norman C., 878
Dalrymple, Dana G., 245, 329n, 331, 334n, 339n, 380
Daly, Herman E., 843, 846n, 850, 851–852, 876, 878, 926
Daniels, F., 466n, 468n, 502
Darity, W. A., 798
Darmstadter, J., 393n, 502
Darwin, Charles, G., 900, 947
David, A., 422n, 423n, 504
David, O., 570n, 612
David, P. A., 879
Davidson, G., 649n, 697
Davidson, John, 879
Davies, J. E., 566n
Davis, G., 700
Davis, J. B., 664n, 698
Davis, J. E., 565n, 566n, 613
Davis, J. H., 565n, 566n, 613
Davis, Kingsley K., 197n, 206, 231–232, 233, 243, 244, 245, 747, 780, 784, 793n, 796, 798, 806
Davis, Nuel P., 818n, 878
Davis, R. W., 609n, 611, 818n, 878
Davison, A. W., 664n, 709
Day, Alice Taylor, 714n, 735, 785n, 792n, 798
Day, L. H., 717n, 735
Day, Samuel H., 919, 947
Deans, J. R., 637n, 697
De Bach, Paul, 634n, 647n, 648n, 649n, 694, 698
Deevey, Edward S., Jr., 71n, 83n, 85n, 86n, 87n, 94, 183, 245, 249n, 280
De Garine, Igor, 335n, 370n, 380
DeHaven, J., 261n, 264n, 265n, 270n, 271n, 272n, 280
Deichmann, W. B., 565n, 566n, 612, 618
Deinzer, M., 557n, 619
Deitz, V. R., 612
de Lappe, B. W., 635n, 706
DeLicardie, E. R., 311n, 380
Delwiche, C. C., 82n, 84n, 85n, 86n, 87n, 94
De Mair, L., 695
DeMarco, S., 321n, 380
Demeny, Paul, 782n, 798
Demko, G. J., 245
Denaeyer-de Smet, S., 93n, 94
DeNike, L., 455n, 502
Denman, D., 285n, 384, 656n, 705
Dennett, Roger D., 47n, 65, 679n, 681n, 683n, 706
Derian, J., 501
De Santo, R. S., 172
Development Dialogue, 947
Deweese, L. R., 637n, 695
De Young, Karen, 924n, 947
Dhua, S. P., 332n, 345n, 380
Dials, G. E., 419n, 502
Diamond, Jared M., 623n, 698
Diamond, M. C., 312n, 384
Dickeman, Mildred, 186n, 191n, 245, 739n, 779, 798
Dickenson, W., 469n, 502
Dickinson, R. E., 706
Dicks, J. B., 480n, 502
Dickson, E. M., 502, 572n, 612
Dickson, W., 662n, 694
Dinneen, G. U., 422n, 423n, 502
Distribution and Abundance of Animals, The, 692
Dittmar, D. S., 379
Dixon, Bernard, 607n, 612, 818n, 879
Dixon, J. A., 289n, 336n, 337–38, 381
Djerassi, Carl, 771n, 799, 932n, 947, 1000n
Doane, Robert R., 149n, 698
Dobben, W. H. van, 173, 174
Dobson, Wendy, 753n, 799
Dobzhansky, T., 173
Dochinger, L. S., 698
Doctor, R., 500
Dolan, Edwin G., 846, 879
Dolinger, P. M., 127n
Doll, Richard, 553n, 613, 615
Domhoff, G. W., 879
Donahue, T., 674n
Donsimoni, M., 501
Dorough, H. W., 633n, 702
Dorst, Jean, 698
Douderoff, M., 72n, 82n
Douglas, L., 791n, 798
Douglas, P. A., 166n
Dovring, Folke, 288n, 380
Dowler, W. M., 335n, 342n, 381
Downes, K., 445n, 502
Doyle, W. S., 502
Dregne, Harold E., 149n
Dritschilo, W., 285n, 286n, 288n, 348n, 350–351, 384, 473n, 509
Dryfoos, Joy G., 745n, 799
Dubos, René, 613, 805, 824n, 879
Duckham, A. N., 380
Duffie, J. A., 502
Dugan, P. R., 698
Duggan, R. E., 563n, 564n, 613
Duke, T. W., 646n, 695
Dulbecco, Renato, 586
Dumond, D. E., 185n, 190n, 208n, 244
Dumont, René, 304, 380
Duncan, D. C., 401n, 418n, 511
Dunham, J. T., 429n, 502
Dunkerley, Joy, 879
Dupré, Louis, 740n, 741n, 797
Durand, J. D., 185n, 245
Durham, W. F., 614
Durston, W. E., 592n, 595n, 610
Duvigneaud, P., 93n, 94
Dwyer, J. T., 313n, 380
Dyson, F. J., 818n, 879
Dyson-Hudson, N., 375n, 380

Dyson-Hudson, R. D., 285n, 375n, 380, 384, 656n, 705
Dytrych, Z., 760n, 799

Eagen, M., 589n, 616
Earl, J. L., 612
Easterlin, Richard A., 212n, 245, 786n, 799, 847, 879
Eastlund, 409n, 458, 503
Eaton, D., 509
Eaton, J., 624n, 695
Echols, J. R., 380
Eckholm, Erik P., 257n, 268n, 269n, 272n, 273n, 276n, 279, 286n, 298n, 302n, 313n, 314, 315n, 322n, 337n, 345n, 351n, 354, 372n, 378, 379, 380, 502, 623n, 628n, 698, 728n, 735, 778n, 792, 799, 899n, 946, 947, 994n
Ecologist, The, 338n, 359n, 922n
Economic Research Service, 971n
Eddy, Charles, 879
Edelson, Barton J., 869n
Edelson, Edward, 590n, 613
Edgecomb, W. G., 637n, 695
Edinger, J. G., 36n, 39n, 42n, 43n, 45n, 53n, 54n, 55n, 57n, 64
Edmondson, W. T., 556n, 613, 665n, 667n
Edsall, J. T., 586n, 613
Edvarson, K., 613
Edwards, Clive A., 641, 698
Edwards, E. O., 947
Edwards, Ron, 367n
Egler, Frank E., 698, 811n, 879
Ehrlich, Anne H., 6, 342n, 731n, 793n, 824n, 825n, 845n, 850n, 876, 887n, 904n, 931n, 947
Ehrlich, Paul R., 6, 73n, 94, 95, 97n, 115n, 116n, 118n, 119n, 124n, 125n, 126n, 127n, 129n, 163n, 172, 245, 270n, 271n, 280, 342n, 359n, 380, 382, 528n, 533, 576n, 602, 604n, 613, 614, 694, 698, 700, 731n, 734, 735, 749n, 750n, 793n, 799, 800, 805n, 818n, 824n, 825n, 828n, 845n, 846n, 850n, 857n, 869n, 875n, 876, 877, 879, 881, 887n, 904n, 905n, 931n, 945, 947, 951
Eichenwald, H. F., 380
Eigner, Joseph, 676n, 698
Eilenstine, D., 748n, 799
Eiseley, Loren, 283
Eisenbud, Merril, 451n, 502, 580n, 582n, 583n, 613
Eisner, T., 656n, 698
El-Deb, M. A., 633n
Elkins, J. W., 675n, 702
Ellingboe, A. H., 343n, 379
Elliot, Charles, 947
Elliott, D., 502
Ellsaesser, H., 624n
Elton, C. S., 138, 173
Emden, H. F. van, 141, 173
Emerson, A. E., 173
Emery, K. O., 27n, 64
Emlen, J. M., 172
Emmerji, Louis, 888, 899
Emmett, J., 459n, 460, 502
Energy Research and Development Administration (ERDA), U.S., 404, 405n, 431, 442n, 450n, 462, 463n, 468n, 493n, 502, 512
Engineering Research Institute, 445n, 502
England, C., 668n, 707
English, T., 546n, 613
Enke, Stephen, 245, 735, 781, 799, 901n, 947
Ennis, W. B., Jr., 335n, 381
Environment, 589n, 660n
Environmental Fund, Inc., 181n, 198–199, 202, 234, 245, 770n, 790n, 798n, 959, 963n
Environmental Mutagen Society, Committee of the Council of the, 576n, 577n, 579n, 612
Environmental Pollution, Royal Commission on, U.K., 456n, 502, 916
Environmental Protection Agency, U.S., 446, 447, 502, 512, 527, 542n, 543n, 552, 557, 558n, 563n, 568n, 599, 620, 671, 879, 883
Epstein, Edward, 879
Epstein, S. S., 544n, 549n, 557n, 589n, 592n, 594n, 613, 616, 617, 670, 698
Epstein, William, 914n, 947
Erb, Guy F., 897n, 947
Ergen, W. K., 448n, 502
Erhart, J. F., 807n
Eriksson, V., 610
Erturk, E., 611
Eshel, Y., 657n, 705
Esposito, J. C., 823n, 879
Etherington, J. R., 173
Euw, J. V., 126n
Evans, C., 571n, 617
Evert, R. F., 145n, 174
Ewell, Raymond, 89n, 95, 333, 381
Eyre, S. R., 157n, 173

Fabacher, D. L., 698
Fagan, R., 615
Fagley, Richard M., 879
Falcon, L. A., 651n
Falk, C. T., 797
Falk, F. D., 946
Falk, H. L., 565n, 615
Falk, Richard A., 939, 940, 947
Family Planning in an Exploding Population (O'Brien), 807
Family Planning Perspectives, 755n, 786n, 799, 993n, 994n, 997n
Famine–1975!, 923
Farm Chemicals, 854
Farmer, F. R., 448n, 502
Farmer, S. A., 61n, 64
Farnsworth, Clyde H., 754n
Farvar, M. T., 698, 899n, 947
Faust, J., 588n, 610
Feacham, Richard, 242n, 245
Fears, R., 381
Federal Energy Administration, 415n, 465n 479, 512
Federation of American Scientists, 910n, 947
Feeley, J. C., 608n, 615
Feiertag, M., 509
Feinberg, Gerald, 825
Feiveson, H. A., 502
Feld, Bernard T., 910n, 911, 913n, 947
Feldman, S., 749n, 750n, 799
Fels, M., 494n, 500, 529n, 533
Fenchel, T., 141n
Ferguson, D. E., 638n, 706
Fetizon, Marcel, 919
Feynmann, R., 15n
Field, J. O., 313n, 381
Fimreite, N., 660n, 698
Finklea, J., 546n, 613
Finlayson, F., 509
Finney, B. C., 502
Finney, J. W., 920n, 947
Firebaugh, M. W., 510, 932n

Firpo, T. H., 745n, 799
First, M. W., 552n, 614
Fischer, D. W., 835n, 879
Fischman, Leonard L., 261n, 269n, 275n, 280, 348n, 532, 722
Fiserova-Bergerova, V., 565n, 566n, 613
Fishbein, L., 565n, 615
Fishbein, W. I., 565n, 614
Fisher, A. C., 877, 879
Fisher, D. W., 695, 702
Fisher, J., 115n, 142n, 698
Fisher, Joseph L., 261n, 269n, 280, 348n, 532, 722, 882
Fisher, N. S., 639n, 640, 698, 704
Fishman, A., 435n, 500
Fitch, W. L., 127n
Fitzgerald, H. Ernest, 948
Fjeld, P., 632n, 697
Flawn, P. T., 601n, 613
Fletcher, K., 502
Fletcher, W. W., 698
Flieger, W., 245
Flohn, Hermann, 677n, 698
Flowers, Sir Brian, 456n, 502, 916n, 948
Fong, J. M., 588n, 619
Food and Agriculture Ministry, Indian, 335
Food and Agriculture Organization of the United Nations (FAO), 280, 286n, 287, 290n, 294, 298, 300, 302, 317n, 322n, 323n, 326n, 328, 332, 333n, 342, 368, 381
Food Task Force, University of California, 250n, 252n, 269n, 281, 315n, 318, 319, 325, 385
Foote, R. S., 572n, 613
Foote, S. R., 698
Forbes, I., 447n, 503
Forbes magazine, 405n, 909
Ford, E. B., 174
Ford, L. A., 572n, 619
Ford Foundation, 1000n; Energy Policy Project, 420n, 485, 491–492, 493n, 497, 498, 499, 504, 859n; Nuclear Energy Policy Study Group, 916–917
Foreign Agricultural Service, 381, 971n
Forrester, Jay W., 604, 613, 730, 732–733, 735
Forster, M. J., 348n, 384, 473n, 509, 669n
Fortune magazine, 859
"Fortune 500" 859n
Foster, G. G., 649n, 698
Fowler, D. P., 675n, 707
Fowler, T. K., 461n, 505, 528n, 533
Fowley, L., Jr., 671n, 708
Fox, R. W., 503, 916n, 948
Franck, J., 133n
Franda, Marcus F., 294n, 769n, 791n, 799, 897n, 948
Frank, C. R., Jr., 898n, 904n, 948
Frank, Jerome, 879, 914n, 945, 948
Frankel, O. H., 343n, 381
Franklin, B. A., 567n, 613
Franklin, J. F., 174
Franklin, W., 494n, 494n, 503
Franks, R. W., 334n, 381
Frantz, Stephen C., 342, 381
Fraumeni, J. F., Jr., 587n, 588n, 614, 615
Frederiksen, Harald, 776n, 778, 799
Freed, V. H., 699
Freedman, Deborah, 245, 786n, 799
Freedman, Jonathan L., 602, 604n, 613
Freedman, R., 190n, 203, 244, 245, 766n, 767n, 772n, 774n, 775n, 776n, 783n, 789n, 797, 799
Freeman, C., 733n
Freeman, David, 859n, 860n, 862n, 879, 894n
Freeman, Orville, 675
Frees, G. F., 695
Freire, P., 947
Frejka, Tomas, 212–214, 218, 219–221, 226, 245, 783n, 799, 959n, 966n
Fremlin, John, 821
French, J. L., 546n, 613
Friberg, L. T., 573n, 611
Fried, E. R., 522n, 533
Friedan, M. H., 572n, 619
Frieden, Earl, 64, 67n, 68n, 73n, 95
Friedman, I., 613
Friedman, Milton, 879
Friends of the Earth, 361n, 362n, 381
Frink, C., 698
Frost, Justin, 698
Frost, P. G. H., 623n, 698
Fry, P. C., 380
Fuhremann, T. W., 633n, 701, 702
Fullarson, W., 571n, 572n, 573n, 620
Fuller, John G., 607n, 613, 879
Fuller, R., 447n, 503
Fuller, S. L. H., 699

Gabica, J., 610
Gage, J. C., 573n, 611
Galbraith, John Kenneth, 846, 879
Gall, Norman, 914n, 948
Galle, O. R., 603n, 604n, 613
Gallese, Liz R., 367n, 369n, 381
Galston, Arthur W., 375n, 381, 567n, 613
Gambell, Ray, 362, 381
Gamberale, Francesco, 613
Garcia, R., 643n
Gardner, Brian, 656n
Gardner, W. R., 701
Garner, Fradley, 948
Garrels, R. M., 33n, 64, 69n, 71n, 79n, 80n, 83n, 84n, 85n, 86n, 87n, 89n, 91n, 92n, 94, 95, 516, 533, 567n, 568n, 569n, 570n, 572n, 613, 658n, 698
Gart, J. J., 565n, 615
Garvey, G., 476n, 503
Gaspar, P. P., 543n, 611, 613
Gass, G. H., 589n, 612
Gates, David, 50n, 64, 76n, 95, 129n
Gatos, Harry C., 822n, 879
Gavan, J. D., 289n, 336n, 337–338, 381
Gay, R., 549n, 620
Gayn, Mark, 341n, 381
General Electric Co., 450n, 503
Genesis Strategy, The, 347, 944
Georgesçy-Rolgen, N., 879
Georghiou, G. P., 647n, 698
Gerasimov, I. P., 260n, 280
Gerba, C. P., 613
German, James, 592n, 613
Geroudet, P., 706
Gerrits, R. J., 589n, 612
Gessell, T., 465n, 503
Gibbons, J. W., 670n, 698, 699
Gibor, Aharon, 36n, 64, 72n, 78n, 79n, 94
Giese, R. L., 650n, 699
Gieseking, John E., 280
Giessner, Klaus, 280
Gifford, Roger M., 852, 884
Gilbert, L. E., 115n, 116n, 119n, 174, 698

Gilbert, R. G., 613
Gilcreas, F., 556n, 614
Gilder, S. S. B., 553n, 613
Gilfillan, S. C., 569n, 614
Gill, R., 649n, 698
Gillette, R., 403n, 435n, 447n, 448n, 454n, 455n, 503
Gillman, Katherine, 879
Gilmour, C. M., 699
Girling, E., 573n, 612
Glackin, James J., 916n, 948
Glaeser, J., 682n, 695
Glaser, P., 471n, 503
Glass, Bentley, 699
Glass, G. E., 612
Glasstone, S., 437n, 503
Glazier, S. C., 126n
Gleria, M., 500
Glooschenko, W. A., 702
Godkin, E. L., 811, 879
Goeller, H. E., 528n, 533, 851n, 879
Gofman, J. W., 443n, 503, 586n, 614
Goldberg, E. D., 568n, 569n, 570n, 571n, 572n, 574n, 611, 614, 620, 632n, 699, 705, 729n
Goldblat, Jozef, 917n, 948
Goldman, M. I., 270n, 280
Goldsmith, Edward, 381, 735, 813n, 879
Goldsmith, J. R., 546n, 570n, 614
Goldsmith, M., 465n, 503
Goldstein, I. S., 503
Goldwater, C. J., 587n, 614
Goldwater, L. G., 573n, 611
Golenpaul, A., 476n, 503
Golueke, C., 474n, 503
Gon, M., 566n, 620
Gonzales, D., 651n
Goodall, D. W., 174
Goodland, R. J. A., 699
Goodman, Daniel, 140, 142
Gordon, A. G., 661n, 661, 699
Gordon, J. E., 384, 614, 777n
Gorham, E., 661, 699
Goss, J. R., 350n, 380
Gough, William, 409n, 458, 458n, 503
Gould, Donald, 791n, 799
Gove, W. R., 603n, 604n, 613
Gradwell, G. R., 173
Graham, Frank, Jr., 638, 694, 699, 879
Granel, L., 311n, 385
Grant, James P., 781n, 789n, 790n, 793n, 799, 875n, 936, 948
Grant, Neville, 573n, 614
Graubard, S. R., 879
Gray, R. A., 652n, 697
Greeley, Andrew, 807, 808n, 879
Green, D. R., 657n, 709
Green, E., 422n, 484n, 485n, 500
Green, Harold P., 820n, 879
Green, Philip, 910n, 914n, 948
Green, Wade, 923n, 948
Greenberg, Daniel S., 317n, 595n, 596, 611
Greenburg, William, 503
Greene, Felix, 948
Greene, N. C., 617
Greenland, D. J., 346n, 378
Greenough, W. B., 614
Greep, R. O., 784n, 800, 1000n
Gregory, D., 482n, 503
Greywood-Hale, E. A., 695
Griffin, J. J., 632n, 705
Griggs, D. T., 601n, 614
Grobecker, A., 674n, 699
Grooms, D. W., 503
Groth, Edward, III, 268n, 280, 350n, 378, 575n, 614, 669n, 699
Gruber, E., 620
Gruchy, I., 660n, 698
Gruen, Victor, 503
Gruener, N., 558n, 614, 699
Guenzi, W. D., 699
Guild, P. W., 523n, 533
Guille, G., 649n, 702
Gulbrandsen, R. A., 89n, 94
Gulland, John A., 352n, 354n, 378, 379
Gumpert, David, 372n
Gunner, S. W., 578, 579n, 619
Gurney, Ramsdell, 913n, 948
Gutenmann, W. H., 610, 660n, 707
Guttmacher, Alan F., 799
Guttmacher Institute, 745n, 756–757, 799, 824n
Gwynne, Peter, 624n, 699
Gyftopolous, E., 494n, 504

Haden-Guest, S., 280
Hadley, R. F., 623n, 696n
Haefele, W., 396n, 441n, 462n, 504
Hagan, Patti, 355n, 381
Hagan, R. M., 476n, 504
Hagen, K. S., 651n
Haines, W. W., 948
Hall, D. B., 454n, 504
Hall, Edward T., 602, 614
Hall, G. A. S., 166n
Hall, J. W., 611, 696
Hall, R. E., 894n, 946
Hall, Ross H., 325n, 381
Hallsworth, E. G., 699
Halsted, T. A., 454n, 504
Hambleton, W. W., 453n, 504
Hamelink, J. L., 630n, 699
Hamilton, D. H., 600n, 614
Hamilton, W. F., II, 879
Hammon, W. M., 607n, 608n, 614
Hammond, A. S., 614
Hammond, Allen L., 410n, 442n, 459n, 463n, 464n, 471n, 474n, 480n, 481n, 504, 674n, 699, 915n, 916n, 948
Hammond, E. C., 588n, 614, 618
Hammond, George S., 879, 932n, 948
Hammond, P., 678, 708
Han Suyin, 772n, 799
Hance, W. A., 245
Handler, Philip, 820n, 879–880, 910
Haney, A., 660n, 661n, 691
Hannon, B., 494n, 498n, 504
Hansen, K. F., 894n
Hansen, Roger D., 887n, 892n, 897n, 946, 948
Hanson, J. A., 381
Hanson, R. P., 607n, 608n, 614
Hanson, W. C., 672n, 699
Haque, R., 699
Hardin, Garrett, 359, 381, 693n, 699, 749n, 760n, 793n, 799, 806, 821, 876, 880, 921–922, 939, 948
Hardmann, M., 841n, 880
Hardy, R. W. F., 82n, 83n, 85n, 86n, 87n, 94, 374n, 381
Harlan, Jack R., 284n, 344n, 381
Harper, J., 699
Harriman, R. L., 846n, 879, 945
Harris, David R., 284n
Harris, R. C., 313n, 385
Harris, R. H., 557n, 617
Harris, R. J. C., 588n, 591n, 614
Harris, S. J., 695
Harris, W., 500, 590n
Harrison, Paul, 937n, 948
Harriss, R. C., 660n, 699, 702
Hart, C. W., Jr., 699
Hart, E. R., 565n, 615
Hart, John, 275n, 280
Hart, R. G., 802
Harte, John, 271n, 279, 433n, 504
Hartley, William D., 769n

Harvard Law Review Association, 880
Harvey, G. R., 630n, 699
Harvey, H. H., 695
Harvey, Robert, 948
Harward, E. D., 507
Harward, M., 664n, 699
Harwood, Robert F., 699, 832n, 880
Harwood, S., 453n, 504
Hasanen, Erkhi 704
Hasiba, H. H., 422n, 423n, 504
Hasler, Arthur D., 699
Hatt, G., 245, 380
Hattis, Dale, 544n, 549n, 578n, 613
Hauser, Philip M., 800
Havelka, U. D., 374n, 381
Hawk, R., 573n, 612
Hawkes, J. G., 343n, 381
Hawrylyshyn, George, 718n
Hay, Edwards, 664n, 699
Hayes, Denis, 880
Hayes, E. T., 530n, 533
Hayes, W. J., Jr., 564n, 565n, 612, 614
Hays J. D., 687n, 699
Hazeltine, W., 700
Heady, Earl O., 381
Healy, J. H., 601n, 614
Healy, T. J., 425n, 504
Heath, A. G., 619, 707
Heath, R. G., 700
Hedberg, Hollis D., 948
Hedgpeth, J. W., 700
Heer, David M., 787, 788n, 800
Heffernan, Patrick, 841n, 853n, 880
Heichel, G. H., 348n, 378
Heilbroner, Robert L., 876, 880, 948–949
Heimburger, Peter, 870n
Hein, R., 481n, 504
Heiser, Charles B., Jr., 284n, 381
Heller, Alfred, 857n, 872n, 880
Heller, Walter, 845, 880
Helminen, M., 660n, 700
Henderson, Hazel, 848, 880
Hendricks, S. B., 381
Hendry, L. B., 656n, 698
Hendry, Peter, 700
Henkin, H., 832n, 880
Henrie, T. A., 429n, 502
Henriques, Affonso, 627n
Henriksson, K., 660n, 700
Hepting, G. H., 688n
Herendeen, R., 504, 505, 862n, 880
Hermalin, A. J., 775n, 776n, 799
Herman, T., 946
Hernberg, S., 570n, 614
Heronemus, W. E., 477n, 504
Herrera, P., 443n, 505, 700, 834n, 880
Hersh, Seymour M., 949
Hershner, C. H., 414n, 501, 658n, 695
Hertz, M., 546n, 613
Hertzig, M. E., 311n, 313n, 381
Hertzog, Arthur, 949
Hess, W. N., 700
Hetter, P., 881
Hewitt, D., 556n, 617
Hexter, A. C., 546n, 570n, 614
Heyerdahl, Thor, 657, 700
Heywood, V. H., 174
Hiatt, V., 574n, 614
Hickey, J., 700
Higgins, G., 422n, 484n, 485n, 500
Hill, Dennis S., 700
Hill, F. B., 90n, 95
Hill, G. R., 133n
Hill, I. D., 615
Hillaby, John, 718n, 890n, 949
Hills, Lawrence D., 669n, 670n, 700
Hinds, W. C., 552n, 614
Hiorns, R. W., 173
Hippocrates, 541
Hirsch, Fred, 846n, 876
Hirsch, R., 458n, 461n, 504
Hirschhorn, N., 614
Hirschleifer, J., 261n, 264n, 265n, 270n, 271n, 272n, 280
Hirshberg, A. S., 468n, 510
Hirst, Eric, 348n, 381, 473n, 493n, 494n, 495n, 504, 558n, 614
Ho, F. K., 121n
Hoagland, Hudson, 949
Hobbes, Thomas, 845
Hocevar, C. J., 505
Hoch, Irving, 604n, 752n, 800
Hodgson, H. J., 289n, 315n, 381
Hoffmann, D., 552n, 618
Hoffman, W. S., 565n, 614
Hofmann, Paul, 869n
Hofs, H. D., 589n, 612
Hofstatter, Ellen, 763n, 801
Hogness, D. S., 609n, 611, 818n, 878
Holaday, D., 431n, 506
Holden, Constance, 647n, 700, 981n
Holdgate, M. W., 121n, 141n
Holdren, John P., 6, 245, 270n, 271n, 280, 380, 382, 393n, 401, 402, 405n, 407, 409n, 421n 429n, 438n, 443n, 446n, 461n, 462n, 463n, 487n, 488n, 490n, 501, 504, 505, 510, 528n, 533, 613, 614, 678, 694, 700, 734, 735, 798, 800, 820n, 834n, 863n, 876, 879, 880, 881, 928n, 929n, 949
Hole, W. H., 589n, 612
Hollaender, A., 589n, 613
Holland, W. W., 553n, 612
Hollander, J. M., 499
Hollick, A. L., 949
Holliday, Robin, 880
Hollin, John T., 700
Holling, C. S., 829
Hollings, Ernest F., 316, 382
Hollocher, T. C., 434n, 451n, 452n, 453n, 503, 505
Holloman, J. H., 894n, 946
Holm, Richard W., 73n, 94, 97, 119n, 124n, 129n, 172, 245, 380, 576n, 613, 694
Holmberg, B., 614, 917n, 949
Holmen, H., 707
Holmes, S., 615
Holsti, P. R., 949
Holsworth, W., 660n, 698
Holt, B. D., 92
Holt, S. J., 121n, 362n, 365, 382
Holt-Jensen, A., 661n, 700
Holton, J. R., 700
Hom, R., 651n, 704
Honnold, Julie A., 858n, 882
Hooker, C. A., 880
Hooven, F. J., 482n, 509
Hoover, E. M., 947
Hoover, R., 587n, 614
Hopkins, J., 873n
Hopper, W. David, 382
Horn, D., 588n, 614
Hottel, H. C., 403n, 421n, 428n, 429n, 480n, 481n, 505
House, Peter W., 846n, 857n, 880
How, S. W., 588n, 619
Howard, J. B., 403n, 421n, 428n, 429n, 480n, 481n, 505
Howe, E. E., 382
Howe, James W., 322n, 790n, 949, 950
Hubbert, M. K., 79n, 95, 401n, 403, 404n, 411n, 413n, 476n, 499, 505
Huber, R. T., 650n, 699
Huber, S. C., 800
Huddle, N., 574n, 609
Hudson, H. E., 556n, 614
Hudson, Norman, 700

Hueckel, Glenn, 874n, 880
Hueper, W. C., 614
Huettner, D. A., 505
Huff, J. E., 574n, 612, 614
Huffaker, C. B., 634n, 651n, 700, 702
Huggett, R. J., 632n, 705
Hughes, J. Donald, 623n, 701, 728n
Hughes, J. M., 557n, 615
Hughes Aircraft Company, 869n
Huisken, Ronald, 918n, 949
Huldt, Lars, 760n, 800
Hulett, H. R., 716, 735
Hulse, J. H., 374n, 382
Humbaraci, A., 656n
Hunt, Charles B., 251n, 255n, 256n, 258, 259, 264n, 265, 269n, 260n, 263n, 279, 280
Hunt, Cynthia, 33n, 64, 69n, 71n, 79n, 80n, 83n, 84n, 85n, 86n, 87n, 91n, 92n, 94, 95, 533, 567n, 568n, 569n, 572n, 613, 658n, 698
Hunt, Eldredge G., 700
Hunt, R., 494n, 503
Hunter, J. R., 382
Hurd, L. E., 140n, 348n, 384, 473n, 509, 669n
Hurlbert, S., 640n, 700
Hurn, R. W., 614
Huschenbeth, E., 630n, 705
Hussey, N. W., 696
Hutchinson, G. E., 174
Hutchinson, J., 947
Hutnik, R. J., 700

Idso, S. B., 681n, 687n, 701
Idyll, C. P., 352n, 354n, 382
Ignoffo, C. M., 648n, 700
Ignotus, Miles, 896n, 909n, 949
Iliad, 874
Illich, Ivan, 807, 824, 828, 868n, 876, 880, 949
Iltis, H. H., 602n, 614, 734
Imbric, John, 687n, 699
Imrie, F., 371n, 382
Inadvertent Modification of the Stratosphere (IMOS), 700
Ingestad, T., 95
Inglis, D. R., 407, 437n, 447n, 462n, 505
Innes, J. R. M., 565n, 615
Institute of Ecology, The (TIE), 85n, 86n, 87n, 95, 423n, 529, 533, 700, 707
Institute of Energy Analysis, 493n, 505
Instituto Brasileiro de Geografia, 627
Interagency Task Force on Inadvertent Modification of the Stratosphere, 674n, 700
Internal Pollution, Special Commission on, U.K., 812n
International Atomic Energy Agency, 455n, 505, 913n, 914n, 949
International Board for Plant Genetic Resources, 382
International Council on Radiation Protection (ICRP), 583, 586
International Food Policy Research Institute, 328
International Institute for Applied Systems Analysis, 505
International Petroleum Encyclopedia, 394, 894n
Iowa State University, 326
Irwin, H.S., 699
Isaacs, J. D., 25n, 64
Isaacson, Peter A., 138
Isaak, L. W., 704
Isensee, A. R., 701
Istock, Conrad E., 880

Jackson, R. D., 681n, 701
Jacobson, M., 701
Jacoby, H. D., 894n, 946
Jacoby, Neil H., 903, 949
Jaffe, Andrew, 375n, 382
Jaffe, Frederick S., 749n, 750n, 784n, 798, 800, 1000n
Jaffee, M., 572n, 619
Jahns, H. O., 682n, 695
Jahns, Richard H., 615, 692, 701
Jahoda, J. C., 627n, 701, 887n, 949
Jahoda, M., 733n
Jain, A. K., 768n
Jalée, Pierre, 889, 949
James, L. W., 471n, 505
Janick, J., 252n, 253, 254n, 255n, 276n, 279, 286n, 300n, 382
Jansen, G. R., 382
Janzen, Daniel H., 143n, 157, 382, 624n, 701
Japan Whaling Association, 359n, 362n
Jaquet, J.-M., 696
Jarrett, Henry, 949
Jasani, Bhupendra M., 917n, 949
Jaworowski, Z., 569n, 615
Jehl, Joseph, R., Jr., 637n, 695
Jelliffe, D. B., 304n, 382
Jelliffe, E. F. P., 304n, 382
Jennings, Peter R., 382
Jensen, C. G., 949
Jensen, S., 630n, 705
Jernelov, A., 573n, 611
Jervis, Robert, 910n, 945
Jet Propulsion Laboratory (JPL), 470n, 496, 506, 554n, 610
Jewczyk, S., 620
Joensu, O., 571n, 615
Johannes, R. E., 622
John, E. C., 530, 533
Johnson, A. W., 172
Johnson, Brian, 791n, 800, 882, 949
Johnson, D. Gale, 335n, 382
Johnson, D. L., 142n
Johnson, H. A., 632n, 709
Johnson, R. H., 948
Johnson, N. M., 702
Johnson, Samuel, 953
Johnson, Stanley, 800
Johnson, W. R., 880
Johnston, Bruce F., 933, 949
Johnston, David W., 637n, 701
Johnston, Harold, 673–674, 675n, 701
Johnston, R., 615, 701
Joint Committee on Atomic Energy (JCAE), U.S., 434n, 443n, 505, 511
Jolly, W. C., 697
Jones, D. P., 701
Jones, M. B., 91n
Jones, R. M., 615
Joseph, K. T., 626n, 709
Joskow, P. L., 894n, 946
Journal of the American Medical Association, 312n, 382
Judson, S., 257n, 280

Kagawa, J., 547n, 615
Kahn, A. R., 798
Kahn, Herman, 5n, 690, 701, 881, 914n, 949
Kalman, Sumner M., 739–740, 800
Kamin, Leon J., 748n, 800
Kammen, H. O., 610
Kammer, W., 448n
Kane, Dorothy Noyes, 544n, 615
Kangas, Lerni W., 800
Kansas Geological Survey, 453n
Kansas State University, 506
Kantrowitz, Arthur, 819, 820n, 881
Karam, R. A., 506

Karas, G., 570n, 612
Karppanen, E., 660n, 700
Kasantzis, G., 573n, 611
Kashyap, S., 600n, 618
Kasper, W., 474n, 506
Kassas, M., 149n, 701
Katagiri, Tameyoshi, 772n, 773n, 800
Katan, J., 633n, 701
Katchadourian, Herant A., 796, 827, 881, 988n
Katz, M., 304n, 311n, 382
Kay, Kingsley, 565n, 615
Kaysen, K., 731n
Kearney, P. C., 701
Keaton, M. J., 419n, 420n, 421n, 429n, 449n, 482n, 484n, 509
Kee, C., 434n, 500
Keeling, C. D., 80n, 94
Keely, Charles B., 232n, 245
Keeney, D. R., 701
Keeny, Spurgeon, 917n, 949
Keith, J., 660n, 698
Keith, V. F., 705
Kelleher, G. G., 916n, 948
Kelley, J. H., 506
Kellock, Sally E., 241n
Kellogg, W. W., 59n, 61n, 62n, 64, 90n, 95, 682n, 683n, 689n, 701, 703
Kelly, N. U., 777n, 778n, 802
Kelso, L. O., 881
Kembrough, R., 612
Kemezis, Paul, 717n
Kemp, A. L. W., 696
Kemp, C., 474n, 510
Kemp, G. E., 607n, 617
Kenaga, E. E., 630n, 701
Kendall, H. W., 446n, 447n, 503, 506
Kendeigh, S. C., 145n, 150n, 174
Kennedy, Robert F., 914n
Keohane, Robert O., 904n, 949
Kermode, G. O., 589n, 615
Kerr, C. B., 916n, 948
Kershaw, K. A., 174
Kessler, G., 504
Ketchel, Melvin, M., 788, 800
Ketchum, Bostwick H., 701, 728n
Keusch, Gerald T., 304n, 311n, 382
Keyfitz, Nathan, 181n, 218, 225n, 240n, 245, 887n, 901n, 904n, 926, 949
Keynes, John Maynard, 743n, 843
Khalil, A. Zaki, 633n, 694
Khan, M. A. Q., 661n, 697, 701
Khera, K. S., 578, 579n, 619
Khoi, L. T., 947
Kier, L. D., 588n, 615
King Must Die, The (Renault), 874
Kirk, D., 226n, 244
Kissinger, Henry A., 896, 907, 949
Kissling, R. E., 607n, 615
Kitto, G. B., 649n, 696
Kitts, F. G., 502
Klare, Michael T., 920n, 949
Klassen, W., 335n, 342n, 381
Klechkovskii, V., 701
Klein, D. H., 568n
Klein, M., 565n, 615
Klein, Richard M., 272, 280
Kleinfeld, M., 587n, 614
Knabe, W., 661n, 701
Knuse, A. V., 533
Knopp, F. D., 697
Knox, J. F., 615
Knudson, A. G., 615
Koblinsky, M. A., 784n, 800, 1000n
Kobori, J., 616
Kocher, James E., 334n, 776n, 777n, 778n, 781n, 789n, 793n, 796, 931n, 933, 934, 935, 945
Kohl, D. H., 701
Koide, M., 571n, 572n, 620
Kolata, G. B., 186n, 208n, 245, 718n
Kolb, C. E., 673n, 675n, 701
Komanoff, Charles, 438n, 486n, 506
Kondratyev, K. Y., 701
Kontogiannis, J. E., 702
Kopf, A., 706
Kothny, E. L., 615
Kouri, R. E., 588n, 610
Koutts, H., 509
Kouyoumjian, H. H., 702
Kovda, V., 269n
Kozlowski, T. T., 174, 703
Kozlowsky, D. G., 133n
Kozol, Jonathan, 881
Kratzer, Myron B., 949
Kraun, G. F., 557n, 615
Krebs, C. J., 98n, 119n, 121n, 161n, 172
Kreitzer, J. F., 700
Krenkel, P., 483n, 508
Krieger, David, 506
Krier, J. E., 834n, 836n, 877
Krishnakumar, S., 800
Kruger, P., 465n, 506
Krummel, J., 285n, 286n, 288n, 348n, 350–351, 384, 473n, 509
Kryter, K. D., 615
Kubo, A. S., 452n, 506
Kuenen, P. H., 26n, 31n, 63
Kuenzler, E. J., 143
Kuhr, R. J., 633n, 702
Kukla, G. J., 64
Kukla, H. J., 64
Kulcinski, G., 461n, 487n, 504, 506
Kummel, B., 174
Kuper, B. H., 445n, 502
Kuratsune, M., 563n, 615
Kutzman, J., 285n, 286n, 288n, 348n, 350–351, 384, 473n, 509
Kwok, L. W., 611
Kyllonen, R. L., 604n, 615

Ladejinsky, W., 334n, 382
Lader, Laurence, 756n, 800
La Force, F. M., 608n, 615
Lagler, K., 476n, 506
Lagunov, L. L., 355n, 382
Laing, David, 529n, 533
Lakshminarayana, V., 269n, 271n, 280
Lam, D. C. L., 696
Lamb, H. H., 59n, 64, 702
Landau, N. J., 620, 881
Landsberg, H. E., 677
Landsberg, Hans H., 261n, 269n, 271n, 279, 280, 348n, 522n, 532, 722, 882
Langer, William L., 186n, 187, 189n, 190, 191n, 245, 607n, 615, 739n, 800
Langley, N., 448n
Lanza, G. R., 611, 696
Lapham, R. J., 766n, 767n, 769n, 803
Lappé, Frances M., 314n, 382, 973n
Lash, T., 453n, 506
Latham, Michael C., 304n, 313n, 378, 382
Laumann, E. A., 506
Lave, L. B., 506, 546n, 549n, 615
Laven, H., 649n, 702
Laws, E. R., Jr., 564n, 615
Lazaradis, L., 494n, 504
Lazlo, Ervin, 945
Lazrus, A., 90n, 95
Leach, G., 350n, 382
Leach, J. H., 667n, 696, 702
Lecomber, Richard, 843n, 881
LeCren, E. D., 121n, 141n
Lederberg, J., 589n, 607n, 608n, 613, 615
Ledogar, Robert J., 891n, 950

Lee, A. M., 588n, 615
Lee, F. D., 592n, 595n, 610
Lee, R. B., 186n, 245
Leeds, A., 290n, 382
Leeper, E. M., 358n, 382
Lees, L., 554n, 555n, 615
Legator, M., 589n, 613
Lehninger, A. L., 71n, 72n, 82n, 95
Lehrer, Tom, 541
Leigh, T. F., 651n
Leighton, R., 15n
Leith, H., 132n
Lelyveld, Joseph, 768n, 772n, 800
Leonard, George B., 881
Leontief, Wassily, 845
Leopold, Aldo, 97
Leopold, Luna B., 64, 260, 279, 280
Lerman, A., 89n, 95
Lerner, I, M., 121n
Leslie, P. H., 121n
Leslie, R., 372n, 382
Lessey, Julian, 929n, 950
Levi-Strauss, Claude, 812
Levin, R., 435n, 506
Levine, R. P., 72n, 95
Levinson, Charles, 597n, 598n, 600, 615
Levinson, F. J., 313n, 381
Levitsky, D. A., 312n, 382
Lewin, Roger, 310n, 311n, 312n, 382n, 595n, 596n, 616, 942n
Lewis, A., 506
Lewis, D. A., 745n, 799
Lewis, D. J., 204, 244
Lewis, H. W., 446n, 506
Lewis, Paul, 894n, 950
Lewis, R., 506, 862n, 881
Lewit, Sarah, 755n, 802
Lewontin, R. C., 174
Liang, T. L., 656n, 702
Libby, W. F., 695
Lichtenberg, A. J., 396n, 483n, 491, 498n, 507, 510, 860n, 881
Lichtenstein, C. P., 633n, 701
Lichtenstein, E. P., 656n, 702
Lichty, R. W., 649n, 697
Lidsky, L. M., 463n, 506
Lieber, M., 617
Lieberman, M. A., 405n, 506
Lieth, H., 174
Lijinsky, W., 589n, 616
Likens, G. E., 74n, 75n, 76n, 93n, 94, 132n, 175, 472n, 624n, 661n, 695, 702
Likosky, W., 572n, 612, 616
Lilius, H., 570n, 614
Limits to Growth, The, 170, 730–733
Lin, C. S., 588n, 619
Lincer, J. L., 635n, 696, 702, 707
Lincoln, C., 702
Lincoln, D. N., 572n, 619
Lincoln, Richard, 756n, 800
Linden, O., 658n, 702
Lindsey, Robert, 866n, 881
Linowitz, Sol, 890
Lipsey, R. L., 660n, 661n, 691
Lipson, A., 500
Lipton, Michael, 297n, 378, 950
Lisk, D. J., 610, 660n, 707
Livingston, R. S., 506
Llaurado, T. P., 947
Lloyd, J. W., 431n, 506, 600n, 618
Lockhart, W. L., 695
Lockie, J. D., 637n, 702
Lockwood, Lee, 950
Loebl, Eugen, 881
Löf, G., 467n, 511
Loftas, Tony, 323n, 382, 658n, 702
Long, T. V., II, 533
Longhurst, A. R., 352n, 379
Loomis, Robert S., 286n, 382
Loomis, W. E., 133n
Loomis, W. F., 307n, 382
Loosli, J. K., 370n, 373n, 382
Lorenz, E. N., 64
Lorraine, John, 768n, 800
Los Angeles Times, 807n
Lotka, A. J., 109n
Loucks, O. L., 602n, 614
Lourimore, G., 546n, 613
Love, Sam, 560n, 616, 669n
Lovelock, J., 95
Lovering, Thomas S., 523n, 533
Lovins, Amory, 488n, 499, 506, 863n, 877, 917n, 945, 950
Low, H. C., 950
Lowe, J. I., 646n, 695
Lowe-McConnell, R. H., 173, 174
Lowrance, W. W., 616, 817n, 877
Lowry, W. P., 677n, 702
Luck, R. T., 643n
Luckman, W. H., 703
Lumsden, M., 616
Lund, R. T., 494n, 506, 529n, 533
Lundberg, Ferdinand, 881
Lunde, Donald T., 796, 828, 881, 988n
Lundin, F., 431n, 506
Luney, P. R., 657n, 707
Lurien, K. K., 768n, 800
Luther, F., 624n
Lynn, David A., 544n, 545n, 547n, 551n, 570n, 610, 727
Lyon, W. S., 571n, 572n, 573n, 620
Lyubimova, I., 355n, 382

MacArthur, R. H., 140, 174
MacAvoy, P. W., 894n, 946
MacDonald, Gordon J. F., 600n, 616, 681n, 689, 690n, 702
MacDonald, R. L., 695
MacDonald, W. E., 566n, 612
Machta, Lester, 80n, 95, 683n, 702
MacIntyre, Ferren, 22n, 64, 71n, 95
Mackenzie, F. T., 33n, 64, 69n, 71n, 79n, 80n, 83n, 84n, 85n, 86n, 87n, 89n, 91n, 92n, 94, 95, 533, 567n, 568n, 569n, 572n, 613, 658n, 698
Mackenzie, James J., 434n, 447n, 493n, 500, 503, 505
MacLeod, D. F., 610
Macrae, Norman, 845n, 881
Maddox, John, 5n, 813n, 879, 881
Maddrey, W. C., 615
Magat, Michel, 919
Magee, P. N., 589n, 616
Magos, L., 573n, 611
Mahoney, J. J., Jr., 638n
Makhijani, Arjun, 350n, 383, 393n, 396n, 472, 474, 475, 491, 499, 506, 507, 879, 932n, 950
Makino, Hiro, 500
Malberg, J. N., 561n, 562n, 618
Malmer, N., 661n, 702
Malone, C. R., 657n, 702
Maltoni, Cesare, 597n, 616
Mamdani, Mahmood, 777–778, 792n, 800
Manabe, S., 683n, 685n, 702
Mandel, J. S., 556n, 617
Manfrin, M., 500
Mangin, W., 241n, 246
Mankind at the Turning Point, 733
Mann, B., 419n, 420n, 421n, 429n, 449n, 482n, 484n, 509
Mann, J. I., 993n
Mann-Borgese, Elizabeth, 941
Manne, A., 441n
Manning, P., 841n, 880
Mao Tse Tung, 737
Marchetti, C., 429n, 482n, 507
Margalef, R., 141n, 174
Margolis, Joseph, 812, 881

Margulis, L., 95
Marigh, T. H., 800, 999n
Marks, P. L., 702
Marmot, M. G., 611
Marolla, F. A., 385, 719n, 735
Marr, P. D., 702
Marsh, George Perkins, 272, 280, 536, 694
Marsh, R. G., 701
Marshall, A. J., 230n
Martell, E. A., 90n, 95, 588n, 616
Martin, H., 702
Martin, H. P., 312n, 380
Martin, J. E., 507
Martin, J. H., 703
Martin, P. S., 142n, 185n, 246, 383
Martin, R. D., 703
Martin, S., 682n, 696
Martin, W. E., 637n
Marx, J. L., 557n, 616, 664n, 703
Marx, Leo, 881
Marx, Wesley, 658n, 703
Masefield, C. B., 380
Mason, Brian, 20n, 64, 95
Mason, T. J., 616
Mass, C., 59n, 65, 686, 687n, 706
Masters, G. M., 427n, 507, 556n, 557n, 558n, 559n, 616, 670n
Mata, L., 304n, 311n, 382
Matson, W. R., 571n, 611
Matsumura, Fumio, 578n, 633n, 703
Matsunaga, Ei, 800
Matthews, W. H., 703
Maugh, T. H., II, 410n, 442n, 459n, 463n, 471n, 474n, 480n, 481n, 504, 507, 568n, 595n, 616, 649n, 674, 699, 703
Mauldin, W. Parker, 774n, 775n, 791n, 792n, 793n, 795n, 800
May, J. M., 688n
May, K., 504
May, R. M., 140, 174
Mayer, A., 324n, 383
Mayer, Jean, 296n, 313n, 315n, 324n, 380, 383
Mayle, Peter, 881
Mayr, E., 174
Mazrui, Ali A., 950
McCabe, L. J., 557n, 615
McCann, J., 578n, 592n, 595n, 616
McCarthy, J. D., 604n, 613
McCarthy, Richard D., 609
McCaull, Julian, 270n, 280, 477n, 507, 881
McClain, C. E., 547n, 619
McCleary, G. F., 743n
McCloskey, William, B., 364n, 383
McConnell, J. C., 676n, 702
McCracken, M., 624n
McCulloh, T. H., 78n, 95, 411n, 506
McDermott, W., 546, 616
McDonald, James E., 64
McElroy, M. B., 675n, 676n, 703, 709
McElroy, William D., 800
McFarlane, R. B., 660n, 699, 702
McGinty, Lawrence, 567n, 616
McGrath, Patricia L., 354, 380, 798, 936, 946, 950
McHale, J., 533
McHugh, J. L., 166n, 280
McIntyre, H. C., 439n, 507
McKay, F. N., 616
McKechnie, S., 115n, 119n
McKenzie, J., 370n, 383
McKeown, T., 190, 192n, 193n, 194, 195, 246
McKinley, D., 706
McKinney, R. W., 607n, 608n, 614
McLaughlin, Martin M., 297n, 383
McLaughlin, S. B., Jr., 664n, 703
McLellan, A. C., 233n, 246
McLeod, J., 857n, 880
McLerney, W. O., 367n, 379
McLin, Jon, 297n, 323n, 328n, 383
McMichael, W. C., 616
McMurtry, J. A., 634n, 700, 703
McNamara, Jack, 895, 952
McNaughton, S. J., 140n, 150n, 174, 375n, 383
McNeil, Mary, 626, 703
McNeill, B., 506
McPhee, J., 453n, 454n, 507
McPherson, V. M., 603n, 613
McQuigg, James, 346–347
Meadows, Dennis L., 170, 507, 730, 731n, 732n, 734, 735, 945
Meadows, Donella, H., 170, 730, 731n, 732n, 734, 735, 945
Means, Richard L., 881
Medvin, N., 859n, 860n, 881
Meeham, R. L., 600n, 614
Meek, Ronald L., 801
Meggers, Betty J., 626n, 627n, 703
Meier, Allan K., 868n
Meier, Richard L., 881
Meinel, A. B., 468n, 470n, 507
Meinel, M. P., 468n, 470n, 507
Meinwald, J., 656n, 698
Meissner, H. P., 894n, 946
Melko, Matthew, 950
Mellin, G., 570n, 614
Mellinger, M. V., 140n
Mellor, John W., 336n, 383
Melman, Seymour, 918, 919, 950
Melnick, J. L., 613
Menard, H. W., 63, 255n, 257n, 260n, 262n, 263n, 264n, 270n, 280, 601n, 616
Mendis, A. B., 343n
Menn, J. J., 650n, 703
Menzee, C. M., 635n, 707
Mercado, Juan L., 374, 383
Merch Index, 578n
Merless, R. R., 616
Merriam, Marshal, 477n, 507
Merrigan, J. A., 507
Merrill, Annabel L., 972n
Merta, M., 832n, 880
Mertz, D. E., 121n
Mesarovic, M., 730, 733, 735, 901n, 950
Meselson, M., 608n, 609n, 616, 697
Mesirow, Lynne E., 321n, 346n, 347, 378, 673n, 686n, 688n, 694, 819, 883, 943n, 944, 945
Metcalf, Robert L., 643n
Metcalf and Eddy, Inc., 269n, 280, 560n, 616
Metz, W. D., 410n, 442n, 459n, 462n, 463n, 471n, 474n, 480n, 481n, 504, 507
Metzger, P., 507, 862n, 881
Meyer, K. K., 313n, 385
Micklin, P., 270n, 280
Miklas, H. P., 630n, 699
Milgrim, J. H., 414n, 501, 658n, 695
Miller, Albert, 64, 703
Miller, Arnold, 419n, 507
Miller, E. C., 595n, 616
Miller, J., 595n, 616
Miller, Judith, 344n, 383
Miller, M. G., 868n, 881
Miller, M. W., 703
Miller, P. C., 172
Miller, R. W., 583n, 616
Miller, Stanton S., 616
Miller, U., 662n, 694
Milliman, J., 261n, 264n, 265n, 270n, 271n, 272n, 280
Milton, J. P., 698, 899n, 947
Miner, F. D., 702
Mintz, M., 881

Mirabito, J. A., 949
Mirov, G. N., 133n
Mirvish, Sidney S., 589n, 616
Misato, T., 703
Mishan, Ezra J., 843–844, 848, 877, 881
Missouri Botanical Garden, 89n, 90n, 91n, 95
Mitchell, H. H., 703
Mitchell, I., 565n, 615
Mitchell, J. M., 683n, 684n, 686, 703
Models of Doom, 733
Moggi, L., 500
Moglewer, S., 446n, 506
Molina, M. J., 703
Moll, K. D., 703
Møller, Aage, R., 597n, 617
Molotch, Harvey L., 871n
Monath, T. P., 607n, 617
Moncrief, Lewis W., 810, 881
Montefiore, Hugh, 881
Montgomery, Johnson C., 829n, 837, 881
Moody, Howard, 801
Moon, R. L., 471n, 505
Moore, E. C., 419n, 502
Moore, Gerald, 881
Moore, J. R., 22n, 64
Moore, N. W., 703
Moore, P. D., 664n, 703
Morales, H. L., 368n, 383
Morgan, E. L., 611, 696
Morgan, J. J., 568n, 617
Morgan, Karl Z., 442n, 506, 507, 584n, 586n, 617
Morgan, R. W., 588n, 618
Moriarty, F., 703
Morris, B. F., 657n, 703
Morris, D., 500
Morris, Desmond, 735, 908
Morris, I., 383
Morris, J. R., 482n, 509
Morris, R. F., 153n, 383
Morrison, Peter A., 237n, 246, 751, 752, 801
Morrow, W., 468n, 470n, 507
Morse, F. H., 507
Moskowitz, Milt, 860n
Moss, Elaine, 871n, 881
Moss, W. D., 573n, 619
Mosser, J. L., 639n, 640n, 704
Mostert, Noel, 415n, 507, 814n, 882
Moumoni, Abdou, 507, 932n, 950
Moyers, J., 493n, 505
Moynihan, Daniel P., 907n
Mudd, J. B., 704
Mulla, M. S., 640n, 700, 703
Muller, Mike, 304n, 323n, 383, 950
Müller, R. E., 891n, 945
Mumford, Lewis, 235n, 244
Munawar, M., 696
Munk, Walter, 64
Murdoch, William, W., 140, 174, 401, 402, 610, 871n, 922n, 950
Murozumi, M., 569n, 617
Murphy, C. B., Jr., 667n, 703
Murphy, F. A., 607n, 615
Murphy, F. X., 807n
Murphy, Garth, J., 364n, 383
Murray, C., 260n, 261n, 265n, 266, 267n, 280
Murray, T. J., 696
Murstein, M. C., 758n, 759n, 761n, 797
Myers, Norman, 362n, 383, 771, 772, 773, 801
Myrdal, Alva, 913n, 918n, 950
Myrdal, Gunnar, 901n, 902–903, 933n, 945, 950

Nader, Ralph, 820
Naill, R. F., 507
Namias, Jerome, 61n, 64–65
Nance, D. K., 879
Nash, R. G., 641n, 704
Nathans, D., 609n, 611, 818n, 878
National Academy of Engineering, 895n
National Academy of Sciences (NAS), 6, 64, 174, 274n, 276n, 280, 343, 344n, 352n, 383, 419, 453, 455n, 492, 496n, 507, 508, 525n, 528n, 533, 558n, 565, 567n, 568n, 569n, 575n, 583n, 584, 617, 643n, 653, 657n, 658n, 669n, 674n, 676n, 691n, 704, 764n, 791n, 801, 855–856, 882, 910, 950; National Research Council, 302, 453n, 499, 975n; *Mineral resources and the environment,* 401n, 405n, 413n, 420n; *Air quality and stationary source emission control,* 428n, 429n, 543n, 546n, 547n, 549n, 550, 551n, 610, 661n, 704; *Effects of herbicides in South Vietnam,* 653n, 655n, 704
National Aeronautics and Space Administration (NASA), 477
National Center for Atmospheric Research (NCAR), 678, 683n, 684n, 704
National Clearinghouse for Smoking and Health, 617
National Commission on Materials Policy, 252n, 266n, 268n, 271n, 280, 516–522, 526, 527n, 532, 571n, 619, 623n, 726n
National Council on Radiation Protection and Measurements, 451n, 508
National Environmental Policy Act of 1969, 833n
National Fertility Study, 742–743, 744
National Science Foundation, 465, 477, 508
National Technical Information Service, 472n
National Times, The (Australia), 294n
Natural Resources Defense Council, 453n
Nature, 649n
Natusch, D., 571n, 617
Naumov, A. G., 355n, 382
Neck, R. W., 649n, 696
Neely, B. S., Jr., 695
Nehring, R., 500
Neiburger, Morris, 36n, 39n, 42n, 43n, 45n, 53n, 54n, 55n, 57n, 64
Neifert, R., 469n, 502
Neilands, J. B., 656n, 704
Nelson, L. D., 858n, 881
Nelson, W., 546n, 613
Nephew, E. A., 418n, 419n, 420n, 508
Nepszy, S. J., 667n, 702
Neri, L. C., 556n, 617
Nero, Anthony V., Jr., 439n, 508, 617
Netboy, Anthony, 364n, 383
Newhouse, V. F., 607n, 617
New Internationalist, 294n, 323n, 383, 792, 898n, 906n, 907n, 950
Newland, Kathleen, 345n, 380, 778n, 792, 799, 950, 994n
Newman, J. E., 777n, 778n, 802
Newman, Lucille F., 801
New Scientist, 311n, 365n, 370n, 383, 472n, 617, 652n, 664n, 704, 801, 999n
Newsom, L. Dale, 651n
Newsweek magazine, 233n, 343n, 344n, 365n, 994n
Newton, C. E., 617
Newton, G. C., Jr., 508

Newton, K. G., 617
New Yorker magazine, 294n
New York Times, 294n, 544n, 628n, 647n, 660n, 892n, 894n, 897n, 914n
Nice, M. M., 116
Nichols, J., 434n, 500
Nicholson, Max, 812n, 882
Nickerson, P. R., 636n
Niering, W. A., 157n
Night Hamburg Died, The (Caidin), 690
Nikkanen, J., 570n, 614
Nisbet, I., 476n, 508
Nitze, Paul H., 913n, 950
Nobbs, C. L., 575n, 617
Noble, Reg, 367n, 383
Noller, C. H., 300n, 382
Norback, D. H., 610
Nordberg, G. F., 573n, 611, 617
Nordhaus, William, 845n, 846, 882
Norgaard, R. D., 270n, 280, 860n, 881
Norman, Lloyd H., 913n
Norman, R., 476n, 508
North, Robert C., 908–909, 945, 949
Nortman, Dorothy, 762n, 763n, 767n, 774n, 790n, 801
Norton, J. J., 409n, 508
Norwood, W. D., 617
Nottingham, J., 617
Nove, Alex, 320n, 383
Nuckolls, J., 459n, 460, 502
Nuclear Fuel Services (NFS), 451n
Nuclear News 405n, 439n, 441n, 443n, 447n, 449n, 508, 585n
Nuclear Regulatory Commission, U.S., 444n, 445n, 446n, 455n, 508, 512, 581n, 583n, 584n, 620
Nuorteva, P., 704
Nutritional Sciences, Canadian Bureau of, 302

Oakley, D. T., (Martin and) 507
Oaten, A., 922n, 950
Oberheu, J. C., 646n, 695
O'Brien, John A., 801, 807, 882
O'Brien, R. D., 561n, 617, 633n
O'Brien, Tom, 791, 801, 889, 950
O'Conner, J. A., 664n, 697
Oden, S., 663
Odum, Eugene P., 73n, 76n, 82n, 95, 131n, 133n, 134, 135n, 144, 145n, 160, 172, 691n, 735
Odum, H. T., 383, 508
Odum, W. E., 623n, 704
Office of Emergency Preparedness, U.S., 491, 493n, 494n, 508
Ogilvie, J., 882
O'Hearn, D. L., 627n, 701, 887n
Ohlin, Goran, 780, 801, 901n, 950
Oil and Gas Journal, 416n, 417
Oka, I. N., 348n, 384, 473n, 509, 656n, 669n, 704
Okorafor, Apia E., 801
Okrent, D., 476n, 508
Okun, Arthur M., 846n, 882
Olander, L., 610
Olembo, Reuben, 344
Olkowski, H., 651n, 704
Olkowski, W., 651n, 704
Olson, B., 660n, 704
Olson, J. S., 135
Olson, M., 882
Omran, Dr. Abdel R., 741n, 792n, 801
O'Neill, Gerard K., 821–823, 882
Onrot, J., 620
Ooms, Van Doorn, 904n, 949
Oort, Abraham H., 65
Oosting, H. J., 174
Ophuls, William, 882
Orians, Gordon H., 142n, 174, 656n, 704
ORNL-NSF Environmental Program, 508
Osborn, Fairfield, 6, 178, 536, 731n, 735, 749n, 801
Ostrand, I., 599n
Oswald, W. J., 474n, 484n, 503, 508, 560n, 617
Otani, Ken, 574n, 617
Othman, M. A., 633n, 694
Othmer, D., 479n, 508
Otte, C., 465n, 506
Otterman, Joseph, 681n, 701, 704
Overgaard-Nielsen, C., 640n
Overseas Development Council, 297
Owen, D. F., 290n, 383
Owen, Henry, 857n, 882

Packard, Vance, 752, 801
Paddock, Elizabeth, 924n, 945, 950
Paddock, Paul, 383, 923
Paddock, William C., 332n, 342n, 383, 923, 924n, 945, 950
Page, S., Jr., 850n, 882
Page, T., 557n, 617
Page, Toby, 525n, 533
Pain, B., 348n
Paine, R. T., 141n
Pal, B., 649n, 704
Pal, Yash, 868n
Pallas, F. M., 650n, 703
Pallmann, A. J., 611
Pallotta, A. J., 565n, 615
Pan American Health Organization, 308n, 383
Para Sema, 627n
Parberg, D. G., 664n, 697
Pariser, E. R., 325n, 380
Park, B., 791n, 798
Park, C. F., 528n, 533
Park, J., 121n
Park, O., 173
Park, T., 121n, 173
Park, W., 494n, 503
Parker, B. C., 611, 696
Parker, F., 483n, 508
Parnell, D. R., 97n, 119n, 124n, 172, 576n, 613
Parr, A. E., 606, 617
Parry, T., 270n, 280
Parsons, Cynthia, 868n
Parsons, Jack A., 126n, 801, 873, 874–875, 882
Patel, I. G., 903, 950
Patel, V. M., 768n, 802
Patrick, J. M., Jr., 646n, 695
Patten, B. C., 174
Patterson, Clair C., 569n, 570n, 617
Patterson, Walter C., 508, 882
Paul VI, Pope, 792n, 801
Paulik, G. J., 383
Pauling, L., 71n, 95, 976
Pavlova, E. V., 133n
Payne, Ian, 368n, 383
Payne, Philip R., 302n, 383, 384, 385
Payne, R., 384
Payne, W. J. A., 385
Pazert, W., 354n, 385
Peakall, D. B., 637, 656n, 698, 704
Pearce, P., 660n, 698
Pearlman, N. E., 547n, 619
Pearsall, W. H., 141n
Pearse, A., 947
Pearson, Lester, 885, 950
Pearson, D., 882
Peart, R. M., 650n, 699
Pecan, E. V., 74n, 75n, 76n, 79n, 87n, 94, 95, 132n, 166n, 175, 472n
Peccei, Aurelio, 951
Peck, E., 786n, 801
Peck, H. D., Jr., 89n, 95
Pell, Claiborne, 941n

Pell, E. J., 705
Penman, H., 76n, 95
Penner, J. E., 676n, 702
Pentagon Capitalism (Melman), 918
People magazine, 993n, 994n
Perelman, Michael J., 348n, 384
Perkins, E. J., 617, 705
Perkle, C. I., 564n, 565n, 614
Perlmutter, M., 617
Perloff, H., 878
Perry, A. M., 508, 509
Perry, H., 420n, 421n, 422n, 508
Persson, Reidar, 273n, 279
Pestel, E., 730, 733, 901n, 950
Pesticides and the Living Landscape (Rudd), 854
Peterle, T. J., 634n, 705
Peterman, W. A., 882
Peters, J., 565n, 615
Peterson, F. M., 879
Peterson, M. R., 565n
Peterson, N., 613
Peterson, Russell W., 835
Petipa, T. S., 133n
Petrucelli, L., 565n, 615
Petruzewicz, K., 155n
Peyton, T. O., 675n, 707
Pfeiffer, E. W., 654n, 656n, 704, 705, 708
Phillips, J., 384
Phipps, R., 348n
Pianka, E. R., 106n, 172
Picardi, A. C., 384
Pichirallo, Joe, 562n, 617
Pielou, E. C., 172, 174
Pierce, D. W., 575n, 617
Pierce, J., 496n, 509
Pierce, P., 573n, 612
Pierce, R. S., 624n, 695, 702
Pigeon, R. F., 133n
Pigford, T. H., 419n, 420n, 421n, 429n, 435n, 443n, 449n, 450n, 482n, 484n, 509
Pillay, T. V. R., 366n, 384
Pilpel, Harriet, 801
Pimentel, David, 127n, 174, 285n, 286n, 288n, 348n, 350–351, 384, 473n, 509, 639n, 642n, 656n, 657n, 669n, 704, 705
Pincus, John A., 951
Pindar, 257
Pinthus, M. J., 657n, 705
Pinto, C. R., 941n
Piotrow, Phyllis Tilson, 746n, 791n, 794n, 801
Pirages, Dennis C., 359n, 806n, 828n, 846n, 857n, 869n, 875n, 877, 882, 905n, 944n, 950
Pirie, N. W., 370n, 371n, 384
Planned Parenthood Federation, International (IPPF), 769n, 770n, 791n, 800, 995n, 998n
Planning and Conservation Foundation, 871n, 872n
Plate, Thomas G., 951
Platt, John, 882, 951
Platts, J., 479n
Polacco, J. C., 373n, 374n, 380
Poland, J. F., 263n, 280
Polikarpov, G., 701
Polunin, Nicholas, 618, 705
Pomeroy, L. R., 174
Pontecorvo, G., 122n, 173
Poole, A., 350n, 383, 393n, 396n, 472, 474, 475, 499, 509, 932n, 950
Poole, R. W., 98n, 174
Pope, Carl, 801
Popovic, B., 707
Population Council Inc., The, 766n, 801
Population Reference Bureau (PRB), 181n, 182, 184n, 196, 198, 200n, 201, 204, 205n, 207, 218n, 230n, 244, 250n, 749n, 750n, 761n, 762, 763n, 766n, 774n, 790n, 796, 801, 936n, 951, 959, 963n, 966n
Population Reports, 801, 994n, 996n, 997n, 998n
Porricelli, J. D., 705
Porter, R. D., 705
Portmann, J. E., 630n, 705
Portola Institute, 509
Posner, Charles, 345n, 384
Post, R. F., 458n, 461n, 480n, 482n, 505, 509, 528n, 533, 882
Post, S. F., 482n, 509, 882
Pott, Sir Percival, 587, 618
Potter, G., 624n
Potts, G. R., 637n, 697
Potts, Malcolm, 801
Powell, N. A., 705
Powers, C. D., 639n, 705
Powers, C. F., 136, 667n
Pradervand, Pierre, 792n, 793n, 801
Pratt, W. P., 94, 95, 499, 532
Pravitt, K., 733n
Precoda, Norman, 623, 705
President's Science Advisory Committee, 248, 250, 280, 308n, 618; Panel on the World Food Supply, 290n, 293, 336n, 342n, 368n, 377, 384, 642
Press, Frank, 14n, 18n, 27n, 64, 70n, 95, 412
Pressman, I., 604n, 618
Pressman, J., 618
Preston, R. C., 589n, 612
Preston, S. B., 530n, 533
Price, John H., 506, 950
Priest, Joseph, 670n, 705
Primack, Joel, 509, 882
Prindle, R. A., 620
Prinn, R., 676n, 694
Prout, T., 649n, 698
Prouty, R. M., 695
Pryde, Philip R., 273n, 280
Pugwash Conference on Science and World Affairs, 509, 951
Puro, H. E., 618
Pyke, M., 384

Quarles, John R., 561n, 618
Quinn, W., 354n, 385
Quirk, W. J., 681, 697

Raats, P. A. C., 272n, 280
Raböl, J., 708
Rabson, R., 373n, 379
Radford, E. P., 573n, 611
Radomski, J. L., 565n, 566n, 613, 618
Rajaratnoam, S., 902
Raleigh, C. B., 601n, 614
Rall, David P., 546n, 618
Ramanathan, N. L., 600n, 618
Ramanathan, V., 677n, 705
Ramel, C., 573n, 611
Rampacek, Carl, 429n, 502
Ramseier, R., 415n, 509
Ramsey, James E., 371n, 384
Ramsey, W., 422n, 484n, 485n, 500
Rand, C. T., 951
Rand Corporation, 911
Randers, J., 170n, 730n, 731n, 734, 945
Rangan, Kasturi, 294n
Ransil, Bernard J., 802
Rappaport, Roy A., 625n, 705
Rasmussen, N., 509
Rasool, S. I., 705
Ratcliffe, D. A., 636, 637n, 702, 705

Rathjens, George W., 951
Rattien, S., 502, 509
Raven, P. H., 125n, 129n, 145n, 174
Ravenholt, A., 384
Ravenholt, R. T., 199, 200n, 222–223, 245, 246
Rawlins, S. L., 272n, 280
Ray, P. M., 129n
Razzell, P. E., 190, 246
Record, F., 298n, 302n, 380
Record, R. G., 190, 192n, 193n, 194, 195, 246
Read, W., 469n, 509
Rechel, W. L., 635n, 707
Reck, R. A., 677n, 705
Redmond, C. K., 600n, 618
Reed, C. A., 185n, 246
Reed, Roy, 237n, 753n, 802
Reeves, A. L., 618
Reeves, E., 260n, 261n, 265n, 266, 267n, 280
Reich, M., 574n, 609
Reichle, D. E., 93n, 95, 146n, 174
Reichstein, T., 126n
Reidinger, R., Jr., 637n, 705
Reifschneider, D., 285n, 384, 656n, 705
Reiger, George, 358n, 367n, 369n, 384
Reilly, Conor, 942n, 951
Reinert, Robert E., 630n, 705
Reiser, D. B., 509
Reitz, L. P., 344n, 380, 384
Remsen, C. C., 640n, 698
Renault, Mary, 874
Renshaw, E. F., 951
Resnikoff, Marvin, 451n, 504, 509
Resources for the Future, 261, 509, 859n, 882
ReVelle, C., 557n, 567n, 571n, 573n, 596n, 610
Revelle, P., 557n, 567n, 571n, 573n, 596n, 610
Revelle, Roger, 269n, 271n, 280, 384, 509, 705, 719n, 728n, 735, 796, 837n
Rey, A., 565n, 618
Reynolds, R. T., 707
Reynolds, W. C., 425n, 437n, 509
Rheingold, P. G., 881
Rhykerd, C. L., 300n, 382
Ribe, F. L., 458n, 480n, 509
Ribicoff, Abraham A., 916n, 951
Rice, R. C., 613
Rice, Richard, 495n, 497, 509
Rice, W., 458n, 461n, 504
Rich, P. H., 166n
Rich, William, 789n, 793n, 802
Richards, P. W., 174, 626n
Richardson, H., 589n, 613
Richardson, John, 925n, 944
Richardson, S. A., 311n, 313n, 381
Richardson, S. D., 280
Ricker, William E., 352n, 353n, 369n, 384
Ricklefs, R. E., 98n, 172
Rider, M. W., 879
Riding, Alan, 892n
Ridker, Ronald G., 261n, 269n, 270n, 281, 533, 785, 802
Rieber, Michael, 428, 509
Rinehart, Ward, 802, 998n
Risebrough, R. W., 630n, 632n, 634n, 637n, 695, 705, 706
Road to Survival (Vogt), 642
Robbins, R. C., 85n
Roberts, E. B., 476n, 504
Robertson, A., 136, 667n
Robinson, Alan S., 649n, 706
Robinson, Clarence A., Jr., 655n
Robinson, E., 85n
Robinson, G. D., 703
Robinson, J., 637n, 697
Robinson, J. P. Perry, 917n, 951
Robinson, R. Q., 607n, 615
Robinson, Sir Robert, 630
Roblin, R., 609n, 611, 818n, 878
Rochereau, S., 285n, 384, 656n, 705
Rochlin, G. I., 452n, 509
Roddewig, R., 841n, 882
Rodin, L. E., 74n, 76n, 95, 132n, 174, 249n
Roe, Frank G., 706
Roelofs, Wendell, 650n, 706
Roels, O., 479n, 508
Rojko, Anthony S., 327n
Rolfe, G. L., 661n, 695
Rona, P. A., 17, 523n, 533
Ronning, M., 289n, 380
Roosevelt, Theodore, 930
Rosató, P., 638n, 706
Rose, D. J., 442n, 452n, 458n, 506, 509
Rose, H. A., 654n
Rose, H. M., 245
Rose, S. P. R., 654n
Rose, William M., 951
Rosenau, D. G., 696
Rosenberg, J. S., 841n, 882
Rosenfield, D., 379
Rosenzweig, M. R., 312n, 384
Rosier, Bernard, 304, 380
Ross, Marc, 491, 492n, 509
Rossman, E. C., 343n, 379
Rosso, A. J., 587n, 614
Rostovsteff, Mikhail, 873n, 882
Rothschild, Emma, 322n, 378, 951
Rothschild, M., 126n
Rotty, R. M., 509
Roughgarden, Jonathan, 98n, 106n, 140–141, 172, 634n, 706
Rounsefell, G. A., 352n, 384
Routley, R., 273n, 281
Routley, V., 273n, 281
Rowland, F. S., 703
Rowland, R. G., 639n, 705
Roy, Robin, 814n, 951
Rozov, N. N., 74n, 76n, 95, 132n, 174, 249n
Rubey, W. W., 601n, 614
Rubin, B., 422n, 484n, 485n, 500
Rubin, H., 592n, 618
Rubin, M., 494n, 510
Rucker, N., 588n, 610
Rudd, Robert L., 642, 694, 706, 854
Ruedisili, L. C., 510, 932n
Rukeyser, William S., 668n, 706
Rush, H. W., 600n, 618
Russell, Bertrand, 811–812, 882
Russell, Richard, 910
Russett, Bruce M., 787n, 802
Ruthenberg, H., 329n, 384
Ruttan, V. W., 252n, 253n, 254n, 255n, 276n, 279, 286n, 382
Ryan, J. W., 502
Ryan, R. G., 657n, 706
Ryder, Norman B., 753n, 802
Ryther, John H., 352, 353, 367, 379, 384

Sabloff, J., 706
Sachs, D. P., 597n, 618
Sacks, S. T., 611
Saenger, G., 385
Sahlins, Marshall, 875n, 882
Sakharov, Andrei D., 925, 951
Salam, Abdus, 902, 942n, 951
Saleem, L. A., 661n, 697
Salisbury, G. W., 802
Samis, R., 285n, 384, 656n, 705
Sampson, Anthony, 951
Samuelson, Paul A., 843, 845, 883

Sanchez, P., 253n, 281, 345n, 384, 626n, 706
Sander, J., 618
Sanders, H. J., 578n, 579n, 618
Sanders, Herman O., 630n, 656n, 706
Sanders, Sol, 951
Sands, M., 15n
San Francisco Chronicle, 239n
Sarkanen, K. V., 527n, 528n, 533
Saulter, Kenneth, 879
Savage, E. P., 561n, 618
Sayce, C. S., 705
Schaeffer, M. B., 384
Schapiro, S., 312n, 384
Scheffer, Victor B., 355n, 356n, 361n, 362–363, 384
Scheinman, L., 503
Schell, W. R., 672n, 706
Schelling, Thomas C., 951
Scherer, H. N., 510
Schery, R. W., 252n, 253n, 254n, 255n, 276n, 279, 286n, 382
Schild, G., 618
Schipper, Lee, 396n, 483n, 491n, 493n, 497n, 498n, 500, 510, 533, 841, 883
Schlesinger, James R., 910
Schlessinger, B., 504
Schlossberg, Kenneth, 316n, 384
Schmeltz, I., 552n, 618
Schmidt, F., 618
Schmidt, K. P., 173
Schmidt, T. T., 635n, 706
Schneider, Stephen H., 47n, 59n, 61n, 62n, 64, 65, 321n, 346, 347, 378, 673n, 679n, 681n, 682n, 683n, 686, 687n, 688n, 689n, 694, 701, 705, 706, 819, 883, 943n, 944, 945
Schneider, William, Jr., 897n, 951
Schnell, G. A., 245
Schoen, R., 468n, 510
Schofield, C. L., 662n, 706
Schreiber, G. B., 556n, 617
Schroeder, H. A., 568n, 618
Schroeder, Richard C., 753n, 763n, 802
Schroll, Henning, 302n
Schuck, P. H., 618
Schultz, K. R., 702
Schultz, V., 706
Schultze, Charles, 857n, 882
Schumacher, E. F., 510, 845n, 852–853, 876n, 877, 893n, 931, 945
Schurgin, A., 503
Schwartz, H., 607n, 618
Schwartz, Herman, 802
Schweinfurth, S. P., 401n, 404n, 418n, 511
Science, 317n, 374n, 384, 473n, 802, 825
Science and Public Policy Program, 421n, 463n, 464, 465n, 472n, 474n, 476n, 477n, 480n, 482n
Scientific American, 510, 586n, 667n, 868n
Scott, A., 380
Scott, J. M., 706
Scotto, J., 706
Scoville, Herbert, 706
Scrimshaw, N. S., 300n, 384, 614
Seaborg, G. T., 510
Sears, Paul, 706
Sebald, A., 504
Sechler, S., 321n, 380
Seckler, David W., 846n, 877
Sedlak, V., 573n, 612
Segal, Sheldon J., 802, 988n
Seiberling, John F., 918
Seif, F., 618
Seifert, W. W., 384
Selander, R. K., 124n
Selikoff, I. J., 588n, 600n, 618
Seliskar, C. E., 698
Sellers, William D., 65, 411n, 510, 706
Selzer, L., 448n
Senderowitz, J., 786n, 801
Serat, W., 632n, 697
Serling, Robert J., 883
Seshachar, B. R., 149n, 706
Seskin, E., 546n, 549n, 615
Sesonshe, A., 437n, 503
Sessions, George S., 811n, 812n, 883
Sessler, G., 419n, 420n, 421n, 429n, 449n, 482n, 484n, 509
Setzer, H. W., 607n, 617
Severson, J. G., Jr., 91n
Sewell, J. W., 888n, 949, 951
Sewell, W., 270n, 281
Seymour, A. H., 706
Shackleton, N. J., 687n, 699
Shaffer, M. L., 623n, 707
Shakespeare, William, 542
Shalita, Ronald, 802, 998n
Shapley, Deborah, 365, 385, 455n, 510, 706, 941n, 951
Sharitz, R., 670n, 698, 699
Shaw, D. T., 695
Shaw, E. A. G., 610
Shawer, M. F., 633n, 694
Shea, Kevin P., 567n, 618, 644, 645, 647n, 706
Shearer, G. B., 701
Sheets, H., 383
Shelford, V. E., 135
Shell, W. R., 706
Shepard, M., 285n, 384, 656n, 705
Shepard, P., 706
Shepherd, Jack, 323n
Sheridan, David, 879
Sherman, William, 594n
Sherrill, Robert, 316n, 385
Sherwood, Martin J., 951
Shettigara, P. T., 588n, 618
Shoemaker, W. J., 385
Shohori, Y., 657n, 705
Sholes, O. D., 348n, 384, 473n, 509, 669n
Short, R. V., 802, 997n
Shubeck, P., 589n, 616
Shubik, Dr. Philippe, 596
Shults, W., 571n, 572n, 573n, 620
Shurcliff, W. A., 510
Shure, D. J., 657n, 706
Shy, C. M., 547n, 618
Siccama, T., 624n, 695
Siegfried, W. R., 623n, 698
Sierra Club Bulletin, 841n, 883
Sidel, R., 771n, 772n, 773, 802
Sidel, V. W., 771n, 772n, 773, 802
Siever, Raymond, 14n, 18n, 27n, 64, 65, 70n, 95, 412
Sigurdson, Tom, 668n, 942n, 951
Silent Spring (Carson), 563, 854
Silverman, L. P., 506, 615
Simberloff, D. S., 174
Simeone, J. B., 175
Simmons, M. K., 499, 507
Simon, N., 115n, 142n, 698, 706
Simons, T. J., 696
Simpson, D. I. H., 618
Simpson, G. G., 174
Simpson, R. L., 657n
Simrad Echo (Norway), 363
Singer, J. D., 951
Singer, M., 115n, 119n
Singer, S. F., 85n, 95, 403n, 510, 707
Singh, H. B., 675n, 707
Singh, Karan, 768
Singh, Kushwant, 294n, 923n
Sinsheimer, Robert, 818, 883
Sioli, Harold, 626n, 707

Sivard, Ruth L., 918n, 951
Skerfving, S., 573n, 611
Skinner, B. F., 883
Skinner, Brian J., 22n, 65, 525n, 534
Sklar, J., 212, 246, 757n, 802
Sladen, W. T. L., 635n, 707
Slesser, M., 385
Slobodkin, L. B., 174, 639, 707
Sly, P. G., 696
Smagorinsky, J., 707
Small Is Beautiful (Schumacher), 852–853, 876
Smil, Vaclav, 930n, 951
Smith, Adam, 859
Smith, B. A., 656n, 705
Smith, C., 510
Smith, C. E. G., 618
Smith, E. A., 285n, 384
Smith, Frank Austin, 525n, 534
Smith, H. H., 175
Smith, J., 431n, 506
Smith, J. W., 707
Smith, K., 421n, 429n, 510
Smith, R. G., 573n, 611, 618
Smith, R. H., 649n, 707
Smith, Ray F., 643, 644n, 707
Smith, W. H., 572n, 618, 661n, 707
Smulyan, M., 502
Snell, F. M., 684n, 708
Snow, D. B., 608n, 615
Snow, Edgar, 763n, 802
Snow, Lord C. P., 923, 925
Snyder, H. A., 707
Snyder, N. F., 707
Sobsey, M. D., 559n, 618
Socolow, Robert H., 271n, 279, 433n, 504, 510
Södergren, A., 708
Solheim, Wilhelm G., 185n
Solomon, M. E., 701
Sommer, John G., 904n, 925n, 951
Sommer, Robert, 602n, 619
Sondheimer, E., 175
Sørenson, B., 477n, 510
Soulé, M., 73n, 94, 129n
Southwood, T. R. E., 175
Sparks, R. E., 611, 612, 619, 696, 707
Sparn, J. W., 700
Spengler, Joseph J., 716n, 735, 748, 802, 883
Speth, J. G., 456n, 510
Spingarn, N. E., 616
Spinrad, B., 438n, 510
Spore, R. L., 419n, 508
Sprague, G. F., 339n, 340n, 350n, 385
Springell, Peter, 951
Sprott, E. R., 380, 629n, 696
Sprout, H., 951
Sprout, M., 951
Spruger, P. T., 696
Spurgeon, D., 374n, 382
Spurr, S. H., 175, 272n, 281
Squires, A. M., 421n, 429n, 500, 510, 527n, 533
Stanford, G., 668n, 707
Stanford Biology Study Group, 653n, 707
Stanier, R. Y., 72n, 82n
Stanley-Miller, J., 507
Stansbury, Jeff, 560n
Stanton, W. R., 385
Staples, J., 832n, 880
Starr, C., 462n, 504
Stauffer, T., 510, 894n, 952
Stauls, W. J., 385
Stavrianos, L. S., 952
Steadman, P., 467n, 468n, 474n, 477n, 493n, 500
Stebbins, G. L., 173, 175
Stecker, Paul G., 619
Steele, J. H., 133n
Stein, J., 468n, 510
Stein, L., 658n
Stein, P. C., 573n, 619
Stein, R., 493n, 510
Stein, Z., 312n, 385
Steiner, G. A., 610
Steinhart, C., 348n, 349, 385, 473n, 500, 510, 859n, 860n, 883
Steinhart, J., 348n, 349, 385, 473n, 500, 510, 859n, 860n
Steinhauer, W. G., 630n, 699
Steneck, N. H., 883
Stephenson, A., 163n
Stephenson, T. A., 163n
Stern, V. M., 651n
Steubing, L., 146n
Stewart, R. J., 510
Stewart, R. W., 26n, 65
Stiskin, N., 574n, 609
Stockholm International Peace Research Institute (SIPRI), 707, 814n, 883, 911n, 912, 913n, 952
Stoewsand, G., 660n, 707
Stokes, Bruce, 354, 380, 798, 936, 946
Stokes, S. L., 608n, 615
Stolarski, S., 697
Stolnitz, George J., 952
Stoltz, D. R., 578, 579n, 619
Stone, Christopher D., 834n, 835, 877, 895, 952
Stone, P. H., 681, 697
Stone, Tabor R., 883
Stonier, Tom, 707
Storch, R. L., 705
Strahler, A. H., 13n, 14n, 27n, 30n, 31n, 56n, 62n, 64, 254n, 255n, 257n, 260n, 263n, 281
Strahler, A. N., 13n, 14n, 17n, 30n, 31n, 56n, 62n, 64, 254n, 255n, 257n, 260n, 263n, 281
Strauss, W., 664n, 697
Streuver, Stuart, 286n, 385
Strong, C. L., 662, 707
Strong, Maurice, 942n, 952
Stroud, R. H., 166n
Stroup, E., 354n, 385
Stryer, Lubert, 94
Study of Critical Environmental Problems (SCEP), 65, 89n, 95, 658n, 666n, 667n, 673n, 694, 707, 728n
Study of Man's Impact on Climate (SMIC), 30n, 43n, 58n, 59n, 62n, 63n, 65, 69n, 95, 260n, 281, 677n, 681n, 682n, 683, 684n, 685n, 707
Stycos, J. Mayone, 791n, 793n, 802
Suess, H. E., 705
Sukhatme, P. V., 385
Sulkin, S. E., 607n, 608n, 614
Sullivan, A. L., 623n, 707
Sullivan, W., 658n
Summers, C., 424, 425n, 510
Susser, M., 385
Suttmeier, R. P., 810n
Sutton, A., 372n, 382
Suzuki, T., 573n, 611
Swartz, L. G., 696
Sweezy, Alan, 212n, 245, 246, 748, 778n, 781n, 782, 786, 792, 798, 802
Swensson, A., 573n, 611
Swift, J. E., 707
Sze, N. D., 709
Szego, G., 474n, 510

Taeuber, Conrad, 749n, 791n, 802
Tait, R. V., 172
Tames, P., 504
Tamm, C. O., 662n, 707

Tamplin, A. R., 443n, 455n, 456n, 503, 510, 586n, 614, 619
Tanesini, Arturo, 816n
Tank, R. W., 280
Tanner, J. T., 572n, 619
Tanner, James, T., 186n
TANSTAAFL: The Economic Strategy for Environmental Crisis (Dolan), 846
Tantawg, G., 633n, 694
Tanton, John H., 234n, 246
Tardiff, R., 557n, 619
Tatum, L. A., 343, 385
Taylor, A., 668, 707
Taylor C. E., 777n, 778n, 802
Taylor, T. B., 453n, 454n, 455n, 462n, 502, 510, 511
Technology Review, 385
Techoff, E. M., 280
Teitelbaum, Michael S., 193n, 244, 781n, 791, 793–794, 796, 802
Tejning, S., 573n, 611
Temkin, R. L., 684n, 708
Teng, T., 639n, 640n, 704
Tepley, Lee, 622
Terborgh, J., 157n
Terhune, E. C., 285n, 384, 656n, 705
Terry, Geraldine B., 802
Tessari, J. D., 561n, 562n, 618
Thakor, V. H., 768n, 802
Thayer, George, 919–920, 952
Theobald, P. K., 401n, 404n, 418n, 511
This Endangered Planet (Falk), 940
Thomas, M. O., 133n
Thomas, R. L., 696
Thomas, W. A., 707
Thomas, William L., Jr., 707
Thompson, Louis M., 327, 346–347, 385
Thompson, R. C., 455n, 500, 586n, 619
Thompson, W. S., 204, 244
Thorndike, E. H., 511
Thrailkill, R. B., 697
Tietze, Christopher, 755n, 758n, 759n, 761n, 797, 802
Tilles, H., 652n, 697
Time magazine, 225, 234n, 285n, 294n, 320n, 321n, 365n, 579n, 627, 752, 887n, 895n, 896n, 907n, 952, 994n
Tinker, Jon, 343n, 552n, 553n, 619, 707, 767n, 803, 899n, 902–903, 952
Tizard, J., 311n, 313n, 381
Tobin, James, 845n, 846, 882
Todd, John, 883
Todd, W. M., 932n, 948
Toeplitz, R., 558n, 614, 699
Tomlinson, P., 620
Topping, G., 619
Total Environmental Action, 511
Toulmin, S. E., 883
Toyama, T., 547n, 615
Toynbee, Arnold, 715
Train, Russell E., 883
Travers, W. B., 657n, 707
Treitel, R., 501
Trenbath, R. B., 346n
Trescher, W. H., 756n, 797
Treshow, M., 664n, 699
Trexler, Richard, 191n
Trijonis, John, 549n, 619
Triplett, G. B., Jr., 656n, 708
Truhaut, R., 573n, 611
Trujillo, P., 573n, 619
Trump, C. G., 561n, 619
Trump, R. P., 422n, 423n, 504
Tseng, W. P., 588n, 619
Tsipis, Kosta, 911n, 952
Tuan, Yi-Fu, 810, 883
Tucker, A., 708
Tucker, J. H., 612
Tucker, Robert W., 896n, 909n, 952
Tuckwell, Sue, 759n, 803
Tudge, Colin, 371n, 385
Tufts, D. F., 705
Tugwell, R. G., 857, 883
Tunney, John, 883
Turner, B. L., II, 626n, 708
Turner, C. B., 798
Turner, F. B., 672n, 708
Turner, Frederick J., 811, 883
Turner, J. S., 579n, 619
Tybout, R., 467n, 511

Udall, Stewart L., 786, 803, 883
Uglow, R. F., 702
Ui, Jun, 563n, 574n, 617, 619
Ulberg, L. C., 589n, 612
Ulfstrand, S., 708
Ullard, B. M., 565n, 615
Ullman, John E., 866n, 883
Unesco Courier, 766n, 803
United Nations, 181n, 198, 199n, 200, 201, 202, 206, 209n, 218n, 222–227, 228, 230, 231, 237n, 238n, 240n, 241n, 244, 246, 250n, 291, 292, 293n, 294n, 298, 299n, 303n, 305, 308–309, 313, 315n, 317n, 326, 327, 328n, 332n, 339n, 363n, 378, 385, 393n, 395, 422n, 511, 534, 717n, 791n, 793n,794n, 803, 929n, 952, 959, 963, 968–972; Scientific Committee on the Effects of Atomic Radiation (UNSCEAR), 583n, 619; World Food Conference, 970n 971n, 972n. *See also* Food and Agriculture Organization of the United Nations (FAO)
United Press International, 322n
United States, Arms Control and Disarmament Agency, 911n, 952
  Bureau of the Census, 192n, 207, 210n, 212, 215, 221, 222n, 233n, 235–237, 246, 339n, 744n, 747n, 803, 959, 963n
  Bureau of Mines, 396, 472, 525, 527n, 532
Commission on Population Growth and the American Future, 735, 744, 748, 751, 756, 797
Congress, 511, 512, 534
Council on International Economic Policy, 534
Department of Agriculture, 250n, 257, 281, 294, 295, 296, 297n, 319n, 320n, 321, 326, 327, 328n, 330, 331, 346, 347, 385, 651n, 708, 972n; Economic Research Service, 293n, 385
Department of Commerce, 89n, 95, 181n, 227n, 251n, 252n, 281, 364n, 385, 393n, 397n, 426, 466n, 512, 534, 574, 720n, 721n, 929n
Department of Defense, 655
Department of Health, Education and Welfare (HEW), 545n, 583n, 588n, 619
Department of Housing and Urban Development (HUD), 880, 883
Department of the Interior, 414n, 476n, 512, 534
Department of State, 233, 895n
Department of Transportation, Climatic Impact Assessment Program (CIAP), 674
Federal Water Pollution Control Admininstration, 619
General Accounting Office, 448, 455
General Services Administration, 585n, 619

Geological Survey, 261, 268, 409–410, 660
National Center for Health Statistics (USNCHS), 112–114, 181n, 184n, 212n, 276
National Commission on Supplies and Shortages, 532
National Committee for the International Biological Program, 94, 95
National Committee of the World Energy Conference, 408n, 512
National Council on Radiation Protection and Measurements, 619
National Fertility Study, 212
Office of Education, 829n
Public Health Service (USPHS), 316, 557, 573, 638
Soil Conservation Service, 255n
Water Resources Council, 281
See also specific governmental units by name

Urbach, F., 706
Urlanis, Boris, 754n, 803
U.S. News & World Report, 890n

Usher, M. B., 175

Vacca, Roberto, 805, 883
Valerier, M. G., 565n, 615
Valéry, Paul, 181
Vallentyne, J. R., 620, 708
van den Bosch, Robert, 643, 644, 645, 646, 651, 708
van den Vrie, M., 634n, 700, 702
van der Leeden, Frits, 620
Van der Schalie, Henry, 900n, 952
van Doren, D. M., Jr., 656n, 708
Van Dyne, G. M., 175
Van Emden, H. F., 140
Van Gelder, G., 570n, 612
Van Hylckama, T., 260n, 263n, 271n
Van Loon, J. C., 695
van Marthens, E., 311n, 385
Van Oberbeek, J., 652n
Vaughan, Paul, 994n
Vayda, A. P., 290n, 382, 625n, 708
Vennema, A., 656n, 704
Vermeer, Donald E., 952
Vernberg, F. J., 708
Vernberg, W. B., 708
Vetz, G., 142n
Viets, Frank G., Jr., 666n, 708
Vijayakumar, A., 635n, 660n, 695
Vincent J., 115n, 142n, 698
Vink, A. P. A., 281
Viorst, Milton, 766n, 803, 808n, 883
Visaria, P., 768n, 777n, 803
Voeller, K., 570n, 612
Voevodsky, John, 952
Vogt, William, 642, 731n, 735
von Borstel, R. C., 649n, 707
von Hippel, Frank, 446n, 462n, 494n, 509, 512, 882
von Humboldt, Alexander, 272
Vonnegut, B., 695
Vonnegut, Kurt, 690n
Vostal, J. J., 573n, 611, 708
Vukovich, K. R., 312n, 384
Vumbaco, Brenda, 754n, 763n, 769n, 803

Wade, Nicholas, 324n, 325n, 332n, 345n, 378, 385, 473n, 589, 590n, 607n, 620, 818n, 883
Wadia, A. B., 768n, 777n, 803
Wagar, J. Alan, 883
Wagner, J. C., 620
Waldheim, Kurt, 907
Waldichuk, M., 661n
Waldron, H. A., 570n, 611
Walford, Cornelius, 187, 188, 246
Walker, W., II, 635n, 706
Wallace, J., 571n, 617
Wallace, Patricia, 312n, 385
Wallace, R. A., 571n, 572n, 572n, 573n, 620
Walleave, L., 589n, 616
Waller, W. T., 611, 612, 696
Wallis, C., 613
Ward, Barbara, 735, 897n, 941n, 952
Ware, B. J., 510
Warnick, S. L., 562n, 620
War on Hunger, 746n, 803
Warren, Charles E., 620, 708, 835n
Warren, K. S., 608n, 620
WASH reports, 445, 453n, 455n, 511
Washington, Booker T., 930
Washington, W. M., 708
Washington Post Service, 366n
Wasserman, A. E., 620
Wasserman, Larry Paul, 708
Wassermann, D., 620
Wassermann, M., 566n, 620
Watanabe, Masao, 810n, 883
Waterbolk, H. T., 246
Waterlow, J. C., 302n, 385
Water Pollution Control Commission, Federal, 667n
Water Resources Council, 271n
Waters, S., 697
Watson, A., 175
Watson, J. D., 73n, 95, 576n, 609n 611, 620, 818n, 878
Watson, M., 448n
Watson, N. H. F., 696
Watson, W. B., 766n 767n, 769n, 803
Watt, Bernice K., 972n
Watt, K. E. F., 120n, 121n, 173, 285n, 385, 608n, 620, 643, 877
Watters, R. L., 672n, 706
Way, M. J., 707
Waybrant, R. C., 630n, 699
Weare, B. C. 684n, 708
Weast, R. C., 581n, 582n, 620
Weatherald, R. T., 685n, 703
Weatherwax, J. R., 509, 563n, 613
Weaver, L., 502
Webb, Walter P., 189, 229n, 246, 874n, 883
Webster's Third New International Dictionary, 541n
Weichart, G., 620
Weinberg, Alvin M., 508, 528n, 533, 678, 708, 851n, 879, 927
Weiner, A. J., 701
Weiner, Myron, 803
Weingart, J., 468n, 471n, 510
Weinraub, Bernard, 294n
Weinstock, Edward, 756n, 803
Weir, John, 533
Weisberg, Barry, 708
Weisbord, Robert G., 750n, 803
Weish, P., 620
Weiss, Edith Brown, 708
Weiss, H. V., 571n, 572n, 620
Weisskopf, Victor, A., 846n
Weisskopf, Walter, 884
Weissman, S., 609n, 611, 818n, 878
Weller, J. M., 175
Wellford, H., 618
Wellhausen, E. J., 385
Wendland, W. M., 684n, 685n, 696
Wenk, Edward, Jr., 22n, 65, 728n, 941n, 952
Went, F. W., 385
Werth, G., 422n, 484n, 485n, 500
West, Barbara, 245, 798
West, G., 660n

Westing, A. H., 654n, 655n, 656n, 697, 708
Westlake, G. F., 611, 696
Westman, Walter E., 852, 884
Westoff, Charles F., 211, 215n, 217, 244, 742n, 743, 744n, 750n, 798, 803, 993n
Westoff, Leslie A., 743n, 750n, 786n, 803, 993n
Westöö, G., 708
Weyant, J., 421n, 429n, 510
Wharton, C. R., Jr., 385
Wheeler, E., 384
Wheeler, H. W., 561n, 562n, 618
Wheeler, Harvey, 884
Wheeler, Judith A., 237n, 246
Whicher, F. W., 671n, 708
White, C. M., 696
White, D. B., 660n, 699
White, D. C., 894n, 946
White, D. E., 410n
White, E. H., 620
White, Lynn, Jr., 809–810, 884
White, R., 115n, 119n
Whiteside, Thomas, 708
Whitfield, S. G., 607n, 615
Whiting, R. L., 413n, 500
Whitman, R., 348n, 384, 473n, 509, 669n
Whittaker, R. H. 74n, 75n, 76n, 93n, 95, 132n, 144, 157n, 173, 175, 472n, 671n, 709
Whitten, Jamie L., 708
Whitten, M. J., 649n, 698, 704
Whittier, G., 701
Whyte, William H., 870n
Wicker, F., 706
Widmer, T., 494n, 504
Widstrand, Carl Gösta, 708
Wiemeyer, S. N., 705
Wiener, A. J., 881
Wiens, J. H., 706
Wigglesworth, V. B., 150n, 708
Wiklander, G., 707
Wilde, Jan de, 708
Wilkniss, P. E., 572n
Willanston, Kim, 913n
Willcox, W. F., 195n
Williams, C. N., 626n, 709
Williams, Carroll M., 650, 709
Williams, D. L., 410n
Williams, E. J., 892n, 952
Williams, Edward R., 857n, 880
Williams, G., 385
Williams, G. F., 141
Williams, J. D. H., 696
Williams, J. R., 466n
Williams, R., 354n, 385
Williams, R. J., 385
Williams, Robert, 491n, 492n, 494n, 509, 879
Williamson, M. H., 175
Willie, Charles V., 803
Willing, Martha Kent, 803
Willrich, Manson, 454n, 455n, 462n
Wilsher, Peter, 242n
Wilson, A. J., Jr., 646n, 695
Wilson, A. T., 709
Wilson, E. O., 98n, 116n, 175, 981
Wilson, H., 640n, 700
Wilson, J. Tuzo, 17n, 65
Wilson, R., 415n
Winell, Margareta, 599n, 600n, 620
Wingate, D. B., 709
Wingo, Lowdon, 847n, 884
Winick, M., 313n, 385
Winkelstein, W., 549n, 620
Wirken, Melanie, 234n
Wite, J. M., 561n, 612
Witherspoon, J. P., 502
Wittwer, S. H., 323n, 352n, 385
Wofsy, S. C., 675n, 676n, 702, 709
Wogan, G. N., 620
Wolf, L. L., 140n, 174
Wolff, H. H., 589n, 613
Wolff, I. A., 620
Wolff, Tony, 373n, 385
Wolkenhaner, W., 452n
Wollman, N., 269n, 270n, 281
Wolman, M. G., 623n, 696
Wolverton, Bill, 669n
Wong, C. S., 657n, 709
Wong, Y. C., 617
Wood, H. Curtis, Jr., 803
Wood, J. M., 568n, 620
Wood, L., 459n, 460, 502
Wood, N., 274n, 276n, 281
Woodcock, John, 813n, 884
Woods, F. W., 252n, 253n, 254n, 255n, 276n, 279, 286n, 382
Woods, L. H., Jr., 637n, 695
Woodson, R., 484n
Woodward, Herbert, 884
Woodwell, George M., 65, 74n, 75n, 76n, 79n, 87n, 94, 95, 131n, 132n, 138, 139, 141, 166n, 175, 472n, 621, 631, 632n, 634, 671n, 672n, 691n, 694, 709
Wooley, M., 479n
Woolson, E. H., 641n, 704
Work, T. H., 607n, 608n, 614
World Bank. *See Atlas* report
World Food Council, 328
World Health Organization, 575n, 620, 741n, 803
Worldwatch Institute, 199, 295, 318
Worthing, C. R., 703
Wortman, Judith, 803, 992n, 996n
Wortman, Sterling, 281, 323n, 328n, 339n, 378, 772n
Wray, J. D., 380, 735, 771n, 772, 778n, 803, 837n
Wright, D. A., 664n, 709
Wright, F. J., 892n, 952
Wright, G., 620
Wright, H. E., 142n, 185n, 246
Wright, J. K., 280
Wright, Quinsy, 952
Wrigley, E. A., 190n, 246
Wuliger, Robert, 709
Wurster, Charles F., 138, 639, 640, 698, 704, 705, 709
Wurtman, R. J., 385
Wyllie, Peter, J., 65
Wynder, E. L., 552n, 618
Wyon, J. B., 777n
Wyrtki, K., 354n, 385

Yadiaroglu, G., 448n
Yamasaki, E., 588n, 592n, 595n, 610, 615, 616
Yarwood, C. E., 385
Yefron, K. M., 260n, 280
Yeh, Shu, 588n, 619
Yellin, J., 446n
Yellot, J. I., 466n
York, Herbert F., 914n, 946, 952
Yoshida, O., 611
Young, Gale, 271n, 281
Young, H., 481n
Young, J. Z., 246
Young, L., 481n

Young, M. M., 547n, 619
Young, V. R., 300n, 384
Yung, Y. L., 675n, 702

Zajonc, R. B., 719n, 735, 837n
Zamenhof, S., 311n, 385
Zanetti, L., 758n, 803
Zare, R. N., 436n
Zeckhauser, Richard, 884, 893n, 952
Zeidberg, L. D., 620
Zelitch, Israel, 374n, 385
Zellermazer, L., 566n, 620
Zener, C., 479n
Zimmerman, David R., 143n
Zimmerman, M. B., 894n, 946
Zimmerman, Margot, 753n, 758n, 803
Zind, R. G., 799
Zinder, N. D., 609n, 611, 818n, 878
Zlotnik, I., 618
Zohary, D., 381

Abbreviations and Acronyms

ABM antiballistic missile
ACDA Arms Control and Disarmament Agency (U.S.)
ACLU American Civil Liberties Union
AEC Atomic Energy Commission (U.S.)
AID Agency for International Development (U.S.)
AMA American Medical Association
APS American Physical Society
ATP adenosine triphosphate
bbl barrel
BHC benzene hexachloride
BHP biological hazard potential
BOD biochemical oxygen demand
Btu British thermal unit
BWR boiling water reactor
bwu blue whale unit
C Celsius
CAB Civil Aeronautics Board (U.S.)
cal calorie
CBW chemical & biological warfare
CEP circular error probability
CEQ Council on Environmental Quality (U.S.)
CIA Central Intelligence Agency (U.S.)
CIAT International Center for Tropical Agriculture
CIMMYT International Maize and Wheat Improvement Center
cm centimeter
CWP coal workers' pneumoconiosis
D deuterium
DC developed country
DDD dichloro-diphenyl-dichloroethane
DDE dichloro-diphenyl-dichloroethylene
DDT dichloro-diphenyl-trichloroethane
DOD Department of Defense (U.S.)
DOI Department of Interior (U.S.)
DOT Department of Transportation (U.S.)
ECCS emergency core cooling system
EDF Environmental Defense Fund
EEC European Economic Community
EIS environmental impact statement
EPA Environmental Protection Agency (U.S.)
ERDA Energy Research and Development Administration (U.S.)
F Fahrenheit
FAO United Nations Food and Agriculture Organization
FCC Federal Communications Commission (U.S.)
FDA Food and Drug Administration (U.S.)
FEA Federal Energy Administration (U.S.)
FOE Friends of the Earth
FPC Federal Power Commission (U.S.)
FPC fish protein concentrate
FWPCA Federal Water Pollution Control Administration (U.S.)
g gram
GNP gross national product
GPP gross primary production
HCB hexachlorobenzene
HEW Department of Health, Education and Welfare (U.S.)
HTGR high temperature gas reactor
HUD Department of Housing and Urban Development (U.S.)
HWR heavy water reactor
HYV high yielding varieties
IAEA International Atomic Energy Agency
ICRP International Commission on Radiological Protection
IEA International Energy Agency
IFAD International Fund for Agricultural Development
IITA International Institute for Tropical Agriculture
ILO International Labor Organization
IMCO Intergovernmental Maritime Consultative Organization
INCAP Institute for Nutrition for Central America and Panama
IPPF International Planned Parenthood Federation
IR infrared
IRI instantaneous rate of increase
IRRI International Rice Research Institute
IUD intrauterine device
IWC International Whaling Commission
J joule
JCAE Joint Committee on Atomic Energy (U.S. Congress)
K Kelvin
K carrying capacity
kcal kilocalorie
kg kilogram
kJ kilojoule
km kilometer
kW kilowatt
kWh kilowatt-hour
l liter

LD_{50}	lethal dose to 50 percent of those exposed
LDC	less developed country
LET	linear energy transfer
LMFBR	liquid-metal fast breeder reactor
LNG	liquefied natural gas
LOCA	loss-of-coolant accident
LWR	light-water reactor
m	meter
MeV	million electron volts
MHD	magnetohydrodynamics
mi	mile
min	minute
MIRV	multiple independently targeted re-entry vehicle
mm	millimeter
MPC	maximum permissible concentration
MPN	most probable number
N	newton
N	population size
NADP	nicotinamide adenine dinucleotide phosphate
NAE	National Academy of Engineering
NAS	National Academy of Sciences (U.S.)
NASA	National Aeronautics and Space Administration (U.S.)
NATO	North Atlantic Treaty Organization
NAWAPA	North American Water and Power Alliance
NCP	net community production
NIH	National Institutes of Health (U.S.)
NPG	negative population growth
NPP	net primary productivity
NPT	Non-Proliferation Treaty
NRC	National Research Council (U.S.)
NRC	Nuclear Regulatory Commission (U.S.)
NRDC	Natural Resources Defense Council
NRR	net reproductive rate
OAS	Organization of American States
ODC	overdeveloped country
OECD	Organization for Economic Cooperation and Development
OMB	Office of Management and Budget (U.S.)
OPEC	Organization of Petroleum Exporting Countries
OSHA	Occupational Safety and Health Act
OTA	Office of Technology Assessment (U.S. Congress)
PAN	peroxyacetl nitrate
PCB	polychlorinated biphenyl
ppb	parts per billion
pphm	parts per hundred million
ppm	parts per million
ppt	parts per trillion
PSAC	President's Science Advisory Committee
PUC	Public Utilities Commission
PVC	polyvinyl chloride
PWR	pressurized-water reactor
QF	quality factor
R	respiration
rad	radiation absorbed dose
RBE	relative biological effectiveness
REA	Rural Electrification Administration (U.S.)
rem	roentgen equivalent man
SALT	Strategic Arms Limitation Talks
SCEP	Study of Critical Environmental Problems
SCP	single cell protein
SEC	Securities and Exchange Commission (U.S.)
SIPRI	Swedish International Peace Research Institute
SLBM	submarine launched ballistic missile
SMIC	Study of Man's Impact on Climate
T	Tritium
ULCC	ultra large crude carrier
UN	United Nations
UNCLOS	U.N. Conference on the Law of the Sea
UNCTAD	U.N. Commission on Trade and Development
UNEP	U.N. Environmental Program
UNESCO	U.N. Educational, Scientific and Cultural Organization
UNFPA	U.N. Fund for Population Activities
USAEC	See AEC
USDA	U.S. Department of Agriculture
USGS	U.S. Geological Survey
USIA	U.S. Information Agency
USPHS	U.S. Public Health Service
UV	ultraviolet
VISTA	Volunteers in Service to America
VLCC	very large crude carrier
WHO	World Health Organization
ZPG	zero population growth or Zero Population Growth, Inc.
α	a helium nucleus emitted in radioactive decay
β	an electron or positron emitted in radioactive decay
γ	electromagnetic radiation emitted in radioactive decay
μ	micron